Children's Literature
Awards and Winners

ISSN 0749-3096

Children's Literature Awards and Winners:

A Directory of Prizes, Authors, and Illustrators

THIRD EDITION

Dolores Blythe Jones
de Grummond Children's Literature Research Collection
The University of Southern Mississippi

Neal-Schuman Publishers, Inc.
in association with

 **Gale Research Inc.** · *DETROIT* · *WASHINGTON, D.C.* · *LONDON*

Dolores Blythe Jones, *Editor*

Printed and manufactured in the United States of America

Published by Neal-Schuman Publishers, Inc.
in association with Gale Research Inc.

Published simultaneously in the United Kingdom by
Gale Research International Limited
(An affiliated company of Gale Research Inc.)

The paper used in this publication meets the minimum requirements of American National Standard for Information Sciences—Permanence Paper for Printed Library Materials, ANSI Z39.48-1984. ∞™

Library of Congress Catalog Card Number 84-643512
ISBN 0-8103-6900-1
ISSN 0749-3096

The trademark **ITP** is used under license.

10 9 8 7 6 5 4 3 2 1

For a third time,
To Gary for his patience and understanding

CONTENTS

Preface   ix

Part One   DIRECTORY OF AWARDS   3

Part Two   AUTHORS AND ILLUSTRATIONS   243

Part Three   SELECTED BIBLIOGRAPHY   579

Part Four   INDEXES

        Author/Illustrator Index   587

        Title Index   623

        Award Index   669

        Subject Index of Awards   673

PREFACE

The third edition of *Children's Literature Awards and Winners* updates and augments the second edition, published in 1988. This is a comprehensive reference source, describing awards granted in English-speaking countries for excellence in children's literature. International awards are included provided that they can be awarded to an author or illustrator from an English-speaking country or to a book written in English. This third edition includes awards granted in the United States, Canada, England, Wales, Australia, Ireland, Scotland, New Zealand, and South Africa.

Children's Literature Awards and Winners is a tool for librarians, teachers, reading specialists, students of children's literature, book collectors, and concerned parents. It provides quick access to the complete award history of an individual author or illustrator. It also documents the award history for a particular title. Readers may compare the criteria and methods of selection utilized for a variety of awards. For example, one might compare the various children's choice awards as to basic criteria, master list formulation, and physical form of the award.

SCOPE OF THE BOOK

Included in *Children's Literature Awards and Winners* are awards presented to an author or illustrator for his or her body of work, awards presented for a particular title, and awards presented for outstanding contributions to the field of children's literature. Children's choice awards are also included. The number of awards for children's literature continues to grow each year. The first edition, published in 1983, contained 144 awards, both current and discontinued. The Supplement, published in 1984, added 32 new awards. The second edition, published in 1988, added another 33 new awards, bringing the total to 211. This third edition contains information on 300 awards, 89 of which are new since the second edition. Information for more than 5,000 titles is included, with nearly 7,000 authors and illustrators indexed.

Each award lists winners from the inception of the award through 1993, when possible. Winners for some 1993 winners have not yet been announced. Every attempt was made to insure an up-to-date listing.

COMPILATION METHODS

Questionnaires were sent to all organizations listed in the second edition, as well as to newly identified award-granting agencies. Follow-up telephone conversations, descriptive brochures, and secondary sources were used when necessary to complete the entries.

ARRANGEMENT

Part One, **Directory of Awards**, is arranged alphabetically by award name. If the award is named in honor of a person, such as the Jane Addams Children's Book Award, the entry is alphabetized by the surname, rather than the first word of the award name. Each listing contains:

- The full name of the award
- The name of the sponsoring agency
- Address of the administering body
- Purpose and history of the award
- Frequency
- Selection criteria
- Award categories
- Rules and regulations
- Form of award

A complete listing of all award recipients for all categories of the award follows the general description. Full bibliographic data is provided for each title:

- title
- author(s)
- illustrator(s)
- translator(s)
- publisher
- date of publication

Part Two, **Authors and Illustrators**, is arranged alphabetically by author, illustrator, and translator. All awards received by the individual are listed under the title of the winning book. This arrangement permits the user to quickly locate all of the children's literature awards won by an author or illustrator throughout his or her career. Awards presented to persons that acknowledge their entire body of work or general contributions to the field are listed before the title entries.

Part Three, **Selected Bibliography**, lists books, book chapters, journal articles, dissertations, and reports on topics germane to children's book awards. There is continued disagreement among professionals concerning the value and relative merits of various award programs. This bibliography provides a starting point for the researcher who wishes to pursue this topic in more depth.

Part Four is comprised of the **Indexes**. The **Author/Illustrator Index** lists each individual who had a part in the creative process of an award-winning title. Cross references are provided for pseudonyms or variant name forms.

The **Title Index** lists each title in Parts One and Two with references to all pages on which the title appears.

The **Award Index**, keyed to the page on which each appears, lists alphabetically the 300 awards covered in Part One. It contains former names, as well as cross references from variant forms of the award name.

The **Subject Index of Awards** provides an additional point of access. Each award is listed under a variety of subject headings, determined by its outstanding features. Therefore, awards may be listed under more than one heading. Subjects include body of work, criticism, international, poetry, children's choice, research, and translation.

SUGGESTIONS ARE WELCOME

The author would like to thank all of those who willingly completed the questionnaires and provided additional information. It is through their assistance that the third edition of *Children's Literature Awards and Winners* could be compiled. I would also like to thank the administration of the University Libraries at the University of Southern Mississippi for their cooperation and assistance.

Although every effort was made to maintain accuracy, errors may occasionally occur. We would be grateful to have any errors, changes, or omissions brought to our attention. We would also welcome any suggestions from users, as well as information on new awards to be included in future editions.

Part One

DIRECTORY OF AWARDS

A

ABINGDON PRESS CHILDREN'S BOOK AWARD

discontinued

Sponsored by the Abingdon Press, this award was first given for a children's title in 1970. The children's category award was presented on a rotating basis, alternating every third year with religious and general books. All writers of fiction suitable for the fourth through sixth grades were eligible. Candidates were nominated by a committee of editors, with the final selection made by a committee of librarians. Manuscripts were judged solely upon their potential value in strengthening Christian faith and promoting Christian living among all people.

1970 *Never Go Anywhere with Digby* by Ethelyn M. Parkinson, illustrated by Leonard Vosburgh; Abingdon, 1971.

JANE ADDAMS CHILDREN'S BOOK AWARD

Ruth Chalmers, Executive Director
Jane Addams Peace Association
77 United Nations Plaza
New York, NY 10017

This annual award was created in 1953 by the United States section of the Women's International League for Peace and Freedom in honor of Jane Addams. The award's purpose is to give recognition to a book that most effectively promotes the cause of peace, social justice, and world community. Honor books may also be chosen. In 1993, a Picture Book category was added.

Publishers are invited to recommend titles to the award committee. Each nominated book is read and evaluated by the committee. The announcement of winning titles is made on September 6, Jane Addams's birthday. The recipient is presented with a hand-illuminated certificate.

1953 *People Are Important* by Eva Knox Evans, illustrated by Vana Earle; Golden, 1951.

1954 *Stick-in-the-Mud: A Tale of a Village, a Custom and a Little Boy* by Jean Ketchum, illustrated by Fred Ketchum; Scott, 1953.

1955 *Rainbow Round the World: A Story of UNICEF* by Elizabeth Yates, illustrated by Betty Alden and Dirk Gringhuis; Bobbs Merrill, 1954.

1956 *Story of the Negro* by Arna Wendell Bontemps, illustrated by Raymond Lufkin; Knopf, 1948.

1957 *Blue Mystery* by Margot Benary-Isbert, translated by Clara Winston and Richard Winston, illustrated by Enrico Arno; Harcourt, 1957.

1958 *The Perilous Road* by William O. Steele, illustrated by Paul Galdone; Harcourt, 1958.

1959 No Award

1960 *Champions of Peace: Winners of the Nobel Peace Prize* by Edith Patterson Meyer, illustrated by Eric von Schmidt; Little Brown, 1959.

1961 *What Then, Raman?* by Shirley L. Arora, illustrated by Hans Guggenheim; Follett, 1960.

1962 *The Road to Agra* by Aimee Sommerfelt, illustrated by Ulf Aas; Criterion, 1961.

1963 *The Monkey and the Wild, Wild Wind* by Ryerson Johnson, illustrated by Lois Lignell; Abelard, 1961.

1964 *Profiles in Courage* by John F. Kennedy, illustrated by Emil Weiss; Harper, 1964. (Young reader's memorial edition)

1965 *Meeting with a Stranger* by Duane Bradley, illustrated by E. Harper Johnson; Lippincott, 1964.

1966 *Berries Goodman* by Emily Cheney Neville, not illustrated; Harper, 1965.

1967 *Queenie Peavy* by Robert Burch, illustrated by Jerry Lazare; Viking, 1966.

1968 *The Little Fishes* by Erik Christian Haugaard, illustrated by Milton Johnson; Houghton Mifflin, 1967.

1969 *The Endless Steppe: Growing up in Siberia* by Esther Hautzig, not illustrated; Crowell, 1968.

1970 No Award

1971 *Jane Addams: Pioneer for Social Justice, a Biography* by Cornelia L. Meigs, illustrated with photographs; Little Brown, 1970.

1972 *The Tamarack Tree* by Mary Betty Underwood, illustrated by Bea Holmes; Houghton Mifflin, 1971.

1973 *The Riddle of Racism* by S. Carl Hirsch, not illustrated; Viking, 1972.

1973 **HONOR** *The Upstairs Room* by Johanna Reiss, not illustrated; Crowell, 1972.

1974 *Nilda* written and illustrated by Nicholasa Mohr; Harper, 1973.

1974 **HONOR** *A Hero Ain't Nothin' but a Sandwich* by Alice Childress, not illustrated; Coward, 1973.

Men Against War by Barbara Habenstreit, not illustrated; Doubleday, 1973.

A Pocket Full of Seeds by Marilyn Sachs, illustrated by Ben Stahl; Doubleday, 1973.

1975 *The Princess and the Admiral* by Charlotte Pomerantz, illustrated by Tony Chen; Addison, 1974.

1975 **HONOR** *My Brother Sam Is Dead* by James L. Collier and Christopher Collier, not illustrated; Four Winds/Scholastic, 1974.

Viva la Raza! The Struggle of the Mexican-American People by Elizabeth Sutherland Martinez and Enriqueta Longeaux y Vasquez, not illustrated; Doubleday, 1974.

The Eye of Conscience: Photographers and Social Change by Milton Meltzer and Bernard Cole, illustrated with photographs; Follett, 1974.

1976 *Paul Robeson* by Eloise Greenfield, illustrated by George Ford; Crowell, 1975.

1976 HONOR *Song of the Trees* by Mildred D. Taylor, illustrated by Jerry Pinkney; Dial, 1975.

Dragonwings by Laurence Yep, not illustrated; Harper, 1975.

Z for Zachariah by Robert C. O'Brien, not illustrated; Atheneum, 1975.

1977 *Never to Forget: The Jews of the Holocaust* by Milton Meltzer, not illustrated; Harper & Row, 1976.

1977 HONOR *Roll of Thunder, Hear My Cry* by Mildred D. Taylor, illustrated by Jerry Pinkney; Dial, 1976.

1978 *Child of the Owl* by Laurence Yep, not illustrated; Harper, 1977.

1978 HONOR *Mischling, Second Degree: My Childhood in Nazi Germany* by Ilse Koehn, not illustrated; Greenwillow, 1977.

Alan and Naomi by Myron Levoy, not illustrated; Harper, 1977.

1978 SPECIAL RECOGNITION *Amifika* by Lucille Clifton, illustrated by Thomas DiGrazia; Dutton, 1977.

The Wheel of King Asoka written and illustrated by Ashok Davar; Follett, 1977.

1979 *Many Smokes, Many Moons: A Chronology of American Indian History through Indian Art* by Jamake Highwater, illustrated with photographs; Lippincott, 1978.

1979 HONOR *Escape to Freedom* by Ossie Davis, not illustrated; Viking, 1978, c1976.

The Great Gilly Hopkins by Katherine Paterson, not illustrated; Crowell, 1978.

1980 *The Road from Home: The Story of an Armenian Girl* by David Kherdian, not illustrated; Greenwillow, 1979.

1980 WEST COAST HONOR BOOK *Woman from Hiroshima* by Toshio Mori, not illustrated; Isthmus Press, 1978.

1980 SPECIAL RECOGNITION *Natural History* written and illustrated by M.B. Goffstein; Farrar, Straus, Giroux, 1979.

1981 *First Woman in Congress: Jeannette Rankin* by Florence Meiman White, illustrated; Messner, 1980.

1981 HONOR *Chase Me, Catch Nobody!* by Erik C. Haugaard, not illustrated; Houghton Mifflin, 1980.

Doing Time: A Look at Crime and Prisons by Phyllis E. Clark and Robert Lehrman, illustrated; Hastings House, 1980.

We Are Mesquakie, We Are One by Hadley Irwin, illustrated with maps; Feminist Press, 1980.

1982 *A Spirit to Ride the Whirlwind* by Athena V. Lord, not illustrated; Macmillan, 1981.

1982 HONOR *Lupita Manana* by Patricia Beatty, not illustrated; Morrow, 1981.

Let the Circle Be Unbroken by Mildred D. Taylor, not illustrated; Dial, 1981.

1983 *Hiroshima no Pika* written and illustrated by Toshi Maruki; Lothrop, Lee & Shepard, 1982.

1983 HONOR *The Bomb* by Sidney Lens, illustrated with photographs; Lodestar/Dutton, 1982.

If I Had a Paka: Poems in Eleven Languages by Charlotte Pomerantz, illustrated by Nancy Tafuri; Greenwillow, 1982.

1983 WEST COAST HONOR BOOK *People at the Edge of the World: The Ohlone of Central California* by Betty Morrow, illustrated by Shahid Naeem; published by the author, 1982.

1983 SPECIAL RECOGNITION *All the Colors of the Race: Poems* by Arnold Adoff, illustrated by John Steptoe; Lothrop, Lee & Shepard, 1982.

Children as Teachers of Peace: By Our Children edited by Gerald G. Jampolsky, foreword by Hugh Prather; illustrated; Celestial Arts, 1982.

1984 *Rain of Fire* by Marion Dane Bauer, not illustrated; Clarion, 1983.

1985 *The Short Life of Sophie Scholl* by Hermann Vinke, translated by Hedwig Pachter, illustrated with photographs; Harper & Row, 1984.

1985 HONOR *The Island on Bird Street* by Uri Orlev, translated by Hillel Halkin, not illustrated; Houghton Mifflin, 1984.

Music, Music for Everyone written and illustrated by Vera B. Williams; Greenwillow, 1984.

1986 *Ain't Gonna Study War No More: The Story of America's Peace Seekers* by Milton Meltzer, illustrated; Harper & Row, 1985.

1986 HONOR *Journey to the Soviet Union* by Samantha Smith, illustrated with photographs; Little Brown, 1985.

1987 *Nobody Wants a Nuclear War* written and illustrated by Judith Vigna; Whitman, 1986.

1987 HONOR *All in a Day* written and illustrated by Mitsumasa Anno; Philomel, 1986.

Children of the Maya: A Guatemalan Indian Odyssey by Brent Ashabranner, photographs by Paul Conklin; Dodd Mead, 1986.

1988 *Waiting for the Rain: A Novel of South Africa* by Sheila Gordon, not illustrated; Orchard, 1987.

1988 HONOR *Trouble at the Mines* by Doreen Rappaport, illustrated by Joan Sandin; Crowell, 1987.

Nicolas, Where Have You Been? written and illustrated by Leo Lionni; Knopf, 1987.

1989 (FICTION AGES 7-UP) *The Most Beautiful Place in the World* by Ann Cameron, illustrated by Thomas B. Allen; Knopf, 1988.

1989 (FICTION AGES 10-14) *Looking Out* by Victoria Boutis, not illustrated; Four Winds, 1988.

1989 (FICTION AGES 10-14 HONOR) *December Stillness* by Mary Downing Hahn, not illustrated; Clarion, 1988.

1989 (FICTIONALIZED BIOGRAPHY AGES 11-UP) *Anthony Burns: The Defeat and Triumph of a Fugitive Slave* by Virginia Hamilton, not illustrated; Knopf, 1988.

1989 (NONFICTION AGES 10-UP) *Rescue: The Story of How Gentiles Saved Jews in the Holocaust* by Milton Meltzer, not illustrated; Harper & Row, 1988.

1990 *A Long Hard Journey: The Story of the Pullman Porter* by Patricia McKissack and Fredrick McKissack, illustrated; Walker, 1989.

1990 HONOR *The Wednesday Surprise* by Eve Bunting, illustrated by Donald Carrick; Clarion, 1989.

Shades of Gray by Carolyn Reeder, not illustrated; Macmillan, 1989.

Number the Stars by Lois Lowry, not illustrated; Houghton Mifflin, 1989.

1991 *The Big Book for Peace* edited by Marilyn Sachs and Ann Durrell, illustrated by various illustrators; Dutton, 1990.

1991 HONOR *The Journey: Japanese Americans, Racism and Renewal* written and illustrated by Sheila Hamanaka; Orchard, 1990.

The Middle of Somewhere by Sheila Gordon, not illustrated; Orchard, 1990.

1992 *Journey of the Sparrows* by Fran Leeper Buss, not illustrated; Lodestar, 1991.

1992 HONOR *Now Is Your Time! The African American Struggle for Freedom* by Walter Dean Myers, illustrated; HarperCollins, 1991.

1993 *A Taste of Salt* by Frances Temple; Orchard, 1992.

1993 HONOR *Letters from a Slave Girl* by Mary E. Lyons, illustrated; Scribner, 1992.

1993 PICTURE BOOK *Aunt Harriet's Underground Railroad in the Sky* written and illustrated by Faith Ringgold; Crown, 1992.

1993 PICTURE BOOK HONOR *Mrs. Katz and the Tush* written and illustrated by Patricia Polacco; Bantam, 1992.

AESOP PRIZE
Children's Folklore Section
American Folklore Society

First awarded in 1993, the prize is awarded by the Children's Folklore Section of the American Folklore Society. The prize honors an English language children's book that best incorporates folklore in text and illustrations.

1993 **Cowinners** *Days of Awe: Stories for Rosh Hashanah and Yom Kippur* adapted by Eric A. Kimmel, illustrated by Erika Weihs; Viking, 1991.

AIM CHILDREN'S BOOK AWARDS
Booksellers New Zealand
John Barr, Marketing Manager
Book House
86 Boulcott St.
P O Box 11-377
Wellington, New Zealand

Established in 1983, this award was originally called the Children's Book Awards. As of 1990, the name changed with the new sponsorship of Lever Rexona through its AIM brand toothpaste and toothbrushes. Administered by the AIM Children's Book Week Management Committee, representing Booksellers New Zealand, the Book Publishers Association of New Zealand,

and the literature programme of the QEII Arts Council, the purpose of the award is to promote excellence in children's literature and to provide recognition for the best children's books published annually in New Zealand.

Each year, awards are offered in the following categories: Book of the Year - 1st, 2nd, and, 3rd prize ($5000, $2000, and $1000 respectively) and Picture Book of the Year - 1st, 2nd, and 3rd prize ($5000, $2000, and $1000 respectively). In the picture book category, the cash award is split between author and illustrator. At the discretion of the judges, an additional award for Best First Book from a previously unpublished author may be awarded. It carries a $1000 award.

In order to qualify, authors and illustrators must be New Zealand citizens by birth, naturalization, or immigration and normally reside in New Zealand. A three-member panel is responsible for the selections. Award presentations are made during AIM Children's Book Week.

1982 STORY BOOK *The Silent One* by Joy Cowley, illustrated by Sherryl Jordan; Whitcoulls, 1981.

1982 PICTURE BOOK *The Kuia and the Spider* by Patricia Grace, illustrated by Robyn Kahukiwa; Longman Paul, 1981.

1983 STORY BOOK *The Halfmen of O* by Maurice Gee, not illustrated; Oxford University Press, 1982.

1983 PICTURE BOOK *Mr. Fox* written and illustrated by Gavin Bishop; Oxford University Press, 1982.

1984 STORY BOOK *Jacky Nobody* by Anne de Roo; Methuen, 1983.

1984 PICTURE BOOK *Hairy Maclary from Donaldson's Dairy* written and illustrated by Lynley Dodd; Mallinson Rendel, 1983; Gareth Stevens, 1985, c1983.

1985 STORY BOOK *Visitors* written and illustrated by Caroline MacDonald; Hodder & Stoughton, 1984.

1985 *The Fish of our Fathers* by Ronald Leonard Bacon, illustrated by Robert H.G. Jahnke; Waiatarua Press, 1984; Child's Play International, 1986.

1986 STORY BOOK No Award

1986 PICTURE BOOK *Hairy Maclary, Scattercat* written and illustrated by Lynley Dodd; Mallinson Rendel, 1985; Gareth Stevens, 1988, c1985.

1987 STORY BOOK *The Keeper* by Barry Faville, not illustrated; Oxford University Press, 1986.

1987 PICTURE BOOK *Taniwha* written and illustrated by Robyn Kahukiwa; Penguin, 1986.

1988 STORY BOOK *Alex* by Tessa Duder, not illustrated; Oxford University Press, 1987.

1988 PICTURE BOOK *Hairy Maclary's Caterwaul Caper* written and illustrated by Lynley Dodd; Mallinson Rendel, 1987.

1989 No Awards

1990 STORY BOOK *Alex in Winter* by Tessa Duder, not illustrated; Oxford University Press, 1989.

1990 STORY BOOK 2ND PRIZE *The Champion* by Maurice Gee, not illustrated; Penguin New Zealand, 1989.

1990 STORY BOOK 3RD PRIZE *The Lake at the End of the World* by Caroline Macdonald, not illustrated; Hodder & Stoughton, 1988; Dial, 1989.

1990 PICTURE BOOK *Annie & Moon* by Miriam Smith, illustrated by Lesley Moyes; Mallinson Rendel, 1988.

1990 PICTURE BOOK 2ND PRIZE *The Story of the Kakapo Parrot of the Night* by Philip Temple, illustrated by Chris Gaskin; Hodder & Stoughton, 1988.

1990 PICTURE BOOK 3RD PRIZE *Hairy Maclary's Rumpus at the Vet* written and illustrated by Lynley Dodd; Mallinson Rendel, 1989.

1991 STORY BOOK *Rocco* by Sherryl Jordan, not illustrated; Ashton Scholastic, 1990.

1991 STORY BOOK 2ND PRIZE *Secrets* by Ruth Corrin, not illustrated; Oxford University Press, 1991.

1991 STORY BOOK 3RD PRIZE *Speaking to Miranda* by Caroline Macdonald, not illustrated; Hodder & Stoughton, 1991.

1991 PICTURE BOOK *My Cat Maisie* written and illustrated by Pamela Allen; Hodder & Stoughton, 1990; Hamish Hamilton, 1990; Viking, 1990.

1991 PICTURE BOOK 2ND PRIZE *Lily and the Bears* written and illustrated by Christine Ross; Angus & Robertson, 1990; Methuen Children's, 1990; Houghton Mifflin, 1991.

1991 PICTURE BOOK 3RD PRIZE *Slinky Malinki* written and illustrated by Lynley Dodd; Mallinson Rendel, 1990; Spindlewood, 1990; Gareth Stevens, 1991.

1991 BEST FIRST BOOK *Water in the Blood* by Alan Bunn; Octopus, 1990.

1992 STORY BOOK *Bow Down Shadrach* by Joy Cowley, not illustrated; Hodder & Stoughton, 1991.

1992 STORY BOOK 2ND PRIZE *The Juniper Game* by Sherryl Jordan, not illustrated; Ashton Scholastic, 1991.

1992 STORY BOOK 3RD PRIZE *Alessandra: Alex in Rome* by Tessa Duder, not illustrated; Oxford University Press, 1991.

1992 PICTURE BOOK *Hairy Maclary's Showbusiness* written and illustrated by Lynley Dodd; Mallinson Rendel, 1991.

1992 PICTURE BOOK 2ND PRIZE *My Aunt Mary Went Shopping* by Roger Hall, illustrated by Trevor Pye; Ashton Scholastic, 1991.

1992 PICTURE BOOK 3RD PRIZE *The One That Got Away* by John Parsons, illustrated by Penny Newman; Arncliffe, 1990.

1992 BEST FIRST BOOK *Out Walked Mel* by Paula Boock, not illustrated; John McIndoe, 1991.

ALAN AWARD
Assembly on Literature for Adolescents of the
 National Council of Teachers of English
1111 Kenyon Rd.
Urbana, IL 61801

The ALAN Award is sponsored by the Assembly on Literature of the National Council of Teachers of English and has been awarded annually since 1974. The award was conceived to honor a person who has made significant contributions to the field of adolescent literature. All who write or provide service in the field of adolescent literature are eligible to be nominated by a member of the sponsoring organization. A plaque is presented at the annual convention of the NCTE.

1974	Stephen Judy, Robert Carlsen
1975	Margaret Edwards
1976	Margaret McElderry, Jerry Weiss
1977	Marguerite Archer
1978	Mary Sucher
1979	Gerri LaRocque
1980	Dwight Burton
1981	Sheila Schwartz
1982	Robert Cormier
1983	Kenneth Donelson
1984	Louise Rosenblatt
1985	Sue Ellen Bridgers
1986	Madeleine L'Engle
1987	Katherine Paterson, Alleen Nilsen
1988	Theodore Hipple
1989	Cynthia Voigt
1990	Richard Peck
1991	Gary Paulsen
1992	Donald Gallo

ALBERTA WRITING FOR YOUTH COMPETITION
Alberta Culture and Multiculturalism
Arts Branch
3rd floor, Beaver House
10158 - 103 St.
Edmonton, Alberta T5J OX6
Canada

Established in 1980, this biennial writing competition is sponsored by the Alberta Culture and Multiculturalism, the Alberta Foundation for the Arts, Tree Frog Press, and ITV to encourage, recognize and develop the diversity of Alberta authors who write fiction for young people. Competition entrants must be residing in Alberta at the time of submission and for a period of not less than twelve of the preceding eighteen months. Entrants must be Canadian citizens or landed immigrants.

An independent panel of qualified judges selects the winning manuscript. First prize for the best publishable manuscript is $4500, consisting of $2000 cash prize from the Alberta Foundation for the Arts, $1000 advance against royalties from the publisher, a $1500 12-month option agreement for motion picture/television rights from ITV, and a publishing contract from Tree Frog Press.

1980 *Hunter in the Dark* by Monica Hughes, not illustrated; Clarke Irwin, 1982.

1982 *Cowboys Don't Cry* by Marilyn Halvorson, not illustrated; Clarke Irwin, 1984; Delacorte, 1985.

1984 No winner

1989 *The Chinese Mirror* by Alice Major, not illustrated; Irwin Publishing, 1988.

1991 *In Such a Place* by Lynne Fairbridge, not illustrated; Doubleday Canada, 1992.

ALCUIN CITATION FOR EXCELLENCE IN BOOK DESIGN IN CANADA

Alcuin Society
P O Box 3216
Vancouver, British Columbia
Canada V6B 3X8

Established in 1983 to promote an awareness of excellence in the book arts, the Alcuin Citation is awarded yearly in May. Citations are issued in many categories, one of them being Juvenile Books. Books published exclusively in Canada or copublished with a publisher in another country are eligible, but the designer must be Canadian. Books are judged on a sound marriage of design and content, appropriate cover design, page layout, typography, and balance of illustration and text. First place juvenile titles are listed below.

1984 *Captain Carp Saves the Sea* written and illustrated by John Larsen; Annick Press, 1983.

1985 *Dinner At Auntie Rose's* by Janet Munsil, illustrated by Scot Ritchie; Annick Press, 1984.

1986 *The Sorcerer's Apprentice* written and illustrated by Robin Muller; Kids Can Press, 1985.

1987 *The Sea Serpent of Grenadier Pond* written and illustrated by David Peacock; Hounslow Press, 1986.

1988 No first place award

1989 *The Wildlife ABC* written and illustrated by Jan Thornhill; Greey de Pencier, 1988.

1990 *The Time Before Dreams* by Stefan Czernecki and Timothy Rhodes, illustrated by Stefan Czernecki; Hyperion, 1989.

1991 *The Sign of the Scales* by Marianne Brandis, illustrated by G. Brender a Brandis; Porcupine's Quill, 1990.

1992 *The Anne of Green Gables Treasury* by Carolyn Strom Collins and Christina Wyss Eriksson; Penguin Books Canada, 1991.

1993 *Hickory, Dickory, Dock* by Robin Muller, illustrated by Suzanne Duranceau; North Winds Press, 1992.

AMERICAN ASSOCIATION OF SCHOOL LIBRARIANS PRESIDENT'S AWARD

American Association of School Librarians
American Library Association
50 East Huron St
Chicago, IL 60611

This annual award was established in 1978 and is cosponsored by the American Association of School Librarians and The Baker and Taylor Co. The purpose of the award is to recognize an individual member of the library profession who has made an outstanding national or international contribution to school librarianship and school library development. Nominations are requested from the membership of the American Association of School Librarians.

Nominees should have demonstrated achievement in such areas as (1) service to the organized profession through AASL, (2) significant and influential research on school library service, (3) publication of a body of scholarly and/or theoretical writing contributing to school library development, or (4) planning and implementing a school library media program of such exemplary quality that it has served as a model for others.

The winning librarian is honored at the American Library Association Annual Conference and receives a $2000 cash award.

1978   Jean E. Lowrie

1979   Frances E. Henney

1980   Mary Virginia Gaver

1981   Mary Helen Maher

1982   D. Philip Baker

1983   Rachel W. De Angelo

1984   Rheta Clark

1985   Frances S. Hatfield

1986   Margaret Hayes Grazier

1987   Suzanne Sutton

1988   Margaret Rufsvold

1989   Virginia Mathews

1990   Ruth V. Bell

1991   Barbara Spriestersbach

1992   Dianne McAfee Hopkins

1993   Marilyn L. Miller

AMERICAN BOOK AWARDS

discontinued
See also **NATIONAL BOOK AWARD**

This annual award, established in 1980 by the Association of American Publishers, replaced the discontinued National Book Award (see entry). The purpose of the American Book Awards was fourfold: (1) to recognize and reward books of literary and artistic merit, (2) to generate public awareness of books, their authors, and the publishing industry, (3) to increase interest in reading, and (4) to find new audiences for books.

In order to be eligible, books must have been written, designed, or translated by U.S. citizens and published in the U.S. during the preceding calendar year. There were seventeen categories of recognition, four of which pertained directly to children's literature: (1) children's fiction (hardback), (2) children's fiction (paperback), (3) children's nonfiction (hardback), and (4) children's nonfiction (paperback). There were also six categories pertaining specifically to graphics in which children's books were considered.

Both the graphic and literary awards consisted of a Louise Nevelson wall sculpture, with literary winners also receiving $1000. The nominees and winners were chosen by an independent group of judges including librarians, authors, publishers, critics, and editors. The awards were presented at a ceremony followed by a reception.

1980   **CHILDREN'S BOOK HARDCOVER** *A Gathering of Days: A New England Girl's Journal, 1830-32* by Joan W. Blos, not illustrated; Scribner, 1979.

1980   **CHILDREN'S BOOK PAPERBACK** *A Swiftly Tilting Planet* by Madeleine L'Engle, not illustrated; Dell, 1979, c1978.

1981   **CHILDREN'S FICTION HARDCOVER** *The Night Swimmers* by Betsy Byars, illustrated by Troy Howell; Delacorte, 1980.

1981   **CHILDREN'S FICTION PAPERBACK** *Ramona and Her Mother* by Beverly Cleary, illustrated by Alan Tiegreen; Morrow, 1979; Dell/Yearling, 1980.

1981   **CHILDREN'S NONFICTION HARDCOVER** *Oh, Boy! Babies!* by Jane Lawrence Mali and Alison Cragin Herzig, illustrated by Katrina Thomas; Little Brown, 1980.

1982 CHILDREN'S FICTION HARDCOVER *Westmark* by Lloyd Alexander, not illustrated; Dutton, 1981.

1982 CHILDREN'S FICTION PAPERBACK *Words by Heart* by Ouida Sebestyen, not illustrated; Little Brown, 1979; Bantam, 1981.

1982 CHILDREN'S NONFICTION *A Penguin Year* written and illustrated by Susan Bonners; Delacorte, 1981.

1982 PICTUREBOOK HARDBACK *Outside Over There* written and illustrated by Maurice Sendak; Harper, 1981.

1982 PICTUREBOOK PAPERBACK *Noah's Ark* written and illustrated by Peter Spier; Doubleday, 1977.

1982 GRAPHIC AWARD FOR BOOK ILLUSTRATION ORIGINAL ART *Jumanji* written and illustrated by Chris Van Allsburg; Houghton Mifflin, 1981.

1983 CHILDREN'S FICTION HARDBACK *Homesick: My Own Story* by Jean Fritz, illustrated with drawings by Margot Tomes and photographs; Putnam, 1982.

1983 CHILDREN'S FICTION PAPERBACK *A Place Apart* by Paula Fox, not illustrated; Farrar, Straus, Giroux, 1980; New American Library 1982.

Marked by Fire by Joyce Carol Thomas, not illustrated; Avon, 1981.

1983 CHILDREN'S NONFICTION *Chimney Sweeps: Yesterday and Today* by James C. Giblin, illustrated by Margot Tomes; Crowell, 1982.

1983 PICTUREBOOK HARDBACK *Doctor DeSoto* written and illustrated by William Steig; Farrar, Straus, Giroux, 1982.

Miss Rumphius written and illustrated by Barbara Cooney; Viking, 1982.

1983 PICTUREBOOK PAPERBACK *A House is a House for Me* by Mary Ann Hoberman, illustrated by Betty Fraser; Viking, 1978; Puffin, 1982.

1983 PICTORIAL DESIGN *Lewis Carroll's Alice's Adventures in Wonderland* illustrated by Barry Moser, text edited by Selwyn H. Goodacre, preface and notes by James R. Kincaid; University of California Press, 1982.

AMERICAN BOOKSELLERS BOOK OF THE YEAR

American Booksellers Association
560 White Plains Rd.
Tarrytown, NY 10591

The American Booksellers Book of the Year (ABBY) was established in 1991 to honor the book that booksellers have most enjoyed handselling. Any book, regardless of subject matter or reading level is eligible to win. Booksellers from ABA member stores vote for the winning title. A $5000 cash award and an ABBY sculpture are awarded annually at the American Booksellers Convention. In 1993, a children's category was added.

1991 *The Education of Little Tree* by Forrest Carter, not illustrated; Delacorte, 1976; University of New Mexico Press, 1986.

1992 *Brother Eagle, Sister Sky* a message from Chief Seattle, illustrated by Susan Jeffers; Dial, 1991.

1993 CHILDREN *Old Turtle* by Douglas Wood, illustrated by Cheng-Khee Chee; Pfeifer-Hamilton, 1992.

AMERICAN INSTITUTE OF GRAPHIC ARTS BOOK SHOW

American Institute of Graphic Arts
1059 Third Ave.
New York, NY 10021

Sponsored by the membership of the AIGA, this annual competition has been held since 1941. Each year the show presents a variety of the best in American publishing. It is hoped that the book show will further the goal of the AIGA, which is to recognize and encourage distinguished graphic work in a variety of forms. Each year a number of juvenile titles are among the books chosen for exhibition in the AIGA Book Show. All books designed and originated in the U.S. or Canada from January 1 to January 31 of the following year are eligible. All award-winning entries will be on exhibit at the AIGA galleries and will be included in the AIGA Graphic Design USA. Those who have participated in the creation of the book will receive the AIGA Certificate of Excellence. The winning books will be added to the permanent collection of all AIGA book-show titles housed at the Low Library, Columbia University.

The yearly winners are too numerous to be included in this listing.

AMERICAN INSTITUTE OF PHYSICS SCIENCE WRITING AWARD IN PHYSICS AND ASTRONOMY FOR ARTICLES, BOOKLETS, OR BOOKS INTENDED FOR CHILDREN

Kenneth W. Ford, Director
American Institute of Physics
335 E. 45th St.
New York, NY 10017

Sponsored by the American Institute of Physics, this unique award seeks to recognize and stimulate distinguished writing and illustration that improves children's understanding and appreciation of physics and astronomy. Begun in 1988, this annual award is aimed at material written for children preschool through 15 years of age, written or translated into English, dealing primarily with physics and astronomy. In order to be eligible for this award, articles, booklets, and books must be accurate, appropriate for the age group, creative, and contain a reasonable amount of information. The winning recipient receives a $3000 cash award, a certificate, and a Windsor chair.

1988 *Splash! All About Baths* by Susan Kovacs Buxbaum, illustrated by Maryann Cocca-Leffler; Little Brown, 1987.

1989 *Micromysteries: Stories of Scientific Detection* by Gail Kay Haines, illustrated with photos; Dodd, Mead, 1988.

1990 *The Way Things Work* written and illustrated by David Macaulay; Houghton Mifflin, 1988.

1991 *Airborne: The Search for the Secret of Flight* by Richard Maurer, illustrated with color photographs; Simon & Schuster, in association with WGBH, Boston, 1990.

1992 *Almost the Real Thing: Simulation in Your High Tech World* by Gloria Skurzynski, illustrated with photos; Bradbury, 1991.

1993 *Stargazers* written and illustrated by Gail Gibbons; Holiday House, 1992.

HANS CHRISTIAN ANDERSEN AWARDS

IBBY Secretariat
Leena Maissen, Director
Nonneweg 12, Postfach
CH-4003
Basel, Switzerland

The most distinguished international prizes in children's literature, the Hans Christian Andersen Awards are given biennially by the International Board on Books for Young People (IBBY) to one author (since 1956) and one illustrator (since 1966) who have made a lasting contribution to literature for children and young people. The prize, a gold medal and a diploma, was originally given for a particular book; since 1962, the author's and illustrator's complete works are taken into consideration. Each national section of IBBY is invited to propose a candidate, living at the time of nomination, for each of the two medals.

The medalists are selected by an international jury (the Hans Christian Andersen Jury) composed of the jury president, the president of IBBY, and eight children's literature experts elected by the executive committee of IBBY from proposals by national sections. No juror is eligible to serve more than two successive terms. The Hans Christian Andersen Jury judges the books submitted for the awards according to literary and artistic criteria. Besides the medal winners, the jury may honor other candidates with a highly commended diploma (since 1966). From 1960 to 1964, the jury selected outstanding books for a runners-up list.

The following regulations govern the awarding of the medals:

1. National sections send the names of candidates for the medals to the president of the Hans Christian Andersen Jury, along with a representative selection of books and other relevant information.

2. When submitting an entry for either of the two medals, the National section must send, for each, the amount of 125 Swiss francs to cover the expenses connected with the awards.

3. Candidates who have been highly commended may be proposed again after an interval of five years.

4. The Hans Christian Andersen Jury judges the books submitted for the Hans Christian Andersen Awards according to literary and artistic criteria. These criteria are to be discussed before each jury meeting. The jury is fully autonomous in its decisions. Members of the jury who are not able to attend a meeting may send their comments and proposals in accordance with the rules established by the president of the Jury. Absent members have no vote. The jury may vote when more than half of the voting members are present. In case of a draw, the president of the Jury will be allowed a vote so that a decision may be reached.

5. The national sections of IBBY will be informed of the jury's decision immediately after the selection has been made. The results will be given the maximum publicity.

1956 *The Little Bookroom* by Eleanor Farjeon, illustrated by Edward Ardizzone; Oxford, 1955.

Jella Lepman for her service to international children's literature.

1958 *Rasmus Pa Luffen* by Astrid Lindgren, illustrated by Eric Palmquist; Raben & Sjogren, 1956.

1960 *Als Ich Ein Kleiher Junge War* by Erich Kastner, illustrated by Horst Lemke; Dressler, 1957.

1960 **RUNNERSUP** *All Together* by Mosche Shamir; Hatzair, 1959.

Along the Seaside by Themos Potaaianos, illustrated by Spyndonos; Greece.

Dede Korkut Masallari by Eflatun Gem Guney, illustrated by Gunal Neset; Dogan Kardes, 1958.

Jan und das Wildpferd by Heinrich-Maria Denneborg, illustrated by Horst Lemke; Dressler, 1957.

Judy and Lakshmi by Naomi Mitchison, illustrated by Avinash Chandra; Collins, 1958.

Lale, Die Turkin by Karl Bruckner, illustrated by E. Wallenta; Jungend u. Volk, 1958.

Manko Kapak by Karel Jeuninckx and Lo Vermeulen, illustrated by Elzavan Hagendoren; De Sikkel, 1957.

Manuel Zigenarpojken by Karl-Rune Nordkvist, illustrated by I. Rossell-Lindahl; Raben & Sjogren, 1958.

Marianne Po Sykehus by Odd Brochman; Aschehoug, 1958.

Mina Olen Lammenpei by Aila Nissinen, illustrated by Maija Karma; Soderstrom, 1958.

Priscilla by Giana Anguissola, illustrated by Gastone Regosta; Mursia, 1958.

Wiplala by Annie Schmidt; Arbeiderspers, 1957.

1962 Meindert DeJong

1962 **RUNNERSUP** *Auf Endlosen Strassen* by Gerhart Ellert, illustrated by Hilde Seidel; Osterreichischer Bundesverlag, 1959.

Baboushka and the Three Kings by Ruth Robbins, illustrated by Nicolas Sidjakov; Parnassus, 1960.

Das Mondgesicht by Gerda Marie Scheidl, illustrated by Lilo Fromm; Obpacher Buch u. Kunstverlag, 1960.

Der Page Orteguill by Adolf Haller, illustrated by Felix Hoffmann; Sauerlander, 1960.

Friday's Tunnel written and illustrated by John Verney; Collins, 1959; Holt, 1966.

Le Avventure de Cinque Ragazzi e un Cane by Renee Reggiani, illustrated by Lionello Zorn Giorni; Cappelli, 1960.

My Side of the Mountain written and illustrated by Jean Craighead George; Dutton, 1959.

Priska Kesasta Kesaan by Merja Otava; Soderstrom, 1959.

The Princess of Tomsobo written and illustrated by Frank Newfeld; Oxford, 1960.

Tapporahat by Erkki Rekimies; Otava, 1959.

1964 Rene Guillot

1964 **RUNNERSUP** *Hannes und Sein Bumpan* by Mira Lobe, illustrated by Susi Weigel; Jugend u. Volk, 1961.

Hokkyoku no Mushika Mishika by Tomiko Inui, illustrated by Yasuko Horioka; Rironsha, 1961.

Illiada by Georgiou Geralis; Kentavros, 1962.

Les Saltimbanques by Jean Ollivier, illustrated by Rene Moreau; La Farandole, 1962.

Mikosch das Karusselpferd written and illustrated by Thomas Zacharias and Wanda Zacharias; Mohn, 1962.

Muru Menee Kalaan written and illustrated by Oili Tanninen; Otava, 1961.

Oscar, Cosmonauta by Carmen Kurtz, illustrated by Carlos Maria Alvarez; E. Juventud, 1962.

Tills Aventyr I Skorstensgrand by Gunnel Linde, illustrated by Ilon Wikland; Bonnier, 1962.

A Wrinkle in Time by Madeleine L'Engle, not illustrated; Farrar, 1962.

1966 AUTHOR Tove Jansson (Finland)

1966 AUTHOR (HIGHLY COMMENDED) Karl Bruckner (Austria); Gianni Rodari (Italy); Jose Maria Sanchez-Silva (Spain)

1966 ILLUSTRATOR Alois Carigiet (Switzerland)

1966 ILLUSTRATOR (HIGHLY COMMENDED) Jiri Trnka (USSR); Brian Wildsmith (Great Britain)

1968 AUTHOR Jose Maria Sanchez-Silva (Spain); James Kruss (German Federal Republic)

1968 AUTHOR (HIGHLY COMMENDED) Elizabeth Coatsworth (United States); Gianni Rodari (Italy)

1968 ILLUSTRATOR Jiri Trnka (USSR)

1968 ILLUSTRATOR (HIGHLY COMMENDED) Roger Duvoisin (United States); Ib Spang Ohlsson (Denmark); Brian Wildsmith (Great Britain)

1970 AUTHOR Gianni Rodari (Italy)

1970 AUTHOR (HIGHLY COMMENDED) Ana Maria Matute (Spain); Ela Peroci (Yugoslavia); E.B. White (United States)

1970 ILLUSTRATOR Maurice Sendak (United States)

1970 ILLUSTRATOR (HIGHLY COMMENDED) Ib Spang Ohlsson (Denmark); Lidija Osterc (Yugoslavia); Daihachi Ota (Japan)

1972 AUTHOR Scott O'Dell (United States)

1972 AUTHOR (HIGHLY COMMENDED) Ana Maria Matute (Spain); Sergei Mikhalkov (USSR); Otfried Preussler (German Federal Republic); Colette Vivier (France); Maria Gripe (Sweden)

1972 ILLUSTRATOR Ib Spang Ohlsson (Denmark)

1972 ILLUSTRATOR (HIGHLY COMMENDED) Felix Hoffmann (Switzerland); Petros Zambellis (Greece); Adolf Zabransky (USSR); Janosch, pseudonym; real name is Horst Eckert (German Federal Republic); Elizabeth Cleaver (Canada); Bjorn Berg (Sweden)

1974 AUTHOR Maria Gripe (Sweden)

1974 AUTHOR (HIGHLY COMMENDED) Cecil Bodker (Denmark); Rosemary Sutcliff (Great Britain); Colette Vivier (France)

1974 ILLUSTRATOR Farshid Mesghali (Iran)

1974 ILLUSTRATOR (HIGHLY COMMENDED) Helga Aichinger (Austria); Nicole Claveloux (France); Charles Keeping (Great Britain)

1976 AUTHOR Cecil Bodker (Denmark)

1976 AUTHOR (HIGHLY COMMENDED) Agnija Barto (USSR); E.B. White (United States)

1976 ILLUSTRATOR Tatjana Mawrina (USSR)

1976 ILLUSTRATOR (HIGHLY COMMENDED) Ludovit Fulla (USSR); Svend Otto S. (Denmark)

1978 AUTHOR Paula Fox (United States)

1978 AUTHOR (HIGHLY COMMENDED) Alan Garner (Great Britain)

1978 ILLUSTRATOR Svend Otto S. (Denmark)

1978 ILLUSTRATOR (HIGHLY COMMENDED) Leo Dillon (United States); Diane Dillon (United States)

1980 AUTHOR Bohumil Riha (USSR)

1980 AUTHOR (HIGHLY COMMENDED) Harry Kullman (Sweden); Lygia Bojunga Nunes (Brazil)

1980 ILLUSTRATOR Suekichi Akaba (Japan)

1980 ILLUSTRATOR (HIGHLY COMMENDED) Etienne Delessert (Switzerland); Tomi Ungerer (France)

1982 AUTHOR Lygia Bojunga Nunes (Brazil)

1982 ILLUSTRATOR Zbigniew Rychlicki (Poland)

1984 AUTHOR Christine Nostlinger

1984 ILLUSTRATOR Mitsumasa Anno (Japan)

1986 AUTHOR Patricia Wrightson (Australia)

1986 ILLUSTRATOR Robert Ingpen (Australia)

1988 AUTHOR Annie M.G. Schmidt (Netherlands)

1988 AUTHOR (HIGHLY COMMENDED) Claude Roy

1988 ILLUSTRATOR Dusan Kallay (Czechoslovakia)

1988 ILLUSTRATOR (HIGHLY COMMENDED) Yasuo Segawa (Japan)

1990 AUTHOR Tormod Haugen (Norway)

1990 ILLUSTRATOR Lisbeth Zwerger (Austria)

1992 AUTHOR Virginia Hamilton (United States)

1992 ILLUSTRATOR Kveta Pacovska (Czechoslovakia)

R. ROSS ANNETT AWARD
Writers Guild of Alberta
10523 100 Avenue
Edmonton, Alberta T5J OA8
Canada

Established in 1982, The R. Ross Annett Award recognizes excellence in children's literature. R. Ross Annett is best known for the publication of seventy-two stories in the Babe and Little Joe series. In order to qualify for this award sponsored by the Writers Guild of Australia, the authors must have been residents of Alberta for twelve of the eighteen months prior to the award date.

Books published in the year preceding the award may be submitted by publishers or authors. A panel of judges read all submissions and choose a winning author to receive the $500 cash award and a leather bound copy of their winning book.

1983 *Hunter in the Dark* by Monica Hughes, not illustrated; Clark Irwin, 1982.

1984 *Space Trap* by Monica Hughes, not illustrated; Groundwood, 1983.

1985   *In the City of the King* by William Pasnak, not illustrated; Douglas & McIntyre, 1984.

1986   *Julie* by Cora Taylor, not illustrated; Western Producer Prairie Books, 1985.

1987   *Blaine's Way* by Monica Hughes, not illustrated; Clark Irwin, 1986.

1988   *Nobody Said It Would Be Easy* by Marilyn Halvorson, not illustrated; Clark Irwin, 1987.

1989   *Under the Eagle's Claw* by William Pasnak, not illustrated; Douglas & McIntyre, 1988.

1990   *Dog Runner* by Don Meredith, not illustrated; Western Producer Prairie Books, 1989.

1991   *Dawnrider* by Jan Hudson, not illustrated; HarperCollins, 1990.

1992   *A Cat of Artimus Pride* by Hazel Hutchins, illustrated by Ruth Ohi; Annick Press, 1991.

1993   *The Crystal Drop* by Monica Hughes, not illustrated; Methuen, 1992; Simon & Schuster, 1993.

ARIZONA YOUNG READERS AWARD

Children's Services Roundtable of the
Arizona State Library Association
13832 N. 32nd St. Suite D1
Phoenix, AZ 85032

Sponsored by the Children's Services Roundtable of the Arizona State Library Association and the Arizona Department of Education, the Arizona Young Readers Award was first presented in 1977. The purpose is to encourage Arizona young readers to become better acquainted with recently published quality books and to honor favorite books and authors of the readers. The common concern of librarians, parents, administrators and teachers to assure interaction between readers and books is a major ingredient in the concept of allowing them to vote for their favorite book and identify it for others to enjoy.

The award is given biennially to Picture Books and Chapter Books (starting in 1993), with a category of Young Adult Books to be added in 1995. A list of ten nominated books for each category is based on recommendations made by teachers and young readers in Arizona. Readers must have been exposed to at least five of the nominated books in order to vote.

Plaques are presented to the winning authors at the Arizona State Library Association annual conference.

1977   *Tales of a Fourth Grade Nothing* by Judy Blume, illustrated by Roy Doty; Dutton, 1972.

1979   *How to Eat Fried Worms* by Thomas Rockwell, illustrated by Emily McCully; Watts, 1973.

1981   *Miss Nelson Is Missing!* by Harry Allard, illustrated by James Marshall; Houghton Mifflin, 1977.

1983   *Superfudge* by Judy Blume, not illustrated; Dutton, 1980.

1985   *The Stupids Die* by Harry Allard, illustrated by James Marshall; Houghton Mifflin, 1981.

1987   *Scary Stories to Tell in the Dark* by Alvin Schwartz, illustrated by Stephen Gammell; Lippincott, 1981.

1989   *The Indian in the Cupboard* by Lynne Reid Banks, illustrated by Brock Cole; Doubleday, 1980.

1991   *Where's Waldo?* written and illustrated by Martin Handford; Little Brown, 1987.

1993   **PICTURE BOOK** *The Very Quiet Cricket* written and illustrated by Eric Carle; Philomel, 1990.

1993   **CHAPTER BOOK** *Wayside School Is Falling Down* by Louis Sachar, illustrated by Joel Schick; Lothrop, Lee & Shepard, 1989.

ART BOOKS FOR CHILDREN CITATIONS
discontinued

This program, initiated by Duncan F. Cameron and Kenneth F. Duchac in 1973, was cosponsored by the Brooklyn Museum and the Brooklyn Public Library. The purpose of the citation was to highlight outstanding verbal and visual achievement in children's books. A prescreening committee was responsible for examining every new picture book and nonfiction title in picture-book format designed for pre-kindergarten through the second grade. Any author or illustrator whose work was published in the U.S. was eligible. Titles could be placed on the winners list more than once. After three years on the list, such titles were permanently added. A committee consisting of curators and art educators of the museum staff and children's services specialists of the library staff were responsible for the final selection. Selected authors and illustrators were presented with citations at an afternoon reception.

The committee's selections were based on the following guidelines and criteria:

1. The work should be innovative and creative.

2. The subject matter must be appropriate for the age group.

3. The illustrations must be appropriate for the text.

4. The appeal to young readers must be evident.

5. The book should stimulate the whole child.

6. The book should help children to see in new ways, expand their growing awareness and aid them in approaching the world with new kinds of understanding.

The Art Books for Children Citations were discontinued with the announcement of the 1979 list.

1973   *Annie and the Old One* by Miska Miles, illustrated by Peter Parnall; Atlantic-Little, 1971.

And Miss Carter Wore Pink: Scenes from an Edwardian Childhood written and illustrated by Helen Bradley; Holt, 1971, 1972.

The Art and Industry of Sandcastles written and illustrated by Jan Adkins; Walker, 1971.

A Boy, a Dog and a Frog written and illustrated by Mercer Mayer; Dial, 1967.

Brian Wildsmith's 1,2,3s written and illustrated by Brian Wildsmith; Watts, 1965.

Cats and Bats and Things with Wings by Conrad Aiken, illustrated by Milton Glaser; Atheneum, 1965.

Changes, Changes written and illustrated by Pat Hutchins; Macmillan, 1971.

Father Fox's Pennyrhymes by Clyde Watson, illustrated by Wendy Watson; Crowell, 1971.

Fletcher and Zenobia by Victoria Chess and Edward Gorey, illustrated by Victoria Chess; Hawthorne, 1967.

Frog and Toad Together written and illustrated by Arnold Lobel; Harper, 1972.

Harriet and the Promised Land written and illustrated by Jacob Lawrence; Windmill/Simon & Schuster, 1968.

How the Mouse Was Hit on the Head by a Stone and so Discovered the World written and illustrated by Etienne Delessert; Doubleday, 1971.

If all the Seas Were One Sea written and illustrated by Janina Domanska; Macmillan, 1971.

In the Night Kitchen written and illustrated by Maurice Sendak; Harper, 1970.

Leo, the Late Bloomer by Robert Kraus, illustrated by Jose Aruego; Windmill, 1973.

Little Blue and Little Yellow written and illustrated by Leo Lionni; Obolensky, 1959.

Look Again! written and illustrated by Tana Hoban; Macmillan, 1971.

Matilda Who Told Lies and Was Burned to Death by Hilaire Belloc, illustrated by Steven Kellogg; Dial, 1970.

Moja Means One: Swahili Counting Book by Muriel Feelings, illustrated by Tom Feelings; Dial, 1971.

Moon Man written and illustrated by Tomi Ungerer; Harper, 1967.

Nothing Ever Happens on My Block written and illustrated by Ellen Raskin; Atheneum, 1966.

One Wide River to Cross by Barbara Emberley, illustrated by Ed Emberley; Prentice Hall, 1966.

Ounce, Dice, Trice by Alastair Reid, illustrated by Ben Shahn; Little Brown, 1958.

Santiago by Pura Belpre, illustrated by Symeon Shimin; Warne, 1969.

The Snowy Day written and illustrated by Ezra Jack Keats; Viking, 1962.

Stevie written and illustrated by John Steptoe; Harper, 1969.

Swimmy written and illustrated by Leo Lionni; Pantheon, 1963.

The Three Robbers written and illustrated by Tomi Ungerer; Atheneum, 1962.

The Tomten by Astrid Lindgren, illustrated by Harald Wiberg; Coward, 1961.

Topsy Turvies: Pictures to Stretch the Imagination written and illustrated by Mitsumasa Anno; Walker/Weatherhill, 1970.

Upside Downers, Downside Uppers: More Pictures to Stretch the Imagination written and illustrated by Mitsumasa Anno; Weatherhill, 1971.

The Very Hungry Caterpillar written and illustrated by Eric Carle; Collins, 1970.

The Wedding Procession of the Rag Doll and the Broom Handle and Who Was in It by Carl Sandburg, illustrated by Harriet Pincus; Harcourt, 1967.

Where the Wild Things Are written and illustrated by Maurice Sendak; Harper, 1963.

Yellow, Yellow by Frank Asch, illustrated by Mark Alan Stamaty; McGraw Hill, 1971.

1974 *The Art and Industry of Sandcastles* written and illustrated by Jan Adkins; Walker, 1971.

Bang, Bang, You're Dead by Sandra Scoppettone and Louise Fitzhugh, illustrated by Louise Fitzhugh; Harper, 1969.

Elvira Everything written and illustrated by Frank Asch; Harper, 1970.

The Emperor's New Clothes by Hans Christian Andersen, adapted by Jean Van Leeuwen, illustrated by Jack Delano and Irene Delano; Random House, 1971.

The Hare and the Tortoise and the Tortoise and the Hare by William Pene du Bois and Lee Po, illustrated by William Pene du Bois; Doubleday, 1972.

Harriet and the Promised Land written and illustrated by Jacob Lawrence; Windmill/Simon & Schuster, 1968.

Hosie's Alphabet by Hosea Baskin, Tobias Baskin, and Lisa Baskin, illustrated by Leonard Baskin; Viking, 1972.

How the Mouse Was Hit on the Head by a Stone and so Discovered the World written and illustrated by Etienne Delessert; Doubleday, 1971.

In the Night Kitchen written and illustrated by Maurice Sendak; Harper, 1970.

Little Blue and Little Yellow written and illustrated by Leo Lionni; Obolensky, 1959.

Look Again! written and illustrated by Tana Hoban; Macmillan, 1971.

The Magic Tree written and illustrated by Gerald McDermott; Holt, 1973.

Milton the Early Riser by Robert Kraus, illustrated by Jose Aruego and Ariane Aruego; Windmill, 1972.

Moja Means One: Swahili Counting Book by Muriel Feelings, illustrated by Tom Feelings; Dial, 1971.

Na-ni written and illustrated by Alexis De Veaux; Harper, 1973.

Red Riding Hood, Retold in Verse for Boys and Girls to Read Themselves by Beatrice Schenck de Regniers, illustrated by Edward Gorey; Atheneum, 1972.

Where the Wild Things Are written and illustrated by Maurice Sendak; Harper, 1963.

Who, Said Sue, Said Whoo? written and illustrated by Ellen Raskin; Atheneum, 1973.

Yellow, Yellow by Frank Asch, illustrated by Mark Alan Stamaty; McGraw Hill, 1971.

1975 *Arrow to the Sun* written and illustrated by Gerald McDermott; Viking, 1974.

The Art and Industry of Sandcastles written and illustrated by Jan Adkins; Walker, 1971.

The Beast of Monsieur Racine written and illustrated by Tomi Ungerer; Farrar, 1971.

Benjamin and Tulip written and illustrated by Rosemary Wells; Dial, 1973.

Charlie Needs a Cloak written and illustrated by Tomie de Paola; Prentice Hall, 1974, c1973.

Father Christmas written and illustrated by Raymond Briggs; Hamilton, 1973; Coward, 1973.

Harriet and the Promised Land written and illustrated by Jacob Lawrence; Windmill/Simon & Schuster, 1968.

Hosie's Alphabet by Hosea Baskin, Tobias Baskin, and Lisa Baskin, illustrated by Leonard Baskin; Viking, 1972.

How the Mouse Was Hit on the Head by a Stone and so Discovered the World written and illustrated by Etienne Delessert; Doubleday, 1971.

In the Night Kitchen written and illustrated by Maurice Sendak; Harper, 1970.

Little Blue and Little Yellow written and illustrated by Leo Lionni; Obolensky, 1959.

Look Again! written and illustrated by Tana Hoban; Macmillan, 1971.

MA NDA LA by Arnold Adoff, illustrated by Emily McCully; Harper, 1971.

Milton the Early Riser by Robert Kraus, illustrated by Jose Aruego and Ariane Aruego; Windmill, 1972.

Moja Means One: Swahili Counting Book by Muriel Feelings, illustrated by Tom Feelings; Dial, 1971.

My Little Hen written and illustrated by Martin Provensen and Alice Provensen; Random House, 1973.

Rhoda's Restaurant written and illustrated by Robert Tallon; Bobbs Merrill, 1973.

The Three Jovial Huntsmen: A Mother Goose Rhyme adapted and illustrated by Susan Jeffers; Bradbury, 1973.

What Do You Do with a Kangaroo? written and illustrated by Mercer Mayer; Scholastic/Four Winds, 1973.

Where the Wild Things Are written and illustrated by Maurice Sendak; Harper, 1963.

Who Needs Donuts? written and illustrated by Mark Alan Stamaty; Dial, 1973.

Yellow, Yellow by Frank Asch, illustrated by Mark Alan Stamaty; McGraw Hill, 1971.

1976 *Anno's Alphabet* written and illustrated by Mitsumasa Anno; Crowell, 1975.

Arrow to the Sun written and illustrated by Gerald McDermott; Viking, 1974.

Benjamin and Tulip written and illustrated by Rosemary Wells; Dial, 1973.

Dawn written and illustrated by Uri Shulevitz; Farrar, 1974.

Everybody Needs a Rock by Byrd Baylor, illustrated by Peter Parnall; Scribner, 1974.

Frog Goes to Dinner written and illustrated by Mercer Mayer; Dial, 1974.

Hosie's Alphabet by Hosea Baskin, Tobias Baskin, and Lisa Baskin, illustrated by Leonard Baskin; Viking, 1972.

Jambo Means Hello: Swahili Alphabet Book by Muriel Feelings, illustrated by Tom Feelings; Dial, 1974.

Milton the Early Riser by Robert Kraus, illustrated by Jose Aruego and Ariane Aruego; Windmill, 1972.

Suho and the White Horse: A Legend of Mongolia by Yuzo Otsuka, translated by Yasuko Hirawa, illustrated by Suekichi Akaba; Bobbs Merrill, 1969.

The Three Jovial Huntsmen: A Mother Goose Rhyme adapted and illustrated by Susan Jeffers; Bradbury, 1973.

1977 *Anno's Alphabet* written and illustrated by Mitsumasa Anno; Crowell, 1975.

Arrow to the Sun written and illustrated by Gerald McDermott; Viking, 1974.

Benjamin and Tulip written and illustrated by Rosemary Wells; Dial, 1973.

Dawn written and illustrated by Uri Shulevitz; Farrar, 1974.

The Desert Is Theirs by Byrd Baylor, illustrated by Peter Parnall; Scribner, 1975.

Frog Goes to Dinner written and illustrated by Mercer Mayer; Dial, 1974.

Great Wolf and the Good Woodsman by Helen Hoover, illustrated by Charles Mikolaycak; Parents, 1967.

Mommy, Buy Me a China Doll by Harve Zemach, illustrated by Margot Zemach; Farrar, 1966.

Piero Ventura's Book of Cities written and illustrated by Piero Ventura; Random House, 1975.

Strega Nona written and illustrated by Tomie de Paola; Prentice Hall, 1975.

Suho and the White Horse: A Legend of Mongolia by Yuzo Otsuka, translated by Yasuko Hirawa, illustrated by Suekichi Akaba; Bobbs Merrill, 1969.

The Three Jovial Huntsmen: A Mother Goose Rhyme adapted and illustrated by Susan Jeffers; Bradbury, 1973.

The Very Hungry Caterpillar written and illustrated by Eric Carle; Collins, 1970.

Why Mosquitos Buzz in People's Ears: A West African Tale by Verna Aardema, illustrated by Leo Dillon and Diane Dillon; Dial, 1975.

1978 *The Amazing Bone* written and illustrated by William Steig; Farrar, 1976.

Anno's Alphabet: An Adventure in Imagination written and illustrated by Mitsumasa Anno; Crowell, 1975.

Dawn written and illustrated by Uri Shulevitz; Farrar, 1974.

Deep in the Forest written and illustrated by Brinton Turkle; Dutton, 1976.

The Desert Is Theirs by Byrd Baylor, illustrated by Peter Parnall; Scribner, 1975.

Friendly Wolf written and illustrated by Paul Goble and Dorothy Goble; Dutton, 1974.

Frog Goes to Dinner written and illustrated by Mercer Mayer; Dial, 1974.

Great Wolf and the Good Woodsman by Helen Hoover, illustrated by Charles Mikolaycak; Parents, 1967.

Hush Little Baby written and illustrated by Margot Zemach; Dutton, 1976.

Merry Ever After: The Story of Two Medieval Weddings written and illustrated by Joe Lasker; Viking, 1976.

The Mother Goose Book written and illustrated by Alice Provensen and Martin Provensen; Random House, 1976.

Piero Ventura's Book of Cities written and illustrated by Piero Ventura; Random House, 1975.

Send Wendell by Genevieve Gray, illustrated by Symeon Shimin; McGraw, 1974.

Simple Pictures Are Best by Nancy Willard, illustrated by Tomie de Paola; Harcourt, 1977.

Strega Nona written and illustrated by Tomie de Paola; Prentice Hall, 1975.

Suho and the White Horse: A Legend of Mongolia by Yuzo Otsuka, translated by Yasuko Hirawa, illustrated by Suekichi Akaba; Bobbs Merrill, 1969.

The Very Hungry Caterpillar written and illustrated by Eric Carle; Collins, 1970.

Why Mosquitos Buzz in People's Ears: A West African Tale by Verna Aardema, illustrated by Leo Dillon and Diane Dillon; Dial, 1975.

1979 *The Amazing Bone* written and illustrated by William Steig; Farrar, 1976.

Anno's Journey written and illustrated by Mitsumasa Anno; Collins-World, 1978.

The Desert Is Theirs by Byrd Baylor, illustrated by Peter Parnall; Scribner, 1975.

Freight Train written and illustrated by Donald Crews; Greenwillow, 1978.

The Girl Who Loved Wild Horses written and illustrated by Paul Goble; Bradbury Press, 1978.

Great Wolf and the Good Woodsman by Helen Hoover, illustrated by Charles Mikolaycak; Parents, 1967.

Hush, Little Baby written and illustrated by Margot Zemach; Dutton, 1976.

Is It Red? Is It Yellow? Is It Blue? written and illustrated by Tana Hoban; Greenwillow, 1978.

Merry Ever After: The Story of Two Medieval Weddings written and illustrated by Joe Lasker; Viking, 1976.

The Mother Goose Book written and illustrated by Alice Provensen and Martin Provensen; Random House, 1976.

Noah's Ark written and illustrated by Peter Spier; Doubleday, 1977.

A Peaceable Kingdom: The Shaker Abecedarius illustrated by Alice Provensen and Martin Provensen; Viking, 1978.

Piero Ventura's Book of Cities written and illustrated by Piero Ventura; Random House, 1975.

The Snowman written and illustrated by Raymond Briggs; Random House, 1978.

Strega Nona written and illustrated by Tomie de Paola; Prentice Hall, 1975.

The Very Hungry Caterpillar written and illustrated by Eric Carle; Collins, 1970.

ARTS COUNCIL OF GREAT BRITAIN NATIONAL BOOK AWARD
discontinued

This award, sponsored by the Arts Council of Great Britain, was first presented in 1979. Awards were presented in several cat-

egories, including children's literature. In the second and final year of the competition, the children's category was not included.

1979 *Animals of Farthing Wood: Escape from Danger* by Colin Dann, illustrated by Jacqueline Tettmar; Heinemann, 1979.

ASHTON SCHOLASTIC AWARD
Australian Book Publishers Association
161 Clarence St.
Sydney, NSW 2000
Australia

Sponsored by the Australian Book Publishers Association, the Ashton Scholastic Award is presented annually for the best designed illustrated children's book.

1987 *Kujuro and the Bears* adapted by Helen Smith, illustrated by Junko Morimoto; Collins, 1986.

1988 *Derek and the Dinosaur* by Mary Blackwood, illustrated by Kerry Argent; Omnibus, 1987.

1989 *Rosie Sips Spiders* written and illustrated by Alison Lester; Oxford, 1988; Houghton Mifflin, 1989.

1990 *The Story of the Falling Star* by Elsie Jones, illustrated by Doug Jones and Karin Donaldson; Aboriginal Studies Press, 1989.

1991 *Magic Beach* written and illustrated by Alison Lester; Allen & Unwin, 1990; Joy Street Books, 1992.

1993 *Spooner or Later* by Paul Jennings, Ted Greenwood and Terry Denton; Viking, 1992.

ASSOCIATION OF JEWISH LIBRARIES SYDNEY TAYLOR BOOK AWARD
see SYDNEY TAYLOR BOOK AWARD

ASSOCIATION OF JEWISH LIBRARIES SYDNEY TAYLOR BODY OF WORK AWARD
see SYDNEY TAYLOR BODY OF WORK AWARD

CLAUDE AUBRY AWARD
IBBY Canada
Virginia K. Davis
National Book service
3269 American Drive
Mississauga, Ontario L4V 1V4
Canada

This biennial award was first given in 1981. Sponsored by the Canadian section of the International Board on Books for Young People (IBBY), the Claude Aubry Award is presented for a distinguished contribution to Canadian children's literature. The award is named for the children's author and former director of the Ottawa Public Library.

Nominations of authors, publishers, teachers, illustrators, librarians, and editors are submitted to the executive committee of the Canadian Section of IBBY. The award is accompanied by a monetary prize.

1981 Irma McDonough Milnes

1983 Sheila Egoff

1985 Paule Daveluy

1987 May Cutler

1989 Irene Aubry

1991 Judy Sarick

AURIANNE AWARD

discontinued

An annual award that was first given in 1958 to the author of the best book about animals, fiction or nonfiction, written for eight to fourteen-year-old children. The criteria was the book's ability to instill a humane attitude toward animals. A bequest from Augustine Aurianne, a New Orleans school librarian, made possible this award, which was managed by the American Library Association. The legacy was to honor the memory of her father, Pierre Aurianne, and that of her sister, Adele. The Aurianne Award, consisting of a donation and a diploma designed by Valenti Angelo, was conferred by a jury of school librarians from the American Library Association. The last award was presented in 1966, when funds provided for by the legacy were depleted.

1958 *Dipper of Copper Creek* by John Lothar George and Jean Craighead George, illustrated by Jean Craighead George; Dutton, 1956.

1959 No Award

1960 *Along Came a Dog* by Meindert DeJong, illustrated by Maurice Sendak; Harper, 1958.

1961 *An Edge of the Forest* by Agnes Smith, illustrated by Roberta Moynihan; Viking, 1959.

1962 *Old Ramon* by Jack Schaefer, illustrated by Harold West; Houghton, 1960.

1963 *The Incredible Journey: A Tale of Three Animals* by Shelia Every Burnford, illustrated by Carl Burger; Little Brown, 1961.

1964 *A Black Bear's Story* by Emil Ernest Liers, illustrated by Ray Sherin; Viking, 1962.

1965 *Rascal: A Memoir of a Better Era* by Sterling North, illustrated by John Schoenherr; Dutton, 1963.

1966 *Big Blue Island* by Wilson Gage, illustrated by Glen Rounds; World, 1964.

AUSTRALIAN CHRISTIAN BOOK OF THE YEAR CHILDREN'S AWARD

Joan M. Shilton
Australian Christian Literature Society
1 Mayfield St.
Greensborough, Victoria 3008
Australia

This annual award was established in 1981 by the Australian Christian Literature Society to encourage Australian writers and publishers. Awards are made for the Best Book, Best Children's Book and Best Design. Fiction, nonfiction, poetry, theological and picture books are eligible, as long as they are authored by an Australian, and published by an Australian publisher.

Books are judged on their contribution to meeting a need in Christian writing for the Australian situation and in the Australian market. Originality, design, layout, cover, text and illustrations are all taken into consideration.

Publishers of the winning book receive a certificate, while the author receives a cash award, as well as a certificate.

1985 *Me and Jeshua* by Eleanor Spence, illustrated by Shane Conroy; Dove Communications, 1985, c1984.

1986 *The Miracle Tree* by Christobel Mattingly, illustrated by Marianne Yamaguchi; Hodder & Stoughton, 1985; Harcourt, Brace, Jovanovich, 1985.

1987 *Stories for Children of the Kingdom*, illustrated; Collins Dove, 1987.

1988 *The Sacramental Programme and Welcome to You.*

1989 *The Little Monster* series by Peter Thamm, illustrated by Robert Roennfeldt; Lutheran Publishing House, 1988.

1990 *Waddayaknow (Workbook, 1,2, Teacher's Manual)* edited by Denise Lake.

1991 *Yonderbeyond* written and illustrated by Thyrza Davey; Hodder & Stoughton, 1990.

1992 **(Joint Winners)** *Inigo: The Adventures of a Saint* by Michael Hansen, illustrated by Tibor David; Lovell, 1991.

Tomb Travellers: Beyond the Gateways and Guardians of Egypt's Underworld by Roy Pond, not illustrated; Albatross Books, 1991.

AUSTRALIAN MULTICULTURAL CHILDREN'S LITERATURE AWARDS

Office of Multicultural Affairs
Dept. of the Prime Minister and Cabinet
3-5 National Circuit
Barton ACT 2600
Australia

Established in 1991 by the Office of Multicultural Affairs in the Department of the Prime Minister and Cabinet to encourage themes of cultural diversity and to promote social harmony in books for Australian children. Entries may take the form of prose, poetry or drama; be written substantially in English, and must have a multicultural theme which focuses on aspects and values of a multicultural society; for example, cultural diversity, community relations and social harmony, or in social justice.

Authors and illustrators must be Australian citizens or residents for two years, and the material must have been published during the preceding calendar year. Books already entered for the Children's Book Council of Australia Awards are judged for the multicultural award.

Prizes of $5000 for each category are awarded during Children's Book Week in late July/early August.

1991 **PICTURE BOOK** *The Rainbow Serpent* by Elaine Sharpe, illustrated by Jennifer Inkamala; Yipirinya School Council, 1990.

1991 **PICTURE BOOK (HIGHLY COMMENDED)** *Scallywag* written and illustrated by Jeannette Rowe; Ashton Scholastic, 1990.

1992 **SENIOR FICTION** *The China Coin* by Allan Baillie, not illustrated; Viking, 1991; Blackie, 1991.

1992 **JUNIOR FICTION** *Do Not Go Around the Edges: Poems* by Daisy Utemorrah, illustrated by Pat Torres; Magabala Books, 1991.

1992 **PICTURE BOOK** *Big Dog* by Libby Gleeson, illustrated by Armin Greder; Ashton Scholastic, 1991.

1993 **SENIOR FICTION** *Looking for Alibrandi* by Melina Marchetta, not illustrated; Puffin, 1992.

1993 **JUNIOR FICTION** *The Fat and Juicy Place* by Diana Kidd, illustrated by Bronwyn Bancroft; Angus & Robertson, 1992.

1993 PICTURE BOOK *Mr. Plunkett's Pool* by Gillian Rubinstein, illustrated by Terry Denton; Random House, 1992.

1993 SPECIAL AWARD *I'm an Australian: A Class Journal* by Dianne Bates.

AUTHOR'S AWARD/JUVENILE/YOUNG ADULT

Alabama Library Association
400 S. Union St.
Suite 255
Montgomery, AL 36104

Sponsored by the Alabama Library Association, the Author's Award was approved in 1978, although the first award was not granted until 1980. Nominations are received from committee members. The selection committee strives to select those books with the greatest literary merit that have been written by an Alabamian in residence for more than five years. A plaque is presented to the winner in each of three areas (Fiction, Nonfiction, and Juvenile/Young Adult). The winners are honored at the annual convention of the Alabama Library Association. Listed below are the winners of the Juvenile/Young Adult category.

1980 *Tiny Bat and the Ball Game* by Margaret Searcy, illustrated by Lu Celia Wise; Portals Press, 1978.

1981 No Award

1982 *LeRoy and the Old Man* by William E. Butterworth, not illustrated; Four Winds, 1980.

1983 *The Brats and Mr. Jack* by Hilary Milton, not illustrated; Beaufort Books, 1980.

1984 *As the Waltz Was Ending* by Emma M. Butterworth, not illustrated; Four Winds, 1982.

1985 No Award

1986 *Marmalade's Christmas Present* written and illustrated by Cindy Wheeler; Knopf, 1984.

1987 No Award

1988 *Count Your Way Around the World* (series) by James Haskins, illustrated by various illustrators; Carolrhoda, 1987- 1992.

1989 *Summer Stories* by Nola Thacker, illustrated by William Low; Lippincott, 1988.

1990 *The Jolly Mon* by Jimmy Buffett and Savannah Jane Buffett, illustrated by Lambert Davis; Harcourt, Brace, Jovanovich, 1988.

1991 *Rainbow Crow: A Lenape Tale* by Nancy Van Laan, illustrated by Beatriz Vidal; Knopf, 1989.

1992 No Award

AVON/FLARE YOUNG ADULT NOVEL COMPETITION

discontinued

The Avon Flare Competition for young adults was begun in 1983. The editors were looking for young writers between the ages of thirteen and eighteen who displayed narrative talent and writing ability. Manuscripts of approximately 125 to 200 pages of a fiction story about and for teenagers were considered. The winning manuscript was published by Avon Flare with an advance of $2500. The award has been discontinued.

1983 *Dragon Fall* by Lee J. Hindle, not illustrated; Avon Flare, 1984.

1985 *Buck* by Tamela Larimer, not illustrated; Avon Flare, 1986.

1987 *At the Edge* by Michael Behrens, not illustrated; Avon, 1988.

1989 *Flute Song Magic* by Andrea Shettle, not illustrated; Avon, 1990.

1991 *Face-off* by Stacy Drumtra, not illustrated; Avon, 1992.

B

MILDRED L. BATCHELDER AWARD

Association for Library Services to Children
American Library Association
50 East Huron St
Chicago, IL 60611

This award was established by the Children's Services Division (now Association for Library Services to Children) of the American Library Association in honor of Mildred L. Batchelder, an outstanding influence on children's librarianship and literature for over thirty years. The purpose of this award is to encourage international exchange of quality children's books by recognizing United States publishers of such books in translation. The award is presented annually to an American publisher for the most outstanding English translation of a children's book originally published in a foreign language in a foreign country during the preceding year. Prior to 1979, there was a lapse of two years between the original publication date and the award date.

The winning publisher receives a citation, which is presented on April 2, International Children's Book Day. The winner of the award is announced at the midwinter meeting of ALA. The award is administered and funded by the Association for Library Services to Children section of the ALA.

According to the definitions set forth by the administrative body, children's book means a U.S. trade publication for which children up to and including age fourteen are a potential audience. The U.S. book must be neither a condensation, excerpt, nor abridgement of the original. The criteria used to judge the most outstanding translation are as follows: (1) Primary attention is to be focused on the text. If a picture book is being considered, the text must substantially contribute to the quality of the book. (2) The translation should be true to the substance (e.g., plot, characterization, setting) and flavor of the original work and should retain the viewpoint of the author. (3) Reflections of the style of the author and of the original language in the translation are considered assets, unless that result in misunderstandings or awkwardness. (4) The book should not be Americanized. The reader should still be able to tell that the book was written in another country. (5) The elements that should be considered in evaluating the textual qualities of the translation are: interpretation of the theme or content; presentation of information including accuracy, clarity and organization; development of plot; delineation of characters; and appropriateness of style. (6) In all cases, committee members must consider the book's manner of presentation and its potential appeal to children. (7) Aspects of the overall design of the book should be considered when they significantly enhance or detract from the text. (8) In some children's books, one of the primary modes of communication is illustration. Special consideration should be given to the importance of retaining in the U.S. edition the original illustrator's work. (From guidelines set forth by ALSC, ALA)

1968 *The Little Man* by Erich Kastner, translated by James Kirkup, illustrated by Rick Schreiter; Knopf, 1966.

1969 *Don't Take Teddy* by Babbis Friis-Baastad, translated by Lise Somme McKinnon; Scribner, 1967.

1970 *Wildcat under Glass* by Alki Zei, translated by Edward Fenton, not illustrated; Holt, 1968.

1971 *In the land of Ur: The Discovery of Ancient Mesopotamia* by Hans Baumann, translated by Stella Humphries, illustrated by Hans Peter Renner; Pantheon, 1969; Oxford, 1969.

1972 *Friedrich* by Hans Peter Richter, translated by Edite Kroll, not illustrated; Holt, 1970.

1973 *Pulga* by Siny Rose Van Iterson, translated by Alexander Gode and Alison Gode, illustrated with maps; Morrow, 1971.

1974 *Petros' War* by Alki Zei, translated by Edward Fenton, not illustrated; Dutton, 1972.

1975 *An Old Tale Carved Out of Stone* by Aleksandr M. Linevski, translated by Maria Polushkin, not illustrated; Crown, 1973.

1976 *The Cat and Mouse Who Shared a House* written and illustrated by Ruth Hurlimann, translated by Anthea Bell; Walck, 1974.

1977 *The Leopard* by Cecil Bodker, illustrated by Gunnar Poulsen; Atheneum, 1975.

1978 No Award

1979 *Konrad* by Christine Nostlinger, translated by Anthea Bell, illustrated by Carol Nicklaus; Watts, 1977.

Rabbit Island by Jorg Steiner, translated by Ann Conrad Lammers, illustrated by Jorg Muller; Harcourt, 1978.

1980 *The Sound of Dragon's Feet* by Alki Zei, translated by Edward Fenton, not illustrated; Dutton, 1979.

1981 *The Winter When Time Was Frozen* by Els Pelgrom, translated by Raphael Rudnik and Maryka Rudnik, not illustrated; Morrow, 1980.

1982 *The Battle Horse* by Harry Kullman, translated by George Blecher and Lone Thygesen-Blecher, not illustrated; Bradbury, 1981.

1983 *Hiroshima no Pika* written and illustrated by Toshi Maruki; Lothrop, Lee & Shepard, 1982.

1984 *Ronia, the Robber's Daughter* by Astrid Lindgren, translated by Patricia Crampton, not illustrated; Viking, 1983.

1985 *The Island on Bird Street* by Uri Orlev, translated by Hillel Halkin, not illustrated; Houghton Mifflin, 1984.

1986 *Rose Blanche* by Christophe Gallaz and Roberto Innocenti, translated by Martha Coventry and Richard Graglia, illustrated by Roberto Innocenti; Creative Education, 1985.

1987 *No Hero for the Kaiser* by Rudolf Frank, translated by Patricia Crampton, illustrated by Klaus Steffans; Lothrop, Lee & Shepard, 1986.

1988 *If You Didn't Have Me* by Ulf Nilsson, illustrated by Eva Eriksson; McElderry, 1987.

1989 *Crutches* by Peter Hartling, not illustrated; Lothrop, Lee & Shepard, 1988.

1990 *Buster's World* by Bjarne Reuter, illustrated by Paul O. Zelinsky; Dutton, 1989.

1991 *A Hand Full of Stars* by Rafik Schami, not illustrated; Dutton, 1990.

1991 **HONOR** *Two Shorts and One Long* by Nina Ring Aamundsen, not illustrated; Houghton Mifflin, 1990.

1992 *The Man From the Other Side* by Uri Orlev, not illustrated; Houghton Mifflin, 1991.

1993 No Award

L. FRANK BAUM MEMORIAL AWARD

The International Wizard of Oz Club
Fred M. Meyer, Secretary
220 N. 11th St.
Escanaba, MI 49829

Founded in 1961 by Justin Schiller, this annual award is presented by the International Wizard of Oz Club. Any person who has made a significant contribution to the work and purpose of the club is eligible. These contributions generally involve regional or national Oz club convention work, creative or editorial work for club publications, assistance with the technical work of the club, or significant scholarship related to Oz and its creators.

Approximately half of the awards have been granted for various kinds of writing, while others have been presented for illustrations, charting the land of Oz on maps, research, and convention work. Nominations are made by past recipients who then vote to determine a winner. A plaque is presented to the winner at the annual convention.

1961 Dick Martin

1962 Russell P. MacFall

1963 Harry Neal Baum

1964 Justin G. Schiller

1965 Douglas G. Greene, David L. Greene

1966 Edna Baum, Elizabeth Baum

1967 James E. Haff

1968 Ruth Plumly Thompson

1969 Ray Powell

1970 John Fricke

1971 Martin Gardner

1972 Matilda J. Gage

1973 Peter E. Hanff

1974 C. Warren Hollister

1975 Bill Eubank

1976 Daniel P. Mannix IV

1977 Barbara S. Koelle

1978 Fred M. Meyer

1979 Jerry V. Tobias

1980 Irene Fisher

1981 John Van Camp

1982 Aljean Harmetz

1983 Eloise Jarvis McGraw and Lauren Lynn McGraw Wagner for authoring Merry Go Round in Oz designed and illustrated by Dick Martin; Reilly & Lee, 1963; and The Forbidden Fountain of Oz illustrated by Dick Martin; International Wizard of Oz Club, 1980.

1984 Ozma Baum Mantele, Dr. Robert A. Baum

1985 Edward Wagenknecht

1986 Jay Delkin

1987 Brenda Baum Turner

1988 Robin Olderman

1989 Marc Lewis

1990 Jean Brockway

1991 Frederick E. Otto

1992 Rob Roy MacVeigh

BAY AREA BOOK REVIEWERS ASSOCIATION AWARD

Bay Area Book Reviewers Association
Jon Sharp
11A Commercial Blvd.
Novato, CA 94949

The Bay Area Book Reviewers Association was founded in 1981 and the first awards were given in 1982 for fiction and nonfiction published in 1981. The first children's literature award was given in 1985 for books published in 1984. Given annually to recognize achievements in children's literature, this award is available to Northern California authors only. A $100 honorarium and a citation are presented at an awards ceremony held in March or April of each year.

1985 *The Fat Girl* by Marilyn Sachs, not illustrated; Dutton, 1984.

1986 *The Happiest Ending* by Yoshiko Uchida, not illustrated; Atheneum, 1985.

1987 *Fish Friday* by Gayle Pearson, not illustrated; Atheneum, 1986.

1988 *Fran Ellen's House* by Marilyn Sachs, not illustrated; Dutton, 1987.

1989 *A Girl From Yamhill: A Memoir* by Beverly Cleary, illustrated with photos; Morrow, 1988.

1990 *Berchick* by Esther Silverstein Blanc, illustrated by Tennessee Dixon; Volcano Press, 1989.

1991 *Stargone* John by Ellen Kindt McKenzie, illustrated by William Low; Henry Holt, 1990.

1992 *Tree of Cranes* written and illustrated by Allen Say; Houghton Mifflin, 1991.

JOHN AND PATRICIA BEATTY AWARD

Mary Sue Ferrell, Executive Director
California Library Association
717 K Street
Suite 300
Sacramento, CA 95814

Sponsored by the California Library Association, the John and Patricia Beatty award was established in 1987 to encourage the writing of quality children's books highlighting California, its culture, heritage and/or future. The initial cash endowment for the award was given by Patricia Beatty in 1987 to honor her husband John Beatty. John and Patricia Beatty co-authored eleven books of fiction for young adults and Patricia wrote 35 other books for young people, ten of which have a California setting.

Any children's or young adult book set in California and published during the calendar year preceding the presentation is eligible. Included are fiction and nonfiction for children and young people of all ages. A prize of $500 as well as an engraved plaque are presented at the California Library Association Annual Conference. The first award was presented in 1989 for a book published in 1988.

1989 *Chang's Paper Pony* by Eleanor Coerr, illustrated by Deborah Kogan Ray; Harper & Row, 1988.

1990 *The Great American Gold Rush* by Rhoda Blumberg, illustrated with photos; Bradbury, 1989.

1991 *Baseball in April and Other Stories* by Gary Soto, not illustrated; Harcourt, Brace, Jovanovich, 1990.

1992 *Sierra* by Diane Siebert, illustrated by Wendell Minor; HarperCollins, 1991.

1993 *Children of the Dust Bowl* by Jerry Stanley, illustrated with photographs; Crown, 1992.

BEAVER TROPHY

discontinued

An award given for the best unpublished manuscript written by a local author which was sponsored by the Hudson's Bay Company of Edmonton, Alberta, Canada. The author must have been a resident of Edmonton or areas within a 100 mile radius for six months immediately preceding January 1 of the competition year. The manuscripts were submitted to the judges by October 1 and not due to be published before December 1 of the same year. Manuscripts for nonfiction, fiction, adult, and juvenile were eligible. The Edmonton Branch of the Canadian Authors' Association was responsible for selection of the judges. An award of $500 and a trophy were presented at a ceremony in November. Listed below are the juvenile award winners.

1967 *Last Voyage of the Unicorn* by Delbert Young, illustrated by Mary Cserepy; Clarke, Irwin, 1969.

1975 *The Quest of the Golden Gannet* by Dorothy P. Barnhouse, illustrated; Breakwater Books, 1979.

1981 *Hunter in the Dark* by Monica Hughes, not illustrated; Clarke, Irwin, 1982.

BEST BOOKS FOR BABIES

discontinued

Discontinued in 1990 due to a lack of sponsorship, Best Book for Babies was initially sponsored by Parents Magazine and administered by the Book Trust. Established in 1985 to recognize excellence in books for the very young and to encourage high standards, eligible books were required to be published in the United Kingdom and be targeted for children under four years of age. Both paperback and hardback books were eligible.

1985 *Peepo!* written and illustrated by Janet Ahlberg and Allan Ahlberg; Viking Kestrel/Puffin, 1983.

1986 *Where Is Bobo?* by Susan Hulme, illustrated by Jan Siegieda; Methuen, 1985.

1987 *Five Minutes' Peace* written and illustrated by Jill Murphy; Walker Books, 1986.

1988 *A Day of Rhymes* written and illustrated by Sarah Pooley; Bodley Head, 1987.

1989 *Wake Up, Dad!* by Sally Grindley, illustrated by Siobhan Dodds; Simon & Schuster (UK), 1988; Doubleday, 1989.

1990 *Rosie's Babies* by Martin Waddell, illustrated by Penny Dale; Walker, 1989.

BIENNALE OF ILLUSTRATIONS BRATISLAVA
The Secretariat BIB
Sprava Kulturnych Zariadeni MK SSR
Dobsinskeho nam. 1
813 49 Bratislava
Czechoslovakia

The Biennale of Illustrations Bratislava (BIB) is an international competitive exposition of original illustrations created for books for children and youth. The competition is held every other year in Bratislava, Czechoslovakia, the headquarters of BIB. First held in 1967, the BIB competition is organized under the auspices of the International Cabinet of Illustrations at the Slovak National Gallery. Selection of participants of BIB is done through central cultural institutions in the participating countries, as well as national committees of the IBBY and BIB.

The biennial awards, which are presented by the international jury, consist of the following: one grand prix (35,000 Kcs.); five golden apples (15,000 Kcs. each); 10 plaques (5000 Kcs. each); and four honorary diplomas.

Some of the important statues governing the BIB are:

1. BIB, conforming with the tasks and aims of UNESCO ... and in cooperation with publishers' organizations, the national committees of the International Board on Books for Young People (IBBY), The national commissions for the cooperation with UNESCO and with organizations of plastic arts, facilitates the presentation of children's book illustrations on an international scale and, by creating a suitable environment for their evaluation, seeks to encourage the development of art in this field.

2. The supreme representative authority of BIB is the international committee. Members of the committee are ad personam representatives of international and national organizations, distinguished artists, scholars, and writers...

3. Prizes of BIB are awarded by an international jury. The international committee determines its territorial composition ... The working committee... will nominate the members of the jury, of which there are fourteen. Jury decisions will be made by a simple majority, with the chairman having the right to use a casting vote in cases of equality of votes. With the exception of the Grand Prix, the jury may decide to withhold prizes.

4. Each artist may participate in BIB by presenting illustrations from one or two books, the total number of illustrations not exceeding ten pieces. Invited artists participating for the first time in BIB shall be entitled to submit book illustrations made in the last five years. Artists taking part repeatedly in BIB are entitled to present only works originating from the period between the two BIBs. Each artist is entitled to two square meters of exhibitional area. Only illustrations published in book form within the fixed period are qualified for the competition.

5. The winner of the Grand Prix BIB shall be entitled to participate in the next BIB with a special exhibition of his illustrations.

6. If participation in the BIB is carried out in the form of a national exhibition, an entry fee of fifty U.S. dollars or fifty Roubles shall be charged. No fee shall be paid by individual exhibitors. (From the statutes passed at Bratislava, September 8, 1979.)

Listed below are all Grand Prix winners and those of Golden Apples and Plaques from English-speaking countries.

1967 **GRAND PRIX** *Taro and a Bamboo Shoot* by Masaku Matsuno, illustrated by Yasuo Segawa; Fukuinkan Shoten, 1963.

1967 **GOLDEN APPLE** *Swimmy* written and illustrated by Leo Lionni; Pantheon, 1963.

1969 **GRAND PRIX** *Chinesische Volksmarchen* by Eva Bednarova; Artia, 1968.

1969 **GOLDEN APPLE** *The Practical Princess* by Jay Williams, illustrated by Friso Henstra; Parents, 1969.

1969 **PLAQUE** *A Book of Ghosts and Goblins* by Ruth Manning-Sanders, illustrated by Robin Jacques; Methuen, 1968.

From King Boggen's Hall to Nothing At All written and illustrated by Blair Lent; Little Brown, 1967.

1971 **GRAND PRIX** *Narzeczony z Morza* by Robert Stieler, illustrated by Ardrezej Strumitto; Nasza Ksiegarnia, 1971.

1973 **GRAND PRIX** *Der Traummacher* by Leiselotte Schwarz; Verlag Heinrich Ellermann, 1972.

1973 **PLAQUE** *Behind the Wheel* written and illustrated by Edward Koren; Holt, 1972.

A Medley of Folk Songs by Janet Archer; Lowe & Brydone, 1971.

The Spider's Web written and illustrated by Charles Keeping; Oxford, 1972.

1975 **GRAND PRIX** *Robinson Crusoe* by Daniel Defoe, illustrated by Nikolaj Popov; Chudozestvenaja Literatura, 1974.

1975 **GOLDEN APPLE** *Railway Passage* written and illustrated by Charles Keeping; Oxford, 1974.

The Three Jovial Huntsmen: A Mother Goose Rhyme adapted and illustrated by Susan Jeffers; Bradbury, 1973.

1977 **GRAND PRIX** *Harlekin* by Ulf Lofgren; Awe/Gebbers, 1977.

1977 **PLAQUE** *Forgetful Fred* by Jay Williams, illustrated by Friso Hentra; Parents, 1974.

1979 **GRAND PRIX** *Der Kleine Daumling* by Klaus Ensikat; Der Kinderbuchverlag, 1977.

Taipi by Herman Melville, illustrated by Klaus Ensikat; Verlag Neues Leben, 1977.

1979 **PLAQUE** *A Christmas Book* by Svend Otto S., translated by J. Tate; Pelham, 1978.

1981 **GRAND PRIX** *Kristoffers Rejse* by Hanne Borner, illustrated by Roald Als; Borgen Denmark, 1980.

1983 **GRAND PRIX** *Alica v Krajine Zazrakov* by Dusan Kallay; Mlade Leta, 1981.

1983 **PLAQUE** *Trouble for Trumpets* by Peter Dallas-Smith, illustrated by Peter Cross; Ernest Benn, 1982; Random House, 1984.

Porcupine Stew by Beverly Major, illustrated by Erick Ingraham; Morrow, 1982.

1985 GRAND PRIX *Bestiare Fableux* by C. Meral, illustrated by Frederic Clement; Editions Magnard.

1985 PLAQUE *It Happened in Pinsk* by Arthur Yorinks, illustrated by Richard Egielski; Farrar, Straus, Giroux, 1983.

1987 GRAND PRIX *Herra Kuningas* by Raija Siekkinen, illustrated by Hannu Taina; Otava, 1986.

1989 GRAND PRIX *Ksiega Bajek Polskich (Book of Polish Fairy Tales)* by Helen Kapelus, illustrated by Marian Murawski; Ludowa Spoldzielnia Wydawnicza, 1988.

1989 HONORABLE MENTION *Jump Again! More Adventures of Brer Rabbit* by Joel Chandler Harris, adapted by Van Dyne Parks, illustrated by Barry Moser; Harcourt Brace Jovanovich, 1987.

1989 HONORABLE MENTION IN MEMORIAM John Steptoe (USA)

1991 *Der Gestiefelte Kater (Puss in Boots)* by Charles Perrault, illustrated by Stasys Eidrigevicius; Nord-Sud Verlag, 1990; North South Books, 1990.

1991 GOLDEN APPLE *A Christmas Carol* by Charles Dickens, illustrated by Roberto Innocenti; Stewart, Tabori & Chang, 1990.

Why the Cangaroo Has Such Long Legs by John Rowe; Neugebauer Press, 1990.

The Big Pets written and illustrated by Lane Smith; Viking, 1991.

GEOFFREY BILSON AWARD FOR HISTORICAL FICTION

The Canadian Children's Book Centre
35 Spadina Rd.
Toronto, Ontario M5R 2S9
Canada

This award was established in 1988 in honor of Geoffrey Bilson, a respected historian and children's author who died in 1987. The purpose of the award is to reward excellence in writing of an outstanding work of historical fiction for young people by a Canadian author. Historical fiction for all ages, published during the preceding year, is eligible. The winning author must be Canadian and have lived in Canada for at least two years prior to the award. This annual award is presented during Canadian Children's Book Week in November and carries with it a $1000 cash award.

1988 *Lisa* by Carol Matas, illustrated with a map; Lester & Orpen Dennys, 1987.

1989 *Mystery in the Frozen Lands* by Martyn Godfrey, not illustrated; Lorimer, 1988.

Rachel's Revolution by Dorothy Perkyns, illustrated; Lancelot Press, 1988.

1990 *The Sky Is Falling* by Kit Pearson, not illustrated; Viking, 1989.

1991 *The Sign of the Scales* by Marianne Brandis, illustrated by G. Brender a Brandis; Porcupine's Quill, 1990.

1992 No Award

BISTO BOOK OF THE YEAR AWARD

Irish Children's Book Trust
Book House Ireland
65 Middle Abbey Street
Dublin 1
Ireland

Presented by the Irish Children's Book Trust and sponsored by R.H.M. Foods (Ireland), this award has a variety of categories. Until a name change in 1991, this award was known as The Young Persons' Bisto Book of the Decade. The purpose of this award is to bring the best of each year's new children's books by Irish writers and illustrators to the attention of readers, parents, teachers and librarians. The winning author and/or illustrator must reside in Ireland or be Irish by birth. Books, in either English or Irish, published during the current year are eligible for the award. The overall winner receives £1500 and a bronze perpetual trophy sculpted by Joseph Slaone. Three awards of £500 each are given to three additional writers or illustrators.

1990 FICTION *Run With the Wind* by Tom McCaughren, illustrated by Jeanette Dunne; Wolfhound Press, 1983.

Run to Earth by Tom McCaughren, illustrated by Jeanette Dunne; Wolfhound Press, 1984.

Run Swift, Run Free by Tom McCaughren, illustrated by Jeanette Dunne; Wolfhound Press, 1986.

1990 INFORMATION BOOK *Exploring the Book of Kells* by George Otto Simms, illustrated by David Rooney; O'Brien Press, 1988.

Brendan the Navigator by George Otto Simms, illustrated by David Rooney; O'Brien Press, 1989.

1991 OVERALL WINNER *The Island of Ghosts* by Eilis Dillon, not illustrated; Faber & Faber, 1990.

1991 ILLUSTRATION *Fairy Tales of Ireland* compiled by W.B. Yeats, illustrated by P.J. Lynch; Collins, 1990.

1991 BOOKS FOR YOUNG READER *Grandma's Bill* by Martin Waddell, illustrated by Jane Johnson; Simon & Schuster, 1990.

1991 FICTION FOR THE YOUNG *Brian Boru: Emperor of the Irish* by Morgan Llywelyn, not illustrated; O'Brien Press, 1990.

1992 BISTO BOOK OF THE YEAR *The Summer of Lily and Esme* by John Quinn; Poolbeg, 1991.

1992 HISTORICAL FICTION *Wildflower Girl* by Marita Conlon-McKenna; O'Brien Press, 1991.

1992 PICTURE STORYBOOK *The Sleeping Giant* written and illustrated by Marie-Louise Fitzpatrick; Brandon Books, 1991.

1992 FIRST CHILDREN'S NOVEL *The Secret of the Ruby Ring* by Yvonne MacGrory; Children's Press, 1991.

1993 BISTO BOOK OF THE YEAR *The Blue Horse* by Marita Conlon-McKenna; O'Brien Press, 1992.

1993 TEENAGE FICTION *Put a Saddle on the Pig* by Sam McBratney; Methuen, 1992.

1993 HISTORICAL FICTION *Strongbow* by Morgan Llywelyn; O'Briend Press, 1992.

IRMA S. and JAMES H. BLACK AWARD

Bank Street College of Education
Linda Greengrass, Librarian
610 West 112th St
New York, NY 10025

This annual award, first presented in 1972, is in memory of Irma Simonton Black, faculty member of the Bank Street College of Education and children's book author and James H. Black. Books published for young children are eligible for this award, which is based on excellence of text and graphics. The judges are the Bank Street College Irma S. and James H. Black Book Award Committee and school children from both urban and nonurban areas. Publishers are encouraged to send books for consideration for the award, which is announced in May. Scrolls are presented to both author and illustrator. A gold seal for award books was designed by Maurice Sendak.

1972 *Mouse Tales* written and illustrated by Arnold Lobel; Harper, 1972.

1973 *Bear Mouse* by Berniece Freschet, illustrated by Donald Carrick; Scribner, 1973.

Harlequin and the Gift of Many Colors by Burton Supree and Remy Charlip, illustrated by Remy Charlip; Parents, 1973.

1974 *She Come Bringing Me that Little Baby Girl* by Eloise Greenfield, illustrated by John Steptoe; Lippincott, 1974.

1975 *The Maggie B.* written and illustrated by Irene Haas; Atheneum, 1975.

Morris's Disappearing Bag: A Christmas Story written and illustrated by Rosemary Wells; Dial, 1975.

1976 *The Easter Egg Artists* written and illustrated by Adrienne Adams; Scribner, 1976.

Everyone Knows What a Dragon Looks Like by Jay Williams, illustrated by Mercer Mayer; Four Winds, 1976.

1977 *The Mysterious Tadpole* written and illustrated by Steven Kellogg; Dial, 1977.

1978 *Felix in the Attic* by Larry Bograd, illustrated by Dirk Zimmer; Harvey House, 1978.

1979 *The Garden of Abdul Gasazi* written and illustrated by Chris Van Allsburg; Houghton Mifflin, 1979.

1980 *Gorky Rises* written and illustrated by William Steig; Farrar, 1980.

1981 *The Stories Julian Tells* by Ann Cameron, illustrated by Ann Strugnell; Pantheon, 1981.

1982 *Mustard* by Charlotte Graeber, illustrated by Donna Diamond; Macmillan, 1982.

1983 *No One Is Going to Nashville* by Mavis Jukes, illustrated by Lloyd Bloom; Knopf, 1983.

1984 *The Mysteries of Harris Burdick* written and illustrated by Chris Van Allsburg; Houghton Mifflin, 1984.

1985 *Chloe and Maude* written and illustrated by Sandra Boynton; Little Brown, 1985.

1986 *Doctor Change* by Joanna Cole, illustrated by Donald Carrick; Morrow, 1986.

1987 *Heckedy Peg* by Audrey Wood, illustrated by Don Wood; Harcourt, Brace, Jovanovich, 1987.

1988 *The Porcupine Mouse* by Bonnie Pryor, illustrated by Maryjane Begin; Morrow, 1988.

1989 *The Talking Eggs* by Robert D. San Souci, illustrated by Jerry Pinkney; Dial, 1989.

1990 *Charlie Anderson* by Barbara Abercrombie, illustrated by Mark Graham; McElderry, 1990.

1991 *The Enchanted Wood* written and illustrated by Ruth Sanderson; Little Brown, 1991.

1992 *The King's Equal* by Katherine Paterson, illustrated by Vladimir Vagin; HarperCollins, 1992.

NANCY BLOCH MEMORIAL AWARD

discontinued

The Nancy Bloch Memorial Award, established by the Downtown Community School to encourage writing, publishing, and reading of children's books that promote understanding between various ethnic and religious groups, was given annually from 1955 to 1971. A committee of students, parents, and teachers of the Downtown Community School surveyed the field of children's literature each year for appropriate books. Their findings were given to a panel of judges for the final selection. A scroll was presented each spring to the author of a children's book that helped foster a sense of understanding among children of various cultures.

1955 *Susan Cornish* by Rebecca Caudill, illustrated by E. Harper Johnson; Viking, 1955.

1956 *Knock at the Door, Emmy* by Florence C. Means, illustrated by Paul Lantz; Houghton Mifflin, 1956.

1957 *The Swimming Pool* by Alice Cobb, illustrated by Joseph Escourido; Friendship Press, 1957.

1958 *Captain of the Planter: The Story of Robert Smalls* by Dorothy Sterling, illustrated by Ernest Crichlow; Doubleday, 1958.

1959 *Mary Jane* by Dorothy Sterling, illustrated by Ernest Crichlow; Doubleday, 1959.

1960 No Award

1961 *Antelope Singer* by Ruth M. Underhill, illustrated by Ursula Koering; Coward, 1961.

1962 No Award

1963 *Roosevelt Grady* by Louisa R. Shotwell, illustrated by Peter Burchard; World, 1963.

1964 No Award

1965 *Jazz Country* by Nat Hentoff, not illustrated; Harper, 1965.

1966 *Lions in the Way* by Bella Rodman, not illustrated; Follett, 1966.

1967 *Zeely* by Virginia Hamilton, illustrated by Symeon Shimin; Macmillan, 1967.

1968 No Award

1969 *The Other City* by Ray Vogel, photographs by William Boyd and others; White, 1969.

1970 No Award

1971 *Voice of the Children* edited by Terri Bush and June Jordan, illustrated with photographs; Holt, 1970.

BLUE SPRUCE: COLORADO YOUNG ADULT BOOK AWARD

Colorado Library Association
Susan Englese, Executive Director
Box 32113
Aurora, CO 80041

This annual children's choice award was established in 1985 by a combined committee of the Colorado Council of the International Reading Association, Colorado Language Arts Society, Colorado Educational Media Association, and the Colorado Library Association. It was established to encourage young adults active involvement with books and reading.

Titles are nominated by Colorado secondary students based on the following guidelines:

1. Fiction or nonfiction, currently in print and published in the ten years preceding the award year;

2. Only one title by each author;

3. Written by a contemporary American author, but not exclusively for a young adult audience;

4. Must meet accepted standards of quality;

5. Must not have appeared first as a movie or television show.

The preceding year's winner and the new ballot selections are announced in February.

1985 *Tiger Eyes* by Judy Blume, not illustrated; Bradbury, 1981.

1986 *Bridge to Terabithia* by Katherine Paterson, illustrated by Donna Diamond; Crowell, 1977.

1987 *The Third Eye* by Lois Duncan, not illustrated; Little Brown, 1984.

1988 *The Other Side of Dark* by Joan Lowery Nixon, not illustrated; Delacorte, 1986.

1989 *The Eyes of the Dragon* by Stephen King, illustrated by David Palladini; Viking, 1987.

1990 *The Cradle Will Fall* by Mary Higgins Clark, not illustrated; Simon & Schuster, 1980.

1992 *Pet Sematary* by Stephen King, not illustrated; Doubleday, 1983.

BOLOGNA CHILDREN'S BOOK FAIR PRIZES

Ente Autonomo per le Fiere di Bologna
Piazza Costituzione, 6
1-40128 Bologna, Italy

Three awards are presented in conjunction with the Bologna Children's Book Fair. First awarded in 1966, they are the Graphics Prize for Children, Graphics Prize for Youth, and the Critici in Erba. The two graphics prizes are awarded to works of remarkable graphic value. A committee appointed by the fair organization made of graphic designers from all over the world evaluate the entries based on graphic, artistic, and technical criteria. The Critici in Erba prize is for the best illustrated book; the winning title is selected by a committee of nine children, ages six through nine, chosen from Bologna schools.

Competition for all three awards is open to any publisher participating in the children's book fair. Each publisher submits one or more works published during the preceding year. The prize, consisting of a gold plaque, is awarded to the winning publisher (rather than author or illustrator). These annual awards are presented on the evening of the opening day of the fair.

1966 **CRITICI IN ERBA** *Album de Bambi* by Felix Salten, illustrated; Societe Nouvelle des Editions Bias, 1966.

1966 **GRAPHICS FOR CHILDREN AND YOUTH** *Gesu Oggi* by Emilio Radius, illustrated; Rizzoli Editore, 1966.

1967 **CRITICI IN ERBA** *Ich Schenk Dir Einen Papagei!* by Franco Barberis; Diogenes Verlag, 1964.

1967 **GRAPHICS FOR CHILDREN AND YOUTH** *Drei Vogel* written and illustrated by Hilde Heyduck-Huth; Otto Maier Verlag.

1968 **CRITIC IN ERBA** *Alla Scoperta Dell'Africa*; Nuova Vallecchi Editore.

1968 **GRAPHICS FOR CHILDREN** *Die Wichtelmanner* by Jacob Grimm and Wilhelm Grimm, illustrated by Katrin Brandt; Atlantis Verlag.

1968 **GRAPHICS FOR YOUTH** *Pribehy* by Anna Hostomska, illustrated by Zdenek Seydl; Albatros, 1969.

1969 **CRITICI IN ERBA** *Pocahontas in London* by Jan Wahl, illustrated by John Alcorn; Delacorte/Seymour Lawrence, 1967.

1969 **GRAPHICS FOR CHILDREN** *The Little Black Fish* by Samad Behrangi, illustrated by Farshid Mesghali; Institute for the Intellectual Development of Children and Young Adults.

1969 **GRAPHICS FOR YOUTH** *La Cite de l'an 2000* by Michel Ragon; Editions Casterman, 1968.

1970 **CRITICI IN ERBA** *La Storia di Francesco e Chiara (Raccontata dai Bimbi di Croce)*; Stadiv I'Aquila.

1970 **GRAPHICS FOR CHILDREN** *1,2,3 Ein Zug Zum Zoo* written and illustrated by Eric Carle; Gerhard Stalling Verlag.

1970 **GRAPHICS FOR YOUTH** *Vertel Het uw Kinderen* by Jac Sinnema and C.M. de Vries; Nederlandsche Zondacsschool Vereniging.

1971 **CRITICI IN ERBA** *Alle Meine Blatter* by Irmgard Lucht, illustrated by Josef Guggenmos; Gertraud Middelhauve Verlag.

1971 **GRAPHICS FOR CHILDREN** *Arm in Arm* written and illustrated by Remy Charlip; Parents, 1969.

1971 **GRAPHICS FOR YOUTH** *Tutto Su Gerusalemme Biblica* by O. Alberti and M. Avi-Yonah, illustrated; C.E. Giunti-Bemporad Marzocco, 1970.

1972 **CRITICI IN ERBA** *Waltzing Mathilda* by Andrew Barton Paterson, illustrated by Desmond Digby; Collins Australia, 1970.

1972 **GRAPHICS FOR CHILDREN** *Stadtmaus und Landmaus* retold and illustrated by Ruth Hurlimann; Atlantis Verlag.

1972 **GRAPHICS FOR YOUTH** *Slavische Marchen* by Vladislav Stanovsky and Oldrich Sirovatka, illustrated by Maria Zelibska; Artia.

1973 **CRITICI IN ERBA** *Snow White and the Seven Dwarfs* by Jacob Grimm and Wilhelm Grimm, translated by Randall Jarrell, illustrated by Nancy Ekholm Burkert; Farrar Straus Giroux, 1972.

1973 **GRAPHICS FOR CHILDREN** *Kopfblumen* by Gianni Rodari, illustrated by Eberhard Binder-Strassfurt; Der Kinderbuchverlag.

1973 GRAPHICS FOR YOUTH *Hodina Nachove Ruze* by Maria Krugernova, illustrated by Jana Sigmundova; Albatros.

1974 CRITICI IN ERBA *A Year in the Woods*; Detskaya Literatura.

1974 GRAPHICS FOR CHILDREN *Rotkappchen* by Jacob Grimm and Wilhelm Grimm; Diogenes Verlag.

1974 GRAPHICS FOR YOUTH *The Last of the Mohicans* by James Fenimore Cooper, illustrated by Christopher Bradbury; Felix Gluck.

1975 CRITICI IN ERBA *Il Principe Felice*; Edizioni Paoline.

1975 GRAPHICS FOR CHILDREN *Trois Petits Flocons* by Bernard Barokas, illustrated by Joelle Boucher; Grasset & Fasquelle, 1974.

1975 GRAPHICS FOR YOUTH *Das Sprachbastelbuch* by Gerri Zotter; Jugend und Volk Verlag.

1976 CRITICI IN ERBA *Das Gelbe Haus*; Carlsen Verlag.

1976 GRAPHICS FOR CHILDREN *Magic for Sale* by Tsuguo Okuda, illustrated by Masakane Yonekura; Kaisei-sha Publishing.

1976 GRAPHICS FOR YOUTH *Il Cavallo di Bronzo* by Aleksandr Sergeevic Puskin, illustrated by Fodor Kontstantinov; Detskaya Literatura.

1977 CRITICI IN ERBA *Die Geschichte Von Babar, Dem Kleine Elefanten*; Diogenes Verlag.

1977 GRAPHICS FOR CHILDREN *Schorschi Schrumpft: Geschichte* by Florence Parry Heide, illustrated by Edward Gorey; Diogenes Verlag, 1976.

1977 GRAPHICS FOR YOUTH *Takeru* written and illustrated by Masakane Yonekura; Kaisei-sha Publishing.

1978 CRITICI IN ERBA *Nicholas and the Moon Eggs* by Mark Way, illustrated; Collins Australia, 1977.

1978 GRAPHICS FOR CHILDREN *Grabianskis Stadtmusikanten* written and illustrated by Janusz Grabianski; Verlag Carl Ueberreuter.

1978 GRAPHICS FOR YOUTH *Anno's Unique World* written and illustrated by Mitsumasa Anno; Kodanska Ltd.

1979 CRITICI IN ERBA *Ein Tag Im Leben der Dorothea Wutz* written and illustrated by Tatjana Hauptmann; Diogenes Verlag, 1978.

1979 GRAPHICS FOR CHILDREN *Histoire du Petit Stephen Girard* by Mark Twain, translated from English by A. Allais, illustrated by Jean-Michel Nicollet; Editions Gallimard, 1978.

1979 GRAPHICS FOR YOUTH *Aurora* by Adela Turin and Annie Goetzinger, illustrated with photographs; Dalla Parte delle Bambine.

1980 CRITICI IN ERBA *Das Buch Vom Dorf*; Fabula Verlag.

1980 GRAPHICS FOR CHILDREN *Anno's Song Book* written and illustrated by Mitsumasa Anno; Kodansha Ltd.

1980 GRAPHICS FOR YOUTH *Himmelszelt und Schneckenhaus* written and illustrated by Rita Muhlbauer and Hanno Rink; Verlag Sauerlander, 1979.

1981 CRITICI IN ERBA *Mr. Squint* written and illustrated by Jenny Partridge; World's Work, 1980.

1981 GRAPHICS FOR CHILDREN *Yok Yok* series by Anne van der Essen, illustrated by Etienne Delessert; Gallimard.

1981 GRAPHICS FOR YOUTH *L'Univers a Deux Voix Insecte* by Marie Perennou, Claude Nuridsany; Jacques Very and children of C.E.S.; La Noria.

1982 CRITICI IN ERBA *The Pixie's Invitation* by T. Nakamura; Kaisei-sha.

1982 GRAPHICS FOR CHILDREN *Les Secrets de L'Image* series; Gallimard.

1982 GRAPHICS FOR YOUTH *City of Gold and Other Stories from the Old Testament* by Peter Dickinson, illustrated by Michael Foreman; Gollancz, 1980.

1983 CRITICI IN ERBA *Our Changing World* by Ingrid Selberg, illustrated by Andrew Muller; Collins, 1982; Philomel, 1982.

1983 GRAPHICS FOR CHILDREN *The Favershams* written and illustrated by Roy Gerrard; Gollancz, 1982; Farrar, 1983.

1983 GRAPHICS FOR YOUTH *Il Etait Une Fois, Les Mots* by Yves Pinguilly, illustrated by Andre Belleguie; Editions la Farandol Messidor, 1981.

1984 CRITICI IN ERBA *Mame's Cats 1,2,3*; Kaisei-sha.

1984 GRAPHICS FOR CHILDREN *Le Petit Chaperon Rouge* by Charles Perrault, illustrated by Sarah Moon; Grasset et Fasquelle.

1984 GRAPHICS FOR YOUTH *Alenka v Kraji Divu* by Lewis Carroll, illustrated by Marketa Prachaticka; Albatros.

1985 CRITICI IN ERBA *Sol Solet* by the Catalonian Theater Company, Comediants; Edicion de l'Eixample.

1985 GRAPHICS FOR CHILDREN *Leaves* by Mahdi Moini, illustrated by Marteza Esmaili-e-Soli; Institute for the Intellectual Development of Children and Young Adults.

1985 GRAPHICS FOR YOUTH [*The Bee on the Comb*] written and illustrated by Kit Williams; Cape, 1984. (The title can be found by solving clues concealed in the illustrations).

1986 CRITICI IN ERBA *Peter und der Wolf* by Sergei Prokofiev, retold by Loriot, illustrated by Jorg Muller; Verlag Sauerlander.

1986 GRAPHICS FOR CHILDREN *One Morning* by Canna Funakoshi, illustrated by Yohiji Izawa; JiShi-Tokyo, 1985.

1986 GRAPHICS FOR YOUTH *Der Hut des Kaminfegers*; BDV Basilius Verlag.

1987 CRITICI IN ERBA *That's My Dad* written and illustrated by Ralph Steadman; Andersen Press, 1986.

1987 GRAPHICS FOR CHILDREN *The Great Games Book [fourteen brilliant board games]*, illustrated by Jez Alborough and others; A&C Black, 1985.

1987 GRAPHICS FOR YOUTH *Decouvertes Gallimard*; Editions Gallimard.

1988 CRITICI IN ERBA *Die Blumenstadt* by Eveline Hasler, illustrated by Stepan Zavrel; Bohem Press, 1987.

1988 GRAPHICS FOR CHILDREN *Animal Numbers* written and illustrated by Bert Kitchen; Lutterworth Press, 1987; Dial, 1987.

1988 GRAPHICS FOR YOUTH *Le Livre de la Creation* by Pierre- Marie Beaude, illustrated by Georges Lemoine; Edition du Centurion, 1987.

1989 CRITICI IN ERBA *Dear Mili* by Wilhelm Grimm, illustrated by Maurice Sendak; Farrar Straus Giroux, 1988.

1989 GRAPHICS FOR CHILDREN *A Long, Long Song* written and illustrated by Etienne Delessert; Farrar Straus Giroux, 1988.

1989 GRAPHICS FOR YOUTH *Les Yeux de la d'ecouverte* series; Editions Gallimard, 1988- .

1990 CRITICI IN ERBA *A Frog Prince* written and illustrated by Alix Berenzy; Henry Holt, 1989.

1990 GRAPHICS FOR CHILDREN *Mijn Held* written and illustrated by Katrien Holland; Em Querido's Uitgeverij.

1990 GRAPHICS FOR YOUTH *Die Geschichte Von der Kleinen Gans, Die Nicht Schnell Genug War* by Hanna Johansen, illustrated by Kathi Bhend; Nagel & Kimche, 1989.

1991 CRITICI IN ERBA *Kleiner Eisbar Nimm Micht Mit!* written and illustrated by Hans De Beer; Nord-Sud Verlag, 1990; North South Books, 1990.

1991 GRAPHICS FOR CHILDREN *An Alphabet of Animals* written and illustrated by Christopher Wormell; HarperCollins, 1990.

1991 GRAPHICS FOR YOUTH *Rue de la Mediterranee*; Hatier.

1992 CRITICI IN ERBA *Que Viene el Iris, Leri*; *Todos los Iris al Iris*; *Desde el Iris Con Amor*; *No Mires Aquel Iris*; *Tantos Iris Como Dragones*; *El Oro de una Iris*; *Un Iris Irritado* (Iris Series) by Miguel Obiols, illustrated by Carme Sole Vendrell; Aura Communicacion.

1992 GRAPHICS FOR CHILDREN *Oh!* written and illustrated by Josse Goffin; Rainbow Grafics International/ Baronian Books.

1992 GRAPHICS FOR YOUTH *Jeder Nach Seiner Art* by Hoffmann von Fallersleben, illustrated by Klaus Ensikat; Beltz & Gelberg.

1993 CRITICI IN ERBA *The Rainbow Fish* by Marcus Pfister; North-South Books, 1992.

A BOOK CAN DEVELOP EMPATHY
Samantha Mullen
New York State Humane Association
P O Box 284
New Paltz, NY 12561

Originally called the Kind Writers Make Kind Readers Award, this award is sponsored by the New York State Humane Association and the Fund for Animals. The award seeks to honor authors, while providing information for parents and others interested in humane education to identify good books that promote empathy for animals.

1990 *Second-hand Dog* written and illustrated by Carol Lee Benjamin; Howell Book House, 1988.

Hoppy the Toad photographs by Jane Burton; Random House, 1989.

Surfer the Seal photographs by Jane Burton; Random House, 1989.

Box Turtle at Long Pond by William T. George, illustrated by Lindsay Barrett George; Greenwillow, 1989.

Walter Warthog written and photographed by Betty Leslie-Melville; Doubleday, 1989.

A Brown Cow written and illustrated by Bijou LeTord; Little Brown, 1989.

Rescue of the Stranded Whales by Andrea Conley and Kenneth Mallory, illustrated with photographs; Simon & Schuster, 1989.

The Lady and the Spider by Faith McNulty, illustrated by Bob Marstall; Harper & Row, 1986.

Scruffy by Peggy Parish, illustrated by Kelly Oechsli; Harper & Row, 1988.

Wild Animals of Africa ABC by Hope Ryden; Dutton, 1989.

Faithful Elephants by Yukio Tsuchiya, illustrated by Ted Lewin; Houghton Mifflin, 1988.

I Love Animals and Broccoli by Debra Wasserman and Charles Stahler, illustrated; Vegetarian Resource Group, 1985.

I'll Always Love You written and illustrated by Hans Wilhelm; Crown, 1985.

Sterling: The Rescue of a Baby Harbor Seal by Sandra Verrill White and Michael Filisky, illustrated; Crown, 1989.

1991 *Animal Babies* by K.K. Ross, illustrated by Lisa McCue; Random House, 1988.

Baby Beluga by Raffi, illustrated by Ashley Wolff; Crown, 1990.

By Day and By Night by Karen Pandell, illustrated by Marty Noble; Kramer, 1991.

Hey, Get Off Our Train written and illustrated by John Burningham; Crown, 1989.

Whales by Seymour Simon, illustrated; Crowell, 1989.

Ibis: A True Whale Story by John Himmelman, illustrated; Scholastic, 1990.

When the Woods Hum by Joanne Ryder, illustrated by Catherine Stock; Morrow, 1991.

Dana Doesn't Like Guns Anymore by Carol W. Moore-Slater, illustrated by Leslie Morales; self published, 1987; Friendship Press, 1991.

Dolphin Adventure: A True Story by Wayne Grover, illustrated by Jim Fowler; Greenwillow, 1990.

A Tale of Antarctica written and illustrated by Ulco Glimmerveen; Scholastic, 1989.

Manatee: On Location by Kathy Darling, photographs by Tara Darling; Lothrop, Lee & Shepard, 1990.

At Home in the Rain Forest by Diane Willow, illustrated by Laura Jacques; Charlesbridge, 1991.

Kids Can Save the Animals: 101 Easy Things To Do by Ingrid Newkirk; Warner, 1991.

Animal Families of the Wild edited by William F. Russell, illustrated by John Butler; Crown, 1990.

The Chosen Puppy by Carol Lea Benjamin, illustrated; Howell Book House, 1990.

Batman: Exploring the World of Bats by Laurence Pringle, photographs by Merlin D. Tuttle; Scribner, 1991.

A White Heron by Sarah Orne Jewett, illustrated by Douglas Alvord; Tillbury House, 1990.

Who Will Speak for the Lamb? by Mildred Ames, not illustrated; HarperCollins, 1989.

The Simon & Schuster Young Readers' Book of Animals by Martin Walters; Simon & Schuster, 1991.

BOOKS I LOVE BEST YEARLY (BILBY) AWARDS

Children's Book Council of Australia
Queensland Branch
P O Box 484
Moorooka, Queensland
4105 Australia

Established by a joint venture of the Queensland Branch of the Children's Book Council of Australia and the Queensland Department of Education, the BILBY Awards are chosen by children. Three categories are chosen annually, Read Alone (Primary); Read Alone (Secondary); and Read Aloud (P-12). The purpose of the award is to promote and encourage children and young adults to read and have their say in a book award. The award is named for the bilby, a rare species of the bandicoot which is a small marsupial. The books are initially nominated by students, with the thirty most nominated titles in each category voted on using a scale of 1-5. The book in each category with the highest number of votes wins.

1990   READ ALONE PRIMARY *Superfudge* by Judy Blume, not illustrated; Bodley Head, 1980.

1990   READ ALONE SECONDARY *The Secret Diary of Adrian Mole Aged 13 3/4* by Sue Townsend, not illustrated; Methuen, 1982.

1990   READ ALOUD PRIMARY-12 *Matilda* by Roald Dahl, illustrated by Quentin Blake; Cape, 1988.

1991   READ ALONE PRIMARY *The BFG* by Roald Dahl, illustrated by Quentin Blake; Cape, 1982.

1991   READ ALONE SECONDARY *The Outsiders* by S. E. Hinton, not illustrated; Collins, 1975.

1991   READ ALOUD PRIMARY-12 *The BFG* by Roald Dahl, illustrated by Quentin Blake; Cape, 1982.

1992   READ ALONE PRIMARY *Unreal! Eight Surprising Stories* by Paul Jennings, not illustrated; Puffin, 1985.

1992   READ ALONE SECONDARY *Where's Wally* written and illustrated by Martin Hanford; Walker, 1987.

1992   READ ALOUD PRIMARY-12 *Charlie and the Chocolate Factory* by Roald Dahl, illustrated by Joseph Schindelman; Penguin, 1973.

BOSTON GLOBE-HORN BOOK AWARDS

Children's Book Editor
The Boston Globe
P O Box 2378
Boston, MA 02107

First given in 1967, this annual award is cosponsored by The Boston Globe and The Horn Book magazine. Awards for text and illustration were given from 1967 through 1975. In 1976, the cate-

gories were changed to fiction, nonfiction, and illustration. The categories are now fiction, nonfiction, and picture book. One award winner is chosen for each category and as many as three honor books may be cited. The winners receive $500 and an engraved silver bowl; honor winners receive a silver plate. Distinctive seals to be placed on the jackets of winning books are made available to the publishers. The awards are presented at the annual meeting of the New England Round Table of Children's Librarians. The books are also displayed at The Boston Globe's book festival in the fall. Although not limited to American authors, the books must be published in the United States.

The following rules govern the selection of the award winning books: (1) Each imprint may submit up to twelve books. A book may be entered for both text and illustration. The category, or categories, must be designated for each book submitted. (2) Three judges are chosen each year and reserve the right to give the award to any children's book published by any publisher in the United States during the designated period (July 1 to June 30). The judges are not restricted to books submitted by publishers. (3) Any book published on a juvenile list is eligible, although new or revised editions, as well as textbooks are excluded.

1967   TEXT *The Little Fishes* by Erik Christian Haugaard, illustrated by Milton Johnson; Houghton Mifflin, 1967.

1967   ILLUSTRATION *London Bridge Is Falling Down!* written and illustrated by Peter Spier; Doubleday, 1967.

1968   TEXT *The Spring Rider* by John Lawson, not illustrated; Crowell, 1968.

1968   TEXT HONOR *Dark Venture* by Audrey W. Beyer, illustrated by Leo Dillon and Diane Dillon; Knopf, 1968.

The Endless Steppe: Growing up in Siberia by Esther Hautzig, not illustrated; Crowell, 1968.

Smith by Leon Garfield, illustrated by Antony Maitland; Pantheon, 1967; Constable, 1967.

Young Mark by E.M. Almedingen, illustrated by Victor Ambrus; Farrar, 1968.

1968   ILLUSTRATION *Tikki Tikki Tembo* by Arlene Mosel, illustrated by Blair Lent; Holt, 1968.

1968   ILLUSTRATION HONOR *All in Free but Janey* by Elizabeth Johnson, illustrated by Trina Schart Hyman; Little Brown, 1968.

Gilgamesh: Man's First Story written and illustrated by Bernarda Bryson; Holt, 1967.

Jorinda and Joringel by Jacob Grimm and Wilhelm Grimm, illustrated by Adrienne Adams; Scribner, 1968.

Rosie's Walk written and illustrated by Pat Hutchins; Macmillan, 1968.

1969   TEXT *The Wizard of Earthsea* by Ursula K. LeGuin, illustrated by Ruth Robbins; Parnassus, 1968.

1969   TEXT HONOR *Flambards* by K.M. Peyton, illustrated by Victor G. Ambrus; Oxford, 1967; World, 1968.

The Pigman by Paul Zindel, not illustrated; Harper, 1968; Dell, 1970.

Turi's Poppa by Elizabeth Borton de Trevino, illustrated by Enrico Arno; Farrar, 1968.

1969   ILLUSTRATION *The Adventures of Paddy Pork* written and illustrated by John S. Goodall; Harcourt, Brace, Jovanovich, 1968.

1969 **ILLUSTRATION HONOR** *Monkey in the Jungle* by Edna Mitchell Preston, illustrated by Clement Hurd; Viking, 1968.

New Moon Cove written and illustrated by Ann Atwood; Scribner, 1969.

Thy Friend, Obadiah written and illustrated by Brinton Turkle; Viking, 1969.

1970 **TEXT** *The Intruder* by John Rowe Townsend, illustrated by Joseph A. Phelan; Lippincott, 1970; Oxford, 1969.

1970 **TEXT HONOR** *Where the Lilies Bloom* by Vera Cleaver and Bill Cleaver, illustrated by Jim Spanfeller; Lippincott, 1969.

1970 **ILLUSTRATION** *Hi, Cat!* written and illustrated by Ezra Jack Keats; Macmillan, 1970.

1970 **ILLUSTRATION HONOR** *A Story, A Story* written and illustrated by Gail E. Haley; Atheneum, 1970.

1971 **TEXT** *A Room Made of Windows* by Eleanor Cameron, illustrated by Trina Schart Hyman; Little Brown, 1971.

1971 **TEXT HONOR** *Beyond the Weir Bridge* by Hester Burton, illustrated by Victor Ambrus; Crowell, 1970.

Come By Here by Olivia Coolidge, illustrated by Milton Johnson; Houghton Mifflin, 1970.

Mrs. Frisby and the Rats of NIMH by Robert C. O'Brien, illustrated by Zena Bernstein; Atheneum, 1971.

1971 **ILLUSTRATION** *If I Built a Village* written and illustrated by Kazue Mizumura; Crowell, 1971.

1971 **ILLUSTRATION HONOR** *The Angry Moon* by William Sleator, illustrated by Blair Lent; Atlantic-Little, 1970.

A Firefly Named Torchy written and illustrated by Bernard Waber; Houghton Mifflin, 1970.

If All the Seas Were One Sea written and illustrated by Janina Domanska; Macmillan, 1971.

1972 **TEXT** *Tristan and Iseult* by Rosemary Sutcliff, not illustrated; Dutton, 1971.

1972 **TEXT HONOR** No Award

1972 **ILLUSTRATION** *Mr. Gumpy's Outing* written and illustrated by John Burningham; Cape, 1970; Holt, 1971.

1972 **ILLUSTRATION HONOR** No Award

1973 **TEXT** *The Dark Is Rising* by Susan Cooper, illustrated by Alan Cober; Atheneum, 1973.

1973 **TEXT HONOR** *The Cat Who Wished To Be a Man* by Lloyd Alexander, not illustrated; Dutton, 1973.

An Island in a Green Sea by Mabel Esther Allan, illustrated by Charles Robinson; Atheneum, 1972.

No Way of Telling by Emma Smith, illustrated with maps; Bodley Head, 1972; Atheneum, 1972.

1973 **ILLUSTRATION** *King Stork* by Howard Pyle, illustrated by Trina Schart Hyman; Little Brown, 1973.

1973 **ILLUSTRATION HONOR** *The Magic Tree* written and illustrated by Gerald McDermott; Holt, 1973.

The Silver Pony written and illustrated by Lynd Ward; Houghton, 1973.

Who, Said Sue, Said Whoo? written and illustrated by Ellen Raskin; Atheneum, 1973.

1974 **TEXT** *M.C. Higgins, the Great* by Virginia Hamilton, not illustrated; Macmillan, 1974.

1974 **TEXT HONOR** *And Then What Happened, Paul Revere?* by Jean Fritz, illustrated by Margot Tomes; Coward, 1973.

The Summer After the Funeral by Jane Gardam, not illustrated; Macmillan, 1973.

Tough Chauncey by Doris Buchanan Smith, illustrated by Michael Eagle; Morrow, 1974.

1974 **ILLUSTRATION** *Jambo Means Hello: Swahili Alphabet Book* by Muriel Feelings, illustrated by Tom Feelings; Dial, 1974.

1974 **ILLUSTRATION HONOR** *All Butterflies: An ABC* written and illustrated by Marcia Brown; Scribner, 1974.

Herman, the Helper by Robert Kraus, illustrated by Jose Aruego and Ariane Dewey; Windmill, 1974.

A Prairie Boy's Winter written and illustrated by William Kurelek; Tundra, 1973; Houghton Mifflin, 1973.

1975 **TEXT** *Transport 7-41-R* by T. Degens, not illustrated; Viking, 1974.

1975 **TEXT HONOR** *The Hundred Penny Box* by Sharon Bell Mathis, illustrated by Leo Dillon and Diane Dillon; Viking, 1975.

1975 **ILLUSTRATION** *Anno's Alphabet: An Adventure in Imagination* written and illustrated by Mitsumasa Anno; Crowell, 1975.

1975 **ILLUSTRATION HONOR** *The Bear's Bicycle* by Emilie Warren McLeod, illustrated by David McPhail; Atlantic-Little, 1975.

Scram, Kid! by Ann McGovern, illustrated by Nola Langner; Viking, 1974.

She Come Bringing Me that Little Baby Girl by Eloise Greenfield, illustrated by John Steptoe; Lippincott, 1974.

1976 **FICTION** *Unleaving* by Jill Paton Walsh, not illustrated; Farrar, 1976.

1976 **FICTION HONOR** *Dragonwings* by Laurence Yep, not illustrated; Harper, 1975.

A Stranger Came Ashore: A Story of Suspense by Mollie Hunter, not illustrated; Harper, 1975.

A String in the Harp by Nancy Bond, illustrated by Allen Davis; Atheneum, 1976.

1976 **NONFICTION** *Voyaging to Cathay: Americans in the China Trade* by Shirley Glubok and Alfred Tamarin, illustrated with photographs and old prints; Viking, 1976.

1976 **NONFICTION HONOR** *Never to Forget: The Jews of the Holocaust* by Milton Meltzer, not illustrated; Harper & Row, 1976.

Pyramid written and illustrated by David Macaulay; Houghton Mifflin, 1975.

Will You Sign Here, John Hancock? by Jean Fritz, illustrated by Trina Schart Hyman; Coward, 1976.

1976 **ILLUSTRATION** *Thirteen* written and illustrated by Jerry Joyner and Remy Charlip; Parents, 1975.

1976 **ILLUSTRATION HONOR** *The Desert Is Theirs* by Byrd Baylor, illustrated by Peter Parnall; Scribner, 1975.

Six Little Ducks written and illustrated by Chris Conover; Crowell, 1976.

Song of the Boat by Lorenz Graham, illustrated by Leo Dillon and Diane Dillon; Crowell, 1975.

1977 FICTION *Child of the Owl* by Laurence Yep, not illustrated; Harper, 1977.

1977 FICTION HONOR *Blood Feud* by Rosemary Sutcliff, not illustrated; Dutton, 1977.

The Machine Gunners by Robert Westall, not illustrated; Macmillan, 1975; Greenwillow, 1976.

Roll of Thunder, Hear My Cry by Mildred D. Taylor, illustrated by Jerry Pinkney; Dial, 1976.

1977 NONFICTION *Chance, Luck and Destiny* by Peter Dickinson, illustrated by Victor Ambrus and David Smee; Atlantic-Little, 1976.

1977 NONFICTION HONOR No Award

1977 ILLUSTRATION *Granfa' Grig had a Pig and other Rhymes without Reason from Mother Goose* written and illustrated by Wallace Tripp; Little Brown, 1976.

1977 ILLUSTRATION HONOR *The Amazing Bone* written and illustrated by William Steig; Farrar, 1976.

Anno's Counting Book written and illustrated by Mitsumasa Anno; Crowell, 1977.

Ashanti to Zulu: African Traditions by Margaret Musgrove, illustrated by Leo Dillon and Diane Dillon; Dial, 1976.

1977 SPECIAL HONORABLE MENTION FOR NON-BOOK ILLUSTRATION *The Changing City* written and illustrated by Jorg Muller; Atheneum, 1977.

The Changing Countryside written and illustrated by Jorg Muller; Atheneum, 1977.

1978 FICTION *The Westing Game* by Ellen Raskin, not illustrated; Dutton, 1978.

1978 FICTION HONOR *Alan and Naomi* by Myron Levoy, not illustrated; Harper, 1977.

Anpao: An American Indian Odyssey by Jamake Highwater, illustrated by Fritz Scholder; Lippincott, 1977.

Ramona and Her Father by Beverly Cleary, illustrated by Alan Tiegreen; Morrow, 1977.

1978 NONFICTION *Mischling, Second Degree: My Childhood in Nazi Germany* by Ilse Koehn, not illustrated; Greenwillow, 1977.

1978 NONFICTION HONOR No Award

1978 ILLUSTRATION *Anno's Journey* written and illustrated by Mitsumasa Anno; Collins, 1978.

1978 ILLUSTRATION HONOR *On to Widecombe Fair* by Patricia Lee Gauch, illustrated by Trina Schart Hyman; Putnam, 1978.

The Story of Edward written and illustrated by Phillipe Dumas; Parents, 1977.

What do you Feed Your Donkey On? Rhymes from a Belfast Childhood by Colette O'Hare, illustrated by Jenny Rodwell; Collins-World, 1978.

1979 FICTION *Humbug Mountain* by Sid Fleischman, illustrated by Eric Von Schmidt; Atlantic-Little, 1978.

1979 FICTION HONOR *All Together Now* by Sue Ellen Bridgers, not illustrated; Knopf, 1979.

Silas and Ben-Godik by Cecil Bodker, translated by Sheila LaFarge; Delacorte/Seymour Lawrence, 1978.

1979 NONFICTION *The Road from Home: The Story of an Armenian Girl* by David Kherdian, not illustrated; Greenwillow, 1979.

1979 NONFICTION HONOR *The Iron Road: A Portrait of American Railroading* by Richard Snow, illustrated with photographs by David Plowden; Four Winds, 1978.

Self-portrait: Margot Zemach written and illustrated by Margot Zemach; Addison-Wesley, 1978.

1979 ILLUSTRATION *The Snowman* written and illustrated by Raymond Briggs; Random House, 1978.

1979 ILLUSTRATION HONOR *Ben's Trumpet* written and illustrated by Rachel Isadora; Greenwillow, 1979.

Cross-Country Cat by Mary Calhoun, illustrated by Erick Ingraham; Morrow, 1979.

1980 FICTION *Conrad's War* by Andrew Davies, not illustrated; Blackie, 1978; Crown, 1980.

1980 FICTION HONOR *The Alfred Summer* by Janice Slepian, not illustrated; Macmillan, 1980.

Me and My Million by Clive King, not illustrated; Kestrel, 1976; Crowell, 1979.

The Night Swimmers by Betsy Byars, illustrated by Troy Howell; Delacorte, 1980.

1980 NONFICTION *Building: The Fight Against Gravity* by Mario Salvadori, illustrated by Saralinda Hooker and Christopher Ragus; Atheneum, 1979.

1980 NONFICTION HONOR *Childtimes* by Eloise Greenfield and Lessie Jones Little, illustrated by Jerry Pinkney; Harper & Row, 1979.

How the Forest Grew by William Jaspersohn, illustrated by Chuck Eckart; Greenwillow, 1979.

Stonewall by Jean Fritz, illustrated by Stephen Gammell; Putnam, 1979.

1980 ILLUSTRATION *The Garden of Abdul Gasazi* written and illustrated by Chris Van Allsburg; Houghton Mifflin, 1979.

1980 ILLUSTRATION HONOR *The Grey Lady and the Strawberry Snatcher* written and illustrated by Molly Bang; Four Winds, 1980.

Why the Tides Ebb and Flow by Joan Chase Bowden, illustrated by Marc Brown; Houghton Mifflin, 1979.

1980 SPECIAL CITATION *Graham Oakley's Magical Changes* written and illustrated by Graham Oakley; Atheneum, 1980.

1981 FICTION *The Leaving* by Lynn Hall, not illustrated; Scribner, 1980.

1981 FICTION HONOR *Flight of the Sparrow* by Julia Cunningham, not illustrated; Pantheon, 1980.

Footsteps by Leon Garfield, not illustrated; Delacorte, 1980.

Ida Early Comes Over the Mountain by Robert Burch, not illustrated; Viking, 1980.

1981   **NONFICTION** *The Weaver's Gift* by Kathryn Lasky, illustrated with photographs by Christopher G. Knight; Warne, 1981.

1981   **NONFICTION HONOR** *Junk Food, Fast Food, Health Food: What America Eats and Why* by Lila Perl, not illustrated; Houghton/Clarion, 1980.

The Hospital Book by James Howe, illustrated with photographs by Mal Warshaw; Crown, 1981.

You Can't Be Timid with a Trumpet: Notes from the Orchestra by Betty Lou English, photographs by Betty Lou English, illustrated by Stan Skardinski; Lothrop, 1980.

1981   **ILLUSTRATION** *Outside Over There* written and illustrated by Maurice Sendak; Harper, 1981.

1981   **ILLUSTRATION HONOR** *Jumanji* written and illustrated by Chris Van Allsburg; Houghton Mifflin, 1981.

On Market Street by Arnold Lobel, illustrated by Anita Lobel; Greenwillow, 1981.

Where the Buffaloes Begin by Olaf Baker, illustrated by Stephen Gammell; Warne, 1981.

1982   **FICTION** *Playing Beatie Bow* by Ruth Park, not illustrated; Kestrel, 1981; Atheneum, 1982.

1982   **FICTION HONOR** *The Voyage Begun* by Nancy Bond, not illustrated; Atheneum, 1981.

Ask Me no Questions by Ann Schlee, not illustrated; Macmillan (London), 1976; Holt, 1982.

The Scarecrows by Robert Westall, not illustrated; Chatto & Windus, 1981; Greenwillow, 1981.

1982   **NONFICTION** *Upon the Head of a Goat: A Childhood in Hungary 1939-1944* by Aranka Siegal, not illustrated; Farrar Straus Giroux, 1981.

1982   **NONFICTION HONOR** *Lobo of the Tasaday* written and photographed by John Nance; Pantheon, 1982.

Dinosaurs of North America by Helen R. Sattler, introduction by John H. Ostrom, illustrated by Anthony Rao; Lothrop, Lee & Shepard, 1981.

1982   **ILLUSTRATION** *A Visit to William Blake's Inn: Poems for Innocent and Experienced Travelers* by Nancy Willard, illustrated by Alice Provensen and Martin Provensen; Harcourt, 1981.

1982   **ILLUSTRATION HONOR** *The Friendly Beasts: An Old English Christmas Carol* illustrated by Tomie dePaola; Putnam, 1981.

1983   **FICTION** *Sweet Whispers, Brother Rush* by Virginia Hamilton, not illustrated; Philomel, 1982.

1983   **FICTION HONOR** *Homesick: My Own Story* by Jean Fritz, illustrated with drawings by Margot Tomes and photographs; Putnam, 1982.

The Road to Camlann by Rosemary Sutcliff, illustrated by Shirley Felts; Dutton, 1982.

Dicey's Song by Cynthia Voigt, not illustrated; Atheneum, 1982.

1983   **NONFICTION** *Behind Barbed Wire: the Imprisonment of Japanese Americans during World War II* by Daniel S. Davis, illustrated; Dutton, 1982.

1983   **NONFICTION HONOR** *Hiroshima no Pika* written and illustrated by Toshi Maruki; Lothrop, Lee & Shepard, 1982.

The Jewish Americans: A History in their Own Words 1650- 1950 edited by Milton Meltzer, illustrated; Crowell, 1982.

1983   **ILLUSTRATION** *A Chair for My Mother* written and illustrated by Vera B. Williams; Greenwillow, 1982.

1983   **ILLUSTRATION HONOR** *Friends* written and illustrated by Helme Heine; Atheneum, 1982.

Yeh-Shen: A Cinderella Story from China retold by Ai-Ling Louie, illustrated by Ed Young; Philomel, 1982.

Doctor De Soto written and illustrated by William Steig; Farrar Straus Giroux, 1982.

1984   **FICTION** *A Little Fear* by Patricia Wrightson, not illustrated; Atheneum, 1983.

1984   **FICTION HONOR** *Archer's Goon* by Diana Wynne Jones, not illustrated; Greenwillow, 1984.

Unclaimed Treasures by Patricia MacLachlan, not illustrated; Harper & Row, 1984.

A Solitary Blue by Cynthia Voigt, not illustrated; Atheneum, 1983.

1984   **NONFICTION** *The Double Life of Pocahontas* by Jean Fritz, illustrated by Ed Young; Putnam, 1983.

1984   **NONFICTION HONOR** *Queen Eleanor, Independent Spirit of the Medieval World* by Polly Brooks, illustrated; Lippincott, 1983.

Children of the Wild West by Russell Freedman, illustrated with photographs; Clarion, 1983.

The Tipi; A Center of Native American Life by Charlotte Yue and David Yue, illustrated by David Yue; Knopf, 1983.

1984   **ILLUSTRATION** *Jonah and the Great Fish* written and illustrated by Warwick Hutton; Atheneum, 1984.

1984   **ILLUSTRATION HONOR** *Dawn* written and illustrated by Molly Bang; Morrow, 1983.

Guinea Pig ABC written and illustrated by Kate Duke; Dutton, 1983.

Rose in My Garden by Arnold Lobel, illustrated by Anita Lobel; Greenwillow, 1984.

1985   **FICTION** *The Moves Make the Man* by Bruce Brooks, not illustrated; Harper & Row, 1984.

1985   **FICTION HONOR** *Babe: The Gallant Pig* by Dick King-Smith, illustrated by Mary Rayner; Crown, 1985.

The Changeover by Margaret Mahy, not illustrated; Atheneum, 1984.

1985   **NONFICTION** *Commodore Perry in the Land of the Shogun* by Rhonda Blumberg, illustrated with photographs; Lothrop, Lee & Shepard, 1985.

1985   **NONFICTION HONOR** *Boy* by Roald Dahl, illustrated with photographs; Farrar Straus Giroux, 1984.

1812: The War Nobody Won by Albert Marrin, illustrated with photographs and prints; Atheneum, 1985.

1985   **ILLUSTRATION** *Mama Don't Allow* written and illustrated by Thacher Hurd; Harper & Row, 1985.

1985 ILLUSTRATION HONOR *Like Jake and Me* by Mavis Jukes, illustrated by Lloyd Bloom; Knopf, 1984.

How Much Is a Million? by David M. Schwartz, illustrated by Steven Kellogg; Lothrop, Lee & Shepard, 1985.

The Mysteries of Harris Burdick written and illustrated by Chris Van Allsburg; Houghton Mifflin, 1984.

1985 SPECIAL CITATION *1,2,3* written and illustrated by Tana Hoban; Greenwillow, 1985.

1986 FICTION *In Summer Light* by Zibby Oneal, not illustrated; Viking Kestrel, 1985.

1986 FICTION HONOR *Prairie Song* by Pam Conrad, illustrated by Darryl S. Zudeck; Harper & Row, 1985.

Howl's Moving Castle by Diana Wynne Jones, not illustrated; Greenwillow, 1986.

1986 NONFICTION *Auks, Rocks and the Odd Dinosaur: Inside Stories from the Smithsonian's Museum of Natural History* by Peggy Thomson, illustrated; Crowell, 1985.

1986 NONFICTION HONOR *Dark Harvest: Migrant Farmworkers in America* by Brent Ashabranner, photographs by Paul Conklin; Dodd Mead, 1985.

The Truth about Santa Claus by James Cross Giblin, illustrated with photographs and prints; Crowell, 1985.

1986 ILLUSTRATION *The Paper Crane* written and illustrated by Molly Bang; Greenwillow, 1985.

1986 ILLUSTRATION HONOR *Gorilla* written and illustrated by Anthony Browne; Knopf, 1985, c1983.

The Trek written and illustrated by Ann Jonas; Greenwillow, 1985.

The Polar Express written and illustrated by Chris Van Allsburg; Houghton Mifflin, 1985.

1987 FICTION *Rabble Starkey* by Lois Lowry, not illustrated; Houghton Mifflin, 1987.

1987 FICTION HONOR *Georgia Music* by Helen V. Griffith, illustrated by James Stevenson; Greenwillow, 1986.

Isaac Campion by Janni Howker, not illustrated; Greenwillow, 1986.

1987 NONFICTION *Pilgrims of Plimoth* written and illustrated by Marcia Sewall; Atheneum, 1986.

1987 NONFICTION HONOR *Being Born* by Sheila Kitzinger, photographs by Lennart Nilsson; Grosset, 1986.

The Magic School Bus at the Waterworks by Joanna Cole, illustrated by Bruce Degen; Scholastic, 1986.

Steamboat in a Cornfield written and illustrated by John Hartford; Crown, 1986.

1987 ILLUSTRATION *Mufaro's Beautiful Daughters* written and illustrated by John Steptoe; Lothrop, Lee & Shepard, 1987.

1987 ILLUSTRATION HONOR *In Coal Country* by Judith Hendershot, illustrated by Thomas B. Allen; Knopf, 1987.

Cherries and Cherry Pits written and illustrated by Vera B. Williams; Greenwillow, 1986.

Old Henry by Joan W. Blos, illustrated by Stephen Gammell; Morrow, 1987.

1988 FICTION *The Friendship* by Mildred D. Taylor, illustrated by Max Ginsburg; Dial, 1987.

1988 FICTION HONOR *Granny Was a Buffer Girl* by Berlie Doherty, not illustrated; Orchard, 1988.

Memory by Margaret Mahy, not illustrated; McElderry, 1988, c1987.

Joyful Noise: Poems for Two Voices by Paul Fleischman, illustrated by Eric Beddows; Harper & Row, 1988.

1988 NONFICTION *Anthony Burns: The Defeat and Triumph of a Fugitive Slave* by Virginia Hamilton, not illustrated; Knopf, 1988.

1988 NONFICTION HONOR *Little by Little: A Writer's Education* by Jean Little, illustrated with photos; Viking Kestrel, 1987.

African Journey by John Chiasson, illustrated with photos; Bradbury, 1987.

1988 PICTURE BOOK *The Boy of the Three-Year Nap* by Dianne Snyder, illustrated by Allen Say; Houghton Mifflin, 1988.

1988 PICTURE BOOK HONOR *Stringbean's Trip to the Shining Sea* by Vera B. Williams, illustrated by Jennifer Williams and Vera B. Williams; Greenwillow, 1988.

Where the Forest Meets the Sea illustrated by Jeannie Baker; Greenwillow, 1987.

1989 FICTION *The Village by the Sea* by Paula Fox, not illustrated; Orchard, 1988.

1989 FICTION HONOR *Eva* by Peter Dickinson, not illustrated; Delacorte, 1989.

Gideon Ahoy! written and illustrated by William Mayne; Delacorte, 1989.

1989 NONFICTION *The Way Things Work* written and illustrated by David Macaulay; Houghton Mifflin, 1988.

1989 NONFICTION HONOR *Round Buildings, Square Buildings and Buildings That Wiggle Like a Fish* by Philip M. Isaacson, illustrated with photographs; Knopf, 1988.

The Rainbow People by Laurence Yep, illustrated by David Wiesner; Harper & Row, 1989.

1989 PICTURE BOOK *Shy Charles* written and illustrated by Rosemary Wells; Dial, 1988.

1989 PICTURE BOOK HONOR *The Nativity* written and illustrated by Julie Vivas; Harcourt, Brace, Jovanovich, 1988.

Island Boy written and illustrated by Barbara Cooney; Viking, 1988.

1990 FICTION *Maniac Magee* by Jerry Spinelli, not illustrated; Little Brown, 1990.

1990 FICTION HONOR *Saturnalia* by Paul Fleischman, not illustrated; Harper & Row, 1990.

Stonewords by Pam Conrad, not illustrated; HarperCollins, 1990.

1990 NONFICTION *The Great Little Madison* by Jean Fritz, illustrated with prints and engravings; Putnam, 1989.

1990 NONFICTION HONOR *Insect Metamorphosis* by Ron Goor and Nancy Goor, illustrated by Ron Goor; Atheneum, 1990.

Shadows and Reflections written and illustrated by Tana Hoban; Greenwillow, 1990.

1990 PICTURE BOOK *Lon Po Po* written and illustrated by Ed Young; Philomel, 1989.

1990 PICTURE BOOK HONOR *Chicka Chicka Boom Boom* by Bill Martin, Jr. and John Archambault, illustrated by Lois Ehlert; Simon & Schuster, 1989.

We're Going on a Bear Hunt by Michael Rosen, illustrated by Helen Oxenbury; McElderry, 1989.

1990 SPECIAL AWARD FOR EXCELLENCE IN BOOK-MAKING *Valentine and Orson* written and illustrated by Nancy Ekholm Burkert; Farrar Straus Giroux, 1989.

1991 FICTION/POETRY *The True Confessions of Charlotte Doyle* by Avi, illustrated by Ruth E. Murray; Orchard, 1990.

1991 FICTION/POETRY HONOR *Judy Scuppernong* by Brenda Seabrooke, illustrated by Ted Lewin; Dutton, 1990.

Paradise Cafe and Other Stories by Martha Brooks, not illustrated; Little Brown, 1990.

1991 NONFICTION *Appalachia: The Voices of Sleeping Birds* by Cynthia Rylant, illustrated by Barry Moser; Harcourt, Brace, Jovanovich, 1991.

1991 NONFICTION HONOR *Good Queen Bess: The Story of Elizabeth I of England* by Diane Stanley and Peter Vennema, illustrated by Diane Stanley; Four Winds, 1990.

The Wright Brothers: How They Invented the Airplane by Russell Freedman, illustrated with photos; Holiday House, 1991.

1991 PICTURE BOOK *The Tale of the Mandarin Ducks* by Katherine Paterson, illustrated by Leo Dillon and Diane Dillon; Dutton, 1990.

1991 PICTURE BOOK HONOR *Sophie and Lou* written and illustrated by Petra Mathers; HarperCollins, 1991.

Aardvarks, Disembark! written and illustrated by Ann Jonas; Greenwillow, 1990.

1992 FICTION *Missing May* by Cynthia Rylant, not illustrated; Orchard, 1992.

1992 FICTION HONOR *Nothing But the Truth* by Avi, not illustrated; Orchard, 1991.

Somewhere in the Darkness by Walter Dean Myers, not illustrated; Scholastic, 1992.

1992 NONFICTION *Talking With Artists* by Pat Cummings, illustrated; Bradbury Press, 1992.

1992 NONFICTION HONOR *The Handmade Alphabet* written and illustrated by Laura Rankin; Dial, 1991.

Red Leaf, Yellow Leaf written and illustrated by Lois Ehlert Lois; Harcourt, Brace, Jovanovich, 1991.

1992 PICTURE BOOK *Seven Blind Mice* written and illustrated by Ed Young; Philomel, 1991.

1992 PICTURE BOOK HONOR *In the Tall, Tall Grass* written and illustrated by Denise Fleming; Henry Holt, 1991.

1993 FICTION *Ajeemah and His Son* by James Berry; HarperCollins, 1992.

1993 FICTION HONOR *The Giver* by Lois Lowry; Houghton Mifflin, 1993.

1993 NONFICTION *Sojourner Truth: Ain't I a Woman* by Patricia McKissack and Fredrick McKissack, illustrated; Scholastic, 1992.

1993 NONFICTION HONOR *Lives of the Musicians: Good Times, Bad Times (And What the Neighbors Thought)* by Kathleen Krull; Harcourt, 1993.

1993 ILLUSTRATION *The Fortune-tellers* by Lloyd Alexander, illustrated by Trina Schart Hyman; Dutton, 1992.

1993 ILLUSTRATION HONOR *Raven: A Trickster Tale from the Pacific Northwest* written and illustrated by Gerald McDermott; Harcourt, 1993.

Komodo! written and illustrated by Peter Sis; Greenwillow, 1993.

BOYS' CLUB JUNIOR BOOK AWARDS
discontinued

First awarded in 1948, the Junior Book Awards were established in 1945 by the Boys' Club of America. The purpose of the award was to encourage wider reading among members of Boys' Clubs and to give them the opportunity of recommending books to be considered for awards by an adult awards committee. There were no limitations placed on the type of literature eligible; fiction, nonfiction, and picture books were among the types considered. Gold medals and certificates were presented to the winning authors and illustrators during National Boys' Club Week. The award program was discontinued in 1969.

1948 *Big Red* by Jim Kjelgaard, illustrated by Bob Kuhn; Holiday House, 1945.

The Black Stallion Returns by Walter Farley, illustrated by Harold Eldridge; Random House, 1945.

Fun with Puzzles by Joseph Leeming, illustrated by Jessie Robinson; Lippincott, 1946.

Guns over Champlain by Leon W. Dean, not illustrated; Rinehart, 1946.

Joe Mason, Apprentice to Audubon by Charlie May Simon, illustrated by Henry C. Pitz; Dutton, 1946.

Mystery Island by Enid Blyton, illustrated by Stuart Tresilian; Macmillan, 1945.

1949 *Great Men of Medicine* by Ruth Fox, illustrated by Dwight Logan; Random House, 1947.

Heart of Danger: A Tale of Adventure on Land and Sea with Tod Moran, Third Mate of the Tramp Steamer Araby by Howard Pease, not illustrated; Doubleday, 1946.

How Much and How Many: The Story of Weights and Measures written and illustrated by Jeanne Bendick; Whittlesey House, 1947.

King of the Stallions by Edward B. Tracy, illustrated by Paul Brown; Dodd Mead, 1947.

Prairie Colt by Stephen Holt, illustrated by Wesley Dennis; Longmans, 1947.

The Rainforest written and illustrated by Armstrong Sperry; Macmillan, 1947.

Wild Animals of the Five Rivers Country by George Cory Franklin, illustrated by Mary Ogden Abbott; Houghton, 1947.

1950 *Albert Einstein* by Elma Ehrlich Levinger, illustrated with photographs; Messner, 1949.

Chains for Columbus by Alfred Powers, not illustrated; Westminster, 1948.

Cruise of the Jeanette by Edward Ellsberg, illustrated by Gerald Foster; Dodd Mead, 1949.

Fourth Down by Robert S. Bowen, not illustrated; Lothrop, 1949.

George Washington: An Initial Biography written and illustrated by Genevieve Foster; Scribner, 1949.

The Green Ginger Jar by Clara Ingram Judson, illustrated by P. Brown; Houghton, 1949.

Hearts Courageous: Twelve Who Achieved by William Herman, illustrated by James MacDonald; Dutton, 1949.

Peter's Pinto: A Story of Utah by Conrad Buff and Mary Buff, illustrated by Conrad Buff; Viking, 1949.

Snakes by Herbert Zim, illustrated by James G. Irving; Morrow, 1949.

You and Atomic Energy by John Lewellen, illustrated by L. Fisher; Childrens Press, 1949.

1951 *Boy of the North: The Story of Pierre Radisson* by Ronald Syme, illustrated by Ralph Ray; Morrow, 1950.

The Ben Lilly Legend by J. Frank Dobie, illustrated with photographs; Little Brown, 1950.

The Big Sky: An Edition for Younger Readers by Alfred B. Guthrie, Jr., illustrated by Jacob Landau; Sloane, 1950.

Hot Rod by Henry Gregor Felsen, not illustrated; Dutton, 1950.

Lost Horse by Glenn Balch, illustrated by Pers Crowell; Grosset & Dunlap, 1950.

Mahatma Gandhi: The Father of Nonviolence by Catherine Owens Peare, illustrated by Paul Frame; Hawthorne, 1950.

The Shining Shooter by Marion Renick, illustrated by Dwight Logan; Scribner, 1950.

The Sky River by Fa-shun Chang, illustrated by Jeanyee Wong; Lothrop, 1950.

Son of the Hawk by Thomas H. Raddall, illustrated by Stanley Turner; Winston, 1950.

1952 *Bucky Forrester* by Leland Silliman, illustrated by Norman Guthrie Rudolph; Winston, 1951.

Bullard of the Space Patrol by Malcolm Jameson, not illustrated; World, 1951.

The Cowboy and His Horse written and illustrated by Sydney E. Fletcher; Grosset, 1951.

Johnny Wants to be a Policeman by Wilbur J. Granberg, illustrated by Alison Cummings; Aladdin, 1951.

The Kid Who Batted 1.000 by Bob Allison and Frank Ernest Hill, illustrated by Paul Galdone; Doubleday, 1951.

A Long Way to Frisco: A Folk Adventure Novel of California and Oregon in 1852 by Alfred Powers, illustrated by James Daugherty; Little Brown, 1951.

Minn of the Mississippi written and illustrated by Holling Clancy Holling; Houghton, 1951.

The Official Encyclopedia of Baseball by Hy Turkin and Sherley Clark Thompson, illustrated with photographs and diagrams; A.S. Barnes, 1951.

Passage to America: The Story of the Great Migrations by Katherine B. Shippen, not illustrated; Harper, 1950.

Phil Sterling, Salesman by Michael Gross, not illustrated; Dodd Mead, 1951.

1953 *Benjie and His Family* by Sally Scott, illustrated by Beth Krush; Harcourt, 1952.

Buffalo Bill written and illustrated by Ingri d'Aulaire and Edgar Parin d'Aulaire; Doubleday, 1952.

Marooned on Mars by Lester del Rey, illustrated by Alex Schomburg; Winston, 1952.

A Place for Peter by Elizabeth Yates, illustrated by Nora S. Unwin; Coward, 1952.

The Trap by Kenneth Gilbert, illustrated by Fred Collins; Holt, 1952.

True Tales of Buried Treasure by Edward Rowe Snow, illustrated with photographs and maps; Dodd Mead, 1951.

1953 **SPECIAL CERTIFICATE OF AWARD FOR A SPECIAL SERIES** *The Real Book* series edited boy Helen Hoke; Doubleday, various years.

1954 *And Now Miguel* by Joseph Krumgold, illustrated by Jean Charlot; Crowell, 1953.

Fast Iron written and illustrated by Victor Mays; Houghton, 1953.

Fast Is not a Ladybug: A Book about Fast and Slow Things by Miriam Schlein, illustrated by Leonard Kessler; Scott, 1953.

The Golden Geography: A Child's Introduction to the World by Elsa Jane Werner, illustrated by Cornelius DeWitt; Simon & Schuster, 1952.

Mr. Revere and I written and illustrated by Robert Lawson; Little, 1953.

1954 **SPECIAL CERTIFICATE OF AWARD FOR A SERIES OF BIOGRAPHIES** *Signature Books* edited by Enid La Monte Meadowcraft; Grosset, various years.

1955 *Alphonse, That Bearded One* by Natalie Savage Carlson, illustrated by Nicolas Mordvinoff; Harcourt, 1954.

High Road Home by William Corbin, not illustrated; Coward, 1954.

Hound Dog Moses and the Promised Land by Walter D. Edmonds, illustrated by William Gropper; Dodd Mead, 1954.

The Little Horse Bus by Graham Greene, illustrated by Dorothy Craigie; Lothrop Lee & Shepard, 1954.

The Secret of the Two Feathers by Ivo Duka and Helena Kolda, illustrated with photographs by Helena Kolda; Harper & Row, 1954.

Squanto, Friend of the White Man by Clyde Robert Bulla, illustrated by Peter Burchard; Crowell, 1954.

1955 **SPECIAL CERTIFICATE OF AWARD FOR SERIES OF BOOKS ABOUT SCIENCE** *All About Books* published by Random House, various years.

1956 *Eddie and His Big Deals* written and illustrated by Carolyn Haywood; Morrow, 1955.

Great Discoverers in Modern Science by Patrick Pringle, illustrated with photographs; Roy, 1955.

Switch on the Night by Ray Bradbury, illustrated by Madeleine Gekiere; Pantheon, 1955.

Wheels: A Pictorial History written and illustrated by Edwin Tunis; World, 1955.

Wings Against the Wind by Natalie Savage Carlson, illustrated by Mircea Vasiliu; Harper & Row, 1955.

1957 *Beaver Water* by Rutherford G. Montgomery, illustrated by Robert Doremus; World, 1956.

The First Lake Dwellers by Chester G. Osborne, illustrated by Richard N. Osborne; Follett, 1956.

Quest of the Snow Leopard by Roy Chapman Andrews, illustrated by Kurt Wiese; Viking, 1955.

The Story of Albert Schweitzer by Jo Manton Gittings, illustrated by Astrid Walford; Abelard, 1955; Methuen, 1955.

Trail Blazer of the Seas by Jean Lee Latham, illustrated by Victor Mays; Houghton Mifflin, 1956.

1958 *The Earth's Satellite: Man's First True Space Adventure* by John Lewellen, illustrated by Ida Scheib; Knopf, 1957.

Hokahey! American Indians Then and Now by Edith Dorian, illustrated by W.N. Wilson; Whittlesey House, 1957.

Prehistoric Man and the Primates written and illustrated by William E. Scheele; World, 1957.

This Is the Story of Faint George Who Wanted to be a Knight written and illustrated by Robert E. Barry; Houghton, 1957.

The Valiant Sailor by Cicely Fox Smith, illustrated by Neville Dear; Criterion, 1957.

The Wonderful World of the Sea by James Fisher, illustrated by Eileen Aplin and others; Doubleday, 1957.

1959 *The Adventure of Light* written and illustrated by Frank Jupo; Prentice Hall, 1958.

All Aboard: Poems by Mary Britton Miller, illustrated by Bill Sokol; Pantheon, 1958.

Avalanche! by A. Rutgers Van der Loeff, illustrated by Gustav Schrotter; Morrow, 1958.

Digging into Yesterday by Estelle E. Friedman, illustrated by Leonard Everett Fisher; Putnam, 1958.

The Golden Impala by Pamela Ropner, illustrated by Ralph Thompson; Criterion, 1958.

Simba of the White Mane by Jocelyn Arundel, illustrated by Wesley Dennis; Whittlesey, 1958.

1960 *The Byzantines* by Thomas C. Chubb, illustrated by Richard M. Powers; World, 1959.

Dinosaurs and Other Prehistoric Animals by Darlene Geis, illustrated by Russell F. Petersen; Grosset, 1959.

The First Book of Color by Herbert P. Paschel, illustrated by Caru Studios; Watts, 1959.

Jets and Rockets and How they Work written and illustrated by William P. Gottlieb; Doubleday, 1959.

The Silver Sword by Ian Serraillier, illustrated by C. Walter Hodges; Cape, 1956; Criterion, 1959.

The Snow Party by Beatrice Schenk deRegniers, illustrated by Reiner Zimnik; Pantheon, 1959.

1961 *The Challenge of the Sea* by Arthur C. Clarke, illustrated by Alex Schomburg; Holt, 1960.

Devil's Hill by Nan Chauncy, illustrated by Geraldine Spence; Oxford, 1958; Watts, 1960.

Grishka and the Bear by Rene Guillot, translated by Gwen Marsh, illustrated by Joan Kiddell-Monroe; Criterion, 1959.

Map Making: The Art that Became a Science by Lloyd A. Brown, illustrated with charts and diagrams; Little, 1960.

Rasmus and the Vagabond by Astrid Lindgren, illustrated by Eric Palmquist; Viking, 1960.

This Is New York written and illustrated by Miroslav Sasek; Macmillan, 1960.

1962 *Digging up America* by Frank Cummings Hibben, illustrated with photographs; Hill & Wang, 1960.

Elsa, the True Story of a Lioness by Joy Adamson, illustrated with photographs; Pantheon, 1961.

The Man Who Sang the Sillies by John Ciardi, illustrated by Edward Gorey; Lippincott, 1961.

Next, Please written and illustrated by Robert E. Barry; Houghton, 1961.

The Road to Agra by Aimee Sommerfelt, illustrated by Ulf Aas; Criterion, 1961.

The Wonderful World of Communication by Lancelot T. Hogben, illustrated with photographs; Doubleday, 1959.

1963 *America's First Army* by Burke Davis, illustrated by Richard Stinely, photographs by John Crane; Rinehart/Colonial Williamsburg, 1962.

The Early Eagles by Frank Donovan, illustrated with photographs; Dodd Mead, 1962.

Owls in the Family by Farley Mowat, illustrated by Robert Frankenberg; Little Brown, 1961.

Robert Boyle, Founder of Modern Chemistry by Harry Sootin, illustrated by Gustav Schrotter; Watts, 1962.

Stars, Mosquitoes and Crocodiles: The American Travels of Alexander von Humboldt edited by Millicent E. Selsam, illustrated by Russell Francis Peterson; Harper & Row, 1962.

The Tide in the Attic by Aleid Van Rhijn, illustrated by Margorie Gill; Criterion, 1962.

1964 *The Boundary Riders* by Joan Phipson, illustrated by Margaret Horder; Harcourt, 1963.

The Bully of Barkham Street by Mary Stolz, illustrated by Leonard Shortall; Harper & Row, 1963.

By the Great Horn Spoon! by Sid Fleischman, illustrated by Eric Von Schmidt; Atlantic-Little, 1963.

Coyote, Come Home by B.F. Beebe, illustrated by Larry Toschik; McKay, 1963.

The North American Indians: Life and Lore written and illustrated by Ernest Berke; Doubleday, 1963.

1965 *Communism, An American's View* by Gerald W. Johnson, illustrated by Leonard Everett Fisher; Morrow, 1964.

Powder and Steel: Notable Battles and Campaigns of the 1800's from New Orleans to the Zulu War written and illustrated by Robert Orbaan; John Day, 1963.

The Pushcart War by Jean Merrill, illustrated by Ronni Solbert; Scott, 1964.

Rain in the Woods and Other Small Matters written and illustrated by Glen Rounds; World, 1964.

The Two Reigns of Tutankhamen by William Wise, illustrated with photographs; Putnam, 1964.

1966 *I Had Trouble in Getting to Solla Sollew* written and illustrated by Dr. Seuss; Random House, 1965.

Jack Holburn by Leon Garfield, illustrated by Antony Maitland; Pantheon, 1965.

North to Freedom by Anne S. Holm, translated by L.W. Kingsland, not illustrated; Harcourt, 1965.

The Quest: A Report on Extraterrestrial Life by Thomas Benton Allen, illustrated with charts; Chilton, 1965.

Ramlal by Albert Theodore William Simeons, illustrated by Robert Shore; Atheneum, 1965.

1966-67 *The Ghost Rock Mystery* by Mary C. Jane, illustrated by Ray Abel; Scholastic, 1966.

Helen Keller's Teacher by Mickie Davidson, illustrated by Wayne Blickenstaff; Scholastic, 1966.

Lions in the Way by Bella Rodman, not illustrated; Follett, 1966.

Mother, Mother, I Feel Sick, Send for the Doctor Quick, Quick, Quick by Burton Supree and Remy Charlip, illustrated by Remy Charlip; Parents, 1966.

The Pushcart War by Jean Merrill, illustrated by Ronni Solbert; Scott, 1964.

The Timid Ghost: or, What Would You Do with a Sackful of Gold? by Anita Brenner, illustrated by Jean Charlot; Scott, 1966.

Who Goes Next? True Stories of Exciting Escapes by Robert Edmond Alter, illustrated by Albert Orbaan; Putnam, 1966.

1966-67 **CERTIFICATE** *The Battle of the Bulge* by John Toland, illustrated by Jerome Kuhl; Random House, 1966.

Benny's Animals and How He Put them in Order by Millicent E. Selsam, illustrated by Arnold Lobel; Harper & Row, 1966.

For Conspicuous Gallantry: Winners of the Medal of Honor by Donald E. Cooke, illustrated by Jack Woodson; Hammond, 1966.

Joseph Strauss: Builder of the Golden Gate Bridge by Michael Chester, illustrated by Tom Hamil; Putnam, 1965.

Max Smart and the Perilous Pellets by William Johnston, not illustrated; Grosset, 1966.

Pecos Bill and the Mustang by Harold W. Felton, illustrated by Leonard Shortall; Prentice Hall, 1965.

Sandy Koufax by Jerry Mitchell, not illustrated; Grosset, 1966.

Willie Mays by Arnold Hano, not illustrated; Grosset, 1966.

1966-67 **SPECIAL CITATION** *Trumpeter of Krakow* by Eric P. Kelly, illustrated by Angela Pruszynska; Macmillan, 1928.

1968 *Charlie the Tramp* by Russell Hoban, illustrated by Lillian Hoban; Scholastic, 1967.

Five-yard Fuller of the N.Y. Gnats by Robert Wells, illustrated by Harold Eldridge; Putnam, 1967.

The Flying Hockey Stick written and illustrated by Roger Bradfield; Rand McNally, 1966.

Three Gold Pieces written and illustrated by Aliki; Pantheon, 1967.

1968 **CERTIFICATE** *And Loving It!* by William Johnston, not illustrated; Grosset, 1967.

Bart Starr by John Devaney, illustrated with photographs; Scholastic, 1967.

The Minstrel and the Mountain: A Tale of Peace by Jane Yolen, illustrated by Anne Rockwell; World, 1967.

The Pai-Pai Pig by Joy Anderson, illustrated by Jay Yang; Harcourt, 1967.

BOYS' LIFE-DODD, MEAD WRITING AWARD
discontinued

This literary competition was begun by the editors of Boys' Life and Dodd, Mead & Company in 1949. This was an annual competition in search of a story of distinctive literary merit and in the American tradition written for boys ages twelve through sixteen. The winning author received $1000 from Boys' Life for first serial rights and $1000 advance against royalties from Dodd, Mead. The award was presented for the last time in 1961.

1950 *The Secret of the Undersea Bell* by John Scott Douglas, not illustrated; Dodd Mead, 1951.

1952 *Sled Dog of Alaska* by Jack Landru, not illustrated; Dodd Mead, 1953.

1953 *Star-crossed Stallion* by Patrick Lawson, not illustrated; Dodd Mead, 1954.

1954 *White Gold in the Cassiar* by William G. Crisp, not illustrated; Dodd Mead, 1955.

1955 *Pony Express Boy* by Marian Talmadge and Iris Gilmore, illustrated; Dodd Mead, 1956.

1956 *Dangerous Deadline* by Mildred Benson, not illustrated; Dodd Mead, 1957.

Trouble at Turtle Bay by Marie Holmstrand, not illustrated; Dodd Mead, 1957.

1957 *Pokes of Gold* by Edesse Peery, not illustrated; Dodd Mead, 1958.

1958 *Missouri River Boy* by William Heuman, illustrated by Robert Handville; Dodd Mead, 1959.

1959 *Ulysses and his Woodland Zoo* by Jim Kjelgaard, illustrated by Kendall Rossi; Dodd Mead, 1960.

1960 *On Guard!* by Diantha Warfel, not illustrated; Dodd Mead, 1961.

1961 *The Bear: Ship of Many Lives* written and illustrated by Stella F. Rapaport; Dodd Mead, 1962.

ANN CONNOR BRIMER AWARD

Nova Scotia Library Association
Ann Connor Brimer Committee
P O Box 36036
Halifax, Nova Scotia
B3J 3S9 Canada

This award is named for Ann Connor Brimer who opened the first children's bookstore in Nova Scotia and was a longtime supporter of Canadian children's literature. This annual award carries a $500 cash prize and is presented for a book published in Canada that has made an outstanding contribution to children's literature.

The author must be a resident in Atlantic Canada and the book, either fiction or nonfiction, must have been published the preceding year. The winning book is representative of the best of its type produced in Atlantic Canada with consistent style, narrative strength, accuracy, and suitability for the intended audience.

1991 *Pit Pony* by Joyce C. Barkhouse, illustrated by Henry Van Der Linde; Gage, 1989.

1992 *Eating Between the Lines* by Kevin Major, not illustrated; Doubleday Canada, 1991.

1993 *Oliver's Wars* by Budge Wilson, not illustrated; Stoddart, 1992.

BRITISH BOOK AWARDS

Merric Davidson
Oakwood
Ashley Park, Tunbridge Wells
Kent TN4 8UA
England

Established in 1989, the British Book Awards were organized by Publishing News. Two categories include Children's Author of the Year and the Illustrated Children's Book of the Year. The Illustrated category was added in 1990. The annual recipients receive the prestigious "Nibbie" trophy. All books published in the United Kingdom are eligible, regardless of the nationality of the author/illustrator. The shortlist is chosen by canvassing over 100 United Kingdom booksellers, nominations from the public, and by direct submissions from publishers.

1989 AUTHOR Roald Dahl

1989 AUTHOR RUNNERUP Allan Ahlberg, Janet Ahlberg, Michael Rosen

1990 AUTHOR Anne Fine

1990 AUTHOR RUNNERUP Dick King-Smith, Joan Aiken

1990 ILLUSTRATED *The Mousehole Cat* by Antonia Barber, illustrated by Nicola Bayley; Walker, 1990; Macmillan, 1990.

1990 ILLUSTRATED RUNNERUP *Alphabeasts* written and illustrated by Quentin Blake; Gollancz, 1990.

Jolly Tall written and illustrated by Jane Hissey; Hutchinson, 1990; Philomel, 1990.

1991 AUTHOR Dick King-Smith

1991 AUTHOR RUNNERUP Allan Ahlberg, Janet Ahlberg, Anne Fine

1991 ILLUSTRATED *Farmer Duck* by Martin Waddell, illustrated by Helen Oxenbury; Walker, 1991; Candlewick, 1992.

1991 ILLUSTRATED RUNNERUP *Jolly Snow* written and illustrated by Jane Hissey; Hutchinson, 1991; Philomel, 1991.

The Minpins by Roald Dahl, illustrated by Patrick Benson; Cape, 1991; Viking, 1991.

1992 AUTHOR Raymond Briggs

1992 AUTHOR RUNNERUP Gillian Cross, Berlie Doherty, Brian Jacques, Robin Jarvis

1992 ILLUSTRATED *Penguin Small* written and illustrated by Mick Inkpen; Hodder & Stoughton, 1992; Harcourt Brace, 1993.

1992 ILLUSTRATED RUNNERUP *Monkey Tricks* written and illustrated by Camilla Ashforth; Walker, 1992; Candlewick, 1992.

Stephen Biesty's Incredible Cross Sections by Richard Platt, illustrated by Stephen Biesty; Viking, 1992; Knopf, 1992.

The Story of Creation illustrated by Jane Ray; Orchard, 1992; Dutton, 1993.

The Bones Book and Skeleton by Stephen Cumbaa, illustrated by Kim LaFave; Workman, 1991.

After the Storm by Nick Butterworth.

BROOKLYN ART BOOKS FOR CHILDREN CITATION
see **ART BOOKS FOR CHILDREN CITATION**

MARY GRANT BRUCE STORY AWARD FOR CHILDREN'S LITERATURE

Secretariat
Fellowship of Australian Writers - Victoria
1/317 Barkers Rd
Kew, Victoria 3101
Australia

This award is sponsored by the city of Sale, which manages the trust fund and is administered by the Victorian Fellowship of Australian Writers. Awarded in honor of Mary Grant Bruce, it recognizes an outstanding manuscript intended for children between ten and fifteen years of age. The monetary prizes are awarded annually.

1986 OPEN $500 *How Casbo Became a Clown* by Luceille Hanley.

1986 WRITER LIVING IN GIPPSLAND $200 *Holly and the Porpoises* by Carole Williams.

1986 ADDITIONAL $100 *Clever Juice* by Edel Wignell.

1989 OPEN $500 *The Terrible Tale of the Vanishing Library* by Adrian Peniston-Bird.

1989 WRITER LIVING IN GIPPSLAND $200 *Lisa of the Lyrebird Creek* by Carole Williams.

1989 ADDITIONAL $100 *The Farmhouse* by Archimede Fusillo.

1990 OPEN $500 *Through the Web* by Ellen Robertson.

1990 WRITER LIVING IN GIPPSLAND $200 *The Second-hand Tongue* by Garry Hurle.

1990 ADDITIONAL $100 *A Cat for Samantha* by Margaret Watts.

1991 OPEN $500 *Best and Fairest* by Helen Manos.

1991 WRITER LIVING IN GIPPSLAND $200 Christine Edwards

1991 ADDITIONAL $100 *Raining Away to Sea* by Kate Walker.

BUCKEYE CHILDREN'S BOOK AWARD

Floyd C. Dickman
The State Library of Ohio
65 South Front St
Room 506
Columbus, OH 43215

This award, first presented in 1982, is sponsored by the Ohio Council International Reading Association, Ohio Council of Teachers of English Language Arts, Ohio Department of Education, Ohio Educational Library Media Association, Ohio Library Association and the State Library of Ohio. From 1982 through 1984 there were two categories, K-3 and 4-8, with winners and honor books in each. As of 1985, the categories were changed to K-2, 3-5, and 6-8. The award was presented annually from 1982 through 1984, with a change to biennial status in 1985.

Books of fiction or nonfiction written by an author in residence in the United States and published within the last five years are eligible to be nominated. Nomination and final voting is done by the children in public and private elementary and middle schools.

This award program was designed to encourage children to read literature critically, encourage teacher involvement in children's literature programs, and to commend authors of this literature. A plaque for the first place winners and a certificate for honor book winners are presented at the annual convention of either OCIRA, OCTELA, OELMA, or OLA on a rotating basis.

1982 GRADES K-3 *The Berenstain Bears and the Spooky Old Tree* written and illustrated by Stan Berenstain and Jan Berenstain; Random House, 1978.

1982 GRADES K-3 HONOR *Miss Nelson Is Missing!* by Harry Allard, illustrated by James Marshall; Houghton Mifflin, 1977; Scholastic, 1978.

Cloudy with a Chance of Meatballs by Judi Barrett, illustrated by Ron Barrett; Atheneum, 1978.

1982 GRADES 4-8 *Superfudge* by Judy Blume, not illustrated; Dutton, 1980.

1982 GRADES 4-8 HONOR *Bunnicula: A Rabbit Tale of Mystery* by Deborah Howe and James Howe, illustrated by Alan Daniel; Atheneum, 1979.

Encyclopedia Brown and the Case of the Midnight Visitor by Donald J. Sobol, illustrated by Lillian Brandi; Nelson, 1977.

1983 GRADES K-3 *Grandpa's Ghost Stories* written and illustrated by James Flora; Atheneum, 1978.

1983 GRADES K-3 HONOR *Cloudy with a Chance of Meatballs* by Judi Barrett, illustrated by Ron Barrett; Atheneum, 1978.

Amelia Bedelia and the Baby by Peggy Parish, illustrated by Lynn Sweat; Greenwillow, 1981.

Jumanji written and illustrated by Chris Van Allsburg; Houghton Mifflin, 1981.

1983 GRADES 4-8 *Tiger Eyes* by Judy Blume, not illustrated; Bradbury, 1981.

1983 GRADES 4-8 HONOR *Light in the Attic* written and illustrated by Shel Silverstein; Harper & Row, 1981.

Nothing's Fair in Fifth Grade by Barthe DeClements, not illustrated; Viking, 1981.

1984 GRADES K-3 *E.T.: Extraterrestrial Storybook* by William Kotzwinkle, based on the screenplay by Melissa Mathison, not illustrated; Putnam, 1982.

1984 GRADES 4-8 *Nothing's Fair in Fifth Grade* by Barthe DeClements, not illustrated; Viking, 1981.

1985 GRADES K-2 *Berenstain Bears Get in a Fight* written and illustrated by Stan Berenstain and Jan Berenstain; Random House, 1982.

1985 GRADES 3-5 *Ramona Quimby, Age 8* by Beverly Cleary, illustrated by Alan Tiegreen; Morrow, 1981.

1985 GRADES 6-8 *Light in the Attic* written and illustrated by Shel Silverstein; Harper & Row, 1981.

1987 GRADES K-2 *In a Dark, Dark Room and other Scary Stories* retold by Alvin Schwartz, illustrated by Dirk Zimmer; Harper & Row, 1984.

1987 GRADES 3-5 *Scary Stories to Tell in the Dark* by Alvin Schwartz, illustrated by Stephen Gammell; Lippincott, 1981.

1987 GRADES 6-8 *Thirteen Ways to Sink a Sub* by Jamie Gilson, illustrated by Linda S. Edwards; Lothrop, Lee & Shepard, 1982.

1989 GRADES K-2 *If You Give a Mouse a Cookie* by Laura J. Numeroff, illustrated by Felicia Bond; Harper & Row, 1985.

1989 GRADES 3-5 *More Scary Stories to Tell in the Dark* by Alvin Schwartz, illustrated by Stephen Gammell; Lippincott, 1984.

1989 GRADES 6-8 *Sixth Grade Can Really Kill You* by Barthe DeClements, not illustrated; Viking Kestrel, 1985.

1991 GRADES K-2 *The Polar Express* written and illustrated by Chris Van Allsburg; Houghton Mifflin, 1985.

1991 GRADES 3-5 *There's a Boy in the Girls' Bathroom* by Louis Sachar, not illustrated; Knopf, 1987.

1991 GRADES 6-8 *Hatchet* by Gary Paulsen, not illustrated; Bradbury, 1987.

1993 GRADES K-2 *The Very Quiet Cricket* written and illustrated by Eric Carle; Philomel, 1990.

1993 GRADES 3-5 *Scary Stories 3: More Tales To Chill Your Bones* retold by Alvin Schwartz, illustrated by Stephen Gammell; HarperCollins, 1991.

1993 GRADES 6-8 *Maniac Magee* by Jerry Spinelli, not illustrated; Little Brown, 1990.

BURNLEY EXPRESS AWARD

discontinued

replaced by **LANCASHIRE COUNTY LIBRARY/ NATIONAL AND PROVINCIAL BUILDING SOCIETY CHILDREN'S BOOK OF THE YEAR AWARD**

This annual award was sponsored by the Burnley Express and the National and Provincial Building Society. A prize of £250 was awarded to a writer of the most outstanding work of fiction for children ages five through fourteen.

1985 *Badger on the Barge and other Stories* by Janni Howker, not illustrated; Julia MacRae, 1984; Greenwillow, 1984.

1986 *Barty* by Janet Collins, not illustrated; Blackie, 1986.

1987 *Granny Was a Buffer Girl* by Berlie Doherty, not illustrated; Methuen, 1986; Orchard, 1988.

1988 *Red Sky in the Morning* by Elizabeth Laird, not illustrated; Heinemann, 1988.

ELIZABETH BURR AWARD

Wisconsin Library Association

Sponsored by the Wisconsin Library Association, this award was first given in 1992. It is presented to an author or illustrator with a Wisconsin connection, for distinguished achievement in children's literature.

1992 *Red Leaf, Yellow Leaf* written and illustrated by Lois Ehlert; Harcourt, Brace, Jovanovich, 1991.

EDITH BUSBY AWARD: DODD, MEAD LIBRARIAN AND TEACHER PRIZE COMPETITION

discontinued

Established by the Dodd, Mead Company in 1954, this award for children's literature was given annually until 1971. Original, unpublished manuscripts consisting of at least 50,000 words and written in English were eligible. The manuscripts were to have been authored by an American librarian or teacher who was working (or who had worked) with children and young people. Manuscripts with an American background and spirit were preferred. The winner received a publishing contract with Dodd, Mead and a $2500 advance against royalties and commissions.

1954 *The Different One* by Pauline H. Coleman, not illustrated; Dodd Mead, 1955.

1955 *The Cornhusk Doll* by Eleanor Reindollar Wilcox, illustrated by Gerald McCann; Dodd Mead, 1956.

1956 *Shadow Across the Campus* by Helen R. Sattley, not illustrated; Dodd Mead, 1957.

1957 *A Business of Their Own* by Lavinia G. Dobler, not illustrated; Dodd Mead, 1958.

1958 *Treasure your Love* by Leona Klipsch, not illustrated; Dodd Mead, 1959.

1959 *This Was Bridget* by Mary Malone, illustrated by Robert Handville; Dodd Mead, 1960.

1960 *Milenka's Happy Summer* by Mary Barker, illustrated by Paul Lantz; Dodd Mead, 1961.

1961 *The Voyage of the Flying Bird* by Margaret Titcomb, illustrated by Joseph Feher; Dodd Mead, 1963.

1962 *Connie Bell, M.D.* by Helen Tann Aschmann, not illustrated; Dodd Mead, 1963.

1963 *The Mystery at Crane's Landing* by Marcella Thum, not illustrated; Dodd Mead, 1964.

1964 *Ghost Hound of Thunder Valley* by Ewart A. Autry, illustrated by Sam Savitt; Dodd Mead, 1965.

1965 *Wheels for Ginny's Chariot* by Earlene W. Luis and Barbara F. Millar, not illustrated; Dodd Mead, 1966.

1966 *Meagher of the Sword: A Dramatization of the Life of Thomas Francis Meagher* by Christian D. Stevens, illustrated with photographs; Dodd Mead, 1967.

1967 No Award

1968 *Midshipman Plowright* by James T. Pole, illustrated with maps; Dodd Mead, 1969.

1969 *Pi Gal* by Valerie King Page, illustrated by Jacques Callaert; Dodd Mead, 1970.

1970 No Award

1971 *Walk in the Sky* by Jack Ishmole, not illustrated; Dodd Mead, 1972.

C

CBC HONORS PROGRAM

Children's Book Council
568 Broadway
New York, NY 10003

Sponsored by the Children's Book Council, the CBC Honors Program was initiated in 1985 and will continue irregularly in association with various Council programming events. The purpose of the program is to salute people whose work in books, communications, and child advocacy, over a sustained period of time, warrants special recognition. The winners for the book and communication categories are listed below.

1985 **BOOKS** Beverly Cleary

1985 **COMMUNICATION** Fred Rogers

1988 Milton Meltzer, Mildred Taylor

RANDOLPH CALDECOTT MEDAL

Association for Library Services for Children
American Library Association
50 East Huron St
Chicago, IL 60611

Frederic Melcher, originator of the Caldecott Medal, suggested in 1937 that an award be given to an illustrator who created the most distinguished picture book for children. The award was named in honor of Randolph Caldecott, the outstanding nineteenth-century English illustrator. The Section for Library Work with Children (now ALSC) of ALA sponsored the program. As with the Newbery Medal, the Melcher family donates the medal.

The Caldecott is given to the artist of the most distinguished American picture book for children published in the U.S. during the preceding year. The award shall go to the artist, who must be a citizen or resident of the U.S., whether or not he/she is the author of the text.

There are no limitations on the age level of the books, although most picture books are intended for young children. The award is made for a picture book in which the pictures, rather than the text, are the heart of the book.

The recipient is chosen by the Caldecott Medal Committee which consists of fifteen members, seven elected and eight appointed. In addition to the winner, an unspecified number of honor books are also cited. The winners receive a gold medal and the honor book recipients are presented with certificates. The winners are announced in January at the ALA Midwinter meeting and the awards are presented at the Newbery-Caldecott Banquet held in June at the ALA annual convention.

The ALSC has provided the following definitions for words and phrases used in the terms of the award: (1) Picture book for children, as distinguished from other books with illustrations, is one that essentially provides the child with a visual experience. A picture book has a collective unity of storyline, theme or concept, developed through the series of pictures of which the book is comprised. (2) Picture book for children is one for which children are a potential audience. The book displays respect for children's understandings, abilities, and appreciations. Children are defined as persons of ages up to and including fourteen and picture books for this entire age range are to be considered. (3) Distinguished is defined as being marked by eminence and distinction, marked by excellence in quality, marked by conspicuous excellence or eminence, or is individually distinct. (4) The artist is the illustrator or co-illustrators. The artist may be awarded the Medal posthumously.

In order to identify a distinguished picture book, the committee needs to consider the following criteria: (1) excellence of execution in the artistic technique employed; (2) excellence of pictorial interpretation of story, theme, or concept; (3) excellence of appropriateness of style of illustrations to the story, theme or concept; (4) excellence of delineation of plot, theme, characters, setting, mood or information through the pictures. (5) the only limitation to graphic form is that the form must be one which may be used in a picture book (e.g., motion picture photography is not at present possible, though still photography is). (6) the committee should keep in mind that the award is for distinguished illustrations in a picture book and for excellence of pictorial presentation for children. The award is not for didactic intent, nor for popularity. (From guidelines adopted by the ALSC Board in January 1978.)

1938 *Animals of the Bible: A Picture Book* by Helen Dean Fish, illustrated by Dorothy P. Lathrop; Stokes, 1937.

1938 **HONOR** *Four and Twenty Blackbirds: Nursery Rhymes of Yesterday Recalled for Children of Today* by Helen Dean Fish, illustrated by Robert Lawson; Lippincott, 1937.

Seven Simeons: A Russian Tale written and illustrated by Boris Artzybasheff; Viking, 1937.

1939 *Mei Li* written and illustrated by Thomas Handforth; Doubleday, Doran, 1938.

1939 **HONOR** *Andy and the Lion* written and illustrated by James Daugherty; Viking, 1938.

Barkis written and illustrated by Clare Turlay Newberry; Harper, 1938.

The Forest Pool written and illustrated by Laura Adams Armer; Longmans, Green, 1938.

Snow White and the Seven Dwarfs translated and illustrated by Wanda Gag; Coward, 1938.

Wee Gillis by Munro Leaf, illustrated by Robert Lawson; Viking, 1938.

1940 *Abraham Lincoln* written and illustrated by Edgar Parin d'Aulaire and Ingri d'Aulaire; Doubleday, Doran, 1939.

1940 **HONOR** *The Ageless Story: With Its Antiphons* written and illustrated by Lauren Ford; Dodd Mead, 1939.

Cock-a-Doodle Doo written and illustrated by Berta Hader and Elmer Hader; Macmillan, 1939.

Madeline written and illustrated by Ludwig Bemelmans; Simon & Schuster, 1939.

1941 *They Were Strong and Good* written and illustrated by Robert Lawson; Viking, 1940.

1941 **HONOR** *April's Kittens* written and illustrated by Clare Turlay Newberry; Harper & Row, 1940.

1942 *Make Way for Ducklings* written and illustrated by Robert McCloskey; Viking, 1941.

1942 **HONOR** *An American ABC* written and illustrated by Miska Petersham and Maud Petersham; Macmillan, 1941.

In My Mother's House by Ann Nolan Clark, illustrated by Velino Herrera; Viking, 1941.

Nothing At All written and illustrated by Wanda Gag; Coward, 1941.

Paddle-to-the-Sea written and illustrated by Holling Clancy Holling; Houghton, 1941.

1943 *The Little House* written and illustrated by Virginia Lee Burton; Houghton, 1942.

1943 **HONOR** *Dash and Dart* written and illustrated by Conrad Buff and Mary Buff; Viking, 1942.

Marshmallow written and illustrated by Clare Turlay Newberry; Harper & Row, 1942.

1944 *Many Moons* by James Thurber, illustrated by Louis Slobodkin; Harcourt, 1943.

1944 **HONOR** *A Child's Good Night Book* by Margaret Wise Brown, illustrated by Jean Charlot; Scott, 1943.

Good Luck Horse by Chih-Yi Chan, illustrated by Plato Chan; Whittlesey House, 1943.

Mighty Hunter written and illustrated by Elmer Hader and Berta Hader; Macmillan, 1943.

Pierre Pidgeon by Lee Kingman, illustrated by Arnold Edwin Bare; Houghton, 1943.

Small Rain: Verses from the Bible by Jessie Orton Jones, illustrated by Elizabeth Orton Jones; Viking, 1943.

1945 *Prayer for a Child* by Rachel Field, illustrated by Elizabeth Orton Jones; Macmillan, 1944.

1945 **HONOR** *The Christmas Anna Angel* by Ruth Sawyer, illustrated by Kate Seredy; Viking, 1944.

In the Forest written and illustrated by Marie Hall Ets; Viking, 1944.

Mother Goose compiled and illustrated by Tasha Tudor; Oxford, 1944.

Yonie Wondernose written and illustrated by Marguerite de Angeli; Doubleday, 1944.

1946 *The Rooster Crows* written and illustrated by Maud Petersham and Miska Petersham; Macmillan, 1945.

1946 **HONOR** *Little Lost Lamb* by Golden MacDonald, illustrated by Leonard Weisgard; Doubleday, Doran, 1945.

My Mother Is the Most Beautiful Woman in the World by Becky Reyher, illustrated by Ruth C. Gannett; Lothrop Lee & Shepard, 1945.

Sing Mother Goose music by Opal Wheeler, illustrated by Marjorie Torrey; Dutton, 1945.

You Can Write Chinese written and illustrated by Kurt Wiese; Viking, 1945.

1947 *The Little Island* by Golden MacDonald, illustrated by Leonard Weisgard; Doubleday, 1946.

1947 **HONOR** *Boats on the River* by Marjorie Flack, illustrated by Jay Hyde Barnum; Viking, 1946.

Pedro, the Angel of Olvera Street written and illustrated by Leo Politi; Scribner, 1946.

Rain Drop Splash by Alvin R. Tresselt, illustrated by Leonard Weisgard; Lothrop Lee & Shepard, 1946.

Sing in Praise: A Collection of the Best Loved Hymns by Opal Wheeler, illustrated by Marjorie Torrey; Dutton, 1946.

Timothy Turtle by Al Graham, illustrated by Tony Palazzo; Robert Welch, 1946.

1948 *White Snow, Bright Snow* by Alvin Tresselt, illustrated by Roger Duvoisin; Lothrop Lee & Shepard, 1947.

1948 **HONOR** *Bambino the Clown* written and illustrated by Georges Schreiber; Viking, 1947.

McElligot's Pool written and illustrated by Dr. Seuss; Random House, 1947.

Roger and the Fox by Lavinia R. Davis, illustrated by Hildegard Woodward; Doubleday, 1947.

Song of Robin Hood edited by Anne B. Malcolmson, illustrated by Virginia Lee Burton; Houghton Mifflin, 1947.

Stone Soup written and illustrated by Marcia Brown; Scribner, 1947.

1949 *The Big Snow* written and illustrated by Elmer Hader and Berta Hader; Macmillan, 1948.

1949 **HONOR** *All around the Town* by Phyllis McGinley, illustrated by Helen Stone; Lippincott, 1948.

Blueberries for Sal written and illustrated by Robert McCloskey; Viking, 1948.

Fish in the Air written and illustrated by Kurt Wiese; Viking, 1948.

Juanita written and illustrated by Leo Politi; Scribner, 1948.

1950 *Song of the Swallows* written and illustrated by Leo Politi; Scribner, 1949.

1950 **HONOR** *America's Ethan Allen* by Stewart Holbrook, illustrated by Lynd Ward; Houghton Mifflin, 1949.

Bartholomew and the Oobleck written and illustrated by Dr. Seuss; Random House, 1949.

The Happy Day by Ruth Krauss, illustrated by Marc Simont; Harper & Row, 1949.

Henry-Fisherman written and illustrated by Marcia Brown; Scribner, 1949.

The Wild Birthday Cake by Lavinia R. Davis, illustrated by Hildegard Woodward; Doubleday, 1949.

1951 *The Egg Tree* written and illustrated by Katherine Milhous; Scribner, 1950.

1951 **HONOR** *Dick Whittington and His Cat* written and illustrated by Marcia Brown; Scribner, 1950.

If I Ran the Zoo written and illustrated by Dr. Seuss; Random House, 1950.

The Most Wonderful Doll in the World by Phyllis McGinley, illustrated by Helen Stone; Lippincott, 1950.

T-Bone, the Baby Sitter written and illustrated by Clare Turlay Newberry; Harper & Row, 1950.

The Two Reds by William Lipkind, illustrated by Nicolas Mordvinoff; Harcourt, 1950.

1952 *Finders Keepers* by William Lipkind, illustrated by Nicolas Mordvinoff; Harcourt, 1951.

1952 **HONOR** *All Falling Down* by Gene Zion, illustrated by Margaret Bloy Graham; Harper & Row, 1951.

Bear Party written and illustrated by William Pene du Bois; Viking, 1951.

Feather Mountain written and illustrated by Elizabeth Olds; Houghton, 1951.

Mr. T.W. Anthony Woo: The Story of a Cat and a Dog and a Mouse written and illustrated by Marie Hall Ets; Viking, 1951.

Skipper John's Cook written and illustrated by Marcia Brown; Scribner, 1951.

1953 *The Biggest Bear* written and illustrated by Lynd Ward; Houghton Mifflin, 1952.

1953 **HONOR** *Ape in a Cape: An Alphabet of Odd Animals* written and illustrated by Fritz Eichenberg; Harcourt, 1952.

Five Little Monkeys written and illustrated by Juliet Kepes; Houghton Mifflin, 1952.

One Morning in Maine written and illustrated by Robert McCloskey; Viking, 1952.

Puss in Boots by Charles Perrault, illustrated by Marcia Brown; Scribner, 1952.

The Storm Book by Charlotte Zolotow, illustrated by Margaret Bloy Graham; Harper & Row, 1952.

1954 *Madeline's Rescue* written and illustrated by Ludwig Bemelmans; Viking, 1953.

1954 **HONOR** *Green Eyes* written and illustrated by Abe Birnbaum; Capitol, 1953.

Journey Cake, Ho! by Ruth Sawyer, illustrated by Robert McCloskey; Viking, 1953.

The Steadfast Tin Soldier by Hans Christian Andersen, illustrated by Marcia Brown; Scribner, 1953.

A Very Special House by Ruth Krauss, illustrated by Maurice Sendak; Harper, 1953.

When Will the World be Mine? The Story of a Snowshoe Rabbit by Miriam Schlein, illustrated by Jean Charlot; Scott, 1953.

1955 *Cinderella; or, The Little Glass Slipper* by Charles Perrault, illustrated by Marcia Brown; Scribner, 1954.

1955 **HONOR** *Marguerite de Angeli's Book of Nursery and Mother Goose Rhymes* compiled and illustrated by Marguerite de Angeli; Doubleday, 1954.

The Thanksgiving Story by Alice Dalgliesh, illustrated by Helen Sewell; Scribner, 1954.

Wheel on the Chimney by Margaret Wise Brown, illustrated by Tibor Gergely; Lippincott, 1954.

1956 *Frog Went A-courtin'* by John Langstaff, illustrated by Feodor Rojankovsky; Harcourt, 1955.

1956 **HONOR** *Crow Boy* written and illustrated by Taro Yashima; Viking, 1955.

Play with Me written and illustrated by Marie Hall Ets; Viking, 1955.

1957 *A Tree Is Nice* by Janice May Udry, illustrated by Marc Simont; Harper, 1956.

1957 **HONOR** *Anatole* by Eve Titus, illustrated by Paul Galdone; Whittlesey, 1956.

Gillespie and the Guards by Benjamin Elkin, illustrated by James Daugherty; Viking, 1956.

Lion written and illustrated by William Pene du Bois; Viking, 1956.

Mr. Penny's Race Horse written and illustrated by Marie Hall Ets; Viking, 1956.

One Is One written and illustrated by Tasha Tudor; Oxford, 1956.

1958 *Time of Wonder* written and illustrated by Robert McCloskey; Viking, 1957.

1958 **HONOR** *Anatole and the Cat* by Eve Titus, illustrated by Paul Galdone; Whittlesey, 1957.

Fly High, Fly Low written and illustrated by Don Freeman; Viking, 1957.

1959 *Chanticleer and the Fox* written and illustrated by Barbara Cooney; Crowell, 1958.

1959 **HONOR** *The House that Jack Built: A Picture Book in Two Languages* written and illustrated by Antonio Frasconi; Harcourt, 1958.

Umbrella written and illustrated by Taro Yashima; Viking, 1958.

What Do You Say, Dear? by Sesyle Joslin, illustrated by Maurice Sendak; Scott, 1958.

1960 *Nine Days to Christmas* by Aurora Labastida and Marie Hall Ets, illustrated by Marie Hall Ets; Viking, 1959.

1960 **HONOR** *Houses from the Sea* by Alice E. Goudey, illustrated by Adrienne Adams; Scribner, 1959.

The Moon Jumpers by Janice May Udry, illustrated by Maurice Sendak; Harper, 1959.

1961 *Baboushka and the Three Kings* by Ruth Robbins, illustrated by Nicolas Sidjakov; Parnassus, 1960.

1961 **HONOR** *Inch by Inch* written and illustrated by Leo Lionni; Obolensky, 1960.

1962 *Once a Mouse* written and illustrated by Marcia Brown; Scribner, 1961.

1962 **HONOR** *The Day We Saw the Sun Come Up* by Alice E. Goudey, illustrated by Adrienne Adams; Scribner, 1961.

The Fox Went Out on a Chilly Night written and illustrated by Peter Spier; Doubleday, 1961.

Little Bear's Visit by Else Holmelund Minarik, illustrated by Maurice Sendak; Harper, 1961.

1963 *The Snowy Day* written and illustrated by Ezra Jack Keats; Viking, 1962.

1963 **HONOR** *Mr. Rabbit and the Lovely Present* by Charlotte Zolotow, illustrated by Maurice Sendak; Harper, 1962.

The Sun Is a Golden Earring by Natalia M. Belting, illustrated by Bernarda Bryson; Holt, 1962.

1964 *Where the Wild Things Are* written and illustrated by Maurice Sendak; Harper, 1963.

1964 **HONOR** *All in the Morning Early* by Sorche Nic Leodhas, illustrated by Evaline Ness; Holt, 1963.

Mother Goose and Nursery Rhymes written and illustrated by Philip Reed; Atheneum, 1963.

Swimmy written and illustrated by Leo Lionni; Pantheon, 1963.

1965 *May I Bring a Friend?* by Beatrice Schenk deRegniers, illustrated by Beni Montresor; Atheneum, 1964.

1965 **HONOR** *A Pocketful of Cricket* by Rebecca Caudill, illustrated by Evaline Ness; Holt, 1964.

Rain Makes Applesauce by Julian Scheer, illustrated by Marvin Bileck; Holiday, 1964.

The Wave by Margaret Hodges, illustrated by Blair Lent; Houghton, 1964.

1966 *Always Room for One More* by Sorche Nic Leodhas, illustrated by Nonny Hogrogian; Holt, 1965.

1966 **HONOR** *Hide and Seek Fog* by Alvin Tresselt, illustrated by Roger Duvoisin; Lothrop Lee & Shepard, 1965.

Just Me written and illustrated by Marie Hall Ets; Viking, 1965.

Tom Tit Tot by Joseph Jacobs, illustrated by Evaline Ness; Scribner, 1965.

1967 *Sam, Bangs, and Moonshine* written and illustrated by Evaline Ness; Holt, 1966.

1967 **HONOR** *One Wide River to Cross* by Barbara Emberley, illustrated by Ed Emberley; Prentice Hall, 1966.

1968 *Drummer Hoff* adapted by Barbara Emberley, illustrated by Ed Emberley; Prentice Hall, 1967.

1968 **HONOR** *The Emperor and the Kite* by Jane Yolen, illustrated by Ed Young; Collins-World, 1967.

Frederick written and illustrated by Leo Lionni; Pantheon, 1967.

Seashore Story written and illustrated by Taro Yashima; Viking, 1967.

1969 *The Fool of the World and the Flying Ship* by Arthur Ransome, illustrated by Uri Shulevitz; Farrar, 1968.

1969 **HONOR** *Why the Sun and the Moon Live in the Sky: An African Folktale* by Elphinstone Dayrell, illustrated by Blair Lent; Houghton, 1968.

1970 *Sylvester and the Magic Pebble* written and illustrated by William Steig; Windmill/Simon & Schuster, 1969.

1970 **HONOR** *Alexander and the Wind-up Mouse* written and illustrated by Leo Lionni; Pantheon, 1969.

Goggles written and illustrated by Ezra Jack Keats; Macmillan, 1969.

The Judge by Harve Zemach, illustrated by Margot Zemach; Farrar, 1969.

Pop Corn and Ma Goodness by Edna Mitchell Preston, illustrated by Robert Andrew Parker; Viking, 1969.

Thy Friend, Obadiah written and illustrated by Brinton Turkle; Viking, 1969.

1971 *A Story, a Story* written and illustrated by Gail E. Haley; Atheneum, 1970.

1971 **HONOR** *The Angry Moon* by William Sleator, illustrated by Blair Lent; Atlantic-Little, 1970.

Frog and Toad Are Friends written and illustrated by Arnold Lobel; Harper, 1970.

In the Night Kitchen written and illustrated by Maurice Sendak; Harper, 1970.

1972 *One Fine Day* written and illustrated by Nonny Hogrogian; Macmillan, 1971.

1972 **HONOR** *Hildilid's Night* by Cheli Duran Ryan, illustrated by Arnold Lobel; Macmillan, 1971.

If All the Seas Were One Sea written and illustrated by Janina Domanska; Macmillan, 1971.

Moja Means One: Swahili Counting Book by Muriel Feelings, illustrated by Tom Feelings; Dial, 1971.

1973 *The Funny Little Woman* by Arlene Mosel, illustrated by Blair Lent; Dutton, 1972.

1973 **HONOR** *Anansi the Spider: A Tale from the Ashanti* written and illustrated by Gerald McDermott; Holt, 1972.

Hosie's Alphabet by Hosea Baskin, Tobias Baskin, and Lisa Baskin, illustrated by Leonard Baskin; Viking, 1972.

Snow White and the Seven Dwarfs by Jacob Grimm and Wilhelm Grimm, translated by Randall Jarrell, illustrated by Nancy Ekholm Burkert; Farrar, 1972.

When Clay Sings by Byrd Baylor, illustrated by Tom Bahti; Scribner, 1972.

1974 *Duffy and the Devil* retold by Harve Zemach, illustrated by Margot Zemach; Farrar, 1973.

1974 **HONOR** *Cathedral: The Story of its Construction* written and illustrated by David Macaulay; Houghton, 1973.

The Three Jovial Huntsmen: A Mother Goose Rhyme adapted and illustrated by Susan Jeffers; Bradbury, 1973.

1975 *Arrow to the Sun: A Pueblo Indian Tale* written and illustrated by Gerald McDermott; Viking, 1974.

1975 **HONOR** *Jambo Means Hello: Swahili Alphabet Book* by Muriel Feelings, illustrated by Tom Feelings; Dial, 1974.

1976 *Why Mosquitos Buzz in People's Ears: A West African Tale* by Verna Aardema, illustrated by Leo Dillon and Diane Dillon; Dial, 1975.

1976 **HONOR** *The Desert Is Theirs* by Byrd Baylor, illustrated by Peter Parnall; Scribner, 1975.

Strega Nona written and illustrated by Tomie de Paola; Prentice Hall, 1975.

1977 *Ashanti to Zulu: African Traditions* by Margaret Musgrove, illustrated by Leo Dillon and Diane Dillon; Dial, 1976.

1977 **HONOR** *The Amazing Bone* written and illustrated by William Steig; Farrar, 1976.

The Contest written and illustrated by Nonny Hogrogian; Greenwillow, 1976.

Fish for Supper written and illustrated by M.B. Goffstein; Dial, 1976.

The Golem: A Jewish Legend written and illustrated by Beverly Brodsky McDermott; Lippincott, 1975.

Hawk, I'm Your Brother by Byrd Baylor, illustrated by Peter Parnall; Scribner, 1976.

1978 *Noah's Ark* written and illustrated by Peter Spier; Doubleday, 1977.

1978 **HONOR** *Castle* written and illustrated by David Macaulay; Houghton Mifflin, 1977.

It Could Always be Worse: A Yiddish Folktale written and illustrated by Margot Zemach; Farrar, 1977.

1979 *The Girl Who Loved Wild Horses* written and illustrated by Paul Goble; Bradbury, 1978.

1979 **HONOR** *Freight Train* written and illustrated by Donald Crews; Greenwillow, 1978.

The Way to Start a Day by Byrd Baylor, illustrated by Peter Parnall; Scribner, 1978.

1980 *Ox-cart Man* by Donald Hall, illustrated by Barbara Cooney; Viking, 1979.

1980 **HONOR** *Ben's Trumpet* written and illustrated by Rachel Isadora; Greenwillow, 1979.

The Garden of Abdul Gasazi written and illustrated by Chris Van Allsburg; Houghton, 1979.

The Treasure written and illustrated by Uri Shulevitz; Farrar, 1979.

1981 *Fables* written and illustrated by Arnold Lobel; Harper, 1980.

1981 **HONOR** *The Bremen-Town Musicians* written and illustrated by Ilse Plume; Doubleday, 1980.

The Grey Lady and the Strawberry Snatcher written and illustrated by Molly Bang; Four Winds, 1980.

Mice Twice written and illustrated by Joseph Low; Atheneum, 1980.

Truck written and illustrated by Donald Crews; Greenwillow, 1980.

1982 *Jumanji* written and illustrated by Chris Van Allsburg; Houghton, 1981.

1982 **HONOR** *On Market Street* by Arnold Lobel, illustrated by Anita Lobel; Greenwillow, 1981.

Outside Over There written and illustrated by Maurice Sendak; Harper, 1981.

A Visit to William Blake's Inn: Poems for Innocent and Experienced Travelers by Nancy Willard, illustrated by Alice Provensen and Martin Provensen; Harcourt, 1981.

Where the Buffaloes Begin by Olaf Baker, illustrated by Stephen Gammell; Warne, 1981.

1983 *Shadow* translated and illustrated by Marcia Brown from the French of Blaise Cendrars; Scribner, 1982.

1983 HONOR *A Chair for My Mother* written and illustrated by Vera B. Williams; Greenwillow, 1982.

When I Was Young in the Mountains by Cynthia Rylant, illustrated by Diane Goode; Dutton, 1982.

1984 *The Glorious Flight: Across the Channel with Louis Bleriot* written and illustrated by Alice Provensen and Martin Provensen; Viking, 1983.

1984 HONOR *Little Red Riding Hood* by Jacob Grimm and Wilhelm Grimm, retold and illustrated by Trina Schart Hyman; Holiday House, 1983.

Ten, Nine, Eight written and illustrated by Molly Bang; Greenwillow, 1983.

1985 *Saint George and the Dragon* adapted by Margaret Hodges from Edmund Spenser's *Faerie Queene*, illustrated by Trina Schart Hyman; Little Brown, 1984.

1985 HONOR *Hansel and Gretel* retold by Rika Lesser, illustrated by Paul O. Zelinsky; Dodd, Mead, 1984.

Have You Seen My Duckling? written and illustrated by Nancy Tafuri; Greenwillow, 1984.

The Story of Jumping Mouse retold and illustrated by John Steptoe; Lothrop, Lee & Shepard, 1984.

1986 *The Polar Express* written and illustrated by Chris Van Allsburg; Houghton Mifflin, 1985.

1986 HONOR *King Bidgood's in the Bathtub* by Audrey Wood, illustrated by Don Wood; Harcourt, 1985.

The Relatives Came by Cynthia Rylant, illustrated by Stephen Gammell; Bradbury, 1985.

1987 *Hey, Al!* by Arthur Yorinks, illustrated by Richard Egielski; Farrar, 1986.

1987 HONOR *Alphabatics* written and illustrated by Suse MacDonald; Bradbury, 1986.

Rumpelstiltskin retold and illustrated by Paul O. Zelinsky; Dutton, 1986.

The Village of Round and Square Houses written and illustrated by Ann Grifalconi; Little Brown, 1986.

1988 *Owl Moon* by Jane Yolen, illustrated by John Schoenherr; Philomel, 1987.

1988 HONOR *Mufaro's Beautiful Daughters* written and illustrated by John Steptoe; Lothrop, Lee & Shepard, 1987.

1989 *Song and Dance Man* by Karen Ackerman, illustrated by Stephen Gammell; Knopf, 1988.

1989 HONOR *The Boy of the Three-Year Nap* by Dianne Snyder, illustrated by Allen Say; Houghton Mifflin, 1988.

Free Fall written and illustrated by David Wiesner; Lothrop, Lee & Shepard, 1988.

Goldilocks and the Three Bears written and illustrated by James Marshall; Dial, 1988.

Mirandy and Brother Wind by Patricia McKissack, illustrated by Jerry Pinkney; Knopf, 1988.

1990 *Lon Po Po* written and illustrated by Ed Young; Philomel, 1989.

1990 HONOR *The Talking Eggs* by Robert D. San Souci, illustrated by Jerry Pinkney; Dial, 1989.

Hershel and the Hanukkah Goblins by Eric Kimmel, illustrated by Trina Schart Hyman; Holiday House, 1989.

Color Zoo written and illustrated by Lois Ehlert; Lippincott, 1989.

Bill Peet: An Autobiography written and illustrated by Bill Peet; Houghton Mifflin, 1989.

1991 *Black and White* written and illustrated by David Macaulay; Houghton Mifflin, 1990.

1991 HONOR *Puss in Boots* by Charles Perrault, illustrated by Fred Marcellino; Farrar Straus Giroux, 1990.

More, More, More, Said the Baby: 3 Love Stories written and illustrated by Vera Williams; Greenwillow, 1990.

1992 *Tuesday* illustrated by David Wiesner; Clarion, 1991.

1992 HONOR *Tar Beach* written and illustrated by Faith Ringgold; Crown, 1991.

1993 *Mirette on the High Wire* written and illustrated by Emily Arnold McCully; Putnam, 1992.

1993 HONOR *Seven Blind Mice* written and illustrated by Ed Young; Philomel, 1992.

The Stinky Cheese Man and Other Fairly Stupid Tales by Jon Scieszka, illustrated by Lane Smith; Viking, 1992.

Working Cotton by Sherley Anne Williams, illustrated by Carole Byard; Harcourt Brace Jovanovich, 1992.

CALIFORNIA YOUNG READER MEDAL
California Reading Association
2790 Harbor Blvd.
Suite 204
Costa Mesa, CA 92626

Founded by the California Reading Association in 1974, the California Young Reader Medal encourages California school children to become better acquainted with good literature and honors distinguished children's book authors. This program is currently sponsored by the California Library Association, California Media and Library Educators Association, the California Association of Teachers of English, as well as the California Reading Association. This award has four possible categories, although not all are used each year. They are Primary (grades K-2), Intermediate (grades 3-6), middle school/junior high (grades 6-9), and young adult (grades 9-12). All titles considered must have been written in the last five years by an author who is still alive. Students in kindergarten through grade twelve vote for their favorite book chosen from a list of nominations drawn up by the students. Each winner receives a bronze medal and a plaque.

1975 INTERMEDIATE *How to Eat Fried Worms* by Thomas Rockwell, illustrated by Emily McCully; Watts, 1973.

1976 PRIMARY *How Droofus the Dragon Lost His Head* written and illustrated by Bill Peet; Houghton Mifflin, 1971.

1977 INTERMEDIATE *Freaky Friday* by Mary Rodgers, not illustrated; Harper, 1972.

1977 HIGH SCHOOL *Watership Down* by Richard Adams, not illustrated; Rex Collings, 1972; Macmillan, 1972; Avon, 1975.

1978 PRIMARY *Little Rabbit's Loose Tooth* by Lucy Bate, illustrated by Diane deGroat; Crown, 1975.

1979 INTERMEDIATE *Danny: the Champion of the World* by Roald Dahl, illustrated by Jill Bennett; Knopf, 1975.

1979 HIGH SCHOOL *The Late Great Me* by Sandra Scoppettone, not illustrated; Putnam, 1976.

1980 PRIMARY *Big Bad Bruce* written and illustrated by Bill Peet; Houghton Mifflin, 1977.

1980 JUNIOR HIGH *The Pinballs* by Betsy Byars, not illustrated; Harper, 1977.

1981 INTERMEDIATE *The Summer of the Monkeys* by Wilson Rawls, not illustrated; Doubleday, 1976.

1981 HIGH SCHOOL *A Summer to Die* by Lois Lowry, illustrated by Jenni Oliver; Houghton Mifflin, 1977.

1982 PRIMARY *Miss Nelson is Missing!* by Harry Allard, illustrated by James Marshall; Houghton Mifflin, 1977; Scholastic, 1978.

1982 JUNIOR HIGH *Hail, Hail, Camp Timberwood* by Ellen Conford, illustrated by Gail Owens; Little Brown, 1978.

1983 PRIMARY *Liza Lou and the Yeller Belly Swamp* written and illustrated by Mercer Mayer; Parents, 1976; Four Winds, 1980.

1983 INTERMEDIATE *Superfudge* by Judy Blume, not illustrated; Dutton, 1980.

1983 JUNIOR HIGH *Tiger Eyes* by Judy Blume, not illustrated; Bradbury, 1981.

1983 HIGH SCHOOL *Summer of Fear* by Lois Duncan, not illustrated; Little Brown, 1976.

1984 PRIMARY *Bagdad Ate It* by Phyllis Green, illustrated by Joel Schick; Watts, 1980.

1984 INTERMEDIATE *The Trouble with Tuck* by Theodore Taylor, not illustrated; Doubleday, 1981.

1984 JUNIOR HIGH *There's a Bat in Bunk Five* by Paula Danziger, not illustrated; Delacorte, 1980.

1984 HIGH SCHOOL *Stranger with my Face* by Lois Duncan, not illustrated; Little Brown, 1981.

1985 PRIMARY *Herbie's Troubles* by Carol Chapman, illustrated by Kelly Oechsli; Dutton, 1981.

1985 INTERMEDIATE *The Indian in the Cupboard* by Lynne Reid Banks, illustrated by Brock Cole; Doubleday, 1980.

1985 JUNIOR HIGH *Taking Terri Mueller* by Norma Fox Mazer, not illustrated; Morrow, 1983.

1985 HIGH SCHOOL *The Truth Trap* by Frances A. Miller, not illustrated; Dutton, 1980.

1986 PRIMARY *Space Case* by Edward Marshall, illustrated by James Marshall; Dial, 1980.

1986 INTERMEDIATE *Nothing's Fair in Fifth Grade* by Barthe DeClements, not illustrated; Viking, 1981.

1986 JUNIOR HIGH *The Girl with the Silver Eyes* by Willo Davis Roberts, not illustrated; Atheneum, 1980.

1986 HIGH SCHOOL *The Darkangel* by Meredith Ann Pierce, not illustrated; Little Brown, 1982.

1987 PRIMARY *The Napping House* by Audrey Wood, illustrated by Don Wood; Harcourt, 1984.

1987 INTERMEDIATE *The Dollhouse Murders* by Betty Ren Wright, not illustrated; Holiday House, 1983.

1987 JUNIOR HIGH *You Shouldn't Have to Say Goodbye* by Patricia Hermes, not illustrated; Harcourt, 1982.

1987 HIGH SCHOOL *Pursuit* by Michael French, not illustrated; Delacorte, 1981; Dell, 1983.

1988 PRIMARY *If You Give a Mouse a Cookie* by Laura J. Numeroff, illustrated by Felicia Bond; Harper & Row, 1985.

1988 INTERMEDIATE *Be a Perfect Person in Just Three Days* by Stephen Manes, illustrated by Tom Huffman; Houghton Mifflin, 1982.

1988 MIDDLE/JUNIOR HIGH *The Root Cellar* by Janet Lunn, illustrated with a map; Scribner, 1983.

1988 YOUNG ADULT *Interstellar Pig* by William Sleator, not illustrated; Dutton, 1984.

1989 PRIMARY *What Happened To Patrick's Dinosaurs?* by Carol Carrick, illustrated by Donald Carrick; Clarion, 1986.

1989 INTERMEDIATE *The Castle in the Attic* by Elizabeth Winthrop, illustrated by Trina Schart Hyman; Holiday House, 1985.

1989 JUNIOR HIGH *The Stalker* by Joan Lowery Nixon, not illustrated; Delacorte, 1985.

1989 SENIOR HIGH *Face at the Edge of the World* by Eve Bunting, not illustrated; Clarion Books, 1985.

1990 PRIMARY *The Eyes of the Dragon* by Margaret Leaf, illustrated by Ed Young; Lothrop, Lee & Shepard, 1987.

1990 INTERMEDIATE *The War With Grandpa* by Robert Kimmel Smith, illustrated by Richard Lauter; Delacorte, 1984.

1990 MIDDLE/JUNIOR HIGH *The Other Side of Dark* by Joan Lowery Nixon, not illustrated; Delacorte, 1986.

1990 YOUNG ADULT *Izzy, Willy-Nilly* by Cynthia Voigt, not illustrated; Atheneum, 1986.

1991 PRIMARY *Tacky the Penguin* by Helen Lester, illustrated by Lynn Munsinger; Houghton Mifflin, 1988.

1991 INTERMEDIATE *Harry's Mad* by Dick King-Smith, illustrated by Jill Bennett; Crown, 1987, c1984; Gollancz, 1984.

1991 MIDDLE/JUNIOR HIGH *December Stillness* by Mary Downing Hahn, not illustrated; Clarion, 1988.

1991 YOUNG ADULT *Night Kites* by M.E. Kerr, not illustrated; Harper & Row, 1986.

1992 PRIMARY *Never Spit on Your Shoes* written and illustrated by Denys Cazet; Orchard, 1990.

1992 INTERMEDIATE *The Sniper* by Theodore Taylor, not illustrated; Harcourt, Brace, Jovanovich, 1989.

All About Sam by Lois Lowry, illustrated by Diane de Groat; Houghton Mifflin, 1988.

1992 YOUNG ADULT *A Sudden Silence* by Eve Bunting, not illustrated; Harcourt, Brace, Jovanovich, 1988.

CALLING ALL GIRLS-DODD, MEAD PRIZE COMPETITION

discontinued

Established in 1954 as a joint effort by Compact, the Young People's Digest and Dodd, Mead Company, this award program was originally called The Seventeenth Summer Literary Competition. It was so named in honor of the famous teen novel Seventeenth Summer by Maureen Daly. In 1960, Calling All Girls became Dodd, Mead's cosponsor for the competition. Manuscripts of mystery and adventure stories written for girls ages eight through fourteen were eligible. American and Canadian authors were encouraged to participate, with the exception of established Dodd, Mead authors or authors with other published books in the same category. The winners received $300 from Calling All Girls for first serial rights and Dodd, Mead offered a $1000 advance against royalties. The competition was discontinued in 1966.

1954 *Uncertain Glory* by Frances Krautter, not illustrated; Dodd Mead, 1954.

1955 *Song of the Voyageur* by Beverly Butler, not illustrated; Dodd Mead, 1955.

1956 *Oasis for Lucy* by Alexander L. Johnson, not illustrated; Dodd Mead, 1956.

1957 *Monica: The Story of a Young Magazine Apprentice* by Ingrid Sladkus and Alberta Eiseman, not illustrated; Dodd Mead, 1957.

1958 *Debutante Hill* by Lois Duncan, not illustrated; Dodd Mead, 1958.

1959 *The Wonderful World Outside* by Dorothy Holder Jones, not illustrated; Dodd Mead, 1959.

1960 *The Morning Side of the Hill* by Jacqueline Reed, not illustrated; Dodd Mead, 1960.

1961 *The Abracadabra Mystery* by Ramona Maher, not illustrated; Dodd Mead, 1961.

1962 *The Summer Ballet Mystery* by Ruth H. Wissman, not illustrated; Dodd Mead, 1962.

1963 *The Mystery of Shadow Walk* by Lucile Morrison, not illustrated; Dodd Mead, 1964.

1964 *The Secret of the Cellars* by Carolyn G. Hart, not illustrated; Dodd Mead, 1964.

1965 *Mystery of the Talking Totem Pole* by Gladys Hall Murray, not illustrated; Dodd Mead, 1965.

1966 *Melissa Finds a Mystery* by Susan Meyers, not illustrated; Dodd Mead, 1966.

CANADA COUNCIL CHILDREN'S LITERATURE PRIZES

see **GOVERNOR GENERAL'S LITERARY AWARD**

CANADIAN LIBRARY ASSOCIATION BOOK OF THE YEAR FOR CHILDREN AWARD

Canadian Library Association
Director of Membership Services
602-200 Elgin St
Ottawa, Ontario K2P 1L5
Canada

The Canadian Association of Children's Librarians of the Canadian Library Association established the Book of the Year Award in 1946. They voted that an annual award be given, by vote of the Canadian Association of Children's Librarians, for an outstanding children's book by a Canadian author or an author resident in Canada, for the purpose of encouraging the writing of books for boys and girls by Canadian authors.

The award consists of a bronze medal bearing Albert Laliberte's figure of Marie Rollet Hebert reading with her children. The medal is gold-plated sterling silver on a dark blue ribbon. From 1954 to 1973, a second medal of bronze was awarded to the most outstanding French-Canadian publication for children (these titles are not listed below). Beginning in 1975, a runnerup book has been chosen. The awards are presented at the annual CLA-ACB meeting.

The following standards apply to works of fiction: (1) The plot should be well constructed, the situations convincing and logically developed. (2) Characters should be alive and believable. (3) The story should be written in acceptable English in a style suited to the themes developed; dialogue should be natural, and the point of view should never condescend. (4) The work should be suitable for the intended audience in terms of subject and level of difficulty. (5) Illustrations should be appropriately integrated with the text.

In nonfiction works, the contents should be accurate and standards 3, 4, and 5 for fiction works should be met. The above standards are only guidelines. The winner will be that book which displays the quality and distinction of a truly creative work of art.

Rules of the competition are as follows: (1) The award may be presented regardless of the number of awards previously won by the author. (2) To merit consideration, the book must have been published in Canada, written by a Canadian citizen, or written on a Canadian subject. (3) If in any year no book is deemed to be of award caliber, the award shall not be made. (4) The Book of the Year Award committee is appointed by the Canadian Association of Children's Librarians executive and since 1974 has consisted of seven children's librarians who are appointed for a three year term.

(From CACL Children's Book Awards, 1947-1978 by Irma McDonough in BOOKBIRD 1979).

1947 *Starbuck Valley Winter* by Roderick Haig-Brown, illustrated by Charles DeFeo; Morrow, 1943; Collins, 1944.

1948 No Award

1949 *Kristli's Trees* by Mabel Dunham, illustrated by Selwyn Dewdney; McClelland & Stewart, 1948.

1950 *Franklin of the Arctic: A Life of Adventure* by Richard S. Lambert, maps by Julius Griffith; McClelland & Stewart, 1949.

1951 No Award

1952 *The Sun Horse* by Catherine Anthony Clark, illustrated by Clare Bice; Macmillan Canada, 1951.

1953-1955 No Award

1956 *Train for Tiger Lily* by Louise Riley, illustrated by Christine Price; Macmillan Canada, 1954.

1957 *Glooskap's Country and Other Indian Tales* by Cyrus Macmillan, illustrated by John A. Hall; Oxford, 1956.

1958 *Lost in the Barrens* by Farley Mowat, illustrated by Charles Geer; Little Brown Canada, 1956.

1959 *The Dangerous Cove: A Story of Early Days in Newfoundland* by John F. Hayes, illustrated by Fred J. Finley; Copp Clark, 1957.

1960 *The Golden Phoenix and other French Canadian Fairy Tales* by Charles Marius Barbeau, retold by Michael Hornyansky, illustrated by Arthur Price; Oxford, 1958.

1961 *The St. Lawrence* by William Toye, illustrated by Leo Rampen; Oxford, 1959.

1962 No Award

1963 *The Incredible Journey: A Tale of Three Animals* by Shelia Every Burnford, illustrated by Carl Burger; Little Brown, 1961.

1964 *The Whale People* by Roderick Haig-Brown, illustrated by Mary Weiler; Collins Canada, 1962.

1965 *Tales of Nanabozho* by Dorothy Reid, illustrated by Donald Grant; Oxford, 1964.

1966 *Tikta'liktak: An Eskimo Legend* written and illustrated by James Houston; Longman, 1965.

The Double Knights: More Tales from Round the World by James McNeill, illustrated by Theo Dimson; Oxford, 1965.

1967 *Raven's Cry* by Christie Harris, illustrated by Bill Reid; McClelland & Stewart, 1966.

1968 *The White Archer: An Eskimo Legend* written and illustrated by James Houston; Longman, 1967.

1969 *And Tomorrow the Stars: The Story of John Cabot* by Kay Hill, illustrated by Laszlo Kubinyi; Dodd Mead, 1968.

1970 *Sally Go Round the Sun* by Edith Fowke, illustrated by Carlos Marchiori; McClelland & Stewart, 1969.

1971 *Cartier Discovers the St. Lawrence* by William Toye, illustrated by Laszlo Gal; Oxford, 1970.

1972 *Mary of Mile 18* written and illustrated by Ann Blades; Tundra, 1971.

1973 *The Marrow of the World* by Ruth Nichols, illustrated by Trina Schart Hyman; Macmillan Canada, 1972.

1974 *The Miraculous Hind* written and illustrated by Elizabeth Cleaver; Holt Canada, 1973.

1974 RUNNERUP *A Prairie Boy's Winter* written and illustrated by William Kurelek; Tundra, 1973.

1975 *Alligator Pie* by Dennis Lee, illustrated by Frank Newfeld; Macmillan Canada, 1974.

1975 RUNNERUP *Slave of Haida* by Doris Andersen, illustrated; Macmillan Canada, 1974.

1976 *Jacob Two-two Meets the Hooded Fang* by Mordecai Richler, illustrated by Fritz Wegner; McClelland & Stewart, 1975.

1976 RUNNERUP *A Prairie Boy's Summer* written and illustrated by William Kurelek; Tundra, 1975.

1977 *Mouse Woman and the Vanished Princesses* by Christie Harris, illustrated by Douglas Tait; McClelland & Stewart, 1976.

1977 RUNNERUP *Simon and the Golden Sword* by Frank Newfeld and William Toye, illustrated by Frank Newfeld; Oxford, 1976.

1978 *Garbage Delight* by Dennis Lee, illustrated by Frank Newfeld; Macmillan Canada, 1977.

1978 RUNNERUP *Underground to Canada* by Barbara Smucker; Clarke, Irwin, 1977.

1979 *Hold Fast* by Kevin Major, not illustrated; Clarke, Irwin, 1978.

1979 RUNNERUP *A Salmon for Simon* by Betty Waterton, illustrated by Ann Blades; Douglas & MacIntyre, 1978.

1980 *River Runners: A Tale of Hardship and Bravery* written and illustrated by James Houston; McClelland & Stewart, 1979.

1980 RUNNERUP *The Olden Days Coat* by Margaret Laurence, illustrated by Muriel Wood; McClelland & Stewart, 1979.

1981 *The Violin Maker's Gift* by Donn Kushner; Macmillan Canada, 1980.

1981 RUNNERUP *The Trouble with Princesses* by Christie Harris, illustrated by Douglas Tait; McClelland & Stewart, 1980; Atheneum, 1980.

1982 *The Root Cellar* by Janet Lunn, illustrated with maps; Lester & Orpen Dennys, 1981.

1982 RUNNERSUP *Ytek and the Arctic Orchid: An Inuit Legend* by Garnet Hewitt, illustrated by Heather Woodall; Douglas & McIntyre, 1981; Vanguard, 1981.

Long Claws: An Arctic Adventure written and illustrated by James Houston; McClelland & Stewart, 1981; Atheneum, 1981.

1983 *Up to Low* by Brian Doyle, not illustrated; Douglas & McIntyre, 1982.

1983 RUNNERUP *Jasmin* by Jan Truss, not illustrated; Douglas & MacIntyre, 1982; Atheneum, 1982.

1984 *Sweetgrass* by Jan Hudson, not illustrated; Tree Frog Press, 1984.

1984 RUNNERUP *Jelly Belly* by Dennis Lee, illustrated by Juan Wijngaard; Macmillan Canada, 1983.

1985 *Mama's Going to Buy You a Mockingbird* by Jean Little, not illustrated; Viking Kestrel, 1984.

1985 RUNNERUP *Witchery Hill* by Welwyn Wilton Katz, not illustrated; Douglas & McIntyre, 1984.

1986 *Julie* by Cora Taylor, not illustrated; Western Producer Prairie Books, 1985.

1986 RUNNERUP *Wild Man of the Woods* by Joan Clark, not illustrated; Penguin Books Canada, 1986.

1987 *Shadow in Hawthorn Bay* by Janet Lunn, not illustrated; Lester & Orpen Dennys, 1986.

1987 RUNNERUP *The Emperor's Panda* by David Day, illustrated by Eric Beddows; McClelland & Stewart, 1986.

1988 *A Handful of Time* by Kit Pearson, not illustrated; Penguin Viking Canada, 1987.

1988 RUNNERUP *Who Is Frances Rain?* by Margaret Buffie, not illustrated; Kids Can Press, 1987.

1989 *Easy Avenue* by Brian Doyle, not illustrated; Douglas & McIntyre, 1988.

1989 RUNNERUP *The Third Magic* by Welwyn Wilton Katz, not illustrated; Douglas & McIntyre, 1988; McElderry, 1989.

Harriet's Daughter by Marlene Nourbese Philip, not illustrated; Women's Press, 1988; Heinemann, 1988.

1990 *The Sky Is Falling* by Kit Pearson, not illustrated; Viking Kestrel, 1989.

1990 **RUNNERUP** *Blood Red Ochre* by Kevin Major, not illustrated; Doubleday Canada, 1989; Delacorte, 1989.

Tales From Gold Mountain by Paul Yee, illustrated by Simon Ng; Douglas & McIntyre, 1989; Macmillan, 1989.

1991 *Redwork* by Michael Bedard, not illustrated; Lester & Orpen Dennys, 1990; Atheneum, 1990.

1991 **RUNNERUP** *Covered Bridge* by Brian Doyle, not illustrated; Douglas & McIntyre, 1990.

Stars Come Out Within by Jean Little, illustrated with photos; Viking, 1990.

1992 *Eating Between the Lines* by Kevin Major, not illustrated; Doubleday Canada, 1991.

1992 **RUNNERUP** *Looking At the Moon* by Kit Pearson, not illustrated; Viking, 1991.

Two Moons in August by Martha Brooks, not illustrated; Groundwood Books, 1991.

1993 *Ticket To Curlew* by Celia Barker Lottridge; Groundwood Books, 1992.

CARNEGIE MEDAL

The Library Association
7 Ridgmount St
London WC1E 7AE
England

Awarded annually since 1936, the Carnegie Medal is given to the outstanding book for children, written in English and published in the United Kingdom. Created to mark the centenary of Andrew Carnegie's birth, it was hoped that the medal would improve the standards of children's books. The Carnegie Medal is administered by the British Library Association and the medal is presented to the winner at a special ceremony in September or October of each year.

Recommendations are made by all members of the Library Association and are given to the selection committee for further discussion and consideration. The selection committee is composed of the chairman and vice chairman of the Youth Libraries Group and eleven other members of the Library Association. The same committee is responsible for the selection of the Greenaway Medal. In addition to the winner, there are also highly commended, commended, and honour books awarded on occasion.

The following guidelines and criteria have been drawn up in an attempt to provide a common basis for discussion of the merits of the books nominated. Fiction, nonfiction and poetry are considered separately. Information on illustrative criteria is listed with the Kate Greenaway Medal (see entry).
Fiction:
Characterization can be revealed through narration, conversation, thoughts of others and actions. The characters should be convincing, credible, and suitable for the ages and backgrounds of intended readers. Style should be appropriate to the subject. Dialogue should be natural and balanced with narration. Sentence patterns should be appropriate. There should be creation of a mood (e.g., mystery, gloom, evil, joy, or security). Settings and styles may vary, including historical, fantasy, social realism, science fiction, or adventure, to name a few. The basic theme must be well constructed in that events and characters progress within the limits of that theme. The plot should be constructive in that it ties up loose ends in a secure and satisfying manner and produces a sense of having extended knowledge. The whole work should provide pleasure from the integration of the plot, style, and characters.

Nonfiction:
The accuracy of factual information, illustrative content, indexes and appendices should be closely checked. Biases and generalizations should be noted. The contents should be assessed in terms of the following points: (1) concepts offered, (2) age of intended readers, (3) use of photographs and illustrations, (4) use of chapter headings, references and readings, (5) scope of the subject, (6) up-to-dateness, (7) use of primary sources where appropriate, and (8) size suitable for use and for best presentation of information.

The style should be appropriate to the subject and to the age of the intended reader. The quality of the binding, paper, and type should be taken into consideration.
Poetry:
Look for imaginative quality, linked rhymes or patterns, and suitable uses of words. Avoid the insipid, the sentimental, and the deadening.

(From Selection Process for Carnegie and Greenaway Awards in Library Association Record 81(3): March 1979.)

1936 *Pigeon Post* written and illustrated by Arthur Ransome; Cape, 1936.

1937 *The Family from One End Street and Some of Their Adventures* written and illustrated by Eve Garnett; Muller, 1937.

1938 *The Circus Is Coming* by Noel Streatfeild, illustrated by Steven Spurrier; Dent, 1938.

1939 *The Radium Woman: A Youth Edition of the Life of Madame Curie* by Eleanor Doorly, illustrated by Robert Gibbings; Heinemann, 1939; Roy, 1955.

1940 *Visitors from London* by Kitty Barne, illustrated by Ruth Gervis; Dent, 1940.

1941 *We Couldn't Leave Dinah* by Mary Treadgold, illustrated by Stuart Tresilian; Cape, 1941.

1942 *The Little Grey Men: A Story for the Young in Heart* written and illustrated by Denys James Watkins-Pitchford; Eyre & Spottiswoode, 1942.

1943 No Award

1944 *The Wind on the Moon: A Story for Children* by Eric Linklater, illustrated by Nicolas Bentley; Macmillan, 1944.

1945 No Award

1946 *The Little White Horse* by Elizabeth Goudge, illustrated by C. Walter Hodges; University of London Press, 1946.

1947 *Collected Stories for Children* by Walter de la Mare, illustrated by Irene Hawkins; Faber, 1947.

1948 *Sea Change* by Richard Armstrong, illustrated by Michael Leszczynski; Dent, 1948.

1949 *The Story of your Home* by Agnes Allen, illustrated by Agnes Allen and Jack Allen; Faber & Faber, 1949.

1950 *The Lark on the Wing* by Elfrida Vipont Foulds, illustrated by Terence Reginald Freeman; Oxford, 1950.

1951 *The Wool-Pack* written and illustrated by Cynthia Harnett; Methuen, 1951.

1952 *The Borrowers* by Mary Norton, illustrated by Diana Stanley; Dent, 1952.

1953 *A Valley Grows Up* written and illustrated by Edward Osmond; Oxford, 1953.

1954 *Knight Crusader* by Ronald Welch, illustrated by William Stobbs; Oxford, 1954.

1954 SPECIAL COMMENDATION *Lavender's Blue* by Kathleen Lines, illustrated by Harold Jones; Watts, 1954.

1954 COMMENDED *The Children of Green Knowe* by L.M. Boston, illustrated by Peter Boston; Faber, 1954; Harcourt, 1955.

The Eagle of the Ninth by Rosemary Sutcliff, illustrated by C. Walter Hodges; Oxford, 1954.

English Fables and Fairy Stories retold by James Reeves, illustrated by Joan Kiddell-Monroe; Oxford, 1954.

The Horse and his Boy by C.S. Lewis, illustrated by Pauline Baynes; Macmillan, 1954.

Lady of the Linden Tree by Barbara Leonie Picard, illustrated by Charles Stewart; Oxford, 1954.

Over the Hills to Fabylon written and illustrated by Nicholas Stuart Gray; Oxford, 1954.

1955 *The Little Bookroom: Eleanor Farjeon's Short Stories for Children Chosen by Herself* by Eleanor Farjeon, illustrated by Edward Ardizzone; Oxford, 1955; Walck, 1956.

1955 COMMENDED *Candidate for Fame* by Margaret Jowett, illustrated by Peggy Fortnum; Oxford, 1955.

Man Must Measure: The Wonderful World of Mathematics by Lancelot T. Hogben, illustrated by Andre and others, maps by Marjorie Saynor; Rathbone Books, 1955.

Minnow on the Say by A. Philippa Pearce, illustrated by Edward Ardizzone; Oxford, 1955.

A Swarm in May by William Mayne, illustrated by C. Walter Hodges; Oxford, 1955.

The Story of Albert Schweitzer by Jo Manton Gittings, illustrated by Astrid Walford; Methuen, 1955; Abelard, 1955.

1956 *The Last Battle: A Story for Children* by C.S. Lewis, illustrated by Pauline Baynes; Bodley Head, 1956.

1956 COMMENDED *Choristers' Cake* by William Mayne, illustrated by C. Walter Hodges; Oxford, 1956.

The Fairy Doll by Rumer Godden, illustrated by Adrienne Adams; Macmillan, 1956.

The Member for the Marsh by William Mayne, illustrated by Lynton Lamb; Oxford, 1956.

Ransom for a Knight by Barbara Leonie Picard, illustrated by C. Walter Hodges; Oxford, 1956.

The Shield Ring by Rosemary Sutcliff, illustrated by C. Walter Hodges; Oxford, 1956, 1957.

The Silver Sword by Ian Serraillier, illustrated by C. Walter Hodges; Cape, 1956; Criterion, 1959.

1957 *A Grass Rope* by William Mayne, illustrated by Lynton Lamb; Oxford, 1957.

1957 COMMENDED *The Blue Boat* by William Mayne, illustrated by Geraldine Spence; Oxford, 1957.

Falconer's Lure: The Story of a Summer Holiday by Antonia Forest, illustrated by Tasha Kallin; Faber, 1957.

The Silver Branch by Rosemary Sutcliff, illustrated by Charles Keeping; Oxford, 1957; Walck, 1958.

Songberd's Grove by Anne Barrett, illustrated by David Knight; Collins, 1957.

Story of the Second World War by Katherine Savage, illustrated with maps; Oxford, 1957.

The Warden's Niece by Gillian Elise Avery, illustrated by Dick Hart; Collins, 1957.

1958 *Tom's Midnight Garden* by A. Philippa Pearce, illustrated by Susan Einzig; Oxford, 1958; Lippincott, 1959.

1958 COMMENDED *The Chimneys of Green Knowe* by Lucy M. Boston, illustrated by Peter Boston; Faber, 1958.

Warrior Scarlet by Rosemary Sutcliff, illustrated by Charles Keeping; Oxford, 1958; Walck, 1958.

1959 *The Lantern Bearers* by Rosemary Sutcliff, illustrated by Charles Keeping; Oxford, 1959.

1959 COMMENDED *The Borrowers Afloat* by Mary Norton, illustrated by Diana Stanley; Dent, 1959.

Friday's Tunnel written and illustrated by John Verney; Collins, 1959; Holt, 1966.

The Load of the Unicorn written and illustrated by Cynthia Harnett; Methuen, 1959.

Quiet as Moss: 36 Poems chosen by Leonard Clark by Andrew Young, illustrated by Joan Hassall; Hart-Davis, 1959.

The Rescuers by Margery Sharp, illustrated by Judith Brook; Collins, 1959.

1960 *The Making of Man* by Ian Wolfram Cornwall, illustrated by M. Maitland Howard; Phoenix House, 1960.

1960 COMMENDED No Award

1961 *A Stranger at Green Knowe* by Lucy M. Boston, illustrated by Peter Boston; Faber, 1961.

1961 COMMENDED *February's Road* written and illustrated by John Verney; Collins, 1961.

Miss Happiness and Miss Flower by Rumer Godden, illustrated by Jean Primrose; Viking, 1961.

Peter's Room by Antonia Forest, not illustrated; Faber, 1961.

Ragged Robin (poems) by James Reeves, illustrated by Jane Paton; Dutton, 1961.

1962 *The Twelve and the Genii* by Pauline Clarke, illustrated by Cecil Leslie; Faber, 1962.

1962 COMMENDED *Armour and Blade* by S. Ernest Ellacott, illustrated; Abelard-Schuman, 1962.

Castors Away! by Hester Burton, illustrated by Victor G. Ambrus; Oxford, 1962.

The Greatest Gresham by Gillian Avery, illustrated by John Verney; Collins, 1962.

The Story of John Keats by Jo Manton Gittings and Robert Gittings, illustrated by Susan Einzig; Methuen, 1962.

The Summer Birds by Penelope Farmer, illustrated by James J. Spanfeller; Harcourt, 1962.

Windfall by K.M. Peyton, illustrated by Victor G. Ambrus; Oxford, 1962.

1963 *Time of Trial* by Hester Burton, illustrated by Victor Ambrus; Oxford, 1963; World, 1964.

1963 COMMENDED *Castaway Christmas* by Margaret J. Baker, illustrated by Richard Kennedy; Methuen, 1963.

Hell's Edge by John Rowe Townsend, not illustrated; Hutchinson, 1963.

Kings, Bishops, Knights, and Pawns: Life in a Feudal Society by Ralph Arnold, illustrated by Hilary Abrahams; Constable, 1963.

The Latchkey Children by Eric Allen, illustrated by Charles Keeping; Oxford, 1963.

The Thursday Kidnapping by Antonia Forest, not illustrated; Faber, 1963.

1964 *Nordy Bank* by Sheena Porter, illustrated by Annette Macarthur-Onslow; Oxford, 1964.

1964 **COMMENDED** *London's River: The Story of a City* by Eric S. De Mare, illustrated by Heather Copley and Christopher Chamberlain; Bodley Head, 1964.

The Maplin Bird by K.M. Peyton, illustrated by Victor G. Ambrus; Oxford, 1964; World, 1965.

The Three Brothers of Ur by Jenny Grace Fyson, illustrated by Victor G. Ambrus; Oxford, 1964.

The Namesake: A Story of King Alfred written and illustrated by C. Walter Hodges; Bell, 1964.

1965 *The Grange at High Force* by Philip Turner, illustrated by William Papas; Oxford, 1965.

1965 **COMMENDED** *The Bus Girls* by Mary Kathleen Harris, illustrated by Eileen Green; Faber, 1965.

Elidor by Alan Garner, illustrated by Charles Keeping; Collins, 1965.

The Journey of the Eldest Son by Jenny Grace Fyson, illustrated by Victor G. Ambrus; Oxford, 1965.

One Is One by Barbara Leonie Picard, illustrated by Victor G. Ambrus; Oxford, 1965.

The Orchestra and its Instruments by Christopher Headington, illustrated by Roy Spencer; Bodley Head, 1965.

The Plan for Birdmarsh by K.M. Peyton, illustrated by Victor G. Ambrus; Oxford, 1965.

1966 No Award

1966 **HIGHLY COMMENDED** *The Bayeux Tapestry: The Story of the Norman Conquest: 1066* by Norman Denny and Josephine Filmer- Sankey, illustrated; Collins, 1966.

1966 **COMMENDED** *Marassa and Midnight* by Morna Stuart, illustrated by Janina Ede; Heinemann, 1966.

Thunder in the Sky by K.M. Peyton, illustrated by Victor Ambrus; Oxford, 1966.

The Wild Horse of Santander by Helen Griffiths, illustrated by Victor G. Ambrus; Hutchinson, 1966.

1967 *The Owl Service* by Alan Garner, not illustrated; Collins, 1967.

1967 **COMMENDED** *The Dream Time* by Henry Treece, illustrated by Charles Keeping; Brockhampton, 1967.

Flambards by K.M. Peyton, illustrated by Victor G. Ambrus; Oxford, 1967; World, 1968.

The Piemakers by Helen Cresswell, illustrated by V.H. Drummond; Faber, 1967.

Smith by Leon Garfield, illustrated by Antony Maitland; Constable, 1967; Pantheon, 1967.

1968 *The Moon in the Cloud* by Rosemary Harris, not illustrated; Faber, 1968; Macmillan, 1970.

1968 **HONOUR** *Black Jack* by Leon Garfield, illustrated by Antony Maitland; Longmans, 1968.

When Jays Fly to Barbmo by Margaret Balderson, illustrated by Victor G. Ambrus; Oxford, 1968.

The Whispering Mountain by Joan Aiken, illustrated by Frank Bozzo; Cape, 1968.

1969 *The Edge of the Cloud* by K.M. Peyton, illustrated by Victor Ambrus; Oxford, 1969.

1969 **HONOUR** *The Intruder* by John Rowe Townsend, illustrated by Graham Humphreys; Oxford, 1969.

The Night Watchmen by Helen Cresswell, illustrated by Gareth Floyd; Faber, 1969.

1970 *The God Beneath the Sea* by Leon Garfield and Edward Blishen, illustrated by Charles Keeping; Longmans, 1970.

1970 **HONOUR** *The Devil's Children* by Peter Dickinson, illustrated by Robert Hales; Gollancz, 1970.

The Drummer Boy by Leon Garfield, illustrated by Antony Maitland; Longmans, 1970.

Ravensgill by William Mayne, not illustrated; Hamilton, 1970.

1971 *Josh* by Ivan Southall, not illustrated; Angus & Robertson, 1971.

1971 **HIGHLY COMMENDED** *A Likely Lad* by Gillian Avery, illustrated by Faith Jacques; Collins, 1971.

Tristan and Iseult by Rosemary Sutcliff, illustrated by Victor Ambrus; Bodley Head, 1971.

Up the Pier by Helen Cresswell, illustrated by Gareth Floyd; Faber, 1971.

1972 *Watership Down* by Richard Adams, not illustrated; Rex Collings, 1972; Macmillan, 1972; Avon, 1975.

1972 **COMMENDED** *Dancing Bear* by Peter Dickinson, illustrated by David Smee; Gollancz, 1972.

No Way of Telling by Emma Smith, illustrated with maps; Bodley Head, 1972; Atheneum, 1972.

1973 *The Ghost of Thomas Kempe* by Penelope Lively, illustrated by Antony Maitland; Heinemann, 1973.

1973 **COMMENDED** *Bongleweed* by Helen Cresswell, illustrated by Ann Strugnell; Faber, 1973.

Carrie's War by Nina Bawden, not illustrated; Gollancz, 1973.

The Dark Is Rising by Susan Cooper, illustrated by Alan Cober; Atheneum, 1973.

1974 *The Stronghold* by Mollie Hunter, not illustrated; Hamilton, 1974.

1974 **COMMENDED** *Battle of Gettysburg, 1-3 July, 1863* written and illustrated by Ian Ribbons; Oxford, 1974.

1975 *The Machine Gunners* by Robert Westall, not illustrated; Macmillan, 1975; Greenwillow, 1976.

1975 **COMMENDED** *Dogsbody* by Diana Wynne Jones, not illustrated; Macmillan, 1975.

The Grey King by Susan Cooper, illustrated by Michael Heslop; Chatto & Windus, 1975; Atheneum, 1975.

1976 *Thunder and Lightnings* by Jan Mark, illustrated by Jim Russell; Kestrel, 1976.

1976 **COMMENDED** *The Blue Hawk* by Peter Dickinson, illustrated by David Smee; Gollancz, 1976.

1977 *The Turbulent Term of Tyke Tiler* by Gene Kemp, illustrated by Carolyn Dinan; Faber, 1977.

1977 **COMMENDED** *A Charmed Life* by Diana Wynne Jones, not illustrated; Macmillan, 1977.

Shadow Cage and other Tales of the Supernatural by A. Philippa Pearce, illustrated by Janet Archer; Kestrel, 1977.

Under Goliath by Peter Carter, illustrated by Ian Ribbons; Oxford, 1977.

1978 *Exeter Blitz* by David Rees, not illustrated; Hamilton, 1978.

1978 **COMMENDED** *The Battle of Bubble and Squeak* by A. Philippa Pearce, illustrated by Alan Baker; Deutsch, 1978.

The Devil on the Road by Robert Westall, not illustrated; Macmillan, 1978.

A Kind of Wild Justice by Bernard Ashley, illustrated by Charles Keeping; Oxford, 1978.

1979 *Tulku* by Peter Dickinson, not illustrated; Unicorn/Dutton, 1979.

1979 **HIGHLY COMMENDED** *The Castle Story* written and illustrated by Sheila Sancha; Kestrel, 1979.

1979 **COMMENDED** *Which Witch?* by Eva Ibbotson, illustrated by Annabel Large; Macmillan, 1979.

The Vandal by Ann Schlee, not illustrated; Macmillan, 1979.

1980 *City of Gold and Other Stories from the Old Testament* by Peter Dickinson, illustrated by Michael Foreman; Gollancz, 1980.

1980 **HIGHLY COMMENDED** *Nothing to Be Afraid of* by Jan Mark, illustrated by David Parkins; Kestrel, 1980.

1980 **COMMENDED** *The Fox in Winter* by John Branfield, not illustrated; Gollancz, 1980.

A Sense of Shame and other Stories by Jan Needle, not illustrated; Deutsch, 1980.

1981 *The Scarecrows* by Robert Westall, not illustrated; Chatto & Windus, 1981; Greenwillow, 1981.

1981 **HIGHLY COMMENDED** *The Hollow Land* by Jane Gardam, illustrated by Janet Rawlins; Julia MacRae, 1981.

1981 **COMMENDED** *Goodnight, Mister Tom* by Michelle Magorian, not illustrated; Kestrel, 1981.

Bridget and William by Jane Gardam, illustrated by Janet Rawlins; Julia MacRae, 1981.

1982 *The Haunting* by Margaret Mahy, not illustrated; Dent, 1982; Atheneum, 1983.

1982 **HIGHLY COMMENDED** *The Dark Behind the Curtains* by Gillian Cross, illustrated by David Parkins; Oxford, 1982.

1982 **COMMENDED** *Wall of Words* by Tim Kennemore, not illustrated; Faber, 1982.

1983 *Handles* by Jan Mark, illustrated by David Parkins; Kestrel, 1983.

1984 *The Changeover* by Margaret Mahy, not illustrated; Dent, 1984.

1984 **HIGHLY COMMENDED** *Brother in the Land* by Robert Swindells, not illustrated; Oxford, 1984.

1985 *Storm* by Kevin Crossley-Holland, illustrated by Alan Marks; Heinemann, 1985.

1985 **HIGHLY COMMENDED** *The Nature of the Beast* by Janni Howker, not illustrated; MacRae, 1985; Greenwillow, 1985.

1986 *Grannie Was a Buffer Girl* by Berlie Doherty, not illustrated; Methuen, 1986.

1986 **HIGHLY COMMENDED** *Isaac Campion* by Janni Howker, not illustrated; MacRae, 1986; Greenwillow, 1986.

1986 **COMMENDED** *Running Scared* by Bernard Ashley, not illustrated; MacRae, 1986.

Chartbreak by Gillian Cross, not illustrated; Oxford, 1986.

The Coal House by Andrew Taylor, not illustrated; Collins, 1986.

1987 *The Ghost Drum* by Susan Price, not illustrated; Faber, 1987; Farrar Straus Giroux, 1987.

1988 *A Pack of Lies: Twelve Stories in One* by Geraldine McCaughrean, not illustrated; Oxford University Press, 1988.

1988 **HIGHLY COMMENDED** *A Map of Nowhere* by Gillian Cross, not illustrated; Oxford University Press, 1988.

Eva by Peter Dickinson, not illustrated; Gollancz, 1988; Delacorte, 1989.

Red Sky in the Morning by Elizabeth Laird, not illustrated; Heinemann, 1988.

1988 **COMMENDED** *The Lives of Christopher Chant* by Diana Wynne Jones, not illustrated; Methuen Children's, 1988.

The Monster Garden by Vivien Alcock, not illustrated; Methuen, 1988.

Awaiting Developments by Judy Allen, not illustrated; Julia MacRae, 1988; Walker, 1989.

1989 *Goggle-eyes* by Anne Fine, not illustrated; Hamish Hamilton, 1989; Joy Street Books, 1989.

1989 **HIGHLY COMMENDED** *The Charlie Barber Treatment* by Carole Lloyd, illustrated; Julia MacRae, 1989.

Bill's New Frock by Anne Fine, illustrated by Philippe Dupasquier; Methuen Children's, 1989.

1989 **COMMENDED** *The Trial of Anna Cotman* by Vivien Alcock, not illustrated; Methuen Children's, 1989; Delacorte, 1990.

1990 *Wolf* by Gillian Cross, not illustrated; Oxford University Press, 1990; Holiday House, 1991.

1990 **HIGHLY COMMENDED** *The Cry of the Wolf* by Melvin Burgess, not illustrated; Andersen Press, 1990; Tambourine Books, 1992.

The Kingdom by the Sea by Robert Westall, not illustrated; Methuen Children's 1990; Farrar, Straus Giroux, 1991.

1991 *Dear Nobody* by Berlie Doherty, not illustrated; Hamish Hamilton, 1991; Orchard, 1992.

1991 **HIGHLY COMMENDED** *The Story of Tracy Beaker* by Jacqueline Wilson, illustrated by Nick Sharratt; Doubleday, 1991.

1991 **COMMENDED** *The Real Tilly Beany* by Annie Dalton, illustrated by Kate Aldous; Methuen, 1991.

The Drowners by Garry Kilworth, not illustrated; Methuen, 1991.

1992 *Flour Babies* by Anne Fine, not illustrated; Hamish Hamilton, 1992.

1992 **HIGHLY COMMENDED** *Gulf* by Robert Westall, not illustrated; Methuen, 1992.

1992 **COMMENDED** *The Great Elephant Chase* by Gillian Cross, not illustrated; Oxford University Press, 1991.

A Bone from a Dry Sea by Peter Dickinson, not illustrated; Gollancz, 1992.

LEWIS CARROLL SHELF AWARD
discontinued

Originated in 1958 by Dr. David C. Davis, the Lewis Carroll Shelf Award was given annually to those titles which possessed enough of the qualities of Alice in Wonderland to enable them to sit on the same book shelf. Each year, publishers of children's literature were invited to submit one title from their list. The final selection was made by a five member committee comprised of editors, librarians, parents, teachers, and writers. Dr. Davis served as the coordinator and sometimes as the final judge. Although there was no limit to the number of books which could be honored each year, all winning titles were unanimously approved by the committee.

The Gold Cheshire Cat Seal was placed on the honored books at the Wisconsin Book Conference, or later, at the Communications for Children Workshop. The Shelf Collection, which grew annually, was exhibited at the conference. Due to the disability of the founder, the Lewis Carroll Shelf Award was discontinued in 1979.

These criteria, all characteristics of Alice in Wonderland, were used by editors in their initial selection of titles to be considered by the committee: (1) imagination and originality, (2) genuine emotion, (3) consistent characters, (4) plausible events (even in fantasy form), and (5) a plot that unfolds gently and logically.

The component analysis selector tool then directed the University of Wisconsin Book Conference Selection Committee to rate the nominated books according to the following factors: (1) Authenticity: author/illustrator depicts his story, episodes, or genre of communication to reflect a genuine identification to the characters, events, or experience communicated. (2) Universals: the book should exhibit an idea, theme focus, thought concept, or behavioral trait that is believed to be part of everyone at all times. (3) Insight: The book should provoke new and distinctive thoughts. (4) Symbol system: the judges should take into account the use of ideation symbol system, page layout, print size, type format, glossaries, jackets and such. (5) Impact: what impact does this work have on its audience? (6) Genre comparison: written literature has developed into many types. Some major types are folklore, fantasy, humor, biography, and poetry. How does the book in question compare with others in its group? (7) Test of time: will this book appeal to children 50 or even 100 years from now? (From Component Analysis Tool developed by Dr. Davis).

It was hoped that the Lewis Carroll Shelf Award would evolve as a tool that could serve as a guide for children, parents, librarians, and teachers in choosing recreational reading materials.

1958 *The Blue Cat of Castle Town* by Catherine C. Coblentz, illustrated by Janice Holland; Longmans, 1949.

Caps for Sale: A Tale of a Peddlar, Some Monkeys and their Monkey Business written and illustrated by Esphyr Slobodkina; Scott, 1947.

Horton Hatches the Egg written and illustrated by Dr. Seuss; Random House, 1940.

The Little Bookroom: Eleanor Farjeon's Short Stories for Children Chosen by Herself by Eleanor Farjeon, illustrated by Edward Ardizzone; Oxford, 1955; Walck, 1956.

The Little Engine That Could by Watty Piper, illustrated by George Hauman and Doris Hauman; Platt, 1954, 1930.

The Little House in the Big Woods by Laura Ingalls Wilder, illustrated by Garth Williams; Harper, 1953.

Millions of Cats written and illustrated by Wanda Gag; Coward, 1928.

Mr. Popper's Penguins by Richard Atwater and Florence Atwater, illustrated by Robert Lawson; Little Brown, 1938.

Ol' Paul, the Mighty Logger written and illustrated by Glen Rounds; Holiday, 1949, 1936.

Pecos Bill, the Greatest Cowboy of All Time by James Cloyd Bowman, illustrated by Laura Bannon; Whitman, 1937.

Prayer for a Child by Rachel Field, illustrated by Elizabeth Orton Jones; Macmillan, 1944.

The Story of Doctor Dolittle written and illustrated by Hugh Lofting; Lippincott, 1948, c1920.

The Tale of Peter Rabbit written and illustrated by Beatrix Potter; Warne, 1903.

The Three Hundred and Ninety-seventh White Elephant by Rene Guillot, translated by Gwen Marsh, illustrated by Moyra Leatham; Phillips, 1957.

The Wind in the Willows by Kenneth Grahame, illustrated by Ernest H. Shepard; Scribner, 1954, c1908.

The World of Pooh by A.A. Milne, illustrated by Ernest H. Shepard; Dutton, 1957.

1959 *Caddie Woodlawn* by Carol Ryrie Brink, illustrated by Kate Seredy; Macmillan, 1935.

Charlotte's Web by E.B. White, illustrated by Garth Williams; Harper, 1952.

The Courage of Sarah Noble by Alice Dalgliesh, illustrated by Leonard Weisgard; Scribner, 1954.

The Five Chinese Brothers by Claire Huchet Bishop, illustrated by Kurt Wiese; Coward, 1938.

Li Lun, Lad of Courage by Carolyn Treffinger, illustrated by Kurt Wiese; Abingdon-Cokesbury, 1947.

The Little House written and illustrated by Virginia Lee Burton; Houghton, 1942.

The Minnow Leads to Treasure by A. Philippa Pearce, illustrated by Edward Ardizzone; World, 1958.

The Secret Garden by Frances Hodgson Burnett, illustrated by N. Unwin; Lippincott, 1938, c1911.

Snipp, Snapp, Snurr and the Red Shoes written and illustrated by Maj Lindman; Whitman, 1936.

The Story of Babar, the Little Elephant written and illustrated by Jean de Brunhoff; translated by Merle S. Haas; Random House, 1933.

This Boy Cody by Leon Wilson, illustrated by Ursula Koering; Watts, 1950.

Tirra Lirra: Rhymes Old and New by Laura E. Richards, illustrated by Marguerite Davis; Little, 1955, c1902.

The White Stag written and illustrated by Kate Seredy; Viking, 1937.

1960 *Blind Colt* written and illustrated by Glen Rounds; Holiday, 1960, 1941.

The Borrowers by Mary Norton, illustrated by Beth Krush and Joe Krush; Harcourt, 1953.

Curious George Takes a Job written and illustrated by H.A. Rey; Houghton, 1947.

Johnny Crow's Garden: A Picture Book written and illustrated by L. Leslie Brooke; Warne, 1903.

The Jungle Book by Rudyard Kipling, illustrated by J.L. Kipling, W.H. Drake, and P. Frenzeny; Doubleday, 1952, c1893.

Lavender's Blue by Kathleen Lines, illustrated by Harold Jones; Watts, 1954.

The Matchlock Gun by Walter D. Edmonds, illustrated by Paul Lantz; Dodd Mead, 1941.

Onion John by Joseph Q. Krumgold, illustrated by Symeon Shimin; Crowell, 1959.

Young Fu of the Upper Yangtze by Elizabeth Foreman Lewis, illustrated by Kurt Wiese; Winston, 1932.

1961 *And to Think that I Saw It on Mulberry Street* written and illustrated by Dr. Seuss; Vanguard, 1937.

Ben and Me written and illustrated by Robert Lawson; Little Brown, 1939.

Blue Willow by Doris Gates, illustrated by Paul Lantz; Viking, 1940.

The Door in the Wall: Story of Medieval London written and illustrated by Marguerite de Angeli; Doubleday, 1949.

Grishka and the Bear by Rene Guillot, translated by Gwen Marsh, illustrated by Joan Kiddell-Monroe; Criterion, 1959.

Hitty, Her First Hundred Years by Rachel Field, illustrated by Dorothy P. Lathrop; Macmillan, 1929.

Island of the Blue Dolphins by Scott O'Dell, not illustrated; Houghton, 1960.

The Moffats by Eleanor Estes, illustrated by Louis Slobodkin; Harcourt, 1941.

Misty of Chincoteague by Marguerite Henry, illustrated by Wesley Dennis; Rand McNally, 1947.

A Roundabout Turn by Robert H. Charles, illustrated by L. Leslie Brooke; Warne, 1930.

When I Was a Boy by Erich Kastner, translated by Isabel McHugh and Florence McHugh, illustrated by Horst Lemke; Watts, 1961.

1962 *The Adventures of Huckleberry Finn* by Samuel Clemens, illustrated by Donald McKay; Grosset, 1948, c1884.

The Dark Frigate by Charles Boardman Hawes, illustrated by A.L. Ripley; Atlantic Monthly Press, 1923; Little Brown, 1934.

Daughter of the Mountains by Louise S. Rankin, illustrated by Kurt Wiese; Viking, 1948.

Inch by Inch written and illustrated by Leo Lionni; Obolensky, 1960.

The Lion, the Witch and the Wardrobe by C.S. Lewis, illustrated by Pauline Baynes; Macmillan, 1950.

Paddle-to-the-Sea written and illustrated by Holling Clancy Holling; Houghton Mifflin, 1941.

Padre Porko: The Gentlemanly Pig by Robert Davis, illustrated by Fritz Eichenberg; Holiday, 1948.

A Penny a Day by Walter de la Mare, illustrated by Paul Kennedy; Knopf, 1960, 1925.

The Tailor of Gloucester written and illustrated by Beatrix Potter; Warne, 1903.

Thistle and Thyme: Tales and Legends from Scotland by Sorche Nic Leodhas, illustrated by Evaline Ness; Holt, 1962.

Thumbelina by Hans Christian Andersen, translated by R.P. Keigwin, illustrated by Adrienne Adams; Scribner, 1961.

Winter Danger by William O. Steele, illustrated by Paul Galdone; Harcourt, 1954.

The World of Christopher Robin by A.A. Milne, illustrated by E.H. Shepard; Dutton, 1958.

1963 *Annuzza: A Girl of Romania* by Hertha Seuberlich, translated by Stella Humphries, illustrated by Gerhard Pallasch; Rand, 1962.

The Art of Ancient Egypt by Shirley Glubok, illustrated by Gerald Nook; Atheneum, 1962.

The Cricket in Times Square by George Selden, illustrated by Garth Williams; Farrar, 1960.

Dwarf Long-nose by Wilhelm Hauff, translated by Doris Orgel, illustrated by Maurice Sendak; Random House, 1960.

The Griffin and the Minor Canon by Frank R. Stockton, illustrated by Maurice Sendak; Holt, 1963.

Invincible Louisa: The Story of the Author of Little Women by Cornelia Meigs, illustrated with photographs; Little Brown, 1961, 1933.

The Man Who Was Don Quixote: The Story of Miguel Cervantes written and illustrated by Rafaello Busoni; Prentice Hall, 1958.

Moccasin Trail by Eloise J. McGraw, illustrated by Paul Galdone; Coward, 1952.

Rabbit Hill written and illustrated by Robert Lawson; Viking, 1962, 1944.

The Reluctant Dragon by Kenneth Grahame, illustrated by Ernest H. Shepard; Holiday, 1953, c1938.

The Superlative Horse by Jean Merrill, illustrated by Ronni Solbert; Scott, 1961.

Tom's Midnight Garden by A. Philippa Pearce, illustrated by Susan Einzig; Oxford, 1958; Lippincott, 1959.

Uncle Remus: His Songs and Sayings by Joel Chandler Harris, illustrated by A.B. Frost; Hawthorne, 1921, c1880.

The Water Babies by Charles Kingsley, illustrated by Harold Jones; Watts, 1961, 1863.

The Wheel on the School by Meindert DeJong, illustrated by Maurice Sendak; Harper, 1954.

The Yearling by Marjorie Kinnan Rawlings, illustrated by N. C. Wyeth; Scribner, 1961, 1939.

1964 *A Little Princess: Being the Whole Story of Sara Crewe now Told for the First Time* by Frances Hodgson Burnett, illustrated by Ethel F. Betts; Scribner, 1938.

Old Wind and Liu Li-San by Aline Glasgow, illustrated by Bernard Glasgow; Harvey, 1962.

Rascal: A Memoir of a Better Era by Sterling North, illustrated by John Schoenherr; Dutton, 1963.

Rifles for Watie by Harold Keith, illustrated by Peter Burchard; Crowell, 1957.

Roller Skates by Ruth Sawyer, illustrated by Valenti Angelo; Viking, 1936.

Roosevelt Grady by Louisa R. Shotwell, illustrated by Peter Burchard; World, 1963.

Where the Wild Things are written and illustrated by Maurice Sendak; Harper, 1963.

1965 *Bond of the Fire* by Anthony T. Fon Eisen, illustrated by W.T. Mars; World, 1965.

The Cock, the Mouse and the Little Red Hen by Felicite LeFevre, illustrated by Tony Sarg; Macrae, 1947.

Joel and the Wild Goose by Helga Sandburg, illustrated by Thomas Daly; Dial, 1963.

My Side of the Mountain written and illustrated by Jean Craighead George; Dutton, 1959.

The Nightingale by Hans Christian Andersen, translated by Eva LeGallienne, illustrated by Nancy Ekholm Burkert; Harper, 1965.

The Pushcart War by Jean Merrill, illustrated by Ronni Solbert; Scott, 1964.

The Return of the Twelves by Pauline Clarke, illustrated by Bernarda Bryson; Coward, 1963.

Smoky, the Cowhorse written and illustrated by Will James; Scribner, 1926.

The Story about Ping by Marjorie Flack, illustrated by Kurt Wiese; Viking, 1933.

The Wolves of Willoughby Chase by Joan Aiken, illustrated by Pat Marriott; Doubleday, 1963.

A Wrinkle in Time by Madeleine L'Engle, not illustrated; Farrar, 1962.

1966 *Across Five Aprils* by Irene Hunt, illustrated by Albert J. Pucci; Follett, 1964.

Banner in the Sky: The Story of a Boy and a Mountain by James Ramsey Ullman, not illustrated; Lippincott, 1954.

A Child's Garden of Verses by Robert Louis Stevenson, illustrated by Brian Wildsmith; Watts, 1966.

An Edge of the Forest by Agnes Smith, illustrated by Roberta Moynihan; Viking, 1959.

Jed: The Story of a Yankee Soldier and a Southern Boy written and illustrated by Peter Burchard; Coward, 1960.

Once a Mouse written and illustrated by Marcia Brown; Scribner, 1961.

Pappa Pellerin's Daughter by Maria Gripe, translated by Kersti French, illustrated by Harald Gripe; Day, 1966.

1967 *More Just So Stories* (phonodisc) by Rudyard Kipling, narrated by Ed Begley; Caedmon R1205.

Tom Sawyer (phonodisc) by Samuel Clemens, narrated by Boris Karloff; Caedmon R1088.

1968 *The Ark* by Margot Benary-Isbert, translated by Clara Winston and Richard Winston; Harcourt, 1953.

Drummer Hoff adapted by Barbara Emberley, illustrated by Ed Emberley; Prentice Hall, 1967.

Earthfasts by William Mayne, not illustrated; Dutton, 1966.

The Emperor and the Kite by Jane Yolen, illustrated by Ed Young; Collins-World, 1967.

The Fiddler of High Lonesome written and illustrated by Brinton Turkle; Viking, 1968.

From the Mixed-up Files of Mrs. Basil E. Frankweiler written and illustrated by E.L. Konigsburg; Atheneum, 1967.

The Hunter I Might Have Been by George Mendoza, illustrated by DeWayne Dalrymple; Astor-Honor, 1968.

My Father's Dragon by Ruth Stiles Gannett, illustrated by Ruth Chrisman Gannett; Random House, 1948.

No Room: An Old Story retold by Rose Dobbs, illustrated by Fritz Eichenberg; McKay, 1944.

Reflections on a Gift of Watermelon Pickle and Other Modern Verse by Edward Lueders, Stephen Dunning and Hugh Smith, illustrated with photographs; Lothrop Lee & Shepard, 1966.

The Wizard of Oz by L. Frank Baum, illustrated by W.W. Denslow; Reilly & Lee, 1956.

1969 *The Children of Green Knowe* by L.M. Boston, illustrated by Peter Boston; Faber, 1954; Harcourt, 1955.

Constance: A Story of Early Plymouth by Patricia Clapp, not illustrated; Lothrop, 1968.

Edge of Two Worlds by Weyman Jones, illustrated by J.C. Kocsis; Dial, 1968.

Little Toot written and illustrated by Hardie Gramatky; Putnam, 1939.

Little Women by Louisa May Alcott, illustrated by Jessie Willcox Smith; Little Brown, 1968, c1868.

McBroom Tells the Truth by Sid Fleischman, illustrated by Kurt Werth; Norton, 1966.

Seventeenth Summer by Maureen Daly, not illustrated; Dodd, 1962, 1942.

The Story of Comock the Eskimo as Told to Robert Flaherty edited by Edmund Carpenter, illustrated with original Eskimo sketches; Simon & Schuster, 1968.

The Storyteller's Pack by Frank R. Stockton, illustrated by Bernarda Bryson; Scribner, 1968.

Usha the Mouse Maiden written and illustrated by Mehlli Gobhai; Hawthorn, 1969.

Wild Horses of the Red Desert written and illustrated by Glen Rounds; Holiday House, 1969.

1970 *The Animal Family* by Randall Jarrell, illustrated by Maurice Sendak; Pantheon, 1965.

The Cay by Theodore Taylor, not illustrated; Doubleday, 1969.

The Egypt Game by Zilpha Keatley Snyder, illustrated by Alton Raible; Atheneum, 1967.

The Enormous Egg by Oliver Butterworth, illustrated by Louis Darling; Little Brown, 1956.

Gautama Buddha, in Life and Legend by Betty Kelen, illustrated with photographs; Lothrop, 1967.

Gone-away Lake by Elizabeth Enright, illustrated by Beth Krush and Joe Krush; Harcourt, 1957.

A Herd of Deer by Eilis Dillon, illustrated by Richard Kennedy; Funk & Wagnalls, 1969.

Honk the Moose by Phil Stong, illustrated by Kurt Wiese; Dodd Mead, 1935.

The Midnight Fox by Betsy Byars, illustrated by Ann Grifalconi; Viking, 1968.

Old Ben by Jesse Stuart, illustrated by Richard Cuffari; McGraw, 1970.

Otto of the Silver Hand written and illustrated by Howard Pyle; Scribner, 1954.

Sounder by William H. Armstrong, illustrated by James Barkley; Harper & Row, 1969.

The Summer I Was Lost by Phillip Viereck, illustrated by Ellen Viereck; Day, 1965.

To Be a Slave by Julius Lester, illustrated by Tom Feelings; Dial, 1968.

The Tomten by Astrid Lindgren, illustrated by Harald Wiberg; Coward, 1961.

The Weirdstone of Brisingamen and a Tale of Alderly by Alan Garner, not illustrated; Walck, 1969.

1971 *Boy Alone* by Reginald Ottley, illustrated by Clyde Pearson; Harcourt, 1966.

Down, Down the Mountain written and illustrated by Ellis Credle; Nelson, 1961, 1934.

The Endless Steppe: Growing Up in Siberia by Esther Hautzig, not illustrated; Crowell, 1968.

Farmer Hoo and the Baboons by Ida Chittum, illustrated by Glen Rounds; Delacorte, 1971.

The Incredible Journey: A Tale of Three Animals by Shelia Every Burnford, illustrated by Carl Burger; Little Brown, 1961.

Journey Outside by Mary Q. Steele, illustrated by Rocco Negri; Viking, 1969.

Lift Every Voice and Sing words and music by J. Rosamund and James Weldon Johnson, illustrated by Mozelle Thompson; Hawthorn, 1970.

The Nonsense Book compiled by Duncan Emrich, illustrated by Ib Spang Ohlsson; Four Winds, 1970.

The Soul Brothers and Sister Lou by Kristin Hunter, not illustrated; Scribner, 1968.

Undine by Friedrich de la Motte Fouque, retold and edited by Gertrude C. Schwebeil, illustrated by Eros Keith; Simon & Schuster, 1971, c1957.

The Velveteen Rabbit: or, How Toys Become Real by Margery Williams, illustrated by William Nicholson; Doubleday, 1958.

The Witch's Brat by Rosemary Sutcliff, illustrated by Richard Lebenson; Walck, 1970.

1972 *The Art and Industry of Sandcastles* written and illustrated by Jan Adkins; Walker, 1971.

Bear Circus written and illustrated by William Pene du Bois; Viking, 1971.

Ceremony of Innocence by James Forman, not illustrated; Hawthorn, 1970.

The Diary of Nina Kosterina by Nina Kosterina, illustrated and translated by Mirra Ginsburg; Crown, 1968.

Dorp Dead by Julia Cunningham, illustrated by James Spanfeller; Pantheon, 1965.

The Duchess Bakes a Cake written and illustrated by Virginia Kahl; Scribner, 1955.

Emmet Otter's Jug-band Christmas by Russell Hoban, illustrated by Lillian Hoban; Parents, 1971.

The Forgotten Door by Alexander Key, not illustrated; Westminster, 1965.

The Hawkstone by Jay Williams, not illustrated; Walck, 1971.

The Little Old Woman Who Used Her Head by Hope Newell, illustrated by Margaret Ruse; Nelson, 1966, 1935.

Long Journey Home: Stories from Black History by Julius Lester, not illustrated; Dial, 1972.

Mrs. Frisby and the Rats of NIMH by Robert C. O'Brien, illustrated by Zena Bernstein; Atheneum, 1971.

The Planet of Junior Brown by Virginia Hamilton, not illustrated; Macmillan, 1971.

Simon Boom Gives a Wedding by Yuri Suhl, illustrated by Margot Zemach; Four Winds, 1972.

1973 *Anansi the Spider: A Tale from the Ashanti* written and illustrated by Gerald McDermott; Holt, 1972.

Cockleburr Quarters by Charlotte Baker, illustrated by Robert Owens; Prentice Hall, 1972.

Four Women in a Violent Time by Deborah Crawford, not illustrated; Crown, 1970.

The Girl Who Loved the Wind by Jane Yolen, illustrated by Ed Young; Crowell, 1972.

Jack Tar by Jean Russell Larson, illustrated by Mercer Mayer; Macrae, 1970.

The Knee-high Man and other Tales by Julius Lester, illustrated by Ralph Pinto; Dial, 1972.

Little Tim and the Brave Sea Captain written and illustrated by Edward Ardizzone; Walck, 1955.

North to Freedom by Anne S. Holm, translated by L.W. Kingsland, not illustrated; Harcourt, 1965.

Pippi Longstocking by Astrid Lindgren, translated by Florence Lamborn, illustrated by Louis Glanzman; Viking, 1950.

The Runaway's Diary by Marilyn Harris, not illustrated; Four Winds, 1971.

The Silver Pony written and illustrated by Lynd Ward; Houghton, 1973.

Snow White and the Seven Dwarfs by Jacob Grimm and Wilhelm Grimm, translated by Randall Jarrell, illustrated by Nancy Ekholm Burkert; Farrar, 1972.

The Stolen Pony written and illustrated by Glen Rounds; Holiday House, 1969, 1948.

1974 No Awards

1975 *Dust of the Earth* by Bill Cleaver and Vera Cleaver, not illustrated; Lippincott, 1975.

A Hero Ain't Nothin' but a Sandwich by Alice Childress, not illustrated; Coward, 1973.

The Pig-tale by Lewis Carroll, illustrated by Leonard B. Lubin; Little Brown, 1975, 1889.

1976 *The Day the Circus Came to Lone Tree* written and illustrated by Glen Rounds; Holiday House, 1973.

Don't Take Teddy by Babbis Friis-Baastad, translated by Lise Somme McKinnon, not illustrated; Scribner, 1967.

Duffy and the Devil retold by Harve Zemach, illustrated by Margot Zemach; Farrar, 1973.

M.C. Higgins, the Great by Virginia Hamilton, not illustrated; Macmillan, 1974.

Saturday, the Twelfth of October by Norma Fox Mazer, not illustrated; Delacorte, 1975.

1977 *Abel's Island* written and illustrated by William Steig; Farrar, 1976.

Sailing to Cythera and other Anatole Stories by Nancy Willard, illustrated by David McPhail; Harcourt, 1974.

Slake's Limbo by Felice Holman, not illustrated; Scribner, 1974.

1978 *Bridge to Terabithia* by Katherine Paterson, illustrated by Donna Diamond; Crowell, 1977.

Come to the Edge by Julia Cunningham, not illustrated; Pantheon, 1977.

Dear Bill, Remember Me? and Other Stories by Norma Fox Mazer, not illustrated; Delacorte, 1976.

Manya's Story by Bettyanne Gray, illustrated with photographs; Lerner, 1978.

Mischling, Second Degree: My Childhood in Nazi Germany by Ilse Koehn, not illustrated; Greenwillow, 1977.

Mr. Yowder and the Giant Bull Snake written and illustrated by Glen Rounds; Holiday House, 1978.

Noah's Ark written and illustrated by Peter Spier; Doubleday, 1977.

The No-Return Trail by Sonia Levitin, not illustrated; Harcourt, 1978.

Stevie written and illustrated by John Steptoe; Harper, 1969.

Sylvester and the Magic Pebble written and illustrated by William Steig; Windmill/Simon & Schuster, 1969.

Tuck Everlasting by Natalie Babbitt, not illustrated; Farrar, 1975.

Who's in Rabbit's House?: A Masai Tale by Verna Aardema, illustrated by Leo Dillon and Diane Dillon; Dial, 1977.

1979 *The Chocolate War* by Robert Cormier, illustrated by Robert Vickery; Pantheon, 1974; Dell, 1975.

Dragonwings by Laurence Yep, not illustrated; Harper, 1975.

The Island of the Grass King: The Further Adventures of Anatole by Nancy Willard, illustrated by David McPhail; Harcourt, 1979.

Lyle, Lyle, Crocodile written and illustrated by Bernard Waber; Houghton, 1965.

The Road from Home: The Story of an Armenian Girl by David Kherdian, not illustrated; Greenwillow, 1979.

The Snowman written and illustrated by Raymond Briggs; Random House, 1978.

The Wizard of Earthsea by Ursula K. LeGuin, illustrated by Ruth Robbins; Parnassus, 1968.

CATHOLIC BOOK AWARDS
discontinued

This award was sponsored by the Catholic Press of the United States and Canada. In the children's categories, the contents of the book must reflect sound Christian and psychological values. The age groups covered were: Children (up to age 12) and Youth (12 years and older). The winners received certificates. The award program was discontinued in 1989.

1984 **CHILDREN** *Story of Brother Francis* by Lene Mayer-Skumanz, illustrated by Alicia Sancha; Ave Maria Press, 1983.

1984 **YOUTH** *No Strangers to Violence, No Strangers to Love* by Boniface Hanley, illustrated with photos; Ave Maria Press, 1983.

1985 **CHILDREN** *Strings and Things: Poems and Other Messages for Children* by Christy Kenneally, illustrated by Gloria Ortiz; Paulist Press, 1984.

1985 **YOUTH** *Mother Teresa of Calcutta* by David Michelinie and Roy M. Gasnick, illustrated by John Tartaglione; Franciscan Communications Office, 1984.

1986 **CHILDREN** *Back-Back and the Lima Bear* by Thomas L. Weck, illustrated by Neil Taylor; Winston Derek, 1985.

1986 **YOUTH** *Hang Tough!* by Matthew Lancaster, illustrated by Pamela Huffman; Paulist Press, 1985.

1987-1988 No Award

REBECCA CAUDILL YOUNG READERS' BOOK AWARD

Illinois School Library Media Association
1342 Gayman Dr.
Decatur, IL 62526

This award is named for children's writer Rebecca Caudill, resident of Urbana, Illinois for nearly fifty years. Established in 1987 by Carol Fox, this children's choice award has the following purposes: (1) to encourage children and young people to read for personal satisfaction; (2) to develop statewide awareness of outstanding literature for children and young people; (3) to promote a desire for literacy; and (4) to encourage cooperation among Illinois agencies providing educational and library services to children.

To be eligible, the book must have literary merit, be of interest and appeal to children, be published in the last five years, and be in print at the time of selection. The award is given to the author of the book voted most outstanding from a master list of titles by students in Illinois schools grades four through eight.

Sponsored by the Illinois School Library Media Association, the Illinois Reading Council, and the Illinois Association of Teachers of English, this award is supported by the Department of Curriculum and Instruction at Northern Illinois University. The winner is announced during National Library Week and the award is presented at the Illinois Library Association spring conference.

1988 *The Indian in the Cupboard* by Lynn Reid Banks, illustrated by Brock Cole; Doubleday, 1980.

1989 *The Dollhouse Murders* by Betty Ren Wright, not illustrated; Holiday House, 1983.

1990 *Wait Til Helen Comes* by Mary Downing Hahn, not illustrated; Clarion, 1986.

1991 *Matilda* by Roald Dahl, illustrated by Quentin Blake; Cape, 1988; Viking Kestrel, 1988.

1992 *Number the Stars* by Lois Lowry, not illustrated; Houghton Mifflin, 1989.

1993 *Maniac Magee* by Jerry Spinelli, not illustrated; Little Brown, 1990.

J. G. CHANDLER REWARD OF MERIT

discontinued

The Chandler Reward of Merit was first awarded in 1962 in honor of John Greene Chandler and his daughter, Alice Greene Chandler. This award was originated by Herbert H. Hosmer for the purpose of giving area residents a chance to hear authors, illustrators, publishers, and collectors of children's books. The event was held at the Lancaster Town Library. A Silver Reward of Merit provided through a family fund was presented to the honored speaker.

1962 Gertrude E. Allen, Ernest Cobb

1963 Tasha Tudor, Thornton Burgess

1964 Barbara Cooney, Joan Walsh Anglund

1965 Isabelle Chang, Shirley Errickson, E.B. Knowlton, Alice B. Cushman, American Antiquarian Society

1966 David McCord

1967 Maurice Sendak

1968 Ed Emberley

1969 Waldo H. Hunt

1970 Jane Yolen

1971 Walter Scherf, William Barass, Paul Heins

1972 Marcus McCorison, d'Alte A. Welch, Benjamin Tighe

1973 Edna Boutwell

1974-1981 Program suspended

1982 Boston Public Library (Juvenile Book Collection), Philip McNiff, Clara G. Dennis (posthumously), Alice M. Jordan (posthumously)

1983 Francelia Butler

1984 Raymond H. Deck, Jr.

CHARLOTTE BOOK AWARD

New York State Reading Association
c/o Susan Lehr
Department of Education
Skidmore College
Saratoga Springs, NY 12866

Established in 1990 to honor the classic children's book, Charlotte's Web, the Charlotte Award is designed to encourage children to read good literature and ultimately become life-long readers. Presented every other year, this children's choice award is presented in categories of K-2, grades 3-5, grades 6-8, and in 1992, grades 9-12 were added. A medal designed by Garth Williams, illustrator of Charlotte's Web, is affixed to the winning titles.

1990 **GRADES K-2** *The Magic School Bus at the Waterworks* by Joanna Cole, illustrated by Bruce Degen; Scholastic, 1986.

1990 **GRADES 3-5** *Piggins* by Jane Yolen, illustrated by Jane Dyer; Harcourt Brace Jovanovich, 1987.

1990 **GRADES 6-8** *The Way Things Work* written and illustrated by David Macaulay; Houghton Mifflin, 1988.

1992 **GRADES K-2** *The Great Kapok Tree: A Tale of the Amazon Rain Forest* written and illustrated by Lynne Cherry; Harcourt, Brace, Jovanovich, 1990.

1992 **GRADES 3-5** *Number the Stars* by Lois Lowry, not illustrated; Houghton Mifflin, 1989.

1992 **GRADES 6-8** *Maniac Magee* by Jerry Spinelli, not illustrated; Little Brown, 1990.

1992 **GRADES 9-12** *Fallen Angels* by Walter Dean Myers, not illustrated; Scholastic, 1988.

NAN CHAUNCY AWARD

Children's Book Council of Australia
Charles Morgan
Box 202
Sandy Bay, TAS 6005
Australia

Sponsored by the Children's Book Council of Australia, this quinquennial award was first presented in 1983. The recipient of the Nan Chauncy Award must be someone of Australian birth or a naturalized citizen, no matter where a resident, or a person normally resident in Australia. Eligible are authors and illustrators whose body of published work has made a distinguished contribution to children's literature and demonstrated an appeal for children. Also considered are people who have made an outstanding contribution to the field of children's literature.

The award is presented to only one person every five years and is given only once to any one recipient. Nominations are made by the state branches of the Council and final selection is made by a panel of three judges chosen by the state branches.

A plaque and $1000 is presented to the recipient at a dinner given by the Federal Executive of the Children's Book Council. A substantial article concerning each recipient will appear in the Australian journal Reading Time.

1983   Marcia Muir

1988   Joyce Oldmeadow

1993   Laurie Copping

CHILD STUDY ASSOCIATION OF AMERICA / WEL-MET CHILDREN'S BOOK AWARD
see **CHILD STUDY CHILDREN'S BOOK AWARD**

CHILD STUDY CHILDREN'S BOOK AWARD

Child Study Children's Book Committee at Bank Street College of Education
610 West 112th St
New York, NY 10025

The Child Study Children's Book Award has been given annually since 1943 to a book for children or young people (ages 8-13) which deals realistically and in a positive way with problems in their world. Both fiction and nonfiction books are eligible, although the award usually has been presented for a fictional work.

The committee that chooses the winning title has approximately thirty members, including teachers, librarians, parents, authors, illustrators, and others experienced in working with children and books. Candidates for the award are selected by the committee from the year's published books reviewed and listed in its annual tabulation, Children's Books of the Year. Each title is read by at least twenty members of the committee and discussed at weekly meetings. The entire committee then votes to determine the award winning title.

A framed scroll and a small monetary prize are presented to the winning author at a reception held at Bank Street College. The award was previously known as the Child Study Association Wel-Met Children's Book Award.

Two of the more detailed criteria used in determining the award-winning title are: (1) The book may concern problems that are universal, such as war and poverty; personal problems such as family distress or death; emotional stress of a boy or girl growing up under difficult circumstances; or problems associated with minority situations, and (2) The book (published in the preceding calendar year) must present its theme realistically, with honesty and insight. It must be well written and addressed specifically to young readers. The character development must be convincing and sensitive and the situations presented must be believable. In addition, it must be a book that young people will want to read.

1943   *Keystone Kids* by John R. Tunis, not illustrated; Harcourt, 1943.

1944   *The House* by Marjorie H. Allee, illustrated by Helen Blair; Houghton, 1944.

1945   *The Moved-outers* by Florence Crannell Means, illustrated by Helen Blair; Houghton, 1945.

1946   *Heart of Danger: A Tale of Adventure on Land and Sea with Tod Moran, Third Mate on the Tramp Steamer Araby* by Howard Pease, not illustrated; Doubleday, 1946.

1947   *Judy's Journey* written and illustrated by Lois Lenski; Lippincott, 1947.

1948   *The Big Wave* by Pearl Buck, illustrated by Nokusai Katsushika and Hiroshige Ando; Day, 1948.

1949   *Paul Tiber: Forester* by Maria Gleit, illustrated by Ralph Ray; Scribner, 1949.

1950   *Partners: The United Nations and Youth* by Helen Ferris and Eleanor Roosevelt, illustrated with photographs; Doubleday, 1950.

1951   No Award

1952   *Jareb* by Miriam Powell, illustrated by Marc Simont; Crowell, 1952.

       Twenty and Ten by Claire Huchet Bishop, illustrated by William Pene du Bois; Viking, 1952.

1953   *In a Mirror* by Mary Stolz, not illustrated; Harper, 1953.

1954   *High Road Home* by William Corbin, not illustrated; Coward 1954.

       The Ordeal of the Young Hunter by Jonreed Lauritzen, illustrated by Hoke Denetsosie; Little Brown, 1954.

1955   *Crow Boy* written and illustrated by Taro Yashima; Viking, 1955.

       Plain Girl by Virginia Sorensen, illustrated by Charles Geer; Harcourt, 1955.

1956   *The House of Sixty Fathers* by Meindert DeJong, illustrated by Maurice Sendak; Harper & Row, 1956.

1957   *Shadow Across the Campus* by Helen R. Sattley, not illustrated; Dodd Mead, 1957.

1958   *Youth Town* by Lorenz Graham, not illustrated; Follett, 1958.

1959   *Jennifer* by Zoa Sherburne, not illustrated; Morrow, 1959.

1960   *Janine* by Robin McKown, not illustrated; Messner, 1960.

1961   *The Girl from Puerto Rico* by Hila Colman, not illustrated; Morrow, 1961.

       The Road to Agra by Aimee Sommerfelt, illustrated by Ulf Aas; Criterion, 1961.

1962   *The Trouble with Terry* by Joan M. Lexau, illustrated by Irene Murray; Dial, 1962.

1963   *The Peaceable Revolution* by Betty Schechter, illustrated with photographs; Houghton, 1963.

       The Rock and the Willow by Mildred Lee, not illustrated; Lothrop, 1963.

1964   *The High Pasture* by Ruth P. Harnden, illustrated by Vee Guthrie; Houghton, 1964.

1965   *The Empty Schoolhouse* by Natalie Savage Carlson, illustrated by John Kaufmann; Harper & Row, 1965.

1966   *Queenie Peavy* by Robert Burch, illustrated by Jerry Lazare; Viking, 1966.

1966   **SPECIAL CITATION** *Curious George Goes to the Hospital* written and illustrated by H.A. and Margret Rey; Houghton, 1966.

1967 *The Contender* by Robert Lipsyte, not illustrated; Harper, 1967.

1968 *What It's all About* by Vadim Frolov, translated by Joseph Barnes, not illustrated; Doubleday, 1968.

1968 **SPECIAL CITATION** *Where is Daddy? The Story of a Divorce* by Beth Goff, illustrated by Susan Perl; Beacon, 1969.

1969 *The Empty Moat* by Margaretha Shemin, not illustrated; Coward, 1969.

1970 *Migrant Girl* by Carli Laklan, not illustrated; McGraw, 1970.

Rock Star by James Lincoln Collier, not illustrated; Four Winds, 1970.

1971 *John Henry McCoy* by Lillie D. Chaffin, illustrated by Emanuel Schongut; Macmillan, 1971.

1971 **SPECIAL CITATION** *The Pair of Shoes* by Aline Glasgow, illustrated by Symeon Shimin; Dial, 1970.

1972 *A Sound of Chariots* by Mollie Hunter, not illustrated; Harper, 1972.

1973 *A Taste of Blackberries* by Doris Buchanan Smith, illustrated by Charles Robinson; Crowell, 1973.

1974 *Luke Was There* by Eleanor Clymer, illustrated by Diane DeGroat; Holt, 1973.

1975 *The Garden Is Doing Fine* by Carol Farley, illustrated by Lynn Sweat; Atheneum, 1975.

1976 *Somebody Else's Child* by Roberta Silman, illustrated by Chris Conover; Warne, 1976.

1977 *The Pinballs* by Betsy Byars, not illustrated; Harper, 1977.

1978 *The Devil in Vienna* by Doris Orgel, not illustrated; Dial, 1978.

1979 *The Whipman Is Watching* by Thomas A. Dyer, not illustrated; Houghton, 1979.

1980 *A Boat to Nowhere* by Maureen Crane Wartski, illustrated by Dick Teicher; Westminster, 1980.

1981 *A Spirit to Ride the Whirlwind* by Athena V. Lord, not illustrated; Macmillan, 1981.

1982 *Homesick: My Own Story* by Jean Fritz, illustrated with drawings by Margot Tomes and photographs; Putnam, 1982.

1983 *The Solomon System* by Phyllis Reynolds Naylor, not illustrated; Atheneum, 1983.

The Sign of the Beaver by Elizabeth George Speare, not illustrated; Houghton Mifflin, 1983.

1984 *One-eyed Cat* by Paula Fox, not illustrated; Bradbury, 1984.

1985 *With Westie and the Tin Man* by C.S. Adler, not illustrated; Macmillan, 1985.

1985 **SPECIAL CITATION** *Ain't Gonna Study War No More: The Story of America's Peace Seekers* by Milton Meltzer; Harper & Row, 1985.

1986 *Journey to Jo'Burg: A South African Story* by Beverly Naidoo, illustrated by Eric Velasquez; Lippincott, 1986.

1987 *Rabble Starky* by Lois Lowry, not illustrated; Houghton Mifflin, 1987.

1988 *The Most Beautiful Place in the World* by Ann Cameron, illustrated by Thomas B. Allen; Knopf, 1988.

December Stillness by Mary Downing Hahn, not illustrated; Clarion, 1988.

1989 *Shades of Gray* by Carolyn Reeder, not illustrated; Macmillan, 1989.

1990 *Secret City, USA* by Felice Holman, not illustrated; Scribner, 1990.

1991 *Shadow Boy* by Susan E. Kirby, not illustrated; Orchard, 1991.

CHILDREN'S BOOK AWARD
(formerly Federation of Children's Book Groups Awards)
Jenny Blanch
Federation of Children's Book Groups
30 Sennerleys Park Rd.
Northfield, Birmingham B31 1AL
England

This award, sponsored by the Federation of Children's Book Groups, was first given in 1980. The award was established to become part of the fight to maintain children's fiction. The award is for a work of fiction for children under fourteen years of age. The recipient is selected by groups of adults and children working together all over the country. Criteria include production, content and illustration. The winning book must have child appeal.

1980 *Mr. Magnolia* written and illustrated by Quentin Blake; Cape, 1980.

1981 *Fair's Fair* by Leon Garfield, illustrated by Margaret Chamberlain; Macdonald, 1981.

1982 *The BFG* by Roald Dahl, illustrated by Quentin Blake; Cape, 1982; Farrar, 1982.

1983 *The Saga of Erik the Viking* by Terry Jones, illustrated by Michael Foreman; Pavilion/Michael Joseph, 1983.

1984 *Brother in the Land* by Robert Swindells, not illustrated; Oxford, 1984.

1985 *Arthur* by Amanda Graham, illustrated by Donna Gynell; Spindlewood, 1985, c1984.

1986 *The Jolly Postman: or, Other People's Letters* written and illustrated by Allan Ahlberg and Janet Ahlberg; Heinemann, 1986.

1987 *Winnie the Witch* by Valerie Thomas and Korky Paul, illustrated by Korky Paul; Oxford University Press, 1987.

1988 *Matilda* by Roald Dahl, illustrated by Quentin Blake; Cape, 1988.

1989-90 *Room 13* by Robert E. Swindells, illustrated by Jon Riley; Doubleday, 1989.

1991 *Threadbear* written and illustrated by Mick Inkpen; Hodder & Stoughton, 1990; Little Brown, 1991.

1992 *Kiss the Dust* by Elizabeth Laird, not illustrated; Heinemann, 1991; Dutton, 1992.

1992 **SHORTER NOVEL** *Find the White Horse* by Dick King-Smith, illustrated by Larry Wilkes; Viking, 1991.

1992 **PICTURE BOOK** *Shhh!* by Sally Grindley, illustrated by Peter Utton; ABC, 1991; Little Brown, 1992.

1993 *The Suitcase Kid* by Jacqueline Wilson, illustrated by Nick Sharratt; Doubleday, 1992.

1993 **LONGER NOVEL** *Gulf* by Robert Westall, not illustrated; Methuen, 1992.

1993 **PICTURE BOOK** *Snowy* by Berlie Doherty, illustrated by Keith Bowen; HarperCollins, 1992.

CHILDREN'S BOOK GUILD NONFICTION AWARD
see WASHINGTON CHILDREN'S BOOK GUILD NONFICTION AWARD

CHILDREN'S BOOK COUNCIL OF AUSTRALIA BOOK OF THE YEAR AWARDS
Children's Book Council of Australia
Chris Donnelly
P O Box 387
Croydon, VIC 3136
Australia

In 1946, the Australian Children's Book Award was established. In 1959, the administration of the award program was assumed by the Australian Children's Book Council. The program is now called the Children's Book Council of Australia Book of the Year Award. A picture book category was added in 1956 and in 1982, a junior book category began. From 1974 to 1976, the Visual Art Board of the Australian Council for the Arts sponsored a competition for the best illustrated children's book of the year. These books are also included in the listing. A council of judges is responsible for the final selection of the winners.

In 1993, the Eve Pownall Award was presented for the first time. It honors an information book of high quality.

1946 *Story of Karrawinga, the Emu* by Leslie Rees, illustrated by Walter Cunningham; Sands, 1946.

1947 No Award

1948 *Shackleton's Argonauts: A Saga of the Antarctic Ice-Packs* written and illustrated by Frank Hurley; Angus & Robertson, 1948.

1949 *Whalers of the Midnight Sun: A Story of Modern Whaling in the Antarctic* by Alan Villiers, illustrated by Charles Pont; Angus & Robertson, 1949.

1950 No Award

1951 *Verity of Sydney Town* by Ruth Williams, illustrated by Rhys Williams; Angus & Robertson, 1950.

1952 *The Australian Book* by Eve Pownall, illustrated by Margaret Senior; Sands, 1953.

1953 *Aircraft of Today and Tomorrow* by James Henry Martin and William Donald Martin, illustrated with photographs; Angus & Robertson, 1953.

Good Luck to the Rider by Joan Phipson, illustrated by Margaret Horder; Angus & Robertson, 1953.

1954 *Australian Legendary Tales* by K. Langloh Parker, illustrated by Elizabeth Durack; Angus & Robertson, 1953.

1955 *The First Walkabout* by Harold Arthur Lindsay and Norman Barnett Tindale, illustrated by Madeleine Boyle; Longmans, 1954.

1956 **BOOK OF THE YEAR** *The Crooked Snake* by Alice Patricia Wrightson, illustrated by Margaret Horder; Angus & Robertson, 1955.

1956 **PICTURE BOOK** *Wish and the Magic Nut* by Peggy Barnard, illustrated by Sheila Hawkins; Sands, 1956.

1957 **BOOK OF THE YEAR** *The Boomerang Book of Legendary Tales* by Enid Moodie-Heddle, illustrated by Nancy Parker; Longmans, 1957.

1957 **PICTURE BOOK** No Award

1958 **BOOK OF THE YEAR** *Tiger in the Bush* by Nan Chauncy, illustrated by Margaret Horder; Oxford, 1957.

1958 **PICTURE BOOK** *Piccaninny Walkabout: A Story of Two Aboriginal Children* by Axel Poignant, illustrated with photographs; Angus & Robertson, 1957.

1959 **BOOK OF THE YEAR** *Devil's Hill* by Nan Chauncy, illustrated by Geraldine Spence; Oxford, 1958; Watts, 1960.

Sea Menace by John Gunn, illustrated by Brian Keogh; Constable, 1958.

1959 **PICTURE BOOK** No Award

1960 **BOOK OF THE YEAR** *All the Proud Tribesmen* by Kylie Tennant, illustrated by Clem Seale; Macmillan (London), 1959.

1960 **PICTURE BOOK** No Award

1961 **BOOK OF THE YEAR** *Tangara, Let Us Set off Again* by Nan Chauncy, illustrated by Brian Wildsmith; Oxford, 1960.

1961 **PICTURE BOOK** No Award

1962 **BOOK OF THE YEAR** *The Racketty Street Gang* by Leonard Herbert Evers, not illustrated; Hodder & Stoughton, 1961.

Rafferty Rides a Winner written and illustrated by Joan Woodbery; Parrish, 1961.

1962 **PICTURE BOOK** No Award

1963 **BOOK OF THE YEAR** *The Family Conspiracy* by Joan M. Phipson, illustrated by Margaret Horder; Angus & Robertson, 1962; Harcourt, 1962, 1964.

1963 **PICTURE BOOK** No Award

1964 **BOOK OF THE YEAR** *The Green Laurel* by Eleanor Spence, illustrated by Geraldine Spence; Oxford, 1963.

1964 **PICTURE BOOK** No Award

1965 **BOOK OF THE YEAR** *Pastures of the Blue Crane* by Hesba Fay Brinsmead, illustrated by Annette Macarthur-Onslow; Oxford, 1964.

1965 **PICTURE BOOK** *Hugo's Zoo* written and illustrated by Elisabeth MacIntyre; Angus & Robertson, 1964.

1966 **BOOK OF THE YEAR** *Ash Road* by Ivan Southall, illustrated by Clem Seale; Angus & Robertson, 1965.

1966 **PICTURE BOOK** No Award

1967 **BOOK OF THE YEAR** *The Min-Min* by Mavis Thorpe Clark, illustrated by Genevieve Melrose; Angus, 1967.

1967 **PICTURE BOOK** No Award

1968 **BOOK OF THE YEAR** *To the Wild Sky* by Ivan Southall, illustrated by Jennifer Tuckwell; Angus & Robertson, 1967.

1968 **PICTURE BOOK** No Award

1969 **BOOK OF THE YEAR** *When Jays Fly to Barbmo* by Margaret Balderson, illustrated by Victor G. Ambrus; Oxford, 1968.

1969 PICTURE BOOK *Sly Old Wardrobe* by Ivan Southall, illustrated by Ted Greenwood; Cheshire, 1968.

1970 BOOK OF THE YEAR *Uhu* written and illustrated by Annette Macarthur-Onslow; Ure Smith, 1969.

1970 PICTURE BOOK No Award

1971 BOOK OF THE YEAR *Bread and Honey* by Ivan Southall, not illustrated; Angus & Robertson, 1970.

1971 PICTURE BOOK *Waltzing Matilda* by Andrew Barton Paterson, illustrated by Desmond Digby; Collins Australia, 1970.

1972 BOOK OF THE YEAR *Longtime Passing* by Hesba Fay Brinsmead, not illustrated; Angus & Robertson, 1971.

1972 PICTURE BOOK No Award

1973 BOOK OF THE YEAR *Family at the Lookout* by Noreen Shelley, illustrated by Robert Micklewright; Oxford, 1972.

1973 PICTURE BOOK No Award

1974 BOOK OF THE YEAR *The Nargun and the Stars* by Patricia Wrightson, not illustrated; Hutchinson, 1973.

1974 PICTURE BOOK *The Bunyip of Berkeley's Creek* by Jenny Wagner, illustrated by Ron Brooks; Longmans Young, 1974.

1974 BEST ILLUSTRATED CHILDREN'S BOOK OF THE YEAR *Mulga Bill's Bycycle* by A.B. Paterson, illustrated by Deborah Niland and Kilmeny Niland; Collins, 1973.

1975 BOOK OF THE YEAR No Award

1975 PICTURE BOOK *The Man from Ironbark* by Andrew Barton Paterson, illustrated by Quentin Hole; Collins Australia, 1974.

1975 BEST ILLUSTRATED CHILDREN'S BOOK OF THE YEAR *The Magpie Island* by Colin Thiele, illustrated by Roger Haldane; Rigby, 1975.

Storm Boy by Colin Thiele, illustrated by Robert Ingpen; Rigby, 1963.

1976 BOOK OF THE YEAR *Fly West* by Ivan Southall, not illustrated; Angus & Robertson, 1974.

1976 PICTURE BOOK *The Rainbow Serpent* written and illustrated by Dick Roughsey; Collins Australia, 1975.

1976 BEST ILLUSTRATED CHILDREN'S BOOK OF THE YEAR *Terry's Brrrmmm GT* written and illustrated by Ted Greenwood; Angus & Robertson, 1976.

1977 BOOK OF THE YEAR *The October Child* by Eleanor Spence, illustrated by Malcolm Green; Oxford, 1976.

1977 PICTURE BOOK *ABC of Monsters* written and illustrated by Deborah Niland and Kilmeny Niland; Hodder and Stoughton Australia, 1977.

1978 BOOK OF THE YEAR *The Ice Is Coming* by Patricia Wrightson, illustrated with maps; Hutchinson Australia, 1977.

1978 PICTURE BOOK *John Brown, Rose and the Midnight Cat* by Jenny Wagner, illustrated by Ron Brooks; Kestrel, 1977.

1979 BOOK OF THE YEAR *The Plum-rain Scroll* by Ruth Manley, illustrated by Marianne Yamaguchi; Hodder & Stoughton Australia, 1978.

1979 PICTURE BOOK *The Quinkins* written and illustrated by Percy J. Trezise and Dick Roughsey; Collins, 1978.

1980 BOOK OF THE YEAR *Displaced Person* by Lee Harding, not illustrated; Hyland House, 1979.

1980 PICTURE BOOK *One Dragon's Dream* written and illustrated by Peter Pavey; Nelson, 1979.

1981 BOOK OF THE YEAR *Playing Beatie Bow* by Ruth Park, not illustrated; Kestrel, 1981, c1980.

1981 PICTURE BOOK No Award

1982 BOOK OF THE YEAR *The Valley Between* by Colin Thiele, not illustrated; Rigby, 1981.

1982 BOOK OF THE YEAR HIGHLY COMMENDED *Behind the Wind* by Patricia Wrightson, not illustrated; Hutchinson, 1981.

1982 BOOK OF THE YEAR COMMENDED *Cannily, Cannily* by Simon French, not illustrated; Angus & Robertson, 1981.

Rummage by Christobel Mattingly, illustrated by Patricia Mullins; Angus & Robertson, 1981.

1982 JUNIOR BOOK OF THE YEAR *Rummage* by Christobel Mattingly, illustrated by Patricia Mullins; Angus & Robertson, 1981.

1982 PICTURE BOOK OF THE YEAR *Sunshine* written and illustrated by Jan Ormerod; Kestrel, 1981; Penguin Australia, 1981; Lothrop, Lee & Shepard, 1981.

1982 PICTURE BOOK OF THE YEAR HIGHLY COMMENDED *The Tram to Bondi Beach* by Elizabeth Hathorn, illustrated by Julie Vivas; Methuen, 1981.

1982 PICTURE BOOK OF THE YEAR COMMENDED *Bumble's Dream* written and illustrated by Bruce Treloar; Bodley Head, 1981.

1983 BOOK OF THE YEAR *Master of the Grove* by Victor Kelleher, not illustrated; Penguin Australia, 1982.

1983 BOOK OF THE YEAR HIGHLY COMMENDED *The Left Overs* by Eleanor Spence, not illustrated; Methuen Australia, 1982.

1983 BOOK OF THE YEAR COMMENDED *Five Times Dizzy* by Nadia Wheatley, illustrated; Oxford, 1982.

Toby's Millions by Morris Lurie; Penguin Australia, 1982.

1983 PICTURE BOOK OF THE YEAR *Who Sank the Boat?* written and illustrated by Pamela Allen; Nelson Australia, 1982; Coward McCann, 1983.

1983 PICTURE BOOK OF THE YEAR HIGHLY COMMENDED *The Train* illustrated by Witold Generowicz; Penguin Australia, 1982; Kestrel, 1982; Dial, 1982.

1983 PICTURE BOOK OF THE YEAR COMMENDED *Tin Lizzie and Little Nell* written and illustrated by David Cox; Aurora Press, 1982; Bodley Head, 1982.

Turramulli the Giant Quinkin written and illustrated by Dick Roughsey and Percy Trezise; Collins, 1982.

1983 JUNIOR BOOK OF THE YEAR *Thing* by Robin Klein, illustrated by Alison Lester; Oxford (London), 1982; Oxford (Melbourne), 1982. (medal awarded to both author and illustrator).

1984 BOOK OF THE YEAR *A Little Fear* by Patricia Wrightson, not illustrated; Hutchinson Australia, 1983; Atheneum, 1983.

1984 BOOK OF THE YEAR HIGHLY COMMENDED *Penny Pollard's Diary* by Robin Klein, illustrated by Ann James; Oxford, 1983.

1984 BOOK OF THE YEAR COMMENDED *The Devil's Stone* by Helen Frances, illustrated; Omnibus Books, 1983.

Breaking Up by Frank Willmott, not illustrated; Fontana Lions, 1983.

1984 JUNIOR BOOK OF THE YEAR *Bernice Knows Best* by Max Dann, illustrated by Ann James; Oxford, 1983.

1984 PICTURE BOOK OF THE YEAR *Bertie and the Bear* written and illustrated by Pamela Allen; Hamish Hamilton, 1983; Coward McCann, 1984, c1983.

1984 PICTURE BOOK OF THE YEAR HIGHLY COMMENDED *Possum Magic* by Mem Fox, illustrated by Julie Vivas; Omnibus Books, 1983.

1984 PICTURE BOOK OF THE YEAR COMMENDED *The White Crane* written and illustrated by Junko Morimoto, adapted by Helen Smith; Collins, 1985.

The Friends of Emily Culpepper by Ann Coleridge, illustrated by Roland Harvey; Five Mile Press, 1983.

1985 BOOK OF THE YEAR *The True Story of Lilli Stubeck* by James Aldridge, not illustrated; Hyland House, 1984.

1985 BOOK OF THE YEAR HIGHLY COMMENDED *Eleanor, Elizabeth* by Libby Gleeson, not illustrated; Angus & Robertson, 1984.

1985 BOOK OF THE YEAR COMMENDED *Me and Jeshua* by Eleanor Spence, illustrated by Shane Conroy; Dove Communications, 1985, c1984.

Dancing in the Anzac Deli by Nadia Wheatley, illustrated by Neil Phillips and Waldemar Buczynski; Oxford, 1984.

1985 PICTURE BOOK OF THE YEAR No Award

1985 PICTURE BOOK OF THE YEAR HIGHLY COMMENDED *The Inch Boy* written and illustrated by Junko Morimoto, adapted by Helen Smith; Collins, 1984.

1985 PICTURE BOOK OF THE YEAR COMMENDED *Home in the Sky* written and illustrated by Jeannie Baker; Julia MacRae, 1984.

Ayu and the Perfect Moon written and illustrated by David Cox; Bodley Head, 1984.

1985 JUNIOR BOOK OF THE YEAR *Something Special* by Emily Rodda, illustrated by Noela Young; Angus & Robertson, 1984.

1986 BOOK OF THE YEAR *The Green Wind* by Thurley Fowler, not illustrated; Rigby, 1985.

1986 BOOK OF THE YEAR HIGHLY COMMENDED *Little Brother* by Allan Baille, not illustrated; Nelson, 1985.

1986 BOOK OF THE YEAR COMMENDED *The House that Was Eureka* by Nadia Wheatley, not illustrated; Viking Kestrel, 1984.

The Changelings of Chaan by David Lake, not illustrated; Hyland House, 1985.

1986 PICTURE BOOK OF THE YEAR *Felix and Alexander* written and illustrated by Terry Denton; Oxford, 1985.

1986 PICTURE BOOK OF THE YEAR HIGHLY COMMENDED *A Piece of Straw* written and illustrated by Junko Morimoto, adapted by Helen Smith; Collins, 1985.

1986 PICTURE BOOK OF THE YEAR COMMENDED *Clive Eats Alligators* written and illustrated by Alison Lester; Oxford, 1985.

First There Was Frances written and illustrated by Bob Graham; Lothian, 1985.

1986 JUNIOR BOOK OF THE YEAR *Arkwright* written and illustrated by Mary Steele; Hyland House, 1985.

1986 CLIFTON PUGH AWARD *Burke and Wills* written and illustrated by Roland Harvey; Five Mile Press, 1985.

1987 BOOK OF THE YEAR OLDER *All We Know* by Simon French, not illustrated; Angus & Robertson; 1986.

1987 BOOK OF THE YEAR OLDER HONOR *Taronga* by Victor Kelleher, not illustrated; Viking Kestrel, 1986.

Space Demons by Gillian Rubinstein, not illustrated; Omnibus/Penguin, 1986.

1987 BOOK OF THE YEAR YOUNGER *Pigs Might Fly* by Emily Rodda, illustrated by Noela Young; Angus & Robertson, 1986.

1987 BOOK OF THE YEAR YOUNGER HONOR *Sister Madge's Book of Nuns* by Doug MacLeod, illustrated by Craig Smith; Omnibus, 1986.

All About Anna and Harriet and Christopher and Me by Elizabeth Hathorn, illustrated by Steve Axelrod; Methuen, 1986.

1987 PICTURE BOOK OF THE YEAR *Kojuro and the Bears* adapted by Helen Smith, illustrated by Junko Morimoto; Collins, 1986.

1987 PICTURE BOOK HONOR *Animalia* written and illustrated by Graeme Base; Viking Kestrel, 1986.

Murgatroyd's Garden by Judy Zavos, illustrated by Drahos Zak; Heinemann, 1986.

1988 BOOK OF THE YEAR OLDER *So Much to Tell You ...* by John Marsden, not illustrated; Walter McVitty Books, 1987; Little Brown, 1989.

1988 BOOK OF THE YEAR OLDER HONOUR *Deezle Boy* by Eleanor Spence, not illustrated; Collins Dove, 1987.

I Am Susannah by Libby Gleeson, not illustrated; Angus & Robertson, 1987.

1988 BOOK OF THE YEAR YOUNGER *My Place* by Nadia Wheatley, illustrated by Donna Rawlins; Collins Dove, 1987.

1988 BOOK OF THE YEAR YOUNGER HONOUR *Looking Out for Sampson* by Libby Hathorn, illustrated by Ann James; Oxford, 1987.

A Paddock of Poems by Max Fatchen, illustrated; Omnibus/Puffin, 1987.

1988 PICTURE BOOK OF THE YEAR *Crusher Is Coming* written and illustrated by Bob Graham; Lothian Publishing, 1987.

1988 PICTURE BOOK OF THE YEAR HONOUR *The Long Red Scarf* by Nette Hilton, illustrated by Margaret Power; Omnibus Books, 1987.

Where the Forest Meets the Sea written and illustrated by Jeannie Baker; Julia McRae, 1987.

1989 BOOK OF THE YEAR OLDER *Beyond the Labyrinth* by Gillian Rubinstein, not illustrated; Hyland House, 1988.

1989 BOOK OF THE YEAR OLDER HONOUR *The Lake at the End of the World* by Caroline Macdonald, not illustrated; Hodder & Stoughton, 1988; Knight, 1992.

Answers to Brut by Gillian Rubinstein, not illustrated; Omnibus/Puffin, 1988; Mammoth, 1991.

1989 BOOK OF THE YEAR YOUNGER *The Best-Kept Secret* by Emily Rodda, illustrated by Noela Young; Angus & Robertson, 1988; Henry Holt, 1990.

1989 BOOK OF THE YEAR YOUNGER HONOUR *The Australopedia* by Joan Grant, illustrated by design students at Phillips Institute; McPhee Gribble/Penguin Books Australia, 1989; Penguin, 1988.

Melanie and the Night Animal by Gillian Rubinstein, not illustrated; Omnibus/Puffin, 1988.

1989 PICTURE BOOK OF THE YEAR *Drac and the Gremlin* by Allan Baillie, illustrated by Jane Tanner; Viking Kestrel, 1988; Dial, 1989.

The Eleventh Hour written and illustrated by Graeme Base; Viking Kestrel, 1988.

1989 PICTURE BOOK OF THE YEAR HONOUR *My Place in Space* by Sally Hirst and Robin Hirst, illustrated by Joe Levine and Roland Harvey; Five Mile Press, 1989.

1990 BOOK OF THE YEAR OLDER *Came Back To Show You I Could Fly* by Robin Klein, not illustrated; Viking Kestrel, 1989.

1990 BOOK OF THE YEAR YOUNGER *Pigs and Honey* written and illustrated by Jeanie Adams; Omnibus Books, 1990.

1990 PICTURE BOOK OF THE YEAR *Very Best of Friends* by Margaret Wild, illustrated by Julie Vivas; Margaret Hamilton, 1989; Harcourt Brace Jovanovich, 1990.

1991 BOOK OF THE YEAR OLDER *Strange Objects* by Gary Crew, not illustrated; Heinemann, 1990.

1991 BOOK OF THE YEAR YOUNGER *Finders Keepers* by Emily Rodda, illustrated by Noela Young; Omnibus, 1990; Greenwillow, 1991.

1991 PICTURE BOOK OF THE YEAR *Greetings From Sandy Beach* written and illustrated by Bob Graham; Lothian, 1990; Blackie, 1990; Kane Miller, 1992.

1992 BOOK OF THE YEAR OLDER *The House Guest* by Eleanor Nilsson, not illustrated; Viking, 1991.

1992 BOOK OF THE YEAR OLDER HONOR *Peter* by Kate Walker, not illustrated; Omnibus Books, 1991.

Change the Locks by Simon French, not illustrated; Ashton Scholastic, 1991.

1992 BOOK OF THE YEAR YOUNGER *Magnificent Nose & Other Marvels* by Anna Fienberg, illustrated by Kim Gamble; Allen & Unwin, 1991.

1992 BOOK OF THE YEAR YOUNGER HONOR *Misery Guts* by Morris Gleitzman, not illustrated; Pan Australia, 1991; Blackie, 1991.

1992 PICTURE BOOK OF THE YEAR *Window* written and illustrated by Jeannie Baker; Julia MacRae, 1991; Greenwillow, 1991.

1992 PICTURE BOOK OF THE YEAR HONOR *Hist!* by Clarence James Dennis, illustrated by Peter J. Gouldthorpe; Walter McVitty, 1991.

William Tell written and illustrated by Margaret Early; Walter McVitty Books, 1991; Abrams, 1991.

1993 PICTURE BOOK OF THE YEAR *Rose Meets Mr. Wintergarten* written and illustrated by Bob Graham; Walker, 1992.

1993 PICTURE BOOK OF THE YEAR HONOR *Belinda* written and illustrated by Pamela Allen; Viking, 1992.

Where's Mum? by Libby Gleeson, illustrated by Craig Smith; Omnibus, 1992.

1993 BOOK OF THE YEAR YOUNGER *The Bamboo Flute* by Garry Disher, illustrated with photographs; Angus & Robertson, 1991; Collins, 1992.

1993 BOOK OF THE YEAR YOUNGER HONOR *Blabber Mouth* by Morris Gleitzman, not illustrated; Pan Macmillan, 1992.

The Web by Nette Hilton, illustrated by Kerry Millard; Collins, 1992.

1993 BOOK OF THE YEAR OLDER *Looking for Alibrandi* by Melina Marchetta, not illustrated; Puffin, 1992.

1993 BOOK OF THE YEAR OLDER HONOR *A Long Way To Tipperary* by Sue Gough, illustrated; University of Queensland Press, 1992.

Galax-Arena by Gillian Rubinstein, not illustrated; Hyland House, 1992.

1993 EVE POWNALL AWARD FOR INFORMATION BOOKS *Tjarany Roughtail* by Gracie Greene and Joe Tramacchi, illustrated by Lucille Gill; Magabala, 1992.

CHILDREN'S BOOK SHOWCASE
discontinued

This annual award was established in 1972 by the Children's Book Council. The purpose of the award was to honor children's books exemplifying particularly thoughtful and creative approaches to design and production. The award winning titles were selected by a panel of experts in children's literature, book production, and graphics. The award was discontinued in 1977.

1972 *Alone in the Wild Forest* by Isaac Bashevis Singer, illustrated by Margot Zemach; Farrar, 1971.

The Alphabeast Book: An Abecedarium written and illustrated by Dorothy Schmiderer; Holt, 1971.

Amos and Boris written and illustrated by William Steig; Farrar, 1971.

Bear Circus written and illustrated by William Pene du Bois; Viking, 1971.

The Beast of Monsieur Racine written and illustrated by Tomi Ungerer; Farrar, 1971.

Changes, Changes written and illustrated by Pat Hutchins; Macmillan, 1971.

Father Fox's Pennyrhymes by Clyde Watson, illustrated by Wendy Watson; Crowell, 1971.

Goody Hall written and illustrated by Natalie Babbitt; Farrar, 1971.

Great Civilizations of Ancient Africa by Lester J. Brooks, illustrated with maps and photographs; Four Winds, 1971.

Hildilid's Night by Cheli Duran Ryan, illustrated by Arnold Lobel; Macmillan, 1971.

Hurray for Captain Jane! by Sam Reavin, illustrated by Emily McCully; Parents, 1971.

I Wrote My Name on the Wall: Sidewalk Songs written and illustrated by Ronni Solbert; Little Brown, 1971.

In the Trail of the Wind: American Indian Poems and Ritual Orations edited by John Bierhorst, illustrated with photographs; Farrar, 1971.

Lions and Lobsters and Foxes and Frogs: Fables from Aesop by Ennis Rees, illustrated by Edward Gorey; Young Scott/Addison Wesley, 1971.

Look Again! written and illustrated by Tana Hoban; Macmillan, 1971.

Look What I Can Do written and illustrated by Jose Aruego; Scribner, 1971.

The Lower East Side: A Portrait in Time by Diane Cavallo, illustrated with photographs by Leo Stashin; Crowell-Collier, 1971.

The Magic Tears by Jack Sendak, illustrated by Mitchell Miller; Harper & Row, 1971.

Mr. Gumpy's Outing written and illustrated by John Burningham; Cape, 1970; Holt, 1971.

The Mother Beaver by Edith Thacher Hurd, illustrated by Clement Hurd; Little Brown, 1971.

The Mysterious Disappearance of Leon (I Mean Noel) written and illustrated by Ellen Raskin; Dutton, 1971.

Nobody Asked Me if I Wanted a Baby Sister written and illustrated by Martha Alexander; Dial, 1971.

On the Day Peter Stuyvesant Sailed into Town written and illustrated by Arnold Lobel; Harper & Row, 1971.

One Dancing Drum by Gail Kredenser and Stanley Mack, illustrated by Stanley Mack; Phillips, 1971.

One Misty Moisty Morning written and illustrated by Mitchell Miller; Farrar, 1971.

The Paper Airplane Book by Seymour Simon, illustrated by Byron Barton; Viking, 1971.

A Penny a Look by Harve Zemach, illustrated by Margot Zemach; Farrar, 1971.

Questions and Answers about Seashore Life by Ilka Katherine List, illustrated by Ilka Katherine List and Arabelle Wheatley; Four Winds, 1971.

Rimes de la Mere Oie: Mother Goose Rendered into French translated by Ormonde deKay, Jr., illustrated by Milton Glaser, Barry Zaid, and Seymour Chwast; Little Brown, 1971.

Sam and Emma by Donald Nelsen, illustrated by Edward Gorey; Parents, 1971.

The Shrinking of Treehorn by Florence Parry Heide, illustrated by Edward Gorey; Holiday, 1971.

The Slightly Irregular Fire Engine: or, The Hithering, Thithering Djinn written and illustrated by Donald Barthelme; Farrar, 1971.

Story Number 3 by Eugene Ionesco, illustrated by Philippe Corentin; Harlin Quist, 1971.

1973 *Authorized Autumn Charts of the Upper Red Canoe River Country* by Peter Zachary Cohen, illustrated by Tomie de Paola; Atheneum, 1972.

Balarin's Goat written and illustrated by Harold Berson; Crown, 1972.

The Blue Bird written and illustrated by Fiona French; Walck, 1972.

The Busy Honeybee by Bernice Kohn, illustrated by Mel Furukawa; Four Winds, 1972.

The Chick and the Ducklings by V. Suteyev, translated and adapted by Mirra Ginsburg, illustrated by Jose Aruego and Ariane Aruego; Macmillan, 1972.

Count and See written and illustrated by Tana Hoban; Macmillan, 1972.

A Crocodile's Tale written and illustrated by Ariane Aruego and Jose Aruego; Scribner, 1972.

Dragonflies written and illustrated by Hilda Simon; Viking, 1972.

Even the Devil Is Afraid of a Shrew adapted by Ray Broekel, retold by Valerie Stalder, illustrated by Richard Brown; Addison- Wesley, 1972.

Farewell to the Farivox by Harry Hartwick, illustrated by Ib Spang Ohlsson; Four Winds, 1972.

Frog and Toad Together written and illustrated by Arnold Lobel; Harper, 1972.

The Funny Little Woman retold by Arlene Mosel, illustrated by Blair Lent; Dutton, 1972.

George and Martha written and illustrated by James Marshall; Houghton, 1972.

The Girl Who Loved the Wind by Jane Yolen, illustrated by Ed Young; Crowell, 1972.

Honschi by Aline Glasgow, illustrated by Tony Chen; Parents, 1972.

Ira Sleeps Over written and illustrated by Bernard Waber; Houghton, 1972.

Jacko written and illustrated by John S. Goodall; Harcourt, 1972.

Noah and the Rainbow: An Ancient Story retold by Max Bolliger, translated by Clyde Robert Bulla, illustrated by Helga Aichinger; Crowell, 1972.

Rebecka written and illustrated by Frank Asch; Harper, 1972.

Red Riding Hood, Retold in Verse for Boys and Girls to Read Themselves by Beatrice Schenk de Regniers, illustrated by Edward Gorey; Atheneum, 1972.

Seahorse by Robert A. Morris, illustrated by Arnold Lobel; Harper, 1972.

Simon Boom Gives a Wedding by Yuri Suhl, illustrated by Margot Zemach; Four Winds, 1972.

Toad written and illustrated by Anne Rockwell and Harlow Rockwell; Doubleday, 1972.

Uncle Harry by Gerlinde Schneider, adapted by Elizabeth Shub, illustrated by Lilo Fromm; Macmillan, 1972.

Where's Al? written and illustrated by Byron Barton; Seabury, 1972.

Wild Green Things in the City: A Book of Weeds written and illustrated by Anne Ophelia T. Dowden; Crowell, 1972.

The Winter Cat written and illustrated by Howard Knotts; Harper, 1972.

The Witch of Fourth Street and other Stories by Myron Levoy, illustrated by Gabriel Lisowski; Harper, 1972.

1974 *All the Way Home* by Lore Segal, illustrated by James Marshall; Farrar, 1973.

Bear Mouse by Berniece Freschet, illustrated by Donald Carrick; Scribner, 1973.

Behind the Back of the Mountain: Black Folktales from Southern Africa by Verna Aardema, illustrated by Leo Dillon and Diane Dillon; Dial, 1973.

A Birthday for the Princess written and illustrated by Anita Lobel; Harper, 1973.

Cathedral written and illustrated by David Macaulay; Houghton, 1973.

The Clay Pot Boy by Cynthia Jameson, illustrated by Arnold Lobel; Coward, 1973.

Duffy and the Devil by Harve Zemach, illustrated by Margot Zemach; Farrar, 1973.

Eclipse: Darkness in Daytime by Franklyn M. Branley, illustrated by Donald Crews; Crowell, 1973.

Escape from the Evil Prophecy by Lee Kingman, illustrated by Richard Cuffari; Houghton, 1973.

Father Christmas written and illustrated by Raymond Briggs; Hamilton, 1973; Coward, 1973.

Gertrude Stein: A Biography by Howard Greenfeld, illustrated with photographs; Crown, 1973.

Great Swedish Fairy Tales by Holger Lundbergh, illustrated by John Bauer; Delacorte/Lawrence, 1973.

Have You Seen Wilhemina Krumpf? by Judith Chasek, illustrated by Sal Murdocca; Lothrop, 1973.

The Juniper Tree and other Tales from Grimm translated by Randall Jarrell and Lore Segal, illustrated by Maurice Sendak; Farrar, 1973.

King Grisly-beard: A Tale from the Brothers Grimm translated by Edgar Taylor, illustrated by Maurice Sendak; Farrar, 1973.

The Magician by I.L. Peretz, adapted and illustrated by Uri Shulevitz; Macmillan, 1973.

A Natural History of Giraffes by Dorcas MacClintock, illustrated by Ugo Mochi; Scribner, 1973.

Noisy Nora written and illustrated by Rosemary Wells; Dial, 1973.

Paddy's Evening Out written and illustrated by John S. Goodall; Atheneum, 1973.

Peter, the Revolutionary Tsar by Peter Brock Putnam, illustrated by Laszlo Kubinyi; Harper, 1973.

Petronella by Jay Williams, illustrated by Friso Henstra; Parents, 1973.

Phoenix Feathers: A Collection of Mythical Monsters by Barbara Silverberg, illustrated with old prints; Dutton, 1973.

A Prairie Boy's Winter written and illustrated by William Kurelek; Tundra, 1973; Houghton, 1973.

Secrets of Redding Glen: The Natural History of a Wooded Valley written and illustrated by Jo Polseno; Western/Golden, 1973.

The Silver Pony written and illustrated by Lynd Ward; Houghton, 1973.

The Tavern at the Ferry written and illustrated by Edwin Tunis; Crowell, 1973.

The Three Jovial Huntsmen: A Mother Goose Rhyme written and illustrated by Susan Jeffers; Bradbury, 1973.

The Throme of the Erril of Sherill by Patricia A. McKillip, illustrated by Julia Noonan; Atheneum, 1973.

Toolchest written and illustrated by Jan Adkins; Walker, 1973.

While the Horses Galloped to London by Mabel Watts, illustrated by Mercer Mayer; Parents, 1971.

Who, Said Sue, Said Whoo? written and illustrated by Ellen Raskin; Atheneum, 1973.

1975 *Albert's Toothache* by Barbara Williams, illustrated by Kay Chorao; Dutton, 1974.

Allumette written and illustrated by Tomi Ungerer; Parents, 1974.

April Fools written and illustrated by Fernando Krahn; Dutton, 1974.

Befana: A Christmas Story written and illustrated by Anne Rockwell; Atheneum, 1974.

Benjamin's Three Hundred and Sixty Five Birthdays by Judi Barrett, illustrated by Ron Barrett; Atheneum, 1974.

Charlie Needs a Cloak written and illustrated by Tomie de Paola; Prentice Hall, 1974, c1973.

City written and illustrated by David Macaulay; Houghton, 1974.

Dawn written and illustrated by Uri Shulevitz; Farrar, 1974.

Don't Feel Sorry for Paul written and illustrated by Bernard Wolf; Lippincott, 1974.

Figgs and Phantoms written and illustrated by Ellen Raskin; Dutton, 1974.

Greedy Mariani and Other Folktales of the Antilles by Dorothy Sharp Carter, illustrated by Trina Schart Hyman; Atheneum, 1974.

A Home by Lennart Rudstrom, illustrated by Carl Larsson; Putnam, 1974.

Indian Harvests by William C. Grimm, illustrated by Ronald Himler; McGraw, 1974.

Lost in the Storm by Carol Carrick, illustrated by Donald Carrick; Seabury, 1974.

Lumberjack written and illustrated by William Kurelek; Houghton, 1974.

The Man Who Took the Indoors Out written and illustrated by Arnold Lobel; Harper, 1974.

The Mouse and the Song by Marilynne K. Roach, illustrated by Joseph Low; Parents, 1974.

The Mushroom Center Disaster by N.M. Bodecker, illustrated by Erik Blegvad; Atheneum, 1974.

The Mystery of the Missing Red Mitten written and illustrated by Steven Kellogg; Dial, 1974.

Owliver by Robert Kraus, illustrated by Jose Aruego and Ariane Dewey; Windmill, 1974.

The Perilous Gard by Elizabeth M. Pope, illustrated by Richard Cuffari; Houghton, 1974.

Pinchpenny Mouse by Robert Kraus, illustrated by Robert Byrd; Windmill, 1974.

Shipwreck by Vera Cumberledge, illustrated by Charles Mikolaycak; Follett, 1974.

The Stupids Step Out by Harry Allard, illustrated by James Marshall; Houghton Mifflin, 1974.

The Two Germanys by John Dornberg, illustrated with photographs; Dial, 1974.

Where's Gomer? by Norma Farber, illustrated by William Pene du Bois; Dutton, 1974.

Whirlwind Is a Ghost Dancing by Natalia M. Belting, illustrated by Leo Dillon and Diane Dillon; Dutton, 1974.

1976 *About Owls* by May Garelick, illustrated by Tony Chen; Four Winds, 1975.

Anno's Alphabet: An Adventure in Imagination written and illustrated by Mitsumasa Anno; Crowell, 1975.

The Art of the Northwest Coast Indians by Shirley Glubok, illustrated by Gerald Nook; Macmillan, 1975.

As I Was Crossing Boston Common by Norma Farber, illustrated by Arnold Lobel; Dutton, 1975.

The Blossom on the Bough: A Book of Trees written and illustrated by Anne Ophelia T. Dowden; Crowell, 1975.

The Blue Lobster: A Life Cycle by Carol Carrick, illustrated by Donald Carrick; Dial, 1975.

Boo to a Goose written and illustrated by Joseph Low; Atheneum, 1975.

Creepy Castle written and illustrated by John S. Goodall; Atheneum, 1975.

Exploring Black America: A History and Guide by Marcella Thum, illustrated with photographs; Atheneum, 1975.

Inside: Seeing Beneath the Surface written and illustrated by Jan Adkins; Walker, 1975.

Lito, the Shoeshine Boy by Lito Chirinos, told to and translated by David Mangurian, photographs by David Mangurian; Four Winds, 1975.

The Little Spotted Fish by Jane Yolen, illustrated by Friso Henstra; Seabury, 1975.

The Maggie B. written and illustrated by Irene Haas; Atheneum, 1975.

Magic in the Mist by Margaret Mary Kimmel, illustrated by Trina Schart Hyman; Atheneum, 1974.

Making our Way: America at the Turn of the Century in the Words of the Poor and Powerless selected by Jacqueline Hunt Katz and William Loren Katz, illustrated with photographs; Dial, 1975.

The Painter and the Bird written and illustrated by Max Velthuijs, translated by Ray Broekel; Addison Wesley, 1975.

The Pig-Tale by Lewis Carroll, illustrated by Leonard Lubin; Little Brown, 1975, c1889.

A Prairie Boy's Summer written and illustrated by William Kurelek; Tundra, 1975.

The Princess and Froggie by Harve Zemach and Kaethe Zemach, illustrated by Margot Zemach; Farrar, 1975.

Pyramid written and illustrated by David Macaulay; Houghton Mifflin, 1975.

Rabbit & Pork: Rhyming Talk written and illustrated by John Lawrence; Crowell, 1975.

Season Songs by Ted Hughes, illustrated by Leonard Baskin; Viking, 1975.

Song of the Boat by Lorenz Graham, illustrated by Leo Dillon and Diane Dillon; Crowell, 1975.

Song of the Trees by Mildred D. Taylor, illustrated by Jerry Pinkney; Dial, 1975.

The Story of Christmas written and illustrated by Felix Hoffmann; Atheneum, 1975.

The Tale of Czar Saltan: or, The Prince and the Swan Princess by Alexander Pushkin, translated and retold by Patricia Tracey Lowe, illustrated by Ivan Bilibin; Crowell, 1975.

The Winter Bear by Ruth Craft, illustrated by Erik Blegvad; Atheneum, 1975.

A Young Person's Guide to Ballet by Noel Streatfeild, illustrated by Georgette Bordier; Warne, 1975.

1977 *Abel's Island* written and illustrated by William Steig; Farrar, 1976.

The Amazing Bone written and illustrated by William Steig; Farrar, 1976.

Amish People: Plain Living in a Complex World by Carolyn Meyer, photographs by Carolyn Meyer, Michael Ramsey and Gerald Dodds; Atheneum, 1976.

As Right as Right Can Be by Anne Rose, illustrated by Arnold Lobel; Dial, 1976.

At Mary Bloom's written and illustrated by Aliki; Greenwillow, 1976.

The Bear and the Fly written and illustrated by Paula Winter; Crown, 1976.

Bonzini! the Tattooed Man by Jeffrey Allen, illustrated by James Marshall; Little Brown, 1976.

The Book of Think: or, How to Solve a Problem Twice your Size by Marilyn Burns, illustrated by Martha Weston; Little Brown, 1976.

A Boy Had a Mother Who Bought Him a Hat written and illustrated by Karla Kushkin; Houghton, 1976.

A Chick Hatches by Joanna Cole, photographs by Jerome Wexler; Morrow, 1976.

Deep in the Forest written and illustrated by Brinton Turkle; Dutton, 1976.

Dragonsong by Anne McCaffrey, illustrated by Laura Lydecker; Atheneum, 1976.

Dupper by Betty Baker, illustrated by Chuck Eckart; Greenwillow, 1976.

A Farm by Lennart Rudstrom, translated by Ernest Edwin Ryden, illustrated by Carl Larsson; Putnam, 1976.

Fly by Night by Randall Jarrell, illustrated by Maurice Sendak; Farrar, 1976.

Free by Sandol Stoddard, illustrated by Jenni Oliver; Houghton, 1976.

From Slave to Abolitionist: The Life of William Wells Brown adapted by Lucille Schulberg Warner, illustrated by Tom Feelings; Dial, 1976.

A Gardening Book: Indoors and Outdoors written and illustrated by Anne Batterberry Walsh; Atheneum, 1976.

Giraffe: the Silent Giant by Miriam Schlein, illustrated by Betty Fraser; Four Winds, 1976.

The Great Balloon Race written and illustrated by Gommaar Timmermans; Addison-Wesley, 1976.

Juanito's Railroad in the Sky written and illustrated by Vic Herman; Golden (Western), 1976.

A Little at a Time by David A. Adler, illustrated by N.M. Bodecker; Random House, 1976.

Little Sister and the Month Brothers by Beatrice Schenk de Regniers, illustrated by Margot Tomes; Seabury, 1976.

Max written and illustrated by Rachel Isadora; Macmillan, 1976.

Meat Pies and Sausages by Dorothy O. Van Woerkom, illustrated by Joseph Low; Greenwillow, 1976.

Mr. Gumpy's Motor Car written and illustrated by John Burningham; Crowell, 1976.

More Small Poems by Valerie Worth, illustrated by Natalie Babbitt; Farrar, 1976.

Nightmares: Poems to Trouble your Sleep by Jack Prelutsky, illustrated by Arnold Lobel; Greenwillow, 1976.

Paddy Pork's Holiday written and illustrated by John S. Goodall; Atheneum, 1976.

Peter Penny's Dance by Janet Quin-Harkin, illustrated by Anita Lobel; Dial, 1976.

The Potlatch Family by Evelyn Sibley Lampman, not illustrated; Atheneum, 1976.

Quebec, Je T'aime : I Love You written and illustrated by Miyuki Tanobe; Tundra, 1976. (in parallel columns of French and English)

The Red Swan: Myths and Tales of the American Indians translated by John Bierhorst, illustrated with photographs and old engravings; Farrar, 1976.

Rotten Ralph by Jack Gantos, illustrated by Nicole Rubel; Houghton, 1976.

Simon Underground by Joanne Ryder, illustrated by John Schoenherr; Harper, 1976.

Smile for Auntie written and illustrated by Diane Paterson; Dial, 1976.

Some Things You Should Know about my Dog written and illustrated by Muriel Batherman; Prentice Hall, 1976.

Tugboat written and illustrated by David Plowden; Macmillan, 1976.

Underground written and illustrated by David Macaulay; Houghton Mifflin, 1976.

Unleaving by Jill Paton Walsh, not illustrated; Farrar, 1976.

What Sadie Sang written and illustrated by Eve Rice; Greenwillow, 1976.

What the Forest Tells Me: 1977 Sierra Club Calendar for Children compiled by Bill Broder, illustrated with photographs; Sierra Club/Scribner, 1976.

CHILDREN'S CHOICE AWARD (ARIZONA)
discontinued

This children's choice award was established in 1981 by the Children's Services staff of the Mesa Public Library. The purpose was to give children ages three through twelve the opportunity to vote for their favorite picture book or juvenile novel without having to choose from a pre-selected list of titles. Winners were chosen annually in the two categories of picture book and juvenile novel. A letter of recognition was given to the authors of the books receiving the most votes. This award was discontinued in 1989.

1981 JUVENILE *Superfudge* by Judy Blume, not illustrated; Dutton, 1980.

1982 PICTURE BOOK *The Little Island* by Golden MacDonald, illustrated by Leonard Weisgard; Doubleday, 1946.

1982 JUVENILE *Nothing's Fair in Fifth Grade* by Barthe DeClements, not illustrated; Viking, 1981.

1983 PICTURE BOOK *One Morning in Maine* written and illustrated by Robert McCloskey; Viking, 1952.

1983 JUVENILE *Superfudge* by Judy Blume, not illustrated; Dutton, 1980.

1984 No Awards presented due to change in voting time

1985 PICTURE BOOK *Where the Wild Things Are* written and illustrated by Maurice Sendak; Harper, 1963.

1985 JUVENILE *Superfudge* by Judy Blume, not illustrated; Dutton, 1980.

1986 PICTURE BOOK *The Adventures of Pinocchio* by Carlo Collodi, illustrated by Attilo Mussino; Macmillan, 1969, c1925.

1986 JUVENILE *Superfudge* by Judy Blume, not illustrated; Dutton, 1980.

1987 PICTURE BOOK *Clifford, the Big Red Dog* written and illustrated by Norman Bridwell; Scholastic, 1985.

Curious George written and illustrated by H.A. Rey; Houghton Mifflin, 1941.

1987 JUVENILE *Superfudge* by Judy Blume, not illustrated; Dutton, 1980.

1988 *Superfudge* by Judy Blume, not illustrated; Dutton, 1980.

CHILDREN'S CHOICE AWARD (TEXAS)

Harris County Public Library
8080 El Rio St.
Houston, TX 77054-4195

The Children's Choice Award was established in 1978 by the children's librarians of the Harris County Public Library in Houston, Texas. The main objective of the program is to encourage children to read and to use the library. Children are given a blank ballot on which they write the name of their favorite author. There are no master lists provided to the children. The election takes place in March and the winner is announced in April during National Library Week. The recipient is presented with a framed certificate.

1978 Dr. Seuss

1979 Judy Blume

1980 Judy Blume

1981 Judy Blume

1982 Judy Blume

1983 Judy Blume

1984 Judy Blume

1985 Judy Blume

1986 Judy Blume

1987 Judy Blume

1988 Judy Blume

1989 Judy Blume

1990 Judy Blume

1991 Judy Blume

1992 Dr. Seuss

CHILDREN'S LITERATURE ASSOCIATION AWARDS FOR EXCELLENCE IN LITERARY CRITICISM

Children's Literature Association
22 Harvest Lane
Battle Creek, MI 49017

This annual award may be given for the best critical essay and also for the best volume of criticism. Nominations and final selection are made by a seven-member committee elected by the membership of the Association. Anyone may submit nominations to the committee, which also screens journals and books in order to make additional nominations. The winner receives a scroll and $100 at the annual conference.

The following criteria have been set forth as guidelines for consideration: (1) The work must exhibit literary excellence; (2) The focus of the piece of criticism must be the literary value of the book discussed; (3) The critical work must be published (papers read at conferences will not be considered); (4) The award will be made on the basis of the calendar year; (5) The award is not limited to an American author; (6) Criticism of adult works considered as children's literature (e.g., Oliver Twist) is acceptable; (7) Criticism of biography or history is acceptable if it throws light on the critical aspects of children's literature. (From guidelines set forth by the Children's Literature Association).

1978 "The Reader in the Book" by Aidan Chambers in *Signal* (May 1977).

1978 RUNNERSUP "What Makes a Fairy Tale Good: The Queer Kindness of the Golden Bird" by Perry M. Nodelman in *Children's Literature in Education* (Autumn 1977).

"Laura Ingalls Wilder's America: An Unflinching Assessment" by Elizabeth Segal in *Children's Literature in Education* (Summer 1977).

"Cracking Open the Geode: the Fiction of Paula Fox" by Alice Bach in *Horn Book* (October 1977).

1979 "Poetry and Children" by Leonard Clark in *Children's Literature in Education* (Autumn 1978).

1979 RUNNERSUP "Fantasy Literature's Evocative Power" by John H. Timmerman in *Christian Century* (May 17, 1978).

"Predicting Children's Choices in Literature: A Developmental Approach" by Norma Schlager in *Children's Literature in Education* (Autumn 1978).

1980 "Tradition and the Individual Talent of Frances Hodgson Burnett: A Generic Analysis of Little Lord Fauntleroy, A Little Princess, and The Secret Garden" by Phyllis Bixler in *Children's Literature* 7 (1979).

1980 RUNNERSUP "'It Is Better Farther On': Laura Ingalls Wilder and The Pioneer Spirit" by Ann Thompson Lee in *The Lion and the Unicorn* (Spring 1979).

1981 "The Development of Consciousness in Lucy Boston's The Children of Green Knowe" by Lynn Rosenthal in *Children's Literature* 8 (1980).

1981 RUNNERSUP "Re-reading The Secret Garden" by Madelon S. Gohlke in *College English* (April 1980).

"Rites of Passage Today: The Cultural Significance of The Wizard of Earthsea" by Jane Murray Walker in *Mosaic*.

"Children's Literature: The Bad Seed?" by Francelia Butler in *The Virginia Quarterly Review* (Summer 1980).

1982 Award not presented

1983 "The Spear and the Piccolo: Heroic and Pastoral Dimensions of William Steig's Dominic and Abel's Island" by Anita Moss in *Children's Literature* 10 (1982).

1984 "The Balancing of Child and Adult" by U.C. Knoepflmacher in *Nineteenth Century Fiction* 37 (March 1983).

1984 RUNNERSUP "The Mirror in the Sea: Treasure Island and the Internalization of Romance" by William Blackburn in *Children's Literature Association Quarterly* 8 (Fall 1983).

"Creation to Civilization" by Hugh Crago in *Signal* (May 1983).

"The Reign of King Babar" by Harry C. Payne in *Children's Literature* 11 (1983).

"Little Girls Without their Curls" by U.C. Knoepflmacher in *Children's Literature* 10 (1983).

1985 "Hans Brinker: Sunny World, Angry Waters" by Jerome Griswold in *Children's Literature* 12 (1984).

1985 RUNNERSUP "The Magic Circle of Laura Ingalls Wilder" by Virginia Wolf in *Children's Literature Association Quarterly* 9 (Winter 1984-85).

"E. Nesbit: Riding the Wave of the Future" by Alison Lurie in *The New York Review* 31 No. 16 (October 25, 1984).

"The Child Reader as Sleuth" by Carol Billman in Children's Literature in *Education* 15 (Spring 1984).

1986 "Charlie and the Chocolate Factory and other Excremental Visions" by Hamida Bosmajian in *The Lion and the Unicorn* 9 (1985).

1986 RUNNERSUP "Growing Up in Earthsea" by Sue Jenkins in *Children's Literature in Education* 58 (Autumn 1985).

"Secrets and Sequences in Children's Stories" by Roderick McGillis in Studies in the *Literary Imagination* 18 (Fall 1985).

"Text as Teacher: the Beginning of Charlotte's Web" by Perry Nodelman in *Children's Literature* 13 (1985).

"The Lion, the Witch and the Wardrobe as Rite of Passage" by Jane Murray Walker in *Children's Literature in Education* 58 (Spring 1985).

1986 BOOK AWARD *A Fine Anger: A Critical Introduction to the Work of Alan Garner* by Neil Philip; Philomel, 1981.

1987 "Impeccable Governesses, Rational Dames, and Moral Mothers" by Mitzi Myers in *Children's Literature* 14 (1986).

1987 RUNNERSUP "Lives and Half-lives: Biographies of Women for Young Adults" by Geraldine DeLucca in *Children's Literature in Education* 17 (Winter 1986).

"Out of the Depths to Joy" by M. Sarah Smedman in *Triumphs of the Human Spirit in Children's Literature* edited by Francelia Butler and Richard Rotert, 1986.

1988 "Narrative Fractures and Fragments" by Margaret R. Higonnet in *Children's Literature* 15 (1987).

1988 RUNNERUP "Enigma Variations: What Feminist Theory Knows about Children's Literature" by Lissa Paul in *Signal* 54 (September 1987).

1988 BOOK AWARD *The Singing Game* by Iona Opie and Peter Opie, illustrated; Oxford University Press, 1988, c1985.

1989 "Ideology and the Children's Book" by Peter Hollindale in *Signal* 55 (January 1988).

1989 RUNNERUP "Fantasy, Nonsense, Parody, and the Status of the Real: The Example of Carroll" by Linda M. Shires in *Victorian Poetry* 26.3 (Fall 1988).

1990 "The Persistence of Riddles" by Richard Wilbur in *Yale Review* 78.3 (December 1989).

1990 RUNNERUP "Dismembering the Text: The Horror of Louisa May Alcott's Little Women" by Angela M. Estes and Kathleen M. Lant in *Children's Literature* 17 (1989).

1991 "Maurice Sendak's Ritual Cooking of the Child in Three Tableaux" by Jean Perrot in *Children's Literature* 18 (1990).

1991 RUNNERUP "Mystical Fantasy for Children: Silence and Community" by Leona W. Fisher in *The Lion and the Unicorn* 14.2 (December 1990).

1991 BOOK AWARD *Nuclear Age Literature for Youth* by Millicent Lenz; American Library Assn., 1990.

CHILDREN'S PEACE LITERATURE AWARD
Psychologists for the Prevention of War
4 Blyth St
Glen Osmond, South Australia
5064 Australia

Psychologists for the Prevention of War (PPOW) is a special interest group of the Australian Psychological Society. Through the Children's Peace Literature Award, the PPOW wishes to recognize authors who promote the peaceful resolution of conflict through their work. They believe that literature has a significant influence on children's attitudes and behaviors.

This biennial award has a cash prize of $2000 and is presented at a public meeting. Nominations are accepted from the publisher or author/illustrator. In order to qualify, the author/illustrator should be Australian or normally reside in Australia and the books theme should encourage the peaceful resolution of conflict and/or promote peace at the global, local, or interpersonal level.

1987 *Space Demons* by Gillian Rubinstein, not illustrated; Omnibus/Puffin, 1986.

1989 *The Makers* by Victor Kelleher, not illustrated; Viking Kestrel, 1987.

1991 *Dodger* by Libby Gleeson, not illustrated; Turton and Chambers, 1990.

CHILDREN'S READING ROUND TABLE AWARD
Children's Reading Round Table of Chicago
1321 East 56th St
Chicago, IL 60637

Known as the Midwest Award from 1953 to 1960, the Children's Reading Round Table Award is given annually in May. This award honors a long-term commitment to children's books and nomination is open for editors, scholars, booksellers, reviewers, and librarians as well as for authors and illustrators. The award recognizes an outstanding person from the Chicago or Midwest area.

Nominations may be made only by members of the Children's Reading Round Table, but nominees are not restricted to membership. The award committee is headed by the second vice-president, who makes a preliminary selection from names suggested by the membership. Final selection is made by a special award committee consisting of five members who are experts in the field of children's books. The honoree receives a individually designed and illustrated citation (done by a member artist) and a cash award. The Children's Reading Round Table of Chicago is the original Round Table, founded in 1931.

1953	Clara Ingram Judson
1954	Agatha Shea
1955	Adah Whitcomb
1956	Dilla W. MacBean
1957	Ruth Harshaw
1958	Martha Bennett King
1959	Jene Barr
1960	Emily Hilsabeck
1961	Marguerite Henry
1962	Laura May Bannon

1963 Charlemae Rollins

1964 Polly Goodwin

1965 Malinda Miller

1966 Miriam E. Peterson

1967 Dorothy Aldus

1968 Isabelle Lawrence

1969 Rebecca Caudill Ayars, James Sterling Ayars

1970 Mary Evans Andrews

1971 Richard Martin

1972 Gladys Berry

1973 S. Carl Hirsch

1974 Sara I. Fenwick

1975 Caroline Rubin

1976 Clementine Skinner

1977 Elizabeth Vogenthaler

1978 Zena Sutherland

1979 Dorothy Haas

1980 Yolanda Federici

1981 Verna Aardema

1982 Betsy Hearne

1983 John Donovan

1984 Florence Parry Heide

1985 Mildred Batchelder

1986 Philip A. Sadler

1987 Barbara Elleman

1988 Ginny Moore Kruse

1989 Hazel Rochman

1990 Tom McGowen

1991 Margaret Hillert

1992 Jamie Gilson

1993 Rochelle Lee

CHILDREN'S SPRING BOOK FESTIVAL AWARDS
see SPRING BOOK FESTIVAL AWARD

CHRISTOPHER AWARDS
The Christophers
12 East 48th St
New York, NY 10017

Awards for children's books were first given in 1970, although the Christopher Award was presented for books in other categories since 1949. This annual award is presented to authors and illustrators whose work is representative of the best achievements in the field. Nominations are solicited from publishers, with a panel of judges making the final decisions. The number of recipients varies each year. In order to be eligible, a book must have been published during the preceding calendar year.

The nominated books are judged on the following criteria: (1) affirmation of the highest values of the human spirit, (2) artis-

tic and technical proficiency, and (3) a significant degree of public acceptance. All titles - picture books, fiction and nonfiction - are eligible. The recipients receive an engraved bronze medallion at annual ceremonies in February.

1970 AGES 4-8 *Alexander and the Wind-up Mouse* written and illustrated by Leo Lionni; Pantheon, 1969.

1970 AGES 8-12 *Tucker's Countryside* by George Selden, illustrated by Garth Williams; Farrar, 1969.

1970 TEENAGE *Brother Can You Spare a Dime? The Great Depression, 1929-1933* by Milton Meltzer, illustrated with photographs; Knopf, 1969.

Escape from Nowhere by Jeannette Eyerly, not illustrated; Lippincott, 1969.

1971 AGES 4-8 *The Erie Canal* written and illustrated by Peter Spier; Doubleday, 1970.

1971 AGES 8-12 *A Moment of Silence* by Pierre Janssen, translated by William R. Tyler, photographs by Hans Samson; Atheneum, 1970.

The Changeling by Zilpha Keatley Snyder, illustrated by Alton Raible; Atheneum, 1970.

1971 TEENAGE *The Guardians* by John Christopher, not illustrated; Macmillan, 1970.

Sea and Earth: The Life of Rachel Carson by Philip Sterling, illustrated with photographs; Crowell, 1970.

1971 ALL AGES *UNICEF Book of Children's Legends* by William I. Kaufman, illustrated with photographs; Stackpole, 1970.

UNICEF Book of Children's Poems by William I. Kaufman, illustrated with photographs; Stackpole, 1970.

UNICEF Book of Children's Prayers by William I. Kaufman, illustrated with photographs; Stackpole, 1970.

UNICEF Book of Children's Songs by William I. Kaufman, illustrated with photographs; Stackpole, 1970.

1972 AGES 4-8 *Emmet Otter's Jug-band Christmas* by Russell Hoban, illustrated by Lillian Hoban; Parents, 1971.

On the Day Peter Stuyvesant Sailed into Town written and illustrated by Arnold Lobel; Harper, 1971.

1972 AGES 8-12 *Annie and the Old One* by Miska Miles, illustrated by Peter Parnall; Atlantic-Little, 1971.

Pocahontas and the Strangers by Clyde Robert Bulla, illustrated by Peter Burchard; Crowell, 1971.

1972 TEENAGE *The Headless Cupid* by Zilpha Keatley Snyder, illustrated by Alton Raible; Atheneum, 1971.

The Rights of the People: The Major Decisions of the Warren Court by Walter Goodman and Elaine Goodman, not illustrated; Farrar, 1971.

1973 AGES 4-8 *The Adventures of Obadiah* written and illustrated by Brinton Turkle; Viking, 1972.

1973 AGES 8-12 *The Book of Giant Stories* by David L. Harrison, illustrated by Philippe Fix; New York American Heritage Press, 1972.

Tracking the Unearthly Creatures of Marsh and Pond by Howard G. Smith, illustrated by Anne Marie Jauss; Abingdon, 1972.

1973 **TEENAGE** *Freaky Friday* by Mary Rodgers, not illustrated; Harper, 1972.

Vanishing Wings: A Tale of Three Birds of Prey by Griffing Bancroft, illustrated by John Hamberger; Watts, 1972.

1973 **YOUNG ADULT** *This Star Shall Abide* by Sylvia L. Engdahl, illustrated by Richard Cuffari; Atheneum, 1972.

1973 **ALL AGES** *Dominic* written and illustrated by William Steig; Farrar, 1972.

1974 **PRE-SCHOOL** *It's Raining, Said John Twaining: Danish Nursery Rhymes* written and illustrated by N.M. Bodecker; Atheneum, 1973.

1974 **AGES 4-8** *Gorilla, Gorilla* by Carol Fenner, illustrated by Symeon Shimin; Random House, 1973.

I'll Protect You from the Jungle Beasts written and illustrated by Martha Alexander; Dial, 1973.

1974 **AGES 8-12** *The Wolf* by Michael Fox, illustrated by Charles Frace; Coward, 1973.

1974 **AGES 12-UP** *Guests in the Promised Land: Stories* by Kristin Hunter, not illustrated; Scribner, 1973.

The Right to Know: Censorship in America by Robert A. Liston, not illustrated; Watts, 1973.

1975 **PRE-SCHOOL** *Dawn* written and illustrated by Uri Shulevitz; Farrar, 1974.

1975 **AGES 4-8** *My Grandson Lew* by Charlotte Zolotow, illustrated by William Pene du Bois; Harper, 1974.

1975 **AGES 8-12** *First Snow* by Helen Coutant, illustrated by Vo- Dinh; Knopf, 1974.

Save the Mustangs! How a Federal Law Is Passed by Ann E. Weiss, illustrated with photographs; Messner, 1974.

1975 **AGES 12-UP** *A Billion for Boris* by Mary Rodgers, not illustrated; Harper, 1974.

1976 **PICTUREBOOK** *Anno's Alphabet: An Adventure in Imagination* written and illustrated by Mitsumasa Anno; Crowell, 1975.

1976 **AGES 7-11** *How the Witch Got Alf* by Cora Annett Scott, illustrated by Steven Kellogg; Watts, 1975.

1976 **AGES 9-12** *Tuck Everlasting* by Natalie Babbitt, not illustrated; Farrar, 1975.

1976 **AGES 12-UP** *Bert Breen's Barn* by Walter D. Edmonds, not illustrated; Little Brown, 1975.

1976 **NONFICTION** *Pyramid* written and illustrated by David Macaulay; Houghton Mifflin, 1975.

1977 **PICTURE BOOK** *Willy Bear* by Mildred Kantrowitz, illustrated by Nancy Winslow Parker; Parents, 1976.

1977 **AGES 6-8** *Frog and Toad All Year* written and illustrated by Arnold Lobel; Harper, 1976.

1977 **AGES 9-12** *The Champion of Merrimack County* by Roger W. Drury, illustrated by Fritz Wegner; Little Brown, 1976.

1977 **AGES 9-UP** *Hurry, Hurry, Mary Dear! and Other Nonsense Poems* written and illustrated by N.M. Bodecker; Atheneum, 1976.

1977 **AGES 12-UP** *Dear Bill, Remember Me? and Other Stories* by Norma Fox Mazer, not illustrated; Delacorte, 1976.

1978 **PICTURE BOOK** *Noah's Ark* written and illustrated by Peter Spier; Doubleday, 1977.

1978 **AGES 6-9** *The Seeing Stick* by Jane Yolen, illustrated by Remy Charlip and Demetra Maraslis; Crowell, 1977.

1978 **AGES 12-UP** *Come to the Edge* by Julia Cunningham, not illustrated; Pantheon, 1977.

Where's Your Head? Psychology for Teenagers by Dale Bick Carlson, illustrated by Carol Nicklaus; Atheneum, 1977.

1978 **ALL AGES** *The Wheel of King Asoka* written and illustrated by Ashok Davar; Follett, 1977.

1979 **PICTURE BOOK** *Panda Cake* written and illustrated by Rosalie Seidler; Parents, 1978.

1979 **AGES 7-9** *Chester Chipmunk's Thanksgiving* by Barbara Williams, illustrated by Kay Chorao; Dutton, 1978.

1979 **AGES 9-12** *The Great Gilly Hopkins* by Katherine Paterson, not illustrated; Crowell, 1978.

1979 **YOUNG ADULT** *Gentlehands* by M. E. Kerr, not illustrated; Harper, 1978.

1980 **AGES 5-8** *Frederick's Alligator* by Esther Allen Peterson, illustrated by Susanna Natti; Crown, 1979.

1980 **AGES 9-12** *What Happened in Hamelin?* by Gloria Skurzynski, not illustrated; Four Winds, 1979.

1980 **AGES 12-UP** *All Together Now* by Sue Ellen Bridgers, not illustrated; Knopf, 1979.

1980 **ALL AGES** *The New York Kid's Book: 170 Children's Writers and Artists Celebrate New York City* by Catherine Edmonds and others, illustrated; Doubleday, 1979.

1981 **PICTUREBOOK** *People* written and illustrated by Peter Spier; Doubleday, 1980.

1981 **AGES 8-12 FICTION** *Son for a Day* by Corrine Gerson, illustrated by Velma Ilsley; Atheneum, 1980.

1981 **AGES 8-12 NONFICTION** *All Times, All Peoples: A World History of Slavery* by Milton Meltzer, illustrated by Leonard Everett Fisher; Harper, 1980.

1981 **AGES 12-UP FICTION** *Encounter at Easton* by Avi, not illustrated; Pantheon, 1980.

1981 **AGES 12-UP NONFICTION** *The Hardest Lesson: Personal Stories of a School Desegregation Crisis* by Pamela Bullard and Judith Stoia, not illustrated; Little Brown, 1980.

1982 **PICTURE BOOK** *My Mom Travels a Lot* by Caroline Feller Bauer, illustrated by Nancy Winslow Parker; Warne, 1981.

1982 **AGES 6-9** *Even If I Did Something Awful* by Barbara S. Hazen, illustrated by Nancy Kincade; Atheneum, 1981.

1982 **AGES 10-14** *A Gift of Mirrorvax* by Malcolm MacCloud, not illustrated; Atheneum, 1981.

1982 **YOUNG ADULT** *The Islanders* by John Rowe Townsend, not illustrated; Lippincott, 1981.

1983 **AGES 4-7** *We Can't Sleep* written and illustrated by James Stevenson; Greenwillow, 1982.

1983 **AGES 8-12** *Homesick: My Own Story* by Jean Fritz, illustrated with drawings by Margot Tomes and photographs; Putnam, 1982.

1983 **AGES 12-UP** *A Formal Feeling* by Zibby Oneal, not illustrated; Viking, 1982; Ballantine, 1983.

1983 **ALL AGES** *Drawing from Nature* written and illustrated by Jim Arnosky; Lothrop, Lee & Shepard, 1982.

1984 **PICTURE BOOK** *Posy* by Charlotte Pomerantz, illustrated by Catherine Stock; Greenwillow, 1983.

1984 **AGES 8-10** *Dear Mr. Henshaw* by Beverly Cleary, illustrated by Paul O. Zelinsky; Morrow, 1983.

1984 **AGES 10-12** *The Sign of the Beaver* by Elizabeth George Speare, not illustrated; Houghton Mifflin, 1983.

1984 **AGES 12-UP** *The Nuclear Arms Race: Can We Survive It?* by Ann E. Weiss, not illustrated; Houghton Mifflin, 1983.

1985 **PICTUREBOOK** *Picnic* written and illustrated by Emily Arnold McCully; Harper, 1984.

1985 **AGES 6-8** *How my Parents Learned to Eat* by Ina Friedman, illustrated by Allen Say; Houghton Mifflin, 1984.

1985 **AGES 8-10** *Secrets of a Small Brother* by Richard J. Margolis, illustrated by Donald Carrick; Macmillan, 1984.

1985 **AGES 10-UP** *One-eyed Cat* by Paula Fox, not illustrated; Bradbury, 1984.

1985 **ALL AGES** *Imagine That! Exploring Make Believe* by Joyce Strauss, illustrated by Jennifer Barrett; Human Sciences Press, 1984.

1986 **AGES 4-8** *The Patchwork Quilt* by Valerie Flournoy, illustrated by Jerry Pinkney; Dial, 1985.

1986 **AGES 8-10** *Sarah, Plain and Tall* by Patricia MacLachlan, not illustrated; Harper, 1985.

1986 **AGES 8-UP** *Promise Not to Tell* by Carolyn Polese, illustrated by Jennifer Barrett; Human Sciences Press, 1985.

1986 **AGES 10-12** *Underdog* by Marilyn Sachs, not illustrated; Doubleday, 1985.

1986 **YOUNG ADULT** *The Mount Rushmore Story* by Judith St. George, illustrated with photographs; Putnam, 1985.

1987 **AGES 4-6** *Duncan & Dolores* written and illustrated by Barbara Samuels; Bradbury, 1986.

1987 **AGES 6-8** *The Purple Coat* by Amy Hest, illustrated by Amy Schwartz; Four Winds, 1986.

1987 **AGES 8-12** *Borrowed Summer* by Marion Walker Doren, not illustrated; Harper & Row, 1986.

1987 **YOUNG ADULT** *Class Dismissed: More High School Poems, No. II* by Mel Glenn, illustrated by Michael J. Bernstein; Clarion, 1986.

1987 **SPECIAL AWARD** Elie Wiesel

1988 **PICTURE BOOK** *Heckedy Peg* by Audrey Wood, illustrated by Don Wood; Harcourt Brace Jovanovich, 1987.

1988 **AGES 6-8** *Humphrey's Bear* by Jan Wahl, illustrated by William Joyce; Holt, 1987.

1988 **AGES 9-12** *The Gold Cadillac* by Mildred D. Taylor, illustrated by Michael Hays; Dial, 1987.

1988 **AGES 12-UP** *Into a Strange Land* by Brent K. Ashabranner and Melissa Ashabranner, illustrated with photos; Dodd Mead, 1987.

1989 **AGES 5-7** *The Good-Bye Book* by Judith Viorst, illustrated by Kay Chorao; Atheneum, 1988.

1989 **AGES 7-10** *Family Farm* written and illustrated by Thomas Locker; Dial, 1988.

1989 **AGES 10-12** *Lies, Deception, and Truth* by Ann E. Weiss, not illustrated; Houghton Mifflin, 1988.

1989 **YOUNG ADULT** *Looking the Tiger in the Eye: Confronting the Nuclear Threat* by Carl B. Feldbaum and Ronald J. Bee, illustrated with photos; Harper & Row, 1988.

1990 **AGES 4-7** *Keeping a Christmas Secret* by Phyllis Reynolds Naylor, illustrated by Lena Shiffman; Atheneum, 1989.

1990 **AGES 8-11** *William and Grandpa* by Alice Schertle, illustrated by Lydia Dabcovich; Lothrop, Lee & Shepard, 1989.

1990 **AGES 10-12** *Can the Whales Be Saved?* by Philip Whitfield, illustrated; Viking Kestrel, 1989.

1990 **YOUNG ADULT** *So Much To Tell You ...* by John Marsden, not illustrated; Little Brown, 1989.

1991 **AGES 9-12** *Mississippi Bridge* by Mildred Taylor, illustrated by Max Ginsburg; Dial, 1990.

1991 **ALL AGES** *Paul Revere's Ride* by Henry Wadsworth Longfellow, illustrated by Ted Rand; Dutton, 1990.

1992 **AGES 4-6** *Somebody Loves You, Mr. Hatch* by Eileen Spinelli, illustrated by Paul Yalowitz; Bradbury, 1991.

1992 **AGES 6-8** *Stephen's Feast* by Jean Richardson, illustrated by Alice Englander; Little Brown, 1991.

1992 **AGES 8-10** *The Gold Coin* by Alma Flor Ada, illustrated by Neil Waldman; Atheneum, 1991.

1992 **AGES 10-UP** *The Star Fisher* by Laurence Yep, not illustrated; Morrow, 1991.

1992 **ALL AGES** *Where Does God Live?* by Thomas Hartman and Marc Gellman, illustrated by William Zdinak; Triumph Books, 1991.

1993 **AGES 5-8** *The Rainbow Fish* written and illustrated by Marcus Pfister; North South Books, 1992.

1993 **AGES 6-8** *Rosie and the Yellow Ribbon* by Paula De Paola, illustrated by Janet Wolf; Little Brown, 1992.

1993 **AGES 8-12** *Letters from Rifka* by Karen Hesse, not illustrated; Henry Holt, 1992.

1993 **AGES 12-UP** *Mississippi Challenge* by Mildred Pitts Walter, illustrated with photos; Bradbury Press, 1992.

CLAREMONT GRADUATE SCHOOL RECOGNITION OF MERIT AWARD

see **GEORGE G. STONE CENTER AWARD**

RUSSELL CLARK AWARD

New Zealand Library Association
20 Brandon St
P O Box 12-212
Wellington, New Zealand

The Russell Clark Award, established by the New Zealand Library Association in 1977, is presented annually for the most distinguished illustrations in a children's books created by a citizen or resident of New Zealand. Nominations are made by publishers, illustrators, or other interested people. A panel of four judges (consisting of two librarians and two experts in the field of illustration) makes the final selection. Judges are expected to take into consideration how children respond to the illustrations. The winner is presented with $250 and an inscribed medal at the annual conference.

1978 *The House of the People* by Ron L. Bacon, illustrated by Robert Jahnke; Collins, 1977.

1979 *Kim* by Bruce Treloar; Collins, 1978.

1980-1981 No Award

1982 *Mrs. McGinty and the Bizarre Plant* written and illustrated by Gavin Bishop; Oxford, 1981.

1983 No Award

1984 *The Tree Witches* written and illustrated by Gwenda Turner; Kestrel, 1983.

1985 *The Duck in the Gun* by Joy Cowley, illustrated by Robyn Belton; Shortland Educational, 1984.

1986 *A Lion in the Night* written and illustrated by Pamela Allen; Hamilton, 1985.

1987 *Taniwha* written and illustrated by Robyn Kahukiwa; Penguin, 1986

1988 *The Magpies* by Denis Glover, illustrated by Dick Frizzell; Century Hutchinson New Zealand, 1987.

1989 *Joseph's Boat* by Caroline Macdonald, illustrated by Chris Gaskin; Hodder & Stoughton, 1988.

1990 *A Walk to the Beach* written and illustrated by Chris Gaskin; Heinemann Reed, 1989.

1991 *Arthur and the Dragon* by Pauline Cartwright, illustrated by David Elliot; Price Milburn, 1990; Steck Vaughn, 1990.

1992 *One Lonely Kakapo* written and illustrated by Sandra Morris; Hodder & Stoughton, 1991.

1993 *Lily and the Present* written and illustrated by Christine Ross; Methuen, 1992.

COKESBURY BOOK STORE AWARD
see **STECK-VAUGHN AWARD**

COLLIER-MACMILLAN AWARD
discontinued

Established by the Collier-Macmillan Publishing Company in Canada, this award was given for the best Canadian juvenile manuscript submitted to the company. To be eligible, an author had to be a citizen of Canada. The award was given on an irregular basis and the manuscripts were evaluated by a panel of independent judges. The award consisted of a $500 prize, as well as a publishing contract with the company.

1974 *Star Maiden: An Ojibwa Legend of the First Water Lily* by Patricia Robins, illustrated by Shirley Day; Cassell & Collier- Macmillan, 1975.

1976 *Alphavegetabet (poems)* by Louise Ellis, illustrated; Collier-Macmillan Canada, 1976.

COLORADO CHILDREN'S BOOK AWARD

This children's choice award was established by Dr. William J. Curtis in 1976 and is presented annually. In the Spring, children are surveyed as to their favorite books. A master list is drawn up for the voting, which is also done by the children. All types of literature are eligible and the authors must be U.S. citizens. The winning author is presented with a commemorative set of bookends at an annual convention.

1976 *How Droofus the Dragon Lost His Head* written and illustrated by Bill Peet; Houghton, 1971.

1977 *A Day no Pigs Would Die* by Robert Newton Peck, not illustrated; Knopf, 1972; Dell, 1974.

1978 *The Sweet Touch* written and illustrated by Lorna Balian; Abingdon, 1976.

1979 *The Great Green Turkey Creek Monster* written and illustrated by James Flora; Atheneum, 1976.

1980 *Cloudy with a Chance of Meatballs* by Judi Barrett, illustrated by Ron Barrett; Atheneum, 1978.

1981 *Cross-country Cat* by Mary Calhoun, illustrated by Erick Ingraham; Morrow, 1979.

1982 *Superfudge* by Judy Blume, not illustrated; Dutton, 1980.

1983 *Space Case* by Edward Marshall, illustrated by James Marshall; Dial, 1980.

1984 *The Unicorn and the Lake* by Marianna Mayer, illustrated by Michael Hague; Dial, 1982.

1985 *Miss Nelson Is Back* by Harry Allard, illustrated by James Marshall; Houghton Mifflin, 1982.

1985 RUNNERUP *Stanleigh's Wrong-side-out Day* by Barbara A. Steiner, illustrated by George Cloven and Ruth Cloven; Children's Press, 1982.

Nothing's Fair in Fifth Grade by Barthe DeClements, not illustrated; Viking, 1981.

1986 *King Bidgood's in the Bathtub* by Audrey Wood, illustrated by Don Wood; Harcourt, 1985.

1988 *If You Give a Mouse a Cookie* by Laura J. Numeroff, illustrated by Felicia Bond; Harper & Row, 1985.

1988 RUNNERUP *There's a Monster Under My Bed* by James Howe, illustrated by David Rose; Atheneum, 1986.

The Little Old Lady Who Was Not Afraid of Anything by Linda Williams, illustrated by Megan Lloyd; Crowell, 1986.

1989 *The Magic School Bus at the Waterworks* by Joanna Cole, illustrated by Bruce Degen; Scholastic, 1986.

1989 RUNNERUP *Meanwhile Back at the Ranch* by Trinka Hakes Noble, illustrated by Tony Ross; Dial, 1987.

Heckedy Peg by Audrey Wood, illustrated by Don Wood; Harcourt, Brace, Jovanovich, 1987.

1990 *Tacky the Penguin* by Helen Lester, illustrated by Lynn Munsinger; Houghton Mifflin, 1988.

1990 RUNNERUP *Two Bad Ants* written and illustrated by Chris Van Allsburg; Houghton Mifflin, 1988.

No Jumping on the Bed! written and illustrated by Tedd Arnold; Dial, 1987.

1991 *The Talking Eggs* by Robert D. San Souci, illustrated by Jerry Pinkney; Dial, 1989.

COMMONWEALTH CLUB OF CALIFORNIA BOOK AWARDS

Michael J. Brassington, Executive Director
Commonwealth Club of California
595 Market St
San Francisco, CA 94105

Each year since 1932, the Commonwealth Club of California has awarded two gold medals and as many as six silver medals to California authors. One of the six silver medals is for the best juvenile title of the year. The first juvenile medal was awarded in 1939. The awards were established to encourage good literature in California. To be considered, an author must be a California resident.

Taken into consideration are juvenile fiction and nonfiction books on any subject. The winning title is chosen by a jury of seven members and the award is presented to the author in June. Listed below are the juvenile titles which have won the silver medal.

1939 *Bright Heritage* by Virginia Provines, illustrated by Sherman C. Hoeflich; Longmans, 1939.

1940 *Blue Willow* by Doris Gates, illustrated by Paul Lantz; Viking, 1940.

1941 No Award

1942 *Long Adventure: The Story of Winston Churchill* by Hildegarde Hawthorne, not illustrated; Appleton, 1942.

1943 *Spurs for Antonia* by Katherine Wigmore Eyre, illustrated by Decie Merwin; Oxford, 1943.

1944 *Thunderbolt House* by Howard Pease, illustrated by Armstrong Sperry; Doubleday, 1944.

1945 *The Singing Cave* by Margaret Leighton, illustrated by Manning de V. Lee; Houghton, 1945.

1946 *Towards Oregon* by E.H. Staffelbach, illustrated by Charles Hargens; Macrae Smith, 1946.

1947 *Sancho of the Long, Long Horns* by Allen R. Bosworth, illustrated by Robert Frankenberg; Doubleday, 1947.

1948 *Seabird* written and illustrated by Holling Clancy Holling; Houghton, 1948.

1949 *At the Palace Gates* by Helen Rand Parrish, illustrated by Leo Politi; Viking, 1949.

1950 *Tomas and the Red-headed Angel* by Marion Garthwaite, illustrated by Lorence F. Bjorklund; Messner, 1950.

1951 *Sandra and the Right Prince* by Mildred N. Anderson, illustrated by J. Paget-Fredericks; Oxford, 1951.

1952 *Wapiti the Elk* by Rutherford Montgomery, illustrated by Gardell Dano Christensen; Little Brown, 1952.

1953 *Roaring River* by Bill Brown, not illustrated; Coward McCann, 1953.

1954 *Epics of Everest* by Leonard Wibberley, illustrated by Genevieve Vaughan-Jackson; Ariel, 1954.

1955 *Westward the Eagle* by Frederick A. Lane, illustrated by E. Harper Johnson; Holt, 1955.

1956 *Spook, the Mustang* by Harlan Thompson, illustrated by Paul Lantz; Doubleday, 1956.

1957 *David and the Phoenix* by Edward Ormondroyd, illustrated by Joan Raysor; Follett, 1957.

1958 *First Scientist of Alaska: William Healey Dall* by Edward A. Herron, not illustrated; Messner, 1958.

1959 *This Is the Desert* by Phillip H. Ault, illustrated by Leonard Everett Fisher; Dodd, 1959.

1960 *Hawaii, the Aloha State* by Helen Bauer, illustrated by Bruce McCurdy; Doubleday, 1960.

1961 *The Gray Sea Raiders* by Gordon D. Shirreffs, not illustrated; Chilton, 1961.

1962 *First Woman Ambulance Surgeon: Emily Barringer* by Iris Noble, not illustrated; Messner, 1962.

1963 *The Keys and the Candle* by Maryhale Woolsey, illustrated by Donald Bolognese; Abingdon, 1963.

1964 *A Spell Is Cast* by Eleanor Cameron, illustrated by Beth Krush and Joe Krush; Atlantic-Little, 1964.

1965 *Campion Towers* by Patricia Beatty and John Beatty, not illustrated; Macmillan, 1965.

1966 *Chancy and the Grand Rascal* by Sid Fleischman, illustrated by Eric von Schmidt; Atlantic-Little, 1966.

1967 *Silent Ship, Silent Sea* by Robb White, not illustrated; Doubleday, 1967.

1968 *Quest for Freedom: Bolivar and the South American Revolution* by Paul Rink, illustrated by Barry Martin; Simon & Schuster, 1968.

1969 *The Cay* by Theodore Taylor, not illustrated; Doubleday, 1969.

1970 *Jonah and the Great Fish* by Clyde Robert Bulla, illustrated by Helga Aichinger; Crowell, 1970.

1971 *Annie and the Old One* by Miska Miles, illustrated by Peter Parnall; Atlantic-Little, 1971.

1972 *Samurai of Gold Hill* by Yoshiko Uchida, illustrated by Ati Forberg; Scribner, 1972.

1973 No Award

1974 *The Paper Party* written and illustrated by Don Freeman; Viking, 1974.

1975 *Coyotes: Last Animals on Earth?* by Harold E. Thomas, illustrated by Lorence F. Bjorklund; Lothrop, 1975.

1976 *The Boy Who Sang the Birds* by John Weston, illustrated by Donna Diamond; Scribner, 1976.

1977 *A Shepherd Watches, a Shepherd Sings* by Louis Irigary and Theodore Taylor, illustrated with photographs; Doubleday, 1977.

1978 *North of Danger* by Dale Fife, illustrated by Haakon Saether; Dutton, 1978.

1979 *The Fool and the Dancing Bear* by Pamela Stearns, illustrated by Ann Strugnell; Little Brown, 1979.

1979 SILVER MEDAL UNCLASSIFIED *Sea Glass* by Laurence Yep, not illustrated; Harper, 1979.

1980 *Flight of the Sparrow* by Julia Cunningham, not illustrated; Pantheon, 1980.

The Half-a-Moon Inn by Paul Fleischman, illustrated by Kathy Jacobi; Harper, 1980.

1981 *A Jar of Dreams* by Yoshiko Uchida, not illustrated; Atheneum, 1981.

1982 *Jake and Honeybunch Go to Heaven* written and illustrated by Margot Zemach; Farrar, 1982.

1983 *Dear Mr. Henshaw* by Beverly Cleary, illustrated by Paul O. Zelinsky; Morrow, 1983.

1984 *Monkey Puzzle and other Poems* by Myra Cohn Livingston, illustrated by Antonio Frasconi; Atheneum, 1984.

1985 *The Willow Maiden* by Meghan Collins, illustrated by Laszlo Gal; Dial, 1985.

1986 *The Secret of the Mountain* by Esther Linfield, not illustrated; Greenwillow, 1986.

1987 *Nell's Quilt* by Susan Terris, not illustrated; Farrar Straus Giroux, 1987.

1988 *Step Into the Night* by Joanne Ryder, illustrated by Dennis Nolan; Four Winds, 1988.

1989 No Award

1990 **AGES 10-UNDER** *Babushka's Doll* written and illustrated by Patricia Polacco; Simon & Schuster, 1990.

1990 **AGES 11-16** *The Fabulous Fifty* by Morton Grosser, not illustrated; Atheneum, 1990.

1991 **AGES 10-UNDER** *Fly Away Home* by Eve Bunting, illustrated by Ronald Himler; Clarion, 1991.

1991 **AGES 11-16** *Jayhawker* by Patricia Beatty, not illustrated; Morrow, 1991.

1992 **AGES 10-UNDER** *A Bowl of Mischief* by Ellen Kindt McKenzie, not illustrated; Henry Holt, 1992.

Chicken Sunday written and illustrated by Patricia Polacco; Philomel, 1992.

1992 **AGES 11-16** *Earthquake at Dawn* by Kristiana Gregory, illustrated with photographs; Harcourt Brace Jovanovich, 1992.

COUNCIL FOR WISCONSIN WRITERS AWARD
discontinued

Sponsored by the writers organizations in Wisconsin, this award was established in 1974. There were numerous categories, including juvenile and picture book. The purpose of the awards was to recognize literary work by living Wisconsin residents published in the preceding year. A panel of judges chosen by the council screened eligible titles to determine the winners. A prize of $500 was made in each category.

1968 Hope Dahle Jordan

1969 Marion Fuller Archer

1970 Hope Dahle Jordan

1971 Mel Ellis

1972 Marion Fuller Archer

1973 Beatrice Smith

1974 Leon McClinton

1975 **JUVENILE** *Cross-country Runner* by Leon McClinton, not illustrated; Dutton, 1974.

1975 **JUVENILE RUNNERUP** *The Friendly Woods* by Charles House, illustrated by Victoria de Larrea; Four Winds, 1973.

Sidewalk Indian by Mel Ellis, not illustrated; Holt, 1974.

1975 **PICTURE BOOK** *Feelings between Brothers and Sisters* by Maureen Reardon and Marcia Maher Conta, photographs by Jules M. Rosenthal; Advanced Learning Concepts, 1974.

1975 **PICTURE BOOK RUNNERUP** *Soft as the Wind* by Edith Eckblad, illustrated by Jim Roberts; Augsburg, 1974.

1976 **JUVENILE** *Icebergs and their Voyages* by Gwen M. Schultz, illustrated with photographs and maps; Morrow, 1975.

1976 **JUVENILE RUNNERUP** *Lady for the Defense: A Biography of Belva Lockwood* by Mary Virginia Fox, illustrated with photographs; Harcourt, 1975.

When the Sad Ones Come to Stay by Florence Parry Heide, not illustrated; Lippincott, 1975.

1976 **PICTURE BOOK** *Ice River* by Phyllis Green, illustrated by James Crowell; Addison Wesley, 1975.

1976 **PICTURE BOOK RUNNERUP** *Brown Mouse and Vole* by Vicki Kimmel Artis, illustrated by Jan Hughes; Putnam, 1975.

1977 **JUVENILE** *Growing Anyway Up* by Florence Parry Heide, not illustrated; Lippincott, 1976.

1977 **JUVENILE RUNNERUP** *The Babe: Mildred Didrikson Zaharias* by Beatrice S. Smith, illustrated with photographs; Raintree, 1976.

The Wild Horse Killers by Mel Ellis, not illustrated; Holt, 1976.

1977 **PICTURE BOOK** *Duane, the Collector* by Eleanor J. Lapp, illustrated by Christine Westerberg; Addison Wesley, 1976.

1977 **PICTURE BOOK RUNNERUP** *The Case of the Missing Bills* by Beatrice S. Smith, illustrated by George Overlie; Carolrhoda, 1976.

The Mice Came in Early this Year by Eleanor J. Lapp, illustrated by David Cunningham; Whitman, 1976.

1978 Award information not available

1979 **JUVENILE** *Edward Troy and the Witch Cat* by Sarah Sargent, illustrated by Emily McCully; Follett, 1978.

1979 **JUVENILE RUNNERUP** *Wisconsin, Forward!* by Marion Fuller Archer, edited by James T. Rutledge, illustrated; McRoberts, 1978.

1979 **PICTURE BOOK** *A New Mother for Martha* by Phyllis Green, illustrated by Margaret Luks; Human Sciences Press, 1978.

1979 **PICTURE BOOK RUNNERUP** *Brimhall Comes to Stay* by Judy Delton, illustrated by Cyndy Szekeres; Lothrop, 1978.

1980 **JUVENILE** *Major Corby and the Unidentified Flapping Object* by Gene DeWeese, not illustrated; Doubleday, 1979.

1980 **JUVENILE RUNNERUP** *Straight Talk about Love and Sex for Teenagers* by Jane Burgess-Kohn, not illustrated; Beacon, 1979.

1980 **PICTURE BOOK** *A Sweetheart for Valentine* written and illustrated by Lorna Balian; Abingdon, 1979.

1980 **PICTURE BOOK RUNNERUP** *I Am an Orthodox Jew* by Laura Greene, illustrated by Lis C. Wesson; Holt, 1979.

COUNCIL ON INTERRACIAL BOOKS FOR CHILDREN AWARD

discontinued

This annual award, sponsored by the Council on Interracial Books for Children, was established in 1968 to encourage the writing and publication of children's books by minority authors. In 1968 and 1969, the awards were offered for categories according to age groups. In 1970, categories such as African American, American Indian, and Puerto Rican were substituted for the age groups. Eligible were manuscripts written by African American, American Indian, Asian American, Chicano, and Puerto Rican authors who had never published a book for children. If none of the submitted manuscripts met the criteria, the award was not given. This award was discontinued in the late 1970s due to lack of support.

1968 **AGES 3-6** *Where Does the Day Go?* by Walter M. Myers, illustrated by Leo Carty; Parents, 1969.

1968 **AGES 7-11** No Award

1968 **AGES 12-16** *The Soul Brothers and Sister Lou* by Kristin Hunter, not illustrated; Scribner, 1968.

1969 **AGES 3-6** "ABC: the Story of the Alphabet" by Virginia Cox; Wayne State University; manuscript.

1969 **AGES 7-11** *Sidewalk Story* by Sharon Bell Mathis, illustrated by Leo Carty; Viking, 1971.

1969 **AGES 12-16** "Letters from Uncle David: Underground Hero" by Margot S. Webb; manuscript.

1970 **AFRICAN AMERICAN** *Sneakers* by Ray Anthony Shepard, not illustrated; Dutton, 1973.

1970 **AMERICAN INDIAN** *Jimmy Yellow Hawk* by Virginia Driving Hawk Sneve, illustrated by Oren Lyons; Holiday House, 1972.

1970 **CHICANO** "I Am Magic" by Juan Valenzuela, Indian Historian Press; manuscript.

1971-72 **AFRICAN AMERICAN** "The Rock Cried Out" by Florenz Webbe Maxwell; manuscript.

1971-72 **ASIAN AMERICAN** "Morning Song" by Minfong Ho; manuscript.

1971-72 **PUERTO RICAN** *The Unusual Puerto Rican* by Theodore Laquer-Francheshi; Lothrop.

1973 **AFRICAN AMERICAN** *Song of the Trees* by Mildred D. Taylor, illustrated by Jerry Pinkney; Dial, 1975.

1973 **AMERICAN INDIAN** *Morning Arrow* by Nanabah Chee Dodge, illustrated by Jeffrey Lunge; Lothrop, 1975.

"Grandfather's Bridge" by Michele P. Robinson; manuscript.

1973 **ASIAN AMERICAN** "Eyak" by Dorothy Tomiye Okamoto; manuscript.

1973 **PUERTO RICAN** "El Pito de Plata de Pito" by Jack Agueros; manuscript.

1974 **AFRICAN AMERICAN** "Midnight: The Stallion of the Night" by Aishah S. Abdullah; manuscript.

"Mweusi" by Aishah S. Abdullah; manuscript.

"Simba" by Aishah S Abdullah; manuscript.

1974 **CHICANO** "My Father Hijacked a Plane" by Abelardo B. Delgado; manuscript.

1974 **PUERTO RICAN** "Yari" by Antonia A. Hernandez; manuscript.

1975 **AFRICAN AMERICAN** "Letters to a Friend on a Brown Paper Bag" by Emily R. Moore; manuscript.

1975 **PUERTO RICAN** "El Mundo Maravilloso de Macu" by Lydia Milagros Gonzalez; manuscript.

CRABbery AWARD

Prince George's County Memorial Library System
Oxon Hill Branch Children's Department
6200 Oxon Hill Road
Oxon Hill, MD 20745
Attn: CRABS

The first CRABbery Award was presented in 1979 in conjunction with a program conceived by Mrs. Birdie Law. CRABs is an acronym for Children Raving About Books. These CRABs nominate titles, both fiction and nonfiction, published in the preceding year, which they have read and enjoyed. The children have hour-long meetings every week to discuss their favorite books. A citation is presented to the winning author at the fall award ceremony.

Following is a list of more detailed specifications governing the award: (1) All books printed in the year preceding the award date are eligible. (2) Nationality of author is not a criterion. (3) The award is given to the book. (4) Only CRABs or members of another book discussion group may nominate. (5) Closing date for nominations is in mid-March. (6) Voting will be in the first week of May. (7) A CRAB may not vote for a book he has not read. (8) Simple majority will determine the winner. (9) Honor books will be the runnersup on the final ballot. (10) Award ceremony is held in September or October.

1979 *The First Two Lives of Lukas-Kaska* by Lloyd Alexander, not illustrated; Dutton, 1978.

1979 **HONOR** *The Great Gilly Hopkins* by Katherine Paterson, not illustrated; Crowell, 1978.

The Westing Game by Ellen Raskin, not illustrated; Dutton, 1978.

1980 *The Magic of the Glits* by Carole S. Adler, illustrated by Ati Forberg; Macmillan, 1979.

1980 **HONOR** *Sport* by Louise Fitzhugh, not illustrated; Delacorte, 1979.

Into the Dream by William Sleator, illustrated by Ruth Sanderson; Dutton, 1979; Scholastic, 1979.

1981 *What if They Knew?* by Patricia Hermes, not illustrated; Harcourt, 1980.

1981 **HONOR** *Superfudge* by Judy Blume, not illustrated; Dutton, 1980.

Jacob Have I Loved by Katherine Paterson, not illustrated; Crowell, 1980.

The Girl with the Silver Eyes by Willo Davis Roberts, not illustrated; Atheneum, 1980.

1982 *There's a Bat in Bunk Five* by Paula Danziger, not illustrated; Delacorte, 1980; Dell, 1982.

1982 HONOR *Tiger Eyes* by Judy Blume, not illustrated; Bradbury, 1981.

The Roquefort Gang written and illustrated by Sandy Clifford; Houghton Mifflin/Parnassus, 1981.

How I Put My Mother Through College by Corinne Gerson, not illustrated; Atheneum, 1981.

1983 *The Animal, the Vegetable & John D. Jones* by Betsy Byars, illustrated by Ruth Sanderson; Delacorte, 1982; Dell, 1983.

1983 HONOR *Captain Hook, That's Me* by Ada B. Litchfield, illustrated by Sonia O. Lisker; Walker, 1982.

The Ghosts of Austwick Manor by Reby E. MacDonald, not illustrated; Atheneum, 1982.

Be a Perfect Person in Just Three Days by Stephen Manes, illustrated by Tom Huffman; Houghton Mifflin, 1982.

1984 *Magnolia's Mixed-up Magic* by Joan Lowery Nixon, illustrated by Linda Bucholtz-Ross; Putnam, 1983.

1984 HONOR *Banana Blitz* by Florence Parry Heide, not illustrated; Holiday House, 1983.

The Celery Stalks at Midnight by James Howe, illustrated by Leslie Morrill; Atheneum, 1983.

The Great Skinner Strike by Stephanie S.Tolan, not illustrated; Macmillan, 1983.

1985-1989 Program Inactive

1990 *The Pizza Monster* by Marjorie Sharmat and Mitchell Sharmat, illustrated by Denise Brunkus; Delacorte, 1989.

1990 HONOR *The Secret Garden* by Frances Hodgson Burnett, illustrated by N. Unwin; Lippincott, 1938, c1911.

Haunted House by Peggy Parish, illustrated by Paul Frame; Macmillan, 1971.

1991 *Willie Pearl* by Michelle Y. Green, illustrated by Steve McCracken; William Ruth & Co., 1990.

1991 HONOR *Libby on Wednesday* by Zilpha Keatley Snyder, not illustrated; Delacorte, 1990; Dell, 1991.

1991 CLASSIC *The Last of the Really Great Whangdoodles* by Julie Edwards, not illustrated; Harper & Row, 1989, c1974.

1992 *Stepping on the Cracks* by Mary Downing Hahn, illustrated with a map; Clarion, 1991.

1992 HONOR *Rats on the Roof and Other Stories* written and illustrated by James Marshall; Dial, 1991.

Song of the Gargoyle by Zilpha Keatley Snyder, not illustrated; Delacorte, 1991.

1992 CLASSIC *Ace: The Very Important Pig* by Dick King-Smith, illustrated by Lynette Hemmant; Crown, 1990.

1993 *Malcolm X: By Any Means Necessary* by Walter Dean Myers, illustrated; Scholastic, 1993.

1993 HONOR *The Great Eggspectations of Lila Fenwick* by Kate McMullan, illustrated by Diane de Groat; Farrar Straus Giroux, 1991.

CRICHTON AWARD FOR CHILDREN'S BOOK ILLUSTRATION

Victorian Branch of the Children's
Book Council of Australia
P O Box 310
Heidelberg, Victoria 3084
Australia

Established in 1988 for Raymond Wallace Crichton, this award is presented in recognition of a new children's book illustrator. This annual award is sponsored by the Victorian Branch of the Children's Book Council. To qualify for the award, it must be the illustrator's first major published work for children and the illustrator must be an Australian citizen or a five-year resident. A certificate and a $1000 cash award are presented to the winner during Children's Book Week.

1988 *Pheasant and Kingfisher* by Catherine Berndt, illustrated by Arone Raymond Meeks; Martin Educational, 1987.

1989 *Australian Dinosaurs and Their Relatives* written and illustrated by Marilyn Pride; Collins, 1988.

1990 *Pigs and Honey* written and illustrated by Jeanie Adams; Omnibus, 1989.

1991 *Bip: The Snapping Bungaroo* by Narelle McRobbie, illustrated by Grace Fielding; Magabala Books, 1990.

1992 *The Magnificent Nose and Other Marvels* by Anna Fienberg, illustrated by Kim Gamble; Allen & Unwin, 1991.

1993 *Alitji in Dreamland* adapted and translated by Nancy Sheppard, illustrated by Donna Leslie, notes by Barbara Ker Wilson; Simon & Schuster Australia, 1992.

D

HARVEY DARTON AWARD

Children's Books History Society
John Coles
15 Rushfield Rd
Liss, Hampshire GU33 7LW
England

Presented by the Children's Books History Society, this award is given for the best book on the history or an aspect of the history of British children's literature published every two years. A prize of £50 is given to the recipient.

1992 *Benjamin Tabart's Juvenile Library* by Marjorie Moon, illustrated with photographs; St. Paul's Bibliographies, 1990.

DELACORTE PRESS PRIZE FOR AN OUTSTANDING FIRST YOUNG ADULT NOVEL

Delacorte Press
Books for Young People
666 Fifth Avenue
New York, NY 10103

The purpose of this award is to gain recognition for the art of the contemporary young adult novel and to confirm its importance. American and Canadian writers who have not previously published a novel for young adults (ages 12 to 18) are eligible.

Foreign language manuscripts and translations are not eligible. The first winners were chosen in 1983 and received contracts for a Delacorte hardcover and a Dell paperback, a $1500 cash prize, and a $6000 advance against royalties. The judges are editors of Delacorte Press Books for Young Readers.

1983 *Center Line* by Joyce Sweeney, not illustrated; Delacorte, 1984.

1983 **HONORABLE MENTION** *The Question Box* by Roberta Hughey, not illustrated; Delacorte, 1984.

1984 *Walk Through Cold Fire* by Cin Forshay-Lunsford, not illustrated; Delacorte, 1985.

1984 **HONORABLE MENTION** *Too Much T.J.* by Jacqueline Shannon, not illustrated; Delacorte, 1986.

The Whole Nine Yards by Dallin Malmgren, not illustrated; Delacorte, 1986.

1985 *The Impact Zone* by Ray Maloney, not illustrated; Delacorte, 1986.

1985 **HONORABLE MENTION** *The Romantic Obsessions and Humiliations of Annie Sehlmeier* by Louise Plummer, not illustrated; Delacorte, 1987.

1986 No Award

1987 *Cal Cameron by Day, Spider-Man by Night* by A.E. (Ann Edwards) Cannon, not illustrated; Delacorte, 1988.

1987 **HONORABLE MENTION** *Children of the River* by Linda Crew, not illustrated; Delacorte, 1989.

Best Friends Tell the Best Lies by Carol Dines, not illustrated; Delacorte, 1989.

1988 *Ozzy on the Outside* by Richard E. Allen, not illustrated; Delacorte, 1989.

1989 *Hank* by James Sauer, not illustrated; Delacorte, 1990.

1989 **HONORABLE MENTION** *Silicon Songs* by Buzz King, not illustrated; Delacorte, 1990.

Mayflower Man by Jean Adair Shriver, not illustrated; Delacorte, 1991.

Mote Herbert R. Reaver, not illustrated; Delacorte, 1990.

1990 *Lizard* by Dennis Covington, not illustrated; Delacorte, 1991.

1990 **HONORABLE MENTION** *The Toom County Mud Race* by Herb Karl, not illustrated; Delacorte, 1992.

Crosses by Shelley Stoehr, not illustrated; Delacorte, 1991.

1991 *Squashed* by Joan Bauer, not illustrated; Delacorte, 1992.

1991 **HONORABLE MENTION** *The Joker and the Thief* by Raymond Obstfeld, not illustrated; Delacorte, 1993.

DIABETES AUSTRALIA ALAN MARSHALL PRIZE FOR CHILDREN'S LITERATURE

Arts Victoria
Private Bag No. 1
City Road Post Office
South Melbourne, Victoria
3205 Australia

Formerly known as the Alan Marshall Prize for Children's Literature, this award is now sponsored by Diabetes Australia, through the Victoria Health Promotion Foundation. This annual award, established in 1988, is given in recognition of an eminent Australian children's book. The book, of any genre, must have been written by an Australian citizen or permanent resident and published during the preceding year.

A $7500 cash award is presented along with a silver letterknife and a Crest Sheaffer fountain pen.

1988 *So Much To Tell You ...* by John Marsden, not illustrated; Walter McVitty Books, 1987; Little Brown, 1989.

1989 *The Lake at the End of the World* by Caroline Macdonald, not illustrated; Hodder & Stoughton, 1988; Dial, 1989; Knight, 1992.

1990 *Onion Tears* by Diana Kidd, illustrated by Dee Huxley; Collins, 1989.

1991 *Strange Objects* by Gary Crew, not illustrated; Heinemann, 1990.

1992 *The House Guest* by Eleanor Nilsson, not illustrated; Viking, 1991.

DR. SEUSS PICTURE-BOOK AWARD

Random House Juvenile Division
225 Park Avenue South
New York, NY 10003

Established in 1993 by Random House, this new award honors the talented Dr. Seuss. The editors at Random House hope to find and nurture the new talents of the future. The winner of the annual award must be both author and illustrator, and a United States citizen over sixteen years of age. Only author/illustrators who have previously published no more than one book or have one book currently under contract are eligible. The winner is announced each year on Dr. Seuss's birthday, March 2.

The books are judged by a panel of independent experts, including an author/illustrator, bookseller, librarian, teacher, and editor. The winner receives a $25,000 cash award as well as a publishing contract.

1993 *Fast Friends: A Tail and Tongue Tale* written and illustrated by Lisa Horstman; to be published by Knopf.

DODD, MEAD LIBRARIAN AND TEACHER PRIZE
see EDITH BUSBY AWARD

DREXEL CITATION

Drexel University
Dr. Shelley G. McNamara
College of Information Studies
32nd and Chestnut Sts.
Rush Building
Philadelphia, PA 19104

Cosponsored by the School of Library and Information Science of Drexel University and the Free Library of Philadelphia, the Drexel Citation was first awarded in 1963. Authors, illustrators, publishers, or others from the Philadelphia area who have made outstanding contributions to literature for children are eligible for this award. A hand-lettered citation is presented to the winner at the annual conference on children's literature, cosponsored by the aforementioned institutions. Prior to 1976, the award was presented at irregular intervals.

1963 Marguerite de Angeli

1967 Katherine Milhous

1970 Carolyn Haywood

1972	Lloyd Alexander
1975	J.B. Lippincott Co.
1976	Elizabeth Janet Gray
1977	Nancy G. Larrick
1978	Catherine Crook de Camp, L. Sprague de Camp
1979	Suzanne Hilton
1980	Kristin Hunter
1981	Joe Krush, Beth Krush
1982	Jan Berenstain, Stan Berenstain
1983	Tana Hoban
1984	Carolyn W. Field
1985	Muriel Feelings
1986	Barbara Bates
1987	Deborah Kogan Ray
1988	Jacqueline Schacter Weiss
1989	Maurice Sendak
1990	Carolyn Croll
1991	Aliki
1992	Jerry Pinkney
1993	Trina Schart Hyman

DROMKEEN MEDAL

Dromkeen Children's Literature Foundation
Pamela Gray, Curator
Riddell's Creek
Victoria 3431
Australia

The Dromkeen Medal is presented annually to a person who has made a significant contribution to the appreciation and development of children's literature in Australia. The recipient is chosen by the Governors of the Dromkeen Foundation. A medal and citation are presented to the recipient at a dinner held at the Dromkeen estate.

1982	Lu Rees (posthumously)
1983	Maurice Saxby
1984	Patricia Wrightson
1985	Anne Bower-Ingram
1986	Albert Ullin
1987	Joan Phipson
1988	Patricia Scott
1989	Robert Ingpen
1990	Mem Fox
1991	Robin Klein
1992	Julie Vivas

DUTTON CHILDREN'S BOOKS PICTURE BOOK COMPETITION

Dutton Children's Books
375 Hudson St.
New York, NY 10014

Established in 1986 to encourage and attract new and talented illustrators, this competition is open to anyone enrolled in an art school, taking an art or design class in a college or university, or a student who graduated within five years. Given to a picture book that displays an imaginative development of story line, treatment of text through art, technical skill, and originality, this award consists of a $1500 1st prize, with $1000 and $500 awarded to 2nd and 3rd place respectively. There is also a possibility that the book will be published. Although the award has not been recently awarded, the competition is still active.

1986 *Minerva Louise* written and illustrated by Janet Morgan Stoeke; Dutton, 1988.

1986 **2ND PRIZE** *Ernst* written and illustrated by Elisa Kleven; Dutton, 1989.

1988 *The Magic Rabbit* written and illustrated by Annette Le Blanc.

DUTTON JUNIOR ANIMAL BOOK AWARD
discontinued

Presented from 1965 to 1969 by E.P. Dutton and Company, this award was given for a fiction or nonfiction children's book about animals. The competition was open to any author, throughout the world, new or established, of a manuscript written in English. The award was a minimum of $3500 as an advance against all earnings.

1965 *Gentle Ben* by Walt Morey, illustrated by John Schoenherr; Dutton, 1965.

1966 *Wild Geese Calling* by Robert Murphy, illustrated by John Kaufmann; Dutton, 1966.

1967 No Award

1968 *Kavik the Wolf Dog* by Walt Morey, illustrated by Peter Parnall; Dutton, 1968.

1969 *A Heritage Restored: America's Wildlife Refuges* by Robert Murphy, illustrated with photographs; Dutton, 1969.

E

EDGAR AWARD
see **EDGAR ALLAN POE AWARD**

EARTHWORM AWARD

Save and Prosper Educational Trust
1 Finsbury Ave.
London EC2M 2QY
England

The Earthworm Children's Book Award was established in 1987 by The Friends of the Earth to encourage the writing and publication of environmentally sensitive children's books. In 1991 the name of the award was changed to the Earthworm Award. Awarded annually in September, this award is open to all types of literature appropriate for the age group, has good values, is environmentally accurate and sensitive, and is inspiring to creativity. A cash award and a trophy are given to the winner.

1987 *The Boy and the Swan* by Catherine Storr, illustrated by Laszlo Acs; Deutsch, 1987.

1988 *Where the Forest Meets the Sea* written and illustrated by Jeannie Baker; Julia McRae, 1987.

1989 *Awaiting Developments* by Judy Allen, not illustrated; Julia MacRae, 1988; Walker, 1989.

1990 *The Young Green Consumer Guide* by John Elkington and Julia Hailes, illustrated by Tony Ross; Gollancz, 1990.

1991 *The Last Rabbit* by Jennifer Curry, illustrated; Methuen, 1990.

1992 *Captain Eco and the Fate of the Earth* by Jonathon Porritt, illustrated by Ellis Nadler; Dorling Kindersley, 1991.

MAX AND GRETEL EBEL MEMORIAL AWARD

discontinued

This award was sponsored by the Canadian Society of Children's Authors, Illustrators, and Performers (CANSCAIP). First given in 1986, the award honored a Canadian author whose work best contributed to a greater understanding among people of different backgrounds, cultures and/or generations. The award carried a $100 prize. It was discontinued in 1990.

1986 *Winners* by Mary-Ellen Lang Collura, not illustrated; Western Producer Prairie Books, 1984.

1987 *Last Chance Summer* by Diana Wieler, not illustrated; Western Producer Prairie Books, 1986.

1988 *False Face* by Welwyn Wilton Katz, not illustrated; Douglas & McIntyre, 1987.

1988 **FIRST RUNNERUP** *Let's Celebrate* written and illustrated by Caroline Parry; Kids Can Press, 1987.

1988 **SECOND RUNNERUP** *A Handful of Time* by Kit Pearson, illustrated with maps; Viking, 1987.

1989 *Whiteout* by James Houston, illustrated with a map; Grey de Pencier Books, 1988.

1990 *Windward Island* by Karleen Bradford, not illustrated; Kids Can Press, 1989.

1990 **RUNNERSUP** *Tales From Gold Mountain* by Paul Yee, illustrated by Simon Ng; Macmillan, 1989.

Blood Red Ochre by Kevin Major, not illustrated; Delacorte, 1989.

THOMAS ALVA EDISON FOUNDATION NATIONAL MASS MEDIA AWARDS

discontinued

This award was established in 1955 to encourage more wholesome influences for youth in the mass media and to interest boys and girls in science. The awards were presented in the following categories: best children's science book (ages 9-13), best science book for youth (ages 13-17), special excellence in contributing to the character development of children (ages 8-12), and for special excellence in portraying America's past (ages 13-16).

All children's trade books published in the U.S. were eligible. The winning titles were determined by a vote of sixty- two national organizations that participated in the Edison foundation program. The honored authors received a scroll and $250; the publisher received a scroll. The presentation ceremony was normally held in January in New York City. The last awards were made in 1967.

1956 **BEST CHILDREN'S SCIENCE BOOK** *The Boy Scientist* by John B. Lewellen, illustrated by Robert Barker; Simon & Schuster, 1955.

1956 **SPECIAL EXCELLENCE IN CONTRIBUTING TO CHARACTER DEVELOPMENT OF CHILDREN** *His Indian Brother* by Hazel Wilson, illustrated by Robert Henneberger; Abingdon, 1955.

1956 **SPECIAL EXCELLENCE IN PORTRAYING AMERICA'S PAST** *The Buffalo Trace* by Virginia S. Eifert, illustrated by Manning de V. Lee; Dodd Mead, 1955.

1957 **BEST CHILDREN'S SCIENCE BOOK** *Exploring the Universe* by Roy A. Gallant, illustrated by Lowell Hess; Garden City Books, 1956.

1957 **SPECIAL EXCELLENCE IN CONTRIBUTING TO CHARACTER DEVELOPMENT OF CHILDREN** *Mr. Justice Holmes* by Clara I. Judson, illustrated by Robert Todd; Follett, 1956.

1957 **SPECIAL EXCELLENCE IN PORTRAYING AMERICA'S PAST** *The Story of the Old Colony of New Plymouth* by Samuel Eliot Morison, illustrated by Charles Overly; Knopf, 1956.

1958 **BEST CHILDREN'S SCIENCE BOOK** *The Wonderful World of Energy* by Lancelot T. Hogben, illustrated by Eileen Aplin and others; Garden City Books, 1957.

1958 **SPECIAL EXCELLENCE IN CONTRIBUTING TO CHARACTER DEVELOPMENT OF CHILDREN** *Armed with Courage* by Lynd Ward and May McNeer, illustrated by Lynd Ward; Abingdon, 1957.

1958 **SPECIAL EXCELLENCE IN PORTRAYING AMERICA'S PAST** *Colonial Living* written and illustrated by Edwin Tunis; World, 1957.

1958 **BEST SCIENCE BOOK FOR YOUTH** *Building Blocks of the Universe* by Isaac Asimov, illustrated with charts; Abelard- Schuman, 1957.

1959 **BEST CHILDREN'S SCIENCE BOOK** *Science in your Own Backyard* written and illustrated by Elizabeth K. Cooper; Harcourt, 1958.

1959 **SPECIAL EXCELLENCE IN CONTRIBUTING TO CHARACTER DEVELOPMENT OF CHILDREN** *That Dunbar Boy* by Jean Gould, illustrated by C. Walker; Dodd Mead, 1958.

1959 **SPECIAL EXCELLENCE IN PORTRAYING AMERICA'S PAST** *The Americans* by Harold Coy, illustrated by William Moyers; Little, 1958.

1959 **BEST SCIENCE BOOK FOR YOUTH** *Elements of the Universe* by Glenn T. Seaborg and Evans G. Valens, illustrated with charts and diagrams; Dutton, 1958.

1960 **BEST CHILDREN'S SCIENCE BOOK** *Experiments in Sky Watching* by Franklyn M. Branley, illustrated by Helmut K. Wimmer; Crowell, 1959.

1960 **SPECIAL EXCELLENCE IN CONTRIBUTING TO CHARACTER DEVELOPMENT OF CHILDREN** *Willie Joe and his Small Change* by Marguerite Vance, illustrated by Robert McAlean; Dutton, 1959.

1960 **SPECIAL EXCELLENCE IN PORTRAYING AMERICA'S PAST** *The Great Dissenters: Guardians of their Country's Laws and Liberties* by Fred Reinfeld, not illustrated; Crowell, 1959.

1960 BEST SCIENCE BOOK FOR YOUTH *IGY: Year of Discovery: The Story of the International Geophysical Year* by Sydney Chapman, illustrated with photographs; University of Michigan Press, 1959.

1961 BEST CHILDREN'S SCIENCE BOOK *Animal Clocks and Compasses: From Animal Migration to Space Travel* by Margaret Hyde, illustrated by P.A. Hutchison; Whittlesey, 1960.

1961 SPECIAL EXCELLENCE IN CONTRIBUTING TO CHARACTER DEVELOPMENT OF CHILDREN *Touched with Fire: Alaska's George William Seller* by Margaret E. Bell, illustrated with maps by Bob Ritter; Morrow, 1960.

1961 SPECIAL EXCELLENCE IN PORTRAYING AMERICA'S PAST *Peter Treegate's War* by Leonard Wibberley, not illustrated; Farrar, 1960.

1961 BEST SCIENCE BOOK FOR YOUTH *Saturday Science* by the Westinghouse Research Laboratories Scientists, edited by Andrew Bluemle, illustrated with diagrams; Dutton, 1960.

1962 BEST CHILDREN'S SCIENCE BOOK *Experiments in Sound* by Nelson F. Beeler, illustrated by George Giusti; Crowell, 1961.

1962 SPECIAL EXCELLENCE IN CONTRIBUTING TO CHARACTER DEVELOPMENT OF CHILDREN *Thomas Jefferson: His Many Talents* by Johanna Johnston, illustrated by Richard Bergere; Dodd, 1961.

1962 SPECIAL EXCELLENCE IN PORTRAYING AMERICA'S PAST *The Fight for Union* by Margaret L. Coit, illustrated with photographs; Houghton, 1961.

1962 BEST SCIENCE BOOK FOR YOUTH *The Atoms within Us* by Ernest Borek, illustrated with photographs; Columbia University Press, 1961.

1963 BEST CHILDREN'S SCIENCE BOOK *Stars, Men and Atoms* by Heinz Haber, illustrated with photographs and diagrams; Golden Press, 1962.

1963 SPECIAL EXCELLENCE IN CONTRIBUTING TO CHARACTER DEVELOPMENT OF CHILDREN *Seeing Fingers: The Story of Louis Braille* by Etta F. De Gering, illustrated by Emil Weiss; McKay, 1962.

1963 SPECIAL EXCELLENCE IN PORTRAYING AMERICA'S PAST *Westward Adventure: The True Stories of Six Pioneers* by William O. Steele, illustrated with maps by Kathleen Voute; Harcourt, 1962.

1963 BEST SCIENCE BOOK FOR YOUTH *Knowledge and Wonder: The Natural World as Man Knows It* by Victor F. Weisskopf, illustrated by R. Paul Larkin; Doubleday, 1962.

1964 BEST CHILDREN'S SCIENCE BOOK *The Globe for the Space Age* by S. Carl Hirsch, illustrated by Burt Silverman; Viking, 1963.

1964 SPECIAL EXCELLENCE IN CONTRIBUTING TO CHARACTER DEVELOPMENT OF CHILDREN *The Peaceable Revolution* by Betty Schechter, illustrated with photographs; Houghton, 1963.

1964 SPECIAL EXCELLENCE IN PORTRAYING AMERICA'S PAST *Voices from America's Past* by James Woodress and Richard B. Morris, illustrated with photographs; Dutton, 1963.

1964 BEST SCIENCE BOOK FOR YOUTH *You and Your Brain* by Judith Groch, illustrated by E.L. Sisley; Harper, 1963.

1965 BEST CHILDREN'S SCIENCE BOOK *The Universe of Galileo and Newton* by Giorgio de Santillana and William Bixby, illustrated with paintings and drawings; American Heritage, 1964.

1965 SPECIAL EXCELLENCE IN CONTRIBUTING TO CHARACTER DEVELOPMENT OF CHILDREN *The White Bungalow* by Aimee Sommerfelt, illustrated by Ulf Aas; Criterion, 1964.

1965 SPECIAL EXCELLENCE IN PORTRAYING AMERICA'S PAST *Yankee Doodle Boy: A Young Soldier's Adventure in the American Revolution Told by Himself* by Joseph Plumb Martin, edited by George F. Scheer, illustrated by Victor Mays; Scott, 1964.

1965 BEST SCIENCE BOOK FOR YOUTH *The Earth Beneath Us* by Kirtley F. Mather, illustrated by Howard Morris, photographs by Josef Muench; Random House, 1964.

1966 BEST CHILDREN'S SCIENCE BOOK *Biography of an Atom* by Millicent E. Selsam and Jacob Bronowski, illustrated by Weimer Pursell; Harper, 1965.

1966 SPECIAL EXCELLENCE IN CONTRIBUTING TO CHARACTER DEVELOPMENT OF CHILDREN *The Summer I Was Lost* by Phillip Viereck, illustrated by Ellen Viereck; Day, 1965.

1966 SPECIAL EXCELLENCE IN PORTRAYING AMERICA'S PAST *In Their Own Words: A History of the American Negro, vol. 2, 1865-1916* edited by Milton Meltzer, illustrated with photographs; Crowell, 1965.

1966 BEST SCIENCE BOOK FOR YOUTH *Explorations in Chemistry* by Charles A. Gray, illustrated with diagrams; Dutton, 1965.

1967 BEST CHILDREN'S SCIENCE BOOK *The Living Community: A Venture into Ecology* by S. Carl Hirsch, illustrated by William Steinel; Viking, 1966.

1967 SPECIAL EXCELLENCE IN CONTRIBUTING TO CHARACTER DEVELOPMENT OF CHILDREN *Boy Alone* by Reginald Ottley, illustrated by Clyde Pearson; Harcourt, 1966.

1967 SPECIAL EXCELLENCE IN PORTRAYING AMERICA'S PAST *Introduction to Tomorrow: The U.S. and the Wider World, 1945-1965* by Robert Abernethy, illustrated with photographs and maps; Harcourt, 1966.

1967 BEST SCIENCE BOOK FOR YOUTH *The Language of Life: An Introduction to the Science of Genetics* by Muriel Beadle and George Beadle, illustrated by Joseph M. Sedacca and others; Doubleday, 1966.

MARGARET A. EDWARDS AWARD
(formerly YASD/SLJ Author Achievement Award)
Young Adult Services Division
American Library Association
50 E. Huron St.
Chicago, IL 60611

The Margaret A. Edwards Award is sponsored by the School Library Journal and administered by the Young Adult Library Services Division of the American Library Association. Presented for the first time in 1988, the award was formerly called the School Library Journal/Young Adult Services Award. The purpose of this annual award is to "give recognition to those authors whose book or books have provided young adults with a window through which they can view the world, and which will help them to grow and understand themselves and their role in society." The award is presented to the winning author during the American Library Association annual conference.

1988   S. E. Hinton

1989   No Award

1990   Richard Peck

1991   Robert Cormier

1992   Lois Duncan

1993   M.E. Kerr

SHEILA A. EGOFF CHILDREN'S PRIZE

West Coast Book Prizes Society
100 West Pender St. Suite 107
Vancouver, British Columbia
V6B 1R8 Canada

Named in honor of children's literature scholar Sheila A. Egoff, this prize is awarded to the author of the best book written for children sixteen years of age and younger in the previous year. It is judged on its content and the originality of the story. The author and/or illustrator must have lived in British Columbia for three of the last five years, but the book may have been published anywhere in the world. Established in 1985 by the West Coast Book Prizes Society, the winner of the children's award receives $1500 and a certificate at the Gala Evening held each spring.

1987   *The Baby Project* by Sarah Ellis, not illustrated; Douglas & McIntyre, 1986; McElderry, 1988.

1988   *Pride of Lions* written and illustrated by Nicola Morgan; Fitzhenry-Whiteside, 1987; Houghton Mifflin, 1992.

1989   *Sunny* by Mary-Ellen Lang Collura, not illustrated; Irwin, 1988.

1990   *Tales From Gold Mountain* by Paul Yee, illustrated by Simon Ng; Douglas & McIntyre, 1989; Macmillan, 1989.

1991   *I Heard My Mother Call My Name* by Nancy Hundal, illustrated by Laura Fernandez; HarperCollins, 1990.

1992   *Siwiti: A Whale's Story* by Alexandra Morton, photos by Alexandra Morton and Robin Morton; Orca, 1991.

EMPHASIS ON READING

Alabama State Department of Education
50 North Ripley St.
Montgomery, AL 36130

Established by Joan Atkinson of the University of Alabama, this award seeks to motivate children to read. The award has three categories K-2, grades 3-5, and grades 6-8 and is sponsored by the Alabama State Department of Education. Fiction and nonfiction books that have been included in ALSC's Notable Books and Booklist Editor's Choices are eligible.

1980-81   **GRADES K-1** *Katy No-Pocket* by Emmy Payne, illustrated by H.A. Rey; Houghton Mifflin, 1944.

1980-81   **GRADES 2-3** *Charlotte's Web* by E.B. White, illustrated by Garth Williams; Harper & Row, 1952.

1980-81   **GRADES 4-6** *The Best Christmas Pageant Ever* by Barbara Robinson, illustrated by Judith Gwyn Brown; Harper, 1972.

1980-81   **GRADES 7-9** *The Hobbit* written and illustrated by J.R.R. Tolkien; Houghton Mifflin, 1938.

1980-81   **GRADES 10-12** *The Acorn People* by Ron Jones, illustrated by Tom Parker; Abingdon, 1978, c1976.

1981-82   **GRADES K-1** *The Runaway Bunny* by Margaret Wise Brown, illustrated by Clement Hurd; Harper & Row, 1942.

1981-82   **GRADES 2-3** *Granny and the Indians* by Peggy Parish, illustrated by Brinton Turkle; Macmillan, 1969.

1981-82   **GRADES 4-6** *Bunnicula: A Rabbit Tale of Mystery* by Deborah Howe and James Howe, illustrated by Alan Daniel; Atheneum, 1979.

1981-82   **GRADES 7-9** *Mayday! Mayday!* by Hilary H. Milton, not illustrated; Watts, 1979.

1981-82   **GRADES 10-12** *Christy* by Catherine Marshall, not illustrated; McGraw Hill, 1967.

1982-83   **GRADES K-1** *Sylvester and the Magic Pebble* written and illustrated by William Steig; Windmill/Simon & Schuster, 1969.

1982-83   **GRADES 2-3** *The Chocolate Chip Mystery* by John McInnes, illustrated by Paul Frame; Garrard, 1972.

1982-83   **GRADES 4-6** *Stuart Little* by E.B. White, illustrated by Garth Williams; Harper & Row, 1945.

1982-83   **GRADES 7-9** *Killing Mr. Griffin* by Lois Duncan, not illustrated; Little Brown, 1978.

1982-83   **GRADES 10-12** *Sunshine* by Norma Klein, not illustrated; Holt, Rinehart & Winston, 1975, c1974.

1983-84   **GRADES K-1** *The Big Orange Splot* written and illustrated by Daniel M. Pinkwater; Hastings House, 1977.

1983-84   **GRADES 2-3** *Ralph S. Mouse* by Beverly Cleary, illustrated by Paul O. Zelinsky; Morrow, 1982.

1983-84   **GRADES 4-6** *Nothing's Fair in Fifth Grade* by Barthe DeClements, not illustrated; Viking, 1981.

1983-84   **GRADES 7-9** *Unicorns in the Rain* by Barbara Cohen, not illustrated; Atheneum, 1980.

1983-84   **GRADES 10-12** *Cages of Glass, Flowers of Time* by Charlotte Culin, not illustrated; Bradbury, 1979.

1984-85   **GRADES K-1** *A Pocket for Corduroy* written and illustrated by Don Freeman; Viking, 1978.

1984-85   **GRADES 2-3** *The Great Green Turkey Creek Monster* written and illustrated by James Flora; Atheneum, 1976.

1984-85   **GRADES 4-6** *The Boxcar Children* by Gertrude Warner, illustrated by L. Kate Deal; Whitman, c1942.

1984-85   **GRADES 7-9** *A Tangle of Roots* by Barbara Girion, not illustrated; Scribner, 1979.

1984-85   **GRADES 10-12** *Grendel* by John Gardner, illustrated by Emil Antonucci; Knopf, 1971.

1985-86 GRADES K-1 *The Pain and the Great One* by Judy Blume, illustrated by Irene Trivas; Bradbury, 1984.

1985-86 GRADES 2-3 *The Adventures of Albert, the Running Bear* by Barbara Isenberg and Susan Wolf, illustrated by Dick Gackenbach; Clarion, 1982.

1985-86 GRADES 4-6 *Superfudge* by Judy Blume, not illustrated; Dutton, 1980.

1985-86 GRADES 7-9 *The Divorce Express* by Paula Danziger, not illustrated; Delacorte, 1982; Dell, 1983.

1985-86 GRADES 10-12 *Him She Loves?* by M.E. Kerr, not illustrated; Harper & Row, 1984.

1986-87 GRADES K-1 *If You Give a Mouse a Cookie* by Laura J. Numeroff, illustrated by Felicia Bond; Harper and Row, 1985.

1986-87 GRADES 2-3 *The New Kid on the Block* by Jack Prelutsky, illustrated by James Stevenson; Greenwillow, 1984.

1986-87 GRADES 4-6 *Stone Fox* by John Reynolds Gardiner, illustrated by Marcia Sewall; Crowell, 1980.

1986-87 GRADES 7-9 *You Never Can Tell* by Ellen Conford, not illustrated; Pocket Books, 1985.

1986-87 GRADES 10-12 *Yeager, an Autobiography* by Chuck Yeager and Leo Janos, illustrated with photographs; Bantam, 1985.

1987-88 GRADES K-1 *My Teacher Sleeps in School* by Leatie Weiss, illustrated by Ellen Weiss; Warne, 1984.

1987-88 GRADES 2-3 *My Mother Never Listens To Me* by Marjorie Weinman Sharmat, illustrated by Lynn Munsinger; Whitman, 1984.

1987-88 GRADES 4-6 *The Dollhouse Murders* by Betty Ren Wright, not illustrated; Holiday House, 1983.

1987-88 GRADES 7-9 *Revenge of the Nerd* by John McNamara, not illustrated; Dell, 1985, c1984.

1987-88 GRADES 10-12 *Wart, Son of Toad* by Alden R. Carter, not illustrated; Pacer/Putnam, 1985.

1988-89 GRADES K-2 *No Jumping on the Bed!* written and illustrated by Tedd Arnold; Dial, 1987.

1988-89 GRADES 3-5 *The War With Grandpa* by Robert Kimmel Smith, illustrated by Richard Lauter; Delacorte, 1984.

1988-89 GRADES 6-8 *No Swimming in Dark Pond and Other Chilling Tales* by Judith Gorog; not illustrated; Philomel, 1987.

1988-89 GRADES 9-12 *The Princess Bride* by William Goldman; Ballantine, 1987.

1989-90 GRADES K-2 *The Little Old Man Who Could Not Read* by Irma S. Black, illustrated by Seymour Fleishman; Whitman, 1968.

1989-90 GRADES 3-5 *In Trouble Again, Zelda Hammersmith?* by Lynn Hall, not illustrated; Harcourt Brace Jovanovich, 1987.

1989-90 GRADES 6-8 *Mad, Mad, Monday* by Herma Silverstein, not illustrated; Dutton, 1988.

1989-90 GRADES 9-12 No Award

1990-91 GRADES K-2 *The Socksnatchers* written and illustrated by Lorna Balian; Abingdon, 1988.

1990-91 GRADES 3-5 *More Scary Stories to Tell in the Dark* by Alvin Schwartz, illustrated by Stephen Gammell; Lippincott, 1984.

1990-91 GRADES 6-8 *The Glory Girl* by Betsy Byars, not illustrated; Viking, 1983.

1990-91 GRADES 9-12 *Walking Across Egypt* by Clyde Edgerton, not illustrated; Algonquin, 1987.

EMPIRE STATE AWARD FOR EXCELLENCE IN LITERATURE FOR YOUNG PEOPLE

New York Library Association
Youth Services Section
252 Hudson Ave.
Albany, NY 11210

Established in 1990, the Empire State Award honors a body of work which represents excellence in children's or young adult literature and has made a significant contribution to literature for young people. The author or illustrator must currently reside in New York state. A medal is presented to the recipient at the annual New York Library Association convention.

1990 Maurice Sendak

1991 Madeleine L'Engle

1992 Leo Dillon, Diane Dillon

1993 Russell Freedman

ETHICAL CULTURE SCHOOL BOOK AWARD

Ethical Culture School
33 Central Park West
New York, NY 10023

Awarded annually in the Spring, this award was originated by Allan Shedlin, Jr. The original idea came from the school children, who were unhappy with the fact that only adults generally pass critical judgment on the merits of children's literature. Books that are considered for the award must have been originally published in the U.S. during the preceding year and written at a level appropriate for grades four through six.

The titles considered must fall into a specific subject category for that particular five-year period. From 1975-1979, humorous fiction was considered. Fantasy was judged from 1980-84. In 1985 the category was Humorous Fiction; 1987 was Mystery; 1988-89 was Humorous Fiction again, with Mystery in 1990.

Fourth through sixth-grade students from the Midtown Ethical Culture School cast votes for their favorite books. All of the procedures involved in choosing the award winner are handled by a committee of fourth-grade students, aided by a librarian. With the help of a drama teacher, the group writes and performs a skit based on a favorite scene from the award winning book. The winning author is invited to attend the ceremony in order to receive the scroll and to visit with the children.

1975 *The Great Christmas Kidnapping Caper* by Jean Van Leeuwen, illustrated by Steven Kellogg; Dial, 1975.

1976 *The Champion of Merrimack County* by Roger W. Drury, illustrated by Fritz Wegner; Little Brown, 1976.

1977 *In Summertime, it's Tuffy* by Judie Angell, not illustrated; Bradbury, 1977.

1978 *Sideways Stories from Wayside School* by Louis Sachar, illustrated by Dennis Hockerman; Follett, 1978.

1979 *A Word from our Sponsor: or, My Friend Alfred* by Judie Angell, not illustrated; Bradbury, 1979.

1980 *King Tut's Game Board* by Leona Ellerby, not illustrated; Lerner, 1980.

1981 *Stranger with my Face* by Lois Duncan, not illustrated; Little Brown, 1981; Dell, 1982.

1982 *Dragon of the Lost Sea* by Laurence Yep, not illustrated; Harper, 1982.

1983 *The Owlstone Crown* by X.J. Kennedy, illustrated by Michele Chessare; Atheneum, 1983.

1984 *Witch Cat* by Joan Carris, illustrated by Beth Peck; Lippincott, 1984.

1985 *Buddies* by Barbara Park, not illustrated; Knopf, 1985.

1986 No Award

1987 *Chelsey and the Green-Haired Kid* by Carol Gorman, not illustrated; Houghton Mifflin, 1987.

1988 *Matilda* by Roald Dahl, illustrated by Quentin Blake; Viking Kestrel, 1988.

1989 *Alice in Rapture, Sort of* by Phyllis Reynolds Naylor, not illustrated; Atheneum, 1989.

1990 *The Dead Man in Indian Creek* by Mary Downing Hahn, not illustrated; Clarion, 1989.

1991 *Wings* by Bill Brittain, not illustrated; HarperCollins, 1991.

F

FABER/JACKANORY/GUARDIAN CHILDREN'S WRITERS COMPETITION
Faber & Faber
3 Queen Square
London WC1N 3AU
England

So far, this prize has been awarded only one time, in 1989, but there are plans to make it an annual competition. The program was set up to discover new writing talent in the area of children's fiction. Any previously unpublished author could submit a manuscript of approximately 25,000 words. The winning manuscript was published by Faber & Faber.

Andi's War by Billi Rosen, illustrated with maps; Faber & Faber, 988; Dutton, 1989.

JEANETTE FAIR AWARD
Tau State
Delta Kappa Gamma

This biennial award was established in 1988 by the Tau State (Minnesota) Delta Kappa Gamma Society to honor Jeanette Fair, a longtime, outstanding elementary school teacher and principal. The award is given to recognize an outstanding book by a Minnesota woman. The book must be creative, with a fresh approach to the subject, contribute to knowledge, and have a wide appeal.

The book must have been published within five years of the award. Both adult and children's books are considered, although text books and picture books are excluded. A cash award is presented to the recipient at the state convention of Delta Kappa Gamma.

1989 *On My Honor* by Marion Dane Bauer, not illustrated; Clarion, 1986.

1991 *The Riddle of Penncroft Farm* by Dorothea Jensen; Harcourt, Brace, Jovanovich, 1989.

1993 presented to an adult book

FAMILY AWARD
New South Wales Family Therapy Association
P O Box 27
Rozelle, New South Wales 2039
Australia

Presented by the New South Wales Family Therapy Association, this award recognizes a book that contains "a realistic and balanced depiction of family life according to what are known to be the characteristics of a healthy family." A $1000 cash prize is presented during Children's Book Week.

1987 *Deezle Boy* by Eleanor Spence, not illustrated; Collins Dove, 1987.

1988 *You Take the High Road* by Mary Pershall, not illustrated; Penguin, 1988.

1989 *The Blue Chameleon* by Katherine Scholes, illustrated by David Wong; Hill of Content, 1989.

1990 *Two Weeks With the Queen* by Morris Gleitzman, not illustrated; Pan, 1990.

1992 *Crossfire* by James Moloney, not illustrated; University of Queensland Press, 1992.

ELEANOR FARJEON AWARD
Children's Book Circle
Awards Committee
Fiona Kenshole
A & C Black Co.
35 Bedford Row
London WC1R 4JH
England

The Eleanor Farjeon Award was established by the Children's Book Circle in 1965 and is also sponsored by Books for Children. This annual award, honoring the well-known children's writer, is presented to a professional of extraordinary achievement involved in any aspect of children's books. The candidates are nominated by members of the Children's Book Circle and seconded by two other members of the Circle. Final selection is made by an eight-member committee. The award, £500, plus a certificate, is presented to the winner at a party held in May or June in London.

1965 Margery Fisher

1966 Jessica Jenkins

1967 Brian Alderson

1968 Anne Wood

1969 Kaye Webb

1970 Margaret Meek

1971   Janet Hill

1972   Eleanor Graham

1973   Leila Berg

1974   Naomi Lewis

1975   Joyce Oldmeadow, Court Oldmeadow

1976   Elaine Moss

1977   Peter Kennerley

1978   Joy Whitby

1979   Dorothy Butler

1980   Margaret Marshall

1981   Virginia Jensen

1982   Aidan Chambers, Nancy Chambers

1983   Jean Russell

1984   Shirley Hughes

1985   Robert Leeson

1986   Judith Elkin

1987   Valerie Bierman

1989   Anna Home

1990   Jill Bennett

1991   Patricia Crampton

1992   Stephanie Nettell

1993   Susan Belgrave

JOAN FASSLER MEMORIAL BOOK AWARD
Association for the Care of Children's Health
7910 Woodmont Ave.
Suite 300
Bethesda, MD 20814

Established in 1989 to honor Joan Fassler, a noted child psychologist and author of seven children's books. The purpose of the award is to recognize outstanding contributions to children's literature dealing with hospitalization, illness, disabling conditions, dying, and death. To be eligible, the book must be commercially published or released in the English language during the preceding two year period.

Selection criteria include accuracy of content, good model for coping and mastery, and must be age and developmentally appropriate. A plaque, a $1000 honorarium, and membership in the ACCH is awarded annually at the organization's conference.

1989   *Saying Goodbye to Grandma* by Jane Resh Thomas, illustrated by Marcia Sewall; Clarion, 1988.

1990   *How It Feels To Fight for Your Life* by Jill Kremetz, illustrated with photographs; Little Brown, 1989.

1991   *The Canada Geese Quilt* by Natalie Kinsey-Warnock, illustrated by Leslie W. Bowman; Dodd Mead, 1988.

1992   *Colt* by Nancy Springer, not illustrated; Dial, 1991.

1993   *I Will Sing Life* by Larry Berger and Dahlia Lithwick and seven campers, photographs by Robert Benson; Little Brown, 1992.

FEATURE A CLASSIC
discontinued

This innovative award, sponsored by the Michigan Council of Teachers of English, was begun in 1980. Any books which were considered "classics" in children's literature, but were "out of phase" with contemporary children's reading were nominated. The award was voted on by teachers, librarians, and children's literature specialists.

1981   *The Yearling* by Marjorie Rawlings, illustrated by N.C. Wyeth; Scribner, 1961, 1939.

1982   *The Incredible Journey: A Tale of Three Animals* by Shelia Every Burnford, illustrated by Carl Burger; Little Brown, 1961.

1983   *The Wind in the Willows* by Kenneth Grahame, illustrated by Ernest H. Shepard; Scribner, 1954, c1908.

1984   *Folk Tales* by Jacob Grimm and Wilhelm Grimm, (various editions and publishers).

FEDERATION OF CHILDREN'S BOOK GROUPS AWARDS
see CHILDREN'S BOOK AWARD

KATHLEEN FIDLER AWARD
Scottish Book Centre
Fountainbridge Library
137 Dundee St.
Edinburgh EH11 1BG
Scotland

The Kathleen Fidler Award was established by Blackie Children's Books in association with the Edinburgh Children's Book Group. The award was named in memory of the Scottish children's book author who died in 1980. The aim of the award is to encourage young Scottish authors to write for eight to twelve year-olds.

Unpublished fiction manuscripts by authors under thirty years of age of Scottish parentage or resident in Scotland are eligible. Manuscripts are submitted by authors. A shortlist of the typescripts is submitted to a panel of children for their comments. These comments are taken into consideration by a panel of judges (adults with an interest in and knowledge of children's literature). The winning author receives a rosewood-and-silver trophy plus £250. Blackie will have the first option to publish the winning manuscript.

1983   *Adrift!* by Allan Baillie, not illustrated; Blackie, 1983.

1984   *No Shelter* by Elizabeth Lutzeier, not illustrated; Blackie, 1984.

1985   *Diamond* by Caroline Pitcher, not illustrated; Blackie, 1987.

1986   *Barty* by Janet Collins, not illustrated; Blackie, 1986.

1987   *Simon's Challenge* by Theresa Breslin, not illustrated; Blackie, 1988.

1988   *Flight of the Solar Ducks* by Charles Morgan, not illustrated; Blackie, 1988.

1989   *Mightier Than the Sword* by Clare Bevan, not illustrated; Blackie, 1989.

1990   *Magic With Everything* by Roger Burt, not illustrated; Blackie, 1990.

1991 *Greg's Revenge* by George Hendry, not illustrated; Blackie, 1991.

1992 *Richard's Castle* by Susan Coon, not illustrated; Blackie, 1992.

CAROLYN W. FIELD AWARD

Margaret S. Bauer, Executive Director
Pennsylvania Library Association
3107 N. Front St.
Harrisburg, PA 17110

The Carolyn W. Field Award is presented annually by the Youth Services Division of the Pennsylvania Library Association for the best book for young people by a Pennsylvania author or illustrator. The goal is to recognize outstanding books of authors or illustrators living in Pennsylvania. This award was established to honor Carolyn W. Field, former Director of the Office of Youth Services, Free Library of Philadelphia.

The following guidelines will be followed by the award committee: (1) given for a single book by any author or illustrator currently residing in Pennsylvania; (2) fiction or nonfiction, preschool through young adult; (3) literary or artistic merit will be the primary aspect considered, although popular appeal will also be recognized; (4) books to be judged will be from the previous year's copyright. Thus, the 1984 award is for books published in 1983.

1984 *Some Things Go Together* by Charlotte Zolotow, illustrated by Karen Gundersheimer; Crowell, 1983.

1985 *Saint George and the Dragon: A Golden Legend* adapted by Margaret Hodges from Edmund Spenser's Faerie Queene, illustrated by Trina Schart Hyman; Little Brown, 1984.

1986 *The New Baby* by Fred Rogers, photographs by Jim Judkis; Putnam, 1985.

1987 *The Illyrian Adventure* by Lloyd Alexander, illustrated with a map; Dutton, 1986.

1988 *Little Tree* by e.e. cummings, illustrated by Deborah Kogan Ray; Crown, 1987.

1989 *Catwings* by Ursula K. Le Guin, illustrated by S.D. Schindler; Orchard, 1988.

1990 *Box Turtle at Long Pond* by William T. George, illustrated by Lindsay Barrett George; Greenwillow, 1989.

1991 *Maniac Magee* by Jerry Spinelli, not illustrated; Little Brown, 1990.

1992 *I Am Regina* by Sally M. Keehn, not illustrated; Philomel, 1991.

HELEN DEAN FISH AWARD

discontinued

Established in honor of Miss Fish, a longtime editor of children's books at Lippincott, this award was first presented in 1953. The award was given to the best book by a new author on the current Lippincott list. A board of judges selected the winner. The winning author received $500 and a parchment scroll.

1953 *Little Witch* by Anna Elizabeth Bennett, illustrated by Helen Stone; Lippincott, 1953.

1954 *Little Angela and her Puppy* written and illustrated by Dorothy Marino; Lippincott, 1954.

1955 *The Whirly Bird* by Aylesa Forsee, illustrated by Tom Two Arrows; Lippincott, 1955.

DOROTHY CANFIELD FISHER CHILDREN'S BOOK AWARD

Vermont Congress of Parents and Teachers
Southwest Regional Library
Pierpont Ave.
Rutland, VT 05701

The purpose of this award, first given in 1957, is to encourage Vermont school children to read more and better books and to honor the memory of one of Vermont's most distinguished and beloved literary figures. The Dorothy Canfield Fisher Children's Book Award is the second oldest state children's book award in the U.S. and is cosponsored by the Vermont Department of Libraries and the Vermont PTA.

A Master List of thirty titles is selected each year by an adult committee of six readers and two consultants. To be eligible for inclusion in the master list, books must be of interest to children in grades four through eight, be written by a living American author, and of the current copyright year. Types of literature eligible include fiction, nonfiction, biography and poetry. In April, this Master List is sent to each school and public library in Vermont.

Children in the fourth through eighth grades are encouraged to read some of the books throughout the year. The following April each child has one vote for his or her favorite book. Announcement of the winner is made in May, with the presentation of an illuminated scroll to the author in June. All librarians, teachers, and participating students are invited to attend the ceremony.

Below are some of the criteria by which the committee composes the Master List. To be distinguished a book should: (1) have established appeal for the children for whom it is written; (2) have literary merit; (3) have qualities of originality, imagination, and vitality; (4) have an element of timelessness; (5) reflect the sincerity of the author in both purpose and treatment; (6) have sound moral values; (7) have a theme or subject worth imparting to, and of interest to, children; (8) have factual accuracy; (9) have clarity and readability; (10) have unity between pictures and text; (11) have a format suitable to content; and (12) be appropriate in subject, treatment, and format. (From Helen Kinsey's restatement of criteria for judging a distinguished book for children).

1957 *Old Bones, the Wonder Horse* by Mildred M. Pace, illustrated by Wesley Dennis; McGraw, 1955.

1958 *Fifteen* by Beverly Cleary, illustrated by Joe Krush and Beth Krush; Morrow, 1956.

1959 *Commanche of the Seventh* by Margaret C. Leighton, illustrated by Elliott Means; Farrar, 1957.

1960 *Double or Nothing* written and illustrated by Phoebe Erickson; Harper, 1958.

1961 *Captain Ghost* by Thelma H. Bell, illustrated by Corydon Bell; Viking, 1959.

1962 *The City under the Back Steps* by Evelyn Lampman, illustrated by Honore Valintcourt; Doubleday, 1960.

1963 *The Incredible Journey: A Tale of Three Animals* by Shelia Every Burnford, illustrated by Carl Burger; Little Brown, 1961.

1964 *Bristle Face* by Zachary Ball, not illustrated; Holiday House, 1962.

1965 *Rascal: A Memoir of a Better Era* by Sterling North, illustrated by John Schoenherr; Dutton, 1963.

1966 *Ribsy* by Beverly Cleary, illustrated by Louis Darling; Morrow, 1964.

1967 *The Summer I Was Lost* by Phillip Viereck, illustrated by Ellen Viereck; Day, 1965.

1968 *The Taste of Spruce Gum* by Jacqueline Jackson, illustrated by Lilian Obligado; Little Brown, 1966.

1969 *Two in the Wilderness* by Mary W. Thompson, illustrated by Tom O'Sullivan; McKay, 1967.

1970 *Kavik the Wolf Dog* by Walt Morey, illustrated by Peter Parnall; Dutton, 1968.

1971 *Go to the Room of the Eyes* by Betty K. Erwin, illustrated by Irene Burns; Little Brown, 1969.

1972 *Flight of the White Wolf* by Mel Ellis, not illustrated; Holt, 1970.

1973 *Never Steal a Magic Cat* by Don Caufield and Joan Caufield, illustrated by Jan Palmer; Doubleday, 1971.

1974 *Catch a Killer* by George A. Woods, not illustrated; Harper, 1972.

1975 *The Eighteenth Emergency* by Betsy Byars, illustrated by Robert Grossman; Viking, 1973.

1976 *The Toothpaste Millionaire* by Jean Merrill, illustrated by Jan Palmer; Houghton, 1974.

1977 *A Smart Kid Like You* by Stella Pevsner, not illustrated; Seabury, 1974.

1978 *Summer of Fear* by Lois Duncan, not illustrated; Little Brown, 1976.

1979 *Kid Power* by Susan Beth Pfeffer, illustrated by Leigh Grant; Watts, 1977.

1980 *Bones on Black Spruce Mountain* by David Budbill, not illustrated; Dial, 1978.

1981 *Bunnicula: A Rabbit Tale of Mystery* by Deborah Howe and James Howe; illustrated by Alan Daniel; Atheneum, 1979, 1980.

1982 *The Hand-me-Down Kid* by Francine Pascal, not illustrated; Viking, 1980.

1983 *Tiger Eyes* by Judy Blume, not illustrated; Bradbury, 1981.

1984 *A Bundle of Sticks* by Pat Rhoads Mauser, illustrated by Gail Owens; Atheneum, 1982.

1985 *Dear Mr. Henshaw* by Beverly Cleary, illustrated by Paul O. Zelinsky; Morrow, 1983.

1986 *The War with Grandpa* by Robert Kimmel Smith, illustrated by Richard Lauter; Delacorte, 1984.

1987 *The Castle in the Attic* by Elizabeth Winthrop, illustrated by Trina Schart Hyman; Holiday House, 1985.

1988 *Wait Til Helen Comes* by Mary Downing Hahn, not illustrated; Clarion, 1986.

1989 *Hatchet* by Gary Paulsen, not illustrated; Bradbury, 1987.

1990 *Where It Stops, Nobody Knows* by Amy Ehrlich, not illustrated; Dial, 1988.

1991 *Number the Stars* by Lois Lowry, not illustrated; Houghton Mifflin, 1989.

1992 *Maniac Magee* by Jerry Spinelli, not illustrated; Little Brown, 1990.

FIT ASTRID LINDGREN TRANSLATION PRIZE

International Federation of Translators
Dr. Rene Haeseryn, Secretary General
Heiveldstraat 245
B-9110 Ghent
St. Amandsberg, Belgium

This international award is sponsored by children's author Astrid Lindgren and administered by the International Federation of Translation. It was established in 1981 to promote the translation of works written for children, improving the quality thereof and drawing attention to the role of the translation in bringing the peoples of the world closer together in the cultural field. Children's literature fiction and poetry translators are eligible for this triennial award. It may be given for a single translation of outstanding quality or for the entire work of a translator. Translators are nominated by a member society of FIT and a diploma and/or a sum of money is presented during the FIT open congresses.

1981 Ake Holmberg (Sweden)

1984 Patricia Crampton (United Kingdom)

1987 Lieselotte Remane (German Democratic Republic)

1990 (tie) Lyudmila Braude (USSR); Anthea Bell (United Kingdom) .

PERCY FITZPATRICK AWARD

South African Institute for Librarianship
 and Information Science
P O Box 36575
Menlo Park, Pretoria 0102
Republic of South Africa

First awarded in 1979, the Percy Fitzpatrick Award was established by the South African Library Association to recognize the best South African children's book in the English language. The award honors Percy Fitzpatrick, author of Jock of the Bushveld, the first South African book for children written in English. A biennial award since 1982, a medal is presented to the author of an English book written by an English author living in South Africa.

1979 *The Mantis and the Moon* by Marguerite Poland, illustrated by Leigh Voight; Raven Press, 1979.

1980-1983 No Award

1984 *The Wood-ash Stars* by Marguerite Poland, illustrated by Shanne Altshuler; David Philip, 1983.

1986 No Award

1988 *The Strollers* by Lesley Beake, illustrated by David Vickers; Maskew Miller Longman, 1987.

1990 *A Cageful of Butterflies* by Lesley Beake, not illustrated; Maskew Miller Longman, 1989.

FLORIDA READING ASSOCIATION (FRA) CHILDREN'S BOOK AWARD

Florida Reading Association

Sponsored by the Florida Reading Association, this children's choice award is given for a book suitable for children preschool through grade two. To be eligible, the book must be published in English during the preceding five years. The Master List is determined by a committee of adults, while the winning title is chosen by the students.

1990 *There's an Alligator Under My Bed* written and illustrated by Mercer Mayer; Dial, 1987.

1991 *The Magic School Bus at the Waterworks* by Joanna Cole, illustrated by Bruce Degen; Scholastic, 1986.

FOCAL (FRIENDS OF CHILDREN AND LITERATURE) AWARD

Children's Services
Los Angeles Public Library
630 West Fifth St
Los Angeles, CA 90071-2097

The FOCAL award was first given in 1980 for excellence in a creative work which enriches a child's appreciation for a knowledge of California. This competition is sponsored by the Los Angeles Public Library. The award is a handcrafted puppet that represents a character from the author's book. A copy of the puppet is also retained by the library. The winning book is adapted for use as a puppet show.

1980 *Pedro, the Angel of Olvera Street* written and illustrated by Leo Politi; Scribner, 1946.

1981 *Island of the Blue Dolphins* by Scott O'Dell, not illustrated; Houghton Mifflin, 1960.

1982 *Blue Willow* by Doris Gates, illustrated by Paul Lantz; Viking, 1940.

1983 *By the Great Horn Spoon!* by Sid Fleischman, illustrated by Eric Von Schmidt; Atlantic-Little, 1963.

1984 *Dragonwings* by Laurence Yep, not illustrated; Harper, 1975.

1985 *Julia and the Hand of God* by Eleanor Cameron, illustrated by Gail Owens; Dutton, 1977.

1986 *A Jar of Dreams* by Yoshiko Uchida, not illustrated; Atheneum, 1981.

1987 *Dear Mr. Henshaw* by Beverly Cleary, illustrated by Paul O. Zelinsky; Morrow, 1983.

1988 *Farewell To Manzanar* by Jeanne Wakatsuki Houston and James D. Houston, not illustrated; Houghton Mifflin, 1973.

1989 *A Room Made of Windows* by Eleanor Cameron, illustrated by Trina Schart Hyman; Little Brown, 1971.

1990 *Come the Morning* by Mark Jonathan Harris, not illustrated; Bradbury, 1989.

1991 *The Great American Gold Rush* by Rhoda Blumberg, illustrated with photos; Bradbury, 1989.

CHARLES W. FOLLETT AWARD

discontinued

Presented annually for a worthy contribution to children's literature, the Charles W. Follett Award was first given in 1950. From 1950 to 1967 the award was given for a manuscript, fiction or nonfiction, written for children eight through twelve years old or for teenage readers. From 1967 to 1972, the award was given for the best children's book published by the Follett Publishing Company during the preceding year. The judging was done by a committee of people who worked with children and children's literature. The winning author received a $3000 cash prize as well as the gold Follett award medal. The presentation was usually made at a luncheon during the ALA annual conference.

1950 *Johnny Texas* by Carol Hoff, illustrated by Bob Meyers; Wilcox & Follett, 1950.

1951 *All-of-a-Kind Family* by Sydney Taylor, illustrated by Helen John; Follett, 1951.

1952 *Thirty-one Brothers and Sisters* by Reba Paeff Mirsky, illustrated by W.T. Mars; Follett, 1952.

1953 *Tornado Jones* By Trella Lamson Dick, illustrated by Mary Stevens; Wilcox & Follett, 1953.

1954 *Little Wu and the Watermelons* by Beatrice Liu, illustrated by Graham Peck; Follett, 1954.

1955 *Minutemen of the Sea* by Tom Cluff, illustrated by Tom O'Sullivan; Follett, 1955.

1956 No Award

1957 *Chucho: The Boy with the Good Name* by Eula Mark Phillips, illustrated by Howard Simon; Follett, 1957.

1958 *South Town* by Lorenz Graham, not illustrated; Follett, 1958.

1959 *Model-A Mule* by Robert J. Willis, illustrated by Victor Mays; Follett, 1959.

1960 *What Then, Raman?* by Shirley Lease Arora, illustrated by Hans Guggenheim; Follett, 1960.

1961 No Award

1962 *Me and Caleb* by Franklyn E. Meyer, illustrated by Lawrence B. Smith; Follett, 1962.

1963 No Award

1964 *Across Five Aprils* by Irene Hunt, illustrated by Albert J. Pucci; Follett, 1964.

1965-1966 No Award

1967 *Lions in the Way* by Bella Rodman, not illustrated; Follett, 1966.

1968 *Marc Chagall* by Howard Greenfeld, illustrated by Marc Chagall; Follett, 1967.

1969 *Banner over Me* by Margery F. Greenleaf, illustrated by Charles Mikolaycak; Follett, 1968.

1970 *The War for the Lot: A Tale of Fantasy and Terror* by Sterling E. Lanier, illustrated by Robert Baumgartner; Follett, 1969.

1971 *No Promises in the Wind* by Irene Hunt, not illustrated; Follett, 1970.

1972 *A Horse Called Dragon* by Lynn Hall, illustrated by Joseph Cellini; Follett, 1971.

FOLLETT BEGINNING-TO-READ AWARD

discontinued

Established by the Follett Publishing Company in 1957, this annual award was first presented in 1958. The purpose of the award was to stimulate authors to provide interesting and lively books for the beginning reader. Any author of a manuscript written for first through third graders to read to themselves was eligible. Follett accepted manuscripts from July 1 until December 31 of the award year. An award of $2000 was made to the author when the manuscript was published.

1958 *Nobody Listens To Andrew* by Elizabeth Guilfoile, illustrated by Mary Stevens; Follett, 1957.

1959 *The Boy Who Would not Say His Name* by Elizabeth Vreekin, illustrated by Leonard Shortall; Follett, 1959.

1960 *The Hole in the Hill* by Marion Seyton, illustrated by Leonard Shortall; Follett, 1960.

1961 *The O'Leary's and Friends* by Jean H. Berg, illustrated by Mary Stevens; Follett, 1961.

JULIA ELLSWORTH FORD FOUNDATION AWARD
discontinued

The Julia Ellsworth Ford Foundation was created in 1934 for the encouragement of unusual and imaginative efforts in the field of children's literature. A yearly competition was sponsored by the Foundation and was open to all U.S. authors. Any unpublished manuscript written in English for children was eligible. The awards were administered by the Julian Messner Company from 1939 to 1950, when the award was discontinued. A cash prize of $3000 accompanied by publication of the manuscript by Julian Messner was awarded to the winning author.

1937 *My Brother Was Mozart* by Claire Lee Purdy and Benson Wheeler, illustrated by Theodore Nadejen; Holt, 1937.

The Stage-Struck Seal written and illustrated by James Hull; Holt, 1937.

1938 *Hello, the Boat!* by Phyllis Crawford, illustrated by Edward Laning; Holt, 1938.

1939 *Falcon, Fly Back* written and illustrated by Elinore Blaisdell; Messner, 1939.

1940 *The Listening Man* by Lucy Embury, illustrated by Russel Hamilton; Messner, 1940.

1941 *Walt Whitman, Builder for America* by Babette Deutsch, illustrated by Raphael Busoni; Messner, 1941.

1942 *Journey Cake* by Isabel McLennan McMeekin, illustrated by Nicholas Panesis; Messner, 1942.

1943 *Valiant Minstrel: The Story of Sir Harry Lauder* by Gladys Malvern, illustrated by Corinne Malvern; Messner, 1943.

1944 *Raymond L. Ditmars: His Exciting Career with Reptiles, Insects and Animals* by Laura Newbold Wood, illustrated with photographs; Messner, 1944.

1945 *The Wonderful Year* by Nancy Barnes, illustrated by Kate Seredy; Messner, 1946.

1946 *A Horse to Remember* by Genevieve T. Eames, illustrated by Paul Brown; Messner, 1947.

1947 *Joe Magarac and his U.S.A. Citizenship Papers* by Irwin Shapiro, illustrated by James Daugherty; Messner, 1948.

1948 *A Canvas Castle* by Alice Rogers Hager, illustrated by Mary Stevens; Messner, 1949.

1949 *Tomas and the Red-headed Angel* by Marion Garthwaite, illustrated by Lorence F. Bjorklund; Messner, 1950.

1950 *The Lost Kingdom* by Chester Bryant, illustrated by Margaret Ayer; Messner, 1951.

FRIENDS OF AMERICAN WRITERS JUVENILE BOOK MERIT AWARD
Friends of American Writers

Sponsored by the Friends of American Writers, these annual awards for juvenile books were first given in 1960. The categories are young adult, middle ages, beginning reader, and author/illus-trator. Books are submitted by publishers and must meet the following criteria to be eligible: (1) The book must have been published during the preceding calendar year; (2) The author must live or have lived in one of the following states: Arkansas, Illinois, Indiana, Iowa, Kansas, Kentucky, Michigan, Minnesota, Mississippi, North Dakota, Nebraska, Ohio, Oklahoma, South Dakota, Tennessee, Wisconsin, or the book must be in one of those regions; (3) The author must have previously published fewer than six books in the juvenile field; (4) The author must have received no previous monetary award of $250 or more or previous award in a duplicate category from the Friends of American Writers; (5) The categories are for readers through high-school age, books for beginning readers, or for reading aloud. Fiction, nonfiction, biographies, histories, etc. (except poetry), in hardcover format will be considered.

Final selection of the winning titles is made by a committee of seven members of the Friends of American Writers (the juvenile awards committee). Each book is judged in the following ten categories and each is scored from one to five with the highest rating being fifty: (1) appearance, (2) well-written for age bracket, (3) plot, (4) setting, (5) theme, (6) characterizations, (7) style, (8) illustration, (9) other considerations, and (10) whether children will read the book.

A certificate of merit along with a $300 cash prize is given to each winning author. The publisher of the book receives a certificate of merit. The awards are presented at a spring awards luncheon in Chicago.

1960 *First Boy on the Moon: A Junior Science Fiction Novel* by Clifford B. Hicks, illustrated by George Wilde; Winston, 1959.

1961 *Sequoyah, Young Cherokee Guide* by Dorothea J. Snow, illustrated by Frank Giacoia; Bobbs-Merrill, 1960.

1962 *Hostage to Alexander* by Mary Evans Andrews, illustrated by Avery Johnson; McKay, 1961.

1963 *Cathie and the Paddy Boy* written and illustrated by Nora Tully MacAlvay; Viking, 1962.

1964 *I Jessie: A Biography of the Girl who Married John Charles Fremont* by Ruth Painter Randall, illustrated with photographs; Little Brown, 1963.

1965 *The Far-off Land* by Rebecca Caudill, illustrated by Brinton Turkle; Viking, 1964.

1966-1968 No Award

1969 *Jud* by Charles Raymond, not illustrated; Houghton, 1968.

1970 *Trailblazer: Negro Nurse in the American Red Cross* by Jean Maddern Pitrone, illustrated with photographs; Harcourt, 1969.

1971 *Touch of Light: The Story of Louis Braille* by Anne E. Neimark, illustrated by Robert Parker; Harcourt, 1970.

1972 *War Work* by Zibby Oneal, illustrated by George Porter; Viking, 1971.

1973 **AGES 4-8** *The Winter Cat* written and illustrated by Howard Knotts; Harper, 1972.

1973 **AGES 10-14** *Foal Creek* by Peter Cohen, illustrated by Allan Moyler; Atheneum, 1972.

1973 **ILLUSTRATOR** *Authorized Autumn Charts of the Upper Red Canoe River Country* by Peter Cohen, illustrated by Tomie de Paola; Atheneum, 1972.

1974 **AGES 4-8** *Six Days from Sunday* by Betty Biesterveld, illustrated by George Armstrong; Rand, 1973.

1974 AGES 10-14 *The Long Hungry Night* by Slim Williams and Elizabeth C. Foster, illustrated by Glo Coalson; Atheneum, 1973.

1974 ILLUSTRATOR *The Long Hungry Night* by Slim Williams and Elizabeth C. Foster; illustrated by Glo Coalson; Atheneum, 1973.

1975 AGES 4-8 No Award

1975 AGES 10-14 *The Tartar's Sword* by Eric A. Kimmel, illustrated with maps; Coward, 1974.

1975 ILLUSTRATOR *Kongo and Kumba: Two Gorillas* by Alice Schick, illustrated by Joseph Cellini; Dial, 1974.

1976 YOUNGER *I'm Moving* by Martha W. Hickman, illustrated by Leigh Grant; Abingdon, 1974.

1976 OLDER *First Step* by Anne Snyder, not illustrated; Holt, 1975.

The Ghost Belonged to Me by Richard Peck, not illustrated; Viking, 1975.

1976 ILLUSTRATOR *The Devil Did It* written and illustrated by Susan Jeschke; Holt, 1975.

1977 YOUNGER No Award

1977 OLDER *Toby, Granny and George* by Robbie Branscum, illustrated by Glen Rounds; Doubleday, 1976.

The Revolutionary Age of Andrew Jackson by Robert V. Remini, illustrated with photographs; Harper, 1976.

1977 ILLUSTRATOR *Little Fox Goes to the End of the World* by Ann Tompert, illustrated by John Wallner; Crown, 1976.

1978 YOUNGER *Loosen your Ears* by Carol Farley, illustrated by Mila Lazarevich; Atheneum, 1977.

1978 OLDER *The Dream Runner* by Audree Distad, not illustrated; Harper, 1977.

1978 ILLUSTRATION No Award

1979 OLDER *A Clearing in the Forest* by Gloria Whelan, not illustrated; Putnam, 1978.

Harvey, the Beer Can King by Jamie Gilson, illustrated by John Wallner; Lothrop Lee & Shepard, 1978.

1979 SPECIAL ARTISTIC AWARD *On the Forest Edge* written and illustrated by Carol Lerner; Morrow, 1978.

1980 OLDER *Between Dark and Daylight* by Crystal Thrasher, not illustrated; Atheneum, 1979.

Grey Cloud by Charlotte Towner Graeber, illustrated by Lloyd Bloom; Four Winds, 1979.

1980 AUTHOR/ILLUSTRATOR *The King at the Door* written and illustrated by Brock Cole; Doubleday, 1979.

1981 OLDER *Weird Henry Berg* by Sarah Sargent, not illustrated; Crown, 1980.

1981 YOUNG ADULT *The Snowbird* by Patricia Calvert, not illustrated; Scribner, 1980.

1981 AUTHOR/ILLUSTRATOR *Stickelwort and Feverfew* written and illustrated by Robert D. Sutherland; Pikestaff Press, 1980.

1982 $500 AWARD *Beyond Two Rivers* by David Kherdian, not illustrated; Greenwillow, 1981.

1982 $350 AWARD *A Matter of Pride* by Emily Crofford, illustrated by Jim LaMarche; Carolrhoda Books, 1981.

1983 $500 AWARD *The Land I Lost: Adventures of a Boy in Vietnam* by Quang Nhuong Huynh, photographs by Vo-Dinh Mai; Harper, 1982.

1983 $350 AWARD *Bloodroot Flower* by Kathy Callaway, not illustrated; Knopf, 1982.

1984 $500 AWARD *Raspberry One* by Charles Ferry, not illustrated; Houghton Mifflin, 1983.

1984 $350 AWARD *Ike and Porker* by Susan E. Kirby, not illustrated; Houghton Mifflin, 1983.

1985 $500 AWARD *Rodeo Summer* by Judie Gulley, not illustrated; Houghton Mifflin, 1984.

1985 $350 AWARD *The Goodnight Circle* by Carolyn Lesser, illustrated by Lorinda Bryan Cauley; Harcourt, 1984.

1986 $500 AWARD *Where the Pirates Are* by Tom Townsend, illustrated; Eakin Press, 1985.

1986 $350 AWARD *Wolf of Shadows* by Whitley Strieber, not illustrated; Sierra Club/Knopf, 1985.

1987 $500 AWARD *Rover and Coo Coo* by John Hay, illustrated by Tim Solliday; Green Tiger Press, 1986.

1987 $350 AWARD *Adventure Beyond the Clouds* by Joseph E. Murphy, illustrated with photographs; Dillon Press, 1986.

1988 *Lighthouse Keeper's Daughter* by Arielle North Olson, illuatrated by Elaine Wentworth; Little Brown, 1987.

Island of Peril by Raboo Rodgers, not illustrated; Houghton Mifflin, 1987.

1989 *Tonia the Tree* by Sandy Stryker, illustrated by Itoko Maeno; Advocacy Press, 1988.

The Secret Friendship by Virginia Brosseit, not illustrated; Winston-Derek, 1988.

1990 *Dying Sun* by Gary L. Blackwood, not illustrated; Atheneum, 1989.

Unlived Affections by George Shannon, not illustrated; Harper & Row, 1989.

1991 *Boy in the Moon* by Ron Koertge, not illustrated; Little Brown, 1990.

Night Owls by Sharon Phillips Denslow, illustrated by Jill Kastner; Bradbury, 1990.

G

GARAVI GUJARAT RACIAL HARMONY BOOK AWARDS

discontinued

The Garavi Gujarat Awards were first presented in 1982 for the adult and children's books which "most effectively contribute to the theme of racial harmony." Any work of fiction, nonfiction, prose or poetry was eligible as long as the theme of the work was racial harmony; for example, human rights, race relations, comparative religions, and ethnic minorities. The winner of the children's category received a 100 pound cash award. The winner in the children's category is listed below.

1982 *The Story of Prince Rama* by Brian Thompson, illustrated by Roy Jeroo and original paintings; Kestrel, 1980.

GARDEN STATE CHILDREN'S BOOK AWARD

Honors & Awards Committee
New Jersey Library Association
Box 1534
Trenton, NJ 08607

The Children's Services Section of the New Jersey Library Association established the Garden State Children's Book Awards in 1977. The purpose of the awards is to show recognition for early and middle grade books and to encourage, stimulate, and captivate the potential readers through the printed word and good illustrations. These annual awards are presented in three categories: Easy to Read (as determined by the publisher), Younger Fiction (grades 2-5), and Younger Nonfiction (grades 2-5).

The awards committee is composed of four members who work directly with children in public libraries. These members are appointed yearly by the children's services executive board to choose the books for the ballot. The eligible books are new American hardcover titles, that have literary merit as well as popularity with readers. The awards are voted on by all section members, who are requested to base their decision on the book's popularity in their library. The books are considered as a whole, thus both author and illustrator are honored. The winners receive a framed certificate at the Children's Services Section dinner at the annual New Jersey Library Association conference.

1977 **EASY TO READ** *Dinosaur Time* by Peggy Parish, illustrated by Arnold Lobel; Harper, 1974.

1977 **YOUNGER FICTION** *Encyclopedia Brown Lends a Hand* by Donald J. Sobol, illustrated by Leonard Shortall; Nelson, 1974.

1977 **YOUNGER NONFICTION** *On the Track of Bigfoot* by Marian T. Place, illustrated with photographs; Dodd, Mead, 1974.

1978 **EASY TO READ** *Owl at Home* written and illustrated by Arnold Lobel; Harper, 1975.

1978 **YOUNGER FICTION** *Dorrie's Book* by Marilyn Sachs, illustrated by Anne Sachs; Doubleday, 1975.

1978 **YOUNGER NONFICTION** *How Kittens Grow* by Millicent E. Selsam, photographs by Esther Bubley; Four Winds, 1975, 1973.

1979 **EASY TO READ** *Hattie Rabbit* written and illustrated by Dick Gackenbach; Harper, 1976.

Heather's Feathers by Leatie Weiss, illustrated by Ellen Weiss; Watts, 1976.

1979 **YOUNGER FICTION** *Nobody Has to Be a Kid Forever* by Hila Colman, not illustrated; Crown, 1976.

1979 **YOUNGER NONFICTION** *A Very Young Dancer* written and illustrated by Jill Krementz; Knopf, 1976.

1980 **EASY TO READ** *Teach Us, Amelia Bedelia* by Peggy Parish, illustrated by Lynn Sweat; Greenwillow, 1977.

1980 **YOUNGER FICTION** *Ramona and Her Father* by Beverly Cleary, illustrated by Alan Tiegreen; Morrow, 1977.

1980 **YOUNGER NONFICTION** *The Quicksand Book* written and illustrated by Tomie de Paola; Holiday, 1977.

1981 **EASY TO READ** *Grasshopper on the Road* written and illustrated by Arnold Lobel; Harper, 1978.

1981 **YOUNGER FICTION** *The Great Gilly Hopkins* by Katherine Paterson, not illustrated; Crowell, 1978.

1981 **YOUNGER NONFICTION** *Tyrannosaurus Rex* by Millicent Selsam, illustrated with photographs; Harper, 1978.

1982 **EASY TO READ** *Mrs. Gaddy and the Ghost* by Wilson Gage, illustrated by Marylin Hafner; Greenwillow, 1979.

1982 **YOUNGER FICTION** *Ramona and her Mother* by Beverly Cleary, illustrated by Alan Tiegreen; Morrow, 1979; Dell/Yearling, 1980.

1982 **YOUNGER NONFICTION** *Mummies Made in Egypt* written and illustrated by Aliki; Harper & Row, 1979.

1983 **EASY TO READ** *Clams Can't Sing* written and illustrated by James Stevenson; Greenwillow, 1980.

Commander Toad in Space by Jane Yolen, illustrated by Bruce Degen; Coward McCann, 1980.

1983 **YOUNGER FICTION** *Superfudge* by Judy Blume, not illustrated; Dutton, 1980.

1983 **YOUNGER NONFICTION** *A Show of Hands: Say It in Sign Language* by Mary Beth and Linda Bourke with Susan Regen, illustrated by Linda Bourke; Addison Wesley, 1980.

1984 **EASY TO READ** *Nate the Great and the Missing Key* by Marjorie Sharmat, illustrated by Marc Simont; Coward, 1981.

1984 **YOUNGER FICTION** *Ramona Quimby, Age 8* by Beverly Cleary, illustrated by Alan Tiegreen; Morrow, 1981.

1984 **YOUNGER NONFICTION** *A Light in the Attic* by Shel Silverstein; Harper & Row, 1981.

1985 **EASY TO READ** *Nate the Great and the Snowy Trail* by Marjorie Sharmat, illustrated by Marc Simont; Coward, 1982.

1985 **YOUNGER FICTION** *Ralph S. Mouse* by Beverly Cleary, illustrated by Paul O. Zelinsky; Morrow, 1982.

1985 **YOUNGER NONFICTION** *It's BASIC: The ABC's of Computer Programming* by Shelley Lipson, illustrated by Janice Stapleton; Holt, 1982.

1986 **EASY TO READ** *M & M and the Bad News Babies* by Pat Ross, illustrated by Marylin Hafner; Knopf, 1983.

1986 **YOUNGER FICTION** *Dear Mr. Henshaw* by Beverly Cleary, illustrated by Paul Zelinsky; Morrow, 1983.

1986 **YOUNGER NONFICTION** *Draw 50 Monsters* written and illustrated by Lee Ames; Doubleday, 1983.

1987 **EASY TO READ** *In a Dark, Dark Room and other Scary Stories* retold by Alvin Schwartz, illustrated by Dirk Zimmer; Harper, 1984.

1987 **YOUNGER FICTION** *Anastasia, Ask your Analyst* by Lois Lowry, not illustrated; Houghton Mifflin, 1984.

1987 **YOUNGER NONFICTION** *The New Kid on the Block* by Jack Prelutsky, illustrated by James Stevenson; Greenwillow, 1984.

1988 EASY TO READ *Amelia Bedelia Goes Camping* by Peggy Parish, illustrated by Lynn Sweat; Greenwillow, 1985.

1988 YOUNGER FICTION *Sarah, Plain and Tall* by Patricia MacLachlan, not illustrated; Harper & Row, 1985.

1988 YOUNGER NONFICTION *How They Built the Statue of Liberty* by Mary J. Shapiro, illustrated by Huck Scarry; Random House, 1985.

1989 EASY TO READ *Merry Christmas, Amelia Bedelia* by Peggy Parish, illustrated by Lynn Sweat; Greenwillow, 1986.

1989 YOUNGER FICTION *Anastasia Has the Answers* by Lois Lowry, illustrated; Houghton Mifflin, 1986.

1989 YOUNGER NONFICTION *To Space and Back* by Sally Ride, illustrated with photos; Lothrop, Lee & Shepard, 1986.

1990 EASY TO READ *Henry and Mudge in Puddle Trouble* by Cynthia Rylant, illustrated by James Stevenson; Bradbury, 1987.

1990 YOUNGER FICTION *Nighty-nightmare* by James Howe, illustrated by Leslie Morrill; Atheneum, 1987.

1990 YOUNGER NONFICTION *Koko's Story* by Francine Patterson, photos by Ronald H. Cohn; Scholastic, 1987.

1991 EASY TO READ *Fox on the Job* written and illustrated by James Marshall ; Dial, 1988.

1991 YOUNGER FICTION *Teacher's Pet* by Johanna Hurwitz, illustrated by Sheila Hamanaka; Morrow, 1988.

The Burning Questions of Bingo Brown by Betsy Byars, illustrated by Cathy Bobak; Viking, 1988.

1991 YOUNGER NONFICTION *Volcanoes* by Seymour Simon, illustrated with photos; Morrow, 1988.

1992 EASY TO READ *Henry and Mudge Get the Cold Shivers* by Cynthia Rylant, illustrated by Sucie Stevenson; Bradbury, 1989.

1992 FICTION *Wayside School Is Falling Down* by Louis Sachar, illustrated by Joel Schick; Lothrop, Lee & Shepard, 1989.

1992 NONFICTION *The Magic School Bus Inside the Human Body* by Joanna Cole, illustrated by Bruce Degen; Scholastic, 1989.

1993 EASY TO READ *Henry and Mudge and the Happy Cat* by Cynthia Rylant, illustrated by Sucie Stevenson; Bradbury Press, 1990.

1993 YOUNGER FICTION *Muggie Maggie* by Beverly Cleary, illustrated by Kay Life; Morrow, 1990.

1993 YOUNGER NONFICTION *The Magic School Bus Lost in the Solar System* by Joanna Cole, illustrated by Bruce Degen; Scholastic, 1990.

GEORGIA CHILDREN'S BOOK AWARD

Carol J. Fisher
College of Education
University of Georgia
125 Aderhold Hall
Athens, GA 30602

The children's choice award program was begun in 1969 to encourage the reading of trade books as a regular part of the curriculum in grades four through eight. The program is sponsored by the University of Georgia College of Education. A master list of twenty titles published in the United States during the last five years (excluding Newbery titles) is composed. Georgia school children in grades four through eight who have read or heard read at least three of the books on the list are eligible to vote for their favorite.

The winning author is honored at the annual conference on children's literature in elementary education at the University and receives a plaque and a $400 award.

1969 *Skinny* by Robert Burch, illustrated by Don Sibley; Viking, 1964.

1970 *Ramona the Pest* by Beverly Cleary, illustrated by Louis Darling; Morrow, 1968.

1971 *Queenie Peavy* by Robert Burch, illustrated by Jerry Lazare; Viking, 1966.

1972 *J.T.* by Jane Wagner, illustrated by Gordon Parks, Jr.; Van Nostrand, 1969.

1973 *Hey, What's Wrong with this One?* by Maia Wojciechowska, illustrated by Joan Sandin; Harper, 1969.

1974 *Doodle and the Go-cart* by Robert Burch, illustrated by Alan Tiegreen; Viking, 1972.

1975 *A Taste of Blackberries* by Doris Buchanan Smith, illustrated by Charles Robinson; Crowell, 1973.

1976 *The Best Christmas Pageant Ever* by Barbara Robinson, illustrated by Judith Gwyn Brown; Harper, 1972.

1977 *Tales of a Fourth Grade Nothing* by Judy Blume, illustrated by Roy Doty; Dutton, 1972.

1978 *Freaky Friday* by Mary Rodgers, not illustrated; Harper, 1972.

1979 *The Pinballs* by Betsy Byars, not illustrated; Harper, 1977.

1980 *The Great Brain Does it Again* by John D. Fitzgerald, illustrated by Mercer Mayer; Dial, 1975.

1981 *The Great Gilly Hopkins* by Katherine Paterson, not illustrated; Crowell, 1978.

1982 *Don't Hurt Laurie!* by Willo Davis Roberts, illustrated by Ruth Sanderson; Atheneum, 1977.

1983 *Superfudge* by Judy Blume, not illustrated; Dutton, 1980.

1984 *Nothing's Fair in Fifth Grade* by Barthe DeClements, not illustrated; Viking, 1981.

1985 *Skinnybones* by Barbara Park, not illustrated; Random House, 1982.

1986 *The Secret Life of the Underwear Champ* by Betty Miles, illustrated by Dan Jones; Knopf, 1981.

1987 *Be a Perfect Person in Just Three Days* by Stephen Manes, not illustrated; Houghton Mifflin, 1982.

1988 *Christina's Ghost* by Betty Ren Wright, not illustrated; Holiday House, 1985.

1989 *The War With Grandpa* by Robert Kimmel Smith, illustrated by Richard Lauter; Delacorte, 1984.

1990 *There's a Boy in the Girls' Bathroom* by Louis Sachar, not illustrated; Knopf, 1987.

1991 *Hatchet* by Gary Paulsen, not illustrated; Bradbury, 1987.

1992 *All About Sam* by Lois Lowry, illustrated by Diane De Groat; Houghton Mifflin, 1988.

GEORGIA CHILDREN'S PICTURE STORYBOOK AWARD

Carol Fisher
College of Education
University of Georgia
125 Aderhold Hall
Athens, GA 30602

This children's choice award program was established in 1976 to encourage the reading of trade books as a regular part of the school curriculum for kindergarten through the third grade. The program is sponsored by the University of Georgia College of Education. A master list of twenty picture storybooks published in the United States during the last five years (excluding Caldecott winners) is selected. Each Georgia school child from kindergarten through third grade who has read or heard read at least ten of the books on the list is eligible to vote for a favorite. The winner is honored at the annual conference on children's literature in elementary education at the University. The author and the illustrator receive a plaque and a $400 award.

1977 *Alexander and the Terrible, Horrible, No Good, Very Bad Day* by Judith Viorst, illustrated by Ray Cruz; Atheneum, 1972.

1978 *The Sweet Touch* written and illustrated by Lorna Balian; Abingdon, 1976.

1979 *Big Bad Bruce* written and illustrated by Bill Peet; Houghton, 1977.

1980 *Miss Nelson is Missing!* by Harry Allard, illustrated by James Marshall; Houghton Mifflin, 1977; Scholastic, 1978.

1981 *The Tailypo: A Ghost Story* by Joanna Galdone, illustrated by Paul Galdone; Houghton/Clarion, 1977.

1982 *Pinkerton Behave!* written and illustrated by Steven Kellogg; Dial, 1979.

1983 *Herbie's Troubles* by Carol Chapman, illustrated by Kelly Oechsli; Dutton, 1981.

1984 *Cloudy with a Chance of Meatballs* by Judith Barrett, illustrated by Ron Barrett; Atheneum, 1978.

1985 *Doctor DeSoto* written and illustrated by William Steig; Farrar, 1981.

1986 *The Unicorn and the Lake* by Marianna Mayer, illustrated by Michael Hague; Dial, 1982.

1987 *My Teacher Sleeps in School* by Leatie Weiss, illustrated by Ellen Weiss; Viking, 1984.

1988 *If You Give a Mouse a Cookie* by Laura J. Numeroff, illustrated by Felicia Bond; Harper & Row, 1985.

1989 *Max, the Bad-Talking Parrot* by Patricia B. Demuth, illustrated by Bo Zaunders; Dodd, Mead, 1986.

1990 *No Jumping on the Bed!* written and illustrated by Tedd Arnold; Dial, 1987.

1991 *We're Back! A Dinosaur's Story* written and illustrated by Hudson Talbott; Crown, 1987.

1992 *Two Bad Ants* written and illustrated by Chris Van Allsburg; Houghton Mifflin, 1988.

ESTHER GLEN AWARD

New Zealand Library Association
20 Brandon St.
P O Box 12-212
Wellington, New Zealand

Awarded annually by the New Zealand Library Association, the Esther Glen Award was first given in 1945. Conceived to honor Esther Glen, New Zealand children's book author and editor, this award is made to a children's author whose literature is considered to be the most distinguished of the year. The author must be a citizen or resident of New Zealand. The nominated books are judged by a three-member committee. A medal and a $50 award are presented to the winner at the annual conference of the New Zealand Library Association. Following is a list of detailed rules and regulations governing the award:

1. There are no limitations on the character of the book except that it be an original work, or, if traditional in origin, new to children's literature and the result of individual research, the retelling and interpretation being the writer's own.

2. The format and physical makeup shall be a consideration.

3. In the financial year ending September 30, the council (of the Association) appoints a panel of three judges to consider books published during the next calendar year ending December 31. The recommendations of the judges are given to the executive officer in July of the following year and the council makes the appropriate award. After studying the recommendations of the committee, it is possible for the council not to make an award that year.

4. Judges may nominate books or they may be submitted directly or through the honorary secretary of the association.

5. If there is a difference of opinion, a majority vote will decide, but a unanimous vote is necessary in the event of a second award to the same writer.

6. Judges are expected to make themselves familiar with the books by discussing them with children in schools and libraries. These discussions should be considered in arriving at the decision.

7. The award shall be announced at any appropriate time, but no later than the annual meeting of the association. (From amendments adopted by the council).

1945 *The Book of Wiremu* by Stella Margery Morice, illustrated by Nancy Bolton; Progress Publication Society, 1944.

1946 No Award

1947 *Myths and Legends of Maoriland* by A.W. Reed, illustrated by George Woods and W. Dittmer; Reed, 1946.

1948-1949 No Awards

1950 *The Adventures of Nimble, Rumble, and Tumble* by Joan Smith, not illustrated; Paul Hamilton, 1950.

1951-1958 No Awards

1959 *Falter Tom and the Water Boy* by Maurice Duggan, illustrated by Kenneth Rowell; Paul's Book Arcade, 1958.

1960-1963 No Awards

1964 *Turi: The Story of a Little Boy* by Lesley Cameron Powell, illustrated by Pius Blank; Paul's Book Arcade, 1964.

1965-1969 No Awards

1970 *A Lion in the Meadow* by Margaret May Mahy, illustrated by Jenny Williams; Watts, 1969.

1971-1972 No Awards

1973 *The First Margaret Mahy Story Book: Stories and Poems* by Margaret May Mahy, illustrated by Shirley Hughes; Dent, 1972.

1974 No Award

1975 *My Cat Likes to Hide in Boxes* by Eve Sutton, illustrated by Lynley Dodd; Hamish Hamilton, 1974.

1976-1977 No Awards

1978 *The Lighthouse Keeper's Lunch* by Ronda Armitage, illustrated by David Armitage; Hutchinson Group NZ Limited, 1977.

1979 *Take the Long Path* by Joan de Hamel, illustrated by Gareth Floyd; Lutterworth Press, 1978.

1980-1981 No Award

1982 *The Year of the Yelvertons* by Katherine O'Brien; Oxford University Press, 1981.

1983 *The Haunting* by Margaret Mahy, not illustrated; Dent, 1982; Atheneum, 1983.

1984 *Elephant Rock* by Caroline MacDonald, not illustrated; Hodder & Stoughton (Aukland), 1983.

1985 *The Changeover* by Margaret Mahy, not illustrated; Dent, 1984.

1986 *Motherstone* by Maurice Gee, not illustrated; Oxford University Press, 1985.

1987 No Award

1988 *Alex* by Tessa Duder, not illustrated; Oxford University Press, 1987.

1989 *The Mangrove Summer* by Jack Lasenby, with maps; Oxford University Press, 1988.

1990 *Alex in Winter* by Tessa Duder, not illustrated; Oxford University Press, 1989.

1991 *Agnes the Sheep* by William Taylor, not illustrated; Ashton Scholastic, 1990; Scholastic, 1990.

1992 *Alessandra: Alex in Rome* by Tessa Duder, not illustrated; Oxford University Press, 1991.

1993 *Underrunners* by Margaret Mahy, not illustrated; Hamish Hamilton, 1992.

GOLD MEDALLION BOOK AWARD

Evangelical Christian Publishers Association
3225 South Hardy Dr. Suite 101
Tempe, AZ 85282

First awarded in 1978, this annual award recognizes the best religious books in a number of categories, children's books being among them. Books published during the preceding year are submitted by publishers and are then screened by a panel of preliminary judges who nominate five titles for consideration by the final judges. The books are judged on the basis of their relevance to Biblical truth and their acceptance, content, and design. The winning author receives a citation and a plaque is presented to the publisher at an awards banquet preceding the annual CBA International Convention each summer.

1978 *Jesus, the Friend of Children* edited by D.C. Cook, illustrated by Richard Hook and Frances Hook; David C. Cook, 1977.

1979 *Family Bible Encyclopedia* by A. Berkeley Mickelsen and Alvera Mickelsen, illustrated; David C. Cook, 1978.

1980 *Our Family Got a Divorce* by Carolyn E. Phillips, designed and illustrated by Roger Bradfield; Gospel Light Publications (GL Regal Books), 1979.

1981 *Who, What, When, Where Book about the Bible* by William L. Coleman, illustrated by Dwight Walles; David C. Cook, 1980.

1982 *Leading Little Ones to God: A Child's Book of Bible Teachings* by Marian M. Schoolland, illustrated by Paul Stoub, rev. ed.; Eerdmans, 1981, c1962.

What Happens When We Die? by Carolyn Nystrom, illustrated by Wayne A. Hanna; Moody Press, 1981.

1983 *Read Aloud Bible Stories* by Ella K. Lindvall, illustrated by Kent Puckett; Moody Press, 1982.

1984 *Tales of the Kingdom* by David Mains and Karen Mains, illustrated by Jack Stockman; David C. Cook, 1983.

1985 *Marvelous Me* by Dr. Anne Townsend, illustrated by Saroj Vaghela; Lion Publishing Co., 1984.

1986 *Potter, Come Fly to the First of the Earth* by Walter Wangerin, Jr., illustrated by Daniel San Souci; Chariot Books, 1985.

Talking Together about Love and Sexuality by Mildred Tengbom, illustrated; Bethany House, 1985.

1987 *The International Children's Bible Handbook* by Lawrence Richards, illustrated; Sweet Publishing, 1986.

What the Bible Is All About for Young Explorers by Frances Blankenbaker, illustrated by Chizuko Yasuda; Reagal Books, 1986.

1988 **PRESCHOOL** *What Does God Do?* adapted from the International Children's Bible, illustrated by Hans Wilhelm; Worthy, 1987.

1988 **ELEMENTARY** *Catherine Marshall's Storybook for Children* by David Hazard, illustrated by Joseph Boddy; Chosen Books, 1987.

1989 **PRESCHOOL** *Katie's Adventure at Blueberry Pond* by Josh McDowell and Dottie McDowell, illustrated by Ann Neilsen; Chariot, 1988.

1989 **ELEMENTARY** *Secrets of the Best Choice* by Lois Johnson, illustrated by Virginia Peck; NavPress, 1988.

You're Worth More Than You Think by Lois Johnson, illustrated by Virginia Peck; NavPress, 1988.

Thanks for Being My Friend by Lois Johnson, illustrated by Virginia Peck; NavPress, 1988.

You Are Wonderfully Made by Lois Johnson, illustrated by Virginia Peck; NavPress, 1988.

1990 **PRESCHOOL** *Do You See Me, God? Prayers for Young Children* by Elspeth Campbell Murphy, illustrated by Bill Duca; Chariot Books, 1989.

1990 **ELEMENTARY** *Destination, Moon* by James Irwin with Al Janssen, illustrated with photos; Multnomah Press, 1989.

1991 PRESCHOOL *King Leonard's Celebration* by Christopher A. Lane, illustrated by Sharon Dahl; Victor Books, 1990.

1991 ELEMENTARY *Treasure in an Oatmeal Box* by Ken Gire, illustrated by Patrick J. Welsh; NavPress, 1990.

1992 PRESCHOOL *What Would Jesus Do?* by Mack Thomas, not illustrated; Questar Publications, 1991.

1992 ELEMENTARY *The Beginner's Devotional* by Stephen T. Barclift, illustrated by Jerry Werner; Questar Publishers, 1991.

1992 YOUTH *If You Really Trust Me, Why Can't I Stay Out Later?* by Lorraine Peterson, illustrated; Bethany House, 1991.

GOLDEN ARCHER AWARD and LITTLE ARCHER AWARD

Department of Library & Learning Resources
University of Wisconsin-Oshkosh
Oshkosh, WI 54901

The idea for the Golden Archer Award was conceived by Marion Fuller Archer and Sally Teresinski in 1973. School children in Wisconsin, grades four through eight, annually vote for their favorite book (fiction or nonfiction) published during the past four years. The children are not limited to a master list of titles, but are given the following criteria to aid them in their choices: The book must have (1) likeable, interesting characters, (2) an exciting plot, (3) a theme that makes one think clearly and have sympathy for people, and (4) words that one remembers for a long time after.

As a result of popular demand, the Little Archer Award was added in 1976. Children in kindergarten through third grade vote for their favorite fiction, nonfiction, or picturebook. The winners receive a hand crafted medal and certificate.

GOLDEN ARCHER

1974 *Are You There God? It's Me, Margaret* by Judy Blume, not illustrated; Bradbury, 1970.

1975 *How to Eat Fried Worms* by Thomas Rockwell, illustrated by Emily McCully; Watts, 1973.

1976 *The Mystery of the Bewitched Bookmobile* by Florence Parry Heide, illustrated by Seymour Fleishman; Whitman, 1975.

1977 *Ramona the Brave* by Beverly Cleary, illustrated by Alan Tiegreen; Morrow, 1975.

Socks by Beverly Cleary, illustrated by Beatrice Darwin; Morrow, 1973.

1978 *The Home Run Trick* by Scott Corbett, illustrated by Paul Galdone; Atlantic-Little, 1973.

1979 *The Summer of the Monkeys* by Wilson Rawls, not illustrated; Doubleday, 1976.

1980 *This School Is Driving Me Crazy* by Nat Hentoff, not illustrated; Delacorte, 1975.

1981 *The Pinballs* by Betsy Byars, not illustrated; Harper, 1977.

1982 *My Sister's Keeper* by Beverly Butler, not illustrated; Dodd Mead, 1980.

1983 S.E. Hinton

1984 *Nothing's Fair in Fifth Grade* by Barthe DeClements, not illustrated; Viking, 1981.

1985 *Tornado!* by Hilary Milton, not illustrated; Watts, 1983.

1986 *Whalesong* by Robert Siegel, not illustrated; Crossways Books, 1981.

1987 *The Whipping Boy* by Sid Fleischman, illustrated by Peter Sis; Greenwillow, 1986.

1988 *On My Honor* by Marion Dane Bauer, not illustrated; Clarion, 1986.

1989 *Hatchet* by Gary Paulsen, not illustrated; Bradbury, 1987.

1990 *Number the Stars* by Lois Lowry, not illustrated; Houghton Mifflin, 1989.

LITTLE ARCHER

1976 The Funny Little Woman retold by Arlene Mosel, illustrated by Blair Lent; Dutton, 1972.

1977 *Cyrus, the Unsinkable Sea Serpent* written and illustrated by Bill Peet; Houghton, 1971.

1978 *Oh, Were They Ever Happy* written and illustrated by Peter Spier; Doubleday, 1978.

1979 *The Sweet Touch* written and illustrated by Lorna Balian; Abingdon, 1976.

1980 *Cross-country Cat* by Mary Calhoun, illustrated by Erick Ingraham; Morrow, 1979.

1981 *Pinkerton, Behave!* written and illustrated by Steven Kellogg; Dial, 1979.

1982 *Henry and the Red Stripes* written and illustrated by Eileen Christelow; Clarion, 1982.

1983 William Steig

1984 *The Butter Battle Book* written and illustrated by Dr. Seuss; Random House, 1984.

1985 *What's Under My Bed?* written and illustrated by James Stevenson; Greenwillow, 1983.

1986 *The Polar Express* written and illustrated by Chris Van Allsburg; Houghton Mifflin, 1985.

1987 *King Bidgood's in the Bathtub* by Audrey Wood, illustrated by Don Wood; Harcourt Brace Jovanovich, 1985.

1988 *Hey, Al!* by Arthur Yorinks, illustrated by Richard Egielski; Farrar Straus Giroux, 1986.

1989 *Underwear!* by Mary Monsell, illustrated by Lynn Munsinger; Whitman, 1988.

1990 *The Tub People* by Pam Conrad, illustrated by Richard Egielski; Harper & Row, 1989.

GOLDEN CAT AWARD

Sjostrands Forlag AB
Hasselby Strandvag 22
S-162 39
Vallingby, Sweden

This international award is presented annually for contributions to children's and young adult literature. Established in 1984 by Ulla-Britt Sjostrand, the Golden Cat recognizes works of distinction and quality in fiction for children and young adults. Authors, illustrators, critics, and publishers are eligible for the award. Recipients receive a statuette and an all expense paid trip to Stockholm.

1984 Lloyd Alexander

1985 Leon Garfield

1986 Patricia Wrightson, Sven-Erik Bergh

1988 Philippa Pearce

1989 No Award

1990 Peter Dickinson

GOLDEN KITE AWARD
Society of Children's Book Writers and Illustrators
P.O. Box 66296
Mar Vista Station
Los Angeles, CA 90066

The Society of Children's Book Writers and Illustrators, a national organization, has sponsored this annual competition since 1973. Prior to 1977, the award was given only to a work of fiction. Honor books were also chosen. In 1977, the competition was broadened to encompass nonfiction titles as well. In 1982 a picture/illustration category was added.

Any work, fiction or nonfiction, for young people using art or photographs as a major part of the book will be eligible. Society members who have published a children's or young adult title during the year are eligible. Submitted books are considered by a jury consisting of two children's book authors, a children's book illustrator or photographer, a children's book editor, and a librarian. The winning titles are those which exhibit excellence in writing and genuinely appeal to the interests and concerns of children. Each winner receives a Golden Kite statuette; the honor award recipients receive a plaque. The award is presented at the Society's conference closest to the recipient's home.

1973 *Summer of my German Soldier* by Bette Greene, not illustrated; Dial, 1973.

1973 HONOR *McBroom the Rainmaker* by Sid Fleischman, illustrated by Kurt Werth; Grosset, 1973.

Red Rock Over the River by Patricia Beatty, illustrated by Robert Quackenbush; Morrow, 1973.

1974 *The Girl Who Cried Flowers and other Tales* by Jane Yolen, illustrated by David Palladini; Crowell, 1974.

1974 HONOR *Meaning Well* by Sheila R. Cole, illustrated by Paul Raynor; Watts, 1974.

The Way Things Are and other Poems by Myra Cohn Livingston, illustrated by Jenni Oliver; Atheneum, 1974.

1975 *The Garden Is Doing Fine* by Carol Farley, illustrated by Lynn Sweat; Atheneum, 1975.

1975 HONOR *Naomi* by Berniece Rabe, not illustrated; Nelson, 1975.

The Transfigured Hart by Jane Yolen, illustrated by Donna Diamond; Crowell, 1975.

1976 *One More Flight* by Eve Bunting, illustrated by Diane de Groat; Warne, 1976.

1976 HONOR *Growing Anyway Up* by Florence Parry Heide, not illustrated; Lippincott, 1976.

The Moon Ribbon and other Tales by Jane Yolen, illustrated by David Palladini; Crowell, 1976.

1977 FICTION *The Girl Who Had no Name* by Berniece Rabe, not illustrated; Dutton, 1977.

1977 FICTION HONOR *Foster Child* by Marion Dane Bauer, not illustrated; Seabury, 1977.

1977 NONFICTION *Peeper, First Voice of Spring* by Robert M. McClung, illustrated by Carol Lerner; Morrow, 1977.

1977 NONFICTION HONOR *Evolution Goes on Everyday* by Dorothy Hinshaw Patent, illustrated by Matthew Kalmenoff; Holiday, 1977.

1978 FICTION *And You Give Me a Pain, Elaine* by Stella Pevsner, not illustrated; Seabury, 1978.

1978 FICTION HONOR *The Devil in Vienna* by Doris Orgel, not illustrated; Dial, 1978.

1978 NONFICTION *How I Came to be a Writer* by Phyllis Reynolds Naylor, illustrated with photographs; Atheneum, 1978.

1978 NONFICTION HONOR *Bionic Parts for People: The Real Story of Artificial Organs and Replacement Parts* by Gloria Skurzynski, illustrated by Frank Schwarz; Four Winds, 1978.

1979 FICTION *The Magic of the Glits* by Carole S. Adler, illustrated by Ati Forberg; Macmillan, 1979.

1979 FICTION HONOR *Cross-country Cat* by Mary Calhoun, illustrated by Erick Ingraham; Morrow, 1979.

1979 NONFICTION *Runaway Teens* by Arnold Madison, not illustrated; Elsevier/Nelson, 1979.

1979 NONFICTION HONOR *America's Endangered Birds: Programs and People Working to Save Them* by Robert M. McClung, illustrated by George Founds; Morrow, 1979.

1980 FICTION *Arthur, for the Very First Time* by Patricia MacLachlan, illustrated by Lloyd Bloom; Harper & Row, 1980.

1980 FICTION HONOR *The Half-a-Moon-Inn* by Paul Fleishman, illustrated by Kathy Jacobi; Harper, 1980.

1980 NONFICTION *The Lives of Spiders* by Dorothy Hinshaw Patent, illustrated with photographs; Holiday House, 1980.

1980 NONFICTION HONOR *Finding Your First Job* by Sue Alexander, photographs by George Ancona; Dutton, 1980.

1981 FICTION *Little Little* by M.E. Kerr, not illustrated; Harper, 1981.

1981 FICTION HONOR *A Visit to William Blake's Inn: Poems for Innocent and Experienced Travelers* by Nancy Willard, illustrated by Alice Provensen and Martin Provensen; Harcourt, 1981.

1981 NONFICTION *Blissymbolics: Speaking Without Speech* by Elizabeth S. Helfman, illustrated; Elsevier/Nelson, 1980.

1981 NONFICTION HONOR *Dinosaurs of North America* by Helen R. Sattler, introduction by John H. Ostrom, illustrated by Anthony Rao; Lothrop, Lee & Shepard, 1981.

1982 FICTION *Ralph S. Mouse* by Beverly Cleary, illustrated by Paul O. Zelinsky; Morrow, 1982.

1982 FICTION HONOR *Class Dismissed: High School Poems* by Mel Glenn, photographs by Michael J. Bernstein; Clarion, 1982.

1982 **NONFICTION** *Chimney Sweeps: Yesterday and Today* by James C. Giblin, illustrated by Margot Tomes; Crowell, 1982.

1982 **NONFICTION HONOR** *The Brooklyn Bridge: They Said It Couldn't Be Built* by Judith St. George, illustrated with photographs; Putnam, 1982.

1982 **PICTURE ILLUSTRATION** *Giorgio's Village* illustrated by Tomie de Paola; Putnam, 1982.

1983 **FICTION** *The Tempering* by Gloria Skurzynski, not illustrated; Clarion, 1983.

1983 **FICTION HONOR** *Path of the Pale Horse* by Paul Fleischman, not illustrated; Harper & Row, 1983.

1983 **NONFICTION** *The Illustrated Dinosaur Dictionary* by Helen R. Sattler, foreword by John H. Ostrom, illustrated by Pamela Carroll, color insert by Anthony Rao and Christopher Santoro; Lothrop, Lee & Shepard, 1983.

1983 **NONFICTION HONOR** *Pets Without Homes* by Caroline Arnold, photographs by Richard Hewett; Clarion, 1983.

1983 **PICTURE ILLUSTRATION** *Little Red Riding Hood* by Jacob Grimm and Wilhelm Grimm, retold and illustrated by Trina Schart Hyman; Holiday House, 1983.

1984 **FICTION** *Tancy* by Belinda Hurmence, not illustrated; Clarion, 1984.

1984 **FICTION HONOR** *Circle of Giving* by Ellen Howard, not illustrated; Atheneum, 1984.

1984 **NONFICTION** *Walls: Defenses throughout History* by James C. Giblin, illustrated with photographs; Little Brown, 1985.

1984 **NONFICTION HONOR** *How You Were Born* by Joanna Cole, illustrated with photographs; Morrow, 1984.

1984 **PICTURE ILLUSTRATION** *The Napping House* by Audrey Wood, illustrated by Don Wood; Harcourt, 1984.

1985 **FICTION** *Sarah Plain and Tall* by Patricia MacLachlan, not illustrated; Harper, 1985.

1985 **FICTION HONOR** *Prairie Songs* by Pam Conrad, illustrated by Darryl S. Zudeck; Harper, 1985.

1985 **NONFICTION** *Commodore Perry in the Land of the Shogun* by Rhoda Blumberg, illustrated with photographs; Lothrop, Lee & Shepard, 1985.

1985 **NONFICTION HONOR** *The Mount Rushmore Story* by Judith St. George, illustrated with photographs; Putnam, 1985.

1985 **ILLUSTRATION** *The Donkey's Dream* written and illustrated by Barbara Helen Berger; Philomel, 1985.

1986 **FICTION** *After the Dancing Days* by Margaret I. Rostkowski, not illustrated; Harper & Row, 1986.

1986 **FICTION HONOR** *The Solitary* by Lynn Hall, not illustrated; Scribner, 1986.

1986 **NONFICTION** *Poverty in America* by Milton Meltzer, illustrated; Morrow, 1986.

1986 **NONFICTION HONOR** *Peter the Great* written and illustrated by Diane Stanley; Four Winds, 1986.

1986 **PICTURE-ILLUSTRATION** *Alphabatics* written and illustrated by Suse MacDonald; Bradbury, 1986.

1986 **PICTURE-ILLUSTRATION HONOR** *Juma and the Magic Jinn* by Joy Anderson, illustrated by Charles Mikolaycak; Lothrop, Lee & Shepard, 1986.

1987 **FICTION** *Rabble Starkey* by Lois Lowry, not illustrated; Houghton Mifflin, 1987.

1987 **FICTION HONOR** *The Great Dimpole Oak* by Janet Taylor Lisle, illustrated by Stephen Gammell; Orchard, 1987.

1987 **NONFICTION** *The Incredible Journey of Lewis and Clark* by Rhoda Blumberg, illustrated with photos and maps, Lothrop, Lee & Shepard, 1987.

1987 **NONFICTION HONOR** *Lincoln: A Photobiography* by Russell Freedman, illustrated with photos; Clarion, 1987.

1987 **PICTURE-ILLUSTRATION** *The Devil & Mother Crump* by Valerie Scho Carey, illustrated by Arnold Lobel; Harper & Row, 1987.

1987 **PICTURE-ILLUSTRATION HONOR** *What the Mailman Brought* by Carolyn Craven, illustrated by Tomie de Paola; Putnam, 1987.

1988 **FICTION** *Borrowed Children* by George Ella Lyon, not illustrated; Orchard, 1988.

1988 **FICTION HONOR** *The Reluctant God* by Pamela F. Service, not illustrated; Atheneum, 1988.

1988 **NONFICTION** *Let There Be Light: a Book About Windows* by James Cross Giblin, illustrated with photos; Crowell, 1988.

1988 **NONFICTION HONOR** *Buffalo Hunt* by Russell Freedman, illustrated with photos; Holiday House, 1988.

1988 **PICTURE-ILLUSTRATION** *Forest of Dreams* by Rosemary Wells, illustrated by Susan Jeffers; Dial, 1988.

1988 **PICTURE-ILLUSTRATION HONOR** *Canterbury Tales* selected by Barbara Cohen, illustrated by Trina Schart Hyman; Lothrop, Lee & Shepard, 1988.

1989 **FICTION** *Jenny of the Tetons* by Kristiana Gregory, not illustrated; Harcourt Brace Jovanovich, 1989.

1989 **FICTION HONOR** *Children of the River* by Linda Crew, not illustrated; Delacorte, 1989.

1989 **NONFICTION** *Panama Canal* by Judith St. George, illustrated with photos; Putnam, 1989.

1989 **NONFICTION HONOR** *Bill Peet: An Autobiography* written and illustrated by Bill Peet; Houghton Mifflin, 1989.

1989 **PICTURE-ILLUSTRATION** *Tom Thumb* written and illustrated by Richard Jesse Watson; Harcourt Brace Jovanovich, 1989.

1989 **PICTURE-ILLUSTRATION HONOR** *Bill Peet: An Autobiography* written and illustrated by Bill Peet; Houghton Mifflin, 1989.

1990 **FICTION** *The True Confessions of Charlotte Doyle* by Avi, illustrated by Ruth E. Murray; Orchard, 1990.

1990 **FICTION HONOR** *Everywhere* by Bruce Brooks, not illustrated; HarperCollins, 1990.

1990 **NONFICTION** *The Boys' War* by Jim Murphy, illustrated with photos; Clarion Books, 1990.

1990 NONFICTION HONOR *Franklin Delano Roosevelt* by Russell Freedman, illustrated with photos; Clarion Books, 1990.

1990 PICTURE-ILLUSTRATION *Home Place* by Crescent Dragonwagon, illustrated by Jerry Pinkney; Macmillan, 1990.

1990 PICTURE-ILLUSTRATION HONOR *Dinosaur Dream* written and illustrated by Dennis Nolan; Macmillan, 1990.

1991 FICTION *The Rain Catchers* by Jean Thesman, not illustrated; Houghton Mifflin, 1991.

1991 FICTION HONOR *The Borning Room* by Paul Fleischman, not illustrated; HarperCollins, 1991.

1991 NONFICTION *The Wright Brothers: How They Invented the Airplane* by Russell Freedman, illustrated with photos; Holiday House, 1991.

1991 NONFICTION HONOR *Now Is Your Time! The African-American Struggle for Freedom* by Walter Dean Myers, illustrated; HarperCollins, 1991.

1991 PICTURE-ILLUSTRATION *Mama, Do You Love Me?* by Barbara M. Joosse, illustrated by Barbara Lavallee; Chronicle Books, 1991.

1991 PICTURE-ILLUSTRATION HONOR *Where Does the Trail Lead?* by Burton Albert, illustrated by Brian Pinkney; Simon & Schuster, 1991.

1992 FICTION *Letters From a Slave Girl* by Mary E. Lyons, illustrated; Scribner, 1992.

1992 FICTION HONOR *Steal Away* by Jennifer Armstrong; Orchard, 1992.

1992 NONFICTION *The Long Road to Gettysburg* by Jim Murphy, illustrated with maps; Clarion, 1992.

1992 NONFICTION HONOR *An Indian Winter* by Russell Freedman, illustrated by Karl Bodmer; Holiday House, 1992.

1992 ILLUSTRATION *Chicken Sunday* written and illustrated by Patricia Polacco; Philomel, 1992.

1992 ILLUSTRATION HONOR *The Fortune-tellers* by Lloyd Alexander, illustrated by Trina Schart Hyman; Dutton, 1992.

GOLDEN MEDALLION AWARD

Romance Writers of America
13700 Veterans Memorial Drive
Suite 315
Houston, TX 77014

In 1982, the Romance Writers of America instituted an awards program to recognize the best published novels by their members. Young Adult Romance is one of the categories. To be eligible, the book must be copyrighted during the preceding year by a member of the Romance Writers of America. A panel of judges chooses the best novel, which is announced at the annual conference. Winning authors receive a walnut book frame with an engraved medallion.

1983 *Andrea* by Jo Steward, not illustrated; New American Library, 1982.

1984 *Julie's Magic Moment* by Barbara Bartholomew, not illustrated; New American Library, 1983.

1985 *The Frog Princess* by Cheryl Zach, not illustrated; Silhouette, 1984.

1986 *Waiting for Amanda* by Cheryl Zach, not illustrated; Silhouette, 1985.

1987 *Video Fever* by Kathleen Garvey, not illustrated; Silhouette, 1986.

1989 *The Ghosts of Stoney Clove* by Eileen Charbonneau; Orchard, 1988.

1990 *Renee* by Vivian Schurfranz; Scholastic, 1989.

1991 No Award

1992 "Summer Nanny" by Donna Jean Tennis; (unpublished manuscript).

1993 *Song of the Buffalo Boy* by Sherry Garland, not illustrated; Harcourt Brace Jovanovich, 1992.

GOLDEN SOWER AWARD

Betty Keefe
Leonard Lawrence School
13204 S. 29 St.
Bellevue, NE 68123

Initiated by Karla Hawkins Wendelin and Denise C. Storey, at the University of Nebraska-Lincoln, this children's choice award was first presented in 1981. The award is sponsored by the Nebraska Library Association. The purposes of the award are to stimulate children's thinking, to introduce them to different types of literature, to encourage them to do independent reading, and to foster library skills.

Two awards are presented annually: one honoring fiction titles appropriate for grades 4-6 and a picture book award including titles appropriate for K-3. The picture book award was initiated in 1983 and in 1993, a young adult category was added.

Nominations are accepted from school children, librarians, teachers and media specialists. From these nominated books, the Golden Sower committee develops two lists of fifteen titles from which the children may choose their favorite.

The following guidelines are used to select the titles which appear on the final lists: (1) The books nominated should exhibit literary merit. (2) Titles published in the three years preceding the current year will be eligible. (3) The titles must be in print. (4) Newbery and Caldecott Award winners are not eligible, however, honor books may be considered. (5) The authors or illustrators should be living in the U.S. at the time of nomination. (6) Only one title of any one author/illustrator will be included on the current list. (7) Authors/illustrators represented on preceding lists may be listed again, but individual titles may not be repeated. (8) The winning author/illustrator will be excluded from competition the following year.

Children whose classroom teachers have agreed to participate are eligible to vote if they have read or heard read at least four titles from the list of nominees. Each child votes for his or her favorite book. The winning authors are presented with plaques at the Nebraska Library Association in the Fall each year. A sticker is available to be placed on the winning book.

1981 *Bunnicula: A Rabbit Tale of Mystery* by James Howe and Deborah Howe, illustrated by Alan Daniel; Atheneum, 1979.

1982 *Yours 'til Niagara Falls, Abby* by Jane O'Connor, illustrated by Margot Apple; Hastings, 1979.

1983 K-3 *Cloudy With a Chance of Meatballs* by Judi Barrett, illustrated by Ron Barrett; Atheneum, 1978.

1983 **GRADES 4-6** *Superfudge* by Judy Blume, not illustrated; Dutton, 1980.

1984 **K-3** *Miss Nelson Is Back* by Harry Allard, illustrated by James Marshall; Houghton Mifflin, 1982.

1984 **GRADES 4-6** *Nothing's Fair in Fifth Grade* by Barthe DeClements, not illustrated; Viking, 1981.

1985 **K-3** *Round Trip* written and illustrated by Ann Jonas; Greenwillow, 1983.

1985 **GRADES 4-6** *A Dog Called Kitty* by Bill Wallace, not illustrated; Holiday House, 1980.

1986 **K-3** *Peabody* written and illustrated by Rosemary Wells; Dial, 1983.

1986 **GRADES 4-6** *Night of the Twisters* by Ivy Ruckman, not illustrated; Crowell, 1984.

1987 **K-3** *Miss Nelson Has a Field Day* by Harry Allard, illustrated by James Marshall; Houghton Mifflin, 1985.

1987 **GRADES 4-6** *The War with Grandpa* by Robert Kimmel Smith, illustrated by Richard Lauter; Delacorte, 1984.

1988 **K-3** *Don't Touch My Room* by Patricia Lakin, illustrated by Patience Brewster; Little Brown, 1985.

1988 **GRADES 4-6** *Sixth Grade Can Really Kill You* by Barthe DeClements, not illustrated; Viking Kestrel, 1985.

1989 **K-3** *Piggins* by Jane Yolen, illustrated by Jane Dyer; Harcourt Brace Jovanovich, 1987.

1989 **GRADES 4-6** *Ferret in the Bedroom, Lizards in the Fridge* by Bill Wallace, not illustrated; Holiday House, 1986.

1990 **K-3** *The Magic School Bus at the Waterworks* by Joanna Cole, illustrated by Bruce Degen; Scholastic, 1986.

1990 **GRADES 4-6** *Wait Til Helen Comes* by Mary Downing Hahn, not illustrated; Clarion, 1986.

1991 **K-3** *Tacky the Penguin* by Helen Lester, illustrated by Lynn Munsinger; Houghton Mifflin, 1988.

1991 **GRADES 4-6** *There's a Boy in the Girls' Bathroom* by Louis Sachar, not illustrated; Knopf, 1987.

1992 **K-3** *The Talking Eggs* by Robert D. San Souci, illustrated by Jerry Pinkney; Dial, 1989.

1992 **GRADES 4-6** *Is Anybody There?* by Eve Bunting, not illustrated; Lippincott, 1988.

1993 **K-3** *Riptide* by Frances Ward Weller, illustrated by Robert J. Blake; Philomel, 1990.

1993 **GRADES 4-6** *Nightmare Mountain* by Peg Kehret, not illustrated; Dutton, 1989.

1993 **YOUNG ADULT** *Whispers from the Dead* by Joan Lowery Nixon, not illustrated; Delacorte, 1989.

GOLDEN SPUR

see **WESTERN WRITERS OF AMERICA SPUR AWARD**

EVA L. GORDON AWARD

American Nature Study Society
c/o Helen R. Russell
44 College Dr
Jersey City, NJ 07305

Founded by the American Nature Study Society in 1964, this annual award is presented to an author of children's science books. The award is given in memory of Eva L. Gordon, author,

reviewer, and professor of children's science literature at Cornell University. The award is presented to an author whose works exemplify Ms. Gordon's high standards of accuracy, readability, sensitivity to interrelationships, timeliness, and joyousness, while they extend either directly or subtly an invitation to the child to become involved. A certificate is presented to the recipient at the annual meeting of the society.

1964 Millicent Selsam

1965 Edwin Way Teale

1966 Robert M. McClung

1967-1969 No Award

1970 Jean Craighead George

1971 Verne Rockcastle

1972-1973 No Award

1974 Phyllis Busch

1975 Jeanne Bendick

1976 Helen Ross Russell

1977 Herman Schneider, Nina Schneider

1978 George Mason, Dorothy Shuttlesworth

1979 Ross E. Hutchins

1980 Glenn O. Blough

1981 Herbert Zim

1982 Peter Parnall

1983 Laurence Pringle

1984 Seymour Simon

1985 Vicki Cobb

1986 Dorothy Hinshaw Patent

1987 Patricia Lauber

1988 Franklyn M. Branley

1989 Ada Graham, Frank Graham

1990 Joanna Cole

1991 Jim Arnosky

1992 Byrd Baylor

GOVERNOR GENERAL'S LITERARY AWARDS

Lise Rochon, Information Officer
The Canada Council
99 Metcalfe St
Box 1047
Ottawa, Ontario K1P 5V8
Canada

This award, established by The Canadian Authors Association in 1937, originally had three categories: fiction, nonfiction, and poetry/drama. In 1947, a juvenile category was added, although a juvenile book was not honored until 1949. In 1959, the Canada Council assumed responsibility for the administration of the awards and reorganized the structure, dropping the juvenile award.

In 1975, the Canada Council established another award, called The Canada Council Children's Literature Prizes, given annually to both English language and French language books. Awards were presented for text and illustration. The name was changed again in 1987, reverting back to the Governor General's Literary Awards.

1949 *Franklin of the Arctic: A Life of Adventure* by Richard S. Lambert, maps by Julius Griffith; McClelland & Stewart, 1949.

1950 *The Great Adventure: An Illustrated History of Canada* by Donalda Dickie, illustrated by Lloyd Scott; Dent, 1950.

1951 *A Land Divided* by John F. Hayes, illustrated by Fred J. Finley; Copp, Clarke, 1951.

1952 *Cargoes on the Great Lakes* by Marie McPhedran, illustrated by Dorothy Ivens; Macmillan Canada, 1952.

1953 *Rebels Ride at Night* by John F. Hayes, illustrated by Fred J. Finley; Copp, Clarke, 1953.

1954 *The Nor'westers: The Fight for the Fur Trade* by Marjorie Campbell, illustrated by Illingworth Kerr; Macmillan Canada, 1954.

1955 *The Map Maker* by Kerry Wood; Macmillan Canada, 1955.

1956 *Lost in the Barrens* by Farley Mowat, illustrated by Charles Geer; Little Brown Canada, 1956.

1957 *The Great Chief: Maskepetoon, Warrior of the Crees* by Kerry Wood, illustrated by John A. Hall; Macmillan Canada, 1957.

1958 *Nkwala* by Edith Lambert Sharp, illustrated by William Winter; Little Brown Canada, 1958.

1975 **AUTHOR** *Shantymen of Cache Lake* by Bill Freeman, illustrated with maps and plates; Lorimer, 1975.

1976 **AUTHOR** *The Wooden People* by Myra Paperny, illustrated by Ken Stampnick; Little Brown, 1976.

1977 **AUTHOR** *Listen for the Singing* by Jean Little, not illustrated; Clarke, Irwin, 1977.

1978 **AUTHOR** *Hold Fast* by Kevin Major, not illustrated; Clarke, Irwin, 1978.

1978 **ILLUSTRATOR** *A Salmon for Simon* by Betty Waterton, illustrated by Ann Blades; Douglas & McIntyre, 1978.

1979 **AUTHOR** *Days of Terror* by Barbara Claassen Smucker, not illustrated; Herald Press, 1979.

1979 **ILLUSTRATOR** *Twelve Dancing Princesses: A Fairy Story* retold by Janet Lunn, illustrated by Laszlo Gal; Methuen, 1979.

1980 **AUTHOR** *The Trouble with Princesses* by Christie Harris, illustrated by Douglas Tait; McClelland & Stewart, 1980; Atheneum, 1980.

1980 **ILLUSTRATOR** *Petrouchka* written and illustrated by Elizabeth Cleaver; Macmillan Canada, 1980; Atheneum, 1980.

1981 **AUTHOR** *The Guardian of Isis* by Monica Hughes, not illustrated; Hamish Hamilton, 1981; Atheneum, 1982.

1981 **ILLUSTRATOR** *Ytek and the Arctic Orchid: An Inuit Legend* by Garnet Hewitt, illustrated by Heather Woodall; Douglas & McIntyre, 1981; Vanguard, 1981.

1982 **AUTHOR** *Hunter in the Dark* by Monica Hughes, not illustrated; Clarke, Irwin, 1982; Atheneum, 1983.

1982 **ILLUSTRATOR** *ABC, 123: The Canadian Alphabet and Counting Book* written and illustrated by Vlasta van Kampen; Hurtig, 1982.

1983 **AUTHOR** *The Ghost Horse of the Mounties* by Sean O. Huigin, not illustrated; Black Moss Press, 1983.

1983 **ILLUSTRATOR** *The Little Mermaid* by Hans Christian Andersen, retold by Margaret Crawford Maloney, illustrated by Laszlo Gal; Methuen, 1983.

1984 **AUTHOR** *Sweetgrass* by Jan Hudson, not illustrated; Tree Frog Press, 1984.

1984 **ILLUSTRATOR** *Lizzy's Lion* by Dennis Lee, illustrated by Marie-Louise Gay; Stoddart, 1984.

1985 **AUTHOR** *Julie* by Cora Taylor, not illustrated; Western Producer Prairie Books, 1985.

1985 **ILLUSTRATOR** *Murdo's Story: A Legend from Northern Manitoba* text by Murdo Scribe, illustrated by Terry Gallagher; Pemmican Publications, 1985.

1986 **AUTHOR** *Shadow in Hawthorn Bay* by Janet Lunn, not illustrated; Lester & Orpen Dennys, 1986.

1986 **ILLUSTRATOR** *Have You Seen Birds?* by Joanne Oppenheim, illustrated by Barbara Reid; North Winds Press, 1986.

1987 **TEXT** *Galahad Schwartz and the Cockroach Army* by Morgan Nyberg, not illustrated; Douglas & McIntyre, 1987.

1987 **ILLUSTRATION** *Rainy Day Magic* written and illustrated by Marie-Louise Gay; Stoddart, 1987.

1988 **TEXT** *The Third Magic* by Welwyn Wilton Katz, not illustrated; Douglas & McIntyre, 1988; McElderry, 1989.

1988 **ILLUSTRATION** *Amos's Sweater* by Janet Lunn, illustrated by Kim LaFave; Douglas & McIntyre, 1988; Scholastic, 1990.

1989 **TEXT** *Bad Boy* by Diana Wieler, not illustrated; Douglas & McIntyre, 1989; Delacorte, 1992.

1989 **ILLUSTRATION** *The Magic Paintbrush* written and illustrated by Robin Muller; Doubleday Canada, 1989.

1990 **TEXT** *Redwork* by Michael Bedard, not illustrated; Lester & Orpen Dennys, 1990; Atheneum, 1990.

1990 **ILLUSTRATION** *The Orphan Boy* by Tololwa M. Mollel, illustrated by Paul Morin; Oxford University Press, 1990.

1991 **TEXT** *Pick-up Sticks* by Sarah Ellis, not illustrated; Douglas & McIntyre, 1991; McElderry, 1992.

1991 **ILLUSTRATION** *Doctor Kiss Says Yes* by Teddy Jam, illustrated by Joanne Fitzgerald; Douglas & McIntyre, 1991.

1992 **TEXT** *Hero of Lesser Causes* by Julie Johnston; Lester Publishing, 1992.

1992 **ILLUSTRATION** *Waiting for the Whales* by Sheryl McFarlane, illustrated by Ron Lightburn; Orca Books, 1992.

GREAT STONE FACE AWARD

Children's Librarians of New Hampshire

This children's choice award was given for the first time in 1980 and is named for a natural rock formation in the White Mountains of New Hampshire. The purpose is to promote reading enjoyment among New Hampshire's students, increase awareness of quality contemporary writing, and to allow children the chance to honor a favorite author. Sponsored by CHILIS, a section of the New Hampshire Library Association, the award is given annually to an author whose book receives the most votes from third through sixth graders throughout the state. The voting takes place each April during National Library Week and the winner is announced in May at the Spring NHLA Conference. Winning authors receive a hand-cut crystal etched with the Great Stone Face design.

1980 *Are You There, God? It's Me, Margaret* by Judy Blume, not illustrated; Bradbury, 1970.

1981 *Superfudge* by Judy Blume, not illustrated; Dutton, 1980.

1982 *Tales of a Fourth Grade Nothing* by Judy Blume, illustrated by Roy Doty; Dutton, 1972.

1983 *The Mouse and the Motorcycle* by Beverly Cleary, illustrated by Louis Darling; Morrow, 1965.

1984 *Superfudge* by Judy Blume, not illustrated; Dutton, 1980.

1985 *Superfudge* by Judy Blume, not illustrated; Dutton, 1980.

1986 *Superfudge* by Judy Blume, not illustrated; Dutton, 1980.

1987 *Superfudge* by Judy Blume, not illustrated; Dutton, 1980.

1988 *Where the Red Fern Grows* by Wilson Rawls, not illustrated; Doubleday, 1961; Bantam, 1974.

1989 *Where the Red Fern Grows* Wilson Rawls, not illustrated; Doubleday, 1961; Bantam, 1974.

1990 *Matilda* by Roald Dahl, illustrated by Quentin Blake; Viking Kestrel, 1988.

1991 *The Secret of the Indian* by Lynne Reid Banks, illustrated by Ted Lewin; Doubleday, 1989.

1992 *Number the Stars* by Lois Lowry, not illustrated; Houghton Mifflin, 1989.

KATE GREENAWAY MEDAL

Ann Hobart
The Library Association
7 Ridgmount St
London WCIE 7AE
England

The Kate Greenaway Medal is awarded annually to an artist who has produced the most distinguished work in the illustration of a children's book which has been published in the preceding year. This award is named after the 19th century British artist who helped to revolutionize children's book illustration. Administered by The [British] Library Association since 1955, the Greenaway Medal is usually presented in September or October of each year. Nominations are invited from all members of The Library Association. These titles are given to the selection committee for final action. The selection committee is composed of the chairman and vice-chairman of the Youth Libraries Group and eleven other Library Association members. In addition to the winning recipient, there are also Highly Commended, Commended, and Honour books cited. This same committee is also responsible for the selection of the Carnegie Medal (see entry). The committee is urged to take into account the design, format and production, as well as artistic merit, when choosing the recipient.

Specifically, with regard to the illustrations, the following points are to be considered: imaginative sympathy with the text, graphic style, consistency, content, relationship to child perception, layout in relationship to text, style of illustration complementing style of writing and theme, and coordination of illustrations with text in depicting character. (From the guidelines set forth by The Library Association).

1955 No Award

1956 *Tim all Alone* written and illustrated by Edward Ardizzone; Oxford, 1956.

1957 *Mrs. Easter and the Storks* written and illustrated by V.H. Drummond; Faber, 1957.

1958 No Award

1959 *A Bundle of Ballads* compiled by Ruth Manning-Sanders, illustrated by William Stobbs; Oxford, 1959.

Kashtanka by Anton Chekhov, translated by Charles Dowsett, illustrated by William Stobbs; Oxford, 1959.

1959 **COMMENDED** *Titus in Trouble* by James Reeves, illustrated by Edward Ardizzone; Bodley Head, 1959.

Wuffles Goes to Town written and illustrated by Gerald Rose and Elizabeth Jane Rose; Faber, 1959.

1960 *Old Winkle and the Seagulls* by Elizabeth Rose, illustrated by Gerald Rose; Faber, 1960.

1960 **COMMENDED** No Award

1961 *Mrs. Cockle's Cat* by A. Philippa Pearce, illustrated by Antony Maitland; Kestrel, 1961.

1961 **COMMENDED** No Award

1962 *Brian Wildsmith's ABC* written and illustrated by Brian Wildsmith; Oxford, 1962.

1962 **COMMENDED** *Achilles the Donkey* by Herbert E. Bates, illustrated by Carol Barker; Dobson, 1962.

1963 *Borka: The Adventures of a Goose With No Feathers* written and illustrated by John Burningham; Cape, 1963.

1963 **COMMENDED** *The Lion and the Rat: A Fable* by Jean de La Fontaine, illustrated by Brian Wildsmith; Oxford, 1963.

The Oxford Book of Poetry for Children compiled by Edward Blishen, illustrated by Brian Wildsmith; Oxford, 1963.

The Royal Navy by Peter Dawlish, illustrated by Victor Ambrus; Oxford, 1963.

Time of Trial by Hester Burton, illustrated by Victor Ambrus; Oxford, 1963; World, 1964.

1964 *Shakespeare's Theatre* written and illustrated by C. Walter Hodges; Oxford, 1964.

1964 **COMMENDED** *Fe Fi Fo Fum: A Picture Book of Nursery Rhymes* written and illustrated by Raymond Briggs; Hamilton, 1964.

Victor G. Ambrus for his work in general

William Papas for his work in general

1965 *Three Poor Tailors* written and illustrated by Victor G. Ambrus; Hamilton, 1965.

1965 **COMMENDED** No Award

1966 *Mother Goose Treasury* written and illustrated by Raymond Briggs; Hamilton, 1966.

1966 **COMMENDED** *The Story of Soul the King* by Doreen Roberts.

1967 *Charley, Charlotte and the Golden Canary* written and illustrated by Charles Keeping; Oxford, 1967.

1967 **COMMENDED** *Birds* written and illustrated by Brian Wildsmith; Oxford, 1967.

The Church by Geoffrey Moorhouse, illustrated by William Papas; Oxford, 1967.

No Mules written and illustrated by William Papas; Oxford, 1967.

1968 *Dictionary of Chivalry* by Grant Uden, illustrated by Pauline Baynes; Kestrel, 1968; Crowell, 1969.

1968 **HONORS LIST** *Flutes and Cymbals (poems)* compiled by Leonard Clark, illustrated by Shirley Hughes; Bodley Head, 1968.

A Letter from India written and illustrated by William Papas; Oxford, 1968.

A Letter from Israel written and illustrated by William Papas; Oxford, 1968.

The Luck Child by Jacob Grimm and Wilhelm Grimm, illustrated by Gaynor Chapman; Hamilton, 1968.

Taresh the Tea Planter written and illustrated by William Papas; Oxford, 1968.

1969 *Dragon of an Ordinary Family* by Margaret Mahy, illustrated by Helen Oxenbury; Heinemann, 1969.

The Quangle-Wangle's Hat by Edward Lear, illustrated by Helen Oxenbury; Heinemann, 1969.

1969 **HONORS LIST** *The Cabbage Princess* written and illustrated by Errol Le Cain; Faber, 1969.

Joseph's Yard written and illustrated by Charles Keeping; Oxford, 1969.

1970 *Mr. Gumpy's Outing* written and illustrated by John Burningham; Cape, 1970; Holt, 1970.

1970 **HONORS LIST** *The God Beneath the Sea* by Edward Blishen and Leon Garfield, illustrated by Charles Keeping; Longmans, 1970.

The Golden Bird by Edith Brill, illustrated by Jan Pienkowski; Dent, 1970.

Pegasus written and illustrated by Krystyna Turska; Hamilton, 1970.

1971 *The Kingdom under the Sea* written and illustrated by Jan Pienkowski; Cape, 1971.

1971 **HIGHLY COMMENDED** *The Owl and the Woodpecker* written and illustrated by Brian Wildsmith; Oxford, 1971.

The Sultan's Bath retold and illustrated by Victor G. Ambrus; Oxford, 1971.

1972 *The Woodcutter's Duck* written and illustrated by Krystyna Turska; Hamilton, 1972; Macmillan, 1973.

1972 **COMMENDED** *The Ghost Downstairs* by Leon Garfield, illustrated by Antony Maitland; Longmans, 1972.

King Midas and the Golden Touch written and illustrated by Carol Barker; Watts, 1972.

Snail and Caterpillar by Helen Piers, illustrated by Pauline Baynes; Longmans, 1972.

1973 *Father Christmas* written and illustrated by Raymond Briggs; Hamilton, 1973; Coward, 1973.

1973 **COMMENDED** *King Tree* written and illustrated by Fiona French; Oxford, 1973.

My Brother Sean by Petronella Breinburg, illustrated by Errol Lloyd; Bodley Head, 1973.

1974 *The Wind Blew* written and illustrated by Pat Hutchins; Bodley Head, 1974.

1974 **HIGHLY COMMENDED** *Railway Passage* written and illustrated by Charles Keeping; Oxford, 1974.

1975 *Horses in Battle* written and illustrated by Victor G. Ambrus; Oxford, 1975.

Mishka written and illustrated by Victor G. Ambrus; Oxford, 1975.

1975 **COMMENDED** *Helpers* written and illustrated by Shirley Hughes; Bodley Head, 1975.

Thorn Rose by Jacob Grimm and Wilhelm Grimm, illustrated by Errol Le Cain; Faber, 1975.

1976 *The Post Office Cat* written and illustrated by Gail E. Haley; Bodley Head, 1976.

1976 **HIGHLY COMMENDED** *The Church Mice Adrift* by Lore Segal, illustrated by Graham Oakley; Macmillan, 1976; Atheneum, 1976.

How the Birds Changed their Feathers retold and illustrated by Joanna Troughton; Blackie, 1976.

Tinker, Tailor, Soldier, Sailor: A Picture Book by Bernard Lodge, illustrated by Maureen Roffey; Bodley Head, 1976.

1977 *Dogger* written and illustrated by Shirley Hughes; Bodley Head, 1977.

1977 **COMMENDED** *Burglar Bill* written and illustrated by Janet Ahlberg and Allan Ahlberg; Heinemann, 1977.

Garth Pig and the Ice Cream Lady written and illustrated by Mary Rayner; Macmillan, 1977.

Each Peach, Pear, Plum written and illustrated by Allan Ahlberg and Janet Ahlberg; Kestrel, 1978.

1978 **HIGHLY COMMENDED** *The Snowman* written and illustrated by Raymond Briggs; Hamilton, 1978; Random House, 1978.

1978 **COMMENDED** *The Brothers Grimm: Popular Folk Tales* by Jacob Grimm and Wilhelm Grimm, newly translated by Brian Alderson, illustrated by Michael Foreman; Gollancz, 1978.

The Twelve Dancing Princesses by Jacob Grimm and Wilhelm Grimm, illustrated by Errol Le Cain; Faber, 1978.

1979 *Haunted House* written and illustrated by Jan Pienkowski; Dutton, 1979.

1979 **HIGHLY COMMENDED** *One-eyed Jake* written and illustrated by Pat Hutchins; Bodley Head, 1979.

The Wild Washerwomen: A New Folktale by John Yeoman, illustrated by Quentin Blake; Hamish Hamilton, 1979.

1980 *Mr. Magnolia* written and illustrated by Quentin Blake; Cape, 1980.

1980 HIGHLY COMMENDED *City of Gold and Other Stories from the Old Testament* by Peter Dickinson, illustrated by Michael Foreman; Gollancz, 1980.

1980 COMMENDED *Peace at Last* written and illustrated by Jill Murphy; Macmillan, 1980.

Seven Years and a Day by Colette O'Hare, illustrated by Beryl Cook; Collins, 1980.

1981 *The Highwayman* by Alfred Noyes, illustrated by Charles Keeping; Oxford, 1981; Oxford (U.S.), 1982.

1981 HIGHLY COMMENDED *Sunshine* written and illustrated by Jan Ormerod; Kestrel, 1981; Lothrop, Lee & Shepard, 1981; Penguin (Australia), 1981.

1981 COMMENDED *The Patchwork Cat* by William Mayne, illustrated by Nicola Bayley; Cape, 1981.

Hansel and Gretel by Jacob Grimm and Wilhelm Grimm, illustrated by Anthony Browne; Julia MacRae, 1981.

1982 *Long Neck and Thunder Foot* by Helen Piers, illustrated by Michael Foreman; Kestrel, 1982.

Sleeping Beauty and other Favourite Fairy Tales chosen and translated by Angela Carter, illustrated by Michael Foreman; Gollancz, 1982.

1982 HIGHLY COMMENDED *The Church Mice in Action* written and illustrated by Graham Oakley; Macmillan, 1982; Atheneum, 1983.

1982 COMMENDED *The Baby's Catalogue* written and illustrated by Janet Ahlberg and Allan Ahlberg; Kestrel, 1982; Little Brown, 1982.

1983 *Gorilla* written and illustrated by Anthony Browne; MacRae, 1983.

1984 *Hiawatha's Childhood* by Henry Wadsworth Longfellow, illustrated by Erroll Le Cain; Faber, 1984.

1985 *Sir Gawain and the Loathly Lady* retold by Selina Hastings, illustrated by Juan Wijngaard; Walker, 1985.

1985 COMMENDED *Seasons of Splendour* by Madhur Jaffrey, illustrated by Michael Foreman; Pavilion Books, 1985.

Tog the Ribber: or, Granny's Tale by Paul Coltman, illustrated by Gillian McClure; Deutsch, 1985.

1986 *Snow White in New York* written and illustrated by Fiona French; Oxford, 1986.

1986 HIGHLY COMMENDED *Happy Christmas, Gemma* written and illustrated by Jan Ormerod; Walker, 1986.

1986 COMMENDED *The Jolly Postman: or, Other People's Letters* written and illustrated by Janet Ahlberg and Allan Ahlberg; Heinemann, 1986.

Are We Nearly There? by Louis Baum, illustrated by Paddy Bouma; Bodley Head, 1986.

Princess Smartypants written and illustrated by Babette Cole; Hamish Hamilton, 1986.

How Many? From 0 to 20 written and illustrated by Fiona Pragoff; Gollancz, 1986.

I Want My Potty written and illustrated by Tony Ross; Andersen Press, 1986.

1987 *Crafty Chameleon* by Mwenye Hadithi, illustrated by Adrienne Kennaway; Hodder & Stoughton, 1987; Little Brown, 1987.

1988 *Can't You Sleep Little Bear?* by Martin Waddell, illustrated by Barbara Firth; Walker, 1988.

1988 HIGHLY COMMENDED *Alice's Adventures in Wonderland* by Lewis Carroll, illustrated by Anthony Browne; Julia MacRae, 1988; Knopf, 1988.

Merlin Dreams by Peter Dickinson, illustrated by Alan Lee; Gollancz, 1988.

The Adventures of Pinocchio by Carlo Collodi, illustrated by Roberto Innocenti; Cape, 1988.

1988 COMMENDED *Wake Up, Mr. B!* written and illustrated by Penny Dale; Walker Books, 1988.

Ladybird, Ladybird written and illustrated by Ruth Brown; Andersen, 1988; Dutton, 1988.

1988 SPECIAL COMMENDATION *Bird* by David Burnie, illustrated by Peter Chadwick and Kim Taylor; Dorling Kindersley/Natural History Museum, 1988; Knopf, 1988.

1989 *War Boy* written and illustrated by Michael Foreman; Pavilion Books in association with Joseph, 1989; Arcade, 1990.

1989 HIGHLY COMMENDED *We're Going on a Bear Hunt* by Michael Rosen, illustrated by Helen Oxenbury; Walker Books, 1989.

Dr. Xargle's Book of Earth Tiggers by Jeanne Willis, illustrated by Tony Ross; Andersen Press, 1990; Dutton, 1991 (*Earth Tigerlets as Explained by Professor Xargle*).

1990 *The Whales' Song* by Dyan Sheldon, illustrated by Gary Blythe; Hutchinson, 1990; Dial, 1991.

1990 COMMENDED *The Mousehole Cat* by Antonia Barber, illustrated by Nicola Bayley; Walker, 1990; Macmillan, 1990.

A Christmas Carol by Charles Dickens, illustrated by Roberto Innocenti; Stewart, Tabori & Chang, 1990.

1991 *The Jolly Christmas Postman* written and illustrated by Allan Ahlberg and Janet Ahlberg; Heinemann, 1991.

1991 HIGHLY COMMENDED *Farmer Duck* by Martin Waddell, illustrated by Helen Oxenbury; Walker, 1991.

1991 COMMENDED *Amazing Grace* by Mary Hoffman, illustrated by Caroline Binch; Frances Lincoln, 1991; Dial, 1991.

1992 *Zoo* written and illustrated by Anthony Browne; MacRae, 1992.

1992 HIGHLY COMMENDED *The Pig in the Pond* by Martin Waddell, illustrated by Jill Barton; Walker, 1992.

GROLIER FOUNDATION AWARD

ALA Awards Committee
American Library Association
50 East Huron St
Chicago, IL 60611

This annual award, first given in 1954, is presented to a librarian in a community or school who has made an unusual contribution to the stimulation and guidance of reading by children and young people. The award is given for outstanding work with children and young people through high-school age, for continued service, or in recognition of one particular contribution of lasting value. A five member jury, appointed by the ALA Awards Committee, chooses the winner. A citation and $1000 is presented to the winner at the ALA annual conference. The award donor is the Grolier Foundation.

1954 Siddie Joe Johnson

1955 Charlemae Hill Rollins

1956 Georgia Sealoff

1957 Margaret Alexander Edwards

1958 Mary Peacock Douglas

1959 Evelyn Sickels

1960 Margaret Scoggin

1961 Della Louise McGregor

1962 Alice McGuire

1963 Carolyn W. Field

1964 Inger Boye

1965 Sarah Lewis Jones

1966 Mildred L. Batchelder

1967 Lura E. Crawford

1968 Augusta Baker

1969 Anne R. Izard

1970 Julia Losinski

1971 Sara Siebert

1972 Ronald W. McCracken

1973 Eleanor Kidder

1974 Regina U. Minudri

1975 Jane B. Wilson

1976 Virginia Haviland

1977 Elizabeth Fast

1978 Dorothy C. McKenzie

1979 Anne Pellowski

1980 Mabel Williams

1981 Jane Ann McGregor

1982 Spencer Shaw

1983 Zena Sutherland

1984 Carolyn Sue Peterson

1985 Mary Kay Chelton

1986 Isabel Schon

1987 Lillian Morrison

1988 Lucille Cole Thomas

1989 Patty Campbell

1990 Patricia Holt

1991 Dorothy Broderick

1992 Effie Lee Morris

1993 Michael L. Printz

GUARDIAN AWARD FOR CHILDREN'S FICTION
The Guardian
119 Farringdon Rd
London EClR 3ER
England

Established in 1967 by the staff of The Guardian, this annual award is presented for an outstanding work of fiction for children by a British or Commonwealth author. The final selection is made by a panel of judges. Commended and runner-up books are also named. The winner receives £50.

1967 *Devil-in-the-Fog* by Leon Garfield, illustrated by Antony Maitland; Kestrel, 1966.

1968 *The Owl Service* by Alan Garner, not illustrated; Collins, 1967.

1969 *The Whispering Mountain* by Joan Aiken, illustrated by Frank Bozzo; Cape, 1968.

1970 *Flambards* by K.M. Peyton, illustrated by Victor G. Ambrus; Oxford, 1967; World, 1968.

1971 *The Guardians* by John Christopher, not illustrated; Macmillan, 1970.

1972 *A Likely Lad* by Gillian E. Avery, illustrated by Faith Jacques; Collins, 1971.

1973 *Watership Down* by Richard Adams, not illustrated; Rex Collings, 1972; Macmillan, 1972; Avon, 1975.

1974 *The Iron Lily* by Barbara Willard, not illustrated; Longmans, 1973.

1975 *Gran at Coalgate* by Winifred Cawley, illustrated by F. Rocker; Oxford, 1974.

1976 *The Peppermint Pig* by Nina Bawden, illustrated by Charles Lilly; Gollancz, 1975.

1976 **COMMENDED** *The Machine Gunners* by Robert Westall, not illustrated; Macmillan, 1975; Greenwillow, 1976.

A Question of Courage by Marjorie Darke, illustrated by Janet Archer; Kestrel, 1975.

Storm Surge by David Rees, illustrated by Trevor Stubley; Lutterworth, 1975.

1977 *The Blue Hawk* by Peter Dickinson, illustrated by David Smee; Gollancz, 1976.

1977 **COMMENDED** *Ask Me no Questions* by Ann Schlee, not illustrated; Macmillan, 1976.

Me and My Million by Clive King, not illustrated; Kestrel, 1976; Crowell, 1979.

Power of Three by Diana Wynne Jones, not illustrated; Macmillan, 1976.

Thunder and Lightnings by Jan Mark, illustrated by Jim Russell; Kestrel, 1976.

1978 *A Charmed Life* by Diana Wynne Jones, not illustrated; Macmillan, 1977.

1978 **COMMENDED** *The First of Midnight* by Marjorie Darke, illustrated by Anthony Morris; Kestrel, 1977.

The Ice Is Coming by Patricia Wrightson, illustrated with maps; Hutchinson Australia, 1977.

John Brown, Rose and the Midnight Cat by Jenny Wagner, illustrated by Ron Brooks; Kestrel, 1977.

1979 *Conrad's War* by Andrew Davies, not illustrated; Blackie, 1978; Crown, 1980.

1979 **COMMENDED** *Moffatt's Road* by Rachel Anderson, illustrated by Pat Marriott; Cape, 1978.

My Mate Shofiq by Jan Needle, not illustrated; Deutsch, 1978.

Scarf Jack by Patrick J. Kavanagh, not illustrated; Bodley Head, 1978.

Silver's Revenge by Robert Leeson, not illustrated; Collins, 1978.

1980 *The Vandal* by Ann Schlee, not illustrated; Macmillan, 1979.

1980 **RUNNERSUP** *Leaving Home* by Alison Morgan, not illustrated; Chatto & Windus, 1979.

Meg and Maxie by Joan G. Robinson, not illustrated; Gollancz, 1978.

1981 *The Sentinels* by Peter Carter, not illustrated; Oxford, 1980.

1981 **RUNNERSUP** *Daggie Dogfoot* by Dick King-Smith, illustrated by Mary Rayner; Gollancz, 1980.

Dear Hill by Gwyneth A. Jones, not illustrated; Macmillan, 1980.

The Hawk of May by Ann Lawrence, not illustrated; Macmillan, 1980.

Tod's Owl by Richard Potts, not illustrated; Hodder, 1980.

1981 **SPECIAL PRIZE** *Nothing to Be Afraid of* by Jan Mark, illustrated by David Parkins; Kestrel, 1980.

1982 *Goodnight, Mister Tom* by Michelle Magorian, not illustrated; Kestrel, 1981.

1982 **RUNNERUP** *Playing Beatie Bow* by Ruth Park, not illustrated; Kestrel, 1981, c1980; Atheneum, 1982.

1983 *The Village by the Sea* by Anita Desai, not illustrated; Heinemann, 1982.

1983 **RUNNERSUP** *Ring-rise Ring-set* by Monica Hughes, not illustrated; Watts, 1982; Julia MacRae, 1982.

The Dark Behind the Curtains by Gillian Cross, illustrated by David Parkins; Oxford, 1982.

1984 *The Sheep-Pig* by Dick King-Smith, illustrated by Mary Rayner; Gollancz, 1983.

1984 **RUNNERUP** *Summer of the Zeppelin* by Elsie McCutcheon, not illustrated; Dent, 1983; Penguin, 1984.

1985 *What is the Truth? A Farmyard Fable for the Young* by Ted Hughes, illustrated by R.J. Lloyd; Faber, 1984.

1985 **RUNNERUP** *The Duck Street Gang* by Denis Murray, not illustrated; Hamish Hamilton, 1984.

1986 *Henry's Leg* by Ann Pilling, illustrated by Rowan Clifford; Viking Kestrel, 1985.

1986 **RUNNERUP** *Trouble Half-way* by Jan Mark, illustrated by David Parkins; Viking Kestrel, 1985.

Mundo and the Weather Child by Joyce Dunbar, not illustrated; Heinemann, 1985.

1987 *The True Story of Spit MacPhee* by James Aldridge, not illustrated; Viking Kestrel, 1986; Viking Penguin Australia, 1986; Viking, 1987.

1987 **RUNNERUP** *Starry Night* by Catherine Sefton, not illustrated; Hamish Hamilton, 1986.

1988 *The Runaways* by Ruth Thomas, not illustrated; Hutchinson Children's, 1987; Lippincott, 1989.

1988 **RUNNERUP** *Madame Doubtfire* by Anne Fine, not illustrated; Hamilton Children's, 1987.

1989 *A Pack of Lies: Twelve Stories in One* by Geraldine McCaughrean, not illustrated; Oxford University Press, 1988.

1989 **RUNNERUP** *Josie Smith* by Magdalen Nabb, illustrated by Pirkko Vainio; Collins, 1988; McElderry, 1989.

1990 *Goggle-eyes* by Anne Fine, not illustrated; Hamish Hamilton, 1989; Joy Street Books, 1989. (published as: *My War with Goggle-eyes* in the United States).

1990 **RUNNERUP** *The Lake at the End of the World* by Caroline Macdonald, not illustrated; Andersen, 1988; Knight, 1992.

1990 **SPECIAL PRAISE** *Blitzcat* by Robert Westall, not illustrated; Macmillan Children's, 1989.

Josephine by Kenneth Lillington, not illustrated; Faber & Faber, 1989.

1991 *The Kingdom by the Sea* by Robert Westall, not illustrated; Methuen Children's, 1990; Farrar Straus Giroux, 1991.

1991 **RUNNERSUP** *Waiting for Anya* by Michael Morpurgo, not illustrated; Heinemann, 1990; Viking, 1991.

No Tigers in Africa by Norman Silver, not illustrated; Faber, 1990; Dutton, 1992.

Against the Storm by Gaye Hicyilmaz, not illustrated; Viking Kestrel, 1990; Little Brown, 1992.

1992 *The Exiles* by Hilary McKay, not illustrated; Gollancz, 1991.

Paper Faces by Rachel Anderson, not illustrated; Oxford University Press, 1991.

1993 *Low Tide* by William Mayne, not illustrated; Cape, 1991.

1993 **RUNNERUP** *The Wheel of Surya* by Jamila Gavin, not illustrated; Methuen, 1992.

H

SUE HEFLY AWARD
discontinued

This children's choice award was begun in 1970 under the direction of the Louisiana Association of School Librarians. From 1973 to 1979, the winner was chosen from a master list of titles provided to the children in grades four through eight. In 1980, the regulations were revised and functioned under the following guidelines: the author must be living; the book could be fiction, biography, or poetry; the copyright must precede the competition by no more than five years; and all students in grades one through eight may participate. In lieu of a master list, the students were polled to ascertain their favorite titles. The last award was given in 1983 using these guidelines.

The award has been renamed to Sue Hefly Educator of the Year Award and as such, no longer falls within the parameters of this listing.

1973 *The Mouse and the Motorcycle* by Beverly Cleary, illustrated by Louis Darling; Morrow, 1965.

1974 *Did You Carry the Flag Today, Charley?* by Rebecca Caudill, illustrated by Nancy Grossman; Holt, 1966.

1975 *Trumpet of the Swan* by E.B. White, illustrated by Edward Frascino; Harper & Row, 1970.

1976 *Sounder* by William H. Armstrong, illustrated by James Barkley; Harper & Row, 1969.

1977 No Award

1978 *A Taste of Blackberries* by Doris Buchanan Smith, illustrated by Charles Robinson; Crowell, 1973.

1979-1981 No Award

1982 *Superfudge* by Judy Blume, not illustrated; Dutton, 1980.

1982 HONOR *Starring Sally J. Freedman as Herself* by Judy Blume, not illustrated; Bradbury, 1977.

Ramona and Her Father by Beverly Cleary, illustrated by Alan Tiegreen; Morrow, 1977.

Tex by S.E. Hinton, not illustrated; Delacorte, 1979.

1983 *Tex* by S.E. Hinton, not illustrated; Delacorte, 1979.

LEE BENNETT HOPKINS POETRY AWARD
Children's Literature Council of Pennsylvania

This award is sponsored by the Children's Literature Council of Pennsylvania and funded by poetry anthologist, Lee Bennett Hopkins. Awarded annually beginning in 1993, the award celebrates the importance of poetry for children and recognizes the work of an American poet or compiler. Eligible are anthologies of poetry or collections of original poems for children published during the preceding year. The recipient receives a $500 cash award and an award seal, bearing the art of Jessie Willcox Smith depicting two children cradled beneath the wings of Mother Goose. The award is made possible by Lee Benett Hopkins in the hopes that poetry will continue "to flow freely in our children's lives."

1993 *Sing to the Sun* written and illustrated by Ashley Bryan; HarperCollins, 1992.

AMELIA FRANCES HOWARD-GIBBON ILLUSTRATOR'S AWARD
Leacy O'Brien
Canadian Association of Children's Librarians
Canadian Library Association
200 Elgin St. Suite 602
Ottawa, Ontario K2P 1L5
Canada

Established in 1969 by the Canadian Association of Children's Literature for the purpose of honoring outstanding illustrations by a Canadian for a work published in Canada, whether picture book, fiction, or nonfiction, in the hope that Canadian artists and illustrators would be stimulated. The award was named after Amelia Frances Howard-Gibbon, illustrator of An Illustrated Comic Alphabet. In order to be eligible for the annual award, the illustrator must have been born in Canada or currently reside there. Members of the CACL are invited to make nominations.

The final selection is made by a five-member committee composed entirely of children's librarians. (Artists are not included among the judges). This committee adheres to the following criteria when making their selection: (1) The text must be worthy of the illustration. (2) Photographic illustrations are ineligible. (3) Illustration is the prime consideration. The total design of the book is secondary. (4) The illustrations must effectively communicate the artist's interpretation of the story and must complement the text, if any. (5) Artistic worth is judged on the basis of color, line, composition, perspective, action and narrative quality, characterization, and medium used. (6) The first-time winner may receive the award for a book published within the last three years. Subsequent awards are made for the preceding year only. (7) A winner may not receive the award more than twice, except in special circumstances. (8) If no work appears worthy, the award may be withheld. (From criteria adopted by the CACL in 1969).

The illustrator of the chosen book receives a monetary award, a citation, and a medal designed by James Houston, a Canadian author and illustrator.

1971 *The Wind Has Wings: Poems from Canada* compiled by Mary Alice Downie and Barbara Robertson, illustrated by Elizabeth Cleaver; Oxford, 1968.

1971 RUNNERUP *How Summer Came to Canada* written and illustrated by Elizabeth Cleaver; Oxford University Press, 1970.

1972 *A Child in Prison Camp* written and illustrated by Shizuye Takashima; Tundra, 1971.

1972 RUNNERUP *The Little Hen of Huronia* by Chip Young; G. McLeod, 1971.

1973 *Beyond the Sun / Au Dela du Soleil* written and illustrated by Jacques de Roussan; Tundra, 1972.

1973 RUNNERUP *Ghost Paddle* by James Houston; Longmans, 1972.

1974 *A Prairie Boy's Winter* written and illustrated by William Kurelek; Tundra, 1973.

1974 RUNNERUP *A Boy of Tache* written and illustrated by Ann Blades; Tundra, 1973.

1975 *The Sleighs of my Childhood / Les Traineaux de mon Enfance* (bilingual text) written and illustrated by Carlo Italiano; Tundra, 1974.

1975 RUNNERUP No Award

1976 *A Prairie Boy's Summer* written and illustrated by William Kurelek; Tundra, 1975.

1976 RUNNERUP *The Witch of the North: Folktales of French Canada* adapted by Mary Alice Downie, illustrated by Elizabeth Cleaver; Oberon Press, 1975.

1977 *Down by Jim Long's Stage: Rhymes for Children and Young Fish* by Al Pittman, illustrated by Pam Hall; Breakwater, 1976.

1977 RUNNERUP *Quebec: Je T'aime: I Love You* written and illustrated by Miyuki Tanobe; Tundra/Northern New York, 1976.

1978 *Loon's Necklace* by William Toye, illustrated by Elizabeth Cleaver; Oxford, 1977.

1978 RUNNERUP *Garbage Delight* by Dennis Lee, illustrated by Frank Newfeld; Macmillan Canada, 1977.

1979 *A Salmon for Simon* by Betty Waterton, illustrated by Ann Blades; Douglas & McIntyre, 1978.

1979 RUNNERUP *The Great Canadian Animal Stories* by Vlasta Van Kampen; Hurtig, 1978.

1980 *Twelve Dancing Princesses: A Fairy Story* retold by Janet Lunn, illustrated by Laszlo Gal; Methuen, 1979.

1980 RUNNERUP *The Great Canadian Adventure Stories* by Vlasta Van Kampen; Hurtig, 1979.

1981 *The Trouble with Princesses* by Christie Harris, illustrated by Douglas Tait; McClelland & Stewart, 1980; Atheneum, 1980.

1981 RUNNERUP *The Buffalo Hunt* by Eleanor Swainson and Donald Swainson, illustrated by James Tughan; PMA Books, 1980.

1982 *Ytek and the Arctic Orchid: An Inuit Legend* by Garnet Hewitt, illustrated by Heather Woodall; Douglas & McIntyre, 1981; Vanguard, 1981.

1982 RUNNERUP *Merchants of the Mysterious East* written and illustrated by John Lim; Tundra, 1981.

1983 *Chester's Barn* written and illustrated by Lindee Climo; Tundra, 1982.

1983 RUNNERUP *A Northern Alphabet* written and illustrated by Ted Harrison; Tundra, 1982.

1984 *Zoom at Sea* by Tim Wynne-Jones, illustrated by Ken Nutt; Douglas & MacIntyre, 1983.

1984 RUNNERUP *The Little Mermaid* by Hans Christian Andersen, retold by Margaret Crawford Maloney, illustrated by Laszlo Gal; Methuen, 1983.

1985 *Chin Chiang and the Dragon's Dance* written and illustrated by Ian Wallace; Douglas & MacIntyre, 1984.

1985 RUNNERUP *The Owl and the Pussycat* by Edward Lear, illustrated by Ron Berg; Scholastic-TAB, 1984.

1986 *Zoom Away* by Tim Wynne-Jones, illustrated by Ken Nutt; Douglas & McIntyre, 1985.

1986 RUNNERUP *By the Sea: An Alphabet Book* written and illustrated by Ann Blades; Kids Can Press, 1985.

1987 *Moonbeam on a Cat's Ear* written and illustrated by Marie-Louise Gay; Stoddart, 1986.

1987 RUNNERUP *Have You Seen Birds?* by Joanne Oppenheim, illustrated by Barbara Reid; North Winds Press, 1986; Scholastic, 1986.

1988 *Rainy Day Magic* written and illustrated by Marie Louise Gay; Stoddart, 1987.

1988 RUNNERUP *Can You Catch Josephine?* written and illustrated by Stephane Poulin; Tundra, 1987.

1989 *Amos's Sweater* by Janet Lunn, illustrated by Kim LaFave; Douglas & McIntyre, 1988; Scholastic, 1990.

1989 RUNNERUP *Night Cars* by Teddy Jam, illustrated by Eric Beddows; Douglas & McIntyre, 1988; Orchard, 1989.

1990 *Til All the Stars Have Fallen: Canadian Poems for Children* by David Booth, illustrated by Kady MacDonald Denton; Kids Can Press, 1989; Viking, 1990.

1990 1st RUNNERUP *Little Fingerling: A Japanese Folktale* by Monica Hughes, illustrated by Brenda Clark; Kids Can Press, 1989.

1990 2nd RUNNERUP *The Name of the Tree* by Celia Barker Lottridge, illustrated by Ian Wallace; Douglas & McIntyre, 1989.

1991 *The Orphan Boy* by Tololwa M. Mollel, illustrated by Paul Morin; Oxford University Press, 1990.

1991 RUNNERUP *Voices on the Wind: Poems for All Seasons* selected by David Booth, illustrated by Michele Lemieux; Kids Can Press, 1990; Morrow, 1990.

1992 *Waiting For the Whales* by Sheryl McFarlane, illustrated by Ron Lightburn; Orca Books, 1991.

1992 RUNNERUP *Aska's Animals* by David Day, illustrated by Warabe Aska; Doubleday Canada, 1991.

1993 *The Dragons Pearls* retold by Julie Lawson, illustrated by Paul Morin; Oxford University Press, 1992.

HUNGRY MIND REVIEW CHILDREN'S BOOKS OF DISTINCTION
Hungry Mind Review
1648 Grand Ave.
St. Paul, MN 55105

Established in 1991 by the Hungry Mind Review, this listing honors outstanding books for young readers from preschool age to young adult level. In order to be eligible, the books must be adhere to the following criteria: (1) books for young readers, receiving their first U.S. publication during the preceding year; (2) books that are compelling to children and adults; (3) books with bold and fresh perspectives, reworking old themes or introducing new ones; (4) books sensitive to issues of culture and gender; (5) books of lasting quality, with special appeal to those building a home library.

Each year, three selections are made in each of six categories. They are Picturebooks/Fiction and Poetry; Picturebooks/Nonfiction; Middle Readers/Fiction and Poetry; Middle Readers/Nonfiction; Young Adults/Fiction and Poetry; and Young Adults/Nonfiction. Publishers are invited to nominate twelve books. A panel of judges makes the final selection. The winners are featured in the May issue of the Hungry Mind Review and on a poster that is distributed to independent bookstores.

1992 PICTUREBOOKS/FICTION *Abuela* by Arthur Dorros, illustrated by Elisa Kleven; Dutton, 1991.

Chicken Man written and illustrated by Michelle Edwards; Lothrop, Lee & Shepard, 1991.

Tar Beach written and illustrated by Faith Ringgold; Crown, 1991.

1992 PICTUREBOOKS/NONFICTION *Diego* by Jonah Winter, illustrated by Jeanette Winter; Knopf, 1991.

The Handmade Alphabet written and illustrated by Laura Rankin; Dial, 1991.

On the Day You Were Born written and illustrated by Debra Frasier; Harcourt Brace Jovanovich, 1991.

1992 MIDDLE READERS/FICTION *Make a Joyful Sound* edited by Deborah Slier, illustrated by Cornelius Van Wright and Ying-Hwa Hu; Checkerboard, 1991.

The Mozart Season by Virginia Euwer Wolff, not illustrated; Henry Holt, 1991.

Wish on a Unicorn by Karen Hesse, not illustrated; Henry Holt, 1991.

1992 MIDDLE READERS/NONFICTION *Living with Dinosaurs* by Patricia Lauber, illustrated by Douglas Henderson; Bradbury, 1991.

A Separate Battle: Women and the Civil War by Ina Chang, illustrated; Lodestar, 1991.

The Wright Brothers by Russell Freedman, illustrated; Holiday House, 1991.

1992 YOUNG ADULTS/FICTION *The Clay Marble* by Minfong Ho, not illustrated; Farrar, Straus & Giroux, 1991.

Face to Face by Marion Dane Bauer, not illustrated; Clarion, 1991.

Journey of the Sparrows by Fran Leeper Buss, with the assistance of Daisy Cubias, not illustrated; Lodestar, 1991.

1992 YOUNG ADULTS/NONFICTION *Frida Kahlo* by Malka Drucker, illustrated; Bantam, 1991.

The Kid's Guide to Social Action by Barbara A. Lewis, illustrated by Steve Michaels; Free Spirit, 1991.

Natural History from A to Z written and illustrated by Tim Arnold; McElderry, 1991.

1993 PICTUREBOOKS/FICTION *Elijah's Angel* by Michael J. Rosen, illustrated by Aminah Brenda Lynn Robinson; Harcourt Brace Jovanovich, 1992.

Sami and the Time of Troubles by Florence Parry Heide and Judith Heide Gilliland, illustrated by Ted Lewin; Clarion, 1992.

Sukey and the Mermaid by Robert D. San Souci, illustrated by Brian Pinkney; Four Winds, 1992.

1993 PICTUREBOOKS/NONFICTION *Saint Valentine* retold and illustrated by Robert Sabuda; Atheneum, 1992.

Jane Yolen's Mother Goose Songbook edited by Jane Yolen, illustrated by Rosekrans Hoffman, music by Adam Stemple; Boyds Mills Press, 1992.

Li'l Sis and Uncle Willie by Gwen Everett, illustrated by William H. Johnson; Rizzoli, 1992.

1993 MIDDLE READERS/FICTION *The Dark-Thirty: Southern Tales of the Supernatural* by Patricia C. McKissack, illustrated by Brian Pinkney; Knopf, 1992.

Missing May by Cynthia Rylant, not illustrated; Orchard, 1992.

Neighborhood Odes by Gary Soto, illustrated by David Diaz; Harcourt Brace Jovanovich, 1992.

1993 MIDDLE READERS/NONFICTION *Science Wizardry for Kids* by Margaret Kenda and Phyllis S. Williams, illustrated by Tim Robinson; Barron's, 1992.

The Sacred Harvest: Ojibway Wild Rice Gathering by Gordon Regguinti, photographs by Dale Kakkak; Lerner, 1992.

Children of the Dust Bowl by Jerry Stanley; Crown, 1992.

1993 YOUNG ADULTS/FICTION *Taste of Salt: A Story of Modern Haiti* by Frances Temple, not illustrated; Orchard, 1992.

Shadow Man by Cynthia D. Grant, not illustrated; Atheneum, 1992.

Against the Storm by Gaye Hicyilmaz, not illustrated; Little Brown, 1992.

1993 YOUNG ADULTS/NONFICTION *Rosa Parks: My Story* by Rosa Parks with Jim Haskins; Dial, 1992.

From Archetype to Zeitgeist: Powerful Ideas for Powerful Thinking by Herbert Kohl; Little Brown, 1992.

The World in 1492 by Jean Fritz, Katherine Paterson, Patricia McKissack, Fredrick McKissack, Margaret Mahy and Jamake Highwater, illustrated by Stefano Vitale; Henry Holt, 1992.

I

INDIAN PAINTBRUSH AWARD
Wyoming Library Association
Box 1387
Cheyenne, WY 82003

This children's choice award was established in 1985 by the Wyoming Library Association for the purpose of promoting reading for Wyoming youth. It is also hoped that program will help students become acquainted with the best contemporary authors, become aware of the qualities that make a good book, and choose the best rather than the mediocre.

The books on the master list are chosen by students in grades four through six. These same children are encouraged to read or listen to as many of the nominated books as possible and to vote for their favorite. The winning author receives an original watercolor that is presented at the annual conference of the Wyoming Library Association.

1986 *Naya Nuki: Girl Who Ran* by Ken Thomasma, illustrated by Eunice Hundley; Baker Book House, 1983.

1987 *The Hot and Cold Summer* by Johanna Hurwitz, illustrated by Gail Owens; Morrow, 1984.

1988 *The Dollhouse Murders* by Betty Ren Wright, not illustrated; Holiday House, 1983.

1989 *The Return of the Indian* by Lynn Reid Banks, illustrated by William Geldart; Doubleday, 1986.

1990 *There's a Boy in the Girls' Bathroom* by Louis Sachar, not illustrated; Knopf, 1987.

1991 *Matilda* by Roald Dahl, illustrated by Quentin Blake; Viking Kestrel, 1988.

1992 *Maniac Magee* by Jerry Spinelli, not illustrated; Little Brown, 1990.

1993 *Pathki Nana: Kootenai Girl Solves a Mystery* by Ken Thomasma, illustrated by Jack Brouwer; Baker House Books, 1991.

INDIANA AUTHOR'S DAY AWARDS
discontinued

In 1950, the Indiana University Writers' Conference established this annual award to recognize the most distinguished Hoosier book of the year in various categories. One of those categories was children's literature, with subdivisions for young children, children, and young adult. The children's awards were given from 1955 to 1972, when the entire award program was discontinued. Books published in the preceding year by authors born or residing in Indiana were eligible. The winning authors received a certificate at the annual Author's Day luncheon on the opening day of National Library Week.

1955 **CHILDREN** *George Rogers Clark: Soldier and Hero* by Jeannette C. Nolan, illustrated by Lee Ames; Messner, 1954.

1956 **CHILDREN** *After-harvest Festival: The Story of a Girl of the Old Kankakee* by Dorothy Fay Arbuckle, illustrated by Maurice Whitman; Dodd, 1955.

1957 **CHILDREN** *Stars for Christy* by Mabel Leigh Hunt, illustrated by Velma Ilsley; Lippincott, 1956.

1958 **CHILDREN** *Benjamin Franklin* by Clara Ingram Judson, illustrated by Robert Frankenberg; Follett, 1957.

1958 **SPECIAL CITATION** Augusta Stevenson

1959 **CHILDREN** *Head High, Ellen Brody* by Elisabeth H. Friermood, not illustrated; Doubleday, 1958.

1960 **YOUNG CHILDREN** *Abe Lincoln Gets his Chance* by Frances Cavanah, illustrated by Paula Hutchison; Rand, 1959.

1960 **YOUNG ADULT** *St. Lawrence Seaway* by Clara Ingram Judson, illustrated by Lorence F. Bjorklund; Follett, 1959.

1961 **YOUNG CHILDREN** *Becky and her Brave Cat, Bluegrass* by Miriam E. Mason, illustrated by Robert MacLean; Macmillan, 1960.

1961 **YOUNG ADULT** *Spy for the Confederacy: Rose O'Neal Greenhow* by Jeannette C. Nolan, not illustrated; Messner, 1960.

1962 **YOUNG Children** *Cupola House* by Mabel Leigh Hunt, illustrated by Nora S. Unwin; Lippincott, 1961.

1962 **YOUNG ADULT** *Secrets of Minos: Sir Arthur Evans' Discoveries at Crete* by Alan Honour, illustrated with photographs and line drawings; Whittlesey House, 1961.

1963 **YOUNG Children** *Tonk and Tonka* by Eugene Ackerman, illustrated by Carl Burger; Dutton, 1962.

1963 **CHILDREN** *Cathie and the Paddy Boy* written and illustrated by Nora Tully MacAlvay; Viking, 1962.

1964 **CHILDREN** *The Shepard of Abu Kush* by Louise A. Stinetorf, not illustrated; Day, 1963.

1964 **YOUNG ADULT** *Glass and Man* written and illustrated by Anne F. Huether; Lippincott, 1963.

1965 **YOUNG CHILDREN** *May I Bring a Friend?* by Beatrice Schenk de Regniers, illustrated by Beni Montresor; Atheneum, 1964.

1965 **YOUNG ADULT** *The Mystery of the Tarnished Trophy* by John F. Carson, not illustrated; Farrar, 1964.

1966 **CHILDREN** *Shoon: Wild Pony of the Moors* written and illustrated by Eunice Young Smith; Bobbs Merrill, 1965.

1966 **YOUNG ADULT** *A Sense of Magic* by Kate McNair, not illustrated; Chilton, 1965.

1967 **CHILDREN** *Cappyboppy* written and illustrated by Bill Peet; Houghton, 1966.

1967 **YOUNG ADULT** *To Survive We Must be Clever* by Gertrude E. Finney, illustrated by Carl Kidwell; McKay, 1966.

1968 **CHILDREN** *Andy and Willie* by Lee Sheridan Cox, not illustrated; Scribner, 1967.

1968 **YOUNG ADULT** *Tormented Genius: The Struggles of Vincent Van Gogh* by Alan Honour, illustrated with photographs; Morrow, 1967.

1968 **SPECIAL CITATION** Jeannette Covert Nolan

1969 **CHILDREN** *Tomahawk Claim* by Dorothea J. Snow, illustrated with maps; Bobbs Merrill, 1968.

1969 **YOUNG ADULT** *A Million Guitars and Other Stories* by Paul Boles, not illustrated; Little Brown, 1967.

1969 **SPECIAL AWARD** *Gemini: A Personal Account of Man's Venture into Space* by Virgil Grissom, illustrated with photographs; Macmillan, 1968.

1970 **CHILDREN** *Clocks, From Shadow to Atom* by Kathryn K. Borland and Helen R. Speicher, illustrated by Robert W. Addison; Follett, 1969.

1970 **YOUNG ADULT** *Lady Queen Anne: A Biography of Queen Anne of England* by Margaret Hodges, illustrated with photographs; Farrar, 1969.

1971 **CHILDREN** *Langston Hughes: Poet of his People* by Elisabeth P. Myers, illustrated by Russell Hoover; Garrard, 1970.

1971 **YOUNG ADULT** *The Castaways* by Jamie Lee Cooper, not illustrated; Bobbs Merrill, 1970.

1972 **CHILDREN** *A Day in the Country* by Willis Barnstone, illustrated by Howard Knotts; Harper & Row, 1971.

1972 **YOUNG ADULT** *American Painter in Paris: A Life of Mary Cassatt* by Ellen Janet Wilson, illustrated with plates; Farrar, 1971.

INFORMATION BOOK AWARD
Children's Literature Roundtables of Canada
c/o Ronald Jobe
Dept. of Language Education
Faculty of Education
University of British Columbia
Vancouver, British Columbia V6T 1Z5
Canada

Sponsored by the Children's Literature Roundtables of Canada, this annual award is presented to the outstanding information book published for children ages five to fifteen. To be eligible, the book must be written by a Canadian citizen or landed immigrant and have been published the preceding year. A cash award of $500 is presented to the winning author.

1987 *Looking At Insects* by David Suzuki with Barbara Hehner, illustrated; Stoddart, 1986.

1988 *Let's Celebrate! Canada's Special Days* by written and illustrated by Caroline Parry; Kids Can Press, 1987.

1989 *Exploring the Sky By Day* by Terence Dickinson, illustrated; Camden House, 1988.

1990 *Wolf Island* by Celia Godkin, illustrated; Fitzhenry & Whiteside, 1989.

1991 *Hands On, Thumbs Up* by Camilla Gryski, illustrated by Pat Cupples; Kids Can Press, 1990.

1992 *A Tree in the Forest* written and illustrated by Jan Thornhill; Greey de Pencier, 1991.

1992 HONOUR *Canadian Garbage Collectors* by Paulette Bourgeois, illustrated by Kim LaFave; Kids Can Press, 1991.

Discover Bones by Lesley Grant, illustrated by Tina Holdcroft; Kids Can Press, 1991.

INTERNATIONAL BOARD ON BOOKS FOR YOUNG PEOPLE (IBBY) HONOUR LIST

Leena Maissen, Director
IBBY Secretariat
Nonnenweg 12
Postfach
CH-4003
Basel, Switzerland

Every two years since 1956, in connection with the Hans Christian Andersen Awards, an IBBY Honour List is announced. These books were originally selected by the same jury which selected the Hans Christian Andersen Medals. At the present time, each national section participates in the final selection. Each national section may submit one entry in each of three categories: excellence in writing, illustration (since 1974), and translation (since 1978). The books nominated for writing and illustration must have been first published no earlier than three years before the awards are presented. For a country with a substantial and continuing production of children's books in more than one language, up to three books may be submitted for writing. One book is cited as an example of the honored translator's work.

Important considerations in selecting the honour list titles are that the books chosen be representative of the best in children's literature from each country and that the books are recommended as suitable for publication throughout the world. This furthers the IBBY goal of encouraging world understanding through children's literature. The diplomas are presented at the biennial congress of IBBY by the president of the IBBY.

The recipients listed below are the winners from English speaking countries only.

1956 GREAT BRITAIN *Lavender's Blue* by Kathleen Lines, illustrated by Harold Jones; Watts, 1954.

Minnow on the Say by A. Philippa Pearce, illustrated by Edward Ardizzone; Oxford, 1955.

1956 USA *Carry on, Mr. Bowditch* by Jean Lee Latham, illustrated by J.O. Cosgrove; Houghton, 1955.

Men, Microscopes and Living Things by Katherine B. Shippen, illustrated by Anthony Ravielli; Viking, 1955.

Play with Me written and illustrated by Marie Hall Ets; Viking, 1955.

1958 CANADA *Lost in the Barrens* by Farley Mowat, illustrated by Charles Geer; Little Brown, 1956.

1958 GREAT BRITAIN *The Fairy Doll* by Rumer Godden, illustrated by Adrienne Adams; Macmillan, 1956.

1958 USA *The House of Sixty Fathers* by Meindert DeJong, illustrated by Maurice Sendak; Harper, 1956.

1960 CANADA *Nkwala* by Edith Lambert Sharp, illustrated by William Winter; Little Brown, 1958.

1960 GREAT BRITAIN *Tom's Midnight Garden* by A. Philippa Pearce, illustrated by Susan Einzig; Oxford, 1958; Lippincott, 1959.

Warrior Scarlet by Rosemary Sutcliff, illustrated by Charles Keeping; Oxford, 1958; Walck, 1958.

1960 USA *Along Came a Dog* by Meindert DeJong, illustrated by Maurice Sendak; Harper, 1958.

The Witch of Blackbird Pond by Elizabeth George Speare, not illustrated; Houghton, 1958.

1962 CANADA *The Sunken City* by James McNeill, illustrated by Theo Dimson; Oxford, 1959.

1962 GREAT BRITAIN *Tangara: Let Us Set off Again* by Nan Chauncy, illustrated by Brian Wildsmith; Oxford, 1960.

The Borrowers Afloat by Mary Norton, illustrated by Diana Stanley; Dent, 1959.

1962 USA *Island of the Blue Dolphins* by Scott O'Dell, not illustrated; Houghton, 1960.

1964 CANADA *The Incredible Journey: A Tale of Three Animals* by Shelia Every Burnford, illustrated by Carl Burger; Little Brown, 1961.

1964 GREAT BRITAIN *The Twelve and the Genii* by Pauline Clarke, illustrated by Cecil Leslie; Faber, 1962.

1964 USA *The Bronze Bow* by Elizabeth George Speare, not illustrated; Houghton, 1961.

1966 GREAT BRITAIN *The Namesake: A Story of King Alfred* written and illustrated by C. Walter Hodges; Bell, 1964.

1966 USA *Where the Wild Things Are* written and illustrated by Maurice Sendak; Harper, 1963.

1968 GREAT BRITAIN *Louie's Lot* by E. W. Hildick, illustrated by Iris Schweitzer; Faber, 1965.

1968 USA *Valley of the Smallest: The Life Story of a Shrew* by Aileen Fisher, illustrated by Jean Zallinger; Crowell, 1966.

1970 AUSTRALIA *I Own the Racecourse* by Patricia Wrightson, illustrated by Margaret Horder; Hutchinson, 1969.

1970 USA *Up a Road Slowly* by Irene Hunt, not illustrated; Follett, 1966.

1972 AUSTRALIA *Blue Fin* by Colin Thiele, illustrated by Roger Haldane; Rigby, 1969.

1972 USA *The Trumpet of the Swan* by E.B. White, illustrated by Edward Frascino; Harper & Row, 1970.

1974 TEXT/AUSTRALIA *Josh* by Ivan Southall, not illustrated; Angus & Robertson, 1971.

1974 TEXT/GREAT BRITAIN *What the Neighbours Did and Other Stories* by A. Philippa Pearce, illustrated by Faith Jacques; Longman, 1972.

1974 TEXT/USA *The Headless Cupid* by Zilpha Keatley Snyder, illustrated by Alton Raible; Atheneum, 1971.

1974 ILLUSTRATION/AUSTRALIA *Joseph and Lulu and the Prindiville House Pigeons* written and illustrated by Ted Greenwood; Angus & Robertson, 1972.

1974 ILLUSTRATION/GREAT BRITAIN *Titch* written and illustrated by Pat Hutchins; Bodley Head, 1972.

1974 ILLUSTRATION/USA *The Funny Little Woman* retold by Arlene Mosel, illustrated by Blair Lent; Dutton, 1972.

1976 TEXT/AUSTRALIA *The Nargun and the Stars* by Patricia Wrightson, not illustrated; Hutchinson, 1973.

1976 TEXT/CANADA *Alligator Pie* by Dennis Lee, illustrated by Frank Newfeld; Macmillan Canada, 1974.

1976 **TEXT/GREAT BRITAIN** *The Ghost of Thomas Kempe* by Penelope Lively, illustrated by Antony Maitland; Heinemann, 1973.

1976 **TEXT/USA** *M.C. Higgins, the Great* by Virginia Hamilton, not illustrated; Macmillan, 1974.

1976 **ILLUSTRATION/AUSTRALIA** *Mulga Bill's Bycycle* by A.B. Paterson, illustrated by Deborah Niland and Kilmeny Niland; Collins, 1973.

1976 **ILLUSTRATION/CANADA** *The Sleighs of my Childhood/ Les Traineaux de mon Enfance* bilingual text written and illustrated by Carlo Italiano; Tundra, 1974.

1976 **ILLUSTRATION/GREAT BRITAIN** *How Tom Beat Captain Najork and his Hired Sportsmen* by Russell Hoban, illustrated by Quentin Blake; Cape, 1974.

1976 **ILLUSTRATION/USA** *Dawn* written and illustrated by Uri Shulevitz; Farrar, 1974.

1978 **TEXT/AUSTRALIAm** *The October Child* by Eleanor Spence, illustrated by Malcolm Green; Oxford, 1976.

1978 **TEXT/CANADA** *Garbage Delight* by Dennis Lee, illustrated by Frank Newfeld; Macmillan Canada, 1977.

Mousewoman and the Vanished Princesses by Christie Harris, illustrated by Douglas Tait; McClelland & Stewart, 1976.

1978 **TEXT/GREAT BRITAIN** *A Year and a Day* by William Mayne, illustrated by Krystyna Turska; Hamilton, 1976.

1978 **TEXT/USA** *Tuck Everlasting* by Natalie Babbitt, not illustrated; Farrar, 1975.

1978 **ILLUSTRATION/AUSTRALIA** *The Runaway Punt* by Michael F. Page, illustrated by Robert R. Ingpen; Rigby, 1976.

1978 **ILLUSTRATION/CANADA** *La Cachette* by Ginette Anfousse, illustrated; La Tamanoir, 1976.

1978 **ILLUSTRATION/GREAT BRITAIN** *Thorn Rose* by Jacob Grimm and Wilhelm Grimm, illustrated by Errol LeCain; Faber, 1975.

1978 **TRANSLATION/GREAT BRITAIN** *The Cucumber King: A Story with a Beginning, a Middle and an End* by Christine Nostlinger, translated by Anthea Bell, illustrated by Werner Maurer; Abelard Schuman, 1975.

1978 **ILLUSTRATION/USA** *Hush, Little Baby* written and illustrated by Margot Zemach; Dutton, 1976.

1978 **TRANSLATION/USA** *Glassblower's Children* by Maria Gripe, translated by Sheila LaFarge, illustrated by Harald Gripe; Delacorte/Lawrence, 1973.

1980 **TEXT/AUSTRALIA** *A Dream of Seas* by Lilith Norman, illustrated by Edwina Bell; Collins, 1978.

1980 **TEXT/CANADA** *Hold Fast* by Kevin Major, not illustrated; Clark, Irwin, 1978.

1980 **TEXT/GREAT BRITAIN** *The Gods in Winter* by Patricia Miles, not illustrated; Hamilton, 1978.

1980 **TEXT/USA** *Ramona and her Father* by Beverly Cleary, illustrated by Alan Tiegreen; Morrow, 1977.

1980 **ILLUSTRATION/AUSTRALIA** *The Quinkins* written and illustrated by Percy J. Trezise and Dick Roughsey; Collins, 1978.

1980 **ILLUSTRATION/CANADA** *La Chicane (The Wrangle)* written and illustrated by Ginette Anfousse; La Courte Echelle, 1978.

1980 **ILLUSTRATION/GREAT BRITAIN** *Each Peach, Pear, Plum* written and illustrated by Janet Ahlberg and Allan Ahlberg; Kestrel, 1978.

1980 **ILLUSTRATION/USA** *Noah's Ark* written and illustrated by Peter Spier; Doubleday, 1977.

1980 **TRANSLATION/CANADA** *Les Chemins Secrets de la Liberte* by Barbara Smucker, translated by Paule C. Daveluy, illustrated by Tom McNeely; Pierre Tisseyire, 1978.

1980 **TRANSLATION/GREAT BRITAIN** *The Sea Lord* by Alet Schouten, translated by Patricia Crampton, illustrated by Rien Poortvliet; Methuen, 1977.

1980 **TRANSLATION/USA** *The Magic Stone* by Leonie Kooiker, translated by Clara Winston and Richard Winston, illustrated by Carl Hollander; Morrow, 1978.

1982 **AUTHOR/AUSTRALIA** *Playing Beatie Bow* by Ruth Park, not illustrated; Kestrel, 1981, c1980; Atheneum, 1982, c1980.

1982 **AUTHOR/CANADA** *The Keeper of the Isis Light* by Monica Hughes, not illustrated; Hamish Hamilton, 1980.

1982 **AUTHOR/GREAT BRITAIN** *Tulku* by Peter Dickinson, not illustrated; Gollancz, 1979; Unicorn/Dutton, 1979.

1982 **AUTHOR/USA** *Autumn Street* by Lois Lowry, not illustrated; Houghton Mifflin, 1980.

1982 **ILLUSTRATION/AUSTRALIA** *The Rainforest Children* by Margaret Pittaway, illustrated by Heather Philpott; Oxford, 1980.

1982 **ILLUSTRATION/AUSTRIA** *Tiny* by Mira Lobe, illustrated by Angelika Kaufmann; Jugend & Volk, 1981.

1982 **ILLUSTRATION/CANADA** *Petrouchka* adapted and illustrated by Elizabeth Cleaver from the work of Igor Stravinsky and Alexandre Benois; Macmillan (Canada), 1980; Atheneum, 1980.

1982 **ILLUSTRATION/GREAT BRITAIN** *Mister Magnolia* written and illustrated by Quentin Blake; Cape, 1980.

1982 **ILLUSTRATION/GREECE** *The Planet Floor* written and illustrated by Yannis Xanthoulis; Asteri Bookshop, 1980.

1982 **ILLUSTRATION/USA** *The Garden of Abdul Gasazi* written and illustrated by Chris Van Allsburg; Houghton Mifflin, 1979.

1982 **TRANSLATION/AUSTRIA** *Am Ende der Spur* by Roy Brown, translated by Wolf Harranth; Benziger und Jungbrunner, 1981.

1982 **TRANSLATION/CANADA** *The King's Daughter* by Suzanne Martel, translated by David Toby Homel and Margaret Rose; Douglas & McIntyre, 1980.

1982 **TRANSLATION/FRANCE** *Incroyables Adventures de Mister MacMiffic* by Sid Fleischman, translated by Jean Queval; Fernand Nathan, 1979. (Original English *Mr. McBroom's Wonderful One-Acre Farm*).

1982 TRANSLATION/GERMAN FEDERAL REPUBLIC *Hinter dem Norwind* by George MacDonald, translated by Sybil Grafin Schonfeldt; Annette Betz, 1981. (Original English *At the Back of the North Wind*).

1982 TRANSLATION/GREAT BRITAIN *The Big Janosch Book of Fun and Verse* by Janosch, translated by Anthea Bell; Andersen Press, 1980.

1982 TRANSLATION/ISRAEL *Pundak Ha-Eima* by Isaac Bashevis Singer, translated by Yehuda Meltzer; Adam, 1980. (Original English *The Fearsome Inn*).

1982 TRANSLATION/NORWAY *Den Fjerneste Kyst* by Ursula K. LeGuin, translated by Jon Bing; Gyldendal Norsk Forlag, 1980. (Original English *The Farthest Shore*).

1982 TRANSLATION/USA *Zlateh the Goat and Other Stories* by Isaac Bashevis Singer, translated by Elizabeth Shub, illustrated by Maurice Sendak; Harper, 1966.

1984 WRITING/AUSTRALIA *The Watcher in the Garden* by Joan Phipson, not illustrated; Methuen, 1982.

1984 WRITING/CANADA *The Root Cellar* by Janet Lunn, illustrated with a map; Lester & Orpen Dennys, 1981.

1984 WRITING/GREAT BRITAIN *All the King's Men* by William Mayne, not illustrated; Cape, 1982.

1984 WRITING/USA *Sweet Whispers, Brother Rush* by Virginia Hamilton; Philomel, 1982.

1984 ILLUSTRATION/AUSTRALIA *Who Sank the Boat?* written and illustrated by Pamela Allen; Nelson Australia, 1982.

1984 ILLUSTRATION/CANADA *A Northern Alphabet* written and illustrated by Ted Harrison; Tundra, 1982.

1984 ILLUSTRATION/GREAT BRITAIN *Hansel and Gretel* by Jacob Grimm and Wilhelm Grimm, illustrated by Anthony Browne; Julia MacRae, 1981.

1984 ILLUSTRATION/USA *Doctor DeSoto* written and illustrated by William Steig; Farrar, 1982.

1984 TRANSLATION/AUSTRIA *Ganesh Oder Eine Neue Welt* by Malcolm J. Bosse, translated by Wolf Harranth (original English: *Ganesh*); Jungbrunner, 1982.

1984 TRANSLATION/CANADA *Je t'Attends a Peggy's Cove* by Brian Doyle, translated by Claude Aubry; Pierre Tisseyre, 1982. (original English *You Can Pick Me Up at Peggy's Cove*).

1984 TRANSLATION/GERMAN FEDERAL REPUBLIC *Der Gelbe Vogel* by Myron Levoy, translated by Fred Schmitz; Benziger, 1981. (original English *Alan and Naomi*).

1984 TRANSLATION/GREAT BRITAIN *The Magic Inkstand and other Stories* by Heinrich Seidel, translated by Elizabeth Watson Taylor; Cape, 1982.

1984 TRANSLATION/ISRAEL *Sefereggel* by Dr. Seuss, translated by Leah Naor; Keter, 1982. (original English *The Foot Book*).

1984 TRANSLATION/ITALY *Storia di una Volpe* by Ruth Manning Sanders, translated by Daniela Camboni; Nouve Edizioni Romane, 1981. (original English *Fox Tales*).

1984 TRANSLATION/JAPAN *Gin no Ude no Otto* by Howard Pyle, translated by Shigeo Watanabe; Kaisei-sha, 1983, rev. ed. (original English *Otto of the Silver Hand*).

1984 TRANSLATION/SWEDEN *Dansa Pa Min Grav* by Aidan Chambers, translated by Ingvar Skogsberg; Awe/Gebbers, 1983. (original English *Dance on my Grave*).

1984 TRANSLATION/USA *The Battle Horse* by Harry Kullman, translated by George Blecher and Lone Thygesen-Blecher; Bradbury, 1981.

1984 TRANSLATION/VENEZUELA *El Diablillo de la Botella* by Robert Louis Stevenson, translated by Ellie; Ediciones Ekare-Banco del Libro, 1981. (original English *The Bottle Imp*).

1986 WRITING/AUSTRALIA *Dancing in the Anzac Deli* by Nadia Wheatley, illustrated by Neil Phillips and Waldemar Buczynski; Oxford, 1984.

1986 WRITING/CANADA *Sweetgrass* by Jan Hudson, not illustrated; Tree Frog Press, 1984.

1986 WRITING/GREAT BRITAIN *The Changeover* by Margaret Mahy, not illustrated; Dent, 1984.

1986 WRITING/NIGERIA *Without a Silver Spoon* by Eddie Iroh, not illustrated; Spectrum Books, 1981.

1986 WRITING/USA *One-Eyed Cat* by Paula Fox, not illustrated; Bradbury, 1984.

1986 ILLUSTRATION/AUSTRALIA *Possum Magic* by Mem Fox, illustrated by Julie Vivas; Omnibus Books, 1983.

1986 ILLUSTRATION/CANADA *Chin Chiang and the Dragon's Dance* written and illustrated by Ian Wallace; Douglas & McIntyre, 1984.

1986 ILLUSTRATION/GREAT BRITAIN *Hiawatha's Childhood* by Henry Wadsworth Longfellow, illustrated by Errol LeCain; Faber, 1984.

1986 ILLUSTRATION/USA *The People Could Fly* by Virginia Hamilton, illustrated by Leo Dillon and Diane Dillon; Knopf, 1985; Walker, 1985.

1986 TRANSLATION/AUSTRIA *Kwajo und das Geheimnis de Trommelmannchens* by Meshack Asare, translated by Kathe Recheis; Verlag Jungbrunner, 1984. (original English: *The Brassman's Secret*).

1986 TRANSLATION/CANADA *Emilie de la Nouvelle Lune* by Lucy Montgomery, translated by Paule Daveluy; Pierre Tisseyre, 1983. (original English: *Emily of the New Moon*).

1986 TRANSLATION/FINLAND *Tuhatkiloinen Kultakala* by Betsy Byars, translated by Pirkko Lokka; WSOY, 1984. (original English: *The Two-Thousand Pound Goldfish*).

1986 TRANSLATION/GERMAN FEDERAL REPUBLIC *Sophiechen und der Riese* by Roald Dahl, translated by Adam Quidam; Rowohlt, 1984. (original English: *The BFG*).

1986 TRANSLATION/GREAT BRITAIN *The Fifth Corner* by Kristina Ehrenstrale, translated by Patricia Crampton; Methuen, 1984.

1986 TRANSLATION/IRAN *Mowje Bozorg* by Pearl S. Buck, translated by Soraya Ghezelayagh; Vaje, 1984. (original English *The Big Wave*).

1986 TRANSLATION/JAPAN *Unmei no Kishi* by Rosemary Sutcliff, translated by Yoko Inokuma; Iwanami-shoten, 1970. (original English *Knight's Fee*).

1986 TRANSLATION/MEXICO *Principio y Fin Tiempo de Vida que Trancurre Entre el Nacer y el Morir* by Bryan Mellonie, translated by Carmen Esteva and Miguel Leon; Compania Editorial Continental, 1984. (original English *Beginnings and Endings with LIFETIMES in Between*).

1986 TRANSLATION/NORWAY *SVK* by Roald Dahl, translated by Tor Edvin Dahl; Gyldendal Norsk Forlag, 1984. (original English *The BFG*).

1986 TRANSLATION/SWEDEN *Den Fortrollade Floden* by Beverly Nichols, translated by Eva Imber Liljeberg; Laseleket, 1985. (original English *The Stream that Stood Still*).

1986 TRANSLATION/USA *Petros' War* by Alki Zei, translated by Edward Fenton, not illustrated; Dutton, 1972.

1986 TRANSLATION/VENEZUELA *El Rojo es el Mejor* by Kathy Stinson, translated by Kiki de la Rosa and Clarisa de la Rosa; Ediciones Ekare-Banco del Libro, 1985. (original English: *Red is Best*).

1988 WRITING/AUSTRALIA *Riverman* by Allan Baillie, not illustrated; Thomas Nelson, 1986.

1988 WRITING/CANADA *Shadow in Hawthorn Bay* by Janet Lunn, not illustrated; Lester & Orpen Dennys, 1986; Scribner's, 1986.

1988 WRITING/GREAT BRITAIN *Woof!* by Allan Ahlberg, illustrated by Fritz Wegner; Viking Kestrel, 1986.

1988 WRITING/USA *Sarah, Plain and Tall* by Patricia MacLachlan, not illustrated; Harper & Row, 1985.

1988 ILLUSTRATION/AUSTRALIA *First There Was Frances* written and illustrated by Bob Graham ; Lothian, 1985.

1988 ILLUSTRATION/CANADA *The Emperor's Panda* by David Day, illustrated by Eric Beddows; McClelland & Stewart, 1986.

1988 ILLUSTRATION/ GREAT BRITAIN *The Jolly Postman: or, Other People's Letters* written and illustrated by Allan Ahlberg and Janet Ahlberg; Heinemann, 1986.

1988 ILLUSTRATION/USA *The Paper Crane* written and illustrated by Molly Bang; Greenwillow, 1985.

1988 TRANSLATION/USA *Don't Say a Word* by Barbara Gehrts, not illustrated; McElderry, 1986.

1990 WRITING/AUSTRALIA *My Place* by Nadia Wheatley, illustrated by Donna Rawlins; Collins Dove, 1987.

1990 WRITING/CANADA *Bad Boy* by Diana Wieler, not illustrated; Douglas & McIntyre, 1989; Delacorte, 1992.

1990 WRITING/GREAT BRITAIN *Slambash Wangs of a Compo Gormer* by Robert Leeson, illustrated by Steve Crisp; Collins, 1987.

1990 WRITING/USA *Lincoln: a Photobiography* by Russell Freedman, illustrated with photographs; Clarion, 1987.

1990 ILLUSTRATION/AUSTRALIA *Where the Forest Meets the Sea* written and illustrated by Jeannie Baker; Julia MacRae Books, 1987.

1990 ILLUSTRATION/CANADA *Could You Stop Josephine?* written and illustrated by Stephane Poulin; Tundra, 1988.

1990 ILLUSTRATION/GREAT BRITAIN *Easter* adapted and illustrated by Jan Pienkowski; William Heinemann, 1989.

1990 ILLUSTRATION/USA *Owl Moon* by Jane Yolen, illustrated by John Schoenherr; Philomel, 1987.

1990 TRANSLATION/USA *Crutches* by Peter Hartling, not illustrated; Lothrop Lee & Shepard, 1988.

1992 WRITING/USA *Shabanu: Daughter of the Wind* by Suzanne Fisher Staples, not illustrated; Knopf, 1989.

1992 ILLUSTRATION/USA *Little Tricker the Squirrel Meets Big Double the Bear* by Ken Chase, illustrated by Barry Moser; Viking, 1990.

1992 TRANSLATION/USA *We Were Not Like Other People* by Efraim Sevela, translated by Antonia W. Bouis, not illustrated; Harper & Row, 1989.

INTERNATIONAL BROTHERS GRIMM AWARD
International Institute for Children's Literature
10-6 Bampaku-Koen
Senri
Suita-Shi 565
Osaka, Japan

This award was established in 1987, the bicentenary of the birth of the Brothers Grimm. The International Brothers Grimm Award is sponsored by the International Institute for Children's Literature in Osaka and supported by the Kinran Foundation. The purpose of the award is to promote research in children's literature.

This biennial award is given to recipients who have performed outstanding work in children's literature research or who have contributed to the promotion of such research. A selection committee of ten members choose the recipient who receives a commemorative prize and a $10,000 cash award.

1987 Dr. Klaus Doderer

1989 Dr. Gote Klingberg

1991 Dr. James Fraser

1993 Shin Torigoe

INTERNATIONAL ORDER OF THE DAUGHTERS OF THE EMPIRE (IODE) BEST CHILDREN'S BOOK OF THE YEAR
Education Secretary
Municipal Chapter of Toronto IODE
40 St. Claire Avenue East
Suite 205
Toronto, Ontario M4T 1M9
Canada

First awarded in 1974, this annual award is sponsored by the Municipal Chapter of Toronto IODE. The purpose of this award is to encourage the publication of books for children between the ages of six and twelve. In order to be eligible, the book must be written or illustrated by a resident of Toronto and must be published by a Canadian publisher in the year preceding the award. The selection committee consists of representatives of the Municipal Chapter of Toronto IODE and staff members of the Toronto Library Board. A prize of $1000 as well as the award is presented to the winning author or illustrator at the annual meeting of the Toronto IODE.

1974 *Alligator Pie* by Dennis Lee, illustrated by Frank Newfeld; Macmillan Canada, 1974.

1975 *A Prairie Boy's Summer* written and illustrated by William Kurelek; Tundra, 1975.

1976 *How the Kookaburra Got his Laugh* by Aviva Layton, illustrated by Robert Smith; McClelland & Stewart, 1976.

1977 *The Loon's Necklace* by William Toye, illustrated by Elizabeth Cleaver; Oxford, 1977.

1978 *My Name Is not Oddessa Yarker* by Marian Engel, illustrated by Laszlo Gal; Kids Can Press, 1977.

The Shirt of the Happy Man by Mariella Bertelli, illustrated by Laszlo Gal; Kids Can Press, 1977.

Why the Man in the Moon Is Happy and Other Eskimo Creation Stories by Ronald Melzack, illustrated by Laszlo Gal; McClelland & Stewart, 1977.

1979 *The Twelve Dancing Princesses* retold by Janet Lunn, illustrated by Laszlo Gal; Methuen, 1979.

1980 *Afraid of the Dark* by Barry Dickson, illustrated by Olena Kassian; Lorimer, 1980.

The Hungry Time by Selwyn Dewdney, illustrated by Olena Kassian; Lorimer, 1980.

1981 *That Scatterbrain Booky* by Bernice Thurman Hunter; Scholastic-TAB, 1981.

1982 *Red Is Best* by Kathy Stinson, illustrated by Robin Baird Lewis; Annick Press, 1982.

1983 *Zoom at Sea* by Tim Wynne-Jones, illustrated by Ken Nutt; Douglas & McIntyre, 1983.

1984 *Chin Chiang and the Dragon's Dance* written and illustrated by Ian Wallace; Douglas & McIntyre, 1984.

1985 *The Sorcerer's Apprentice* written and illustrated by Robin Muller; Kids Can Press, 1985.

1986 *Have You Seen Birds?* by Joanne Oppenheim, illustrated by Barbara Reid; North Winds Press, 1986; Scholastic, 1986.

1987 *Let's Celebrate! Canada's Special Days* written and illustrated by Caroline Parry; Kids Can Press, 1987.

1988 *Night Cars* by Teddy Jam, illustrated by Eric Beddows; Douglas & MacIntyre, 1988; Orchard, 1989.

1989 *Little Fingerling: A Japanese Folktale* by Monica Hughes, illustrated by Brenda Clark; Kids Can Press, 1989.

1990 *Voices on the Wind: Poems for all Seasons* selected by David Booth, illustrated by Michele Lemieux; Kids Can Press, 1990; Morrow, 1990.

INTERNATIONAL READING ASSOCIATION CHILDREN'S BOOK AWARD

Patricia C. DuBois
International Reading Association
800 Barksdale Road
Box 8139
Newark, DE 19714-8139

Sponsored by the International Reading Association, this annual award was first presented in 1975. In order to be eligible for this award, a book must be the author's first or second title for a juvenile audience. Fiction or nonfiction books written in any language for children or young adolescents will be considered. Beginning in 1987, there are two awards, at US $1000 each; one for a primary book and the other for a young adult book.

Appropriate titles may be entered for consideration by the author or publisher by sending seven copies of the book to the IRA Children's Book Award subcommittee. This committee considers all nominations and makes the final decision. A plaque and $1000 are awarded to the winning authors at the annual convention of the International Reading Association each spring.

Following are the more detailed eligibility and selection criteria developed by the International Reading Association: (1) The books are submitted only during the year of publication. 2) Both fiction and nonfiction are eligible; each will be rated according to characteristics that are specifically appropriate to the genre. (3) The winning book should serve as a literary standard by which readers can measure other books. (4) If appropriate to the genre, the winning book should provide believable and intriguing characters growing naturally out of the events and actions in the story. (5) The winning book should be truthful and authentic in its presentation of information and attitudes. (6) The characters and events in the book should be appropriate to the experience and expectations of the intended audience. (7) The winning book will be nonracist and nonsexist. (8) The winning book should encourage young readers to read by providing them with something they will delight in and profit from. (9) Entries submitted in a language other than English must include a one-page abstract of the book in English and a translation into English of one chapter or a similar selection that in the submitter's estimation is representative of the book. (From the standards set by the International Reading Association in February 1981.)

1975 *Transport 7-41-R* by T. Degens, not illustrated; Viking, 1974.

1976 *Dragonwings* by Laurence Yep, not illustrated; Harper, 1975.

1977 *A String in the Harp* by Nancy Bond, illustrated by Allen Davis; Atheneum, 1976.

1978 *A Summer to Die* by Lois Lowry, illustrated by Jenni Oliver; Houghton, 1977.

1979 *Reserved for Mark Anthony Crowder* by Alison Smith, not illustrated; Dutton, 1978.

1980 *Words by Heart* by Ouida Sebestyen, not illustrated; Little Brown, 1979.

1981 *My own Private Sky* by Delores Beckman, not illustrated; Dutton, 1980.

1982 *Goodnight, Mister Tom* by Michelle Magorian, not illustrated; Kestrel, 1981.

1983 *The Darkangel* by Meredith Ann Pierce, not illustrated; Little Brown, 1982.

1984 *Ratha's Creature* by Clare Bell, not illustrated; Atheneum, 1983.

1985 *Badger on the Barge and Other Stories* by Janni Howker, not illustrated; Julia MacRae, 1984; Greenwillow, 1984.

1986 *Prairie Songs* by Pam Conrad, illustrated by Darryl S. Zudeck; Harper, 1985.

1987 **PRIMARY** *The Line Up Book* written and illustrated by Marisabina Russo; Greenwillow, 1986.

1987 **YOUNG ADULT** *After the Dancing Days* by Margaret I. Rostkowski, not illustrated; Harper & Row, 1986.

1988 YOUNGER *The Third-Story Cat* written and illustrated by Leslie Baker; Little Brown, 1987.

1988 OLDER *The Ruby in the Smoke* by Philip Pullman, not illustrated; Knopf, 1985.

1989 YOUNGER *Rechenka's Eggs* written and illustrated by Patricia Polacco; Philomel, 1988.

1989 OLDER *Probably Still Nick Swansen* by Virginia Euwer Wolff, not illustrated; Henry Holt, 1988.

1990 YOUNGER *No Star Nights* by Anna Egan Smucker, illustrated by Steve Johnson; Knopf, 1989.

1990 OLDER *Children of the River* by Linda Crew, not illustrated; Delacorte, 1989.

1991 YOUNGER *Is This a House for Hermit Crab?* by Megan McDonald, illustrate by S.D. Schindler; Orchard, 1990.

1991 OLDER *Under the Hawthorn Tree* by Marita Conlon-McKenna, illustrated by Donald Teskey; Holiday House, 1990.

1992 YOUNGER *Ten Little Rabbits* by Virginia Grossman, illustrated by Sylvia Long; Chronicle Books, 1991.

1992 OLDER *Rescue Josh McGuire* by Ben Mikaelsen, not illustrated; Hyperion, 1991.

1993 YOUNGER *Old Turtle* by Douglas Wood, illustrated by Cheng-Kee Chee; Pfeiffer-Hamilton, 1992.

1993 OLDER *Letters from Rifka* by Karen Hesse, not illustrated; Holt, 1992.

IOWA CHILDREN'S CHOICE AWARD

Iowa Educational Media Association
2406 North Shore Dr.
Clear Lake, IA 50428

The Iowa Children's Choice Award is sponsored by the Iowa Educational Media Association and was first awarded in 1980. The purpose of the award is fourfold: to encourage children to read more and better books; to discriminate in choosing worthwhile books; to provide an avenue for positive dialogue between teacher, parent, and children about books and authors; and to give recognition to those who write books for children.

Nominations for the annual master list are accepted from students, teachers, media specialists, and administrators. Final selection of the master-list titles is made by a committee of media specialists. Books chosen for the master list must be written by American authors during the last five years. Both fiction and nonfiction titles appropriate for children in grades three through six are eligible. No textbooks are included. Except for the winning title, books may be reconsidered in succeeding years.

The students must read at least two titles from the master list in order to be eligible to vote. The students may read the book themselves or have heard it read by a teacher or parent. Students may vote for only one title and may not vote for a book they have not read. The voting results are sent to the book selection committee of the Iowa Educational Media Association for tabulation.

The winning author is invited to attend the awards ceremony at the IEMA spring conference, where he or she will be presented with an engraved bell.

1980 *How to Eat Fried Worms* by Thomas Rockwell, illustrated by Emily McCully; Watts, 1973.

1981 *The Great Gilly Hopkins* by Katherine Paterson, not illustrated; Crowell, 1978.

1982 *Bunnicula: A Rabbit Tale of Mystery* by Deborah Howe and James Howe, illustrated by Alan Daniel; Atheneum, 1980, c1979.

1983 *Superfudge* by Judy Blume, not illustrated; Dutton, 1980.

1984 *Nothing's Fair in Fifth Grade* by Barthe DeClements, not illustrated; Viking, 1981.

1985 *Ralph S. Mouse* by Beverly Cleary, illustrated by Paul O. Zelinsky; Morrow, 1982.

1986 *When the Boys Ran the House* by Joan Carris, illustrated by Carol Newsom; Lippincott, 1982.

1987 *Ramona Forever* by Beverly Cleary, illustrated by Alan Tiegreen; Morrow, 1984.

1988 *The Dollhouse Murders* by Betty Ren Wright, not illustrated; Holiday House, 1983.

1989 *The Night of the Twisters* by Ivy Ruckman, not illustrated; Crowell, 1984.

1990 *Wait Til Helen Comes* by Mary Downing Hahn, not illustrated; Clarion, 1986.

1991 *There's a Boy in the Girls' Bathroom* by Louis Sachar, not illustrated; Knopf, 1987.

1992 *Fudge* by Charlotte T. Graeber, illustrated by Cheryl Harness; Lothrop, Lee & Shepard, 1987.

IOWA TEEN AWARD

Iowa Educational Media Association
2406 North Shore Dr.
Clear Lake, IA 50428

First awarded in 1985, the purposes of the Iowa Teen Award are to encourage students to read more and better books, to discriminate in choosing worthwhile books, to provide an avenue for positive dialogue between teachers, parents and students about books and authors, and to give recognition to those who write books for early teens. This award is unique in that it gives early teens an opportunity to choose the book to receive the award and to suggest books for the yearly reading list.

The following guidelines govern the award procedure: (1) books must be published within the last six years, (2) fiction or nonfiction of interest to students in grades six through nine, (3) all titles except the winner may be repeated on the master list in succeeding years, and (4) students must read at least three titles. The winning author receives a brass apple.

1985 *Tiger Eyes* by Judy Blume, not illustrated; Bradbury; 1981.

1986 *When We First Met* by Norma Fox Mazer, not illustrated; Scholastic, 1984.

1987 *You Shouldn't Have to Say Good-Bye* by Patricia Heimes, not illustrated; Harcourt, 1982.

1988 *Abby, My Love* by Hadley Irwin, not illustrated; Atheneum, 1985.

1989 *The Other Side of Dark* by Joan Lowery Nixon, not illustrated; Delacorte, 1986.

1990 *Hatchet* by Gary Paulsen, not illustrated; Bradbury, 1987.

1991 *Silver* by Norma Fox Mazer, not illustrated; Morrow, 1988.

1992 *Don't Look Behind You* by Lois Duncan, not illustrated; Delacorte, 1989.

WASHINGTON IRVING CHILDREN'S BOOK CHOICE AWARD

Westchester Library Association
Jane Marino
White Plains Public Library
100 Martine Ave
White Plains, NY 10601-2599

This biennial award was established in 1982 by Betsy Seerman and Sara Miller for the Westchester Library Association. The purpose is to honor Westchester authors of children's books and to encourage reading and reading aloud throughout the county. In 1984 and 1986 a winner was chosen in both a fiction and nonfiction category. In 1988 illustration and younger fiction were added. Books for the master list are chosen on the basis of literary quality and popular appeal. Books must be published within two years preceding the award date. Children vote for their favorite book in each category. Winning authors are presented with a medal at a ceremony in May.

1984 **FICTION** *Zucchini* by Barbara Dana, illustrated by Eileen Christelow; Harper & Row, 1982.

1984 **NONFICTION** *The Secret Life of School Supplies* by Vicki Cobb, illustrated by Bill Morrison; Harper, 1981.

1986 **FICTION** *Peabody* written and illustrated by Rosemary Wells; Dial/Dutton, 1983.

1986 **NONFICTION** Hercules by Bernard Evslin; Morrow, 1984.

1988 **ILLUSTRATION** *Max's Christmas* written and illustrated by Rosemary Wells; Dial, 1986.

1988 **ALL AGES** *The Macmillan Book of Greek Gods and Heroes* by Alice Low, illustrated by Arvis Stewart; Macmillan, 1985.

1988 **YOUNGER FICTION** *There's a Monster under my Bed* by James Howe, illustrated by David Rose; Atheneum, 1986.

1988 **OLDER FICTION** *The Twenty-five Cent Miracle* by Theresa Nelson, not illustrated; Bradbury, 1986.

1990 **NONFICTION** *One Day in the Woods* by Jean Craighead George, illustrated by Gary Allen; Crowell, 1988.

1990 **ILLUSTRATION** *Bring Back the Deer* by Jeffrey Prusski, illustrated by Neil Waldman; Harcourt Brace Jovanovich, 1988.

1990 **OLDER FICTION** *Too Much Magic* by Samuel Sterman and Betsy Sterman, illustrated by Judy Glasser; Lippincott, 1987.

1990 **YOUNGER FICTION** *Dinosaur Cousins?* written and illustrated by Bernard Most; Harcourt Brace Jovanovich, 1987.

1992 **NONFICTION** *For Your Own Protection: Science Stories Photos Tell* by Vicki Cobb, illustrated with photos; Lothrop, Lee & Shepard, 1989.

1992 **NOVEL** *On the Far Side of the Mountain* written and illustrated by Jean Craighead George; Dutton, 1990.

1992 **ILLUSTRATION** *The Highwayman* by Alfred Noyes, illustrated by Neil Waldman; Harcourt, Brace, Jovanovich, 1990.

1992 **YOUNGER FICTION** *Max's Chocolate Chicken* written and illustrated by Rosemary Wells; Dial, 1989.

J

LELAND B. JACOBS AWARD

discontinued

This award, named in honor of Leland B. Jacobs, critic and poet, was sponsored jointly by the Friends of Leland B. Jacobs and the Columbia University School of Library Service. These annual awards were presented for the first time in 1980.

1980 Award information not available

1981 Louise M. Rosenblatt

1984 Jean Karl

JEFFERSON CUP AWARD

Deborah Trocchi, Executive Director
Virginia Library Association
669 S. Washington St
Alexandria, VA 22314

Sponsored by the Children's and Young Adult Round Table of the Virginia Library Association, the Jefferson Cup Award was first presented in 1983. The purpose of this award is to honor distinguished writing in American history, historical fiction, or biography for young people. The award is presented at the annual conference of the Virginia Library Association.

1983 *The Jewish Americans: A History in Their Own Words, 1650-1950* edited by Milton Meltzer, illustrated; Crowell, 1982.

1984 *Who Speaks for Wolf* by Paula Underwood Spencer, illustrated by Frank Howell; Tribe of Two Press, 1983.

1985 *In the Year of the Boar and Jackie Robinson* by Betty Lord, illustrated by Marc Simont; Harper, 1986.

1986 *Sarah, Plain and Tall* by Patricia MacLachlan, not illustrated; Harper, 1985.

1987 *After the Dancing Days* by Margaret I. Rostkowski, not illustrated; Harper, 1986.

1988 *Lincoln: A Photobiography* by Russell Freedman, illustrated with photos; Clarion, 1987.

1989 *Anthony Burns: The Defeat and Triumph of a Fugitive Slave* by Virginia Hamilton, not illustrated; Knopf, 1988.

1990 *Shades of Gray* by Carolyn Reeder, not illustrated; Macmillan, 1989.

1991 *Franklin Delano Roosevelt* by Russell Freedman, illustrated with photos; Clarion, 1990.

1992 *The Wright Brothers: How They Invented the Airplane* by Russell Freedman, illustrated with photos; Holiday House, 1991.

1993 *Children of the Dust Bowl* by Jerry Stanley, illustrated with photographs; Crown, 1992.

JEWISH BOOK COUNCIL NATIONAL JEWISH BOOK AWARDS

Paula Gribetz Gottlieb, Director
Jewish Book Council
15 East 26th St
New York, NY 10010-1579

Included in the nine categories of the Jewish Book Council Awards are two for children's literature. Since its inception in

1952, this award has been known by a variety of names (depending on the donor of the funds for the award). The award for the best Jewish children's book was known as the Isaac Siegel Memorial Award from 1952-1956 and again from 1959-1967. In 1957, the donor was the Temple B'nai Jeshurun and in 1958 the Pioneer Women sponsored the Hayim Greenburg Memorial. In 1967 and 1968, the award was not presented due to a lack of funding. In 1970, the Charles and Bertie G. Schwartz Juvenile Award was instituted and continued through 1980. The William (Zev) Frank Memorial Award for Children's Literature presented by Ellen and David Scheinfeld was given for the first time in 1981.

These annual awards are given to a book which combines literary merit with an affirmative expression of Jewish values. Awards have also been given for a body of work rather than a specific title. The award of $500 to the author or translator is presented at an annual ceremony held in the spring. A panel of three judges determines the winning title.

Following are the rules that govern the selection of the annual recipient: (1) These awards will be given to authors or translators of books of outstanding scholarship and literary merit according to the specific criteria described by children's literature authorities (character development, plot development, setting, theme, and style). (2) Books published during the preceding calendar year will be eligible. (3) The books must be written and published in English. (4) The author or translator must be a resident or citizen of the U.S. or Canada, although he may hold a dual Israeli citizenship. (5) If an award is given for a translated work, the translator receives honorable mention. (6) Anthologies, prayerbooks, textbooks, collections, reprints, and revised editions are not eligible. (7) Posthumous awards shall be presented only in the event of the author's death within the year of the publication of the book. (8) An author or translator shall not receive the award more than twice. (9) The award will not be given if there is no suitable book. The Jewish Book Council may select an author for his cumulative works. (10) The announcements of the winners will be made at the public ceremony in New York City that will take place in the spring each year.

(From guidelines set by the Jewish Book Council).

1951 *All-of-a-Kind Family* by Sydney Taylor, illustrated by Helen John; Follett, 1951.

1952 *Star Light Stories: Holiday and Sabbath Tales* by Lillian Simon Freehof, illustrated by Jessie B. Robinson; Bloch, 1952.

Stories of King David by Lillian Simon Freehof, illustrated by Seymour R. Kaplan; Jewish Publications, 1952.

1953 *The Jewish People: Book Three* by Deborah Pessin, illustrated by Ruth Levin; United Synagogue of America, 1952.

1954 *King Solomon's Navy* written and illustrated by Nora Benjamin Kubie; Harper, 1954.

1955 Sadie Rose Weilerstein for her body of work

1956 Elma E. Levinger for her body of work

1957 *Junior Jewish Encyclopedia* by Naomi Ben-Asher and Hayim Leaf, illustrated with photographs; Shengold, 1957.

1958 *Border Hawk: August Bondi* by Lloyd Alexander, illustrated by Bernard Krigstein; Farrar, 1958.

1959 *Keys to a Magic Door* by Sylvia Rothchild, illustrated by Bernard Krigstein; Farrar, 1959.

1960 *Discovering Israel* written and illustrated by Regina Tor; Random House, 1960.

1961 *Ten and a Kid* by Sadie Rose Weilerstein, illustrated by Janina Domanska; Doubleday, 1961.

1962 *Return to Freedom* by Josephine Kamm, illustrated by William Stobbs; Abelard-Schuman, 1962.

1963 *A Boy of Old Prague* by Sulamith Ish-Kishor, illustrated by Ben Shahn; Pantheon, 1963.

1964 *Worlds Lost and Found* by Dov Peretz Elkins and Azriel Eisenberg, illustrated by Charles Pickard; Abelard, 1964.

1965 *The Dreyfus Affair: A National Scandal* by Betty Schechter, not illustrated; Houghton, 1965.

1966 *The Story of Israel* by Meyer Levin, illustrated by Eli Levin; Putnam, 1966.

1967-1968 No Award

1969 *Martin Buber: Wisdom in our Time* by Charlie May Simon, illustrated with photographs; Dutton, 1969.

The Story of Masada by Yigael Yadin, retold by Gerald Gottlieb, illustrated with photographs; Random House, 1969.

1970 *Journey to America* by Sonia Levitin, illustrated by Charles Robinson; Atheneum, 1970.

1971 *The Master of Miracle: A New Novel of the Golem* by Sulamith Ish-Kishor, illustrated by Arnold Lobel; Harper, 1971.

1972 *The Upstairs Room* by Johanna Reiss, not illustrated; Crowell, 1972.

1973 *Uncle Misha's Partisans* by Yuri Suhl, not illustrated; Four Winds, 1973.

1974 *The Holocaust: A History Of Courage and Resistance* by Bea Stadtler, illustrated by David Stone Martin; Behrman, 1974.

1975 *Haym Salomon: Liberty's Son* by Shirley G. Milgrim, illustrated by Richard Fish; Jewish Publication Society, 1975.

1976 *Rifka Grows Up* written and illustrated by Chaya Burstein; Bonim Books, 1976.

1977 *Never to Forget: The Jews of the Holocaust* by Milton Meltzer, not illustrated; Harper, 1976.

1978 *Joshua: Fighter for Bar Kochba* by Irena Narell, not illustrated; Akiba Press, 1978.

1979 *Dita Saxova* by Arnost Lustig, translated by Jeanne Nemcova, not illustrated; Harper, 1979.

1980 *A Russian Farewell* written and illustrated by Leonard Everett Fisher; Four Winds, 1980.

1982 **CHILDREN** *The Night Journey* by Kathryn Lasky, illustrated by Trina Schart Hyman; Warne, 1981.

1983 **CHILDREN (WILLIAM 'ZEV' FRANK MEMORIAL AWARD)** *King of the Seventh Grade* by Barbara Cohen, not illustrated; Lothrop, Lee & Shepard, 1982.

1983 **CHILDREN'S PICTURE BOOK (MARCIA LOUIS POSNER AWARD)** *Yussel's Prayer: A Yom Kippur Story* by Barbara Cohen, illustrated by Michael J. Deraney; Lothrop, Lee & Shepard, 1981.

1984 WILLIAM 'ZEV' FRANK MEMORIAL AWARD FOR CHILDREN'S LITERATURE *The Jewish Kids Catalog* written and illustrated by Chaya M. Burstein; Jewish Publication Society of America, 1983.

1985 ILLUSTRATED CHILDREN'S BOOK *Mrs. Moskowitz and the Sabbath Candlesticks* written and illustrated by Amy Schwartz; Jewish Publication Society of America, 1983.

1985 CHILDREN'S LITERATURE *Good if it Goes* by Gary Provost and Gail Levine-Freidus, not illustrated; Bradbury, 1984.

1986 CHILDREN'S LITERATURE *In Kindling Flame: The Story of Hannah Senesh, 1921-1944* by Linda Atkinson, not illustrated; Lothrop, Lee & Shepard, 1985.

1986 ILLUSTRATION *Brothers* retold by Florence B. Freedman, illustrated by Robert Andrew Parker; Harper & Row, 1985.

1987 CHILDREN'S LITERATURE *Monday in Odessa* by Eileen Bluestone Sherman, not illustrated; Jewish Publication Society, 1986.

1987 ILLUSTRATED CHILDREN'S BOOK *Poems for Jewish Holidays* by Myra Cohn Livingston, illustrated by Lloyd Bloom; Holiday House, 1986.

1988 CHILDREN'S LITERATURE *The Return* by Sonia Levitin, not illustrated; Atheneum, 1987.

1988 CHILDREN'S PICTURE BOOK *Exodus* adapted from the Bible by Miriam Chaikin, illustrated by Charles Mikolaycak; Holiday House, 1987.

1989 CHILDREN'S LITERATURE *The Devil's Arithmetic* by Jane Yolen, not illustrated; Viking Kestrel, 1988.

1989 CHILDREN'S PICTURE BOOK *Just Enough Is Plenty: A Hanukkah Tale* by Barbara Diamond Goldin, illustrated by Seymour Chwast; Viking Kestrel, 1988.

1990 CHILDREN'S LITERATURE *Number the Stars* by Lois Lowry, not illustrated; Houghton Mifflin, 1989.

1990 CHILDREN'S PICTURE BOOK *Berchick* by Esther Silverstein Blanc, illustrated by Tennessee Dixon; Volcano Press, 1989.

1991 CHILDREN'S LITERATURE *Becoming Gershona* by Nava Semel, not illustrated; Viking, 1990.

1991 CHILDREN'S PICTURE BOOK *Hannukkah* by Roni Schotter, illustrated by Marylin Hafner; Little Brown, 1990.

1992 ONCE UPON A TIME BOOKSTORE AWARD *The Man From the Other Side* by Uri Orlev, not illustrated; Houghton Mifflin, 1991.

1992 MARCIA & LOUIS POSNER AWARD *Chicken Man* written and illustrated by Michelle Edwards; Lothrop, Lee & Shepard, 1991.

CLARA INGRAM JUDSON AWARD

discontinued

Sponsored by the Society of Midland Authors beginning in 1966, this award was named after the Midwestern author.

1966 *A Certain Small Shepherd* by Rebecca Caudill, illustrated by William Pene du Bois; Holt, 1965.

1967 *The Living Community: A Venture into Ecology* by S. Carl Hirsch, illustrated by William Steinel; Viking, 1966.

1978 *And You Give Me a Pain, Elaine* by Stella Pevsner, not illustrated; Seabury, 1978.

The Orphans by Berniece Rabe, not illustrated; Dutton, 1978.

JUNIOR BOOK AWARDS
see BOYS' CLUB JUNIOR BOOK AWARDS

K

KC THREE AWARD
Greater Kansas City
Association of School Librarians

This children's choice award was established in 1985 by the Greater Kansas City Association of School Librarians (GKCASL) in Missouri. It's purpose is to promote reading by students of third grade and appropriate levels of special education by providing them with book selections which represent quality for a variety of tastes and interests. Selections are intended to bridge the gap between picture books and chapter books encouraging both read-aloud and read alone strategies. This award was created to provide a program for third graders when their grade was eliminated from the Mark Twain Award program in Missouri.

Approximately ten books are chosen by a committee of the CKCASL. To qualify for inclusion on the list the author must reside in the United States and the book must have a copyright date two years prior to the issuance of the list. The book may be either fiction or nonfiction.

Books are read throughout the school year and in March, all third grade students vote for their favorite title. A statue engraved with the name of the book and the name of the author is presented at the Spring Banquet of the GKCASL.

1985-86 *Rich Mitch* by Marjorie Weinman Sharmat, illustrated by Loretta Lustig; Morrow, 1983.

1986-87 *The Flunking of Joshua T. Bates* by Susan Shreve, illustrated by Diane de Groat; Knopf, 1984.

1987-88 *Christina's Ghost* by Betty Ren Wright, not illustrated; Holiday House, 1985.

1988-89 *What's the Matter With Herbie Jones* by Suzy Kline, illustrated by Richard Williams; Putnam, 1986.

1989-90 *Fudge* by Charlotte T. Graeber, illustrated by Cheryl Harness; Lothrop, Lee & Shepard, 1987.

1990-91 *How to Survive Third Grade* by Laurie Lawlor, illustrated by Joyce Audy Zarins; Whitman, 1988.

1991-92 *Snot Stew* by Bill Wallace, not illustrated; Holiday House, 1980.

1992-93 *The High Rise Glorious Skittle Skat Roarious Sky Pie Angel Food Cake* by Nancy Willard, illustrated by Richard Jesse Watson; Harcourt Brace Jovanovich, 1990.

EZRA JACK KEATS AWARD
see UNICEF-EZRA JACK KEATS INTERNATIONAL
AWARD FOR CHILDREN'S BOOK ILLUSTRATION
EZRA JACK KEATS NEW WRITER'S AWARD

Mrs. Hanna Nuba
New York Public Library
Early Childhood Information and Resource Center
66 LeRoy St.
New York, NY 10014

This award was established in 1986 in honor of author/illustrator Ezra Jack Keats to perpetuate his values of multiculturalism and family in books for children. A silver medal and $500 is awarded to a new children's book writer of promise with no more than five published books. Awarded biennially on the last Thursday in March, this award was established by the Ezra Jack Keats Foundation and the New York Public Library.

1986 *The Patchwork Quilt* by Valerie Flournoy, illustrated by Jerry Pinkney; Dial, 1985.

1987 *Jamaica's Find* by Juanita Havill, illustrated by Anne Sibley O'Brien; Houghton Mifflin, 1986.

1989 *Anna's Special Present* by Yoriko Tsutsui, illustrated by Akiko Hayashi; Viking Kestrel, 1988; Puffin, 1990.

1991 *Tell Me a Story, Mama* by Angela Johnson, illustrated by David Soman; Orchard, 1989.

1993 *Tar Beach* written and illustrated by Faith Ringgold; Crown, 1991.

KEENE (NEW HAMPSHIRE) STATE COLLEGE CHILDREN'S LITERATURE FESTIVAL AWARD

Dr. David E. White
Keene State College
229 Main St.
Keene, NH 03431

This award recognizes an individual who has demonstrated continued excellence in the field of children's literature over a period of at least ten years. The individual must be currently working in the field and the body of work must show variety and diversity while maintaining the highest standards of literature for children. Nominations for the award are accepted from participants in the Keene State College Children's Literature Festival. The honored individual receives an engraved pewter Revere bowl along with a cash award at the spring Festival.

1986 Maurice Sendak

1987 Katherine Paterson

1988 Leo Dillon, Diane Dillon

1989 Barbara Cooney

1990 Betsy Byars

1991 Trina Schart Hyman

1992 Eric Carle

1993 Natalie Babbitt

A KELPIE FOR THE NINETIES
discontinued
Originally called Quest for a Kelpie, this biennial award was discontinued after the 1990 award was presented. The award was established in 1986 by BBC Scotland, Canongate Publishing, and the Scottish Libraries Association to honor the best fiction book written by an adult for children eight through twelve years of age. The author had to live in Scotland or be of Scottish descent. The winning manuscript was published and serialized as a radio drama. The winner was selected by a jury of authors, publishers, and children.

1986 *Quest for a Kelpie* by Frances Hendry, not illustrated; Canongate, 1986.

1988 *The Dark Shadow* by Mary Rhind, not illustrated; Canongate, 1988.

1990 *The Baillie's Daughter* by Donald Lightwood, not illustrated; Canongate, 1990.

KENTUCKY BLUEGRASS AWARD

Jennifer Smith
Northern Kentucky University
Learning Resource Center
BEP-268
Highland Heights, KY 41076

The Kentucky Bluegrass Award is an annual presentation that was established in 1982 and first awarded in 1983. The program's goal is to encourage Kentucky children to read and enjoy a variety of books and select their favorite from a list of recently published books. Two divisions comprise the Kentucky Bluegrass Award. Books frequently used in grades K-3 and grades 4-8 are considered. Between 15-25 titles are selected from each division. From 1983 to 1987, the author of the collectively favorite book from both divisions received the award. As of 1988, winners are determined in both categories.

1983 *Jumanji* written and illustrated by Chris Van Allsburg; Houghton Mifflin, 1981.

1984 *Move Over, Twerp* written and illustrated by Martha G. Alexander; Dial, 1981.

1985 *Angelina Ballerina* by Katharine Holabird, illustrated by Helen Craig; Crown, 1983.

1986 *Badger's Parting Gifts* written and illustrated by Susan Varley; Lothrop, Lee & Shepard, 1984.

1987 *Polar Express* written and illustrated by Chris Van Allsburg; Houghton Mifflin, 1985.

1988 GRADES K-3 *Hey, Al!* by Arthur Yorinks, illustrated by Richard Egielski; Farrar Straus Giroux, 1986.

1988 GRADES 4-8 *Who Needs a Bratty Brother?* by Linda Gondosch, illustrated by Helen Cogancherry; Dutton, 1985.

1989 GRADES K-3 *Wolf's Chicken Stew* written and illustrated by Keiko Kasza; Putnam, 1987.

1989 GRADES 4-8 *Class Clown* by Johanna Hurwitz, illustrated by Sheila Hamanaka; Morrow, 1987.

1990 GRADES K-3 *The Lady With the Alligator Purse* written and illustrated by Nadine Bernard Westcott; Little Brown, 1988.

1990 GRADES 4-8 *The Stranger* written and illustrated by Chris Van Allsburg; Houghton Mifflin, 1986.

1991 GRADES K-3 *Chicka Chicka Boom Boom* by John Archambault and Bill Martin, Jr., illustrated by Lois Ehlert; Simon & Schuster, 1989.

1991 GRADES 4-8 *The Butterfly Jar: Poems* by Jeff Moss, illustrated by Chris Demarest; Bantam, 1989.

1992 **GRADES K-3** *The Basket* by George Ella Lyon, illustrated by Mary Szilagyi; Orchard, 1990.

1992 **GRADES 4-8** *Something Big Has Been Here* by Jack Prelutsky, illustrated by James Stevenson; Greenwillow, 1988.

KERLAN AWARD
Dr. Karen Nelson Hoyle, Curator
Children's Literature Research Collections
109 Walter Library
University of Minnesota
Minneapolis, MN 55455

The Kerlan Award was established by the Kerlan Collection 25th Anniversary Committee in 1975. This annual award is given in recognition of singular attainments in the creation of children's literature and in appreciation for generous donations of unique resources to the Kerlan Collection for the study of children's literature.

There is a public call for nominations, which are considered by the Kerlan Award committee. The committee consists of five members representing the Minnesota Library Association and the University of Minnesota College of Education, Library School, Kerlan Collection, and an alternating department or college. The winner is presented with a plaque.

1975 Elizabeth Coatsworth, Marie Hall Ets, Marguerite Henry

1976 Roger Duvoisin

1977 Wanda Gag

1978 Carol Ryrie Brink

1979 Margot Zemach

1980 Glen Rounds

1981 Tomie de Paola

1982 Jean Craighead George

1983 Katherine Paterson

1984 Margaret Wise Brown and her editors and illustrators

1985 Eleanor Cameron

1986 Charlotte Zolotow

1987 Charles Mikolaycak

1988 Jane Yolen

1989 Gail E. Haley

1990 Madeleine L'Engle

1991 Leonard Everett Fisher

1992 Barbara Cooney

1993 Mary Stolz

KEYSTONE TO READING BOOK AWARD
Keystone State Reading Association

This children's choice award is presented by the Keystone State Reading Association in Pennsylvania. Each year's Master List has at least ten titles which are available in classrooms and libraries throughout the state. Children vote for their favorite title.

1988 *The Little Old Lady Who Was Not Afraid of Anything* by Linda Williams, illustrated by Megan Lloyd; Crowell, 1986.

1989 *More Surprises* by Lee Bennett Hopkins, illustrated by Megan Lloyd; Harper & Row, 1987.

1990 *Chester's Way* written and illustrated by Kevin Henkes; Greenwillow, 1988.

KIDS OWN AUSTRALIAN LITERATURE (KOALA)
KOALA Committee

The KOALA Award is a joint project of the New South Wales branches of the Schools and Children's Sections of the Library association, Australian Reading Association, Primary English Teachers Association, School Library Association, Children's Book Council, Australian Book Publishers Association, and the English Teachers Association. The award is presented in two categories, Primary and Secondary. Students throughout the state of New South Wales have the opportunity to vote for their favorite book from a shortlist of approximately 30 titles for each category.

1987 **PRIMARY** *Possum Magic* by Mem Fox, illustrated by Julie Vivas; Omnibus, 1983.

1987 **SECONDARY** *Hating Alison Ashley* by Robin Klein, not illustrated; Penguin, 1984.

1988 **PRIMARY** *Sister Madge's Book of Nuns* by Doug McLeod, illustrated by Craig Smith; Omnibus, 1986.

1988 **SECONDARY** *Animalia* written and illustrated by Graeme Base; Viking Kestrel, 1988.

1988 **(One time only Bicentennial Award)** *The Complete Adventures of Snugglepot and Cuddlepie* written and illustrated by May Gibbs; Angus & Robertson, 1981.

1989 **PRIMARY** *The Eleventh Hour* written and illustrated by Graeme Base; Viking Kestrel, 1988.

1989 **SECONDARY** *So Much To Tell You ...* by John Marsden, not illustrated; Walter McVitty, 1987.

1990 **PRIMARY** *Where the Forest Meets the Sea* written and illustrated by Jeannie Baker; Julia MacRae, 1987.

1990 **SECONDARY** *Unreal! Eight Surprising Stories* by Paul Jennings, not illustrated; Puffin, 1985.

CORETTA SCOTT KING AWARD
Social Responsibilities Round Table
American Library Association
50 E Huron Street
Chicago, IL 60611

Established in 1969, the Coretta Scott King Award has the following purposes: to commemorate the life and works of the late Dr. Martin Luther King, Jr.; to honor Mrs. King for her courage to continue to fight for peace and world brotherhood; to encourage creative artists and authors to promote the cause of peace and brotherhood through their work; and to inspire children and youth to dedicate their talents and energies to help achieve these goals.

This annual award is presented at the annual American Library Association conference. Since 1979, an additional award for illustration has been made.

1970 *Martin Luther King, Jr.: Man of Peace* by Lillie Patterson, illustrated by Victor Mays; Garrard, 1969.

1971 *Black Troubador: Langston Hughes* by Charlemae Rollins, illustrated with photographs; Rand, 1970.

1972 *Seventeen Black Artists* by Elton Clay Fax, illustrated with photographs; Dodd Mead, 1971.

1973 *I Never Had It Made* by Jackie Robinson as told to Alfred Duckett; illustrated with photographs; Putnam, 1972.

1974 *Ray Charles* by Sharon Bell Mathis, illustrated by George Ford; Crowell, 1973.

1975 *The Legend of Africania* by Dorothy Robinson, illustrated by Herbert Temple; Johnson, 1974.

1976 *Duey's Tale* by Pearl Bailey, photographs by Arnold Skolnick and Gary Azon; Harcourt, 1975.

1977 *The Story of Stevie Wonder* by James Haskins, illustrated with photographs; Lothrop, 1976.

1978 *African Dream* by Eloise Greenfield, illustrated by Carole Byard; Day/Crowell, 1977.

1979 *Escape to Freedom* by Ossie Davis, not illustrated; Viking, 1978, c1976.

1979 **SPECIAL AWARD FOR ILLUSTRATION** *Something on My Mind* by Nikki Grimes, illustrated by Tom Feelings; Dial, 1978.

1980 *The Young Landlords* by Walter D. Myers, not illustrated; Viking, 1979.

1980 **ILLUSTRATION** *Corn Rows* by Camile Yarbrough, illustrated by Carole Byard; Coward, 1979.

1981 *This Life* by Sidney Poitier, not illustrated; Knopf, 1980.

1981 **ILLUSTRATION** *Beat the Story-drum, Pum-pum* written and illustrated by Ashley Bryan; Atheneum, 1980.

1982 **AUTHOR** *Let the Circle Be Unbroken* by Mildred D. Taylor, not illustrated; Dial, 1981.

1982 **ILLUSTRATOR** *Mother Crocodile = Maman-Caiman* by Birago Diop, translated and adapted by Rosa Guy, illustrated by John Steptoe; Delacorte, 1981.

1983 **AUTHOR** *Sweet Whispers, Brother Rush* by Virginia Hamilton, not illustrated; Philomel, 1982.

1983 **AUTHOR HONORABLE MENTION** *This Strange New Feeling* by Julius Lester, not illustrated; Dial, 1982.

1983 **ILLUSTRATOR** *Black Child* written and photographed by Peter Magubane; Knopf, distributed by Random House, 1982.

1983 **ILLUSTRATOR HONORABLE MENTION** *I'm Going to Sing: Black American Spirituals, vol. 2* selected and illustrated by Ashley Bryan; Atheneum, 1982.

1984 **AUTHOR** *Everett Anderson's Goodbye* by Lucille Clifton, illustrated by Ann Grifalconi; Holt, 1983.

1984 **ILLUSTRATOR** *My Mama Needs Me* by Mildred Pitts Walter, illustrated by Pat Cummings; Lothrop, Lee & Shepard, 1983.

1984 **HONORABLE MENTION** *Because We Are* by Mildred Pitts Walter, not illustrated; Lothrop, Lee & Shepard, 1983.

Bright Shadow by Joyce Carol Thomas; Avon, 1983.

Lena Horne by James Haskins, illustrated with photographs; Coward McCann, 1983.

The Magical Adventures of Pretty Pearl by Virginia Hamilton, not illustrated; Harper, 1983.

1984 **SPECIAL CITATION** *The Words of Martin Luther King, Jr.* selected by Coretta Scott King, illustrated; Newmarket Press, 1983.

1985 **LITERATURE** *Motown and Didi: A Love Story* by Walter Dean Myers, not illustrated; Viking Kestrel, 1984.

1985 **LITERATURE HONORABLE MENTION** *Little Love* by Virginia Hamilton, not illustrated; Philomel, 1984.

The Circle of Gold by Candy Dawson Boyd, not illustrated; Apple Paperbacks/Scholastic, 1984.

1985 **ILLUSTRATION** No Award

1986 **LITERATURE** *The People Could Fly: American Black Folktales* by Virginia Hamilton, illustrated by Leo and Diane Dillon; Knopf, 1985.

1986 **LITERATURE HONORABLE MENTION** *Junius Over Far* by Virginia Hamilton, not illustrated; Harper, 1985.

Trouble's Child by Mildred Pitts Walter, not illustrated; Lothrop, Lee & Shepard, 1985.

1986 **ILLUSTRATION** *The Patchwork Quilt* by Valerie Flournoy, illustrated by Jerry Pinkney; Dial, 1985.

1986 **ILLUSTRATION HONORABLE MENTION** *The People Could Fly* by Virginia Hamilton, illustrated by Leo and Diane Dillon; Knopf, 1985.

1987 **LITERATURE** *Justin and the Best Biscuits in the World* by Mildred Pitts Walter, illustrated by Catherine Stock; Lothrop, Lee & Shepard, 1986.

1987 **LITERATURE HONORABLE MENTION** *Which Way Freedom?* by Joyce Hansen, not illustrated; Walker, 1986.

The Lion and the Ostrich Chicks written and illustrated by Ashley Bryan; Atheneum, 1986.

1987 **ILLUSTRATION** *Half a Moon and One Whole Star* by Crescent Dragonwagon, illustrated by Jerry Pinkney; Macmillan, 1986.

1987 **ILLUSTRATION HONORABLE MENTION** *C.L.O.U.D.S.* written and illustrated by Pat Cummings; Lothrop, Lee & Shepard, 1986.

1988 **TEXT** *The Friendship* by Mildred D. Taylor, illustrated by Max Ginsburg; Dial, 1987.

1988 **TEXT HONOR** *An Enchanted Hair Tale* by Alexis De Veaux, illustrated by Cheryl Hanna; Harper & Row, 1987.

The Tales of Uncle Remus by Joel Chandler Harris, adapted by Julius Lester, illustrated by Jerry Pinkney; Dial, 1987.

1988 **ILLUSTRATION** *Mufaro's Beautiful Daughters* written and illustrated by John Steptoe; Lothrop, Lee & Shepard, 1987.

1988 **ILLUSTRATION HONOR** *The Invisible Hunters* by Harriet Rohmer, illustrated by Joe Sam; Children's Book Press, 1987.

What a Morning! The Christmas Story in Black Spirituals by John Langstaff, illustrated by Ashley Bryan; McElderry, 1987.

1989 **TEXT** *Fallen Angels* by Walter Dean Myers, not illustrated; Scholastic, 1988.

1989 **TEXT HONOR** *A Thief in the Village* by James Berry, not illustrated; Orchard, 1988, c1987.

Anthony Burns: The Defeat and Triumph of a Fugitive Slave by Virginia Hamilton, not illustrated; Knopf, 1988.

1989   **ILLUSTRATION** *Mirandy and Brother Wind* by Patricia McKissack, illustrated by Jerry Pinkney; Knopf, 1988.

1989   **ILLUSTRATION HONOR** *Under the Sunday Tree* by Eloise Greenfield, illustrated by Amos Ferguson; Harper & Row, 1988.

Storm in the Night by Mary Stolz, illustrated by Pat Cummings; Harper & Row, 1988.

1990   **TEXT** *A Long Hard Journey: The Story of the Pullman Porter* by Patricia McKissack and Fredrick McKissack, illustrated; Walker, 1989.

1990   **TEXT HONOR** *The Bells of Christmas* by Virginia Hamilton, illustrated by Lambert Davis; Harcourt, Brace, Jovanovich, 1989.

Nathaniel Talking by Eloise Greenfield, illustrated by Jan Spivey Gilchrist; Black Butterfly Children's Books, 1988.

Martin Luther King, Jr. and the Freedom Movement by Lillie Patterson, illustrated; Facts on File, 1989.

1990   **ILLUSTRATION** *Nathaniel Talking* by Eloise Greenfield, illustrate by Jan Spivey Gilchrist; Black Butterfly Children's Books, 1988.

1990   **ILLUSTRATION HONOR** *The Talking Eggs* by Robert D. San Souci, illustrated by Jerry Pinkney; Dial, 1989.

1991   **TEXT** *The Road to Memphis* by Mildred D. Taylor, not illustrated; Dial, 1990.

1991   **TEXT HONOR** *Black Dance in America: A History Through Its People* by James Haskins, illustrated with photos; Crowell, 1990.

1991   **ILLUSTRATION** *Aida* by Leontyne Price, illustrated by Leo Dillon and Diane Dillon; Harcourt, Brace, Jovanovich, 1990.

1991   **ILLUSTRATION HONOR** *When I Am Old With You* by Angela Johnson, illustrated by David Soman; Orchard, 1990.

Night on Neighborhood Street by Eloise Greenfield, illustrated by Jan Spivey Gilchrist; Dial, 1991.

1992   **TEXT** *Now Is Your Time! The African American Struggle for Freedom* by Walter Dean Myers, illustrated; HarperCollins, 1991.

1992   **TEXT HONOR** *Night on Neighborhood Street* by Eloise Greenfield, illustrated by Jan Spivey Gilchrist; Dial, 1991.

1992   **ILLUSTRATION** *Tar Beach* written and illustrated by Faith Ringgold; Crown, 1991.

1992   **ILLUSTRATION HONOR** *All Night, All Day: A Child's First Book of African American Spirituals* written and illustrated by Ashley Bryan; Atheneum, 1991.

1993   **TEXT** *The Dark-Thirty* by Patricia McKissack, not illustrated; Knopf, 1992.

1993   **TEXT HONOR** *Sojourner Truth: Ain't I a Woman?* by Patricia McKissack and Fredrick McKissack, illustrated; Scholastic, 1992.

Mississippi Challenge by Mildred Pitts Walter, illustrated with photos; Bradbury Press, 1992.

Somewhere in the Darkness by Walter Dean Myers, not illustrated; Scholastic, 1992.

1993   **ILLUSTRATION** *The Origin of Life on Earth: An African Creation Myth* retold by David A. Anderson, illustrated by Kathleen Atkins Wilson; Sight Productions, 1992.

1993   **ILLUSTRATION HONOR** *Working Cotton* by Sherley Anne Williams, illustrated by Carole Byard; Harcourt Brace Jovanovich, 1992.

Sukey and the Mermaid by Robert D. San Souci, illustrated by Brian Pinkney; Four Winds, 1992.

Little Eight John by Jan Wahl, illustrated by Will Clay; Lodestar Books, 1992.

KNICKERBOCKER AWARD FOR JUVENILE LITERATURE
School Library Media Section of the
New York Library Association
252 Hudson Ave.
Albany, NY 12210-1802

The Knickerbocker Award, established in 1990, honors an author who has demonstrated through a body of work a consistent superior quality which has assisted in the support of the educational needs of the elementary, middle, and secondary students in New York State. Eligible are authors currently residing in New York whose literature is of consistent quality and useful in an educational setting.

The word Knickerbocker comes from a group of writers who flourished in New York in the early 1800s. Its members shared literary tastes and a wish to nurture a national literature.

A crystal trophy, embossed with the award symbol and created by Tiffany's, is presented annually at the Spring Conference for the School Library Media Section of the New York Library Association.

1991   Jean Craighead George

1992   Jean Fritz

1993   Russell Freedman

JANUSZ KORCZAK LITERARY AWARDS FOR CHILDREN'S BOOKS
Janusz Korczak Literary Award Committee
Anti-Defamation League of B'nai B'rith
823 United Nations Plaza
New York, NY 10017

This award has been sponsored by the International Center for Holocaust Studies of the Anti-Defamation League of B'nai B'rith since 1981. Books are judged on the way they exemplify the courage, humanitarianism and leadership of Dr. Korczak, a Polish physician, educator, author and orphan home administrator. A first prize of $1000 and a plaque is awarded to authors of the best books in two categories: fiction or nonfiction for young readers at the elementary or secondary school level and books directed to parents and educators on the welfare and nurturing of children.

1981   **FOR CHILDREN** *Black as I Am* by Zindzi Mandela and Peter Magubane, foreword by Andrew Young, illustrated; Guild of Tudors Press, 1978.

1981   **ABOUT CHILDREN** *Will to Live* by Hugh Franks, not illustrated; Routledge & Kegan Paul, 1979.

1982   **FOR CHILDREN** *Upon the Head of a Goat: A Childhood in Hungary 1939-1944* by Aranka Siegal; not illustrated; Farrar Straus Giroux, 1981.

1982 ABOUT CHILDREN *Responsible Parenthood: The Child's Psyche through the Six-Year Pregnancy* by Gilbert Kliman and Albert Rosen, not illustrated; Holt, Rinehart & Winston, 1980.

1984 FOR CHILDREN *Seaward* by Susan Cooper, not illustrated; Atheneum, 1983.

1984 ABOUT CHILDREN *If We Could Hear the Grass Grow* by Eleanor Craig, illustrated; Simon & Schuster, 1983.

1986 FOR CHILDREN *Days of Honey: The Tunisian Boyhood of Raphael Uzan* by Irene Awret, illustrated with plates; Schocken, 1984.

1986 ABOUT CHILDREN *Thou Shalt not be Aware: Society's Betrayal of the Child* by Alice Miller, translated by Hildegarde Hannum and Hunter Hannum, not illustrated; Farrar, 1984.

1988 FOR CHILDREN *Eliezer Ben-Yehuda, the Father of Modern Hebrew* by Malka Drucker, illustrated with photos; Lodestar, 1987.

1988 ABOUT CHILDREN *Covenant House* by Bruce Ritter, not illustrated; Doubleday, 1987.

1989-91 Temporarily suspended for reorganization

1992 FOR CHILDREN *Shadow of the Wall* by Christa Laird, illustrated with a map; MacRae, 1989; Greenwillow, 1990.

1992 FOR CHILDREN HONORABLE MENTION *The Mozart Season* by Virginia Euwer Wolff, not illustrated; Henry Holt, 1991.

1992 ABOUT CHILDREN *Before Their Time: Four Generations of Teenage Mothers* by Joelle Sander, not illustrated; Harcourt, Brace, Jovanovich, 1991.

1992 ABOUT CHILDREN HONORABLE MENTION *Unfulfilled Promise: Rescue and Resettlement of Jewish Refugee Children in the United States, 1934-1945* by Judith Tydor Baumel, illustrated; Denali Press, 1990.

JANUSZ KORCZAK INTERNATIONAL LITERARY AWARD

IBBY - Polish Section
Hipoteczua 2
00-950 Warsaw
Poland

Established in 1979 by the Polish Section of the International Board on Books for Young People, this award honors the late Janusz Korczak. Korczak was a physician and writer who established a home for orphans in Warsaw in 1927. He died at Treblinka, a German extermination camp, with all of his foster children.

The purpose of this biennial award is to promote humanitarian values in books for children. All IBBY National Sections are invited to submit titles that promote understanding and friendship among children all over the world. The winning author receives a cash award and a citation.

1979 *The Brothers Lionheart* by Astrid Lindgren (Sweden)

1981 *Endless History* by Michael Ende (German Federal Republic)

1983 *Day, Night and Nobody's Time* by Ewa Nowacka (Poland)

1985 *The Wrong Step* by Latchesar Stantchev (Bulgaria)

1987 *Where Kite Balloons Come Back* by Maria Borowa (Poland)

1990 *The Island on Bird Street* by Uri Orlev (Israel)

1992 *The Year of the Dragon* by Joanna Rudnianska (Poland)

L

EVELYN SIBLEY LAMPMAN AWARD

Sandi Olmstead
City of Newberg Public Library
503 E. Hancock St.
Newberg, OR 97132

The Lampman Award is presented annually in honor of children's writer Evelyn Sibley Lampman, a life-long resident of Oregon. The award is sponsored by the Children's Section of the Oregon Library Association to honor an Oregon author, librarian, or educator who has made a significant contribution in the fields of children's literature and/or library services to children.

Nominations are made by the membership of the Children's Section of the Oregon Library Association. A committee chooses the finalists who are then voted on by the entire membership of the Children's Section. A plaque is presented to the recipient at the Oregon Library Association Awards Luncheon in the Spring.

1982 Walt Morey

1983 Patricia Feehan

1984 Eloise Jarvis McGraw

1985 Nonny Hogrogian

1986 Irene Brady

1987 Ursula K. LeGuin

1988 Irene Bennett Brown

1989 Peggy Sharp

1990 B.J. Quinlin

1991 Eric Kimmel

1992 Walter Minkel

LANCASHIRE COUNTY LIBRARY/NATIONAL WESTMINSTER BANK CHILDREN'S BOOK OF THE YEAR AWARD

David Lightfoot
Asst. County Librarian
Lancashire County Council
County Library Headquarters
143 Corporation St.
Preston PR1 2UQ
England

This children's choice award was established in 1986 by David Lightfoot, County Librarian and first awarded in 1987. Original fiction, written by residents of the United Kingdom and suitable for the 11-14 year old age group is submitted by publishers. The winning book is selected by a judging panel consisting of 13 and 14 year old Lancashire County secondary school students. This annual award, consisting of £300 and an engraved glass decanter, is presented to the winning author at a ceremony in the main council chamber of Lancashire County Council in Preston.

1987   *The Ruby in the Smoke* by Philip Pullman, not illustrated; Oxford, 1985; Knopf, 1985.

1988   *Redwall* by Brian Jacques, illustrated by Gary Chalk; Hutchinson Children's, 1986; Philomel, 1986.

1989   *Groosham Grange* by Anthony Horowitz, illustrated by Cathy Simpson; Methuen, 1988.

1990   *Plague 99* by Jean Ure, not illustrated; Methuen Teen Collection, 1989.

1991   *Mattimeo* by Brian Jacques, illustrated by Gary Chalk; Hutchinson, 1989; Philomel, 1990.

1992   *The Whitby Witches* by Robin Jarvis, not illustrated; Simon & Schuster, 1991.

LAND OF ENCHANTMENT CHILDREN'S BOOK AWARD

New Mexico Library Association
2838-32 Paseo de Los Pueblos
Santa Fe, NM 87501

Jointly sponsored by the New Mexico Library Association and the New Mexico State International Reading Association, this children's choice award was first presented in 1981. Children in grades four through eight vote for their favorite book from a master list of twenty-five titles created by the selection committee. Eligible books include fiction, poetry, and nonfiction published within the last five years, whose author lives in the United States. A name plaque with a medallion in the center is presented to the winner at the state convention of either sponsoring organization.

1981   *Ramona and Her Father* by Beverly Cleary, illustrated by Alan Tiegreen; Morrow, 1977.

1982   *Bunnicula: A Rabbit Tale of Mystery* by James Howe and Deborah Howe, illustrated by Alan Daniel; Atheneum, 1979.

1983   *Summer of Fear* by Lois Duncan, not illustrated; Little Brown, 1976.

1984   Judy Blume

1985   *Nothing's Fair in Fifth Grade* by Barthe DeClements, not illustrated; Viking, 1981.

1986   *Zucchini* by Barbara Dana, illustrated by Eileen Christelow; Harper & Row, 1982.

1989   *Sixth Grade Can Really Kill You* by Barthe DeClements, not illustrated; Viking Kestrel, 1985.

1990   *There's a Boy in the Girls' Bathroom* by Louis Sachar, not illustrated; Knopf, 1987.

1991   *Pecos Bill* retold and illustrated by Steven Kellogg; Morrow, 1986.

1992   *Wayside School Is Falling Down* by Louis Sachar, illustrated by Joel Schick; Lothrop, Lee & Shepard, 1989.

ELLIOTT LANDAU AWARD

discontinued

This award was established in 1975 to honor Elliott Landau, founder of the Intermountain Conference on Children's and Young Adult Literature. The biennial award was designed to honor a college or university professor of children's literature who inspired students to be lifelong lovers and promoters of this genre of literature. The awards program was cosponsored by the Salt Lake City County Library System and the Department of Education, University of Utah.

Nominations were made by letter, explaining the impact of the instructor on the nominator. All college instructors of children's literature were eligible. The Salt Lake County Librarians made the final decision. A plaque was presented to the honoree at the Intermountain Conference on Children's and Young Adult Literature at the University of Utah. The last award was given in 1987.

1975   Virginia Westerberg

1977   M. Jerry (Morton Jerome) Weiss

1979   Charlotte Huck

1981   Mae Durham Roger

1983   Sheila Egoff

1985   Clara O. Jackson

1987   Theodore W. Hipple

LITTLE ARCHER

see **GOLDEN ARCHER AND LITTLE ARCHER AWARDS**

LITTLE BROWN CANADIAN CHILDREN'S BOOK AWARD

discontinued

This children's literature award was jointly established by Little, Brown (Boston) and Little, Brown (Canada) in 1957. It was intermittently given to Canadian authors for a previously unpublished fiction or nonfiction manuscript for children. Little Brown published the winning manuscript as well as awarding a $4500 prize.

1957   *Nkwala* by Edith Lambert Sharp, illustrated by William Winter; Little, Brown Canada, 1958.

1961   *Mine for Keeps* by Jean Little, illustrated by Lewis Parker; Little Brown, 1962.

1964   *The White Calf* by Cliff Faulknor, illustrated by Gerald Tailfeathers; Little Brown, 1965.

1967   *Strange Summer in Stratford* by Norah A. Perez, illustrated by Robert Ihrig; Little, Brown, 1968.

1975   *The Wooden People* by Myra Paperny, illustrated by Ken Stampnick; Little, Brown, 1976.

1977   *The Snailman* by Brenda Sivers, illustrated by Shirley Hughes; Little, Brown, 1978.

JUDY LOPEZ MEMORIAL AWARD

Los Angeles Chapter
Women's National Book Association

This award honors the memory of Judy Lopez, one of the founding members of the Los Angeles Chapter of the Women's National Book Association. Works eligible for this award include those "of literary excellence for nine to twelve year olds, written by a citizen or resident of the United States."

1986   *Prairie Songs* by Pam Conrad, illustrated by Darryl S. Zudeck; Harper & Row, 1985.

1987 *Come a Stranger* by Cynthia Voigt, not illustrated; Atheneum, 1986.

1988 *M.E. and Morton* by Sylvia Cassedy, not illustrated; Crowell, 1987.

1989 *The Trouble with Gramary* by Betty Levin, not illustrated; Greenwillow, 1988.

1990 *The Winter Room* by Gary Paulsen, not illustrated; Orchard, 1989.

1991 *The True Confessions of Charlotte Doyle* by Avi, illustrated by Ruth E. Murray; Orchard, 1990.

MAUD HART LOVELACE BOOK AWARD

Friends of the Minnesota Valley Regional Library
100 East Main Street
Box 3446
Mankato, MN 56001

This annual award is sponsored by the Friends of the Minnesota Valley Regional Library to honor Maud Hart Lovelace, author of the Betsy-Tacy books. The winning titles are chosen by the school children of Minnesota in grades three through eight. A plaque is presented to the winning author.

1982 *The Best Christmas Pageant Ever* by Barbara Robinson, illustrated by Judith Gwyn Brown; Harper, 1972.

1983 *It Can't Hurt Forever* by Marilyn Singer, illustrated by Leigh Grant; Harper, 1978.

1984 *Nothing's Fair in Fifth Grade* by Barthe DeClements, not illustrated; Viking, 1981.

1985 *Skinnybones* by Barbara Park, not illustrated; Random House, 1982.

1986 *Zucchini* by Barbara Dana, illustrated by Eileen Christelow; Harper & Row, 1982.

1987 *Stone Fox* by John Reynolds Gardiner, illustrated by Marcia Sewall; Harper, 1983.

1988 *The Night of the Twisters* by Ivy Ruckman, not illustrated; Crowell, 1984.

1989 *Eating Ice Cream With a Werewolf* by Phyllis Green, illustrated by Patti Stren; Harper and Row, 1983.

1990 *Wait Til Helen Comes* by Mary Downing Hahn, not illustrated; Clarion, 1986.

1991 *Hatchet* by Gary Paulsen, not illustrated; Bradbury, 1987.

1992 *This Island Isn't Big Enough for the Four of Us* by Bob Ruddick and Gery Greer, not illustrated; Crowell, 1987.

LUCKY BOOK CLUB FOUR-LEAF CLOVER AWARD

discontinued

First awarded in 1971, the Lucky Book Club Four-Leaf Clover Award was presented in recognition of an author's contribution to the reading pleasures of seven- and eight-year olds. In order to be eligible for the award, authors must have been familiar to and popular with the readers of the Lucky Book Club books. At least two of their books must have been offered by the Club in the year preceding the award. The author of the year was determined by the editors of the Lucky Book Club. The Four Leaf Clover Award consisted of a photograph of the author which was published and sent to teachers so that it could be posted on classroom bulletin boards. A copy of this photograph was framed and presented to the winning author at a reception at the Scholastic offices. The award was discontinued in 1983.

1971 Norman Bridwell

1972 Ann McGovern

1973 Millicent E. Selsam

1974 John Peterson

1975 Ruth Belov Gross

1976 Margaret Davidson

1977 Ruth Chew

1978 Clare Gault, Frank Gault

1979 Bernice Myers

1980 Carla Stevens

1981 Nancy K. Robinson

1982 Gary Tong

1983 Arnold Lobel

JEREMIAH LUDINGTON MEMORIAL AWARD

Educational Paperback Association
Marilyn Abel
Box 1399
East Hampton, NY 11937

First awarded in 1978, the Jeremiah Ludington Award is given to an individual who has made a significant contribution to children and paperback books. An awards committee receives nominations from the Board of Directors of the Educational Paperback Association. A final selection is made by both the Board and the committee. A plaque is awarded to the recipient at the annual meeting of the Educational Paperback Association in June of each year.

1978- Information unavailable

1980

1981 Mary Kay Chelton

1982 Ruth Graves

1983 Judy Blume

1984 Marilyn Abel

1986 Edward Packard, R.A. Montgomery

1987 Beverly Cleary

1988 *Read-Aloud Handbook* by Jim Trelease, illustrated by Joanne Rathe; Penguin, 1982.

1989 Stan Berenstain, Jan Berenstain

1990 Patricia Reilly Giff

LUPINE AWARD

Children's and Young Adults' Services Section
Maine Library Association
Local Government Center
RFD 4 Box 35
Augusta, ME 04330

Established in 1990 by the Children's and Young Adults' Services Section of the Maine Library Association, to honor a living author or illustrator who is a resident of Maine or who has created a work of outstanding merit, the focus of which is Maine. The word "Lupine" comes from and is in honor of the lupine in Miss Rumphius by Barbara Cooney. All types of literature appropriate for children 17 years of age and younger are eligible for this annual award. A commemorative plaque and the gift of a copy of the award winning book to a library of the recipient's choice is presented annually at the Maine Library Association Conference.

1990 *Brickyard Summer: Poems* by Paul B. Janeczko, illustrated by Ken Rush; Orchard, 1989.

1991 *Hattie and the Wild Waves* written and illustrated by Barbara Cooney; Viking, 1990.

1992 *Rosebud & Red Flannel* by Ethel Pochocki, illustrated by Mary Beth Owens; Henry Holt, 1991.

M

DAVID McCORD CHILDREN'S LITERATURE CITATION

Curriculum Library
Framingham State College
Framingham, MA 01701

This annual award is sponsored by Framingham State College and the Nobscot Reading Council of the International Reading Association and recognizes significant contributions to excellence in the field of children's books. The award was established to honor poet David McCord and is presented to those whose work continues the tradition he initiated. The recipient receives a citation, an engraved Jefferson cup and an honorarium.

1986 Tomie de Paola

1987 Steven Kellogg

1988 Jean Fritz

1989 Peter Spier

1990 Barbara Cooney

1991 Rosemary Wells

1992 Jerry Pinkney

1993 Jan Brett

MACMILLAN OF CANADA CONTEST

discontinued

Sponsored by the Macmillan Publishing Company in Canada, this competition was first held in 1962. Eligible for the $500 first prize were stories suitable for readers aged eight through ten based on exciting incidents in Canada's past. It was planned to publish these stories in Macmillan's series of Buckskin Books. The contest was discontinued shortly after the 1962 award was made.

1962 *The Great Canoe* by Adelaide Leitch, illustrated by Clare Bice; Macmillan Canada, 1962.

MACMILLAN PRIZE

Michael Wace, Publishing Director
Pan Macmillan Children's Books
Cavaye Place
London SW10 9PG
England

This annual competition was established in 1986 by Macmillan Children's Books in order to stimulate new work from young illustrators in art schools and to help them start their professional lives. The competition is open to all art students in higher education establishments in the United Kingdom. The jury appreciates that art students may not be skilled writers; they will look for evidence of the imaginative visual development of a story-line rather than assessing the quality of the text. However, preference will be given to a wholly original work. Prizes of £1000, £500, and £250 will be awarded for work which the jury considers to be an original contribution to the field and which children will enjoy. Macmillan Children's Books reserves the right to publish any of the winning titles.

1986 **FIRST PRIZE** *Shh! It's the Secret Club!* written and illustrated by John Watson; Macmillan, 1987; Henry Holt, 1987.

1986 **SECOND PRIZE** *The White Cat* by Mark Southgate; to be published by Macmillan.

1986 **THIRD PRIZE** *Imagine* by Andrew Midgley; to be published by Macmillan.

1987 **FIRST PRIZE** *Bush Vark's First Day Out* written and illustrated by Charles Fuge; Macmillan, 1988.

1987 **SECOND PRIZE** *Portly's Hat* written and illustrated by Lucy Cousins; Macmillan, 1988; Dutton, 1988.

1987 **THIRD PRIZE** *To Become a Man* by Kathleen Childs; to be published by Macmillan.

Captain Bilgerbelly's Treasure by Leo Hartas; to be published by Macmillan.

1988 **FIRST PRIZE** *Alphabet City* by Mark Hudson; to be published by Macmillan.

1988 **SECOND PRIZE** *A Gardener's Alphabet* written and illustrated by Elizabeth Harbour; Michael Joseph, 1990.

1988 **THIRD PRIZE** *The Great Zoo Hunt* written and illustrated by Pippa Unwin; Macmillan, 1989; Doubleday, 1990.

1989 **FIRST PRIZE** *A Close Call* written and illustrated by Amanda Harvey; Macmillan Children's, 1990.

1989 **SECOND PRIZE** *Alec and His Flying Bed* written and illustrated by Simon Buckingham; Macmillan, 1990; Lothrop, Lee & Shepard, 1991.

1989 **THIRD PRIZE** Emma Phillips, Patrick Yee

1990 **FIRST PRIZE** No Award

1990 **SECOND PRIZE** *Donald and the Singing Fish* written and illustrated by Peter Lubach; Macmillan, 1992; Hyperion, 1992.

Helen Balmer

1990 **THIRD PRIZE** Alice Dumas

The Tiger and the Traveler by Patrick Yee.

1991 **FIRST PRIZE** *My Grampa has Big Pockets* written and illustrated by Selina Young; forthcoming from Macmillan.

1991 **SECOND PRIZE** *Animal A to Z* by Nicole Zivkovic.

1991 THIRD PRIZE *Woof Miaow* by Sara Fanelli.

1992 FIRST PRIZE *Botton* written and illustrated by Sara Fanelli.

1992 SECOND PRIZE *Ten Dogs* written and illustrated by Rebecca Gibbon.

1992 THIRD PRIZE *Rabbit and Wolf* written and illustrated by Sandra Banks.

1993 FIRST PRIZE *Look Out, Look Out, Mad Animals About* written and illustrated by Joanne Kouyoumdjian.

MAGAZINE MERIT AWARD

Society of Children's Book Writers and Illustrators
P O Box 66296
Mar Vista Station
Los Angeles, CA 90066

This award for original magazine work for young people has been sponsored by the Society of Children's Book Writers and Illustrators (SCBWI) since 1988. Three plaques, one for fiction, one for nonfiction, and one for illustration are awarded each year for outstanding original magazine work for young people published during that year. The author or illustrator must be a member of the SCBWI. Honor certificates may also be awarded in each category. The panel of judges consists of two full members of the SCBWI and a children's magazine editor.

1988 FICTION Peggy King Anderson for a story in *Pockets*.

1988 NONFICTION Rosalie Maggio for a story in *Cricket*.

1988 ILLUSTRATION Carol Heyer for a cover illustration in *Dragon Magazine*.

1989 FICTION Elaine Marie Alphin for a story in *Young and Alive*

1989 NONFICTION Elizabeth R. Hennefrund for a story in *Ranger Rick*.

1989 ILLUSTRATION Bianca Lavies for a story in *Ranger Rick*.

1990 FICTION Eileen Spinelli for a story in *Highlights*.

1990 FICTION HONOR Maureen Crane Wartski for a story in *Boys Life*.

1990 NONFICTION Mary Glucksman for a story in *Highlights*.

1990 NONFICTION HONOR Peter K. Lourie for a story in *Highlights*.

1990 ILLUSTRATION Mary Kurnick Maass for an illustration in *Wee Wisdom*.

1990 ILLUSTRATION HONOR Evelyn Gallardo for an illustration in *Ranger Rick*.

1991 FICTION Marlys G. Stapelbroek for a story in *Boys Life*.

1991 FICTION HONOR Deborah Hopkinson for a story in *Cricket*.

1991 NONFICTION Elizabeth S. Wall for a story in *Highlights*.

1991 NONFICTION HONOR Margaret S. Ross for a story in *Fantastic Flyer*.

1991 ILLUSTRATION Judith A. Moffatt for an illustration in *Children's Playmate*.

1991 ILLUSTRATION HONOR Bonnie MacKain for an illustration in *Cricket*.

ALLIE BETH MARTIN AWARD

Public Library Association
American Library Association
50 E. Huron St.
Chicago, IL 60611

The Allie Beth Martin Award was established in 1978 by the Public Library Association and is partially funded by the Baker & Taylor Company. Allie Beth Martin was the director of the Tulsa City County Library and a President of the American Library Association. An annual award is presented to a librarian who, in a public library setting, has demonstrated (1) extraordinary range and depth of knowledge about books or other library materials and (2) distinguished ability to share that knowledge.

Nominations are submitted in writing to the jury chairperson. The jury is guided by, but not confined to, the nominations. The jury consists of five members appointed for a one-year term by the president of the Public Library Association. The winner is announced and presented with a citation and a $2000 cash award at Public Library Association meeting at the annual ALA conference. The honoree is also allowed to select the speaker for the award function.

1979 Harriett Bard

1980 Mary Louise Rheay

1981 Birdie Law

1982 Murray L. Bob

1983 Dr. Hardy R. Franklin

1984 Cecil P. Beach

1985 Junivee Black

1986 Suzanne Sutton

1987 Susan B. Madden

1988 Daniel Robles

1989 Joyce G. Saricks

1990 Nyla Ching Fujii

1991 Sandra M. Neerman

MARYLAND CHILDREN'S CHOICE BOOK AWARD

Maryland International Reading Association Council

Sponsored by the Maryland International Reading Association Council, this children's choice award was first given in 1988. The purpose of the award is to foster an interest in reading among students in grades three through six. Titles previously winning a Newbery or Caldecott Medal are excluded, as are picture books. Authors must be currently living in the United States at the time of nomination and only one title per author may appear on the list. The winning author is excluded from the following year's list.

1988 *Cracker Jackson* by Betsy Byars, not illustrated; Viking Kestrel, 1985.

1989 *Switcharound* by Lois Lowry, not illustrated; Houghton Mifflin, 1985.

1990 *The Haunting of Cabin 13* by Kristi D. Hall, illustrated; Atheneum, 1987.

1991 *The Doll in the Garden* by Mary Downing Hahn, not illustrated; Clarion, 1989.

KURT MASCHLER AWARD

Celia Parry-Jones
Publicity Officer
Book House
45 East Hill
London SW18 2QZ
England

Founded by Kurt Maschler in 1982 in memory of Erich Kastner and Walter Trier, this annual award is administered by the Book Trust. The award is made for a work of imagination in the children's field, for excellence in text and illustration, where each enhances, yet balances, the other. Eligible are authors and illustrators of British nationality or United Kingdom residents of 10 years. Entries are submitted by publishers and screened by a three-judge panel which makes the final selection. The winning author and/or illustrator receives a cash award of £1000 as well an Emil. The Emil is a small bronze statue sculpted by Diana Welch, the design of which is based on Walter Trier's illustration of Erich Kastner's famous detective hero from Emil and the Detectives.

1982 *Sleeping Beauty and other Favourite Fairy Tales* chosen and translated by Angela Carter, illustrated by Michael Foreman; Gollancz, 1982.

1982 **RUNNERSUP** *The Church Mice in Action* written and illustrated by Graham Oakley; Macmillan, 1982; Atheneum, 1983.

Pelican written and illustrated by Brian Wildsmith; Oxford, 1982; Pantheon, 1982.

Rumbelow's Dance by John Yeoman, illustrated by Quentin Blake; Hamish Hamilton, 1982.

1983 *Gorilla* written and illustrated by Anthony Browne; Julia MacRae, 1983; Knopf, 1983.

1983 **RUNNERSUP** *Copycats* by Marianne Ford, diagrams by Anna Pugh; Deutsch, 1983.

The Troublesome Pig retold and illustrated by Priscilla Lamont; Hamish Hamilton, 1983.

The Wind in the Willows by Kenneth Grahame, illustrated by John Burningham; Kestrel, 1983; Penguin, 1983.

The Mouldy by William Mayne, illustrated by Nicola Bayley; Cape, 1983; Knopf, 1983.

1984 *Granpa* written and illustrated by John Burningham; Cape, 1984.

1984 **RUNNERSUP** *The Story of the Dancing Frog* written and illustrated by Quentin Blake; Cape, 1984.

Alice's Adventures in Wonderland by Lewis Carroll, illustrated by Justin Todd; Gollancz, 1984.

Christmas: The King James Version written and illustrated by Jan Pienkowski; Hutchinson, 1984.

The Woman in the Moon and other Tales of Forgotten Heroines by James Riordan, illustrated by Angela Barrett; Hutchinson, 1984.

1985 *The Iron Man* by Ted Hughes, illustrated by Andrew Davidson; Faber, 1985.

1985 **RUNNERSUP** *The Giraffe and the Pelly and Me* by Roald Dahl, illustrated by Quentin Blake; Cape, 1985.

Shakespeare Stories by Leon Garfield, illustrated by Michael Foreman; Gollancz, 1985.

The Wedding Ghost by Leon Garfield, illustrated by Charles Keeping; Oxford, 1985.

Chips and Jessie written and illustrated by Shirley Hughes; Bodley Head, 1985.

The Helen Oxenbury Nursery Story Book written and illustrated by Helen Oxenbury; Heinemann, 1985.

1986 *The Jolly Postman: or, Other People's Letters* written and illustrated by Alan Ahlberg and Janet Ahlberg; Heinemann, 1986.

1986 **RUNNERSUP** *Where's Julius?* written and illustrated by John Burningham; Cape, 1986.

Early in the Morning: A Collection of New Poems by Charles Causley, illustrated by Michael Foreman; Viking Kestrel, 1986.

The Rain Door by Russell Hoban, illustrated by Quentin Blake; Gollancz, 1986.

The Doorbell Rang written and illustrated by Pat Hutchins; Bodley Head, 1986.

Stanley Bagshaw and the Short-Sighted Goal Keeper by Bob Wilson, illustrated; Hamish Hamilton, 1986.

1987 *Jack the Treacle Eater* by Charles Causley, illustrated by Charles Keeping; Macmillan, 1987.

1988 *Alice's Adventures in Wonderland* by Lewis Carroll, illustrated by Anthony Browne; Julia MacRae, 1988; Knopf, 1988.

1989 *The Park in the Dark* by Martin Waddell, illustrated by Barbara Firth; Walker Books, 1989; Lothrop, Lee & Shepard, 1989.

1990 *All Join In* written and illustrated by Quentin Blake; Cape, 1990; Little Brown, 1991.

1991 *Have You Seen Who's Just Moved in Next Door to Us?* written and illustrated by Colin McNaughton; Walker, 1991; Random House, 1991.

1992 *The Man* written and illustrated by Raymond Briggs; Julia MacRae, 1992.

MASSACHUSETTS CHILDREN'S BOOK AWARD

Dr. Helen Constant
Division of Graduate and Continuing Education
Salem State College
352 Lafayette St.
Salem, MA 01970

Established by Dr. Helen Constant in 1976, the Massachusetts Children's Book Award is sponsored by the Education Department of Salem State College in Salem, Massachusetts. From 1978 to 1982 this annual award was presented to two book categories: grades 4-6 and grades 7-9. In 1983, the category for grades 7-9 was dropped. Master lists for both groups are drawn from nominations received from students, teachers, librarians, and reading specialists throughout the Commonwealth. The books must be of high quality and must broaden the children's horizons. Books that are intended simply to amuse and entertain are considered along with more serious or literary works. Children throughout the Commonwealth vote for their favorite book. A Paul Revere bowl is presented to the winner at a conference in June.

Criteria used to compose the master list are: (1) books of high literary quality and those appealing to children; (2) primarily fiction, of various genres, in paperback; (3) books within the reading range of slow readers as well as those for the more advanced; (4) old favorites and contemporary books; (5) both boys and girls as major characters; (6) primarily books written by living U.S. resi-

dents (but not necessarily so); (7) books about minorities written by minorities; (8) classics, and (9) books on the Holocaust.
    (Taken from the criteria set forth by Dr. Helen Constant.)

1976 *How to Eat Fried Worms* by Thomas Rockwell, illustrated by Emily McCully; Watts, 1973.

1977 *Tales of a Fourth Grade Nothing* by Judy Blume, illustrated by Roy Doty; Dutton, 1972.

1978 **GRADES 4-6** *Mrs. Frisby and the Rats of NIMH* by Robert C. O'Brien, illustrated by Zena Bernstein; Atheneum, 1971.

1978 **GRADES 7-9** *That Was Then, This Is Now* by S.E. Hinton, illustrated by Hal Siegel; Viking, 1971.

1979 **GRADES 4-6** *The Cricket in Times Square* by George Selden, illustrated by Garth Williams; Farrar, 1960.

1979 **GRADES 7-9** *The Cat Ate My Gymsuit* by Paula Danziger, not illustrated; Delacorte, 1974.

The Outsiders by S.E. Hinton, not illustrated; Viking, 1967; Dell, 1968.

1980 **ELEMENTARY** *Chocolate Fever* by Robert Kimmel Smith, illustrated by Gioia Fiammenghi; Dell, 1978.

1980 **YOUNG ADULT** *Summer of my German Soldier* by Bette Greene, not illustrated; Dial, 1973.

1981 **ELEMENTARY** *The Great Gilly Hopkins* by Katherine Paterson, not illustrated; Crowell, 1978.

1981 **YOUNG ADULT** *A Summer to Die* by Lois Lowry, illustrated by Jenni Oliver; Houghton, 1977.

1982 **ELEMENTARY** *James and the Giant Peach: A Children's Story* by Roald Dahl, illustrated by Nancy Ekholm Burkert; Knopf, 1961; Bantam, 1978.

1982 **YOUNG ADULT** *Killing Mr. Griffin* by Lois Duncan, not illustrated; Little Brown, 1978; Dell, 1979.

1983 **ELEMENTARY** *Tales of a Fourth Grade Nothing* by Judy Blume, illustrated by Roy Doty; Dutton, 1972.

1983 **YOUNG ADULT** *Stranger With My Face* by Lois Duncan, not illustrated; Little Brown, 1981.

1984 *Charlotte's Web* by E.B. White, illustrated by Garth Williams; Harper, 1952.

1985 *Nothing's Fair in Fifth Grade* by Barthe DeClements, not illustrated; Viking, 1981.

1986 *Dear Mr. Henshaw* by Beverly Cleary, illustrated by Paul O. Zelinsky; Morrow, 1983.

1987 *Where the Red Fern Grows* by Wilson Rawls, not illustrated; Doubleday, 1961.

1988 *The Indian in the Cupboard* by Lynn Reid Banks, illustrated by Brock Cole; Doubleday, 1980.

1989 *The Chocolate Touch* by Patrick Catling, illustrated by Margot Apple; Morrow, 1979.

1990 No Award

1991 *There's a Boy in the Girls' Bathroom* by Louis Sachar, not illustrated; Knopf, 1987.

1992 *Matilda* by Roald Dahl, illustrated by Quentin Blake; Viking Kestrel, 1988.

1993 *Maniac Magee* by Jerry Spinelli, not illustrated; Little Brown, 1990.

MEDIA & METHODS MAXI AWARD
discontinued

Media & Methods Maxi Awards were instituted to encourage excellence in materials developed for contemporary classroom use. First awarded in 1973, these awards were sponsored by Media & Methods, a publication of the American Society of Educators.

Readers of Media & Methods were urged to vote for materials which they felt had a maximum educational effectiveness. It was hoped that the poll results would encourage producers to be more responsive to the needs of today's teachers and students. It was also hoped that the award could foster critical evaluation and national acclaim for materials endorsed most often by Media & Methods readers. The awards were presented at the ALA annual convention.

Listed below are the titles that received the most votes for the textbook and paperback categories.

1973 **TEXTBOOK** *Exploring the Film* by Robert Stanley and William Kuhns; Pflaum/Standard, 1969.

Language of Man series edited by Joseph Fletcher Littell, illustrated; McDougall-Littell, 1971-1972.

1973 **PAPERBACK** *Go Ask Alice* (anonymous); Avon, 1972.

The Pigman by Paul Zindel, not illustrated; Harper, 1968; Dell, 1970.

1974 **TEXTBOOK** *Coping with Television* edited by Joseph Fletcher Littell, illustrated; McDougall-Littell, 1973.

1974 **PAPERBACK** *I'm OK, You're OK: A Practical Guide to Transactional Analysis* by Thomas Harris, not illustrated; Avon, 1973.

1975 **TEXTBOOK** *Mass Media* by M. Lawrence Reuter, Elizabeth Conley and Ann Heintz, illustrated; Loyola University Press, 1972.

The Media Works by Jeanne Crow and Joan Valdes; Pflaum/Standard, 1973.

TV Action Book by Jeffrey Schrank, illustrated with charts, diagrams; McDougall-Littell, 1974.

1975 **PAPERBACK** *A Day No Pigs Would Die* by Robert Newton Peck, not illustrated; Knopf, 1972; Dell, 1974.

Hatter Fox by Marilyn Harris; Bantam, 1974.

The Outsiders by S. E. Hinton, not illustrated; Viking, 1967; Dell, 1968.

Sunshine by Norma Klein, not illustrated; Holt Rinehart & Winston, 1975, c1974; Avon, 1974.

1976 **TEXTBOOK** *Film: Real to Reel* revised ed. by David Coynik, illustrated with photographs and movie stills; McDougall-Littell, 1972.

1976 **PAPERBACK** *Alive* by Piers Paul Read; Avon, 1975.

The Chocolate War by Robert Cormier, illustrated by Robert Vickery; Pantheon, 1974; Dell, 1975.

Watership Down by Richard Adams, not illustrated; Rex Collings, 1972; Macmillan, 1972; Avon, 1975.

Zen and the Art of Motorcycle Maintenance: An Inquiry into Values by Robert M. Pirsig; Bantam, 1976.

M E R PRIZE FOR YOUTH LITERATURE

Dr. Annari van der Merwe
Tafelberg Publishers
P O Box 879
8000 Cape Town
South Africa

The M E R Prize for Youth Literature was established in 1984 by the Nasionale Boekhandel Limited in memory of Mrs. M E Rothman (pen name M E R), one of the most beloved Afrikaans writers. The annual prize is awarded in recognition of the most deserving book for children or young people in English or Afrikaans during the preceding year by the publishing houses of the Nasionale Boekhandel Publishing Group.

Eligible books include fiction, nonfiction, picture books and poetry for children 8 to 15 years of age. The recipient receives and monetary prize of R5000 (South African Rand) and a gold medal. Listed below are the English language winners.

1988   *Place Among the Stones* by Jenny Seed; Tafelberg, 1987.

1990   *Down Street* by Lawrence Bransby; Tafelberg, 1989.

1991   *Tintinyane: The Girl Who Sang Like a Magic Bird* by Corlia Fourie, illustrated by Alida Bothma; Human & Rousseau, 1990.

VICKY METCALF AWARD

Jeffrey Holmes
Canadian Authors Association
275 Slater St. Suite 500
Ottawa, Ontario K1P 5B9
Canada

Founded by Vicky Metcalf in 1963, this annual award is administered by the Canadian Authors Association. The purpose of the award as stated by Vicky Metcalf is "to stimulate writing for children. We do not have enough children's books that are written by Canadians, and I do not think we should lag so far behind the U.S. in this respect. The prize is intended for a number of strictly children's books by any Canadian author. The books may be fiction, nonfiction, or even picture books. There is no set formula."

Nominations may be made by any individual or association by letter in triplicate listing the published works (at least four books) of the nominee. The only criterion is that the writing be wholesome. The deadline is March 31 of each year. A committee of three judges familiar with Canadian children's literature selects the recipient, who is awarded $10,000 donated by Vicky Metcalf. The award is made at the annual conference of the Canadian Authors Association.

1963   Kerry Wood

1964   John F. Hayes

1965   Roderick Haig-Brown

1966   Fred Swayze

1967   John Patrick Gillese

1968   Lorrie McLaughlin

1969   Audrey McKim

1970   Farley Mowat

1971   Kay Hill

1972   William Toye

1973   Christie Harris

1974   Jean Little

1975   Lyn Harrington

1976   Suzanne Martel

1977   James Houston

1978   Lyn Cook

1979   Cliff Faulknor

1980   John Craig

1981   Monica Hughes

1982   Janet Lunn

1983   Claire Mackay

1984   Bill Freeman

1985   Edith Fowke

1986   Dennis Lee

1987   Robert Munsch

1988   Barbara Smucker

1989   Stephane Poulin

1990   Bernice Thurman Hunter

1991   Brian Doyle

1992   Kevin Major

VICKY METCALF SHORT STORY AWARD

Jeffrey Holmes
Canadian Authors Association
275 Slater St. Suite 500
Ottawa, Ontario K1P 5B9
Canada

First awarded in 1979, this annual award is given to the best children's short story first published in a Canadian periodical or anthology during the previous calendar year. The story must be fiction of interest to children ages seven through seventeen and written by a Canadian author. The only criterion is that the story be wholesome. Anyone may nominate a story by submitting the story, with dateline, in triplicate. A committee of three judges (including the previous winner) selects the winner. The prize of $3000 is presented at the Canadian Authors Association annual conference.

1979   *The Kingdom of the Riddles* by Marina McDougall in *Ready or Not* edited by Jack Booth (Language Patterns Impressions, Reading Series); Holt, 1978.

1980   *Blind Date* by Estelle Salata in *Time Enough* edited by Jack Booth; Holt, Rinehart & Winston, 1979.

1981   *Long Claws* by James Houston in *The Winter Fun Book* by Laima Dingwall; Greey de Pencier Books, 1980.

1982   *Major Resolution* by Barbara Greenwood in *Contexts*; Nelson, 1981.

1983   *Iron Barred Door* by Monica Hughes in *Anthology Two*; Nelson, 1982.

1984   *Dog Who Wanted to Die* by P.C. Archer in *Jam Magazine* v.4#1, Sept/Oct 1983.

1985   *Here She Is, Ms. Teeny-Wonderful!* by Martyn Godfrey in *Crackers Magazine* #12 Spring 1984.

1986   *Boy Who Walked Backwards* by Diana J. Weiler; *Western Producer Prairie*, 1985.

1987 *Viking Dagger* by Isabel Reiner in *Of the Jigsaw*; Peguis, 1986.

1988 *Marvin & Me & the Flies* by Claire Mackay in *Canadian Children's Annual* 1987; Grolier, 1987.

1989 *Paradise Cafe and Other Stories* by Martha Brooks, not illustrated; Thistledown Press, 1988; Little Brown, 1990.

1990 *Choose Your Grandma* by Patricia Armstrong; Cateau Books, 1989.

1991 No Award

1992 *Adventure on Thunder Island* by Edna King in *Adventure on Thunder Island* by E. King and J. Wheeler; Lorimer, 1991.

MICHIGAN YOUNG READER'S AWARD
discontinued

The Michigan Young Reader's Award was first presented in 1979 for the purpose of interesting children preschool through eighth grade in reading literature and in expressing their feelings and ideas. Any type of literature, in English, written by a living author, was eligible for this annual children's choice award. The award was made in two categories: Division I (K-3) and Division II (4-8). Each year, the children voted for their favorite title from a list of ten titles in their division. They also nominated a favorite book to be placed on the list for next year's award. The book with the most votes in each category was the winner. The winner was announced at the Michigan Council of Teachers of English regional meeting and in the Michigan English Teacher.

Specific rules governing the contest included: (1) The winning author of this year's MYRA will not appear on next year's list. (2) No books that appear on this year's list may appear on next year's list. (3) Only one title of any one author will be included. (4) The author should be living. (5) The book must have originally been written in English. (6) The book must have been published within the last ten years.

1979 *Charlotte's Web* by E.B. White, illustrated by Garth Williams; Harper, 1952.

1980 **DIVISION I** *Freckle Juice* by Judy Blume, illustrated by Sonia O. Lisker; Four Winds, 1971.

1980 **DIVISION I RUNNERUP** *Fish Is Fish* written and illustrated by Leo Lionni; Pantheon, 1970.

1980 **DIVISION II** *Where the Red Fern Grows* by Wilson Rawls, not illustrated; Doubleday, 1961.

1980 **DIVISION II RUNNERUP** *Bridge to Terabithia* by Katherine Paterson, illustrated by Donna Diamond; Crowell, 1977.

The House With a Clock in its Walls by John Bellairs, illustrated by Edward Gorey; Dial, 1973.

1981 **DIVISION I** *Bears in the Night* written and illustrated by Stan Berenstain and Jan Berenstain; Random House, 1971.

1981 **DIVISION II** *Where the Sidewalk Ends* written and illustrated by Shel Silverstein; Harper, 1974.

1982 **DIVISION I** *Beauty and the Beast* retold by Marianna Mayer, illustrated by Mercer Mayer; Four Winds, 1978.

1982 **DIVISION II** *The Westing Game* by Ellen Raskin, not illustrated; Dutton, 1978.

1983 **DIVISION I** *The Island of the Skog* written and illustrated by Steven Kellogg; Dial, 1973.

1983 **DIVISION II** *Anastasia Krupnick* by Lois Lowry, not illustrated; Houghton Mifflin, 1979.

1984 *Ramona Quimby, Age 8* by Beverly Cleary, illustrated by Alan Tiegreen; Morrow, 1981.

Soup by Robert Newton Peck, illustrated by Charles Gehm; Knopf, 1974.

MILNER AWARD
Rennie Davant, Executive Director
Friends of the Atlanta-Fulton Public Library
One Margaret Mitchell Square
Atlanta, GA 30303

Sponsored by the Friends of the Atlanta Public Library, the Milner Award was founded by Miss Vera Milner in 1983. Grammar school children of Atlanta vote for their favorite living American author. The chosen author must be able to attend the award ceremonies held at the Central Atlanta Library each Spring. A $1000 honorarium and a specially commissioned work of the internationally famous glass sculptor, Hans Frabel are presented to the author.

1983 Judy Blume

1984 Peggy Parish

1985 Paula Danziger

1986 Barbara Park

1987 Lois Lowry

1988 Francine Pascal

1989 John Steptoe

1990 Louis Sachar

1991 Marc Brown

1992 Barthe DeClements

MINNESOTA BOOK AWARDS
Minnesota Center for the Book
226 Metro Square
7th and Robert Sts.
St. Paul, MN 55101

This annual award was established in 1988 to recognize, celebrate, and promote the contributions that resident authors, illustrators and editors make to the quality of life. These contributions strengthen the linkages among the Minnesota community of the book. In order to be eligible, the nominee must be a resident of the state at time of authorship or publication and the book must be published during the preceding year.

Children's categories vary each year, but typical categories are younger children and older children. Nominees are selected as outstanding representatives of the year. Award recipients are selected by panels of three judges in each category. A framed certificate is presented to the winners at a public ceremony during National Book Week at the end of January.

1988 **FINALIST** *The Star Maiden: An Ojibway Tale* retold by Barbara Juster Esbensen, illustrated by Helen K. Davie; Little Brown, 1988.

Hatchet by Gary Paulsen, not illustrated; Viking, 1988.

1989 **CHILDREN** *Going the Moose Way Home* by Jim Latimer, illustrated by Donald Carrick; Scribner, 1988.

1991 YOUNGER CHILDREN *How the Guinea Fowl Got Her Spots* retold and illustrated by Barbara Knutson; Carolrhoda, 1990.

1991 OLDER CHILDREN *Woodsong* by Gary Paulsen, illustrated by Ruth Wright Paulsen; Bradbury, 1990.

1992 YOUNGER CHILDREN *The Salamander Room* by Anne Mazer, illustrated by Steve Johnson; Knopf, 1991.

Old Turtle by Douglas Wood, illustrated by Cheng-Khee Chee; Pfeifer-Hamilton, 1992.

1992 OLDER CHILDREN *Face To Face* by Marion Dane Bauer, not illustrated; Clarion, 1991.

1993 YOUNGER CHILDREN *Old Black Fly* by Jim Aylesworth, illustrated by Stephen Gammell; Holt, 1992.

Dreamcatcher by Audrey Osofsky, illustrated by Ed Young; Orchard, 1992.

1993 OLDER CHILDREN *What's Your Story? A Young Person's Guide to Writing Fiction* by Marion Dane Bauer; Clarion, 1992.

MISSISSIPPI CHILDREN'S BOOK AWARD

discontinued

This children's choice award was established in 1989 by Vandelia Van Meter and Jeannine Laughlin of the School of Library Service and Dee Jones and Anne Lundin of the de Grummond Collection of the University of Southern Mississippi. Financial assistance was provided by the Mississippi Power Foundation and the University of Southern Mississippi. The purpose of the annual Mississippi Children's Book Award (MCBA) was to promote reading and cultural literacy, to encourage young Mississippi readers to become acquainted with good literature and to present reading as a joyful and menaingful experience.

The books on each year's Master List were chosen by the MCBA Committee from the lists of notable fiction books honored by the American Library Association and the School Library Journal during the preceding two years.

Mississippi school children in grades four through six voted for their favorite title from the Master List. The winning author was honored at the annual conference of the Mississippi Library Association with an engraved plaque and an appropriate gift. The award program was discontinued in 1990.

1989 *Class Clown* by Johanna Hurwitz, illustrated by Sheila Hamanaka; Morrow, 1987.

1990 *All About Sam* by Lois Lowry, illustrated by Diane de Groat; Houghton Mifflin, 1988.

MR. CHRISTIE'S BOOK AWARD PROGRAM

Christie Brown & Co.
2150 Lakeshore Blvd. West
Toronto, Ontario M8V 1A5
Canada

Awarded annually since 1989, the Mr. Christie's Book Award is a national competition which honors excellence in writing and illustration of Canadian children's literature and is designed to encourage the development and publishing of high quality children's books. The program is supported by the Canadian Children's Book Centre and Communications Jeunesse.

Six awards of $7500 each are presented in the following categories: English Text (under 8 years of age); English Text (Ages 9-14); English Illustration; French Text (under 8 years of age); French Text (Ages 9-14); French Illustration. Four books in each category are selected for the short list. The short list as well as the winning titles will be announced at the award ceremony.

Two judging panels, one French and one English, consist of five members each and serve a two year term. Criteria considered in the judging include the ability to inspire the imagination of the winner; to recognize the importance of play; represent the highest standard of integrity; to bring delight and edification; and to help children understand the world both intellectually and emotionally.

Only the English language titles are listed below.

1989 ENGLISH TEXT *The Sky Is Falling* by Kit Pearson, not illustrated; Viking, 1989.

1989 ENGLISH ILLUSTRATION *The Name of the Tree* retold by Celia Barker Lottridge, illustrated by Ian Wallace; Douglas & MacIntyre, 1989; McElderry, 1989.

1990 ENGLISH TEXT *Covered Bridge* by Brian Doyle, illustrated with maps; Douglas & MacIntyre, 1990.

1990 ENGLISH ILLUSTRATION *The Story of Little Quack* written by Betty Gibson, illustrated by Kady MacDonald Denton; Kids Can Press, 1990.

1991 ENGLISH TEXT *The Ice Cream Store* by Dennis Lee, illustrated by David McPhail; HarperCollins, 1991.

1991 ENGLISH ILLUSTRATION *Zoe's Rainy Day* illustrated by Barbara Reid; HarperCollins, 1991.

Zoe's Sunny Day illustrated by Barbara Reid; HarperCollins, 1991.

Zoe's Windy Day illustrated by Barbara Reid; HarperCollins, 1991.

Zoe's Snowy Day illustrated by Barbara Reid; HarperCollins, 1991.

1992 ENGLISH TEXT AGES 8 AND UNDER *There Were Monkeys In My Kitchen!* by Sheree Fitch and Marc Mongeau; Doubleday Canada, 1992.

1992 ENGLISH TEXT AGES 9-14 *The Story of Canada* by Janet Lunn and Christopher Moore, illustrated by Alan Daniel; Lester Publishing, 1992.

1992 ENGLISH ILLUSTRATION *A Prairie Alphabet, ABC* by Jo Bannatyne-Cugnet, illustrated by Yvette Moore; Tundra, 1992.

MOTHER GOOSE AWARD

Books for Children
c/o Angela Hart
Whiteway Court
The Whiteway
Cirencester
Gloucestershire GL7 7BA
England

This annual award was first presented in 1979 to the most exciting newcomer to British children's book illustration. It is sponsored by the book club Books for Children. The award takes the form of a bronze goose egg, a scroll, and £500 for the winner. The runnersup receive a scroll and a bottle of champagne.

1979 *Pippin and Pod* written and illustrated by Michelle Cartlidge; Heinemann, 1978.

1979 RUNNERSUP *Hepzibah* by Peter Dickinson, illustrated by Sue Porter; Eel Pie, 1978.

The Most Amazing Hide and Seek Alphabet Book written and illustrated by Robert Crowther; Kestrel, 1977.

My Brother Sammy written and illustrated by Atie Van Der Meer and Ronald Van der Meer; Hamilton, 1978.

Sammy and Mara written and illustrated by Atie Van Der Meer and Ronald Van Der Meer; Hamilton, 1978.

1980 *Mr. Potter's Pigeon* by Patrick Kinmouth, illustrated by Reg Cartwright; Hutchinson, 1979.

1980 RUNNERSUP *Abbey-lubbers, Banshees and Boggarts: An Illustrated Encyclopedia of Fairies* by Katherine M. Briggs, illustrated by Yvonne Gilbert; Kestrel, 1979.

Sybil and the Blue Rabbit written and illustrated by Jane Johnson; Benn, 1979.

1981 *Green Finger House* by Rosemary Harris, illustrated by Juan Wijngaard; Eel Pie, 1980.

1981 RUNNERSUP *Cousin Blodwyn's Visit* written and illustrated by Amanda Vesey; Methuen, 1980.

I Believe in Unicorns by Adam John Munthe, illustrated by Elizabeth Falconer; Chatto, 1979.

Where's Spot? written and illustrated by Eric Hill; Methuen, 1980.

1982 *Sunshine* written and illustrated by Jan Ormerod; Kestrel, 1981; Penguin (Australia), 1981; Lothrop, Lee & Shepard, 1981.

1982 RUNNERSUP *Matilda* Jane by Jean Gerrard, illustrated by Roy Gerrard; Gollancz, 1981.

The Fox and the Circus Bear written and illustrated by Terry McKenna; Gollancz, 1982.

Only the Best by Meguido Zola, illustrated by Valerie Littlewood; Julia MacRae, 1981.

1983 *Angry Arthur* by Hiawyn Oram, illustrated by Satoshi Kitamura; Andersen Press, 1982; Harcourt, 1982.

1983 RUNNERSUP *Trouble for Trumpets* by Peter Dallas-Smith, illustrated by Peter Cross; Ernest Benn, 1982; Random House, 1984.

On Friday Something Funny Happened written and illustrated by John Prater; Bodley Head, 1982.

Outlawed Inventions by Chris Winn and Jeremy Beadle; illustrated; Pepper Press, 1982.

The Great Smile Robbery by Roger McGough, illustrated by Tony Blundell; Kestrel, 1982.

1984 *The Blue Book of Hob Stories* by William Mayne, illustrated by Patrick Benson; Walker, 1984.

The Green Book of Hob Stories by William Mayne, illustrated by Patrick Benson; Walker, 1984.

The Red Book of Hob Stories by William Mayne, illustrated by Patrick Benson; Walker, 1984.

The Yellow Book of Hob Stories by William Mayne, illustrated by Patrick Benson; Walker, 1984.

1984 RUNNERSUP *The King, the Cat and the Fiddle* by Yehudi Menuhin and Christopher Hope, illustrated by Angela Barrett; Benn, 1983.

Rufus the Fox written and illustrated by Graeme Sims; Warne, 1983.

Your Body: Skin and Bone by Dr. Gwynne Vevers, illustrated by Sarah Pooley; Bodley Head, 1983.

1985 *Badger's Parting Gifts* written and illustrated by Susan Varley; Andersen Press, 1984.

1985 RUNNERSUP *The Sheep and the Rowan Tree* written and illustrated by Julia Butcher; Methuen, 1984.

Zoo Walk written and illustrated by Gregg Reyes; Oxford, 1984.

Bare Bear written and illustrated by Jez Alborough; Benn, 1984.

1986 No Award

1987 *A Bag of Moonshine* by Alan Garner, illustrated by Patrick James Lynch; Collins, 1986.

1987 RUNNERSUP *The Selfish Giant* by Oscar Wilde, illustrated by Dom Mansell; Walker, 1986.

Little Pickle written and illustrated by Peter Collington; Methuen, 1986.

Miss Fanshawe and the Great Dragon Adventure written and illustrated by Sue Scullard; Macmillan Children's, 1986.

Big Baby by Jon Ward, illustrated by Claudio Munoz; Walker, 1986.

1988 *Listen to This* by Laura Cecil, illustrated by Emma Chichester Clark; Bodley Head, 1987.

1988 RUNNERSUP *Busy Baby's Day - Afternoon* written and illustrated by Carol Thompson; Macdonald, 1987.

Busy Baby's Day - Wake up Time written and illustrated by Carol Thompson; Macdonald, 1987.

Busy Baby's Day - Morning written and illustrated by Carol Thompson; Macdonald, 1987.

Busy Baby's Day - Bedtime written and illustrated by Carol Thompson; Macdonald, 1987.

Ottoline at the British Museum by Sally Craddock, illustrated by Corinne Pearlman; Macdonald, 1987; Simon & Schuster, 1990.

Where's Wally? written and illustrated by Martin Handford; Walker Books, 1987.

Manhattan written and illustrated by Jean Christian Knaff; Faber, 1987.

1989 *Bush Vark's First Day Out* written and illustrated by Charles Fuge; Macmillan, 1988.

1990 *Strat and Chatto* by Jan Mark, illustrated by David Hughes; Walker Books, 1989.

1990 RUNNERSUP *The Witch's Hand* written and illustrated by Peter Utton; Aurum Books for Children, 1989; Farrar Straus Giroux, 1989.

1991 *A Close Call* written and illustrated by Amanda Harvey; Macmillan Children's, 1990.

1991 RUNNERSUP *Squeak-a-Lot* by Martin Waddell, illustrated by Virginia Miller; Walker, 1991; Greenwillow, 1991.

The Whales' Song by Dyan Sheldon, illustrated by Gary Blythe; Hutchinson, 1991; Dial, 1991.

Eddie and Teddy written and illustrated by Gus Clarke; Andersen Press, 1990.

1992 *Inside the Whale and Other Animals* by Steve Parker, illustrated by Ted Dewan; Dorling Kindersley, 1992.

1992 RUNNERSUP *A Tale of Two Kings* written and illustrated by Carol Morley; ABC, 1991.

The Moonlit Journey written and illustrated by Peter O'Donnell; All Books for Children, 1991; Scholastic, 1991.

Quacky, Quack-quack! by Ian Whybrow, illustrated by Russell Ayto; Walker, 1991; Four Winds, 1991.

1993 *The Seashell Song* by Susie Jenkin-Pearce, illustrated by Claire Fletcher; Bodley Head, 1992; Lothrop, Lee & Shepard, 1992.

1993 RUNNERSUP *Paul Hunt's Night Diary* written and illustrated by Paul Hunt; Child's Play, 1992.

When Grandma Came by Jill Paton Walsh, illustrated by Sophy Williams; Viking, 1992.

Maybe It's a Pirate by Judy Hindley, illustrated by Selina Young; ABC, 1992.

1993 HONORABLE MENTION *But No Cheese!* by Saviour Pirotta, illustrated by Kate Simpson; Hodder & Stoughton, 1992.

ELIZABETH MRAZIK-CLEAVER CANADIAN PICTURE BOOK AWARD

Canadian Children's Book Centre
35 Spadina Rd.
Toronto, Ontario M5R 2S9
Canada

Established in 1986 in memory of Canadian illustrator Elizabeth Mrazik-Cleaver, this award recognizes the best picture book of the year. To be eligible, the picture book (as opposed to illustrated book) must be published in Canada, in English or French, during the previous calendar year. It must be a first edition and contain original illustrations. The award is made each year unless no book is judged deserving. The $1000 prize is intended to help enable the illustrator to continue in their work.

The following criteria have been established: (1) the pictures should recreate the significant ideas of the story and reflect the mood. (2) The pictures speak to a young child and are understood by them. (3) The pictures have warmth and depth of emotion with a storytelling quality. (4) The color is well applied and suitable to the text. (5) If black and white, shading and contrasts are used so that figures stand out and action is portrayed. An adequate degree of warmth and vitality is expressed. (6) The line expresses movement and is in keeping with the mood of the story. (7) The shapes fill, but do not clutter the page. (8) Elements of each page are well arranged, the parts have balance so that there is a focus. (9) The pictures are well drawn. (10) The overall effect is good - story, pictures and graphic presentation are all one and pleasing to observe.

1986 *By the Sea: An Alphabet Book* written and illustrated by Ann Blades; Kids Can Press, 1985.

1987 *Have You Seen Birds?* by Joanne Oppenheim, illustrated by Barbara Reid; North Winds Press, 1986.

1988 *Can You Catch Josephine?* written and illustrated by Stephane Poulin; Tundra, 1987.

1989 *Night Cars* by Teddy Jam, illustrated by Eric Beddows; Douglas & McIntyre, 1988; Orchard, 1989.

1990 *The Name of the Tree* by Celia Barker Lottridge, illustrated by Ian Wallace; Groundwood Books, 1989; McElderry, 1989.

1991 *The Orphan Boy* by Tololwa M. Mollel, illustrated by Paul Morin; Oxford University Press, 1990.

1992 *Waiting for the Whales* by Sheryl McFarlane, illustrated by Ron Lightburn; Orca, 1991.

N

NATIONAL BOOK AWARDS
discontinued
see also **AMERICAN BOOK AWARDS**

The Association of American Publishers established the National Book Awards in 1950 to give recognition to the most distinguished books of the preceding year. In 1969, a children's category was added to recognize the most distinguished book written by an American citizen and published in the United States for children. A $1000 prize along with a citation was awarded to the recipient. The award was administered by the National Book Awards committee until 1975, when the American Academy and Institute of Arts and Letters assumed responsibility until 1977. From 1977 to 1979, the award was sponsored by the Association of American Publishers. In 1979, the award was discontinued and replaced by the American Book Awards (see entry) in 1980.

1969 *Journey from Peppermint Street* by Meindert DeJong, illustrated by Emily McCully; Harper, 1968.

1969 FINALISTS *Constance: A Story of Early Plymouth* by Patricia Clapp, not illustrated; Lothrop, 1968.

The Endless Steppe: Growing Up in Siberia by Esther Hautzig, not illustrated; Crowell, 1968.

The High King by Lloyd Alexander, not illustrated; Holt, 1968.

Langston Hughes: A Biography by Milton Meltzer, not illustrated; Crowell, 1968.

1970 *A Day of Pleasure: Stories of a Boy Growing Up in Warsaw* by Isaac Bashevis Singer, illustrated by Roman Vishniac; Farrar, 1969.

1970 FINALISTS *Pop Corn and Ma Goodness* by Edna Mitchell Preston, illustrated by Robert Andrew Parker; Viking, 1969.

Sylvester and the Magic Pebble written and illustrated by William Steig; Windmill/Simon & Schuster, 1969.

Where the Lilies Bloom by Bill Cleaver and Vera Cleaver, illustrated by Jim Spanfeller; Lippincott, 1969.

The Young United States: 1783-1830 written and illustrated by Edwin Tunis; World, 1969.

1971 *The Marvelous Misadventures of Sebastian: Grand Extravaganza, including a Performance by the Entire Cast of the Gallimaufry-Theatricus* by Lloyd Alexander, not illustrated; Dutton, 1970.

1971 FINALISTS *Blowfish Live in the Sea* by Paula Fox, not illustrated; Bradbury, 1970.

Frog and Toad Are Friends written and illustrated by Arnold Lobel; Harper, 1970.

Grover by Bill Cleaver and Vera Cleaver, illustrated by Frederic Marvin; Lippincott, 1970.

The Trumpet of the Swan by E.B. White, illustrated by Edward Frascino; Harper, 1970.

1972 *The Slightly Irregular Fire Engine: or, The Hithering, Thithering Djinn* written and illustrated by Donald Barthelme; Farrar, 1971.

1972 FINALISTS *Amos and Boris* written and illustrated by William Steig; Farrar, 1971.

The Art and Industry of Sandcastles written and illustrated by Jan Adkins; Walker, 1971.

The Bears' House by Marilyn Sachs, illustrated by Louis Glanzman; Doubleday, 1971.

Father Fox's Pennyrhymes by Clyde Watson, illustrated by Wendy Watson; Crowell, 1971.

Hildilid's Night by Cheli Duran Ryan, illustrated by Arnold Lobel; Macmillan, 1971.

His Own Where by June Jordan, not illustrated; Crowell, 1971.

Mrs. Frisby and the Rats of NIMH by Robert C. O'Brien, illustrated by Zena Bernstein; Atheneum, 1971.

The Planet of Junior Brown by Virginia Hamilton, not illustrated; Macmillan, 1971.

The Tombs of Atuan by Ursula K. LeGuin, illustrated by Gail Garraty; Atheneum, 1971.

Wild in the World by John Donovan, not illustrated; Harper, 1971.

1973 *The Farthest Shore* by Ursula K. LeGuin, illustrated by Gail Garraty; Atheneum, 1972.

1973 FINALISTS *Children of Vietnam* by Betty Jean Lifton and Thomas C. Fox, illustrated by Thomas C. Fox; Atheneum, 1972.

D'Aulaires' Trolls written and illustrated by Edgar Parin d'Aulaire and Ingri d'Aulaire; Doubleday, 1972.

Dominic written and illustrated by William Steig; Farrar, 1972.

The House of Wings by Betsy Byars, illustrated by Daniel Schwartz; Viking, 1972.

The Impossible People: A History Natural and Unnatural of Beings Terrible and Wonderful by Georgess McHargue, illustrated by Frank Bozzo; Holt, 1972.

Julie of the Wolves by Jean Craighead George, illustrated by John Schoenherr; Harper, 1972.

Long Journey Home: Stories from Black History by Julius Lester, not illustrated; Dial, 1972.

The Witches of Worm by Zilpha Keatley Snyder, illustrated by Alton Raible; Atheneum, 1972.

1974 *The Court of the Stone Children* by Eleanor Cameron, not illustrated; Dutton, 1973.

1974 FINALISTS *Duffy and the Devil* by Harve Zemach, illustrated by Margot Zemach; Farrar, 1973.

A Figure of Speech by Norma Fox Mazer, not illustrated; Delacorte, 1973.

Guests in the Promised Land: Stories by Kristin Hunter, not illustrated; Scribner, 1973.

A Hero Ain't Nothin' but a Sandwich by Alice Childress, not illustrated; Coward, 1973.

Poor Richard in France by F.N. Monjo, illustrated by Brinton Turkle; Holt, 1973.

A Proud Taste for Scarlet and Miniver written and illustrated by E.L. Konigsburg; Atheneum, 1973.

Summer of my German Soldier by Bette Greene, not illustrated; Dial, 1973.

The Treasure is the Rose by Julia Cunningham, illustrated by Judy Graese; Pantheon, 1973.

The Whys and Wherefores of Littabelle Lee by Bill Cleaver and Vera Cleaver, not illustrated; Atheneum, 1973.

1975 *M.C. Higgins, the Great* by Virginia Hamilton, not illustrated; Macmillan, 1974.

1975 FINALISTS *The Devil's Storybook* written and illustrated by Natalie Babbitt; Farrar, 1974.

Doctor in the Zoo written and illustrated by Bruce Buchenholz, illustrated with photographs; Studio/Viking, 1974.

The Edge of Next Year by Mary Stolz, not illustrated; Harper, 1974.

The Girl Who Cried Flowers and other Tales by Jane Yolen, illustrated by David Palladini; Crowell, 1974.

I Tell a Lie Every So Often by Bruce Clements, not illustrated; Farrar, 1974.

Joi Bangla! The Children of Bangladesh by Ettagale Laure and Jason Laure; Farrar, 1974.

My Brother Sam is Dead by James L. Collier and Christopher Collier; Four Winds/Scholastic, 1974.

Remember the Days: A Short History of the Jewish American by Milton Meltzer, illustrated by Harvey Dinnerstein; Zenith/Doubleday, 1974.

Wings by Adrienne Richard, not illustrated; Atlantic-Little, 1974.

World of Our Fathers: The Jews of Eastern Europe by Milton Meltzer, illustrated with photographs; Farrar, 1974.

1976 *Bert Breen's Barn* by Walter D. Edmonds, not illustrated; Little Brown, 1975.

1976 FINALISTS *As I Was Crossing Boston Common* by Norma Farber, illustrated by Arnold Lobel; Dutton, 1975.

El Bronx Remembered: A Novella and Stories by Nicholasa Mohr, not illustrated; Harper, 1975.

Ludell by Brenda Wilkinson, not illustrated; Harper, 1975.

Of Love and Death and Other Journeys by Isabelle Holland, not illustrated; Lippincott, 1975.

The Star in the Pail by David McCord, illustrated by Marc Simont; Little Brown, 1975.

To the Green Mountains by Eleanor Cameron, not illustrated; Dutton, 1975.

1977 *The Master Puppeteer* by Katherine Paterson, illustrated by Haru Wells; Crowell, 1976.

1977 FINALISTS *Never to Forget: The Jews of the Holocaust* by Milton Meltzer, not illustrated; Harper, 1976.

Ox Under Pressure by John Ney, not illustrated; Lippincott, 1976.

Roll of Thunder, Hear My Cry by Mildred D. Taylor, illustrated by Jerry Pinkney; Dial, 1976.

Tunes for a Small Harmonica by Barbara Wersba, not illustrated; Harper, 1976.

1978 *The View from the Oak* by Herbert Kohl and Judith Kohl, illustrated by Roger Bayless; Sierra Club/Scribner, 1977.

1978 FINALISTS *Caleb and Kate* written and illustrated by William Steig; Farrar, 1977.

Hew Against the Grain by Betty Sue Cummings, not illustrated; Atheneum, 1977.

Mischling, Second Degree: My Childhood in Nazi Germany by Ilse Koehn, not illustrated; Greenwillow, 1977.

One at a Time: His Collected Poems for the Young by David McCord, illustrated by Henry B. Kane; Little Brown, 1977.

1979 *The Great Gilly Hopkins* by Katherine Paterson, not illustrated; Crowell, 1978.

1979 FINALISTS *The First Two Lives of Lukas-Kasha* by Lloyd Alexander, not illustrated; Dutton, 1978.

Humbug Mountain by Sid Fleischman, illustrated by Eric Von Schmidt; Atlantic-Little, 1978.

The Little Swineherd and other Tales by Paula Fox, illustrated by Leonard Lubin; Dutton, 1978.

Queen of Hearts by Bill Cleaver and Vera Cleaver, not illustrated; Lippincott, 1978.

NATIONAL CHAPTER OF CANADA IODE VIOLET DOWNEY BOOK AWARD

The National Chapter of Canada IODE
40 Orchard View Blvd.
Suite 254
Toronto, Ontario M4R 1B9
Canada

Named after its benefactor, the late Violet Downey, this award is offered annually to recognize the best English language book, containing at least 500 words of text, in any category, suitable for children aged 13 and under. Fairy tales, anthologies and books adapted from another source are not eligible. To be eligible, the book must have been written by a Canadian citizen, and must have been published in Canada during the calendar year immediately preceding the National Chapter meeting.

Established in 1985, the award of not more than $3000 can be divided between two people. A five-member panel of judges includes the National President, the National Education Officer, a third IODE member to be appointed annually, and two non-members who are recognized specialists in children's literature.

1985 *Winners* by Mary-Ellen Lang Collura, not illustrated; Western Producer Prairie Books, 1984.

1986 *The Quarter-pie Window* by Marianne Brandis, illustrated by G. Brender a Brandis; Porcupine's Quill, 1985.

1987 *Shadow in Hawthorn Bay* by Janet Lunn, not illustrated; Lester & Orpen Dennys, 1986; Scribner, 1986.

1988 *A Book Dragon* by Donn Kushner, illustrated by Nancy Ruth Jackson; Macmillan of Canada, 1987.

1989 No Award

1990 *Tales From Gold Mountain* by Paul Yee, illustrated by Simon Ng; Douglas & McIntyre, 1989; Macmillan, 1989.

1991 *Redwork* by Michael Bedard, not illustrated; Lester & Orpen Dennys, 1990; Atheneum, 1990.

Incredible Jumbo by Barbara Smucker, not illustrated; Viking, 1990.

1992 *Waiting for the Whales* by Sheryl McFarlane, illustrated by Ron Lightburn; Orca Books, 1991.

1993 *Hero of Lesser Causes* by Julie Johnston; Lester Publishing, 1992.

NATIONAL CHILDREN'S LITERATURE AWARD

South Australian Department for the Arts
and Cultural Heritage
GPO Box 2308
Adelaide 5001 South Australia
Australia

Awarded for the best Australian children's book of the preceding two years, either fiction or nonfiction, the National Children's Literature Award was established in 1986 by the South Australian Department for the Arts and Cultural Heritage. This biennial award provides for a cash award of $12,000 (Australian) and is presented at Writers' Week of the Adelaide Festival of the Arts.

1986 *The Long Night Watch* by Ivan Southall, not illustrated; Methuen, 1983.

1988 *Space Demons* by Gillian Rubinstein, not illustrated; Omnibus/Penguin, 1986.

1990 *Beyond the Labyrinth* by Gillian Rubinstein, not illustrated; Hyland House, 1988.

1992 *The House Guest* by Eleanor Nilsson, not illustrated; Viking, 1991.

NATIONAL COUNCIL OF TEACHERS OF ENGLISH ACHIEVEMENT AWARD FOR POETRY FOR CHILDREN

National Council of Teachers of English
1111 Kenyon Rd
Urbana, IL 61801

First awarded in 1977, this program is sponsored by the National Council of Teachers of English (NCTE). The award is presented for the aggregate body of poetry for children by a living American author. Nominations are received from all members of NCTE. The Poetry Award selection committee considers all nominations and makes their final selection. A plaque is presented to the winner at the Books for Children luncheon at the annual convention of the National Council of Teachers of English. After 1982, the award was presented every three years.

1977 David McCord

1978 Aileen Fisher

1979 Karla Kuskin

1980 Myra Cohn Livingston

1981 Eve Merriam

1982　John Ciardi

1985　Lilian Moore

1988　Arnold Adoff

1991　Valerie Worth

NATIONAL JEWISH BOOK AWARD
see **JEWISH WELFARE BOARD**

NATIONAL MASS MEDIA AWARDS
see **THOMAS ALVA EDISON FOUNDATION MASS MEDIA AWARDS**

NATIONAL RELIGIOUS BOOK AWARD
discontinued

The National Religious Book Award was cosponsored by The Religious Book Review and Omni Communications. The aim of this award was to highlight the contributions made by religious publications. Several categories of literature were honored including children's literature. Nominations were made by the publishers; a committee of booksellers, editors, librarians, and book reviewers selected the winning titles. Listed below are the children's literature winners.

1978　*Noah's Ark* written and illustrated by Peter Spier; Doubleday, 1977.

1979　*Book of the Dun Cow* by Walter Wangerin, Jr., not illustrated; Harper, 1978.

NEBRASKA CHILDREN'S BOOK AWARD
see **GOLDEN SOWER AWARD**

NENE AWARD
Hawaii Association of School Librarians
Box 23019
Honolulu, HI 96822

This annual children's choice award was founded by Cynthia Geiser in 1964. The purposes of the award are to help the children of Hawaii become acquainted with the best contemporary writers of fiction for children, to become aware of the qualities that make a good book, to choose the best rather than the mediocre, and to honor an author whose book has been enjoyed by the children of Hawaii. This award is cosponsored by the Hawaii Association of School Librarians and the children's section of the Hawaii Library Association. The Nene Award honors fiction titles that are suitable for grades four through six. The author must be living and the book must have been published in the last six years. The winning author is not eligible again for five years (this rule took effect after 1972). Nominations are made by the Nene committee and all children in grades four through six in Hawaii vote for their favorite book. Announcement of the winner is made during National Library Week and the winner receives a carved koa wood platter.

1964　*Island of the Blue Dolphins* by Scott O'Dell, not illustrated; Houghton, 1960.

1965　*Mary Poppins* by Pamela L. Travers, illustrated by Mary Shepard; Harcourt, 1962.

1966　*Old Yeller* by Fred Gipson, illustrated by Carl Burger; Harper, 1956.

1967　No Award

1968　*Ribsy* by Beverly Cleary, illustrated by Louis Darling; Morrow, 1964.

1969　*The Mouse and the Motorcycle* by Beverly Cleary, illustrated by Louis Darling; Morrow, 1965.

1970　*Henry Reed's Baby-sitting Service* by Keith Robertson, illustrated by Robert McCloskey; Viking, 1966.

1971　*Ramona the Pest* by Beverly Cleary, illustrated by Louis Darling; Morrow, 1968.

1972　*Runaway Ralph* by Beverly Cleary, illustrated by Louis Darling; Morrow, 1970.

1973　*Sounder* by William H. Armstrong, illustrated by James Barkley; Harper & Row, 1969.

1974　*Jonathan Livingston Seagull* by Richard Bach, illustrated with photographs; Macmillan, 1970.

1975　*Are You There, God? It's Me, Margaret* by Judy Blume, not illustrated; Bradbury, 1970.

1976　*How to Eat Fried Worms* by Thomas Rockwell, illustrated by Emily McCully; Watts, 1973.

1977　*Freaky Friday* by Mary Rodgers, not illustrated; Harper, 1972.

1978　*Charlie and the Great Glass Elevator* by Roald Dahl, illustrated by Joseph Schindelman; Knopf, 1972.

1979　*Ramona and her Father* by Beverly Cleary, illustrated by Alan Tiegreen; Morrow, 1977.

1980　*The Cat Ate my Gymsuit* by Paula Danziger, not illustrated; Delacorte, 1974.

1981　*My Robot Buddy* by Robert Slote, illustrated by Joel Schick; Lippincott, 1975.

1982　*Superfudge* by Judy Blume, not illustrated; Dutton, 1980.

1982　**RUNNERUP** *Bunnicula: A Rabbit Tale of Mystery* by Deborah Howe and James Howe, illustrated by Alan Daniel; Atheneum, 1980, c1979.

1983　*Bunnicula: A Rabbit Tale of Mystery* by Deborah Howe and James Howe, illustrated by Alan Daniel; Atheneum, 1980, c1979.

1983　**RUNNERUP** *The Pinballs* by Betsy Byars, not illustrated; Harper, 1977.

1984　*Nothing's Fair in Fifth Grade* by Barthe DeClements, not illustrated; Viking, 1981.

1985　*Jelly Belly* by Robert Kimmel Smith, illustrated by Bob Jones; Delacorte, 1981.

1986　*Be a Perfect Person in Just Three Days!* by Stephen Manes, illustrated by Tom Huffman; Clarion/Houghton Mifflin, 1982.

1986　**RUNNERUP** *You Shouldn't Have to Say Good-Bye* by Patricia Hermes, not illustrated; Harcourt, 1982.

1987　*Karen Kepplewhite is the World's Best Kisser* by Eve Bunting, not illustrated; Clarion, 1983.

1988　*You Shouldn't Have to Say Goodbye* by Patricia Hermes, not illustrated; Harcourt Brace Jovanovich, 1982.

1989　*Dear Mr. Henshaw* by Beverly Cleary, illustrated by Paul O. Zelinsky; Morrow, 1983.

1990　*Fudge* by Charlotte T. Graeber, illustrated by Cheryl Harness; Lothrop, Lee & Shepard, 1987.

1991　*There's a Boy in the Girls' Bathroom* by Louis Sachar, not illustrated; Knopf, 1987.

1992　*The Whipping Boy* by Sid Fleischman, illustrated by Peter Sis; Greenwillow, 1986.

NEVADA YOUNG READERS' AWARD

Nevada Department of Education
Jody Gehrig
400 W. King St.
Carson City, NV 89710

This children's choice award was established in 1987 by Bill Abrams and is cosponsored by the Nevada Department of Education and the Nevada Library Association. The purpose of the award is to encourage the children in Nevada to improve their reading skills by reading from the best modern children's literature. The award is presented in three categories, Primary, Intermediate, and Young Adult. The winning book in each category is a book nominated, read, and voted on by young readers.

In order to be eligible, a book must appeal to the age group for which the nomination is made; be a title most often read or requested by young readers; and have been published within the last five years.

A plaque is presented annually at the Nevada Library Association Convention to winning authors.

1987-88 PRIMARY *The Polar Express* written and illustrated by Chris Van Allsburg; Houghton Mifflin, 1985.

1987-88 INTERMEDIATE *Sixth Grade Can Really Kill You* by Barthe De Clements, not illustrated; Viking Kestrel, 1985.

1988-89 PRIMARY *If You Give a Mouse a Cookie* by Laura J. Numeroff, illustrated by Felicia Bond; Harper & Row, 1985.

1988-89 INTERMEDIATE *Babysitting Is a Dangerous Job* by Willo Davis Roberts, not illustrated; Atheneum, 1985.

1988-89 YOUNG ADULT *Locked In Time* by Lois Duncan, not illustrated; Little Brown, 1985.

1989-90 PRIMARY *Heckedy Peg* by Audrey Wood, illustrated by Don Wood; Harcourt, Brace, Jovanovich, 1987.

1989-90 INTERMEDIATE *There's a Boy in the Girls' Bathroom* by Louis Sachar, not illustrated; Knopf, 1987.

1989-90 YOUNG ADULT *Experiment in Terror* by Bernal C. Payne, Jr., not illustrated; Houghton Mifflin, 1987.

1990-91 PRIMARY *We're Back: A Dinosaur Story* written and illustrated by Hudson Talbott; Crown, 1987.

1990-91 INTERMEDIATE *My Teacher Is an Alien* by Bruce Coville, illustrated by Mike Wimmer; Pocket Books, 1989.

1990-91 YOUNG ADULT *Princess Ashley* by Richard Peck, not illustrated; Delacorte, 1987.

1991-92 PRIMARY *Call of the Wolves* by Jim Murphy, illustrated by Mark Alan Weatherby; Scholastic, 1989.

1991-92 INTERMEDIATE *Matilda* by Roald Dahl, illustrated by Quentin Blake; Viking Kestrel, 1988.

1991-92 YOUNG ADULT *Whispers From the Dead* by Joan Lowery Nixon, not illustrated; Delacorte, 1989.

NEW ENGLAND ROUND TABLE OF CHILDREN'S LIBRARIANS AWARDS

discontinued

This award was sponsored by the New England Round Table and was first presented in 1972.

1972 *Charlie and the Chocolate Factory* by Roald Dahl, illustrated by Joseph Schindelman; Knopf, 1964.

1976 *The Witch of Blackbird Pond* by Elizabeth George Speare, not illustrated; Houghton Mifflin, 1958.

NEW JERSEY INSTITUTE OF TECHNOLOGY NEW JERSEY AUTHORS AWARD

discontinued

This annual award was founded by Dr. Herman A. Estrin in 1960 for the purpose of honoring able writers born in or living in New Jersey. Many types of writing were honored by the award, including children's literature. All types of children's literature were eligible. Publishers were asked to submit appropriate books to the director, who made the final selection. Honored authors received citations at a ceremony in conjunction with the annual New Jersey Authors luncheon. The last awards were given in 1990.

1961 *Beth Hilton: Model* by Lee Wyndham, not illustrated; Messner, 1961.

Big Tracks, Little Tracks by Franklyn M. Branley, illustrated by Leonard Kessler; Crowell, 1960.

Buffalo and Beaver by Stephen W. Meader, illustrated by Charles Beck; Harcourt, 1960.

Cathy Leonard Calling by Catherine Woolley, illustrated by Liz Dauber; Morrow, 1961.

Exploring by Satellite: The Story of Project Vanguard by Franklyn M. Branley, illustrated by Helmut K. Wimmer; Crowell, 1957.

Find Out by Touching by Paul Showers, illustrated by Robert Galster; Crowell, 1961.

God Made the World written and illustrated by Pelagie Doane; Lippincott, 1960.

The Happy Lion's Quest by Louise Fatio, illustrated by Roger Duvoisin; McGraw Hill, 1961.

I Met a Man by John Ciardi, illustrated by Robert Osborn; Houghton Mifflin, 1961.

In the Night by Paul Showers, illustrated by Ezra Jack Keats; Crowell, 1961.

The Listening Walk by Paul Showers, illustrated by Aliki; Crowell, 1961.

Man Against Earth: The Story of Tunnels and Tunnel Builders by Don Murray, illustrated by Lili Rethi; Lippincott, 1961.

The Moon: Earth's Natural Satellite by Franklyn M. Branley, illustrated by Helmut K. Wimmer; Crowell, 1960.

The Moon Seems to Change by Franklyn M. Branley, illustrated by Helen Borten; Crowell, 1960.

Otto in Africa written and illustrated by William Pene du Bois; Viking, 1961.

Our Fifty States by Earl Schenck Miers, illustrated by Eleanor Mill, maps by Leonard Darwin; Grosset, 1961.

Rockets and Satellites by Franklyn M. Branley, illustrated by Bill Sokol; Crowell, 1961.

Snow on Blueberry Mountain by Stephen W. Meader, illustrated by Don Sibley; Harcourt, 1961.

The Sun: Our Nearest Star by Franklyn M. Branley, illustrated by Helen Borten; Crowell, 1961.

The Three Policemen written and illustrated by William Pene du Bois; Viking, 1938.

The Twenty Miracles of Saint Nicholas written and illustrated by Bernarda Bryson; Little, 1960.

What Makes Day and Night? by Franklyn M. Branley, illustrated by Helen Borten; Crowell, 1961.

1962 AGES 3-5 *A Is for Anything: An ABC Book of Pictures and Rhymes* written and illustrated by Katharina Barry; Harcourt, 1961.

1962 AGES 12 UP *Phantom of the Blockade* by Stephen W. Meader, illustrated by Victor Mays; Harcourt, 1962.

1962 AGES 14 UP *Seashore Summer* by Adele Hall, not illustrated; Harper, 1962.

1962 ILLUSTRATION *The Miller, his Son, and their Donkey* written and illustrated by Roger Duvoisin; Whittlesey House, 1962.

1963 *The American Indian Story* by May McNeer, illustrated by Lynd Ward; Ariel, 1963.

America's Mark Twain by May McNeer, illustrated by Lynd Ward; Houghton, 1962.

A Drink for Little Red Diker by Catherine Woolley, illustrated by W.T. Mars; Morrow, 1963.

Ginnie and her Juniors by Catherine Woolley, illustrated by Liz Dauber; Morrow, 1963.

How Hospitals Help Us by Alice M. Meeker, illustrated by Jack Faulkner; Beckley-Cardy, 1962.

Look Alive, Libby by Catherine Woolley, illustrated by Liz Dauber; Morrow, 1962.

The Party Book for Boys and Girls by Bernice Wells Carlson, illustrated by Faith C. Minnerly; Abingdon, 1963.

Rascal: Memoir of a Better Era by Sterling North, illustrated by John Schoenherr; Dutton, 1963.

Sad Day, Glad Day by Vivian Laubach Thompson, illustrated by Lilian Obligado; Holiday House, 1962.

1963 SCIENCE *Firefly* by Paul M. Sears, illustrated by Glen Rounds; Holiday House, 1956.

Monarch Butterfly by Marion W. Marcher, illustrated by Barbara Latham; Hale, 1954.

In Prehistoric Seas by Mildred A. Fenton and Carroll Lane Fenton, illustrated by Carroll Lane Fenton; Doubleday, 1963.

The World of the White-tailed Deer by Leonard Lee Rue, III, illustrated with photographs; Lippincott, 1962.

1964 AGES 3-5 *The Alphabet Tale* by Jan Garten, illustrated by Muriel Batherman; Random House, 1964.

1964 ART *Junior Flower Shows: A Complete Guide to the Planning, Staging and Judging of Children's Flower Shows* by Katherine Cutler, not illustrated; Barrows, 1963.

1964 BIOGRAPHY - AGES 7-9 *George Washington* by Vivian L. Thompson, illustrated by Frank Aloise; Putnam, 1964.

1964 BIOGRAPHY - AGES 12 UP *Portraits of Nobel Laureates in Medicine and Physiology* by Sarah Riedman and Elton T. Gustafson, illustrated with photographs; Abelard-Schuman, 1964.

1964 BIOGRAPHY - TEENS *John J. Pershing* by Arch Whitehouse, not illustrated; Putnam, 1964.

1964 ECONOMICS *Taxation* by Edith G. Stull and J. Woodrow Sayre; Watts, 1963.

1964 HISTORY *Where the Raritan Flows* by Earl Schenk Miers, illustrated by Charles Waterhouse; Rutgers University Press, 1964.

1964 HISTORY - AGES 6-12 *Stars and Stripes: The Story of the American Flag* by Mae Blacker Freeman, illustrated by Lorence F. Bjorklund; Random House, 1964.

1964 HISTORY - TEENS *The Story of World War II* by Robert Leckie, illustrated with photographs and maps; Random House, 1964.

The War in Korea, 1950-53 by Robert Leckie, illustrated with photographs; Random House, 1963.

1964 ILLUSTRATION *Lonely Veronica* written and illustrated by Roger Duvoisin; Knopf, 1963.

Veronica's Smile written and illustrated by Roger Duvoisin; Knopf, 1964.

1964 LATE TEENAGE NOVEL *The Natives Are Always Restless* by Gerald Raftery, illustrated by Charles Geer; Vanguard, 1964.

1964 RELIGIOUS *The Quiet Flame: Mother Marianne of Molokai* by Eva K. Betz, illustrated by Lloyd Ostendorf; Bruce, 1963.

1964 SCIENCE - AGES 5-8 *Bees and Beelines* by Judy Hawes, illustrated by Aliki; Crowell, 1964.

A Book of Astronauts for You by Franklyn M. Branley, illustrated by Leonard Kessler; Crowell, 1963.

1964 SCIENCE - AGES 8-12 *Birds We Live With* by Carroll Lane Fenton and Herminie B. Kitchen, illustrated by Carroll Lane Fenton; Day, 1963.

The Wonders of Astronomy by William E. Butterworth, illustrated by Dallas Pasco; Putnam, 1964.

The Wonders of Rockets and Missiles by William E. Butterworth, illustrated with photographs and diagrams; Putnam, 1964.

1964 SCIENCE - AGES 12-14 *Inventor's Notebook: Entirely New Do-it-Yourself Toy Inventions* written and illustrated by Robert E. Mueller; Day, 1963.

1964 SHORT STORY - AGES 6-14 *The Polished Diamond and other Stories* by Reinold Shubert, illustrated; Vantage, 1963.

1964 SHORT STORY - AGES 9-12 *Legends and Folk Tales of Holland* by Adele de Leeuw, illustrated by Paul Kennedy; Nelson, 1963.

1964 SOCIAL SCIENCES *World's Fairs: Yesterday, Today, and Tomorrow* by Roberta F. Roesch, illustrated with photographs; Day, 1964.

1964 TEENAGE NOVEL *Wisdom to Know* by Regina J. Woody, not illustrated; Funk & Wagnalls, 1964.

The Wider Heart by Norma Johnston, not illustrated; Funk & Wagnalls, 1964.

1964   NEW JERSEY CHILDREN'S BOOK WRITER OF THE YEAR Catherine Woolley (pseudonym for Jane Thayer)

1965   *ABC of Buses* by Dorothy Shuttlesworth, illustrated by Leonard Shortall; Doubleday, 1965.

All About Light and Radiation by Ira M. Freeman, illustrated by George T. Resch; Random House, 1965.

The Alligator Case written and illustrated by William Pene du Bois; Harper, 1965.

Benjamin Rush: Physician, Patriot, Founding Father by Sarah R. Riedman and Clarence C. Green, illustrated with photographs; Abelard-Schuman, 1964.

Fast Green Car by William E. Butterworth, not illustrated; Norton, 1965.

Great Quarterbacks of the NFL by Dave Anderson, illustrated with photographs; Random House, 1965.

Hong Kong Altar Boy by Joseph E. Hanson, not illustrated; Bruce, 1965.

I Like Trains by Catherine Woolley, illustrated by George Fonseca; Harper, 1965.

Little Rascal by Sterling North, illustrated by Carl Burger; Dutton, 1965.

Ready or Not by Norma Johnston, not illustrated; Funk and Wagnalls, 1965.

The Story of Ants by Dorothy Shuttlesworth, illustrated by Su Zan Swain; Doubleday, 1964.

The Story of Football by Robert Leckie, illustrated with photographs and diagrams; Random House, 1965.

Styles by Suzy by Karla H. Wiley, illustrated by Genia; McKay, 1965.

1965   AGES K-3 *Watch Out!* by Norah Smaridge, illustrated by Susan Perl; Abingdon, 1965.

1965   AGES 6-14 *You Can't Measure My Love with a Teaspoon* by Reinold Shubert, illustrated; Vantage, 1965.

1965   SCIENCE *Moon Moth* by Carleen Maley Hutchins, illustrated by Douglas Howland; Coward, 1965.

1965   NEW JERSEY'S CHILDREN'S HISTORY AUTHOR OF THE YEAR Earl Schenk Miers

1965   SPECIAL CITATION John Ciardi

1965   SPECIAL CITATION (AGES 5-12) *Listen! and Help Tell the Story* by Bernice Wells Carlson, illustrated by Burmah Burris; Abingdon, 1965.

1965   NEW JERSEY'S MOST DISTINGUISHED HUSBAND-WIFE TEAM OF WRITERS FOR ADULTS, YOUNG ADULTS, TEENAGERS AND OLDER, MIDDLE AGE AND YOUNG CHILDREN Mary Elting and Franklin Folsom

1966   *Animal Camouflage* by Dorothy Shuttlesworth, illustrated by Matthew Kalmenoff; Doubleday, 1966.

Fashion as a Career by Edith Heal, illustrated by Bob Walker; Messner, 1966.

No Girls Allowed and other Stories by Reinold Shubert; Vantage, 1967.

Topsail Island Treasure by Stephen W. Meader, illustrated by Marbury Brown; Harcourt, 1966.

Why the Russians Are the Way They Are by Benjamin Appel, illustrated by Samuel H. Bryant; Little Brown, 1966.

The Wishing Night by Carole Vetter, illustrated by Beverly Komoda; Macmillan, 1966.

The Wonders of Sand written and illustrated by Christie McFall; Dodd, 1966.

Young Miss Josie Delaney, Detective by Mary Malone, illustrated by R.S. Horne; Dodd, 1966.

The Upside Down Man written and illustrated by Shan Ellentuck; Doubleday, 1965.

1966   AGES 11-14 *Voyage of the Vagabond* by Richard Thruelsen, illustrated with maps; Harcourt, 1965.

1966   AGES 12 UP *Miss Fix-it* by Adele De Leeuw, not illustrated; Macmillan, 1966.

Mystery at Love's Creek by Betty Cavanna, not illustrated; Morrow, 1965.

Tiger Rookie by Edmund O. Scholefield, illustrated by Paul Frame; World, 1966.

1966   AGES 12-16 *The Night Workers* by Alvin Schwartz, photographs by Ulli Steltzer; Dutton, 1966.

1966   AGES 15-16 *A Blow for Liberty* by Stephen W. Meader, illustrated by Victor Mays; Harcourt, 1965.

1966   BIOGRAPHY *Fifty Useful Americans* by Wheeler McMillen, not illustrated; Putnam, 1966.

1966   SCIENCE *Cottontail: Children's Pet, Gardener's Pest, and Hunter's Favorite* by Leonard Lee Rue III, illustrated with photographs; Crowell, 1965.

How Man Discovered His Body by Sarah R. Riedman, illustrated by Frances Wells; Abelard-Schuman, 1966.

Science and the Secret of Man's Past by Franklin Folsom, illustrated by Ursula Koering; Harvey House, 1966.

1966   NEW JERSEY'S CHILDREN'S BOOKS WRITER OF THE YEAR Sterling North

1967   *All Kinds of Bees* by Dorothy Shuttlesworth, illustrated by Su Zan Noguchi Swain; Random House, 1967.

The Answer Book of History by Franklin Folsom and Mary Elting, illustrated by W.K. Plummer; Grosset, 1966.

Be Good, Harry written and illustrated by Mary Chalmers; Harper, 1967.

The Bridge Between by Norma Johnston, not illustrated; Funk & Wagnalls, 1966.

Famous Mathematicians by Frances B. Stonaker, not illustrated; Lippincott, 1966.

A Guide to Nature Projects by Ted S. Pettit, illustrated by Walt Wenzel; Norton, 1966.

The Horse in the Camel Suit written and illustrated by William Pene du Bois; Harper & Row, 1967.

The King of Hermits and other Stories by Jack Sendak, illustrated by Margot Zemach; Farrar, 1967.

The King Who Saved Himself from Being Saved by John Ciardi, illustrated by Edward Gorey; Lippincott, 1965.

Man and Magic by Benjamin Appel, illustrated by Jacob Landau; Pantheon, 1966.

Monster Den; or, Look What Happened at my House - and To It by John Ciardi, illustrated by Edward Gorey; Lippincott, 1966.

Not Very Much of a House by M. Jean Craig, illustrated by Don Almquist; Norton, 1967.

Phaethon by Merrill Pollack, illustrated by William Hoffmann; Lippincott, 1966.

Pick a Peck of Puzzles written and illustrated by Arnold Roth; Norton, 1966.

Samantha's Masquerade by Charles W. Pierce, illustrated by Erwin Schachner; McKay, 1967.

The Secret of the Sea Rocks by Carol Reuter, illustrated by Vera Bock; McKay, 1967.

Spies and More Spies by Robert Arthur, illustrated by Saul Lambert; Random House, 1967.

The Trouble with Lucy by Jean Capron, not illustrated; Dodd, 1967.

The True Story of Okee the Otter by Dorothy Wisbeski, illustrated with photographs; Farrar, 1967.

Vicky Barnes, Junior Hospital Volunteer: The Story of a Candy Striper by Alice Ross Colver, not illustrated; Dodd, 1966.

We Read: A to Z written and illustrated by Donald Crews; Harper, 1967.

What a Silly Thing to Do by Norah Smaridge, illustrated by Susan Perl; Abingdon, 1967.

The Wonders of Sand written and illustrated by Christie McFall; Dodd, 1966.

You Know What? I Like Animals by Bernice Wells Carlson, illustrated by Ruth Van Sciver; Abingdon, 1967.

1967   NEW JERSEY'S WRITER OF CHILDREN'S BOOKS Janet Lambert, Stephen W. Meader

1968 *Assignment: Latin America - A Story of the Peace Corps* by Karla H. Wiley, not illustrated; McKay, 1968.

Aunt Agatha, There's a Lion under the Couch written and illustrated by Harry Devlin; Van Nostrand, 1968.

The Barn written and illustrated by John Schoenherr; Little Brown, 1968.

Hear a Different Drummer by Theodora J. Koob, not illustrated; Lippincott, 1968.

Helpful Microorganisms by Daniel Lapedes, illustrated with photographs; World, 1968.

Martze by Jack Sendak, illustrated by Mitchell Miller; Farrar, 1968.

Mystery of the Old Musket by Patience Zawadsky, illustrated by D. McMains; Putnam, 1967.

The Pasture written and illustrated by Anne Marie Jauss; McKay, 1968.

Poetry for Autumn by Leland B. Jacobs, illustrated by Stina Nagel; Garrard, 1968.

Poetry for Chuckles and Grins by Leland B. Jacobs, illustrated by Tomie dePaola; Garrard, 1968.

Rags, Rugs and Wool Pictures: A First Book of Rug Hooking by Ann Wisemann, illustrated with photographs; Scribner, 1968.

Twelve at War: Great Photographers under Fire by Robert E. Hood, illustrated with photographs; Putnam, 1967.

The Walloping Window Blind written and illustrated by Harry Devlin; Van Nostrand, 1968.

Weeny Witch by Ida DeLage, illustrated by Kelly Oechsli; Garrard, 1968.

What a Silly Thing To Do by Norah Smaridge, illustrated by Susan Perl; Abingdon, 1967.

Why the Chinese Are the Way They Are by Benjamin Appel, illustrated by Samuel H. Bryant; Little, 1968.

1968   BIOGRAPHY *Dorothea Dix: Hospital Founder* by Mary Malone, illustrated by Katharine Sampson; Garrard, 1968.

1968   EDUCATION *Freedom Builders: Great Teachers from Socrates to John Dewey* by Rose Friedman, not illustrated; Little Brown, 1968.

1968   GAMES *The Rainy Day Book* written and illustrated by Alvin Schwartz; Simon & Schuster/Trident, 1968.

1968   SCIENCE *Before You Were a Baby* by Kay Showers and Paul S. Showers, illustrated by Ingrid Fetz; Crowell, 1968.

A Book of Mars for You by Franklyn M. Branley, illustrated by Leonard Kessler; Crowell, 1968.

A Book of Stars for You by Franklyn M. Branley, illustrated by Leonard Kessler; Crowell, 1967.

A Drop of Blood by Paul Showers, illustrated by Don Madden; Crowell, 1967.

Floating and Sinking by Franklyn M. Branley, illustrated by Robert Galster; Crowell, 1967.

Hear your Heart by Paul Showers, illustrated by Joseph Low; Crowell, 1968.

High Sounds, Low Sounds by Franklyn M. Branley, illustrated by Paul Galdone; Crowell, 1967.

How You Talk by Paul Showers, illustrated by Robert Galster; Crowell, 1967.

I Wanna Be a Lady Plumber and other Stories by Reinold Shubert; Vantage, 1968.

Ladybug, Ladybug, Fly Away Home by Judy Hawes, illustrated by Ed Emberley; Crowell, 1967.

The Right Size: Why some Creatures Survive and others are Extinct by Hal Hellman, illustrated by Sam Salant; Putnam, 1968.

Shrimps by Judy Hawes, illustrated by Joseph Low; Crowell, 1967.

Why Frogs Are Wet by Judy Hawes, illustrated by Don Madden; Crowell, 1968.

1968   NEW JERSEY'S WRITERS OF CHILDREN'S BOOKS Adele DeLeeuw, Earl Schenck Miers

1969 *Aspire to the Heavens: A Portrait of George Washington* by Mary Higgins Clark, not illustrated; Meredith, 1969.

Babushka and the Pig by Ann Trofimuk, illustrated by Jerry Pinkney; Houghton, 1969.

City Critters by Helen R. Russell, illustrated by Marcia Erickson; Meredith, 1969.

Freedom Builders: Great Teachers from Socrates to John Dewey by Rose Friedman, not illustrated; Little Brown, 1968.

The Invisible Giants: Atoms, Nuclei and Radioisotopes by Vivian Grey, illustrated with photographs; Little, 1969.

The Land and People of Malaysia by Mary Louise Clifford, illustrated with photographs; Lippincott, 1968.

The Money Machine by Keith Robertson, illustrated by George Porter; Viking, 1969.

New Jersey by Keith Robertson, illustrated by Donald T. Pitcher; Coward, 1969.

A Paper Zoo by Renee Weiss, illustrated by Ellen Raskin; Macmillan, 1968.

Porko von Popbutton written and illustrated by William Pene du Bois; Harper, 1969.

Scary Things by Norah Smaridge, illustrated by Ruth Van Sciver; Abingdon, 1969.

Sunday Morning by Judith Viorst, illustrated by Hilary Knight; Harper, 1968.

University: The Students, Faculty and Campus Life at One University by Alvin Schwartz, illustrated with photographs; Viking, 1969.

Up to the Quarterback by William Butterworth, not illustrated; Four Winds, 1969.

The Witches' Secret by Frances C. Allen, illustrated by Laura J. Allen; Harper, 1968.

The Witchy Broom by Ida DeLage, illustrated by Walt Peaver; Garrard, 1969.

The World of Chocolate by Norah Smaridge, illustrated by Don Lambo; Messner, 1969.

1969 NEW JERSEY AUTHOR AWARDS SPECIAL CITATION Harriet Stratemeyer Adams (pseudonyms are Carolyn Keene and Laura Lee Hope); Andrew Svenson (pseudonyms are Jerry West, Alan Stone and Laura Lee Hope)

1969 NEW JERSEY WRITER OF CHILDREN'S BOOKS Maia Wojchiechowska

1969 SPECIAL CITATION FOR HUSBAND-WIFE WRITERS OF CHILDREN'S BOOKS Harry Devlin and Wende Devlin; Mary Elting and Franklin Folsom; Lee Wyndham and Robert Wyndham

1970 *Andrew Carnegie: Giant of Industry* by Mary Malone, illustrated by Marvin Besunder; Garrard, 1969.

Animal Atlas of the World by Emil L. Jordan, illustrated by Melvin R. Bolden; Hammond, 1969.

Benedict Arnold: Hero and Traitor by Cateau DeLeeuw, illustrated; Putnam, 1970.

Binky Brothers and the Fearless Four by James Lawrence, illustrated by Leonard Kessler; Harper, 1970.

Don't Play Dead Before You Have To by Maia Wojciechowska, not illustrated; Harper, 1970.

Elvira Everything written and illustrated by Frank Asch; Harper, 1970.

Eric: The Tale of a Red Tempered Viking by Susan Bond, illustrated by Sally Trinkle; Grove Press, 1968.

Flags of all Nations and the People Who Live under Them by Franklin Folsom and Mary Elting, illustrated with photographs; Grosset, 1969.

The Goats Who Killed the Leopard by Judy Hawes, illustrated by Ric Estrada; Crowell, 1970.

How Fletcher Was Hatched! written and illustrated by Wende Devlin and Harry Devlin; Parents, 1969.

If You Lived in the Days of the Wild Mammoth Hunters by Franklin Folsom and Mary Elting, illustrated by John Moodie; Four Winds, 1969.

I'll Fix Anything by Judith Viorst, illustrated by Arnold Lobel; Harper, 1969.

Join Hands with the Ghosts by Mary Canty, illustrated by Ragna T. Goddard; McKay, 1969.

Lindbergh: Lone Eagle by Adele DeLeeuw, illustrated with photographs; Doubleday, 1969.

The Manners Zoo by Susan Bond, illustrated by Sally Trinkle; Follett, 1969.

Marie Curie: Woman of Genius by Adele DeLeeuw, illustrated by Cary; Garrard, 1970.

The Old Witch and the Snores by Ida DeLage, illustrated by Gil Miret; Garrard, 1970.

The Old Witch Goes to the Ball by Ida DeLage, illustrated by Gustave E. Nebel; Garrard, 1969.

The Only Earth We Have by Laurence Pringle, illustrated by Philip Lohman; Macmillan, 1969.

Paul Bunyan Finds a Wife by Adele DeLeeuw, illustrated by Ted Schroeder; Garrard, 1969.

Peter Stuyvesant by Adele DeLeeuw, illustrated by Vincent Colabella; Garrard, 1970.

Poetry for Winter by Leland B. Jacobs, illustrated by Kelly Oechsli; Garrard, 1970.

Poetry of Witches, Elves, and Goblins by Leland B. Jacobs, illustrated by Frank Aloise; Garrard, 1970.

The Polly Cameron Picture Book written and illustrated by Polly Cameron; Coward, 1970.

Ride with Me through ABC by Susan Bond, illustrated by Horst Lemke; Scroll Press, 1969.

Russian Tales of Fabulous Beasts and Marvels by Lee Wyndham, illustrated by Charles Mikolaycak; Parents, 1969.

Tales the People Tell in Russia by Lee Wyndham, illustrated by Andrew Antal; Messner, 1970.

We Are the Government by Margaret Gossett and Mary Elting, illustrated by Angio Culfogienis; Doubleday, 1967.

What I Like about Toads by Judy Hawes, illustrated by James McCrea and Ruth McCrea; Crowell, 1969.

What Kind of a House Is That? written and illustrated by Harry Devlin; Parents, 1969.

The Winter Child by Lee Wyndham, illustrated by Yaroslava; Parents, 1970.

1970   NEW JERSEY CHILDREN'S BOOK WRITER OF THE YEAR Franklyn M. Branley

1971 *Animals Made by Me* written and illustrated by Margery W. Brown; Putnam, 1970.

Annie Sullivan by Mary Malone, illustrated by Lydia Rosier; Putnam, 1971.

Arnold Roth's Crazy Book of Science written and illustrated by Arnold Roth; Grosset, 1971.

The Bird from the Sea by Renee Karol Weiss, illustrated by Ed Young; Crowell, 1970.

Christina Katerina and the Box by Patricia Lee Gauch, illustrated by Doris Burn; Coward, 1971.

Colonial New Jersey by John T. Cunningham, illustrated with photographs; Nelson, 1971.

Finding the Forgotten: Adventures in the Discovery of the Past by Steven Frimmer, not illustrated; Putnam, 1971.

The Galapagos Kid: or, The Spirit of 1976 by Luke Walton, not illustrated; Nautilus, 1971.

Genius with a Scalpel: Harvey Cushing by Justin F. Denzel, not illustrated; Messner, 1971.

Hello, Come In by Ida DeLage, illustrated by John Mardon; Garrard, 1971.

I'm Glad I'm Me by Elberta Stone, illustrated by Margery W. Brown; Putnam, 1971.

Indians of the Southern Plains by William Powers, illustrated with photographs; Putnam, 1971.

Man in Space to the Moon by Franklyn M. Branley, illustrated by Louis Glanzman; Crowell, 1970.

Milton Hershey: Chocolate King by Mary Malone, illustrated by William Hutchinson; Garrard, 1971.

A Secret House by Patricia Lee Gauch, illustrated by Margot Tomes; Coward, 1970.

Soot Devil written and illustrated by Charles Geer; Grosset, 1971.

Tales the People Tell in China by Robert Wyndham, edited by Doris K. Coburn, illustrated by Jay Yang; Messner, 1971.

That Jefferson Boy by Earl Schenck Miers, illustrated by Kurt Werth; World, 1970.

Two Straws in a Soda by Reinold Shubert, not illustrated; Vantage, 1970.

What Does a Witch Need? by Ida DeLage, illustrated by Ted Schroeder; Garrard, 1971.

1971   NEW JERSEY AUTHOR CITATION WRITER OF CHILDREN'S BOOKS OF THE YEAR Adele DeLeeuw, Leland B. Jacobs

1972 *Aaron and the Green Mountain Boys* by Patricia Lee Gauch, illustrated by Margot Tomes; Coward, 1972.

The Ball That Wouldn't Bounce by Mel Cebulash, illustrated by Tom Eaton; Scholastic, 1972.

Benny's Nose by Mel Cebulash, illustrated by Ib Ohlsson; Scholastic, 1972.

Beware! Beware! A Witch Won't Share by Ida DeLage, illustrated by Ted Schroeder; Garrard, 1972.

The Boy with Wings by Adele DeLeeuw, illustrated by Leonard Vosburgh; Nautilus, 1971.

The Carp in the Bathtub by Barbara Cohen, illustrated by Joan Halpern; Lothrop, 1972.

Catbird written and illustrated by Ellen Galinsky; Coward, 1971.

Charley the Mouse Finds Christmas by Wayne Carley, illustrated by Ruth Bagshaw; Garrard, 1972.

Corvus the Cow by Franklin Russell, illustrated by Richard Cuffari; Four Winds, 1972.

Dic-tion-ar-y Skilz by Mel Cebulash, not illustrated; Scholastic, 1972.

Freedom Eagle written and illustrated by Bette J. Davis; Lothrop, 1972.

Grandpa and Me by Patricia Lee Gauch, illustrated by Symeon Shimin; Coward, 1972.

Guinea Pigs: All about Them by Alvin Silverstein and Virginia Silverstein, illustrated by Roger Kerkham; Lothrop, 1972.

Helicopters at Work by Mary Elting and Judith Steigler, illustrated by Ursula Koering; Harvey House, 1972.

Hello, People by Leland B. Jacobs, illustrated by Edward Malsberg; Garrard, 1972.

Holiday Happenings in Limerick Land by Leland B. Jacobs, illustrated by Edward Malsberg; Garrard, 1972.

I Was a 98-pound Duckling by Jean Van Leeuwen, not illustrated; Dial, 1972.

Indians of the Southern Plains by William Powers, illustrated with photographs; Putnam, 1971.

It's Not the End of the World by Judy Blume, not illustrated; Bradbury, 1972.

Kids Gardening: A First Indoor Gardening Book for Children by Aileen Paul, illustrated by Arthur Hawkins; Doubleday, 1972.

The Life and Death of a Brave Bull by Maia Wojciechowska, illustrated by John Groth; Harcourt, 1972.

Life in a Bucket of Soil by Richard Rhine, illustrated by Elsie Wrigley; Lothrop, 1972.

Lotor the Raccoon by Franklin Russell, illustrated by Richard Cuffari; Four Winds, 1972.

Otherwise Known as Sheila the Great by Judy Blume, not illustrated; Dutton, 1972.

Tales of a Fourth Grade Nothing by Judy Blume, illustrated by Roy Doty; Dutton, 1972.

Then Again, Maybe I Won't by Judy Blume, not illustrated; Bradbury, 1971.

Through the Broken Mirror with Alice: Including Parts of Through the Looking Glass by Lewis Carroll by Maia Wojciechowska, not illustrated; Harcourt, 1972.

A Twister of Twists, a Tangler of Tongues by Alvin Schwartz, illustrated by Glen Rounds; Lippincott, 1972.

Two Boys of Baghdad by Bahija Fattuhi Lovejoy, illustrated with photographs; Lothrop, 1972.

Under Christopher's Hat by Dorothy Callahan, illustrated by Carole M. Byard; Scribner, 1972.

Who Will Clean the Air? by Wallace Orlowsky and Thomas B. Perera, illustrated by Richard Cuffari; Coward, 1971.

A Woggle of Witches written and illustrated by Adrienne Adams; Scribner, 1971.

1973 *Aaron and the Green Mountain Boys* by Patricia Lee Gauch, illustrated by Margot Tomes; Coward, 1972.

April Fool! by Leland B. Jacobs, illustrated by Lou Cunette; Garrard, 1973.

Catch a Killer by George A. Woods, not illustrated; Harper, 1972.

Civil War Nurse: Mary Ann Bickerdyke by Adele DeLeeuw, not illustrated; Messner, 1973.

Cow for Jaya by Eva Grant, illustrated by Michael Hampshire; Coward, 1973.

Energy in the World of the Future by Hal Hellman, not illustrated; Evans, 1973.

Funny Bone Ticklers in Verse and Rhyme by Leland B. Jacobs, illustrated by Edward Malsberg; Garrard, 1973.

Grandpa and Me by Patricia Lee Gauch, illustrated by Symeon Shimin; Coward, 1972.

In the Eye of the Teddy written and illustrated by Frank Asch; Harper, 1973.

Jumbo: Giant Circus Elephant by Justin F. Denzel, illustrated by Richard Amundsen; Garrard, 1973.

Let's Pretend It Happened to You by Bernice Wells Carlson, illustrated by Ralph McDonald; Abingdon, 1973.

Moke and Poki in the Rain Forest written and illustrated by Mamoru Funai; Harper & Row, 1972.

The Moon Is Like a Silver Sickle: A Celebration of Poetry by Russian Children compiled by Miriam Morton, illustrated by Eros Keith; Simon & Schuster, 1972.

Penny Tunes and Princesses by Myron Levoy, illustrated by Ezra Jack Keats; Harper, 1972.

Pink Pink by Ida DeLage, illustrated by Benton Mahan; Garrard, 1973.

Rebecka written and illustrated by Frank Asch; Harper, 1972.

The Story of George Washington by May McNeer, illustrated by Lynd Ward; Abingdon, 1973.

The World Turned Upside Down: The Story of the American Revolution by Robert Leckie, illustrated with maps by Theodore R. Miller; Putnam, 1973.

1975 *Anthony Wayne: Washington's General* by Adele DeLeeuw and Cateau DeLeeuw, illustrated by Andrew Snyder; Westminster, 1974.

Black Kettle: King of the Wild Horses by Justin F. Denzel, illustrated by Richard E. Amundsen; Garrard, 1974.

Blubber by Judy Blume, not illustrated; Bradbury, 1974.

Civil War Nurse: Mary Ann Bickerdyke by Adele DeLeeuw, not illustrated; Messner, 1973.

A Comick Book of Sports written and illustrated by Arnold Roth; Scribner, 1974.

Fat Eliot and the Gorilla written and illustrated by Manus Pinkwater; Four Winds, 1974.

Funny Bone Dramatics by Bernice Wells Carlson, illustrated by Charles Cox; Abingdon, 1974.

Good Morning, Lady by Ida DeLage, illustrated by Tracy McVay; Garrard, 1974.

The Green Isle by Philip Burton, illustrated by Robert A. Parker; Dial, 1974.

The Halloween Party by Lonzo Anderson, illustrated by Adrienne Adams; Scribner, 1974.

Jumbo: Giant Circus Elephant by Justin F. Denzel, illustrated by Richard Amundsen; Garrard, 1973.

The Old Witch and the Wizard by Ida DeLage, illustrated by Mimi Korach; Garrard, 1974.

Too Hot for Ice Cream by Jean Van Leeuwen, illustrated by Martha Alexander; Dial, 1974.

Why the Chinese Are the Way They Are by Benjamin Appel, illustrated with maps by Samuel Bryant; Little Brown, 1973.

The World Beneath Our Feet: The Story of Soil by Martin Keen, illustrated by Haris Petie; Messner, 1974.

1975 **NEW JERSEY'S OUTSTANDING AUTHORS SPECIAL CITATION** Adele DeLeeuw and Cateau DeLeeuw

1976 *Anthony Wayne: Washington's General* by Adele deLeeuw and Cateau DeLeeuw, illustrated by Andrew Snyder; Westminster, 1974.

A Bicycle from Bridgetown by Dawn Thomas, illustrated by Don Miller; McGraw, 1975.

A Bunny Ride by Ida DeLage, illustrated by Tracy McVay; Garrard, 1975.

The Cat Ate my Gymsuit by Paula Danziger, not illustrated; Delacorte, 1974.

Catchpenny Street by Betty Cavanna, not illustrated; Westminster, 1975.

El Bronx Remembered by Nicholasa Mohr, not illustrated; Harper, 1975.

Emma's Dilemma by Gen LeRoy, not illustrated; Harper, 1975.

Good Morning, Lady by Ida DeLage, illustrated by Tracy McVay; Garrard, 1974.

Holidays in Scandinavia by Lee Wyndham, illustrated by Gordon Laite; Garrard, 1975.

I Hate Books and other Stories by Reinold Shubert, illustrated; Vantage, 1975.

Liliuokalani: Queen of Hawaii by Mary Malone, illustrated by Louis F. Cary; Garrard, 1975.

Little Owl, Keeper of the Trees by Ronald Himler and Ann Himler, illustrated by Ronald Himler; Harper & Row, 1974.

Marc and Pixie and the Walls in Mrs. Jones' Garden by Louise Fatio and Roger Duvoisin, illustrated by Roger Duvoisin; McGraw, 1975.

The Mystery Waters of Tonbridge Wells by Teri Martini, illustrated by Linda Boehm; Westminster, 1975.

Sports and Games in Verse and Rhyme by Leland B. Jacobs and Allan D. Jacobs, illustrated by George DeLara; Garrard, 1975.

Tales of Thunder and Lightning written and illustrated by Harry Devlin; Parents, 1975.

Then and Now by George Zappler and Lisbeth Zappler, illustrated by Sy Barlowe and Dorothea Barlowe; McGraw, 1974.

Too Hot for Ice Cream by Jean Van Leeuw, illustrated by Martha Alexander; Dial, 1974.

Trying Hard to Hear You by Sandra Scoppettone, not illustrated; Harper, 1974.

Wild Wing: Great Hunting Eagle by Justin F. Denzel, illustrated by Herman B. Vestal; Garrard, 1975.

1977 *All Because of Jill* by Teri Martini, not illustrated; Westminster, 1976.

Bunny School by Ida DeLage, illustrated by Tracy McVay; Garrard, 1976.

Bitter Herbs and Honey by Barbara Cohen, not illustrated; Lothrop, 1976.

Carlos P. Romulo: The Barefoot Boy of Diplomacy by Adele DeLeeuw, illustrated; Westminster, 1976.

Death: Everyone's Heritage by Elaine Landau, not illustrated; Messner, 1976.

Every Vote Counts: A Teenage Guide to the Electoral Process by James J. O'Donnell, not illustrated; Messner, 1976.

Hidden Heroines: Women in American History by Elaine Landau, illustrated with photographs; Messner, 1975.

Integration of Mary-Larkin Thornhill by Ann Wood Waldron, not illustrated; Dutton, 1975.

Journal of Madame Royale by Elizabeth Powers, illustrated with old engravings; Walker, 1976.

Kickle Snifters and other Fearsome Critters by Alvin Schwartz, illustrated by Glen Rounds; Lippincott, 1976.

Kids Cooking Without a Stove: A Cookbook for Young Children by Aileen Paul, illustrated by Carol Inouye; Doubleday, 1975.

Let's Make Soup by Hannah Lyons Johnson, illustrated by Daniel Dorn, Jr.; Lothrop, 1976.

The Old Witch's Party by Ida DeLage, illustrated by Mimi Korach; Garrard, 1976.

Only Silly People Waste by Norah Smaridge, illustrated by Mary Carrithers; Abingdon, 1973.

Partnership of Mind and Body: Biofeedback by Larry Kettelkamp, illustrated with photographs; Morrow, 1976.

Pele, The King of Soccer by Frank Gault and Clare Gault, illustrated with photographs; Walker, 1975.

A Poetic Look at Aesop's Fables by Betty Sullivan; Carleton Press.

Snowfoot: White Reindeer of the Arctic by Justin F. Denzel, illustrated by Taylor Oughton; Garrard, 1976.

Stories from the Olympics from 776 B.C. to Now by Frank Gault and Clare Gault, illustrated with photographs; Walker, 1976.

Sudden Steps, Small Stones by Betty Sullivan; Carleton Press.

Teeny Tiny by Leland B. Jacobs, illustrated by Marilyn Lucey; Garrard, 1976.

Where's Florrie? by Barbara Cohen, illustrated by John Halpern; Lothrop, 1976.

1978 *ABC Fire Dogs* by Ida DeLage, illustrated by Ellen Sloan; Garrard, 1977.

ABC Halloween Witch by Ida DeLage, illustrated by Lou Cunette; Garrard, 1977.

ABC Pigs Go to Market by Ida DeLage, illustrated by Kelly Oeschli; Garrard, 1977.

ABC Pirate Adventure by Ida DeLage, illustrated by Buck Brown; Garrard, 1977.

Alan and Naomi by Myron Levoy, not illustrated; Harper, 1977.

Are You in the House Alone? by Richard Peck, not illustrated; Viking, 1976.

The Birthday Trombone written and illustrated by Margaret Hartelius; Doubleday, 1977.

Bony by Fran Zweifel, illustrated by Whitney Darrow, Jr.; Harper, 1977.

Comick Book of Pets: Found, Raised, Washed, Curried, Combed, Fed, and Cared for in Every other Way written and illustrated by Arnold Roth; Scribner, 1976.

Crafting with Newspapers by William Shisler and Vivienne Eisner, illustrated by Guy Brison-Stack; Sterling, 1977.

Fireflies by Joanne Ryder, illustrated by Don Bolognese; Harper, 1977.

The Grouch and the Tower and other Sillies written and illustrated by John O'Brien; Harper, 1977.

Hector and Christina by Louise Fatio, illustrated by Roger Duvoisin; McGraw Hill, 1977.

Hotheads by Gen LeRoy, not illustrated; Harper, 1977.

In Nueva York by Nicholasa Mohr, not illustrated; Dial, 1977.

The Jewish Holiday Book by Wendy Lazar, illustrated with photographs; Doubleday, 1977.

Merry Christmas, Harry written and illustrated by Mary Chalmers; Harper & Row, 1977.

Mr. Slim Goodbody Presents the Inside Story by John Burstein, illustrated by Paul Kirouac; McGraw, 1977.

One Fat Summer by Robert Lipsyte, not illustrated; Harper, 1977.

Scat: The Movie Cat by Justin F. Denzel, illustrated by Herman B. Vestal; Garrard, 1977.

School Is not a Missile Range by Norah Smaridge, illustrated by Ron Martin; Abingdon, 1977.

The Secret of the Brownstone House by Norah A. Smaridge, illustrated by Michael Hampshire; Dodd, 1977.

Thursday's Daughters: The Story of Women Working in America by Janet Harris, illustrated with photographs; Harper, 1977.

1980 *Aging* by Alvin Silverstein and Virginia Silverstein, illustrated with photographs; Watts, 1979.

Animals that Use Tools by Barbara Ford, illustrated by Janet D'Amato; Messner, 1978.

The Battlestar Galactica Storybook by Glen A. Larson and Robert Thurston, adapted by Charles Mercer, illustrated with photographs; Putnam, 1979.

Be a Rockhound written and illustrated by Martin Keen; Messner, 1979.

Bill of Rights by Ernest B. Fincher, illustrated with photographs; Watts, 1978.

Can You Sue Your Parents for Malpractice? by Paula Danziger, not illustrated; Delacorte, 1979.

Chin Music: Tall Talk and other Talk by Alvin Schwartz, illustrated by John O'Brien; Lippincott, 1979.

City Cop by Fred Cook, not illustrated; Doubleday, 1979.

Effective English by Susan Carnell Poskanzer, illustrated; Silver Burdett, 1979.

Farms for Today and Tomorrow: The Wonders of Food Production by Dorothy E. Shuttlesworth and Gregory Shuttlesworth, not illustrated; Doubleday, 1979.

Fog in the Meadow by Joanne Ryder, illustrated by Gail Owens; Harper, 1979.

Frannie's Flower by Ida DeLage, illustrated by Ellen Sloan; Garrard, 1979.

It's Time to Go to Bed by Joyce Segal, illustrated by Robin Eaton; Doubleday, 1979.

Jimmy: The Story of Young Jimmy Carter by Dorothy Callahan, illustrated with photographs; Doubleday, 1979.

The Old Witch Finds a New House by Ida DeLage, illustrated by Pat Paris; Garrard, 1979.

On a Picnic by Judy Delton, illustrated by Mamoru Funai; Doubleday, 1979.

Pet Safety by Joseph J. McCoy, illustrated by Bette J. Davis; Watts, 1979.

Pickle in the Middle and other Easy Snacks written and illustrated by Frances Zweifel; Harper, 1979.

Pumpkin Personalities by Ruth J. Katz, illustrated by Sharon Tondreau; Walker, 1979.

Quick Wits and Nimble Fingers by Bernice Wells Carlson, illustrated by Dolores M. Rowland; Abingdon, 1979.

Run, Don't Walk by Harriet May Savitz, not illustrated; Watts, 1979.

Sleep and Dreams by Rae Lindsay, illustrated by Leigh Grant; Watts, 1978.

Snail in the Woods by Joanne Ryder and Harold S. Feinberg, illustrated by Jo Polseno; Harper & Row, 1979.

The Story of Cake by Norah A. Smaridge, illustrated with photographs; Abingdon, 1979.

Superplanes by John Gabriel Navarra, illustrated with photographs; Doubleday, 1979.

Turtle Tale written and illustrated by Frank Asch; Dial, 1978.

When I Grew Up Long Ago by Alvin Schwartz, illustrated by Harold Berson; Lippincott, 1978.

Winners on the Ice by Frank Litsky, illustrated with photographs; Watts, 1979.

You'd Better Not Tell by Curt Schleier, not illustrated; Westminster, 1979.

1981 *ABC Triplets at the Zoo* by Ida DeLage, illustrated by Lori Pierson; Garrard, 1980.

The Alfred Summer by Jan Slepian, not illustrated; Macmillan, 1980.

Be a Rockhound written and illustrated by Martin Keen; Messner, 1979.

The Book of Pets by Stanley Leinwoll, illustrated with photographs; Messner, 1980.

Chin Music: Tall Talk and other Talk by Alvin Schwartz, illustrated by John O'Brien; Lippincott, 1979.

Exploring the Sun written and illustrated by William Jaber; Messner, 1980.

Fire! It's Many Faces and Moods by James O'Donnell, not illustrated; Messner, 1980.

The French Detection by Ann Waldron, not illustrated; Dutton, 1979.

A Frost in the Night: A Childhood on the Eve of the Third Reich by Edith Baer, not illustrated; Pantheon, 1980.

I Carve Stone by Joan Fine, photographs by David Anderson; Crowell, 1979.

I Hate My Name by Eva Grant, illustrated by Gretchen Mayo; Raintree, 1980.

If Wishes Were Horses and other Rhymes by Mother Goose illustrated by Susan Jeffers; Dutton, 1979.

The Ku Klux Klan: America's Recurring Nightmare by Fred J. Cook, illustrated; Messner, 1980.

Manners Matter by Norah Smaridge, illustrated by Imbior Kudrna; Abingdon, 1980.

Occult Visions: A Mystical Gaze into the Future by Elaine Landau, illustrated by Carol Gjertsen; Messner, 1979.

Our Wild Wetlands by Sheila Cowing, illustrated by Deborah Cowing; Messner, 1980.

Pickle in the Middle and Other Easy Snacks written and illustrated by Frances W. Zweifel; Harper, 1979.

Pilgrim Children on the Mayflower by Ida DeLage, illustrated by Bert Dodson; Garrard, 1980.

The S.S. Valentine by Terry Wolfe Phelan, illustrated by Judy Glassner; Four Winds, 1979.

Sampson: Yankee Stallion by Justin F. Denzel, illustrated by William Hutchinson; Garrard, 1980.

Superfudge by Judy Blume, not illustrated; Dutton, 1980.

The Teen Guide to Dating by Elaine Landau, not illustrated; Messner, 1980.

Ten Copycats in a Boat and other Riddles by Alvin Schwartz, illustrated by Marc Simont; Harper, 1980.

The Treasure Trap by Virginia Masterman-Smith, illustrated by Roseanne Litzinger; Four Winds, 1979.

1983 *Alanna: The First Adventure* by Tamora Pierce, illustrated with a map; Atheneum, 1983.

Alive & Starting Over by Sheila Solomon Klass, not illustrated; Scribner, 1983.

Bible Crafts by Joyce Becker, illustrated; Holiday House, 1982.

The Bollo Caper: A Furry Tale for all Ages by Art Buchwald, illustrated by Elise Primavera; Putnam, 1983.

Bummer Summer by Ann M. Martin, not illustrated; Holiday House, 1983.

Caught in the Turtle by Judith Gorog, illustrated by Ruth Sanderson; Philomel, 1983.

The Christmas Camel written and illustrated by Nancy Winslow Parker; Dodd, Mead, 1983.

Confessions of a Teenage TV Addict by Ellen Leroe, not illustrated; Lodestar/Dutton, 1983.

The Demon Who Would not Die retold by Barbara Cohen, illustrated by Anatoly Ivanov; Atheneum, 1982.

Do You See What I See? by Judith St. George, not illustrated; Putnam, 1982.

Final Grades by Anita Heyman, not illustrated; Dodd, Mead, 1983.

Footfalls by Elizabeth Harlan, not illustrated; Atheneum, 1982.

The Halloween Costume Party written and illustrated by Ron Wegen; Clarion, 1983.

Hansy's Mermaid written and illustrated by Trinka Hakes Noble; Dial, 1983.

Hiawatha by Henry Wadsworth Longfellow, illustrated by Susan Jeffers; Dial, 1983.

Hugo and the Spacedog written and illustrated by Lee Lorenz; Prentice Hall, 1983.

Ike and Mama and the Trouble at School by Carol Snyder, illustrated by Charles Robinson; Coward McCann, 1983.

In the Middle of a Rainbow by Barbara Girion, not illustrated; Scribner, 1983.

In the Shadow of the Bear by Judith St. George, not illustrated; Putnam, 1983.

The Indy 500 by Jim Murphy, illustrated with photographs; Clarion, 1983.

It's BASIC: The ABC's of Computer Programming by Shelley Lipson, illustrated by Janice Stapleton; Holt, 1982.

Keeping it Secret by Penny Pollock, illustrated by Donna Diamond; Putnam, 1982.

A Lion for Lewis written and illustrated by Rosemary Wells; Dial, 1982.

Love from Aunt Betty written and illustrated by Nancy Winslow Parker; Dodd, Mead, 1983.

Lovers' Games by Barbara Cohen, not illustrated; Atheneum, 1983.

Mary Anne by Mary Mapes Dodge, illustrated by June Amos Grammer; Lothrop Lee & Shepard, 1983.

Matthew and his Dad story and photographs by Arlene Alda; Little Simon (Simon & Schuster), 1983.

Meet the Opossum by Leonard Lee Rue III with William Owen, illustrated with photographs by Leonard Lee Rue III; Dodd, Mead, 1983.

Memo: To Myself When I Have a Teenage Kid by Carol Snyder, not illustrated; Coward McCann, 1983.

Molly's Pilgrim by Barbara Cohen, illustrated by Michael J. Deraney; Lothrop Lee & Shepard, 1983.

The Mysteries in the Commune by Norah Smaridge, illustrated by Robert Handville; Dodd, Mead, 1982.

The Night of the Bozos by Jan Slepian, not illustrated; Dutton, 1983.

Night Talks by Patricia Gauch, not illustrated; Putnam, 1983.

Peabody written and illustrated by Rosemary Wells; Dial, 1983.

Red Bird of Ireland by Sondra Gordon Langford, not illustrated; Atheneum, 1983.

The Robots Are Here by Alvin Silverstein and Virginia B. Silverstein, illustrated with photographs and drawings; Prentice Hall, 1983.

Ruth Marini: Dodger Ace by Mel Cebulash, not illustrated; Lerner, 1983.

Ruth Marini of the Dodgers by Mel Cebulash, not illustrated; Lerner, 1983.

Shadrach's Crossing by Avi, not illustrated; Pantheon, 1983.

The Story of Your Mouth by Alvin Silverstein and Virginia B. Silverstein, illustrated by Karen Ackoff; Coward McCann, 1983.

The Summerboy: A Novel by Robert Lipsyte, not illustrated; Harper, 1982.

Super Stitches: A Book of Superstitions by Ann Nevins, illustrated by Dan Nevins; Holiday House, 1983.

Tales of a Dead King by Walter Dean Myers, not illustrated; Morrow, 1983.

A Taste for Quiet and Other Disquieting Tales by Judith Gorog, illustrated by Jean Titherington; Philomel, 1982.

Timewarp Summer by Norma Johnston, not illustrated; Atheneum, 1983.

True or False? Amazing Art Forgeries by Ann Waldron, illustrated; Hastings House, 1983.

What's on your Plate? by Norah Smaridge, illustrated by C. Imbior Kudrna; Abingdon Press, 1982.

Wonders of Sheep by Sigmund A. Lavine and Vincent Scuro, illustrated with photographs and old prints; Dodd, Mead, 1983.

Yeh-Shen: A Cinderella Story from China retold by Ai-Ling Louie, illustrated by Ed Young; Philomel, 1982.

1987 *Back-Back and the Lima Bear* by Thomas L. Weck, illustrated by Neil Taylor; Winston-Derek, 1985.

Cranberry Valentine written and illustrated by Wende Devlin and Harry Devlin; Four Winds, 1986.

The Forbidden Door by Jeanne K. Norweb, illustrated by George Laws; David C. Cook, 1985.

The Giant Egg by Charles Damitz; Weekly Reader Books, 1986.

Happily May I Walk: American Indians and Alaska Natives Today by Arlene Hirschfelder, illustrated; Scribner, 1986.

Making Music text and photographs by Arthur Paxton, concept by Helen Sive Paxton; Scribner, 1986.

Max's Christmas written and illustrated by Rosemary Wells; Dial, 1986.

Missing Since Monday by Ann M. Martin, not illustrated; Holiday House, 1986.

Nelson Malone Meets the Man from Mushnut by Louise Hawes, illustrated by Bert Dodson; Dutton, 1986.

Never Say Yes to a Stranger by Susan Newman, photographs by George Tiboni; Putnam, 1985.

Sarah's Questions by Harriet Ziefert, illustrated by Susan Bonners; Lothrop Lee & Shepard, 1986.

The Small Potatoes' Busy Beach Day by Harriet Ziefert, illustrated by Richard Brown; Dell, 1986.

Tales of Trickery: From the Land of Spoof by Alvin Schwartz, illustrated by David Christiana; Farrar Straus Giroux, 1985.

The Tamarack Tree by Patricia Clapp, not illustrated; Lothrop Lee & Shepard, 1986.

This Is a Crocodile written and illustrated by Evhy Constable; Bradbury, 1986.

Time Enough for Drums by Ann Rinaldi, illustrated with maps; Holiday House, 1986.

Water is Wet by Penny Pollock, photographs by Barbara Beirne; Putnam, 1985.

You Can Say No to a Drink or a Drug by Susan Newman, photographs by George Tiboni; Putnam, 1986.

1988 *The Bennington Stitch* by Sheila Solomon Klass, not illustrated; Scribner, 1985.

Donald Says Thumb Down by Nancy Evans Cooney, illustrated by Maxie Chambliss; Putnam, 1987.

Footsteps in the Ocean: Careers in Diving by Denise V. Lang, illustrated with photographs; Dutton, 1987.

Knight on Horseback by Ann Rabinowitz, not illustrated; Macmillan, 1987.

Leave It To Christy by Pamela Curtis Swallow, not illustrated; Putnam, 1987; Scholastic, 1988, c1987.

Making Music written and illustrated by Arthur K. Paxton, concept by Helen Sive Paxton; Atheneum, 1986.

Max and Diana and the Beach Day by Harriet Ziefert, illustrated by Lonni Sue Johnson; Harper & Row, 1987.

Max and Diana and the Birthday Present by Harriet Ziefert, illustrated by Lonni Sue Johnson; Harper & Row, 1987.

Max and Diana and the Snowy Day by Harriet Ziefert, illustrated by Lonni Sue Johnson; Harper & Row, 1987.

Meanwhile Back at the Ranch by Trinka Hakes Noble, illustrated by Tony Ross; Dial, 1987.

Meet the Beaver written and illustrated by Leonard Lee Rue III; Dodd Mead, 1986.

A New Coat for Anna by Harriet Ziefert, illustrated by Anita Lobel; Harper & Row, 1986.

People Like Us by Barbara Cohen, not illustrated; Bantam Books, 1989, c1987.

Shadow of a Unicorn by Norma Johnston, not illustrated; Bantam, 1987.

So Hungry! by Harriet Ziefert, illustrated by Carol Nicklaus; Random House, 1987.

Under the Sun written and illustrated by Ellen Kandoian; Dodd Mead, 1987.

Uneasy Money by Robin Brancato, not illustrated; Random House, 1986; Knopf, 1989.

What I Heard by Mark Geller; not illustrated; Harper & Row, 1987.

Where's the Cat? by Harriet Ziefert, illustrated by Arnold Lobel; Harper & Row, 1987.

Where's the Dog? by Harriet Ziefert, illustrated by Arnold Lobel; Harper & Row, 1987.

Where's the Guinea Pig? by Harriet Ziefert, illustrated by Arnold Lobel; Harper & Row, 1987.

I Won't Go To Bed by Harriet Ziefert, illustrated by Andrea Baruffi; Little Brown, 1987.

Story of Your Foot by Alvin Silverstein and Virginia Silverstein, illustrated by Greg Wenzel; Putnam, 1987.

The Good Side of My Heart by Ann Rinaldi, not illustrated; Holiday House, 1987.

Good Night, Jessie! by Harriet Ziefert, illustrated by Mavis Smith; Random House, 1987.

Just As Long As We're Together by Judy Blume, not illustrated; Orchard, 1987.

No Swimming in Dark Pond and Other Chilling Tales by Judith Gorog, not illustrated; Philomel, 1987.

Credit-Card Carole by Sheila Solomon Klass, not illustrated; Scribner, 1987.

Something Beyond Paradise by Jan Slepian, not illustrated; Philomel, 1987.

Who's Scared, Not Me by Judith St. George, not illustrated; Putnam, 1987.

Pet Day by Harriet Ziefert, illustrated by Richard Brown; Little Brown, 1987.

Fat Santa by Margery Cuyler, illustrated by Marsha Winborn; Henry Holt, 1987.

Telling Fortunes by Alvin Schwartz, illustrated by Tracey Cameron; Lippincott, 1987.

The Automobile by Barbara Ford, illustrated with photos; Walker, 1987.

What's Happening To My Junior Year? by Judith St. George, not illustrated; Putnam, 1986.

The Runaway Teddy Bear written and illustrated by Ginnie Hofmann; Random House, 1986.

Happily May I Walk by Arlene Hirschfelder, illustrated with photos; Scribner, 1986.

Hurry Up, Jessie! by Harriet Ziefert, illustrated by Mavis Smith; Random House, 1987.

The Boy Who Held Back the Sea retold by Lenny Hort, illustrated by Thomas Locker; Dial, 1987.

Worm Day by Harriet Ziefert, illustrated by Richard Brown; Harper & Row, 1987.

Trip Day by Harriet Ziefert, illustrated by Richard Brown; Little Brown, 1987.

Christina Katerina and the Time She Quit the Family by Patricia Lee Gauch, illustrated by Elise Primavera; Putnam, 1987.

Boat Song by Frances Ward Weller, not illustrated; Macmillan, 1987.

Leave Me Alone, Ma by Carol Snyder, not illustrated; Bantam Books, 1987.

Napoleon by Manfred Weidhorn, illustrated; Atheneum, 1986.

1989 *The Picture Life of Whitney Houston* by Gene Busnar, illustrated with photos; Watts, 1988.

Florida by Suzanne M. Coil, illustrated with photos; Watts, 1987.

The Picture Life of Tina Turner by Gene Busnar, illustrated with photos; Watts, 1988.

The Good-Bye Book by Judith Viorst, illustrated by Kay Chorao; Atheneum, 1988.

When the Boys Ran the House by Joan Carris, illustrated by Carol Newsom; Lippincott, 1982.

Under the Lights: A Child Model at Work by Barbara Beirne, illustrated with photos; Carolrhoda Books, 1988.

Hedgehogs in the Closet by Joan Davenport Carris, illustrated by Carol Newsom; Lippincott, 1988; Dell, 1990, c1988.

Pets, Vets and Marty Howard by Joan Davenport Carris, illustrated by Carol Newsom; Lippincott, 1984.

The Dark Corridor by Jay Bennett, not illustrated; Watts, 1988.

Return to Morocco by Norma Johnston, not illustrated; Four Winds, 1988.

Rusty Timmons' First Million by Joan Carris, illustrated by Kim Mulkey; Lippincott, 1985.

Pollen Pie written and illustrated by Louise Argiroff; Atheneum, 1988.

Wanted: One New Dad by Carol H. Behrman, not illustrated; Field Publications, 1988.

My Very Own Animated Jewish Holiday Activity Book by Jacqueline Pliskin; Shapolsky Publishers.

Panama Canal by Judith St. George, illustrated with photos; Putnam, 1989.

Cranberry Birthday written and illustrated by Harry Devlin and Wende Devlin; Four Winds, 1988.

Fallen Angels by Walter Dean Myers, not illustrated; Scholastic, 1988.

Alzheimer's Disease by Elaine Landau, illustrated with photos; Watts, 1987.

The Jewish Holiday Game & Workbook written and illustrated by Jacqueline Jacobson Pliskin; Shapolsky Publishers, 1987.

Surrogate Mothers by Elaine Landau, illustrated; Watts, 1988.

1990 *Staying With Grandma* by Eileen Roe, illustrated by Jacqueline Rogers; Bradbury Press, 1989.

Your Best Friend, Kate by Pat Brisson, illustrated by Rick Brown; Bradbury, 1989.

Uneasy Money by Robin Brancato, not illustrated; Random House, 1986; Knopf, 1989.

The Delphic Choice by Norma Johnston, not illustrated; Four Winds, 1989.

Operation Grizzly Bear by Marian Calabro, illustrated with photos; Four Winds, 1989.

Where Babies Come From by Martin Silverman and Harriet Ziefert, illustrated by Claire Schumacher; Random House, 1989.

Computer Graphics: How It Works, What It Does by Larry Kettelkamp, illustrated; Morrow, 1989.

Jimmy's Boa and the Big Splash Birthday Bash by Trinka Hakes Noble, illustrated by Steven Kellogg; Dial, 1989.

Is Your Mama a Llama? by Deborah Guarino, illustrated by Steven Kellogg; Scholastic, 1989.

Playing It Smart by Tova Navarra, illustrated by Tom Kerr; Barron's Press, 1989.

Winning by Robin Brancato, not illustrated; Knopf, 1988.

Petunia written and illustrated by Roger Duvoisin; Knopf, 1950.

Alessandra In Love by Robert Kaplow, not illustrated; Lippincott, 1989.

Curse of Claudia written and illustrated by Edward Miller; Crown, 1989.

Mr. Jordan in the Park written and illustrated by Laura Jane Coats; Macmillan, 1989.

Just One More written and illustrated by Michelle Koch; Greenwillow, 1989.

Glasses and Contact Lenses by Alvin Silverstein and Virginia Silverstein, illustrated with photos; Lippincott, 1989.

Look Closer! written and illustrated by Peter Ziebel; Clarion, 1989.

Canterbury Tales selected by Barbara Cohen, illustrated by Trina Schart Hyman; Lothrop, Lee & Shepard, 1988.

Custom Car: A Nuts-and-Bolts Guide to Creating One by Jim Murphy, illustrated with photos; Clarion, 1989.

I Saw You in the Bathtub and Other Folk Rhymes by Alvin Schwartz, illustrated by Syd Hoff; Harper & Row, 1989.

Bethie by Ann Rabinowitz, not illustrated; Macmillan, 1989.

NEW SOUTH WALES STATE LITERARY AWARDS
Australia-New South Wales Ministry for the Arts
Evan Williams, Secretary
P O Box 810
Darlington, New South Wales 2010
Australia

These annual awards were inaugurated by the New South Wales Government in 1979 to honor distinguished achievement by Australian writers. Until 1987 they were called the Premier's Literary Awards. The award for children's literature is judged by a three member panel. Writers whose works are nominated must be living Australian citizens or person's holding permanent resident status.

1979 **SPECIAL CHILDREN'S** *The Dark Bright Water* by Patricia Wrightson, not illustrated; Atheneum, 1979, c1978.

1979 **CHILDREN'S** *John Brown, Rose and the Midnight Cat* by Jenny Wagner, illustrated by Ron Brooks; Kestrel, 1977; Bradbury, 1978.

1980 *Mr. Archimedes' Bath* written and illustrated by Pamela Allen; Bodley Head, 1980; Lothrop, Lee & Shepard, 1980.

1980 **SPECIAL CHILDREN'S** *Land of the Rainbow Snake* by Catherine Berndt, illustrated by Djoki Yunupingu; Collins, 1979.

1981 **SPECIAL CHILDREN'S** *Seventh Pebble* by Eleanor Spence, illustrated by Sisca Verwoert; Oxford University Press, 1980.

1981 *When the Wind Changed* by Ruth Park, illustrated by Deborah Niland; Collins, 1982.

1982 *Whistle Up the Chimney* by Nan Hunt and Craig Smith, illustrated by Craig Smith; Collins, 1982.

1983 *Who Sank the Boat?* written and illustrated by Pamela Allen; Nelson Australia, 1983; Coward-McCann, 1983.

1983 **SPECIAL CHILDREN'S** *Five Times Dizzy* by Nadia Wheatley; Oxford University Press, 1983, c1982.

1984 *Possum Magic* by Mem Fox, illustrated by Julie Vivas; Omnibus Books, 1983; Harcourt, Brace, Jovanovich, 1983.

1985 *The House That Was Eureka* by Nadia Wheatley, not illustrated; Viking Kestrel, 1984.

1986 *The True Story of Spit MacPhee* by James Aldridge, not illustrated; Viking Penguin Australia, 1986; Viking Kestrel, 1986; Viking, 1987.

1987 *A Rabbit Named Harris* by Nan Hunt, illustrated by Betina Ogden; William Collins, 1991; Collins/Angus & Robertson, 1991.

1988 *Answers to Brut* by Gillian Rubinstein, not illustrated; Omnibus Books, 1988; Mammoth, 1991.

1988 **SPECIAL AWARD** Patricia Wrightson

1989 *You Take the High Road* by Mary Pershall, not illustrated; Penguin Books Australia, 1988; Dial, 1990.

1990 *The Blue Chameleon* by Katherine Scholes, illustrated by David Wong; Hill of Content, 1989.

1991 *Strange Objects* by Gary Crew, not illustrated; Heinemann, 1990.

1992 *All in the Blue Unclouded Weather* by Robin Klein, not illustrated; Penguin Books Australia, 1991.

NEW VOICES, NEW WORLD
Little Brown
34 Beacon St.
Boston, MA 02108

The purpose of this award, established in 1990 by Joy Street Books/Little Brown & Co., is to encourage submissions from minority writers and to create a more ethnically diverse list. Writers from ethnic minority backgrounds who have never published a children's book are eligible to submit manuscripts for picture books, middle grade and young adult readers. The winner will receive a $5000 cash award and a contract for publication to be negotiated with Joy Street Books/Little Brown and Company.

1990 *Dumpling Soup* by Jama Kim Rattigan, illustrated by Lillian Hsu-Flanders; Little Brown, 1992.

NEW YORK ACADEMY OF SCIENCES CHILDREN'S SCIENCE BOOK AWARDS
discontinued

Founded in 1970 by Dr. Joel Lebowitz of Rutgers University, the Children's Science Book Award has been presented annually since 1972 to encourage the writing and publication of high-quality science books for children. Since 1973, there have been two nonfiction categories: younger (ages five through nine) and older (ages nine through sixteen). All trade children's science books were eligible and were submitted by the publishers. A group of scientists formed a committee to make the final decision. The winners each received a citation and $500 at the awards luncheon in March or April. Honorable-mention books were also named for each category. The award program was suspended after the 1989 winners were chosen.

1972 *The Stars and Serendipity* written and illustrated by Robert S. Richardson; Pantheon, 1971.

1973 **YOUNGER** *City Leaves, City Trees* written and illustrated by Edward Gallob; Scribner, 1972.

1973 **OLDER** *Reading the Past: The Story of Deciphering Ancient Languages* by Leonard Cottrell, illustrated with photographs and line drawings; Crowell-Collier, 1971.

1974 **YOUNGER** *The Web in the Grass* by Berniece Freschet, illustrated by Roger Duvoisin; Scribner, 1972.

1974 **YOUNGER HONOR** *City Rocks, City Blocks and the Moon* written and illustrated by Edward Gallob; Scribner, 1973.

Discovering Cycles by Glenn O. Blough, illustrated by Jeanne Bendick; McGraw, 1973.

From Afar it is an Island translated and adapted by Pierrette Fleutiaux, illustrated by Bruno Munari; World, 1972.

1974 **OLDER** *A Natural History of Giraffes* by Dorcas MacClintock, illustrated by Ugo Mochi; Scribner, 1973.

1974 **OLDER HONOR** *It's Fun to Know Why: Experiments with Things Around Us* by Julius Schwartz, illustrated by Anne Marie Jauss and Edwin Herron; McGraw, 1973.

Vultures by Anne W. Turner, illustrated by Marian G. Warren; McKay, 1973.

X-raying the Pharaohs by Kent R. Weeks and James E. Harris, illustrated with photographs; Scribner, 1973.

1974 **SPECIAL HONORABLE MENTION TO A PUBLISHER** *The Walck Archaeology* published by Walck, 1973.

1975 **YOUNGER** *See What I Am* written and illustrated by Roger Duvoisin; Lothrop, 1974.

1975 **YOUNGER HONOR** *Circles, Triangles, and Squares* written and illustrated by Tana Hoban; Macmillan, 1974.

Handtalk: An ABC of Finger Spelling and Sign Language by Mary Beth Miller, Remy Charlip and George Ancona, photographs by George Ancona; Parents, 1974.

Sunlight by Sally Cartwright, illustrated by Marylin Hafner; Coward, 1974.

1975 **OLDER** *Hunters of the Whale: An Adventure in Northwest Coast Archaeology* by Richard D. Daugherty with Ruth Kirk, photographs by Ruth Kirk and Louis Kirk; Morrow, 1974.

1975 **OLDER HONOR** *Fever: The Hunt for a New Killer Virus* by John G. Fuller, illustrated with maps; Reader's Digest Press, 1974.

Gypsy Moth: Its History in America written and illustrated by Robert M. McClung; Morrow, 1974.

Summer Gold: A Camper's Guide to Amateur Prospecting by John N. Dwyer, illustrated with maps; Scribner, 1974.

Treasure Keepers by John FitzMaurice Mills, illustrated with photographs; Doubleday, 1973.

Wrapped for Eternity: The Story of the Egyptian Mummies by Mildred Mastin Pace, illustrated by Tom Huffman; McGraw, 1974.

1975 **SPECIAL HONORABLE MENTION FOR A PUBLISHER** *Ancient China* by John Hay, illustrated by Rosemonde Nairac and Pippa Brand; Walck, 1974.

The Archaeology of Ships by Paul Johnstone, illustrated by Pippa Brand; Walck, 1974.

Rand McNally Atlas of World Wildlife illustrated with photographs and paintings; Rand McNally, 1973.

1976 **YOUNGER** *Emperor Penguin: Bird of the Antarctic* by Jean-Claude Deguine, illustrated with photographs; Stephen Greene Press, 1974.

1976 **YOUNGER HONOR** *The Blue Lobster: A Life Cycle* by Carol Carrick, illustrated by Donald Carrick; Dial, 1975.

The Desert Is Theirs by Byrd Baylor, illustrated by Peter Parnall; Scribner, 1975.

The Lobster: It's Life Cycle by Herb Taylor, illustrated with photographs; Sterling, 1975.

Paper Movie Machines by Budd Wentz, illustrated with photographs; Troubadour, 1975.

Spring Peepers by Judy Hawes, illustrated by Graham Booth; Crowell, 1975.

1976 **OLDER** *Doctor in the Zoo* written and illustrated by Bruce Buchenholz; Studio/Viking, 1974.

1976 **OLDER HONOR** *A Life of Their Own: An Indian Family in Latin America* by Lisa W. Kroeber and Aylette Jenness, illustrated by Susan Votaw, photographs by the authors; Crowell, 1975.

Look how Many People Wear Glasses: The Magic of Lenses by Ruth Brindze, illustrated with photographs and drawings; Atheneum, 1975.

Sounds and Signals: How We Communicate by Charles T. Meadow, illustrated with photographs; Westminster, 1975.

The Story of Oceanography by Robert E. Boyer, illustrated with photographs and diagrams; Harvey, 1975.

1977 **YOUNGER** *Corn Is Maize: The Gift of the Indians* written and illustrated by Aliki; Crowell, 1976.

1977 **YOUNGER HONOR** *A Foal Is Born* by Hans-Heinrich Isenbart, translated by Catherine Edwards, photographs by Hanns-Jorg Anders; Putnam, 1976.

Iceberg Alley by Madelyn Klein Anderson, illustrated with maps; Messner, 1976.

The Milkweed and Its World of Animals by Ada Graham and Frank Graham, photographs by Les Line; Doubleday, 1976.

1977 **OLDER** *Watching the Wild Apes: The Primate Studies of Goodall, Fossey, and Galdikas* by Bettyann Kevles, illustrated with photographs; Dutton, 1976.

1977 **OLDER HONOR** *The Cave Bear Story: Life and Death of a Vanished Animal* by Bjorn Hurten, illustrated by Margaret Lambert; Columbia University Press, 1976.

Exploring the World of Leaves written and illustrated by Raymond A. Wohlrabe; Crowell, 1976.

Potatoes: All About Them by Alvin Silverstein and Virginia B. Silverstein, illustrated by Shirley Chan; Prentice Hall, 1976.

Windows Into a Nest by Geraldine Lux Flanagan, illustrated with photographs by Sean Morris; Kestrel, 1975; Houghton, 1976.

1977 **SPECIAL AWARD TO A PUBLISHER ON THE TWENTIETH ANNIVERSARY OF** *Cosmic View: The Universe in 40 Jumps* by Kees Boeke; illustrated with drawings; Day, 1957.

1978 **YOUNGER** *Wild Mouse* written and illustrated by Irene Brady; Scribner, 1976.

1978 **YOUNGER HONOR** *Anno's Counting Book* written and illustrated by Mitsumasa Anno; Crowell, 1977.

Castle written and illustrated by David Macaulay; Houghton, 1977.

Hanging On: How Animals Carry Their Young by Russell Freedman, illustrated with photographs; Holiday House, 1977.

1978 **OLDER** *Grains: An Illustrated History with Recipes* by Elizabeth Burton Brown, illustrated with photographs; Prentice Hall, 1977.

1978 **OLDER HONOR** *Epidemic! The Story of the Disease Detectives* by Jules Archer, illustrated with photographs; Harcourt, 1977.

The Microbes, Our Unseen Friends by Harold W. Rossmoore, illustrated with photographs; Wayne State University Press, 1976.

3-Dimensional Optical Illusions to Color and Construct written and illustrated by Larry Evans; Troubadour, 1977.

The Versatile Satellite by Richard W. Porter, illustrated with photographs and line drawings; Oxford, 1977.

1979 **YOUNGER** *The Smallest Life Around Us* by Lucia Anderson, illustrated by Leigh Grant; Crown, 1978.

1979 YOUNGER HONOR *The Bakery Factory: Who Puts the Bread on Your Table* written and illustrated by Aylette Jenness; Crowell, 1978.

Dr. Beaumont and the Man With the Hole in His Stomach by Beryl Epstein and Sam Epstein, illustrated by Joseph Scrofani; Coward, 1978.

Hyena Day by Robert Caputo and Miriam Hsia, photographs by Robert Caputo; Coward, 1978.

Winning with Numbers: A Kid's Guide to Statistics by Manfred G. Riedel, illustrated by Paul Coker, Jr.; Prentice Hall, 1978.

1979 OLDER *Laser Light* by Herman Schneider, illustrated by Radu Vero; McGraw, 1978.

1979 OLDER HONOR *Color in Plants and Flowers* by John Proctor and Susan Proctor, illustrated with photographs; Everest House, 1978.

Insect Magic by Michael Emsley, illustrated with photographs by Kjell Sandved; Viking, 1978.

The Magic Orange Tree and Other Haitian Folktales by Diane Wolkstein, illustrated by Elsa Henriquez; Knopf, 1978.

Worlds Within Worlds: A Journey into the Unknown by John Chesterman, John May, John Trux, and Michael Marten, illustrated with photographs; Holt, 1977.

1979 SPECIAL AWARD FOR A SERIES ON ENGINEER-ING AND TECHNOLOGY *Jet Journey* by Mike Wilson and Robin Scagell, illustrated with photographs; Viking, 1978.

Space Frontiers by Heather Couper and Nigel Henbest, illustrated with photographs; Viking, 1978.

Supermachines by Ralph Hancock, edited by Tony Palumbo, illustrated with photographs; Viking, 1978.

Television Magic by Eufron Gwynne Jones, illustrated with diagrams and photographs; Viking, 1978.

1980 YOUNGER *A Space Story* by Karla Kuskin, illustrated by Marc Simont; Harper, 1978.

1980 YOUNGER HONOR *Bubbles* by Bernie Zubrowski, illustrated by Joan Drescher; Little, 1979.

Natural Fire: It's Ecology in Forests by Laurence Pringle, illustrated with photographs; Morrow, 1979.

What Do Animals Do When it Rains? by J. Fred Dice, illustrated by Teppy Williams; Crescent, 1978.

The Wild Inside: A Sierra Club Guide to the Great Indoors written and illustrated by Linda Allison; Sierra Club/Scribner, 1979.

1980 OLDER *Building: The Fight Against Gravity* by Mario Salvadori, illustrated by Saralinda Hooker and Christopher Ragus; Atheneum, 1979.

1980 OLDER HONOR *Archosauria: A New Look at the Old Dinosaur* written and illustrated by John C. McLoughlin; Viking, 1979.

The Crab Nebula by Simon Mitton, illustrated with photographs; Scribner, 1978, 1979.

Morse, Marconi and You: Understanding and Building Telegraph, Telephone and Radio Sets by Irwin Math, illustrated by Hal Keith; Scribner, 1979.

Time and Clocks for the Space Age by Jane Fitz-Randolph and James Jespersen, not illustrated; Atheneum, 1979.

1980 SPECIAL AWARD FOR A REFERENCE BOOK SERIES *Wildlife of the Forests* by Myron Sutton and Ann Sutton, illustrated with photographs; Abrams, 1979.

Wildlife of the Oceans by Albert C. Jensen, illustrated with photographs; Abrams, 1979.

Wildlife of the Mountains by Edward R. Ricciuti, illustrated with photographs; Abrams, 1979.

1981 YOUNGER *Bet You Can't! Science Impossibilities to Fool You* by Vicki Cobb and Kathy Darling, illustrated by Martha Weston; Lothrop, 1980.

1981 YOUNGER HONOR *Max, the Music Maker* by Miriam B. Stecher, photographs by Alice S. Kandell; Lothrop, 1980.

Sunflower! written and illustrated by Martha McKeen Welch; Dodd, 1980.

Unbuilding written and illustrated by David Macaulay; Houghton, 1980.

1981 OLDER *Moving Heavy Things* written and illustrated by Jan Adkins: Houghton, 1980.

1981 OLDER HONOR *Careers in Conservation* by Frank Graham and Ada Graham, illustrated by Drake Jordan; Sierra Club/Scribner, 1980.

Magic in the Movies: The Story of Special Effects by Jane O'Connor and Katy Hall, illustrated with photographs; Doubleday, 1980.

Our Urban Planet by Ellen Switzer, photographs by Michael Switzer and Jeffrey Switzer; Atheneum, 1980.

Stones: Their Collection, Identification and Uses by Richard Vincent Dietrich, illustrated with sketches; Freeman, 1980.

1982 YOUNGER *Messing Around with Water Pumps and Siphons* by Bernie Zubrowski, illustrated by Steve Lindblom; Little Brown, 1981.

1982 YOUNGER HONOR *Hieroglyphs: The Writing of Ancient Egypt* written and illustrated by Norma Jean Katan, with Barbara Mintz; Atheneum, 1981.

The President's Car written and illustrated by Nancy Winslow Parker, introduction by Betty Ford; Crowell Jr. Books, 1981.

1982 OLDER *The Tree of Animal Life: A Tale of Changing Forms and Fortunes* written and illustrated by John C. McLoughlin; Dodd, Mead, 1981.

1983 YOUNGER *The Snail's Spell* by Joanne Ryder, illustrated by Lynne Cherry; Warne, 1982.

1983 YOUNGER HONOR *Animals that Migrate* by Caroline Arnold, illustrated by Michele Zylman; Carolrhoda, 1982.

Chickens Aren't the Only Ones written and illustrated by Ruth Heller; Grosset & Dunlap, 1981.

Elephant School written and illustrated by John Stewart; Pantheon, 1982.

1983 OLDER *The Brooklyn Bridge: They Said It Couldn't Be Built* by Judith St. George, illustrated with photographs; Putnam, 1982.

1983 OLDER HONOR *Drawing From Nature* written and illustrated by Jim Arnosky; Lothrop Lee & Shepard, 1982.

Nature's Clean-up Crew: The Burying Beetles written and photographed by Lorus Johnson Milne and Margery Milne; Dodd, Mead, 1982.

Our Modern Stone Age by Robert L. Bates and Julia Jackson, illustrated; William Kaufmann, 1982.

Tingambato: Adventures in Archaeology by Iris Noble, illustrated; Messner/Simon & Schuster, 1982.

1983 SPECIAL AWARD To Lerner Science Books for a beautifully photographed series of reference books for younger children:

Ants by Cynthia Overbeck, photographs by Satoshi Kuribayashi; Lerner, 1982.

Apple Trees by Sylvia A. Johnson, photographs by Hiroo Koike; Lerner, 1983.

Beetles by Sylvia A. Johnson, photographs by Isao Kishida; Lerner, 1982.

Cactus by Cynthia Overbeck, photographs by Shabo Hani; Lerner, 1982.

Carnivorous Plants by Cynthia Overbeck, photographs by Kiyoshi Shimizu; Lerner, 1982.

Cats by Cynthia Overbeck, photographs by Shin Yoshino; Lerner, 1983.

Crabs by Sylvia A. Johnson, photographs by Atsushi Sakurai; Lerner, 1982.

Dragonflies by Cynthia Overbeck, photographs by Yuko Sato; Lerner, 1982.

Elephants by Cynthia Overbeck, photographs by Tokumitsu Iwago; Lerner, 1981.

Frogs and Toads by Jane Dallinger and Sylvia A. Johnson, photographs by Hiroshi Tanemura; Lerner, 1982.

Grasshoppers by Jane Dallinger, photographs by Yuko Sato; Lerner, 1981.

How Seeds Travel by Cynthia Overbeck, photographs by Shabo Hani; Lerner, 1982.

Inside an Egg by Sylvia A. Johnson, photographs by Kiyoshi Shimizu; Lerner, 1982.

Ladybugs by Sylvia A. Johnson, photographs by Yuko Sato; Lerner, 1983.

Lions by Cynthia Overbeck, photographs by Tokumitsu Iwago; Lerner, 1981.

Monkeys: The Japanese Macaques by Cynthia Overbeck, photographs by Osamu Nishikawa; Lerner, 1981.

Mosses by Sylvia A. Johnson, photographs by Masana Izawa; Lerner, 1983.

Mushrooms by Sylvia A. Johnson, photographs by Masana Izawa; Lerner, 1982.

Penguins by Sylvia A. Johnson, illustrated with photographs; Lerner, 1981.

Silkworms by Sylvia A. Johnson, photographs by Isao Kishida; Lerner, 1982.

Snails by Sylvia A. Johnson, photographs by Modoki Masuda; Lerner, 1982.

Spiders by Jane Dallinger, photographs by Satoshi Kuribayashi; Lerner, 1981.

Sunflowers by Cynthia Overbeck, photographs by Susumu Kanozawa; Lerner, 1981.

Swallowtail Butterflies by Jane Dallinger and Cynthia Overbeck, photographs by Yuko Sato; Lerner, 1982.

1984 YOUNGER *Oak & Company* by Richard Mabey, illustrated by Clare Roberts; Greenwillow, 1983.

1984 YOUNGER HONOR *Anno's Mysterious Multiplying Jar* by Masaichiro Anno and Mitsumasa Anno, illustrated by Mitsumasa Anno; Philomel, 1983.

The Cranberry Book by Elizabeth Gemming, illustrated with prints and photographs; Coward McCann, 1983.

Ferris Wheels by Walter R. Brown and Norman D. Anderson, illustrated; Pantheon, 1983.

Hidden Worlds: Pictures of the Invisible by Seymour Simon, illustrated with photographs; Morrow, 1983.

1984 OLDER *Volcano Weather: The Story of 1816, the Year Without a Summer* by Henry Stommel and Elizabeth Stommel, illustrated; Seven Seas Press, 1983.

1984 OLDER HONOR *Dinosaurs: An Illustrated History* by Edwin H. Colbert, illustrated; Hammond, 1983.

Kites: The Science and Wonder by Toshio Ito and Hirotsuga Komura, illustrated; Japan Publications (distributed by Kodansha International through Harper), 1983.

Zounds! The Kids' Guide to Sound Making by Frederick R. Newman, illustrated by Elwood H. Smith; Random House, 1983.

1984 ELLIOTT MONTROLL SPECIAL AWARD *From Hand Axe to Laser: Man's Growing Mastery of Energy* by John Purcell, illustrated by Judy Skorpil; Vanguard, 1982.

1985 YOUNGER *The Secret Language of Snow* by Terry Tempest Williams and Ted Major, illustrated by Jennifer Dewey; Sierra Club/Pantheon, 1984.

1985 YOUNGER HONOR *Is It Rough? Is It Smooth? Is It Shiny?* written and illustrated by Tana Hoban; Greenwillow, 1984.

Potatoes by Sylvia A. Johnson, photographs by Masaharu Suzuki; Lerner, 1984.

Project Panda Watch by Miriam Schlein, illustrated by Robert Shetterly and photographs; Atheneum, 1984.

The Rising of the Wind: Adventures Along the Beaufort Scale by Jacques Yvart, illustrated by Claire Forgeot; Green Tiger Press, 1984.

1985 OLDER *The Daywatchers* written and illustrated by Peter Parnall; Macmillan, 1984.

1985 OLDER HONOR *Exploring the Night Sky With Binoculars* by David Chandler, illustrated by David Chandler and Don Davis; David Chandler, 1983.

The Invisible World of the Infrared by Jack R. White, illustrated; Dodd, Mead, 1984.

Rainbows, Snowflakes and Quarks: Physics and the World Around Us by Hans Christian Von Baeyer, illustrated by Laura Hartman; McGraw Hill, 1984.

The Whale Watchers' Guide by Robert Gardner, illustrated by Don Sineti; Messner, 1984.

Woodworks: Experiments with Common Wood and Tools by William F. Brown, illustrated by Mary G. Brown; Atheneum, 1984.

1985 ELLIOTT MONTROLL SPECIAL AWARD *Dreamers and Doers: Inventors who Changed our World* by Norman Richards, illustrated; Atheneum, 1984.

1985 SPECIAL AWARD *Macmillan Illustrated Animal Encyclopedia* edited by Philip Whitfield; Macmillan, 1984.

1986 YOUNGER *The Big Stretch: The Complete Book of the Amazing Rubber Band* by Ada Graham and Frank Graham, illustrated by Richard Rosenblum; Knopf, 1985.

1986 YOUNGER HONOR *Is It Larger? Is It Smaller?* written and illustrated by Tana Hoban; Greenwillow, 1985.

Koko's Kitten by Dr. Francine Patterson, photographs by Dr. Ronald H. Cohn; Scholastic, 1985.

The Mirror Puzzle Book written and illustrated by Marion Walter; Tarquin Publications, 1985.

Night of Ghosts and Hermits by Mary Stolz, illustrated by Susan Gallagher; Harcourt, 1985.

1986 OLDER *Breakthrough: The True Story of Penicillin* by Francine Jacobs, illustrated with photographs; Dodd, Mead, 1985.

1986 OLDER HONOR *Leaves* by Ghilean Tolmie Prance, photographs by Kjell B. Sandved; Crown, 1985.

Spaceshots by Timothy Ferris and Carolyn Zecca, illustrated with photographs; Pantheon, 1984.

Tales Mummies Tell by Patricia Lauber, illustrated with photographs; Crowell, 1985.

The Third Experiment by David E. Fisher, illustrated; Atheneum, 1985.

1986 ELLIOTT MONTROLL SPECIAL AWARD *Comet Halley: Once in a Lifetime* by Mark Littmann and Donald K. Yeomans, illustrated; American Chemical Society, 1985.

1987 YOUNGER *When Sheep Cannot Sleep* written and illustrated by Satoshi Kitamura; Farrar, 1986.

1987 YOUNGER HONOR *Earthworms, Dirt and Rotten Leaves* by Molly McLaughlin, illustrated by Robert Shetterly; Atheneum, 1986.

The Giant Panda written and illustrated by Xuqi Jin and Markus Kappeler, translated by Noel Simon; Putnam, 1986.

Pumpkin, Pumpkin written and illustrated by Jeanne Titherington; Greenwillow, 1986.

River and Canal written and illustrated by Edward Boyer; Holiday House, 1986.

Shapes, Shapes, Shapes written and illustrated by Tana Hoban; Greenwillow, 1986.

1987 OLDER *The Evolution Book* by Sara Stein, photographs by Rona Beame; Workman, 1986.

1987 OLDER HONOR *An Explorer's Handbook* by Christina Dodwell, illustrated; Facts on File, 1986.

The Practical Archaeologist by Jane McIntosh, illustrated; Facts on File, 1986.

Surely You're Joking, Mr. Feynman! by Richard P. Feynman as told to Ralph Leighton, edited by Edward Hutchings, not illustrated; Bantam, 1986.

Volcano: The Eruption and Healing of Mt. St. Helens by Patricia Lauber, illustrated with photographs; Bradbury Press, 1986.

1987 ELLIOTT MONTROLL SPECIAL AWARD *Atlas of North America* edited by Wilbur E. Garret, illustrations; National Geographic Society, 1985.

1987 SPECIAL PRIZE AS AN EXHIBITION CATALOGUE OF EXCELLENCE AND EXTRAORDINARY INTEREST *Puzzles Old and New* by Jerry Slocum and Jack Botermans, text by Carla van Splunteren and Tony Burrett; Plenary Publications International, distributed by University of Washington Press, 1986.

1988 YOUNGER *Icebergs and Glaciers* by Seymour Simon, illustrated; Morrow, 1987.

1988 YOUNGER HONOR *Turtle Watch* written and illustrated by George Ancona; Macmillan, 1987.

OPT: An Illusionary Tale written and illustrated by Joseph Baum and Arline Baum; Viking Kestrel, 1987.

Trapped in Tar: Fossils From the Ice Age by Caroline Arnold, illustrated by Richard Hewett; Clarion, 1987.

From Flower to Flower by Patricia Lauber, illustrated by Jerome Wexler; Crown, 1986.

1988 OLDER *Exploring the Night Sky* by Terence Dickinson, illustrated by John Bianchi; Camden House, 1987.

1988 OLDER HONOR *Bridging the Golden Gate* by Kathy Pelta, illustrated with photos; Lerner Publications, 1987.

A Shovelful of Earth by Margery Milne and Lorus J. Milne, illustrated by Margaret LaFarge; Henry Holt, 1987.

Optics: Light for a New Age by Jeff Hecht, illustrated; Scribners, 1987.

The Genius of China by Robert K.G. Temple, illustrated with photos; Simon & Schuster, 1986.

The Naturalists' Year by Scott Camazine, illustrated by Cynthia Camazine and Scott Camazine; Wiley, 1987.

1988 SPECIAL AWARD *Tana Hoban Golden Guides series*; Golden Press.

1988 ELLIOTT MONTROLL AWARD *The Media Lab: Inventing the Future at MIT* by Stewart Brand, illustrated; Viking Kestrel, 1987.

1989 YOUNGER *The Sierra Club Wayfinding Book* by Vicki McVey, illustrated by Martha Weston; Little Brown, 1989.

1989 YOUNGER HONOR *The Big Rock* written and illustrated by Bruce Hiscock; Atheneum, 1988.

Simple Machines by Anne Horvatic, illustrated by Stephen Bruner; Dutton, 1989.

The Igloo written and illustrated by Charlotte Yue and David Yue; Houghton Mifflin, 1988.

Plant Families written and illustrated by Carol Lerner; Morrow, 1989.

The News About Dinosaur written and illustrated by Patricia Lauber; Bradbury, 1989.

Tree Trunk Traffic written and illustrated by Bianca Lavies; Dutton, 1989.

More Wires and Watts by Irwin Math, illustrated by Hal Keith; Scribner, 1988.

1989 OLDER *Digging Dinosaurs* by James Gorman and John R. Horner, illustrated by Kris Ellingsen and Donna Braginetz; Workman Publishers, 1988.

1989 OLDER HONOR *Small Energy Sources* by Augusta Goldin, illustrated with photos; Harcourt, Brace, Jovanovich, 1988.

In Two Worlds: A Yup'ik Eskimo Family by Aylette Jenness and Alice Rivers, illustrated by Aylette Jenness; Houghton Mifflin, 1989.

Wonders of Speech by Virginia Silverstein and Alvin Silverstein, illustrated by Gordon Tomei; Morrow, 1988.

Through the Telescope by Michael R. Porcellino, illustrated; Tab Books, 1989.

Hominids: A Look Back at Our Ancestors by Helen Roney Sattler, illustrated by Christopher Santoro; Lothrop, Lee & Shepard, 1988.

1989 SPECIAL AWARD TO FIELD GUIDES - YOUNGER *No Bones* by Elizabeth Shepard, illustrated by Ippy Patterson; Macmillan, 1988.

1989 SPECIAL AWARD TO FIELD GUIDES - OLDER *The Field Guide to Geology* by David Lambert, illustrated; Facts on File, 1988.

1989 SPECIAL AWARD - YOUNGER Young Discovery Library (series)

1989 SPECIAL AWARD - OLDER Eyewitness Books (series) Knopf

1989 ELLIOTT AND SHIRLEY MONTROLL AWARD *Log of Christopher Columbus* edited by Robert H. Fuson, illustrated; International Marine Publishing Co., 1987.

NEW YORK HERALD TRIBUNE SPRING BOOK FESTIVAL AWARDS
see **SPRING BOOK FESTIVAL AWARD**

THE NEW YORK TIMES CHOICE OF BEST ILLUSTRATED CHILDREN'S BOOKS OF THE YEAR
The New York Times
Children's Book Editor
229 West 43rd Street
New York, NY 10036

First awarded in 1952, the *New York Times's Choice of Best Illustrated Children's Book of the Year* was established to honor the highest quality illustrations in children's books. The children's book editor, along with an artist and a critic, review all illustrated children's books published in the United States during the year. From these, they choose the award winning books. The number chosen varies from year to year, but is approximately ten. The children's books special supplement to *The New York Times Book Review* in mid-November announces the winners.

1952 *The Animal Farm* written and illustrated by Alice Provensen and Martin Provensen; Simon & Schuster, 1952.

Beasts and Nonsense written and illustrated by Marie Hall Ets; Viking, 1952.

The Dogcatcher's Dog written and illustrated by Andre Dugo; Holt, 1952.

Five Little Monkeys written and illustrated by Juliet Kepes; Houghton, 1952.

The Happy Place written and illustrated by Ludwig Bemelmans; Little, 1952.

A Hole Is to Dig by Ruth Krauss, illustrated by Maurice Sendak; Harper, 1952.

The Magic Currant Bun by John Symonds, illustrated by Andre Francois; Lippincott, 1952.

1953 *Fast Is not a Ladybug: A Book about Fast and Slow Things* by Miriam Schlein, illustrated by Leonard Kessler; Scott, 1953.

Florinda and the Wild Bird by Selina Chonz, translated by Anne Serraillier and Ian Serraillier, illustrated by Alois Carigiet; Walck, 1952.

The Golden Bible for Children: The New Testament edited by Elsa Jane Werner, illustrated by Alice and Martin Provensen; Golden, 1953.

Green Eyes written and illustrated by Abe Birnbaum; Capitol, 1953.

A Hero by Mistake by Anita Brenner, illustrated by Jean Charlot; Scott, 1953.

Lucky Blacky by Eunice Lackey, illustrated by Winifred Greene; Watts, 1953.

Madeline's Rescue written and illustrated by Ludwig Bemelmans; Viking, 1953.

Mother Goose Riddle Rhymes by Ruth Low and Joseph Low, illustrated by Joseph Low; Harcourt, 1953.

Pitschi: The Kitten Who Always Wanted to be Something Else written and illustrated by Hans Fischer; Harcourt, 1953.

Who Gave Us . . . Peacocks? Planes? and Ferris Wheels? written and illustrated by Madeleine Gekiere; Pantheon, 1953.

1954 *Andy Says ... Bonjour!* by Pat Diska, illustrated by Chris Jenkyns; Vanguard, 1954.

The Animal Frolic illustrated by Toba Sojo, adapted by Velma Varner; Putnam, 1954.

Circus Ruckus by William Lipkind, illustrated by Nicolas Mordvinoff; Harcourt, 1954.

The Happy Lion by Louise Fatio, illustrated by Roger Duvoisin; McGraw Hill, 1954.

Heavy Is a Hippopotamus by Miriam Schlein, illustrated by Leonard Kessler; Scott, 1954.

I'll Be You and You Be Me by Ruth Krauss, illustrated by Maurice Sendak; Harper, 1954.

Jenny's Birthday Book written and illustrated by Esther Averill; Harper, 1954.

A Kiss Is Round: Verses by Blossom Budney, illustrated by Vladimir Bobri; Lothrop, 1954.

The Sun Looks Down by Miriam Schlein, illustrated by Abner Graboff; Abelard-Schuman, 1954.

The Wet World by Norma Simon, illustrated by Jane Miller; Lippincott, 1954.

1955 *Beasts from a Brush* written and illustrated by Juliet Kepes; Pantheon, 1955.

Chaga by William Lipkind, illustrated by Nicolas Mordvinoff; Harcourt, 1955.

The Happy Lion in Africa by Louise Fatio, illustrated by Roger Duvoisin; McGraw Hill, 1955.

A Little House of Your Own by Beatrice Schenk de Regniers, illustrated by Irene Haas; Harcourt, 1955.

Parsley written and illustrated by Ludwig Bemelmans; Harper, 1955.

Rumpelstiltskin by Jacob Grimm and Wilhelm Grimm, adapted by Patricia Jones, illustrated by Jan B. Balet; Rand McNally, 1955.

See and Say: A Picture Book in Four Languages written and illustrated by Antonio Frasconi; Harcourt, 1955.

Switch on the Night by Ray Bradbury, illustrated by Madeleine Gekiere; Pantheon, 1955.

The Three Kings of Saba by Alf Evers, illustrated by Helen Sewell; Lippincott, 1955.

Uncle Ben's Whale by Walter D. Edmonds, illustrated by William Gropper; Dodd Mead, 1955.

1956 *Babar's Fair Will Be Opened next Sunday* written and illustrated by Laurent de Brunhoff, translated by Merle Haas; Random House, 1954.

Crocodile Tears written and illustrated by Andre Francois; Universe, 1956.

I Know a Lot of Things by Ann Rand and Paul Rand, illustrated by Paul Rand; Harcourt, 1956.

I Want to Paint My Bathroom Blue by Ruth Krauss, illustrated by Maurice Sendak; Harper, 1956.

I Will Tell You of a Town by Alastair Reid, illustrated by Walter Lorraine; Houghton, 1956.

Jonah the Fisherman written and illustrated by Reiner Zimnik, translated by Richard Winston and Clara Winston; Pantheon, 1956.

Little Big-Feather by Joseph Longstreth, illustrated by Helen Borten; Abelard, 1956.

The Little Elephant written and illustrated by Ylla; Harper, 1956.

Really Spring by Gene Zion, illustrated by Margaret Bloy Graham; Harper, 1956.

Was It a Good Trade? by Beatrice Schenk de Regniers, illustrated by Irene Haas; Harcourt, 1956.

1957 *Big Red Bus* by Ethel Kessler, illustrated by Leonard Kessler; Doubleday, 1957.

The Birthday Party by Ruth Krauss, illustrated by Maurice Sendak; Harper, 1957.

Curious George Gets a Medal written and illustrated by H.A. Rey; Houghton, 1957.

Dear Garbage Man by Gene Zion, illustrated by Margaret Bloy Graham; Harper, 1957.

The Fisherman and his Wife by Jacob Grimm and Wilhelm Grimm, illustrated by Madeleine Gekiere; Pantheon, 1957.

The Friendly Beasts by Laura Baker, illustrated by Nicholas Sidjakov; Parnassus, 1957.

The Red Balloon by Albert Lamorisse, illustrated with photographs; Doubleday, 1957.

Sparkle and Spin: A Book about Words by Ann Rand and Paul Rand, illustrated by Paul Rand; Harcourt, 1957.

This Is the Story of Faint George Who Wanted to Be a Knight written and illustrated by Robert E. Barry; Houghton, 1957.

The Unhappy Hippopotamus by Nancy Moore, illustrated by Edward Leight; Vanguard, 1957.

1958 *All Aboard: Poems* by Mary Britton Miller, illustrated by Bill Sokol; Pantheon, 1958.

Chouchou written and illustrated by Francoise; Scribner, 1958.

The Daddy Days by Norma Simon, illustrated by Abner Graboff; Abelard-Schuman, 1958.

A Friend Is Someone Who Likes You written and illustrated by Joan Walsh Anglund; Harcourt, 1958.

The Golden Book of Animals by Anne Terry White, photographs by W. Suschitzky; Simon & Schuster, 1958.

The House that Jack Built: A Picture Book in Two Languages written and illustrated by Antonio Frasconi; Harcourt, 1958.

How to Hide a Hippopotamus written and illustrated by Volney Crowell; Dodd, 1958.

The Magic Feather Duster by William Lipkind, illustrated by Nicolas Mordvinoff; Harcourt, 1958.

Roland by Nelly Stephane, illustrated by Andre Francois; Harcourt, 1958.

What Do You Say, Dear? by Sesyle Joslin, illustrated by Maurice Sendak; Scott, 1958.

1959 *Animal Babies* by Arthur Gregor, illustrated by Arthur Gregor and Ylla; Harper, 1959.

Father Bear Comes Home by Else Holmelund Minarik, illustrated by Maurice Sendak; Harper, 1959.

The First Noel: The Birth of Christ from the Gospel According to St. Luke illustrated by Alice Provensen and Martin Provensen; Golden, 1959.

Full of Wonder written and illustrated by Ann Kirn; World, 1959.

The Girl in the White Hat written and illustrated by W.T. Cummings; McGraw, 1959.

Kasimir's Journey by Monroe Stearns, illustrated by Marlene Reidel; Lippincott, 1959.

Little Blue and Little Yellow written and illustrated by Leo Lionni; Obolensky, 1959.

Pablo Paints a Picture by Warren Miller, illustrated by Edward Sorel; Little, 1959.

The Reason for the Pelican by John Ciardi, illustrated by Madeleine Gekiere; Lippincott, 1959.

This Is London written and illustrated by Miroslav Sasek; Macmillan, 1959.

1960 *The Adventures of Ulysses* by Jacques Lemarchand, translated by E.M. Hatt, illustrated by Andre Francois; Criterion, 1960.

Baboushka and the Three Kings by Ruth Robbins, illustrated by Nicolas Sidjakov; Parnassus, 1960.

Bruno Munari's ABC written and illustrated by Bruno Munari; World, 1960.

Inch by Inch written and illustrated by Leo Lionni; Obolensky, 1960.

Open House for Butterflies by Ruth Krauss, illustrated by Maurice Sendak; Harper, 1960.

Scrappy the Pup by John Ciardi, illustrated by Jane Miller; Lippincott, 1960.

The Shadow Book by Beatrice Schenk de Regniers and Isabel Gordon, illustrated by Isabel Gordon; Harcourt, 1960.

This Is New York written and illustrated by Miroslav Sasek; Macmillan, 1960.

Twenty Six Ways To Be Somebody Else written and illustrated by Devorah Boxer; Pantheon, 1960.

Two Little Birds and Three written and illustrated by Juliet Kepes; Houghton, 1960.

1961 *The Big Book of Animal Stories* edited by Margaret Green, illustrated by Janusz Grabianski; Watts, 1961.

Dear Rat by Julia Cunningham, illustrated by Walter Lorraine; Houghton, 1961.

The Happy Hunter written and illustrated by Roger Duvoisin; Lothrop, 1961.

Listen - the Birds by Mary Britton Miller, illustrated by Evaline Ness, Pantheon, 1961.

My Time of Year by Katharine Dow, illustrated by Walter Erhard; Walck, 1961.

Once a Mouse written and illustrated by Marcia Brown; Scribner, 1961.

Sandpipers by Edith Thacher Hurd, illustrated by Lucienne Bloch; Crowell, 1961.

The Snow and the Sun: A South American Folk Rhyme in Two Languages written and illustrated by Antonio Frasconi; Harcourt, 1961.

Umbrellas, Hats and Wheels by Jerome Snyder and Ann Rand, illustrated by Jerome Snyder; Harcourt, 1961.

The Wing on a Flea: A Book about Shapes written and illustrated by Ed Emberley; Little Brown, 1961.

1962 *Books!* by Murray McCain, illustrated by John Alcorn; Simon & Schuster, 1962.

The Emperor and the Drummer Boy by Ruth Robbins, illustrated by Nicolas Sidjakov; Parnassus, 1962.

Gennarino written and illustrated by Nicola Simbari; Lippincott, 1962.

The Island of Fish in the Trees by Eva-Lis Wuorio, illustrated by Edward Ardizzone; World, 1962.

Kay-Kay Comes Home by Nicholas Samstag, illustrated by Ben Shahn; Obolensky, 1962.

Little Owl by Hanne Axmann and Reiner Zimnik, illustrated by Hanne Axmann; Atheneum, 1962.

The Princesses: Sixteen Stories about Princesses edited by Sally P. Johnson, illustrated by Beni Montresor; Harper, 1962.

The Singing Hill by Meindert DeJong, illustrated by Maurice Sendak; Harper, 1962.

The Tale of a Wood written and illustrated by Henry B. Kane; Knopf, 1962.

The Three Robbers written and illustrated by Tomi Ungerer; Atheneum, 1962.

1963 *The Great Picture Robbery* by Leon Harris, illustrated by Joseph Schindelman; Atheneum, 1963.

Gwendolyn and the Weathercock by Nancy Sherman, illustrated by Edward Sorel; Golden, 1963.

A Holiday for Mister Muster written and illustrated by Arnold Lobel; Harper, 1963.

Hurly Burly and the Knights by Milton Rugoff, illustrated by Emanuele Luzzati; Platt, 1963.

John J. Plenty and Fiddler Dan by John Ciardi, illustrated by Madeleine Gekiere; Lippincott, 1963.

Karen's Curiosity written and illustrated by Alice Provensen and Martin Provensen; Golden, 1963.

Once Upon a Totem by Christie Harris, illustrated by John Frazer Mills; Atheneum, 1963.

Plunkety Plunk written and illustrated by Peter J. Lippman; Farrar, 1963.

Swimmy written and illustrated by Leo Lionni; Pantheon, 1963.

Where the Wild Things Are written and illustrated by Maurice Sendak; Harper, 1963.

1964 *The Bat-Poet* by Randall Jarrell, illustrated by Maurice Sendak; Macmillan, 1964.

Casey at the Bat by Ernest L. Thayer, illustrated by Leonard Everett Fisher; Watts, 1964.

The Charge of the Light Brigade by Alfred Tennyson, illustrated by Alice Provensen and Martin Provensen; Golden, 1964.

Exactly Alike written and illustrated by Evaline Ness; Scribner, 1964.

The Giraffe of King Charles X written and illustrated by Miche Wynants; McGraw, 1964.

The Happy Owls written and illustrated by Celestino Piatti; Atheneum, 1964.

I'll Show You Cats by C.N. Bonsall, illustrated by Ylla; Harper, 1964.

The Life of a Queen written and illustrated by Colette Portal, translated by Marcia Nardi; Braziller, 1964.

Rain Makes Applesauce by Julian Scheer, illustrated by Marvin Bileck; Holiday, 1964.

The Wave by Margaret Hodges, illustrated by Blair Lent; Houghton, 1964.

1965 *Alberic the Wise and other Journeys* by Norton Juster, illustrated by Domenico Gnoli; Pantheon, 1965.

The Animal Family by Randall Jarrell, illustrated by Maurice Sendak; Pantheon, 1965.

A Double Discovery written and illustrated by Evaline Ness; Scribner, 1965.

Hide and Seek Fog by Alvin Tresselt, illustrated by Roger Duvoisin; Lothrop, 1965.

Kangaroo & Kangaroo by Kathy Braun, illustrated by Jim McMullan; Doubleday, 1965.

Please Share That Peanut! A Preposterous Pageant in Fourteen Acts by Sesyle Joslin and Simms Taback, illustrated by Simms Taback; Harcourt, 1965.

Punch and Judy: A Play for Puppets illustrated by Ed Emberley; Little Brown, 1965.

Sven's Bridge written and illustrated by Anita Lobel; Harper, 1965.

1966 *Ananse the Spider: Tales from an Ashanti Village* by Peggy Appiah, illustrated by Peggy Wilson; Pantheon, 1966.

A Boy Went out to Gather Pears written and illustrated by Felix Hoffmann; Harcourt, 1966.

Celestino Piatti's Animal ABC written and illustrated by Celestino Piatti; Atheneum, 1966.

The Jazz Man by Mary Hays Weik, illustrated by Ann Grifalconi; Atheneum, 1966.

The Magic Flute by Stephen Spender, illustrated by Beni Montresor; Putnam, 1966.

The Monster Den: or, Look What Happened at my House - and to It by John Ciardi, illustrated by Edward Gorey; Lippincott, 1966.

Nothing Ever Happens on my Block written and illustrated by Ellen Raskin; Atheneum, 1966.

Shaw's Fortune: The Picture Story of a Colonial Plantation written and illustrated by Edwin Tunis; World, 1966.

Wonderful Time by Phyllis McGinley, illustrated by John Alcorn; Lippincott, 1966.

Zlateh the Goat and other Stories by Isaac Bashevis Singer, translated by Elizabeth Shub, illustrated by Maurice Sendak; Harper & Row, 1966.

1967 *Animals of Many Lands* edited by Hanns Reich, illustrated with photographs; Hill & Wang, 1967.

Brian Wildsmith's Birds written and illustrated by Brian Wildsmith; Watts, 1967.

A Dog's Book of Bugs by Elizabeth Griffen, illustrated by Peter Parnall; Atheneum, 1967.

Fables of Aesop by Sir Roger L'Estrange, illustrated by Alexander Calder; Dover, 1967.

Frederick written and illustrated by Leo Lionni; Pantheon, 1967.

The Honeybees by Franklin Russell, illustrated by Collette Portal; Knopf, 1967.

Hubert, the Caterpillar Who Thought He Was a Moustache by Susan Richards and Wendy Stang, illustrated by Robert L. Anderson; Quist, 1967.

Knee-deep in Thunder by Sheila Moon, illustrated by Peter Parnall; Atheneum, 1967.

Seashore Story written and illustrated by Taro Yashima; Viking, 1967.

1968 *Harriet and the Promised Land* written and illustrated by Jacob Lawrence; Windmill/Simon & Schuster, 1968.

A Kiss for Little Bear by Else Holmelund Minarik, illustrated by Maurice Sendak; Harper, 1968.

Malachi Mudge by Edward Cecil, illustrated by Peter Parnall; McGraw, 1968.

Mister Corbett's Ghost by Leon Garfield, illustrated by Alan Cober; Pantheon, 1968.

The Real Tin Flower: Poems about the World at Nine by Aliki Barnstone, illustrated by Paul Giovanopoulos; Crowell-Collier, 1968.

The Secret Journey of Hugo the Brat by Francois Ruy-Vidal, illustrated by Nicole Claveloux; Quist, 1968.

Spectacles written and illustrated by Ellen Raskin; Atheneum, 1968.

Story Number 1 by Eugene Ionesco, illustrated by Etienne Delessert; Quist, 1968.

Talking Without Words written and illustrated by Marie Hall Ets; Viking, 1968.

The Very Obliging Flowers by Claude Roy, translated by Gerald Bertin, illustrated by Alain LeFoll; Grove, 1968.

1969 *Arm in Arm* written and illustrated by Remy Charlip; Parents, 1969.

Bang, Bang You're Dead by Louise Fitzhugh and Sandra Scoppettone, illustrated by Louise Fitzhugh; Harper, 1969.

Birds written and illustrated by Juliet Kepes; Walker, 1968.

The Circus in the Mist written and illustrated by Bruno Munari; World, 1969.

The Dong with a Luminous Nose by Edward Lear, illustrated by Edward Gorey; Scott, 1969.

Free as a Frog by Elizabeth J. Hodges, illustrated by Paul Giovanopoulos; Addison-Wesley, 1969.

The Light Princess by George MacDonald, illustrated by Maurice Sendak; Farrar, 1969.

Sara's Granny and the Groodle by Joan Gill, illustrated by Seymour Chwast; Doubleday, 1969.

What Is It For? written and illustrated by Henry Humphrey; Simon & Schuster, 1969.

Winter's Eve by Natalia M. Belting, illustrated by Alan E. Cober; Holt, 1969.

1970 *Alala* by Guy Monreal, illustrated by Nicole Claveloux; Quist, 1970.

Finding a Poem by Eve Merriam, illustrated by Seymour Chwast; Atheneum, 1970.

The Gnu and the Guru Go Behind the Beyond by Peggy Clifford, illustrated by Eric Von Schmidt; Houghton, 1970.

Help, Help, the Globolinks! by Gian-Carlo Menotti, adapted by Leigh Dean, illustrated by Milton Glaser; McGraw, 1970.

In the Night Kitchen written and illustrated by Maurice Sendak; Harper, 1970.

Lift Every Voice and Sing words and music by J. Rosamund and James Weldon Johnson, illustrated by Mozelle Thompson; Hawthorn, 1970.

Matilda Who Told Lies and Was Burned to Death by Hilaire Belloc, illustrated by Steven Kellogg; Dial, 1970.

Timothy's Horse by Vladimir Mayakovsky, adapted by Guy Daniels, illustrated by Flavio Constantini; Pantheon, 1970.

Topsy Turvies: Pictures to Stretch the Imagination written and illustrated by Mitsumasa Anno; Walker/Weatherhill, 1970.

You Are Ri-di-cu-lous written and illustrated by Andre Francois; Pantheon, 1970.

1971 *Amos and Boris* written and illustrated by William Steig; Farrar, 1971.

Bear Circus written and illustrated by William Pene du Bois; Viking, 1971.

The Beast of Monsieur Racine written and illustrated by Tomi Ungerer; Farrar, 1971.

Changes, Changes written and illustrated by Pat Hutchins; Macmillan, 1971.

Look Again! written and illustrated by Tana Hoban; Macmillan, 1971.

Look What I Can Do written and illustrated by Jose Aruego; Scribner, 1971.

The Magic Tears by Jack Sendak, illustrated by Mitchell Miller; Harper, 1971.

Mr. Gumpy's Outing written and illustrated by John Burningham; Holt, 1971.

One Dancing Drum by Gail Kredenser and Stanley Mack, illustrated by Stanley Mack; Phillips, 1971.

The Shrinking of Treehorn by Florence Parry Heide, illustrated by Edward Gorey; Holiday, 1971.

1972 *Behind the Wheel* written and illustrated by Edward Koren; Holt, 1972.

Count and See written and illustrated by Tana Hoban; Macmillan, 1972.

George and Martha written and illustrated by James Marshall; Houghton, 1972.

Hosie's Alphabet by Hosea, Tobias, and Lisa Baskin, illustrated by Leonard Baskin; Viking, 1972.

Just So Stories by Rudyard Kipling, illustrated by Etienne Delessert; Doubleday, 1972.

A Little Schubert written and illustrated by M.B. Goffstein; Harper, 1972.

Miss Jaster's Garden written and illustrated by N.M. Bodecker; Golden, 1972.

Mouse Cafe written and illustrated by Patricia Coombs; Lothrop, 1972.

Simon Boom Gives a Wedding by Yuri Suhl, illustrated by Margot Zemach; Four Winds, 1972.

Where's Al? written and illustrated by Byron Barton; Seabury, 1972.

1973 *Cathedral: The Story of its Construction* written and illustrated by David Macaulay; Houghton, 1973.

The Emperor's New Clothes: A Fairy Tale by Hans Christian Andersen, illustrated by a Monika Laimgruber; Addison-Wesley, 1973.

Hector Penguin by Louise Fatio, illustrated by Roger Duvoisin; McGraw Hill, 1973.

The Juniper Tree and other Tales from Grimm translated by Lore Segal and Randall Jarrell, illustrated by Maurice Sendak; Farrar, 1973.

King Grisly-Beard: A Tale from the Brothers Grimm translated by Edgar Taylor, illustrated by Maurice Sendak; Farrar, 1973.

The Number 24 written and illustrated by Guy Billout; Quist, 1973.

A Prairie Boy's Winter written and illustrated by William Kurelek; Houghton, 1973.

The Silver Pony written and illustrated by Lynd Ward; Houghton, 1973.

Tim's Last Voyage written and illustrated by Edward Ardizzone; Walck, 1973.

1974 *The Girl Who Cried Flowers* by Jane Yolen, illustrated by David Palladini; Crowell, 1974.

A Home by Lennart Rudstrom, illustrated by Carl Larsson; Putnam, 1974.

Lumberjack written and illustrated by William Kurelek; Houghton, 1974.

The Man Who Took the Indoors Out written and illustrated by Arnold Lobel; Harper, 1974.

Miss Suzy's Birthday by Miriam Young, illustrated by Arnold Lobel; Parents, 1974.

A Storybook edited and illustrated by Tomi Ungerer; Watts, 1974.

There Was an Old Woman written and illustrated by Steven Kellogg; Parents, 1974.

1975 *Anno's Alphabet: An Adventure in Imagination* written and illustrated by Mitsumasa Anno; Crowell, 1975.

A Book of A-maze-ments by Jean Seisser; Quist, 1974.

Mr. Michael Mouse Unfolds His Tale written and illustrated by Walter Crane; Merrimack, 1975.

The Pig-tale by Lewis Carroll, illustrated by Leonard B. Lubin; Little Brown, 1975, 1889.

There's a Sound in the Sea: A Child's Eye View of the Whale compiled by Tamar Griggs, illustrated with paintings by school children; Scrimshaw, 1975.

Thirteen written and illustrated by Jerry Joyner and Remy Charlip; Parents, 1975.

The Tutti-Frutti Case: Starring the Four Doctors of Goodge by Harry Allard, illustrated by James Marshall; Prentice Hall, 1975.

1976 *As Right as Right Can Be* by Anne Rose, illustrated by Arnold Lobel; Dial, 1976.

Ashanti to Zulu: African Traditions by Margaret Musgrove, illustrated by Leo and Diane Dillon; Dial, 1976.

The Bear and the Fly written and illustrated by Paula Winter; Crown, 1976.

Everyone Knows What a Dragon Looks Like by Jay Williams, illustrated by Mercer Mayer; Four Winds, 1976.

Fly by Night by Randall Jarrell, illustrated by Maurice Sendak; Farrar, 1976.

Little Though I Be written and illustrated by Joseph Low; McGraw Hill, 1976.

Merry Ever After: The Story of Two Medieval Weddings written and illustrated by Joe Lasker; Viking, 1976.

The Mother Goose Book written and illustrated by Alice Provensen and Martin Provensen; Random House, 1976.

A Near Thing for Captain Najork by Russell Hoban, illustrated by Quentin Blake; Atheneum, 1976.

1977 *The Church Mice Adrift* by Lore Segal, illustrated by Graham Oakley; Atheneum, 1977.

Come Away from the Water, Shirley written and illustrated by John Burningham; Crowell, 1977.

It Could Always Be Worse: A Yiddish Folk Tale retold and illustrated by Margot Zemach; Farrar, 1977.

Jack and the Wonder Beans by James Still, illustrated by Margot Tomes; Putnam, 1977.

Merry, Merry FIBruary by Doris Orgel, illustrated by Arnold Lobel; Parents, 1977.

My Village, Sturbridge by Gary Bowen, illustrated by Gary Bowen and Randy Miller; Farrar, 1977.

Noah's Ark written and illustrated by Peter Spier; Doubleday, 1977.

The Surprise Picnic written and illustrated by John S. Goodall; Atheneum, 1977.

When the Wind Blew by Margaret Wise Brown, illustrated by Geoffrey Hayes; Harper, 1977.

1978 *Cloudy with a Chance of Meatballs* by Judi Barrett, illustrated by Ron Barrett; Atheneum, 1978.

The Forbidden Forest written and illustrated by William Pene du Bois; Harper, 1978.

The Great Song Book edited by Timothy John, music edited by Peter Hankey, illustrated by Tomi Ungerer; Doubleday, 1978.

Hanukah Money by Sholem Aleichem, adapted and illustrated by Uri Shulevitz; Greenwillow, 1978.

The Legend of Scarface: A Blackfoot Indian Tale by Robert San Souci, illustrated by Daniel San Souci; Doubleday, 1978.

This Little Pig-a-wig and other Rhymes about Pigs by Lenore Blegvad, illustrated by Erik Blegvad; Atheneum/McElderry, 1978.

The Nutcrackers and the Sugar-tongs by Edward Lear, illustrated by Marcia Sewall; Atlantic-Little, 1978.

Odette: A Bird in Paris by Kay Fender, illustrated by Phillipe Dumas; Prentice Hall, 1978.

A Peaceable Kingdom: The Shaker Abecedarius illustrated by Alice Provensen and Martin Provensen; Viking, 1978.

There Once Was a Woman Who Married a Man by Norma Farber, illustrated by Lydia Dabcovich; Addison, 1978.

1979 *By Camel or by Car: A Look at Transportation* written and illustrated by Guy Billout; Prentice Hall, 1979.

The Garden of Abdul Gasazi written and illustrated by Chris Van Allsburg; Houghton, 1979.

Happy Birthday, Oliver! written and illustrated by Pierre Le-Tan; Random House, 1979.

King Krakus and the Dragon written and illustrated by Janina Domanska; Greenwillow, 1979.

The Long Dive written and illustrated by Catriona Smith and Ray Smith; Atheneum/Jonathan Cape, 1979.

Natural History written and illustrated by M.B. Goffstein; Farrar, 1979.

Ox-Cart Man by Donald Hall, illustrated by Barbara Cooney; Viking, 1979.

The Tale of Fancy Nancy: A Spanish Folk Tale adapted by Marion Koenig, illustrated by Klaus Ensikat; Chatto, 1978.

Tilly's House written and illustrated by Faith Jacques; Atheneum, 1979.

The Treasure written and illustrated by Uri Shulevitz; Farrar, 1979.

1980 *An Artist* written and illustrated by M.B. Goffstein; Harper, 1980.

A Child's Christmas in Wales by Dylan Thomas, illustrated by Edward Ardizzone; Godine, 1980.

Gorky Rises written and illustrated by William Steig; Farrar, 1980.

The Headless Horseman Rides Tonight: More Poems to Trouble your Sleep by Jack Prelutsky, illustrated by Arnold Lobel; Greenwillow, 1980.

Howard written and illustrated by James Stevenson; Greenwillow, 1980.

The Lucky Yak by Annetta Lawson, illustrated by Allen Say; Parnassus/Houghton Mifflin, 1980.

Mr. Miller the Dog written and illustrated by Helme Heine; Atheneum, 1980.

Stone and Steel: A Look at Engineering written and illustrated by Guy Billout; Prentice Hall, 1980.

Unbuilding written and illustrated by David Macaulay; Houghton, 1980.

The Wonderful Travels and Adventures of Baron Munchhausen by Peter Nickl, translated by Elizabeth Buchanan Taylor, illustrated by Binette Schroeder; Chatto & Windus, 1979.

1981 *My Mom Travels a Lot* by Caroline Feller Bauer, illustrated by Nancy Winslow Parker; Warne, 1981.

On Market Street by Arnold Lobel, illustrated by Anita Lobel; Greenwillow, 1981.

The Maid and the Mouse and the Odd-Shaped House: A Story in Rhyme adapted and illustrated by Paul O. Zelinsky; Dodd, Mead, 1981.

The Story of Old Mrs. Brubeck and How She Looked for Trouble and Where She Found Him by Lore Segal, illustrated by Marcia Sewall; Pantheon, 1979.

The Crane Wife retold by Sumiko Yagawa, translated by Katherine Paterson, illustrated by Suekichi Akaba; Morrow, 1981.

Flight: A Panorama of Aviation by Melvin B. Zisfein, illustrated by Robert Andrew Parker; Pantheon, 1979.

Jumanji written and illustrated by Chris Van Allsburg; Houghton Mifflin, 1981.

Outside Over There written and illustrated by Maurice Sendak; Harper, 1981.

The Nose Tree adapted and illustrated by Warwick Hutton; Atheneum, 1980; Julia MacRae, 1981.

Where the Buffaloes Begin by Olaf Baker, illustrated by Stephen Gammell; Warne, 1981.

1982 *The Strange Appearance of Howard Cranebill, Jr.* written and illustrated by Henrik Drescher; Lothrop, 1982.

Smile, Ernestine and Celestine written and illustrated by Gabrielle Vincent; Greenwillow, 1982.

Anno's Britain written and illustrated by Mitsumasa Anno; Philomel, 1982, c1981.

My Uncle written and illustrated by Jenny Thorne; Atheneum, 1982.

Ben's Dream written and illustrated by Chris Van Allsburg; Houghton Mifflin, 1982.

The Tiny Visitor written and illustrated by Oscar de Mejo; Pantheon, 1982.

Paddy Goes Traveling written and illustrated by John S. Goodall; Atheneum, 1982.

Rainbows Are Made: Poems by Carl Sandburg, edited by Lee Bennett Hopkins, illustrated by Fritz Eichenberg; Harcourt, 1982.

The Gift of the Magi by O. Henry, illustrated by Lisbeth Zwerger, lettering by Michael Neugebauer; Neugebauer Press distributed by Alphabet Press, 1982.

Squid and Spider: A Look at the Animal Kingdom written and illustrated by Guy Billout; Prentice Hall, 1982.

1983 *Twelve Cats for Christmas* written and illustrated by Martin Leman; Pelham/Merrimack Publishers Circle, 1982.

Round Trip written and illustrated by Ann Jonas; Greenwillow, 1983.

Little Red Cap by Jacob Grimm and Wilhelm Grimm, translated by Elizabeth D. Crawford, illustrated by Lisbeth Zwerger; Morrow, 1983.

Leonard Baskin's Miniature Natural History: First Series written and illustrated by Leonard Baskin; Pantheon, 1983.

The Wreck of the Zephyr written and illustrated by Chris Van Allsburg; Houghton Mifflin, 1983.

Simon's Book written and illustrated by Henrik Drescher; Lothrop, 1983.

Tools written and photographed by Ken Robbins; Four Winds, 1983.

The Favershams written and illustrated by Roy Gerrard; Gollancz, 1982; Farrar, 1983.

Up a Tree written and illustrated by Ed Young; Harper & Row, 1983.

1984 *Saint George and the Dragon* adapted by Margaret Hodges from Edmund Spenser's *Faerie Queene*, illustrated by Trina Schart Hyman; Little Brown, 1984.

Animal Alphabet written and illustrated by Bert Kitchen; Dial, 1984.

Sir Cedric written and illustrated by Roy Gerrard; Farrar, 1984.

The Mysteries of Harris Burdick written and illustrated by Chris Van Allsburg; Houghton Mifflin, 1984.

The Napping House by Audrey Wood, illustrated by Don Wood; Harcourt, 1984.

Where the River Begins written and illustrated by Thomas Locker; Dial, 1984.

If There Were Dreams to Sell by Barbara Lalicki, illustrated by Margot Tomes; Lothrop, Lee & Shepard, 1984.

Babushka written and illustrated by Charles Mikolaycak; Holiday House, 1984.

Jonah and the Great Fish written and illustrated by Warwick Hutton; Atheneum, 1984.

Nutcracker by E.T.A. Hoffmann, translated by Ralph Manheim, illustrated by Maurice Sendak; Crown, 1984.

1985 *Gorilla* written and illustrated by Anthony Browne; Knopf, 1985.

Granpa written and illustrated by John Burningham; Crown, 1985.

Hazel's Amazing Mother written and illustrated by Rosemary Wells; Dial, 1985.

The Inside-Outside Book of New York City written and illustrated by Roxie Munro; Dodd, Mead, 1985.

The Legend of Rosepetal by Clemens Brentano, illustrated by Lisbeth Zwerger; Picture Book Studio, 1985.

The Nightingale by Hans Christian Andersen, illustrated by Demi; Harcourt, 1985.

The Polar Express written and illustrated by Chris Van Allsburg; Houghton Mifflin, 1985.

The People Could Fly: American Black Folktales by Virginia Hamilton, illustrated by Leo Dillon and Diane Dillon; Knopf, 1985.

The Relatives Came by Cynthia Rylant, illustrated by Stephen Gammell; Bradbury, 1985.

The Story of Mrs. Lovewright and Purrless, Her Cat by Lore Segal, illustrated by Paul O. Zelinsky; Knopf, 1985.

1986 *The Stranger* written and illustrated by Chris Van Allsburg; Houghton Mifflin, 1986.

The Ugly Duckling by Hans Christian Andersen, illustrated by Robert Van Nutt; Knopf, 1986.

Flying written and illustrated by Donald Crews; Greenwillow, 1986.

The Owl-Scatterer by Howard Norman, illustrated by Michael McCurdy; Atlantic Monthly Press, 1986.

Rembrandt Takes a Walk by Mark Strand, illustrated by Red Grooms; Clarkson N. Potter, 1986.

Cherries and Cherry Pits written and illustrated by Vera B. Williams; Greenwillow, 1986.

Molly's New Washing Machine by Laura Geringer, illustrated by Petra Mathers; Harper, 1986.

Brave Irene written and illustrated by William Steig; Farrar, 1986.

Pigs from A to Z written and illustrated by Arthur Geisert; Houghton Mifflin, 1986.

One Morning by Canna Funakoshi, illustrated by Yohiji Izawa; Picture Book Studio, 1986.

1987 *Rainbow Rhino* written and illustrated by Peter Sis; Knopf, 1987.

Halloween ABC by Eve Merriam, illustrated by Lane Smith; Macmillan, 1987.

In Coal Country by Judith Hendershot, illustrated by Thomas B. Allen; Knopf, 1987.

Fox's Dream written and illustrated by Keizaburo Tejima; Philomel, 1987.

Handtalk Birthday by Remy Charlip and Mary Beth Miller, photographs by George Ancona; Four Winds, 1987.

The Mountains of Tibet written and illustrated by Mordicai Gerstein; Harper, 1987.

The Yellow Umbrella written and illustrated by Henrik Drescher; Bradbury, 1987.

Seventeen Kings and Forty-two Elephants by Margaret Mahy, illustrated by Patricia MacCarthy; Dial, 1987.

Jump Again! More Adventures of Brer Rabbit by Joel Chandler Harris, adapted by Van Dyne Parks, illustrated by Barry Moser; Harcourt, 1987.

The Cremation of Sam McGee by Robert W. Service, illustrated by Ted Harrison; Greenwillow, 1987.

1988 *A River Dream* written and illustrated by Allen Say; Houghton Mifflin, 1988.

Cats Are Cats: Poems by Nancy Larrick, illustrated by Ed Young; Philomel, 1988.

Theodor and Mr. Balbini written and illustrated by Petra Mathers; Harper & Row, 1988.

Shaka: King of the Zulus by Peter Vennema and Diane Stanley, illustrated by Diane Stanley; Morrow, 1988.

Swan Sky written and illustrated by Tejima; Philomel, 1988.

Look! Look! Look! written and illustrated by Tana Hoban; Greenwillow, 1988.

Fire Came to the Earth People written and illustrated by Susan L. Roth; St. Martin's Press, 1988.

Sir Francis Drake: His Daring Deeds written and illustrated by Roy Gerrard; Farrar Straus Giroux, 1988.

Stringbean's Trip to the Shining Sea by Vera B. Williams, illustrated by Vera B. Williams and Jennifer Williams; Greenwillow, 1988.

I Want To Be an Astronaut written and illustrated by Byron Barton; Crowell, 1988.

1989 *Turtle in July* by Marilyn Singer, illustrated by Jerry Pinkney; Macmillan, 1989.

Heartaches of a French Cat written and illustrated by Barbara McClintock; Godine, 1989.

Nicholas Cricket by Joyce Maxner, illustrated by William Joyce; Harper & Row, 1989.

Olson's Meat Pies by Peter Cohen, illustrated by Olof Landstrom; Farrar Straus Giroux, 1989.

Peacock Pie: A Book of Rhymes by Walter De La Mare, illustrated by Louise Brierley; Henry Holt, 1989.

Theseus and the Minotaur written and illustrated by Warwick Hutton; McElderry, 1989.

Whales by Seymour Simon, illustrated with photos; Crowell, 1989.

Dancing Skelton by Cynthia C. DeFelice, illustrated by Robert Andrew Parker; Macmillan, 1989.

Does God Have a Big Toe? Stories About Stories in the Bible by Marc Gellman, illustrated by Oscar de Mejo; Harper & Row, 1989.

How Pizza Came to Queens written and illustrated by Dayal Kaur Khalsa; Clarkson Potter (Crown), 1989.

1990 *One Gorilla: A Counting Book* written and illustrated by Atsuko Morozumi; Farrar Straus Giroux, 1990.

Fish Eyes: A Book You Can Count On written and illustrated by Lois Ehlert; Harcourt Brace Jovanovich, 1990.

The Fool and the Fish: A Tale From Russia by Alexander Nikolayevich Afanasyev, illustrated by Gennady Spirin; Dial, 1990.

I'm Flying! by Alan Wade, illustrated by Petra Mathers; Knopf, 1990.

The Tale of the Mandarin Ducks by Katherine Paterson, illustrated by Leo Dillon and Diane Dillon; Dutton, 1990.

A Christmas Carol by Charles Dickens, illustrated by Roberto Innocenti; Stewart, Tabori & Chang, 1990.

War Boy written and illustrated by Michael Foreman; Arcade, 1990, c1989.

The Dancing Palm Tree and Other Nigerian Folktales by Barbara K. Walker, illustrated by Helen Siegl; Texas Tech University Press, 1990.

Beneath a Blue Umbrella by Jack Prelutsky, illustrated by Garth Williams; Greenwillow, 1990.

Beach Ball written and illustrated by Peter Sis; Greenwillow, 1990.

1991 *Follow the Dream* written and illustrated by Peter Sis; Knopf, 1991.

Another Celebrated Dancing Bear by Gladys Scheffrin-Falk, illustrated by Barbara Garrison; Scribner, 1991.

Punch in New York written and illustrated by Alice Provensen; Viking, 1991.

Ooh La La (Max in Love) written and illustrated by Maira Kalman; Viking, 1991.

Diego by Jonah Winter, illustrated by Jeanette Winter; Knopf, 1991.

Old Mother Hubbard and Her Wonderful Dog by Sarah Catherine Martin, illustrated by James Marshall; Farrar, Straus, Giroux, 1991.

What Can Rabbit Hear? written and illustrated by Lucy Cousins; Tambourine Books, 1991.

Tar Beach written and illustrated by Faith Ringgold; Crown, 1991.

The Marvelous Journey Through the Night written and illustrated by Helme Heine; Farrar, Straus, Giroux, 1990.

Little Red Riding Hood retold and illustrated by Beni Montresor; Doubleday, 1991.

1992 *Li'l Sis and Uncle Willie* by Gwen Everett, illustrated by William H. Johnson; Rizzoli, 1992.

Oscar deMejo's ABC written and illustrated by Oscar deMejo; HarperCollins, 1992.

Boodil my Dog written and illustrated by Pija Lindenbaum; Holt, 1992.

The Stinky Cheese Man and Other Fairly Stupid Tales by Jon Scieszka, illustrated by Lane Smith; Viking, 1992.

Mirette on the High Wire written and illustrated by Emily Arnold McCully; Putnam, 1992.

The Cataract of Lodore by Robert Southey, illustrated by David Catrow; Holt, 1992.

Martha Speaks written and illustrated by Susan Meddaugh; Houghton Mifflin, 1992.

The Fortune-Tellers by Lloyd Alexander, illustrated by Trina Schart Hyman; Dutton, 1992.

Where Does It Go? written and illustrated by Margaret Miller; Greenwillow, 1992.

Why the Sky Is Far Away by Mary-Joan Gerson, illustrated by Carla Golembe; Little Brown, 1992.

NEW YORK TIMES NOTABLE BOOKS

Children's Book Editor
New York Times Book Review
229 West 43 Street
New York, NY 10036

This is an annual list of the best of the books which appeared in the New York Times Book Review throughout the year. Prior to 1971, the juvenile titles were listed separately in the children's book column of the same issue. The list was previously called "New York Times Outstanding Books."

1971 *About Wise Men and Simpletons: Twelve Tales from Grimm* translated by Elizabeth Shub, illustrated by Nonny Hogrogian; Macmillan, 1971.

Amos and Boris written and illustrated by William Steig; Farrar, 1971.

The Bear and the People written and illustrated by Reiner Zimnik, translated by Nina Ignatowicz; Harper, 1971.

Bear Circus written and illustrated by William Pene duBois; Viking, 1971.

The Bear's House by Marilyn Sachs, illustrated by Louis Glanzman; Doubleday, 1971.

Father Fox's Pennyrhymes by Clyde Watson, illustrated by Wendy Watson; Crowell, 1971.

Gone and Back by Nathaniel Benchley, not illustrated; Harper, 1971.

The Master of Miracle: A New Novel of the Golem by Sulamith Ish-Kishor, illustrated by Arnold Lobel; Harper, 1971.

Mr. Gumpy's Outing written and illustrated by John Burningham; Cape, 1970; Holt, 1971.

A Room Made of Windows by Eleanor Cameron, illustrated by Trina Schart Hyman; Little Brown, 1971.

Wild in the World by John Donovan, not illustrated; Harper, 1971.

1972 *D'Aulaire's Trolls* written and illustrated by Edgar Parin D'Aulaire and Ingri D'Aulaire; Doubleday, 1972.

Fog by Mildred Lee, not illustrated; Seabury, 1972.

Frog and Toad Together written and illustrated by Arnold Lobel; Harper, 1972.

The Funny Little Woman by Arlene Mosel, illustrated by Blair Lent; Dutton, 1972.

George and Martha written and illustrated by James Marshall; Houghton Mifflin, 1972.

Goldengrove by Jill Paton Walsh, not illustrated; Farrar, 1972.

The Haunted Mountain by Mollie Hunter, illustrated by Laszlo Kubinyi; Harper, 1972.

Milton the Early Riser by Robert Kraus, illustrated by Ariane Aruego and Jose Aruego; Windmill, 1972.

Snow White and the Seven Dwarfs by Jacob Grimm and Wilhelm Grimm, translated by Randall Jarrell, illustrated by Nancy Ekholm Burkert; Farrar, 1972.

A Sound of Chariots by Mollie Hunter, not illustrated; Harper, 1972.

A Twister of Twists, a Tangler of Tongues by Alvin Schwartz, illustrated by Glen Rounds; Lippincott, 1972.

The Upstairs Room by Johanna Reiss, not illustrated; Crowell, 1972.

The Witches of Worm by Zilpha Keatley Snyder, illustrated by Alton Raible; Atheneum, 1972.

Zeek Silver Moon by Amy Ehrlich, illustrated by Robert A. Parker; Dial, 1972.

1973 *Duffy and the Devil* retold by Harve Zemach, illustrated by Margot Zemach; Farrar, 1973.

The Friends by Rosa Guy, not illustrated; Holt, 1973.

A Hero Ain't Nothin' but a Sandwich by Alice Childress, not illustrated; Coward McCann, 1973.

The House with a Clock in its Walls by John Bellairs, illustrated by Edward Gorey; Dial, 1973.

Nilda written and illustrated by Nicholasa Mohr; Harper, 1973.

A Prairie Boy's Winter written and illustrated by William Kurelek; Houghton Mifflin, 1973.

The Satanic Mill by Otfried Preussler, translated by Anthea Bell, not illustrated; Abelard-Schuman (London), 1972; Macmillan, 1973.

Summer of my German Soldier by Bette Greene, not illustrated; Dial, 1973.

Tomfoolery, Trickery and Foolery with Words collected by Alvin Schwartz, illustrated by Glen Rounds; Lippincott, 1973.

The Treasure Is the Rose by Julia Cunningham, illustrated by Judy Graese; Pantheon, 1973.

The Whys and Wherefores of Littabelle Lee by Bill Cleaver and Vera Cleaver; Atheneum, 1973.

1974 *A Carrot for a Nose* by M.J. Gladstone, illustrated with photographs and drawings; Scribner, 1974.

Child of Fire by Scott O'Dell, not illustrated; Houghton Mifflin, 1974.

Dawn written and illustrated by Uri Shulevitz; Farrar, 1974.

The Chocolate War by Robert Cormier, not illustrated; Pantheon, 1974; Dell, 1975.

Jenny's Corner by Frederic Bell, illustrated by Zenowij Onyshkewych; Random House, 1974.

Lumberjack written and illustrated by William Kurelek; Houghton Mifflin, 1974.

M.C. Higgins, the Great by Virginia Hamilton, not illustrated; Macmillan, 1974.

Midnight Is a Place by Joan Aiken, not illustrated; Viking, 1974.

The Nargun and the Stars by Patricia Wrightson, not illustrated; Hutchinson, 1973.

Philip Hall Likes Me: I Reckon Maybe by Bette Greene, illustrated by Charles Lilly; Dial, 1974.

Squawk to the Moon, Little Goose by Edna Mitchell Preston, illustrated by Barbara Cooney; Viking, 1974.

Where the Sidewalk Ends poems and drawings by Shel Silverstein; Harper, 1974.

1975 *Anno's Alphabet: An Adventure in Imagination* written and illustrated by Mitsumasa Anno; Crowell, 1975.

Are All the Giants Dead? by Mary Norton, illustrated by Brian Froud; Harcourt, 1975.

Bert Breen's Barn by Walter D. Edmonds, not illustrated; Little, Brown, 1975.

Cakes and Custards: Children's Rhymes compiled by Brian Alderson, illustrated by Helen Oxenbury; Morrow, 1975.

The Dark Didn't Catch Me by Crystal Thrasher, not illustrated; Atheneum, 1975.

The Drac: French Tales of Dragons and Demons by Felice Holman and Nanine Valen, illustrated by Stephen Walker; Scribner, 1975.

Dragon, Dragon and other Timeless Tales by John Gardner, illustrated by Charles Shields; Knopf, 1975.

Dust of the Earth by Vera Cleaver and Bill Cleaver, not illustrated; Lippincott, 1975.

The Hundred Penny Box by Sharon Bell Mathis, illustrated by Leo Dillon and Diane Dillon; Viking, 1975.

Is That You, Miss Blue? by M.E. Kerr, not illustrated; Harper, 1975; Dell, 1976.

Jacob Two-Two Meets the Hooded Fang by Mordecai Richler, illustrated by Fritz Wegner; McClelland & Stewart, 1975.

The Kidnapping of the Coffee Pot by Kay Saari, illustrated by Henri Galeron; Quist, 1975.

One Winter Night in August and other Nonsense Jingles by X.J. Kennedy, illustrated by David McPhail; Atheneum, 1975.

Owl at Home written and illustrated by Arnold Lobel; Harper, 1975.

A Stranger Came Ashore: A Story of Suspense by Mollie Hunter, not illustrated; Harper, 1975.

Tuck Everlasting by Natalie Babbitt, not illustrated; Farrar, 1975.

When the Sky is Like Lace by Elinor Lander Horwitz, illustrated by Barbara Cooney; Harper, 1975.

Why Mosquitos Buzz in People's Ears: A West African Tale by Verna Aardema, illustrated by Leo Dillon and Diane Dillon; Dial, 1975.

1976 *Abel's Island* written and illustrated by William Steig; Farrar, 1976.

The Amazing Bone written and illustrated by William Steig; Farrar, 1976.

Battle in the Arctic Seas: The Story of Convoy PQ17 by Theodore Taylor, illustrated by Robert A. Parker; Harper, 1976.

Bible Stories You Can't Forget by Marshall Efron and Alfa-Betty Olsen, illustrated by Ron Barrett; Dutton, 1976; Dell, 1979.

Dear Bill, Remember Me? and other Stories by Norma Fox Mazer, not illustrated; Delacorte, 1976.

Diving for Roses by Patricia Windsor, not illustrated; Harper, 1976.

Freelon Starbird: Being a Narrative of the Extraordinary Hardships Suffered by an Accidental Soldier in a Beaten Army During the Autumn and Winter of 1776 by Richard F. Snow, illustrated by Ben F. Stahl; Houghton Mifflin, 1976.

Frog and Toad All Year written and illustrated by Arnold Lobel; Harper, 1976.

The Golem: A Jewish Legend written and illustrated by Beverly Brodsky McDermott; Lippincott, 1975.

The Lemming Condition by Alan Arkin, illustrated by Joan Sandin; Harper, 1976.

Merry Ever After: The Story of Two Medieval Weddings written and illustrated by Joe Lasker; Viking, 1976.

Mr. and Mrs. Pig's Evening Out written and illustrated by Mary Rayner; Atheneum, 1976.

The Mother Goose Book written and illustrated by Martin Provensen and Alice Provensen; Random House; Random House, 1976.

Peter Penny's Dance by Janet Quin-Harkin, illustrated by Anita Lobel; Dial, 1976.

A Year and a Day by William Mayne, illustrated by Krystyna Turska; Hamish Hamilton, 1976.

1977   No Juvenile titles chosen

1978   *Book of the Dun Cow* by Walter Wangerin, Jr., not illustrated; Harper, 1978.

Bored - Nothing to Do written and illustrated by Peter Spier; Doubleday, 1978.

Gentlehands by M.E. Kerr, not illustrated; Harper, 1978.

The Last Guru written and illustrated by Daniel Pinkwater; Dodd, Mead, 1978.

A Peaceable Kingdom: The Shaker Abecedarius written and illustrated by Martin Provensen and Alice Provensen; Viking, 1978.

Tawny by Chas Carner, illustrated by Donald Carrick; Macmillan, 1978.

To the Tune of the Hickory Stick by Robbie Branscum, not illustrated; Doubleday, 1978.

1979   *After the First Death* by Robert Cormier, not illustrated; Pantheon, 1979.

All Together Now by Sue Ellen Bridgers, not illustrated; Knopf, 1979.

The Disappearance by Rosa Guy, not illustrated; Delacorte, 1979.

The Garden of Abdul Gasazi written and illustrated by Chris Van Allsburg; Houghton, Mifflin, 1979.

Good-bye Chicken Little by Betsy Byars, not illustrated; Harper, 1979.

Inside my Feet: The Story of a Giant by Richard Kennedy, illustrated by Ronald Himler; Harper, 1979.

King Krakus and the Dragon written and illustrated by Janina Domanska; Greenwillow, 1979.

The Last Mission by Harry Mazer, not illustrated; Delacorte, 1979.

The New York Kid's Book: 170 Children's Writers and Artists Celebrate New York City by Catherine Edmonds and others, illustrated; Doubleday, 1979.

Ox-cart Man by Donald Hall, illustrated by Barbara Cooney; Viking, 1979.

The Pig's Wedding written and illustrated by Helme Heine; Atheneum, 1979, c1978.

Stonewall by Jean Fritz, illustrated by Stephen Gammell; Putnam, 1979.

Turkeylegs Thompson by Jean McCord, not illustrated; Atheneum, 1979.

Words by Heart by Ouida Sebestyen, not illustrated; Little, Brown, 1979; Bantam, 1981.

1980   *Anno's Italy* written and illustrated by Mitsumasa Anno; Collins, 1980.

Fables written and illustrated by Arnold Lobel; Harper, 1980.

Gorky Rises written and illustrated by William Steig; Farrar, 1980.

The Half-a-Moon Inn by Paul Fleischman, illustrated by Kathy Jacobi; Harper, 1980.

The Headless Horseman Rides Tonight: More Poems to Trouble Your Sleep by Jack Prelutsky, illustrated by Arnold Lobel; Harper, 1980.

Howard written and illustrated by James Stevenson; Greenwillow, 1980.

Jacob Have I Loved by Katherine Paterson, not illustrated; Crowell, 1980.

The Pigman's Legacy by Paul Zindel, not illustrated; Harper, 1980.

A Place Apart by Paula Fox, not illustrated; Farrar, 1980; Dent, 1981; New American Library, 1982.

Stone Fox by John Reynolds Gardiner, illustrated by Marcia Sewall; Crowell, 1980.

Three Days by Paxton Davis, illustrated; Atheneum, 1980.

Unbuilding written and illustrated by David Macaulay; Houghton Mifflin, 1980.

The War Between the Pitiful Teachers and the Splendid Kids by Stanley Kiesel, edited by Emilie McLeod, not illustrated; Dutton, 1980.

1981   *The Crane Wife* retold by Sumiko Yagawa, translated by Katherine Paterson, illustrated by Suekichi Akaba; Morrow, 1981.

A Fabulous Creature by Zilpha Keatley Snyder, not illustrated; Atheneum, 1981.

Flight: A Panorama of Aviation by Melvin B. Zisfein, illustrated by Robert Andrew Parker; Pantheon, 1979.

Homecoming by Cynthia Voigt, not illustrated; Atheneum, 1981.

The Indian in the Cupboard by Lynne Reid Banks, illustrated by Brock Cole; Doubleday, 1981.

Jumanji written and illustrated by Chris Van Allsburg; Houghton Mifflin, 1981.

Let the Circle Be Unbroken by Mildred D. Taylor, not illustrated; Dial, 1981.

McGoogan Moves the Mighty Rock written and illustrated by Dick Gackenbach; Harper, 1981.

The Marzipan Moon by Nancy Willard, illustrated by Marcia Sewall; Harcourt, 1981.

On Market Street by Arnold Lobel, illustrated by Anita Lobel; Greenwillow, 1981.

Outside Over There written and illustrated by Maurice Sendak; Harper, 1981.

Rainbow Jordan by Alice Childress, not illustrated; Coward McCann, 1981.

Stranger with my Face by Lois Duncan, not illustrated; Little Brown, 1981; Dell, 1982.

Traitor: The Case of Benedict Arnold by Jean Fritz, illustrated by John Andre; Putnam, 1981.

Where the Buffaloes Begin by Olaf Baker, illustrated by Stephen Gammell; Warne, 1981.

1982   *Airport* written and illustrated by Byron Barton; Crowell Jr. Books, 1982.

The Brooklyn Bridge: They Said it Couldn't Be Built by Judith St. George, illustrated with photographs; Putnam, 1982.

The Darkangel by Meredith Ann Pierce, not illustrated; Little, Brown, 1982.

Doctor DeSoto written and illustrated by William Steig; Farrar, 1982.

The Golem by Isaac Bashevis Singer, illustrated by Uri Shulevitz; Farrar, 1982.

Help! Let Me Out! by David Lord Porter, illustrated by David Macaulay; Houghton Mifflin, 1982.

Herbert Rowbarge by Natalie Babbitt, not illustrated; Farrar, 1982.

Homesick: My Own Story by Jean Fritz, illustrated with drawings by Margot Tomes and photographs; Putnam, 1982.

Jake and Honeybunch go to Heaven written and illustrated by Margot Zemach; Farrar, 1982.

Journey to the Planets by Patricia Lauber, illustrated with photographs; Crown, 1982.

Marked by Fire by Joyce Carol Thomas, not illustrated; Avon, 1982.

The Murder of Hound Dog Bates: a novel by Robbie Branscum, not illustrated; Viking, 1982.

The Philharmonic Gets Dressed by Karla Kuskin, illustrated by Marc Simont; Harper, 1982.

Sweet Whispers, Brother Rush by Virginia Hamilton, not illustrated; Philomel, 1982.

Terpin by Tor Seidler, not illustrated; Farrar, 1982.

The Two-thousand-pound Goldfish by Betsy Byars, not illustrated; Harper, 1982.

1983   *Anno's U.S.A.* written and illustrated by Mitsumasa Anno; Philomel, 1983.

Arnold of the Ducks written and illustrated by Mordicai Gerstein; Harper, 1983.

Beyond the Divide by Kathryn Lasky, illustrated with a map; Macmillan, 1983.

Dear Mr. Henshaw by Beverly Cleary, illustrated by Paul O. Zelinsky; Morrow, 1983.

The Glorious Flight: Across the Channel with Louis Bleriot written and illustrated by Alice Provensen and Martin Provensen; Viking, 1983.

I Will Call it Georgie's Blues: A novel by Suzanne Newton, not illustrated; Viking, 1983.

The Sign of the Beaver by Elizabeth George Speare, not illustrated; Houghton Mifflin, 1983.

The Silver Cow retold by Susan Cooper, illustrated by Warwick Hutton; Atheneum, 1983.

The Witches by Roald Dahl, illustrated by Quentin Blake; Cape, 1983; Farrar, 1983.

The Wreck of the Zephyr written and illustrated by Chris Van Allsburg; Houghton Mifflin, 1983.

1984   *The Butter Battle Book* written and illustrated by Dr. Seuss; Random House, 1984.

Downtown by Norma Fox Mazer, not illustrated; Morrow, 1984.

I Walk and Read written and illustrated by Tana Hoban; Greenwillow, 1984.

The Iron Lion by Peter Dickinson, illustrated by Pauline Baynes; Bedrick/Blackie, 1984.

Jonah and the Great Fish written and illustrated by Warwick Hutton; Atheneum, 1984.

The Moves Make the Man by Bruce Brooks, not illustrated; Harper, 1984.

One-eyed Cat by Paula Fox, not illustrated; Bradbury, 1984.

Ramona Forever by Beverly Cleary, illustrated by Alan Tiegreen; Morrow, 1984.

Stories for Children by Isaac Bashevis Singer, not illustrated; Farrar, 1984.

Where the River Begins written and illustrated by Thomas Locker; Dial, 1984.

1985   *Beyond the Chocolate War* by Robert Cormier, not illustrated; Knopf, 1985.

Come Sing, Jimmy Jo by Katherine Paterson, not illustrated; Lodestar, 1985.

Once There Was a Tree by Natalia Romanov, illustrated by Gennady Spirin; Dial, 1985.

The People Could Fly by Virginia Hamilton, illustrated by Leo Dillon and Diane Dillon; Knopf, 1985.

Sarah, Plain and Tall by Patricia MacLachlan, not illustrated; Harper, 1985.

Seasons of Splendour by Madhur Jaffrey, illustrated by Michael Foreman; Atheneum, 1985.

The Story of Mrs. Lovewright and Purrless her Cat by Lore Segal, illustrated by Paul O. Zelinsky; Knopf, 1985.

What's Inside: The Alphabet Book written and illustrated by Satoshi Kitamura; Farrar, 1985.

Whiskers and Rhymes written and illustrated by Arnold Lobel; Greenwillow, 1985.

The Year it Rained by Crescent Dragonwagon, not illustrated; Macmillan, 1985.

1986   *Dinosaurs Divorce: A Guide for Changing Families* written and illustrated by Laurene Krasny Brown and Marc Brown; Atlantic Monthly, 1986.

Hugh Pine and the Good Place by Janwillem Van de Wetering, illustrated by Lynn Munsinger; Houghton Mifflin, 1986.

Make Way for Sam Houston by Jean Fritz, illustrated by Elise Primavera; Putnam, 1986.

The Moonlight Man by Paula Fox, not illustrated; Bradbury, 1986.

Moses in the Bulrushes written and illustrated by Warwick Hutton; Atheneum, 1986.

Pigs from A to Z written and illustrated by Arthur Geisert; Houghton Mifflin, 1986.

The Random House Book of Mother Goose written and illustrated by Arnold Lobel; Random House, 1986.

The Return of the Indian by Lynn Reid Banks, illustrated by William Geldart; Doubleday, 1986.

Tales of a Gambling Grandma written and illustrated by Dayal Kaur Khalsa; Clarkson N. Potter, 1986.

What Happened to Patrick's Dinosaurs by Carol Carrick, illustrated by Donald Carrick; Clarion Books, 1986.

1987 *The Book of Adam to Moses* by Lore Segal, illustrated by Leonard Baskin; Knopf, 1987.

Fox's Dream written and illustrated by [Keizaburo] Tejima; Philomel, 1987.

The Goats written and illustrated by Brock Cole; Farrar, 1987.

The Gold Cadillac by Mildred D. Taylor, illustrated by Michael Hays; Dial, 1987.

In Coal Country by Judith Hendershot, illustrated by Thomas B. Allen; Knopf, 1987.

Isaac Campion written and illustrated by Janni Howker; Greenwillow, 1986.

The Mountains of Tibet written and illustrated by Mordicai Gerstein; Harper, 1987.

The Ridiculous Story of Gammer Gurton's Needle by David Lloyd, illustrated by Charlotte Voake; Clarkson N. Potter/Crown, 1987.

The Shadowmaker by Ron Hansen, illustrated by Margot Tomes; Harper, 1987.

The Tricksters by Margaret Mahy, not illustrated; McElderry, 1987.

NEW ZEALAND LIBRARY ASSOCIATION YOUNG PEOPLE'S NON FICTION MEDAL

New Zealand Library Association
20 Brandon St.
P O Box 12-212
Wellington, New Zealand

Established by the New Zealand Library Association in 1986 to honor a work that is considered to be a distinguished contribution to non fiction for young people. Eligible are non fiction works published in the preceding calendar year by writers and artists who are citizens of, or resident in New Zealand. The winner receives a medal, accompanied by a monetary prize.

1987 *Gaijain: Foreign Children of Japan* by Olive Hill and Ngaio Hill.

1988 No Award

1989 *It's OK To Be You! Feeling Good About Growing Up* by Claire Patterson, illustrated by Lindsay Quilter; Century Hutchinson, 1988.

1990 *The Web: The Triumph of a New Zealand Girl Over Anorexia* by Deborah Furley; Collins, 1989.

1991 *Model Boats that Really Go* by John Reid, illustrated; Random Century New Zealand, 1990.

1992 *The Damselfly* by Peter Garland; Arncliffe, 1990.

1993 *Albatross Adventure* by Kim Westerskov.

JOHN NEWBERY MEDAL

Association for Library Services to Children
American Library Association
50 East Huron Street
Chicago, IL 60611

Awarded annually since 1922, the Newbery Medal is administered by the Association for Library Services to Children (ALSC) of the American Library Association. Donated by the Frederic G. Melcher family, the award is named for the 18th century English publisher and bookseller John Newbery. The original purpose of the Newbery Medal is to encourage original and creative work in the field of books for children and to emphasize to the public that literature for children deserves recognition.

The Newbery Medal is presented to the author of the most distinguished contribution to American literature for children published in the United States during the preceding year. The award is restricted to citizens or residents of the U.S., although there are no limitations as to the character of the book. The recipient is chosen by a selection committee consisting of eight elected and seven appointed members from the ALSC. In addition to the winner, honor books are also cited. The winners are announced in January at the ALA Midwinter meeting and the awards are presented at the Newbery-Caldecott banquet held in June at the ALA annual convention. The winner receives a gold medal and the honor-book recipients are presented with certificates.

The ALSC has provided the following definitions for words and phrases used in the terms of the award. They are as follows: (1) "Contribution to American literature" indicates the text of the book. This also implies that fiction, nonfiction, and poetry are to be considered. Reprints and compilations are not eligible. (2) "Literature for children" indicates that the books selected were written for children as a potential audience. The book should have respect for children's understandings, abilities, and appreciations. Children are defined as up to and including age fourteen. (3) "Distinguished" is defined as being marked by eminence and distinction, excellence in quality, or conspicuous excellence or eminence. The book may be individually distinct.

In order to identify distinguished writing in a book for children the committee members need to consider the following criteria: interpretation of theme or concept; presentation of information including accuracy, clarity, and organization; development of plot; delineation of characters; delineation of setting, and appropriateness of style.

Each book is to be considered as a contribution to literature. The committee is to make its decision primarily on the text. Other aspects are to be considered only if they distract from the text. Such other aspects might include illustration or book design. The award is for literary quality and quality of presentation for children. It is not for didactic intent or popularity. (From criteria adopted by the ALSC Board in January 1978).

1922 *The Story of Mankind* written and illustrated by Hendrik Willem Van Loon; Boni & Liveright, 1921.

1922 **HONOR** *Cedric the Forester* by Bernard G. Marshall, not illustrated; Appleton, 1921.

The Golden Fleece and the Heroes Who Lived before Achilles by Padraic Colum, illustrated by Willy Pogany; Macmillan, 1921.

The Great Quest!: A Romance of 1826 by Charles Boardman Hawes, illustrated by George Varian; Little, 1921.

The Old Tobacco Shop: A True Account of what Befell a Little Boy in Search of Adventure written and illustrated by William A. Bowen; Macmillan, 1921.

Windy Hill by Cornelia Meigs, not illustrated; Macmillan, 1921.

1923 *The Voyages of Doctor Dolittle* written and illustrated by Hugh Lofting; Stokes, 1922.

1923 **HONOR** No Record

1924 *The Dark Frigate* by Charles Boardman Hawes, illustrated by A.L. Ripley; Atlantic Monthly Press, 1923; Little, 1934.

1924 **HONOR** No Record

1925 *Tales from Silver Lands* by Charles J. Finger, illustrated by Paul Honore; Doubleday, 1924.

1925 **HONOR** *Dream Coach* written and illustrated by Anne Parrish and Dillwyn Parrish; Macmillan, 1924.

Nicholas: A Manhattan Christmas Story by Anne Carroll Moore, illustrated by Jan Van Everen; Putnam, 1924.

1926 *Shen of the Sea: A Book for Children* by Arthur Bowie Chrisman, illustrated by Else Hasselriis; Dutton, 1925.

1926 **HONOR** *The Voyagers: Being Legends and Romances of Atlantic Discovery* by Padraic Colum, illustrated by Wilfred Jones; Macmillan, 1925.

1927 *Smoky, the Cowhorse* written and illustrated by Will James; Scribner, 1926.

1927 **HONOR** No Record

1928 *Gay-neck: The Story of a Pigeon* by Dhan Gopal Mukerji, illustrated by Boris Artzybasheff; Dutton, 1927.

1928 **HONOR** *Downright Dencey* by Caroline Dale Snedeker, illustrated by Maginel W. Barney; Doubleday, 1927.

The Wonder-smith and His Son: A Tale from the Golden Childhood of the World by Ella Young, illustrated by Boris Artzybasheff; Longmans, 1927.

1929 *Trumpeter of Krakow* by Eric P. Kelly, illustrated by Angela Pruszynska; Macmillan, 1928.

1929 **HONOR** *The Boy Who Was* by Grace T. Hallock, illustrated by Harrie Wood; Dutton, 1928.

Clearing Weather by Cornelia Meigs, illustrated by Frank Dobias; Little, 1928.

Millions of Cats written and illustrated by Wanda Gag; Coward, 1928.

The Pigtail of Ah Lee Ben Loo with Seventeen other Laughable Tales and 200 Comical Silhouettes written and illustrated by John Bennett; Longmans, 1928.

The Runaway Papoose by Grace P. Moon, illustrated by Carl Moon; Doubleday, 1928.

Tod of the Fens by Elinor Whitney, illustrated by Warwick Goble; Macmillan, 1928.

1930 *Hitty, her First Hundred Years* by Rachel Field, illustrated by Dorothy P. Lathrop; Macmillan, 1929.

1930 **HONOR** *A Daughter of the Seine: The Life of Madame Roland* by Jeanette Eaton, not illustrated; Harper, 1929.

Jumping-off Place by Marian Hurd McNeely, illustrated by William Siegel; Longmans, 1929.

Little Blacknose: The Story of a Pioneer by Hildegarde Swift, illustrated by Lynd Ward; Harcourt, 1929.

Pran of Albania by Elizabeth C. Miller, illustrated by Maud Petersham and Miska Petersham; Doubleday, 1929.

Tangle-coated Horse and other Tales: Episodes from the Fionn Saga by Ella Young, illustrated by Vera Bock; Longmans, 1929.

Vaino, a Boy of New Finland by Julia Davis Adams, illustrated by Lempi Ostman; Dutton, 1929.

1931 *The Cat Who Went to Heaven* by Elizabeth Coatsworth, illustrated by Lynd Ward; Macmillan, 1930.

1931 **HONOR** *The Dark Star of Itza* by Alida Malkus, illustrated by Lowell Houser; Harcourt, 1930.

Floating Island written and illustrated by Anne Parrish; Harper, 1930.

Garram the Hunter: A Boy of the Hill Tribes by Herbert Best, illustrated by Erick Berry; Doubleday, Doran, 1930.

Meggy MacIntosh by Elizabeth Janet Gray, illustrated by Marguerite de Angeli; Doubleday, 1930.

Mountains are Free by Julia Davis Adams, illustrated by Theodore Nadejen; Dutton, 1930.

Ood-Le-Uk the Wanderer by Alice Lide and Margaret Johansen, illustrated by Raymond Lufkin; Little, 1930.

Queer Person by Ralph Hubbard, illustrated by Harold Von Schmidt; Doubleday, 1930.

Spice and the Devil's Cave by Agnes D. Hewes, illustrated by Lynd Ward; Knopf, 1930.

1932 *Waterless Mountain* by Laura Adams Armer, illustrated by Sidney Armer and Laura Adams Armer; Longmans, 1931.

1932 **HONOR** *Boy of the South Seas* by Eunice Tietjens, illustrated by Myrtle Sheldon; Coward, 1931.

Calico Bush by Rachel Field, illustrated by Allen Lewis; Macmillan, 1931.

The Fairy Circus written and illustrated by Dorothy P. Lathrop; Macmillan, 1931.

Jane's Island by Marjorie Hill Allee, illustrated by Maitland de Gogorza; Houghton, 1931.

Out of the Flame by Eloise Lownsbery, illustrated by Elizabeth T. Wolcott; Longmans, 1931.

Truce of the Wolf and other Tales of Old Italy by Mary Gould Davis, illustrated by Jay Van Everen; Harcourt, 1931.

1933 *Young Fu of the Upper Yangtze* by Elizabeth Foreman Lewis, illustrated by Kurt Wiese; Winston, 1932.

1933 **HONOR** *Children of the Soil: A Story of Scandinavia* by Nora Burglon, illustrated by E. Parin d'Aulaire; Doubleday, Doran, 1932.

The Railroad to Freedom: A Story of the Civil War by Hildegarde Swift, illustrated by James Daugherty; Harcourt, 1932.

Swift Rivers by Cornelia Meigs, illustrated by Peter Hurd; Little, 1932.

1934 *Invincible Louisa: The Story of the Author of Little Women* by Cornelia Meigs, illustrated with photographs; Little, 1961, 1933.

1934 **HONOR** *ABC Bunny* written and illustrated by Wanda Gag; Coward, 1933.

Apprentices of Florence by Anne Kyle, illustrated by Erick Berry; Houghton, 1933.

Big Tree of Bunlahy: Stories of my Own Countryside by Padraic Colum, illustrated by Jack Yeats; Macmillan, 1933.

Forgotten Daughter by Caroline Dale Snedeker, illustrated by Dorothy P. Lathrop; Doubleday, 1933.

Glory of the Seas by Agnes Hewes, illustrated by N.C. Wyeth; Knopf, 1933.

New Land by Sarah L. Schmidt, illustrated by Frank Dobias; McBride, 1933.

Swords of Steel: The Story of a Gettysburg Boy by Elsie Singmaster, illustrated by David Hendrickson; Houghton, 1933.

Winged Girl of Knossos written and illustrated by Erick Berry; Appleton-Century, 1933.

1935 *Dobry* by Monica Shannon, illustrated by Atanas Katchamakoff; Viking, 1934.

1935 HONOR *Davy Crockett* by Constance Rourke, illustrated by James MacDonald; Harcourt, 1934.

A Day on Skates: The Story of a Dutch Picnic written and illustrated by Hilda Van Stockum; Harper, 1934.

The Pageant of Chinese History by Elizabeth Seeger, illustrated by Bernard Watkins; Longmans, 1934.

1936 *Caddie Woodlawn* by Carol Ryrie Brink, illustrated by Kate Seredy; Macmillan, 1935.

1936 HONOR *All Sail Set: A Romance of the "Flying Cloud"* written and illustrated by Armstrong Sperry; Winston, 1935.

The Good Master written and illustrated by Kate Seredy; Viking, 1935.

Honk the Moose by Phil Stong, illustrated by Kurt Wiese; Dodd, 1935.

Young Walter Scott by Elizabeth Janet Gray, illustrated by Kate Seredy; Viking, 1935.

1937 *Roller Skates* by Ruth Sawyer, illustrated by Valenti Angelo; Viking, 1936.

1937 HONOR *Audubon* by Constance M. Rourke, illustrated by James MacDonald; Harcourt, 1936.

The Codfish Musket by Agnes D. Hewes, illustrated by Armstrong Sperry; Doubleday, 1936.

The Golden Basket written and illustrated by Ludwig Bemelmans; Viking, 1936.

Phebe Fairchild: Her Book written and illustrated by Lois Lenski; Lippincott, 1936.

Whistler's Van by Idwal Jones, illustrated by Zhenya Gay; Viking, 1936.

Winterbound by Margery Bianco, illustrated by Kate Seredy; Viking, 1936.

1938 *The White Stag* written and illustrated by Kate Seredy; Viking, 1937.

1938 HONOR *Bright Island* by Mabel L. Robinson, illustrated by Lynd Ward; Random House, 1937.

On the Banks of Plum Creek by Laura Ingalls Wilder, illustrated by Mildred Boyle and Helen Sewell; Harper, 1937.

Pecos Bill: The Greatest Cowboy of all Time by James Cloyd Bowman, illustrated by Laura Bannon; Whitman, 1937.

1939 *Thimble Summer* written and illustrated by Elizabeth Enright; Farrar, 1938.

1939 HONOR *Hello, the Boat!* by Phyllis Crawford, illustrated by Edward Laning; Holt Rinehart & Winston, 1938.

Leader by Destiny: George Washington, Man and Patriot by Jeanette Eaton, illustrated by J.M. Rose; Harcourt, 1938.

Mr. Popper's Penguins by Richard Atwater and Florence Atwater, illustrated by Robert Lawson; Little Brown, 1938.

Nino written and illustrated by Valenti Angelo; Viking, 1938.

Penn by Elizabeth Janet Gray, illustrated by George G. Whitney; Viking, 1938.

1940 *Daniel Boone* written and illustrated by James H. Daugherty; Viking, 1939.

1940 HONOR *Boy with a Pack* by Stephen W. Meader, illustrated by Edward Shenton; Harcourt, 1939.

By the Shores of Silver Lake by Laura Ingalls Wilder, illustrated by Helen Sewell and Mildred Boyle; Harper, 1939.

Runner of the Mountain Tops: The Life of Louis Agassiz by Mabel L. Robinson; illustrated by Lynd Ward; Random House, 1939.

The Singing Tree written and illustrated by Kate Seredy; Viking, 1939.

1941 *Call It Courage* written and illustrated by Armstrong Sperry; Macmillan, 1940.

1941 HONOR *Blue Willow* by Doris Gates, illustrated by Paul Lantz; Viking, 1940.

The Long Winter by Laura Ingalls Wilder, illustrated by Helen Sewell and Mildred Boyle; Harper, 1940.

Nansen by Anna Gertrude Hall, illustrated by Boris Artzybasheff; Viking, 1940.

Young Mac of Fort Vancouver by Mary Jane Carr, illustrated by Richard Holberg; Crowell, 1940.

1942 *The Matchlock Gun* by Walter D. Edmonds, illustrated by Paul Lantz; Dodd, 1941.

1942 HONOR *Down Ryton Water* by Eva Roe Gaggin, illustrated by Elmer Hader; Viking, 1941.

George Washington's World written and illustrated by Genevieve Foster; Scribner, 1941.

Indian Captive: The Story of Mary Jemison written and illustrated by Lois Lenski; Stokes, 1941.

Little Town on the Prairie by Laura Ingalls Wilder, illustrated by Mildred Boyle and Helen Sewell; Harper, 1941.

1943 *Adam of the Road* by Elizabeth Janet Gray, illustrated by Robert Lawson; Viking, 1942.

1943 HONOR *Have You Seen Tom Thumb?* by Mabel Leigh Hunt, illustrated by Fritz Eichenberg; Stokes, 1942.

The Middle Moffat by Eleanor Estes, illustrated by Louis Slobodkin; Harcourt, 1942.

1944 *Johnny Tremain* by Esther Forbes, illustrated by Lynd Ward; Houghton Mifflin, 1943.

1944 HONOR *Fog Magic* by Julia L. Sauer, illustrated by Lynd Ward; Viking, 1943.

Mountain Born by Elizabeth Yates, illustrated by Nora S. Unwin; Coward, 1943.

Rufus M. by Eleanor Estes, illustrated by Louis Slobodkin; Harcourt, 1943.

These Happy Golden Years by Laura Ingalls Wilder, illustrated by Mildred Boyle and Helen Sewell; Harper, 1943.

1945 *Rabbit Hill* written and illustrated by Robert Lawson; Viking, 1944.

1945 HONOR *Abraham Lincoln's World* written and illustrated by Genevieve Foster; Scribner, 1944.

The Hundred Dresses by Eleanor Estes, illustrated by Louis Slobodkin; Harcourt, 1944.

Lone Journey: The Life of Roger Williams by Jeanette Eaton, illustrated by Woodi Ishmael; Harcourt, 1944.

The Silver Pencil by Alice Dalgliesh, illustrated by Katherine Milhous; Scribner, 1944.

1946 *Strawberry Girl* written and illustrated by Lois Lenski; Lippincott, 1945.

1946 HONOR *Bhimsa, the Dancing Bear* by Christine Weston, illustrated by Roger Duvoisin; Scribner, 1945.

Justin Morgan Had a Horse by Marguerite Henry, illustrated by Wesley Dennis; Wilcox & Follett, 1945.

The Moved-outers by Florence Crannell Means, illustrated by Helen Blair; Houghton, 1945.

New Found World by Katherine B. Shippen, illustrated by C. B. Falls; Viking, 1945.

1947 *Miss Hickory* by Carolyn Sherwin Bailey, illustrated by Ruth Chrisman Gannett; Viking, 1946.

1947 HONOR *The Avion my Uncle Flew* by Cyrus Fisher, illustrated by Richard Floethe; Appleton, 1946.

Big Tree written and illustrated by Mary Buff and Conrad Buff; Viking, 1946.

The Heavenly Tenants by William Maxwell, illustrated by Ilonka Karasz; Harper, 1946.

The Hidden Treasure of Glaston by Eleanore Myers Jewett, illustrated by Frederick T. Chapman; Viking, 1946.

The Wonderful Year by Nancy Barnes, illustrated by Kate Seredy; Messner, 1946.

1948 *The Twenty One Balloons* written and illustrated by William Pene du Bois; Viking, 1947.

1948 HONOR *Cow-tail Switch and other West African Stories* by George Herzog and Harold Courlander, illustrated by Madye Lee Chastain; Holt, 1947.

Li Lun, Lad of Courage by Carolyn Treffinger, illustrated by Kurt Wiese; Abingdon-Cokesbury, 1947.

Misty of Chincoteague by Marguerite Henry, illustrated by Wesley Dennis; Rand McNally, 1947.

Pancakes-Paris by Claire H. Bishop, illustrated by Georges Schreiber; Viking, 1947.

The Quaint and Curious Quest of Johnny Longfoot, the Shoe King's Son by Catherine Besterman, illustrated by Warren Chappell; Bobb-Merrill, 1947.

1949 *King of the Wind* by Marguerite Henry, illustrated by Wesley Dennis; Rand McNally, 1948.

1949 HONOR *Daughter of the Mountains* by Louise S. Rankin, illustrated by Kurt Wiese; Viking, 1948.

My Father's Dragon by Ruth Stiles Gannett, illustrated by Ruth Chrisman Gannett; Random House, 1948.

Seabird written and illustrated by Holling Clancy Holling; Houghton, 1948.

Story of the Negro by Arna Wendall Bontemps, illustrated by Raymond Lufkin; Knopf, 1948.

1950 *The Door in the Wall: Story of Medieval London* written and illustrated by Marguerite de Angeli; Doubleday, 1949.

1950 HONOR *The Blue Cat of Castle Town* by Catherine C. Coblentz, illustrated by Janice Holland; Longmans, 1949.

George Washington: An Initial Biography written and illustrated by Genevieve Foster; Scribner, 1949.

Kildee House by Rutherford G. Montgomery, illustrated by Barbara Cooney; Doubleday, 1949.

Song of the Pines: A Story of Norwegian Lumbering in Wisconsin by Walter Havighurst and Marion Havighurst, illustrated by Richard Floethe; Winston, 1949.

Tree of Freedom by Rebecca Caudill, illustrated by Dorothy B. Morse; Viking, 1949.

1951 *Amos Fortune, Free Man* by Elizabeth Yates, illustrated by Nora S. Unwin; Aladdin, 1950.

1951 HONOR *Abraham Lincoln, Friend of the People* by Clara Ingram Judson, illustrated by Robert Frankenberg; Wilcox & Follett, 1950.

Better Known as Johnny Appleseed by Mabel Leigh Hunt, illustrated by James Daugherty; Lippincott, 1950.

Gandhi, Fighter without a Sword by Jeanette Eaton, illustrated by Ralph Ray; Morrow, 1950.

The Story of Appleby Capple written and illustrated by Anne Parrish; Harper, 1950.

1952 *Ginger Pye* written and illustrated by Eleanor Estes; Harcourt, 1951.

1952 HONOR *Americans Before Columbus* by Elizabeth Chesley Baity, illustrated by C.B. Falls; Viking, 1951.

The Apple and the Arrow written and illustrated by Conrad Buff and Mary Buff; Houghton, 1951.

The Defender by Nicholas Kalashnikoff, illustrated by Claire Louden and George Louden; Scribner, 1951.

The Light at Tern Rock by Julia L. Sauer, illustrated by Georges Schreiber; Viking, 1951.

Minn of the Mississippi written and illustrated by Holling Clancy Holling; Houghton, 1951.

1953 *Secret of the Andes* by Ann Nolan Clark, illustrated by Jean Charlot; Viking, 1952.

1953 HONOR *The Bears on Hemlock Mountain* by Alice Dalgliesh, illustrated by Helen Sewell; Scribner, 1952.

Birthdays of Freedom: America's Heritage from the Ancient World written and illustrated by Genevieve Foster; Scribner, 1952.

Charlotte's Web by E.B. White, illustrated by Garth Williams; Harper, 1952.

Moccasin Trail by Eloise Jarvis McGraw, illustrated by Paul Galdone; Coward, 1952.

Red Sails to Capri by Ann Weil, illustrated by C.B. Falls; Viking, 1952.

1954 *And Now Miguel* by Joseph Krumgold, illustrated by Jean Charlot; Crowell, 1953.

1954 **HONOR** *All Alone* by Claire Huchet Bishop, illustrated by Feodor Rojankovsky; Viking, 1953.

Hurry Home, Candy by Meindert DeJong, illustrated by Maurice Sendak; Harper, 1953.

Magic Maize written and illustrated by Conrad Buff and Mary Buff; Houghton, 1953.

Shadrach by Meindert DeJong, illustrated by Maurice Sendak; Harper, 1953.

Theodore Roosevelt, Fighting Patriot by Clara Ingram Judson, illustrated by Lorence F. Bjorklund; Follett, 1953.

1955 *The Wheel on the School* by Meindert DeJong, illustrated by Maurice Sendak; Harper, 1954.

1955 **HONOR** *Banner in the Sky: The Story of a Boy and a Mountain* by James Ramsey Ullman, not illustrated; Lippincott, 1954.

The Courage of Sarah Noble by Alice Dalgliesh, illustrated by Leonard Weisgard; Scribner, 1954.

1956 *Carry On, Mr. Bowditch* by Jean Lee Latham, illustrated by J. O. Cosgrove; Houghton, 1955.

1956 **HONOR** *The Golden Name Day* by Jennie D. Lindquist, illustrated by Garth Williams; Harper, 1955.

Men, Microscopes and Living Things by Katherine B. Shippen, illustrated by Anthony Ravielli; Viking, 1955.

The Secret River by Marjorie Kinnan Rawlings, illustrated by Leonard Weisgard; Scribner, 1955.

1957 *Miracles on Maple Hill* by Virginia Sorensen, illustrated by Beth Krush and Joe Krush; Harcourt, 1956.

1957 **HONOR** *The Black Fox of Lorne* written and illustrated by Marguerite de Angeli; Doubleday, 1956.

The Corn Grows Ripe by Dorothy Rhoads, illustrated by Jean Charlot; Viking, 1956.

The House of Sixty Fathers by Meindert DeJong, illustrated by Maurice Sendak; Harper, 1956.

Mr. Justice Holmes by Clara Ingram Judson, illustrated by Robert Todd; Follett, 1956.

Old Yeller by Fred Gipson, illustrated by Carl Burger; Harper, 1956.

1958 *Rifles for Watie* by Harold Keith, illustrated by Peter Burchard; Crowell, 1957.

1958 **HONOR** *Gone-away Lake* by Elizabeth Enright, illustrated by Beth Krush and Joe Krush; Harcourt, 1957.

The Great Wheel written and illustrated by Robert Lawson; Viking, 1957.

The Horsecatcher by Mari Sandoz, not illustrated; Westminster, 1957.

Tom Paine, Freedom's Apostle by Leo Gurko, illustrated by Fritz Kredel; Crowell, 1957.

1959 *The Witch of Blackbird Pond* by Elizabeth George Speare, not illustrated; Houghton, 1958.

1959 **HONOR** *Along Came a Dog* by Meindert DeJong, illustrated by Maurice Sendak; Harper, 1958.

Chucaro: Wild Pony of the Pampa by Francis Kalnay, illustrated by Julian DeMiskey; Harcourt, 1958.

The Family under the Bridge by Natalie Savage Carlson, illustrated by Garth Williams; Harper, 1958.

The Perilous Road by William O. Steele, illustrated by Paul Galdone; Harcourt, 1958.

1960 *Onion John* by Joseph Krumgold, illustrated by Symeon Shimin; Crowell, 1959.

1960 **HONOR** *America Is Born: A History for Peter* by Gerald W. Johnson, illustrated by Leonard Everett Fisher; Morrow, 1959.

The Gammage Cup by Carol Kendall, illustrated by Erik Blegvad; Harcourt, 1959.

My Side of the Mountain written and illustrated by Jean Craighead George; Dutton, 1959.

1961 *Island of the Blue Dolphins* by Scott O'Dell, not illustrated; Houghton, 1960.

1961 **HONOR** *America Moves Forward: A History for Peter* by Gerald W. Johnson, illustrated by Leonard Everett Fisher; Morrow, 1960.

The Cricket in Times Square by George Selden, illustrated by Garth Williams; Farrar, 1960.

Old Ramon by Jack Schaefer, illustrated by Harold West; Houghton, 1960.

1962 *The Bronze Bow* by Elizabeth George Speare, not illustrated; Houghton, 1961.

1962 **HONOR** *Belling the Tiger* by Mary Stolz, illustrated by Beni Montresor; Harper, 1961.

Frontier Living written and illustrated by Edwin Tunis; World, 1961.

The Golden Goblet by Eloise Jarvis McGraw, not illustrated; Coward, 1961.

1963 *A Wrinkle in Time* by Madeleine L'Engle, not illustrated; Farrar, 1962.

1963 **HONOR** *Men of Athens* by Olivia Coolidge, illustrated by Milton Johnson; Houghton, 1962.

Thistle and Thyme: Tales and Legends from Scotland by Sorche Nic Leodhas, illustrated by Evaline Ness; Holt, 1962.

1964 *It's Like This, Cat* by Emily Cheney Neville, illustrated by Emil Weiss; Harper, 1963.

1964 **HONOR** *The Loner* by Ester Wier, illustrated by Christine Price; McKay, 1963.

Rascal: A Memoir of a Better Era by Sterling North, illustrated by John Schoenherr; Dutton, 1963.

1965 *Shadow of a Bull* by Maia Wojciechowska, illustrated by Alvin Smith; Atheneum, 1964.

1965 HONOR *Across Five Aprils* by Irene Hunt, illustrated by Albert J. Pucci; Follett, 1964.

1966 *I, Juan de Pareja* by Elizabeth Borton de Trevino, not illustrated; Farrar, 1965.

1966 HONOR *The Animal Family* by Randall Jarrell, illustrated by Maurice Sendak; Pantheon, 1965.

The Black Cauldron by Lloyd Alexander, not illustrated; Holt, 1965.

The Noonday Friends by Mary Stolz, illustrated by Louis Glanzman; Harper, 1965.

1967 *Up a Road Slowly* by Irene Hunt, not illustrated; Follett, 1966.

1967 HONOR *The Jazz Man* by Mary Hays Weik, illustrated by Ann Grifalconi; Atheneum, 1966.

The King's Fifth by Scott O'Dell, illustrated by Samuel Bryant; Houghton, 1966.

Zlateh the Goat and other Stories by Isaac Bashevis Singer, illustrated by Maurice Sendak; Harper, 1966.

1968 *From the Mixed-up Files of Mrs. Basil E. Frankweiler* written and illustrated by E.L. Konigsburg; Atheneum, 1967.

1968 HONOR *The Black Pearl* by Scott O'Dell, illustrated by Milton Johnson; Houghton, 1967.

The Egypt Game by Zilpha Keatley Snyder, illustrated by Alton Raible; Atheneum, 1967.

The Fearsome Inn by Isaac Bashevis Singer, illustrated by Nonny Hogrogian; Scribner, 1967.

Jennifer, Hecate, Macbeth, William McKinley, and Me, Elizabeth written and illustrated by E.L. Konigsburg; Atheneum, 1967.

1969 *The High King* by Lloyd Alexander, not illustrated; Holt, 1968.

1969 HONOR *To Be a Slave* by Julius Lester, illustrated by Tom Feelings; Dial, 1968.

When Schlemiel Went to Warsaw and other Stories by Isaac Bashevis Singer, illustrated by Margot Zemach; Farrar, 1968.

1970 *Sounder* by William H. Armstrong, illustrated by James Barkley; Harper, 1969.

1970 HONOR *Journey Outside* by Mary Q. Steele, illustrated by Rocco Negri; Viking, 1969.

The Many Ways of Seeing: An Introduction to the Pleasures of Art written and illustrated by Janet Gaylord Moore; Collins World, 1969.

Our Eddie by Sulamith Ish-Kishor, not illustrated; Pantheon, 1969.

1971 *Summer of the Swans* by Betsy Byars, illustrated by Ted CoConis; Viking, 1970.

1971 HONOR *Enchantress from the Stars* by Sylvia L. Engdahl, illustrated by Rodney Shackell; Atheneum, 1970.

Knee-knock Rise written and illustrated by Natalie Babbitt; Farrar, 1970.

Sing Down the Moon by Scott O'Dell, not illustrated; Houghton, 1970.

1972 *Mrs. Frisby and the Rats of NIMH* by Robert C. O'Brien, illustrated by Zena Bernstein; Atheneum, 1971.

1972 HONOR *Annie and the Old One* by Miska Miles, illustrated by Peter Parnall; Atlantic-Little, 1971.

The Headless Cupid by Zilpha Keatley Snyder, illustrated by Alton Raible; Atheneum, 1971.

Incident at Hawk's Hill by Allan W. Eckert, illustrated by John Schoenherr; Little, 1971.

The Planet of Junior Brown by Virginia Hamilton, not illustrated; Macmillan, 1971.

The Tombs of Atuan by Ursula K. LeGuin, illustrated by Gail Garraty; Atheneum, 1971.

1973 *Julie of the Wolves* by Jean Craighead George, illustrated by John Schoenherr; Harper, 1972.

1973 HONOR *Frog and Toad Together* written and illustrated by Arnold Lobel; Harper, 1972.

The Upstairs Room by Johanna Reiss, not illustrated; Crowell, 1972.

The Witches of Worm by Zilpha Keatley Snyder, illustrated by Alton Raible; Atheneum, 1972.

1974 *The Slave Dancer* by Paula Fox, illustrated by Eros Keith; Bradbury, 1973.

1974 HONOR *The Dark Is Rising* by Susan Cooper, illustrated by Alan Cober; Atheneum, 1973.

1975 *M.C. Higgins, the Great* by Virginia Hamilton, not illustrated; Macmillan, 1974.

1975 HONOR *Figgs and Phantoms* written and illustrated by Ellen Raskin; Dutton, 1974.

My Brother Sam Is Dead by James L. Collier and Christopher Collier, not illustrated; Four Winds/Scholastic, 1974.

The Perilous Gard by Elizabeth M. Pope, illustrated by Richard Cuffari; Houghton, 1974.

Philip Hall Likes Me: I Reckon Maybe by Bette Greene, illustrated by Charles Lilly; Dial, 1974.

1976 *The Grey King* by Susan Cooper, illustrated by Michael Heslop; Chatto & Windus, 1975; Atheneum, 1975.

1976 HONOR *Dragonwings* by Laurence Yep, not illustrated; Harper, 1975.

The Hundred Penny Box by Sharon Bell Mathis, illustrated by Leo Dillon and Diane Dillon; Viking, 1975.

1977 *Roll of Thunder, Hear My Cry* by Mildred D. Taylor, illustrated by Jerry Pinkney; Dial, 1976.

1977 HONOR *Abel's Island* written and illustrated by William Steig; Farrar, 1976.

A String in the Harp by Nancy Bond, illustrated by Allen Davis; Atheneum, 1976.

1978 *Bridge to Terabithia* by Katherine Paterson, illustrated by Donna Diamond; Crowell, 1977.

1978 HONOR *Anpao: An American Indian Odyssey* by Jamake Highwater, illustrated by Fritz Scholder; Lippincott, 1977.

Ramona and her Father by Beverly Cleary, illustrated by Alan Tiegreen; Morrow, 1977.

1979 *The Westing Game* by Ellen Raskin, not illustrated; Dutton, 1978.

1979 HONOR *The Great Gilly Hopkins* by Katherine Paterson, not illustrated; Crowell, 1978.

1980 *A Gathering of Days: A New England Girl's Journal, 1830-32* by Joan W. Blos, not illustrated; Scribner, 1979.

1980 HONOR *The Road from Home: The Story of an Armenian Girl* by David Kherdian, not illustrated; Greenwillow, 1979.

1981 *Jacob Have I Loved* by Katherine Paterson, not illustrated; Crowell, 1980.

1981 HONOR *The Fledgling* by Jane Langton, illustrated by Erik Blegvad; Harper, 1980.

Ring of Endless Light by Madeleine L'Engle, not illustrated; Farrar, 1980.

1982 *A Visit to William Blake's Inn: Poems for Innocent and Experienced Travelers* by Nancy Willard, illustrated by Alice Provensen and Martin Provensen; Harcourt, 1981.

1982 HONOR *Ramona Quimby, Age 8* by Beverly Cleary, illustrated by Alan Tiegreen; Morrow, 1981.

Upon the Head of a Goat: A Childhood in Hungary, 1939-1944 by Aranka Siegal, not illustrated; Farrar, 1981.

1983 *Dicey's Song* by Cynthia Voigt, not illustrated; Atheneum, 1982.

1983 HONOR *The Blue Sword* by Robin McKinley, not illustrated; Greenwillow, 1982.

Doctor DeSoto written and illustrated by William Steig; Farrar, 1982.

Graven Images: Three Stories by Paul Fleishman, illustrated by Andrew Glass; Harper, 1982.

Homesick: My Own Story by Jean Fritz, illustrated with drawings by Margot Tomes and photographs; Putnam, 1982.

Sweet Whispers, Brother Rush by Virginia Hamilton, not illustrated ; Philomel, 1982.

1984 *Dear Mr. Henshaw* by Beverly Cleary, illustrated by Paul O. Zelinsky; Morrow, 1983.

1984 HONOR *The Sign of the Beaver* by Elizabeth George Speare, not illustrated; Houghton Mifflin, 1983.

A Solitary Blue by Cynthia Voigt, not illustrated; Atheneum, 1983.

Sugaring Time by Kathryn Lasky, photographs by Christopher G. Knight; Macmillan, 1983.

The Wish Giver: Three Tales of Coven Tree by William Brittain, illustrated by Andrew Glass; Harper, 1983.

1985 *The Hero and the Crown* by Robin McKinley, not illustrated; Greenwillow, 1984.

1985 HONOR *Like Jake and Me* by Mavis Jukes, illustrated by Lloyd Bloom; Knopf, 1984.

The Moves Make the Man by Bruce Brooks, not illustrated; Harper, 1984.

One-eyed Cat by Paula Fox, not illustrated; Bradbury, 1984.

1986 *Sarah, Plain and Tall* by Patricia MacLachlan, not illustrated; Harper, 1985.

1986 HONOR *Commodore Perry in the Land of the Shogun* by Rhoda Blumberg, illustrated with photographs; Lothrop Lee & Shepard, 1985.

Dogsong by Gary Paulsen, not illustrated; Bradbury, 1985.

1987 *The Whipping Boy* by Sid Fleischman, illustrated by Peter Sis; Greenwillow, 1986.

1987 HONOR *On My Honor* by Marion Dane Bauer, not illustrated; Clarion, 1986.

Volcano: The Eruption and Healing of Mount St. Helens by Patricia Lauber, illustrated with photographs; Bradbury, 1986.

A Fine White Dust by Cynthia Rylant, not illustrated; Bradbury, 1986.

1988 *Lincoln: A Photobiography* by Russell Freedman, illustrated with photographs; Clarion, 1987.

1988 HONOR *After the Rain* by Norma Fox Mazer, not illustrated; Morrow, 1987.

Hatchet by Gary Paulsen, not illustrated; Bradbury, 1987.

1989 *Joyful Noise: Poems for Two Voices* by Paul Fleischman, illustrated by Eric Beddows; Harper & Row, 1988.

1989 HONOR *In the Beginning: Creation Stories from Around the World* by Virginia Hamilton, illustrated by Barry Moser; Harcourt Brace Jovanovich, 1988.

Scorpions by Walter Dean Myers, not illustrated; Harper & Row, 1988.

1990 *Number the Stars* by Lois Lowry, not illustrated; Houghton Mifflin, 1989.

1990 HONOR *Shabanu: Daughter of the Wind* by Suzanne Fisher Staples, not illustrated; Knopf, 1989.

Afternoon of the Elves by Janet Taylor Lisle, not illustrated; Orchard, 1989.

The Winter Room by Gary Paulsen, not illustrated; Orchard, 1989.

1991 *Maniac Magee* by Jerry Spinelli, not illustrated; Little Brown, 1990.

1991 HONOR *The True Confessions of Charlotte Doyle* by Avi, illustrated by Ruth E. Murray; Orchard, 1990.

1992 *Shiloh* by Phyllis Reynolds Naylor, not illustrated; Atheneum, 1991.

1992 HONOR *Nothing But the Truth* by Avi, not illustrated; Orchard, 1991.

The Wright Brothers: How They Invented the Airplane by Russell Freedman, illustrated with photos; Holiday House, 1991.

1993 *Missing May* by Cynthia Rylant, not illustrated; Orchard, 1992.

1993 HONOR *The Dark-Thirty* by Patricia McKissack, not illustrated; Knopf, 1992.

Somewhere in the Darkness by Walter Dean Myers, not illustrated; Scholastic, 1992.

What Hearts by Bruce Brooks, not illustrated; HarperCollins, 1992.

NORTH CAROLINA DIVISION OF AMERICAN ASSOCIATION OF UNIVERSITY WOMEN AWARD IN JUVENILE LITERATURE

Henry T. Dawkins, Assistant Secretary
North Carolina Department of Cultural Resources
Raleigh, NC 27601-2807

First awarded in 1953, this annual award is sponsored by the North Carolina Literary and Historical Association for the purpose of stimulating among the people of the state an interest in their own literature. Any author who has maintained legal residence in North Carolina for three years is eligible. Juvenile literature, either fiction or nonfiction, will be judged according to its creative and imaginative quality, excellence of style, universality of appeal, and relevance to North Carolina and its people.

The entry must be an original work published during the twelve months ending June 30 of the year for which the award is given. Technical and scientific works are excluded. Three copies of each entry must be submitted. A committee of five judges is responsible for the selection of the winner. Presentation of a cup is made to the winner at the annual meeting of the North Carolina Literary and Historical Association during Culture Week in November. A plaque, inscribed with award winners' names is kept at the North Carolina Museum of History in Raleigh.

1953 *Peanut* by Ruth Carroll and Latrobe Carroll, illustrated by Ruth Carroll; Walck, 1951.

1954 *Penny Rose* by Mebane H. Burgwyn, not illustrated; Walck, 1952.

1955 *Digby, the Only Dog* by Ruth Carroll and Latrobe Carroll, illustrated by Ruth Carroll; Walck, 1955.

1956 *Fiddler's Fancy* by Julia Montgomery Street, illustrated by Don Sibley; Follett, 1955.

1957 *Taffy of Torpedo Junction* by Nell Wise Wechter, illustrated by Mary Walker Sparks; Blair, 1957.

1958 *The Secret Circle* by Ina B. Forbus, illustrated by Corydon Bell; Viking, 1958.

1959 *Captain Ghost* by Thelma H. Bell, illustrated by Corydon Bell; Viking, 1959.

1960 *Stonewall Jackson* by Jonathan Daniels, illustrated by William Moyers; Random House, 1959.

1961 *Beaver Business: An Almanac* written and illustrated by Glen Rounds; Prentice Hall, 1960.

1962 *Rifles at Ramsour's Mill: A Tale of the Revolutionary War* by Manly Wade Wellman, not illustrated; Washburn, 1961.

1963 *Dulcie's Whale* by Julia Montgomery Street, illustrated by Anthony D'Adamo; Bobbs Merrill, 1963.

1964 *The Bat-poet* by Randall Jarrell, illustrated by Maurice Sendak; Macmillan, 1964.

1965 *The Forgotten Door* by Alexander Key, not illustrated; Westminster, 1965.

1966 *North Carolina Parade: Stories of History and People* by Richard Walser and Julia Street, illustrated by D.B. Browning; University of North Carolina Press, 1966.

1967 *The Snake Tree* written and illustrated by Glen Rounds; World, 1966.

1968 *A Biography of Thomas Wolfe* by Neal F. Austin, illustrated with photographs; Roger Beacham, 1968.

1969 *Bugles at the Border* by Mary Gillett, illustrated by B. Tucker; Blair, 1968.

1970 *The Crackajack Pony* by Mebane H. Burgwyn, illustrated by Dale Payson; Lippincott, 1969.

1971 *Purro and the Prattleberries* by Suzanne Newton, illustrated by James Puskas; Westminster, 1971.

1972 No Award

1973 *The People of North Carolina* by Barbara M. Parramore, illustrated; Sadlier, 1972.

1974 *c/o Arnold's Corners* by Suzanne Newton, not illustrated; Westminster, 1974.

1975 *The Magic Meadow* by Alexander Key, not illustrated; Westminster, 1975.

1976 *Mr. Yowder and the Lion Roar Capsules* written and illustrated by Glen Rounds; Holiday House, 1976.

1977 *The City Rose* by Ruth White Miller, not illustrated; McGraw, 1977.

1978 *What Are You Up To, William Thomas?* by Suzanne Newton, not illustrated; Westminster, 1977.

1979 *Reubella and the Old Focus Home* by Suzanne Newton, not illustrated; Westminster, 1978.

1980 *Safe as the Grave* by Caroline B. Cooney, illustrated by Gail Owens; Coward, 1979.

1981 No Award

1982 *M.V. Sexton Speaking: A Novel* by Suzanne Newton, not illustrated; Viking, 1981.

1983 *Wild Appaloosa* written and illustrated by Glen Rounds; Holiday House, 1983.

1984 *Tancy* by Belinda Hurmence, not illustrated; Clarion, 1984.

1985 *The Summer that Lasted Forever* by Catherine Petroski, not illustrated; Houghton Mifflin, 1984.

1986 *Golden Girl* by Nancy Tilly, not illustrated; Farrar, 1985.

1987 *Permanent Connections* by Sue Ellen Bridgers, not illustrated; Harper & Row, 1987.

1988 *Eating Crow* by Lila Hopkins, not illustrated; Watts, 1988.

1989 *The Nightwalker* by Belinda Hurmence, not illustrated; Clarion, 1988.

1990 *Talking Turkey* by Lila Hopkins, not illustrated; Watts, 1989.

1991 *Where Are You When I Need You?* by Suzanne Newton, not illustrated; Viking, 1991.

1992 *Wings* by Bill Brittain, not illustrated; HarperCollins, 1991.

NORTH DAKOTA CHILDREN'S CHOICE AWARD
North Dakota Library Association
Marcella Schmaltz
Bismarck State College Library
1500 Edwards Ave.
Bismarck, ND 58501

Founded in 1978 by Darrel Hildebrant, the North Dakota Children's Choice Award is sponsored by the Youth Services section of the North Dakota Library Association. The award is presented in two categories: younger than fourth grade and older than fourth grade. In 1989, the categories changed to Picture Book and Juvenile Fiction. By mid-February, the children cast a vote for their favorite book read within the last year. The only titles excluded are past winners. All titles receiving more than one vote are placed on a list which is sent back to the schools. The children vote again for their favorite from this list. A plaque is presented to the author of the book receiving the largest number of votes. If the author is unable to attend the North Dakota Library Association convention to accept the plaque, it is mailed.

1978 *The Star Wars: From the Adventures of Luke Skywalker* by George Lucas, illustrated; Ballantine, 1976.

1979 *Are You There, God? It's Me, Margaret* by Judy Blume, not illustrated; Bradbury, 1970.

1980 YOUNGER *My Mom Hates Me in January* by Judy Delton, illustrated by John Faulkner; Whitman, 1977.

1980 OLDER *Tales of a Fourth Grade Nothing* by Judy Blume, illustrated by Roy Doty; Dutton, 1972.

1981 YOUNGER *Curious George* written and illustrated by H.A. Rey; Houghton Mifflin, 1973, 1941.

1981 OLDER *Where the Red Fern Grows* by Wilson Rawls, not illustrated; Doubleday, 1961.

1982 YOUNGER *The Fox and the Hound* by Walt Disney Productions from the film; Golden Press, 1981.

1982 OLDER *Superfudge* by Judy Blume, not illustrated; Dutton, 1980.

1983 YOUNGER *E.T.: The Extra-Terrestrial Storybook* by William Kotzwinkle, based on the screenplay by Melissa Mathison, not illustrated; Putnam, 1982.

1983 OLDER *Blubber* by Judy Blume, not illustrated; Bradbury, 1974.

1984 YOUNGER *A Sister for Sam* by Evelyn Mason, illustrated by Tom Cooke; Children's Press, 1983.

1984 OLDER *Return of the Jedi: The Storybook* based on the movie adapted by Joan D. Vinge; Random House, 1983.

1985 YOUNGER *Miss Nelson Is Missing!* by Harry Allard, illustrated by James Marshall; Houghton Mifflin, 1977.

1985 OLDER *Charlie and the Chocolate Factory* by Roald Dahl, illustrated by Joseph Schindelman; Knopf, 1964.

1986 No Awards

1987 YOUNGER *The Day Jimmy's Boa Ate the Wash* by Trinka Hakes Noble, illustrated by Steven Kellogg; Dial, 1980.

1987 OLDER *Superfudge* by Judy Blume, not illustrated; Dutton, 1980.

1988 YOUNGER *Miss Nelson Has a Field Day* by Harry Allard, illustrated by James Marshall; Houghton Mifflin, 1985.

1988 OLDER *Nothing's Fair in Fifth Grade* by Barthe DeClements, not illustrated; Viking, 1981.

1989 PICTURE BOOK *Love You Forever* by Robert N. Munsch, illustrated by Sheila McGraw; Firefly, 1986.

1989 JUVENILE FICTION *On My Honor* by Marion Dane Bauer, not illustrated; Clarion, 1986.

1990 PICTURE BOOK *Meanwhile Back at the Ranch* by Trinka Hakes Noble, illustrated by Tony Ross; Dial, 1987.

1990 JUVENILE FICTION *Hatchet* by Gary Paulsen, not illustrated; Bradbury, 1987.

1991 PICTURE BOOK *No Jumping on the Bed!* written and illustrated by Tedd Arnold; Dial, 1987.

1991 JUVENILE FICTION *How To Fight a Girl* by Thomas Rockwell, illustrated by Gioia Fiammenghi; Dell, 1988, c1987.

1992 PICTURE BOOK *Harold and Chester in Scared Silly: A Halloween Treat* by James Howe, illustrated by Leslie Morrill; Morrow, 1989.

1992 JUVENILE FICTION *Maniac Magee* by Jerry Spinelli, not illustrated; Little Brown, 1990.

NOTTINGHAMSHIRE CHILDREN'S BOOK AWARD

Nottinghamshire Libraries
Glaisdale Parkway
Nottingham NG8 49P
England

The Nottinghamshire Children's Book Award is jointly organized and promoted by Nottinghamshire Libraries and Dillons Bookstore. The aim of the award is to encourage reading, to draw attention to the range of exciting new children's books, and to involve children in enjoying and evaluating new books.

The award is presented annually in two categories, The Acorn Award for an outstanding book written and illustrated for children up to 7 years of age and The Oak Tree Award for the 8-12 year old group. A shortlist of eight titles is selected from those published during the preceding year in the United Kingdom. The winning books are chosen by children who vote for their favorites during March, April, and May. Winners are announced in July, with each winner receiving a cash prize of £250.

1989 ACORN *Sidney the Monster* by David Wood, illustrated by Clive Scruton; Walker, 1988.

1989 OAK TREE *Matilda* by Roald Dahl, illustrated by Quentin Blake; Cape, 1988.

1990 ACORN *Knickerless Nicola* by Kara May, illustrated by Doffy Weir; Macmillan, 1989.

1990 OAK TREE *Bill's New Frock* by Anne Fine, illustrated by Philippe Dupasquier; Methuen, 1989.

1991 ACORN *Threadbear* written and illustrated by Mick Inkpen; Hodder & Stoughton, 1990.

1991 OAK TREE *The Afterdark Princess* by Annie Dalton, illustrated by Kate Aldous; Methuen, 1990.

1992 ACORN *Kipper* written and illustrated by Mick Inkpen; Walker, 1991.

1992 OAK TREE *The Story of Tracy Beaker* by Jacqueline Wilson, illustrated by Nick Sharratt; Doubleday, 1991.

1993 ACORN *Jonpanda* by Gwen Grant, illustrated by Elaine Mills; Heinemann, 1992.

1993 OAK TREE *Pongwiffy and the Spell of the Year* by Kaye Umansky, illustrated by Chris Smedley; Viking, 1992.

O

OBSERVER TEENAGE FICTION PRIZE
(*formerly* YOUNG OBSERVER)
discontinued

Sponsored by The Observer, this annual award was presented from 1981 to 1987. The aims of the award were to encourage better literary standards among teenage readers, to encourage publishers to recognize this segment of the reading public, to encourage teenagers to read, and to persuade them that there are books written especially with them in mind. Only full-length novels were considered and nominations were made by publishers. A committee of judges considered all nominations. The winning author received a monetary prize.

1981 *Moses Beech* by Ian Strachan, not illustrated; Oxford, 1981.

1982 *The Watcher Bee* by Mary Melwood, not illustrated; Deutsch, 1982.

Aquarius by Jan Mark, not illustrated; Kestrel, 1982.

1983 *Children of the Book* by Peter Carter, illustrated by Richard Jervis, maps by Barry Rowe; Oxford, 1982.

1984 *A Little Fear* by Patricia Wrightson, not illustrated; Hutchinson, 1983; Atheneum, 1983.

1985 *The Nature of the Beast* by Janni Howker, not illustrated; MacRae, 1985; Greenwillow, 1985.

1986 *Bury the Dead* by Peter Carter, not illustrated; Oxford, 1986.

1987 *Memory* by Margaret Mahy, not illustrated; Dent, 1987.

SCOTT O'DELL AWARD FOR HISTORICAL FICTION
Scott O'Dell Foundation
c/o Zena Sutherland
1418 E. 37th St.
Chicago, IL 60637

Conceived by the Scott O'Dell Foundation, this award was established in 1981 and first awarded in 1983. Books of historical fiction written by U.S. citizens are considered for this annual award. In addition, the story must be set in the New World (U.S., Canada, Central or South America, any islands off those shores, etc.). The story must have historical significance and must meet all the usual literary criteria for the genre and be potentially appealing to readers. All eligible books for the year are considered by the award committee.

1983 *The Sign of the Beaver* by Elizabeth George Speare, not illustrated; Houghton Mifflin, 1983.

1984 *The Fighting Ground* by Avi, not illustrated; Lippincott, 1984.

1985 *Sarah, Plain and Tall* by Patricia MacLachlan, not illustrated; Harper, 1985.

1986 *Streams to the River, River to the Sea: A Novel of Sacagewea* by Scott O'Dell, not illustrated; Houghton Mifflin, 1986.

1987 *Charley Skedaddle* by Patricia Beatty, not illustrated; Morrow, 1987.

1988 *The Honorable Prison* by Lyll Becerra de Jenkins, not illustrated; Dutton, 1988.

1989 *Shades of Gray* by Carolyn Reeder, not illustrated; Macmillan, 1989.

1990 *A Time of Troubles* by Pieter Van Raven, not illustrated; Scribners, 1990.

1991 *Stepping on the Cracks* by Mary Downing Hahn, illustrated with a map; Clarion, 1991.

1992 *Morning Girl* by Michael Dorris, not illustrated; Hyperion, 1992.

LUCILLE E. OGLE LITERARY AWARDS
discontinued

This award was established by the Western Publishing Company in 1969 to honor Lucille Ogle, an originator of the Little Golden Books. The purpose was to encourage and stimulate aspiring writers seeking a first juvenile book publication. Original unpublished manuscripts for children were eligible. Members of the faculty of Bank Street College of Education were responsible for choosing the award winning manuscript in each of two categories: ages three through seven and eight through twelve. $1000 was awarded to each winning author and the Western Publishing Company had the first option to publish the manuscript.

1970 AGES 3-7 No Award

1970 AGES 8-12 *Lost in the Everglades* by Lucy Salamanca, illustrated by Jo Polseno; Western, 1971.

OHIOANA BOOK AWARDS
Linda Hengst, Director
Ohioana Library Association
1105 Ohio Departments Building
65 South Front St
Columbus, OH 43215

This annual award was established by Martha Kinney Cooper. The purpose of the award is threefold: to honor Ohio writers, to acquaint the public with their books, and to assemble a collection of these books. Each year, the Ohioana Book Awards jury considers all books received since the preceding jury met. It normally selects four books for Ohioana Book Awards and one book for the Florence Roberts Head Book Award (for a book on the Ohio scene). These selections are made from all types of literature received, both adult and juvenile. The jury's only instruction is to select the best books. It is not required to select the possible total of five books, but it usually does so. It is not required to select books in any special classification, such as juvenile, but one or two juveniles are usually included. Eligible are authors born in Ohio or who have lived there for at least five years, and writers of books about Ohio and Ohioans.

In 1990, the Alice Louise Wood Ohioana Award was established to honor an author for his or her body of work or a lifetime contribution to children's literature. A $1000 award is made annually.

The winning authors are presented with a medallion and certificate at an annual awards luncheon in October. Listed below are the juvenile award winning titles.

1943 *Bibi: the Baker's Horse* by Anna Bird Stewart, illustrated by Catherine M. Richter; Lippincott, 1942.

1943 **HONORABLE MENTION** *Mr. Totter and the Five Black Cats* by Eleanor Thomas, illustrated by Charlotte Becker; Scribner, 1942.

The Story of the Great Lakes by Marie Emilie Gilchrist, illustrated by C.H. DeWitt; Harper, 1942.

1944 *Bayou Suzette* written and illustrated by Lois Lenski; Stokes, 1943.

1945 *One God: The Ways We Worship Him* by Florence Mary Fitch, illustrated with photographs; Lothrop, 1944.

1945 **SECOND PLACE** *The Great Quillow* by James Thurber, illustrated by Doris Lee; Harcourt, 1944.

1945 **THIRD PLACE** *Mount Delightful: The Story of Ellen Evans and her Dog Taffy* by Eleanor Youmans, illustrated by Sandra James; Bobbs Merrill, 1944.

1946 *The White Deer* by James Thurber, illustrated by Don Freeman; Harcourt, 1945.

1946 **HONORABLE MENTION** *The Mystery of the Creaking Windmill* written and illustrated by Harriet T. Evatt; Bobbs Merrill, 1945.

Splasher by Fleming Crew and Alice Crew Gall, illustrated by Else Bostelmann; Oxford, 1945.

1947 *The Snow Owl's Secret* written and illustrated by Harriet Torrey Evatt; Bobbs Merrill, 1946.

1947 **HONORABLE MENTION** *Meriwether Lewis: Boy Explorer* by Charlotta M. Bebenroth, illustrated by Edward Caswell; Bobbs Merrill, 1946.

1948 *Li Lun, Lad of Courage* by Carolyn Treffinger, illustrated by Kurt Wiese; Abingdon-Cokesbury, 1947.

1948 **HONORABLE MENTION** *David Livingston, Foe of Darkness* by Jeanette Eaton, illustrated by Ralph Ray; Morrow, 1947.

1949 *Blueberries for Sal* written and illustrated by Robert McCloskey; Viking, 1948.

1949 **HONORABLE MENTION** *Boom Town Boy* written and illustrated by Lois Lenski; Lippincott, 1948.

1950 *Song of the Pines: A Story of Norwegian Lumbering in Wisconsin* by Marion Havighurst and Walter Havighurst, illustrated by Richard Floethe; Winston, 1949.

1950 **HONORABLE MENTION** *Island Summer* by Hazel Wilson, illustrated by Richard Floethe; Abingdon-Cokesbury, 1949.

Sword in Sheath by Andre Norton, illustrated by Lorence F. Bjorklund; Harcourt, 1949.

1951 No Award

1952 *Enter David* Garrick by Anna Bird Stewart, illustrated by Ernest H. Shepard; Lippincott, 1951.

1953 No Award

1954 *Tinker's Tim and the Witches* by Bertha C. Anderson, illustrated by Lloyd Coe; Little Brown, 1953.

1955 *Prehistoric Animals* written and illustrated by William E. Scheele; World, 1954.

1956 *The Fabulous Firework Family* written and illustrated by James Flora; Harcourt, 1955.

1957 *Knight's Castle* by Edward Eager, illustrated by N. M. Bodecker; Harcourt, 1956.

1958 *Time of Wonder* written and illustrated by Robert McCloskey; Viking, 1957.

1959 *America's Own Mark Twain* by Jeanette Eaton, illustrated by Leonard Everett Fisher; Morrow, 1958.

1960 *The Gammage Cup* by Carol Kendall, illustrated by Erik Blegvad; Harcourt, 1959.

1961 *Old Ramon* by Jack Schaefer, illustrated by Harold West; Houghton, 1960.

1962 *Ships, Shoals and Amphoras: The Story of Underwater Archaeology* by Suzanne De Borhegyi, illustrated by Alex Schomburg; Holt, 1961.

1962 **BODY OF WORK** Marguerite Vance

1963 *Seven-day Magic* by Edward Eager, illustrated by N. M. Bodecker; Harcourt, 1962.

1964-1966 No Award

1967 *Walk a Narrow Bridge* by Dale Fife, not illustrated; Coward, 1966.

1968 *Focus the Bright Land* by Elisabeth H. Friermood, not illustrated; Doubleday, 1967.

1969 *The House of Dies Drear* by Virginia Hamilton, illustrated by Eros Keith; Macmillan, 1968.

1970 *The Norman Rockwell Storybook* by Jan Wahl, illustrated by Norman Rockwell; Windmill/Simon & Schuster, 1969.

1971 **FICTION** *Dave's Song* by Robert McKay, not illustrated; Meredith, 1969.

1971 **NONFICTION** *Ohio* by Marion Lewis Renick, illustrated with photographs and old plates; Coward, 1970.

1972 *Winds* by Mary O'Neill, illustrated by James Barclay; Doubleday, 1971.

1973-1975 No Award

1976 *Witch of the Cumberlands* by Mary Jo Stephens, illustrated by Arvis Stewart; Houghton, 1974.

1977 *Deep in the Forest* written and illustrated by Brinton Turkle; Dutton, 1976.

Island Time by Bette Lamont, illustrated by Brinton Turkle; Lippincott, 1976.

1978 *Poor Tom's Ghost* by Jane Louise Curry, illustrated by Janet Archer; Atheneum, 1977.

1979 **FLORENCE HEAD AWARD** *Zoar Blue* by Janet Hickman, not illustrated; Macmillan, 1978.

1980 **BODY OF WORK** Andre Norton

1981 *The Liberation of Tansy Warner* by Stephanie S. Tolan, not illustrated ; Scribner, 1980.

1982 *Another Heaven, Another Earth* by H.M. Hoover, not illustrated; Viking, 1981.

1983 No Award

1984 **BODY OF WORK** Virginia Hamilton

1985-1986 No Award

1987 *The Lotus Cup* by Jane Louise Curry, not illustrated; Atheneum, 1986.

1988 No Award

1988 CITATION FOR CHILDREN'S LITERATURE Joseph Slate

1989 *The Tsar and the Amazing Cow* by J. Patrick Lewis, illustrated by Friso Henstra; Dial, 1988.

1990 *But I'll Be Back Again: An Album* by Cynthia Rylant, illustrated with photos; Orchard, 1989.

1991 *With a Name Like Lulu, Who Needs More Trouble?* by Tricia Springstubb, illustrated by Jill Kastner; Delacorte, 1989.

1991 ALICE L. WOOD MEMORIAL Mildred Taylor

1991 CAREER MEDAL Virginia Hamilton

1992 *Appalachia: The Voices of Sleeping Birds* by Cynthia Rylant, illustrated by Barry Moser; Harcourt, Brace, Jovanovich, 1991.

1992 ALICE L. WOOD MEMORIAL Virginia Hamilton

OKLAHOMA BOOK AWARD

Oklahoma Center for the Book
200 NE 18th St.
Oklahoma City, OK 73105

Established in 1990 by the Oklahoma Center for the Book, this annual award recognizes achievement in books written by Oklahomans or books with an Oklahoma theme. One of the categories is for Children/Young Adult and eligible books include fiction, nonfiction, poetry, and picture books. A panel of judges representing a broad spectrum of expertise in writing and publishing will consider all entries based on the quality of writing. Winners are announced at an awards ceremony and are presented with a medal. Only the Children/Young Adult category winners are listed below.

1990 *Tyrannosaurus Rex and Its Kin* by Helen Roney Sattler, illustrated by Joyce Powzyk; Lothrop Lee & Shepard, 1989.

1991 *A Capital for the Nation* by Stan Hoig, illustrated with photographs; Cobblehill Books, 1990.

1992 *Hillback to Boggy* told by Jess Willard Speer, written by Bonnie Speer, illustrated; Reliance Press, 1991.

1993 *Red-dirt Jessie* by Anna Myers, not illustrated; Walker, 1992.

ORBIS PICTUS AWARD FOR OUTSTANDING NON-FICTION FOR CHILDREN

National Council of Teachers of English
1111 Kenyon Rd.
Urbana, IL 61801

This award, established in 1990, commemorates the work of Johannes Amos Comenius, author of Orbis Pictus (1657), considered to be the first picture book planned for a child audience. A purpose of the award is to recognize the large and growing body of nonfiction and informational books, often neglected and overlooked in their potential for classroom teaching application.

Members of the National Council of Teachers of English, as well as the educational community at large, may nominate titles of nonfiction or informational literature for consideration of the award committee. One book is chosen to win the award and as many as five honor books may also be recognized. The award is presented each November at the annual NCTE convention.

1989 *The Great Little Madison* by Jean Fritz, illustrated with prints and engravings; Putnam, 1989.

1989 HONOR *The News About Dinosaurs* written and illustrated by Patricia Lauber; Bradbury, 1989.

The Great American Gold Rush by Rhoda Blumberg, illustrated with photos; Bradbury, 1989.

1990 *Franklin Delano Roosevelt* by Russell Freedman, illustrated with photos; Clarion Books, 1990.

1991 HONOR *Arctic Memories* by Normee Ekoomiak, illustrated with photos; Henry Holt, 1990, c1988.

Seeing Earth From Space by Patricia Lauber, illustrated; Orchard, 1990.

1992 *Flight: The Journey of Charles Lindbergh* by Robert Burleigh, illustrated by Mike Wimmer; Philomel, 1991.

1992 HONOR *Now Is Your Time! The African-American Struggle for Freedom* by Walter Dean Myers, illustrated; HarperCollins, 1991.

Prairie Visions: The Life and Times of Solomon Butcher by Pam Conrad, illustrated with photos; HarperCollins, 1991.

1993 *Children of the Dust Bowl* by Jerry Stanley, illustrated with photographs; Crown, 1992.

1993 HONOR *Talking with Artists* by Pat Cummings, illustrated; Bradbury Press, 1992.

Come Back, Salmon by Molly Cone, photographs by Sidnee Wheelwright; Sierra, 1992.

OTHER AWARD

discontinued

The Other Award was an alternative children's book award for nonbiased books of literary merit. It was begun in 1975 in an attempt to draw attention to important new writing and illustration for children and to give due recognition to those writers and illustrators who were taking positive steps to widen the literary experience of young people. The Other Award was inaugurated by Rosemary Stones and Andrew Mann, coeditors of the Children's Book Bulletin. All types of children's books published in Britain from July 1 to June 30, including reprints and paperback editions, were eligible. Approximately three winners were chosen each year by a panel consisting of the editors of Children's Book Bulletin and invited specialists in and practitioners of children's literature. Publishers and authors could also submit titles for consideration. The Other Award took the form of a commendation that was presented to the winners at a yearly celebration.

In selecting the award-winning books, the panel determined those books which: (1) children will enjoy; (2) have literary merit (i.e. imaginative, interesting story line, rounded characterizations, credible and recognizable situations, natural sequencing); (3) contains realistic depictions of all people, whatever their culture, background or occupation; (4) contain balanced depictions of sex roles; (5) are historically correct, and if historical fiction, present a people's history of events, not just that of rulers and elites; (6) do not condone or take for granted the explicit or implicit values of competitive individualism, the accumulation of wealth, hierarchical social organization, or the inevitability of superior and inferior social categories.

(From the criteria set by the Children's Book Bulletin).

1975 *Hal* by Jean MacGibbon, not illustrated; Heinemann, 1974.

Joe and Timothy Together by Dorothy Edwards, illustrated by Reintje Venema; Methuen, 1971.

Twopence a Tub by Susan Price, not illustrated; Faber, 1975.

1976 *Helpers* written and illustrated by Shirley Hughes; Bodley Head, 1975.

Nobody's Family Is Going to Change by Louise Fitzhugh, not illustrated; Gollancz, 1976.

The Trouble with Donovan Croft by Bernard Ashley, illustrated by Fermin Rocker; Oxford, 1974.

1977 *East End at Your Feet* by Farrakh Dhondy, not illustrated; Macmillan, 1976.

Building Worker by Sarah Cox, illustrated by Robert Golden; Kestrel, 1976.

Hospital Worker by Sarah Cox, illustrated by Robert Golden; Kestrel, 1976.

Railway Worker by Sarah Cox, illustrated by Robert Golden; Kestrel, 1976.

Textile Worker by Sarah Cox, illustrated by Robert Golden; Kestrel, 1976.

The Turbulent Term of Tyke Tiler by Gene Kemp, illustrated by Carolyn Dinan; Faber, 1977.

Frederick Grice- Special commendation for body of work

1978 *Discovering Africa's Past* by Basil Davidson, illustrated with maps; Longman, 1978.

The Goalkeeper's Revenge and other Stories by Bill Naughton, illustrated by Dick de Wilde; Brockhampton Press, 1971.

Gypsy Family by Mary Waterson, photographs by Lance Browne; Black, 1978.

Song for a Dark Queen by Rosemary Sutcliff, not illustrated; Pelham, 1978.

1979 *Come to Mecca and other Stories* by Farrukh Dhondy, not illustrated; Collins, 1978.

A Comprehensive Education, 1965-1975 by Roger Mills, not illustrated; Centerprise Trust, Ltd., 1978.

Old Dog, New Tricks by Dick Cate, illustrated by Trevor Stubley; Hamilton, 1978.

Two Victorian Families by Sue Wagstaff, illustrated with photographs; Black, 1979.

1980 *Aborigines* by Virginia Luling, illustrated with photographs and maps; Macdonald & Janes, 1979.

The Green Bough of Liberty by David Rees, illustrated with old prints and maps; Dobson, 1980.

The Machine Breakers: The Story of the Luddites by Angela Bull, illustrated with photographs; Collins, 1980.

Mrs. Plug the Plumber by Allan Ahlberg, illustrated by Joe Wright; Kestrel, 1980.

1981 *A Strong and Willing Girl* by Dorothy Edwards, not illustrated; Methuen, 1980.

What Is a Union? by Althea, illustrated by Chris Evans; Dinosaur Publications, 1981; Rourke Enterprises, 1981.

Have You Started Yet? by Ruth Thomson, illustrated by C. Beaton; Heinemann, 1980.

Terraced House Books: Set D by Peter Heaslip, illustrated by Anne Griffiths; Methuen Educational, 1980.

1981 SPECIAL COMMENDATION Young World Books

1982 *Into the Past: Parts 1-4* by Sallie Purkis and Elizabeth Merson, illustrated with photographs (*At Home and in the Street in 1900*; *At Home in 1900*; *At School and in the Country in 1900*; *At School in 1900*); Longman, 1981.

Black Lives, White Worlds edited by Keith Ajegbo; Cambridge University Press, 1982.

Girls Are Powerful: Young Women's Writings from Spare Rib edited by Susan Hemmings; Sheba Feminist Publishers, 1982.

Welcome Home, Jellybean by Marlene Fanta Shyer, not illustrated; Granada, 1981.

When the Wind Blows written and illustrated by Raymond Briggs; Hamish Hamilton, 1982.

1983 *Nowhere to Play* written and illustrated by Kurusa, translated by Judith Elkin; A&C Black, 1982.

Will of Iron by Gerard Melia; Longman Knockouts.

Everybody Here! by Michael Rosen, illustrated with photographs and line drawings; Bodley Head, 1982.

Talking in Whispers by James Watson, not illustrated; Gollancz, 1983.

1984 *Brother in the Land* by Robert Swindells, not illustrated; Oxford, 1984.

Who Lies Inside by Timothy Ireland, not illustrated; Gay Men's Press, 1984.

Wheel Around the World by Chris Searle, illustrated by Katinka Kew; Macdonald, 1983.

A Chair for My Mother written and illustrated by Vera B. Williams; MacRae, 1983; Greenwillow, 1982.

1985 *Our Kids* by Mothers of the Children; Peckham Publishing Project, 1984.

Journey to Jo'burg by Beverly Naidoo, illustrated by Eric Velasquez; Longman, 1984.

Comfort Herself by Geraldine Kaye, illustrated by Jenny Northway; Deutsch, 1984.

Vila: An Adventure Story by Sarah Baylis, not illustrated; Brillance Books, 1984.

Motherland: West Indian Women to Britain in the 1950s by Elyse Dodgson, illustrated; Heinemann Educational, 1984.

Coalmining Women by Angela V. John; Cambridge Educational, 1984.

1986 *Say it Again, Granny!* by John Agard, illustrated by Susanna Gretz; Bodley Head, 1985.

The Bus Driver by Anne Stewart, photographs by Chris Fairclough; Hamish Hamilton, 1986.

Starry Night by Catherine Sefton, not illustrated; Hamish Hamilton, 1986.

The People Could Fly by Virginia Hamilton, illustrated by Leo Dillon and Diane Dillon; Walker Books, 1985; Knopf, 1985.

1987 Rosa Guy for her body of work

Grandma's Favourite written and illustrated by Peter C. Heaslip; Methuen Children's, 1987.

Which Twin Wins? written and illustrated by Peter C. Heaslip; Methuen Children's, 1987.

Wok's Cooking? written and illustrated by Peter C. Heaslip; Methuen Children's, 1987.

Chapatis, Not Chips written and illustrated by Peter C. Heaslip; Methuen Children's, 1987.

The Palestinians by David McDowall, illustrated by Ron Howard Associates; Watts, 1986.

Push Me, Pull Me by Sandra Chick, not illustrated; Women's Press, 1987.

HELEN KEATING OTT AWARD FOR OUTSTANDING CONTRIBUTION TO CHILDREN'S LITERATURE

Executive Director
Church and Synagogue Library Association
Box 19357
Portland, OR 97219

This annual award has been presented since 1980 and is sponsored by the Church and Synagogue Library Association. Any person or institution who has made a significant contribution to promoting high moral and ethical values through children's literature may be considered, including authors, illustrators, educators, librarians, clergy, editors, and publishers.

Anyone may send a nomination to the CSLA awards committee. A citation is presented to the winner at the annual conference awards banquet.

1980 Arch Book series edited by Patricia McKissock; Concordia Publishing House.

1981 *Win Me and You Lose* by Phyllis Anderson Wood, not illustrated; Westminster, 1977.

This Time Count Me In by Phyllis Anderson Wood, not illustrated; Westminster, 1980.

1982 No Award

1983 *Abbie's God Book* by Isabelle Holland, illustrated by James McLaughlin; Westminster, 1982.

God, Mrs. Muskrat and Aunt Dot by Isabelle Holland, illustrated by Beth Krush and Joe Krush; Westminster, 1983.

1984 Nancy Larrick

1985 Lillie G. Patterson

1986 No Award

1987 Lloyd Alexander

1988 Carolyn Field, Jacqueline S. Weiss

1989 Edith Patterson Meyer

1990 Elizabeth A. Van Steenwyck

1991 Miriam L. Johnson

1992 Boone County Board of Education "I Love To Read" Program

OUTSTANDING ARIZONA AUTHOR

Arizona State Library Association
c/o Cathy Bonnell
Ironwood Elementary School
14850 N. 39th Ave.
Phoenix, AZ 85023

Established in 1983 by Libraries Unlimited, the Outstanding Arizona Author Award is administered by the Arizona State Library Association. The award recognizes the contribution of a living writer who is closely identified with Arizona and whose works are intended primarily for children and young adults. The honored author receives a citation and a commemorative gift at the Arizona State Library Association annual conference.

1983 Sister Eulalie Bourne

1984 Ann Nolan Clark

1985 Byrd Baylor

1986 Don Schellie

1987 Lynn Gessner

1988 Betty Baker

1989 Elizabeth Q. White (Elizabeth Polingaysi Qoyawayma)

1990 Gisela Jernigan, E. Wesley Jernigan

1991 Michael Lacapa

OUTSTANDING PENNSYLVANIA AUTHOR

Pennsylvania School Librarians Association
c/o Susan Wolfe
1201 Yverdon Dr. A7
Camp Hill, PA 17011

Established in 1975 by the Pennsylvania School Library Association, this annual award provides recognition to an author living in and/or writing about Pennsylvania and who has made a notable contribution to the field of children's literature. All types of literature, K-12 are eligible. A certificate is awarded to the selected author at the Pennsylvania Library Association annual conference.

1975 Marguerite de Angeli

1976 Lloyd Alexander

1977 Margaret Hodges

1978 Jean Fritz

1979 Carolyn Haywood

1980 Walter Farley

1981 Harriet May Savitz

1982 James Michener

1983 Robin Brancato

1984 Muriel Feelings

1985 Barbara Robinson

1986 Barbara Brenner

1987 Lucille Wallower

1989 Marc Brown

1990 Carolyn Mayer

1991 Aliki

1992 Jerry Spinelli

OWL PRIZE

discontinued

The Owl Prize, now discontinued, was sponsored by Shiko-Sha Co. and Maruzen Co. Visitors to the Exhibition of Original Pictures of International Children's Picture Books, held each summer in Tokyo since 1976, voted for the book they considered to be the best illustrated. The illustrator whose work was chosen as the best received a cash award of 200,000 yen, a diploma, and a seal with the illustrator's name in Chinese characters carved into a water buffalo horn. The Owl Prize was terminated with the 25th exhibition in 1990.

1976 *Crocodile, Crocodile* by Peter Nickl, illustrated by Binette Schroeder; Nord-Sud Verlag, 1975; Tundra, 1976.

1977 *The Maggie B.* written and illustrated by Irene Haas; Atheneum, 1975.

1978 *Das Schonste Geschenk* by Cornelis Wilkeshuis and Rita Van Bilsen, illustrated; Bohem Press, 1977.

1979 *Wie Tierkinder Schlafen* illustrated by Erika Dietzsch-Capelle; K. Thienemanns Verlag.

1980 *Carrie Hepple's Garden* by Ruth Craft, illustrated by Irene Haas; McElderry, 1979.

1981 *Spring Story* (Brambly Hedge series) written and illustrated by Jill Barklem; Collins, 1980.

1982 *Viktor, das Fliegende Nilpferd* by Guy Counhaye, illustrated by Marie-Jose Sacre; Everest, 1982.

1983 *Freunde* written and illustrated by Helme Heine; Gertraud Middelhauve, 1982; Atheneum, 1985.

1984 *Die Geschichte Vom Guten Wolf* by Peter Nickl, illustrated by Jozef Wilkon; Nord-Sud Verlag, 1985, c1982.

1985 *Spatzen Brauchen Keinen Schirm* by Ursel Scheffler, illustrated by Ulises Wensell; Methuen Children's, 1984.

1986 *Das Kleine Madchen mit den Schwefelholzchen* by Hans Christian Andersen, illustrated by Bernadette Watts; Nord-Sud, 1983.

1987 *Der Rabe Im Schnee* written and illustrated by Erwin Moser; Adama Books, 1986.

1988 *Kleiner Eisbar, Wohin Fahrst Du?* written and illustrated by Hans de Beer; Nord-Sud, 1987.

1989 *Simon and the Snowflakes* written and illustrated by Gilles Tibo; Tundra Books, 1988.

1990 *George and Matilda Mouse and the Floating School* written and illustrated by Heather S. Buchanan; Methuen, 1990.

P

PACIFIC NORTHWEST LIBRARY ASSOCIATION YOUNG READER'S CHOICE AWARD

see YOUNG READER'S CHOICE AWARD

LUCILE MICHEELS PANNELL AWARD

Women's National Book Association
Ann Heidbreder Eastman
3583 S. Via del Jilguero
Green Valley, AZ 85614-4841

The Lucile Micheels Pannell Award was established by the Women's National Book Association to honor this distinguished bookshop owner and high-school librarian. The aim of the award is to recognize the creative uses of books with children. Since 1983, the award has been presented to bookstores for the most dynamic programs to bring books and children together. Winners receive $2500 and an original piece of art created by a children's book illustrator.

Applicants for the award are asked to submit an application form and various other materials as directed by the committee. Leaders in book selling, publishing and professional associations evaluate the application and select the winner.

1983 Raphael P. Martin

1984 Jim McLaughlin, Meg Risser

1985 Anne Bustard

1986 Diane Etherington

1987 Andrew G. Laties, Christine F. Bluhm

1988 Sheilah Egan, Marilyn Dugan

1989 Margaret Walker, Jan Barstow, Robin Walker, Judi Baxter

1990 Ann La Pietra, Clifford F. Wohl

1991 Rosemary Stimola, Michael Stimola, Janet E. Grojean

1993 Karen Creech

PARENTS' CHOICE AWARD FOR CHILDREN'S BOOKS

Parents' Choice Foundation
Box 185
Newton, MA 02168

First awarded in 1980, this children's literature award is sponsored by the Parents' Choice Foundation. The original purpose of the award was to recognize children's books with illustrations of more than remarkable charm. In 1982, a category for Literature was added and the purpose was expanded to include literary merit. Nominations are made by parents, who have enjoyed a particular book with their children. The final selection is made by the Parents' Choice board. A ribbon is presented to the award winners. The award is presented on an irregular basis and the results are announced in Parents' Choice magazine.

1980 **ILLUSTRATION** *Anno's Italy* written and illustrated by Mitsumasa Anno; Collins, 1980.

Beat the Story-drum, Pum-pum written and illustrated by Ashley Bryan; Atheneum, 1980.

The Bremen-town Musicians written and illustrated by Ilse Plume; Doubleday, 1980.

Crazy in Love by Richard Kennedy, illustrated by Marcia Sewall; Unicorn/Dutton, 1980.

The Green Man written and illustrated by Gail E. Haley; Scribner, 1980.

Once Upon a Time in a Pigpen by Margaret Wise Brown, illustrated by Ann Strugnell; Addison-Wesley, 1980.

Paddy's New Hat written and illustrated by John S. Goodall; Atheneum, 1980.

Petrouchka written and illustrated by Elizabeth Cleaver; Atheneum, 1980.

Roadrunner by Naomi John, illustrated by Peter Parnall and Virginia Parnall; Unicorn/Dutton, 1980.

Taking Care of Melvin by Marjorie Weinman Sharmat, illustrated by Victoria Chess; Holiday House, 1980.

Three is Company written and illustrated by Friedrich Karl Waechter, translated by Harry Allard; Doubleday, 1979.

Unbuilding written and illustrated by David Macaulay; Houghton, 1980.

1982 ILLUSTRATION *The Tiny Visitor* written and illustrated by Oscar de Mejo; Pantheon, 1982.

Ming Lo Moves the Mountain written and illustrated by Arnold Lobel; Greenwillow, 1982.

The Dwindling Party written and illustrated by Edward Gorey, paper engineering by Ib Penick; Random House, 1982.

Ben's Dream written and illustrated by Chris Van Allsburg; Houghton Mifflin, 1982.

Selina, The Mouse and the Giant Cat written and illustrated by Susi Bohdal, translated by Lucy Meredith; Faber & Faber in association with Nord-Sud Verlag, 1982.

Porcupine Stew by Beverly Major, illustrated by Erick Ingraham; Morrow, 1982.

The Castle on Hester Street written and illustrated by Linda Heller; Jewish Publication Society of America, 1982.

My Uncle written and illustrated by Jenny Thorne; Atheneum, 1982.

Peter and the Wolf by Sergei Prokofiev, translated by Maria Carlson, illustrated by Charles Mikolaycak; Viking, 1982.

The Giant Fish and other Stories written and illustrated by Svend Otto S., translated by Joan Tate; Larousse, 1982.

The First Tulips in Holland by Phyllis Krasilovsky, illustrated by S.D. Schindler; Doubleday, 1982.

A Winter Place by Ruth Yaffe Radin, illustrated by Mattie Lou O'Kelley; Little Brown, 1982.

The Swineherd by Hans Christian Andersen, translated by Anthea Bell, illustrated by Lisbeth Zwerger; Morrow, 1982.

The Farm Book written and illustrated by E. Boyd Smith, introduction by Barbara Bader; Houghton Mifflin, 1982, c1938.

Sparrow Song written and illustrated by Ben Shecter; Harper, 1981.

1982 LITERATURE *That Julia Redfern* by Eleanor Cameron, illustrated by Gail Owens; Dutton, 1982.

Ralph S. Mouse by Beverly Cleary, illustrated by Paul O. Zelinsky; Morrow, 1982.

The Kestrel by Lloyd Alexander, not illustrated; Dutton, 1982; Dell, 1983.

The Divorce Express by Paula Danziger, not illustrated; Delacorte, 1982; Dell, 1983.

Kept in the Dark by Nina Bawden, not illustrated; Lothrop Lee & Shepard, 1982.

Miss Nelson Is Back by Harry Allard, illustrated by James Marshall; Houghton Mifflin, 1982.

The Animal, the Vegetable, and John D. Jones by Betsy Byars, illustrated by Ruth Sanderson; Delacorte, 1982; Dell, 1983.

A Girl Called Boy by Belinda Hurmence, not illustrated; Ticknor & Fields, 1982.

The Rabbi's Girls by Johanna Hurwitz, illustrated by Pamela Johnson; Morrow, 1982.

Tallyho, Pinkerton! written and illustrated by Steven Kellogg; Dial, 1982.

The Firelings by Carol Kendall, map and illustrations by Felicia Bond; Atheneum, 1982.

This Strange New Feeling by Julius Lester, not illustrated; Dial, 1982.

Great Cat written and illustrated by David McPhail; Dutton, 1982.

Won't Know Till I Get There by Walter Dean Myers, not illustrated; Viking, 1982.

Playing Beatie Bow by Ruth Park, not illustrated; Kestrel, 1981; Atheneum, 1982.

The Darkangel by Meredith Ann Pierce, not illustrated; Little Brown, 1982.

Roger's Umbrella by Daniel Pinkwater, illustrated by James Marshall; Dutton, 1982.

Oliver, Clarence and Violet written and illustrated by James Stevenson; Greenwillow, 1982.

Dragon's Blood: A Fantasy by Jane Yolen, not illustrated; Delacorte, 1980.

1983 ILLUSTRATION *Leonard Baskin's Miniature Natural History: First Series* written and illustrated by Leonard Baskin; Pantheon, 1983.

Simon's Book written and illustrated by Henrik Drescher; Lothrop, 1983.

The Favershams written and illustrated by Roy Gerrard; Gollancz, 1982; Farrar, 1983.

If You Take a Pencil written and illustrated by Fulvio Testa; Dial, 1982.

The Silver Cow retold by Susan Cooper, illustrated by Warwick Hutton; Atheneum, 1983.

The Glorious Flight: Across the Channel with Louis Bleriot written and illustrated by Martin Provensen and Alice Provensen; Viking, 1983.

Mill written and illustrated by David Macaulay; Houghton Mifflin, 1983.

Pigs in Hiding written and illustrated by Arlene Dubanevich; Four Winds, 1983.

Up a Tree illustrated by Ed Young; Harper, 1983.

Anno's Mysterious Multiplying Jar by Masaichiro Anno and Mitsumasa Anno, illustrated by Mitsumasa Anno; Philomel, 1983.

The Tale of John Barleycorn: or, From Barley to Beer: A Traditional English Ballad written and illustrated by Mary Azarian; Godine, 1982.

The Magnificent Moo written and illustrated by Victoria Forrester; Atheneum, 1983.

Doctor DeSoto written and illustrated by William Steig; Farrar, 1982.

Little Red Riding Hood by Jacob Grimm and Wilhelm Grimm, retold and illustrated by Trina Schart Hyman; Holiday House, 1983.

Pelican written and illustrated by Brian Wildsmith; Oxford, 1982; Pantheon, 1982.

1983 LITERATURE *A Solitary Blue* by Cynthia Voigt, not illustrated; Atheneum, 1983.

The Curse of the Blue Figurine by John Bellairs, illustrated by Edward Gorey; Dial, 1983.

The Silver Cow retold by Susan Cooper, illustrated by Warwick Hutton; Atheneum, 1983.

Cecelia and the Blue Mountain Boy by Ellen H. Showell, illustrated by Margot Tomes; Lothrop, 1983.

The Birds of Summer by Zilpha Keatley Snyder, not illustrated; Atheneum, 1983.

Dear Mr. Henshaw by Beverly Cleary, illustrated by Paul O. Zelinsky; Morrow, 1983.

Courage, Dana by Susan Pfeffer, illustrated by Jenny Rutherford; Delacorte, 1983.

Rebels of the Heavenly Kingdom by Katherine Paterson, not illustrated; Lodestar/Dutton, 1983.

Taking Care of Terrific by Lois Lowry, not illustrated; Houghton Mifflin, 1983.

The Magical Adventures of Pretty Pearl by Virginia Hamilton, not illustrated; Harper, 1983.

Lenny Kandell, Smart Aleck by Ellen Conford, illustrated by Walter Gaffney-Kessell; Little Brown, 1983.

New Found Land by John Christopher, not illustrated; Dutton, 1983.

Why Am I Grown So Cold? Poems of the Unknowable edited by Myra Cohn Livingston, not illustrated; Atheneum, 1982.

New Guys Around the Block by Rosa Guy, not illustrated; Delacorte, 1983.

The Golem by Isaac Bashevis Singer, illustrated by Uri Shulevitz; Farrar, 1982.

Rapscallion Jones written and illustrated by James Marshall; Viking, 1983.

Path of the Pale Horse by Paul Fleischman, not illustrated; Harper, 1983.

Them that Glitter and Them That Don't by Bette Greene, not illustrated; Knopf, 1983.

Ronia, the Robber's Daughter by Astrid Lindgren, translated by Patricia Crampton, not illustrated; Viking, 1983.

1984 LITERATURE *When the Dark Comes Dancing* compiled by Nancy Larrick, illustrated by John Wallner; Philomel, 1983.

The Hot and Cold Summer by Johanna Hurwitz, illustrated by Gail Owens; Morrow, 1984.

The Outside Shot by Walter Dean Myers, not illustrated; Delacorte, 1984.

Always, Always by Crescent Dragonwagon, illustrated by Arieh Zeldich; Macmillan, 1984.

The Beggar Queen by Lloyd Alexander, not illustrated; Dutton, 1984.

Because We Are by Mildred Pitts Walter, not illustrated; Lothrop, 1983.

Sky Songs by Myra Cohn Livingston, illustrated by Leonard Everett Fisher; Holiday House, 1984.

The Morning the Sun Refused to Shine written and illustrated by Glen Rounds; Holiday House, 1984.

The War with Grandpa by Robert Kimmel Smith, illustrated by Richard Lauter; Delacorte, 1984.

Moon-Flash by Patricia McKillip, not illustrated; Atheneum, 1984.

The Crack-of-Dawn Walkers by Amy Hest, illustrated by Amy Schwartz; Macmillan, 1984.

The Stone Silenus by Jane Yolen, not illustrated; Philomel, 1984.

Oh, Kojo! How Could You! by Verna Aardema, illustrated by Marc Brown; Dial, 1984.

Thursday's Children by Rumer Godden, not illustrated; Viking, 1984.

Born to Dance Samba by Miriam Cohen, illustrated by Gioia Fiammenghi; Harper, 1984.

Julia's Magic by Eleanor Cameron, illustrated by Gail Owens; Dutton, 1984.

The Way to Sattin Shore by Philippa Pearce, illustrated by Charlotte Voake; Greenwillow, 1984.

Ramona Forever by Beverly Cleary, illustrated by Alan Tiegreen; Morrow, 1984.

Alexandra by Scott O'Dell, not illustrated; Houghton Mifflin, 1984.

The Frog Princess by Elizabeth Isele, illustrated by Michael Hague; Crowell, 1984.

1985 LITERATURE *Amy's Eyes* by Richard Kennedy, illustrated by Richard Egielski; Harper, 1985.

Buddies by Barbara Park, not illustrated; Knopf, 1985.

Bimwili and the Zimwi by Verna Aardema, illustrated by Susan Meddaugh; Dial, 1985.

Watch the Stars Come Out by Riki Levinson, illustrated by Diane Goode; Dutton, 1985.

The Woman who Loved Reindeer by Meredith Ann Pierce, not illustrated; Atlantic, 1985.

Sirens and Spies by Janet Lisle, not illustrated; Bradbury, 1985.

Blackberry Ink by Eve Merriam, illustrated by Hans Wilhelm; Morrow, 1985.

The Willow Maiden by Meghan Collins, illustrated by Laszlo Gal; Dial, 1985.

It's an Aardvark-Eat-Turtle World by Paula Danziger, not illustrated; Delacorte, 1985.

Babe, the Gallant Pig by Dick King-Smith, illustrated by Mary Rayner; Crown, 1985.

Dog Song by Gary Paulsen, not illustrated; Bradbury, 1985.

The Finding by Nina Bawden, not illustrated; Lothrop, 1985.

Brother to the Wind by Mildred Pitts Walter, illustrated by Leo Dillon and Diane Dillon; Lothrop, 1985.

Come Sing, Jimmy Jo by Katherine Paterson, not illustrated; Lodestar, 1985.

Imogene's Antlers written and illustrated by David Small; Crown, 1985.

Tales for the Perfect Child by Florence Heide, illustrated by Victoria Chess; Lothrop, 1985.

Cracker Jackson by Betsy Byars, not illustrated; Viking Kestrel, 1985.

The Everlasting Hills by Irene Hunt, not illustrated; Scribner, 1985.

Rosie Cole's Great American Guilt Club written and illustrated by Sheila Greenwald; Atlantic, 1985.

Why Me? by Ellen Conford, not illustrated; Little Brown, 1985.

Washday on Noah's Ark written and illustrated by Glen Rounds; Holiday House, 1985.

1986 **LITERATURE** *Not So Fast, Songololo* written by Niki Daly; Atheneum, 1986.

Angel's Mother's Boyfriend by Judy Delton, illustrated by Margot Apple; Houghton Mifflin, 1985.

No Hero for the Kaiser by Rudolph Frank, translated by Patricia Crampton, illustrated by Klaus Steffens; Lothrop, 1986.

The Return of the Indian by Lynne Reid Banks, illustrated by William Geldart; Doubleday, 1986.

Tales of Pan written and illustrated by Mordicai Gerstein; Harper, 1986.

Yellow Bird and Me by Joyce Hansen, not illustrated; Clarion, 1986.

Up From Jericho Tell by E.L. Konigsburg, not illustrated; Atheneum, 1986.

The Not-Just-Anybody Family by Betsy Byars, illustrated by Jacqueline Rogers;Delacorte, 1986.

A Fine White Dust by Cynthia Rylant, not illustrated; Bradbury, 1986.

Return to Bitter Creek by Doris Buchanan Smith, not illustrated; Viking Kestrel, 1986.

The Giant's Toe written and illustrated by Brock Cole; Farrar, 1986.

So Far from the Bamboo Grove by Yoko Kawashima Watkins, introduction by Jean Fritz; Lothrop, Lee & Shepard, 1986.

More Stories Julian Tells by Ann Cameron, illustrated by Ann Strugnell; Knopf, 1986.

A Royal Pain by Ellen Conford, not illustrated; Scholastic, 1986.

Streams to the River, River to the Sea by Scott O'Dell, not illustrated; Houghton Mifflin, 1986.

The Illyrian Adventure by Lloyd Alexander, illustrated with a map; Dutton, 1986.

The Dallas Titans Get Ready for Bed by Karla Kuskin, illustrated by Marc Simont; Harper, 1986.

Best Friends written and illustrated by Steven Kellogg; Dial, 1986.

1987 **PICTURE BOOK** *The Devil & Mother Crump* by Valerie Scho Carey, illustrated by Arnold Lobel; Harper & Row, 1987.

Mufaro's Beautiful Daughters written and illustrated by John Steptoe; Lothrop, Lee & Shepard, 1987.

How Dog Began written and illustrated by Pauline Baynes; Henry Holt, 1987, c1985; Methuen, 1985.

The Zabajaba Jungle written and illustrated by William Steig; Farrar, Straus, Giroux, 1987.

Little Nino's Pizzeria written and illustrated by Karen Barbour; Harcourt, Brace, Jovanovich, 1987.

The Tongue-Cut Sparrow by Momoko Ishii, illustrated by Suekichi Akaba; Lodestar, 1987.

The Z Was Zapped written and illustrated by Chris Van Allsburg; Houghton Mifflin, 1987.

The Magic Leaf by Winifred Morris, illustrated by Ju-Hong Chen; Atheneum, 1987.

The Eyes of the Dragon by Margaret Leaf, illustrated by Ed Young; Lothrop, Lee & Shepard, 1987.

Grandaddy's Place by Helen V. Griffith, illustrated by James Stevenson; Greenwillow, 1987.

Why the Chicken Crossed the Road written and illustrated by David Macaulay; Houghton Mifflin, 1987.

Gunga Din by Rudyard Kipling, illustrated by Robert Andrew Parker; Gulliver Books, 1987.

The Three Bears Rhyme Book by Jane Yolen, illustrated by Jane Dyer; Harcourt, Brace, Jovanovich, 1987.

Adam and Eve: The Bible Story adapted and illustrated by Warwick Hutton; McElderry, 1987.

Four Brave Sailors by Mirra Ginsburg, illustrated by Nancy Tafuri; Greenwillow, 1987.

Higher on the Door written and illustrated by James Stevenson; Greenwillow, 1987.

Piggybook written and illustrated by Anthony Browne; Knopf, 1986.

Random House Book of Mother Goose selected and illustrated by Arnold Lobel; Random House, 1986.

The Book of Adam To Moses by Lore Segal, illustrated by Leonard Baskin; Knopf, 1987.

Bossyboots written and illustrated by David Cox; Crown, 1987, c1985.

In Coal Country by Judith Hendershot, illustrated by Thomas B. Allen; Knopf, 1987.

I Have a Friend written and illustrated by Keiko Narahashi; McElderry, 1987.

Big, Small, Short, Tall written and illustrated by Loreen Leedy; Holiday House, 1987.

The Cremation of Sam McGee by Robert W. Service, illustrated by Ted Harrison; Greenwillow, 1987.

Peter and the Wolf retold by Selina Hastings, illustrated by Reg Cartwright; Holt, Rinehart & Winston, 1987.

1987 STORY BOOK *Fat Chance, Claude* by Joan Lowery Nixon, illustrated by Tracy Campbell Pearson; Viking Kestrel, 1987.

The Devil's Other Storybook written and illustrated by Natalie Babbitt; Farrar, Straus, Giroux, 1987.

Grandaddy's Place by Helen V. Griffith, illustrated by James Stevenson; Greenwillow, 1987.

The Tales of Uncle Remus by Joel Chandler Harris, adapted by Julius Lester, illustrated by Jerry Pinkney; Dial, 1987.

The Eyes of the Dragon by Margaret Leaf, illustrated by Ed Young; Lothrop, Lee & Shepard, 1987.

Brave Irene written and illustrated by William Steig; Farrar, Straus, Giroux, 1986.

Harry's Mad by Dick King-Smith, illustrated by Jill Bennett; Crown, 1987, c1984; Gollancz, 1984.

Ghost's Hour, Spook's Hour by Eve Bunting, illustrated by Donald Carrick; Clarion, 1987.

Who Stole the Apples? written and illustrated by Sigrid Heuck; Knopf, 1986.

Mrs. Pig Gets Cross and Other Stories written and illustrated by Mary Rayner; Dutton, 1986.

I Had a Friend Named Peter by Janice Cohn, illustrated by Gail Owens; Morrow, 1987.

Crystal by Walter Dean Myers, not illustrated; Viking Kestrel, 1987.

Orvis by H.M. Hoover, not illustrated; Viking Kestrel, 1987.

The Two Foolish Cats by Yoshiko Uchida, illustrated by Margot Zemach; McElderry, 1987.

There's a Boy in the Girls' Bathroom by Louis Sachar, not illustrated; Knopf, 1987.

Blade of the Poisoner by Douglas Hill, not illustrated; McElderry, 1987.

The Kid In the Red Jacket by Barbara Park, not illustrated; Knopf, 1987.

The Ivory Lyre by Shirley Rousseau Murphy, not illustrated; Harper & Row, 1987.

The El Dorado Adventure by Lloyd Alexander, not illustrated; Dutton, 1987.

Cat Poems by Myra Cohn Livingston, illustrated by Trina Schart Hyman; Holiday House, 1987.

Piggins by Jane Yolen, illustrated by Jane Dyer; Harcourt, Brace, Jovanovich, 1987.

The Tongue-Cut Sparrow by Momoko Ishii, illustrated by Suekichi Akaba; Lodestar, 1987.

Permanent Connections by Sue Ellen Bridgers, not illustrated; Harper & Row, 1987.

Jerusalem Shining Still by Karla Kuskin, illustrated by David Frampton; Harper & Row, 1987.

Devils Who Learned To Be Good written and illustrated by Michael McCurdy; Little Brown, 1987.

Ridiculous Story of Gammar Gurton's Needle by David Lloyd, written and illustrated by Charlotte Voake; Clarkson Potter, 1987.

The Twisted Window by Lois Duncan, not illustrated; Delacorte, 1987.

The Secret of Gumbo Grove by Eleanora E. Tate, not illustrated; Watts, 1987.

Fran Ellen's House by Marilyn Sachs, not illustrated; Dutton, 1987.

The Return by Sonia Levitin, not illustrated; Atheneum, 1987.

1988 PICTURE BOOK *Seven Wild Pigs* written and illustrated by Helme Heine; McElderry, 1988.

The Man Who Wanted To Live Forever by Selina Hastings, illustrated by Reg Cartwright; Holt, 1988.

Goldilocks and the Three Bears retold and illustrated by James Marshall; Dial, 1988.

The Enchanter's Daughter by Antonia Barber, illustrated by Errol Le Cain; Farrar, Straus, Giroux, 1988, c1987.

Sleepers written and illustrated by Dayal Kaur Khalsa; Clarkson Potter, 1988.

The Rumor of Pavel and Paali adapted by Carole Kismaric, illustrated by Charles Mikolaycak; Harper & Row, 1988.

John Patrick Norman McHennessey, The Boy Who Was Always Late written and illustrated by John Burningham; Crown, 1988, c1987.

Flamboyan by Arnold Adoff, illustrated by Karen Barbour; Harcourt, Brace, Jovanovich, 1988.

The Dove's Letter written and illustrated by Keith Baker; Harcourt, Brace, Jovanovich, 1988.

At the Cafe Splendid written and illustrated by Terry Denton; Houghton Mifflin, 1988.

Step Into the Night by Joanne Ryder, illustrated by Dennis Nolan; Four Winds, 1988.

The Secret in the Matchbox by Val Willis, illustrated by John Shelley; Farrar, Straus Giroux, 1988.

Just Enough Is Plenty: A Hanukkah Tale by Barbara Diamond Goldin, illustrated by Seymour Chwast; Viking Kestrel, 1988.

1988 STORY BOOK *The Boy of the Three-Year Nap* by Dianne Snyder, illustrated by Allen Say; Houghton Mifflin, 1988.

Stringbean's Trip to the Shining Sea by Vera B. Williams, illustrated by Vera Williams and Jennifer Williams; Greenwillow, 1989.

Alias Madame Doubtfire by Anne Fine, not illustrated; Little Brown, 1988.

Children of Long Ago: Poems by Lessie Jones Little, illustrated by Jan Spivey Gilchrist; Philomel, 1988.

Runaway Mittens by Jean Rogers, illustrated by Rie Munoz; Greenwillow, 1988.

Storm in the Night by Mary Stolz, illustrated by Pat Cummings; Harper & Row, 1988.

The Honorable Prison by Lyll Becerra de Jenkins, not illustrated; Dutton, 1988.

The Private World of Julia Redfern by Eleanor Cameron, not illustrated; Dutton, 1988.

The Fox Busters by Dick King-Smith, illustrated by Jon Miller; Delacorte, 1988, c1978.

Fallen Angels by Walter Dean Myers, not illustrated; Scholastic, 1988.

Facts and Fictions of Minna Pratt by Patricia MacLachlan, not illustrated; Harper & Row, 1988.

Henry by Nina Bawden, illustrated by Joyce Powzyk; Lothrop, Lee & Shepard, 1988.

The Burning Questions of Bingo Brown by Betsy Byars, illustrated by Cathy Bobak; Viking, 1988.

1989 PICTURE BOOK *Alice's Adventures in Wonderland* by Lewis Carroll, illustrated by Anthony Browne; Knopf, 1988.

William and Grandpa by Alice Schertle, illustrated by Lydia Dabcovich; Lothrop, Lee & Shepard, 1989.

Anno's Math Games II written and illustrated by Mitsumasa Anno; Philomel, 1989.

Hey Willie, See the Pyramids written and illustrated by Maira Kalman; Viking, 1988.

Ragtime Tumpie by Alan Schroeder, illustrated by Bernie Fuchs; Little Brown, 1989.

Rosie and the Rustlers written and illustrated by Roy Gerrard; Farrar, Straus, Giroux, 1989.

The Tub People by Pam Conrad, illustrated by Richard Egielski; Harper & Row, 1989.

The Talking Eggs by Robert D. San Souci, illustrated by Jerry Pinkney; Dial, 1989.

Valentine and Orson written and illustrated by Nancy Ekholm Burkert; Farrar, Straus, Giroux, 1989.

Aesop's Fables illustrated by Lisbeth Zwerger; Picture Book Studios, 1989.

We're Going on a Bear Hunt by Michael Rosen, illustrated by Helen Oxenbury; McElderry, 1989.

The Lady Who Put Salt in Her Coffee by Lucretia Hale, adapted and illustrated by Amy Schwartz; Harcourt Brace Jovanovich, 1989.

As: A Surfeit of Similes by Norton Juster, illustrated by David Small; Morrow, 1989.

1989 STORY BOOK *Shy Charles* written and illustrated by Rosemary Wells; Dial, 1988.

Nettie Jo's Friends by Patricia McKissack, illustrated by Scott Cook; Knopf, 1989.

Sweetgrass by Jan Hudson, not illustrated; Philomel, 1989.

Rabbit Makes a Monkey Out of a Lion by Verna Aardema, illustrated by Jerry Pinkney; Dial, 1989.

Wayside School Is Falling Down by Louis Sachar, illustrated by Joel Schick; Lothrop, Lee & Shepard, 1989.

Turtle Knows Your Name written and illustrated by Ashley Bryan; Atheneum, 1989.

Everyone Else's Parents Said Yes by Paula Danziger, illustrated with line drawings; Delacorte, 1989.

Afternoon of the Elves by Janet Taylor Lisle, not illustrated; Orchard, 1989.

Don't Look Behind You by Lois Duncan, not illustrated; Delacorte, 1989.

The Chalk Doll by Charlotte Pomerantz, illustrated by Frane Lessac; Lippincott, 1989.

The Shimmershine Queens by Camille Yarbrough, not illustrated; Putnam, 1989.

Tell Me a Story, Mama by Angela Johnson, illustrated by David Soman; Orchard, 1989.

The Big Alfie and Annie Rose Storybook written and illustrated by Shirley Hughes; Lothrop, Lee & Shepard, 1989, c1988.

Shark Beneath the Reef by Jean Craighead George, not illustrated; Harper & Row, 1989.

1990 PICTURE BOOK *Possum Come a-Knockin'* by Nancy Van Laan, illustrated by George Booth; Knopf, 1990.

The Adventures of Taxi Dog by Sal Barracca and Debra Barracca, illustrated by Mark Buehner; Dial, 1990.

Shadows and Reflections written and illustrated by Tana Hoban; Greenwillow, 1990.

Ducks Fly written and illustrated by Lydia Dabcovich; Dutton, 1990.

Shrek! written and illustrated by William Steig; Farrar, Straus, Giroux, 1990.

Box and Cox by Grace Chetwin, illustrated by David Small; Bradbury, 1990.

Uncle Wizzmo's New Used Car written and illustrated by Rodney A. Greenblat; Harper & Row, 1990.

Puss In Boots by Charles Perrault, illustrated by Fred Marcellino; Farrar, Straus, Giroux, 1990.

Hey! Get Off Our Train! written and illustrated by John Burningham; Crown, 1989.

Crow and Weasel by Barry Lopez, illustrated by Tom Pohrt; North Point Press, 1990; Random House of Canada, 1990.

More Bugs in Boxes: A Pop-up book about Color written and illustrated by David A. Carter; Simon & Schuster, 1990.

The Wheels on the Bus adapted and illustrated by Paul O. Zelinsky; Dutton, 1990.

1990 STORY BOOK *Maxie, Rosie and Earl: Partners in Grime* by Barbara Park, illustrated by Alexander Strogart; Knopf, 1990.

The Mouse Rap by Walter Dean Myers, not illustrated; Harper & Row, 1990.

Rice Without Rain by Minfong Ho, not illustrated; Lothrop, Lee & Shepard, 1990.

The Squeaky Wheel by Robert Kimmell Smith, not illustrated; Delacorte, 1990.

Laura Charlotte by Katherine Galbraith, illustrated by Floyd Cooper; Philomel, 1990.

Stonewords by Pam Conrad, not illustrated; HarperCollins, 1990.

Elizabeth and Larry by Marilyn Sadler, illustrated by Roger Bollen; Simon & Schuster, 1990.

Nessa's Fish by Nancy Leunn, illustrated by Neil Waldman; Atheneum, 1990.

Bingo Brown, Gypsy Lover by Betsy Byars, illustrated by Cathy Bobak; Viking, 1990.

Further Tales of Uncle Remus by Joel Chandler Harris, adapted by Julius Lester, illustrated by Jerry Pinkney; Dial, 1990.

My Daddy Was a Soldier: A World War II Story written and illustrated by Deborah Kogan Ray; Holiday House, 1990.

I Hate English! by Ellen Levine, illustrated by Steve Bjorkman; Scholastic, 1989.

The Midnight Horse by Sid Fleischman, illustrated by Peter Sis; Greenwillow, 1990.

1991 PICTURE BOOK *Tigress* written and illustrated by Helen Cowcher; Farrar, Straus, Giroux, 1991.

Randolph's Dream by Judith Mellecker, illustrated by Robert Andrew Parker; Knopf, 1991.

Aunt Flossie's Hats (and Crab Cakes Later) by Elizabeth Fitzgerald Howard, illustrated by James Ransome; Clarion, 1990.

Witch Hazel by Alice Schertle, illustrated by Margot Tomes; HarperCollins, 1991.

Bridges written and illustrated by Ken Robbins; Dial, 1991.

Tar Beach written and illustrated by Faith Ringgold; Crown, 1991.

Anno's Math Games III written and illustrated by Mitsumasa Anno; Philomel, 1991.

The Alphabet Parade written and illustrated by Seymour Chwast; Harcourt, Brace, Jovanovich, 1991.

Appalachia: The Voices of Sleeping Birds by Cynthia Rylant, illustrated by Barry Moser; Harcourt, Brace, Jovanovich, 1991.

Brother Eagle, Sister Sky: A Message from Chief Seattle illustrated by Susan Jeffers; Dial, 1991.

Glasses: Who Needs 'Em? written and illustrated by Lane Smith; Viking, 1991.

Diego by Jonah Winter, written and illustrated by Jeanette Winter; Knopf, 1991.

The Night Ones by Patricia Grossman, illustrated by Lydia Dabcovich; Harcourt, Brace, Jovanovich, 1991.

Just So Stories by Rudyard Kipling, illustrated by David Frampton; HarperCollins, 1991.

A Day With Wilbur Robinson written and illustrated by William Joyce; Harper and Row, 1990.

Cactus Hotel by Brenda Z. Guiberson, illustrated by Megan Lloyd; Henry Holt, 1991.

On the Pampas written and illustrated by Maria Cristina Brusca; Henry Holt, 1991.

1991 STORY BOOK *Reluctantly Alice* by Phyllis Reynolds Naylor, not illustrated; Atheneum, 1991.

Boy Who Owned the School: A Comedy of Love by Gary Paulsen, not illustrated; Orchard, 1990.

The Mozart Season by Virginia Euwer Wolff, not illustrated; Henry Holt, 1991.

Dakota of the White Flats by Philip Ridley, not illustrated; Knopf, 1991.

Fat Glenda Turns Fourteen by Lila Perl, not illustrated; Clarion, 1991.

The New Creatures written and illustrated by Mordicai Gerstein; HarperCollins, 1991.

Little Red Riding Hood retold and illustrated by Beni Montresor; Doubleday, 1991.

A Wave In Her Pocket: Stories From Trinidad by Lynn Joseph, illustrated by Brian Pinkney; Clarion, 1991.

Abuela by Arthur Dorros, illustrated by Elisa Kleven; Dutton, 1991.

Rats on the Roof and Other Stories written and illustrated by James Marshall; Dial, 1991.

Magic Carpet by Pat Brisson, illustrated by Amy Schwartz; Bradbury, 1991.

Pedro & the Padre by Verna Aardema, illustrated by Friso Henstra; Dial, 1991.

On the Day You Were Born written and illustrated by Debra Frasier; Harcourt, Brace, Jovanovich, 1991.

Remarkable Journey of Prince Jen by Lloyd Alexander, map by Bebby L. Carter; Dutton, 1991.

Antler, Bear, Canoe: A Northwoods Alphabet Year written and illustrated by Betsy Bowen; Little Brown, 1991.

Short, Short, Short Stories written and illustrated by William Accorsi; Greenwillow, 1991.

Gretchen's ABC written and illustrated by Gretchen Dow Simpson; HarperCollins, 1991.

Long Is a Dragon: Chinese Writing For Children written and illustrated by Peggy Goldstein; China Books & Periodicals, 1991.

Dogs Don't Tell Jokes by Louis Sachar, not illustrated; Knopf, 1991.

At the Crossroads written and illustrated by Rachel Isadora; Greenwillow, 1991.

Anancy and Mr. Dry-Bone written and illustrated by Fiona French; Little Brown, 1991.

The Adventures of Isabel by Ogden Nash, illustrated by James Marshall; Little Brown, 1991.

Sophie and Lou written and illustrated by Petra Mathers; HarperCollins, 1991.

An Auto Mechanic written and illustrated by Douglas Florian; Greenwillow, 1991.

The Boy and the Samurai by Erik Christian Haugaard, not illustrated; Houghton Mifflin, 1991.

The Wright Brothers: How They Invented the Airplane by Russell Freedman, illustrated with photos; Holiday House, 1991.

Wolf by Gillian Cross, not illustrated; Holiday House, 1991.

If You Give a Moose a Muffin by Laura Joffe Numeroff, illustrated by Felicia Bond; HarperCollins, 1991.

Rosie Swanson: Fourth-Grade Geek For President by Barbara Park, not illustrated; Knopf, 1989.

1992   PICTURE BOOK *Will's New Cap* by Olof Landstrom, illustrated by Lena Landstrom; R & S Books, 1992.

I Saw Esau by Iona Opie and Peter Opie, illustrated by Maurice Sendak; Candlewick Press, 1992.

Klara's New World written and illustrated by Jeanette Winter; Knopf, 1992.

Shortcut written and illustrated by Donald Crews; Greenwillow, 1992.

June 29, 1999 illustrated by David Wiesner; Clarion, 1992.

The Golden Locket by Carol Greene, illustrated by Marcia Sewall; Harcourt Brace Jovanovich, 1992.

An Indian Winter by Russell Freedman, illustrated by Karl Bodmer; Holiday House, 1992.

I Spy: An Alphabet In Art written and illustrated by Lucy Micklethwait; Greenwillow, 1992.

The Steadfast Tin Soldier by Hans Christian Andersen, illustrated by Fred Marcellino; HarperCollins, 1992.

Tigers by Roland Edwards, illustrated by Judith Riches; Tambourine Books, 1992.

Back Home by Gloria Jean Pinkney, illustrated by Jerry Pinkney; Dial, 1992.

An Ocean World written and illustrated by Peter Sis; Greenwillow, 1992.

My Little Red Car written and illustrated by Chris L. Demarest; Caroline House/Boyds Mills, 1992.

The Return of Freddy LeGrand written and illustrated by Jon Agee; Farrar Straus Giroux, 1992.

Rosa Parks: My Story by Rosa Parks, with Jim Haskins, illustrated; Dial, 1992.

The Righteous Revenge of Artemis Bonner by Walter Dean Myers, not illustrated; HarperCollins, 1992.

A Twilight Struggle: The Life of John Fitzgerald Kennedy by Daniel Terris and Barbara Harrison, illustrated; Lothrop, Lee & Shepard; 1992.

Don't You Know There's a War On? written and illustrated by James Stevenson; Greenwillow, 1992.

The Widow's Broom written and illustrated by Chris Van Allsburg; Houghton Mifflin, 1992.

1992   STORY BOOK *Oh, Those Harper Girls!* by Kathleen Karr, not illustrated; Farrar Straus Giroux, 1992.

A Ride on the Red Mare's Back by Ursula K. Le Guin, illustrated by Julie Downing; Orchard, 1992.

Blue Skin of the Sea: A Novel in Stories by Graham Salisbury, not illustrated; Delacorte, 1992.

Humbug by Nina Bawden, not illustrated; Clarion, 1992.

Missing May by Cynthia Rylant, not illustrated; Orchard, 1992.

The Fortune-Tellers by Lloyd Alexander, illustrated by Trina Schart Hyman; Dutton, 1992.

Jim Ugly by Sid Fleischman, illustrated by Joseph A. Smith; Greenwillow, 1992.

Talk, Talk: An Ashanti Legend by Deborah Newton Chocolate, illustrated by David Albers; Troll, 1992.

Slither McCreep and His Brother Joe by Tony Johnston, illustrated by Victoria Chess; Harcourt, Brace, Jovanovich, 1992.

Through the Mickle Woods by Valiska Gregory, illustrated by Barry Moser; Little Brown, 1992.

Sing to the Sun written and illustrated by Ashley Bryan; HarperCollins, 1992.

Soap Soup and Other Verses by Karla Kuskin; HarperCollins, 1992.

PEN CENTER USA WEST LITERARY AWARD IN CHILDREN'S LITERATURE

PEN Center USA West
672 S. Lafayette Park Place #41
Los Angeles, CA 90057

Established in 1983 and awarded annually, the Pen Center USA West Literary Award recognizes outstanding children's books by western writers. The author must live west of the Mississippi River and the book must be published in the year of eligibility. All categories, from picture books to young adult are eligible. The winning author receives a $500 cash prize and a plaque.

1983   *The Birds of Summer* by Zilpha Keatley Snyder, not illustrated; Atheneum, 1983.

Ratha's Creature by Clare Bell, not illustrated; Atheneum, 1983.

1986   *King Bidgood's in the Bathtub* by Audrey Wood, illustrated by Don Wood; Harcourt, 1985.

Top Secret by John Reynolds Gardiner, illustrated by Marc simont; Little Brown, 1984.

1987   *The Girl* by Robbie Branscum, not illusrtated; Harper & Row, 1986.

Israel by Helen Hinkley Jones, illustrated with photographs; Children's Press, 1986.

1988   *Street Family* by Adrienne Jones, not illustrated; Harper & Row, 1987.

The Return by Sonia Levitin, illustrated with a map; Atheneum, 1987.

1989   *Her Own Song* by Ellen Howard, not illustrated; Atheneum, 1988.

Probably Still Nick Swansen by Virginia Euwer Wolff, not illustrated; Henry Holt, 1988.

1990 *The Forty-third War* by Louise Moeri, not illustrated; Houghton Mifflin, 1989.

The Five-Finger Discount by Barthe DeClements, not illustrated; Delacorte, 1989.

1991 *The Dragon's Robe* written and illustrated by Deborah Nourse Lattimore; Harper & Row, 1990.

1992 *Tree of Cranes* written and illustrated by Allen Say; Houghton Mifflin, 1991.

1993 *Is Kissing a Girl Who Smokes Like Licking an Ashtray?* by Randy Powell, not illustrated; Farrar Straus Giroux, 1992.

PEN/NORMA KLEIN AWARD

PEN American Center
568 Broadway
New York, NY 10012

This biennial prize, first awarded in 1991, was established in memory of Norma Klein, the late PEN member and distinguished children's book author. The prize recognizes an emerging voice of literary merit among American writers of children's fiction. Candidates for the award are new authors whose books (for elementary school to young adult readers) demonstrate the adventuresome and innovative spirit that characterizes the best children's literature and Norma Klein's own work, but need not resemble her novels stylistically. The winner receive a $3000 cash award.

1991 Cynthia D. Grant

1991 CITATION Rita Williams-Garcia

PHOENIX AWARD

Children's Literature Association
22 Harvest Lane
Grand Rapids, MI 49017

This annual award is given to the author, or the estate of the author, of a book for children first published twenty years earlier which did not win a major award at the time of its publication but which, from the perspective of time, is deemed worthy of special recognition for its literary quality.

The Children's Literature Association created the award in 1985 to recognize books of merit. The Phoenix Award is named after the fabled bird who rose from its ashes with renewed life and beauty. Phoenix books also rise from the ashes of neglect and obscurity and enrich the lives of those who read them. The recipient is chosen by an elected committee of Children's Literature Association members and others interested in literature for children. The award was designed by Trina Schart Hyman and sculpted by Diane Davis. Each year's winner receives an individually cast, two dimensional brass statue inscribed with their name.

1985 *The Mark of the Horse Lord* by Rosemary Sutcliff, illustrated with a map; Walck, 1965; Oxford, 1975; Penguin, 1983.

1986 *Queenie Peavy* by Robert Burch, illustrated by Jerry Lazare; Viking, 1966; Dell, 1975.

1987 *Smith* by Leon Garfield, illustrated by Antony Maitland; Constable, 1967; Pantheon, 1967; Penguin, 1968; Dell, 1987.

1988 *The Rider and His Horse* by Erik Christian Haugaard, illustrated by Leo Dillon and Diane Dillon; Houghton Mifflin, 1968.

1989 *The Night Watchmen* by Helen Cresswell, illustrated by Gareth Floyd; Macmillan, 1969.

1990 *Enchantress From the Stars* by Sylvia L. Engdahl, illustrated by Rodney Shackell; Atheneum, 1970; Collier Books, 1989.

1991 *A Long Way From Verona* by Jane Gardam, not illustrated; Macmillan, 1971.

1992 *A Sound of Chariots* by Mollie Hunter, not illustrated; Harper & Row, 1972.

1993 *Carrie's War* by Nina Bawden, illustrated by Coleen Browning; Lippincott, 1973.

PLEASE TOUCH BOOK AWARD

Curator of Education
Please Touch Museum for Children
210 N 21 St
Philadelphia, PA 19103

Awarded annually since 1985, the Please Touch Award was created to recognize and encourage the publication of books for young children that are of the highest quality and will aid them in enjoying the art of learning. The winning book should be particularly imaginative and effective in exploring and clarifying a concept for children three years of age or older (i.e. alphabet, numbers, shapes, sizes, etc.). It must be published in the previous year by an American publisher and be distinguished in both text and illustration.

The following criteria apply: (1) The content must be age appropriate, original, develop concepts and provide a point of view or values. (2) The book design must complement the text and reinforce the concept. (3) The book should display an overall excellence.

A medal is awarded to the recipient.

1985 *What's Inside?* illustrated by Duanne Daughtry; Knopf, 1984.

1986 *Is It Larger? Is It Smaller?* written and illustrated by Tana Hoban; Greenwillow, 1985.

1986 HONORABLE MENTION *Hello, Clouds!* by Dalia H. Renberg, illustrated by Alona Frankel; Harper, 1985.

1987 *Who's Counting?* written and illustrated by Nancy Tafuri; Greenwillow, 1986.

1987 HONORABLE MENTION *Have You Ever Seen...? An ABC Book* written and illustrated by Beau Gardner; Dodd Mead, 1986.

1988 *Claude and Sun* by Matt Novak, not illustrated; Bradbury, 1987.

1989 *Who's Sick Today?* written and illustrated by Lynne Cherry; Dutton, 1988.

1990 *Dinosaurs, Dinosaurs* written and illustrated by Byron Barton; Crowell, 1989.

1991 *Maisy Goes to Bed* written and illustrated by Lucy Cousins; Little Brown, 1990.

1992 *In the Tall, Tall Grass* written and illustrated by Denise Fleming; Henry Holt, 1991.

EDGAR ALLAN POE AWARD

Mystery Writers of America
17 East 47th St.
6th Floor
New York, NY 10017

Established and sponsored by the Mystery Writers of America since 1945, the Edgar Allan Poe Award has numerous categories, one of which is juvenile mystery. This award, given for the best juvenile mystery of the preceding year, was presented for the first time in 1961. There are few limitations placed on the nominees. A committee is appointed to make the final selection. The winning author receives a ceramic bust of Poe, known as the Edgar, at a dinner held in New York City. In 1989, a Young Adult category was added.

1961 *The Mystery of the Haunted Pool* by Phyllis A. Whitney, illustrated by H. Tom Hall; Westminster, 1960.

1962 *The Phantom of Walkaway Hill* by Edward Fenton, illustrated by Jo Ann Stover; Doubleday, 1961.

1962 RUNNERSUP *The Secret of the Tiger Eyes* by Phyllis A. Whitney, not illustrated; Westminster, 1961.

1963 *Cutlass Island* by Scott Corbett, illustrated by Leonard Shortall; Atlantic-Little, 1962.

1963 RUNNERSUP *The House on Charlton Street* by Dola deJong, illustrated by Gilbert Riswold; Scribner, 1962.

The Diamond in the Window by Jane Langton, illustrated by Erik Blegvad; Harper, 1962.

The Mystery of Ghost Valley by Harriet Carr, not illustrated; Macmillan, 1962.

1964 *The Mystery of the Hidden Hand* by Phyllis A. Whitney, illustrated by H. Tom Hall; Westminster, 1963.

1964 RUNNERSUP *Honor Bound* by Frank Bonham, not illustrated; Crowell, 1963.

Mystery of the Velvet Box by Margaret Scheft, illustrated by Charles Geer; Watts, 1963.

1965 *The Mystery at Crane's Landing* by Marcella Thum, not illustrated; Dodd, Mead, 1964.

1965 RUNNERSUP *A Spell Is Cast* by Eleanor Cameron, illustrated by Beth Krush and Joe Krush; Little Brown, 1964.

Treasure River by Hal Evarts, illustrated with a map; Scribner, 1964.

Private Eyes: Adventures with the Saturday Gang by Lee Kingman, illustrated by Burt Silverman; Doubleday, 1964.

1966 *The Mystery of 22 East* by Leon Ware, not illustrated; Westminster, 1965.

1966 RUNNERSUP *The Apache Gold Mystery* by Eileen Thompson, illustrated by James Russell; Abelard-Schuman, 1965.

The Secret of the Simple Code by Nancy Faulkner, illustrated by Mimi Korach; Doubleday, 1965.

Secret of Haunted Crags by Lawrence J. Hunt, not illustrated; Funk & Wagnalls, 1965.

1967 *Sinbad and Me* by Kin Platt, not illustrated; Chilton, 1966.

1967 RUNNERSUP *Ransom* by Lois Duncan, not illustrated; Doubleday, 1966.

Danger Beats the Drum by Arnold Madison, not illustrated; Holt, 1966.

The Mystery of the Red Tide by Frank Bonham, not illustrated; Dutton, 1966.

1968 *Signpost to Terror* by Gretchen Sprague, not illustrated; Dodd Mead, 1967.

1968 RUNNERSUP *The Secret of the Missing Boat* by Paul Berna, translated by John Buchanan-Brown, illustrated by Barry Wilkinson; Pantheon, 1967, c1966.

The Witches Bridge by Barbee Oliver Carleton, not illustrated; Holt, 1967.

1969 *The House of Dies Drear* by Virginia Hamilton, illustrated by Eros Keith; Macmillan, 1968.

1969 RUNNERSUP *Mystery of the Fat Cat* by Frank Bonham, illustrated by Alvin Smith; Dutton, 1968.

Smugglers Road by Hal G. Evarts, not illustrated; Scribner, 1968.

Forgery! by Phyllis Bentley, not illustrated; Doubleday, 1968.

1970 *Danger at Black Dyke* written and illustrated by Winifred Finlay; Phillips, 1968.

1970 RUNNERSUP *They Never Came Home* by Lois Duncan, not illustrated; Doubleday, 1969.

Spice Island Mystery by Betty Cavanna, not illustrated; Morrow, 1969.

Mystery of the Witch Who Wouldn't by Kin Platt, not illustrated; Chilton, 1969.

1971 *The Intruder* by John Rowe Townsend, illustrated by Joseph A. Phelan; Lippincott, 1970.

1971 RUNNERSUP *The Mystery Man* by Scott Corbett, illustrated by Nathan Goldstein; Little Brown, 1970.

The Secret of the Missing Footprint by Phyllis A. Whitney, illustrated by Alex Stein; Westminster, 1969.

1972 *Night Fall* by Joan Aiken, not illustrated; Holt, 1971.

1972 RUNNERSUP *The Ghost of Ballyhooly* by Betty Cavanna, not illustrated; Morrow, 1971.

Goody Hall written and illustrated by Natalie Babbitt; Farrar, 1971.

Mystery in Wales by Mabel Esther Allan, not illustrated; Vanguard, 1971.

1973 *Deathwatch* by Robb White, not illustrated; Doubleday, 1972.

1973 RUNNERSUP *Catch a Killer* by George A. Woods, not illustrated; Harper, 1972.

Elizabeth's Tower by A.C. Stewart, not illustrated; S.G. Phillips, 1972.

Uncle Robert's Secret by Wylly Folk St. John, illustrated by Frank Aloise; Viking, 1972.

1974 *The Long Black Coat* by Jay Bennett, not illustrated; Delacorte, 1973.

1974 RUNNERSUP *Dreamland Lake* by Richard Peck, not illustrated; Holt, 1973.

Mystery of the Scowling Boy by Phyllis A. Whitney, illustrated by John Gretzer; Westminster, 1973.

The Secret of the Seven Crows by Wylly Folk St. John, illustrated by Judith Gwyn Brown; Viking, 1973.

1975 *The Dangling Witness: A Mystery* by Jay Bennett, not illustrated; Delacorte, 1974.

1975 **RUNNERSUP** *The Fire in the Stone* by Colin Thiele, not illustrated; Harper, 1974.

The Girl in the Grove by David Severn, not illustrated; Harper, 1974.

Here Lies the Body by Scott Corbett, illustrated by Geff Gerlach; Little Brown, 1974.

The Mysterious Red Tape Gang by Joan Lowery Nixon, illustrated by Joan Sandin; Putnam, 1974.

1975 **SPECIAL EDGAR** Donald J. Sobol for the *Encyclopedia Brown* books

1976 *Z for Zachariah* by Robert C. O'Brien, not illustrated; Atheneum, 1975.

1976 **RUNNERSUP** *No More Magic* by Avi, not illustrated; Pantheon, 1975.

The Great Steamboat Mystery written and illustrated by Richard Scarry; Random House, 1975.

The Tattooed Potato and other Clues by Ellen Raskin, not illustrated; Dutton, 1975.

1977 *Are You in the House Alone?* by Richard Peck, not illustrated; Viking, 1976.

1977 **RUNNERSUP** *The Master Puppeteer* by Katherine Paterson, illustrated by Haru Wells; Crowell, 1975.

Wiley and the Hairy Man written and illustrated by Molly Garrett Bang; Macmillan, 1976.

Mr. Moon's Last Case by Brian Patten, illustrated by Mary Moore; Scribner, 1975.

The Chalk Cross by Berthe Amoss, not illustrated; Seabury, 1976.

1978 *A Really Weird Summer* by Eloise Jarvis McGraw, not illustrated; Atheneum, 1977.

1978 **RUNNERSUP** *Miss Nelson Is Missing!* by Harry Allard, illustrated by James Marshall; Houghton Mifflin, 1977; Scholastic, 1978.

Poor Tom's Ghost by Jane L. Curry, not illustrated; Atheneum, 1977.

Night Spell by Robert Newman, illustrated by Peter Burchard; Atheneum, 1977.

1979 *Alone in Wolf Hollow* by Dana Brookins, not illustrated; Seabury, 1978.

1979 **RUNNERSUP** *The Bassumtyte Treasure* by Jane L. Curry, not illustrated; Atheneum, 1978.

Emily Upham's Revenge: or, How Deadwood Dick Saved the Banker's Niece: A Massachusetts Adventure by Avi, illustrated by Paul O. Zelinsky; Pantheon, 1978.

The Halloween Pumpkin Smasher by Judith St. George, illustrated by Margot Tomes; Putnam, 1978.

The Case of the Secret Scribbler by E.W. Hildick, illustrated by Lisl Weil; Macmillan, 1978.

1980 *Kidnapping of Christine Lattimore* by Joan Lowery Nixon, not illustrated; Harcourt, 1979.

1980 **RUNNERSUP** *Mystery Cottage in Left Field* by Remus F. Caroselli, not illustrated; Putnam, 1979.

The Whispered Horse by Lynn Hall, not illustrated; Follett, 1979.

Chameleon Was a Spy written and illustrated by Diane Redfield Massie; Crowell, 1979.

Mystery of the Eagle's Claw by Frances Wosmek, not illustrated; Westminster, 1979.

1981 *The Seance* by Joan Lowery Nixon, not illustrated; Harcourt, 1980; Dell, 1981.

1981 **RUNNERSUP** *When No One Was Looking* by Rosemary Wells, not illustrated; Dial, 1980.

We Dare Not Go A-Hunting by Charlotte MacLeod, illustrated with a map; Atheneum, 1980.

More Minden Curses by Willo David Roberts, illustrated by Sherry Streeter; Atheneum, 1980.

The Doggone Mystery by Mary Blount Christian, illustrated by Irene Trivas; Whitman, 1980.

1982 *Taking Terri Mueller* by Norma Fox Mazer, not illustrated; Avon, 1981; Morrow, 1983.

1982 **RUNNERSUP** *Detective Mole and the Halloween Mystery* written and illustrated by Robert Quackenbush; Lothrop, 1981.

Detour to Danger by Eva-Lis Wuorio, not illustrated; Delacorte, 1981.

Hoops by Walter Dean Myers, not illustrated; Delacorte, 1981.

Village of the Vampire Cat by Lensey Namioka, not illustrated; Delacorte, 1981.

1983 *The Murder of Hound Dog Bates: A Novel* by Robbie Branscum, not illustrated; Viking, 1982.

1983 **RUNNERSUP** *Cadbury's Coffin* by Glendon Swarthout and Kathryn Swarthout, illustrated by Frank Mayo; Doubleday, 1982.

The Baker Street Irregulars in the Case of the Cop Catchers by Terrance Dicks, not illustrated; Lodestar/Dutton, 1981.

Clone Catcher by Alfred Slote, illustrated by Elizabeth Slote; Lippincott, 1982.

Kept in the Dark by Nina Bawden, not illustrated; Lothrop Lee & Shepard, 1982.

1984 *The Callendar Papers* by Cynthia Voigt, not illustrated; Atheneum, 1983.

1984 **RUNNERSUP** *The Dollhouse Murders* by Betty Ren Wright, not illustrated; Holiday House, 1983.

The Griffin Legacy by Jan O'Donnell Klaveness, not illustrated; Macmillan, 1983.

Shadrach's Crossing by Avi, not illustrated; Pantheon, 1983.

1985 *Night Cry* by Phyllis Reynolds Naylor, not illustrated; Atheneum, 1984.

1985 **RUNNERSUP** *Chameleon the Spy and the Case of the Vanishing Jewels* written and illustrated by Diane R. Massie; Crowell, 1984.

The Ghosts of Now by Joan Lowery Nixon, not illustrated; Delacorte, 1984.

The Island on Bird Street by Uri Orlev, translated by Hillel Halkin, not illustrated; Houghton Mifflin, 1984.

The Third Eye by Lois Duncan, not illustrated; Little Brown, 1984.

1986 *The Sandman's Eyes* by Patricia Windsor, not illustrated; Delacorte, 1985.

1986 **RUNNERSUP** *Locked in Time* by Lois Duncan, not illustrated; Little Brown, 1985.

On the Edge by Gillian Cross, not illustrated; Holiday House, 1985.

Playing Murder by Sandra Scoppettone, not illustrated; Harper, 1985.

Screaming High by David Line, not illustrated; Little Brown, 1985.

1987 *The Other Side of Dark* by Joan Lowery Nixon, not illustrated; Delacorte, 1986.

1987 **RUNNERSUP** *Floating Illusions* by Chelsea Quinn Yarbro, not illustrated; Harper, 1986.

The Secret Life of Dilly McBean by Dorothy Haas, not illustrated; Bradbury, 1986.

The Skeleton Man by Jay Bennett, not illustrated; Watts, 1986.

1988 *Lucy Forever & Miss Rosetree, Shrinks* by Susan Shreve, not illustrated; Henry Holt, 1987.

1989 **JUVENILE** *Megan's Island* by Willo Davis Roberts, not illustrated; Atheneum, 1988.

1989 **YOUNG ADULT** *Incident at Loring Groves* by Sonia Levitin, not illustrated; Dial, 1988.

1990 **JUVENILE** No Award

1990 **YOUNG ADULT** *Show Me the Evidence* by Alane Ferguson, not illustrated; Bradbury, 1989.

1991 **JUVENILE** *Stonewords* by Pam Conrad, not illustrated; HarperCollins, 1990.

1991 **YOUNG ADULT** *Mote* by Herbert R. Reaver, not illustrated; Delacorte, 1990.

PRESENT TENSE/JOEL H. CAVIOR LITERARY AWARDS

(formerly Kenneth B. Smilen/Present Tense Literary Awards)
discontinued

This annual award was founded in 1980 by the Present Tense magazine. The purpose of the award was to encourage the flourishing of Jewish literary and intellectual life by stimulating the writing of significant, serious works with Jewish themes. The award had several categories including fiction, biography/autobiography, history, and juvenile. The juvenile category was discontinued in 1983. Only the juvenile winners are listed below.

Any book for juveniles with a Jewish content and interest, published in English in the United States during the year preceding the award was eligible. Nominations were made by a committee; final selection was made by a panel of judges. A $500 cash award as well as a plaque was presented to the winner at the annual awards ceremony.

1980 *The Power of Light: Eight Stories for Hanukkah* by Isaac Bashevis Singer, illustrated by Irene Lieblich; Farrar, 1980.

1981 No Award

1982 *King of the Seventh Grade* by Barbara Cohen, not illustrated; Lothrop, 1982.

G. P. PUTNAM'S SONS FICTION PRIZE
discontinued

The G. P. Putnam's Sons Fiction Prize was a one-time award presented for a first work of fiction for middle grade readers. Sponsored by G. P. Putnam's Sons, it was awarded in 1987.

1987 *Good-Bye, My Wishing Star* by Vicki Grove, not illustrated; Putnam, 1988.

1987 **RUNNERUP** *After the Fortune Cookies* by Ann Blakeslee, not illustrated; Putnam, 1989.

Q

QUEST FOR A KELPIE
see **KELPIE FOR THE 90s**

R

READING ASSOCIATION OF IRELAND (RAI) CHILDREN'S BOOK AWARD
Reading Association of Ireland
Educational Research Centre
St. Patrick's College
Dumcondra
Dublin 9 Ireland

The Reading Association of Ireland established this biennial award in 1985 to encourage the writing and publication of children's books in Ireland. In 1989 a Special Merit category was added to honor a book making a unique contribution to children's publishing in Ireland. Both works of fiction and nonfiction are considered, while textbooks are ineligible. The winning books carry the official RAI Book Award stamps.

1985 *Run Swift, Run Free* by Tom McCaughren, illustrated by Jeanette Dunne; Wolfhound Press, 1986.

1987 *Cyril: The Quest of an Orphan Squirrel* by Eugene McCabe, illustrated by Al O'Donnell; O'Brien Press, 1986.

1989 *An Chanail* by Marie-Louise Fitzpatrick; An Gum, 1988.

1989 **SPECIAL MERIT** *Exploring the Book of Kells* by George Otto Simms, illustrated by David Rooney; O'Brien Press, 1988.

1991 *Under the Hawthorn Tree* by Marita Conlon-McKenna, illustrated by Donald Teskey; O'Brien Press, 1990.

1991 **SPECIAL MERIT** *Daisy Chain War* by Joan O'Neill, not illustrated; Attic Press, 1990.

READING MAGIC AWARDS
Parenting Magazine
301 Howard St.
17th Floor
San Francisco, CA 94105

Instituted in 1988 by Parenting Magazine, the purpose of this annual award is to help parents choose wisely from among the abundance of enticing, colorful new offerings from children's book publishers. A panel of experts in children's literature reviews hundreds of books published during the year, narrowing the list to approximately forty titles. From this, an overall top ten list is chosen. Books in all age ranges are represented.

1988 *Tom and Pippo* series written and illustrated by Helen Oxenbury; Aladdin/Macmillan, 1988-.

A Girl From Yamhill: A Memoir by Beverly Cleary, illustrated with photos; Morrow, 1988.

More Tales of Uncle Remus: Further Adventures of Brer Rabbit by Joel Chandler Harris, adapted by Julius Lester, illustrated by Jerry Pinkney; Dial, 1988.

Henry by Nina Bawden, illustrated by Joyce Powzyk; Lothrop, Lee & Shepard, 1988.

Catwings by Ursula K. Le Guin, illustrated by S.D. Schindler; Orchard, 1988.

The Three and Many Wishes of Jason Reid by Hazel J. Hutchins, illustrated by Julie Tennent; Viking Kestrel, 1988.

Dear Mili by Wilhelm Grimm, illustrated by Maurice Sendak; Farrar, Straus, Giroux, 1988.

The Boy of the Three-Year Nap by Dianne Snyder, illustrated by Allen Say; Houghton Mifflin, 1988.

A Caribou Alphabet written and illustrated by Mary Beth Owens; Dog Ear Press, 1988.

Where the Forest Meets the Sea written and illustrated by Jeannie Baker; Greenwillow, 1987.

1989 *Bill Peet: An Autobiography* written and illustrated by Bill Peet; Houghton Mifflin, 1989.

Young Lions written and illustrated by Toshi Yoshida; Philomel, 1989.

The Rainbow People by Laurence Yep, illustrated by David Wiesner; Harper & Row, 1989.

The Pup Grew Up! by Samuel Marshak, illustrated by Vladimir Radunsky; Henry Holt, 1989.

Quentin Blake's ABC written and illustrated by Quentin Blake; Knopf, 1989.

Inspirations: Stories About Women Artists by Leslie Sills, illustrated with photos; Whitman, 1989.

Eating the Alphabet written and illustrated by Lois Ehlert; Harcourt, Brace, Jovanovich, 1989.

Valentine and Orson written and illustrated by Nancy Ekholm Burkert; Farrar, Straus, Giroux, 1989.

We're Going On a Bear Hunt by Michael Rosen, illustrated by Helen Oxenbury; Walker, 1989; McElderry, 1989.

Mouse Paint written and illustrated by Ellen Stoll Walsh; Harcourt, Brace, Jovanovich, 1989.

1990 *The Buck Stops Here* written and illustrated by Alice Provensen; HarperCollins, 1990.

Puss in Boots by Charles Perrault, illustrated by Fred Marcellino; Farrar, Straus, Giroux, 1990.

White Peak Farm by Berlie Doherty, not illustrated; Orchard, 1990.

The Wheels on the Bus written and illustrated by Paul O. Zelinsky; Dutton, 1990.

Baseball in April and Other Stories by Gary Soto, not illustrated; Harcourt, Brace, Jovanovich, 1990.

Tehanu by Ursula K. Le Guin, not illustrated; Atheneum, 1990.

Cousins by Virginia Hamilton, not illustrated; Philomel, 1990.

Shrek! written and illustrated by William Steig; Farrar, Straus, Giroux, 1990.

Good Queen Bess by Diane Stanley and Peter Vennema, illustrated by Diane Stanley; Four Winds, 1990.

El Chino written and illustrated by Allen Say; Houghton Mifflin, 1990.

1991 *The Wright Brothers: How They Invented the Airplane* by Russell Freedman, illustrated with photos; Holiday House, 1991.

Stars Come out Within by Jean Little, not illustrated; Viking, 1991.

Duck written and illustrated by Juan Wijngaard; Crown, 1991.

Punch in New York written and illustrated by Alice Provensen; Viking, 1991.

Aki and the Fox written and illustrated by Akiko Hayashi; Doubleday, 1991.

A Wave in her Pocket: Stories From Trinidad by Lynn Joseph, illustrated by Brian Pinkney; Clarion, 1991.

Clowning Around written and illustrated by Cathryn Falwell; Orchard, 1991.

Bear written and illustrated by Juan Wijngaard; Crown, 1991.

How the Ox Star Fell From Heaven written and illustrated by Lily Toy Hong; Whitman, 1991.

Strider by Beverly Cleary, illustrated by Paul O. Zelinsky; Morrow, 1991.

Dog written and illustrated by Juan Wijngaard; Crown, 1991.

Cat written and illustrated by Juan Wijngaard; Crown, 1991.

1992 *Bard of Avon: The Story of William Shakespeare* by Diane Stanley and Peter Vennema, illustrated by Diane Stanley; Morrow, 1992.

An Indian Winter by Russell Freedman, illustrated by Karl Bodmer; Holiday House, 1992.

Bently & Egg written and illustrated by William Joyce; HarperCollins, 1992.

Missing May by Cynthia Rylant, not illustrated; Orchard, 1992.

I Saw Esau by Iona Opie and Peter Opie, illustrated by Maurice Sendak; Candlewick, 1992.

Drylongso by Virginia Hamilton, illustrated by Brian Pinkney; Harcourt, Brace, Jovanovich, 1992.

Seven Blind Mice written and illustrated by Ed Young; Philomel, 1992.

Circus written and illustrated by Lois Ehlert; HarperCollins, 1992.

Sukey and the Mermaid by Robert D. San Souci, illustrated by Brian Pinkney; Four Winds, 1992.

Farmer Duck by Martin Waddell, illustrated by Helen Oxenbury; Candlewick, 1992.

REDBOOK'S TOP TEN CHILDREN'S PICTURE BOOKS

Redbook Magazine
224 W 57 St
New York, NY 10019

Established in 1984 by the Redbook Fiction Department, this annual award was created to assist readers in selecting books of quality for their children. Fiction and nonfiction picturebooks which display an overall excellence in design and text are chosen from all American imprints of the calendar year. The goal is to choose books with lasting appeal, that children will want to read again and again, and that parents will enjoy sharing with them. The books may be whimsical, instructive, timely, or fantastical - what is most important is that they captivate.

The winning titles are listed in the December issue of Redbook and the author/illustrator receives a citation. Stickers to be attached to winning books are provided.

1984 **HARDBACK** *I'm Coming to Get You!* written and illustrated by Tony Ross; Dial, 1984.

Yellow & Pink written and illustrated by William Steig; Farrar, 1984.

I Know a Lady by Charlotte Zolotow, illustrated by James Stevenson; Greenwillow, 1984.

1984 **SPECIAL MENTION** *The Mysteries of Harris Burdick* written and illustrated by Chris Van Allsburg; Houghton Mifflin, 1984.

1984 **PAPERBACK** *The Emperor's New Clothes* by Hans Christian Andersen, retold and illustrated by Nadine Bernard Westcott; Little Brown, 1984.

Where the Wild Things Are written and illustrated by Maurice Sendak; Harper Trophy, 1984.

Moon Man written and illustrated by Tomi Ungerer; Harper Trophy, 1984.

1984 **POP-UP** *Sailing Ships* by Ron Van Der Meer and Dr. Alan McGowan, paintings by Borje Svensson; Viking Kestrel, 1984.

Leonardo DaVinci written and illustrated by Alice Provensen and Martin Provensen; Viking Kestrel, 1984.

The Car: Watch it Work by Operating the Moving Diagrams! by Ray Marshall and John Bradley; Viking Kestrel, 1984.

1985 *The Polar Express* written and illustrated by Chris Van Allsburg; Houghton Mifflin, 1985.

Solomon the Rusty Nail written and illustrated by William Steig; Farrar, 1985.

In the Night Kitchen written and illustrated by Maurice Sendak; Harper Trophy, 1985.

Annie and the Wild Animals written and illustrated by Jan Brett; Houghton Mifflin, 1985.

Freight Train written and illustrated by Donald Crews; Greenwillow, 1978; Viking/Puffin, 1985.

There Was an Old Woman by Stephen Wyllie, illustrated by Maureen Roffey, paper engineering by Ray Marshall; Harper, 1985.

In Our House written and illustrated by Anne Rockwell; Crowell, 1985.

Miss Rumphius written and illustrated by Barbara Cooney; Viking, 1982; Viking/Puffin, 1985.

William's Doll by Charlotte Zolotow, illustrated by William Pene du Bois; Harper & Row, 1972; Harper Trophy, 1985.

Watch the Stars Come Out by Riki Levinson, illustrated by Diane Goode; Dutton, 1985.

1986 *Abiyoyo* by Pete Seeger, illustrated by Michael Hays; Macmillan, 1986.

The Snowman written and illustrated by Raymond Briggs; Random House, 1986.

A Year of Beasts written and illustrated by Ashley Wolff; Dutton, 1986.

Rumpelstiltskin retold and illustrated by Paul O. Zelinsky; Dutton, 1986.

The Guinea Pig ABC written and illustrated by Kate Duke; Dutton, 1986.

A Tournament of Knights written and illustrated by Joe Lasker; Crowell, 1986.

What Do You Say, Dear? by Sesyle Joslin, illustrated by Maurice Sendak; Harper Trophy, 1986.

Anno's Counting Book written and illustrated by Mitsumasa Anno; Harper, 1977; Macmillan, 1985.

Brave Irene written and illustrated by William Steig; Farrar, 1985.

The Little Bookmobile: Colors, Numbers, and Shapes on Wheels by Suzanne Green, illustrated by Daisuke Yokoi; Doubleday, 1986.

1986 **HONORABLE MENTION** *Tomie de Paola's Favorite Nursery Tales* illustrated by Tomie de Paola; Putnam, 1986.

Twelve Days of Christmas illustrated by Sophie Windham; Putnam, 1986.

1987 *Creatures of the Desert World* by Jennifer C. Urquhart, illustrated by Barbara Gibson; National Geographic Society, 1987.

Higher on the Door written and illustrated by James Stevenson; Greenwillow, 1987.

Humphrey's Bear by Jan Wahl, illustrated by William Joyce; Holt, 1987.

Jump Again! by Joel Chandler Harris, adapted by Van Dyne Parks, illustrated by Barry Moser; Harcourt, 1987.

The Loathsome Dragon retold by David Wiesner and Kim Kahng, illustrated by David Wiesner; Putnam, 1987.

The Midnight Farm by Reeve Lindbergh, illustrated by Susan Jeffers; Dial, 1987.

Monkey's Crazy Hotel by Stephen Wyllie, illustrated by Maureen Roffey; Harper, 1987.

The Monster Bed by Jeanne Willis, illustrated by Susan Varley; Lothrop, 1987.

A Place for Ben written and illustrated by Jeanne Titherington; Greenwillow, 1987.

Strange Animals of the Sea by Jane H. Buxton, illustrated by Jerry Pinkney; National Geographic Society, 1987.

The Wild Swans by Hans Christian Andersen, retold by Amy Ehrlich, illustrated by Susan Jeffers; Dial, 1987, c1981.

1988 *Animals Showing Off* by Jane R. McCauley, illustrated by Tony Chen; National Geographic, 1988.

Tail Feathers from Mother Goose: The Opie Rhyme Book by Iona Opie, illustrated; Little Brown, 1988.

How Many Bugs in a Box? written and illustrated by David A. Carter; Little Simon (Simon & Schuster), 1988.

The Enchanter's Daughter by Antonia Barber, illustrated by Errol Le Cain; Farrar, Straus, Giroux, 1988, c1987.

Creatures of Long Ago: Dinosaurs by Peggy Winston, illustrated by John Sibbick; National Geographic, 1988.

The Scarebird by Sid Fleischman, illustrated by Peter Sis; Greenwillow, 1988.

Blossom Comes Home by James Herriot, illustrated by Ruth Brown; St. Martin's Press, 1988.

Company's Coming by Arthur Yorinks, illustrated by David Small; Crown, 1988.

Junglewalk written and illustrated by Nancy Tafuri; Greenwillow, 1988.

Spinky Sulks written and illustrated by William Steig; Farrar, Straus, Giroux, 1988.

The Incredible Painting of Felix Clousseau written and illustrated by Jon Agee; Farrar, Straus, Giroux, 1988.

1989 *Night Noises* by Mem Fox, illustrated by Terry Denton; Harcourt Brace Jovanovich, 1989.

Annabel's House written and illustrated by Norman Messenger; Orchard, 1989.

Skip To My Lou written and illustrated by Nadine Bernard Westcott; Little Brown, 1989.

Tenrec's Twigs written and illustrated by Bert Kitchen; Philomel, 1989.

Animals, Animals written and illustrated by Eric Carle; Philomel, 1989.

Child's Garden of Verses by Robert Louis Stevenson, illustrated; Chronicle Books, 1989.

The Little Mermaid by Hans Christian Andersen, illustrated by Katie Thamer Treherne; Harcourt, Brace, Jovanovich, 1989.

My First Cook Book by Angela Wilkes, illustrated; Knopf, 1989.

1990 *Benjamin's Barn* by Reeve Lindbergh, illustrated by Susan Jeffers; Dial, 1990.

Very Quiet Cricket written and illustrated by Eric Carle; Philomel, 1990.

Feathers for Lunch written and illustrated by Lois Ehlert; Harcourt, Brace, Jovanovich, 1990.

Train Song by Diane Siebert, illustrated by Mike Wimmer; Crowell, 1990.

Teammates by Peter Golenbock, illustrated by Paul Bacon; Harcourt, Brace, Jovanovich, 1990.

Charlie Anderson by Barbara Abercrombie, illustrated by Mark Graham; McElderry, 1990.

Aesop's Fables compiled by Russell Ash and Bernard Higton, illustrated; Chronicle, 1990.

Ugly Duckling by Hans Christian Andersen, illustrated by Troy Howell; Dodd, Mead, 1987; Putnam, 1990.

The Wheels on the Bus written and illustrated by Paul O. Zelinsky; Orchard, 1990.

Many Moons by James Thurber, illustrated by Marc Simont; Harcourt, Brace, Jovanovich, 1990.

1991 *Kitten* by Angela Royston, illustrated by Jane Burton; Lodestar, 1991.

Borreguita and the Coyote by Verna Aardema, illustrated by Petra Mathers; Knopf, 1991.

In the Tall, Tall Grass written and illustrated by Denise Fleming; Henry Holt, 1991.

A Is For Animals: 26 Pop-up Surprises: An Animal ABC written and illustrated by David Pelham; Simon & Schuster, 1991.

The Story of Christmas: Words from the Gospels of Matthew and Luke illustrated by Jane Ray; Dutton, 1991.

Puppy by Angela Royston, illustrated by Jane Burton; Lodestar, 1991.

Frog by Angela Royston, illustrated by Kim Taylor; Lodestar, 1991.

The Fish Who Could Wish by John Bush, illustrated by Korky Paul; Kane Miller, 1991.

Duck by Angela Royston, illustrated by Barrie Watts; Lodestar, 1991.

Ten Little Rabbits by Virginia Grossman, illustrated by Sylvia Long; Chronicle Books, 1991.

The Minpins by Roald Dahl, illustrated by Patrick Benson; Viking, 1991.

Polar Bear, Polar Bear, What Do You Hear? by Bill Martin, Jr., illustrated by Eric Carle; Holt, 1991.

REGINA MEDAL
The Catholic Library Association
461 West Lancaster Ave
Haverford, PA 19041

The Regina Medal Award was established in 1959 by the Catholic Library Association to dramatize the timeless standards and ideals for the writing of good literature for children. Funds for the project are provided by the generosity of an anonymous donor. The award is administered by the Children's Libraries Section of the Catholic Library Association through the Regina Medal committee. The only criteria for the award is excellence. The recipient must be a living person who has had a consistent, sustained quality of work and has met with approval of their work as a whole. The works must have been originally written in English.

The Regina Medal Committee is a standing committee of the Catholic Library Association consisting of a chairman, vice chairman, the members of the executive board of the children's libraries section and five members-at-large. Suggestions are made to the committee from members of the Children's Libraries Section. Each member of the committee also places in nomination a name of a worthy recipient. A slate of candidates is drawn up and voted on by the Regina Medal Committee. Public announcement of the recipient is made in the January issue of Catholic Library World.

An oval-shaped silver medal designed by Sister M. Owen is presented to the winner at a special luncheon during the Catholic Library Association annual convention.

1959   Eleanor Farjeon

1960   Anne Carroll Moore

1961   Padraic Colum

1962   Frederic Melcher

1963   Ann Nolan Clark

1964   May Hill Arbuthnot

1965   Ruth Sawyer

1966   Leo Politi

1967   Bertha Mahony Miller

1968   Marguerite de Angeli

1969   Lois Lenski

1970   Edgar Parin d'Aulaire, Ingri d'Aulaire

1971   Tasha Tudor

1972   Meindert DeJong

1973   Frances Clarke Sayers

1974   Robert McCloskey

1975   May McNeer, Lynd Ward

1976   Virginia Haviland

1977   Marcia Brown

1978   Scott O'Dell

1979   Morton Schindel

1980   Beverly Cleary

1981   Augusta Baker

1982   Theodor Geisel (Dr. Seuss)

1983   Tomie de Paola

1984   Madeleine L'Engle

1985   Jean Fritz

1986   Lloyd Alexander

1987   Betsy Byars

1988   Katherine Paterson

1989   Steven Kellogg

1990   Virginia Hamilton

1991   Leonard Everett Fisher

1992   Jane Yolen

1993   Chris Van Allsburg

RHODE ISLAND CHILDREN'S BOOK AWARD

State Library Services
300 Richmond St.
Providence, RI 02903

The Rhode Island Children's Book Award is a children's choice award, sponsored by the Rhode Island Educational Media Association, Rhode Island Library Association, and the Rhode Island State Council of the International Reading Association. The purpose is to encourage children in grades three through six to read. A master list is compiled, and students are encouraged to vote for their favorite book. Fiction and nonfiction books selected for the master list are published during the two years preceding the award and must be written by a person currently living in the United States. A trophy is presented to the winning author.

1991   *Something Upstairs: A Tale of Ghosts* by Avi, not illustrated; Orchard, 1988.

1992   *Maniac Magee* by Jerry Spinelli, not illustrated; Little Brown, 1990.

1993   *The Houdini Box* by Brian Selznick, illustrated; Knopf, 1991.

FRANCES E. RUSSELL AWARD

IBBY - Canadian Section
Canadian Children's Book Centre
35 Spadina Rd.
Toronto Ontario M5R 2S9
Canada

In memory of her sister, Frances, Marjorie Russell of Toronto has donated an annual grant of $1000 to further the work of IBBY Canadian Section. One of the aims of IBBY is to initiate and encourage research in young people's literature in all forms. The Frances E. Russell Award will promote this ideal. The award is made for the purpose of research for a publishable work (book or paper) on Canadian children's literature. The applicant must be a Canadian citizen or landed immigrant. A committee selects the winning applicant who is required to submit a detailed report of the research conducted, within one year of receipt of the award.

1982   Dr. Corinne Davies and Dr. Catherine Ross, University of Western Ontario

1983   Professor Shirley Wright, University of Alberta

1984   Dr. Jacques LaMothe, University of Quebec in Montreal

1985   Andre Gagnon

1986   Judith Saltman

1987   Joan Weller

1988   Dave Jenkinson

1989   Judy Arter

1990   Linda Granfield

RUTGERS AWARD FOR DISTINGUISHED CONTRIBUTION TO CHILDREN'S LITERATURE

discontinued

The Rutgers Award was founded in 1966 by Mary V. Gaver. The purpose of the award was to honor New Jersey authors and illustrators of excellent children's books. The award was presented on an irregular basis through 1979. All New Jersey authors and illustrators of children's literature were eligible for this award. Nomination and final selection was made by a committee. A medal was presented to the winner.

1966   John Ciardi, Roger Duvoisin

1969   Lynd Ward

1973   Adrienne Adams

1979   Dorothy Shuttlesworth

S

CARL SANDBURG AWARD

Friends of the Chicago Public Library
400 South State St.
Chicago, IL 60605

Sponsored by the Friends of the Chicago Public Library, this award was presented for the first time in 1979. There are several categories of awards, including children's literature. It is awarded for outstanding achievement in literature for children by a Chicago author. Only the children's literature winners are listed below.

1980   *Cute Is a Four Letter Word* by Stella Pevsner, not illustrated; Houghton/Clarion, 1980.

1981   *Do Bananas Chew Gum?* by Jamie Gilson, not illustrated; Lothrop Lee & Shepard, 1980.

1982   *Behind the Scenes at the Horse Hospital* by Fern G. Brown, edited by Kathleen Tucker, photographs by Roger Ruhlin; Whitman, 1981.

1983   *Wait, Skates!* by Mildred D. Johnson, illustrated by Tom Dunnington, prepared under the direction of Robert Hillerich; Children's Press, 1983.

1984   *Pitcher Plants: The Elegant Insect Traps* written and illustrated by Carol Lerner; Morrow, 1983.

1985   *The Search for Grissi* by Mary Frances Shura, illustrated by Ted Lewin; Dodd, Mead, 1985.

1986   *Thatcher-Payne-in-the-Neck* by Betty Bates, illustrated by Linda Strauss Edwards; Holiday House, 1985.

1987   *Eli's Ghost* by Betsy Hearne, illustrated by Ronald Himler; McElderry, 1987.

1988   *The Goats* written and illustrated by Brock Cole; Farrar Straus Giroux, 1987.

1989   *A Circle Unbroken* by Sollace Hotze, not illustrated; Clarion, 1988.

1990   *The House on Walenska Street* by Charlotte Herman, illustrated by Susan Avishai; Dutton, 1990.

1991   *The Bridge Dancers* by Carol Saller, illustrated by Gerald Talifero; Carolrhoda, 1991.

1992   *Knee Holes* by Jerome Brooks, not illustrated; Orchard, 1992.

SCHOOL LIBRARY MEDIA SPECIALISTS OF SOUTH EASTERN NEW YORK (SLMSSNY) AWARD

New York Library Association
6294 Rivka Rd.
Saugerties, NY 12477

This award, sponsored and established by the School Library Media Specialists of South Eastern New York, was presented for the first time in 1979. The recipients are recognized for outstanding contributions to the field of children's literature.

1979   Leonard Everett Fisher

1980   Eleanor Clymer

1981   Jean Craighead George

1982   Leonard Kessler

1983   Susan Beth Pfeffer

1984   Jean Fritz

1985   Paul Galdone

1986   Alice Provensen, Martin Provensen

1988   Judie Angell

1989   Scott O'Dell

1990   Lilian Moore

1992   Nancy Willard

1993   Vicki Cobb

RUTH SCHWARTZ CHILDREN'S BOOK AWARD

Ontario Arts Council
151 Bloor Street West
Suite 500
Toronto, Ontario
M5S 1T6 Canada

Founded in 1976 by the Ruth Schwartz Foundation, the aim of this children's book award is to reward the best creative effort in children's literature for the particular year. All children's books published in Canada are eligible to be nominated by members of the Canadian Booksellers Association. The final selection is made by a jury of high school children. The winning author receives a cash award of $2000 at the Canadian Booksellers Convention.

1976   *Jacob Two-two Meets the Hooded Fang* by Mordecai Richler, illustrated by Fritz Wegner; McClelland & Stewart, 1975.

1977   *The Violin* by Robert Thomas Allen, illustrated by George Pastic; McGraw-Hill/Ryerson, 1976.

1978   *Garbage Delight* by Dennis Lee, illustrated by Frank Newfeld; Macmillan Canada, 1977.

1979   *Hold Fast* by Kevin Major, not illustrated; Clarke, Irwin, 1978.

1980   *Days of Terror* by Barbara Claassen Smucker, not illustrated; Herald Press, 1979.

1981   *The King's Daughter* by Suzanne Martell, translated by David Toby Homel and Margaret Rose; Douglas & MacIntyre, 1980.

1982   *One Proud Summer* by Claire Mackay and Marsha Hewitt, not illustrated; The Women's Press, 1981.

1983   *Jasmin* by Jan Truss, not illustrated; Douglas & McIntyre, 1982; Atheneum, 1982.

1984 *Zoom at Sea* by Tim Wynne-Jones, illustrated by Ken Nutt; Groundwood, 1983.

1985 *Mama's Going to Buy You a Mockingbird* by Jean Little, not illustrated; Viking Kestrel, 1984.

1986 *Thomas' Snowsuit* by Robert Munsch, illustrated by Michael Martchenko; Annick Press, 1985.

1987 *Have You Seen Birds?* by Joanne Oppenheim, illustrated by Barbara Reid; North Winds Press, 1986.

1988 *The Doll* by Cora Taylor, not illustrated; Western Producer Prairie Books, 1987.

1989 *Amos's Sweater* by Janet Lunn, illustrated by Kim LaFave; Douglas & McIntyre, 1988; Scholastic, 1990.

1990 *Bad Boy* by Diana Wieler, not illustrated; Douglas & McIntyre, 1989; Delacorte, 1992.

1991 *Forbidden City* by William Bell, illustrated with maps; Doubleday Canada, 1990.

SCIENCE BOOK PRIZES
COPUS
c/o The Royal Society
6 Carlton House Terrace
London SW1Y 5AG
England

In 1988 the Committee on the Public Understanding of Science (COPUS) and the Science Museum established the Science Book Prizes to reward books that have contributed most to the public understanding of science. Eligible for this annual prize are popular nonfiction science and technology books, published in the United Kingdom in the year preceding the prize. Awards are made in two categories, one for books aimed at a general audience and the other for those books written for young people under the age of fourteen. Sponsored by Rhone Poulenic, a prize of £10,000 is awarded in each category. Award winners in the Younger category are listed below.

1988 *Science Alive: Living Things* by Roger Kerrod, illustrated; Macdonalds Children's Books, 1987.

1989 *The Way Things Work* written and illustrated by David Macaulay; Dorling Kindersley, 1988; Houghton Mifflin, 1988.

1990 *What Makes a Flower Grow?* by Susan Mayes, illustrated by Brin Edwards and Mike Pringle; Usborne, 1989.

What Makes It Rain? by Susan Mayes, illustrated by Richard Deverell and Mike Pringle; Usborne, 1989.

What's Under the Ground? by Susan Mayes, illustrated by Mike Pringle, Brin Edwards and John Scorey; Usborne, 1989.

Where Does Electricity Come From? by Susan Mayes, illustrated by John Shackell and John Scorey; Usborne, 1989.

1990 **(UNDER 8 YEARS OF AGE)** *The Giant Book of Space* by Ian Redpath, illustrated; Hamlyn, 1989.

1991 *Cells Are Us* by Fran Balkwill, illustrated by Mic Rolph; HarperCollins, 1990.

Cell Wars by Fran Balkwill, illustrated by Mic Rolph; HarperCollins, 1990.

1992 *The Amazing Voyage of the Cucumber Sandwich* by Peter Rowan, illustrated by Polly Noakes; Cape, 1991.

How Nature Works by David Burnie, illustrated; Dorling Kindersley, 1991.

1993 *Mighty Microbes* by Thompson Yardley, illustrated; Cassell, 1992.

SEQUOYAH CHILDREN'S BOOK AWARD
Oklahoma Library Association
Library and Learning Resources Division
Oliver Hodge Building
2500 North Lincoln Blvd.
Oklahoma City, OK 73105-4599

Founded in 1959 by the Oklahoma Library Association, the Sequoyah Children's Book Award winner is chosen annually by children in grades three through six. The Sequoyah Children's Book Award committee chooses 100 titles for the preliminary list. The members then read and evaluate the merits of each book before choosing the 20 to 25 titles which appear on the final master list.

The following selection criteria are applied to the titles chosen (textbooks are excluded): (1) The author must be an American currently living in the U.S.; (2) The interest and reading level must be appropriate for grades three through six; (3) The year of copyright must precede the date of the Sequoyah master list by no more than three years; (4) Evaluation of the titles will be based on the literary standard adopted by the Association of Library Services to Children for their Notable Books listing.

To be considered notable the book should have literary merit, qualities of originality, imagination, and vitality; an element of timelessness; sincerity; sound values; a theme or subject worth imparting to and of interest to children; factual accuracy; clarity; readability; and must be appropriate in subject, treatment, and format to the age group for which it was intended. (From the guidelines developed by the Sequoyah Children's Book Award Committee).

Children in grades three through six who have read at least two titles are eligible to vote for their favorite book. A plaque is presented to the winning author at the annual Sequoyah luncheon held during the Oklahoma Library Association spring convention.

1959 *Old Yeller* by Fred Gipson, illustrated by Carl Burger; Harper, 1956.

1960 *Black Gold* by Marguerite Henry, illustrated by Wesley Dennis; Rand, 1957.

1961 *Have Space Suit - Will Travel* by Robert Heinlein, not illustrated; Scribner, 1958.

1962 *The Helen Keller Story* by Catherine O. Peare, not illustrated; Crowell, 1959.

1963 *The Mystery of the Haunted Pool* by Phyllis A. Whitney, illustrated by H. Tom Hall; Westminster, 1960.

1964 *Where the Panther Screams* by William Powell Robinson, illustrated by Lorence F. Bjorklund; World, 1961.

1965 *A Wrinkle in Time* by Madeleine L'Engle, not illustrated; Farrar, Straus, Giroux; 1962.

1966 *Rascal: A Memoir of a Better Era* by Sterling North, illustrated by John Schoenherr; Dutton, 1963.

1967 *Harriet the Spy* written and illustrated by Louise Fitzhugh; Harper, 1964.

1968 *Gentle Ben* by Walt Morey, illustrated by John Schoenherr; Dutton, 1965.

1969 *Blackbeard's Ghost* written and illustrated by Ben Stahl; Houghton, 1965.

1970 *Mustang: Wild Spirit of the West* by Marguerite Henry, illustrated by Robert Lougheed; Rand, 1966.

1971 *Ramona the Pest* by Beverly Cleary, illustrated by Louis Darling; Morrow, 1968.

1972 *The Man in the Box: A Story from Vietnam* by Mary Lois Dunn, not illustrated; McGraw, 1968.

1973 *The Trumpet of the Swan* by E.B. White, illustrated by Edward Frascino; Harper, 1970.

1974 *Flight of the White Wolf* by Melvin Richard Ellis, not illustrated; Holt, 1970.

1975 *Tales of a Fourth Grade Nothing* by Judy Blume, illustrated by Roy Doty; Dutton, 1972.

1976 *How to Eat Fried Worms* by Thomas Rockwell, illustrated by Emily McCully; Watts, 1973.

1977 *The Toothpaste Millionaire* by Jean Merrill, illustrated by Jan Palmer; Houghton, 1974.

1978 *Shoeshine Girl* by Clyde Robert Bulla, illustrated by Leigh Grant; Crowell, 1975.

1979 *Summer of the Monkeys* by Wilson Rawls, not illustrated; Doubleday, 1976.

1980 *Kid Power* by Susan Beth Pfeffer, illustrated by Leigh Grant; Watts, 1977.

1981 *The Get-away Car* by Eleanor Clymer, not illustrated; Dutton, 1978.

1982 *Bunnicula: A Rabbit Tale of Mystery* by Deborah Howe and James Howe, illustrated by Alan Daniel; Atheneum, 1980.

1983 *A Dog Called Kitty* by Bill Wallace, not illustrated; Holiday House, 1980.

1984 *The Cybil War* by Betsy Byars, illustrated by Gail Owens; Viking, 1981.

1985 *Thirteen Ways to Sink a Sub* by Jamie Gilson, illustrated by Linda S. Edwards; Lothrop Lee & Shepard, 1982.

1986 *Dear Mr. Henshaw* by Beverly Cleary, illustrated by Paul O. Zelinsky; Morrow, 1983.

Just Tell Me When We're Dead! by Eth Clifford, illustrated by George Hughes; Houghton Mifflin, 1983.

1987 *The Night of the Twisters* by Ivy Ruckman, not illustrated; Crowell, 1984.

1988 *Christina's Ghost* by Betty Ren Wright, not illustrated; Holiday House, 1985.

1989 *Sixth Grade Sleepover* by Eve Bunting, not illustrated; Harcourt Brace Jovanovich, 1986.

1990 *Fudge* by Charlotte T. Graeber, illustrated by Cheryl Harness; Lothrop, Lee & Shepard, 1987.

1991 *Beauty* by Bill Wallace, not illustrated; Holiday House, 1988.

1992 *The Doll in the Garden* by Mary Downing Hahn, illustrated; Clarion, 1989.

1993 *Weasel* by Cynthia DeFelice, not illustrated; Macmillan, 1990.

SEQUOYAH YOUNG ADULT AWARD

Oklahoma Library Association
Library and Learning Resources Division
Oliver Hodge Building
2500 North Lincoln Blvd.
Oklahoma City, OK 73105-4599

Named after Sequoyah, creator of the Cherokee alphabet, this young adult award was established in 1986 by the Oklahoma Library Association. The purpose is to encourage the young people (grades 7-9) of Oklahoma to read books of literary quality.

Fiction and nonfiction titles appropriate for young adults are eligible as long as they have literary merit, qualities of originality, imagination, and vitality. They must have an element of timeliness and have a theme or subject of interest to young adults. A selection committee prepares a Master List of 12-15 titles that have received favorable reviews in major reviewing media. Students must read or hear at least three books from the list to be eligible to vote. A trophy and citation are presented annually to the winner at the Oklahoma Library Association conference.

1988 *Abby, My Love* by Hadley Irwin, not illustrated; Atheneum, 1985.

1989 *The Other Side of Dark* by Joan Lowery Nixon, not illustrated; Delacorte, 1986.

1990 *Hatchet* by Gary Paulsen, not illustrated; Bradbury, 1987.

1991 *A Sudden Silence* by Eve Bunting, not illustrated; Harcourt Brace Jovanovich, 1988.

1992 *Appointment With a Stranger* by Jean Thesman, not illustrated; Houghton Mifflin, 1989.

1993 *The Silver Kiss* by Annette Curtis Klause, not illustrated; Delacorte, 1990.

SIGNAL POETRY AWARD

Signal Approaches to Children's Books
Nancy Chambers, Editor
Lockwood, Station Road
South Woodchester
Stroud Glos. GL5 5EQ
England

The Signal Poetry Award was established in 1979 by Adrian and Nancy Chambers for the purpose of highlighting excellence in poetry published for children and in the work done to prompt poetry with children. The award is presented annually for excellence in any one of the following categories: single-poet collection published for children, poetry anthologies published for children, the body of work for children by a contemporary poet, or educational or critical activity which enhance the cause of poetry for children.

A committee of selectors is appointed by Signal to make the final determination. The most significant aspect of the award is the writing that it prompts; the award selectors are given as much space as they require in each May issue of Signal to discuss their views, not only on the winner, but on other poetry in books published during the year. It is hoped that this regular critical activity will help to sharpen response generally to the poetry published for children. The honored author receives £100.

1979 *Moon-bells and other Poems* by Ted Hughes, not illustrated; Chatto & Windus, 1978.

1980-1981 No Award

1982 *You Can't Catch Me!* by Michael Rosen, illustrated by Quentin Blake; Deutsch, 1981.

1983 *The Rattle Bag: An Anthology of Poetry* by Ted Hughes and Seamus Heaney, not illustrated; Faber & Faber, 1982.

1984 *Sky in the Pie* by Roger McGough, illustrated by Satoshi Kitamura; Kestrel, 1983.

1985 *What Is the Truth? A Farmyard Fable for the Young* by Ted Hughes, illustrated by R.J. Lloyd; Faber, 1984.

1986 *Song of the City* by Gareth Owen, illustrated by Jonathan Hills; Fontana Young Lions Original, 1985.

1987 *Early in the Morning: A Collection of New Poems* by Charles Causley, illustrated by Michael Foreman; Viking Kestrel, 1986.

1988 *Boo To a Goose* by John Mole, illustrated by Mary Norman; Peterloo Poets, 1987.

1989 *When I Dance* by James Berry, illustrated by Sonia Boyce; Hamish Hamilton, 1988; Harcourt Brace Jovanovich, 1991.

1990 *Heard It In the Playground* by Allan Ahlberg, illustrated by Fritz Wegner; Viking Kestrel, 1989.

1991 *This Poem Doesn't Rhyme* by Gerard Benson, illustrated by Sarah-Jane Stewart; Viking, 1990.

1992 *Shades of Green* by Anne Harvey, illustrated by John Lawrence; MacRae, 1991; Greenwillow, 1992.

1993 *Two's Company* by Jackie Kay, illustrated by Shirley Tourret; Blackie, 1992.

CHARLIE MAY SIMON CHILDREN'S BOOK AWARD

James A. Hester, Secretary/Treasurer
Arkansas Elementary School Council
Arkansas Department of Education
4 State Capitol Mall
Little Rock, AR 72201-1071

This children's choice award was established in 1970 by the Arkansas Elementary School Council to encourage more critical reading by Arkansas elementary school children. A reading list is compiled by the book selection committee which is composed of representatives from various Arkansas educational organizations. This list, which includes easy as well as more advanced books, is presented to the children in grades four through six. Each child who has read or heard read at least two titles from the reading list is eligible to vote for his or her favorite book. The author of the award-winning book is honored at a banquet with the presentation of a medallion.

1970-71 *Striped Ice Cream* by Joan M. Lexau, illustrated by John Wilson; Lippincott, 1968.

1971-72 *Big Ben* by David Walker, illustrated by Victor G. Ambrus; Houghton, 1969.

1972-73 *Runaway Ralph* by Beverly Cleary, illustrated by Louis Darling; Morrow, 1970.

1973-74 *The Runt of Rogers School* by Harold Keith, not illustrated; Lippincott, 1971.

1974-75 *Tales of a Fourth Grade Nothing* by Judy Blume, illustrated by Roy Doty; Dutton, 1972.

1975-76 *Bigfoot* by Hal G. Evarts, not illustrated; Scribner, 1973.

1976-77 *The Ghost on Saturday Night* by Sid Fleischman, illustrated by Eric Von Schmidt; Atlantic-Little, 1974.

1977-78 *Shoeshine Girl* by Clyde Robert Bulla, illustrated by Leigh Grant; Crowell, 1975.

1978-79 *Alvin's Swap Shop* by Clifford Hicks, illustrated by Bill Sokol; Holt, 1976.

1979-80 *The Pinballs* by Betsy Byars, not illustrated; Harper, 1977.

1980-1981 *Banana Twist* by Florence Parry Heide, not illustrated; Holiday House, 1978.

1981-1982 *All the Money in the World* by William Brittain, illustrated by Charles Robinson; Harper, 1979.

1982-1983 *Do Bananas Chew Gum?* by Jamie Gilson, not illustrated; Lothrop Lee & Shepard, 1980.

1983-1984 *Ramona Quimby, Age 8* by Beverly Cleary, illustrated by Alan Tiegreen; Morrow, 1981.

1984-1985 *Be a Perfect Person in Just Three Days!* by Stephen Manes, illustrated by Tom Huffman; Houghton Mifflin, 1982.

1985-1986 *My Horrible Secret* by Stephen Roos, illustrated by Carol Newsom; Delacorte, 1983.

1986-1987 *The Computer Nut* by Betsy Byars, computer graphics by Guy Byars; Viking Kestrel, 1984.

1987-1988 *Sarah, Plain and Tall* by Patricia MacLachlan, not illustrated; Harper & Row, 1985.

1988-1989 *The Whipping Boy* by Sid Fleischman, illustrated by Peter Sis; Greenwillow, 1986.

1989-1990 *There's a Boy in the Girls' Bathroom* by Louis Sachar, not illustrated; Knopf, 1987.

1990-1991 *All About Sam* by Lois Lowry, illustrated by Diane de Groat; Houghton Mifflin, 1988.

1991-92 *Number the Stars* by Lois Lowry, not illustrated; Houghton Mifflin, 1989.

CONSTANCE LINDSAY SKINNER AWARD
see WOMEN'S NATIONAL BOOK AWARD

SMARTIES PRIZE FOR CHILDREN'S BOOKS

Celia Parry-Jones
Book Trust
45 East Hill
London SW18 2QZ
England

The Smarties Prize was established in 1985 by the Rowntree Mackintosh Co. to encourage high standards and stimulate interest in books for children. The award is open to any children's books written in English by a citizen of or author resident in the United Kingdom, and published there. A panel of judges chosen by Rowntree Mackintosh compiles a shortlist of not more than five books and not less than three books for each category. The prize money totals £10,000 and is awarded to the authors of the best children's books in the following categories: (1) £1000 for 5 years and under; (2) £1000 for 6-8 years; (3) £1000 for 9-11 years; and (4) £7000 grand prix - overall winner chosen from the above three category winners. The Smarties Prize is administered by the Book Trust.

1985 **GRAND PRIX** *Gaffer Samson's Luck* by Jill Paton Walsh, illustrated by Brock Cole; Viking Kestrel, 1985.

1985 **AGES 7-11** *Gaffer Samson's Luck* by Jill Paton Walsh, illustrated by Brock Cole; Viking Kestrel, 1985.

1985 **6 AND UNDER** *It's Your Turn, Roger!* written and illustrated by Susanna Gretz; Bodley Head, 1985.

1985 **INNOVATION** *Watch It Work! The Plane* by Ray Marshall and John Bradley; Viking Kestrel, 1985.

1986 **GRAND PRIX** *The Snow Spider* by Jenny Nimmo, illustrated by Joanna Carey; Methuen Children's, 1986.

1986 **AGES 7-11** *The Snow Spider* by Jenny Nimmo, illustrated by Joanna Carey; Methuen Children's, 1986.

1986 **6 AND UNDER** *The Goose That Laid the Golden Egg* written and illustrated by Geoffrey Patterson; Deutsch, 1986.

1986 **INNOVATION** *The Mirrorstone* by Michael Palin, illustrated by Alan Lee, design by Richard Seymour; Cape, 1986; Knopf, 1986.

Village Heritage by Miss Pinnell and the children of Sapperton School, introduction by Michael Wood, illustrated; Alan Sutton, 1986.

1987 **GRAND PRIX** *A Thief in the Village* by James Berry, not illustrated; Hamish Hamilton, 1987; Orchard, 1988.

1987 **AGES 9-11** *A Thief in the Village* by James Berry, not illustrated; Hamish Hamilton, 1987; Orchard, 1988.

1987 **AGES 6-8** *Tangle and the Firesticks* written and illustrated by Benedict Blathwayt; Julia MacRae, 1987; Knopf, 1987.

1987 **AGES 0-5** *The Angel and the Soldier Boy* written and illustrated by Peter Collington; Methuen Children's, 1987; Knopf, 1987.

1988 **GRAND PRIX** *Can't You Sleep Little Bear?* by Martin Waddell, illustrated by Barbara Firth; Walker, 1988.

1988 **AGES 0-5** *Can't You Sleep Little Bear?* by Martin Waddell, illustrated by Barbara Firth; Walker, 1988.

1988 **AGES 9-11** *Rushavenn Time* by Theresa Whistler, illustrated by Anne Jope; Brixworth V C Primary School, 1988.

1988 **AGES 6-8** *Can It Be True?* by Susan Hill, illustrated by Angela Barrett; Hamish Hamilton, 1988.

1989 **GRAND PRIX** *We're Going on a Bear Hunt* by Michael Rosen, illustrated by Helen Oxenbury; Walker Books, 1989.

1989 **AGES 0-5** *We're Going on a Bear Hunt* by Michael Rosen, illustrated by Helen Oxenbury; Walker Books, 1989.

1989 **AGES 9-11** *Blitzcat* by Robert Westall, not illustrated; Macmillan Children's, 1989.

1989 **AGES 6-8** *Bill's New Frock* by Anne Fine, illustrated by Philippe Dupasquier; Methuen Children's, 1989.

1990 **GRAND PRIX** *Midnight Blue* by Pauline Fisk, not illustrated; Lion Publishing, 1990.

1990 **AGES 0-5** *Six Dinner Sid* written and illustrated by Inga Moore; Simon & Schuster, 1990.

1990 **AGES 9-11** *Midnight Blue* by Pauline Fisk, not illustrated; Lion Publishing, 1990.

1990 **AGES 6-8** *Esio Trot* by Roald Dahl, illustrated by Quentin Blake; Cape, 1990; Viking, 1990.

1991 **GRAND PRIX** *Farmer Duck* by Martin Waddell, illustrated by Helen Oxenbury; Walker, 1991; Candlewick Press, 1992.

1991 **AGES 6-8** *Josie Smith and Eileen* by Magdalen Nabb, illustrated by Pirkko Vainio; Collins, 1991; HarperCollins, 1991; McElderry, 1992.

1991 **AGES 0-5** *Farmer Duck* by Martin Waddell, illustrated by Helen Oxenbury; Walker, 1991; Candlewick Press, 1992.

1991 **AGES 9-11** *Krindlekrax* by Philip Ridley, illustrated by Mark Robinson; Cape, 1991; Knopf, 1992.

1992 **AGES 9-11** *The Great Elephant Chase* by Gillian Cross, not illustrated; Oxford University Press, 1991.

1992 **GRAND PRIX** *The Great Elephant Chase* by Gillian Cross, not illustrated; Oxford University Press, 1991.

1992 **AGES 0-5** *Nice Work, Little Wolf!* written and illustrated by Hilda Offen; Hamish Hamilton, 1991; Dutton, 1992.

1992 **AGES 6-8** *The Story of the Creation: Words From Genesis* illustrated by Jane Ray; Dutton, 1991; Orchard UK, 1992.

KENNETH B. SMILEN/PRESENT TENSE LITERARY AWARDS
see **PRESENT TENSE/JOEL H. CAVIOR LITERARY AWARDS**

W. H. SMITH ILLUSTRATION AWARD
formerly **FRANCIS WILLIAMS ILLUSTRATION AWARD**

Celia Parry-Jones
Book Trust
45 East Hill
London SW18 2QZ
England

Since 1972, the Victoria and Albert Museum has organized a competition, originally named after its benefactor Francis Williams, for excellence in illustration. The award has been presented once every five years. As of 1987, new funding from W. H. Smith has enabled the Museum to supplement the original bequest so that the more valuable awards may be offered annually. A premier award of £3000, two secondary awards of £1000 each and a number of commended awards of £500 are given. The Museum stages an exhibition, known as the Francis Williams Exhibition of Illustration, of the best work to be submitted. A panel of qualified judges assess printed and published illustrations submitted by both book and periodical publishers on behalf of their artists. Submissions are handled by the Book Trust.

1972 *The Great Sleigh Robbery* by Michael Foreman; Hamish Hamilton, 1968.

Horatio by Michael Foreman; Hamish Hamilton, 1969.

1977 **£100** *Rabbit & Pork: Rhyming Talk* written and illustrated by John Lawrence; Hamilton, 1975.

The Wildman by Kevin Crossley-Holland, illustrated by Charles Keeping; Deutsch, 1976.

Monkey and the Three Wizards by Cheng-en Wu, translated by Peter Harris, illustrated by Michael Foreman; Collins, 1976.

1977 £50 *Father Christmas* written and illustrated by Raymond Briggs; Hamilton, 1973.

King Wilbur the Third and the Bicycle by James Rogerson, illustrated by George Him; Dent, 1976.

The Adventures of King Midas by Lynne Reid Banks, illustrated by George Him; Dent, 1976.

Runaway Danny written and illustrated by Celia Berridge; Deutsch, 1975.

1982 **BEST CHILDREN'S BOOK** *The Snowman* written and illustrated by Raymond Briggs; Hamilton, 1978.

1987 **FIRST PRIZE** *I, Leonardo* written and illustrated by Ralph Steadman; Cape, 1983.

1987 **SECOND PRIZE** *Alice's Adventures in Wonderland* by Lewis Carroll, illustrated by Justin Todd; Gollancz, 1984.

Through the Looking Glass and What Alice Found there by Lewis Carroll, illustrated by Justin Todd; Gollancz, 1986.

1988 **FIRST PRIZE** *Charles Keeping's Classic Tales of the Macabre* written and illustrated by Charles Keeping; Blackie Children's, 1987.

1988 **SECOND PRIZE** *Fred* written and illustrated by Posy Simmonds; Cape, 1987; Knopf, 1987.

The Blemyahs by William Mayne, illustrated by Juan Wijngaard; Walker, 1987.

The Baron All at Sea by Adrian Mitchell, illustrated by Patrick Benson; Walker, 1987; Philomel, 1987.

1989 **SECOND PRIZE** *The Mighty Slide* by Allan Ahlberg, illustrated by Charlotte Voake; Viking Kestrel, 1988.

1990 *Aesop's Fables* retold in verse by James Michie, illustrated by John Vernon Lord; Cape, 1989.

1990 **SECOND PRIZE** *War Boy* written and illustrated by Michael Foreman; Pavilion in association with Joseph, 1989.

1991 *The Hidden House* by Martin Waddell, illustrated by Angela Barrett; Walker Books, 1989.

1991 **SECOND PRIZE** *An Alphabet of Animals* written and illustrated by Christopher Wormell; Collins, 1990; Dial, 1990.

SOARING EAGLE BOOK AWARD

Wyoming Library Association
6123 Weaver Rd.
Cheyenne, WY 82009

The Soaring Eagle Book Award is sponsored by the Wyoming Council of the International Reading Association and the Wyoming Educational Media Association to encourage students' active involvement with books and reading. Given since 1989, this award is similar to the Wyoming Indian Paintbrush Award for grades 4-6, but is designed for grades 7-12.

This award is unique in that students nominate the books as well as vote for their favorite. In order to be eligible, the book must have been published in the last ten years and must not have appeared first as a movie or television show.

1989 **(GRADES 7-9)** *Superfudge* by Judy Blume, not illustrated; Dutton, 1980.

1990 **(GRADES 7-9)** *Someone Is Hiding on Alcatraz Island* by Eve Bunting, not illustrated; Clarion, 1984.

1990 **(GRADES 10-12)** *Of Love and Shadows* by Isabel Allende, translated from Spanish by Margarte Sayers Peder, not illustrated; Knopf, 1987.

1991 **(GRADES 7-9)** *Trapped in Death Cave* by Bill Wallace, not illustrated; Holiday House, 1984.

1991 **(GRADES 10-12)** *Princess Ashley* by Richard Peck, not illustrated; Delacorte, 1987.

1992 **(GRADES 7-12)** *Dances With Wolves* by Michael Blake, not illustrated; Fawcett Gold Medal 1988.

1993 **(GRADES 7-12)** *Hugh Glass, Mountain Man* by Robert McClung, illustrated; Morrow, 1990.

SOCIETY OF MIDLAND AUTHORS AWARD

Society of Midland Authors
See Also **CLARA INGRAM JUDSON AWARD**

This award was originally called the Clara Ingram Judson Award after the famous Midwestern author.

1980 *The Other Shore* by Lucinda Mays, not illustrated; Atheneum, 1979.

1981 *Snowbird* by Patricia Calvert, not illustrated; Scribner, 1980.

1982 *Moon and Me* by Hadley Irwin, not illustrated; Atheneum, 1981.

1983 *Joel, Growing Up a Farm Man* by Patricia Demuth, photographs by Jack Demuth; Dodd, Mead, 1982.

1984 *Love in a Different Key* by Marjorie Franco, not illustrated; Houghton Mifflin, 1983.

1985 *Tracker* by Gary Paulsen, not illustrated; Bradbury, 1984.

Waiting to Waltz by Cynthia Rylant, illustrated by Stephen Gammell; Bradbury, 1984.

1986 *Prairie Songs* by Pam Conrad, illustrated by Darryl S. Zudeck; Harper, 1985.

1987 *Mrs. Portree's Pony* by Lynn Hall, not illustrated; Scribners, 1986.

1989 **Juvenile Fiction** *Song and Dance Man* by Karen Ackerman, illustrated by Stephen Gammell; Knopf, 1988.

1989 **Juvenile Nonfiction** *Allosaurus* by Janet Riehecky, illustrated by Llyn Hunter; Child's World, 1988.

Apatosaurus by Janet Riehecky, illustrated by Lydia Halverson; Child's World, 1988.

Stegosaurus by Janet Riehecky, illustrated by Diana Magnuson; Child's World, 1988.

Triceratops by Janet Riehecky, illustrated by Diana Magnuson; Child's World, 1988.

Tyrannosaurus by Janet Riehecky, illustrated by Diana Magnuson; Child's World, 1988.

1990 *Robodad* by Alden R. Carter, not illustrated; Putnam, 1990.

SOUTH CAROLINA CHILDREN'S BOOK AWARD

South Carolina Association of School Librarians
Box 2442
Columbia, SC 29202

The South Carolina Children's Book Award was established by the South Carolina Association of School Librarians in 1975 to stimulate an interest in reading among school children. A committee of librarians, parents, teachers and school administrators selects a master list of books consisting of twenty works published in the previous five years. Students in grades four through eight who have read at least three of the nominated books are eligible to vote for their favorite. A medallion is presented to the winning author at the annual meeting of the South Carolina Association of School Librarians.

1976 *How to Eat Fried Worms* by Thomas Rockwell, illustrated by Emily McCully; Watts, 1973.

1977 *Tales of a Fourth Grade Nothing* by Judy Blume, illustrated by Roy Doty; Dutton, 1972.

1978 *Otherwise Known as Sheila the Great* by Judy Blume, not illustrated; Dutton, 1972.

1979 *The Great Christmas Kidnapping Caper* by Jean Van Leeuwen, illustrated by Steven Kellogg; Dial, 1975.

1980 *Shoeshine Girl* by Clyde Robert Bulla, illustrated by Leigh Grant; Crowell, 1975.

1981 *Bunnicula: A Rabbit Tale of Mystery* by Deborah Howe and James Howe, illustrated by Alan Daniel; Atheneum, 1980.

1982 *The Ghost of Tillie Jean Cassaway* by Ellen H. Showell, illustrated by Stephen Gammell; Four Winds, 1978.

1983 *Prisoners at the Kitchen Table* by Barbara Holland, not illustrated; Houghton Mifflin/Clarion, 1979.

1984 *Jelly Belly* by Robert Kimmel Smith, illustrated by Bob Jones; Delacorte, 1981.

1985 *The Monster's Ring* by Bruce Coville, illustrated by Katherine Coville; Pantheon, 1982.

1986 *The War with Grandpa* by Robert Kimmel Smith, illustrated by Richard Lauter; Delacorte, 1984.

1987 *Cracker Jackson* by Betsy Byars, not illustrated; Viking Kestrel, 1985.

1988 *Babysitting Is a Dangerous Job* by Willo Davis Roberts, not illustrated; Atheneum, 1985.

1989 *Ferret in the Bedroom, Lizards in the Fridge* by Bill Wallace, not illustrated; Holiday House, 1986.

1990 *Class Clown* by Johanna Hurwitz, illustrated by Sheila Hamanaka; Morrow, 1987.

1991 *Is Anybody There?* by Eve Bunting, not illustrated; Lippincott, 1988.

1992 *Snot Stew* by Bill Wallace, illustrated by Lisa McCue; Holiday House, 1989.

SOUTH CAROLINA YOUNG ADULT BOOK AWARD

South Carolina Association of School Librarians
Box 2442
Columbia, SC 29202

First awarded in 1980, this young adult's choice award is sponsored by the South Carolina Association of School Librarians, with the cooperation of the South Carolina Department of Education and the College of Library and Information Science, University of South Carolina. The purposes of this award are to encourage young adults to read good, contemporary literature which gives an understanding of the human experience and which provides information and to honor the author of the book annually chosen the favorite by students.

A master list is drawn up, containing twenty fiction or nonfiction titles published in the last three years. Newbery winners are excluded. Each title on the list should have two positive reviews from recognized reviewers. Students in grades nine through twelve in public or private school in South Carolina who have read at least three of the listed books will be eligible to vote for their favorite. The winning author receives a medallion at the spring conference of the South Carolina Association of School Librarians.

1980 *Amityville Horror* by Jay Anson, not illustrated; Prentice Hall, 1977; Bantam, 1978.

1981 *A Shining Season* by William J. Buchanan, illustrated with photographs; Coward McCann, 1978; Bantam, 1979.

1982 *The Boy Who Drank Too Much* by Shep Greene, not illustrated; Viking, 1979; Dell, 1980.

1983 *About David* by Susan Beth Pfeffer, not illustrated; Delacorte, 1980; Dell, 1982.

1984 *Stranger with My Face* by Lois Duncan, not illustrated; Little Brown, 1981; Dell, 1982.

1985 *The Divorce Express* by Paula Danziger, not illustrated; Delacorte, 1982.

1986 *A String of Chances* by Phyllis Reynolds Naylor, not illustrated; Atheneum, 1982.

1987 *If This Is Love, I'll Take Spaghetti* by Ellen Conford, not illustrated; Four Winds, 1983.

1988 *Locked in Time* by Lois Duncan, not illustrated; Little Brown, 1985.

1989 *Face at the Edge of the World* by Eve Bunting, not illustrated; Clarion, 1985.

1990 *The Year Without Michael* by Susan Beth Pfeffer, not illustrated; Bantam, 1987.

1991 *Fallen Angels* by Walter Dean Myers, not illustrated; Scholastic, 1988.

1992 *On the Devil's Court* by Carl Deuker, not illustrated; Little Brown (Joy Street), 1988.

SOUTH DAKOTA PRAIRIE PASQUE AWARD

South Dakota Library Association
800 Governor's Dr.
Pierre, SD 57501

The South Dakota Prairie Pasque Award is a reader's choice award to recognize an American author whose nominated work is considered to be of high literary quality and which is popular with young readers in South Dakota. First awarded in 1987, the winner of this annual award is chosen by students in grades four through six. Fiction, nonfiction and poetry published one to two years prior to the award is eligible.

1987 *Night of the Twisters* by Ivy Ruckman, not illustrated; Crowell, 1984.

1988 *Switcharound* by Lois Lowry, not illustrated; Houghton Mifflin, 1985.

1989 *Royal Pain* by Ellen Conford, not illustrated; Scholastic, 1986.

1990 *This Island Isn't Big Enough for the Four of Us* by Gery Greer and Bob Ruddick, not illustrated; Crowell, 1987.

1991 *All About Sam* by Lois Lowry, illustrated by Diane de Groat; Houghton Mifflin, 1988.

1992 *The Doll in the Garden* by Mary Downing Hahn, illustrated; Clarion, 1989; Avon, 1990.

SOUTHERN CALIFORNIA COUNCIL ON LITERATURE FOR CHILDREN AND YOUNG PEOPLE (SCCLCYP) ANNUAL CHILDREN'S LITERATURE AWARDS
SCCLCYP

Lynn Mook, Publicity Chair
8724 Portafino Place
Whittier, CA 90603

This children's literature award has been presented since 1961 to promote greater interest in literature for children and young people and to encourage excellence in the field. The awards recognize outstanding books, illustrations, and bodies of work by Southern Californians. In addition, the Dorothy C. McKenzie Award, named for the founder of the council, honors an individual for significant endeavors on behalf of children and books.

Nominations are recommended by the board of the council from lists compiled throughout the previous year of works published by Southern California authors and illustrators. Final selections are made by a committee consisting of board members and organization members. A plaque is presented to the honored authors and illustrators at an annual awards luncheon.

1961 **NOTABLE BOOK** *Island of the Blue Dolphins* by Scott O'Dell, not illustrated; Houghton, 1960.

1961 **SIGNIFICANT CONTRIBUTION IN THE FIELD OF ILLUSTRATION** *Moy Moy* written and illustrated by Leo Politi; Scribner, 1960.

1961 **COMPREHENSIVE CONTRIBUTION OF LASTING VALUE** Conrad Buff, Mary Buff, Lucille Holling, Holling Clancy Holling

1962 **NOTABLE BOOK** *Legend of Billy Bluesage* by Jonreed Lauritzen, illustrated by Edward Chavez; Little Brown, 1961.

1962 **ILLUSTRATION** *Come Again, Pelican* written and illustrated by Don Freeman; Viking, 1961.

1962 **DISTINGUISHED CONTRIBUTION TO THE FIELD OF CHILDREN'S LITERATURE** Clyde Robert Bulla

1963 **NOTABLE BOOK** *From the Eagle's Wing: A Biography of John Muir* by Hildegarde Hoyt Swift, illustrated by Lynd Ward; Morrow, 1962.

1963 **DISTINGUISHED CONTRIBUTION TO THE FIELD OF CHILDREN'S LITERATURE** Irene Robinson, W.W. Robinson

1964 **NOTABLE BOOK** *By the Great Horn Spoon!* by Sid Fleischman, illustrated by Eric von Schmidt; Atlantic-Little, 1963.

1964 **ILLUSTRATION** *Wild Wings over the Marshes* by Lucille N. Stratton and William D. Stratton, illustrated by Bernard Garbutt; Golden Gate Books, 1964.

1964 **ILLUSTRATION AND WRITING** Taro Yashima

1964 **DISTINGUISHED CONTRIBUTION TO THE FIELD OF LITERATURE FOR CHILDREN AND YOUNG PEOPLE AND FOR OUTSTANDING COMMUNITY SERVICE** Dorothy McKenzie

1965 **NOTABLE BOOK** *A Dawn in the Trees: Thomas Jefferson, the Years 1776 to 1789* by Leonard Wibberley, not illustrated; Ariel, 1964.

1965 **DISTINGUISHED CONTRIBUTION TO THE FIELD OF CHILDREN'S LITERATURE** Eleanor Cameron

1966 **NOTABLE BOOK** *Dorp Dead* by Julia Cunningham, illustrated by James Spanfeller; Pantheon, 1965.

1966 **COMPREHENSIVE CONTRIBUTION OF LASTING VALUE TO THE FIELD OF CHILDREN'S LITERATURE** Carol Ryrie Brink

1966 **DISTINGUISHED CONTRIBUTION TO THE FIELD OF CHILDREN'S LITERATURE** Mary Rogers Smith

1967 **NOTABLE BOOK** *The Royal Dirk* by John Beatty and Patricia Beatty, illustrated by Franz Altschuler; Morrow, 1966.

1967 **ILLUSTRATION** *Farewell to Shady Glade* written and illustrated by Bill Peet; Houghton, 1966.

1967 **COMPREHENSIVE CONTRIBUTION OF LASTING VALUE TO THE FIELD OF CHILDREN'S LITERATURE** Margot Benary-Isbert

1967 **DISTINGUISHED CONTRIBUTION TO THE FIELD OF CHILDREN'S LITERATURE** Rosemary Livsey

1968 **SIGNIFICANT CONTRIBUTION TO THE FIELD OF LITERATURE FOR YOUNG PEOPLE** Lorenz Graham

1968 **ILLUSTRATION** *Seashore Story* written and illustrated by Taro Yashima; Viking, 1967.

1968 **SIGNIFICANT CONTRIBUTION IN INFORMATIONAL BOOKS** Charles Coombs

1968 **COMPREHENSIVE CONTRIBUTION OF LASTING VALUE IN THE FIELD OF LITERATURE FOR CHILDREN AND YOUNG PEOPLE** Myra Cohn Livingston

1969 **NOTABLE BOOK** *The Bears and I: Raising Three Cubs in the North Woods* by Robert Franklin Leslie, illustrated by Theodore A. Xaras; Dutton, 1968.

1969 **COMPREHENSIVE CONTRIBUTION OF LASTING VALUE** Harriet Huntington

1969 **DISTINGUISHED CONTRIBUTION OF LASTING VALUE** Frances Clarke Sayers

1970 **NOTABLE BOOK** *The Cay* by Theodore Taylor, not illustrated; Doubleday, 1969.

1970 **ILLUSTRATION** *New Moon Cove* written and illustrated by Ann Atwood; Scribner, 1969.

1970 **DISTINGUISHED CONTRIBUTION TO THE FIELD OF FOLKLORE** Richard Chase

1970 **OUTSTANDING COMMUNITY SERVICE** Blanche Campbell

1971 **NOTABLE BOOK** *The Daybreakers* by Jane L. Curry, illustrated by Charles Robinson; Harcourt, 1970.

1971 **ILLUSTRATION** *Bobby Shafto's Gone to Sea* by Mark Taylor, illustrated by Graham Booth; Golden Gate Junior Books, 1970.

1971 **COMPREHENSIVE CONTRIBUTION OF LASTING VALUE** Margaret Leighton

1971 **DISTINGUISHED CONTRIBUTION TO THE FIELD OF CHILDREN'S LITERATURE AND OUTSTANDING COMMUNITY SERVICE** Laramee Haynes

1972 **NOTABLE BOOK** *Another Place, Another Spring* by Adrienne Jones, not illustrated; Houghton, 1971.

1972 **COMPREHENSIVE CONTRIBUTION OF LASTING VALUE** Sid Fleischman

1972 **DISTINGUISHED CONTRIBUTION FOR OUTSTANDING COMMUNITY SERVICE** Lloyd Severe

1972 **DISTINGUISHED CONTRIBUTION EXHIBITING THE FUSION OF POETRY AND PHOTOGRAPHY** Ann Atwood, Mark Pines

1973 **NOTABLE BOOK** *The Malibu and other Poems* by Myra Cohn Livingston, illustrated by James J. Spanfeller; Atheneum, 1972.

1973 **COMPREHENSIVE CONTRIBUTION OF LASTING VALUE** Marguerite Henry

1973 **DISTINGUISHED CONTRIBUTION TO THE FIELD OF CHILDREN'S LITERATURE** Betty Kalagian

1974 **FICTION** *Chloris and the Creeps* by Kin Platt, not illustrated; Chilton, 1973.

1974 **NONFICTION** *Juarez: A Son of the People* by Jean Rouverol, not illustrated; Crowell-Collier, 1973.

1974 **COMPREHENSIVE CONTRIBUTION OF LASTING VALUE** Patricia Beatty

1974 **SPECIAL CONTRIBUTION TO CHILDREN'S LITERATURE** Dr. Seuss (Theodor Geisel)

1975 **FICTION** *So, Nothing Is Forever* by Adrienne Jones, illustrated by Richard Cuffari; Houghton, 1974.

1975 **NONFICTION** *Before the Supreme Court: The Story of Belva Ann Lockwood* by Terry Dunnahoo, illustrated by Bea Holmes; Houghton, 1974.

1975 **ILLUSTRATION** *Son of Thunder: An Old Lapp Tale* retold by Ethel K. McHale, illustrated by Ruth Bornstein; Childrens, 1974.

1975 **DISTINGUISHED CONTRIBUTION FOR OUTSTANDING COMMUNITY SERVICE** Edith Wynn Horton

1976 **NOTABLE BOOK** *Shoeshine Girl* by Clyde Robert Bulla, illustrated by Leigh Grant; Crowell, 1975.

1976 **ILLUSTRATION** *Little Pieces of the West Wind* by Christian Garrison, illustrated by Diane Goode; Bradbury, 1975.

Selchie's Seed by Sulamith Oppenheim, illustrated by Diane Goode; Bradbury, 1975.

1976 **SIGNIFICANT CONTRIBUTION FOR TOTAL CONCEPT AND ILLUSTRATION** *Will's Quill* written and illustrated by Don Freeman; Viking, 1975.

1976 **EXCELLENCE IN A SERIES** Mark Taylor (for the Henry series)

1976 **DISTINGUISHED CONTRIBUTION** Helen Hinckley Jones

1977 **NOTABLE BOOK** *The Mark of Conte* by Sonia Levitin, illustrated by Bill Negron; Atheneum, 1976.

1977 **ILLUSTRATION** *Little Gorilla* written and illustrated by Ruth Bornstein; Seabury, 1976.

1977 **EXCELLENCE IN A SERIES** *The Treegate Chronicles* by Leonard Wibberley, not illustrated; Farrar, 1976.

1977 **DISTINGUISHED CONTRIBUTION FOR OUTSTANDING SERVICE** Sylvia Ziskind

1978 **FICTION** *Ghost of Summer* by Eve Bunting, illustrated by W.T. Mars; Warne, 1977.

1978 **BODY OF WORK** Theodore Taylor

1978 **INTERPRETATION OF LITERATURE THROUGH FILM** Martin Tahse

1978 **DOROTHY C. McKENZIE AWARD** Helen Fuller

1979 **FICTION** *Alone in Wolf Hollow* by Dana Brookins, not illustrated; Seabury, 1978.

1979 **ILLUSTRATION** *Dream Eater* by Christian Garrison, illustrated by Diane Goode; Bradbury, 1978.

1979 **BODY OF WORK** Jane Louise Curry

1979 **DISTINGUISHED CONTRIBUTION FOR OUTSTANDING COMMUNITY SERVICE** Nettie Frishman

1980 **NONFICTION** *The Snow Monkey at Home* by Margaret Rau, illustrated by Eva Hulsmann; Knopf, 1979.

1980 **SPECIAL RECOGNITION FOR A CONTRIBUTION OF CULTURAL SIGNIFICANCE** *Beyond the East Wind: Legends and Folktales of Vietnam* told by Duong Van Quyen, written by Jewell Reinhart Coburn, illustrated by Nena Grigorian Ullberg; Burn, Hart, 1976.

Encircled Kingdom: Legends and Folktales of Laos by Jewell Reinhart Coburn, illustrated by Nena Grigorian Ullberg; Burn, Hart, 1979.

Khmers, Tigers and Talismans: From the History and Legends of Mysterious Cambodia by Jewell Rinehart Coburn, illustrated by Nena Grigorian Ullberg; Burn, Hart, 1978.

1980 **BODY OF WORK** Frank Bonham

1980 **DOROTHY C. McKENZIE AWARD** Sue Alexander

1981 **NOTABLE WORK OF FICTION** *Stone Fox* by John Reynolds Gardiner, illustrated by Marcia Sewall; Crowell, 1980.

1981 **DISTINGUISHED BODY OF WORK** Sonia Levitin

1981 **DOROTHY C. McKENZIE AWARD** Miriam S. Cox

1982 **DISTINGUISHED WORK OF FICTION** *Which Way Courage* by Eileen Weiman, not illustrated; Atheneum, 1981.

1982 **DISTINGUISHED BODY OF WORK** Julia Cunningham

1982 **DOROTHY C. McKENZIE AWARD** Ruth Radlauer, Edward Radlauer

1982 SIGNIFICANT CONTRIBUTION FOR EXCEL-LENCE IN A SERIES *Hanukkah: Eight Nights, Eight Lights* by Malka Drucker, illustrated by Brom Hoban; Holiday House, 1980.

Passover: A Season of Freedom by Malka Drucker, illustrated by Brom Hoban; Holiday House, 1981.

Rosh Hashanah and Yom Kippur: Sweet Beginnings by Malka Drucker, illustrated by Brom Hoban; Holiday House, 1981.

Sukkot: A Time to Rejoice by Malka Drucker, illustrated by Brom Hoban; Holiday House, 1982.

1983 CONTRIBUTION OF CULTURAL SIGNIFICANCE *Story for a Black Night* by Clayton Bess, not illustrated; Houghton Mifflin, 1982.

1983 DISTINGUISHED WORK OF FICTION *Jonathan Down Under* by Patricia Beatty, not illustrated; Morrow, 1982.

1983 DISTINGUISHED WORK OF NONFICTION *Windows in Space* by Ann Elwood and Linda C. Wood, illustrated; Walker, 1982.

1983 SIGNIFICANT CONTRIBUTION FOR EXCEL-LENCE IN A SERIES T. Ernesto Bethancourt for Doris Fein Mysteries; Holiday House, 1978-1983.

1983 DOROTHY C. McKENZIE AWARD Michael Cart

1984 RECOGNITION OF MERIT FOR FIRST NOVEL *Element of Time* by Kathy Livoni, not illustrated; Harcourt, 1983.

1984 DISTINGUISHED WORK OF FICTION *Nadia the Willful* by Sue Alexander, illustrated by Lloyd Bloom; Pantheon, 1983.

1984 DISTINGUISHED BODY OF WORK Adrienne Jones

1984 DOROTHY C. McKENZIE AWARD Winifred Ragsdale

1985 NOTABLE WORK OF FICTION *Prune* by Ramon Royal Ross, illustrated by Susan Sarabasha; Atheneum, 1984.

1985 NOTABLE WORK OF NONFICTION *Too Fat? Too Thin? Do You Have a Choice?* by Caroline Arnold, foreword by Tony Greenberg, not illustrated; Morrow, 1984.

1985 SIGNIFICANT CONTRIBUTION IN ILLUSTRA-TION *The Napping House* by Audrey Wood, illustrated by Don Wood; Harcourt, 1984.

1985 DOROTHY C. McKENZIE AWARD Clifton Fadiman

1986 DISTINGUISHED WORK OF FICTION *A Place for Allie* by Mary V. Carey, not illustrated; Dodd, Mead, 1985.

1986 DISTINGUISHED WORK OF NONFICTION *The Comet and You* by Edwin C. Krupp, illustrated by Robin Rector Krupp; Macmillan, 1985.

1986 EXCELLENCE IN A SERIES Eve Bunting for Lippincott Page Turners - Cloverdale Switch, 1979; *Ghosts of Departure Point*, 1982; *Haunting of Safekeep*, 1985; *If I Asked You Would You Stay?* 1984; *Waiting Game*, 1981.

1986 DOROTHY C. McKENZIE AWARD Caroline Feller Bauer

1987 NOTABLE ACHIEVEMENT IN PHOTOJOURNAL-ISM *Motorcycle on Patrol: The Story of a Highway Officer* by Joan Hewett, illustrated by Richard Hewett; Clarion, 1986.

1987 DISTINGUISHED WORK OF NONFICTION *I Lift My Lamp: Emma Lazarus and the Statue of Liberty* by Nancy Smiler Levinson, illustrated; Lodestar Books, 1986.

1987 OUTSTANDING CONTRIBUTION OF LASTING VALUE IN A BODY OF WORK Clyde Robert Bulla

1987 DOROTHY C. McKENZIE AWARD Carolyn Johnson

1988 EXCELLENCE IN ILLUSTRATION *The Flame of Peace: A Tale of the Aztecs* written and illustrated by Deborah Nourse Lattimore; Harper & Row, 1987.

1988 OUTSTANDING WORK OF FICTION FOR YOUNG ADULTS *Invincible Summer* by Jean Ferris, not illustrated; Farrar, Straus, Giroux, 1987.

1988 OUTSTANDING WORK OF FICTION FOR CHIL-DREN *Lila on the Landing* by Sue Alexander, illustrated by Ellen Eagle; Clarion, 1987.

1988 DOROTHY C. McKENZIE AWARD Terry Dunnahoo

1989 SPECIAL RECOGNITION FOR EXCELLENCE IN A POETRY QUARTET *Earth Songs* by Myra Cohn Livingston, illustrated by Leonard Everett Fisher; Holiday House, 1986.

Space Songs by Myra Cohn Livingston, illustrated by Leonard Everett Fisher; Holiday House, 1988.

Sky Songs by Myra Cohn Livingston, illustrated by Leonard Everett Fisher; Holiday House, 1984.

Sea Songs by Myra Cohn Livingston, illustrated by Leonard Everett Fisher; Holiday House, 1986.

1989 OUTSTANDING WORK OF FICTION FOR CHIL-DREN *Dear Baby* by Joanne Rocklin, illustrated by Eileen McKeating; Macmillan, 1988.

1989 OUTSTANDING WORK OF FICTION FOR YOUNG ADULTS *A Sudden Silence* by Eve Bunting, not illustrated; Harcourt Brace Jovanovich, 1988.

1989 OUTSTANDING LITERARY QUALITY IN A PIC-TURE BOOK *Yonder* by Tony Johnston, illustrated by Lloyd Bloom; Dial, 1988.

1989 DOROTHY C. McKENZIE AWARD Betsy Brown

1990 NONFICTION *Once Upon a Horse* by Suzanne Jurmain, illustrated with photos; Lothrop, Lee & Shepard, 1989.

1990 FICTION FOR YOUNG ADULTS *Wrestling With Honor* by David Klass, not illustrated; Dutton, 1989.

1990 NOTABLE BOOK CELEBRATING A CREATIVE LIFE *Bill Peet: An Autobiography* written and illustrated by Bill Peet; Houghton Mifflin, 1989.

1990 FICTION *The Wednesday Surprise* by Eve Bunting, illustrated by Donald Carrick; Clarion, 1989.

1990 DOROTHY C. McKENZIE AWARD Betty Takeuchi

1991 DISTINGUISHED WORK OF NONFICTION *Christopher Columbus: Voyager to the Unknown* by Nancy Smiler Levinson, illustrated with maps; Lodestar, 1990.

1991 DISTINGUISHED WORK OF FICTION *The Wall* by Eve Bunting, illustrated by Ronald Himler; Clarion, 1990.

1991 DISTINGUISHED ILLUSTRATING AND WRITING
The Dragon's Robe written and illustrated by Deborah Nourse Lattimore; HarperCollins, 1990.

1991 DISTINGUISHED WORK OF FICTION FOR YOUNG ADULTS *Dixie Storms* by Barbara Hall, not illustrated; Harcourt Brace Jovanovich, 1990.

1991 DOROTHY MCKENZIE AWARD Barbara Karlin

1992 SIGNIFICANT CONTRIBUTION TO FIELD OF BIOGRAPHY *Native American Doctor: The Story of Susan LaFlesche Picotte* by Jeri Ferris, illustrated; Carolrhoda, 1991.

1992 NOTABLE PICTURE BOOK *Piggies* written and illustrated by Don Wood and Audrey Wood; Harcourt Brace Jovanovich, 1991.

1992 OUTSTANDING FICTION FOR YOUNG ADULTS *What Daddy Did* by Neal Shusterman, not illustrated; Little Brown, 1991.

1992 NOTABLE WORK OF FICTION *Blue Skye* by Lael Littke, not illustrated; Scholastic, 1990.

1992 DOROTHY MCKENZIE AWARD Peggy Miller

SOUTHWEST BOOK AWARD

Border Regional Library Association
El Paso Public Library
501 N. Oregon
El Paso, TX 79901

This annual award is sponsored by the Border Regional Library Association and recognizes the best books written about the Southwest. The winning author receives a certificate at an awards banquet.

1985 *The Pueblo* written and illustrated by Charlotte Yue and David Yue; Houghton Mifflin, 1986.

1986 *Doctor Coyote: A Native American Aesop's Fable* retold by John Bierhorst, illustrated by Wendy Watson; Macmillan, 1987.

1988 *The Dawn Seekers* by Carol Hamilton, illustrated by Abby Levine; Whitman, 1987.

1989 *Born To the Land: An American Portrait* by Brent Ashabranner, photographs by Paul Conklin; Putnam, 1989.

Desert Giant by Barbara Bash, illustrated; Sierra Club/Little Brown, 1989.

1990 *Agave Blooms Just Once* by Giselda Jernigan, illustrated by E. Wesley Jernigan; Harbinger House, 1989.

SPRING BOOK FESTIVAL AWARDS

discontinued

This children's book award was originally sponsored by *The New York Herald Tribune*. Awards were presented annually in the categories of younger children (later, picture book), middle ages, and older children. The first awards were presented in 1937 for the purpose of encouraging the publication and sale of children's books in the spring. Any children's book published from January through June of the award year was eligible. Judges for the competition were authors, illustrators and others prominent in the field.

The following guidelines determined the winning books: (1) Books for children must be interesting. (2) The books must have validity. (3) The books should have beauty not only of thought, but of appearance. (4) They should have the harmony of conscious design, holding together text, illustration, and all departments and details of mechanical production.

The New York Herald Tribune sponsored the annual competition from 1937 until 1967, when the paper ceased publication. Book World, published by *The Chicago Tribune* and *The Washington Post*, assumed sponsorship from 1968 through 1973, when the award was discontinued.

1937 YOUNGER *Seven Simeons: A Russian Tale* written and illustrated by Boris Artzybasheff; Viking, 1937.

1937 YOUNGER HONOR *Blaze and the Gypsies* written and illustrated by Clarence W. Anderson; Macmillan, 1937.

Claudius the Bee by John F. Leeming, illustrated by Richard B. Ogle; Viking, 1937.

Drusilla written and illustrated by Emma L. Brock; Macmillan, 1937.

Harry in England by Laura E. Richards, illustrated by Reginald Birch; Appleton Century Crofts, 1937.

The Wonderful Wonders of One-Two-Three by David Eugene Smith, illustrated by Barbara Irvins; McFarlane, Warde & McFarlane, 1937.

1937 OLDER *Smuggler's Sloop* by Robb White, illustrated by Andrew Wyeth; Little, 1937.

1937 OLDER HONOR *Bright Island* by Mabel L. Robinson, illustrated by Lynd Ward; Random House, 1937.

The Insect Man: Jean Henri Fabre by Eleanor Doorly, illustrated by Robert Gibbings; Appleton Century Crofts, 1937.

Pecos Bill, the Greatest Cowboy of all Times by James Cloyd Bowman, illustrated by Laura Bannon; Whitman, 1937.

Wind of the Vikings by Maribelle Cormack, illustrated by Robert Lawson; Appleton Century Crofts, 1937.

1938 YOUNGER *The Hobbitt* written and illustrated by J.R.R. Tolkien; Houghton Mifflin, 1938.

1938 YOUNGER HONOR *Adventures of Misha* by Sergei Rozanov, illustrated by Alexander Mogilevsky; Stokes, 1938.

The Cautious Carp and other Fables in Pictures written and illustrated by Nicholas Radlov, translated by Helen Black; Coward McCann, 1938.

The Jumping Lions of Borneo by John William Dunne, illustrated by Irene Robinson; Holt, 1938.

The Magic Spear and other Stories of China's Famous Heroes by Louise Crane, illustrated by Yenchi Tiao T'u and Ching Chi Yee; Random House, 1938.

Runaway Balboa by Enid Johnson, illustrated by Anne Merriman Peck; Harper, 1938.

1938 OLDER *Iron Duke* by John R. Tunis, illustrated by Johan Bull; Harcourt, 1938.

1938 OLDER HONOR *Five Proud Riders* by Ann Stafford, illustrated by Bobri; Knopf, 1938.

Give a Man a Horse by Charles J. Finger, illustrated by Henry C. Pitz; Winston, 1938.

Sailing for Gold by Clifton Johnson, illustrated by James Reid; Putnam, 1938.

Sons of the Hurricane by J.J. Floherty, illustrated with photographs; Lippincott, 1938.

Storms on the Labrador written and illustrated by Hepburn Dinwoodie; Oxford, 1938.

1939 **YOUNGER** *The Story of Horace* written and illustrated by Alice M. Coats; Coward, 1939.

1939 **YOUNGER HONOR** *A Book of Wild Flowers* by Margaret McKenny, illustrated by Edith F. Johnson; Macmillan, 1939.

An Ear for Uncle Emil by Eva Rose Gaggin, illustrated by Kate Seredy; Viking, 1939.

The Little French Farm by Lida Guertik, translated by Louise Raymond, illustrated by Helene Guertik; Harper, 1939.

Travels of a Snail by Eleanor Hoffmann, illustrated by Zhenya Gay; Stokes, 1939.

The Young Aunts by Alice Dalgliesh, illustrated by Charlotte Becker; Scribner, 1939.

1939 **OLDER** *The Hired Man's Elephant* by Phil Stong, illustrated by Doris Lee; Dodd, 1939.

1939 **OLDER HONOR** *Bat: The Story of a Bull Terrier* by Stephen W. Meader, illustrated by Edward Shenton; Harcourt, 1939.

Land for My Sons: A Frontier Tale of the American Revolution by Maribelle Cormack and William P. Alexander, illustrated by Lyle Justis; Appleton-Century, 1939.

Long Wharf: A Story of Young San Francisco by Howard Pease, illustrated by Manning de V. Lee; Dodd, 1939.

Phantom on Skis by Helen Girvan, illustrated by Alan Haemer; Farrar, 1939.

The Sword of Roland Arnot by Agnes Danforth Hewes, illustrated by Paul Strayer; Houghton, 1939.

1940 **YOUNGER** *That Mario* written and illustrated by Lucy H. Crockett; Holt, 1940.

1940 **YOUNGER HONOR** *The Far-away Trail* by Charlie May Simon, illustrated by Howard Simon; Dutton, 1940.

A Good House for a Mouse by Irmengarde Eberle, illustrated by Eloise Wilkin; Messner, 1940.

The Great Geppy written and illustrated by William Pene du Bois; Viking, 1940.

The Littlest House by Elizabeth Coatsworth, illustrated by Marguerite Davis; Macmillan, 1940.

Whistle for Good Fortune by Margery Bailey, illustrated by Alice B. Preston; Little Brown, 1940.

1940 **OLDER** *Cap'n Ezra, Privateer* by James D. Adams, illustrated by I.B. Hazelton; Harcourt, 1940.

1940 **OLDER HONOR** *The Golden Knight* by George Challis, illustrated by Steele Savage; Greystone Press, 1940.

The Kid from Tomkinsville by John R. Tunis, illustrated by Jay Hyde Barnum; Harcourt, 1940.

The Lost Baron by Allen French, illustrated by Andrew Wyeth; Houghton, 1940.

Nansen by Anna Gertrude Hall, illustrated by Boris Artzybasheff; Viking, 1940.

Voices from the Grass by Julie Closson Kenly, illustrated by Henry Kenly; Appleton Century Crofts, 1940.

1941 **YOUNGER** *In My Mother's House* by Ann Nolan Clark, illustrated by Velino Herrera; Viking, 1941.

1941 **YOUNGER HONOR** *Billy Button's Butter'd Biscuit* by Mabel Leigh Hunt, illustrated by Katherine Milhous; Stokes, 1941.

Flip written and illustrated by Wesley Dennis; Viking, 1941.

Story of the Mississippi by Marshall MacClintock, illustrated by C.H. DeWitt; Harper, 1941.

A Tale for Easter written and illustrated by Tasha Tudor; Oxford, 1941.

1941 **MIDDLE** *Pete* by Tom Robinson, illustrated by Morgan Dennis; Viking, 1941.

1941 **MIDDLE HONOR** *Captain Kidd's Cow* by Phil Stong, illustrated by Kurt Wiese; Dodd, 1941.

Hilla of Finland by Geneva de Malroy, illustrated by Frederick Andersen; Nelson, 1941.

Lottie's Valentine by Katherine Wigmore Eyre, illustrated by Susanne Suba; Oxford, 1941.

A Name for Obed by Ethel Calvert Phillips, illustrated by Lois Lenski; Houghton, 1941.

1941 **OLDER** *Clara Barton* by Mildred M. Pace, illustrated by Robert Ball; Scribner, 1941.

1941 **OLDER HONOR** *Finlandia, the Story of Sibelius* by Elliott Arnold, illustrated by Lolita Granahan; Holt, 1941.

The Middle Button by Kathryn Worth, illustrated by Dorothy Bayley; Doubleday-Doran, 1941.

Renfrew Flies Again by Laurie York Erskine, illustrated by Edward Shenton; Appleton Century Crofts, 1941.

Smoke Eater by Howard M. Brier, illustrated by Louis Cunette; Random House, 1941.

1942 **PICTURE BOOK** *Mr. Tootwhistle's Invention* written and illustrated by Peter Wells; Winston, 1942.

1942 **PICTURE BOOK HONOR** *The Donkey from Dorking* by Frances F. Neilson, illustrated by Janet Hopkins and Lidia Vitale; Dutton, 1942.

Johnny Jump-up by John Hooper, illustrated by Regina Bode; Macmillan, 1942.

The Truck That Flew written and illustrated by Dudley Morris; Putnam, 1942.

Whitney's First Round-up written and illustrated by Glen Rounds; Grosset, 1942.

1942 **MIDDLE** *I Have Just Begun to Fight: The Story of John Paul Jones* by Edward Ellsberg, illustrated by G. Foster; Dodd Mead, 1942.

1942 **MIDDLE HONOR** *Adam of the Road* by Elizabeth Janet Gray, illustrated by Robert Lawson; Viking, 1942.

The Boy Who Could Do Anything, and other Mexican Folk Tales by Anita Brenner, illustrated by Jean Charlot; Young Scott Books, 1942.

Lions on the Hunt by Theodore J. Waldeck, illustrated by Kurt Wiese; Viking, 1942.

Steppin and Family by Hope Newell, illustrated by Anne Merriman Peck; Oxford, 1942.

1942 OLDER *None but the Brave: A Story of Holland* by Rosamund Van der Zee Marshall, illustrated by Gregor Duncan; Houghton, 1942.

1942 OLDER HONOR *Carolina Caravan* by Christine Noble Govan, illustrated by Helen Blair; Houghton, 1942.

Street of Ships written and illustrated by Charles M. Daugherty; Holt, 1942.

They Loved to Laugh by Kathryn Worth, illustrated by Marguerite de Angeli; Doubleday, 1942.

War Horse by Fairfax Downey, illustrated by Paul Brown; Dodd, 1942.

1943 YOUNGER *Five Golden Wrens* written and illustrated by Hugh Troy; Oxford, 1943.

1943 YOUNGER HONOR *Corporal Keeperupper* written and illustrated by Katherine Milhous; Scribner, 1943.

Michael the Colt by Katharine K. Garbutt, illustrated by Bernard Garbutt; Houghton, 1943.

The Peddler's Clock by Mabel Leigh Hunt, illustrated by Elizabeth Orton Jones; Grosset, 1943.

Pito's House written and illustrated by Catherine Bryan and Mabra Madden; Macmillan, 1943.

1943 MIDDLE *These Happy Golden Years* by Laura Ingalls Wilder, illustrated by Mildred Boyle and Helen Sewell; Harper, 1943.

1943 MIDDLE HONOR *Green Wagons* by Oskar Seidlin and Senta Rypins, illustrated by Barbara Cooney; Houghton, 1943.

Mischief in Fez by Eleanor Hoffmann, illustrated by Fritz Eichenberg; Holiday House, 1943.

Mounted Messenger by Cornelia Meigs, illustrated by John Wonsetler; Macmillan, 1943.

Spotlight for Danny by Lorraine Beim and Jerrold Beim, illustrated by Corinne Malvern; Harcourt, 1943.

1943 OLDER *Patterns on the Wall* by Elizabeth Yates, illustrated by Warren Chappell; Knopf, 1943.

1943 OLDER HONOR *Here Is Alaska* by Evelyn Stefansson, maps by Raymond Lufkin, photographs by Frederick Machetanz; Scribner, 1943.

Stand By - Mark! The Career Story of a Naval Officer by Frederic M. Gardiner, illustrated with photographs; Dodd Mead, 1943.

Vast Horizons by Mary Seymour Lucas, illustrated by C.B. Falls; Viking, 1943.

Walter Reed: Doctor in Uniform by Laura Newbold Wood, illustrated by Douglas Duer; Messner, 1943.

1944 YOUNGER *A Ring and a Riddle* by M. Ilin and E.A. Segal, translated by Beatrice Kinkead, illustrated by Vera Bock; Lippincott, 1944.

1944 YOUNGER HONOR *Clarinda* by Frances Duncombe, illustrated by Angela Straeter; Holt, 1944.

The Golden Almanac by Dorothy Agnes Bennett, illustrated by Marie Stern; Simon & Schuster, 1944.

Molly the Rogue by Mary R. Walsh, illustrated by Henry C. Pitz; Knopf, 1944.

Susan Who Lives in Australia written and illustrated by Elisabeth MacIntyre; Scribner, 1944.

1944 MIDDLE *They Put Out To Sea: The Story of the Map* written and illustrated by Roger Duvoisin; Knopf, 1943.

1944 MIDDLE HONOR *Far from Marlborough Street* by Elizabeth Philbrook, illustrated by Marjorie Torrey; Viking, 1944.

High Prairie by Walter Havighurst and Marion Havighurst, illustrated by Gertrude Howe; Farrar & Rinehart, 1944.

Rex of the Coast Patrol written and illustrated by Helen Lossing Johnson and Margaret S. Johnson; Harcourt, 1944.

Three and a Pigeon by Kitty Barne, illustrated by Stuart Tresilian; Dodd Mead, 1944.

1944 OLDER *Storm Canvas* written and illustrated by Armstrong Sperry; Winston, 1944.

1944 OLDER HONOR *Dorinda* by Elizabeth Howard, illustrated by Leonard Weisgard; Lothrop, 1944.

Road to Down Under by Maribelle Cormack, illustrated by Edward Shenton; Appleton Century, 1944.

Some Follow the Sea by Henry Gregor Felsen, illustrated with photographs; Dutton, 1944.

Young Willkie by Alden Hatch, illustrated with photographs; Harcourt, 1944.

1945 YOUNGER *Little People in a Big Country* by Norma Cohn, illustrated by the children of Soviet Russia; Oxford, 1945.

1945 YOUNGER HONOR *The Carrot Seed* by Ruth Krauss, illustrated by Crockett Johnson; Harper, 1945.

Nine Cry-baby Dolls by Josephine B. Bernhard, illustrated by Irena Lowentowicz; Roy, 1945.

Valery by Elizabeth Conger, illustrated by Bill Crawford; Holt, 1944.

The Wizard and his Magic Powder by Alfred S. Campbell, illustrated by Kurt Wiese; Knopf, 1945.

1945 MIDDLE *The Gulf Stream* by Ruth Brindze, illustrated by Helene Carter; Vanguard, 1945.

1945 MIDDLE HONOR *Mickey, the Horse that Volunteered* by Carl Glick, illustrated by Bill Crawford; Whittlesey House, 1945.

Nathan, Boy of Capernaum by Amy Morris Lillie, illustrated by Nedda Walker; Dutton, 1944.

Orange on Top by Henrietta Van der Haas, illustrated by Lucille Wallower; Harcourt, 1945.

Sky Highways: Geography from the Air by Trevor Lloyd, illustrated by Armstrong Sperry; Houghton, 1945.

1945 OLDER *Sandy* by Elizabeth Janet Gray, illustrated by Robert Hallock; Viking, 1945.

1945 OLDER HONOR *Give Me Liberty* by Hildegarde Hawthorne, illustrated by Woodi Ishmael; Appleton Century Crofts, 1945.

New Found World by Katherine B. Shippen, illustrated by C. B. Falls; Viking, 1945.

A Sea Between by Lavinia R. Davis, not illustrated; Doubleday, 1945.

Stocky, Boy of West Texas by Elizabeth Baker, illustrated by Charles Hargens; Winston, 1945.

Within the Circle by Evelyn Stefansson, illustrated by Richard Edes Harrison; Scribner, 1945.

1946 YOUNGER *Farm Stories* by Kathryn Byron Jackson, illustrated by Gustaf Tenggren; Simon & Schuster, 1946.

1946 YOUNGER HONOR *Chicken Little Count-to-Ten* by Margaret R. Friskey, illustrated by Katherine Evans; Childrens Press, 1946.

Keep Singing, Keep Humming: A Collection of Play and Story Songs by Margaret Bradford, accompaniments by Barbara Woodruff, illustrated by Lucienne Bloch; Scott, 1946.

The Runaway Shuttle Train by Muriel Fuller, illustrated by Dorathea Dana; McKay, 1946.

Who Likes the Dark? by Virginia Howell, illustrated by Marjorie Thompson; Howell, Soskin, 1945.

1946 MIDDLE *The Thirteenth Stone* by Jean Bothwell, illustrated by Margaret Ayer; Harcourt, 1946.

1946 MIDDLE HONOR *The Beginning Was a Dutchman* by Isla Mitchell, illustrated by Richard Kennedy; Dodd, 1946.

Bright April written and illustrated by Marguerite deAngeli; Doubleday, 1946.

Harriet by Charles McKinley, Jr., illustrated by William Pene du Bois; Viking, 1946.

Let's Find Out: A Picture Science Book by Nina Schneider and Herman Schneider, illustrated by Jeanne Bendick; Scott, 1946.

1946 OLDER *The Quest of the Golden Condor* written and illustrated by Clayton Knight; Knopf, 1946.

1946 OLDER HONOR *Bright Spurs* by Armine von Tempski, illustrated by Paul Brown; Dodd, 1946.

Going on Sixteen by Betty Cavanna, illustrated by John Gretzer; Westminster, 1946.

Made in India by Cornelia Spencer, illustrated by Allen Lewis; Knopf, 1946.

Mistress of the White House by Helen L. Morgan, illustrated by Phyllis Cote; Westminster, 1946.

1947 YOUNGER *Oley the Sea Monster* written and illustrated by Marie Hall Ets; Viking, 1947.

1947 YOUNGER HONOR *The Bad Little Duck-hunter* by Margaret Wise Brown, illustrated by Clement Hurd; Scott, 1947.

Dot for Short by Frieda Friedman, illustrated by Carolyn Haywood; Morrow, 1947.

Taffy and Joe by Earl Burton and Linette Burton, illustrated by Helen Stone; Whittlesey House, 1947.

Wee Willow Whistle by Kay Avery, illustrated by Winifred Bromhall; Knopf, 1947.

1947 MIDDLE *Pancakes-Paris* by Claire Huchet Bishop, illustrated by Georges Schreiber; Viking, 1947.

1947 MIDDLE HONOR *The Rainforest* written and illustrated by Armstrong Sperry; Macmillan, 1947.

The Secret of the Porcelain Fish by Margaret Evernden, illustrated by Thomas Handforth; Random House, 1947.

Secret Passage by Betty Cavanna, illustrated by Jean McLaughlin; Winston, 1946.

Sugar Bush written and illustrated by Dorathea Dana; Nelson, 1947.

1947 OLDER *The Twenty-one Balloons* written and illustrated by William Pene du Bois; Viking, 1947.

1947 OLDER HONOR *Discovering Design* by Marion Downer, illustrated with photographs and drawings; Lothrop, 1947.

The Little White Horse by Elizabeth Goudge, illustrated by C. Walter Hodges; University of London Press, 1946; Coward, 1947.

North Star Shining by Hildegarde Hoyt Swift, illustrated by Lynd Ward; Morrow, 1947.

Willow Hill by Phyllis A. Whitney, not illustrated; Reynal & Hitchcock, 1947; McKay, 1947.

1948 YOUNGER *My Father's Dragon* by Ruth Stiles Gannett, illustrated by Ruth Chrisman Gannett; Random House, 1948.

1948 YOUNGER HONOR *Fish in the Air* written and illustrated by Kurt Wiese; Viking, 1948.

Juanita written and illustrated by Leo Politi; Scribner, 1948.

Mr. and Mrs. Noah written and illustrated by Lois Lenski; Crowell, 1948.

Tiny Animal Stories (series) by Dorothy Kunhardt, illustrated by Garth Williams; Simon & Schuster, various years.

1948 MIDDLE *Daughter of the Mountains* by Louise S. Rankin, illustrated by Kurt Wiese; Viking, 1948.

1948 MIDDLE HONOR *Appleseed Farm* by Emily Taft Douglas, illustrated by Anne Vaughan; Abingdon-Cokesbury, 1948.

The Bewitched Caverns by Leona Rienow, illustrated by Allen Pope; Scribner, 1948.

The Castle of Grumpy Grouch by Mary Dickerson Donahey, illustrated by Pelagie Doane; Random House, 1948.

River Dragon by Carl D. Lane, illustrated by Charles Banks Wilson; Little, 1948.

1948 OLDER *Crimson Anchor: A Sea Mystery* by Felix Riesenberg, not illustrated; Dodd, 1948.

1948 OLDER HONOR *Bittersweet* by Martha Barnhart Harper, illustrated by Erick Berry; Longmans, 1948.

Highpockets by John R. Tunis, illustrated by Charles Beck; Morrow, 1948.

The Secret of the Buried Tomb written and illustrated by Clayton Knight; Knopf, 1948.

Your Kind Indulgence by Gladys Malvern, illustrated by Corrine Malvern; Messner, 1948.

1949 YOUNGER *Bonnie Bess: The Weathervane Horse* by Alvin Tresselt, illustrated by Marylin Hafner; Lothrop, 1949.

1949 **YOUNGER HONOR** *Hodie* by Katharine Garbutt and Bernard Garbutt, illustrated by Bernard Garbutt; Aladdin, 1949.

The Little Cowboy by Margaret Wise Brown, illustrated by Esphyr Slobodkina; Scott, 1948, 1949.

Sonny-boy Sim by Elizabeth Baker, illustrated by Susanne Suba; Rand McNally, 1948.

Susie, the Cat written and illustrated by Tony Palazzo; Viking, 1949.

1949 **UNDER 12** *Bush Holiday* by Stephen Fennimore, illustrated by Ninon MacKnight; Doubleday, 1949.

1949 **UNDER 12 HONOR** *At the Palace Gates* by Helen Rand Parrish, illustrated by Leo Politi; Viking, 1949.

Movie Shoes by Noel Streatfeild, illustrated by Susanne Suba; Random House, 1949.

Sea Boots by Robert C. DuSoe, illustrated by Arthur Harper; Longmans, 1949.

A Sundae with Judy by Frieda Friedman, illustrated by Carolyn Haywood; Morrow, 1949.

1949 **OLDER** *Start of the Trail: The Story of a Young Maine Guide* by Louise Dickinson Rich, not illustrated; Lippincott, 1949.

1949 **OLDER HONOR** *Albert Einstein* by Elma Ehrlich Levinger, illustrated with photographs; Messner, 1949.

Son of the Valley by John R. Tunis, not illustrated; Morrow, 1949.

Song of the Pines: A Story of Norwegian Lumbering in Wisconsin by Walter Havighurst and Marion Havighurst, illustrated by Richard Floethe; Winston, 1949.

Tree of Freedom by Rebecca Caudill, illustrated by Dorothy B. Morse; Viking, 1949.

1950 **PICTURE BOOK** *Sunshine: A Story about the City of New York* written and illustrated by Ludwig Bemelmans; Simon & Schuster, 1950.

1950 **PICTURE BOOK HONOR** *Charley the Horse* written and illustrated by Tony Palazzo; Viking, 1950.

The Egg Tree written and illustrated by Katherine Milhous; Scribner, 1950.

Pawnee by Thelma Harrington Bell, illustrated by Corydon Bell; Viking, 1950.

Pictures of France by her Children selected by Marion B. Cothren, illustrated with photographs of paintings; Oxford, 1950.

1950 **AGES 8-12** *Windfall Fiddle* by Carl L. Carmer, illustrated by Arthur Conrad; Knopf, 1950.

1950 **AGES 8-12 HONOR** *Herbert* by Hazel H. Wilson, illustrated by John N. Barron; Knopf, 1950.

Homer the Tortoise by Margaret J. Baker, illustrated by Leo Bates; Whittlesey House, 1949, 1950.

The Radio Imp by Archie Binns, illustrated by Rafaello Busoni; Winston, 1950.

The Tune Is in the Tree by Maud Hart Lovelace, illustrated by Eloise Wilkin; Crowell, 1950.

1950 **OLDER** *Amos Fortune, Free Man* by Elizabeth Yates, illustrated by Nora S. Unwin; Aladdin, 1950.

1950 **OLDER HONOR** *Debbie of the Green Gate* by Helen Fern Daringer, illustrated by Edward Goodwin; Harcourt, 1950.

Farm Boy written and illustrated by Douglas Gorsline; Viking, 1950.

Quest in the Desert by Roy Chapman Andrews, illustrated by Kurt Wiese; Viking, 1950.

The Story of Irving Berlin by David Ewen, illustrated by Jane Castle; Holt, 1950.

1951 **PICTURE BOOK** *Jeanne-Marie Counts Her Sheep* written and illustrated by Francoise; Scribner, 1951.

1951 **PICTURE BOOK HONOR** *The Big Book of Real Building and Wrecking Machines* written and illustrated by George J. Zaffo; Grosset, 1951.

I Can Fly by Ruth Krauss, illustrated by Mary Blair; Simon & Schuster, 1950.

Mr. T.W. Anthony Woo: The Story of a Dog, a Cat, and a Mouse written and illustrated by Marie Hall Ets; Viking, 1951.

The Mousewife by Rumer Godden, illustrated by William Pene du Bois; Viking, 1951.

1951 **AGES 8-12** *Ginger Pye* written and illustrated by Eleanor Estes; Harcourt, 1951.

1951 **AGES 8-12 HONOR** *Let Them Live* written and illustrated by Dorothy P. Lathrop; Macmillan, 1951.

Lonesome Longhorn written and illustrated by John Latham; Westminster, 1951.

Summerfield Farm by Mary Martin Black, illustrated by Wesley Dennis; Viking, 1951.

Wild Hunter by Kenneth Charles Randall, illustrated by Manning de V. Lee; Watts, 1951.

1951 **OLDER** *Americans before Columbus* by Elizabeth C. Baity, illustrated by C.B. Falls; Viking, 1951.

1951 **OLDER HONOR** *Crown Fire* by Eloise Jarvis McGraw, not illustrated; Coward, 1951.

Francie by Emily Hahn, not illustrated; Watts, 1951.

North Woods Whammy by Clyde Brion Davis, not illustrated; Lippincott, 1951.

Ride Out the Storm by Margaret E. Bell, not illustrated; Morrow, 1951.

1952 **PICTURE BOOK** *Looking-for-Something* by Ann Nolan Clark, illustrated by Leo Politi; Viking, 1952.

1952 **PICTURE BOOK HONOR** *Indian, Indian* by Charlotte Zolotow, illustrated by Leonard Weisgard; Simon, 1952.

One Morning in Maine written and illustrated by Robert McCloskey; Viking, 1952.

The Stable that Stayed by Josephine Balfour Payne, illustrated by Joan Balfour Payne; Pellegrini & Cudahy, 1952.

Too Many Pets by Mary M. Aldrich, illustrated by Barbara Cooney; Macmillan, 1952.

1952 **AGES 8-12** *The Talking Cat* by Natalie Savage Carlson, illustrated by Roger Duvoisin; Harper & Row, 1952.

1952 **AGES 8-12 HONOR** *Busby & Co.* by Herbert Coggins, illustrated by Roger Duvoisin; Whittlesey House, 1952.

Jareb by Miriam Powell, illustrated by Marc Simont; Crowell, 1952.

Secret of the Andes by Ann Nolan Clark, illustrated by Jean Charlot; Viking, 1952.

Zuska of the Burning Hills by Alvena Seckar, illustrated by Kathleen Voute; Oxford, 1952.

1952 OLDER *Big Mutt* by John Reese, illustrated by Rod Ruth; Westminster, 1952.

1952 OLDER HONOR *The Haunted Reef* by Frank Crisp, illustrated by Richard M. Powers; Coward, 1952.

Jeb Ellis of Candlemas Bay by Ruth Moore, illustrated by William N. Wilson; Morrow, 1952.

String Lug the Fox by David Stephen, illustrated by Nina Scott Langley; Little, 1952.

Trail of the Little Paiute by Mabel O'Moran, illustrated by Claire Davison; Lippincott, 1952.

1953 AGES 4-8 *Pet of the Met* by Don Freeman and Lydia Freeman, illustrated by Don Freeman; Viking, 1953.

1953 AGES 4-8 HONOR *A Bear Named Grumms* by Bessie F. White, illustrated by Sari; Houghton, 1953.

A Hero by Mistake by Anita Brenner, illustrated by Jean Charlot; Scott, 1953.

The Journey of Josiah Talltatters by Josephine Balfour Payne, illustrated by Joan Balfour Payne; Ariel, 1953.

When the Moon Is New written and illustrated by Laura Bannon; Whitman, 1953.

1953 AGES 8-12 *Captain Ramsey's Daughter* by Elizabeth Fraser Torjesen, illustrated by Adrienne Adams; Lothrop, 1953.

1953 AGES 8-12 HONOR *All Alone* by Claire Huchet Bishop, illustrated by Feodor Rojankovsky; Viking, 1953.

The First Book of Space Travel written and illustrated by Jeanne Bendick; Watts, 1953.

Martin Luther by May McNeer and Lynd Ward, illustrated by Lynd Ward; Abingdon-Cokesbury, 1953.

The School Train by Helen Acker, illustrated by Janet Smalley; Abelard, 1953.

1953 OLDER *The Ark* by Margot Benary-Isbert, translated by Clara Winston and Richard Winston, not illustrated; Harcourt, 1953.

1953 OLDER HONOR *Girl Trouble* by James L. Summers, not illustrated; Westminster, 1953.

Ready or Not by Mary Stolz, not illustrated; Harper & Row, 1953.

The Story of People by May Edel, illustrated by Herbert Danska; Little Brown, 1953.

William Crawford Gorgas: Tropic Fever Fighter by Samuel Epstein and Beryl Williams Epstein, illustrated by Robert Burns; Messner, 1953.

1954 AGES 4-8 *Alphonse, That Bearded One* by Natalie Savage Carlson, illustrated by Nicolas Mordvinoff; Harcourt, 1954.

1954 AGES 4-8 HONOR *Away Went Wolfgang!* written and illustrated by Virginia Kahl; Scribner, 1954.

In Came Horace by Janet Beattie, illustrated by Anne Marie Jauss; Lippincott, 1954.

The Piebald Princess written and illustrated by Joan Balfour Payne; Ariel, 1954.

The Tin Fiddle by Edward Tripp, illustrated by Maurice Sendak; Oxford, 1954.

1954 MIDDLE *Winter Danger* by William O. Steele, illustrated by Paul Galdone; Harcourt, 1954.

1954 MIDDLE HONOR *The Courage of Sarah Noble* by Alice Dalgliesh, illustrated by Leonard Weisgard; Scribner, 1954.

Half Magic by Edward Eager, illustrated by N.M. Bodecker; Harcourt, 1954.

My Brother Bird by Evelyn Ames, illustrated by William Pene du Bois; Dodd, 1954.

Tales of Christophilos by Joice M. Nankivell, illustrated by Panos Ghikas; Houghton, 1954.

1954 OLDER *Engineer's Dreams* by Willy Ley, illustrated by Isami Kashiwagi; Viking, 1954.

1954 OLDER HONOR *The Caves of the Great Hunters* by Hans Baumann, illustrated with reproductions of cave paintings; Pantheon, 1954.

The Drawbridge Gate written and illustrated by Cynthia Harnett; Putnam, 1953.

Egyptian Adventures by Olivia E. Coolidge, illustrated by Joseph Low; Houghton, 1954.

The House of the Fifers by Rebecca Caudill, illustrated by Genia; Longmans, 1954.

1955 AGES 4-8 *Frog Went A-courtin'* by John Langstaff, illustrated by Feodor Rojankovsky; Harcourt, 1955.

1955 AGES 4-8 HONOR *The Duchess Bakes a Cake* written and illustrated by Virginia Kahl; Scribner, 1955.

A Little House of Your Own by Beatrice Schenk deRegniers, illustrated by Irene Haas; Harcourt, 1955.

Little Red Nose by Miriam Schlein, illustrated by Roger Duvoisin; Abelard, 1955.

World Full of Horses written and illustrated by Dahlov Ipcar; Doubleday, 1955.

1955 MIDDLE *Crystal Mountain* by Belle Dorman Rugh, illustrated by Ernest Shepard; Houghton, 1955.

1955 MIDDLE HONOR *Amikuk* by Rutherford G. Montgomery, illustrated by Marie Nonnast; World, 1955.

Junket by Anne H. White, illustrated by Robert McCloskey; Viking, 1955.

The Magic Listening Cap: More Folk Tales from Japan written and illustrated by Yoshiko Uchida; Harcourt, 1955.

Wings Against the Wind by Natalie Savage Carlson, illustrated by Mircea Vasiliu; Harper & Row, 1955.

1955 OLDER *The Buffalo Trace* by Virginia S. Eifert, illustrated by Manning De V. Lee; Dodd Mead, 1955.

1955 OLDER HONOR *The Land and People of South Africa* by Alan Paton, illustrated with photographs; Lippincott, 1955.

Men, Microscopes, and Living Things by Katherine B. Shippen, illustrated by Anthony Ravielli; Viking, 1955.

The Radium Woman: A Youth Edition of the Life of Madame Curie by Eleanor Doorly, illustrated by Robert Gibbings; Heinemann, 1939; Roy, 1955.

Santiago by Ann Nolan Clark, illustrated by Lynd Ward; Viking, 1955.

1956 AGES 4-8 *Lion* written and illustrated by William Pene du Bois; Viking, 1956.

1956 AGES 4-8 HONOR *Davy Crockett's Earthquake* by William O. Steele, illustrated by Nicolas Mordvinoff; Harcourt, 1956.

Georgie to the Rescue written and illustrated by Robert Bright; Doubleday, 1956.

The House of Four Seasons written and illustrated by Roger Duvoisin; Lothrop, 1956.

Kenny's Window written and illustrated by Maurice Sendak; Harper, 1956.

1956 MIDDLE *Beaver Water* by Rutherford G. Montgomery, illustrated by Robert Doremus; World, 1956.

1956 MIDDLE HONOR *Janitor's Girl* by Frieda Friedman, illustrated by Mary Stevens; Morrow, 1956.

The Pilgrim Goose by Keith Robertson, illustrated by Erick Berry; Viking, 1956.

Ten Tall Texans by Lee McGiffin, illustrated by John Maxwell; Lothrop, 1956.

Tony of the Ghost Towns by Marie H. Bloch, illustrated by Dorothy Marino; Coward, 1956.

1956 OLDER *Cold Hazard* by Richard Armstrong, illustrated by C. Walter Hodges; Houghton, 1956.

1956 OLDER HONOR *Abe Lincoln: Log Cabin to White House* by Sterling North, illustrated by Lee Ames; Random House, 1956.

The Day and the Way We Met by Mary Stolz, not illustrated; Harper, 1956.

Jacobin's Daughter by Joanne S. Williamson, illustrated by Charles Clement; Knopf, 1956.

The Rainbow Book of Art by Thomas Craven, illustrated with photographs; World, 1956.

1957 AGES 4-8 *Madeleine and the Bad Hat* written and illustrated by Ludwig Bemelmans; Viking, 1957.

1957 AGES 4-8 HONOR *Cheerful* written and illustrated by Palmer Brown; Harper & Row, 1957.

Kevin written and illustrated by Mary Chalmers; Harper, 1957.

The March Wind by Inez Rice, illustrated by Vladimir Bobri; Lothrop, 1957.

The Mellops Go Flying written and illustrated by Tomi Ungerer; Harper, 1957.

1957 MIDDLE *Gone-away Lake* by Elizabeth Enright, illustrated by Beth Krush and Joe Krush; Harcourt, 1957.

1957 MIDDLE HONOR *Fairwater* by Alastair Reid, illustrated by Walter Lorraine; Houghton, 1957.

Flaming Arrows by William O. Steele, illustrated by Paul Galdone; Harcourt, 1957.

Hortense, the Cow for a Queen by Natalie Savage Carlson, illustrated by Nicolas; Harcourt, 1957.

The Walt Disney Story of Our Friend the Atom by Heinz Haber, illustrated by Walt Disney Studio; Simon & Schuster, 1957.

1957 OLDER *Because of Madeleine* by Mary Stolz, not illustrated; Harper, 1957.

1957 OLDER HONOR *Gunilla, an Arctic Adventure* by Albert Viksten, translated by Gustaf Lannestock, illustrated by Rus Anderson; Nelson, 1957.

The Horsecatcher by Mari Sandoz, not illustrated; Westminster, 1957.

The Shield Ring by Rosemary Sutcliff, illustrated by C. Walter Hodges; Oxford, 1956, 1957.

Tom Paine: Freedom's Apostle by Leo Gurko, illustrated by Fritz Kredel; Crowell, 1957.

1958 AGES 4-8 *Crictor* written and illustrated by Tomi Ungerer; Harper, 1958.

1958 AGES 4-8 HONOR *Cats, Cats, Cats, Cats, Cats* by Beatrice Schenk de Regniers, illustrated by Bill Sokol; Pantheon, 1958.

Umbrella written and illustrated by Taro Yashima; Viking, 1958.

The Whiskers of Ho Ho by William Littlefield, illustrated by Vladimir Bobri; Lothrop, 1958.

Whispers and other Poems by Myra Cohn Livingston, illustrated by Jacqueline Chwast; Harcourt, 1958.

1958 MIDDLE *Chucaro: Wild Pony of the Pampa* by Francis Kalnay, illustrated by Julian DeMiskey; Harcourt, 1958.

1958 MIDDLE HONOR *Avalanche!* by A. Rutgers Van der Loeff, illustrated by Gustav Schrotter; Morrow, 1958.

Me and Frumpet: An Adventure with Size and Science written and illustrated by Evans G. Valens, illustrated with photographs; Dutton, 1958.

The Minnow Leads to Treasure by A. Philippa Pearce, illustrated by Edward Ardizzone; World, 1958.

The Ship that Flew by Hilda Lewis, illustrated by Nora Lavrin; Criterion, 1958.

1958 OLDER *Sons of the Steppe* by Hans Baumann, illustrated by Heiner Rothfuchs; Walck, 1958.

1958 OLDER HONOR *Chingo Smith of the Erie Canal* by Samuel Hopkins Adams, illustrated by Leonard Vosburgh; Random House, 1958.

Shadows into Mist by Ellen Turngren, illustrated by Vera Bock; Longmans, 1958.

The Sherwood Ring by Elizabeth Marie Pope, illustrated by Evaline Ness; Houghton, 1958.

The Silver Branch by Rosemary Sutcliff, illustrated by Charles Keeping; Oxford, 1957; Walck, 1958.

1959 AGES 4-8 *Sia Lives on Kilimanjaro* by Astrid Lindgren, photographs by Anna Riwkin-Brick; Macmillan, 1959.

1959 AGES 4-8 HONOR *The Blackbird in the Lilac* by James Reeves, illustrated by Edward Ardizzone; Dutton, 1959.

How St. Francis Tamed the Wolf by Elizabeth Rose, illustrated by Gerald Rose; Harcourt, 1959.

The Pointed Brush by Patricia Miles Martin, illustrated by Roger Duvoisin; Lothrop, 1959.

The Raggle-Taggle Fellow by Miriam Schlein, illustrated by Harvey Weiss; Abelard-Schuman, 1959.

1959 MIDDLE *The Long-nosed Princess* by Priscilla Hallowell, illustrated by Rita Fava; Viking, 1959.

1959 MIDDLE HONOR *The Borrowers Afloat* by Mary Norton, illustrated by Joe Krush and Beth Krush; Harcourt, 1959.

The Colt from the Dark Forest by Anna Belle Loken, illustrated by Donald Bolognese; Lothrop, 1959.

Magic or Not? by Edward Eager, illustrated by N.M. Bodecker; Harcourt, 1959.

Treasure of the High Country by Jonreed Lauritzen, illustrated by Eric von Schmidt; Little, 1959.

1959 OLDER *An Edge of the Forest* by Agnes Smith, illustrated by Roberta Moynihan; Viking, 1959.

1959 OLDER HONOR *The Black Symbol* by Annabell Johnson and Edgar Johnson, illustrated by Brian Saunders; Harper, 1959.

Land of Foam by Ivan Yefremov, not illustrated; Houghton, 1959.

The Lion's Whiskers: Tales of High Africa by Brent Ashabranner and Russell Davis, illustrated by James G. Teason; Little Brown, 1959.

The Silver Sword by Ian Serraillier, illustrated by C. Walter Hodges; Cape, 1956; Criterion, 1959.

1960 AGES 4-8 *The Secret Hiding Place* written and illustrated by Rainey Bennett; World, 1960.

1960 AGES 4-8 HONOR *Candy Floss* by Rumer Godden, illustrated by Adrienne Adams; Viking, 1960.

Emile written and illustrated by Tomi Ungerer; Harper, 1960.

A Jungle in the Wheat Field written and illustrated by Egon Mathiesen; McDowell, Obolensky, 1960.

Kap the Kappa by Betty Jean Lifton, illustrated by Eiichi Mitsui; Morrow, 1960.

1960 MIDDLE *The Trouble with Jenny's Ear* by Oliver Butterworth, illustrated by Julian De Miskey; Atlantic-Little, 1960.

1960 MIDDLE HONOR *Ondine: The Story of a Bird Who Was Different* by Maurice Machado Osborne, Jr., illustrated by Evaline Ness; Houghton, 1960.

The Secret of Fiery Gorge by Wilson Gage, illustrated by Mary Stevens; World, 1960.

The Secret Pencil by Patricia Ward, illustrated by Nicole Hornby; Random, 1960.

The Talking Dog and the Barking Man by Elizabeth Seeman, illustrated by James Flora; Watts, 1960.

1960 OLDER *The Walls of Windy Troy: A Biography of Heinrich Schliemann* by Marjorie Braymer, illustrated with photographs; Harcourt, 1960.

1960 OLDER HONOR *America Grows Up: A History for Peter* by Gerald W. Johnson, illustrated by Leonard Everett Fisher; Morrow, 1960.

Old Ramon by Jack Schaefer, illustrated by Harold West; Houghton, 1960.

The Singing Cave by Eilis Dillon, illustrated by Stan Campbell; Funk & Wagnalls, 1960.

Torrie by Edgar Johnson and Annabell Johnson, illustrated by Pearl Falconer; Harper, 1960.

1961 AGES 4-8 *Gwendolyn the Miracle Hen* by Nancy Sherman, illustrated by Edward Sorel; Golden, 1961.

1961 AGES 4-8 HONOR *Barto Takes the Subway* by Barbara Brenner, photographs by Sy Katzoff; Knopf, 1961.

I Met a Man by John Ciardi, illustrated by Robert Osborn; Houghton, 1961.

Let's Be Enemies by Janice May Udry, illustrated by Maurice Sendak; Harper, 1961.

The Remarkable Harry by Evan Hunter, illustrated by Richard Hunter, Ted Hunter, and Mark Hunter; Abelard-Schuman, 1961.

1961 MIDDLE *Norwegian Folk Tales* by Jorgen Moe and Peter Christen Asbjornsen, illustrated by Erik Werenskiold and Theodor Kittelsen; Viking, 1961.

1961 MIDDLE HONOR *Children of the Red King* by Madeleine Polland, illustrated by Annette Macarthur-Onslow; Holt, 1961.

Miss Happiness and Miss Flower by Rumer Godden, illustrated by Jean Primrose; Viking, 1961.

Pencil, Pen and Brush written and illustrated by Harvey Weiss; Scott, 1961.

The Robber Ghost by Karin Anckarsvard, translated by Annabelle MacMillan, illustrated by Paul Galdone; Harcourt, 1961.

1961 OLDER *Adventures in the Desert* by Herbert Kaufmann, translated by Stella Humphries, illustrated by Eugene Karlin; Obolensky, 1961.

1961 OLDER HONOR *A Poppy in the Corn* by Stella Weaver, not illustrated; Pantheon, 1960.

Secrets of Minos: Sir Arthur Evans' Discoveries at Crete by Alan Honour, illustrated with photographs and line drawings; Whittlesey House, 1961.

Stephen Crane: The Story of an American Writer by Ruth Franchere, not illustrated; Crowell, 1961.

Valentine by Evan Carroll Commager, not illustrated; Harper, 1961.

1962 PICTURE BOOK *Adam's Book of Odd Creatures* written and illustrated by Joseph Low; Atheneum, 1962.

1962 PICTURE BOOK HONOR *The House on East 88th Street* written and illustrated by Bernard Waber; Houghton, 1962.

Jeremiah Octopus by Margaret Stone Zilboorg, illustrated by Hilary Knight; Golden, 1962.

The New Nutcracker Suite and other Innocent Verses by Ogden Nash, illustrated by Ivan Chermayeff; Little Brown, 1962.

Snail, Where Are You? written and illustrated by Tomi Ungerer; Harper, 1962.

1962 **MIDDLE** *The Orphans of Simitra* by Paul-Jacques Bonzon, translated by Thelma Niklaus, illustrated by Simon Jeruchim; Criterion, 1962.

1962 **MIDDLE HONOR** *Beorn the Proud* by Madeleine Polland, illustrated by William Stobbs; Holt, 1962.

Bonifacius the Green by Karin Anckarsvard, illustrated by Ingrid Rosell; Abelard-Schuman, 1961.

Mr. Mysterious & Co. by Sid Fleischman, illustrated by Eric Von Schmidt; Atlantic-Little, 1962.

The Presidency by Gerald W. Johnson, illustrated by Leonard Everett Fisher; Morrow, 1962.

1962 **OLDER** *Dawn Wind* by Rosemary Sutcliff, illustrated by Charles Keeping; Walck, 1962.

1962 **OLDER HONOR** *Bristle Face* by Zachary Ball, not illustrated; Holiday House, 1962.

I Marched with Hannibal by Hans Baumann, translated by K. Potts, illustrated by Ulrik Schramm; Walck, 1962.

Kaiulani: Crown Princess of Hawaii by Jean Francis Webb and Nancy Webb, not illustrated; Viking, 1962.

Lost Cities and Vanished Civilizations by Robert Silverberg, illustrated with photographs; Chilton, 1962.

1963 **PICTURE BOOK** *The Seven Ravens* by Jacob Grimm and Wilhelm Grimm, illustrated by Felix Hoffmann; Harcourt, 1963.

1963 **PICTURE BOOK HONOR** *The Bear on the Motorcycle* written and illustrated by Reiner Zimnik; Atheneum, 1963.

Gilberto and the Wind written and illustrated by Marie Hall Ets; Viking, 1963.

Josefina February written and illustrated by Evaline Ness; Scribner, 1963.

Karen's Opposites written and illustrated by Martin Provensen and Alice Provensen; Golden, 1963.

1963 **MIDDLE** *A Dog So Small* by A. Philippa Pearce, illustrated by Antony Maitland; Lippincott, 1963.

1963 **MIDDLE HONOR** *A Dog Called Scholar* by Anne H. White, illustrated by Lilian Obligado; Viking, 1963.

Joy Is Not Herself by Josephine Lee, illustrated by Pat Marriott; Harcourt, 1963.

Naughty Children by Christianna Brand, illustrated by Edward Ardizzone; Dutton, 1963.

Tatsinda by Elizabeth Enright, illustrated by Irene Haas; Harcourt, 1963.

1963 **OLDER** *The Cossacks* by Barbara Bartos-Hoeppner, illustrated by Victor G. Ambrus; Walck, 1963.

1963 **OLDER HONOR** *Hakon of Rogen's Saga* by Erik Haugaard, illustrated by Diane Dillon and Leo Dillon; Houghton, 1963.

In Love and War by Barbara Ker Wilson, not illustrated; World, 1962.

The Plainsmen by Jack Schaefer, illustrated by Lorence F. Bjorklund; Houghton, 1963.

Portrait of Lisette by Elisabeth Kyle, illustrated by Charles Mozley; Nelson, 1963.

1964 **PICTURE BOOK** *The Coconut Thieves* by Catharine Fournier, illustrated by Janina Domanska; Scribner, 1964.

1964 **PICTURE BOOK HONOR** *The Alphabet Tale* by Jan Garten, illustrated by Muriel Batherman; Random House, 1964.

Lady Bird, Quickly written and illustrated by Juliet Kepes; Atlantic-Little, 1964.

More Tongue Tanglers and a Rigmarole by Charles Francis Potter, illustrated by William Wiesner; World, 1964.

Sophie written and illustrated by Alain Trez and Denise Trez, translated by Douglas McKee; World, 1964.

1964 **MIDDLE** *The Family Conspiracy* by Joan M. Phipson, illustrated by Margaret Horder; Harcourt, 1962, 1964; Angus & Robertson, 1962.

1964 **MIDDLE HONOR** *Fifer for the Union* by Lorenzo Allen, illustrated by Brian Wildsmith; Morrow, 1964.

Out of Hand by Emma Smith, illustrated by Antony Maitland; Harcourt, 1964.

The Return of the Twelves by Pauline Clarke, illustrated by Bernarda Bryson; Coward, 1963.

Skinny by Robert Burch, illustrated by Don Sibley; Viking, 1964.

1964 **OLDER** *The Story of Design* by Marion Downer, illustrated with photographs; Lothrop, 1963.

1964 **OLDER HONOR** *The Coriander* by Eilis Dillon, illustrated by Vic Donahue; Funk & Wagnalls, 1965.

Girl with a Pen: Charlotte Bronte by Elisabeth Kyle, illustrated by Charles Mozley; Holt, 1964.

Shadow of a Bull by Maia Wojciechowska, illustrated by Alvin Smith; Atheneum, 1964.

Time of Trial by Hester Burton, illustrated by Victor G. Ambrus; Oxford, 1963; World, 1964.

1965 **PICTURE BOOK** *Salt: A Russian Tale* by Harve Zemach, illustrated by Margot Zemach; Follett, 1965.

1965 **PICTURE BOOK HONOR** *Hide and Seek Fog* by Alvin Tresselt, illustrated by Roger Duvoisin; Lothrop, 1965.

The Nightingale by Hans Christian Andersen, translated by Eva LeGallienne, illustrated by Nancy Ekholm Burkert; Harper, 1965.

Spaghetti for Breakfast and other Useful Phrases in Italian and English by Sesyle Joslin, illustrated by Katharina Barry; Harcourt, 1965.

A Turtle, and a Loon, and other Fables written and illustrated by Diane Redfield Massie; Atheneum, 1965.

1965 **MIDDLE** *Dorp Dead* by Julia Cunningham, illustrated by James Spanfeller; Pantheon, 1965.

1965 **MIDDLE HONOR** *Black Magic, White Magic* by Gary Jennings, illustrated by Barbara Begg; Dial, 1965.

I Saw You from Afar: A Visit to the Bushmen of the Kalahari Desert by Richard Marlin Perkins and Carol Morse Perkins, illustrated with photographs; Atheneum, 1965.

Lean Out of the Window: An Anthology of Modern Poetry compiled by Sara Hannum and Gwendolyn E. Reed, illustrated by Ragna Tischler; Atheneum, 1965.

String, Straight-edge and Shadow: The Story of Geometry by Julia E. Diggins, illustrated by Corydon Bell; Viking, 1965.

1965 OLDER *Jazz Country* by Nat Hentoff, not illustrated; Harper, 1965.

1965 OLDER HONOR *Colonial Craftsmen and the Beginnings of American Industry* written and illustrated by Edwin Tunis; World, 1965.

Emily Dickinson: Her Letter to the World by Polly Longworth, not illustrated; Crowell, 1965.

The Maplin Bird by K.M. Peyton, illustrated by Victor G. Ambrus; Oxford, 1964; World, 1965.

Ring the Judas Bell by James Forman, not illustrated; Farrar, 1965.

1966 PICTURE BOOK *Nothing Ever Happens on My Block* written and illustrated by Ellen Raskin; Atheneum, 1966.

1966 PICTURE BOOK HONOR *Baba Yaga* by Ernest Small, illustrated by Blair Lent; Houghton, 1966.

The Day the Sun Danced by Edith Thacher Hurd, illustrated by Clement Hurd; Harper, 1966.

The Gats! written and illustrated by M.B. Goffstein; Pantheon, 1966.

The Good Bird written and illustrated by Peter Wezel; Harper, 1966.

1966 MIDDLE *Boy Alone* by Reginald Ottley, illustrated by Clyde Pearson; Harcourt, 1966.

1966 MIDDLE HONOR *Friday's Tunnel* written and illustrated by John Verney; Collins, 1959; Holt, 1966.

My Name Is Pablo by Aimee Sommerfelt, illustrated by Hans Norman Dahl; Criterion, 1965.

Smudge of the Fells by Joyce Gard, not illustrated; Holt, 1966.

Woody and Me by Mary Neville, illustrated by Ronni Solbert; Pantheon, 1966.

1966 OLDER *This is Your Century* by Geoffrey Trease, not illustrated; Harcourt, 1965.

1966 OLDER HONOR *The Hunt for the Whooping Cranes* by J.J. McCoy, illustrated by Rey Abruzzi; Lothrop, 1966.

The King of Men by Olivia Coolidge, illustrated by Ellen Raskin; Houghton, 1966.

Pappa Pellerin's Daughter by Maria Gripe, translated by Kersti French, illustrated by Harald Gripe; Day, 1966.

Tormented Angel: A Life of John Henry Newman by Emmeline Garnett, not illustrated; Farrar, 1966.

1967 PICTURE BOOK *Moon Man* written and illustrated by Tomi Ungerer; Harper, 1967.

1967 PICTURE BOOK HONOR *The Dragon* by Archibald Marshall, illustrated by Edward Ardizzone; Dutton, 1967.

Palmiero and the Ogre written and illustrated by Janina Domanska; Macmillan, 1967.

Too Much Nose by Harve Zemach, illustrated by Margot Zemach; Holt, 1967.

The Wedding Procession of the Rag Doll and the Broom Handle and Who Was in It by Carl Sandburg, illustrated by Harriet Pincus; Harcourt, 1967.

1967 MIDDLE *The Egypt Game* by Zilpha Keatley Snyder, illustrated by Alton Raible; Atheneum, 1967.

1967 MIDDLE HONOR *Don't Take Teddy* by Babbis Friis-Baastad, translated by Lise Somme McKinnon, not illustrated; Scribner, 1967.

Jennifer, Hecate, Macbeth, William McKinley and Me, Elizabeth written and illustrated by E.L. Konigsburg; Atheneum, 1967.

The Sea Egg by Lucy M. Boston, illustrated by Peter Boston; Harcourt, 1967.

The Spider of Brooklyn Heights by Nancy Veglahn, illustrated with photographs by Andreas Feininger; Scribner, 1967.

1967 OLDER *The Little Fishes* by Erik Christian Haugaard, illustrated by Milton Johnson; Houghton, 1967.

1967 OLDER HONOR *The Auk, the Dodo, and the Oryx: Vanished and Vanishing Creatures* by Robert Silverberg, illustrated by Jacques Hnizdovsky; Crowell, 1967.

Fierce and Gentle Warriors by Mikhail Sholokhov, translated by Miriam Morton, illustrated by Milton Glaser; Doubleday, 1967.

The Outsiders by S.E. Hinton, not illustrated; Viking, 1967; Dell, 1968.

Red Lion and Gold Dragon: A Novel of the Norman Conquest by Rosemary Sprague, not illustrated; Chilton, 1967.

1968 PICTURE BOOK *Why the Sun and the Moon Live in the Sky: An African Folktale* by Elphinstone Dayrell, illustrated by Blair Lent; Houghton, 1968.

1968 PICTURE BOOK HONOR *The Biggest House in the World* written and illustrated by Leo Lionni; Pantheon, 1968.

1968 PICTURE BOOK HONOR *The Brave Little Goat of Monsieur Seguin* by Alphonse Daudet, illustrated by Chiyoko Nakatani; World, 1968.

The Prancing Pony: Nursery Rhymes from Japan by Charlotte B. De Forest, illustrated by Keiko Hida; Walker, 1968.

A Sunflower as Big as the Sun written and illustrated by Shan Ellentuck; Doubleday, 1968.

1968 MIDDLE *A Racecourse for Andy* by Patricia Wrightson, illustrated by Margaret Horder; Harcourt, 1968.

1968 MIDDLE HONOR *The Battle of St. George Without* by Janet McNeill, illustrated by Mary Russon; Little, 1968.

The Flight of the Doves by Walter Macken, not illustrated; Macmillan, 1968.

Out of the Earth I Sing: Poetry and Songs of Primitive Peoples of the World by Richard Lewis, illustrated with photographs; Norton, 1968.

Traveler from a Small Kingdom by Emily Cheney Neville, illustrated by George Mocniak; Harper, 1968.

1968 **OLDER** *Young Mark* by E.M. Almedingen, illustrated by Victor Ambrus; Farrar, 1968.

1968 **OLDER HONOR** *The Endless Steppe: Growing Up in Siberia* by Esther Hautzig, not illustrated; Crowell, 1968.

Mount Joy by Daisy Newman, illustrated with photographs; Atheneum, 1968.

The Pit by Reginald Maddock, illustrated by Douglas Hall; Little, 1968.

The Young Unicorn by Madeleine L'Engle, not illustrated; Farrar, 1968.

1969 **PICTURE BOOK** *Thy Friend, Obadiah* written and illustrated by Brinton Turkle; Viking, 1969.

1969 **PICTURE BOOK HONOR** *Dominique and the Dragon* by Jurgen Tamchina, translated by Elizabeth D. Crawford, illustrated by Heidrun Petrides; Harcourt, 1968.

How, Hippo! written and illustrated by Marcia Brown; Scribner, 1969.

The Magic Balloon written and illustrated by Iela Mari; Phillips, 1969.

Sylvester and the Magic Pebble written and illustrated by William Steig; Windmill/Simon & Schuster, 1969.

1969 **MIDDLE** *Whose Town?* by Lorenz Graham, not illustrated; Crowell, 1969.

1969 **MIDDLE HONOR** *A Girl Called Al* by Constance Greene, illustrated by Byron Barton; Viking, 1969.

The Liverpool Cats by Sylvia Sherry, illustrated by Ilse Koehn; Lippincott, 1969.

My Village, My World by David E. Sandford, illustrated by Gustave Nebel; Crown, 1969.

A Walk Out of the World by Ruth Nichols, illustrated by Trina Schart Hyman; Harcourt, 1969.

1969 **OLDER** *My Enemy, My Brother* by James Forman, not illustrated; Meredith, 1969.

1969 **OLDER HONOR** *Dictionary of Chivalry* by Grant Uden, illustrated by Pauline Baynes; Kestrel, 1968; Crowell, 1969.

I'll Get There. It Better Be Worth the Trip by John Donovan, not illustrated; Harper, 1969.

Lorenzo De'Medici and the Renaissance by John Walker and Charles L. Mee, Jr., illustrated with photographs; American Heritage, 1969.

The Skating Rink by Mildred Lee, not illustrated; Seabury, 1969.

1970 **PICTURE BOOK** *Tell Me a Mitzi* by Lore Segal, illustrated by Harriet Pincus; Farrar, 1970.

1970 **PICTURE BOOK HONOR** *Catfish* by Edith Thacher Hurd, illustrated by Clement Hurd; Viking, 1970.

The Elephant and the Bad Baby by Elfrida Vipont, illustrated by Raymond Briggs; Coward, 1970.

The Hat written and illustrated by Tomi Ungerer; Parents, 1970.

Return to Hiroshima by Betty Jean Lifton, illustrated by Eikoh Hosoe; Atheneum, 1970.

Topsy Turvies: Pictures to Stretch the Imagination written and illustrated by Mitsumasa Anno; Walker/Wetherhill, 1970.

1970 **MIDDLE** *Sundiata: The Epic of the Lion King* by Roland Bertol, illustrated by Gregorio Prestopino; Crowell, 1970.

1970 **MIDDLE HONOR** *The Daybreakers* by Jane Louise Curry, illustrated by Charles Robinson; Harcourt, 1970.

The Little Man and the Big Thief by Erich Kastner, illustrated by Stanley Mack; Knopf, 1970.

A Snake Lover's Diary by Barbara Brenner, illustrated with photographs; Young Scott, 1970.

The Trumpet of the Swan by E.B. White, illustrated by Edward Frascino; Harper, 1970.

1970 **OLDER** *Fireweed* by Jill Paton Walsh, not illustrated; Farrar, 1969, 1970.

1970 **OLDER HONOR** *Dwellers of the Tundra: Life in an Alaskan Eskimo Village* by Aylette Jenness, illustrated by Jonathan Jenness; Crowell-Collier, 1970.

A Herd of Deer by Eilis Dillon, illustrated by Richard Kennedy; Funk & Wagnalls, 1969.

The Lothian Run by Mollie Hunter, not illustrated; Funk and Wagnalls, 1970.

The Moon in the Cloud by Rosemary Harris, not illustrated; Faber, 1968; Macmillan, 1970.

1971 **PICTURE BOOK** *All Upon a Stone* by Jean Craighead George, illustrated by Don Bolognese; Crowell, 1971.

1971 **PICTURE BOOK HONOR** *Changes, Changes* written and illustrated by Pat Hutchins; Macmillan, 1971.

Do You Want To Be My Friend? written and illustrated by Eric Carle; Crowell, 1971.

Sabrina written and illustrated by Martha Alexander; Dial, 1971.

Under the Green Willow by Elizabeth Coatsworth, illustrated by Janina Domanska; Macmillan, 1971.

1971 **MIDDLE** No Award

1971 **MIDDLE HONOR** *Beaver Valley* by Walter D. Edmonds, illustrated by Leslie Morrill; Little Brown, 1971.

Goody Hall written and illustrated by Natalie Babbitt; Farrar, 1971.

Jingo Django by Sid Fleischman, illustrated by Eric von Schmidt; Atlantic-Little, 1971.

The Three Toymakers by Ursula Moray Williams, illustrated by Shirley Hughes; Nelson, 1971.

1971 **OLDER** *Reggie and Nilma: A New York City Story* by Louise Tanner, not illustrated; Farrar, 1971.

1971 **OLDER HONOR** *Out There* by Adrien Stoutenburg, illustrated by Donald A. Mackay; Viking, 1971.

Pendragon: Arthur and His Britain by Joseph P. Clancy, illustrated with maps and diagrams; Praeger, 1971.

A Room Made of Windows by Eleanor Cameron, illustrated by Trina Schart Hyman; Atlantic-Little, 1971.

That Was Then, This Is Now by S.E. Hinton, illustrated by Hal Siegel; Viking, 1971.

1972 **PICTURE BOOK** *Little John* by Theodor Storm, illustrated by Anita Lobel; Farrar, 1972.

1972 **PICTURE BOOK HONOR** *Frog and Toad Together* written and illustrated by Arnold Lobel; Harper, 1972.

Soldier and Tsar in the Forest: A Russian Tale by Richard Lourie, illustrated by Uri Shulevitz; Farrar, 1972.

The Squirrel-wife by A. Philippa Pearce, illustrated by Derek Collard; Crowell, 1972.

We Are Having a Baby written and illustrated by Viki Holland; Scribner, 1972.

1972 **AGES 8-12** *Cockleburr Quarters* by Charlotte Baker, illustrated by Robert Owens; Prentice Hall, 1972.

1972 **AGES 8-12 HONOR** *Anna (Anna Khlebnikova de Poltaratzky, 1770- 1840)* by E.M. Almedingen, not illustrated; Farrar, 1972.

The Impossible People: A History Natural and Unnatural of Beings Terrible and Wonderful by Georgess McHargue, illustrated by Frank Bozzo; Holt, 1972.

When Hitler Stole Pink Rabbit written and illustrated by Judith Kerr; Coward, 1972.

The Witch of Fourth Street and other Stories by Myron Levoy, illustrated by Gabriel Lisowski; Harper, 1972.

1972 **AGES 12 TO 16** *Freaky Friday* by Mary Rodgers, not illustrated; Harper, 1972.

1972 **AGES 12 TO 16 HONOR** *The Fog Comes on Little Pig Feet* written and illustrated by Rosemary Wells; Dial, 1972.

A Long Way from Verona by Jane Gardam, not illustrated; Macmillan, 1971.

The Mountain of Truth by Dale Carlson, illustrated by Charles Robinson; Atheneum, 1972.

Oh, Lizzie: The Life of Elizabeth Cady Stanton by Doris Faber, illustrated with photographs; Lothrop, 1972.

1973 **YOUNGER** *The Magician* by I.L. Peretz, adapted and illustrated by Uri Shulevitz; Macmillan, 1973.

1973 **YOUNGER HONOR** *Duffy and the Devil* by Harve Zemach and Margot Zemach, illustrated by Margot Zemach; Farrar, 1973.

The Midnight Adventures of Kelly, Dot, and Esmeralda written and illustrated by John S. Goodall; Atheneum, 1972.

Mine's the Best written and illustrated by Crosby Bonsall; Harper, 1973.

The Woodcutter's Duck written and illustrated by Krystyna Turska; Hamilton, 1972.

1973 **MIDDLE** *Gildaen: The Heroic Adventures of a Most Unusual Rabbit* by Emilie Buchwald, illustrated by Barbara Flynn; Harcourt, 1973.

1973 **MIDDLE HONOR** *The Driftway* by Penelope Lively, not illustrated; Dutton, 1972, 1973.

Opposites written and illustrated by Richard Wilbur; Harcourt, 1973.

She, the Adventuress by Dorothy Crayder, illustrated by Velma Ilsley; Atheneum, 1973.

Time Ago Lost: More Tales of Jahdu by Virginia Hamilton, illustrated by Ray Prather; Macmillan, 1973.

1973 **OLDER** *Guests in the Promised Land: Stories* by Kristin Hunter, not illustrated; Scribner, 1973.

1973 **OLDER HONOR** *Black Images: The Art of West Africa* by Penelope Naylor, illustrated with photographs by Lisa Little; Doubleday, 1973.

A Day No Pigs Would Die by Robert Newton Peck, not illustrated; Knopf, 1973.

If I Love You, Am I Trapped Forever? by M.E. Kerr, not illustrated; Harper, 1973.

The Summer Before by Patricia Windsor, not illustrated; Harper, 1973.

The Writing on the Hearth by Cynthia Harnett, illustrated by Gareth Floyd; Viking, 1973.

STATE HISTORICAL SOCIETY OF WISCONSIN'S BOOK AWARD OF MERIT

State Historical Society of Wisconsin
816 State St.
Madison, WI 53706

Presented for the first time in 1966, this award is given for either a juvenile or adult book that contributes to the knowledge of the history of Wisconsin. Selection of the award recipients is made by the State Relations Committee of the State Historical Society Board of Curators.

When juvenile books are nominated, they are considered separately and if one is judged worthy, it is given a separate award. The awards are presented at the Annual Meeting of the Society. Listed below are those juvenile titles that have won the award.

1966 *Feather in the Wind* by Beverly Butler, not illustrated; Dodd Mead, 1965.

1967 *Span Across a River* by Donald Emerson, not illustrated; McKay, 1966.

1969 *Nine Lives of Moses on the Oregon Trail* by Marion Fuller Archer, illustrated by George Armstrong; Whitman, 1968.

1971 *Higgins of the Railroad Museum* by Ethelyn M. Parkinson, illustrated by Bill McPheeters; Abingdon, 1970.

1975 *Songs of the Chippewa* adapted by John Bierhorst, illustrated by Joe Servello; Farrar Straus Giroux, 1974.

1977 *Cutover Country: Jolie's Story* by Jolie Paylin, illustrated by Judy Appenzeller La Motte; Iowa State University Press, 1976.

1981 *My Sister's Keeper* by Beverly Butler, not illustrated; Dodd Mead, 1980.

1983 *First Farm in the Valley: Anna's Story* by Anne Pellowski, illusrtated by Wendy Watson; Philomel, 1982.

1984 *The Child of Two Mothers* by Malcolm Rosholt and Margaret Rosholt, illustrated by Lynn Larson; Rosholt House, 1983.

1986 *Railroads of Southern and Southwestern Wisconsin* by Daniel J. Lanz, illustrated; D J Lanz, 1985.

1988 *The Story of Old Abe* by Malcolm Rosholt and Margaret Rosholt, illustrated by Don Mullen; Rosholt House, 1987.

1991 *The Disappearing Stranger* by Lois Walfrid Johnson, not illustrated; Bethany House, 1990.

The Hidden Message by Lois Walfrid Johnson, not illustrated; Bethany House, 1990.

STECK-VAUGHN AWARD

discontinued

Formerly known as the Cokesbury Book Store Award, this children's award was presented annually to a Texas author or for a book on a Texas subject. First presented in 1951, this award was chosen by a three-member committee appointed by the Texas Institute of Letters.

1951 *Sonny-boy Sim* by Elizabeth Baker, illustrated by Susanne Suba; Rand McNally, 1948.

1952 *Johnny Texas* by Carol Hoff, illustrated by Bob Meyers; Wilcox & Follett, 1950.

1953 *Lonesome Longhorn* written and illustrated by John Latham; Westminster, 1951.

1954 *A Month of Christmases* by Siddie Joe Johnson, illustrated by Henrietta Jones Moon; Longmans, 1952.

1955 *Magic for Mary M.* written and illustrated by Charlotte Baker Montgomery; McKay, 1953.

1956 *Lone Star Fight* by Irmengarde Eberle, illustrated by Lee Townsend; Dodd, 1954.

1957 *The Trail Driving Rooster* by Fred Gipson, illustrated by Marc Simont; Harper, 1955.

1958 *How Medicine Man Cured Paleface Woman: An Easy Reading Story in Indian Picture Writing and Paleface Words* written and illustrated by Jessie Brewer McGaw; Scott, 1956.

1959 *Tame the Wild Stallion* by J.R. Williams, not illustrated; Prentice, 1957.

1960 *Coronado and his Captains* by Camilla Campbell, illustrated by Harve Stein; Follett, 1958.

1961 *Beef for Beauregard!* by Byrd Hooper, illustrated by Charles Geer; Putnam, 1959.

1962 *Throw Stone: The First American Boy, 25,000 Years Ago* by M. E. Stevens and Edwin B. Sayles; illustrated by Barton Wright; Reilly & Lee, 1960.

1963 *I'm Hiding* by Myra Cohn Livingston and Erik Blegvad, illustrated by Erik Blegvad; Harcourt, 1961.

Pony Soldier by Lee McGiffin, illustrated; Dutton, 1961.

1964 *Ten Cousins* by Wanda Jay Campbell, illustrated by Leonard Shortall; Dutton, 1963.

1965 *Love, Bid Me Welcome* by Janette Sebring Lowrey, not illustrated; Harper, 1964.

1966 No Award

1967 *A Man of the Family* by Elizabeth Burleson, not illustrated; Follett, 1965.

1968 *Young Readers Book of Christian Symbolism* by Michael Daves, illustrated by Gordon Laite; Abingdon, 1967.

1969 *Ride the Pale Stallion* by Gus Tavo, illustrated by Lorence F. Bjorklund; Knopf, 1968.

1970 *Pebbles from a Broken Jar: Fables and Hero Stories from Old China* by Frances Alexander, illustrated by students in Cheefu, China; Bobbs Merrill, 1969.

1971 *Indians Who Lived in Texas* written and illustrated by Betsy Warren; Steck-Vaughn, 1970.

1972 *Good Old Boy* by Willie Morris, not illustrated; Harper, 1971.

1973 *When Clay Sings* by Byrd Baylor, illustrated by Tom Bahti; Scribner, 1972.

1974 *A Bluebird Will Do* by Loula Grace Erdman, not illustrated; Dodd Mead, 1973.

1975 *The Alligator Under the Bed* by Joan L. Nixon, illustrated by Jan Hughes; Putnam, 1974.

1976 *The Desert Is Theirs* by Byrd Baylor, illustrated by Peter Parnall; Scribner, 1975.

1977 No Award

1978 *Guess Who My Favorite Person Is* by Byrd Baylor, illustrated by Robert A. Parker; Scribner, 1977.\

GEORGE G. STONE CENTER FOR CHILDREN'S BOOKS RECOGNITION OF MERIT AWARD

Carolyn Angus, Assistant Director
George G. Stone Center for Children's Books
Claremont Graduate School
131 East 10 Street
Claremont, CA 91711-6188

Established in 1964 by Priscilla Neff Fenn, the Recognition of Merit Award is cosponsored by the George G. Stone Center for Children's Books and the Claremont Reading Conference. This award is given annually to an author or illustrator of a children's book that has been recommended for its power to please and to heighten the awareness of children and teachers as they have shared the book in their classrooms; for a book or body of works that have the capacity to arouse in children an awareness of the complexity and the beauty of the expanding universe. There are no restrictions on the type of literature, except that it is limited to books for children up to the age of twelve or thirteen. Nominations are made by classroom teachers and librarians; the final selection is made by a special committee composed of librarians, teachers, and children's literature specialists from Southern California. The winning author or illustrator receives a hand-lettered scroll executed by Dick Beasley, an eminent contemporary calligrapher.

1965 *Cricket Songs: Japanese Haiku* translated by Harry Behn, illustrated by Sesshu and others; Harcourt, 1964.

1966 *Calendar Moon* by Natalia M. Belting, illustrated by Bernarda Bryson; Holt, 1964.

1967 *Durango Street* by Frank Bonham, not illustrated; Dutton, 1965.

1968 *White Bird* by Clyde Robert Bulla, illustrated by Leonard Weisgard; Crowell, 1966.

1969 *My Side of the Mountain* written and illustrated by Jean Craighead George; Dutton, 1959.

1970 *Charlotte's Web* by E.B. White, illustrated by Garth Williams; Harper, 1952.

1971 *The Phantom Tollbooth* by Norton Juster, illustrated by Jules Feiffer; Random House, 1961.

1972 *By the Great Horn Spoon!* by Sid Fleischman, illustrated by Eric Von Schmidt; Atlantic-Little, 1963.

1973 *The Egypt Game* by Zilpha Keatley Snyder, illustrated by Alton Raible; Atheneum, 1967.

1974 *Queenie Peavy* by Robert Burch, illustrated by Jerry Lazare; Viking, 1966.

1975 *Incident at Hawk's Hill* by Allan W. Eckert, illustrated by John Schoenherr; Little, 1971.

1976 Collected works of Leo Lionni

1977 The White Mountains trilogy (*The White Mountains*, 1967; *The City of Gold and Lead*, 1967; *The Pool of Fire*, 1968) by John Christopher, not illustrated; Macmillan.

1978 *Frog and Toad* books written and illustrated by Arnold Lobel; Harper, various years.

1979 Collected works of Natalie Babbitt

1980 Collected works of Theodore Taylor

1981 No Award

1982 Collected works of Mary Stolz

1983 Collected works of Beverly Cleary

1984 *A Light in the Attic* written and illustrated by Shel Silverstein; Harper, 1981.

Where the Sidewalk Ends written and illustrated by Shel Silverstein; Harper, 1974.

1985 Collected works of Bill Peet

1986 Collected works of Tana Hoban

1987 *Stone Fox* by John Reynolds Gardiner, illustrated by Marcia Sewall; Harper, 1983.

1988 *Alexander and the Terrible, Horrible, No-good, Very Bad Day* by Judith Viorst, illustrated by Ray Cruz; Athenuem, 1972.

1989 *Fran Ellen's House* by Marilyn Sachs, not illustrated; Dutton, 1987.

The Bears' House by Marilyn Sachs, illustrated by Louis Glanzman; Doubleday, 1971.

1990 *Honey, I Love and Other Love Poems* by Eloise Greenfield, illustrated by Leo Dillon and Diane Dillon; Crowell, 1978.

1991 *Let the Circle Be Unbroken* by Mildred D. Taylor, not illustrated; Dial, 1981.

The Road to Memphis by Mildred D. Taylor, not illustrated; Dial, 1990.

Roll of Thunder, Hear My Cry by Mildred D. Taylor, illustrated by Jerry Pinkney; Dial, 1976.

1992 Mitsumasa Anno

1993 *Baseball in April and Other Stories* by Gary Soto, not illustrated; Harcourt Brace Jovanovich, 1990.

JESSE STUART MEDIA AWARD

Kentucky School Media Association
Neata Wiley, President
701 Carter Lane
Bowling Green, KY 42103

Awarded annually since 1972, this award recognizes the creative development of media relating to Kentucky. Any type of media or combination of media is eligible. A plaque is presented

to the winner at the annual meeting of the Kentucky School Media Association. Listed below are the books that have won this award.

1974 *Kentucky: A Pictorial History* edited by J. Winston Coleman, Jr., illustrated; University of Kentucky Press, 1971.

1976 Kentucky Bicentennial Bookshop; University of Kentucky Press.

1978 *Atlas of Kentucky* edited by P. P. Karen and Cotton Mather, illustrated; University Press of Kentucky, 1977.

1980 *Shanty Boat* written and illustrated by Harlan Hubbard; Dodd Mead, 1953.

1981 Works of Jesse Stuart

1982 Works of Robert Powell; Works of Lillie Chaffin

1983 Works of Rebecca Caudill

1984 Works of Dr. Thomas D. Clark

JOAN G. SUGARMAN CHILDREN'S BOOK AWARD

Washington Independent Writers Legal and Educational Fund
220 Woodward Building
733 Fifteenth St. N.W.
Washington, DC 20005

Recognizing excellence in children's literature, this award was established in 1987 by Joan G. Sugarman, a children's book author and librarian from Washington, DC, to honor her late husband Norman A. Sugarman. This regional book award requires that all books submitted, both fiction and nonfiction, be written by authors residing in Washington, DC, Maryland, or Virginia and be geared to children ages 15 and under.

The award is administered under a grant to the Washington Independent Writers Legal and Educational Fund, a nonprofit organization founded in 1980 to defend First Amendment cases and address concerns of independent writers.

The winning book must be original and have universal appeal, having content that is meaningful and appropriate for its intended age group. A cash prize of $1000 is awarded to the winning author. The award was originally given every year, but is now presented biennially.

1988 *Beetles, Lightly Toasted* by Phyllis Reynolds Naylor, not illustrated; Atheneum, 1987.

1989 *Tree by Leaf* by Cynthia Voigt, not illustrated; Atheneum, 1988.

1990 *Shabanu: Daughter of the Wind* by Suzanne Fisher Staples, not illustrated; Knopf, 1989.

1992 *Stepping on the Cracks* by Mary Downing Hahn, illustrated with a map; Clarion, 1991.

SUNSHINE STATE YOUNG READERS AWARD

Sandy Ulm, Program Director
School Library Media Services
Department of Education
Tallahassee, FL 32399-0400

Cosponsored by the Florida Association for Media in Education and the School Library Media Services, this children's choice award was first given in 1984. Florida grade school students choose their favorite book of the year.

1984 *Bunnicula: A Rabbit Tale of Mystery* by Deborah Howe and James Howe, illustrated by Alan Daniel; Atheneum, 1980.

1984 RUNNERSUP *Ramona Quimby, Age 8* by Beverly Cleary, illustrated by Alan Tiegreen; Morrow, 1981.

The Great Gilly Hopkins by Katherine Paterson, not illustrated; Crowell, 1978.

1985 *Superfudge* by Judy Blume, not illustrated; Dutton, 1980.

1985 RUNNERSUP *Nothing's Fair in Fifth Grade* by Barthe DeClements, not illustrated; Viking, 1981.

Ralph S. Mouse by Beverly Cleary, illustrated by Paul O. Zelinsky; Morrow, 1982.

1986 *Be a Perfect Person in Just Three Days!* by Stephen Manes, illustrated by Tom Huffman; Clarion/Houghton Mifflin, 1982.

1987 *Thirteen Ways to Sink a Sub* by Jamie Gilson, illustrated by Linda S. Edwards; Lothrop Lee & Shepard, 1982.

1988 GRADES 3-5 and 6-8 *Sixth Grade Can Really Kill You* by Barthe DeClements, not illustrated; Viking Kestrel, 1985.

1989 GRADES 3-5 *Sixth Grade Sleepover* by Eve Bunting, not illustrated; Harcourt Brace Jovanovich, 1986.

1989 GRADES 6-8 *Sixth Grade Sleepover* by Eve Bunting, not illustrated; Harcourt Brace Jovanovich, 1986.

1990 GRADES 3-5 *Teacher's Pet* by Johanna Hurwitz, illustrated by Sheila Hamanaka; Morrow, 1988.

1990 GRADES 6-8 *Trapped in Death Cave* by Bill Wallace, not illustrated; Holiday House, 1984.

1991 GRADES 3-5 *There's a Boy in the Girls' Bathroom* by Louis Sachar, not illustrated; Knopf, 1987.

1991 GRADES 6-8 *There's a Boy in the Girls' Bathroom* by Louis Sachar, not illustrated; Knopf, 1987.

1992 GRADES 3-5 *Fudge* by Charlotte T. Graeber, illustrated by Cheryl Harness; Lothrop, Lee & Shepard, 1987.

1992 GRADES 6-8 *Something Upstairs: A Tale of Ghosts* by Avi, not illustrated; Orchard Books, 1988.

SURREY SCHOOL BOOK OF THE YEAR AWARD

Surrey School District 36
14225-56th Ave
Surrey, British Columbia
V3W lH9 Canada

Given since 1972 by the Surrey School Librarians of Surrey, British Columbia, this annual award is determined by the school children of Surrey School District #36. Each child voting is expected to have read at least two of the titles on the final ballot drawn up by a committee of librarians. Titles eligible for the balloting are recently published works of fiction at the intermediate-grade level. The voting takes place during the last week in January and the winning author is notified by letter. A decal is affixed to all copies of the award-winning book in the district.

1972 *Charlotte's Web* by E.B. White, illustrated by Garth Williams; Harper, 1952.

1973 *Charlie and the Chocolate Factory* by Roald Dahl, illustrated by Joseph Schindelman; Knopf, 1964.

1974 *The Mouse and the Motorcycle* by Beverly Cleary, illustrated by Louis Darling; Morrow, 1965.

1975 *Charlie and the Great Glass Elevator* by Roald Dahl, illustrated by Joseph Schindelman; Knopf, 1972.

1976 *Me and My Little Brain* by John D. Fitzgerald, illustrated by Sara Silcock; Dial, 1974.

1977 *Freaky Friday* by Mary Rodgers, not illustrated; Harper, 1972.

1978 *Danny: The Champion of the World* by Roald Dahl, illustrated by Jill Bennett; Knopf, 1975.

1979 *The Goof that Won the Pennant* by Jonah Kalb, illustrated by Sandy Kossin; Houghton, 1976.

1980 *The Pinballs* by Betsy Byars, not illustrated; Harper, 1977.

1981 *Hail, Hail, Camp Timberwood* by Ellen Conford, illustrated by Gail Owens; Little Brown, 1978.

1982 *Ramona and Her Mother* by Beverly Cleary, illustrated by Alan Tiegreen; Morrow, 1979; Dell/Yearling, 1980.

1983 *The Toothpaste Genie* by Frances Duncan; Scholastic-TAB, 1981.

1984 *The Secret of Spirit Mountain* by Helen Kronberg Olson, illustrated by Hameed Benjamin; Dodd, Mead, 1980.

1985 *Be a Perfect Person in Just Three Days* by Stephen Manes, illustrated by Tom Huffman; Houghton Mifflin, 1982 .

1986 *Ralph S. Mouse* by Beverly Cleary, illustrated by Paul O. Zelinsky; Morrow, 1982.

1987 *Sixth Grade Sleepover* by Eve Bunting, not illustrated; Harcourt, Brace, Jovanovich, 1986.

1988 *Pop Bottles* by Ken Roberts, not illustrated; Groundwood Books, 1987.

1989 *Hatchet* by Gary Paulsen, not illustrated; Bradbury, 1987.

1990 *There's a Boy in the Girls' Washroom* by Louis Sachar, not illustrated.

1991-92 *Secret of the Cards* by Sonia Craddock, not illustrated; Scholastic Canada, 1990.

T

SYDNEY TAYLOR BOOK AWARD

Association of Jewish Libraries
c/o National Foundation for Jewish Culture
330 Seventh Ave., 21st Floor
New York, NY 10001

This annual award, sponsored by the Association of Jewish Libraries, was first presented in 1968. The author or illustrator of a book deemed to have made the most outstanding contribution in the field of Jewish literature for children and young people during the past year is presented with a plaque at the annual convention of the Association of Jewish Libraries. Fiction, nonfiction, and picture books of interest to children are eligible. A committee reviews all books published during the year and recommends five titles. One winner is then selected.

The following criteria and guidelines are observed by the committee members in making their decision: (1) The book must have general literary merit (as defined by Charlotte Huck and/or Arbuthnot). (2) The book must have a positive Jewish focus and stress positive Jewish values. (3) The book must be engaging and entertaining, rather than didactic. (4) The book must add to the reader's understanding of Jewish life. (5) The book must be suitable in style, vocabulary, format, and illustrations for the intended age level. (6) Whether fiction or nonfiction, the book must be solidly rooted in authentic detail and accurate scholarship and research. Any scene, period of history, or aspect of ancient or modern life may be depicted. (7) No award will be given if there is no publication of suitable merit.

1969 *Our Eddie* by Sulamith Ish-Kishor, not illustrated; Pantheon, 1969.

1970 *The Year* by Suzanne Lange, not illustrated; Phillips, 1970.

1971 Isaac Bashevis Singer for his general contributions

1972 Molly Cone for her general contributions

1973 *Uncle Misha's Partisans* by Yuri Suhl, not illustrated; Four Winds, 1973.

1974 No Award

1975 *Waiting for Moma* by Marietta Moskins, illustrated by Richard Lebenson; Coward, 1975.

1976 *Never to Forget: The Jews of the Holocaust* by Milton Meltzer, not illustrated; Harper, 1976.

1977 *Exit from Home* by Anita Heyman, not illustrated; Crown, 1977.

1978 *The Endless Steppe: Growing Up in Siberia* by Esther Hautzig, not illustrated; Crowell, 1968.

1979 *The Devil in Vienna* by Doris Orgel, not illustrated; Dial, 1978.

1980 *Ike and Mama and the Block Wedding* by Carol Snyder, illustrated by Charles Robinson; Coward, 1979.

1981 *A Russian Farewell* written and illustrated by Leonard Everett Fisher; Four Winds, 1980.

1982 **CHILDREN** *Yussel's Prayer: A Yom Kippur Story* by Barbara Cohen, illustrated by Michael J. Deraney; Lothrop, Lee & Shepard, 1981.

1982 **OLDER CHILDREN** *The Night Journey* by Kathryn Lasky, illustrated by Trina Schart Hyman; Warne, 1981.

1983 **CHILDREN** *The Castle on Hester Street* written and illustrated by Linda Heller; Jewish Publication Society of America, 1982.

1983 **OLDER CHILDREN** *Call Me Ruth* by Marilyn Sachs, not illustrated; Doubleday, 1982.

1984 **YOUNGER READERS** *Bubby, Me and Memories* by Barbara Pomerantz, photographs by Leon Lurie; Union of American Hebrew Congregations, 1983.

1984 **OLDER READERS** *In the Mouth of the Wolf* by Rose Zar, not illustrated; Jewish Publication Society of America, 1983.

1985 **PICTURE BOOK** *Mrs. Moskowitz and the Sabbath Candlesticks* written and illustrated by Amy Schwartz; Jewish Publication Society, 1983.

1985 **OLDER** *The Island on Bird Street* by Uri Orlev, translated from the Hebrew by Hillel Halkin, not illustrated; Houghton Mifflin, 1984, c1983.

1986 **PICTURE BOOK** *Brothers* retold by Florence B. Freedman, illustrated by Robert Andrew Parker; Harper & Row, 1985.

1986 **OLDER** *Ike and Mama and the Seven Surprises* by Carol Snyder, illustrated by Charles Robinson; Lothrop, 1985.

1987 **PICTURE BOOK** *Joseph Who Loved the Sabbath* by Marilyn Hirsh, illustrated by Devis Grebu; Viking Kestrel, 1986.

1987 **OLDER** *Beyond the High White Wall* by Nancy Pitt, not illustrated; Scribner, 1986.

1988 **PICTURE BOOK** *The Number on my Grandfather's Arm* by David A. Adler, photographs by Rose A. Eichenbaum; Union of American Hebrew Congregations, 1987.

1988 **OLDER** *The Return* by Sonia Levitin, not illustrated; Atheneum, 1987.

1989 **PICTURE BOOK** *The Keeping Quilt* written and illustrated by Patricia Polacco; Simon & Schuster, 1988.

1989 **OLDER** *The Devil's Arithmetic* by Jane Yolen, not illustrated; Viking Kestrel, 1988.

1990 **PICTURE BOOK** *Berchick* by Esther Silverstein Blanc, illustrated by Tennessee Dixon; Volcano Press, 1989.

1990 **OLDER** *Number the Stars* by Lois Lowry, not illustrated; Houghton Mifflin, 1989.

1991 **PICTURE BOOK** *The Chanukkah Guest* by Eric Kimmel, illustrated by Giori Carmi; Holiday House, 1990.

1991 **OLDER** *My Grandmother's Stories* by Adele Geras, illustrated by Jael Jordan; Knopf, 1990; Heinemann, 1990.

1992 **PICTURE BOOK** *Daddy's Chair* by Sandy Lanton, illustrated by Shelly O. Haas; KarBen Copies, 1991.

Cakes and Miracles: A Purim Tale by Barbara Diamond Goldin, illustrated by Erika Weihs; Viking, 1991.

1992 **OLDER** *The Diamond Tree: Jewish Tales From Around the World* by Howard Schwartz and Barbara Rush, illustrated by Uri Shulevitz; HarperCollins, 1991.

SYDNEY TAYLOR BODY OF WORK AWARD

Association of Jewish Libraries
c/o National Foundation for Jewish Culture
330 Seventh Ave., 21st floor
New York, NY 10001

First given posthumously to Sydney Taylor in 1979, this award honors an author's entire body of work. Nominations are received by the awards committee from members of the Association of Jewish Libraries. The body of work must have withstood time and have had a positive effect on its readers. The criteria used in selection of the Association of Jewish Libraries Sydney Taylor Book Award (see entry) is employed here also. The final selection of the committee is disclosed at the annual convention where the winning author is presented with a plaque.

1979 Sydney Taylor

1980 Marilyn Hirsh

1981 Sadie Rose Weilerstein

1982 Barbara Cohen

1983 No Award

1985 Miriam Chaikin

1986-1989 No Award

1990 Yaffa Ganz

1991-1992 No Award

SYDNEY TAYLOR MANUSCRIPT AWARD

Association of Jewish Libraries
c/o National Foundation for Jewish Culture
330 Seventh Ave., 21st floor
New York, NY 10001

This award was established in 1985 by Ralph Taylor in memory of his wife Sydney Taylor to encourage the writing of children's literature with universal values and Jewish content. Previously unpublished authors who have written a fiction story suitable for children ages 8-12 are eligible. A $1000 cash prize and a certificate are presented to the winning author at the June convention of the Association of Jewish Libraries.

1986 "Spirit" by Rosalie Fleischer.

1987 "Cubs of the Lion of Judah" by E.M. Solowey.

1988 *The Streets Are Paved with Gold* by Fran Weissenberg, not illustrated; Harbinger House, 1990.

1989 "Borders" by Suzi Wizowaty.

1990-1991 No Award

1992 "Leaving Egypt" by Lois Roisman.

TENNESSEE CHILDREN'S CHOICE AWARD
see **VOLUNTEER STATE BOOK AWARD**

TEXAS BLUEBONNET AWARD

Patricia H. Smith, Executive Director
Texas Library Association
3355 Bee Cave Road
Suite 603
Austin, TX 78746-6763

The Texas Bluebonnet Award was officially established in April 1979 through the efforts of Dr. Janelle A. Paris. The state of Texas superimposed on an open book and flanked by bluebonnets, the state flower, is depicted as the official logo of the award. This design is the result of a statewide contest held in 1979 among Texas schoolchildren in grades three through six.

The purpose of this award is to recognize the books most preferred by children and to honor writers of creative and enjoyable books. Cosponsored by the Texas Library Association Children's Round Table and the Texas Association of School Librarians, this award encourages Texas children to read more books, explore a variety of books, and develop powers of discrimination.

A master list of fifteen to twenty titles is prepared annually by the seven-member TBA administrative committee (three school librarians, three public librarians, and one library educator). The committee also accepts nominations from librarians, teachers, parents, and students.

Following are the guidelines for choosing the titles on the master list:

(1) Books must have a copyright date within three years prior to the election. (2) The author must be a living United States citizen. (3) The books must be published in the U.S. (4) The books should be judged for their literary content. (5) The appropriateness of the book's contents should be considered. (6) There should be a variety of book types, both fiction and nonfiction. (7) The books should be on a third-grade through sixth-grade level. (8) The following will be ineligible for the list: textbooks, new editions, adaptations, and abridged editions. (9) The books must be favorably reviewed by at least one standard reviewing tool.

Texas students in grades three through six who have read or heard read aloud at least five titles from the master list are eligible to vote. They are allowed to cast one vote for their favorite book.

The author whose book receives the most votes is the winner. They are honored at a breakfast meeting at the Texas Library Association conference. A medallion mounted inside a lucite square, with the name of the author, book title, and date inscribed on the back, is presented to the winner.

1981 *Ramona and her Father* by Beverly Cleary, illustrated by Alan Tiegreen; Morrow, 1977.

1982 *Superfudge* by Judy Blume, not illustrated; Dutton, 1980.

1983 *A Dog Called Kitty* by Bill Wallace, not illustrated; Holiday House, 1980.

1984 *Nothing's Fair in Fifth Grade* by Barthe DeClements, not illustrated; Viking, 1981.

1985 *Skinnybones* by Barbara Park, not illustrated; Knopf, 1982.

1986 *The Dollhouse Murders* by Betty Ren Wright, not illustrated; Holiday House, 1983.

1987 *The Hot and Cold Summer* by Johanna Hurwitz, illustrated by Gail Owens; Morrow, 1984.

1988 *Christina's Ghost* by Betty Ren Wright, not illustrated; Holiday House, 1985.

1989 *Wait Til Helen Comes* by Mary Downing Hahn, not illustrated; Clarion, 1986.

1990 *There's a Boy in the Girls' Bathroom* by Louis Sachar, not illustrated; Knopf, 1987.

1991 *Aliens for Breakfast* by Jonathan Etra and Stephanie Spinner, illustrated by Steve Bjorkman; Random House, 1988.

1992 *Snot Stew* by Bill Wallace, illustrated by Lisa McCue; Holiday House, 1989.

1993 *The Houdini Box* by Brian Selznick, illustrated; Knopf, 1991.

TEXAS INSTITUTE OF LETTERS TEXAS PUBLISHERS AWARD FOR BEST BOOK FOR CHILDREN

Texas Institute of Letters
James Hoggard
Secretary-Treasurer
Box 9032
Wichita Falls, TX 76308-9032

This award is funded by the Texas Publishers Association. Books for children which are written by Texans or have a Texas setting are eligible. Only books published for the first time in the year preceding the award are considered. Entries are made by authors or by their publishers. The winning book is determined by a panel of three judges. A $250 cash award is presented to the winner at the annual spring meeting of the Texas Institute of Letters. This award is presented irregularly.

1983 *The Once-upon-a-Time Dragon* written and illustrated by Jack Kent; Harcourt, 1982.

IOU's by Ouida Sebestyen, not illustrated; Little Brown, 1982.

1985 *Luke and the Van Zandt County War* by Judith M. Alter, illustrated by Walli Conoly; Texas Christian University, 1984.

1986-1989 No Awards

1990 *Introducing Birds to Young Naturalists* by Ilo Hiller, illustrated; Texas A & M University Press, 1989.

1991 *The Last Innocent Summer* by Zinita Fowler; Texas Christian University Press, 1990.

TIMES EDUCATIONAL SUPPLEMENT INFORMATION BOOK AWARD

The Times Educational Supplement
Priory House
St. John's Lane
London EC1M 4BX
England

The Times Educational Supplement has sponsored this award program since 1972. In 1973, the program was expanded to include two categories: junior (up to age nine) and senior (ages ten through sixteen). In 1986 a third category of schoolbooks was added. The books are chosen on the basis of distinction in context and presentation of information. Trade books originally published in the United Kingdom or Commonwealth countries are eligible. Each winning author receives £150.

1972 *Introducing Archaeology* by Magnus Magnusson, illustrated by Martin Simmons; Bodley Head, 1972.

1973 **JUNIOR** No Award

1973 **SENIOR** *Human Populations* by David Hay, illustrated with photographs and maps; Penguin, 1972.

1974 **JUNIOR** *Frogs, Toads and Newts* by Francis D. Ommanney, illustrated by Deborah Fulfold; Bodley Head, 1973.

1974 **SENIOR** *Understanding Art: The Uses of Space, Form and Structure* by Betty Churcher, illustrated with photographs; McDougall, 1973.

1975 **JUNIOR** *Spiders* by Ralph Whitlock, illustrated with photographs; Wayland & Priory Press, 1975.

1975 **SENIOR** *Windows into a Nest* by Geraldine Lux Flanagan, photographs by Sean Morris; Kestrel, 1975; Houghton, 1976.

1976 **JUNIOR** *Wash and Brush Up* by Eleanor Allen, illustrated with photographs; A&C Black, 1976.

1976 **SENIOR** *MacDonald's Encyclopedia of Africa* illustrated with photographs; MacDonald Educational, 1976.

1977 **JUNIOR** *Street Flowers* by Richard Mabey, illustrated by Sarah Kensington; Kestrel, 1976.

1977 **SENIOR** *Man and Machines. The Mitchell Beazley Joy of Knowledge Library* edited by James Mitchell, illustrated with photographs; Mitchell Beazley, 1977.

1978 **JUNIOR** *Tournaments* by Richard Barber, illustrated by Anne Dalton; Kestrel, 1978.

1978 **SENIOR** *Butterflies on my Mind: Their Life and Conservation in Britain Today* by Dulcie Gray, illustrated by Brian Hargreaves; Angus & Robertson, 1978.

1979 **JUNIOR** *The Common Frog* by Oxford Scientific Films, Ltd., photographs by George Bernard; Whizzard/Deutsch, 1979.

1979 **SENIOR** *Make it Happy: What Sex Is All About* by Jane Cousins, illustrated by Susan Hunter; Virago, 1978.

1980 **JUNIOR** *Earthquakes and Volcanoes* written and illustrated by Robert Updegraff and Imelda Updegraff; Methuen, 1980.

1980 **SENIOR** *Oxford Junior Companion to Music* based on the original published by Percy Scholes, 2nd edition by Michael Hurd, illustrated with photographs; Oxford, 1979.

1981 **JUNIOR** No Award

1981 **SENIOR** *Skulls!* by Richard Steel, illustrated by Gerry Gaskin; Heinemann, 1980.

1982 **JUNIOR** *A Day with a Miner* by Phillippa Aston, photographs by Chris Fairclough; Wayland, 1981.

1982 **SENIOR** *The Easy Way to Bird Recognition* by John Kilbracken, illustrated; Kingfisher Books, 1982.

1983 **JUNIOR** *Mum - I Feel Funny!* by Ann McPherson and Aidan Macfarlane, illustrated by Nicholas Garland; Chatto & Windus, 1982.

1983 **SENIOR** *Defence* by Charles Freeman, illustrated with portraits; Batsford Academic & Educational, 1983.

Just Imagine - Ideas in Painting by Robert Cummming, illustrated with photographs; Kestrel, 1982; Scribner, 1982.

1984 **JUNIOR** No Award

1984 **SENIOR** *In Deutschland* by Rod Nash, illustrated by David Parkins; Thomas Nelson/Chancerel, 1984.

1985 **JUNIOR** *KwaZulu South Africa* by Nancy Durrell McKenna, illustrated; A&C Black, 1984.

1985 **SENIOR** *The Sunday Times Countryside Companion* by Geoffrey Young; illustrated; Country Life Books, 1985.

Growing Up by Susan Meredith, illustrated by Sue Stitt, Kuo Kang Chen and Rob McCaig; Usborne, 1985.

1986 **JUNIOR** *Polar Regions* by Terry Jennings, illustrated; Oxford, 1986.

1986 **SENIOR** *Legend of Odysseus* by Peter Connolly, illustrated; Oxford, 1986.

1986 **SCHOOLBOOK** *Scientific Eye* by Adam Hart-Davis; Bell & Hyman, 1986.

1987 **JUNIOR** *Being Born* by Sheila Kitzinger, photographs by Lennart Nilsson; Dorling Kindersley, 1986.

1987 **SENIOR** *The Ultimate Alphabet* written and illustrated by Mike Wilks; Pavilion, 1987, c1986; Henry Holt, 1986.

Galaxies and Quasars by Nigel Henbest and Heather Couper, illustrated; Watts, 1986.

1987 **SCHOOLBOOK** *The American West 1840-1895* by S.J. Styles and R.A. Rees, illustrated with photos; Longman, 1986.

New Perspectives Book 1: An English Course by Hugh Knight and Angela Bell, illustrated; Oxford, 1987.

1988 **JUNIOR** *Conker* written and illustrated by Barrie Watts; A & C Black, 1987.

Making a Book by Ruth Thomson, illustrated by Chris Fairclough; Watts, 1987.

1988 **SENIOR** *Martin Luther King: America's Great Non-Violent Leader* by Pam Brown and Valerie Schloredt, illustrated; Exley Publications, 1988; Longman, 1988.

1988 SCHOOLBOOK *Active Science 1* by Richard Gott, Tony Thornley, and Michael Coles, illustrated; Collins Educational, 1988.

1989 JUNIOR *Why Do People Smoke?* by Pete Sanders, illustrated with photos; Gloucester Press, 1989.

1989 SENIOR *The Way Things Work* written and illustrated by David Macaulay; Dorling Kindersley, 1988.

1989 SCHOOLBOOK *Arc-en-ciel 2* by Ann Miller, Liz Roselman and Marie-Therese Bougard; Mary Glasgow, 1989.

1990 JUNIOR *The Tree* by Judy Hindley, illustrated by Alison Wisenfeld; Aurum, 1990; Potter, 1990.

1990 SENIOR *The New Oxford School Atlas* by Patrick Weigand, illustrated; Oxford University Press, 1990.

1990 SCHOOLBOOK *National Mathematics Project: Mathematics for Secondary Schools Year 5* by Eon Harper, illustrated; Longman, 1990.

1991 JUNIOR *Ian and Fred's Big Green Book* by Fred Pearce, illustrated by Ian Winton; Kingfisher, 1991.

1991 SENIOR *An Egyptian Pyramid* by Jacqueline Morley, John James, and Mark Bergin, illustrated; Simon & Schuster, 1991; Peter Bedrick, 1991.

1991 SCHOOLBOOK *After the Bomb: Brother in the Land* by Elaine Scarratt, Guy Dickens, and Nick Williams; English & Media Centre, 1991.

1991 SCHOOLBOOK SECONDARY *Thin Ice: A Poetry Anthology* by David Kitchen, illustrated; Oxford University Press, 1991.

1992 JUNIOR *My First Book of Time* by Claire Llewellyn, illustrated; Dorling Kindersley, 1992.

1992 SENIOR *Black and British* by David Bygott, illustrated; Oxford University Press, 1992.

TIR NA N'OG

Menna Lloyd Williams
Welsh National Centre for Children's Literature
Castell Brychan, Heol-y-Bryn
Aberysthwyth, Dyfed, Cymru SY23 2JB
Wales

The Tir Na n'Og Award was created to acknowledge the work of authors and illustrators, to raise the standard of writing for children and young people, and to encourage book buying and reading by bringing these books to the attention of readers. These annual awards are presented for a Welsh language book and also for an English language book with an authentic Welsh setting. Only the English language winners are listed here.

1976 *The Grey King* by Susan Cooper, illustrated by Michael Heslop; Chatto & Windus, 1975; Atheneum, 1975.

1977 *A String in the Harp* by Nancy Bond, illustrated by Allen Davis; Atheneum, 1976.

1978 *Silver on the Tree* by Susan Cooper, not illustrated; Atheneum, 1977.

1979 *Time Circles* by Bette Meyrick, not illustrated; Abelard, 1978.

1980 No Award

1981 *The Blindfold Track* by Frances Thomas, not illustrated; Macmillan, 1980.

1982 No Award

1983 *Bluestones* by Mary John, not illustrated; Barn Owl Press, 1982.

1984 *The Prize* by Irma Chilton, not illustrated; Barn Owl Press, 1983.

1985 No Award

1986 *The Region of the Summer Stars* by Frances Thomas, not illustrated; Barn Owl Press, 1985.

1987 *The Snow Spider* by Jenny Nimmo, illustrated by Joanna Carey; Methuen Children's, 1986.

1988 *Steel Town Cats* by Celia Lucas, illustrated by Susan Cutting; Tabb House, 1987.

1989-1991 Award withheld

1992 *Who Stole a Bloater?* by Frances Thomas, not illustrated; Seren Books, 1991.

1993 Award withheld

MARK TWAIN AWARD

Judy Mahoney
Missouri Association of School Librarians
Box 22476
Kansas City, MO 64113-2476

Founded by Marnie Neal in 1972, the Mark Twain Award is sponsored by the Missouri Association of School Librarians. The purpose of this annual award is to introduce children to the best in current literature and to promote reading. Missouri school children in grades four through eight vote for their favorite book from a master list compiled by a committee of librarians and reader/selectors who represent many participating organizations in Missouri. Books eligible for inclusion on the master list must have been written by an author living in the U.S., be of interest to children in grades four through eight, and be of literary value to enrich the children's lives. Both fiction and nonfiction titles are eligible. A bronze bust of Mark Twain sculpted by Barbara Shanklin is presented to the winning author at the spring conference of the Missouri Association of School Librarians.

1972 *Sounder* by William H. Armstrong, illustrated by James Barkley; Harper & Row, 1969.

1973 *Mrs. Frisby and the Rats of NIMH* by Robert C. O'Brien, illustrated by Zena Bernstein; Atheneum, 1971.

1974 *It's a Mile from Here to Glory* by Robert C. Lee, not illustrated; Little, 1972.

1975 *How to Eat Fried Worms* by Thomas Rockwell, illustrated by Emily McCully; Watts, 1973.

1976 *The Home Run Trick* by Scott Corbett, illustrated by Paul Galdone; Atlantic-Little, 1973.

1977 *The Ghost on Saturday Night* by Sid Fleischman, illustrated by Eric von Schmidt; Atlantic-Little, 1974.

1978 *Ramona the Brave* by Beverly Cleary, illustrated by Alan Tiegreen; Morrow, 1975.

1979 *The Champion of Merrimack County* by Roger W. Drury, illustrated by Fritz Wegner; Little Brown, 1976.

1980 *Pinballs* by Betsy Byars, not illustrated; Harper, 1977.

1981 *Soup for President* by Robert Newton Peck, illustrated by Ted Lewin; Knopf, 1978.

1982 *The Boy Who Saw Bigfoot* by Marian T. Place, not illustrated; Dodd, Mead, 1979.

1983 *The Girl with the Silver Eyes* by Willo David Roberts, not illustrated; Atheneum, 1980.

1984 *The Secret Life of the Underwear Champ* by Betty Miles, illustrated by Dan Jones; Knopf, 1981.

1985 *A Bundle of Sticks* by Pat Rhoads Mauser, illustrated by Gail Owens; Atheneum, 1982.

1986 *The Dollhouse Murders* by Betty Ren Wright, not illustrated; Holiday House, 1983.

1987 *The War with Grandpa* by Robert Kimmel Smith, illustrated by Richard Lauter; Delacorte, 1984.

1988 *Baby-sitting Is a Dangerous Job* by Willo Davis Roberts, not illustrated; Atheneum, 1985.

1989 *Sixth Grade Sleepover* by Eve Bunting, not illustrated; Harcourt Brace Jovanovich, 1986.

1990 *There's a Boy in the Girls' Bathroom* by Louis Sachar, not illustrated; Knopf, 1987.

1991 *All About Sam* by Lois Lowry, illustrated by Diane de Groat; Houghton Mifflin, 1988.

1992 *The Doll in the Garden* by Mary Downing Hahn, illustrated; Clarion, 1989.

1993 *Maniac Magee* by Jerry Spinelli, not illustrated; Little Brown, 1990.

U

UNICEF-EZRA JACK KEATS INTERNATIONAL AWARD FOR CHILDREN'S BOOK ILLUSTRATION
(formerly USBBY-UNICEF EZRA JACK KEATS AWARD)

UNICEF
c/o Kathryne Andrews
Greeting Card Operation
331 E. 38th St. 3rd floor
New York, NY 10016

This award is given in memory of the well-known children's author/illustrator, Ezra Jack Keats, to encourage outstanding artists to illustrate children's books so that children are inspired to read. This biennial award was established in 1989 and is funded by the Ezra Jack Keats Foundation and administered by UNICEF. Any artist who has no more than five published children's books is eligible for this award which is based on quality illustrations. A $5000 cash award and a silver medallion are awarded to the winning illustrator.

1986 Felipe Davalos

1988 Barbara Reid

1990 *The Wildlife 1-2-3: A Nature Counting Book* written and illustrated by Jan Thornhill; Grey de Pencier Books, 1989; Simon & Schuster, 1989.

1992 *Enora and the Black Crane* written and illustrated by Arone Raymond Meeks; Ashton Scholastic, 1991; Scholastic, 1993.

UNICEF-EZRA JACK KEATS NATIONAL AWARD FOR CHILDREN'S BOOK ILLUSTRATION

U.S. Committee for UNICEF
c/o Mrs. Elizabeth Schalk
331 E. 38th St. 3rd floor
New York, NY 10016

Established in 1989 by the Ezra Jack Keats Foundation and the U.S. Committee for UNICEF, the purpose of this national award is to select the United States' winner for submission to the UNICEF-EZRA JACK KEATS INTERNATIONAL AWARD FOR CHILDREN'S BOOK ILLUSTRATION (see entry). The same criteria apply for eligibility. The winner receives a silver medallion.

1989 *The Magic Fan* written and illustrated by Keith Baker; Harcourt Brace Jovanovich, 1989.

1991 *Another Celebrated Dancing Bear* by Gladys Scheffrin-Falk, illustrated by Barbara Garrison; Scribner, 1991.

UNIVERSE LITERARY PRIZE
discontinued

Begun in 1984 by the National Book League in England, The Universe Literary Prize was offered for only a year before it was discontinued. A 500 pound prize was awarded for a fiction or nonfiction title aimed at young people ages ten through fourteen which best made a real contribution to their Christian moral development.

1984 *A Parcel of Patterns* by Jill Paton Walsh, not illustrated; Farrar, 1983.

1984 **RUNNERSUP** *Redemption Greenback* by David Johnstone, illustrated by Antony Maitland; Methuen Children's, 1983.

Seaward by Susan Cooper, not illustrated; Atheneum, 1983.

UNIVERSITY OF SOUTHERN MISSISSIPPI MEDALLION

School of Library and Information Science
University of Southern Mississippi
Box 5146
Hattiesburg, MS 39406-5146

This annual award was established in 1969 to honor an author or illustrator who has made an outstanding contribution to the field of children's literature. The author or illustrator's entire body of work is taken into consideration. Nominations are received from publishers, authors, illustrators, professors, and others interested in children's literature. A committee composed of authors, librarians, and children's literature specialists make their choices from a ballot consisting of all nominations. The author or illustrator with the highest number of votes wins. A silver medallion with the likeness of the recipient on one side and a representative book character on the other is presented to the winner. Additional silver medallions are struck and retained in the permanent collection housed at the de Grummond Children's Literature Research Collection at the University of Southern Mississippi. The medallion is presented in conjunction with the Children's Book Festival held each March at the University.

1969 Lois Lenski

1970 Ernest H. Shepard

1971 Roger Duvoisin

1972 Marcia Brown

1973 Lynd Ward

1974 Taro Yashima

1975 Barbara Cooney

1976 Scott O'Dell

1977 Adrienne Adams

1978 Madeleine L'Engle

1979 Leonard Everett Fisher

1980 Ezra Jack Keats

1981 Maurice Sendak

1982 Beverly Cleary

1983 Katherine Paterson

1984 Peter Spier

1985 Arnold Lobel

1986 Jean Craighead George

1987 Paula Fox

1988 Jean Fritz

1989 Lee Bennett Hopkins

1990 Charlotte Zolotow

1991 Richard Peck

1992 James Marshall

1993 Quentin Blake

1994 Ashley Bryan

UTAH CHILDREN'S BOOK AWARD

Lillian Heil
Children's Literature Association of Utah Executive Board
210-L MCKB
Brigham Young University
Provo, UT 84602

Sponsored by the Utah Children's Literature Association, this children's choice award was begun in 1980. The purpose is to encourage the love of reading on the part of children and to introduce children (and the adults in their lives) to good books by outstanding authors that are both appealing to their interest and well written.

The following criteria are used in selecting nominations: (1) Must be appropriate for grades three through six; (2) Caldecott and Newbery winners are ineligible; (3) Only one title of any one author will be included; (4) Titles published in the five years preceding the award are eligible; (5) Title must be in print; (6) A title may appear only once on a list; (7) The winning author will be excluded from competition the following year; (8) The author must be living in the U.S. at the time of nomination; (9) Picture books are ineligible; (10) All books should be worthy of an award from a literary standpoint.

The annual list of twenty titles is selected by parents, teachers, librarians, and others interested in children's books. Schools may participate if they have at least twelve of the twenty nominated titles. Children in grades three through six are eligible to vote if they have read or heard at least three of the titles.

1980 *Ramona and her Father* by Beverly Cleary, illustrated by Alan Tiegreen; Morrow, 1977.

1981 *Eddie's Menagerie* by Carolyn Haywood, illustrated by Ingrid Fetz; Morrow, 1978.

     The Letter, the Witch and the Ring by John Bellairs, illustrated by Richard Egielski; Dial, 1976.

1982 *Superfudge* by Judy Blume, not illustrated; Dutton, 1980.

1983 *The Chocolate Touch* by Patrick Catling, illustrated by Margot Apple; Morrow, 1979.

1984 *Lost in the Devil's Desert* by Gloria Skurzynski, illustrated by Joseph M. Scrofani; Lothrop, Lee & Shepard, 1982.

1985 *Stone Fox* by John Reynolds Gardiner, illustrated by Marcia Sewall; Crowell, 1980.

1986 *Me and the Weirdos* by Jane Sutton, illustrated by Sandy Kossin; Houghton Mifflin, 1981.

1987 *Skinnybones* by Barbara Park, not illustrated; Knopf, 1982.

1988 *Wait Til Helen Comes* by Mary Downing Hahn, not illustrated; Clarion, 1986.

1989 *Trapped in Death Cave* by Bill Wallace, not illustrated; Holiday House, 1984.

1990 *This Island Isn't Big Enough for the Four of Us* by Gery Greer and Bob Ruddick, not illustrated; Crowell, 1987.

1991 *Matilda* by Roald Dahl, illustrated by Quentin Blake; Viking Kestrel, 1988.

1992 *There's a Boy in the Girls' Bathroom* by Louis Sachar, not illustrated; Knopf, 1987.

UTAH CHILDREN'S INFORMATIONAL BOOK AWARD

Lillian Heil
Children's Literature Association of Utah Executive Board
210-L MCKB
Brigham Young University
Provo, UT 84602

This award for an informational book was begun in 1986 by the Children's Literature Association of Utah. For the first award in 1986, the Executive Board chose a winner from a short list of eight titles. In succeeding years, the winner has been chosen by the children.

In order to be eligible for the master list, books (1) Must have been published within the preceding two years of the year of nomination; (2) Newbery Medal winners are excluded; (3) Must be appropriate for use by children up to and including age 12; (4) Must appeal to children of usual interests and reading abilities; (5) Should present subjects in a unique way to create excitement; (6) Should be outstanding examples of concept, writing, art, and bookmaking; (7) Winning author is ineligible for nomination for two years.

1986 *Great Painters* written and illustrated by Piero Venturo; Putnam, 1984.

1987 No Award

1988 *How Much Is a Million?* by David Schwartz, illustrated by Steven Kellogg; Lothrop, Lee & Shepard, 1985.

1989 *Your Amazing Senses* written and illustrated by Ron Van Der Meer and Atie Van Der Meer; Child's Play, 1987.

1990 *How To Make Pop-Ups* by Joan Irvine, illustrated by Barbara Reid; Morrow, 1988.

1991 *Bill Peet: An Autobiography* written and illustrated by Bill Peet; Houghton Mifflin, 1989.

1992 *An Ant Colony* by Andreas Fischer-Nagel and Heiderose Fischer-Nagel, illustrated; Carolrhoda, 1989.

UTAH YOUNG ADULTS' BOOK AWARD
Lillian Heil
Children's Literature Association of Utah Executive Board
210-L MCKB
Brigham Young University
Provo, UT 84602
   This young adult's choice award was begun in 1991 and is sponsored by the Children's Literature Association of Utah.

1991 *The Other Side of Dark* by Joan Lowery Nixon, not illustrated; Delacorte, 1986.

1992 *Don't Look Behind You* by Lois Duncan, not illustrated; Delacorte, 1989.

V

VIRGINIA YOUNG READERS PROGRAM
Virginia State Reading Association
   Sponsored by the Virginia State Reading Association, this children's choice award was designed to encourage reading for pleasure among Virginia's students. When the program began in 1982, the only category was for the Elementary level. In 1984, the category was changed to Middle School and in 1985, it changed to High School. In 1986 and 1987, all three categories were covered. In 1988, a Primary category was added.

1982 **ELEMENTARY** *Island of the Blue Dolphins* by Scott O'Dell, not illustrated; Houghton Mifflin, 1960.

1983 **ELEMENTARY** *Bridge to Terabithia* by Katherine Paterson, illustrated by Donna Diamond; Crowell, 1977.

1984 **MIDDLE SCHOOL** *The Westing Game* by Ellen Raskin, not illustrated; Dutton, 1978.

1985 **HIGH SCHOOL** *The Outsiders* by S.E. Hinton, not illustrated; Viking, 1967; Dell, 1968.

1986 **ELEMENTARY** *Superfudge* by Judy Blume, not illustrated; Dutton, 1980.

1986 **MIDDLE SCHOOL** *The Cat Ate My Gymsuit* by Paula Danziger, not illustrated; Delacorte, 1974.

1986 **HIGH SCHOOL** *The Third Eye* by Mollie Hunter, not illustrated; Harper & Row, 1979.

1987 **ELEMENTARY** *My Friend, the Vampire* by Angela Sommer-Bodenburg, illustrated by Amelie Glienke; Dial, 1984.

1987 **MIDDLE SCHOOL** *The Curse of the Blue Figurine* by John Bellairs, illustrated by Edward Gorey; Dial, 1983.

1987 **HIGH SCHOOL** *The Man in the Woods* by Rosemary Wells, not illustrated; Dial, 1984.

1988 **PRIMARY** *In a Dark, Dark Room and Other Scary Stories* by Alvin Schwartz, illustrated by Dirk Zimmer; Harper & Row, 1984.

1988 **ELEMENTARY** *The Indian in the Cupboard* by Lynne Reid Banks, illustrated by Brock Cole; Doubleday, 1980.

1988 **MIDDLE SCHOOL** *The Ghost in my Soup* by Judi Miller, not illustrated; Bantam, 1985.

1988 **HIGH SCHOOL** *Izzy, Willy-Nilly* by Cynthia Voigt, not illustrated; Atheneum, 1986.

1989 **PRIMARY** *Heckedy Peg* by Audrey Wood, illustrated by Don Wood; Harcourt Brace Jovanovich, 1987.

1989 **ELEMENTARY** *Wait Til Helen Comes* by Mary Downing Hahn, not illustrated; Clarion, 1986.

1989 **MIDDLE SCHOOL** *The Other Side of Dark* by Joan Lowery Nixon, not illustrated; Delacorte, 1986.

1989 **HIGH SCHOOL** *The Face at the Edge of the World* by Eve Bunting, not illustrated; Clarion, 1985.

1990 **PRIMARY** *The Magic School Bus Inside the Earth* by Joanna Cole, illustrated by Bruce Degen; Scholastic, 1987.

1990 **ELEMENTARY** *Christina's Ghost* by Betty Ren Wright, not illustrated; Holiday House, 1985.

1990 **MIDDLE SCHOOL** *Hatchet* by Gary Paulsen, not illustrated; Bradbury, 1987.

1990 **HIGH SCHOOL** *A Tale of Terror* by Avi, not illustrated; Bradbury, 1986.

1991 **PRIMARY** *Two Bad Ants* written and illustrated by Chris Van Allsburg; Houghton Mifflin, 1988.

1991 **ELEMENTARY** *Matilda* by Roald Dahl, illustrated by Quentin Blake; Viking Kestrel, 1988.

1991 **MIDDLE SCHOOL** *Good Night, Mr. Tom* by Michelle Magorian, not illustrated; Harper & Row, 1981.

1991 **HIGH SCHOOL** *Say Goodnight, Gracie* by Julie Reece Deaver, not illustrated; Harper & Row, 1988.

1992 **PRIMARY** *The Great White Man-Eating Shark* by Margaret Mahy, illustrated by Jonathan Allen; Dial, 1990.

1992 **ELEMENTARY** *The Doll in the Garden* by Mary Downing Hahn, illustrated; Clarion, 1989.

1992 **MIDDLE SCHOOL** *A Family Apart* by Joan Lowery Nixon, not illustrated; Bantam, 1987.

1992 **HIGH SCHOOL** *Don't Look Behind You* by Lois Duncan, not illustrated; Delacorte, 1989.

VOLUNTEER STATE BOOK AWARD
(formerly Tennessee Children's Choice Book Award)

Dr. Beverly Youree
YESPS Dept.
Middle Tennessee State University
Murfreesboro, TN 37132
   This annual children's choice award was first presented in 1979, when it was known as the Tennessee Children's Choice Award. The award program was created to promote increasing awareness, interest, and enjoyment of good, new children's literature. It was also hoped that children of all reading levels would enjoy the same books as their peers through the community effort of reading the selected books aloud.
   Since 1989, when the name changed, the award has been given in four categories, Primary (K-3); Intermediate (grades 4-6); Middle/Junior High (grades 7-9); and High School (grades 10-12).

Each year a master list for each category is chosen by school and public librarians and library educators. Students are encouraged to read or have read aloud books from this list. Each child votes for his or her favorite book. A plaque is presented to the author of the winning titles at the Tennessee Library Association convention.

Some of the specific criteria follow: (1) Only one title of any one author will be included on the list; (2) Titles published in the five years prior to the year of voting are eligible; (3) Only books written by authors residing in the U.S. will be considered; and (4) Textbooks, anthologies, translations, and books from foreign publishers are not eligible.

1979 *How to Eat Fried Worms* by Thomas Rockwell, illustrated by Emily McCully; Watts, 1973.

1980 *Ramona and her Father* by Beverly Cleary, illustrated by Alan Tiegreen; Morrow, 1977.

1981 *Shadows* by Lynn Hall, illustrated by Joseph Cellini; Follett, 1977.

1982 *Superfudge* by Judy Blume, not illustrated; Dutton, 1980.

1983 *The Cybil War* by Betsy Byars, illustrated by Gail Owens; Viking, 1981.

1984 *Howliday Inn* by James Howe, illustrated by Lynn Munsinger; Atheneum, 1982.

1985 *When the Boys Ran the House* by Joan Carris, illustrated by Carol Newsom; Lippincott, 1982.

1986 *Operation: Dump the Chump* by Barbara Park, not illustrated; Knopf, 1982.

1987 *Skinnybones* by Barbara Park, not illustrated; Knopf, 1982.

1988 *The War With Grandpa* by Robert Kimmel Smith, illustrated by Richard Lauter; Delacorte, 1984.

1989 GRADES K-3 *In a Dark, Dark Room and Other Scary Stories* by Alvin Schwartz, illustrated by Dirk Zimmer; Harper & Row, 1984.

1989 GRADES 4-6 *Wait Til Helen Comes* by Mary Downing Hahn, not illustrated; Clarion, 1986.

1989 GRADES 7-9 *Dogsong* by Gary Paulsen, not illustrated; Bradbury, 1985.

1989 GRADES 10-12 *Izzy, Willy-Nilly* by Cynthia Voigt, not illustrated; Atheneum, 1986.

1990 GRADES K-3 *The Magic School Bus at the Waterworks* by Joanna Cole, illustrated by Bruce Degen; Scholastic, 1986.

1990 GRADES 4-7 *Beetles, Lightly Toasted* by Phyllis Reynolds Naylor, not illustrated; Atheneum, 1987.

1990 GRADES 7-9 *Shadow Club* by Neal Shusterman, not illustrated; Little Brown, 1988.

1990 GRADES 10-12 *Say Goodnight, Gracie* by Julie Reece Deaver, not illustrated; Harper & Row, 1988.

1991-92 GRADES K-3 *No Jumping on the Bed* written and illustrated by Tedd Arnold; Dial, 1987.

1991-92 GRADES 4-6 *There's a Boy In the Girls' Bathroom* by Louis Sachar, not illustrated; Knopf, 1987.

1991-92 GRADES 7-9 *Something Upstairs: A Tale of Ghosts* by Avi, not illustrated; Orchard, 1988.

W

WASHINGTON CHILDREN'S CHOICE PICTURE BOOK AWARD

Washington Library Media Association
Kathy Leland
Box 1413
Bothell, WA 98041

Established in 1982 by Barbara Jean Yonck, this award allows children, from kindergarten through third grade, in the state of Washington, to select their favorite book. Nominations of picture books are made to a committee which compiles a ballot from which the children vote. Each child casts one vote for their favorite picture book.

The following criteria govern the ballot composition: (1) Titles must be published three or four years prior to the award year; (2) Only picture book format. Not limited to fiction; may include photography and wordless books; (3) The winning book may not reappear on the following year's ballot, but no restriction is placed on non-winning titles; (4) Books published or distributed in the U.S. and are still in print; (5) Ballot may contain no more than twenty titles.

The winning author receives a plate with the book award logo at the Washington Library Media Association conference in October.

1982 *Cross-country Cat* by Mary Calhoun, illustrated by Erick Ingraham; Morrow, 1979.

1983 *Space Case* by Edward Marshall, illustrated by James Marshall; Dial, 1980.

1984 *Jumanji* written and illustrated by Chris Van Allsburg; Houghton Mifflin, 1981.

1985 *Nimby* written and illustrated by Jasper Tomkins; Green Tiger Press, 1982.

1986 *The Unicorn and the Lake* by Marianna Mayer, illustrated by Michael Hague; Dial, 1982.

1987 *In a Dark, Dark Room and Other Scary Stories* by Alvin Schwartz, illustrated by Dirk Zimmer; Harper & Row, 1984.

1988 *King Bidgood's in the Bathtub* by Audrey Wood, illustrated by Don Wood; Harcourt, Brace, Jovanovich, 1985.

1989 *The Magic School Bus at the Waterworks* by Joanna Cole, illustrated by Bruce Degen; Scholastic, 1986.

1990 *Amos: The Story of an Old Dog and His Couch* written by Howie Schneider and Susan Seligson, illustrated by Howie Schneider; Joy Street Books, 1987.

1991 *Two Bad Ants* written and illustrated by Chris Van Allsburg; Houghton Mifflin, 1988.

1992 *Hershel and the Hanukkah Goblins* by Eric Kimmel, illustrated by Trina Schart Hyman; Holiday House, 1989.

THE WASHINGTON POST/CHILDREN'S BOOK GUILD NONFICTION AWARD

Patricia M. Markun
Public Relations Coordinator
4405 W St., NW
Washington, DC 23185-1626

This annual award for nonfiction literature was established in 1977 by the Washington Children's Book Guild and is co sponsored by The Washington Post. The award is presented to an author for the creation of a substantial body of outstanding nonfiction books. A committee discusses the eligible candidates and makes the final decision. The winner is presented with a monetary award and a crystal cube at the Children's Book Week luncheon held in Washington, D.C.

1977 David Macaulay

1978 Millicent Selsam

1979 Jean Fritz

1980 Shirley Glubok

1981 Milton Meltzer

1982 Tana Hoban

1983 Patricia Lauber

1984 Jill Krementz

1985 Isaac Asimov

1986 Kathryn Lasky

1987 Gail Gibbons

1988 Jim Arnosky

1989 Leonard Everett Fisher

1990 Brent Ashabranner

1991 Joanna Cole

1992 Russell Freedman

1993 Seymour Simon

FRANKLIN WATTS JUVENILE FICTION AWARD

discontinued

Presented for a distinguished contribution to children's literature, the Franklin Watts Juvenile Fiction Award was first given in 1958. This annual award, sponsored by the Franklin Watts Publishing Company, was given for a manuscript that children ages eight through twelve could read themselves. The winning author received a $1000 prize and a $2500 advance on royalties.

1958 *The Cabin at Medicine Springs* by Lulita Crawford Pritchett, illustrated by Anthony D'Adamo; Watts, 1958.

1959 *The Tent Under the Spider Tree* by Gene Inyart, illustrated by Carol Beech; Watts, 1959.

1960 No Award

1961 *Adam Gray, Stowaway: A Story of the China Trade* by Herbert E. Arntson, illustrated by Henry S. Gillette; Watts, 1961.

WEEKLY READER CHILDREN'S BOOK CLUB AWARD

First presented in 1992, this award is sponsored by the Weekly Reader Book Club. Members of the book club vote for their favorite picture book via a survey. The winning author/illustrator receives a plaque and a $1000 cash award.

1992 *Arthur's Baby* written and illustrated by Marc Brown; Little Brown, 1987.

WEST AUSTRALIAN YOUNG READERS BOOK AWARD

Australian Library and Information Association
Box E441
Queen Victoria Terrace
Canberra, ACT 2600
Australia

First awarded in 1980, this children's choice award is organized on a statewide basis for young readers aged nine through fifteen. The purpose of the award is to generate enthusiasm for pleasure reading, to enrich children's reading experiences, and to develop their powers of discrimination in comparing quality literature. It also provides a balance to the adult selected awards, which are not always popular with children.

The West Australian Young Readers Book Award is modeled on similar programs in the U.S., particularly the Georgia Children's Book Award. The award is presented in two categories: primary (ages 9-12) and secondary (ages 13-15). The winning authors receive a trophy crafted by a local artist in Western Australian jarrah in the form of a book.

1980 **PRIMARY** *Tales of a Fourth Grade Nothing* by Judy Blume, illustrated by Roy Doty; Dutton, 1972; Bodley Head, 1982.

1980 **SECONDARY** *My Darling Villain* by Lynne Reid Banks, not illustrated; Bodley Head, 1977; Harper, 1977.

1981 **PRIMARY** *Sadako and the Thousand Paper Cranes* by Eleanor Coerr, illustrated by Ronald Himler; Putnam, 1977; Dell, 1979.

1981 **SECONDARY** *Don't Hurt Laurie!* by Willo Davis Roberts, illustrated by Ruth Sanderson; Atheneum, 1977.

1982 **PRIMARY** *Superfudge* by Judy Blume, not illustrated; Dutton, 1980; Bodley Head, 1982.

1982 **SECONDARY** *Forbidden Paths of Thual* by Victor Kelleher, illustrated by Antony Maitland; Kestrel, 1981.

1983 **PRIMARY** *Samantha on Stage* by Susan Clement Farrar, illustrated by Ruth Sanderson; Dial, 1979.

1983 **SECONDARY** *Goodnight, Mr. Tom* by Michelle Magorian, not illustrated; Kestrel, 1981.

1984 **PRIMARY** *George's Marvellous Medicine* by Roald Dahl, illustrated by Quentin Blake; Cape, 1981.

1984 **SECONDARY** *Did You Hear What Happened to Andrea?* by Gloria Miklowitz, not illustrated; Delacorte, 1979.

1985 **PRIMARY** *The BFG* by Roald Dahl, illustrated by Quentin Blake; Cape, 1982.

1985 **SECONDARY** *The Secret Diary of Adrian Mole, Aged 13 3/4* by Sue Townsend, not illustrated; Methuen, 1982.

1986 **OVERSEAS PRIMARY** *The Witches* by Roald Dahl, illustrated by Quentin Blake; Farrar, 1983.

1986 **OVERSEAS SECONDARY** *The Growing Pains of Adrian Mole* by Sue Townsend, illustrated by Caroline Holden; Methuen, 1984.

1986 **AUSTRALIAN PRIMARY** *Hating Alison Ashley* by Robin Klein, not illustrated; Penguin, 1984.

1986 **AUSTRALIAN SECONDARY** *People Might Hear You* by Robin Klein, not illustrated; Puffin, 1983.

1987 **PRIMARY** *Selby's Secret* by Duncan Ball, illustrated by Allan Stomann; Angus & Robertson, 1985.

1987 SECONDARY *The eyes of Karen Connors* by Lois Duncan, not illustrated; Hamilton, 1985.

Back Home by Michelle Magorian, not illustrated; Viking, 1985; Harper & Row, 1984.

1988 PRIMARY *Grandma Cadbury's Trucking Tales* by Dianne Bates, illustrated by Kevin Burgemeestre; Angus & Robertson, 1988.

1988 SECONDARY *Dead Birds Singing* by Marc Talbert, not illustrated; Hamilton, 1986; Little Brown, 1985.

1989 PRIMARY *Matilda* by Roald Dahl, illustrated by Quentin Blake; Cape, 1988.

1989 SECONDARY *When the Phone Rang* by Harry Mazer, not illustrated; Scholastic, 1985.

1990 PRIMARY *Selby Speaks* by Duncan Ball, illustrated by Allan Stomann; Angus & Robertson, 1988.

1990 SECONDARY *Redwall* by Brian Jacques, illustrated by Gary Chalk; Hutchinson Children's, 1986.

1991 PRIMARY *Selby Screams* by Duncan Ball, illustrated by Allan Stomann; Angus & Robertson, 1989.

1991 SECONDARY *Mossflower* by Brian Jacques, illustrated by Gary Chalk; Hutchinson, 1988; Philomel, 1988.

1992 PRIMARY *Uncanny! Even More Surprising Stories* by Paul Jennings, not illustrated; Puffin, 1988.

1992 SECONDARY *Mattimeo* by Brian Jacques, illustrated by Gary Chalk; Hutchinson, 1989; Philomel, 1990.

1992 HOFFMAN AWARD *Brother Night* by Victor Kelleher, illustrated by Peter Clarke; Julia MacRae, 1990.

WEST VIRGINIA CHILDREN'S BOOK AWARD

West Virginia Educational Media Assn.
Linda Freeman, President
RFD 2, Box 264
Elkins, WV 26241

Established in the Fall of 1984 by Patricia Benedum, Elizabeth Howard, Joyce Lang, and Barbara Mertins, this children's choice award is selected by students in grades three through six. The award's purpose is to enrich the lives of children by encouraging the reading of books of literary quality. The award provides a personal relationship and interaction between authors and readers in order to increase children's enjoyment of the books. Fiction books published in the United States within the last three years and still in print are considered for inclusion on the master list. An inscribed plaque is presented to the winning author annually in the spring.

1984-1985 *Jumanji* written and illustrated by Chris Van Allsburg; Houghton Mifflin, 1981.

1985-1986 *Mustard* by Charlotte Graeber, illustrated by Donna Diamond; Macmillan, 1982.

1986-1987 *Ralph S. Mouse* by Beverly Cleary, illustrated by Paul O. Zelinsky; Morrow, 1982.

1987-88 *Herbie Jones* by Suzy Kline, illustrated by Richard Williams; Putnam, 1985.

1987-88 HONOR BOOK *Eddie and the Fairy Godpuppy* by Willo Davis Roberts, illustrated by Leslie Morrill; Atheneum, 1984.

King Bidgood's in the Bathtub by Audrey Wood, illustrated by Don Wood; Harcourt Brace Jovanovich, 1985.

1988-89 *Class Clown* by Johanna Hurwitz, illustrated by Sheila Hamanaka; Morrow, 1987.

1988-89 HONOR BOOK *The Castle in the Attic* by Elizabeth Winthrop, illustrated by Trina Schart Hyman; Holiday House, 1985.

On My Honor by Marion Dane Bauer, not illustrated; Clarion, 1986.

1989-90 *Fudge* by Charlotte T. Graeber, illustrated by Cheryl Harness; Lothrop, Lee & Shepard, 1987.

1989-90 HONOR BOOK *The Kid in the Red Jacket* by Barbara Park, not illustrated; Knopf, 1987.

1990-91 *There's a Boy in the Girls' Bathroom* by Louis Sachar, not illustrated; Knopf, 1987.

WESTERN HERITAGE CHILDREN'S BOOK AWARD

National Cowboy Hall of Fame and Western Heritage Center
1700 N.E. 63 Street
Oklahoma City, OK 73111

Sponsored by the National Cowboy Hall of Fame since 1961, the Western Heritage Awards have twelve different categories. One of the categories is juvenile literature, which was first recognized in 1962. Any juvenile book published in the preceding year is eligible. Each entry is judged by a panel of experts for artistic merit, integrity and outstanding achievement in portraying the spirit of the pioneers of the developing West. The Wrangler Trophy (a replica of a C. M. Russell bronze) is presented to the winner in April at the Cowboy Hall of Fame in Oklahoma City.

1962 *King of the Mountain Men: The Life of Jim Bridger* by Gene Caesar, illustrated with maps; Dutton, 1961.

1963 *The Book of the West: An Epic of America's Wild Frontier* by Charles Chilton, illustrated by Eric Tansley; Bobbs Merrill, 1962.

1964 *Killer-of-Death* by Betty Baker, illustrated by John Kaufmann; Harper, 1963.

1965 *The Greatest Cattle Drive* by Paul I. Wellman, illustrated by Lorence F. Bjorklund; Houghton, 1964.

1966 *Land Rush* by Carl G. Hodges, illustrated by John Martinez; Duell-Sloan, 1965.

1967 *Mustang: Wild Spirit of the West* by Marguerite Henry, illustrated by Robert Lougheed; Rand, 1966.

1968 *Down the River, Westward Ho!* by Eric Scott, not illustrated; Meredith, 1967.

1969 *Edge of Two Worlds* by Weyman Jones, illustrated by J.C. Kocsis; Dial, 1968.

1970 *An Awful Name to Live Up To* by Jossie Hosford, illustrated by Charles Geer; Meredith, 1969.

1971 *And One Was a Wooden Indian* by Betty Baker, not illustrated; Macmillan, 1970.

1972 *The Black Mustanger* by Richard Wormser, illustrated by Donald Bolognese; Morrow, 1971.

1973 *Famous American Explorers* by Bern Keating, illustrated by Lorence F. Bjorklund; Rand, 1972.

1974 No Award

1975 *Susy's Scoundrel* by Harold Keith, illustrated by John Schoenherr; Crowell, 1974.

1976 *Owl in the Cedar Tree* by Natachee Scott Momaday, illustrated by Don Perceval; Northland Press, 1975.

1977-1978 No Award

1979 *The Obstinate Land* by Harold Keith, not illustrated; Crowell, 1977.

1980 *The Little House Cookbook* by Barbara M. Walker, illustrated by Garth Williams; Harper, 1979.

1981-1983 No Award

1984 *Children of the Wild West* by Russell Freedman, illustrated with photographs; Clarion, 1983.

1985 No Award

1986 *Prairie Songs* by Pam Conrad, illustrated by Darryl S. Zudeck; Harper, 1985.

1987 *Happily May I Walk: American Indians and Alaska Natives Today* by Arlene Hirschfelder, illustrated; Scribner, 1986.

1988 *The Covered Wagon & Other Adventures* by Lynn H. Scott, illustrated; University of Nebraska Press, 1987.

1989 *Stay Put, Robbie McAmis* by Frances G. Tunbo, illustrated by Charles Shaw; Texas Christian University Press, 1988.

1990 *Letters To Oma: A Young German Girl's Account of Her First Year in Texas, 1847* by Marj Gurasich, illustrated by Barbara Whitehead; Texas Christian University Press, 1989.

1991 *Bunkhouse Journal* by Diane Johnston Hamm, not illustrated; Scribner, 1990.

1992 *Monster Slayer: A Navajo Folktale* by Vee Browne, illustrated by Baje Whitethorne; Northland Publishing, 1991.

WESTERN WRITERS OF AMERICA SPUR AWARD
(formerly GOLDEN SPUR AWARD)

Barbara Ketcham, Secretary-Treasurer
Western Writers of America
Box 823
Sheridan, WY 82801

Sponsored by the Western Writers of America since 1954, the Spur Award has six different categories, one for children's literature. The Spur Award was established to further the cause of western literature and to upgrade and improve the quality. Fiction and nonfiction titles may be submitted by authors or publishers. Three judges in each category make the final selection. The winning author receives a plaque with a mounted golden spur.

Some years, a separate prize is given for fiction and nonfiction; other years, the two categories have been combined.

1954 *Sagebrush Sorrel* by Frank C. Robertson, illustrated by Lee Townsend; Nelson, 1953.

1955 *Young Hero of the Range* by Stephen Payne, illustrated by Charles H. Geer; Lantern Press, 1954.

1956 No Award

1957 *Trapping the Silver Beaver* by Charles Niehuis, illustrated by Chris Kenyon; Dodd Mead, 1956.

1958 *Wolf Brother* by James Kjelgaard, not illustrated; Holiday House, 1957.

1959 *Steamboat Up the Missouri* by Dale White, illustrated by Charles H. Geer; Viking, 1958.

1960 FICTION *Their Shining Hour: Based on Events in the life of Susanna Dickenson at the Siege of the Alamo* by Ramona Maher, not illustrated; Day, 1960.

1960 NONFICTION *Hold Back the Hunter* by Dale White, not illustrated; Day, 1959.

1961 FICTION *The Horse-talker* by J.R. Williams, not illustrated; Prentice Hall, 1960.

1961 NONFICTION *South Pass - 1868 (His) Journal of the Wyoming Gold Rush* written and illustrated by James Chisholm, edited by Lola M. Homsher; University of Nebraska Press, 1960.

1962 FICTION No Award

1962 NONFICTION No Award

1963 FICTION No Award

1963 NONFICTION *The Western Horse: A Handbook* by Natlee P. Kenoyer, illustrated by Randy Steffen; Meredith, 1962.

1964 FICTION *By the Great Horn Spoon!* by Sid Fleischman, illustrated by Eric Von Schmidt; Atlantic-Little, 1963.

The Story Catcher by Mari Sandoz, illustrated by Elsie J. McCorkell; Westminster, 1963.

1964 NONFICTION No Award

1965 FICTION *Ride a Northbound Horse* by Richard Wormser, illustrated by Charles Geer; Morrow, 1964.

1965 NONFICTION No Award

1966 FICTION *The Stubborn One* by Rutherford Montgomery, illustrated by Don Miller; Duell-Sloan-Pearce, 1965.

1966 NONFICTION No Award

1967 FICTION *The Burning Glass* by Edgar Johnson and Annabell Johnson, not illustrated; Harper, 1966.

1967 NONFICTION *Valley of the Smallest: The Life Story of a Shrew* by Aileen Fisher, illustrated by Jean Zallinger; Crowell, 1966.

1968 FICTION *Half Breed* by Evelyn S. Lampman, illustrated by Ann Grifalconi; Doubleday, 1967.

The Dunderhead War by Betty Baker, not illustrated; Harper & Row, 1967.

1968 NONFICTION *To the Pacific with Lewis and Clark* by Edwin R. Bingham and Ralph K. Andrist, illustrated with photographs, maps and drawings; Harper & Row, 1967.

1969 FICTION *Middl'un* by Elizabeth Burleson, illustrated by George Roth; Follett, 1968.

1969 NONFICTION *Rifles and Warbonnets* by Marian Templeton Place, not illustrated; Washburn, 1968.

1970 FICTION *The Meeker Massacre* by Lewis B. Patten and Wayne D. Overholser, illustrated with photographs; Cowles, 1969.

1970 NONFICTION *Conquistadores and Pueblos: The Story of the American Southwest 1540-1848* by Olga W. Hall-Quest, illustrated by Marian Ebert; Dutton, 1969.

1971 FICTION *A Shield of Clover* by Peggy Simson Curry, not illustrated; McKay, 1970.

1971 NONFICTION *Indian Foe, Indian Friend: The Story of William S. Harney* by Jules Archer, illustrated with photographs; Crowell- Collier, 1970.

1972 FICTION *The Black Mustanger* by Richard Wormser, illustrated by Don Bolognese; Morrow, 1971.

1972 NONFICTION *Lords of the Earth: The History of the Navajo Indians* by Jules Loh, illustrated with photographs; Crowell- Collier, 1971.

1973 FICTION *Only Earth and Sky Last Forever* by Nathaniel Benchley, not illustrated; Harper, 1972.

1973 NONFICTION *The Tiguas: The Lost Tribe of City Indians* by Stan Steiner, illustrated with photographs; Crowell-Collier, 1972.

1974 FICTION *Freedom Trail* by Jeanne Williams, not illustrated; Putnam, 1973.

1974 NONFICTION *Red Power on the Rio Grande: The Native American Revolution of 1680* by Franklin Folsom, illustrated by J.D. Roybal; Follett, 1973.

1975 FICTION *Dust of the Earth* by Bill Cleaver and Vera Cleaver, not illustrated; Lippincott, 1975.

1975 NONFICTION *Ride 'em Cowgirl* by Lynn Haney, illustrated by Peter Burchard; Putnam, 1975.

1976 *All Aboard! The Story of Passenger Trains in America* by Phil Ault, illustrated with photographs and old prints; Dodd, 1976.

1977 *A Shepherd Watches, a Shepherd Sings* by Louis Irigary and Theodore Taylor, illustrated with photographs; Doubleday, 1977.

1978 *The No-return Trail* by Sonia Levitin, not illustrated; Harcourt, 1978.

1979 No Award

1980 *Getting There: Frontier Travel without Power* by Suzanne Hilton, illustrated; Westminster, 1980.

1981 JUVENILE FICTION *The Last Run* by Mark Jonathan Harris, not illustrated; Lothrop, Lee & Shepard, 1981.

1981 JUVENILE NONFICTION No Award

1982 JUVENILE FICTION *Before the Lark* by Irene Bennett Brown, not illustrated; Atheneum, 1982.

1982 JUVENILE NONFICTION No Award

1984 *Thunder on the Tennessee* by Gary Clifton Wisler, not illustrated; Lodestar, 1983.

1985 *Trapped in Sliprock Canyon* by Gloria Skurzynski, illustrated by Daniel San Souci; Lothrop, Lee & Shepard, 1984.

1986 *Prairie Songs* by Pam Conrad, illustrated by Darryl S. Zudeck; Harper, 1985.

1987 *Make Way for Sam Houston* by Jean Fritz, illustrated by Elise Primavera; Putnam, 1986.

1988 *A Family Apart* by Joan Lowery Nixon, not illustrated; Bantam, 1987.

1989 *In the Face of Danger* by Joan Lowery Nixon, not illustrated; Bantam, 1988.

1990 *My Daniel* by Pam Conrad, not illustrated; Harper & Row, 1989.

1991 JUVENILE FICTION *Honey Girl* by Madge Harrah, illustrated; Avon, 1990.

1991 JUVENILE NONFICTION *Woodsong* by Gary Paulsen, with photographs by Ruth Wright Paulsen; Bradbury, 1990.

1992 JUVENILE FICTION *Rescue* Josh McGuire by Ben Mikaelsen, not illustrated; Hyperion, 1991.

WHITBREAD LITERARY AWARDS

The Booksellers Association of Great Britain and Ireland
Alice Kennelly
Kellaway, Limited
2 Portland Rd.
Holland Park
London W11 4LA
England

Founded by the Whitbread Brewery in 1971, the Whitbread Literary Awards are administered by the Booksellers Association of Great Britain and Ireland. This annual award has five different categories, including children's literature. The aim of the Whitbread Awards is to promote a high standard of English literature.

Eligible authors include those who have lived in the United Kingdom or Ireland for three years and who have had a book published in the United Kingdom or Ireland during the award year. Eligible books are to be submitted directly by the publishers. Each category winner receives a prize of £1250. The overall winner of the Whitbread Book of the Year receives an additional £18,750. Total prize money is £25,000.

1972 *The Diddakoi* by Rumer Godden, illustrated by Creina Glegg; Macmillan, 1972.

1973 *The Butterfly Ball and the Grasshopper's Feast* by William Plomer, illustrated by Alan Aldridge; Cape, 1973.

1974 *The Emperor's Winding Sheet* by Jill Paton Walsh, not illustrated; Macmillan, 1974.

How Tom Beat Captain Najork and his Hired Sportsmen by Russell Hoban, illustrated by Quentin Blake; Cape, 1974.

1975 No Award

1976 *A Stitch in Time* by Penelope Lively, not illustrated; Heinemann, 1976.

1977 *No End to Yesterday* by Shelagh Macdonald, not illustrated; Deutsch, 1977.

1978 *The Battle of Bubble and Squeak* by A. Philippa Pearce, illustrated by Alan Baker; Deutsch, 1978.

1979 *Tulku* by Peter Dickinson, not illustrated; Unicorn/Dutton, 1979.

1980 *John Diamond* by Leon Garfield, illustrated by Antony Maitland; Kestrel, 1980.

1981 *The Hollow Land* by Jane Gardam, illustrated by Janet Rawlins; MacRae, 1981.

1982 *The Song of Pentecost* by William J. Corbett, illustrated by Martin Unsell; Methuen, 1982.

1982 RUNNERSUP *The Secret World of Polly Flint* by Helen Cresswell, illustrated by Shirley Felts; Faber, 1982.

War Horse by Michael Morpurgo, not illustrated; Kaye & Ward, 1982; Greenwillow, 1983.

1983 *The Witches* by Roald Dahl, illustrated by Quentin Blake; Cape, 1982; Farrar, 1983.

1983 **RUNNERSUP** *Donkey's Crusade* by Jean Morris, not illustrated; Chatto & Windus, 1983.

A Parcel of Patterns by Jill Paton Walsh, not illustrated; Kestrel, 1983; Farrar, 1983.

1984 *The Queen of Pharisees' Children* by Barbara Willard, not illustrated; MacRae, 1983.

1984 **RUNNERSUP** *On the Edge* by Gillian Cross, not illustrated; Oxford, 1984; Holiday House, 1985.

Charlie Lewis Plays for Time by Gene Kemp, illustrated by Vanessa Julian-Ottie; Faber, 1984.

1985 *The Nature of the Beast* by Janni Howker, not illustrated; MacRae, 1985; Greenwillow, 1985.

1986 *The Coal House* by Andrew Taylor, not illustrated; Collins, 1986.

1987 *A Little Lower than the Angels* by Geraldine McCaughrean, not illustrated; Oxford University Press, 1987.

1988 *Awaiting Developments* by Judy Allen, not illustrated; Julia MacRae, 1988; Walker, 1989.

1989 *Why Weeps the Brogan?* by Hugh Scott, not illustrated; Walker Books, 1989.

1990 *AK* by Peter Dickinson, not illustrated; Gollancz, 1990.

1991 *Harvey Angell* by Diana Hendry, not illustrated; Julia MacRae, 1991.

1992 *The Great Elephant Chase* by Gillian Cross; Oxford University Press, 1992.

WILLIAM ALLEN WHITE CHILDREN'S BOOK AWARD

Mary Bogan, Executive Secretary
William Allen White Library
Box 51 / 1200 Commercial
Emporia State University
Emporia, KS 66801

The William Allen White Children's Book Award Program, founded in 1952 by Ruth Garver Gagliardo, was the first statewide reader's choice award program. This award honors the memory of William Allen White by encouraging the boys and girls of Kansas to read and enjoy good books. Established and directed by Emporia State University, this program has stimulated the development of reader's choice award programs throughout the U.S.

Children in grades four through eight vote for their favorite book from a master list compiled by the White Award Book Selection Committee. Eligible for inclusion on the master list are trade books (not texts), fiction, nonfiction, biography and poetry. Anthologies, translations, and books by foreign publishers are ineligible. To be eligible for inclusion on the annual White Award Master List a book must have been first published in the United States within the calendar year immediately preceding the year when the master list is selected. Authors selected must reside in The United States, Canada, or Mexico.

The following criteria are used in selection of titles for the master list: (1) qualities of originality and vitality, (2) clarity, (3) factual accuracy in the case of nonfiction, (4) sincerity of author and respect for reader, and (5) acceptance by children.

The winning author receives a bronze medal designed by Elden Tefft.

1953 *Amos Fortune, Free Man* by Elizabeth Yates, illustrated by Nora S. Unwin; Aladdin, 1950.

1954 *Little Vic* by Doris Gates, illustrated by Kate Seredy; Viking, 1951.

1955 *Cherokee Bill: Oklahoma Pacer* by Jean Bailey, illustrated by Pers Crowell; Abingdon-Cokesbury, 1952.

1956 *Brighty of the Grand Canyon* by Marguerite Henry, illustrated by Welsey Dennis; Rand McNally, 1953.

1957 *Daniel 'Coon: The Story of a Pet Raccoon* written and illustrated by Phoebe Erickson; Knopf, 1954.

1958 *White Falcon* by Elliott Arnold, illustrated by Frederick T. Chapman; Knopf, 1955.

1959 *Old Yeller* by Fred Gipson, illustrated by Carl Burger; Harper, 1956.

1960 *Flaming Arrows* by William O. Steele, illustrated by Paul Galdone; Harcourt, 1957.

1961 *Henry Reed, Inc.* by Keith Robertson, illustrated by Robert McCloskey; Viking, 1958.

1962 *The Helen Keller Story* by Catherine O. Peare, not illustrated; Crowell, 1959.

1963 *Island of the Blue Dolphins* by Scott O'Dell, not illustrated; Houghton, 1960.

1964 *The Incredible Journey: A Tale of Three Animals* by Shelia Every Burnford, illustrated by Carl Burger; Little Brown, 1961.

1965 *Bristle Face* by Zachary Ball, not illustrated; Holiday House, 1962.

1966 *Rascal: A Memoir of a Better Era* by Sterling North, illustrated by John Schoenherr; Dutton, 1963.

1967 *The Grizzly* by Annabel Johnson and Edgar Johnson, illustrated by Gilbert Riswold; Harper, 1964.

1968 *The Mouse and the Motorcycle* by Beverly Cleary, illustrated by Louis Darling; Morrow, 1965.

1969 *Henry Reed's Babysitting Service* by Keith Robertson, illustrated by Robert McCloskey; Viking, 1966.

1970 *From the Mixed-up Files of Mrs. Basil E. Frankweiler* written and illustrated by E.L. Konigsburg; Atheneum, 1967.

1971 *Kavik, the Wolf Dog* by Walt Morey, illustrated by Peter Parnall; Dutton, 1968.

1972 *Sasha, my Friend* by Barbara Corcoran, illustrated by Richard L. Shell; Atheneum, 1969.

1973 *The Trumpet of the Swan* by E.B. White, illustrated by Edward Frascino; Harper, 1970.

1974 *The Headless Cupid* by Zilpha Keatley Snyder, illustrated by Alton Raible; Atheneum, 1971.

Mrs. Frisby and the Rats of NIMH by Robert C. O'Brien, illustrated by Zena Bernstein; Atheneum, 1971.

1975 *Dominic* written and illustrated by William Steig; Farrar, 1972.

1976 *Socks* by Beverly Cleary, illustrated by Beatrice Darwin; Morrow, 1973.

1977 *Harry Cat's Pet Puppy* by George Selden, illustrated by Garth Williams; Farrar, 1974.

1978 *The Great Christmas Kidnapping Caper* by Jean Van Leeuwen, illustrated by Steven Kellogg; Dial, 1975.

1979 *The Summer of the Monkeys* by Wilson Rawls, not illustrated; Doubleday, 1976.

1980 *The Pinballs* by Betsy Byars, not illustrated; Harper, 1977.

1981 *The Great Gilly Hopkins* by Katherine Paterson, not illustrated; Crowell, 1978.

1982 *The Magic of the Glits* by Carole S. Adler, illustrated by Ati Forberg; Macmillan, 1979.

1983 *Peppermints in the Parlor* by Barbara Brooks Wallace, not illustrated; Atheneum, 1980.

1984 *A Light in the Attic* written and illustrated by Shel Silverstein; Harper, 1981.

1985 *The Land I Lost: Adventures of a Boy in Vietnam* by Huynh Quang Nhuong, illustrated by Vo-Dinh Mai; Harper, 1982.

1986 *Daphne's Book* by Mary Downing Hahn, not illustrated; Clarion Books, 1983.

1987 *The War with Grandpa* by Robert Kimmel Smith, illustrated by Richard Lauter; Delacorte, 1984.

1988 *Cracker Jackson* by Betsy Byars, not illustrated; Viking Kestrel, 1985.

1989 *On My Honor* by Marion Dane Bauer, not illustrated; Clarion, 1986.

1990 *Hatchet* by Gary Paulsen, not illustrated; Bradbury, 1987.

1991 *Beauty* by Bill Wallace, not illustrated; Holiday House, 1988.

1992 *The Doll in the Garden* by Mary Downing Hahn, illustrated; Clarion, 1989.

1993 *Maniac Magee* by Jerry Spinelli, not illustrated; Little Brown, 1990.

WHITLEY AWARDS
Royal Zoological Society of New South Wales
P O Box 20
Mosman 2088
New South Wales, Australia

This award was established in 1978 by the Royal Zoological Society of New South Wales for the purpose of honoring excellence in Australasian zoological literature. The award was named for Gilbert Whitley, a well-known Australian zoologist. Eligible is Australasian zoological literature published within eighteen months of the May 31 deadline each year. The award covers all areas of zoology including field guides, historical zoology, children's books, symposium proceedings, text books limited editions, and periodicals, including children's magazines.

A Silver Medal is given for the best contribution to the natural history of Australasian animals or to the history of zoological studies in Australasia.

1980 *The Gould League Book of Australian Birds* by Don Goodsir, illustrated by Tony Oliver; Golden Press, 1979.

1981 *Feathers, Fur and Frills* written and illustrated by Kilmeny Niland; Hodder & Stoughton, 1980.

1982 *The Friends of Burramys* by June Epstein, illustrated by Pamela Conder; Oxford, 1981.

1983 *The Gould League Book of Australian Mammals* by Don Goodsir, illustrated by Tony Oliver; Golden Press, 1981.

1984 *Australian Animals* by Peter Sloan, illustrated by Ross Latham; Methuen Australia, 1983.

1985 *Australia's Prehistoric Animals* by Peter Murray, illustrated; Methuen Australia, 1984.

1986 *Sebastian Lives in a Hat* by Thelma Catterwall, illustrated by Kerry Argent; Omnibus, 1985.

1987 *The Arrow Book of Backyard Creatures* by Brian Macness; Ashton Scholastic, 1986.

1988 *Animal Tracks* by Carson Creagh and Kathie Atkinson, illustrated by Richard Hassall; Methuen Australia, 1986.

1989 **CHILDREN'S BOOK** *Aldita and the Forest* by Thelma Catterwall, illustrated by Derek Stone; Dent, 1988; Houghton Mifflin, 1989, c1988.

1989 **ZOOLOGICAL PHOTO ESSAY** *The Australian Echidna* by Eleanor Stodart, illustrated; Houghton Mifflin Australia, 1989; Houghton Mifflin, 1991.

1989 **EDUCATIONAL SERIES** *An Introduction To Insects* by Bettina Bird and Joan Short, illustrated by Deborah Savin.

Crocodilians; Martin Educational Bookshelf.

1990 *Australian Junior Field Guides* (series) by Eleanor Stodart; Weldon.

1991 **CHILDREN'S BOOK** *Tom's Friend* written and illustrated by Pat Reynolds; Allen & Unwin, 1990.

1991 **CHILDREN'S EDUCATIONAL SERIES** *Australian Museum's Young Naturalist* series by a variety of authors; Reed Books.

1991 **ILLUSTRATED CHILDREN'S BOOK** *Bush Song* written and illustrated by Tricia Oktober; Hodder & Stoughton, 1991.

1992 **CHILDREN'S EDUCATIONAL SERIES** *Picture Roo Books* series by Pauline Reilly, illustrated by Will Roland; Kangaroo Press, 1989-1992.

LAURA INGALLS WILDER AWARD
Association for Library Services to Children
American Library Association
50 East Huron St
Chicago, IL 60611

The Laura Ingalls Wilder Award was established in 1954 to honor the much loved creator of the Little House books. It is administered by the Association of Library Services to Children (ALSC). From 1954 to 1980, the award was presented every five years. Since 1980, the Wilder Award has been presented every three years to an author or illustrator whose books, published in the United States, have over a period of years made a substantial and lasting contribution to literature for children.

The ALSC has provided detailed definitions of the words and phrases used in the terms of the award. They are as follows: (1) "Author" or "illustrator" means co-authors or co-illustrators and persons who both write and illustrate. The person may be nominated posthumously. Some portion of the nominee's active career in books for children must have occurred in the twenty- five years prior to nomination. Citizenship or residence of the potential nominee is not to be considered. Honors and awards received in earlier years do not preclude consideration. (2) "Published in the United States" does not indicate that first publication had to be have been in the United States. It means that children's books written and/or illustrated by the nominee have been published in the United States, and it is those books that are to be considered. (3) "Over a period of years" means that at least some of the books by the nominee have been available to children for at least ten years. (4) "A substantial and lasting contribution" means that the books occupy an important place in literature for American children and that over the years children have read the books and that the books continue to be requested and read by children. (5) "Literature for children" indicates that the committee is to direct its attention only to that part of the potential nominee's total work which consists of books for children up to and including age fourteen. It further indicates that the committee is to select on the basis of the literary or artistic merit of the books for children.

A committee of six ALSC members receives nominations from the ALSC membership and selects a slate of nominees. The winner is chosen by a mail ballot of all ALSC members. The committee is asked to consider the following points when comprising the slate: (1) Whether some or all of the books are exceptionally notable and leading examples of the genre to which they belong; (2) Whether some or all of the books have established a new type of book or new trends in books available for children; (3) The committee should be aware of the entire body of work for children of the potential nominee, and may base its decision for nomination on the total body of work for children or on those portions of the total body of work which are of a substantial and lasting nature. (Taken from the guidelines adopted by the ALSC Board, January 1978).

A medal, designed by Garth Williams, an illustrator of the Little House series, is presented to the winner at the ALA summer conference.

1954 Laura Ingalls Wilder

1960 Clara Ingram Judson

1965 Ruth Sawyer

1970 E.B. White

1975 Beverly Cleary

1980 Theodor Geisel (Dr. Seuss)

1983 Maurice Sendak

1986 Jean Fritz

1989 Elizabeth George Speare

1992 Marcia Brown

FRANCIS WILLIAMS ILLUSTRATION AWARD
see **W. H. SMITH ILLUSTRATION AWARD**

PAUL A. WITTY SHORT STORY AWARD

Patricia C. Du Bois
International Reading Association
800 Barksdale Rd.
P O Box 8139
Newark, DE 19714-8139

This short story award was established in 1986 by the International Reading association in memory of Paul A. Witty. An annual award of $1000 will be given to the author of an original short story which serves as a literary standard that encourages young people to read periodicals.

1986 *Cleopatra's Revenge* by Ruth Kelley; in *Ranger Rick* Magazine.

1987 *Family Cracks* by Leslie Wolfe-Cundiff; in Short Story International: Seedlings series No. 24.

1988 *The Scarebird* by Sid Fleischman; in *Cricket* (November 1987).

1989 *The Innkeeper's Boy* by Diane Brooks Pleninger, illustrated by Leonard Everett Fisher; in *Cricket* (November 1988).

1990 *Four Dollars and Fifty Cents* by Eric Kimmel; in *Cricket* (September and October 1989).

1991 *Chen-Li and the River Spirit* by Anthony Holcroft, illustrated by Donna Diamond; in *Cricket* (August 1990).

1992 *Five Words* by Pnina Kass; in *Cricket* (September 1991).

1993 *The Day Mother Sold the Family Swords* by Shizuko Obo in *Cricket* (August 1992).

WOMEN'S NATIONAL BOOK ASSOCIATION AWARD
(formerly Constance Lindsay Skinner Award)
Women's National Book Association
160 Fifth Avenue
New York, NY 10010

Sponsored by the Women's National Book Association since 1940, this award was established to honor Constance Lindsay Skinner, distinguished American author and editor. Although this is not an award specifically for children's literature, many of the recipients are outstanding authors, educators, and other professionals in this field. The award-winning women are honored for their notable efforts in their chosen field. In order to be eligible, the woman must be a resident of the U.S. and earn part or all of her income from books and the allied arts. Listed below are those winners who were active in the field of children's literature.

1940 Anne Carroll Moore, librarian

1943 Mary Graham Bonner, author

1945 Lillian Smith, author

1948 May Lamberton Becker, book reviewer

1949 Lucile Pannell, bookseller

1950 May Massee, children's book editor

1951 Dorothy Canfield Fisher, author

1952 Margaret C. Scoggin, young people's librarian

1954 Elizabeth Janet Gray, author and teacher

1955 Bertha Mahony Miller, author and editor

1959 May Hill Arbuthnot, educator and critic; Marchette Chute, author

1962 Catherine Drinker Bowen

1964 Polly Goodwin, children's book reviewer

1965 Virginia Mathews, school and library consultant

1967 Mildred L. Batchelder, children's librarian

1968 Ruth Hill Viguers, author and librarian

1970 Charlemae Hill Rollins, librarian and author

1971 Augusta Baker, school and public librarian

1972 Ursula Nordstrom, publisher

1973 Mary V. Gaver, librarian and author

1975 Margaret K. McElderry, children's book editor

1976 Frances Neal Cheney, professor

1980 Anne Pellowski, author

1982 Barbara Tuchman

1984 Effie Lee Morris, children's librarian

1985- Information unavailable from award sponsors

CARTER G. WOODSON BOOK AWARD

National Council for the Social Studies
3501 Newark Street, NW
Washington, D.C. 20016

This award was established in 1973 by the National Council for the Social Studies to honor Carter G. Woodson, a black historian and educator. The purpose of the award is to encourage the writing, publishing, and dissemination of outstanding social science books for young readers that treat topics related to ethnic minorities and race relations sensitively and accurately.

Eligible are nonfiction books with a U.S. setting and published in the U.S. during the preceding year. The final decision is made by a selection committee consisting of members of the American Library Association's Council on Interracial Books for Children, Children's Book Council, the National Council for the Social Studies Board of Directors, and the NCSS Racism and Social Justice Committee. A plaque is presented to the honored author at the yearly convention.

1974 *Rosa Parks* by Eloise Greenfield, illustrated by Eric Marlow; Crowell, 1973.

1975 *Make a Joyful Noise unto the Lord! The life of Mahalia Jackson, Queen of the Gospel Singers* by Jesse Jackson, illustrated with photographs; Crowell, 1974.

1976 *Dragonwings* by Laurence Yep, not illustrated; Harper, 1975.

1977 *The Trouble They Seen: Black People Tell the Story of Reconstruction* edited by Dorothy Sterling, illustrated with photographs; Doubleday, 1976.

1978 *The Biography of Daniel Inouye* by Jane Goodsell, illustrated by Haru Wells; Crowell, 1977.

1979 *Native American Testimony: An Anthology of Indian and White Relations: First Encounter to Dispossession* by Peter Nabokov, illustrated with maps and photographs; Crowell, 1978.

1980 *War Cry on a Prayer Feather: Prose and Poetry of the Ute Indians* by Nancy Wood, illustrated with photographs; Doubleday, 1979.

1980 **OUTSTANDING MERIT BOOKS** *A Cry from Earth: Music of the North American Indians* written and illustrated by John Bierhorst; Four Winds, 1979.

James Van Der Zee: The Picture-Takin' Man by Jim Haskins, illustrated with photographs by James Van Der Zee; Dodd, Mead, 1979.

Childtimes by Eloise Greenfield and Lessie Jones Little, illustrated by Jerry Pinkney; Harper, 1979.

1981 *The Chinese Americans* by Milton Meltzer, illustrated; Crowell, 1980.

1981 **OUTSTANDING MERIT BOOKS** *The Hardest Lesson: Personal Accounts of a School Desegregation Crisis* by Pamela Bullard and Judith Stoia, not illustrated; Little Brown, 1980.

1982 *Coming to North America from Mexico, Cuba & Puerto Rico* by Susan Garver and Paula McGuire, illustrated with photographs; Delacorte, 1981.

1983 *Morning Star, Black Sun: The Northern Cheyenne Indians and America's Energy Crisis* by Brent Ashabranner, photographs by Paul Conklin; Dodd, Mead, 1982.

1984 *Mexico and the United States* by E. B. Fincher, illustrated with photos; Crowell, 1983.

1985 *To Live in Two Worlds: American Indian Youth Today* by Brent Ashabranner, photographs by Paul Conklin; Dodd Mead, 1984.

1985 **OUTSTANDING MERIT BOOKS** *Our Golda: The Story of Golda Meir* by David A. Adler, illustrated by Donna Ruff; Viking, 1984.

1986 *Dark Harvest: Migrant Farmworkers in America* by Brent Ashabranner, photographs by Paul Conklin; Dodd Mead, 1985.

1986 **OUTSTANDING MERIT BOOKS** *Racial Prejudice* by Elaine Pascoe, illustrated with photos; Franklin Watts, 1985.

1987 *Happily May I Walk: American Indians and Alaska Natives Today* by Arlene Hirschfelder, illustrated with photos; Scribner, 1986.

1987 **OUTSTANDING MERIT** *Children of the Maya: A Guatemalan Indian Odyssey* by Brent Ashabranner, photographs by Paul Conklin; Dodd Mead, 1986.

Living in Two Worlds by Maxine B. Rosenberg, photographs by George Ancona; Lothrop, Lee & Shepard, 1986.

1988 *Black Music In America: A History Through Its People* by James Haskins, illustrated with photos; Crowell, 1987.

1988 **OUTSTANDING MERIT BOOKS** *American Indians Today: Issues and Conflicts* by Judith Harlan, illustrated with photos; Watts, 1987.

Into a Strange Land by Brent K. Ashabranner and Melissa Ashabranner, illustrated with photos; Dodd Mead, 1987.

You May Plow Here: The Narrative of Sarah Brooks by Thordis Simonsen, illustrated with photos; Norton, 1986.

1989 **ELEMENTARY** *Walking the Road to Freedom: A Story about Sojourner Truth* by Jeri Ferris, illustrated by Peter E. Hanson; Carolrhoda, 1988.

1989 **OUTSTANDING MERIT - ELEMENTARY** *Buffalo Hunt* by Russell Freedman, illustrated with photos; Holiday House, 1988.

1989 **SECONDARY** *Marian Anderson* by Charles Patterson, illustrated; Watts, 1988.

1989 **OUTSTANDING MERIT BOOKS - SECONDARY** *Pride Against Prejudice: The Biography of Larry Doby* by Joseph Thomas Moore, illustrated with photos; Greenwood, 1988.

Hispanic Voters: A Voice in American Politics by Judith Harlan, illustrated with photos; Watts, 1988.

1990 **ELEMENTARY** *In Two Worlds: A Yup'ik Eskimo Family* by Alice Rivers and Aylette Jenness, illustrated by Aylette Jenness; Houghton Mifflin, 1989.

1990 OUTSTANDING MERIT - ELEMENTARY *Arctic Explorer: The Story of Matthew Henson* by Jeri Ferris, illustrated; Carolrhoda, 1989.

Vilma Martinez by Corinn Codye, illustrated by Susi Kilgore; Raintree, 1989.

1990 SECONDARY *Paul Robeson: Hero Before His Time* by Rebecca Larsen, illustrated with photos; Watts, 1989.

1990 OUTSTANDING MERIT - SECONDARY *New Kids on the Block* by Janet Bode, illustrated; Watts, 1989.

A Long Hard Journey: The Story of the Pullman Porter by Fredrick McKissack and Patricia McKissack, illustrated; Walker, 1989.

1991 ELEMENTARY *Shirley Chisholm: Teacher and Congresswoman* by Catherine Scheader, illustrated with photos; Enslow, 1990.

1991 OUTSTANDING MERIT - ELEMENTARY *Hector Lives in the United States Now* by Joan Hewett, illustrated by Richard Hewett; Lippincott, 1990.

Teammates by Peter Golenbock, illustrated by Paul Bacon; Harcourt Brace Jovanovich, 1990.

1991 SECONDARY *Sorrow's Kitchen: The Life and Folklore of Zora Neale Hurston* by Mary E. Lyons, illustrated; Scribner, 1990.

1991 OUTSTANDING MERIT - SECONDARY *Breaking the Chains: African- American Slave Resistance* by William Loren Katz, illustrated with photos; Atheneum, 1990.

W.E.B. DuBois by Patricia McKissack and Fredrick McKissack, illustrated; Watts, 1990.

1992 SECONDARY *Native American Doctor: The Story of Susan LaFlesche Picotte* by Jeri Ferris, illustrated; Carolrhoda, 1991.

WOODWARD PARK SCHOOL ANNUAL BOOK AWARD

Gertrude Goldstein, Executive Director
Woodward Park School
50 Prospect Park West
Brooklyn, NY 11215

This annual award was first presented in 1958. The children of the Woodward Park School sponsor this program, highlighting a book for children that best demonstrates good human relations.

1958 *The House of Sixty Fathers* by Meindert DeJong, illustrated by Maurice Sendak; Harper, 1956.

1959 *To Build a Land* by Sally Watson, illustrated by Lili Cassel; Holt, 1957.

1960 *Mary Jane* by Dorothy Sterling, illustrated by Ernest Crichlow; Doubleday, 1959.

1961 *What Then, Raman?* by Shirley Lease Arora, illustrated by Hans Guggenheim; Follett, 1960.

1962 *The Road to Agra* by Aimee Sommerfelt, illustrated by Ulf Aas; Criterion, 1961.

1963 *The Shepherd of Abu Kush* by Louise A. Stinetorf, not illustrated; Day, 1963.

1964 *Roosevelt Grady* by Louisa R. Shotwell, illustrated by Peter Burchard; World, 1963.

1965 *Meeting with a Stranger* by Duane Bradley, illustrated by E. Harper Johnson; Lippincott, 1964.

1966 *Jazz Country* by Nat Hentoff, not illustrated; Harper, 1965.

1967 *The Bushbabies* by William Stevenson, illustrated by Victor G. Ambrus; Houghton, 1965.

1968 *My Brother Stevie* by Eleanor Clymer, illustrated by Esta Nesbitt; Holt, 1967.

1969 *Ann, Aurelia and Dorothy* by Natalie Savage Carlson, illustrated by Dale Payson; Harper & Row, 1968.

1970 *The Cay* by Theodore Taylor, not illustrated; Doubleday, 1969.

1971 *Friedrich* by Hans Peter Richter, translated by Edite Kroll; Holt, 1970.

Viva Chicano by Frank Bonham, not illustrated; Dutton, 1970.

1972 *Annie and the Old One* by Miska Miles, illustrated by Peter Parnall; Atlantic-Little, 1971.

1973 *Black Pilgrimage* written and illustrated by Tom Feelings; Lothrop, 1972.

1974 *A Hero Ain't Nothin' but a Sandwich* by Alice Childress, not illustrated; Coward, 1973.

1975 *A Book for Jodan* by Marcia Newfield, illustrated by Diane de Groat; Atheneum, 1975.

1976 *Fast Sam, Cool Clyde and Stuff* by Walter Dean Myers, not illustrated; Viking, 1975.

Ludell by Brenda Wilkinson, not illustrated; Harper, 1975.

1977 *The Pinballs* by Betsy Byars, not illustrated; Harper, 1977.

1978 *Alan and Naomi* by Myron Levoy, not illustrated; Harper, 1977.

I Am the Cheese by Robert Cormier, illustrated by Robert Vickery; Pantheon, 1977.

1979 No Award

1980 *Charlotte & Charles* by Ann Tompert, illustrated by John Wallner; Crown, 1979.

1981 *Joshua Fortune* by Cynthia D. Grant, not illustrated; Atheneum, 1980.

1982 *A Shadow Like a Leopard* by Myron Levoy, not illustrated; Harper, 1981.

Just Like Everybody Else by Lillian Rosen, not illustrated; Harcourt, 1981.

1982 HONORABLE MENTION *My Sister* by Karen Hirsch, illustrated by Nancy Inderieden; Carolrhoda, 1977.

1983 *Run, Run, as Fast as You Can* by Mary Pope Osborne, not illustrated; Dial, 1982.

The Divorce Express by Paula Danziger, not illustrated; Delacorte, 1982; Dell, 1983.

1984 No Award

1985 *Gleanings* by Lou Willet Stanek, not illustrated; Harper, 1985.

1989 *Black Star, Bright Dawn* by Scott O'Dell, illustrated with maps; Houghton Mifflin, 1988.

1990 *Silver Days* by Sonia Levitin, not illustrated; Atheneum, 1989.

1991 *Code Name Kris* by Carol Matas, not illustrated; Scribner, 1990.

Send No Blessings by Phyllis Reynolds Naylor, not illustrated; Atheneum, 1990.

Letters From Atlantis by Robert Silverberg, illustrated by Robert Gould; Atheneum, 1990.

WRITERS AWARD
discontinued

This children's literature award was established in 1973 by Lilith Norman and Patricia Wrightson for the purpose of allowing writers to unite in support of their own professional standards. A jury of three or four writers evaluated the eligible novels written for children ages eight through fourteen by a resident of Australia.

1973 *The Fire in the Stone* by Colin Thiele, not illustrated; Rigby, 1973.

1974 *Matt and Jo* by Ivan Southall, not illustrated; Angus & Robertson, 1973.

1975 *Helping Horse* by Joan Phipson, not illustrated; Macmillan, 1974.

1976 *A Dog Called George* by Margaret Balderson, illustrated by Nikki Jones; Oxford, 1975.

Y

YOUNG ADULT CANADIAN BOOK AWARD
Young Adult Caucus
Canadian Library Association
200 Elgin St. Suite 602
Ottawa, Ontario K2P 1L5
Canada

This annual award was first given in 1981. It is sponsored by the Young Adult Caucus of the Saskatchewan Library Association. The award honors the best Canadian book for young adults written in the previous year. Honor books are also named.

1981 *Far from Shore* by Kevin Major, not illustrated; Clarke Irwin, 1980.

1981 **HONORABLE MENTION** *Wilted* by Paul Kropp, not illustrated; Coward, 1980.

1982 *Superbike!* by Jamie Brown, not illustrated; Clarke Irwin, 1981.

1982 **HONORABLE MENTION** *Freshie* by Pat Krause; Potlatch Publications, 1981.

1983 *Hunter in the Dark* by Monica Hughes, not illustrated; Clarke Irwin, 1982; Atheneum, 1983.

1984 *The Druid's Tune* by O.R. Melling, illustrated with maps; Penguin, 1983.

1985 *Winners* by Mary-Ellen Lang Collura, not illustrated; Western Producer Prairie Books, 1984.

1986 *The Quarter-pie Window* by Marianne Brandis, illustrated by G. Brender a Brandis; Porcupine's Quill, 1985.

1987 *Shadow in Hawthorn Bay* by Janet Lunn, not illustrated; Lester & Orpen Dennys, 1986.

1988 *Who Is Frances Rain?* by Margaret Buffie, not illustrated; Kids Can Press, 1987.

1989 *January, February, June, or July* by Helen Fogwell Porter, not illustrated; Breakwater Books, 1988.

1989 **RUNNERSUP** *Mystery in the Frozen Lands* by Martyn Godfrey, not illustrated; Lorimer, 1988.

Paradise Cafe and Other Stories by Martha Brooks, not illustrated; Thistledown Press, 1988; Little Brown (Joy Street), 1990.

The Cripples' Club by William Bell, not illustrated; Irwin, 1988.

1989 **HONORABLE MENTION** *Unlocking the Doors* by Nicole Luiken, not illustrated; Scholastic-TAB, 1988.

Escape to the Overworld by Nicole Luiken, not illustrated; Tree Frog Press, 1988.

1990 *Bad Boy* by Diana Wieler, not illustrated; Douglas & McIntyre, 1989; Delacorte, 1992.

1990 **RUNNERSUP** *Blood Red Ochre* by Kevin Major, not illustrated; Doubleday Canada, 1989; Delacorte, 1989.

Jesper by Carol Matas, not illustrated; Lester & Orpen Dennys, 1989.

1991 *The Leaving* by Budge Wilson, not illustrated; Anansi Press, 1990; Philomel, 1992.

1991 **RUNNERSUP** *Redwork* by Michael Bedard, not illustrated; Lester & Orpen Dennys, 1990; Atheneum, 1990.

The Whalesinger by Welwyn Wilton Katz, illustrated with map; Douglas & McIntyre, 1990; McElderry, 1990.

Forbidden City by William Bell, illustrated with maps; Doubleday Canada, 1990.

1991 **HONORABLE MENTION** *Dawnrider* by Jan Hudson, not illustrated; HarperCollins, 1990; Philomel, 1990.

1992 *Strandia* by Susan Lynn Reynolds, not illustrated; HarperCollins (Canada), 1991; Farrar, Straus, Giroux, 1991.

1992 **RUNNERSUP** *Two Moons in August* by Martha Brooks, not illustrated; Groundwood Books, 1991.

Eating Between the Lines by Kevin Major, not illustrated; Doubleday Canada, 1991.

On My Own by Mitzi Dale, not illustrated; Douglas & McIntyre, 1991.

1992 **HONORABLE MENTION** *Yuletide Blues* by Rod MacIntyre, not illustrated; Thistledown Press, 1991.

Escape To Freedom by Vancy Kasper, not illustrated; Stoddart, 1991.

1993 *There Will Be Wolves* by Karleen Bradford; HarperCollins, 1992.

YOUNG ADULT NOVEL OF THE YEAR/MICHIGAN LIBRARY ASSOCIATION
Michigan Library Association
1000 Long Blvd., Suite 1
Lansing, MI 48911

Established in 1987 by the Young Adult Caucus of the Michigan Library Association, this award recognizes a work of fiction by an American author that makes a permanent contribution to the genre and appeals to young adults. The winning author is recognized at the annual award ceremony in September.

1987 *The Flight of the Cassowary* by John LeVert, not illustrated; Atlantic Monthly Press, 1986.

1988 *The Year of the Gopher* by Phyllis Reynolds Naylor, not illustrated; Atheneum, 1987; Bantam, 1988.

1989 *Sex Education* by Jenny Davis, not illustrated; Orchard, 1988; Watts, 1988.

1990 *The Road to Memphis* by Mildred D. Taylor, not illustrated; Dial, 1990.

1990 **HONOR** *The Silver Kiss* by Annette Curtis Klause, not illustrated; Delacorte, 1990.

1991 *Athletic Shorts: Six Short Stories* by Chris Crutcher, not illustrated; Greenwillow, 1991.

YOUNG AUSTRALIAN'S BEST BOOK AWARD

Young Australian's Best Book Award Council
P O Box 238
Kew, Victoria
Australia 3101

This award was established in 1986 to recognize the best books of the year as voted by the young readers of Victoria, Australia. Children from grades one to nine may each nominate one Australian fiction book. A voting list is compiled from these nominations with titles grouped into three categories: picture book, junior fiction, and older fiction. Each child may cast a vote for one title from the appropriate section. Citations are given to the winning authors of this annual award.

1986 **PICTURE BOOK** *When the Wind Changed* by Ruth Park, illustrated by Deborah Niland; Collins, 1981.

1986 **FICTION FOR YOUNG READERS** *The Twenty-seventh Annual African Hippopotamus Race* by Morris Lurie, illustrated by Elizabeth Honey; Penguin, 1977.

1986 **FICTION FOR OLDER READERS** *Hating Alison Ashley* by Robin Klein, not illustrated; Penguin, 1984.

1987 **PICTURE BOOK** *Animalia* written and illustrated by Graeme Base; Abrams, 1987, c1986.

1987 **FICTION YOUNGER READER** *Sister Madge's Book of Nuns* by Doug MacLeod, illustrated by Craig Smith; Omnibus, 1986.

1987 **FICTION OLDER READER** *Unreal! Eight Surprising Stories* by Paul Jennings, not illustrated; Puffin, 1985; Viking, 1991.

1988 **PICTURE BOOK** *Where the Forest Meets the Sea* written and illustrated by Jeannie Baker; Julia McRae, 1987.

1988 **FICTION YOUNGER READER** *My Place* by Nadia Wheatley, illustrated by Donna Rawlins; Collins Dove, 1987.

1988 **FICTION OLDER READER** *Unbelievable! More Surprising Stories* by Paul Jennings, not illustrated; Puffin, 1986.

1989 **PICTURE BOOK** *The Eleventh Hour* written and illustrated by Graeme Base; Viking Kestrel, 1988.

1989 **FICTION YOUNGER READER** *The Cabbage Patch Fib* by Paul Jennings, illustrated by Craig Smith; Puffin, 1988.

1989 **FICTION OLDER READER** *Uncanny! Even More Surprising Stories* by Paul Jennings, not illustrated; Puffin, 1988.

1990 **PICTURE BOOK** *The Monster Who Ate Australia* written and illustrated by Michael Salmon; Lamont, 1986.

1990 **FICTION YOUNGER READER** *The Paw Thing* by Paul Jennings, illustrated by Keith McEwan; Puffin, 1989.

1990 **FICTION OLDER READER** *Space Demons* by Gillian Rubinstein, not illustrated; Omnibus, 1986.

1991 **PICTURE BOOK** *Counting On Frank* written and illustrated by Rod Clement; Collins, in association with Anne Ingram Books, 1990; Gareth Stevens, 1991.

1991 **FICTION YOUNGER READER** *Finders Keepers* by Emily Rodda, illustrated by Noela Young; Omnibus, 1990; Greenwillow, 1991.

1991 **FICTION OLDER READER** *Round the Twist* by Paul Jennings, illustrated; Puffin, 1990.

1992 **PICTURE BOOK** *Window* written and illustrated by Jeannie Baker; Julia MacRae, 1991; Greenwillow, 1991.

1992 **FICTION FOR YOUNG READERS** *Quirky Tails! More Oddball Stories* by Paul Jennings, illustrated; Puffin, 1987.

1992 **FICTION FOR OLDER READERS** *Unmentionable! More Amazing Stories* by Paul Jennings, not illustrated; Puffin, 1991.

YOUNG HOOSIER BOOK AWARD

Association for Indiana Media Educators
Dr. Lawrence Reck
AIME Executive Secretary
Indiana State University
School of Education
Terre Haute, IN 47809

As a response to the Right-to-Read program, the Young Hoosier Book Award was first presented in 1975. This yearly program is sponsored by the Association for Indiana Media Educators for the purpose of stimulating the recreational reading of children in grades four through six and six through eight. Books can be nominated by students, teachers, and librarians. Of those titles nominated, twenty are selected for a master list. In order to be eligible, titles must be fiction, appropriate for grades four through eight, published in the last five years, in print at the time of selection, and the author must be living in the United States.

Students in grades four through six and six through eight who have read at least three of the titles on the master list are eligible to vote for their favorite book. Prior to 1986, there was only the category of grades four through six. In 1992, a Picture Book category was added. The winning authors are presented a plaque bearing the seal of the Young Hoosier Book Award. The plaque is presented to the recipients at the spring convention of the AIME.

1975 **GRADES 4-6** *The Trumpet of the Swan* by E.B. White, illustrated by Edward Frascino; Harper & Row, 1970.

1976 **GRADES 4-6** *Are You There, God? It's Me, Margaret* by Judy Blume, not illustrated; Bradbury, 1970.

1977 **GRADES 4-6** *How to Eat Fried Worms* by Thomas Rockwell, illustrated by Emily McCully; Watts, 1973.

1978 **GRADES 4-6** *The Best Christmas Pageant Ever* by Barbara Robinson, illustrated by Judith Gwyn Brown; Harper, 1972.

1979 GRADES 4-6 *The Ghost on Saturday Night* by Sid Fleischman, illustrated by Eric Von Schmidt; Atlantic-Little, 1974.

1980 GRADES 4-6 *Don't Hurt Laurie* by Willo Davis Roberts, illustrated by Ruth Sanderson; Atheneum, 1977.

1981 GRADES 4-6 *The Goof that Won the Pennant* by Jonah Kalb, illustrated by Sandy Kossin; Houghton Mifflin, 1976.

1982 GRADES 4-6 *Help! I'm a Prisoner in the Library* by Eth Clifford, illustrated by George Hughes; Houghton Mifflin, 1979.

1983 GRADES 4-6 *Superfudge* by Judy Blume, not illustrated; Dutton, 1980.

1984 GRADES 4-6 *Jelly Belly* by Robert Kimmel Smith, illustrated by Bob Jones; Delacorte, 1981.

1985 GRADES 4-6 *Operation: Dump the Chump* by Barbara Park, not illustrated; Knopf, 1982.

1986 GRADES 4-6 *When the Boys Ran the House* by Joan Carris, illustrated by Carol Newsom; Lippincott, 1982.

1986 GRADES 6-8 *Stranger with My Face* by Lois Duncan, not illustrated; Little Brown, 1981; Dell, 1982.

1987 GRADES 4-6 *The War With Grandpa* by Robert Kimmel Smith, illustrated by Richard Lauter; Delacorte, 1984.

1987 GRADES 6-8 *The Third Eye* by Lois Duncan, not illustrated; Little Brown, 1984.

1988 GRADES 4-6 *Babysitting Is a Dangerous Job* by Willo Davis Roberts, not illustrated; Atheneum, 1985.

1988 GRADES 6-8 *A Deadly Game of Magic* by Joan Lowery Nixon, not illustrated; Harcourt, Brace, Jovanovich, 1983.

1989 GRADES 4-6 *Christina's Ghost* by Betty Ren Wright, not illustrated; Holiday House, 1985.

1989 GRADES 6-8 *Wait Til Helen Comes* by Mary Downing Hahn, not illustrated; Clarion, 1986.

1990 GRADES 4-6 *Fudge* by Charlotte T. Graeber, illustrated by Cheryl Harness; Lothrop, Lee & Shepard, 1987.

1990 GRADES 6-8 *The Dark and Deadly Pool* by Joan Lowery Nixon, not illustrated; Delacorte, 1987.

1991 GRADES 4-6 *Ten Kids, No Pets* by Ann M. Martin, not illustrated; Holiday House, 1988.

1991 GRADES 6-8 *Hatchet* by Gary Paulsen, not illustrated; Bradbury, 1987.

1992 PICTURE BOOK GRADES K-3 *Heckedy Peg* by Audrey Wood, illustrated by Don Wood; Harcourt, Brace, Jovanovich, 1987.

1992 GRADES 4-6 *Nightmare Mountain* by Peg Kehret, not illustrated; Dutton, 1989.

1992 GRADES 6-8 *Don't Look Behind You* by Lois Duncan, not illustrated; Delacorte, 1989.

YOUNG OBSERVER RANK TEENAGE FICTION PRIZE
see **OBSERVER TEENAGE FICTION PRIZE**

YOUNG READER MEDAL
see **CALIFORNIA YOUNG READER MEDAL**

YOUNG READER'S CHOICE AWARD
Pacific Northwest Library Association
Carol Doll
Graduate School of Library & Information Science
University of Washington
133 Suzzallo Library FM-30
Seattle, WA 98195

At the suggestion of Harry Hartman, a Seattle bookseller, The Young Reader's Choice Award was established in 1940. The competition is sponsored annually by the Pacific Northwest Library Association. This is a children's choice award, conducted in Alaska, Alberta, British Columbia, Idaho, Montana, Oregon, and Washington. School children in grades four through eight are eligible to vote for their favorite book. A Senior Division was added in 1991. All types of literature (fiction, nonfiction, poetry) published in the U.S. and Canada are considered for inclusion on the master list. A committee consisting of representatives from five states and two provinces, including children, nominates titles published three years prior to the voting.

Each representative submits to the Chair a list of titles considered appropriate for the ballot. The final ballot of twelve to fifteen titles are voted on in schools and libraries by children who have read, or had read to them, at least two titles. The winning author is presented with a medal at the annual conference of the association.

1940 *Paul Bunyan Swings His Axe* written and illustrated by Dell J. McCormick; Caxton, 1936.

1941 *Mr. Popper's Penguins* by Florence Atwater and Richard Atwater; illustrated by Robert Lawson; Little Brown, 1938.

1942 *By the Shores of Silver Lake* by Laura Ingalls Wilder, illustrated by Mildred Boyle and Helen Sewell; Harper, 1939.

1943 *Lassie Come Home* by Eric Knight, illustrated by Cyrus L. Baldridge; Holt, 1940.

1944 *The Black Stallion* by Walter Farley, illustrated by Keith Ward; Random House, 1941.

1945 *Snow Treasure* by Marie McSwigan, illustrated by Mary Reardon; Dutton, 1942.

1946 *The Return of Silver Chief* by Jack O'Brien, illustrated by Kurt Wiese; Holt, 1943.

1947 *Homer Price* written and illustrated by Robert McCloskey; Viking, 1943.

1948 *The Black Stallion Returns* by Walter Farley, illustrated by Harold Eldridge; Random House, 1945.

1949 *Cowboy Boots* by Doris Shannon Garst, illustrated by Charles Hargens; Abingdon, 1946.

1950 *McElligot's Pool* written and illustrated by Dr. Seuss; Random House, 1947.

1951 *King of the Wind* by Marguerite Henry, illustrated by Wesley Dennis; Rand McNally, 1948.

1952 *Sea Star: Orphan of Chincoteague* by Marguerite Henry, illustrated by Wesley Dennis; Rand McNally, 1949.

1953-1955   No Award

1956 *Miss Pickerell Goes to Mars* by Ellen MacGregor, illustrated by Paul Galdone; McGraw, 1951.

1957 *Henry and Ribsy* by Beverly Cleary, illustrated by Louis Darling; Morrow, 1954.

1958 *Golden Mare* by William Corbin, illustrated by Pers Crowell; Coward, 1955.

1959 *Old Yeller* by Fred Gipson, illustrated by Carl Burger; Harper, 1956.

1960 *Henry and the Paper Route* by Beverly Cleary, illustrated by Louis Darling; Morrow, 1957.

1961 *Danny Dunn and the Homework Machine* by Jay Williams and Raymond Abrashkin, illustrated by Ezra Jack Keats; Whittlesey House, 1958.

1962 *The Swamp Fox of the Revolution* by Stewart Holbrook, illustrated by Ernest Richardson; Random House, 1959.

1963 *Danny Dunn on the Ocean Floor* by Jay Williams and Raymond Abrashkin, illustrated by Brinton Turkle; McGraw, 1960.

1964 *The Incredible Journey: A Tale of Three Animals* by Shelia Every Burnford, illustrated by Carl Burger; Little Brown, 1961.

1965 *John F. Kennedy and PT-109* by Richard Tregaskis, illustrated with photographs; Random House, 1962.

1966 *Rascal: A Memoir of a Better Era* by Sterling North, illustrated by John Schoenherr; Dutton, 1963.

1967 *Chitty-Chitty-Bang-Bang* by Ian Fleming, illustrated by John Burningham; Random House, 1964.

1968 *The Mouse and the Motorcycle* by Beverly Cleary, illustrated by Louis Darling; Morrow, 1965.

1969 *Henry Reed's Babysitting Service* by Keith Robertson, illustrated by Robert McCloskey; Viking, 1966.

1970 *Smoke* by William Corbin, not illustrated; Coward, 1967.

1971 *Ramona the Pest* by Beverly Cleary, illustrated by Louis Darling; Morrow, 1968.

1972 *Encyclopedia Brown Keeps the Peace* by Donald J. Sobol, illustrated by Leonard Shortall; Nelson, 1969.

1973   No Award

1974 *Mrs. Frisby and the Rats of NIMH* by Robert C. O'Brien, illustrated by Zena Bernstein; Atheneum, 1971.

1975 *Tales of a Fourth Grade Nothing* by Judy Blume, illustrated by Roy Doty; Dutton, 1972.

1976 *The Great Brain Reforms* by John D. Fitzgerald, illustrated by Mercer Mayer; Dial, 1973.

1977 *Blubber* by Judy Blume, not illustrated; Bradbury, 1974.

1978 *Great Brain Does It Again* by John D. Fitzgerald, illustrated by Mercer Mayer; Dial, 1975.

1979 *Roll of Thunder, Hear My Cry* by Mildred D. Taylor, illustrated by Jerry Pinkney; Dial, 1976.

1980 *Ramona and her Father* by Beverly Cleary, illustrated by Allen Tiegreen; Morrow, 1977.

1981 *Hail, Hail, Camp Timberwood* by Ellen Conford, illustrated by Gail Owens; Little, 1978.

1982 *Bunnicula: A Rabbit Tale of Mystery* by Deborah Howe and James Howe, illustrated by Alan Daniel; Atheneum, 1980.

1983 *Superfudge* by Judy Blume, not illustrated; Dutton, 1980.

1984 *The Indian in the Cupboard* by Lynn Reid Banks, illustrated by Brock Cole; Doubleday, 1981.

1985 *Thirteen Ways to Sink a Sub* by Jamie Gilson, illustrated by Linda S. Edwards; Lothrop Lee & Shepard, 1982.

1986 *The Dollhouse Murders* by Betty Ren Wright, not illustrated; Holiday House, 1983.

1987 *The War with Grandpa* by Robert Kimmel Smith, illustrated by Richard Lauter; Delacorte, 1984.

1988 *Sixth Grade Can Really Kill You* by Barthe DeClements, not illustrated; Viking Kestrel, 1985.

1989 *Wait Til Helen Comes* by Mary Downing Hahn, not illustrated; Clarion, 1986.

1990 *There's a Boy in the Girls' Bathroom* by Louis Sachar, not illustrated; Knopf, 1987.

1991 *Ten Kids, No Pets* by Ann M. Martin, not illustrated; Holiday House, 1988.

1991 **SENIOR** *Sex Education* by Jenny Davis, not illustrated; Watts, 1988; Orchard, 1988.

1992 *Danger in Quicksand Swamp* by Bill Wallace, not illustrated; Holiday House, 1989.

1992 **SENIOR** *Eva* by Peter Dickinson, not illustrated; Delacorte, 1989.

YOUNG TEENS CHILDREN'S LITERATURE AWARD
Central School Library
Coolidge Unified School District 21
P O Box 1499
Coolidge, AZ 85228

The Young Teens Children's Literature Award was established in 1989 through the Coolidge school librarians' Need-To-Read program. The award is given annually to well reviewed and popular books found in a school library that encourage pleasure reading at home, sustained silent reading in school, and shared book experiences throughout the community.

The winners are chosen by a volunteer committee of 5th through 8th grade students who represent a broadly pluralistic community and who read widely. The primary selection category for novels focuses on young characters and the courage, determination, and resourcefulness they reveal when solving problems that could be real for children.

1989 *Babysitters on Board!* by Ann M. Martin, not illustrated; Apple, 1988.

Flowers in the Attic by V. C. Andrews, not illustrated; Pocket Books, 1982.

Old Yeller by Fred Gipson, illustrated by Carl Burger; Harper & Row, 1956.

1990 *Superfudge* by Judy Blume, not illustrated; Dutton, 1980.

Chronicles of Narnia by C. S. Lewis, illustrated by Pauline Baynes; Macmillan, 1983.

1991 *Charlie and the Chocolate Factory* by Roald Dahl, illustrated by Joseph Schindelman; Knopf, 1964.

Tales of a Fourth Grade Nothing by Judy Blume, illustrated by Roy Doty; Dutton, 1972.

It by Stephen King; Signet Books, 1990.

Bo Knows Bo: The Autobiography of a Ballplayer by Bo Jackson and Dick Shaap; Doubleday, 1990.

Part Two

AUTHORS AND ILLUSTRATORS

A

AAMUNDSEN, NINA RING

Two Shorts and One Long by Nina Ring Aamundsen, not illustrated; Houghton Mifflin, 1990. **Awarded:** Mildred Batchelder (Honor) 1991.

AARDEMA, VERNA

Awarded: Children's Reading Round Table 1981.

Behind the Back of the Mountain: Black Folktales from Southern Africa by Verna Aardema, illustrated by Leo and Diane Dillon; Dial, 1973. **Awarded:** Children's Book Showcase 1974.

Bimwili and the Zimwi by Verna Aardema, illustrated by Susan Meddaugh; Dial, 1985. **Awarded:** Parents' Choice (literature) 1985.

Borreguita and the Coyote by Verna Aardema, illustrated by Petra Mathers; Knopf, 1991. **Awarded:** Redbook 1991.

Oh, Kojo! How Could You! by Verna Aardema, illustrated by Marc Brown; Dial, 1984. **Awarded:** Parents' Choice (literature) 1984.

Pedro & the Padre by Verna Aardema, illustrated by Friso Henstra; Dial, 1991. **Awarded:** Parents' Choice (Story Book) 1991.

Rabbit Makes a Monkey Out of a Lion by Verna Aardema, illustrated by Jerry Pinkney; Dial, 1989. **Awarded:** Parents' Choice (Story Book) 1989.

Who's in Rabbit's House? A Masai Tale by Verna Aardema, illustrated by Leo and Diane Dillon; Dial, 1977. **Awarded:** Lewis Carroll Shelf 1978.

Why Mosquitos Buzz in People's Ears: A West African Tale by Verna Aardema, illustrated by Leo and Diane Dillon; Dial, 1975. **Awarded:** Art Books for Children 1977, 1978; Caldecott 1976; New York Times Notable Books 1975.

AAS, ULF

The Road to Agra by Aimee Sommerfelt, illustrated by Ulf Aas; Criterion, 1961. **Awarded:** Jane Addams 1962; Boys Club 1962; Child Study 1961; Woodward Park School 1962.

The White Bungalow by Aimee Sommerfelt, illustrated by Ulf Aas; Criterion, 1964. **Awarded:** Edison Mass Media (character development in children) 1965.

ABBOTT, MARY OGDEN

Wild Animals of the Five Rivers Country by George Cory Franklin, illustrated by Mary O. Abbott; Houghton, 1947. **Awarded:** Boys Club 1949.

ABDULLAH, AISHAH S.

"Midnight: the Stallion of the Night" by Aishah S. Abdullah; unpublished manuscript. **Awarded:** Council on Interracial Books (African American) 1974.

"Mweusi" by Aishah S. Abdullah; unpublished manuscript. **Awarded:** Council on Interracial Books (African American) 1974.

"Simba" by Aishah S. Abdullah, unpublished manuscript. **Awarded:** Council on Interracial Books (African American) 1974.

ABEL, MARILYN

Awarded: Jeremiah Ludington 1984.

ABEL, RAYMOND

The Ghost Rock Mystery by Mary C. Jane, illustrated by Ray Abel; Scholastic, 1966. **Awarded:** Boys Club 1966-67.

ABERCROMBIE, BARBARA

Charlie Anderson by Barbara Abercrombie, illustrated by Mark Graham; McElderry, 1990. **Awarded:** Redbook 1990; Irma S. and James H. Black 1990.

ABERNETHY, ROBERT GORDON

Introduction to Tomorrow: The U.S. and the Wider World, 1945-1965 by Robert G. Abernethy, illustrated with photographs and maps; Harcourt, 1966. **Awarded:** Edison Mass Media (America's past) 1967.

ABRAHAMS, HILARY RUTH

Kings, Bishops, Knights, and Pawns: Life in a Feudal Society by Ralph Arnold, illustrated by Hilary Abrahams; Constable, 1963. **Awarded:** Carnegie (commended) 1963.

ABRASHKIN, RAYMOND

Danny Dunn and the Homework Machine by Raymond Abrashkin and Jay Williams, illustrated by Ezra Jack Keats; Whittlesey House, 1958. **Awarded:** Young Readers Choice 1961.

Danny Dunn on the Ocean Floor by Raymond Abrashkin and Jay Williams, illustrated by Brinton Turkle; McGraw, 1960. **Awarded:** Young Readers Choice 1963.

ABRUZZI, REY

The Hunt for the Whooping Cranes by Joseph J. McCoy, illustrated by Rey Abruzzi; Lothrop, 1966. **Awarded:** Spring Book Festival (older honor) 1966.

ACCORSI, WILLIAM

Short, Short, Short Stories written and illustrated by William Accorsi; Greenwillow, 1991. **Awarded:** Parents' Choice (Story Book) 1991.

ACKER, HELEN

The School Train by Helen Acker, illustrated by Janet Smalley; Abelard, 1953. **Awarded:** Spring Book Festival (ages 8-12 honor) 1953.

ACKERMAN, EUGENE FRANCIS

Tonk and Tonka by Eugene Ackerman, illustrated by Carl Burger; Dutton, 1962. **Awarded:** Indiana Author's Day (young children) 1963.

ACKERMAN, KAREN
Song and Dance Man by Karen Ackerman, illustrated by Stephen Gammell; Knopf, 1988. **Awarded:** Caldecott 1989; Society of Midland Authors (Juvenile Fiction) 1989.

ACKOFF, KAREN
The Story of Your Mouth by Alvin and Virginia B. Silverstein, illustrated by Karen Ackoff; Coward McCann, 1983. **Awarded:** New Jersey Institute of Technology 1983.

ACS, LASZLO
The Boy and the Swan by Catherine Storr, illustrated by Laszlo Acs; Deutsch, 1987. **Awarded:** Earthworm Award 1987.

ADA, ALMA FLOR
The Gold Coin by Alma Flor Ada, illustrated by Neil Waldman; Atheneum, 1991. **Awarded:** Christopher Award (Ages 8-10) 1992.

ADAMS, ADRIENNE
Awarded: Rutgers 1973; University of Southern Mississippi 1977.

Candy Floss by Rumer Godden, illustrated by Adrienne Adams; Viking, 1960. **Awarded:** Spring Book Festival (ages 4-8 honor) 1960.

Captain Ramsey's Daughter by Elizabeth Fraser Torjesen, illustrated by Adrienne Adams; Lothrop, 1953. **Awarded:** Spring Book Festival (ages 8-12) 1953.

The Day We Saw the Sun Come Up by Alice E. Goudey, illustrated by Adrienne Adams; Scribner, 1961. **Awarded:** Caldecott (honor) 1962.

The Easter Egg Artists written and illustrated by Adrienne Adams; Scribner, 1976. **Awarded:** Irma Simonton Black 1976.

The Fairy Doll by Rumer Godden, illustrated by Adrienne Adams; Macmillan, 1956. **Awarded:** Carnegie (commended) 1956; International Board on Books for Young People (honour list/Great Britain) 1958.

The Halloween Party by Lonzo Anderson, illustrated by Adrienne Adams; Scribner, 1974. **Awarded:** New Jersey Institute of Technology 1975.

Houses From the Sea by Alice E. Goudey, illustrated by Adrienne Adams; Scribner, 1959. **Awarded:** Caldecott (honor) 1960.

Jorinda and Joringel by Jacob and Wilhelm Grimm, illustrated by Adrienne Adams; Scribner, 1968. **Awarded:** Boston Globe Horn Book (illustration honor) 1968.

Thumbelina by Hans Christian Andersen, translated by R. P. Keigwin, illustrated by Adrienne Adams; Scribner, 1961. **Awarded:** Lewis Carroll Shelf 1962.

A Woggle of Witches written and illustrated by Adrienne Adams; Scribner, 1971. **Awarded:** New Jersey Institute of Technology 1972.

ADAMS, HARRIET STRATEMEYER
(pseudonyms are Carolyn Keene and Laura Lee Hope)

Awarded: New Jersey Institute of Technology (New Jersey author awards special citation) 1969.

ADAMS, JAMES D.
Cap'n Ezra, Privateer by James D. Adams, illustrated by I. B. Hazelton; Harcourt, 1940. **Awarded:** Spring Book Festival (older) 1940.

ADAMS, JEANIE
Pigs and Honey written and illustrated by Jeanie Adams; Omnibus Books, 1990. **Awarded:** Children's Book Council of Australia (Book of the Year Younger) 1990; Crichton 1990.

ADAMS, JULIA DAVIS
see DAVIS, JULIA

ADAMS, RICHARD
Watership Down by Richard Adams, not illustrated; Rex Collings, 1972; Macmillan, 1972; Avon, 1975. **Awarded:** California Young Reader Medal (high school) 1977; Carnegie 1972; Guardian 1973; Media & Methods (paperback) 1976.

ADAMS, SAMUEL HOPKINS
Chingo Smith of the Erie Canal by Samuel H. Adams, illustrated by Leonard Vosburgh; Random House, 1958. **Awarded:** Spring Book Festival (older honor) 1958.

ADAMSON, JOY
Elsa, the True Story of a Lioness by Joy Adamson, illustrated with photographs; Pantheon, 1961. **Awarded:** Boys Club 1962.

ADDISON, ROBERT W.
Clocks: From Shadow to Atom by Kathryn K. Borland and Helen R. Speicher, illustrated by Robert W. Addison; Follett, 1969. **Awarded:** Indiana Authors Day (Children) 1970.

ADKINS, JAN
The Art and Industry of Sandcastles written and illustrated by Jan Adkins; Walker, 1971. **Awarded:** Art Books for Children 1973, 1974, 1975; Lewis Carroll Shelf 1972; National Book Awards (finalist) 1972.

Inside: Seeing Beneath the Surface written and illustrated by Jan Adkins; Walker, 1975. **Awarded:** Children's Book Showcase 1976.

Moving Heavy Things written and illustrated by Jan Adkins; Houghton, 1980. **Awarded:** New York Academy of Sciences (older) 1981.

Toolchest written and illustrated by Jan Adkins; Walker, 1973. **Awarded:** Children's Book Showcase 1974.

ADLER, CAROLE S.
The Magic of the Glits by Carole S. Adler, illustrated by Ati Forberg; Macmillan, 1979. **Awarded:** CRABbery 1980; Golden Kite (fiction) 1979; William Allen White 1982.

With Westie and the Tin Man by C. S. Adler, not illustrated; Macmillan, 1985. **Awarded:** Child Study 1985.

ADLER, DAVID A.
A Little at a Time by David A. Adler, illustrated by N. M. Bodecker; Random House, 1976. **Awarded:** Children's Book Showcase 1977.

The Number on My Grandfather's Arm by David A. Adler, illustrated by Rose Eichenbaum; Union of American Hebrew Congregations, 1987. **Awarded:** Sydney Taylor Book Award (Picture Book) 1988.

Our Golda: The Story of Golda Meir by David A. Adler, illustrated by Donna Ruff; Viking, 1984. **Awarded:** Carter G. Woodson (Outstanding Merit) 1985.

ADOFF, ARNOLD
Awarded: National Council of Teachers of English 1988.

All the Colors of the Race: Poems by Arnold Adoff, illustrated by John Steptoe; Lothrop, Lee & Shepard, 1982. **Awarded:** Jane Addams (special recognition) 1983.

Flamboyan by Arnold Adoff, illustrated by Karen Barbour; Harcourt Brace Jovanovich, 1988. **Awarded:** Parents' Choice (Picture Book) 1988.

MA NDA LA by Arnold Adoff, illustrated by Emily McCully; Harper, 1971. **Awarded:** Art Books for Children 1975.

AFANASYEV, ALEXANDER NIKOLAYEVICH
The Fool and the Fish: A Tale From Russia by Alexander Nikolayevich Afanasyev, illustrated by Gennady Spirin; Dial, 1990. **Awarded:** New York Times Best Illustrated 1990.

AGARD, JOHN
Say it Again, Granny! by John Agard, illustrated by Susanna Gretz; Bodley Head, 1985. **Awarded:** Other Award 1986.

AGEE, JON
The Incredible Painting of Felix Clousseau written and illustrated by Jon Agee; Farrar Straus Giroux, 1988. **Awarded:** Redbook 1988.

The Return of Freddy LeGrand written and illustrated by Jon Agee; Farrar Straus Giroux, 1992. **Awarded:** Parents Choice (Picture Books) 1992.

AGUEROS, JACK
El Pito de Plata de Pito by Jack Agueros; manuscript. **Awarded:** Council on Interracial Books (Puerto Rican) 1973.

AHLBERG, ALLAN
Awarded: British Book Awards (Author runnerup) 1989, 1991

The Baby's Catalogue written and illustrated by Allan Ahlberg and Janet Ahlberg; Kestrel, 1982; Little Brown, 1982. **Awarded:** Greenaway (commended) 1982.

Burglar Bill written and illustrated by Allan Ahlberg and Janet Ahlberg; Heinemann, 1977. **Awarded:** Greenaway (commended) 1977.

Each Peach, Pear, Plum written and illustrated by Allan Ahlberg and Janet Ahlberg; Kestrel, 1978. **Awarded:** Greenaway 1978; International Board on Books for Young People (illustration/Great Britain) 1980.

Heard It In the Playground by Allan Ahlberg, illustrated by Fritz Wegner; Viking Kestrel, 1989. **Awarded:** Signal Poetry Award 1990.

The Jolly Christmas Postman written and illustrated by Allan Ahlberg and Janet Ahlberg; Heinemann, 1991. **Awarded:** Greenaway 1991.

The Jolly Postman: or, Other People's Letters written and illustrated by Allan Ahlberg and Janet Ahlberg; Heinemann, 1986. **Awarded:** Children's Book Award 1986; Greenaway (commended) 1986; International Board on Books for Young People (Illustration/Great Britain) 1988; Maschler 1986.

The Mighty Slide by Allan Ahlberg, illustrated by Charlotte Voake; Viking Kestrel, 1988. **Awarded:** W. H. Smith (Second Prize) 1989.

Mrs. Plug the Plumber by Allan Ahlberg, illustrated by Joe Wright; Kestrel, 1980. **Awarded:** Other Award 1980.

Peepo! written and illustrated by Janet Ahlberg and Allan Ahlberg; Viking Kestrel/Puffin, 1983. **Awarded:** Best Books for Babies 1985.

Woof! by Allan Ahlberg, illustrated by Fritz Wegner; Viking Kestrel, 1986. **Awarded:** International Board on Books for Young People (Writing/Great Britain) 1988.

AHLBERG, JANET
Awarded: British Book Awards (Author runnerup) 1989, 1991.

The Baby's Catalogue written and illustrated by Allan Ahlberg and Janet Ahlberg; Kestrel, 1982; Little Brown, 1982. **Awarded:** Greenaway (commended) 1982.

Burglar Bill written and illustrated by Allan Ahlberg and Janet Ahlberg; Heinemann, 1977. **Awarded:** Greenaway (commended) 1977.

Each Peach, Pear, Plum written and illustrated by Allan Ahlberg and Janet Ahlberg; Kestrel, 1978. **Awarded:** Greenaway 1978; International Board on Books for Young People (illustration/Great Britain) 1980.

The Jolly Christmas Postman written and illustrated by Allan Ahlberg and Janet Ahlberg; Heinemann, 1991. **Awarded:** Greenaway 1991.

The Jolly Postman: or, Other People's Letters written and illustrated by Allan Ahlberg and Janet Ahlberg; Heinemann, 1986. **Awarded:** Children's Book Award 1986; Greenaway (commended) 1986; International Board on Books for Young People (Illustration/Great Britain) 1988; Maschler 1986.

Peepo! written and illustrated by Janet Ahlberg and Allan Ahlberg; Viking Kestrel/Puffin, 1983. **Awarded:** Best Books for Babies 1985.

AICHINGER, HELGA
Awarded: Hans Christian Andersen (highly commended illustrator/Austria) 1974.

Jonah and the Great Fish by Clyde Robert Bulla, illustrated by Helga Aichinger; Crowell, 1970. **Awarded:** Commonwealth Club of California 1970.

Noah and the Rainbow: An Ancient Story retold by Max Bolliger, translated by Clyde Robert Bulla, illustrated by Helga Aichinger; Crowell, 1972. **Awarded:** Children's Book Showcase 1973.

AIKEN, CONRAD
Cats and Bats and Things with Wings by Conrad Aiken, illustrated by Milton Glaser; Atheneum, 1965. **Awarded:** Art Books for Children 1973.

AIKEN, JOAN
Awarded: British Book Awards (Author runnerup) 1990.

Midnight Is a Place by Joan Aiken, not illustrated; Viking, 1974. (British edition published by Cape in 1974 is illustrated by Pat Marriott). **Awarded:** New York Times Notable Books 1974.

Night Fall by Joan Aiken, not illustrated; Holt, 1971. **Awarded:** Edgar Allan Poe 1972.

The Whispering Mountain by Joan Aiken, illustrated by Frank Bozzo; Cape, 1968. **Awarded:** Carnegie (honour) 1968; Guardian 1969.

The Wolves of Willoughby Chase by Joan Aiken, illustrated by Pat Marriott; Doubleday, 1963. **Awarded:** Lewis Carroll Shelf 1965.

AJEGBO, KEITH
Black Lives, White Worlds edited by Keith Ajegbo; Cambridge University Press, 1982. **Awarded:** Other Award 1982.

AKABA, SUEKICHI
Awarded: Hans Christian Andersen (illustrator) 1980.

The Crane Wife retold by Sumiko Yagawa, translated by Katherine Paterson, illustrated by Suekichi Akaba; Morrow,

1981. **Awarded:** New York Times Best Illustrated 1981; New York Times Notable Book 1981.

Suho and the White Horse: A Legend of Mongolia by Yuzo Otsuka, translated by Yasuko Hirawa, illustrated by Suekichi Akaba; Bobbs Merrill, 1969. **Awarded:** Art Books for Children 1976, 1977, 1978.

The Tongue-Cut Sparrow by Momoko Ishii, illustrated by Suekichi Akaba; Lodestar, 1987. **Awarded:** Parents' Choice (Picture Book) 1987; Parents' Choice (Story Book) 1987.

ALBERS, DAVID
Talk, Talk: An Ashanti Legend by Deborah Newton Chocolate, illustrated by David Albers; Troll, 1992. **Awarded:** Parents Choice (Story Book) 1992.

ALBERT, BURTON
Where Does the Trail Lead? by Burton Albert, illustrated by Brian Pinkney; Simon & Schuster, 1991. **Awarded:** Golden Kite (Picture-Illustration honor) 1991.

ALBERTI, O.
Tutto Su Gerusalemme Biblica by O. Alberti and M. Avi-Yonah, illustrated; C. E. Giunti-Bemporad Marzocca, 1970; **Awarded:** Bologna (Graphics for Youth) 1971.

ALBOROUGH, JEZ
Bare Bear written and illustrated by Jez Alborough; Benn, 1984. **Awarded:** Mother Goose (runnerup) 1985.

The Great Games Book [fourteen brilliant board games] illustrated by Jez Alborough and others; A&C Black, 1985. **Awarded:** Bologna (graphics for children) 1987.

ALCOCK, VIVIEN
The Monster Garden by Vivien Alcock, not illustrated; Methuen, 1988. **Awarded:** Carnegie (Commended) 1988.

The Trial of Anna Cotman by Vivien Alcock, not illustrated; Methuen Children's, 1989; Delacorte, 1990. **Awarded:** Carnegie (Commended) 1989.

ALCORN, JOHN
Books! by Murray McCain, illustrated by John Alcorn; Simon & Schuster, 1962. **Awarded:** New York Times Best Illustrated 1962.

Pocahontas in London by Jan Wahl, illustrated by John Alcorn; Delacorte/Seymour Lawrence, 1967. **Awarded:** Bologna (critici in erba) 1969.

Wonderful Time by Phyllis McGinley, illustrated by John Alcorn; Lippincott, 1966. **Awarded:** New York Times Best Illustrated 1966.

ALCOTT, LOUISA MAY
Little Women by Louisa May Alcott, illustrated by Jessie Willcox Smith; Little Brown, 1968, c1868. **Awarded:** Lewis Carroll Shelf 1969.

ALDA, ARLENE
Matthew and His Dad story and photographs by Arlene Alda; Little Simon (Simon & Schuster), 1983. **Awarded:** New Jersey Institute of Technology 1983.

ALDEN, BETTY
Rainbow Round the World: A Story of UNICEF by Elizabeth Yates, illustrated by Betty Alden and Dirk Gringhuis; Bobbs Merrill, 1954. **Awarded:** Jane Addams 1955.

ALDERSON, BRIAN
Awarded: Eleanor Farjeon 1967

The Brothers Grimm: Popular Folk Tales newly translated by Brian Alderson, illustrated by Michael Foreman; Gollancz, 1978. **Awarded:** Greenaway (commended) 1978.

Cakes and Custard: Children's Rhymes compiled by Brian Alderson, illustrated by Helen Oxenbury; Morrow, 1975. **Awarded:** New York Times Notable Books 1975.

ALDOUS, KATE
The Afterdark Princess by Annie Dalton, illustrated by Kate Aldous; Methuen, 1990. **Awarded:** Nottinghamshire (Oak Tree) 1991.

The Real Tilly Beany by Annie Dalton, illustrated by Kate Aldous; Methuen, 1991. **Awarded:** Carnegie (Commended) 1991.

ALDRICH, MARY M.
Too Many Pets by Mary M. Aldrich, illustrated by Barbara Cooney; Macmillan, 1952. **Awarded:** Spring Book Festival (picture book honor) 1952.

ALDRIDGE, ALAN
The Butterfly Ball and the Grasshopper's Feast by William Plomer, illustrated by Alan Aldridge; Cape, 1973. **Awarded:** Whitbread 1973.

ALDRIDGE, JAMES
The True Story of Lilli Stubeck by James Aldridge, not illustrated; Hyland House, 1984. **Awarded:** Children's Book Council of Australia (book of the year) 1985.

The True Story of Spit MacPhee by James Aldridge, not illustrated; Viking Penguin Australia, 1986; Viking Kestrel, 1986; Viking, 1987. **Awarded:** Guardian 1987; New South Wales State Literary Awards (Children's) 1986.

ALDUS, DOROTHY
Awarded: Children's Reading Round Table 1967.

ALEICHEM, SHOLEM
Hanukah Money by Sholem Aleichem, adapted and illustrated by Uri Shulevitz; Greenwillow, 1978. **Awarded:** New York Times Best Illustrated 1978.

ALEXANDER, FRANCES
Pebbles from a Broken Jar: Fables and Hero Stories from Old China by Frances Alexander, illustrated by students of Cheefu, China; Bobbs Merrill, 1969. **Awarded:** Steck-Vaughn 1970.

ALEXANDER, JOCELYN ANNE ARUNDEL
see ARUNDEL, JOYCELYN

ALEXANDER, LLOYD CHUDLEY
Awarded: Drexel 1972; Golden Cat 1984; Helen Keating Ott 1987; Outstanding Pennsylvania Author 1976; Regina 1986.

The Beggar Queen by Lloyd Alexander, not illustrated; Dutton, 1984. **Awarded:** Parents' Choice (literature) 1984.

The Black Cauldron by Lloyd Alexander, not illustrated; Holt, 1965. **Awarded:** Newbery (honor) 1966.

Border Hawk: August Bondi by Lloyd Alexander, illustrated by Bernard Krigstein; Farrar, 1958. **Awarded:** Jewish Book Council 1958.

The Cat Who Wished to be a Man by Lloyd Alexander, not illustrated; Dutton, 1973. **Awarded:** Boston Globe Horn Book (text honor) 1973.

The El Dorado Adventure by Lloyd Alexander, not illustrated; Dutton, 1987. **Awarded:** Parents' Choice (Story Book) 1987.

The First Two Lives of Lukas-Kasha by Lloyd Alexander, not illustrated; Dutton, 1978. **Awarded:** CRABbery 1979; National Book Award (finalist) 1979.

The Fortune-Tellers by Lloyd Alexander, illustrated by Trina Schart Hyman; Dutton, 1992. **Awarded:** Boston Globe Horn Book (Illustration) 1993; Golden Kite (Illustration honor) 1992; New York Times Best Illustrated 1992; Parents Choice (Story Book) 1992.

The High King by Lloyd Alexander, not illustrated; Holt, 1968. **Awarded:** National Book Award (finalist) 1969; Newbery 1969.

The Illyrian Adventure by Lloyd Alexander, illustrated with a map; Dutton, 1986. **Awarded:** Carolyn W. Field 1987; Parents' Choice (literature) 1986.

The Kestrel by Lloyd Alexander, not illustrated; Dutton, 1982; Dell, 1983. **Awarded:** Parents' Choice (literature) 1982.

The Marvelous Misadventures of Sebastian: Grand Extravaganza, Including a Performance by the Entire Cast of the Gallimaufry-Theatricus by Lloyd Alexander, not illustrated; Dutton, 1970. **Awarded:** National Book Award 1971.

The Remarkable Journey of Prince Jen by Lloyd Alexander, map by Bebby L. Carter; Dutton, 1991. **Awarded:** Parents' Choice (Story Book) 1991.

Westmark by Lloyd Alexander, not illustrated; Dutton, 1981. **Awarded:** American Book Awards (children's fiction hardcover) 1982.

ALEXANDER, MARTHA

I'll Protect You from the Jungle Beasts written and illustrated by Martha Alexander; Dial, 1973. **Awarded:** Christopher (ages 4-8) 1974.

Move Over, Twerp written and illustrated by Martha G. Alexander; Dial, 1981. **Awarded:** Kentucky Bluegrass 1984.

Nobody Asked Me if I Wanted a Baby Sister written and illustrated by Martha Alexander; Dial, 1971. **Awarded:** Children's Book Showcase 1972.

Sabrina written and illustrated by Martha Alexander; Dial, 1971. **Awarded:** Spring Book Festival (picture book honor) 1971.

Too Hot for Ice Cream by Jean van Leeuwen, illustrated by Martha Alexander; Dial, 1974. **Awarded:** New Jersey Institute of Technology 1975, 1976.

ALEXANDER, SUE

Awarded: Southern California Council (Dorothy C. McKenzie Award) 1980.

Finding Your First Job by Sue Alexander, photographs by George Ancona; Dutton, 1980. **Awarded:** Golden Kite (nonfiction honor) 1980.

Lila on the Landing by Sue Alexander, illustrated by Ellen Eagle; Clarion, 1987. **Awarded:** Southern California Council (Outstanding Work of Fiction for Children) 1988.

Nadia the Willful by Sue Alexander, illustrated by Lloyd Bloom; Pantheon, 1983. **Awarded:** Southern California Council (distinguished work of fiction) 1984.

ALEXANDER, WILLIAM P.

Land for My Sons: A Frontier Tale of the American Revolution by William P. Alexander and Maribelle Cormack, illustrated by Lyle Justis; Appleton-Century, 1939. **Awarded:** Spring Book Festival (older honor) 1939.

ALGER, LECLAIRE GOWANS
see NIC LEODHAS, SORCHE

ALIKI (pseudonym for Aliki Brandenberg)
Awarded: Drexel Citation 1991; Outstanding

Pennsylvania Author 1991.

At Mary Bloom's written and illustrated by Aliki; Greenwillow, 1976. **Awarded:** Children's Book Showcase 1977.

Bees and Beelines by Judy Hawes, illustrated by Aliki; Crowell, 1964. **Awarded:** New Jersey Institute of Technology (science, ages 5-8) 1964.

Corn is Maize: The Gift of the Indians written and illustrated by Aliki; Crowell, 1976. **Awarded:** New York Academy of Sciences (younger) 1977.

The Listening Walk by Paul Showers, illustrated by Aliki; Crowell, 1961. **Awarded:** New Jersey Institute of Technology 1961.

Mummies Made in Egypt written and illustrated by Aliki; Harper & Row, 1979. **Awarded:** Garden State Children's Book Award (younger nonfiction) 1982.

Three Gold Pieces written and illustrated by Aliki; Pantheon, 1967. **Awarded:** Boys Club 1968.

ALLAIS, ALPHONSE
Histoire du Petit Stephen Girard by Mark Twain, translated from English by Alphonse Allais, illustrated by Jean Michel Nicollet; Editions Gallimard, 1978. **Awarded:** Bologna (graphics for children) 1979.

ALLAN, MABEL ESTHER
An Island in a Green Sea by Mabel E. Allan, illustrated by Charles Robinson; Atheneum, 1972. **Awarded:** Boston Globe Horn Book (text honor) 1973.

Mystery in Wales by Mabel Esther Allan, not illustrated; Vanguard, 1971. **Awarded:** Edgar Allan Poe (runnerup) 1972.

ALLARD, HARRY
Miss Nelson Has a Field Day by Harry Allard, illustrated by James Marshall; Houghton-Mifflin, 1985. **Awarded:** Golden Sower (K-3) 1987; North Dakota Children's Choice (Younger) 1988.

Miss Nelson Is Back by Harry Allard, illustrated by James Marshall; Houghton-Mifflin, 1982. **Awarded:** Colorado 1985; Golden Sower (K-3) 1984; Parents' Choice (literature) 1982.

Miss Nelson Is Missing! by Harry Allard, illustrated by James Marshall; Houghton Mifflin, 1977; Scholastic 1978. **Awarded:** Arizona 1981; Buckeye (K-3 honor) 1982; California Young Reader Medal (primary) 1982; Georgia Children's Picture Storybook 1980; North Dakota Children's Choice (Younger) 1985; Edgar Allan Poe (runnerup) 1978.

The Stupids Die by Harry Allard, illustrated by James Marshall; Houghton Mifflin, 1981. **Awarded:** Arizona 1985.

The Stupids Step Out by Harry Allard, illustrated by James Marshall; Houghton Mifflin, 1974. **Awarded:** Children's Book Showcase 1975.

Three Is Company written and illustrated by Friedrich Karl Waechter, translated by Harry Allard; Doubleday, 1979. **Awarded:** Parents' Choice (Illustration) 1980.

The Tutti-Frutti Case: Starring the Four Doctors of Goodge by Harry Allard, illustrated by James Marshall; Prentice Hall, 1975. **Awarded:** New York Times Best Illustrated 1975.

ALLEE, MARJORIE HILL
The House by Marjorie Allee, illustrated by Helen Blair; Houghton, 1944. **Awarded:** Child Study 1944.

Jane's Island by Marjorie Hill Allee, illustrated by Maitland de Gogorza; Houghton, 1931. **Awarded:** Newbery (honor) 1932.

ALLEN, AGNES
The Story of Your Home by Agnes Allen, illustrated by Agnes Allen and Jack Allen; Faber and Faber, 1949. **Awarded:** Carnegie 1949.

ALLEN, ELEANOR
Wash and Brush Up by Eleanor Allen, illustrated with photographs; A&C Black, 1976. **Awarded:** Times Educational Supplement (junior) 1976.

ALLEN, ERIC
The Latchkey Children by Eric Allen, illustrated by Charles Keeping; Oxford, 1963. **Awarded:** Carnegie (commended) 1963.

ALLEN, FRANCES C.
The Witches' Secret by Frances C. Allen, illustrated by Laura J. Allen; Harper, 1968. **Awarded:** New Jersey Institute of Technology 1969.

ALLEN, GARY
One Day in the Woods by Jean Craighead George, illustrated by Gary Allen; Crowell, 1988. **Awarded:** Washington Irving (Nonfiction) 1990.

ALLEN, GERTRUDE E.
Awarded: Chandler Reward of Merit 1962.

ALLEN, JACK
The Story of Your Home by Agnes Allen, illustrated by Agnes Allen and Jack Allen; Faber and Faber, 1949. **Awarded:** Carnegie 1949.

ALLEN, JEFFREY
Bonzini! The Tattooed Man by Jeffrey Allen, illustrated by James Marshall; Little Brown, 1976. **Awarded:** Children's Book Showcase 1977.

ALLEN, JONATHAN
The Great White Man-Eating Shark by Margaret Mahy, illustrated by Jonathan Allen; Dial, 1990. **Awarded:** Virginia Young Readers (Primary) 1992.

ALLEN, JUDY
Awaiting Developments by Judy Allen, not illustrated; Julia MacRae, 1988; Walker, 1989. **Awarded:** Carnegie (Commended) 1988; Earthworm Award 1989; Whitbread 1988.

ALLEN, LAURA J.
The Witches' Secret by Frances C. Allen, illustrated by Laura J. Allen; Harper, 1968. **Awarded:** New Jersey Institute of Technology 1969.

ALLEN, LORENZO
Fifer for the Union by Lorenzo Allen, illustrated by Brian Wildsmith; Morrow, 1964. **Awarded:** Spring Book Festival (middle honor) 1964.

ALLEN, PAMELA
Belinda written and illustrated by Pamela Allen; Viking, 1992. **Awarded:** Children's Book Council of Australia (Picture Book of the Year honor) 1993.

Bertie and the Bear written and illustrated by Pamela Allen; Hamish-Hamilton, 1983; Coward-McCann, 1984, c1983. **Awarded:** Children's Book Council of Australia (picture book of the year) 1984.

A Lion in the Night written and illustrated by Pamela Allen; Hamilton, 1985. **Awarded:** Russell Clark 1986.

Mr. Archimedes' Bath written and illustrated by Pamela Allen; Bodley Head, 1980; Lothrop, Lee & Shepard, 1980. **Awarded:** New South Wales State Literary Awards (Children's) 1980.

My Cat Maisie written and illustrated by Pamela Allen; Hodder & Stoughton, 1990; Hamish Hamilton, 1990; Viking, 1990. **Awarded:** Aim Children's Book Awards (Picture Book) 1991.

Who Sank the Boat? written and illustrated by Pamela Allen; Nelson Australia, 1982; Coward McCann, 1983. **Awarded:** Children's Book Council of Australia (picture book of the year) 1983; International Board on Books for Young People (illustration/Australia) 1984; New South Wales State Literary Awards (Children's) 1983.

ALLEN, RICHARD E.
Ozzy on the Outside by Richard E. Allen, not illustrated; Delacorte, 1989. **Awarded:** Delacorte Press Prize 1988.

ALLEN, ROBERT THOMAS
The Violin by Robert Thomas Allen, illustrated by George Pastic; McGraw-Hill/Ryerson, 1976. **Awarded:** Ruth Schwartz 1977.

ALLEN, THOMAS B.
In Coal Country by Judith Hendershot, Illustrated by Thomas B. Allen; Knopf, 1987. **Awarded:** Boston Globe Horn Book (Illustration honor) 1987; New York Times Best Illustrated 1987; New York Times Notable 1987; Parents' Choice (Picture Book) 1987.

The Most Beautiful Place in the World by Ann Cameron, illustrated by Thomas B. Allen; Knopf, 1988. **Awarded:** Addams (Fiction Ages 7-up) 1989; Child Study 1988.

ALLEN, THOMAS BENTON
The Quest: A Report on Extra-terrestrial Life by Thomas Benton Allen, illustrated with charts; Chilton, 1965. **Awarded:** Boys Club 1966.

ALLENDE, ISABEL
Of Love and Shadows by Elizabeth Allende, translated from Spanish by Margaret Sayers Peder, not illustrated; Knopf, 1987. **Awarded:** Soaring Eagle (Grades 10-12) 1990.

ALLISON, BOB
The Kid Who Batted 1.000 by Bob Allison and Frank Ernest Hill, illustrated by Paul Galdone; Doubleday, 1951. **Awarded:** Boys Club 1952.

ALLISON, LINDA
The Wild Inside: A Sierra Club Guide to the Great Indoors written and illustrated by Linda Allison; Sierra Club/Scribner, 1979. **Awarded:** New York Academy of Sciences (younger honor) 1980.

ALLSBURG, CHRIS VAN
see VAN ALLSBURG, CHRIS

ALMEDINGEN, E.M.
Anna (Anna Khlebnikova de Poltaratzky, 1770-1840) by E. M. Almedingen, not illustrated; Farrar, 1972. **Awarded:** Spring Book Festival (ages 8-12 honor) 1972.

Young Mark by E.M. Almedingen, illustrated by Victor Ambrus; Farrar, 1968. **Awarded:** Boston Globe Horn Book (text honor) 1968; Spring Book Festival (older) 1968.

ALMEDINGEN, MARTHA EDITH VON
see ALMEDINGEN, E. M.

ALMQUIST, DON
Not Very Much of a House by M. Jean Craig, illustrated by Don Almquist; Norton, 1967. **Awarded:** New Jersey Institute of Technology 1967.

ALOISE, FRANK
George Washington by Vivian L. Thompson, illustrated by Frank Aloise; Putnam, 1964. **Awarded:** New Jersey Institute of Technology (biography, ages 7-9) 1964.

Poetry of Witches, Elves, and Goblins by Leland B. Jacobs, illustrated by Frank Aloise; Garrard, 1970. **Awarded:** New Jersey Institute of Technology 1970.

Uncle Robert's Secret by Wylly Folk St. John, illustrated by Frank Aloise; Viking, 1972. **Awarded:** Edgar Allan Poe (runnerup) 1973.

ALPHIN, ELAINE MARIE
Story in *Young and Alive* magazine. **Awarded:** Magazine Merit Award (Fiction) 1989.

ALS, ROALD
Kristoffers Rejse by Hanne Borner, illustrated by Roald Als; Borgen Denmark, 1980. **Awarded:** Biennale Illustrations Bratislava (grand prix) 1981.

ALTER, JUDITH M.
Luke and the Van Zandt County War by Judith M. Alter, illustrated by Walli Conoly; Texas Christian University, 1984. **Awarded:** Texas Institute of Letters 1985.

ALTER, ROBERT EDMOND
Who Goes Next? True Stories of Exciting Escapes by Robert Edmond Alter, illustrated by A. Orbaan; Putnam, 1966. **Awarded:** Boys Club 1966-67.

ALTHEA
What Is a Union? by Althea, illustrated by Chris Evans; Dinosaur Publications, 1981; Rourke Enterprises, 1981. **Awarded:** Other Award 1981.

ALTSCHULER, FRANZ
The Royal Dirk by Patricia Beatty and John Beatty, illustrated by Franz Altschuler; Morrow, 1966. **Awarded:** Southern California Council (Notable) 1967.

ALTSHULER, SHANNE
The Wood-ash Stars by Marguerite Poland, illustrated by Shanne Altshuler; David Philip, 1983. **Awarded:** Percy Fitzpatrick 1984.

ALVAREZ, CARLOS MARIA
Oscar, Cosmonauta by Carmen Kurtz, illustrated by Carlos Maria Alvarez; E. Juventud (Spain), 1962. **Awarded:** Hans Christian Andersen (runnerup) 1964.

ALVORD, DOUGLAS
A White Heron by Sarah Orne Jewett, illustrated by Douglas Alvord; Tillbury House, 1990. **Awarded:** Book Can Develop Empathy 1990.

AMBRUS, VICTOR G.
Awarded: Greenaway (commended for work in general) 1964.

Beyond the Weir Bridge by Hester Burton, illustrated by Victor G. Ambrus; Crowell, 1970. **Awarded:** Boston Globe Horn Book (text honor) 1971.

Big Ben by David Walker, illustrated by Victor G. Ambrus; Houghton, 1969. **Awarded:** Charlie May Simon 1971-72.

The Bushbabies by William Stevenson, illustrated by Victor G. Ambrus; Houghton, 1965. **Awarded:** Woodward Park School 1967.

Castors Away! by Hester Burton, illustrated by Victor G. Ambrus; Oxford, 1962. **Awarded:** Carnegie (commended) 1962.

Chance, Luck and Destiny by Peter Dickinson, illustrated by Victor G. Ambrus and David Smee; Atlantic-Little, 1976. **Awarded:** Boston Globe Horn Book (nonfiction) 1977.

The Cossacks by Barbara Bartos-Hoeppner, illustrated by Victor G. Ambrus; Walck, 1963. **Awarded:** Spring Book Festival (older) 1963.

The Edge of the Cloud by K. M. Peyton, illustrated by Victor G. Ambrus; Oxford, 1969. **Awarded:** Carnegie 1969.

Flambards by K. M. Peyton, illustrated by Victor G. Ambrus; Oxford, 1967; World, 1968. **Awarded:** Boston Globe Horn Book (text honor) 1969; Carnegie (commended) 1967; Guardian 1970.

Horses in Battle written and illustrated by Victor G. Ambrus; Oxford, 1975. **Awarded:** Greenaway 1975.

The Journey of the Eldest Son by Jenny Grace Fyson, illustrated by Victor G. Ambrus; Oxford, 1965. **Awarded:** Carnegie (commended) 1965.

The Maplin Bird by K. M. Peyton, illustrated by Victor G. Ambrus; Oxford, 1964; World, 1965. **Awarded:** Carnegie (commended) 1964; Spring Book Festival (older honor) 1965.

Mishka written and illustrated by Victor G. Ambrus; Oxford, 1975. **Awarded:** Greenaway 1975.

One is One by Barbara L. Picard, illustrated by Victor G. Ambrus; Oxford, 1965. **Awarded:** Carnegie (commended) 1965.

The Plan for Birdmarsh by K. M. Peyton, illustrated by Victor G. Ambrus; Oxford, 1965. **Awarded:** Carnegie (commended) 1965.

The Royal Navy by Peter Dawlish, illustrated by Victor G. Ambrus; Oxford, 1963. **Awarded:** Greenaway (commended) 1963.

The Sultan's Bath retold and illustrated by Victor G. Ambrus; Oxford, 1971. **Awarded:** Greenaway (highly commended) 1971.

The Three Brothers of Ur by Jenny Grace Fyson, illustrated by Victor G. Ambrus; Oxford, 1964. **Awarded:** Carnegie (commended) 1964.

Three Poor Tailors written and illustrated by Victor G. Ambrus, Hamilton, 1965. **Awarded:** Greenaway 1965.

Thunder in the Sky by K. M. Peyton, illustrated by Victor G. Ambrus; Oxford, 1966. **Awarded:** Carnegie (commended) 1966.

Time of Trial by Hester Burton, illustrated by Victor G. Ambrus; Oxford, 1963; World, 1964. **Awarded:** Carnegie 1963; Greenaway (commended) 1963; Spring Book Festival (older honor) 1964.

Tristan and Iseult by Rosemary Sutcliff, illustrated by Victor G. Ambrus; Bodley Head, 1971. **Awarded:** Carnegie (highly commended) 1971.

When Jays Fly to Barbmo by Margaret Balderson; illustrated by Victor G. Ambrus; Oxford, 1968. **Awarded:** Children's Book Council of Australia (book of the year) 1969; Carnegie (honour) 1968.

The Wild Horse of Santander by Helen Griffiths, illustrated by Victor G. Ambrus; Hutchinson, 1966. **Awarded:** Carnegie (commended) 1966.

Windfall by K. M. Peyton, illustrated by Victor G. Ambrus; Oxford, 1962. **Awarded:** Carnegie (commended) 1962.

Young Mark by E. M. Almedingen, illustrated by Victor G. Ambrus; Farrar, 1968. **Awarded:** Boston Globe Horn Book (text honor) 1968; Spring Book Festival (older) 1968.

AMERICAN ANTIQUARIAN SOCIETY
Awarded: Chandler Reward of Merit 1965.

AMES, EVELYN
My Brother Bird by Evelyn Ames, illustrated by William Pene du Bois; Dodd, 1954. **Awarded:** Spring Book Festival (middle honor) 1954.

AMES, LEE JUDAH
Abe Lincoln: Log Cabin to White House by Sterling North, illustrated by Lee Ames; Random House, 1956. **Awarded:** Spring Book Festival (older honor) 1956.

George Rogers Clark: Soldier and Hero by Jeannette C. Nolan, illustrated by Lee Ames; Messner, 1954. **Awarded:** Indiana Authors Day (children) 1955.

Draw 50 Monsters written and illustrated by Lee Ames; Doubleday, 1983. **Awarded:** Garden State Children's Book Award (younger nonfiction) 1986.

AMES, MILDRED
Who Will Speak for the Lamb? by Mildred Ames, not illustrated; HarperCollins, 1989. **Awarded:** Book Can Develop Empathy 1991.

AMOSS, BERTHE
The Chalk Cross by Berthe Amoss, not illustrated; Seabury, 1976. **Awarded:** Edgar Allan Poe (runnerup) 1977.

AMUNDSEN, RICHARD E.
Black Kettle: King of the Wild Horses by Justin F. Denzel, illustrated by Richard Amundsen; Garrard, 1974. **Awarded:** New Jersey Institute of Technology 1975.

Jumbo: Giant Circus Elephant by Justin F. Denzel, illustrated by Richard Amundsen; Garrard, 1973. **Awarded:** New Jersey Institute of Technology 1973, 1975.

ANCKARSVARD, KARIN INEZ MARIA
Bonifacius the Green by Karin Anckarsvard, illustrated by Ingrid Rosell; Abelard-Schuman, 1961. **Awarded:** Spring Book Festival (middle honor) 1962.

The Robber Ghost by Karin Anckarsvard, translated by Annabelle MacMillan, illustrated by Paul Galdone; Harcourt, 1961. **Awarded:** Spring Book Festival (middle honor) 1961.

ANCONA, GEORGE
Finding Your First Job by Sue Alexander, photographs by George Ancona; Dutton, 1980. **Awarded:** Golden Kite (nonfiction honor) 1980.

Handtalk: An ABC of Finger Spelling and Sign Language by George Ancona, Mary Beth Miller and Remy Charlip, photographs by George Ancona; Parents, 1974. **Awarded:** New York Academy of Sciences (younger honor) 1975.

Handtalk Birthday by Remy Charlip and Mary Beth Miller, photographs by George Ancona; Four Winds, 1987. **Awarded:** New York Times Best Illustrated 1987.

Living in Two Worlds by Maxine B. Rosenberg, illustrated by George Ancona; Lothrop, Lee & Shepard, 1986. **Awarded:** Woodson, Carter G. (Outstanding Merit) 1987.

Turtle Watch written and illustrated by George Ancona; Macmillan, 1987. **Awarded:** New York Academy of Sciences (Younger honorable mention) 1988.

ANDERS, HANNS-JORG
A Foal Is Born by Hans-Heinrich Isenbart, translated by Catherine Edwards, photographs by Hanns-Jorg Anders; Putnam, 1976. **Awarded:** New York Academy of Sciences (younger honor) 1977.

ANDERSEN, DORIS
Slave of the Haida by Doris Andersen, illustrated; Macmillan Canada, 1974. **Awarded:** Canadian Library Assn. (runnerup) 1975.

ANDERSEN, FREDERICK
Hilla of Finland by Geneva de Malroy, illustrated by Frederick Andersen; Nelson, 1941. **Awarded:** Spring Book Festival (middle honor) 1941.

ANDERSEN, HANS CHRISTIAN
The Emperor's New Clothes: A Fairy Tale by Hans Christian Andersen, illustrated by Monika Laimgruber; Addison-Wesley, 1973. **Awarded:** New York Times Best Illustrated 1973.

The Emperor's New Clothes by Hans Christian Andersen, adapted by Jean Van Leeuwen, illustrated by Jack Delano and Irene Delano; Random House, 1971. **Awarded:** Art Books for Children 1974.

The Emperor's New Clothes by Hans Christian Andersen, retold and illustrated by Nadine Bernard Westcott; Little, Brown, 1984. **Awarded:** Redbook (paperback) 1984.

Das Kleine Madchen mit den Schwefelholzchen by Hans Christian Andersen, illustrated by Bernadette Watts; Nord-Sud, 1983. **Awarded:** Owl Prize 1986.

The Little Mermaid by Hans Christian Andersen, retold by Margaret Crawford Maloney, illustrated by Laszlo Gal; Methuen, 1983. **Awarded:** Governor General (illustrator) 1983; Amelia Frances Howard-Gibbon (runnerup) 1984.

The Little Mermaid by Hans Christian Andersen, illustrated by Katie Thamer Treherne; Harcourt Brace Jovanovich, 1989. **Awarded:** Redbook 1989.

The Nightingale by Hans Christian Andersen, translated by Eva Le Gallienne, illustrated by Nancy Ekholm Burkert; Harper, 1965. **Awarded:** Lewis Carroll Shelf 1965; Spring Book Festival (picture book honor) 1965.

The Nightingale by Hans Christian Andersen, illustrated by Demi; Harcourt Brace Jovanovich, 1985. **Awarded:** New York Times Best Illustrated 1985.

The Steadfast Tin Soldier by Hans Christian Andersen, illustrated by Marcia Brown; Scribner, 1953. **Awarded:** Caldecott (honor) 1954.

The Steadfast Tin Soldier by Hans Christian Andersen, illustrated by Fred Marcellino; HarperCollins, 1992. **Awarded:** Parents Choice (Picture Book) 1992.

The Swineherd by Hans Christian Andersen, translated by Anthea Bell, illustrated by Lisbeth Zwerger; Morrow, 1982. **Awarded:** Parents' Choice (illustration) 1982.

Thumbelina by Hans Christian Andersen, translated by R. P. Keigwin, illustrated by Adrienne Adams; Scribner, 1961. **Awarded:** Lewis Carroll Shelf 1962.

The Ugly Duckling by Hans Christian Andersen, illustrated by Robert Van Nutt; Knopf, 1986. **Awarded:** New York Times Best Illustrated 1986.

Ugly Duckling by Hans Christian Andersen, illustrated by Troy Howell; Dodd, Mead, 1987; Putnam, 1990. **Awarded:** Redbook 1990.

The Wild Swans by Hans Christian Andersen, retold by Amy Ehrlich, illustrated by Susan Jeffers; Dial, 1987, c1981. **Awarded:** Redbook 1987.

ANDERSON, BERTHA C.
Tinker's Tim and the Witches by Bertha C. Anderson, illustrated by Lloyd Coe; Little Brown, 1953. **Awarded:** Ohioana 1954.

ANDERSON, CLARENCE WILLIAM
Blaze and the Gypsies written and illustrated by Clarence W. Anderson; Macmillan, 1937. **Awarded:** Spring Book Festival (younger honor) 1937.

ANDERSON, DAVE
Great Quarterbacks of the NFL by Dave Anderson, illustrated with photographs; Random House, 1965. **Awarded:** New Jersey Institute of Technology 1965.

ANDERSON, DAVID A.
The Origin of Life on Earth: An African Creation Myth retold by David A. Anderson, illustrated by Kathleen Atkins Wilson; Sight Productions, 1992. **Awarded:** Coretta Scott King (Illustration) 1993.

ANDERSON, DAVID
I Carve Stone by Joan Fine, photographs by David Anderson; Crowell, 1979. **Awarded:** New Jersey Institute of Technology 1981.

ANDERSON, JOY
The Pai-pai Pig by Joy Anderson, illustrated by Jay Yang; Harcourt, 1967. **Awarded:** Boys Club (certificate) 1968.

Juma and the Magic Jinn by Joy Anderson, illustrated by Charles Mikolaycak; Lothrop, Lee & Shepard, 1986. **Awarded:** Golden Kite (picture illustration honor) 1986.

ANDERSON, LONZO
The Halloween Party by Lonzo Anderson, illustrated by Adrienne Adams; Scribner, 1974. **Awarded:** New Jersey Institute of Technology 1975.

ANDERSON, LUCIA
The Smallest Life Around Us by Lucia Anderson, illustrated by Leigh Grant; Crown, 1978. **Awarded:** New York Academy of Sciences (younger) 1979.

ANDERSON, MADELYN KLEIN
Iceberg Alley by Madelyn K. Anderson, illustrated with maps; Messner, 1976. **Awarded:** New York Academy of Sciences (younger honor) 1977.

ANDERSON, MILDRED N.
Sandra and the Right Prince by Mildred N. Anderson, illustrated by J. Pajet-Fredericks; Oxford, 1951. **Awarded:** Commonwealth Club of California 1951.

ANDERSON, NORMAN D.
Ferris Wheels by Norman D. Anderson and Walter R. Brown, illustrated with photographs; Pantheon, 1983. **Awarded:** New York Academy of Sciences (younger honor) 1984.

ANDERSON, PEGGY KING
Story in *Pockets* magazine. **Awarded:** Magazine Merit Award (Fiction) 1988.

ANDERSON, RACHEL
Moffatt's Road by Rachel Anderson, illustrated by Pat Marriott; Cape, 1978. **Awarded:** Guardian (commended) 1979.

Paper Faces by Rachel Anderson, not illustrated; Oxford University Press, 1991. **Awarded:** Guardian 1992.

ANDERSON, ROBERT L.
Hubert, the Caterpillar Who Thought He Was a Moustache by Wendy Stang and Susan Richards, illustrated by Robert L. Anderson; Quist, 1967. **Awarded:** New York Times Best Illustrated 1967.

ANDERSON, RUS
Gunilla, an Arctic Adventure by Albert Viksten, translated by Gustaf Lannestock, illustrated by Rus Anderson; Nelson, 1957. **Awarded:** Spring Book Festival (older honor) 1957.

ANDO, HIROSHIGE
The Big Wave by Pearl Buck, illustrated by Hiroshige Ando and Nokusai Katsushika; Day, 1948. **Awarded:** Child Study 1948.

ANDRE
Man Must Measure: The Wonderful World of Mathematics by Lancelot T. Hogben, illustrated by Andre and others, maps by Marjorie Saynor; Rathbone Books, 1955. **Awarded:** Carnegie (commended) 1955.

ANDRE, JOHN
Traitor: The Case of Benedict Arnold by Jean Fritz, illustrated by John Andre; Putnam, 1981. **Awarded:** New York Times Notable Books 1981.

ANDREWS, MARY EVANS
Awarded: Children's Reading Round Table 1970.

Hostage to Alexander by Mary Evans Andrews, illustrated by Avery Johnson; McKay, 1961. **Awarded:** Friends of American Writers 1962.

ANDREWS, ROY CHAPMAN
Quest in the Desert by Roy Chapman Andrews, illustrated by Kurt Wiese; Viking, 1950. **Awarded:** Spring Book Festival (older honor) 1950.

Quest of the Snow Leopard by Roy Chapman Andrews, illustrated by Kurt Wiese; Viking, 1955. **Awarded:** Boys Club 1957.

ANDREWS, V.C.
Flowers in the Attic by V. C. Andrews, not illustrated; Pocket Books, 1982. **Awarded:** Young Teens 1989.

ANDRIST, RALPH K.
To the Pacific With Lewis and Clark by Ralph K. Andrist and Edwin R. Bingham, illustrated with photographs, maps, and drawings; Harper and Row, 1967. **Awarded:** Western Writers (nonfiction) 1968

ANFOUSSE, GINETTE
La Cachette by Ginette Anfousse, illustrated; Le Tamanoir, 1976. **Awarded:** International Board on Books for Young People (illustration/Canada) 1978.

La Chicane (The Wrangle) written and illustrated by Ginette Anfousse; La Courte Echelle, 1978. **Awarded:** International Board on Books for Young People (illustration/Canada) 1980.

ANGELL, JUDIE
Awarded: School Library Media Specialists of New York 1988.

In Summertime, It's Tuffy by Judie Angell, not illustrated; Bradbury, 1977. **Awarded:** Ethical Culture School 1977.

A Word from Our Sponsor: or, My Friend Alfred by Judie Angell, not illustrated; Bradbury, 1979. **Awarded:** Ethical Culture School 1979.

ANGELO, VALENTI
Nino written and illustrated by Valenti Angelo; Viking, 1938. **Awarded:** Newbery (honor) 1939.

Roller Skates by Ruth Sawyer, illustrated by Valenti Angelo; Viking, 1936. **Awarded:** Lewis Carroll Shelf 1964; Newbery 1937.

ANGLUND, JOAN WALSH
Awarded: Chandler Reward of Merit 1964.

A Friend Is Someone Who Likes You written and illustrated by Joan Walsh Anglund; Harcourt, 1958. **Awarded:** New York Times Best Illustrated 1958.

ANGUISSOLA, GIANA
Priscilla by Giana Anguissola, illustrated by Gastone Regosta; Mursia, 1958. **Awarded:** Hans Christian Andersen (runnerup) 1960.

ANNETT, CORA
see SCOTT, CORA ANNETT PIPITONE

ANNO, MASAICHIRO
Anno's Mysterious Multiplying Jar by Masaichiro and Mitsumasa Anno, illustrated by Mitsumasa Anno; Philomel, 1983. **Awarded:** New York Academy of Sciences (younger honor) 1984; Parents' Choice (illustration) 1983.

ANNO, MITSUMASA
Awarded: Hans Christian Andersen (illustrator) 1984; George G. Stone 1992.

All in a Day written and illustrated by Mitsumasa Anno; Philomel, 1986. **Awarded:** Jane Addams (honor) 1987.

Anno's Alphabet: an Adventure in Imagination written and illustrated by Mitsumasa Anno; Crowell, 1975. **Awarded:** Art Books for Children 1976, 1977, 1978; Boston Globe Horn Book (illustration) 1975; Children's Book Showcase 1976; Christopher (picturebook) 1976; New York Times Best Illustrated 1975; New York Times Notable Books 1975.

Anno's Britain illustrated by Mitsumasa Anno; Philomel, 1982, c1981. **Awarded:** New York Times Best Illustrated 1982.

Anno's Counting Book written and illustrated by Mitsumasa Anno; Crowell, 1977. **Awarded:** Boston Globe Horn Book (illustration honor) 1977; New York Academy of Sciences (younger honor) 1978; Redbook 1986.

Anno's Italy written and illustrated by Mitsumasa Anno; Collins, 1980. **Awarded:** New York Times Notable Books 1980; Parents' Choice (illustration) 1980.

Anno's Journey written and illustrated by Mitsumasa Anno; Collins, 1978. **Awarded:** Art Books for Children 1979; Boston Globe Horn Book (illustration) 1978.

Anno's Math Games II written and illustrated by Mitsumasa Anno; Philomel, 1989. **Awarded:** Parents' Choice (Picture Book) 1989.

Anno's Math Games III written and illustrated by Mitsumasa Anno; Philomel, 1991. **Awarded:** Parents' Choice (Picture Book) 1991.

Anno's Mysterious Multiplying Jar by Masaichiro and Mitsumasa Anno, illustrated by Mitsumasa Anno; Philomel, 1983. **Awarded:** New York Academy of Sciences (younger honor) 1984; Parents' Choice (illustration) 1983.

Anno's Song Book written and illustrated by Mitsumasa Anno; Kodansha. **Awarded:** Bologna (graphics for children) 1980.

Anno's Unique World written and illustrated by Mitsumasa Anno; Kodansha. **Awarded:** Bologna (graphics for youth) 1978.

Anno's U.S.A. written and illustrated by Mitsumasa Anno; Philomel, 1983. **Awarded:** New York Times Notable Books 1983.

Topsy Turvies: Pictures to Stretch the Imagination written and illustrated by Mitsumasa Anno; Walker/Weatherhill, 1970. **Awarded:** Art Books for Children 1973; New York Times Best Illustrated 1970; Spring Book Festival (picture book honor) 1970.

Upside Downers, Downside Uppers: More Pictures to Stretch the Imagination written and illustrated by Mitsumasa Anno; Weatherhill, 1971. **Awarded:** Art Book for Children 1973.

ANSON, JAY
Amityville Horror by Jay Anson, not illustrated; Prentice Hall, 1977; Bantam, 1978. **Awarded:** South Carolina Young Adult 1980.

ANTAL, ANDREW
Tales the People Tell in Russia by Lee Wyndham, illustrated by Andrew Antal; Messner, 1970. **Awarded:** New Jersey Institute of Technology 1970.

ANTONUCCI, EMIL
Grendel by John Gardner, illustrated by Emil Antonucci; Knopf, 1971. **Awarded:** Emphasis on Reading (Grades 10-12) 1984-85.

APLIN, EILEEN
The Wonderful World of Energy by Lancelot T. Hogben, illustrated by Eileen Aplin and others; Garden City Books, 1957. **Awarded:** Edison Mass Media (science books) 1958.

The Wonderful World of the Sea by James Fisher, illustrated by Eileen Aplin and others; Doubleday, 1957. **Awarded:** Boys Club 1958.

APPEL, BENJAMIN
Man and Magic by Benjamin Appel, illustrated by Jacob Landau; Pantheon, 1966. **Awarded:** New Jersey Institute of Technology 1967.

Why the Chinese Are the Way They Are by Benjamin Appel, illustrated by Samuel H. Bryant; Little Brown, 1968; rev. ed., 1973. **Awarded:** New Jersey Institute of Technology 1968, 1975.

Why the Russians Are the Way They Are by Benjamin Appel, illustrated by Samuel H. Bryant; Little Brown, 1966. **Awarded:** New Jersey Institute of Technology 1966.

APPIAH, PEGGY
Ananse the Spider: Tales from an Ashanti Village by Peggy Appiah, illustrated by Peggy Wilson; Pantheon, 1966. **Awarded:** New York Times Best Illustrated 1966.

APPLE, MARGOT
Angel's Mother's Boyfriend by Judy Delton, illustrated by Margot Apple; Houghton Mifflin, 1985. **Awarded:** Parents' Choice (literature) 1986.

The Chocolate Touch by Patrick Catling, illustrated by Margot Apple; Morrow, 1979. **Awarded:** Massachusetts Children's 1989; Utah Children's Choice 1983.

Yours 'Til Niagara Falls, Abby by Jane O'Connor, illustrated by Margot Apple; Hastings, 1979. **Awarded:** Golden Sower 1982.

ARBUCKLE, DOROTHY FAY
After-harvest Festival: The Story of a Girl of the Old Kankakee by Dorothy Fay Arbuckle, illustrated by Maurice Whitman; Dodd, 1955. **Awarded:** Indiana Authors Day (children) 1956.

ARBUTHNOT, MAY HILL
Awarded: Regina 1964; Women's National Book Assn. 1959.

ARCHAMBAULT, JOHN
Chicka Chicka Boom Boom by John Archambault and Bill Martin, Jr., illustrated by Lois Ehlert; Simon & Schuster, 1989. **Awarded:** Kentucky Bluegrass (K-3) 1991; Boston Globe (Picture Book Honor) 1990.

ARCHER, JANET
A Medley of Folk Songs by Janet Archer; Lowe and Brydone, 1971. **Awarded:** Biennale Illustrations Bratislava (plaque) 1973.

Poor Tom's Ghost by Jane Louise Curry, illustrated by Janet Archer; Atheneum, 1977. **Awarded:** Ohioana 1978.

A Question of Courage by Marjorie Darke, illustrated by Janet Archer; Kestrel, 1975. **Awarded:** Guardian (commended) 1976.

Shadow Cage and Other Tales of the Supernatural by A. Philippa Pearce, illustrated by Janet Archer; Kestrel, 1977. **Awarded:** Carnegie (commended) 1977.

ARCHER, JULES
Epidemic! The Story of the Disease Detectives by Jules Archer, illustrated with photographs; Harcourt, 1977. **Awarded:** New York Academy of Sciences (older honor) 1978.

Indian Foe, Indian Friend: the Story of William S. Harney by Jules Archer, illustrated with photographs; Crowell-Collier, 1970. **Awarded:** Western Writers (nonfiction) 1971.

ARCHER, MARGUERITE
Awarded: ALAN 1977.

ARCHER, MARION FULLER
Awarded: Council for Wisconsin Writers (juvenile) 1969, 1972.

Nine Lives of Moses on the Oregon Trail by Marion Fuller Archer, illustrated by George Armstrong; Whitman, 1968. **Awarded:** State Historical Society of Wisconsin 1969.

Wisconsin, Forward! by Marion Fuller Archer, edited by James T. Rutledge, illustrated; McRoberts, 1978. **Awarded:** Council of Wisconsin Writers (juvenile runnerup) 1979.

ARCHER, P.C.
Dog Who Wanted to Die by P. C. Archer in Jam Magazine (v.4 #1 Sept/ Oct 1983). **Awarded:** Vicky Metcalf Short Story 1984.

ARDIZZONE, EDWARD
The Blackbird in the Lilac by James Reeves, illustrated by Edward Ardizzone; Dutton, 1959. **Awarded:** Spring Book Festival (ages 4-8 honor) 1959.

A Child's Christmas in Wales by Dylan Thomas, illustrated by Edward Ardizzone; Godine, 1980. **Awarded:** New York Times Best Illustrated 1980.

The Dragon by Archibald Marshall, illustrated by Edward Ardizzone; Dutton, 1967. **Awarded:** Spring Book Festival (picture book honor) 1967.

The Island of Fish in the Trees by Eva-Lis Wuorio, illustrated by Edward Ardizzone; World, 1962. **Awarded:** New York Times Best Illustrated 1962.

The Little Bookroom: Eleanor Farjeon's Short Stories for Children chosen by herself, by Eleanor Farjeon, illustrated by Edward Ardizzone; Oxford, 1955; Walck, 1956. **Awarded:** Andersen 1956; Carnegie 1955; Lewis Carroll Shelf 1958.

Little Tim and the Brave Sea Captain written and illustrated by Edward Ardizzone; Walck, 1955. **Awarded:** Lewis Carroll Shelf 1973.

The Minnow Leads to Treasure by A. Philippa Pearce, illustrated by Edward Ardizzone; World, 1958. **Awarded:** Lewis Carroll Shelf 1959; Spring Book Festival (middle honor) 1958.

Minnow on the Say by A. Philippa Pearce, illustrated by Edward Ardizzone; Oxford, 1955. **Awarded:** Carnegie (commended) 1955; International Board on Books for Young People (honour list/Great Britain) 1956.

Naughty Children by Christianna Brand, illustrated by Edward Ardizzone; Dutton, 1963. **Awarded:** Spring Book Festival (middle honor) 1963.

Tim All Alone written and illustrated by Edward Ardizzone; Oxford, 1956. **Awarded:** Greenaway 1956.

Tim's Last Voyage written and illustrated by Edward Ardizzone; Walck, 1973. **Awarded:** New York Times Best Illustrated 1973.

Titus in Trouble by James Reeves, illustrated by Edward Ardizzone; Bodley Head, 1959. **Awarded:** Greenaway (commended) 1959.

ARGENT, KERRY
Derek and the Dinosaur by Mary Blackwood, illustrated by Kerry Argent; Omnibus, 1987. **Awarded:** Ashton Scholastic 1988.

Sebastian Lives in a Hat by Thelma Catterwall, illustrated by Kerry Argent; Omnibus, 1985. **Awarded:** Whitley Awards 1986.

ARGIROFF, LOUISE
Pollen Pie written and illustrated by Louise Argiroff; Atheneum, 1988. **Awarded:** New Jersey Institute of Technology 1989.

ARKIN, ALAN
The Lemming Condition by Alan Arkin, illustrated by Joan Sandin; Harper & Row, 1976. **Awarded:** New York Times Notable Books 1976.

ARMER, LAURA ADAMS
The Forest Pool written and illustrated by Laura Adams Armer; Longmans Green, 1938. **Awarded:** Caldecott (honor) 1939.

Waterless Mountain by Laura Adams Armer, illustrated by Laura Adams Armer and Sidney Armer; Longmans, 1931. **Awarded:** Newbery 1932.

ARMER, SIDNEY
Waterless Mountain by Laura Adams Armer, illustrated by Laura Adams Armer and Sidney Armer; Longmans, 1931. **Awarded:** Newbery 1932.

ARMITAGE, DAVID
The Lighthouse Keeper's Lunch by Ronda Armitage, illustrated by David Armitage; Hutchinson Group NZ Limited, 1977. **Awarded:** Esther Glen 1978.

ARMITAGE, RONDA
The Lighthouse Keeper's Lunch by Ronda Armitage, illustrated by David Armitage; Hutchinson Group NZ Limited, 1977. **Awarded:** Esther Glen 1978.

ARMSTRONG, GEORGE
Six Days from Sunday by Betty Biesterveld, illustrated by George Armstrong; Rand, 1973. **Awarded:** Friends of American Writers (ages 4-8) 1974.

Nine Lives of Moses on the Oregon Trail by Marion Fuller Archer, illustrated by George Armstrong; Whitman, 1968. **Awarded:** State Historical Society of Wisconsin 1969.

ARMSTRONG, JENNIFER
Steal Away by Jennifer Armstrong; Orchard, 1992. **Awarded:** Golden Kite (Fiction honor) 1992.

ARMSTRONG, PATRICIA
Choose Your Grandma by Patricia Armstrong; Cateau Books, 1989. **Awarded:** Vicky Metcalf Short Story 1990.

ARMSTRONG, RICHARD
Cold Hazard by Richard Armstrong, illustrated by C. Walter Hodges; Houghton, 1956. **Awarded:** Spring Book Festival (older) 1956.

Sea Change by Richard Armstrong, illustrated by Michael Leszczynski; Dent, 1948. **Awarded:** Carnegie 1948.

ARMSTRONG, WILLIAM HOWARD
Sounder by William H. Armstrong, illustrated by James Barkley; Harper and Row, 1969. **Awarded:** Lewis Carroll Shelf 1970; Sue Hefly 1976; Nene 1973; Newbery 1970; Mark Twain 1972.

ARNO, ENRICO
Blue Mystery by Margot Benary-Isbert, translated by Clara Winston and Richard Winston, illustrated by Enrico Arno; Harcourt, 1957. **Awarded:** Jane Addams 1957.

Turi's Poppa by Elizabeth Borton de Trevino, illustrated by Enrico Arno; Farrar, 1968. **Awarded:** Boston Globe Horn Book (text honor) 1969.

ARNOLD, CAROLINE
Animals That Migrate by Caroline Arnold, illustrated by Michele Zylman; Carolrhoda, 1982. **Awarded:** New York Academy of Sciences (younger honor) 1983.

Pets Without Homes by Caroline Arnold, photographs by Richard Hewett; Clarion, 1983. **Awarded:** Golden Kite (nonfiction honor) 1983.

Too Fat? Too Thin? Do You Have a Choice? by Caroline Arnold, foreword by Tony Greenberg, not illustrated; Morrow, 1984. **Awarded:** Southern California Council (notable work of nonfiction) 1985.

Trapped in Tar: Fossils From the Ice Age by Caroline Arnold, illustrated by Richard Hewett; Clarion, 1987. **Awarded:** New York Academy of Sciences (Younger honorable mention) 1988.

ARNOLD, ELLIOTT
Finlandia, the Story of Sibelius by Elliott Arnold, illustrated by Lolita Granahan; Holt, 1941. **Awarded:** Spring Book Festival (older honor) 1941.

White Falcon by Elliott Arnold, illustrated by Frederick T. Chapman; Knopf, 1955. **Awarded:** William Allen White 1958.

ARNOLD, RALPH
Kings, Bishops, Knights and Pawns: Life in a Feudal Society by Ralph Arnold, illustrated by Hilary Abrahams; Constable, 1963. **Awarded:** Carnegie (commended) 1963.

ARNOLD, TEDD
No Jumping on the Bed! written and illustrated by Tedd Arnold; Dial, 1987. **Awarded:** Colorado Children's Book Award (Runnerup) 1990; Emphasis on Reading (K-2) 1988-89; Georgia Children's Picture Storybook 1990; North Dakota Children's Choice (Picture Book) 1991; Volunteer State Book Awards (K-3) 1991-92.

ARNOLD, TIM
Natural History from A to Z written and illustrated by Tim Arnold; McElderry, 1991. **Awarded:** Hungry Mind (Young Adult Nonfiction) 1992.

ARNOSKY, JIM
Awarded: Eva L. Gordon 1991; Washington Post Nonfiction Award 1988.

Drawing from Nature written and illustrated by Jim Arnosky; Lothrop, Lee & Shepard, 1982. **Awarded:** Christopher (all ages) 1983; New York Academy of Sciences (older honor) 1983.

ARNTSON, HERBERT E.
Adam Gray, Stowaway: A Story of the China Trade by Herbert E. Arntson, illustrated by Henry S. Gillette; Watts, 1961. **Awarded:** Franklin Watts Juvenile Fiction 1961.

ARORA, SHIRLEY LEASE
What Then, Raman? by Shirley Lease Arora, illustrated by Hans Guggenheim; Follett, 1960. **Awarded:** Jane Addams 1961; Follett 1960; Woodward Park School 1961.

ARQUETTE, LOIS S.
see DUNCAN, LOIS

ARTER, JUDY
Awarded: Frances E. Russell 1989.

ARTHUR, ROBERT
Spies and More Spies by Robert Arthur, illustrated by Saul Lambert; Random House, 1967. **Awarded:** New Jersey Institute of Technology 1967.

ARTIS, VICKI KIMMEL
Brown Mouse and Vole by Vicki Kimmel Artis, illustrated by Jan Hughes; Putnam, 1975. **Awarded:** Council of Wisconsin Writers (picture book runnerup) 1976.

ARTZYBASHEFF, BORIS MIKHAILOVIC
Gay-Neck: The Story of a Pigeon by Dhan Gopal Mukerji, illustrated by Boris Artzybasheff; Dutton, 1927. **Awarded:** Newbery 1928.

Nansen by Anna Gertrude Hall, illustrated by Boris Artzybasheff; Viking, 1940. **Awarded:** Newbery (honor) 1941; Spring Book Festival (older honor) 1940.

Seven Simeons: A Russian Tale written and illustrated by Boris Artzybasheff; Viking, 1937. **Awarded:** Caldecott (honor) 1938; Spring Book Festival(Younger) 1937.

The Wonder-Smith and his Son: A Tale from the Golden Childhood of the World by Ella Young, illustrated by Boris Artzybasheff; Longmans, 1927. **Awarded:** Newbery (honor) 1928.

ARUEGO, ARIANE DEWEY
The Chick and the Ducklings by V. Suteyev, translated and adapted by Mirra Ginsburg, illustrated by Ariane Aruego and Jose Aruego; Macmillan, 1972. **Awarded:** Children's Book Showcase 1973.

A Crocodile's Tale written and illustrated by Ariane Aruego and Jose Aruego; Scribner, 1972. **Awarded:** Children's Book Showcase 1973.

Herman the Helper by Robert Kraus, illustrated by Ariane Dewey and Jose Aruego; Windmill, 1974. **Awarded:** Boston Globe Horn Book (illustration honor) 1974.

Milton the Early Riser by Robert Kraus, illustrated by Ariane Aruego and Jose Aruego; Windmill, 1972. **Awarded:** Art Books for Children 1974, 1975, 1976; New York Times Notable Books 1972.

Owliver by Robert Kraus, illustrated by Ariane Dewey and Jose Aruego; Windmill, 1974. **Awarded:** Children's Book Showcase 1975.

ARUEGO, JOSE

The Chick and the Ducklings by V. Suteyev, translated and adapted by Mirra Ginsburg, illustrated by Ariane Aruego and Jose Aruego; Macmillan, 1972. **Awarded:** Children's Book Showcase 1973.

A Crocodile's Tale written and illustrated by Jose Aruego and Ariane Aruego; Scribner, 1972. **Awarded:** Children's Book Showcase 1973.

Herman the Helper by Robert Kraus, illustrated by Jose Aruego and Ariane Dewey; Windmill, 1974. **Awarded:** Boston Globe Horn Book (illustration honor) 1974.

Leo, the Late Bloomer by Robert Kraus, illustrated by Jose Aruego; Windmill, 1973. **Awarded:** Art Books for Children 1973.

Look What I Can Do written and illustrated by Jose Aruego; Scribner, 1971. **Awarded:** Children's Book Showcase 1972; New York Times Best Illustrated 1971.

Milton the Early Riser by Robert Kraus, illustrated by Jose Aruego and Ariane Aruego; Windmill, 1972. **Awarded:** Art Books for Children 1974, 1975, 1976; New York Times Notable Books 1972.

Owliver by Robert Kraus, illustrated by Jose Aruego and Ariane Dewey; Windmill, 1974. **Awarded:** Children's Book Showcase 1975.

ARUNDEL, JOCELYN

Simba of the White Mane by Jocelyn Arundel, illustrated by Wesley Dennis; Whittlesey, 1958. **Awarded:** Boys Club 1959.

ASARE, MESHACK

Kwajo und das Geheimnis des Trommelmannchens by Meshack Asare, translated by Kathe Recheis; Verlag Jungbrunner, 1984. (original English, *The Brassman's Secret*) **Awarded:** International Board on Books for Young People (translation/Austria) 1986.

ASBJORNSEN, PETER CHRISTEN

Norwegian Folk Tales by Peter Christen Asbjornsen and Jorgen Moe, illustrated by Erik Werenskiold and Theodor Kittelsen; Viking, 1961. **Awarded:** Spring Book Festival (middle) 1961.

ASCH, FRANK

Elvira Everything written and illustrated by Frank Asch; Harper, 1970. **Awarded:** Art Books for Children 1974; New Jersey Institute of Technology 1970.

In the Eye of the Teddy written and illustrated by Frank Asch; Harper, 1973. **Awarded:** New Jersey Institute of Technology 1973.

Rebecka written and illustrated by Frank Asch; Harper, 1972. **Awarded:** Children's Book Showcase 1973; New Jersey Institute of Technology 1973.

Turtle Tale written and illustrated by Frank Asch; Dial, 1978. **Awarded:** New Jersey Institute of Technology 1980.

Yellow, Yellow by Frank Asch, illustrated by Mark Alan Stamaty; McGraw Hill, 1971. **Awarded:** Art Books for Children 1973, 1974, 1975.

ASCHMANN, HELEN TANN

Connie Bell, M.D. by Helen Tann Aschmann, not illustrated; Dodd, 1963. **Awarded:** Edith Busby 1962.

ASH, RUSSELL

Aesop's Fables compiled by Russell Ash and Bernard Higton, illustrated; Chronicle, 1990. **Awarded:** Redbook 1990.

ASHABRANNER, BRENT

Awarded: Washington Post Nonfiction Award 1990.

Born to the Land: An American Portrait by Brent Ashabranner, photographs by Paul Conklin; Putnam, 1989. **Awarded:** Southwest 1989.

Children of the Maya: A Guatemalan Indian Odyssey by Brent Ashabranner, photographs by Paul Conklin; Dodd, Mead, 1986. **Awarded:** Jane Addams (honor) 1987; Woodson (Outstanding Merit) 1987.

Dark Harvest: Migrant Farmworkers in America by Brent Ashabranner, photographs by Paul Conklin; Dodd, Mead, 1985. **Awarded:** Boston Globe Horn Book (nonfiction honor) 1986; Woodson 1986.

Into a Strange Land by Brent K. Ashabranner and Melissa Ashabranner, illustrated with photos; Dodd Mead, 1987. **Awarded:** Christopher (Ages 12-up) 1988; Woodson (Outstanding Merit) 1988.

The Lion's Whiskers: Tales of High Africa by Brent Ashabranner and Russell Davis, illustrated by James G. Teason; Little Brown, 1959. **Awarded:** Spring Book Festival (older honor) 1959.

Morning Star, Black Sun: The Northern Cheyenne Indians and America's Energy Crisis by Brent Ashabranner, photographs by Paul Conklin; Dodd Mead, 1982. **Awarded:** Woodson 1983.

To Live in Two Worlds: American Indian Youth Today by Brent Ashabranner, photographs by Paul Conklin; Dodd, Mead, 1984. **Awarded:** Woodson 1985.

ASHABRANNER, MELISSA

Into a Strange Land by Brent K. Ashabranner and Melissa Ashabranner, illustrated with photos; Dodd Mead, 1987. **Awarded:** Christopher (Ages 12-up) 1988; Woodson (Outstanding Merit) 1988.

ASHFORTH, CAMILLA

Monkey Tricks written and illustrated by Camilla Ashforth; Walker, 1992; Candlewick, 1992. **Awarded:** British Book Awards (Illustrated runnerup) 1992.

ASHLEY, BERNARD

A Kind of Wild Justice by Bernard Ashley, illustrated by Charles Keeping; Oxford, 1978. **Awarded:** Carnegie (commended) 1978.

Running Scared by Bernard Ashley, not illustrated; MacRae, 1986. **Awarded:** Carnegie (commended) 1986.

The Trouble with Donovan Croft by Bernard Ashley, illustrated by Fermin Rocker; Oxford, 1974. **Awarded:** Other Award 1976.

ASIMOV, ISAAC

Awarded: Washington Post/Children's Book Guild 1985.

Building Blocks of the Universe by Isaac Asimov, illustrated with charts; Abelard-Schuman, 1957. **Awarded:** Edison Mass Media (science books for youth) 1958.

ASKA, WARABE

Aska's Animals by David Day, illustrated by Warabe Aska; Doubleday Canada, 1991. **Awarded:** Amelia Frances Howard-Gibbon (Runnerup) 1992.

ASTON, PHILLIPPA
A Day with a Miner by Phillippa Aston, photographs by Chris Fairclough; Wayland, 1981. **Awarded:** Times Educational Supplement (junior) 1982.

ATKINSON, KATHIE
Animal Tracks by Carson Creagh and Kathie Atkinson, illustrated by Richard Hassall; Methuen Australia, 1986. **Awarded:** Whitley Awards 1988.

ATKINSON, LINDA
In Kindling Flame: The Story of Hannah Senesh, 1921-1944 by Linda Atkinson, not illustrated; Lothrop, Lee & Shepard, 1985. **Awarded:** Jewish Book Council (children's literature) 1986.

ATWATER, FLORENCE HASSELTINE
Mr. Popper's Penguins by Florence Atwater and Richard Atwater, illustrated by Robert Lawson; Little Brown, 1938. **Awarded:** Lewis Carroll Shelf 1958; Newbery (honor) 1939; Young Readers Choice 1941.

ATWATER, RICHARD TUPPER
Mr. Popper's Penguins by Richard Atwater and Florence Atwater, illustrated by Robert Lawson; Little Brown, 1938. **Awarded:** Lewis Carroll Shelf 1958; Newbery (honor) 1939; Young Readers Choice 1941.

ATWOOD, ANN
Awarded: Southern California Council (distinguished contribution exhibiting the fusion of poetry and photography) 1972.

New Moon Cove written and illustrated by Ann Atwood; Scribner, 1969. **Awarded:** Boston Globe Horn Book (illustration honor) 1969; Southern California Council (illustration) 1970.

AUBRY, CLAUDE
Je t'attends a Peggy's Cove (original English: *You Can Pick Me up at Peggy's Cove*) by Brian Doyle, translated by Claude Aubry; Pierre Tisseyre, 1982. **Awarded:** International Board on Books for Young People (translator/Canada) 1984.

AUBRY, IRENE
Awarded: Claude Aubry Award 1989.

AULAIRE, EDGAR PARIN d'
see D'AULAIRE, EDGAR PARIN

AULAIRE, INGRI d'
see D'AULAIRE, INGRI

AULT, PHILLIP H.
All Aboard! The Story of Passenger Trains in America by Phil Ault, illustrated with photographs and old prints; Dodd Mead, 1976. **Awarded:** Western Writers 1976.

This is the Desert by Phillip H. Ault, illustrated by Leonard E. Fisher; Dodd Mead, 1959. **Awarded:** Commonwealth Club of California 1959.

AUSTIN, NEAL FULLER
A Biography of Thomas Wolfe by Neal F. Austin, illustrated with photographs; Roger Beacham, 1968. **Awarded:** North Carolina AAUW 1968.

AUTRY, EWART ARTHUR
Ghost Hound of Thunder Valley by Ewart A. Autry, illustrated by Sam Savitt; Dodd Mead, 1965. **Awarded:** Edith Busby 1964.

AVERILL, ESTHER HOLDEN
Jenny's Birthday Book written and illustrated by Esther Averill; Harper, 1954. **Awarded:** New York Times Best Illustrated 1954.

AVERY, GILLIAN ELISE
The Greatest Gresham by Gillian Avery, illustrated by John Verney; Collins, 1962. **Awarded:** Carnegie (commended) 1962.

A Likely Lad by Gillian Avery, illustrated by Faith Jacques; Collins, 1971. **Awarded:** Carnegie (highly commended) 1971; Guardian 1972.

The Warden's Niece by Gillian Avery, illustrated by Dick Hart; Collins, 1957. **Awarded:** Carnegie (commended) 1957.

AVERY, KAY
Wee Willow Whistle by Kay Avery, illustrated by Winifred Bromhall; Knopf, 1947. **Awarded:** Spring Book Festival (younger honor) 1947.

AVI (pseudonym for Avi Wortis)
Emily Upham's Revenge: or, How Deadwood Dick Saved the Banker's Niece: A Massachusetts Adventure by Avi, illustrated by Paul O. Zelinsky; Pantheon, 1978. **Awarded:** Edgar Allan Poe (runnerup) 1979.

Encounter at Easton by Avi, not illustrated; Pantheon, 1980. **Awarded:** Christopher (ages 12-up fiction) 1981.

The Fighting Ground by Avi, not illustrated; Lippincott, 1984. **Awarded:** Scott O'Dell 1984.

No More Magic by Avi, not illustrated; Pantheon, 1975. **Awarded:** Edgar Allan Poe (runnerup) 1976.

Nothing But the Truth by Avi, not illustrated; Orchard, 1991. **Awarded:** Boston Globe Horn Book (Fiction Honor) 1992; Newbery (honor) 1992.

Shadrach's Crossing by Avi, not illustrated; Pantheon, 1983. **Awarded:** New Jersey Institute of Technology 1983; Edgar Allan Poe (runnerup) 1984.

Something Upstairs: A Tale of Ghosts by Avi, not illustrated; Orchard Books, 1988. **Awarded:** Rhode Island 1991; Sunshine State (grades 6-8) 1992; Volunteer State Book Awards (grades 7-9) 1991-92.

A Tale of Terror by Avi; Bradbury, 1986. **Awarded:** Virginia Young Readers (High School) 1990.

The True Confessions of Charlotte Doyle by Avi, illustrated by Ruth E. Murray; Orchard, 1990. **Awarded:** Boston Globe Horn Book (Fiction/Poetry) 1991; Judy Lopez 1991; Newbery (Honor) 1991; Golden Kite (Fiction) 1990.

AVI-YONAH, M.
Tutto Su Gerusalemme Biblica by O. Alberti and M. Avi-Yonah, illustrated; C. E. Giunti-Bemporad Marzocco, 1970. **Awarded:** Bologna (Graphics for Youth) 1971.

AVISHAI, SUSAN
The House on Walenska Street by Charlotte Herman, illustrated by Susan Avishai; Dutton, 1990. **Awarded:** Carl Sandburg 1990.

AWRET, IRENE
Days of Honey: The Tunisian Boyhood of Rafael Uzan by Irene Awret, illustrated with plates; Schocken, 1984. **Awarded:** Korczak (for children) 1986.

AXELROD, STEVE
All About Anna and Harriet and Christopher and Me by Elizabeth Hathorn, illustrated by Steve Axelrod; Methuen, 1986. **Awarded:** Children's Book Council of Australia (book of the year younger honor) 1987.

AXMANN, HANNE
Little Owl by Hanne Axmann and Reiner Zimnik, illustrated by Hanne Axmann; Atheneum, 1962. **Awarded:** New York Times Best Illustrated 1962.

AYARS, JAMES STERLING
Awarded: Children's Reading Round Table 1969.

AYARS, REBECCA CAUDILL
see CAUDILL, REBECCA

AYER, MARGARET
The Lost Kingdom by Chester Bryant, illustrated by Margaret Ayer; Messner, 1951. **Awarded:** Julia Ellsworth Ford 1950.

The Thirteenth Stone by Jean Bothwell, illustrated by Margaret Ayer; Harcourt, 1946. **Awarded:** Spring Book Festival (middle) 1946.

AYLESWORTH, JIM
Old Black Fly by Jim Aylesworth, illustrated by Stephen Gammell; Holt, 1992. **Awarded:** Minnesota (Younger Children) 1993.

AYTO, RUSSELL
Quacky, Quack-quack! by Ian Whybrow, illustrated by Russell Ayto; Walker, 1991; Four Winds, 1991. **Awarded:** Mother Goose (runnersup) 1992.

AZARIAN, MARY
The Tale of John Barleycorn: or, From Barley to Beer: a Traditional English Ballad written and illustrated by Mary Azarian; Godine, 1982. **Awarded:** Parents' Choice (illustration) 1983.

AZON, GARY
Duey's Tale by Pearl Bailey, photographs by Gary Azon and Arnold Skolnick; Harcourt, 1975. **Awarded:** Coretta Scott King 1976.

B

B. B.
see WATKINS-PITCHFORD, DENYS JAMES

BABBITT, NATALIE
Awarded: Keene State College Award 1993; George G. Stone (for her body of work) 1979.

The Devil's Other Storybook written and illustrated by Natalie Babbitt; Farrar, Straus, Giroux, 1987. **Awarded:** Parents' Choice (Story Book) 1987.

The Devil's Storybook written and illustrated by Natalie Babbitt; Farrar, 1974. **Awarded:** National Book Award (finalist) 1975.

Goody Hall written and illustrated by Natalie Babbitt; Farrar, 1971. **Awarded:** Children's Book Showcase 1972; Edgar Allan Poe (runnerup) 1972; Spring Book Festival (middle honor) 1971.

Herbert Rowbarge by Natalie Babbitt, not illustrated; Farrar, 1982. **Awarded:** New York Times Notable Books 1982.

Knee-knock Rise written and illustrated by Natalie Babbitt; Farrar, 1970. **Awarded:** Newbery (honor) 1971.

More Small Poems by Valerie Worth, illustrated by Natalie Babbitt; Farrar, 1976. **Awarded:** Children's Book Showcase 1977.

Tuck Everlasting by Natalie Babbitt, not illustrated; Farrar, 1975. **Awarded:** Lewis Carroll Shelf 1978; Christopher (ages 9-12) 1976; International Board on Books for Young People (Text) 1978; New York Times Notable Books 1975.

BACH, ALICE
Cracking Open the Geode: the Fiction of Paula Fox by Alice Bach in Horn Book October 1977. **Awarded:** Children's Literature Assn. Excellence in Literary Criticism (runnerup) 1978.

BACH, RICHARD
Jonathan Livingston Seagull by Richard Bach, illustrated with photographs; Macmillan, 1970. **Awarded:** Nene 1974.

BACON, PAUL
Teammates by Peter Golenbock, illustrated by Paul Bacon; Harcourt Brace Jovanovich, 1990. **Awarded:** Redbook 1990; Carter G. Woodson (Outstanding Merit - Elementary) 1991.

BACON, RONALD LEONARD
The Fish of our Fathers by Ronald Leonard Bacon, illustrated by Robert H. G. Jahnke; Waiatarua Press, 1984; Child's Play International, 1986. **Awarded:** AIM Children's Book Award 1985.

The House of the People by Ron L. Bacon, illustrated by Robert Jahnke; Collins, 1977. **Awarded:** Russell Clark 1978.

BADER, BARBARA
Aesop and Company prepared by Barbara Bader, illustrated by Arthur Geisert; Houghton Mifflin, 1991. **Awarded:** Aesop Prize 1993.

The Farm Book written and illustrated by E. Boyd Smith, introduction by Barbara Bader; Houghton Mifflin, 1982, c1938. **Awarded:** Parents' Choice (Illustration) 1982.

BAER, EDITH
A Frost in the Night: a Childhood on the Eve of the Third Reich by Edith Baer, not illustrated; Pantheon, 1980. **Awarded:** New Jersey Institute of Technology 1981.

BAGSHAW, RUTH
Charley the Mouse Finds Christmas by Wayne Carley, illustrated by Ruth Basgshaw; Garrard, 1972. **Awarded:** New Jersey Institute of Technology 1972.

BAHTI, TOM
When Clay Sings by Byrd Baylor, illustrated by Tom Bahti; Scribner, 1972. **Awarded:** Caldecott (honor) 1973; Steck-Vaughn 1973.

BAILEY, CAROLYN SHERWIN
Miss Hickory by Carolyn Sherwin Bailey, illustrated by Ruth Chrisman Gannett; Viking, 1946. **Awarded:** Newbery 1947.

BAILEY, JEAN
Cherokee Bill: Oklahoma Pacer by Jean Bailey, illustrated by Pers Crowell; Abingdon-Cokesbury, 1952. **Awarded:** William Allen White 1955.

BAILEY, MARGERY
Whistle for Good Fortune by Margery Bailey, illustrated by Alice B. Preston; Little, Brown, 1940. **Awarded:** Spring Book Festival (younger honor) 1940.

BAILEY, PEARL
Duey's Tale by Pearl Bailey, photographs by Gary Azon and Arnold Skolnick; Harcourt, 1975. **Awarded:** Coretta Scott King 1976.

BAILLIE, ALLAN

Adrift! by Allan Baillie, not illustrated; Blackie, 1983. **Awarded:** Kathleen Fidler 1983.

The China Coin by Allan Baillie, not illustrated; Viking, 1991; Blackie, 1991. **Awarded:** Australian Multicultural Children's Literature Award (Senior Fiction) 1992.

Drac and the Gremlin by Allan Baillie, illustrated by Jane Tanner; Viking Kestrel, 1988; Dial, 1989. **Awarded:** Children's Book Council of Australia (Picture Book of the Year) 1989.

Little Brother by Allan Baillie, not illustrated; Blackie, 1985. **Awarded:** Children's Book Council of Australia (book of the year highly commended) 1986.

Riverman by Allan Baillie, not illustrated; Thomas Nelson, 1986. **Awarded:** International Board on Books for Young People (Writing/Australia) 1988.

BAITY, ELIZABETH CHESLEY

Americans Before Columbus by Elizabeth Chesley Baity, illustrated by C. B. Falls; Viking, 1951. **Awarded:** Newbery (honor) 1952; Spring Book Festival (older) 1951.

BAKER, ALAN

The Battle of Bubble and Squeak by A. Philippa Pearce, illustrated by Alan Baker; Deutsch, 1978. **Awarded:** Carnegie (commended) 1978; Whitbread 1978.

BAKER, AUGUSTA

Awarded: Grolier 1968; Regina 1981; Women's National Book Assn. 1971.

BAKER, BETTY

Awarded: Outstanding Arizona Author Award 1988.

And One Was a Wooden Indian by Betty Baker, not illustrated; Macmillan, 1970. **Awarded:** Western Heritage 1971

The Dunderhead War by Betty Baker, not illustrated; Harper & Row, 1967. **Awarded:** Western Writers (fiction) 1968

Dupper by Betty Baker, illustrated by Chuck Eckart; Greenwillow, 1976. **Awarded:** Children's Book Showcase 1977.

Killer-of-Death by Betty Baker, illustrated by John Kaufmann; Harper, 1963. **Awarded:** Western Heritage 1964.

BAKER, CHARLOTTE

Cockleburr Quarters by Charlotte Baker, illustrated by Robert Owens; Prentice Hall, 1972. **Awarded:** Lewis Carroll Shelf 1973; Spring Book Festival (ages 8-12) 1972.

BAKER, D. PHILIP

Awarded: American Assn. of School Librarians 1982.

BAKER, ELIZABETH

Sonny-boy Sim by Elizabeth Baker, illustrated by Susanne Suba; Rand McNally, 1948. **Awarded:** Spring Book Festival (younger honor) 1949; Steck-Vaughn 1951.

Stocky, Boy of West Texas by Elizabeth Baker, illustrated by Charles Hargens; Winston, 1945. **Awarded:** Spring Book Festival (older honor) 1945.

BAKER, JEANNIE

Home in the Sky written and illustrated by Jeannie Baker; Julia MacRae, 1984. **Awarded:** Children's Book Council of Australia (picture book of the year commended) 1985.

Where the Forest Meets the Sea written and illustrated by Jeannie Baker; Julia McRae, 1987; Greenwillow, 1987. **Awarded:** Boston Globe (Picture Book honor) 1988; Children's Book Council of Australia (Picture Book Honour) 1988; Earthworm Award 1988; International Board on Books for Young People (Illustration/Australia) 1990; KOALA (Primary) 1990; Reading Magic Award 1988; Young Australian Best Book (Picture Book) 1988.

Window written and illustrated by Jeannie Baker; Julia MacRae, 1991; Greenwillow, 1991. **Awarded:** Children's Book Council of Australia (Picture Book) 1992; Young Australian Best Book (Picture Book) 1992.

BAKER, KEITH

The Dove's Letter written and illustrated by Keith Baker; Harcourt Brace Jovanovich, 1988. **Awarded:** Parents' Choice (Picture Book) 1988.

The Magic Fan written and illustrated by Keith Baker; Harcourt Brace Jovanovich, 1989. **Awarded:** UNICEF-Ezra Jack Keats National Award for Children's Book Illustration 1989.

BAKER, LAURA

The Friendly Beasts by Laura Baker, illustrated by Nicholas Sidjakov; Parnassus, 1957. **Awarded:** New York Times Best Illustrated 1957.

BAKER, LESLIE

The Third-Story Cat written and illustrated by Leslie Baker; Little Brown, 1987. **Awarded:** International Reading Assn. (Younger) 1988.

BAKER, MARGARET JOYCE

Castaway Christmas by Margaret J. Baker, illustrated by Richard Kennedy; Methuen, 1963. **Awarded:** Carnegie (commended) 1963.

Homer the Tortoise by Margaret J. Baker, illustrated by Leo Bates; Whittlesey House, 1949, 1950. **Awarded:** Spring Book Festival (ages 8-12 honor) 1950.

BAKER, OLAF

Where the Buffaloes Begin by Olaf Baker, illustrated by Stephen Gammell; Warne, 1981. **Awarded:** Boston Globe Horn Book (illustration honor) 1981; Caldecott (honor) 1982; New York Times Best Illustrated 1981; New York Times Notable Books 1981.

BALCH, GLENN

Lost Horse by Glenn Balch, illustrated by Pers Crowell; Grosset & Dunlap, 1950. **Awarded:** Boys Club 1951.

BALDERSON, MARGARET

A Dog Called George by Margaret Balderson, illustrated by Nikki Jones; Oxford, 1975. **Awarded:** Writers Award 1976.

When Jays Fly to Barbmo by Margaret Balderson, illustrated by Victor G. Ambrus; Oxford, 1968. **Awarded:** Carnegie (honour) 1968; Children's Book Council of Australia (book of the year) 1969.

BALDRIDGE, CYRUS LeROY

Lassie Come Home by Eric Knight, illustrated by Cyrus L. Baldridge; Holt, 1940. **Awarded:** Young Reader's Choice 1943.

BALET, JAN B.

Rumpelstiltskin by Jacob and Wilhelm Grimm, adapted by Patricia Jones, illustrated by Jan B. Balet; Rand McNally, 1955. **Awarded:** New York Times Best Illustrated 1955.

BALIAN, LORNA

The Socksnatchers written and illustrated by Lorna Balian; Abingdon, 1988. **Awarded:** Emphasis on Reading (Grades K-2) 1990-91.

The Sweet Touch written and illustrated by Lorna Balian; Abingdon, 1976. **Awarded:** Colorado Children's Book

Award 1978; Georgia Picture Story Book Award 1978; Little Archer 1979.

A Sweetheart for Valentine written and illustrated by Lorna Balian; Abingdon, 1979. **Awarded:** Council for Wisconsin Writers (picture book) 1980.

BALKWILL, FRAN
Cells Are Us by Fran Balkwill, illustrated by Mic Rolph; HarperCollins, 1990. **Awarded:** Science Book Prizes 1991.

Cell Wars by Fran Balkwill, illustrated by Mic Rolph; HarperCollins, 1990. **Awarded:** Science Book Prizes 1991.

BALL, DUNCAN
Selby Screams by Duncan Bell, illustrated by Allan Stomann; Angus & Robertson, 1989. **Awarded:** West Australian (Primary) 1991.

Selby Speaks by Duncan Ball, illustrated by Allan Stomann; Angus & Robertson, 1988. **Awarded:** West Australian (Primary) 1990.

Selby's Secret by Duncan Ball, illustrated by Allan Stomann; Angus & Robertson, 1985. **Awarded:** West Australian (Primary) 1987.

BALL, ROBERT
Clara Barton by Mildred M. Pace, illustrated by Robert Ball; Scribner, 1941. **Awarded:** Spring Book Festival (older) 1941.

BALL, ZACHARY
Bristle Face by Zachary Ball, not illustrated; Holiday House, 1962. **Awarded:** Dorothy Canfield Fisher 1964; Spring Book Festival (older honor) 1962; William Allen White 1965.

BALMER, HELEN
Awarded: Macmillan Prize (2nd prize) 1990.

BANCROFT, BRONWYN
The Fat and Juicy Place by Diana Kidd, illustrated by Bronwyn Bancroft; Angus & Robertson, 1992. **Awarded:** Australian Multicultural (Junior) 1993.

BANCROFT, GRIFFING
Vanished Wings: a Tale of Three Birds of Prey by Griffing Bancroft, illustrated by John Hamberger; Watts, 1972. **Awarded:** Christopher (teenage) 1973.

BANG, MOLLY
Dawn written and illustrated by Molly Bang; Morrow, 1983. **Awarded:** Boston Globe Horn Book (illustration honor) 1984.

The Grey Lady and the Strawberry Snatcher written and illustrated by Molly Bang; Four Winds, 1980. **Awarded:** Boston Globe Horn Book (illustration honor) 1980; Caldecott (honor) 1981.

The Paper Crane written and illustrated by Molly Bang; Greenwillow, 1985. **Awarded:** Boston Globe Horn Book (illustration) 1986; International Board on Books for Young People (Illustration/USA) 1988.

Ten, Nine, Eight written and illustrated by Molly Bang; Greenwillow, 1983. **Awarded:** Caldecott (honor) 1984.

Wiley and the Hairy Man written and illustrated by Molly Garrett Bang; Macmillan, 1976. **Awarded:** Edgar Allan Poe (runnerup) 1977.

BANKS, LYNNE REID
The Adventures of King Midas by Lynne Reid Banks, illustrated by George Him; Dent, 1976. **Awarded:** W. H. Smith (£50) 1977.

The Indian in the Cupboard by Lynne Reid Banks, illustrated by Brock Cole; Doubleday, 1980. **Awarded:** Arizona Young Readers Award 1989; California Young Reader (Intermediate) 1985; Caudill Young Reader's Book Award 1988; Massachusetts Children's Book Award 1988; New York Times Notable Books 1981; Virginia Young Readers (Elementary) 1988; Young Readers Choice 1984.

My Darling Villain by Lynne Reid Banks, not illustrated; Bodley Head, 1977; Harper, 1977. **Awarded:** West Australian Young Readers (secondary) 1980.

The Return of the Indian by Lynne Reid Banks, illustrated by William Geldart; Doubleday, 1986. **Awarded:** Indian Paintbrush 1989; New York Times Notable 1986; Parents Choice (Literature) 1986.

The Secret of the Indian by Lynne Reid Banks, illustrated by Ted Lewin; Doubleday, 1989. **Awarded:** Great Stone Face 1991.

BANKS, SANDRA
Rabbit and Wolf written and illustrated by Sandra Banks. **Awarded:** Macmillan Prize (Third Prize) 1992.

BANNATYNE-CUGNET, JO
A Prairie Alphabet, ABC by Jo Bannatyne-Cugnet, illustrated by Yvette Moore; Tundra, 1992. **Awarded:** Mr. Christie's (English Illustration) 1992.

BANNON, LAURA MAY
Awarded: Children's Reading Round Table 1962.

Pecos Bill, the Greatest Cowboy of All Times by James Cloyd Bowman, illustrated by Laura Bannon; Whitman, 1937. **Awarded:** Lewis Carroll Shelf 1958; Newbery (honor) 1938; Spring Book Festival (older honor) 1937.

When the Moon Is New written and illustrated by Laura Bannon; Whitman, 1953. **Awarded:** Spring Book Festival (picture book honor) 1953.

BARASS, WILLIAM
Awarded: Chandler Reward of Merit 1971.

BARBEAU, CHARLES MARIUS
The Golden Phoenix and Other French Canadian Fairy Tales by Charles Marius Barbeau, retold by Michael Hornyansky, illustrated by Arthur Price; Oxford, 1958. **Awarded:** Canadian Library Assn. 1960.

BARBER, ANTONIA
The Enchanter's Daughter by Antonia Barber, illustrated by Errol Le Cain; Farrar, Straus, Giroux, 1988, c1987. **Awarded:** Parents' Choice (Picture Book) 1988; Redbook 1988.

The Mousehole Cat by Antonia Barber, illustrated by Nicola Bayley; Walker, 1990; Macmillan, 1990. **Awarded:** British Book Awards (Illustrated) 1990; Greenaway (Commended) 1990.

BARBER, RICHARD
Tournaments by Richard Barber, illustrated by Anne Dalton; Kestrel, 1978. **Awarded:** Times Educational Supplement (junior) 1978.

BARBERIS, FRANCO
Ich Schenk Dir Einen Papagei! by Franco Barberis; Diogenes Verlag, 1964. **Awarded:** Bologna (critici in erba) 1967.

BARBOUR, KAREN
Flamboyan by Arnold Adoff, illustrated by Karen Barbour; Harcourt Brace Jovanovich, 1988. **Awarded:** Parents' Choice (Picture Book) 1988.

Little Nino's Pizzeria written and illustrated by Karen Barbour; Harcourt Brace Jovanovich, 1987. **Awarded:** Parents' Choice (Picture Book) 1987.

BARCLAY, JAMES
Winds by Mary O'Neill, illustrated by James Barclay; Doubleday, 1971. **Awarded:** Ohioana 1972.

BARCLIFT, STEPHEN T.
The Beginner's Devotional by Stephen T. Barclift, illustrated by Jerry Werner; Questar Publishers, 1991. **Awarded:** Gold Medallion (Elementary) 1992.

BARE, ARNOLD EDWIN
Pierre Pidgeon by Lee Kingman, illustrated by Arnold Edwin Bare; Houghton, 1943. **Awarded:** Caldecott (honor) 1944.

BARKER, CAROL M.
Achilles the Donkey by Herbert E. Bates, illustrated by Carol Barker; Dobson, 1962. **Awarded:** Greenaway (commended) 1962.

King Midas and the Golden Touch written and illustrated by Carol Barker; Watts, 1972. **Awarded:** Greenaway (commended) 1972.

BARKER, MARY
Milenka's Happy Summer by Mary Barker, illustrated by Paul Lantz; Dodd, 1961. **Awarded:** Edith Busby 1960.

BARKER, ROBERT
The Boy Scientist by John B. Lewellen, illustrated by Robert Barker; Simon and Schuster, 1955. **Awarded:** Edison Mass Media (science books) 1956.

BARKHOUSE, JOYCE C.
Pit Pony by Joyce C. Barkhouse, illustrated by Henry Van Der Linde; Gage, 1989. **Awarded:** Brimer 1991.

BARKLEM, JILL
Spring Story (Brambly Hedge series) written and illustrated by Jill Barklem; Collins, 1980. **Awarded:** Owl Prize 1981.

BARKLEY, JAMES EDWARD
Sounder by William H. Armstrong, illustrated by James Barkley; Harper & Row, 1969. **Awarded:** Lewis Carroll Shelf 1970; Sue Hefly 1976; Nene 1973; Newbery 1970; Mark Twain 1972.

BARLOWE, DOROTHEA
Then and Now by George Zappler and Lisbeth Zappler, illustrated by Dorothea Barlowe and Sy Barlowe; McGraw Hill, 1974. **Awarded:** New Jersey Institute of Technology 1976.

BARLOWE, SY
Then and Now by George Zappler and Lisbeth Zappler, illustrated by Dorothea Barlowe and Sy Barlowe; McGraw Hill, 1974. **Awarded:** New Jersey Institute of Technology 1976.

BARNARD, PEGGY
Wish and the Magic Nut by Peggy Barnard, illustrated by Sheila Hawkins; Sands, 1956. **Awarded:** Children's Book Council of Australia (picture book) 1956.

BARNE, KITTY
Three and a Pigeon by Kitty Barne, illustrated by Stuart Tresilian; Dodd Mead, 1944. **Awarded:** Spring Book Festival (middle honor) 1944.

Visitors from London by Kitty Barne, illustrated by Ruth Gervis; Dent, 1940. **Awarded:** Carnegie 1940.

BARNES, JOSEPH
What It's All About by Vadim Frolov, translated by Joseph Barnes, not illustrated; Doubleday, 1968. **Awarded:** Child Study 1968.

BARNES, NANCY
The Wonderful Year by Nancy Barnes, illustrated by Kate Seredy; Messner, 1946. **Awarded:** Julia Ellsworth Ford 1945; Newbery (honor) 1947.

BARNEY, MAGINEL WRIGHT
Downright Dencey by Caroline Dale Snedeker, illustrated by Maginel W. Barney; Doubleday, 1927. **Awarded:** Newbery (honor) 1928.

BARNHOUSE, DOROTHY P.
The Quest of the Golden Gannet by Dorothy P. Barnhouse, illustrated; Breakwater Books, 1979. **Awarded:** Beaver Trophy 1975.

BARNSTONE, ALIKI
The Real Tin Flower: Poems About the World at Nine by Aliki Barnstone, illustrated by Paul Giovanopoulos; Crowell-Collier, 1968. **Awarded:** New York Times Best Illustrated 1968.

BARNSTONE, WILLIS
A Day in the Country by Willis Barnstone, illustrated by Howard Knotts; Harper & Row, 1971. **Awarded:** Indiana Author's Day (children) 1972.

BARNUM, JAY HYDE
Boats on the River by Marjorie Flack, illustrated by Jay Hyde Barnum; Viking, 1946. **Awarded:** Caldecott (honor) 1947.

The Kid from Tomkinsville by John R. Tunis, illustrated by Jay Hyde Barnum; Harcourt, 1940. **Awarded:** Spring Book Festival (older honor) 1940.

BAROKAS, BERNARD
Trois Petits Flocons by Bernard Barokas and Joelle Boucher, illustrated; Grasset & Fasquelle, 1974. **Awarded:** Bologna (graphics for children) 1975.

BARR, JENE
Awarded: Children's Reading Round Table 1959.

BARRACCA, DEBRA
The Adventures of Taxi Dog by Debra Barracca and Sal Barracca, illustrated by Mark Buehner; Dial, 1990. **Awarded:** Parents' Choice (Picture Book) 1990.

BARRACCA, SAL
The Adventures of Taxi Dog by Sal Barracca and Debra Barracca, illustrated by Mark Buehner; Dial, 1990. **Awarded:** Parents' Choice (Picture Book) 1990.

BARRETT, ANGELA
Can It Be True? by Susan Hill, illustrated by Angela Barrett; Hamish Hamilton, 1988. **Awarded:** Smarties (6-8s) 1988.

The Hidden House by Martin Waddell, illustrated by Angela Barrett; Walker Books, 1989. **Awarded:** W. H. Smith 1991.

The King, the Cat and the Fiddle by Yehudi Menuhin and Christopher Hope, illustrated by Angela Barrett; Benn, 1983. **Awarded:** Mother Goose (runnerup) 1984.

The Woman in the Moon and Other Tales of Forgotten Heroines by James Riordan, illustrated by Angela Barrett; Hutchinson, 1984. **Awarded:** Maschler (runnerup) 1984.

BARRETT, ANNE
Songberd's Grove by Anne Barrett, illustrated by David Knight; Collins, 1957. **Awarded:** Carnegie (commended) 1957.

BARRETT, JENNIFER
Imagine That! Exploring Make-believe by Joyce Strauss, illustrated by Jennifer Barrett; Human Sciences Press, 1984. **Awarded:** Christopher (All Ages) 1985.

Promise Not to Tell by Carolyn Polese, illustrated by Jennifer Barrett; Human Sciences Press, 1985. **Awarded:** Christopher (8-up) 1986.

BARRETT, JUDI
Benjamin's Three Hundred and Sixty Five Birthdays by Judi Barrett, illustrated by Ron Barrett; Atheneum, 1974. **Awarded:** Children's Book Showcase 1975.

Cloudy With a Chance of Meatballs by Judi Barrett, illustrated by Ron Barrett; Atheneum, 1978. **Awarded:** Buckeye (K-3 honor) 1982; Buckeye (K-3 honor) 1983; Colorado Children's Book Award 1980; Georgia Picture Storybook 1984; Golden Sower (K-3) 1983; New York Times Best Illustrated 1978.

BARRETT, RON
Benjamin's Three Hundred and Sixty Five Birthdays by Judi Barrett, illustrated by Ron Barrett; Atheneum, 1974. **Awarded:** Children's Book Showcase 1975.

Bible Stories You Can't Forget by Marshall Efron and Alpha-Betty Olsen, illustrated by Ron Barrett; Dutton, 1976; Dell, 1979. **Awarded:** New York Times Notable Books 1976.

Cloudy With a Chance of Meatballs by Judi Barrett, illustrated by Ron Barrett; Atheneum, 1978. **Awarded:** Buckeye (K-3 honor) 1982; Buckeye (K-3 honor) 1983; Colorado Children's Book Award 1980; Georgia Picture Storybook 1984; Golden Sower (K-3) 1983; New York Times Best Illustrated 1978.

BARRON, JOHN N.
Herbert by Hazel H. Wilson, illustrated by John N. Barron; Knopf, 1950. **Awarded:** Spring Book Festival (8-12 honor) 1950.

BARRY, KATHARINA WATJEN
A Is for Anything: An ABC Book of Pictures and Rhymes written and illustrated by Katharina Barry; Harcourt, 1961. **Awarded:** New Jersey Institute of Technology (ages 3-5) 1962.

Spaghetti for Breakfast and Other Useful Phrases in Italian and English by Sesyle Joslin, illustrated by Katharina Barry; Harcourt, 1965. **Awarded:** Spring Book Festival (picture book honor) 1965.

BARRY, ROBERT E.
Next, Please written and illustrated by Robert E. Barry; Houghton, 1961. **Awarded:** Boys Club 1962.

This Is the Story of Faint George Who Wanted to Be a Knight written and illustrated by Robert E. Barry; Houghton, 1957. **Awarded:** Boys Club 1958; New York Times Best Illustrated 1957.

BARSTOW, JAN
Awarded: Lucile M. Pannell 1989.

BARTHELME, DONALD
The Slightly Irregular Fire Engine: or, The Hithering Thithering Djinn written and illustrated by Donald Barthelme; Farrar, 1971. **Awarded:** Children's Book Showcase 1972; National Book Award 1972.

BARTHOLOMEW, BARBARA
Julie's Magic Moment by Barbara Bartholomew, not illustrated; New American Library, 1983. **Awarded:** Golden Medallion 1984.

BARTO, AGNIJA
Awarded: Hans Christian Andersen (highly commended author) 1976.

BARTON, BYRON
Airport written and illustrated by Byron Barton; Crowell Jr. Books, 1982. **Awarded:** New York Times Notable Books 1982.

Dinosaurs, Dinosaurs written and illustrated by Byron Barton; Crowell, 1989. **Awarded:** Please Touch 1990.

A Girl Called Al by Constance Greene, illustrated by Byron Barton; Viking, 1969. **Awarded:** Spring Book Festival (middle honor) 1969.

I Want To Be an Astronaut written and illustrated by Byron Barton; Crowell, 1988. **Awarded:** New York Times Best Illustrated 1988.

The Paper Airplane Book by Seymour Simon, illustrated by Byron Barton; Viking, 1971. **Awarded:** Children's Book Showcase 1972.

Where's Al? written and illustrated by Byron Barton, Seabury, 1972. **Awarded:** Children's Book Showcase 1973; New York Times Best Illustrated 1972.

BARTON, JILL
The Pig in the Pond by Martin Waddell, illustrated by Jill Barton; Walker, 1992. **Awarded:** Greenaway (Highly Commended) 1992.

BARTOS-HOEPPNER, BARBARA
The Cossacks by Barbara Bartos-Hoeppner, illustrated by Victor G. Ambrus; Walck, 1963. **Awarded:** Spring Book Festival (older) 1963.

BARUFFI, ANDREA
I Won't Go To Bed by Harriet Ziefert, illustrated by Andrea Baruffi; Little Brown, 1987. **Awarded:** New Jersey Institute of Technology (Children's) 1988.

BASE, GRAEME
Animalia written and illustrated by Graeme Base; Viking Kestrel, 1986; Abrams, 1987. **Awarded:** Children's Book Council of Australia (picture book of the year honor) 1987; KOALA (Secondary) 1988; Young Australian Best Book (Picture Book) 1987.

The Eleventh Hour written and illustrated by Graeme Base; Viking Kestrel, 1988. **Awarded:** Children's Book Council of Australia (Picture Book of the Year) 1989; KOALA (Primary) 1989; Young Australian Best Book (Picture Book) 1989.

BASH, BARBARA
Desert Giant by Barbara Bash, illustrated; Sierra Club/Little Brown, 1989. **Awarded:** Southwest 1989.

BASKIN, HOSEA
Hosie's Alphabet by Hosea, Tobias, and Lisa Baskin, illustrated by Leonard Baskin; Viking, 1972. **Awarded:** Art Books for Children 1974, 1975, 1976; Caldecott (honor) 1973; New York Times Best Illustrated 1972.

BASKIN, LEONARD
The Book of Adam to Moses by Lore Segal, illustrated by Leonard Baskin; Knopf, 1987. **Awarded:** New York Times Notable 1987; Parents' Choice (Picture Book) 1987.

Hosie's Alphabet by Hosea, Tobias, and Lisa Baskin, illustrated by Leonard Baskin; Viking, 1972. **Awarded:** Art Books for Children 1974, 1975, 1976; Caldecott (honor) 1973; New York Times Best Illustrated 1972.

Leonard Baskin's Miniature Natural History: First Series written and illustrated by Leonard Baskin; Pantheon, 1983. **Awarded:** New York Times Best Illustrated 1983; Parents' Choice (illustration) 1983.

Season Songs by Ted Hughes, illustrated by Leonard Baskin; Viking, 1975. **Awarded:** Children's Book Showcase 1976.

BASKIN, LISA
Hosie's Alphabet by Hosea, Tobias, and Lisa Baskin, illustrated by Leonard Baskin; Viking, 1972. **Awarded:** Art Books for Children 1974, 1975, 1976; Caldecott (honor) 1973; New York Times Best Illustrated 1972.

BASKIN, TOBIAS
Hosie's Alphabet by Hosea, Tobias, and Lisa Baskin, illustrated by Leonard Baskin; Viking, 1972. **Awarded:** Art Books for Children 1974, 1975, 1976; Caldecott (honor) 1973; New York Times Best Illustrated 1972.

BATCHELDER, MILDRED L.
Awarded: Children's Reading Round Table 1985; Grolier 1966; Women's National Book Assn. 1967.

BATE, LUCY
Little Rabbit's Loose Tooth by Lucy Bate, illustrated by Diane de Groat; Crown, 1975. **Awarded:** California Young Reader Medal (primary) 1978.

BATES, BARBARA S.
see ROBERTS, JIM

BATES, BARBARA
Awarded: Drexel 1986.

BATES, BETTY
Thatcher Payne-in-the-Neck by Betty Bates, illustrated by Linda Strauss Edwards; Holiday House, 1985. **Awarded:** Carl Sandburg 1986.

BATES, DIANNE
Grandma Cadbury's Trucking Tales by Dianne Bates, illustrated by Kevin Burgemeestre; Angus & Robertson, 1988. **Awarded:** West Australian (Primary) 1988.

I'm an Australian: A Class Journal by Dianne Bates. **Awarded:** Australian Multicultural (Special Award) 1993.

BATES, HERBERT ERNEST
Achilles the Donkey by Herbert E. Bates, illustrated by Carol Barker; Dobson, 1962. **Awarded:** Greenaway (commended) 1962.

BATES, LEO
Homer the Tortoise by Margaret J. Baker, illustrated by Leo Bates; Whittlesey, 1949, 1950. **Awarded:** Spring Book Festival (8-12 honor) 1950.

BATES, ROBERT L.
Our Modern Stone Age by Robert L. Bates and Julia Jackson, illustrated; William Kaufmann, 1982. **Awarded:** New York Academy of Sciences (older honor) 1983.

BATHERMAN, MURIEL
The Alphabet Tale by Jan Garten, illustrated by Muriel Batherman; Random House, 1964. **Awarded:** New Jersey Institute of Technology (ages 3-5) 1964; Spring Book Festival (picture book honor) 1964.

Some Things You Should Know About My Dog written and illustrated by Muriel Batherman; Prentice Hall, 1976. **Awarded:** Children's Book Showcase 1977.

BAUER, CAROLINE FELLER
Awarded: Southern California Council (Dorothy McKenzie Award) 1986.

My Mom Travels a Lot by Caroline Feller Bauer, illustrated by Nancy Winslow Parker; Warne, 1981. **Awarded:** Christopher (picture book) 1982; New York Times Best Illustrated 1981.

BAUER, HELEN
Hawaii, the Aloha State by Helen Bauer, illustrated by Bruce McCurdy; Doubleday, 1960. **Awarded:** Commonwealth Club of California 1960.

BAUER, JOAN
Squashed by Joan Bauer, not illustrated; Delacorte, 1992. **Awarded:** Delacorte Press Prize 1991.

BAUER, JOHN
Great Swedish Fairy Tales by Holger Lundbergh, illustrated by John Bauer; Delacorte/Lawrence, 1973. **Awarded:** Children's Book Showcase 1974.

BAUER, MARION DANE
Face To Face by Marion Dane Bauer, not illustrated; Clarion, 1991. **Awarded:** Hungry Mind (Young Adult (Fiction) 1992; Minnesota (Older Children) 1992.

Foster Child by Marion Dane Bauer, not illustrated; Seabury, 1977. **Awarded:** Golden Kite (fiction honor) 1977.

On My Honor by Marion Dane Bauer, not illustrated; Clarion, 1986. **Awarded:** Jeanette Fair 1989; Golden Archer 1988; Newbery (honor) 1987; North Dakota Children's Choice (Juvenile Fiction) 1989; West Virginia Children's (Honor book) 1988-89; William Allen White 1989.

Rain of Fire by Marion Dane Bauer, not illustrated; Clarion, 1983. **Awarded:** Jane Addams 1984.

What's Your Story? A Young Person's Guide to Writing Fiction by Marion Dane Bauer; Clarion, 1992. **Awarded:** Minnesota (Older Children) 1993.

BAUM, ARLINE
OPT: An Illusionary Tale written and illustrated by Arline Baum and Joseph Baum; Viking Kestrel, 1987. **Awarded:** New York Academy of Sciences (Younger honorable mention) 1988.

BAUM, EDNA
Awarded: L. Frank Baum 1966.

BAUM, ELIZABETH
Awarded: L. Frank Baum 1966.

BAUM, HARRY NEAL
Awarded: L. Frank Baum 1963.

BAUM, JOSEPH
OPT: An Illusionary Tale written and illustrated by Joseph Baum and Arline Baum; Viking Kestrel, 1987. **Awarded:** New York Academy of Sciences (Younger honorable mention) 1988.

BAUM, LOUIS
Are We Nearly There? by Louis Baum, illustrated by Paddy Bouma; Bodley Head, 1986. **Awarded:** Greenaway (commended) 1986.

BAUM, LYMAN FRANK
The Wizard of Oz by L. Frank Baum, illustrated by W. W. Denslow; Reilly & Lee, 1956. **Awarded:** Lewis Carroll Shelf 1968.

BAUM, ROBERT A., DR.
Awarded: L. Frank Baum 1984.

BAUMANN, HANS

The Caves of the Great Hunters by Hans Baumann, illustrated with reproductions of cave paintings; Pantheon, 1954. **Awarded:** Spring Book Festival (older honor) 1954.

I Marched with Hannibal by Hans Baumann, translated by K. Potts, illustrated by Ulrik Schramm; Walck, 1962. **Awarded:** Spring Book Festival (older honor) 1962.

In the Land of Ur: the Discovery of Ancient Mesopotamia by Hans Baumann, translated by Stella Humphries, illustrated by Hans Peter Renner; Pantheon, 1969. **Awarded:** Mildred L. Batchelder 1971.

Sons of the Steppe by Hans Baumann, illustrated by Heiner Rothfuchs; Walck, 1958. **Awarded:** Spring Book Festival (older) 1958.

BAUMEL, JUDITH TYDOR

Unfulfilled Promise: Rescue and Resettlement of Jewish Refugee Children in the United States, 1934-1945 by Judith Tydor Baumel, illustrated; Denali Press, 1990. **Awarded:** Korczak Literary Awards (Book for Adults About Children Honorable Mention) 1992.

BAUMGARTNER, ROBERT

The War for the Lot: A Tale of Fantasy and Terror by Sterling E. Lanier, illustrated by Robert Baumgartner; Follett, 1969. **Awarded:** Charles W. Follett 1970.

BAWDEN, NINA

Carrie's War by Nina Bawden, not illustrated; Gollancz, 1973; Lippincott, 1973 (illustrated by Coleen Browning). **Awarded:** Carnegie (commended) 1973; Phoenix 1993.

The Finding by Nina Bawden, not illustrated; Lothrop, Lee & Shepard, 1985. **Awarded:** Parents' Choice (literature) 1985.

Henry by Nina Bawden, illustrated by Joyce Powzyk; Lothrop, Lee & Shepard, 1988. **Awarded:** Parents' Choice (Story Book) 1988; Reading Magic Award 1988.

Humbug by Nina Bawden, not illustrated; Clarion, 1992. **Awarded:** Parents Choice (Story Book) 1992.

Kept in the Dark by Nina Bawden, not illustrated; Lothrop, Lee & Shepard, 1982. **Awarded:** Parents' Choice (literature) 1982; Edgar Allan Poe (runnerup) 1983.

The Peppermint Pig by Nina Bawden, illustrated by Charles Lilly; Gollancz, 1975. **Awarded:** Guardian 1976.

BAXTER, JUDI

Awarded: Lucile M. Pannell 1989.

BAYLESS, ROGER

The View from the Oak by Herbert and Judith Kohl, illustrated by Roger Bayless; Sierra Club/Scribner, 1977. **Awarded:** National Book Award 1978.

BAYLEY, DOROTHY

The Middle Button by Kathryn Worth, illustrated by Dorothy Bayley; Doubleday/Doran, 1941. **Awarded:** Spring Book Festival (older honor) 1941.

BAYLEY, NICOLA

The Mouldy by William Mayne, illustrated by Nicola Bayley; Cape, 1983; Knopf, 1983. **Awarded:** Maschler (runnerup) 1983.

The Mousehole Cat by Antonia Barber, illustrated by Nicola Bayley; Walker, 1990; Macmillan, 1990. **Awarded:** British Book Awards (Illustrated) 1990; Greenaway (Commended) 1990.

The Patchwork Cat by William Mayne, illustrated by Nicola Bayley; Cape, 1981. **Awarded:** Greenaway (commended) 1981.

BAYLIS, SARAH

Vila: An Adventure Story by Sarah Baylis, not illustrated; Brilliance Books, 1984. **Awarded:** Other Award 1985.

BAYLOR, BYRD

Awarded: Eva L. Gordon 1992; Outstanding Arizona Author 1985.

The Desert Is Theirs by Byrd Baylor, illustrated by Peter Parnall; Scribner, 1975. **Awarded:** Art Books for Children 1977, 1978, 1979; Boston Globe Horn Book (illustration honor) 1976Caldecott (honor) 1976; New York Academy of Sciences (younger honor) 1976; Steck-Vaughn 1976.

Everybody Needs a Rock by Byrd Baylor, illustrated by Peter Parnall; Scribner, 1974. **Awarded:** Art Books for Children 1976.

Guess Who My Favorite Person Is by Byrd Baylor, illustrated by Robert A. Parker; Scribner, 1977. **Awarded:** Steck-Vaughn 1978.

Hawk, I'm Your Brother by Byrd Baylor, illustrated by Peter Parnall; Scribner, 1976. **Awarded:** Caldecott (honor) 1977.

The Way to Start a Day by Byrd Baylor, illustrated by Peter Parnall; Scribner, 1978. **Awarded:** Caldecott (honor) 1979.

When Clay Sings by Byrd Baylor, illustrated by Tom Bahti; Scribner, 1972. **Awarded:** Caldecott (honor) 1973; Steck-Vaughn 1973.

BAYNES, PAULINE DIANA

Chronicles of Narnia by C. S. Lewis, illustrated by Pauline Baynes; Macmillan, 1983. **Awarded:** Young Teens 1990.

Dictionary of Chivalry by Grant Uden, illustrated by Pauline Baynes; Kestrel, 1968; Crowell, 1969. **Awarded:** Greenaway 1968; Spring Book Festival (older honor) 1969.

The Horse and His Boy by C. S. Lewis, illustrated by Pauline Baynes; Macmillan, 1954. **Awarded:** Carnegie (commended) 1954.

How Dog Began written and illustrated by Pauline Baynes; Henry Holt, 1987, c1985; Methuen, 1985. **Awarded:** Parents' Choice (Picture Book) 1987.

The Iron Lion by Peter Dickinson, illustrated by Pauline Baynes; Bedrick/Blackie, 1984. **Awarded:** New York Times Notable 1984.

The Last Battle: a Story for Children by C. S. Lewis, illustrated by Pauline Baynes; Bodley Head, 1956. **Awarded:** Carnegie 1956.

The Lion, the Witch and the Wardrobe by C. S. Lewis, illustrated by Pauline Baynes; Macmillan, 1950. **Awarded:** Lewis Carroll Shelf 1962.

Snail and Caterpillar by Helen Piers, illustrated by Pauline Baynes; Longmans, 1972. **Awarded:** Greenaway (commended) 1972.

BEADLE, GEORGE

The Language of Life: an Introduction to the Science of Genetics by George Beadle and Muriel Beadle, illustrated by Joseph M. Sedacca and others; Doubleday, 1966. **Awarded:** Edison Mass Media (best science book for youth) 1967.

BEADLE, JEREMY
Outlawed Inventions by Jeremy Beadle and Chris Winn, illustrated; Pepper Press, 1982. **Awarded:** Mother Goose (runnerup) 1983.

BEADLE, MURIEL
The Language of Life: an Introduction to the Science of Genetics by George Beadle and Muriel Beadle, illustrated by Joseph M. Sedacca and others; Doubleday, 1966. **Awarded:** Edison Mass Media (best science book for youth) 1967.

BEAKE, LESLEY
A Cageful of Butterflies by Lesley Beake, not illustrated; Maskew Miller Longman, 1989. **Awarded:** Percy Fitzpatrick 1990.

The Strollers by Lesley Beake, illustrated by David Vickers; Maskew Miller Longman, 1987. **Awarded:** Percy Fitzpatrick 1988.

BEAME, RONA
The Evolution Book written and illustrated by Sara Stein, photographs by Rona Beame; Workman, 1986. **Awarded:** New York Academy of Sciences (older) 1987.

BEATON, C.
Have You Started Yet? by Ruth Thomson, illustrated by C. Beaton; Heinemann, 1980. **Awarded:** Other Award 1981.

BEATTIE, JANET
In Came Horace by Janet Beattie, illustrated by Anne Marie Jauss; Lippincott, 1954. **Awarded:** Spring Book Festival (ages 4-8 honor) 1954.

BEATTY, JOHN
Campion Towers by John Beatty and Patricia Beatty, not illustrated; Macmillan, 1965. **Awarded:** Commonwealth Club of California 1965.

The Royal Dirk by John Beatty and Patricia Beatty, illustrated by Franz Altschuler; Morrow, 1966. **Awarded:** Southern California Council (notable) 1967.

BEATTY, PATRICIA
Awarded: Southern California Council (comprehensive contribution of lasting value to the field of children's literature) 1974.

Charley Skedaddle by Patricia Beatty, not illustrated; Morrow, 1987. **Awarded:** Scott O'Dell 1987.

Campion Towers by Patricia Beatty and John Beatty, not illustrated; Macmillan, 1965. **Awarded:** Commonwealth Club of California 1965.

Jayhawker by Patricia Beatty, not illustrated; Morrow, 1991. **Awarded:** Commonwealth Club of California (Ages 11-16) 1991.

Jonathan Down Under by Patricia Beatty, not illustrated; Morrow, 1982. **Awarded:** Southern California Council (Distinguished work of fiction) 1983.

Lupita Manana by Patricia Beatty, not illustrated; Morrow, 1981. **Awarded:** Jane Addams (honor) 1982.

Red Rock Over the River by Patricia Beatty, illustrated by Robert Quackenbush; Morrow, 1973. **Awarded:** Golden Kite (honor) 1973.

The Royal Dirk by Patricia Beatty and John Beatty, illustrated by Franz Altschuler; Morrow, 1966. **Awarded:** Southern California Council (notable) 1967.

BEAUDE, PIERRE-MARIE
Le Livre de la Creation by Pierre-Marie Beaude, illustrated by Georges Lemoine; Edition du Centurion, 1987. **Awarded:** Bologna (Graphic for Youth) 1988.

BEBENROTH, CHARLOTTA M.
Meriwether Lewis: Boy Explorer by Charlotta M. Bebenroth, illustrated by Edward Caswell; Bobbs Merrill, 1946. **Awarded:** Ohioana (honorable mention) 1947.

BECK, CHARLES
Buffalo and Beaver by Stephen W. Meader, illustrated by Charles Beck; Harcourt, 1960. **Awarded:** New Jersey Institute of Technology 1961.

Highpockets by John R. Tunis, illustrated by Charles Beck; Morrow, 1948. **Awarded:** Spring Book Festival (older honor) 1948.

BECKER, CHARLOTTE
Mr. Totter and the Five Black Cats by Eleanor Thomas, illustrated by Charlotte Becker; Scribner, 1942. **Awarded:** Ohioana (honorable mention) 1943.

The Young Aunts by Alice Dalgliesh, illustrated by Charlotte Becker; Scribner, 1939. **Awarded:** Spring Book Festival (younger honor) 1939.

BECKER, JOYCE
Bible Crafts by Joyce Becker, illustrated; Holiday House, 1982. **Awarded:** New Jersey Institute of Technology 1983.

BECKER, MAY LAMBERTON
Awarded: Women's National Book Assn. 1948.

BECKMAN, DELORES
My Own Private Sky by Delores Beckman, not illustrated; Dutton, 1980. **Awarded:** International Reading Assn. 1981.

BEDARD, MICHAEL
Redwork by Michael Bedard, not illustrated; Lester & Orpen Dennys, 1990; Atheneum, 1990. **Awarded:** Canadian Library Assn. Book of the Year 1991; Governor General's Literary Award (Text) 1990; National Chapter of Canada IODE Violet Downey 1991; Young. Adult Canadian (runnersup) 1991

BEDDOWS, ERIC
The Emperor's Panda by David Day, illustrated by Eric Beddows; McClelland & Stewart, 1986. **Awarded:** Canadian Library Assn. (runnerup) 1987; International Board on Books for Young People (Illustration/Canada) 1988.

Joyful Noise: Poems for Two Voices by Paul Fleischman, illustrated by Eric Beddows; Harper & Row, 1988. **Awarded:** Boston Globe (Fiction honor) 1988; Newbery 1989.

Night Cars by Teddy Jam, illustrated by Eric Beddows; Douglas & McIntyre, 1988; Orchard, 1989. **Awarded:** Amelia Frances Howard-Gibbon (runnerup) 1989; IODE 1988; Elizabeth Mrazik- Cleaver 1989.

BEDNAROVA, EVA
Chinesische Volksmarcken by Eva Bednarova; Artia, 1968.Biennale Illustrations Bratislava (grand prix) 1969

BEE, RONALD J.
Looking the Tiger in the Eye: Confronting the Nuclear Threat by Ronald J. Bee and Carl B. Feldbaum, illustrated with photos; Harper & Row, 1988. **Awarded:** Christopher (Young Adult) 1989.

BEEBE, BURDETTA FAYE
Coyote, Come Home by B. F. Beebe, illustrated by Larry Toschik; McKay, 1963. **Awarded:** Boys Club 1964.

BEECH, CAROL
The Tent Under the Spider Tree by Gene Inyart, illustrated by Carol Beech; Watts, 1959. **Awarded:** Franklin Watts Juvenile Fiction 1959.

BEELER, NELSON FREDERICK
Experiments in Sound by Nelson F. Beeler, illustrated by George Giusti; Crowell, 1961. **Awarded:** Edison Mass Media (best science book) 1962.

BEER, HANS DE
Kleiner Eisbar, Wohin Fahrst Du? written and illustrated by Hans de Beer; Nord-Sud, 1987. **Awarded:** Owl Prize 1988.

BEGG, BARBARA
Black Magic, White Magic by Gary Jennings, illustrated by Barbara Begg; Dial, 1965. **Awarded:** Spring Book Festival (middle honor) 1965.

BEGIN, MARYJANE
The Porcupine Mouse by Bonnie Pryor, illustrated by Maryjane Begin; Morrow, 1988. **Awarded:** Irma S. and James H. Black 1988.

BEGLEY, ED
More Just So Stories [phonodisc] by Rudyard Kipling, narrated by Ed Begley; Caedmon R 1205. **Awarded:** Lewis Carroll Shelf 1967.

BEHN, HARRY
Cricket Songs: Japanese Haiku translated by Harry Behn, illustrated by Sesshu and others; Harcourt, 1964. **Awarded:** George G. Stone 1965.

BEHRANGI, SAMAD
The Little Black Fish by Samad Behrangi, illustrated by Farshid Mesghali; Institute for the Intellectual Development of Children and Young Adults. **Awarded:** Bologna (Graphic for Children) 1969.

BEHRENS, MICHAEL
At the Edge by Michael Behrens, not illustrated; Avon, 1988. **Awarded:** Avon Flare Competition 1987.

BEHRMAN, CAROL H.
Wanted: One New Dad by Carol H. Behrman, not illustrated; Field Publications, 1988. **Awarded:** New Jersey Institute of Technology 1989.

BEIM, JERROLD
Spotlight for Danny by Jerrold Beim and Lorraine Beim, illustrated by Corinne Malvern; Harcourt, 1943. **Awarded:** Spring Book Festival (middle honor) 1943.

BEIM, LORRAINE
Spotlight for Danny by Lorraine Beim and Jerrold Beim, illustrated by Corinne Malvern; Harcourt, 1943. **Awarded:** Spring Book Festival (middle honor) 1943.

BEIRNE, BARBARA
Under the Lights: A Child Model at Work by Barbara Beirne, illustrated with photos; Carolrhoda Books, 1988. **Awarded:** New Jersey Institute of Technology 1989.

Water is Wet by Penny Pollock, photographs by Barbara Beirne; Putnam, 1985. **Awarded:** New Jersey Institute of Technology 1987.

BELGRAVE, SUSAN
Awarded: Eleanor Farjeon 1993

BELL, ANGELA
New Perspectives Book 1: An English Course by Angela Bell and Hugh Knight, illustrated; Oxford, 1987. **Awarded:** Times Educational Supplement (Schoolbook) 1987.

BELL, ANTHEA
Awarded: FIT Astrid Lindgren Translation 1990.

The Big Janosch Book of Fun and Verse by Janosch, translated by Anthea Bell; Andersen Press, 1980. (Original German:

Die Maus Hat Rote Strumpfe an by Janosch). **Awarded:** International Board on Books for Young People (translation/Great Britain) 1982.

The Cat and the Mouse Who Shared a House written and illustrated by Ruth Hurlimann, translated by Anthea Bell; Walck, 1974. **Awarded:** Batchelder 1976.

The Cucumber King: A Story with a Beginning, a Middle and an End by Christine Nostlinger, translated by Anthea Bell, illustrated by Werner Maurer; Abelard-Schuman, 1975. **Awarded:** International Board on Books for Young People (translation/Great Britain) 1978.

Konrad by Christine Nostlinger, translated by Anthea Bell, illustrated by Carol Nicklaus; Watts, 1977. **Awarded:** Batchelder 1979.

The Satanic Mill by Otfried Preussler, translated by Anthea Bell, not illustrated; Abelard-Schuman (London), 1972; Macmillan, 1973. **Awarded:** New York Times Notable Books 1973.

The Swineherd by Hans Christian Andersen, translated by Anthea Bell, illustrated by Lisbeth Zwerger; Morrow, 1982. **Awarded:** Parents' Choice (illustration) 1982.

BELL, CLARE
Ratha's Creature by Clare Bell, not illustrated; Atheneum, 1983. **Awarded:** International Reading Assn. 1984; PEN Center USA West 1983.

BELL, CORYDON WHITTEN
Captain Ghost by Thelma H. Bell, illustrated by Corydon Bell; Viking, 1959. **Awarded:** Dorothy Canfield Fisher 1961; North Carolina AAUW 1959

Pawnee by Thelma Harrington Bell, illustrated by Corydon Bell; Viking, 1950. **Awarded:** Spring Book Festival (picture book honor) 1950.

The Secret Circle by Ina B. Forbus, illustrated by Corydon Bell; Viking, 1958. **Awarded:** North Carolina AAUW 1958.

String, Straight-edge and Shadow: The Story of Geometry by Julia E. Diggins, illustrated by Corydon Bell; Viking, 1965. **Awarded:** Spring Book Festival (middle honor) 1965.

BELL, EDWINA
A Dream of Seas by Lilith Norman, illustrated by Edwina Bell; Collins, 1978. **Awarded:** International Board on Books for Young People (text/Australia) 1980.

BELL, FREDERIC
Jenny's Corner by Frederic Bell, illustrated by Zenowij Onyshkewych; Random House, 1974. **Awarded:** New York Times Notable Books 1974.

BELL, MARGARET E.
Ride out the Storm by Margaret E. Bell, not illustrated; Morrow, 1951. **Awarded:** Spring Book Festival (older honor) 1951.

Touched with Fire: Alaska's George William Seller by Margaret E. Bell, maps by Bob Ritter; Morrow, 1960. **Awarded:** Edison Mass Media (character development of children) 1961.

BELL, RUTH V.
Awarded: American Association of School Librarians 1990.

BELL, THELMA HARRINGTON

Captain Ghost by Thelma H. Bell, illustrated by Corydon Bell; Viking, 1959. **Awarded:** Dorothy Canfield Fisher 1961; North Carolina AAUW 1959.

Pawnee by Thelma Harrington Bell, illustrated by Corydon Bell; Viking, 1950. **Awarded:** Spring Book Festival (picture book honor) 1950.

BELL, WILLIAM

The Cripples' Club by William Bell, not illustrated; Irwin, 1988. **Awarded:** Young Adult Canadian (Runnersup) 1989.

Forbidden City by William Bell, illustrated with maps; Doubleday Canada, 1990. **Awarded:** Ruth Schwartz 1991; Young Adult Canadian (runnersup) 1991.

BELLAIRS, JOHN

The Curse of the Blue Figurine by John Bellairs, illustrated by Edward Gorey; Dial, 1983. **Awarded:** Parents' Choice (literature) 1983; Virginia Young Readers (Middle School) 1987.

The House with a Clock in Its Walls by John Bellairs, illustrated by Edward Gorey; Dial, 1973. **Awarded:** Michigan Young Readers (Division II runnerup) 1980; New York Times Notable Books 1973.

The Letter, the Witch and the Ring by John Bellairs, illustrated by Richard Egielski; Dial, 1976. **Awarded:** Utah Children's Choice 1981.

BELLEGUIE, ANDRE

Il Etait Une Fois, les Mots by Yves Pinguilly, illustrated by Andre Belleguie; Editions la Farandol Messidor, 1981. **Awarded:** Bologna (graphics for youth) 1983.

BELLOC, HILAIRE

Matilda Who Told Lies and Was Burned to Death by Hilaire Belloc, illustrated by Steven Kellogg; Dial, 1970. **Awarded:** Art Books for Children 1973; New York Times Best Illustrated 1970.

BELPRE, PURA

Santiago by Pura Belpre, illustrated by Symeon Shimin; Warne, 1969. **Awarded:** Art Books for Children 1973.

BELTING, NATALIA MAREE

Calendar Moon by Natalia M. Belting, illustrated by Bernarda Bryson; Holt, 1964. **Awarded:** George G. Stone 1966.

The Sun Is a Golden Earring by Natalia M. Belting, illustrated by Bernarda Bryson; Holt, 1962. **Awarded:** Caldecott (honor) 1963.

Whirlwind Is a Ghost Dancing by Natalia M. Belting, illustrated by Leo Dillon and Diane Dillon; Dutton, 1974. **Awarded:** Children's Book Showcase 1975.

Winter's Eve by Natalia M. Belting, illustrated by Alan E. Cober; Holt, 1969. **Awarded:** New York Times Best Illustrated 1969.

BELTON, ROBYN

The Duck in the Gun by Joy Cowley, illustrated by Robyn Belton; Shortland Educational, 1984. **Awarded:** Russell Clark 1985.

BEMELMANS, LUDWIG

The Golden Basket written and illustrated by Ludwig Bemelmans; Viking, 1936. **Awarded:** Newbery (honor) 1937.

The Happy Place written and illustrated by Ludwig Bemelmans; Little, 1952. **Awarded:** New York Times Best Illustrated 1952.

Madeline written and illustrated by Ludwig Bemelmans; Simon & Schuster, 1939. **Awarded:** Caldecott (honor) 1940.

Madeline and the Bad Hat written and illustrated by Ludwig Bemelmans; Viking, 1957. **Awarded:** Spring Book Festival (ages 4-8) 1957.

Madeline's Rescue written and illustrated by Ludwig Bemelmans; Viking, 1953. **Awarded:** Caldecott 1954; New York Times Best Illustrated 1953.

Parsley written and illustrated by Ludwig Bemelmans; Harper, 1955. **Awarded:** New York Times Best Illustrated 1955.

Sunshine: a Story About the City of New York written and illustrated by Ludwig Bemelmans; Simon & Schuster, 1950. **Awarded:** Spring Book Festival (picture book) 1950.

BEN-ASHER, NAOMI

Junior Jewish Encyclopedia by Naomi Ben-Asher and Hayim Leaf, illustrated with photographs; Shengold, 1957. **Awarded:** Jewish Book Council 1957.

BENARY-ISBERT, MARGOT

Awarded: Southern California Council (comprehensive contribution of lasting value to the field of children's literature) 1967.

The Ark by Margot Benary-Isbert, translated by Clara Winston and Richard Winston; Harcourt, 1953. **Awarded:** Lewis Carroll Shelf 1968; Spring Book Festival (older) 1953.

Blue Mystery by Margot Benary-Isbert, translated by Clara Winston and Richard Winston, illustrated by Enrico Arno; Harcourt, 1957. **Awarded:** Jane Addams 1957.

BENCHLEY, NATHANIEL

Gone and Back by Nathaniel Benchley, not illustrated; Harper & Row, 1971. **Awarded:** New York Times Notable Books 1971.

Only Earth and Sky Last Forever by Nathaniel Benchley, not illustrated; Harper, 1972. **Awarded:** Western Writers (fiction) 1973.

BENDICK, JEANNE

Awarded: Eva L. Gordon 1975.

Discovering Cycles by Glenn O. Blough, illustrated by Jeanne Bendick; McGraw, 1973. **Awarded:** New York Academy of Sciences (younger honor) 1974.

The First Book of Space Travel written and illustrated by Jeanne Bendick; Watts, 1953. **Awarded:** Spring Book Festival (8-12 honor) 1953.

How Much and How Many: The Story of Weights and Measures written and illustrated by Jeanne Bendick; Whittlesey House, 1947. **Awarded:** Boys Club 1949.

Let's Find Out: A Picture Science Book by Herman Schneider and Nina Schneider, illustrated by Jeanne Bendick; Scott, 1946. **Awarded:** Spring Book Festival (middle honor) 1946.

BENJAMIN, CAROL LEE

The Chosen Puppy by Carol Lee Benjamin, illustrated; Howell Book House, 1990. **Awarded:** Book Can Develop Empathy 1991.

Second-hand Dog written and illustrated by Carol Lee Benjamin; Howell Book House, 1988. **Awarded:** Book Can Develop Empathy 1990.

BENJAMIN, HAMEED

The Secret of Spirit Mountain by Helen Kronberg Olson, illustrated by Hameed Benjamin; Dodd, Mead, 1980. **Awarded:** Surrey School 1984.

BENNETT, ANNA ELIZABETH
Little Witch by Anna Elizabeth Bennett, illustrated by Helen Stone; Lippincott, 1953. **Awarded:** Helen Dean Fish 1953.

BENNETT, DOROTHY AGNES
The Golden Almanac by Dorothy Agnes Bennett, illustrated by Marie Stern; Simon and Schuster, 1944. **Awarded:** Spring Book Festival (younger honor) 1944.

BENNETT, JAY
The Dangling Witness: A Mystery by Jay Bennett, not illustrated; Delacorte, 1974. **Awarded:** Edgar Allen Poe 1975.

The Dark Corridor by Jay Bennett, not illustrated; Watts, 1988. **Awarded:** New Jersey Institute of Technology 1989.

The Long Black Coat by Jay Bennett, not illustrated; Delacorte, 1973. **Awarded:** Edgar Allan Poe 1974.

The Skeleton Man by Jay Bennett, not illustrated; Watts, 1986. **Awarded:** Edgar Allan Poe (runnerup) 1987.

BENNETT, JILL
Awarded: Eleanor Farjeon 1990.

Danny: the Champion of the World by Roald Dahl, illustrated by Jill Bennett; Knopf, 1975. **Awarded:** Surrey School Book of the Year 1978; California Young Reader Medal (intermediate) 1979.

Harry's Mad by Dick King-Smith, illustrated by Jill Bennett; Crown, 1987, c1984; Gollancz, 1984. **Awarded:** California Young Reader (Intermediate) 1991; Parents' Choice (Story Book) 1987.

BENNETT, JOHN
The Pigtail of Ah Lee Ben Loo: With Seventeen Other Laughable Tales and 200 Comical Silhouettes written and illustrated by John Bennett; Longmans, 1928. **Awarded:** Newbery (honor) 1929.

BENNETT, RAINEY
The Secret Hiding Place written and illustrated by Rainey Bennett; World, 1960. **Awarded:** Spring Book Festival (ages 4-8) 1960.

BENOIS, ALEXANDRE
Petrouchka adapted and illustrated by Elizabeth Cleaver from the work of Alexandre Benois and Igor Stravinsky; Macmillan (Canada), 1980; Atheneum, 1980. **Awarded:** International Board on Books for Young People (illustration/Canada) 1982.

BENSON, GERARD
This Poem Doesn't Rhyme by Gerard Benson, illustrated by Sarah-Jane Stewart; Viking, 1990. **Awarded:** Signal Poetry Award 1991.

BENSON, MILDRED
Dangerous Deadline by Mildred Benson, not illustrated; Dodd Mead, 1957. **Awarded:** Boys Life- Dodd Mead Writing Award 1956.

BENSON, PATRICK
The Baron All at Sea by Adrian Mitchell, illustrated by Patrick Benson; Walker, 1987; Philomel, 1987. **Awarded:** W. H. Smith (Second Prize) 1988.

The Blue Book of Hob Stories by William Mayne, illustrated by Patrick Benson; Walker, 1984. **Awarded:** Mother Goose 1984.

The Green Book of Hob Stories by William Mayne, illustrated by Patrick Benson; Walker, 1984. **Awarded:** Mother Goose 1984.

The Minpins by Roald Dahl, illustrated by Patrick Benson; Viking, 1991. **Awarded:** British Book Awards (Illustrated runnerup) 1991Redbook 1991.

The Red Book of Hob Stories by William Mayne, illustrated by Patrick Benson; Walker, 1984. **Awarded:** Mother Goose 1984.

The Yellow Book of Hob Stories by William Mayne, illustrated by Patrick Benson; Walker, 1984. **Awarded:** Mother Goose 1984.

BENSON, ROBERT
I Will Sing Life by Larry Berger and Dahlia Lithwick and seven campers, photographs by Robert Benson; Little Brown, 1992. **Awarded:** Fassler 1993.

BENTLEY, NICOLAS CLERIHEW
The Wind on the Moon: A Story for Children by Eric Linklater, illustrated by Nicolas Bentley; Macmillan, 1944. **Awarded:** Carnegie 1944.

BENTLEY, PHYLLIS
Forgery! by Phyllis Bentley, not illustrated; Doubleday, 1968. **Awarded:** Edgar Allan Poe (runnerup) 1969.

BERENSTAIN, JAN
Awarded: Drexel 1982; Jeremiah Ludington 1989.

Bears in the Night written and illustrated by Jan Berenstain and Stan Berenstain; Random House, 1971. **Awarded:** Michigan Young Readers (division I) 1981.

The Berenstain Bears and the Spooky Old Tree written and illustrated by Jan Berenstain and Stan Berenstain; Random House, 1978. **Awarded:** Buckeye (K-3) 1982.

Berenstain Bears Get in a Fight written and illustrated by Jan Berenstain and Stan Berenstain; Random House, 1982. **Awarded:** Buckeye (K-2) 1985.

BERENSTAIN, STAN
Awarded: Drexel 1982; Jeremiah Ludington 1989.

Bears in the Night written and illustrated by Jan Berenstain and Stan Berenstain; Random House, 1971. **Awarded:** Michigan Young Readers (division I) 1981.

The Berenstain Bears and the Spooky Old Tree written and illustrated by Jan Berenstain and Stan Berenstain; Random House, 1978. **Awarded:** Buckeye (K-3) 1982.

Berenstain Bears Get in a Fight written and illustrated by Jan Berenstain and Stan Berenstain; Random House, 1982. **Awarded:** Buckeye (K-2) 1985.

BERENZY, ALIX
A Frog Prince written and illustrated by Alix Berenzy; Henry Holt, 1989. **Awarded:** Bologna (Critici in Erba) 1990.

BERG, BJORN
Awarded: Hans Christian Andersen (highly commended illustrator/ Sweden) 1972.

BERG, JEAN H.
The O'Learys and Friends by Jean H. Berg, illustrated by Mary Stevens; Follett, 1961. **Awarded:** Follett Beginning to Read 1961.

BERG, LEILA
Awarded: Eleanor Farjeon 1973.

BERG, RON
The Owl and the Pussycat by Edward Lear, illustrated by Ron Berg; Scholastic-TAB, 1984. **Awarded:** Amelia Frances Howard-Gibbon (runnerup) 1985.

BERGER, BARBARA HELEN
The Donkey's Dream written and illustrated by Barbara Helen Berger; Philomel, 1985. **Awarded:** Golden Kite (illustration) 1985.

BERGER, LARRY
I Will Sing Life by Larry Berger and Dahlia Lithwick and seven campers, photographs by Robert Benson; Little Brown, 1992. **Awarded:** Fassler 1993.

BERGERE, RICHARD
Thomas Jefferson: His Many Talents by Johanna Johnston, illustrated by Richard Bergere; Dodd, 1961. **Awarded:** Edison Mass Media (character development in children) 1962.

BERGH, SVEN-ERIK
Awarded: Golden Cat 1986.

BERGIN, MARK
An Egyptian Pyramid by Mark Bergin, John James and Jacqueline Morley, illustrated; Simon & Schuster, 1991; Peter Bedrick, 1991. **Awarded:** Times Educational Supplement (Senior Information) 1991.

BERKE, ERNEST
The North American Indians: Life and Lore written and illustrated by Ernest Berke; Doubleday, 1963. **Awarded:** Boys Club 1964.

BERNA, PAUL
The Secret of the Missing Boat by Paul Berna, translated by John Buchanan-Brown, illustrated by Barry Wilkinson; Pantheon, 1967, c1966. **Awarded:** Edgar Allan Poe (runnerup) 1968.

BERNARD, GEORGE
The Common Frog by Oxford Scientific Films, Ltd., photographs by George Bernard; Whizzard/Deutsch, 1979. **Awarded:** Times Educational Supplement (junior) 1979.

BERNDT, CATHERINE
Land of the Rainbow Snake by Catherine Berndt, illustrated by Djoki Yunupingu; Collins, 1979. **Awarded:** New South Wales State Literary Awards (Special Children's) 1980.

BERNHARD, JOSEPHINE B.
Nine Cry-baby Dolls by Josephine B. Bernhard, illustrated by Irena Lowentowicz; Roy, 1945. **Awarded:** Spring Book Festival (younger honor) 1945.

BERNSTEIN, MICHAEL J.
Class Dismissed: High School Poems by Mel Glenn, photographs by Michael J. Bernstein; Clarion, 1982. **Awarded:** Golden Kite (fiction honor) 1982.

Class Dismissed: More High School Poems, No. II by Mel Glenn, photographs by Michael J. Bernstein; Clarion, 1986. **Awarded:** Christopher (Young Adult) 1987.

BERNSTEIN, ZENA
Mrs. Frisby and the Rats of NIMH by Robert C. O'Brien, illustrated by Zena Bernstein; Atheneum, 1971. **Awarded:** Boston Globe Horn Book (text honor) 1971; Lewis Carroll Shelf 1972; Massachusetts Children's (Grades 4-6) 1978; National Book Award (finalist) 1972; Newbery 1972; Mark Twain 1973; William Allen White 1974; Young Readers Choice 1974.

BERRIDGE, CELIA
Runaway Danny written and illustrated by Celia Berridge; Deutsch, c1975. **Awarded:** W. H. Smith (£500) 1977.

BERRY, ERICK
Apprentices of Florence by Anne Kyle, illustrated by Erick Berry; Houghton, 1933. **Awarded:** Newbery (honor) 1934.

Bittersweet by Martha Barnhart Harper, illustrated by Erick Berry; Longmans, 1948. **Awarded:** Spring Book Festival (older honor) 1948.

Garram the Hunter, a Boy of the Hill Tribes by Herbert Best, illustrated by Erick Berry; Doubleday-Doran, 1930. **Awarded:** Newbery (honor) 1931.

The Pilgrim Goose by Keith Robertson, illustrated by Erick Berry; Viking, 1956. **Awarded:** Spring Book Festival (middle honor) 1956.

Winged Girl of Knossos written and illustrated by Erick Berry; Appleton Century, 1933. **Awarded:** Newbery (honor) 1934.

BERRY, GLADYS
Awarded: Children's Reading Round Table 1972.

BERRY, JAMES
Ajeemah and His Son by James Berry; HarperCollins, 1992. **Awarded:** Boston Globe (Fiction) 1993.

A Thief in the Village by James Berry, not illustrated; Hamish Hamilton, 1987; Orchard, 1988, c1987. **Awarded:** Coretta Scott King (Text honor) 1989; Smarties (Ages 9-11) 1987; Smarties (Grand Prix) 1987.

When I Dance by James Berry, illustrated by Sonia Boyce; Hamish Hamilton, 1988; Harcourt Brace Jovanovich, 1991. **Awarded:** Signal Poetry Award 1989.

BERSON, HAROLD
Balarin's Goat written and illustrated by Harold Berson; Crown, 1972. **Awarded:** Children's Book Showcase 1973.

When I Grew Up Long Ago by Alvin Schwartz, illustrated by Harold Berson; Lippincott, 1978. **Awarded:** New Jersey Institute of Technology 1980.

BERTELLI, MARIELLA
The Shirt of the Happy Man by Mariella Bertelli, illustrated by Laszlo Gal; Kids Can Press, 1977. **Awarded:** IODE 1978.

BERTIN, GERALD
The Very Obliging Flowers by Claude Roy, translated by Gerald Bertin, illustrated by Alain Le Foll; Grove, 1968. **Awarded:** New York Times Best Illustrated 1968.

BERTOL, ROLAND
Sundiata: the Epic of the Lion King by Roland Bertol, illustrated by Gregorio Prestopino; Crowell, 1970. **Awarded:** Spring Book Festival (middle) 1970.

BESS, CLAYTON
Story for a Black Night by Clayton Bess, not illustrated; Houghton Mifflin, 1982. **Awarded:** Southern California Council (contribution of cultural significance) 1983.

BEST, ALLENA CHAMPLIN
see BERRY, ERICK

BEST, HERBERT
Garram the Hunter, a Boy of the Hill Tribes by Herbert Best, illustrated by Erick Berry; Doubleday-Doran, 1930. **Awarded:** Newbery (honor) 1931.

BEST, OSWALD HERBERT
see BEST, HERBERT

BESTERMAN, CATHERINE
The Quaint and Curious Quest of Johnny Longfoot, the Shoe King's Son by Catherine Besterman, illustrated by Warren Chappell; Bobbs Merrill, 1947. **Awarded:** Newbery (honor) 1948.

BESUNDER, MARVIN
Andrew Carnegie: Giant of Industry by Mary Malone, illustrated by Marvin Besunder; Garrard, 1969. **Awarded:** New Jersey Institute of Technology 1970.

BETHANCOURT, T. ERNESTO
Doris Fein Mysteries (series) by T. Ernesto Bethancourt; Holiday House, 1978-83. **Awarded:** Southern California Council (excellence in a series) 1983.

BETTS, ETHEL FRANKLIN
A Little Princess: Being the Whole Story of Sara Crewe Now Told for the First Time by Frances Hodgson Burnett, illustrated by Ethel F. Betts; Scribner, 1938. **Awarded:** Lewis Carroll Shelf 1964.

BETZ, EVA K.
The Quiet Flame: Mother Marianne of Molokai by Eva K. Betz, illustrated by Lloyd Ostendorf; Bruce, 1963. **Awarded:** New Jersey Institute of Technology (religious) 1964.

BEVAN, CLARE
Mightier Than the Sword by Clare Bevan, not illustrated; Blackie, 1989. **Awarded:** Kathleen Fidler 1989.

BEYER, AUDREY WHITE
Dark Venture by Audrey W. Beyer, illustrated by Leo Dillon and Diane Dillon; Knopf, 1968. **Awarded:** Boston Globe Horn Book (text honor) 1968.

BHEND, KATHI
Die Geschichte Von der Kleinen Gans, Die Nicht Schnell Genug War by Hanna Johansen, illustrated by Kathi Bhend; Nagel & Kimche, 1989. **Awarded:** Bologna (Graphics for youth) 1990.

BIANCHI, JOHN
Exploring the Night Sky by Terence Dickinson, illustrated by John Bianchi; Camden House, 1987. **Awarded:** New York Academy of Sciences (Older) 1988.

BIANCO, MARGERY WILLIAMS
The Velveteen Rabbit: or, How Toys Become Real by Margery Williams, illustrated by William Nicholson; Doubleday, 1958. **Awarded:** Lewis Carroll Shelf 1971.

Winterbound by Margery Williams Bianco, illustrated by Kate Seredy; Viking, 1936. **Awarded:** Newbery (honor) 1937.

BICE, CLARE
The Great Canoe by Adelaide Leitch, illustrated by Clare Bice; Macmillan Canada, 1962. **Awarded:** Macmillan of Canada 1962.

The Sun Horse by Catherine Anthony Clark, illustrated by Clare Bice; Macmillan Canada, 1951. **Awarded:** Canadian Library Assn. 1952.

BIERHORST, JOHN
A Cry from the Earth: Music of the North American Indians written and illustrated by John Bierhorst; Four Winds, 1979. **Awarded:** Woodson (outstanding merit) 1980.

Doctor Coyote: A Native American Aesop's Fable retold by John Bierhorst, illustrated by Wendy Watson; Macmillan, 1987. **Awarded:** Southwest 1986.

In the Trail of the Wind: American Indian Poems and Ritual Orations edited by John Bierhorst, illustrated with photographs; Farrar, 1971. **Awarded:** Children's Book Showcase 1972.

The Red Swan: Myths and Tales of the American Indians translated by John Bierhorst, illustrated with photographs and old engravings; Farrar, 1976. **Awarded:** Children's Book Showcase 1977.

Song of the Chippewa adapted by John Bierhorst, illustrated by Joe Servello; Farrar Straus Giroux, 1974. **Awarded:** State Historical Society of Wisconsin 1975.

BIERMAN, VALERIE
Awarded: Eleanor Farjeon 1987.

BIESTERVELD, BETTY PARSONS
Six days from Sunday by Betty Biesterveld, illustrated by George Armstrong; Rand, 1973. **Awarded:** Friends of American Writers (ages 4-8) 1974.

BIESTY, STEPHEN
Stephen Biesty's Incredible Cross Sections by Richard Platt, illustrated by Stephen Biesty; Viking, 1992; Knopf, 1992. **Awarded:** British Book Awards (Illustrated Runnerup) 1992.

BILECK, MARVIN
Rain Makes Applesauce by Julian Scheer, illustrated by Marvin Bileck; Holiday, 1964. **Awarded:** Caldecott (honor) 1965; New York Times Best Illustrated 1964.

BILIBIN, IVAN
The Tale of Czar Saltan: or, The Prince and the Swan Princess by Alexander Pushkin, translated and retold by Patricia Tracey Lowe, illustrated by Ivan Bilibin; Crowell, 1975. **Awarded:** Children's Book Showcase 1976.

BILLMAN, CAROL
The Child Reader as Sleuth by Carol Billman in *Children's Literature in Education* 15 (Spring 1984). **Awarded:** Children's Literature Assn. Excellence in Criticism (runnerup) 1985.

BILLOUT, GUY RENE
By Camel or By Car: A Look at Transportation written and illustrated by Guy Billout; Prentice Hall, 1979. **Awarded:** New York Times Best Illustrated 1979.

The Number 24 written and illustrated by Guy Billout; Harlin Quist, 1973. **Awarded:** New York Times Best Illustrated 1973.

Squid and Spider: A Look at the Animal Kingdom written and illustrated by Guy Billout; Prentice Hall, 1982. **Awarded:** New York Times Best Illustrated 1982.

Stone and Steel: A Look at Engineering written and illustrated by Guy Billout; Prentice Hall, 1980. **Awarded:** New York Times Best Illustrated 1980.

BINCH, CAROLINE
Amazing Grace by Mary Hoffman, illustrated by Caroline Binch; Frances Lincoln, 1991; Dial, 1991. **Awarded:** Greenaway (Commended) 1991.

BINDER-STRASSFURT, EBERHARD
Kopfblumen by Gianni Rodari, illustrated by Eberhard Binder-Strassfurt; Der Kinderbuchverlag. **Awarded:** Bologna (Graphics for Children) 1973.

BING, JON
Den Fjerneste Kyst (Original English

The Farthest Shore) by Ursula K. LeGuin, translated by Jon Bing; Gyldendal Norsk Forlag, 1980. **Awarded:** International Board on Books for Young People (honour list/translation/Norway) 1982.

BINGHAM, EDWIN RALPH
To the Pacific with Lewis and Clark by Edwin R. Bingham and Ralph K. Andrist, illustrated with photographs, maps and

drawings; Harper and Row, 1967. **Awarded:** Western Writers (nonfiction) 1968.

BINNS, ARCHIE
The Radio Imp by Archie Binns, illustrated by Rafaello Busoni; Winston, 1950. **Awarded:** Spring Book Festival (8-12 honor) 1950.

BIRCH, REGINALD
Harry in England by Laura E. Richards, illustrated by Reginald Birch; Appleton Century Crofts, 1937. **Awarded:** Spring Book Festival (younger honor) 1937.

BIRD, BETTINA
An Introduction to Insects by Bettina Bird and Joan Short, illustrated by Deborah Savin. **Awarded:** Whitley Awards (Educational Series) 1989.

BIRNBAUM, ABE
Green Eyes written and illustrated by Abe Birnbaum; Capitol, 1953. **Awarded:** Caldecott (honor) 1954; New York Times Best Illustrated 1953.

BISHOP, CLAIRE HUCHET
All Alone by Claire Huchet Bishop, illustrated by Feodor Rojankovsky; Viking, 1953. **Awarded:** Newbery (honor) 1954; Spring Book Festival (Ages 8-12 honor) 1953.

The Five Chinese Brothers by Claire Huchet Bishop, illustrated by Kurt Wiese; Coward, 1938. **Awarded:** Lewis Carroll Shelf 1959.

Pancakes-Paris by Claire Huchet Bishop, illustrated by Georges Schreiber; Viking, 1947. **Awarded:** Newbery (honor) 1948; Spring Book Festival (middle) 1947.

Twenty and Ten by Claire Huchet Bishop, illustrated by William Pene du Bois; Viking, 1952. **Awarded:** Child Study 1952.

BISHOP, GAVIN
Mrs. McGinty and the Bizarre Plant written and illustrated by Gavin Bishop; Oxford, 1981. **Awarded:** Russell Clark 1982.

Mr. Fox written and illustrated by Gavin Bishop; Oxford University Press, 1982. **Awarded:** AIM Children's Book Award 1983.

BIXBY, WILLIAM
The Universe of Galileo and Newton by William Bixby and Giorgio de Santillana, illustrated with paintings and documents of the period; American Heritage, 1964. **Awarded:** Edison Mass Media (best children's science book) 1965.

BIXLER, PHYLLIS KOPPES
Tradition and the Individual Talent of Frances Hodgson Burnett: A Generic Analysis of Little Lord Fauntleroy, A Little Princess, and The Secret Garden by Phyllis Bixler in Children's Literature 7 (1979). **Awarded:** Children's Literature Assn. Award for Literary Criticism 1980.

BJORKLUND, LORENCE F.
Coyotes: Last Animals on Earth? by Harold E. Thomas, illustrated by Lorence F. Bjorkland; Lothrop, 1975. **Awarded:** Commonwealth Club of California 1975.

Famous American Explorers by Bern Keating, illustrated by Lorence F. Bjorklund; Rand, 1972. **Awarded:** Western Heritage 1973

The Greatest Cattle Drive by Paul I. Wellman, illustrated by Lorence F. Bjorklund; Houghton, 1964. **Awarded:** Western Heritage 1965.

The Plainsmen by Jack Schaefer, illustrated by Lorence F. Bjorklund; Houghton, 1963. **Awarded:** Spring Book Festival (older honor) 1963.

Ride the Pale Stallion by Gus Tavo, illustrated by Lorence F. Bjorklund; Knopf, 1968. **Awarded:** Steck-Vaughn 1969.

St. Lawrence Seaway by Clara Ingram Judson, illustrated by Lorence F. Bjorklund; Follett, 1959. **Awarded:** Indiana Authors Day (young adult) 1960.

Stars and Stripes: the Story of the American Flag by Mae Blacker Freeman, illustrated by Lorence F. Bjorklund; Random House, 1964. **Awarded:** New Jersey Institute of Technology (history 6-12) 1964.

Sword in Sheath by Andre Norton, illustrated by Lorence F. Bjorklund; Harcourt, 1949. **Awarded:** Ohioana (honorable mention) 1950.

Theodore Roosevelt, Fighting Patriot by Clara Ingram Judson, illustrated by Lorence F. Bjorklund; Follett, 1953. **Awarded:** Newbery (honor) 1954.

Tomas and the Red-headed Angel by Marion Garthwaite, illustrated by Lorence F. Bjorklund; Messner, 1950. **Awarded:** Commonwealth Club of California 1950; Julia Ellsworth Ford 1949.

Where the Panther Screams by William Powell Robinson, illustrated by Lorence F. Bjorklund; World, 1961. **Awarded:** Sequoyah 1964.

BJORKMAN, STEVE
Aliens for Breakfast by Jonathan Etra and Stephanie Spinner, illustrated by Steve Bjorkman; Random House, 1988. **Awarded:** Texas Bluebonnet 1991.

I Hate English! by Ellen Levine, illustrated by Steve Bjorkman; Scholastic, 1989. **Awarded:** Parents' Choice (Story Book) 1990.

BLACK, HELEN
The Cautious Carp and other Fables in Pictures written and illustrated by Nicholas Radlov, translated by Helen Black; Coward McCann, 1938. **Awarded:** Spring Book Festival (younger honor) 1938.

BLACK, IRMA SIMONTON
The Little Old Man Who Could Not Read by Irma Simonton Black, illustrated by Seymour Fleishman; Whitman, 1968. **Awarded:** Emphasis on Reading (Grades K-2) 1989-90.

BLACK, MARY MARTIN
Summerfield Farm by Mary Martin Black, illustrated by Wesley Dennis; Viking, 1951. **Awarded:** Spring Book Festival (8-12 honor) 1951.

BLACKBURN, WILLIAM
The Mirror in the Sea: Treasure Island and the Internalization of Romance by William Blackburn in Children's Literature Assn. Quarterly 8 (Fall 1983). **Awarded:** Children's Literature Assn. Excellence in Criticism (runnerup) 1984.

BLACKWOOD, GARY L.
Dying Sun by Gary L. Blackwood, not illustrated; Atheneum, 1989. **Awarded:** Friends of American Writers 1990.

BLACKWOOD, MARY
Derek and the Dinosaur by Mary Blackwood, illustrated by Kerry Argent; Omnibus, 1987. **Awarded:** Ashton Scholastic 1988.

BLADES, ANN
A Boy of Tache written and illustrated by Ann Blades; Tundra, 1973. **Awarded:** Amelia Frances Howard-Gibbon (runnerup) 1974.

By the Sea: An Alphabet Book written and illustrated by Ann Blades; Kids Can Press, 1985. **Awarded:** Amelia Frances

Howard-Gibbon (runnerup) 1986; Elizabeth Mrazik-Cleaver 1986.

Mary of Mile 18 written and illustrated by Ann Blades; Tundra, 1971. **Awarded:** Canadian Library Assn. 1972.

A Salmon for Simon by Betty Waterton, illustrated by Ann Blades; Douglas & MacIntyre, 1978. **Awarded:** Canadian Library Assn. (Runnerup) 1979; Governor General (illustrator) 1978; Amelia Frances Howard-Gibbon 1979.

BLAIR, HELEN
Carolina Caravan by Christine Noble Govan, illustrated by Helen Blair; Houghton, 1942. **Awarded:** Spring Book Festival (older honor) 1942.

The House by Marjorie H. Allee, illustrated by Helen Blair; Houghton, 1944. **Awarded:** Child Study 1944.

The Moved-outers by Florence Crannell Means, illustrated by Helen Blair; Houghton, 1945. **Awarded:** Child Study 1945; Newbery (honor) 1946.

BLAIR, MARY
I Can Fly by Ruth Krauss, illustrated by Mary Blair; Simon and Schuster, 1950. **Awarded:** Spring Book Festival (picture book honor) 1951.

BLAISDELL, ELINORE
Falcon, Fly Back written and illustrated by Elinore Blaisdell; Messner, 1939. **Awarded:** Julia Ellsworth Ford 1939.

BLAKE, MICHAEL
Dances With Wolves by Michael Blake, not illustrated; Fawcett Gold Medal, 1988. **Awarded:** Soaring Eagle (Grades 7-12) 1992.

BLAKE, QUENTIN
Awarded: University of Southern Mississippi Medallion 1993.

All Join In written and illustrated by Quentin Blake; Cape, 1990; Little Brown, 1991. **Awarded:** Maschler 1990.

Alphabeasts written and illustrated by Quentin Blake; Gollancz, 1990. **Awarded:** British Book Awards (Illustrated runnerup) 1990.

The BFG by Roald Dahl, illustrated by Quentin Blake; Cape, 1982; Farrar, 1982. **Awarded:** Books I Love Best Yearly (Read Alone Primary) 1991; Books I Love Best Yearly (Read Aloud Primary-12) 1991; Children's Book Award (Federation) 1982; West Australian (Primary) 1985.

Esio Trot by Roald Dahl, illustrated by Quentin Blake; Cape, 1990; Viking, 1990. **Awarded:** Smarties (Ages 6-8) 1990.

George's Marvellous Medicine by Roald Dahl, illustrated by Quentin Blake; Cape, 1981. **Awarded:** West Australian (Primary) 1984.

The Giraffe and the Pelly and Me by Roald Dahl, illustrated by Quentin Blake; Cape, 1985. **Awarded:** Maschler (runnerup) 1985.

How Tom Beat Captain Najork and His Hired Sportsmen by Russell Hoban, illustrated by Quentin Blake; Cape, 1974. **Awarded:** International Board on Books for Young People (illustrator/Great Britain) 1976; Whitbread 1974.

Matilda by Roald Dahl, illustrated by Quentin Blake; Cape, 1988; Viking Kestrel, 1988. **Awarded:** Books I Love Best Yearly (Read Aloud Primary-12) 1990; Caudill Young Reader's Book Award 1991; Children's Book Award (Federation of) 1988; Ethical Culture School 1988; Great Stone Face 1990; Indian Paintbrush 1991; Massachusetts Children's 1992; Nevada Young Reader (Intermediate) 1991-92; Nottinghamshire (Oak Tree) 1989; Utah Children's Choice 1991; Virginia Young Readers (Elementary) 1991; West Australian (Primary) 1989.

Mister Magnolia written and illustrated by Quentin Blake; Cape, 1980. **Awarded:** Children's Book Award (Federation) 1980; Greenaway 1980; International Board on Books for Young People (illustration/Great Britain) 1982.

A Near Thing for Captain Najork by Russell Hoban, illustrated by Quentin Blake; Atheneum, 1976. **Awarded:** New York Times Best Illustrated 1976.

Quentin Blake's ABC written and illustrated by Quentin Blake; Knopf, 1989. **Awarded:** Reading Magic 1989.

The Rain Door by Russell Hoban, illustrated by Quentin Blake; Gollancz, 1986. **Awarded:** Maschler (runnerup) 1986.

Rumbelow's Dance by John Yeoman, illustrated by Quentin Blake; Hamish Hamilton, 1982. **Awarded:** Maschler (runnerup) 1982.

The Story of the Dancing Frog written and illustrated by Quentin Blake; Cape, 1984. **Awarded:** Maschler (runnerup) 1984.

The Wild Washerwomen: A New Folktale by John Yeoman, illustrated by Quentin Blake; Hamish Hamilton, 1979. **Awarded:** Greenaway (highly commended) 1979.

The Witches by Roald Dahl, illustrated by Quentin Blake; Cape, 1983; Farrar, 1983. **Awarded:** New York Times Notable Books 1983; West Australia (overseas primary) 1986; Whitbread 1983.

You Can't Catch Me! by Michael Rosen, illustrated by Quentin Blake; Deutsch, 1981. **Awarded:** Signal Poetry 1982.

BLAKE, ROBERT J.
Riptide by Frances Ward Weller, illustrated by Robert J. Blake; Philomel, 1990. **Awarded:** Golden Sower (K-3) 1993.

BLAKESLEE, ANN
After the Fortune Cookies by Ann Blakeslee, not illustrated; Putnam, 1989. **Awarded:** Putnam's Fiction (runnerup) 1987.

BLANC, ESTHER SILVERSTEIN
Berchick by Esther Silverstein Blanc, illustrated by Tennessee Dixon; Volcano Press, 1989. **Awarded:** Bay Area Book Reviewers Assn. 1990; Jewish Book Council (Children's Picture Book) 1990; Sydney Taylor Book Award (Picture Book) 1990.

BLANK, PIUS
Turi: The Story of a Little Boy by Lesley Cameron Powell, illustrated by Pius Blank; Paul's Book Arcade (Angus), 1964. **Awarded:** Esther Glen 1964.

BLANKENBAKER, FRANCES
What the Bible Is All About for Young Explorers by Frances Blankenbaker, illustrated by Chizuko Yasuda; Reagal Books, 1986. **Awarded:** Gold Medallion (Children's) 1987.

BLATHWAYT, BENEDICT
Tangle and the Firesticks written and illustrated by Benedict Blathwayt; Julia MacRae, 1987; Knopf, 1987. **Awarded:** Smarties (Ages 6-8) 1987.

BLECHER, GEORGE
The Battle Horse by Harry Kullman, translated by George Blecher and Lone Thygesen-Blecher, not illustrated; Bradbury, 1981. **Awarded:** Batchelder 1982; International Board on Books for Young People (translation/USA) 1984.

BLEGVAD, ERIK
The Diamond in the Window by Jane Langton, illustrated by Erik Blegvad; Harper, 1962. **Awarded:** Edgar Allan Poe (runnerup) 1963.

The Fledgling by Jane Langton, illustrated by Erik Blegvad; Harper, 1980. **Awarded:** Newbery (honor) 1981.

The Gammage Cup by Carol Kendall, illustrated by Erik Blegvad; Harcourt, 1959. **Awarded:** Newbery (honor) 1960; Ohioana 1960.

I'm Hiding by Erik Blegvad and Myra Cohn Livingston, illustrated by Erik Blegvad; Harcourt, 1961. **Awarded:** Steck-Vaughn 1963.

The Little Pig-a-wig and Other Rhymes About Pigs by Lenore Blegvad, illustrated by Erik Blegvad; Atheneum, 1978. **Awarded:** New York Times Best Illustrated 1978.

The Mushroom Center Disaster by N. M. Bodecker, illustrated by Erik Blegvad; Atheneum, 1974. **Awarded:** Children's Book Showcase 1975.

The Winter Bear by Ruth Craft, illustrated by Erik Blegvad; Atheneum, 1975. **Awarded:** Children's Book Showcase 1976.

BLEGVAD, LENORE
The Little Pig-a-wig and Other Rhymes About Pigs by Lenore Blegvad, illustrated by Erik Blegvad; Atheneum, 1978. **Awarded:** New York Times Best Illustrated 1978.

BLICKENSTAFF, WAYNE
Helen Keller's Teacher by Mickie Davidson, illustrated by Wayne Blickenstaff; Scholastic, 1966. **Awarded:** Boys Club 1966-67.

BLISHEN, EDWARD
The God Beneath the Sea by Edward Blishen and Leon Garfield, illustrated by Charles Keeping; Longmans, 1970. **Awarded:** Carnegie 1970; Greenaway (commended) 1970.

The Oxford Book of Poetry for Children compiled by Edward Blishen, illustrated by Brian Wildsmith; Oxford, 1963. **Awarded:** Greenaway (commended) 1963.

BLOCH, LUCIENNE
Keep Singing, Keep Humming: A Collection of Play and Story Songs by Margaret Bradford, accompaniments by Barbara Woodruff, illustrated by Lucienne Bloch; Scott, 1946. **Awarded:** Spring Book Festival (younger honor) 1946.

Sandpipers by Edith Thacher Hurd, illustrated by Lucienne Bloch; Crowell, 1961. **Awarded:** New York Times Best Illustrated 1961.

BLOCH, MARIE HALUN
Tony of the Ghost Towns by Marie H. Bloch, illustrated by Dorothy Marino; Coward, 1956. **Awarded:** Spring Book Festival (middle honor) 1956.

BLOOM, LLOYD
Arthur, for the Very First Time by Patricia MacLachlan, illustrated by Lloyd Bloom; Harper & Row, 1980. **Awarded:** Golden Kite (fiction) 1980.

Grey Cloud by Charlotte Towner Graeber, illustrated by Lloyd Bloom; Four Winds, 1979. **Awarded:** Friends of American Writers 1980.

Like Jake and Me by Mavis Jukes, illustrated by Lloyd Bloom; Knopf, 1984. **Awarded:** Boston Globe Horn Book (illustration honor) 1985; Newbery (honor) 1985.

Nadia the Willful by Sue Alexander, illustrated by Lloyd Bloom; Pantheon, 1983. **Awarded:** Southern California Council (distinguished work of fiction) 1984.

No One is Going to Nashville by Mavis Jukes, illustrated by Lloyd Bloom; Knopf, 1983. **Awarded:** Irma Simonton Black 1983.

Poems for Jewish Holidays by Myra Cohn Livingston, illustrated by Lloyd Bloom; Holiday House, 1986. **Awarded:** Jewish Book Council (illustrated children's book) 1987.

Yonder by Tony Johnston, illustrated by Lloyd Bloom; Dial, 1988. **Awarded:** Southern California Council (Outstanding Literary Quality in a Picture Book) 1989.

BLOS, JOAN W.
A Gathering of Days: A New England Girl's Journal, 1830-32 by Joan W. Blos, not illustrated; Scribner, 1979. **Awarded:** American Book Awards (hardcover) 1980; Newbery 1980.

Old Henry by Joan W. Blos, illustrated by Stephen Gammell; Morrow, 1987. **Awarded:** Boston Globe Horn Book (Illustration honor) 1987.

BLOUGH, GLENN ORLANDO
Awarded: Eva L. Gordon 1980.

Discovering Cycles by Glenn O. Blough, illustrated by Jeanne Bendick; McGraw, 1973. **Awarded:** New York Academy of Sciences (younger honor) 1974.

BLUEMLE, ANDREW
Saturday Science by Westinghouse Research Laboratories Scientists, edited by Andrew Bluemle, illustrated with diagrams; Dutton, 1960. **Awarded:** Edison Mass Media (best science book for youth) 1961.

BLUHM, CHRISTINE F.
Awarded: Lucile M. Pannell 1987.

BLUMBERG, RHODA
Commodore Perry in the Land of the Shogun by Rhoda Blumberg, illustrated with photographs; Lothrop, Lee & Shepard, 1985. **Awarded:** Boston Globe Horn Book (nonfiction) 1985; Golden Kite (nonfiction) 1985; Newbery (honor) 1986.

The Great American Gold Rush by Rhoda Blumberg, illustrated with photos; Bradbury, 1989. **Awarded:** John and Patricia Beatty 1990; FOCAL 1991; Orbis Pictus Award for Outstanding Nonfiction for Children (Honor) 1989.

The Incredible Journey of Lewis and Clark by Rhoda Blumberg, illustrated with photos and maps; Lothrop, Lee & Shepard, 1987. **Awarded:** Golden Kite (Nonfiction) 1987.

BLUME, JUDY
Awarded: Children's Choice (Texas) (1st place) 1979, 1980, 1981, 1982, 1983, 1984, 1985, 1986, 1987, 1988, 1989, 1990, 1991; Land of Enchantment 1984; Jeremiah Ludington 1983; Milner 1983.

Are You There God? It's Me, Margaret by Judy Blume, not illustrated; Bradbury, 1970. **Awarded:** Golden Archer 1974; Great Stone Face 1980; Nene Award 1975; North Dakota Children's Choice 1979; Young Hoosier (Grades 4-6) 1976.

Blubber by Judy Blume, not illustrated; Bradbury, 1974. **Awarded:** New Jersey Institute of Technology 1975; North Dakota Children's Choice (older) 1983; Young Readers' Choice 1977.

Freckle Juice by Judy Blume, illustrated by Sonia O. Lisker; Four Winds, 1971. **Awarded:** Michigan Young Readers (division I) 1980.

It's Not the End of the World by Judy Blume, not illustrated; Bradbury, 1972. **Awarded:** New Jersey Institute of Technology 1972.

Just As Long As We're Together by Judy Blume, not illustrated; Orchard, 1987. **Awarded:** New Jersey Institute of Technology 1988

Otherwise Known as Sheila the Great by Judy Blume, not illustrated; Dutton, 1972. **Awarded:** New Jersey Institute of Technology 1972; South Carolina Children's Book Award 1978.

The Pain and the Great One by Judy Blume, illustrated by Irene Trivas; Bradbury, 1984. **Awarded:** Emphasis on Reading (Grades K-1) 1985-86.

Starring Sally J. Freedman as Herself by Judy Blume, not illustrated; Bradbury, 1977. **Awarded:** Sue Hefly (honor) 1982.

Superfudge by Judy Blume, not illustrated; Dutton, 1980. **Awarded:** Arizona 1983; Books I Love Best Yearly (Read Alone Primary) 1990; Buckeye (grades 4-8) 1982; California Young Reader Medal (intermediate) 1983; Children's Choice (Arizona) Juvenile category 1981, 1983, 1985, 1986, 1987, 1988; Colorado Children's 1982; CRABbery (honor) 1981; Emphasis on Reading (Grades 4-6) 1985-86; Garden State Children's (younger fiction) 1983; Georgia Children's 1983; Golden Sower (grades 4-6) 1983; Great Stone Face 1981, 1984, 1985, 1986, 1987; Sue Hefly 1982; Iowa Children's Choice 1983; Nene 1982; New Jersey Institute of Technology 1981; North Dakota Children's Choice (older) 1982, 1987; Soaring Eagle (Grades 7-9) 1989; Sunshine 1985; Texas Bluebonnet 1982; Utah Children's Choice 1982; Virginia (Elementary) 1986; Volunteer State 1982; West Australian Young Reader's (primary) 1982; Young Hoosier (grades 4-6) 1983; Young Reader's Choice 1983; Young Teens 1990.

Tales of a Fourth Grade Nothing by Judy Blume, illustrated by Roy Doty; Dutton, 1972. **Awarded:** Arizona 1977; Georgia Children's 1977; Great Stone Face 1982; Massachusetts Children's 1977; Massachusetts Children's (elementary) 1983; New Jersey Institute of Technology 1972; North Dakota Children's Choice (older) 1980; Sequoyah 1975; Charlie May Simon 1974-75; South Carolina Children's Book Award 1977; West Australian Young Readers' (primary) 1980; Young Readers' Choice 1975; Young Teens 1991.

Then Again, Maybe I Won't by Judy Blume, not illustrated; Bradbury, 1971. **Awarded:** New Jersey Institute of Technology 1972.

Tiger Eyes by Judy Blume, not illustrated; Bradbury, 1981. **Awarded:** Blue Spruce 1985; Buckeye (grades 4-8) 1983; California Young Reader Medal (junior high) 1983; CRABbery (honor) 1982; Dorothy Canfield Fisher 1983; Iowa Teen 1985.

BLUNDELL, TONY
The Great Smile Robbery by Roger McGough, illustrated by Tony Blundell; Kestrel, 1982. **Awarded:** Mother Goose (runnerup) 1983.

BLYTHE, GARY
The Whales' Song by Dyan Sheldon, illustrated by Gary Blythe; Hutchinson, 1990; Dial, 1991. **Awarded:** Greenaway 1990; Mother Goose (runnerup) 1991.

BLYTON, ENID
Mystery Island by Enid Blyton, illustrated by Stuart Tresilian; Macmillan, 1945. (Published in London as *The Island of Adventure*, Macmillan, 1944.) **Awarded:** Boys Club 1948.

BOBAK, CATHY
Bingo Brown, Gypsy Lover by Betsy Byars, illustrated by Cathy Bobak; Viking, 1990. **Awarded:** Parents' Choice (Story Book) 1990.

The Burning Questions of Bingo Brown by Betsy Byars, illustrated by Cathy Bobak; Viking, 1988. **Awarded:** Garden State

Children's (Younger Fiction) 1991; Parents' Choice (Story Book) 1988.

BOBRI (pseudonym)
see BOBRITSKY, VLADIMIR

BOBRI, VLADIMIR
see BOBRITSKY, VLADIMIR

BOBRITSKY, VLADIMIR
(pseudonyms are Bobri and Vladimir Bobri)

Five Proud Riders by Ann Stafford, illustrated by Bobri; Knopf, 1938. **Awarded:** Spring Book Festival (older honor) 1938.

A Kiss Is Round: Verses by Blossom Budney, illustrated by Vladimir Bobri; Lothrop, 1954. **Awarded:** New York Times Best Illustrated 1954.

The March Wind by Inez Rice, illustrated by Vladimir Bobri; Lothrop, 1957. **Awarded:** Spring Book Festival (ages 4-8 honor) 1957.

The Whiskers of Ho Ho by William Littlefield, illustrated by Vladimir Bobri; Lothrop, 1958. **Awarded:** Spring Book Festival (ages 4-8 honor) 1958.

BOCK, VERA
A Ring and a Riddle by M. Ilin and E. A. Segal, translated by Beatrice Kinkead, illustrated by Vera Bock; Lippincott, 1944. **Awarded:** Spring Book Festival (younger) 1944

The Secret of the Sea Rocks by Carol Reuter, illustrated by Vera Bock; McKay, 1967. **Awarded:** New Jersey Institute of Technology 1967.

Shadows into Mist by Ellen Turngren, illustrated by Vera Bock; Longmans, 1958. **Awarded:** Spring Book Festival (older honor) 1958.

Tangle-coated Horse and Other Tales: Episodes from the Fionn Saga by Ella Young, illustrated by Vera Bock; Longmans, 1929. **Awarded:** Newbery (honor) 1930.

BODDY, JOSEPH
Catherine Marshall's Storybook for Children by David Hazard, illustrated by Joseph Boddy; Chosen Books, 1987. **Awarded:** Gold Medallion (Elementary) 1988.

BODE, JANET
New Kids on the Block by Janet Bode, illustrated; Watts, 1989. **Awarded:** Woodson (Outstanding Merit - Secondary) 1990.

BODE, REGINA
Johnny Jump-up by John Hooper, illustrated by Regina Bode; Macmillan, 1942. **Awarded:** Spring Book Festival (picture book honor) 1942.

BODECKER, N. M. (NILS MOGENS)
Half Magic by Edward Eager, illustrated by N. M. Bodecker; Harcourt, 1954. **Awarded:** Spring Book Festival (Middle honor) 1954.

Hurry, Hurry, Mary Dear! and Other Nonsense Poems written and illustrated by N. M. Bodecker; Atheneum, 1976. **Awarded:** Christopher (ages 9-up) 1977.

It's Raining, Said John Twaining: Danish Nursery Rhymes written and illustrated by N. M. Bodecker; Atheneum, 1973. **Awarded:** Christopher (preschool) 1974.

Knight's Castle by Edward Eager, illustrated by N. M. Bodecker; Harcourt, 1956. **Awarded:** Ohioana 1957.

A Little at a Time by David A. Adler, illustrated by N. M. Bodecker; Random House, 1976. **Awarded:** Children's Book Showcase 1977.

Magic or Not? by Edward Eager, illustrated by N. M. Bodecker; Harcourt, 1959. **Awarded:** Spring Book Festival (middle honor) 1959.

Miss Jaster's Garden written and illustrated by N. M. Bodecker; Golden, 1972. **Awarded:** New York Times Best Illustrated 1972.

The Mushroom Center Disaster by N. M. Bodecker, illustrated by Erik Blegvad; Atheneum, 1974. **Awarded:** Children's Book Showcase 1975.

Seven-day Magic by Edward Eager, illustrated by N. M. Bodecker; Harcourt, 1962. **Awarded:** Ohioana 1963.

BODKER, CECIL
Awarded: Hans Christian Andersen (highly commended author/Denmark) 1974; Hans Christian Andersen (author) 1976.

The Leopard by Cecil Bodker, translated by Gunnar Poulsen; Atheneum, 1975. **Awarded:** Batchelder 1977.

Silas and Ben-Godik by Cecil Bodker, translated by Sheila LaFarge; Delacorte/Seymour Lawrence, 1978. **Awarded:** Boston Globe Horn Book (fiction honor) 1979.

BODMER, KARL
An Indian Winter by Russell Freedman, illustrated by Karl Bodmer; Holiday House, 1992. **Awarded:** Golden Kite (Nonfiction honor) 1992; Parents Choice (Picture Book) 1992; Reading Magic Award 1992.

BOEHM, LINDA
The Mystery Waters of Tonbridge Wells by Teri Martini, illustrated by Linda Boehm; Westminster, 1975. **Awarded:** New Jersey Institute of Technology 1976.

BOEKE, KEES
Cosmic View: the Universe in 40 Jumps by Kees Boeke, illustrated with drawings; Day, 1957. **Awarded:** New York Academy of Sciences (special award to John Day Co. on the 20th anniversary of the publication of above book) 1977.

BOGRAD, LARRY
Felix in the Attic by Larry Bograd, illustrated by Dirk Zimmer; Harvey House, 1978. **Awarded:** Irma Simonton Black 1978.

BOHDAL, SUSI
Selina, the Mouse and the Giant Cat written and illustrated by Susi Bohdal, translated by Lucy Meredith (from *Selina Pumpernickel und die Katz Flora*); Faber & Faber in association with Nord Sud Verlag, 1982. **Awarded:** Parents' Choice (illustration) 1982.

BOLDEN, MELVIN R.
Animal Atlas of the World by Emil L. Jordan, illustrated by Melvin R. Bolden; Hammond, 1969. **Awarded:** New Jersey Institute of Technology 1970.

BOLES, PAUL DARCY
A Million Guitars and Other Stories by Paul Boles, not illustrated; Little Brown, 1967. **Awarded:** Indiana Authors Day (young adult) 1969.

BOLLEN, ROGER
Elizabeth and Larry by Marilyn Sadler, illustrated by Roger Bollen; Simon & Schuster, 1990. **Awarded:** Parents' Choice (Story Book) 1990.

BOLLIGER, MAX
Noah and the Rainbow: an Ancient Story retold by Max Bolliger, translated by Clyde Robert Bulla, illustrated by Helga Aichinger; Crowell, 1972. **Awarded:** Children's Book Showcase 1973.

BOLOGNESE, DONALD
All Upon a Stone by Jean Craighead George, illustrated by Don Bolognese; Crowell, 1971. **Awarded:** Spring Book Festival (picture book) 1971.

The Black Mustanger by Richard Wormser, illustrated by Donald Bolognese; Morrow, 1971. **Awarded:** Western Heritage 1972; Western Writers (fiction) 1972.

The Colt from the Dark Forest by Anna Belle Loken, illustrated by Donald Bolognese; Lothrop, 1959. **Awarded:** Spring Book Festival (middle honor) 1959.

Fireflies by Joanne Ryder, illustrated by Donald Bolognese; Harper, 1977. **Awarded:** New Jersey Institute of Technology 1978.

The Keys and the Candle by Maryhale Woolsey, illustrated by Donald Bolognese; Abingdon, 1963. **Awarded:** Commonwealth Club of California 1963.

BOLTON, NANCY
The Book of Wiremu by Stella Margery Morice, illustrated by Nancy Bolton; Progressive Publication Society, 1944. **Awarded:** Esther Glen 1945.

BOND, FELICIA
The Firelings by Carol Kendall, map and illustrations by Felicia Bond; Atheneum, 1982. **Awarded:** Parents' Choice (literature) 1982.

If You Give a Moose a Muffin by Laura Joffe Numeroff, illustrated by Felicia Bond; HarperCollins, 1991. **Awarded:** Parents' Choice (Story Book) 1991.

If You Give a Mouse a Cookie by Laura J. Numeroff, illustrated by Felicia Bond; Harper & Row, 1985. **Awarded:** Buckeye (K-2) 1989; California Young Reader (Primary) 1988; Colorado Children's Book Award 1988; Emphasis on Reading (K-1) 1986-87; Georgia Children's Picture Storybook 1988; Nevada Young Reader Award (Primary) 1988-89.

BOND, NANCY
A String in the Harp by Nancy Bond, illustrated by Allen Davis; Atheneum, 1976. **Awarded:** Boston Globe Horn Book (fiction honor) 1976; International Reading Assn. 1977; Newbery (honor) 1977; Tir Na n-Og (English) 1977.

The Voyage Begun by Nancy Bond, not illustrated; Atheneum, 1981. **Awarded:** Boston Globe Horn Book (fiction honor) 1982.

BOND, SUSAN
Eric: The Tale of a Red Tempered Viking by Susan Bond, illustrated by Sally Trinkle; Grove Press, 1968. **Awarded:** New Jersey Institute of Technology 1970.

The Manners Zoo by Susan Bond, illustrated by Sally Trinkle; Follett, 1969. **Awarded:** New Jersey Institute of Technology 1970.

Ride With Me Through ABC by Susan Bond, illustrated by Horst Lemke; Scroll Press, 1969. **Awarded:** New Jersey Institute of Technology 1970.

BONHAM, FRANK
Awarded: Southern California Council (for body of work) 1980.

Durango Street by Frank Bonham, not illustrated; Dutton, 1965. **Awarded:** George G. Stone 1967.

Honor Bound by Frank Bonham, not illustrated; Crowell, 1963. **Awarded:** Edgar Allan Poe (runnerup) 1964.

Mystery of the Fat Cat by Frank Bonham, illustrated by Alvin Smith; Dutton, 1968. **Awarded:** Edgar Allan Poe (runnerup) 1969.

The Mystery of the Red Tide by Frank Bonham, not illustrated; Dutton, 1966. **Awarded:** Edgar Allan Poe (runnerup) 1967.

Viva Chicano by Frank Bonham, not illustrated; Dutton, 1970. **Awarded:** Woodward Park School 1971.

BONNER, MARY GRAHAM
Awarded: Women's National Book Assn. 1943.

BONNERS, SUSAN
A Penguin Year written and illustrated by Susan Bonners; Delacorte, 1981. **Awarded:** American Book Award (children's nonfiction) 1982.

Sarah's Questions by Harriet Ziefert, illustrated by Susan Bonners; Lothrop, Lee & Shepard, 1986. **Awarded:** New Jersey Institute of Technology 1987.

BONSALL, CROSBY NEWELL
I'll Show You Cats by C. N. Bonsall, illustrated by Ylla; Harper, 1964. **Awarded:** New York Times Best Illustrated 1964.

Mine's the Best written and illustrated by Crosby Bonsall; Harper, 1973. **Awarded:** Spring Book Festival (younger honor) 1973.

BONTEMPS, ARNA WENDELL
Story of the Negro by Arna Wendell Bontemps, illustrated by Raymond Lufkin; Knopf, 1948. **Awarded:** Jane Addams 1956; Newbery (honor) 1949.

BONZON, PAUL-JACQUES
The Orphans of Simitra by Paul-Jacques Bonzon, translated by Thelma Niklaus, illustrated by Simon Jeruchim; Criterion, 1962. **Awarded:** Spring Book Festival (middle) 1962.

BOOCK, PAULA
Out Walked Mel by Paula Boock, not illustrated; John McIndoe, 1991. **Awarded:** AIM Children's Book Award (Best First Book Award) 1992.

BOONE COUNTY BOARD OF EDUCATION
Awarded: Helen Keating Ott 1992.

BOOTH, DAVID
Til All the Stars Have Fallen: Canadian Poems for Children by David Booth, illustrated by Kady MacDonald Denton; Kids Can Press, 1989; Viking, 1990. **Awarded:** Amelia Frances Howard-Gibbon 1990.

Voices on the Wind: Poems for All Seasons selected by David Booth, illustrated by Michele Lemieux; Kids Can Press, 1990; Morrow, 1990. **Awarded:** Amelia Frances Howard-Gibbon (runnerup) 1991; IODE 1990.

BOOTH, GEORGE
Possum Come a-Knockin' by Nancy Van Laan, illustrated by George Booth; Knopf, 1990. **Awarded:** Parents' Choice (Picture Book) 1990.

BOOTH, GRAHAM
Bobby Shafto's Gone to Sea by Mark Taylor, illustrated by Graham Booth; Golden Gate Junior Books, 1970. **Awarded:** Southern California Council (distinguished contribution to illustration) 1971.

Spring Peepers by Judy Hawes, illustrated by Graham Booth; Crowell, 1975. **Awarded:** New York Academy of Sciences (younger honor) 1976.

BORDIER, GEORGETTE
A Young Person's Guide to Ballet by Noel Streatfeild, illustrated by Georgette Bordier; Warne, 1975. **Awarded:** Children's Book Showcase 1976.

BOREK, ERNEST
The Atoms Within Us by Ernest Borek, illustrated with photographs; Columbia University Press, 1961. **Awarded:** Edison Mass Media (best science book for youth) 1962.

BORLAND, KATHRYN K.
Clocks, from Shadow to Atom by Kathryn K. Borland and Helen R. Speicher, illustrated by Robert W. Addison; Follett, 1969. **Awarded:** Indiana Authors Day (children) 1970.

BORNER, HANNE
Kristoffers Rejse by Hanne Borner, illustrated by Roald Als; Borgen Denmark, 1980. **Awarded:** Biennale Illustrations Bratislava (grand prix) 1981.

BORNSTEIN, RUTH
Little Gorilla written and illustrated by Ruth Bornstein; Seabury, 1976. **Awarded:** Southern California Council (distinguished contribution to illustration) 1977.

Son of Thunder: An Old Lapp Tale retold by Ethel K. McHale, illustrated by Ruth Bornstein; Childrens, 1974. **Awarded:** Southern California Council (distinguished contribution to illustration) 1975.

BORTEN, HELEN
Little Big-feather by Joseph Longstreth, illustrated by Helen Borten; Abelard, 1956. **Awarded:** New York Times Best Illustrated 1956.

The Moon Seems to Change by Franklyn M. Branley, illustrated by Helen Borten; Crowell, 1960. **Awarded:** New Jersey Institute of Technology 1961.

The Sun: Our Nearest Star by Franklyn M. Branley, illustrated by Helen Borten; Crowell, 1961. **Awarded:** New Jersey Institute of Technology 1961.

What Makes Day and Night? by Franklyn M. Branley, illustrated by Helen Borten; Crowell, 1961. **Awarded:** New Jersey Institute of Technology 1961.

BOSMAJIAN, HAMIDA
Charlie and the Chocolate Factory and Other Excremental Visions by Hamida Bosmajian in The Lion and the Unicorn 9 (1985). **Awarded:** Children's Literature Assn. Excellence in Criticism 1986.

BOSSE, MALCOM J.
Ganesh Oder Eine Neue Welt (original English

Ganesh) by Malcom J. Bosse, translated by Wolf Harranth; Jungbrunner, 1982. **Awarded:** International Board on Books for Young People (translation/Austria) 1984.

BOSTELMANN, ELSE
Splasher by Fleming Crew and Alice Crew Gall, illustrated by Else Bostelmann; Oxford, 1945. **Awarded:** Ohioana (honorable mention) 1946.

BOSTON, LUCY MARIA
The Children of Green Knowe by L. M. Boston, illustrated by Peter Boston; Faber, 1954; Harcourt, 1955. **Awarded:** Carnegie (commended) 1954; Lewis Carroll Shelf 1969.

The Chimneys of Green Knowe by Lucy M. Boston, illustrated by Peter Boston; Faber, 1958. (Published in the U.S. as *Treasure of Green Knowe* in 1958 by Harcourt). **Awarded:** Carnegie (commended) 1958.

The Sea Egg by Lucy M. Boston, illustrated by Peter Boston; Harcourt, 1967. **Awarded:** Spring Book Festival (middle honor) 1967.

A Stranger at Green Knowe by Lucy M. Boston, illustrated by Peter Boston; Faber, 1961. **Awarded:** Carnegie 1961.

BOSTON, PETER
The Children of Green Knowe by L. M. Boston, illustrated by Peter Boston; Faber, 1954; Harcourt, 1955. **Awarded:** Carnegie (commended) 1954; Lewis Carroll Shelf 1969.

The Chimneys of Green Knowe by Lucy M. Boston, illustrated by Peter Boston; Faber, 1958. (Published in the U.S. as *Treasure of Green Knowe* in 1958 by Harcourt.) **Awarded:** Carnegie (commended) 1958.

The Sea Egg by Lucy M. Boston, illustrated by Peter Boston; Harcourt, 1967. **Awarded:** Spring Book Festival (middle honor) 1967.

A Stranger at Green Knowe by Lucy Boston, illustrated by Peter Boston; Faber, 1961. **Awarded:** Carnegie 1961.

BOSTON PUBLIC LIBRARY JUVENILE BOOK COLLECTION
Awarded: Chandler Reward of Merit 1982.

BOSWORTH, ALLAN R.
Sancho of the Long, Long Horns by Allan R. Bosworth, illustrated by Robert Frankenberg; Doubleday, 1947. **Awarded:** Commonwealth Club of California 1947.

BOTERMANS, JACK
Puzzles Old & New by Jerry Slocum and Jack Botermans, text by Carla Van Splunteren and Tony Burrett; Plenary Publications International, distributed by the University of Washington Press, 1986. **Awarded:** New York Academy of Sciences (prize as an exhibition catalogue of excellence and extraordinary interest) 1987.

BOTHWELL, JEAN
The Thirteenth Stone by Jean Bothwell, illustrated by Margaret Ayer; Harcourt, 1946. **Awarded:** Spring Book Festival (middle) 1946.

BOUCHER, JOELLE
Trois Petits Flocons by Joelle Boucher and Bernard Barokas; Grasset & Fasquelle, 1974. **Awarded:** Bologna (graphics for children) 1975.

BOUGARD, MARIE-THERESE
Arc-en-ciel 2 by Marie-Therese Bougard, Ann Miller and Liz Roselman; Mary Glasgow, 1989. **Awarded:** Times Educational Supplement (Schoolbook) 1989.

BOUIS, ANTONIA W.
We Were Not Like Other People by Efraim Sevela, translated by Antonia W. Bouis, not illustrated; Harper & Row, 1989. **Awarded:** International Board on Books for Young People (Translation/USA) 1992.

BOUMA, PADDY
Are We Nearly There? by Louis Baum, illustrated by Paddy Bouma; Bodley Head, 1986. **Awarded:** Greenaway (commended) 1986.

BOURGEOIS, PAULETTE
Canadian Garbage Collectors by Paulette Bourgeois, illustrated by Kim LaFave; Kids Can Press, 1991. **Awarded:** Information Book Award (Honour) 1992.

BOURKE, LINDA
A Show of Hands: Say It in Sign Language by Linda Bourke and Mary Beth, with Susan Regan, illustrated by Linda Bourke;

Addison Wesley, 1980. **Awarded:** Garden State Children's Book Award (younger nonfiction) 1983.

BOURNE, EULALIE, SISTER
Awarded: Outstanding Arizona Author 1983.

BOUTIS, VICTORIA
Looking Out by Victoria Boutis, not illustrated; Four Winds, 1988. **Awarded:** Addams (Fiction Ages 10-14) 1989.

BOUTWELL, EDNA
Awarded: Chandler Reward of Merit 1973.

BOWDEN, JOAN CHASE
Why the Tides Ebb and Flow by Joan Chase Bowden, illustrated by Marc Brown; Houghton Mifflin, 1979. **Awarded:** Boston Globe Horn Book (illustration honor) 1980.

BOWEN, BETSY
Antler, Bear, Canoe: A Northwoods Alphabet Year written and illustrated by Betsy Bowen; Little Brown, 1991. **Awarded:** Parents' Choice (Story Book) 1991.

BOWEN, CATHERINE DRINKER
Awarded: Women's National Book Assn. 1962.

BOWEN, GARY
My Village, Sturbridge by Gary Bowen, illustrated by Gary Bowen and Randy Miller; Farrar, 1977. **Awarded:** New York Times Best Illustrated 1977.

BOWEN, KEITH
Snowy by Berlie Doherty, illustrated by Keith Bowen; HarperCollins, 1992. **Awarded:** Children's Book Award (Picture Book) 1993.

BOWEN, ROBERT SYDNEY
Fourth Down by Robert S. Bowen, not illustrated; Lothrop, 1949. **Awarded:** Boys Club 1950.

BOWEN, WILLIAM ALVIN
The Old Tobacco Shop: A True Account of What Befell a Little Boy in Search of Adventure written and illustrated by William A. Bowen; Macmillan, 1921. **Awarded:** Newbery (honor) 1922.

BOWER-INGRAM, ANNE
Awarded: Dromkeen 1985.

BOWMAN, JAMES CLOY
Pecos Bill, the Greatest Cowboy of All Time by James Cloyd Bowman, illustrated by Laura Bannon; Whitman, 1937. **Awarded:** Lewis Carroll Shelf 1958; Newbery (honor) 1938; Spring Book Festival (older honor) 1937.

BOWMAN, LESLIE W.
The Canada Geese Quilt by Natalie Kinsey-Warnock, illustrated by Leslie W. Bowman; Dodd Mead, 1988. **Awarded:** Fassler 1991.

BOXER, DEVORAH
Twenty-six Ways to Be Somebody Else written and illustrated by Devorah Boxer; Pantheon, 1960. **Awarded:** New York Times Best Illustrated 1960.

BOYCE, MADELEINE
The First Walkabout by Norman Barnett Tindale and Harold Arthur Lindsay, illustrated by Madeleine Boyce; Longmans, 1954. **Awarded:** Children's Book Council of Australia (book of the year) 1955.

BOYCE, SONIA
When I Dance by James Berry, illustrated by Sonia Boyce; Hamish Hamilton, 1988; Harcourt Brace Jovanovich, 1991. **Awarded:** Signal Poetry Award 1989.

BOYD, CANDY DAWSON
The Circle of Gold by Candy Dawson Boyd, not illustrated; Apple Paperbacks/Scholastic, 1984. **Awarded:** Coretta Scott King (literature honorable mention) 1985.

BOYD, WILLIAM
The Other City by Ray Vogel, photographs by William Boyd and others; White, 1969. **Awarded:** Nancy Bloch 1969.

BOYE, INGER
Awarded: Grolier 1964.

BOYER, EDWARD
River and Canal written and illustrated by Edward Boyer; Holiday House, 1986. **Awarded:** New York Academy of Sciences (younger honor) 1987.

BOYER, ROBERT E.
The Story of Oceanography by Robert E. Boyer, illustrated with photographs and diagrams; Harvey, 1975. **Awarded:** New York Academy of Sciences (older honor) 1976.

BOYLE, MILDRED
By the Shores of Silver Lake by Laura Ingalls Wilder, illustrated by Mildred Boyle and Helen Sewell; Harper, 1939. **Awarded:** Newbery (honor) 1940; Young Readers' Choice 1942.

Little Town on the Prairie by Laura Ingalls Wilder, illustrated by Mildred Boyle and Helen Sewell; Harper, 1941. **Awarded:** Newbery (honor) 1942.

The Long Winter by Laura Ingalls Wilder, illustrated by Mildred Boyle and Helen Sewell; Harper, 1940. **Awarded:** Newbery (honor) 1941.

On the Banks of Plum Creek by Laura Ingalls Wilder, illustrated by Mildred Boyle and Helen Sewell; Harper, 1937. **Awarded:** Newbery (honor) 1938.

These Happy Golden Years by Laura Ingalls Wilder, illustrated by Mildred Boyle and Helen Sewell; Harper, 1943. **Awarded:** Newbery (honor) 1944; Spring Book Festival (middle) 1943.

BOYNTON, SANDRA
Chloe and Maude written and illustrated by Sandra Boynton; Little Brown, 1985. **Awarded:** Irma Simonton Black 1985.

BOZZO, FRANK
The Impossible People: a History Natural and Unnatural of Beings Terrible and Wonderful by Georgess McHargue, illustrated by Frank Bozzo; Holt, 1972. **Awarded:** National Book Award (finalist) 1973; Spring Book Festival (ages 8-12 honor) 1972.

The Whispering Mountain by Joan Aiken, illustrated by Frank Bozzo; Cape, 1968. **Awarded:** Carnegie (honour) 1968; Guardian 1969.

BRADBURY, CHRISTOPHER
The Last of the Mohicans by James Fenimore Cooper, illustrated by Christopher Bradbury; Felix Gluck. **Awarded:** Bologna (Graphics for Youth) 1974.

BRADBURY, RAY
Switch on the Night by Ray Bradbury, illustrated by Madeleine Gekiere; Pantheon, 1955. **Awarded:** Boys Club 1956; New York Times Best Illustrated 1955.

BRADFIELD, ROGER
The Flying Hockey Stick written and illustrated by Roger Bradfield; Rand McNally, 1966. **Awarded:** Boys Club 1968.

Our Family Got a Divorce by Carolyn E. Phillips, designed and illustrated by Roger Bradfield; Gospel Light Publications (GL Regal Books), 1979. **Awarded:** Gold Medallion 1980.

BRADFORD, KARLEEN
There Will Be Wolves by Karleen Bradford; HarperCollins, 1992. **Awarded:** Young Adult Canadian 1993.

BRADFORD, MARGARET
Keep Singing, Keep Humming: a Collection of Play and Story Songs by Margaret Bradford, accompaniments by Barbara Woodruff, illustrated by Lucienne Bloch; Scott, 1946. **Awarded:** Spring Book Festival (younger honor) 1946.

BRADLEY, DUANE
Meeting with a Stranger by Duane Bradley, illustrated by E. Harper Johnson; Lippincott, 1964. **Awarded:** Jane Addams 1965; Woodward Park School 1965.

BRADLEY, HELEN
And Miss Carter Wore Pink: Scenes from an Edwardian Childhood written and illustrated by Helen Bradley; Holt, 1971, 1972. **Awarded:** Art Books for Children 1973.

BRADLEY, JOHN
The Car: Watch it Work by Operating the Moving Diagrams! by Ray Marshall and John Bradley, illustrated; Viking Kestrel, 1984. **Awarded:** Redbook (popup) 1984.

Watch it Work! The Plane by Ray Marshall and John Bradley; illustrated; Viking Kestrel, 1985. **Awarded:** Smarties (innovation) 1985.

BRADY, IRENE
Awarded: Evelyn Sibley Lampman 1986.

Wild Mouse written and illustrated by Irene Brady; Scribner, 1976. **Awarded:** New York Academy of Sciences (younger) 1978.

BRAGINETZ, DONNA
Digging Dinosaurs by John R. Horner and James Gorman, illustrated by Donna Braginetz and Chris Ellingsen; Workman Publishers, 1988. **Awarded:** New York Academy of Sciences (Older) 1989.

BRANCATO, ROBIN
Awarded: Outstanding Pennsylvania Author 1983.

Uneasy Money by Robin Brancato, not illustrated; Random House, 1986; Knopf, 1989. **Awarded:** New Jersey Institute of Technology 1988, 1990.

Winning by Robin Brancato, not illustrated; Knopf, 1988. **Awarded:** New Jersey Institute of Technology 1990.

BRAND, CHRISTIANNA
Naughty Children by Christianna Brand, illustrated by Edward Ardizzone; Dutton, 1963. **Awarded:** Spring Book Festival (middle honor) 1963.

BRAND, PIPPA
Ancient China by John Hay, illustrated by Pippa Brand and Rosemonde Nairac; Walck, 1974. **Awarded:** New York Academy of Sciences (special honorable mention for publisher) 1975.

The Archaeology of Ships by Paul Johnstone, illustrated by Pippa Brand; Walck, 1974. **Awarded:** New York Academy of Sciences (special honorable mention for publisher) 1975.

BRAND, STEWART
The Media Lab: Inventing the Future at MIT by Stewart Brand, illustrated; Viking Kestrel, 1987. **Awarded:** New York Academy of Sciences (Elliott Montroll Award) 1988.

BRANDENBERG, ALIKI
see ALIKIBRANDI, LILLIAN

Encyclopedia Brown and the Case of the Midnight Visitor by Donald J. Sobol, illustrated by Lillian Brandi; Nelson, 1977. **Awarded:** Buckeye (grades 4-8 honor) 1982.

BRANDIS, MARIANNE
The Quarter-pie Window by Marianne Brandis, illustrated by G. Brender a Brandis; Porcupine's Quill, 1985. **Awarded:** National Chapter of Canada IODE Violet Downey 1986; Young Adult Canadian 1986.

The Sign of the Scales by Marianne Brandis, illustrated by G. Brender a Brandis; Porcupine's Quill, 1990. **Awarded:** Alcuin 1991; Bilson 1991.

BRANDT, KATRIN
Die Wichtelmanner by Jacob Grimm and Wilhelm Grimm, illustrated by Katrin Brandt; Atlantis Verlag. **Awarded:** Bologna (Graphics for Children) 1968.

BRANFIELD, JOHN
The Fox in Winter by John Branfield, not illustrated; Gollancz, 1980. **Awarded:** Carnegie (commended) 1980.

BRANLEY, FRANKLYN MANSFIELD
Awarded: Gordon, Eva L. 1988; New Jersey Institute of Technology (New Jersey children's book writer of the year) 1970.

Big Tracks, Little Tracks by Franklyn M. Branley, illustrated by Leonard Kessler; Crowell, 1960. **Awarded:** New Jersey Institute of Technology 1961.

A Book of Astronauts for You by Franklyn M. Branley, illustrated by Leonard Kessler; Crowell, 1963. **Awarded:** New Jersey Institute of Technology (ages 5-8 science books) 1964.

A Book of Mars for You by Franklyn M. Branley, illustrated by Leonard Kessler; Crowell, 1968. **Awarded:** New Jersey Institute of Technology (science) 1968.

A Book of Stars for You by Franklyn M. Branley, illustrated by Leonard Kessler; Crowell, 1967. **Awarded:** New Jersey Institute of Technology (science) 1968

Eclipse: Darkness in Daytime by Franklyn M. Branley, illustrated by Donald Crews; Crowell, 1973. **Awarded:** Children's Book Showcase 1974.

Experiments in Sky Watching by Franklyn M. Branley, illustrated by Helmut K. Wimmer; Crowell, 1959. **Awarded:** Edison Mass Media (best children's science book) 1960.

Exploring by Satellite: the Story of Project Vanguard by Franklyn M. Branley, illustrated by Helmut K. Wimmer; Crowell, 1957. **Awarded:** New Jersey Institute of Technology 1961.

Floating and Sinking by Franklyn M. Branley, illustrated by Robert Galster; Crowell, 1967. **Awarded:** New Jersey Institute of Technology (science) 1968.

High Sounds, Low Sounds by Franklyn M. Branley, illustrated by Paul Galdone; Crowell, 1967. **Awarded:** New Jersey Institute of Technology (science) 1968.

Man in Space to the Moon by Franklyn M. Branley, illustrated by Louis Glanzman; Crowell, 1970. **Awarded:** New Jersey Institute of Technology 1971.

The Moon: Earth's Natural Satellite by Franklyn M. Branley, illustrated by Helmut K. Wimmer; Crowell, 1960. **Awarded:** New Jersey Institute of Technology 1961.

The Moon Seems to Change by Franklyn M. Branley, illustrated by Helen Borten; Crowell, 1960. **Awarded:** New Jersey Institute of Technology 1961.

Rockets and Satellites by Franklyn M. Branley, illustrated by Bill Sokol; Crowell, 1961. **Awarded:** New Jersey Institute of Technology 1961.

The Sun: Our Nearest Star by Franklyn M. Branley, illustrated by Helen Borten; Crowell, 1961. **Awarded:** New Jersey Institute of Technology 1961.

What Makes Day and Night? by Franklyn M. Branley, illustrated Helen Borten; Crowell, 1961. **Awarded:** New Jersey Institute of Technology 1961.

BRANSCUM, ROBBIE
The Girl by Robbie Branscum, not illustrated; Harper & Row, 1986. **Awarded:** PEN Center USA West 1987.

The Murder of Hound Dog Bates: a Novel by Robbie Branscum, not illustrated; Viking, 1982. **Awarded:** New York Times Notable Books 1982; Edgar Allan Poe 1983.

To the Tune of the Hickory Stick by Robbie Branscum, not illustrated; Doubleday, 1978. **Awarded:** New York Times Notable Books 1978.

Toby, Granny and George by Robbie Branscum, illustrated by Glen Rounds; Doubleday, 1976. **Awarded:** Friends of American Writers (older) 1977.

BRAUDE, LYUDMILA
Awarded: FIT Astrid Lindgren Translation 1990.

BRAUN, KATHY
Kangaroo & Kangaroo by Kathy Braun, illustrated by Jim McMullan; Doubleday, 1965. **Awarded:** New York Times Best Illustrated 1965.

BRAYMER, MARJORIE
The Walls of Windy Troy: a Biography of Heinrich Schliemann by Marjorie Braymer, illustrated with photographs; Harcourt, 1960. **Awarded:** Spring Book Festival (older) 1960.

BREINBURG, PETRONELLA
My Brother Sean by Petronella Breinburg, illustrated by Errol Lloyd; Bodley Head, 1973. **Awarded:** Greenaway (commended) 1973.

BRENDER A BRANDIS, G.
The Quarter-Pie Window by Marianne Brandis, illustrated by G. Brender a Brandis; Porcupine's Quill, 1985. **Awarded:** National Chapter of Canada IODE Violet Downey 1986; Young Adult Canadian 1986.

The Sign of the Scales by Marianne Brandis, illustrated by G. Brender a Brandis; Porcupine's Quill, 1990. **Awarded:** Alcuin 1991; Bilson 1991.

BRENNER, ANITA
The Boy Who Could Do Anything and Other Mexican Folktales by Anita Brenner, illustrated by Jean Charlot; Young Scott Books, 1942. **Awarded:** Spring Book Festival (middle honor) 1942.

A Hero by Mistake by Anita Brenner, illustrated by Jean Charlot; Scott, 1953. **Awarded:** New York Times Best Illustrated 1953; Spring Book Festival (4-8 honor) 1953.

The Timid Ghost: or, What Would You Do with a Sackful of Gold? by Anita Brenner, illustrated by Jean Charlot; Scott, 1966. **Awarded:** Boys Club 1966-67.

BRENNER, BARBARA
Awarded: Outstanding Pennsylvania Author 1986.

Barto Takes the Subway by Barbara Brenner, photographs by Sy Katzoff; Knopf, 1961. **Awarded:** Spring Book Festival (ages 4-8 honor) 1961.

A Snake-lover's Diary by Barbara Brenner, illustrated with photographs; Young Scott, 1970. **Awarded:** Spring Book Festival (middle honor) 1970.

BRENTANO, CLEMENS
The Legend of Rosepetal by Clemens Brentano, illustrated by Lisbeth Zwerger; Picture Book Studio, 1985. **Awarded:** New York Times Best Illustrated 1985.

BRESLIN, THERESA
Simon's Challenge by Theresa Breslin, not illustrated; Blackie, 1988. **Awarded:** Fidler 1987.

BRETT, JAN
Awarded: David McCord 1993.

Annie and the Wild Animals written and illustrated by Jan Brett; Houghton Mifflin, 1985. **Awarded:** Redbook 1985.

BREWSTER, PATIENCE
Don't Touch My Room by Patricia Lakin, illustrated by Patience Brewster; Little Brown, 1985. **Awarded:** Golden Sower (K-3) 1988.

BRIDGERS, SUE ELLEN
Awarded: ALAN 1985.

All Together Now by Sue Ellen Bridgers, not illustrated; Knopf, 1979. **Awarded:** Boston Globe Horn Book (fiction honor) 1979; Christopher (ages 12-up) 1980; New York Times Notable Books 1979.

Permanent Connections by Sue Ellen Bridgers, not illustrated; Harper & Row, 1987. **Awarded:** North Carolina AAUW 1987; Parents' Choice (Story Book) 1987.

The Man written and illustrated by Raymond Briggs; Julia MacRae, 1992. **Awarded:** Kurt Maschler 1992.

BRIDWELL, NORMAN
Awarded: Lucky Book Club Four-Leaf Clover 1971.

Clifford, the Big Red Dog written and illustrated by Norman Bridwell; Scholastic, 1985. **Awarded:** Children's Choice [Arizona] (picture book) 1987.

BRIER, HOWARD M.
Smoke Eater by Howard M. Brier, illustrated by Louis Cunette; Random House, 1941. **Awarded:** Spring Book Festival (older honor) 1941.

BRIERLEY, LOUISE
Peacock Pie: A Book of Rhymes by Walter De La Mare, illustrated by Louise Brierley; Henry Holt, 1989. **Awarded:** New York Times Best Illustrated 1989.

BRIGGS, KATHARINE M.
Abbey-lubbers, Banshees and Boggarts: an Illustrated Encyclopedia of Fairies by Katharine M. Briggs, illustrated by Yvonne Gilbert; Kestrel, 1979. **Awarded:** Mother Goose (runnerup) 1980.

BRIGGS, RAYMOND REDVERS
Awarded: British Book Awards (Author) 1992.

The Elephant and the Bad Baby by Elfrida Vipont, illustrated by Raymond Briggs; Coward, 1970. **Awarded:** Spring Book Festival (picture book honor) 1970.

Father Christmas written and illustrated by Raymond Briggs; Hamilton, 1973; Coward, 1973. **Awarded:** Art Books for Children 1975; Children's Book Showcase 1974; Greenaway 1973; W. H. Smith (£50) 1977.

Fee Fi Fo Fum: a Picture Book of Nursery Rhymes written and illustrated by Raymond Briggs; Hamilton, 1964. **Awarded:** Greenaway (commended) 1964.

Mother Goose Treasury written and illustrated by Raymond Briggs; Hamilton, 1966. **Awarded:** Greenaway 1966.

The Snowman written and illustrated by Raymond Briggs; Random House, 1978; Hamilton, 1978. **Awarded:** Art Books for Children 1979; Boston Globe Horn Book (illustration) 1979; Lewis Carroll Shelf 1979; Greenaway (highly commended) 1978; Redbook 1986; W. H. Smith (best children's book) 1982.

When the Wind Blows written and illustrated by Raymond Briggs; Hamish Hamilton, 1982. **Awarded:** Other Award 1982.

BRIGHT, ROBERT
Georgie to the Rescue written and illustrated by Robert Bright; Doubleday, 1956. **Awarded:** Spring Book Festival (ages 4-8 honor) 1956.

BRILL, EDITH
The Golden Bird by Edith Brill, illustrated by Jan Pienkowski; Dent, 1970. **Awarded:** Greenaway (honour) 1970.

BRINDZE, RUTH
The Gulf Stream by Ruth Brindze, illustrated by Helene Carter; Vanguard, 1945. **Awarded:** Spring Book Festival (middle) 1945.

Look How Many People Wear Glasses: The Magic of Lenses by Ruth Brindze, illustrated with photographs and diagrams; Atheneum, 1975. **Awarded:** New York Academy of Sciences (older honor) 1976.

BRINK, CAROL RYRIE
Awarded: Southern California Council (comprehensive contribution of lasting value to the field of children's literature) 1966; Kerlan 1978.

Caddie Woodlawn by Carol Ryrie Brink, illustrated by Kate Seredy; Macmillan, 1935. **Awarded:** Lewis Carroll Shelf 1959; Newbery 1936

BRINSMEAD, HESBA FAY
Longtime Passing by Hesba Fay Brinsmead, not illustrated; Angus & Robertson, 1971. **Awarded:** Children's Book Council of Australia (book of the year) 1972.

Pastures of the Blue Crane by Hesba Fay Brinsmead, illustrated by Annette Macarthur-Onslow; Oxford, 1964. **Awarded:** Children's Book Council of Australia (book of the year) 1965.

BRISON-STACK, GUY
Crafting with Newspapers by Vivienne Eisner and William Shisler, illustrated by Guy Brison-Stack; Sterling, 1977. **Awarded:** New Jersey Institute of Technology 1978.

BRISSON, PAT
Magic Carpet by Pat Brisson, illustrated by Amy Schwartz; Bradbury, 1991. **Awarded:** Parents' Choice (Story Book) 1991.

Your Best Friend, Kate by Pat Brisson, illustrated by Rick Brown; Bradbury, 1989. **Awarded:** New Jersey Institute of Technology (Children's) 1990.

BRITTAIN, BILL
Wings by Bill Brittain, not illustrated; HarperCollins, 1991. **Awarded:** Ethical Culture School 1991; North Carolina AAUW 1992.

BRITTAIN, WILLIAM
All the Money in the World by William Brittain, illustrated by Charles Robinson; Harper, 1979. **Awarded:** Charlie May Simon 1981-82.

The Wish Giver: Three Tales of Coven Tree by William Brittain, illustrated by Andrew Glass; Harper, 1983. **Awarded:** Newbery (honor) 1984.

BROCHMAN, ODD
Marianne Po Sykehus by Odd Brochman; Aschehoug, 1958. **Awarded:** Hans Christian Andersen (runnerup) 1960.

BROCK, EMMA L.
Drusilla written and illustrated by Emma L. Brock; Macmillan, 1937. **Awarded:** Spring Book Festival (younger honor) 1937.

BROCKWAY, JEAN
Awarded: L. Frank Baum 1990.

BRODER, BILL
What the Forest Tells Me: 1977 Sierra Club Calendar for Children compiled by Bill Broder, illustrated with photographs; Sierra Club/Scribner, 1976. **Awarded:** Children's Book Showcase 1977.

BRODERICK, DOROTHY
Awarded: Grolier 1991.

BROEKEL, RAY
Even the Devil Is Afraid of a Shrew adapted by Ray Broekel, retold by Valerie Stalder, illustrated by Richard Brown; Addison-Wesley, 1972. **Awarded:** Children's Book Showcase 1973.

The Painter and the Bird written and illustrated by Max Velthuijs, translated by Ray Broekel; Addison-Wesley, 1975. **Awarded:** Children's Book Showcase 1976.

BRONOWSKI, JACOB
Biography of an Atom by Jacob Bronowski and Millicent E. Selsam, illustrated by Weimer Pursell; Harper, 1965. **Awarded:** Edison Mass Media (best children's science book) 1966.

BRONSON, LYNN
see LAMPMAN, EVELYN SIBLEY

BROOK, JUDITH
The Rescuers by Margery Sharp, illustrated by Judith Brook; Collins, 1959. **Awarded:** Carnegie (commended) 1959.

BROOKE, LEONARD LESLIE
Johnny Crow's Garden: a Picture Book written and illustrated by L. Leslie Brooke; Warne, 1903. **Awarded:** Lewis Carroll Shelf 1960.

A Roundabout Turn by Robert H. Charles, illustrated by L. Leslie Brooke; Warne, 1930. **Awarded:** Lewis Carroll Shelf 1961.

BROOKINS, DANA
Alone in Wolf Hollow by Dana Brookins, not illustrated; Seabury, 1978. **Awarded:** Edgar Allan Poe 1979; Southern California Council (distinguished contribution in the field of fiction) 1979.

BROOKS, BRUCE
Everywhere by Bruce Brooks, not illustrated; HarperCollins, 1990. **Awarded:** Golden Kite (Fiction Honor) 1990.

The Moves Make the Man by Bruce Brooks, not illustrated; Harper & Row, 1984. **Awarded:** Boston Globe (fiction) 1985; New York Times Notable 1984; Newbery (honor) 1985.

What Hearts by Bruce Brooks, not illustrated; HarperCollins, 1992. **Awarded:** Newbery (honor) 1993.

BROOKS, JEROME
Knee Holes by Jerome Brooks, not illustrated; Orchard, 1992. **Awarded:** Carl Sandburg 1992.

BROOKS, LESTER J.
Great Civilizations of Ancient Africa by Lester J. Brooks, illustrated with photographs and maps; Four Winds, 1971. **Awarded:** Children's Book Showcase 1972.

BROOKS, MARTHA
Paradise Cafe and Other Stories by Martha Brooks, not illustrated; Thistledown Press, 1988; Little Brown (Joy Street), 1990. **Awarded:** Boston Globe Horn Book (Fiction/Poetry Honor) 1991; Vicky Metcalf Short Story 1989; Young Adult Canadian (Runnersup) 1989.

Two Moons in August by Martha Brooks, not illustrated; Groundwood Books, 1991. **Awarded:** Canadian Library Assn. Book of the Year (Runnerup) 1992; Young Adult Canadian (Runnerup) 1992.

BROOKS, POLLY SCHOYER
Queen Eleanor, Independent Spirit of the Medieval World by Polly Brooks, illustrated; Lippincott, 1983. **Awarded:** Boston Globe (nonfiction honor) 1984.

BROOKS, RON
The Bunyip of Berkeley's Creek by Jenny Wagner, illustrated by Ron Brooks; Longmans Young, 1974. **Awarded:** Children's Book Council of Australia (picture book of the year) 1974.

John Brown, Rose and the Midnight Cat by Jenny Wagner, illustrated by Ron Brooks; Kestrel, 1977; Bradbury, 1978. **Awarded:** Children's Book Council of Australia (picture book of the year) 1978; Guardian (commended) 1978; New South Wales State Literary Awards (Children's) 1979.

BROOMHALL, WINIFRED
Wee Willow Whistle by Kay Avery, illustrated Winifred Broomhall; Knopf, 1947. **Awarded:** Spring Book Festival (younger honor) 1947.

BROSSEIT, VIRGINIA
The Secret Friendship by Virginia Brosseit, not illustrated; Winston-Derek, 1988. **Awarded:** Friends of American Writers 1989.

BROUWER, JACK
Pathki Nana: Kootenai Girl Solves a Mystery by Thomasma, illustrated by Jack Brouwer; Baker Book House, 1991. **Awarded:** Indian Paintbrush 1993.

BROWN, BETSY
Awarded: Southern California Council (Dorothy C. McKenzie Award) 1989.

BROWN, BILL
Roaring River by Bill Brown, not illustrated; Coward McCann, 1953. **Awarded:** Commonwealth Club of California 1953.

BROWN, BUCK
ABC Pirate Adventure by Ida DeLage, illustrated by Buck Brown; Garrard, 1977. **Awarded:** New Jersey Institute of Technology 1978.

BROWN, ELIZABETH BURTON
Grains: An Illustrated History with Recipes by Elizabeth Burton Brown, illustrated with photographs; Prentice Hall, 1977. **Awarded:** New York Academy of Sciences (older) 1978.

BROWN, FERN G.

Behind the Scenes at the Horse Hospital by Fern G. Brown, edited by Kathleen Tucker, photographs by Roger Ruhlin; Whitman, 1981. **Awarded:** Sandburg 1982.

BROWN, IRENE BENNETT

Awarded: Evelyn Sibley Lampman 1988.

Before the Lark by Irene Bennett Brown, not illustrated; Atheneum, 1982. **Awarded:** Western Writers of America Spur (juvenile fiction) 1982.

BROWN, JAMIE

Superbike! by Jamie Brown, not illustrated; Clarke, Irwin, 1981. **Awarded:** Young Adult Canadian 1982.

BROWN, JUDITH GWYN

The Best Christmas Pageant Ever by Barbara Robinson, illustrated by Judith Gwyn Brown; Harper, 1972. **Awarded:** Emphasis on Reading (Grades 4-6) 1980-81; Georgia Children's 1976; Maud Hart Lovelace 1982; Young Hoosier (4-6) 1978.

The Secret of the Seven Crows by Wylly Folk St. John, illustrated by Judith Gwyn Brown; Viking, 1973. **Awarded:** Edgar Allan Poe (runnerup) 1974.

BROWN, LAURENE KRASNY

Dinosaurs Divorce: A Guide for Changing Families written and illustrated by Laurene Krasny Brown and Marc Brown; Atlantic Monthly, 1986. **Awarded:** New York Times Notable 1986.

BROWN, LLOYD A.

Map Making: The Art that Became a Science by Lloyd A. Brown, illustrated with charts and diagrams; Little, 1960. **Awarded:** Boys Club 1961.

BROWN, MARBURY

Topsail Island Treasure by Stephen W. Meader, illustrated by Marbury Brown; Harcourt, 1966. **Awarded:** New Jersey Institute of Technology 1966.

BROWN, MARC

Awarded: Milner Award 1991; Outstanding Pennsylvania Author 1989.

Arthur's Baby written and illustrated by Marc Brown; Little Brown, 1987. **Awarded:** Weekly Reader Children's Book Club Award 1992.

Dinosaurs Divorce: A Guide for Changing Families written and illustrated by Laurene Krasny Brown and Marc Brown; Atlantic Monthly, 1986. **Awarded:** New York Times Notable 1986.

Oh, Kojo! How Could You! by Verna Aardema, illustrated by Marc Brown; Dial, 1984. **Awarded:** Parents' Choice (literature) 1984.

Why the Tides Ebb and Flow by Joan Chase Bowden, illustrated by Marc Brown; Houghton Mifflin, 1979. **Awarded:** Boston Globe Horn Book (illustration honor) 1980.

BROWN, MARCIA

Awarded: Regina 1977; University of Southern Mississippi 1972; Laura Ingalls Wilder 1992.

All Butterflies: An ABC written and illustrated by Marcia Brown; Scribner, 1974. **Awarded:** Boston Globe Horn Book (illustration honor) 1974.

Cinderella: or, The Little Glass Slipper by Charles Perrault, illustrated by Marcia Brown; Scribner, 1954. **Awarded:** Caldecott 1955.

Dick Whittington and his Cat written and illustrated by Marcia Brown; Scribner, 1950. **Awarded:** Caldecott (honor) 1951.

Henry-Fisherman written and illustrated by Marcia Brown; Scribner, 1949. **Awarded:** Caldecott (honor) 1950.

How, Hippo! written and illustrated by Marcia Brown; Scribner, 1969. **Awarded:** Spring Book Festival (picture book honor) 1969.

Once a Mouse written and illustrated by Marcia Brown; Scribner, 1961. **Awarded:** Caldecott 1962; Lewis Carroll Shelf 1966; New York Times Best Illustrated 1961.

Puss in Boots by Charles Perrault, illustrated by Marcia Brown; Scribner, 1952. **Awarded:** Caldecott (honor) 1953.

Shadow translated and illustrated by Marcia Brown from the French of Blaise Cendrars; Scribner, 1982. **Awarded:** Caldecott 1983.

Skipper John's Cook written and illustrated by Marcia Brown; Scribner, 1951. **Awarded:** Caldecott (honor) 1952.

The Steadfast Tin Soldier by Hans Christian Andersen, illustrated by Marcia Brown; Scribner, 1953. **Awarded:** Caldecott (honor) 1954.

Stone Soup written and illustrated by Marcia Brown; Scribner, 1947. **Awarded:** Caldecott (honor) 1948.

BROWN, MARGARET WISE

(pseudonym is Golden MacDonald) **Awarded:** Kerlan 1984 (to Brown, her editors, and illustrators).

The Bad Little Duck-hunter by Margaret Wise Brown, illustrated by Clement Hurd; Scott, 1947. **Awarded:** Spring Book Festival (younger honor) 1947.

A Child's Good Night Book by Margaret Wise Brown, illustrated by Jean Charlot; Scott, 1943. **Awarded:** Caldecott (honor) 1944.

The Little Cowboy by Margaret Wise Brown, illustrated by Esphyr Slobodkina; Scott, 1948, 1949. **Awarded:** Spring Book Festival (younger honor) 1949.

The Little Island by Golden MacDonald, illustrated by Leonard Weisgard; Doubleday, 1946. **Awarded:** Caldecott 1947; Children's Choice (picture book) 1982.

Little Lost Lamb by Golden MacDonald, illustrated by Leonard Weisgard; Doubleday, Doran, 1945. **Awarded:** Caldecott (honor) 1946.

Once Upon a Time in a Pigpen by Margaret Wise Brown, illustrated by Ann Strugnell; Addison- Wesley, 1980. **Awarded:** Parents' Choice (illustration) 1980.

The Runaway Bunny by Margaret Wise Brown, illustrated by Clement Hurd; Harper & Row, 1942. **Awarded:** Emphasis on Reading (Grades K-1) 1981-82.

Wheel on the Chimney by Margaret Wise Brown, illustrated by Tibor Gergely; Lippincott, 1954. **Awarded:** Caldecott (honor) 1955.

When the Wind Blew by Margaret Wise Brown, illustrated by Geoffrey Hayes; Harper, 1977. **Awarded:** New York Times Best Illustrated 1977.

BROWN, MARGERY W.

Animals Made by Me written and illustrated by Margery W. Brown; Putnam, 1970. **Awarded:** New Jersey Institute of Technology 1971.

I'm Glad I'm Me by Elberta Stone, illustrated by Margery W. Brown; Putnam, 1971. **Awarded:** New Jersey Institute of Technology 1971.

BROWN, MARY GEIGER
Woodworks: Experiments with Common Wood and Tools by William F. Brown, illustrated by Mary G. Brown; Atheneum, 1984. **Awarded:** New York Academy of Sciences (older honor) 1985.

BROWN, P.
The Green Ginger Jar by Clara Ingram Judson, illustrated by P. Brown; Houghton, 1949. **Awarded:** Boys Club 1950.

BROWN, PALMER
Cheerful written and illustrated by Palmer Brown; Harper, 1957. **Awarded:** Spring Book Festival (ages 4-8 honor) 1957.

BROWN, PAM
Martin Luther King: America's Great Non-Violent Leader by Pam Brown and Valerie Schloredt, illustrated; Exley Publications, 1988; Longman, 1988. **Awarded:** Times Educational Supplement (Senior Information Book) 1988.

BROWN, PAUL
Bright Spurs by Armine von Tempski, illustrated by Paul Brown; Dodd, 1946. **Awarded:** Spring Book Festival (older honor) 1946.

A Horse to Remember by Genevieve Torrey Eames, illustrated by Paul Brown; Messner, 1947. **Awarded:** Julia Ellsworth Ford 1946.

King of the Stallions by Edward B. Tracy, illustrated by Paul Brown; Dodd, 1947. **Awarded:** Boys Club 1949.

War Horse by Fairfax Downey, illustrated by Paul Brown; Dodd, 1942. **Awarded:** Spring Book Festival (older honor) 1942.

BROWN, RICHARD
Even the Devil Is Afraid of a Shrew retold by Valerie Stalder, adapted by Ray Broekel, illustrated by Richard Brown; Addison-Wesley, 1972. **Awarded:** Children's Book Showcase 1973.

BROWN, RICHARD
Pet Day by Harriet Ziefert, illustrated by Richard Brown; Little Brown, 1987. **Awarded:** New Jersey Institute of Technology 1988.

The Small Potatoes' Busy Beach Day by Harriet Ziefert, illustrated by Richard Brown; Dell, 1986. **Awarded:** New Jersey Institute of Technology 1987.

Trip Day by Harriet Ziefert, illustrated by Richard Brown; Little Brown, 1987. **Awarded:** New Jersey Institute of Technology 1988.

Worm Day by Harriet Ziefert, illustrated by Richard Brown; Harper & Row, 1987. **Awarded:** New Jersey Institute of Technology 1988.

BROWN, RICK
Your Best Friend, Kate by Pat Brisson, illustrated by Rick Brown; Bradbury, 1989. **Awarded:** New Jersey Institute of Technology 1990.

BROWN, ROY
Am Ende der Spur by Roy Brown, translated by Wolf Harranth; Benziger und Jungbrunner, 1981. **Awarded:** International Board on Books for Young People (Translation/Austria) 1982.

BROWN, RUTH
Blossom Comes Home by James Herriot, illustrated by Ruth Brown; St. Martin's Press, 1988. **Awarded:** Redbook 1988.

Ladybird, Ladybird written and illustrated by Ruth Brown; Andersen, 1988; Dutton, 1988. **Awarded:** Greenaway (Commended) 1988.

BROWN, WALTER R.
Ferris Wheels by Walter R. Brown and Norman D. Anderson, illustrated with photographs; Pantheon, 1983. **Awarded:** New York Academy of Sciences (younger honor) 1984.

BROWN, WILLIAM F.
Woodworks: Experiments with Common Wood and Tools by William F. Brown, illustrated by Mary G. Brown; Atheneum, 1984. **Awarded:** New York Academy of Sciences (older honor) 1985.

BROWNE, ANTHONY
Alice's Adventures in Wonderland by Lewis Carroll, illustrated by Anthony Browne; Julia MacRae, 1988; Knopf, 1988. **Awarded:** Greenaway (Highly Commended) 1988; Kurt Maschler 1988; Parents' Choice (Picture Book) 1989.

Gorilla written and illustrated by Anthony Browne; Julia MacRae, 1983; Knopf, 1985. **Awarded:** Boston Globe Horn Book (illustration honor) 1986; Greenaway 1983; Maschler 1983; New York Times Best Illustrated 1985.

Hansel and Gretel by Jacob Grimm and Wilhelm Grimm, illustrated by Anthony Browne; Julia MacRae, 1981; Watts, 1981. **Awarded:** Greenaway (commended) 1981; International Board on Books for Young People (illustration/Great Britain) 1984.

Piggybook written and illustrated by Anthony Browne; Knopf, 1986. **Awarded:** Parents' Choice (Picture Book) 1987.

Zoo written and illustrated by Anthony Browne; MacRae, 1992. **Awarded:** Greenaway 1992.

BROWNE, LANCE
Gypsy Family by Mary Waterson, photographs by Lance Browne; Black, 1978. **Awarded:** Other Award 1978.

BROWNE, VEE
Monster Slayer: A Navajo Folktale by Vee Browne, illustrated by Baje Whitethorne; Northland Publishing, 1991. **Awarded:** Western Heritage 1992.

BROWNING, COLEEN
Carrie's War by Nina Bawden, illustrated by Coleen Browning; Lippincott, 1973. **Awarded:** Phoenix 1993.

BROWNING, D. B.
North Carolina Parade: Stories of History and People by Richard Walser and Julia Street, illustrated by D. B. Browning; University of North Carolina, 1966. **Awarded:** North Carolina AAUW 1966.

BRUCKNER, KARL
Awarded: Hans Christian Andersen (highly commended Author/Austria) 1966.

Lale, Die Turkin by Karl Bruckner, illustrated by E. Wallenta; Jungend u. Volk, 1958. **Awarded:** Hans Christian Andersen (runnerup) 1960.

BRUNER, STEPHEN
Simple Machines by Anne Horvatic, illustrated by Stephen Bruner; Dutton, 1989. **Awarded:** New York Academy of Sciences (Younger Honor) 1989.

BRUNHOFF, JEAN de
The Story of Babar, the Little Elephant written and illustrated by Jean de Brunhoff, translated by Merle S. Haas; Random House, 1933. **Awarded:** Lewis Carroll Shelf 1959.

BRUNHOFF, LAURENT de
Babar's Fair Will Be Opened Next Sunday written and illustrated by Laurent de Brunhoff, translated by Merle Haas; Random

House, 1954. **Awarded:** New York Times Best Illustrated 1956.

BRUNKUS, DENISE
The Pizza Monster by Mitchell Sharmat and Marjorie Sharmat, illustrated by Denise Brunkus; Delacorte, 1989. **Awarded:** CRABbery 1990.

BRUSCA, MARIA CRISTINA
On the Pampas written and illustrated by Maria Cristina Brusca; Henry Holt, 1991. **Awarded:** Parents' Choice (Picture Book) 1991.

BRYAN, ASHLEY
Awarded: University of Southern Mississippi 1994.

All Night, All Day: A Child's First Book of African American Spirituals written and illustrated by Ashley Bryan; Atheneum, 1991. **Awarded:** Coretta Scott King (Illustrator honor) 1992.

Beat the Story-drum, Pum-pum written and illustrated by Ashley Bryan; Atheneum, 1980. **Awarded:** Coretta Scott King (illustration) 1981; Parents' Choice (illustration) 1980.

I'm Going to Sing: Black American Spirituals vol. 2 selected and illustrated by Ashley Bryan; Atheneum, 1982. **Awarded:** Coretta Scott King (illustration honorable mention) 1983.

The Lion and the Ostrich Chicks written and illustrated by Ashley Bryan; Atheneum, 1986. **Awarded:** Coretta Scott King (literature honorable mention) 1987.

Sing to the Sun written and illustrated by Ashley Bryan; HarperCollins, 1992. **Awarded:** Lee Bennett Hopkins Poetry 1993; Parents Choice (Story Book) 1992.

Turtle Knows Your Name written and illustrated by Ashley Bryan; Atheneum, 1989. **Awarded:** Parents' Choice (Story Book) 1989.

What a Morning! The Christmas Story in Black Spirituals by John Langstaff, illustrated by Ashley Bryan; McElderry, 1987. **Awarded:** Coretta Scott King (Illustration honor) 1988.

BRYAN, CATHERINE
Pito's House written and illustrated by Catherine Bryan and Mabra Madden; Macmillan, 1943. **Awarded:** Spring Book Festival (younger honor) 1943.

BRYANT, CHESTER
The Lost Kingdom by Chester Bryant, illustrated by Margaret Ayer; Messner, 1951. **Awarded:** Julia Ellsworth Ford 1950.

BRYANT, SAMUEL
The King's Fifth by Scott O'Dell, illustrated by Samuel Bryant; Houghton, 1966. **Awarded:** Newbery (honor) 1967.

Why the Chinese Are the Way They Are by Benjamin Appel, illustrated by Samuel H. Bryant; Little Brown, 1968, 1973. **Awarded:** New Jersey Institute of Technology 1968, 1975.

Why the Russians Are the Way They Are by Benjamin Appel, illustrated by Samuel H. Bryant; Little Brown, 1966. **Awarded:** New Jersey Institute of Technology 1966.

BRYSON, BERNARDA
Calendar Moon by Natalia M. Belting, illustrated by Bernarda Bryson; Holt, 1964. **Awarded:** George G. Stone 1966.

Gilgamesh: Man's First Story written and illustrated by Bernarda Bryson; Holt, 1964. **Awarded:** Boston Globe Horn Book (illustration honor) 1968.

The Return of the Twelves by Pauline Clarke, illustrated by Bernarda Bryson; Coward, 1963. **Awarded:** Lewis Carroll Shelf 1965; Spring Book Festival (middle honor) 1964.

The Storyteller's Pack by Frank R. Stockton, illustrated by Bernarda Bryson; Scribner, 1968. **Awarded:** Lewis Carroll Shelf 1969.

The Sun Is a Golden Earring by Natalia M. Belting, illustrated by Bernarda Bryson; Holt, 1962. **Awarded:** Caldecott (honor) 1963.

The Twenty Miracles of Saint Nicholas written and illustrated by Bernarda Bryson; Little, 1960. **Awarded:** New Jersey Institute of Technology 1961.

BUBLEY, ESTHER
How Kittens Grow by Millicent Selsam, photographs by Esther Bubley; Four Winds, 1975, 1973. **Awarded:** Garden State Children's (young nonfiction) 1978.

BUCHANAN, HEATHER S.
George and Matilda Mouse and the Floating School written and illustrated by Heather S. Buchanan; Methuen, 1990; Simon & Schuster, 1990. **Awarded:** Owl Prize 1990.

BUCHANAN, WILLIAM J.
A Shining Season by William J. Buchanan, illustrated with photographs; Coward, McCann, 1978; Bantam, 1979. **Awarded:** South Carolina Young Adult 1981.

BUCHANAN-BROWN, JOHN
The Secret of the Missing Boat by Paul Berna, translated by John Buchanan-Brown, illustrated by Barry Wilkinson; Pantheon, 1967, c1966. **Awarded:** Edgar Allan Poe (runnerup) 1968.

BUCHENHOLZ, BRUCE
Doctor in the Zoo written and illustrated by Bruce Buchenholz; Studio/Viking, 1974. **Awarded:** National Book Award (finalist) 1975; New York Academy of Sciences (older) 1976.

BUCHOLTZ-ROSS, LINDA
Magnolia's Mixed-up Magic by Joan Lowery Nixon, illustrated by Linda Bucholtz-Ross; Putnam, 1983. **Awarded:** CRABbery 1984.

BUCHWALD, ART
The Bollo Caper: A Furry Tale for All Ages by Art Buchwald, illustrated by Elise Primavera; Putnam, 1983. **Awarded:** New Jersey Institute of Technology 1983.

BUCHWALD, EMILIE
Gildean: the Heroic Adventures of a Most Unusual Rabbit by Emilie Buchwald, illustrated by Barbara Flynn; Harcourt, 1973. **Awarded:** Spring Book Festival (middle) 1973.

BUCK, PEARL SYDENSTRICKER
The Big Wave by Pearl Buck, illustrated by Hiroshige Ando and Nokusai Katsushika; Day, 1948. **Awarded:** Child Study 1948.

Mowje Bozorg (original English:

The Big Wave) by Pearl S. Buck, translated by Soraya Ghezelayagh; Vaje, 1984. **Awarded:** International Board on Books for Young People (translation/Iran) 1986.

BUCKINGHAM, SIMON
Alec and His Flying Bed written and illustrated by Simon Buckingham; Macmillan, 1990; Lothrop, Lee & Shepard, 1991. **Awarded:** Macmillan Prize (2nd prize) 1989.

BUCZYNSKI, WALDEMAR
Dancing in the Anzac Deli by Nadia Wheatley, illustrated by Neil Phillips and Waldemar Buczynski; Oxford, 1984. **Awarded:** Children's Book Council of Australia (book of the year commended) 1985; International Board on Books for Young People (writing/Australia) 1986.

BUDBILL, DAVID
Bones on Black Spruce Mountain by David Budbill, not illustrated; Dial, 1978. **Awarded:** Dorothy Canfield Fisher 1980.

BUDNEY, BLOSSOM
A Kiss Is Round: Verses by Blossom Budney, illustrated by Vladimir Bobri; Lothrop, 1954. **Awarded:** New York Times Best Illustrated 1954.

BUEHNER, MARK
The Adventures of Taxi Dog by Debra Barracca and Sal Barracca, illustrated by Mark Buehner; Dial, 1990. **Awarded:** Parents' Choice (Picture Book) 1990.

BUFF, CONRAD
Awarded: Southern California Council (comprehensive contribution of lasting value) 1961.

The Apple and the Arrow written and illustrated by Conrad Buff and Mary Buff; Houghton, 1951. **Awarded:** Newbery (honor) 1952.

Big Tree written and illustrated by Conrad Buff and Mary Buff; Viking, 1946. **Awarded:** Newbery (honor) 1947.

Dash and Dart written and illustrated by Conrad Buff and Mary Buff; Viking, 1942. **Awarded:** Caldecott (honor) 1943.

Magic Maize written and illustrated by Conrad Buff and Mary Buff; Houghton, 1953. **Awarded:** Newbery (honor) 1954.

Peter's Pinto: A Story of Utah by Conrad Buff and Mary Buff, illustrated by Conrad Buff; Viking, 1949. **Awarded:** Boys Club 1950.

BUFF, MARY MARSH
Awarded: Southern California Council (comprehensive contribution of lasting value) 1961.

The Apple and the Arrow written and illustrated by Conrad Buff and Mary Buff; Houghton, 1951. **Awarded:** Newbery (honor) 1952.

Big Tree written and illustrated by Conrad Buff and Mary Buff; Viking, 1946. **Awarded:** Newbery (honor) 1947.

Dash and Dart written and illustrated by Conrad Buff and Mary Buff; Viking, 1942. **Awarded:** Caldecott (honor) 1943.

Magic Maize written and illustrated by Conrad Buff and Mary Buff; Houghton, 1953. **Awarded:** Newbery (honor) 1954.

Peter's Pinto: a Story of Utah by Conrad Buff and Mary Buff, illustrated by Conrad Buff; Viking, 1949. **Awarded:** Boys Club 1950.

BUFFETT, JIMMY
The Jolly Mon by Jimmy Buffett and Savannah Jane Buffett, illustrated by Lambert Davis; Harcourt Brace Jovanovich, 1988. **Awarded:** Author's Award (Alabama) 1990.

BUFFETT, SAVANNAH JANE
The Jolly Mon by Savannah Jane Buffett and Jimmy Buffett, illustrated by Lambert Davis; Harcourt Brace Jovanovich, 1988. **Awarded:** Author's Award (Alabama) 1990.

BUFFIE, MARGARET
Who Is Frances Rain? by Margaret Buffie, not illustrated; Kids Can Press, 1987. **Awarded:** Canadian Library Assn. Book of Year (Runner up) 1988; Young Adult Canadian 1988.

BULL, ANGELA
The Machine Breakers: the Story of the Luddites by Angela Bull, illustrated with photographs; Collins, 1980. **Awarded:** Other Award 1980.

BULL, JOHAN
Iron Duke by John R. Tunis, illustrated by Johan Bull; Harcourt, 1938. **Awarded:** Spring Book Festival (older) 1938.

BULLA, CLYDE ROBERT
Awarded: Southern California Council (distinguished contribution to the field of children's literature) 1962; Southern California Council (outstanding contribution of lasting value in a body of work) 1987.

Jonah and the Great Fish by Clyde Robert Bulla, illustrated by Helga Aichinger; Crowell, 1970. **Awarded:** Commonwealth Club of California 1970.

Noah and the Rainbow: an Ancient Story retold by Max Bolliger, translated by Clyde Robert Bulla, illustrated by Helga Aichinger; Crowell, 1972. **Awarded:** Children's Book Showcase 1973.

Pocahontas and the Stranger by Clyde Robert Bulla, illustrated by Peter Burchard; Crowell, 1971. **Awarded:** Christopher (ages 8-12) 1972.

Shoeshine Girl by Clyde Robert Bulla, illustrated by Leigh Grant; Crowell, 1975. **Awarded:** Sequoyah 1978; Charlie May Simon 1977-78; South Carolina Children's 1980; Southern California Council (notable) 1976.

Squanto, Friend of the White Man by Clyde Robert Bulla, illustrated by Peter Burchard; Crowell, 1954. **Awarded:** Boys Club 1955.

White Bird by Clyde Robert Bulla, illustrated by Leonard Weisgard; Crowell, 1966. **Awarded:** George G. Stone 1968.

BULLARD, PAMELA
The Hardest Lesson: Personal Stories of a School Desegregation Crisis by Pamela Bullard and Judith Stoia, not illustrated; Little Brown, 1980. **Awarded:** Christopher (ages 12-up nonfiction) 1981; Woodson (outstanding merit) 1981.

BUNN, ALAN
Water in the Blood by Alan Bunn; Octopus, 1990. **Awarded:** AIM (Best First Book) 1991.

BUNTING, EVE
Face at the Edge of the World by Eve Bunting, not illustrated; Clarion Books, 1985. **Awarded:** California Young Reader (Senior High) 1989; South Carolina Young Adult 1989; Virginia Young Readers (High School) 1989.

Fly Away Home by Eve Bunting, illustrated by Ronald Himler; Clarion, 1991. **Awarded:** Commonwealth Club of California (Ages 10-under) 1991.

Ghost of Summer by Eve Bunting, illustrated by W. T. Mars; Warne, 1977. **Awarded:** Southern California Council (fiction) 1978.

Ghost's Hour, Spook's Hour by Eve Bunting, illustrated by Donald Carrick; Clarion, 1987. **Awarded:** Parents' Choice (Story Book) 1987.

Is Anybody There? by Eve Bunting, not illustrated; Lippincott, 1988. **Awarded:** Golden Sower (Grades 4-6) 1992; South Carolina Children's 1991.

Karen Kepplewhite Is the World's Best Kisser by Eve Bunting, not illustrated; Clarion, 1983. **Awarded:** Nene 1987. Lippincott Page Turners series includes

Cloverdale Switch 1979;

Waiting Game 1981;

Ghosts of Departure Point 1982;

If I Asked You, Would You Stay? 1984;

Haunting of Safekeep 1985. **Awarded:** Southern California Council (excellence in a series) 1986.

One More Flight by Eve Bunting, illustrated by Diane de Groat; Warne, 1976. **Awarded:** Golden Kite 1976.

Sixth Grade Sleepover by Eve Bunting, not illustrated; Harcourt Brace Jovanovich, 1986. **Awarded:** Sequoyah Children's 1989; Sunshine State Young Reader's Award (grades 3-5) 1989; Sunshine State Young Reader's Award (grades 6-8) 1989; Surrey School 1987; Mark Twain 1989.

Someone Is Hiding on Alcatraz Island by Eve Bunting, not illustrated; Clarion, 1984. **Awarded:** Soaring Eagle (Grades 7-9) 1990.

A Sudden Silence by Eve Bunting, not illustrated; Harcourt Brace Jovanovich, 1988. **Awarded:** California Young Reader (Young Adult) 1992; Southern California Council (Outstanding Work of Fiction for Young Adults) 1989; Sequoyah Young Adult Award 1991.

The Wall by Eve Bunting, illustrated by Ronald Himler; Clarion, 1990. **Awarded:** Southern California Council (Distinguished Work of Fiction) 1991.

The Wednesday Surprise by Eve Bunting, illustrated by Donald Carrick; Clarion, 1989. **Awarded:** Jane Addams (Honor) 1990; Southern California Council (Fiction) 1990.

BURCH, ROBERT

Doodle and the Go-cart by Robert Burch, illustrated by Alan Tiegreen; Viking, 1972. **Awarded:** Georgia Children's 1974.

Ida Early Comes over the Mountain by Robert Burch, not illustrated; Viking, 1980. **Awarded:** Boston Globe Horn Book (fiction honor) 1981.

Queenie Peavy by Robert Burch, illustrated by Jerry Lazare; Viking, 1966; Dell, 1975. **Awarded:** Jane Addams 1967; Child Study 1966; Georgia Children's 1971; Phoenix 1986; George G. Stone 1974.

Skinny by Robert Burch, illustrated by Don Sibley; Viking, 1964. **Awarded:** Georgia Children's 1969; Spring Book Festival (middle honor) 1964.

BURCHARD, PETER DUNCAN

Jed: The Story of a Yankee Soldier and a Southern Boy written and illustrated by Peter Burchard; Coward, 1960. **Awarded:** Lewis Carroll Shelf 1966.

Night Spell by Robert Newman, illustrated by Peter Burchard; Atheneum, 1977. **Awarded:** Edgar Allan Poe (runnerup) 1978.

Pocahontas and the Strangers by Clyde Robert Bulla, illustrated by Peter Burchard; Crowell, 1971. **Awarded:** Christopher (ages 8-12) 1972.

Ride 'Em Cowgirl by Lynn Haney, photographs by Peter Burchard; Putnam, 1975. **Awarded:** Western Writers (nonfiction) 1975.

Rifles for Watie by Harold Keith, illustrated by Peter Burchard; Crowell, 1957. **Awarded:** Lewis Carroll Shelf 1964; Newbery 1958.

Roosevelt Grady by Louisa R. Shotwell, illustrated by Peter Burchard; World, 1963. **Awarded:** Nancy Bloch 1963; Lewis Carroll Shelf 1964; Woodward Park School 1964.

Squanto, Friend of the White Man by Clyde Robert Bulla, illustrated by Peter Burchard; Crowell, 1954. (Published as *Squanto, Friend of the Pilgrims* by Crowell, 1969.) **Awarded:** Boys Club 1955.

BURGER, CARL VICTOR

The Incredible Journey: A Tale of Three Animals by Shelia Every Burnford, illustrated by Carl Burger; Little Brown, 1961. **Awarded:** Aurianne 1963; Lewis Carroll Shelf 1971; Canadian Library Assn. 1963; Feature a Classic 1982; Dorothy Canfield Fisher 1963; International Board on Books for Young People (honour list/Canada) 1964; William Allen White 1964; Young Reader's Choice 1964.

Little Rascal by Sterling North, illustrated by Carl Burger; Dutton, 1965. **Awarded:** New Jersey Institute of Technology 1965.

Old Yeller by Fred Gipson, illustrated by Carl Burger; Harper, 1956. **Awarded:** Nene 1966; Newbery (honor) 1957; Sequoyah 1959; William Allen White 1959; Young Reader's Choice 1959; Young Teens 1989.

Tonk and Tonka by Eugene Ackerman, illustrated by Carl Burger; Dutton, 1962. **Awarded:** Indiana Author's Day (young children) 1963.

BURGESS, MELVIN

The Cry of the Wolf by Melvin Burgess, not illustrated; Andersen Press, 1990; Tambourine Books, 1992. **Awarded:** Carnegie (Highly Commended) 1990.

BURGESS, THORNTON

Awarded: Chandler Reward of Merit 1963.

BURGESS-KOHN, JANE

Straight Talk about Love and Sex for Teenagers by Jane Burgess-Kohn, not illustrated; Beacon, 1979. **Awarded:** Council of Wisconsin Writers (juvenile runnerup) 1980.

BURGLON, NORA

Children of the Soil: A Story of Scandinavia by Nora Burglon, illustrated by Edgar Parin d'Aulaire; Doubleday, Doran, 1932. **Awarded:** Newbery (honor) 1933.

BURGWYN, MEBANE HOLOMAN

The Crackajack Pony by Mebane H. Burgwyn, illustrated by Dale Payson; Lippincott, 1969. **Awarded:** North Carolina AAUW 1970.

Penny Rose by Mebane H. Burgwyn, not illustrated; Walck, 1952. **Awarded:** North Carolina AAUW 1954.

BURKERT, NANCY EKHOLM

James and the Giant Peach: A Children's Story by Roald Dahl, illustrated by Nancy Ekholm Burkert; Knopf, 1961; Bantam, 1978. **Awarded:** Massachusetts Children's (elementary) 1982.

The Nightingale by Hans Christian Andersen, translated by Eva Le Gallienne, illustrated by Nancy Ekholm Burkert; Harper, 1965. **Awarded:** Lewis Carroll Shelf 1965; Spring Book Festival (picture book honor) 1965

Snow White and the Seven Dwarfs by Jacob Grimm and Wilhelm Grimm, translated by Randall Jarrell, illustrated by Nancy Ekholm Burkert; Farrar, 1972. **Awarded:** Bologna (critici in erba) 1973; Caldecott (honor) 1973; Lewis Carroll Shelf 1973; New York Times Notable Books 1972.

Valentine and Orson written and illustrated by Nancy Ekholm Burkert; Farrar Straus Giroux, 1989. **Awarded:** Boston Globe (Special Award for Excellence in Bookmaking) 1990; Parents' Choice (Picture Book) 1989; Reading Magic 1989.

BURLEIGH, ROBERT

Flight: The Journey of Charles Lindbergh by Robert Burleigh, illustrated by Mike Wimmer; Philomel, 1991. **Awarded:** Orbis Pictus 1992.

BURLESON, ELIZABETH

A Man of the Family by Elizabeth Burleson, not illustrated; Follett, 1965. **Awarded:** Steck-Vaughn 1967.

Middl'un by Elizabeth Burleson, illustrated by George Roth; Follett, 1968. **Awarded:** Western Writers (fiction) 1969.

BURN, DORIS

Christina Katerina and the Box by Patricia Lee Gauch, illustrated by Doris Burn; Coward, 1971. **Awarded:** New Jersey Institute of Technology 1971.

BURNETT, FRANCES HODGSON

A Little Princess: Being the Whole Story of Sara Crewe Now Told for the First Time by Frances Hodgson Burnett, illustrated by Ethel F. Betts; Scribner, 1938. **Awarded:** Lewis Carroll Shelf 1964.

The Secret Garden by Frances Hodgson Burnett, illustrated by N. Unwin; Lippincott, 1938, c1911. **Awarded:** Lewis Carroll Shelf 1959; CRABbery (Honor) 1990.

BURNFORD, SHELIA EVERY

The Incredible Journey: a Tale of Three Animals by Shelia Every Burnford, illustrated by Carl Burger; Little Brown, 1961. **Awarded:** Aurianne 1963; Lewis Carroll Shelf 1971; Canadian Library Assn. 1963; Feature a Classic 1982; Dorothy Canfield Fisher 1963; International Board on Books for Young People (honour list/Canada) 1964; William Allen White 1964; Young Reader's Choice 1964.

BURNIE, DAVID

Bird by David Burnie, illustrated by Peter Chadwick and Kim Taylor; Dorling Kindersley/Natural History Museum, 1988; Knopf, 1988. **Awarded:** Greenaway (Special Commendation) 1988.

How Nature Works by David Burnie, illustrated; Dorling Kindersley, 1991. **Awarded:** Science Book Prizes 1992.

BURNINGHAM, HELEN OXENBURY
   see OXENBURY, HELEN

BURNINGHAM, JOHN

Borka: the Adventures of a Goose with No Feathers written and illustrated by John Burningham; Cape, 1963. **Awarded:** Greenaway 1963.

Chitty-Chitty-Bang-Bang by Ian Fleming, illustrated by John Burningham; Random House, 1964. **Awarded:** Young Reader's Choice 1967.

Come Away from the Water, Shirley written and illustrated by John Burningham; Crowell, 1977. **Awarded:** New York Times Best Illustrated 1977.

Granpa written and illustrated by John Burningham; Cape, 1984; Crown, 1985. **Awarded:** Maschler 1984; New York Times Best Illustrated 1985.

Hey! Get Off Our Train! written and illustrated by John Burningham; Crown, 1989. **Awarded:** Book Can Develop Empathy 1991; Parents' Choice (Picture Book) 1990.

John Patrick Norman McHennessey, The Boy Who Was Always Late written and illustrated by John Burningham; Crown, 1988, c1987. **Awarded:** Parents' Choice (Picture Book) 1988.

Mr. Gumpy's Motor Car written and illustrated by John Burningham; Crowell, 1976. **Awarded:** Children's Book Showcase 1977.

Mr. Gumpy's Outing written and illustrated by John Burningham; Cape, 1970; Holt, 1971. **Awarded:** Boston Globe Horn Book (illustration) 1972; Children's Book Showcase 1972; Greenaway 1970; New York Times Best Illustrated 1971; New York Times Notable Books 1971.

Where's Julius? written and illustrated by John Burningham; Cape, 1986. **Awarded:** Maschler (runnerup) 1986.

The Wind in the Willows by Kenneth Grahame, illustrated by John Burningham; Kestrel, 1983; Penguin, 1983. **Awarded:** Maschler (runnerup) 1983.

BURNS, IRENE

Go to the Room of the Eyes by Betty K. Erwin, illustrated by Irene Burns; Little Brown, 1969. **Awarded:** Dorothy Canfield Fisher 1971.

BURNS, MARILYN

The Book of Think: or, How to Solve a Problem Twice Your Size by Marilyn Burns, illustrated by Martha Weston; Little Brown, 1976. **Awarded:** Children's Book Showcase 1977.

BURNS, ROBERT

William Crawford Gorgas: Tropic Fever Fighter by Samuel Epstein and Beryl Williams Epstein, illustrated by Robert Burns; Messner, 1953. **Awarded:** Spring Book Festival (older honor) 1953.

BURRETT, TONY

Puzzles Old and New by Jerry Slocum and Jack Botermans, text by Carla Van Splunteren and Tony Burrett; Plenary Publications International, distributed by the University of Washington Press, 1986. **Awarded:** New York Academy of Sciences (prize as an exhibition catalogue of excellence and extraordinary interest) 1987.

BURRIS, BURMAH

Listen! and Help Tell the Story by Bernice Wells Carlson, illustrated by Burmah Burris; Abingdon, 1965. **Awarded:** New Jersey Institute of Technology (Special citation, ages 5-12) 1965.

BURSTEIN, CHAYA

The Jewish Kids Catalog written and illustrated by Chaya M. Burstein; Jewish Publication Society of America, 1983. **Awarded:** Jewish Book Council (William Zev Frank) 1984.

Rifka Grows Up written and illustrated by Chaya Burstein; Bonim Books, 1976. **Awarded:** Jewish Book Council 1976.

BURSTEIN, JOHN

Mr. Slim Goodbody Presents the Inside Story by John Burstein, illustrated by Paul Kirouac; McGraw Hill, 1977. **Awarded:** New Jersey Institute of Technology 1978.

BURT, ROGER

Magic With Everything by Roger Burt, not illustrated; Blackie, 1990. **Awarded:** Kathleen Fidler 1990.

BURTON, DWIGHT
   Awarded: ALAN 1980.

BURTON, EARL

Taffy and Joe by Earl Burton and Linette Burton, illustrated by Helen Stone; Whittlesey House, 1947. **Awarded:** Spring Book Festival (younger honor) 1947.

BURTON, HESTER

Beyond the Weir Bridge by Hester Burton, illustrated by Victor G. Ambrus; Crowell, 1970. **Awarded:** Boston Globe Horn Book (text honor) 1971.

Castors Away! by Hester Burton, illustrated by Victor Ambrus; Oxford, 1962. **Awarded:** Carnegie (commended) 1962.

Time of Trial by Hester Burton, illustrated by Victor Ambrus; Oxford, 1963; World, 1964. **Awarded:** Carnegie 1963;

Greenaway (commended) 1963; Spring Book Festival (older honor) 1964.

BURTON, JANE

Hoppy the Toad photographs by Jane Burton; Random House, 1989. **Awarded:** Book Can Develop Empathy 1990.

Kitten by Angela Royston, illustrated by Jane Burton; Lodestar, 1991. **Awarded:** Redbook 1991.

Puppy by Angela Royston, illustrated by Jane Burton; Lodestar, 1991. **Awarded:** Redbook 1991.

Surfer the Seal photographs by Jane Burton; Random House, 1989. **Awarded:** Book Can Develop Empathy 1990.

BURTON, LINETTE

Taffy and Joe by Linette Burton and Earl Burton, illustrated by Helen Stone; Whittlesey House, 1947. **Awarded:** Spring Book Festival (younger honor) 1947.

BURTON, PHILIP

The Green Isle by Philip Burton, illustrated by Robert A. Parker; Dial, 1974. **Awarded:** New Jersey Institute of Technology 1975.

BURTON, VIRGINIA LEE

The Little House written and illustrated by Virginia Lee Burton; Houghton, 1942. **Awarded:** Caldecott 1943; Lewis Carroll Shelf 1959.

Song of Robin Hood edited by Anne B. Malcolmson, illustrated by Virginia Lee Burton; Houghton, 1947. **Awarded:** Caldecott (honor) 1948.

BUSCH, PHYLLIS

Awarded: Eva L. Gordon 1974.

BUSH, JOHN

The Fish Who Could Wish by John Bush, illustrated by Korky Paul; Kane Miller, 1991. **Awarded:** Redbook 1991.

BUSH, TERRI

Voice of the Children edited by Terri Bush and June Jordan, illustrated with photographs; Holt, 1970. **Awarded:** Nancy Bloch 1971.

BUSNAR, GENE

The Picture Life of Tina Turner by Gene Busnar, illustrated with photos; Watts, 1988. **Awarded:** New Jersey Institute of Technology 1989.

The Picture Life of Whitney Houston by Gene Busnar, illustrated with photos; Watts, 1988. **Awarded:** New Jersey Institute of Technology 1989.

BUSONI, RAFAELLO

The Man Who Was Don Quixote: the Story of Miguel Cervantes written and illustrated by Rafaello Busoni; Prentice Hall, 1958. **Awarded:** Lewis Carroll Shelf 1963.

The Radio Imp by Archie Binns, illustrated by Rafaello Busoni; Winston, 1950. **Awarded:** Spring Book Festival (8-12 honor) 1950.

Walt Whitman, Builder for America by Babette Deutsch, illustrated by Raphael Busoni; Messner, 1941. **Awarded:** Julia Ellsworth Ford 1941.

BUSS, FRAN LEEPER

Journey of the Sparrows by Fran Leeper Buss, with the assistance of Daisy Cubias, not illustrated; Lodestar, 1991. **Awarded:** Jane Addams 1992; Hungry Mind (Young Adult/Fiction) 1992.

BUSTARD, ANNE

Awarded: Lucile M. Pannell 1985.

BUTCHER, JULIA

The Sheep and the Rowan Tree written and illustrated by Julia Butcher; Methuen, 1984. **Awarded:** Mother Goose (runnerup) 1985.

BUTLER, BEVERLY

Feather in the Wind by Beverly Butler, not illustrated; Dodd Mead, 1965. **Awarded:** State Historical Society of Wisconsin 1966.

My Sister's Keeper by Beverly Butler, not illustrated; Dodd Mead, 1980. **Awarded:** Golden Archer 1982; State Historical Society of Wisconsin 1981.

Song of the Voyageur by Beverly Butler, not illustrated; Dodd, 1955. **Awarded:** Calling All Girls - Dodd, Mead 1955.

BUTLER, DOROTHY

Awarded: Eleanor Farjeon 1979.

BUTLER, FRANCELIA

Awarded: Chandler Reward of Merit 1983.

Children's Literature: the Bad Seed? by Francelia Butler in The Virginia Quarterly Review Summer 1980. **Awarded:** Children's Literature Assn. Awards for excellence in the field of literary criticism (runnerup) 1981.

BUTLER, JOHN

Animal Families of the Wild edited by William F. Russell, illustrated by John Butler; Crown, 1990. **Awarded:** Book Can Develop Empathy 1991.

BUTTERWORTH, BILL

see SCHOLEFIELD, EDMUND O.

BUTTERWORTH, EMMA MACALIK

As the Waltz Was Ending by Emma M. Butterworth, not illustrated; Four Winds, 1982. **Awarded:** Author's Award [Alabama] 1984.

BUTTERWORTH, NICK

After the Storm by Nick Butterworth. **Awarded:** British Book Awards (Illustrated runnerup) 1992.

BUTTERWORTH, OLIVER

The Enormous Egg by Oliver Butterworth, illustrated by Louis Darling; Little Brown, 1956. **Awarded:** Lewis Carroll Shelf 1970.

The Trouble with Jenny's Ear by Oliver Butterworth, illustrated by Julian de Miskey; Atlantic- Little, 1960. **Awarded:** Spring Book Festival (middle) 1960.

BUTTERWORTH, WILLIAM E.

Fast Green Car by W. E. Butterworth, not illustrated; Norton, 1965. **Awarded:** New Jersey Institute of Technology 1965.

LeRoy and the Old Man by William E. Butterworth, not illustrated; Four Winds, 1980. **Awarded:** Author's Award [Alabama] 1982.

Up to the Quarterback by William Butterworth, not illustrated; Four Winds, 1969. **Awarded:** New Jersey Institute of Technology 1969.

The Wonders of Astronomy by William E. Butterworth, illustrated by Dallas Pasco; Putnam, 1964. **Awarded:** New Jersey Institute of Technology (science ages 8-12) 1964.

The Wonders of Rockets and Missiles by William E. Butterworth, illustrated with photographs and diagrams; Putnam, 1964. **Awarded:** New Jersey Institute of Technology (science ages 8-12) 1964.

BUXBAUM, SUSAN KOVACS

Splash! All About Baths by Susan Kovacs Buxbaum, illustrated by Maryann Cocca-Leffler; Little Brown, 1987. **Awarded:** American Institute of Physics 1988.

BUXTON, JANE H.

Strange Animals of the Sea by Jane H. Buxton, illustrated by Jerry Pinkney; National Geographic Society, 1987. **Awarded:** Redbook 1987.

BYARD, CAROLE

Africa Dream by Eloise Greenfield, illustrated by Carole Byard; Day, 1977. **Awarded:** Coretta Scott King 1978.

Corn Rows by Camile Yarbrough, illustrated by Carole Byard; Coward, 1979. **Awarded:** Coretta Scott King (illustration) 1980.

Under Christopher's Hat by Dorothy Callahan, illustrated by Carole M. Byard; Scribner, 1972. **Awarded:** New Jersey Institute of Technology (illustration) 1972.

Working Cotton by Sherley Anne Williams, illustrated by Carole Byard; Harcourt Brace Jovanovich, 1992. **Awarded:** Caldecott (honor) 1993; Coretta Scott King (Illustration honor) 1993.

BYARS, BETSY CROMER

Awarded: Keene State College Festival 1990; Regina 1987.

The Animal, the Vegetable, and John D. Jones by Betsy Byars, illustrated by Ruth Sanderson; Delacorte, 1982; Dell, 1983. **Awarded:** CRABbery 1983; Parents' Choice (literature) 1982.

Bingo Brown, Gypsy Lover by Betsy Byars, illustrated by Cathy Bobak; Viking, 1990. **Awarded:** Parents' Choice (Story Book) 1990.

The Burning Questions of Bingo Brown by Betsy Byars, illustrated by Cathy Bobak; Viking, 1988. **Awarded:** Garden State Children's (Younger Fiction) 1991; Parents' Choice (Story Book) 1988.

The Computer Nut by Betsy Byars, computer graphics by Guy Byars; Viking Kestrel, 1984. **Awarded:** Simon 1986-87.

Cracker Jackson by Betsy Byars, not illustrated; Viking Kestrel, 1985. **Awarded:** Maryland 1988; Parents' Choice (literature) 1985; South Carolina Children 1987; William Allen White 1988.

The Cybil War by Betsy Byars, illustrated by Gail Owens; Viking, 1981. **Awarded:** Sequoyah 1984; Volunteer State 1983.

The Eighteenth Emergency by Betsy Byars, illustrated by Robert Grossman; Viking, 1973. **Awarded:** Dorothy Canfield Fisher 1975.

The Glory Girl by Betsy Byars, not illustrated; Viking, 1983. **Awarded:** Emphasis on Reading (Grades 6-8) 1990-91.

Good-bye Chicken Little by Betsy Byars, not illustrated; Harper, 1979. **Awarded:** New York Times Notable Books 1979.

The House of Wings by Betsy Byars, illustrated by Daniel Schwartz; Viking, 1972. **Awarded:** National Book Award (finalist) 1973.

The Midnight Fox by Betsy Byars, illustrated by Ann Grifalconi; Viking, 1968. **Awarded:** Lewis Carroll Shelf 1970.

The Night Swimmers by Betsy Byars, illustrated by Troy Howell; Delacorte, 1980. **Awarded:** American Book Award (children's fiction hardcover) 1981; Boston Globe Horn Book (fiction honor) 1980.

The Not-Just-Anybody Family by Betsy Byars, illustrated by Jacqueline Rogers; Delacorte, 1986. **Awarded:** Parents Choice (literature) 1986.

The Pinballs by Betsy Byars, not illustrated; Harper, 1977. **Awarded:** California Young Reader (junior high) 1980; Child Study 1977; Georgia Children's 1979; Golden Archer 1981; Nene (runnerup) 1983; Charlie May Simon 1979-80; Surrey School 1980; Mark Twain 1980; William Allen White 1980; Woodward Park School 1977.

Summer of the Swans by Betsy Byars, illustrated by Ted CoConis; Viking, 1970. **Awarded:** Newbery 1971.

Tuhatkiloinen Kultakala (original English:

The Two-thousand-pound Goldfish) by Betsy Byars, translated by Piekko Lokka; WSOY, 1984. **Awarded:** International Board on Books for Young People (translation/Finland) 1986.

The Two-thousand-pound Goldfish by Betsy Byars, not illustrated; Harper, 1982. **Awarded:** New York Times Notable 1982.

BYARS, GUY

The Computer Nut by Betsy Byars, computer graphics by Guy Byars; Viking Kestrel, 1984. **Awarded:** Charlie May Simon 1986-87.

BYGOTT, DAVID

Black and British by David Bygott, illustrated; Oxford University Press, 1992. **Awarded:** Times Educational Supplement (Senior) 1992.

BYRD, ROBERT

Pinchpenny Mouse by Robert Kraus, illustrated by Robert Byrd; Windmill, 1974. **Awarded:** Children's Book Showcase 1975.

C

CAESAR, EUGENE

King of the Mountain Men: The Life of Jim Bridger by Gene Caesar, illustrated with maps; Dutton, 1961. **Awarded:** Western Heritage 1962.

CALABRO, MARIAN

Operation Grizzly Bear by Marian Calabro, illustrated with photos; Four Winds, 1989. **Awarded:** New Jersey Institute of Technology 1990.

CALDER, ALEXANDER

Fables of Aesop by Sir Roger L'Estrange, illustrated by Alexander Calder; Dover, 1967. **Awarded:** New York Times Best Illustrated 1967.

CALHOUN, MARY

Cross-country Cat by Mary Calhoun, illustrated by Erick Ingraham; Morrow, 1979. **Awarded:** Boston Globe Horn Book (illustration honor) 1979; Colorado Children's 1981; Golden Kite (fiction honor) 1979; Little Archer 1980; Washington Children's Choice 1982.

CALLAERT, JACQUES

Pi Gal by Valerie King Page, illustrated by Jacques Callaert; Dodd Mead, 1970. **Awarded:** Edith Busby 1969.

CALLAHAN, DOROTHY

Jimmy: The Story of the Young Jimmy Carter by Dorothy Callahan, illustrated with photographs; Doubleday, 1979. **Awarded:** New Jersey Institute of Technology 1980.

Under Christopher's Hat by Dorothy Callahan, illustrated by Carole M. Byard; Scribner, 1972. **Awarded:** New Jersey Institute of Technology (illustration) 1972.

CALLAWAY, KATHY
Bloodroot Flower by Kathy Callaway, not illustrated; Knopf, 1982. **Awarded:** Friends of American Writers ($350) 1983.

CALVERT, JOHN
see LEAF, MUNRO

CALVERT, PATRICIA
The Snowbird by Patricia Calvert, not illustrated; Scribner, 1980. **Awarded:** Friends of American Writers (young adult) 1981; Society of Midland Authors 1981.

CAMAZINE, CYNTHIA
The Naturalists' Year by Scott Camazine, illustrated by Cynthia Camazine and Scott Camazine; Wiley, 1987. **Awarded:** New York Academy of Sciences (Older honor) 1988.

CAMAZINE, SCOTT
The Naturalists' Year by Scott Camazine, illustrated by Cynthia & Scott Camazine; Wiley, 1987. **Awarded:** New York Academy of Sciences (Older honor) 1988.

CAMBONI, DANIELA
Storia di una Volpe (original English: *Fox Tales*) by Ruth Manning Sanders, translated by Daniela Camboni; Nuove Edizioni Romane, 1981. **Awarded:** International Board on Books for Young People (translator/Italy) 1984.

CAMERON, ANN
More Stories Julian Tells by Ann Cameron, illustrated by Ann Strugnell; Knopf, 1986. **Awarded:** Parents' Choice (literature) 1986.

The Most Beautiful Place in the World by Ann Cameron, illustrated by Thomas B. Allen; Knopf, 1988. **Awarded:** Addams (Fiction Ages 7- up) 1989; Child Study 1988.

The Stories Julian Tells by Ann Cameron, illustrated by Ann Strugnell; Pantheon, 1981. **Awarded:** Irma Simonton Black 1981.

CAMERON, ELEANOR BUTLER
Awarded: Kerlan 1985; Southern California Council (distinguished contribution to the field of children's literature) 1965.

The Court of the Stone Children by Eleanor Cameron, not illustrated; Dutton, 1973. **Awarded:** National Book Award 1974.

Julia and the Hand of God by Eleanor Cameron, illustrated by Gail Owens; Dutton, 1977. **Awarded:** FOCAL 1985.

Julia's Magic by Eleanor Cameron, illustrated by Gail Owens; Dutton, 1984. **Awarded:** Parents' Choice (literature) 1984.

The Private World of Julia Redfern by Eleanor Cameron, not illustrated; Dutton, 1988. **Awarded:** Parents' Choice (Story Book) 1988.

A Room Made of Windows by Eleanor Cameron, illustrated by Trina Schart Hyman; Little Brown, 1971. **Awarded:** Boston Globe Horn Book (text) 1971; FOCAL 1989; New York Times Notable Books 1971; Spring Book Festival (older honor) 1971.

A Spell Is Cast by Eleanor Cameron, illustrated by Beth Krush and Joe Krush; Little Brown, 1964. **Awarded:** Commonwealth Club of California 1964; Edgar Allan Poe (runnerup) 1965.

That Julia Redfern by Eleanor Cameron, illustrated by Gail Owens; Dutton, 1982. **Awarded:** Parents' Choice (literature) 1982.

To the Green Mountains by Eleanor Cameron, not illustrated; Dutton, 1975. **Awarded:** National Book Award (finalist) 1976.

CAMERON, POLLY
The Polly Cameron Picture Book written and illustrated by Polly Cameron; Coward, 1970. **Awarded:** New Jersey Institute of Technology 1970.

CAMERON, TRACEY
Telling Fortunes by Alvin Schwartz, illustrated by Tracey Cameron; Lippincott, 1987. **Awarded:** New Jersey Institute of Technology 1988.

CAMPBELL, ALFRED S.
The Wizard and His Magic Powder by Alfred S. Campbell, illustrated by Kurt Wiese; Knopf, 1945. **Awarded:** Spring Book Festival (younger honor) 1945.

CAMPBELL, BLANCHE
Awarded: Southern California Council (outstanding community service) 1970.

CAMPBELL, CAMILLA
Coronado and His Captains by Camilla Campbell, illustrated by Harve Stein; Follett, 1958. **Awarded:** Steck-Vaughn 1960.

CAMPBELL, MARJORIE WILKINS
The Nor'westers: the Fight for the Fur Trade by Marjorie Campbell, illustrated by Illingsworth Kerr; Macmillan Canada, 1954. **Awarded:** Governor-General's 1954.

CAMPBELL, PATTY
Awarded: Grolier 1989.

CAMPBELL, STAN
The Singing Cave by Eilis Dillon, illustrated by Stan Campbell; Funk & Wagnalls, 1960. **Awarded:** Spring Book Festival (older honor) 1960.

CAMPBELL, WANDA JAY
Ten Cousins by Wanda Jay Campbell, illustrated by Leonard Shortall; Dutton, 1963. **Awarded:** Steck-Vaughn 1964.

CANNON, ANN EDWARDS
Cal Cameron by Day, Spider-Man by Night by A. E. (Ann Edwards) Cannon, not illustrated; Delacorte, 1988. **Awarded:** Delacorte Press Prize 1987.

CANTY, MARY
Join Hands with the Ghosts by Mary Canty, illustrated by Ragna T. Goddard; McKay, 1969. **Awarded:** New Jersey Institute of Technology 1970.

CAPRON, JEAN F.
The Trouble with Lucy by Jean Capron, not illustrated; Dodd, 1967. **Awarded:** New Jersey Institute of Technology 1967.

CAPUTO, ROBERT
Hyena Day by Robert Caputo and Miriam Hsia, photographs by Robert Caputo; Coward, 1978. **Awarded:** New York Academy of Sciences (younger honor) 1979.

CARDOZA, LOIS S.
see DUNCAN, LOIS

CAREY, JOANNA
The Snow Spider by Jenny Nimmo, illustrated by Joanna Carey; Methuen Children's, 1986. **Awarded:** Smarties (grand prix) 1986; Smarties (Ages 7-11) 1986; Tir Na n-Og (Anglo-Welsh) 1987.

CAREY, MARY V.
A Place for Allie by Mary V. Carey, not illustrated; Dodd, Mead, 1985. **Awarded:** Southern California Council (fiction) 1986.

CAREY, VALERIE SCHO
The Devil & Mother Crump by Valerie Scho Carey, illustrated by Arnold Lobel; Harper & Row, 1987. **Awarded:** Golden Kite (Picture- Illustration) 1987; Parents' Choice (Picture Book) 1987.

CARIGIET, ALOIS
Awarded: Hans Christian Andersen (illustrator) 1966.

Florinda and the Wild Bird by Selina Chonz, translated by Anne Serraillier and Ian Serraillier, illustrated by Alois Carigiet; Walck, 1952. **Awarded:** New York Times Best Illustrated 1953.

CARLE, ERIC
Awarded: Keene State College Festival 1992.

Animals, Animals written and illustrated by Eric Carle; Philomel, 1989. **Awarded:** Redbook 1989.

Do You Want to Be My Friend? written and illustrated by Eric Carle; Crowell, 1971. **Awarded:** Spring Book Festival (picture book honor) 1971.

1,2,3 Ein Zug Zum Zoo written and illustrated by Eric Carle; Gerhard Stalling Verlag. **Awarded:** Bologna (Graphics for Children) 1970.

Polar Bear, Polar Bear, What Do You Hear? by Bill Martin, Jr., illustrated by Eric Carle; Holt, 1991. **Awarded:** Redbook 1991.

The Very Hungry Caterpillar written and illustrated by Eric Carle; Collins, 1970. **Awarded:** Art Books for Children 1973, 1977, 1978, 1979.

The Very Quiet Cricket written and illustrated by Eric Carle; Philomel, 1990. **Awarded:** Arizona Young Readers (Picture Book) 1993; Buckeye (Grades K-2) 1993; Redbook 1990.

CARLETON, BARBEE OLIVER
The Witches Bridge by Barbee Oliver Carleton, not illustrated; Holt, 1967. **Awarded:** Edgar Allan Poe (runnerup) 1968.

CARLEY, WAYNE
Charley the Mouse Finds Christmas by Wayne Carley, illustrated by Ruth Bagshaw; Garrard, 1972. **Awarded:** New Jersey Institute of Technology 1972.

CARLSEN, ROBERT
Awarded: ALAN 1974.

CARLSON, BERNICE WELLS
Funny Bone Dramatics by Bernice Wells Carlson, illustrated by Charles Cox; Abingon, 1974. **Awarded:** New Jersey Institute of Technology 1975.

Let's Pretend It Happened to You by Bernice Wells Carlson, illustrated by Ralph McDonald; Abingdon, 1973. **Awarded:** New Jersey Institute of Technology 1973.

Listen! and Help Tell the Story by Bernice Wells Carlson, illustrated by Burmah Burris; Abingdon, 1965. **Awarded:** New Jersey Institute of Technology (special citation ages 5-12) 1965.

The Party Book for Boys and Girls by Bernice Wells Carlson, illustrated by Faith C. Minnerly; Abingdon, 1963. **Awarded:** New Jersey Institute of Technology 1963.

Quick Wits and Nimble Fingers by Bernice Wells Carlson, illustrated by Dolores M. Rowland; Abingdon, 1979. **Awarded:** New Jersey Institute of Technology 1980.

You Know What? I Like Animals by Bernice Wells Carlson, illustrated by Ruth Van Sciver; Abingdon, 1967. **Awarded:** New Jersey Institute of Technology 1967.

CARLSON, DALE BICK
The Mountain of Truth by Dale Carlson, illustrated by Charles Robinson; Atheneum, 1972. **Awarded:** Spring Book Festival (ages 12- 16 honor) 1972.

Where's Your Head? Psychology for Teenagers by Dale Bick Carlson, illustrated by Carol Nicklaus; Atheneum, 1977. **Awarded:** Christopher (ages 12-up) 1978.

CARLSON, MARIA
Peter and the Wolf by Sergei Prokofiev, translated by Maria Carlson, illustrated by Charles Mikolaycak; Viking, 1982. **Awarded:** Parents' Choice (illustration) 1982.

CARLSON, NATALIE SAVAGE
Alphonse, That Bearded One by Natalie Savage Carlson, illustrated by Nicolas Mordvinoff; Harcourt, 1954. **Awarded:** Boys Club 1955; Spring Book Festival (ages 4-8) 1954.

Ann, Aurelia and Dorothy by Natalie Savage Carlson, illustrated by Dale Payson; Harper & Row, 1968. **Awarded:** Woodward Park School 1969.

The Empty Schoolhouse by Natalie Savage Carlson, illustrated by John Kaufmann; Harper & Row, 1965. **Awarded:** Child Study 1965.

The Family Under the Bridge by Natalie Savage Carlson, illustrated by Garth Williams; Harper, 1958. **Awarded:** Newbery (honor) 1959.

Hortense, the Cow for a Queen by Natalie Savage Carlson, illustrated by Nicolas; Harcourt, 1957. **Awarded:** Spring Book Festival (middle honor) 1957.

The Talking Cat by Natalie Savage Carlson, illustrated by Roger Duvoisin; Harper & Row, 1952. **Awarded:** Spring Book Festival (ages 8-12) 1952.

Wings Against the Wind by Natalie Savage Carlson, illustrated by Mircea Vasiliu; Harper & Row, 1955. **Awarded:** Boys Club 1956; Spring Book Festival (middle honor) 1955.

CARMER, CARL L.
Windfall Fiddle by Carl L. Carmer, illustrated by Arthur Conrad; Knopf, 1950. **Awarded:** Spring Book Festival (ages 8-12) 1950.

CARMI, GIORI
The Chanukkah Guest by Eric Kimmel, illustrated by Giori Carmi; Holiday House, 1990. **Awarded:** Sydney Taylor Book Award (Picture Book) 1991.

CARNER, CHAS
Tawny by Chas Carner, illustrated by Donald Carrick; Macmillan, 1978. **Awarded:** New York Times Notable Books 1978.

CAROSELLI, REMUS F.
Mystery Cottage in Left Field by Remus F. Caroselli, not illustrated; Putnam, 1979. **Awarded:** Edgar Allan Poe (runnerup) 1980.

CARPENTER, EDMUND
The Story of Comock the Eskimo, as Told to Robert Flaherty edited by Edmund Carpenter, illustrated with original Eskimo sketches; Simon & Schuster, 1968. **Awarded:** Lewis Carroll Shelf 1969.

CARR, HARRIET
The Mystery of Ghost Valley by Harriet Carr, not illustrated; Macmillan, 1962. **Awarded:** Edgar Allan Poe (runnerup) 1963.

CARR, MARY JANE

Young Mac of Fort Vancouver by Mary Jane Carr, illustrated by Richard Holberg; Crowell, 1940. **Awarded:** Newbery (honor) 1941.

CARRICK, CAROL

The Blue Lobster: A Life Cycle by Carol Carrick, illustrated by Donald Carrick; Dial, 1975. **Awarded:** Children's Book Showcase 1976; New York Academy of Sciences (younger honor) 1976.

Lost in the Storm by Carol Carrick, illustrated by Donald Carrick; Seabury, 1974. **Awarded:** Children's Book Showcase 1975.

What Happened to Patrick's Dinosaurs? by Carol Carrick, illustrated by Donald Carrick; Clarion, 1986. **Awarded:** California Young Reader (Primary) 1989; New York Times Notable 1986.

CARRICK, DONALD

Bear Mouse by Berniece Freschet, illustrated by Donald Carrick; Scribner, 1973. **Awarded:** Irma Simonton Black 1973; Children's Book Showcase 1974.

The Blue Lobster: A Life Cycle by Carol Carrick, illustrated by Donald Carrick; Dial, 1975. **Awarded:** Children's Book Showcase 1976; New York Academy of Sciences (younger honor) 1976.

Doctor Change by Joanna Cole, illustrated by Donald Carrick; Morrow, 1986. **Awarded:** Irma Simonton Black 1986.

The Ghost's Hour, Spook's Hour by Eve Bunting, illustrated by Donald Carrick; Clarion, 1987. **Awarded:** Parents' Choice (Story Book) 1987.

Going the Moose Way Home by Jim Latimer, illustrated by Donald Carrick; Scribner, 1988. **Awarded:** Minnesota (Children) 1989.

Lost in the Storm by Carol Carrick, illustrated by Donald Carrick; Seabury, 1974. **Awarded:** Children's Book Showcase 1975.

Secrets of a Small Brother by Richard J. Margolis, illustrated by Donald Carrick; Macmillan, 1984. **Awarded:** Christopher (Ages 8-10) 1985.

Tawny by Chas Carner, illustrated by Donald Carrick; Macmillan, 1978. **Awarded:** New York Times Notable Books 1978.

The Wednesday Surprise by Eve Bunting, illustrated by Donald Carrick; Clarion, 1989. **Awarded:** Addams (Honor) 1990; Southern California Council (Fiction) 1990.

What Happened to Patrick's Dinosaurs? by Carol Carrick, illustrated by Donald Carrick; Clarion, 1986. **Awarded:** California Young Reader (Primary) 1989; New York Times Notable 1986.

CARRIS, JOAN

Hedgehogs in the Closet by Joan Davenport Carris, illustrated by Carol Newsom; Lippincott, 1988; Dell, 1990, c1988. **Awarded:** New Jersey Institute of Technology 1989.

Pets, Vets and Marty Howard by Joan Davenport Carris, illustrated by Carol Newsom; Lippincott, 1984. **Awarded:** New Jersey Institute of Technology 1989.

Rusty Timmons' First Million by Joan Carris, illustrated by Kim Mulkey; Lippincott, 1985. **Awarded:** New Jersey Institute of Technology 1989.

When the Boys Ran the House by Joan Carris, illustrated by Carol Newsom; Lippincott, 1982. **Awarded:** Iowa Children 1986; New Jersey Institute of Technology 1989; Volunteer State 1985; Young Hoosier (grades 4-6) 1986.

Witch Cat by Joan Carris, illustrated by Beth Peck; Lippincott, 1984. **Awarded:** Ethical Culture 1984.

CARRITHERS, MARY

Only Silly People Waste by Norah Smaridge, illustrated by Mary Carrithers; Abingdon, 1973. **Awarded:** New Jersey Institute of Technology 1977.

CARROLL, LATROBE

Digby, the Only Dog by Latrobe Carroll and Ruth Carroll, illustrated by Ruth Carroll; Walck, 1955. **Awarded:** North Carolina AAUW 1955.

Peanut by Ruth Carroll and Latrobe Carroll, illustrated by Ruth Carroll; Walck, 1951. **Awarded:** North Carolina AAUW 1953.

CARROLL, LEWIS

Alenka v Kraji Divu by Lewis Carroll, illustrated by Marketa Prachaticka; Albatros, 1983. **Awarded:** Bologna (graphics for youth) 1984.

Alice's Adventures in Wonderland by Lewis Carroll, illustrated by Justin Todd; Gollancz, 1984. **Awarded:** Kurt Maschler (runnerup) 1984; W. H. Smith Illustration (2nd prize) 1987.

Alice's Adventures in Wonderland by Lewis Carroll, illustrated by Anthony Browne; Julia MacRae, 1988; Knopf, 1988. **Awarded:** Greenaway (Highly Commended) 1988; Kurt Maschler 1988; Parents' Choice (Picture Book) 1989.

Lewis Carroll's Alice's Adventures in Wonderland illustrated by Barry Moser, preface and notes by James R. Kincaid, text edited by Selwyn H. Goodacre; University of California Press, 1982. **Awarded:** American Book Award (pictorial design) 1983.

The Pig-tale by Lewis Carroll, illustrated by Leonard Lubin; Little Brown, 1975, 1889. **Awarded:** Lewis Carroll Shelf 1975; Children's Book Showcase 1976; New York Times Best Illustrated 1975.

Through the Broken Mirror with Alice: Including Parts of Through the Looking Glass by Lewis Carroll by Maia Wojciechowska, not illustrated; Harcourt Brace Jovanovich, 1972. **Awarded:** New Jersey Institute of Technology 1972.

Through the Looking Glass and What Alice Found There by Lewis Carroll, illustrated by Justin Todd; Gollancz, 1986. **Awarded:** W. H. Smith Illustration (2nd prize) 1987.

CARROLL, PAMELA

The Illustrated Dinosaur Dictionary by Helen R. Sattler, foreword by John H. Ostrom, illustrated by Pamela Carroll, color insert by Anthony Rao and Christopher Santoro; Lothrop, Lee & Shepard, 1983. **Awarded:** Golden Kite (nonfiction) 1983.

CARROLL, RUTH

Digby, the Only Dog by Latrobe Carroll and Ruth Carroll, illustrated by Ruth Carroll; Walck, 1955. **Awarded:** North Carolina AAUW 1955.

Peanut by Ruth Carroll and Latrobe Carroll, illustrated by Ruth Carroll; Walck, 1951. **Awarded:** North Carolina AAUW 1953.

CARSON, JOHN F.

The Mystery of the Tarnished Trophy by John F. Carson, not illustrated; Farrar, 1964. **Awarded:** Indiana Authors Day (young adult) 1965.

CART, MICHAEL

Awarded: Southern California Council (Dorothy C. McKenzie Award) 1983.

CARTER, ALDEN R.
Robodad by Alden R. Carter, not illustrated; Putnam, 1990. **Awarded:** Society of Midland Authors 1990.

Wart, Son of Toad by Alden R. Carter, not illustrated; Pacer/Putnam, 1985. **Awarded:** Emphasis on Reading (Grades 10-12) 1987-88.

CARTER, ANGELA
Sleeping Beauty and Other Favourite Fairy Tales chosen and translated by Angela Carter, illustrated by Michael Foreman; Gollancz, 1982. **Awarded:** Greenaway (co-winner) 1982; Maschler 1982.

CARTER, BEBBY L.
Remarkable Journey of Prince Jen by Lloyd Alexander, map by Bebby L. Carter; Dutton, 1991. **Awarded:** Parents' Choice (Story Book) 1991.

CARTER, DAVID A.
How Many Bugs in a Box? written and illustrated by David A. Carter; Little Simon (Simon & Schuster), 1988. **Awarded:** Redbook 1988.

More Bugs in Boxes: A Pop-up Book about Color written and illustrated by David A. Carter; Simon & Schuster, 1990. **Awarded:** Parents' Choice (Picture Book) 1990.

CARTER, DOROTHY SHARP
Greedy Mariani and Other Folktales of the Antilles by Dorothy Sharp Carter, illustrated by Trina Schart Hyman; Atheneum, 1974. **Awarded:** Children's Book Showcase 1975.

CARTER, FORREST
The Education of Little Tree by Forrest Carter, not illustrated; Delacorte, 1976; University of New Mexico Press, 1986. **Awarded:** American Booksellers Book of the Year 1991.

CARTER, HELENE
The Gulf Stream by Ruth Brindze, illustrated by Helene Carter; Vanguard, 1945. **Awarded:** Spring Book Festival (middle) 1945.

CARTER, JAMES
see MAYNE, WILLIAM

CARTER, PETER
Bury the Dead by Peter Carter, not illustrated; Oxford, 1986. **Awarded:** Observer 1986.

Children of the Book by Peter Carter, illustrated by Richard Jervis, maps by Barry Rowe; Oxford, 1982. **Awarded:** Observer 1983.

The Sentinels by Peter Carter, not illustrated; Oxford, 1980. **Awarded:** Guardian 1981.

Under Goliath by Peter Carter, illustrated by Ian Ribbons; Oxford, 1977. **Awarded:** Carnegie (commended) 1977.

CARTER, PHYLLIS ANN
see EBERLE, IRMENGARDE

CARTLIDGE, MICHELLE
Pipin and Pod written and illustrated by Michelle Cartlidge; Heinemann, 1978. **Awarded:** Mother Goose 1979.

CARTWRIGHT, PAULINE
Arthur and the Dragon by Pauline Cartwright, illustrated by David Elliot; Price Milburn, 1990. **Awarded:** Steck-Vaughn 1990; Russell Clark 1991.

CARTWRIGHT, REG
The Man Who Wanted To Live Forever by Selina Hastings, illustrated by Reg Cartwright; Holt, 1988. **Awarded:** Parents' Choice (Picture Book) 1988.

Mr. Potter's Pigeon by Patrick Kinmouth, illustrated by Reg Cartwright; Hutchinson, 1979. **Awarded:** Mother Goose 1980.

Peter and the Wolf retold by Selina Hastings, illustrated by Reg Cartwright; Holt, Rinehart & Winston, 1987. **Awarded:** Parents' Choice (Picture Book) 1987.

CARTWRIGHT, SALLY
Sunlight by Sally Cartwright, illustrated by Marylin Hafner; Coward, 1974. **Awarded:** New York Academy of Sciences (younger honor) 1975.

CARTY, LEO
Sidewalk Story by Sharon Bell Mathis, illustrated by Leo Carty; Viking, 1971. **Awarded:** Council on Interracial Books (ages 7-11) 1969.

Where Does the Day Go? by Walter M. Myers, illustrated by Leo Carty; Parents, 1969. **Awarded:** Council on Interracial Books (ages 3-6) 1968.

CARU STUDIOS
The First Book of Color by Herbert P. Paschel, illustrated by Caru Studios; Watts, 1959. **Awarded:** Boys Club 1960.

CARY
see CARY, LOUIS FAVREAU

CARY, LOUIS FAVREAU
Liliuokalani: Queen of Hawaii by Mary Malone, illustrated by Cary; Garrard, 1975. **Awarded:** New Jersey Institute of Technology 1976.

Marie Curie: Woman of Genius by Adele de Leeuw, illustrated by Cary; Garrard, 1970. **Awarded:** New Jersey Institute of Technology 1970.

CASSEDY, SYLVIA
M. E. and Morton by Sylvia Cassedy, not illustrated; Crowell, 1987. **Awarded:** Judy Lopez 1988.

CASSEL, LILI
To Build a Land by Sally Watson, illustrated by Lili Cassel; Holt, 1957. **Awarded:** Woodward Park School 1959.

CASTLE, JANE
The Story of Irving Berlin by David Ewen, illustrated by Jane Castle; Holt, 1950. **Awarded:** Spring Book Festival (older honor) 1950.

CASWELL, EDWARD
Meriwether Lewis: Boy Explorer by Charlotta M. Bebenroth, illustrated by Edward Caswell; Bobbs-Merrill, 1946. **Awarded:** Ohioana (honorable mention) 1947.

CATALONIAN THEATER COMPANY
Sol Solet by the Catalonian Theater Company; Eixample, Spain. **Awarded:** Bologna (critici in erba) 1985.

CATE, DICK
Old Dog, New Tricks by Dick Cate, illustrated by Trevor Stubley; Hamilton, 1978. **Awarded:** Other Award 1979.

CATLING, PATRICK
The Chocolate Touch by Patrick Catling, illustrated by Margot Apple; Morrow, 1979. **Awarded:** Massachusetts Children's 1989; Utah Children's Choice 1983.

CATROW, DAVID
The Cataract of Lodore by Robert Southey, illustrated by David Catrow; Holt, 1992. **Awarded:** New York Times Best Illustrated 1992.

CATTERWALL, THELMA
Aldita and the Forest by Thelma Catterwall, illustrated by Derek Stone; Dent, 1988; Houghton Mifflin, 1989, c1988. **Awarded:** Whitley (Children's Book) 1989.

Sebastian Lives in a Hat by Thelma Catterwall, illustrated by Kerry Argent; Omnibus, 1985. **Awarded:** Whitley 1986.

CAUDILL, REBECCA
Awarded: Children's Reading Round Table 1969; Jesse Stuart 1983.

A Certain Small Shepherd by Rebecca Caudill, illustrated by William Pene du Bois; Holt, 1965. **Awarded:** Clara Ingram Judson 1966.

Did You Carry the Flag Today, Charley? by Rebecca Caudill, illustrated by Nancy Grossman; Holt, 1966. **Awarded:** Sue Hefly 1974.

The Far-off Land by Rebecca Caudill, illustrated by Brinton Turkle; Viking, 1964. **Awarded:** Friends of American Writers 1965.

The House of the Fifers by Rebecca Caudill, illustrated by Genia; Longmans, 1954. **Awarded:** Spring Book Festival (older honor) 1954.

A Pocketful of Cricket by Rebecca Caudill, illustrated by Evaline Ness; Holt, 1964. **Awarded:** Caldecott (honor) 1965.

Susan Cornish by Rebecca Caudill, illustrated by E. Harper Johnson; Viking, 1955. **Awarded:** Nancy Bloch 1955.

Tree of Freedom by Rebecca Caudill, illustrated by Dorothy B. Morse; Viking, 1949. **Awarded:** Newbery (honor) 1950; Spring Book Festival (older honor) 1949.

CAUFIELD, DON
Never Steal a Magic Cat by Don Caufield and Joan Caufield, illustrated by Jan Palmer; Doubleday, 1971. **Awarded:** Dorothy Canfield Fisher 1973.

CAUFIELD, JOAN
Never Steal a Magic Cat by Don Caufield and Joan Caufield, illustrated by Jan Palmer; Doubleday, 1971. **Awarded:** Dorothy Canfield Fisher 1973.

CAULEY, LORINDA BRYAN
The Goodnight Circle by Carolyn Lesser, illustrated by Lorinda Bryan Cauley; Harcourt Brace Jovanovich, 1984. **Awarded:** Friends of American Writers ($350) 1985.

CAUSLEY, CHARLES
Early in the Morning: A Collection of New Poems by Charles Causley, illustrated by Michael Foreman; Viking Kestrel, 1986. **Awarded:** Kurt Maschler (runnerup) 1986; Signal 1987.

Jack the Treacle Eater by Charles Causley, illustrated by Charles Keeping; Macmillan, 1987. **Awarded:** Kurt Maschler 1987.

CAVALLO, DIANA
The Lower East Side: A Portrait in Time by Diane Cavallo, photographs by Leo Stashin; Crowell-Collier, 1971. **Awarded:** Children's Book Showcase 1972.

CAVANAH, FRANCES
Abe Lincoln Gets His Chance by Frances Cavanah, illustrated by Paula Hutchison; Rand, 1959. **Awarded:** Indiana Authors Day (young children) 1960.

CAVANNA, BETTY
Catchpenny Street by Betty Cavanna, not illustrated; Westminster, 1975. **Awarded:** New Jersey Institute of Technology 1976.

The Ghost of Ballyhooly by Betty Cavanna, not illustrated; Morrow, 1971. **Awarded:** Edgar Allan Poe (runnerup) 1972.

Going on Sixteen by Betty Cavanna, illustrated by John Gretzner; Westminster, 1946. **Awarded:** Spring Book Festival (older honor) 1946.

Mystery at Love's Creek by Betty Cavanna, not illustrated; Morrow, 1965. **Awarded:** New Jersey Institute of Technology (ages 12-up) 1966.

Secret Passage by Betty Cavanna, illustrated by Jean McLaughlin; Winston, 1946. **Awarded:** Spring Book Festival (middle honor) 1947.

Spice Island Mystery by Betty Cavanna, not illustrated; Morrow, 1969. **Awarded:** Edgar Allan Poe (runnerup) 1970.

CAWLEY, WINIFRED
Gran at Coalgate by Winifred Cawley, illustrated by F. Rocker; Oxford, 1974. **Awarded:** Guardian 1975.

CAZET, DENYS
Never Spit on Your Shoes written and illustrated by Denys Cazet; Orchard, 1990. **Awarded:** California Young Reader (Primary) 1992.

CEBULASH, MEL
The Ball That Wouldn't Bounce by Mel Cebulash, illustrated by Tom Eaton; Scholastic, 1972. **Awarded:** New Jersey Institute of Technology 1972.

Benny's Nose by Mel Cebulash, illustrated by Ib Ohlsson; Scholastic, 1972. **Awarded:** New Jersey Institute of Technology 1972.

Dic-tion-ar-y Skilz by Mel Cebulash, not illustrated; Scholastic, 1972. **Awarded:** New Jersey Institute of Technology 1972.

Ruth Marini: Dodger Ace by Mel Cebulash, not illustrated; Lerner, 1983. **Awarded:** New Jersey Institute of Technology 1983.

Ruth Marini of the Dodgers by Mel Cebulash, not illustrated; Lerner, 1983. **Awarded:** New Jersey Institute of Technology 1983.

CECIL, EDWARD
Malachi Mudge by Edward Cecil, illustrated by Peter Parnall; McGraw, 1968. **Awarded:** New York Times Best Illustrated 1968.

CECIL, LAURA
Listen to This by Laura Cecil, illustrated by Emma Chichester Clark; Bodley Head, 1987. **Awarded:** Mother Goose 1988.

CELLINI, JOSEPH
A Horse Called Dragon by Lynn Hall, illustrated by Joseph Cellini; Follett, 1971. **Awarded:** Charles W. Follett 1972.

Kongo and Kumba: Two Gorillas by Alice Schick, illustrated by Joseph Cellini; Dial, 1974. **Awarded:** Friends of American Writers (illustration) 1975.

Shadows by Lynn Hall, illustrated by Joseph Cellini; Follett, 1977. **Awarded:** Volunteer State 1981.

CENDRARS, BLAISE
Shadow translated and illustrated by Marcia Brown from the French of Blaise Cendrars; Scribner, 1982. **Awarded:** Caldecott 1983.

CHADWICK, PETER
Bird by David Burnie, illustrated by Peter Chadwick and Kim Taylor; Dorling Kindersley/Natural History Museum, 1988; Knopf, 1988. **Awarded:** Greenaway (Special Commendation) 1988.

CHAFFIN, LILLIE D.
   Awarded: Jesse Stuart 1982.

John Henry McCoy by Lillie D. Chaffin, illustrated by Emanuel Schongut; Macmillan, 1971. **Awarded:** Child Study 1971.

CHAGALL, MARC
Marc Chagall by Howard Greenfeld, illustrated by Marc Chagall; Follett, 1967. **Awarded:** Charles W. Follett 1968.

CHAIKIN, MIRIAM
   Awarded: Sydney Taylor Body of Work 1985.

Exodus adapted from the Bible by Miriam Chaikin, illustrated by Charles Mikolaycak; Holiday House, 1987. **Awarded:** Jewish Book Council (Children's Picture Book) 1988.

CHALK, GARY
Mattimeo by Brian Jacques, illustrated by Gary Chalk; Hutchinson, 1989; Philomel, 1990. **Awarded:** Lancashire County Library 1991; West Australian (Secondary) 1992.

Mossflower by Brian Jacques, illustrated by Gary Chalk; Hutchinson, 1988; Philomel, 1988. **Awarded:** West Australian (Secondary) 1991.

Redwall by Brian Jacques, illustrated by Gary Chalk; Hutchinson Children's, 1986; Philomel, 1986. **Awarded:** Lancashire County Library 1988; Western Australian (Secondary) 1990.

CHALLIS, GEORGE
The Golden Knight by George Challis, illustrated by Steel Savage; Greystone Press, 1940. **Awarded:** Spring Book Festival (older honor) 1940.

CHALMERS, MARY
Be Good, Harry written and illustrated by Mary Chalmers; Harper, 1967. **Awarded:** New Jersey Institute of Technology 1967.

Kevin written and illustrated by Mary Chalmers; Harper & Row, 1957. **Awarded:** Spring Book Festival (ages 4-8 honor) 1957.

Merry Christmas, Harry written and illustrated by Mary Chalmers; Harper & Row, 1977. **Awarded:** New Jersey Institute of Technology 1978.

CHAMBERLAIN, CHRISTOPHER
London's River: The Story of a City by Eric S. De Mare, illustrated by Christopher Chamberlain and Heather Copley; Bodley Head, 1964. **Awarded:** Carnegie (commended) 1964.

CHAMBERLAIN, MARGARET
Fair's Fair by Leon Garfield, illustrated by Margaret Chamberlain; Macdonald, 1981. **Awarded:** Children's Book Award (Federation) 1981.

CHAMBERS, AIDAN
   Awarded: Eleanor Farjeon 1982.

Dansa Pa Min Grav (original English: *Dance on My Grave*) by Aidan Chambers, translated by Ingvar Skogsberg; Awe/Gebbers, 1983. **Awarded:** International Board on Books for Young People (translation/Sweden) 1984.

The Reader in the Book by Aidan Chambers in Signal May 1977. **Awarded:** Children's Literature Assn. Literary Criticism 1978.

CHAMBERS, NANCY
   Awarded: Eleanor Farjeon 1982.

CHAMBLISS, MAXIE
Donald Says Thumb Down by Nancy Evans Cooney, illustrated by Maxie Chambliss; Putnam, 1987. **Awarded:** New Jersey Institute of Technology 1988.

CHAN, CHIH-YI
Good Luck Horse by Chih-Yi Chan, illustrated by Plato Chan; Whittlesey House, 1943. **Awarded:** Caldecott (honor) 1944.

CHAN, PLATO
Good Luck Horse by Chih-Yi Chan, illustrated by Plato Chan; Whittlesey House, 1943. **Awarded:** Caldecott (honor) 1944.

CHAN, SHIRLEY
Potatoes: All About Them by Alvin Silverstein and Virginia B. Silverstein, illustrated by Shirley Chan; Prentice Hall, 1976. **Awarded:** New York Academy of Sciences (older honor) 1977.

CHANDLER, DAVID
Exploring the Night Sky with Binoculars by David Chandler, illustrated by David Chandler and Don Davis; David Chandler, 1983. **Awarded:** New York Academy of Sciences (older honor) 1985.

CHANDRA, AVINASH
Judy and Lakshmi by Naomi Mitchison, illustrated by Avinash Chandra; Collins, 1958. **Awarded:** Hans Christian Andersen (runnerup) 1960.

CHANG, FA-SHUN
The Sky River by Fa-Shun Chang, illustrated by Jeanyee Wong; Lothrop, 1950. **Awarded:** Boys Club 1951.

CHANG, INA
A Separate Battle: Women and the Civil War by Ina Chang, illustrated; Lodestar, 1991. **Awarded:** Hungry Mind (Middle Readers/Nonfiction) 1992.

CHANG, ISABELLE
   Awarded: Chandler Reward of Merit 1965.

CHAPMAN, CAROL
Herbie's Troubles by Carol Chapman, illustrated by Kelly Oechsli; Dutton, 1981. **Awarded:** California Young Reader (primary) 1985; Georgia Children's Picture Storybook 1983.

CHAPMAN, FREDERICK TRENCH
The Hidden Treasure of Glaston by Eleanore Myers Jewett, illustrated by Frederick T. Chapman; Viking, 1946. **Awarded:** Newbery (honor) 1947.

White Falcon by Elliott Arnold, illustrated by Frederick T. Chapman; Knopf, 1955. **Awarded:** William Allen White 1958.

CHAPMAN, GAYNOR
The Luck Child by Jacob Grimm and Wilhelm Grimm, illustrated by Gaynor Chapman; Hamilton, 1968. **Awarded:** Greenaway (honour) 1968.

CHAPMAN, SYDNEY
IGY: Year of Discovery: The Story of the International Geophysical Year by Sydney Chapman, illustrated with photographs; University of Michigan Press, 1959. **Awarded:** Edison Mass Media (best science book for youth) 1960.

CHAPPELL, WARREN
Patterns on the Wall by Elizabeth Yates, illustrated by Warren Chappell; Knopf, 1943. **Awarded:** Spring Book Festival (older) 1943.

The Quaint and Curious Quest of Johnny Longfoot, the Shoe King's Son by Catherine Besterman, illustrated by Warren Chappell; Bobbs-Merrill, 1947. **Awarded:** Newbery (honor) 1948.

CHARBONNEAU, EILEEN
The Ghosts of Stoney Clove by Eileen Charbonneau; Orchard, 1988. **Awarded:** Golden Medallion 1989.

CHARLES, ROBERT H.

A Roundabout Turn by Robert H. Charles, illustrated by L. Leslie Brooke; Warne, 1930. **Awarded:** Lewis Carroll Shelf 1961.

CHARLIP, REMY

Arm In Arm written and illustrated by Remy Charlip; Parents, 1969. **Awarded:** Bologna (graphics for children) 1971; New York Times Best Illustrated 1969.

Handtalk: an ABC of Finger Spelling and Sign Language by Remy Charlip, Mary Beth Miller, and George Ancona, photographs by George Ancona; Parents, 1974. **Awarded:** New York Academy of Sciences (younger honor) 1975

Handtalk Birthday by Remy Charlip and Mary Beth Miller, photographs by George Ancona; Four Winds, 1987. **Awarded:** New York Times Best Illustrated 1987.

Harlequin and the Gift of Many Colors by Remy Charlip and Burton Supree, illustrated by Remy Charlip; Parents, 1973. **Awarded:** Irma Simonton Black 1973.

Mother, Mother I Feel Sick, Send for the Doctor Quick, Quick, Quick by Remy Charlip and Burton Supree, illustrated by Remy Charlip; Parents, 1966. **Awarded:** Boys Club 1966-67.

The Seeing Stick by Jane Yolen, illustrated by Remy Charlip and Demetra Maraslis; Crowell, 1977. **Awarded:** Christopher (ages 6-9) 1978.

Thirteen written and illustrated by Remy Charlip and Jerry Joyner; Parents, 1975. **Awarded:** Boston Globe Horn Book (illustration) 1976; New York Times Best Illustrated 1975.

CHARLOT, JEAN

And Now Miguel by Joseph Krumgold, illustrated by Jean Charlot; Crowell, 1953. **Awarded:** Boys Club 1954; Newbery 1954.

The Boy Who Could Do Anything and Other Mexican Folk Tales by Anita Brenner, illustrated by Jean Charlot; Young Scott Books, 1942. **Awarded:** Spring Book Festival (middle honor) 1942.

A Child's Good Night Book by Margaret Wise Brown, illustrated by Jean Charlot; Scott, 1943. **Awarded:** Caldecott (honor) 1944.

The Corn Grows Ripe by Dorothy Rhoads, illustrated by Jean Charlot; Viking, 1956. **Awarded:** Newbery (honor) 1957.

A Hero by Mistake by Anita Brenner, illustrated by Jean Charlot; Scott, 1953. **Awarded:** New York Times Best Illustrated 1953; Spring Book Festival (ages 4-8 honor) 1953.

Secret of the Andes by Ann Nolan Clark, illustrated by Jean Charlot; Viking, 1952. **Awarded:** Newbery 1953; Spring Book Festival (ages 8-12 honor) 1952.

The Timid Ghost: or, What Would You Do with a Sackful of Gold? by Anita Brenner, illustrated by Jean Charlot; Scott, 1966. **Awarded:** Boys Club 1966-67.

When Will the World Be Mine? The Story of a Snowshoe Rabbit by Miriam Schlein, illustrated by Jean Charlot; Scott, 1953. **Awarded:** Caldecott (honor) 1954.

CHASE, ALICE

see McHARGUE, GEORGESS

CHASE, RICHARD

Awarded: Southern California Council (distinguished contribution to the field of folklore) 1970.

CHASEK, JUDITH

Have You Seen Wilhemina Krumpf? by Judith Chasek, illustrated by Sal Murdocca; Lothrop, 1973. **Awarded:** Children's Book Showcase 1974.

CHASTAIN, MADYE LEE

Cow-tail Switch, and Other West African Stories by Harold Courlander and George Herzog; illustrated by Madye Lee Chastain; Holt, 1947. **Awarded:** Newbery (honor) 1948.

CHAUNCY, NANCEN BERYL MASTERMAN

Devil's Hill by Nan Chauncy, illustrated by Geraldine Spence; Oxford, 1958; Watts, 1960. **Awarded:** Boys Club 1961; Children's Book Council of Australia (book of the year) 1959.

Tangara: Let Us Set Off Again by Nan Chauncy, illustrated by Brian Wildsmith; Oxford, 1960. (Published as *The Secret Friends* in 1962 by Watts). **Awarded:** Children's Book Council of Australia (book of the year) 1961; International Board on Books for Young People (honour list/Great Britain) 1962.

Tiger in the Bush by Nan Chauncy, illustrated by Margaret Horder; Oxford, 1957. **Awarded:** Children's Book Council of Australia (book of the year) 1958.

CHAVEZ, EDWARD

Legend of Billy Bluesage by Jonreed Lauritzen, illustrated by Edward Chavez; Little Brown, 1961. **Awarded:** Southern California Council (notable) 1962.

CHEE, CHENG-KHEE

Old Turtle by Douglas Wood, illustrated by Cheng-Khee Chee; Pfeifer-Hamilton, 1992. **Awarded:** American Bookseller's Book of the Year (Children's Book) 1993; International Reading Assn. (Younger) 1993; Minnesota (Younger children) 1992.

CHEKHOV, ANTON

Kashtanka by Anton Chekhov, translated by Charles Dowsett, illustrated by William Stobbs; Oxford, 1959. **Awarded:** Greenaway 1959.

CHELTON, MARY KAY

Awarded: Grolier 1985; Jeremiah Ludington 1981.

CHEN, JU-HONG

The Magic Leaf by Winifred Morris, illustrated by Ju-Hong Chen; Atheneum, 1987. **Awarded:** Parents' Choice (Picture Book) 1987.

CHEN, KUO KANG

Growing Up by Susan Meredith, illustrated by Sue Stitt, Kuo Kang Chen and Rob McCaig; Usborne, 1985. **Awarded:** Times Educational Supplement (senior) 1985.

CHEN, TONY

About Owls by May Garelick, illustrated by Tony Chen; Four Winds, 1975. **Awarded:** Children's Book Showcase 1976.

Animals Showing Off by Jane R. McCauley, illustrated by Tony Chen; National Geographic, 1988. **Awarded:** Redbook 1988.

Honschi by Aline Glasgow, illustrated by Tony Chen; Parents, 1972. **Awarded:** Children's Book Showcase 1973.

The Princess and the Admiral by Charlotte Pomerantz, illustrated by Tony Chen; Addison, 1974. **Awarded:** Jane Addams 1975.

CHENEY, FRANCES NEAL

Awarded: Women's National Book Assn. 1976.

CHERMAYEFF, IVAN
The New Nutcracker Suite and Other Innocent Verses by Ogden
Nash, illustrated by Ivan Chermayeff; Little Brown, 1962.
Awarded: Spring Book Festival (picture book honor) 1962.

CHERRY, LYNNE
The Great Kapok Tree: A Tale of the Amazon Rain Forest written
and illustrated by Lynne Cherry; Harcourt Brace Jovanovich,
1990. **Awarded:** Charlotte Book Award (K-2) 1992.

The Snail's Spell by Joanne Ryder, illustrated by Lynne Cherry;
Warne, 1982. **Awarded:** New York Academy of Sciences
(younger) 1983.

Who's Sick Today? written and illustrated by Lynne Cherry;
Dutton, 1988. **Awarded:** Please Touch 1989.

CHESS, VICTORIA
Fletcher and Zenobia by Victoria Chess and Edward Gorey, illus-
trated by Victoria Chess; Hawthorne, 1967. **Awarded:** Art
Books for Children 1973.

Slither McCreep and His Brother Joe by Tony Johnston, illustrated by Victoria Chess; Harcourt Brace Jovanovich, 1992.
Awarded: Parents Choice (Story Book) 1992.

Taking Care of Melvin by Marjorie Weiman Sharmat, illustrated
by Victoria Chess; Holiday House, 1980. **Awarded:** Parents'
Choice (illustration) 1980.

Tales for the Perfect Child by Florence Heide, illustrated by
Victoria Chess; Lothrop, Lee & Shepard, 1985. **Awarded:**
Parents' Choice (literature) 1985.

CHESSARE, MICHELE
The Owlstone Crown by X. J. Kennedy, illustrated by Michele
Chessare; Atheneum, 1983. **Awarded:** Ethical Culture 1983.

CHESTER, MICHAEL
Joseph Strauss - Builder of the Golden Gate Bridge by Michael
Chester, illustrated by Tom Hamil; Putnam, 1965. **Awarded:**
Boys Club (certificate) 1966-67.

CHESTERMAN, JOHN
Worlds Within Worlds: a Journey into the Unknown by John
Chesterman, John May, John Trux, and Michael Marten, illus-
trated with photographs; Holt, 1977. **Awarded:** New York
Academy of Sciences (older honor) 1979.

CHETWIN, GRACE
Box and Cox by Grace Chetwin, illustrated by David Small;
Bradbury, 1990. **Awarded:** Parents' Choice (Picture Book)
1990.

CHEW, RUTH
Awarded: Lucky Book Club Four-leaf Clover 1977.

CHIASSON, JOHN
African Journey by John Chiasson, illustrated with photos;
Bradbury, 1987. **Awarded:** Boston Globe (Nonfiction
Honor) 1988.

CHICK, SANDRA
Push Me, Pull Me by Sandra Chick; not illustrated; Women's
Press, 1987. **Awarded:** Other Award 1987.

CHIEF SEATTLE
Brother Eagle, Sister Sky: A Message from Chief Seattle, illustrat-
ed by Susan Jeffers; Dial, 1991. **Awarded:** American
Booksellers Book of the Year 1992; Parents' Choice (Picture
Book) 1991.

CHILDRESS, ALICE
A Hero Ain't Nothin' But a Sandwich by Alice Childress, not
illustrated; Coward, 1973. **Awarded:** Jane Addams (honor)

1974; Lewis Carroll Shelf 1975; National Book Award (finalist) 1974; New York Times Notable Books 1973; Woodward
Park School 1974.

Rainbow Jordan by Alice Childress, not illustrated; Coward
McCann, 1981. **Awarded:** New York Times Notable Books
1981.

CHILDS, KATHERINE
To Become a Man by Katherine Childs; to be published by
Macmillan. **Awarded:** Macmillan (3rd prize) 1987.

CHILTON, CHARLES
The Book of the West: An Epic of America's Wild Frontier by
Charles Chilton, illustrated by Eric Tansley; Bobbs-Merrill,
1962. **Awarded:** Western Heritage 1963.

CHILTON, IRMA
The Prize by Irma Chilton, not illustrated; Barn Owl Press, 1983.
Awarded: Tir Na n-Og (Anglo Welsh) 1984

CHIMAERA
see FARJEON, ELEANOR

CHIRINOS, LITO
Lito, the Shoeshine Boy by Lito Chirinos, told to and translated by
David Mangurian, photographs by David Mangurian; Four
Winds, 1975. **Awarded:** Children's Book Showcase 1976.

CHISHOLM, JAMES
South Pass - 1868 (His) Journal of the Wyoming Gold Rush writ-
ten and illustrated by James Chisholm, edited by Lola M.
Homsher; University of Nebraska Press, 1960. **Awarded:**
Western Writers (nonfiction) 1961.

CHITTUM, IDA
Farmer Hoo and the Baboons by Ida Chittum, illustrated by Glen
Rounds; Delacorte, 1971. **Awarded:** Lewis Carroll Shelf
1971.

CHOCOLATE, DEBORAH NEWTON
Talk, Talk: An Ashanti Legend by Deborah Newton Chocolate,
illustrated by David Albers; Troll, 1992. **Awarded:** Parents
Choice (Story Book) 1992.

CHONZ, SELINA
Florinda and the Wild Bird by Selina Chonz, translated by Anne
Serraillier and Ian Serraillier, illustrated by Alois Carigiet;
Walck, 1952. **Awarded:** New York Times Best Illustrated
1953.

CHORAO, KAY
Albert's Toothache by Barbara Williams, illustrated by Kay
Chorao; Dutton, 1974. **Awarded:** Children's Book Showcase
1975.

Chester Chipmunk's Thanksgiving by Barbara Williams, illustrated by Kay Chorao; Dutton, 1978. **Awarded:** Christopher
(ages 7-9) 1979.

The Good-Bye Book by Judith Viorst, illustrated by Kay Chorao;
Atheneum, 1988. **Awarded:** Christopher (Ages 5-7) 1989;
New Jersey Institute of Technology 1989.

CHRISMAN, ARTHUR BOWIE
Shen of the Sea: a Book for Children by Arthur Bowie Chrisman,
illustrated by Else Hasselriis; Dutton, 1925. **Awarded:**
Newbery 1926.

CHRISTELOW, EILEEN
Henry and the Red Stripes written and illustrated by Eileen
Christelow; Clarion, 1982. **Awarded:** Little Archer 1982.

Zucchini by Barbara Dana, illustrated by Eileen Christelow; Harper & Row, 1982. **Awarded:** Washington Irving (Fiction) 1984; Land of Enchantment 1986; Maud Hart Lovelace 1986.

CHRISTENSEN, GARDELL DANO
Wapiti the Elk by Rutherford Montgomery, illustrated by Gardell Dano Christensen; Little Brown, 1952. **Awarded:** Commonwealth Club of California 1952.

CHRISTIAN, MARY BLOUNT
The Doggone Mystery by Mary Blount Christian, illustrated by Irene Trivas; Whitman, 1980. **Awarded:** Edgar Allan Poe (runnerup) 1981.

CHRISTIANA, DAVID
Tales of Trickery from the Land of Spoof by Alvin Schwartz, illustrated by David Christiana; Farrar, Straus & Giroux, 1985. **Awarded:** New Jersey Institute of Technology 1987.

CHRISTOPHER, JOHN
The City of Gold and Lead by John Christopher, not illustrated; Macmillan, 1967. **Awarded:** George G. Stone 1977.

The Guardians by John Christopher, not illustrated; Macmillan, 1970. **Awarded:** Christopher (Teenage) 1971; Guardian 1971.

New Found Land by John Christopher, not illustrated; Dutton, 1983. **Awarded:** Parents' Choice (literature) 1983.

The Pool of Fire by John Christopher, not illustrated; Macmillan, 1968. **Awarded:** George G. Stone 1977.

The White Mountains by John Christopher, not illustrated; Macmillan, 1967. **Awarded:** George G. Stone 1977.

CHUBB, THOMAS CALDECOT
The Byzantines by Thomas C. Chubb, illustrated by Richard M. Powers; World, 1959. **Awarded:** Boys Club 1960.

CHURCHER, BETTY
Understanding Art: the Use of Space, Form, and Structure by Betty Churcher, illustrated with photographs; McDougall, 1973. **Awarded:** Times Educational Supplement (Senior) 1974.

CHUTE, MARCHETTE
Awarded: Women's National Book Assn. 1959.

CHWAST, JACQUELINE
Whispers and Other Poems by Myra Cohn Livingston, illustrated by Jacqueline Chwast; Harcourt, 1958. **Awarded:** Spring Book Festival (ages 4-8 honor) 1958.

CHWAST, SEYMOUR
The Alphabet Parade written and illustrated by Seymour Chwast; Harcourt Brace Jovanovich, 1991. **Awarded:** Parents' Choice (Picture Book) 1991.

Finding a Poem by Eve Merriam, illustrated by Seymour Chwast; Atheneum, 1970. **Awarded:** New York Times Best Illustrated 1970.

Just Enough Is Plenty: A Hanukkah Tale by Barbara Diamond Goldin, illustrated by Seymour Chwast; Viking Kestrel, 1988. **Awarded:** Jewish Book Council (Illustration) 1989; Parents' Choice (Picture Book) 1988.

Rimes de la Mere Oie: Mother Goose Rendered into French translated by Ormonde deKay, Jr., illustrated by Milton Glaser, Barry Zaid, and Seymour Chwast; Little Brown, 1971. **Awarded:** Children's Book Showcase 1972.

Sara's Granny and the Groodle by Joan Gill, illustrated by Seymour Chwast; Doubleday, 1969. **Awarded:** New York Times Best Illustrated 1969.

CIARDI, JOHN
Awarded: National Council of Teachers of English Poetry Award 1982; New Jersey Institute of Technology (special citation) 1965; Rutgers 1966.

I Met a Man by John Ciardi, illustrated by Robert Osborn; Houghton, 1961. **Awarded:** New Jersey Institute of Technology 1961; Spring Book Festival (ages 4-8 honor) 1961.

John J. Plenty and Fiddler Dan by John Ciardi, illustrated by Madeleine Gekiere; Lippincott, 1963. **Awarded:** New York Times Best Illustrated 1963.

The King Who Saved Himself from Being Saved by John Ciardi, illustrated by Edward Gorey; Lippincott, 1965. **Awarded:** New Jersey Institute of Technology 1967.

The Man who Sang the Sillies by John Ciardi, illustrated by Edward Gorey; Lippincott, 1961. **Awarded:** Boys Club 1962.

The Monster Den: or, Look What Happened at My House - and to It by John Ciardi, illustrated by Edward Gorey; Lippincott, 1966. **Awarded:** New Jersey Institute of Technology 1967; New York Times Best Illustrated 1966.

The Reason for the Pelican by John Ciardi, illustrated by Madeleine Gekiere; Lippincott, 1959. **Awarded:** New York Times Best Illustrated 1959.

Scrappy the Pup by John Ciardi, illustrated by Jane Miller; Lippincott, 1960. **Awarded:** New York Times Best Illustrated 1960.

CLANCY, JOSEPH P.
Pendragon: Arthur and His Britain by Joseph P. Clancy, illustrated with maps and diagrams; Praeger, 1971. **Awarded:** Spring Book Festival (older honor) 1971.

CLAPP, PATRICIA
Constance: A Story of Early Plymouth by Patricia Clapp, not illustrated; Lothrop, 1968. **Awarded:** Lewis Carroll Shelf 1969; National Book Award (finalist) 1969.

The Tamarack Tree by Patricia Clapp; Lothrop, Lee & Shepard, 1986. **Awarded:** New Jersey Institute of Technology 1987.

CLARE, HELEN
see HUNTER BLAIR, PAULINE CLARKE

CLARK, ANN NOLAN
Awarded: Outstanding Arizona Author 1984; Regina 1963.

In My Mother's House by Ann Nolan Clark, illustrated by Velino Herrera; Viking, 1941. **Awarded:** Caldecott (honor) 1942; Spring Book Festival (younger) 1941.

Looking-for-Something by Ann Nolan Clark, illustrated by Leo Politi; Viking, 1952. **Awarded:** Spring Book Festival (picture book) 1952.

Santiago by Ann Nolan Clark, illustrated by Lynd Ward; Viking, 1955. **Awarded:** Spring Book Festival (older honor) 1955.

Secret of the Andes by Ann Nolan Clark, illustrated by Jean Charlot; Viking, 1952. **Awarded:** Newbery 1953; Spring Book Festival (ages 8-12 honor) 1952.

CLARK, BRENDA
Little Fingerling: A Japanese Folktale by Monica Hughes, illustrated by Brenda Clark; Kids Can Press, 1989. **Awarded:** Amelia Frances Howard-Gibbon (1st runnerup) 1990; IODE 1989.

CLARK, CATHERINE ANTHONY
The Sun Horse by Catherine Anthony Clark, illustrated by Clare Bice; Macmillan Canada, 1951. **Awarded:** Canadian Library Assn. 1952.

CLARK, EMMA CHICHESTER
Listen to This by Laura Cecil, illustrated by Emma Chichester Clark; Bodley Head, 1987. **Awarded:** Mother Goose 1988.

CLARK, JOAN
Wild Man of the Woods by Joan Clark; Penguin Books Canada, 1986. **Awarded:** Canadian Library Assn. (runnerup) 1986.

CLARK, LEONARD
Flutes and Cymbals (Poems) compiled by Leonard Clark, illustrated by Shirley Hughes; Bodley Head, 1968. **Awarded:** Greenaway (honour) 1968.

Poetry and Children by Leonard Clark in Children's Literature in Education Autumn 1978. **Awarded:** Children's Literature Assn. Award for Literary Criticism 1979.

Quiet as Moss: 36 Poems chosen by Leonard Clark by Andrew Young, illustrated by Joan Hassall; Hart-Davis, 1959. **Awarded:** Carnegie (commended) 1959.

CLARK, MARY HIGGINS
Aspire to the Heavens: a Portrait of George Washington by Mary Higgins Clark, not illustrated; Meredith, 1969. **Awarded:** New Jersey Institute of Technology 1969.

The Cradle Will Fall by Mary Higgins Clark, not illustrated; Simon & Schuster, 1980. **Awarded:** Blue Spruce 1990.

CLARK, MAVIS THORPE
The Min-min by Mavis Thorpe Clark, illustrated by Genevieve Melrose; Angus, 1967. **Awarded:** Children's Book Council of Australia (book of the year) 1967.

CLARK, PHYLLIS E.
Doing Time: a Look at Crime and Prisons by Phyllis E. Clark and Robert Lehrman, illustrated; Hastings House, 1980. **Awarded:** Jane Addams (honor) 1981.

CLARK, RHETA
Awarded: American Association of School Librarians 1984.

CLARK, THOMAS D., DR.
Awarded: Jesse Stuart 1984.

CLARKE, ARTHUR C.
The Challenge of the Sea by Arthur C. Clarke, illustrated by Alex Schomburg; Holt, 1960. **Awarded:** Boys Club 1961.

CLARKE, GUS
Eddie and Teddy written and illustrated by Gus Clarke; Andersen Press, 1990. **Awarded:** Mother Goose (runnerup) 1991.

CLARKE, PAULINE
The Return of the Twelves by Pauline Clarke, illustrated by Bernarda Bryson; Coward, 1963. **Awarded:** Lewis Carroll Shelf 1965; Spring Book Festival (middle honor) 1964.

The Twelve and the Genii by Pauline Clarke, illustrated by Cecil Leslie; Faber, 1962. (Published in the U.S. as *The Return of the Twelves* in 1963). **Awarded:** Carnegie 1962; International Board on Books for Young People (honour list/Great Britain) 1964

CLARKE, PETER
Brother Night by Victor Kelleher, illustrated by Peter Clarke; Julia MacRae, 1990. **Awarded:** West Australian (Hoffman Award) 1992.

CLAVELOUX, NICOLE
Awarded: Hans Christian Andersen (highly commended illustrator/France) 1974.

Alala by Guy Monreal, illustrated by Nicole Claveloux; Quist, 1970. **Awarded:** New York Times Best Illustrated 1970.

The Secret Journey of Hugo the Brat by Francois Ruy-Vidal, illustrated by Nicole Claveloux; Quist, 1968. **Awarded:** New York Times Best Illustrated 1968.

CLAY, WILL
Little Eight John by Jan Wahl, illustrated by Will Clay; Lodestar Books, 1992. **Awarded:** Coretta Scott King (Illustration honor) 1993.

CLEARY, BEVERLY BUNN
Awarded: CBC Honors Program (books) 1985; Jeremiah Ludington 1987; Regina 1980; George G. Stone 1983; University of Southern Mississippi 1982; Laura Ingalls Wilder 1975.

Dear Mr. Henshaw by Beverly Cleary, illustrated by Paul O. Zelinsky; Morrow, 1983. **Awarded:** Christopher (ages 8-10) 1984; Commonwealth Club of California 1983; Dorothy Canfield Fisher 1985; FOCAL 1987; Garden State (younger fiction) 1986; Massachusetts 1986; Nene 1989; New York Times Notable Books 1983; Newbery 1984; Parents' Choice (literature) 1983; Sequoyah 1986.

Fifteen by Beverly Cleary, illustrated by Beth Krush and Joe Krush; Morrow, 1956. **Awarded:** Dorothy Canfield Fisher 1958.

A Girl From Yamhill: A Memoir by Beverly Cleary, illustrated with photographs; Morrow, 1988. **Awarded:** Bay Area Book Reviewers Assn. 1989; Reading Magic Award 1988.

Henry and Ribsy by Beverly Cleary, illustrated by Louis Darling; Morrow, 1954. **Awarded:** Young Reader's Choice 1957.

Henry and the Paper Route by Beverly Cleary, illustrated by Louis Darling; Morrow, 1957. **Awarded:** Young Readers' Choice 1960.

The Mouse and the Motorcycle by Beverly Cleary, illustrated by Louis Darling; Morrow, 1965. **Awarded:** Great Stone Face 1983; Sue Hefly 1973; Nene 1969; Surrey School 1974; William Allen White 1968; Young Reader's Choice 1968.

Muggie Maggie by Beverly Cleary, illustrated by Kay Life; Morrow, 1990. **Awarded:** Garden State (Younger fiction) 1993.

Ralph S. Mouse by Beverly Cleary, illustrated by Paul O. Zelinsky; Morrow, 1982. **Awarded:** Emphasis on Reading (Grades 2-3) 1983-84; Garden State (younger fiction) 1985; Golden Kite (fiction) 1982; Iowa Children 1985; Parents' Choice (literature) 1982; Sunshine (runnerup) 1985; Surrey School 1986; West Virginia 1986-87.

Ramona and Her Father by Beverly Cleary, illustrated by Alan Tiegreen; Morrow, 1977. **Awarded:** Boston Globe Horn Book (fiction honor) 1978; Sue Hefly (honor) 1982; Garden State Children's (young fiction) 1980; International Board on Books for Young People (text/USA) 1980; Land of Enchantment 1981; Nene 1979; Newbery (honor) 1978; Volunteer State 1980; Texas Bluebonnet 1981; Utah Children's Choice 1980; Young Reader's Choice 1980.

Ramona and Her Mother by Beverly Cleary, illustrated by Alan Tiegreen; Morrow, 1979; Dell/Yearling, 1980. **Awarded:** American Book Award (children's fiction paperback) 1981; Garden State Children's (younger fiction) 1982; Surrey School 1982.

Ramona Forever by Beverly Cleary, illustrated by Alan Tiegreen; Morrow, 1984. **Awarded:** Iowa Children's Choice 1987; New York Times Notable 1984; Parents' Choice (literature) 1984.

Ramona Quimby, Age 8 by Beverly Cleary, illustrated by Alan Tiegreen; Morrow, 1981. **Awarded:** Buckeye (grades 3-5) 1985; Garden State (younger fiction) 1984; Michigan Young Readers 1984; Newbery (honor) 1982; Charlie May Simon 1983-84; Sunshine (runnerup) 1984.

Ramona the Brave by Beverly Cleary, illustrated by Alan Tiegreen; Morrow, 1975. **Awarded:** Golden Archer 1977; Mark Twain 1978.

Ramona the Pest by Beverly Cleary, illustrated by Louis Darling; Morrow, 1968. **Awarded:** Georgia Children's 1970; Nene 1971; Sequoyah 1971; Young Reader's Choice 1971.

Ribsy by Beverly Cleary, illustrated by Louis Darling; Morrow, 1964. **Awarded:** Dorothy Canfield Fisher 1966; Nene 1968.

Runaway Ralph by Beverly Cleary, illustrated by Louis Darling; Morrow, 1970. **Awarded:** Nene 1972; Charlie May Simon 1972-73.

Socks by Beverly Cleary, illustrated by Beatrice Darwin; Morrow, 1973. **Awarded:** Golden Archer 1977; William Allen White 1976.

Strider by Beverly Cleary, illustrated by Paul O. Zelinsky; Morrow, 1991. **Awarded:** Reading Magic Award 1991.

CLEAVER, BILL
see CLEAVER, WILLIAM

CLEAVER, ELIZABETH
Awarded: Hans Christian Andersen (highly commended illustrator/Canada) 1972.

How Summer Came to Canada written and illustrated by Elizabeth Cleaver; Oxford University Press, 1970. **Awarded:** Amelia Frances Howard-Gibbon (runnerup) 1971.

The Loon's Necklace by William Toye, illustrated by Elizabeth Cleaver; Oxford, 1977. **Awarded:** Amelia Frances Howard-Gibbon 1978; IODE 1977.

The Miraculous Hind written and illustrated by Elizabeth Cleaver; Holt Canada, 1973. **Awarded:** Canadian Library Assn. 1974.

Petrouchka written and illustrated by Elizabeth Cleaver; Macmillan (Canada), 1980; Atheneum, 1980. **Awarded:** Governor General's (illustrator) 1980; International Board on Books for Young People (illustration/Canada) 1982; Parents' Choice (illustration) 1980.

The Wind Has Wings: Poems from Canada compiled by Barbara Robertson and Mary Alice Downie, illustrated by Elizabeth Cleaver; Oxford, 1968. **Awarded:** Amelia Frances Howard-Gibbon 1971.

The Witch of the North: Folk Tales of French Canada adapted by Mary Alice Downie, illustrated by Elizabeth Cleaver; Oberon Press, 1975. **Awarded:** Amelia Frances Howard-Gibbon (runnerup) 1976.

CLEAVER, VERA
Dust of the Earth by Bill Cleaver and Vera Cleaver, not illustrated; Lippincott, 1975. **Awarded:** Lewis Carroll Shelf 1975; New York Times Notable Books 1975; Western Writers (fiction) 1975.

Grover by Bill Cleaver and Vera Cleaver, illustrated by Frederic Marvin; Lippincott, 1970. **Awarded:** National Book Award (finalist) 1971.

Queen of Hearts by Bill Cleaver and Vera Cleaver, not illustrated; Lippincott, 1978. **Awarded:** National Book Award (finalist) 1979.

Where the Lilies Bloom by Bill Cleaver and Vera Cleaver, illustrated by Jim Spanfeller; Lippincott, 1969. **Awarded:** Boston Globe Horn Book (text honor) 1970; National Book Award (finalist) 1970.

The Whys and Wherefores of Littabelle Lee by Bill Cleaver and Vera Cleaver, not illustrated; Atheneum, 1973. **Awarded:** National Book Award (finalist) 1974; New York Times Notable Books 1973.

CLEAVER, WILLIAM
Dust of the Earth by Bill Cleaver and Vera Cleaver, not illustrated; Lippincott, 1975. **Awarded:** Lewis Carroll Shelf 1975; New York Times Notable Books 1975; Western Writers (fiction) 1975.

Grover by Bill Cleaver and Vera Cleaver, illustrated by Frederic Marvin; Lippincott, 1970. **Awarded:** National Book Award (finalist) 1971.

Queen of Hearts by Bill Cleaver and Vera Cleaver, not illustrated; Lippincott, 1978. **Awarded:** National Book Award (finalist) 1979.

Where the Lilies Bloom by Bill Cleaver and Vera Cleaver, illustrated by Jim Spanfeller; Lippincott, 1969. **Awarded:** Boston Globe Horn Book (text honor) 1970; National Book Award (finalist) 1970.

The Whys and Wherefores of Littabelle Lee by Bill Cleaver and Vera Cleaver, not illustrated; Atheneum, 1973. **Awarded:** National Book Award (finalist) 1974; New York Times Notable Books 1973.

CLEMENS, SAMUEL (pseudonym Mark Twain)
The Adventures of Huckleberry Finn by Samuel Clemens, illustrated by Donald McKay; Grosset, 1948, c1884. **Awarded:** Lewis Carroll Shelf 1962.

Histoire du Petit Stephen Girard by Mark Twain, translated from the English by A. Allais, illustrated by Jean Michel Nicollet; Editions Gallimard, 1978. **Awarded:** Bologna (graphics for children) 1979.

Tom Sawyer (phonodisc) by Samuel Clemens, narrated by Boris Karloff; Caedmon R1088. **Awarded:** Lewis Carroll Shelf 1967.

CLEMENT, CHARLES
Jacobin's Daughter by Joanne S. Williamson, illustrated by Charles Clement; Knopf, 1956. **Awarded:** Spring Book Festival (older honor) 1956.

CLEMENT, FREDERIC
Bestiare Fableux by C. Meral, illustrated by Frederic Clement; Editions Magnard. **Awarded:** Biennale Illustrations Bratislava (grand prix) 1985.

CLEMENT, ROD
Counting On Frank written and illustrated by Rod Clement; Collins, in assoc. with Anne Ingram Books, 1990; Gareth Stevens, 1991. **Awarded:** Young Australian Best Book (Picture Book) 1991.

CLEMENTS, BRUCE
I Tell a Lie Every So Often by Bruce Clements, not illustrated; Farrar, 1974. **Awarded:** National Book Award (finalist) 1975.

CLERK, N. W.
see LEWIS, CLIVE STAPLES

CLIFFORD, ETH

Help! I'm a Prisoner in the Library by Eth Clifford, illustrated by George Hughes; Houghton Mifflin, 1979. **Awarded:** Young Hoosier (Grades 5-6) 1982.

Just Tell Me When We're Dead! by Eth Clifford, illustrated by George Hughes; Houghton Mifflin, 1983. **Awarded:** Sequoyah 1986.

CLIFFORD, MARGARET CORT

(pseudonym is Peggy Clifford)

The Gnu and the Guru Go Behind the Beyond by Peggy Clifford, illustrated by Eric Von Schmidt; Houghton, 1970. **Awarded:** New York Times Best Illustrated 1970.

CLIFFORD, MARY LOUISE

The Land and People of Malaysia by Mary Louise Clifford, illustrated with photographs; Lippincott, 1968. **Awarded:** New Jersey Institute of Technology 1969.

CLIFFORD, PEGGY

see CLIFFORD, MARGARET CORT

CLIFFORD, ROWAN

Henry's Leg by Ann Pilling, illustrated by Rowan Clifford; Viking Kestrel, 1985. **Awarded:** Guardian 1986.

CLIFFORD, SANDY

The Roquefort Gang written and illustrated by Sandy Clifford; Houghton Mifflin/Parnassus, 1981. **Awarded:** CRABbery (honor) 1982.

CLIFTON, LUCILLE

Amifika by Lucille Clifton, illustrated by Thomas DiGrazia; Dutton, 1977. **Awarded:** Jane Addams (special recognition) 1978.

Everett Anderson's Goodbye by Lucille Clifton, illustrated by Ann Grifalconi; Holt, 1983. **Awarded:** Coretta Scott King (author) 1984.

CLIMO, LINDEE

Chester's Barn written and illustrated by Lindee Climo; Tundra, 1982. **Awarded:** Amelia Frances Howard-Gibbon 1983.

CLOVEN, GEORGE

Stanleigh's Wrong-side-out Day by Barbara A. Steiner, illustrated by George Cloven and Ruth Cloven; Children's Press, 1982. **Awarded:** Colorado (runnerup) 1985.

CLOVEN, RUTH

Stanleigh's Wrong-side-out Day by Barbara A. Steiner, illustrated by George Cloven and Ruth Cloven; Children's Press, 1982. **Awarded:** Colorado (runnerup) 1985.

CLUFF, TOM

Minutemen of the Sea by Tom Cluff, illustrated by Tom O'Sullivan; Follett, 1955. **Awarded:** Charles W. Follett 1955.

CLYMER, ELEANOR

Awarded: School Library Media Specialists, New York 1980.

The Get-away Car by Eleanor Clymer, not illustrated; Dutton, 1978. **Awarded:** Sequoyah 1981.

Luke Was There by Eleanor Clymer, illustrated by Diane deGroat; Holt, 1973. **Awarded:** Child Study 1974.

My Brother Stevie by Eleanor Clymer, illustrated by Esta Nesbitt; Holt, 1967. **Awarded:** Woodward Park School 1968.

COALSON, GLO

The Long Hungry Night by Elizabeth C. Foster and Slim Williams, illustrated by Glo Coalson; Atheneum, 1973.

Awarded: Friends of American Writers (illustration) 1974; Friends of American Writers (ages 10-14) 1974.

COATS, ALICE M.

The Story of Horace written and illustrated by Alice M. Coats; Coward, 1939. **Awarded:** Spring Book Festival (younger) 1939.

COATS, LAURA JANE

Mr. Jordan in the Park written and illustrated by Laura Jane Coats; Macmillan, 1989. **Awarded:** New Jersey Institute of Technology 1990.

COATSWORTH, ELIZABETH JANE

Awarded: Hans Christian Andersen (highly commended author/U.S.) 1968; Kerlan 1975.

The Cat Who Went to Heaven by Elizabeth Coatsworth, illustrated by Lynd Ward; Macmillan, 1930. **Awarded:** Newbery 1931.

The Littlest House by Elizabeth Coatsworth, illustrated by Marguerite Davis; Macmillan, 1940. **Awarded:** Spring Book Festival (younger honor) 1940.

Under the Green Willow by Elizabeth Coatsworth, illustrated by Janina Domanska; Macmillan, 1971. **Awarded:** Spring Book Festival (picture book honor) 1971.

COBB, ALICE

The Swimming Pool by Alice Cobb, illustrated by Joseph Escourido; Friendship Press, 1957. **Awarded:** Nancy Bloch 1957.

COBB, ERNEST

Awarded: Chandler Reward of Merit 1962.

COBB, VICKI

Awarded: Eva L. Gordon 1985; School Library Media Specialists of Southeastern New York 1993.

Bet You Can't! Science Impossibilities to Fool You by Vicki Cobb and Kathy Darling, illustrated by Martha Weston; Lothrop, 1980. **Awarded:** New York Academy of Sciences (younger) 1981.

The Secret Life of School Supplies by Vicki Cobb, illustrated by Bill Morrison; Harper, 1981. **Awarded:** Washington Irving (nonfiction) 1984.

For Your Own Protection: Science Stories Photos Tell by Vicki Cobb, illustrated with photos; Lothrop, Lee & Shepard, 1989. **Awarded:** Washington Irving (Nonfiction) 1992.

COBER, ALAN EDWIN

The Dark Is Rising by Susan Cooper, illustrated by Alan Cober; Atheneum, 1973; Chatto, 1973. **Awarded:** Boston Globe Horn Book (text) 1973; Carnegie (commended) 1973; Newbery (honor) 1974.

Mister Corbett's Ghost by Leon Garfield, illustrated by Alan E. Cober; Pantheon, 1968. **Awarded:** New York Times Best Illustrated 1968.

Winter's Eve by Natalia M. Belting, illustrated by Alan E. Cober; Holt, 1969. **Awarded:** New York Times Best Illustrated 1969.

COBLENTZ, CATHERINE CATE

The Blue Cat of Castle Town by Catherine C. Coblentz, illustrated by Janice Holland; Longmans, 1949. **Awarded:** Lewis Carroll Shelf 1958; Newbery (honor) 1950.

COBURN, DORIS K.

Tales the People Tell in China by Robert Wyndham, edited by Doris K. Coburn, illustrated Jay Yang; Messner, 1971. **Awarded:** New Jersey Institute of Technology 1971.

COBURN, JEWELL REINHART

Beyond the East Wind: Legends and Folktales of Vietnam told by Duong Van Quyen, written by Jewell R. Coburn, illustrated by Nena Grigorian Ullberg; Burn, Hart, 1976. **Awarded:** Southern California Council (special recognition for a contribution of cultural significance) 1980.

Encircled Kingdom: Legends and Folktales of Laos by Jewell R. Coburn, illustrated by Nena Grigorian Ullberg; Burn, Hart, 1979. **Awarded:** Southern California Council (special recognition for a contribution of cultural significance) 1980.

Khmers, Tigers and Talismans: From the History and Legends of Mysterious Cambodia by Jewell R. Coburn, illustrated by Nena Grigorian Ullberg; Burn, Hart, 1978. **Awarded:** Southern California Council (special recognition for a contribution of cultural significance) 1980.

COCCA-LEFFLER, MARYANN

Splash! All About Baths by Susan Kovacs Buxbaum, illustrated by Maryann Cocca-Leffler; Little Brown, 1987. **Awarded:** American Institute of Physics 1988.

COCONIS, TED

Summer of the Swans by Betsy Byars, illustrated by Ted CoConis; Viking, 1970. **Awarded:** Newbery 1971.

CODYE, CORINN

Vilma Martinez by Corinn Codye, illustrated by Susi Kilgore; Raintree, 1989. **Awarded:** Woodson (Outstanding Merit - Elementary) 1990.

COE, LLOYD

Tinker's Tim and the Witches by Bertha C. Anderson, illustrated by Lloyd Coe; Little Brown, 1953. **Awarded:** Ohioana 1954.

COERR, ELEANOR

Chang's Paper Pony by Eleanor Coerr, illustrated by Deborah Kogan Ray; Harper & Row, 1988. **Awarded:** John and Patricia Beatty Award 1989.

Sadako and the Thousand Paper Cranes by Eleanor Coerr, illustrated by Ronald Himler; Putnam, 1977; Dell, 1979. **Awarded:** West Australian Young Readers (primary) 1981.

COGANCHERRY, HELEN

Who Needs a Bratty Brother? by Linda Gondosch, illustrated by Helen Cogancherry; Dutton, 1985. **Awarded:** Kentucky Bluegrass (4- 8) 1988.

COGGINS, HERBERT LEONARD

Busby & Co. by Herbert Coggins, illustrated by Roger Duvoisin; Whittlesey House, 1952. **Awarded:** Spring Book Festival (ages 8-12 honor) 1952.

COHEN, BARBARA

Awarded: Sydney Taylor Body of Work Award 1982.

Bitter Herbs and Honey by Barbara Cohen, not illustrated; Lothrop, 1976. **Awarded:** New Jersey Institute of Technology 1977.

Canterbury Tales selected by Barbara Cohen, illustrated by Trina Schart Hyman; Lothrop, Lee & Shepard, 1988. **Awarded:** Golden Kite (Picture-Illustration honor) 1988; New Jersey Institute of Technology 1990.

The Carp in the Bathtub by Barbara Cohen, illustrated by Joan Halpern; Lothrop, 1972. **Awarded:** New Jersey Institute of Technology 1972.

The Demon who Would not Die retold by Barbara Cohen, illustrated by Anatoly Ivanov; Atheneum, 1982. **Awarded:** New Jersey Institute of Technology 1983.

King of the Seventh Grade by Barbara Cohen, not illustrated; Lothrop, Lee & Shepard, 1982. **Awarded:** Jewish Book Council (children) 1983; Present Tense 1982.

Lovers' Games by Barbara Cohen, not illustrated; Atheneum, 1983. **Awarded:** New Jersey Institute of Technology 1983.

Molly's Pilgrim by Barbara Cohen, illustrated by Michael J. Deraney; Lothrop, Lee & Shepard, 1983. **Awarded:** New Jersey Institute of Technology 1983.

People Like Us by Barbara Cohen, not illustrated; Bantam Books, 1989, c1987. **Awarded:** New Jersey Institute of Technology 1988.

Unicorns in the Rain by Barbara Cohen, not illustrated; Atheneum, 1980. **Awarded:** Emphasis on Reading (Grades 7-9) 1983-84.

Where's Florrie? by Barbara Cohen, illustrated by Joan Halpern; Lothrop, 1976. **Awarded:** New Jersey Institute of Technology 1977.

Yussel's Prayer: A Yom Kippur Story by Barbara Cohen, illustrated by Michael J. Deraney; Lothrop, Lee & Shepard, 1981. **Awarded:** Sydney Taylor Book Award (children) 1982; Jewish Book Council (children's picture book) 1983.

COHEN, MIRIAM

Born to Dance Samba by Miriam Cohen, illustrated by Gioia Fiammenghi; Harper & Row, 1984. **Awarded:** Parents' Choice (literature) 1984.

COHEN, PETER

Authorized Autumn Charts of the Upper Red Canoe River Country by Peter Cohen, illustrated by Tomie de Paola; Atheneum, 1972. **Awarded:** Children's Book Showcase 1973; Friends of American Writers (illustrator) 1973.

Foal Creek by Peter Zachary Cohen, illustrated by Allan Moyler; Atheneum, 1972. **Awarded:** Friends of American Writers (ages 10-14) 1973.

Olson's Meat Pies by Peter Cohen, illustrated by Olof Landstrom; Farrar Straus Giroux, 1989. **Awarded:** New York Times Best Illustrated 1989.

COHN, JANICE

I Had a Friend Named Peter by Janice Cohn, illustrated by Gail Owens; Morrow, 1987. **Awarded:** Parents' Choice (Story Book) 1987.

COHN, NORMA

Little People in a Big Country by Norma Cohn, illustrated by the children of Soviet Russia; Oxford, 1945. **Awarded:** Spring Book Festival (younger) 1945.

COHN, RONALD H., DR.

Koko's Kitten by Dr. Francine Patterson, photographs by Dr. Ronald H. Cohn; Scholastic, 1985. **Awarded:** New York Academy of Sciences (younger honor) 1986.

Koko's Story by Francine Patterson, photos by Ronald H. Cohn; Scholastic, 1987. **Awarded:** Garden State Children's Book Award (Younger Nonfiction) 1990.

COIL, SUZANNE M.

Florida by Suzanne M. Coil, illustrated with photos; Watts, 1987. **Awarded:** New Jersey Institute of Technology 1989.

COIT, MARGARET L.

The Fight for Union by Margaret L. Coit, illustrated with photographs; Houghton, 1961. **Awarded:** Edison Mass Media (America's past) 1962.

COKER, PAUL, JR.
Winning with Numbers: A Kid's Guide to Statistics by Manfred G. Riedel, illustrated by Paul Coker, Jr.; Prentice Hall, 1978. **Awarded:** New York Academy of Sciences (younger honor) 1979.

COLABELLA, VINCENT
Peter Stuyvesant by Adele DeLeeuw, illustrated by Vincent Colabella; Garrard, 1970. **Awarded:** New Jersey Institute of Technology 1970.

COLBERT, EDWIN H.
Dinosaurs: An Illustrated History by Edwin H. Colbert, illustrated; Hammond, 1983. **Awarded:** New York Academy of Sciences (older honor) 1984.

COLE, BABETTE
Princess Smartypants written and illustrated by Babette Cole; Hamish Hamilton, 1986. **Awarded:** Greenaway (commended) 1986.

COLE, BERNARD
The Eye of Conscience: Photographers and Social Change by Milton Meltzer and Bernard Cole, illustrated with photos; Follett, 1974. **Awarded:** Jane Addams (honor) 1975.

COLE, BROCK
Gaffer Samson's Luck by Jill Paton Walsh, illustrated by Brock Cole; Viking Kestrel, 1985. **Awarded:** Smarties (grand prix) 1985; Smarties (7-11) 1985.

The Giant's Toe written and illustrated by Brock Cole; Farrar, 1986. **Awarded:** Parents' Choice (literature) 1986.

The Goats written and illustrated by Brock Cole; Farrar, 1987. **Awarded:** New York Times Notable 1987; Carl Sandburg 1988.

The Indian in the Cupboard by Lynne Reid Banks, illustrated by Brock Cole; Doubleday, 1981. **Awarded:** Arizona Young Readers' Award 1989; California Young Reader (intermediate) 1985; Caudill Young Reader's Book Award 1988; Massachusetts Children's Book Award 1988; New York Times Notable Books 1981; Virginia Young Readers (Elementary) 1988; Young Readers Choice 1984.

The King at the Door written and illustrated by Brock Cole; Doubleday, 1979. **Awarded:** Friends of American Writers (juvenile author/illustrator) 1980.

COLE, JOANNA
Awarded: Gordon, Eva L. 1990; Washington Post/Nonfiction Award 1991.

A Chick Hatches by Joanna Cole, photographs by Jerome Wexler; Morrow, 1976. **Awarded:** Children's Book Showcase 1977.

Doctor Change by Joanna Cole, illustrated by Donald Carrick; Morrow, 1986. **Awarded:** Irma Simonton Black 1986.

How You Were Born by Joanna Cole, illustrated with photographs; Morrow, 1984. **Awarded:** Golden Kite (nonfiction honor) 1984.

The Magic School Bus at the Waterworks by Joanna Cole, illustrated by Bruce Degen; Scholastic, 1986. **Awarded:** Boston Globe Horn Book (nonfiction honor) 1987; Charlotte Book Award (K- 2) 1990; Colorado Children's Book Award 1989; Florida Reading Assn. 1991; Golden Sower (K-3) 1990; Volunteer State Book Awards (K-3) 1990; Washington Children's Choice 1989.

The Magic School Bus Inside the Earth by Joanna Cole, illustrated by Bruce Degen; Scholastic, 1987. **Awarded:** Virginia Young Readers (Primary) 1990.

The Magic School Bus Inside the Human Body by Joanna Cole, illustrated by Bruce Degen; Scholastic, 1989. **Awarded:** Garden State (Nonfiction) 1992.

The Magic School Bus Lost in the Solar System by Joanna Cole, illustrated by Bruce Degen; Scholastic, 1990. **Awarded:** Garden State (Younger nonfiction) 1993.

COLE, SHEILA R.
Meaning Well by Sheila R. Cole, illustrated by Paul Raynor; Watts, 1974. **Awarded:** Golden Kite (honor) 1974.

COLEMAN, J. WINSTON, JR.
Kentucky: A Pictorial History edited by J. Winston Coleman, Jr., illustrated; University of Kentucky Press, 1971. **Awarded:** Jesse Stuart 1974.

COLEMAN, PAULINE H.
The Different One by Pauline H. Coleman, not illustrated; Dodd Mead, 1955. **Awarded:** Edith Busby 1954.

COLEMAN, WILLIAM L.
Who, What, When, Where Book about the Bible by William L. Coleman, illustrated by Dwight Walles; David C. Cook, 1980. **Awarded:** Gold Medallion 1981.

COLERIDGE, ANN
The Friends of Emily Culpepper by Ann Coleridge, illustrated by Roland Harvey; Five Mile Press, 1983. **Awarded:** Children's Book Council of Australia (picture book of the year commended) 1984.

COLES, MICHAEL
Active Science I by Michael Coles, Richard Gott, and Tony Thornley, illustrated; Collins Educational, 1988. **Awarded:** Times Educational Supplement (Schoolbook) 1988.

COLLARD, DEREK
The Squirrel-wife by A. Philippa Pearce, illustrated by Derek Collard; Crowell, 1972. **Awarded:** Spring Book Festival (picture book honor) 1972.

COLLIER, CHRISTOPHER
My Brother Sam Is Dead by Christopher Collier and James L. Collier, not illustrated; Four Winds/Scholastic, 1974. **Awarded:** Jane Addams (honor) 1975; National Book Award (finalist) 1975; Newbery (honor) 1975.

COLLIER, JAMES LINCOLN
My Brother Sam Is Dead by James L. Collier and Christopher Collier, not illustrated; Four Winds/Scholastic, 1974. **Awarded:** Jane Addams (honor) 1975; National Book Award (finalist) 1975; Newbery (honor) 1975.

Rock Star by James Lincoln Collier, not illustrated; Four Winds, 1970. **Awarded:** Child Study 1970.

COLLINGTON, PETER
The Angel and the Soldier Boy written and illustrated by Peter Collington; Methuen Children's, 1987; Knopf, 1987. **Awarded:** Smarties (Under 5s) 1987.

Little Pickle written and illustrated by Peter Collington; Methuen, 1986. **Awarded:** Mother Goose (runnerup) 1987.

COLLINS, CAROLYN STROM
The Anne of Green Gables Treasury by Carolyn Strom Collins and Christina Wyss Eriksson; Penguin Canada, 1991. **Awarded:** Alcuin 1992.

COLLINS, FRED
The Trap by Kenneth Gilbert, illustrated by Fred Collins; Holt, 1952. **Awarded:** Boys Club 1953.

COLLINS, JANET
Barty by Janet Collins, not illustrated; Blackie, 1986. **Awarded:** Burnley Express 1986; Fidler 1986.

COLLINS, MEGHAN
The Willow Maiden by Meghan Collins, illustrated by Laszlo Gal; Dial, 1985. **Awarded:** Commonwealth Club of California 1985; Parents' Choice (literature) 1985.

COLLODI, CARLO
The Adventures of Pinocchio by Carlo Collodi, illustrated by Attilio Mussino; Macmillan, 1969, c1925. **Awarded:** Children's Choice [Arizona] (picture book) 1986.

The Adventures of Pinocchio by Carlo Collodi, illustrated by Roberto Innocenti; Cape, 1988. **Awarded:** Greenaway (Highly Commended) 1988.

COLLURA, MARY-ELLEN LANG
Sunny by Mary-Ellen Lang Collura, not illustrated; Irwin, 1988. **Awarded:** Egoff 1989.

Winners by Mary-Ellen Lang Collura, not illustrated; Western Producer Prairie Books, 1984. **Awarded:** National Chapter of Canada IODE Violet Downey 1985; Young Adult Canadian 1985.

COLMAN, HILA
The Girl from Puerto Rico by Hila Colman, not illustrated; Morrow, 1961. **Awarded:** Child Study 1961.

Nobody Has to Be a Kid Forever by Hila Colman, not illustrated; Crown, 1976. **Awarded:** Garden State Children's (young fiction) 1979.

COLTMAN, PAUL
Tog the Ribber: or, Granny's Tale by Paul Coltman, illustrated by Gillian McClure; Deutsch, 1985. **Awarded:** Greenaway (commended) 1985.

COLUM, PADRAIC
Awarded: Regina 1961.

Big Tree of Bunlahy: Stories of My Own Countryside by Padraic Colum, illustrated by Jack Yeats; Macmillan, 1933. **Awarded:** Newbery (honor) 1934.

The Golden Fleece and the Heroes Who Lived Before Achilles by Padraic Colum, illustrated by Willy Pogany; Macmillan, 1921. **Awarded:** Newbery (honor) 1922.

The Voyagers: Being Legends and Romances of Atlantic Discovery by Padraic Colum, illustrated by Wilfred Jones; Macmillan, 1925. **Awarded:** Newbery (honor) 1926.

COLVER, ALICE ROSS
Vicky Barnes, Junior Hospital Volunteer: The Story of a Candy Striper by Alice Ross Colver, not illustrated; Dodd, 1966. **Awarded:** New Jersey Institute of Technology 1967.

COMMAGER, EVAN CARROLL
Valentine by Evan Carroll Commager, not illustrated; Harper, 1961. **Awarded:** Spring Book Festival (older honor) 1961.

CONDER, PAMELA
The Friends of Burramys by June Epstein, illustrated by Pamela Conder; Oxford, 1981. **Awarded:** Whitley Awards 1982.

CONE, MOLLY
Awarded: Sydney Taylor Book Award (for general contributions) 1972.

Come Back, Salmon by Molly Cone, photographs by Sidnee Wheelwright; Sierra, 1992. **Awarded:** Orbis Pictus (honor) 1993.

CONFORD, ELLEN
Hail, Hail Camp Timberwood by Ellen Conford, illustrated by Gail Owens; Little, 1978. **Awarded:** California Young Reader Medal (junior high) 1982; Surrey School 1981; Young Reader's Choice 1981.

If This Is Love, I'll Take Spaghetti by Ellen Conford, not illustrated; Four Winds, 1983. **Awarded:** South Carolina Young Adult 1987.

Lenny Kandell, Smart Aleck by Ellen Conford, illustrated by Walter Gaffney-Kessell; Little Brown, 1983. **Awarded:** Parents Choice (literature) 1983.

A Royal Pain by Ellen Conford, not illustrated; Scholastic, 1986. **Awarded:** Parents' Choice (literature) 1986; South Dakota Prairie Pasque 1989.

Why Me? by Ellen Conford, not illustrated; Little, Brown, 1985. **Awarded:** Parents' Choice (literature) 1985.

You Never Can Tell by Ellen Conford, not illustrated; Pocket Books, 1985. **Awarded:** Emphasis on Reading (Grades 7-9) 1986-87.

CONGER, ELIZABETH MALLETT
Valery by Elizabeth Conger, illustrated by Bill Crawford; Holt, 1944. **Awarded:** Spring Book Festival (younger honor) 1945.

CONKLIN, PAUL
Born To the Land: An American Portrait by Brent Ashabranner, photographs by Paul Conklin; Putnam, 1989. **Awarded:** Southwest 1989.

Children of the Maya: A Guatemalan Indian Odyssey by Brent Ashabranner, photographs by Paul Conklin; Dodd, Mead, 1986. **Awarded:** Jane Addams (honor) 1987; Woodson (Outstanding Merit) 1987

Dark Harvest: Migrant Farmworkers in America by Brent Ashabranner, photographs by Paul Conklin; Dodd, Mead, 1985. **Awarded:** Boston Globe Horn Book (nonfiction honor) 1986; Woodson 1986.

Morning Star, Black Sun: The Northern Cheyenne Indians and America's Energy Crisis by Brent Ashabranner, photographs by Paul Conklin; Dodd, Mead, 1982. **Awarded:** Woodson 1983.

To Live in Two Worlds: American Indian Youth Today by Brent Ashabranner, photographs by Paul Conklin; Dodd, Mead, 1984. **Awarded:** Woodson 1985.

CONLEY, ANDREA
Rescue of the Stranded Whales by Andrea Conley and Kenneth Mallory, illustrated with photographs; Simon & Schuster, 1989. **Awarded:** Book Can Develop Empathy 1990.

CONLEY, ELIZABETH
Mass Media by Elizabeth Conley, Ann Heintz and M. Lawrence Reuter, illustrated; Loyola University Press, 1972. **Awarded:** Media & Methods (textbook) 1975.

CONLON-McKENNA, MARITA
The Blue Horse by Marita Conlon-McKenna; O'Brien Press, 1992. **Awarded:** Bisto (Book of the Year) 1992.

Under the Hawthorn Tree by Marita Conlon-McKenna, illustrated by Donald Teskey; Holiday House, 1990; O'Brien Press, 1990. **Awarded:** International Reading Assn. (Older) 1991; Reading Association of Ireland 1991.

Wildflower Girl by Marita Conlon-McKenna; O'Brien Press, 1991. **Awarded:** Bisto (Historical Fiction) 1992.

CONLY, ROBERT LESLIE
see O'BRIEN, ROBERT C.

CONNOLLY, PETER
Legend of Odysseus by Peter Connolly, illustrated with maps; Oxford, 1986. **Awarded:** Times Educational Supplement (senior) 1986.

CONOLY, WALLI
Luke and the Van Zandt County War by Judith M. Alter, illustrated by Walli Conoly; Texas Christian University, 1984. **Awarded:** Texas Institute of Letters 1985.

CONOVER, CHRIS
Six Little Ducks written and illustrated by Chris Conover; Crowell, 1976. **Awarded:** Boston Globe Horn Book (illustration honor) 1976.

Somebody Else's Child by Roberta Silman, illustrated by Chris Conover; Warne, 1976. **Awarded:** Child Study 1976.

CONRAD, ARTHUR
Windfall Fiddle by Carl L. Carmer, illustrated by Arthur Conrad; Knopf, 1950. **Awarded:** Spring Book Festival (8-12) 1950.

CONRAD, PAM
My Daniel by Pam Conrad, not illustrated; Harper & Row, 1989. **Awarded:** Western Writers of America 1990.

Prairie Songs by Pam Conrad, illustrated by Darryl S. Zudeck; Harper & Row, 1985. **Awarded:** Boston Globe Horn Book (fiction honor) 1986; Golden Kite (fiction honor) 1985; International Reading Assn. 1986; Judy Lopez 1986; Society of Midland Authors 1986; Western Heritage 1986; Western Writers 1986.

Prairie Visions: The Life and Times of Solomon Butcher by Pam Conrad, illustrated by with photos; HarperCollins, 1991. **Awarded:** Orbis Pictus (Honor) 1992.

Stonewords by Pam Conrad, not illustrated; HarperCollins, 1990. **Awarded:** Boston Globe (Fiction Honor) 1990; Parents' Choice (Story Book) 1990; Edgar Allan Poe (Juvenile) 1991.

The Tub People by Pam Conrad, illustrated by Richard Egielski; Harper & Row, 1989. **Awarded:** Little Archer 1990; Parents' Choice (Picture Book) 1989.

CONROY, SHANE
Me and Jeshua by Eleanor Spence, illustrated by Shane Conroy; Dove Communications, 1985, c1984. **Awarded:** Children's Book Council of Australia (book of the year commended) 1985; Australian Christian Book of the Year Children's Award 1985.

CONSTABLE, EVHY
This Is a Crocodile written and illustrated by Evhy Constable; Bradbury, 1986. **Awarded:** New Jersey Institute of Technology 1987.

CONSTANTINI, FLAVIO
Timothy's Horse by Vladimir Mayakovsky, adapted by Guy Daniels, illustrated by Flavio Constantini; Pantheon, 1970. **Awarded:** New York Times Best Illustrated 1970.

CONTA, MARCIA MAHER
Feelings Between Brothers and Sisters by Marcia Maher Conta and Maureen Reardon, photographs by Jules M. Rosenthal; Advanced Learning Concepts, 1974. **Awarded:** Council for Wisconsin Writers (picture book) 1975.

COOK, BERYL
Seven Years and a Day by Colette O'Hare, illustrated by Beryl Cook; Collins, 1980. **Awarded:** Greenaway (commended) 1980.

COOK, D.C.
Jesus, the Friend of Children edited by D. C. Cook, illustrated by Frances Hook and Richard Hook; David C. Cook, 1977. **Awarded:** Gold Medallion 1978.

COOK, FRED
City Cop by Fred Cook, not illustrated; Doubleday, 1979. **Awarded:** New Jersey Institute of Technology 1980.

The Ku Klux Klan: America's Recurring Nightmare by Fred J. Cook, illustrated; Messner, 1980. **Awarded:** New Jersey Institute of Technology 1981.

COOK, LYN
Awarded: Vicky Metcalf 1978.

COOK, SCOTT
Nettie Jo's Friends by Patricia McKissack, illustrated by Scott Cook; Knopf, 1989. **Awarded:** Parents' Choice (Story Book) 1989.

COOKE, DONALD E.
For Conspicuous Gallantry: Winners of the Medal of Honor by Donald E. Cooke, illustrated by Jack Woodson; Hammond, 1966. **Awarded:** Boys Club (certificate) 1966-67.

COOKE, TOM
A Sister for Sam by Evelyn Mason, illustrated by Tom Cooke; Children's Press, 1983. **Awarded:** North Dakota Children's Choice (younger) 1984.

COOLIDGE, OLIVIA ENSOR
Come by Here by Olivia Coolidge, illustrated by Milton Johnson; Houghton, 1970. **Awarded:** Boston Globe Horn Book (text honor) 1971.

Egyptian Adventures by Olivia E. Coolidge, illustrated by Joseph Low; Houghton, 1954. **Awarded:** Spring Book Festival (older honor) 1954.

The King of Men by Olivia Coolidge, illustrated by Ellen Raskin; Houghton, 1966. **Awarded:** Spring Book Festival (older honor) 1966.

Men of Athens by Olivia Coolidge, illustrated by Milton Johnson; Houghton, 1962. **Awarded:** Newbery (honor) 1963.

COOMBS, CHARLES
Awarded: Southern California Council (significant contribution to the field of informational books for children and young people) 1968.

COOMBS, PATRICIA
Mouse Cafe written and illustrated by Patricia Coombs; Lothrop, 1972. **Awarded:** New York Times Best Illustrated 1972.

COON, SUSAN
Richard's Castle by Susan Coon, not illustrated; Blackie, 1992. **Awarded:** Kathleen Fidler 1992.

COONEY, BARBARA
Awarded: Chandler Reward of Merit 1964; Keene State College Festival 1989; Kerlan 1992; McCord Children's Literature Citation 1990; University of Southern Mississippi 1975.

Chanticleer and the Fox written and illustrated by Barbara Cooney; Crowell, 1958. **Awarded:** Caldecott 1959.

Green Wagons by Oskar Seidlin and Senta Rypins, illustrated by Barbara Cooney; Houghton, 1943. **Awarded:** Spring Book Festival (middle honor) 1943.

Hattie and the Wild Waves written and illustrated by Barbara Cooney; Viking, 1990. **Awarded:** Lupine Award 1991.

Island Boy written and illustrated by Barbara Cooney; Viking, 1988. **Awarded:** Boston Globe (Picture Book honor) 1989.

Kildee House by Rutherford Montgomery, illustrated by Barbara Cooney; Doubleday, 1949. **Awarded:** Newbery (honor) 1950.

Miss Rumphius written and illustrated by Barbara Cooney; Viking, 1982; Viking Puffin, 1985. **Awarded:** American Book Award (children's picturebook hardback) 1983; Redbook 1985.

Ox-cart Man by Donald Hall, illustrated by Barbara Cooney; Viking, 1979. **Awarded:** Caldecott 1980; New York Times Best Illustrated 1979; New York Times Notable Books 1979.

Squawk to the Moon, Little Goose by Edna Mitchell Preston, illustrated by Barbara Cooney; Viking, 1974. **Awarded:** New York Times Notable Books 1974.

Too Many Pets by Mary M. Aldrich, illustrated by Barbara Cooney; Macmillan, 1952. **Awarded:** Spring Book Festival (picture book honor) 1952.

When the Sky Is Like Lace by Elinor Lander Horwitz, illustrated by Barbara Cooney; Harper, 1975. **Awarded:** New York Times Notable Books 1975.

COONEY, CAROLINE B.
Safe as the Grave by Caroline B. Cooney, illustrated by Gail Owens; Coward, 1979. **Awarded:** North Carolina AAUW 1980.

COONEY, NANCY EVANS
Donald Says Thumb Down by Nancy Evans Cooney, illustrated by Maxie Chambliss; Putnam, 1987. **Awarded:** New Jersey Institute of Technology 1988.

COOPER, ELIZABETH K.
Science in Your Own Backyard written and illustrated by Elizabeth K. Cooper; Harcourt, 1958. **Awarded:** Edison Mass Media (science book) 1959.

COOPER, FLOYD
Laura Charlotte by Katherine Galbraith, illustrated by Floyd Cooper; Philomel, 1990. **Awarded:** Parents' Choice (Story Book) 1990.

COOPER, JAMES FENIMORE
The Last of the Mohicans by James Fenimore Cooper, illustrated by Christopher Bradbury; Felix Gluck, 1973. **Awarded:** Bologna (graphics for youth) 1974.

COOPER, JAMIE LEE
The Castaways by Jamie Lee Cooper, not illustrated; Bobbs-Merrill, 1970. **Awarded:** Indiana Authors Day (young adult) 1971.

COOPER, SUSAN MARY
The Dark Is Rising by Susan Cooper, illustrated by Alan Cober; Atheneum, 1973; Chatto, 1973. **Awarded:** Boston Globe Horn Book (text) 1973; Carnegie (commended) 1973; Newbery (honor) 1974.

The Grey King by Susan Cooper, illustrated by Michael Heslop; Chatto & Windus, 1975; Atheneum, 1975. **Awarded:** Carnegie (commended) 1975; Newbery 1976; Tir Na n-Og 1976.

Seaward by Susan Cooper, not illustrated; Atheneum, 1983. **Awarded:** Janusz Korczak (for children) 1984; Universe (runnerup) 1984.

The Silver Cow retold by Susan Cooper, illustrated by Warwick Hutton; Atheneum, 1983. **Awarded:** New York Times

Notable Books 1983; Parents' Choice (illustration) 1983; Parents' Choice (literature) 1983.

Silver on the Tree by Susan Cooper, not illustrated; Atheneum, 1977. **Awarded:** Tir Na n-Og 1978.

COPLEY, HEATHER
London's River: The Story of a City by Eric S. De Mare, illustrated by Heather Copley and Christopher Chamberlain; Bodley Head, 1964. **Awarded:** Carnegie (commended) 1964.

COPPING, LAURIE
Awarded: Nan Chauncy 1993.

CORBETT, SCOTT
Awarded: Golden Archer 1978.

Cutlass Island by Scott Corbett, illustrated by Leonard Shortall; Atlantic-Little, 1962. **Awarded:** Edgar Allan Poe 1963.

Here Lies the Body by Scott Corbett, illustrated by Geff Gerlach; Little Brown, 1974. **Awarded:** Edgar Allan Poe (runnerup) 1975.

The Home Run Trick by Scott Corbett, illustrated by Paul Galdone; Atlantic-Little, 1973. **Awarded:** Golden Archer 1978; Mark Twain 1976.

The Mystery Man by Scott Corbett, illustrated by Nathan Goldstein; Little Brown, 1970. **Awarded:** Edgar Allan Poe (runnerup) 1971.

CORBETT, WILLIAM J.
The Song of Pentecost by William J. Corbett, illustrated by Martin Unsell; Methuen, 1982. **Awarded:** Whitbread 1982.

CORBIN, WILLIAM
Golden Mare by William Corbin, illustrated by Pers Crowell; Coward, 1955. **Awarded:** Young Readers Choice 1958.

High Road Home by William Corbin, not illustrated; Coward, 1954. **Awarded:** Boys Club 1955; Child Study 1954.

Smoke by William Corbin, not illustrated; Coward, 1967. **Awarded:** Young Readers Choice 1970.

CORCORAN, BARBARA
Sasha, My Friend by Barbara Corcoran, illustrated by Richard L. Shell; Atheneum, 1969. **Awarded:** William Allen White 1972.

CORENTIN, PHILIPPE
Story Number 3 by Eugene Ionesco, illustrated by Philippe Corentin; Harlin Quist, 1971. **Awarded:** Children's Book Showcase 1972.

CORMACK, MARIBELLE
Land for My Sons: A Frontier Tale of the American Revolution by Maribelle Cormack and William P. Alexander, illustrated by Lyle Justis; Appleton Century, 1939. **Awarded:** Spring Book Festival (older honor) 1939.

Road to Down Under by Maribelle Cormack, illustrated by Edward Shenton; Appleton Century, 1944. **Awarded:** Spring Book Festival (older honor) 1944.

Wind of the Vikings by Maribelle Cormack, illustrated by Robert Lawson; Appleton Century Crofts, 1937. **Awarded:** Spring Book Festival (older honor) 1937.

CORMIER, ROBERT
Awarded: ALAN 1982; Margaret A. Edwards 1991.

After the First Death by Robert Cormier, not illustrated; Pantheon, 1979. **Awarded:** New York Times Notable Books 1979.

Beyond the Chocolate War by Robert Cormier, not illustrated; Knopf, 1985. **Awarded:** New York Times Notable 1985.

The Chocolate War by Robert Cormier, illustrated by Robert Vickery; Pantheon, 1974; Dell, 1975. **Awarded:** Lewis Carroll Shelf 1979; Media & Methods (paperback) 1976; New York Times Notable Books 1974.

I Am the Cheese by Robert Cormier, illustrated by Robert Vickery; Pantheon, 1977. **Awarded:** Woodward Park School 1978.

CORNWALL, IAN WOLFRAM
The Making of Man by Ian Wolfram Cornwall, illustrated by M. Maitland Howard; Phoenix House, 1960. **Awarded:** Carnegie 1960.

CORRIN, RUTH
Secrets by Ruth Corrin, not illustrated; Oxford University Press, 1991. **Awarded:** AIM Children's Book Awards (Story Book 2nd Prize) 1991.

COSGROVE, JOHN O'HARA
Carry on Mr. Bowditch by Jean Lee Latham, illustrated by J. O. Cosgrove; Houghton, 1955. **Awarded:** International Board on Books for Young People 1956; Newbery 1956.

COTE, PHYLLIS
Mistress of the White House by Helen L. Morgan, illustrated by Phyllis Cote; Westminster, 1946. **Awarded:** Spring Book Festival (older honor) 1946.

COTHREN, MARION B.
Pictures of France by Her Children (text in English and French) selected by Marion B. Cothren, illustrated with photographs of paintings; Oxford, 1950. **Awarded:** Spring Book Festival (picture book honor) 1950.

COTTRELL, LEONARD
Reading the Past: The Story of Deciphering Ancient Languages by Leonard Cottrell, illustrated with photographs and line drawings; Crowell-Collier, 1971. **Awarded:** New York Academy of Sciences (older) 1973.

COUNHAYE, GUY
Viktor, das Fliegende Nilpferd by Guy Counhaye, illustrated by Marie-Jose Sacre; Everest, 1982. **Awarded:** Owl Prize 1982.

COUPER, HEATHER
Galaxies and Quasars by Heather Couper and Nigel Henbest, illustrated; Watts, 1986. **Awarded:** Times Educational Supplement (Senior) 1987.

Space Frontiers by Heather Couper and Nigel Henbest, illustrated with photographs; Viking, 1978. **Awarded:** New York Academy of Sciences (special award for series in engineering and technology) 1979.

COURLANDER, HAROLD
Cow-tail Switch and Other West African Stories by Harold Courlander and George Herzog, illustrated by Madye Lee Chastain; Holt, 1947. **Awarded:** Newbery (honor) 1948.

COUSINS, JANE
Make It Happy: What Sex Is All About by Jane Cousins, illustrated by Susan Hunter; Virago, 1978. **Awarded:** Times Educational Supplement (senior) 1979.

COUSINS, LUCY
Maisy Goes to Bed written and illustrated by Lucy Cousins; Little Brown, 1990. **Awarded:** Please Touch 1991.

Portly's Hat written and illustrated by Lucy Cousins; Macmillan, 1988; Dutton, 1988. **Awarded:** Macmillan (2nd prize) 1987.

What Can Rabbit Hear? written and illustrated by Lucy Cousins; Tambourine Books, 1991. **Awarded:** New York Times Best Illustrated 1991.

COUTANT, HELEN
First Snow by Helen Coutant, illustrated by Vo-Dinh; Knopf, 1974. **Awarded:** Christopher (Ages 4-8) 1975.

COVENTRY, MARTHA
Rose Blanche by Roberto Innocenti and Christophe Gallaz, English translation by Martha Coventry and Richard Graglia, illustrated by Roberto Innocenti; Creative Education, 1986. **Awarded:** Batchelder 1986.

COVILLE, BRUCE
The Monster's Ring by Bruce Coville, illustrated by Katherine Coville; Pantheon, 1982. **Awarded:** South Carolina Children 1985.

My Teacher Is an Alien by Bruce Coville, illustrated by Mike Wimmer; Pocket Books, 1989. **Awarded:** Nevada Young Reader Award (Intermediate) 1990-91.

COVILLE, KATHERINE
The Monster's Ring by Bruce Coville, illustrated by Katherine Coville; Pantheon, 1982. **Awarded:** South Carolina Children 1985.

COVINGTON, DENNIS
Lizard by Dennis Covington, not illustrated; Delacorte, 1991. **Awarded:** Delacorte Press Prize 1990.

COWCHER, HELEN
Tigress written and illustrated by Helen Cowcher; Farrar, Straus, Giroux, 1991. **Awarded:** Parents' Choice (Picture Book) 1991.

COWING, DEBORAH
Our Wild Wetlands by Sheila Cowing, illustrated by Deborah Cowing; Messner, 1980. **Awarded:** New Jersey Institute of Technology 1981.

COWING, SHEILA
Our Wild Wetlands by Sheila Cowing, illustrated by Deborah Cowing; Messner, 1980. **Awarded:** New Jersey Institute of Technology 1981.

COWLEY, JOY
Bow Down Shadrach by Joy Cowley, not illustrated; Hodder & Stoughton, 1991. **Awarded:** AIM Children's Book Award (Story Book) 1992.

The Duck in the Gun by Joy Cowley, illustrated by Robyn Belton; Shortland Educational, 1984. **Awarded:** Russell Clark 1985.

The Silent One by Joy Cowley, illustrated by Sherryl Jordan; Whitcoulls, 1981. **Awarded:** AIM (Story Book) 1982.

COX, CHARLES
Funny Bone Dramatics by Bernice Wells Carlson, illustrated by Charles Cox; Abingdon, 1974. **Awarded:** New Jersey Institute of Technology 1975.

COX, DAVID
Ayu and the Perfect Moon written and illustrated by David Cox; Bodley Head, 1984. **Awarded:** Children's Book Council of Australia (picture book of the year commended) 1985.

Bossyboots written and illustrated by David Cox; Crown, 1987, c1985. **Awarded:** Parents' Choice (Picture Book) 1987.

Tin Lizzie and Little Nell written and illustrated by David Cox; Aurora Press, 1982; Bodley Head, 1982. **Awarded:** Children's Book Council of Australia (picture book of the year commended) 1983.

COX, LEE SHERIDAN
Andy and Willie by Lee Sheridan Cox, not illustrated; Scribner, 1967. **Awarded:** Indiana Authors Day (children) 1968.

COX, MIRIAM S.
Awarded: Southern California Council (Dorothy C. McKenzie Award) 1981.

COX, SARAH
Building Worker by Sarah Cox, illustrated by Robert Golden; Kestrel, 1976. **Awarded:** Other Award 1977.

Hospital Worker by Sarah Cox, illustrated by Robert Golden; Kestrel, 1976. **Awarded:** Other Award 1977.

Railway Worker by Sarah Cox, illustrated by Robert Golden; Kestrel, 1976. **Awarded:** Other Award 1977.

Textile Worker by Sarah Cox, illustrated by Robert Golden; Kestrel, 1976. **Awarded:** Other Award 1977.

COX, VIRGINIA
ABC: The Story of the Alphabet by Virginia Cox; Wayne State University, (manuscript). **Awarded:** Council on Interracial Books for Children (ages 3-6) 1969.

COY, HAROLD
The Americans by Harold Coy, illustrated by William Moyers; Little, 1958. **Awarded:** Edison Mass Media (America's past) 1959.

COYNIK, DAVID
Film: Real to Reel by David Coynik, illustrated with movie stills and photographs; rev. ed.; McDougal-Littell, 1972. **Awarded:** Media & Methods (textbook) 1976.

CRADDOCK, SALLY
Ottoline at the British Museum by Sally Craddock, illustrated by Corinne Pearlman; Macdonald, 1987; Simon & Schuster, 1990. **Awarded:** Mother Goose (runner-up) 1988.

CRADDOCK, SONIA
Secret of the Cards by Sonia Craddock, not illustrated; Scholastic Canada, 1990. **Awarded:** Surrey School 1991-92.

CRAFT, RUTH
Carrie Hepple's Garden by Ruth Craft, illustrated by Irene Haas; McElderry, 1979. **Awarded:** Owl Prize 1980.

The Winter Bear by Ruth Craft, illustrated by Erik Blegvad; Atheneum, 1975. **Awarded:** Children's Book Showcase 1976.

CRAGO, HUGH
Creation to Civilization by Hugh Crago in *Signal* (May 1983). **Awarded:** Children's Literature Assn. Excellence in Criticism (runnerup) 1984.

CRAIG, ELEANOR
If We Could Hear the Grass Grow by Eleanor Craig, illustrated; Simon & Schuster, 1983. **Awarded:** Korczak (about children) 1984.

CRAIG, HELEN
Angelina Ballerina by Katharine Holabird, illustrated by Helen Craig; Crown, 1983. **Awarded:** Kentucky Bluegrass 1985.

CRAIG, JOHN
Awarded: Vicky Metcalf 1980.

CRAIG, M. JEAN
Not Very Much of a House by M. Jean Craig, illustrated by Don Almquist; Norton, 1967. **Awarded:** New Jersey Institute of Technology 1967.

CRAIGIE, DOROTHY
The Little Horse Bus by Graham Greene, illustrated by Dorothy Craigie; Lothrop Lee & Shepard, 1954. **Awarded:** Boys Club 1955.

CRAMPTON, PATRICIA
Awarded: Eleanor Farjeon 1991; FIT Translation 1984.

Det Femte Hornet (The Fifth Corner) by Kristina Ehrenstrale, translated by Patricia Crampton; Methuen, 1984. **Awarded:** International Board on Books for Young People (translator/Great Britain) 1986.

No Hero for the Kaiser by Rudolf Frank, translated by Patricia Crampton, illustrated by Klaus Steffans; Lothrop Lee & Shepard, 1986. **Awarded:** Batchelder 1987; Parents Choice (literature) 1986.

Ronia, the Robber's Daughter by Astrid Lindgren, translated by Patricia Crampton, not illustrated; Viking, 1983. **Awarded:** Batchelder 1984; Parents' Choice (literature) 1983.

The Sea Lord by Alet Schouten, translated by Patricia Crampton, illustrated by Rien Poortvliet; Methuen, 1977. **Awarded:** International Board on Books for Young People (translation/Great Britain) 1980.

CRANE, JOHN
America's First Army by Burke Davis, illustrated by Richard Stinely, photographs by John Crane; Rinehart/Colonial Williamsburg, 1962. **Awarded:** Boys Club 1963.

CRANE, LOUISE
The Magic Spear and Other Stories of China's Famous Heroes by Louise Crane, illustrated by Ching Chi Yee and Yenchi Tiao T'u, Random House, 1938. **Awarded:** Spring Book Festival (younger honor) 1938.

CRANE, WALTER
Mr. Michael Mouse Unfolds His Tale written and illustrated by Walter Crane; Merrimack, 1975. **Awarded:** New York Times Best Illustrated 1975.

CRAVEN, CAROLYN
What the Mailman Brought by Carolyn Craven, illustrated by Tomie de Paola; Putnam, 1987. **Awarded:** Golden Kite (Picture- Illustration honor) 1987.

CRAVEN, THOMAS
The Rainbow Book of Art by Thomas Craven, illustrated with photographs; World, 1956. **Awarded:** Spring Book Festival (older honor) 1956.

CRAWFORD, BILL
Mickey, the Horse That Volunteered by Carl Glick, illustrated by Bill Crawford; Whittlesey House, 1945. **Awarded:** Spring Book Festival (middle honor) 1945.

Valery by Elizabeth Mallett Conger, illustrated by Bill Crawford; Holt, 1944. **Awarded:** Spring Book Festival (younger honor) 1945.

CRAWFORD, DEBORAH
Four Women in a Violent Time by Deborah Crawford, not illustrated; Crown, 1970. **Awarded:** Lewis Carroll Shelf 1973.

CRAWFORD, ELIZABETH D.
Dominique and the Dragon by Jurgen Tamchina, translated by Elizabeth D. Crawford, illustrated by Heidrun Petrides; Harcourt, 1968. **Awarded:** Spring Book Festival (picture book honor) 1969.

Little Red Cap by Jacob Grimm and Wilhelm Grimm, translated by Elizabeth D. Crawford, illustrated by Lisbeth Zwerger;

Morrow, 1983. **Awarded:** New York Times Best Illustrated 1983.

CRAWFORD, LURA E.
Awarded: Grolier 1967.

CRAWFORD, PHYLLIS
Hello, the Boat! by Phyllis Crawford, illustrated by Edward Laning; Holt, 1938. **Awarded:** Julia Ellsworth Ford 1938; Newbery (honor) 1939.

CRAYDER, DOROTHY
She, the Adventuress by Dorothy Crayder, illustrated by Velma Ilsley; Atheneum, 1973. **Awarded:** Spring Book Festival (middle honor) 1973.

CREAGH, CARSON
Animal Tracks by Carson Creagh and Kathie Atkinson, illustrated by Richard Hassall; Methuen Australia, 1986. **Awarded:** Whitley Awards 1988.

CREDLE, ELLIS
Down, Down the Mountain written and illustrated by Ellis Credle; Nelson, 1961, c1934. **Awarded:** Lewis Carroll Shelf 1971.

CREECH, KAREN
Awarded: Lucile M. Pannell 1993.

CRESSWELL, HELEN
Bongleweed by Helen Cresswell, illustrated by Ann Strugnell; Faber, 1973. **Awarded:** Carnegie (commended) 1973.

The Night Watchmen by Helen Cresswell, illustrated by Gareth Floyd; Faber, 1969; Macmillan, 1969. **Awarded:** Carnegie (honour) 1969; Phoenix Award 1989.

The Piemakers by Helen Cresswell, illustrated by V. H. Drummond; Faber, 1967. **Awarded:** Carnegie (commended) 1967.

The Secret World of Polly Flint by Helen Cresswell, illustrated by Shirley Felts; Faber, 1982. **Awarded:** Whitbread (runnerup) 1982.

Up the Pier by Helen Cresswell, illustrated by Gareth Floyd; Faber, 1971. **Awarded:** Carnegie (highly commended) 1971.

CREW, FLEMING
Splasher by Fleming Crew and Alice Crew Gall, illustrated by Else Bostelmann; Oxford, 1945. **Awarded:** Ohioana (honorable mention) 1946.

CREW, GARY
Strange Objects by Gary Crew, not illustrated; Heinemann, 1990. **Awarded:** Children's Book Council of Australia (Book of the Year Older) 1991; Diabetes Australia Alan Marshall 1991; New South Wales State Literary Awards (Children's) 1991.

CREW, LINDA
Children of the River by Linda Crew, not illustrated; Delacorte, 1989. **Awarded:** Delacorte Press Prize (Honorable Mention) 1987; Golden Kite (Fiction honor) 1989; International Reading Assn. (Older) 1990.

CREWS, DONALD
Eclipse: Darkness in Daytime by Franklyn M. Branley, illustrated by Donald Crews; Crowell, 1973. **Awarded:** Children's Book Showcase 1974.

Flying written and illustrated by Donald Crews; Greenwillow, 1986. **Awarded:** New York Times Best Illustrated 1986.

Freight Train written and illustrated by Donald Crews; Greenwillow, 1978; Viking Puffin, 1985. **Awarded:** Art Books for Children 1979; Caldecott (honor) 1979; Redbook 1985.

Shortcut written and illustrated by Donald Crews; Greenwillow, 1992. **Awarded:** Parents Choice (Picture Book) 1992.

Truck written and illustrated by Donald Crews; Greenwillow, 1980. **Awarded:** Caldecott (honor) 1981.

We Read: A to Z written and illustrated by Donald Crews; Harper, 1967. **Awarded:** New Jersey Institute of Technology 1967.

CRICHLOW, ERNEST
Captain of the Planter: The Story of Robert Smalls by Dorothy Sterling, illustrated by Ernest Crichlow; Doubleday, 1958. **Awarded:** Nancy Bloch 1958.

Mary Jane by Dorothy Sterling, illustrated by Ernest Crichlow; Doubleday, 1959. **Awarded:** Nancy Bloch 1959; Woodward Park School 1960.

CRISP, FRANK
The Haunted Reef by Frank Crisp, illustrated by Richard M. Powers; Coward, 1952. **Awarded:** Spring Book Festival (older honor) 1952.

CRISP, STEVE
Slambash Wangs of a Compo Gormer by Robert Leeson, illustrated by Steve Crisp; Collins, 1987. **Awarded:** International Board on Books for Young People (Writing/Great Britain) 1990.

CRISP, WILLIAM G.
White Gold in the Cassiar by William G. Crisp, not illustrated; Dodd Mead, 1955. **Awarded:** Boy's Life - Dodd, Mead 1954.

CROCKETT, LUCY HERNDON
That Mario written and illustrated by Lucy H. Crockett; Holt, 1940. **Awarded:** Spring Book Festival (younger) 1940.

CROFFORD, EMILY
A Matter of Pride by Emily Crofford, illustrated by Jim LaMarche; Carolrhoda Books, 1981. **Awarded:** Friends of American Writers ($350) 1982.

CROLL, CAROLYN
Awarded: Drexel Citation 1990.

CROSS, GILLIAN
Awarded: British Book Awards (Author runnerup) 1992.

Chartbreak by Gillian Cross, not illustrated; Oxford, 1986. **Awarded:** Carnegie (commended) 1986.

The Dark Behind the Curtains by Gillian Cross, illustrated by David Parkins; Oxford, 1982. **Awarded:** Carnegie (highly commended) 1982; Guardian (runnerup) 1983.

The Great Elephant Chase by Gillian Cross, not illustrated; Oxford University Press, 1991. **Awarded:** Carnegie (Commended) 1992; Smarties (Ages 9-11) 1992; Smarties (Grand Prix) 1992; Whitbread 1992.

A Map of Nowhere by Gillian Cross, not illustrated; Oxford University Press, 1988. **Awarded:** Carnegie (Highly Commended) 1988.

On the Edge by Gillian Cross, not illustrated; Holiday House, 1985; Oxford, 1984. **Awarded:** Edgar Allan Poe (runnerup) 1986; Whitbread (runnerup) 1984.

Wolf by Gillian Cross, not illustrated; Oxford University Press, 1990; Holiday House, 1991. **Awarded:** Carnegie 1990; Parents' Choice (Story Book) 1991.

CROSS, PETER
Trouble for Trumpets by Peter Dallas-Smith, illustrated by Peter Cross; Ernest Benn, 1982; Random House, 1984. **Awarded:**

Biennale Illustrations Bratislava (plaque) 1983; Mother Goose (runnerup) 1983.

CROSSLEY-HOLLAND, KEVIN
Storm by Kevin Crossley-Holland, illustrated by Alan Marks; Heinemann, 1985. **Awarded:** Carnegie 1985.

The Wildman by Kevin Crossley-Holland, illustrated by Charles Keeping; Deutsch, 1976. **Awarded:** W. H. Smith (£100) 1977.

CROSWELL, VOLNEY
How to Hide a Hippopotamus written and illustrated by Volney Croswell; Dodd, 1958. **Awarded:** New York Times Best Illustrated 1958.

CROW, JEANNE
The Media Works by Jeanne Crow and Joan Valdes; Pflaum/Standard, 1973. **Awarded:** Media & Methods (textbook) 1975.

CROWELL, JAMES
Ice River by Phyllis Green, illustrated by James Crowell; Addison-Wesley, 1975. **Awarded:** Council of Wisconsin Writers (picture book) 1976.

CROWELL, PERS
Cherokee Bill: Oklahoma Pacer by Jean Bailey, illustrated by Pers Crowell; Abingdon-Cokesbury, 1952. **Awarded:** William Allen White 1955.

Golden Mare by William Corbin, illustrated by Pers Crowell; Coward, 1955. **Awarded:** Young Readers' Choice 1958.

Lost Horse by Glenn Balch, illustrated by Pers Crowell; Grosset & Dunlap, 1950. **Awarded:** Boys Club 1951.

CROWTHER, ROBERT
The Most Amazing Hide and Seek Alphabet Book written and illustrated by Robert Crowther; Kestrel, 1977. **Awarded:** Mother Goose (runnerup) 1979.

CRUTCHER, CHRIS
Athletic Shorts: Six Short Stories by Chris Crutcher, not illustrated; Greenwillow, 1991. **Awarded:** Young Adult Novel of the Year / Michigan Library Assn. 1991.

CRUZ, RAY
Alexander and the Terrible, Horrible, No Good, Very Bad Day by Judith Viorst, illustrated by Ray Cruz; Atheneum, 1972. **Awarded:** Georgia Children's Picture Storybook 1977; George G. Stone 1988.

CSEREPY, MARY
Last Voyage of the Unicorn by Delbert Young, illustrated by Mary Cserepy; Clarke, Irwin, 1969. **Awarded:** Beaver 1967.

CUBIAS, DAISY
Journey of the Sparrows by Fran Leeper Buss, with the assistance of Daisy Cubias, not illustrated; Lodestar, 1991. **Awarded:** Hungry Mind (Young Adult/Fiction) 1992.

CUFFARI, RICHARD
Corvus the Cow by Franklin Russell, illustrated by Richard Cuffari; Four Winds, 1972. **Awarded:** New Jersey Institute of Technology 1972.

Escape from the Evil Prophecy by Lee Kingman, illustrated by Richard Cuffari; Houghton, 1973. **Awarded:** Children's Book Showcase 1974.

Lotor the Raccoon by Franklin Russell, illustrated by Richard Cuffari; Four Winds, 1972. **Awarded:** New Jersey Institute of Technology 1972.

Old Ben by Jesse Stuart, illustrated by Richard Cuffari; McGraw Hill, 1970. **Awarded:** Lewis Carroll Shelf 1970.

The Perilous Gard by Elizabeth M. Pope, illustrated by Richard Cuffari; Houghton Mifflin, 1974. **Awarded:** Children's Book Showcase 1975; Newbery (honor) 1975.

So, Nothing Is Forever by Adrienne Jones, illustrated by Richard Cuffari; Houghton Mifflin, 1974. **Awarded:** Southern California Council (distinguished fiction) 1975.

This Star Shall Abide by Sylvia L. Engdahl, illustrated by Richard Cuffari; Atheneum, 1972. **Awarded:** Christopher (young adult) 1973.

Who Will Clean the Air? by Wallace Orlowsky and Thomas B. Perera, illustrated by Richard Cuffari; Coward, 1971. **Awarded:** New Jersey Institute of Technology 1972.

CULFOGIENIS, ANGIO
We Are the Government by Mary Elting and Margaret Gossett, illustrated by Angio Culfogienis; Doubleday, 1967. **Awarded:** New Jersey Institute of Technology 1970.

CULIN, CHARLOTTE
Cages of Glass, Flowers of Time by Charlotte Culin, not illustrated; Bradbury, 1979. **Awarded:** Emphasis on Reading (Grades 10-12) 1983-84.

CUMBAA, STEPHEN
The Bones Book and Skeleton by Stephen Cumbaa, illustrated by Kim LaFave; Workman, 1991. **Awarded:** British Book Awards (Illustrated runnerup) 1992.

CUMBERLEGE, VERA
Shipwreck by Vera Cumberlege, illustrated by Charles Mikolaycak; Follett, 1974. **Awarded:** Children's Book Showcase 1975.

CUMMING, ROBERT
Just Imagine - Ideas in Painting by Robert Cumming, illustrated with photographs; Kestrel, 1982; Scribner, 1982. **Awarded:** Times Educational Supplement (senior) 1983.

CUMMINGS, ALISON
Johnny Wants to Be a Policeman by Wilbur J. Granberg, illustrated by Alison Cummings; Aladdin, 1951. **Awarded:** Boys Club 1952.

CUMMINGS, BETTY SUE
Hew Against the Grain by Betty Sue Cummings, not illustrated; Atheneum, 1977. **Awarded:** National Book Award (finalist) 1978.

CUMMINGS, E. E.
Little Tree by E. E. cummings, illustrated by Deborah Kogan Ray; Crown, 1987. **Awarded:** Carolyn W. Field 1988.

CUMMINGS, PAT
C.L.O.U.D.S. by Pat Cummings, illustrated; Lothrop, Lee & Shepard, 1986. **Awarded:** Coretta Scott King (illustration honorable mention) 1987.

My Mama Needs Me by Mildred Pitts Walter, illustrated by Pat Cummings; Lothrop, Lee & Shepard, 1983. **Awarded:** Coretta Scott King (illustrator) 1984.

Storm in the Night by Mary Stolz, illustrated by Pat Cummings; Harper & Row, 1988. **Awarded:** Coretta Scott King (Illustration honor) 1989; Parents' Choice (Story Book) 1988.

Talking With Artists by Pat Cummings, illustrated; Bradbury Press, 1992. **Awarded:** Boston Globe Horn Book (Nonfiction) 1992; Orbis Pictus (honor) 1993.

CUMMINGS, WALTER THIES
The Girl in the White Hat written and illustrated by W. T. Cummings; McGraw, 1959. **Awarded:** New York Times Best Illustrated 1959.

CUNETTE, LOUIS
ABC Halloween Witch by Ida De Lage, illustrated by Lou Cunette; Garrard, 1977. **Awarded:** New Jersey Institute of Technology 1978.

April Fool! by Leland B. Jacobs, illustrated by Lou Cunette; Garrard, 1973. **Awarded:** New Jersey Institute of Technology 1973.

Smoke Eater by Howard M. Brier, illustrated by Louis Cunette; Random House, 1941. **Awarded:** Spring Book Festival (older honor) 1941.

CUNNINGHAM, DAVID
The Mice Came in Early This Year by Eleanor J. Lapp, illustrated by David Cunningham; Whitman, 1976. **Awarded:** Council of Wisconsin Writers (picture book runnerup) 1977.

CUNNINGHAM, JOHN T.
Colonial New Jersey by John T. Cunningham, illustrated with photographs; Nelson, 1971. **Awarded:** New Jersey Institute of Technology 1971.

CUNNINGHAM, JULIA
Awarded: Southern California Council (distinguished body of work) 1982.

Come to the Edge by Julia Cunningham, not illustrated; Pantheon, 1977. **Awarded:** Lewis Carroll Shelf 1978; Christopher (ages 12-up) 1978.

Dear Rat by Julia Cunningham, illustrated by Walter Lorraine; Houghton, 1961. **Awarded:** New York Times Best Illustrated 1961.

Dorp Dead by Julia Cunningham, illustrated by James Spanfeller; Pantheon, 1965. **Awarded:** Lewis Carroll Shelf 1972; Southern California Council (notable) 1966; Spring Book Festival (middle) 1965.

Flight of the Sparrow by Julia Cunningham, not illustrated; Pantheon, 1980. **Awarded:** Boston Globe Horn Book (fiction honor) 1981; Commonwealth Club of California 1980.

The Treasure Is the Rose by Julia Cunningham, illustrated by Judy Graese; Pantheon, 1973. **Awarded:** National Book Award (finalist) 1974; New York Times Notable Books 1973.

CUNNINGHAM, WALTER
Story of Karrawinga, the Emu by Leslie Rees, illustrated by Walter Cunningham; Sands, 1946. **Awarded:** Children's Book Council of Australia (book of the year) 1946.

CUPPLES, PAT
Hands On, Thumbs Up by Camilla Gryski, illustrated by Pat Cupples; Kids Can Press, 1990. **Awarded:** Information Book Award 1991.

CURRY, JANE LOUISE
Awarded: Southern California Council (significant contribution for a body of work) 1979.

The Bassumtyte Treasure by Jane L. Curry, not illustrated; Atheneum, 1978. **Awarded:** Edgar Allan Poe (runnerup) 1979.

The Daybreakers by Jane L. Curry, illustrated by Charles Robinson; Harcourt, 1970. **Awarded:** Southern California Council (notable) 1971; Spring Book Festival (middle honor) 1970.

The Lotus Cup by Jane Louise Curry, not illustrated; Atheneum, 1986. **Awarded:** Ohioana 1987.

Poor Tom's Ghost by Jane Louise Curry, illustrated by Janet Archer; Atheneum, 1977. **Awarded:** Ohioana 1978; Edgar Allan Poe (runnerup) 1978.

CURRY, JENNIFER
The Last Rabbit by Jennifer Curry, illustrated; Methuen, 1990. **Awarded:** Earthworm 1991.

CURRY, PEGGY SIMSON
A Shield of Clover by Peggy Simson Curry, not illustrated; McKay, 1970. **Awarded:** Western Writers (fiction) 1971.

CUSHMAN, ALICE B.
Awarded: Chandler Reward of Merit 1965.

CUTLER, KATHERINE
Junior Flower Shows: A Complete Guide to the Planning, Staging, and Judging of Children's Flower Shows by Katherine Cutler, not illustrated; Barrows, 1963. **Awarded:** New Jersey Institute of Technology (art) 1964.

CUTLER, MAY
Awarded: Claude Aubry Award 1987.

CUTTING, SUSAN
Steel Town Cats by Celia Lucas, illustrated by Susan Cutting; Tabb House, 1987. **Awarded:** Tir Na N'og 1988.

CUYLER, MARGERY
Fat Santa by Margery Cuyler, illustrated by Marsha Winborn; Henry Holt, 1987. **Awarded:** New Jersey Institute of Technology 1988.

CZERNECKI, STEFAN
The Time Before Dreams by Stefan Czernecki and Timothy Rhodes, illustrated by Stefan Czernecki; Hyperion, 1989. **Awarded:** Alcuin 1990.

D

DABCOVICH, LYDIA
Ducks Fly written and illustrated by Lydia Dabcovich; Dutton, 1990. **Awarded:** Parents' Choice (Picture Book) 1990.

The Night Ones by Patricia Grossman, illustrated by Lydia Dabcovich; Harcourt Brace Jovanovich, 1991. **Awarded:** Parents' Choice (Picture Book) 1991.

There Once Was a Woman Who Married a Man by Norma Farber, illustrated by Lydia Dabcovich; Addison, 1978. **Awarded:** New York Times Best Illustrated 1978.

William and Grandpa by Alice Schertle, illustrated by Lydia Dabcovich; Lothrop, Lee & Shepard, 1989. **Awarded:** Christopher (Ages 8-11) 1990; Parents' Choice (Picture Book) 1989.

D'ADAMO, ANTHONY
The Cabin at Medicine Springs by Lulita Crawford Pritchett, illustrated by Anthony D'Adamo; Watts, 1958. **Awarded:** Franklin Watts Juvenile Fiction 1958.

Dulcie's Whale by Julia Montgomery Street, illustrated by Anthony D'Adamo; Bobbs-Merrill, 1963. **Awarded:** North Carolina AAUW 1963.

DAHL, HANS NORMAN
My Name Is Pablo by Aimee Sommerfelt, illustrated by Hans Norman Dahl; Criterion, 1965. **Awarded:** Spring Book Festival (middle honor) 1966.

DAHL, ROALD
   Awarded: British Book Awards (Author) 1989.

The BFG by Roald Dahl, illustrated by Quentin Blake; Cape, 1982; Farrar, 1982. **Awarded:** Books I Love Best Yearly (Read Alone Primary) 1991; Books I Love Best Yearly (Read Aloud Primary-12) 1991; Children's Book Award (Federation) 1982; West Australian (Primary) 1985.

Boy: Tales of Childhood by Roald Dahl, illustrated with photographs; Farrar, Straus and Giroux, 1984. **Awarded:** Boston Globe Horn Book (nonfiction honor) 1985.

Charlie and the Chocolate Factory by Roald Dahl, illustrated by Joseph Schindelman; Knopf, 1964. **Awarded:** Books I Love Best Yearly (Read Aloud Primary-12) 1992; New England Round Table of Children's Librarians 1972; North Dakota Children's Choice (Older) 1985; Surrey School 1973; Young Teens 1991.

Charlie and the Great Glass Elevator by Roald Dahl, illustrated by Joseph Schindelman; Knopf, 1972. **Awarded:** Nene 1978; Surrey School 1975.

Danny: The Champion of the World by Roald Dahl, illustrated by Jill Bennett; Knopf, 1975. **Awarded:** California Young Reader Medal (intermediate) 1979; Surrey School 1978.

Esio Trot by Roald Dahl, illustrated by Quentin Blake; Cape, 1990; Viking, 1990. **Awarded:** Smarties (Ages 6-8) 1990.

George's Marvellous Medicine by Roald Dahl, illustrated by Quentin Blake; Cape, 1981. **Awarded:** West Australian (Primary) 1984.

The Giraffe and the Pelly and Me by Roald Dahl, illustrated by Quentin Blake; Cape, 1985. **Awarded:** Maschler (runnerup) 1985.

James and the Giant Peach by Roald Dahl, illustrated by Nancy Ekholm Burkert; Knopf, 1961; Bantam, 1978. **Awarded:** Massachusetts Children's (elementary) 1982.

Matilda by Roald Dahl, illustrated by Quentin Blake; Cape, 1988; Viking Kestrel, 1988. **Awarded:** Books I Love Best Yearly (Read Aloud Primary-12) 1990; Caudill Young Reader's Book Award 1991; Children's Book Award (Federation of...) 1988; Ethical Culture School 1988; Great Stone Face 1990; Indian Paintbrush 1991; Massachusetts Children's 1992; Nevada Young Reader (Intermediate) 1991-92; Nottinghamshire (Oak Tree) 1989; Utah Children's Choice 1991; Virginia Young Readers (Elementary) 1991; West Australian (Primary) 1989.

The Minpins by Roald Dahl, illustrated by Patrick Benson; Cape, 1991; Viking, 1991. **Awarded:** British Book Awards (Illustrated runnerup) 1991; Redbook 1991.

Sophiechen und der Riese (Original English *The BFG*) by Roald Dahl, translated by Adam Quidam; Rowohlt, 1984. **Awarded:** International Board on Books for Young People (translation/German Federal Republic) 1986.

SVK (original English *The BFG*) by Roald Dahl, translated by Tor Edvin Dahl; Gyldendal Norsk Forlag, 1984. **Awarded:** International Board on Books for Young People (translation/Norway) 1986.

The Witches by Roald Dahl, illustrated by Quentin Blake; Cape, 1983; Farrar, 1983. **Awarded:** New York Times Notable Books 1983; West Australian (overseas primary) 1986; Whitbread 1983.

DAHL, SHARON
King Leonard's Celebration by Christopher A. Lane, illustrated by Sharon Dahl; Victor Books, 1990. **Awarded:** Gold Medallion (Preschool) 1991.

DAHL, TOR EDVIN
SVK (original English *The BFG*) by Roald Dahl, translated by Tor Edvin Dahl; Gyldendal Norsk Forlag, 1984. **Awarded:** International Board on Books for Young People (translator/Norway) 1986

DALE, MITZI
On My Own by Mitzi Dale, not illustrated; Douglas & McIntyre, 1991. **Awarded:** Young Adult Canadian (Runnerup) 1992.

DALE, PENNY
Rosie's Babies by Martin Waddell, illustrated by Penny Dale; Walker, 1989. **Awarded:** Best Books for Babies 1990.

Wake Up, Mr. B! written and illustrated by Penny Dale; Walker Books, 1988. **Awarded:** Greenaway (Commended) 1988.

DALGLIESH, ALICE
The Bears on Hemlock Mountain by Alice Dalgliesh, illustrated by Helen Sewell; Scribner, 1952. **Awarded:** Newbery (honor) 1953.

The Courage of Sarah Noble by Alice Dalgliesh, illustrated by Leonard Weisgard; Scribner, 1954. **Awarded:** Lewis Carroll Shelf 1959; Newbery (honor) 1955; Spring Book Festival (middle honor) 1954.

The Silver Pencil by Alice Dalgliesh, illustrated by Katherine Milhous; Scribner, 1944. **Awarded:** Newbery (honor) 1945.

The Thanksgiving Story by Alice Dalgliesh, illustrated by Helen Sewell; Scribner, 1954. **Awarded:** Caldecott (honor) 1955.

The Young Aunts by Alice Dalgliesh, illustrated by Charlotte Becker; Scribner, 1939. **Awarded:** Spring Book Festival (younger honor) 1939.

DALLAS-SMITH, PETER
Trouble for Trumpets by Peter Dallas-Smith, illustrated by Peter Cross; Ernest Benn, 1982; Random House, 1984. **Awarded:** Biennale Illustrations Bratislava (plaque) 1983; Mother Goose (runnerup) 1983.

DALLINGER, JANE
Frogs and Toads by Jane Dallinger and Sylvia A. Johnson, photographs by Hiroshi Tanemura; Lerner, 1982. **Awarded:** New York Academy of Sciences (special award) 1983.

Grasshoppers by Jane Dallinger, photographs by Yuko Sato; Lerner, 1981. **Awarded:** New York Academy of Sciences (special award) 1983.

Spiders by Jane Dallinger, photographs by Satoshi Kuribayashi; Lerner, 1981. **Awarded:** New York Academy of Sciences (special award) 1983.

Swallowtail Butterflies by Jane Dallinger and Cynthia Overbeck, photographs by Yuko Sato; Lerner, 1982. **Awarded:** New York Academy of Sciences (special award) 1983.

DALRYMPLE, DE WAYNE
The Hunter I Might Have Been by George Mendoza, illustrated by De Wayne Dalrymple; Astor-Honor, 1968. **Awarded:** Lewis Carroll Shelf 1968.

DALTON, ANNE
Tournaments by Richard Barber, illustrated by Anne Dalton; Kestrel, 1978. **Awarded:** Times Educational Supplement (junior) 1978.

DALTON, ANNIE

The Afterdark Princess by Annie Dalton, illustrated by Kate Aldous; Methuen, 1990. **Awarded:** Nottinghamshire (Oak Tree) 1991.

The Real Tilly Beany by Annie Dalton, illustrated by Kate Aldous; Methuen, 1991. **Awarded:** Carnegie (Commended) 1991.

DALY, MAUREEN

Seventeenth Summer by Maureen Daly, not illustrated; Dodd, Mead, 1962, c1942. **Awarded:** Lewis Carroll Shelf 1969.

DALY, NIKI

Not so Fast, Songololo written and illustrated by Niki Daly; Atheneum, 1986. **Awarded:** Parents' Choice (literature) 1986.

DALY, THOMAS

Joel and the Wild Goose by Helga Sandburg, illustrated by Thomas Daly; Dial, 1963. **Awarded:** Lewis Carroll Shelf 1965.

D'AMATO, JANET

Animals That Use Tools by Barbara Ford, illustrated by Janet D'Amato; Messner, 1978. **Awarded:** New Jersey Institute of Technology 1980.

DAMITZ, CHARLES

The Giant Egg by Charles Damitz; Weekly Reader Books, 1987. **Awarded:** New Jersey Institute of Technology 1987.

DANA, BARBARA

Zucchini by Barbara Dana, illustrated by Eileen Christelow; Harper & Row, 1982. **Awarded:** Washington Irving (fiction) 1984; Land of Enchantment 1986; Maud Hart Lovelace 1986.

DANA, DORATHEA

The Runaway Shuttle Train by Muriel Fuller, illustrated by Dorathea Dana; McKay, 1946. **Awarded:** Spring Book Festival (younger honor) 1946.

Sugar Bush written and illustrated by Dorathea Dana; Nelson, 1947. **Awarded:** Spring Book Festival (middle honor) 1947.

DANIEL, ALAN

Bunnicula: A Rabbit Tale of Mystery by James Howe and Deborah Howe, illustrated by Alan Daniel; Atheneum, 1980, 1979. **Awarded:** Buckeye (grades 4-8 honor) 1982; Emphasis on Reading (Grades 4-6) 1981-82; Dorothy Canfield Fisher 1981; Golden Sower 1981; Iowa Children's Choice 1982; Land of Enchantment 1982; Nene (runnerup) 1982; Nene 1983; Sequoyah 1982; South Carolina Children's 1981; Sunshine State 1984; Young Reader's Choice 1982.

The Story of Canada by Janet Lunn and Christopher Moore, illustrated by Alan Daniel; Lester Publishing, 1992. **Awarded:** Mr. Christie's (English Text Ages 9-14) 1992.

DANIELS, GUY

Timothy's Horse by Vladimir Mayakovsky, adapted by Guy Daniels, illustrated by Flavio Constantini; Pantheon, 1970. **Awarded:** New York Times Best Illustrated 1970.

DANIELS, JONATHAN

Stonewall Jackson by Jonathan Daniels, illustrated by William Moyers; Random House, 1959. **Awarded:** North Carolina AAUW 1960.

DANKOVSZKY, DORATHEA
     see DANA, DORATHEA

DANN, COLIN

Animals of Farthing Wood: Escape from Danger by Colin Dann, illustrated by Jacqueline Tettmar; Heinemann, 1979. **Awarded:** Arts Council of Great Britain 1979.

DANN, MAX

Bernice Knows Best by Max Dann, illustrated by Ann James; Oxford University Press (Australia), 1983. **Awarded:** Children's Book Council of Australia (junior book of the year) 1984.

DANSKA, HERBERT

The Story of People by May Edel, illustrated by Herbert Danska; Little, 1953. **Awarded:** Spring Book Festival (older honor) 1953.

DANZIGER, PAULA
     Awarded: Milner 1985.

Can You Sue Your Parents for Malpractice? by Paula Danziger, not illustrated; Delacorte, 1979. **Awarded:** New Jersey Institute of Technology 1980.

The Cat Ate My Gymsuit by Paula Danziger, not illustrated; Delacorte, 1974. **Awarded:** Massachusetts Children's (grades 7-9) 1979; Nene 1980; New Jersey Institute of Technology 1976; Virginia Young Readers (Middle School) 1986.

The Divorce Express by Paula Danziger, not illustrated; Delacorte, 1982; Dell, 1983. **Awarded:** Emphasis on Reading (Grades 7-9) 1985-86; Parents' Choice (literature) 1982; South Carolina Young Adult 1985; Woodward Park School 1983.

Everyone Else's Parents Said Yes by Paula Danziger, illustrated with line drawings; Delacorte, 1989. **Awarded:** Parents' Choice (Story Book) 1989.

It's an Aardvark-Eat-Turtle World by Paula Danziger, not illustrated; Delacorte, 1985. **Awarded:** Parents' Choice (literature) 1985.

There's a Bat in Bunk Five by Paula Danziger, not illustrated; Delacorte, 1980; Dell, 1982. **Awarded:** California Young Readers (junior high) 1984; CRABbery 1982.

DARINGER, HELEN FERN

Debbie of the Green Gate by Helen Fern Daringer, illustrated by Edward Goodwin; Harcourt, 1950. **Awarded:** Spring Book Festival (older honor) 1950.

DARKE, MARJORIE

The First of Midnight by Marjorie Darke, illustrated by Anthony Morris; Kestrel, 1977. **Awarded:** Guardian (commended) 1978.

A Question of Courage by Marjorie Darke, illustrated by Janet Archer; Kestrel, 1975. **Awarded:** Guardian (commended) 1976.

DARLING, KATHY

Bet You Can't! Science Impossibilities to Fool You by Kathy Darling and Vicki Cobb, illustrated by Martha Weston; Lothrop, 1980. **Awarded:** New York Academy of Sciences (younger) 1981.

Manatee: On Location by Kathy Darling, photographs by Tara Darling; Lothrop Lee & Shepard, 1990. **Awarded:** Book Can Develop Empathy 1991.

DARLING, LOUIS

The Enormous Egg by Oliver Butterworth, illustrated by Louis Darling; Little Brown, 1956. **Awarded:** Lewis Carroll Shelf 1970.

Henry and Ribsy by Beverly Cleary, illustrated by Louis Darling; Morrow, 1954. **Awarded:** Young Reader's Choice 1957.

Henry and the Paper Route by Beverly Cleary, illustrated by Louis Darling; Morrow, 1957. **Awarded:** Young Readers' Choice 1960.

The Mouse and the Motorcycle by Beverly Cleary, illustrated by Louis Darling; Morrow, 1965. **Awarded:** Great Stone Face 1983; Sue Hefly 1973; Nene 1969; Surrey School 1974; William Allen White 1968; Young Reader's Choice 1968.

Ramona the Pest by Beverly Cleary, illustrated by Louis Darling; Morrow, 1968. **Awarded:** Georgia Children's 1970; Nene 1971; Sequoyah 1971; Young Readers' Choice 1971.

Ribsy by Beverly Cleary, illustrated by Louis Darling; Morrow, 1964. **Awarded:** Dorothy Canfield Fisher 1966; Nene 1968.

Runaway Ralph by Beverly Cleary, illustrated by Louis Darling; Morrow, 1970. **Awarded:** Nene 1972; Charlie May Simon 1972-73.

DARLING, TARA
Manatee: On Location by Kathy Darling, photographs by Tara Darling; Lothrop Lee & Shepard, 1990. **Awarded:** Book Can Develop Empathy 1991.

DARROW, WHITNEY, JR.
Bony by Fran Zweifel, illustrated by Whitney Darrow, Jr.; Harper, 1977. **Awarded:** New Jersey Institute of Technology 1978.

DARWIN, BEATRICE
Socks by Beverly Cleary, illustrated by Beatrice Darwin; Morrow, 1973. **Awarded:** Golden Archer 1977; William Allen White 1976.

DARWIN, LEONARD
Our Fifty States by Earl Schenck Miers, illustrated by Eleanor Mill, maps by Leonard Darwin; Grosset, 1961. **Awarded:** New Jersey Institute of Technology 1961.

DAUBER, LIZ
Cathy Leonard Calling by Catherine Woolley, illustrated by Liz Dauber; Morrow, 1961. **Awarded:** New Jersey Institute of Technology 1961.

Ginnie and Her Juniors by Catherine Woolley, illustrated by Liz Dauber; Morrow, 1963. **Awarded:** New Jersey Institute of Technology 1963.

Look Alive, Libby by Catherine Woolley, illustrated by Liz Dauber; Morrow, 1962. **Awarded:** New Jersey Institute of Technology 1963.

DAUDET, ALPHONSE
The Brave Little Goat of Monsieur Seguin by Alphonse Daudet, illustrated by Chiyoko Nakatani; World, 1968. **Awarded:** Spring Book Festival (picture book honor) 1968.

DAUGHERTY, CHARLES M.
Street of Ships written and illustrated by Charles M. Daugherty; Holt, 1942. **Awarded:** Spring Book Festival (older honor) 1942.

DAUGHERTY, JAMES HENRY
Andy and the Lion written and illustrated by James Daugherty; Viking, 1938. **Awarded:** Caldecott (honor) 1939.

Better Known as Johnny Appleseed by Mabel Leigh Hunt, illustrated by James Daugherty; Lippincott, 1950. **Awarded:** Newbery (honor) 1951.

Daniel Boone written and illustrated by James H. Daugherty; Viking, 1939. **Awarded:** Newbery 1940.

Gillespie and the Guards by Benjamin Elkin, illustrated by James Daugherty; Viking, 1956. **Awarded:** Caldecott (honor) 1957.

Joe Magarac and his U.S.A. Citizenship Papers by Irwin Shapiro, illustrated by James Daugherty; Messner, 1948. **Awarded:** Julia Ellsworth Ford 1947.

A Long Way to Frisco: A Folk Adventure Novel of California and Oregon in 1852 by Alfred Powers, illustrated by James Daugherty; Little Brown, 1951. **Awarded:** Boys Club 1952.

The Railroad to Freedom: A Story of the Civil War by Hildegarde Swift, illustrated by James Daugherty; Harcourt, 1932. **Awarded:** Newbery (honor) 1933.

DAUGHERTY, RICHARD D.
Hunters of the Whale: An Adventure in Northwest Coast Archaeology by Richard D. Daugherty with Ruth Kirk, photographs by Ruth Kirk and Louis Kirk; Morrow, 1974. **Awarded:** New York Academy of Sciences (older) 1975.

DAUGHTRY, DUANNE
What's Inside? illustrated by Duanne Daughtry; Knopf, 1984. **Awarded:** Please Touch Award 1985.

d'AULAIRE, EDGAR
Awarded: Regina 1970.

Abraham Lincoln written and illustrated by Ingri d'Aulaire and Edgar Parin d'Aulaire; Doubleday-Doran, 1939. **Awarded:** Caldecott 1940.

Buffalo Bill written and illustrated by Ingri d'Aulaire and Edgar Parin d'Aulaire; Doubleday, 1952. **Awarded:** Boys Club 1953.

Children of the Soil: a Story of Scandinavia by Nora Burglon, illustrated by Edgar Parin d'Aulaire; Doubleday-Doran, 1932. **Awarded:** Newbery (honor) 1933.

D'Aulaires' Trolls written and illustrated by Ingri and Edgar Parin d'Aulaire; Doubleday, 1972. **Awarded:** National Book Award (finalist) 1973; New York Times Notable Books 1972.

d'AULAIRE, INGRI
Awarded: Regina 1970.

Abraham Lincoln written and illustrated by Ingri d'Aulaire and Edgar Parin d'Aulaire; Doubleday-Doran, 1939. **Awarded:** Caldecott 1940.

Buffalo Bill written and illustrated by Ingri d'Aulaire and Edgar Parin d'Aulaire; Doubleday, 1952. **Awarded:** Boys Club 1953.

D'Aulaires' Trolls written and illustrated by Ingri and Edgar Parin d'Aulaire; Doubleday, 1972. **Awarded:** National Book Award (finalist) 1973; New York Times Notable Books 1972.

DAVALOS, FELIPE
Awarded: UNICEF-Ezra Jack Keats International 1986.

DAVAR, ASHOK
The Wheel of King Asoka written and illustrated by Ashok Davar; Follett, 1977. **Awarded:** Jane Addams (special recognition) 1978; Christopher (all ages) 1978.

DAVELUY, PAULE C.
Awarded: Claude Aubry 1985.

Les Chemins Secrets de la Liberte by Barbara Smucker, translated by Paule C. Daveluy, illustrated by Tom McNeely; Pierre Tisseyire, 1978. (originally published in English as *Underground to Canada*, Clarke, Irwin, 1977). **Awarded:** International Board on Books for Young People (translation/Canada) 1980.

Emilie de la Nouvelle Lune (original English *Emily of the New Moon*) by Lucy Montgomery, translated by Paule Daveluy; Pierre Tisseyre, 1983. **Awarded:** International Board on Books for Young People (translation/Canada) 1986.

DAVES, MICHAEL
Young Readers Book of Christian Symbolism by Michael Daves, illustrated by Gordon Laite; Abingdon, 1967. **Awarded:** Steck- Vaughn 1968.

DAVEY, THYRZA
Yonderbeyond written and illustrated by Thyrza Davey; Hodder & Stoughton, 1990. **Awarded:** Australian Christian Book of the Year 1991.

DAVID, TIBOR
Inigo: The Adventures of a Saint by Michael Hansen, illustrated by Tibor David; Lovell, 1991. **Awarded:** Australian Christian Book of the Year 1992.

DAVIDSON, ANDREW
The Iron Man by Ted Hughes, illustrated by Andrew Davidson; Faber & Faber, 1985. **Awarded:** Maschler 1985.

DAVIDSON, BASIL
Discovering Africa's Past by Basil Davidson, illustrated with maps; Longmans, 1978. **Awarded:** Other Award 1978.

DAVIDSON, MARGARET
Awarded: Lucky Book Club Four-Leaf Clover 1976.

Helen Keller's Teacher by Mickie Davidson, illustrated by Wayne Blickenstaff; Scholastic, 1966. **Awarded:** Boys Club 1966-67.

DAVIDSON, MICKIE
see DAVIDSON, MARGARET

DAVIE, HELEN K.
The Star Maiden: An Ojibway Tale retold by Barbara Juster Esbensen, illustrated by Helen K. Davie; Little Brown, 1988. **Awarded:** Minnesota (Finalist) 1988.

DAVIES, ANDREW
Conrad's War by Andrew Davies, not illustrated; Blackie, 1978; Crown, 1980. **Awarded:** Boston Globe Horn Book (fiction) 1980; Guardian 1979.

DAVIES, CORINNE, DR.
Awarded: Frances E. Russell 1982.

DAVIS, ALLEN
A String in the Harp by Nancy Bond, illustrated by Allen Davis; Atheneum, 1976. **Awarded:** Boston Globe Horn Book (fiction honor) 1976; International Reading Assn. 1977; Newbery (honor) 1977; Tir Na n-Og 1977.

DAVIS, BETTE J.
Freedom Eagle written and illustrated by Bette J. Davis; Lothrop, 1972. **Awarded:** New Jersey Institute of Technology 1972.

Pet Safety by Joseph J. McCoy, illustrated by Bette J. Davis; Watts, 1979. **Awarded:** New Jersey Institute of Technology 1980.

DAVIS, BURKE
America's First Army by Burke Davis, illustrated by Richard Stinely, photographs by John Crane; Rinehart/Colonial Williamsburg, 1962. **Awarded:** Boys Club 1963.

DAVIS, CLYDE BRION
North Woods Whammy by Clyde Brion Davis, not illustrated; Lippincott, 1951. **Awarded:** Spring Book Festival (older honor) 1951.

DAVIS, DANIEL S.
Behind Barbed Wire: The Imprisonment of Japanese Americans During World War II by Daniel S. Davis, illustrated; Dutton, 1982. **Awarded:** Boston Globe Horn Book (nonfiction) 1983.

DAVIS, DON
Exploring the Night Sky with Binoculars by David Chandler, illustrated by David Chandler and Don Davis; David Chandler, 1983. **Awarded:** New York Academy of Sciences (older honor) 1985.

DAVIS, JENNY
Sex Education by Jenny Davis, not illustrated; Watts, 1988; Orchard, 1988. **Awarded:** Young Adult Novel of the Year / Michigan Library Assn. 1989; Young Reader's Choice (Senior) 1991.

DAVIS, JULIA
Mountains Are Free by Julia Davis Adams, illustrated by Theodore Nadejen; Dutton, 1930. **Awarded:** Newbery (honor) 1931.

Vaino: A Boy of New Finland by Julia Davis Adams, illustrated by Lempi Ostman; Dutton, 1929. **Awarded:** Newbery (honor) 1930.

DAVIS, LAMBERT
The Bells of Christmas by Virginia Hamilton, illustrated by Lambert Davis; Harcourt Brace Jovanovich, 1989. **Awarded:** Coretta Scott King (Text honor) 1990.

The Jolly Mon by Jimmy Buffett and Savannah Jane Buffett, illustrated by Lambert Davis; Harcourt Brace Jovanovich, 1988. **Awarded:** Author's Award (Alabama) 1990.

DAVIS, LAVINIA RIKER
Roger and the Fox by Lavinia R. Davis, illustrated by Hildegard Woodward; Doubleday, 1947. **Awarded:** Caldecott (honor) 1948.

A Sea Between by Lavinia R. Davis, not illustrated; Doubleday, 1945. **Awarded:** Spring Book Festival (older honor) 1945.

The Wild Birthday Cake by Lavinia R. Davis, illustrated by Hildegard Woodward; Doubleday, 1949. **Awarded:** Caldecott (honor) 1950.

DAVIS, MARGUERITE
Tirra Lirra: Rhymes Old and New by Laura E. Richards, illustrated by Marguerite Davis; Little, 1955, c1902. **Awarded:** Lewis Carroll Shelf 1959.

The Littlest House by Elizabeth Coatsworth, illustrated by Marguerite Davis; Macmillan, 1940. **Awarded:** Spring Book Festival (younger honor) 1940.

DAVIS, MARY GOULD
Truce of the Wolf and Other Tales of Old Italy by Mary Gould Davis, illustrated by Jay Van Everen; Harcourt, 1931. **Awarded:** Newbery (honor) 1932.

DAVIS, OSSIE
Escape to Freedom by Ossie Davis, not illustrated; Viking, 1978, c1976. **Awarded:** Jane Addams (honor) 1979; Coretta Scott King 1979.

DAVIS, PAXTON
Three Days by Paxton Davis, illustrated; Atheneum, 1980. **Awarded:** New York Times Notable Books 1980.

DAVIS, ROBERT
Padre Porko: The Gentlemanly Pig by Robert Davis, illustrated by Fritz Eichenberg; Holiday, 1948. **Awarded:** Lewis Carroll Shelf 1962.

DAVIS, RUSSELL

The Lion's Whiskers: Tales of High Africa by Russell Davis and Brent Ashabranner, illustrated by James G. Teason; Little, Brown, 1959. **Awarded:** Spring Book Festival (older honor) 1959.

DAVISON, CLAIRE

Trail of the Little Paiute by Mabel O'Moran, illustrated by Claire Davison; Lippincott, 1952. **Awarded:** Spring Book Festival (older honor) 1952.

DAWLISH, PETER

The Royal Navy by Peter Dawlish, illustrated by Victor G. Ambrus; Oxford, 1963. **Awarded:** Greenaway (commended) 1963.

DAY, DAVID

Aska's Animals by David Day, illustrated by Warabe Aska; Doubleday Canada, 1991. **Awarded:** Amelia Frances Howard-Gibbon (Runnerup) 1992.

The Emperor's Panda by David Day, illustrated by Eric Beddows; McClelland & Stewart, 1986. **Awarded:** Canadian Library Assn. (runnerup) 1987; International Board on Books for Young People (Illustration/Canada) 1988.

DAY, SHIRLEY

Star Maiden: An Ojibwa Legend of the First Water Lily by Patricia Robins, illustrated by Shirley Day; Cassell & Collier-Macmillan, 1975. **Awarded:** Collier-Macmillan 1974.

DAYRELL, ELPHINSTONE

Why the Sun and the Moon Live in the Sky: An African Folktale by Elphinstone Dayrell, illustrated by Blair Lent; Houghton, 1968. **Awarded:** Caldecott (honor) 1969; Spring Book Festival (picture book) 1968.

DEAL, L. KATE

The Boxcar Children by Gertrude Warner, illustrated by L. Kate Deal; Whitman, c1942. **Awarded:** Emphasis on Reading (Grades 4-6) 1984-85.

DEAN, LEIGH

Help, Help, the Globolinks! by Gian-Carlo Menotti, adapted by Leigh Dean, illustrated by Milton Glaser; McGraw, 1970. **Awarded:** New York Times Best Illustrated 1970.

DEAN, LEON

Guns Over Champlain by Leon W. Dean, not illustrated; Rinehart, 1946. **Awarded:** Boys Club 1948.

de ANGELI, MARGUERITE LOFFT

Awarded: Drexel 1963; Outstanding Pennsylvania Author 1975; Regina 1968.

The Black Fox of Lorne written and illustrated by Marguerite de Angeli; Doubleday, 1956. **Awarded:** Newbery (honor) 1957.

Bright April written and illustrated by Marguerite de Angeli; Doubleday, 1946. **Awarded:** Spring Book Festival (middle honor) 1946.

The Door in the Wall: Story of Medieval London written and illustrated by Marguerite de Angeli; Doubleday, 1949. **Awarded:** Lewis Carroll Shelf 1961; Newbery 1950.

Marguerite de Angeli's Book of Nursery and Mother Goose Rhymes compiled and illustrated by Marguerite de Angeli; Doubleday, 1954. **Awarded:** Caldecott (honor) 1955.

Meggy MacIntosh by Elizabeth Janet Gray, illustrated by Marguerite de Angeli; Doubleday, 1930. **Awarded:** Newbery (honor) 1931.

They Loved to Laugh by Kathryn Worth, illustrated by Marguerite de Angeli; Doubleday, 1942. **Awarded:** Spring Book Festival (older honor) 1942.

Yonie Wondernose written and illustrated by Marguerite de Angeli; Doubleday, 1944. **Awarded:** Caldecott (honor) 1945.

De ANGELO, RACHEL W.

Awarded: American Association of School Librarians 1983.

DEAR, NEVILLE

The Valiant Sailor by Cicely Fox Smith, illustrated by Neville Dear; Criterion, 1957. **Awarded:** Boys Club 1958.

DEAVER, JULIE REECE

Say Goodnight, Gracie by Julie Reece Deaver, not illustrated; Harper & Row, 1988. **Awarded:** Virginia Young Readers (High School) 1991; Volunteer State Book Awards (grades 10-12) 1990.

DE BEER, HANS

Kleiner Eisbar Nimm Micht Mit! written and illustrated by Hans De Beer; Nord-Sud Verlag, 1990; North South Books, 1990. **Awarded:** Bologna (Critici in Erba) 1991.

De BORHEGYI, SUZANNE SIMS

Ships, Shoals and Amphoras: The Story of Underwater Archaeology by Suzanne de Borhegyi, illustrated by Alex Schomburg; Holt, 1961. **Awarded:** Ohioana 1962.

de CAMP, CATHERINE CROOK

Awarded: Drexel 1978.

de CAMP, L. SPRAGUE

Awarded: Drexel 1978.

DECK, RAYMOND H., JR.

Awarded: Chandler Reward of Merit 1984.

DE CLEMENTS, BARTHE

Awarded: Milner 1992.

The Five-finger Discount by Barthe DeClements, not illustrated; Delacorte, 1989. **Awarded:** PEN Center USA West 1990.

Nothing's Fair in Fifth Grade by Barthe DeClements, not illustrated; Viking, 1981. **Awarded:** Buckeye (grades 4-8 honor) 1983; Buckeye (grades 4-8) 1984; California Young Reader (intermediate) 1986; Children's Choice [Arizona] (juvenile) 1982; Colorado (runnerup) 1985; Emphasis on Reading (Grades 4-6) 1983-84; Georgia Children's 1984; Golden Archer 1984; Golden Sower (grades 4-6) 1984; Iowa 1984; Land of Enchantment 1985; Maud Hart Lovelace 1984; Massachusetts 1985; Nene 1984; North Dakota Children's Choice (Older) 1988; Sunshine (runnerup) 1985; Texas Bluebonnet 1984.

Sixth Grade Can Really Kill You by Barthe DeClements, not illustrated; Viking Kestrel, 1985. **Awarded:** Buckeye (grades 6-8) 1989; Golden Sower (grades 4-6) 1988; Land of Enchantment 1989; Nevada Young Reader Award (Intermediate) 1987-88; Sunshine State (grades 3-5) 1988; Sunshine State (grades 6-8) 1988; Young Reader's Choice 1988.

DE FELICE, CYNTHIA C.

Dancing Skelton by Cynthia C. DeFelice, illustrated by Robert Andrew Parker; Macmillan, 1989. **Awarded:** New York Times Best Illustrated 1989.

Weasel by Cynthia DeFelice, not illustrated; Macmillan, 1990. **Awarded:** Sequoyah Children's 1993.

De FEO, CHARLES
Starbuck Valley Winter by Roderick Haig-Brown, illustrated by Charles De Feo; Morrow, 1943; Collins, 1944. **Awarded:** Canadian Library Assn. 1947.

DEFOE, DANIEL
Robinson Crusoe by Daniel Defoe, illustrated by Nikolaj Popov; Chudozestvenaja Literatura, 1974. **Awarded:** Biennale Illustrations Bratislava (grand prix) 1975.

De FOREST, CHARLOTTE B.
The Prancing Pony: Nursery Rhymes from Japan by Charlotte B. De Forest, illustrated by Keiko Hida; Walker, 1968. **Awarded:** Spring Book Festival (picture book honor) 1968.

DEGEN, BRUCE
Commander Toad in Space by Jane Yolen, illustrated by Bruce Degen; Coward McCann, 1980. **Awarded:** Garden State Children's (Easy to Read) 1983.

The Magic School Bus at the Waterworks by Joanna Cole, illustrated by Bruce Degen; Scholastic, 1986. **Awarded:** Boston Globe Horn Book (nonfiction honor) 1987; Charlotte Book Award (K- 2) 1990; Colorado Children's Book Award 1989; Florida Reading Association 1991; Golden Sower (K-3) 1990; Volunteer State Book Awards (K-3) 1990; Washington Children's Choice 1989.

The Magic School Bus Inside the Earth by Joanna Cole, illustrated by Bruce Degen; Scholastic, 1987. **Awarded:** Virginia Young Readers (Primary) 1990.

The Magic School Bus Inside the Human Body by Joanna Cole, illustrated by Bruce Degen; Scholastic, 1989. **Awarded:** Garden State (Nonfiction) 1992.

The Magic School Bus Lost in the Solar System by Joanna Cole, illustrated by Bruce degen; Scholastic, 1990. **Awarded:** Garden State (Younger Nonfiction) 1993.

DEGENS, T.
Transport 7-41-R by T. Degens, not illustrated; Viking, 1974. **Awarded:** Boston Globe Horn Book (text) 1975. International Reading Assn. 1975.

De GERING, ETTA F.
Seeing Fingers: The Story of Louis Braille by Etta F. De Gering, illustrated by Emil Weiss; McKay, 1962. **Awarded:** Edison Mass Media (character development in children) 1963.

de GOGORZA, MAITLAND
June's Island by Marjorie Hill Allee, illustrated by Maitland de Gogorza; Houghton, 1931. **Awarded:** Newbery (honor) 1932.

de GROAT, DIANE
All About Sam by Lois Lowry, illustrated by Diane de Groat; Houghton Mifflin, 1988. **Awarded:** California Young Reader (Intermediate) 1992; Georgia Children's Book Award 1992; Mississippi Children's Book Award 1990; Charlie May Simon 1990- 91; South Dakota Prairie Pasque 1991; Mark Twain 1991.

A Book for Jodan by Marcia Newfield, illustrated by Diane de Groat; Atheneum, 1975. **Awarded:** Woodward Park School 1975.

The Flunking of Joshua T. Bates by Susan Shreve, illustrated by Diane de Groat; Knopf, 1984. **Awarded:** KC Three 1986-87.

The Great Eggspectations of Lila Fenwick by Kate McMullan, illustrated by Diane de Groat; Farrar Straus Giroux, 1991. **Awarded:** CRABbery (honor) 1993.

Little Rabbit's Loose Tooth by Lucy Bate, illustrated by Diane de Groat; Crown, 1975. **Awarded:** California Young Reader Medal (primary) 1978.

Luke Was There by Eleanor Clymer, illustrated by Diane de Groat; Holt, 1973. **Awarded:** Child Study 1974.

One More Flight by Eve Bunting, illustrated by Diane de Groat; Warne, 1976. **Awarded:** Golden Kite 1976.

DEGUINE, JEAN-CLAUDE
Emperor Penguin: Bird of the Antarctic by Jean-Claude Deguine, illustrated with photographs; Stephen Greene Press, 1974. **Awarded:** New York Academy of Sciences (younger) 1976.

de HAMEL, JOAN
Take the Long Path by Joan de Hamel, illustrated by Gareth Floyd; Lutterworth Press, 1978. **Awarded:** Esther Glen 1979.

DeJONG, DOLA
The House on Charlton Street by Dola deJong, illustrated by Gilbert Riswold; Scribner, 1962. **Awarded:** Edgar Allan Poe (runnerup) 1963.

DeJONG, MEINDERT
Awarded: Hans Christian Andersen 1962; Regina 1972.

Along Came a Dog by Meindert DeJong, illustrated by Maurice Sendak; Harper, 1958. **Awarded:** Aurianne 1960; International Board on Books for Young People (USA) 1960; Newbery (honor) 1959.

The House of Sixty Fathers by Meindert DeJong, illustrated by Maurice Sendak; Harper, 1956. **Awarded:** Child Study 1956; International Board on Books for Young People (USA) 1958; Newbery (honor) 1957; Woodward Park School 1958.

Hurry Home, Candy by Meindert DeJong, illustrated by Maurice Sendak; Harper, 1953. **Awarded:** Newbery (honor) 1954.

Journey from Peppermint Street by Meindert DeJong, illustrated by Emily McCully; Harper & Row, 1968. **Awarded:** National Book Award 1969.

Shadrach by Meindert DeJong, illustrated by Maurice Sendak; Harper, 1953. **Awarded:** Newbery (honor) 1954.

The Singing Hill by Meindert DeJong, illustrated by Maurice Sendak; Harper, 1962. **Awarded:** New York Times Best Illustrated 1962.

The Wheel on the School by Meindert DeJong, illustrated by Maurice Sendak; Harper, 1954. **Awarded:** Lewis Carroll Shelf 1963; Newbery 1955.

de KAY, ORMONDE, JR.
Rimes de la Mere Oie: Mother Goose Rendered into French translated by Ormonde de Kay, Jr., illustrated by Seymour Chwast, Milton Glaser, and Barry Zaid; Little Brown, 1971. **Awarded:** Children's Book Showcase 1972.

DE LAGE, IDA
ABC Fire Dogs by Ida De Lage, illustrated by Ellen Sloan; Garrard, 1977. **Awarded:** New Jersey Institute of Technology 1978.

ABC Halloween Witch by Ida De Lage, illustrated by Lou Cunette; Garrard, 1977. **Awarded:** New Jersey Institute of Technology 1978.

ABC Pigs Go to Market by Ida De Lage, illustrated by Kelly Oechsli; Garrard, 1977. **Awarded:** New Jersey Institute of Technology 1978.

ABC Pirate Adventure by Ida De Lage, illustrated by Buck Brown; Garrard, 1977. **Awarded:** New Jersey Institute of Technology 1978.

ABC Triplets at the Zoo by Ida De Lage, illustrated by Lori Pierson; Garrard, 1980. **Awarded:** New Jersey Institute of Technology 1981.

Beware! Beware! A Witch Won't Share by Ida De Lage, illustrated by Ted Schroeder; Garrard, 1972. **Awarded:** New Jersey Institute of Technology 1972.

A Bunny Ride by Ida De Lage, illustrated by Tracy McVay; Garrard, 1975. **Awarded:** New Jersey Institute of Technology 1976.

Bunny School by Ida De Lage, illustrated by Tracy McVay; Garrard, 1976. **Awarded:** New Jersey Institute of Technology 1977.

Frannie's Flower by Ida De Lage, illustrated by Ellen Sloan; Garrard, 1979. **Awarded:** New Jersey Institute of Technology 1980.

Good Morning, Lady by Ida De Lage, illustrated by Tracy McVay; Garrard, 1974. **Awarded:** New Jersey Institute of Technology 1975, 1976.

Hello, Come In by Ida De Lage, illustrated by John Mardon; Garrard, 1971. **Awarded:** New Jersey Institute of Technology 1971.

The Old Witch and the Snores by Ida De Lage, illustrated by Gil Miret; Garrard, 1970. **Awarded:** New Jersey Institute of Technology 1970.

The Old Witch and the Wizard by Ida De Lage, illustrated by Mimi Korach; Garrard, 1974. **Awarded:** New Jersey Institute of Technology 1975.

The Old Witch Finds a New House by Ida De Lage, illustrated by Pat Paris; Garrard, 1979. **Awarded:** New Jersey Institute of Technology 1980.

The Old Witch Goes to the Ball by Ida De Lage, illustrated by Gustave E. Nebel; Garrard, 1969. **Awarded:** New Jersey Institute of Technology 1970.

The Old Witch's Party by Ida De Lage, illustrated by Mimi Korach; Garrard, 1976. **Awarded:** New Jersey Institute of Technology 1977.

Pilgrim Children on the Mayflower by Ida De Lage, illustrated by Bert Dodson; Garrard, 1980. **Awarded:** New Jersey Institute of Technology 1981.

Pink Pink by Ida De Lage, illustrated by Benton Mahan; Garrard, 1973. **Awarded:** New Jersey Institute of Technology 1973.

Weeny Witch by Ida De Lage, illustrated by Kelly Oechsli; Garrard, 1968. **Awarded:** New Jersey Institute of Technology 1968.

What Does a Witch Need? by Ida De Lage, illustrated by Ted Schroeder; Garrard, 1971. **Awarded:** New Jersey Institute of Technology 1971.

The Witchy Broom by Ida De Lage, illustrated by Walt Peaver; Garrard, 1969. **Awarded:** New Jersey Institute of Technology 1969.

de la MARE, WALTER

Collected Stories for Children by Walter de la Mare, illustrated by Irene Hawkins; Faber, 1947. **Awarded:** Carnegie 1947.

Peacock Pie: A Book of Rhymes by Walter De La Mare, illustrated by Louise Brierley; Henry Holt, 1989. **Awarded:** New York Times Best Illustrated 1989.

A Penny a Day by Walter de la Mare, illustrated by Paul Kennedy; Knopf, 1960, c1925. **Awarded:** Lewis Carroll Shelf 1962.

DELANO, IRENE

The Emperor's New Clothes by Hans Christian Andersen, adapted by Jean van Leeuwen, illustrated by Irene Delano and Jack Delano; Random House, 1971. **Awarded:** Art Books for Children 1974.

DELANO, JACK

The Emperor's New Clothes by Hans Christian Andersen, adapted by Jean van Leeuwen, illustrated by Jack Delano and Irene Delano; Random House, 1971. **Awarded:** Art Books for Children 1974.

De LARA, GEORGE

Sports and Games in Verse and Rhyme by Allan D. Jacobs and Leland B. Jacobs, illustrated by George De Lara; Garrard, 1975. **Awarded:** New Jersey Institute of Technology 1976.

De LARREA, VICTORIA

The Friendly Woods by Charles House, illustrated by Victoria De Larrea; Four Winds, 1973. **Awarded:** Council of Wisconsin Writers (juvenile runnerup) 1975.

De LEEUW, ADELE

Awarded: New Jersey Institute of Technology (New Jersey's outstanding authors special citation) 1968, 1971, 1975.

Anthony Wayne: Washington's General by Adele De Leeuw and Cateau De Leeuw, illustrated by Andrew Snyder; Westminster, 1974. **Awarded:** New Jersey Institute of Technology 1975, 1976.

The Boy with Wings by Adele De Leeuw, illustrated by Leonard Vosburgh; Nautilus, 1971. **Awarded:** New Jersey Institute of Technology (illustrator) 1972.

Carlos P. Romulo: The Barefoot Boy of Diplomacy by Adele DeLeeuw, illustrated; Westminster, 1976. **Awarded:** New Jersey Institute of Technology 1977.

Civil War Nurse: Mary Ann Bickerdyke by Adele De Leeuw, not illustrated; Messner, 1973. **Awarded:** New Jersey Institute of Technology 1973, 1975.

Legends and Folk Tales of Holland by Adele De Leeuw, illustrated by Paul Kennedy; Nelson, 1963. **Awarded:** New Jersey Institute of Technology (short stories, ages 9-12) 1964.

Lindbergh: Lone Eagle by Adele De Leeuw, illustrated with photographs; Doubleday, 1969. **Awarded:** New Jersey Institute of Technology 1970.

Marie Curie: Woman of Genius by Adele De Leeuw, illustrated by Cary; Garrard, 1970. **Awarded:** New Jersey Institute of Technology 1970.

Miss Fix-it by Adele De Leeuw, not illustrated; Macmillan, 1966. **Awarded:** New Jersey Institute of Technology (ages 12-up) 1966.

Paul Bunyan Finds a Wife by Adele De Leeuw, illustrated by Ted Schroeder; Garrard, 1969. **Awarded:** New Jersey Institute of Technology 1970.

Peter Stuyvesant by Adele De Leeuw, illustrated by Vincent Colabella; Garrard, 1970. **Awarded:** New Jersey Institute of Technology 1970.

De LEEUW, CATEAU

Awarded: New Jersey Institute of Technology (New Jersey's outstanding authors special citation) 1975.

Anthony Wayne: Washington's General by Cateau De Leeuw and Adele De Leeuw, illustrated by Andrew Snyder; Westminster, 1974. **Awarded:** New Jersey Institute of Technology 1975, 1976.

Benedict Arnold: Hero and Traitor by Cateau DeLeeuw, illustrated; Putnam, 1970. **Awarded:** New Jersey Institute of Technology 1970.

DELESSERT, ETIENNE
Awarded: Hans Christian Andersen (highly commended Illustrator/ Switzerland) 1980.

How the Mouse Was Hit on the Head by a Stone and So Discovered the World written and illustrated by Etienne Delessert; Doubleday, 1971. **Awarded:** Art Books for Children 1973, 1974, 1975.

Just So Stories by Rudyard Kipling, illustrated by Etienne Delessert; Doubleday, 1972. **Awarded:** New York Times Best Illustrated 1972.

A Long, Long Song written and illustrated by Etienne Delessert; Farrar Straus Giroux, 1988. **Awarded:** Bologna (Graphics for Children) 1989.

Story Number 1 by Eugene Ionesco, illustrated by Etienne Delessert; Quist, 1968. **Awarded:** New York Times Best Illustrated 1968.

Yok Yok series by Anne van der Essen, illustrated by Etienne Delessert; Gallimard. **Awarded:** Bologna (graphics for children) 1981.

DELGADO, ABELARDO B.
My Father Hijacked a Plane by Abelardo B. Delgado; manuscript. **Awarded:** Council on Interracial Books (Chicano) 1974.

DELKIN, JAY
Awarded: L. Frank Baum 1986.

DEL REY, LESTER
Marooned on Mars by Lester del Rey, illustrated by Alex Schomberg; Winston, 1952. **Awarded:** Boys Club 1953.

DELTON, JUDY
Brimhall Comes to Stay by Judy Delton, illustrated by Cyndy Czekeres; Lothrop, 1978. **Awarded:** Council of Wisconsin Writers (picture book runnerup) 1979.

On a Picnic by Judy Delton, illustrated by Mamoru Funai; Doubleday, 1979. **Awarded:** New Jersey Institute of Technology 1980.

Angel's Mother's Boyfriend by Judy Delton, illustrated by Margot Apple; Houghton Mifflin, 1985. **Awarded:** Parents' Choice (literature) 1986.

My Mom Hates Me in January by Judy Delton, illustrated by John Faulkner; Whitman, 1977. **Awarded:** North Dakota Children's Choice (younger) 1980.

DE LUCCA, GERALDINE
Lives and Half-Lives: Biographies of Women for Young Adults by Geraldine DeLucca in Children's Literature in Education 17 (Winter 1986): 241-252. **Awarded:** Children's Literature Assn. Criticism (Most Significant Article runnerup) 1987.

de MALROY, GENEVA
Hilla of Finland by Geneva de Malroy, illustrated by Frederick Andersen; Nelson, 1941. **Awarded:** Spring Book Festival (middle honor) 1941.

De MARE, ERIC S.
London's River: The Story of a City by Eric S. De Mare, illustrated by Heather Copley and Christopher Chamberlain; Bodley Head, 1964. **Awarded:** Carnegie (commended) 1964.

DE MEJO, OSCAR
Does God Have a Big Toe? Stories About Stories in the Bible by Marc Gellman, illustrated by Oscar de Mejo; Harper & Row, 1989. **Awarded:** New York Times Best Illustrated 1989.

Oscar de Mejo's ABC written and illustrated by Oscar de Mejo; HarperCollins, 1992. **Awarded:** New York Times Best Illustrated 1992.

The Tiny Visitor written and illustrated by Oscar de Mejo; Pantheon, 1982. **Awarded:** New York Times Best Illustrated 1982; Parents' Choice (illustration) 1982.

DEMAREST, CHRIS
The Butterfly Jar: Poems by Jeff Moss, illustrated by Chris Demarest; Bantam, 1989. **Awarded:** Kentucky Bluegrass (grades 4-8) 1991.

My Little Red Car written and illustrated by Chris L. Demarest; Caroline House/Boyds Mills, 1992. **Awarded:** Parents Choice (Picture Book) 1992.

DEMI
The Nightingale by Hans Christian Andersen, illustrated by Demi; Harcourt Brace Jovanovich, 1985. **Awarded:** New York Times Best Illustrated 1985.

De MISKEY, JULIAN
Chucaro: Wild Pony of the Pampa by Francis Kalnay, illustrated by Julian De Miskey; Harcourt, 1958. **Awarded:** Newbery (honor) 1959; Spring Book Festival (middle) 1958.

The Trouble with Jenny's Ear by Oliver Butterworth, illustrated by Julian De Miskey; Atlantic Little, 1960. **Awarded:** Spring Book Festival (middle) 1960.

DEMUTH, JACK
Joel, Growing Up a Farm Man by Patricia Demuth, photographs by Jack Demuth; Dodd Mead, 1982. **Awarded:** Society of Midland Authors 1983.

DEMUTH, PATRICIA
Joel, Growing Up a Farm Man by Patricia Demuth, photographs by Jack Demuth; Dodd Mead, 1982. **Awarded:** Society of Midland Authors 1983.

Max, the Bad-Talking Parrot by Patricia B. Demuth, illustrated by Bo Zaunders; Dodd Mead, 1986. **Awarded:** Georgia Children's Picture Storybook 1989.

DENETSOSIE, HOKE
The Ordeal of the Young Hunter by Jonreed Lauritzen, illustrated by Hoke Denetsosie; Little Brown, 1954. **Awarded:** Child Study 1954.

DENNEBORG, HEINRICH-MARIA
Jan und das Wildpferd by Heinrich-Maria Denneborg, illustrated by Horst Lemke; Dressler, 1957. **Awarded:** Hans Christian Andersen (runnerup) 1960.

DENNIS, CLARA G.
Awarded: Chandler Reward of Merit 1982 (posthumously).

DENNIS, CLARENCE JAMES
Hist! by Clarence James Dennis, illustrated by Peter J. Gouldthorpe; Walter McVitty, 1991. **Awarded:** Children's Book Council of Australia (Picture Book honor) 1992.

DENNIS, MORGAN
Pete by Tom Robinson, illustrated by Morgan Dennis; Viking, 1941. **Awarded:** Spring Book Festival (middle) 1941.

DENNIS, WESLEY
Black Gold by Marguerite Henry, illustrated by Wesley Dennis; Rand McNally, 1957. **Awarded:** Sequoyah 1960.

Brighty of the Grand Canyon by Marguerite Henry, illustrated by Wesley Dennis; Rand, 1953. **Awarded:** William Allen White 1956.

Flip written and illustrated by Wesley Dennis; Viking, 1941. **Awarded:** Spring Book Festival (younger honor) 1941.

Justin Morgan Had a Horse by Marguerite Henry, illustrated by Wesley Dennis; Wilcox & Follett, 1945. **Awarded:** Newbery (honor) 1946.

King of the Wind by Marguerite Henry, illustrated by Wesley Dennis; Rand McNally, 1948. **Awarded:** Newbery 1949; Young Readers Choice 1951.

Misty of Chincoteague by Marguerite Henry, illustrated by Wesley Dennis; Rand McNally, 1947. **Awarded:** Lewis Carroll Shelf 1961; Newbery (honor) 1948.

Old Bones, the Wonder Horse by Mildred M. Pace, illustrated by Wesley Dennis; McGraw, 1955. **Awarded:** Dorothy Canfield Fisher 1957.

Prairie Colt by Stephen Holt, illustrated by Wesley Dennis; Longmans, 1947. **Awarded:** Boys Club 1949.

Sea Star: Orphan of Chincoteague by Marguerite Henry, illustrated by Wesley Dennis; Rand McNally, 1949. **Awarded:** Young Readers Choice 1952.

Simba of the White Mane by Jocelyn Arundel, illustrated by Wesley Dennis; Whittlesey House, 1958. **Awarded:** Boys Club 1959.

Summerfield Farm by Mary Martin Black, illustrated by Wesley Dennis; Viking, 1951. **Awarded:** Spring Book Festival (8-12 honor) 1951.

DENNY, NORMAN
The Bayeaux Tapestry: The Story of the Norman Conquest: 1066 by Norman Denny and Josephine Filmer-Sankey, illustrated; Collins, 1966. **Awarded:** Carnegie (highly commended) 1966.

DENSLOW, SHARON PHILLIPS
Night Owls by Sharon Phillips Denslow, illustrated by Jill Kastner; Bradbury, 1990. **Awarded:** Friends of American Writers 1991.

DENSLOW, W. W. (WILLIAM WALLACE)
The Wizard of Oz by L. Frank Baum, illustrated by W. W. Denslow; Reilly & Lee, 1956. **Awarded:** Lewis Carroll Shelf 1968.

DENTON, KADY MACDONALD
The Story of Little Quack by Betty Gibson, illustrated by Kady MacDonald Denton; Kids Can Press, 1990. **Awarded:** Mr. Christie's (English Illustration) 1990.

Til All the Stars Have Fallen: Canadian Poems for Children by David Booth, illustrated by Kady MacDonald Denton; Kids Can Press, 1989; Viking, 1990. **Awarded:** Amelia Frances Howard-Gibbon 1990.

DENTON, TERRY
At the Cafe Splendid written and illustrated by Terry Denton; Houghton Mifflin, 1988. **Awarded:** Parents' Choice (Picture Book) 1988.

Felix & Alexander written and illustrated by Terry Denton; Oxford, 1985. **Awarded:** Children's Book Council of Australia (picture book) 1986.

Mr. Plunkett's Pool by Gillian Rubinstein, illustrated by Terry Denton; Random House, 1992. **Awarded:** Australian Multicultural (Picturebook) 1993.

Night Noises by Mem Fox, illustrated by Terry Denton; Harcourt Brace Jovanovich, 1989. **Awarded:** Redbook 1989.

Spooner or Later by Paul Jennings, Ted Greenwood and Terry Denton; Viking, 1992. **Awarded:** Ashton Scholastic 1993.

DENZEL, JUSTIN F.
Black Kettle: King of the Wild Horses by Justin F. Denzel, illustrated by Richard Amundsen; Garrard, 1974. **Awarded:** New Jersey Institute of Technology 1975.

Genius with a Scalpel: Harvey Cushing by Justin F. Denzel, not illustrated; Messner, 1971. **Awarded:** New Jersey Institute of Technology 1971.

Jumbo: Giant Circus Elephant by Justin F. Denzel, illustrated by Richard Amundsen; Garrard, 1973. **Awarded:** New Jersey Institute of Technology 1973, 1975.

Sampson: Yankee Stallion by Justin F. Denzel, illustrated by William Hutchinson; Garrard, 1980. **Awarded:** New Jersey Institute of Technology 1981.

Scat: the Movie Cat by Justin F. Denzel, illustrated by Herman B. Vestal; Garrard, 1977. **Awarded:** New Jersey Institute of Technology 1978.

Snowfoot: White Reindeer of the Arctic by Justin F. Denzel, illustrated by Taylor Oughton; Garrard, 1976. **Awarded:** New Jersey Institute of Technology 1977.

Wild Wing: Great Hunting Eagle by Justin F. Denzel, illustrated by Herman B. Vestal; Garrard, 1975. **Awarded:** New Jersey Institute of Technology 1976.

DePAOLA, PAULA
Rosie and the Yellow Ribbon by Paula DePaola, illustrated by Janet Wolf; Little Brown, 1992. **Awarded:** Christopher (Ages 6-8) 1993.

de PAOLA, TOMIE
Awarded: Kerlan 1981; David McCord 1986; Regina 1983.

Authorized Autumn Charts of the Upper Red Canoe River Country by Peter Cohen, illustrated by Tomie de Paola; Atheneum, 1972. **Awarded:** Children's Book Showcase 1973; Friends of American Writers (illustration) 1973.

Charlie Needs a Cloak written and illustrated by Tomie de Paola; Prentice Hall, 1974, c1973. **Awarded:** Art Books for Children 1975; Children's Book Showcase 1975.

The Friendly Beasts: an Old English Christmas Carol illustrated by Tomie de Paola; Putnam, 1981. **Awarded:** Boston Globe Horn Book (illustration honor) 1982.

Giorgio's Village illustrated by Tomie De Paola; Putnam, 1982. **Awarded:** Golden Kite (picture illustration) 1982.

Poetry for Chuckles and Grins by Leland B. Jacobs, illustrated by Tomie de Paola; Garrard, 1968. **Awarded:** New Jersey Institute of Technology 1968.

The Quicksand Book written and illustrated by Tomie de Paola; Holiday, 1977. **Awarded:** Garden State Children's (younger nonfiction) 1980.

Simple Pictures Are Best by Nancy Willard, illustrated by Tomie de Paola; Harcourt, 1977. **Awarded:** Art Books for Children 1978.

Strega Nona written and illustrated by Tomie de Paola; Prentice Hall, 1975. **Awarded:** Art Books for Children 1977, 1978, 1979; Caldecott (honor) 1976.

Tomie de Paola's Favorite Nursery Tales illustrated by Tomie de Paola; Putnam, 1986. **Awarded:** Redbook (honorable mention) 1986.

What the Mailman Brought by Carolyn Craven, illustrated by Tomie de Paola; Putnam, 1987. **Awarded:** Golden Kite (Picture- Illustration honor) 1987.

DERANEY, MICHAEL J.

Molly's Pilgrim by Barbara Cohen, illustrated by Michael J. Deraney; Lothrop, Lee & Shepard, 1983. **Awarded:** New Jersey Institute of Technology 1983.

Yussel's Prayer: A Yom Kippur Story by Barbara Cohen, illustrated by Michael J. Deraney; Lothrop, Lee & Shepard, 1981. **Awarded:** Sydney Taylor Book (children) 1982; Jewish Book Council (children's picture book) 1983.

de REGNIERS, BEATRICE SCHENK

Cats, Cats, Cats, Cats, Cats by Beatrice Schenk de Regniers, illustrated by Bill Sokol; Pantheon, 1958. **Awarded:** Spring Book Festival (ages 4-8 honor) 1958.

A Little House of Your Own by Beatrice Schenk de Regniers, illustrated by Irene Haas; Harcourt, 1955. **Awarded:** New York Times Best Illustrated 1955; Spring Book Festival (ages 4-8 honor) 1955.

Little Sister and the Month Brothers by Beatrice Schenk de Regniers, illustrated by Margot Tomes; Seabury, 1976. **Awarded:** Children's Book Showcase 1977.

May I Bring a Friend? by Beatrice Schenk de Regniers, illustrated by Beni Montresor; Atheneum, 1964. **Awarded:** Caldecott 1965; Indiana Authors Day (young children) 1965.

Red Riding Hood, Retold in Verse for Boys and Girls to Read Themselves by Beatrice Schenk de Regniers, illustrated by Edward Gorey; Atheneum, 1972. **Awarded:** Art Books for Children 1974; Children's Book Showcase 1973.

The Shadow Book by Beatrice Schenk de Regniers and Isabel Gordon, illustrated by Isabel Gordon; Harcourt, 1960. **Awarded:** New York Times Best Illustrated 1960.

The Snow Party by Beatrice Schenk de Regniers, illustrated by Reiner Zimnik; Pantheon, 1959. **Awarded:** Boys Club 1960.

Was It a Good Trade? by Beatrice Schenk de Regniers, illustrated by Irene Haas; Harcourt, 1956. **Awarded:** New York Times Best Illustrated 1956.

DE ROO, ANNE

Jacky Nobody by Anne de Roo; Methuen, 1983. **Awarded:** AIM (Story Book) 1984.

DESAI, ANITA

The Village by the Sea by Anita Desai, not illustrated; Heinemann, 1982. **Awarded:** Guardian 1983.

de SANTILLANA, GIORGIO

The Universe of Galileo and Newton by Giorgio de Santillana and William Bixby, illustrated with paintings and drawings; American Heritage, 1964. **Awarded:** Edison Mass Media (best children's science book) 1965.

de TREVINO, ELIZABETH BORTON

see TREVINO, ELIZABETH BORTON

DEDEUKER, CARL

On the Devil's Court by Carl Deuker, not illustrated; Little Brown (Joy Street), 1988. **Awarded:** South Carolina Young Adult 1992.

DEUTSCH, BABETTE

Walt Whitman, Builder for America by Babette Deutsch, illustrated by Raphael Busoni; Messner, 1941. **Awarded:** Julia Ellsworth Ford 1941.

DEVANEY, JOHN

Bart Starr by John Devaney, illustrated with photographs; Scholastic, 1967. **Awarded:** Boys Club (certificate) 1968.

DE VEAUX, ALEXIS

An Enchanted Hair Tale by Alexis De Veaux, illustrated by Cheryl Hanna; Harper & Row, 1987. **Awarded:** Coretta Scott King (Text honor) 1988.

Na-ni written and illustrated by Alexis De Veaux; Harper, 1973. **Awarded:** Art Books for Children 1974.

DEVERELL, RICHARD

What Makes It Rain? by Susan Mayes, illustrated by Richard Deverell and Mike Pringle; Usborne, 1989. **Awarded:** Science Book Prizes 1990.

DEVLIN, HARRY

Awarded: New Jersey Institute of Technology (New Jersey author awards, special citation for husband-wife writers of children's books) 1969.

Aunt Agatha, There's a Lion under the Couch written and illustrated by Harry Devlin; Van Nostrand, 1968. **Awarded:** New Jersey Institute of Technology 1968.

Cranberry Birthday written and illustrated by Harry Devlin and Wende Devlin; Four Winds, 1988. **Awarded:** New Jersey Institute of Technology 1989.

Cranberry Valentine written and illustrated by Harry and Wende Devlin; Four Winds, 1986. **Awarded:** New Jersey Institute of Technology 1987.

How Fletcher Was Hatched! written and illustrated by Harry and Wende Devlin; Parents', 1969. **Awarded:** New Jersey Institute of Technology 1970.

Tales of Thunder and Lightning written and illustrated by Harry Devlin; Parents, 1975. **Awarded:** New Jersey Institute of Technology 1976.

The Walloping Window Blind written and illustrated by Harry Devlin; Van Nostrand, 1968. **Awarded:** New Jersey Institute of Technology 1968.

What Kind of House Is That? written and illustrated by Harry Devlin; Parents, 1969. **Awarded:** New Jersey Institute of Technology 1970.

DEVLIN, WENDE

Awarded: New Jersey Institute of Technology (New Jersey author awards, special citation for husband-wife writers of children's books) 1969.

Cranberry Birthday written and illustrated by Wende Devlin and Harry Devlin; Four Winds, 1988. **Awarded:** New Jersey Institute of Technology 1989.

Cranberry Valentine written and illustrated by Wende and Harry Devlin; Four Winds, 1986. **Awarded:** New Jersey Institute of Technology 1987.

How Fletcher Was Hatched! written and illustrated by Harry and Wende Devlin; Parents, 1969. **Awarded:** New Jersey Institute of Technology 1970.

DE VRIES, C.M.

Vertel Het uw Kinderen by Jac Sinnema and C. M. de Vries; Nederlandsche Zondacsschool Vereniging. **Awarded:** Bologna (Graphics for Youth) 1970.

DEWAN, TED

Inside the Whale and Other Animals by Steve Parker, illustrated by Ted Dewan; Dorling Kindersley, 1992. **Awarded:** Mother Goose 1992.

DEWDNEY, SELWYN

The Hungry Time by Selwyn Dewdney, illustrated by Olena Kassian; Lorimer, 1980. **Awarded:** IODE 1980.

Kristli's Trees by Mabel Dunham, illustrated by Selwyn Dewdney; McClelland & Stewart, 1948. **Awarded:** Canadian Library Assn. 1949.

DeWEESE, GENE

Major Corby and the Unidentified Flapping Object by Gene DeWeese, not illustrated; Doubleday, 1979. **Awarded:** Council for Wisconsin Writers (juvenile) 1980.

DEWEY, ARIANE

see ARUEGO, ARIANE DEWEY

DEWEY, JENNIFER

The Secret Language of Snow by Terry Tempest Williams and Ted Major, illustrated by Jennifer Dewey; Sierra Club/Pantheon, 1984. **Awarded:** New York Academy of Sciences (younger) 1985.

de WILDE, DICK

The Goalkeeper's Revenge and Other Stories by Bill Naughton, illustrated by Dick de Wilde; Brockhampton Press, 1971. **Awarded:** Other Award 1978.

DeWITT, CORNELIUS HUGH

The Story of the Great Lakes by Marie Emilie Gilchrist, illustrated by C. H. DeWitt; Harper, 1942. **Awarded:** Ohioana (honorable mention) 1943.

Story of the Mississippi by Marshall McClintock, illustrated by C. H. DeWitt; Harper, 1941. **Awarded:** Spring Book Festival (younger honor) 1941.

The Golden Geography: a Child's Introduction to the World by Elsa Jane Werner, illustrated by Cornelius DeWitt; Simon & Schuster, 1952. **Awarded:** Boys Club 1954.

DHONDY, FARRUKH

Come to Mecca and Other Stories by Farrukh Dhondy, not illustrated; Collins, 1978. **Awarded:** Other Award 1979.

East End at Your Feet by Farrukh Dhondy, not illustrated Macmillan, 1976. **Awarded:** Other Award 1977.

DIAMOND, DONNA

The Boy Who Sang the Birds by John Weston, illustrated by Donna Diamond; Scribner, 1976. **Awarded:** Commonwealth Club of California 1976.

Bridge to Terabithia by Katherine Paterson, illustrated by Donna Diamond; Crowell, 1977. **Awarded:** Blue Spruce 1986; Lewis Carroll Shelf 1978; Michigan Young Readers (division II runnerup) 1980; Newbery 1978; Virginia Young Readers (Elementary) 1983.

Chen-Li and the River Spirit by Anthony Holcroft, illustrated by Donna Diamond; in Cricket, August 1990. **Awarded:** Witty Short Story Award 1991.

Keeping it Secret by Penny Pollock, illustrated by Donna Diamond; Putnam, 1982. **Awarded:** New Jersey Institute of Technology 1983.

Mustard by Charlotte Graeber, illustrated by Donna Diamond; Macmillan, 1982. **Awarded:** Irma Simonton Black 1982; West Virginia 1985-86.

The Transfigured Hart by Jane Yolen, illustrated by Donna Diamond; Crowell, 1975. **Awarded:** Golden Kite (honor) 1975.

DIAZ, DAVID

Neighborhood Odes by Gary Soto, illustrated by David Diaz; Harcourt Brace Jovanovich, 1992. **Awarded:** Hungry Mind (Middle Readers/Fiction) 1993.

DICE, J. FRED

What Do Animals Do When It Rains? by J. Fred Dice, illustrated by Teppy Williams; Crescent, 1978. **Awarded:** New York Academy of Sciences (younger honor) 1980.

DICK, TRELLA LAMSON

Tornado Jones by Trella Lamson Dick, illustrated by Mary Stevens; Wilcox & Follett, 1953. **Awarded:** Charles W. Follett 1953.

DICKENS, CHARLES

A Christmas Carol by Charles Dickens, illustrated by Roberto Innocenti; Stewart, Tabori & Chang, 1990. **Awarded:** Biennale Illustrations Bratislava (Golden Apple) 1991; Greenaway (Commended) 1990; New York Times Best Illustrated 1990.

DICKENS, GUY

After the Bomb: Brother in the Land by Guy Dickens, Elaine Scarratt, and Nick Williams; English & Media Centre, 1991. **Awarded:** Times Educational Supplement (Schoolbook Award) 1991.

DICKIE, DONALDA

The Great Adventure: An Illustrated History of Canada by Donalda Dickie, illustrated by Lloyd Scott; Dent, 1950. **Awarded:** Governor-General 1950.

DICKINSON, PETER

Awarded: Golden Cat 1990.

AK by Peter Dickinson, not illustrated; Gollancz, 1990. **Awarded:** Whitbread 1990.

The Blue Hawk by Peter Dickinson, illustrated by David Smee; Gollancz, 1976. **Awarded:** Carnegie (commended) 1976; Guardian 1977.

A Bone From a Dry Sea by Peter Dickinson, not illustrated; Gollancz, 1992. **Awarded:** Carnegie (commended) 1992.

Chance, Luck and Destiny by Peter Dickinson, illustrated by Victor Ambrus and David Smee; Atlantic-Little, 1976. **Awarded:** Boston Globe Horn Book (nonfiction) 1977.

Eva by Peter Dickinson, not illustrated; Gollancz, 1988, Delacorte, 1989. **Awarded:** Boston Globe (Fiction honor) 1989; Carnegie (Highly Commended) 1988; Young Reader's Choice (Senior) 1992.

City of Gold and Other Stories from the Old Testament by Peter Dickinson, illustrated by Michael Foreman; Gollancz, 1980. **Awarded:** Bologna (graphics for youth) 1982; Carnegie 1980; Greenaway (highly commended) 1980.

Dancing Bear by Peter Dickinson, illustrated by David Smee; Gollancz, 1972. **Awarded:** Carnegie (commended) 1972.

The Devil's Children by Peter Dickinson, illustrated by Robert Hales; Gollancz, 1970. **Awarded:** Carnegie (honour) 1970.

Hepzibah by Peter Dickinson, illustrated by Sue Porter; Eel Pie, 1978. **Awarded:** Mother Goose (runnerup) 1979.

The Iron Lion by Peter Dickinson, illustrated by Pauline Baynes; Bedrick/Blackie, 1984. **Awarded:** New York Times Notable 1984.

Merlin Dreams by Peter Dickinson, illustrated by Alan Lee; Gollancz, 1988. **Awarded:** Greenaway (Highly Commended) 1988.

Tulku by Peter Dickinson, not illustrated; Gollancz, 1979; Unicorn/Dutton, 1979. **Awarded:** Carnegie 1979; International Board on Books for Young People (author/Great Britain) 1982; Whitbread 1979.

DICKINSON, TERENCE
Exploring the Night Sky by Terence Dickinson, illustrated by John Bianchi; Camden House, 1987. **Awarded:** New York Academy of Sciences (Older) 1988.

Exploring the Sky by Day by Terence Dickinson, illustrated; Camden House, 1988. **Awarded:** Information Book Award 1989.

DICKS, TERRANCE
The Baker Street Irregulars in the Case of the Cop Catchers by Terrance Dicks, not illustrated; Lodestar/Dutton, 1981. **Awarded:** Edgar Allan Poe (runnerup) 1983.

DICKSON, BARRY
Afraid of the Dark by Barry Dickson, illustrated by Olena Kassian; Lorimer, 1980. **Awarded:** IODE 1980.

DIETRICH, RICHARD VINCENT
Stones: Their Collection, Identification and Uses by Richard Vincent Dietrich; illustrated with sketches; Freeman, 1980. **Awarded:** New York Academy of Sciences (older honor) 1981.

DIETZCH-CAPELLE, ERIKA
Wie Tierkinder Schlafen illustrated by Erika Dietzsch-Capelle; K. Thienemanns Verlag. **Awarded:** Owl Prize 1979.

DIGBY, DESMOND
Waltzing Matilda by Andrew Barton Paterson, illustrated by Desmond Digby; Collins Australia, 1970. **Awarded:** Children's Book Council of Australia (picture book) 1971; Bologna (critici in erba) 1972.

DIGGINS, JULIA E.
String, Straight-edge and Shadow: The Story of Geometry by Julia E. Diggins, illustrated by Corydon Bell; Viking, 1965. **Awarded:** Spring Book Festival (middle honor) 1965.

DI GRAZIA, THOMAS
Amifika by Lucille Clifton, illustrated by Thomas DiGrazia; Dutton, 1977. **Awarded:** Jane Addams (special recognition) 1978.

DILLON, DIANE
Awarded: Hans Christian Andersen (highly commended illustrator/USA) 1978; Empire State Award for Excellence in Literature for Young People 1992; Keene State College Festival 1988.

Aida by Leontyne Price, illustrated by Diane Dillon and Leo Dillon; Harcourt Brace Jovanovich, 1990. **Awarded:** Coretta Scott King (Illustration) 1991.

Ashanti to Zulu: African Traditions by Margaret Musgrove, illustrated by Diane Dillon and Leo Dillon; Dial, 1976. **Awarded:** Boston Globe Horn Book (illustrator honor) 1977; Caldecott 1977; New York Times Best Illustrated 1976.

Behind the Back of the Mountain: Black Folktales from Southern Africa by Verna Aardema, illustrated by Diane Dillon and Leo Dillon; Dial, 1973. **Awarded:** Children's Book Showcase 1974.

Brother to the Wind by Mildred Pitts Walter, illustrated by Leo Dillon and Diane Dillon; Lothrop, Lee & Shepard, 1985. **Awarded:** Parents' Choice (literature) 1985.

Dark Venture by Audrey W. Beyer, illustrated by Diane Dillon and Leo Dillon; Knopf, 1968. **Awarded:** Boston Globe Horn Book (text honor) 1968.

Hakon of Rogen's Saga by Erik Haugaard, illustrated by Diane Dillon and Leo Dillon; Houghton, 1963. **Awarded:** Spring Book Festival (older honor) 1963.

Honey, I Love and Other Love Poems by Eloise Greenfield, illustrated by Diane Dillon and Leo Dillon; Crowell, 1978. **Awarded:** George G. Stone 1990.

The Hundred Penny Box by Sharon Bell Mathis, illustrated by Diane Dillon and Leo Dillon; Viking, 1975. **Awarded:** Boston Globe Horn Book (text honor) 1975; New York Times Notable 1975; Newbery (honor) 1976.

The People Could Fly: American Black Folktales by Virginia Hamilton, illustrated by Leo Dillon and Diane Dillon; Knopf, 1985; Walker, 1985. **Awarded:** International Board on Books for Young People (illustrator/USA 1986; Coretta Scott King (literature) 1986; Coretta Scott King (illustrator honorable mention) 1986; New York Times Best Illustrated 1985; New York Times Notable 1985; Other Award 1986.

The Rider and His Horse by Erik Christian Haugaard, illustrated by Diane Dillon and Leo Dillon; Houghton Mifflin, 1968. **Awarded:** Phoenix Award 1988.

Song of the Boat by Lorenz Graham, illustrated by Diane Dillon and Leo Dillon; Crowell, 1975. **Awarded:** Boston Globe Horn Book (illustration honor) 1976; Children's Book Showcase 1976.

The Tale of the Mandarin Ducks by Katherine Paterson, illustrated by Diane Dillon and Leo Dillon; Dutton, 1990. **Awarded:** Boston Globe Horn Book (Picture Book) 1991; New York Times Best Illustrated 1990.

Whirlwind is a Ghost Dancing by Natalia M. Belting, illustrated by Diane Dillon and Leo Dillon; Dutton, 1974. **Awarded:** Children's Book Showcase 1975.

Who's in Rabbit's House? A Masai Tale by Verna Aardema, illustrated by Diane Dillon and Leo Dillon; Dial, 1979. **Awarded:** Lewis Carroll Shelf 1978.

Why Mosquitos Buzz in People's Ears: A West African Tale by Verna Aardema, illustrated by Diane Dillon and Leo Dillon; Dial, 1975. **Awarded:** Art Books for Children 1977, 1978; Caldecott 1976; New York Times Notable 1975.

DILLON, EILIS
The Coriander by Eilis Dillon, illustrated by Vic Donahue; Funk & Wagnall, 1965. **Awarded:** Spring Book Festival (older honor) 1964.

A Herd of Deer by Eilis Dillon, illustrated by Richard Kennedy; Funk & Wagnalls, 1969. **Awarded:** Lewis Carroll Shelf 1970; Spring Book Festival (older honor) 1970.

The Island of Ghosts by Eilis Di!lon, not illustrated; Faber & Faber, 1990. **Awarded:** Bisto (Overall winner) 1991.

The Singing Cave by Eilis Dillon, illustrated by Stan Campbell; Funk & Wagnalls, 1960. **Awarded:** Spring Book Festival (older honor) 1960.

DILLON, LEO
Awarded: Hans Christian Andersen (highly commended illustrator/USA) 1978; Empire State Award for Excellence in Literature for Young People 1992; Keene State College Festival 1988.

Aida by Leontyne Price, illustrated by Leo Dillon and Diane Dillon; Harcourt Brace Jovanovich, 1990. **Awarded:** Coretta Scott King (Illustration) 1991.

Ashanti to Zulu: African Traditions by Margaret Musgrove, illustrated by Diane Dillon and Leo Dillon; Dial, 1976. **Awarded:** Boston Globe Horn Book (illustrator honor) 1977; Caldecott 1977; New York Times Best Illustrated 1976.

Behind the Back of the Mountain: Black Folktales from Southern Africa by Verna Aardema, illustrated by Diane Dillon and Leo Dillon; Dial, 1973. **Awarded:** Children's Book Showcase 1974.

Brother to the Wind by Mildred Pitts Walter, illustrated by Leo Dillon and Diane Dillon; Lothrop, Lee & Shepard, 1985. **Awarded:** Parents' Choice (literature) 1985.

Dark Venture by Audrey White Beyer, illustrated by Diane Dillon and Leo Dillon; Knopf, 1968. **Awarded:** Boston Globe Horn Book (text honor) 1968.

Hakon of Rogen's Saga by Erik Haugaard, illustrated by Diane Dillon and Leo Dillon; Houghton, 1963. **Awarded:** Spring Book Festival (older honor) 1963.

Honey, I Love and Other Love Poems by Eloise Greenfield, illustrated by Leo Dillon and Diane Dillon; Crowell, 1978. **Awarded:** George G. Stone 1990.

The Hundred Penny Box by Sharon Bell Mathis, illustrated by Diane Dillon and Leo Dillon; Viking, 1975. **Awarded:** Boston Globe Horn Book (text honor) 1975; New York Times Notable 1975; Newbery (honor) 1976.

The People Could Fly: American Black Folktales by Virginia Hamilton, illustrated by Leo Dillon and Diane Dillon; Knopf, 1985; Walker, 1985. **Awarded:** International Board on Books for Young People (illustrator/USA) 1986; Coretta Scott King (literature) 1986; Coretta Scott King (illustrator honorable mention) 1986; New York Times Best Illustrated 1985; New York Times Notable 1985; Other Award 1986.

The Rider and His Horse by Erik Christian Haugaard, illustrated by Leo Dillon and Diane Dillon; Houghton Mifflin, 1968. **Awarded:** Phoenix Award 1988.

Song of the Boat by Lorenz Graham, illustrated by Diane Dillon and Leo Dillon; Crowell, 1975. **Awarded:** Boston Globe Horn Book (illustration honor) 1976; Children's Book Showcase 1976.

The Tale of the Mandarin Ducks by Katherine Paterson, illustrated by Leo Dillon and Diane Dillon; Dutton, 1990. **Awarded:** Boston Globe Horn Book (Picture Book) 1991; New York Times Best Illustrated 1990.

Whirlwind Is a Ghost Dancing by Natalia M. Belting, illustrated by Diane Dillon and Leo Dillon; Dutton, 1974. **Awarded:** Children's Book Showcase 1975.

Who's in Rabbit's House? A Masai Tale by Verna Aardema, illustrated by Diane Dillon and Leo Dillon; Dial, 1979. **Awarded:** Lewis Carroll Shelf 1978.

Why Mosquitos Buzz in People's Ears: A West African Tale by Verna Aardema, illustrated by Diane Dillon and Leo Dillon; Dial, 1975. **Awarded:** Art Books for Children 1977, 1978; Caldecott 1976; New York Times Notable 1975.

DIMSON, THEO
The Double Knights: More Tales from Round the World by James McNeill, illustrated by Theo Dimson; Oxford, 1965. **Awarded:** Canadian Library Assn. 1966.

The Sunken City by James McNeill, illustrated by Theo Dimson; Oxford, 1959. **Awarded:** International Board on Books for Young People (honour list/Canada) 1962.

DINAN, CAROLYN
The Turbulent Term of Tyke Tiler by Gene Kemp, illustrated by Carolyn Dinan; Faber, 1977. **Awarded:** Carnegie 1977; Other Award 1977.

DINES, CAROL
Best Friends Tell the Best Lies by Carol Dines, not illustrated; Delacorte, 1989. **Awarded:** Delacorte Press Prize (Honorable Mention) 1987.

DINNERSTEIN, HARVEY
Remember the Days: A Short History of the Jewish American by Milton Meltzer, illustrated by Harvey Dinnerstein; Zenith/Doubleday, 1974. **Awarded:** National Book Award (finalist) 1975.

DINWOODIE, HEPBURN
Storms on the Labrador written and illustrated by Hepburn Dinwoodie; Oxford, 1938. **Awarded:** Spring Book Festival (older honor) 1938.

DIOP, BIRAGO
Mother Crocodile = Maman-Caiman by Birago Diop, translated and adapted by Rosa Guy, illustrated by John Steptoe; Delacorte, 1981. **Awarded:** Coretta Scott King (illustrator) 1982.

DISHER, GARRY
The Bamboo Flute by Garry Disher, illustrated with photographs; Angus & Robertson, 1991; Collins, 1992. **Awarded:** Children's Book Council of Australia (Book of the Year Younger) 1993.

DISKA, PAT
Andy Says ... Bonjour! by Pat Diska, illustrated by Chris Jenkyns; Vanguard, 1954. **Awarded:** New York Times Best Illustrated 1954.

DISNEY, WALT PRODUCTIONS
The Fox and the Hound by Walt Disney Productions from the film; Golden Press, 1981. **Awarded:** North Dakota Children's Choice (Younger) 1982.

DISTAD, AUDREE
The Dream Runner by Audree Distad, not illustrated; Harper, 1977. **Awarded:** Friends of American Writers (older) 1978.

DITTMER, W.
Myths and Legends of Maoriland by A. W. Reed, illustrated by W. Dittmer and George Woods; Reed, 1946. **Awarded:** Esther Glen 1947.

DIXON, TENNESSEE
Berchick by Esther Silverstein Blanc, illustrated by Tennessee Dixon; Volcano Press, 1989. **Awarded:** Bay Area Book Reviewers Assn. 1990; Jewish Book Council (Children's Picture Book) 1990; Sydney Taylor Book Award (Picture Book) 1990.

DOANE, PELAGIE
The Castle of Grumpy Grouch by Mary Dickerson Donahey, illustrated by Pelagie Doane; Random House, 1948. **Awarded:** Spring Book Festival (middle honor) 1948.

God Made the World written and illustrated by Pelagie Doane; Lippincott, 1960. **Awarded:** New Jersey Institute of Technology 1961.

DOBBS, ROSE

No Room: An Old Story retold by Rose Dobbs, illustrated by Fritz Eichenberg; McKay, 1944. **Awarded:** Lewis Carroll Shelf 1968.

DOBIAS, FRANK

Clearing Weather by Cornelia Meigs, illustrated by Frank Dobias, Little, Brown, 1928. **Awarded:** Newbery (honor) 1929.

New Land by Sarah L. Schmidt, illustrated by Frank Dobias; McBride, 1933. **Awarded:** Newbery (honor) 1934.

DOBIE, JAMES FRANK

The Ben Lilly Legend by J. Frank Dobie, illustrated with photographs; Little, Brown, 1950. **Awarded:** Boys Club 1951.

DOBLER, LAVINIA G.

A Business of Their Own by Lavinia G. Dobler, not illustrated; Dodd, 1958. **Awarded:** Edith Busby 1957.

DOCTOR SEUSS

see SEUSS, DR.

DODD, LYNLEY

Hairy Maclary from Donaldson's Dairy written and illustrated by Lynley Dodd; Mallinson Rendel, 1983; Gareth Stevens, 1985, c1983. **Awarded:** AIM Children's Book Award (Picture Book) 1984.

Hairy Maclary's Caterwaul Caper written and illustrated by Lynley Dodd; Mallinson Rendel, 1987. **Awarded:** AIM Children's Book Award (Picture Book) 1988.

Hairy Maclary's Rumpus at the Vet written and illustrated by Lynley Dodd; Mallinson Rendel, 1989. **Awarded:** AIM Children's Book Award (Picture Book 3rd prize) 1990.

Hairy Maclary's Showbusiness written and illustrated by Lynley Dodd; Mallinson Rendel, 1991. **Awarded:** AIM Children's Book Award (Picture Book) 1992.

Hairy Maclary, Scattercat written and illustrated by Lynley Dodd; Mallinson Rendel, 1985; Gareth Stevens, 1988, c1985. **Awarded:** AIM Children's Book Award (Picture Book) 1986.

My Cat Likes to Hide in Boxes by Eve Sutton, illustrated by Lynley Dodd; Hamish Hamilton, 1974. **Awarded:** Esther Glen 1975.

Slinky Malinki written and illustrated by Lynley Dodd; Mallinson Rendel, 1990; Spindlewood, 1990; Gareth Stevens, 1991. **Awarded:** AIM Children's Book Award (Picture Book 3rd prize) 1991.

DODDS, GERALD

Amish People: Plain Living in a Complex World by Carolyn Meyer, photographs by Gerald Dodds, Michael Ramsey, and Carolyn Meyer; Atheneum, 1976. **Awarded:** Children's Book Showcase 1977.

DODDS, SIOBHAN

Wake Up, Dad! by Sally Grindley, illustrated by Siobhan Dodds; Simon & Schuster (UK), 1988; Doubleday, 1989. **Awarded:** Best Books for Babies 1989.

DODERER, KLAUS, DR.

Awarded: International Brothers Grimm 1987.

DODGE, MARY MAPES

Mary Anne by Mary Mapes Dodge, illustrated by June Amos Grammer; Lothrop, Lee & Shepard, 1983. **Awarded:** New Jersey Institute of Technology 1983.

DODGE, NANABAH CHEE

Morning Arrow by Nanabah Chee Dodge, illustrated by Jeffrey Lunge; Lothrop, 1975. **Awarded:** Council on Interracial Books (American Indian) 1973.

DODGSON, CHARLES LUTWIDGE

see CARROLL, LEWIS

DODGSON, ELYSE

Motherland: West Indian Women to Britain in the 1950s by Elyse Dodgson, illustrated; Heinemann Educational, 1984. **Awarded:** Other Award 1985.

DODSON, BERT

Nelson Malone Meets the Man from Mushnut by Louise Hawes, illustrated by Bert Dodson; Dutton, 1986. **Awarded:** New Jersey Institute of Technology 1987.

Pilgrim Children on the Mayflower by Ida De Lage, illustrated by Bert Dodson; Garrard, 1980. **Awarded:** New Jersey Institute of Technology 1981.

DODWELL, CHRISTINA

An Explorer's Handbook by Christina Dodwell, illustrated; Facts on File, 1986. **Awarded:** New York Academy of Sciences (older honor) 1987.

DOHERTY, BERLIE

Awarded: British Book Award (Author runnerup) 1992.

Dear Nobody by Berlie Doherty, not illustrated; Hamish Hamilton, 1991; Orchard, 1992. **Awarded:** Carnegie 1991.

Granny Was a Buffer Girl by Berlie Doherty, not illustrated; Methuen, 1986, Orchard, 1988. **Awarded:** Boston Globe (Fiction Honor) 1988; Burnley Express 1987; Carnegie 1986.

Snowy by Berlie Doherty, illustrated by Keith Bowen; HarperCollins, 1992. **Awarded:** Children's Book Award (Picture Book) 1993.

White Peak Farm by Berlie Doherty, not illustrated; Orchard, 1990. **Awarded:** Reading Magic Award 1990.

DOMANSKA, JANINA

The Coconut Thieves by Catharine Fournier, illustrated by Janina Domanska; Scribner, 1964. **Awarded:** Spring Book Festival (picture book) 1964.

If All the Seas Were One Sea written and illustrated by Janina Domanska; Macmillan, 1971. **Awarded:** Art Books for Children 1973; Boston Globe Horn Book (illustration honor) 1971; Caldecott (honor) 1972.

King Krakus and the Dragon written and illustrated by Janina Domanska; Greenwillow, 1979. **Awarded:** New York Times Best Illustrated 1979; New York Times Notable 1979.

Palmiero and the Ogre written and illustrated by Janina Domanska; Macmillan, 1967. **Awarded:** Spring Book Festival (picture book honor) 1967.

Ten and a Kid by Sadie Rose Weilerstein, illustrated by Janina Domanska; Doubleday, 1961. **Awarded:** Jewish Book Council 1961.

Under the Green Willow by Elizabeth Coatsworth, illustrated by Janina Domanska; Macmillan, 1971. **Awarded:** Spring Book Festival (picture book honor) 1971.

DONAHEY, MARY DICKERSON

The Castle of Grumpy Grouch by Mary Dickerson Donahey, illustrated by Pelagie Doane; Random House, 1948. **Awarded:** Spring Book Festival (middle honor) 1948.

DONAHUE, VIC

The Coriander by Eilis Dillon, illustrated by Vic Donahue; Funk & Wagnall, 1965. **Awarded:** Spring Book Festival (older honor) 1964.

DONALDSON, KARIN
The Story of the Falling Star by Elsie Jones, illustrated by Doug Jones and Karin Donaldson; Aboriginal Studies Press, 1989. **Awarded:** Ashton Scholastic 1990.

DONELSON, KENNETH
Awarded: ALAN 1983.

DONOVAN, FRANK
The Early Eagles by Frank Donovan, illustrated with photographs; Dodd, Mead, 1962. **Awarded:** Boys Club 1963.

DONOVAN, JOHN
Awarded: Children's Reading Round Table 1983.

I'll Get There. It Better Be Worth the Trip by John Donovan, not illustrated; Harper, 1969. **Awarded:** Spring Book Festival (older honor) 1969.

Wild in the World by John Donovan, not illustrated; Harper, 1971. **Awarded:** National Book Award (finalist) 1972; New York Times Notable 1971.

DOORLY, ELEANOR
The Insect Man: Jean Henri Fabre by Eleanor Doorly, illustrated by Robert Gibbings; Appleton Century Crofts, 1937. **Awarded:** Spring Book Festival (older honor) 1937.

The Radium Woman: a Youth Edition of the Life of Madame Curie by Eleanor Doorly, illustrated by Robert Gibbings; Heinemann, 1939; Roy, 1955. **Awarded:** Carnegie 1939; Spring Book Festival (older honor) 1955.

DOREMUS, ROBERT
Beaver Water by Rutherford G. Montgomery, illustrated by Robert Doremus; World, 1956. **Awarded:** Boys Club 1957; Spring Book Festival (middle) 1956.

DOREN, MARION WALKER
Borrowed Summer by Marion Walker Doren, not illustrated; Harper & Row, 1986. **Awarded:** Christopher (Ages 8-12) 1987.

DORIAN, EDITH
Hokahey! American Indians Then and Now by Edith Dorian, illustrated by W. N. Wilson; Whittlesey, 1957. **Awarded:** Boys Club 1958.

DORN, DANIEL, JR.
Let's Make Soup by Hannah Lyons Johnson, illustrated by Daniel Dorn, Jr.; Lothrop, 1976. **Awarded:** New Jersey Institute of Technology 1977.

DORNBERG, JOHN
The Two Germanys by John Dornberg, illustrated with photographs; Dial, 1974. **Awarded:** Children's Book Showcase 1975.

DORRIS, MICHAEL
Morning Girl by Michael Dorris, not illustrated; Hyperion, 1992. **Awarded:** Scott O'Dell 1992.

DORROS, ARTHUR
Abuela by Arthur Dorros, illustrated by Elisa Kleven; Dutton, 1991. **Awarded:** Hungry Mind (Picturebooks/Fiction) 1992; Parents' Choice (Story Book) 1991.

DOTY, ROY
Tales of a Fourth Grade Nothing by Judy Blume, illustrated by Roy Doty; Dutton, 1972; Bodley Head, 1982. **Awarded:** Arizona 1977; Georgia Children's 1977; Great Stone Face 1982; Massachusetts Children's 1977; Massachusetts Children's (Elementary) 1983; New Jersey Institute of Technology 1972; North Dakota Children's Choice 1980; Sequoyah 1975; Charlie May Simon 1974-75; South Carolina Children's 1977; West Australian Young Readers 1980; Young Readers Choice 1975; Young Teens 1991.

DOUGLAS, EMILY TAFT
Appleseed Farm by Emily Taft Douglas, illustrated by Anne Vaughan; Abingdon-Cokesbury, 1948. **Awarded:** Spring Book Festival (middle honor) 1948.

DOUGLAS, JOHN SCOTT
The Secret of the Undersea Bell by John Scott Douglas, not illustrated; Dodd, 1951. **Awarded:** Boys Life - Dodd, Mead 1950.

DOUGLAS, MARY PEACOCK
Awarded: Grolier 1958.

DOW, KATHARINE
My Time of Year by Katharine Dow, illustrated by Walter Erhard; Walck, 1961. **Awarded:** New York Times Best Illustrated 1961

DOWDEN, ANNE OPHELIA T.
The Blossom on the Bough: A Book of Trees written and illustrated by Anne Ophelia T. Dowden; Crowell, 1975. **Awarded:** Children's Book Showcase 1976.

Wild Green Things in the City: A Book of Weeds written and illustrated by Anne Ophelia T. Dowden; Crowell, 1972. **Awarded:** Children's Book Showcase 1973.

DOWNER, MARION
Discovering Design by Marion Downer, illustrated with photographs and drawings; Lothrop, 1947. **Awarded:** Spring Book Festival (older honor) 1947.

The Story of Design by Marion Downer, illustrated with photographs; Lothrop, 1963. **Awarded:** Spring Book Festival (older) 1964.

DOWNEY, FAIRFAX
War Horse by Fairfax Downey, illustrated by Paul Brown; Dodd, 1942. **Awarded:** Spring Book Festival (older honor) 1942.

DOWNIE, MARY ALICE
The Wind Has Wings: Poems from Canada compiled by Mary Alice Downie and Barbara Robertson, illustrated by Elizabeth Cleaver; Oxford, 1968. **Awarded:** Amelia Frances Howard-Gibbon 1971.

The Witch of the North: Folk Tales of French Canada adapted by Mary Alice Downie, illustrated by Elizabeth Cleaver; Oberon Press, 1975. **Awarded:** Amelia Frances Howard-Gibbon (runnerup) 1976.

DOWNING, JULIE
A Ride on the Red Mare's Back by Ursula K. Le Guin, illustrated by Julie Downing; Orchard, 1992. **Awarded:** Parents Choice (Story Book) 1992.

DOWSETT, CHARLES
Kashtanka by Anton Chekhov, translated by Charles Dowsett, illustrated by William Stobbs; Oxford, 1959. **Awarded:** Greenaway 1959.

DOYLE, BRIAN
Awarded: Vicky Metcalf 1991.

Covered Bridge by Brian Doyle, illustrated with a map; Douglas & McIntyre, 1990. **Awarded:** Canadian Library Assn. (Runnerup) 1991; Mr. Christie's (English Text) 1990.

Easy Avenue by Brian Doyle, not illustrated; Douglas & McIntyre, 1988. **Awarded:** Canadian Library Assn. 1989.

Je T'Attends a Peggy's Cove by Brian Doyle, translated by Claude Aubry (original English: *You Can Pick Me Up at Peggy's Cove*) Pierre Tisseyre, 1982. **Awarded:** International Board on Books for Young People (translator/Canada) 1984.

Up To Low by Brian Doyle, not illustrated; Douglas & McIntyre, 1982. **Awarded:** Canadian Library Assn. 1983.

DRAGONWAGON, CRESCENT

Always, Always by Crescent Dragonwagon, illustrated by Arieh Zeldich; Macmillan, 1984. **Awarded:** Parents' Choice (literature) 1984.

Half a Moon and One Whole Star by Crescent Dragonwagon, illustrated by Jerry Pinkney; Macmillan, 1986. **Awarded:** Coretta Scott King (illustration) 1987.

Home Place by Crescent Dragonwagon, illustrated by Jerry Pinkney; Macmillan, 1990. **Awarded:** Golden Kite (Picture-Illustration) 1990.

The Year it Rained by Crescent Dragonwagon, not illustrated; Macmillan, 1985. **Awarded:** New York Times Notable 1985.

DRAKE, WILLIAM HENRY

The Jungle Book by Rudyard Kipling, illustrated by W. H. Drake, J. L. Kipling, and P. Frenzeny; Doubleday, 1952, c1893. **Awarded:** Lewis Carroll Shelf 1960.

DRESCHER, HENRIK

Simon's Book written and illustrated by Henrik Drescher; Lothrop Lee & Shepard, 1983. **Awarded:** New York Times Best Illustrated 1983; Parents Choice (Illustration) 1983.

The Strange Appearance of Howard Cranebill, Jr. written and illustrated by Henrik Drescher; Lothrop Lee & Shepard, 1982. **Awarded:** New York Times Best Illustrated 1982.

The Yellow Umbrella written and illustrated by Henrik Drescher; Bradbury, 1987. **Awarded:** New York Times Best Illustrated 1987.

DRESCHER, JOAN

Bubbles by Bernie Zubrowski, illustrated by Joan Drescher; Little, 1979. **Awarded:** New York Academy of Sciences (younger honor) 1980.

DRUCKER, MALKA

Eliezer Ben-Yehuda, the Father of Modern Hebrew by Malka Drucker, illustrated with photos; Lodestar, 1987. **Awarded:** Janusz Korczak (Books for Young Readers) 1988.

Frido Kahlo by Malka Drucker, illustrated; Bantam, 1991. **Awarded:** Hungry Mind (Young Adult/Nonfiction) 1992.

Hanukkah: Eight Nights, Eight Lights by Malka Drucker, illustrated by Brom Hoban; Holiday House, 1980. **Awarded:** Southern California Council (significant contribution of excellence in a series) 1982.

Passover: A Season of Freedom by Malka Drucker, illustrated by Brom Hoban; Holiday House, 1981. **Awarded:** Southern California Council (significant contribution of excellence in a series) 1982.

Rosh Hashanah and Yom Kippur: Sweet Beginnings by Malka Drucker, illustrated by Brom Hoban; Holiday House, 1981. **Awarded:** Southern California Council (significant contribution of excellence in a series) 1982.

Sukkot: A Time to Rejoice by Malka Drucker, illustrated by Brom Hoban; Holiday House, 1982. **Awarded:** Southern California Council (significant contribution of excellence in a series) 1982.

DRUMMOND, VIOLET HILDA

Mrs. Easter and the Storks written and illustrated by V. H. Drummond; Faber, 1957. **Awarded:** Greenaway 1957.

The Piemakers by Helen Cresswell, illustrated by V. H. Drummond; Faber, 1967. **Awarded:** Carnegie (commended) 1967.

DRUMTRA, STACY

Face-off by Stacy Drumtra, not illustrated; Avon, 1992. **Awarded:** Avon Flare 1991.

DRURY, ROGER W.

The Champion of Merrimack County by Roger W. Drury, illustrated by Fritz Wegner; Little Brown, 1976. **Awarded:** Christopher (ages 9-12) 1977; Ethical Culture School 1976; Mark Twain 1979.

DUBANEVICH, ARLENE

Pigs in Hiding written and illustrated by Arlene Dubanevich; Four Winds, 1983. **Awarded:** Parents' Choice (illustration) 1983.

du BOIS, WILLIAM PENE

The Alligator Case written and illustrated by William Pene du Bois; Harper, 1965. **Awarded:** New Jersey Institute of Technology 1965.

Bear Circus written and illustrated by William Pene du Bois; Viking, 1971. **Awarded:** Lewis Carroll Shelf 1972; Children's Book Showcase 1972; New York Times Best Illustrated 1971; New York Times Notable 1971.

Bear Party written and illustrated by William Pene du Bois; Viking, 1951. **Awarded:** Caldecott (honor) 1952.

A Certain Small Shepherd by Rebecca Caudill, illustrated by William Pene du Bois; Holt, 1965. **Awarded:** Clara Ingram Judson 1966.

The Forbidden Forest written and illustrated by William Pene du Bois; Harper, 1978. **Awarded:** New York Times Best Illustrated 1978.

The Great Geppy written and illustrated by William Pene du Bois; Viking, 1940. **Awarded:** Spring Book Festival (younger honor) 1940.

Harriet by Charles Frederick McKinley, Jr., illustrated by William Pene du Bois; Viking, 1946. **Awarded:** Spring Book Festival (middle honor) 1946.

The Hare and the Tortoise and the Tortoise and the Hare by William Pene du Bois and Lee Po, illustrated by William Pene du Bois; Doubleday, 1972. **Awarded:** Art Books for Children 1974.

The Horse in the Camel Suit written and illustrated by William Pene du Bois; Harper, 1967. **Awarded:** New Jersey Institute of Technology 1967.

Lion written and illustrated by William Pene du Bois; Viking, 1956. **Awarded:** Caldecott (honor) 1957; Spring Book Festival (ages 4-8) 1956.

The Mousewife by Rumer Godden, illustrated by William Pene du Bois; Viking, 1951. **Awarded:** Spring Book Festival (picture book honor) 1951.

My Brother Bird by Evelyn Ames, illustrated by William Pene du Bois; Dodd, 1954. **Awarded:** Spring Book Festival (middle honor) 1954.

My Grandson Lew by Charlotte Zolotow, illustrated by William Pene du Bois; Harper, 1974. **Awarded:** Christopher (ages 4-8) 1975.

Otto in Africa written and illustrated by William Pene du Bois; Viking, 1961. **Awarded:** New Jersey Institute of Technology 1961.

Porko von Popbutton written and illustrated by William Pene du Bois; Harper, 1969. **Awarded:** New Jersey Institute of Technology 1969.

The Three Policemen written and illustrated by William Pene du Bois; Viking, 1938. **Awarded:** New Jersey Institute of Technology 1961.

Twenty and Ten by Claire Huchet Bishop, illustrated William Pene du Bois; Dutton, 1952. **Awarded:** Child Study 1952.

The Twenty-one Balloons written and illustrated by William Pene du Bois; Viking, 1947. **Awarded:** Newbery 1948; Spring Book Festival (older) 1947.

Where's Gomer? by Norma Farber, illustrated by William Pene du Bois; Dutton, 1974. **Awarded:** Children's Book Showcase 1975.

William's Doll by Charlotte Zolotow, illustrated by William Pene du Bois; Harper Trophy, 1985, c1972. **Awarded:** Redbook 1985.

DUCA, BILL
Do You See Me, God? Prayers for Young Children by Elspeth Campbell Murphy, illustrated by Bill Duca; Chariot Books, 1989. **Awarded:** Gold Medallion (Preschool) 1990.

DUCHACEK, IVO
see DUKA, IVO (pseudonym)

DUCKETT, ALFRED
I Never Had It Made by Jackie Robinson as told to Alfred Duckett, illustrated with photographs; Putnam, 1972. **Awarded:** Coretta Scott King 1973.

DUDER, TESSA
Alessandra: Alex in Rome by Tessa Duder, not illustrated; Oxford University Press, 1991. **Awarded:** AIM Children's Book Award (Story Book 3rd Prize) 1992; Esther Glen 1992.

Alex by Tessa Duder, not illustrated; Oxford University Press, 1987. **Awarded:** AIM Children's Book Award (Story Book) 1988; Esther Glen 1988.

Alex in Winter by Tessa Duder, not illustrated; Oxford University Press, 1989. **Awarded:** AIM Children's Book Award (Story Book) 1990; Esther Glen 1990.

DUER, DOUGLAS
Walter Reed: Doctor in Uniform by Laura Newbold Wood, illustrated by Douglas Duer; Messner, 1943. **Awarded:** Spring Book Festival (older honor) 1943.

DUFAULT, JOSEPH ERNEST NEPHTALI
see JAMES, WILL

DUGAN, MARILYN
Awarded: Lucile M. Pannell 1988.

DUGGAN, MAURICE
Falter Tom and the Water Boy by Maurice Duggan, illustrated by Kenneth Rowell; Paul's Book Arcade, 1958. **Awarded:** Esther Glen 1959.

DUGO, ANDRE
The Dogcatcher's Dog written and illustrated by Andre Dugo; Holt, 1952. **Awarded:** New York Times Best Illustrated 1952.

DUKA, IVO
The Secret of the Two Feathers by Ivo Duka and Helena Kolda, photographs by Helena Kolda; Harper, 1954. **Awarded:** Boys Club 1955.

DUKE, KATE
The Guinea Pig ABC written and illustrated by Kate Duke; Dutton, 1983. **Awarded:** Boston Globe (illustration honor) 1984; Redbook 1986.

DUMAS, ALICE
Awarded: Macmillan Prize (3rd prize) 1990.

DUMAS, PHILLIPE
Odette: a Bird in Paris by Kay Fender, illustrated by Phillipe Dumas; Prentice Hall, 1978. **Awarded:** New York Times Best Illustrated 1978.

The Story of Edward written and illustrated by Phillipe Dumas; Parents, 1977. **Awarded:** Boston Globe Horn Book (illustration honor) 1978.

DUNBAR, JOYCE
Mundo and the Weather-child by Joyce Dunbar, not illustrated; Heinemann, 1985. **Awarded:** Guardian (runnerup) 1986.

DUNCAN, FRANCES
The Toothpaste Genie by Frances Duncan; Scholastic-TAB, 1981. **Awarded:** Surrey School 1983.

DUNCAN, GREGOR
None But the Brave: A Story of Holland by Rosamund Van der Zee Marshall, illustrated by Gregor Duncan; Houghton, 1942. **Awarded:** Spring Book Festival (older) 1942.

DUNCAN, LOIS
Awarded: Margaret A. Edwards 1992.

Debutante Hill by Lois Duncan, not illustrated; Dodd Mead, 1958. **Awarded:** Calling All Girls - Dodd, Mead 1958.

Don't Look Behind You by Lois Duncan, not illustrated; Delacorte, 1989. **Awarded:** Iowa Teen Award 1992; Parents' Choice (Story Book) 1989; Utah Young Adults' Book Award 1992; Virginia Young Readers (High School) 1992; Young Hoosier (grades 6-8) 1992.

The Eyes of Karen Connors by Lois Duncan, not illustrated; Hamish Hamilton, 1985. **Awarded:** West Australian (Secondary) 1987.

Killing Mr. Griffin by Lois Duncan, not illustrated; Little Brown, 1978. **Awarded:** Emphasis on Reading (Grades 7-9) 1982-83; Massachusetts (Young Adult) 1982.

Locked In Time by Lois Duncan, not illustrated; Little Brown, 1985. **Awarded:** Nevada Young Reader Award (Young Adult) 1988-89; Edgar Allan Poe (runnerup) 1986; South Carolina Young Adult 1988.

Ransom by Lois Duncan, not illustrated; Doubleday, 1966. **Awarded:** Edgar Allan Poe (runnerup) 1967.

Stranger With my Face by Lois Duncan, not illustrated; Little Brown, 1981; Dell, 1982. **Awarded:** California Young Reader (high school) 1984; Ethical Culture School 1981; Massachusetts Children's (Young Adult) 1983; New York Times Notable 1981; South Carolina Young Adult 1984; Young Hoosier (grades 6-8) 1986.

Summer of Fear by Lois Duncan, not illustrated; Little Brown, 1976. **Awarded:** California Young Reader (High School) 1983; Dorothy Canfield Fisher 1978; Land of Enchantment 1983.

The Third Eye by Lois Duncan, not illustrated; Little, Brown, 1984. **Awarded:** Blue Spruce 1987; Edgar Allan Poe (honor) 1985; Young Hoosier (Grades 6-8) 1987.

They Never Came Home by Lois Duncan, not illustrated; Doubleday, 1969. **Awarded:** Edgar Allan Poe (runnerup) 1970.

The Twisted Window by Lois Duncan, not illustrated; Delacorte, 1987. **Awarded:** Parents' Choice (Story Book) 1987.

DUNCOMBE, FRANCES
Clarinda by Frances Duncombe, illustrated by Angela Straeter; Holt, 1944. **Awarded:** Spring Book Festival (younger honor) 1944.

DUNHAM, MABEL
Kristli's Trees by Mabel Dunham, illustrated by Selwyn Dewdney; McClelland & Stewart, 1948. **Awarded:** Canadian Library Assn. 1949.

DUNLOP, AGNES MARY ROBERTSON
see KYLE, ELISABETH (pseudonym)

DUNN, MARY LOIS
The Man in the Box: A Story from Vietnam by Mary Lois Dunn, not illustrated; McGraw, 1968. **Awarded:** Sequoyah 1972.

DUNNAHOO, TERRY
Awarded: Southern California Council (Dorothy C. McKenzie Award) 1988.

Before the Supreme Court: the Story of Belva Ann Lockwood by Terry Dunnahoo, illustrated by Bea Holmes; Houghton, 1974. **Awarded:** Southern California Council (distinguished nonfiction) 1975.

DUNNE, JEANETTE
Run Swift, Run Free by Tom McCaughren, illustrated by Jeanette Dunne; Wolfhound Press, 1986. **Awarded:** Bisto (Fiction) 1990; Reading Association of Ireland 1985.

Run To Earth by Tom McCaughren, illustrated by Jeanette Dunne; Wolfhound Press, 1984. **Awarded:** Bisto (Fiction) 1990.

Run With the Wind by Tom McCaughren, illustrated by Jeanette Dunne; Wolfhound Press, 1983. **Awarded:** Bisto (Fiction) 1990.

DUNNE, JOHN WILLIAM
The Jumping Lions of Borneo by John William Dunne, illustrated by Irene Robinson; Holt, 1938. **Awarded:** Spring Book Festival (younger honor) 1938.

DUNNING, STEPHEN
Reflections on a Gift of Watermelon Pickle and Other Modern Verse by Stephen Dunning, Edward Lueders, and Hugh Smith, illustrated with photographs; Lothrop, 1966. **Awarded:** Lewis Carroll Shelf 1968.

DUNNINGTON, TOM
Wait, Skates! by Mildred D. Johnson, illustrated by Tom Dunnington, prepared under the direction of Robert Hillerich; Children's Press, 1983. **Awarded:** Sandburg 1983.

DUPASQUIER, PHILIPPE
Bill's New Frock by Anne Fine, illustrated by Philippe Dupasquier; Methuen Children's, 1989. **Awarded:** Carnegie (Highly Commended) 1989; Nottinghamshire (Oak Tree) 1990; Smarties (ages 6-8) 1989.

DURACK, ELIZABETH
Australian Legendary Tales by K. Langloh Parker, illustrated by Elizabeth Durack; Angus & Robertson, 1953. **Awarded:** Children's Book Council of Australia 1954.

DURANCEAU, SUZANNE
Hickory, Dickory Dock by Robin Muller, illustrated by Suzanne Duranceau; North Winds Press, 1992. **Awarded:** Alcuin 1993.

DURRELL, ANN
The Big Book for Peace by Ann Durrell and Marilyn Sachs, illustrated by various illustrators; Dutton, 1990. **Awarded:** Jane Addams 1991.

DuSOE, ROBERT C.
Sea Boots by Robert C. DuSoe, illustrated by Arthur Harper, Longman, 1949. **Awarded:** Spring Book Festival (under 12 honor) 1949.

DUVOISIN, ROGER ANTOINE
Awarded: Hans Christian Andersen (highly commended illustrator/U.S.) 1968; Kerlan 1976; Rutgers 1966; University of Southern Mississippi 1971.

Bhimsa, the Dancing Bear by Christine Weston, illustrated by Roger Duvoisin; Scribner, 1945. **Awarded:** Newbery (honor) 1946.

Busby & Co. by Herbert L. Coggins, illustrated by Roger Duvoisin; Whittlesey House, 1952. **Awarded:** Spring Book Festival (ages 8-12 honor) 1952.

The Happy Hunter written and illustrated by Roger Duvoisin; Lothrop, 1961. **Awarded:** New York Times Best Illustrated 1961.

The Happy Lion by Louise Fatio, illustrated by Roger Duvoisin; McGraw, 1954. **Awarded:** New York Times Best Illustrated 1954.

The Happy Lion in Africa by Louise Fatio, illustrated by Roger Duvoisin; McGraw, 1955. **Awarded:** New York Times Best Illustrated 1955.

The Happy Lion's Quest by Louise Fatio, illustrated by Roger Duvoisin; McGraw, 1961. **Awarded:** New Jersey Institute of Technology 1961.

Hector and Christina by Louise Fatio, illustrated by Roger Duvoisin; McGraw, 1977. **Awarded:** New Jersey Institute of Technology 1978.

Hector Penguin by Louise Fatio, illustrated by Roger Duvoisin; McGraw, 1973. **Awarded:** New York Times Best Illustrated 1973.

Hide and Seek Fog by Alvin Tresselt, illustrated by Roger Duvoisin; Lothrop, 1965. **Awarded:** Caldecott (honor) 1966; New York Times Best Illustrated 1965; Spring Book Festival (picture book honor) 1965.

The House of Four Seasons written and illustrated by Roger Duvoisin; Lothrop, 1956. **Awarded:** Spring Book Festival (ages 4-8 honor) 1956.

Little Red Nose by Miriam Schlein, illustrated by Roger Duvoisin; Abelard, 1955. **Awarded:** Spring Book Festival (ages 4-8 honor) 1955.

Lonely Veronica written and illustrated by Roger Duvoisin; Knopf, 1963. **Awarded:** New Jersey Institute of Technology (illustration) 1964.

Marc and Pixie and the Walls in Mrs. Jones' Garden by Roger Duvoisin and Louise Fatio, illustrated by Roger Duvoisin;

McGraw, 1975. **Awarded:** New Jersey Institute of Technology 1976.

The Miller, His Son, and Their Donkey written and illustrated by Roger Duvoisin; Whittlesey House, 1962. **Awarded:** New Jersey Institute of Technology (illustration) 1962.

Petunia written and illustrated by Roger Duvoisin; Knopf, 1950. **Awarded:** New Jersey Institute of Technology 1990.

The Pointed Brush by Patricia Miles Martin, illustrated by Roger Duvoisin; Lothrop, 1959. **Awarded:** Spring Book Festival (ages 4-8 honor) 1959.

See What I Am written and illustrated by Roger Duvoisin; Lothrop, 1974. **Awarded:** New York Academy of Sciences (younger) 1975.

The Talking Cat by Natalie Savage Carlson, illustrated by Roger Duvoisin; Harper & Row, 1952. **Awarded:** Spring Book Festival (ages 8-12) 1952.

They Put Out to Sea: The Story of the Map written and illustrated by Roger Duvoisin; Knopf, 1943. **Awarded:** Spring Book Festival (ages 8-12) 1944.

Veronica's Smile written and illustrated by Roger Duvoisin; Knopf, 1964. **Awarded:** New Jersey Institute of Technology (illustration) 1964.

The Web in the Grass by Berniece Freschet, illustrated by Roger Duvoisin; Scribner, 1972. **Awarded:** New York Academy of Sciences (younger) 1974.

White Snow, Bright Snow by Alvin Tresselt, illustrated by Roger Duvoisin; Lothrop, 1947. **Awarded:** Caldecott 1948.

DWYER, JOHN N.
Summer Gold: A Camper's Guide to Amateur Prospecting by John N. Dwyer, illustrated with maps; Scribner, 1974. **Awarded:** New York Academy of Sciences (older honor) 1975.

DYER, JANE
Piggins by Jane Yolen, illustrated by Jane Dyer; Harcourt Brace Jovanovich, 1987. **Awarded:** Charlotte Book Award (3-5) 1990; Golden Sower (K-3) 1989; Parents' Choice (Story Book) 1987.

The Three Bears Rhyme Book by Jane Yolen, illustrated by Jane Dyer; Harcourt Brace Jovanovich, 1987. **Awarded:** Parents' Choice (Picture Book) 1987.

DYER, THOMAS A.
The Whipman Is Watching by Thomas A. Dyer, not illustrated; Houghton Mifflin, 1979. **Awarded:** Child Study 1979.

E

EAGER, EDWARD McMAKEN
Half Magic by Edward Eager, illustrated by N. M. Bodecker; Harcourt, 1954. **Awarded:** Spring Book Festival (middle honor) 1954.

Knight's Castle by Edward Eager, illustrated by N. M. Bodecker; Harcourt, 1956. **Awarded:** Ohioana 1957.

Magic or Not? by Edward Eager, illustrated by N. M. Bodecker; Harcourt, 1959. **Awarded:** Spring Book Festival (middle honor) 1959.

Seven-day Magic by Edward Eager, illustrated by N. M. Bodecker; Harcourt, 1962. **Awarded:** Ohioana 1963.

EAGLE, ELLEN
Lila on the Landing by Sue Alexander, illustrated by Ellen Eagle; Clarion, 1987. **Awarded:** Southern California Council (Outstanding Work of Fiction for Children) 1988.

EAGLE, MICHAEL
Tough Chauncey by Doris Buchanan Smith, illustrated by Michael Eagle; Morrow, 1974. **Awarded:** Boston Globe Horn Book (text honor) 1974.

EAMES, GENEVIEVE TORREY
A Horse to Remember by Genevieve Eames, illustrated by Paul Brown; Messner, 1947. **Awarded:** Julia Ellsworth Ford 1946.

EARLE, VANA
People Are Important by Eva Knox Evans, illustrated by Vana Earle; Golden Press, 1951. **Awarded:** Jane Addams 1953.

EARLY, MARGARET
William Tell written and illustrated by Margaret Early; Walter McVitty Books, 1991; Abrams, 1991. **Awarded:** Children's Book Council of Australia (Picture Book honor) 1992.

EATON, JEANETTE
America's Own Mark Twain by Jeanette Eaton, illustrated by Leonard Everett Fisher; Morrow, 1958. **Awarded:** Ohioana 1959.

A Daughter of the Seine: The Life of Madame Roland by Jeanette Eaton, not illustrated; Harper & Row, 1929. **Awarded:** Newbery (honor) 1930.

David Livingston, Foe of Darkness by Jeanette Eaton, illustrated by Ralph Ray; Morrow, 1947. **Awarded:** Ohioana (honorable mention) 1948.

Gandhi, Fighter Without a Sword by Jeanette Eaton, illustrated by Ralph Ray; Morrow, 1950. **Awarded:** Newbery (honor) 1951.

Leader by Destiny: George Washington, Man and Patriot by Jeanette Eaton, illustrated by J. M. Rose; Harcourt, 1938. **Awarded:** Newbery (honor) 1939.

Lone Journey: the Life of Roger Williams by Jeanette Eaton, illustrated by Woodi Ishmael; Harcourt, 1944. **Awarded:** Newbery (honor) 1945.

EATON, ROBIN
It's Time to Go to Bed by Joyce Segal, illustrated by Robin Eaton; Doubleday, 1979. **Awarded:** New Jersey Institute of Technology 1980.

EATON, TOM
The Ball That Wouldn't Bounce by Mel Cebulash, illustrated by Tom Eaton; Scholastic, 1972. **Awarded:** New Jersey Institute of Technology 1972.

EBERLE, IRMENGARDE
A Good House for a Mouse by Irmengarde Eberle, illustrated by Eloise Wilkin; Messner, 1940. **Awarded:** Spring Book Festival (younger honor) 1940.

Lone Star Fight by Irmengarde Eberle, illustrated by Lee Townsend; Dodd, 1954. **Awarded:** Steck-Vaughn 1956.

EBERT, MARIAN
Conquistadores and Pueblos: The Story of the American Southwest 1540-1848 by Olga W. Hall-Quest, illustrated by Marian Ebert; Dutton, 1969. **Awarded:** Western Writers (nonfiction) 1970.

EBY, LOIS C.
see LAWSON, PATRICK

ECKART, CHUCK
Dupper by Betty Baker, illustrated by Chuck Eckart; Greenwillow, 1976. **Awarded:** Children's Book Showcase 1977.

How the Forest Grew by William Jaspersohn, illustrated by Chuck Eckart; Greenwillow, 1979. **Awarded:** Boston Globe Horn Book (nonfiction honor) 1980.

ECKBLAD, EDITH
Soft as the Wind by Edith Eckblad, illustrated by Jim Roberts; Augsburg, 1974. **Awarded:** Council of Wisconsin Writers (picture book runnerup) 1975.

ECKERT, ALLAN W.
Incident at Hawk's Hill by Allan W. Eckert, illustrated by John Schoenherr; Little, 1971. **Awarded:** Newbery (honor) 1972; George G. Stone 1975.

ECKERT, HORST (pseudonym is Janosch)
Awarded: Hans Christian Andersen (highly commended illustrator/German Federal Republic) 1972.
The Big Janosch Book of Fun and Verse by Janosch (Horst Eckert), translated by Anthea Bell; Andersen Press, 1980. **Awarded:** International Board on Book for Young People (translation/Great Britain) 1982.

EDE, JANINA
Marassa and Midnight by Morna Stuart, illustrated by Janina Ede; Heinemann, 1966. **Awarded:** Carnegie (commended) 1966.

EDEL, MAY
The Story of People by May Edel, illustrated by Herbert Danska; Little Brown, 1953. **Awarded:** Spring Book Festival (older honor) 1953.

EDGERTON, CLYDE
Walking Across Egypt by Clyde Edgerton, not illustrated; Algonquin, 1987. **Awarded:** Emphasis on Reading (Grades 9-12) 1990-91.

EDMONDS, CATHARINE
The New York Kid's Book: 170 Children's Writers and Artists Celebrate New York City by Catharine Edmonds and others, illustrated; Doubleday, 1979. **Awarded:** Christopher (all ages) 1980; New York Times Notable Books 1979.

EDMONDS, WALTER DUMAUX
Beaver Valley by Walter D. Edmonds, illustrated by Leslie Morrill; Little Brown, 1971. **Awarded:** Spring Book Festival (middle honor) 1971.

Bert Breen's Barn by Walter D. Edmonds, not illustrated; Little Brown, 1975. **Awarded:** Christopher (ages 12-up) 1976; National Book Award 1976; New York Times Notable Books 1975.

Hound Dog Moses and the Promised Land by Walter D. Edmonds, illustrated by William Gropper; Dodd, Mead, 1954. **Awarded:** Boys Club 1955.

The Matchlock Gun by Walter D. Edmonds, illustrated by Paul Lantz; Dodd, 1941. **Awarded:** Lewis Carroll Shelf 1960; Newbery 1942.

Uncle Ben's Whale by Walter D. Edmonds, illustrated by William Gropper; Dodd, 1955. **Awarded:** New York Times Best Illustrated 1955.

EDWARDS, BRIN
What Makes a Flower Grow? by Susan Mayes, illustrated by Brin Edwards and Mike Pringle; Usborne, 1989. **Awarded:** Science Book Prizes 1990.

What's Under the Ground? by Susan Mayes, illustrated by Mike Pringle, Brin Edwards and John Scorey; Usborne, 1989. **Awarded:** Science Book Prizes 1990.

EDWARDS, CATHERINE
A Foal Is Born by Hans-Heinrich Isenbart, translated by Catherine Edwards, photographs by Hans-Jorg Anders; Putnam, 1976. **Awarded:** New York Academy of Sciences (younger honor) 1977.

EDWARDS, CHRISTINE
Awarded: Mary Grant Bruce Story Award (Writer Living in Gippsland $200) 1991.

EDWARDS, DOROTHY
Joe and Timothy Together by Dorothy Edwards, illustrated by Reintje Venema; Methuen, 1971. **Awarded:** Other Award 1975.

A Strong and Willing Girl by Dorothy Edwards, not illustrated; Methuen, 1980. **Awarded:** Other Award 1981.

EDWARDS, JULIE
The Last of the Really Great Whangdoodles by Julie Edwards, not illustrated; Harper & Row, 1989, c1974. **Awarded:** CRABbery Award (Classic) 1991.

EDWARDS, LINDA STRAUSS
Thatcher Payne-in-the-Neck by Betty Bates, illustrated by Linda Strauss Edwards; Holiday House, 1985. **Awarded:** Sandburg 1986.

Thirteen Ways to Sink a Sub by Jamie Gilson, illustrated by Linda S. Edwards; Lothrop, Lee & Shepard, 1982. **Awarded:** Buckeye (grades 6-8) 1987; Sequoyah 1985; Sunshine State 1987; Young Readers Choice 1985.

EDWARDS, MARGARET ALEXANDER
Awarded: ALAN 1975; Grolier 1957.

EDWARDS, MICHELLE
Chicken Man written and illustrated by Michelle Edwards; Lothrop, Lee & Shepard, 1991. **Awarded:** Hungry Mind (Picturebooks/Fiction) 1992; Jewish Book Council (Marcia & Louis Posner Award) 1992.

EDWARDS, ROLAND
Tigers by Roland Edwards, illustrated by Judith Riches; Tambourine Books, 1992. **Awarded:** Parents Choice (Picture Book) 1992.

EFRON, MARSHALL
Bible Stories You Can't Forget by Marshall Efron and Alfa-Betty Olsen, illustrated by Ron Barrett; Dutton, 1976; Dell, 1979. **Awarded:** New York Times Notable Books 1976.

EGAN, SHEILAH
Awarded: Lucile M. Pannell 1988.

EGIELSKI, RICHARD
Amy's Eyes by Richard Kennedy, illustrated by Richard Egielski; Harper & Row, 1985. **Awarded:** Parents' Choice (literature) 1985.

Hey, Al! by Arthur Yorinks, illustrated by Richard Egielski; Farrar, Straus and Giroux, 1986. **Awarded:** Caldecott 1987; Kentucky Bluegrass (K-3) 1988; Little Archer 1988.

It Happened in Pinsk by Arthur Yorinks, illustrated by Richard Egielski; Farrar, 1983. **Awarded:** Biennale Illustrations Bratislava (plaque) 1985.

The Letter, the Witch and the Ring by John Bellairs, illustrated by Richard Egielski; Dial, 1976. **Awarded:** Utah Children's Choice 1981.

The Tub People by Pam Conrad, illustrated by Richard Egielski; Harper & Row, 1989. **Awarded:** Little Archer 1990; Parents' Choice (Picture Book) 1989.

EGOFF, SHEILA
Awarded: Claude Aubry 1983; Elliott Landau 1983.

EHLERT, LOIS
Chicka Chicka Boom Boom by John Archambault and Bill Martin, Jr., illustrated by Lois Ehlert; Simon & Schuster, 1989. **Awarded:** Boston Globe (Picture Book Honor) 1990; Kentucky Bluegrass (K-3) 1991.

Circus written and illustrated by Lois Ehlert; HarperCollins, 1992. **Awarded:** Reading Magic Award 1992.

Color Zoo written and illustrated by Lois Ehlert; Lippincott, 1989. **Awarded:** Caldecott (honor) 1990.

Eating the Alphabet written and illustrated by Lois Ehlert; Harcourt Brace Jovanovich, 1989. **Awarded:** Reading Magic 1989.

Feathers for Lunch written and illustrated by Lois Ehlert; Harcourt Brace Jovanovich, 1990. **Awarded:** Redbook 1990.

Fish Eyes: A Book You Can Count On written and illustrated by Lois Ehlert; Harcourt Brace Jovanovich, 1990. **Awarded:** New York Times Best Illustrated 1990.

Red Leaf, Yellow Leaf written and illustrated by Lois Ehlert; Harcourt Brace Jovanovich, 1991. **Awarded:** Boston Globe Horn Book (Nonfiction Honor) 1992; Elizabeth Burr 1992.

EHRENSTRALE, KRISTINA
Det Femte Hornet (translated to *The Fifth Corner*) by Kristina Ehrenstrale, translated by Patricia Crampton; Methuen, 1984. **Awarded:** International Board on Books for Young People (translation/Great Britain) 1986.

EHRLICH, AMY
Where It Stops, Nobody Knows by Amy Ehrlich, not illustrated; Dial, 1988. **Awarded:** Dorothy Canfield Fisher 1990.

The Wild Swans by Hans Christian Andersen, retold by Amy Ehrlich, illustrated by Susan Jeffers; Dial, 1987, c1981. **Awarded:** Redbook 1987.

Zeek Silver Moon by Amy Ehrlich, illustrated by Robert A. Parker; Dial, 1972. **Awarded:** New York Times Notable Books 1972.

EICHENBAUM, ROSE
The Number on My Grandfather's Arm by David A. Adler, illustrated by Rose Eichenbaum; Union of American Hebrew Congregations, 1987. **Awarded:** Sydney Taylor Book Award (Picture Book) 1988.

EICHENBERG, FRITZ
Ape in a Cape: An Alphabet of Odd Animals written and illustrated by Fritz Eichenberg; Harcourt, 1952. **Awarded:** Caldecott (honor) 1953.

Have You Seen Tom Thumb? by Mabel Leigh Hunt, illustrated by Fritz Eichenberg; Stokes, 1942. **Awarded:** Newbery (honor) 1943.

Mischief in Fez by Eleanor Hoffmann, illustrated by Fritz Eichenberg; Holiday House, 1943. **Awarded:** Spring Book Festival (middle honor) 1943.

No Room: An Old Story Retold by Rose Dobbs, illustrated by Fritz Eichenberg; McKay, 1944. **Awarded:** Lewis Carroll Shelf 1968.

Padre Porko: The Gentlemanly Pig by Robert Davis, illustrated by Fritz Eichenberg; Holiday, 1948. **Awarded:** Lewis Carroll Shelf 1962.

Rainbows Are Made: Poems by Carl Sandburg, edited by Lee Bennett Hopkins, illustrated by Fritz Eichenberg; Harcourt, 1982. **Awarded:** New York Times Best Illustrated 1982.

EIDRIGEVICIUS, STASYS
Der Gestiefelte Kater (Puss in Boots) by Charles Perrault, illustrated by Stasys Eidrigevicius; Nord-Sud Verlag, 1990; North South Books, 1990. **Awarded:** Biennale Illustrations Bratislava (Grand Prix) 1991.

EIFERT, VIRGINIA SNIDER
The Buffalo Trace by Virginia S. Eifert, illustrated by Manning de V. Lee; Dodd, Mead, 1955. **Awarded:** Edison Mass Media (America's past) 1956; Spring Book Festival (older) 1955.

EINZIG, SUSAN
The Story of John Keats by Robert Gittings and Jo Manton, illustrated by Susan Einzig; Methuen, 1962. **Awarded:** Carnegie (commended) 1962.

Tom's Midnight Garden by A. Philippa Pearce, illustrated by Susan Einzig; Oxford, 1958; Lippincott, 1959. **Awarded:** Carnegie 1958; Lewis Carroll Shelf 1963; International Board on Books for Young People (honour list/Great Britain) 1960.

EISEMAN, ALBERTA
Monica: the Story of a Young Magazine Apprentice by Alberta Eiseman and Ingrid Sladkus, not illustrated; Dodd, Mead, 1957. **Awarded:** Calling All Girls - Dodd, Mead 1957.

EISENBERG, AZRIEL
Worlds Lost and Found by Azriel Eisenberg and Dov Peretz Elkins, illustrated by Charles Pickard; Abelard, 1964. **Awarded:** Jewish Book Council 1964.

EISNER, VIVIENNE
Crafting with Newspapers by Vivienne Eisner and William Shisler, illustrated by Guy Brison-Stack; Sterling, 1977. **Awarded:** New Jersey Institute of Technology 1978.

EKOOMIAK, NORMEE
Arctic Memories by Normee Ekoomiak, illustrated with photos; Henry Holt, 1990, c1988. **Awarded:** Orbis Pictus (Honor) 1991.

ELDRIDGE, HAROLD
The Black Stallion Returns by Walter Farley, illustrated by Harold Eldridge; Random House, 1945. **Awarded:** Boys Club 1948; Young Readers Choice 1948.

Five-yard Fuller of the N.Y. Gnats by Robert Wells, illustrated by Harold Eldridge; Putnam, 1967. **Awarded:** Boys Club 1968.

ELKIN, BENJAMIN
Gillespie and the Guards by Benjamin Elkin, illustrated by James Daugherty; Viking, 1956. **Awarded:** Caldecott (honor) 1957.

ELKIN, JUDITH
Awarded: Eleanor Farjeon 1986.

Nowhere to Play written and illustrated by Kurusa, translated by Judith Elkin; A & C Black, 1982. **Awarded:** Other Award 1983.

ELKINGTON, JOHN
The Young Green Consumer Guide by John Elkington and Julia Hailes, illustrated by Tony Ross; Gollancz, 1990. **Awarded:** Earthworm Award 1990.

ELKINS, DOV PERETZ
Worlds Lost and Found by Dov Peretz Elkins and Azriel Eisenberg, illustrated by Charles Pickard; Abelard, 1964. **Awarded:** Jewish Book Council 1964.

ELLACOTT, SAMUEL ERNEST
Armour and Blade by S. Ernest Ellacott, illustrated; Abelard-Schuman, 1962. **Awarded:** Carnegie (commended) 1962.

ELLENTUCK, SHAN
A Sunflower as Big as the Sun written and illustrated by Shan Ellentuck; Doubleday, 1968. **Awarded:** Spring Book Festival (picture book honor) 1968.

The Upside-down Man written and illustrated by Shan Ellentuck; Doubleday, 1965. **Awarded:** New Jersey Institute of Technology 1966.

ELLEMAN, BARBARA
Awarded: Children's Reading Round Table 1987.

ELLERBY, LEONA
King Tut's Game Board by Leona Ellerby, not illustrated; Lerner, 1980. **Awarded:** Ethical Culture School 1980.

ELLERT, GERHART
Auf Endlosen Strassen by Gerhart Ellert, illustrated by Hilde Seidel; Osterreichischer Bundesverlag, 1959. **Awarded:** Hans Christian Andersen (runnerup) 1962.

ELLIE
El Diablillo de la Botella (original English *The Bottle Imp*) by Robert Louis Stevenson, translated by Ellie; Ediciones Ekare-Banco del Libro, 1981. **Awarded:** International Board on Books for Young People (translation/Venezuela) 1984.

ELLINGSEN, KRIS
Digging Dinosaurs by James Gorman and John R. Horner, illustrated by Kris Ellingsen and Donna Braginetz; Workman Publishers, 1988. **Awarded:** New York Academy of Sciences (Older) 1989.

ELLIOT, DAVID
Arthur and the Dragon by Pauline Cartwright, illustrated by David Elliot; Price Milburn, 1990; Steck Vaughn, 1990. **Awarded:** Russell Clark 1991.

ELLIS, LOUISE
Alphavegetabet (Poems) by Louise Ellis, illustrated; Collier-Macmillan Canada, 1976. **Awarded:** Collier-Macmillan 1976.

ELLIS, MELVIN RICHARD
Awarded: Council for Wisconsin Writers (juvenile) 1971.

Flight of the White Wolf by Mel Ellis, not illustrated; Holt, 1970. **Awarded:** Dorothy Canfield Fisher 1972; Sequoyah 1974.

Sidewalk Indian by Mel Ellis, not illustrated; Holt, 1974. **Awarded:** Council for Wisconsin Writers (juvenile runnerup) 1975.

The Wild Horse Killers by Mel Ellis, not illustrated; Holt, 1976. **Awarded:** Council for Wisconsin Writers (juvenile runnerup) 1977.

ELLIS, SARAH
The Baby Project by Sarah Ellis, not illustrated; Douglas & McIntyre, 1986; McElderry, 1988. **Awarded:** Egoff Prize for Children's Literature 1987.

Pick-up Sticks by Sarah Ellis, not illustrated; Douglas & McIntyre, 1991; McElderry, 1992. **Awarded:** Governor General's Literary Awards (Children's Literature-Text) 1991.

ELLISON, VIRGINIA HOWELL
see HOWELL, VIRGINIA

ELLSBERG, EDWARD
Cruise of the Jeanette by Edward Ellsberg, illustrated by Gerald Foster; Dodd, Mead, 1949. **Awarded:** Boys Club 1950.

I Have Just Begun to Fight: The Story of John Paul Jones by Edward Ellsberg, illustrated by G. Foster; Dodd, Mead, 1942. **Awarded:** Spring Book Festival (middle) 1942.

ELTING, MARY
Awarded: New Jersey Institute of Technology (New Jersey's most distinguished husband-wife team of writers for adults, young adults, teenagers and older, middle age and younger children) 1965; New Jersey Institute of Technology (New Jersey author awards special citation for husband-wife writers of children's books) 1969.

The Answer Book of History by Mary Elting and Franklin Folsom, illustrated by W. K. Plummer; Grosset, 1966. **Awarded:** New Jersey Institute of Technology 1967.

Flags of All Nations and the People Who Live under Them by Mary Elting and Franklin Folsom, illustrated with photographs; Grosset, 1969. **Awarded:** New Jersey Institute of Technology 1970.

Helicopters at Work by Mary Elting and Judith Steigler, illustrated by Ursula Koering; Harvey House, 1972. **Awarded:** New Jersey Institute of Technology 1972.

If You Lived in the Days of the Wild Mammoth Hunters by Mary Elting and Franklin Folsom, illustrated by John Moodie; Four Winds, 1969. **Awarded:** New Jersey Institute of Technology 1970.

We Are the Government by Mary Elting and Margaret Gossett, illustrated by Angio Culfogienis; Doubleday, 1967. **Awarded:** New Jersey Institute of Technology 1970.

ELWOOD, ANN
Windows in Space by Ann Elwood and Linda C. Wood, illustrated; Walker, 1982. **Awarded:** Southern California Council (distinguished work of nonfiction) 1983.

EMBERLEY, BARBARA A.
Drummer Hoff adapted by Barbara Emberley, illustrated by Ed Emberley; Prentice Hall, 1967. **Awarded:** Caldecott 1968; Lewis Carroll Shelf 1968.

One Wide River to Cross by Barbara Emberley, illustrated by Ed Emberley; Prentice Hall, 1966. **Awarded:** Art Books for Children 1973; Caldecott (honor) 1967.

EMBERLEY, EDWARD
Awarded: Chandler Reward of Merit 1968.

Drummer Hoff adapted by Barbara Emberley, illustrated by Ed Emberley; Prentice Hall, 1967. **Awarded:** Caldecott 1968; Lewis Carroll Shelf 1968.

Ladybug, Ladybug, Fly Away Home by Judy Hawes, illustrated by Ed Emberley; Crowell, 1967. **Awarded:** New Jersey Institute of Technology (science) 1968.

One Wide River to Cross by Barbara Emberley, illustrated by Ed Emberley; Prentice Hall, 1966. **Awarded:** Art Books for Children 1973; Caldecott (honor) 1967.

Punch and Judy: A Play for Puppets illustrated by Ed Emberley; Little, Brown, 1965. **Awarded:** New York Times Best Illustrated 1965.

The Wing on a Flea: A Book about Shapes written and illustrated by Ed Emberley; Little, Brown, 1961. **Awarded:** New York Times Best Illustrated 1961.

EMBURY, LUCY
The Listening Man by Lucy Embury, illustrated by Russel Hamilton; Messner, 1940. **Awarded:** Julia Ellsworth Ford 1940.

EMERSON, DONALD
Span Across a River by Donald Emerson, not illustrated; McKay, 1966. **Awarded:** State Historical Society of Wisconsin 1967.

EMRICH, DUNCAN
The Nonsense Book compiled by Duncan Emrich, illustrated by Ib Spang Ohlsson; Four Winds, 1970. **Awarded:** Lewis Carroll Shelf 1971.

EMSLEY, MICHAEL
Insect Magic by Michael Emsley, photographs by Kjell Sandved; Viking, 1978. **Awarded:** New York Academy of Sciences (older honor) 1979.

ENGDAHL, SYLVIA LOUISE
Enchantress from the Stars by Sylvia L. Engdahl, illustrated by Rodney Shackell; Atheneum, 1970; Collier Books, 1989. **Awarded:** Newbery (honor) 1971; Phoenix Award 1990

This Star Shall Abide by Sylvia L. Engdahl, illustrated by Richard Cuffari; Atheneum, 1972. **Awarded:** Christopher (young adult) 1973.

ENGEL, MARIAN
My Name is Not Oddessa Yarker by Marian Engel, illustrated by Laszlo Gal; Kids Can Press, 1977. **Awarded:** IODE 1978.

ENGLISH, BETTY LOU
You Can't be Timid with a Trumpet: Notes from the Orchestra by Betty Lou English, photographs by Betty Lou English, illustrated by Stan Skardinski; Lothrop, 1980. **Awarded:** Boston Globe Horn Book (nonfiction honor) 1981.

ENGLANDER, ALICE
Stephen's Feast by Jean Richardson, illustrated by Alice Englander; Little Brown, 1991. **Awarded:** Christopher Award (Ages 6-8) 1992.

ENRIGHT, ELIZABETH
Gone-away Lake by Elizabeth Enright, illustrated by Beth Krush and Joe Krush; Harcourt, 1957. **Awarded:** Lewis Carroll Shelf 1970; Newbery (honor) 1958; Spring Book Festival (middle) 1957.

Tatsinda by Elizabeth Enright, illustrated by Irene Haas; Harcourt, 1963. **Awarded:** Spring Book Festival (middle honor) 1963.

Thimble Summer written and illustrated by Elizabeth Enright; Farrar, 1938. **Awarded:** Newbery 1939.

ENSIKAT, KLAUS
Der Kleine Daumling by Klaus Ensikat; Der Kinderbuchverlag, 1977. **Awarded:** Biennale Illustrations Bratislava (grand prix) 1979.

Jeder Nach Seiner Art by Hoffmann von Fallersleben, illustrated by Klaus Ensikat; Beltz & Gelberg. **Awarded:** Bologna (Graphics for Youth) 1992.

Taipi by Herman Melville, illustrated by Klaus Ensikat; Verlag Neues Leben, 1977. **Awarded:** Biennale Illustrations Bratislava (Grand Prix) 1979.

The Tale of Fancy Nancy: A Spanish Folk Tale adapted by Marion Koenig, illustrated by Klaus Ensikat; Chatto, 1978. **Awarded:** New York Times Best Illustrated 1979.

EPSTEIN, BERYL WILLIAMS
Dr. Beaumont and the Man with the Hole in His Stomach by Beryl Epstein and Sam Epstein, illustrated by Joseph Scrofani; Coward, 1978. **Awarded:** New York Academy of Sciences (younger honor) 1979.

William Crawford Gorgas: Tropic Fever Fighter by Samuel Epstein and Beryl Epstein, illustrated by Robert Burns; Messner, 1953. **Awarded:** Spring Book Festival (older honor) 1953.

EPSTEIN, JUNE
The Friends of Burramys by June Epstein, illustrated by Pamela Conder; Oxford, 1981. **Awarded:** Whitley Awards 1982.

EPSTEIN, SAM
Dr. Beaumont and the Man with the Hole in His Stomach by Sam Epstein and Beryl Epstein, illustrated by Joseph Scrofani; Coward, 1978. **Awarded:** New York Academy of Sciences (younger honor) 1979.

William Crawford Gorgas: Tropic Fever Fighter by Samuel Epstein and Beryl Epstein, illustrated by Robert Burns; Messner, 1953. **Awarded:** Spring Book Festival (older honor) 1953.

ERDMAN, LOULA GRACE
A Bluebird Will Do by Loula Grace Erdman, not illustrated; Dodd, Mead, 1973. **Awarded:** Steck-Vaughn 1974.

ERHARD, WALTER
My Time of Year by Katherine Dow, illustrated by Walter Erhard; Walck, 1961. **Awarded:** New York Times Best Illustrated 1961.

ERICKSON, MARCIA
City Critters by Helen R. Russell, illustrated by Marcia Erickson; Meredith, 1969. **Awarded:** New Jersey Institute of Technology 1969.

ERICKSON, PHOEBE
Daniel 'Coon: The Story of a Pet Raccoon written and illustrated by Phoebe Erickson; Knopf, 1954. **Awarded:** William Allen White 1957.

Double or Nothing written and illustrated by Phoebe Erickson; Harper, 1958. **Awarded:** Dorothy Canfield Fisher 1960.

ERIKSSON, CHRISTINA WYSS
The Anne of Green Gables Treasury by Carolyn Strom Collins and Christina Wyss Eriksson; Penguin Canada, 1991. **Awarded:** Alcuin 1992.

ERIKSSON, EVA
If You Didn't Have Me by Ulf Nilsson, illustrated by Eva Eriksson; McElderry, 1987. **Awarded:** Batchelder 1988.

ERRICKSON, SHIRLEY
Awarded: Chandler Reward of Merit 1965.

ERSKINE, LAURIE YORK
Renfrew Flies Again by Laurie York Erskine, illustrated by Edward Shenton; Appleton Century Crofts, 1941. **Awarded:** Spring Book Festival (older honor) 1941.

ERWIN, BETTY K.
Go to the Room of the Eyes by Betty K. Erwin, illustrated by Irene Burns; Little Brown, 1969. **Awarded:** Dorothy Canfield Fisher 1971.

ESBENSEN, BARBARA JUSTER
The Star Maiden: An Ojibway Tale retold by Barbara Juster Esbensen, illustrated by Helen K. Davie; Little Brown, 1988. **Awarded:** Minnesota (Finalist) 1988.

ESCOURIDO, JOSEPH
The Swimming Pool by Alice Cobb, illustrated by Joseph Escourido; Friendship Press, 1957. **Awarded:** Nancy Bloch 1957.

ESMAILI-E-SOLI, MARTEZA
Leaves by Mahdi Moini, illustrated by Marteza Esmaili-e-Soli; Institute for the Intellectual Development of Children and Young Adults. **Awarded:** Bologna (graphics for children) 1985.

ESTES, ANGELA M.
"Dismembering the Text: The Horror of Louisa May Alcott's Little Women" by Angela M. Estes and Kathleen M. Lant in Children's Literature 17 (1989): 98-123. **Awarded:** Children's Literature Assn. Criticism Award (runnerup) 1990.

ESTES, ELEANOR RUTH
Ginger Pye written and illustrated by Eleanor Estes; Harcourt, 1951. **Awarded:** Newbery 1952; Spring Book Festival (ages 8-12) 1951.

The Hundred Dresses by Eleanor Estes, illustrated by Louis Slobodkin; Harcourt, 1944. **Awarded:** Newbery (honor) 1945.

The Middle Moffat by Eleanor Estes, illustrated by Louis Slobodkin; Harcourt, 1942. **Awarded:** Newbery (honor) 1943.

The Moffats by Eleanor Estes, illustrated by Louis Slobodkin; Harcourt, 1941. **Awarded:** Lewis Carroll Shelf 1961.

Rufus M. by Eleanor Estes, illustrated by Louis Slobodkin; Harcourt, 1943. **Awarded:** Newbery (honor) 1944.

ESTEVA, CARMEN
Principio y Fin Tiempo de Vida que Transcurre Entre el Nacer y el Morir (original English *Beginnings and Endings with LIFETIMES in Between*) by Bryan Mellonie, translated by Carmen Esteva and Miguel Leon; Compania Editorial Continental, 1984. **Awarded:** International Board on Books for Young People (translation/Mexico) 1986.

ESTRADA, RIC
The Goats Who Killed the Leopard by Judy Hawes, illustrated by Ric Estrada; Crowell, 1970. **Awarded:** New Jersey Institute of Technology 1970.

ETHERINGTON, DIANE
Awarded: Lucile M. Pannell 1986.

ETRA, JONATHAN
Aliens for Breakfast by Jonathan Etra and Stephanie Spinner, illustrated by Steve Bjorkman; Random House, 1988. **Awarded:** Texas Bluebonnet 1991.

ETS, MARIE HALL
Awarded: Kerlan 1975.

Beasts and Nonsense written and illustrated by Marie Hall Ets; Viking, 1952. **Awarded:** New York Times Best Illustrated 1952.

Gilberto and the Wind written and illustrated by Marie Hall Ets; Viking, 1963. **Awarded:** Spring Book Festival (picture book honor) 1963.

In the Forest written and illustrated by Marie Hall Ets; Viking, 1944. **Awarded:** Caldecott (honor) 1945.

Just Me written and illustrated by Marie Hall Ets; Viking, 1965. **Awarded:** Caldecott (honor) 1966.

Mr. Penny's Race Horse written and illustrated by Marie Hall Ets; Viking, 1956. **Awarded:** Caldecott (honor) 1957.

Mr. T. W. Anthony Woo: The Story of a Cat and a Dog and a Mouse written and illustrated by Marie Hall Ets; Viking, 1951. **Awarded:** Caldecott (honor) 1952; Spring Book Festival (picture book honor) 1951.

Nine Days to Christmas by Marie Hall Ets and Aurora Labastida, illustrated by Marie Hall Ets; Viking, 1959. **Awarded:** Caldecott 1960.

Oley the Sea Monster written and illustrated by Marie Hall Ets; Viking, 1947. **Awarded:** Spring Book Festival (younger) 1947.

Play with Me written and illustrated by Marie Hall Ets; Viking, 1955. **Awarded:** Caldecott (honor) 1956; International Board on Books for Young People (USA) 1956.

Talking Without Words written and illustrated by Marie Hall Ets; Viking, 1968. **Awarded:** New York Times Best Illustrated 1968.

EUBANK, BILL
Awarded: L. Frank Baum 1975

EVANS, CHRIS
What is a Union? by Althea, illustrated by Chris Evans; Dinosaur Publications, 1981; Rourke Enterprises, 1981. **Awarded:** Other Award 1981.

EVANS, EVA KNOX
People Are Important by Eva Knox Evans, illustrated by Vana Earle; Golden, 1951. **Awarded:** Jane Addams 1953.

EVANS, KATHERINE
Chicken Little Count-to-Ten by Margaret Friskey, illustrated by Katherine Evans; Children's Press, 1946. **Awarded:** Spring Book Festival (younger honor) 1946.

EVANS, LARRY
3-Dimensional Optical Illusions to Color and Construct written and illustrated by Larry Evans; Troubadour, 1977. **Awarded:** New York Academy of Sciences (older honor) 1978.

EVARTS, HAL G.
Bigfoot by Hal G. Evarts, not illustrated; Scribner, 1973. **Awarded:** Charlie May Simon 1975-76.

Smuggler's Road by Hal G. Evarts, not illustrated; Scribner, 1968. **Awarded:** Edgar Allan Poe (runnerup) 1969.

Treasure River by Hal Evarts, illustrated with a map; Scribner, 1964. **Awarded:** Edgar Allan Poe (runnerup) 1965.

EVATT, HARRIET TORREY
The Mystery of the Creaking Windmill written and illustrated by Harriet T. Evatt; Bobbs-Merrill, 1945. **Awarded:** Ohioana (honorable mention) 1946.

The Snow Owl's Secret written and illustrated by Harriet Torrey Evatt; Bobbs-Merrill, 1946. **Awarded:** Ohioana 1947.

EVERETT, GWEN
Li'l Sis and Uncle Willie by Gwen Everett, illustrated by William H. Johnson; Rizzoli, 1992. **Awarded:** Hungry Mind (Picturebook/Nonfiction) 1993; New York Times Best Illustrated 1992.

EVERNDEN, MARGARET
The Secret of the Porcelain Fish by Margaret Evernden, illustrated by Thomas Handforth; Random House, 1947. **Awarded:** Spring Book Festival (middle honor) 1947.

EVERS, ALF
The Three Kings of Saba by Alf Evers, illustrated by Helen Sewell; Lippincott, 1955. **Awarded:** New York Times Best Illustrated 1955.

EVERS, LEONARD HERBERT

The Racketty Street Gang by Leonard Herbert Evers, not illustrated; Hodder & Stoughton, 1961. **Awarded:** Children's Book Council of Australia (book of the year) 1962.

EVERY, PHILIP COCHRANE

see BURNFORD, SHELIA

EVERYEVSLIN, BERNARD

Hercules by Bernard Evslin; Morrow, 1984. **Awarded:** Washington Irving (nonfiction) 1986

EWEN, DAVID

The Story of Irving Berlin by David Ewen, illustrated by Jane Castle; Holt, 1950. **Awarded:** Spring Book Festival (older honor) 1950.

EYERLY, JEANNETTE HYDE

Escape from Nowhere by Jeannette Eyerly, not illustrated; Lippincott, 1969. **Awarded:** Christopher (teenage) 1970.

EYRE, KATHERINE WIGMORE

Lottie's Valentine by Katherine Wigmore Eyre, illustrated by Susanne Suba; Oxford, 1941. **Awarded:** Spring Book Festival (middle honor) 1941.

Spurs for Antonia by Katherine Wigmore Eyre, illustrated by Decie Merwin; Oxford, 1943. **Awarded:** Commonwealth Club of California 1943.

F

FABER, DORIS

Oh, Lizzie: The Life of Elizabeth Cady Stanton by Doris Faber, illustrated with photographs; Lothrop, 1972. **Awarded:** Spring Book Festival (ages 12-16 honor) 1972.

FADIMAN, CLIFTON

Awarded: Southern California Council (Dorothy McKenzie Award) 1985.

FAIRBRIDGE, LYNNE

In Such a Place by Lynne Fairbridge, not illustrated; Doubleday Canada, 1992. **Awarded:** Alberta Writing for Youth 1991.

FAIRCLOUGH, CHRIS

The Bus Driver by Anne Stewart, photographs by Chris Fairclough; Hamish Hamilton, 1986. **Awarded:** Other Award 1986.

A Day with a Miner by Phillippa Aston, photographs by Chris Fairclough; Wayland, 1981. **Awarded:** Times Educational Supplement (junior) 1982.

Making a Book by Ruth Thomson, illustrated by Chris Fairclough; Watts, 1987. **Awarded:** Times Educational Supplement (Junior) 1988.

FALCONER, ELIZABETH

I Believe in Unicorns by Adam John Munthe, illustrated by Elizabeth Falconer; Chatto, 1979. **Awarded:** Mother Goose (runnerup) 1981.

FALCONER, PEARL

Torrie by Annabel Johnson and Edgar Johnson, illustrated by Pearl Falconer; Harper, 1960. **Awarded:** Spring Book Festival (older honor) 1960.

FALLERSLEBEN, HOFFMANN VON

Jeder Nach Seiner Art by Hoffmann von Fallersleben, illustrated by Klaus Ensikat; Beltz & Gelberg. **Awarded:** Bologna (Graphics for Youth) 1992.

FALLS, CHARLES BUCKLES

Americans Before Columbus by Elizabeth Chesley Baity, illustrated by C. B. Falls; Viking, 1951. **Awarded:** Newbery (honor) 1952; Spring Book Festival (older) 1951.

New Found World by Katherine B. Shippen, illustrated by C. B. Falls; Viking, 1945. **Awarded:** Newbery (honor) 1946; Spring Book Festival (older honor) 1945.

Red Sails to Capri by Ann Weil, illustrated by C. B. Falls; Viking, 1952. **Awarded:** Newbery (honor) 1953.

Vast Horizons by Mary Seymour Lucas, illustrated by C. B. Falls; Viking, 1943. **Awarded:** Spring Book Festival (older honor) 1943.

FALWELL, CATHRYN

Clowning Around written and illustrated by Cathryn Falwell; Orchard, 1991. **Awarded:** Reading Magic Award 1991.

FANELLI, SARA

Awarded: Macmillan Prize (3rd prize) 1991.

Botton written and illustrated by Sara Fanelli. **Awarded:** Macmillan Prize (First Prize) 1992.

FARBER, NORMA

As I Was Crossing Boston Common by Norma Farber, illustrated by Arnold Lobel; Dutton, 1975. **Awarded:** Children's Book Showcase 1976; National Book Award (finalist) 1976.

There Once Was a Woman Who Married a Man by Norma Farber, illustrated by Lydia Dabcovich; Addison, 1978. **Awarded:** New York Times Best Illustrated 1978.

Where's Gomer? by Norma Farber, illustrated by William Pene du Bois; Dutton, 1974. **Awarded:** Children's Book Showcase 1975.

FARJEON, ELEANOR

Awarded: Regina 1959.

The Little Bookroom by Eleanor Farjeon, illustrated by Edward Ardizzone; Oxford, 1955; Walck, 1956. **Awarded:** Hans Christian Andersen 1956; Carnegie 1955; Lewis Carroll Shelf 1958.

FARLEY, CAROL

The Garden Is Doing Fine by Carol Farley, illustrated by Lynn Sweat; Atheneum, 1975. **Awarded:** Child Study 1975; Golden Kite 1975.

Loosen Your Ears by Carol Farley, illustrated by Mila Lazarevich; Atheneum, 1977. **Awarded:** Friends of American Writers (younger) 1978.

FARLEY, WALTER

Awarded: Outstanding Pennsylvania Author 1980.

The Black Stallion by Walter Farley, illustrated by Keith Ward; Random House, 1941. **Awarded:** Young Readers Choice 1944.

The Black Stallion Returns by Walter Farley, illustrated by Harold Eldridge; Random House, 1945. **Awarded:** Boys Club 1948; Young Readers Choice 1948.

FARMER, PENELOPE

The Summer Birds by Penelope Farmer, illustrated by James J. Spanfeller; Harcourt, 1962. **Awarded:** Carnegie (commended) 1962.

FARRAR, SUSAN CLEMENT
Samantha on Stage by Susan Clement Farrar, illustrated by Ruth Sanderson; Dial, 1979. **Awarded:** West Australian Young Readers' (primary) 1983.

FAST, ELIZABETH
Awarded: Grolier 1977.

FATCHEN, MAX
A Paddock of Poems by Max Fatchen, illustrated; Omnibus/Puffin, 1987. **Awarded:** Children's Book Council of Australia (Book of the Year Younger Honour) 1988.

FATIO, LOUISE
The Happy Lion by Louise Fatio, illustrated by Roger Duvoisin; McGraw Hill, 1954. **Awarded:** New York Times Best Illustrated 1954.

The Happy Lion in Africa by Louise Fatio, illustrated by Roger Duvoisin; McGraw Hill, 1955. **Awarded:** New York Times Best Illustrated 1955.

The Happy Lion's Quest by Louise Fatio, illustrated by Roger Duvoisin; McGraw Hill, 1961. **Awarded:** New Jersey Institute of Technology 1961.

Hector and Christina by Louise Fatio, illustrated by Roger Duvoisin; McGraw Hill, 1977. **Awarded:** New Jersey Institute of Technology 1978.

Hector Penguin by Louise Fatio, illustrated by Roger Duvoisin; McGraw Hill, 1973. **Awarded:** New York Times Best Illustrated 1973.

Marc & Pixie & the Walls in Mrs. Jones' Garden by Louise Fatio and Roger Duvoisin, illustrated by Roger Duvoisin; McGraw Hill, 1975. **Awarded:** New Jersey Institute of Technology 1976.

FAULKNER, JACK
How Hospitals Help Us by Alice M. Meeker, illustrated by Jack Faulkner; Beckley-Cardy, 1962. **Awarded:** New Jersey Institute of Technology 1963.

FAULKNER, JOHN
My Mom Hates Me in January by Judy Delton, illustrated by John Faulkner; illustrated by Mimi Korach; Whitman, 1977. **Awarded:** North Dakota Children's Choice (younger) 1980.

FAULKNER, NANCY
The Secret of the Simple Code by Nancy Faulkner, illustrated by Mimi Korach; Doubleday, 1965. **Awarded:** Edgar Allan Poe (runnerup) 1966.

FAULKNOR, CLIFF
Awarded: Vicky Metcalf 1979.

The White Calf by Cliff Faulknor, illustrated by Gerald Tailfeathers; Little, Brown, 1965. **Awarded:** Little Brown Canadian Children's Book Award 1964.

FAVA, RITA
The Long-nosed Princess by Priscilla Hallowell, illustrated by Rita Fava; Viking, 1959. **Awarded:** Spring Book Festival (middle) 1959.

FAVILLE, BARRY
The Keeper by Barry Faville, not illustrated; Oxford, 1986. **Awarded:** AIM (Story Book) 1987.

FAX, ELTON CLAY
Seventeen Black Artists by Elton Clay Fax, illustrated with photographs; Dodd, Mead, 1971. **Awarded:** Coretta Scott King 1972.

FEDERICI, YOLANDA
Awarded: Children's Reading Round Table 1980.

FEEHAN, PATRICIA
Awarded: Evelyn Sibley Lampman 1983.

FEELINGS, MURIEL
Awarded: Drexel 1985; Outstanding Pennsylvania Author 1984.

Jambo Means Hello: Swahili Alphabet Book by Muriel Feelings, illustrated by Tom Feelings; Dial, 1974. **Awarded:** Art Books for Children 1976; Boston Globe Horn Book (illustration) 1974; Caldecott (honor) 1975.

Moja Means One: Swahili Counting Book by Muriel Feelings, illustrated by Tom Feelings; Dial, 1971. **Awarded:** Art Books for Children 1973, 1974, 1975; Caldecott (honor) 1972.

FEELINGS, THOMAS
Black Pilgrimage written and illustrated by Tom Feelings; Lothrop, 1972. **Awarded:** Woodward Park 1973.

From Slave to Abolitionist: the Life of William Wells Brown adapted by Lucille Schulberg Warner, illustrated by Tom Feelings; Dial, 1976. **Awarded:** Children's Book Showcase 1977.

Jambo Means Hello: Swahili Alphabet Book by Muriel Feelings, illustrated by Tom Feelings; Dial, 1974. **Awarded:** Art Books for Children 1976; Boston Globe Horn Book (illustration) 1974; Caldecott (honor) 1975.

Moja Means One: Swahili Counting Book by Muriel Feelings, illustrated by Tom Feelings; Dial, 1971. **Awarded:** Art Books for Children 1973, 1974, 1975; Caldecott (honor) 1972.

Something on My Mind by Nikki Grimes, illustrated by Tom Feelings; Dial, 1978. **Awarded:** Coretta Scott King (special illustration) 1979.

To Be a Slave by Julius Lester, illustrated by Tom Feelings; Dial, 1968. **Awarded:** Lewis Carroll Shelf 1970; Newbery (honor) 1969.

FEHER, JOSEPH
The Voyage of the Flying Bird by Margaret Titcomb, illustrated by Joseph Feher; Dodd, Mead, 1963. **Awarded:** Edith Busby 1961.

FEIFFER, JULES
The Phantom Tollbooth by Norton Juster, illustrated by Jules Feiffer; Random House, 1961. **Awarded:** George G. Stone 1971.

FEINBERG, HAROLD S.
Snail in the Woods by Harold S. Feinberg and Joanne Ryder, illustrated by Jo Polseno; Harper & Row, 1979. **Awarded:** New Jersey Institute of Technology 1980.

FEININGER, ANDREAS
The Spider of Brooklyn Heights by Nancy Veglahn, photographs by Andreas Feininger; Scribner, 1967. **Awarded:** Spring Book Festival (middle honor) 1967.

FELDBAUM, CARL B.
Looking the Tiger in the Eye: Confronting the Nuclear Threat by Carl B. Feldbaum and Ronald J. Bee, illustrated with photos; Harper & Row, 1988. **Awarded:** Christopher 1989.

FELSEN, HENRY GREGOR
Hot Rod by Henry Gregor Felsen, not illustrated; Dutton, 1950. **Awarded:** Boys Club 1951.

Some Follow the Sea by Henry Gregor Felsen, illustrated with photographs; Dutton, 1944. **Awarded:** Spring Book Festival (older honor) 1944.

FELTON, HAROLD W.
Pecos Bill and the Mustang by Harold W. Felton, illustrated by Leonard Shortall; Prentice Hall, 1965. **Awarded:** Boys Club (certificate) 1966-67.

FELTON, RONALD OLIVER
see WELCH, RONALD

FELTS, SHIRLEY
The Road to Camlann by Rosemary Sutcliff, illustrated by Shirley Felts; Dutton, 1982. **Awarded:** Boston Globe Horn Book (fiction honor) 1983.

The Secret World of Polly Flint by Helen Cresswell, illustrated by Shirley Felts; Faber, 1982. **Awarded:** Whitbread (runnerup) 1982.

FENDER, KAY
Odette: a Bird in Paris by Kay Fender, illustrated by Phillipe Dumas; Prentice Hall, 1978. **Awarded:** New York Times Best Illustrated 1978.

FENNER, CAROL ELIZABETH
Gorilla, Gorilla by Carol Fenner, illustrated by Symeon Shimin; Random House, 1973. **Awarded:** Christopher (ages 4-8) 1974 .

FENNIMORE, STEPHEN
Bush Holiday by Stephen Fennimore, illustrated by Ninon MacKnight; Doubleday, 1949. **Awarded:** Spring Book Festival (under 12) 1949.

FENTON, CARROLL LANE
Birds We Live With by Carroll Lane Fenton and Herminie B. Kitchen, illustrated by Carroll Lane Fenton; Day, 1963. **Awarded:** New Jersey Institute of Technology (science ages 8-12) 1964.

In Prehistoric Seas by Carroll Lane Fenton and Mildred A. Fenton, illustrated by Carroll Lane Fenton; Doubleday, l963. **Awarded:** New Jersey Institute of Technology (science) 1963.

FENTON, EDWARD
Petros' War by Alki Zei, not illustrated, translated by Edward Fenton; Dutton, 1972. **Awarded:** Batchelder 1974; International Board on Book for Young People (translation/USA) 1986.

The Phantom of Walkaway Hill by Edward Fenton, illustrated by Jo Ann Stover; Doubleday, 1961. **Awarded:** Edgar Allan Poe 1962.

The Sound of Dragon's Feet by Alki Zei, translated by Edward Fenton, not illustrated; Dutton, 1979. **Awarded:** Batchelder 1980.

Wildcat under Glass by Alki Zei, translated by Edward Fenton, not illustrated; Holt, 1968. **Awarded:** Batchelder 1970.

FENTON, MILDRED A.
In Prehistoric Seas by Mildred A. Fenton and Carroll Lane Fenton, illustrated by Carroll Lane Fenton; Doubleday, 1963. **Awarded:** New Jersey Institute of Technology (science) 1963.

FENWICK, SARA I.
Awarded: Children's Reading Round Table 1974.

FERGUSON, ALANE
Show Me the Evidence by Alane Ferguson, not illustrated; Bradbury, 1989. **Awarded:** Edgar Allan Poe (Young Adult) 1990.

FERGUSON, AMOS
Under the Sunday Tree by Eloise Greenfield, illustrated by Amos Ferguson; Harper & Row, 1988. **Awarded:** Coretta Scott King (Illustration honor) 1989.

FERNANDEZ, LAURA
I Heard My Mother Call My Name by Nancy Hundal, illustrated by Laura Fernandez; HarperCollins, 1990. **Awarded:** Egoff Prize for Children's Literature 1991.

FERRIS, HELEN
Partners: The United Nations and Youth by Helen Ferris and Eleanor Roosevelt, illustrated with photographs; Doubleday, 1950. **Awarded:** Child Study 1950.

FERRIS, JEAN
Invincible Summer by Jean Ferris, not illustrated; Farrar Straus Giroux, 1987. **Awarded:** Southern California Council (Outstanding Work of Fiction for Young Adults) 1988.

FERRIS, JERI
Arctic Explorer: The Story of Matthew Henson by Jeri Ferris, illustrated; Carolrhoda, 1989. **Awarded:** Woodson (Outstanding Merit - Elementary) 1990.

Native American Doctor: The Story of Susan LaFlesche Picotte by Jeri Ferris, illustrated; Carolrhoda, 1991. **Awarded:** Southern California Council (Significant Contribution to Field of Biography) 1992; Woodson (Secondary) 1992.

Walking the Road to Freedom: A Story about Sojourner Truth by Jeri Ferris, illustrated by Peter E. Hanson; Carolrhoda, 1988. **Awarded:** Woodson (Elementary) 1989.

FERRIS, TIMOTHY
Spaceshots by Timothy Ferris and Carolyn Zecca, illustrated with photographs; Pantheon, 1984. **Awarded:** New York Academy of Sciences (older honor) 1986.

FERRY, CHARLES
Raspberry One by Charles Ferry, not illustrated; Houghton Mifflin, 1983. **Awarded:** Friends of American Writers ($500) 1984.

FETZ, INGRID
Before You Were a Baby by Paul Showers and Kay S. Showers, illustrated by Ingrid Fetz; Crowell, 1968. **Awarded:** New Jersey Institute of Technology (science) 1968.

Eddie's Menagerie by Carolyn Haywood, illustrated by Ingrid Fetz; Morrow, 1978. **Awarded:** Utah Children's Choice 1981.

FEYNMAN, RICHARD P.
Surely You're Joking, Mr. Feynman! by Richard P. Feynman as told to Ralph Leighton, edited by Edward Hutchings, not illustrated; Bantam, 1986. **Awarded:** New York Academy of Sciences (older honor) 1987.

FIAMMENGHI, GIOIA
Born to Dance Samba by Miriam Cohen, illustrated by Gioia Fiammenghi; Harper & Row, 1984. **Awarded:** Parents' Choice (literature) 1984.

Chocolate Fever by Robert Kimmel Smith, illustrated by Gioia Fiammenghi; Dell, 1978. **Awarded:** Massachusetts Children's (Elementary) 1980.

How To Fight a Girl by Thomas Rockwell, illustrated by Gioia Fiammenghi; Dell, 1988, c1987. **Awarded:** North Dakota Children's Choice (Juvenile Fiction) 1991.

FIELD, CAROLYN W.
Awarded: Drexel 1984; Grolier 1963; Helen Keating Ott 1988.

FIELD, RACHEL LYMAN
Calico Bush by Rachel Field, illustrated by Allen Lewis; Macmillan, 1931. **Awarded:** Newbery (honor) 1932.

Hitty, Her First Hundred Years by Rachel Field, illustrated by Dorothy P. Lathrop; Macmillan, 1929. **Awarded:** Lewis Carroll Shelf 1961; Newbery 1930.

Prayer for a Child by Rachel Field, illustrated by Elizabeth Orton Jones; Macmillan, 1944. **Awarded:** Caldecott 1945; Lewis Carroll Shelf 1958.

FIENBERG, ANNA
The Magnificent Nose and Other Marvels by Anna Fienberg, illustrated by Kim Gamble; Allen & Unwin, 1991. **Awarded:** Children's Book Council of Australia (Book of the Year Younger) 1992; Crichton 1992.

FIFE, DALE
North of Danger by Dale Fife, illustrated by Haakon Saether; Dutton, 1978. **Awarded:** Commonwealth Club of California 1978.

Walk a Narrow Bridge by Dale Fife, not illustrated; Coward, 1966. **Awarded:** Ohioana 1967.

FILISKY, MICHAEL
Sterling: The Rescue of a Baby Harbor Seal by Sandra Verrill White and Michael Filisky, illustrated; Crown, 1989. **Awarded:** Book Can Develop Empathy 1990.

FILMER-SANKEY, JOSEPHINE
The Bayeux Tapestry: The Story of the Norman Conquest 1066 by Josephine Filmer-Sankey and Norman Denny, illustrated; Collins, 1966. **Awarded:** Carnegie (highly commended) 1966.

FINCHER, E. B. (ERNEST B.)
Bill of Rights by Ernest B. Fincher, illustrated with photographs; Watts, 1978. **Awarded:** New Jersey Institute of Technology 1980.

Mexico and the United States by E. B. Fincher, illustrated with photos; Crowell, 1983. **Awarded:** Woodson 1984.

FINE, ANNE
Awarded: British Book Awards (Author) 1990; British Book Awards (Author runnerup) 1991.

Alias Madame Doubtfire by Anne Fine, not illustrated; Little Brown, 1988. **Awarded:** Parents' Choice (Story Book) 1988.

Bill's New Frock by Anne Fine, illustrated by Philippe Dupasquier; Methuen Children's, 1989. **Awarded:** Carnegie (Highly Commended) 1989; Nottinghamshire (Oak Tree) 1990; Smarties (ages 6-8) 1989.

Flour Babies by Anne Fine, not illustrated; Hamish Hamilton, 1992. **Awarded:** Carnegie 1992.

Goggle-eyes by Anne Fine, not illustrated; Hamish Hamilton, 1989; Joy Street Books, 1989. (U.S. title: *My War With Goggle Eyes*). **Awarded:** Carnegie 1989; Guardian Award 1990.

Madame Doubtfire by Anne Fine, not illustrated; Hamilton Children's, 1987. **Awarded:** Guardian Award (runnerup) 1988.

FINE, JOAN
I Carve Stone by Joan Fine, photographs by David Anderson; Crowell, 1979. **Awarded:** New Jersey Institute of Technology 1981.

FINGER, CHARLES JOSEPH
Give a Man a Horse by Charles J. Finger, illustrated by Henry C. Pitz; Winston, 1938. **Awarded:** Spring Book Festival (older honor) 1938.

Tales from Silver Lands by Charles J. Finger, illustrated by Paul Honore; Doubleday, 1924. **Awarded:** Newbery 1925.

FINLAY, WINIFRED
Danger at Black Dyke written and illustrated by Winifred Finlay; Phillips, 1968. **Awarded:** Edgar Allan Poe 1970.

FINLEY, FRED J.
The Dangerous Cove: A Story of Early Days in Newfoundland by John Francis Hayes, illustrated by Fred J. Finley; Copp Clark, 1957. **Awarded:** Canadian Library Assn. 1959.

A Land Divided by John F. Hayes, illustrated by Fred J. Finley; Copp Clarke, 1951. **Awarded:** Governor-General's Literary Award 1951.

Rebels Ride at Night by John F. Hayes, illustrated Fred J. Finley; Copp Clarke, 1953. **Awarded:** Governor-General's Literary Award 1953.

FINNEY, GERTRUDE E.
To Survive We Must be Clever by Gertrude E. Finney, illustrated by Carl Kidwell; McKay, 1966. **Awarded:** Indiana Authors Day (young adult) 1967.

FIRTH, BARBARA
Can't You Sleep Little Bear? by Martin Waddell, illustrated by Barbara Firth; Walker, 1988. **Awarded:** Greenaway 1988; Smarties (Grand Prix) 1988; Smarties (ages 0-5) 1988.

The Park in the Dark by Martin Waddell, illustrated by Barbara Firth; Walker Books, 1989; Lothrop, Lee & Shepard, 1989. **Awarded:** Kurt Maschler 1989.

FISCHER, HANS
Pitschi: The Kitten Who Always Wanted to Be Something Else written and illustrated by Hans Fischer; Harcourt, 1953. **Awarded:** New York Times Best Illustrated 1953.

FISCHER-NAGEL, ANDREAS
An Ant Colony by Andreas Fischer-Nagel and Heiderose Fischer-Nagel, illustrated; Carolrhoda, 1989. **Awarded:** Utah Children's Informational Book Award 1992.

FISCHER-NAGEL, HEIDEROSE
An Ant Colony by Andreas Fischer-Nagel and Heiderose Fischer-Nagel, illustrated; Carolrhoda, 1989. **Awarded:** Utah Children's Informational Book Award 1992.

FISCHTROM, HARVEY
see ZEMACH, HARVE

FISH, HELEN DEAN
Animals of the Bible: A Picture Book by Helen Dean Fish, illustrated by Dorothy P. Lathrop; Stokes, 1937. **Awarded:** Caldecott 1938.

Four and Twenty Blackbirds: Nursery Rhymes of Yesterday Recalled for Children of Today by Helen Dean Fish, illustrated by Robert Lawson; Lippincott, 1937. **Awarded:** Caldecott (honor) 1938.

FISH, RICHARD
Haym Salomon: Liberty's Son by Shirley G. Milgrim, illustrated by Richard Fish; Jewish Publication Society, 1975. **Awarded:** Jewish Book Council 1975.

FISHER, AILEEN
Awarded: National Council of Teachers of English Award for Excellence in Poetry for Children 1978.

Valley of the Smallest: The Life Story of a Shrew by Aileen Fisher, illustrated by Jean Zallinger; Crowell, 1966. **Awarded:** International Board on Book for Young People (USA) 1968; Western Writers (nonfiction) 1967.

FISHER, CYRUS
The Avion My Uncle Flew by Cyrus Fisher, illustrated by Richard Floethe; Appleton, 1946. **Awarded:** Newbery (honor) 1947.

FISHER, DAVID E.
The Third Experiment by David E. Fisher, illustrated; Atheneum, 1985. **Awarded:** New York Academy of Sciences (older honor) 1986.

FISHER, DOROTHY CANFIELD
   Awarded: Women's National Book Assn. 1951.

FISHER, IRENE
   Awarded: L. Frank Baum 1980.

FISHER, JAMES
The Wonderful World of the Sea by James Fisher, illustrated by Eileen Aplin and others; Doubleday, 1957. **Awarded:** Boys Club 1958.

FISHER, L.
You and Atomic Energy by John Lewellen, illustrated by L. Fisher; Children's Press, 1949. **Awarded:** Boys Club 1950.

FISHER, LEONA W.
Mystical Fantasy for Children: Silence and Community by Leona W. Fisher in The Lion and the Unicorn 14.2 December 1990. **Awarded:** Children's Literature Assn. Criticism 1991.

FISHER, LEONARD EVERETT
   Awarded: Kerlan Award 1991; Regina Medal 1991; School Library Media Section of the New York Library Assn. 1979; University of Southern Mississippi 1979; Washington Post Nonfiction Award 1989.

All Times, All Peoples: A World History of Slavery by Milton Meltzer, illustrated by Leonard Everett Fisher; Harper, 1980. **Awarded:** Christopher (ages 8-12 nonfiction) 1981.

America Grows Up: A History for Peter by Gerald W. Johnson, illustrated by Leonard Everett Fisher; Morrow, 1960. **Awarded:** Spring Book Festival (Older honor) 1960.

America Is Born: A History for Peter by Gerald W. Johnson, illustrated by Leonard Everett Fisher; Morrow, 1959. **Awarded:** Newbery (honor) 1960

America Moves Forward: A History for Peter by Gerald W. Johnson, illustrated by Leonard Everett Fisher; Morrow, 1960. **Awarded:** Newbery (honor) 1961.

America's Own Mark Twain by Jeanette Eaton, illustrated by Leonard Everett Fisher; Morrow, 1958. **Awarded:** Ohioana 1959.

Casey at the Bat by Ernest L. Thayer, illustrated by Leonard Everett Fisher; Watts, 1964. **Awarded:** New York Times Best Illustrated 1964.

Communism, an American's View by Gerald W. Johnson, illustrated by Leonard Everett Fisher; Morrow, 1964. **Awarded:** Boys Club 1965.

Digging into Yesterday by Estelle Friedman, illustrated by Leonard Everett Fisher; Putnam, 1958. **Awarded:** Boys Club 1959.

Earth Songs by Myra Cohn Livingston, illustrated by Leonard Everett Fisher; Holiday House, 1986. **Awarded:** Southern California Council (Special Recognition for Excellence in a Poetry Quartet) 1989.

The Innkeeper's Boy by Diane Brooks Pleninger, illustrated by Leonard Everett Fisher in Cricket, November 1988. **Awarded:** Witty Short Story Award 1989.

The Presidency by Gerald W. Johnson, illustrated by Leonard Everett Fisher; Morrow, 1962. **Awarded:** Spring Book Festival (middle honor) 1962.

A Russian Farewell written and illustrated by Leonard Everett Fisher; Four Winds, 1980. **Awarded:** Jewish Book Council 1980; Sydney Taylor Book Award 1981.

Sea Songs by Myra Cohn Livingston, illustrated by Leonard Everett Fisher; Holiday House, 1986. **Awarded:** Southern California Council (Special Recognition for Excellence in a Poetry Quartet) 1989.

Sky Songs by Myra Cohn Livingston, illustrated by Leonard Everett Fisher; Holiday House, 1984. **Awarded:** Parents' Choice (literature) 1984; Southern California Council (Special Recognition for Excellence in a Poetry Quartet) 1989.

Space Songs by Myra Cohn Livingston, illustrated by Leonard Everett Fisher; Holiday House, 1988. **Awarded:** Southern California Council (Special Recognition for Excellence in a Poetry Quartet) 1989.

This is the Desert by Phillip H. Ault, illustrated by Leonard Everett Fisher; Dodd, Mead, 1959. **Awarded:** Commonwealth Club of California 1959.

FISHER, MARGERY
   Awarded: Eleanor Farjeon 1965.

FISK, PAULINE
Midnight Blue by Pauline Fisk, not illustrated; Lion Publishing, 1990. **Awarded:** Smarties (ages 9-11) 1990; Smarties (Grand Prix) 1990.

FITCH, FLORENCE MARY
One God: The Ways We Worship Him by Florence Mary Fitch, illustrated with photographs; Lothrop, 1944. **Awarded:** Ohioana 1945.

FITCH, SHEREE
There Were Monkeys in My Kitchen! by Sheree Fitch and Marc Mongeau; Doubleday Canada, 1992. **Awarded:** Mr. Christie's (English Text ages 8 and under) 1992.

FITZGERALD, JOANNE
Doctor Kiss Says Yes by Teddy Jam, illustrated by Joanne Fitzgerald; Douglas & McIntyre, 1991. **Awarded:** Governor General's Literary Awards (Illustration) 1991.

FITZGERALD, JOHN D.
The Great Brain Does It Again by John D. Fitzgerald, illustrated by Mercer Mayer; Dial, 1975. **Awarded:** Georgia Children's 1980; Young Readers Choice 1978.

The Great Brain Reforms by John D. Fitzgerald, illustrated by Mercer Mayer; Dial, 1973. **Awarded:** Young Readers Choice 1976.

Me and My Little Brain by John D. Fitzgerald, illustrated by Sara Silcock; Dent, 1974. **Awarded:** Surrey School 1976.

FITZHARDINGE, JOAN MARGARET
   see PHIPSON, JOAN

FITZHUGH, LOUISE
Bang, Bang, You're Dead by Louise Fitzhugh and Sandra Scoppettone, illustrated by Louise Fitzhugh; Harper, 1969. **Awarded:** Art Books for Children 1974; New York Times Best Illustrated 1969.

Harriet the Spy written and illustrated by Louise Fitzhugh; Harper, 1964. **Awarded:** Sequoyah 1967.

Nobody's Family Is Going to Change by Louise Fitzhugh, not illustrated; Gollancz, 1976. **Awarded:** Other Award 1976.

Sport by Louise Fitzhugh, not illustrated; Delacorte, 1979. **Awarded:** CRABbery (honor) 1980.

FITZPATRICK, MARIE-LOUISE
An Chanail by Marie-Louise Fitzpatrick; An Gum, 1988. **Awarded:** Reading Association of Ireland 1989.

The Sleeping Giant written and illustrated by Marie-Louise Fitzpatrick; Brandon Books, 1991. **Awarded:** Bisto (Picture Storybook) 1992.

FITZ-RANDOLPH, JANE
Time and Clocks for the Space Age by Jane Fitz-Randolph and James Jespersen; not illustrated; Atheneum, 1979. **Awarded:** New York Academy of Sciences (older honor) 1980.

FIX, PHILIPPE
The Book of Giant Stories by David L. Harrison, illustrated by Philippe Fix; New York American Heritage Press, 1972. **Awarded:** Christopher (ages 8-12) 1973.

FLACK, MARJORIE
Boats on the River by Marjorie Flack, illustrated by Jay Hyde Barnum; Viking, 1946. **Awarded:** Caldecott (honor) 1947.

The Story about Ping by Marjorie Flack, illustrated by Kurt Wiese; Viking, 1933. **Awarded:** Lewis Carroll Shelf 1965.

FLANAGAN, GERALDINE LUX
Window into a Nest by Geraldine Lux Flanagan, photographs by Sean Morris; Kestrel, 1975; Houghton, 1976. **Awarded:** New York Academy of Sciences (older honor) 1977; Times Educational Supplement (senior) 1975.

FLEISCHER, ROSALIE
Spirit by Rosalie Fleischer. **Awarded:** Sydney Taylor Manuscript Awards 1986.

FLEISCHMAN, ALBERT SIDNEY
see FLEISCHMAN, SID

FLEISCHMAN, PAUL
The Borning Room by Paul Fleischman, not illustrated; HarperCollins, 1991. **Awarded:** Golden Kite (Fiction honor) 1991.

Joyful Noise: Poems for Two Voices by Paul Fleischman, illustrated by Eric Beddows; Harper & Row, 1988. **Awarded:** Boston Globe (Fiction Honor) 1988; Newbery 1989.

Graven Images: Three Stories by Paul Fleischman, illustrated by Andrew Glass; Harper & Row, 1982. **Awarded:** Newbery (honor) 1983.

The Half-a-Moon Inn by Paul Fleischman, illustrated by Kathy Jacobi; Harper, 1980. **Awarded:** Commonwealth Club of California 1980; Golden Kite (fiction honor) 1980; New York Times Notable Books 1980.

Path of the Pale Horse by Paul Fleischman, not illustrated; Harper & Row, 1983. **Awarded:** Golden Kite (fiction honor) 1983; Parents' Choice (literature) 1983.

Saturnalia by Paul Fleischman, not illustrated; Harper & Row, 1990. **Awarded:** Boston Globe (Fiction Honor) 1990.

FLEISCHMAN, SID
Awarded: Southern California Council (comprehensive contribution of lasting value to the literature for children and young people) 1972.

By the Great Horn Spoon! by Sid Fleischman, illustrated by Eric Von Schmidt; Atlantic-Little, 1963. **Awarded:** Boys Club 1964; FOCAL 1983; Southern California Council (notable) 1964; George G. Stone 1972; Western Writers (fiction) 1964.

Chancy and the Grand Rascal by Sid Fleischman, illustrated by Eric Von Schmidt; Atlantic-Little, 1966. **Awarded:** Commonwealth Club of California 1966.

The Ghost on Saturday Night by Sid Fleischman, illustrated by Eric Von Schmidt; Atlantic-Little, 1974. **Awarded:** Charlie May Simon 1976-77; Mark Twain 1977; Young Hoosier (4-6) 1979.

Humbug Mountain by Sid Fleischman, illustrated by Eric Von Schmidt; Atlantic-Little, 1978. **Awarded:** Boston Globe Horn Book (fiction) 1979; National Book Award (finalist) 1979.

Incroyables Adventures de Mister Mac Miffic by Sid Fleischman, translated by Jean Queval; Fernand Nathan, 1979. **Awarded:** International Board on Books for Young People (Translation/France) 1982.

Jim Ugly by Sid Fleischman, illustrated by Joseph A. Smith; Greenwillow, 1992. **Awarded:** Parents Choice (Story Book) 1992.

Jingo Django by Sid Fleischman, illustrated by Eric Von Schmidt; Atlantic-Little, 1971. **Awarded:** Spring Book Festival (middle honor) 1971.

McBroom Tells the Truth by Sid Fleischman, illustrated by Kurt Werth; Norton, 1966. **Awarded:** Lewis Carroll Shelf 1969.

McBroom the Rainmaker by Sid Fleischman, illustrated by Kurt Werth; Grosset, 1973. **Awarded:** Golden Kite (honor) 1973.

The Midnight Horse by Sid Fleischman, illustrated by Peter Sis; Greenwillow, 1990. **Awarded:** Parents' Choice (Story Book) 1990.

Mr. Mysterious & Co. by Sid Fleischman, illustrated by Eric Von Schmidt; Atlantic-Little, 1962. **Awarded:** Spring Book Festival (middle honor) 1962.

The Scarebird by Sid Fleischman, illustrated by Peter Sis; Greenwillow, 1988. **Awarded:** Redbook 1988.

The Scarebird by Sid Fleischman in *Cricket* (November 1987). **Awarded:** Witty Short Story Award 1988.

The Whipping Boy by Sid Fleischman, illustrated by Peter Sis; Greenwillow, 1986. **Awarded:** Golden Archer 1987; Nene 1992; Newbery 1987; Charlie May Simon 1988-89.

FLEISHMAN, SEYMOUR
The Little Old Man Who Could Not Read by Irma Simonton Black, illustrated by Seymour Fleishman; Whitman, 1968. **Awarded:** Emphasis on Reading (Grades K-2) 1989-90.

The Mystery of the Bewitched Bookmobile by Florence Parry Heide, illustrated by Seymour Fleishman; Whitman, 1975. **Awarded:** Golden Archer 1976.

FLEMING, DENISE
In the Tall, Tall Grass written and illustrated by Denise Fleming; Henry Holt, 1991. **Awarded:** Boston Globe Horn Book (Picture Book Honor) 1992; Please Touch Museum 1992; Redbook 1991.

FLEMING, IAN
Chitty-Chitty-Bang-Bang by Ian Fleming, illustrated by John Burningham; Random House, 1964. **Awarded:** Young Readers Choice 1967.

FLETCHER, CHARLIE MAY HOGUE
see SIMON, CHARLIE MAY

FLETCHER, CLAIRE
The Seashell Song by Susie Jenkin-Pearce, illustrated by Claire Fletcher; Bodley Head, 1992; Lothrop, Lee & Shepard, 1992. **Awarded:** Mother Goose 1993.

FLETCHER, SYDNEY E.
The Cowboy and His Horse written and illustrated by Sydney E. Fletcher; Grosset, 1951. **Awarded:** Boys Club 1952.

FLEUR, ANNE ELIZABETH
see SARI

FLEUTIAUX, PIERRETTE
From Afar It Is an Island translated and adapted by Pierrette Fleutiaux, illustrated by Bruno Munari; World, 1972. **Awarded:** New York Academy of Sciences (younger honor) 1974.

FLOETHE, RICHARD
The Avion My Uncle Flew by Cyrus Fisher, illustrated by Richard Floethe; Appleton, 1946. **Awarded:** Newbery (honor) 1947.

Island Summer by Hazel Wilson, illustrated by Richard Floethe; Abingdon-Cokesbury, 1949. **Awarded:** Ohioana (honorable mention) 1950.

Song of the Pines: A Story of Norwegian Lumbering in Wisconsin by Walter Havighurst and Marion Havighurst; illustrated by Richard Floethe; Winston, 1949. **Awarded:** Newbery (honor) 1950; Ohioana 1950; Spring Book Festival (older honor) 1949.

FLOHERTY, JOHN JOSEPH
Sons of the Hurricane by J. J. Floherty, illustrated with photographs; Lippincott, 1938. **Awarded:** Spring Book Festival (older honor) 1938.

FLORA, JAMES
The Fabulous Firework Family written and illustrated by James Flora; Harcourt, 1955. **Awarded:** Ohioana 1956.

Grandpa's Ghost Stories written and illustrated by James Flora; Atheneum, 1978. **Awarded:** Buckeye (K-3) 1983.

The Great Green Turkey Creek Monster written and illustrated by James Flora; Atheneum, 1976. **Awarded:** Colorado Children's 1979; Emphasis on Reading (Grades 2-3) 1984-85.

The Talking Dog and the Barking Man by Elizabeth Seeman, illustrated by James Flora; Watts, 1960. **Awarded:** Spring Book Festival (middle honor) 1960.

FLORIAN, DOUGLAS
An Auto Mechanic written and illustrated by Douglas Florian; Greenwillow, 1991. **Awarded:** Parents' Choice (Story Book) 1991.

FLOURNOY, VALERIE
The Patchwork Quilt by Valerie Flournoy, illustrated by Jerry Pinkney; Dial, 1985. **Awarded:** Christopher (ages 4-8) 1986; Ezra Jack Keats New Writer Award 1986; Coretta Scott King (illustration) 1986.

FLOYD, GARETH
The Night Watchmen by Helen Cresswell, illustrated by Gareth Floyd; Faber, 1969; Macmillan, 1969. **Awarded:** Carnegie (honour) 1969; Phoenix 1989.

Take the Long Path by Joan de Hamel, illustrated by Gareth Floyd; Lutterworth Press, 1978. **Awarded:** Esther Glen 1979.

Up the Pier by Helen Cresswell, illustrated by Gareth Floyd; Faber, 1971. **Awarded:** Carnegie (highly commended) 1971.

The Writing on the Hearth by Cynthia Harnett, illustrated by Gareth Floyd; Viking, 1973. **Awarded:** Spring Book Festival (older honor) 1973.

FLYNN, BARBARA
Gildaen: The Heroic Adventures of a Most Unusual Rabbit by Emilie Buchwald, illustrated by Barbara Flynn; Harcourt, 1973. **Awarded:** Spring Book Festival (middle) 1973.

FOLSOM, FRANKLIN
Awarded: New Jersey Institute of Technology (New Jersey author awards special citation for husband-wife writers of children's books) 1969; New Jersey Institute of Technology (New Jersey's most distinguished husband-wife team of writers for adults, young adults, teenagers, and older, middle age and young children) 1965.

The Answer Book of History by Franklin Folsom and Mary Elting, illustrated by W. K. Plummer; Grosset, 1966. **Awarded:** New Jersey Institute of Technology 1967.

Flags of All Nations and the People Who Live under Them by Franklin Folsom and Mary Elting, illustrated with photographs; Grosset, 1969. **Awarded:** New Jersey Institute of Technology 1970.

If You Lived in the Days of the Wild Mammoth Hunters by Franklin Folsom and Mary Elting; illustrated by John Moodie; Four Winds, 1969. **Awarded:** New Jersey Institute of Technology 1970.

Red Power on the Rio Grande: The Native American Revolution of 1680 by Frank Folsom, illustrated by J. D. Roybal; Follett, 1973. **Awarded:** Western Writers (nonfiction) 1974.

Science and the Secret of Man's Past by Franklin Folsom, illustrated by Ursula Koering; Harvey House, 1966. **Awarded:** New Jersey Institute of Technology (science) 1966.

FON EISEN, ANTHONY T.
Bond of the Fire by Anthony T. Fon Eisen, illustrated by W. T. Mars; World, 1965. **Awarded:** Lewis Carroll Shelf 1965.

FONSECA, GEORGE
I Like Trains by Catherine Woolley, illustrated by George Fonseca; Harper, 1965. **Awarded:** New Jersey Institute of Technology 1965.

FORBERG, ATI
The Magic of the Glits by Carole S. Adler, illustrated by Ati Forberg; Macmillan, 1979. **Awarded:** CRABbery 1980; Golden Kite (fiction) 1979; William Allen White 1982.

Samurai of Gold Hill by Yoshiko Uchida, illustrated by Ati Forberg; Scribner, 1972. **Awarded:** Commonwealth Club of California 1972.

FORBES, ESTHER
Johnny Tremain by Esther Forbes, illustrated by Lynd Ward; Houghton-Mifflin, 1943. **Awarded:** Newbery 1944.

FORBUS, INA B.
The Secret Circle by Ina B. Forbus, illustrated by Corydon Bell; Viking, 1958. **Awarded:** North Carolina AAUW 1958.

FORD, BARBARA
Animals That Use Tools by Barbara Ford, illustrated by Janet D'Amato; Messner, 1978. **Awarded:** New Jersey Institute of Technology 1980.

The Automobile by Barbara Ford, illustrated with photos; Walker, 1987. **Awarded:** New Jersey Institute of Technology 1988.

FORD, BETTY
The President's Car written and illustrated by Nancy Winslow Parker, introduction by Betty Ford; Crowell Jr. Books, 1981.

Awarded: New York Academy of Sciences (younger honor) 1982.

FORD, GEORGE
Paul Robeson by Eloise Greenfield, illustrated by George Ford; Crowell, 1975. **Awarded:** Jane Addams 1976.

Ray Charles by Sharon Bell Mathis, illustrated by George Ford; Crowell, 1973. **Awarded:** Coretta Scott King 1974.

FORD, LAUREN
The Ageless Story: With It's Antiphons written and illustrated by Lauren Ford; Dodd, Mead, 1939. **Awarded:** Caldecott (honor) 1940.

FORD, MARIANNE
Copycats by Marianne Ford, diagrams by Anna Pugh; Deutsch, 1983. **Awarded:** Maschler (runnerup) 1983.

FOREMAN, MICHAEL
The Brothers Grimm: Popular Folk Tales by Jacob Grimm and Wilhelm Grimm, newly translated by Brian Alderson, illustrated by Michael Foreman; Gollancz, 1978. **Awarded:** Greenaway (commended) 1978.

City of Gold and Other Stories from the Old Testament by Peter Dickinson, illustrated by Michael Foreman; Gollancz, 1980. **Awarded:** Bologna (graphics for youth) 1982; Carnegie 1980; Greenaway (highly commended) 1980.

Early in the Morning: A Collection of New Poems by Charles Causley, illustrated by Michael Foreman; Viking Kestrel, 1986. **Awarded:** Maschler (runnerup) 1986; Signal 1987.

The Great Sleigh Robbery by Michael Foreman; Hamilton, 1968. **Awarded:** W. H. Smith 1972.

Horatio by Michael Foreman; Hamilton, 1969. **Awarded:** W. H. Smith 1972.

Long Neck and Thunder Foot by Helen Piers, illustrated by Michael Foreman; Kestrel, 1982. **Awarded:** Greenaway (cowinner) 1982.

Monkey and the Three Wizards by Cheng-en Wu, translated by Peter Harris, illustrated by Michael Foreman; Collins, 1976. **Awarded:** W. H. Smith (£100) 1977

The Saga of Erik the Viking by Terry Jones, illustrated by Michael Foreman; Pavilion/Michael Joseph, 1983. **Awarded:** Children's Book Award 1983.

Seasons of Splendour by Madhur Jaffrey, illustrated by Michael Foreman; Pavilion Books, 1985; Atheneum, 1985. **Awarded:** Greenaway (commended) 1985; New York Times Notable 1985.

Shakespeare Stories by Leon Garfield, illustrated by Michael Foreman; Gollancz, 1985. **Awarded:** Maschler (runnerup) 1985.

Sleeping Beauty and Other Favourite Fairy Tales chosen and translated by Angela Carter, illustrated by Michael Foreman; Gollancz, 1982. **Awarded:** Greenaway (cowinner) 1982; Maschler 1982.

War Boy written and illustrated by Michael Foreman; Pavilion Books in association with Joseph, 1989; Arcade, 1990. **Awarded:** Greenaway 1989; New York Times Best Illustrated 1990; W. H. Smith (2nd prize) 1990.

FOREST, ANTONIA
Falconer's Lure: The Story of a Summer Holiday by Antonia Forest, illustrated by Tasha Kallin; Faber, 1957. **Awarded:** Carnegie (commended) 1957.

Peter's Room by Antonia Forest, not illustrated; Faber, 1961. **Awarded:** Carnegie (commended) 1961.

The Thursday Kidnapping by Antonia Forest, not illustrated; Faber, 1963. **Awarded:** Carnegie (commended) 1963.

FORGEOT, CLAIRE
The Rising of the Wind: Adventures Along the Beaufort Scale by Jacques Yvart, illustrated by Claire Forgeot; Green Tiger Press, 1984. **Awarded:** New York Academy of Sciences (younger honor) 1985.

FORMAN, JAMES
Ceremony of Innocence by James Forman, not illustrated; Hawthorn, 1970. **Awarded:** Lewis Carroll Shelf 1972.

My Enemy, My Brother by James Forman, not illustrated; Meredith, 1969. **Awarded:** Spring Book Festival (older) 1969.

Ring the Judas Bell by James Forman, not illustrated; Farrar, 1965. **Awarded:** Spring Book Festival (older honor) 1965.

FORRESTER, VICTORIA
The Magnificent Moo written and illustrated by Victoria Forrester; Atheneum, 1983. **Awarded:** Parents Choice (illustration) 1983.

FORSEE, AYLESA
The Whirly Bird by Aylesa Forsee, illustrated by Tom Two Arrows; Lippincott, 1955. **Awarded:** Helen Dean Fish 1955.

FORSHAY-LUNSFORD, CIN
Walk Through Cold Fire by Cin Forshay-Lunsford, not illustrated; Delacorte, 1985. **Awarded:** Delacorte Press Prize 1984.

FORTNUM, PEGGY
Candidate for Fame by Margaret Jowett, illustrated by Peggy Fortnum; Oxford, 1955. **Awarded:** Carnegie (commended) 1955.

FOSTER, ELIZABETH C.
The Long Hungry Night by Elizabeth C. Foster and Slim Williams, illustrated by Glo Coalson; Atheneum, 1973. **Awarded:** Friends of American Writers (illustrator) 1974; Friends of American Writers (ages 10-14) 1974.

FOSTER, GENEVIEVE
Abraham Lincoln's World written and illustrated by Genevieve Foster; Scribner, 1944. **Awarded:** Newbery (honor) 1945.

Birthdays of Freedom: America's Heritage from the Ancient World written and illustrated by Genevieve Foster; Scribner, 1952. **Awarded:** Newbery (honor) 1953.

George Washington: an Initial Biography written and illustrated by Genevieve Foster; Scribner, 1949. **Awarded:** Boys Club 1950; Newbery (honor) 1950.

George Washington's World written and illustrated by Genevieve Foster; Scribner, 1941. **Awarded:** Newbery (honor) 1942.

FOSTER, GERALD
Cruise of the Jeanette by Edward Ellsberg, illustrated by Gerald Foster; Dodd, Mead, 1949. **Awarded:** Boys Club 1950.

I Have Just Begun to Fight: The Story of John Paul Jones by Edward Ellsberg, illustrated by G. Foster; Dodd, Mead, 1942. **Awarded:** Spring Book Festival (middle) 1942.

FOULDS, ELFRIDA VIPONT
The Elephant and the Bad Baby by Elfrida Vipont, illustrated by Raymond Briggs; Coward, 1970. **Awarded:** Spring Book Festival (picture book honor) 1970.

The Lark on the Wing by Elfrida Vipont Foulds, illustrated by Terence Reginald Freeman; Oxford, 1950. **Awarded:** Carnegie 1950.

FOUNDS, GEORGE
America's Endangered Birds: Programs and People Working to Save Them by Robert M. McClung, illustrated by George Founds; Morrow, 1979. **Awarded:** Golden Kite (nonfiction honor) 1979.

FOUQUE, FRIEDRICH HEINRICH DE LA MOTTE
Undine by Friedrich de La Motte Fouque, retold and edited by Gertrude C. Schwebeil, illustrated by Eros Keith; Simon & Schuster, 1971, c1957. **Awarded:** Lewis Carroll Shelf 1971.

FOURNIER, CATHARINE
The Coconut Thieves by Catharine Fournier, illustrated by Janina Domanska; Scribner, 1964. **Awarded:** Spring Book Festival (picture book) 1964.

FOWKE, EDITH
Awarded: Vicky Metcalf 1985.

Sally Go Round the Sun by Edith Fowke, illustrated by Carlos Marchiori; McClelland & Stewart, 1969. **Awarded:** Canadian Library Assn. 1970.

FOWLER, JIM
Dolphin Adventure: A True Story by Wayne Grover, illustrated by Jim Fowler; Greenwillow, 1990. **Awarded:** Book Can Develop Empathy 1991.

FOWLER, THURLEY
The Green Wind by Thurley Fowler, not illustrated; Rigby, 1985. **Awarded:** Children's Book Council of Australia (book of the year) 1986.

FOWLER, ZINITA
The Last Innocent Summer by Zinita Fowler; Texas Christian University Press, 1990. **Awarded:** Texas Institute of Letters 1991.

FOX, MARY VIRGINIA
Lady for the Defense: A Biography of Belva Lockwood by Mary Virginia Fox, illustrated with photographs; Harcourt, 1975. **Awarded:** Council for Wisconsin Writers (juvenile runnerup) 1976.

FOX, MEM
Awarded: Dromkeen Medal 1990.

Night Noises by Mem Fox, illustrated by Terry Denton; Harcourt Brace Jovanovich, 1989. **Awarded:** Redbook 1989.

Possum Magic by Mem Fox, illustrated by Julie Vivas; Omnibus Books, 1983; Harcourt Brace Jovanovich, 1983. **Awarded:** Children's Book Council of Australia (picture book of the year highly commended) 1984; International Board on Book for Young People (illustration/Australia) 1986; KOALA (Primary) 1987; New South Wales State Literary Awards (Children's) 1984.

FOX, MICHAEL
The Wolf by Michael Fox, illustrated by Charles Frace; Coward, 1973. **Awarded:** Christopher (ages 8-12) 1974.

FOX, PAULA
Awarded: Hans Christian Andersen (author) 1978; University of Southern Mississippi 1987.

A Place Apart by Paula Fox, not illustrated; Farrar, 1980; Dent, 1981; New American Library, 1982. **Awarded:** American Book Award (children's fiction paperback) 1983; New York Times Notable Books 1980.

Blowfish Live in the Sea by Paula Fox, not illustrated; Bradbury, 1970. **Awarded:** National Book Award (finalist) 1971.

The Little Swineherd and Other Tales by Paula Fox, illustrated by Leonard Lubin; Dutton, 1978. **Awarded:** National Book Award (finalist) 1979.

The Moonlight Man by Paula Fox, not illustrated; Bradbury, 1986. **Awarded:** New York Times Notable 1986.

One-eyed Cat by Paula Fox, not illustrated; Bradbury, 1984. **Awarded:** Child Study 1984; Christopher (Ages 10-up) 1985; International Board on Book for Young People (writing/U.S.) 1986; New York Times Notable 1984; Newbery (honor) 1985.

The Slave Dancer by Paula Fox, illustrated by Eros Keith; Bradbury, 1973. **Awarded:** Newbery 1974.

The Village by the Sea by Paula Fox, not illustrated; Orchard, 1988. **Awarded:** Boston Globe (Fiction) 1989.

FOX, RUTH
Great Men of Medicine by Ruth Fox, illustrated by Dwight Logan; Random House, 1947. **Awarded:** Boys Club 1949.

FOX, THOMAS C.
Children of Vietnam by Thomas C. Fox and Betty Jean Lifton, illustrated by Thomas C. Fox; Atheneum, 1972. **Awarded:** National Book Award (finalist) 1973.

FRACE, CHARLES
The Wolf by Michael Fox, illustrated by Charles Frace; Coward, 1973. **Awarded:** Christopher (ages 8-12) 1974.

FRAME, PAUL
The Chocolate Chip Mystery by John McInnes, illustrated by Paul Frame; Garrard, 1972. **Awarded:** Emphasis on Reading (Grades 2-3) 1982-83.

Haunted House by Peggy Parish, illustrated by Paul Frame; Macmillan, 1971. **Awarded:** CRABbery (Honor) 1990.

Mahatma Gandhi: the Father of Nonviolence by Catherine Owens Peare, illustrated by Paul Frame; Hawthorne, 1950. **Awarded:** Boys Club 1951.

Tiger Rookie by Edmund O. Scholefield, illustrated by Paul Frame; World, 1966. **Awarded:** New Jersey Institute of Technology (ages 12-up) 1966.

FRAMPTON, DAVID
Jerusalem Shining Still by Karla Kuskin, illustrated by David Frampton; Harper & Row, 1987. **Awarded:** Parents' Choice (Story Book) 1987.

Just So Stories by Rudyard Kipling, illustrated by David Frampton; HarperCollins, 1991. **Awarded:** Parents' Choice (Picture Book) 1991.

FRANCES, HELEN
The Devil's Stone by Helen Frances, illustrated; Omnibus Books, 1983. **Awarded:** Children's Book Council of Australia (book of the year commended) 1984.

FRANCHERE, RUTH
Stephen Crane: The Story of an American Writer by Ruth Franchere, not illustrated; Crowell, 1961. **Awarded:** Spring Book Festival (older honor) 1961.

FRANCO, MARJORIE
Love In a Different Key by Marjorie Franco, not illustrated; Houghton Mifflin, 1983. **Awarded:** Society of Midland Authors 1984.

FRANCOIS, ANDRE
The Adventures of Ulysses by Jacques Lemarchand, translated by E. M. Hatt, illustrated by Andre Francois; Criterion, 1960. **Awarded:** New York Times Best Illustrated 1960.

Crocodile Tears written and illustrated by Andre Francois; Universe, 1956. **Awarded:** New York Times Best Illustrated 1956.

The Magic Currant Bun by John Symonds, illustrated by Andre Francois; Lippincott, 1952. **Awarded:** New York Times Best Illustrated 1952.

Roland by Nelly Stephane, illustrated by Andre Francois; Harcourt, 1958. **Awarded:** New York Times Best Illustrated 1958.

You Are Ri-di-cu-lous written and illustrated by Andre Francois; Pantheon, 1970. **Awarded:** New York Times Best Illustrated 1970.

FRANCOISE
see SEIGNOBOSC, FRANCOISE

FRANK, RUDOLF
No Hero for the Kaiser by Rudolf Frank, translated by Patricia Crampton, illustrated by Klaus Steffans; Lothrop, Lee & Shepard, 1986. **Awarded:** Batchelder 1987; Parents Choice (literature) 1986.

FRANKEL, ALONA
Hello, Clouds! by Dalia H. Renberg, illustrated by Alona Frankel; Harper & Row, 1985. **Awarded:** Please Touch (honorable mention) 1986.

FRANKENBERG, ROBERT CLINTON
Abraham Lincoln, Friend of the People by Clara Ingram Judson, illustrated by Robert Frankenberg; Wilcox & Follett, 1950. **Awarded:** Newbery (honor) 1951.

Benjamin Franklin by Clara Ingram Judson, illustrated by Robert Frankenberg; Follett, 1957. **Awarded:** Indiana Authors Day (children) 1958.

Owls in the Family by Farley Mowat, illustrated by Robert Frankenberg; Little, Brown, 1961. **Awarded:** Boys Club 1963.

Sancho of the Long, Long Horns by Allen R. Bosworth, illustrated by Robert Frankenberg; Doubleday, 1947. **Awarded:** Commonwealth Club of California 1947.

FRANKLIN, GEORGE CORY
Wild Animals of the Five Rivers Country by George Cory Franklin, illustrated by Mary Ogden Abbott; Houghton, 1947. **Awarded:** Boys Club 1949.

FRANKS, HUGH
Will to Live by Hugh Franks, not illustrated; Routledge & Kegan Paul, 1979. **Awarded:** Korczak (about children) 1981.

FRASCINO, EDWARD
The Trumpet of the Swan by E. B. White, illustrated by Edward Frascino; Harper, 1970. **Awarded:** Sue Hefly 1975; International Board on Books for Young People (USA) 1972; National Book Award (finalist) 1971; Sequoyah 1973; Spring Book Festival (middle honor) 1970; William Allen White 1973; Young Hoosier (grades 4-6) 1975.

FRASCONI, ANTONIO
The House That Jack Built: A Picture Book in Two Languages written and illustrated by Antonio Frasconi; Harcourt, 1958. **Awarded:** Caldecott (honor) 1959; New York Times Best Illustrated 1958.

Monkey Puzzle and Other Poems by Myra Cohn Livingston, illustrated by Antonio Frasconi; Atheneum, 1984. **Awarded:** Commonwealth Club of California 1984.

See and Say: A Picture Book in Four Languages written and illustrated by Antonio Frasconi; Harcourt, 1955. **Awarded:** New York Times Best Illustrated 1955.

The Snow and the Sun: A South American Folk Rhyme in Two Languages written and illustrated by Antonio Frasconi; Harcourt, 1961. **Awarded:** New York Times Best Illustrated 1961.

FRASER, BETTY
Giraffe: the Silent Giant by Miriam Schlein, illustrated by Betty Fraser; Four Winds, 1976. **Awarded:** Children's Book Showcase 1977.

A House Is a House for Me by Mary Ann Hoberman, illustrated by Betty Fraser; Viking, 1978; Puffin, 1982. **Awarded:** American Book Award (picturebook paperback) 1983.

FRASIER, DEBRA
On the Day You Were Born written and illustrated by Debra Frasier; Harcourt Brace Jovanovich, 1991. **Awarded:** Hungry Mind (Picturebooks/Nonfiction) 1992; Parents' Choice (Story Book) 1991.

FREEDMAN, FLORENCE B.
Brothers retold by Florence B. Freedman, illustrated by Robert Andrew Parker; Harper & Row, 1985. **Awarded:** Jewish Book Council (illustration) 1986; Sydney Taylor Book Award (Picture book) 1986.

FREEDMAN, RUSSELL
Awarded: Empire State 1993; Knickerbocker 1993; Washington Post Nonfiction 1992.

Buffalo Hunt by Russell Freedman, illustrated with photos; Holiday House, 1988. **Awarded:** Golden Kite (Nonfiction honor) 1988; Woodson (Outstanding Merit - Elementary) 1989.

Children of the Wild West by Russell Freedman, illustrated with photographs; Clarion, 1983. **Awarded:** Boston Globe Horn Book (nonfiction honor) 1984; Western Heritage 1984.

Franklin Delano Roosevelt by Russell Freedman, illustrated with photos; Clarion Books, 1990. **Awarded:** Golden Kite (Nonfiction Honor) 1990; Jefferson Cup 1991; Orbis Pictus 1990.

Hanging On: How Animals Carry Their Young by Russell Freedman, illustrated with photographs; Holiday, 1977. **Awarded:** New York Academy of Sciences (younger honor) 1978.

An Indian Winter by Russell Freedman, illustrated by Karl Bodmer; Holiday House, 1992. **Awarded:** Golden Kite (nonfiction honor) 1992; Parents Choice (Picture Book) 1992; Reading Magic Award 1992.

Lincoln: A Photobiography by Russell Freedman, illustrated with photos; Clarion, 1987. **Awarded:** Golden Kite (Nonfiction honor) 1987; International Board on Book for Young People (Writing/United States) 1990; Jefferson Cup 1988; Newbery 1988.

The Wright Brothers: How They Invented the Airplane by Russell Freedman, illustrated with photos; Holiday House, 1991. **Awarded:** Boston Globe Horn Book (Nonfiction Honor) 1991; Golden Kite (Nonfiction) 1991; Hungry Mind (Middle Readers/Nonfiction) 1992; Jefferson Cup 1992; Newbery (honor) 1992; Parents' Choice (Story Book) 1991; Reading Magic Award 1991.

FREEHOF, LILLIAN SIMON

Star Light Stories: Holiday and Sabbath Tales by Lillian Simon Freehof, illustrated by Jessie B. Robinson; Bloch, 1952. **Awarded:** Jewish Book Council 1952.

Stories of King David by Lillian Simon Freehof, illustrated by Seymour R. Kaplan; Jewish Publications, 1952. **Awarded:** Jewish Book Council 1952.

FREEMAN, ANNE FRANCES
see HUETHER, ANNE F.

FREEMAN, BILL
Awarded: Vicky Metcalf 1984.

Shantymen of Cache Lake by Bill Freeman, illustrated with maps and plates; Lorimer, 1975. **Awarded:** Governor General (author) 1975.

FREEMAN, CHARLES
Defence by Charles Freeman, illustrated with portraits; Batsford Academic & Educational, 1983. **Awarded:** Times Educational Supplement (senior) 1983.

FREEMAN, DON
Come Again, Pelican written and illustrated by Don Freeman; Viking, 1961. **Awarded:** Southern California Council (significant contribution to illustration) 1962.

Fly High, Fly Low written and illustrated by Don Freeman; Viking, 1957. **Awarded:** Caldecott (honor) 1958.

The Paper Party written and illustrated by Don Freeman; Viking, 1974. **Awarded:** Commonwealth Club of California 1974.

Pet of the Met by Don Freeman and Lydia Freeman, illustrated by Don Freeman; Viking, 1953. **Awarded:** Spring Book Festival (ages 4- 8) 1953.

A Pocket for Corduroy written and illustrated by Don Freeman; Viking, 1978. **Awarded:** Emphasis on Reading (grades K-1) 1984-85.

The White Deer by James Thurber, illustrated by Don Freeman; Harcourt, 1945. **Awarded:** Ohioana 1946.

Will's Quill written and illustrated by Don Freeman; Viking, 1975. **Awarded:** Southern California Council (total concept and illustration) 1976.

FREEMAN, IRA M.
All About Light and Radiation by Ira M. Freeman, illustrated by George T. Resch; Random House, 1965. **Awarded:** New Jersey Institute of Technology 1965.

FREEMAN, LYDIA
Pet of the Met by Lydia Freeman and Don Freeman, illustrated by Don Freeman; Viking, 1953. **Awarded:** Spring Book Festival (ages 4- 8) 1953.

FREEMAN, MAE BLACKER
Stars and Stripes: The Story of the American Flag by Mae Blacker Freeman, illustrated by Lorence F. Bjorklund; Random House, 1964. **Awarded:** New Jersey Institute of Technology (history ages 6-12) 1964.

FREEMAN, TERENCE REGINALD
The Lark on the Wing by Elfrida Vipont Foulds, ill. by T. R. Freeman; Oxford, 1950. **Awarded:** Carnegie 1950.

FRENCH, ALLEN
The Lost Baron by Allen French, illustrated by Andrew Wyeth; Houghton, 1940. **Awarded:** Spring Book Festival (older honor) 1940.

FRENCH, FIONA
Anancy and Mr. Dry-Bone written and illustrated by Fiona French; Little Brown, 1991. **Awarded:** Parents' Choice (Story Book) 1991.

The Blue Bird written and illustrated by Fiona French; Walck, 1972. **Awarded:** Children's Book Showcase 1973.

King Tree written and illustrated by Fiona French; Oxford, 1973. **Awarded:** Greenaway (commended) 1973.

Snow White in New York written and illustrated by Fiona French; Oxford University Press, 1986. **Awarded:** Greenaway 1986.

FRENCH, KERSTI
Pappa Pellerin's Daughter by Maria Gripe, translated by Kersti French, illustrated by Harald Gripe; John Day, 1966. **Awarded:** Lewis Carroll Shelf 1966; Spring Book Festival (older honor) 1966.

FRENCH, MICHAEL
Pursuit by Michael French, not illustrated; Delacorte, 1982; Dell, 1983. **Awarded:** California Young Reader (high school) 1987.

FRENCH, SIMON
All We Know by Simon French, not illustrated; Angus & Robertson, 1986. **Awarded:** Children's Book Council of Australia (book of the year older) 1987.

Cannily, Cannily by Simon French, not illustrated; Angus & Robertson, 1981. **Awarded:** Children's Book Council of Australia (book of the year commended) 1982.

Change the Locks by Simon French, not illustrated; Ashton Scholastic, 1991. **Awarded:** Children's Book Council of Australia (Book of the year Older Honor) 1992.

FRENZENY, P.
The Jungle Book by Rudyard Kipling, illustrated by P. Frenzeny, J. L. Kipling, and W. H. Drake; Doubleday, 1952, c1893. **Awarded:** Lewis Carroll Shelf 1960.

FRESCHET, BERNIECE
Bear Mouse by Berniece Freschet, illustrated by Donald Carrick; Scribner, 1973. **Awarded:** Irma Simonton and James H. Black 1973; Children's Book Showcase 1974.

The Web in the Grass by Berniece Freschet, illustrated by Roger Duvoisin; Scribner, 1972. **Awarded:** New York Academy of Sciences (younger) 1974.

FRICKE, JOHN
Awarded: L. Frank Baum 1970.

FRIEDMAN, ESTELLE E.
Digging into Yesterday by Estelle E. Friedman, illustrated by Leonard Everett Fisher; Putnam, 1958. **Awarded:** Boys Club 1959.

FRIEDMAN, FRIEDA
Dot for Short by Frieda Friedman, illustrated by Carolyn Haywood; Morrow, 1947. **Awarded:** Spring Book Festival (younger honor) 1947.

Janitor's Girl by Frieda Friedman, illustrated by Mary Stevens; Morrow, 1956. **Awarded:** Spring Book Festival (middle honor) 1956.

A Sundae with Judy by Frieda Friedman, illustrated by Carolyn Haywood; Morrow, 1949. **Awarded:** Spring Book Festival (under 12 honor) 1949.

FRIEDMAN, INA
How My Parents Learned to Eat by Ina Friedman, illustrated by Allen Say; Houghton Mifflin, 1984. **Awarded:** Christopher (ages 6-8) 1985.

FRIEDMAN, ROSE
Freedom Builders: Great Teachers from Socrates to John Dewey by Rose Friedman, not illustrated; Little, Brown, 1968. **Awarded:** New Jersey Institute of Technology (education) 1968, 1969.

FRIERMOOD, ELISABETH HAMILTON
Focus the Bright Land by Elisabeth H. Friermood, not illustrated; Doubleday, 1967. **Awarded:** Ohioana 1968.

Head High, Ellen Brody by Elisabeth H. Friermood, not illustrated; Doubleday, 1958. **Awarded:** Indiana Authors Day (children) 1959.

FRIIS-BAASTAD, BABBIS
Don't Take Teddy by Babbis Friis-Baastad, translated by Lise Somme McKinnon, not illustrated; Scribner, 1967. **Awarded:** Batchelder 1969; Lewis Carroll Shelf 1976; Spring Book Festival (middle honor) 1967.

FRIMMER, STEVEN
Finding the Forgotten: Adventures in the Discovery of the Past by Steven Frimmer, not illustrated; Putnam, 1971. **Awarded:** New Jersey Institute of Technology 1971.

FRISHMAN, NETTIE
Awarded: Southern California Council (distinguished contribution for outstanding community service in the field of children's literature) 1979.

FRISKEY, MARGARET RICHARDS
Chicken Little Count-to-Ten by Margaret R. Friskey, illustrated by Katherine Evans; Children's Press, 1946. **Awarded:** Spring Book Festival (Younger Honor) 1946.

FRITZ, JEAN
Awarded: Knickerbocker 1992; David McCord Children's Literature Citation 1988; Outstanding Pennsylvania Author 1978; Regina 1985; School Library Media Specialist of South Eastern New York 1984; University of Southern Mississippi 1988; Washington Post Children's Book Guild Nonfiction Award 1979; Wilder 1986.

And Then What Happened, Paul Revere? by Jean Fritz, illustrated by Margot Tomes; Coward, 1973. **Awarded:** Boston Globe Horn Book (text honor) 1974.

The Double Life of Pocahontas by Jean Fritz, illustrated by Ed Young; Putnam, 1983. **Awarded:** Boston Globe Horn Book (nonfiction) 1984.

The Great Little Madison by Jean Fritz, illustrated with prints and engravings; Putnam, 1989. **Awarded:** Boston Globe (Nonfiction) 1990; Orbis Pictus 1989.

Homesick, My Own Story by Jean Fritz, illustrated with drawings by Margot Tomes and photographs; Putnam, 1982. **Awarded:** American Book Award (children's fiction hardback) 1983; Boston Globe Horn Book (fiction honor) 1983; Child Study 1982; Christopher (ages 8- 12) 1983; New York Times Notable Books 1982; Newbery (honor) 1983.

Make Way for Sam Houston by Jean Fritz, illustrated by Elise Primavera; Putnam, 1986. **Awarded:** New York Times Notable 1986; Western Writers Spur Award 1987.

So Far from the Bamboo Grove by Yoko Kawashima Watkins, introduction by Jean Fritz; Lothrop Lee & Shepard, 1986. **Awarded:** Parents Choice (literature) 1986.

Stonewall by Jean Fritz, illustrated by Stephen Gammell; Putnam, 1979. **Awarded:** Boston Globe Horn Book (nonfiction honor) 1980; New York Times Notable Books 1979.

Traitor: The Case of Benedict Arnold by Jean Fritz, illustrated by John Andre; Putnam, 1981. **Awarded:** New York Times Notable Books 1981.

Will You Sign Here, John Hancock? by Jean Fritz, illustrated by Trina Schart Hyman; Coward, 1976. **Awarded:** Boston Globe Horn Book (nonfiction honor) 1976.

The World in 1492 by Jean Fritz, Katherine Paterson, Patricia McKissack, Fredrick McKissack, Margaret Mahy and Jamake Highwater, illustrated by Stefano Vitale; Henry Holt, 1992. **Awarded:** Hungry Mind (Young Adult/Nonfiction) 1993.

FRIZZELL, DICK
The Magpies by Denis Glover, illustrated by Dick Frizzell; Century Hutchinson New Zealand, 1987. **Awarded:** Russell Clark 1988.

FROLOV, VADIM
What It's All About by Vadim Frolov, translated by Joseph Barnes, not illustrated; Doubleday, 1968. **Awarded:** Child Study 1968.

FROMM, LILO
Das Mondgesicht by Gerda Marie Scheidl, illustrated by Lilo Fromm; Obpacher Buch u. Kunstverlag, 1960. **Awarded:** Hans Christian Andersen (runnerup) 1962.

Uncle Harry by Gerlinde Schneider, adapted by Elizabeth Shub, illustrated by Lilo Fromm; Macmillan, 1972. **Awarded:** Children's Book Showcase 1973.

FROST, ARTHUR BURDETT
Uncle Remus: His Songs and Sayings by Joel Chandler Harris, illustrated by A. B. Frost; Hawthorne, 1921, c1880. **Awarded:** Lewis Carroll Shelf 1963.

FROUD, BRIAN
Are All the Giants Dead? by Mary Norton, illustrated by Brian Froud; Harcourt, 1975. **Awarded:** New York Times Notable Books 1975.

FUCHS, BERNIE
Ragtime Tumpie by Alan Schroeder, illustrated by Bernie Fuchs; Little Brown, 1989. **Awarded:** Parents' Choice (Picture Book) 1989.

FUGE, CHARLES
Bush Vark's First Day Out written and illustrated by Charles Fuge; Macmillan, 1988. **Awarded:** Macmillan Prize (1st prize) 1987; Mother Goose 1989.

FULFOLD, DEBORAH
Frogs, Toads, and Newts by Francis D. Ommanney, illustrated by Deborah Fulfold; Bodley Head, 1973. **Awarded:** Times Educational Supplement (junior) 1974.

FULLA, LUDOVIT
Awarded: Hans Christian Andersen (highly commended illustrator/USSR) 1976.

FULLER, HELEN
Awarded: Southern California Council (Dorothy C. McKenzie Award) 1978.

FULLER, JOHN G.
Fever: the Hunt for a New Killer Virus by John G. Fuller, illustrated with maps; Reader's Digest Press, 1974. **Awarded:** New York Academy of Sciences (older honor) 1975.

FULLER, MURIEL
The Runaway Shuttle Train by Muriel Fuller, illustrated by Dorathea Dana; McKay, 1946. **Awarded:** Spring Book Festival (younger honor) 1946.

FUNAI, MAMORU
Moke and Poki in the Rain Forest written and illustrated by Mamoru Funai; Harper & Row, 1972. **Awarded:** New Jersey Institute of Technology 1973.

On a Picnic by Judy Delton, illustrated by Mamoru Funai; Doubleday, 1979. **Awarded:** New Jersey Institute of Technology 1980.

FUNAKOSHI, CANNA
One Morning by Canna Funakoshi, illustrated by Yohiji Izawa; Picture Book Studio, 1986; JiShi-Tokyo, 1985. **Awarded:** Bologna (graphics for children) 1986; New York Times Best Illustrated 1986.

FURLEY, DEBORAH
The Web: The Triumph of a New Zealand Girl Over Anorexia by Deborah Furley, Collins, 1989. **Awarded:** New Zealand Library Assn. Young People's Non Fiction 1990.

FURUKAWA, MEL
The Busy Honeybee by Bernice Kohn, illustrated by Mel Furukawa; Four Winds, 1972. **Awarded:** Children's Book Showcase 1973.

FUSILLO, ARCHIMEDE
The Farmhouse by Archimede Fusillo. **Awarded:** Mary Grant Bruce Story Award ($100) 1989.

FUSON, ROBERT H.
Log of Christopher Columbus edited by Robert H. Fuson, illustrated; International Marine Publishing Co., 1987. **Awarded:** New York Academy of Sciences (Elliott and Shirley Montroll Award) 1989.

FYSON, JENNY GRACE
The Journey of the Eldest Son by Jenny Grace Fyson, illustrated by Victor G. Ambrus; Oxford, 1965. **Awarded:** Carnegie (commended) 1965.

The Three Brothers of Ur by Jenny Grace Fyson, illustrated by Victor G. Ambrus; Oxford, 1964. **Awarded:** Carnegie (commended) 1964,

G

GACKENBACH, DICK
The Adventures of Albert, the Running Bear by Barbara Isenberg and Susan Wolf, illustrated by Dick Gackenbach; Clarion, 1982. **Awarded:** Emphasis on Reading (Grades 2-3) 1985-86.

Hattie Rabbit written and illustrated by Dick Gackenbach; Harper, 1976. **Awarded:** Garden State Children's (easy to read) 1979.

McGoogan Moves the Mighty Rock written and illustrated by Dick Gackenbach; Harper, 1981. **Awarded:** New York Times Notable Books 1981.

GAFFNEY-KESSELL, WALTER
Lenny Kandell, Smart Aleck by Ellen Conford, illustrated by Walter Gaffney-Kessell; Little Brown, 1983. **Awarded:** Parents' Choice (literature) 1983.

GAG, WANDA HAZEL
Awarded: Kerlan 1977.

ABC Bunny written and illustrated by Wanda Gag; Coward, 1933. **Awarded:** Newbery (honor) 1934.

Millions of Cats written and illustrated by Wanda Gag; Coward, 1928. **Awarded:** Lewis Carroll Shelf 1958; Newbery (honor) 1929.

Nothing At All written and illustrated by Wanda Gag; Coward, 1941. **Awarded:** Caldecott (honor) 1942.

Snow White and the Seven Dwarfs translated and illustrated by Wanda Gag; Coward, 1938. **Awarded:** Caldecott (honor) 1939.

GAGE, MATILDA J.
Awarded: L. Frank Baum 1972.

GAGE, WILSON
see STEELE, MARY QUINTARD GOVAN

GAGGIN, EVA ROE
Down Ryton Water by Eva Roe Gaggin, illustrated by Elmer Hader; Viking, 1941. **Awarded:** Newbery (honor) 1942.

An Ear for Uncle Emil by Eva Roe Gaggin, illustrated by Kate Seredy; Viking, 1939. **Awarded:** Spring Book Festival (younger honor) 1939.

GAGNON, ANDRE
Awarded: Frances E. Russell 1985.

GAL, LASZLO
Cartier Discovers the St. Lawrence by William Toye, illustrated by Laszlo Gal; Oxford, 1970. **Awarded:** Canadian Library Assn. 1971.

The Little Mermaid by Hans Christian Andersen, retold by Margaret Crawford Maloney, illustrated by Laszlo Gal; Methuen, 1983. **Awarded:** Governor General (illustrator) 1983; Amelia Frances Howard-Gibbon (runnerup) 1984.

My Name Is Not Odessa Yarker by Marian Engel, illustrated by Laszlo Gal; Kids Can Press, 1977. **Awarded:** IODE 1978.

The Shirt of the Happy Man by Mariella Bertelli, illustrated by Laszlo Gal; Kids Can Press, 1977. **Awarded:** IODE 1978.

The Twelve Dancing Princesses: A Fairy Story retold by Janet Lunn, illustrated by Laszlo Gal; Methuen, 1979. **Awarded:** Governor General (illustrator) 1979; Amelia Frances Howard-Gibbon 1980; IODE 1979.

Why the Man in the Moon Is Happy and Other Eskimo Creation Stories by Ronald Melzack, illustrated by Laszlo Gal; McClelland & Stewart, 1977. **Awarded:** IODE 1978.

The Willow Maiden by Meghan Collins, illustrated by Laszlo Gal; Dial, 1985. **Awarded:** Commonwealth Club of California 1985; Parents' Choice (literature) 1985.

GALBRAITH, KATHERINE
Laura Charlotte by Katherine Galbraith, illustrated by Floyd Cooper; Philomel, 1990. **Awarded:** Parents' Choice (Story Book) 1990.

GALDONE, JOANNA
The Tailypo: A Ghost Story by Joanna Galdone, illustrated by Paul Galdone; Houghton-Mifflin/Clarion, 1977. **Awarded:** Georgia Children's Picture Story Book 1981.

GALDONE, PAUL
Awarded: School Library Media Specialist of South Eastern New York 1985.

Anatole by Eve Titus, illustrated by Paul Galdone; Whittlesey, 1956. **Awarded:** Caldecott (honor) 1957.

Anatole and the Cat by Eve Titus, illustrated by Paul Galdone; Whittlesey, 1957. **Awarded:** Caldecott (honor) 1958.

Flaming Arrows by William O. Steele, illustrated by Paul Galdone; Harcourt, 1957. **Awarded:** Spring Book Festival (middle honor) 1957; William Allen White 1960.

High Sounds, Low Sounds by Franklyn M. Branley, illustrated by Paul Galdone; Crowell, 1967. **Awarded:** New Jersey Institute of Technology (science) 1968.

The Home Run Trick by Scott Corbett, illustrated by Paul Galdone; Atlantic-Little, 1973. **Awarded:** Golden Archer 1978; Mark Twain 1976.

The Kid Who Batted 1.000 by Bob Allison and Frank Ernest Hill, illustrated by Paul Galdone; Doubleday, 1951. **Awarded:** Boys Club 1952.

Miss Pickerell Goes to Mars by Ellen MacGregor, illustrated by Paul Galdone; McGraw, 1951. **Awarded:** Young Readers Choice 1956.

Moccasin Trail by Eloise J. McGraw, illustrated by Paul Galdone; Coward, 1952. **Awarded:** Lewis Carroll Shelf 1963; Newbery (honor) 1953.

The Perilous Road by William O. Steele, illustrated by Paul Galdone; Harcourt, 1958. **Awarded:** Jane Addams 1958; Newbery (honor) 1959.

The Robber Ghost by Karin Anckarsvard, translated by Annabelle MacMillan, illustrated by Paul Galdone; Harcourt, 1961. **Awarded:** Spring Book Festival (middle honor) 1961.

The Tailypo: A Ghost Story by Joanna Galdone, illustrated by Paul Galdone; Houghton-Mifflin/Clarion, 1977. **Awarded:** Georgia Picture Book 1981.

Winter Danger by William O. Steele, illustrated by Paul Galdone; Harcourt, 1954. **Awarded:** Lewis Carroll Shelf 1962; Spring Book Festival (middle) 1954.

GALERON, HENRI
The Kidnapping of the Coffee Pot by Kay Saari, illustrated by Henri Galeron; Quist, 1975. **Awarded:** New York Times Notable Books 1975.

GALINSKY, ELLEN
Catbird written and illustrated by Ellen Galinsky; Coward, 1971. **Awarded:** New Jersey Institute of Technology 1972.

GALL, ALICE CREW
Splasher by Alice Crew Gall and Fleming Crew, illustrated by Else Bostelmann; Oxford, 1945. **Awarded:** Ohioana (honorable mention) 1946.

GALLAGHER, SUSAN
Night of Ghosts and Hermits by Mary Stolz, illustrated by Susan Gallagher; Harcourt Brace Jovanovich, 1985. **Awarded:** New York Academy of Sciences (younger honor) 1986.

GALLAGHER, TERRY
Murdo's Story by Murdo Scribe, illustrated by Terry Gallagher; Pemmican Publications, 1985. **Awarded:** Governor General (illustrator) 1985.

GALLANT, ROY A.
Exploring the Universe by Roy A. Gallant, illustrated by Lowell Hess; Garden City Books, 1956. **Awarded:** Edison Mass Media (best children's science book) 1957.

GALLARDO, EVELYN
Illustration in *Ranger Rick* magazine. Awarded: Magazine Merit (Illustration Honor) 1990.

GALLAZ, CHRISTOPHE
Rose Blanche by Christophe Gallaz and Roberto Innocenti, illustrated by Roberto Innocenti, translated by Martha Coventry and Richard Graglia; Creative Education, 1985. **Awarded:** Batchelder 1986.

GALLO, DONALD
Awarded: ALAN Award 1992

GALLOB, EDWARD
City Leaves, City Trees written and illustrated by Edward Gallob; Scribner, 1972. **Awarded:** New York Academy of Sciences (younger) 1973.

City Rocks, City Blocks and the Moon written and illustrated by Edward Gallob; Scribner, 1973. **Awarded:** New York Academy of Sciences (younger honor) 1974.

GALSTER, ROBERT
Find Out by Touching by Paul Showers, illustrated by Robert Galster; Crowell, 1961. **Awarded:** New Jersey Institute of Technology 1961.

Floating and Sinking by Franklyn M. Branley, illustrated by Robert Galster; Crowell, 1967. **Awarded:** New Jersey Institute of Technology (science) 1968.

How You Talk by Paul Showers, illustrated by Robert Galster; Crowell, 1967. **Awarded:** New Jersey Institute of Technology (science) 1968.

GAMBLE, KIM
The Magnificent Nose and Other Marvels by Anna Fienberg, illustrated by Kim Gamble; Allen & Unwin, 1991. **Awarded:** Children's Book Council of Australia (Book of the Year Younger) 1992; Crichton 1992.

GAMMELL, STEPHEN
The Ghost of Tillie Jean Cassaway by Ellen H. Showell, illustrated by Stephen Gammell; Four Winds, 1978. **Awarded:** South Carolina Children's 1982.

The Great Dimpole Oak by Janet Taylor Lisle, illustrated by Stephen Gammell; Orchard, 1987. **Awarded:** Golden Kite (Fiction honor) 1987.

More Scary Stories to Tell in the Dark by Alvin Schwartz, illustrated by Stephen Gammell; Lippincott, 1984. **Awarded:** Buckeye (grades 3-5) 1989; Emphasis on Reading (grades 3-5) 1990-91.

Old Black Fly by Jim Aylesworth, illustrated by Stephen Gammell; Holt, 1992. **Awarded:** Minnesota (Younger children) 1993.

Old Henry by Joan W. Blos, illustrated by Stephen Gammell; Morrow, 1987. **Awarded:** Boston Globe Horn Book (illustration honor) 1987.

The Relatives Came by Cynthia Rylant, illustrated by Stephen Gammell; Bradbury, 1985. **Awarded:** Caldecott (honor) 1986; New York Times Best Illustrated 1985.

Scary Stories 3: More Tales To Chill Your Bones retold by Alvin Schwartz, illustrated by Stephen Gammell; Collins, 1991. **Awarded:** Buckeye (grades 3-5) 1993.

Scary Stories to Tell in the Dark by Alvin Schwartz, illustrated by Stephen Gammell; Lippincott, 1981. **Awarded:** Arizona 1987; Buckeye (grades 3-5) 1987.

Song and Dance Man by Karen Ackerman, illustrated by Stephen Gammell; Knopf, 1988. **Awarded:** Caldecott 1989; Society of Midland Authors (Juvenile Fiction) 1989.

Stonewall by Jean Fritz, illustrated by Stephen Gammell; Putnam, 1979. **Awarded:** Boston Globe Horn Book (nonfiction honor) 1980; New York Times Notable Books 1979.

Waiting to Waltz by Cynthia Rylant, illustrated by Stephen Gammell; Bradbury, 1984. **Awarded:** Society of Midland Authors 1985.

Where the Buffaloes Begin by Olaf Baker, illustrated by Stephen Gammell; Warne, 1981. **Awarded:** Boston Globe Horn Book (illustration honor) 1981; Caldecott (honor) 1982; New York Times Best Illustrated 1981; New York Times Notable Books 1981.

GANNETT, RUTH CHRISMAN ARENS
Miss Hickory by Carolyn Sherwin Bailey, illustrated by Ruth Chrisman Gannett; Viking, 1946. **Awarded:** Newbery 1947.

My Father's Dragon by Ruth Stiles Gannett, illustrated by Ruth Chrisman Gannett; Random House, 1948. **Awarded:** Lewis Carroll Shelf 1968; Newbery (honor) 1949; Spring Book Festival (younger) 1948.

My Mother Is the Most Beautiful Woman in the World by Becky Reyher, illustrated by Ruth C. Gannett; Lothrop, 1945. **Awarded:** Caldecott (honor) 1946.

GANNETT, RUTH STILES
My Father's Dragon by Ruth Stiles Gannett, illustrated by Ruth Chrisman Gannett; Random House, 1948. **Awarded:** Lewis Carroll Shelf 1968; Newbery (honor) 1949; Spring Book Festival (younger) 1948.

GANTOS, JACK
Rotten Ralph by Jack Gantos, illustrated by Nicole Rubel; Houghton, 1976. **Awarded:** Children's Book Showcase 1977.

GANZ, YAFFA
Awarded: Sydney Taylor Award (Body of Work) 1990.

GARBUTT, BERNARD
Hodie by Bernard Garbutt and Katharine Garbutt, illustrated by Bernard Garbutt; Aladdin, 1949. **Awarded:** Spring Book Festival (younger honor) 1949.

Michael the Colt by Katharine K. Garbutt, illustrated by Bernard Garbutt; Houghton, 1943. **Awarded:** Spring Book Festival (younger honor) 1943.

Wild Wings over the Marshes by Lucille N. Stratton and William D. Stratton, illustrated by Bernard Garbutt; Golden Gate Books, 1964. **Awarded:** Southern California Council (illustration) 1964.

GARBUTT, KATHARINE K.
Hodie by Bernard Garbutt and Katharine Garbutt, illustrated by Bernard Garbutt; Aladdin, 1949. **Awarded:** Spring Book Festival (younger honor) 1949.

Michael the Colt by Katharine K. Garbutt, illustrated by Bernard Garbutt; Houghton, 1943. **Awarded:** Spring Book Festival (younger honor) 1943.

GARD, JANICE
see LATHAM, JEAN LEE

GARD, JOYCE
Smudge of the Fells by Joyce Gard, not illustrated; Holt, 1966. **Awarded:** Spring Book Festival (middle honor) 1966.

GARDAM, JANE
Bridget and William by Jane Gardam, illustrated by Janet Rawlins; Julia MacRae, 1981. **Awarded:** Carnegie (commended) 1981.

The Hollow Land by Jane Gardam, illustrated by Janet Rawlins; Julia MacRae, 1981. **Awarded:** Carnegie (highly commended) 1981; Whitbread 1981.

A Long Way From Verona by Jane Gardam, not illustrated; Macmillan, 1971. **Awarded:** Phoenix Award 1991; Spring Book Festival (ages 12-16 honor) 1972.

The Summer after the Funeral by Jane Gardam, not illustrated; Macmillan, 1973. **Awarded:** Boston Globe Horn Book (text honor) 1974.

GARDINER, FREDERIC M.
Stand By - Mark! The Career Story of a Naval Officer by Frederic M. Gardiner, illustrated with photographs; Dodd, Mead, 1943. **Awarded:** Spring Book Festival (older honor) 1943.

GARDINER, JOHN REYNOLDS
Stone Fox by John Reynolds Gardiner, illustrated by Marcia Sewall; Crowell, 1980; Harper & Row, 1983. **Awarded:** Emphasis on Reading (grades 4-6) 1986-87; Maud Hart Lovelace 1987; New York Times Notable Books 1980; Southern California Council (notable work of fiction) 1981; George G. Stone 1987; Utah Children's 1985.

Top Secret by John Reynolds Gardiner, illustrated by Marc Simont; Little Brown, 1984. **Awarded:** PEN Center USA West 1986.

GARDNER, BEAU
Have You Ever Seen...? An ABC Book written and illustrated by Beau Gardner; Dodd Mead, 1986. **Awarded:** Please Touch (honorable mention) 1987.

GARDNER, JOHN
Dragon, Dragon and Other Timeless Tales by John Gardner, illustrated by Charles Shields; Knopf, 1975. **Awarded:** New York Times Notable Books 1975.

Grendel by John Gardner, illustrated by Emil Antonucci; Knopf, 1971. **Awarded:** Emphasis on Reading (grades 10-12) 1984-85.

GARDNER, MARTIN
Awarded: L. Frank Baum 1971.

GARDNER, ROBERT
The Whale Watchers' Guide by Robert Gardner, illustrated by Don Sineti; Messner, 1984. **Awarded:** New York Academy of Sciences (older honor) 1985.

GARELICK, MAY
About Owls by May Garelick, illustrated by Tony Chen; Four Winds, 1975. **Awarded:** Children's Book Showcase 1976.

GARFIELD, LEON
Awarded: Golden Cat 1985.

Black Jack by Leon Garfield, illustrated by Antony Maitland; Longmans, 1968. **Awarded:** Carnegie (honour) 1968.

Devil-in-the-Fog by Leon Garfield, illustrated by Antony Maitland; Kestrel, 1966. **Awarded:** Guardian 1967.

The Drummer Boy by Leon Garfield, illustrated by Antony Maitland; Longmans, 1970. **Awarded:** Carnegie (honour) 1970.

Fair's Fair by Leon Garfield, illustrated by Margaret Chamberlain; Macdonald, 1981. **Awarded:** Children's Book Award 1981.

Footsteps by Leon Garfield, not illustrated; Delacorte, 1980. **Awarded:** Boston Globe Horn Book (fiction honor) 1981.

The Ghost Downstairs by Leon Garfield, illustrated by Antony Maitland; Longmans, 1972. **Awarded:** Greenaway (commended) 1972.

The God Beneath the Sea by Leon Garfield and Edward Blishen, illustrated by Charles Keeping; Longmans, 1970. **Awarded:** Carnegie 1970; Greenaway (honors list) 1970.

Jack Holburn by Leon Garfield, illustrated by Antony Maitland; Pantheon, 1965. **Awarded:** Boys Club 1966.

John Diamond by Leon Garfield, illustrated by Antony Maitland; Kestrel, 1980. **Awarded:** Whitbread 1980.

Mister Corbett's Ghost by Leon Garfield, illustrated by Alan E. Cober; Pantheon, 1968. **Awarded:** New York Times Best Illustrated 1968.

Shakespeare Stories by Leon Garfield, illustrated by Michael Foreman; Gollancz, 1985. **Awarded:** Maschler (runnerup) 1985.

Smith by Leon Garfield, illustrated by Antony Maitland; Pantheon, 1967; Constable, 1967; Penguin, 1968; Dell, 1987. **Awarded:** Boston Globe Horn Book (text honor) 1968; Carnegie (commended) 1967; Phoenix 1987.

The Wedding Ghost by Leon Garfield, illustrated by Charles Keeping; Oxford University Press, 1985. **Awarded:** Maschler (runnerup) 1985.

GARLAND, NICHOLAS
Mum - I Feel Funny! by Aidan Macfarlane and Ann McPherson, illustrated by Nicholas Garland; Chatto & Windus, 1982. **Awarded:** Times Educational Supplement (junior) 1983.

GARLAND, PETER
The Damselfly by Peter Garland; Arncliffe, 1990. **Awarded:** New Zealand Library Assn. Nonfiction for Young People 1992.

GARLAND, SHERRY
Song of the Buffalo Boy by Sherry Garland, not illustrated; Harcourt Brace Jovanovich, 1992. **Awarded:** Golden Medallion 1993.

GARNER, ALAN
Awarded: Hans Christian Andersen (highly commended author/Great Britain) 1978.

A Bag of Moonshine by Alan Garner, illustrated by Patrick James Lynch; Collins, 1986. **Awarded:** Mother Goose 1987.

Elidor by Alan Garner, illustrated by Charles Keeping; Collins, 1965. **Awarded:** Carnegie (commended) 1965.

The Owl Service by Alan Garner, not illustrated; Collins, 1967. **Awarded:** Carnegie 1967; Guardian 1968.

The Weirdstone of Brisingamen and a Tale of Alderly by Alan Garner, not illustrated; Walck, 1969. **Awarded:** Lewis Carroll Shelf 1970.

GARNETT, EMMELINE
Tormented Angel: A Life of John Henry Newman by Emmeline Garnett, not illustrated; Farrar, 1966. **Awarded:** Spring Book Festival (older honor) 1966.

GARNETT, EVE C.R.
The Family from One End Street and Some of Their Adventures written and illustrated by Eve Garnett; Muller, 1937. **Awarded:** Carnegie 1937.

GARRATY, GAIL
The Farthest Shore by Ursula K. LeGuin, illustrated by Gail Garraty; Atheneum, 1972. **Awarded:** National Book Award 1973.

The Tombs of Atuan by Ursula K. LeGuin, illustrated by Gail Garraty; Atheneum, 1971. **Awarded:** National Book Award (finalist) 1972; Newbery (honor) 1972.

GARRET, WILBUR E.
Atlas of North America edited by Wilbur E. Garret, color illustrations; National Geographic Society, 1985. **Awarded:** New York Academy of Sciences (Elliott Montroll special award) 1987.

GARRISON, BARBARA
Another Celebrated Dancing Bear by Gladys Scheffrin-Falk, illustrated by Barbara Garrison; Scribner, 1991. **Awarded:** New York Times Best Illustrated 1991; UNICEF-Ezra Jack Keats National Award for Children's Book Illustration 1991.

GARRISON, CHRISTIAN
Dream Eater by Christian Garrison, illustrated by Diane Goode; Bradbury, 1978. **Awarded:** Southern California Council (contribution to illustration) 1979.

Little Pieces of the West Wind by Christian Garrison, illustrated by Diane Goode; Bradbury, 1975. **Awarded:** Southern California Council (contribution to illustration) 1976.

GARST, DORIS SHANNON
Cowboy Boots by Doris Shannon Garst, illustrated by Charles Hargens; Abingdon, 1946. **Awarded:** Young Readers Choice 1949.

GARTEN, JAN
The Alphabet Tale by Jan Garten, illustrated by Muriel Batherman; Random House, 1964. **Awarded:** New Jersey Institute of Technology (ages 3-5) 1964; Spring Book Festival (picture book honor) 1964.

GARTHWAITE, MARION HOOK
Tomas and the Red-headed Angel by Marion Garthwaite, illustrated by Lorence F. Bjorklund; Messner, 1950. **Awarded:** Commonwealth Club of California 1950; Julia Ellsworth Ford 1949.

GARVER, SUSAN
Coming to North America from Mexico, Cuba & Puerto Rico by Susan Garver and Paula McGuire, illustrated with photographs; Delacorte, 1981. **Awarded:** Woodson 1982.

GARVEY, KATHLEEN
Video Fever by Kathleen Garvey, not illustrated; Silhouette Books, 1986. **Awarded:** Golden Medallion 1987.

GASKIN, CHRIS
Joseph's Boat by Caroline Macdonald, illustrated by Chris Gaskin; Hodder & Stoughton, 1988. **Awarded:** Russell Clark 1989.

The Story of the Kakapo Parrot of the Night by Philip Temple, illustrated by Chris Gaskin; Hodder & Stoughton, 1988. **Awarded:** AIM Children's Book Award (Picture Book 2nd prize) 1990.

A Walk to the Beach written and illustrated by Chris Gaskin; Heinemann Reed, 1989. **Awarded:** Russell Clark 1990.

GASKIN, GERRY

Skulls! by Richard Steel, illustrated by Gerry Gaskin; Heinemann, 1980. **Awarded:** Times Educational Supplement (senior) 1981.

GASNICK, ROY M.

Mother Teresa of Calcutta by Roy M. Gasnick and David Michelinie, illustrated by John Tartaglione; Franciscan Communications Office, 1984. **Awarded:** Catholic Book Awards (Youth) 1985.

GATES, DORIS

Blue Willow by Doris Gates, illustrated by Paul Lantz; Viking, 1940. **Awarded:** Lewis Carroll Shelf 1961; Commonwealth Club of California 1940; FOCAL 1982; Newbery (honor) 1941.

Little Vic by Doris Gates, illustrated by Kate Seredy; Viking, 1951. **Awarded:** William Allen White 1954.

GAUCH, PATRICIA LEE

Aaron and the Green Mountain Boys by Patricia Lee Gauch, illustrated by Margot Tomes; Coward, 1972. **Awarded:** New Jersey Institute of Technology 1972, 1973.

Christina Katerina and the Box by Patricia Lee Gauch, illustrated by Doris Burn; Coward, 1971. **Awarded:** New Jersey Institute of Technology 1971.

Christina Katerina and the Time She Quit the Family by Patricia Lee Gauch, illustrated by Elise Primavera; Putnam, 1987. **Awarded:** New Jersey Institute of Technology 1988.

Grandpa and Me by Patricia L. Gauch, illustrated by Symeon Shimin; Coward, 1972. **Awarded:** New Jersey Institute of Technology 1972, 1973.

Night Talks by Patricia Gauch, not illustrated; Putnam, 1983. **Awarded:** New Jersey Institute of Technology 1983.

On to Widecombe Fair by Patricia Lee Gauch, illustrated by Trina Schart Hyman; Putnam, 1978. **Awarded:** Boston Globe Horn Book (illustration honor) 1978.

A Secret House by Patricia Lee Gauch, illustrated by Margot Tomes; Coward, 1970. **Awarded:** New Jersey Institute of Technology 1971.

GAULT, CLARE

Awarded: Lucky Book Club Four-Leaf Clover 1978.

Pele, the King of Soccer by Clare Gault and Frank Gault, illustrated with photographs; Walker, 1975. **Awarded:** New Jersey Institute of Technology 1977.

Stories from the Olympics from 776 B.C. to Now by Clare Gault and Frank Gault, illustrated with photographs; Walker, 1976. **Awarded:** New Jersey Institute of Technology 1977.

GAULT, FRANK

Awarded: Lucky Book CLub Four-Leaf Clover 1978.

Pele, the King of Soccer by Frank Gault and Clare Gault, illustrated with photographs; Walker, 1975. **Awarded:** New Jersey Institute of Technology 1977.

Stories from the Olympics from 776 B.C. to Now by Frank Gault and Clare Gault; illustrated with photographs; Walker, 1976. **Awarded:** New Jersey Institute of Technology 1977.

GAVER, MARY VIRGINIA

Awarded: American Association of School Librarians 1980; Women's National Book Assn. 1973.

GAVIN, JAMILA

The Wheel of Surya by Jamila Gavin, not illustrated; Methuen, 1992. **Awarded:** Guardian (runnerup) 1993.

GAY, MARIE-LOUISE

Lizzy's Lion by Dennis Lee, illustrated by Marie-Louise Gay; Stoddart, 1984. **Awarded:** Governor General (illustration) 1984.

Moonbeam on a Cat's Ear written and illustrated by Marie-Louise Gay; Stoddart, 1986. **Awarded:** Amelia Frances Howard-Gibbon 1987.

Rainy Day Magic written and illustrated by Marie-Louise Gay; Stoddart, 1987. **Awarded:** Governor General (Illustration) 1987; Amelia Frances Howard-Gibbon 1988.

GAY, ZHENYA

Travels of a Snail by Eleanor Hoffmann, illustrated by Zhenya Gay; Stokes, 1939. **Awarded:** Spring Book Festival (younger honor) 1939.

Whistler's Van by Idwal Jones, illustrated by Zhenya Gay; Viking, 1936. **Awarded:** Newbery (honor) 1937.

GEE, MAURICE

The Champion by Maurice Gee, not illustrated; Penguin New Zealand, 1989. **Awarded:** AIM Children's Book Award (Story Book 2nd prize) 1990.

The Halfmen of O by Maurice Gee, not illustrated; Oxford, 1982. **Awarded:** AIM (Story Book) 1983.

Motherstone by Maurice Gee, not illustrated; Oxford University Press, 1985. **Awarded:** Esther Glen 1986.

GEER, CHARLES

An Awful Name to Live Up To by Jossie Hosford, illustrated by Charles Geer; Meredith, 1969. (original title: *Prairie Child*). **Awarded:** Western Heritage 1970.

Beef for Beauregard! by Byrd Hooper, illustrated by Charles Geer; Putnam, 1959. **Awarded:** Steck-Vaughn 1961.

Lost in the Barrens by Farley Mowat, illustrated by Charles Geer; Little Brown Canada, 1956. **Awarded:** Canadian Library Assn. 1958; International Board on Books for Young People (honour list/Canada) 1958; Governor General 1956.

Mystery of the Velvet Box by Margaret Scheft, illustrated by Charles Geer; Watts, 1963. **Awarded:** Edgar Allan Poe (runnerup) 1964.

The Natives Are Always Restless by Gerald Raftery, illustrated by Charles Geer; Vanguard Press, 1964. **Awarded:** New Jersey Institute of Technology (late teenage novel) 1964.

Plain Girl by Virginia Sorensen, illustrated by Charles Geer; Harcourt, 1955. **Awarded:** Child Study 1955.

Ride a Northbound Horse by Richard Wormser, illustrated by Charles Geer; Morrow, 1964. **Awarded:** Western Writers of America (fiction) 1965.

Soot Devil written and illustrated by Charles Geer; Grosset, 1971. **Awarded:** New Jersey Institute of Technology 1971.

Steamboat up the Missouri by Dale White, illustrated by Charles H. Geer; Viking, 1958. **Awarded:** Western Writers 1959.

Young Hero of the Range by Stephen Payne, illustrated by Charles H. Geer; Lantern Press, 1954. **Awarded:** Western Writers 1955.

GEHM, CHARLES

Soup by Robert Newton Peck, illustrated by Charles Gehm; Knopf, 1974; Dell, 1979. **Awarded:** Michigan Young Readers 1984.

GEHRTS, BARBARA
Don't Say a Word by Barbara Gehrts, not illustrated; McElderry, 1986. **Awarded:** International Board on Books for Young People (Translation/USA) 1988.

GEIS, DARLENE
Dinosaurs and Other Prehistoric Animals by Darlene Geis, illustrated by Russell F. Petersen; Grosset, 1959. **Awarded:** Boys Club 1960.

GEISEL, THEODOR SEUSS
see SEUSS, DR.

GEISERT, ARTHUR
Aesop and Company prepared by Barbara Bader, illustrated by Arthur Geisert; Houghton Mifflin, 1991. **Awarded:** Aesop Prize 1993.

Pigs from A to Z written and illustrated by Arthur Geisert; Houghton Mifflin, 1986. **Awarded:** New York Times Best Illustrated 1986; New York Times Notable 1986.

GEKIERE, MADELEINE
The Fisherman and His Wife by Wilhelm Grimm and Jacob Grimm, illustrated by Madeleine Gekiere; Pantheon, 1957. **Awarded:** New York Times Best Illustrated 1957.

John J. Plenty and Fiddler Dan by John Ciardi, illustrated by Madeleine Gekiere; Lippincott, 1963. **Awarded:** New York Times Best Illustrated 1963.

The Reason for the Pelican by John Ciardi, illustrated by Madeleine Gekiere; Lippincott, 1959. **Awarded:** New York Times Best Illustrated 1959.

Switch on the Night by Ray Bradbury, illustrated by Madeleine Gekiere; Pantheon, 1955. **Awarded:** Boys Club 1956; New York Times Best Illustrated 1955.

Who Gave Us ... Peacocks? Planes? and Ferris Wheels? written and illustrated by Madeleine Gekiere; Pantheon, 1953. **Awarded:** New York Times Best Illustrated 1953.

GELDART, WILLIAM
The Return of the Indian by Lynn Reid Banks, illustrated by William Geldart; Doubleday, 1986. **Awarded:** Indian Paintbrush 1989; New York Times Notable 1986; Parents' Choice (literature) 1986.

GELLER, MARK
What I Heard by Mark Geller, not illustrated; Harper & Row, 1987. **Awarded:** New Jersey Institute of Technology 1988.

GELLMAN, MARC
Does God Have a Big Toe? Stories About Stories in the Bible by Marc Gellman, illustrated by Oscar de Mejo; Harper & Row, 1989. **Awarded:** New York Times Best Illustrated 1989.

Where Does God Live? by Marc Gellman and Thomas Hartman, illustrated by William Zdinak; Triumph Books, 1991. **Awarded:** Christopher Award (All Ages) 1992.

GEMMING, ELIZABETH
The Cranberry Book by Elizabeth Gemming, illustrated with prints and photographs; Coward McCann, 1983. **Awarded:** New York Academy of Sciences (younger honor) 1984.

GENEROWICZ, WITOLD
The Train illustrated by Witold Generowicz; Penguin Australia, 1982; Kestrel, 1982; Dial, 1982. **Awarded:** Children's Book Council of Australia (picture book of the year highly commended) 1983.

GENIA
The House of the Fifers by Rebecca Caudill, illustrated by Genia; Longmans, 1954. **Awarded:** Spring Book Festival (older honor) 1954.

Styles by Suzy by Karla H. Wiley, illustrated by Genia; McKay, 1965. **Awarded:** New Jersey Institute of Technology 1965.

GEORGE, JEAN CRAIGHEAD
Awarded: Eva L. Gordon 1970; Kerlan 1982; Knickerbocker 1991; School Library Media Specialists of Southeastern New York 1981; University of Southern Mississippi 1986.

All upon a Stone by Jean Craighead George, illustrated by Don Bolognese; Crowell, 1971. **Awarded:** Spring Book Festival (picture book) 1971.

Dipper of Copper Creek by Jean Craighead George and John Lothar George, illustrated by Jean Craighead George; Dutton, 1956. **Awarded:** Aurianne 1958.

Julie of the Wolves by Jean Craighead George, illustrated by John Schoenherr; Harper, 1972. **Awarded:** National Book Award (finalist) 1973; Newbery 1973.

My Side of the Mountain written and illustrated by Jean Craighead George; Dutton, 1959. **Awarded:** Hans Christian Andersen (runnerup) 1962; Lewis Carroll Shelf 1965; Newbery (honor) 1960; George G. Stone 1969.

On the Far Side of the Mountain written and illustrated by Jean Craighead George; Dutton, 1990. **Awarded:** Washington Irving (Novel) 1992.

One Day in the Woods by Jean Craighead George, illustrated by Gary Allen; Crowell, 1988. **Awarded:** Washington Irving (Nonfiction) 1990.

Shark Beneath the Reef by Jean Craighead George, not illustrated; Harper & Row, 1989. **Awarded:** Parents' Choice (Story Book) 1989.

GEORGE, JOHN LOTHAR
Dipper of Copper Creek by Jean Craighead George and John Lothar George, illustrated by Jean Craighead George; Dutton, 1956. **Awarded:** Aurianne 1958.

GEORGE, LINDSAY BARRETT
Box Turtle at Long Pond by William T. George, illustrated by Lindsay Barrett George; Greenwillow, 1989. **Awarded:** Book Can Develop Empathy 1990; Carolyn Field 1990.

GEORGE, WILLIAM T.
Box Turtle at Long Pond by William T. George, illustrated by Lindsay Barrett George; Greenwillow, 1989. **Awarded:** Book Can Develop Empathy 1990; Carolyn Field 1990.

GERALIS, GEORGIOU
Illiada by Georgiou Geralis; Kentavros, 1962. **Awarded:** Hans Christian Andersen (runnerup) 1964.

GERAS, ADELE
My Grandmother's Stories by Adele Geras, illustrated by Jael Jordan; Knopf, 1990; Heinemann, 1990. **Awarded:** Sydney Taylor Book Award (Older) 1991.

GERGELY, TIBOR
Wheel on the Chimney by Margaret Wise Brown, illustrated by Tibor Gergely; Lippincott, 1954. **Awarded:** Caldecott (honor) 1955.

GERINGER, LAURA
Molly's New Washing Machine by Laura Geringer, illustrated by Petra Mathers; Harper & Row, 1986. **Awarded:** New York Times Best Illustrated 1986.

GERLACH, GEFF

Here Lies the Body by Scott Corbett, illustrated by Geff Gerlach; Little Brown, 1974. **Awarded:** Edgar Allan Poe (runnerup) 1975.

GERRARD, JEAN

Matilda Jane by Jean Gerrard, illustrated by Roy Gerrard; Gollancz, 1981. **Awarded:** Mother Goose (runnerup) 1982.

GERRARD, ROY

The Favershams written and illustrated by Roy Gerrard; Gollancz, 1982; Farrar, Straus, Giroux, 1983. **Awarded:** Bologna (children's graphic prize) 1983; New York Times Best Illustrated 1983; Parents' Choice (illustration) 1983.

Matilda Jane by Jean Gerrard, illustrated by Roy Gerrard; Gollancz, 1981. **Awarded:** Mother Goose (runnerup) 1982.

Rosie and the Rustlers written and illustrated by Roy Gerrard; Farrar, Straus, Giroux, 1989. **Awarded:** Parents' Choice (Picture Book) 1989.

Sir Cedric written and illustrated by Roy Gerrard; Farrar, Straus, Giroux, 1984. **Awarded:** New York Times Best Illustrated 1984.

Sir Francis Drake: His Daring Deeds written and illustrated by Roy Gerrard; Farrar Straus Giroux, 1988. **Awarded:** New York Times Best Illustrated 1988.

GERSON, CORRINE

How I Put My Mother Through College by Corinne Gerson, not illustrated; Atheneum, 1981. **Awarded:** CRABbery (honor) 1982.

Son for a Day by Corrine Gerson, illustrated by Velma Ilsley; Atheneum, 1980. **Awarded:** Christopher (ages 8-12 fiction) 1981.

GERSON, MARY-JOAN

Why the Sky Is Far Away by Mary-Joan Gerson, illustrated by Carla Golembe; Little Brown, 1992. **Awarded:** New York Times Best Illustrated 1992.

GERSTEIN, MORDICAI

Arnold of the Ducks written and illustrated by Mordicai Gerstein; Harper, 1983. **Awarded:** New York Times Notable Books 1983.

The Mountains of Tibet written and illustrated by Mordicai Gerstein; Harper, 1987. **Awarded:** New York Times Best Illustrated 1987; New York Times Notable 1987.

The New Creatures written and illustrated by Mordicai Gerstein; HarperCollins, 1991. **Awarded:** Parents' Choice (Story Book) 1991.

Tales of Pan written and illustrated by Mordicai Gerstein; Harper & Row, 1986. **Awarded:** Parents' Choice (literature) 1986.

GERVIS, RUTH S.

Visitors from London by Kitty Barne, illustrated by Ruth Gervis; Dent, 1940. **Awarded:** Carnegie 1940.

GESSNER, LYNN

Awarded: Outstanding Arizona Author 1987.

GHEZELAYAGH, SORAYA

Mowje Bozorg by Pearl S. Buck (original English: *The Big Wave*) translated by Soraya Ghezelayagh; Vaje (Fatemi), 1984. **Awarded:** International Board on Books for Young People (translator/Iran) 1986.

GHIKAS, PANOS

Tales of Christophilos by Joice M. Nankivell, illustrated by Panos Ghikas; Houghton, 1954. **Awarded:** Spring Book Festival (middle honor) 1954.

GIACOIA, FRANK

Sequoyah, Young Cherokee Guide by Dorothea J. Snow, illustrated by Frank Giacoia; Bobbs Merrill, 1960. **Awarded:** Friends of American Writers 1961.

GIBBINGS, ROBERT

The Insect Man: Jean Henri Fabre by Eleanor Doorly, illustrated by Robert Gibbings; Appleton Century Crofts, 1937. **Awarded:** Spring Book Festival (older honor) 1937.

The Radium Woman: A Youth Edition of the Life of Madame Curie by Eleanor Doorly, illustrated by Robert Gibbings; Heinemann, 1939; Roy, 1955. **Awarded:** Carnegie 1939; Spring Book Festival (older honor) 1955.

GIBBON, REBECCA

Ten Dogs by Rebecca Gibbon. **Awarded:** Macmillan Prize (Second Prize) 1992.

GIBBONS, GAIL

Awarded: Washington Post/Children's Book Guild 1987.

Stargazers written and illustrated by Gail Gibbons; Holiday House, 1992. **Awarded:** American Institute of Physics 1993.

GIBBS, MAY

The Complete Adventures of Snugglepot and Cuddlepie written and illustrated by May Gibbs; Angus & Robertson, 1981. **Awarded:** KOALA (one time Bicentennial award) 1988.

GIBLIN, JAMES CROSS

Chimney Sweeps: Yesterday and Today by James C. Giblin, illustrated by Margot Tomes; Crowell, 1982. **Awarded:** American Book Award (children's nonfiction) 1983; Golden Kite (nonfiction) 1982.

Let There Be Light: A Book About Windows by James Cross Giblin, illustrated with photos; Crowell, 1988. **Awarded:** Golden Kite (Nonfiction) 1988.

The Truth about Santa Claus by James Cross Giblin, illustrated with photographs and prints; Crowell, 1985. **Awarded:** Boston Globe Horn Book (nonfiction honor) 1986.

Walls: Defenses Throughout History by James C. Giblin, illustrated with photographs; Little Brown, 1985. **Awarded:** Golden Kite (nonfiction) 1984.

GIBSON, BARBARA

Creatures of the Desert World by Jennifer C. Urquhart, illustrated by Barbara Gibson; National Geographic Society, 1987. **Awarded:** Redbook 1987.

GIBSON, BETTY

The Story of Little Quack by Betty Gibson, illustrated by Kady Macdonald Denton; Kids Can Press, 1990. **Awarded:** Mr. Christie's (English illustration) 1990.

GIFF, PATRICIA REILLY

Awarded: Jeremiah Ludington 1990.

GILBERT, KENNETH

The Trap by Kenneth Gilbert, illustrated by Fred Collins; Holt, 1952. **Awarded:** Boys Club 1953.

GILBERT, YVONNE

Abbey-Lubbers, Banshees and Boggarts: An Illustrated Encyclopedia of Fairies by Katharine Briggs, illustrated by Yvonne Gilbert; Kestrel, 1979. **Awarded:** Mother Goose (runnerup) 1980.

GILCHRIST, JAN SPIVEY

Children of Long Ago: Poems by Lessie Jones Little, illustrated by Jan Spivey Gilchrist; Philomel, 1988. **Awarded:** Parents' Choice (Story Book) 1988.

Nathaniel Talking by Eloise Greenfield, illustrated by Jan Spivey Gilchrist; Black Butterfly Children's Books, 1988. **Awarded:** Coretta Scott King (Illustration) 1990; Coretta Scott King (Text honor) 1990.

Night on Neighborhood Street by Eloise Greenfield, illustrated by Jan Spivey Gilchrist; Dial, 1991. **Awarded:** Coretta Scott King (Text honor) 1992; Coretta Scott King (Illustrator honor) 1992.

GILCHRIST, MARIE EMILIE

The Story of the Great Lakes by Marie Emilie Gilchrist, illustrated by C. H. DeWitt; Harper, 1942. **Awarded:** Ohioana (honorable mention) 1943.

GILL, JOAN

Sara's Granny and the Groodle by Joan Gill, illustrated by Seymour Chwast; Doubleday, 1969. **Awarded:** New York Times Best Illustrated 1969.

GILL, LUCILLE

Tjarany Roughtail by Gracie Greene and Joe Tramacchi, illustrated by Lucille Gill; Magabala, 1992. **Awarded:** Children's Book Council of Australia (Eve Pownall award) 1993.

GILL, MARGORIE

The Tide in the Attic by Aleid Van Rhijn, illustrated by Margorie Gill; Criterion, 1962. **Awarded:** Boys Club 1963.

GILLESE, JOHN PATRICK

Awarded: Vicky Metcalf 1967.

GILLETT, MARY

Bugles at the Border by Mary Gillett, illustrated by B. Tucker; Blair, 1968. **Awarded:** North Carolina AAUW 1969.

GILLETTE, HENRY S.

Adam Gray, Stowaway: A Story of the China Trade by Herbert E. Arntson, illustrated by Henry S. Gillette; Watts, 1961. **Awarded:** Watts 1961.

GILLILAND, JUDITH HEIDE

Sami and the Time of Troubles by Florence Parry Heide and Judith Heide Gilliland, illustrated by Ted Lewin; Clarion, 1992. **Awarded:** Hungry Mind (Picturebook Nonfiction) 1993.

GILMORE, IRIS

Pony Express Boy by Iris Gilmore and Marian Talmadge, illustrated; Dodd Mead, 1956. **Awarded:** Boys Life - Dodd Mead 1955.

GILSON, JAMIE

Awarded: Children's Reading Round Table 1992.

Do Bananas Chew Gum? by Jamie Gilson, not illustrated; Lothrop, Lee & Shepard, 1980. **Awarded:** Carl Sandburg 1981; Charlie May Simon 1982-83.

Harvey, the Beer Can King by Jamie Gilson, illustrated by John Wallner; Lothrop Lee & Shepard, 1978. **Awarded:** Friends of American Writers (older) 1979.

Thirteen Ways to Sink a Sub by Jamie Gilson, illustrated by Linda S. Edwards; Lothrop, Lee & Shepard, 1982. **Awarded:** Buckeye (grades 6-8) 1987; Sequoyah 1985; Sunshine 1987; Young Readers Choice 1985.

GINSBURG, MAX

The Friendship by Mildred D. Taylor, illustrated by Max Ginsburg; Dial, 1987. **Awarded:** Boston Globe (Fiction) 1988; Coretta Scott King (Text) 1988.

Mississippi Bridge by Mildred Taylor, illustrated by Max Ginsburg; Dial, 1990. **Awarded:** Christopher (Ages 9-12) 1991.

GINSBURG, MIRRA

The Chick and the Duckling by V. Suteyev, translated and adapted by Mirra Ginsburg, illustrated by Ariane Aruego and Jose Aruego; Macmillan, 1972. **Awarded:** Children's Book Showcase 1973.

The Diary of Nina Kosterina by Nina Kosterina, translated and illustrated by Mirra Ginsburg; Crown, 1968. **Awarded:** Lewis Carroll Shelf 1972.

Four Brave Sailors by Mirra Ginsburg, illustrated by Nancy Tafuri; Greenwillow, 1987. **Awarded:** Parents' Choice (Picture Book) 1987.

GIORNI, LIONELLO ZORN

Le Avventure de Cinque Ragazzi e un Cane by Renee Reggiani, illustrated by Lionelle Zorn Giorni; Cappelli, 1960. **Awarded:** Hans Christian Andersen (runnerup) 1962.

GIOVANOPOULOS, PAUL

Free as a Frog by Elizabeth J. Hodges, illustrated by Paul Giovanopoulos; Addison-Wesley, 1969. **Awarded:** New York Times Best Illustrated 1969.

The Real Tin Flower: Poems about the World at Nine by Aliki Barnstone, illustrated by Paul Giovanopoulos; Crowell-Collier, 1968. **Awarded:** New York Times Best Illustrated 1968.

GIPSON, FREDERICK BENJAMIN

Old Yeller by Fred Gipson, illustrated by Carl Burger; Harper, 1956. **Awarded:** Nene 1966; Newbery (honor) 1957; Sequoyah 1959; William Allen White 1959; Young Readers Choice 1959; Young Teens 1989.

The Trail Driving Rooster by Fred Gipson, illustrated by Marc Simont; Harper, 1955. **Awarded:** Steck-Vaughn 1957.

GIRE, KEN

Treasure in an Oatmeal Box by Ken Gire, illustrated by Patrick J. Welsh; NavPress, 1990. **Awarded:** Gold Medallion (Elementary) 1991.

GIRION, BARBARA

In the Middle of a Rainbow by Barbara Girion, not illustrated; Scribner, 1983. **Awarded:** New Jersey Institute of Technology 1983.

A Tangle of Roots by Barbara Girion, not illustrated; Scribner, 1979. **Awarded:** Emphasis on Reading (grades 7-9) 1984-85.

GIRVAN, HELEN

Phantom on Skis by Helen Girvan, illustrated by Alan Haemer; Farrar, 1939. **Awarded:** Spring Book Festival (older honor) 1939.

GITTINGS, JO MANTON

The Story of Albert Schweitzer by Jo Manton Gittings, illustrated by Astrid Walford; Methuen, 1955; Abelard, 1955. **Awarded:** Boys Club 1957; Carnegie (commended) 1955.

The Story of John Keats by Jo Manton Gittings and Robert Gittings, illustrated by Susan Einzig; Methuen, 1962. **Awarded:** Carnegie (commended) 1962.

GITTINGS, ROBERT
The Story of John Keats by Robert Gittings and Jo Manton Gittings, illustrated by Susan Einzig; Methuen, 1962. **Awarded:** Carnegie (commended) 1962.

GIUSTI, GEORGE
Experiments in Sound by Nelson F. Beeler, illustrated by George Giusti; Crowell, 1961. **Awarded:** Edison Mass Media (best children's science book) 1962.

GJERTSEN, CAROL
Occult Visions: A Mystical Gaze into the Future by Elaine Landau, illustrated by Carol Gjertsen; Messner, 1979. **Awarded:** New Jersey Institute of Technology 1981.

GLADSTONE, M. J.
A Carrot for a Nose by M. J. Gladstone, illustrated with photographs and drawings; Scribner, 1974. **Awarded:** New York Times. Notable Books 1974

GLANZMAN, LOUIS
The Bear's House by Marilyn Sachs, illustrated by Louis Glanzman; Doubleday, 1971. **Awarded:** National Book Award (finalist) 1972; New York Times Notable Books 1971; George G. Stone 1989.

Man in Space to the Moon by Franklyn M. Branley, illustrated by Louis Glanzman; Crowell, 1970. **Awarded:** New Jersey Institute of Technology 1971.

The Noonday Friends by Mary Stolz, illustrated by Louis Glanzman; Harper, 1965. **Awarded:** Newbery (honor) 1966.

Pippi Longstocking by Astrid Lindgren, translated by Florence Lamborn, illustrated by Louis Glanzman; Viking, 1950. **Awarded:** Lewis Carroll Shelf 1973.

GLASER, MILTON
Cats and Bats and Things with Wings by Conrad Aiken, illustrated by Milton Glaser; Atheneum, 1965. **Awarded:** Art Books for Children 1973.

Fierce and Gentle Warriors by Mikhail Sholokhov; translated by Miriam Morton, illustrated by Milton Glaser; Doubleday, 1967. **Awarded:** Spring Book Festival (older honor) 1967.

Help, Help, the Globolinks! by Gian-Carlo Menotti, adapted by Leigh Dean, illustrated by Milton Glaser; McGraw Hill, 1970. **Awarded:** New York Times Best Illustrated 1970.

Rimes de la Mere Oie: Mother Goose Rendered into French translated by Ormonde deKay, Jr., illustrated by Milton Glaser, Barry Zaid, and Seymour Chwast; Little, Brown, 1971. **Awarded:** Children's Book Showcase 1972.

GLASGOW, ALINE
Honschi by Aline Glasgow, illustrated by Tony Chen; Parents, 1972. **Awarded:** Children's Book Showcase 1973.

The Pair of Shoes by Aline Glasgow, illustrated by Symeon Shimin; Dial, 1970. **Awarded:** Child Study (special citation) 1971.

Old Wind and Liu Li-San by Aline Glasgow, illustrated by Bernard Glasgow; Harvey, 1962. **Awarded:** Lewis Carroll Shelf 1964.

GLASGOW, BERNARD
Old Wind and Liu Li-San by Aline Glasgow, illustrated by Bernard Glasgow; Harvey, 1962. **Awarded:** Lewis Carroll Shelf 1964.

GLASS, ANDREW
Graven Images: Three Stories by Paul Fleischman, illustrated by Andrew Glass; Harper & Row, 1982. **Awarded:** Newbery (honor) 1983.

The Wish Giver: Three Tales of Coven Tree by William Brittain, illustrated by Andrew Glass; Harper, 1983. **Awarded:** Newbery (honor) 1984.

GLASSER, JUDY
Too Much Magic by Samuel Sterman and Betsy Sterman, illustrated by Judy Glasser; Lippincott, 1987. **Awarded:** Washington Irving (Older Fiction) 1990.

GLASSNER, JUDY
The S.S. Valentine by Terry Wolfe Phelan, illustrated by Judy Glassner; Four Winds, 1979. **Awarded:** New Jersey Institute of Technology 1981.

GLEESON, LIBBY
Big Dog by Libby Gleeson, illustrated by Armin Greder; Ashton Scholastic, 1991. **Awarded:** Australian Multicultural Children's Literature Award (Picture Book) 1992.

Dodger by Libby Gleeson, not illustrated; Turton and Chambers, 1990. **Awarded:** Children's Peace Literature 1991.

Eleanor, Elizabeth by Libby Gleeson, not illustrated; Angus & Robertson, 1984. **Awarded:** Children's Book Council of Australia (book of the year highly commended) 1985.

I Am Susannah by Libby Gleeson, not illustrated; Angus & Robertson, 1987. **Awarded:** Children's Book Council of Australia (Book of the Year Older Honour) 1988.

Where's Mum? by Libby Gleeson, illustrated by Craig Smith; Omnibus, 1992. **Awarded:** Children's Book Council of Australia (Picture Book of the Year Honour) 1993.

GLEGG, CREINA
The Diddakoi by Rumer Godden, illustrated by Creina Glegg; Macmillan, 1972. **Awarded:** Whitbread 1972.

GLEIT, MARIA
Paul Tiber, Forester by Maria Gleit, illustrated by Ralph Ray; Scribner, 1949. **Awarded:** Child Study 1949.

GLEITSMANN, HERTHA
see GLEIT, MARIA

GLEITZMAN, MORRIS
Blabber Mouth by Morris Gleitzman, not illustrated; Pan Macmillan, 1992. **Awarded:** Children's Book Council of Australia (Book of the Year Younger Honour) 1993.

Misery Guts by Morris Gleitzman, not illustrated; Pan Australia, 1991; Blackie, 1991. **Awarded:** Children's Book Council of Australia (Younger honor) 1992.

Two Weeks With the Queen by Morris Gleitzman; Pan, 1990. **Awarded:** Family Award 1990.

GLENN, MEL
Class Dismissed: High School Poems by Mel Glenn, photographs by Michael J. Bernstein; Clarion, 1982. **Awarded:** Golden Kite (fiction honor) 1982.

Class Dismissed: More High School Poems, No. II by Mel Glenn, illustrated by Michael J. Bernstein; Clarion, 1986. **Awarded:** Christopher (Young Adult) 1987.

GLICK, CARL
Mickey, the Horse That Volunteered by Carl Glick, illustrated by Bill Crawford; Whittlesey House, 1945. **Awarded:** Spring Book Festival (middle honor) 1945.

GLIENKE, AMELIE
My Friend, the Vampire by Angela Sommer-Bodenburg, illustrated by Amelie Glienke; Dial, 1984. **Awarded:** Virginia Young Readers (Elementary) 1987.

GLIMMERVEEN, ULCO
A Tale of Antarctica written and illustrated by Ulco Glimmerveen; Scholastic, 1989. **Awarded:** Book Can Develop Empathy 1991.

GLOVER, DENIS
The Magpies by Denis Glover, illustrated by Dick Frizzell; Century Hutchinson New Zealand, 1987. **Awarded:** Russell Clark 1988.

GLUBOK, SHIRLEY
Awarded: Washington Post/Children's Book Guild Nonfiction Award 1980.

The Art of Ancient Egypt by Shirley Glubok, illustrated by Gerald Nook; Atheneum, 1962. **Awarded:** Lewis Carroll Shelf 1963.

The Art of the Northwest Coast Indians by Shirley Glubok, illustrated by Gerald Nook; Macmillan, 1975. **Awarded:** Children's Book Showcase 1976.

Voyaging to Cathay: Americans in the China Trade by Shirley Glubok and Alfred Tamarin, illustrated with photographs and old prints; Viking, 1976. **Awarded:** Boston Globe Horn Book (nonfiction) 1976.

GLUCKSMAN, MARY
Article in *Highlights* magazine. Awarded: Magazine Merit Award (Nonfiction) 1990.

GNOLI, DOMENICO
Alberic the Wise and Other Journeys by Norton Juster, illustrated by Domenico Gnoli; Pantheon, 1965. **Awarded:** New York Times Best Illustrated 1965.

GOBHAI, MEHLLI
Usha the Mouse Maiden written and illustrated by Mehlli Gobhai; Hawthorn, 1969. **Awarded:** Lewis Carroll Shelf 1969.

GOBLE, DOROTHY
Friendly Wolf written and illustrated Dorothy Goble and Paul Goble; Dutton, 1974. **Awarded:** Art Books for Children 1978.

GOBLE, PAUL
Friendly Wolf written and illustrated Paul Goble and Dorothy Goble; Dutton, 1974. **Awarded:** Art Books for Children 1978.

The Girl Who Loved Wild Horses written and illustrated by Paul Goble; Bradbury, 1978. **Awarded:** Art Books for Children 1979; Caldecott 1979.

GOBLE, WARWICK
Tod of the Fens by Elinor Whitney, illustrated by Warwick Goble; Macmillan, 1928. **Awarded:** Newbery (honor) 1929.

GODDARD, RAGNA T.
Join Hands with the Ghosts by Mary Canty, illustrated by Ragna T. Goddard; McKay, 1969. **Awarded:** New Jersey Institute of Technology 1970.

GODDEN, RUMER
Candy Floss by Rumer Godden, illustrated by Adrienne Adams; Viking, 1960. **Awarded:** Spring Book Festival (ages 4-8 honor) 1960.

The Diddakoi by Rumer Godden, illustrated by Creina Glegg; Macmillan, 1972. **Awarded:** Whitbread 1972.

The Fairy Doll by Rumer Godden, illustrated by Adrienne Adams; Macmillan, 1956. **Awarded:** Carnegie (commended) 1956; International Board on Books for Young People (honour list/Great Britain) 1958.

Miss Happiness and Miss Flower by Rumer Godden, illustrated by Jean Primrose; Viking, 1961. **Awarded:** Carnegie (commended) 1961; Spring Book Festival (middle honor) 1961.

The Mousewife by Rumer Godden, illustrated by William Pene du Bois; Viking, 1951. **Awarded:** Spring Book Festival (picture book honor) 1951.

Thursday's Child by Rumer Godden, not illustrated; Viking, 1984. **Awarded:** Parents' Choice (literature) 1984.

GODE, ALEXANDER
Pulga by Siny Rose Van Iterson, translated by Alexander Gode and Alison Gode, illustrated with maps; Morrow, 1971. **Awarded:** Batchelder 1973.

GODE, ALISON
Pulga by Siny Rose Van Iterson, translated by Alison Gode and Alexander Gode, illustrated with maps; Morrow, 1971. **Awarded:** Batchelder 1973.

GODFREY, MARTYN
Here She Is, Ms. Teeny-Wonderful! by Martyn Godfrey in *Crackers Magazine* #12 Spring 1984. **Awarded:** Vicky Metcalf Short Story 1985.

Mystery in the Frozen Lands by Martyn Godfrey, not illustrated; Lorimer, 1988. **Awarded:** Bilson 1989; Young Adult Canadian (Runnerup) 1989.

GODKIN, CELIA
Wolf Island by Celia Godkin, illustrated; Fitzhenry & Whiteside, 1989. **Awarded:** Information Book Award 1990.

GOETZINGER, ANNIE
Aurora by Annie Goetzinger and Adela Turin, illustrated with photographs; Dalla Parte delle Bambine. **Awarded:** Bologna (graphics for youth) 1979.

GOFF, BETH
Where Is Daddy? The Story of a Divorce by Beth Goff, illustrated by Susan Perl; Beacon, 1969. **Awarded:** Child Study (special citation) 1968.

GOFFIN, JOSSE
Oh! written and illustrated by Josse Goffin; Rainbow Grafics International/Baronian Books. **Awarded:** Bologna (Graphics for Children) 1992.

GOFFSTEIN, MARILYN BROOKE
An Artist written and illustrated by M. B. Goffstein; Harper, 1980. **Awarded:** New York Times Best Illustrated 1980.

Fish for Supper written and illustrated by M. B. Goffstein; Dial, 1976. **Awarded:** Caldecott (honor) 1977.

The Gats! written and illustrated by M. B. Goffstein; Pantheon, 1966. **Awarded:** Spring Book Festival (picture book honor) 1966.

A Little Schubert written and illustrated by M. B. Goffstein; Harper, 1972. **Awarded:** New York Times Best Illustrated 1972.

Natural History written and illustrated by M. B. Goffstein; Farrar Straus Giroux, 1979. **Awarded:** Jane Addams (special recognition) 1980; New York Times Best Illustrated 1979.

GOHLKE, MADELON S.
Re-reading the Secret Garden by Madelon S. Gohlke in College English April 1980. **Awarded:** Children's Literature Assn. Awards for excellence in the field of Literary criticism (runnerup) 1981.

GOLDEN, ROBERT

Building Worker by Sarah Cox, illustrated by Robert Golden; Kestrel, 1976. **Awarded:** Other Award 1977.

Hospital Worker by Sarah Cox, illustrated by Robert Golden; Kestrel, 1976. **Awarded:** Other Award 1977.

Railway Worker by Sarah Cox, illustrated by Robert Golden; Kestrel, 1976. **Awarded:** Other Award 1977.

Textile Worker by Sarah Cox, illustrated by Robert Golden; Kestrel, 1976. **Awarded:** Other Award 1977.

GOLDIN, AUGUSTA

Small Energy Sources by Augusta Goldin, illustrated with photos; Harcourt Brace Jovanovich, 1988. **Awarded:** New York Academy of Sciences (Older Honor) 1989.

GOLDIN, BARBARA DIAMOND

Cakes and Miracles: A Purim Tale by Barbara Diamond Goldin, illustrated by Erika Weihs; Viking, 1991. **Awarded:** Sydney Taylor Book Award (Picture Book) 1992.

Just Enough Is Plenty: A Hanukkah Tale by Barbara Diamond Goldin, illustrated by Seymour Chwast; Viking Kestrel, 1988. **Awarded:** Jewish Book Council (Children's Picturebook) 1989; Parents' Choice (Picture Book) 1988.

GOLDMAN, WILLIAM

The Princess Bride by William Goldman; Ballantine, 1987. **Awarded:** Emphasis on Reading (grades 9-12) 1988-89.

GOLDSTEIN, NATHAN

The Mystery Man by Scott Corbett, illustrated by Nathan Goldstein; Little, Brown, 1970. **Awarded:** Edgar Allan Poe (runnerup) 1971.

GOLDSTEIN, PEGGY

Long Is a Dragon: Chinese Writing For Children written and illustrated by Peggy Goldstein; China Books & Periodicals, 1991. **Awarded:** Parents' Choice (Story Book) 1991.

GOLEMBE, CARLA

Why the Sky Is Far Away by Mary-Joan Gerson, illustrated by Carla Golembe; Little Brown, 1992. **Awarded:** New York Times Best Illustrated 1992.

GOLENBOCK, PETER

Teammates by Peter Golenbock, illustrated by Paul Bacon; Harcourt Brace Jovanovich, 1990. **Awarded:** Redbook 1990; Woodson (Outstanding Merit - Elementary) 1991.

GONDOSCH, LINDA

Who Needs a Bratty Brother? by Linda Gondosch, illustrated by Helen Cogancherry; Dutton, 1985. **Awarded:** Kentucky Bluegrass (grades 4-8) 1988.

GONZALEZ, LYDIA MILAGROS

El Mundo Maravilloso de Macu by Lydia Milagros Gonzalez, manuscript. **Awarded:** Council on Interracial Books (Puerto Rican) 1975.

GOODACRE, SELWYN H.

Lewis Carroll's Alice's Adventures in Wonderland by Lewis Carroll, illustrated by Barry Moser, text edited by Selwyn H. Goodacre, preface and notes by James R. Kincaid; University of California Press, 1982. **Awarded:** American Book Award (pictorial design) 1983.

GOODALL, JOHN STRICKLAND

The Adventures of Paddy Pork written and illustrated by John S. Goodall; Harcourt, 1968. **Awarded:** Boston Globe Horn Book (illustration) 1969.

Creepy Castle written and illustrated by John S. Goodall; Atheneum, 1975. **Awarded:** Children's Book Showcase 1976.

Jacko written and illustrated by John S. Goodall; Harcourt, 1972. **Awarded:** Children's Book Showcase 1973.

The Midnight Adventures of Kelly, Dot, and Esmeralda written and illustrated by John S. Goodall; Atheneum, 1972. **Awarded:** Spring Book Festival (younger honor) 1973.

Paddy Goes Traveling written and illustrated by John S. Goodall; Atheneum, 1982. **Awarded:** New York Times Best Illustrated 1982.

Paddy Pork's Holiday written and illustrated by John S. Goodall; Atheneum, 1976. **Awarded:** Children's Book Showcase 1977.

Paddy's Evening Out written and illustrated by John S. Goodall; Atheneum, 1973. **Awarded:** Children's Book Showcase 1974.

Paddy's New Hat written and illustrated by John S. Goodall; Atheneum, 1980. **Awarded:** Parents' Choice (illustration) 1980.

The Surprise Picnic written and illustrated by John S. Goodall; Atheneum, 1977. **Awarded:** New York Times Best Illustrated 1977.

GOODE, DIANE

Dream Eater by Christian Garrison, illustrated by Diane Goode; Bradbury, 1978. **Awarded:** Southern California Council (contribution to illustration) 1979.

Little Pieces of the West Wind by Christian Garrison, illustrated by Diane Goode; Bradbury, 1975. **Awarded:** Southern California Council (contribution to illustration) 1976.

Selchie's Seed by Sulamith Oppenheim, illustrated by Diane Goode; Bradbury, 1975. **Awarded:** Southern California Council (contribution to illustration) 1976.

Watch the Stars Come Out by Riki Levinson, illustrated by Diane Goode; Dutton, 1985. **Awarded:** Parents' Choice (literature) 1985; Redbook 1985.

When I Was Young in the Mountains by Cynthia Rylant, illustrated by Diane Goode; Dutton, 1982. **Awarded:** Caldecott (honor) 1983.

GOODMAN, ELAINE

The Rights of the People: The Major Decisions of the Warren Court by Elaine Goodman and Walter Goodman, not illustrated; Farrar, 1971. **Awarded:** Christopher (teenage) 1972.

GOODMAN, WALTER

The Rights of the People: The Major Decisions of the Warren Court by Walter Goodman and Elaine Goodman, not illustrated; Farrar, 1971. **Awarded:** Christopher (teenage) 1972.

GOODSELL, JANE

The Biography of Daniel Inouye by Jane Goodsell, illustrated by Haru Wells; Crowell, 1977. **Awarded:** Carter G. Woodson 1978.

GOODSIR, DON

The Gould League Book of Australian Birds by Don Goodsir, illustrated by Tony Oliver; Golden Press, 1979. **Awarded:** Whitley Awards 1980.

The Gould League Book of Australian Mammals by Don Goodsir, illustrated by Tony Oliver; Golden Press, 1981. **Awarded:** Whitley Awards 1983.

GOODWIN, EDWARD
Debbie of the Green Gate by Helen Fern Daringer, illustrated by Edward Goodwin; Harcourt, 1950. **Awarded:** Spring Book Festival (older honor) 1950.

GOODWIN, POLLY
Awarded: Children's Reading Round Table 1964; Women's National Book Assn. 1964.

GOOR, NANCY
Insect Metamorphosis by Ron Goor and Nancy Goor, illustrated by Ron Goor; Atheneum, 1990. **Awarded:** Boston Globe (Nonfiction honor) 1990.

GOOR, RON
Insect Metamorphosis by Ron Goor and Nancy Goor, illustrated by Ron Goor; Atheneum, 1990. **Awarded:** Boston Globe (Nonfiction honor) 1990.

GORDON, ISABEL
The Shadow Book by Isabel Gordon and Beatrice Schenk de Regniers, illustrated by Isabel Gordon; Harcourt, 1960. **Awarded:** New York Times Best Illustrated 1960.

GORDON, SHEILA
The Middle of Somewhere by Sheila Gordon, not illustrated; Orchard, 1990. **Awarded:** Addams (Honor) 1991.

Waiting for the Rain: A Novel of South Africa by Sheila Gordon, not illustrated; Orchard, 1987. **Awarded:** Addams 1988.

GOREY, EDWARD ST. JOHN
The Curse of the Blue Figurine by John Bellairs, illustrated by Edward Gorey; Dial, 1983; Bantam, 1984. **Awarded:** Parents Choice (literature) 1983; Virginia Young Readers (Middle School) 1987.

The Dong with a Luminous Nose by Edward Lear, illustrated by Edward Gorey; Scott, 1969. **Awarded:** New York Times Best Illustrated 1969.

The Dwindling Party written and illustrated by Edward Gorey, paper engineering by Ib Penick; Random House, 1982. **Awarded:** Parents' Choice (illustration) 1982.

Fletcher and Zenobia by Edward Gorey and Victoria Chess, illustrated by Victoria Chess; Hawthorne, 1967. **Awarded:** Art Books for Children 1973.

The House with a Clock in Its Walls by John Bellairs, illustrated by Edward Gorey; Dial, 1973. **Awarded:** Michigan Young Readers (division II runnerup) 1980; New York Times Notable Books 1973.

The King Who Saved Himself from Being Saved by John Ciardi, illustrated by Edward Gorey; Lippincott, l965. **Awarded:** New Jersey Institute of Technology 1967.

Lions and Lobsters and Foxes and Frogs: Fables from Aesop by Ennis Rees, illustrated by Edward Gorey; Young Scott/Addison- Wesley, 1971. **Awarded:** Children's Book Showcase 1972.

The Man Who Sang the Sillies by John Ciardi, illustrated by Edward Gorey; Lippincott, 1961. **Awarded:** Boys Club 1962.

The Monster Den: or, Look What Happened at My House - and to It by John Ciardi, illustrated by Edward Gorey; Lippincott, 1966. **Awarded:** New Jersey Institute of Technology 1967; New York Times Best Illustrated 1966.

Red Riding Hood, Retold in Verse for Boys and Girls to Read Themselves by Beatrice Schenk de Regniers, illustrated by Edward Gorey; Atheneum, 1972. **Awarded:** Art Books for Children 1974; Children's Book Showcase 1973.

Sam and Emma by Donald Nelsen, illustrated by Edward Gorey; Parents, 1971. **Awarded:** Children's Book Showcase 1972.

Schorschi Schrumpft: Geschichte by Florence Parry Heide, illustrated by Edward Gorey; Diogenes Verlag, 1976. **Awarded:** Bologna (graphics for children) 1977.

The Shrinking of Treehorn by Florence Parry Heide, illustrated by Edward Gorey; Holiday, 1971. **Awarded:** Children's Book Showcase 1972; New York Times Best Illustrated 1971.

GORMAN, CAROL
Chelsey and the Green-Haired Kid by Carol Gorman, not illustrated; Houghton Mifflin, 1987. **Awarded:** Ethical Culture School 1987.

GORMAN, JAMES
Digging Dinosaurs by James Gorman and John R. Horner, illustrated by Kris Ellingsen and Donna Braginetz; Workman, 1988. **Awarded:** New York Academy of Sciences (Older) 1989.

GOROG, JUDITH
Caught in the Turtle by Judith Gorog, illustrated by Ruth Sanderson; Philomel, 1983. **Awarded:** New Jersey Institute of Technology 1983.

No Swimming in Dark Pond and Other Chilling Tales by Judith Gorog, not illustrated; Philomel, 1987. **Awarded:** Emphasis on Reading (grades 6-8) 1988-89; New Jersey Institute of Technology 1988.

A Taste for Quiet and Other Disquieting Tales by Judith Gorog, illustrated by Jean Titherington; Philomel, 1982. **Awarded:** New Jersey Institute of Technology 1983.

GORSLINE, DOUGLAS
Farm Boy written and illustrated by Douglas Gorsline; Viking, 1950. **Awarded:** Spring Book Festival (older honor) 1950.

GOSSETT, MARGARET
We Are the Government by Margaret Gossett and Mary Elting, illustrated by Angio Culfogienis; Doubleday, 1967. **Awarded:** New Jersey Institute of Technology 1970.

GOTT, RICHARD
Active Science I by Michael Coles, Richard Gott, and Tony Thornley, illustrated; Collins Educational, 1988. **Awarded:** Times Educational Supplement (Schoolbook) 1988.

GOTTLIEB, GERALD
The Story of Masada by Yigael Yadin, retold by Gerald Gottlieb, illustrated with photographs; Random House, 1969. **Awarded:** Jewish Book Council 1969.

GOTTLIEB, WILLIAM P.
Jets and Rockets and How They Work written and illustrated by William P. Gottlieb; Doubleday, 1959. **Awarded:** Boys Club 1960.

GOUDEY, ALICE E.
The Day We Saw the Sun Come Up by Alice E. Goudey, illustrated by Adrienne Adams; Scribner, 1961. **Awarded:** Caldecott (honor) 1962.

Houses from the Sea by Alice E. Goudey, illustrated by Adrienne Adams; Scribner, 1959. **Awarded:** Caldecott (honor) 1960.

GOUDGE, ELIZABETH
The Little White Horse by Elizabeth Goudge, illustrated by C. Walter Hodges; University of London Press, 1946; Coward, 1947. **Awarded:** Carnegie 1946; Spring Book Festival (older honor) 1947.

GOUGH, SUE
A Long Way From Tipperary by Sue Gough, illustrated; University of Queensland Press, 1992. **Awarded:** Children's Book Council of Australia (Book of the Year Older) 1993.

GOULD, JEAN
That Dunbar Boy by Jean Gould, illustrated by C. Walker; Dodd Mead, 1958. **Awarded:** Edison Mass Media (character development in children) 1959.

GOULD, ROBERT
Letters from Atlantis by Robert Silverberg, illustrated by Robert Gould; Atheneum, 1990. **Awarded:** Woodward Park 1991.

GOULDTHORPE, PETER J.
Hist! by Clarence James Dennis, illustrated by Peter J. Gouldthorpe; Walter McVitty, 1991. **Awarded:** Children's Book Council of Australia (Picture Book honor) 1992.

GOVAN, CHRISTINE NOBLE
Carolina Caravan by Christine Noble Govan, illustrated by Helen Blair; Houghton, 1942. **Awarded:** Spring Book Festival (older honor) 1942.

GRABIANSKI, JANUSZ
The Big Book of Animal Stories by Margaret Green, illustrated by Janusz Grabianski; Watts, 1961. **Awarded:** New York Times Best Illustrated 1961.

Grabianskis Stadtmusikanten written and illustrated by Janusz Grabianski; Verlag Carl Ueberreuter. **Awarded:** Bologna (Graphics for Children) 1978.

GRABOFF, ABNER
The Daddy Days by Norma Simon, illustrated by Abner Graboff; Abelard-Schuman, 1958. **Awarded:** New York Times Best Illustrated 1958.

The Sun Looks Down by Miriam Schlein, illustrated by Abner Graboff; Abelard-Schuman, 1954. **Awarded:** New York Times Best Illustrated 1954.

GRACE, PATRICIA
The Kuia and the Spider by Patricia Grace, illustrated by Robyn Kahukiwa; Longmans Paul, 1981. **Awarded:** AIM (Picture Book) 1982.

GRAEBER, CHARLOTTE TOWNER
Fudge by Charlotte T. Graeber, illustrated by Cheryl Harness; Lothrop, Lee & Shepard, 1987. **Awarded:** Iowa Children's Choice 1992; KC Three 1989-90; Nene Award 1990; Sequoyah Children's 1990; Sunshine State (grades 3-5) 1992; West Virginia Children's 1989-90; Young Hoosier (Grades 4-6) 1990.

Grey Cloud by Charlotte Towner Graeber, illustrated by Lloyd Bloom; Four Winds, 1979. **Awarded:** Friends of American Writers (Older) 1980.

Mustard by Charlotte Graeber, illustrated by Donna Diamond; Macmillan, 1982. **Awarded:** Irma Simonton Black 1982; West Virginia 1985-86.

GRAESE, JUDY
The Treasure Is the Rose by Julia Cunningham, illustrated by Judy Graese; Pantheon, 1973. **Awarded:** National Book Award (finalist) 1974; New York Times Notable Books 1973.

GRAGLIA, RICHARD
Rose Blanche by Roberto Innocenti and Christophe Gallaz, translated by Martha Coventry and Richard Graglia, illustrated by Roberto Innocenti; Creative Education, 1985. **Awarded:** Batchelder 1986.

GRAHAM, ADA
Awarded: Eva Gordon 1989.

The Big Stretch: The Complete Book of the Amazing Rubber Band by Ada Graham and Frank Graham, illustrated by Richard Rosenblum; Knopf, 1985. **Awarded:** New York Academy of Sciences (younger) 1986.

Careers in Conservation by Ada Graham and Frank Graham, illustrated by Drake Jordan; Sierra Club/Scribner, 1980. **Awarded:** New York Academy of Sciences (older honor) 1981.

The Milkweed and Its World of Animals by Ada Graham and Frank Graham, photographs by Les Line; Doubleday, 1976. **Awarded:** New York Academy of Sciences (younger honor) 1977.

GRAHAM, AL
Timothy Turtle by Al Graham, illustrated by Tony Palazzo; Welch, 1946. **Awarded:** Caldecott (honor) 1947.

GRAHAM, AMANDA
Arthur by Amanda Graham, illustrated by Donna Gynell; Spindlewood, 1985, c1984; Keystone Picture Books, 1984. **Awarded:** Children's Book Award 1985.

GRAHAM, BOB
Crusher Is Coming written and illustrated by Bob Graham; Lothian Publishing, 1987. **Awarded:** Children's Book Council of Australia (Picture Book) 1988.

First There Was Frances written and illustrated by Bob Graham; Lothian, 1985. **Awarded:** Children's Book Council of Australia (picture book of the year commended) 1986; International Board on Books for Young People (Illustration/Australia) 1988.

Greetings From Sandy Beach written and illustrated by Bob Graham; Lothian, 1990; Blackie, 1990; Kane Miller, 1992. **Awarded:** Children's Book Council of Australia (Picture Book) 1991.

Rosie Meets Mr. Wintergarten written and illustrated by Bob Graham; Walker, 1992. **Awarded:** Children's Book Council of Australia (Picture Book of the Year) 1993.

GRAHAM, ELEANOR
Awarded: Eleanor Farjeon 1972.

GRAHAM, FRANK
Awarded: Eva L. Gordon 1989.

The Big Stretch: The Complete Book of the Amazing Rubber Band by Ada Graham and Frank Graham, illustrated by Richard Rosenblum; Knopf, 1985. **Awarded:** New York Academy of Sciences (younger) 1986.

Careers in Conservation by Frank Graham and Ada Graham, illustrated by Drake Jordan; Sierra Club/Scribner, 1980. **Awarded:** New York Academy of Sciences (older honor) 1981.

The Milkweed and Its World of Animals by Frank Graham and Ada Graham, photographs by Les Line; Doubleday, 1976. **Awarded:** New York Academy of Sciences (younger honor) 1977.

GRAHAM, LORENZ
Awarded: Southern California Council (significant contribution to the field of literature for young people) 1968.

Song of the Boat by Lorenz Graham, illustrated by Leo Dillon and Diane Dillon; Crowell, 1975. **Awarded:** Boston Globe Horn Book (illustration honor) 1976; Children's Book Showcase 1976.

South Town by Lorenz Graham, not illustrated; Follett, 1958. **Awarded:** Child Study 1958; Charles W. Follett 1958.

Whose Town? by Lorenz Graham, not illustrated; Crowell, 1969. **Awarded:** Spring Book Festival (middle) 1969.

GRAHAM, MARGARET BLOY

All Falling Down by Gene Zion, illustrated by Margaret Bloy Graham; Harper, 1951. **Awarded:** Caldecott (honor) 1952.

Dear Garbage Man by Gene Zion, illustrated by Margaret Bloy Graham; Harper, 1957. **Awarded:** New York Times Best Illustrated 1957.

Really Spring by Gene Zion, illustrated by Margaret Bloy Graham; Harper, 1956. **Awarded:** New York Times Best Illustrated 1956.

The Storm Book by Charlotte Zolotow, illustrated by Margaret Bloy Graham; Harper, 1952. **Awarded:** Caldecott (honor) 1953.

GRAHAM, MARK

Charlie Anderson by Barbara Abercrombie, illustrated by Mark Graham; McElderry, 1990. **Awarded:** Irma S. and James H. Black 1990; Redbook 1990.

GRAHAME, KENNETH

The Reluctant Dragon by Kenneth Grahame, illustrated by Ernest H. Shepard; Holiday, 1953, c1938. **Awarded:** Lewis Carroll Shelf 1963.

The Wind in the Willows by Kenneth Grahame, illustrated by Ernest H. Shepard; Scribner, 1954, c1908. **Awarded:** Lewis Carroll Shelf 1958; Feature a Classic 1983.

The Wind in the Willows by Kenneth Grahame, illustrated by John Burningham; Kestrel, 1983; Penguin, 1983. **Awarded:** Maschler (runnerup) 1983.

GRAMATKY, HARDIE

Little Toot written and illustrated by Hardie Gramatky; Putnam, 1939. **Awarded:** Lewis Carroll Shelf 1969.

GRAMMER, JUNE AMOS

Mary Anne by Mary Mapes Dodge, illustrated by June Amos Grammer; Lothrop, Lee & Shepard, 1983. **Awarded:** New Jersey Institute of Technology 1983.

GRANAHAN, LOLITA

Finlandia, the Story of Sibelius by Elliott Arnold, illustrated by Lolita Granahan; Holt, 1941. **Awarded:** Spring Book Festival (older honor) 1941.

GRANBERG, WILBUR J.

Johnny Wants to Be a Policeman by Wilbur J. Granberg, illustrated by Alison Cummings; Aladdin, 1951. **Awarded:** Boys Club 1952.

GRANFIELD, LINDA

Awarded: Frances E. Russell 1990.

GRANT, CYNTHIA D.

Awarded: PEN/Norma Klein Award 1991.

Joshua Fortune by Cynthia D. Grant, not illustrated; Atheneum, 1980. **Awarded:** Woodward Park 1981.

Shadow Man by Cynthia Grant, not illustrated; Atheneum, 1992. **Awarded:** Hungry Mind (Young Adult/Fiction) 1993.

GRANT, DONALD

Tales of Nanabozho by Dorothy Reid, illustrated by Donald Grant; Oxford, 1964. **Awarded:** Canadian Library Assn. 1965.

GRANT, EVA

Cow for Jaya by Eva Grant, illustrated by Michael Hampshire; Coward, 1973. **Awarded:** New Jersey Institute of Technology 1973.

I Hate My Name by Eva Grant, illustrated by Gretchen Mayo; Raintree, 1980. **Awarded:** New Jersey Institute of Technology 1981.

GRANT, GWEN

Jonpanda by Gwen Grant, illustrated by Elaine Mills; Heinemann, 1992. **Awarded:** Nottinghamshire (Acorn) 1993.

GRANT, JOAN

The Australopedia by Joan Grant, illustrated by design students at Phillips Institute; McPhee Gribble/Penguin Books Australia, 1989; Penguin, 1988. **Awarded:** Children's Book Council of Australia (Book of the Year Younger Honour) 1989.

GRANT, LEIGH

I'm Moving by Martha Whitmore Hickman, illustrated by Leigh Grant; Abingdon, 1974. **Awarded:** Friends of American Writers (younger) 1976.

It Can't Hurt Forever by Marilyn Singer, illustrated by Leigh Grant; Harper, 1978; Harper Trophy, 1981. **Awarded:** Maud Hart Lovelace 1983.

Kid Power by Susan Beth Pfeffer, illustrated by Leigh Grant; Watts, 1977. **Awarded:** Dorothy Canfield Fisher 1979; Sequoyah 1980.

Shoeshine Girl by Clyde Robert Bulla, illustrated by Leigh Grant; Crowell, 1975. **Awarded:** Sequoyah 1978; Charlie May Simon 1977-78; South Carolina Children's 1980; Southern California Council (notable) 1976.

Sleep and Dreams by Rae Lindsay, illustrated by Leigh Grant; Watts, 1978. **Awarded:** New Jersey Institute of Technology 1980.

The Smallest Life Around Us by Lucia Anderson, illustrated by Leigh Grant; Crown, 1978. **Awarded:** New York Academy of Sciences (younger) 1979.

GRANT, LESLEY

Discover Bones by Lesley Grant, illustrated by Tina Holdcroft; Kids Can Press, 1991. **Awarded:** Information Book Award (Honour) 1992.

GRAVES, RUTH

Awarded: Jeremiah Ludington 1982.

GRAY, BETTYANNE

Manya's Story by Bettyanne Gray, illustrated with photographs; Lerner, 1978. **Awarded:** Lewis Carroll Shelf 1978.

GRAY, CHARLES A.

Explorations in Chemistry by Charles A. Gray, illustrated with diagrams; Dutton, 1965. **Awarded:** Edison Mass Media (best science book for youth) 1966.

GRAY, DULCIE

Butterflies on My Mind: Their Life and Conservation in Britain Today by Dulcie Gray, illustrated by Brian Hargreaves; Angus & Robertson, 1978. **Awarded:** Times Educational Supplement (senior) 1978.

GRAY, ELIZABETH JANET

Awarded: Drexel 1976; Women's National Book Assn. 1954.

Adam of the Road by Elizabeth Janet Gray, illustrated by Robert Lawson; Viking, 1942. **Awarded:** Newbery 1943; Spring Book Festival (middle honor) 1942.

Meggy MacIntosh by Elizabeth Janet Gray, illustrated by Marguerite de Angeli; Doubleday, 1930. **Awarded:** Newbery (honor) 1931.

Penn by Elizabeth Janet Gray, illustrated by George G. Whitney; Viking, 1938. **Awarded:** Newbery (honor) 1939.

Sandy by Elizabeth Janet Gray, illustrated by Robert Hallock; Viking, 1945. **Awarded:** Spring Book Festival (older) 1945.

Young Walter Scott by Elizabeth Janet Gray, illustrated by Kate Seredy; Viking, 1935. **Awarded:** Newbery (honor) 1936.

GRAY, GENEVIEVE
Send Wendell by Genevieve Gray, illustrated by Symeon Shimin; McGraw, 1974. **Awarded:** Art Books for Children 1978.

GRAY, NICHOLAS STUART
Over the Hills to Fabylon written and illustrated by Nicholas Stuart Gray; Oxford, 1954. **Awarded:** Carnegie (commended) 1954.

GRAZIER, MARGARET HAYES
Awarded: American Association of School Librarians 1986.

GREBU, DEVIS
Joseph Who Loved the Sabbath by Marilyn Hirsh, illustrated by Devis Grebu; Viking Kestrel, 1986. **Awarded:** Sydney Taylor Book Award (picture book) 1987.

GREDER, ARMIN
Big Dog by Libby Gleeson, illustrated by Armin Greder; Ashton Scholastic, 1991. **Awarded:** Australian Multicultural Children's Literature Award (Picture Book) 1992.

GREEN, CLARENCE C.
Benjamin Rush: Physician, Patriot, Founding Father by Clarence C. Green and Sarah R. Reidman, illustrated with photographs; Abelard-Schuman, 1964. **Awarded:** New Jersey Institute of Technology 1965.

GREEN, EILEEN
The Bus Girls by Mary Kathleen Harris, illustrated by Eileen Green; Faber, 1965. **Awarded:** Carnegie (commended) 1965.

GREEN, MALCOLM
The October Child by Eleanor Spence, illustrated by Malcolm Green; Oxford, 1976. **Awarded:** Children's Book Council of Australia (book of the year) 1977; International Board on Books for Young People (text/Australia) 1978.

GREEN, MARGARET
The Big Book of Animal Stories by Margaret Green, illustrated by Janusz Grabianski; Watts, 1961. **Awarded:** New York Times Best Illustrated 1961.

GREEN, MICHELLE Y.
Willie Pearl by Michelle Y. Green, illustrated by Steve McCracken; William Ruth & Co., 1990. **Awarded:** CRABbery Award 1991.

GREEN, PHYLLIS
Bagdad Ate It by Phyllis Green, illustrated by Joel Schick; Watts, 1980. **Awarded:** California Young Reader (primary) 1984.

Eating Ice Cream With a Werewolf by Phyllis Green, illustrated by Patti Stren; Harper and Row, 1983. **Awarded:** Maud Hart Lovelace 1989.

Ice River by Phyllis Green, illustrated by James Crowell; Addison Wesley, 1975. **Awarded:** Council for Wisconsin Writers (picture book) 1976.

A New Mother for Martha by Phyllis Green, illustrated by Margaret Luks; Human Sciences Press, 1978. **Awarded:** Council for Wisconsin Writers (picture book) 1979.

GREEN, SUZANNE
The Little Bookmobile: Colors, Numbers, and Shapes on Wheels by Suzanne Green, illustrated by Daisuke Yokoi; Doubleday, 1986. **Awarded:** Redbook 1986.

GREENBERG, TONY
Too Fat? Too Thin? Do You Have a Choice? by Caroline Arnold, foreword by Tony Greenberg, not illustrated; Morrow, 1984. **Awarded:** Southern California Council (notable work of nonfiction) 1985.

GREENBLAT, RODNEY A.
Uncle Wizzmo's New Used Car written and illustrated by Rodney A. Greenblat; Harper & Row, 1990. **Awarded:** Parents' Choice (Picture Book) 1990.

GREENE, BETTE
Philip Hall Likes Me: I Reckon Maybe by Bette Greene, illustrated by Charles Lilly; Dial, 1974. **Awarded:** New York Times Notable Books 1974; Newbery (honor) 1975.

Summer of My German Soldier by Bette Greene, not illustrated; Dial, 1973. **Awarded:** Golden Kite 1973; Massachusetts Children's (young adult) 1980; National Book Award (finalist) 1974; New York Times Notable Books 1973.

Them That Glitter and Them That Don't by Bette Greene, not illustrated; Knopf, 1983. **Awarded:** Parents' Choice (literature) 1983.

GREENE, CAROL
The Golden Locket by Carol Greene, illustrated by Marcia Sewall; Harcourt Brace Jovanovich, 1992. **Awarded:** Parents Choice (Picture Book) 1992.

GREENE, CONSTANCE
A Girl Called Al by Constance Greene, illustrated by Byron Barton; Viking, 1969. **Awarded:** Spring Book Festival (middle honor) 1969.

GREENE, DAVID L.
Awarded: L. Frank Baum 1965.

GREENE, DOUGLAS G.
Awarded: L. Frank Baum 1965.

GREENE, GRACIE
Tjarany Roughtail by Gracie Greene and Joe Tramacchi, illustrated by Lucille Gill; Magabala, 1992. **Awarded:** Children's Book Council of Australia (Eve Pownall Award) 1993.

GREENE, GRAHAM
The Little Horse Bus by Graham Greene, illustrated by Dorothy Craigie; Lothrop Lee & Shepard, 1954. **Awarded:** Boys Club 1955.

GREENE, LAURA
I Am an Orthodox Jew by Laura Greene, illustrated by Lis C. Wesson; Holt, 1979. **Awarded:** Council for Wisconsin Writers (picture book runnerup) 1980.

GREENE, SHEP
The Boy Who Drank Too Much by Shep Greene, not illustrated; Viking, 1979; Dell, 1980. **Awarded:** South Carolina Young Adult 1982.

GREENE, WINIFRED
Lucky Blacky by Eunice Lackey, illustrated by Winifred Greene; Watts, 1953. **Awarded:** New York Times Best Illustrated 1953.

GREENFELD, HOWARD
Gertrude Stein: A Biography by Howard Greenfeld, illustrated with photographs; Crown, 1973. **Awarded:** Children's Book Showcase 1974.

Marc Chagall by Howard Greenfeld, illustrated by Marc Chagall; Follett, 1967. **Awarded:** Charles W. Follett 1968.

GREENFIELD, ELOISE

Africa Dream by Eloise Greenfield, illustrated by Carole Byard; Day/Crowell, 1977. **Awarded:** Coretta Scott King 1978.

Childtimes by Eloise Greenfield and Lessie Jones Little, illustrated by Jerry Pinkney; Harper, 1979. **Awarded:** Boston Globe Horn Book (nonfiction honor) 1980; Woodson (outstanding merit) 1980.

Honey, I Love and other Love Poems by Eloise Greenfield, illustrated by Diane Dillon and Leo Dillon; Crowell, 1978. **Awarded:** George G. Stone 1990.

Nathaniel Talking by Eloise Greenfield, illustrated by Jan Spivey Gilchrist; Black Butterfly Children's Books, 1988. **Awarded:** Coretta Scott King (Illustration) 1990; Coretta Scott King (Text honor) 1990.

Night on Neighborhood Street by Eloise Greenfield, illustrated by Jan Spivey Gilchrist; Dial, 1991. **Awarded:** Coretta Scott King (Author honor) 1992; Coretta Scott King (Illustrator honor) 1992.

Paul Robeson by Eloise Greenfield, illustrated by George Ford; Crowell, 1975. **Awarded:** Jane Addams 1976

Rosa Parks by Eloise Greenfield, illustrated by Eric Marlow; Crowell, 1973. **Awarded:** Carter G. Woodson 1974.

She Come Bringing Me That Little Baby Girl by Eloise Greenfield, illustrated by John Steptoe; Lippincott, 1974. **Awarded:** Irma Simonton Black 1974; Boston Globe Horn Book (illustration honor) 1975.

Under the Sunday Tree by Eloise Greenfield, illustrated by Amos Ferguson; Harper & Row, 1988. **Awarded:** Coretta Scott King (Illustration honor) 1989.

GREENLEAF, MARGERY F.

Banner Over Me by Margery F. Greenleaf, illustrated by Charles Mikolaycak; Follett, 1968. **Awarded:** Charles W. Follett 1969.

GREENWALD, SHEILA

Rosie Cole's Great American Guilt Club written and illustrated by Sheila Greenwald; Atlantic, 1985. **Awarded:** Parents Choice (literature) 1985.

GREENWOOD, BARBARA

Major Resolution by Barbara Greenwood in Contexts; Nelson, 1981. **Awarded:** Vicky Metcalf Short Story 1982.

GREENWOOD, TED

Joseph and Lulu and the Prindiville House Pigeons written and illustrated by Ted Greenwood; Angus & Robertson, 1972. **Awarded:** International Board on Books for Young People (illustration/Australia) 1974.

Sly Old Wardrobe by Ivan Southall, illustrated by Ted Greenwood; Cheshire, 1968. **Awarded:** Children's Book Council of Australia (picture book) 1969.

Spooner or Later by Paul Jennings, Ted Greenwood and Terry Denton; Viking, 1992. **Awarded:** Ashton Scholastic 1993.

Terry's Brrrmmm GT written and illustrated by Ted Greenwood; Angus & Robertson, 1976. **Awarded:** Children's Book Council of Australia (best illustrated) 1976.

GREER, GERY

This Island Isn't Big Enough for the Four of Us by Gery Greer and Bob Ruddick, not illustrated; Crowell, 1987. **Awarded:** Maud Hart Lovelace 1992; South Dakota Prairie Pasque 1990; Utah Children's 1990.

GREGOR, ARTHUR

Animal Babies by Arthur Gregor, illustrated by Arthur Gregor and Ylla; Harper, 1959. **Awarded:** New York Times Best Illustrated 1959.

GREGORY, KRISTIANA

Earthquake at Dawn by Kristiana Gregory, illustrated with photographs; Harcourt Brace Jovanovich, 1992. **Awarded:** Commonwealth Club of California (Ages 11-16) 1992.

Jenny of the Tetons by Kristiana Gregory, not illustrated; Harcourt Brace Jovanovich, 1989. **Awarded:** Golden Kite (Fiction) 1989.

GREGORY, VALISKA

Through the Mickle Woods by Valiska Gregory, illustrated by Barry Moser; Little Brown, 1992. **Awarded:** Parents Choice (Story Book) 1992.

GRETZ, SUSANNA

It's Your Turn, Roger! written and illustrated by Susanna Gretz; Bodley Head, 1985. **Awarded:** Smarties (ages 6 and under) 1985.

Say it Again, Granny! by John Agard, illustrated by Susanna Gretz; Bodley Head, 1985. **Awarded:** Other Award 1986.

GRETZER, JOHN

Going on Sixteen by Betty Cavanna, illustrated by John Gretzer; Westminster, 1946. **Awarded:** Spring Book Festival (older honor) 1946.

Mystery of the Scowling Boy by Phyllis A. Whitney, illustrated by John Gretzer; Westminster, 1973. **Awarded:** Edgar Allan Poe (runnerup) 1974.

GREY, VIVIAN

The Invisible Giants: Atoms, Nuclei and Radioisotopes by Vivian Grey, illustrated with photographs; Little, 1969. **Awarded:** New Jersey Institute of Technology 1969.

GRICE, FREDERICK

Awarded: Other Award (special commendation for body of work) 1977.

GRIFALCONI, ANN

Everett Anderson's Goodbye by Lucille Clifton, illustrated by Ann Grifalconi; Holt, 1983. **Awarded:** Coretta Scott King (author) 1984.

Half-Breed by Evelyn S. Lampman, illustrated by Ann Grifalconi; Doubleday, 1967. **Awarded:** Western Writers (fiction) 1968.

The Jazz Man by Mary Hays Weik, illustrated by Ann Grifalconi; Atheneum, 1966. **Awarded:** New York Times Best Illustrated 1966; Newbery (honor) 1967.

The Midnight Fox by Betsy Byars, illustrated by Ann Grifalconi; Viking, 1968. **Awarded:** Lewis Carroll Shelf 1970.

The Village of Round and Square Houses written and illustrated by Ann Grifalconi; Little, Brown, 1986. **Awarded:** Caldecott (honor) 1987.

GRIFFEN, ELIZABETH

A Dog's Book of Bugs by Elizabeth Griffen, illustrated by Peter Parnall; Atheneum, 1967. **Awarded:** New York Times Best Illustrated 1967.

GRIFFITH, HELEN V.

Georgia Music by Helen V. Griffith, illustrated by James Stevenson; Greenwillow, 1986. **Awarded:** Boston Globe Horn Book (fiction honor) 1987.

Grandaddy's Place by Helen V. Griffith, illustrated by James Stevenson; Greenwillow, 1987. **Awarded:** Parents' Choice (Picture Book) 1987; Parents' Choice (Story Book) 1987.

GRIFFITH, JULIUS
Franklin of the Arctic: A Life of Adventure by Richard S. Lambert, illustrated with maps by Julius Griffith; McClelland & Stewart, 1949. **Awarded:** Canadian Library Assn. 1950; Governor- General's Literary Award 1949.

GRIFFITHS, ANNE
Terraced House Books: Set D by Peter Heaslip, illustrated by Anne Griffiths; Methuen Educational, 1980. **Awarded:** Other Award 1981.

GRIFFITHS, HELEN
The Wild Horse of Santander by Helen Griffiths, illustrated by Victor G. Ambrus; Hutchinson, 1966. **Awarded:** Carnegie (commended) 1966.

GRIGGS, FRANKIE LEE
see BALL, ZACHARY

GRIGGS, TAMAR
There's a Sound in the Sea: A Child's Eye View of the Whale compiled by Tamar Griggs, illustrated with paintings by school children; Scrimshaw, 1975. **Awarded:** New York Times Best Illustrated 1975.

GRIMES, NIKKI
Something on My Mind by Nikki Grimes, illustrated by Tom Feelings; Dial, 1978. **Awarded:** Coretta Scott King (special illustration) 1979.

GRIMM, JACOB
About Wise Men and Simpletons: Twelve Tales from Grimm translated by Elizabeth Shub, illustrated by Nonny Hogrogian; Macmillan, 1971. **Awarded:** New York Times Notable Books 1971.

The Brothers Grimm: Popular Folk Tales by Jacob Grimm and Wilhelm Grimm, newly translated by Brian Alderson, illustrated by Michael Foreman; Gollancz, 1978. **Awarded:** Greenaway (commended) 1978.

The Fisherman and His Wife by Jacob Grimm and Wilhelm Grimm, illustrated by Madeleine Gekiere; Pantheon, 1957. **Awarded:** New York Times Best Illustrated 1957.

Folk Tales by Jacob Grimm and Wilhelm Grimm (various editions and publishers). **Awarded:** Feature a Classic 1984.

Hansel and Gretel by Wilhelm Grimm and Jacob Grimm, illustrated by Anthony Browne; Julia MacRae, 1981. **Awarded:** Greenaway (commended) 1981; International Board on Books for Young People (illustration/Great Britain) 1984.

Jorinda and Joringel by Jacob Grimm and Wilhelm Grimm, illustrated by Adrienne Adams; Scribner, 1968. **Awarded:** Boston Globe Horn Book (illustration honor) 1968.

Little Red Cap by Jacob Grimm and Wilhelm Grimm, translated by Elizabeth D. Crawford, illustrated by Lisbeth Zwerger; Morrow, 1983. **Awarded:** New York Times Best Illustrated 1983.

Little Red Riding Hood by Jacob Grimm and Wilhelm Grimm, retold and illustrated by Trina Schart Hyman; Holiday House, 1983. **Awarded:** Caldecott (honor) 1984; Golden Kite (picture illustration) 1983; Parents' Choice (illustration) 1983.

The Luck Child based on a story of the Brothers Grimm by Jacob Grimm and Wilhelm Grimm, illustrated by Gaynor Chapman; Hamilton, 1968. **Awarded:** Greenaway (honour) 1968.

Rotkappchen by Jacob Grimm and Wilhelm Grimm; Diogenes Verlag. **Awarded:** Bologna (Graphics for Children) 1974.

Rumpelstiltskin by Jacob Grimm and Wilhelm Grimm, adapted by Patricia Jones, illustrated by Jan B. Balet; Rand McNally, 1955. **Awarded:** New York Times Best Illustrated 1955.

The Seven Ravens by Jacob Grimm and Wilhelm Grimm, illustrated by Felix Hoffmann; Harcourt, 1963. **Awarded:** Spring Book Festival (picture book) 1963.

Snow White and the Seven Dwarfs by Jacob Grimm and Wilhelm Grimm, translated by Randall Jarrell, illustrated by Nancy Ekholm Burkert; Farrar, 1972. **Awarded:** Bologna (critici in erba) 1973; Caldecott (honor) 1973; Lewis Carroll Shelf 1973; New York Times Notable Books 1972.

Thorn Rose by Jacob Grimm and Wilhelm Grimm, illustrated by Errol Le Cain; Faber, 1975. **Awarded:** Greenaway (commended) 1975; International Board on Books for Young People (illustration/Great Britain) 1978.

The Twelve Dancing Princesses by Jacob Grimm and Wilhelm Grimm, illustrated by Errol Le Cain; Faber, 1978. **Awarded:** Greenaway (commended) 1978.

Die Wichtelmanner by Jacob Grimm and Wilhelm Grimm, illustrated by Katrin Brandt; Atlantis Verlag. **Awarded:** Bologna (Graphics for Children) 1968.

GRIMM, WILHELM
About Wise Men and Simpletons: Twelve Tales from Grimm translated by Elizabeth Shub, illustrated by Nonny Hogrogian; Macmillan, 1971. **Awarded:** New York Times Notable Books 1971.

The Brothers Grimm: Popular Folk Tales by Jacob Grimm and Wilhelm Grimm, newly translated by Brian Alderson, illustrated by Michael Foreman; Gollancz, 1978. **Awarded:** Greenaway (commended) 1978.

Dear Mili by Wilhelm Grimm, illustrated by Maurice Sendak; Farrar Straus Giroux, 1988. **Awarded:** Bologna (Critici in Erba) 1989; Reading Magic Award 1988.

The Fisherman and His Wife by Jacob Grimm and Wilhelm Grimm, illustrated by Madeleine Gekiere; Pantheon, 1957. **Awarded:** New York Times Best Illustrated 1957.

Folk Tales by Jacob Grimm and Wilhelm Grimm (various editions and publishers). **Awarded:** Feature a Classic 1984.

Hansel and Gretel by Wilhelm Grimm and Jacob Grimm, illustrated by Anthony Browne; Julia MacRae, 1981. **Awarded:** Greenaway (commended) 1981; International Board on Books for Young People (illustration/Great Britain) 1984.

Jorinda and Joringel by Jacob Grimm and Wilhelm Grimm, illustrated by Adrienne Adams; Scribner, 1968. **Awarded:** Boston Globe Horn Book (illustration honor) 1968.

Little Red Cap by Jacob Grimm and Wilhelm Grimm, translated by Elizabeth D. Crawford, illustrated by Lisbeth Zwerger; Morrow, 1983. **Awarded:** New York Times Best Illustrated 1983.

Little Red Riding Hood by Jacob Grimm and Wilhelm Grimm, retold and illustrated by Trina Schart Hyman; Holiday House, 1983. **Awarded:** Caldecott (honor) 1984; Golden Kite (picture illustration) 1983; Parents' Choice (illustration) 1983.

The Luck Child based on a story by Jacob Grimm and Wilhelm Grimm, illustrated by Gaynor Chapman; Hamilton, 1968. **Awarded:** Greenaway (honour) 1968.

Rotkappchen by Jacob Grimm and Wilhelm Grimm; Diogenes Verlag. **Awarded:** Bologna (Graphics for Children) 1974.

Rumpelstiltskin by Jacob Grimm and Wilhelm Grimm, adapted by Patricia Jones, illustrated by Jan B. Balet; Rand McNally, 1955. **Awarded:** New York Times Best Illustrated 1955.

The Seven Ravens by Jacob Grimm and Wilhelm Grimm, illustrated by Felix Hoffmann; Harcourt, 1963. **Awarded:** Spring Book Festival (picture book) 1963.

Snow White and the Seven Dwarfs by Jacob Grimm and Wilhelm Grimm, translated by Randall Jarrell, illustrated by Nancy Ekholm Burkert; Farrar, 1972. **Awarded:** Bologna (critici in erba) 1973; Caldecott (honor) 1973; Lewis Carroll Shelf 1973; New York Times Notable Books 1972.

Thorn Rose by Jacob Grimm and Wilhelm Grimm, illustrated by Errol Le Cain; Faber, 1975. **Awarded:** Greenaway (commended) 1975; International Board on Books for Young People (illustration/Great Britain) 1978.

The Twelve Dancing Princesses by Jacob Grimm and Wilhelm Grimm, illustrated by Errol Le Cain; Faber, 1978. **Awarded:** Greenaway (commended) 1978.

Die Wichtelmanner by Jacob Grimm and Wilhelm Grimm, illustrated by Katrin Brandt; Atlantis Verlag. **Awarded:** Bologna (Graphics for Children) 1968.

GRIMM, WILLIAM C.
Indian Harvests by William C. Grimm, illustrated by Ronald Himler; McGraw, 1974. **Awarded:** Children's Book Showcase 1975.

GRINDLEY, SALLY
Shhh! by Sally Grindley, illustrated by Peter Utton; ABC, 1991; Little Brown (Joy Street), 1992. **Awarded:** Children's Book Award (Picture Book) 1992.

Wake Up, Dad! by Sally Grindley, illustrated by Siobhan Dodds; Simon & Schuster (UK), 1988; Doubleday, 1989. **Awarded:** Best Books for Babies 1989.

GRINGHUIS, DIRK
Rainbow Round the World: A Story of UNICEF by Elizabeth Yates, illustrated by Dirk Gringhuis and Betty Alden; Bobbs-Merrill, 1954. **Awarded:** Jane Addams 1955.

GRIPE, HARALD
Glassblower's Children by Maria Gripe, translated by Sheila LaFarge, illustrated by Harald Gripe; Delacorte/Lawrence, 1973. **Awarded:** International Board on Books for Young People (translation/USA) 1978.

Pappa Pellerin's Daughter by Maria Gripe, translated by Kersti French, illustrated by Harald Gripe; Day, 1966. **Awarded:** Lewis Carroll Shelf 1966; Spring Book Festival (older honor) 1966.

GRIPE, MARIA
Awarded: Hans Christian Andersen (highly commended author/Sweden) 1972; Hans Christian Andersen (author) 1974.

Glassblower's Children by Maria Gripe, translated by Sheila La Farge, illustrated by Harald Gripe; Delacorte/Lawrence, 1973. **Awarded:** International Board on Books for Young People (translation/USA) 1978.

Pappa Pellerin's Daughter by Maria Gripe, translated by Kersti French, illustrated by Harald Gripe; Day, 1966. **Awarded:** Lewis Carroll Shelf 1966; Spring Book Festival (older honor) 1966.

GRISSOM, VIRGIL
Gemini: A Personal Account of Man's Venture into Space by Virgil Grissom, illustrated with photographs; Macmillan, 1968. **Awarded:** Indiana Authors Day (special award) 1969.

GRISWOLD, JEROME
Hans Brinker: Sunny World, Angry Waters by Jerome Griswold in Children's Literature 12 (1984). **Awarded:** Children's Literature Assn. Excellence in Criticism 1985.

GROCH, JUDITH
You and Your Brain by Judith Groch, illustrated by E. L. Sisley; Harper, 1963. **Awarded:** Edison Mass Media (best science book youth) 1964.

GROJEAN, JANET E.
Awarded: Lucile M. Pannell 1991.

GROOMS, RED
Rembrandt Takes a Walk by Mark Strand, illustrated by Red Grooms; Clarkson N. Potter, 1986. **Awarded:** New York Times Best Illustrated 1986.

GROPPER, WILLIAM
Hound Dog Moses and the Promised Land by Walter D. Edmonds, illustrated by William Gropper; Dodd, Mead, 1955. **Awarded:** Boys Club 1955.

Uncle Ben's Whale by Walter D. Edmonds, illustrated by William Gropper; Dodd, Mead, 1955. **Awarded:** New York Times Best Illustrated 1955.

GROSS, MICHAEL
Phil Sterling, Salesman by Michael Gross, not illustrated; Dodd, Mead, 1951. **Awarded:** Boys Club 1952.

GROSS, RUTH BELOV
Awarded: Lucky Book Club Four-Leaf Clover 1975.

GROSSER, MORTON
The Fabulous Fifty by Morton Grosser, not illustrated; Atheneum, 1990. **Awarded:** Commonwealth Club of California (ages 11-16) 1990.

GROSSMAN, NANCY
Did You Carry the Flag Today, Charley? by Rebecca Caudill, illustrated by Nancy Grossman; Holt, 1966. **Awarded:** Sue Hefly 1974.

GROSSMAN, PATRICIA
The Night Ones by Patricia Grossman, illustrated by Lydia Dabcovich; Harcourt Brace Jovanovich, 1991. **Awarded:** Parents' Choice (Picture Book) 1991.

GROSSMAN, ROBERT
The Eighteenth Emergency by Betsy Byars, illustrated by Robert Grossman; Viking, 1973. **Awarded:** Dorothy Canfield Fisher 1975.

GROSSMAN, VIRGINIA
Ten Little Rabbits by Virginia Grossman, illustrated by Sylvia Long; Chronicle Books, 1991. **Awarded:** International Reading Assn. (Younger) 1992; Redbook 1991.

GROTH, JOHN
The Life and Death of a Brave Bull by Maia Wojciechowska, illustrated by John Groth; Harcourt, 1972. **Awarded:** New Jersey Institute of Technology 1972.

GROVE, VICKI
Good-bye My Wishing Star by Vicki Grove, not illustrated Putnam, 1988. **Awarded:** Putnam's Fiction 1987.

GROVER, WAYNE
Dolphin Adventure: A True Story by Wayne Grover, illustrated by Jim Fowler; Greenwillow, 1990. **Awarded:** Book Can Develop Empathy 1991.

GRYSKI, CAMILLA
Hands On, Thumbs Up by Camilla Gryski, illustrated by Pat Cupples; Kids Can Press, 1990. **Awarded:** Information Book Award 1991.

GUARINO, DEBORAH
Is Your Mama a Llama? by Deborah Guarino, illustrated by Steven Kellogg; Scholastic, 1989. **Awarded:** New Jersey Institute of Technology 1990.

GUERTIK, HELENE
The Little French Farm by Lida Guertik, illustrated by Helene Guertik, translated by Louise Raymond; Harper, 1939. **Awarded:** Spring Book Festival (younger honor) 1939.

GUERTIK, LIDA
The Little French Farm by Lida Guertik, illustrated by Helene Guertik, translated by Louise Raymond; Harper, 1939. **Awarded:** Spring Book Festival (younger honor) 1939.

GUGGENHEIM, HANS
What Then, Raman? by Shirley Lease Arora, illustrated by Hans Guggenheim; Follett, 1960. **Awarded:** Jane Addams 1961; Charles W. Follett 1960; Woodward Park School 1961.

GUGGENMOS, JOSEF
Alle Meine Blatter by Irmgard Lucht, illustrated by Josef Guggenmos; Gertraud Middelhauve Verlag. **Awarded:** Bologna (critici in erba) 1971.

GUIBERSON, BRENDA Z.
Cactus Hotel by Brenda Z. Guiberson, illustrated by Megan Lloyd; Henry Holt, 1991. **Awarded:** Parents' Choice (Picture Book) 1991.

GUILFOILE, ELIZABETH
Nobody Listens to Andrew by Elizabeth Guilfoile, illustrated by Mary Stevens; Follett, 1957. **Awarded:** Follett Beginning to Read 1958.

GUILLOT, RENE
Awarded: Hans Christian Andersen 1964.

Grishka and the Bear by Rene Guillot, translated by Gwen Marsh, illustrated by Joan Kidell-Monroe; Criterion, 1959. **Awarded:** Boys Club 1961; Lewis Carroll Shelf 1961.

The Three Hundred and Ninety-Seventh White Elephant by Rene Guillot, translated by Gwen Marsh, illustrated by Moyra Leatham; Phillips, 1957. **Awarded:** Lewis Carroll Shelf 1958.

GULLEY, JUDIE
Rodeo Summer by Judie Gulley, not illustrated; Houghton Mifflin, 1984. **Awarded:** Friends of American Writers ($500) 1985.

GUNDERSHEIMER, KAREN
Some Things Go Together by Charlotte Zolotow, illustrated by Karen Gundersheimer; Crowell, 1983. **Awarded:** Carolyn W. Field 1984.

GUNEY, EFLATUN GEM
Dede Korkut Masallari by Eflatun Gem Guney, illustrated by Gunal Neset; Dogan Kardes, 1958. **Awarded:** Hans Christian Andersen (runnerup) 1960.

GUNN, JOHN
Sea Menace by John Gunn, illustrated by Brian Keogh; Constable, 1958. **Awarded:** Children's Book Council of Australia (book of the year) 1959.

GURASICH, MARJ
Letters To Oma: A Young German Girl's Account of Her First Year in Texas, 1847 by Marj Gurasich, illustrated by Barbara Whitehead; Texas Christian University Press, 1989. **Awarded:** Western Heritage 1990.

GURKO, LEO
Tom Paine: Freedom's Apostle by Leo Gurko, illustrated by Fritz Kredel; Crowell, 1957. **Awarded:** Newbery (honor) 1958; Spring Book Festival (older honor) 1957.

GUSTAFSON, ELTON T.
Portraits of Nobel Laureates in Medicine and Physiology by Elton Gustafson and Sarah Reidman, illustrated with photographs; Abelard-Schuman, 1964. **Awarded:** New Jersey Institute of Technology (biography ages 12-up) 1964.

GUTHRIE, ALFRED B., JR.
The Big Sky: An Edition for Younger Readers by Alfred B. Guthrie, Jr., illustrated by Jacob Landau; Sloane, 1950. **Awarded:** Boys Club 1951.

GUTHRIE, VEE
The High Pasture by Ruth P. Harnden, illustrated by Vee Guthrie; Houghton, 1964. **Awarded:** Child Study 1964.

GUY, ROSA
Awarded: Other Award 1987.

The Disappearance by Rosa Guy, not illustrated; Delacorte, 1979. **Awarded:** New York Times Notable Books 1979.

The Friends by Rosa Guy, not illustrated; Holt, 1973. **Awarded:** New York Times Notable Books 1973.

Mother Crocodile = Maman-Caiman by Birago Diop, translated and adapted by Rosa Guy, illustrated by John Steptoe; Delacorte, 1981. **Awarded:** Coretta Scott King (illustrator) 1982.

New Guys Around the Block by Rosa Guy, not illustrated; Delacorte, 1983. **Awarded:** Parents' Choice (literature) 1983.

GYNELL, DONNA
Arthur by Amanda Graham, illustrated by Donna Gynell; Spindlewood, 1985; Keystone Picture Books, 1984. **Awarded:** Children's Book Award 1985.

H

HAAS, DOROTHY
Awarded: Children's Reading Round Table 1979.

The Secret Life of Dilly McBean by Dorothy Haas, not illustrated; Bradbury, 1986. **Awarded:** Edgar Allan Poe (runnerup) 1987.

HAAS, IRENE
Carrie Hepple's Garden by Ruth Craft, illustrated by Irene Haas; McElderry, 1979. **Awarded:** Owl Prize 1980.

A Little House of Your Own by Beatrice Schenk de Regniers, illustrated by Irene Haas; Harcourt, 1955. **Awarded:** New York Times Best Illustrated 1955; Spring Book Festival (ages 4-8 honor) 1955.

The Maggie B written and illustrated by Irene Haas; Atheneum, 1975. **Awarded:** Irma Simonton Black 1975; Children's Book Showcase 1976; Owl Prize 1977.

Tatsinda by Elizabeth Enright, illustrated by Irene Haas; Harcourt, 1963. **Awarded:** Spring Book Festival (middle honor) 1963.

Was It a Good Trade? by Beatrice Schenk de Regniers, illustrated by Irene Haas; Harcourt, 1956. **Awarded:** New York Times Best Illustrated 1956.

HAAS, MERLE
Babar's Fair Will Be Opened Next Sunday written and illustrated by Laurent de Brunhoff, translated by Merle Haas; Random House, 1954. **Awarded:** New York Times Best Illustrated 1956.

The Story of Babar, the Little Elephant written and illustrated by Jean de Brunhoff, translated by Merle Haas; Random House, 1933. **Awarded:** Lewis Carroll Shelf 1959.

HAAS, SHELLY O.
Daddy's Chair by Sandy Lanton, illustrated by Shelly O. Haas; KarBen Copies, 1991. **Awarded:** Sydney Taylor Book Award (Picture Book) 1992.

HABENSTREIT, BARBARA
Men Against War by Barbara Habenstreit, not illustrated; Doubleday, 1973. **Awarded:** Jane Addams (honor) 1974.

HABER, HEINZ
Stars, Men and Atoms by Heinz Haber, illustrated with photographs and diagrams; Golden Press, 1962. **Awarded:** Edison Mass Media (science book) 1963.

The Walt Disney Story of Our Friend the Atom by Heinz Haber, illustrated by Walt Disney Studios; Simon, 1957. **Awarded:** Spring Book Festival (middle honor) 1957.

HADER, BERTA HOERNER
The Big Snow written and illustrated by Berta Hader and Elmer Hader; Macmillan, 1948. **Awarded:** Caldecott 1949.

Cock-a-Doodle-Doo written and illustrated by Berta Hader and Elmer Hader; Macmillan, 1939. **Awarded:** Caldecott (honor) 1940.

Mighty Hunter written and illustrated by Berta Hader and Elmer Hader; Macmillan, 1943. **Awarded:** Caldecott (honor) 1944.

HADER, ELMER STANLEY
The Big Snow written and illustrated by Berta Hader and Elmer Hader; Macmillan, 1948. **Awarded:** Caldecott 1949.

Cock-a-Doodle-Doo written and illustrated by Berta Hader and Elmer Hader; Macmillan, 1939. **Awarded:** Caldecott (honor) 1940.

Down Ryton Water by Eva Roe Gaggin, illustrated by Elmer Hader; Viking, 1941. **Awarded:** Newbery (honor) 1942.

Mighty Hunter written and illustrated by Berta Hader and Elmer Hader; Macmillan, 1943. **Awarded:** Caldecott (honor) 1944.

HADITHI, MWENYE
Crafty Chameleon by Mwenye Hadithi, illustrated by Adrienne Kennaway; Hodder & Stoughton, 1987; Little Brown, 1987. **Awarded:** Greenaway 1987.

HAEMER, ALAN
Phantom on Skis by Helen Girvan, illustrated by Alan Haemer; Farrar, 1939. **Awarded:** Spring Book Festival (older honor) 1939.

HAFF, JAMES E.
Awarded: L. Frank Baum 1967.

HAFNER, MARYLIN
Bonnie Bess: The Weathervane Horse by Alvin Tresselt, illustrated by Marylin Hafner; Lothrop, 1949. **Awarded:** Spring Book Festival (younger) 1949.

Hannukkah by Roni Schotter, illustrated by Marylin Hafner; Little Brown, 1990. **Awarded:** Jewish Book Council (Children's Picture Book) 1991.

M&M and the Bad News Babies by Pat Ross, illustrated by Marylin Hafner; Knopf, 1983. **Awarded:** Garden State Children's Book Award (easy to read) 1986.

Mrs. Gaddy and the Ghost by Wilson Gage, illustrated by Marylin Hafner; Greenwillow, 1979. **Awarded:** Garden State Children's (easy to read) 1982.

Sunlight by Sally Cartwright, illustrated by Marylin Hafner; Coward, 1974. **Awarded:** New York Academy of Sciences (younger honor) 1975.

HAGENDOREN, ELZAVAN
Manko Kapak by Lo Vermeulen and Karel Jeuninckx, illustrated by Elzavan Hagendoren; De Sikkel, 1957. **Awarded:** Hans Christian Andersen (runnerup) 1960.

HAGER, ALICE ROGERS
A Canvas Castle by Alice Rogers Hager, illustrated by Mary Stevens; Messner, 1949. **Awarded:** Julia Ellsworth Ford 1948.

HAGUE, MICHAEL
The Frog Princess by Elizabeth Isele, illustrated by Michael Hague; Crowell, 1984. **Awarded:** Parents' Choice (literature) 1984.

The Unicorn and the Lake by Marianna Mayer, illustrated by Michael Hague; Dial, 1982. **Awarded:** Colorado 1984; Georgia Children's Picture Storybook 1986; Washington Children's Choice 1986.

HAHN, EMILY
Francie by Emily Hahn, not illustrated; Watts, 1951. **Awarded:** Spring Book Festival (older honor) 1951.

HAHN, MARY DOWNING
Daphne's Book by Mary Downing Hahn, not illustrated; Clarion, 1983. **Awarded:** William Allen White 1986.

The Dead Man in Indian Creek by Mary Downing Hahn, not illustrated; Clarion, 1989. **Awarded:** Ethical Culture School 1990.

December Stillness by Mary Downing Hahn, not illustrated; Clarion, 1988. **Awarded:** Addams (Fiction Ages 10-14 Honor) 1989; California Young Reader (Middle/Junior High) 1991; Child Study 1988.

The Doll in the Garden by Mary Downing Hahn, illustrated; Clarion, 1989. **Awarded:** Maryland 1991; Sequoyah Children's 1992; South Dakota Prairie Pasque 1992; Mark Twain 1992; Virginia Young Readers (Elementary) 1992; William Allen White 1992.

Stepping on the Cracks by Mary Downing Hahn, illustrated with a map; Clarion, 1991. **Awarded:** CRABbery 1992; Scott O'Dell 1991; Sugarman Children's Book Award 1992.

Wait Til Helen Comes by Mary Downing Hahn, not illustrated; Clarion, 1986. **Awarded:** Caudill Young Reader's Book Award 1990; Dorothy Canfield Fisher 1988; Golden Sower (grades 4-6) 1990; Iowa Children's Choice 1990; Maud Hart Lovelace 1990; Texas Bluebonnet 1989; Utah Children's 1988; Virginia Young Readers (Elementary) 1989; Volunteer State Book Awards (grades 4-6) 1989; Young Hoosier (Grades 6-8) 1989; Young Reader's Choice 1989.

HAIG-BROWN, RODERICK
Awarded: Vicky Metcalf 1965.

Starbuck Valley Winter by Roderick Haig-Brown, illustrated by Charles De Feo; Morrow, 1943; Collins, 1944. **Awarded:** Canadian Library Assn. 1947.

The Whale People by Roderick Haig-Brown, illustrated by Mary Weiler; Collins Canada, 1962. **Awarded:** Canadian Library Assn. 1964.

HAILES, JULIA
The Young Green Consumer Guide by Julia Hailes and John Elkington, illustrated by Tony Ross; Gollancz, 1990. **Awarded:** Earthworm Award 1990.

HAINES, GAIL KAY
Micromysteries: Stories of Scientific Detection by Gail Kay Haines, illustrated with photos; Dodd, Mead, 1988. **Awarded:** American Institute of Physics 1989.

HALDANE, ROGER
Blue Fin by Colin Thiele, illustrated by Roger Haldane; Rigby, 1969. **Awarded:** International Board on Books for Young People (honour list/Australia) 1972.

The Magpie Island by Colin Thiele, illustrated by Roger Haldane; Rigby, 1975. **Awarded:** Children's Book Council of Australia (best illustrated) 1975.

HALE, LUCRETIA
The Lady Who Put Salt in Her Coffee by Lucretia Hale, adapted and illustrated by Amy Schwartz; Harcourt Brace Jovanovich, 1989. **Awarded:** Parents' Choice (Picture Book) 1989.

HALES, ROBERT
The Devil's Children by Peter Dickinson, illustrated by Robert Hales; Gollancz, 1970. **Awarded:** Carnegie (honour) 1970.

HALEY, GAIL EINHART
Awarded: Kerlan Award 1989.

The Green Man written and illustrated by Gail E. Haley; Scribner, 1980. **Awarded:** Parents Choice (illustration) 1980.

The Post Office Cat written and illustrated by Gail E. Haley; Bodley Head, 1976. **Awarded:** Greenaway 1976.

A Story, a Story written and illustrated by Gail E. Haley; Atheneum, 1970. **Awarded:** Boston Globe Horn Book (illustration honor) 1970; Caldecott 1971.

HALKIN, HILLEL
The Island on Bird Street by Uri Orlev, translated by Hillel Halkin, not illustrated; Houghton Mifflin, 1984. **Awarded:** Jane Addams (honor) 1985; Batchelder 1985; Edgar Allan Poe (runnerup) 1985; Sydney Taylor Book (older) 1985.

HALL, ADELE
Seashore Summer by Adele Hall, not illustrated; Harper, 1962. **Awarded:** New Jersey Institute of Technology (ages 14-up) 1962.

HALL, ANNA GERTRUDE
Nansen by Anna Gertrude Hall, illustrated by Boris Artzybasheff; Viking, 1940. **Awarded:** Newbery (honor) 1941; Spring Book Festival (older honor) 1940.

HALL, BARBARA
Dixie Storms by Barbara Hall, not illustrated; Harcourt Brace Jovanovich, 1990. **Awarded:** Southern California Council (Distinguished Work of Fiction for Young Adults) 1991.

HALL, DONALD ANDREW
Ox-Cart Man by Donald Hall, illustrated by Barbara Cooney; Viking, 1979. **Awarded:** Caldecott 1980; New York Times Best Illustrated 1979; New York Times Notable Books 1979.

HALL, DOUGLAS
The Pit by Reginald Maddock, illustrated by Douglas Hall; Little, 1968. **Awarded:** Spring Book Festival (older honor) 1968.

HALL, H. TOM
The Mystery of the Haunted Pool by Phyllis A. Whitney, illustrated by H. Tom Hall; Westminster, 1960. **Awarded:** Edgar Allan Poe 1961; Sequoyah 1963.

The Mystery of the Hidden Hand by Phyllis A. Whitney, illustrated by H. Tom Hall; Westminster, 1963. **Awarded:** Edgar Allan Poe 1964.

HALL, JOHN A.
Glooskap's Country and Other Indian Tales by Cyrus Macmillan, illustrated by John A. Hall; Oxford, 1956. **Awarded:** Canadian Library Assn. 1957.

The Great Chief: Maskepetoon, Warrior of the Crees by Kerry Wood, illustrated by John A. Hall; Macmillan Canada, 1957. **Awarded:** Governor-General's Literary Award 1957.

HALL, KATY
Magic in the Movies: The Story of Special Effects by Katy Hall and Jane O'Connor; illustrated with photographs; Doubleday, 1980. **Awarded:** New York Academy of Sciences (older honor) 1981.

HALL, LYNN
A Horse Called Dragon by Lynn Hall, illustrated by Joseph Cellini; Follett, 1971. **Awarded:** Charles W. Follett 1972.

In Trouble Again, Zelda Hammersmith? by Lynn Hall, not illustrated; Harcourt Brace Jovanovich, 1987. **Awarded:** Emphasis on Reading (grades 3-5) 1989-90.

The Leaving by Lynn Hall, not illustrated; Scribner, 1980. **Awarded:** Boston Globe Horn Book (fiction) 1981.

Mrs. Portree's Pony by Lynn Hall, not illustrated; Scribners, 1986. **Awarded:** Society of Midland Authors 1987.

Shadows by Lynn Hall, illustrated by Joseph Cellini; Follett, 1977. **Awarded:** Volunteer State 1981.

The Solitary by Lynn Hall, not illustrated; Scribner, 1986. **Awarded:** Golden Kite (fiction honor) 1986.

The Whispered Horse by Lynn Hall, not illustrated; Follett, 1979. **Awarded:** Edgar Allan Poe (runnerup) 1980.

HALL, PAM
Down by Jim Long's Stage: Rhymes for Children and Young Fish by Al Pittman, illustrated by Pam Hall; Breakwater, 1976. **Awarded:** Amelia Frances Howard-Gibbon 1977.

HALL, ROGER
My Aunt Mary Went Shopping by Roger Hall, illustrated by Trevor Pye; Ashton Scholastic, 1991. **Awarded:** AIM Children's Book Award (Picture Book 2nd Prize) 1992.

HALL-QUEST, OLGA W.
Conquistadores and Pueblos: The Story of the American Southwest 1540-1848 by Olga W. Hall-Quest, illustrated by Marian Ebert; Dutton, 1969. **Awarded:** Western Writers (nonfiction) 1970.

HALLER, ADOLF
Der Page Orteguill by Adolf Haller, illustrated by Felix Hoffmann; Sauerlander, 1960. **Awarded:** Hans Christian Andersen (runnerup) 1962.

HALLOCK, GRACE T.
The Boy Who Was by Grace T. Hallock, illustrated by Harrie Wood; Dutton, 1928. **Awarded:** Newbery (honor) 1929.

HALLOCK, ROBERT
Sandy by Elizabeth Janet Gray, illustrated by Robert Hallock; Viking, 1945. **Awarded:** Spring Book Festival (older) 1945.

HALLOWELL, PRISCILLA
The Long-Nosed Princess by Priscilla Hallowell, illustrated by Rita Fava; Viking, 1959. **Awarded:** Spring Book Festival (middle) 1959.

HALPERN, JOAN
The Carp in the Bathtub by Barbara Cohen, illustrated by Joan Halpern; Lothrop, 1972. **Awarded:** New Jersey Institute of Technology 1972.

Where's Florrie? by Barbara Cohen, illustrated by Joan Halpern; Lothrop, 1976. **Awarded:** New Jersey Institute of Technology 1977.

HALVERSON, LYDIA
Apatosaurus by Janet Riehecky, illustrated by Lydia Halverson; Child's World, 1988. **Awarded:** Society of Midland Authors (Juvenile Nonfiction) 1989.

HALVORSON, MARILYN
Cowboys Don't Cry by Marilyn Halvorson, not illustrated; Clarke Irwin, 1984; Delacorte, 1985. **Awarded:** Alberta Writing for Youth 1982.

Nobody Said it Would be Easy by Marilyn Halvorson, not illustrated; Clark Irwin, 1987. **Awarded:** R. Ross Annett 1988.

HAMANAKA, SHEILA
Class Clown by Johanna Hurwitz, illustrated by Sheila Hamanaka; Morrow, 1987. **Awarded:** Kentucky Bluegrass (grades 4-8) 1989; Mississippi Children's Book Award 1989; South Carolina Children's 1990; West Virginia Children's 1988-89.

The Journey: Japanese Americans, Racism and Renewal written and illustrated by Sheila Hamanaka; Orchard, 1990. **Awarded:** Jane Addams (Honor) 1991.

Teacher's Pet by Johanna Hurwitz, illustrated by Sheila Hamanaka; Morrow, 1988. **Awarded:** Garden State Children's (Younger Fiction) 1991; Sunshine State Young Reader's Award (grades 3-5) 1990.

HAMBERGER, JOHN F.
Vanishing Wings: A Tale of Three Birds of Prey by Griffing Bancroft, illustrated by John Hamberger; Watts, 1972. **Awarded:** Christopher (teenage) 1973.

HAMIL, TOM
Joseph Strauss: Builder of the Golden Gate Bridge by Michael Chester, illustrated by Tom Hamil; Putnam, 1965. **Awarded:** Boys Club (certificate) 1966-67.

HAMILTON, CAROL
The Dawn Seekers by Carol Hamilton, illustrated by Abby Levine; Whitman, 1987. **Awarded:** Southwest 1988.

HAMILTON, GAIL
see CORCORAN, BARBARA

HAMILTON, RUSSEL
The Listening Man by Lucy Embury, illustrated by Russel Hamilton; Messner, 1940. **Awarded:** Julia Ellsworth Ford 1940.

HAMILTON, VIRGINIA
Awarded: Hans Christian Andersen (Author) 1992; Ohioana (body of work) 1984; Ohioana (Alice L. Wood Memorial) 1992; Ohioana Award for Children's Literature (Career Medal) 1992; Regina Medal 1990.

Anthony Burns: The Defeat and Triumph of a Fugitive Slave by Virginia Hamilton, not illustrated; Knopf, 1988. **Awarded:** Addams (Fictionalized Biography Ages 11-up) 1989; Boston Globe (Nonfiction) 1988; Jefferson Cup 1989; Coretta Scott King (Text honor) 1989.

The Bells of Christmas by Virginia Hamilton, illustrated by Lambert Davis; Harcourt Brace Jovanovich, 1989. **Awarded:** Coretta Scott King (Text honor) 1990.

Cousins by Virginia Hamilton, not illustrated; Philomel, 1990. **Awarded:** Reading Magic Award 1990.

Drylongso by Virginia Hamilton, illustrated by Brian Pinkney; Harcourt Brace Jovanovich, 1992. **Awarded:** Reading Magic Award 1992.

The House of Dies Drear by Virginia Hamilton, illustrated by Eros Keith; Macmillan, 1968. **Awarded:** Ohioana 1969; Edgar Allan Poe 1969.

In the Beginning: Creation Stories from Around the World by Virginia Hamilton, illustrated by Barry Moser; Harcourt Brace Jovanovich, 1988. **Awarded:** Newbery (Honor) 1989.

Junius Over Far by Virginia Hamilton, not illustrated; Harper, 1985. **Awarded:** Coretta Scott King (literature honorable mention) 1986.

Little Love by Virginia Hamilton, not illustrated; Philomel, 1984. **Awarded:** Coretta Scott King (literature honorable mention) 1985.

M. C. Higgins, the Great by Virginia Hamilton, not illustrated; Macmillan, 1974. **Awarded:** Boston Globe Horn Book (text) 1974; Lewis Carroll Shelf 1976; International Board on Books for Young People (text/USA) 1976; National Book Award 1975; New York Times Notable Books 1974; Newbery 1975.

The Magical Adventures of Pretty Pearl by Virginia Hamilton, not illustrated; Harper, 1983. **Awarded:** Coretta Scott King (honorable mention) 1984; Parents' Choice (literature) 1983.

The People Could Fly: American Black Folktales by Virginia Hamilton, illustrated by Leo and Diane Dillon; Knopf, 1985. **Awarded:** International Board on Books for Young People (illustration/USA) 1986; Coretta Scott King (illustration honorable mention) 1986; Coretta Scott King (literature) 1986; New York Times Best Illustrated 1985; New York Times Notable 1985; Other Award 1986.

The Planet of Junior Brown by Virginia Hamilton, not illustrated; Macmillan, 1971. **Awarded:** Lewis Carroll Shelf 1972; National Book Award (finalist) 1972; Newbery (honor) 1972.

Sweet Whispers, Brother Rush by Virginia Hamilton, not illustrated; Philomel, 1982. **Awarded:** Boston Globe Horn Book (fiction) 1983; International Board on Books for Young People (writing/USA) 1984; Coretta Scott King (author) 1983; New York Times Notable Books 1982; Newbery (honor) 1983.

Time-Ago Lost: More Tales of Jahdu by Virginia Hamilton, illustrated by Ray Prather; Macmillan, 1973. **Awarded:** Spring Book Festival (middle honor) 1973.

Zeely by Virginia Hamilton, illustrated by Symeon Shimin; Macmillan, 1967. **Awarded:** Nancy Bloch 1967.

HAMM, DIANE JOHNSTON
Bunkhouse Journal by Diane Johnston Hamm, not illustrated; Scribner, 1990. **Awarded:** Western Heritage 1991.

HAMPSHIRE, MICHAEL
Cow for Jaya by Eva Grant, illustrated by Michael Hampshire; Coward, 1973. **Awarded:** New Jersey Institute of Technology 1973.

The Secret of the Brownstone House by Norah A. Smaridge, illustrated by Michael Hampshire; Dodd, 1977. **Awarded:** New Jersey Institute of Technology 1978.

HANCOCK, RALPH
Supermachines by Ralph Hancock, edited by Toni Palumbo, illustrated with photographs and diagrams; Viking, 1978. **Awarded:** New York Academy of Sciences (special award for series on engineering and technology) 1979.

HANDFORD, MARTIN
Where's Waldo? written and illustrated by Martin Handford; Little Brown, 1987. **Awarded:** Arizona 1991.

Where's Wally? written and illustrated by Martin Handford; Walker Books, 1987. **Awarded:** Books I Love Best Yearly (Read Aloud Secondary) 1992; Mother Goose (runner-up) 1988.

HANDFORTH, THOMAS S.
Mei Li written and illustrated by Thomas Handforth; Doubleday, Doran, 1938. **Awarded:** Caldecott 1939.

The Secret of the Porcelain Fish by Margaret Everden, illustrated by Thomas Handforth; Random House, 1947. **Awarded:** Spring Book Festival (middle honor) 1947.

HANDVILLE, ROBERT
Missouri River Boy by William Heuman, illustrated by Robert Handville; Dodd Mead, 1959. **Awarded:** Boys Life - Dodd, Mead 1958.

The Mysteries in the Commune by Norah Smaridge, illustrated by Robert Handville; Dodd Mead, 1982. **Awarded:** New Jersey Institute of Technology 1983.

This Was Bridget by Mary Malone, illustrated by Robert Handville; Dodd Mead, 1960. **Awarded:** Edith Busby 1959.

HANEY, LYNN
Ride 'Em Cowgirl by Lynn Haney, photographs by Peter Burchard; Putnam, 1975. **Awarded:** Western Writers (non-fiction) 1975.

HANFF, PETER E.
Awarded: L. Frank Baum 1973.

HANI, SHABO
Cactus by Cynthia Overbeck, photographs by Shabo Hani; Lerner, 1982. **Awarded:** New York Academy of Sciences (special award) 1983.

How Seeds Travel by Cynthia Overbeck, photographs by Shabo Hani; Lerner, 1982. **Awarded:** New York Academy of Sciences (special award) 1983.

HANKEY, PETER
The Great Song Book by Timothy John, music edited by Peter Hankey, illustrated by Tomi Ungerer; Doubleday, 1978. **Awarded:** New York Times Best Illustrated 1978.

HANLEY, BONIFACE
No Strangers to Violence, No Strangers to Love by Boniface Hanley, illustrated with photos; Ave Maria Press, 1983. **Awarded:** Catholic Book Awards (Youth) 1984.

HANLEY, LUCEILLE
How Casbo Became a Clown by Luceille Hanley. **Awarded:** Mary Grant Bruce ($500) 1986.

HANNA, CHERYL
An Enchanted Hair Tale by Alexis De Veaux, illustrated by Cheryl Hanna; Harper & Row, 1987. **Awarded:** Coretta Scott King (Text honor) 1988.

HANNA, WAYNE A.
What Happens When We Die? by Carolyn Nystrom, illustrated by Wayne A. Hanna; Moody Press, 1981. **Awarded:** Gold Medallion (co- winner) 1982.

HANNUM, HILDEGARDE
Thou Shalt not be Aware: Society's Betrayal of the Child by Alice Miller, not illustrated, translated by Hildegarde Hannum and Hunter Hannum; Farrar, 1984. **Awarded:** Korczak (about children) 1986.

HANNUM, HUNTER
Thou Shalt not be Aware: Society's Betrayal of the Child by Alice Miller, not illustrated, translated by Hildegarde Hannum and Hunter Hannum; Farrar, 1984. **Awarded:** Korczak (about children) 1986.

HANNUM, SARA
Lean Out of the Window: An Anthology of Modern Poetry compiled by Sara Hannum and Gwendolyn E. Reed, illustrated by Ragna Tischler; Atheneum, 1965. **Awarded:** Spring Book Festival (middle honor) 1965.

HANO, ARNOLD
Willie Mays by Arnold Hano, not illustrated; Grosset, 1966. **Awarded:** Boys Club (certificate) 1966-67.

HANSEN, JOYCE
Which Way Freedom? by Joyce Hansen, not illustrated; Walker, 1986. **Awarded:** Coretta Scott King (literature honorable mention) 1987.

Yellow Bird and Me by Joyce Hansen, not illustrated; Clarion Books, 1986. **Awarded:** Parents Choice (literature) 1986.

HANSEN, MICHAEL
Inigo: The Adventures of a Saint by Michael Hansen, illustrated by Tibor David; Lovell, 1991. **Awarded:** Australian Christian Book of the Year Children's 1992.

HANSEN, RON
The Shadowmaker by Ron Hansen, illustrated by Margot Tomes; Harper, 1987. **Awarded:** New York Times Notable 1987.

HANSON, JOSEPH E.
Hong Kong Altar Boy by Joseph E. Hanson, not illustrated; Bruce, 1965. **Awarded:** New Jersey Institute of Technology 1965.

HANSON, PETER E.
Walking the Road to Freedom: A Story about Sojourner Truth by Jeri Ferris, illustrated by Peter E. Hanson; Carolrhoda, 1988. **Awarded:** Woodson (Elementary) 1989.

HARBOUR, ELIZABETH
A Gardener's Alphabet written and illustrated by Elizabeth Harbour; Michael Joseph, 1990. **Awarded:** Macmillan Prize (2nd Prize) 1988.

HARDING, LEE
Displaced Person by Lee Harding, not illustrated; Hyland House, 1979. (Published in the U.S. as *Misplaced Persons*). **Awarded:** Children's Book Council of Australia (book of the year) 1980.

HARGENS, CHARLES
Cowboy Boots by Doris Shannon Garst, illustrated by Charles Hargens; Abingdon, 1946. **Awarded:** Young Readers Choice 1949.

Stocky, Boy of West Texas by Elizabeth Baker, illustrated by Charles Hargens; Winston, 1945. **Awarded:** Spring Book Festival (older honor) 1945.

Towards Oregon by E. H. Staffelbach, illustrated by Charles Hargens; Macrae Smith, 1946. **Awarded:** Commonwealth Club of California 1946.

HARGREAVES, BRIAN
Butterflies on My Mind: Their Life and Conservation in Britain Today by Dulcie Gray, illustrated by Brian Hargreaves; Angus & Robertson, 1978. **Awarded:** Times Educational Supplement (senior) 1978.

HARLAN, ELIZABETH
Footfalls by Elizabeth Harlan, not illustrated; Atheneum, 1982. **Awarded:** New Jersey Institute of Technology 1983.

HARLAN, JUDITH
American Indians Today: Issues and Conflicts by Judith Harlan, illustrated with photos; Watts, 1987. **Awarded:** Woodson (Outstanding Merit) 1988.

Hispanic Voters: A Voice in American Politics by Judith Harlan, illustrated with photos; Watts, 1988. **Awarded:** Woodson (Outstanding Merit - Secondary) 1989.

HARMETZ, ALJEAN
Awarded: L. Frank Baum 1982.

HARNDEN, RUTH P.
The High Pasture by Ruth P. Harnden, illustrated by Vee Guthrie; Houghton, 1964. **Awarded:** Child Study 1964.

HARNESS, CHERYL
Fudge by Charlotte T. Graeber, illustrated by Cheryl Harness; Lothrop, Lee & Shepard, 1987. **Awarded:** Iowa Children's Choice 1992; KC Three 1989-90; Nene Award 1990; Sequoyah Children's 1990; Sunshine State (grades 3-5) 1992; West Virginia Children's 1989-90; Young Hoosier (Grades 4-6) 1990.

HARNETT, CYNTHIA
The Drawbridge Gate written and illustrated by Cynthia Harnett; Putnam, 1953. **Awarded:** Spring Book Festival (older honor) 1954.

The Load of the Unicorn written and illustrated by Cynthia Harnett; Methuen, 1959. (Published in the U.S. as *Caxton's Challenge*; World, 1960). **Awarded:** Carnegie (commended) 1959.

The Wool-Pack written and illustrated by Cynthia Harnett; Methuen, 1951. **Awarded:** Carnegie 1951.

The Writing on the Hearth by Cynthia Harnett, illustrated by Gareth Floyd; Viking, 1973. **Awarded:** Spring Book Festival (older honor) 1973.

HARPER, ARTHUR
Sea Boots by Robert C. DuSoe, illustrated by Arthur Harper; Longmans, 1949. **Awarded:** Spring Book Festival (under 12 honor) 1949.

HARPER, EON
National Mathematics Project: Mathematics for Secondary Schools Year 5 by Eon Harper, illustrated; Longman, 1990. **Awarded:** Times Educational Supplement (Schoolbook) 1990.

HARPER, MARTHA BARNHART
Bittersweet by Martha Barnhart Harper, illustrated by Erick Berry; Longmans, 1948. **Awarded:** Spring Book Festival (older honor) 1948.

HARRAH, MADGE
Honey Girl by Madge Harrah, illustrated; Avon, 1990. **Awarded:** Western Writers of America Spur (Juvenile Fiction) 1991.

HARRANTH, WOLF
Am Ende der Spur by Roy Brown, translated by Wolf Harranth; Benziger und Jungbrunner, 1981. **Awarded:** International Board on Books for Young People (translation/Austria) 1982.

Ganesh Oder Eine Neue Welt by Malcom J. Bosse (original English: *Ganesh*) translated by Wolf Harranth; Jungbrunner, 1982. **Awarded:** International Board on Books for Young People (translation/Austria) 1984.

HARRINGTON, LYN DAVIS
Awarded: Vicky Metcalf 1975.

HARRIS, CHRISTIE LUCY IRWIN
Awarded: Vicky Metcalf 1973.

Mouse Woman and the Vanished Princesses by Christie Harris, illustrated by Douglas Tait; McClelland & Stewart, 1976. **Awarded:** Canadian Library Assn. 1977; International Board on Books for Young People (honour list/text/Canada) 1978.

Once Upon a Totem by Christie Harris, illustrated by John Frazer Mills; Atheneum, 1963. **Awarded:** New York Times Best Illustrated 1963.

Raven's Cry by Christie Harris, illustrated by Bill Reid; McClelland & Stewart, 1966. **Awarded:** Canadian Library Assn. 1967.

The Trouble with Princesses by Christie Harris, illustrated by Douglas Tait; McClelland & Stewart, 1980; Atheneum, 1980. **Awarded:** Canadian Library Assn. (runnerup) 1981; Governor General (author) 1980; Amelia Frances Howard-Gibbon 1981.

HARRIS, JAMES E.
X-raying the Pharoahs by James E. Harris and Kent R. Weeks, illustrated with photographs; Scribner, 1973. **Awarded:** New York Academy of Sciences (older honor) 1974.

HARRIS, JANET
Thursday's Daughters: The Story of Women Working in America by Janet Harris, illustrated with photographs; Harper, 1977. **Awarded:** New Jersey Institute of Technology 1978.

HARRIS, JOEL CHANDLER
Further Tales of Uncle Remus by Joel Chandler Harris, adapted by Julius Lester, illustrated by Jerry Pinkney; Dial, 1990. **Awarded:** Parents Choice (Story book) 1990.

Jump Again! More Adventures of Brer Rabbit by Joel Chandler Harris, adapted by Van Dyke Parks, illustrated by Barry Moser; Harcourt Brace Jovanovich, 1987. **Awarded:** Biennale Illustrations Bratislava (honorable mention) 1989; New York Times Best Illustrated 1987; Redbook 1987.

More Tales of Uncle Remus: Further Adventures of Brer Rabbit by Joel Chandler Harris, adapted by Julius Lester, illustrated by Jerry Pinkney; Dial, 1988. **Awarded:** Reading Magic 1988.

The Tales of Uncle Remus by Joel Chandler Harris, adapted by Julius Lester, illustrated by Jerry Pinkney; Dial, 1987. **Awarded:** Coretta Scott King (Text honor) 1988; Parents Choice (Storybook) 1987.

Uncle Remus: His Songs and Sayings by Joel Chandler Harris, illustrated by A. B. Frost; Hawthorne, 1921, c1880. **Awarded:** Lewis Carroll Shelf 1963.

HARRIS, LEON
The Great Picture Robbery by Leon Harris, illustrated by Joseph Schindelman; Atheneum, 1963. **Awarded:** New York Times Best Illustrated 1963.

HARRIS, MARILYN

Hatter Fox by Marilyn Harris; Bantam, 1974. **Awarded:** Media & Methods (paperback) 1975.

The Runaway's Diary by Marilyn Harris, not illustrated; Four Winds, 1971. **Awarded:** Lewis Carroll Shelf 1973.

HARRIS, MARK JONATHAN

Come the Morning by Mark Jonathan Harris, not illustrated; Bradbury, 1989. **Awarded:** FOCAL 1990.

The Last Run by Mark Jonathan Harris, not illustrated; Lothrop, 1981. **Awarded:** Western Writers (juvenile fiction) 1981.

HARRIS, MARY KATHLEEN

The Bus Girls by Mary Kathleen Harris, illustrated by Eileen Green; Faber, 1965. **Awarded:** Carnegie (commended) 1965.

HARRIS, PETER

Monkey and the Three Wizards by Cheng-en Wu, translated by Peter Harris, illustrated by Michael Foreman; Collins, 1976. **Awarded:** W. H. Smith (£50) 1977.

HARRIS, ROSEMARY JEANNE

Green Finger House by Rosemary Harris, illustrated by Juan Wijngaard; Eel Pie, 1980. **Awarded:** Mother Goose 1981.

The Moon in the Cloud by Rosemary Harris, not illustrated; Faber, 1968; Macmillan, 1970. **Awarded:** Carnegie 1968; Spring Book Festival (older honor) 1970.

HARRIS, THOMAS

I'm OK, You're OK: A Practical Guide to Transactional Analysis by Thomas Harris, not illustrated; Avon, 1973. **Awarded:** Media & Methods (paperback) 1974.

HARRISON, BARBARA

A Twilight Struggle: The Life of John Fitzgerald Kennedy by Barbara Harrison and Daniel Terris, illustrated; Lothrop, Lee & Shepard, 1992. **Awarded:** Parents Choice (Picture Book) 1992.

HARRISON, DAVID L.

The Book of Giant Stories by David L. Harrison, illustrated by Philippe Fix; New York American Heritage Press, 1972. **Awarded:** Christopher (ages 8-12) 1973.

HARRISON, RICHARD EDES

Within the Circle by Evelyn Stefansson illustrated by Richard Edes Harrison; Scribner, 1945. **Awarded:** Spring Book Festival (older honor) 1945.

HARRISON, TED

The Cremation of Sam McGee by Robert W. Service, illustrated by Ted Harrison; Greenwillow, 1987. **Awarded:** New York Times Best Illustrated 1987; Parents' Choice (Picture Book) 1987.

A Northern Alphabet written and illustrated by Ted Harrison; Tundra, 1982. **Awarded:** Amelia Frances Howard-Gibbon (runnerup) 1983; International Board on Books for Young People (illustration/Canada) 1984.

HARSHAW, RUTH

Awarded: Children's Reading Round Table 1957.

HART, CAROLYN G.

The Secret of the Cellars by Carolyn G. Hart, not illustrated; Dodd Mead, 1964. **Awarded:** Calling All Girls - Dodd, Mead 1964.

HART, DICK

The Warden's Niece by Gillian Elise Avery, illustrated by Dick Hart; Collins, 1957. **Awarded:** Carnegie (commended) 1957.

HART-DAVIS, ADAM

Scientific Eye by Adam Hart-Davis; Bell & Hyman, 1986. **Awarded:** Times Educational Supplement (schoolbook) 1986.

HARTAS, LEO

Captain Bilgerbelly's Treasure by Leo Hartas; to be published by Macmillan. **Awarded:** Macmillan (3rd prize) 1987.

HARTELIUS, MARGARET

The Birthday Trombone written and illustrated by Margaret Hartelius; Doubleday, 1977. **Awarded:** New Jersey Institute of Technology 1978.

HARTFORD, JOHN

Steamboat in a Cornfield written and illustrated by John Hartford; Crown, 1986. **Awarded:** Boston Globe Horn Book (nonfiction honor) 1987.

HARTLING, PETER

Crutches by Peter Hartling, not illustrated; Lothrop, Lee & Shepard, 1988. **Awarded:** Batchelder 1989; International Board on Books for Young People (Translation/USA) 1990.

HARTMAN, LAURA

Rainbows, Snowflakes and Quarks: Physics and the World Around Us by Hans Christian Von Baeyer, illustrated by Laura Hartman; McGraw Hill, 1984. **Awarded:** New York Academy of Sciences (older honor) 1985.

HARTMAN, THOMAS

Where Does God Live? by Thomas Hartman and Marc Gellman, illustrated by William Zdinak; Triumph Books, 1991. **Awarded:** Christopher Award (All Ages) 1992.

HARTWICK, HARRY

Farewell to the Farivox by Harry Hartwick, illustrated by Ib Spang Ohlsson; Four Winds, 1972. **Awarded:** Children's Book Showcase 1973.

HARVEY, AMANDA

A Close Call written and illustrated by Amanda Harvey; Macmillan Children's, 1990. **Awarded:** Macmillan Prize (1st prize) 1989; Mother Goose 1991.

HARVEY, ANNE

Shades of Green by Anne Harvey, illustrated by John Lawrence; MacRae, 1991; Greenwillow, 1992. **Awarded:** Signal Poetry 1992.

HARVEY, ROLAND

Burke and Wills written and illustrated by Roland Harvey; Five Mile Press, 1985. **Awarded:** Children's Book Council of Australia (Clifton Pugh award) 1986.

The Friends of Emily Culpepper by Ann Coleridge, illustrated by Roland Harvey; Five Mile Press, 1983. **Awarded:** Children's Book Council of Australia (picture book of the year commended) 1984.

My Place in Space by Robin Hirst and Sally Hirst, illustrated by Roland Harvey and Joe Levine; Five Mile Press, 1989. **Awarded:** Children's Book Council of Australia (Picture Book of the Year Honour) 1989.

HASKINS, JAMES

Black Dance in America: A History Through Its People by James Haskins, illustrated with photos; Crowell, 1990. **Awarded:** Coretta Scott King (Text honor) 1991.

Black Music In America: A History Through Its People by James Haskins, illustrated with photos; Crowell, 1987. **Awarded:** Woodson 1988.

Count Your Way Around the World (series) by James Haskins, with various illustrators; Carolrhoda, 1987-1992. **Awarded:** Author's Award (Alabama) 1988.

James Van Der Zee: The Picture-Takin' Man by Jim Haskins, illustrated with photographs by James Van Der Zee; Dodd, Mead, 1979. **Awarded:** Woodson (outstanding merit) 1980.

Lena Horne by James Haskins, illustrated with photographs; Coward McCann, 1983. **Awarded:** Coretta Scott King (honorable mention) 1984.

Rosa Parks: My Story by Rosa Parks with Jim Haskins, illustrated; Dial, 1992. **Awarded:** Hungry Mind (Young Adult/Nonfiction) 1993; Parents Choice (Picture Books) 1992.

The Story of Stevie Wonder by James Haskins, illustrated with photographs; Lothrop, 1976. **Awarded:** Coretta Scott King 1977.

HASLER, EVELINE
Die Blumenstadt by Eveline Hasler, illustrated by Stepan Zavrel; Bohem Press, 1987. **Awarded:** Bologna (Critici in Erba) 1988.

HASSALL, JOAN
Quiet as Moss: 36 Poems Chosen by Leonard Clark by Andrew Young, illustrated by Joan Hassall; Hart-Davis, 1959. **Awarded:** Carnegie (commended) 1959.

HASSALL, RICHARD
Animal Tracks by Carson Creagh and Kathie Atkinson, illustrated by Richard Hassall; Methuen Australia, 1986. **Awarded:** Whitley 1988.

HASSELRIIS, ELSE
Shen of the Sea: A Book for Children by Arthur Bowie Chrisman, illustrated by Else Hasselriis; Dutton, 1925. **Awarded:** Newbery 1926.

HASTINGS, SELINA
The Man Who Wanted To Live Forever by Selina Hastings, illustrated by Reg Cartwright; Holt, 1988. **Awarded:** Parents' Choice (Picture Book) 1988.

Peter and the Wolf retold by Selina Hastings, illustrated by Reg Cartwright; Holt, Rinehart & Winston, 1987. **Awarded:** Parents' Choice (Picture Book) 1987.

Sir Gawain and the Loathly Lady retold by Selina Hastings, illustrated by Juan Wijngaard; Walker, 1985. **Awarded:** Greenaway 1985.

HATCH, ALDEN
Young Willkie by Alden Hatch, illustrated with photographs; Harcourt, 1944. **Awarded:** Spring Book Festival (older honor) 1944.

HATFIELD, FRANCES S.
Awarded: American Association of School Librarians 1985.

HATHORN, ELIZABETH
All About Anna and Harriet and Christopher and Me by Elizabeth Hathorn, illustrated by Steve Axelrod; Methuen, 1986. **Awarded:** Children's Book Council of Australia (book of the year younger honor) 1987.

The Tram to Bondi Beach by Elizabeth Hathorn, illustrated by Julie Vivas; Methuen, 1981. **Awarded:** Children's Book Council of Australia (picture book of the year highly commended) 1982.

HATHORN, LIBBY
Looking Out for Sampson by Libby Hathorn, illustrated by Ann James; Oxford, 1987. **Awarded:** Children's Book Council of Australia (Book of the Year Younger Honour) 1988.

HATT, E. M.
The Adventures of Ulysses by Jacques Lemarchand, translated by E. M. Hatt; illustrated by Andre Francois; Criterion, 1960. **Awarded:** New York Times Best Illustrated 1960.

HAUFF, WILHELM
Dwarf Long-Nose by Wilhelm Hauff, translated by Doris Orgel, illustrated by Maurice Sendak; Random House, 1960. **Awarded:** Lewis. Carroll Shelf 1963

HAUGAARD, ERIK CHRISTIAN
The Boy and the Samurai by Erik Christian Haugaard, not illustrated; Houghton Mifflin, 1991. **Awarded:** Parents' Choice (Story Book) 1991.

Chase Me, Catch Nobody! by Erik C. Haugaard, not illustrated; Houghton Mifflin, 1980. **Awarded:** Jane Addams (honor) 1981.

Hakon of Rogen's Saga by Erik Haugaard, illustrated by Leo and Diane Dillon; Houghton, 1963. **Awarded:** Spring Book Festival (older honor) 1963.

The Little Fishes by Erik Christian Haugaard, illustrated by Milton Johnson; Houghton Mifflin, 1967. **Awarded:** Jane Addams 1968; Boston Globe Horn Book (text) 1967; Spring Book Festival (older) 1967.

The Rider and His Horse by Erik Christian Haugaard, illustrated by Leo Dillon and Diane Dillon; Houghton Mifflin, 1968. **Awarded:** Phoenix Award 1988.

HAUGEN, TORMOD
Awarded: Hans Christian Andersen (Author) 1990.

HAUMAN, DORIS
The Little Engine That Could by Piper Watty, illustrated by Doris Hauman and George Hauman; Platt, 1954, c1930. **Awarded:** Lewis Carroll Shelf 1958.

HAUMAN, GEORGE
The Little Engine That Could by Piper Watty, illustrated by George Hauman and Doris Hauman; Platt, 1954, c1930. **Awarded:** Lewis Carroll Shelf 1958.

HAUPTMANN, TATJANA
Ein Tag im Leben der Dorothea Wutz written and illustrated by Tatjana Hauptmann; Diogenes Verlag, 1978. **Awarded:** Bologna (critic in erba) 1979.

HAUTZIG, ESTHER RUDOMIN
The Endless Steppe: Growing Up in Siberia by Esther Hautzig, not illustrated; Crowell, 1968. **Awarded:** Jane Addams 1969; Boston Globe Horn Book (text honor) 1968; Lewis Carroll Shelf 1971; National Book Award (finalist) 1969; Spring Book Festival (older honor) 1968; Sydney Taylor Book 1978.

HAVIGHURST, MARION BOYD
High Prairie by Marion Havighurst and Walter Havighurst, illustrated by Gertrude Howe; Farrar & Rinehart, 1944. **Awarded:** Spring Book Festival (middle honor) 1944.

Song of the Pines: A Story of Norwegian Lumbering in Wisconsin by Marion Havighurst and Walter Havighurst, illustrated by Richard Floethe; Winston, 1949. **Awarded:** Newbery (honor) 1950; Ohioana 1950; Spring Book Festival (older honor) 1949.

HAVIGHURST, WALTER EDWIN
High Prairie by Walter Havighurst and Marion Havighurst, illustrated by Gertrude Howe; Farrar & Rinehart, 1944. **Awarded:** Spring Book Festival (middle honor) 1944.

Song of the Pines: A Story of Norwegian Lumbering in Wisconsin by Walter Havighurst and Marion Havighurst, illustrated by

Richard Floethe; Winston, 1949. **Awarded:** Newbery (honor) 1950; Ohioana 1950; Spring Book Festival (older honor) 1949.

HAVILAND, VIRGINIA
Awarded: Grolier 1976; Regina 1976.

HAVILL, JUANITA
Jamaica's Find by Juanita Havill, illustrated by Anne Sibley O'Brien; Houghton Mifflin, 1986. **Awarded:** Ezra Jack Keats New Writer Award 1987.

HAWES, CHARLES BOARDMAN
The Dark Frigate by Charles Boardman Hawes, illustrated by A. L. Ripley; Atlantic Monthly Press, 1923; Little, Brown, 1934. **Awarded:** Lewis Carroll Shelf 1962; Newbery 1924.

The Great Quest: A Romance of 1826 by Charles Boardman Hawes, illustrated by George Varian; Little Brown, 1921. **Awarded:** Newbery (honor) 1922.

HAWES, JUDY
Bees and Beelines by Judy Hawes, illustrated by Aliki; Crowell, 1964. **Awarded:** New Jersey Institute of Technology (science ages 5-8) 1964.

The Goats Who Killed the Leopard by Judy Hawes, illustrated by Ric Estrada; Crowell, 1970. **Awarded:** New Jersey Institute of Technology 1970.

Ladybug, Ladybug, Fly Away Home by Judy Hawes, illustrated by Ed Emberley; Crowell, 1967. **Awarded:** New Jersey Institute of Technology (science) 1968.

Shrimps by Judy Hawes, illustrated by Joseph Low; Crowell, 1967. **Awarded:** New Jersey Institute of Technology (science) 1968.

Spring Peepers by Judy Hawes, illustrated by Graham Booth; Crowell, 1975. **Awarded:** New York Academy of Sciences (younger honor) 1976.

What I Like about Toads by Judy Hawes, illustrated by James and Ruth McCrea; Crowell, 1969. **Awarded:** New Jersey Institute of Technology 1970.

Why Frogs Are Wet by Judy Hawes, illustrated by Don Madden; Crowell, 1968. **Awarded:** New Jersey Institute of Technology (science) 1968.

HAWES, LOUISE
Nelson Malone Meets the Man from Mushnut by Louise Hawes, illustrated by Bert Dodson; Dutton, 1986. **Awarded:** New Jersey Institute of Technology 1987.

HAWKINS, ARTHUR
Kids Gardening: A First Indoor Gardening Book for Children by Aileen Paul, illustrated by Arthur Hawkins; Doubleday, 1972. **Awarded:** New Jersey Institute of Technology 1972.

HAWKINS, IRENE BEATRICE
Collected Stories for Children by Walter de la Mare, illustrated by Irene Hawkins; Faber, 1947. **Awarded:** Carnegie 1947.

HAWKINS, SHEILA
Wish and the Magic Nut by Peggy Barnard, illustrated by Sheila Hawkins; Sands, 1956. **Awarded:** Children's Book Council of Australia (picture book) 1956.

HAWTHORNE, HILDEGARDE
Give Me Liberty by Hildegarde Hawthorne, illustrated by Woodi Ishmael; Appleton Century Crofts, 1945. **Awarded:** Spring Book Festival (older honor) 1945.

Long Adventure: The Story of Winston Churchill by Hildegarde Hawthorne, not illustrated; Appleton, 1942. **Awarded:** Commonwealth Club of California 1942.

HAY, DAVID
Human Populations by David Hay, illustrated with photographs and maps; Penguin, 1972. **Awarded:** Times Educational Supplement (senior) 1973.

HAY, JOHN
Ancient China by John Hay, illustrated by Rosemonde Nairac and Pippa Brand; Walck, 1974. **Awarded:** New York Academy of Sciences (special honorable mention for publication of the book) 1975.

Rover and Coo Coo by John Hay, illustrated by Tim Solliday; Green Tiger Press, 1986. **Awarded:** Friends of American Writers ($500) 1987.

HAYASHI, AKIKO
Aki and the Fox written and illustrated by Akiko Hayashi; Doubleday, 1991. **Awarded:** Reading Magic Award 1991.

Anna's Special Present by Yoriko Tsutsui, illustrated by Akiko Hayashi; Viking Kestrel, 1988; Puffin, 1990. **Awarded:** Ezra Jack Keats New Writer's Award 1989.

HAYES, GEOFFREY
When the Wind Blew by Margaret Wise Brown, illustrated by Geoffrey Hayes; Harper, 1977. **Awarded:** New York Times Best Illustrated 1977.

HAYES, JOHN F.
Awarded: Vicky Metcalf 1964.

The Dangerous Cove: A Story of Early Days in Newfoundland by John F. Hayes, illustrated by Fred J. Finley; Copp Clark, 1957. **Awarded:** Canadian Library Assn. 1959.

A Land Divided by John F. Hayes, illustrated by Fred J. Finley; Copp Clark, 1951. **Awarded:** Governor-General's Literary Award 1951.

Rebels Ride at Night by John F. Hayes, illustrated by Fred J. Finley; Copp Clark, 1953. **Awarded:** Governor-General's Literary Award 1953.

HAYES, SARAH
Happy Christmas, Gemma by Sarah Hayes, illustrated by Jan Ormerod; Walker Books, 1986. **Awarded:** Greenaway (highly commended) 1986.

HAYNES, LARAMEE.
Awarded: Southern California Council (distinguished contribution to the field of children's literature and outstanding community services) 1971.

HAYS, MICHAEL
Abiyoyo by Pete Seeger, illustrated by Michael Hays; Macmillan, 1986. **Awarded:** Redbook 1986.

The Gold Cadillac by Mildred D. Taylor, illustrated by Michael Hays; Dial, 1987. **Awarded:** Christopher (ages 9-12) 1988; New York Times Notable 1987.

HAYWOOD, CAROLYN
Awarded: Drexel 1970; Outstanding Pennsylvania Author 1979.

Dot for Short by Frieda Friedman, illustrated by Carolyn Haywood; Morrow, 1947. **Awarded:** Spring Book Festival (younger honor) 1947.

Eddie and His Big Deals written and illustrated by Carolyn Haywood; Morrow, 1955. **Awarded:** Boys Club 1956.

Eddie's Menagerie by Carolyn Haywood, illustrated by Ingrid Fetz; Morrow, 1978. **Awarded:** Utah Children's Choice 1981.

A Sundae with Judy by Frieda Friedman, illustrated by Carolyn Haywood; Morrow, 1949. **Awarded:** Spring Book Festival (under 12 honor) 1949.

HAZARD, DAVID
Catherine Marshall's Storybook for Children by David Hazard, illustrated by Joseph Boddy; Chosen Books, 1987. **Awarded:** Gold Medallion (Elementary) 1988.

HAZELTON, I.B.
Cap'n Ezra, Privateer by James D. Adams, illustrated by I. B. Hazelton; Harcourt, 1940. **Awarded:** Spring Book Festival (older) 1940.

HAZEN, BARBARA SHOOK
Even if I Did Something Awful by Barbara S. Hazen, illustrated by Nancy Kincade; Atheneum, 1981. **Awarded:** Christopher (ages 6-9) 1982.

HEADINGTON, CHRISTOPHER
The Orchestra and Its Instruments by Christopher Headington, illustrated by Roy Spencer; Bodley Head, 1965. **Awarded:** Carnegie (commended) 1965.

HEAL, EDITH
Fashion as a Career by Edith Heal, illustrated by Bob Walker; Messner, 1966. **Awarded:** New Jersey Institute of Technology 1966.

HEANEY, SEAMUS
The Rattle Bag: An Anthology of Poetry by Seamus Heaney and Ted Hughes, not illustrated; Faber & Faber, 1982. **Awarded:** Signal Poetry 1983.

HEARNE, BETSY
Awarded: Children's Reading Round Table 1982.

Eli's Ghost by Betsy Hearne, illustrated by Ronald Himler; McElderry, 1987. **Awarded:** Carl Sandburg 1987.

HEASLIP, PETER
Chapatis, Not Chips written and illustrated by Peter C. Heaslip; Methuen Children's, 1987. **Awarded:** Other Award 1987.

Grandma's Favourite written and illustrated by Peter C. Heaslip; Methuen Children's, 1987. **Awarded:** Other Award 1987.

Terraced House Books: Set D by Peter Heaslip, illustrated by Anne Griffiths; Metheun Educational, 1980. **Awarded:** Other Award 1981.

Which Twin Wins? written and illustrated by Peter C. Heaslip; Methuen Children's, 1987. **Awarded:** Other Award 1987.

Wok's Cooking? written and illustrated by Peter C. Heaslip; Methuen Children's, 1987. **Awarded:** Other Award 1987.

HECHT, JEFF
Optics: Light for a New Age by Jeff Hecht, illustrated; Scribners, 1987. **Awarded:** New York Academy of Sciences (Older honor) 1988.

HEHNER, BARBARA
Looking at Insects by David Suzuki, with Barbara Hehner, illustrated; Stoddart, 1986. **Awarded:** Information Book Award 1987.

HEIDE, FLORENCE PARRY
Awarded: Children's Reading Round Table 1984.

Banana Blitz by Florence Parry Heide, not illustrated; Holiday House, 1983. **Awarded:** CRABbery (honor) 1984.

Banana Twist by Florence Parry Heide, not illustrated; Holiday House, 1978. **Awarded:** Charlie May Simon 1980-81.

Growing Anyway Up by Florence Parry Heide, not illustrated; Lippincott, 1976. **Awarded:** Council of Wisconsin Writers (juvenile) 1977; Golden Kite (honor) 1976.

The Mystery of the Bewitched Bookmobile by Florence Parry Heide, illustrated by Seymour Fleischman; Whitman, 1975. **Awarded:** Golden Archer 1976.

Sami and the Time of Troubles by Florence Parry Heide and Judith Heide Gilliland, illustrated by Ted Lewin; Clarion, 1992. **Awarded:** Hungry Mind (Picturebook/Fiction) 1993.

Schorschi Schrumpft: Geschichte by Florence Parry Heide, illustrated by Edward Gorey; Diogenes Verlag, 1976. **Awarded:** Bologna (graphics for children) 1977.

The Shrinking of Treehorn by Florence Parry Heide, illustrated by Edward Gorey; Holiday, 1971. **Awarded:** Children's Book Showcase 1972; New York Times Best Illustrated 1971.

Tales for the Perfect Child by Florence Heide, illustrated by Victoria Chess; Lothrop, Lee & Shepard, 1985. **Awarded:** Parents' Choice (literature) 1985.

When the Sad Ones Come to Stay by Florence Parry Heide, not illustrated; Lippincott, 1975. **Awarded:** Council of Wisconsin Writers (juvenile runnerup) 1976.

HEIMES, PATRICIA
You Shouldn't Have To Say Good-Bye by Patricia Heimes, not illustrated; Harcourt Brace Jovanovich, 1982. **Awarded:** Iowa Teen 1987.

HEINE, HELME
Freunde written and illustrated by Helme Heine; Gertraud Middelhauve, 1982; Atheneum, 1985. **Awarded:** Owl Prize 1983.

Friends written and illustrated by Helme Heine; Atheneum, 1982. **Awarded:** Boston Globe Horn Book (illustration honor) 1983.

The Marvelous Journey Through the Night written and illustrated by Helme Heine; Farrar, Straus, Giroux, 1990. **Awarded:** New York Times Best Illustrated 1991.

Mr. Miller the Dog written and illustrated by Helme Heine; Atheneum, 1980. **Awarded:** New York Times Best Illustrated 1980.

The Pig's Wedding written and illustrated by Helme Heine; Atheneum, 1979, c1978. **Awarded:** New York Times Notable Books 1979.

Seven Wild Pigs written and illustrated by Helme Heine; McElderry, 1988. **Awarded:** Parents' Choice (Picture Book) 1988.

HEINLEIN, ROBERT
Have Space Suit - Will Travel by Robert Heinlein, not illustrated; Scribner, 1958. **Awarded:** Sequoyah 1961.

HEINS, PAUL
Awarded: Chandler Reward of Merit 1971.

HEINTZ, ANN
Mass Media by Ann Heintz, M. Lawrence Reuter, and Elizabeth Conley, illustrated; Loyola University Press, 1972. **Awarded:** Media & Methods (textbook) 1975.

HELFMAN, ELIZABETH S.
Blissymbolics: Speaking Without Speech by Elizabeth S. Helfman, illustrated ; Elsevier/Nelson, 1980. **Awarded:** Golden Kite (nonfiction) 1981.

HELLER, LINDA
The Castle on Hester Street written and illustrated by Linda Heller; Jewish Publication Society of America, 1982.

Awarded: Sydney Taylor Book Award (children) 1983; Parents' Choice (illustration) 1982.

HELLER, RUTH

Chickens Aren't the Only Ones written and illustrated by Ruth Heller; Grosset & Dunlap, 1981. **Awarded:** New York Academy of Sciences (younger honor) 1983.

HELLMAN, HAL

Energy in the World of the Future by Hal Hellman, not illustrated; Evans, 1973. **Awarded:** New Jersey Institute of Technology 1973.

The Right Size: Why Some Creatures Survive and Others Are Extinct by Hal Hellman, illustrated by Sam Salant; Putnam, 1968. **Awarded:** New Jersey Institute of Technology (science) 1968.

HEMMANT, LYNETTE

Ace: The Very Important Pig by Dick King-Smith, illustrated by Lynette Hemmant; Crown, 1990. **Awarded:** CRABbery (Classic) 1992.

HEMMINGS, SUSAN

Girls Are Powerful: Young Women's Writings from Spare Rib edited by Susan Hemmings; Sheba Feminist Publishers, 1982. **Awarded:** Other Award 1982.

HENBEST, NIGEL

Galaxies and Quasars by Nigel Henbest and Heather Couper, illustrated; Watts, 1986. **Awarded:** Times Educational Supplement (Senior) 1987.

Space Frontiers by Nigel Henbest and Heather Couper, illustrated with photographs and diagrams; Viking, 1978. **Awarded:** New York Academy of Sciences (special award for series on engineering and technology) 1979.

HENDERSHOT, JUDITH

In Coal Country by Judith Hendershot, illustrated by Thomas B. Allen; Knopf, 1987. **Awarded:** Boston Globe Horn Book (illustration honor) 1987; New York Times Best Illustrated 1987; New York Times Notable 1987; Parents' Choice (Picture Book) 1987.

HENDERSON, DOUGLAS

Living With Dinosaurs by Patricia Lauber, illustrated by Douglas Henderson; Bradbury, 1991. **Awarded:** Hungry Mind (Middle Reader/Nonfiction) 1992.

HENDRICKSON, DAVID

Swords of Steel: The Story of a Gettysburg Boy by Elsie Singmaster, illustrated by David Hendrickson; Houghton, 1933. **Awarded:** Newbery (honor) 1934.

HENDRY, DIANA

Harvey Angell by Diana Hendry, not illustrated; Julia MacRae, 1991. **Awarded:** Whitbread 1991.

HENDRY, FRANCES

Quest for a Kelpie by Frances Hendry, not illustrated; Canongate Publishing, 1986. **Awarded:** Quest for a Kelpie 1986.

HENDRY, GEORGE

Greg's Revenge by George Hendry, not illustrated; Blackie, 1991. **Awarded:** Kathleen Fidler 1991.

HENKES, KEVIN

Chester's Way written and illustrated by Kevin Henkes; Greenwillow, 1988. **Awarded:** Keystone To Reading 1990.

HENNEBERGER, ROBERT

His Indian Brother by Hazel Wilson, illustrated by Robert Henneberger; Abingdon, 1955. **Awarded:** Edison Mass Media (character development) 1956.

HENNEFRUND, ELIZABETH R.

Story in *Ranger Rick* magazine. **Awarded:** Magazine Merit Award (Nonfiction) 1989.

HENNEY, FRANCES E.

Awarded: American Assn. of School Librarians 1979.

HENRIQUEZ, ELSA

The Magic Orange Tree and Other Haitian Folktales by Diane Wolkstein, illustrated by Elsa Henriquez; Knopf, 1978. **Awarded:** New York Academy of Sciences (older honor) 1979.

HENRY, MARGUERITE

Awarded: Children's Reading Round Table 1961; Kerlan 1975; Southern California Council (comprehensive contribution of lasting value to the field of children's literature) 1973.

Black Gold by Marguerite Henry, illustrated by Wesley Dennis; Rand, 1957. **Awarded:** Sequoyah 1960.

Brighty of the Grand Canyon by Marguerite Henry, illustrated by Wesley Dennis; Rand, 1953. **Awarded:** William Allen White 1956.

Justin Morgan Had a Horse by Marguerite Henry, illustrated by Wesley Dennis; Wilcox & Follett, 1945. **Awarded:** Newbery (honor) 1946.

King of the Wind by Marguerite Henry, illustrated by Wesley Dennis; Rand McNally, 1948. **Awarded:** Newbery 1949; Young Readers' Choice 1951.

Misty of Chincoteague by Marguerite Henry, illustrated by Wesley Dennis; Rand McNally, 1947. **Awarded:** Lewis Carroll Shelf 1961; Newbery (honor) 1948.

Mustang: Wild Spirit of the West by Marguerite Henry, illustrated by Robert Lougheed; Rand, 1966. **Awarded:** Sequoyah 1970; Western Heritage 1967.

Sea Star: Orphan of Chincoteague by Marguerite Henry, illustrated by Wesley Dennis; Rand, 1949. **Awarded:** Young Readers' Choice 1952.

HENSTRA, FRISO

Forgetful Fred by Jay Williams, illustrated by Friso Henstra; Parents, 1974. **Awarded:** Biennale Illustrations Bratislava (Plaque) 1977.

The Little Spotted Fish by Jane Yolen, illustrated by Friso Henstra; Seabury, 1975. **Awarded:** Children's Book Showcase 1976.

Pedro & the Padre by Verna Aardema, illustrated by Friso Henstra; Dial, 1991. **Awarded:** Parents' Choice (Story Book) 1991.

Petronella by Jay Williams, illustrated by Friso Henstra; Parents', 1973. **Awarded:** Children's Book Showcase 1974.

The Practical Princess by Jay Williams, illustrated by Friso Henstra; Parents, 1969. **Awarded:** Biennale Illustrations Bratislava (Golden Apple) 1969.

The Tsar and the Amazing Cow by J. Patrick Lewis, illustrated by Friso Henstra; Dial, 1988. **Awarded:** Ohioana 1989.

HENRY, O.

The Gift of the Magi by O. Henry, illustrated by Lisbeth Zwerger, lettering by Michael Neugebauer; Neugebauer Press distributed by Alphabet Press, 1982. **Awarded:** New York Times Best Illustrated 1982.

HENTOFF, NAT
Jazz Country by Nat Hentoff, not illustrated; Harper, 1965. **Awarded:** Nancy Bloch 1965; Spring Book Festival (older) 1965; Woodward Park School 1966.

This School Is Driving Me Crazy by Nat Hentoff, not illustrated; Delacorte, 1975. **Awarded:** Golden Archer 1980.

HERALD, KATHLEEN
see PEYTON, K.M.

HERMAN, CHARLOTTE
The House on Walenska Street by Charlotte Herman, illustrated by Susan Avishai; Dutton, 1990. **Awarded:** Carl Sandburg 1990.

HERMAN, VIC
Juanito's Railroad in the Sky written and illustrated by Vic Herman; Golden (Western), 1976. **Awarded:** Children's Book Showcase 1977.

HERMAN, WILLIAM
Hearts Courageous: Twelve Who Achieved by William Herman, illustrated by James MacDonald; Dutton, 1949. **Awarded:** Boys Club 1950.

HERMES, PATRICIA
What if They Knew? by Patricia Hermes, not illustrated; Harcourt, 1980. **Awarded:** CRABbery 1981.

You Shouldn't Have to Say Good-bye by Patricia Hermes, not illustrated; Harcourt, 1982. **Awarded:** California Young Reader (junior high) 1987; Iowa Teen 1987; Nene (runnerup) 1986; Nene Award 1988.

HERNANDEZ, ANTONIA A.
Yari by Antonia A. Hernandez, manuscript. **Awarded:** Council on Interracial Books for Children (Puerto Rican) 1974.

HERRERA, VELINO
In My Mother's House by Ann Nolan Clark, illustrated by Velino Herrera; Viking, 1941. **Awarded:** Caldecott (honor) 1942; Spring Book Festival (younger children) 1941.

HERRIOT, JAMES
Blossom Comes Home by James Herriot, illustrated by Ruth Brown; St. Martin's Press, 1988. **Awarded:** Redbook 1988.

HERRON, EDWARD A.
First Scientist of Alaska: William Healey Dall by Edward A. Herron, not illustrated; Messner, 1958. **Awarded:** Commonwealth Club of California 1958.

HERRON, EDWIN
It's Fun to Know Why: Experiments with Things Around Us by Julius Schwartz, illustrated by Edwin Herron and Anne Marie Jauss; McGraw, 1973. **Awarded:** New York Academy of Sciences (older honor) 1974.

HERZIG, ALISON CRAGIN
Oh, Boy! Babies! by Alison Cragin Herzig and Jane Lawrence Mali, illustrated by Katrina Thomas; Little Brown, 1980. **Awarded:** American Book Award (nonfiction hardcover) 1981.

HERZOG, GEORGE
Cow-tail Switch and Other West African Stories by George Herzog and Harold Courlander, illustrated by Madye Lee Chastain; Holt, 1947. **Awarded:** Newbery (honor) 1948.

HESLOP, MICHAEL
The Grey King by Susan Cooper, illustrated by Michael Heslop; Chatto & Windus, 1975; Atheneum, 1975. **Awarded:** Carnegie (commended) 1975; Newbery 1976; Tir Na n-Og 1976.

HESS, LOWELL
Exploring the Universe by Roy A. Gallant, illustrated by Lowell Hess; Garden City Books, 1956. **Awarded:** Edison Mass Media (children's science book) 1957.

HESSE, KAREN
Letters from Rifka by Karen Hesse, not illustrated; Henry Holt, 1992. **Awarded:** Christopher (ages 8-12) 1993; International Reading Assn. (Older) 1993.

Wish on a Unicorn by Karen Hesse, not illustrated; Henry Holt, 1991. **Awarded:** Hungry Mind (Middle Readers/Fiction) 1992.

HEST, AMY
The Crack-of-Dawn Walkers by Amy Hest, illustrated by Amy Schwartz; Macmillan, 1984. **Awarded:** Parents' Choice (literature) 1984.

The Purple Coat by Amy Hest, illustrated by Amy Schwartz; Four Winds, 1986. **Awarded:** Christopher (Ages 6-8) 1987.

HEUCK, SIGRID
Who Stole the Apples? written and illustrated by Sigrid Heuck; Knopf, 1986. **Awarded:** Parents' Choice (Story Book) 1987.

HEUMAN, WILLIAM
Missouri River Boy by William Heuman, illustrated by Robert Handville; Dodd Mead, 1959. **Awarded:** Boys' Life - Dodd, Mead 1958.

HEWES, AGNES DANFORTH
The Codfish Musket by Agnes D. Hewes, illustrated by Armstrong Sperry; Doubleday, 1936. **Awarded:** Newbery (honor) 1937.

Glory of the Seas by Agnes Hewes, illustrated by N. C. Wyeth; Knopf, 1933. **Awarded:** Newbery (honor) 1934.

Spice and the Devil's Cave by Agnes D. Hewes, illustrated by Lynd Ward; Knopf, 1930. **Awarded:** Newbery (honor) 1931.

The Sword of Roland Arnot by Agnes D. Hewes, illustrated by Paul Strayer; Houghton, 1939. **Awarded:** Spring Book Festival (older honor) 1939.

HEWETT, JOAN
Hector Lives in the United States Now by Joan Hewett, illustrated by Richard Hewett; Lippincott, 1990. **Awarded:** Woodson (Outstanding Merit - Elementary) 1991.

Motorcycle on Patrol: The Story of a Highway Officer by Joan Hewett, illustrated by Richard Hewett; Clarion, 1986. **Awarded:** Southern California Council (notable achievement in photojournalism) 1987.

HEWETT, RICHARD
Hector Lives in the United States Now by Joan Hewett, illustrated by Richard Hewett; Lippincott, 1990. **Awarded:** Woodson (Outstanding Merit - Elementary) 1991.

Motorcycle on Patrol: The Story of a Highway Officer by Joan Hewett, illustrated by Richard Hewett; Clarion, 1986. **Awarded:** Southern California Council (notable achievement in photojournalism) 1987.

Pets without Homes by Caroline Arnold, photographs by Richard Hewett; Clarion, 1983. **Awarded:** Golden Kite (nonfiction honor) 1983.

Trapped in Tar: Fossils From the Ice Age by Caroline Arnold, illustrated by Richard Hewett; Clarion, 1987. **Awarded:** New York Academy of Sciences (Younger honor) 1988.

HEWITT, GARNET
Ytek and the Arctic Orchid: An Inuit Legend by Garnet Hewitt, illustrated by Heather Woodall; Douglas & McIntyre, 1981; Vanguard, 1981. **Awarded:** Governor General (illustrator) 1981; Canadian Library Assn. (runnerup) 1982; Amelia Frances Howard- Gibbon 1982.

HEWITT, MARSHA
One Proud Summer by Marsha Hewitt and Claire Mackay, not illustrated; The Women's Press, 1981. **Awarded:** Ruth Schwartz 1982.

HEYDUCK-HUTH, HILDE
Drei Vogel by Hilde Heyduck-Huth; Otto Maier Verlag. **Awarded:** Bologna (graphics for children and youth) 1967.

HEYER, CAROL
Illustration in *Dragon Magazine*. **Awarded:** Magazine Merit Award (Illustration) 1988.

HEYMAN, ANITA
Exit from Home by Anita Heyman, not illustrated; Crown, 1977. **Awarded:** Sydney Taylor Book Award 1977.

Final Grades by Anita Heyman, not illustrated; Dodd, Mead, 1983. **Awarded:** New Jersey Institute of Technology 1983.

HIBBEN, FRANK CUMMINGS
Digging up America by Frank Cummings Hibben, illustrated with photographs; Hill & Wang, 1960. **Awarded:** Boys Club 1962.

HICKMAN, JANET
Zoar Blue by Janet Hickman, not illustrated; Macmillan, 1978. **Awarded:** Ohioana (Florence Head Award) 1979.

HICKMAN, MARTHA WHITMORE
I'm Moving by Martha W. Hickman, illustrated by Leigh Grant; Abingdon, 1974. **Awarded:** Friends of American Writers (younger) 1976.

HICKS, CLIFFORD B.
Alvin's Swap Shop by Clifford Hicks, illustrated by Bill Sokol; Holt, 1976. **Awarded:** Charlie May Simon 1978-79.

First Boy on the Moon: A Junior Science Fiction Novel by Clifford B. Hicks, illustrated by George Wilde; Winston, 1959. **Awarded:** Friends of American Writers 1960.

HICYILMAZ, GAYE
Against the Storm by Gaye Hicyilmaz, not illustrated; Viking Kestrel, 1990; Little Brown, 1992. **Awarded:** Guardian (runnerup) 1991; Hungry Mind (Young Adult/Fiction) 1993.

HIDA, KEIKO
The Prancing Pony: Nursery Rhymes from Japan by Charlotte B. De Forest, illustrated by Keiko Hida; Walker, 1968. **Awarded:** Spring Book Festival (picture book honor) 1968.

HIGHWATER, JAMAKE
Anpao: An American Indian Odyssey by Jamake Highwater, illustrated by Fritz Scholder; Lippincott, 1977. **Awarded:** Boston Globe Horn Book (fiction honor) 1978; Newbery (honor) 1978.

Many Smokes, Many Moons: A Chronology of American Indian History through Indian Art by Jamake Highwater, illustrated with photographs; Lippincott, 1978. **Awarded:** Jane Addams 1979.

The World in 1492 by Jean Fritz, Katherine Paterson, Patricia McKissack, Fredrick McKissack, Margaret Mahy and Jamake Highwater, illustrated by Stefano Vitale; Henry Holt, 1992. **Awarded:** Hungry Mind (Young Adult/Nonfiction) 1993.

HIGONNET, MARGARET R.
Narrative Fractures and Fragments by Margaret R. Higonnet in Children's Literature 15 (1987). **Awarded:** Children's Literature Assn. Criticism Award 1988.

HIGTON, BERNARD
Aesop's Fables compiled by Russell Ash and Bernard Higton, various illustrators; Chronicle, 1990. **Awarded:** Redbook 1990.

HILDICK, EDMUND WALLACE
The Case of the Secret Scribbler by E. W. Hildick, illustrated by Lisl Weil; Macmillan, 1978. **Awarded:** Edgar Allan Poe (runnerup) 1979.

Louie's Lot by E. W. Hildick, illustrated by Iris Schweitzer; Faber, 1965. **Awarded:** International Board on Books for Young People (honour list/Great Britain) 1968.

HILL, DOUGLAS
Blade of the Poisoner by Douglas Hill, not illustrated; McElderry, 1987. **Awarded:** Parents' Choice (Story Book) 1987.

HILL, ERIC
Where's Spot? written and illustrated by Eric Hill; Heinemann, 1980. **Awarded:** Mother Goose (runnerup) 1981.

HILL, FRANK ERNEST
The Kid Who Batted 1.000 by Frank Ernest Hill and Bob Allison, illustrated by Paul Galdone; Doubleday, 1951. **Awarded:** Boys Club 1952.

HILL, JANET
Awarded: Eleanor Farjeon 1971.

HILL, KAY
Awarded: Vicky Metcalf 1971.

And Tomorrow the Stars: The Story of John Cabot by Kay Hill, illustrated by Laszlo Kubinyi; Dodd Mead, 1968. **Awarded:** Canadian Library Assn. 1969.

HILL, NGAIO
Gaijain: Foreign Children of Japan by Olive Hill and Ngaio Hill. **Awarded:** New Zealand Library Association Nonfiction Award 1987.

HILL, OLIVE
Gaijain: Foreign Children of Japan by Olive Hill and Ngaio Hill. **Awarded:** New Zealand Library Association Nonfiction Award 1987.

HILL, SUSAN
Can It Be True? by Susan Hill, illustrated by Angela Barrett; Hamish Hamilton, 1988. **Awarded:** Smarties (ages 6-8) 1988.

HILLER, ILO
Introducing Birds to Young Naturalists by Ilo Hiller, illustrated; Texas A & M University Press, 1989. **Awarded:** Texas Institute of Letters 1990.

HILLERICH, ROBERT
Wait, Skates! by Mildred D. Johnson, illustrated by Tom Dunnington, prepared under the direction of Robert Hillerich; Children's Press, 1983. **Awarded:** Sandburg 1983.

HILLERT, MARGARET
Awarded: Children's Reading Round Table 1991.

HILLS, JONATHAN

Song of the City by Gareth Owen, illustrated by Jonathan Hills; Fontana Young Lions Original, 1985. **Awarded:** Signal 1986.

HILSABECK, EMILY

Awarded: Children's Reading Round Table 1960.

HILTON, NETTE

The Long Red Scarf by Nette Hilton, illustrated by Margaret Power; Omnibus Books, 1987. **Awarded:** Children's Book Council of Australia (Picture Book Honour) 1988.

The Web by Nette Hilton, illustrated by Kerry Millard; Collins, 1992. **Awarded:** Children's Book Council of Australia (Book of the Year Younger honor) 1993.

HILTON, SUZANNE

Awarded: Drexel 1979.

Getting There: Frontier Travel without Power by Suzanne Hilton, illustrated; Westminster, 1980. **Awarded:** Western Writers 1980.

HIM, GEORGE

The Adventures of King Midas by Lynne Reid Banks, illustrated by George Him; Dent, 1976. **Awarded:** W. H. Smith (£50) 1977.

King Wilbur the Third and the Bicycle by James Rogerson, illustrated by George Dent; 1976. **Awarded:** W. H. Smith (£50) 1977.

HIMLER, ANN

Little Owl, Keeper of the Trees by Ann Himler and Ronald Himler, illustrated by Ronald Himler; Harper, 1974. **Awarded:** New Jersey Institute of Technology 1976.

HIMLER, RONALD

Eli's Ghost by Betsy Hearne, illustrated by Ronald Himler; McElderry, 1987. **Awarded:** Sandburg 1987.

Fly Away Home by Eve Bunting, illustrated by Ronald Himler; Clarion, 1991. **Awarded:** Commonwealth Club of California (ages 10- under) 1991.

Indian Harvests by William C. Grimm, illustrated by Ronald Himler; McGraw, 1974. **Awarded:** Children's Book Showcase 1975.

Inside My Feet: The Story of a Giant by Richard Kennedy, illustrated by Ronald Himler; Harper, 1979. **Awarded:** New York Times Notable Books 1979.

Little Owl, Keeper of the Trees by Ronald Himler and Ann Himler, illustrated by Ronald Himler; Harper, 1974. **Awarded:** New Jersey Institute of Technology 1976.

Sadako and the Thousand Paper Cranes by Eleanor Coerr, illustrated by Ronald Himler; Putnam, 1977; Dell, 1979. **Awarded:** West Australian Young Readers (primary) 1981.

The Wall by Eve Bunting, illustrated by Ronald Himler; Clarion, 1990. **Awarded:** Southern California Council (Distinguished Work of Fiction) 1991.

HIMMELMAN, JOHN

Ibis: A True Whale Story by John Himmelman, illustrated; Scholastic, 1990. **Awarded:** Book Can Develop Empathy 1991.

HINDLE, LEE J.

Dragon Fall by Lee J. Hindle, not illustrated; Avon Flare, 1984. **Awarded:** Avon/Flare 1983.

HINDLEY, JUDY

Maybe It's a Pirate by Judy Hindley, illustrated by Selina Young; ABC, 1992. **Awarded:** Mother Goose (runnerup) 1993.

The Tree by Judy Hindley, illustrated by Alison Wisenfeld; Aurum, 1990; Potter, 1990. **Awarded:** Times Educational Supplement (Junior) 1990.

HINTON, S. E. (SUSAN ELOISE)

Awarded: Margaret A. Edwards Award 1988; Golden Archer 1983.

The Outsiders by S. E. Hinton, not illustrated; Viking, 1967; Dell, 1968; Collins, 1975. **Awarded:** Massachusetts Children's (grades 7-9) 1979; Media & Methods (paperback) 1975; Spring Book Festival (older honor) 1967; Virginia Young Readers (High School) 1985.

Tex by S. E. Hinton, not illustrated; Delacorte, 1979. **Awarded:** Books I Love Best Yearly (Read Alone Secondary) 1991; Sue Hefly Award (honor) 1982; Sue Hefly Award 1983.

That Was Then, This Is Now by S. E. Hinton, illustrated by Hal Siegel; Viking, 1971. **Awarded:** Massachusetts Children's (grades 7-9) 1978; Spring Book Festival (older honor) 1971.

HIPPLE, THEODORE W.

Awarded: ALAN Award 1988; Landau 1987.

HIRAWA, YASUKO

Suho and the White Horse: A Legend of Mongolia by Yuzo Otsuka, translated by Yasuko Hirawa, illustrated by Suekichi Akaba; Bobbs Merrill, 1969. **Awarded:** Art Books for Children 1976, 1977, 1978.

HIRSCH, KAREN

My Sister by Karen Hirsch, illustrated by Nancy Inderieden; Carolrhoda, 1977. **Awarded:** Woodward Park (honorable mention) 1982.

HIRSCH, S. CARL

Awarded: Children's Reading Round Table 1973.

The Globe for the Space Age by S. Carl Hirsch, illustrated by Burt Silverman; Viking, 1963. **Awarded:** Edison Mass Media (science book) 1964.

The Living Community: A Venture into Ecology by S. Carl Hirsch, illustrated by William Steinel; Viking, 1966. **Awarded:** Edison Mass Media (science book) 1967; Clara Ingram Judson 1967.

The Riddle of Racism by S. Carl Hirsch, not illustrated; Viking, 1972. **Awarded:** Jane Addams 1973.

HIRSCHFELDER, ARLENE

Happily May I Walk: American Indians and Alaska Natives Today by Arlene Hirschfelder, illustrated; Scribner, 1986. **Awarded:** New Jersey Institute of Technology 1987, 1988; Western Heritage 1987; Woodson 1987.

HIRSH, MARILYN

Awarded: Sydney Taylor Body of Work Award 1980

Joseph Who Loved the Sabbath by Marilyn Hirsh, illustrated by Davis Grebu; Viking Kestrel, 1986. **Awarded:** Sydney Taylor Book Award (picture book) 1987.

HIRST, ROBIN

My Place in Space by Robin Hirst and Sally Hirst, illustrated by Roland Harvey and Joe Levine; Five Mile Press, 1989. **Awarded:** Children's Book Council of Australia (Picture Book of the Year Honour) 1989.

HIRST, SALLY

My Place in Space by Sally Hirst and Robin Hirst, illustrated by Joe Levine and Roland Harvey; Five Mile Press, 1989. **Awarded:** Children's Book Council of Australia (Picture Book of the Year Honour) 1989.

HISCOCK, BRUCE

The Big Rock written and illustrated by Bruce Hiscock; Atheneum, 1988. **Awarded:** New York Academy of Sciences (Younger Honor) 1989.

HISSEY, JANE

Jolly Snow written and illustrated by Jane Hissey; Hutchinson, 1991; Philomel, 1991. **Awarded:** British Book Awards (Illustrated runnerup) 1991.

Jolly Tall written and illustrated by Jane Hissey; Hutchinson, 1990; Philomel, 1990. **Awarded:** British Book Awards (Illustrated runnerup) 1990.

HNIZDOVSKY, JACQUES

The Auk, the Dodo, and the Oryx: Vanished and Vanishing Creatures by Robert Silverberg, illustrated by Jacques Hnizdovsky; Crowell, 1967. **Awarded:** Spring Book Festival (older honor) 1967.

HO, MINFONG

The Clay Marble by Minfong Ho, not illustrated; Farrar Straus Giroux, 1991. **Awarded:** Hungry Mind (Young Adult/Fiction) 1992.

Morning Song by Minfong Ho, manuscript. **Awarded:** Council on Interracial Books for Children (Asian American) 1971-72.

Rice Without Rain by Minfong Ho, not illustrated; Lothrop, Lee & Shepard, 1990. **Awarded:** Parents' Choice (Story Book) 1990.

HOBAN, BROM

Hanukkah: Eight Nights, Eight Lights by Malka Drucker, illustrated by Brom Hoban; Holiday House, 1980. **Awarded:** Southern California Council (significant contribution of excellence in a series) 1982.

Passover: A Season of Freedom by Malka Drucker, illustrated by Brom Hoban; Holiday House, 1981. **Awarded:** Southern California Council (significant contribution of excellence in a series) 1982.

Rosh Hashanah and Yom Kippur: Sweet Beginnings by Malka Drucker, illustrated by Brom Hoban; Holiday House, 1981. **Awarded:** Southern California Council (significant contribution of excellence in a series) 1982.

Sukkot: A Time To Rejoice by Malka Drucker, illustrated by Brom Hoban; Holiday House, 1982. **Awarded:** Southern California Council (significant contribution of excellence in a series) 1982.

HOBAN, LILLIAN

Charlie the Tramp by Russell Hoban, illustrated by Lillian Hoban; Scholastic, 1967. **Awarded:** Boys Club 1968.

Emmet Otter's Jug-band Christmas by Russell Hoban, illustrated by Lillian Hoban; Parents, 1971. **Awarded:** Lewis Carroll Shelf 1972; Christopher (ages 4-8) 1972.

HOBAN, RUSSELL

Charlie the Tramp by Russell Hoban, illustrated by Lillian Hoban; Scholastic, 1967. **Awarded:** Boys Club 1968.

Emmet Otter's Jug-band Christmas by Russell Hoban, illustrated by Lillian Hoban; Parents, 1971. **Awarded:** Lewis Carroll Shelf 1972; Christopher (ages 4-8) 1972.

How Tom Beat Captain Najork and His Hired Sportsmen by Russell Hoban, illustrated by Quentin Blake; Cape, 1974. **Awarded:** International Board on Books for Young People (honour list/illustration/Great Britain) 1976; Whitbread 1974.

A Near Thing for Captain Najork by Russell Hoban, illustrated by Quentin Blake; Atheneum, 1976. **Awarded:** New York Times Best Illustrated 1976.

The Rain Door by Russell Hoban, illustrated by Quentin Blake; Gollancz, 1986. **Awarded:** Kurt Maschler (runnerup) 1986.

HOBAN, TANA

Awarded: Drexel 1983; New York Academy of Sciences (Special Award) 1988; George G. Stone 1986; Washington Post/Children's Book Guild Nonfiction 1982.

Circles, Triangles, and Squares written and illustrated by Tana Hoban; Macmillan, 1974. **Awarded:** New York Academy of Sciences (younger honor) 1975.

Count and See written and illustrated by Tana Hoban; Macmillan, 1972. **Awarded:** Children's Book Showcase 1973; New York Times Best Illustrated 1972.

I Walk and Read written and illustrated by Tana Hoban; Greenwillow, 1984. **Awarded:** New York Times Notable 1984.

Is it Larger? Is it Smaller? written and illustrated by Tana Hoban; Greenwillow, 1985. **Awarded:** New York Academy of Sciences (younger honor) 1986; Please Touch 1986.

Is it Red? Is it Yellow? Is it Blue? written and illustrated by Tana Hoban; Greenwillow, 1978. **Awarded:** Art Books for Children 1979.

Is it Rough? Is it Smooth? Is it Shiny? written and illustrated by Tana Hoban; Greenwillow, 1984. **Awarded:** New York Academy of Sciences (younger honor) 1985.

Look Again! written and illustrated by Tana Hoban; Macmillan, 1971. **Awarded:** Art Books for Children 1973, 1974, 1975; Children's Book Showcase 1972; New York Times Best Illustrated 1971.

Look! Look! Look! written and illustrated by Tana Hoban; Greenwillow, 1988. **Awarded:** New York Times Best Illustrated 1988.

1,2,3 written and illustrated by Tana Hoban; Greenwillow, 1985. **Awarded:** Boston Globe Horn Book (special citation) 1985.

Shadows and Reflections written and illustrated by Tana Hoban; Greenwillow, 1990. **Awarded:** Boston Globe (Nonfiction honor) 1990; Parents' Choice (Picture Book) 1990.

Shapes, Shapes, Shapes written and illustrated by Tana Hoban; Greenwillow, 1986. **Awarded:** New York Academy of Sciences (younger honor) 1987.

HOBERMAN, MARY ANN

A House Is a House for Me by Mary Ann Hoberman, illustrated by Betty Fraser; Viking, 1978; Puffin, 1982. **Awarded:** American Book Award (picturebook paperback) 1983.

HOCKERMAN, DENNIS

Sideways Stories from Wayside School by Louis Sachar, illustrated by Dennis Hockerman; Follett, 1978. **Awarded:** Ethical Culture School 1978.

HODGES, CARL G.

Land Rush by Carl G. Hodges, illustrated by John Martinez; Duell- Sloan, 1965. **Awarded:** Western Heritage 1966.

HODGES, CYRIL WALTER

Choristers' Cake by William Mayne, illustrated by C. Walter Hodges; Oxford, 1956. **Awarded:** Carnegie (commended) 1956.

Cold Hazard by Richard Armstrong, illustrated by C. Walter Hodges; Houghton, 1956. **Awarded:** Spring Book Festival (older) 1956.

The Eagle of the Ninth by Rosemary Sutcliff, illustrated by C. Walter Hodges; Oxford, 1954. **Awarded:** Carnegie (commended) 1954.

The Little White Horse by Elizabeth Goudge, illustrated by C. Walter Hodges; University of London Press, 1946; Coward, 1947. **Awarded:** Carnegie 1946; Spring Book Festival (older honor) 1947.

The Namesake: A Story of King Alfred written and illustrated by C. Walter Hodges; Bell, 1964. **Awarded:** Carnegie (commended) 1964; International Board on Books for Young People (honour list/Great Britain) 1966.

Ransom for a Knight by Barbara Leonie Picard, illustrated by C. Walter Hodges; Oxford, 1956. **Awarded:** Carnegie (commended) 1956.

Shakespeare's Theatre written and illustrated by C. Walter Hodges; Oxford, 1964. **Awarded:** Greenaway 1964.

The Shield Ring by Rosemary Sutcliff, illustrated by C. Walter Hodges; Oxford, 1956, 1957. **Awarded:** Carnegie (commended) 1956; Spring Book Festival (older honor) 1957.

The Silver Sword by Ian Serraillier, illustrated by C. Walter Hodges; Cape, 1956; Criterion, 1959. **Awarded:** Boys Club 1960; Carnegie (commended) 1956; Spring Book Festival (older honor) 1959.

A Swarm in May by William Mayne, illustrated by C. Walter Hodges; Oxford, 1955. **Awarded:** Carnegie (commended) 1955.

HODGES, ELIZABETH J.

Free as a Frog by Elizabeth J. Hodges, illustrated by Paul Giovanopoulos; Addison-Wesley, 1969. **Awarded:** New York Times Best Illustrated 1969.

HODGES, MARGARET MOORE

Awarded: Outstanding Pennsylvania Author 1977.

Lady Queen Anne: A Biography of Queen Anne of England by Margaret Hodges, illustrated with photographs; Farrar, 1969. **Awarded:** Indiana Authors Day (young adult) 1970.

Saint George and the Dragon adapted by Margaret Hodges from Edmund Spenser's Faerie Queene, illustrated by Trina Schart Hyman; Little, Brown, 1984. **Awarded:** Caldecott 1985; Carolyn W. Field 1985; New York Times Best Illustrated 1984.

The Wave by Margaret Hodges, illustrated by Blair Lent; Houghton, 1964. **Awarded:** Caldecott (honor) 1965; New York Times Best Illustrated 1964.

HOEFLICH, SHERMAN C.

Bright Heritage by Virginia Provines, illustrated by Sherman C. Hoeflich; Longmans, 1939. **Awarded:** Commonwealth Club of California 1939.

HOFF, CAROL

Johnny Texas by Carol Hoff, illustrated by Bob Meyers; Wilcox & Follett, 1950. **Awarded:** Charles W. Follett 1950; Steck-Vaughn 1952.

HOFF, SYD

I Saw You in the Bathtub and Other Folk Rhymes by Alvin Schwartz, illustrated by Syd Hoff; Harper & Row, 1989. **Awarded:** New Jersey Institute of Technology 1990.

HOFFMAN, MARY

Amazing Grace by Mary Hoffman, illustrated by Caroline Binch; Frances Lincoln, 1991; Dial, 1991. **Awarded:** Greenaway (Commended) 1991.

HOFFMAN, ROSEKRANS

Jane Yolen's Mother Goose Songbook edited by Jane Yolen, illustrated by Rosekrans Hoffman, music by Adam Stemple; Boyds Mills Press, 1992. **Awarded:** Hungry Mind (Picture-books/Nonfiction) 1993.

HOFFMANN, E. T. A.

Nutcracker by E. T. A. Hoffmann, illustrated by Maurice Sendak, translated by Ralph Manheim; Crown, 1984. **Awarded:** New York Times Best Illustrated 1984.

HOFFMANN, ELEANOR

Mischief in Fez by Eleanor Hoffmann, illustrated by Fritz Eichenberg; Holiday House, 1943. **Awarded:** Spring Book Festival (middle honor) 1943.

Travels of a Snail by Eleanor Hoffmann, illustrated by Zhenya Gay; Stokes, 1939. **Awarded:** Spring Book Festival (younger honor) 1939.

HOFFMANN, FELIX

Awarded: Hans Christian Andersen (highly commended illustrator/ Switzerland) 1972.

A Boy Went out to Gather Pears written and illustrated by Felix Hoffmann; Harcourt, 1966. *Der Page Orteguill* by Adolf Haller, illustrated by Felix Hoffmann; Sauerlander, 1960. **Awarded:** Hans Christian Andersen (runnerup) 1962.

The Seven Ravens by Jacob and Wilhelm Grimm, illustrated by Felix Hoffmann; Harcourt, 1963. **Awarded:** Spring Book Festival (picture book) 1963.

The Story of Christmas written and illustrated by Felix Hoffmann; Atheneum, 1975. **Awarded:** Children's Book Showcase 1976.

HOFFMANN, WILLIAM

Phaethon by Merrill Pollack, illustrated by William Hoffmann; Lippincott, 1966. **Awarded:** New Jersey Institute of Technology 1967. **Awarded:** New York Times Best Illustrated 1966.

HOFFNER, DOROTHY
see DOANE, PELAGIE

HOFMANN, GINNIE

The Runaway Teddy Bear written and illustrated by Ginnie Hofmann; Random House, 1986. **Awarded:** New Jersey Institute of Technology 1988.

HOGBEN, LANCELOT THOMAS

Man Must Measure: The Wonderful World of Mathematics by Lancelot T. Hogben, illustrated by Andre and others, maps by Marjorie Saynor; Rathbone Books, 1955. **Awarded:** Carnegie (commended) 1955.

The Wonderful World of Communication by Lancelot T. Hogben, illustrated with photographs; Doubleday, 1959. **Awarded:** Boys Club 1962.

The Wonderful World of Energy by Lancelot T. Hogben, illustrated by Eileen Aplin and others; Garden City Books, 1957.

Awarded: Edison Mass Media (children's science book) 1958.

HOGROGIAN, NONNY
Awarded: Evelyn Sibley Lampman 1985.

About Wise Men and Simpletons: Twelve Tales from Grimm translated by Elizabeth Shub, illustrated by Nonny Hogrogian; Macmillan, 1971. **Awarded:** New York Times Outstanding Books 1971.

Always Room for One More by Sorche Nic Leodhas, illustrated by Nonny Hogrogian; Holt, 1965. **Awarded:** Caldecott 1966.

The Contest written and illustrated by Nonny Hogrogian; Greenwillow, 1976. **Awarded:** Caldecott (honor) 1977.

The Fearsome Inn by Isaac Bashevis Singer, illustrated by Nonny Hogrogian; Scribner, 1967. **Awarded:** Newbery (honor) 1968.

One Fine Day written and illustrated by Nonny Hogrogian; Macmillan, 1971. **Awarded:** Caldecott 1972.

HOIG, STAN
A Capital for the Nation by Stan Hoig, illustrated with photographs; Cobblehill Books, 1990. **Awarded:** Oklahoma Book Award 1991.

HOKE, HELEN
The Real Book series edited by Helen Hoke; Doubleday. **Awarded:** Boys Club (special certificate of award for special series) 1953.

HOLABIRD, KATHARINE
Angelina Ballerina by Katharine Holabird, illustrated by Helen Craig; Crown, 1983. **Awarded:** Kentucky Bluegrass 1985.

HOLBERG, RICHARD A.
Young Mac of Fort Vancouver by Mary Jane Carr, illustrated by Richard Holberg; Crowell, 1940. **Awarded:** Newbery (honor) 1941.

HOLBROOK, STEWART HALL
America's Ethan Allen by Stewart Holbrook, illustrated by Lynd Ward; Houghton, 1949. **Awarded:** Caldecott (honor) 1950.

The Swamp Fox of the Revolution by Stewart Holbrook, illustrated by Ernest Richardson; Random House, 1959. **Awarded:** Young Readers Choice 1962.

HOLCROFT, ANTHONY
Chen-Li and the River Spirit by Anthony Holcroft, illustrated by Donna Diamond in Cricket, August 1990. **Awarded:** Witty Short Story Award 1991.

HOLDCROFT, TINA
Discover Bones by Lesley Grant, illustrated by Tina Holdcroft; Kids Can Press, 1991. **Awarded:** Information Book Award (Honour) 1992.

HOLDEN, CAROLINE
The Growing Pains of Adrian Mole by Sue Townsend, illustrated by Caroline Holden; Methuen, 1984. **Awarded:** West Australian (overseas secondary) 1986.

HOLE, QUENTIN
The Man from Ironbark by Andrew Barton Paterson, illustrated by Quentin Hole; Collins Australia, 1974. **Awarded:** Children's Book Council of Australia (Picture Book) 1975.

HOLL, KRISTI D.
The Haunting of Cabin 13 by Kristi D. Holl, illustrated; Atheneum, 1987. **Awarded:** Maryland 1990.

HOLLAND, BARBARA
Prisoners at the Kitchen Table by Barbara Holland, not illustrated; Houghton Mifflin/Clarion, 1979. **Awarded:** South Carolina Children's Award 1983.

HOLLAND, ISABELLE
Abbie's God Book by Isabelle Holland, illustrated by James McLaughlin; Westminster, 1982. **Awarded:** Helen Keating Ott 1983.

God, Mrs. Muskrat and Aunt Dot by Isabelle Holland, illustrated by Beth and Joe Krush; Westminster, 1983. **Awarded:** Helen Keating Ott 1983.

Of Love and Death and Other Journeys by Isabelle Holland, not illustrated; Lippincott, 1975. **Awarded:** National Book Award (finalist) 1976.

HOLLAND, JANICE
The Blue Cat of Castle Town by Catherine C. Coblentz, illustrated by Janice Holland; Longmans, 1949. **Awarded:** Lewis Carroll Shelf 1958; Newbery (honor) 1950.

HOLLAND, KATRIEN
Mijn Held (My Hero) written and illustrated by Katrien Holland; Em Querido's Uitgeverij. **Awarded:** Bologna (Graphic Prize for Children) 1990.

HOLLAND, VIKI
We Are Having a Baby written and illustrated by Viki Holland; Scribner, 1972. **Awarded:** Spring Book Festival (picture book honor) 1972.

HOLLANDER, CARL
The Magic Stone by Leonie Kooiker, translated by Richard Winston and Clara Winston, illustrated by Carl Hollander; Morrow, 1978. **Awarded:** International Board on Books for Young People (translation\USA) 1980.

HOLLINDALE, PETER
Ideology and the Children's Book by Peter Hollindale in Signal 55 (January 1988). **Awarded:** Children's Literature Assn. Criticism Award 1989.

HOLLING, HOLLING CLANCY
Awarded: Southern California Council (comprehensive contribution of lasting value) 1961.

Minn of the Mississippi written and illustrated by Holling Clancy Holling; Houghton Mifflin, 1951. **Awarded:** Boys Club 1951; Newbery (honor) 1952.

Paddle-to-the-Sea written and illustrated by Holling Clancy Holling; Houghton, 1941. **Awarded:** Caldecott (honor) 1942; Lewis Carroll Shelf 1962.

Seabird written and illustrated by Holling Clancy Holling; Houghton, 1948. **Awarded:** Commonwealth Club of California 1948; Newbery (honor) 1949.

HOLLING, LUCILLE
Awarded: Southern California Council (comprehensive contribution of lasting value) 1961.

HOLLISTER, C. WARREN
Awarded: L. Frank Baum 1974.

HOLM, ANNE S.
North to Freedom by Anne S. Holm, translated by L. W. Kingsland, not illustrated; Harcourt, 1965. **Awarded:** Boys Club 1966; Lewis Carroll Shelf 1973.

HOLMAN, FELICE
The Drac: French Tales of Dragons and Demons by Felice Holman and Nanine Valen, illustrated by Stephen Walker;

Scribner, 1975. **Awarded:** New York Times Notable Books 1975.

Secret City, USA by Felice Holman, not illustrated; Scribner, 1990. **Awarded:** Child Study 1990.

Slake's Limbo by Felice Holman, not illustrated; Scribner, 1974. **Awarded:** Lewis Carroll Shelf 1977.

HOLMBERG, AKE
Awarded: FIT Translation 1981.

HOLMES, BEA
Before the Supreme Court: The Story of Belva Ann Lockwood by Terry Dunnahoo, illustrated by Bea Holmes; Houghton, 1974. **Awarded:** Southern California Council (distinguished nonfiction) 1975.

The Tamarack Tree by Betty Underwood, illustrated by Bea Holmes; Houghton Mifflin, 1971. **Awarded:** Jane Addams 1972.

HOLMSTRAND, MARIE
Trouble at Turtle Bay by Marie Holmstrand, not illustrated; Dodd, 1957. **Awarded:** Boys Life - Dodd, Mead 1956.

HOLT, PATRICIA
Awarded: Grolier 1990.

HOLT, STEPHEN
see THOMPSON, HARLAN H.

HOME, ANNA
Awarded: Eleanor Farjeon Award 1989.

HOMEL, DAVID TOBY
The King's Daughter by Suzanne Martel, translated by David Toby Homel and Margaret Rose; Douglas & McIntyre, 1980. **Awarded:** International Board on Books for Young People (translation/Canada) 1982; Schwartz 1981.

HOMSHER, LOLA M.
South Pass - 1868 (His) Journal of the Wyoming Gold Rush written and illustrated by James Chisholm, edited by Lola M. Homsher; University of Nebraska Press, 1960. **Awarded:** Western Writers (nonfiction) 1961.

HONEY, ELIZABETH
The Twenty-seventh Annual African Hippopotamus Race by Morris Lurie, illustrated by Elizabeth Honey; Penguin, 1977. **Awarded:** Young Australian's Best Book Award (fiction young reader) 1986.

HONG, LILY TOY
How the Ox Star Fell From Heaven written and illustrated by Lily Toy Hong; Whitman, 1991. **Awarded:** Reading Magic Award 1991.

HONORE, PAUL
Tales from Silver Lands by Charles J. Finger, illustrated by Paul Honore; Doubleday, 1924. **Awarded:** Newbery 1925.

HONOUR, ALAN
Secrets of Minos: Sir Arthur Evans' Discoveries at Crete by Alan Honour, illustrated with photographs and line drawings; Whittlesey House, 1961. **Awarded:** Indiana Authors Day (young adult) 1962; Spring Book Festival (older honor) 1961.

Tormented Genius: The Struggles of Vincent Van Gogh by Alan Honour, illustrated with photographs; Morrow, 1967. **Awarded:** Indiana Authors Day (young adult) 1968.

HOOD, ROBERT E.
Twelve at War: Great Photographers Under Fire by Robert E. Hood, illustrated with photographs; Putnam, 1967. **Awarded:** New Jersey Institute of Technology 1968.

HOOK, FRANCES
Jesus, the Friend of Children edited by D. C. Cook, illustrated by Frances Hook and Richard Hook; David C. CAwarded: Gold Medallion 1978.ook, 1977.

HOOK, RICHARD
Jesus, the Friend of Children edited by D. C. Cook, illustrated by Frances Hook and Richard Hook; David C. Cook, 1977. **Awarded:** Gold Medallion 1978.

HOOKER, SARALINDA
Building: The Fight Against Gravity by Mario Salvadori, illustrated by Saralinda Hooker and Christopher Ragus; Atheneum, 1979. **Awarded:** Boston Globe Horn Book (nonfiction) 1980; New York Academy of Sciences (older) 1980.

HOOPER, BYRD
Beef for Beauregard! by Byrd Hooper, illustrated by Charles Geer; Putnam, 1959. **Awarded:** Steck-Vaughn 1961.

HOOPER, JOHN
Johnny Jump-up by John Hooper, illustrated by Regina Bode; Macmillan, 1942. **Awarded:** Spring Book Festival (picture book honor) 1942.

HOOVER, H. M.
Another Heaven, Another Earth by H. M. Hoover, not illustrated; Viking, 1981. **Awarded:** Ohioana 1982.

Orvis by H. M. Hoover, not illustrated; Viking Kestrel, 1987. **Awarded:** Parents' Choice (Story Book) 1987.

HOOVER, HELEN
Great Wolf and the Good Woodsman by Helen Hoover, illustrated by Charles Mikolaycak; Parents, 1967. **Awarded:** Art Books for Children 1977, 1978, 1979.

HOOVER, RUSSELL
Langston Hughes: Poet of His People by Elisabeth P. Myers, illustrated by Russell Hoover; Garrard, 1970. **Awarded:** Indiana Authors Day (children) 1971.

HOPE, CHRISTOPHER
The King, the Cat and the Fiddle by Yehudi Menuhin and Christopher Hope, illustrated by Angela Barrett; Benn, 1983. **Awarded:** Mother Goose (runnerup) 1984.

HOPE, LAURA LEE
see ADAMS, HARRIET S.

HOPKINS, DIANNE McAFEE
Awarded: American Association of School Librarians 1992.

HOPKINS, JANET
The Donkey from Dorking by Frances F. Neilson, illustrated by Janet Hopkins and Lidia Vitale; Dutton, 1942. **Awarded:** Spring Book Festival (picture book honor) 1942.

HOPKINS, LEE BENNETT
Awarded: University of Southern Mississippi 1989.

More Surprises by Lee Bennett Hopkins, illustrated by Megan Lloyd; Harper & Row, 1987. **Awarded:** Keystone to Reading 1989.

Rainbows Are Made: Poems by Carl Sandburg edited by Lee Bennett Hopkins, illustrated by Fritz Eichenberg; Harcourt, Brace Jovanovich, 1982. **Awarded:** New York Times Best Illustrated 1982.

HOPKINS, LILA
Eating Crow by Lila Hopkins, not illustrated; Watts, 1988. **Awarded:** North Carolina AAUW 1988.

Talking Turkey by Lila Hopkins, not illustrated; Watts, 1989. **Awarded:** North Carolina AAUW 1990.

HOPKINSON, DEBORAH
Story in *Cricket* magazine. Awarded: Magazine Merit (Fiction Honor) 1991.

HORDER, MARGARET
The Boundary Riders by Joan Phipson, illustrated by Margaret Horder; Harcourt, 1963. **Awarded:** Boys Club 1964.

The Crooked Snake by Alice Patricia Wrightson, illustrated by Margaret Horder; Angus & Robertson, 1955. **Awarded:** Children's Book Council of Australia (book of the year) 1956.

The Family Conspiracy by Joan Phipson, illustrated by Margaret Horder; Harcourt, 1962, 1964; Angus & Robertson, 1962. **Awarded:** Children's Book Council of Australia (book of the year) 1963; Spring Book Festival (middle) 1964.

Good Luck to the Rider by Joan Phipson, illustrated by Margaret Horder; Angus & Robertson, 1953. **Awarded:** Children's Book Council of Australia 1953.

I Own the Racecourse by Patricia Wrightson, illustrated by Margaret Horder; Hutchinson, 1969. **Awarded:** International Board on Books for Young People (honour list/Australia) 1970.

A Racecourse for Andy by Patricia Wrightson, illustrated by Margaret Horder; Harcourt, 1968. **Awarded:** Spring Book Festival (middle) 1968.

Tiger in the Bush by Nan Chauncy, illustrated by Margaret Horder; Oxford, 1957. **Awarded:** Children's Book Council of Australia (book of the year) 1958.

HORIOKA, YASUKO
Hokkyoku no Mushika Mishika by Tomiko Inui, illustrated by Yasuko Horioka; Rironsha, 1961. **Awarded:** Hans Christian Andersen (runnerup) 1964.

HORNBY, NICOLE
The Secret Pencil by Patricia Ward, illustrated by Nicole Hornby; Random House, 1960. **Awarded:** Spring Book Festival (middle honor) 1960.

HORNE, R. S.
Young Miss Josie Delaney, Detective by Mary Malone, illustrated by R. S. Horne; Dodd, Mead, 1966. **Awarded:** New Jersey Institute of Technology 1966.

HORNER, JOHN R.
Digging Dinosaurs by John R. Horner and James Gorman, illustrated by Kris Ellingsen and Donna Braginetz; Workman Publishers, 1988. **Awarded:** New York Academy of Sciences (Older) 1989.

HORNYANSKY, MICHAEL
The Golden Phoenix and Other French Canadian Fairy Tales by Charles Marius Barbeau, retold by Michael Hornyansky, illustrated by Arthur Price; Oxford, 1958. **Awarded:** Canadian Library Assn. 1960.

HOROWITZ, ANTHONY
Groosham Grange by Anthony Horowitz, illustrated by Cathy Simpson; Methuen, 1988. **Awarded:** Lancashire County Library 1989.

HORSTMAN, LISA
Fast Friends: A Tail and Tongue Tale written and illustrated by Lisa Horstman, Knopf. **Awarded:** Dr. Seuss Picture Book Award 1993.

HORT, LENNY
The Boy Who Held Back the Sea retold by Lenny Hort, illustrated by Thomas Locker; Dial, 1987. **Awarded:** New Jersey Institute of Technology 1988.

HORTON, EDITH WYNN
Awarded: Southern California Council (distinguished contribution for outstanding community service in the field of children's literature) 1975.

HORVATIC, ANNE
Simple Machines by Anne Horvatic, illustrated by Stephen Bruner; Dutton, 1989. **Awarded:** New York Academy of Sciences (Younger Honor) 1989.

HORWITZ, ELINOR LANDER
When the Sky Is Like Lace by Elinor Lander Horwitz, illustrated by Barbara Cooney; Harper, 1975. **Awarded:** New York Times Notable Books 1975.

HOSFORD, JOSSIE
An Awful Name to Live Up to by Jossie Hosford, illustrated by Charles Geer; Meredith, 1969. (originally titled *Prairie Child*). **Awarded:** Western Heritage 1970.

HOSOE, EIKOH
Return to Hiroshima by Betty Jean Lifton, illustrated by Eikoh Hosoe; Atheneum, 1970. **Awarded:** Spring Book Festival (picture book honor) 1970.

HOSTOMSKA, ANNA
Pribehy by Anna Hostomska, illustrated by Zdenek Seydl; Albatros, 1969. **Awarded:** Bologna (Graphics for youth) 1968.

HOTZE, SOLLACE
A Circle Unbroken by Sollace Hotze, not illustrated; Clarion, 1988. **Awarded:** Carl Sandburg 1989.

HOUSE, CHARLES
The Friendly Woods by Charles House, illustrated by Victoria de Larrea; Four Winds, 1973. **Awarded:** Council of Wisconsin Writers (juvenile runnerup) 1975.

HOUSER, LOWELL
The Dark Star of Itza by Alida Malkus, illustrated by Lowell Houser; Harcourt, 1930. **Awarded:** Newbery (honor) 1931

HOUSTON, JAMES
Awarded: Vicky Metcalf 1977.

Ghost Paddle by James Houston; Longmans, 1972. **Awarded:** Amelia Frances Howard-Gibbon (runnerup) 1973.

Long Claws by James Houston in The Winter Fun Book by Laima Dingwall; Greey de Pencier, 1980. **Awarded:** Vicky Metcalf Short Story 1981.

Long Claws: An Arctic Adventure written and illustrated by James Houston; McClelland & Stewart, 1981; Atheneum, 1981. **Awarded:** Canadian Library Assn. (runnerup) 1982.

River Runners: A Tale of Hardship and Bravery written and illustrated by James Houston; McClelland & Stewart, 1979. **Awarded:** Canadian Library Assn. 1980.

Tikta'liktak: An Eskimo Legend written and illustrated by James Houston; Longmans, 1965. **Awarded:** Canadian Library Assn. 1966.

The White Archer: An Eskimo Legend written and illustrated by James Houston; Longmans, 1967. **Awarded:** Canadian Library Assn. 1968.

HOUSTON, JAMES D.
Farewell To Manzanar by James D. Houston and Jeanne Wakatsuki Houston, not illustrated; Houghton Mifflin, 1973. **Awarded:** FOCAL. 1988

HOUSTON, JEANNE WAKATSUKI
Farewell To Manzanar by Jeanne Wakatsuki Houston and James
D. Houston, not illustrated; Houghton Mifflin, 1973.
Awarded: FOCAL 1988.

HOWARD, ELIZABETH
Dorinda by Elizabeth Howard, illustrated by Leonard Weisgard;
Lothrop, Lee & Shepard, 1944. **Awarded:** Spring Book
Festival (older honor) 1944.

HOWARD, ELIZABETH FITZGERALD
Aunt Flossie's Hats (and Crab Cakes Later) by Elizabeth
Fitzgerald Howard, illustrated by James Ransome; Clarion,
1990. **Awarded:** Parents' Choice (Picture Book) 1991.

HOWARD, ELLEN
Circle of Giving by Ellen Howard, not illustrated; Atheneum,
1984. **Awarded:** Golden Kite (fiction honor) 1984.

Her Own Story by Ellen Howard, not illustrated; Atheneum, 1988.
Awarded: PEN Center USA West 1989.

HOWARD, M. MAITLAND
The Making of Man by Ian Wolfram Cornwall, illustrated by M.
Maitland Howard; Phoenix House, 1960. **Awarded:**
Carnegie 1960.

HOWARD ASSOCIATES, RON
The Palestinians by David McDowall, illustrated by Ron Howard
Associates; Watts, 1986. **Awarded:** Other Award 1987.

HOWE, DEBORAH
Bunnicula: A Rabbit Tale of Mystery by Deborah Howe and
James Howe, illustrated by Alan Daniel; Atheneum, 1979.
Awarded: Buckeye (grades 4-8 honor) 1982; Emphasis on
Reading (grades 4-6) 1981-82; Dorothy Canfield Fisher 1981;
Golden Sower 1981; Iowa Children's Choice 1982; Land of
Enchantment 1982; Nene (runnerup) 1982; Nene 1983;
Sequoyah 1982; South Carolina Children's 1981; Sunshine
1984; Young Readers Choice 1982,

HOWE, GERTRUDE
High Prairie by Walter Havighurst and Marion Havighurst, illus-
trated by Gertrude Howe; Farrar, 1944. **Awarded:** Spring
Book Festival (middle honor) 1944.

HOWE, JAMES
Bunnicula: A Rabbit Tale of Mystery by Deborah Howe and
James Howe, illustrated by Alan Daniel; Atheneum, 1979.
Awarded: Buckeye (grades 4-8 honor) 1982; Emphasis on
Reading (grades 4-6) 1981-82; Dorothy Canfield Fisher 1981;
Golden Sower 1981; Iowa Children's Choice 1982; Land of
Enchantment 1982; Nene (runnerup) 1982; Nene 1983;
Sequoyah 1982; South Carolina Children's 1981; Sunshine
1984; Young Readers Choice 1982.

The Celery Stalks at Midnight by James Howe, illustrated by
Leslie Morrill; Atheneum, 1983. **Awarded:** CRABbery
(honor) 1984.

Harold and Chester in Scared Silly: A Halloween Treat by James
Howe, illustrated by Leslie Morrill; Morrow, 1989.
Awarded: North Dakota Children's Choice (Picture Book)
1992.

The Hospital Book by James Howe, illustrated with photographs
by Mal Warshaw; Crown, 1981. **Awarded:** Boston Globe
Horn Book (nonfiction honor) 1981.

Howliday Inn by James Howe, illustrated by Lynn Munsinger;
Atheneum, 1982. **Awarded:** Volunteer State 1984.

Nighty-nightmare by James Howe, illustrated by Leslie Morrill;
Atheneum, 1987. **Awarded:** Garden State Children's Book
Award (Younger Fiction) 1990.

There's a Monster Under My Bed by James Howe, illustrated by
David Rose; Atheneum, 1986. **Awarded:** Colorado
Children's Book Award (Runnerup) 1988; Washington Irving
(Younger fiction) 1988.

HOWELL, FRANK
Who Speaks for Wolf by Paula Underwood Spencer, illustrated by
Frank Howell; Tribe of Two Press, 1983. **Awarded:**
Jefferson Cup 1984.

HOWELL, TROY
The Night Swimmers by Betsy Byars, illustrated by Troy Howell;
Delacorte, 1980. **Awarded:** American Book Award (children's fiction hardcover) 1981; Boston Globe Horn Book (fiction honor) 1980.

Ugly Duckling by Hans Christian Andersen, illustrated by Troy
Howell; Dodd, Mead, 1987; Putnam, 1990. **Awarded:**
Redbook 1990.

HOWELL, VIRGINIA
Who Likes the Dark? by Virginia Howell, illustrated by Marjorie
Thompson; Howell, Soskin, 1945. **Awarded:** Spring Book
Festival (younger honor) 1946.

HOWKER, JANNI
Badger on the Barge and Other Stories by Janni Howker, not
illustrated; Julia MacRae, 1984; Greenwillow, 1984.
Awarded: Burnley Express 1985; International Reading Assn.
1985.

Isaac Campion by Janni Howker, not illustrated; Greenwillow,
1986; Julia MacRae, 1986. **Awarded:** Boston Globe Horn
Book (fiction honor) 1987; Carnegie (highly commended)
1986; New York Times Notable 1987

The Nature of the Beast by Janni Howker, not illustrated;
MacRae, 1985; Greenwillow, 1985. **Awarded:** Carnegie
(highly commended) 1985; Observer Teenage Fiction 1985;
Whitbread 1985.

HOWLAND, DOUGLAS
Moon Moth by Carleen Maley Hutchins, illustrated by Douglas
Howland; Coward, 1965. **Awarded:** New Jersey Institute of
Technology (science) 1965.

HSIA, MIRIAM
Hyena Day by Miriam Hsia and Robert Caputo; photographs by
Robert Caputo; Coward, 1978. **Awarded:** New York
Academy of Sciences (younger honor) 1979.

HSU-FLANDERS, LILLIAN
Dumpling Soup by Jama Kim Rattigan, illustrated by Lillian Hsu-
Flanders; Little Brown, 1992. **Awarded:** New Voices New
World 1990.

HU, YING-HWA
Make a Joyful Sound edited by Deborah Slier, illustrated by
Cornelius Van Wright and Ying-Hwa Hu; Checkerboard,
1991. **Awarded:** Hungry Mind (Middle Reader/Fiction)
1992.

HUBBARD, HARLAN
Shanty Boat written and illustrated by Harlan Hubbard; Dodd
Mead, 1953. **Awarded:** Jesse Stuart 1980.

HUBBARD, RALPH
Queer Person by Ralph Hubbard, illustrated by Harold Von
Schmidt; Doubleday, 1930. **Awarded:** Newbery (honor)
1931.

HUCK, CHARLOTTE
Awarded: Landau 1979.

HUDSON, JAN

Dawnrider by Jan Hudson, not illustrated; HarperCollins, 1990; Philomel, 1990. **Awarded:** R. Ross Annett 1991; Young Adult Canadian (honorable mention) 1991.

Sweetgrass by Jan Hudson, not illustrated; Tree Frog Press, 1984; Philomel, 1989. **Awarded:** Governor General (author) 1984; Canadian Library Assn. 1984; International Board on Books for Young People (Writing/Canada) 1986; Parents' Choice (story book) 1989.

HUDSON, MARK

Alphabet City by Mark Hudson, to be published by Macmillan. **Awarded:** Macmillan Prize (1st Prize) 1988.

HUETHER, ANNE FRANCES

Glass and Man written and illustrated by Anne F. Huether; Lippincott, 1963. **Awarded:** Indiana Authors Day (young adult) 1964.

HUFFMAN, PAMELA

Hang Toughf by Matthew Lancaster, illustrated by Pamela Huffman; Paulist Press, 1985. **Awarded:** Catholic Book Awards (Youth) 1986.

HUFFMAN, TOM

Be a Perfect Person in Just Three Days by Stephen Manes, illustrated by Tom Huffman; Houghton Mifflin, 1982; Bantam, 1983. **Awarded:** California Young Reader (Intermediate) 1988; CRABbery (honor) 1983; Georgia Children's 1987; Nene 1986; Charlie May Simon 1984-85; Sunshine State 1986; Surrey School 1985.

Wrapped for Eternity: The Story of the Egyptian Mummies by Mildred Mastin Pace, illustrated by Tom Huffman; McGraw, 1974. **Awarded:** New York Academy of Sciences (older honor) 1975.

HUGHES, DAVID

Strat and Chatto by Jan Mark, illustrated by David Hughes; Walker Books, 1989. **Awarded:** Mother Goose 1990.

HUGHES, GEORGE

Help! I'm a Prisoner in the Library by Eth Clifford, illustrated by George Hughes; Houghton Mifflin, 1979. **Awarded:** Young Hoosier (grades 4-6) 1982.

Just Tell Me When We're Dead! by Eth Clifford, illustrated by George Hughes; Houghton Mifflin, 1983. **Awarded:** Sequoyah 1986.

HUGHES, JAN

The Alligator under the Bed by Joan Lowry Nixon, illustrated by Jan Hughes; Putnam, 1974. **Awarded:** Steck-Vaughn 1975.

Brown Mouse and Vole by Vicki Kimmel Artis, illustrated by Jan Hughes; Putnam, 1975. **Awarded:** Council of Wisconsin Writers (picture book runnerup) 1976.

HUGHES, MONICA

Awarded: Vicky Metcalf 1981.

Blaine's Way by Monica Hughes, not illustrated; Clark Irwin, 1986. **Awarded:** R. Ross Annett 1987.

The Guardian of Isis by Monica Hughes, not illustrated; Hamish Hamilton, 1981; Atheneum, 1982. **Awarded:** Governor General (author) 1981.

Hunter in the Dark by Monica Hughes, not illustrated; Clarke, Irwin, 1982; Atheneum, 1983. **Awarded:** Alberta Writing for Youth 1980; R.Ross Annett 1983; Beaver Trophy 1981; Governor General (author) 1982; Young Adult Canadian Book Award 1983.

Iron Barred Door by Monica Hughes in Anthology Two; Nelson, 1982. **Awarded:** Vicky Metcalf Short Story 1983.

The Keeper of the Isis Light by Monica Hughes, not illustrated; Hamish Hamilton, 1980. **Awarded:** International Board on Books for Young People (honour list/author/Canada) 1982.

Little Fingerling: A Japanese Folktale by Monica Hughes, illustrated by Brenda Clark; Kids Can Press, 1989. **Awarded:** Amelia Frances Howard-Gibbon (1st runnerup) 1990; IODE 1989.

Ring-rise Ring-set by Monica Hughes, not illustrated; Watts, 1982; McRae, 1982. **Awarded:** Guardian (runnerup) 1983.

Space Trap by Monica Hughes, not illustrated; Groundwood, 1983. **Awarded:** R. Ross Annett 1984.

HUGHES, SHIRLEY

Awarded: Eleanor Farjeon 1984.

The Big Alfie and Annie Rose Storybook written and illustrated by Shirley Hughes; Lothrop, Lee & Shepard, 1989, c1988. **Awarded:** Parents' Choice (Story Book) 1989.

Chips and Jessie written and illustrated by Shirley Hughes; Bodley Head, 1985. **Awarded:** Kurt Maschler (runnerup) 1985.

Dogger written and illustrated by Shirley Hughes; Bodley Head, 1977. **Awarded:** Greenaway 1977.

The First Margaret Mahy Story Book: Stories and Poems by Margaret Mahy, illustrated by Shirley Hughes; Dent, 1972. **Awarded:** Esther Glen 1973.

Flutes and Cymbals (Poems) compiled by Leonard Clark, illustrated by Shirley Hughes; Bodley Head, 1968. **Awarded:** Greenaway (honour) 1968.

Helpers written and illustrated by Shirley Hughes; Bodley Head, 1975. **Awarded:** Greenaway (commended) 1975; Other Award 1976.

The Snailman by Brenda Sivers, illustrated by Shirley Hughes; Little, Brown, 1978. **Awarded:** Little Brown Canadian 1977.

The Three Toymakers by Ursula Moray Williams, illustrated by Shirley Hughes; Thomas Nelson, 1971. **Awarded:** Spring Book Festival (middle honor) 1971.

HUGHES, TED

The Iron Man by Ted Hughes, illustrated by Andrew Davidson; Faber & Faber, 1985. **Awarded:** Kurt Maschler 1985.

Moon-bells and Other Poems by Ted Hughes, not illustrated; Chatto & Windus, 1978. **Awarded:** Signal Poetry 1979.

The Rattlebag: An Anthology of Poetry by Ted Hughes and Seamus Heaney, not illustrated; Faber, 1982. **Awarded:** Signal Poetry 1983.

Season Songs by Ted Hughes, illustrated by Leonard Baskin; Viking, 1975. **Awarded:** Children's Book Showcase 1976.

What Is the Truth? A Farmyard Fable for the Young by Ted Hughes, illustrated by R. J. Lloyd; Faber & Faber, 1984. **Awarded:** Guardian 1985; Signal Poetry 1985.

HUGHEY, ROBERTA

The Question Box by Roberta Hughey, not illustrated; Delacorte, 1984. **Awarded:** Delacorte (honorable mention) 1983.

HUIGIN, SEAN O.

The Ghost Horse of the Mounties by Sean O. Huigin, not illustrated; Black Moss Press, 1983. **Awarded:** Governor General (author) 1983.

HULL, JAMES
The Stage-struck Seal written and illustrated by James Hull; Holt, 1937. **Awarded:** Julia Ellsworth Ford 1937.

HULME, SUSAN
Where is Bobo? by Susan Hulme, illustrated by Jan Siegieda; Methuen, 1985. **Awarded:** Best Book for Babies 1986.

HULSMANN, EVA
The Snow Monkey at Home by Margaret Rau, illustrated by Eva Hulsmann; Knopf, 1979. **Awarded:** Southern California Council (distinguished work of nonfiction) 1980.

HUMPHREY, HENRY
What Is it For? written and illustrated by Henry Humphrey; Simon & Schuster, 1969. **Awarded:** New York Times Best Illustrated 1969.

HUMPHREYS, GRAHAM
The Intruder by John Rowe Townsend, illustrated by Graham Humphreys; Oxford, 1969. **Awarded:** Carnegie (honour) 1969.

HUMPHRIES, STELLA
Adventures in the Desert by Herbert Kaufmann, translated by Stella Humphries, illustrated by Eugene Karlin; Obolensky, 1961. **Awarded:** Spring Book Festival (older) 1961.

Annuzza, a Girl of Romania by Hertha Seuberlich, translated by Stella Humphries, illustrated by Gerhard Pallasch; Rand, 1962. **Awarded:** Lewis Carroll Shelf 1963.

In the Land of Ur: The Discovery of Ancient Mesopotamia by Hans Baumann, translated by Stella Humphries, illustrated by Hans Peter Renner; Pantheon, 1969; Oxford, 1969. **Awarded:** Batchelder 1971.

HUNDAL, NANCY
I Heard My Mother Call My Name by Nancy Hundal, illustrated by Laura Fernandez; HarperCollins, 1990. **Awarded:** Egoff Prize for Children's Literature 1991.

HUNDLEY, EUNICE
Naya Nuki: Girl Who Ran by Ken Thomasma, illustrated by Eunice Hundley; Baker Book House, 1983. **Awarded:** Indian Paintbrush 1986.

HUNT, IRENE
Across Five Aprils by Irene Hunt, illustrated by Albert J. Pucci; Follett; 1964. **Awarded:** Lewis Carroll Shelf 1966; Charles W. Follett 1964; Newbery (honor) 1965.

The Everlasting Hills by Irene Hunt, not illustrated; Scribner, 1985. **Awarded:** Parents' Choice (literature) 1985.

No Promises in the Wind by Irene Hunt, not illustrated; Follett, 1970. **Awarded:** Charles W. Follett 1971.

Up a Road Slowly by Irene Hunt, not illustrated; Follett, 1966. **Awarded:** International Board on Books for Young People (USA) 1970; Newbery 1967.

HUNT, LAWRENCE J.
Secret of Haunted Crags by Lawrence J. Hunt, not illustrated; Funk & Wagnalls, 1965. **Awarded:** Edgar Allan Poe (runnerup) 1966.

HUNT, MABEL LEIGH
Better Known as Johnny Appleseed by Mabel Leigh Hunt, illustrated by James Daugherty; Lippincott, 1950. **Awarded:** Newbery (honor) 1951.

Billy Button's Butter'd Biscuit by Mabel Leigh Hunt, illustrated by Katherine Milhous; Stokes, 1941. **Awarded:** Spring Book Festival (younger honor) 1941.

Cupola House by Mabel Leigh Hunt, illustrated by Nora S. Unwin; Lippincott, 1961. **Awarded:** Indiana Authors Day (young children) 1962.

Have You Seen Tom Thumb? by Mabel Leigh Hunt, illustrated by Fritz Eichenberg; Stokes, 1942. **Awarded:** Newbery (honor) 1943.

The Peddler's Clock by Mabel Leigh Hunt, illustrated by Elizabeth Orton Jones; Grosset, 1943. **Awarded:** Spring Book Festival (younger honor) 1943.

Stars for Christy by Mabel Leigh Hunt, illustrated by Velma Ilsley; Lippincott, 1956. **Awarded:** Indiana Authors Day (children) 1957.

HUNT, NAN
A Rabbit Named Harris by Nan Hunt, illustrated by Betina Ogden; William Collins, 1991; Collins/Angus & Robertson, 1991. **Awarded:** New South Wales State Literary Awards (Children's) 1987.

Whistle Up the Chimney by Nan Hunt and Craig Smith, illustrated by Craig Smith; Collins, 1982. **Awarded:** New South Wales State Literary Awards (Children's) 1982.

HUNT, PAUL
Paul Hunt's Night Diary written and illustrated by Paul Hunt; Child's Play, 1992. **Awarded:** Mother Goose (runnerup) 1993.

HUNT, WALDO H.
Awarded: Chandler Reward of Merit 1969.

HUNTER, BERNICE THURMAN
Awarded: Vicky Metcalf 1990.

That Scatterbrain Booky by Bernice Thurman Hunter; Scholastic-TAB, 1981. **Awarded:** IODE 1981.

HUNTER, EVAN
The Remarkable Harry by Evan Hunter, illustrated by Ted Hunter, Mark Hunter, and Richard Hunter; Abelard-Schuman, 1961. **Awarded:** Spring Book Festival (ages 4-8 honor) 1961.

HUNTER, KRISTIN
Awarded: Drexel 1980.

Guests in the Promised Land: Stories by Kristin Hunter, not illustrated; Scribner, 1973. **Awarded:** Christopher (ages 12-up) 1974; National Book Award (finalist) 1974; Spring Book Festival (older) 1973.

The Soul Brothers and Sister Lou by Kristin Hunter, not illustrated; Scribner, 1968. **Awarded:** Lewis Carroll Shelf 1971; Council on Interracial Books (ages 12-16) 1968.

HUNTER, LLYN
Allosaurus by Janet Riehecky, illustrated by Llyn Hunter; Child's World, 1988. **Awarded:** Society of Midland Authors (Juvenile Nonfiction) 1989.

HUNTER, MARK
The Remarkable Harry by Evan Hunter, illustrated by Mark Hunter, Ted Hunter, and Richard Hunter; Abelard-Schuman, 1961. **Awarded:** Spring Book Festival (ages 4-8 honor) 1961.

HUNTER, MOLLIE
(pseudonym for Maureen Mollie Hunter McIlwraith)

The Haunted Mountain by Mollie Hunter, illustrated by Laszlo Kubinyi; Harper, 1972. **Awarded:** New York Times Notable Books 1972.

The Lothian Run by Mollie Hunter, not illustrated; Funk and Wagnalls, 1970. **Awarded:** Spring Book Festival (older honor) 1970.

A Sound of Chariots by Mollie Hunter, not illustrated; Harper, 1972. **Awarded:** Child Study 1972; New York Times Notable Books 1972; Phoenix Award 1992.

A Stranger Came Ashore: A Story of Suspense by Mollie Hunter, not illustrated; Harper, 1975. **Awarded:** Boston Globe Horn Book (fiction honor) 1976; New York Times Notable Books 1975.

The Stronghold by Mollie Hunter, not illustrated; Hamilton, 1974. **Awarded:** Carnegie 1974.

The Third Eye by Mollie Hunter, not illustrated; Harper & Row, 1979. **Awarded:** Virginia Young Readers (High School) 1986.

HUNTER, RICHARD
The Remarkable Harry by Evan Hunter, illustrated by Richard Hunter, Ted Hunter, and Mark Hunter; Abelard-Schuman, 1961. **Awarded:** Spring Book Festival (ages 4-8 honor) 1961.

HUNTER, SUSAN
Make It Happy: What Sex Is All About by Jane Cousins, illustrated by Susan Hunter; Virago, 1978. **Awarded:** Times Educational Supplement (senior) 1979.

HUNTER, TED
The Remarkable Harry by Evan Hunter, illustrated by Ted Hunter, Mark Hunter, and Richard Hunter; Abelard-Schuman, 1961. **Awarded:** Spring Book Festival (ages 4-8 honor) 1961.

HUNTER BLAIR, PAULINE CLARKE
see CLARKE, PAULINE

HUNTINGTON, HARRIET
Awarded: Southern California Council (comprehensive contribution of lasting value for children and young people) 1969.

HURD, CLEMENT
The Bad Little Duck-hunter by Margaret Wise Brown, illustrated by Clement Hurd; Scott, 1947. **Awarded:** Spring Book Festival (younger honor) 1947.

Catfish by Edith Thacher Hurd, illustrated by Clement Hurd; Viking, 1970. **Awarded:** Spring Book Festival (picture book honor) 1970.

The Day the Sun Danced by Edith Thacher Hurd, illustrated by Clement Hurd; Harper, 1966. **Awarded:** Spring Book Festival (picture book honor) 1966.

Monkey in the Jungle by Edna Mitchell Preston, illustrated by Clement Hurd; Viking, 1968. **Awarded:** Boston Globe Horn Book (illustration honor) 1969.

The Mother Beaver by Edith Thacher Hurd, illustrated by Clement Hurd; Little, Brown, 1971. **Awarded:** Children's Book Showcase 1972.

The Runaway Bunny by Margaret Wise Brown, illustrated by Clement Hurd; Harper & Row, 1942. **Awarded:** Emphasis on Reading (grades K-1) 1981-82.

HURD, EDITH THACHER
Catfish by Edith Thacher Hurd, illustrated by Clement Hurd; Viking, 1970. **Awarded:** Spring Book Festival (picture book honor) 1970.

The Day the Sun Danced by Edith Thacher Hurd, illustrated by Clement Hurd; Harper, 1966. **Awarded:** Spring Book Festival (picture book honor) 1966.

The Mother Beaver by Edith Thacher Hurd, illustrated by Clement Hurd; Little, Brown, 1971. **Awarded:** Children's Book Showcase 1972.

Sandpipers by Edith Thacher Hurd, illustrated by Lucienne Bloch; Crowell, 1961. **Awarded:** New York Times Best Illustrated 1961.

HURD, MICHAEL
Oxford Junior Companion to Music by Michael Hurd, based on the original published by Percy Scholes, 2nd ed.; illustrated with photographs; Oxford, 1979. **Awarded:** Times Educational Supplement (senior) 1980.

HURD, PETER
Swift Rivers by Cornelia Meigs, illustrated by Peter Hurd; Little Brown, 1932. **Awarded:** Newbery (honor) 1933.

HURD, THACHER
Mama Don't Allow written and illustrated by Thacher Hurd; Harper & Row, 1985. **Awarded:** Boston Globe Horn Book (illustration) 1985.

HURLE, GARRY
The Second-Hand Tongue by Garry Hurle. **Awarded:** Mary Grant Bruce (Writer in Gippsland) 1990.

HURLEY, FRANK
Shackleton's Argonauts: A Saga of the Antarctic Ice-packs written and illustrated by Frank Hurley; Angus & Robertson, 1948. **Awarded:** Children's Book Council of Australia 1948.

HURLIMANN, RUTH
The Cat and Mouse Who Shared a House written and illustrated by Ruth Hurlimann, translated by Anthea Bell; Walck, 1974. **Awarded:** Batchelder 1976.

Stadtmaus und Landmaus retold and illustrated by Ruth Hurlimann; Atlantis Verlag. **Awarded:** Bologna (Graphics for Children) 1972.

HURMENCE, BELINDA
A Girl Called Boy by Belinda Hurmence, not illustrated; Ticknor & Fields, 1982. **Awarded:** Parents' Choice (literature) 1982.

The Nightwalker by Belinda Hurmence, not illustrated; Clarion, 1988. **Awarded:** North Carolina AAUW 1989.

Tancy by Belinda Hurmence, not illustrated; Clarion, 1984. **Awarded:** Golden Kite (fiction) 1984; North Carolina AAUW 1984.

HURWITZ, JOHANNA
Class Clown by Johanna Hurwitz, illustrated by Sheila Hamanaka; Morrow, 1987. **Awarded:** Kentucky Bluegrass (grades 4-8) 1989; Mississippi Children's Book Award 1989; South Carolina Children's 1990; West Virginia Children's 1988-89.

The Hot and Cold Summer by Johanna Hurwitz, illustrated by Gail Owens; Morrow, 1984. **Awarded:** Indian Paintbrush 1987; Parents' Choice (literature) 1984; Texas Bluebonnet 1987.

The Rabbi's Girls by Johanna Hurwitz, illustrated by Pamela Johnson; Morrow, 1982. **Awarded:** Parents' Choice (literature) 1982.

Teacher's Pet by Johanna Hurwitz, illustrated by Sheila Hamanaka; Morrow, 1988. **Awarded:** Garden State Children's (Younger Fiction) 1991; Sunshine State Young Reader's Award (grades 3-5) 1990.

HUTCHINGS, EDWARD
Surely You're Joking, Mr. Feynman! by Richard P. Feynman as told to Ralph Leighton, edited by Edward Hutchings; not illustrated; Bantam, 1986. **Awarded:** New York Academy of Sciences (older honor) 1987.

HUTCHINS, CARLEEN MALEY
Moon Moth by Carleen Maley Hutchins, illustrated by Douglas Howland; Coward, 1965. **Awarded:** New Jersey Institute of Technology (science) 1965.

HUTCHINS, HAZEL J.
The Three and Many Wishes of Jason Reid by Hazel J. Hutchins, illustrated by Julie Tennent; Viking Kestrel, 1988. **Awarded:** Reading Magic Award 1988.

HUTCHINS, PAT
Changes, Changes written and illustrated by Pat Hutchins; Macmillan, 1971. **Awarded:** Art Books for Children 1973; Children's Book Showcase 1972; New York Times Best Illustrated 1971; Spring Book Festival (picture book honor) 1971.

The Doorbell Rang written and illustrated by Pat Hutchins; Bodley Head, 1986. **Awarded:** Kurt Maschler (runnerup) 1986.

One-eyed Jake written and illustrated by Pat Hutchins; Bodley Head, 1979. **Awarded:** Greenaway (highly commended) 1979.

Rosie's Walk written and illustrated by Pat Hutchins; Macmillan, 1968. **Awarded:** Boston Globe Horn Book (illustration honor) 1968.

Titch written and illustrated by Pat Hutchins; Bodley Head, 1972. **Awarded:** International Board on Books for Young People (honour list/illustration/Great Britain) 1974.

The Wind Blew written and illustrated by Pat Hutchins; Bodley Head, 1974. **Awarded:** Greenaway 1974.

HUTCHINS, ROSS E.
Awarded: Eva L. Gordon 1979.

HUTCHINSON, WILLIAM
Milton Hershey: Chocolate King by Mary Malone, illustrated by William Hutchinson; Garrard, 1971. **Awarded:** New Jersey Institute of Technology 1971.

Sampson: Yankee Stallion by Justin F. Denzel, illustrated by William Hutchinson; Garrard, 1980. **Awarded:** New Jersey Institute of Technology 1981.

HUTCHISON, P. A.
Animal Clocks and Compasses: From Animal Migration to Space Travel by Margaret Hyde, illustrated by P. A. Hutchison; Whittlesey, 1960. **Awarded:** Edison Mass Media (science book) 1961.

HUTCHISON, PAULA
Abe Lincoln Gets His Chance by Frances Cavanah, illustrated by Paula Hutchison; Rand, 1959. **Awarded:** Indiana Authors Day (young children) 1960.

HUTTON, WARWICK
Adam and Eve: The Bible Story adapted and illustrated by Warwick Hutton; McElderry, 1987. **Awarded:** Parents' Choice (Picture Book) 1987.

Jonah and the Great Fish written and illustrated by Warwick Hutton; Atheneum, 1984. **Awarded:** Boston Globe Horn Book (illustration) 1984; New York Times Best Illustrated 1984; New York Times Notable 1984.

Moses in the Bulrushes written and illustrated by Warwick Hutton; Atheneum, 1986. **Awarded:** New York Times Notable 1986.

The Nose Tree adapted and illustrated by Warwick Hutton; Atheneum, 1980; McRae, 1981. **Awarded:** New York Times Best Illustrated 1981.

The Silver Cow retold by Susan Cooper, illustrated by Warwick Hutton; Atheneum, 1983. **Awarded:** New York Times Notable Books 1983; Parents' Choice (illustration) 1983; Parents' Choice (Literature) 1983.

Theseus and the Minotaur written and illustrated by Warwick Hutton; McElderry, 1989. **Awarded:** New York Times Best Illustrated 1989.

HUXLEY, DEE
Onion Tears by Diana Kidd, illustrated by Dee Huxley; Collins, 1989. **Awarded:** Diabetes Australia 1990.

HUYNH, QUANG NHUONG
The Land I Lost: Adventures of a Boy in Vietnam by Quang Nhuong Huynh, photographs by Vo-Dinh Mai; Harper, 1982. **Awarded:** Friends of American Writers ($500 award) 1983.

HYDE, MARGARET
Animal Clocks and Compasses: From Animal Migration to Space Travel by Margaret Hyde, illustrated by P. A. Hutchison; Whittlesey, 1960. **Awarded:** Edison Mass Media (science books) 1961.

HYMAN, TRINA SCHART
Awarded: Drexel Citation 1993; Keene State College Festival 1991.

All in Free But Janey by Elizabeth Johnson, illustrated by Trina Schart Hyman; Little Brown, 1968. **Awarded:** Boston Globe Horn Book (illustration honor) 1968.

Canterbury Tales selected by Barbara Cohen, illustrated by Trina Schart Hyman; Lothrop, Lee & Shepard, 1988. **Awarded:** Golden Kite (Picture-Illustration honor) 1988; New Jersey Institute of Technology 1990.

The Castle in the Attic by Elizabeth Winthrop, illustrated by Trina Schart Hyman; Holiday House, 1985. **Awarded:** California Young Reader (Intermediate) 1989; Dorothy Canfield Fisher 1987; West Virginia Children's (Honor book) 1988-89.

Cat Poems by Myra Cohn Livingston, illustrated by Trina Schart Hyman; Holiday House, 1987. **Awarded:** Parents' Choice (Story Book) 1987.

The Fortune-Tellers by Lloyd Alexander, illustrated by Trina Schart Hyman; Dutton, 1992. **Awarded:** Boston Globe Horn Book (Illustration) 1993; Golden Kite (Illustration honor) 1992; New York Times Best Illustrated 1992; Parents Choice (Story Book) 1992.

Greedy Mariana and Other Folktales of the Antilles by Dorothy Sharp Carter, illustrated by Trina Schart Hyman; Atheneum, 1974. **Awarded:** Children's Book Showcase 1975.

Hershel and the Hanukkah Goblins by Eric Kimmel, illustrated by Trina Schart Hyman; Holiday House, 1989. **Awarded:** Caldecott (honor) 1990; Washington Children's Choice 1992.

King Stork by Howard Pyle, illustrated by Trina Schart Hyman; Little Brown, 1973. **Awarded:** Boston Globe Horn Book (illustration) 1973.

Little Red Riding Hood by Jacob Grimm and Wilhelm Grimm, retold and illustrated by Trina Schart Hyman; Holiday House, 1983. **Awarded:** Caldecott (honor) 1984; Golden Kite (picture illustration) 1983; Parents' Choice (illustration) 1983.

Magic in the Mist by Margaret Mary Kimmel, illustrated by Trina Schart Hyman; Atheneum, 1974. **Awarded:** Children's Book Showcase 1976.

The Marrow of the World by Ruth Nichols, illustrated by Trina Schart Hyman; Macmillan Canada, 1972. **Awarded:** Canadian Library Assn. 1973.

The Night Journey by Kathryn Lasky, illustrated by Trina Schart Hyman; Warne, 1981. **Awarded:** Sydney Taylor Book (older children) 1982; Jewish Book Council (children) 1982.

On to Widecombe Fair by Patricia Lee Gauch, illustrated by Trina Schart Hyman; Putnam, 1978. **Awarded:** Boston Globe Horn Book (illustration honor) 1978.

A Room Made of Windows by Eleanor Cameron, illustrated by Trina Schart Hyman; Atlantic-Little, 1971. **Awarded:** Boston Globe Horn Book (text) 1971; FOCAL 1989; New York Times Notable Books 1971; Spring Book Festival (older honor) 1971.

Saint George and the Dragon: A Golden Legend adapted by Margaret Hodges from Edmund Spenser's Faerie Queene, illustrated by Trina Schart Hyman; Little Brown, 1984. **Awarded:** Caldecott 1985; Carolyn W. Field 1985; New York Times Best Illustrated 1984.

A Walk Out of the World by Ruth Nichols, illustrated by Trina Schart Hyman; Harcourt, 1969. **Awarded:** Spring Book Festival (middle honor) 1969.

Will You Sign Here, John Hancock? by Jean Fritz, illustrated by Trina Schart Hyman; Coward, 1976. **Awarded:** Boston Globe Horn Book (nonfiction honor) 1976.

I

IBBOTSON, EVA
Which Witch? by Eva Ibbotson, illustrated by Annabel Large; Macmillan, 1979. **Awarded:** Carnegie (commended) 1979.

IGNATOWICZ, NINA
The Bear and the People written and illustrated by Reiner Zimnik, translated by Nina Ignatowicz; Harper, 1971. **Awarded:** New York Times Notable Books 1971.

IHRIG, ROBERT
Strange Summer in Stratford by Norah A. Perez, illustrated by Robert Ihrig; Little, Brown, 1968. **Awarded:** Little Brown Canadian 1967.

ILIN, M.
(Pseudonym for MARSHAK, ILIA IAKOVLEVICH)

A Ring and a Riddle by M. Ilin and E. A. Segal, translated by Beatrice Kinkead, illustrated by Vera Bock; Lippincott, 1944. **Awarded:** Spring Book Festival (younger) 1944.

ILSLEY, VELMA
She, the Adventuress by Dorothy Crayder, illustrated by Velma Ilsley; Atheneum, 1973. **Awarded:** Spring Book Festival (middle honor) 1973.

Son for a Day by Corrine Gerson, illustrated by Velma Ilsley; Atheneum, 1980. **Awarded:** Christopher (fiction ages 8-12) 1981.

Stars for Christy by Mabel Leigh Hunt, illustrated by Velma Ilsley; Lippincott, 1956. **Awarded:** Indiana Authors Day (children) 1957.

INDERIEDEN, NANCY
My Sister by Karen Hirsch, illustrated by Nancy Inderieden; Carolrhoda, 1977. **Awarded:** Woodward Park School (honorable mention) 1982.

INGPEN, ROBERT R.
Awarded: Hans Christian Andersen (illustrator) 1986; Dromkeen Medal 1989.

The Runaway Punt by Michael F. Page, illustrated by Robert R. Ingpen; Rigby, 1976. **Awarded:** International Board on Books for Young People (illustration/Australia) 1978.

Storm Boy by Colin Thiele, illustrated by Robert Ingpen; Rigby, 1963. **Awarded:** Children's Book Council of Australia (best illustrated) 1975.

INGRAHAM, ERICK
Cross-country Cat by Mary Calhoun, illustrated by Erick Ingraham; Morrow, 1979. **Awarded:** Boston Globe Horn Book (illustration honor) 1979; Colorado Children's Book Award 1981; Golden Kite (fiction honor) 1979; Little Archer 1980; Washington Children's Choice 1982

Porcupine Stew by Beverly Major, illustrated by Erick Ingraham; Morrow, 1982. **Awarded:** Biennale Illustrations Bratislava (plaque) 1983; Parents' Choice (illustration) 1982.

INKAMALA, JENNIFER
The Rainbow Serpent by Elaine Sharpe, illustrated by Jennifer Inkamala; Yipirinya School Council, 1990. **Awarded:** Australian Multicultural Children's Literature Award (Picture Book) 1991.

INKPEN, MICK
Kipper written and illustrated by Mick Inkpen; Hodder & Stoughton, 1991. **Awarded:** Nottinghamshire (Acorn) 1992.

Penguin Small written and illustrated by Mick Inkpen; Hodder & Stoughton, 1992; Harcourt Brace, 1993. **Awarded:** British Book Awards (Illustrated runnerup) 1992.

Threadbear written and illustrated by Mick Inkpen; Hodder & Stoughton, 1990; Little Brown, 1991. **Awarded:** Children's Book Award (Federation) 1991; Nottinghamshire (Acorn) 1991.

INNOCENTI, ROBERTO
The Adventures of Pinocchio by Carlo Collodi, illustrated by Roberto Innocenti; Cape, 1988. **Awarded:** Greenaway (Highly Commended) 1988.

A Christmas Carol by Charles Dickens, illustrated by Roberto Innocenti; Stewart, Tabori & Chang, 1990; Creative Education, 1990. **Awarded:** Biennale Illustrations Bratislava (Golden Apple) 1991; Greenaway (Commended) 1990; New York Times Best Illustrated 1990.

Rose Blanche by Roberto Innocenti and Christophe Gallaz, illustrated by Roberto Innocenti, translated by Martha Coventry and Richard Graglia; Creative Education, 1985. **Awarded:** Batchelder 1986.

INOKUMA, YOKO
Unmei no Kishi (original English: *Knight's Fee*) by Rosemary Sutcliff, translated by Yoko Inokuma; Iwanami-shoten, 1970. **Awarded:** International Board on Books for Young People (translation/Japan) 1986.

INOUYE, CAROL
Kids Cooking without a Stove: A Cookbook for Young Children by Aileen Paul, illustrated by Carol Inouye; Doubleday, 1975. **Awarded:** New Jersey Institute of Technology 1977.

INUI, TOMIKO
Hokkyoju no Mushika Mishika by Tomiko Inui, illustrated by Yasuko Horioka; Rironsha, 1961. **Awarded:** Hans Christian Andersen (runnerup) 1964.

INYART, GENE
The Tent under the Spider Tree by Gene Inyart, illustrated by Carol Beech; Watts, 1959. **Awarded:** Franklin Watts 1959.

IONESCO, EUGENE
Story Number 1 by Eugene Ionesco, illustrated by Etienne Delessert; Quist, 1968. **Awarded:** New York Times Best Illustrated 1968.

Story Number 3 by Eugene Ionesco, illustrated by Philippe Corentin; Quist, 1971. **Awarded:** Children's Book Showcase 1971.

IPCAR, DAHLOV
World Full of Horses written and illustrated by Dahlov Ipcar; Doubleday, 1955. **Awarded:** Spring Book Festival (ages 4-8 honor) 1955.

IRELAND, TIMOTHY
Who Lies Inside by Timothy Ireland, not illustrated; Gay Men's Press, 1984. **Awarded:** Other Award 1984.

IRIGARY, LOUIS
A Shepherd Watches, a Shepherd Sings by Louis Irigary and Theodore Taylor, illustrated with photographs; Doubleday, 1977. **Awarded:** Commonwealth Club of California 1977; Western Writers 1977.

IROH, EDDIE
Without a Silver Spoon by Eddie Iroh, not illustrated; Spectrum Books, 1981. **Awarded:** International Board on Books for Young People (writing/Nigeria) 1986.

IRVINE, JOAN
How To Make Pop-Ups by Joan Irvine, illustrated by Barbara Reid; Morrow, 1988. **Awarded:** Utah Children's Informational 1990.

IRVING, JAMES G.
Snakes by Herbert Zim, illustrated by James G. Irving; Morrow, 1949. **Awarded:** Boys Club 1950.

IRVINS, BARBARA
The Wonderful Wonders of One-Two-Three by David Eugene Smith, illustrated by Barbara Irvins; McFarlane, Warde & McFarlane, 1937. **Awarded:** Spring Book Festival (younger honor) 1937.

IRWIN, HADLEY
Abby, My Love by Hadley Irwin, not illustrated; Atheneum, 1985. **Awarded:** Iowa Teen 1988; Sequoyah Young Adult 1988.

Moon and Me by Hadley Irwin, not illustrated; Atheneum, 1981. **Awarded:** Society of Midland Authors 1982.

We Are Mesquakie, We Are One by Hadley Irwin, illustrated with maps; Feminist Press, 1980. **Awarded:** Addams (honor) 1981.

IRWIN, JAMES
Destination, Moon by James Irwin with Al Janssen, illustrated with photos; Multnomah Press, 1989. **Awarded:** Gold Medallion (Elementary) 1990.

ISAACSON, PHILIP
Round Buildings, Square Buildings and Buildings That Wiggle Like a Fish by Philip M. Isaacson, illustrated with photos; Knopf, 1988. **Awarded:** Boston Globe Horn Book (Nonfiction Honor) 1989.

ISADORA, RACHEL
At the Crossroads written and illustrated by Rachel Isadora; Greenwillow, 1991. **Awarded:** Parents' Choice (Story Book) 1991.

Ben's Trumpet written and illustrated by Rachel Isadora; Greenwillow, 1979. **Awarded:** Boston Globe Horn Book (illustration honor) 1979; Caldecott (honor) 1980.

Max written and illustrated by Rachel Isadora; Macmillan, 1976. **Awarded:** Children's Book Showcase 1977.

ISELE, ELIZABETH
The Frog Princess by Elizabeth Isele, illustrated by Michael Hague; Crowell, 1984. **Awarded:** Parents' Choice (literature) 1984.

ISENBART, HANS-HEINRICH
A Foal Is Born by Hans-Heinrich Isenbart, translated by Catherine Edwards, photographs by Hanns-Jorg Anders; Putnam, 1976. **Awarded:** New York Academy of Sciences (younger honor) 1977.

ISENBERG, BARBARA
The Adventures of Albert, the Running Bear by Barbara Isenberg and Susan Wolf, illustrated by Dick Gackenbach; Clarion, 1982. **Awarded:** Emphasis on Reading (Grades 2-3) 1985-86.

ISHII, MOMOKO
The Tongue-Cut Sparrow by Momoko Ishii, illustrated by Suekichi Akaba; Lodestar, 1987. **Awarded:** Parents' Choice (Picture Book) 1987; Parents' Choice (Story Book) 1987.

ISH-KISHOR, SULAMITH
A Boy of Old Prague by Sulamith Ish-Kishor, illustrated by Ben Shahn; Pantheon, 1963. **Awarded:** Jewish Book Council 1963.

The Master of Miracle: A New Novel of the Golem by Sulamith Ish-Kishor, illustrated by Arnold Lobel; Harper, 1971. **Awarded:** Jewish Book Council 1971; New York Times Notable Books 1971.

Our Eddie by Sulamith Ish-Kishor, not illustrated; Pantheon, 1969. **Awarded:** Sydney Taylor Book Award 1969; Newbery (honor) 1970.

ISHMAEL, WOODI
Give Me Liberty by Hildegarde Hawthorne, illustrated by Woodi Ishmael; Appleton Century Crofts, 1945. **Awarded:** Spring Book Festival (older honor) 1945.

Lone Journey: The Life of Roger Williams by Jeanette Eaton, illustrated by Woodi Ishmael; Harcourt, 1944. **Awarded:** Newbery (honor) 1945.

ISHMOLE, JACK
Walk in the Sky by Jack Ishmole, not illustrated; Dodd Mead, 1972. **Awarded:** Edith Busby 1971.

ITALIANO, CARLO
The Sleighs of my Childhood/Les Traineaux de Mon Enfance (bilingual text) written and illustrated by Carlo Italiano; Tundra, 1974. **Awarded:** Amelia Frances Howard-Gibbon 1975; International Board on Books for Young People (illustration/Canada) 1976.

ITO, TOSHIO
Kites: The Science and Wonder by Toshio Ito and Hirotsuga Komura; Japan Publications (distributed by Kodansha International through Harper), 1983. **Awarded:** New York Academy of Sciences (older honor) 1984.

IVANOV, ANATOLY
The Demon Who Would Not Die retold by Barbara Cohen, illustrated by Anatoly Ivanov; Atheneum, 1982. **Awarded:** New Jersey Institute of Technology 1983.

IVENS, DOROTHY
Cargoes on the Great Lakes by Marie McPhedran, illustrated by Dorothy Ivens; Macmillan Canada, 1952. **Awarded:** Governor- General's Literary Award 1952.

IWAGO, TOKUMITSU
Elephants by Cynthia Overbeck, photographs by Tokumitsu Iwago; Lerner, 1981. **Awarded:** New York Academy of Sciences (special award) 1983.

Lions by Cynthia Overbeck, photographs by Tokumitsu Iwago; Lerner, 1981. **Awarded:** New York Academy of Sciences (special award) 1983.

IZARD, ANNE R.
Awarded: Grolier 1969.

IZAWA, MASANA
Mosses by Sylvia A. Johnson, photographs by Masana Izawa; Lerner, 1983. **Awarded:** New York Academy of Sciences (special award) 1983.

Mushrooms by Sylvia A. Johnson, photographs by Masana Izawa; Lerner, 1982. **Awarded:** New York Academy of Scences (special award) 1983.

IZAWA, YOHIJI
One Morning by Canna Funakoshi, illustrated by Yohiji Izawa; Picture Book Studio, 1986. **Awarded:** Bologna (graphics for children) 1986; New York Times Best Illustrated 1986.

J

JABER, WILLIAM
Exploring the Sun written and illustrated by William Jaber; Messner, 1980. **Awarded:** New Jersey Institute of Technology 1981/

JACKSON, BO
Bo Knows Bo: The Autobiography of a Ballplayer by Bo Jackson and Dick Shaap; Doubleday, 1990. **Awarded:** Young Teens 1991.

JACKSON, CLARA O.
Awarded: Landau 1985.

JACKSON, JACQUELINE
The Taste of Spruce Gum by Jacqueline Jackson, illustrated by Lillian Obligado; Little, 1966. **Awarded:** Dorothy Canfield Fisher 1968.

JACKSON, JESSE
Make a Joyful Noise Unto the Lord! The Life of Mahalia Jackson, Queen of the Gospel Singers by Jesse Jackson, illustrated with photographs; Crowell, 1974. **Awarded:** Carter G. Woodson 1975.

JACKSON, JULIA A.
Our Modern Stone Age by Julia Jackson and Robert L. Bates, illustrated; William Kaufmann, 1982. **Awarded:** New York Academy of Sciences (older honor) 1983.

JACKSON, KATHRYN BYRON
Farm Stories by Kathryn Byron Jackson, illustrated by Gustaf Tenggren; Simon & Schuster, 1946. **Awarded:** Spring Book Festival (younger) 1946.

JACKSON, NANCY RUTH
A Book of Dragon by Donn Kushner, illustrated by Nancy Ruth Jackson; Macmillan of Canada, 1987. **Awarded:** National Chapter of Canada IODE Violet Downey 1988.

JACOBI, KATHY
The Half-a-Moon Inn by Paul Fleischman, illustrated by Kathy Jacobi; Harper, 1980. **Awarded:** Commonwealth Club of California 1980; Golden Kite (fiction honor) 1980; New York Times Notable Books 1980.

JACOBS, ALLAN D.
Sports and Games in Verse and Rhyme by Allan D. Jacobs and Leland B. Jacobs; illustrated by George deLara; Garrard, 1975. **Awarded:** New Jersey Institute of Technology 1976.

JACOBS, FRANCINE
Breakthrough: The True Story of Penicillin by Francine Jacobs, illustrated with photographs; Dodd, Mead, 1985. **Awarded:** New York Academy of Sciences (older) 1986.

JACOBS, JOSEPH
Tom Tit Tot by Joseph Jacobs, illustrated by Evaline Ness; Scribner, 1965. **Awarded:** Caldecott (honor) 1966.

JACOBS, LELAND B.
Awarded: New Jersey Institute of Technology (New Jersey author citation for writer of children's book of the year) 1971.

April Fool! by Leland B. Jacobs, illustrated by Lou Cunette; Garrard, 1973. **Awarded:** New Jersey Institute of Technology 1973.

Funny Bone Ticklers in Verse and Rhyme by Leland B. Jacobs, illustrated by Edward Malsberg; Garrard, 1973. **Awarded:** New Jersey Institute of Technology 1973.

Hello, People by Leland B. Jacobs, illustrated by Edward Malsberg; Garrard, 1972. **Awarded:** New Jersey Institute of Technology 1972.

Holiday Happenings in Limerick Land by Leland B. Jacobs, illustrated by Edward Malsberg; Garrard, 1972. **Awarded:** New Jersey Institute of Technology 1972.

Poetry for Autumn by Leland B. Jacobs, illustrated by Stina Nagel; Garrard, 1968. **Awarded:** New Jersey Institute of Technology 1968.

Poetry for Chuckles and Grins by Leland B. Jacobs, illustrated by Tomie de Paola; Garrard, 1968. **Awarded:** New Jersey Institute of Technology 1968.

Poetry for Winter by Leland B. Jacobs, illustrated by Kelly Oeschli; Garrard, 1970. **Awarded:** New Jersey Institute of Technology 1970.

Poetry of Witches, Elves, and Goblins by Leland B. Jacobs, illustrated by Frank Aloise; Garrard, 1970. **Awarded:** New Jersey Institute of Technology 1970.

Sports and Games in Verse and Rhyme by Leland B. Jacobs and Allan D. Jacobs; Garrard, 1975. **Awarded:** New Jersey Institute of Technology 1976.

Teeny-tiny by Leland B. Jacobs, illustrated by Marilyn Lucey; Garrard, 1976. **Awarded:** New Jersey Institute of Technology 1977.

JACQUES, BRIAN
Awarded: British Book Awards (Author runnerup) 1992.

Mattimeo by Brian Jacques, illustrated by Gary Chalk; Hutchinson, 1989; Philomel, 1990. **Awarded:** Lancashire County Library 1991; West Australian (Secondary) 1992.

Mossflower by Brian Jacques, illustrated by Gary Chalk; Hutchinson, 1988; Philomel, 1988. **Awarded:** West Australian (Secondary) 1991.

Redwall by Brian Jacques, illustrated by Gary Chalk; Hutchinson Children's, 1986; Philomel, 1986. **Awarded:** Lancashire County Library 1988; Western Australia (Secondary) 1990.

JACQUES, FAITH

A Likely Lad by Gillian Avery, illustrated by Faith Jacques; Collins, 1971. **Awarded:** Carnegie (highly commended) 1971; Guardian 1972.

Tilly's House written and illustrated by Faith Jacques; Atheneum, 1979. **Awarded:** New York Times Best Illustrated 1979.

What the Neighbors Did and Other Stories by A. Philippa Pearce, illustrated by Faith Jacques; Longmans, 1972. **Awarded:** International Board on Books for Young People (honour list/text/Great Britain) 1974.

JACQUES, LAURA

At Home in the Rain Forest by Diane Willow, illustrated by Laura Jacques; Charlesbridge, 1991. **Awarded:** Book Can Develop Empathy 1991.

JACQUES, ROBIN

A Book of Ghosts and Goblins by Ruth Manning-Sanders, illustrated by Robin Jacques; Methuen, 1968. **Awarded:** Biennale Illustrations Bratislava (Plaque) 1969.

JAFFREY, MADHUR

Seasons of Splendour: Tales, Myths, and Legends of India by Madhur Jaffrey, illustrated by Michael Foreman; Pavilion Books, 1985; Atheneum, 1985. **Awarded:** Greenaway (commended) 1985; New York Times Notable 1985.

JAHNKE, ROBERT H.G.

The Fish of our Fathers by R. L. (Ronald Leonard) Bacon, illustrated by R. H. G. (Robert H. G.) Jahnke; Waiatarua Press, 1984; Child's Play International, 1986. **Awarded:** AIM Children's Book Award 1985.

The House of the People by Ron L. Bacon, illustrated by Robert Jahnke; Collins, 1977. **Awarded:** Russell Clark 1978.

JAM, TEDDY

Doctor Kiss Says Yes by Teddy Jam, illustrated by Joanne Fitzgerald; Douglas & McIntyre, 1991. **Awarded:** Governor General's Literary Awards (Illustration) 1991.

Night Cars by Teddy Jam, illustrated by Eric Beddows; Douglas & McIntyre, 1988; Orchard, 1989. **Awarded:** Amelia Frances Howard- Gibbon (runnerup) 1989; IODE 1988; Elizabeth Mrazik-Cleaver 1989.

JAMES, ANN

Bernice Knows Best by Max Dann, illustrated by Ann James; Oxford (Australia), 1983. **Awarded:** Children's Book Council of Australia (junior book of the year) 1984.

Looking Out for Sampson by Libby Hathorn, illustrated by Ann James; Oxford, 1987. **Awarded:** Children's Book Council of Australia (Book of the Year Younger Honour) 1988.

Penny Pollard's Diary by Robin Klein, illustrated by Ann James; Oxford, 1983. **Awarded:** Children's Book Council of Australia (book of the year highly commended) 1984.

JAMES, JOHN

An Egyptian Pyramid by John James, Mark Bergin and Jacqueline Morley, illustrated; Simon & Schuster, 1991; Peter Bedrick,

1991. **Awarded:** Times Educational Supplement (Senior) 1991.

JAMES, SANDRA

Mount Delightful: The Story of Ellen Evans and Her Dog Taffy by Eleanor Youmans, illustrated by Sandra James; Bobbs-Merrill, 1944. **Awarded:** Ohioana (3rd place) 1945.

JAMES, WILL

Smoky, the Cowhorse written and illustrated by Will James; Scribner, 1926. **Awarded:** Lewis Carroll Shelf 1965; Newbery 1927.

JAMESON, CYNTHIA

The Clay Pot Boy by Cynthia Jameson, illustrated by Arnold Lobel; Coward, 1973. **Awarded:** Children's Book Showcase 1974.

JAMESON, MALCOLM

Bullard of the Space Patrol by Malcolm Jameson, not illustrated; World, 1951. **Awarded:** Boys Club 1952.

JAMPOLSKY, GERALD G.

Children as Teachers of Peace: By Our Children edited by Gerald G. Jampolsky, forward by Hugh Prather, illustrated; Celestial Arts, 1982. **Awarded:** Jane Addams (special recognition) 1983.

JANE, MARY C.

The Ghost Rock Mystery by Mary C. Jane, illustrated by Ray Abel; Scholastic, 1956. **Awarded:** Boys Club 1966-67.

JANECZKO, PAUL B.

Brickyard Summer: Poems by Paul B. Janeczko, illustrated by Ken Rush; Orchard, 1989. **Awarded:** Lupine Award 1990.

JANOS, LEO

Yeager: An Autobiography by Chuck Yeager and Leo Janos, illustrated with photographs; Bantam, 1985. **Awarded:** Emphasis on Reading (Grades 10-12) 1986-87.

JANOSCH

see ECKERT, HORST

JANSSEN, AL

Destination, Moon by James Irwin with Al Janssen, illustrated with photos; Multnomah Press, 1989. **Awarded:** Gold Medallion (Elementary) 1990.

JANSSEN, PIERRE

A Moment of Silence by Pierre Janssen, translated by William R. Tyler, photographs by Hans Samson; Atheneum, 1970. **Awarded:** Christopher (ages 8-12) 1971.

JANSSON, TOVE

Awarded: Hans Christian Andersen (author) 1966.

JARRELL, RANDALL

The Animal Family by Randall Jarrell, illustrated by Maurice Sendak; Pantheon, 1965. **Awarded:** Lewis Carroll Shelf 1970; New York Times Best Illustrated 1965; Newbery (honor) 1966.

The Bat-poet by Randall Jarrell, illustrated by Maurice Sendak; Macmillan, 1964. **Awarded:** New York Times Best Illustrated 1964; North Carolina AAUW 1964.

Fly by Night by Randall Jarrell, illustrated by Maurice Sendak; Farrar, 1976. **Awarded:** Children's Book Showcase 1977; New York Times Best Illustrated 1976.

The Juniper Tree and Other Tales from Grimm translated by Randall Jarrell and Lore Segal, illustrated by Maurice Sendak; Farrar, 1973. **Awarded:** Children's Book Showcase 1974; New York Times Best Illustrated 1973.

Snow White and the Seven Dwarfs by Jacob Grimm and Wilhelm Grimm, translated by Randall Jarrell, illustrated by Nancy Ekholm Burkert; Farrar, 1972. **Awarded:** Bologna (critici in erba) 1973; Caldecott (honor) 1973; Lewis Carroll Shelf 1973; New York Times Notable Books 1972.

JARVIS, ROBIN
Awarded: British Book Awards (Author runnerup) 1992.

The Whitby Witches by Robin Jarvis, not illustrated; Simon & Schuster, 1991. **Awarded:** Lancashire County Library 1992.

JASPERSOHN, WILLIAM
How the Forest Grew by William Jaspersohn, illustrated by Chuck Eckart; Greenwillow, 1979. **Awarded:** Boston Globe Horn Book (nonfiction honor) 1980.

JAUSS, ANNE MARIE
In Came Horace by Janet Beattie, illustrated by Anne Marie Jauss; Lippincott, 1954. **Awarded:** Spring Book Festival (ages 4-8 honor) 1954.

It's Fun to Know Why: Experiments with Things around Us by Julius Schwartz, illustrated by Anne Marie Jauss and Edwin Herron; McGraw, 1973. **Awarded:** New York Academy of Sciences (older honor) 1974.

The Pasture written and illustrated by Anne Marie Jauss; McKay, 1968. **Awarded:** New Jersey Institute of Technology 1968.

Tracking the Unearthly Creatures of Marsh and Pond by Howard G. Smith, illustrated by Anne Marie Jauss; Abingdon, 1972. **Awarded:** Christopher (ages 8-12) 1973.

JEFFERS, SUSAN
Benjamin's Barn by Reeve Lindbergh, illustrated by Susan Jeffers; Dial, 1990. **Awarded:** Redbook 1990.

Brother Eagle, Sister Sky: A Message from Chief Seattle, illustrated by Susan Jeffers; Dial, 1991. **Awarded:** American Booksellers Book of the Year 1992; Parents' Choice (Picture Book) 1991.

Forest of Dreams by Rosemary Wells, illustrated by Susan Jeffers; Dial, 1988. **Awarded:** Golden Kite (Picture-Illustration) 1988.

Hiawatha by Henry Wadsworth Longfellow, illustrated by Susan Jeffers; Dial, 1983. **Awarded:** New Jersey Institute of Technology 1983.

If Wishes Were Horses and Other Rhymes by Mother Goose, illustrated by Susan Jeffers; Dutton, 1979. **Awarded:** New Jersey Institute of Technology 1981.

The Midnight Farm by Reeve Lindbergh, illustrated by Susan Jeffers; Dial, 1987. **Awarded:** Redbook 1987.

The Three Jovial Huntsmen: A Mother Goose Rhyme adapted and illustrated by Susan Jeffers; Bradbury, 1973. **Awarded:** Art Books for Children 1975, 1976, 1977; Biennale Illustrations Bratislava (golden apple) 1975; Caldecott (honor) 1974; Children's Book Showcase 1974.

The Wild Swans by Hans Christian Andersen, retold by Amy Ehrlich, illustrated by Susan Jeffers; Dial, 1987, c1981. **Awarded:** Redbook 1987.

JENKIN-PEARCE, SUSIE
The Seashell Song by Susie Jenkin-Pearce, illustrated by Claire Fletcher; Bodley Head, 1992; Lothrop Lee & Shepard, 1992. **Awarded:** Mother Goose 1993.

JENKINS, JESSICA
Awarded: Eleanor Farjeon 1976.

JENKINS, LYLL BECERRA DE
The Honorable Prison by Lyll Becerra de Jenkins, not illustrated; Dutton, 1988. **Awarded:** Scott O'Dell 1988; Parents' Choice (Story Book) 1988.

JENKINS, SUE
Growing up in Earthsea by Sue Jenkins in Children's Literature in Education 58 (Autumn 1985). **Awarded:** Children's Literature Assn. Excellence in Criticism (runnerup) 1986.

JENKINSON, DAVE
Awarded: Frances E. Russell 1988.

JENKYNS, CHRIS
Andy Says ... Bonjour! by Pat Diska, illustrated by Chris Jenkyns; Vanguard, 1954. **Awarded:** New York Times Best Illustrated 1954.

JENNESS, AYLETTE
The Bakery Factory: Who Puts the Bread on Your Table written and illustrated by Aylette Jenness; Crowell, 1978. **Awarded:** New York Academy of Sciences (younger honor) 1979.

Dwellers of the Tundra: Life in an Alaskan Eskimo Village by Aylette Jenness, photographs by Jonathan Jenness; Crowell-Collier, 1970. **Awarded:** Spring Book Festival (older honor) 1970.

In Two Worlds: A Yup'ik Eskimo Family by Aylette Jenness and Alice Rivers, illustrated by Aylette Jenness; Houghton Mifflin, 1989. **Awarded:** New York Academy of Sciences (Older Honor) 1989; Carter G. Woodson (Elementary) 1990.

A Life of Their Own: An Indian Family in Latin America by Aylette Jenness and Lisa W. Kroeber, photographs by the authors, drawings by Susan Votaw; Crowell, 1975. **Awarded:** New York Academy of Sciences (older honor) 1976.

JENNESS, JONATHAN
Dwellers of the Tundra: Life in an Alaskan Eskimo Village by Aylette Jenness, photos by Jonathan Jenness; Crowell-Collier, 1970. **Awarded:** Spring Book Festival (older honor) 1970.

JENNINGS, GARY
Black Magic, White Magic by Gary Jennings, illustrated by Barbara Begg; Dial, 1965. **Awarded:** Spring Book Festival (middle honor) 1965.

JENNINGS, PAUL
The Cabbage Patch Fib by Paul Jennings, illustrated by Craig Smith; Puffin, 1988. **Awarded:** Young Australian Best Book (Fiction Younger Reader) 1989.

The Paw Thing by Paul Jennings, illustrated by Keith McEwan; Puffin, 1989. **Awarded:** Young Australian Best Book (Fiction Younger Reader) 1990.

Quirky Tails! More Oddball Stories by Paul Jennings, illustrated; Puffin, 1987. **Awarded:** Young Australian Best Book (Fiction for Young Readers) 1992.

Round the Twist by Paul Jennings, illustrated; Puffin, 1990. **Awarded:** Young Australian Best Book (Fiction Older Reader) 1991.

Spooner or Later by Paul Jennings, Ted Greenwood and Terry Denton; Viking, 1992. **Awarded:** Ashton Scholastic 1993.

Unbelievable! More Surprising Stories by Paul Jennings, not illustrated; Puffin, 1986. **Awarded:** Young Australian Best Book (Fiction Older Reader) 1988.

Uncanny! Even More Surprising Stories by Paul Jennings, not illustrated; Puffin, 1988. **Awarded:** West Australian

(Primary) 1992; Young Australian Best Book (Fiction Older Reader) 1989.

Unmentionable! More Amazing Stories by Paul Jennings, not illustrated; Puffin, 1991. **Awarded:** Young Australian Best Book (Fiction for Older Readers) 1992.

Unreal! Eight Surprising Stories by Paul Jennings, not illustrated; Puffin, 1985; Viking, 1991. **Awarded:** Books I Love Best Yearly (Read Alone Primary) 1992; KOALA (Secondary) 1990; Young Australian Best Book (Fiction Older Reader) 1987.

JENNINGS, TERRY
Polar Regions by Terry Jennings, illustrated; Oxford, 1986. **Awarded:** Times Educational Supplement (junior) 1986.

JENSEN, ALBERT C.
Wildlife of the Oceans by Albert C. Jensen, illustrated with photographs and maps; Abrams, 1979. **Awarded:** New York Academy of Sciences (special award to a publisher for a reference book series) 1980.

JENSEN, DOROTHEA
The Riddle of Pennecroft Farm by Dorothea Jensen; Harcourt Brace Jovanovich 1989. **Awarded:** Jeanette Fair 1991.

JENSEN, VIRGINIA
Awarded: Eleanor Farjeon 1981.

JERNIGAN, E. WESLEY
Awarded: Outstanding Arizona Author 1990.

Agave Blooms Just Once by Giselda Jernigan, illustrated by E. Wesley Jernigan; Harbinger House, 1989. **Awarded:** Southwest 1990.

JERNIGAN, GISELDA
Awarded: Outstanding Arizona Author 1990.

Agave Blooms Just Once by Giselda Jernigan, illustrated by E. Wesley Jernigan; Harbinger House, 1989. **Awarded:** Southwest 1990.

JEROO, ROY
The Story of Prince Rama by Brian Thompson, illustrated by Roy Jeroo and original paintings; Kestrel, 1980. **Awarded:** Garavi Gujarat (children) 1982.

JERUCHIM, SIMON
The Orphans of Simitra by Paul-Jacques Bonzon, translated by Thelma Niklaus, illustrated by Simon Jeruchim; Criterion, 1962. **Awarded:** Spring Book Festival (middle) 1962.

JERVIS, RICHARD
Children of the Book by Peter Carter, illustrated by Richard Jervis, maps by Barry Rowe; Oxford, 1982. **Awarded:** Young Observer Teenage Fiction 1983

JESCHKE, SUSAN
The Devil Did It written and illustrated by Susan Jeschke; Holt, 1975. **Awarded:** Friends of American Writers (illustrator) 1976.

JESPERSEN, JAMES
Time and Clocks for the Space Age by James Jespersen and Jane Fitz-Randolph, not illustrated; Atheneum, 1979. **Awarded:** New York Academy of Sciences (older honor) 1980.

JEUNINCKX, KAREL
Manko Kapak by Karel Jeuninckx and Lo Vermeulen, illustrated by Elzaven Hagendorn; De Sikkel, 1957. **Awarded:** Hans Christian Andersen (runnerup) 1960.

JEWETT, ELEANORE MYERS
The Hidden Treasure of Glaston by Eleanore Myers Jewett, illustrated by Frederick T. Chapman; Viking, 1946. **Awarded:** Newbery (honor) 1947.

JEWETT, SARAH ORNE
A White Heron by Sarah Orne Jewett, illustrated by Douglas Alford; Tillbury House, 1990. **Awarded:** Book Can Develop Empathy 1991.

JIN, XUQI
The Giant Panda written and illustrated by Xuqi Jin and Markus Kappeler, translated by Noel Simon; Putnam, 1986. **Awarded:** New. York Academy of Sciences (younger honor) 1987

JOHANSEN, HANNA
Die Geschichte Von der Kleinen Gans, Die Nicht Schnell Genug War by Hanna Johansen, illustrated by Kathi Bhend; Nagel & Kimche, 1989. **Awarded:** Bologna (Graphic Prize for Youth) 1990.

JOHANSEN, MARGARET
Ood-le-Uk the Wanderer by Margaret Johansen and Alice Lide, illustrated by Raymond Lufkin; Little, 1930. **Awarded:** Newbery (honor) 1931.

JOHN, ANGELA V.
Coalmining Women by Angela V. John; Cambridge Educational, 1984. **Awarded:** Other Award 1985.

JOHN, HELEN
All-of-a-Kind Family by Sydney Taylor, illustrated by Helen John; Follett, 1951. **Awarded:** Charles W. Follett 1951; Jewish Book Council 1951.

JOHN, MARY
Bluestones by Mary John, not illustrated; Barn Owl Press, 1982. **Awarded:** Tir Na n-Og (English) 1983.

JOHN, NAOMI
Roadrunner by Naomi John, illustrated by Peter Parnall and Virginia Parnall; Unicorn/Dutton, 1980. **Awarded:** Parents' Choice (illustration) 1980.

JOHN, TIMOTHY
The Great Song Book edited by Timothy John, music edited by Peter Hankey, illustrated by Tomi Ungerer; Doubleday, 1978. **Awarded:** New York Times Best Illustrated 1978.

JOHNSON, A.E.
see JOHNSON, ANNABELL JONES

JOHNSON, ALEXANDER L.
Oasis for Lucy by Alexander L. Johnson, not illustrated; Dodd Mead, 1956. **Awarded:** Calling All Girls - Dodd, Mead 1956.

JOHNSON, ANGELA
Tell Me a Story, Mama by Angela Johnson, illustrated by David Soman; Orchard, 1989. **Awarded:** Ezra Jack Keats New Writer 1991; Parents' Choice (Story Book) 1989.

When I Am Old With You by Angela Johnson, illustrated by David Soman; Orchard, 1990. **Awarded:** Coretta Scott King (Illustration honor) 1991.

JOHNSON, ANNABELL JONES
The Black Symbol by Annabell Johnson and Edgar Johnson, illustrated by Brian Saunders; Harper, 1959. **Awarded:** Spring Book Festival (older honor) 1959.

The Burning Glass by Annabell Johnson and Edgar Johnson, not illustrated; Harper, 1966. **Awarded:** Western Writers (fiction) 1967.

The Grizzly by Annabell Johnson and Edgar Johnson, illustrated by Gilbert Riswold; Harper, 1964. **Awarded:** William Allen White 1967.

Torrie by Annabell Johnson and Edgar Johnson, illustrated by Pearl Falconer; Harper, 1960. **Awarded:** Spring Book Festival (older honor) 1960.

JOHNSON, AVERY
Hostage to Alexander by Mary Evans Andrews, illustrated by Avery Johnson; McKay, 1961. **Awarded:** Friends of American Writers 1962.

JOHNSON, CAROLYN
Awarded: Southern California Council (Dorothy C. McKenzie) 1987.

JOHNSON, CLIFTON
Sailing for Gold by Clifton Johnson, illustrated by James Reid; Putnam, 1938. **Awarded:** Spring Book Festival (older honor) 1938.

JOHNSON, CROCKETT
The Carrot Seed by Ruth Krauss, illustrated by Crockett Johnson; Harper, 1945. **Awarded:** Spring Book Festival (younger honor) 1945.

JOHNSON, MRS. CROCKETT
see KRAUSS, RUTH IDA

JOHNSON, E. HARPER
Meeting with a Stranger by Duane Bradley, illustrated by E. Harper Johnson; Lippincott, 1964. **Awarded:** Jane Addams 1965; Woodward Park 1965.

Susan Cornish by Rebecca Caudill, illustrated by E. Harper Johnson; Viking, 1955. **Awarded:** Nancy Bloch 1955.

Westward the Eagle by Frederick A. Lane, illustrated by E. Harper Johnson; Holt, 1955. **Awarded:** Commonwealth Club of California 1955.

JOHNSON, EDGAR
The Black Symbol by Annabell Johnson and Edgar Johnson, illustrated by Brian Saunders; Harper, 1959. **Awarded:** Spring Book Festival (older honor) 1959.

The Burning Glass by Annabell Johnson and Edgar Johnson, not illustrated; Harper, 1966. **Awarded:** Western Writers (fiction) 1967.

The Grizzly by Annabell Johnson and Edgar Johnson, illustrated by Gilbert Riswold; Harper, 1964. **Awarded:** William Allen White 1967.

Torrie by Annabell Johnson and Edgar Johnson, illustrated by Pearl Falconer; Harper, 1960. **Awarded:** Spring Book Festival (older honor) 1960.

JOHNSON, EDITH F.
A Book of Wild Flowers by Margaret McKenny, illustrated by Edith F. Johnson; Macmillan, 1939. Spring Book Festival (Younger honor) 1939.

JOHNSON, ELIZABETH
All in Free But Janey by Elizabeth Johnson, illustrated by Trina Schart Hyman; Little Brown, 1968. **Awarded:** Boston Globe Horn Book (illustration honor) 1968.

JOHNSON, ENID
Runaway Balboa by Enid Johnson, illustrated by Anne Merriman Peck; Harper, 1938. **Awarded:** Spring Book Festival (younger honor) 1938.

JOHNSON, GERALD WHITE
America Grows Up: A History for Peter by Gerald W. Johnson, illustrated by Leonard Everett Fisher; Morrow, 1960. **Awarded:** Spring Book Festival (older honor) 1960.

America Is Born: A History for Peter by Gerald W. Johnson, illustrated by Leonard E. Fisher; Morrow, 1959. **Awarded:** Newbery (honor) 1960.

America Moves Forward: A History for Peter by Gerald W. Johnson, illustrated by Leonard E. Fisher; Morrow, 1960. **Awarded:** Newbery (honor) 1961.

Communism: An American's View by Gerald W. Johnson, illustrated by Leonard Everett Fisher; Morrow, 1964. **Awarded:** Boys Club 1965.

The Presidency by Gerald W. Johnson, illustrated by Leonard Everett Fisher; Morrow, 1962. **Awarded:** Spring Book Festival (middle honor) 1962.

JOHNSON, HANNAH LYONS
Let's Make Soup by Hannah Lyons Johnson, illustrated by Daniel Dorn, Jr; Lothrop, 1976. **Awarded:** New Jersey Institute of Technology 1977.

JOHNSON, HELEN LOSSING
Rex of the Coast Patrol written and illustrated by Helen Lossing Johnson and Margaret S. Johnson; Harcourt, 1944. **Awarded:** Spring Book Festival (middle honor) 1944.

JOHNSON, JAMES WELDON
Lift Every Voice and Sing words and music by James Weldon Johnson and J. Rosamund, illustrated by Mozelle Thompson; Hawthorn, 1970. **Awarded:** Lewis Carroll Shelf 1971; New York Times Best Illustrated 1970.

JOHNSON, JANE
Grandma's Bill by Martin Waddell, illustrated by Jane Johnson; Simon & Schuster, 1990. **Awarded:** Bisto (Books for Young Readers) 1991.

Sybil and the Blue Rabbit written and illustrated by Jane Johnson; Benn, 1979. **Awarded:** Mother Goose (runnerup) 1980.

JOHNSON, LOIS
Secrets of the Best Choice by Lois Johnson, illustrated by Virginia Peck; NavPress, 1988. **Awarded:** Gold Medallion (Elementary) 1989.

Thanks for Being My Friend by Lois Johnson, illustrated by Virginia Peck; NavPress, 1988. **Awarded:** Gold Medallion (Elementary) 1989.

You Are Wonderfully Made by Lois Johnson, illustrated by Virginia Peck; NavPress, 1988. **Awarded:** Gold Medallion (Elementary) 1989.

You're Worth More Than You Think by Lois Johnson, illustrated by Virginia Peck; NavPress, 1988. **Awarded:** Gold Medallion (Elementary) 1989.

JOHNSON, LOIS WALFRID
The Disappearing Stranger by Lois Walfrid Johnson, not illustrated; Bethany House, 1990. **Awarded:** State Historical Society of Wisconsin 1991.

The Hidden Message by Lois Walfrid Johnson, not illustrated; Bethany House, 1990. **Awarded:** State Historical Society of Wisconsin 1991.

JOHNSON, LONNI SUE
Max and Diana and the Beach Day by Harriet Ziefert, illustrated by Lonni Sue Johnson; Harper & Row, 1987. **Awarded:** New Jersey Institute of Technology 1988.

Max and Diana and the Birthday Present by Harriet Ziefert, illustrated by Lonni Sue Johnson; Harper & Row, 1987. **Awarded:** New Jersey Institute of Technology 1988.

Max and Diana and the Snowy Day by Harriet Ziefert, illustrated by Lonni Sue Johnson; Harper & Row, 1987. **Awarded:** New Jersey Institute of Technology 1988.

JOHNSON, MARGARET S.
Rex of the Coast Patrol written and illustrated by Margaret S. Johnson and Helen Lossing Johnson; Harcourt, 1944. **Awarded:** Spring Book Festival (middle honor) 1944.

JOHNSON, MILDRED D.
Wait, Skates! by Mildred D. Johnson, illustrated by Tom Dunnington, prepared under the direction of Robert Hillerich; Children's Press, 1983. **Awarded:** Sandburg 1983.

JOHNSON, MILTON
The Black Pearl by Scott O'Dell, illustrated by Milton Johnson; Houghton Mifflin, 1967. **Awarded:** Newbery (honor) 1968.

Come by Here by Olivia Coolidge, illustrated by Milton Johnson; Houghton Mifflin, 1970. **Awarded:** Boston Globe Horn Book (text honor) 1971.

The Little Fishes by Erik Christian Haugaard, illustrated by Milton Johnson; Houghton Mifflin, 1967. **Awarded:** Jane Addams 1968; Boston Globe Horn Book (text) 1967; Spring Book Festival (older) 1967.

Men of Athens by Olivia Coolidge, illustrated by Milton Johnson; Houghton Mifflin, 1962. **Awarded:** Newbery (honor) 1963.

JOHNSON, MIRIAM L.
Awarded: Helen Keating Ott 1991.

JOHNSON, PAMELA
The Rabbi's Girls by Johanna Hurwitz, illustrated by Pamela Johnson; Morrow, 1982. **Awarded:** Parents' Choice (literature) 1982.

JOHNSON, RYERSON
The Monkey and the Wild, Wild Wind by Ryerson Johnson, illustrated by Lois Lignell; Abelard, 1961. **Awarded:** Jane Addams 1963.

JOHNSON, SALLY P.
The Princesses: Sixteen Stories about Princesses edited by Sally P. Johnson, illustrated by Beni Montresor; Harper, 1962. **Awarded:** New York Times Best Illustrated 1962.

JOHNSON, SIDDIE JOE
Awarded: Grolier 1954.

A Month of Christmases by Siddie Joe Johnson, illustrated by Henrietta Jones Moon; Longmans, 1952. **Awarded:** Steck-Vaughn 1954.

JOHNSON, STEVE
No Star Nights by Anna Egan Smucker, illustrated by Steve Johnson; Knopf, 1989. **Awarded:** International Reading Assn. (Younger) 1990.

The salamander Room by Anne Mazer, illustrated by Steve Johnson; Knopf, 1991. **Awarded:** Minnesota (Younger children) 1992.

JOHNSON, SYLVIA A.
Apple Trees by Sylvia A. Johnson, photographs by Hiroo Koike; Lerner, 1983. **Awarded:** New York Academy of Sciences (special award) 1983.

Beetles by Sylvia A. Johnson, photographs by Isao Kishida; Lerner, 1982. **Awarded:** New York Academy of Sciences (special award) 1983.

Crabs by Sylvia A. Johnson, photographs by Atsushi Sakurai; Lerner, 1982. **Awarded:** New York Academy of Sciences (special award) 1983.

Frogs and Toads by Sylvia A. Johnson and Jane Dallinger, photographs by Hiroshi Tanemura; Lerner, 1982. **Awarded:** New York Academy of Sciences (special award) 1983.

Inside an Egg by Sylvia A. Johnson, photographs by Kiyoshi Shimuzu; Lerner, 1982. **Awarded:** New York Academy of Sciences (special award) 1983.

Ladybugs by Sylvia A. Johnson, photographs by Yuko Sato; Lerner, 1982. **Awarded:** New York Academy of Sciences (special award) 1983.

Mosses by Sylvia A. Johnson, photographs by Masana Izawa; Lerner, 1983. **Awarded:** New York Academy of Sciences (special award) 1983.

Mushrooms by Sylvia A. Johnson, photographs by Masana Izawa; Lerner, 1982. **Awarded:** New York Academy of Sciences (special award) 1983.

Penguins by Sylvia A. Johnson, illustrated with photographs; Lerner, 1981. **Awarded:** New York Academy of Sciences (special award) 1983.

Potatoes by Sylvia A. Johnson, photographs by Masaharu Suzuki; Lerner, 1984. **Awarded:** New York Academy of Sciences (younger honor) 1985.

Silkworms by Sylvia A. Johnson, photographs by Isao Kishida; Lerner, 1982. **Awarded:** New York Academy of Sciences (special award) 1983.

Snails by Sylvia A. Johnson, photographs by Modoki Masuda; Lerner, 1982. **Awarded:** New York Academy of Sciences (special award) 1983.

JOHNSON, WILLIAM H.
Li'l Sis and Uncle Willie by Gwen Everett, illustrated by William H. Johnson; Rizzoli, 1992. **Awarded:** Hungry Mind (Picturebook/Fiction) 1993; New York Times Best Illustrated 1992.

JOHNSTON, EDITH F.
A Book of Wild Flowers by Margaret McKenny, illustrated by Edith F. Johnston; Macmillan, 1939. **Awarded:** Spring Book Festival (younger honor) 1939.

JOHNSTON, JOHANNA
Thomas Jefferson: His Many Talents by Johanna Johnston, illustrated by Richard Bergere; Dodd Mead, 1961. **Awarded:** Edison Mass Media (character development for children) 1962.

JOHNSTON, JULIE
Hero of Lesser Causes by Julie Johnston; Lester Publishing, 1992. **Awarded:** Governor General's Literary Award (Text) 1992; National Chapter of Canada IODE Violet Downey 1993.

JOHNSTON, NORMA
The Delphic Choice by Norma Johnston, not illustrated; Four Winds, 1989. **Awarded:** New Jersey Institute of Technology 1990.

Return to Morocco by Norma Johnston, not illustrated; Four Winds, 1988. **Awarded:** New Jersey Institute of Technology 1989.

Shadow of a Unicorn by Norma Johnston, not illustrated; Bantam, 1987. **Awarded:** New Jersey Institute of Technology 1988.

The Bridge Between by Norma Johnston, not illustrated; Funk & Wagnalls, 1966. **Awarded:** New Jersey Institute of Technology 1967.

Ready or Not by Norma Johnston, not illustrated; Funk & Wagnalls, 1965. **Awarded:** New Jersey Institute of Technology 1965.

Timewarp Summer by Norma Johnston, not illustrated; Atheneum, 1983. **Awarded:** New Jersey Institute of Technology 1983.

The Wider Heart by Norma Johnston, not illustrated; Funk & Wagnalls, 1964. **Awarded:** New Jersey Institute of Technology (teenage novel) 1964.

JOHNSTON, TONY
Slither McCreep and His Brother Joe by Tony Johnston, illustrated by Victoria Chess; Harcourt Brace Jovanovich, 1992. **Awarded:** Parents Choice (Story Book) 1992.

Yonder by Tony Johnston, illustrated by Lloyd Bloom; Dial, 1988. **Awarded:** Southern California Council (Outstanding Literary Quality in a Picture Book) 1989.

JOHNSTON, WILLIAM
And Loving It! by William Johnston, not illustrated; Grosset, 1967. **Awarded:** Boys Club (certificate) 1968.

Max Smart and the Perilous Pellets by William Johnston, not illustrated; Grosset, 1966. **Awarded:** Boys Club (certificate) 1966-67.

JOHNSTONE, DAVID
Redemption Greenback by David Johnstone, illustrated by Antony Maitland; Methuen Children's, 1983. **Awarded:** Universe (runnerup) 1984.

JOHNSTONE, PAUL
The Archaeology of Ships by Paul Johnstone, illustrated by Pippa Brand; Walck, 1974. **Awarded:** New York Academy of Sciences (special honorable mention for publisher of series) 1975.

JONAS, ANN
Aardvarks, Disembark! written and illustrated by Ann Jonas; Greenwillow, 1990. **Awarded:** Boston Globe Horn Book (Picture Book Honor) 1991.

Round Trip written and illustrated by Ann Jonas; Greenwillow, 1983. **Awarded:** Golden Sower (K-3) 1985; New York Times Best Illustrated 1983.

The Trek written and illustrated by Ann Jonas; Greenwillow, 1985. **Awarded:** Boston Globe Horn Book (illustration honor) 1986.

JONES, ADRIENNE
Awarded: Southern California Council (distinguished body of work) 1984.

Another Place, Another Spring by Adrienne Jones, not illustrated; Houghton, 1971. **Awarded:** Southern California Council (notable) 1972.

So, Nothing Is Forever by Adrienne Jones, illustrated by Richard Cuffari; Houghton, 1974. **Awarded:** Southern California Council (distinguished fiction) 1975.

Street Family by Adrienne Jones, not illustrated; Harper & Row, 1987. **Awarded:** PEN Center USA West 1988.

JONES, ALUN L.
Gardd o Gerddi by Alun L. Jones and John Pinion Jones; Gomer, 1986. **Awarded:** Tir Na n-Og (Welsh) 1987.

JONES, BOB
Jelly Belly by Robert Kimmel Smith, illustrated by Bob Jones; Delacorte, 1981. **Awarded:** Nene 1985; South Carolina Children's 1984; Young Hoosier (grades 4-6) 1984.

JONES, D. CYRIL
Herio'r Cestyll by Gwen Redvers Jones, illustrated by D. Cyril Jones and Malcolm M. Jones; Gwasg Prifysgol Cymru, 1983. **Awarded:** Tir Na n-Og (Welsh) 1984.

JONES, DAN
The Secret Life of the Underwear Champ by Betty Miles, illustrated by Dan Jones; Knopf, 1981. **Awarded:** Georgia Children's 1986; Mark Twain 1984.

JONES, DIANA WYNNE
Archer's Goon by Diana Wynne Jones, not illustrated; Greenwillow, 1984; Methuen, 1984. **Awarded:** Boston Globe Horn Book (fiction honor) 1984.

A Charmed Life by Diane Wynne Jones, not illustrated; Macmillan, 1977. **Awarded:** Carnegie (commended) 1977; Guardian 1978.

Dogsbody by Diane Wynne Jones, not illustrated; Macmillan, 1975. **Awarded:** Carnegie (commended) 1975.

Howl's Moving Castle by Diana Wynne Jones, not illustrated; Greenwillow, 1986. **Awarded:** Boston Globe Horn Book (fiction honor) 1986.

The Lives of Christopher Chant by Diana Wynne Jones, not illustrated; Methuen Children's, 1988. **Awarded:** Carnegie (Commended) 1988.

Power of Three by Diana Wynne Jones, not illustrated; Macmillan, 1976. **Awarded:** Guardian (commended) 1977.

JONES, DOROTHY HOLDER
The Wonderful World Outside by Dorothy H. Jones, not illustrated; Dodd, 1959. **Awarded:** Calling All Girls - Dodd, Mead 1959.

JONES, DOUG
The Story of the Falling Star by Elsie Jones, illustrated by Doug Jones and Karin Donaldson; Aboriginal Studies Press, 1989. **Awarded:** Ashton Scholastic 1990.

JONES, ELIZABETH ORTON
The Peddler's Clock by Mabel Leigh Hunt, illustrated by Elizabeth Orton Jones; Grosset, 1943. **Awarded:** Spring Book Festival (younger honor) 1943

Prayer for a Child by Rachel Field, illustrated by Elizabeth Orton Jones; Macmillan, 1944. **Awarded:** Caldecott 1945; Lewis. Carroll Shelf 1958.

Small Rain: Verses from the Bible by Jessie Orton Jones, illustrated by Elizabeth Orton Jones; Viking, 1943. **Awarded:** Caldecott (honor) 1944.

JONES, ELSIE
The Story of the Falling Star by Elsie Jones, illustrated by Doug Jones and Karin Donaldson; Aboriginal Studies Press, 1989. **Awarded:** Ashton Scholastic 1990.

JONES, EUFRON GWYNNE
Television Magic by Eufron Gwynne Jones, illustrated with diagrams and photographs; Viking, 1978. **Awarded:** New York Academy of Sciences (special award for series on engineering and technology) 1979.

JONES, GWEN REDVERS
Herio'r Cestyll by Gwen Redvers Jones, illustrated by Cyril Jones and Malcolm M. Jones; Gwasg Prifysgol Cymru, 1983. **Awarded:** Tir Na n-Og (Welsh) 1984.

Y Llinyn Arian by Mair Wynn Hughes and Gwen Redvers Jones, not illustrated; Gomer, 1983. **Awarded:** Tir Na n-Og (Welsh) 1984.

JONES, GWYNETH A.
Dear Hill by Gwyneth A. Jones, not illustrated; Macmillan, 1980. **Awarded:** Guardian (runnerup) 1981.

JONES, HAROLD
Lavender's Blue by Kathleen Lines, illustrated by Harold Jones; Watts, 1954. **Awarded:** Carnegie (special commendation) 1954; Lewis Carroll Shelf 1960; International Board on Books for Young People (honour list/Great Britain) 1956.

The Water Babies by Charles Kingsley, illustrated by Harold Jones; Watts, 1961, c1863. **Awarded:** Lewis Carroll Shelf 1963.

JONES, HELEN HINCKLEY
Awarded: Southern California Council (distinguished contribution to the field of children's literature) 1976.

Israel by Helen Hinkley Jones, illustrated with photographs; Children's Press, 1986. **Awarded:** PEN Center USA West 1987.

JONES, IDWAL
Whistler's Van by Idwal Jones, illustrated by Zhenya Gay; Viking, 1936. **Awarded:** Newbery (honor) 1937.

JONES, JESSIE ORTON
Small Rain: Verses from the Bible by Jessie Orton Jones, illustrated by Elizabeth Orton Jones; Viking, 1943. **Awarded:** Caldecott (honor) 1944.

JONES, JOHN PINION
Gardd o Gerddi by Alun L. Jones and J. Pinion Jones; Gomer, 1986. **Awarded:** Tir Na n-Og (Welsh) 1987.

JONES, MALCOLM M.
Herio'r Cestyll by Gwen Redvers Jones, illustrated by D. Cyril Jones and Malcolm M. Jones; Gwasg Prifysgol Cymru, 1983. **Awarded:** Tir Na n-Og (Welsh) 1984.

JONES, NIKKI
A Dog Called George by Margaret Balderson, illustrated by Nikki Jones; Oxford, 1975. **Awarded:** Writers Award 1976.

JONES, PATRICIA
Rumpelstiltskin by Jacob Grimm and Wilhelm Grimm, adapted by Patricia Jones, illustrated by Jan B. Balet; Rand McNally, 1955. **Awarded:** New York Times Best Illustrated 1955.

JONES, PENRI
Jabas by Penri Jones; Gwasg Dwyfor, 1986. **Awarded:** Tir Na n-Og (Welsh) 1987.

JONES, RON
The Acorn People by Ron Jones, illustrated by Tom Parker; Abingdon, 1978, c1976. **Awarded:** Emphasis on Reading (Grades 10-12) 1980-81.

JONES, SARAH LEWIS
Awarded: Grolier 1965.

JONES, T. LLEW
Tan Ar y Comin by T. Llew Jones; Gomer, 1975. **Awarded:** Tir Na n- Og (Welsh) 1976.

JONES, TERRY
The Saga of Erik the Viking by Terry Jones, illustrated by Michael Foreman; Pavilion/Michael Joseph, 1983. **Awarded:** Children's Book Award 1983.

JONES, WEYMAN
Edge of Two Worlds by Weyman Jones, illustrated by J. C. Kocsis; Dial, 1968. **Awarded:** Lewis Carroll Shelf 1969; Western Heritage 1969.

JONES, WILFRED J.
The Voyagers: Being Legends and Romances of Atlantic Discovery by Padraic Colum, illustrated by Wilfred Jones; Macmillan, 1925. **Awarded:** Newbery (honor) 1926.

JOOSSE, BARBARA
Mama, Do You Love Me? by Barbara M. Joosse, illustrated by Barbara Lavallee; Chronicle Books, 1991. **Awarded:** Golden Kite (Picture-Illustration) 1991.

JOPE, ANNE
Rushavenn Time by Theresa Whistler, illustrated by Anne Jope; Brixworth V C Primary School, 1988. **Awarded:** Smarties (ages 9-11) 1988.

JORDAN, ALICE M.
Awarded: Chandler Reward of Merit 1982 (posthumously).

JORDAN, DRAKE
Careers in Conservation by Frank Graham and Ada Graham, illustrated by Drake Jordan; Sierra Club/Scribner, 1980. **Awarded:** New York Academy of Sciences (older honor) 1981.

JORDAN, EMIL L.
Animal Atlas of the World by Emil L. Jordan, illustrated by Melvin R. Bolden; Hammond, 1969. **Awarded:** New Jersey Institute of Technology 1970.

JORDAN, HOPE DAHLE
Awarded: Council for Wisconsin Writers (juvenile) 1968, 1970.

JORDAN, JAEL
My Grandmother's Stories by Adele Geras, illustrated by Jael Jordan; Knopf, 1990; Heinemann, 1990. **Awarded:** Sydney Taylor Book Award (Older) 1991.

JORDAN, JUNE MEYER
His Own Where by June Jordan, not illustrated; Crowell, 1971. **Awarded:** National Book Award (finalist) 1972.

Voice of the Children edited by June Jordan and Terri Bush, illustrated with photographs; Holt, 1970. **Awarded:** Nancy Bloch 1971.

JORDAN, SHERRYL
The Juniper Game by Sherryl Jordan, not illustrated; Ashton Scholastic, 1991. **Awarded:** AIM Children's Book Award (Story Book 2nd Prize) 1992.

Rocco by Sherryl Jordan, not illustrated; Ashton Scholastic, 1990. **Awarded:** AIM Children's Book Awards (Story Book) 1991.

The Silent One by Joy Cowley, illustrated by Sherryl Jordan; Whitcoulls, 1981. **Awarded:** AIM (Story Book) 1982.

JOSEPH, LYNN
A Wave In Her Pocket: Stories From Trinidad by Lynn Joseph, illustrated by Brian Pinkney; Clarion, 1991. **Awarded:** Parents' Choice (Story Book) 1991; Reading Magic Award 1991.

JOSLIN, SESYLE
Please Share That Peanut! A Preposterous Pageant in Fourteen Acts by Sesyle Joslin and Simms Taback, illustrated by Simms Taback; Harcourt, 1965. **Awarded:** New York Times Best Illustrated 1965.

Spaghetti for Breakfast and other Useful Phrases in Italian and English by Sesyle Joslin, illustrated by Katharina Barry; Harcourt, 1965. **Awarded:** Spring Book Festival (picture book honor) 1965.

What Do You Say, Dear? by Sesyle Joslin, illustrated by Maurice Sendak; Scott, 1958; Harper Trophy, 1986. **Awarded:** Caldecott (honor) 1959; New York Times Best Illustrated 1958; Redbook 1986.

JOWETT, MARGARET
Candidate for Fame by Margaret Jowett, illustrated by Peggy Fortnum; Oxford, 1955. **Awarded:** Carnegie (commended) 1955.

JOYCE, WILLIAM
Bently & Egg written and illustrated by William Joyce; HarperCollins, 1992. **Awarded:** Reading Magic Award 1992.

A Day With Wilbur Robinson written and illustrated by William Joyce; Harper and Row, 1990. **Awarded:** Parents' Choice (Picture Book) 1991.

Humphrey's Bear by Jan Wahl, illustrated by William Joyce; Holt, 1987. **Awarded:** Christopher (ages 6-8) 1988; Redbook 1987.

Nicholas Cricket by Joyce Maxner, illustrated by William Joyce; Harper & Row, 1989. **Awarded:** New York Times Best Illustrated 1989.

JOYNER, JERRY
Thirteen written and illustrated by Jerry Joyner and Remy Charlip; Parents, 1975. **Awarded:** Boston Globe Horn Book (illustration) 1976; New York Times Best Illustrated 1975.

JUDKIS, JIM
The New Baby by Fred Rogers, photographs by Jim Judkis; Putnam, 1985. **Awarded:** Carolyn W. Field 1986.

JUDSON, CLARA INGRAM
Awarded: Children's Reading Round Table 1953; Laura Ingalls Wilder 1960.

Abraham Lincoln, Friend of the People by Clara Ingram Judson, illustrated by Robert Frankenberg; Wilcox & Follet, 1950. **Awarded:** Newbery (honor) 1951.

Benjamin Franklin by Clara Ingram Judson, illustrated by Robert Frankenberg; Follett, 1957. **Awarded:** Indiana Authors Day (children) 1958.

The Green Ginger Jar by Clara Ingram Judson, illustrated by P. Brown; Houghton, 1949. **Awarded:** Boys Club 1950.

Mr. Justice Holmes by Clara Ingram Judson, illustrated by Robert Todd; Follett, 1956. **Awarded:** Edison Mass Media (character development in children) 1957; Newbery (honor) 1957.

St. Lawrence Seaway by Clara Ingram Judson, illustrated by Lorence F. Bjorklund; Follet, 1959. **Awarded:** Indiana Authors Day (young adult) 1960.

Theodore Roosevelt, Fighting Patriot by Clara Ingram Judson, illustrated by Lorence F. Bjorklund; Follett, 1953. **Awarded:** Newbery (honor) 1954.

JUDY, STEPHEN
Awarded: ALAN 1974.

JUKES, MAVIS
Like Jake and Me by Mavis Jukes, illustrated by Lloyd Bloom; Knopf, 1984. **Awarded:** Boston Globe Horn Book (illustration honor) 1985; Newbery (honor) 1985.

No One Is Going to Nashville by Mavis Jukes, illustrated by Lloyd Bloom; Knopf, 1983. **Awarded:** Irma Simonton Black 1983.

JULIAN-OTTIE, VANESSA
Charlie Lewis Plays for Time by Gene Kemp, illustrated by Vanessa Julian-Ottie; Faber, 1984. **Awarded:** Whitbread (runnerup) 1984.

JUPO, FRANK
The Adventure of Light written and illustrated by Frank Jupo; Prentice Hall, 1958. **Awarded:** Boys Club 1959.

JURMAIN, SUZANNE
Once Upon a Horse by Suzanne Jurmain, illustrated with photos; Lothrop, Lee & Shepard, 1989. **Awarded:** Southern California Council (Nonfiction) 1990.

JUSTER, NORTON
Alberic the Wise and Other Journeys by Norton Juster, illustrated by Domenico Gnoli; Pantheon, 1965. **Awarded:** New York Times Best Illustrated 1965.

As: A Surfeit of Similes by Norton Juster, illustrated by David Small; Morrow, 1989. **Awarded:** Parents' Choice (Picture Book) 1989.

The Phantom Tollbooth by Norton Juster, illustrated by Jules Feiffer; Random House, 1961. **Awarded:** George G. Stone 1971.

JUSTIS, LYLE
Land for My Sons: A Frontier Tale of the American Revolution by Maribelle Cormack and William P. Alexander, illustrated by Lyle Justis; Appleton-Century, 1939. **Awarded:** Spring Book Festival (older honor) 1939.

K

KAHL, VIRGINIA
Away Went Wolfgang! written and illustrated by Virginia Kahl; Scribner, 1954. **Awarded:** Spring Book Festival (ages 4-8 honor) 1954.

The Duchess Bakes a Cake written and illustrated by Virginia Kahl; Scribner, 1955. **Awarded:** Lewis Carroll Shelf 1972; Spring Book Festival (ages 4-8 honor) 1955.

KAHNG, KIM
The Loathsome Dragon retold by David Wiesner and Kim Kahng, illustrated by Barry Moser; Harcourt, 1987. **Awarded:** Redbook 1987.

KAHUKIWA, ROBYN
The Kuia and the Spider by Patricia Grace, illustrated by Robin Kahukiwa; Longman Paul, 1981. **Awarded:** AIM (Picture Book) 1982.

Taniwha written and illustrated by Robyn Kahukiwa; Penguin, 1986. **Awarded:** AIM Children's Book Award 1987; Clark, Russell 1987.

KAKKAK, DALE
The Sacred Harvest: Ojibway Wild Rice Gathering by Gordon Regguinti, photographs by Dale Kakkak; Lerner, 1992. **Awarded:** Hungry Mind (Middle Readers/Nonfiction) 1993.

KALAGIAN, BETTY
Awarded: Southern California Council (distinguished contribution to the field of children's literature) 1973.

KALASHNIKOFF, NICHOLAS
The Defender by Nicholas Kalashnikoff, illustrated by Claire Louden and George Louden; Scribner, 1951. **Awarded:** Newbery (honor) 1952.

KALB, JONAH
The Goof That Won the Pennant by Jonah Kalb, illustrated by Sandy Kossin; Houghton, 1976. **Awarded:** Surrey School 1979; Young Hoosier (grades 4-6) 1981.

KALLAY, DUSAN
Awarded: Andersen (Illustrator) 1988.

Alica v Krajine Zazrakov by Dusan Kallay; Mlade Leta, 1981. **Awarded:** Biennale Illustrations Bratislava (grand prix) 1983.

KALLIN, TASHA
Falconer's Lure: The Story of a Summer Holiday by Antonia Forest, illustrated by Tasha Kallin; Faber, 1957. **Awarded:** Carnegie (commended) 1957.

KALMAN, MAIRA
Hey Willie, See the Pyramids written and illustrated by Maira Kalman; Viking, 1988. **Awarded:** Parents' Choice (Picture Book) 1989.

Ooh La La (Max in Love) written and illustrated by Maira Kalman; Viking, 1991. **Awarded:** New York Times Best Illustrated 1991.

KALMENOFF, MATTHEW
Animal Camouflage by Dorothy Shuttlesworth, illustrated by Matthew Kalmenoff; Doubleday, 1966. **Awarded:** New Jersey Institute of Technology 1966.

Evolution Goes on Everyday by Dorothy Hinshaw Patent, illustrated by Matthew Kalmenoff; Holiday, 1977. **Awarded:** Golden Kite (nonfiction honor) 1977.

KALNAY, FRANCIS
Chucaro: Wild Pony of the Pampa by Francis Kalnay, illustrated by Julian De Miskey; Harcourt, 1958. **Awarded:** Newbery (honor) 1959; Spring Book Festival (middle) 1958.

KAMM, JOSEPHINE
Return to Freedom by Josephine Kamm, illustrated by William Stobbs; Abelard-Schuman, 1962. **Awarded:** Jewish Book Council 1962.

KANDELL, ALICE S.
Max, the Music Maker by Miriam B. Stecher, photographs by Alice S. Kandell; Lothrop, 1980. **Awarded:** New York Academy of Sciences (younger honor) 1981.

KANDOIAN, ELLEN
Under the Sun written and illustrated by Ellen Kandoian; Dodd Mead, 1987. **Awarded:** New Jersey Institute of Technology 1988.

KANE, HENRY BUGBEE
One at a Time: His Collected Poems for the Young by David McCord, illustrated by Henry B. Kane; Little Brown, 1977. **Awarded:** National Book Award (finalist) 1978.

The Tale of a Wood written and illustrated by Henry B. Kane; Knopf, 1962. **Awarded:** New York Times Best Illustrated 1962.

KANOZAWA, SUSUMU
Sunflowers by Cynthia Overbeck, photographs by Susumu Kanozawa; Lerner, 1981. **Awarded:** New York Academy of Sciences (special award) 1983.

KANTROWITZ, MILDRED
Willy Bear by Mildred Kantrowitz, illustrated by Nancy Winslow Parker; Parents', 1976. **Awarded:** Christopher (picture book) 1977.

KAPELUS, HELENA
Ksiega Bajek Polskich (Book of Polish Fairy Tales) by Helena Kapelus, illustrated by Marian Murawski; Ludowa Spoldzielnia Wydawnicza, 1988. **Awarded:** Biennale Illustrations Bratislava (Grand Prix) 1989.

KAPLAN, SEYMOUR
Stories of King David by Lillian Simon Freehof, illustrated by Seymour R. Kaplan; Jewish Publications, 1952. **Awarded:** Jewish Book Council 1952.

KAPLOW, ROBERT
Alessandra In Love by Robert Kaplow, not illustrated; Lippincott, 1989. **Awarded:** New Jersey Institute of Technology 1990.

KAPPELER, MARKUS
The Giant Panda written and illustrated by Xuqi Jin and Marcus Kappeler, translated by Noel Simon; Putnam, 1986. **Awarded:** New York Academy of Sciences (younger honor) 1987.

KARASZ, ILONKA
The Heavenly Tenants by William Maxwell, illustrated by Ilonka Karasz; Harper, 1946. **Awarded:** Newbery (honor) 1947.

KAREN, P. P.
Atlas of Kentucky by P. P. Karen and Cotton Mather, illustrated; University Press of Kentucky, 1977. **Awarded:** Jesse Stuart 1978.

KARL, HERB
The Toom County Mud Race by Herb Karl, not illustrated; Delacorte, 1992. **Awarded:** Delacorte Press Prize (Honorable Mention) 1990.

KARL, JEAN
Awarded: Jacobs 1984.

KARLIN, BARBARA
Awarded: Southern California Council (Dorothy McKenzie) 1991.

KARLIN, EUGENE
Adventures in the Desert by Herbert Kaufmann, translated by Stella Humphries, illustrated by Eugene Karlin; Obolensky, 1961. **Awarded:** Spring Book Festival (older) 1961.

KARLOFF, BORIS
Tom Sawyer (phonodisc) by Samuel Clemens, narrated by Boris Karloff; Caedmon R1088. **Awarded:** Lewis Carroll Shelf 1967.

KARMA, MAIJA
Mina Olen Lammenpei by Aila Nissinen, illustrated by Maija Karma; Soderstrom, 1958. **Awarded:** Hans Christian Andersen (runnerup) 1960.

KARR, KATHLEEN
Oh, Those Harper Girls! by Kathleen Karr, not illustrated; Farrar Straus Giroux, 1992. **Awarded:** Parents Choice (Story Book) 1992.

KASHIWAGI, ISAMI
Engineer's Dream by Willy Ley, illustrated by Isami Kashiwagi; Viking, 1954. **Awarded:** Spring Book Festival (older) 1954.

KASPER, VANCY

Escape To Freedom by Vancy Kasper, not illustrated; Stoddart, 1991. **Awarded:** Young Adult Canadian (Honorable Mention) 1992.

KASS, PNINA

Five Words by Pnina Kass in Cricket (September 1991). **Awarded:** Witty Short Story Award 1992.

KASSIAN, OLENA

Afraid of the Dark by Barry Dickson, illustrated by Olena Kassian; Lorimer, 1980. **Awarded:** IODE 1980.

The Hungry Time by Selwyn Dewdney, illustrated by Olena Kassian; Lorimer, 1980. **Awarded:** IODE 1980.

KASTNER, ERICH

Als Ich Kleiher Junge War by Erich Kastner, illustrated by Horst Lemke; Dressler, 1957. **Awarded:** Hans Christian Andersen 1960.

The Little Man by Erich Kastner, translated by James Kirkup, illustrated by Rick Schreiter; Knopf, 1966. **Awarded:** Batchelder 1968.

The Little Man and the Big Thief by Erich Kastner, illustrated by Stanley Mack; Knopf, 1970. **Awarded:** Spring Book Festival (middle honor) 1970.

When I Was a Boy by Erich Kastner, translated by Isabel McHugh and Florence McHugh, illustrated by Horst Lemke; Watts, 1961. **Awarded:** Lewis Carroll Shelf 1961.

KASTNER, JILL

Night Owls by Sharon Phillips Denslow, illustrated by Jill Kastner; Bradbury, 1990. **Awarded:** Friends of American Writers 1991.

With a Name Like Lulu, Who Needs More Trouble? by Tricia Springstubb, illustrated by Jill Kastner; Delacorte, 1989. **Awarded:** Ohioana 1991.

KASZA, KEIKO

Wolf's Chicken Stew written and illustrated by Keiko Kasza; Putnam, 1987. **Awarded:** Kentucky Bluegrass (grades K-3) 1989.

KATAN, NORMA JEAN

Hieroglyphs: The Writing of Ancient Egypt written and illustrated by Norma Jean Katan, with Barbara Mintz; Atheneum, 1981. **Awarded:** New York Academy of Sciences (younger honor) 1982.

KATCHAMAKOFF, ATANAS

Dobry by Monica Shannon, illustrated by Atanas Katchamakoff; Viking, 1934. **Awarded:** Newbery 1935.

KATSUSHIKA, NOKUSAI

The Big Wave by Pearl Buck, illustrated by Nokusai Katsushika and Hiroshige Ando; Day, 1948. **Awarded:** Child Study 1948.

KATZ, JACQUELINE HUNT

Making Our Way: America at the Turn of the Century in the Words of the Poor and Powerless selected by Jacqueline Hunt Katz and William Loren Katz, illustrated with photographs; Dial, 1975. **Awarded:** Children's Book Showcase 1976.

KATZ, RUTH J.

Pumpkin Personalities by Ruth J. Katz, illustrated by Sharon Tondreau; Walker, 1979. **Awarded:** New Jersey Institute of Technology 1980.

KATZ, WELWYN WILTON

The Third Magic by Welwyn Wilton Katz, not illustrated; Douglas & McIntyre, 1988; McElderry, 1989. **Awarded:** Canadian Library Assn. (runnerup) 1989; Governor General's Literary Award (Text) 1988.

The Whalesinger by Welwyn Wilton Katz, illustrated with map; Douglas & McIntyre, 1990; McElderry, 1990. **Awarded:** Young Adult Canadian (runnersup) 1991.

Witchery Hill by Welwyn Wilton Katz, not illustrated; Douglas & MacIntyre, 1984. **Awarded:** Canadian Library Assn. (runnerup) 1985.

KATZ, WILLIAM LOREN

Breaking the Chains: African-American Slave Resistance by William Loren Katz, illustrated with photos; Atheneum, 1990. **Awarded:** Woodson (Outstanding Merit - Secondary) 1991.

Making Our Way: America at the Turn of the Century in the Words of the Poor and Powerless selected by William Loren Katz and Jacqueline Hunt Katz; illustrated with photographs; Dial, 1975. **Awarded:** Children's Book Showcase 1976,

KATZOFF, SY

Barto Takes the Subway by Barbara Brenner, photographs by Sy Katzoff; Knopf, 1961. **Awarded:** Spring Book Festival (ages 4-8 honor) 1961.

KAUFMAN, WILLIAM I.

UNICEF Book of Children's Legends by William I. Kaufman, illustrated with photographs; Stackpole, 1970. **Awarded:** Christopher (all ages) 1971.

UNICEF Book of Children's Poems by William I. Kaufman, illustrated with photographs; Stackpole, 1970. **Awarded:** Christopher (all ages) 1971.

UNICEF Book of Children's Prayers by William I. Kaufman, illustrated with photographs; Stackpole, 1970. **Awarded:** Christopher (all ages) 1971.

UNICEF Book of Children's Songs by William I. Kaufman, illustrated with photographs; Stackpole, 1970. **Awarded:** Christopher (all ages) 1971.

KAUFMANN, ANGELIKA

Tiny by Mira Lobe, illustrated by Angelika Kaufmann; Jugend & Volk, 1981. **Awarded:** International Board on Books for Young People (illustration/Austria) 1982.

KAUFMANN, HERBERT

Adventures in the Desert by Herbert Kaufmann, translated by Stella Humphries, illustrated by Eugene Karlin; Obolensky, 1961. **Awarded:** Spring Book Festival (older) 1961.

KAUFMANN, JOHN

The Empty Schoolhouse by Natalie Savage Carlson, illustrated by John Kaufmann; Harper & Row, 1965. **Awarded:** Child Study 1965.

Killer-of-Death by Betty Baker, illustrated by John Kaufmann; Harper, 1963. **Awarded:** Western Heritage 1964.

Wild Geese Calling by Robert Murphy, illustrated by John Kaufmann; Dutton, 1966. **Awarded:** Dutton Junior Animal Book 1966.

KAVANAGH, PATRICK JOSEPH

Scarf Jack by Patrick J. Kavanagh, not illustrated; Bodley Head, 1978. **Awarded:** Guardian (commended) 1979.

KAYE, GERALDINE

Comfort Herself by Geraldine Kaye, illustrated by Jenny Northway; Deutsch, 1984. **Awarded:** Other Award 1985.

KAY, JACKIE
Two's Company by Jackie Kay, illustrated by Shirley Tourret; Blackie, 1992. **Awarded:** Signal 1993.

KEATING, BERN
Famous American Explorers by Bern Keating, illustrated by Lorence F. Bjorklund; Rand, 1972. **Awarded:** Western Heritage 1973.

KEATS, EZRA JACK
    Awarded: University of Southern Mississippi 1980.

Danny Dunn and the Homework Machine by Raymond Abrashkin and Jay Williams, illustrated by Ezra Jack Keats; Whittlesey House, 1958. **Awarded:** Young Readers Choice 1961.

Goggles written and illustrated by Ezra Jack Keats; Macmillan, 1969. **Awarded:** Caldecott (honor) 1970.

Hi, Cat! written and illustrated by Ezra Jack Keats; Macmillan, 1970. **Awarded:** Boston Globe Horn Book (illustration) 1970.

In the Night by Paul Showers, illustrated by Ezra Jack Keats; Crowell, 1961. **Awarded:** New Jersey Institute of Technology 1961.

Penny Tunes and Princesses by Myron Levoy, illustrated by Ezra Jack Keats; Harper, 1972. **Awarded:** New Jersey Institute of Technology 1973.

The Snowy Day written and illustrated by Ezra Jack Keats; Viking, 1962. **Awarded:** Art Books for Children 1973; Caldecott 1963.

KEEHN, SALLY M.
I Am Regina by Sally M. Keehn, not illustrated; Philomel, 1991. **Awarded:** Carolyn W. Field 1992.

KEEN, MARTIN
Be a Rockhound written and illustrated by Martin Keen; Messner, 1979. **Awarded:** New Jersey Institute of Technology 1980, 1981.

The World Beneath Our Feet: The Story of Soil by Martin Keen, illustrated by Haris Petie; Messner, 1974. **Awarded:** New Jersey Institute of Technology 1975.

KEENE, CAROLYN (pseudonym)
    see ADAMS, HARRIET S.

KEEPING, CHARLES
    Awarded: Hans Christian Andersen (highly commended illustrator/Great Britain) 1974.

Charles Keeping's Classic Tales of the Macabre illustrated by Charles Keeping; Blackie Children's, 1987. **Awarded:** W. H. Smith (£1000) 1988.

Charley, Charlotte and the Golden Canary written and illustrated by Charles Keeping; Oxford, 1967. **Awarded:** Greenaway 1967.

Dawn Wind by Rosemary Sutcliff, illustrated by Charles Keeping; Walck, 1962. **Awarded:** Spring Book Festival (older) 1962.

The Dream Time by Henry Treece, illustrated by Charles Keeping; Brockhampton, 1967. **Awarded:** Carnegie (commended) 1967.

Elidor by Alan Garner, illustrated by Charles Keeping; Collins, 1965. **Awarded:** Carnegie (commended) 1965.

The God Beneath the Sea by Edward Blishen and Leon Garfield, illustrated by Charles Keeping; Longmans, 1970. **Awarded:** Carnegie 1970; Greenaway (commended) 1970.

The Highwayman by Alfred Noyes, illustrated by Charles Keeping; Oxford, 1981; Oxford (U.S.), 1982. **Awarded:** Greenaway 1981.

Jack the Treacle Eater by Charles Causley, illustrated by Charles Keeping; Macmillan, 1987. **Awarded:** Kurt Maschler 1987.

Joseph's Yard written and illustrated by Charles Keeping; Oxford, 1969. **Awarded:** Greenaway (honour) 1969.

A Kind of Wild Justice by Bernard Ashley, illustrated by Charles Keeping; Oxford, 1978. **Awarded:** Carnegie (commended) 1978.

The Lantern Bearers by Rosemary Sutcliff, illustrated by Charles Keeping; Oxford, 1959. **Awarded:** Carnegie 1959.

The Latchkey Children by Eric Allen, illustrated by Charles Keeping; Oxford, 1963. **Awarded:** Carnegie (commended) 1963.

Railway Passage written and illustrated by Charles Keeping; Oxford, 1974. **Awarded:** Biennale Illustrations Bratislava (golden apple) 1975; Greenaway (highly commended) 1974.

The Silver Branch by Rosemary Sutcliff, illustrated by Charles Keeping; Oxford, 1957; Walck, 1958. **Awarded:** Carnegie (commended) 1957; Spring Book Festival (older honor) 1958.

The Spider's Web written and illustrated by Charles Keeping; Oxford, 1972. **Awarded:** Biennale Illustrations Bratislava (plaque) 1973.

Warrior Scarlet by Rosemary Sutcliff, illustrated by Charles Keeping; Oxford, 1958; Walck, 1958. **Awarded:** Carnegie (commended) 1958; International Board on Books for Young People (honour list/Great Britain) 1960.

The Wedding Ghost by Leon Garfield, illustrated by Charles Keeping; Oxford, 1985. **Awarded:** Maschler (runnerup) 1985.

The Wildman by Kevin Crossley-Holland, illustrated by Charles Keeping; Deutsch, 1976. **Awarded:** W. H. Smith (£100) 1977.

KEHRET, PEG
Nightmare Mountain by Peg Kehret, not illustrated; Dutton, 1989. **Awarded:** Golden Sower (grades 4-6) 1993; Young Hoosier (grades 4-6) 1992.

KEIGWIN, R.P.
Thumbelina by Hans Christian Andersen, translated by R. P. Keigwin, illustrated by Adrienne Adams; Scribner, 1961. **Awarded:** Lewis Carroll Shelf 1962.

KEITH, CARLTON
    see ROBERTSON, KEITH CHARLTON

KEITH, EROS
The House of Dies Drear by Virginia Hamilton, illustrated by Eros Keith; Macmillan, 1968. **Awarded:** Ohioana 1969; Edgar Allan Poe 1969.

The Moon Is Like a Silver Sickle: A Celebration of Poetry by Russian Children compiled by Miriam Morton, illustrated by Eros Keith; Simon & Schuster, 1972. **Awarded:** New Jersey Institute of Technology 1973.

The Slave Dancer by Paula Fox, illustrated by Eros Keith; Bradbury, 1973. **Awarded:** Newbery 1974.

Undine by Friedrich de la Motte Fouque, retold and edited by Gertrude C. Schwebeil, illustrated by Eros Keith; Simon & Schuster, 1971, c1957. **Awarded:** Lewis Carroll Shelf 1971.

KEITH, HAL

More Wires and Watts by Irwin Math, illustrated by Hal Keith; Scribner, 1988. **Awarded:** New York Academy of Sciences (Younger Honor) 1989.

Morse, Marconi and You: Understanding and Building Telegraph, Telephone and Radio Sets by Irwin Math, illustrated by Hal Keith; Scribner, 1979. **Awarded:** New York Academy of Sciences (older honor) 1980.

KEITH, HAROLD VERNE

The Obstinate Land by Harold Keith, not illustrated; Crowell, 1977. **Awarded:** Western Heritage 1979.

Rifles for Watie by Harold Keith, illustrated by Peter Burchard; Crowell, 1957. **Awarded:** Lewis Carroll Shelf 1964; Newbery 1958.

The Runt of Rogers School by Harold Keith, not illustrated; Lippincott, 1971. **Awarded:** Charlie May Simon 1973-74.

Suzy's Scoundrel by Harold Keith, illustrated by John Schoenherr; Crowell, 1974. **Awarded:** Western Heritage 1975.

KELEN, BETTY

Gautama Buddha, in Life and Legend by Betty Kelen, illustrated with photographs; Lothrop, 1967. **Awarded:** Lewis Carroll Shelf 1970.

KELLEHER, VICTOR

Brother Night by Victor Kelleher, illustrated by Peter Clarke; Julia MacRae, 1990. **Awarded:** West Australian (Hoffman Award) 1992.

Forbidden Paths of Thual by Victor Kelleher, illustrated by Anthony Maitland; Kestrel, 1981. **Awarded:** West Australian Young Readers' (Secondary) 1982.

The Makers by Victor Kelleher, not illustrated; Viking Kestrel, 1987. **Awarded:** Children's Peace Literature 1989.

Master of the Grove by Victor Kelleher, not illustrated; Penguin (Australia), 1982. **Awarded:** Children's Book Council of Australia (book of the year) 1983.

Taronga by Victor Kelleher, not illustrated; Viking Kestrel, 1986. **Awarded:** Children's Book Council of Australia (book of the year older honor) 1987.

KELLEY, RUTH

Cleopatra's Revenge by Ruth Kelley, in *Ranger Rick* Magazine. **Awarded:** Witty Short Story Award 1986.

KELLOGG, STEVEN

Awarded: David McCord Children's Literature Citation 1987; Regina Medal 1989.

Best Friends written and illustrated by Steven Kellogg; Dial, 1986. **Awarded:** Parents' Choice (literature) 1986.

The Day Jimmy's Boa Ate the Wash by Trinka Hakes Noble, illustrated by Steven Kellogg; Dial, 1980. **Awarded:** North Dakota Children's Choice (Younger) 1987.

The Great Christmas Kidnapping Caper by Jean Van Leeuwen, illustrated by Steven Kellogg; Dial, 1975. **Awarded:** Ethical Culture School 1975; South Carolina Children's 1979; William Allen White 1978.

How Much Is a Million? by David M. Schwartz, illustrated by Steven Kellogg; Lothrop, Lee & Shepard, 1985. **Awarded:** Boston Globe Horn Book (illustration honor) 1985; Utah Children's Informational Book Award 1988.

How the Witch Got Alf by Cora Annett, illustrated by Steven Kellogg; Watts, 1975. **Awarded:** Christopher (ages 7-11) 1976.

Is Your Mama a Llama? by Deborah Guarino, illustrated by Steven Kellogg; Scholastic, 1989. **Awarded:** New Jersey Institute of Technology 1990.

The Island of the Skog written and illustrated by Steven Kellogg; Dial, 1973. **Awarded:** Michigan Young Reader's (division I) 1983.

Jimmy's Boa and the Big Splash Birthday Bash by Trinka Hakes Noble, illustrated by Steven Kellogg; Dial, 1989. **Awarded:** New Jersey Institute of Technology 1990.

Matilda Who Told Lies and Was Burned to Death by Hilaire Belloc, illustrated by Steven Kellogg; Dial, 1970. **Awarded:** Art Books for Children 1973; New York Times Best Illustrated 1970.

The Mysterious Tadpole written and illustrated by Steven Kellogg; Dial, 1977. **Awarded:** Irma Simonton Black 1977.

The Mystery of the Missing Red Mitten written and illustrated by Steven Kellogg; Dial, 1974. **Awarded:** Children's Book Showcase 1975.

Pecos Bill retold and illustrated by Steven Kellogg; Morrow, 1986. **Awarded:** Land of Enchantment 1991.

Pinkerton, Behave! written and illustrated by Steven Kellogg; Dial, 1979. **Awarded:** Georgia Children's Picture Storybook 1982; Little Archer 1981.

Tallyho, Pinkerton! written and illustrated by Steven Kellogg; Dial, 1982. **Awarded:** Parents' Choice (literature) 1982.

There Was an Old Woman written and illustrated by Steven Kellogg; Parents', 1974. **Awarded:** New York Times Best Illustrated 1974.

KELLY, ERIC PHILBROOK

Trumpeter of Krakow by Eric P. Kelly, illustrated by Angela Pruszynska; Macmillan, 1928. **Awarded:** Boys Club (special citation) 1966-67; Newbery 1929.

KEMP, GENE

Charlie Lewis Plays for Time by Gene Kemp, illustrated by Vanessa Julian-Ottie; Faber & Faber, 1984. **Awarded:** Whitbread (runnerup) 1984.

The Turbulent Term of Tyke Tiler by Gene Kemp, illustrated by Carolyn Dinan; Faber, 1977. **Awarded:** Carnegie 1977; Other Award 1977.

KENDA, MARGARET

Science Wizardry for Kids by Margaret Kenda and Phyllis S. Williams, illustrated by Tim Robinson; Barron's, 1992. **Awarded:** Hungry Mind (Middle Readers/Nonfiction) 1993.

KENDALL, CAROL SEEGER

The Firelings by Carol Kendall, illustrated by Felicia Bond; Atheneum, 1982. **Awarded:** Parents' Choice (literature) 1982.

The Gammage Cup by Carol Kendall, illustrated by Erik Blegvad; Harcourt, 1959. **Awarded:** Newbery (honor) 1960; Ohioana 1960.

KENLY, HENRY

Voices from the Grass by Julie Closson Kenly, illustrated by Henry Kenly; Appleton Century Crofts, 1940. **Awarded:** Spring Book Festival (older honor) 1940.

KENLY, JULIE CLOSSON

Voices from the Grass by Julie Closson Kenly, illustrated by Henry Kenly; Appleton Century Crofts, 1940. **Awarded:** Spring Book Festival (older honor) 1940.

KENNAWAY, ADRIENNE
Crafty Chameleon by Mwenye Hadithi, illustrated by Adrienne Kennaway; Hodder & Stoughton, 1987; Little Brown, 1987. **Awarded:** Greenaway 1987.

KENNEALLY, CHRISTY
Strings and Things: Poems and Other Messages for Children by Christy Kenneally, illustrated by Gloria Ortiz; Paulist Press, 1984. **Awarded:** Catholic Book Awards (Children's) 1985.

KENNEDY, JOHN F.
Profiles in Courage by John F. Kennedy, illustrated by Emil Weiss; Harper, 1964. (young reader's memorial edition). **Awarded:** Jane Addams 1964.

KENNEDY, PAUL
Legends and Folk Tales of Holland by Adele de Leeuw, illustrated by Paul Kennedy; Nelson, 1963. **Awarded:** New Jersey Institute of Technology (short stories ages 9-12) 1964.

A Penny a Day by Walter De la Mare, illustrated by Paul Kennedy; Knopf, 1960, c1925. **Awarded:** Lewis Carroll Shelf 1962.

KENNEDY, RICHARD
The Beginning Was a Dutchman by Isla Mitchell, illustrated by Richard Kennedy; Dodd Mead, 1946. **Awarded:** Spring Book Festival (middle honor) 1946.

Castaway Christmas by Margaret Joyce Baker, illustrated by Richard Kennedy; Methuen, 1963. **Awarded:** Carnegie (commended) 1963.

A Herd of Deer by Eilis Dillon, illustrated by Richard Kennedy; Funk & Wagnall, 1969. **Awarded:** Lewis Carroll Shelf 1970; Spring Book Festival (older honor) 1970.

KENNEDY, RICHARD
Amy's Eyes by Richard Kennedy, illustrated by Richard Egielski; Harper & Row, 1985. **Awarded:** Parents' Choice (literature) 1985.

Crazy in Love by Richard Kennedy, illustrated by Marcia Sewall; Unicorn/Dutton, 1980. **Awarded:** Parents' Choice (illustration) 1980.

Inside My Feet: The Story of a Giant by Richard Kennedy, illustrated by Ronald Himler; Harper, 1979. **Awarded:** New York Times Notable Books 1979.

KENNEDY, X. J.
One Winter Night in August and Other Nonsense Jingles by X. J. Kennedy, illustrated by David McPhail; Atheneum, 1975. **Awarded:** New York Times Notable Books 1975.

The Owlstone Crown by X. J. Kennedy, illustrated by Michele Chessare; Atheneum, 1983. **Awarded:** Ethical Culture 1983.

KENNEMORE, TIM
Wall of Words by Tim Kennemore, not illustrated; Faber, 1982. **Awarded:** Carnegie (commended) 1982.

KENNERLEY, PETER
Awarded: Eleanor Farjeon 1977.

KENOYER, NATLEE P.
The Western Horse: A Handbook by Natlee P. Kenoyer, illustrated by Randy Steffen; Meredith, 1962. **Awarded:** Western Writers (nonfiction) 1963.

KENSINGTON, SARAH
Street Flowers by Richard Mabey, illustrated by Sarah Kensington; Kestrel, 1976. **Awarded:** Times Educational Supplement (junior) 1977.

KENT, JACK
The Once-upon-a-Time Dragon written and illustrated by Jack Kent; Harcourt, 1982. **Awarded:** Texas Institute of Letters 1983.

KENYON, CHRIS
Trapping the Silver Beaver by Charles Niehuis, illustrated by Chris Kenyon; Dodd Mead, 1956. **Awarded:** Western Writers 1957.

KEOGH, BRIAN
Sea Menace by John Gunn, illustrated by Brian Keogh; Constable, 1958. **Awarded:** Children's Book Council of Australia (book of the year) 1959.

KEPES, JULIET
Beasts from a Brush written and illustrated by Juliet Kepes; Pantheon, 1955. **Awarded:** New York Times Best Illustrated 1955.

Birds written and illustrated by Juliet Kepes; Walker, 1968. **Awarded:** New York Times Best Illustrated 1969.

Five Little Monkeys written and illustrated by Juliet Kepes; Houghton Mifflin, 1952. **Awarded:** Caldecott (honor) 1953; New York Times Best Illustrated 1952.

Lady Bird, Quickly written and illustrated by Juliet Kepes; Atlantic, 1964. **Awarded:** Spring Book Festival (picture book honor) 1964.

Two Little Birds and Three written and illustrated by Juliet Kepes; Houghton, 1960. **Awarded:** New York Times Best Illustrated 1960.

KERKHAM, ROGER
Guinea Pigs: All about Them by Alvin Silverstein and Virginia Silverstein, photographs by Roger Kerkham; Lothrop, 1972. **Awarded:** New Jersey Institute of Technology 1972.

KERR, ILLINGSWORTH
The Nor'westers: The Fight for the Fur Trade by Marjorie W. Campbell, illustrated by Illingsworth Kerr; Macmillan Canada, 1954. **Awarded:** Governor-General's Literary Award 1954.

KERR, JUDITH
When Hitler Stole Pink Rabbit written and illustrated by Judith Kerr; Coward, 1972. **Awarded:** Spring Book Festival (ages 8-12 honor) 1972.

KERR, LENNOX
see DAWLISH, PETER (pseudonym)

KERR, M. E.
Awarded: Margaret A. Edwards 1993.

Gentlehands by M. E. Kerr, not illustrated; Harper, 1978. **Awarded:** Christopher (young adult) 1979; New York Times Notable Books 1978.

Him, she Loves? by M. E. Kerr, not illustrated; Harper & Row, 1984. **Awarded:** Emphasis on Reading (grades 10-12) 1985-86.

If I Love You, Am I Trapped Forever? by M. E. Kerr, not illustrated; Harper, 1973. **Awarded:** Spring Book Festival (older honor) 1973.

Is that You, Miss Blue? by M. E. Kerr, not illustrated; Harper, 1975; Dell, 1976. **Awarded:** New York Times Notable Books 1975.

Little Little by M. E. Kerr, not illustrated; Harper, 1981. **Awarded:** Golden Kite (fiction) 1981.

Night Kites by M. E. Kerr, not illustrated; Harper & Row, 1986. **Awarded:** California Young Reader (Young Adult) 1991.

KERR, TOM
Playing It Smart by Tova Navarra, illustrated by Tom Kerr; Barron's Press, 1989. **Awarded:** New Jersey Institute of Technology 1990.

KERROD, ROGER
Science Alive: Living Things by Roger Kerrod, illustrated; Macdonalds Children's Books, 1987. **Awarded:** Science Book Prizes 1988.

KESEY, KEN
Little Tricker the Squirrel Meets Big Trouble the Bear by Ken Kesey, illustrated by Barry Moser; Viking, 1990. **Awarded:** International Board on Books for Young People (Illustration/USA) 1992.

KESSLER, ETHEL
Big Red Bus by Ethel Kessler, illustrated by Leonard Kessler; Doubleday, 1957. **Awarded:** New York Times Best Illustrated 1957.

KESSLER, LEONARD
Awarded: School Library Media Specialists of Southeastern New York 1982.

Big Red Bus by Ethel Kessler, illustrated by Leonard Kessler; Doubleday, 1957. **Awarded:** New York Times Best Illustrated 1957.

Big Tracks, Little Tracks by Franklyn M. Branley, illustrated by Leonard Kessler; Crowell, 1960. **Awarded:** New Jersey Institute of Technology 1961.

Binky Brothers and the Fearless Four by James Lawrence, illustrated by Leonard Kessler; Harper, 1970. **Awarded:** New Jersey Institute of Technology 1970.

A Book of Astronauts for You by Franklyn M. Branley, illustrated by Leonard Kessler; Crowell, 1963. **Awarded:** New Jersey Institute of Technology (science ages 5-8) 1964.

A Book of Mars for You by Franklyn M. Branley, illustrated by Leonard Kessler; Crowell, 1968. **Awarded:** New Jersey Institute of Technology (science) 1968.

A Book of Stars for You by Franklyn M. Branley, illustrated by Leonard Kessler; Crowell, 1967. **Awarded:** New Jersey Institute of Technology (science) 1968.

Fast Is Not a Ladybug: A Book about Fast and Slow Things by Miriam Schlein, illustrated by Leonard Kessler; Scott, 1953. **Awarded:** Boys Club 1954; New York Times Best Illustrated 1953.

Heavy Is a Hippopotamus by Miriam Schlein, illustrated by Leonard Kessler; Scott, 1954. **Awarded:** New York Times Best Illustrated 1954.

KETCHUM, FRED
Stick-in-the-Mud: A Tale of a Village, a Custom and a Little Boy by Jean Ketchum, illustrated by Fred Ketchum; Scott, 1953. **Awarded:** Jane Addams 1954.

KETCHUM, JEAN
Stick-in-the-Mud: A Tale of a Village, a Custom and a Little Boy by Jean Ketchum, illustrated by Fred Ketchum; Scott, 1953. **Awarded:** Jane Addams 1954.

KETTELKAMP, LARRY
Computer Graphics: How It Works, What It Does by Larry Kettelkamp, illustrated; Morrow, 1989. **Awarded:** New Jersey Institute of Technology 1990.

Partnership of Mind and Body: Biofeedback by Larry Kettelkamp, illustrated with photographs; Morrow, 1976. **Awarded:** New Jersey Institute of Technology 1977.

KEVLES, BETTYANN
Watching the Wild Apes: The Primate Studies of Goodall, Fossey, and Galdikas by Bettyann Kevles, illustrated with photographs; Dutton, 1976. **Awarded:** New York Academy of Sciences (older) 1977.

KEW, KATINKA
Wheel Around the World by Chris Searle, illustrated by Katinka Kew; Macdonald, 1983. **Awarded:** Other Award 1984.

KEY, ALEXANDER
The Forgotten Door by Alexander Key, not illustrated; Westminster, 1965. **Awarded:** Lewis Carroll Shelf 1972; North Carolina AAUW 1965.

The Magic Meadow by Alexander Key, not illustrated; Westminster, 1975. **Awarded:** North Carolina AAUW 1975.

KHALSA, DAYAL KAUR
How Pizza Came to Queens written and illustrated by Dayal Kaur Khalsa; Clarkson Potter (Crown), 1989. **Awarded:** New York Times Best Illustrated 1989.

Sleepers written and illustrated by Dayal Kaur Khalsa; Clarkson Potter, 1988. **Awarded:** Parents' Choice (Picture Book) 1988.

Tales of a Gambling Grandma written and illustrated by Dayal Kaur Khalsa; Clarkson N. Potter, 1986. **Awarded:** New York Times Notable 1986.

KHERDIAN, DAVID
Beyond Two Rivers by David Kherdian, not illustrated; Greenwillow, 1981. **Awarded:** Friends of American Writers ($500 award) 1982.

The Road from Home: The Story of an Armenian Girl by David Kherdian, not illustrated; Greenwillow, 1979. **Awarded:** Jane Addams 1980; Boston Globe Horn Book (nonfiction) 1979; Lewis Carroll Shelf 1979' Newbery (honor) 1980.

KIDD, DIANA
The Fat and Juicy Place by Diana Kidd, illustrated by Bronwyn Bancroft; Angus & Robertson, 1992. **Awarded:** Australian Multicultural (Junior) 1993.

Onion Tears by Diana Kidd, illustrated by Dee Huxley; Collins, 1989. **Awarded:** Diabetes Australia Alan Marshall 1990.

KIDDELL-MONROE, JOAN
English Fables and Fairy Stories retold by James Reeves, illustrated by Joan Kiddell-Monroe; Oxford, 1954. **Awarded:** Carnegie (commended) 1954.

Grishka and the Bear by Rene Guillot, translated by Gwen Marsh, illustrated by Joan Kiddell-Monroe; Criterion, 1959. **Awarded:** Boys Club 1961; Lewis Carroll Shelf 1961.

KIDDER, ELEANOR
Awarded: Grolier 1973.

KIDWELL, CARL
To Survive We must Be Clever by Gertrude E. Finney, illustrated by Carl Kidwell; McKay, 1966. **Awarded:** Indiana Authors Day (young adult) 1967.

KIESEL, STANLEY
The War Between the Pitiful Teachers and the Splendid Kids by Stanley Kiesel, edited by Emilie McLeod, not illustrated; Dutton, 1980. **Awarded:** New York Times Notable Books 1980.

KILBRACKEN, JOHN
The Easy Way to Bird Recognition by John Kilbracken, illustrated; Kingfisher Books, 1982. **Awarded:** Times Educational Supplement (senior) 1982.

KILGORE, SUSI
Vilma Martinez by Corinn Codye, illustrated by Susi Kilgore; Raintree, 1989. **Awarded:** Woodson (Outstanding Merit - Elementary) 1990.

KILWORTH, GARRY
The Drowners by Garry Kilworth, not illustrated; Methuen, 1991. **Awarded:** Carnegie (Commended) 1991.

KIMMEL, ERIC A.
Awarded: Evelyn Sibley Lampman 1991.

The Chanukkah Guest by Eric Kimmel, illustrated by Giori Carmi; Holiday House, 1990. **Awarded:** Sydney Taylor Book Award (Picture Book) 1991.

Days of Awe: Stories for Rosh Hashanah and Yom Kippur adapted by Eric A. Kimmel, illustrated by Erika Weihs; Viking, 1991. **Awarded:** Aesop Prize 1993.

Four Dollars and Fifty Cents by Eric Kimmel in Cricket, September and October, 1989. **Awarded:** Witty Short Story Award 1990.

Hershel and the Hanukkah Goblins by Eric Kimmel, illustrated by Trina Schart Hyman; Holiday House, 1989. **Awarded:** Caldecott (honor) 1990; Washington Children's Choice 1992.

The Tartar's Sword by Eric A. Kimmel, illustrated with maps; Coward, 1974. **Awarded:** Friends of American Writers (ages 10-14) 1975.

KIMMEL, MARGARET MARY
Magic in the Mist by Margaret Mary Kimmel, illustrated by Trina Schart Hyman; Atheneum, 1974. **Awarded:** Children's Book Showcase 1976.

KINCADE, NANCY
Even If I Did Something Awful by Barbara S. Hazen, illustrated by Nancy Kincade; Atheneum, 1981. **Awarded:** Christopher (ages 6-9) 1982.

KINCAID, JAMES R.
Lewis Carroll's Alice's Adventures in Wonderland illustrated by Barry Moser, text edited by Selwyn Goodacre, preface and notes by James R. Kincaid; University of California Press, 1982. **Awarded:** American Book Award (pictorial design) 1983.

KING, BUZZ
Silicon Songs by Buzz King, not illustrated; Delacorte, 1990. **Awarded:** Delacorte Press Prize (Honorable Mention) 1989.

KING, CLIVE
Me and My Million by Clive King, not illustrated; Kestrel, 1976; Crowell, 1979. **Awarded:** Boston Globe Horn Book (fiction honor) 1980; Guardian (commended) 1977.

KING, CORETTA SCOTT
The Words of Martin Luther King, Jr. selected by Coretta Scott King, illustrated; Newmarket Press, 1983. **Awarded:** Coretta Scott King (special citation) 1984.

KING, EDNA
Adventure on Thunder Island by Edna King in Adventure on Thunder Island by E. King and J. Wheeler; Lorimer, 1991. **Awarded:** Vicky Metcalf Short Story 1992.

KING, MARTHA BENNETT
Awarded: Children's Reading Round Table 1958.

KING, STEPHEN
The Eyes of the Dragon by Stephen King, illustrated by David Palladini; Viking, 1987. **Awarded:** Blue Spruce 1989.

It by Stephen King; Signet Books, 1990. **Awarded:** Young Teens 1991.

Pet Sematary by Stephen King, not illustrated; Doubleday, 1983. **Awarded:** Blue Spruce 1992.

KING-SMITH, DICK
Awarded: British Book Awards (Author runnerup) 1990; British Book Awards (Author) 1991.

Ace: The Very Important Pig by Dick King-Smith, illustrated by Lynette Hemmant; Crown, 1990. **Awarded:** CRABbery (Classic) 1992.

Babe: The Gallant Pig by Dick King-Smith, illustrated by Mary Rayner; Crown, 1985. **Awarded:** Boston Globe Horn Book (fiction honor) 1985; Parents' Choice (literature) 1985.

Daggie Dogfoot by Dick King-Smith, illustrated by Mary Rayner; Gollancz, 1980. **Awarded:** Guardian (runnerup) 1981.

Find the White Horse by Dick King-Smith, illustrated by Larry Wilkes; Viking, 1991. **Awarded:** Children's Book Award (Shorter Novel) 1992.

The Fox Busters by Dick King-Smith, illustrated by Jon Miller; Delacorte, 1988, c1978. **Awarded:** Parents' Choice (Story Book) 1988.

Harry's Mad by Dick King-Smith, illustrated by Jill Bennett; Crown, 1987, c1984; Gollancz, 1984. **Awarded:** California Young Reader (Intermediate) 1991; Parents' Choice (Story Book) 1987.

The Sheep-pig by Dick King-Smith, illustrated by Mary Rayner; Gollancz, 1983. **Awarded:** Guardian 1984.

KINGMAN, LEE
Escape from the Evil Prophecy by Lee Kingman, illustrated by Richard Cuffari; Houghton, 1973. **Awarded:** Children's Book Showcase 1974.

Pierre Pidgeon by Lee Kingman, illustrated by Arnold Edwin Bare; Houghton, 1943. **Awarded:** Caldecott (honor) 1944.

Private Eyes: Adventures with the Saturday Gang by Lee Kingman, illustrated by Burt Silverman; Doubleday, 1964. **Awarded:** Edgar. Allan Poe (runnerup) 1965

KINGMAN, MARY LEE
see KINGMAN, LEE

KINGSLAND, LESLIE WILLIAM
North to Freedom by Anne S. Holm, translated by L. W. Kingsland, not illustrated; Harcourt, 1965. **Awarded:** Boys Club 1966; Lewis Carroll Shelf 1973.

KINGSLEY, CHARLES
The Water Babies by Charles Kingsley, illustrated by Harold Jones; Watts, 1961, c1863. **Awarded:** Lewis Carroll Shelf 1963.

KINKEAD, BEATRICE
A Ring and a Riddle by E. A. Segal and M. Ilin, translated by Beatrice Kinkead, illustrated by Vera Bock; Lippincott, 1944. **Awarded:** Spring Book Festival (younger) 1944.

KINMOUTH, PATRICK
Mr. Potter's Pigeon by Patrick Kinmouth, illustrated by Reg Cartwright; Hutchinson, 1979. **Awarded:** Mother Goose 1980.

KINSEY-WARNOCK, NATALIE
The Canada Geese Quilt by Natalie Kinsey-Warnock, illustrated by Leslie W. Bowman; Dodd Mead, 1988. **Awarded:** Fassler 1991.

KIPLING, JOHN LOCKWOOD
The Jungle Book by Rudyard Kipling, illustrated by J. L. Kipling, W. H. Drake, and P. Frenzeny; Doubleday, 1952, c1893. **Awarded:** Lewis Carroll Shelf 1960.

KIPLING, RUDYARD
Gunga Din by Rudyard Kipling, illustrated by Robert Andrew Parker; Gulliver Books, 1987. **Awarded:** Parents' Choice (Picture Book) 1987.

The Jungle Book by Rudyard Kipling, illustrated by J. L. Kipling, W. H. Drake, and P. Frenzeny; Doubleday, 1952, c1893. **Awarded:** Lewis Carroll Shelf 1960.

Just So Stories by Rudyard Kipling, illustrated by Etienne Delessert; Doubleday, 1972. **Awarded:** New York Times Best Illustrated 1972.

Just So Stories by Rudyard Kipling, illustrated by David Frampton; HarperCollins, 1991. **Awarded:** Parents' Choice (Picture Book) 1991.

More Just So Stories by Rudyard Kipling, narrated by Ed Begley (phonodisc); Caedmon Records R1205. **Awarded:** Lewis Carroll Shelf 1967.

KIRBY, SUSAN E.
Ike and Porker by Susan E. Kirby, not illustrated; Houghton Mifflin, 1983. **Awarded:** Friends of American Writers ($350) 1984.

Shadow Boy by Susan E. Kirby, not illustrated; Orchard, 1991. **Awarded:** Child Study 1991.

KIRK, LOUIS
Hunters of the Whale: An Adventure in Northwest Coast Archaeology by Ruth Kirk and Richard D. Daugherty, illustrated with photographs by Louis Kirk and Ruth Kirk; Morrow, 1974. **Awarded:** New York Academy of Sciences (older) 1975.

KIRK, RUTH
Hunters of the Whale: An Adventure in Northwest Coast Archaeology by Ruth Kirk and Richard D. Daugherty, illustrated with photographs by Louis Kirk and Ruth Kirk; Morrow, 1974. **Awarded:** New York Academy of Sciences (older) 1975.

KIRKUP, JAMES
The Little Man by Erich Kastner, translated by James Kirkup, illustrated by Rick Schreiter; Knopf, 1966. **Awarded:** Batchelder 1968.

KIRN, ANN
Full of Wonder written and illustrated by Ann Kirn; World, 1959. **Awarded:** New York Times Best Illustrated 1959.

KIROUAC, PAUL
Mr. Slim Goodbody Presents the Inside Story by John Burstein, illustrated by Paul Kirouac; McGraw, 1977. **Awarded:** New Jersey Institute of Technology 1978.

KISHIDA, ISAO
Beetles by Sylvia A. Johnson, photographs by Isao Kishida; Lerner, 1982. **Awarded:** New York Academy of Sciences (special award) 1983.

Silkworms by Sylvia A. Johnson, photographs by Isao Kishida; Lerner, 1982. **Awarded:** New York Academy of Sciences (special award) 1983.

KISMARIC, CAROLE
The Rumor of Pavel and Paali adapted by Carole Kismaric, illustrated by Charles Mikolaycak; Harper & Row, 1988. **Awarded:** Parents' Choice (Picture Book) 1988.

KITAMURA, SATOSHI
Angry Arthur by Hiawyn Oram, illustrated by Satoshi Kitamura; Andersen Press, 1982; Harcourt, 1982. **Awarded:** Mother Goose 1983.

Sky in the Pie by Roger McGough, illustrated by Satoshi Kitamura; Kestrel, 1983. **Awarded:** Signal 1984.

What's Inside: The Alphabet Book written and illustrated by Satoshi Kitamura; Farrar, 1985. **Awarded:** New York Times Notable 1985.

When Sheep Cannot Sleep written and illustrated by Satoshi Kitamura; Farrar, Straus, Giroux, 1986. **Awarded:** New York Academy of Sciences (younger) 1987.

KITCHEN, BERT
Animal Alphabet written and illustrated by Bert Kitchen; Dial, 1984. **Awarded:** New York Times Best Illustrated 1984.

Animal Numbers written and illustrated by Bert Kitchen; Lutterworth Press, 1987; Dial, 1987. **Awarded:** Bologna (Graphic Prize for Children) 1988.

Tenrec's Twigs written and illustrated by Bert Kitchen; Philomel, 1989. **Awarded:** Redbook 1989.

KITCHEN, DAVID
Thin Ice by David Kitchen, illustrated; Oxford, 1991. **Awarded:** Times Educational Supplement (Schoolbook-Secondary) 1991.

KITCHEN, HERMINIE B.
Birds We Live With by Herminie B. Kitchen and Carroll Lane Fenton; illustrated by Carroll Lane Fenton; Day, 1963. **Awarded:** New Jersey Institute of Technology (science ages 8-12) 1964.

KITTELSEN, THEODOR
Norwegian Folk Tales by Peter Christen Asbjornsen and Jorgen Moe, illustrated by Theodor Kittelsen and Erik Werenskiold; Viking, 1961. **Awarded:** Spring Book Festival (middle) 1961.

KITZINGER, SHEILA
Being Born by Sheila Kitzinger, photographs by Lennart Nilsson; Dorling Kindersley, 1986; Grosset, 1986. **Awarded:** Boston Globe Horn Book (nonfiction honor) 1987; Times Educational Supplement (Junior) 1987.

KJELGAARD, JAMES ARTHUR
Big Red by Jim Kjelgaard, illustrated by Bob Kuhn; Holiday House, 1945. **Awarded:** Boys Club 1948.

Ulysses and His Woodland Zoo by Jim Kjelgaard, illustrated by Kendall Rossi; Dodd, 1960. **Awarded:** Boys Life - Dodd Mead 1959.

Wolf Brother by James Kjelgaard, not illustrated; Holiday House, 1957. **Awarded:** Western Writers 1958.

KLASS, DAVID
Wrestling With Honor by David Klass, not illustrated; Dutton, 1989. **Awarded:** Southern California Council (Fiction for Young Adults) 1990.

KLASS, SHEILA SOLOMON
Alive & Starting Over by Sheila Solomon Klass, not illustrated; Scribner, 1983. **Awarded:** New Jersey Institute of Technology 1983.

The Bennington Stitch by Sheila Solomon Klass, not illustrated; Scribner, 1985. **Awarded:** New Jersey Institute of Technology 1988.

Credit-Card Carole by Sheila Solomon Klass, not illustrated; Scribner, 1987. **Awarded:** New Jersey Institute of Technology 1988.

KLAUSE, ANNETTE CURTIS
The Silver Kiss by Annette Curtis Klause, not illustrated; Delacorte, 1990. **Awarded:** Sequoyah Young Adult 1993; Young Adult Novel of the Year / Michigan Library Assn. (honor) 1990.

KLAVENESS, JAN O'DONNELL
The Griffin Legacy by Jan O'Donnell Klaveness, not illustrated; Macmillan, 1983. **Awarded:** Edgar Allan Poe (runnerup) 1984.

KLEIN, NORMA
Sunshine by Norma Klein, not illustrated; Avon, 1974; Holt Rinehart and Winston, 1975, c1974. **Awarded:** Emphasis on Reading (grades 10-12) 1982-83; Media & Methods (paperback) 1975.

Treasure Your Love by Leona Klipsch, not illustrated; Dodd, 1959. **Awarded:** Edith Busby 1958.

KLEIN, ROBIN
Awarded: Dromkeen Medal 1991.

All in the Blue Unclouded Weather by Robin Klein, not illustrated; Penguin Books Australia, 1991. **Awarded:** New South Wales State Literary Awards (Children's) 1992.

Came Back To Show You I Could Fly by Robin Klein, not illustrated; Viking Kestrel, 1989. **Awarded:** Children's Book Council of Australia (Book of the Year Older) 1990.

Hating Alison Ashley by Robin Klein, not illustrated; Penguin, 1984. **Awarded:** KOALA (Secondary) 1987; West Australian (Australian primary) 1986; Young Australian's Best Book (fiction for older readers) 1986.

Penny Pollard's Diary by Robin Klein, illustrated by Ann James; Oxford University Press, 1983. **Awarded:** Children's Book Council of Australia (book of the year highly commended) 1984.

People Might Hear You by Robin Klein, not illustrated; Puffin, 1983. **Awarded:** West Australian (Australian secondary) 1986.

Thing by Robin Klein, illustrated by Alison Lester; Oxford (London), 1982; Oxford (Melbourne), 1982. **Awarded:** Children's Book Council of Australia (junior book of the year) 1983.

KLEVEN, ELISA
Abuela by Arthur Dorros, illustrated by Elisa Kleven; Dutton, 1991. **Awarded:** Hungry Mind (Picturebooks/Fiction) 1992; Parents' Choice (Story Book) 1991.

Ernst written and illustrated by Elisa Kleven; Dutton, 1989. **Awarded:** Dutton Children's Books Picture Book (2nd prize) 1986.

KLIMAN, GILBERT
Responsible Parenthood: The Child's Psyche through the Six-Year Pregnancy by Gilbert Kliman and Albert Rosen, not illustrated; Holt Rinehart and Winston, 1980. **Awarded:** Korczak (about children) 1982.

KLINE, SUZY
Herbie Jones by Suzy Kline, illustrated by Richard Williams; Putnam, 1985. **Awarded:** West Virginia Children's 1987-88.

What's the Matter with Herbie Jones? by Suzy Kline, illustrated by Richard Williams; Putnam, 1986. **Awarded:** KC Three 1988-89.

KLIPSCH, LEONA
Treasure your Love by Leona Klipsch, not illustrated; Dodd Mead, 1959. **Awarded:** Edith Busby 1958.

KNAFF, JEAN CHRISTIAN
Manhattan written and illustrated by Jean Christian Knaff; Faber, 1987. **Awarded:** Mother Goose (runner-up) 1988.

KNIGHT, CHRISTOPHER G.
Sugaring Time by Kathryn Lasky, photographs by Christopher G. Knight; Macmillan, 1983. **Awarded:** Newbery (honor) 1984.

The Weaver's Gift by Kathryn Lasky, illustrated with photographs by Christopher G. Knight; Warne, 1981. **Awarded:** Boston Globe Horn Book (Nonfiction) 1981.

KNIGHT, CLAYTON
The Quest of the Golden Condor written and illustrated by Clayton Knight; Knopf, 1946. **Awarded:** Spring Book Festival (older) 1946.

The Secret of the Buried Tomb written and illustrated by Clayton Knight; Knopf, 1948. **Awarded:** Spring Book Festival (older honor) 1948.

KNIGHT, DAVID
Songberd's Grove by Anne Barrett, illustrated by David Knight; Collins, 1957. **Awarded:** Carnegie (commended) 1957.

KNIGHT, ERIC
Lassie Come Home by Eric Knight, illustrated by Cyrus L. Baldredge; Holt, 1940. **Awarded:** Young Readers Choice 1943.

KNIGHT, HILARY
Jeremiah Octopus by Margaret Stone Zilboorg, illustrated by Hilary Knight; Golden, 1962. **Awarded:** Spring Book Festival (picture book honor) 1962.

Sunday Morning by Judith Viorst, illustrated by Hilary Knight; Harper, 1968. **Awarded:** New Jersey Institute of Technology 1969.

KNIGHT, HUGH
New Perspectives Book 1: An English Course by Hugh Knight and Angela Bell, illustrated; Oxford, 1987. **Awarded:** Times Educational Supplement (Schoolbook) 1987.

KNOEPFLMACHER, U. C.
The Balancing of Child and Adult by U. C. Knoepflmacher in Nineteenth Century Fiction 37 (Mar 1983). **Awarded:** Children's Literature Assn. Excellence in Criticism 1984.

Little Girls without Their Curls by U. C. Knoepflmacher in Children's Literature 10 (1983). **Awarded:** Children's Literature Assn. Excellence in Criticism (runnerup) 1984.

KNOTTS, HOWARD
A Day in the Country by Willis Barnstone, illustrated by Howard Knotts; Harper, 1971. **Awarded:** Indiana Authors Day (children) 1972.

The Winter Cat written and illustrated by Howard Knotts; Harper, 1972. **Awarded:** Children's Book Showcase 1973; Friends of American Writers (ages 4-8) 1973.

KNOWLTON, E.B.
Awarded: Chandler Reward of Merit 1965.

KNUTSON, BARBARA
How the Guinea Fowl Got Her Spots retold and illustrated by Barbara Knutson; Carolrhoda, 1990. **Awarded:** Minnesota (younger children) 1991.

KOBAYASHI, MASAKO MATSUNO
see MATSUNO, MASAKO

KOCH, CHARLOTTE AND RAYMOND
see RAYMOND, CHARLES

KOCH, MICHELLE
Just One More written and illustrated by Michelle Koch; Greenwillow, 1989. **Awarded:** New Jersey Institute of Technology 1990.

KOCSIS, JAMES C.
Edge of Two Worlds by Weyman Jones, illustrated by J. C. Kocsis; Dial, 1968. **Awarded:** Lewis Carroll Shelf 1969; Western Heritage 1969.

KOEHN, ILSE
The Liverpool Cats by Sylvia Sherry, illustrated by Ilse Koehn; Lippincott, 1969. **Awarded:** Spring Book Festival (middle honor) 1969.

Mischling, Second Degree: My Childhood in Nazi Germany by Ilse Koehn, not illustrated; Greenwillow, 1977. **Awarded:** Jane Addams (honor) 1978; Boston Globe Horn Book (nonfiction) 1978; Lewis Carroll Shelf 1978; National Book Award (finalist) 1978.

KOELLE, BARBARA S.
Awarded: L. Frank Baum 1977.

KOENIG, MARION
The Tale of Fancy Nancy: A Spanish Folk Tale by Marion Koenig, illustrated by Klaus Ensikat; Chatto, 1978. **Awarded:** New York Times Best Illustrated 1979.

KOERING, URSULA
Antelope Singer by Ruth M. Underhill, illustrated by Ursula Koering; Coward, 1961. **Awarded:** Nancy Bloch 1961.

Helicopters at Work by Mary Elting and Judith Steigler, illustrated by Ursula Koering; Harvey House, 1972. **Awarded:** New Jersey Institute of Technology 1972.

Science and the Secret of Man's Past by Franklin Folsom, illustrated by Ursula Koering; Harvey House, 1966. **Awarded:** New Jersey Institute of Technology (science) 1966.

This Boy Cody by Leon Wilson, illustrated by Ursula Koering; Watts, 1950. **Awarded:** Lewis Carroll Shelf 1959.

KOERTGE, RON
Boy in the Moon by Ron Koertge, not illustrated; Little Brown, 1990. **Awarded:** Friends of American Writers 1991.

KOFFLER, CAMILLA
see YLLAKOHL, HERBERT

From Archetype to Zeitgeist: Powerful Ideas for Powerful Thinking by Herbert Kohl; Little Brown, 1992. **Awarded:** Hungry Mind (Young Adult/Nonficiton) 1993.

The View from the Oak by Herbert Kohl and Judith Kohl, illustrated by Roger Bayless; Sierra Club/Scribner, 1977. **Awarded:** National Book Award 1978.

KOHL, JUDITH
The View from the Oak by Judith Kohl and Herbert Kohl, illustrated by Roger Bayless; Sierra Club/ Scribner, 1977. **Awarded:** National Book Award 1978.

KOHN, BERNICE
The Busy Honeybee by Bernice Kohn, illustrated by Mel Furukawa; Four Winds, 1972. **Awarded:** Children's Book Showcase 1973.

KOIKE, HIROO
Apple Trees by Sylvia A. Johnson, photographs by Hiroo Koike; Lerner, 1983. **Awarded:** New York Academy of Sciences (special award) 1983.

KOLDA, HELENA
The Secret of the Two Feathers by Helena Kolda and Ivo Duka, photographs by Helena Kolda; Harper & Row, 1954. **Awarded:** Boys Club 1955.

KOMODA, BEVERLY
The Wishing Night by Carole Vetter, illustrated by Beverly Komoda; Macmillan, 1966. **Awarded:** New Jersey Institute of Technology 1966.

KOMURA, HIROTSUGA
Kites, the Science and the Wonder by Hirotsuga Komura and Toshio Ito; Japan Publications (Distributed by Kodansha International through Harper), 1983. **Awarded:** New York Academy of Sciences (older honor) 1984.

KONIGSBURG, ELAINE LOBL
From the Mixed-up Files of Mrs. Basil E. Frankweiler written and illustrated by E. L. Konigsburg; Atheneum, 1967. **Awarded:** Lewis Carroll Shelf 1968; Newbery 1968; William Allen White 1970.

Jennifer, Hecate, Macbeth, William McKinley, & Me, Elizabeth written and illustrated by E. L. Konigsburg; Atheneum, 1967. **Awarded:** Newbery (honor) 1968; Spring Book Festival (middle honor) 1967.

A Proud Taste for Scarlet and Miniver written and illustrated by E. L. Konigsburg; Atheneum, 1973. **Awarded:** National Book Award (finalist) 1974.

Up from Jerich Tell by E. L. Konigsburg, not illustrated; Atheneum, 1986. **Awarded:** Parents' Choice (literature) 1986.

KONSTANTINOV, FODOR
Il Cavallo di Bronzo by Aleksandr Sergeevic Puskin, illustrated by Fodor Konstantinov; Detskaya Literatura. **Awarded:** Bologna (Graphics for Youth) 1976.

KOOB, THEODORA JOHANNA FOTH
Hear a Different Drummer by Theodora Koob, not illustrated; Lippincott, 1968. **Awarded:** New Jersey Institute of Technology 1968.

KOOIKER, LEONIE
The Magic Stone by Leonie Kooiker, translated by Clara Winston and Richard Winston, illustrated by Carl Hollander; Morrow, 1978. **Awarded:** International Board on Books for Young People (Translation/USA) 1980.

KORACH, MIMI
The Old Witch and the Wizard by Ida De Lage, illustrated by Mimi Korach; Garrard, 1974. **Awarded:** New Jersey Institute of Technology 1975.

The Old Witch's Party by Ida De Lage, illustrated by Mimi Korach; Garrard, 1976. **Awarded:** New Jersey Institute of Technology 1977.

The Secret of the Simple Code by Nancy Faulkner, illustrated by Mimi Korach; Doubleday, 1965. **Awarded:** Edgar Allan Poe (runnerup) 1966.

KOREN, EDWARD
Behind the Wheel written and illustrated by Edward Koren; Holt, 1972. **Awarded:** Biennale Illustrations Bratislava (plaque) 1973; New York Times Best Illustrated 1972.

KOSSIN, SANDY
The Goof That Won the Pennant by Jonah Kalb, illustrated by Sandy Kossin; Houghton, 1976. **Awarded:** Surrey School 1979; Young Hoosier (grades 4-6) 1981.

Me and the Weirdos by Jane Sutton, illustrated by Sandy Kossin; Houghton Mifflin, 1981. **Awarded:** Utah Children's 1986.

KOSTERINA, NINA
The Diary of Nina Kosterina by Nina Kosterina, translated and illustrated by Mirra Ginsburg; Crown, 1968. **Awarded:** Lewis Carroll Shelf 1972.

KOTZWINKLE, WILLIAM
E.T.: Extra-terrestrial Storybook by William Kotzwinkle, based on the screenplay by Melissa Mathison, not illustrated; Putnam, 1982. **Awarded:** Buckeye (grades K-3) 1984; North Dakota Children's Choice (younger) 1983.

KOUYOUMDJIAN, JOANNE
Look Out, Look Out, Mad Animals About written and illustrated by Joanne Kouyoumdjian. **Awarded:** Macmillan (1st Prize) 1993.

KRAHN, FERNANDO
April Fools written and illustrated by Fernando Krahn; Dutton, 1974. **Awarded:** Children's Book Showcase 1975.

KRASILOVSKY, PHYLLIS
The First Tulips in Holland by Phyllis Krasilovsky, illustrated by S. D. Schindler; Doubleday, 1982. **Awarded:** Parents' Choice (illustration) 1982.

KRAUS, ROBERT
Herman the Helper by Robert Kraus, illustrated by Jose Aruego and Ariane Dewey; Windmill, 1974. **Awarded:** Boston Globe Horn Book (illustrator honor) 1974.

Leo the Late Bloomer by Robert Kraus, illustrated by Jose Aruego; Windmill, 1973. **Awarded:** Art Books for Children 1973.

Milton the Early Riser by Robert Kraus, illustrated by Jose Aruego and Ariane Aruego; Windmill, 1972. **Awarded:** Art Books for Children 1974, 1975, 1976; New York Times Notable Books 1972.

Owliver by Robert Kraus, illustrated by Jose Aruego and Ariane Dewey; Windmill, 1974. **Awarded:** Children's Book Showcase 1975.

Pinchpenny Mouse by Robert Kraus, illustrated by Robert Byrd; Windmill, 1974. **Awarded:** Children's Book Showcase 1975.

KRAUSE, PAT
Freshie by Pat Krause; Potlatch Publications, 1981. **Awarded:** Young Adult Canadian Book Award (honorable mention) 1982.

KRAUSS, RUTH IDA
The Birthday Party by Ruth Krauss, illustrated by Maurice Sendak; Harper, 1957. **Awarded:** New York Times Best Illustrated 1957.

The Carrot Seed by Ruth Krauss, illustrated by Crockett Johnson; Harper, 1945. **Awarded:** Spring Book Festival (younger honor) 1945.

The Happy Day by Ruth Krauss, illustrated by Marc Simont; Harper & Row, 1949. **Awarded:** Caldecott (honor) 1950.

A Hole Is To Dig by Ruth Krauss, illustrated by Maurice Sendak; Harper, 1952. **Awarded:** New York Times Best Illustrated 1952.

I Can Fly by Ruth Krauss, illustrated by Mary Blair; Simon & Schuster, 1950. **Awarded:** Spring Book Festival (picture book honor) 1951.

I Want to Paint My Bathroom Blue by Ruth Krauss, illustrated by Maurice Sendak; Harper, 1956. **Awarded:** New York Times Best Illustrated 1956.

I'll Be You and You Be Me by Ruth Krauss, illustrated by Maurice Sendak; Harper, 1954. **Awarded:** New York Times Best Illustrated 1954.

Open House for Butterflies by Ruth Krauss, illustrated by Maurice Sendak; Harper, 1960. **Awarded:** New York Times Best Illustrated 1960.

A Very Special House by Ruth Krauss, illustrated by Maurice Sendak; Harper, 1953. **Awarded:** Caldecott (honor) 1954.

KRAUTTER, FRANCES
Uncertain Glory by Frances Krautter, not illustrated; Dodd, 1954. **Awarded:** Calling All Girls - Dodd, Mead 1954.

KREDEL, FRITZ
Tom Paine, Freedom's Apostle by Leo Gurko, illustrated by Fritz Kredel; Crowell, 1957. **Awarded:** Newbery (honor) 1958; Spring Book Festival (older honor) 1957.

KREDENSER, GAIL
One Dancing Drum by Gail Kredenser and Stanley Mack, illustrated by Stanley Mack; Phillips, 1971. **Awarded:** Children's Book Showcase 1972; New York Times Best Illustrated 1971.

KREMENTZ, JILL
Awarded: Washington Post/Children's Book Guild Nonfiction 1984.

How It Feels To Fight for Your Life by Jill Krementz, illustrated with photographs; Little Brown, 1989. **Awarded:** Fassler 1990.

A Very Young Dancer written and illustrated by Jill Krementz; Knopf, 1976. **Awarded:** Garden State Children's (younger nonfiction) 1979.

KRIGSTEIN, BERNARD
Border Hawk: August Bondi by Lloyd Alexander, illustrated by Bernard Krigstein; Farrar, 1958. **Awarded:** Jewish Book Council 1958.

Keys to a Magic Door by Sylvia Rothchild, illustrated by Bernard Krigstein; Farrar, 1959. **Awarded:** Jewish Book Council 1959.

KROEBER, LISA W.
A Life of Their Own: An Indian Family in Latin America by Lisa W. Kroeber and Aylette Jeness, photographs by the authors, illustrated by Susan Votaw; Crowell, 1975. **Awarded:** New York Academy of Sciences (older honor) 1976.

KROLL, EDITE
Friedrich by Hans Peter Richter, translated by Edite Kroll, not illustrated; Holt, 1970. **Awarded:** Batchelder 1972; Woodward Park School 1971.

KROPP, PAUL
Wilted by Paul Kropp, not illustrated; Coward, 1980. **Awarded:** Young Adult Book Award (honorable mention) 1981.

KRUGERNOVA, MARIA
Hodina Nachove Ruze by Maria Krugernova, illustrated by Jana Sigmundova; Albatros. **Awarded:** Bologna (Graphics for Youth) 1973.

KRULL, KATHLEEN
Lives of the Musicians: Good Times, Bad Times (And What the neighbors Thought) by Kathleen Krull; Harcourt, 1993. **Awarded:** Boston Globe Horn Book (Nonfiction honor) 1993.

KRUMGOLD, JOSEPH
And Now Miguel by Joseph Krumgold, illustrated by Jean Charlot; Crowell, 1953. **Awarded:** Boys Club 1954; Newbery 1954.

Onion John by Joseph Krumgold, illustrated by Symeon Shimin; Crowell, 1959. **Awarded:** Lewis Carroll Shelf 1960; Newbery 1970.

KRUPP, EDWIN C.
The Comet and You by Edwin C. Krupp, illustrated by Robin Rector Krupp; Macmillan, 1985. **Awarded:** Southern California Council (nonfiction) 1986.

KRUPP, ROBIN RECTOR
The Comet and You by Edwin C. Krupp, illustrated by Robin Rector Krupp; Macmillan, 1985. **Awarded:** Southern California Council (nonfiction) 1986.

KRUSE, GINNY MOORE
Awarded: Children's Reading Round Table 1988.

KRUSH, BETH
Awarded: Drexel 1980.

Benjie and His Family by Sally Scott, illustrated by Beth Krush; Harcourt, 1952. **Awarded:** Boys Club 1953.

The Borrowers by Mary Norton, illustrated by Beth Krush and Joe Krush; Harcourt, 1953. **Awarded:** Lewis Carroll Shelf 1960.

The Borrowers Afloat by Mary Norton, illustrated by Beth Krush and Joe Krush; Harcourt, 1959. **Awarded:** Spring Book Festival (middle honor) 1959.

Fifteen by Beverly Cleary, illustrated by Beth Krush and Joe Krush; Morrow, 1956. **Awarded:** Dorothy Canfield Fisher 1958.

God, Mrs. Muskrat and Aunt Dot by Isabelle Holland, illustrated by Beth Krush and Joe Krush; Westminster, 1983. **Awarded:** Helen Keating Ott 1983.

Gone Away Lake by Elizabeth Enright, illustrated by Beth Krush and Joe Krush; Harcourt, 1957. **Awarded:** Lewis Carroll Shelf 1970; Newbery (honor) 1958; Spring Book Festival (middle) 1957.

Miracles on Maple Hill by Virginia Sorensen, illustrated by Beth Krush and Joe Krush; Harcourt, 1956. **Awarded:** Newbery 1957.

A Spell Is Cast by Eleanor Cameron, illustrated by Beth Krush and Joe Krush; Atlantic-Little, 1964. **Awarded:** Commonwealth Club of California 1964; Edgar Allan Poe (runnerup) 1965.

KRUSH, JOE
Awarded: Drexel 1980.

The Borrowers by Mary Norton, illustrated by Beth Krush and Joe Krush; Harcourt, 1953. **Awarded:** Lewis Carroll Shelf 1960.

The Borrowers Afloat by Mary Norton, illustrated by Beth Krush and Joe Krush; Harcourt, 1959. **Awarded:** Spring Book Festival (middle honor) 1959.

Fifteen by Beverly Cleary, illustrated by Beth Krush and Joe Krush; Morrow, 1956. **Awarded:** Dorothy Canfield Fisher 1958.

God, Mrs. Muskrat and Aunt Dot by Isabelle Holland, illustrated by Beth Krush and Joe Krush; Westminster, 1983. **Awarded:** Helen Keating Ott 1983.

Gone Away Lake by Elizabeth Enright, illustrated by Beth Krush and Joe Krush; Harcourt, 1957. **Awarded:** Lewis Carroll Shelf 1970; Newbery (honor) 1958; Spring Book Festival (middle) 1957.

Miracles on Maple Hill by Virginia Sorensen, illustrated by Beth Krush and Joe Krush; Harcourt, 1956. **Awarded:** Newbery 1957.

A Spell Is Cast by Eleanor Cameron, illustrated by Beth Krush and Joe Krush; Atlantic-Little, 1964. **Awarded:** Commonwealth Club of California 1964; Edgar Allan Poe (runnerup) 1965.

KRUSS, JAMES
Awarded: Hans Christian Andersen (author) 1968.

KUBIE, NORA GOTTHEIL BENJAMIN
King Solomon's Navy written and illustrated by Nora Benjamin Kubie; Harper, 1954. **Awarded:** Jewish Book Club 1954.

KUBINYI, LASZLO
The Haunted Mountain by Mollie Hunter, illustrated by Laszlo Kubinyi; Harper, 1972. **Awarded:** New York Times Notable Books 1972.

And Tomorrow the Stars: The Story of John Cabot by Kay Hill, illustrated by Laszlo Kubinyi; Dodd Mead, 1968. **Awarded:** Canadian Library Assn. 1969.

Peter the Revolutionary Tsar by Peter Brock Putnam, illustrated by Laszlo Kubinyi; Harper, 1973. **Awarded:** Children's Book Showcase 1974.

KUDRNA, C. IMBIOR
Manners Matter by Norah Smaridge, illustrated by Imbior Kudrna; Abingdon, 1980. **Awarded:** New Jersey Institute of Technology 1981.

What's on Your Plate? by Norah Smaridge, illustrated by C. Imbior Kudrna; Abingdon Press, 1982. **Awarded:** New Jersey Institute of Technology 1983.

KUHL, JEROME
The Battle of the Bulge by John Toland, illustrated by Jerome Kuhl; Random House, 1966. **Awarded:** Boys Club (certificate) 1966- 67.

KUHN, BOB
Big Red by Jim Kjelgaard, illustrated by Bob Kuhn; Holiday House, 1945. **Awarded:** Boys Club 1948.

KUHNS, WILLIAM
Exploring the Film by William Kuhns and Robert Stanley; Pflaum/Standard, 1969. **Awarded:** Media & Methods (textbook) 1973.

KULLMAN, HARRY
Awarded: Hans Christian Andersen (highly commended author/Sweden). 1980

The Battle Horse by Harry Kullman, translated by George Blecher and Lone Thygesen-Blecher, not illustrated; Bradbury, 1981. **Awarded:** Batchelder 1982.

KRUSS, JAMES
Awarded: Hans Christian Andersen (author) 1968.

KUBIE, NORA GOTTHEIL BENJAMIN
King Solomon's Navy written and illustrated by Nora Benjamin Kubie; Harper, 1954. **Awarded:** Jewish Book Club 1954.

KUBINYI, LASZLO
The Haunted Mountain by Mollie Hunter, illustrated by Laszlo Kubinyi; Harper, 1972. **Awarded:** New York Times Notable Books 1972.

And Tomorrow the Stars: The Story of John Cabot by Kay Hill, illustrated by Laszlo Kubinyi; Dodd Mead, 1968. **Awarded:** Canadian Library Assn. 1969.

Peter the Revolutionary Tsar by Peter Brock Putnam, illustrated by Laszlo Kubinyi; Harper, 1973. **Awarded:** Children's Book Showcase 1974.

KUDRNA, C. IMBIOR
Manners Matter by Norah Smaridge, illustrated by Imbior Kudrna; Abingdon, 1980. **Awarded:** New Jersey Institute of Technology 1981.

What's on Your Plate? by Norah Smaridge, illustrated by C. Imbior Kudrna; Abingdon Press, 1982. **Awarded:** New Jersey Institute of Technology 1983.

KUHL, JEROME
The Battle of the Bulge by John Toland, illustrated by Jerome Kuhl; Random House, 1966. **Awarded:** Boys Club (certificate) 1966- 67.

KUHN, BOB
Big Red by Jim Kjelgaard, illustrated by Bob Kuhn; Holiday House, 1945. **Awarded:** Boys Club 1948.

KUHNS, WILLIAM
Exploring the Film by William Kuhns and Robert Stanley; Pflaum/Standard, 1969. **Awarded:** Media & Methods (textbook) 1973.

KULLMAN, HARRY
Awarded: Hans Christian Andersen (highly commended author/Sweden). 1980

The Battle Horse by Harry Kullman, translated by George Blecher and Lone Thygesen-Blecher, not illustrated; Bradbury, 1981. **Awarded:** Batchelder 1982.

KUNHARDT, DOROTHY
Tiny Animal Stories (series) by Dorothy Kunhardt, illustrated by Garth Williams; Simon & Schuster, various years. **Awarded:** Spring Book Festival (younger honor) 1948.

KURELEK, WILLIAM
Lumberjack written and illustrated by William Kurelek; Houghton, 1974. **Awarded:** Children's Book Showcase 1975; New York Times Best Illustrated 1974; New York Times Notable Books 1974.

A Prairie Boy's Summer written and illustrated by William Kurelek; Tundra, 1975. **Awarded:** Canadian Library Assn. (runnerup) 1976; Children's Book Showcase 1976; Amelia Frances Howard-Gibbon 1976; IODE 1975.

A Prairie Boy's Winter written and illustrated by William Kurelek; Tundra, 1973; Houghton Mifflin, 1973. **Awarded:** Boston Globe Horn Book (illustrator honor) 1974; Canadian Library Assn. (runnerup) 1974; Children's Book Showcase 1974; Amelia Frances Howard-Gibbon 1974; New York Times Best Illustrated 1973; New York Times Notable Books 1973.

KURIBAYASHI, SATOSHI
Ants by Cynthia Overbeck, photographs by Satoshi Kuribayashi; Lerner, 1982. **Awarded:** New York Academy of Sciences (special award) 1983.

Spiders by Jane Dallinger, photographs by Satoshi Kuribayashi; Lerner, 1981. **Awarded:** New York Academy of Sciences (special award) 1983.

KURTEN, BJORN
The Cave Bear Story: Life and Death of a Vanished Animal by Bjorn Kurten, illustrated by Margaret Lambert; Columbia University Press, 1976. **Awarded:** New York Academy of Sciences (older honor) 1977.

KURTZ, CARMEN
Oscar, Cosmonauta by Carmen Kurtz, illustrated by Carlos Maria Alvarez; E. Juventud, 1962. **Awarded:** Hans Christian Andersen (runnerup) 1964.

KURUSA
Nowhere to Play written and illustrated by Kurusa, translated by Judith Elkin; A&C Black, 1982. **Awarded:** Other Award 1983.

KUSHNER, DONN
A Book Dragon by Donn Kushner, illustrated by Nancy Ruth Jackson; Macmillan, 1987. **Awarded:** National Chapter of Canada IODE Violet Downey 1988.

The Violin Maker's Gift by Donn Kushner; Macmillan Canada, 1981. **Awarded:** Canadian Library Assn. 1981.

KUSKIN, KARLA
Awarded: National Council of Teachers of English Award for Excellence in Poetry for Children 1979.

A Boy Had a Mother Who Bought Him a Hat written and illustrated by Karla Kuskin; Houghton, 1976. **Awarded:** Children's Book Showcase 1977.

The Dallas Titans Get Ready for Bed by Karla Kuskin, illustrated by Marc Simont; Harper, 1986. **Awarded:** Parents' Choice (literature) 1986.

Jerusalem Shining Still by Karla Kuskin, illustrated by David Frampton; Harper & Row, 1987. **Awarded:** Parents' Choice (Story Book) 1987.

The Philharmonic Gets Dressed by Karla Kuskin, illustrated by Marc Simont; Harper, 1982. **Awarded:** New York Times Notable Books 1982.

Soap Soup and Other Verses by Karla Kuskin; HarperCollins, 1992. **Awarded:** Parents Choice (Story Book) 1992.

A Space Story by Karla Kuskin, illustrated by Marc Simont; Harper, 1978. **Awarded:** New York Academy of Sciences (younger) 1980.

KYLE, ANNE D.
Apprentices of Florence by Anne Kyle, illustrated by Erick Berry; Houghton, 1933. **Awarded:** Newbery (honor) 1934.

KYLE, ELISABETH
Girl with a Pen: Charlotte Bronte by Elisabeth Kyle, illustrated by Charles Mozley; Holt, 1964. **Awarded:** Spring Book Festival (older honor) 1964.

Portrait of Lisette by Elisabeth Kyle, illustrated by Charles Mozley; Nelson, 1963. **Awarded:** Spring Book Festival (older honor) 1963.

L

LABASTIDA, AURORA
Nine Days to Christmas by Aurora Labastida and Marie Hall Ets, illustrated by Marie Hall Ets; Viking, 1959. **Awarded:** Caldecott 1960.

LACAPA, MICHAEL
Awarded: Outstanding Arizona Author 1991.

LACKEY, EUNICE
Lucky Blacky by Eunice Lackey, illustrated by Winifred Greene; Watts, 1953. **Awarded:** New York Times Best Illustrated 1953.

LAFARGE, MARGARET
A Shovelful of Earth by Lorus J. Milne and Margery Milne, illustrated by Margaret LaFarge; Henry Holt, 1987. **Awarded:** New York Academy of Sciences (Older honorable mention) 1988.

LA FARGE, SHEILA
Glassblower's Children by Maria Gripe, translated by Sheila La Farge, illustrated by Harald Gripe; Delacorte/Lawrence, 1973. **Awarded:** International Board on Books for Young People (translation/USA) 1978.

Silas and Ben-Godik by Cecil Bodker, translated by Sheila La Farge; Delacorte/Seymour Lawrence, 1978. **Awarded:** Boston Globe Horn Book (fiction honor) 1979.

LAFAVE, KIM
Amos's Sweater by Janet Lunn, illustrated by Kim LaFave; Douglas & McIntyre, 1988; Scholastic, 1990. **Awarded:** Governor General's Literary Award (Illustration) 1988; Amelia Frances Howard-Gibbon 1989; Ruth Schwartz 1989.

The Bones Book and Skeleton by Stephen Cumbaa, illustrated by Kim LaFave; Workman, 1991. **Awarded:** British Book Awards (Illustrated runnerup) 1992.

Canadian Garbage Collectors by Paulette Bourgeois, illustrated by Kim LaFave; Kids Can Press, 1991. **Awarded:** Information Book Award (Honour) 1992.

LA FONTAINE, JEAN DE
The Lion and the Rat: A Fable by Jean de la Fontaine, illustrated by Brian Wildsmith; Oxford, 1963. **Awarded:** Greenaway (commended) 1963.

LAIMGRUBER, MONIKA
The Emperor's New Clothes: A Fairy Tale by Hans Christian Andersen, illustrated by Monika Laimgruber; Addison-Wesley, 1973. **Awarded:** New York Times Best Illustrated 1973.

LAIRD, CHRISTA
Shadow of the Wall by Christa Laird, illustrated with a map; MacRae, 1989; Greenwillow, 1990. **Awarded:** Janusz Korczak Literary Awards (Children) 1992.

LAIRD, ELIZABETH
Kiss the Dust by Elizabeth Laird, not illustrated; Heinemann, 1991; Dutton, 1992. **Awarded:** Children's Book Award (Federation) 1992.

Red Sky in the Morning by Elizabeth Laird, not illustrated; Heinemann, 1988. **Awarded:** Burnley Express 1988; Carnegie (Highly Commended) 1988.

LAITE, GORDON
Holidays in Scandinavia by Lee Wyndham, illustrated by Gordon Laite; Garrard, 1975. **Awarded:** New Jersey Institute of Technology 1976.

Young Readers Book of Christian Symbolism by Michael Daves, illustrated by Gordon Laite; Abingdon, 1967. **Awarded:** Steck- Vaughn 1968.

LAKE, DAVID
The Changelings of Chaan by David Lake, not illustrated; Hyland House, 1985. **Awarded:** Children's Book Council of Australia (Book of the Year commended) 1986.

LAKE, DENISE
Waddayaknow (Workbook, 1,2, Teacher's Manual) edited by Denise Lake. **Awarded:** Australian Christian Book of the Year Children's Award 1990.

LAKIN, PATRICIA
Don't Touch My Room by Patricia Lakin, illustrated by Patience Brewster; Little Brown, 1985. **Awarded:** Golden Sower (K-3) 1988.

LAKLAN, CARLI
Migrant Girl by Carli Laklan, not illustrated; McGraw, 1970. **Awarded:** Child Study 1970.

LALICKI, BARBARA
If There Were Dreams to Sell by Barbara Lalicki, illustrated by Margot Tomes; Lothrop, Lee & Shepard, 1984. **Awarded:** New York Times Best Illustrated 1984.

LA MARCHE, JIM
A Matter of Pride by Emily Crofford, illustrated by Jim LaMarche; Carolrhoda Books, 1981. **Awarded:** Friends of American Writers ($350 award) 1982.

LAMB, LYNTON HAROLD
A Grass Rope by William Mayne, illustrated by Lynton Lamb; Oxford, 1957. **Awarded:** Carnegie 1957.

The Member for the Marsh by William Mayne, illustrated by Lynton Lamb; Oxford, 1956. **Awarded:** Carnegie (commended) 1956.

LAMBERT, DAVID
The Field Guide to Geology by David Lambert, illustrated; Facts on File, 1988. **Awarded:** New York Academy of Sciences (Special Award to Field Guides - Older) 1989.

LAMBERT, JANET
Awarded: New Jersey Institute of Technology (New Jersey writers of children's books) 1967.

LAMBERT, MARGARET
The Cave Bear Story: Life and Death of a Vanished Animal by Bjorn Kurten, illustrated by Margaret Lambert; Columbia University Press, 1976. **Awarded:** New York Academy of Sciences (older honor) 1977.

LAMBERT, RICHARD STANTON
Franklin of the Arctic: A Life of Adventure by Richard S. Lambert, maps by Julius Griffith; McClelland & Stewart, 1949. **Awarded:** Canadian Library Assn. 1950; Governor-General's Literary Awards 1949.

LAMBERT, SAUL
Spies and More Spies by Robert Arthur, illustrated by Saul Lambert; Random House, 1967. **Awarded:** New Jersey Institute of Technology 1967.

LAMBO, DON
The World of Chocolate by Norah Smaridge, illustrated by Don Lambo; Messner, 1969. **Awarded:** New Jersey Institute of Technology 1969.

LAMBORN, FLORENCE
Pippi Longstocking by Astrid Lindgren, translated by Florence Lamborn, illustrated by Louis Glanzman; Viking, 1950. **Awarded:** Lewis Carroll Shelf 1973.

LAMMERS, ANN CONRAD
Rabbit Island by Jorg Steiner, translated by Ann Conrad Lammers, illustrated by Jorg Muller; Harcourt, 1978. **Awarded:** Batchelder 1979.

LAMONT, BETTE
Island Time by Bette Lamont, illustrated by Brinton Turkle; Lippincott, 1976. **Awarded:** Ohioana 1977.

LAMONT, PRISCILLA
The Troublesome Pig retold and illustrated by Priscilla Lamont; Hamish Hamilton, 1983. **Awarded:** Maschler (runnerup) 1983.

LAMORISSE, ALBERT
The Red Balloon by Albert Lamorisse, illustrated with photographs; Doubleday, 1957. **Awarded:** New York Times Best Illustrated 1957.

La MOTHE, JACQUES, DR.
Awarded: Frances E. Russell 1984.

LA MOTTE, JUDY APPENZELLER
Cutover Country: Jolie's Story by Jolie Paylin, illustrated by Judy Appenzeller La Motte; Iowa State University Press, 1976. **Awarded:** State Historical Society of Wisconsin 1977.

LAMPMAN, EVELYN SIBLEY
The City under the Back Steps by Evelyn Lampman, illustrated by Honore Valintcourt; Doubleday, 1960. **Awarded:** Dorothy Canfield Fisher 1962.

Half-breed by Evelyn S. Lampman, illustrated by Ann Grifalconi; Doubleday, 1967. **Awarded:** Western Writers of America (Fiction) 1968.

The Potlatch Family by Evelyn Sibley Lampman, not illustrated; Atheneum, 1976. **Awarded:** Children's Book Showcase 1977.

LANCASTER, MATTHEW
Hang Toughf by Matthew Lancaster, illustrated by Pamela Huffman; Paulist Press, 1985. **Awarded:** Catholic Book Awards (Youth) 1986.

LANDAU, ELAINE
Alzheimer's Disease by Elaine Landau, illustrated with photos; Watts, 1987. **Awarded:** New Jersey Institute of Technology 1989.

Death: Everyone's Heritage by Elaine Landau, not illustrated; Messner, 1976. **Awarded:** New Jersey Institute of Technology 1977.

Hidden Heroines: Women in American History by Elaine Landau, illustrated with photographs and prints; Messner, 1975. **Awarded:** New Jersey Institute of Technology 1977.

Occult Visions: A Mystical Gaze into the Future by Elaine Landau, illustrated by Carol Gjertsen; Messner, 1979. **Awarded:** New Jersey Institute of Technology 1981.

Surrogate Mothers by Elaine Landau, illustrated; Watts, 1988. **Awarded:** New Jersey Institute of Technology 1989.

The Teen Guide to Dating by Elaine Landau, not illustrated; Messner, 1980. **Awarded:** New Jersey Institute of Technology 1981.

LANDAU, JACOB
The Big Sky: An Edition for Young Readers by Alfred B. Guthrie, Jr., illustrated by Jacob Landau; Sloane, 1950. **Awarded:** Boys Club 1951.

Man and Magic by Benjamin Appel, illustrated by Jacob Landau; Pantheon, 1966. **Awarded:** New Jersey Institute of Technology 1967.

LANDRU, HORTENSE PARKER
see LANDRU, JACK (pseudonym)

LANDRU, JACK
Sled Dog of Alaska by Jack Landru, not illustrated; Dodd, Mead, 1953. **Awarded:** Boys Life 1952.

LANDSTROM, LENA
Will's New Cap by Olof Landstrom, illustrated by Lena Landstrom; R & S Books, 1992. **Awarded:** Parents Choice (Picture Book) 1992.

LANDSTROM, OLOF
Olson's Meat Pies by Peter Cohen, illustrated by Olof Landstrom; Farrar Straus Giroux, 1989. **Awarded:** New York Times Best Illustrated 1989.

Will's New Cap by Olof Landstrom, illustrated by Lena Landstrom; R & S Books, 1992. **Awarded:** Parents Choice (Picture Book) 1992.

LANE, CARL D.
River Dragon by Carl D. Lane, illustrated by Charles Banks Wilson; Little, Brown, 1948. **Awarded:** Spring Book Festival (middle honor) 1948.

LANE, CHRISTOPHER A.
King Leonard's Celebration by Christopher A. Lane, illustrated by Sharon Dahl; Victor Books, 1990. **Awarded:** Gold Medallion (Preschool) 1991.

LANE, FREDERICK A.
Westward the Eagle by Frederick A. Lane, illustrated by E. Harper Johnson; Holt, 1955. **Awarded:** Commonwealth Club of California 1955.

LANG, DENISE V.
Footsteps in the Ocean: Careers in Diving by Denise V. Lang, illustrated with photographs; Dutton, 1987. **Awarded:** New Jersey Institute of Technology 1988.

LANGE, SUZANNE
The Year by Suzanne Lange, not illustrated; Phillips, 1970. **Awarded:** Sydney Taylor Book Award 1970.

LANGFORD, SONDRA GORDON
Red Bird of Ireland by Sondra Gordon Langford, not illustrated; Atheneum, 1983. **Awarded:** New Jersey Institute of Technology 1983.

LANGLEY, NINA SCOTT
String Lug the Fox by David Stephen, illustrated by Nina Scott Langley; Little, Brown, 1952. **Awarded:** Spring Book Festival (older honor) 1952.

LANGNER, NOLA
Scram, Kid! by Ann McGovern, illustrated by Nola Langner; Viking, 1974. **Awarded:** Boston Globe Horn Book (Illustration honor) 1975.

LANGSTAFF, JOHN MEREDITH
Frog Went A-courtin' by John Langstaff, illustrated by Feodor Rojankovsky; Harcourt, 1955. **Awarded:** Caldecott 1956; Spring Book Festival (ages 4-8) 1955.

What a Morning! The Christmas Story in Black Spirituals by John Langstaff, illustrated by Ashley Bryan; McElderry, 1987. **Awarded:** Coretta Scott King (illustration honor) 1988.

LANGTON, JANE
The Diamond in the Window by Jane Langton, illustrated by Erik Blegvad; Harper, 1962. **Awarded:** Edgar Allan Poe (runnerup) 1963.

The Fledgling by Jane Langton, illustrated by Erik Blegvad; Harper, 1980. **Awarded:** Newbery (honor) 1981.

LANIER, STERLING E.
The War for the Lot: A Tale of Fantasy and Terror by Sterling E. Lanier, illustrated by Robert Baumgartner; Follett, 1969. **Awarded:** Charles W. Follett 1970.

LANING, EDWARD
Hello, the Boat! by Phyllis Crawford, illustrated by Edward Laning; Holt, 1938. **Awarded:** Julia Ellsworth Ford 1938; Newbery. (honor) 1939

LANNESTOCK, GUSTAF
Gunilla, an Arctic Adventure by Albert Viksten, translated by Gustaf Lannestock, illustrated by Rus Anderson; Nelson, 1957. **Awarded:** Spring Book Festival (older honor) 1957.

LANT, KATHLEEN M.
Dismembering the Text: The Horror of Louisa May Alcott's Little Women by Kathleen M. Lant and Angela M. Estes in Children's Literature 17 (1989). **Awarded:** Children's Literature Assn. Criticism Award (runnerup) 1990.

LANTON, SANDY
Daddy's Chair by Sandy Lanton, illustrated by Shelly O. Haas; KarBen Copies, 1991. **Awarded:** Sydney Taylor Book Award (Picture Book) 1992.

LANTZ, PAUL
Blue Willow by Doris Gates, illustrated by Paul Lantz; Viking, 1940. **Awarded:** Lewis Carroll Shelf 1961; Commonwealth Club of California 1940; FOCAL 1982; Newbery (honor) 1941.

Knock at the Door, Emmy by Florence C. Means, illustrated by Paul Lantz; Houghton Mifflin, 1956. **Awarded:** Nancy Bloch 1956.

The Matchlock Gun by Walter D. Edmonds, illustrated by Paul Lantz; Dodd Mead, 1941. **Awarded:** Lewis Carroll Shelf 1960; Newbery 1942.

Milenka's Happy Summer by Mary Barker, illustrated by Paul Lantz; Dodd Mead, 1961. **Awarded:** Edith Busby 1960.

Spook, the Mustang by Harlan Thompson, illustrated by Paul Lantz; Doubleday, 1956. **Awarded:** Commonwealth Club of California 1956.

LANZ, DANIEL J.
Railroads of Southern and Southwestern Wisconsin by Daniel J. Lanz, illustrated; D. J. Lanz, 1985. **Awarded:** State Historical Society of Wisconsin 1986.

LAPEDES, DANIEL N.
Helpful Microorganisms by Daniel Lapedes, illustrated with photographs and diagrams; World, 1968. **Awarded:** New Jersey Institute of Technology 1968.

LA PIETRA, ANN
Awarded: Lucile M. Pannell 1990.

LAPP, ELEANOR J.
Duane, the Collector by Eleanor J. Lapp, illustrated by Christine Westerberg; Addison Wesley, 1976. **Awarded:** Council of Wisconsin Writers (picture book) 1977.

The Mice Came in Early this Year by Eleanor J. Lapp, illustrated by David Cunningham; Whitman, 1976. **Awarded:** Council of Wisconsin Writers (picture book runnerup) 1977.

LAQUER-FRANCHESHI,THEODORE
The Unusual Puerto Rican by Theodore Laquer-Francheshi; Lothrop Lee & Shepard. **Awarded:** Council on Interracial Books (Puerto Rican) 1971-72.

LARGE, ANNABEL
Which Witch? by Eva Ibbotson, illustrated by Annabel Large; Macmillan, 1979. **Awarded:** Carnegie (commended) 1979.

LARIMER, TAMELA
Buck by Tamela Larimer, not illustrated; Avon/Flare, 1986. **Awarded:** Avon/Flare 1985.

LARKIN, R. PAUL
Knowledge and Wonder: The Natural World as Man Knows It by Victor F. Weisskopf, illustrated by R. Paul Larkin; Doubleday, 1962. **Awarded:** Edison Mass Media (science book youth) 1963.

LAROCQUE, GERRI
Awarded: ALAN 1979.

LARRICK, NANCY G.
Awarded: Drexel 1977; Helen Keating Ott 1984.

Cats Are Cats: Poems by Nancy Larrick, illustrated by Ed Young; Philomel, 1988. **Awarded:** New York Times Best Illustrated 1988.

When the Dark Comes Dancing compiled by Nancy Larrick, illustrated by John Wallner; Philomel, 1983. **Awarded:** Parents' Choice (literature) 1984.

LARSEN, JOHN
Captain Carp Saves the Sea written and illustrated by John Larsen; Annick Press, 1983. **Awarded:** Alcuin 1984.

LARSEN, REBECCA
Paul Robeson: Hero Before His Time by Rebecca Larsen, illustrated with photos; Watts, 1989. **Awarded:** Woodson (Secondary) 1990.

LARSON, GLEN A.
The Battlestar Galactica Storybook by Glen A. Larson and Robert Thurston, adapted by Charles Mercer, illustrated with photographs; Putnam, 1979. **Awarded:** New Jersey Institute of Technology 1980.

LARSON, JEAN RUSSELL
Jack Tar by Jean Russell Larson, illustrated by Mercer Mayer; Macrae, 1970. **Awarded:** Lewis Carroll Shelf 1973.

LARSON, LYNN
The Child of Two Mothers by Malcolm Rosholt and Margaret Rosholt, illustrated by Lynn Larson; Rosholt House, 1983. **Awarded:** State Historical Society of Wisconsin 1984.

LARSSON, CARL
A Farm by Lennart Rudstrom, translated by Ernest Edwin Ryden, illustrated by Carl Larsson; Putnam, 1976. **Awarded:** Children's Book Showcase 1977.

A Home by Lennart Rudstrom, illustrated by Carl Larsson; Putnam, 1974. **Awarded:** Children's Book Showcase 1975; New York Times Best Illustrated 1974.

LASENBY, JACK
The Mangrove Summer by Jack Lasenby, illustrated with maps; Oxford University Press, 1988. **Awarded:** Esther Glen Award 1989.

LASKER, JOE
Merry Ever After: The Story of Two Medieval Weddings written and illustrated by Joe Lasker; Viking, 1976. **Awarded:** Art Books for Children 1978, 1979; New York Times Best Illustrated 1976; New York Times Notable 1976.

A Tournament of Knights written and illustrated by Joe Lasker; Crowell, 1986. **Awarded:** Redbook 1986.

LASKOWSKI, JANINA DOMANSKA
see DOMANSKA, JANINA

LASKY, KATHRYN
Awarded: Washington Post/Children's Book Guild Nonfiction 1986.

Beyond the Divide by Kathryn Lasky, illustrated with a map; Macmillan, 1983. Awarded: New York Times Notable 1983.

The Night Journey by Kathryn Lasky, illustrated by Trina Schart Hyman; Warne, 1981. Awarded: Sydney Taylor Book Award (older children) 1982; Jewish Book Council (children) 1982.

Sugaring Time by Kathryn Lasky, photographs by Christopher G. Knight; Macmillan, 1983. Awarded: Newbery (honor) 1984.

The Weaver's Gift by Kathryn Lasky, illustrated with photographs by Christopher G. Knight; Warne, 1981. Awarded: Boston Globe Horn Book (nonfiction) 1981.

LATHAM, BARBARA
Monarch Butterfly by Marion W. Marcher, illustrated by Barbara Latham; Hale, 1954. Awarded: New Jersey Institute of Technology (science) 1963.

LATHAM, JEAN LEE
Carry On, Mr. Bowditch by Jean Lee Latham, illustrated by J. O. Cosgrove; Houghton, 1955. Awarded: International Board on Books for Young People (USA) 1956; Newbery 1956.

Trail Blazer of the Seas by Jean Lee Latham, illustrated by Victor Mays; Houghton Mifflin, 1956. Awarded: Boys Club 1957.

LATHAM, JOHN
Lonesome Longhorn written and illustrated by John Latham; Westminster, 1951. Awarded: Spring Book Festival (older honor) 1951; Steck-Vaughn 1953.

LATHAM, ROSS
Australian Animals by Peter Sloan, illustrated by Ross Latham; Methuen Australia, 1983. Awarded: Whitley Awards 1984.

LATHROP, DOROTHY PULIS
Animals of the Bible: A Picture Book by Helen Dean Fish, illustrated by Dorothy P. Lathrop; Stokes, 1937. Awarded: Caldecott 1938.

The Fairy Circus written and illustrated by Dorothy P. Lathrop; Macmillan, 1931. Awarded: Newbery (honor) 1932.

Forgotten Daughter by Caroline Dale Snedeker, illustrated by Dorothy P. Lathrop; Doubleday, 1933. Awarded: Newbery (honor) 1934.

Hitty: Her First Hundred Years by Rachel Field, illustrated by Dorothy P. Lathrop; Macmillan, 1929. Awarded: Lewis Carroll Shelf 1961; Newbery 1930.

Let Them Live written and illustrated by Dorothy P. Lathrop; Macmillan, 1951. Awarded: Spring Book Festival (8-12 honor) 1951.

LATIES, ANDREW G.
Awarded: Lucile M. Pannell 1987.

LATIMER, JIM
Going the Moose Way Home by Jim Latimer, illustrated by Donald Carrick; Scribner, 1988. Awarded: Minnesota (Children) 1989.

LATTIMORE, DEBORAH NOURSE
The Dragon's Robe written and illustrated by Deborah Nourse Lattimore; HarperCollins, 1990. Awarded: PEN Center USA West 1991; Southern California Council (Distinguished Illustrating and Writing) 1991.

The Flame of Peace: A Tale of the Aztecs written and illustrated by Deborah Nourse Lattimore; Harper & Row, 1987. Awarded: Southern California Council (Excellence in Illustration) 1988.

LAUBER, PATRICIA
Awarded: Eva L. Gordon 1987; Washington Post/Children's Book Guild Nonfiction 1983.

From Flower to Flower by Patricia Lauber, illustrated by Jerome Wexler; Crown, 1986. Awarded: New York Academy of Sciences (Younger) 1988.

Journey to the Planets by Patricia Lauber, illustrated with photographs; Crown, 1982. Awarded: New York Times Notable 1982.

Living With Dinosaurs by Patricia Lauber, illustrated by Douglas Henderson; Bradbury, 1991. Awarded: Hungry Mind (Middle Readers/Nonfiction) 1992.

The News About Dinosaurs written and illustrated by Patricia Lauber; Bradbury, 1989. Awarded: New York Academy of Sciences (Younger Honorable Mention) 1989; Orbis Pictus (Honor) 1989.

Seeing Earth From Space by Patricia Lauber, illustrated; Orchard, 1990. Awarded: Orbis Pictus (Honor) 1991.

Tales Mummies Tell by Patricia Lauber, illustrated with photographs; Crowell, 1985. Awarded: New York Academy of Sciences (older honor) 1986.

Volcano: The Eruption and Healing of Mt. St. Helens by Patricia Lauber, illustrated; Bradbury Press, 1986. Awarded: New York Academy of Sciences (older honor) 1987; Newbery (honor) 1987.

LAURE, ETTAGALE
Joi Bangla! The Children of Bangladesh by Ettagale Laure and Jason Laure, illustrated by Jason Laure; Farrar, 1974. Awarded: National Book Award (finalist) 1975.

LAURE, JASON
Joi Bangla! The Children of Bangladesh by Jason Laure and Ettagale Laure, illustrated by Jason Laure; Farrar, 1974. Awarded: National Book Award (finalist) 1975.

LAURENCE, MARGARET
The Olden Days Coat by Margaret Laurence, illustrated by Muriel Wood; McClelland & Stewart, 1979. Awarded: Canadian Library Assn. (runnerup) 1980.

LAURITZEN, JONREED
Legend of Billy Bluesage by Jonreed Lauritzen, illustrated by Edward Chavez; Little, Brown, 1961. Awarded: Southern California Council (notable) 1962.

The Ordeal of the Young Hunter by Jonreed Lauritzen, illustrated by Hoke Denetsosie; Little, Brown, 1954. Awarded: Child Study 1954.

Treasure of the High Country by Jonreed Lauritzen, illustrated by Eric von Schmidt; Little, Brown, 1959. Awarded: Spring Book Festival (middle honor) 1959.

LAUTER, RICHARD
The War with Grandpa by Robert Kimmel Smith, illustrated by Richard Lauter; Delacorte, 1984. Awarded: California Young Reader (Intermediate) 1990; Emphasis on Reading (grades 3-5) 1988-89; Dorothy Canfield Fisher 1986; Georgia Children's Book Award 1989; Golden Sower (grades 4-6) 1987; Parents' Choice (literature) 1984; South Carolina Children's 1986; Mark Twain 1987; William Allen White

1987; Volunteer State Book Awards 1988; Young Hoosier (Grades 4-6) 1987; Young Readers Choice 1987.

LAVALLEE, BARBARA
Mama, Do You Love Me? by Barbara M. Joosse, illustrated by Barbara Lavallee; Chronicle Books, 1991. **Awarded:** Golden Kite (Picture-Illustration) 1991.

LAVIES, BIANCA
Illustration in *Ranger Rick* magazine. **Awarded:** Magazine Merit Award (Illustration) 1989.

Tree Trunk Traffic written and illustrated by Bianca Lavies; Dutton, 1989. **Awarded:** New York Academy of Sciences (Younger Honor) 1989.

LAVINE, SIGMUND A.
Wonders of Sheep by Sigmund A. Lavine and Vincent Scuro, illustrated with photographs and old prints; Dodd Mead, 1983. **Awarded:** New Jersey Institute of Technology 1983.

LAVRIN, NORA
The Ship that Flew by Hilda Lewis, illustrated by Nora Lavrin; Criterion, 1958. **Awarded:** Spring Book Festival (middle honor) 1958.

LAW, BIRDIE
Awarded: Allie Beth Martin 1981.

LAWLOR, LAURIE
How To Survive Third Grade by Laurie Lawlor, illustrated by Joyce Audy Zarins; Whitman, 1988. **Awarded:** KC Three 1990-91.

LAWRENCE, ANN
The Hawk of May by Ann Lawrence, not illustrated; Macmillan, 1980. **Awarded:** Guardian (runnerup) 1981.

LAWRENCE, ISABELLE
Awarded: Children's Reading Round Table 1968.

LAWRENCE, JACOB
Harriet and the Promised Land written and illustrated by Jacob Lawrence; Windmill/Simon & Schuster, 1968. **Awarded:** Art Books for Children 1973, 1974, 1975; New York Times Best Illustrated 1968.

LAWRENCE, JAMES
Binky Brothers and the Fearless Four by James Lawrence, illustrated by Leonard Kessler; Harper, 1970. **Awarded:** New Jersey Institute of Technology 1970.

LAWRENCE, JOHN
Rabbit & Pork: Rhyming Talk written and illustrated by John Lawrence; Hamish Hamilton, 1975; Crowell, 1975. **Awarded:** Children's Book Showcase 1976; W. H. Smith (£100) 1977.

Shades of Green by Anne Harvey, illustrated by John Lawrence; MacRae, 1991; Greenwillow, 1992. **Awarded:** Signal Poetry 1992.

LAWS, GEORGE
The Forbidden Door by Jeanne K. Norweb, illustrated by George Laws; David C. Cook, 1985. **Awarded:** New Jersey Institute of Technology 1987.

LAWSON, ANNETTA
The Lucky Yak by Annetta Lawson, illustrated by Allen Say; Parnassus/Houghton, 1980. **Awarded:** New York Times Best Illustrated 1980.

LAWSON, JOHN
The Spring Rider by John Lawson, not illustrated; Crowell, 1968. **Awarded:** Boston Globe Horn Book (text) 1968.

LAWSON, JULIE
The Dragons Pearls retold by Julie Lawson, illustrated by Paul Morin; Oxford University Press, 1992; Clarion, 1992. **Awarded:** Amelia Frances Howard-Gibbon 1993.

LAWSON, PATRICK
Star-crossed Stallion by Patrick Lawson, not illustrated; Dodd, Mead, 1954. **Awarded:** Boys' Life - Dodd, Mead 1953.

LAWSON, ROBERT
Adam of the Road by Elizabeth Janet Gray, illustrated by Robert Lawson; Viking, 1942. **Awarded:** Newbery 1943; Spring Book Festival (middle honor) 1942.

Ben and Me written and illustrated by Robert Lawson; Little, Brown, 1939. **Awarded:** Lewis Carroll Shelf 1961.

Four and Twenty Blackbirds: Nursery Rhymes of Yesterday Recalled for Children of Today by Helen Dean Fish, illustrated by Robert Lawson; Lippincott, 1937. **Awarded:** Caldecott (honor) 1938.

The Great Wheel written and illustrated Robert Lawson, Viking, 1957. **Awarded:** Newbery (honor) 1958.

Mr. Popper's Penguins by Florence Atwater and Richard Atwater, illustrated by Robert Lawson; Little, Brown, 1938. **Awarded:** Lewis Carroll Shelf 1958; Newbery (honor) 1939; Young Readers Choice 1941.

Mr. Revere and I written and illustrated by Robert Lawson; Little, Brown, 1953. **Awarded:** Boys Club 1954.

Rabbit Hill written and illustrated by Robert Lawson; Viking, 1962, 1944. **Awarded:** Lewis Carroll Shelf 1963; Newbery 1945.

They Were Strong and Good written and illustrated by Robert Lawson; Viking, 1940. **Awarded:** Caldecott 1941.

Wee Gillis by Munro Leaf, illustrated by Robert Lawson; Viking, 1938. **Awarded:** Caldecott (honor) 1939.

Wind of the Vikings by Maribelle Cormack, illustrated by Robert Lawson; Appleton Century Crofts, 1937. **Awarded:** Spring Book Festival (older honor) 1937.

LAYTON, AVIVA
How the Kookaburra Got His Laugh by Aviva Layton, illustrated by Robert Smith; McClelland & Stewart, 1976. **Awarded:** IODE 1976.

LAZAR, WENDY
The Jewish Holiday Book by Wendy Lazar, illustrated with photographs; Doubleday, 1977. **Awarded:** New Jersey Institute of Technology 1978.

LAZARE, JERRY
Queenie Peavy by Robert Burch, illustrated by Jerry Lazare; Viking, 1966; Dell, 1975. **Awarded:** Jane Addams 1967; Child Study 1966; Georgia Children's 1971; Phoenix 1986; George G. Stone 1974.

LAZAREVICH, MILA
Loosen your Ears by Carol Farley, illustrated by Mila Lazarevich; Atheneum, 1977. **Awarded:** Friends of American Writers (younger) 1978.

LEAF, HAYIM
Junior Jewish Encyclopedia by Hayim Leaf and Naomi Ben-Asher, illustrated with photographs; Shengold, 1957. **Awarded:** Jewish Book Council 1957.

LEAF, MARGARET
The Eyes of the Dragon by Margaret Leaf, illustrated by Ed Young; Lothrop, Lee & Shepard, 1987. **Awarded:** California

Young Reader (Primary) 1990; Parents' Choice (Picture Book) 1987; Parents' Choice (Story Book) 1987.

LEAF, MUNRO
Wee Gillis by Munro Leaf, illustrated by Robert Lawson; Viking, 1938. **Awarded:** Caldecott (honor) 1939.

LEAR, EDWARD
The Dong with a Luminous Nose by Edward Lear, illustrated by Edward Gorey; Scott, 1969. **Awarded:** New York Times Best Illustrated 1969.

The Nutcrackers and the Sugar-tongs by Edward Lear, illustrated by Marcia Sewall; Atlantic, 1978. **Awarded:** New York Times Best Illustrated 1978.

The Owl and the Pussycat by Edward Lear, illustrated by Ron Berg; Scholastic-TAB, 1984. **Awarded:** Amelia Frances Howard-Gibbon (runnerup) 1985.

The Quangle-wangle's Hat by Edward Lear, illustrated by Helen Oxenbury; Heinemann, 1969. **Awarded:** Greenaway 1969.

LEATHAM, MOYRA
Three Hundred and Ninety-seventh White Elephant by Rene Guillot, translated by Gwen Marsh, illustrated by Moyra Leatham; Phillips, 1957. **Awarded:** Lewis Carroll Shelf 1958.

LEBENSON, RICHARD
Waiting for Moma by Marietta Moskins, illustrated by Richard Lebenson; Coward, 1975. **Awarded:** Sydney Taylor Book Award 1975.

The Witch's Brat by Rosemary Sutcliff, illustrated by Richard Lebenson; Walck, 1970. **Awarded:** Lewis Carroll Shelf 1971.

LE BLANC, ANNETTE
The Magic Rabbit by Annette Le Blanc. **Awarded:** Dutton Children's Books Picture Book 1988.

LE CAIN, ERROL
The Cabbage Princess written and illustrated by Errol Le Cain; Faber, 1969. **Awarded:** Greenaway (honour) 1969.

The Enchanter's Daughter by Antonia Barber, illustrated by Errol Le Cain; Farrar, Straus, Giroux, 1988, c1987. **Awarded:** Parents' Choice (Picture Book) 1988; Redbook 1988.

Hiawatha's Childhood by Henry Wadsworth Longfellow, illustrated by Errol Le Cain; Faber, 1984. Greenaway 1984; International Board on Books for Young People (illustration/Great Britain) 1986.

Thorn Rose by Wilhelm Grimm and Jacob Grimm, illustrated by Errol Le Cain; Faber, 1975. **Awarded:** Greenaway (commended) 1975; International Board on Books for Young People (honour list/Great Britain/illustrator) 1978.

The Twelve Dancing Princesses by Jacob and Wilhelm Grimm, illustrated by Errol Le Cain; Faber, 1978. **Awarded:** Greenaway (commended) 1978.

LECKIE, ROBERT
The Story of Football by Robert Leckie, illustrated with photographs and diagrams; Random House, 1965. **Awarded:** New Jersey Institute of Technology 1965.

The Story of World War II by Robert Leckie, illustrated with photographs and maps; Random House, 1964. **Awarded:** New Jersey Institute of Technology (history teens) 1964.

The War in Korea, 1950-53 by Robert Leckie, illustrated with photographs; Random House, 1963. **Awarded:** New Jersey Institute of Technology (history teens) 1964.

The World Turned Upside Down: The Story of the American Revolution by Robert Leckie, illustrated with maps by Theodore R. Miller; Putnam, 1973. **Awarded:** New Jersey Institute of Technology 1973.

LEE, ALAN
Merlin Dreams by Peter Dickinson, illustrated by Alan Lee; Gollancz, 1988. **Awarded:** Greenaway (Highly Commended) 1988.

The Mirrorstone by Michael Palin, illustrated by Alan Lee, design by Richard Seymour; Cape, 1986; Knopf, 1986. **Awarded:** Smarties (innovation) 1986.

LEE, ANN THOMPSON
It Is Better Farther On: Laura Ingalls Wilder and The Pioneer Spirit by Ann Thompson Lee in *The Lion and the Unicorn* Spring 1979. **Awarded:** Children's Literature Assn. Award for Literary Criticism (runnerup) 1980.

LEE, DENNIS
Awarded: Vicky Metcalf 1986.

Alligator Pie by Dennis Lee, illustrated by Frank Newfeld; Macmillan Canada, 1974. **Awarded:** Canadian Library Assn. 1975; International Board on Books for Young People (honour list/text/Canada) 1976; IODE 1974.

Garbage Delight by Dennis Lee, illustrated by Frank Newfeld; Macmillan Canada, 1977. **Awarded:** Canadian Library Assn. 1978; Amelia Frances Howard-Gibbon (runnerup) 1978; International Board on Books for Young People (honour list/text/Canada) 1978; Ruth Schwartz 1978.

The Ice Cream Store by Dennis Lee, illustrated by David McPhail; HarperCollins, 1991. **Awarded:** Mr. Christie's (English Text) 1991.

Jelly Belly by Dennis Lee, illustrated by Juan Wijngaard; Macmillan of Canada, 1983; Blackie, 1983. **Awarded:** Canadian Library Assn. (runnerup) 1984.

Lizzy's Lion by Dennis Lee, illustrated by Marie-Louise Gay; Stoddart, 1984. **Awarded:** Governor General (illustrator) 1984.

LEE, DORIS
The Great Quillow by James Thurber, illustrated by Doris Lee; Harcourt, 1944. **Awarded:** Ohioana (2nd place) 1945.

The Hired Man's Elephant by Phil Stong, illustrated by Doris Lee; Dodd, 1939. **Awarded:** Spring Book Festival (older) 1939.

LEE, JOSEPHINE
Joy Is Not Herself by Josephine Lee, illustrated by Pat Marriott; Harcourt, 1963. **Awarded:** Spring Book Festival (middle honor) 1963.

LEE, MANNING DE V.
The Buffalo Trace by Virginia S. Eifert, illustrated by Manning De V. Lee; Dodd Mead, 1955. **Awarded:** Edison Mass Media (America's past) 1956; Spring Book Festival (older) 1955.

Long Wharf: A Story of Young San Francisco by Howard Pease, illustrated by Manning De V. Lee; Dodd, Mead, 1939. **Awarded:** Spring Book Festival (older honor) 1939.

The Singing Cave by Margaret Leighton, illustrated by Manning De V. Lee; Houghton, 1945. **Awarded:** Commonwealth Club of California 1945.

Wild Hunter by Kenneth Charles Randall, illustrated by Manning De V. Lee; Watts, 1951. **Awarded:** Spring Book Festival (ages 8-12 honor) 1951.

LEE, MILDRED

Fog by Mildred Lee, not illustrated; Seabury, 1972. **Awarded:** New York Times Notable 1972.

The Rock and the Willow by Mildred Lee, not illustrated; Lothrop, 1963. **Awarded:** Child Study 1963.

The Skating Rink by Mildred Lee, not illustrated; Seabury, 1969. **Awarded:** Spring Book Festival (older honor) 1969.

LEE, ROBERT C.

It's a Mile from Here to Glory by Robert C. Lee, not illustrated; Little, Brown, 1972. **Awarded:** Mark Twain 1974.

LEE, ROCHELLE

Awarded: Children's Reading Round Table 1993.

LEEDY, LOREEN

Big, Small, Short, Tall written and illustrated by Loreen Leedy; Holiday House, 1987. **Awarded:** Parents' Choice (Picture Book) 1987.

LEEMING, JOHN F.

Claudius the Bee by John F. Leeming, illustrated by Richard B. Ogle; Viking, 1937. **Awarded:** Spring Book Festival (younger honor) 1937.

LEEMING, JOSEPH

Fun with Puzzles by Joseph Leeming, illustrated by Jessie Robinson; Lippincott, 1946. **Awarded:** Boys Club 1948.

LEESON, ROBERT

Awarded: Eleanor Farjeon 1985.

Silver's Revenge by Robert Leeson, not illustrated; Collins, 1978. **Awarded:** Guardian (commended) 1979.

Slambash Wangs of a Compo Gormer by Robert Leeson, illustrated by Steve Crisp; Collins, 1987. **Awarded:** International Board on Books for Young People (Writing/Great Britain) 1990.

LeFEVRE, FELICITE

The Cock, the Mouse and the Little Red Hen by Felicite LeFevre, illustrated by Tony Sarg; Macrae, 1947. **Awarded:** Lewis Carroll Shelf 1965.

Le FOLL, ALAIN

The Very Obliging Flowers by Claude Roy, translated by Gerald Bertin, illustrated by Alain Le Foll; Grove, 1968. **Awarded:** New York Times Best Illustrated 1968.

Le GALLIENNE, EVA

The Nightingale by Hans Christian Andersen, translated by Eva LeGallienne, illustrated by Nancy Ekholm Burkert; Harper, 1965. **Awarded:** Lewis Carroll Shelf 1965; Spring Book Festival (picture book honor) 1965.

Le GUIN, URSULA KROEBER

Awarded: Evelyn Sibley Lampman 1987.

Catwings by Ursula K. Le Guin, illustrated by S. D. Schindler; Orchard, 1988. **Awarded:** Carolyn W. Field 1989; Reading Magic Award 1988.

Den Fjerneste Kyst by Ursula K. Le Guin, translated by Jon Bing; Gyldendal Norsk Forlag, 1980. **Awarded:** International Board on Books for Young People (translation/Norway) 1982.

The Farthest Shore by Ursula K. Le Guin, illustrated by Gail Garraty; Atheneum, 1972. **Awarded:** National Book Award 1973.

A Ride on the Red Mare's Back by Ursula K. Le Guin, illustrated by Julie Downing; Orchard, 1992. **Awarded:** Parents Choice (Story Book) 1992.

Tehanu by Ursula K. Le Guin, not illustrated; Atheneum, 1990. **Awarded:** Reading Magic Award 1990.

The Tombs of Atuan by Ursula K. Le Guin, illustrated by Gail Garraty; Atheneum, 1971. **Awarded:** National Book Award (finalist) 1972; Newbery (honor) 1972.

The Wizard of Earthsea by Ursula K. Le Guin, illustrated by Ruth Robbins; Parnassus, 1968. **Awarded:** Boston Globe Horn Book (text) 1969; Lewis Carroll Shelf 1979.

LEHRMAN, ROBERT

Doing Time: A Look at Crime and Prisons by Phyllis E. Clark and Robert Lehrman, illustrated; Hastings House, 1980. **Awarded:** Jane Addams (honor) 1981.

LEIGHT, EDWARD

The Unhappy Hippopotamus by Nancy Moore, illustrated by Edward Leight; Vanguard, 1957. **Awarded:** New York Times Best Illustrated 1957.

LEIGHTON, MARGARET CARVER

Awarded: Southern California Council (comprehensive contribution of lasting value to the field of children's literature) 1971.

Commanche of the Seventh by Margaret C. Leighton, illustrated by Elliott Means; Farrar, 1957. **Awarded:** Dorothy Canfield Fisher 1959.

The Singing Cave by Margaret Leighton, illustrated by Manning De V. Lee; Houghton, 1945. **Awarded:** Commonwealth Club of California 1945.

LEIGHTON, RALPH

Surely You're Joking, Mr. Feynman! by Richard P. Feynman as told to Ralph Leighton, edited by Edward Hutchings, not illustrated; Bantam, 1986. **Awarded:** New York Academy of Sciences (older honor) 1987.

LEINWOLL, STANLEY

The Book of Pets by Stanley Leinwoll, illustrated with photographs: Messner, 1980. **Awarded:** New Jersey Institute of Technology 1981.

LEISK, DAVID JOHNSON

see JOHNSON, CROCKETT

LEITCH, ADELAIDE

The Great Canoe by Adelaide Leitch, illustrated by Clare Bice; Macmillan Canada, 1962. **Awarded:** Macmillan of Canada 1962.

LEMAN, MARTIN

Twelve Cats for Christmas written and illustrated by Martin Leman; Pelham/Merrimack Publishers' Circle, 1982. **Awarded:** New York Times Best Illustrated 1983.

LEMARCHAND, JACQUES

The Adventures of Ulysses by Jacques Lemarchand, translated by E. M. Hatt; illustrated by Andre Francois; Criterion, 1960. **Awarded:** New York Times Best Illustrated 1960.

LEMIEUX, MICHELE

Voices on the Wind: Poems for All Seasons selected by David Booth, illustrated by Michele Lemieux; Kids Can Press, 1990; Morrow, 1990. **Awarded:** Amelia Frances Howard-Gibbon (runnerup) 1991; IODE 1990.

LEMKE, HORST

Als Ich Ein Kleiher Junge War by Erich Kastner, illustrated by Horst Lemke; Dressler, 1957. **Awarded:** Hans Christian Andersen 1960.

Jan und das Wildpferd by Heinrich-Maria Denneborg, illustrated Horst Lemke; Dressler, 1957. **Awarded:** Hans Christian Andersen (runnerup) 1960.

Ride with me through ABC by Susan Bond, illustrated by Horst Lemke; Scroll Press, 1969. **Awarded:** New Jersey Institute of Technology 1970.

When I Was a Boy by Erich Kastner, translated by Isabel McHugh and Florence McHugh, illustrated by Horst Lemke; Watts, 1961. **Awarded:** Lewis Carroll Shelf 1961.

LEMOINE, GEORGES
Le Livre de la Creation by Pierre-Marie Beaude, illustrated by Georges Lemoine; Edition du Centurion, 1987. **Awarded:** Bologna (Graphic Prize for Youth) 1988.

L'ENGLE MADELEINE
Awarded: ALAN 1986; Empire State Award 1991; Kerlan Award 1990; Regina 1984; University of Southern Mississippi 1978.

Ring of Endless Light by Madeleine L'Engle, not illustrated; Farrar, 1980. **Awarded:** Newbery (honor) 1981.

A Swiftly Tilting Planet by Madeleine L'Engle; Dell, 1979, c1978. **Awarded:** American Book Award (Paperback) 1980.

A Wrinkle in Time by Madeleine L'Engle, not illustrated; Farrar, 1962. **Awarded:** Hans Christian Andersen (runnerup) 1964; Lewis Carroll Shelf 1965; Newbery 1963; Sequoyah 1965.

The Younq Unicorns by Madeleine L'Engle, not illustrated; Farrar, 1968. **Awarded:** Spring Book Festival (Older honor) 1968.

LENS, SIDNEY
The Bomb by Sidney Lens, illustrated with photographs; Lodestar/Dutton, 1982. **Awarded:** Jane Addams (honor) 1983.

LENSKI, LOIS
Awarded: Regina 1969; University of Southern Mississippi 1969.

Bayou Suzette written and illustrated by Lois Lenski; Stokes, 1943. **Awarded:** Ohioana 1944.

Boom Town Boy written and illustrated by Lois Lenski; Lippincott, 1948. **Awarded:** Ohioana (honorable mention) 1949.

Indian Captive: The Story of Mary Jemison written and illustrated by Lois Lenski; Stokes, 1941. **Awarded:** Newbery (honor) 1942.

Judy's Journey written and illustrated by Lois Lenski; Lippincott, 1947. **Awarded:** Child Study 1947.

Mr. and Mrs. Noah written and illustrated by Lois Lenski; Crowell, 1948. **Awarded:** Spring Book Festival (younger honor) 1948.

A Name for Obed by Ethel Calvert Phillips, illustrated by Lois Lenski; Houghton, 1941. **Awarded:** Spring Book Festival (middle honor) 1941.

Phebe Fairchild: Her Book written and illustrated by Lois Lenski; Lippincott, 1936. **Awarded:** Newbery (honor) 1937.

Strawberry Girl written and illustrated by Lois Lenski; Lippincott, 1945. **Awarded:** Newbery 1946.

LENT, BLAIR
The Angry Moon by William Sleator, illustrated by Blair Lent; Atlantic-Little, 1970. **Awarded:** Boston Globe Horn Book (illustration honor) 1971; Caldecott (honor) 1971.

Baba Yaga by Ernest Small, illustrated by Blair Lent; Houghton, 1966. **Awarded:** Spring Book Festival (picture book honor) 1966.

From King Boggen's Hall To Nothing At All written and illustrated by Blair Lent; Little Brown, 1967. **Awarded:** Biennale Illustrations Bratislava (plaque) 1969.

The Funny Little Woman retold by Arlene Mosel, illustrated by Blair Lent; Dutton, 1972. **Awarded:** Caldecott 1973; Children's Book Showcase 1973; International Board on Books for Young People (illustration/USA) 1974; Little Archer 1976; New York Times Notable Books 1972.

Tikki Tikki Tembo by Arlene Mosel, illustrated by Blair Lent; Holt, 1968. **Awarded:** Boston Globe Horn Book (illustration) 1968.

The Wave by Margaret Hodges, illustrated by Blair Lent; Houghton, 1964. **Awarded:** Caldecott (honor) 1965; New York Times Best Illustrated 1964.

Why the Sun and the Moon Live in the Sky: An African Folktale by Elphinstone Dayrell, illustrated by Blair Lent; Houghton, 1968. **Awarded:** Caldecott (honor) 1969; Spring Book Festival (picture book) 1968.

LENZ, MILLICENT
Nuclear Age Literature for Youth by Millicent Lenz; American Library Association, 1990. **Awarded:** Children's Literature Association Criticism (Book) 1991.

LEON, MIGUEL
Principio y Fin Tiempo de Vida que Transcurre Entre el Nacer y el Morir (original English: *Beginnings and Endings with LIFETIMES in Between*) by Bryan Mellonie, translated by Carmen Esteva and Miguel Leon; Compania Editorial Continental, 1984. **Awarded:** International Board on Books for Young People (translation/Mexico) 1986.

LEPMAN, JELLA
Awarded: Hans Christian Andersen (for service to international children's literature) 1956.

LERNER, CAROL
On the Forest Edge written and illustrated by Carol Lerner; Morrow, 1978. **Awarded:** Friends of American Writers (special artistic award) 1979.

Peeper, First Voice of Spring by Robert M. McClung, illustrated by Carol Lerner; Morrow, 1977. **Awarded:** Golden Kite (nonfiction) 1977.

Pitcher Plants: The Elegant Insect Traps written and illustrated by Carol Lerner; Morrow, 1983. **Awarded:** Carl Sandburg 1984.

Plant Families written and illustrated by Carol Lerner; Morrow, 1989. **Awarded:** New York Academy of Sciences (Younger Honor) 1989.

LEROE, ELLEN
Confessions of a Teenage TV Addict by Ellen Leroe, not illustrated; Lodestar/Dutton, 1983. **Awarded:** New Jersey Institute of Technology 1983.

LeROY, GEN
Emma's Dilemma by Gen LeRoy, not illustrated; Harper & Row, 1975. **Awarded:** New Jersey Institute of Technology 1976.

Hotheads by Gen LeRoy, not illustrated; Harper & Row, 1977. **Awarded:** New Jersey Institute of Technology 1978.

LeSIEG, THEO
see SEUSS, DR. LESLIE, CECIL

The Twelve and the Genii by Pauline Clarke, illustrated by Cecil Leslie; Faber, 1962. (Published in the U.S. in 1964 as The Return of the Twelves). **Awarded:** Carnegie 1962; International Board on Books for Young People (honour list/Great Britain) 1964.

LESLIE, DONNA
Alitji in Dreamland adapted and translated by Nancy Sheppard, illustrated by Donna Leslie, notes by Barbara Ker Wilson; Simon & Schuster Australia, 1992.

LESLIE, ROBERT FRANKLIN
The Bears and I: Raising Three Cubs in the North Woods by Robert Franklin Leslie, illustrated by Theodore A. Xaras; Dutton, 1968. **Awarded:** Southern California Council (notable) 1969.

LESLIE-MELVILLE, BETTY
Walter Warthog written and photographed by Betty Leslie-Melville; Doubleday, 1989. **Awarded:** Book Can Develop Empathy 1990.

LESSAC, FRANE
The Chalk Doll by Charlotte Pomerantz, illustrated by Frane Lessac; Lippincott, 1989. **Awarded:** Parents' Choice (Story Book) 1989.

LESSER, CAROLYN
The Goodnight Circle by Carolyn Lesser, illustrated by Lorinda Bryan Cauley; Harcourt Brace Jovanovich, 1984. **Awarded:** Friends of American Writers ($350) 1985.

LESSER, RIKA
Hansel and Gretel retold by Rika Lesser, illustrated by Paul O. Zelinsky; Dodd, Mead, 1984. **Awarded:** Caldecott (honor) 1985.

LESTER, ALISON
Clive Eats Alligators written and illustrated by Alison Lester; Oxford University Press, 1985. **Awarded:** Children's Book Council of Australia Picture Book of the Year (commended) 1986.

Magic Beach written and illustrated by Alison Lester; Allen & Unwin, 1990; Joy Street Books, 1992. **Awarded:** Ashton Scholastic 1991.

Rosie Sips Spiders written and illustrated by Alison Lester; Oxford University Press, 1988; Houghton Mifflin, 1989. **Awarded:** Ashton Scholastic 1989.

Thing by Robin Klein, illustrated by Alison Lester; Oxford University Press, 1982. **Awarded:** Children's Book Council of Australia (Junior Book of the Year) 1983.

LESTER, HELEN
Tacky the Penguin by Helen Lester, illustrated by Lynn Munsinger; Houghton Mifflin, 1988. **Awarded:** California Young Reader (Primary) 1991; Colorado Children's 1990; Golden Sower (K-3) 1991.

LESTER, JULIUS B.
Further Tales of Uncle Remus by Joel Chandler Harris, adapted by Julius Lester, illustrated by Jerry Pinkney; Dial, 1990. **Awarded:** Parents' Choice (Story Book) 1990.

The Knee-high Man and Other Tales by Julius Lester, illustrated by Ralph Pinto; Dial, 1972. **Awarded:** Lewis Carroll Shelf 1973.

Long Journey Home: Stories from Black History by Julius Lester, not illustrated; Dial, 1972. **Awarded:** Lewis Carroll Shelf 1972; National Book Award (finalist) 1973.

More Tales of Uncle Remus: Further Adventures of Brer Rabbit by Joel Chandler Harris, adapted by Julius Lester, illustrated by Jerry Pinkney; Dial, 1988. **Awarded:** Reading Magic Award 1988.

The Tales of Uncle Remus by Joel Chandler Harris, adapted by Julius Lester, illustrated by Jerry Pinkney; Dial, 1987. **Awarded:** Coretta Scott King (Text honor) 1988; Parents' Choice (Story Book) 1987.

This Strange New Feeling by Julius Lester, not illustrated; Dial, 1982. **Awarded:** Coretta Scott King (Author honorable mention) 1983; Parents Choice (Literature) 1982.

To Be a Slave by Julius Lester, illustrated by Tom Feelings; Dial, 1968. **Awarded:** Nancy Bloch 1968; Lewis Carroll Shelf 1970; Newbery (honor) 1969.

L'ESTRANGE, SIR ROGER
Fables of Aesop by Sir Roger L'Estrange, illustrated by Alexander Calder; Dover, 1967. **Awarded:** New York Times Best Illustrated 1967.

LESZCZYNSKI, MICHAEL
Sea Change by Richard Armstrong, illustrated by Michael Leszczynski; Dent, 1948. **Awarded:** Carnegie 1948.

LE-TAN, PIERRE
Happy Birthday, Oliver! written and illustrated by Pierre Le-Tan; Random House, 1979. **Awarded:** New York Times Best Illustrated 1979.

LeTORD, BIJOU
A Brown Cow written and illustrated by Bijou LeTord; Little Brown, 1989. **Awarded:** Book Can Develop Empathy 1990.

LEUNN, NANCY
Nessa's Fish by Nancy Leunn, illustrated by Neil Waldman; Atheneum, 1990. **Awarded:** Parents' Choice (Story Book) 1990.

LEVERT, JOHN
The Flight of the Cassowary by John LeVert, not illustrated; Atlantic Monthly Press, 1986. **Awarded:** Young Adult Novel of the Year / Michigan Library Assn. 1987.

LEVIN, BETTY
The Trouble with Gramary by Betty Levin, not illustrated; Greenwillow, 1988. **Awarded:** Judy Lopez 1989.

LEVIN, ELI
The Story of Israel by Meyer Levin, illustrated by Eli Levin; Putnam, 1966. **Awarded:** Jewish Book Council 1966.

LEVIN, MEYER
The Story of Israel by Meyer Levin, illustrated by Eli Levin; Putnam, 1966. **Awarded:** Jewish Book Council 1966.

LEVIN, RUTH
The Jewish People: Book Three by Deborah Pessin, illustrated by Ruth Levin; United Synagogue of America, 1952. **Awarded:** Jewish Book Council 1953.

LEVINE, ABBY
The Dawn Seekers by Carol Hamilton, illustrated by Abby Levine; Whitman, 1987. **Awarded:** Southwest 1988.

LEVINE, ELLEN
I Hate English! by Ellen Levine, illustrated by Steve Bjorkman; Scholastic, 1989. **Awarded:** Parents' Choice (Story Book) 1990.

LEVINE, JOE
My Place in Space by Sally Hirst and Robin Hirst, illustrated by Joe Levine and Roland Harvey; Five Mile Press, 1989.

Awarded: Children's Book Council of Australia (Picture Book of the Year Honour) 1989.

LEVINE-FREIDUS, GAIL
Good if it Goes by Gary Provost and Gail Levine-Freidus, not illustrated; Bradbury, 1984. **Awarded:** Jewish Book Council (children's literature) 1985.

LEVINGER, ELMA E.
Awarded: Jewish Book Council (for her body of work) 1956.

Albert Einstein by Elma Ehrlich Levinger, illustrated with photographs; Messner, 1949. **Awarded:** Boys Club 1950; Spring Book Festival (older honor) 1949.

LEVINSON, NANCY SMILER
Christopher Columbus: Voyager to the Unknown by Nancy Smiler Levinson, illustrated with maps; Lodestar, 1990. **Awarded:** Southern California Council (Distinguished Work of Nonfiction) 1991.

I Lift My Lamp: Emma Lazarus and the Statue of Liberty by Nancy Smiler Levinson, illustrated; Lodestar Books, 1986. **Awarded:** Southern California Council (distinguished work of nonfiction) 1987.

LEVINSON, RIKI
Watch the Stars Come Out by Riki Levinson, illustrated by Diane Goode; Dutton, 1985. **Awarded:** Parents' Choice (literature) 1985; Redbook 1985.

LEVITIN, SONIA
Awarded: Southern California Council (Distinguished Body of Work) 1981.

Incident at Loring Groves by Sonia Levitin, not illustrated; Dial, 1988. **Awarded:** Edgar Allan Poe (Young Adult) 1989.

Journey to America by Sonia Levitin, illustrated by Charles Robinson; Atheneum, 1970. **Awarded:** Jewish Book Council 1970.

The Mark of Conte by Sonia Levitin, illustrated by Bill Negron; Atheneum, 1976. **Awarded:** Southern California Council (notable) 1977.

The No-return Trail by Sonia Levitin, not illustrated; Harcourt Brace, 1978. **Awarded:** Lewis Carroll Shelf 1978; Western Writers of America 1978.

The Return by Sonia Levitin, not illustrated; Atheneum, 1987. **Awarded:** Jewish Book Council (Children's Literature) 1988; Parents' Choice (Story Book) 1987; PEN Center USA West 1988; Sydney Taylor Book Award (Older) 1988.

Silver Days by Sonia Levitin, not illustrated; Atheneum, 1989. **Awarded:** Woodward Park School 1990.

LEVOY, MYRON
Alan and Naomi by Myron Levoy, not illustrated; Harper, 1977. **Awarded:** Jane Addams (honor) 1978; Boston Globe Horn Book (fiction honor) 1978; New Jersey Institute of Technology 1978; Woodward Park School 1978.

Der Gelbe Vogel (Original English: *Alan and Naomi*) by Myron Levoy, translated by Fred Schmitz; Benziger, 1981. **Awarded:** International Board on Books for Young People (translation/German Federal Republic) 1984.

Penny Tunes and Princesses by Myron Levoy, illustrated by Ezra Jack Keats; Harper, 1972. **Awarded:** New Jersey Institute of Technology 1973.

A Shadow Like a Leopard by Myron Levoy, not illustrated; Harper & Row, 1981. **Awarded:** Woodward Park School 1982.

The Witch of Fourth Street and Other Stories by Myron Levoy, illustrated by Gabriel Lisowski; Harper, 1972. **Awarded:** Children's Book Showcase 1973; Spring Book Festival (ages 8-12 honor) 1972.

LEWELLEN, JOHN B.
The Boy Scientist by John B. Lewellen, illustrated by Robert Barker; Simon & Schuster, 1955. **Awarded:** Edison Mass Media (children's science book) 1956.

The Earth's Satellite: Man's First True Space Adventure by John Lewellen, illustrated by Ida Scheib; Knopf, 1957. **Awarded:** Boys Club 1958.

You and Atomic Energy by John Lewellen, illustrated by L. Fisher; Children's Press, 1949. **Awarded:** Boys Club 1950.

LEWIN, TED
Faithful Elephants by Yukio Tsuchiya, illustrated by Ted Lewin; Houghton Mifflin, 1988. **Awarded:** Book Can Develop Empathy 1990.

Judy Scuppernong by Brenda Seabrooke, illustrated by Ted Lewin; Dutton, 1990. **Awarded:** Boston Globe Horn Book (Fiction/Poetry Honor) 1991.

Sami and the Time of Troubles by Florence Parry Heide and Judith Heide Gilliland, illustrated by Ted Lewin; Clarion, 1992. **Awarded:** Hungry Mind (Picturebook/Fiction) 1993.

The Search for Grissi by Mary Frances Shura, illustrated by Ted Lewin; Dodd, Mead, 1985. **Awarded:** Sandburg 1985.

The Secret of the Indian by Lynne Reid Banks, illustrated by Ted Lewin; Doubleday, 1989. **Awarded:** Great Stone Face 1991.

Soup for President by Robert Newton Peck, illustrated by Ted Lewin; Knopf, 1978. **Awarded:** Mark Twain 1981.

LEWIS, ALLEN
Calico Bush by Rachel L. Field, illustrated by Allen Lewis; Macmillan, 1931. **Awarded:** Newbery (honor) 1932.

Made in India by Cornelia Spencer, illustrated by Allen Lewis; Knopf, 1946. **Awarded:** Spring Book Festival (older honor) 1946.

LEWIS, BARBARA A.
The Kid's Guide to Social Action by Barbara Lewis, illustrated by Steve Michaels; Free Spirit, 1991. **Awarded:** Hungry Mind (Young Adult/Nonfiction) 1992.

LEWIS, C. S. (CLIVE STAPLES)
Chronicles of Narnia by C. S. Lewis, illustrated by Pauline Baynes; Macmillan, 1983. **Awarded:** Young Teens 1990.

The Horse and His Boy by C. S. Lewis, illustrated by Pauline Baynes; Macmillan, 1954. **Awarded:** Carnegie (commended) 1954.

The Last Battle: A Story for Children by C. S. Lewis, illustrated by Pauline Baynes; Bodley Head, 1956. **Awarded:** Carnegie 1956.

The Lion, the Witch and the Wardrobe by C. S. Lewis, illustrated by Pauline Baynes; Macmillan, 1950. **Awarded:** Lewis Carroll Shelf 1962.

LEWIS, ELIZABETH FOREMAN
Young Fu of the Upper Yangtze by Elizabeth Foreman Lewis, illustrated by Kurt Wiese; Winston, 1932. **Awarded:** Lewis Carroll Shelf 1960; Newbery 1933.

LEWIS, HILDA
The Ship that Flew by Hilda Lewis, illustrated by Nora Lavrin; Criterion, 1958. **Awarded:** Spring Book Festival (middle honor) 1958.

LEWIS, J. PATRICK
The Tsar and the Amazing Cow by J. Patrick Lewis, illustrated by Friso Henstra; Dial, 1988. **Awarded:** Ohioana 1989.

LEWIS, MARC
Awarded: L. Frank Baum 1989.

LEWIS, MARY CHRISTIANNA MILNE
see BRAND, CHRISTIANNA

LEWIS, NAOMI
Awarded: Eleanor Farjeon 1974.

LEWIS, RICHARD
Out of the Earth I Sing: Poetry and Songs of Primitive Peoples of the World by Richard Lewis, illustrated with photographs; Norton, 1968. **Awarded:** Spring Book Festival (middle honor) 1968.

LEWIS, ROBIN BAIRD
Red Is Best by Kathy Stinson, illustrated by Robin Baird Lewis; Annick Press, 1982. **Awarded:** IODE 1982.

LEXAU, JOAN M.
Striped Ice Cream by Joan M. Lexau, illustrated by John Wilson; Lippincott, 1968. **Awarded:** Charlie May Simon 1970-71.

The Trouble with Terry by Joan M. Lexau, illustrated by Irene Murray; Dial, 1962. **Awarded:** Child Study 1962.

LEY, WILLY
Engineer's Dream by Willy Ley, illustrated by Isami Kashigawi; Viking, 1954. **Awarded:** Spring Book Festival (older) 1954.

LIDE, ALICE
Ood-Le-Uk the Wanderer by Alice Lide and Margaret Johansen, illustrated by Raymond Lufkin; Little, Brown, 1930. **Awarded:** Newbery (honor) 1931.

LIEBLICH, IRENE
The Power of Light: Eight Stories for Hanukkah by Isaac Bashevis Singer, illustrated by Irene Lieblich; Farrar Straus Giroux, 1980. **Awarded:** Present Tense 1980.

LIERS, EMIL ERNEST
A Black Bear's Story by Emil Ernest Liers, illustrated by Ray Sherin; Viking, 1962. **Awarded:** Aurianne 1964.

LIFE, KAY
Muggie Maggie by Beverly Cleary, illustrated by Kay Life; Morrow, 1990. **Awarded:** Garden State (Younger Fiction) 1993.

LIFTON, BETTY JEAN
Children of Vietnam by Betty Jean Lifton and Thomas C. Fox, illustrated by Thomas C. Fox; Atheneum, 1972. **Awarded:** National Book Award (finalist) 1973.

Kap the Kappa by Betty Jean Lifton, illustrated by Eiichi Mitsui; Morrow, 1960. **Awarded:** Spring Book Festival (ages 4-8 honor) 1960.

Return to Hiroshima by Betty Jean Lifton, illustrated by Eikoh Hosoe; Atheneum, 1970. **Awarded:** Spring Book Festival (picture book honor) 1970.

LIGHTBURN, RON
Waiting for the Whales by Sheryl McFarlane, illustrated by Ron Lightburn; Orca Books, 1991. **Awarded:** Governor General's Literary Award (Illustration) 1992; Amelia Frances Howard-Gibbon 1992; Elizabeth Mrazik-Cleaver 1992; National Chapter of Canada IODE Violet Downey 1992.

LIGHTWOOD, DONALD
The Baillie's Daughter by Donald Lightwood, not illustrated; Canongate, 1990. **Awarded:** Kelpie for the Nineties 1990.

LIGNELL, LOIS
The Monkey and the Wild, Wild Wind by Ryerson Johnson, illustrated by Lois Lignell; Abelard, 1961. **Awarded:** Jane Addams 1963.

LILJEBERG, EVA IMBER
Den Fortrollade Floden (original English: *The Stream that Stood Still*) by Beverly Nichols, translated by Eva Imber Liljeberg; Laseleket, 1985. **Awarded:** International Board on Books for Young People (translation/Sweden) 1986.

LILLIE, AMY MORRIS
Nathan, Boy of Capernaum by Amy Morris Lillie, illustrated by Nedda Walker; Dutton, 1944. **Awarded:** Spring Book Festival (middle honor) 1945.

LILLINGTON, KENNETH
Josephine by Kenneth Lillington, not illustrated; Faber & Faber, 1989. **Awarded:** Guardian Award (Special Praise) 1990.

LILLY, CHARLES
The Peppermint Pig by Nina Bawden, illustrated by Charles Lilly; Gollancz, 1975. **Awarded:** Guardian 1976.

Philip Hall Likes Me: I Reckon Maybe by Bette Greene, illustrated by Charles Lilly; Dial, 1974. **Awarded:** New York Times Notable 1974; Newbery (honor) 1975.

LILLY, GWENETH
Y Drudwy Dewr by Gweneth Lilly; Gomer, 1980. **Awarded:** Tir Na n-Og (Welsh) 1981.

LIM, JOHN
Merchants of the Mysterious East written and illustrated by John Lim; Tundra, 1981. **Awarded:** Amelia Frances Howard-Gibbon (runnerup) 1982.

LINDBERGH, REEVE
Benjamin's Barn by Reeve Lindbergh, illustrated by Susan Jeffers; Dial, 1990. **Awarded:** Redbook 1990.

The Midnight Farm by Reeve Lindbergh, illustrated by Susan Jeffers; Dial, 1987. **Awarded:** Redbook 1987.

LINDBLOM, STEVE
Messing Around with Water Pumps and Siphons by Bernie Zubrowski, illustrated by Steve Lindblom; Little Brown, 1981. **Awarded:** New York Academy of sciences (Younger) 1982.

LINDE, GUNNEL
Tills Aventyr I Skorstensgrand by Gunnel Linde, illustrated by Ilon Wikland; Bonnier, 1962. **Awarded:** Hans Christian Andersen (runnerup) 1964.

LINDENBAUM, PIJA
Boodil my Dog written and illustrated by Pija Lindenbaum; Holt, 1992. **Awarded:** New York Times Best Illustrated 1992.

LINDGREN, ASTRID
Pippi Longstocking by Astrid Lindgren, translated by Florence Lamborn, illustrated by Louis S. Glanzman; Viking, 1950. **Awarded:** Lewis Carroll Shelf 1973.

Rasmus and the Vagabond by Astrid Lindgren, illustrated by Eric Palmquist; Viking, 1960. **Awarded:** Boys Club 1961.

Rasmus Pa Luffen by Astrid Lindgren, illustrated by Eric Palmquist; Raben & Sjogren, 1956. **Awarded:** Hans Christian Andersen 1958.

Ronia, the Robber's Daughter by Astrid Lindgren, translated by Patricia Crampton, not illustrated; Viking, 1983. **Awarded:** Batchelder 1984; Parents Choice (Literature) 1983.

Sia lives on Kilimanjaro by Astrid Lindgren, photographs by Anna Riwkin-Brick; Macmillan, 1959. **Awarded:** Spring Book Festival (ages 4-8) 1959.

The Tomten by Astrid Lindgren, illustrated by Harald Wiberg; Coward, 1961. **Awarded:** Art Books for Children 1973; Lewis Carroll Shelf 1970.

LINDMAN, MAJ
Snipp, Snapp, Snurr and the Red Shoes written and illustrated by Maj Lindman; Whitman, 1936. **Awarded:** Lewis Carroll Shelf 1959.

LINDQUIST, JENNIE DOROTHEA
The Golden Name Day by Jennie D. Lindquist, illustrated by Garth Williams; Harper, 1955. **Awarded:** Newbery (honor) 1956.

LINDSAY, HAROLD ARTHUR
The First Walkabout by Harold Arthur Lindsay and Norman Barnett Tindale, illustrated by Madeleine Boyce; Longmans, 1954. **Awarded:** Children's Book Council of Australia 1955.

LINDSAY, RAE
Sleep and Dreams by Rae Lindsay, illustrated by Leigh Grant; Watts, 1978. **Awarded:** New Jersey Institute of Technology 1980.

LINDVALL, ELLA K.
Read Aloud Bible Stories by Ella K. Lindvall, illustrated by Kent Puckett; Moody Press, 1982. **Awarded:** Gold Medallion 1983.

LINE, DAVID
Screaming High by David Line, not illustrated; Little, Brown, 1985. **Awarded:** Edgar Allan Poe (runnerup) 1986.

LINE, LES
The Milkweed and Its World of Animals by Ada Graham and Frank Graham, photographs by Les Line; Doubleday, 1976. **Awarded:** New York Academy of Sciences (younger honor) 1977.

LINES, KATHLEEN
Lavender's Blue by Kathleen Lines, illustrated by Harold Jones; Watts, 1954. **Awarded:** Carnegie (special commendation) 1954; Lewis Carroll Shelf 1960; International Board on Books for Young People (honour list/Great Britain) 1956.

LINEVSKI, ALEKSANDR M.
An Old Tale Carved Out of Stone by Aleksandr M. Linevski, translated by Maria Polushkin, not illustrated; Crown, 1973. **Awarded:** Batchelder 1975.

LINFIELD, ESTHER
The Secret of the Mountain by Esther Linfield, not illustrated; Greenwillow, 1986. **Awarded:** Commonwealth Club of California 1986.

LINKLATER, ERIC
The Wind on the Moon: A Story for Children by Eric Linklater, illustrated by Nicolas Bentley; Macmillan, 1944. **Awarded:** Carnegie 1944.

LIONNI, LEO
Awarded: George G. Stone (for his body of work) 1976.

Alexander and the Windup Mouse written and illustrated by Leo Lionni; Pantheon, 1969. **Awarded:** Caldecott (honor) 1970; Christopher (ages 4-8) 1970.

The Biggest House in the World written and illustrated by Leo Lionni; Pantheon, 1968. **Awarded:** Spring Book Festival (picture book honor) 1968.

Fish Is Fish written and illustrated by Leo Lionni; Pantheon, 1970. **Awarded:** Michigan Young Reader (division I runnerup) 1980.

Frederick written and illustrated by Leo Lionni; Pantheon, 1967. **Awarded:** Caldecott (honor) 1968; New York Times Best illustrated 1967.

Inch by Inch written and illustrated by Leo Lionni; Obolensky, 1960. **Awarded:** Caldecott (Honor) 1961; Lewis Carroll Shelf 1962; New York Times Best Illustrated 1960.

Little Blue and Little Yellow written and illustrated by Leo Lionni; Obolensky, 1959. **Awarded:** Art Books for Children 1973, 1974, 1975; New York Times Best Illustrated 1959.

Nicolas, Where Have You Been? written and illustrated by Leo Lionni; Knopf, 1987. **Awarded:** Jane Addams (honor) 1988.

Swimmy written and illustrated by Leo Lionni; Pantheon, 1963. **Awarded:** Art Books for Children 1973; Biennale Illustrations Bratislava (golden apple) 1967; Caldecott (honor) 1964; New York Times Best Illustrated 1963.

LIPKIND, WILLIAM
Chaga by William Lipkind, illustrated by Nicolas Mordvinoff; Harcourt, 1955. **Awarded:** New York Times Best Illustrated 1955.

Circus Ruckus by William Lipkind, illustrated by Nicolas Mordvinoff; Harcourt, 1954. **Awarded:** New York Times Best Illustrated 1954.

Finders Keepers by William Lipkind, illustrated by Nicolas Mordvinoff; Harcourt, 1951. **Awarded:** Caldecott 1952.

The Magic Feather Duster by William Lipkind and Nicolas Mordvinoff, illustrated by Nicolas Mordvinoff; Harcourt, 1958. **Awarded:** New York Times Best Illustrated 1958.

The Two Reds by William Lipkind, illustrated by Nicolas Mordvinoff; Harcourt, 1950. **Awarded:** Caldecott (honor) 1951.

LIPPINCOTT CO.
Awarded: Drexel 1973.

LIPPMAN, PETER J.
Plunkety Plunk written and illustrated by Peter J. Lippman; Farrar, 1963. **Awarded:** New York Times Best Illustrated 1963.

LIPSON, SHELLEY
It's BASIC: The ABC's of Computer Programming by Shelley Lipson, illustrated by Janice Stapleton; Holt, Rinehart and Winston, 1982. **Awarded:** Garden State (younger nonfiction) 1985; New Jersey Institute of Technology 1983.

LIPSYTE, ROBERT
The Contender by Robert Lipsyte, not illustrated; Harper, 1967. **Awarded:** Child Study 1967.

One Fat Summer by Robert Lipsyte, not illustrated; Harper, 1977. **Awarded:** New Jersey Institute of Technology 1978.

The Summerboy by Robert Lipsyte, not illustrated; Harper & Row, 1982. **Awarded:** New Jersey Institute of Technology 1983.

LISKER, SONIA O.
Captain Hook, That's Me by Ada B. Litchfield, illustrated by Sonia O. Lisker; Walker, 1982. **Awarded:** CRABbery (honor) 1983.

Freckle Juice by Judy Blume, illustrated by Sonia O. Lisker; Four Winds, 1971. **Awarded:** Michigan Young Readers (Division I) 1980.

LISLE, JANET TAYLOR

Afternoon of the Elves by Janet Taylor Lisle, not illustrated; Orchard, 1989. **Awarded:** Newbery (Honor) 1990; Parents' Choice (Story Book) 1989.

The Great Dimpole Oak by Janet Taylor Lisle, illustrated by Stephen Gammell; Orchard, 1987. **Awarded:** Golden Kite (Fiction honor) 1987.

Sirens and Spies by Janet Lisle, not illustrated; Bradbury, 1985. **Awarded:** Parents' Choice (literature) 1985.

LISOWSKI, GABRIEL

The Witch of Fourth Street and Other Stories by Myron Levoy, illustrated by Gabriel Lisowski; Harper, 1972. **Awarded:** Children's Book Showcase 1973; Spring Book Festival (ages 8-12 honor) 1972.

LIST, ILKA KATHERINE

Questions and Answers about Seashore Life by Ilka Katherine List, illustrated by Ilka Katherine List and Arabelle Wheatley; Four Winds, 1971. **Awarded:** Children's Book Showcase 1972.

LISTON, ROBERT A.

The Right to Know: Censorship in America by Robert A. Liston, not illustrated; Watts, 1973. **Awarded:** Christopher (12-up) 1974.

LITCHFIELD, ADA B.

Captain Hook, That's Me by Ada B. Litchfield, illustrated by Sonia O. Lisker; Walker, 1982. **Awarded:** CRABbery (honor) 1983.

LITHWICK, DAHLIA

I Will Sing Life by Larry Berger and Dahlia Lithwick and seven campers, photographs by Robert Benson; Little Brown, 1992. **Awarded:** Fassler 1993.

LITSKY, FRANK

Winners on the Ice by Frank Litsky, illustrated with photographs; Watts, 1979. **Awarded:** New Jersey Institute of Technology 1980.

LITTELL, JOSEPH FLETCHER

Coping with Television edited by Joseph Fletcher Littell, illustrated; McDougall-Littell, 1973. **Awarded:** Media & Methods (textbook) 1974.

Language of Man series edited by Joseph Fletcher Littell, illustrated; McDougall-Littell, 1971, 1972. **Awarded:** Media & Methods (textbook) 1973.

LITTKE, LAEL

Blue Skye by Lael Littke, not illustrated; Scholastic, 1990. **Awarded:** Southern California Council (Notable Work of Fiction) 1992.

LITTLE, JEAN

Awarded: Vicky Metcalf 1974.

Listen for the Singing by Jean Little, not illustrated; Clarke, Irwin, 1977. **Awarded:** Governor General (author) 1977.

Little by Little: A Writer's Education by Jean Little, illustrated with photos; Viking Kestrel, 1987. **Awarded:** Boston Globe (Nonfiction Honor) 1988.

Mama's Going to Buy You a Mockingbird by Jean Little, not illustrated; Viking Kestrel, 1984. **Awarded:** Canadian Library Assn. 1985; Ruth Schwartz 1985.

Mine for Keeps by Jean Little, illustrated by Lewis Parker; Little, Brown, 1962. **Awarded:** Little-Brown Canadian 1961.

Stars Come Out Within by Jean Little, illustrated with photos; Viking, 1990, Viking, 1991. **Awarded:** Canadian Library Assn. (Runnerup) 1991; Reading Magic Award 1991.

LITTLE, LESSIE JONES

Children of Long Ago: Poems by Lessie Jones Little, illustrated by Jan Spivey Gilchrist; Philomel, 1988. **Awarded:** Parents' Choice (Story Book) 1988.

Childtimes by Lessie Jones Little and Eloise Greenfield, illustrated by Jerry Pinkney; Harper & Row, 1979. **Awarded:** Boston Globe Horn Book (nonfiction honor) 1980; Woodson (Outstanding Merit) 1980.

LITTLE, LISA

Black Images: The Art of West Africa by Penelope Naylor, photographs by Lisa Little; Doubleday, 1973. **Awarded:** Spring Book Festival (older honor) 1973.

LITTLEFIELD, WILLIAM

The Whiskers of Ho Ho by William Littlefield, illustrated by Vladimir Bobri; Lothrop, 1958. **Awarded:** Spring Book Festival (ages 4-8 honor) 1958.

LITTLEWOOD, VALERIE

Only the Best by Meguido Zola, illustrated by Valerie Littlewood; Julia MacRae, 1981. **Awarded:** Mother Goose (runnerup) 1982.

LITTMANN, MARK

Comet Halley: Once in a Lifetime by Mark Littmann and Donald K. Yeomans, illustrated; American Chemical Society, 1985. **Awarded:** New York Academy of Sciences (Elliott Montroll special award) 1986.

LITZINGER, ROSEANNE

The Treasure Trap by Virginia Masterman-Smith, illustrated by Roseanne Litzinger; Four Winds, 1979. **Awarded:** New Jersey Institute of Technology 1981.

LIU, BEATRICE

Little Wu and the Watermelons by Beatrice Liu, illustrated by Graham Peck; Follett, 1954. **Awarded:** Charles W. Follett 1954.

LIVELY, PENELOPE

The Driftway by Penelope Lively, not illustrated; Dutton, 1972, 1973. **Awarded:** Spring Book Festival (middle honor) 1973.

The Ghost of Thomas Kempe by Penelope Lively, illustrated by Antony Maitland; Heinemann, 1973. **Awarded:** Carnegie 1973; International Board on Books for Young People (text/Great Britain) 1976.

A Stitch in Time by Penelope Lively, not illustrated; Heinemann, 1976. **Awarded:** Whitbread 1976.

Treasures of Time by Penelope Lively, not illustrated; Doubleday, 1979, 1980. **Awarded:** Arts Council of Great Britain 1979.

LIVINGSTON, MYRA COHN

Awarded: National Council of Teachers of English Award for Excellence in Poetry for Children 1980; Southern California Council (comprehensive contribution of lasting value in the field of literature for children and young people) 1968.

Cat Poems by Myra Cohn Livingston, illustrated by Trina Schart Hyman; Holiday House, 1987. **Awarded:** Parents' Choice (Story Book) 1987.

Earth Songs by Myra Cohn Livingston, illustrated by Leonard Everett Fisher; Holiday House, 1986. **Awarded:** Southern California Council (Special Recognition for Excellence in a Poetry Quartet) 1989.

I'm Hiding by Myra Cohn Livingston and Erik Blegvad, illustrated by Erik Blegvad; Harcourt, 1961. **Awarded:** Steck-Vaughn 1963.

The Malibu and Other Poems by Myra Cohn Livingston, illustrated by James J. Spanfeller; Atheneum, 1972. **Awarded:** Southern California Council (notable) 1973.

Monkey Puzzle and Other Poems by Myra Cohn Livingston, illustrated by Antonio Frasconi; Atheneum/McElderry, 1984. **Awarded:** Commonwealth Club of California 1984.

Poems for Jewish Holidays by Myra Cohn Livingston, illustrated by Lloyd Bloom; Holiday House, 1986. **Awarded:** Jewish Book Council (illustrated children's book) 1987.

Sea Songs by Myra Cohn Livingston, illustrated by Leonard Everett Fisher; Holiday House, 1986. **Awarded:** Southern California Council (Special Recognition for Excellence in a Poetry Quartet) 1989.

Sky Songs by Myra Cohn Livingston, illustrated by Leonard Everett Fisher; Holiday House, 1984. **Awarded:** Parents Choice (literature) 1984; Southern California Council (Special Recognition for Excellence in a Poetry Quartet) 1989.

Space Songs by Myra Cohn Livingston, illustrated by Leonard Everett Fisher; Holiday House, 1988. **Awarded:** Southern California Council (Special Recognition for Excellence in a Poetry Quartet) 1989.

The Way Things Are and other Poems by Myra Cohn Livingston, illustrated by Jenni Oliver; Atheneum, 1974. **Awarded:** Golden Kite (honor) 1974.

Whispers and Other Poems by Myra Cohn Livingston, illustrated by Jacqueline Chwast; Harcourt, 1958. **Awarded:** Spring Book Festival (ages 4-8 honor) 1958.

Why Am I Grown So Cold? Poems of the Unknowable edited by Myra Cohn Livingston, not illustrated; Atheneum, 1982. **Awarded:** Parents Choice (Literature) 1983.

LIVONI, CATHY
Element of Time by Cathy Livoni, not illustrated; Harcourt, 1983. **Awarded:** Southern California Council (recognition of merit for first novel) 1984.

LIVSEY, ROSEMARY
Awarded: Southern California Council (distinguished contribution to the field of children's literature) 1967.

LLEWELLYN, CLAIRE
My First Book of Time by Claire Llewellyn, illustrated; Dorling Kindersley, 1992. **Awarded:** Times Educational Supplement (Junior) 1992.

LLOYD, CAROLE
The Charlie Barber Treatment by Carole Lloyd, illustrated; Julia MacRae, 1989. **Awarded:** Carnegie (Highly Commended) 1989.

LLOYD, DAVID
The Ridiculous Story of Gammer Gurton's Needle by David Lloyd, illustrated by Charlotte Voake; Clarkson N. Potter/Crown, 1987. **Awarded:** New York Times Notable 1987; Parents Choice (Story Book) 1987.

LLOYD, ERROL
My Brother Sean by Petronella Breinburg, illustrated by Errol Lloyd; Bodley Head, 1973. **Awarded:** Greenaway (commended) 1973.

LLOYD, J. SELWYN
Trysor Bryniau Caspar by J. Selwyn Lloyd; Gomer, 1976. **Awarded:** Tir Na n-Og (Welsh) 1977.

LLOYD, MEGAN
Cactus Hotel by Brenda Z. Guiberson, illustrated by Megan Lloyd; Henry Holt, 1991. **Awarded:** Parents' Choice (Picture Book) 1991.

The Little Old Lady Who Was Not Afraid of Anything by Linda Williams, illustrated by Megan Lloyd; Crowell, 1986. **Awarded:** Colorado Children's Book Award (Runnerup) 1988; Keystone To Reading 1988.

More Surprises by Lee Bennett Hopkins, illustrated by Megan Lloyd; Harper & Row, 1987. **Awarded:** Keystone To Reading 1989.

LLOYD, R. J.
What Is the Truth? A Farmyard Fable for the Young by Ted Hughes, illustrated by R. J. Lloyd; Faber, 1984. **Awarded:** Guardian 1985; Signal 1985.

LLOYD, TREVOR
Sky Highways: Geography from the Air by Trevor Lloyd, illustrated by Armstrong Sperry; Houghton, 1945. **Awarded:** Spring Book Festival (middle honor) 1945.

LLYWELYN, MORGAN
Brian Boru: Emperor of the Irish by Morgan Llywelyn; O'Brien Press, 1990. **Awarded:** Bisto (Fiction for the Young) 1991.

Strongbow by Morgan Llywelyn; O'Brien Press, 1992. **Awarded:** Bisto (Historical Fiction) 1992.

LOBE, MIRA
Hannes und Sein Bumpan by Mira Lobe, illustrated by Susi Weigel; Jugend u. Volk, 1961. **Awarded:** Hans Christian Andersen (runnerup) 1964.

Tiny by Mira Lobe, illustrated by Angelika Kaufmann; Jugend & Volk, 1981. **Awarded:** International Board on Books for Young People (Illustrator/Austria) 1982.

LOBEL, ANITA
A Birthday for the Princess written and illustrated by Anita Lobel; Harper, 1973. **Awarded:** Children's Book Showcase 1974.

Little John by Theodor Storm, illustrated by Anita Lobel; Harper, 1972. **Awarded:** Spring Book Festival (picture book) 1972.

A New Coat for Anna by Harriet Ziefert, illustrated by Anita Lobel; Harper & Row, 1986. **Awarded:** New Jersey Institute of Technology 1988.

On Market Street by Arnold Lobel, illustrated by Anita Lobel; Greenwillow, 1981. **Awarded:** Boston Globe Horn Book (illustration honor) 1981; Caldecott (honor) 1982; New York Times Best Illustrated 1981; New York Times Notable 1981.

Peter Penny's Dance by Janet Quin-Harkin, illustrated by Anita Lobel; Dial, 1976. **Awarded:** Children's Book Showcase 1977; New York Times Notable 1976.

The Rose in my Garden by Arnold Lobel, illustrated by Anita Lobel; Greenwillow, 1984. **Awarded:** Boston Globe Horn Book (illustration honor) 1984.

Sven's Bridge written and illustrated by Anita Lobel; Harper, 1965. **Awarded:** New York Times Best Illustrated 1965.

LOBEL, ARNOLD
Awarded: Lucky Book Club 1983; University of Southern Mississippi 1985.

As I Was Crossing Boston Common by Norma Farber, illustrated by Arnold Lobel; Dutton, 1975. **Awarded:** Children's Book Showcase 1976; National Book Award (finalist) 1976.

As Right As Right Can Be by Anne Rose, illustrated by Arnold Lobel; Dial, 1976. **Awarded:** Children's Book Showcase 1977; New York Times Best Illustrated 1976.

Benny's Animals and How He Put Them in Order by Millicent E. Selsam, illustrated by Arnold Lobel; Harper & Row, 1966. **Awarded:** Boys Club (certificate) 1966-67.

The Clay Pot Boy by Cynthia Jameson, illustrated by Arnold Lobel; Coward, 1973. **Awarded:** Children's Book Showcase 1974.

The Devil & Mother Crump by Valerie Scho Carey, illustrated by Arnold Lobel; Harper & Row, 1987. **Awarded:** Golden Kite (Picture- Illustration) 1987; Parents Choice (Picture Book) 1987.

Dinosaur Time by Peggy Parish, illustrated by Arnold Lobel; Harper, 1974. **Awarded:** Garden State Children's (easy to read) 1977.

Fables written and illustrated by Arnold Lobel; Harper, 1980. **Awarded:** Caldecott 1981; New York Times Notable 1980.

Frog and Toad series written and illustrated by Arnold Lobel; Harper, various years. **Awarded:** George G. Stone 1978.

Frog and Toad All Year written and illustrated by Arnold Lobel; Harper, 1976. **Awarded:** Christopher (ages 6-8) 1977; New York Times Notable 1976.

Frog and Toad Are Friends written and illustrated by Arnold Lobel; Harper, 1970. **Awarded:** Caldecott (honor) 1971; National Book Award (finalist) 1971.

Frog and Toad Together written and illustrated by Arnold Lobel; Harper, 1972. **Awarded:** Art Books for Children 1973; Children's Book Showcase 1973; New York Times Notable 1972; Newbery (honor) 1973; Spring Book Festival (picture book honor) 1972.

Grasshopper on the Road written and illustrated by Arnold Lobel; Harper, 1978. **Awarded:** Garden State Children's (easy to read) 1981.

The Headless Horseman Rides Tonight: More Poems to Trouble Your Sleep by Jack Prelutsky, illustrated by Arnold Lobel; Greenwillow, 1980. **Awarded:** New York Times Best Illustrated 1980; New York Times Notable 1980.

Hildilid's Night by Cheli Duran Ryan, illustrated by Arnold Lobel; Macmillan, 1971. **Awarded:** Caldecott (honor) 1972; Children's Book Showcase 1972; National Book Award (finalist) 1972.

A Holiday for Mister Muster written and illustrated by Arnold Lobel; Harper, 1963. **Awarded:** New York Times Best Illustrated 1963.

I'll Fix Anything by Judith Viorst, illustrated by Arnold Lobel; Harper, 1969. **Awarded:** New Jersey Institute of Technology 1970.

The Man Who Took the Indoors Out written and illustrated by Arnold Lobel; Harper 1974. **Awarded:** Children's Book Showcase 1975; New York Times Best Illustrated 1974.

The Master of Miracle: A New Novel of the Golem by Sulamith Ish- Kishor, illustrated by Arnold Lobel; Harper, 1971. **Awarded:** Jewish Book Council 1971; New York Times Notable 1971.

Merry, Merry FIBruary by Doris Orgel, illustrated by Arnold Lobel; Parents, 1977. **Awarded:** New York Times Best Illustrated 1977.

Ming Lo Moves the Mountain written and illustrated by Arnold Lobel; Greenwillow, 1982. **Awarded:** Parents Choice (Illustration) 1982.

Miss Suzy's Birthday by Miriam Young, illustrated by Arnold Lobel; Parents, 1974. **Awarded:** New York Times Best Illustrated 1974.

Mouse Tales written and illustrated by Arnold Lobel; Harper, 1972. **Awarded:** Irma Simonton Black 1972.

Nightmares: Poems to Trouble Your Sleep by Jack Prelutsky, illustrated by Arnold Lobel; Greenwillow, 1976. **Awarded:** Children's Book Showcase 1977.

On Market Street by Arnold Lobel, illustrated by Anita Lobel; Greenwillow, 1981. **Awarded:** Boston Globe Horn Book (illustration honor) 1981; Caldecott (honor) 1982; New York Times Best Illustrated 1981; New York Times Notable 1981.

On the Day Peter Stuyvesant Sailed into Town written and illustrated by Arnold Lobel; Harper, 1971. **Awarded:** Children's Book Showcase 1972; Christopher (ages 4-8) 1972.

Owl at Home written and illustrated Arnold Lobel; Harper, 1975. **Awarded:** Garden State Children's (easy to read) 1978; New York Times Notable 1975.

The Random House Book of Mother Goose selected and illustrated by Arnold Lobel; Random House, 1986. **Awarded:** New York Times Notable 1986; Parents' Choice (Picture Book) 1987.

The Rose in My Garden by Arnold Lobel, illustrated by Anita Lobel; Greenwillow, 1984. **Awarded:** Boston Globe Horn Book (illustration honor) 1984.

Seashore by Robert A. Morris, illustrated by Arnold Lobel; Harper, 1972. **Awarded:** Children's Book Showcase 1973.

Where's the Cat? by Harriet Ziefert, illustrated by Arnold Lobel; Harper & Row, 1987. **Awarded:** New Jersey Institute of Technology 1988.

Where's the Dog? by Harriet Ziefert, illustrated by Arnold Lobel; Harper & Row, 1987. **Awarded:** New Jersey Institute of Technology 1988.

Where's the Guinea Pig? by Harriet Ziefert, illustrated by Arnold Lobel; Harper & Row, 1987. **Awarded:** New Jersey Institute of Technology 1988.

Whiskers & Rhymes written and illustrated by Arnold Lobel; Greenwillow, 1985. **Awarded:** New York Times Notable 1985.

LOCKER, THOMAS

The Boy Who Held Back the Sea retold by Lenny Hort, illustrated by Thomas Locker; Dial, 1987. **Awarded:** New Jersey Institute of Technology 1988.

Family Farm written and illustrated by Thomas Locker; Dial, 1988. **Awarded:** Christopher (Ages 7-10) 1989.

Where the River Begins written and illustrated by Thomas Locker; Dial, 1984. **Awarded:** New York Times Best Illustrated 1984; New York Times Notable 1984.

LODGE, BERNARD

Tinker, Tailor, Soldier, Sailor: A Picture Book by Bernard Lodge, illustrated by Maureen Roffey, Bodley Head, 1976. **Awarded:** Greenaway (highly commended) 1976.

LOFGREN, ULF

Harlekin by Ulf Lofgren; Awe/Gebbers, 1977. **Awarded:** Biennale Illustrations Bratislava (grand prix) 1977.

LOFTING, HUGH JOHN
The Story of Doctor Dolittle written and illustrated by Hugh Lofting; Lippincott, 1948, c1920. **Awarded:** Lewis Carroll Shelf 1958.

The Voyages of Doctor Dolittle written and illustrated by Hugh Lofting; Stokes, 1922. **Awarded:** Newbery 1923.

LOGAN, DWIGHT
Great Men of Medicine by Ruth Fox, illustrated by Dwight Logan; Random House, 1947. **Awarded:** Boys Club 1949.

The Shining Shooter by Marion Renick, illustrated by Dwight Logan; Scribner, 1950. **Awarded:** Boys Club 1951.

LOH, JULES
Lords of the Earth: The History of the Navajo Indians by Jules Loh, illustrated with photographs; Crowell-Collier, 1971. **Awarded:** Western Writers (nonfiction) 1972.

LOHMAN, PHILIP
The Only Earth We Have by Laurence Pringle, illustrated by Philip Lohman; Macmillan, 1969. **Awarded:** New Jersey Institute of Technology 1970.

LOKEN, ANNA BELLE
The Colt from the Dark Forest by Anna Belle Loken, illustrated by Donald Bolognese; Lothrop, 1959. **Awarded:** Spring Book Festival (middle honor) 1959.

LOKKA, PIRKKO
Tuhatkiloinen Kultakala (original English *The Two-thousand-pound Goldfish*) by Betsy Byars, translated by Pirkko Lokka; WSOY, 1984. **Awarded:** International Board on Books for Young People (translation/Finland) 1986.

LONG, SYLVIA
Ten Little Rabbits by Virginia Grossman, illustrated by Sylvia Long; Chronicle Books, 1991. **Awarded:** International Reading Assn. (Younger) 1992; Redbook 1991.

LONGEUX Y VASQUEZ, ENRIQUETA
Viva la Raza! The Struggle of the Mexican-American People by Elizabeth Sutherland Martinez and Enriqueta Longeaux y Vasquez, not illustrated; Doubleday, 1974. **Awarded:** Jane Addams (honor) 1975.

LONGFELLOW, HENRY WADSWORTH
Hiawatha by Henry Wadsworth Longfellow, illustrated by Susan Jeffers; Dial, 1983. **Awarded:** New Jersey Institute of Technology 1983.

Hiawatha's Childhood by Henry Wadsworth Longfellow, illustrated by Errol Le Cain; Faber & Faber, 1984. **Awarded:** Greenaway 1984; International Board on Books for Young People (illustration/Great Britain) 1986.

Paul Revere's Ride by Henry Wadsworth Longfellow, illustrated by Ted Rand; Dutton, 1990. **Awarded:** Christopher (All ages) 1991.

LONGSTRETH, JOSEPH
Little Big-Feather by Joseph Longstreth, illustrated by Helen Borten; Abelard, 1956. **Awarded:** New York Times Best Illustrated 1956.

LONGWORTH, POLLY
Emily Dickinson: Her Letter to the World by Polly Longworth, not illustrated; Crowell, 1965. **Awarded:** Spring Book Festival (older honor) 1965.

LOPEZ, BARRY
Crow and Weasel by Barry Lopez, illustrated by Tom Pohrt; North Point Press, 1990; Random House of Canada, 1990. **Awarded:** Parents' Choice (Picture Book) 1990.

LORD, ATHENA V.
A Spirit To Ride the Whirlwind by Athena V. Lord, not illustrated; Macmillan, 1981. **Awarded:** Jane Addams 1982; Child Study 1981.

LORD, BETTY
In the Year of the Boar and Jackie Robinson by Betty Lord, illustrated by Marc Simont; Harper & Row, 1986. **Awarded:** Jefferson Cup 1985.

LORD, JOHN VERNON
Aesop's Fables retold in verse by James Michie, selected and illustrated by John Vernon Lord; Cape, 1989. **Awarded:** W. H. Smith 1990.

LORENZ, LEE
Hugo and the Spacedog written and illustrated by Lee Lorenz; Prentice Hall, 1983. **Awarded:** New Jersey Institute of Technology 1983.

LORIOT
Peter und der Wolf by Sergei Prokofiev, retold by Loriot, illustrated by Jorg Muller; Verlag Sauerlander. **Awarded:** Bologna (critici in erba) 1986.

LORRAINE, WALTER
Dear Rat by Julia Cunningham, illustrated by Walter Lorraine; Houghton, 1961. **Awarded:** New York Times Best Illustrated 1961.

Fairwater by Alastair Reid, illustrated by Walter Lorraine; Houghton, 1957. **Awarded:** Spring Book Festival (middle honor) 1957.

I Will Tell You of a Town by Alastair Reid, illustrated by Walter Lorraine; Houghton, 1956. **Awarded:** New York Times Best Illustrated 1956.

LOSINSKI, JULIA
Awarded: Grolier 1970.

LOTTRIDGE, CELIA BARKER
The Name of the Tree by Celia Barker Lottridge, illustrated by Ian Wallace; Douglas & McIntyre, 1989; McElderry, 1989. **Awarded:** Amelia Frances Howard-Gibbon (2nd runnerup) 1990; Mr. Christie's (English Illustration) 1989; Elizabeth Mrazik-Cleaver 1990.

Ticket to Curlew by Celia Barker Lottridge; Groundwood, 1992. **Awarded:** Canadian Library Assn. Book of the Year 1993.

LOUDEN, CLAIRE
The Defender by Nicholas Kalashnikoff, illustrated by Claire Louden and George Louden; Scribner, 1951. **Awarded:** Newbery (honor) 1952.

LOUDEN, GEORGE
The Defender by Nicholas Kalashnikoff, illustrated by George Louden and Claire Louden; Scribner, 1951. **Awarded:** Newbery (honor) 1952.

LOUGHEED, ROBERT
Mustang: Wild Spirit of the West by Marguerite Henry, illustrated by Robert Lougheed; Rand, 1966. **Awarded:** Sequoyah 1970; Western Heritage 1967.

LOUIE, AI-LING
Yeh-Shen: A Cinderella Story from China retold by Ai-Ling Louie, illustrated by Ed Young; Philomel, 1982. **Awarded:** Boston Globe Horn Book (Illustration honor) 1983; New Jersey Institute of Technology 1983.

LOURIE, PETER K.
Story by Peter K. Lourie in Highlights magazine. **Awarded:** Magazine Merit (Nonfiction Honor) 1990.

LOURIE, RICHARD

Soldier and Tsar in the Forest: A Russian Tale by Richard Lourie, illustrated by Uri Shulevitz; Farrar, 1972. **Awarded:** Spring Book Festival (picture book honor) 1972.

LOVEJOY, BAHIJA FATTUHI

Two Boys of Baghdad by Bahija Fattuhi Lovejoy, illustrated with photographs; Lothrop, 1972. **Awarded:** New Jersey Institute of Technology 1972.

LOVELACE, MAUD HART

The Tune is in the Tree by Maud Hart Lovelace, illustrated by Eloise Wilkin; Crowell, 1950. **Awarded:** Spring Book Festival (ages 8-12 honor) 1950.

LOW, ALICE

The Macmillan Book of Greek Gods and Heroes by Alice Low, illustrated by Arvis Stewart; Macmillan, 1985. **Awarded:** Washington Irving (All Ages) 1988.

LOW, JOSEPH

Adam's Book of Odd Creatures written and illustrated by Joseph Low; Atheneum, 1962. **Awarded:** Spring Book Festival (picture book) 1962.

Boo to a Goose written and illustrated by Joseph Low; Atheneum, 1975. **Awarded:** Children's Book Showcase 1976.

Egyptian Adventures by Olivia E. Coolidge, illustrated by Joseph Low; Houghton, 1954. **Awarded:** Spring Book Festival (older honor) 1954.

Hear Your Heart by Paul Showers, illustrated by Joseph Low; Crowell, 1968. **Awarded:** New Jersey Institute of Technology (science) 1968.

Little Though I Be written and illustrated by Joseph Low; McGraw, 1976. **Awarded:** New York Times Best Illustrated 1976.

Meat Pies and Sausages by Dorothy O. Van Woerkom, illustrated by Joseph Low; Greenwillow, 1976. **Awarded:** Children's Book Showcase 1977.

Mice Twice written and illustrated by Joseph Low; Atheneum, 1980. **Awarded:** Caldecott (honor) 1981.

Mother Goose Riddle Rhymes by Joseph Low and Ruth Low, illustrated by Joseph Low; Harcourt, 1953. **Awarded:** New York Times Best Illustrated 1953.

The Mouse and the Song by Marilynne K. Roach, illustrated by Joseph Low; Parents, 1974. **Awarded:** Children's Book Showcase 1975.

Shrimps by Judy Hawes, illustrated by Joseph Low; Crowell, 1967. **Awarded:** New Jersey Institute of Technology (science) 1968.

LOW, RUTH

Mother Goose Riddle Rhymes by Ruth Low and Joseph Low, illustrated by Joseph Low; Harcourt, 1953. **Awarded:** New York Times Best Illustrated 1953.

LOW, WILLIAM

Stargone John by Ellen Kindt McKenzie, illustrated by William Low; Henry Holt, 1990. **Awarded:** Bay Area Book Reviewers Assn. (Children's Book) 1991.

Summer Stories by Nola Thacker, illustrated by William Low; Lippincott, 1988. **Awarded:** Author's Award (Alabama) 1989.

LOWE, PATRICIA TRACY

The Tale of Czar Saltan: or, The Prince and the Swan Princess by Alexander Pushkin, translated and retold by Patricia Tracy

Lowe, illustrated by Ivan Bilibin; Crowell, 1975. **Awarded:** Children's Book Showcase 1976.

LOWENTOWICZ, IRENA

Nine Cry-baby Dolls by Josephine B. Bernhard, illustrated by Irena Lowentowicz; Roy, 1945. **Awarded:** Spring Book Festival (younger honor) 1945.

LOWNSBERY, ELOISE

Out of the Flame by Eloise Lownsbery, illustrated by Elizabeth Tyler Wolcott; Longmans, 1931. **Awarded:** Newbery (honor) 1932.

LOWREY, JANETTE SEBRING

Love, Bid Me Welcome by Janette Sebring Lowrey, not illustrated; Harper, 1964. **Awarded:** Steck-Vaughn 1965.

LOWRIE, JEAN E.

Awarded: American Assn. of School Librarians 1978.

LOWRY, LOIS

Awarded: Milner 1987.

All About Sam by Lois Lowry, illustrated by Diane de Groat; Houghton Mifflin, 1988. **Awarded:** California Young Reader (Intermediate) 1992; Georgia Children's Book Award 1992; Mississippi Children's Book Award 1990; Charlie May Simon 1990-91; South Dakota Prairie Pasque 1991; Mark Twain 1991.

Anastasia, Ask Your Analyst by Lois Lowry, not illustrated; Houghton Mifflin, 1984. **Awarded:** Garden State (younger fiction) 1987.

Anastasia Has the Answers by Lois Lowry, illustrated; Houghton Mifflin, 1986. **Awarded:** Garden State Children's Book Award (Younger Fiction) 1989.

Anastasia Krupnik by Lois Lowry, not illustrated; Houghton Mifflin, 1979. **Awarded:** Michigan Young Readers (Division II) 1983.

Autumn Street by Lois Lowry, not illustrated; Houghton Mifflin, 1980. **Awarded:** International Board on Books for Young People (Author/USA) 1982.

The Giver by Lois Lowry; Houghton Mifflin, 1993. **Awarded:** Boston Globe (fiction honor) 1993.

Number the Stars by Lois Lowry, not illustrated; Houghton Mifflin, 1989. **Awarded:** Addams (Honor) 1990; Caudill Young Reader's Book Award 1992; Charlotte Book Award (grades 3-5) 1992; Dorothy Canfield Fisher 1991; Golden Archer 1990; Great Stone Face 1992; Jewish Book Council (Children's Literature) 1990; Newbery 1990; Charlie May Simon 1991-92; Sydney Taylor Book Award (Older) 1990.

Rabble Starkey by Lois Lowry, not illustrated; Houghton Mifflin, 1987. **Awarded:** Boston Globe Horn Book (fiction) 1987; Child Study 1987; Golden Kite (Fiction) 1987.

A Summer to Die by Lois Lowry, illustrated by Jenni Oliver; Houghton, 1977. **Awarded:** California Young Reader (high school) 1981; International Reading Assn. 1978; Maryland 1989; Massachusetts Children's (young adult) 1981.

Switcharound by Lois Lowry, not illustrated; Houghton Mifflin, 1985. **Awarded:** South Dakota Prairie Pasque 1988.

Taking Care of Terrific by Lois Lowry, not illustrated; Houghton Mifflin, 1983. **Awarded:** Parents Choice (literature) 1983.

LUBACH, PETER

Donald and the Singing Fish written and illustrated by Peter Lubach; Macmillan, 1992; Hyperion, 1992. **Awarded:** Macmillan Prize (2nd prize) 1990.

LUBIN, LEONARD

The Little Swineherd and Other Tales by Paula Fox, illustrated by Leonard Lubin; Dutton, 1978. **Awarded:** National Book Award (finalist) 1979.

The Pig-tale by Lewis Carroll, illustrated by Leonard B. Lubin; Little, Brown, 1975, 1889. **Awarded:** Lewis Carroll Shelf 1975; Children's Book Showcase 1976' New York Times Best Illustrated 1975.

LUCAS, CELIA

Steel Town Cats by Celia Lucas, illustrated by Susan Cutting; Tabb House, 1987. **Awarded:** Tir Na n-og 1988.

LUCAS, GEORGE

The Star Wars: From the Adventures of Luke Skywalker by George Lucas, illustrated; Ballantine Books, 1976. **Awarded:** North Dakota Children's Choice 1978.

LUCAS, MARY SEYMOUR

Vast Horizons by Mary Seymour Lucas, illustrated by C. B. Falls; Viking, 1943. **Awarded:** Spring Book Festival (older honor) 1943.

LUCEY, MARILYN

Teeny-tiny by Leland B. Jacobs, illustrated by Marilyn Lucey; Garrard, 1976. **Awarded:** New Jersey Institute of Technology 1977.

LUCHT, IRMGARD

Alle Meine Blatter by Irmgard Lucht, illustrated by Josef Guggenmos; Gertraud Middeuve Verlag. **Awarded:** Bologna (critici in erba) 1971.

LUEDERS, EDWARD

Reflections on a Gift of Watermelon Pickle and Other Modern Verse by Edward Lueders, Stephen Dunning, and Hugh Smith, illustrated with photographs; Lothrop Lee & Shepard, 1966. **Awarded:** Lewis Carroll Shelf 1968.

LUFKIN, RAYMOND

Here Is Alaska by Evelyn Stefansson, maps by Raymond Lufkin, photographs by Frederick Machetanz; Scribner, 1943. **Awarded:** Spring Book Festival (older honor) 1943.

Ood-Le-Uk the Wanderer by Alice Lide and Margaret Johansen, illustrated by Raymond Lufkin; Little, Brown, 1930. **Awarded:** Newbery (honor) 1931.

Story of the Negro by Arna Wendell Bontemps, illustrated by Raymond Lufkin; Knopf, 1948. **Awarded:** Jane Addams 1956; Newbery (honor) 1949.

LUIKEN, NICOLE

Escape to the Overworld by Nicole Luiken, not illustrated; Tree Frog Press, 1988. **Awarded:** Young Adult Canadian (Honorable Mention) 1989.

Unlocking the Doors by Nicole Luiken, not illustrated; Scholastic-TAB, 1988. **Awarded:** Young Adult Canadian (Honorable Mention) 1989.

LUIS, EARLENE W.

Wheels for Ginny's Chariot by Earlene W. Luis and Barbara F. Millar; not illustrated; Dodd, Mead, 1966. **Awarded:** Edith Busby 1965.

LUKS, MARGARET

A New Mother for Martha by Phyllis Green, illustrated by Margaret Luks; Human Sciences Press, 1978. **Awarded:** Council of Wisconsin Writers (picture book) 1979.

LULING, VIRGINIA

Aborigines by Virginia Luling, illustrated with maps and photographs; Macdonald & Janes, 1979. **Awarded:** Other Award 1980.

LUNDBERGH, HOLGER

Great Swedish Fairy Tales by Holger Lundbergh, illustrated by John Bauer; Delacorte/Lawrence, 1973. **Awarded:** Children's Book Showcase 1974.

LUNGE, JEFFREY

Morning Arrow by Nanabah Chee Dodge, illustrated by Jeffrey Lunge; Lothrop, 1975. **Awarded:** Council on Interracial Books (American Indian) 1973.

LUNN, JANET

Awarded: Vicky Metcalf 1982.

Amos's Sweater by Janet Lunn, illustrated by Kim LaFave; Douglas & McIntyre, 1988; Scholastic, 1990. **Awarded:** Governor General's Literary Award (Illustration) 1988; Amelia Frances Howard-Gibbon 1989; Ruth Schwartz 1989.

The Root Cellar by Janet Lunn, illustrated with a map; Lester & Orpen Dennys, 1981; Scribner, 1983. **Awarded:** California Young Reader (Middle/Junior High) 1988; Canadian Library Association 1982; International Board on Books for Young People (writing/Canada) 1984.

Shadow in Hawthorn Bay by Janet Lunn, not illustrated; Lester & Orpen Dennys, 1986; Scribner, 1986. **Awarded:** Governor General (author) 1986; Canadian Library Assn. 1987; International Board on Books for Young People (Writing/Canada) 1988; National Chapter of Canada IODE Violet Downey 1987; Young Adult Canadian 1987.

The Story of Canada by Janet Lunn and Christopher Moore, illustrated by Alan Daniel; Lester Publishing Co., 1992. **Awarded:** Mr. Christie's (English Text ages 9-14) 1992.

The Twelve Dancing Princesses: A Fairy Story retold by Janet Lunn, illustrated by Laszlo Gal; Methuen, 1979. **Awarded:** Governor General (illustrator) 1979; Amelia Frances Howard-Gibbon 1980; IODE 1979.

LURIE, ALISON

E. Nesbit: Riding the Wave of the Future by Alison Lurie in The New York Review 31 (No. 16 Oct. 25, 1984). **Awarded:** Children's Literature Assn. Excellence in Criticism (runnerup) 1985.

LURIE, LEON

Bubby, Me and Memories by Barbara Pomerantz, photographs by Leon Lurie; Union of American Hebrew Congregations, 1983. **Awarded:** Sydney Taylor Book Award (younger readers) 1984.

LURIE, MORRIS

Toby's Millions by Morris Lurie; Penguin Australia, 1982. **Awarded:** Children's Book Council of Australia (Book of the year commended) 1983.

The Twenty-seventh Annual African Hippopotamus Race by Morris Lurie, illustrated by Elizabeth Honey; Penguin, 1977. **Awarded:** Young Australian's Best Book Award (fiction for young readers) 1986.

LUSTIG, ARNOST

Dita Saxova by Arnost Lustig, translated by Jeanne Nemcova, not illustrated; Harper, 1979. **Awarded:** Jewish Book Council 1979.

LUSTIG, LORETTA

Rich Mitch by Marjorie Weinman Sharmat, illustrated by Loretta Lustig; Morrow, 1983. **Awarded:** KC Three 1985-86.

LUTZEIER, ELIZABETH
No Shelter by Elizabeth Lutzeier, not illustrated; Blackie, 1984. **Awarded:** Kathleen Fidler 1984.

LUZZATI, EMANUELE
Hurly Burly and the Knights by Milton Rugoff, illustrated by Emanuele Luzzati; Platt, 1963. **Awarded:** New York Times Best Illustrated 1963.

LYDECKER, LAURA
Dragonsong by Anne McCaffrey, illustrated by Laura Lydecker; Atheneum, 1976. **Awarded:** Children's Book Showcase 1977.

LYNCH, PATRICK JAMES
A Bag of Moonshine by Alan Garner, illustrated by Patrick James Lynch; Collins, 1986. **Awarded:** Mother Goose 1987.

Fairy Tales of Ireland by W. B. Yeats, illustrated by P. J. Lynch; Collins, 1990. **Awarded:** Bisto (Illustration) 1991.

LYON, GEORGE ELLA
The Basket by George Ella Lyon, illustrated by Mary Szilagyi; Orchard, 1990. **Awarded:** Kentucky Bluegrass (grades K-3) 1992.

Borrowed Children by George Ella Lyon, not illustrated; Orchard, 1988. **Awarded:** Golden Kite (Fiction) 1988.

LYONS, MARY E.
Letters from a Slave Girl by Mary E. Lyons, illustrated; Scribner, 1992. **Awarded:** Jane Addams (honor) 1993; Golden Kite (fiction) 1992.

Sorrow's Kitchen: The Life and Folklore of Zora Neale Hurston by Mary E. Lyons, illustrated; Scribner, 1990. **Awarded:** Woodson (Secondary) 1991.

LYONS, OREN
Jimmy Yellow Hawk by Virginia Driving Hawk Sneve, illustrated by Oren Lyons; Holiday House, 1972. **Awarded:** Council on Interracial Books (American Indian) 1970.

M

MAASS, MARY KURNICK
Illustrations by Mary Kurnick Maass in *Wee Wisdom* magazine. **Awarded:** Magazine Merit Award (Illustration) 1990.

MABEY, RICHARD
Oak & Company by Richard Mabey, illustrated by Clare Roberts; Greenwillow, 1983. **Awarded:** New York Academy of Sciences (younger) 1984.

Street Flowers by Richard Mabey, illustrated by Sarah Kensington; Kestrel, 1976. **Awarded:** Times Educational Supplement (junior) 1977.

MacALVAY, NORA TULLY
Cathie and the Paddy Boy written and illustrated by Nora Tully MacAlvay; Viking, 1962. **Awarded:** Friends of American Writers 1963; Indiana Authors Day (children) 1963.

MACARTHUR-ONSLOW, ANNETTE
Children of the Red King by Madeleine Polland, illustrated by Annette Macarthur-Onslow; Holt, 1961. **Awarded:** Spring Book Festival (middle honor) 1961.

Nordy Bank by Sheena Porter, illustrated by Annette Macarthur-Onslow; Oxford, 1964. **Awarded:** Carnegie 1964.

Pastures of the Blue Crane by Hesba Fay Brinsmead, illustrated by Annette Macarthur-Onslow; Oxford, 1964. **Awarded:** Children's Book Council of Australia (book of the year) 1965.

Uhu written and illustrated by Annette Macarthur-Onslow; Ure Smith, 1969. **Awarded:** Children's Book Council of Australia (book of the year) 1970.

MACAULAY, DAVID
Awarded: Washington Post/Children's Book Guild Nonfiction Award 1977.

Black and White written and illustrated by David Macaulay; Houghton Mifflin, 1990. **Awarded:** Caldecott 1991.

Castle written and illustrated by David Macaulay; Houghton Mifflin, 1977. **Awarded:** Caldecott (honor) 1978; New York Academy of Sciences (younger honor) 1978.

Cathedral: The Story of Its Construction written and illustrated by David Macaulay; Houghton Mifflin, 1973. **Awarded:** Caldecott (honor) 1974; Children's Book Showcase 1974; New York Times Best Illustrated 1973.

City written and illustrated by David Macaulay; Houghton, 1974. **Awarded:** Children's Book Showcase 1975.

Help! Let Me Out! by David Lord Porter, illustrated by David Macaulay; Houghton Mifflin, 1982. **Awarded:** New York Times Notable Books 1982.

Mill written and illustrated by David Macaulay; Houghton Mifflin, 1983. **Awarded:** Parents' Choice (literature) 1983.

Pyramid written and illustrated by David Macaulay; Houghton Mifflin, 1975. **Awarded:** Boston Globe Horn Book (nonfiction honor) 1976; Children's Book Showcase 1976; Christopher (nonfiction) 1976.

Unbuilding written and illustrated by David Macaulay; Houghton Mifflin, 1980. **Awarded:** New York Academy of Sciences (younger honor) 1981; New York Times Best Illustrated 1980; New York Times Notable Books 1980; Parents' Choice (illustration) 1980.

Underground written and illustrated by David Macaulay; Houghton, 1976. **Awarded:** Children's Book Showcase 1977.

The Way Things Work written and illustrated by David Macaulay; Houghton Mifflin, 1988; Dorling Kindersley, 1988. **Awarded:** American Institute of Physics 1990; Boston Globe (Nonfiction) 1989; Charlotte Book Award (grades 6-8) 1990; Science Book Prizes 1989; Times Educational Supplement (Senior) 1989.

Why the Chicken Crossed the Road written and illustrated by David Macaulay; Houghton Mifflin, 1987. **Awarded:** Parents' Choice (Picture Book) 1987.

MacBEAN, DILLA W.
Awarded: Children's Reading Round Table 1956.

MacCARTHY, PATRICIA
Seventeen Kings and Forty-two Elephants by Margaret Mahy, illustrated by Patricia MacCarthy; Dial, 1987. **Awarded:** New York Times Best Illustrated 1987.

MacCLINTOCK, DORCAS
A Natural History of Giraffes by Dorcas MacClintock, illustrated by Ugo Mochi; Scribner, 1973. **Awarded:** Children's Book Showcase 1974; New York Academy of Sciences (older) 1974.

MacCLINTOCK, MARSHALL
Story of the Mississippi by Marshall MacClintock, illustrated by C. H. DeWitt; Harper, 1941. **Awarded:** Spring Book Festival (younger honor) 1941.

MacCLOUD, MALCOLM
A Gift of Mirrovax by Malcolm MacCloud, not illustrated; Atheneum, 1981. **Awarded:** Christopher (ages 10-14) 1982.

MACDONALD, CAROLINE
Elephant Rock by Caroline Macdonald, not illustrated; Hodder & Stoughton Aukland, 1983. **Awarded:** Esther Glen 1984.

Joseph's Boat by Caroline Macdonald, illustrated by Chris Gaskin; Hodder & Stoughton, 1988. **Awarded:** Russell Clark 1989.

The Lake at the End of the World by Caroline Macdonald, not illustrated; Hodder & Stoughton, 1988; Dial, 1989; Knight, 1992. **Awarded:** AIM Children's Book Award (Story Book 3rd prize) 1990; Children's Book Council of Australia (Book of the Year Older Honour) 1989; Diabetes Australian Alan Marshall 1989; Guardian Award (runnerup) 1990.

Speaking to Miranda by Caroline Macdonald, not illustrated; Hodder & Stoughton, 1991. **Awarded:** AIM Children's Book Awards (Story Book 3rd prize) 1991.

Visitors written and illustrated by Caroline Macdonald; Hodder & Stoughton, 1984. **Awarded:** AIM Children's Book Award (Story Book) 1985.

MacDONALD, GEORGE
Hinter Dem Norwind by George MacDonald, translated by Sybil Grafin Schonfeldt; Annette Betz, 1981. (original English: *At the Back of the north Wind*). **Awarded:** International Board on Books for Young People (translation/German Federal Republic) 1982.

The Light Princess by George MacDonald, illustrated by Maurice Sendak; Farrar, 1969. **Awarded:** New York Times Best Illustrated 1969.

MacDONALD, GOLDEN
see BROWN, MARGARET WISE

MacDONALD, JAMES
Audubon by Constance M. Rourke, illustrated by James MacDonald; Harcourt, 1936. **Awarded:** Newbery (honor) 1937.

Davy Crockett by Constance Rourke, illustrated by James MacDonald; Harcourt, 1934. **Awarded:** Newbery (honor) 1935.

Hearts Courageous: Twelve Who Achieved by William Herman, illustrated by James MacDonald; Dutton, 1949. **Awarded:** Boys Club 1950.

MacDONALD, REBY EDMOND
The Ghosts of Austwick Manor by Reby E. MacDonald, not illustrated; Atheneum, 1982. **Awarded:** CRABbery (honor) 1983.

MacDONALD, SHELAGH
No End to Yesterday by Shelagh Macdonald, not illustrated; Deutsch, 1977. **Awarded:** Whitbread 1977.

MacDONALD, SUSE
Alphabatics written and illustrated by Suse MacDonald; Bradbury, 1986. **Awarded:** Caldecott (honor) 1987; Golden Kite (picture illustration) 1986.

MACFARLANE, AIDAN
Mum - I Feel Funny! by Aidan Macfarlane and Ann McPherson, illustrated by Nicholas Garland; Chatto & Windus, 1982. **Awarded:** Times Educational Supplement (junior) 1983.

MacGIBBON, JEAN
Hal by Jean MacGibbon, not illustrated; Heinemann, 1974. **Awarded:** Other Award 1975.

MacGREGOR, ELLEN
Miss Pickerell Goes to Mars by Ellen MacGregor, illustrated by Paul Galdone; McGraw, 1951. **Awarded:** Young Readers Choice 1956.

MacGRORY, YVONNE
The Secret of the Ruby Ring by Yvonne MacGrory; Children's Press, 1991. **Awarded:** Bisto (First Children's Novel) 1991.

MACHETANZ, FREDERICK
Here Is Alaska by Evelyn Stefansson, maps by Raymond Lufkin, photographs by Frederick Machetanz; Scribner, 1943. **Awarded:** Spring Book Festival (older honor) 1943.

MacINTYRE, ELISABETH
Hugo's Zoo written and illustrated by Elisabeth MacIntyre; Angus & Robertson, 1964. **Awarded:** Children's Book Council of Australia (picture book) 1965.

Susan Who Lives in Australia written and illustrated by Elisabeth MacIntyre; Scribner, 1944. **Awarded:** Spring Book Festival (younger honor) 1944.

MacINTYRE, ROD
Yuletide Blues by Rod MacIntyre, not illustrated; Thistledown Press, 1991. **Awarded:** Young Adult Canadian (Honorable Mention) 1992.

MACK, STANLEY
The Little Man and the Big Thief by Erich Kastner, illustrated by Stanley Mack; Knopf, 1970. **Awarded:** Spring Book Festival (middle honor) 1970.

One Dancing Drum by Gail Kredenser and Stanley Mack, illustrated by Stanley Mack; Phillips, 1971. **Awarded:** Children's Book Showcase 1972; New York Times Best Illustrated 1971.

MacKAIN, BONNIE
Illustration by Bonnie MacKain in *Cricket* magazine. **Awarded:** Magazine Merit (Illustration Honor) 1991.

MACKAY, CLAIRE
Awarded: Vicky Metcalf 1983.

Marvin & Me & the Flies by Claire Mackay in Canadian Children's Annual 1987; Grolier, 1987. **Awarded:** Vicky Metcalf Short Story 1988.

One Proud Summer by Claire Mackay and Marsha Hewitt, not illustrated; The Women's Press, 1981. **Awarded:** Ruth Schwartz 1982.

MacKAY, DONALD A.
The Adventures of Huckleberry Finn by Samuel Clemens, illustrated by Donald MacKay; Grosset, 1948, 1884. **Awarded:** Lewis Carroll Shelf 1962.

Out There by Adrien Stoutenburg, illustrated by Donald A. MacKay; Viking, 1971. **Awarded:** Spring Book Festival (older honor) 1971.

MACKEN, WALTER
The Flight of the Doves by Walter Macken, not illustrated; Macmillan, 1968. **Awarded:** Spring Book Festival (middle honor) 1968.

MacKNIGHT, NINON
Bush Holiday by Stephen Fennimore, illustrated by Ninon MacKnight; Doubleday, 1949. **Awarded:** Spring Book Festival (under 12) 1949.

MacLACHLAN, PATRICIA
Arthur, for the Very First Time by Patricia MacLachlan, illustrated by Lloyd Bloom; Harper & Row, 1980. **Awarded:** Golden Kite (fiction) 1980.

Facts and Fictions of Minna Pratt by Patricia MacLachlan, not illustrated; Harper & Row, 1988. **Awarded:** Parents' Choice (Story Book) 1988.

Sarah, Plain and Tall by Patricia MacLachlan, not illustrated; Harper & Row, 1985. **Awarded:** Christopher (ages 8-10) 1986; Garden State Children's (Younger Fiction) 1988; Golden Kite (fiction) 1985; International Board on Books for Young People (Writing/USA) 1988; Jefferson Cup 1986; New York Times Notable 1985; Newbery 1986; Scott O'Dell 1985; Charlie May Simon 1987-88.

Unclaimed Treasures by Patricia MacLachlan, not illustrated; Harper & Row, 1984. **Awarded:** Boston Globe Horn Book (fiction honor) 1984.

MacLEAN, ROBERT
Becky and Her Brave Cat, Bluegrass by Miriam E. Mason, illustrated by Robert MacLean; Macmillan, 1960. **Awarded:** Indiana Authors Day (young children) 1961.

Willie Joe and His Small Change by Marguerite Vance, illustrated by Robert MacLean; Dutton, 1959. **Awarded:** Edison Mass Media (character development of children) 1960.

MacLEOD, CHARLOTTE
We Dare Not Go A-Hunting by Charlotte MacLeod, illustrated with a map; Atheneum, 1980. **Awarded:** Edgar Allan Poe (runnerup) 1981.

MacLEOD, DOUG
Sister Madge's Book of Nuns by Doug MacLeod, illustrated by Craig Smith; Omnibus, 1986. **Awarded:** Children's Book Council of Australia (book of the year younger honor) 1987; KOALA (Primary) 1988; Young Australian Best Book (Fiction Younger Reader) 1987.

MacMILLAN, ANNABELLE
The Robber Ghost by Karin Anckarsvard, translated by Annabelle MacMillan, illustrated by Paul Galdone; Harcourt, 1961. **Awarded:** Spring Book Festival (middle honor) 1961.

MACMILLAN, CYRUS
Glooskap's Country and Other Indian Tales by Cyrus Macmillan, illustrated by John A. Hall; Oxford, 1956. **Awarded:** Canadian Library Assn. 1957.

MACNESS, BRIAN
The Arrow Book of Backyard Creatures by Brian Macness; Ashton Scholastic, 1986. **Awarded:** Whitley Awards 1987.

MacVEIGH, ROB ROY
Awarded: L. Frank Baum 1992.

MADDEN, DON
A Drop of Blood by Paul Showers, illustrated by Don Madden; Crowell, 1967. **Awarded:** New Jersey Institute of Technology (science) 1968.

Why Frogs Are Wet by Judy Hawes, illustrated by Don Madden; Crowell, 1968. **Awarded:** New Jersey Institute of Technology (science) 1968.

MADDEN, MABRA
Pito's House written and illustrated by Mabra Madden and Catherine Bryan; Macmillan, 1943. **Awarded:** Spring Book Festival (younger honor) 1943.

MADDEN, SUSAN
Awarded: Allie Beth Martin 1987.

MADDOCK, REGINALD
The Pit by Reginald Maddock, illustrated by Douglas Hall; Little, 1968. **Awarded:** Spring Book Festival (older honor) 1968.

MADISON, ARNOLD
Danger Beats the Drum by Arnold Madison, not illustrated; Holt, 1966. **Awarded:** Edgar Allan Poe (runnerup) 1967.

Runaway Teens by Arnold Madison, not illustrated; Elsevier/Nelson, 1979. **Awarded:** Golden Kite (nonfiction) 1979.

MAENO, ITOKO
Tonia the Tree by Sandy Stryker, illustrated by Itoko Maeno; Advocacy Press, 1988. **Awarded:** Friends of American Writers 1989.

MAGGIO, ROSALIE
Story by Rosalie Maggio in Cricket magazine. **Awarded:** Magazine Merit Award (Nonfiction) 1988.

MAGNUSON, DIANA
Stegosaurus by Janet Riehecky, illustrated by Diana Magnuson; Child's World, 1988. **Awarded:** Society of Midland Authors (Juvenile Nonfiction) 1989.

Triceratops by Janet Riehecky, illustrated by Diana Magnuson; Child's World, 1988. **Awarded:** Society of Midland Authors (Juvenile Nonfiction) 1989.

Tyrannosaurus by Janet Riehecky, illustrated by Diana Magnuson; Child's World, 1988. **Awarded:** Society of Midland Authors (Juvenile Nonfiction) 1989.

MAGNUSSON, MAGNUS
Introducing Archaeology by Magnus Magnusson, illustrated by Martin Simmons; Bodley Head, 1972. **Awarded:** Times Educational Supplement 1972.

MAGORIAN, MICHELLE
Back Home by Michelle Magorian, not illustrated; Harper & Row, 1984; Viking, 1985. **Awarded:** West Australian (Secondary) 1987.

Goodnight, Mister Tom by Michelle Magorian, not illustrated; Kestrel, 1981; Harper & Row, 1981. **Awarded:** Carnegie (commended) 1981; Guardian 1982; International Reading Assn. 1982; Virginia Young Readers (Middle School) 1991; West Australian Young Readers' (secondary) 1983.

MAGUBANE, PETER
Black as I Am by Zindzi Mandela and Peter Magubane, foreword by Andrew Young, illustrated; Guild of Tudors Press, 1978. **Awarded:** Korczak (for children) 1981.

Black Child written and photographed by Peter Magubane; Knopf, 1982. **Awarded:** Coretta Scott King (illustrator) 1983.

MAHAN, BENTON
Pink Pink by Ida DeLage, illustrated by Benton Mahan; Garrard, 1973. **Awarded:** New Jersey Institute of Technology 1973.

MAHER, MARY HELEN
Awarded: American Assn. of School Librarians 1981.

MAHER, RAMONA
The Abracadabra Mystery by Ramona Maher, not illustrated; Dodd Mead, 1961. **Awarded:** Calling All Girls - Dodd, Mead 1961.

Their Shining Hour: Based on Events in the Life of Susanna Dickenson at the Siege of the Alamo by Ramona Maher, not illustrated; Day, 1960. **Awarded:** Western Writers (fiction) 1960.

MAHY, MARGARET MAY

The Changeover by Margaret Mahy, not illustrated; Dent, 1984; Atheneum, 1984. **Awarded:** Boston Globe Horn Book (fiction honor) 1985; Carnegie 1984; Esther Glen 1985; International Board on Books for Young People (Writing/Great Britain) 1986.

Dragon of an Ordinary Family by Margaret May Mahy, illustrated by Helen Oxenbury; Heinemann, 1969. **Awarded:** Greenaway 1969.

The First Margaret Mahy Story Book: Stories and Poems by Margaret Mahy, illustrated by Shirley Hughes; Dent, 1972. **Awarded:** Esther Glen 1973.

The Great White Man-Eating Shark by Margaret Mahy, illustrated by Jonathan Allen; Dial, 1990. **Awarded:** Virginia Young Readers (Primary) 1992.

The Haunting by Margaret Mahy, not illustrated; Dent, 1982; Atheneum, 1983. **Awarded:** Carnegie 1982; Esther Glen 1983.

A Lion in the Meadow by Margaret May Mahy, illustrated by Jenny Williams; Watts, 1969. **Awarded:** Esther Glen 1970.

Memory by Margaret Mahy, not illustrated; Dent, 1987; McElderry, 1988. **Awarded:** Boston Globe (Fiction Honor) 1988; Observer Teenage Fiction Prize 1987.

Seventeen Kings and Forty-two Elephants by Margaret Mahy, illustrated by Patricia MacCarthy; Dial, 1987. **Awarded:** New York Times Best Illustrated 1987.

The Tricksters by Margaret Mahy, not illustrated; McElderry, 1987. **Awarded:** New York Times Notable 1987.

Underrunners by Margaret Mahy, not illustrated; Hamish Hamilton, 1992. **Awarded:** Esther Glen 1993.

The World in 1492 by Jean Fritz, Katherine Paterson, Patricia McKissack, Fredrick McKissack, Margaret Mahy and Jamake Highwater, illustrated by Stefano Vitale; Henry Holt, 1992. **Awarded:** Hungry Mind (Young Adult Nonfiction) 1993.

MAI, VO-DINH

The Land I Lost: Adventures of a Boy in Vietnam by Quang Nhuong Huynh, photographs by Vo-Dinh Mai; Harper, 1982. **Awarded:** Friends of American Writers ($500 award) 1983; William Allen White 1985.

MAINS, DAVID

Tales of the Kingdom by David Mains and Karen Mains, illustrated by Jack Stockman; David C. Cook, 1983. **Awarded:** Gold Medallion 1984.

MAINS, KAREN

Tales of the Kingdom by David Mains and Karen Mains, illustrated by Jack Stockman; David C. Cook, 1983. **Awarded:** Gold Medallion 1984.

MAITLAND, ANTONY JASPER

Black Jack by Leon Garfield, illustrated by Antony Maitland; Longmans, 1968. **Awarded:** Carnegie (honour) 1968.

Devil-in-the-Fog by Leon Garfield, illustrated by Antony Maitland; Kestrel, 1966. **Awarded:** Guardian 1967.

A Dog so Small by A. Philippa Pearce, illustrated by Antony Maitland; Lippincott, 1963. **Awarded:** Spring Book Festival (middle) 1963.

The Drummer Boy by Leon Garfield, illustrated by Antony Maitland; Longmans, 1970. **Awarded:** Carnegie (honour) 1970.

Forbidden Paths of Thual by Victor Kelleher, illustrated by Antony Maitland; Kestrel, 1981. **Awarded:** West Australian Young Readers' (secondary) 1982.

The Ghost Downstairs by Leon Garfield, illustrated by Antony Maitland; Longmans, 1972. **Awarded:** Greenaway (commended) 1972.

The Ghost of Thomas Kempe by Penelope Lively, illustrated by Antony Maitland; Heinemann, 1973. **Awarded:** Carnegie 1973; International Board on Books for Young People (honour list/text/Great Britain) 1976.

Jack Holburn by Leon Garfield, illustrated by Antony Maitland; Pantheon, 1965. **Awarded:** Boys Club 1966.

John Diamond by Leon Garfield, illustrated by Antony Maitland; Kestrel, 1980. **Awarded:** Whitbread 1980.

Mrs. Cockle's Cat by A. Philippa Pearce, illustrated by Antony Maitland; Kestrel, 1961. **Awarded:** Greenaway 1961.

Out of Hand by Emma Smith, illustrated by Antony Maitland; Harcourt, 1964. **Awarded:** Spring Book Festival (middle honor) 1964.

Redemption Greenback by David Johnstone, illustrated by Antony Maitland; Methuen Children's, 1983. **Awarded:** Universe (runnerup) 1984.

Smith by Leon Garfield, illustrated by Antony Maitland; Pantheon, 1967; Constable, 1967; Dell, 1987; Penguin, 1968. **Awarded:** Boston Globe Horn Book (text honor) 1968; Carnegie (commended) 1967; Phoenix 1987.

MAJOR, ALICE

The Chinese Mirror by Alice Major, not illustrated; Irwin Publishing, 1988. **Awarded:** Alberta Writing for Youth 1989.

MAJOR, BEVERLY

Porcupine Stew by Beverly Major, illustrated by Erick Ingraham; Morrow, 1982. **Awarded:** Biennale Illustrations Bratislava (plaque) 1983; Parents' Choice (illustration) 1982.

MAJOR, KEVIN

Awarded: Vicky Metcalf 1992.

Blood Red Ochre by Kevin Major, not illustrated; Doubleday Canada, 1989; Delacorte, 1989. **Awarded:** Canadian Library Assn. (runnerup) 1990; Young Adult Canadian (runnerup) 1990.

Eating Between the Lines by Kevin Major, not illustrated; Doubleday Canada, 1991. **Awarded:** Brimer 1992; Canadian Library Assn. 1992; Young Adult Canadian (runnerup) 1992.

Far from Shore by Kevin Major, not illustrated; Clarke, Irwin, 1980. **Awarded:** Young Adult Canadian Book Award 1981.

Hold Fast by Kevin Major, not illustrated; Clarke, Irwin, 1978. **Awarded:** Canadian Library Assn. 1979; Governor General (author) 1978; International Board on Books for Young People (honour list/text/Canada) 1980; Ruth Schwartz 1978.

MAJOR, TED

The Secret Language of Snow by Terry Tempest Williams and Ted Major, illustrated by Jennifer Dewey; Sierra Club/Pantheon, 1984. **Awarded:** New York Academy of Sciences (Younger) 1985.

MALCOLMSON, ANNE ELIZABETH

Song of Robin Hood edited by Anne B. Malcolmson, illustrated by Virginia Lee Burton; Houghton Mifflin, 1947. **Awarded:** Caldecott (honor) 1948.

MALI, JANE LAWRENCE
Oh, Boy! Babies! by Jane Lawrence Mali and Alison Cragin Herzig, illustrated by Katrina Thomas; Little, Brown, 1980. **Awarded:** American Book Awards (nonfiction hardcover) 1981.

MALKUS, ALIDA WRIGHT SIMS
The Dark Star of Itza by Alida Malkus, illustrated by Lowell Houser; Harcourt, 1930. **Awarded:** Newbery (honor) 1931.

MALLORY, KENNETH
Rescue of the Stranded Whales by Andrea Conley and Kenneth Mallory, illustrated with photographs; Simon & Schuster, 1989. **Awarded:** Book Can Develop Empathy 1990.

MALMGREN, DALLIN
The Whole Nine Yards by Dallin Malmgren, not illustrated; Delacorte, 1986. **Awarded:** Delacorte (honorable mention) 1984.

MALONE, MARY
Andrew Carnegie: Giant of Industry by Mary Malone, illustrated by Marvin Besunder; Garrard, 1969. **Awarded:** New Jersey Institute of Technology 1970.

Annie Sullivan by Mary Malone, illustrated by Lydia Rosier; Putnam, 1971. **Awarded:** New Jersey Institute of Technology 1971.

Dorothea Dix: Hospital Founder by Mary Malone, illustrated by Katherine Sampson; Garrard, 1968. **Awarded:** New Jersey Institute of Technology (biography) 1968.

Liliuokalani: Queen of Hawaii by Mary Malone, illustrated by Louis F. Cary; Garrard, 1975. **Awarded:** New Jersey Institute of Technology 1976.

Milton Hershey: Chocolate King by Mary Malone, illustrated by William Hutchinson; Garrard, 1971. **Awarded:** New Jersey Institute of Technology 1971.

This Was Bridget by Mary Malone, illustrated by Robert Handville; Dodd, Mead, 1960. **Awarded:** Edith Busby 1959.

Young Miss Josie Delaney, Detective by Mary Malone, illustrated by R. S. Horne; Dodd, Mead, 1966. **Awarded:** New Jersey Institute of Technology 1966.

MALONEY, MARGARET CRAWFORD
The Little Mermaid by Hans Christian Andersen retold by Margaret Crawford Maloney, illustrated by Laszlo Gal; Methuen, 1983. **Awarded:** Governor General (illustrator) 1983; Amelia Frances Howard-Gibbon (runnerup) 1984.

MALONEY, RAY
The Impact Zone by Ray Maloney, not illustrated; Delacorte, 1986. **Awarded:** Delacorte 1985.

MALSBERG, EDWARD
Funny Bone Ticklers in Verse and Rhyme by Leland B. Jacobs, illustrated by Edward Malsberg; Garrard, 1973. **Awarded:** New Jersey Institute of Technology 1973.

Hello, People by Leland B. Jacobs, illustrated by Edward Malsberg; Garrard, 1972. **Awarded:** New Jersey Institute of Technology 1972.

Holiday Happenings in Limerick Land by Leland B. Jacobs, illustrated by Edward Malsberg; Garrard, 1972. **Awarded:** New Jersey Institute of Technology 1972.

MALVERN, CORINNE
Spotlight for Danny by Lorraine Beim and Jerrold Beim, illustrated by Corinne Malvern; Harcourt, 1943. **Awarded:** Spring Book Festival (middle honor) 1943.

Valiant Minstrel: The Story of Sir Harry Lauder by Gladys Malvern, illustrated by Corinne Malvern; Messner, 1943. **Awarded:** Julia Ellsworth Ford 1943.

Your Kind Indulgence by Gladys Malvern, illustrated by Corinne Malvern; Messner, 1948. **Awarded:** Spring Book Festival (older honor) 1948.

MALVERN, GLADYS
Valiant Minstrel: The Story of Sir Harry Lauder by Gladys Malvern, illustrated by Corinne Malvern; Messner, 1943. **Awarded:** Julia Ellsworth Ford 1943.

Your Kind Indulgence by Gladys Malvern, illustrated by Corinne Malvern; Messner, 1948. **Awarded:** Spring Book Festival (older honor) 1948.

MANDELA, ZINDZI
Black as I Am by Zindzi Mandela and Peter Magubane, foreword by Andrew Young, illustrated; Guild of Tudors Press, 1978. **Awarded:** Korczak (for children) 1981.

MANES, STEPHEN
Be a Perfect Person in Just Three Days by Stephen Manes, illustrated by Tom Huffman; Houghton Mifflin, 1982. **Awarded:** California Young Reader (Intermediate) 1988; CRABbery (honor) 1983; Georgia Children's 1987; Nene 1986; Charlie May Simon 1984-85; Sunshine 1986; Surrey School 1985.

MANGURIAN, DAVID
Lito, the Shoeshine Boy by Lito Chirinos, told to and translated by David Mangurian, photographs by David Mangurian; Four Winds, 1975. **Awarded:** Children's Book Showcase 1976.

MANHEIM, RALPH
Nutcracker by E. T. A. Hoffmann, translated by Ralph Manheim, illustrated by Maurice Sendak; Crown, 1984. **Awarded:** New York Times Best Illustrated 1984.

MANLEY, RUTH
The Plum-rain Scroll by Ruth Manley, illustrated by Marianne Yamaguchi; Hodder & Stoughton Australia, 1978. **Awarded:** Children's Book Council of Australia (book of the year) 1979.

MANNING-SANDERS, RUTH
A Book of Ghosts and Goblins by Ruth Manning-Sanders, illustrated by Robin Jacques; Methuen, 1968. **Awarded:** Biennale Illustrations Bratislava (plaque) 1969.

A Bundle of Ballads compiled by Ruth Manning-Sanders, illustrated by William Stobbs; Oxford, 1959. **Awarded:** Greenaway 1959.

MANNIX, DANIEL P.
Awarded: L. Frank Baum 1976.

MANOS, HELEN
Best and Fairest by Helen Manos. **Awarded:** Mary Grant Bruce Story Award (Open $500) 1991.

MANSELL, DOM
The Selfish Giant by Oscar Wilde, illustrated by Dom Mansell; Walker Books, 1986. **Awarded:** Mother Goose (runnerup) 1987.

MANTELE, OZMA BAUM
Awarded: L. Frank Baum 1984.

MANTON, JO
see GITTINGS, JO MANTON

MARASLIS, DEMETRA
The Seeing Stick by Jane Yolen, illustrated by Demetra Maraslis and Remy Charlip; Crowell, 1977. **Awarded:** Christopher (ages 6-9) 1978.

MARCELLINO, FRED
Puss in Boots by Charles Perrault, illustrated by Fred Marcellino; Farrar Straus Giroux, 1990. **Awarded:** Caldecott (Honor) 1991; Parents' Choice (Picture Book) 1990; Reading Magic Award 1990.

The Steadfast Tin Soldier by Hans Christian Andersen, illustrated by Fred Marcellino; HarperCollins, 1992. **Awarded:** Parents Choice (Picture Books) 1992.

MARCHER, MARION W.
Monarch Butterfly by Marion W. Marcher, illustrated by Barbara Latham; Hale, 1954. **Awarded:** New Jersey Institute of Technology (science) 1963.

MARCHETTA, MELINA
Looking for Alibrandi by Melina Marchetta, not illustrated; Puffin, 1992. **Awarded:** Australian Multicultural (senior) 1993; Children's Book Council of Australia (book of the year older) 1993.

MARCHIORI, CARLOS
Sally Go Round the Sun by Edith Fowke, illustrated by Carlos Marchiori; McClelland & Stewart, 1969. **Awarded:** Canadian Library Assn. 1970.

MARDON, JOHN
Hello, Come In by Ida DeLage, illustrated by John Mardon; Garrard, 1971. **Awarded:** New Jersey Institute of Technology 1971.

MARGOLIS, RICHARD J.
Secrets of a Small Brother by Richard J. Margolis, illustrated by Donald Carrick; Macmillan, 1984. **Awarded:** Christopher (ages 8-10) 1985.

MARI, IELA
The Magic Balloon written and illustrated by Iela Mari; Phillips, 1969. **Awarded:** Spring Book Festival (picture book honor) 1969.

MARINO, DOROTHY
Little Angela and Her Puppy written and illustrated by Dorothy Marino; Lippincott, 1954. **Awarded:** Helen Dean Fish 1954.

Tony of the Ghost Towns by Marie H. Bloch, illustrated by Dorothy Marino; Coward, 1956. **Awarded:** Spring Book Festival (middle honor) 1956.

MARK, JAN
Aquarius by Jan Mark, not illustrated; Kestrel, 1982. **Awarded:** Observer Teenage Fiction (cowinner) 1982.

Handles by Jan Mark, illustrated by David Parkins; Kestrel, 1983; Atheneum, 1985. **Awarded:** Carnegie 1983.

Nothing to Be Afraid of by Jan Mark, illustrated by David Parkins; Kestrel, 1980. **Awarded:** Carnegie (highly commended) 1980; Guardian (special prize) 1981.

Strat and Chatto by Jan Mark, illustrated by David Hughes; Walker Books, 1989. **Awarded:** Mother Goose 1990.

Thunder and Lightnings by Jan Mark, illustrated by Jim Russell; Kestrel, 1976. **Awarded:** Carnegie 1976; Guardian (commended) 1977.

Trouble Half-Way by Jan Mark, illustrated by David Parkins; Viking Kestrel, 1985. **Awarded:** Guardian (runnerup) 1986.

MARKS, ALAN
Storm by Kevin Crossley-Holland, illustrated by Alan Marks; Heinemann, 1985. **Awarded:** Carnegie 1985.

MARLOW, ERIC
Rosa Parks by Eloise Greenfield, illustrated by Eric Marlow; Crowell, 1973. **Awarded:** Carter G. Woodson 1974.

MARRAY, DENIS
Duck Street Gang by Denis Marray, not illustrated; Hamish Hamilton, 1984. **Awarded:** Guardian (runnerup) 1985.

MARRIN, ALBERT
1812: The War Nobody Won by Albert Marrin, illustrated with photographs and prints; Atheneum, 1985. **Awarded:** Boston Globe Horn Book (nonfiction honor) 1985.

MARRIOTT, PAT
Joy Is Not Herself by Josephine Lee, illustrated by Pat Marriott; Harcourt, 1963. **Awarded:** Spring Book Festival (middle honor) 1963.

Midnight is a Place by Joan Aiken, illustrated by Pat Marriott; Viking, 1974; Cape, 1974. (only the Cape edition is illustrated). **Awarded:** New York Times Notable Books 1974.

Moffatt's Road by Rachel Anderson, illustrated by Pat Marriott; Cape, 1978. **Awarded:** Guardian (commended) 1979.

The Wolves of Willoughby Chase by Joan Aiken, illustrated by Pat Marriott; Doubleday, 1963. **Awarded:** Lewis Carroll Shelf 1965.

MARS, WITOLD TADEUSZ
Bond of the Fire by Anthony T. Fon Eisen, illustrated by W. T. Mars; World, 1965. **Awarded:** Lewis Carroll Shelf 1965.

A Drink for Little Red Diker by Catherine Woolley, illustrated by W. T. Mars; Morrow, 1963. **Awarded:** New Jersey Institute of Technology 1963.

Ghost of Summer by Eve Bunting, illustrated by W. T. Mars; Warne, 1977. **Awarded:** Southern California Council (best fiction) 1978.

Thirty-one Brothers and Sisters by Reba Paeff Mirsky, illustrated by W. T. Mars; Follett, 1952. **Awarded:** Charles W. Follett 1952.

MARSDEN, JOHN
So Much to Tell You by John Marsden, not illustrated; Walter McVitty Books, 1987; Little Brown (Joy Street), 1989. **Awarded:** Children's Book Council of Australia (Book of the Year Older) 1988; Christopher (young adult) 1990; Diabetes Australia Alan Marshall 1988; KOALA (Secondary) 1989.

MARSH, GWEN
Grishka and the Bear by Rene Guillot, translated by Gwen Marsh, illustrated by Joan Kiddell-Monroe; Criterion, 1959. **Awarded:** Boys Club 1961; Lewis Carroll Shelf 1961.

Three Hundred Ninety-seventh White Elephant by Rene Guillot, translated by Gwen Marsh, illustrated by Moyra Leatham; Phillips, 1957. **Awarded:** Lewis Carroll Shelf 1958.

MARSHAK, ILIA IAKOVLEVICH
see ILIM, M.

MARSHAK, SAMUEL
The Pup Grew Up! by Samuel Marshak, illustrated by Vladimir Radunsky; Henry Holt, 1989. **Awarded:** Reading Magic 1989.

MARSHALL, ARCHIBALD
The Dragon by Archibald Marshall, illustrated by Edward Ardizzone; Dutton, 1967. **Awarded:** Spring Book Festival (picture book honor) 1967.

MARSHALL, BERNARD G.

Cedric the Forester by Bernard G. Marshall, not illustrated; Appleton, 1921. **Awarded:** Newbery (honor) 1922.

MARSHALL, CATHERINE

Christy by Catherine Marshall, not illustrated; McGraw Hill, 1967. **Awarded:** Emphasis on Reading (grades 10-12) 1981-82.

MARSHALL, EDWARD

(pseudonym of James Marshall)

Space Case by Edward Marshall, illustrated by James Marshall; Dial, 1980. **Awarded:** California Young Reader (primary) 1986; Colorado Children's 1983; Washington Children's Choice 1983.

MARSHALL, JAMES

Awarded: University of Southern Mississippi 1992.

The Adventures of Isabel by Ogden Nash, illustrated by James Marshall; Little Brown, 1991. **Awarded:** Parents' Choice (Story Book) 1991.

All the Way Home by Lore Segal, illustrated by James Marshall; Farrar, 1973. **Awarded:** Children's Book Showcase 1974.

Bonzini! The Tattooed Man by Jeffrey Allen, illustrated by James Marshall; Little, Brown, 1976. **Awarded:** Children's Book Showcase 1977.

Fox on the Job written and illustrated by James Marshall; Dial, 1988. **Awarded:** Garden State Children's (Easy to Read) 1991.

George and Martha written and illustrated by James Marshall; Houghton, 1972. **Awarded:** Children's Book Showcase 1973; New York Times Best Illustrated 1972; New York Times Notable Books 1972.

Goldilocks and the Three Bears written and illustrated by James Marshall; Dial, 1988. **Awarded:** Caldecott (honor) 1989; Parents' Choice (Picture Book) 1988.

Miss Nelson Has a Field Day by Harry Allard, illustrated by James Marshall; Houghton Mifflin, 1985. **Awarded:** Golden Sower (K-3) 1987; North Dakota Children's Choice (Younger) 1988.

Miss Nelson Is Back by Harry Allard, illustrated by James Marshall; Houghton Mifflin, 1982. **Awarded:** Colorado 1985; Golden Sower (K-3) 1984; Parents' Choice (literature) 1982.

Miss Nelson Is Missing! by Harry Allard, illustrated by James Marshall; Houghton Mifflin, 1977; Scholastic, 1978. **Awarded:** Arizona 1981; Buckeye (K-3 honor) 1982; California Young Reader Medal (primary) 1982; Georgia Children's Picture Storybook 1980; North Dakota Children's Choice (Younger) 1985; Edgar Allan Poe (runnerup) 1978.

Old Mother Hubbard and Her Wonderful Dog by Sarah Catherine Martin, illustrated by James Marshall; Farrar, Straus, Giroux, 1991. **Awarded:** New York Times Best Illustrated 1991.

Rapscallion Jones written and illustrated by James Marshall; Viking, 1983. **Awarded:** Parents' Choice (literature) 1983.

Rats on the Roof and Other Stories written and illustrated by James Marshall; Dial, 1991. **Awarded:** CRABbery (Honor) 1992; Parents' Choice (Story Book) 1991.

Roger's Umbrella by Daniel Pinkwater, illustrated by James Marshall; Dutton, 1982. **Awarded:** Parents' Choice (literature) 1982.

Space Case by Edward Marshall, illustrated by James Marshall; Dial, 1980. **Awarded:** California Young Reader (primary) 1986; Colorado Children's 1983; Washington Children's Choice 1983.

The Stupids Die by Harry Allard, illustrated by James Marshall; Houghton Mifflin, 1981. **Awarded:** Arizona 1985.

The Stupids Step Out by Harry Allard, illustrated by James Marshall; Houghton, 1974. **Awarded:** Children's Book Showcase 1975.

The Tutti-Frutti Case: Starring the Four Doctors of Goodge by Harry Allard, illustrated by James Marshall; Prentice Hall, 1975. **Awarded:** New York Times Best Illustrated 1975.

MARSHALL, MARGARET

Awarded: Eleanor Farjeon 1980.

MARSHALL, RAY

The Car: Watch it Work by Operating the Moving Diagrams! by Ray Marshall and John Bradley; Viking, 1984. **Awarded:** Redbook (pop- up) 1984.

There Was an Old Woman by Stephen Wyllie, illustrated by Maureen Roffey, paper engineering by Ray Marshall; Harper, 1985. **Awarded:** Redbook 1985.

Watch it Work! The Plane by Ray Marshall and John Bradley; Viking Kestrel, 1985. **Awarded:** Smarties (innovation) 1985.

MARSHALL, ROSAMUND VAN DER ZEE

None but the Brave: A story of Holland by Rosamond Van der Zee Marshall, illustrated by Gregor Duncan; Houghton, 1942. **Awarded:** Spring Book Festival (older) 1942.

MARSTALL, BOB

The Lady and the Spider by Faith McNulty, illustrated by Bob Marstall; Harper & Row, 1986. **Awarded:** Book Can Develop Empathy 1990.

MARTCHENKO, MICHAEL

Thomas' Snowsuit by Robert Munsch, illustrated by Michael Martchenko; Annick Press, 1985. **Awarded:** Schwartz 1986.

MARTELL, SUZANNE

Awarded: Vicky Metcalf 1976.

The King's Daughter by Suzanne Martell, translated by David Toby Homel and Margaret Rose; Douglas & MacIntyre, 1980. **Awarded:** International Board on Books for Young People (translation/Canada) 1982; Schwartz 1981.

MARTEN, MICHAEL

Worlds Within Worlds: A Journey into the Unknown by Michael Marten, John Chesterman, John May, and John Trux, illustrated with photographs; Holt, 1977. **Awarded:** New York Academy of Sciences (older honor) 1979.

MARTIN, ANN M.

Bummer Summer by Ann M. Martin, not illustrated; Holiday House, 1983. **Awarded:** New Jersey Institute of Technology 1983.

Babysitters on Board! by ann M. Martin, not illustrated; Apple, 1988. **Awarded:** Young Teens 1989.

Missing Since Monday by Ann M. Martin, not illustrated; Holiday House, 1986. **Awarded:** New Jersey Institute of Technology 1987.

Ten Kids, No Pets by Ann M. Martin, not illustrated; Holiday House, 1988. **Awarded:** Young Hoosier (grades 4-6) 1991; Young Reader's Choice 1991.

MARTIN, BARRY

Quest for Freedom: Bolivar and the South American Revolution by Paul Rink, illustrated by Barry Martin; Simon & Schuster, 1968. **Awarded:** Commonwealth Club of California 1968.

MARTIN, JR., BILL

Chicka Chicka Boom Boom by Bill Martin, Jr. and John Archambault, illustrated by Lois Ehlert; Simon & Schuster, 1989. **Awarded:** Boston Globe (Picture Book Honor) 1990; Kentucky Bluegrass (grades K-3) 1991.

Polar Bear, Polar Bear, What Do You Hear? by Bill Martin, Jr., illustrated by Eric Carle; Holt, 1991. **Awarded:** Redbook 1991.

MARTIN, DAVID STONE

The Holocaust: A History of Courage and Resistance by Bea Stadtler, illustrated by David Stone Martin; Behrman, 1974. **Awarded:** Jewish Book Council 1974.

MARTIN, DICK

Awarded: L. Frank Baum 1961.

The Forbidden Fountain of Oz by Lauren Lynn McGraw and Eloise Jarvis McGraw, illustrated by Dick Martin; International Wizard of Oz Club, 1980. **Awarded:** L. Frank Baum (cowinner) 1983.

Merry Go Round in Oz by Lauren McGraw Wagner and Eloise Jarvis McGraw, designed and illustrated by Dick Martin; Reilly & Lee, 1963. **Awarded:** L. Frank Baum (co-winner) 1983.

MARTIN, JAMES HENRY

Aircraft of Today and Tomorrow by James Henry Martin and William Donald Martin, illustrated with photographs; Angus & Robertson, 1953. **Awarded:** Children's Book Council of Australia 1953.

MARTIN, JOSEPH PLUMB

Yankee Doodle Boy: A Young Soldier's Adventure in the American Revolution told by himself by Joseph Plumb Martin, edited by George F. Scheer, illustrated by Victor Mays; Scott, 1964. **Awarded:** Edison Mass Media (America's past) 1965.

MARTIN, PATRICIA MILES

(pseudonyms are Patricia Miles and Miska Miles)

Annie and the Old One by Miska Miles, illustrated by Peter Parnall; Atlantic-Little, 1971. **Awarded:** Art Books for Children 1973; Christopher (ages 8-12) 1972; Commonwealth Club of California 1971; Newbery (honor) 1972; Woodward Park School 1972.

The Gods in Winter by Patricia Miles, not illustrated; Hamish Hamilton, 1978. **Awarded:** International Board on Books for Young People (text/Great Britain) 1980.

The Pointed Brush by Patricia Miles Martin, illustrated by Roger Duvoisin; Lothrop, 1959. **Awarded:** Spring Book Festival (ages 4-8 honor) 1959.

MARTIN, RAPHAEL P.

Awarded: Lucile M. Pannell 1983.

MARTIN, RICHARD

Awarded: Children's Reading Round Table 1971.

MARTIN, RON

School Is not a Missile Range by Norah Smaridge, illustrated by Ron Martin; Abingdon, 1977. **Awarded:** New Jersey Institute of Technology 1978.

MARTIN, SARAH CATHERINE

Old Mother Hubbard and Her Wonderful Dog by Sarah Catherine Martin, illustrated by James Marshall; Farrar, Straus, Giroux, 1991. **Awarded:** New York Times Best Illustrated 1991.

MARTIN, WILLIAM DONALD

Aircraft of Today and Tomorrow by William Donald Martin and James Henry Martin; illustrated with photographs; Angus & Robertson, 1953. **Awarded:** Children's Book Council of Australia 1953.

MARTINEZ, ELIZABETH SUTHERLAND

Viva la Raza! The Struggle of the Mexican-American People by Elizabeth Sutherland Martinez and Enriqueta Longeaux y Vasquez, not illustrated; Doubleday, 1974. **Awarded:** Jane Addams (honor) 1975.

MARTINEZ, JOHN

Land Rush by Carl G. Hodges, illustrated by John Martinez; Duell- Sloan, 1965. **Awarded:** Western Heritage 1966.

MARTINI, TERI

All Because of Jill by Teri Martini, not illustrated; Westminster, 1976. **Awarded:** New Jersey Institute of Technology 1977.

The Mystery Waters of Tonbridge Wells by Teri Martini, illustrated by Linda Boehm; Westminster, 1975. **Awarded:** New Jersey Institute of Technology 1976.

MARUKI, TOSHI

Hiroshima no Pika written and illustrated by Toshi Maruki; Lothrop, Lee & Shepard, 1982. **Awarded:** Jane Addams 1983; Batchelder 1983; Boston Globe Horn Book (nonfiction honor) 1983.

MARVIN, FREDERIC

Grover by Bill Cleaver and Vera Cleaver, illustrated by Frederic Marvin; Lippincott, 1970. **Awarded:** National Book Award (finalist) 1971.

MASHA

see STERN, MARIE SIMCHOW

MASON, EVELYN

A Sister for Sam by Evelyn Mason, illustrated by Tom Cooke; Children's Press, 1983. **Awarded:** North Dakota Children's Choice (younger) 1984.

MASON, GEORGE

Awarded: Eva L. Gordon 1978.

MASON, MIRIAM E.

Becky and Her Brave Cat, Bluegrass by Miriam E. Mason, illustrated by Robert MacLean; Macmillan, 1960. **Awarded:** Indiana Authors Day (young children) 1961.

MASSEE, MAY

Awarded: Women's National Book Assn. 1950.

MASSIE, DIANE REDFIELD

Chameleon the Spy and the Case of the Vanishing Jewels written and illustrated by Diane R. Massie; Crowell, 1984. **Awarded:** Edgar Allan Poe (runnerup) 1985.

Chameleon Was a Spy written and illustrated by Diane Redfield Massie; Crowell, 1979. **Awarded:** Edgar Allan Poe (runnerup) 1980.

A Turtle, and a Loon, and other Fables by Diane Redfield Massie; Atheneum, 1965. **Awarded:** Spring Book Festival (picture book honor) 1965.

MASTERMAN-SMITH, VIRGINIA
The Treasure Trap by Virginia Masterman-Smith, illustrated by Roseanne Litzinger; Four Winds, 1979. **Awarded:** New Jersey Institute of Technology 1981.

MASTERS, KELLY RAY
see BALL, ZACHARY

MASUDA, MODOKI
Snails by Sylvia A. Johnson, photographs by Modoki Masuda; Lerner, 1982. **Awarded:** New York Academy of Sciences (special award) 1983.

MATAS, CAROL
Code Name Kris by Carol Matas, not illustrated; Scribner, 1990. **Awarded:** Woodward Park 1991.

Jesper by Carol Matas, not illustrated; Lester & Orpen Dennys, 1989. **Awarded:** Young Adult Canadian (Runnersup) 1990.

Lisa by Carol Matas, illustrated with maps; Lester & Orpen Dennys, 1987. **Awarded:** Bilson 1988.

MATH, IRWIN
More Wires and Watts by Irwin Math, illustrated by Hal Keith; Scribner, 1988. **Awarded:** New York Academy of Sciences (Younger Honor) 1989.

Morse, Marconi and You: Understanding and Building Telegraph, Telephone and Radio Sets by Irwin Math, illustrated by Hal Keith; Scribner, 1979. **Awarded:** New York Academy of Sciences (older honor) 1980.

MATHER, COTTON
Atlas of Kentucky edited by P. P. Karen and Cotton Mather, illustrated; University Press of Kentucky, 1977. **Awarded:** Jesse Stuart 1978.

MATHER, KIRTLEY F.
The Earth Beneath Us by Kirtley F. Mather, illustrated by Howard Morris, photographs by Josef Muench; Random House, 1964. **Awarded:** Edison Mass Media (science book youth) 1965.

MATHERS, PETRA
Borreguita and the Coyote by Verna Aardema, illustrated by Petra Mathers; Knopf, 1991. **Awarded:** Redbook 1991.

I'm Flying! by Alan Wade, illustrated by Petra Mathers; Knopf, 1990. **Awarded:** New York Times Best Illustrated 1990.

Molly's New Washing Machine by Laura Geringer, illustrated by Petra Mathers; Harper & Row, 1986. **Awarded:** New York Times Best Illustrated 1986.

Sophie and Lou written and illustrated by Petra Mathers; HarperCollins, 1991. **Awarded:** Boston Globe Horn Book (Picture Book Honor) 1991; Parents' Choice (Story Book) 1991.

Theodor and Mr. Balbini written and illustrated by Petra Mathers; Harper & Row, 1988. **Awarded:** New York Times Best Illustrated 1988.

MATHEWS, VIRGINIA
Awarded: American Association of School Librarians 1989; Women's National Book Assn. 1965.

MATHIESEN, EGON
A Jungle in the Wheat Field written and illustrated by Egon Mathiesen; McDowell, Obolensky, 1960. **Awarded:** Spring Book Festival (ages 4-8 honor) 1960.

MATHIS, SHARON BELL
The Hundred Penny Box by Sharon Bell Mathis, illustrated by Leo Dillon and Diane Dillon; Viking, 1975. **Awarded:** Boston Globe Horn Book (text honor) 1975; New York Times Notable Books 1975; Newbery (honor) 1976.

Ray Charles by Sharon Bell Mathis, illustrated by George Ford; Crowell, 1973. **Awarded:** Coretta Scott King 1974.

Sidewalk Story by Sharon Bell Mathis, illustrated by Leo Carty; Viking, 1971. **Awarded:** Council on Interracial Books (ages 7-11) 1969.

MATHISON, MELISSA
E. T.: Extra-Terrestrial Storybook by William Kotzwinkle, based on the screenplay by Melissa Mathison, not illustrated; Putnam, 1982. **Awarded:** Buckeye (grades K-3) 1984; North Dakota Children's Choice (younger) 1983.

MATSUNO, MASAKU
Taro and a Bamboo Shoot by Masaku Matsuno, illustrated by Yasuo Segawa; Fukuinkan Shoten, 1963. **Awarded:** Biennale Illustrations Bratislava (grand prix) 1967.

MATTINGLY, CHRISTOBEL
The Miracle Tree by Christobel Mattingly, illustrated by Marianne Yamaguchi; Hodder & Stoughton, 1985; Harcourt Brace Jovanovich, 1985. **Awarded:** Australian Christian Book of the Year Children's Award 1986.

Rummage by Christobel Mattingly, illustrated by Patricia Mullins; Angus & Robertson, 1981. **Awarded:** Children's Book Council of Australia (book of the year commended) 1982; Children's Book Council of Australia (junior book of the year) 1982.

MATUTE, ANA MARIA
Awarded: Hans Christian Andersen (highly commended author/Spain) 1970, 1972.

MAURER, RICHARD
Airborne: The Search for the Secret of Flight by Richard Maurer, illustrated with color photographs; Simon & Schuster, in association with WGBH, Boston, 1990. **Awarded:** American Institute of Physics 1991.

MAURER, WERNER
The Cucumber King: A Story with a Beginning, a Middle and an End by Christine Nostlinger, translated by Anthea Bell, illustrated by Werner Maurer; Abelard Schuman, 1975. **Awarded:** International Board on Books for Young People (translation/Great Britain) 1978.

MAUSER, PAT RHOADS
A Bundle of Sticks by Pat Rhoads Mauser, illustrated by Gail Owens; Atheneum, 1982. **Awarded:** Dorothy Canfield Fisher 1984; Mark Twain 1985.

MAWRINA, TATJANA
Awarded: Hans Christian Andersen (illustrator) 1976.

MAXNER, JOYCE
Nicholas Cricket by Joyce Maxner, illustrated by William Joyce; Harper & Row, 1989. **Awarded:** New York Times Best Illustrated 1989.

MAXWELL, FLORENZ WEBBE
The Rock Cried Out by Florenz Webbe Maxwell; manuscript. **Awarded:** Council on Interracial Books (African-American) 1971-72.

MAXWELL, JOHN
Ten Tall Texans by Lee McGiffin, illustrated by John Maxwell; Lothrop, 1956. **Awarded:** Spring Book Festival (middle honor) 1956.

MAXWELL, WILLIAM
The Heavenly Tenants by William Maxwell, illustrated by Ilonka Karasz; Harper, 1946. **Awarded:** Newbery (honor) 1947.

MAY, JOHN
Worlds within Worlds: A Journey into the Unknown by John May, John Trux, Michael Marten, and John Chesterman, illustrated with photographs; Holt, 1977. **Awarded:** New York Academy of Sciences (older honor) 1979.

MAY, KARA
Knickerlass Nicola by Kara May, illustrated by Doffy Weir; Macmillan, 1989. **Awarded:** Nottinghamshire (Acorn) 1990.

MAYAKOVSKY, VLADIMIR
Timothy's Horse by Vladimir Mayakovsky, adapted by Guy Daniels, illustrated by Flavio Constantini; Pantheon, 1970. **Awarded:** New York Times Best Illustrated 1970.

MAYES, SUSAN
What Makes a Flower Grow? by Susan Mayes, illustrated by Brin Edwards and Mike Pringle; Usborne, 1989. **Awarded:** Science Book Prizes 1990.

What Makes It Rain? by Susan Mayes, illustrated by Richard Deverell and Mike Pringle; Usborne, 1989. **Awarded:** Science Book Prizes 1990.

What's Under the Ground? by Susan Mayes, illustrated by Mike Pringle, Brin Edwards, and John Scorey; Usborne, 1989. **Awarded:** Science Book Prizes 1990.

Where Does Electricity Come From? by Susan Mayes, illustrated by John Shackell and John Scorey; Usborne, 1989. **Awarded:** Science Book Prizes 1990.

MAYER, CAROLYN
Awarded: Outstanding Pennsylvania Author 1990.

MAYER, MARIANNA
Beauty and the Beast retold by Marianna Mayer, illustrated by Mercer Mayer; Four Winds, 1978. **Awarded:** Michigan Young Readers (division I) 1982.

The Unicorn and the Lake by Marianna Mayer, illustrated by Michael Hague; Dial, 1982. **Awarded:** Colorado Children's 1984; Georgia Children's Picture Storybook 1986; Washington Children's Choice 1986.

MAYER, MERCER
Beauty and the Beast retold by Marianna Mayer, illustrated by Mercer Mayer; Four Winds, 1978. **Awarded:** Michigan Young Readers (division I) 1982.

A Boy, a Dog, and a Frog written and illustrated by Mercer Mayer; Dial, 1967. **Awarded:** Art Books for Children 1973.

Everyone Knows What a Dragon Looks Like by Jay Williams, illustrated by Mercer Mayer; Four Winds, 1976. **Awarded:** Irma Simonton Black 1976; New York Times Best Illustrated 1976.

Frog Goes to Dinner written and illustrated by Mercer Mayer; Dial, 1974. **Awarded:** Art Books for Children 1976, 1977, 1978.

The Great Brain Does it Again by John D. Fitzgerald, illustrated by Mercer Mayer; Dial, 1975. **Awarded:** Georgia Children's 1980; Young Readers Choice 1978.

Great Brain Reforms by John D. Fitzgerald, illustrated by Mercer Mayer; Dial, 1973. **Awarded:** Young Readers Choice 1976.

Jack Tar by Jean Russell Larson, illustrated by Mercer Mayer; Macrae, 1970. **Awarded:** Lewis Carroll Shelf 1973.

Liza Lou and the Yeller Belly Swamp written and illustrated by Mercer Mayer; Parents Magazine Press, 1976; Four Winds, 1980. **Awarded:** California Young Reader Medal (primary) 1983.

There's an Alligator Under My Bed written and illustrated by Mercer Mayer; Dial, 1987. **Awarded:** Florida Reading Association 1990.

What Do You Do with a Kangaroo? written and illustrated by Mercer Mayer; Scholastic/Four Winds, 1973. **Awarded:** Art Books for Children 1975.

While the Horses Galloped to London by Mabel Watts, illustrated by Mercer Mayer; Parents, 1971. **Awarded:** Children's Book Showcase 1974.

MAYER-SKUMANZ, LENE
Story of Brother Francis by Lene Mayer-Skumanz, illustrated by Alicia Sancha; Ave Maria Press, 1983. **Awarded:** Catholic Book Awards (Children's) 1984.

MAYNE, WILLIAM
All the King's Men by William Mayne, not illustrated; Jonathan Cape, 1982. **Awarded:** International Board on Books for Young People (writing/Great Britain) 1984.

The Blemyahs by William Mayne, illustrated by Juan Wijngaard; Walker, 1987. **Awarded:** W. H. Smith (2nd prize) 1988.

The Blue Boat by William Mayne, illustrated by Geraldine Spence; Oxford, 1957. **Awarded:** Carnegie (commended) 1957.

The Blue Book of Hob Stories by William Mayne, illustrated by Patrick Benson; Walker Books, 1984. **Awarded:** Mother Goose 1984.

Choristers' Cake by William Mayne, illustrated by C. Walter Hodges; Oxford, 1956. **Awarded:** Carnegie (commended) 1956.

Earthfasts by William Mayne, not illustrated; Dutton, 1966. **Awarded:** Lewis Carroll Shelf 1968.

Gideon Ahoy! written and illustrated by William Mayne; Delacorte, 1989. **Awarded:** Boston Globe (Fiction honor) 1989.

A Grass Rope by William Mayne, illustrated by Lynton Lamb; Oxford, 1957. **Awarded:** Carnegie 1957.

The Green Book of Hob Stories by William Mayne, illustrated by Patrick Benson; Walker, 1984. **Awarded:** Mother Goose 1984.

Low Tide by William Mayne, not illustrated; Cape, 1991; Delacorte, 1993. **Awarded:** Guardian 1993.

The Member for the Marsh by William Mayne, illustrated by Lynton Lamb; Oxford, 1956. **Awarded:** Carnegie (commended) 1956.

The Mouldy by William Mayne, illustrated by Nicola Bayley; Cape, 1983; Knopf, 1983. **Awarded:** Maschler (runnerup) 1983.

The Patchwork Cat by William Mayne, illustrated by Nicola Bayley; Cape, 1981. **Awarded:** Greenaway (commended) 1981.

Ravensgill by William Mayne, not illustrated; Hamilton, 1970. **Awarded:** Carnegie (honour) 1970.

The Red Book of Hob Stories by William Mayne, illustrated by Patrick Benson; Walker Books, 1984. **Awarded:** Mother Goose 1984.

A *Swarm in May* by William Mayne, illustrated by C. Walter Hodges; Oxford, 1955. **Awarded:** Carnegie (commended) 1955.

A *Year and a Day* by William Mayne, illustrated by Krystyna Turska; Hamish Hamilton, 1976. **Awarded:** International Board on Books for Young People (text/Great Britain) 1978; New York Times Notable Books 1976.

The Yellow Book of Hob Stories by William Mayne, illustrated by Patrick Benson; Walker, 1984. **Awarded:** Mother Goose 1984.

MAYO, FRANK
Cadbury's Coffin by Glendon Swarthout and Kathryn Swarthout, illustrated by Frank Mayo; Doubleday, 1982. **Awarded:** Edgar Allan Poe (runnerup) 1983.

MAYO, GRETCHEN
I Hate My Name by Eva Grant, illustrated by Gretchen Mayo; Raintree, 1980. **Awarded:** New Jersey Institute of Technology 1981.

MAYS, LUCINDA
The Other Shore by Lucinda Mays, not illustrated; Atheneum, 1979. **Awarded:** Society of Midland Authors 1980.

MAYS, VICTOR
A Blow for Victory by Stephen W. Meader, illustrated by Victor Mays; Harcourt, 1965. **Awarded:** New Jersey Institute of Technology (ages 15-16) 1966.

Fast Iron written and illustrated by Victor Mays; Houghton, 1953. **Awarded:** Boys Club 1954.

Martin Luther King, Jr.: Man of Peace by Lillie Patterson, illustrated by Victor Mays; Garrard, 1969. **Awarded:** Coretta Scott King 1970.

Model-A Mule by Robert J. Willis, illustrated by Victor Mays; Follett, 1959. **Awarded:** Charles W. Follett 1959.

Phantom of the Blockade by Stephen W. Meader, illustrated by Victor Mays; Harcourt, 1962. **Awarded:** New Jersey Institute of Technology (ages 12-up) 1962.

Trail Blazer of the Seas by Jean Lee Latham, illustrated by Victor Mays; Houghton Mifflin, 1956. **Awarded:** Boys Club 1957.

Yankee Doodle Boy: A Young Soldier's Adventure in the American Revolution Told by Himself by Joseph Plumb Martin, edited by George F. Scheer, illustrated by Victor Mays; Scott, 1964. **Awarded:** Edison Mass Media (America's past) 1965.

MAZER, ANNE
The Salamander Room by Anne Mazer, illustrated by Steve Johnson; Knopf, 1991. **Awarded:** Minnesota (younger children) 1992.

MAZER, HARRY
The Last Mission by Harry Mazer, not illustrated; Delacorte, 1979. **Awarded:** New York Times Notable Books 1979.

When the Phone Rang by Harry Mazer, not illustrated; Scholastic, 1985. **Awarded:** West Australian (Secondary) 1989.

MAZER, NORMA FOX
After the Rain by Norma Fox Mazer, not illustrated; Morrow, 1987. **Awarded:** Newbery (honor) 1988.

Dear Bill, Remember Me? And Other Stories by Norma Fox Mazer, not illustrated; Delacorte, 1976. **Awarded:** Lewis Carroll Shelf 1978; Christopher (ages 12-up) 1977; New York Times Notable Books 1976.

Downtown by Norma Fox Mazer, not illustrated; Morrow, 1984. **Awarded:** New York Times Notable 1984.

A Figure of Speech by Norma Fox Mazer, not illustrated; Delacorte, 1973. **Awarded:** National Book Award (finalist) 1974.

Saturday, the Twelfth of October by Norma Fox Mazer, not illustrated; Delacorte, 1975. **Awarded:** Lewis Carroll Shelf 1976.

Silver by Norma Fox Mazer, not illustrated; Morrow, 1988. **Awarded:** Iowa Teen 1991.

Taking Terri Mueller by Norma Fox Mazer, not illustrated; Avon, 1981; Morrow, 1983. **Awarded:** California Young Reader (junior high) 1985; Edgar Allan Poe 1982.

When We First Met by Norma Fox Mazer, not illustrated; Scholastic, 1984. **Awarded:** Iowa Teen 1986.

McBRATNEY, SAM
Put the Saddle on the Pig by Sam McBratney; Methuen, 1992. **Awarded:** Bisto (Teenage Fiction) 1993.

McCABE, EUGENE
Cyril: The Quest of an Orphan Squirrel by Eugene McCabe, illustrated by Al O'Donnell; O'Brien Press, 1986. **Awarded:** Reading Association of Ireland 1987.

McCAFFREY, ANNE
Dragonsong by Anne McCaffrey, illustrated by Laura Lydecker; Atheneum, 1976. **Awarded:** Children's Book Showcase 1977.

McCAIG, ROB
Growing Up by Susan Meredith, illustrated by Sue Stitt, Kuo Kang Chen and Rob McCaig; Usborne, 1985. **Awarded:** Times Educational Supplement (senior) 1985.

McCAIN, MURRAY
Books! by Murray McCain, illustrated by John Alcorn; Simon & Schuster, 1962. **Awarded:** New York Times Best Illustrated 1962.

McCANN, GERALD
The Cornhusk Doll by Eleanor Reindollar Wilcox, illustrated by Gerald McCann; Dodd, Mead, 1956. **Awarded:** Edith Busby 1955.

McCAUGHREAN, GERALDINE
A Little Lower Than the Angels by Geraldine McCaughrean, not illustrated; Oxford University Press, 1987. **Awarded:** Whitbread 1987.

A Pack of Lies: Twelve Stories in One by Geraldine McCaughrean, not illustrated; Oxford University Press, 1988. **Awarded:** Carnegie 1988; Guardian Award 1989.

McCAUGHREN, TOM
Run Swift, Run Free by Tom McCaughren, illustrated by Jeanette Dunne; Wolfhound Press, 1986. **Awarded:** Bisto (Fiction) 1990; Reading Association of Ireland 1985.

Run To Earth by Tom McCaughren, illustrated by Jeanette Dunne; Wolfhound Press, 1984. **Awarded:** Bisto (Fiction) 1990.

Run With the Wind by Tom McCaughren, illustrated by Jeanette Dunne; Wolfhound Press, 1983. **Awarded:** Bisto (Fiction) 1990.

McCAULEY, JANE R.
Animals Showing Off by Jane R. McCauley, illustrated by Tony Chen; National Geographic, 1988. **Awarded:** Redbook 1988.

McCLINTOCK, BARBARA

Heartaches of a French Cat written and illustrated by Barbara McClintock; Godine, 1989. **Awarded:** New York Times Best Illustrated 1989.

McCLINTON, LEON

Awarded: Council for Wisconsin Writers (juvenile) 1974.

Cross-country Runner by Leon McClinton, not illustrated; Dutton, 1974. **Awarded:** Council for Wisconsin Writers (juvenile) 1975.

McCLOSKEY, ROBERT

Awarded: Regina 1974.

Blueberries for Sal written and illustrated by Robert McCloskey; Viking, 1948. **Awarded:** Caldecott (honor) 1949; Ohioana 1949.

Henry Reed, Inc. by Keith Robertson, illustrated by Robert McCloskey; Viking, 1958. **Awarded:** William Allen White 1961.

Henry Reed's Baby-sitting Service by Keith Robertson, illustrated by Robert McCloskey; Viking, 1966. **Awarded:** Nene 1970; William Allen White 1969; Young Readers Choice 1969.

Homer Price written and illustrated by Robert McCloskey; Viking, 1943. **Awarded:** Young Readers Choice 1947.

Journey Cake, Ho! by Ruth Sawyer, illustrated by Robert McCloskey; Viking, 1953. **Awarded:** Caldecott (honor) 1954.

Junket by Anne H. White, illustrated by Robert McCloskey; Viking, 1955. **Awarded:** Spring Book Festival (middle honor) 1955.

Make Way for Ducklings written and illustrated by Robert McCloskey; Viking, 1941. **Awarded:** Caldecott 1942.

One Morning in Maine written and illustrated by Robert McCloskey; Viking, 1952. **Awarded:** Caldecott (honor) 1953; Children's Choice [Arizona] (picture book) 1983; Spring Book Festival (picture book honor) 1952.

Time of Wonder written and illustrated by Robert McCloskey; Viking, 1957. **Awarded:** Caldecott 1958; Ohioana 1958.

McCLUNG, ROBERT M.

Awarded: Eva L. Gordon 1966.

America's Endangered Birds: Programs and People Working to Save Them by Robert M. McClung, illustrated by George Founds; Morrow, 1979. **Awarded:** Golden Kite (nonfiction honor) 1979.

Gypsy Moth: It's History in America written and illustrated by Robert M. McClung; Morrow, 1974. **Awarded:** New York Academy of Sciences (older honor) 1975.

Hugh Glass, Mountain Man by Robert McClung, illustrated; Morrow, 1990. **Awarded:** Soaring Eagle (Grades 7-12) 1993.

Peeper, First Voice of Spring by Robert M. McClung, illustrated by Carol Lerner; Morrow, 1977. **Awarded:** Golden Kite (nonfiction) 1977.

McCLURE, GILLIAN

Tog the Ribber: or, Granny's Tale by Paul Coltman, illustrated by Gillian McClure; Deutsch, 1985. **Awarded:** Greenaway (commended) 1985.

McCORD, DAVID

Awarded: Chandler Reward of Merit 1966; National Council of Teachers of English Award for Excellence in Poetry for Children 1977.

One at a Time: His collected Poems for the Young by David McCord, illustrated by Henry B. Kane; Little, Brown, 1977. **Awarded:** National Book Award (finalist) 1978.

The Star in the Pail by David McCord, illustrated by Marc Simont; Little, Brown, 1975. **Awarded:** National Book Award (finalist) 1976.

McCORD, JEAN

Turkeylegs Thompson by Jean McCord, not illustrated; Atheneum, 1979. **Awarded:** New York Times Notable Books 1979.

McCORISON, MARCUS

Awarded: Chandler Reward of Merit 1972.

McCORKELL, ELSIE J.

The Story Catcher by Mari Sandoz, illustrated by Elsie J. McCorkell; Westminster, 1963. **Awarded:** Western Writers (fiction) 1964.

McCORMICK, DELL J.

Paul Bunyan Swings his Axe written and illustrated by Dell J. McCormick; Caxton, 1936. **Awarded:** Young Readers Choice 1940.

McCOY, JOSEPH JEROME

The Hunt for the Whooping Crane by J. J. McCoy, illustrated by Rey Abruzzi; Lothrop, 1966. **Awarded:** Spring Book Festival (older honor) 1966.

Pet Safety by Joseph J. McCoy, illustrated by Bette J. Davis; Watts, 1979. **Awarded:** New Jersey Institute of Technology 1980.

McCRACKEN, RONALD W.

Awarded: Grolier 1972.

McCRACKEN, STEVE

Willie Pearl by Michelle Y. Green, illustrated by Steve McCracken; William Ruth & Co., 1990. **Awarded:** CRABbery Award 1991.

McCREA, JAMES

What I Like about Toads by Judy Hawes, illustrated by James McCrea and Ruth McCrea; Crowell, 1969. **Awarded:** New Jersey Institute of Technology 1970.

McCREA, RUTH

What I Like about Toads by Judy Hawes, illustrated by Ruth McCrea and James McCrea; Crowell, 1969. **Awarded:** New Jersey Institute of Technology 1970.

McCUE, LISA

Animal Babies by K. K. Ross, illustrated by Lisa McCue; Random House, 1988. **Awarded:** Book Can Develop Empathy 1991.

Snot Stew by Bill Wallace, illustrated by Lisa McCue; Holiday House, 1989. **Awarded:** South Carolina Children's 1992; Texas Bluebonnet 1992.

McCULLY, EMILY ARNOLD

Edward Troy and the Witch Cat by Sarah Sargent, illustrated by Emily McCully; Follett, 1978. **Awarded:** Council of Wisconsin Writers (juvenile) 1979.

How to Eat Fried Worms by Thomas Rockwell, illustrated by Emily McCully; Watts, 1973. **Awarded:** Arizona 1979; California Young Reader Medal (Intermediate) 1975; Golden Archer 1975; Iowa Children's Choice 1980; Massachusetts Children's 1976; Nene 1976; Sequoyah 1976; South Carolina Children's 1976; Mark Twain 1975; Volunteer State 1979; Young Hoosier (grades 4-6) 1977.

Hurray for Captain Jane! by Sam Reavin, illustrated by Emily McCully; Parents, 1971. **Awarded:** Children's Book Showcase 1972.

Journey from Peppermint Street by Meindert De Jong, illustrated by Emily A. McCully; Harper, 1968. **Awarded:** National Book Award 1969.

MA NDA LA by Arnold Adoff, illustrated by Emily McCully; Harper, 1971. **Awarded:** Art Books for Children 1975.

Mirette on the High Wire written and illustrated by Emily Arnold McCully; Putnam, 1992. **Awarded:** Caldecott 1993; New York Times Best Illustrated 1992.

Picnic written and illustrated by Emily Arnold McCully; Harper & Row, 1984. **Awarded:** Christopher (Picturebook) 1985.

McCURDY, BRUCE
Hawaii, the Aloha State by Helen Bauer, illustrated by Bruce McCurdy; Doubleday, 1960. **Awarded:** Commonwealth Club of California 1960.

McCURDY, MICHAEL
Devils Who Learned To Be Good written and illustrated by Michael McCurdy; Little Brown, 1987. **Awarded:** Parents' Choice (Story Book) 1987.

The Owl-scatterer by Howard Norman, illustrated by Michael McCurdy; Atlantic Monthly Press, 1986. **Awarded:** New York Times Best Illustrated 1986.

McCUTCHEON, ELSIE
Summer of the Zeppelin by Elsie McCutcheon, not illustrated; Dent, 1983; Penguin, 1984. **Awarded:** Guardian (runnerup) 1984.

McDERMOTT, BEVERLY BRODSKY
The Golem: A Jewish Legend written and illustrated by Beverly Brodsky McDermott; Lippincott, 1975. **Awarded:** Caldecott (honor) 1977; New York Times Notable Books 1976.

McDERMOTT, GERALD
Anansi the Spider: A Tale from the Ashanti written and illustrated by Gerald McDermott; Holt, 1972. **Awarded:** Caldecott (honor) 1973; Lewis Carroll Shelf 1973.

Arrow to the Sun: A Pueblo Indian Tale written and illustrated by Gerald McDermott; Viking, 1974. **Awarded:** Art Books for Children 1975, 1976, 1977; Caldecott 1975.

The Magic Tree written and illustrated by Gerald McDermott; Holt, 1973. **Awarded:** Art Books for Children 1974; Boston Globe Horn Book (illustration honor) 1973.

Raven: A Trickster Tale from the Pacific Northwest written and illustrated by Gerald McDermott; Harcourt Brace, 1993. **Awarded:** Boston Globe (Illustration honor) 1993.

McDONALD, MEGAN
Is This a House for Hermit Crab? by Megan McDonald, illustrated by S. D. Schindler; Orchard, 1990. **Awarded:** International Reading Assn. (Younger) 1991.

McDONALD, RALPH
Let's Pretend It Happened to You by Bernice Wells Carlson, illustrated by Ralph McDonald; Abingdon, 1973. **Awarded:** New Jersey Institute of Technology 1973.

McDOUGALL, MARINA
The Kingdom of the Riddles by Marina McDougall in Ready or Not edited by Jack Booth (Language Patterns Impressions, Reading Series) Holt, 1978. **Awarded:** Vicky Metcalf Short Story 1979.

McDOWALL, DAVID
The Palestinians by David McDowall, illustrated by Ron Howard Associates; Watts, 1986. **Awarded:** Other Award 1987.

McDOWELL, DOTTIE
Katie's Adventure at Blueberry Pond by Dottie McDowell and Josh McDowell, illustrated by Ann Neilsen; Chariot, 1988. **Awarded:** Gold Medallion (Preschool) 1989.

McDOWELL, JOSH
Katie's Adventure at Blueberry Pond by Josh McDowell and Dottie McDowell, illustrated by Ann Neilsen; Chariot, 1988. **Awarded:** Gold Medallion (Preschool) 1989.

McELDERRY, MARGARET K.
Awarded: ALAN 1976; Women's National Book Assn. 1975.

McEWAN, KEITH
The Paw Thing by Paul Jennings, illustrated by Keith McEwan; Puffin, 1989. **Awarded:** Young Australian Best Book (Fiction Younger Reader) 1990.

McFALL, CHRISTIE
The Wonders of Sand written and illustrated by Christie McFall; Dodd, Mead, 1966. **Awarded:** New Jersey Institute of Technology 1966, 1967.

McFALL, RUSSELL P.
Awarded: L. Frank Baum 1962.

McFARLANE, SHERYL
Waiting for the Whales by Sheryl McFarlane, illustrated by Ron Lightburn; Orca Books, 1991. **Awarded:** Governor General's Literary Award (Illustration) 1992; Amelia Frances Howard-Gibbon 1992; Elizabeth Mrazik-Cleaver 1992; National Chapter of Canada IODE Violet Downey 1992.

McGAW, JESSIE BREWER
How Medicine Man Cured Paleface Woman: An Easy Reading Story in Indian Picture Writing and Paleface Words written and illustrated by Jessie Brewer McGaw; Scott, 1956. **Awarded:** Steck-Vaughn 1958.

McGIFFIN, LEE
Pony Soldier by Lee McGiffin, illustrated; Dutton, 1961. **Awarded:** Steck-Vaughn 1963.

Ten Tall Texans by Lee McGiffin, illustrated by John Maxwell; Lothrop Lee & Shepard, 1956. **Awarded:** Spring Book Festival (middle honor) 1956.

McGILLIS, RODERICK
Secrets and Sequences in Children's Stories by Roderick McGillis in *Studies in the Literary Imagination* 18 (Fall 1985). **Awarded:** Children's Literature Assn. Excellence in Criticism (runnerup) 1986.

McGINLEY, PHYLLIS
All Around the Town by Phyllis McGinley, illustrated by Helen Stone; Lippincott, 1948. **Awarded:** Caldecott (honor) 1949.

The Most Wonderful Doll in the World by Phyllis McGinley, illustrated by Helen Stone; Lippincott, 1950. **Awarded:** Caldecott (honor) 1951.

Wonderful Time by Phyllis McGinley, illustrated by John Alcorn; Lippincott, 1966. **Awarded:** New York Times Best Illustrated 1966.

McGOUGH, ROGER
The Great Smile Robbery by Roger McGough, illustrated by Tony Blundell; Kestrel, 1982. **Awarded:** Mother Goose (runnerup) 1983.

Sky in the Pie by Roger McGough, illustrated by Satoshi Kitamura; Kestrel, 1983. **Awarded:** Signal Poetry 1984.

McGOVERN, ANN
Awarded: Lucky Book Club Four-Leaf Clover 1972.

Scram, Kid! by Ann McGovern, illustrated by Nola Langner; Viking, 1974. **Awarded:** Boston Globe Horn Book (illustration honor) 1975.

McGOWAN, ALAN, DR.
Sailing Ships by Ron Van der Meer and Dr. Alan McGowan, paintings by Borje Svensson; Viking, 1984. **Awarded:** Redbook (popup) 1984.

MCGOWEN, TOM
Awarded: Children's Reading Round Table 1990.

McGRAW, ELOISE JARVIS
Awarded: Evelyn Sibley Lampman 1984.

Crown Fire by Eloise Jarvis McGraw, not illustrated; Coward, 1951. **Awarded:** Spring Book Festival (older honor) 1951.

The Forbidden Fountain of Oz by Eloise Jarvis McGraw and Lauren Lynn McGraw, illustrated by Dick Martin; International Wizard of Oz Club, 1980. **Awarded:** L. Frank Baum (cowinner) 1983.

The Golden Goblet by Eloise Jarvis McGraw, not illustrated; Coward, 1961. **Awarded:** Newbery (honor) 1962.

Merry Go Round in Oz by Eloise Jarvis McGraw and Lauren McGraw Wagner, designed and illustrated by Dick Martin; Reilly & Lee, 1963. **Awarded:** L. Frank Baum (cowinner) 1983.

Moccasin Trail by Eloise Jarvis McGraw, illustrated by Paul Galdone; Coward, 1952. **Awarded:** Lewis Carroll Shelf 1963; Newbery (honor) 1953.

A Really Weird Summer by Eloise Jarvis McGraw, not illustrated; Atheneum/McElderry, 1977. **Awarded:** Edgar Allen Poe 1978.

McGRAW, LAUREN LYNN
see also WAGNER, LAUREN LYNN McGRAW

The Forbidden Fountain of Oz by Lauren Lynn McGraw and Eloise Jarvis McGraw; illustrated by Dick Martin; International Wizard of Oz Club, 1980. **Awarded:** L. Frank Baum (cowinner) 1983.

McGRAW, SHEILA
Love You Forever by Robert N. Munsch, illustrated by Sheila McGraw; Firefly Books, 1986. **Awarded:** North Dakota Children's Choice (Picture Book) 1989.

McGRAW, WILLIAM CORBIN
see CORBIN, WILLIAM

McGREGOR, DELLA LOUISE
Awarded: Grolier 1961.

McGREGOR, JANE ANN
Awarded: Grolier 1981.

McGUIRE, ALICE
Awarded: Grolier 1962.

McGUIRE, PAULA
Coming to North America from Mexico, Cuba & Puerto Rico by Paula McGuire and Susan Garver, illustrated with photographs; Delacorte, 1981. **Awarded:** Woodson 1982.

McHALE, ETHEL K.
Son of Thunder: An Old Lapp Tale retold by Ethel K. McHale, illustrated by Ruth Bornstein; Children's Press, 1974. **Awarded:** Southern California Council (contribution to illustration) 1975.

McHARGUE, GEORGESS
The Impossible People: A History Natural and Unnatural of Beings Terrible and Wonderful by Georgess McHargue, illustrated by Frank Bozzo; Holt, 1972. **Awarded:** National Book Award (finalist) 1973; Spring Book Festival (ages 8-12 honor) 1972.

McHUGH, FLORENCE
When I Was a Boy by Erich Kastner, translated by Florence McHugh and Isabel McHugh, illustrated by Horst Lemke; Watts, 1961. **Awarded:** Lewis Carroll Shelf 1961.

McHUGH, ISABEL
When I Was a Boy by Erich Kastner, translated by Isabel McHugh and Florence McHugh, illustrated by Horst Lemke; Watts, 1961. **Awarded:** Lewis Carroll Shelf 1961.

McILWRAITH, MAUREEN MOLLIE HUNTER
see HUNTER, MOLLIE

McINNES, JOHN
The Chocolate Chip Mystery by John McInnes, illustrated by Paul Frame; Garrard, 1972. **Awarded:** Emphasis on Reading (grades 2-3) 1982-83.

McINTOSH, JANE
The Practical Archaeologist by Jane McIntosh, illustrated; Facts on File, 1986. **Awarded:** New York Academy of Sciences (older honor) 1987.

McKAY, HILARY
The Exiles by Hilary McKay, not illustrated; Gollancz, 1991. **Awarded:** Guardian 1992.

McKAY, ROBERT
Dave's Song by Robert McKay, not illustrated; Meredith, 1969. **Awarded:** Ohioana (fiction) 1971.

McKEATING, EILEEN
Dear Baby by Joanne Rocklin, illustrated by Eileen McKeating; Macmillan, 1988. **Awarded:** Southern California Council (Outstanding Work of Fiction for Children) 1989.

McKEE, DOUGLAS
Sophie written and illustrated by Denise Trez and Alain Trez, translated by Douglas McKee; World, 1964. **Awarded:** Spring Book Festival (picture book honor) 1964.

McKENNA, NANCY DURRELL
KwaZulu, South Africa by Nancy Durell McKenna, illustrated; A&C Black, 1984. **Awarded:** Times Educational Supplement (junior) 1985.

McKENNA, TERRY
The Fox and the Circus Bear written and illustrated by Terry McKenna; Gollancz, 1982. **Awarded:** Mother Goose (runnerup) 1982.

McKENNY, MARGARET
A Book of Wild Flowers by Margaret McKenny, illustrated by Edith F. Johnson; Macmillan, 1939. **Awarded:** Spring Book Festival (younger honor) 1939.

McKENZIE, DOROTHY
Awarded: Southern California Council (distinguished contribution to the field of literature for children and young people and for outstanding community service) 1964; Grolier 1978.

McKENZIE, ELLEN KINDT
A Bowl of Mischief by Ellen Kindt McKenzie, not illustrated; Henry Holt, 1992. **Awarded:** Commonwealth Club of California (Ages 10-under) 1992.

Stargone John by Ellen Kindt McKenzie, illustrated by William Low; Henry Holt, 1990. **Awarded:** Bay Area Book Reviewers Assn. (Children's Book) 1991.

McKILLIP, PATRICIA A.
Moon-flash by Patricia McKillip, not illustrated; Atheneum, 1984. **Awarded:** Parents' Choice (literature) 1984.

The Throme of the Erril of Sherill by Patricia A. McKillip, illustrated by Julia Noonan; Atheneum, 1973. **Awarded:** Children's Book Showcase 1974.

McKIM, AUDREY
Awarded: Vicky Metcalf 1969.

McKINLEY, CHARLES FREDERICK, JR.
Harriet by Charles McKinley, Jr., illustrated by William Pene du Bois; Viking, 1946. **Awarded:** Spring Book Festival (middle honor) 1946.

McKINLEY, ROBIN
The Blue Sword by Robin McKinley, not illustrated; Greenwillow, 1982. **Awarded:** Newbery (honor) 1983.

The Hero and the Crown by Robin McKinley, not illustrated; Greenwillow, 1984. **Awarded:** Newbery 1985.

McKINNON, LISE
Don't Take Teddy by Babbis Friis-Baastad, translated by Lise Somme McKinnon, not illustrated; Scribner, 1967. **Awarded:** Batchelder 1969; Lewis Carroll Shelf 1976; Spring Book Festival (middle honor) 1967.

McKISSACK, FREDRICK
A Long Hard Journey: The Story of the Pullman Porter by Patricia McKissack and Fredrick McKissack, illustrated; Walker, 1989. **Awarded:** Addams 1990; Coretta Scott King (Text) 1990; Woodson (Outstanding Merit - Secondary) 1990.

Sojourner Truth: Ain't I a Woman? by Patricia McKissack and Fredrick McKissack, illustrated; Scholastic, 1992. **Awarded:** Boston Globe Horn Book (Nonfiction) 1993; Coretta Scott King (text honor) 1993.

W. E. B. DuBois by Patricia McKissack and Fredrick McKissack, illustrated; Watts, 1990. **Awarded:** Woodson (Outstanding Merit - Secondary) 1991.

The World in 1492 by Jean Fritz, Katherine Paterson, Patricia McKissack, Fredrick McKissack, Margaret Mahy and Jamake Highwater, illustrated by Stefano Vitale; Henry Holt, 1992. **Awarded:** Hungry Mind (Young Adult/Nonfiction) 1993.

McKISSACK, PATRICIA
The Dark-Thirty by Patricia McKissack, not illustrated; Knopf, 1992. **Awarded:** Hungry Mind (Middle Readers/Fiction) 1993; Coretta Scott King (Text) 1993; Newbery (Honor) 1993.

A Long Hard Journey: The Story of the Pullman Porter by Patricia McKissack and Fredrick McKissack, illustrated; Walker, 1989. **Awarded:** Addams 1990; Coretta Scott King (Text) 1990; Woodson (Outstanding Merit - Secondary) 1990.

Mirandy and Brother Wind by Patricia McKissack, illustrated by Jerry Pinkney; Knopf, 1988. **Awarded:** Caldecott (honor) 1989; Coretta Scott King (Illustration) 1989.

Nettie Jo's Friends by Patricia McKissack, illustrated by Scott Cook; Knopf, 1989. **Awarded:** Parents' Choice (Story Book) 1989.

Sojourner Truth: Ain't I a Woman? by Patricia McKissack and Fredrick McKissack, illustrated; Scholastic, 1992. **Awarded:** Boston Globe Horn Book (nonfiction) 1993; Coretta Scott King (Text Honor) 1993.

W. E. B. DuBois by Patricia McKissack and Fredrick McKissack, illustrated; Watts, 1990. **Awarded:** Woodson (Outstanding Merit - Secondary) 1991.

The World in 1492 by Jean Fritz, Katherine Paterson, Patricia McKissack, Fredrick McKissack, Margaret Mahy and Jamake Highwater, illustrated by Stefano Vitale; Henry Holt, 1992. **Awarded:** Hungry Mind (Young Adult/Nonfiction) 1993.

McKISSOCK, PATRICIA
Arch Book series edited by Patricia McKissock; Concordia Publishing House. **Awarded:** Helen Keating Ott 1980.

McKOWN, ROBIN
Janine by Robin McKown, not illustrated; Messner, 1960. **Awarded:** Child Study 1960.

McLAUGHLIN, JAMES
Abbie's God Book by Isabelle Holland, illustrated by James McLaughlin; Westminster, 1982. **Awarded:** Helen Keating Ott 1983.

McLAUGHLIN, JEAN
Secret Passage by Betty Cavanna, illustrated by Jean McLaughlin; Winston, 1946. **Awarded:** Spring Book Festival (middle honor) 1947.

McLAUGHLIN, JIM
Awarded: Lucile M. Pannell 1984.

McLAUGHLIN, LORRIE
Awarded: Vicky Metcalf 1968.

McLAUGHLIN, MOLLY
Earthworms, Dirt and Rotten Leaves: An Exploration in Ecology by Molly McLaughlin, illustrated by Robert Shetterly; Atheneum, 1986. **Awarded:** New York Academy of Sciences (younger honor) 1987.

McLEOD, EMILIE WARREN
The Bear's Bicycle by Emilie Warren McLeod, illustrated by David McPhail; Atlantic-Little, 1975. **Awarded:** Boston Globe Horn Book (illustration honor) 1975.

The War Between the Pitiful Teachers and the Splendid Kids by Stanley Kiesel, edited by Emilie McLeod, not illustrated; Dutton, 1980. **Awarded:** New York Times Notable Books 1980.

McLOUGHLIN, JOHN C.
Archosauria: A New Look at the Old Dinosaur written and illustrated by John C. McLoughlin; Viking, 1979. **Awarded:** New York Academy of Sciences (older honor) 1980.

The Tree of Animal Life: A Tale of Changing Forms and Fortunes written and illustrated by John C. McLoughlin; Dodd, Mead, 1981. **Awarded:** New York Academy of Sciences (older) 1982.

McMAINS, D.
Mystery of the Old Musket by Patience Zawadsky, illustrated by D. McMains; Putnam, 1967. **Awarded:** New Jersey Institute of Technology 1968.

McMEEKIN, ISABEL McLENNAN
Journey Cake by Isabel McLennan McMeekin, illustrated by Nicholas Panesis; Messner, 1942. **Awarded:** Julia Ellsworth Ford 1942.

McMILLEN, WHEELER
Fifty Useful Americans by Wheeler McMillen, not illustrated; Putnam, 1966. **Awarded:** New Jersey Institute of Technology (biography) 1966.

McMULLAN, JIM
Kangaroo & Kangaroo by Kathy Braun, illustrated by Jim McMullan; Doubleday, 1965. **Awarded:** New York Times Best Illustrated 1965.

McMULLAN, KATE
The Great Eggspectations of Lila Fenwick by Kate McMullan, illustrated by Diane deGroat; Farrar Straus Giroux, 1991. **Awarded:** CRABbery honor) 1993.

McNAIR, KATE
A Sense of Magic by Kate McNair, not illustrated; Chilton, 1965. **Awarded:** Indiana Authors Day (young adult) 1966.

McNAMARA, JOHN
Revenge of the Nerd by John McNamara, not illustrated; Dell, 1985, c1984. **Awarded:** Emphasis on Reading (grades 7-9) 1987-88.

McNAUGHTON, COLIN
Have You Seen Who's Just Moved in Next Door to Us? written and illustrated by Colin McNaughton; Walker, 1991; Random House, 1991. **Awarded:** Maschler 1991.

McNEELY, MARIAN HURD
Jumping-off Place by Marian Hurd McNeely, illustrated by William Siegel; Longmans, 1929. **Awarded:** Newbery (honor) 1930.

McNEELY, TOM
Les Chemins Secrets de la Liberte by Barbara Smucker, translated by Paule C. Daveluy, illustrated by Tom McNeely; Pierre Tisseyire, 1978. **Awarded:** International Board on Books for Young People (translation/Canada) 1980.

McNEER, MAY YONGE
Awarded: Regina 1975.

The American Indian Story by May McNeer, illustrated by Lynd Ward; Ariel, 1963. **Awarded:** New Jersey Institute of Technology 1963.

America's Mark Twain by May McNeer, illustrated by Lynd Ward; Houghton, 1962. **Awarded:** New Jersey Institute of Technology 1963.

Armed with Courage by May McNeer and Lynd Ward, illustrated by Lynd Ward; Abingdon, 1957. **Awarded:** Edison Mass Media (character development for children) 1958.

Martin Luther by May McNeer and Lynd Ward, illustrated by Lynd Ward; Abingdon-Cokesbury, 1953. **Awarded:** Spring Book Festival (8- 12 honor) 1953.

The Story of George Washington by May McNeer, illustrated by Lynd Ward; Abingdon, 1973. **Awarded:** New Jersey Institute of Technology 1973.

McNEILL, JAMES
The Double Knights: More Tales from Round the World by James McNeill, illustrated by Theo Dimson; Oxford, 1965. **Awarded:** Canadian Library Assn. 1966.

The Sunken City by James McNeill, illustrated by Theo Dimson; Oxford, 1959. **Awarded:** International Board on Books for Young People (honour list/Canada) 1962.

McNEILL, JANET
The Battle of St. George Without by Janet McNeill, illustrated by Mary Russon; Little, 1968. **Awarded:** Spring Book Festival (middle honor) 1968.

McNIFF, PHILIP
Awarded: Chandler Reward of Merit 1982.

McNULTY, FAITH
The Lady and the Spider by Faith McNulty, illustrated by Bob Marstall; Harper & Row, 1986. **Awarded:** Book Can Develop Empathy 1990.

McPHAIL, DAVID
The Bear's Bicycle by Emilie Warren McLeod, illustrated by David McPhail; Atlantic-Little, 1975. **Awarded:** Boston Globe Horn Book (illustration honor) 1975.

Great Cat written and illustrated by David McPhail; Dutton, 1982. **Awarded:** Parents' Choice (literature) 1982.

The Ice Cream Store by Dennis Lee, illustrated by David McPhail; HarperCollins, 1991. **Awarded:** Mr. Christie's (English Text) 1991.

The Island of the Grass King: The Further Adventures of Anatole by Nancy Willard, illustrated by David McPhail; Harcourt, 1979. **Awarded:** Lewis Carroll Shelf 1979.

One Winter Night in August and Other Nonsense Jingles by X. J. Kennedy, illustrated by David McPhail; Atheneum, 1975. **Awarded:** New York Times Notable Books 1975.

Sailing to Cythera and Other Anatole Stories by Nancy Willard, illustrated by David McPhail; Harcourt, 1974. **Awarded:** Lewis Carroll Shelf 1977.

McPHEDRAN, MARIE
Cargoes on the Great Lakes by Marie McPhedran, illustrated by Dorothy Ivens; Macmillan Canada, 1952. **Awarded:** Governor- General's Literary Award 1952.

McPHEETERS, BILL
Higgins of the Railroad Museum by Ethelyn M. Parkinson, illustrated by Bill McPheeters; Abingdon, 1970. **Awarded:** State Historical Society of Wisconsin 1971.

McPHERSON, ANN
Mum - I Feel Funny! by Ann McPherson and Aidan Macfarlane; illustrated by Nicholas Garland; Chatto & Windus, 1982. **Awarded:** Times Educational Supplement (junior) 1983.

McSWIGAN, MARIE
Snow Treasure by Marie McSwigan, illustrated by Mary Reardon; Dutton, 1942. **Awarded:** Young Readers Choice 1945.

McVAY, TRACY
A Bunny Ride by Ida DeLage, illustrated by Tracy McVay; Garrard, 1975. **Awarded:** New Jersey Institute of Technology 1976.

Bunny School by Ida DeLage, illustrated by Tracy McVay; Garrard, 1976. **Awarded:** New Jersey Institute of Technology 1977.

Good Morning, Lady by Ida DeLage, illustrated by Tracy McVay; Garrard, 1974. **Awarded:** New Jersey Institute of Technology 1975, 1976.

McVEY, VICKI
The Sierra Club Wayfinding Book by Vicki McVey, illustrated by Martha Weston; Little Brown, 1989. **Awarded:** New York Academy of Sciences (Younger) 1989.

MEADER, STEPHEN WARREN
Awarded: New Jersey Institute of Technology (New Jersey's writers of children's books) 1967.

Bat: The Story of a Bull Terrier by Stephen W. Meader, illustrated by Edward Shenton; Harcourt, 1939. **Awarded:** Spring Book Festival (older honor) 1939.

A Blow for Liberty by Stephen W. Meader, illustrated by Victor Mays; Harcourt, 1965. **Awarded:** New Jersey Institute of Technology (ages 15-16) 1966.

Boy with a Pack by Stephen W. Meader, illustrated by Edward Shenton; Harcourt, 1939. **Awarded:** Newbery (honor) 1940.

Buffalo and Beaver by Stephen W. Meader, illustrated by Charles Beck; Harcourt, 1960. **Awarded:** New Jersey Institute of Technology 1961.

Phantom of the Blocade by Stephen W. Meader, illustrated by Victor Mays; Harcourt, 1962. **Awarded:** New Jersey Institute of Technology (ages 12-up) 1962.

Snow on Blueberry Mountain by Stephen W. Meader, illustrated by Don Sibley; Harcourt, 1961. **Awarded:** New Jersey Institute of Technology 1961.

Topsail Island Treasure by Stephen W. Meader, illustrated by Marbury Brown; Harcourt, 1966. **Awarded:** New Jersey Institute of Technology 1966.

MEADOW, CHARLES T.
Sounds and Signals: How We Communicate by Charles T. Meadow, illustrated with photographs; Westminster, 1975. **Awarded:** New York Academy of Sciences (older honor) 1976.

MEADOWCROFT, ENID LA MONTE
Signature Books edited by Enid La Monte Meadowcroft, Grosset. **Awarded:** Boys Club Junior Book Awards (special certificate of award for a series of biographies by different authors for readers ages 8-12) 1954.

MEAKER, MARIJANE
see KERR, M. E.

MEANS, ELLIOTT
Commanche of the Seventh by Margaret C. Leighton, illustrated by Elliott Means; Farrar, 1957. **Awarded:** Dorothy Canfield Fisher 1959.

MEANS, FLORENCE CRANNELL
Knock at the Door, Emmy by Florence C. Means, illustrated by Paul Lantz; Houghton Mifflin, 1956. **Awarded:** Nancy Bloch 1956.

The Moved-Outers by Florence Crannell Means, illustrated by Helen Blair; Houghton, 1945. **Awarded:** Child Study 1945; Newbery (honor) 1946.

MEDDAUGH, SUSAN
Bimwili and the Zimwi by Verna Aardema, illustrated by Susan Meddaugh; Dial, 1985. **Awarded:** Parents' Choice (literature) 1985.

Martha Speaks written and illustrated by Susan Meddaugh; Houghton Mifflin, 1992. **Awarded:** New York Times Best Illustrated 1992.

MEE, CHARLES L., JR.
Lorenzo De'Medici and the Renaissance by Charles L. Mee, Jr. and John Walker, illustrated with photographs; American Heritage, 1969. **Awarded:** Spring Book Festival (older honor) 1969.

MEEK, MARGARET
Awarded: Eleanor Farjeon 1970.

MEEKER, ALICE M.
How Hospitals Help Us by Alice M. Meeker, illustrated by Jack Faulkner; Beckley-Cardy, 1962. **Awarded:** New Jersey Institute of Technology 1963.

MEEKS, ARONE RAYMOND
Enora and the Black Crane written and illustrated by Arone Raymond Meeks; Ashton Scholastic, 1991; Scholastic, 1993. **Awarded:** UNICEF-Ezra Jack Keats International Award for Children's Book Illustration 1992.

MEIGS, CORNELIA L.
Clearing Weather by Cornelia Meigs, illustrated by Frank Dobias; Little, Brown, 1928. **Awarded:** Newbery (honor) 1929.

Invincible Louisa: The Story of the Author of Little Women by Cornelia Meigs, illustrated with photographs; Little, Brown, 1961, 1933. **Awarded:** Lewis Carroll Shelf 1963; Newbery 1934.

Jane Addams: Pioneer for Social Justice, a Biography by Cornelia L. Meigs, illustrated with photographs; Little, Brown, 1970. **Awarded:** Jane Addams 1971.

Mounted Messenger by Cornelia Meigs, illustrated by John Wonsetler; Macmillan, 1943. **Awarded:** Spring Book Festival (middle honor) 1943.

Swift Rivers by Cornelia Meigs, illustrated by Peter Hurd; Little, Brown, 1932. **Awarded:** Newbery (honor) 1933.

Windy Hill by Cornelia Meigs, not illustrated; Macmillan, 1921. **Awarded:** Newbery (honor) 1922.

MELCHER, FREDERIC
Awarded: Regina 1962.

MELIA, GERARD
Will of Iron by Gerard Melia; Longman Knockouts. **Awarded:** Other Award 1983.

MELLECKER, JUDITH
Randolph's Dream by Judith Mellecker, illustrated by Robert Andrew Parker; Knopf, 1991. **Awarded:** Parents' Choice (Picture Book) 1991.

MELLING, O. R.
The Druid's Tune by O. R. Melling, illustrated with maps; Penguin, 1983. **Awarded:** Young Adult Canadian 1984.

MELLONIE, BRYAN
Principio y Fin Tiempo de Vida que Trancurre Entre el Nacer y el Morir (original English *Beginnings and Endings with LIFE-TIMES in Between*) by Bryan Mellonie, translated by Carmen Esteva and Miguel Leon; Compania Editorial Continental, 1984. **Awarded:** International Board on Books for Young People (translation/Mexico) 1986.

MELROSE, GENEVIEVE
The Min-Min by Mavis Thorpe Clark, illustrated by Genevieve Melrose; Angus, 1967. **Awarded:** Children's Book Council of Australia (book of the year) 1967.

MELTZER, MILTON
Awarded: CBC Honors Program 1988; Washington Post/Children's Book Guild Nonfiction 1981.

Ain't Gonna Study War No More: The Story of America's Peace Seekers by Milton Meltzer, illustrated; Harper & Row, 1985. **Awarded:** Jane Addams 1986; Child Study (special citation) 1985.

All Times, All Peoples: A World History of Slavery by Milton Meltzer, illustrated by Leonard Everett Fisher; Harper & Row, 1980. **Awarded:** Christopher (ages 8-12 nonfiction) 1981.

Brother, Can You Spare a Dime? The Great Depression, 1929-1933 by Milton Meltzer, illustrated with photographs; Knopf, 1969. **Awarded:** Christopher (teenage) 1970.

The Chinese Americans by Milton Meltzer, illustrated; Crowell, 1980. **Awarded:** Woodson 1981.

The Eye of Conscience: Photographers and Social Change by Milton Meltzer and Bernard Cole, illustrated with photographs; Follett, 1974. **Awarded:** Jane Addams (honor) 1975.

In Their Own Words: A History of the American Negro: Vol. 2, 1865-1916 edited by Milton Meltzer, illustrated with photographs; Crowell, 1965. **Awarded:** Edison Mass Media (America's past) 1966.

The Jewish Americans: A History in Their Own Words, 1650-1950 edited by Milton Meltzer, illustrated; Crowell, 1982. **Awarded:** Boston Globe Horn Book (Nonfiction honor) 1983; Jefferson Cup 1983.

Langston Hughes: A Biography by Milton Meltzer, not illustrated; Crowell, 1968. **Awarded:** National Book Awards (finalist) 1969.

Never to Forget: The Jews of the Holocaust by Milton Meltzer, not illustrated; Harper & Row, 1976. **Awarded:** Jane Addams 1977; Boston Globe Horn Book (nonfiction honor) 1976; Jewish Book Council 1977; National Book Award (finalist) 1977; Sydney Taylor Book Award 1976.

Poverty in America by Milton Meltzer, illustrated; Morrow, 1986. **Awarded:** Golden Kite (nonfiction) 1986.

Remember the Days: A Short History of the Jewish American by Milton Meltzer, illustrated by Harvey Dinnerstein; Zenith/Doubleday, 1974. **Awarded:** National Book Award (finalist) 1975.

Rescue: The Story of How Gentiles Saved Jews in the Holocaust by Milton Meltzer, not illustrated; Harper & Row, 1988. **Awarded:** Addams (Nonfiction Ages 10-up) 1989.

World of Our Fathers: The Jews of Eastern Europe by Milton Meltzer, illustrated with photographs; Farrar, 1974. **Awarded:** National Book Awards (finalist) 1975.

MELTZER, YEHUDA
Pundak Ha-Eima by Isaac Bashevis Singer, translated by Yehuda Meltzer; Adam, 1980. (original English: *The Fearsome Inn* by Isaac Bashevis Singer). **Awarded:** International Board on Books for Young People (translation/Israel) 1982.

MELVILLE, HERMAN
Taipi by Herman Melville, illustrated by Klaus Ensikat; Verlag Neues Leben, 1977. **Awarded:** Biennale Illustrations Bratislava (grand prix) 1979.

MELWOOD, MARY
The Watcher Bee by Mary Melwood, not illustrated; Deutsch, 1982. **Awarded:** Observer Teenage Fiction (cowinner) 1982.

MELZACK, RONALD
Why the Man in the Moon is Happy and Other Eskimo Creation Stories by Ronald Melzack, illustrated by Laszlo Gal; McClelland & Stewart, 1977. **Awarded:** IODE 1978.

MENDOZA, GEORGE
The Hunter I Might Have Been by George Mendoza, illustrated by DeWayne Dalrymple; Astor-Honor, 1968. **Awarded:** Lewis Carroll Shelf 1968.

MENOTTI, GIAN-CARLO
Help, Help, the Globolinks! by Gian-Carlo Menotti, adapted by Leigh Dean, illustrated by Milton Glaser; McGraw, 1970. **Awarded:** New York Times Best Illustrated 1970.

MENUHIN, YEHUDI
The King, the Cat and the Fiddle by Yehudi Menuhin and Christopher Hope, illustrated by Angela Barrett; Benn, 1983. **Awarded:** Mother Goose (runnerup) 1984.

MERAL, C.
Bestiare Fableux by C. Meral, illustrated by Frederic Clement; Editions Magnard. **Awarded:** Biennale Illustrations Bratislava (grand prix) 1985.

MERCER, CHARLES
The Battlestar Galactica Storybook by Glen A. Larson and Robert Thurston, adapted by Charles Mercer, illustrated with photographs; Putnam, 1979. **Awarded:** New Jersey Institute of Technology 1980.

MEREDITH, DON
Dog Runner by Don Meredith, not illustrated; Western Producer Prairie Books, 1989. **Awarded:** R. Ross Annett 1990.

MEREDITH, LUCY
Selina, the Mouse and the Giant Cat written and illustrated by Susi Bohdal, translated by Lucy Meredith; Faber & Faber in association with Nord-Sud Verlag, 1982. **Awarded:** Parents' Choice (illustration) 1982.

MEREDITH, SUSAN
Growing Up by Susan Meredith, illustrated by Sue Stitt, Kuo Kang Chen and Rob McCaig; Usborne, 1985. **Awarded:** Times Educational Supplement (senior) 1985.

MERRIAM, EVE
Awarded: National Council of Teachers of English Award for Excellence in Poetry for Children 1981.

Blackberry Ink by Eve Merriam, illustrated by Hans Wilhelm; Morrow, 1985. **Awarded:** Parents' Choice (literature) 1985.

Finding a Poem by Eve Merriam, illustrated by Seymour Chwast; Atheneum, 1970. **Awarded:** New York Times Best Illustrated 1970.

Halloween ABC by Eve Merriam, illustrated by Lane Smith; Macmillan, 1987. **Awarded:** New York Times Best Illustrated 1987.

MERRILL, JEAN FAIRBANKS
The Pushcart War by Jean Merrill, illustrated by Ronni Solbert; Scott, 1964. **Awarded:** Boys Club 1965, 1966-67; Lewis Carroll Shelf 1965.

The Superlative Horse by Jean Merrill, illustrated by Ronni Solbert; Scott, 1961. **Awarded:** Lewis Carroll Shelf 1963.

The Toothpaste Millionaire by Jean Merrill, illustrated by Jan Palmer; Houghton, 1974. **Awarded:** Dorothy Canfield Fisher 1976; Sequoyah 1977.

MERSON, ELIZABETH
Into the Past: 1-4 by Elizabeth Merson and Sallie Purkis, illustrated with photographs; Longman, 1981. (*At Home and in the Street in 1900*; *At Home in 1900*; *At School and in the Country in 1900*; *At School in 1900*) **Awarded:** Other Award 1982.

MERWIN, DECIE
Spurs for Antonia by Katherine Wigmore Eyre, illustrated by Decie Merwin; Oxford, 1943. **Awarded:** Commonwealth Club of California 1943.

MESGHALI, FARSHID
Awarded: Hans Christian Andersen Award (illustrator) 1974.

The Little Black Fish by Samad Behrangi, illustrated by Farshid Mesghali; Institute for the Intellectual Development of Children and Young Adults. **Awarded:** Bologna (Graphics for Children) 1969.

MESSENGER, NORMAN
Annabel's House written and illustrated by Norman Messenger; Orchard, 1989. **Awarded:** Redbook 1989.

MEYER, CAROLYN
Amish People: Plain Living in a Complex World by Carolyn Meyer, photographs by Carolyn Meyer, Michael Ramsey, Gerald Dodds; Atheneum, 1976. **Awarded:** Children's Book Showcase 1977.

MEYER, EDITH PATTERSON
Awarded: Helen Keating Ott 1989.

Champions of Peace: Winners of the Nobel Peace Prize by Edith Patterson Meyer, illustrated by Eric von Schmidt; Little, Brown, 1959. **Awarded:** Jane Addams 1960.

MEYER, FRANKLYN E.
Me and Caleb by Franklyn E. Meyer, illustrated by Lawrence Beall Smith; Follett, 1962. **Awarded:** Charles W. Follett 1962.

MEYER, FRED M.
Awarded: L. Frank Baum 1978.

MEYERS, BOB
Johnny Texas by Carol Hoff, illustrated by Bob Meyers; Wilcox & Follett, 1950. **Awarded:** Charles W. Follett 1950; Steck-Vaughn 1952.

MEYERS, SUSAN
Melissa Finds a Mystery by Susan Meyers, not illustrated; Dodd Mead, 1966. **Awarded:** Calling All Girls - Dodd, Mead 1966.

MEYRICK, BETTE
Time Circles by Bette Meyrick, not illustrated; Abelard, 1978. **Awarded:** Tir Na n-Og (English) 1979.

MICHAELS, STEVE
The Kid's Guide to Social Action by Barbara A. Lewis, illustrated by Steve Michaels; Free Spirit, 1991. **Awarded:** Hungry Mind (Young Adult/Nonfiction) 1992.

MICHELINIE, DAVID
Mother Teresa of Calcutta by David Michelinie and Roy M. Gasnick, illustrated by John Tartaglione; Franciscan Communications Office, 1984. **Awarded:** Catholic Book Awards (Youth) 1985.

MICHENER, JAMES
Awarded: Outstanding Pennsylvania Author 1982.

MICHIE, JAMES
Aesop's Fables retold in verse by James Michi, illustrated by John Vernon Lord; Cape, 1989. **Awarded:** W. H. Smith 1990.

MICKELSEN, A. BERKELEY
Family Bible Encyclopedia by A. Berkeley Mickelsen and Alvera Mickelsen, illustrated; David C. Cook, 1978. **Awarded:** Gold Medallion 1979.

MICKELSEN, ALVERA
Family Bible Encyclopedia by A. Berkeley Mickelsen and Alvera Mickelsen, illustrated; David C. Cook, 1978. **Awarded:** Gold Medallion 1979.

MICKLETHWAIT, LUCY
I Spy: An Alphabet In Art written and illustrated by Lucy Micklethwait; Greenwillow, 1992. **Awarded:** Parents Choice (Picture Books) 1992.

MICKLEWRIGHT, ROBERT
Family at the Lookout by Noreen Shelly, illustrated by Robert Micklewright; Oxford, 1972. **Awarded:** Children's Book Council of Australia (book of the year) 1973.

MIDGLEY, ANDREW
Imagine by Andrew Midgley; to be published by Macmillan. **Awarded:** Macmillan (3rd prize) 1986.

MIERS, EARL SCHENCK
Awarded: New Jersey Institute of Technology (New Jersey's writers of children's books) 1968; New Jersey Institute of Technology (New Jersey's children's history author of the year) 1965.

Our Fifty States by Earl Schenck Miers, illustrated by Eleanor Mill, maps by Leonard Darwin; Grosset, 1961. **Awarded:** New Jersey Institute of Technology 1961.

That Jefferson Boy by Earl Schenck Miers, illustrated by Kurt Werth; World, 1970. **Awarded:** New Jersey Institute of Technology 1971.

Where the Raritan Flows by Earl Schenck Miers, illustrated by Charles Waterhouse; Rutgers University Press, 1964. **Awarded:** New Jersey Institute of Technology (history) 1964.

MIKAELSEN, BEN
Rescue Josh McGuire by Ben Mikaelsen, not illustrated; Hyperion, 1991. **Awarded:** International Reading Assn. (Older) 1992; Western Writers of America Spur (Juvenile Fiction) 1992.

MIKHALKOV, SERGEI
Awarded: Hans Christian Andersen (highly commended author/USSR) 1972.

MIKLOWITZ, GLORIA
Did You Hear What Happened To Andrea? by Gloria Miklowitz, not illustrated; Delacorte, 1979. **Awarded:** West Australian (Secondary) 1984.

MIKOLAYCAK, CHARLES
Awarded: Kerlan 1987.

Babushka written and illustrated by Charles Mikolaycak; Holiday House, 1984. **Awarded:** New York Times Best Illustrated 1984.

Banner Over Me by Margery F. Greenleaf, illustrated by Charles Mikolaycak; Follett, 1968. **Awarded:** Charles W. Follett 1969.

Exodus adapted from the Bible by Miriam Chaikin, illustrated by Charles Mikolaycak; Holiday House, 1987. **Awarded:** Jewish Book Council (Children's Picture Book) 1988.

Great Wolf and the Good Woodsman by Helen Hoover, illustrated by Charles Mikolaycak; Parents, 1967. **Awarded:** Art Books for Children 1977, 1978, 1979.

Juma and the Magic Jinn by Joy Anderson, illustrated by Charles Mikolaycak; Lothrop, Lee & Shepard, 1986. **Awarded:** Golden Kite (picture illustration honor) 1986.

Peter and the Wolf by Sergei Prokofiev, translated by Maria Carlson, illustrated by Charles Mikolaycak; Viking, 1982. **Awarded:** Parents' Choice (illustration) 1982.

The Rumor of Pavel and Paali adapted by Carole Kismaric, illustrated by Charles Mikolaycak; Harper & Row, 1988. **Awarded:** Parents' Choice (Picture Book) 1988.

Russian Tales of Fabulous Beasts and Marvels by Lee Wyndham, illustrated by Charles Mikolaycak; Parents, 1969. **Awarded:** New Jersey Institute of Technology 1970.

Shipwreck by Vera Cumberledge, illustrated by Charles Mikolaycak; Follett, 1974. **Awarded:** Children's Book Showcase 1975.

MILES, BETTY
The Secret Life of the Underwear Champ by Betty Miles, illustrated by Dan Jones; Knopf, 1981. **Awarded:** Georgia Children's 1986; Mark Twain 1984.

MILES, MISKA
see MARTIN, PATRICIA MILES

MILES, PATRICIA
see MARTIN, PATRICIA MILES

MILGRIM, SHIRLEY G.
Haym Salomon: Liberty's Son by Shirley G. Milgrim, illustrated by Richard Fish; Jewish Publication Society, 1975. **Awarded:** Jewish Book Council 1975.

MILHOUS, KATHERINE
    Awarded: Drexel 1967.

Billy Button's Butter'd Biscuit by Mabel Leigh Hunt, illustrated by Katherine Milhous; Stokes, 1941. **Awarded:** Spring Book Festival (younger honor) 1941.

Corporal Keeperupper written and illustrated by Katherine Milhous; Scribner, 1943. **Awarded:** Spring Book Festival (younger honor) 1943.

The Egg Tree written and illustrated by Katherine Milhous; Scribner, 1950. **Awarded:** Caldecott 1951; Spring Book Festival (picture book honor) 1950.

The Silver Pencil by Alice Dalgliesh, illustrated by Katherine Milhous; Scribner, 1944. **Awarded:** Newbery (honor) 1945.

MILL, ELEANOR
Our Fifty States by Earl Schenck Miers, illustrated by Eleanor Mill, maps by Leonard Darwin; Grosset, 1961. **Awarded:** New Jersey Institute of Technology 1961.

MILLAR, BARBARA F.
Wheels for Ginny's Chariot by Barbara F. Millar and Earlene W. Luis, not illustrated; Dodd Mead, 1966. **Awarded:** Edith Busby 1965.

MILLARD, KERRY
The Web by Nette Hilton, illustrated by Kerry Millard; Collins, 1992. **Awarded:** Children's Book Council of Australia (Book of the Year younger honor) 1993.

MILLER, ALICE
Thou Shalt Not Be Aware: Society's Betrayal of the Child by Alice Miller, translated by Hildegarde Hannum and Hunter Hannum, not illustrated; Farrar, Straus, Giroux, 1984. **Awarded:** Korczak (about children) 1986.

MILLER, ANDREW
Our Changing World by Ingrid Selberg, illustrated by Andrew Miller; Collins, 1982; Philomel, 1982. **Awarded:** Bologna (critici in erba) 1983.

MILLER, ANN
Arc-en-ciel 2 by Marie-Therese Bougard, Ann Miller and Liz Roselman; Mary Glasgow, 1989. **Awarded:** Times Educational Supplement (Schoolbook) 1989.

MILLER, BERTHA MAHONY
    Awarded: Regina 1967; Women's National Book Assn. 1955.

MILLER, DON
A Bicycle from Bridgetown by Dawn Thomas, illustrated by Don Miller; McGraw, 1975. **Awarded:** New Jersey Institute of Technology 1976.

The Stubborn One by Rutherford Montgomery, illustrated by Don Miller; Duell-Sloan-Pearce, 1965. **Awarded:** Western Writers (fiction) 1966.

MILLER, EDWARD
Curse of Claudia written and illustrated by Edward Miller; Crown, 1989. **Awarded:** New Jersey Institute of Technology 1990.

MILLER, ELIZABETH CLEVELAND
Pran of Albania by Elizabeth C. Miller, illustrated by Maud Petersham and Miska Petersham; Doubleday, 1929. **Awarded:** Newbery (honor) 1930.

MILLER, FRANCES A.
The Truth Trap by Frances A. Miller, not illustrated; Dutton, 1980. **Awarded:** California Young Reader (high school) 1985.

MILLER, JANE
Scrappy the Pup by John Ciardi, illustrated by Jane Miller; Lippincott, 1960. **Awarded:** New York Times Best Illustrated 1960.

The Wet World by Norma Simon, illustrated by Jane Miller; Lippincott, 1954. **Awarded:** New York Times Best Illustrated 1954.

MILLER, JON
The Fox Busters by Dick King-Smith, illustrated by Jon Miller; Delacorte, 1988, c1978. **Awarded:** Parents' Choice (Story Book) 1988.

MILLER, JUDI
The Ghost in my Soup by Judi Miller, not illustrated; Bantam, 1985. **Awarded:** Virginia Young Readers (Middle) 1988.

MILLER, MALINDA
    Awarded: Children's Reading Round Table 1965.

MILLER, MARGARET
Where Does It Go? written and illustrated by Margaret Miller; Greenwillow, 1992. **Awarded:** New York Times Best Illustrated 1992.

MILLER, MARILYN
    Awarded: American Association of School Librarians 1993.

MILLER, MARY BETH
Handtalk: An ABC of Finger Spelling and Sign Language by George Ancona, Mary Beth Miller and Remy Charlip, photographs by George Ancona; Parents, 1974. **Awarded:** New York Academy of Sciences (younger honor) 1975.

Handtalk Birthday by Remy Charlip and Mary Beth Miller, photographs by George Ancona; Four Winds, 1987. **Awarded:** New York Times Best Illustrated 1987.

A Show of Hands: Say it in Sign Language by Mary Beth Miller and Linda Bourke with Susan Regan, illustrated by Linda Bourke; Addison Wesley, 1980. **Awarded:** Garden State (younger nonfiction) 1983.

MILLER, MARY BRITTON
All Aboard: Poems by Mary Britton Miller, illustrated by Bill Sokol; Pantheon, 1958. **Awarded:** Boys Club 1959; New York Times Best Illustrated 1958.

Listen - the Birds by Mary Britton Miller, illustrated by Evaline Ness; Pantheon, 1961. **Awarded:** New York Times Best Illustrated 1961.

MILLER, MITCHELL

The Magic Tears by Jack Sendak, illustrated by Mitchell Miller; Harper, 1971. **Awarded:** Children's Book Showcase 1972; New York Times Best Illustrated 1971.

Martze by Jack Sendak, illustrated by Mitchell Miller; Farrar, 1968. **Awarded:** New Jersey Institute of Technology 1968.

One Misty Moisty Morning written and illustrated by Mitchell Miller; Farrar, 1971. **Awarded:** Children's Book Showcase 1972.

MILLER, PEGGY

Awarded: Southern California Council (Dorothy McKenzie) 1992.

MILLER, RANDY

My Village, Sturbridge by Gary Bowen, illustrated by Randy Miller and Gary Bowen; Farrar, 1977. **Awarded:** New York Times Best Illustrated 1977.

MILLER, RUTH WHITE

The City Rose by Ruth White Miller, not illustrated; McGraw, 1977. **Awarded:** North Carolina AAUW 1977.

MILLER, THEODORE R.

The World Turned Upside Down: The Story of the American Revolution by Robert Leckie, illustrated with maps by Theodore R. Miller; Putnam, 1973. **Awarded:** New Jersey Institute of Technology 1973.

MILLER, VIRGINIA

Squeak-a-Lot by Martin Waddell, illustrated by Virginia Miller; Walker, 1991; Greenwillow, 1991. **Awarded:** Mother Goose (runnerup) 1991.

MILLER, WARREN

Pablo Paints a Picture by Warren Miller, illustrated by Edward Sorel; Little, Brown, 1959. **Awarded:** New York Times Best Illustrated 1959.

MILLS, ELAINE

Jonpanda by Gwen Grant, illustrated by Elaine Mills; Heinemann, 1992. **Awarded:** Nottinghamshire (Acorn) 1993.

MILLS, JOHN FITZMAURICE

Treasure Keepers by John FitzMaurice Mills, illustrated with photographs; Doubleday, 1973. **Awarded:** New York Academy of Sciences (older honor) 1975.

MILLS, JOHN FRAZER

Once Upon a Totem by Christie Harris, illustrated by John Frazer Mills; Atheneum, 1963. **Awarded:** New York Times Best Illustrated 1963.

MILLS, ROGER

A Comprehensive Education, 1965-1975 by Roger Mills, not illustrated; Centerprise Trust, Ltd., 1978. **Awarded:** Other Award 1979.

MILNE, A. A. (ALAN ALEXANDER)

The World of Christopher Robin by A. A. Milne, illustrated by E. H. Shepard: Dutton, 1958. **Awarded:** Lewis Carroll Shelf 1962.

The World of Pooh by A. A. Milne, illustrated by Ernest H. Shepard; Dutton, 1957. **Awarded:** Lewis Carroll Shelf 1958.

MILNE, LORUS JOHNSON

Nature's Clean-up Crew: The Burying Beetles written and photographed by Lorus J. Milne and Margery Milne; Dodd, Mead, 1982. **Awarded:** New York Academy of Sciences (older honor) 1983.

A Shovelful of Earth by Lorus J. Milne and Margery Milne, illustrated by Margaret LaFarge; Henry Holt, 1987. **Awarded:** New York Academy of Sciences (Older honor) 1988.

MILNE, MARGERY

Nature's Clean-up Crew: The Burying Beetles written and photographed by Lorus J. Milne and Margery Milne; Dodd, Mead, 1982. **Awarded:** New York Academy of Sciences (older honor) 1983.

A Shovelful of Earth by Lorus J. Milne and Margery Milne, illustrated by Margaret LaFarge; Henry Holt, 1987. **Awarded:** New York Academy of Sciences (Older honor) 1988.

MILNES, IRMA McDONOUGH

Awarded: Claude Aubry 1981.

MILTON, HILARY

The Brats and Mr. Jack by Hilary Milton, not illustrated; Beaufort Books, 1980. **Awarded:** Author's Award/Alabama 1983.

Mayday! Mayday! by Hilary H. Milton, not illustrated; Watts, 1979. **Awarded:** Emphasis on Reading (grades 7-9) 1981-82.

Tornado! by Hilary Milton, not illustrated; Watts, 1983. **Awarded:** Golden Archer 1985.

MINARIK, ELSE HOLMELUND

Father Bear Comes Home by Else Holmelund Minarik, illustrated by Maurice Sendak; Harper, 1959. **Awarded:** New York Times Best Illustrated 1959.

A Kiss for Little Bear by Else Holmelund Minarik, illustrated by Maurice Sendak; Harper, 1968. **Awarded:** New York Times Best Illustrated 1968.

Little Bear's Visit by Else Holmelund Minarik, illustrated by Maurice Sendak; Harper, 1961. **Awarded:** Caldecott (honor) 1962.

MINKEL, WALTER

Awarded: Evelyn Sibley Lampman 1992.

MINNERLY, FAITH C.

The Party Book for Boys and Girls by Bernice Wells Carlson, illustrated by Faith C. Minnerly; Abingdon, 1963. **Awarded:** New Jersey Institute of Technology 1963.

MINOR, WENDELL

Sierra by Diane Siebert, illustrated by Wendell Minor; HarperCollins, 1991. **Awarded:** John & Patricia Beatty 1992.

MINTZ, BARBARA

Hieroglyphs, the Writing of Ancient Egypt written and illustrated by Norma Jean Katan, with Barbara Mintz; Atheneum, 1981. **Awarded:** New York Academy of Sciences (younger honor) 1982.

MINUDRI, REGINA U.

Awarded: Grolier 1974.

MIRET, GIL

The Old Witch and the Snores by Ida DeLage, illustrated by Gil Miret; Garrard, 1970. **Awarded:** New Jersey Institute of Technology 1970.

MIRSKY, REBA PAEFF

Thirty-one Brothers and Sisters by Reba Paeff Mirsky, illustrated by W. T. Mars; Follett, 1952. **Awarded:** Charles W. Follett 1952.

MITCHELL, ADRIAN

The Baron All at Sea by Adrian Mitchell, illustrated by Patrick Benson; Walker, 1987; Philomel, 1987. **Awarded:** W. H. Smith (2nd prize) 1988.

MITCHELL, ISLA
The Beginning Was a Dutchman by Isla Mitchell, illustrated by Richard Kennedy; Dodd, Mead, 1946. **Awarded:** Spring Book Festival (middle honor) 1946.

MITCHELL, JAMES
Man and Machines. The Mitchell Beazley Joy of Knowledge Library edited by James Mitchell, illustrated with photographs; Mitchell Beazley, 1977. **Awarded:** Times Educational Supplement (Senior) 1977.

MITCHELL, JERRY
Sandy Koufax by Jerry Mitchell, not illustrated; Grosset, 1966. **Awarded:** Boys Club (certificate) 1966-67.

MITCHISON, NAOMI
Judy and Lakshmi by Naomi Mitchison, illustrated by Avinash Chandra; Collins, 1958. **Awarded:** Hans Christian Andersen (runnerup) 1960.

MITSUI, EIICHI
Kap the Kappa by Betty Jean Lifton, illustrated by Eiichi Mitsui; Morrow, 1960. **Awarded:** Spring Book Festival (ages 4-8 honor) 1960.

MITTON, SIMON
The Crab Nebula by Simon Mitton, illustrated with photographs and diagrams; Scribner, 1978, 1979. **Awarded:** New York Academy of Sciences (older honor) 1980.

MIZUMURA, KAZUE
If I Built a Village written and illustrated by Kazue Mizumura; Crowell, 1971. **Awarded:** Boston Globe Horn Book (illustration) 1971.

MOCHI, UGO
A Natural History of Giraffes by Dorcas MacClintock, illustrated by Ugo Mochi; Scribner, 1973. **Awarded:** Children's Book Showcase 1974; New York Academy of Sciences (older) 1974.

MOCNIAK, GEORGE
Traveler from a Small Kingdom by Emily Cheney Neville, illustrated by George Mocniak; Harper, 1968. **Awarded:** Spring Book Festival (middle honor) 1968.

MOE, JORGEN
Norwegian Folk Tales by Jorgen Moe and Peter Christen Asbjornsen, illustrated by Erik Werenskiold and Theodor Kittelsen; Viking, 1961. **Awarded:** Spring Book Festival (middle) 1961.

MOERI, LOUISE
The Forty-third War by Louise Moeri, not illustrated; Houghton Mifflin, 1989. **Awarded:** PEN Center USA West 1990.

MOFFATT, JUDITH A.
Illustration by Judith A. Moffatt in *Children's Playmate* magazine. **Awarded:** Magazine Merit (Illustration) 1991.

MOGILEVSKY, ALEXANDER
Adventures of Misha by Sergei Rozanov, illustrated by Alexander Mogilevsky; Stokes, 1938. **Awarded:** Spring Book Festival (younger honor) 1938.

MOHR, NICHOLASA
El Bronx Remembered: A Novella and Stories by Nicholasa Mohr, not illustrated; Harper, 1975. **Awarded:** National Book Award (finalist) 1976; New Jersey Institute of Technology 1976.

In Nueva York by Nicholasa Mohr, not illustrated; Dial, 1977. **Awarded:** New Jersey Institute of Technology 1978.

Nilda written and illustrated by Nicholasa Mohr; Harper, 1973. **Awarded:** Jane Addams 1974; New York Times Notable Books 1973.

MOINI, MAHDI
Leaves by Mahdi Moini, illustrated by Marteza Esmaili-e-Soli; Institute for the Intellectual Development of Children and Young Adults. **Awarded:** Bologna (graphics for children) 1985.

MOLE, JOHN
Boo To a Goose by John Mole, illustrated by Mary Norman; Peterloo Poets, 1987. **Awarded:** Signal Poetry Award 1988.

MOLLEL, TOLOLWA M.
The Orphan Boy by Tololwa M. Mollel, illustrated by Paul Morin; Oxford University Press, 1990. **Awarded:** Governor General's Literary Award (Children's Literature-Illustration) 1990; Amelia Frances Howard-Gibbon 1991; Elizabeth Mrazik-Cleaver 1991.

MOLONEY, JAMES
Crossfire by James Moloney, not illustrated; University of Queensland Press, 1992. **Awarded:** Family Award 1992.

MOMADAY, NATACHEE SCOTT
Owl in the Cedar Tree by Natachee Scott Momaday, illustrated by Don Perceval; Northland Press, 1975. **Awarded:** Western Heritage 1976.

MONGEAU, MARC
There Were Monkeys in my Kitchen! by Sheree Fitch and Marc Mongeau; Doubleday Canada, 1992. **Awarded:** Mr. Christie's (English text ages 8 and under) 1992.

MONJO, FERDINAND NICOLAS, III
Poor Richard in France by F. N. Monjo, illustrated by Brinton Turkle; Holt, 1973. **Awarded:** National Book Award (finalist) 1974.

MONREAL, GUY
Alala by Guy Monreal, illustrated by Nicole Claveloux; Quist, 1970. **Awarded:** New York Times Best Illustrated 1970.

MONSELL, MARY
Underwear! by Mary Monsell, illustrated by Lynn Munsinger; Whitman, 1988. **Awarded:** Little Archer 1989.

MONTGOMERY, CHARLOTTE BAKER
Magic for Mary M. written and illustrated by Charlotte Baker Montgomery; McKay, 1953. **Awarded:** Steck-Vaughn 1955.

MONTGOMERY, LUCY
Emilie de la Nouvelle Lune (original English *Emily of the New Moon*) by Lucy Montgomery, translated by Paule Daveluy; Pierre Tisseyre, 1983. **Awarded:** International Board on Books for Young People (translation/Canada) 1986.

MONTGOMERY, R. A.
Awarded: Jeremiah Ludington 1986.

MONTGOMERY, RUTHERFORD GEORGE
Amikuk by Rutherford G. Montgomery, illustrated by Marie Nonnast; World, 1955. **Awarded:** Spring Book Festival (Middle honor) 1955.

Beaver Water by Rutherford G. Montgomery, illustrated by Robert Doremus; World, 1956. **Awarded:** Boys Club 1957; Spring Book Festival (middle) 1956.

Kildee House by Rutherford G. Montgomery, illustrated by Barbara Cooney; Doubleday, 1949. **Awarded:** Newbery (honor) 1950.

The Stubborn One by Rutherford Montgomery, illustrated by Don Miller; Duell-Sloan-Pearce, 1965. **Awarded:** Western Writers (fiction) 1966.

Wapiti the Elk by Rutherford Montgomery, illustrated by Gardell Dano Christensen; Little, Brown, 1952. **Awarded:** Commonwealth Club of California 1952.

MONTRESOR, BENI
Belling the Tiger by Mary Stolz, illustrated by Beni Montresor; Harper, 1961. **Awarded:** Newbery (honor) 1962.

Little Red Riding Hood retold and illustrated by Beni Montresor; Doubleday, 1991. **Awarded:** New York Times Best Illustrated 1991; Parents' Choice (Story Book) 1991.

The Magic Flute by Stephen Spender, illustrated by Beni Montresor; Putnam, 1966. **Awarded:** New York Times Best Illustrated 1966.

May I Bring a Friend? by Beatrice Schenk de Regniers, illustrated by Beni Montresor; Atheneum, 1964. **Awarded:** Caldecott 1965; Indiana Authors Day (Young Children) 1965.

The Princesses: Sixteen Stories About Princesses edited by Sally P. Johnson, illustrated by Beni Montresor; Harper, 1962. **Awarded:** New York Times Best Illustrated 1962.

MOODIE, JOHN
If You Lived in the Days of the Wild Mammoth Hunters by Mary Elting and Franklin Folsom, illustrated by John Moodie; Four Winds, 1969. **Awarded:** New Jersey Institute of Technology 1970.

MOODIE-HEDDLE, ENID
The Boomerang Book of Legendary Tales by Enid Moodie-Heddle, illustrated by Nancy Parker; Longmans, 1957. **Awarded:** Children's Book Council of Australia (book of the year) 1957.

MOON, CARL
The Runaway Papoose by Grace P. Moon, illustrated by Carl Moon; Doubleday, 1928. **Awarded:** Newbery (honor) 1929.

MOON, GRACE PURDIE
The Runaway Papoose by Grace P. Moon, illustrated by Carl Moon; Doubleday, 1928. **Awarded:** Newbery (honor) 1929.

MOON, HENRIETTA JONES
A Month of Christmases by Siddie Joe Johnson, illustrated by Henrietta Jones Moon; Longmans, 1952. **Awarded:** Steck-Vaughn 1954.

MOON, MARJORIE
Benjamin Tabart's Juvenile Library by Marjorie Moon, illustrated with photos; St. Paul's Bibliographies, 1990. **Awarded:** Harvey Darton Award 1992.

MOON, SARAH
Le Petit Chaperon Rouge by Charles Perrault, illustrated by Sarah Moon; Grasset et Fasquelle, 1983. **Awarded:** Bologna (graphics for children) 1984.

MOON, SHEILA
Knee-deep in Thunder by Sheila Moon, illustrated by Peter Parnall; Atheneum, 1967. **Awarded:** New York Times Best Illustrated 1967.

MOORE, ANNE CARROLL
Awarded: Women's National Book Assn. 1940; Regina 1960.

Nicholas: A Manhattan Christmas Story by Anne Carroll Moore, illustrated by Jay Van Everen; Putnam, 1924. **Awarded:** Newbery (honor) 1925.

MOORE, CHRISTOPHER
The Story of Canada by Janet Lunn and Christopher Moore, illustrated by Alan Daniel; Lester Publishing, 1992. **Awarded:** Mr. Christie's (English text ages 9-14) 1992.

MOORE, EMILY R.
Letters to a Friend on a Brown Paper Bag by Emily R. Moore, manuscript. **Awarded:** Council on Interracial Books (African American) 1975.

MOORE, INGA
Six Dinner Sid written and illustrated by Inga Moore; Simon & Schuster, 1990. **Awarded:** Smarties (Ages 0-5) 1990.

MOORE, JANET GAYLORD
The Many Ways of Seeing: An Introduction to the Pleasures of Art written and illustrated by Janet Gaylord Moore; Collins World, 1969. **Awarded:** Newbery (honor) 1970.

MOORE, JOSEPH THOMAS
Pride Against Prejudice: The Biography of Larry Doby by Joseph Thomas Moore, illustrated with photos; Greenwood, 1988. **Awarded:** Woodson (Outstanding Merit - Secondary) 1989.

MOORE, LILIAN
Awarded: National Council of Teachers of English Poetry 1985; School Library Media Specialists... New York 1990.

MOORE, MARY
Mr. Moon's Last Case by Brian Patten, illustrated by Mary Moore; Scribner, 1975. **Awarded:** Edgar Allan Poe (runnerup) 1977.

MOORE, NANCY
The Unhappy Hippopotamus by Nancy Moore, illustrated by Edward Leight; Vanguard, 1957. **Awarded:** New York Times Best Illustrated 1957.

MOORE, RUTH
Jeb Ellis of Candlemas Bay by Ruth Moore, illustrated by William N. Wilson; Morrow, 1952. **Awarded:** Spring Book Festival (older honor) 1952.

MOORE, YVETTE
A Prairie Alphabet, ABC by Jo Bannatyne-Gugnet, illustrated by Yvette Moore; Tundra, 1992. **Awarded:** Mr. Christie's (English illustration) 1992.

MOORE-SLATER, CAROL W.
Dana Doesn't Like Guns Anymore by Carol W. Moore-Slater, illustrated by Leslie Morales; self-published, 1987; Friendship Press, 1991. **Awarded:** Book Can Develop Empathy 1991.

MOORHOUSE, GEOFFREY
The Church by Geoffrey Moorhouse, illustrated by William Papas; Oxford, 1967. **Awarded:** Greenaway (commended) 1967.

MORALES, LESLIE
Dana Doesn't Like Guns Anymore by Carol W. Moore-Slater, illustrated by Leslie Morales; self published, 1987; Friendship Press, 1991. **Awarded:** Book Can Develop Empathy 1991.

MORAN, MABEL O'CONNOR
see O'MORAN, MABEL

MORDVINOFF, NICOLAS
(pseudonym is Nicolas)

Alphonse, that Bearded One by Natalie Savage Carlson, illustrated by Nicolas Mordvinoff; Harcourt, 1954. **Awarded:** Boys Club 1955; Spring Book Festival (ages 4-8) 1954.

Chaga by William Lipkind, illustrated by Nicolas Mordvinoff; Harcourt, 1955. **Awarded:** New York Times Best Illustrated 1955.

Circus Ruckus by William Lipkind, illustrated by Nicolas Mordvinoff; Harcourt, 1954. **Awarded:** New York Times Best Illustrated 1954.

Davy Crockett's Earthquake by William O. Steele, illustrated by Nicolas Mordvinoff; Harcourt, 1956. **Awarded:** Spring Book Festival (ages 4-8 honor) 1956.

Finders Keepers by William Lipkind, illustrated by Nicolas Mordvinoff; Harcourt, 1951. **Awarded:** Caldecott 1952.

Hortense, the Cow for a Queen by Natalie Savage Carlson, illustrated by Nicolas; Harcourt, 1957. **Awarded:** Spring Book Festival (middle honor) 1957.

The Magic Feather Duster by William Lipkind and Nicolas Mordvinoff, illustrated by Nicolas Mordvinoff; Harcourt, 1958. **Awarded:** New York Times Best Illustrated 1958.

The Two Reds by William Lipkind, illustrated by Nicolas Mordvinoff; Harcourt, 1950. **Awarded:** Caldecott (honor) 1951.

MOREAU, RENE
Les Saltimbanques by Jean Ollivier, illustrated by Rene Moreau; La Farandole, 1962. **Awarded:** Hans Christian Andersen (runnerup) 1964.

MOREY, WALTER NELSON
Awarded: Evelyn Sibley Lampman 1982.

Gentle Ben by Walt Morey, illustrated by John Schoenherr; Dutton, 1965. **Awarded:** Dutton Junior Animal 1965; Sequoyah 1968.

Kavik, the Wolf Dog by Walt Morey, illustrated by Peter Parnall; Dutton, 1968. **Awarded:** Dutton Junior Animal 1968; Dorothy Canfield Fisher 1970; William Allen White 1971.

MORGAN, ALISON
Leaving Home by Alison Morgan, not illustrated; Chatto & Windus, 1979. **Awarded:** Guardian (runnerup) 1980.

MORGAN, CHARLES
Flight of the Solar Ducks by Charles Morgan, not illustrated; Blackie, 1988. **Awarded:** Kathleen Fidler 1988.

MORGAN, HELEN L.
Mistress of the White House by Helen L. Morgan, illustrated by Phyllis Cote; Westminster, 1946. **Awarded:** Spring Book Festival (older honor) 1946.

MORGAN, NICOLA
Pride of Lions written and illustrated by Nicola Morgan; Fitzhenry Whiteside, 1987; Houghton Mifflin, 1992. **Awarded:** Egoff 1988.

MORI, TOSHIO
Woman from Hiroshima by Toshio Mori, not illustrated; Isthmus Press, 1978. **Awarded:** Jane Addams (West Coast honor book) 1980.

MORICE, STELLA MARGERY
The Book of Wiremu by Stella M. Morice, illustrated by Nancy Bolton; Progressive Publication Society, 1944. **Awarded:** Esther Glen 1945.

MORIMOTO, JUNKO
The Inch Boy written and illustrated by Junko Morimoto, English adaptation by Helen Smith; Collins, 1984; Viking Kestrel, 1986. **Awarded:** Children's Book Council of Australia (Picture Book of the Year highly commended) 1985.

Kojuro and the Bears adapted by Helen Smith, illustrated by Junko Morimoto; Collins, 1986. **Awarded:** Ashton Scholastic 1987; Children's Book Council of Australia (picture book of the year) 1987.

A Piece of Straw written and illustrated by Junko Morimoto, English adaptation by Helen Smith; Collins, 1985. **Awarded:** Children's Book Council of Australia (Picture Book of the Year highly commended) 1986.

The White Crane written and illustrated by Junko Morimoto, English adaptation by Helen Smith; Collins, 1985. **Awarded:** Children's Book Council of Australia (Picture Book of the Year commended) 1984.

MORIN, PAUL
The Dragon's Pearls retold by Julie Lawson, illustrated by Paul Morin; Oxford University Press, 1992; Clarion, 1992. **Awarded:** Amelia Frances Howard-Gibbon 1993.

The Orphan Boy by Tololwa M. Mollel, illustrated by Paul Morin; Oxford University Press, 1990. **Awarded:** Governor General's Literary Award (Illustration) 1990; Amelia Frances Howard-Gibbon 1991; Elizabeth Mrazik-Cleaver 1991.

MORISON, SAMUEL ELIOT
The Story of the Old Colony of New Plymouth by Samuel Eliot Morison, illustrated by Charles Overly; Knopf, 1956. **Awarded:** Edison Mass Media (America's past) 1957.

MORLEY, CAROL
A Tale of Two Kings written and illustrated by Carol Morley; ABC, 1991. **Awarded:** Mother Goose (runnersup) 1992.

MORLEY, JACQUELINE
An Egyptian Pyramid by Jacqueline Morley, John James, and Mark Bergin, illustrated; Simon & Schuster, 1991; Peter Bedrick, 1991. **Awarded:** Times Educational Supplement (Senior) 1991.

MOROZUMI, ATSUKO
One Gorilla: A Counting Book written and illustrated by Atsuko Morozumi; Farrar Straus Giroux, 1990. **Awarded:** New York Times Best Illustrated 1990.

MORPURGO, MICHAEL
Waiting for Anya by Michael Morpurgo, not illustrated; Heinemann, 1990; Viking, 1991. **Awarded:** Guardian (runnerup) 1991.

War Horse by Michael Morpurgo, not illustrated; Kaye & Ward, 1982; Greenwillow, 1983, c1982. **Awarded:** Whitbread (runnerup) 1982.

MORRILL, LESLIE
Beaver Valley by Walter D. Edmonds, illustrated Leslie Morrill; Little, Brown, 1971. **Awarded:** Spring Book Festival (middle honor) 1971.

The Celery Stalks at Midnight by James Howe, illustrated by Leslie Morrill; Atheneum, 1983; Avon, 1984. **Awarded:** CRABbery (honor) 1984.

Eddie and the Fairy Godpuppy by Willo Davis Roberts, illustrated by Leslie Morrill; Atheneum, 1984. **Awarded:** West Virginia Children's (Honor book) 1987-88.

Harold and Chester in Scared Silly: A Halloween Treat by James Howe, illustrated by Leslie Morrill; Morrow, 1989. **Awarded:** North Dakota Children's Choice (Picture Book) 1992.

Nighty-nightmare by James Howe, illustrated by Leslie Morrill; Atheneum, 1987. **Awarded:** Garden State Children's Book Award (Younger Fiction) 1990.

MORRIS, ANTHONY
The First of Midnight by Marjorie Darke, illustrated by Anthony Morris; Kestrel, 1977. **Awarded:** Guardian (commended) 1978.

MORRIS, DUDLEY
The Truck that Flew written and illustrated by Dudley Morris; Putnam, 1942. **Awarded:** Spring Book Festival (picture book honor) 1942.

MORRIS, EFFIE LEE
Awarded: Grolier 1992; Women's National Book Assn. 1984.

MORRIS, HOWARD
The Earth Beneath Us by Kirtley F. Mather, illustrated by Howard Morris, photographs by Josef Muench; Random House, 1964. **Awarded:** Edison Mass Media (science book for youth) 1965.

MORRIS, JEAN
Donkey's Crusade by Jean Morris, not illustrated; Chatto & Windus, 1983. **Awarded:** Whitbread (runnerup) 1983.

MORRIS, RICHARD B.
Voices from America's Past by Richard B. Morris and James Woodress, illustrated with photographs; Dutton, 1963. **Awarded:** Edison Mass Media (America's past) 1964.

MORRIS, ROBERT A.
Seashore by Robert A. Morris, illustrated by Arnold Lobel; Harper, 1972. **Awarded:** Children's Book Showcase 1973.

MORRIS, SANDRA
One Lonely Kakapo written and illustrated by Sandra Morris; Hodder & Stoughton, 1991. **Awarded:** Clark, Russell 1992.

MORRIS, SEAN
Window into a Nest by Geraldine Lux Flanagan, photographs by Sean Morris; Kestrel, 1975; Houghton, 1976. **Awarded:** New York Academy of Sciences (older honor) 1977; Times Educational Supplement (senior) 1975.

MORRIS, WILLIE
Good Old Boy by Willie Morris, not illustrated; Harper, 1971. **Awarded:** Steck-Vaughn 1972.

MORRIS, WINIFRED
The Magic Leaf by Winifred Morris, illustrated by Ju-Hong Chen; Atheneum, 1987. **Awarded:** Parents' Choice (Picture Book) 1987.

MORRISON, BILL
The Secret Life of School Supplies by Vicki Cobb, illustrated by Bill Morrison; Harper, 1981. **Awarded:** Washington Irving (nonfiction) 1984.

MORRISON, FRANCES
Awarded: Canadian Library Association's Outstanding Service to Librarianship Award 1981.

MORRISON, LILLIAN
Awarded: Grolier 1987.

MORRISON, LUCILE
The Mystery of Shadow Walk by Lucile Morrison, not illustrated; Dodd Mead, 1964. **Awarded:** Calling All Girls - Dodd, Mead 1963.

MORROW, BETTY
People at the Edge of the World: The Ohlone of Central California by Betty Morrow, illustrated by Shahid Naeem; published by the author, 1982. **Awarded:** Jane Addams (West Coast honor book) 1983.

MORSE, DOROTHY BAYLEY
Tree of Freedom by Rebecca Caudill, illustrated by Dorothy B. Morse; Viking, 1949. **Awarded:** Newbery (honor) 1950; Spring Book Festival (older honor) 1949.

MORTON, ALEXANDRA
Siwiti: A Whale's Story by Alexandra Morton, illustrated by Alexandra Morton and Robin Morton; Orca, 1991. **Awarded:** Egoff Prize 1992.

MORTON, MIRIAM
Fierce and Gentle Warriors by Mikhail Sholokhov, translated by Miriam Morton, illustrated by Milton Glaser; Doubleday, 1967. **Awarded:** Spring Book Festival (older honor) 1967.

The Moon Is Like a Silver Sickle: A Celebration of Poetry by Russian Children by Miriam Morton, illustrated by Eros Keith; Simon & Schuster, 1972. **Awarded:** New Jersey Institute of Technology 1973.

MORTON, ROBIN
Siwiti: A Whale's Story by Alexandra Morton, illustrated by Robin Morton and Alexandra Morton; Orca, 1991. **Awarded:** Egoff Prize 1992.

MOSEL, ARLENE TICHY
The Funny Little Woman retold by Arlene Mosel, illustrated by Blair Lent; Dutton, 1972. **Awarded:** Caldecott 1973; Children's Book Showcase 1973; International Board on Books for Young People (illustration/USA) 1974; Little Archer 1976; New York Times Notable Books 1972.

Tikki Tikki Tembo by Arlene Mosel, illustrated by Blair Lent; Holt, 1968. **Awarded:** Boston Globe Horn Book (illustration) 1968.

MOSER, BARRY
Appalachia: the Voices of Sleeping Birds by Cynthia Rylant, illustrated by Barry Moser; Harcourt Brace Jovanovich, 1991. **Awarded:** Boston Globe Horn Book (Nonfiction) 1991; Ohioana 1992; Parents' Choice (Picture Book) 1991.

In the Beginning: Creation Stories from Around the World by Virginia Hamilton, illustrated by Barry Moser; Harcourt Brace Jovanovich, 1988. **Awarded:** Newbery (Honor) 1989.

Jump Again! More Adventures of Brer Rabbit by Joel Chandler Harris, adapted by Van Dyne Parks, illustrated by Barry Moser; Harcourt Brace Jovanovich, 1987. **Awarded:** Biennale Illustrations Bratislava (Honorable Mention) 1989; New York Times Best Illustrated 1987; Redbook 1987.

Lewis Carroll's Alice's Adventures in Wonderland illustrated by Barry Moser, text edited by Selwyn H. Goodacre, preface and notes by James R. Kincaid; University of California Press, 1982. **Awarded:** American Book Awards (pictorial design) 1983.

Little Tricker the Squirrel Meets Big Trouble the Bear by Ken Kesey, illustrated by Barry Moser; Viking, 1990. **Awarded:** International Board on Books for Young People (Illustration/USA) 1992.

Through the Mickle Woods by Valiska Gregory, illustrated by Barry Moser; Little Brown, 1992. **Awarded:** Parents Choice (Story Book) 1992.

MOSER, ERWIN
Der Rabe Im Schnee written and illustrated by Erwin Moser; Adama Books, 1986. **Awarded:** Owl Prize 1987.

MOSKINS, MARIETTA
Waiting for Moma by Marietta Moskins, illustrated by Richard Lebenson; Coward, 1975. **Awarded:** Sydney Taylor Book Award 1975.

MOSS, ANITA

The Spear and the Piccolo: Heroic and Pastoral Dimensions of William Steig's Dominic and Abel's Island by Anita Moss in *Children's Literature* 10 (1982). **Awarded:** Children's Literature Association Excellence in Criticism 1983.

MOSS, ELAINE

Awarded: Eleanor Farjeon 1976.

MOSS, JEFF

The Butterfly Jar: Poems by Jeff Moss, illustrated by Chris Demarest; Bantam, 1989. **Awarded:** Kentucky Bluegrass (grades 4-8) 1991.

MOST, BERNARD

Dinosaur Cousins? written and illustrated by Bernard Most; Harcourt Brace Jovanovich, 1987. **Awarded:** Irving, Washington (Younger Fiction) 1990.

MOTHERS OF THE CHILDREN

Our Kids by Mothers of the Children; Peckham Publishing Project, 1984. **Awarded:** Other Award 1985.

MOWAT, FARLEY

Awarded: Vicky Metcalf 1970.

Lost in the Barrens by Farley Mowat, illustrated by Charles Geer; Little Brown Canada, 1956. **Awarded:** Canadian Library Assn. 1958; Governor General 1956; International Board on Books for Young People (honour list/Canada) 1958.

Owls in the Family by Farley Mowat, illustrated by Robert Frankenberg; Little, Brown, 1961. **Awarded:** Boys Club 1963.

MOYERS, WILLIAM

The Americans by Harold Coy, illustrated by William Moyers; Little, Brown, 1958. **Awarded:** Edison Mass Media (America's past) 1959.

Stonewall Jackson by Jonathan Daniels, illustrated by William Moyers; Random House, 1959. **Awarded:** North Carolina AAUW 1960.

MOYES, LESLEY

Annie & Moon by Miriam Smith, illustrated by Lesley Moyes; Mallinson Rendel, 1988. **Awarded:** AIM Children's Book Award (Picture Book) 1990.

MOYLER, ALLAN

Foal Creek by Peter Zachary Cohen, illustrated by Allan Moyler; Atheneum, 1972. **Awarded:** Friends of American Writers (ages 10-14) 1973.

MOYNIHAN, ROBERTA

An Edge of the Forest by Agnes Smith, illustrated by Roberta Moynihan; Viking, 1959. **Awarded:** Aurianne 1961; Lewis Carroll Shelf 1966; Spring Book Festival (older) 1959.

MOZLEY, CHARLES

Girl with a Pen: Charlotte Bronte by Elisabeth Kyle, illustrated by Charles Mozley; Holt, 1964. **Awarded:** Spring Book Festival (older honor) 1964.

Portrait of Lisette by Elisabeth Kyle, illustrated by Charles Mozley; Nelson, 1963. **Awarded:** Spring Book Festival (older honor) 1963.

MUELLER, ROBERT E.

Inventor's Notebook: Entirely New Do-it-Yourself Toy Inventions written and illustrated by Robert E. Mueller; John Day, 1963. **Awarded:** New Jersey Institute of Technology (science ages 12-14) 1964.

MUENCH, JOSEF

The Earth beneath Us by Kirtley F. Mather, illustrated by Howard Morris, photographs by Josef Muench; Random House, 1964. **Awarded:** Edison Mass Media (science books for youth) 1965.

MUHLBAUER, RITA

Himmelszelt und Schneckenhaus written and illustrated by Rita Muhlbauer and Hanno Rink; Verlag Sauerlander, 1979. **Awarded:** Bologna (graphics for youth) 1980.

MUIR, MARCIA

Awarded: Nan Chauncy 1983.

MUKERJI, DHAN GOPAL

Gay-Neck: The Story of a Pigeon by Dhan Gopal Mukerji, illustrated by Boris Artzybasheff; Dutton, 1927. **Awarded:** Newbery 1928.

MULKEY, KIM

Rusty Timmons' First Million by Joan Carris, illustrated by Kim Mulkey; Lippincott, 1985. **Awarded:** New Jersey Institute of Technology 1989.

MULLEN, DON

The Story of Old Abe by Malcolm Rosholt and Margaret Rosholt, illustrated by Don Mullen; Rosholt House, 1987. **Awarded:** State Historical Society of Wisconsin 1988.

MULLER, ANDREW

Our Changing World by Ingrid Selberg, illustrated by Andrew Muller; Collins, 1982; Philomel, 1982. **Awarded:** Bologna (Critici in erba) 1983.

MULLER, JORG

The Changing City written and illustrated by Jorg Muller; Atheneum, 1977. **Awarded:** Boston Globe Horn Book (special honorable mention for nonbook illustration) 1977.

The Changing Countryside written and illustrated by Jorg Muller; Atheneum, 1977. **Awarded:** Boston Globe Horn Book (special honorable mention for nonbook illustration) 1977.

Peter und der Wolf by Sergei Prokofiev, retold by Loriot, illustrated by Jorg Muller; Verlag Sauerlander. **Awarded:** Bologna (critici in erba) 1986.

Rabbit Island by Jorg Steiner, translated by Ann Conrad Lammers, illustrated by Jorg Muller; Harcourt, 1978. **Awarded:** Batchelder 1979.

MULLER, ROBIN

Hickory, Dickory, Dock by Robin Muller, illustrated by Suzanne Duranceau; North Winds Press, 1992. **Awarded:** Alcuin 1993.

The Magic Paintbrush written and illustrated by Robin Muller; Doubleday Canada, 1989. **Awarded:** Governor General's Literary Award (Illustration) 1989.

The Sorcerer's Apprentice written and illustrated by Robin Muller; Kids Can Press, 1985. **Awarded:** Alcuin 1986; IODE 1985.

MULLINS, PATRICIA

Rummage by Christobel Mattingly, illustrated by Patricia Mullins; Angus & Robertson, 1981. **Awarded:** Children's Book Council of Australia (book of the year commended) 1982; Children's Book Council of Australia (junior book of the year) 1982.

MUNARI, BRUNO

Bruno Munari's ABC written and illustrated by Bruno Munari; World, 1960. **Awarded:** New York Times Best Illustrated 1960.

The Circus in the Mist written and illustrated by Bruno Munari; World, 1969. **Awarded:** New York Times Best Illustrated 1969.

From Afar It Is an Island translated and adapted by Pierrette Fleutiaux, illustrated by Bruno Munari; World, 1972. **Awarded:** New York Academy of Sciences (younger honor) 1974.

MUNOZ, CLAUDIO
Big Baby by Jon Ward, illustrated by Claudio Munoz; Walker Books, 1986. **Awarded:** Mother Goose (runnerup) 1987.

MUNOZ, RIE
Runaway Mittens by Jean Rogers, illustrated by Rie Munoz; Greenwillow, 1988. **Awarded:** Parents' Choice (Story Book) 1988.

MUNRO, ROXIE
The Inside-Outside Book of New York City written and illustrated by Roxie Munro; Dodd, Mead, 1985. **Awarded:** New York Times Best Illustrated 1985.

MUNSCH, ROBERT
Awarded: Vicky Metcalf 1987.

Love You Forever by Robert N. Munsch, illustrated by Sheila McGraw; Firefly Books, 1986. **Awarded:** North Dakota Children's Choice (Picture Book) 1989.

Thomas' Snowsuit by Robert Munsch, illustrated by Michael Martchenko; Annick Press, 1985. **Awarded:** Ruth Schwartz 1986.

MUNSIL, JANET
Dinner at Aunt Rose's by Janet Munsil, illustrated by Scot Ritchie; Annick Press, 1984. **Awarded:** Alcuin 1985.

MUNSINGER, LYNN
Howliday Inn by James Howe, illustrated by Lynn Munsinger; Atheneum, 1982. **Awarded:** Volunteer State 1984.

Hugh Pine and the Good Place by Jamwillem Van de Wetering, illustrated by Lynn Munsinger; Houghton Mifflin, 1986. **Awarded:** New York Times Notable 1986.

My Mother Never Listens To Me by Marjorie Weinman Sharmat, illustrated by Lynn Munsinger; Whitman, 1984. **Awarded:** Emphasis on Reading (grades 2-3) 1987-88.

Tacky the Penguin by Helen Lester, illustrated by Lynn Munsinger; Houghton Mifflin, 1988. **Awarded:** California Young Reader (Primary) 1991; Colorado Children's Book Award 1990; Golden Sower (K-3) 1991.

Underwear! by Mary Monsell, illustrated by Lynn Munsinger; Whitman, 1988. **Awarded:** Little Archer 1989.

MUNTHE, ADAM JOHN
I Believe in Unicorns by Adam John Munthe, illustrated by Elizabeth Falconer; Chatto, 1979. **Awarded:** Mother Goose (runnerup) 1981.

MURAWSKI, MARIAN
Ksiega Bajek Polskich (Book of Polish Fairy Tales) by Helena Kapelus, illustrated by Marian Murawski; Ludowa Spoldzielnia Wydawnicza, 1988. **Awarded:** Biennale Illustrations Bratislava (Grand Prix) 1989.

MURDOCCA, SAL
Have You Seen Wilhelmina Krumpf? by Judith Chasek, illustrated by Sal Murdocca; Lothrop, 1973. **Awarded:** Children's Book Showcase 1981.

MURPHY, ELSPETH CAMPBELL
Do You See Me, God? Prayers for Young Children by Elspeth Campbell Murphy, illustrated by Bill Duca; Chariot Books, 1989. **Awarded:** Gold Medallion (Preschool) 1990.

MURPHY, JILL
Five Minutes' Peace written and illustrated by Jill Murphy; Walker Books, 1986. **Awarded:** Best Books for Babies 1987.

Peace at Last written and illustrated by Jill Murphy; Macmillan, 1980. **Awarded:** Greenaway (commended) 1980.

MURPHY, JIM
The Boys' War by Jim Murphy, illustrated with photos; Clarion Books, 1990. **Awarded:** Golden Kite (Nonfiction) 1990.

Call of the Wolves by Jim Murphy, illustrated by Mark Alan Weatherby; Scholastic, 1989. **Awarded:** Nevada Young Reader (Primary) 1991-92.

Custom Car: A Nuts-and-Bolts Guide to Creating One by Jim Murphy, illustrated with photos; Clarion, 1989. **Awarded:** New Jersey Institute of Technology 1990.

The Indy 500 by Jim Murphy, illustrated with photographs; Clarion, 1983. **Awarded:** New Jersey Institute of Technology 1983.

The Long Road to Gettysburg by Jim Murphy, illustrated with maps; Clarion, 1992. **Awarded:** Golden Kite (Nonfiction) 1992.

MURPHY, JOSEPH E.
Adventure Beyond the Clouds by Joseph E. Murphy, illustrated with photographs; Dillon Press, 1986. **Awarded:** Friends of American Writers ($350) 1987.

MURPHY, ROBERT
A Heritage Restored: America's Wildlife Refuges by Robert Murphy, illustrated with photographs; Dutton, 1969. **Awarded:** Dutton Junior Animal 1969.

Wild Geese Calling by Robert Murphy, illustrated by John Kaufmann; Dutton, 1966. **Awarded:** Dutton Junior Animal 1966.

MURPHY, SHIRLEY ROUSSEAU
The Ivory Lyre by Shirley Rousseau Murphy, not illustrated; Harper & Row, 1987. **Awarded:** Parents' Choice (Story Book) 1987.

MURRAY, DENIS
The Duck Street Gang by Denis Murray, not illustrated; Hamish Hamilton, 1984. **Awarded:** Guardian (runnerup) 1985.

MURRAY, DON
Man against Earth: The Story of Tunnels and Tunnel Builders by Don Murray, illustrated by Lili Rethi; Lippincott, 1961. **Awarded:** New Jersey Institute of Technology 1961.

MURRAY, GLADYS HALL
Mystery of the Talking Totem Pole by Gladys Hall Murray; not illustrated; Dodd, Mead, 1965. **Awarded:** Calling All Girls - Dodd, Mead 1965.

MURRAY, IRENE
The Trouble with Terry by Joan M. Lexau, illustrated by Irene Murray; Dial, 1962. **Awarded:** Child Study 1962.

MURRAY, PETER
Australia's Prehistoric Animals by Peter Murray, illustrated; Methuen Australia, 1984. **Awarded:** Whitley Awards 1985.

MURRAY, RUTH E.
The True Confessions of Charlotte Doyle by Avi, illustrated by Ruth E. Murray; Orchard, 1990. **Awarded:** Boston Globe

Horn Book (Fiction/Poetry) 1991; Golden Kite (Fiction) 1990; Judy Lopez 1991; Newbery (Honor) 1991.

MUSGROVE, MARGARET WYNKOOP

Ashanti to Zulu: African Traditions by Margaret Musgrove, illustrated by Leo Dillon and Diane Dillon; Dial, 1976. **Awarded:** Boston Globe Horn Book (illustration honor) 1977; Caldecott 1977; New York Times Best Illustrated 1976.

MUSSINO, ATTILIO

The Adventure of Pinocchio by Carlo Collodi, illustrated by Attilio Mussino; Macmillan, 1969, c1925. **Awarded:** Children's Choice [Arizona] (picture book) 1986.

MYERS, ANNA

Red-Dirt Jessie by Anna Myers, not illustrated; Walker, 1992. **Awarded:** Oklahoma Book Award 1993.

MYERS, BERNICE

Awarded: Lucky Book Club Four-Leaf Clover 1979.

MYERS, ELISABETH P.

Langston Hughes: Poet of His People by Elisabeth P. Myers; illustrated by Russell Hoover; Garrard, 1970. **Awarded:** Indiana Authors Day (children) 1971.

MYERS, MITZI

Impeccable Governesses, Rational Dames, and Moral Mothers by Mitzi Myers in Children's Literature 14 (1986). **Awarded:** Children's Literature Assn. Criticism 1987.

MYERS, WALTER DEAN

Crystal by Walter Dean Myers, not illustrated; Viking Kestrel, 1987. **Awarded:** Parents' Choice (Story Book) 1987.

Fallen Angels by Walter Dean Myers, not illustrated; Scholastic, 1988. **Awarded:** Charlotte Book Award (grades 9-12) 1992; Coretta Scott King (Text) 1989; New Jersey Institute of Technology 1989; Parents' Choice (Story Book) 1988; South Carolina Young Adult 1991.

Fast Sam, Cool Clyde and Stuff by Walter Dean Myers, not illustrated; Viking, 1975. **Awarded:** Woodward Park School 1976.

Hoops by Walter Dean Myers, not illustrated; Delacorte, 1981. **Awarded:** Edgar Allan Poe (runnerup) 1982.

Malcolm X: By Any Means Necessary by Walter Dean Myers, illustrated; Scholastic, 1993. **Awarded:** CRABbery 1993.

Motown and Didi: A Love Story by Walter Dean Myers, not illustrated; Viking Kestrel, 1984. **Awarded:** Coretta Scott King (literature) 1985.

The Mouse Rap by Walter Dean Myers, not illustrated; Harper & Row, 1990. **Awarded:** Parents' Choice (Story Book) 1990.

Now Is Your Time! The African-American Struggle for Freedom by Walter Dean Myers, illustrated; HarperCollins, 1991. **Awarded:** Addams (Honor) 1992; Golden Kite (Nonfiction honor) 1991; Coretta Scott King (Text) 1992; Orbis Pictus (Honor) 1992.

The Outside Shot by Walter Dean Myers, not illustrated; Delacorte, 1984. **Awarded:** Parents' Choice (literature) 1984.

The Righteous Revenge of Artemis Bonner by Walter Dean Myers, not illustrated; HarperCollins, 1992. **Awarded:** Parents Choice (Picture Books) 1992.

Scorpions by Walter Dean Myers, not illustrated; Harper & Row, 1988. **Awarded:** Newbery (Honor) 1989.

Somewhere in the Darkness by Walter Dean Myers, not illustrated; Scholastic, 1992. **Awarded:** Boston Globe Horn Book

(Fiction Honor) 1992; Coretta Scott King (Text honor) 1993; Newbery (honor) 1993.

Tales of a Dead King by Walter Dean Myers, not illustrated; Morrow, 1983. **Awarded:** New Jersey Institute of Technology 1983.

Won't Know Till I Get There by Walter Dean Myers, not illustrated; Viking, 1982. **Awarded:** Parents' Choice (literature) 1982.

The Young Landlords by Walter D. Myers; not illustrated; Viking, 1979. **Awarded:** Coretta Scott King 1980.

MYERS, WALTER M.

Where Does the Day Go? by Walter M. Myers, illustrated by Leo Carty; Parents, 1969. **Awarded:** Council on Interracial Books for Children (ages 3-6) 1968.

N

NABB, MAGDALEN

Josie Smith by Magdalen Nabb, illustrated by Pirkko Vainio; Collins, 1988; McElderry, 1989. **Awarded:** Guardian Award (runnerup) 1989.

Josie Smith and Eileen by Magdalen Nabb, illustrated by Pirkko Vainio; Collins, 1991; HarperCollins, 1991; McElderry, 1992. **Awarded:** Smarties (6-8 years) 1991.

NABOKOV, PETER

Native American Testimony: An Anthology of Indian and White Relations: First Encounter to Disposession by Peter Nabokov, illustrated with maps and photographs; Crowell, 1978. **Awarded:** Carter G. Woodson 1979.

NADEJEN, THEODORE

Mountains are Free by Julia Davis Adams, illustrated by Theodore Nadejen; Dutton, 1930. **Awarded:** Newbery (honor) 1931.

My Brother Was Mozart by Claire Lee Purdy and Benson Wheeler, illustrated by Theodore Nadejen; Holt, 1937. **Awarded:** Julia Ellsworth Ford 1937.

NADLER, ELLIS

Captain Eco and the Fate of the Earth by Jonathon Porritt, illustrated by Ellis Nadler; Dorling Kindersley, 1991. **Awarded:** Earthworm Award 1992.

NAEEM, SHAHID

People at the Edge of the World: The Ohlone of Central California by Betty Morrow, illustrated by Shahid Naeem; published by the author, 1982. **Awarded:** Jane Addams (West Coast honor book) 1983.

NAGEL, STINA

Poetry for Autumn by Leland B. Jacobs, illustrated by Stina Nagel; Garrard, 1968. **Awarded:** New Jersey Institute of Technology 1968.

NAIDOO, BEVERLY

Journey to Jo'burg: A South African Story by Beverly Naidoo, illustrated by Eric Velasquez; Lippincott, 1986. **Awarded:** Child Study 1986; Other Award 1985.

NAIRAC, ROSEMONDE

Ancient China by John Hay, illustrated by Rosemonde Nairac and Pippa Brand; Walck, 1974. **Awarded:** New York Academy of Sciences (special honorable mention for publisher) 1975.

NAKAMURA, T.

The Pixie's Invitation by T. Nakamura; Kaisei-sha. **Awarded:** Bologna (critici in erba) 1982.

NAKATANI, CHIYOKO

The Brave Little Goat of Monsieur Seguin by Alphonse Daudet, illustrated by Chiyoko Nakatani; World, 1968. **Awarded:** Spring Book Festival (picture book honor) 1968.

NAMIOKA, LENSEY

Village of the Vampire Cat by Lensey Namioka, not illustrated; Delacorte, 1981. **Awarded:** Edgar Allan Poe (runnerup) 1982.

NANCE, JOHN

Lobo of the Tasaday written and photographed by John Nance; Pantheon, 1982. **Awarded:** Boston Globe Horn Book (non-fiction honor) 1982.

NANKIVELL, JOICE M.

Tales of Christophilos by Joice M. Nankivell, illustrated by Panos Ghikas; Houghton, 1954. **Awarded:** Spring Book Festival (middle honor) 1954.

NAOR, LEAH

Sefereggel (original English *The Foot Book*) by Dr. Seuss, translated by Leah Naor; Keter, 1982. **Awarded:** International Board on Books for Young People (translation/Israel) 1984.

NARAHASHI, KEIKO

I Have a Friend written and illustrated by Keiko Narahashi; McElderry, 1987. **Awarded:** Parents' Choice (Picture Book) 1987.

NARDI, MARCIA

The Life of a Queen written and illustrated by Colette Portal, translated by Marcia Nardi; Braziller, 1964. **Awarded:** New York Times Best Illustrated 1964.

NARELL, IRENA

Joshua: Fighter for Bar Kochba by Irena Narell, not illustrated; Akiba Press, 1978. **Awarded:** Jewish Book Council 1978.

NASH, OGDEN

The Adventures of Isabel by Ogden Nash, illustrated by James Marshall; Little Brown, 1991. **Awarded:** Parents' Choice (Story Book) 1991.

The New Nutcracker Suite and Other Innocent Verses by Ogden Nash, illustrated by Ivan Chermayeff; Little, Brown, 1962. **Awarded:** Spring Book Festival (picture book honor) 1962.

NASH, ROD

In Deutschland by Rod Nash, illustrated by David Parkins; Thomas Nelson/Chancerel, 1984. **Awarded:** Times Educational Supplement (senior) 1984.

NATTI, SUSANNA

Frederick's Alligator by Esther Allen Peterson, illustrated by Susanna Natti; Crown, 1979. **Awarded:** Christopher (ages 5-8) 1980.

NAUGHTON, BILL

The Goalkeeper's Revenge and Other Stories by Bill Naughton, illustrated by Dick de Wilde; Brockhampton Press, 1971. **Awarded:** Other Award 1978.

NAVARRA, JOHN GABRIEL

Superplanes by John Gabriel Navarra, illustrated with photographs; Doubleday, 1979. **Awarded:** New Jersey Institute of Technology 1980.

NAVARRA, TOVA

Playing It Smart by Tova Navarra, illustrated by Tom Kerr; Barron's Press, 1989. **Awarded:** New Jersey Author Awards (Children's) 1990.

NAYLOR, PENELOPE

Black Images: The Art of West Africa by Penelope Naylor, photographs by Lisa Little; Doubleday, 1973. **Awarded:** Spring Book Festival (older honor) 1973.

NAYLOR, PHYLLIS REYNOLDS

Alice in Rapture, Sort of by Phyllis Reynolds Naylor, not illustrated; Atheneum, 1989. **Awarded:** Ethical Culture School 1989.

Beetles, Lightly Toasted by Phyllis Reynolds Naylor, not illustrated; Atheneum, 1987. **Awarded:** Sugarman Children's Book Award 1988; Volunteer State Book Awards (grades 4-7) 1990.

How I Came to Be a Writer by Phyllis Reynolds Naylor, illustrated with photographs; Atheneum, 1978. **Awarded:** Golden Kite (nonfiction) 1978.

Keeping a Christmas Secret by Phyllis R. Naylor, illustrated by Lena Shiffman; Atheneum, 1989. **Awarded:** Christopher (ages 4-7) 1990.

Night Cry by Phyllis Reynolds Naylor, not illustrated; Atheneum, 1984. **Awarded:** Edgar Allan Poe 1985.

Reluctantly Alice by Phyllis Reynolds Naylor, not illustrated; Atheneum, 1991. **Awarded:** Parents' Choice (Story Book) 1991.

Send no Blessings by Phyllis Reynolds Naylor, not illustrated; Atheneum, 1990. **Awarded:** Woodward Park 1991.

Shiloh by Phyllis Reynolds Naylor, not illustrated; Atheneum, 1991. **Awarded:** Newbery 1992.

The Solomon System by Phyllis Reynolds Naylor, not illustrated; Atheneum, 1983. **Awarded:** Child Study 1983.

A String of Chances by Phyllis Reynolds Naylor, not illustrated; Atheneum, 1982. **Awarded:** South Carolina Young Adult 1986.

The Year of the Gopher by Phyllis Reynolds Naylor, not illustrated; Atheneum, 1987; Bantam, 1988. **Awarded:** Young Adult Novel of the Year / Michigan Library Assn. 1988.

NEBEL, GUSTAVE

My Village, My World by David E. Sanford, illustrated by Gustave Nebel; Crown, 1969. **Awarded:** Spring Book Festival (middle honor) 1969.

The Old Witch Goes to the Ball by Ida DeLage, illustrated by Gustave E. Nebel; Garrard, 1969. **Awarded:** New Jersey Institute of Technology 1970.

NEEDLE, JAN

My Mate Shofiq by Jan Needle, not illustrated; Deutsch, 1978. **Awarded:** Guardian (commended) 1979.

A Sense of Shame and Other Stories by Jan Needle, not illustrated; Deutsch, 1980. **Awarded:** Carnegie (commended) 1980.

NEGRI, ROCCO

Journey Outside by Mary Q. Steele, illustrated by Rocco Negri; Viking, 1969. **Awarded:** Lewis Carroll Shelf 1971; Newbery (honor) 1970.

NEGRON, BILL

The Mark of Conte by Sonia Levitin, illustrated by Bill Negron; Atheneum, 1976. **Awarded:** Southern California Council (notable) 1977.

NEILSEN, ANN
Katie's Adventure at Blueberry Pond by Josh McDowell and Dottie McDowell, illustrated by Ann Neilsen; Chariot, 1988. **Awarded:** Gold Medallion (Preschool) 1989.

NEILSON, FRANCES F.
The Donkey from Dorking by Frances F. Neilson, illustrated by Lidia Vitale and Janet Hopkins; Dutton, 1942. **Awarded:** Spring Book Festival (picture book honor) 1942.

NEIMARK, ANNE M.
Touch of Light: The Story of Louis Braille by Anne E. Neimark, illustrated by Robert Parker; Harcourt, 1970. **Awarded:** Friends of American Writers 1971.

NELSEN, DONALD
Sam and Emma by Donald Nelsen, illustrated by Edward Gorey; Parents, 1971. **Awarded:** Children's Book Showcase 1972.

NELSON, THERESA
The Twenty-five Cent Miracle by Theresa Nelson, not illustrated; Bradbury, 1986. **Awarded:** Washington Irving (Older fiction) 1988.

NEMCOVA, JEANNE
Dita Saxova by Arnost Lustig, translated by Jeanne Nemcova, not illustrated; Harper, 1979. **Awarded:** Jewish Book Council 1979.

NESBITT, ESTA
My Brother Stevie by Eleanor Clymer, illustrated by Esta Nesbitt; Holt, 1967. **Awarded:** Woodward Park School 1968.

NESET, GUNAL
Dede Korkut Masallari by Eflatun Gem Guney, illustrated by Gunal Neset; Dogan Kardes, 1958. **Awarded:** Hans Christian Andersen (runnerup) 1960.

NESS, EVALINE
All in the Morning Early by Sorche Nic Leodhas, illustrated by Evaline Ness; Holt, 1963. **Awarded:** Caldecott (honor) 1964.

A Double Discovery written and illustrated by Evaline Ness; Scribner, 1965. **Awarded:** New York Times Best Illustrated 1965.

Exactly Alike written and illustrated by Evaline Ness; Scribner, 1964. **Awarded:** New York Times Best Illustrated 1964.

Josefina February written and illustrated by Evaline Ness; Scribner, 1963. **Awarded:** Spring Book Festival (picture book honor) 1963.

Listen - the Birds by Mary Britton Miller, illustrated by Evaline Ness; Pantheon, 1961. **Awarded:** New York Times Best Illustrated 1961.

Ondine: The Story of a Bird Who Was Different by Maurice Machado Osborne, Jr., illustrated by Evaline Ness; Houghton, 1960. **Awarded:** Spring Book Festival (middle honor) 1960.

A Pocketful of Cricket by Rebecca Caudill, illustrated by Evaline Ness; Holt, 1964. **Awarded:** Caldecott (honor) 1965.

Sam, Bangs & Moonshine written and illustrated by Evaline Ness; Holt, 1966. **Awarded:** Caldecott 1967.

The Sherwood Ring by Elizabeth Marie Pope, illustrated by Evaline Ness; Houghton, 1958. **Awarded:** Spring Book Festival (older honor) 1958.

Thistle and Thyme: Tales and Legends from Scotland by Sorche Nic Leodhas, illustrated by Evaline Ness; Holt, 1962. **Awarded:** Lewis Carroll Shelf 1962; Newbery (honor) 1963.

Tom Tit Tot by Joseph Jacobs, illustrated by Evaline Ness; Scribner, 1965. **Awarded:** Caldecott (honor) 1966.

NETTELL, STEPHANIE
Awarded: Farjeon 1992.

NEUGEBAUER, MICHAEL
The Gift of the Magi by O. Henry, illustrated by Lisbeth Zwerger, lettering by Michael Nugebauer; Neugebauer Press distributed by Alphabet Press, 1982. **Awarded:** New York Times Best Illustrated 1982.

NEVILLE, EMILY CHENEY
Berries Goodman by Emily Cheney Neville, not illustrated; Harper, 1965. **Awarded:** Jane Addams 1966.

It's Like This, Cat by Emily Cheney Neville, illustrated by Emil Weiss; Harper, 1963. **Awarded:** Newbery 1964.

Traveler from a Small Kingdom by Emily Cheney Neville, illustrated by George Mocniak; Harper, 1968. **Awarded:** Spring Book Festival (middle honor) 1968.

NEVILLE, MARY
Woody and Me by Mary Neville, illustrated by Ronni Solbert; Pantheon, 1966. **Awarded:** Spring Book Festival (middle honor) 1966.

NEVINS, ANN
Super Stitches: A Book of Superstitions by Ann Nevins, illustrated by Dan Nevins; Holiday House, 1983. **Awarded:** New Jersey Institute of Technology 1983.

NEVINS, DAN
Super Stitches: A Book of Superstitions by Ann Nevins, illustrated by Dan Nevins; Holiday House, 1983. **Awarded:** New Jersey Institute of Technology 1983.

NEWBERRY, CLARE TURLAY
April's Kittens written and illustrated by Clare Turlay Newberry; Harper & Row, 1940. **Awarded:** Caldecott (honor) 1941.

Barkis written and illustrated by Clare Turlay Newberry; Harper & Row, 1938. **Awarded:** Caldecott (honor) 1939.

Marshamallow written and illustrated by Clare Turlay Newberry; Harper & Row, 1942. **Awarded:** Caldecott (honor) 1943.

T-Bone, the Baby Sitter written and illustrated by Clare Turlay Newberry; Harper & Row, 1950. **Awarded:** Caldecott (honor) 1951.

NEWELL, CROSBY
see BONSALL, CROSBY BARBARA NEWELL

NEWELL, HOPE
The Little Old Woman Who Used Her Head by Hope Newell, illustrated by Margaret Ruse; Nelson, 1966, 1935. **Awarded:** Lewis Carroll Shelf 1972.

Steppin and Family by Hope Newell, illustrated by Anne Merriman Peck; Oxford, 1942. **Awarded:** Spring Book Festival (middle honor) 1942.

NEWFELD, FRANK
Alligator Pie by Dennis Lee, illustrated by Frank Newfeld; Macmillan Canada, 1974. **Awarded:** Canadian Library Assn. 1975; International Board on Books for Young People (text/Canada) 1976; IODE 1974.

Garbage Delight by Dennis Lee, illustrated by Frank Newfeld; Macmillan Canada, 1977. **Awarded:** Canadian Library Assn. 1978; Amelia Frances Howard-Gibbon (runnerup) 1978; International Board on Books for Young People (text/Canada) 1978; Ruth Schwartz 1978.

The Princess of Tomsobo written and illustrated by Frank Newfeld; Oxford (Canada), 1960. **Awarded:** Hans Christian Andersen (runnerup) 1962.

Simon and the Golden Sword by Frank Newfeld and William Toye, illustrated by Frank Newfeld; Oxford, 1976. **Awarded:** Canadian Library Assn. (runnerup) 1977.

NEWFIELD, MARCIA
A Book for Jodan by Marcia Newfield, illustrated by Diane de Groat; Atheneum, 1975. **Awarded:** Woodward Park School 1975.

NEWKIRK, INGRID
Kids Can Save the Animals: 101 Easy Things To Do by Ingrid Newkirk; Warner, 1991. **Awarded:** Book Can Develop Empathy 1991.

NEWMAN, DAISY
Mount Joy by Daisy Newman, illustrated with photographs; Atheneum, 1968. **Awarded:** Spring Book Festival (older honor) 1968.

NEWMAN, FREDERICK R.
Zounds! The Kids' Guide to Sound Making by Frederick R. Newman, illustrated by Elwood H. Smith; Random House, 1983. **Awarded:** New York Academy of Sciences (older honor) 1984.

NEWMAN, PENNY
The One That Got Away by John Parsons, illustrated by Penny Newman; Arncliffe, 1990. **Awarded:** AIM Children's Book Award (Picture Book 3rd Prize) 1992.

NEWMAN, ROBERT
Night Spell by Robert Newman, illustrated by Peter Burchard; Atheneum, 1977. **Awarded:** Edgar Allan Poe (runnerup) 1978.

NEWMAN, SUSAN
Never Say Yes to a Stranger by Susan Newman, photographs by George Tiboni; Putnam, 1985. **Awarded:** New Jersey Institute of Technology 1987.

You Can Say No to a Drink or a Drug: What Every Kid Should Know by Susan Newman, photographs by George Tiboni; Putnam, 1986. **Awarded:** New Jersey Institute of Technology 1987.

NEWSOM, CAROL
Hedgehogs in the Closet by Joan Davenport Carris, illustrated by Carol Newsom; Lippincott, 1988; Dell, 1990, c1988. **Awarded:** New Jersey Institute of Technology 1989.

My Horrible Secret by Stephen Roos, illustrated by Carol Newsom; Delacorte, 1983. **Awarded:** Charlie May Simon 1985-86.

Pets, Vets and Marty Howard by Joan Davenport Carris, illustrated by Carol Newsom; Lippincott, 1984. **Awarded:** New Jersey Institute of Technology 1989.

When the Boys Ran the House by Joan Carris, illustrated by Carol Newsom; Lippincott, 1982. **Awarded:** Iowa Children's 1986; New Jersey Institute of Technology 1989; Volunteer State 1985; Young Hoosier (grades 4-6) 1986.

NEWTON, SUZANNE
c/o Arnold's Corners by Suzanne Newton, not illustrated; Westminster, 1974. **Awarded:** North Carolina AAUW 1974.

I Will Call it Georgie's Blues: A Novel by Suzanne Newton, not illustrated; Viking, 1983. **Awarded:** New York Times Notable Books 1983.

M. V. Sexton Speaking: A Novel by Suzanne Newton, not illustrated; Viking, 1981. **Awarded:** North Carolina AAUW 1982.

Purro and the Prattleberries by Suzanne Newton, illustrated by James Puskas; Westminster, 1971. **Awarded:** North Carolina AAUW 1971.

Reubella and the Old Focus Home by Suzanne Newton, not illustrated; Westminster, 1978. **Awarded:** North Carolina AAUW 1979.

What Are You Up To, William Thomas? by Suzanne Newton, not illustrated; Westminster, 1977. **Awarded:** North Carolina AAUW 1978.

Where Are You When I Need You? by Suzanne Newton, not illustrated; Viking, 1991. **Awarded:** North Carolina AAUW 1991.

NEY, JOHN
Ox Under Pressure by John Ney, not illustrated; Lippincott, 1976. **Awarded:** National Book Award (finalist) 1977.

NG, SIMON
Tales From Gold Mountain by Paul Yee, illustrated by Simon Ng; Douglas & McIntyre, 1989; Macmillan, 1989. **Awarded:** Canadian Library Assn. (runnerup) 1990; Egoff 1990; National Chapter of Canada IODE Violet Downey 1990.

NHUONG, HUYNH QUANG
The Land I Lost: Adventures of a Boy in Vietnam by Huynh Quang Nhuong, illustrated by Vo-Dinh Mai; Harper, 1982. **Awarded:** William Allen White 1985.

NICHOLS, BEVERLY
Den Fortrollade Floden (original English *The Stream that Stood Still*) by Beverly Nichols, translated by Eva Imber Liljeberg; Laseleket, 1985. **Awarded:** International Board on Books for Young People (Translation/Sweden) 1986.

NICHOLS, RUTH
The Marrow of the World by Ruth Nichols, illustrated by Trina Schart Hyman; Macmillan Canada, 1972. **Awarded:** Canadian Library Assn. 1973.

A Walk Out of the World by Ruth Nichols, illustrated by Trina Schart Hyman; Harcourt, 1969. **Awarded:** Spring Book Festival (middle honor) 1969.

NICHOLSON, WILLIAM
The Velveteen Rabbit: or, How Toys Become Real by Margery Williams, illustrated by William Nicholson; Doubleday, 1958. **Awarded:** Lewis Carroll Shelf 1971.

NICKL, PETER
Crocodile, Crocodile by Peter Nickl, illustrated by Binette Schroeder; Nord-Sud Verlag, 1975; Tundra, 1976. **Awarded:** Owl Prize 1976.

Die Geschichte Vom Guten Wolf by Peter Nickl, illustrated by Jozef Wilkon; Nord-Sud Verlag, 1985, c1982. **Awarded:** Owl Prize 1984.

The Wonderful Travels and Adventures of Baron Munchhausen by Peter Nickl, translated by Elizabeth Buchanan Taylor, illustrated by Binette Schroeder; Chatto & Windus, 1979. **Awarded:** New York Times Best Illustrated 1980.

NICKLAUS, CAROL
Konrad by Christine Nostlinger, translated by Anthea Bell, illustrated by Carol Nicklaus; Watts, 1977. **Awarded:** Batchelder 1979.

So Hungry! by Harriet Ziefert, illustrated by Carol Nicklaus; Random House, 1987. **Awarded:** New Jersey Institute of Technology 1988.

Where's Your Head? Psychology for Teenagers by Dale Bick Carlson, illustrated by Carol Nicklaus; Atheneum, 1977. **Awarded:** Christopher (ages 12-up) 1978.

NIC LEODHAS, SORCHE

All in the Morning Early by Sorche Nic Leodhas, illustrated by Evaline Ness; Holt, 1963. **Awarded:** Caldecott (honor) 1964.

Always Room for One More by Sorche Nic Leodhas, illustrated by Nonny Hogrogian; Holt, 1965. **Awarded:** Caldecott 1966.

Thistle and Thyme: Tales and Legends from Scotland by Sorche Nic Leodhas, illustrated by Evaline Ness; Holt, 1962. **Awarded:** Lewis Carroll Shelf 1962; Newbery (honor) 1963.

NICOLAS

see MORDVINOFF, NICOLAS

NICOLLET, JEAN MICHEL

Histoire du Petit Stephen Girard by Mark Twain, translated from English by A. Allais, illustrated by Jean-Michel Nicollet; Editions Gallimard, 1978. **Awarded:** Bologna (graphics for children) 1979.

NIEHUIS, CHARLES

Trapping the Silver Beaver by Charles Niehuis, illustrated by Chris Kenyon; Dodd, Mead, 1956. **Awarded:** Western Writers of America 1957.

NIKLAUS, THELMA

The Orphans of Simitra by Paul-Jacques Bonzon, translated by Thelma Niklaus, illustrated by Simon Jeruchim; Criterion, 1962. **Awarded:** Spring Book Festival (middle) 1962.

NILAND, DEBORAH

ABC of Monsters written and illustrated by Deborah Niland and Kilmeny Niland; Hodder and Stoughton Australia, 1977. **Awarded:** Children's Book Council of Australia (picture book) 1977.

Mulga Bill's Bycycle by A. B. Paterson, illustrated by Deborah Niland and Kilmeny Niland; Collins, 1973. **Awarded:** Children's Book Council of Australia (best illustrated) 1974; International Board on Books for Young People (illustrator/Australia) 1976.

When the Wind Changed by Ruth Park, illustrated by Deborah Niland; Collins, 1981. **Awarded:** New South Wales State Literary Awards (Children's) 1981; Young Australian Best Book Award (picture book) 1986.

NILAND, KILMENY

ABC of Monsters written and illustrated by Deborah Niland and Kilmeny Niland; Hodder and Stoughton Australia, 1977. **Awarded:** Children's Book Council of Australia (picture book) 1977.

Feathers, Fur and Frills written and illustrated by Kilmeny Niland; Hodder & Stoughton, 1980. **Awarded:** Whitley Awards 1981.

Mulga Bill's Bycycle by A. B. Paterson, illustrated by Deborah Niland and Kilmeny Niland; Collins, 1973. **Awarded:** Children's Book Council of Australia (best illustrated) 1974; International Board on Books for Young People (illustrator/Australia) 1976.

NILSEN, ALLEEN

Awarded: ALAN 1987.

NILSSON, ELEANOR

The House Guest by Eleanor Nilsson, not illustrated; Viking, 1991. **Awarded:** Children's Book Council of Australia (Book of the Year Older) 1992; Diabetes Australia Alan Marshall 1992; National Children's Literature Award 1992.

NILSSON, LENNART

Being Born by Sheila Kitzinger, photographs by Lennart Nilsson; Dorling Kindersley, 1986; Grosset, 1986. **Awarded:** Boston Globe Horn Book (nonfiction honor) 1987; Times Educational Supplement (Junior) 1987.

NILSSON, ULF

If You Didn't Have Me by Ulf Nilsson, illustrated by Eva Eriksson; McElderry, 1987. **Awarded:** Batchelder 1988.

NIMMO, JENNY

The Snow Spider by Jenny Nimmo, illustrated by Joanna Carey; Methuen Children's, 1986. **Awarded:** Smarties (grand prix) 1986; Smarties (ages 7-11) 1986; Tir Na n-Og 1987.

NISHIKAWA, OSAMU

Monkeys: The Japanese Macaques by Cynthia Overbeck, photographs by Osamu Nishikawa; Lerner, 1981. **Awarded:** New York Academy of Sciences (special award) 1983.

NISSINEN, AILA

Mina Olen Lammenpei by Aila Nissinen, illustrated by Maija Karma; Soderstrom, 1958. **Awarded:** Hans Christian Andersen (runnerup) 1960.

NIXON, JOAN LOWERY

The Alligator under the Bed by Joan L. Nixon, illustrated by Jan Hughes; Putnam, 1974. **Awarded:** Steck-Vaughn 1975.

The Dark and Deadly Pool by Joan Lowery Nixon, not illustrated; Delacorte, 1987. **Awarded:** Young Hoosier (Grades 6-8) 1990.

A Deadly Game of Magic by Joan Lowery Nixon, not illustrated; Harcourt Brace Jovanovich, 1983. **Awarded:** Young Hoosier (Grades 6-8) 1988.

A Family Apart by Joan Lowery Nixon, not illustrated; Bantam, 1987. **Awarded:** Virginia Young Readers (Middle School) 1992; Western Writers of America Spur 1988.

Fat Chance, Claude by Joan Lowery Nixon, illustrated by Tracy Campbell Pearson; Viking Kestrel, 1987. **Awarded:** Parents' Choice (Story Book) 1987.

The Ghosts of Now by Joan Lowery Nixon, not illustrated; Delacorte, 1984. **Awarded:** Edgar Allan Poe (runnerup) 1985.

In the Face of Danger by Joan Lowery Nixon, not illustrated; Bantam, 1988. **Awarded:** Western Writers of America Spur 1989.

Kidnapping of Christine Lattimore by Joan Lowery Nixon, not illustrated; Harcourt, 1979. **Awarded:** Edgar Allan Poe 1980.

Magnolia's Mixed-up Magic by Joan Lowery Nixon, illustrated by Linda Bucholtz-Ross; Putnam, 1983. **Awarded:** CRABbery 1984.

The Mysterious Red Tape Gang by Joan Lowery Nixon, illustrated by Joan Sandin; Putnam, 1974. **Awarded:** Edgar Allan Poe (runnerup) 1975.

The Other Side of Dark by Joan Lowery Nixon, not illustrated; Delacorte, 1986. **Awarded:** Blue Spruce 1988; California Young Reader (Middle/Junior High) 1990; Edgar Allan Poe 1987; Iowa Teen 1989; Sequoyah Young Adult 1989; Utah Young Adults Book Award 1991; Virginia Young Readers (Middle School) 1989.

The Seance by Joan Lowery Nixon, not illustrated; Harcourt, 1980; Dell, 1981. **Awarded:** Edgar Allan Poe 1981.

The Stalker by Joan Lowery Nixon, not illustrated; Delacorte, 1985. **Awarded:** California Young Reader (Junior High) 1989.

Whispers From the Dead by Joan Lowery Nixon, not illustrated; Delacorte, 1989. **Awarded:** Golden Sower (Young Adult) 1993; Nevada Young Reader (Young Adult) 1991-92,

NOAKES, POLLY
The Amazing Voyage of the Cucumber Sandwich by Peter Rowan, illustrated by Polly Noakes; Cape, 1991. **Awarded:** Science Book Prizes 1992.

NOBLE, IRIS
First Woman Ambulance Surgeon: Emily Barringer by Iris Noble, not illustrated; Messner, 1962. **Awarded:** Commonwealth Club of California 1962.

Tingambato: Adventure in Archaeology by Iris Noble, illustrated; Messner/Simon & Schuster, 1982. **Awarded:** New York Academy of Sciences (older honor) 1983.

NOBLE, MARTY
By Day and By Night by Karen Pandell, illustrated by Marty Noble; Kramer, 1991. **Awarded:** Book Can Develop Empathy 1991.

NOBLE, TRINKA HAKES
The Day Jimmy's Boa Ate the Wash by Trinka Hakes Noble, illustrated by Steven Kellogg; Dial, 1980. **Awarded:** North Dakota Children's Choice (Younger) 1987.

Hansy's Mermaid written and illustrated by Trinka Hakes Noble; Dial, 1983. **Awarded:** New Jersey Institute of Technology 1983.

Jimmy's Boa and the Big Splash Birthday Bash by Trinka Hakes Noble, illustrated by Steven Kellogg; Dial, 1989. **Awarded:** New Jersey Institute of Technology 1990.

Meanwhile Back at the Ranch by Trinka Hakes Noble, illustrated by Tony Ross; Dial, 1987. **Awarded:** Colorado Children's Book Award (runner up) 1989; New Jersey Institute of Technology 1988; North Dakota Children's Choice (Picture Book) 1990.

NODELMAN, PERRY M.
What Makes a Fairy Tale Good: The Queer Kindness of the Golden Bird by Perry M. Nodelman in *Children's Literature in Education* Autumn 1977. **Awarded:** Children's Literature Assn. Award for Literary Criticism (runnerup) 1978.

Text as Teacher: The Beginning of Charlotte's Web by Perry Nodelman in *Children's Literature* 13 (1985). **Awarded:** Children's Literature Assn. Excellence in Criticism (runnerup) 1986.

NOLAN, DENNIS
Dinosaur Dream written and illustrated by Dennis Nolan; Macmillan, 1990. **Awarded:** Golden Kite (Picture-Illustration Honor) 1990.

Step Into the Night by Joanne Ryder, illustrated by Dennis Nolan; Four Winds, 1988. **Awarded:** Commonwealth Club of California 1988; Parents' Choice (Picture Book) 1988.

NOLAN, JEANNETTE COVERT
Awarded: Indiana Authors Day (special citation) 1968.

George Rogers Clark: Soldier and Hero by Jeannette C. Nolan, illustrated by Lee Ames; Messner, 1954. **Awarded:** Indiana Authors Day (children) 1955.

Spy for the Confederacy: Rose O'Neal Greenhow by Jeannette C. Nolan, not illustrated; Messner, 1960. **Awarded:** Indiana Authors Day (young adult) 1961.

NONNAST, MARIE
Amikuk by Rutherford G. Montgomery, illustrated by Marie Nonnast; World, 1955. **Awarded:** Spring Book Festival (middle honor) 1955.

NOOK, GERALD
The Art of Ancient Egypt by Shirley Glubok, illustrated by Gerald Nook; Atheneum, 1962. **Awarded:** Lewis Carroll Shelf 1963.

The Art of the Northwest Coast Indians by Shirley Glubok, illustrated by Gerald Nook; Macmillan, 1975. **Awarded:** Children's Book Showcase 1976.

NOONAN, JULIA
The Throme of the Errill of Sherill by Patricia A. McKillip, illustrated by Julia Noonan; Atheneum, 1973. **Awarded:** Children's Book Showcase 1974.

NORDKVIST, KARL-RUNE
Manuel Zigenarpojken by Karl-Rune Nordkvist, illustrated by I. Rossell-Lindhal; Raben & Sjogren, 1958. **Awarded:** Hans Christian Andersen (runnerup) 1960.

NORDSTROM, URSULA
Awarded: Women's National Book Assn. 1972.

NORMAN, HOWARD
The Owl-Scatterer by Howard Norman, illustrated by Michael McCurdy; Atlantic Monthly Press, 1986. **Awarded:** New York Times Best Illustrated 1986.

NORMAN, LILITH
A Dream of Seas by Lilith Norman, illustrated by Edwina Bell; Collins, 1978. **Awarded:** International Board on Books for Young People (honour list/text/Australia) 1980.

NORMAN, MARY
Boo To a Goose by John Mole, illustrated by Mary Norman; Peterloo Poets, 1987. **Awarded:** Signal Poetry Award 1988.

NORTH, STERLING
Awarded: New Jersey Institute of Technology (New Jersey's children's book writer of the year) 1966.

Abe Lincoln: Log Cabin to White House by Sterling North, illustrated by Lee Ames; Random House, 1956. **Awarded:** Spring Book Festival (older honor) 1956.

Little Rascal by Sterling North, illustrated by Carl Burger; Dutton, 1965. **Awarded:** New Jersey Institute of Technology 1965.

Rascal: A Memoir of a Better Era by Sterling North, illustrated by John Schoenherr; Dutton, 1963. **Awarded:** Aurianne 1965; Lewis Carroll Shelf 1964; Dorothy Canfield Fisher 1965; New Jersey Institute of Technology 1963; Newbery (honor) 1964; Sequoyah 1966; William Allen White 1966; Young Readers Choice 1966.

NORTHWAY, JENNY
Comfort Herself by Geraldine Kaye, illustrated by Jenny Northway; Deutsch, 1984. **Awarded:** Other Award 1985.

NORTON, ALICE MARY
see NORTON, ANDRE

NORTON, ANDRE
Awarded: Ohioana (for body of work) 1980.

Sword in Sheath by Andre Norton, illustrated by Lorence Bjorklund; Harcourt, 1949. **Awarded:** Ohioana (honor) 1950.

NORTON, MARY

Are All the Giants Dead? by Mary Norton, illustrated by Brian Froud; Harcourt, 1975. **Awarded:** New York Times Notable Books 1975.

The Borrowers by Mary Norton, illustrated by Diana Stanley; Dent, 1952. **Awarded:** Carnegie 1952.

The Borrowers by Mary Norton, illustrated by Beth Krush and Joe Krush; Harcourt, 1953. **Awarded:** Lewis Carroll Shelf 1960.

The Borrowers Afloat by Mary Norton, illustrated by Beth Krush and Joe Krush; Harcourt, 1959. **Awarded:** Spring Book Festival (middle honor) 1959.

The Borrowers Afloat by Mary Norton, illustrated by Diana Stanley; Dent, 1959. **Awarded:** Carnegie (commended) 1959; International Board on Books for Young People (honour list/Great Britain) 1962.

NORWEB, JEANNE K.

The Forbidden Door by Jeanne K. Norweb, illustrated by George Laws; David C. Cook, 1985. **Awarded:** New Jersey Institute of Technology 1987.

NOSTLINGER, CHRISTINE

Awarded: Hans Christian Andersen (author) 1984.

The Cucumber King: A Story with a Beginning, a Middle and an End by Christine Nostlinger, translated by Anthea Bell, illustrated by Werner Maurer; Abelard-Schuman, 1975. **Awarded:** International Board on Books for Young People (translation/Great Britain) 1978.

Konrad by Christine Nostlinger, translated by Anthea Bell, illustrated by Carol Nicklaus; Watts, 1977. **Awarded:** Batchelder 1979.

NOVAK, MATT

Claude and Sun by Matt Novak, not illustrated; Bradbury, 1987. **Awarded:** Please Touch 1988.

NOYES, ALFRED

The Highwayman by Alfred Noyes, illustrated by Neil Waldman; Harcourt Brace Jovanovich, 1990. **Awarded:** Washington Irving (Illustration) 1992.

The Highwayman by Alfred Noyes, illustrated by Charles Keeping; Oxford, 1981; Oxford (U.S.), 1982. **Awarded:** Greenaway 1981.

NUMEROFF, LAURA J.

If You Give a Mouse a Cookie by Laura J. Numeroff, illustrated by Felicia Bond; Harper & Row, 1985. **Awarded:** Buckeye (K-2) 1989; California Young Reader (Primary) 1988; Colorado Children's 1988; Emphasis on Reading (K-1) 1986-87; Georgia Children's Picture Storybook 1988; Nevada Young Reader Award (Primary) 1988-89.

If You Give a Moose a Muffin by Laura Joffe Numeroff, illustrated by Felicia Bond; HarperCollins, 1991. **Awarded:** Parents' Choice (Story Book) 1991.

NUNES, LYGIA BOJUNGA

Awarded: Hans Christian Andersen Medal (author) 1982; Hans Christian Andersen (highly commended author/Brazil) 1980.

NURIDSANY, CLAUDE

L'Univers a Deux Voix Insecte by Marie Perennou, Claude Nuridsany, Jacques Very and children of C.E.S.; La Noria. **Awarded:** Bologna (graphics for youth) 1981.

NUTT, KEN

Zoom at Sea by Tim Wynne-Jones, illustrated by Ken Nutt; Douglas & McIntyre, 1983. **Awarded:** Amelia Frances Howard-Gibbon 1984; IODE 1983; Schwartz 1984.

Zoom Away by Tim Wynne-Jones, illustrated by Ken Nutt; Douglas & McIntyre, 1985. **Awarded:** Amelia Frances Howard-Gibbon 1986.

NYBERG, MORGAN

Galahad Schwartz and the Cockroach Army by Morgan Nyberg, not illustrated; Douglas & McIntyre, 1987. **Awarded:** Governor General's Literary Award (Text) 1987.

NYSTROM, CAROLYN

What Happens When We Die? by Carolyn Nystrom, illustrated by Wayne A. Hanna; Moody Press, 1981. **Awarded:** Gold Medallion (cowinner) 1982.

O

OAKLEY, GRAHAM

The Church Mice Adrift by Lore Segal, illustrated by Graham Oakley; Macmillan, 1976; Atheneum, 1976. **Awarded:** Greenaway (highly commended) 1976; New York Times Best Illustrated 1977.

The Church Mice in Action written and illustrated by Graham Oakley; Macmillan, 1982; Atheneum, 1983. **Awarded:** Greenaway (highly commended) 1982; Maschler (runnerup) 1982.

Graham Oakley's Magical Changes written and illustrated by Graham Oakley; Atheneum, 1980. **Awarded:** Boston Globe Horn Book (illustration special citation) 1980.

OBIOLS, MIGUEL

Desde el Iris Con Amor (Iris Series) by Miguel Obiols, illustrated by Carme Sole Vendrell; Aura Communicacion (Barcelona). **Awarded:** Bologna (Critici in Erba) 1992.

Un Iris Irritado (Iris Series) by Miguel Obiols, illustrated by Carme Sole Vendrell; Aura Communicacion (Barcelona). **Awarded:** Bologna (Critici in Erba) 1992.

No Mires Aquel Iris (Iris Series) by Miguel Obiols, illustrated by Carme Sole Vendrell; Aura Communicacion (Barcelona). **Awarded:** Bologna (Critici in Erba) 1992.

El Oro de una Iris (Iris Series) by Miguel Obiols, illustrated by Carme Sole Vendrell; Aura Communicacion (Barcelona). **Awarded:** Bologna (Critici in Erba) 1992.

Que Viene el Iris, Leri (Iris Series) by Miguel Obiols, illustrated by Carme Sole Vendrell; Aura Communicacion (Barcelona). **Awarded:** Bologna (Critici in Erba) 1992.

Tantos Iris Como Dragones (Iris Series) by Miguel Obiols, illustrated by Carme Sole Vendrell; Aura Communicacion (Barcelona). **Awarded:** Bologna (Critici in Erba) 1992.

Todos los Iris al Iris (Iris Series) by Miguel Obiols, illustrated by Carme Sole Vendrell; Aura Communicacion (Barcelona). **Awarded:** Bologna (Critici in Erba) 1992.

OBLIGADO, LILIAN ISABEL

A Dog Called Scholar by Anne H. White, illustrated by Lilian Obligado; Viking, 1963. **Awarded:** Spring Book Festival (middle honor) 1963.

Sad Day, Glad Day by Vivian Laubach Thompson, illustrated by Lilian Obligado; Holiday House, 1962. **Awarded:** New Jersey Institute of Technology 1963.

The Taste of Spruce Gum by Jacqueline Jackson, illustrated by Lilian Obligado; Little Brown, 1966. **Awarded:** Dorothy Canfield Fisher 1968.

O'BRIEN, ANNE SIBLEY
Jamaica's Find by Juanita Havill, illustrated by Anne Sibley O'Brien; Houghton Mifflin, 1986. **Awarded:** Ezra Jack Keats New Writer Award 1987.

O'BRIEN, JACK
The Return of Silver Chief by Jack O'Brien, illustrated by Kurt Wiese; Holt, 1943. **Awarded:** Young Readers Choice 1946.

OBO, SHIZUKO
The Day Mother Sold the Family Swords by Shizuko Obo in Cricket (August 1992). **Awarded:** Witty Short Story 1993.

O'BRIEN, JOHN
Chin Music: Tall Talk and Other Talk by Alvin Schwartz, illustrated by John O'Brien; Lippincott, 1979. **Awarded:** New Jersey Institute of Technology 1980, 1981.

The Grouch and the Tower and Other Sillies written and illustrated by John O'Brien; Harper, 1977. **Awarded:** New Jersey Institute of Technology 1978.

O'BRIEN, KATHERINE
The Year of the Yelvertons by Katherine O'Brien; Oxford University Press, 1981. **Awarded:** Esther Glen 1982.

O'BRIEN, ROBERT C.
Mrs. Frisby and the Rats of NIMH by Robert C. O'Brien, illustrated by Zena Bernstein; Atheneum, 1971. **Awarded:** Boston Globe Horn Book (text honor) 1971; Lewis Carroll Shelf 1972; Massachusetts (grades 4-6) 1978; National Book Award (finalist) 1972; Newbery 1972; Mark Twain 1973; William Allen White 1974; Young Readers Choice 1974.

Z for Zachariah by Robert C. O'Brien, not illustrated; Atheneum, 1975. **Awarded:** Jane Addams (honor) 1976; Edgar Allen Poe 1976.

OBSTFELD, RAYMOND
The Joker and the Thief by Raymond Obstfeld, not illustrated; Delacorte, 1993. **Awarded:** Delacorte Press Prize (Honorable Mention) 1991.

O'CONNOR, JANE
Magic in the Movies: The Story of Special Effects by Jane O'Connor and Katy Hall, illustrated with photographs; Doubleday, 1980. **Awarded:** New York Academy of Sciences (older honor) 1981.

Yours Til Niagara Falls, Abby by Jane O'Connor, illustrated by Margot Apple; Hastings, 1979. **Awarded:** Golden Sower 1982.

O'DELL, SCOTT
Awarded: Hans Christian Andersen (author) 1972; Regina 1978; School Library Media Specialists of New York 1989; University of Southern Mississippi 1976.

Alexandra by Scott O'Dell, not illustrated; Houghton Mifflin, 1984. **Awarded:** Parents Choice (literature) 1984.

The Black Pearl by Scott O'Dell, illustrated by Milton Johnson; Houghton, 1967. **Awarded:** Newbery (honor) 1968.

Black Star, Bright Dawn by Scott O'Dell, illustrated with maps; Houghton Mifflin, 1988. **Awarded:** Woodward Park School 1989.

Child of Fire by Scott O'Dell, not illustrated; Houghton Mifflin, 1974. **Awarded:** New York Times Notable Books 1974.

Island of the Blue Dolphins by Scott O'Dell, not illustrated; Houghton Mifflin, 1960. **Awarded:** Lewis Carroll Shelf 1961; FOCAL 1981; International Board on Books for Young People (USA) 1962; Nene 1964; Newbery 1961; Southern California Council (notable) 1961; Virginia (Elementary) 1982; William Allen White 1963.

The King's Fifth by Scott O'Dell, illustrated by Samuel Bryant; Houghton, 1966. **Awarded:** Newbery (honor) 1967.

Sing Down the Moon by Scott O'Dell, not illustrated; Houghton, 1970. **Awarded:** Newbery (honor) 1971.

Streams to the River, River to the Sea: A Novel of Sacagewea by Scott O'Dell, not illustrated; Houghton Mifflin, 1986. **Awarded:** Scott O'Dell 1986; Parents' Choice (literature) 1986.

O'DONNELL, AL
Cyril: The Quest of an Orphan Squirrel by Eugene McCabe, illustrated by Al O'Donnell; O'Brien Press, 1986. **Awarded:** Reading Association of Ireland 1987.

O'DONNELL, JAMES J.
Every Vote Counts: A Teenage Guide to the Electoral Process by James J. O'Donnell, not illustrated; Messner, 1976. **Awarded:** New Jersey Institute of Technology 1977.

Fire! Its Many Faces and Moods by James O'Donnell, not illustrated; Messner, 1980. **Awarded:** New Jersey Institute of Technology 1981.

O'DONNELL, PETER
The Moonlit Journey written and illustrated by Peter O'Donnell; All Books for Children, 1991; Scholastic, 1991. **Awarded:** Mother Goose (runnersup) 1992.

OECHSLI, KELLY
ABC Pigs Go to Market by Ida DeLage, illustrated by Kelly Oechsli; Garrard, 1977. **Awarded:** New Jersey Institute of Technology 1978.

Herbie's Troubles by Carol Chapman, illustrated by Kelly Oechsli; Dutton, 1981. **Awarded:** California Young Reader (primary) 1985; Georgia Children's Picture Storybook 1983.

Poetry for Winter by Leland B. Jacobs, illustrated by Kelly Oechsli; Garrard, 1970. **Awarded:** New Jersey Institute of Technology 1970.

Scruffy by Peggy Parish, illustrated by Kelly Oechsli; Harper & Row, 1988. **Awarded:** Book Can Develop Empathy 1990.

Weeny Witch by Ida DeLage, illustrated by Kelly Oechsli; Garrard, 1968. **Awarded:** New Jersey Institute of Technology 1968.

OFFEN, HILDA
Nice Work, Little Wolf! written and illustrated by Hilda Offen; Hamish Hamilton, 1991; Dutton, 1992. **Awarded:** Smarties (0-5 years) 1992.

OGDEN, BETINA
A Rabbit Named Harris by Nan Hunt, illustrated by Betina Ogden; William Collins, 1991; Collins/Angus & Robertson, 1991. **Awarded:** New South Wales State Literary Awards (Children's) 1987.

OGLE, RICHARD B.
Claudius the Bee by John F. Leeming, illustrated by Richard B. Ogle; Viking, 1937. **Awarded:** Spring Book Festival (younger honor) 1937.

O'HARE, COLETTE
Seven Years and a Day by Colette O'Hare, illustrated by Beryl Cook; Collins, 1980. **Awarded:** Greenaway (commended) 1980.

What Do You Feed Your Donkey On? Rhymes from a Belfast Childhood by Colette O'Hare, illustrated by Jenny Rodwell; Collins-World, 1978. **Awarded:** Boston Globe Horn Book (illustration honor) 1978.

O. HENRY
The Gift of the Magi by O. Henry, illustrated by Lisbeth Zwerger, lettering by Michael Neugebauer; Alphabet Press/Picture Book Studio, 1982. **Awarded:** New York Times Best Illustrated 1982.

OHLSSON, IB SPANG
Awarded: Hans Christian Andersen (highly commended illustrator/Denmark) 1968, 1970; Hans Christian Andersen (illustrator) 1972.

Benny's Nose by Mel Cebulash, illustrated by Ib Ohlsson; Scholastic, 1972. **Awarded:** New Jersey Institute of Technology 1972.

Farewell to the Farivox by Harry Hartwick, illustrated by Ib Spang Ohlsson; Four Winds, 1972. **Awarded:** Children's Book Showcase 1973.

The Nonsense Book compiled by Duncan Emrich, illustrated by Ib Spang Ohlsson; Four Winds, 1970. **Awarded:** Lewis Carroll Shelf 1971.

OKAMOTO, DOROTHY TOMIYE
Eyak by Dorothy Tomiye Okamoto, manuscript. **Awarded:** Council on Interracial Books (Asian American) 1973

O'KELLEY, MATTIE LOU
A Winter Place by Ruth Yaffe Radin, illustrated by Mattie Lou O'Kelley; Little, Brown, 1982. **Awarded:** Parents' Choice (illustration) 1982.

OKTOBER, TRICIA
Bush Song written and illustrated by Tricia Oktober; Hodder & Stoughton, 1991. **Awarded:** Whitley Awards (Illustrated Children's Book) 1991.

OKUDA, TSUGUO
Magic for Sale by Tsuguo Okuda, illustrated by Masakane Yonekura; Kaisei-sha Publishing. **Awarded:** Bologna (Graphics for Children) 1976.

OLDERMAN, ROBIN
Awarded: L. Frank Baum 1988.

OLDMEADOW, COURT
Awarded: Eleanor Farjeon 1975.

OLDMEADOW, JOYCE
Awarded: Nan Chauncy 1988; Eleanor Farjeon 1975.

OLDS, ELIZABETH
Feather Mountain written and illustrated by Elizabeth Olds; Houghton, 1951. **Awarded:** Caldecott (honor) 1952.

OLIVER, JENNI
Free by Sandol Stoddard, illustrated by Jenni Oliver; Houghton, 1976. **Awarded:** Children's Book Showcase 1977.

A Summer to Die by Lois Lowry, illustrated by Jenni Oliver; Houghton, 1977. **Awarded:** California Young Reader Medal (high school) 1981; International Reading Assn. 1978; Massachusetts Children's (young adult) 1981.

The Way Things Are and Other Poems by Myra Livingston Cohn, illustrated by Jenni Oliver; Atheneum, 1974. **Awarded:** Golden Kite (honor) 1974.

OLIVER, TONY
The Gould League Book of Australian Birds by Don Goodsir, illustrated by Tony Oliver; Golden Press, 1979. **Awarded:** Whitley Awards 1980.

The Gould League Book of Australian Mammals by Don Goodsir, illustrated by Tony Oliver; Golden Press, 1981. **Awarded:** Whitley Awards 1983.

OLLIVIER, JEAN
Les Saltimbanques by Jean Ollivier, illustrated by Rene Moreau; La Farandole, 1962. **Awarded:** Hans Christian Andersen (runnerup) 1964.

OLSEN, ALFA-BETTY
Bible Stories You Can't Forget by Alfa-Betty Olsen and Marshall Efron, illustrated by Ron Barrett; Dutton, 1976; Dell, 1979. **Awarded:** New York Times Notable Books 1976.

OLSON, ARIELLE NORTH
Lighthouse Keeper's Daughter by Arielle North Olson, illustrated by Elaine Wentworth; Little Brown, 1987. **Awarded:** Friends of American Writers 1988.

OLSON, HELEN KRONBERG
The Secret of Spirit Mountain by Helen Kronberg Olson, illustrated by Hameed Benjamin; Dodd, Mead, 1980. **Awarded:** Surrey School 1984.

OMMANNEY, FRANCIS DOWNES
Frogs, Toads and Newts by F. D. Ommanney, illustrated by Deborah Fulfold; Bodley Head, 1973. **Awarded:** Times Educational Supplement (junior) 1974.

O'MORAN, MABEL
Trail of the Little Paiute by Mabel O'Moran, illustrated by Claire Davison; Lippincott, 1952. **Awarded:** Spring Book Festival (older honor) 1952.

ONEAL, ZIBBY
A Formal Feeling: A Novel by Zibby Oneal, not illustrated; Viking, 1982; Ballantine, 1983. **Awarded:** Christopher (ages 12-up) 1983.

In Summer Light by Zibby Oneal, not illustrated; Viking Kestrel, 1985. **Awarded:** Boston Globe Horn Book (fiction) 1986.

War Work by Zibby Oneal, illustrated by George Porter; Viking, 1971. **Awarded:** Friends of American Writers 1972.

O'NEILL, JOAN
Daisy Chain War by Joan O'Neill, not illustrated; Attic Press, 1990. **Awarded:** Reading Association of Ireland (Special Merit) 1991.

O'NEILL, MARY
Winds by Mary O'Neill, illustrated by James Barclay; Doubleday, 1971. **Awarded:** Ohioana 1972.

ONYSHKEWYCH, ZENOWIJ
Jenny's Corner by Frederic Bell, illustrated by Zenowij Onyshkewych; Random House, 1974. **Awarded:** New York Times Notable Books 1974.

OPIE, IONA
I Saw Esau by Iona Opie and Peter Opie, illustrated by Maurice Sendak; Candlewick Press, 1992. **Awarded:** Parents Choice (Picture Book) 1992; Reading Magic Award 1992.

The Singing Game by Iona Opie and Peter Opie, illustrated; Oxford University Press, 1988, c1985. **Awarded:** Children's Literature Assn. Criticism (Book) 1988.

Tail Feathers from Mother Goose: The Opie Rhyme Book by Iona Opie, illustrated; Little Brown, 1988. **Awarded:** Redbook 1988.

OPIE, PETER
I Saw Esau by Peter Opie and Iona Opie, illustrated by Maurice Sendak; Candlewick, 1992. **Awarded:** Parents Choice (Picture Book) 1992; Reading Magic Award 1992.

The Singing Game by Peter Opie and Iona Opie, illustrated; Oxford University Press, 1988, c1985. **Awarded:** Children's Literature Assn. Criticism (Book) 1988.

OPPENHEIM, JOANNE
Have You Seen Birds? by Joanne Oppenheim, illustrated by Barbara Reid; North Winds Press, 1986; Scholastic, 1986. **Awarded:** Governor General (illustrator) 1986; Amelia Frances Howard-Gibbon (runnerup) 1987; IODE 1986; Elizabeth Mrazik-Cleaver 1987; Ruth Schwartz 1987.

OPPENHEIM, SULAMITH
Selchie's Seed by Sulamith Oppenheim, illustrated by Diane Goode; Bradbury, 1975. **Awarded:** Southern California Council (contribution to illustration) 1976.

ORAM, HIAWYN
Angry Arthur by Hiawyn Oram, illustrated by Satoshi Kitamura; Andersen Press, 1982; Harcourt, 1982. **Awarded:** Mother Goose 1983.

ORBAAN, ALBERT
Who Goes Next? True Stories of Exciting Escapes by Robert Edmonds Alter, illustrated by Albert Orbaan; Putnam, 1966. **Awarded:** Boys Club 1966-67.

ORBAAN, ROBERT
Powder and Steel: Notable Battles and Campaigns of the 1800s from New Orleans to the Zulu War written and illustrated by Robert Orbaan; John Day, 1963. **Awarded:** Boys Club 1965.

ORGEL, DORIS
The Devil in Vienna by Doris Orgel, not illustrated; Dial, 1978. **Awarded:** Child Study 1978; Golden Kite (fiction honor) 1978; Sydney Taylor Book Award 1979.

Dwarf Long-Nose by Wilhelm Hauff, translated by Doris Orgel, illustrated by Maurice Sendak; Random House, 1960. **Awarded:** Lewis Carroll Shelf 1963.

Merry, Merry FIBruary by Doris Orgel, illustrated by Arnold Lobel; Parents, 1977. **Awarded:** New York Times Best Illustrated 1977.

ORLEV, URI
The Island on Bird Street by Uri Orlev, translated by Hillel Halkin, not illustrated; Houghton Mifflin, 1984, c1983. **Awarded:** Addams (honor) 1985; Batchelder 1985; Edgar Allan Poe (honor) 1985; Sydney Taylor Book Award 1985.

The Man From the Other Side by Uri Orlev, not illustrated; Houghton Mifflin, 1991. **Awarded:** Batchelder 1992; Jewish Book Council (Once Upon a Time Bookstore Award) 1992.

ORLOWSKY, WALLACE
Who Will Clean the Air? by Wallace Orlowsky and Thomas B. Perera, illustrated by Richard Cuffari; Coward, 1971. **Awarded:** New Jersey Institute of Technology 1972.

ORMEROD, JAN
Happy Christmas, Gemma by Sarah Hayes, illustrated by Jan Ormerod; Walker Books, 1986. **Awarded:** Greenaway (highly commended) 1986.

Sunshine written and illustrated by Jan Ormerod; Kestrel, 1981; Penguin (Australia), 1981; Lothrop, Lee & Shepard, 1981. **Awarded:** Children's Book Council of Australia (picture book of the year) 1982; Greenaway (highly commended) 1981; Mother Goose 1982.

ORMONDROYD, EDWARD
David and the Phoenix by Edward Ormondroyd, illustrated by Joan Raysor; Follett, 1957. **Awarded:** Commonwealth Club of California 1957.

ORTIZ, GLORIA
Strings and Things: Poems and Other Messages for Children by Christy Kenneally, illustrated by Gloria Ortiz; Paulist Press, 1984. **Awarded:** Catholic Book Awards (Children's) 1985.

OSBORN, ROBERT
I Met a Man by John Ciardi, illustrated by Robert Osborn; Houghton Mifflin, 1961. **Awarded:** New Jersey Institute of Technology 1961; Spring Book Festival (ages 4-8 honor) 1961.

OSBORNE, CHESTER G.
The First Lake Dwellers by Chester G. Osborne, illustrated by Richard N. Osborne; Follett, 1956. **Awarded:** Boys Club 1957.

OSBORNE, MARY POPE
Run, Run, as Fast as You Can by Mary Pope Osborne, not illustrated; Dial, 1982. **Awarded:** Woodward Park School 1983.

OSBORNE, MAURICE MACHADO, JR.
Ondine: The Story of a Bird Who Was Different by Maurice Machado Osborne, Jr., illustrated by Evaline Ness; Houghton, 1960. **Awarded:** Spring Book Festival (middle honor) 1960.

OSBORNE, RICHARD N.
The First Lake Dwellers by Chester G. Osborne, illustrated by Richard N. Osborne; Follett, 1956. **Awarded:** Boys Club 1957.

OSOFSKY, AUDREY
Dreamcatcher by Audrey Osofsky, illustrated by Ed Young; Orchard, 1992. **Awarded:** Minnesota (younger children) 1993.

OSMOND, EDWARD
A Valley Grows Up written and illustrated by Edward Osmond; Oxford, 1953. **Awarded:** Carnegie 1953.

OSTENDORF, LLOYD
The Quiet Flame: Mother Marianne of Molokai by Eva K. Betz, illustrated by Lloyd Ostendorf; Bruce, 1963. **Awarded:** New Jersey Institute of Technology (religious) 1964,

OSTERC, LIDIJA
Awarded: Hans Christian Andersen (highly commended illustrator/Yugoslavia) 1970.

OSTMAN, LEMPI
Vaino, a Boy of New Finland by Julia Davis Adams, illustrated by Lempi Ostman; Dutton, 1929. **Awarded:** Newbery (honor) 1930.

OSTROM, JOHN H.
Dinosaurs of North America by Helen R. Sattler, introduction by John H. Ostrom, illustrated by Anthony Rao; Lothrop, Lee & Shepard, 1981. **Awarded:** Boston Globe Horn Book (nonfiction honor) 1982; Golden Kite (nonfiction honor) 1981.

The Illustrated Dinosaur Dictionary by Helen R. Sattler, foreword by John H. Ostrom, illustrations by Pamela Carroll, color insert by Anthony Rao and Christopher Santoro; Lothrop, Lee & Shepard, 1983. **Awarded:** Golden Kite (nonfiction) 1983.

O'SULLIVAN, TOM
Minutemen of the Sea by Tom Cluff, illustrated by Tom O'Sullivan; Follett, 1955. **Awarded:** Charles W. Follett 1955.

Two in the Wilderness by Mary W. Thompson, illustrated by Tom O'Sullivan; McKay, 1967. **Awarded:** Dorothy Canfield Fisher 1969.

OTA, DAIHACHI
Awarded: Hans Christian Andersen (highly commended illustrator/Japan) 1970.

OTAVO, MERJA
Priska Kesasta Kesaan by Merja Otava; Soderstrom, 1959. **Awarded:** Hans Christian Andersen (runnerup) 1962.

OTSUKA, YUZO
Suho and the White Horse: A Legend of Mongolia by Yuzo Otsuka, translated by Yasuko Hirawa, illustrated by Suekichi Akaba; Bobbs Merrill, 1969. **Awarded:** Art Books for Children 1976, 1977, 1978.

OTTLEY, REGINALD
Boy Alone by Reginald Ottley, illustrated by Clyde Pearson; Harcourt, 1966. **Awarded:** Lewis Carroll Shelf 1971; Edison Mass Media (character development in children) 1967; Spring Book Festival (middle) 1966.

OTTO, FREDERICK E.
Awarded: L. Frank Baum 1991.

OUGHTON, TAYLOR
Snowfoot: White Reindeer of the Arctic by Justin F. Denzel, illustrated by Taylor Oughton; Garrard, 1976. **Awarded:** New Jersey Institute of Technology 1977.

OVERBECK, CYNTHIA
Ants by Cynthia Overbeck, photos by Satoshi Kuribayashi; Lerner, 1982. **Awarded:** New York Academy of Sciences (special award) 1983.

Cactus by Cynthia Overbeck, photos by Shabo Hani; Lerner, 1982. **Awarded:** New York Academy of Sciences (special award) 1983.

Carnivorous Plants by Cynthia Overbeck, photos by Kiyoshi Shimizu; Lerner, 1982. **Awarded:** New York Academy of Sciences (special award) 1983.

Cats by Cynthia Overbeck, photos by Shin Yoshino; Lerner, 1983. **Awarded:** New York Academy of Sciences (special award) 1983.

Dragonflies by Cynthia Overbeck, photos by Yuko Sato; Lerner, 1982. **Awarded:** New York Academy of Sciences (special award) 1983.

Elephants by Cynthia Overbeck, photos by Tokumitsu Iwago; Lerner, 1981. **Awarded:** New York Academy of Sciences (special award) 1983.

How Seeds Travel by Cynthia Overbeck, photos by Shabo Hani; Lerner, 1982. **Awarded:** New York Academy of Sciences (special award) 1983.

Lions by Cynthia Overbeck, photos by Tokumitsu Iwago; Lerner, 1981. **Awarded:** New York Academy of Sciences (special award) 1983.

Monkeys: The Japanese Macaques by Cynthia Overbeck, photos by Osamu Nishikawa; Lerner, 1981. **Awarded:** New York Academy of Sciences (special award) 1983.

Sunflowers by Cynthia Overbeck, photos by Susumu Kanozawa; Lerner, 1981. **Awarded:** New York Academy of Sciences (special award) 1983.

Swallowtail Butterflies by Cynthia Overbeck and Jane Dallinger, photos by Yuko Sato; Lerner, 1982. **Awarded:** New York Academy of Sciences (special award) 1983.

OVERHOLSER, WAYNE D.
The Meeker Massacre by Wayne D. Overholser and Lewis B. Patten, illustrated with photographs; Cowles, 1969. **Awarded:** Western Writers (fiction) 1970.

OVERLIE, GEORGE
The Case of the Missing Bills by Beatrice S. Smith, illustrated by George Overlie; Carolrhoda, 1976. **Awarded:** Council of Wisconsin Writers (picture book runnerup) 1977.

OVERLY, CHARLES
The Story of the Old Colony of New Plymouth by Samuel Eliot Morison, illustrated by Charles Overly; Knopf, 1956. **Awarded:** Edison Mass Media (America's past) 1957.

OWEN, CAROLINE DALE
see SNEDEKER, CAROLINE DALE PARKER

OWEN, DYDDGU
Y Flwyddyn Honno by Dyddgu Owen; Christopher Davies, 1978. **Awarded:** Tir Na n-Og (Welsh) 1979.

OWEN, GARETH
Song of the City by Gareth Owen, illustrated by Jonathan Hills; Fontana Young Lions Original, 1985. **Awarded:** Signal Poetry 1986.

OWEN, WILLIAM
Meet the Opossum by Leonard Lee Rue III, with William Owen, photographs by Leonard Lee Rue III; Dodd, Mead, 1983. **Awarded:** New Jersey Institute of Technology 1983.

OWENS, GAIL
A Bundle of Sticks by Pat Rhoads Mauser, illustrated by Gail Owens; Atheneum, 1982. **Awarded:** Dorothy Canfield Fisher 1984; Mark Twain 1985.

The Cybil War by Betsy Byars, illustrated by Gail Owens; Viking, 1981. **Awarded:** Sequoyah 1984; Volunteer State 1983.

Fog in the Meadow by Joanne Ryder, illustrated by Gail Owens; Harper, 1979. **Awarded:** New Jersey Institute of Technology 1980.

Hail, Hail, Camp Timberwood by Ellen Conford, illustrated by Gail Owens; Little, Brown, 1978. **Awarded:** California Young Reader Medal (junior high) 1982; Surrey School 1981; Young Reader's Choice 1981.

The Hot and Cold Summer by Johanna Hurwitz, illustrated by Gail Owens; Morrow, 1984. **Awarded:** Indian Paintbrush 1987; Parents' Choice (literature) 1984; Texas Bluebonnet 1987.

I Had a Friend Named Peter by Janice Cohn, illustrated by Gail Owens; Morrow, 1987. **Awarded:** Parents' Choice (Story Book) 1987.

Julia and the Hand of God by Eleanor Cameron, illustrated by Gail Owens; Dutton, 1977. **Awarded:** FOCAL 1985.

Julia's Magic by Eleanor Cameron, illustrated by Gail Owens; Dutton, 1984. **Awarded:** Parents' Choice (literature) 1984.

Safe as the Grave by Caroline B. Cooney, illustrated by Gail Owens; Coward, 1979. **Awarded:** North Carolina AAUW 1980.

That Julia Redfern by Eleanor Cameron, illustrated by Gail Owens; Dutton, 1982. **Awarded:** Parents' Choice (literature) 1982.

OWENS, MARY BETH

A Caribou Alphabet written and illustrated by Mary Beth Owens; Dog Ear Press, 1988. **Awarded:** Reading Magic Award 1988.

Rosebud & Red Flannel by Ethel Pochocki, illustrated by Mary Beth Owens; Henry Holt, 1991. **Awarded:** Lupine Award 1992.

OWENS, ROBERT

Cockleburr Quarters by Charlotte Baker, illustrated by Robert Owens; Prentice Hall, 1972. **Awarded:** Lewis Carroll Shelf 1973; Spring Book Festival (ages 8-12) 1972.

OXENBURY, HELEN

Cakes and Custards: Children's Rhymes compiled by Brian Alderson, illustrated by Helen Oxenbury; Morrow, 1975. **Awarded:** New York Times Notable Books 1975.

Dragon of an Ordinary Family by Margaret Mahy, illustrated by Helen Oxenbury; Heinemann, 1969. **Awarded:** Greenaway 1969.

Farmer Duck by Martin Waddell, illustrated by Helen Oxenbury; Walker, 1991; Candlewick, 1992. **Awarded:** British Book Awards (Illustrated) 1991; Greenaway (Highly Commended) 1991; Reading Magic Award 1992; Smarties (0-5 years) 1991; Smarties (Grand Prix) 1991.

The Helen Oxenbury Nursery Story Book written and illustrated by Helen Oxenbury; Heinemann, 1985. **Awarded:** Maschler (runnerup) 1985.

The Quangle-Wangle's Hat by Edward Lear, illustrated by Helen Oxenbury; Heinemann, 1969. **Awarded:** Greenaway 1969.

Tom and Pippo series written and illustrated by Helen Oxenbury; Aladdin/Macmillan, 1988- **Awarded:** Reading Magic Award 1988.

We're Going on a Bear Hunt by Michael Rosen, illustrated by Helen Oxenbury; McElderry, 1989. **Awarded:** Boston Globe (Picture Book Honor) 1990; Greenaway (Highly Commended) 1989; Parents' Choice (Picture Book) 1989; Reading Magic 1989; Smarties (Grand Prix) 1989; Smarties (Ages 0-5) 1989.

OXFORD SCIENTIFIC FILMS, LTD.

The Common Frog by Oxford Scientific Films, photographs by George Bernard; Whizzard/Deutsch, 1979. **Awarded:** Times Educational Supplement (junior) 1979.

P

PACE, MILDRED MASTIN

Clara Barton by Mildred M. Pace, illustrated by Robert Ball; Scribner, 1941. **Awarded:** Spring Book Festival (older) 1941.

Old Bones, the Wonder Horse by Mildred M. Pace, illustrated by Wesley Dennis; McGraw, 1955. **Awarded:** Dorothy Canfield Fisher 1957.

Wrapped for Eternity: The Story of the Egyptian Mummies by Mildred Mastin Pace, illustrated by Tom Huffman; McGraw,

1974. **Awarded:** New York Academy of Sciences (older honor) 1975.

PACHTER, HEDWIG

The Short Life of Sophie Scholl by Hermann Vinke, translated by Hedwig Pachter, illustrated with photographs; Harper & Row, 1984. **Awarded:** Addams 1985.

PACKARD, EDWARD

Awarded: Jeremiah Ludington 1986.

PACOVSKA, KVETA

Awarded: Hans Christian Andersen (Illustrator) 1992.

PAGE, KENNETH CALVIN (pseudonym)
see HOGBEN, LANCELOT THOMAS

PAGE, MICHAEL F.

The Runaway Punt by Michael F. Page, illustrated by Robert R. Ingpen; Rigby, 1976. **Awarded:** International Board on Books for Young People (illustration/Australia) 1978.

PAGE, VALERIE KING

Pi Gal by Valerie King Page, illustrated by Jacques Callaert; Dodd, Mead, 1970. **Awarded:** Edith Busby 1969.

PAGET-FREDERICKS, JOSEPH

Sandra and the Right Prince by Mildred N. Anderson, illustrated by Joseph Paget-Fredericks; Oxford, 1951. **Awarded:** Commonwealth Club of California 1951.

PALAZZO, TONY

Charley the Horse written and illustrated by Tony Palazzo; Viking, 1950. **Awarded:** Spring Book Festival (picture book honor) 1950.

Susie the Cat written and illustrated by Tony Palazzo; Viking, 1949. **Awarded:** Spring Book Festival (younger honor) 1949.

Timothy Turtle by Al Graham, illustrated by Tony Palazzo; Robert Welch, 1946. **Awarded:** Caldecott (honor) 1947.

PALIN, MICHAEL

The Mirrorstone by Michael Palin, illustrated by Alan Lee, design by Richard Seymour; Cape, 1986; Knopf, 1986. **Awarded:** Smarties (Innovation) 1986.

PALLADINI, DAVID

The Eyes of the Dragon by Stephen King, illustrated by David Palladini; Viking, 1987. **Awarded:** Blue Spruce 1989.

The Girl Who Cried Flowers and Other Tales by Jane Yolen, illustrated by David Palladini; Crowell, 1974. **Awarded:** Golden Kite 1974; National Book Award (finalist) 1975; New York Times Best Illustrated 1974.

The Moon Ribbon and Other Tales by Jane Yolen, illustrated by David Palladini; Crowell, 1976. **Awarded:** Golden Kite (honor) 1976.

PALLASCH, GERHARD

Annuzza: A Girl of Romania by Hertha Seuberlich, translated by Stella Humphries, illustrated by Gerhard Pallasch; Rand, 1962. **Awarded:** Lewis Carroll Shelf 1963.

PALMER, JAN

Never Steal a Magic Cat by Don Caufield and Joan Caufield, illustrated by Jan Palmer; Doubleday, 1971. **Awarded:** Dorothy Canfield Fisher 1973.

The Toothpaste Millionaire by Jean Merrill, illustrated by Jan Palmer; Houghton, 1974. **Awarded:** Dorothy Canfield Fisher 1976; Sequoyah 1977.

PALMQUIST, ERIC
Rasmus and the Vagabond by Astrid Lindgren, illustrated by Eric Palmquist; Viking, 1960. **Awarded:** Boys Club 1961.

Rasmus Pa Luffen by Astrid Lindgren, illustrated by Eric Palmquist; Raben & Sjogren, 1956. **Awarded:** Hans Christian Andersen 1958.

PALUMBO, TONI
Supermachines by Ralph Hancock, edited by Toni Palumbo, illustrated with photographs and diagrams; Viking, 1978. **Awarded:** New York Academy of Sciences (special award for series in engineering and technology) 1979.

PANDELL, KAREN
By Day and By Night by Karen Pandell, illustrated by Marty Noble; Kramer, 1991. **Awarded:** Book Can Develop Empathy 1991.

PANESIS, NICHOLAS
Journey Cake by Isabel McLennan McMeekin, illustrated by Nicholas Panesis; Messner, 1942. **Awarded:** Julia Ellsworth Ford 1942.

PANNELL, LUCILE
Awarded: Women's National Book Assn. 1949.

PAPAS, WILLIAM
Awarded: Greenaway (for his body of work) 1964.

The Church by Geoffrey Moorhouse, illustrated by William Papas; Oxford, 1967. **Awarded:** Greenaway (commended) 1967.

The Grange at High Force by Philip Turner, illustrated by William Papas; Oxford, 1965. **Awarded:** Carnegie 1965.

A Letter from India written and illustrated by William Papas; Oxford, 1968. **Awarded:** Greenaway (honour) 1968.

A Letter from Israel written and illustrated by William Papas; Oxford, 1968. **Awarded:** Greenaway (honour) 1968.

No Mules written and illustrated by William Papas; Oxford, 1967. **Awarded:** Greenaway (commended) 1967.

Taresh the Tea Planter written and illustrated by William Papas; Oxford, 1968. **Awarded:** Greenaway (honour) 1968.

PAPERNY, MYRA
The Wooden People by Myra Paperny, illustrated by Ken Stampnick; Little, Brown, 1976. **Awarded:** Governor General (author) 1976; Little Brown Canadian 1975.

PARIS, PAT
The Old Witch Finds a New House by Ida DeLage, illustrated by Pat Paris; Garrard, 1979. **Awarded:** New Jersey Institute of Technology 1980.

PARISH, PEGGY
Awarded: Milner 1984.

Amelia Bedelia and the Baby by Peggy Parish, illustrated by Lynn Sweat; Greenwillow, 1981. **Awarded:** Buckeye (K-3 honor) 1983.

Amelia Bedelia Goes Camping by Peggy Parish, illustrated by Lynn Sweat; Greenwillow, 1985. **Awarded:** Garden State Children's Book Award (Easy to Read) 1988.

Dinosaur Time by Peggy Parish, illustrated by Arnold Lobel; Harper, 1974. **Awarded:** Garden State Children's (easy to read) 1977.

Granny and the Indians by Peggy Parish, illustrated by Brinton Turkle; Macmillan, 1969. **Awarded:** Emphasis on Reading (grades 2-3) 1981-82.

Haunted House by Peggy Parish, illustrated by Paul Frame; Macmillan, 1971. **Awarded:** CRABbery (Honor) 1990.

Merry Christmas, Amelia Bedelia by Peggy Parish, illustrated by Lynn Sweat; Greenwillow, 1986. **Awarded:** Garden State Children's Book Award (Easy to Read) 1989.

Scruffy by Peggy Parish, illustrated by Kelly Oechsli; Harper & Row, 1988. **Awarded:** Book Can Develop Empathy 1990.

Teach Us, Amelia Bedelia by Peggy Parish, illustrated by Lynn Sweat; Greenwillow, 1977. **Awarded:** Garden State Children's (easy to read) 1980.

PARK, BARBARA
Awarded: Milner 1986.

Buddies by Barbara Park, not illustrated; Knopf, 1985. **Awarded:** Ethical Culture 1985; Parents' Choice (literature) 1985.

The Kid In the Red Jacket by Barbara Park, not illustrated; Knopf, 1987. **Awarded:** Parents' Choice (Story Book) 1987; West Virginia Children's (Honor Book) 1989-90.

Maxie, Rosie and Earl: Partners in Grime by Barbara Park, illustrated by Alexander Strogart; Knopf, 1990. **Awarded:** Parents' Choice (Story Book) 1990.

Operation: Dump the Chump by Barbara Park, not illustrated; Knopf, 1982. **Awarded:** Volunteer State 1986; Young Hoosier (grades 4-6) 1985.

Rosie Swanson: Fourth-Grade Geek For President by Barbara Park, not illustrated; Knopf, 1989. **Awarded:** Parents' Choice (Story Book) 1991.

Skinnybones by Barbara Park, not illustrated; Random House, 1982. **Awarded:** Georgia Children's 1985; Maud Hart Lovelace 1985; Texas Bluebonnet 1985; Utah Children's 1987; Volunteer State 1987.

PARK, RUTH
Playing Beatie Bow by Ruth Park, not illustrated; Kestrel, 1981, c1980; Atheneum, 1982, c1980. **Awarded:** Children's Book Council of Australia (book of the year) 1981; Boston Globe Horn Book (fiction) 1982; Guardian (runnerup) 1982; International Board on Books for Young People (honour list/author/Australia) 1982; Parents' Choice (literature) 1982.

When the Wind Changed by Ruth Park, illustrated by Deborah Niland; Collins, 1981. **Awarded:** New South Wales State Literary Awards (Children's) 1981; Young Australian's Best Book (picture book) 1986.

PARKER, K. LANGLOH
Australian Legendary Tales by K. Langloh Parker, illustrated by Elizabeth Durack; Angus & Robertson, 1953. **Awarded:** Children's Book Council of Australia 1954.

PARKER, LEWIS
Mine for Keeps by Jean Little, illustrated by Lewis Parker; Little, Brown, 1962. **Awarded:** Little Brown Canadian 1961.

PARKER, NANCY
The Boomerang Book of Legendary Tales by Enid Moodie-Heddle, illustrated by Nancy Parker; Longmans, 1957. **Awarded:** Children's Book Council of Australia (book of the year) 1957.

PARKER, NANCY WINSLOW
The Christmas Camel written and illustrated by Nancy Winslow Parker; Dodd, Mead, 1983. **Awarded:** New Jersey Institute of Technology 1983.

Love from Aunt Betty written and illustrated by Nancy Winslow Parker; Dodd, Mead, 1983. **Awarded:** New Jersey Institute of Technology 1983.

My Mom Travels a Lot by Caroline Feller Bauer, illustrated by Nancy Winslow Parker; Warne, 1981. **Awarded:** Christopher (picture book) 1982; New York Times Best Illustrated 1981.

The President's Car written and illustrated by Nancy Winslow Parker, introduction by Betty Ford; Crowell Jr. Books, 1981. **Awarded:** New York Academy of Sciences (younger honor) 1982.

Willy Bear by Mildred Kantrowitz, illustrated by Nancy Winslow Parker; Parents, 1976. **Awarded:** Christopher (picture book) 1977.

PARKER, ROBERT ANDREW
Battle in the Arctic Seas: The Story of Convoy PQ17 by Theodore Taylor, illustrated by Robert A. Parker; Harper, 1976. **Awarded:** New York Times Notable Books 1976.

Brothers retold by Florence B. Freedman, illustrated by Robert Andrew Parker; Harper, 1985. **Awarded:** Jewish Book Council (illustration) 1986; Sydney Taylor Book Award (picture book) 1986.

Dancing Skelton by Cynthia C. DeFelice, illustrated by Robert Andrew Parker; Macmillan, 1989. **Awarded:** New York Times Best Illustrated 1989.

Flight: A Panorama of Aviation by Melvin B. Zisfein, illustrated by Robert Andrew Parker; Pantheon, 1979. **Awarded:** New York Times Best Illustrated 1981; New York Times Notable Books 1981.

The Green Isle by Philip Burton, illustrated by Robert A. Parker; Dial, 1974. **Awarded:** New Jersey Institute of Technology 1975.

Gunga Din by Rudyard Kipling, illustrated by Robert Andrew Parker; Gulliver Books, 1987. **Awarded:** Parents' Choice (Picture Book) 1987.

Guess Who My Favorite Person Is by Byrd Baylor, illustrated by Robert A. Parker; Scribner, 1977. **Awarded:** Steck-Vaughn 1978.

Pop Corn and Ma Goodness by Edna Mitchell Preston, illustrated by Robert Andrew Parker; Viking, 1969. **Awarded:** Caldecott (honor) 1970; National Book Award (finalist) 1970.

Randolph's Dream by Judith Mellecker, illustrated by Robert Andrew Parker; Knopf, 1991. **Awarded:** Parents' Choice (Picture Book) 1991.

Touch of Light: The story of Louis Braille by Anne E. Neimark, illustrated by Robert Parker; Harcourt, 1970. **Awarded:** Friends of American Writers 1971.

Zeek Silver Moon by Amy Ehrlich, illustrated by Robert A. Parker; Dial, 1972. **Awarded:** New York Times Notable Books 1972.

PARKER, STEVE
Inside the Whale and Other Animals by Steve Parker, illustrated by Ted Dewan; Dorling Kindersley, 1992. **Awarded:** Mother Goose 1992.

PARKER, TOM
The Acorn People by Ron Jones, illustrated by Tom Parker; Abingdon, 1978, c1976. **Awarded:** Emphasis on Reading (Grades 10-12) 1980-81.

PARKINS, DAVID
The Dark Behind the Curtains by Gillian Cross, illustrated by David Parkins; Oxford, 1982. **Awarded:** Carnegie (highly commended) 1982; Guardian (runnerup) 1983.

Handles by Jan Mark, illustrated by David Parkins; Kestrel, 1983; Atheneum, 1985. **Awarded:** Carnegie 1983.

In Deutschland by Rod Nash, illustrated by David Parkins; Thomas Nelson/Chancerel, 1984. **Awarded:** Times Educational Supplement (senior) 1984.

Nothing to Be Afraid of by Jan Mark, illustrated by David Parkins; Kestrel, 1980. **Awarded:** Carnegie (highly commended) 1980; Guardian (special prize) 1981.

Trouble Half-way by Jan Mark, illustrated by David Parkins; Viking Kestrel, 1985. **Awarded:** Guardian (runnerup) 1986.

PARKINSON, ETHELYN M.
Higgins of the Railroad Museum by Ethelyn M. Parkinson, illustrated by Bill McPheeters; Abingdon, 1970. **Awarded:** State Historical Society of Wisconsin 1971.

Never Go Anywhere with Digby by Ethelyn M. Parkinson, illustrated by Leonard Vosburgh; Abingdon, 1971. **Awarded:** Abingdon 1970.

PARKS, GORDON, JR.
J.T. by Jane Wagner, illustrated by Gordon Parks, Jr.; Van Nostrand, 1969. **Awarded:** Georgia Children's 1972.

PARKS, ROSA
Rosa Parks: My Story by Rosa Parks with Jim Haskins, illustrated; Dial, 1992. **Awarded:** Hungry Mind (Young Adult Nonfiction) 1993; Parents Choice (Picture Book) 1992.

PARKS, VAN DYNE
Jump Again! More Adventures of Brer Rabbit by Joel Chandler Harris, adapted by Van Dyne Parks, illustrated by Barry Moser; Harcourt, 1987. **Awarded:** Biennale Illustrations Bratislava (Honorable Mention) 1989; New York Times Best Illustrated 1987Redbook 1987.

PARNALL, PETER
Awarded: Eva L. Gordon 1982.

Annie and the Old One by Miska Miles, illustrated by Peter Parnall; Atlantic-Little, 1971. **Awarded:** Art Books for Children 1973; Christopher (ages 8-12) 1972; Commonwealth Club of California 1971; Newbery (honor) 1972; Woodward Park School 1972.

The Daywatchers written and illustrated by Peter Parnall; Macmillan, 1984. **Awarded:** New York Academy of Sciences (older) 1985.

The Desert Is Theirs by Byrd Baylor, illustrated by Peter Parnall; Scribner, 1975. **Awarded:** Art Books for Children 1977, 1978, 1979; Boston Globe Horn Book (illustration honor) 1976; Caldecott (honor) 1976; New York Academy of Sciences (younger honor) 1976; Steck-Vaughn 1976.

A Dog's Book of Bugs by Elizabeth Griffen, illustrated by Peter Parnall; Atheneum, 1967. **Awarded:** New York Times Best Illustrated 1967.

Everybody Needs a Rock by Byrd Baylor, illustrated by Peter Parnall; Scribner, 1974. **Awarded:** Art Books for Children 1976.

Hawk, I'm Your Brother by Byrd Baylor, illustrated by Peter Parnall; Scribner, 1976. **Awarded:** Caldecott (honor) 1977.

Kavik the Wolf Dog by Walt Morey, illustrated by Peter Parnall; Dutton, 1968. **Awarded:** Dutton Junior Animal 1968; Dorothy Canfield Fisher 1970; William Allen White 1971.

Knee-deep in Thunder by Sheila Moon, illustrated by Peter Parnall; Atheneum, 1967. **Awarded:** New York Times Best Illustrated 1967.

Malachi Mudge by Edward Cecil, illustrated by Peter Parnall; McGraw, 1968. **Awarded:** New York Times Best Illustrated 1968.

Roadrunner by Naomi John, illustrated by Peter Parnall and Virginia Parnall; Unicorn/Dutton, 1980. **Awarded:** Parents' Choice (illustration) 1980.

The Way to Start a Day by Byrd Baylor, illustrated by Peter Parnall; Scribner, 1978. **Awarded:** Caldecott (honor) 1979.

PARNALL, VIRGINIA
Roadrunner by Naomi John, illustrated by Virginia Parnall and Peter Parnall; Unicorn/Dutton, 1980. **Awarded:** Parents' Choice (illustration) 1980.

PARRAMORE, BARBARA M.
The People of North Carolina by Barbara M. Parramore, illustrated; Sadlier, 1972. **Awarded:** North Carolina AAUW 1973.

PARRISH, ANNE
Dream Coach written and illustrated by Anne Parrish and Dillwyn Parrish; Macmillan, 1924. **Awarded:** Newbery (honor) 1925.

Floating Island written and illustrated by Anne Parrish; Harper, 1930. **Awarded:** Newbery (honor) 1931.

The Story of Appleby Capple written and illustrated by Anne Parrish; Harper, 1950. **Awarded:** Newbery (honor) 1951.

PARRISH, DILLWYN
Dream Coach written and illustrated by Dillwyn Parrish and Anne Parrish; Macmillan, 1924. **Awarded:** Newbery (honor) 1925.

PARRISH, HELEN RAND
At the Palace Gates by Helen Rand Parrish, illustrated by Leo Politi; Viking, 1949. **Awarded:** Commonwealth Club of California 1949; Spring Book Festival (under 12 honor) 1949.

PARRY, CAROLINE
Let's Celebrate! Canada's Special Days written and illustrated by Caroline Parry; Kids Can Press, 1987. **Awarded:** Information Book Award 1988; IODE 1987.

PARSONS, JOHN
The One That Got Away by John Parsons, illustrated by Penny Newman; Arncliffe, 1990. **Awarded:** AIM Children's Book Award (Picture Book 3rd Prize) 1992.

PARTRIDGE, JENNY
Mr. Squint written and illustrated by Jenny Partridge; World's Work, 1980. **Awarded:** Bologna (critici in erba) 1981.

PASCAL, FRANCINE
Awarded: Milner 1988.

The Hand-me-Down Kid by Francine Pascal, not illustrated; Viking, 1980. **Awarded:** Dorothy Canfield Fisher 1982.

PASCHEL, HERBERT P.
The First Book of Color by Herbert P. Paschel, illustrated by Caru Studios; Watts, 1959. **Awarded:** Boys Club 1960.

PASCO, DALLAS
The Wonders of Astronomy by William E. Butterworth, illustrated by Dallas Pasco; Putnam, 1964. **Awarded:** New Jersey Institute of Technology (science ages 8-12) 1964.

PASCOE, ELAINE
Racial Prejudice by Elaine Pascoe, illustrated with photos; Franklin Watts, 1985. **Awarded:** Woodson (Outstanding Merit) 1986.

PASNAK, WILLIAM
In the City of the King by William Pasnak, not illustrated; Douglas & MacIntyre, 1984. **Awarded:** R. Ross Annett 1985.

Under the Eagle's Claw by William Pasnak, not illustrated; Douglas & MacIntyre, 1988. **Awarded:** R. Ross Annett 1989.

PASTIC, GEORGE
The Violin by Robert Thomas Allen, illustrated by George Pastic; McGraw, 1976. **Awarded:** Ruth Schwartz 1977.

PATENT, DOROTHY HINSHAW
Awarded: Eva L. Gordon 1986.

Evolution Goes on Everyday by Dorothy Hinshaw Patent, illustrated by Matthew Kalmenoff; Holiday, 1977. **Awarded:** Golden Kite (nonfiction honor) 1977.

The Lives of Spiders by Dorothy Hinshaw Patent, illustrated with photographs; Holiday House, 1980. **Awarded:** Golden Kite (nonfiction) 1980.

PATERSON, A. B. (ANDREW BARTON)
The Man from Ironbark by Andrew Barton Paterson, illustrated by Quentin Hole; Collins Australia, 1974. **Awarded:** Children's Book Council of Australia (picture book) 1975.

Mulga Bill's Bycycle by A. B. Paterson, illustrated by Deborah Niland and Kilmeny Niland; Collins, 1973. **Awarded:** Children's Book Council of Australia (best illustrated) 1974; International Board on Books for Young People (illustration/Australia) 1976.

Waltzing Matilda by Andrew Barton Paterson, illustrated by Desmond Digby; Collins Australia, 1970. **Awarded:** Children's Book Council of Australia (picture book) 1971; Bologna (critici in erba) 1972.

PATERSON, DIANE
Smile for Auntie written and illustrated by Diane Paterson; Dial, 1976. **Awarded:** Children's Book Showcase 1977.

PATERSON, KATHERINE
Awarded: ALAN 1987; Keene State College 1987; Kerlan 1983; Regina Medal 1988; University of Southern Mississippi 1983.

Bridge to Terabithia by Katherine Paterson, illustrated by Donna Diamond; Crowell, 1977. **Awarded:** Blue Spruce 1986; Lewis Carroll Shelf 1978; Michigan Young Readers (division II runnerup) 1980; Newbery 1978; Virginia Young Readers (Elementary) 1983.

Come Sing, Jimmy Jo by Katherine Paterson, not illustrated; Lodestar, 1985. **Awarded:** New York Times Notable 1985; Parents' Choice (literature) 1985.

The Crane Wife retold by Sumiko Yagawa, translated by Katherine Paterson, illustrated by Suekichi Akaba; Morrow, 1981. **Awarded:** New York Times Best Illustrated 1981; New York Times Notable Books 1981.

The Great Gilly Hopkins by Katherine Paterson, not illustrated; Crowell, 1978. **Awarded:** Jane Addams (honor) 1979; Christopher (ages 9-12) 1979; CRABbery (honor) 1979; Garden State Children's (younger fiction) 1981; Georgia Children's 1981; Iowa Children's Choice 1981; Massachusetts Children's (elementary) 1981; National Book Award 1979;

Newbery (honor) 1979; Sunshine (runnerup) 1984; William Allen White 1981.

Jacob Have I Loved by Katherine Paterson, not illustrated; Crowell, 1980. **Awarded:** CRABbery (honor) 1981; New York Times Notable Books 1980; Newbery 1981.

The King's Equal by Katherine Paterson, illustrated by Vladimir Vagin; HarperCollins, 1992. **Awarded:** Irma S. and James H. Black 1992.

The Master Puppeteer by Katherine Paterson, illustrated by Haru Wells; Crowell, 1976. **Awarded:** National Book Award 1977; Edgar Allan Poe (runnerup) 1977.

Rebels of the Heavenly Kingdom by Katherine Paterson, not illustrated; Lodestar/Dutton, 1983. **Awarded:** Parents' Choice (literature) 1983.

The Tale of the Mandarin Ducks by Katherine Paterson, illustrated by Leo Dillon and Diane Dillon; Dutton, 1990. **Awarded:** Boston Globe Horn Book (Picture Book) 1991; New York Times Best Illustrated 1990.

The World in 1492 by Jean Fritz, Katherine Paterson, Patricia McKissack, Fredrick McKissack, Margaret Mahy and Jamake Highwater, illustrated by Stefano Vitale; Henry Holt, 1992. **Awarded:** Hungry Mind (Young Adult/Nonfiction) 1993.

PATON, ALAN
The Land and People of South Africa by Alan Paton, illustrated with photographs; Lippincott, 1955. **Awarded:** Spring Book Festival (older honor) 1955.

PATON, JANE
Ragged Robin (poems) by James Reeves, illustrated by Jane Paton; Dutton, 1961. **Awarded:** Carnegie (commended) 1961.

PATON WALSH, GILLIAN
see PATON WALSH, JILL

PATON WALSH, JILL
The Emperor's Winding Sheet by Jill Paton Walsh, not illustrated; Macmillan, 1974. **Awarded:** Whitbread 1974.

Fireweed by Jill Paton Walsh, not illustrated; Farrar, 1969, 1970. **Awarded:** Spring Book Festival (older) 1970.

Gaffer Samson's Luck by Jill Paton Walsh, illustrated by Brock Cole; Viking Kestrel, 1985. **Awarded:** Smarties (Grand Prix) 1985; Smarties (ages 7-11) 1985.

Goldengrove by Jill Paton Walsh, not illustrated; Farrar, 1972. **Awarded:** New York Times Notable Books 1972.

A Parcel of Patterns by Jill Paton Walsh, not illustrated; Kestrel, 1983; Farrar, 1983. **Awarded:** Universe 1984; Whitbread (runnerup) 1983.

Unleaving by Jill Paton Walsh, not illustrated; Farrar, 1976. **Awarded:** Boston Globe Horn Book (fiction) 1976; Children's Book Showcase 1977.

When Grandma Came by Jill Paton Walsh, illustrated by Sophy Williams; Viking, 1992. **Awarded:** Mother Goose (runnerup) 1993.

PATTEN, BRIAN
Mr. Moon's Last Case by Brian Patten, illustrated by Mary Moore; Scribner, 1975. **Awarded:** Edgar Allan Poe (runnerup) 1977.

PATTEN, LEWIS B.
The Meeker Massacre by Lewis B. Patten and Wayne D. Overholser, illustrated with photographs; Cowles, 1969. **Awarded:** Western Writers of America (fiction) 1970.

PATTERSON, CHARLES
Marian Anderson by Charles Patterson, illustrated; Watts, 1988. **Awarded:** Woodson (Secondary) 1989.

PATTERSON, CLAIRE
It's OK To Be You! Feeling Good About Growing Up by Claire Patterson, illustrated by Lindsay Quilter; Century Hutchinson, 1988. **Awarded:** New Zealand Library Assn. Non Fiction for Young People 1989.

PATTERSON, FRANCINE, DR.
Koko's Kitten by Dr. Francine Patterson, photographs by Dr. Ronald H. Cohn; Scholastic, 1985. **Awarded:** New York Academy of Sciences (younger honor) 1986.

Koko's Story by Francine Patterson, photographs by Ronald H. Cohn; Scholastic, 1987. **Awarded:** Garden State Children's Book Award (Younger Nonfiction) 1990.

PATTERSON, GEOFFREY
The Goose that Laid the Golden Egg written and illustrated by Geoffrey Patterson; Deutsch, 1986. **Awarded:** Smarties (ages 6 and under) 1986.

PATTERSON, IPPY
No Bones by Elizabeth Shepard, illustrated by Ippy Patterson; Macmillan, 1988. **Awarded:** New York Academy of Sciences (Special Award to Field Guides - Younger) 1989.

PATTERSON, LILLIE G.
Awarded: Helen Keating Ott 1985.

Martin Luther King, Jr.: A Man of Peace by Lillie Patterson, illustrated by Victor Mays; Garrard, 1969. **Awarded:** Coretta Scott King 1970.

Martin Luther King, Jr. and the Freedom Movement by Lillie Patterson, illustrated; Facts on File, 1989. **Awarded:** Coretta Scott King (Text honor) 1990.

PAUL, AILEEN
Kids Cooking Without a Stove: A Cookbook for Young Children by Aileen Paul, illustrated by Carol Inouye; Doubleday, 1975. **Awarded:** New Jersey Institute of Technology 1977.

Kids Gardening: A First Indoor Gardening Book for Children by Aileen Paul, illustrated by Arthur Hawkins; Doubleday, 1972. **Awarded:** New Jersey Institute of Technology 1972.

PAUL, KORKY
The Fish Who Could Wish by John Bush, illustrated by Korky Paul; Kane Miller, 1991. **Awarded:** Redbook 1991.

Winnie the Witch by Valerie Thomas and Korky Paul, illustrated by Korky Paul; Oxford University Press, 1987. **Awarded:** Children's Book Award (Federation) 1987.

PAUL, LISSA
Enigma Variations: What Feminist Theory Knows About Children's Literature by Lissa Paul in *Signal 54* (September 1987). **Awarded:** Children's Literature Assn. Criticism Award (runner-up) 1988.

PAULSEN, GARY
Awarded: ALAN Award 1991.

Boy Who Owned the School: A Comedy of Love by Gary Paulsen, not illustrated; Orchard, 1990. **Awarded:** Parents' Choice (Story Book) 1991.

Dogsong by Gary Paulsen, not illustrated; Bradbury, 1985. **Awarded:** Newbery (honor) 1986; Parents' Choice (literature) 1985; Volunteer State Book Awards (grades 7-9) 1989.

Hatchet by Gary Paulsen, not illustrated; Bradbury, 1987. **Awarded:** Buckeye (grades 6-8) 1991; Dorothy Canfield

Fisher 1989; Georgia Children's Book Award 1991; Golden Archer 1989; Iowa Teen 1990; Maud Hart Lovelace 1991; Minnesota (finalist) 1988; Newbery (honor) 1988; North Dakota Children's Choice (Juvenile Fiction) 1990; Sequoyah Young Adult 1990; Surrey School 1989; Virginia Young Readers (Middle School) 1990; William Allen White 1990; Young Hoosier (grades 6-8) 1991.

Tracker by Gary Paulsen, not illustrated; Bradbury, 1984. **Awarded:** Society of Midland Authors 1985.

The Winter Room by Gary Paulsen, not illustrated; Orchard, 1989. **Awarded:** Judy Lopez 1990; Newbery (Honor) 1990.

Woodsong by Gary Paulsen, illustrated by Ruth Wright Paulsen; Bradbury, 1990. **Awarded:** Minnesota (Older children) 1991; Western Writers of America Spur (Juvenile Nonfiction) 1991.

PAULSEN, RUTH WRIGHT
Woodsong by Gary Paulsen, illustrated by Ruth Wright Paulsen; Bradbury, 1990. **Awarded:** Minnesota (Older children) 1991; Western Writers of America Spur (Juvenile Nonfiction) 1991.

PAVEY, PETER
One Dragon's Dream written and illustrated by Peter Pavey; Nelson, 1979. **Awarded:** Children's Book Council of Australia (picture book) 1980.

PAXTON, ARTHUR
Making Music text and photographs by Arthur Paxton, concept by Helen Sive Paxton; Atheneum, 1986. **Awarded:** New Jersey Institute of Technology 1987, 1988.

PAXTON, HELEN SIVE
Making Music text and photographs by Arthur Paxton, concept by Helen Sive Paxton; Atheneum, 1986. **Awarded:** New Jersey Institute of Technology 1987, 1988.

PAYLIN, JOLIE
Cutover Country: Jolie's Story by Jolie Paylin, illustrated by Judy Appenzeller La Motte; Iowa State University Press, 1976. **Awarded:** State Historical Society of Wisconsin 1977.

PAYNE, BERNAL C., JR.
Experiment in Terror by Bernal C. Payne, Jr., not illustrated; Houghton Mifflin, 1987. **Awarded:** Nevada Young Reader Award (Young Adult) 1989-90.

PAYNE, EMMY
Katy No-Pocket by Emmy Payne, illustrated by H. A. Rey; Houghton Mifflin, 1944. **Awarded:** Emphasis on Reading (grades K-1) 1980-81.

PAYNE, HARRY C.
The Reign of King Babar by Harry C. Payne in *Children's Literature* 11 (1983). **Awarded:** Children's Literature Excellence in Criticism (runnerup) 1984.

PAYNE, JOAN BALFOUR
The Journey of Josiah Talltatters by Josephine Balfour Payne, illustrated by Joan Balfour Payne; Ariel, 1953. **Awarded:** Spring Book Festival (ages 4-8 honor) 1953.

The Piebald Princess written and illustrated by Joan Balfour Payne; Ariel, 1954. **Awarded:** Spring Book Festival (ages 4-8 honor) 1954.

The Stable that Stayed by Josephine Balfour Payne, illustrated by Joan Balfour Payne; Pellegrini & Cudahy, 1952. **Awarded:** Spring Book Festival (picture book honor) 1952.

PAYNE, JOSEPHINE BALFOUR
The Journey of Josiah Talltatters by Josephine Balfour Payne, illustrated by Joan Balfour Payne; Ariel, 1953. **Awarded:** Spring Book Festival (ages 4-8 honor) 1953.

The Stable that Stayed by Josephine Balfour Payne, illustrated by Joan Balfour Payne; Pellegrini & Cudahy, 1952. **Awarded:** Spring Book Festival (picture book honor) 1952.

PAYNE, STEPHEN
Young Hero of the Range by Stephen Payne, illustrated by Charles H. Geer; Lantern Press, 1954. **Awarded:** Western Writers of America 1955.

PAYSON, DALE
Ann, Aurelia and Dorothy by Natalie Savage Carlson, illustrated by Dale Payson; Harper, 1968. **Awarded:** Woodward Park School 1969.

The Crackajack Pony by Mebane H. Burgwyn, illustrated by Dale Payson; Lippincott, 1969. **Awarded:** North Carolina AAUW 1970.

PEACOCK, DAVID
The Sea Serpent of Grenadier Pond written and illustrated by David Peacock; Hounslow, 1986. **Awarded:** Alcuin 1987.

PEARCE, A. (ANN) PHILIPPA
Awarded: Golden Cat 1988.

The Battle of Bubble and Squeak by A. Philippa Pearce, illustrated by Alan Baker; Deutsch, 1978. **Awarded:** Carnegie (commended) 1978; Whitbread 1978.

A Dog so Small by A. Philippa Pearce, illustrated by Antony Maitland; Lippincott, 1963. **Awarded:** Spring Book Festival (middle) 1963.

The Minnow Leads to Treasure by A. Philippa Pearce, illustrated by Edward Ardizzone; World, 1958. **Awarded:** Lewis Carroll Shelf 1959; Spring Book Festival (middle honor) 1958.

Minnow on the Say by A. Philippa Pearce, illustrated by Edward Ardizzone; Oxford, 1955. **Awarded:** Carnegie (commended) 1955; International Board on Books for Young People (Great Britain) 1956.

Mrs. Cockle's Cat by A. Philippa Pearce, illustrated by Antony Maitland; Kestrel, 1961. **Awarded:** Greenaway 1961.

Shadow Cage and Other Tales of the Supernatural by A. Philippa Pearce, illustrated by Janet Archer; Kestrel, 1977. **Awarded:** Carnegie (commended) 1977.

The Squirrel-Wife by A. Philippa Pearce, illustrated by Derek Collard; Crowell, 1972. **Awarded:** Spring Book Festival (picture book honor) 1972.

Tom's Midnight Garden by A. Philippa Pearce, illustrated by Susan Einzig; Lippincott, 1959; Oxford, 1958. **Awarded:** Carnegie 1958; Lewis Carroll Shelf 1963; International Board on Books for Young People (honour list/Great Britain) 1960.

The Way to Sattin Shore by Philippa Pearce, illustrated by Charlotte Voake; Greenwillow, 1984. **Awarded:** Parents Choice (literature) 1984.

What the Neighbours Did and Other Stories by A. Philippa Pearce, illustrated by Faith Jacques; Longman Young Books, 1972. **Awarded:** International Board on Books for Young People (honour list/text/Great Britain) 1974.

PEARCE, FRED
Ian and Fred's Big Green Book by Fred Pearce, illustrated by Ian Winton; Kingfisher, 1991. **Awarded:** Times Educational Supplement (Junior) 1991.

PEARE, CATHERINE OWENS
The Helen Keller Story by Catherine O. Peare, not illustrated; Crowell, 1959. **Awarded:** Sequoyah 1962; William Allen White 1962.

Mahatma Gandhi: The Father of Nonviolence by Catherine Owens Peare, illustrated by Paul Frame; Hawthorne, 1969. **Awarded:** Boys Club 1951.

PEARLMAN, CORINNE
Ottoline at the British Museum by Sally Craddock, illustrated by Corinne Pearlman; Macdonald, 1987; Simon & Schuster, 1990. **Awarded:** Mother Goose (runner-up) 1988.

PEARSON, CLYDE
Boy Alone by Reginald Ottley, illustrated by Clyde Pearson; Harcourt, 1966. **Awarded:** Lewis Carroll Shelf 1971; Edison Mass Media (character development in children) 1967; Spring Book Festival (middle) 1966.

PEARSON, GAYLE
Fish Friday by Gayle Pearson, not illustrated; Atheneum, 1986. **Awarded:** Bay Area Book Reviewers Assn. (Children's Book) 1987.

PEARSON, KIT
A Handful of Time by Kit Pearson, not illustrated; Penguin Viking Canada, 1987. **Awarded:** Canadian Library Assn. 1988.

Looking At the Moon by Kit Pearson, not illustrated; Viking, 1991. **Awarded:** Canadian Library Assn. (Runnerup) 1992.

The Sky Is Falling by Kit Pearson, not illustrated; Viking Kestrel, 1989. **Awarded:** Bilson 1990; Canadian Library Assn. 1990; Mr. Christie's (English text) 1989.

PEARSON, TRACY CAMPBELL
Fat Chance, Claude by Joan Lowery Nixon, illustrated by Tracy Campbell Pearson; Viking Kestrel, 1987. **Awarded:** Parents' Choice (Story Book) 1987.

PEASE, HOWARD
Heart of Danger: A Tale of Adventure on Land and Sea with Tod Moran, Third Mate of the Tramp Steamer Araby by Howard Pease, not illustrated; Doubleday, 1946. **Awarded:** Boys Club 1949; Child Study 1946.

Long Wharf: A Story of Young San Francisco by Howard Pease, illustrated by Manning de V. Lee; Dodd, 1939. **Awarded:** Spring Book Festival (older honor) 1939.

Thunderbolt House by Howard Pease, illustrated by Armstrong Sperry; Doubleday, 1944. **Awarded:** Commonwealth Club of California 1944.

PEAVER, WALT
The Witchy Broom by Ida DeLage, illustrated by Walt Peaver; Garrard, 1969. **Awarded:** New Jersey Institute of Technology 1969.

PECK, ANNE MERRIMAN
Runaway Balboa by Enid Johnson, illustrated by Anne Merriman Peck; Harper, 1938. **Awarded:** Spring Book Festival (younger honor) 1938.

Steppin and Family by Hope Newell, illustrated by Anne Merriman Peck; Oxford, 1942. **Awarded:** Spring Book Festival (middle honor) 1942.

PECK, BETH
Witch Cat by Joan Carris, illustrated by Beth Peck; Lippincott, 1984. **Awarded:** Ethical Culture 1984.

PECK, GRAHAM
Little Wu and the Watermelons by Beatrice Liu, illustrated by Graham Peck; Follett, 1954. **Awarded:** Charles W. Follett 1954.

PECK, RICHARD
Awarded: ALAN Award 1990; Margaret A. Edwards 1990; University of Southern Mississippi 1991.

Are You in the House Alone? by Richard Peck, not illustrated; Viking, 1976. **Awarded:** New Jersey Institute of Technology 1978; Edgar Allen Poe 1977.

Dreamland Lake by Richard Peck, not illustrated; Holt, 1973. **Awarded:** Edgar Allan Poe (runnerup) 1974.

The Ghost Belonged to Me by Richard Peck, not illustrated; Viking, 1975. **Awarded:** Friends of American Writers (older) 1976.

Princess Ashley by Richard Peck, not illustrated; Delacorte, 1987. **Awarded:** Nevada Young Reader Award (Young Adult) 1990-91; Soaring Eagle (Grades 10-12) 1991.

PECK, ROBERT NEWTON
A Day No Pigs Would Die by Robert Newton Peck, not illustrated; Knopf, 1972; Dell, 1974. **Awarded:** Colorado Children's 1977; Media & Methods (paperback) 1975; Spring Book Festival (older honor) 1973.

Soup by Robert Newton Peck, illustrated by Charles Gehm; Knopf, 1974; Dell, 1979, c1974. **Awarded:** Michigan Young Readers 1984.

Soup for President by Robert Newton Peck, illustrated by Ted Lewin; Knopf, 1978. **Awarded:** Mark Twain 1981.

PECK, VIRGINIA
Secrets of the Best Choice by Lois Johnson, illustrated by Virginia Peck; NavPress, 1988. **Awarded:** Gold Medallion (Elementary) 1989.

Thanks for Being My Friend by Lois Johnson, illustrated by Virginia Peck; NavPress, 1988. **Awarded:** Gold Medallion (Elementary) 1989.

You Are Wonderfully Made by Lois Johnson, illustrated by Virginia Peck; NavPress, 1988. **Awarded:** Gold Medallion (Elementary) 1989.

You're Worth More Than You Think by Lois Johnson, illustrated by Virginia Peck; NavPress, 1988. **Awarded:** Gold Medallion (Elementary) 1989.

PEDER, MARGARET SAYERS
Of Love and Shadows by Isabel Allende, translated from Spanish by Margaret Sayers Peder, not illustrated; Knopf, 1987. **Awarded:** Soaring Eagle (Grades 10-12) 1990.

PEET, BILL
Awarded: George G. Stone for collected works 1985.

Big Bad Bruce written and illustrated by Bill Peet; Houghton Mifflin, 1977. **Awarded:** California Young Reader Medal (primary) 1980; Georgia Picture Book 1979.

Bill Peet: An Autobiography written and illustrated by Bill Peet; Houghton Mifflin, 1989. **Awarded:** Caldecott (honor) 1990; Golden Kite (Nonfiction honor) 1989; Golden Kite (Picture-Illustration honor) 1989; Reading Magic 1989; Southern California Council (Notable Book Celebrating a Creative Life) 1990; Utah Children's Informational Book Award 1991.

Cappyboppy written and illustrated by Bill Peet; Houghton, 1966. **Awarded:** Indiana Authors Day (children) 1967.

Cyrus, the Unsinkable Sea Serpent written and illustrated by Bill Peet; Houghton, 1975. **Awarded:** Little Archer 1977.

Farewell to Shady Glade written and illustrated by Bill Peet; Houghton, 1966. **Awarded:** Southern California Council (contribution to illustration) 1967.

How Droofus the Dragon Lost His Head written and illustrated by Bill Peet; Houghton, 1971. **Awarded:** California Young Reader Medal (primary) 1976; Colorado Children's 1976.

PELGROM, ELS
The Winter When Time Was Frozen by Els Pelgrom, translated by Raphael Rudnik and Maryka Rudnik, not illustrated; Morrow, 1980. **Awarded:** Batchelder 1981.

PELHAM, DAVID
A Is For Animals: 26 Pop-up Surprises: An Animal ABC written and illustrated by David Pelham; Simon & Schuster, 1991. **Awarded:** Redbook 1991.

PELLOWSKI, ANNE
Awarded: Grolier 1979; Women's National Book Assn. 1980.

First Farm in the Valley: Anna's Story by Anne Pellowski, illustrated by Wendy Watson; Philomel, 1982. **Awarded:** State Historical Society of Wisconsin 1983.

PELTA, KATHY
Bridging the Golden Gate by Kathy Pelta, illustrated with photos; Lerner Publications, 1987. **Awarded:** New York Academy of Sciences (Older honor) 1988.

PENICK, IB
The Dwindling Party written and illustrated by Edward Gorey, paper engineering by Ib Penick; Random House, 1982. **Awarded:** Parents' Choice (illustration) 1982.

PENISTON-BIRD, ADRIAN
The Terrible Tale of the Vanishing Library by Adrian Peniston-Bird. **Awarded:** Mary Grant Bruce Story Award (Open $500) 1989.

PERCEVAL, DON
Owl in the Cedar Tree by Natachee Scott Momaday, illustrated by Don Perceval; Northland Press, 1975. **Awarded:** Western Heritage 1976.

PERENNOU, MARIE
L'Univers a Deux Voix Insecte by Marie Perennou, Claude Nuridsany, Jacques Very and children of C.E.S.; La Noria. **Awarded:** Bologna (graphics for youth) 1981.

PERERA, THOMAS B.
Who Will Clean the Air? by Thomas B. Perera and Wallace Orlowsky, illustrated by Richard Cuffari; Coward, 1971. **Awarded:** New Jersey Institute of Technology 1972.

PERETZ, I. L.
The Magician by I. L. Peretz, adapted and illustrated by Uri Shulevitz; Macmillan, 1973. **Awarded:** Children's Book Showcase 1974; Spring Book Festival (younger) 1973.

PEREZ, NORAH A.
Strange Summer in Stratford by Norah A. Perez, illustrated by Robert Ihrig; Little, Brown, 1968. **Awarded:** Little Brown Canadian 1967.

PERKINS, CAROL MORSE
I Saw You from Afar: A Visit to the Bushmen of the Kalahari Desert by Carol Morse Perkins and Richard Marlin Perkins, illustrated with photographs; Atheneum, 1965. **Awarded:** Spring Book Festival (middle honor) 1965.

PERKINS, RICHARD MARLIN
I Saw You from Afar: A Visit to the Bushmen of the Kalahari Desert by Richard Marlin Perkins and Carol Morse Perkins, illustrated with photographs; Atheneum, 1965. **Awarded:** Spring Book Festival (middle honor) 1965.

PERKYNS, DOROTHY
Rachel's Revolution by Dorothy Perkyns, illustrated; Lancelot Press, 1988. **Awarded:** Bilson 1989.

PERL, LILA
Fat Glenda Turns Fourteen by Lila Perl, not illustrated; Clarion, 1991. **Awarded:** Parents' Choice (Story Book) 1991.

Junk Food, Fast Food, Health Food: What America Eats and Why by Lila Perl, not illustrated; Houghton/Clarion, 1980. **Awarded:** Boston Globe Horn Book (nonfiction honor) 1981.

PERL, SUSAN
Watch Out! by Norah Smaridge, illustrated by Susan Perl; Abingdon, 1965. **Awarded:** New Jersey Institute of Technology (grades K-3) 1965.

What a Silly Thing to Do by Norah Smaridge, illustrated by Susan Perl; Abingdon, 1967. **Awarded:** New Jersey Institute of Technology 1967, 1968.

Where Is Daddy? The Story of a Divorce by Beth Goff, illustrated by Susan Perl; Beacon, 1969. **Awarded:** Child Study (special citation) 1968.

PEROCI, ELA
Awarded: Hans Christian Andersen (highly commended author/Yugoslavia) 1970.

PERRAULT, CHARLES
Cinderella: or, The Little Glass Slipper by Charles Perrault, illustrated by Marcia Brown; Scribner, 1954. **Awarded:** Caldecott 1955.

Der Gestiefelte Kater (Puss in Boots) by Charles Perrault, illustrated by Stasys Eidrigevicius; Nord-Sud Verlag, 1990; North South Books, 1990. **Awarded:** Biennale Illustrations Bratislava (Grand Prix) 1991.

Le Petit Chaperon Rouge by Charles Perrault, illustrated by Sarah Moon; Grasset et Fasquelle, 1983. **Awarded:** Bologna (graphics for children) 1984.

Puss in Boots by Charles Perrault, illustrated by Marcia Brown; Scribner, 1952. **Awarded:** Caldecott (honor) 1953.

Puss in Boots by Charles Perrault, illustrated by Fred Marcellino; Farrar Straus Giroux, 1990. **Awarded:** Caldecott (Honor) 1991; Parents' Choice (Picture Book) 1990; Reading Magic Award 1990.

PERROT, JEAN
Maurice Sendak's Ritual Cooking of the Child in Three Tableaux by Jean Perrot in *Children's Literature* 18 (1990). **Awarded:** Children's Literature Assn. Criticism 1991.

PERSHALL, MARY
You Take the High Road by Mary Pershall, not illustrated; Penguin Books Australia, 1988; Dial, 1990. **Awarded:** Family Award 1988; New South Wales State Literary Awards (Children's) 1989.

PESSIN, DEBORAH
The Jewish People: Book Three by Deborah Pessin, illustrated by Ruth Levin; United Synagogue of America, 1952. **Awarded:** Jewish Book Council 1953.

PETERSEN, RUSSELL F.
Dinosaurs and Other Pre-Historic Animals by Darlene Geis, illustrated by Russell F. Petersen; Grosset, 1959. **Awarded:** Boys Club 1960.

PETERSHAM, MAUD
An American ABC written and illustrated by Maud Petersham and Miska Petersham; Macmillan, 1941. **Awarded:** Caldecott (honor) 1942/

Pran of Albania by Elizabeth C. Miller, illustrated by Maud Petersham and Miska Petersham; Doubleday, 1929. **Awarded:** Newbery (honor) 1930.

The Rooster Crows written and illustrated by Maud Petersham and Miska Petersham; Macmillan, 1945. **Awarded:** Caldecott 1946.

PETERSHAM, MISKA

An American ABC written and illustrated by Miska Petersham and Maud Petersham; Macmillan, 1941. **Awarded:** Caldecott (honor) 1942.

Pran of Albania by Elizabeth C. Miller, illustrated by Miska Petersham and Maud Petersham; Doubleday, 1929. **Awarded:** Newbery (honor) 1930.

The Rooster Crows written and illustrated by Miska Petersham and Maud Petersham; Macmillan, 1945. **Awarded:** Caldecott 1946.

PETERSON, CAROLYN SUE
Awarded: Grolier 1984.

PETERSON, ESTHER ALLEN

Frederick's Alligator by Esther Allen Peterson, illustrated by Susanna Natti; Crown, 1979. **Awarded:** Christopher (ages 5-8) 1980.

PETERSON, JOHN
Awarded: Lucky Book Club Four-Leaf Clover Award 1974.

PETERSON, LORRAINE

If You Really Trust Me, Why Can't I Stay Out Later? by Lorraine Peterson, illustrated; Bethany House, 1991. **Awarded:** Gold Medallion (Youth) 1992.

PETERSON, MIRIAM E.
Awarded: Children's Reading Round Table 1966.

PETERSON, RUSSELL FRANCIS

Stars, Mosquitos and Crocodiles: The American Travels of Alexander von Humboldt edited by Millicent E. Selsam, illustrated by Russell Francis Peterson; Harper & Row, 1962. **Awarded:** Boys Club 1963.

PETIE, HARIS

The World Beneath our Feet: The Story of Soil by Martin L. Keen, illustrated by Haris Petie; Messner, 1974. **Awarded:** New Jersey Institute of Technology 1975.

PETRIDES, HEIDRUN

Dominique and the Dragon by Jurgen Tamchina, translated by Elizabeth D. Crawford, illustrated by Heidrun Petrides; Harcourt, 1968. **Awarded:** Spring Book Festival (picture book honor) 1969.

PETROSKI, CATHERINE

The Summer that Lasted Forever by Catherine Petroski, not illustrated; Houghton Mifflin, 1984. **Awarded:** North Carolina AAUW 1985.

PETTIT, TED S.

A Guide to Nature Projects by Ted S. Pettit, illustrated by Walt Wenzel; Norton, 1966. **Awarded:** New Jersey Institute of Technology 1967.

PEVSNER, STELLA

And You Give Me a Pain, Elaine by Stella Pevsner, not illustrated; Seabury, 1978. **Awarded:** Golden Kite (fiction) 1978; Clara Ingram Judson 1978.

Cute Is a Four-Letter Word by Stella Pevsner, not illustrated; Houghton/Clarion, 1980. **Awarded:** Sandburg 1980.

A Smart Kid like You by Stella Pevsner, not illustrated; Seabury, 1974. **Awarded:** Dorothy Canfield Fisher 1977.

PEYTON, K. M.
(pseudonyms for Kathleen Peyton and Michael Peyton)

The Edge of the Cloud by K. M. Peyton, illustrated by Victor G. Ambrus; Oxford, 1969. **Awarded:** Carnegie 1969.

Flambards by K. M. Peyton, illustrated by Victor G. Ambrus; Oxford, 1967; World, 1968. **Awarded:** Boston Globe Horn Book (text honor) 1969; Carnegie (commended) 1967; Guardian 1970.

The Maplin Bird by K. M. Peyton, illustrated by Victor G. Ambrus; Oxford, 1964; World, 1965. **Awarded:** Carnegie (commended) 1964; Spring Book Festival (older honor) 1965.

The Plan for Birdmarsh by K. M. Peyton, illustrated by Victor G. Ambrus; Oxford, 1965. **Awarded:** Carnegie (commended) 1965.

Thunder in the Sky by K. M. Peyton, illustrated by Victor G. Ambrus; Oxford, 1966. **Awarded:** Carnegie (commended) 1966.

Windfall by K. M. Peyton, illustrated by Victor G. Ambrus; Oxford, 1962. **Awarded:** Carnegie (commended) 1962.

PEYTON, KATHLEEN
see PEYTON, K. M.

PEYTON, MICHAEL
see PEYTON, K. M.

PFEFFER, SUSAN BETH
Awarded: School Library Media Specialists, New York 1983.

About David by Susan Beth Pfeffer, not illustrated; Delacorte, 1980; Dell, 1982. **Awarded:** South Carolina Young Adult 1983.

Courage Dana by Susan Pfeffer, illustrated by Jenny Rutherford; Delacorte, 1983. **Awarded:** Parents' Choice (literature) 1983.

Kid Power by Susan Beth Pfeffer, illustrated by Leigh Grant; Watts, 1977. **Awarded:** Dorothy Canfield Fisher 1979; Sequoyah 1980.

The Year Without Michael by Susan Beth Pfeffer, not illustrated; Bantam, 1987. **Awarded:** South Carolina Young Adult 1990.

PFISTER, MARCUS

The Rainbow Fish written and illustrated by Marcus Pfister; North-South Books, 1992. **Awarded:** Bologna (Critici in Erba) 1993; Christopher (ages 5-8) 1993.

PHELAN, JOSEPH A.

The Intruder by John Rowe Townsend, illustrated by Joseph A. Phelan; Lippincott, 1970; Oxford, 1969. **Awarded:** Boston Globe Horn Book (text) 1970; Edgar Allan Poe 1971.

PHELAN, TERRY WOLFE

The S. S. Valentine by Terry Wolfe Phelan, illustrated by Judy Glasser; Four Winds, 1979. **Awarded:** New Jersey Institute of Technology 1981.

PHILBROOK, ELIZABETH

Far from Marlborough Street by Elizabeth Philbrook, illustrated by Marjorie Torrey; Viking, 1944. **Awarded:** Spring Book Festival (middle honor) 1944.

PHILIP, MARLENE NOURBESE
Harriet's Daughter by Marlene Nourbese Philip, not illustrated; Women's Press, 1988; Heinemann, 1988. **Awarded:** Canadian Library Assn. (runnerup) 1989.

PHILIP, NEIL
A Fine Anger: A Critical Introduction to the Work of Alan Garner by Neil Philip, not illustrated; Philomel, 1981. **Awarded:** Children's Literature Assn. Excellence in Criticism (book) 1986.

PHILLIPS, CAROLYN E.
Our Family got a Divorce by Carolyn E. Phillips, designed and illustrated by Roger Bradfield; Gospel Light Publications (GL Regal Books), 1979. **Awarded:** Gold Medallion 1980.

PHILLIPS, EMMA
Awarded: Macmillan Prize (3rd prize) 1989.

PHILLIPS, ETHEL CALVERT
A Name for Obed by Ethel Calvert Phillips, illustrated by Lois Lenski; Houghton, 1941. **Awarded:** Spring Book Festival (middle honor) 1941.

PHILLIPS, EULA MARK
Chucho: The Boy with the Good Name by Eula Mark Phillips, illustrated by Howard Simon; Follett, 1957. **Awarded:** Charles W. Follett 1957.

PHILLIPS, NEIL
Dancing in the Anzac Deli by Nadia Wheatley, illustrated by Neil Phillips and Waldemar Buczynski; Oxford, 1984. **Awarded:** Children's Book Council of Australia (book of the year commended) 1985; International Board on Books for Young People (writing/Australia) 1986.

PHILPOTT, HEATHER
The Rainforest Children by Margaret Pittaway, illustrated by Heather Philpott; Oxford, 1980. **Awarded:** International Board on Books for Young People (illustration/Australia) 1982.

PHIPSON, JOAN
Awarded: Dromkeen Medal 1987.

The Boundary Riders by Joan Phipson, illustrated by Margaret Horder; Harcourt, 1963. **Awarded:** Boys Club 1964.

The Family Conspiracy by Joan M. Phipson, illustrated by Margaret Horder; Angus & Robertson, 1962; Harcourt, 1964, 1962. **Awarded:** Children's Book Council of Australia (book of the year) 1963; Spring Book Festival (middle) 1964.

Good Luck to the Rider by Joan Phipson, illustrated by Margaret Horder; Angus & Robertson, 1953. **Awarded:** Children's Book Council of Australia (book of the year) 1953.

Helping Horse by Joan Phipson, not illustrated; Macmillan, 1974. **Awarded:** Writers Award 1975.

The Watcher in the Garden by Joan Phipson, not illustrated; Methuen, 1982. **Awarded:** International Board on Books for Young People (writing/Australia) 1984.

PIATTI, CELESTINO
Celestino Piatti's Animal ABC written and illustrated by Celestino Piatti; Atheneum, 1966. **Awarded:** New York Times Best Illustrated 1966.

The Happy Owls written and illustrated by Celestino Piatti; Atheneum, 1964. **Awarded:** New York Times Best Illustrated 1964.

PICARD, BARBARA LEONIE
Lady of the Linden Tree by Barbara Leonie Picard, illustrated by Charles Stewart; Oxford, 1954. **Awarded:** Carnegie (commended) 1954.

One Is One by Barbara Leonie Picard, illustrated by Victor G. Ambrus; Oxford, 1965. **Awarded:** Carnegie (commended) 1965.

Ransom for a Knight by Barbara Leonie Picard, illustrated by C. Walter Hodges; Oxford, 1956. **Awarded:** Carnegie (commended) 1956.

PICKARD, CHARLES
Worlds Lost and Found by Dov Peretz Elkins and Azriel Eisenberg, illustrated by Charles Pickard; Abelard, 1964. **Awarded:** Jewish Book Council 1964.

PIENKOWSKI, JAN

Christmas: The King James Version illustrated by Jan Pienkowski; Heinemann, 1984. **Awarded:** Kurt Maschler (runnerup) 1984.

Easter adapted and illustrated by Jan Pienkowski; William Heinemann, 1989. **Awarded:** International Board on Books for Young People (Illustration/Great Britain) 1990.

The Golden Bird by Edith Brill, illustrated by Jan Pienkowski; Dent, 1970. **Awarded:** Greenaway (honour) 1970.

Haunted House written and illustrated by Jan Pienkowski; Dutton, 1979. **Awarded:** Greenaway 1979.

The Kingdom under the Sea written and illustrated by Jan Pienkowski; Cape, 1971. **Awarded:** Greenaway 1971.

PIERCE, CHARLES W.
Samantha's Masquerade by Charles W. Pierce, illustrated by Erwin Schachner; McKay, 1967. **Awarded:** New Jersey Institute of Technology 1967.

PIERCE, MEREDITH ANN
The Darkangel by Meredith Ann Pierce, not illustrated; Little, Brown, 1982. **Awarded:** California Young Reader (high school) 1986; International Reading Assn. 1983; New York Times Notable Books 1982; Parents' Choice (literature) 1982.

The Woman Who Loved Reindeer by Meredith Ann Pierce, not illustrated; Atlantic, 1985. **Awarded:** Parents' Choice (literature) 1985.

PIERCE, TAMORA
Alanna: The First Adventure by Tamora Pierce, illustrated with a map; Atheneum, 1983. **Awarded:** New Jersey Institute of Technology 1983.

PIERS, HELEN
Long Neck and Thunder Foot by Helen Piers, illustrated by Michael Foreman; Kestrel, 1982. **Awarded:** Greenaway (cowinner) 1982.

Snail and Caterpillar by Helen Piers, illustrated by Pauline Baynes; Longmans, 1972. **Awarded:** Greenaway (commended) 1972.

PIERSON, LORI
ABC Triplets at the Zoo by Ida DeLage, illustrated by Lori Pierson; Garrard, 1980. **Awarded:** New Jersey Institute of Technology 1981.

PILLING, ANN
Henry's Leg by Ann Pilling, illustrated by Rowan Clifford; Viking Kestrel, 1985. **Awarded:** Guardian 1986.

PINCUS, HARRIET

Tell Me a Mitzi by Lore Segal, illustrated by Harriet Pincus; Farrar, 1970. **Awarded:** Spring Book Festival (picture book) 1970.

The Wedding Procession of the Rag Doll and the Broom Handle and Who Was in It by Carl Sandburg, illustrated by Harriet Pincus; Harcourt, 1967. **Awarded:** Art Books for Children 1973; Spring Book Festival (picture book honor) 1967.

PINES, MARK

Awarded: Southern California Council (distinguished contribution exhibiting the fusion of poetry and photography) 1972.

PINGUILLY, YVES

Il Etait Une Fois, Les Mots by Yves Pinguilly, illustrated by Andre Belleguie; Editions la Farandole, 1981. **Awarded:** Bologna (graphics for youth) 1983.

PINKNEY, BRIAN

The Dark-Thirty: Southern Tales of the Supernatural by Patricia C. McKissack, illustrated by Brian Pinkney; Knopf, 1992. **Awarded:** Hungry Mind (Middle Readers/Fiction) 1993.

Drylongso by Virginia Hamilton, illustrated by Brian Pinkney; Harcourt Brace Jovanovich, 1992. **Awarded:** Reading Magic Award 1992.

Sukey and the Mermaid by Robert D. San Souci, illustrated by Brian Pinkney; Four Winds, 1992. **Awarded:** Hungry Mind (Picturebook/Fiction) 1993; Coretta Scott King (Illustration Honor) 1993; Reading Magic Award 1992.

A Wave In Her Pocket: Stories From Trinidad by Lynn Joseph, illustrated by Brian Pinkney; Clarion, 1991. **Awarded:** Parents' Choice (Story Book) 1991; Reading Magic Award 1991.

Where Does the Trail Lead? by Burton Albert, illustrated by Brian Pinkney; Simon & Schuster, 1991. **Awarded:** Golden Kite (Picture- Illustration honor) 1991.

PINKNEY, GLORIA JEAN

Back Home by Gloria Jean Pinkney, illustrated by Jerry Pinkney; Dial, 1992. **Awarded:** Parents Choice (Picture Book) 1992.

PINKNEY, JERRY

Awarded: Drexel Citation 1992; David McCord Children's Literature Citation 1992.

Babushka and the Pig by Ann Trofimuk, illustrated by Jerry Pinkney; Houghton, 1969. **Awarded:** New Jersey Institute of Technology 1969.

Back Home by Gloria Jean Pinkney, illustrated by Jerry Pinkney; Dial, 1992. **Awarded:** Parents Choice (Picture Book) 1992.

Childtimes by Eloise Greenfield and Lessie Jones Little, illustrated by Jerry Pinkney; Harper & Row, 1979. **Awarded:** Boston Globe Horn Book (nonfiction honor) 1980; Woodson (outstanding merit) 1980.

Further Tales of Uncle Remus by Joel Chandler Harris, retold by Julius Lester, illustrated by Jerry Pinkney; Dial, 1990. **Awarded:** Parents' Choice (Story Book) 1990.

Half a Moon and One Whole Star by Crescent Dragonwagon, illustrated by Jerry Pinkney; Macmillan, 1986. **Awarded:** Coretta Scott King (illustration) 1987.

Home Place by Crescent Dragonwagon, illustrated by Jerry Pinkney; Macmillan, 1990. **Awarded:** Golden Kite (Picture-Illustration) 1990.

Mirandy and Brother Wind by Patricia McKissack, illustrated by Jerry Pinkney; Knopf, 1988. **Awarded:** Caldecott (honor) 1989; Coretta Scott King (Illustration) 1989.

More Tales of Uncle Remus: Further Adventures of Brer Rabbit by Joel Chandler Harris, adapted by Julius Lester, illustrated by Jerry Pinkney; Dial, 1988. **Awarded:** Reading Magic Award 1988.

The Patchwork Quilt by Valerie Flournoy, illustrated by Jerry Pinkney; Dial, 1985. **Awarded:** Christopher (ages 4-8) 1986; Ezra Jack Keats New Writer Award 1986; Coretta Scott King (illustration) 1986.

Rabbit Makes a Monkey Out of a Lion by Verna Aardema, illustrated by Jerry Pinkney; Dial, 1989. **Awarded:** Parents' Choice (Story Book) 1989.

Roll of Thunder, Hear My Cry by Mildred D. Taylor, illustrated by Jerry Pinkney; Dial, 1976. **Awarded:** Jane Addams (honor) 1977; Boston Globe Horn Book (fiction honor) 1977; National Book Award (finalist) 1977; Newbery 1977; George G. Stone 1991; Young Readers Choice 1979.

Song of the Trees by Mildred D. Taylor, illustrated by Jerry Pinkney; Dial, 1975. **Awarded:** Jane Addams (honor) 1976; Children's Book Showcase 1976; Council on Interracial Books (African American) 1973.

Strange Animals of the Sea by Jane H. Buxton, illustrated by Jerry Pinkney; National Geographic Society, 1987. **Awarded:** Redbook 1987.

The Tales of Uncle Remus by Joel Chandler Harris, adapted by Julius Lester, illustrated by Jerry Pinkney; Dial, 1987. **Awarded:** Coretta Scott King (Text honor) 1988; Parents Choice (Storybook) 1987.

The Talking Eggs by Robert D. San Souci, illustrated by Jerry Pinkney; Dial, 1989. **Awarded:** Irma S. and James H. Black 1989; Caldecott (honor) 1990; Colorado Children's 1991; Golden Sower (K-3) 1992; Coretta Scott King (Illustration honor) 1990; Parents' Choice (Picture Book) 1989.

Turtle in July by Marilyn Singer, illustrated by Jerry Pinkney; Macmillan, 1989. **Awarded:** New York Times Best Illustrated 1989.

PINKWATER, DANIEL

The Big Orange Splot written and illustrated by Daniel M. Pinkwater; Hastings House, 1977. **Awarded:** Emphasis on Reading (grades K-1) 1983-84.

The Last Guru written and illustrated by Daniel Pinkwater; Dodd, Mead, 1978. **Awarded:** New York Times Notable Books 1978.

Roger's Umbrella by Daniel Pinkwater, illustrated by James Marshall; Dutton, 1982. **Awarded:** Parents' Choice (literature) 1982.

PINKWATER, MANUS

Fat Elliot and the Gorilla written and illustrated by Manus Pinkwater; Four Winds, 1974. **Awarded:** New Jersey Institute of Technology 1975.

PINNELL, MISS

Village Heritage by Miss Pinnell and the children of Sapperton School, introduction by Michael Wood, illustrated; Alan Sutton, 1986. **Awarded:** Smarties (Innovation) 1986.

PINTO, RALPH

The Knee-high man and Other Tales by Julius Lester, illustrated by Ralph Pinto; Dial, 1972. **Awarded:** Lewis Carroll Shelf 1973.

PIPER, WATTY
The Little Engine that Could by Watty Piper, illustrated by George Hauman and Doris Hauman; Platt, 1954, 1930. **Awarded:** Lewis Carroll Shelf 1958.

PIROTTA, SAVIOUR
But No Cheese! by Saviour Pirotta, illustrated by Kate Simpson; Hodder & Stoughton, 1992. **Awarded:** Mother Goose (honorable mention) 1993.

PIRSIG, ROBERT M.
Zen and the Art of Motorcycle Maintenance: An Inquiry into Values by Robert M. Pirsig; Bantam, 1976. **Awarded:** Media & Methods (paperback) 1976.

PITCHER, CAROLINE
Diamond by Caroline Pitcher, not illustrated; Blackie Children's, 1987. **Awarded:** Fidler 1985.

PITCHER, DONALD T.
New Jersey by Keith Robertson, illustrated by Donald T. Pitcher; Coward, 1969. **Awarded:** New Jersey Institute of Technology 1969.

PITRONE, JEAN MADDERN
Trailblazer: Negro Nurse in the American Red Cross by Jean Maddern Pitrone, illustrated with photographs; Harcourt, 1969. **Awarded:** Friends of American Writers 1970.

PITT, NANCY
Beyond the High White Wall by Nancy Pitt, not illustrated; Scribner, 1986. **Awarded:** Sydney Taylor Book Award (older) 1987.

PITTAWAY, MARGARET
The Rainforest Children by Margaret Pittaway, illustrated by Heather Philpott; Oxford, 1980. **Awarded:** International Board on Books for Young People (illustration/Australia) 1982.

PITTMAN, AL
Down by Jim Long's Stage: Rhymes for Children and Young Fish by Al Pittman, illustrated by Pam Hall; Breakwater, 1976. **Awarded:** Amelia Frances Howard Gibbon 1977.

PITZ, HENRY C.
Give a Man a Horse by Charles J. Finger, illustrated by Henry C. Pitz; Winston, 1938. **Awarded:** Spring Book Festival (older honor) 1938.

Joe Mason, Apprentice to Audubon by Charlie May Simon, illustrated by Henry C. Pitz; Dutton, 1946. **Awarded:** Boys Club 1948.

Molly the Rogue by Mary R. Walsh, illustrated by Henry C. Pitz; Knopf, 1944. **Awarded:** Spring Book Festival (younger honor) 1944.

PLACE, MARIAN TEMPLETON
(pseudonym is Dale White)

The Boy Who Saw Bigfoot by Marian T. Place, not illustrated; Dodd, Mead, 1979. **Awarded:** Mark Twain 1982.

Hold Back the Hunter by Dale White, not illustrated; Day, 1959. **Awarded:** Western Writers of America (nonfiction) 1960.

On the Track of Bigfoot by Marian T. Place, illustrated with photographs; Dodd, Mead, 1974. **Awarded:** Garden State Children's (young nonfiction) 1977.

Rifles and Warbonnets by Marian Templeton Place, not illustrated; Washburn, 1968. **Awarded:** Western Writers of America (nonfiction) 1969.

Steamboat Up the Missouri by Dale White, illustrated by Charles H. Geer; Viking, 1958. **Awarded:** Western Writers of America 1959.

PLATT, KIN
Chloris and the Creeps by Kin Platt, not illustrated; Chilton, 1973. **Awarded:** Southern California Council (distinguished fiction) 1974.

Mystery of the Witch who Wouldn't by Kin Platt, not illustrated; Chilton, 1969. **Awarded:** Edgar Allan Poe (runnerup) 1970.

Sinbad and Me by Kin Platt, not illustrated; Chilton, 1966. **Awarded:** Edgar Allan Poe 1967.

PLATT, RICHARD
Stephen Biesty's Incredible Cross Sections by Richard Platt, illustrated by Stephen Biesty; Viking, 1992; Knopf, 1992. **Awarded:** British Book Awards (Illustrated runnerup) 1992.

PLENINGER, DIANE BROOKS
The Innkeeper's Boy by Diane Brooks Pleninger, illustrated by Leonard Everett Fisher in Cricket (November 1988). **Awarded:** Witty Short Story Award 1989.

PLISKIN, JACQUELINE JACOBSON
My Very Own Animated Jewish Holiday Activity Book by Jacqueline Pliskin; Shapolsky Publishers. **Awarded:** New Jersey Institute of Technology 1989.

The Jewish Holiday Game & Workbook written and illustrated by Jacqueline Jacobson Pliskin; Shapolsky Publishers, 1987. **Awarded:** New Jersey Institute of Technology 1989.

PLOMER, WILLIAM
The Butterfly Ball and the Grasshopper's Feast by William Plomer, illustrated by Alan Aldridge; Cape, 1973. **Awarded:** Whitbread 1973.

PLOWDEN, DAVID
The Iron Road: A Portrait of American Railroading by Richard Snow, photographs by David Plowden; Four Winds, 1978. **Awarded:** Boston Globe Horn Book (nonfiction honor) 1979.

Tugboat written and illustrated by David Plowden; Macmillan, 1976. **Awarded:** Children's Book Showcase 1977.

PLUME, ILSE
The Bremen-town Musicians written and illustrated by Ilse Plume; Doubleday, 1980. **Awarded:** Caldecott (honor) 1981; Parents' Choice (illustration) 1980.

PLUMMER, LOUISE
The Romantic Obsessions and Humiliations of Annie Sehlmeier by Louise Plummer, not illustrated; Delacorte, 1987. **Awarded:** Delacorte (honorable mention) 1985.

PLUMMER, WILLIAM KIRTMAN
The Answer Book of History by Franklin Folsom and Mary Elting, illustrated by W. K. Plummer; Grosset, 1966. **Awarded:** New Jersey Institute of Technology 1967.

PO, LEE
The Hare and the Tortoise and the Tortoise and the Hare by Lee Po and William Pene du Bois, illustrated by William Pene du Bois; Doubleday, 1972. **Awarded:** Art Books for Children 1974.

POCHOCKI, ETHEL
Rosebud & Red Flannel by Ethel Pochocki, illustrated by Mary Beth Owens; Henry Holt, 1991. **Awarded:** Lupine Award 1992.

POGANY, WILLY
The Golden Fleece and the Heroes Who Lived Before Achilles by Padraic Colum, illustrated by Willy Pogany; Macmillan, 1921. **Awarded:** Newbery (honor) 1922.

POHRT, TOM
Crow and Weasel by Barry Lopez, illustrated by Tom Pohrt; North Point Press, 1990; Random House of Canada, 1990. **Awarded:** Parents' Choice (Picture Book) 1990.

POIGNANT, AXEL
Piccaninny Walkabout: A Story of Two Aboriginal Children by Axel Poignant, illustrated with photographs; Angus & Robertson, 1957. **Awarded:** Children's Book Council of Australia (Picture Book) 1958.

POITIER, SIDNEY
This Life by Sidney Poitier, not illustrated; Knopf, 1980. **Awarded:** Coretta Scott King 1981.

POLACCO, PATRICIA
Babushka's Doll written and illustrated by Patricia Polacco; Simon & Schuster, 1990. **Awarded:** Commonwealth Club of California (Ages 10-under) 1990.

Chicken Sunday written and illustrated by Patricia Polacco; Philomel, 1992. **Awarded:** Commonwealth Club of California (Ages 10-under) 1992; Golden Kite (Illustration) 1992.

The Keeping Quilt written and illustrated by Patricia Polacco; Simon & Schuster, 1988. **Awarded:** Sydney Taylor Book Awards (Picture Book) 1989.

Mrs. Katz and Tush written and illustrated by Patricia Polacco; Bantam, 1992. **Awarded:** Jane Addams (picture book honor) 1993.

Rechenka's Eggs written and illustrated by Patricia Polacco; Philomel, 1988. **Awarded:** International Reading Assn. (Younger) 1989.

POLAND, MARGUERITE
The Mantis and the Moon by Marguerite Poland, illustrated by Leigh Voight; Raven Press, 1979. **Awarded:** Percy Fitzpatrick 1979.

The Wood-ash Stars by Marguerite Poland, illustrated by Shanne Altshuler; David Philip, 1983. **Awarded:** Percy Fitzpatrick 1984.

POLE, JAMES T.
Midshipman Plowright by James T. Pole, illustrated with maps; Dodd, Mead, 1969. **Awarded:** Edith Busby 1968.

POLESE, CAROLYN
Promise Not to Tell by Carolyn Polese, illustrated by Jennifer Barrett; Human Sciences Press, 1985. **Awarded:** Christopher (ages 8-up) 1986.

POLITI, LEO
Awarded: Regina 1966.

At the Palace Gates by Helen Rand Parrish, illustrated by Leo Politi; Viking, 1949. **Awarded:** Commonwealth Club of California 1949; Spring Book Festival (under 12 honor) 1949.

Juanita written and illustrated by Leo Politi; Scribner, 1948. **Awarded:** Caldecott (honor) 1949; Spring Book Festival (younger honor) 1948.

Looking for Something by Ann Nolan Clark, illustrated by Leo Politi; Viking, 1952. **Awarded:** Spring Book Festival (picture book) 1952.

Moy Moy written and illustrated by Leo Politi; Scribner, 1960. **Awarded:** Southern California Council (contribution to illustration) 1961.

Pedro, the Angel of Olvera St. written and illustrated by Leo Politi; Scribner, 1946. **Awarded:** Caldecott (honor) 1947; FOCAL 1980.

Song of the Swallows written and illustrated by Leo Politi; Scribner, 1949. **Awarded:** Caldecott 1950.

POLLACK, MERRILL
Phaethon by Merrill Pollack, illustrated by William Hoffmann; Lippincott, 1966. **Awarded:** New Jersey Institute of Technology 1967.

POLLAND, MADELEINE
Beorn the Proud by Madeleine Polland, illustrated by William Stobbs; Holt, 1962. **Awarded:** Spring Book Festival (middle honor) 1962.

Children of the Red King by Madeleine Polland, illustrated by Annette Macarthur-Onslow; Holt, 1961. **Awarded:** Spring Book Festival (middle honor) 1961.

POLLOCK, PENNY
Keeping it Secret by Penny Pollock, illustrated by Donna Diamond; Putnam, 1982. **Awarded:** New Jersey Institute of Technology 1983.

Water Is Wet by Penny Pollock, photographs by Barbara Beirne; Putnam, 1985. **Awarded:** New Jersey Institute of Technology 1987.

POLSENO, JO
Lost in the Everglades by Lucy Salamanca, illustrated by Jo Polseno; Western, 1971. **Awarded:** Lucille E. Ogle 1970.

Secrets of Redding Glen: The Natural History of a Wooded Valley written and illustrated by Jo Polseno; Western/Golden, 1973. **Awarded:** Children's Book Showcase 1974.

Snail in the Woods by Joanne Ryder and Harold S. Feinberg, illustrated by Jo Polseno; Harper, 1979. **Awarded:** New Jersey Institute of Technology 1980.

POLUSHKIN, MARIA
An Old Tale Carved Out of Stone by Aleksandr M. Linevski, translated by Maria Polushkin, not illustrated; Crown, 1973. **Awarded:** Batchelder 1975.

POMERANTZ, BARBARA
Bubby, Me, and Memories by Barbara Pomerantz, photographs by Leon Lurie; Union of American Hebrew Congregations, 1983. **Awarded:** Sydney Taylor Book Award (younger readers) 1984.

POMERANTZ, CHARLOTTE
The Chalk Doll by Charlotte Pomerantz, illustrated by Frane Lessac; Lippincott, 1989. **Awarded:** Parents' Choice (Story Book) 1989.

If I Had a Paka: Poems in Eleven Languages by Charlotte Pomerantz, illustrated by Nancy Tafuri; Greenwillow, 1982. **Awarded:** Jane Addams (honor) 1983.

Posy by Charlotte Pomerantz, illustrated by Catherine Stock; Greenwillow, 1983. **Awarded:** Christopher (picture book) 1984.

The Princess and the Admiral by Charlotte Pomerantz, illustrated by Tony Chen; Addison, 1974. **Awarded:** Jane Addams 1975.

POND, ROY
Tomb Travellers: Beyond the Gateways and Guardians of Egypt's Underworld by Roy Pond, not illustrated; Albatross Books, 1991. **Awarded:** Australian Christian Book of the Year (Children's) 1992.

PONT, CHARLES
Whalers of the Midnight Sun: A Story of Modern Whaling in the Antarctic by Alan Villiers, illustrated by Charles Pont; Angus & Robertson, 1949. **Awarded:** Children's Book Council of Australia 1949.

POOLEY, SARAH
A Day of Rhymes written and illustrated by Sarah Pooley; Bodley Head, 1987. **Awarded:** Best Books for Babies 1988.

Your Body: Skin and Bone by Dr. Gwynne Vevers, illustrated by Sarah Pooley; Bodley Head, 1983. **Awarded:** Mother Goose (runnerup) 1984.

POORTVLIET, RIEN
The Sea Lord by Alet Schouten, translated by Patricia Crampton, illustrated by Rien Poortvliet; Methuen, 1977. **Awarded:** International Board on Books for Young People (translation/Great Britain) 1980.

POPE, ALLEN
The Bewitched Caverns by Leona Rienow, illustrated by Allen Pope; Scribner, 1948. **Awarded:** Spring Book Festival (middle honor) 1948.

POPE, ELIZABETH MARIE
The Perilous Gard by Elizabeth M. Pope, illustrated by Richard Cuffari; Houghton, 1974. **Awarded:** Children's Book Showcase 1975; Newbery (honor) 1975.

The Sherwood Ring by Elizabeth Marie Pope, illustrated by Evaline Ness; Houghton, 1958. **Awarded:** Spring Book Festival (older honor) 1958.

POPOV, NIKOLAJ
Robinson Crusoe by Daniel Defoe, illustrated by Nikolaj Popov; Chudozestvenaja Literatura, 1974. **Awarded:** Biennale Illustrations Bratislava (grand prix) 1975.

PORCELLINO, MICHAEL R.
Through the Telescope by Michael R. Porcellino, illustrated; Tab Books, 1989. **Awarded:** New York Academy of Sciences (Older Honor) 1989.

PORRITT, JONATHON
Captain Eco and the Fate of the Earth by Jonathon Porritt, illustrated by Ellis Nadler; Dorling Kindersley, 1991. **Awarded:** Earthworm Award 1992.

PORTAL, COLETTE
The Honeybees by Franklin Russell, illustrated by Colette Portal; Knopf, 1967. **Awarded:** New York Times Best Illustrated 1967.

The Life of a Queen written and illustrated by Colette Portal, translated by Marcia Nardi; Braziller, 1964. **Awarded:** New York Times Best Illustrated 1964.

PORTER, DAVID LORD
Help! Let Me Out! by David Lord Porter, illustrated by David Macaulay; Houghton Mifflin, 1982. **Awarded:** New York Times Notable Books 1982.

PORTER, GEORGE
The Money Machine by Keith Robertson, illustrated by George Porter; Viking, 1969. **Awarded:** New Jersey Institute of Technology 1969.

War Work by Zibby Oneal, illustrated by George Porter; Viking, 1971. **Awarded:** Friends of American Writers 1972.

PORTER, HELEN FOGWELL
January, February, June, or July by Helen Fogwell Porter, not illustrated; Breakwater Books, 1988. **Awarded:** Young Adult Canadian 1989.

PORTER, RICHARD W.
The Versatile Satellite by Richard W. Porter, illustrated with photographs and drawings; Oxford, 1977. **Awarded:** New York Academy of Sciences (older honor) 1978.

PORTER, SHEENA
Nordy Bank by Sheena Porter, illustrated by Annette Macarthur-Onslow; Oxford, 1964. **Awarded:** Carnegie 1964.

PORTER, SUE
Hepzibah by Peter Dickinson, illustrated by Sue Porter; Eel Pie Publishing, 1978. **Awarded:** Mother Goose (runnerup) 1979.

POSKANZER, SUSAN C.
Effective English by Susan C. Poskanzer, illustrated; Silver Burdett, 1979. **Awarded:** New Jersey Institute of Technology 1980.

POTAAIANOS, THEMOS
Along the Seaside by Themos Potaaianos, illustrated by Spyndonos; Greece. **Awarded:** Hans Christian Andersen (runnerup) 1960.

POTTER, BEATRIX
The Tailor of Gloucester written and illustrated by Beatrix Potter; Warne, 1903. **Awarded:** Lewis Carroll Shelf 1962.

The Tale of Peter Rabbit written and illustrated by Beatrix Potter; Warne, 1903. **Awarded:** Lewis Carroll Shelf 1958.

POTTER, CHARLES FRANCIS
More Tongue Tanglers and a Rigmarole by Charles F. Potter, illustrated by William Wiesner; World, 1964. **Awarded:** Spring Book Festival (picture book honor) 1964.

POTTS, K.
I Marched with Hannibal by Hans Baumann, translated by K. Potts, illustrated by Ulrik Schramm; Walck, 1962. **Awarded:** Spring Book Festival (older honor) 1962.

POTTS, RICHARD
Tod's Owl by Richard Potts, not illustrated; Hodder, 1980. **Awarded:** Guardian (runnerup) 1981.

POULIN, STEPHANE
Awarded: Vicky Metcalf 1989.

Can You Catch Josephine? written and illustrated by Stephane Poulin; Tundra, 1987. **Awarded:** Amelia Frances Howard-Gibbon (runnerup) 1988; Elizabeth Mrazik-Cleaver 1988.

Could You Stop Josephine? written and illustrated by Stephane Poulin; Tundra, 1988. **Awarded:** International Board on Books for Young People (Illustration/Canada) 1990.

POULSEN, GUNNAR
The Leopard by Cecil Bodker, translated by Gunnar Poulsen; Atheneum, 1975. **Awarded:** Batchelder 1977.

POWELL, LESLEY CAMERON
Turi: The Story of a Little Boy by Lesley Cameron Powell, illustrated by Pius Blank; Paul's Book Arcade, 1964. **Awarded:** Esther Glen 1964.

POWELL, MIRIAM
Jareb by Miriam Powell, illustrated by Marc Simont; Crowell, 1952. **Awarded:** Child Study 1952; Spring Book Festival (ages 8-12 honor) 1952.

POWELL, RANDY
Is Kissing a Girl Who Smokes Like Licking an Ashtray? by Randy Powell, not illustrated; Farrar Straus Giroux, 1992. **Awarded:** PEN Center USA West 1993.

POWELL, RAY
Awarded: L. Frank Baum 1969.

POWELL, ROBERT
Awarded: Jesse Stuart 1982.

POWER, MARGARET
The Long Red Scarf by Nette Hilton, illustrated by Margaret Power; Omnibus Books, 1987. **Awarded:** Children's Book Council of Australia (Picture Book Honour) 1988.

POWERS, ALFRED
Chains for Columbus by Alfred Powers, not illustrated; Westminster, 1948. **Awarded:** Boys Club 1950.

A Long Way to Frisco: A Folk Adventure Novel of California and Oregon in 1852 by Alfred Powers, illustrated by James Daugherty; Little, Brown, 1951. **Awarded:** Boys Club 1952.

POWERS, ELIZABETH
Journal of Madame Royale by Elizabeth Powers, illustrated with old engravings; Walker, 1976. **Awarded:** New Jersey Institute of Technology 1977.

POWERS, RICHARD M.
The Byzantines by Thomas C. Chubb, illustrated by Richard M. Powers; World, 1959. **Awarded:** Boys Club 1960.

The Haunted Reef by Frank Crisp, illustrated by Richard M. Powers; Coward, 1952. **Awarded:** Spring Book Festival (older honor) 1952.

POWERS, WILLIAM
Indians of the Southern Plains by William Powers, illustrated with photographs; Putnam, 1971. **Awarded:** New Jersey Institute of Technology 1971, 1972.

POWNALL, EVE
The Australia Book by Eve Pownall, illustrated by Margaret Senior; Sands, 1953. **Awarded:** Children's Book Council of Australia 1952.

POWZYK, JOYCE
Henry by Nina Bawden, illustrated by Joyce Powzyk; Lothrop, Lee & Shepard, 1988. **Awarded:** Parents' Choice (Story Book) 1988; Reading Magic Award 1988.

Tyrannosaurus Rex and Its Kin by Helen Roney Sattler, illustrated by Joyce Powzyk; Lothrop Lee & Shepard, 1989. **Awarded:** Oklahoma Book Award 1990.

PRACHATICKA, MARKETA
Alenka v Kraji Divu by Lewis Carroll, illustrated by Marketa Prachaticka; Albatros, 1983. **Awarded:** Bologna (graphics for youth) 1984.

PRAGOFF, FIONA
How Many? From 0 to 20 written and illustrated by Fiona Pragoff; Gollancz, 1986. **Awarded:** Greenaway (commended) 1986.

PRANCE, GHILLEAN TOLMIE
Leaves by Ghillean Tolmie Prance, photographs by Kjell B. Sandved; Crown, 1985. **Awarded:** New York Academy of Science (older honor) 1986.

PRATER, JOHN
On Friday Something Funny Happened written and illustrated by John Prater; Bodley Head, 1982. **Awarded:** Mother Goose (runnerup) 1983.

PRATHER, HUGH
Children as Teachers of Peace: By Our Children edited by Gerald G. Jampolsky, foreword by Hugh Prather, illustrated; Celestial Arts, 1982. **Awarded:** Jane Addams (special recognition) 1983.

PRATHER, RAY
Time-ago Lost: More Tales of Jahdu by Virginia Hamilton, illustrated by Ray Prather; Macmillan, 1973. **Awarded:** Spring Book Festival (middle honor) 1973.

PRELUTSKY, JACK
Beneath a Blue Umbrella by Jack Prelutsky, illustrated by Garth Williams; Greenwillow, 1990. **Awarded:** New York Times Best Illustrated 1990.

The Headless Horseman Rides Tonight: More Poems to Trouble Your Sleep by Jack Prelutsky, illustrated by Arnold Lobel; Greenwillow, 1980. **Awarded:** New York Times Best Illustrated 1980; New York Times Notable Books 1980.

The New Kid on the Block by Jack Prelutsky, illustrated by James Stevenson; Greenwillow, 1984. **Awarded:** Emphasis on Reading (grades 2-3) 1986-87; Garden State (younger nonfiction) 1987.

Nightmares: Poems to Trouble Your Sleep by Jack Prelutsky, illustrated by Arnold Lobel; Greenwillow, 1976. **Awarded:** Children's Book Showcase 1977.

Something Big Has Been Here by Jack Prelutsky, illustrated by James Stevenson; Greenwillow, 1988. **Awarded:** Kentucky Bluegrass (grades 4-8) 1992.

PRESTON, ALICE B.
Whistle for Good Fortune by Margery Bailey, illustrated by Alice B. Preston; Little, Brown, 1940. **Awarded:** Spring Book Festival (younger honor) 1940.

PRESTON, EDNA MITCHELL
Monkey in the Jungle by Edna Mitchell Preston, illustrated by Clement Hurd; Viking, 1968. **Awarded:** Boston Globe Horn Book (illustration honor) 1969.

Pop Corn and Ma Goodness by Edna Mitchell Preston, illustrated by Robert Andrew Parker; Viking, 1969. **Awarded:** Caldecott (honor) 1970; National Book Award (finalist) 1970.

Squawk to the Moon, Little Goose by Edna Mitchell Preston, illustrated by Barbara Cooney; Viking, 1974. **Awarded:** New York Times Notable Books 1974.

PRESTOPINO, GREGORIO
Sundiata: The Epic of the Lion King by Roland Bertol, illustrated by Gregorio Prestopino; Crowell, 1970. **Awarded:** Spring Book Festival (middle) 1970.

PREUSSLER, OTFRIED
Awarded: Hans Christian Andersen (highly commended author/German Federal Republic) 1972.

The Satanic Mill by Otfried Preussler, translated by Anthea Bell, not illustrated; Abelard-Schuman (London), 1972; Macmillan, 1973. **Awarded:** New York Times Notable Books 1973.

PRICE, ARTHUR
The Golden Phoenix and Other French Canadian Fairy Tales by Charles Marius Barbeau, retold by Michael Hornyansky, illustrated by Arthur Price; Oxford, 1958. **Awarded:** Canadian Library Assn. 1960.

PRICE, CHRISTINE HILDA
The Loner by Ester Wier, illustrated by Christine Price; McKay, 1963. **Awarded:** Newbery (honor) 1964.

Train for Tiger Lily by Louise Riley, illustrated by Christine Price; Macmillan Canada, 1954. **Awarded:** Canadian Library Assn. 1956.

PRICE, LEONTYNE
Aida by Leontyne Price, illustrated by Diane Dillon and Leo Dillon; Harcourt Brace Jovanovich, 1990. **Awarded:** Coretta Scott King (Illustration) 1991.

PRICE, SUSAN
The Ghost Drum by Susan Price, not illustrated; Faber, 1987; Farrar Straus Giroux, 1987. **Awarded:** Carnegie 1987.

Twopence a Tub by Susan Price, not illustrated; Faber, 1975. **Awarded:** Other Award 1975.

PRIDE, MARILYN
Australian Dinosaurs and Their Relatives written and illustrated by Marilyn Pride; Collins, 1988. **Awarded:** Crichton 1989.

PRIMAVERA, ELISE
The Bollo Caper: A Furry Tale for all Ages by Art Buchwald, illustrated by Elise Primavera; Putnam, 1983. **Awarded:** New Jersey Institute of Technology 1983.

Christina Katerina and the Time She Quit the Family by Patricia Lee Gauch, illustrated by Elise Primavera; Putnam, 1987. **Awarded:** New Jersey Institute of Technology 1988.

Make Way for Sam Houston by Jean Fritz, illustrated by Elise Primavera; Putnam, 1986. **Awarded:** New York Times Notable 1986; Western Writers of America Spur Award 1987.

PRIMROSE, JEAN
Miss Happiness and Miss Flower by Rumer Godden, illustrated by Jean Primrose; Viking, 1961. **Awarded:** Carnegie (commended) 1961; Spring Book Festival (middle honor) 1961.

PRINGLE, LAURENCE
Awarded: Eva L. Gordon 1983.

Batman: Exploring the World of Bats by Laurence Pringle, photographs by Merlin D. Tuttle; Scribner, 1991. **Awarded:** Book Can Develop Empathy 1991.

Natural Fire: Its Ecology in Forests by Laurence Pringle, illustrated with photographs; Morrow, 1979. **Awarded:** New York Academy of Sciences (younger honor) 1980.

The Only Earth We Have by Laurence Pringle, illustrated by Philip Lohman; Macmillan, 1969. **Awarded:** New Jersey Institute of Technology 1970.

PRINGLE, MIKE
What Makes a Flower Grow? by Susan Mayes, illustrated by Brin Edwards and Mike Pringle; Usborne, 1989. **Awarded:** Science Book Prizes 1990.

What Makes It Rain? by Susan Mayes, illustrated by Richard Deverell and Mike Pringle; Usborne, 1989. **Awarded:** Science Book Prizes 1990.

What's Under the Ground? by Susan Mayes, illustrated by Mike Pringle, Brin Edwards and John Scorey; Usborne, 1989. **Awarded:** Science Book Prizes 1990.

PRINGLE, PATRICK
Great Discoveries in Modern Science by Patrick Pringle, illustrated with photographs; Roy, 1955. **Awarded:** Boys Club 1956.

PRITCHETT, LULITA CRAWFORD
The Cabin at Medicine Springs by Lulita Crawford Pritchett, illustrated by Anthony D'Adamo; Watts, 1958. **Awarded:** Watts 1958.

PRINTZ, MICHAEL L.
Awarded: Grolier 1993.

PROCTOR, JOHN
Color in Plants and Flowers by John Proctor and Susan Proctor, illustrated with photographs and diagrams; Everest House, 1978. **Awarded:** New York Academy of Sciences (older honor) 1979.

PROCTOR, SUSAN
Color in Plants and Flowers by John Proctor and Susan Proctor, illustrated with photographs and diagrams; Everest House, 1978. **Awarded:** New York Academy of Sciences (older honor) 1979.

PROKOFIEV, SERGEI
Peter und der Wolf by Sergei Prokofiev, retold by Loriot, illustrated by Jorg Muller; Verlag Sauerlander. **Awarded:** Bologna (critici in erba) 1986.

Peter and the Wolf by Sergei Prokofiev, translated by Maria Carlson, illustrated by Charles Mikolaycak; Viking, 1982. **Awarded:** Parents' Choice (illustration) 1982.

PROVENSEN, ALICE
Awarded: School Library Media Specialist of South Eastern New York 1986.

The Animal Fair written and illustrated by Alice Provensen and Martin Provensen; Simon & Schuster, 1952. New York Times Best Illustrated 1952.

The Buck Stops Here written and illustrated by Alice Provensen; HarperCollins, 1990. **Awarded:** Reading Magic Award 1990.

The Charge of the Light Brigade by Lord Alfred Tennyson, illustrated by Alice Provensen and Martin Provensen; Golden, 1964. **Awarded:** New York Times Best Illustrated 1964.

The First Noel: The Birth of Christ from the Gospel According to St. Luke illustrated by Alice Provensen and Martin Provensen; Golden, 1959. **Awarded:** New York Times Best Illustrated 1959.

The Glorious Flight: Across the Channel with Louis Bleriot written and illustrated by Alice Provensen and Martin Provensen; Viking, 1983. **Awarded:** Caldecott 1984; New York Times Notable Books 1983; Parents' Choice (illustration) 1983.

The Golden Bible for Children: The New Testament edited by Elsa Jane Werner, illustrated by Alice Provensen and Martin Provensen; Golden, 1953. **Awarded:** New York Times Best Illustrated 1953.

Karen's Curiosity written and illustrated by Alice Provensen and Martin Provensen; Golden, 1963. **Awarded:** New York Times Best Illustrated 1963.

Karen's Opposites written and illustrated by Alice Provensen and Martin Provensen; Golden, 1963. **Awarded:** Spring Book Festival (picture book honor) 1963.

Leonardo Da Vinci written and illustrated by Alice Provensen and Martin Provensen; Viking, 1984. **Awarded:** Redbook (pop-up) 1984.

The Mother Goose Book written and illustrated by Alice Provensen and Martin Provensen; Random House, 1976. **Awarded:** Art Books for Children 1978, 1979; New York Times Best Illustrated 1976; New York Times Notable 1976.

My Little Hen written and illustrated by Alice Provensen and Martin Provensen; Random House, 1973. **Awarded:** Art Books for Children 1975.

A Peaceable Kingdom: The Shaker Abecedarius illustrated by Alice Provensen and Martin Provensen; Viking, 1978.

Awarded: Art Books for Children 1979; New York Times Best Illustrated 1978; New York Times Notable 1978.

Punch in New York written and illustrated by Alice Provensen; Viking, 1991. **Awarded:** New York Times Best Illustrated 1991; Reading Magic Award 1991.

A Visit to William Blake's Inn: Poems for Innocent and Experienced Travelers by Nancy Willard, illustrated by Alice Provensen and Martin Provensen; Harcourt, 1981. **Awarded:** Boston Globe Horn Book (illustration) 1982; Caldecott (honor) 1982; Golden Kite (fiction honor) 1981; Newbery 1982.

PROVENSEN, MARTIN

Awarded: School Library Media Specialists of South Eastern New York 1986.

The Animal Fair written and illustrated by Alice Provensen and Martin Provensen; Simon & Schuster, 1952. **Awarded:** New York Times Best Illustrated 1952.

The Charge of the Light Brigade by Lord Alfred Tennyson, illustrated by Alice Provensen and Martin Provensen; Golden, 1964. **Awarded:** New York Times Best Illustrated 1964.

The First Noel: The Birth of Christ from the Gospel According to St. Luke illustrated by Alice Provensen and Martin Provensen; Golden, 1959. **Awarded:** New York Times Best Illustrated 1959.

The Glorious Flight: Across the Channel with Louis Bleriot written and illustrated by Alice Provensen and Martin Provensen; Viking, 1983. **Awarded:** Caldecott 1984; New York Times Notable Books 1983; Parents' Choice (illustration) 1983.

The Golden Bible for Children: The New Testament edited by Elsa Jane Werner, illustrated by Alice Provensen and Martin Provensen; Golden, 1953. **Awarded:** New York Times Best Illustrated 1953.

Karen's Curiosity written and illustrated by Alice Provensen and Martin Provensen; Golden, 1963. **Awarded:** New York Times Best Illustrated 1963.

Karen's Opposites written and illustrated by Alice Provensen and Martin Provensen; Golden, 1963. **Awarded:** Spring Book Festival (picture book honor) 1963.

Leonardo Da Vinci written and illustrated by Alice Provensen and Martin Provensen; Viking, 1984. **Awarded:** Redbook (pop-up) 1984.

The Mother Goose Book written and illustrated by Alice Provensen and Martin Provensen; Random House, 1976. **Awarded:** Art Books for Children 1978, 1979; New York Times Best Illustrated 1976; New York Times Notable Books 1976.

My Little Hen written and illustrated by Alice Provensen and Martin Provensen; Random House, 1973. **Awarded:** Art Books for Children 1975.

A Peaceable Kingdom: The Shaker Abecedarius illustrated by Alice Provensen and Martin Provensen; Viking, 1978. **Awarded:** Art Books for Children 1979; New York Times Best Illustrated 1978; New York Times Notable Books 1978.

A Visit to William Blake's Inn: Poems for Innocent and Experienced Travelers by Nancy Willard, illustrated by Alice Provensen and Martin Provensen; Harcourt, 1981. **Awarded:** Boston Globe Horn Book (illustration) 1982; Caldecott (honor) 1982; Golden Kite (fiction honor) 1981; Newbery 1982.

PROVINES, VIRGINIA

Bright Heritage by Virginia Provines, illustrated by Sherman C. Hoeflich, Longmans, 1939. **Awarded:** Commonwealth Club of California 1939.

PROVOST, GARY

Good if it Goes by Gary Provost and Gail Levine-Freidus, not illustrated; Bradbury, 1984. **Awarded:** Jewish Book Council (children's literature) 1985.

PRUSSKI, JEFFREY

Bring Back the Deer by Jeffrey Prusski, illustrated by Neil Waldman; Harcourt Brace Jovanovich, 1988. **Awarded:** Washington Irving (Illustration) 1990.

PRUSZYNSKA, ANGELA

Trumpeter of Krakow by Eric P. Kelly, illustrated by Angela Pruszynska; Macmillan, 1928. **Awarded:** Boys Club (Special Citation) 1966-67; Newbery 1929.

PRYOR, BONNIE

The Porcupine Mouse by Bonnie Pryor, illustrated by Maryjane Begin; Morrow, 1988. **Awarded:** Irma S. and James H. Black 1988.

PUCCI, ALBERT JOHN

Across Five Aprils by Irene Hunt, illustrated by Albert J. Pucci; Follett, 1964. **Awarded:** Lewis Carroll Shelf 1966; Charles W. Follett 1964; Newbery (honor) 1965.

PUCKETT, KENT

Read Aloud Bible Stories by Ella K. Lindvall, illustrated by Kent Puckett; Moody Press, 1982. **Awarded:** Gold Medallion 1983.

PUGH, ANNA

Copycats by Marianne Ford, diagrams by Anna Pugh; Deutsch, 1983. **Awarded:** Maschler (runnerup) 1983.

PULLMAN, PHILIP

The Ruby in the Smoke by Philip Pullman, not illustrated; Oxford, 1985; Knopf, 1985. **Awarded:** International Reading Assn. (Older) 1988; Lancashire County Library 1987.

PURCELL, JOHN

From Hand Ax to Laser: Man's Growing Mastery of Energy by John Purcell, illustrated by Judy Skorpil; Vanguard, 1982. **Awarded:** New York Academy of Sciences (Elliott Montroll special award) 1984.

PURDY, CLAIRE LEE

My Brother Was Mozart by Claire Lee Purdy and Benson Wheeler, illustrated by Theodore Nadejen; Holt, 1937. **Awarded:** Julia Ellsworth Ford 1937.

PURKIS, SALLIE

Into the Past: Parts 1-4 by Sallie Purkis and Elizabeth Merson, illustrated with photographs; Longmans, 1981. (*At Home and in the Street in 1900*; *At Home in 1900*; *At School and in the Country in 1900*; *At School in 1900*). **Awarded:** Other Award 1982.

PURSELL, WEIMER

Biography of an Atom by J. Bronowski and Millicent E. Selsam, illustrated by Weimer Pursell; Harper, 1965. **Awarded:** Edison Mass Media (science book) 1966.

PUSHKIN, ALEXANDER

Il Cavallo di Bronzo by Aleksandr Sergeevic Pushkin, illustrated by Fodor Kontstantinov; Detskaya Literatura. **Awarded:** Bologna (Graphics for Youth) 1976.

The Tale of Czar Saltan: or, The Prince and the Swan Princess by Alexander Pushkin, translated and retold by Patricia Tracy

Lowe, illustrated by Ivan Bilibin; Crowell, 1975. **Awarded:** Children's Book Showcase 1976.

PUSKAS, JAMES
Purro and the Prattleberries by Suzanne Newton, illustrated by James Puskas; Westminster, 1971. **Awarded:** North Carolina AAUW 1971.

PUTNAM, PETER BROCK
Peter, the Revolutionary Tsar by Peter Brock Putnam, illustrated by Laszlo Kubinyi; Harper, 1973. **Awarded:** Children's Book Showcase 1974.

PYE, TREVOR
My Aunt Mary Went Shopping by Roger Hall, illustrated by Trevor Pye; Ashton Scholastic, 1991. **Awarded:** AIM Children's Book Award (Picture Book 2nd Prize) 1992.

PYLE, HOWARD
Gin No Ude no Otto (original English: *Otto of the Silver Hand*) by Howard Pyle, translated by Shigeo Watanabe; Kaisei-sha, 1983 rev. ed. **Awarded:** International Board on Books for Young People (translation/Japan) 1984.

King Stork by Howard Pyle, illustrated by Trina Schart Hyman; Little, Brown, 1973. **Awarded:** Boston Globe Horn Book (illustration) 1973.

Otto of the Silver Hand written and illustrated by Howard Pyle; Scribner, 1954. **Awarded:** Lewis Carroll Shelf 1970.

Q

QUACKENBUSH, ROBERT
Detective Mole and the Halloween Mystery written and illustrated by Robert Quackenbush; Lothrop, Lee & Shepard, 1981. **Awarded:** Edgar Allan Poe (runnerup) 1982.

Red Rock over the River by Patricia Beatty, illustrated by Robert Quackenbush; Morrow, 1973. **Awarded:** Golden Kite (honor) 1973.

QUEVAL, JEAN
Incroyables Adventures de Mister MacMiffic by Sid Fleischman, translated by Jean Queval; Fernand Nathan, 1979. **Awarded:** International Board on Books for Young People (translation/France) 1982.

QUICK, ANNABELLE
see MACMILLAN, ANNABELLE

QUIDAM, ADAM
Sophiechen und der Riese (original English: *The BFG*) by Roald Dahl, translated by Adam Quidam; Rowohlt, 1984. **Awarded:** International Board on Books for Young People (translation/German Federal Republic) 1986.

QUILTER, LINDSAY
It's OK To Be You! Feeling Good About Growing Up by Claire Patterson, illustrated by Lindsay Quilter; Century Hutchinson, 1988. **Awarded:** New Zealand Library Assn. Non Fiction for Young People 1989.

QUIN-HARKIN, JANET
Peter Penny's Dance by Janet Quin-Harkin, illustrated by Anita Lobel; Dial, 1976. **Awarded:** Children's Book Showcase 1977; New York Times Notable 1976.

QUINLIN, B. J.
Awarded: Evelyn Sibley Lampman 1990.

QUINN, JOHN
The Summer of Lily and Esme by John Quinn; Poolbeg, 1991. **Awarded:** Bisto (Book of the Year) 1992.

R

RABE, BERNIECE
The Girl Who Had no Name by Berniece Rabe, not illustrated; Dutton, 1977. **Awarded:** Golden Kite (fiction) 1977.

Naomi by Berniece Rabe, not illustrated; Nelson, 1975. **Awarded:** Golden Kite (honor) 1975.

The Orphans by Berniece Rabe, not illustrated; Dutton, 1978. **Awarded:** Clara Ingram Judson 1978.

RABINOWITZ, ANN
Bethie by Ann Rabinowitz, not illustrated; Macmillan, 1989. **Awarded:** New Jersey Institute of Technology 1990.

Knight on Horseback by Ann Rabinowitz, not illustrated; Macmillan, 1987. **Awarded:** New Jersey Institute of Technology 1988.

RADDALL, THOMAS HEAD
Son of the Hawk by Thomas H. Raddall, illustrated by Stanley Turner; Winston, 1950. **Awarded:** Boys Club 1951.

RADIN, RUTH YAFFE
A Winter Place by Ruth Yaffe Radin, illustrated by Mattie Lou O'Kelley; Little, Brown, 1982. **Awarded:** Parents' Choice (illustration) 1982.

RADIUS, EMILIO
Gesu Oggi by Emilio Radius, illustrated; Rizzoli Editore, 1966. **Awarded:** Bologna (graphics for children and youth) 1966.

RADLAUER, EDWARD
Awarded: Southern California Council (Dorothy C. McKenzie) 1982.

RADLAUER, RUTH
Awarded: Southern California Council (Dorothy C. McKenzie) 1982.

RADLOV, NICHOLAS
The Cautious Carp and Other Fables in Pictures written and illustrated by Nicholas Radlov, translated by Helen Black; Coward, 1938. **Awarded:** Spring Book Festival (younger honor) 1938.

RADUNSKY, VLADIMIR
The Pup Grew Up! by Samuel Marshak, illustrated by Vladimir Radunsky; Henry Holt, 1989. **Awarded:** Reading Magic 1989.

RAFFI
Baby Beluga by Raffi, illustrated by Ashley Wolff; Crown, 1990. **Awarded:** Book Can Develop Empathy 1991.

RAFTERY, GERALD
The Natives Are Always Restless by Gerald Raftery, illustrated by Charles Geer; Vanguard Press, 1964. **Awarded:** New Jersey Institute of Technology (late teenage novel) 1964.

RAGON, MICHEL
La Cite de l'an 2000 by Michel Ragon; Editions Casterman, 1968. **Awarded:** Bologna (graphics for youth) 1969.

RAGSDALE, WINIFRED
Awarded: Southern California Council (Dorothy McKenzie) 1984.

RAGUS, CHRISTOPHER
Building: The Fight Against Gravity by Mario Salvadori, illustrated by Christopher Ragus and Saralinda Hooker; Atheneum, 1979. **Awarded:** Boston Globe Horn Book (nonfiction) 1980; New York. Academy of Sciences (older) 1980.

RAIBLE, ALTON ROBERT
The Changeling by Zilpha Keatley Snyder, illustrated by Alton Raible; Atheneum, 1970. **Awarded:** Christopher (ages 8-12) 1971.

The Egypt Game by Zilpha Keatley Snyder, illustrated by Alton Raible; Atheneum, 1967. **Awarded:** Lewis Carroll Shelf 1970; Newbery (honor) 1968; Spring Book Festival (middle) 1967; George G. Stone 1973.

The Headless Cupid by Zilpha Keatley Snyder, illustrated by Alton Raible; Atheneum, 1971. **Awarded:** Christopher (teenage) 1972; International Board on Books for Young People (text/USA) 1974; Newbery (honor) 1972; William Allen White 1974.

The Witches of Worm by Zilpha Keatley Snyder, illustrated by Alton Raible; Atheneum, 1972. **Awarded:** National Book Award (finalist) 1973; New York Times Notable Books 1972; Newbery (honor) 1973.

RAMPEN, LEO
The St. Lawrence by William Toye, illustrated by Leo Rampen; Oxford, 1959. **Awarded:** Canadian Library Assn. 1961.

RAMSEY, MICHAEL
Amish People: Plain Living in a Complex World by Carolyn Meyer, photographs by Michael Ramsey, Gerald Dodds and Carolyn Meyer; Atheneum, 1976. **Awarded:** Children's Book Showcase 1977.

RAND, ANN
I Know a Lot of Things by Ann Rand and Paul Rand, illustrated by Paul Rand; Harcourt, 1956. **Awarded:** New York Times Best Illustrated 1956.

Sparkle and Spin: A Book about Words by Ann Rand and Paul Rand, illustrated by Paul Rand; Harcourt, 1957. **Awarded:** New York Times Best Illustrated 1957.

Umbrellas, Hats and Wheels by Ann Rand and Jerome Snyder, illustrated by Jerome Snyder; Harcourt, 1961. **Awarded:** New York Times Best Illustrated 1961.

RAND, PAUL
I Know a Lot of Things by Paul Rand and Ann Rand, illustrated by Paul Rand; Harcourt, 1956. **Awarded:** New York Times Best Illustrated 1956.

Sparkle and Spin: A Book about Words by Paul Rand and Ann Rand, illustrated by Paul Rand; Harcourt, 1957. **Awarded:** New York Times Best Illustrated 1957.

RAND, TED
Paul Revere's Ride by Henry Wadsworth Longfellow, illustrated by Ted Rand; Dutton, 1990. **Awarded:** Christopher (All ages) 1991.

RANDALL, KENNETH CHARLES
Wild Hunter by Kenneth Charles Randall, illustrated by Manning deV. Lee; Watts, 1951. **Awarded:** Spring Book Festival (8-12 honor) 1951.

RANDALL, RUTH PAINTER
I Jessie: A Biography of the Girl Who Married John Charles Fremont by Ruth Painter Randall, illustrated with photographs; Little Brown, 1963. **Awarded:** Friends of American Writers 1964.

RANKIN, LAURA
The Handmade Alphabet written and illustrated by Laura Rankin; Dial, 1991. **Awarded:** Boston Globe Horn Book (Nonfiction Honor) 1992; Hungry Mind (Picturebooks/Nonfiction) 1992.

RANKIN, LOUISE S.
Daughter of the Mountains by Louise S. Rankin, illustrated by Kurt Wiese; Viking, 1948. **Awarded:** Lewis Carroll Shelf 1962; Newbery (honor) 1949; Spring Book Festival (middle) 1948.

RANSOME, ARTHUR
The Fool of the World and the Flying Ship by Arthur Ransome, illustrated by Uri Shulevitz; Farrar, 1968. **Awarded:** Caldecott 1969.

Pigeon Post written and illustrated by Arthur Ransome; Cape, 1936. **Awarded:** Carnegie 1936.

RANSOME, JAMES
Aunt Flossie's Hats (and Crab Cakes Later) by Elizabeth Fitzgerald Howard, illustrated by James Ransome; Clarion, 1990. **Awarded:** Parents' Choice (Picture Book) 1991.

RAO, ANTHONY
Dinosaurs of North America by Helen R. Sattler, introduction by John H. Ostrom, illustrated by Anthony Rao; Lothrop, Lee & Shepard, 1981. **Awarded:** Boston Globe Horn Book (nonfiction honor) 1982; Golden Kite (nonfiction honor) 1981.

The Illustrated Dinosaur Dictionary by Helen R. Sattler, foreword by John H. Ostrom, illustrated by Pamela Carroll, color insert by Anthony Rao and Christopher Santoro; Lothrop, Lee & Shepard, 1983. **Awarded:** Golden Kite (nonfiction) 1983.

RAPAPORT, STELLA F.
The Bear: Ship of Many Lives written and illustrated by Stella F. Rapaport; Dodd, Mead, 1962. **Awarded:** Boys' Life 1961.

RAPPAPORT, DOREEN
Trouble at the Mines by Doreen Rappaport, illustrated by Joan Sandin; Crowell, 1987. **Awarded:** Addams (Honor) 1988.

RASKIN, ELLEN
Figgs and Phantoms written and illustrated by Ellen Raskin; Dutton, 1974. **Awarded:** Children's Book Showcase 1975; Newbery (honor) 1975.

The King of Men by Olivia Coolidge, illustrated by Ellen Raskin; Houghton, 1966. **Awarded:** Spring Book Festival (older honor) 1966.

The Mysterious Disappearance of Leon (I Mean Noel) written and illustrated by Ellen Raskin; Dutton, 1971. **Awarded:** Children's Book Showcase 1972.

Nothing Ever Happens on My Block written and illustrated by Ellen Raskin; Atheneum, 1966. **Awarded:** Art Books for Children 1973; New York Times Best Illustrated 1966; Spring Book Festival (picture book) 1966.

A Paper Zoo by Renee Weiss, illustrated by Ellen Raskin; Macmillan, 1968. **Awarded:** New Jersey Institute of Technology 1969.

Spectacles written and illustrated by Ellen Raskin; Atheneum, 1968. **Awarded:** New York Times Best Illustrated 1968.

The Tattooed Potato and Other Clues by Ellen Raskin, not illustrated; Dutton, 1975. **Awarded:** Edgar Allan Poe (runnerup) 1976.

The Westing Game by Ellen Raskin, not illustrated; Dutton, 1978. **Awarded:** Boston Globe Horn Book (fiction) 1978; CRABbery (honor) 1979; Michigan Young Readers (division II) 1982; Newbery 1979; Virginia (Middle School) 1984.

Who, Said Sue, Said Whoo? written and illustrated by Ellen Raskin; Atheneum, 1973. **Awarded:** Art Books for Children 1974; Boston Globe Horn Book (illustration honor) 1973; Children's Book Showcase 1974.

RATHE, JOANNE

Read-Aloud Handbook by Jim Trelease, illustrated by Joanne Rathe; Penguin, 1982. **Awarded:** Jeremiah Ludington 1988.

RATTIGAN, KIM

Dumpling Soup by Jama Kim Rattigan, illustrated by Lillian Hsu-Flanders; Little Brown, 1992. **Awarded:** New Voices, New World 1990.

RAU, MARGARET

The Snow Monkey at Home by Margaret Rau, illustrated by Eva Hulsmann; Knopf, 1979. **Awarded:** Southern California Council (distinguished work of nonfiction) 1980.

RAVIELLI, ANTHONY

Men, Microscopes and Living Things by Katherine B. Shippen, illustrated by Anthony Ravielli; Viking, 1955. **Awarded:** International Board on Books for Young People (USA) 1956; Newbery (honor) 1956; Spring Book Festival (older honor) 1955.

RAWLINGS, MARJORIE KINNAN

The Secret River by Margaret Kinnan Rawlings, illustrated by Leonard Weisgard; Scribner, 1955. **Awarded:** Newbery (honor) 1956.

The Yearling by Marjorie Kinnan Rawlings, illustrated by N. C. Wyeth; Scribner, 1961, 1939. **Awarded:** Lewis Carroll Shelf 1963; Feature a Classic 1981.

RAWLINS, DONNA

My Place by Nadia Wheatley, illustrated by Donna Rawlins; Collins Dove, 1987. **Awarded:** Children's Book Council of Australia (Book of the Year Younger) 1988; International Board on Books for Young People (Writing/Australia) 1990; Young Australian Best Book (Fiction Younger Reader) 1988.

RAWLINS, JANET

Bridget and William by Jane Gardam, illustrated by Janet Rawlins; Julia MacRae, 1981. **Awarded:** Carnegie (commended) 1981.

The Hollow Land by Jane Gardam, illustrated by Janet Rawlins; Julia MacRae, 1981. **Awarded:** Carnegie (highly commended) 1981; Whitbread 1981.

RAWLS, WILSON

The Summer of the Monkeys by Wilson Rawls, not illustrated; Doubleday, 1976. **Awarded:** California Young Reader Medal (intermediate) 1981; Golden Archer 1979; Sequoyah 1979; William Allen White 1979.

Where the Red Fern Grows by Wilson Rawls, not illustrated; Doubleday, 1961. **Awarded:** Great Stone Face 1988; Great Stone Face 1989; Massachusetts 1987; Michigan Young Readers (division II) 1980; North Dakota Children's (older) 1981.

RAY, DEBORAH KOGAN

Awarded: Drexel 1987.

Chang's Paper Pony by Eleanor Coerr, illustrated by Deborah Kogan Ray; Harper & Row, 1988. **Awarded:** John and Patricia Beatty 1989.

Little Tree by E. E. Cummings, illustrated by Deborah Kogan Ray; Crown, 1987. **Awarded:** Carolyn W. Field 1988.

My Daddy Was a Soldier: A World War II Story written and illustrated by Deborah Kogan Ray; Holiday House, 1990. **Awarded:** Parents' Choice (Story Book) 1990.

RAY, JANE

The Story of Christmas: Words from the Gospels of Matthew and Luke illustrated by Jane Ray; Dutton, 1991. **Awarded:** Redbook 1991.

The Story of the Creation: Words From Genesis, illustrated by Jane Ray; Orchard, 1992; Dutton, 1993. **Awarded:** British Book Awards (illustrated runnerup) 1992; Smarties (6-8 years) 1992.

RAY, RALPH

Boy of the North: The Story of Pierre Radisson by Ronald Syme, illustrated by Ralph Ray; Morrow, 1950. **Awarded:** Boys Club 1951.

David Livingston, Foe of Darkness by Jeanette Eaton, illustrated by Ralph Ray; Morrow, 1947. **Awarded:** Ohioana (honorable mention) 1948.

Gandhi, Fighter without a Sword by Jeanette Eaton, illustrated by Ralph Ray; Morrow, 1950. **Awarded:** Newbery (honor) 1951.

Paul Tiber, Forester by Maria Gleit, illustrated by Ralph Ray; Scribner, 1949. **Awarded:** Child Study 1949.

RAYMOND, CHARLES

(pseudonym for Charlotte and Raymond Koch)

Jud by Charles Raymond, not illustrated; Houghton, 1968. **Awarded:** Friends of American Writers 1969.

RAYMOND, LOUISE

The Little French Farm by Lida Guertik, translated by Louise Raymond, illustrated by Helene Guertik; Harper, 1939. **Awarded:** Spring Book Festival (younger honor) 1939.

RAYMOND, ROBERT

see ALTER, ROBERT EDMOND

RAYNER, MARY

Babe: the Gallant Pig by Dick King-Smith, illustrated by Mary Rayner; Crown, 1985. **Awarded:** Boston Globe Horn Book (fiction honor) 1985; Parents' Choice (literature) 1985.

Daggie Dogfoot by Dick King-Smith, illustrated by Mary Rayner; Gollancz, 1980. **Awarded:** Guardian (runnerup) 1981.

Garth Pig and the Ice Cream Lady written and illustrated by Mary Rayner; Macmillan, 1977. **Awarded:** Greenaway (commended) 1977.

Mr. and Mrs. Pig's Evening Out written and illustrated by Mary Rayner; Atheneum, 1976. **Awarded:** New York Times Notable Books 1976.

Mrs. Pig Gets Cross and Other Stories written and illustrated by Mary Rayner; Dutton, 1986. **Awarded:** Parents' Choice (Story Book) 1987.

The Sheep-pig by Dick King-Smith, illustrated by Mary Rayner; Gollancz, 1983. **Awarded:** Guardian 1984.

RAYNOR, PAUL

Meaning Well by Sheila R. Cole, illustrated by Paul Raynor; Watts, 1974. **Awarded:** Golden Kite (honor) 1974.

RAYSOR, JOAN
David and the Phoenix by Edward Ormondroyd, illustrated by Joan Raysor; Follett, 1957. **Awarded:** Commonwealth Club of California 1957.

READ, PIERS PAUL
Alive by Piers Paul Reid; Avon, 1975. **Awarded:** Media & Methods (paperback) 1976.

REARDON, MARY
Snow Treasure by Marie McSwigan, illustrated by Mary Reardon; Dutton, 1942. **Awarded:** Young Readers Choice 1945.

REARDON, MAUREEN
Feelings between Brothers and Sisters by Maureen Reardon and Marcia Maher Conta, photographs by Jules M. Rosenthal; Advanced Learning Concepts, 1974. **Awarded:** Council of Wisconsin Writers (picture book) 1975.

REAVER, HERBERT R.
Mote by Herbert R. Reaver, not illustrated; Delacorte, 1990. **Awarded:** Delacorte Press Prize (Honorable Mention) 1989; Edgar Allan Poe (Young Adult) 1991.

REAVIN, SAM
Hurray for Captain Jane! by Sam Reavin, illustrated by Emily McCully; Parents, 1971. **Awarded:** Children's Book Showcase 1972.

RECHEIS, KATHE
Kwajo und das Geheimnis de Trommelmanncheno by Meshack Asare, translated by Kathe Recheis; Verlag Jungbrunner, 1984. (Original English: *The Brassman's Secret*) **Awarded:** International Board on Books for Young People (translation/Austria) 1986.

REDPATH, IAN
The Giant Book of Space by Ian Redpath, illustrated; Hamlyn, 1989. **Awarded:** Science Book Prizes (Under 8 years of age) 1990.

REED, ALEXANDER WYCLIF
Myths and Legends of Maoriland by A. W. Reed, illustrated by George Woods and W. Dittmer; Reed, 1946. **Awarded:** Esther Glen 1947.

REED, GWENDOLYN E.
Lean out of the Window: An Anthology of Modern Poetry by Gwendolyn E. Reed and Sara Hannum, illustrated by Ragna Tischler; Atheneum, 1965. **Awarded:** Spring Book Festival (middle honor) 1965.

REED, JACQUELINE
The Morning Side of the Hill by Jacqueline Reed, not illustrated; Dodd, Mead, 1960. **Awarded:** Calling All Girls - Dodd, Mead 1960.

REED, PHILIP G.
Mother Goose and Nursery Rhymes written and illustrated by Philip Reed; Atheneum, 1963. **Awarded:** Caldecott (honor) 1964.

REEDER, CAROLYN
Shades of Gray by Carolyn Reeder, not illustrated; Macmillan, 1989. **Awarded:** Addams (Honor) 1990; Child Study 1989; Jefferson Cup 1990; Scott O'Dell 1989.

REES, DAVID
Exeter Blitz by David Rees, not illustrated; Hamilton, 1978. **Awarded:** Carnegie 1978.

The Green Bough of Liberty by David Rees, illustrated with old prints and maps; Dobson, 1980. **Awarded:** Other Award 1980.

Storm Surge by David Rees, illustrated by Trevor Stubley; Lutterworth, 1975. **Awarded:** Guardian (commended) 1976.

REES, ENNIS
Lions and Lobsters and Foxes and Frogs: Fables from Aesop by Ennis Rees, illustrated by Edward Gorey; Young Scott/Addison Wesley, 1971. **Awarded:** Children's Book Showcase 1972.

REES, LESLIE
Story of Karrawingi, the Emu by Leslie Rees, illustrated by Walter Cunningham; Sands, 1946. **Awarded:** Children's Book Council of Australia 1946.

REES, LU
Awarded: Dromkeen Medal 1982 (posthumously).

REES, R. A.
The American West 1840-1895 by R. A. Rees and S. J. Styles, illustrated with photos; Longman, 1986. **Awarded:** Times Educational Supplement (Schoolbook) 1987.

REESE, JOHN
Big Mutt by John Reese, illustrated by Rod Ruth; Westminster, 1952. **Awarded:** Spring Book Festival (older) 1952.

REEVES, JAMES
The Blackbird in the Lilac by James Reeves, illustrated by Edward Ardizzone; Dutton, 1959. **Awarded:** Spring Book Festival (ages 4-8 honor) 1959.

English Fables and Fairy Stories retold by James Reeves, illustrated by Joan Kiddell-Monroe; Oxford, 1954. **Awarded:** Carnegie (commended) 1954.

Ragged Robin (poems) by James Reeves, illustrated by Jane Paton; Dutton, 1961. **Awarded:** Carnegie (commended) 1961.

Titus in Trouble by James Reeves, illustrated by Edward Ardizzone; Bodley Head, 1959. **Awarded:** Greenaway (commended) 1959.

REGEN, SUSAN
A Show of Hands: Say it in Sign Language by Linda Bourke and Mary Beth Miller, with Susan Regen, illustrated by Linda Bourke; Addison Wesley, 1980. **Awarded:** Garden State Children's (younger nonfiction) 1983.

REGGIANI, RENEE
Le Avventure de Cinque Ragazzi e un Cane by Renee Reggiani, illustrated by Lionello Zorn Giorni; Cappelli, 1960. **Awarded:** Hans Christian Andersen (runnerup) 1962.

REGGUINTI, GORDON
The Sacred Harvest: Ojibway Wild Rice Gathering by Gordon Regguinti, photographs by Dale Kakkak; Lerner, 1992. **Awarded:** Hungry Mind (Middle Readers/Nonfiction) 1993.

REGOSTA, GASTONE
Priscilla by Giana Anguissola, illustrated by Gastone Regosta; Mursia, 1958. **Awarded:** Hans Christian Andersen (runnerup) 1960.

REICH, HANNS
Animals of Many Lands edited by Hanns Reich, illustrated with photographs; Hill & Wang, 1967. **Awarded:** New York Times Best Illustrated 1967.

REID, ALASTAIR
Fairwater by Alastair Reid, illustrated by Walter Lorraine; Houghton, 1957. **Awarded:** Spring Book Festival (middle honor) 1957.

I Will Tell You of a Town by Alastair Reid, illustrated by Walter Lorraine; Houghton, 1956. **Awarded:** New York Times Best Illustrated 1956.

Ounce, Dice, Trice by Alastair Reid, illustrated by Ben Shahn; Little, Brown, 1958. **Awarded:** Art Books for Children 1973.

REID, BARBARA
Awarded: UNICEF-Ezra Jack Keats International Award for Children's Book Illustration 1988.

Have You Seen Birds? by Joanne Oppenheim, illustrated by Barbara Reid; North Winds Press, 1986; Scholastic, 1986. **Awarded:** Governor General (illustration) 1986; Amelia Frances Howard- Gibbon (runnerup) 1987; IODE 1986; Elizabeth Mrazik-Cleaver 1987; Ruth Schwartz 1987.

How To Make Pop-ups by Joan Irvine, illustrated by Barbara Reid; Morrow, 1988. **Awarded:** Utah Children's Informational 1990.

Zoe's Rainy Day illustrated by Barbara Reid; HarperCollins, 1991. **Awarded:** Mr. Christie's (English Illustration) 1991.

Zoe's Snowy Day illustrated by Barbara Reid; HarperCollins, 1991. **Awarded:** Mr. Christie's (English Illustration) 1991.

Zoe's Sunny Day illustrated by Barbara Reid; HarperCollins, 1991. **Awarded:** Mr. Christie's (English Illustration) 1991.

Zoe's Windy Day illustrated by Barbara Reid; HarperCollins, 1991. **Awarded:** Mr. Christie's (English Illustration) 1991.

REID, BILL
Raven's Cry by Christie Harris, illustrated by Bill Reid; McClelland & Stewart, 1966. **Awarded:** Canadian Library Assn. 1967.

REID, DOROTHY
Tales of Nanabozho by Dorothy Reid, illustrated by Donald Grant; Oxford, 1964. **Awarded:** Canadian Library Assn. 1965.

REID, JAMES
Sailing for Gold by Clifton Johnson, illustrated by James Reid; Putnam, 1938. **Awarded:** Spring Book Festival (older honor) 1938.

REID, JOHN
Model Boats that Really Go by John Reid, illustrated; Random Century New Zealand, 1990. **Awarded:** New Zealand Library Assn. Nonfiction for Young People 1991.

REIDEL, MARLENE
Kasimir's Journey by Monroe Stearns, illustrated by Marlene Reidel; Lippincott, 1959. **Awarded:** New York Times Best Illustrated 1959.

REILLY, PAULINE
Picture Roo Books series by Pauline Reilly, illustrated by Will Roland; Kangaroo Press, 1989-1992. **Awarded:** Whitley (Children's Educational Series) 1992.

REINER, ISABEL
Viking Dagger by Isabel Reiner in *Of the Jigsaw*; Peguin, 1986. **Awarded:** Vicky Metcalf Short Story 1987.

REINFELD, FRED
The Great Dissenters: Guardians of Their Country's Laws and Liberties by Fred Reinfeld, not illustrated; Crowell, 1959. **Awarded:** Edison Mass Media (America's past) 1960.

REISS, JOHANNA
The Upstairs Room by Johanna Reiss, not illustrated; Crowell, 1972. **Awarded:** Jane Addams (honor) 1973; Jewish Book Council 1972; New York Times Notable Books 1972; Newbery (honor) 1973.

REKIMIES, ERKKI
Tapporahat by Erkki Rekimies; Otava, 1959. **Awarded:** Hans Christian Andersen (runnerup) 1962.

REMANE, LIESELOTTE
Awarded: FIT Translation 1987.

REMINI, ROBERT V.
The Revolutionary Age of Andrew Jackson by Robert V. Remini, illustrated with photographs; Harper, 1976. **Awarded:** Friends of American Writers (older) 1977.

RENBERG, DALIA H.
Hello, Clouds! by Dalia H. Renberg, illustrated by Alona Frankel; Harper & Row, 1985. **Awarded:** Please Touch (honorable mention) 1986.

RENICK, MARION LEWIS
Ohio by Marion Lewis Renick, illustrated with old plates and photographs; Coward, 1970. **Awarded:** Ohioana (nonfiction) 1971.

The Shining Shooter by Marion Renick, illustrated by Dwight Logan; Scribner, 1950. **Awarded:** Boys Club 1951.

RENNER, HANS PETER
In the Land of Ur: The Discovery of Ancient Mesopotamia by Hans Baumann, translated by Stella Humphries, illustrated by Hans Peter Renner; Pantheon, 1969; Oxford, 1969. **Awarded:** Batchelder 1971.

RESCH, GEORGE T.
All about Light and Radiation by Ira M. Freeman, illustrated by George T. Resch; Random House, 1965. **Awarded:** New Jersey Institute of Technology 1965.

RETHI, LILI
Man against Earth: The Story of Tunnels and Tunnel Builders by Don Murray, illustrated by Lili Rethi; Lippincott, 1961. **Awarded:** New Jersey Institute of Technology 1961.

RETLA, ROBERT
see ALTER, ROBERT EDMOND

REUTER, BJARNE
Buster's World by Bjarne Reuter, illustrated by Paul O. Zelinsky; Dutton, 1989. **Awarded:** Batchelder 1990.

REUTER, CAROL
The Secret of the Sea Rocks by Carol Reuter, illustrated by Vera Bock; McKay, 1967. **Awarded:** New Jersey Institute of Technology 1967.

REUTER, M. LAWRENCE
Mass Media by M. Lawrence Reuter, Elizabeth Conley and Ann Heintz, illustrated; Loyola University Press, 1972. **Awarded:** Media & Methods (Textbook) 1975.

REY, H. A. (HANS AUGUSTO)
Curious George written and illustrated by H. A. Rey; Houghton Mifflin, 1973, 1941. **Awarded:** Children's Choice [Arizona] (picture book) 1987; North Dakota Children's Choice (younger) 1981.

Curious George Gets a Medal written and illustrated by H. A. Rey; Houghton, 1957. **Awarded:** New York Times Best Illustrated 1957.

Curious George Goes to the Hospital written and illustrated by H. A. Rey and Margret Rey; Houghton, 1966. **Awarded:** Child Study (special citation) 1966.

Curious George Takes a Job written and illustrated by H. A. Rey; Houghton, 1947. **Awarded:** Lewis Carroll Shelf 1960.

Katy No-Pocket by Emmy Payne, illustrated by H. A. Rey; Houghton Mifflin, 1944. **Awarded:** Emphasis on Reading (grades K-1) 1980-81.

REY, MARGRET
Curious George Goes to the Hospital written and illustrated by Margret Rey and H. A. Rey; Houghton, 1966. **Awarded:** Child Study (special citation) 1966.

REYES, GREGG
Zoo Walk written and illustrated by Gregg Reyes; Oxford, 1984. **Awarded:** Mother Goose (runnerup) 1985.

REYHER, BECKY
My Mother is the Most Beautiful Woman in the World by Becky Reyher, illustrated by Ruth C. Gannett; Lothrop Lee & Shepard, 1945. **Awarded:** Caldecott (honor) 1946.

REYNOLDS, PAT
Tom's Friend written and illustrated by Pat Reynolds; Allen & Unwin, 1990. **Awarded:** Whitley (Children's Books) 1991.

REYNOLDS, SUSAN LYNN
Strandia by Susan Lynn Reynolds, not illustrated; HarperCollins (Canada), 1991; Farrar, Straus, Giroux, 1991. **Awarded:** Young Adult Canadian 1992.

RHEAY, MARY LOUISE
Awarded: Allie Beth Martin 1980.

RHIND, MARY
The Dark Shadow by Mary Rhind, not illustrated; Canongate, 1988. **Awarded:** Kelpie for the Nineties 1988.

RHINE, RICHARD
Life in a Bucket of Soil by Richard Rhine, illustrated by Elsie Wrigley; Lothrop, 1972. **Awarded:** New Jersey Institute of Technology 1972.

RHOADS, DOROTHY MARY
The Corn Grows Ripe by Dorothy Rhoads, illustrated by Jean Charlot; Viking, 1956. **Awarded:** Newbery (honor) 1957.

RIBBONS, IAN
Battle of Gettysburg, 1-3 July, 1863 written and illustrated by Ian Ribbons; Oxford, 1974. **Awarded:** Carnegie (commended) 1974.

Under Goliath by Peter Carter, illustrated by Ian Ribbons; Oxford, 1977. **Awarded:** Carnegie (commended) 1977.

RICCIUTI, EDWARD R.
Wildlife of the Mountains by Edward R. Ricciuti, illustrated with photographs and maps; Abrams, 1979. **Awarded:** New York Academy of Sciences (special award for reference book series to publisher) 1980.

RICE, EVE
What Sadie Sang written and illustrated by Eve Rice; Greenwillow, 1976. **Awarded:** Children's Book Showcase 1977.

RICE, INEZ
The March Wind by Inez Rice, illustrated by Vladimir Bobri; Lothrop, 1957. **Awarded:** Spring Book Festival (ages 4-8 honor) 1957.

RICH, LOUISE DICKINSON
Start of the Trail: The Story of a Young Maine Guide by Louise Dickinson Rich, not illustrated; Lippincott, 1949. **Awarded:** Spring Book Festival (older) 1949.

RICHARD, ADRIENNE
Wings by Adrienne Richard, not illustrated; Atlantic-Little, 1974. **Awarded:** National Book Award (finalist) 1975.

RICHARDS, LAURA E.
Harry in England by Laura E. Richards, illustrated by Reginald Birch; Appleton Century Crofts, 1937. **Awarded:** Spring Book Festival (younger honor) 1937.

Tirra Lirra: Rhymes Old and New by Laura E. Richards, illustrated by Marguerite Davis; Little, 1955, 1902. **Awarded:** Lewis Carroll Shelf 1959.

RICHARDS, LAWRENCE
The International Children's Bible Handbook by Lawrence Richards, illustrated; Sweet Publishing, 1986. **Awarded:** Gold Medallion 1987.

RICHARDS, NORMAN
Dreamers and Doers: Inventors who Changed our World by Norman Richards, illustrated; Atheneum, 1984. **Awarded:** New York Academy of Sciences (Elliott Montroll special award) 1985.

RICHARDS, SUSAN
Hubert, the Caterpillar who Thought He Was a Moustache by Susan Richards and Wendy Stang, illustrated by Robert L. Anderson; Quist, 1967. **Awarded:** New York Times Best Illustrated 1967.

RICHARDSON, ERNEST
The Swamp Fox of the Revolution by Stewart Holbrook, illustrated by Ernest Richardson; Random House, 1959. **Awarded:** Young Readers Choice 1962.

RICHARDSON, JEAN
Stephen's Feast by Jean Richardson, illustrated by Alice Englander; Little Brown, 1991. **Awarded:** Christopher Award (Ages 6-8) 1992.

RICHARDSON, ROBERT S.
The Stars and Serendipity written and illustrated by Robert S. Richardson; Pantheon, 1971. **Awarded:** New York Academy of Sciences 1972

RICHES, JUDITH
Tigers by Roland Edwards, illustrated by Judith Riches; Tambourine Books, 1992. **Awarded:** Parents Choice (Picture Books) 1992.

RICHLER, MORDECAI
Jacob Two-two Meets the Hooded Fang by Mordecai Richler, illustrated by Fritz Wegner; McClelland & Stewart, 1975. **Awarded:** Canadian Library Assn. 1976; New York Times Notable Books 1975; Ruth Schwartz 1976.

RICHTER, CATHERINE M.
Bibi: The Baker's Horse by Anna Bird Stewart, illustrated by Catherine M. Richter; Lippincott, 1942. **Awarded:** Ohioana 1943.

RICHTER, HANS PETER
Friedrich by Hans Peter Richter, translated by Edite Kroll, not illustrated; Holt, 1970. **Awarded:** Batchelder 1972; Woodward Park School 1971.

RIDE, SALLY
To Space and Back by Sally Ride, illustrated with photos; Lothrop, Lee & Shepard, 1986. **Awarded:** Garden State Children's Book Award (Younger Nonfiction) 1989.

RIDLEY, PHILIP
Dakota of the White Flats by Philip Ridley, not illustrated; Knopf, 1991. **Awarded:** Parents' Choice (Story Book) 1991.

Krindlekrax by Philip Ridley, illustrated by Mark Robinson; Cape, 1991; Knopf, 1992. **Awarded:** Smarties (9-11 years) 1991.

RIEDEL, MANFRED G.

Winning with Numbers: A Kid's Guide to Statistics by Manfred G. Riedel, illustrated by Paul Coker, Jr.; Prentice-Hall, 1978. **Awarded:** New York Academy of Sciences (younger honor) 1979.

RIEDMAN, SARAH R.

Benjamin Rush: Physician, Patriot, Founding Father by Sarah R. Riedman and Clarence C. Green, illustrated with photographs; Abelard-Schuman, 1964. **Awarded:** New Jersey Institute of Technology 1965.

How Man Discovered His Body by Sarah R. Riedman, illustrated by Frances Wells; Abelard Schuman, 1966. **Awarded:** New Jersey Institute of Technology (science) 1966.

Portraits of Nobel Laureates in Medicine and Physiology by Sarah Riedman and Elton T. Gustafson, illustrated with portraits; Abelard-Schuman, 1964. **Awarded:** New Jersey Institute of Technology (biography ages 12-up) 1964.

RIEHECKY, JANET

Allosaurus by Janet Riehecky, illustrated by Llyn Hunter; Child's World, 1988. **Awarded:** Society of Midland Authors (Juvenile Nonfiction) 1989.

Apatosaurus by Janet Riehecky, illustrated by Lydia Halverson; Child's World, 1988. **Awarded:** Society of Midland Authors (Juvenile Nonfiction) 1989.

Stegosaurus by Janet Riehecky, illustrated by Diana Magnuson; Child's World, 1988. **Awarded:** Society of Midland Authors (Juvenile Nonfiction) 1989.

Triceratops by Janet Riehecky, illustrated by Diana Magnuson; Child's World, 1988. **Awarded:** Society of Midland Authors (Juvenile Nonfiction) 1989.

Tyrannosaurus by Janet Riehecky, illustrated by Diana Magnuson; Child's World, 1988. **Awarded:** Society of Midland Authors (Juvenile Nonfiction) 1989.

RIENOW, LEONA

The Bewitched Caverns by Leona Rienow, illustrated by Allen Pope, Scribner, 1948. **Awarded:** Spring Book Festival (middle honor) 1948.

RIESENBERG, FELIX

Crimson Anchor: A Sea Mystery by Felix Riesenberg, not illustrated; Dodd, Mead, 1948. **Awarded:** Spring Book Festival (older) 1948.

RIHA, BOHUMIL

Awarded: Hans Christian Andersen (author) 1980.

RILEY, JON

Room 13 by Robert E. Swindells, illustrated by Jon Riley; Doubleday, 1989. **Awarded:** Children's Book Award (Federation) 1989-90.

RILEY, LOUISE

Train for Tiger Lily by Louise Riley, illustrated by Christine Price; Macmillan Canada, 1954. **Awarded:** Canadian Library Assn. 1956.

RINALDI, ANN

The Good Side of My Heart by Ann Rinaldi, not illustrated; Holiday House, 1987. **Awarded:** New Jersey Institute of Technology 1988.

Time Enough for Drums by Ann Rinaldi, illustrated with maps; Holiday House, 1986. **Awarded:** New Jersey Institute of Technology 1987.

RINGGOLD, FAITH

Aunt Harriet's Underground Railroad in the Sky written and illustrated by Faith Ringgold; Crown, 1992. **Awarded:** Jane Addams (picture book) 1993.

Tar Beach written and illustrated by Faith Ringgold; Crown, 1991. **Awarded:** Caldecott (Honor) 1992; Hungry Mind (Picturebooks/Fiction) 1992; Ezra Jack Keats New Writer Award 1993; Coretta Scott King (Illustration) 1992; New York Times Best Illustrated 1991; Parents' Choice (Picture Book) 1991.

RINK, HANNO

Himmelszelt und Schneckenhaus written and illustrated by Rita Muhlbauer and Hanno Rink; Verlag Sauerlander, 1979. **Awarded:** Bologna (Graphics for Youth) 1980.

RINK, PAUL

Quest for Freedom: Bolivar and The South American Revolution by Paul Rink, illustrated by Barry Martin; Simon & Schuster, 1968. **Awarded:** Commonwealth Club of California 1968.

RIORDAN, JAMES

The Woman in the Moon and Other Tales of Forgotten Heroines by James Riordan, illustrated by Angela Barrett; Hutchinson, 1984. **Awarded:** Kurt Maschler (runnerup) 1984.

RIPLEY, A. L.

The Dark Frigate by Charles Boardman Hawes, illustrated by A. L. Ripley; Atlantic Monthly Press, 1923; Little, Brown, 1934. **Awarded:** Lewis Carroll Shelf 1962; Newbery 1924.

RISSER, MEG

Awarded: Lucile M. Pannell 1984.

RISWOLD, GILBERT

The Grizzly by Annabel Johnson and Edgar Johnson, illustrated by Gilbert Riswold; Harper, 1964. **Awarded:** William Allen White 1967.

The House on Charlton Street by Dola de Jong, illustrated by Gilbert Riswold; Scribner, 1962. **Awarded:** Edgar Allan Poe (runnerup) 1963.

RITCHIE, SCOT

Dinner at Aunt Rose's by Janet Munsil, illustrated by Scot Ritchie; Annick Press, 1984. **Awarded:** Alcuin 1985.

RITTER, BOB

Touched with Fire: Alaska's George William Seller by Margaret E. Bell, maps by Bob Ritter; Morrow, 1960. **Awarded:** Edison Mass Media (character development for children) 1961.

RITTER, BRUCE

Covenant House by Bruce Ritter, not illustrated; Doubleday, 1987. **Awarded:** Janusz Korczak (About Children) 1988.

RIVERS, ALICE

In Two Worlds: A Yup'ik Eskimo Family by Alice Rivers and Aylette Jenness, illustrated by Aylette Jenness; Houghton Mifflin, 1989. **Awarded:** New York Academy of Sciences (Older Honor) 1989; Woodson (elementary) 1990.

RIWKIN-BRICK, ANNA

Sia Lives on Kilimanjaro by Astrid Lindgren, illustrated with photographs by Anna Riwkin-Brick; Macmillan, 1959. **Awarded:** Spring Book Festival (ages 4-8) 1959.

ROACH, MARILYNNE K.
The Mouse and the Song by Marilynne K. Roach, illustrated by Joseph Low; Parents, 1974. **Awarded:** Children's Book Showcase 1975.

ROBBINS, KEN
Bridges written and illustrated by Ken Robbins; Dial, 1991. **Awarded:** Parents' Choice (Picture Book) 1991.

Tools written and illustrated by Ken Robbins; Four Winds, 1983. **Awarded:** New York Times Best Illustrated 1983.

ROBBINS, RUTH
Baboushka and the Three Kings by Ruth Robbins, illustrated by Nicolas Sidjakov; Parnassus, 1960. **Awarded:** Hans Christian Andersen (runnerup) 1962; Caldecott 1961; New York Times Best Illustrated 1960.

The Emperor and the Drummer Boy by Ruth Robbins, illustrated by Nicolas Sidjakov; Parnassus, 1962. **Awarded:** New York Times Best Illustrated 1962.

The Wizard of Earthsea by Ursula K. LeGuin, illustrated by Ruth Robbins; Parnassus, 1968. **Awarded:** Boston Globe Horn Book (text) 1969; Lewis Carroll Shelf 1979.

ROBERTS, CLARE
Oak & Company by Richard Mabey, illustrated by Clare Roberts; Greenwillow, 1983. **Awarded:** New York Academy of Sciences (younger) 1984.

ROBERTS, DOREEN
The Story of Soul the King by Doreen Roberts. **Awarded:** Greenaway (commended) 1966.

ROBERTS, JIM
Soft as the Wind by Edith Eckblad, illustrated by Jim Roberts; Augsburg, 1974. **Awarded:** Council for Wisconsin Writers (picture book runnerup) 1975.

ROBERTS, KEN
Pop Bottles by Ken Roberts, not illustrated; Groundwood Books, 1987. **Awarded:** Surrey School 1988.

ROBERTS, WILLO DAVIS
Babysitting Is a Dangerous Job by Willo Davis Roberts, not illustrated; Atheneum, 1985. **Awarded:** Nevada Young Reader Award (Intermediate) 1988-89; South Carolina Children's Choice 1988; Mark Twain 1988; Young Hoosier (Grades 4-6) 1988.

Don't Hurt Laurie! by Willo Davis Roberts, illustrated by Ruth Sanderson; Atheneum, 1977. **Awarded:** Georgia Children's 1982; West Australian Young Readers (secondary) 1981; Young Hoosier (grades 4-6) 1980.

Eddie and the Fairy Godpuppy by Willo Davis Roberts, illustrated by Leslie Morrill; Atheneum, 1984. **Awarded:** West Virginia Children's (Honor book) 1987-88.

The Girl with the Silver Eyes by Willo Davis Roberts, not illustrated; Atheneum, 1980. **Awarded:** California Young Reader (junior high) 1986; CRABbery (honor) 1981; Mark Twain 1983.

Megan's Island by Willo Davis Roberts, not illustrated; Atheneum, 1988. **Awarded:** Edgar Allan Poe (Juvenile) 1989.

More Minden Curses by Willo Davis Roberts, illustrated by Sherry Streeter; Atheneum, 1980. **Awarded:** Edgar Allan Poe (runnerup) 1981.

ROBERTSON, BARBARA
The Wind Has Wings: Poems from Canada compiled by Barbara Robertson and Mary Alice Downie, illustrated by Elizabeth Cleaver; Oxford, 1968. **Awarded:** Amelia Frances Howard-Gibbon 1971.

ROBERTSON, ELLEN
Through the Web by Ellen Robertson. **Awarded:** Mary Grant Bruce (Open $500) 1990.

ROBERTSON, FRANK C.
Sagebrush Sorrel by Frank C. Robertson, illustrated by Lee Townsend; Nelson, 1953. **Awarded:** Western Writers of America 1954.

ROBERTSON, KEITH
Henry Reed, Inc. by Keith Robertson, illustrated by Robert McCloskey; Viking, 1958. **Awarded:** William Allen White 1961.

Henry Reed's Baby-sitting Service by Keith Robertson, illustrated by Robert McCloskey; Viking, 1966. **Awarded:** Nene 1970; William Allen White 1969; Young Readers Choice 1969.

The Money Machine by Keith Robertson, illustrated by George Porter; Viking, 1969. **Awarded:** New Jersey Institute of Technology 1969.

New Jersey by Keith Robertson, illustrated by Donald T. Pitcher; Coward, 1969. **Awarded:** New Jersey Institute of Technology 1969.

The Pilgrim Goose by Keith Robertson, illustrated by Erick Berry; Viking, 1956. **Awarded:** Spring Book Festival (middle honor) 1956.

ROBINS, PATRICIA
Star Maiden: An Ojibwa Legend of the First Water Lily by Patricia Robins, illustrated by Shirley Day; Cassell & Collier-Macmillan, 1975. **Awarded:** Collier-Macmillan 1974.

ROBINSON, AMINAH BRENDA LYNN
Elijah's Angels by Michael J. Rosen, illustrated by Aminah Brenda Lynn Robinson; Harcourt Brace Jovanovich, 1992. **Awarded:** Hungry Mind (Picturebooks/Fiction) 1993.

ROBINSON, BARBARA
Awarded: Outstanding Pennsylvania Author 1985.

The Best Christmas Pageant Ever by Barbara Robinson, illustrated by Judith Gwyn Brown; Harper, 1972. **Awarded:** Georgia Children's 1976; Emphasis on Reading (grades 4-6) 1980-81; Maud Hart Lovelace 1982; Young Hoosier (grades 4-6) 1978.

ROBINSON, CHARLES
All the Money in the World by William Brittain, illustrated by Charles Robinson; Harper, 1979. **Awarded:** Charlie May Simon 1981-82.

The Daybreakers by Jane Louise Curry, illustrated by Charles Robinson; Harcourt, 1970. **Awarded:** Southern California Council (notable) 1971; Spring Book Festival (middle honor) 1970.

Ike and Mama and the Block Wedding by Carol Snyder, illustrated by Charles Robinson; Coward, 1979. **Awarded:** Sydney Taylor Book Award 1980.

Ike and Mama and the Seven Surprises by Carol Snyder, illustrated by Charles Robinson; Lothrop, Lee & Shepard, 1985. **Awarded:** Sydney Taylor Book Award 1986.

Ike and Mama and the Trouble at School by Carol Snyder, illustrated by Charles Robinson; Coward McCann, 1983. **Awarded:** New Jersey Institute of Technology 1983.

An Island in a Green Sea by Mabel Esther Allan, illustrated by Charles Robinson; Atheneum, 1972. **Awarded:** Boston Globe Horn Book (text honor) 1973.

Journey to America by Sonia Levitin, illustrated by Charles Robinson; Atheneum, 1970. **Awarded:** Jewish Book Council 1970.

The Mountain of Truth by Dale Carlson, illustrated by Charles Robinson; Atheneum, 1972. **Awarded:** Spring Book Festival (ages 6- 12 honor) 1972.

A Taste of Blackberries by Doris Buchanan Smith, illustrated by Charles Robinson; Crowell, 1973. **Awarded:** Child Study 1973; Georgia Children's 1975; Sue Hefly 1979.

ROBINSON, DOROTHY
The Legend of Africania by Dorothy Robinson, illustrated by Herbert Temple; Johnson, 1974. **Awarded:** Coretta Scott King 1975.

ROBINSON, IRENE
Awarded: Southern California Council (distinguished contribution to the field of children's literature) 1963.

The Jumping Lions of Borneo by John William Dunne, illustrated by Irene Robinson; Holt, 1938. **Awarded:** Spring Book Festival (younger honor) 1938.

ROBINSON, JACKIE
I Never Had it Made by Jackie Robinson as told to Alfred Duckett, illustrated with photographs; Putnam, 1972. **Awarded:** Coretta Scott King 1973.

ROBINSON, JESSIE B.
Fun with Puzzles by Joseph Leeming, illustrated by Jessie Robinson; Lippincott, 1946. **Awarded:** Boys Club 1948.

Star Light Stories: Holiday and Sabbath Tales by Lillian Simon Freehof, illustrated by Jessie B. Robinson; Bloch, 1952. **Awarded:** Jewish Book Council 1952.

ROBINSON, JOAN G.
Meg and Maxie by Joan G. Robinson, not illustrated; Gollancz, 1978. **Awarded:** Guardian (runnerup) 1980.

ROBINSON, JOHN ROOSEVELT
see ROBINSON, JACKIE

ROBINSON, MABEL LOUISE
Bright Island by Mabel L. Robinson, illustrated by Lynd Ward; Random House, 1937. **Awarded:** Newbery (honor) 1938; Spring Book Festival (older honor) 1937.

Runner of the Mountain Tops: The Life of Louis Agassiz by Mabel L. Robinson, illustrated by Lynd Ward; Random House, 1939. **Awarded:** Newbery (honor) 1940.

ROBINSON, MARK
Krindlekrax by Philip Ridley, illustrated by Mark Robinson; Cape, 1991; Knopf, 1992. **Awarded:** Smarties (9-11 years) 1991.

ROBINSON, MICHELE P.
Grandfather's Bridge by Michele P. Robinson; manuscript. **Awarded:** Council on Interracial Books for Children (American Indian) 1973.

ROBINSON, NANCY K.
Awarded: Lucky Book Club Four-Leaf Clover 1981.

ROBINSON, TIM
Science Wizardry for Kids by Margaret Kenda and Phyllis S. Williams, illustrated by Tim Robinson; Barron's, 1992. **Awarded:** Hungry Mind (Middle Readers/Nonfiction) 1993.

ROBINSON, TOM
Pete by Tom Robinson, illustrated by Morgan Dennis; Viking, 1941. **Awarded:** Spring Book Festival (middle) 1941.

ROBINSON, W. W.
Awarded: Southern California Council (distinguished contribution to the field of children's literature) 1963.

ROBINSON, WILLIAM POWELL
Where the Panther Screams by William Powell Robinson, illustrated by Lorence F. Bjorklund; World, 1961. **Awarded:** Sequoyah 1964.

ROCHMAN, HAZEL
Awarded: Children's Reading Round Table 1989.

ROCKCASTLE, VERNE
Awarded: Eva L. Gordon 1971.

ROCKER, F.
Gran at Coalgate by Winifred Cawley, illustrated by F. Rocker; Oxford, 1974. **Awarded:** Guardian 1975.

ROCKER, FERMIN
The Trouble with Donovan Croft by Bernard Ashley, illustrated by Fermin Rocker; Oxford, 1974. **Awarded:** Other Award 1976.

ROCKLIN, JOANNE
Dear Baby by Joanne Rocklin, illustrated by Eileen McKeating; Macmillan, 1988. **Awarded:** Southern California Council (Outstanding Work of Fiction for Children) 1989.

ROCKWELL, ANNE
Befana: A Christmas Story written and illustrated by Anne Rockwell; Atheneum, 1974. **Awarded:** Children's Book Showcase 1975.

In Our House written and illustrated by Anne Rockwell; Crowell, 1985. **Awarded:** Redbook 1985.

The Minstrel and the Mountain: A Tale of Peace by Jane Yolen, illustrated by Anne Rockwell; World, 1967. **Awarded:** Boys Club (certificate) 1968.

Toad written and illustrated by Anne Rockwell and Harlow Rockwell; Doubleday, 1972. **Awarded:** Children's Book Showcase 1973.

ROCKWELL, HARLOW
Toad written and illustrated by Harlow Rockwell and Anne Rockwell; Doubleday, 1972. **Awarded:** Children's Book Showcase 1973.

ROCKWELL, NORMAN
The Norman Rockwell Storybook by Jan Wahl, illustrated by Norman Rockwell; Windmill/Simon & Schuster, 1969. **Awarded:** Ohioana 1970.

ROCKWELL, THOMAS
How to Eat Fried Worms by Thomas Rockwell, illustrated by Emily McCully; Watts, 1973. **Awarded:** Arizona 1979; California Young Reader Medal (Intermediate) 1975; Golden Archer 1975; Iowa Children's Choice 1980; Mark Twain 1975; Massachusetts Children's 1976; Nene 1976; Sequoyah 1976; South Carolina Children's 1976; Volunteer State 1979; Young Hoosier (grades 4-6) 1977.

How To Fight a Girl by Thomas Rockwell, illustrated by Gioia Fiammenghi; Dell, 1988, c1987. **Awarded:** North Dakota Children's Choice (Juvenile Fiction) 1991.

RODARI, GIANNI
Awarded: Hans Christian Andersen (highly commended author/Italy) 1966, 1968; Hans Christian Andersen (author) 1970.

Kopfblumen by Gianni Rodari, illustrated by Eberhard Binder-Strassfurt; Der Kinderbuchverlag. **Awarded:** Bologna (Graphics for Children) 1973.

RODDA, EMILY

The Best-Kept Secret by Emily Rodda, illustrated by Noela Young; Angus & Robertson, 1988; Henry Holt, 1990. **Awarded:** Children's Book Council of Australia (Book of the Year Younger) 1989.

Finders Keepers by Emily Rodda, illustrated by Noela Young; Omnibus, 1990; Greenwillow, 1991. **Awarded:** Children's Book Council of Australia (Book of the Year Younger) 1991; Young Australian Best Book (Fiction Younger Reader) 1991.

Pigs Might Fly by Emily Rodda, illustrated by Noela Young; Angus & Robertson, 1986. **Awarded:** Children's Book Council of Australia (book of the year younger) 1987.

Something Special by Emily Rodda, illustrated by Noela Young; Angus & Robertson, 1984. **Awarded:** Children's Book Council of Australia (Junior Book of the Year) 1985.

RODGERS, MARY

A Billion for Boris by Mary Rodgers, not illustrated; Harper, 1974. **Awarded:** Christopher (ages 12-up) 1975.

Freaky Friday by Mary Rodgers, not illustrated; Harper, 1972. **Awarded:** California Young Reader Medal (intermediate) 1977; Christopher (teenage) 1973; Georgia Children's 1978; Nene 1977; Sequoyah 1976; South Carolina Children's 1976; Spring Book Festival (ages 12-16) 1972; Surrey School 1977.

RODGERS, RABOO

Island of Peril by Raboo Rodgers, not illustrated; Houghton Mifflin, 1987. **Awarded:** Friends of American Writers 1988.

RODMAN, BELLA

Lions in the Way by Bella Rodman, not illustrated; Follett, 1966. **Awarded:** Nancy Bloch 1966; Boys Club 1966-67; Charles W. Follett 1967.

RODMAN, MAIA

see WOJCIECHOWSKA, MAIA

RODWELL, JENNY

What Do You Feed Your Donkey On? Rhymes from a Belfast Childhood by Colette O'Hare, illustrated by Jenny Rodwell; Collins-World, 1978. **Awarded:** Boston Globe Horn Book (illustration honor) 1978.

ROE, EILEEN

Staying With Grandma by Eileen Roe, illustrated by Jacqueline Rogers; Bradbury Press, 1989. **Awarded:** New Jersey Institute of Technology 1990.

ROENNFELDT, ROBERT

The Little Monster series by Peter Thamm, illustrated by Robert Roennfeldt; Lutheran Publishing House, 1988. **Awarded:** Australian Christian Book of the Year Children's Award 1989.

ROESCH, ROBERTA FLEMING

World's Fairs: Yesterday, Today and Tomorrow by Roberta F. Roesch, illustrated with photographs; Day, 1964. **Awarded:** New Jersey Institute of Technology (social sciences) 1964.

ROFFEY, MAUREEN

Monkey's Crazy Hotel by Stephen Wyllie, illustrated by Maureen Roffey; Harper, 1987. **Awarded:** Redbook 1987.

There Was an Old Woman by Stephen Wyllie, illustrated by Maureen Roffey, paper engineering by Ray Marshall; Harper & Row, 1985. **Awarded:** Redbook 1985.

Tinker, Tailor, Soldier, Sailor: A Picture Book by Bernard Lodge, illustrated by Maureen Roffey; Bodley Head, 1976. **Awarded:** Greenaway (highly commended) 1976.

ROGER, MAE DURHAM

Awarded: Landau 1981.

ROGERS, FRED

Awarded: CBC Honors Program (Communication) 1985.

The New Baby by Fred Rogers, photographs by Jim Judkis; Putnam, 1985. **Awarded:** Carolyn W. Field 1986.

ROGERS, JACQUELINE

The Not-just-Anybody Family by Betsy Byars, illustrated by Jacqueline Rogers; Delacorte, 1986. **Awarded:** Parents' Choice (literature) 1986.

Staying With Grandma by Eileen Roe, illustrated by Jacqueline Rogers; Bradbury Press, 1989. **Awarded:** New Jersey Institute of Technology 1990.

ROGERS, JEAN

Runaway Mittens by Jean Rogers, illustrated by Rie Munoz; Greenwillow, 1988. **Awarded:** Parents' Choice (Story Book) 1988.

ROGERSON, JAMES

King Wilbur the Third and the Bicycle by James Rogerson, illustrated by George Him; Dent, 1976. **Awarded:** W. H. Smith (£50) 1977.

ROHMER, HARRIET

The Invisible Hunters by Harriet Rohmer, illustrated by Joe Sam; Children's Book Press, 1987. **Awarded:** Coretta Scott King (Illustration honor) 1988.

ROISMAN, LOIS

Leaving Egypt by Lois Roisman. **Awarded:** Sydney Taylor Manuscript Award 1992.

ROJANKOVSKY, FEODOR STEPANOVICH

All Alone by Claire Huchet Bishop, illustrated by Feodor Rojankovsky; Viking, 1953. **Awarded:** Newbery (honor) 1954; Spring Book Festival (ages 8-12 honor) 1953.

Frog Went A-Courtin' by John Langstaff, illustrated by Feodor Rojankovsky; Harcourt, 1955. **Awarded:** Caldecott 1956; Spring Book Festival (ages 4-8) 1955.

ROLAND, WILL

Picture Roo Books series by Pauline Reilly, illustrated by Will Roland; Kangaroo Press, 1989-1992. **Awarded:** Whitley (Children's Educational Series) 1992.

ROLLINS, CHARLEMAE HILL

Awarded: Children's Reading Round Table 1963; Grolier 1955; Women's National Book Assn. 1970.

Black Troubador, Langston Hughes by Charlemae Rollins, illustrated with photographs; Rand, 1970. **Awarded:** Coretta Scott King 1971.

ROLPH, MIC

Cells Are Us by Fran Balkwill, illustrated by Mic Rolph; HarperCollins, 1990. **Awarded:** Science Book Prizes 1991.

Cells Wars by Fran Balkwill, illustrated by Mic Rolph; HarperCollins, 1990. **Awarded:** Science Book Prizes 1991.

ROMANOV, NATALIA

Once There Was a Tree by Natalia Romanov, illustrated by Gennady Spirin; Dial, 1985. **Awarded:** New York Times Notable 1985.

ROONEY, DAVID
Brendan the Navigator by George Otto Simms, illustrated by David Rooney; O'Brien Press, 1989. **Awarded:** Bisto (Information Book) 1990.

Exploring the Book of Kells by George Otto Simms, illustrated by David Rooney; O'Brien Press, 1988. **Awarded:** Bisto (Information Book) 1990; Reading Association of Ireland (Special Merit) 1989.

ROOS, STEPHEN
My Horrible Secret by Stephen Roos, illustrated by Carol Newsom; Delacorte, 1983. **Awarded:** Charlie May Simon 1985-86.

ROOSEVELT, ELEANOR
Partners: The United Nations and Youth by Eleanor Roosevelt and Helen Ferris, illustrated with photographs; Doubleday, 1950. **Awarded:** Child Study 1950.

ROPNER, PAMELA
The Golden Impala by Pamela Ropner, illustrated by Ralph Thompson; Criterion, 1958. **Awarded:** Boys Club 1959.

ROSA, CLARISA DE LA
El Rojo es el Mejor (original English: *Red is Best*) by Kathy Stinson, translated by Kiki de la Rosa and Clarisa de la Rosa; Ediciones Ekare-Banco de Libro, 1985. **Awarded:** International Board on Books for Young People (translation/Venezuela) 1986.

ROSA, KIKI DE LA
El Rojo es el Mejor (original English: *Red is Best*) by Kathy Stinson, translated by Kiki de la Rosa and Clarisa de la Rosa; Ediciones Ekare-Banco de Libro, 1985. **Awarded:** International Board on Books for Young People (translation/Venezuela) 1986.

ROSAMUND, J.
Lift Every Voice and Sing words and music by J. Rosamund and James Weldon Johnson, illustrated by Mozelle Thompson; Hawthorn, 1970. **Awarded:** Lewis Carroll Shelf 1971; New York Times Best Illustrated 1970.

ROSE, ANNE
As Right as Right Can Be by Anne Rose, illustrated by Arnold Lobel; Dial, 1976. **Awarded:** Children's Book Showcase 1977; New York Times Best Illustrated 1976.

ROSE, DAVID
There's a Monster Under My Bed by James Howe, illustrated by David Rose; Atheneum, 1986. **Awarded:** Colorado Children's Book Award (Runnerup) 1988; Washington Irving (Younger fiction) 1988.

ROSE, ELIZABETH JANE
How St. Francis Tamed the Wolf by Elizabeth Rose, illustrated by Gerald Rose; Harcourt, 1959. **Awarded:** Spring Book Festival (ages 4-8 honor) 1959.

Old Winkle and the Seagulls by Elizabeth Rose, illustrated by Gerald Rose; Faber, 1960. **Awarded:** Greenaway 1960.

Wuffles Goes to Town written and illustrated by Elizabeth Jane Rose and Gerald Rose; Faber, 1959. **Awarded:** Greenaway (Commended) 1959.

ROSE, GERALD
How St. Francis Tamed the Wolf by Elizabeth Rose, illustrated by Gerald Rose; Harcourt, 1959. **Awarded:** Spring Book Festival (ages 4-8 honor) 1959.

Old Winkle and the Seagulls by Elizabeth Rose, illustrated by Gerald Rose; Faber, 1960. **Awarded:** Greenaway 1960.

Wuffles Goes to Town written and illustrated by Gerald Rose and Elizabeth Jane Rose; Faber, 1959. **Awarded:** Greenaway (commended) 1959.

ROSE, J. M.
Leader by Destiny: George Washington, Man and Patriot by Jeanette Eaton, illustrated by J. M. Rose; Harcourt, 1938. **Awarded:** Newbery (honor) 1939.

ROSE, MARGARET
The King's Daughter by Suzanne Martel translated by Margaret Rose and David Toby Homel; Douglas & McIntyre, 1980. **Awarded:** International Board on Books for Young People (translation/Canada) 1982; Ruth Schwartz 1981.

ROSELL, INGRID
Bonifacius the Green by Karin Anckarsvard, illustrated by Ingrid Rosell; Abelard-Schuman, 1961. **Awarded:** Spring Book Festival (middle honor) 1962.

ROSELMAN, LIZ
Arc-en-ciel 2 by Marie-Therese Bougard, Ann Miller and Liz Roselman; Mary Glasgow, 1989. **Awarded:** Times Educational Supplement (Schoolbook) 1989.

ROSEN, ALBERT
Responsible Parenthood: The Child's Psyche through the Six-Year Pregnancy by Gilbert Kliman and Albert Rosen, not illustrated; Holt Rinehart & Winston, 1980. **Awarded:** Korczak (about children) 1982.

ROSEN, BILLI
Andi's War by Billi Rosen, illustrated with maps; Faber & Faber, 1988; Dutton, 1989. **Awarded:** Faber/Jackanory/Guardian 1989.

ROSEN, LILLIAN
Just Like Everybody Else by Lillian Rosen, not illustrated; Harcourt, 1981. **Awarded:** Woodward Park 1982.

ROSEN, MICHAEL
Awarded: British Book Awards (Author runnerup) 1989.

Everybody Here! by Michael Rosen, illustrated with photographs and line drawings; Bodley Head, 1982. **Awarded:** Other Award 1983.

We're Going on a Bear Hunt by Michael Rosen, illustrated by Helen Oxenbury; Walker, 1989; McElderry, 1989. **Awarded:** Boston Globe (Picture Book Honor) 1990; Greenaway (Highly Commended) 1989; Parents' Choice (Picture Book) 1989; Reading Magic 1989; Smarties (Grand Prix) 1989; Smarties (ages 0-5) 1989.

You Can't Catch Me! by Michael Rosen, illustrated by Quentin Blake; Deutsch, 1981. **Awarded:** Signal 1982.

ROSEN, MICHAEL J.
Elijah's Angels by Michael J. Rosen, illustrated by Aminah Brenda Lynn Robinson; Harcourt Brace Jovanovich, 1992. **Awarded:** Hungry Mind (Picturebooks/Fiction) 1993.

ROSENBERG, MAXINE B.
Living in Two Worlds by Maxine B. Rosenberg, illustrated by George Ancona; Lothrop, Lee & Shepard, 1986. **Awarded:** Woodson (Outstanding Merit) 1987.

ROSENBLATT, LOUISE M.
Awarded: ALAN 1984; Leland B. Jacobs 1981.

ROSENBLUM, RICHARD
The Big Stretch: The Complete Book of the Amazing Rubber Band by Ada Graham and Frank Graham, illustrated by Richard Rosenblum; Knopf, 1985. **Awarded:** New York Academy of Sciences (younger) 1986.

ROSENTHAL, JULES M.

Feelings Between Brothers and Sisters by Marcia Maher Conta and Maureen Reardon, photographs by Jules M. Rosenthal; Advanced Learning Concepts, 1974. **Awarded:** Council of Wisconsin Writers (picture book) 1975.

ROSENTHAL, LYNN

The Development of Consciousness in Lucy Boston's The Children of Green Knowe by Lynn Rosenthal in *Children's Literature* 8 (1980). **Awarded:** Children's Literature Assn. Awards for Excellence in the Field of Literary Criticism 1981.

ROSHOLT, MALCOLM

The Child of Two Mothers by Malcolm Rosholt and Margaret Rosholt, illustrated by Lynn Larson; Rosholt House, 1983. **Awarded:** State Historical Society of Wisconsin 1984.

The Story of Old Abe by Malcolm Rosholt and Margaret Rosholt, illustrated by Don Mullen; Rosholt House, 1987. **Awarded:** State Historical Society of Wisconsin 1988.

ROSHOLT, MARGARET

The Child of Two Mothers by Malcolm Rosholt and Margaret Rosholt, illustrated by Lynn Larson; Rosholt House, 1983. **Awarded:** State Historical Society of Wisconsin 1984.

Lily and the Present written and illustrated by Christine Ross; Methuen, 1992. **Awarded:** Russell Clark 1993.

The Story of Old Abe by Malcolm Rosholt and Margaret Rosholt, illustrated by Don Mullen; Rosholt House, 1987. **Awarded:** State Historical Society of Wisconsin 1988.

ROSIER, LYDIA

Annie Sullivan by Mary Malone, illustrated by Lydia Rosier; Putnam, 1971. **Awarded:** New Jersey Institute of Technology 1971.

ROSS, CATHERINE, DR.

Awarded: Frances E. Russell 1982.

ROSS, CHRISTINE

Lily and the Bears written and illustrated by Christine Ross; Angus & Robertson, 1990; Methuen Children's, 1990; Houghton Mifflin, 1991. **Awarded:** AIM Children's Book Awards (Picture Book 2nd prize) 1991.

ROSS, K. K.

Animal Babies by K. K. Ross, illustrated by Lisa McCue; Random House, 1988. **Awarded:** Book Can Develop Empathy 1991.

ROSS, MARGARET S.

Story by Margaret S. Ross in Fantastic Flyer magazine. **Awarded:** Magazine Merit (Nonfiction Honor) 1991.

ROSS, PAT

M & M and the Bad News Babies by Pat Ross, illustrated by Marylin Hafner; Knopf, 1983. **Awarded:** Garden State Children's (easy to read) 1986.

ROSS, RAMON ROYAL

Prune by Ramon Royal Ross, illustrated by Susan Sarabasha; Atheneum, 1984. **Awarded:** Southern California Council (notable work of fiction) 1985.

ROSS, TONY

Dr. Xargle's Book of Earth Tiggers by Jeanne Willis, illustrated by Tony Ross; Andersen Press, 1990; Dutton, 1991. **Awarded:** Greenaway (Highly Commended) 1990.

I Want my Potty written and illustrated by Tony Ross; Andersen Press, 1986. **Awarded:** Greenaway (commended) 1986.

I'm Coming to Get You! written and illustrated by Tony Ross; Dial, 1984. **Awarded:** Redbook (hardback) 1984.

Meanwhile Back at the Ranch by Trinka Hakes Noble, illustrated by Tony Ross; Dial, 1987. **Awarded:** Colorado Children's (runner up) 1989; New Jersey Institute of Technology 1988; North Dakota Children's Choice (Picture Book) 1990.

The Young Green Consumer Guide by John Elkington and Julia Hailes, illustrated by Tony Ross; Gollancz, 1990. **Awarded:** Earthworm Award 1990.

ROSSELL-LINDHAHL, I.

Manuel Zigenarpojken by Karl-Rune Nordkvist, illustrated by I. Rossell-Lindahl; Raben & Sjogren, 1958. **Awarded:** Hans Christian Andersen (runnerup) 1960.

ROSSI, KENDALL

Ulysses and his Woodland Zoo by Jim Kjelgaard, illustrated by Kendall Rossi; Dodd, Mead, 1960. **Awarded:** Boys Life 1959.

ROSSMORE, HAROLD W.

The Microbes, our Unseen Friends by Harold W. Rossmore, illustrated with photographs; Wayne State University Press, 1976. **Awarded:** New York Academy of Sciences (older honor) 1978.

ROSTKOWSKI, MARGARET I.

After the Dancing Days by Margaret I. Rostkowski, not illustrated; Harper & Row, 1986. **Awarded:** Golden Kite (fiction) 1986; International Reading Assn. (young adult) 1987; Jefferson Cup 1987.

ROTH, ARNOLD

Arnold Roth's Crazy Book of Science written and illustrated by Arnold Roth; Grosset, 1971. **Awarded:** New Jersey Institute of Technology 1971.

Comick Book of Pets: Found, Raised, Washed, Curried, Combed, Fed and Cared for in Every Other Way written and illustrated by Arnold Roth; Scribner, 1976. **Awarded:** New Jersey Institute of Technology 1978.

A Comick Book of Sports written and illustrated by Arnold Roth; Scribner, 1974. **Awarded:** New Jersey Institute of Technology 1975.

Pick a Peck of Puzzles written and illustrated by Arnold Roth; Norton, 1966. **Awarded:** New Jersey Institute of Technology 1967.

ROTH, GEORGE

Middl'un by Elizabeth Burleson, illustrated by George Roth; Follett, 1968. **Awarded:** Western Writers (fiction) 1969.

ROTH, SUSAN L.

Fire Came to the Earth People written and illustrated by Susan L. Roth; St. Martin's Press, 1988. **Awarded:** New York Times Best Illustrated 1988.

ROTHCHILD, SYLVIA

Keys to a Magic Door by Sylvia Rothchild, illustrated by Bernard Krigstein; Farrar, 1959. **Awarded:** Jewish Book Council 1959.

ROTHFUCHS, HEINER

Sons of the Steppe by Hans Baumann, illustrated by Heiner Rothfuchs; Walck, 1958. **Awarded:** Spring Book Festival (older) 1958.

ROUGHSEY, DICK

The Quinkins written and illustrated by Dick Roughsey and Percy J. Trezise; Collins, 1978. **Awarded:** Children's Book

Council of Australia (picture book) 1979; International Board on Books for Young People (illustration/Australia) 1980.

The Rainbow Serpent written and illustrated by Dick Roughsey; Collins Australia, 1975. **Awarded:** Children's Book Council of Australia (picture book) 1976.

Turramulli the Giant Quinkin written and illustrated by Dick Roughsey and Percy Trezise; Collins, 1982. **Awarded:** Children's Book Council of Australia (picture book of the year commended) 1983.

ROUNDS, GLEN
Awarded: Kerlan 1980.

Beaver Business: An Almanac written and illustrated by Glen Rounds; Prentice Hall, 1960. **Awarded:** North Carolina AAUW 1961.

Big Blue Island by Wilson Gage, illustrated by Glen Rounds; World, 1964. **Awarded:** Aurianne 1966.

Blind Colt written and illustrated by Glen Rounds; Holiday, 1960, 1941. **Awarded:** Lewis Carroll Shelf 1960.

The Day the Circus Came to Lone Tree written and illustrated by Glen Rounds; Holiday House, 1973. **Awarded:** Lewis Carroll Shelf 1976.

Farmer Hoo and the Baboons by Ida Chittum, illustrated by Glen Rounds, Delacorte, 1971. **Awarded:** Lewis Carroll Shelf 1971.

Firefly by Paul M. Sears, illustrated by Glen Rounds; Holiday House, 1956. **Awarded:** New Jersey Institute of Technology (science) 1963.

Kickle Snifters and Other Fearsome Critters by Alvin Schwartz, illustrated by Glen Rounds; Lippincott, 1976. **Awarded:** New Jersey Institute of Technology 1977.

Mr. Yowder and the Giant Bull Snake written and illustrated by Glen Rounds; Holiday House, 1978. **Awarded:** Lewis Carroll Shelf 1978.

Mr. Yowder and the Lion Roar Capsules written and illustrated by Glen Rounds; Holiday House, 1976. **Awarded:** North Carolina AAUW 1976.

The Morning the Sun Refused to Shine written and illustrated by Glen Rounds; Holiday House, 1984. **Awarded:** Parents' Choice (literature) 1984.

Ol' Paul, the Mighty Logger written and illustrated by Glen Rounds; Holiday House, 1949, c1936. **Awarded:** Lewis Carroll Shelf 1958.

Rain in the Woods and Other Small Matters written and illustrated by Glen Rounds; World, 1964. **Awarded:** Boys Club 1965.

The Snake Tree written and illustrated by Glen Rounds; World, 1966. **Awarded:** North Carolina AAUW 1967.

The Stolen Pony written and illustrated by Glen Rounds; Holiday House, 1969, 1948. **Awarded:** Lewis Carroll Shelf 1973.

Toby, Granny and George by Robbie Branscum, illustrated by Glen Rounds; Doubleday, 1976. **Awarded:** Friends of American Writers (older) 1977.

Tomfoolery, Trickery and Foolery with Words collected by Alvin Schwartz, illustrated by Glen Rounds; Lippincott, 1973. **Awarded:** New York Times Notable Books 1973.

A Twister of Twists, a Tangler of Tongues by Alvin Schwartz, illustrated by Glen Rounds; Lippincott, 1972. **Awarded:** New Jersey Institute of Technology 1972; New York Times Notable Books 1972.

Washday on Noah's Ark written and illustrated by Glen Rounds; Holiday House, 1985. **Awarded:** Parents' Choice (literature) 1985.

Whitney's First Round-up written and illustrated by Glen Rounds; Grosset, 1942. **Awarded:** Spring Book Festival (picture book honor) 1942.

Wild Appaloosa written and illustrated by Glen Rounds; Holiday House, 1983. **Awarded:** North Carolina AAUW 1983.

Wild Horses of the Red Desert written and illustrated by Glen Rounds; Holiday House, 1969. **Awarded:** Lewis Carroll Shelf 1969.

ROURKE, CONSTANCE MAYFIELD
Audubon by Constance M. Rourke, illustrated by James MacDonald; Harcourt, 1936. **Awarded:** Newbery (honor) 1937.

Davy Crockett by Constance Rourke, illustrated by James MacDonald; Harcourt, 1934. **Awarded:** Newbery (honor) 1935.

ROUSSAN, JACQUES DE
Beyond the Sun/Au dela du Soleil written and illustrated by Jacques de Roussan; Tundra, 1972. **Awarded:** Amelia Frances Howard-Gibbon 1973.

ROUVEROL, JEAN
Juarez: A Son of the People by Jean Rouverol, not illustrated; Crowell-Collier, 1973. **Awarded:** Southern California Council (distinguished contribution to nonfiction) 1974.

ROWAN, PETER
The Amazing Voyage of the Cucumber Sandwich by Peter Rowan, illustrated by Polly Noakes; Cape, 1991. **Awarded:** Science Book Prizes 1992.

ROWE, BARRY
Children of the Book by Peter Carter, illustrated by Richard Jervis, maps by Barry Rowe; Oxford, 1982. **Awarded:** Observer Teenage Fiction 1983.

ROWE, JEANNETTE
Scallywag written and illustrated by Jeannette Rowe; Ashton Scholastic, 1990. **Awarded:** Australian Multicultural Children's Literature Award (Picture Book Highly commended) 1991.

ROWE, JOHN
Why the Cangaroo Has Such Long Legs by John Rowe; Neugebauer Press, 1990. **Awarded:** Biennale Illustrations Bratislava (Golden Apple) 1991.

ROWELL, KENNETH
Falter Tom and the Water Boy by Maurice Duggan, illustrated by Kenneth Rowell; Paul's Book Arcade, 1958. **Awarded:** Esther Glen 1959.

ROWLAND, DOLORES M.
Quick Wits and Nimble Fingers by Bernice Wells Carlson, illustrated by Dolores M. Rowland; Abingdon, 1979. **Awarded:** New Jersey Institute of Technology 1980.

ROY, CLAUDE
Awarded: Andersen (Author Highly Commended) 1988.

The Very Obliging Flowers by Claude Roy, translated by Gerald Bertin, illustrated by Alain LeFoll; Grove 1968. **Awarded:** New York Times Best Illustrated 1968.

ROYBAL, J. D.
Red Power on the Rio Grande: The Native American Revolution of 1680 by Franklin Folsom, illustrated by J. D. Roybal;

Follett, 1973. **Awarded:** Western Writers of America (nonfiction) 1974.

ROYSTON, ANGELA

Duck by Angela Royston, illustrated by Barrie Watts; Lodestar, 1991. **Awarded:** Redbook 1991.

Frog by Angela Royston, illustrated by Kim Taylor; Lodestar, 1991. **Awarded:** Redbook 1991.

Kitten by Angela Royston, illustrated by Jane Burton; Lodestar, 1991. **Awarded:** Redbook 1991.

Puppy by Angela Royston, illustrated by Jane Burton; Lodestar, 1991. **Awarded:** Redbook 1991.

ROZANOV, SERGEI

Adventures of Misha by Sergei Rozanov, illustrated by Alexander Mogilevsky; Stokes, 1938. **Awarded:** Spring Book Festival (younger honor) 1938.

RUBEL, NICOLE

Rotten Ralph by Jack Gantos, illustrated by Nicole Rubel; Houghton, 1976. **Awarded:** Children's Book Showcase 1977.

RUBIN, CAROLINE

Awarded: Children's Reading Round Table 1975.

RUBINSTEIN, GILLIAN

Answers to Brut by Gillian Rubinstein, not illustrated; Omnibus/Puffin, 1988; Mammoth, 1991. **Awarded:** Children's Book Council of Australia (Book of the Year Older Honour) 1989; New South Wales State Literary Awards (Children's) 1988.

Beyond the Labyrinth by Gillian Rubinstein, not illustrated; Hyland House, 1988. **Awarded:** Children's Book Council of Australia (Book of the Year Older) 1989; National Children's Literature Award 1990.

Galax-Arena by Gillian Rubinstein, not illustrated; Hyland House, 1992. **Awarded:** Children's Book Council of Australia (Book of the Year Older Honor) 1993.

Melanie and the Night Animal by Gillian Rubinstein, not illustrated; Omnibus/Puffin, 1988. **Awarded:** Children's Book Council of Australia (Book of the Year Younger Honour) 1989.

Mr. Plunkett's Pool by Gillian Rubinstein, illustrated by Terry Denton; Random House, 1992. **Awarded:** Australian Multicultural (Picture book) 1993.

Space Demons by Gillian Rubinstein, not illustrated; Omnibus/Penguin, 1986. **Awarded:** Children's Book Council of Australia (book of the year older honor) 1987; Children's Peace Literature 1987; National Children's Literature Award 1988; Young Australian Best Book (Fiction Older Reader) 1990.

RUCKMAN, IVY

Night of the Twisters by Ivy Ruckman, not illustrated; Crowell, 1984. **Awarded:** Golden Sower (grades 4-6) 1986; Iowa Children's Choice 1989; Maud Hart Lovelace 1988; Sequoyah 1987; South Dakota Prairie Pasque 1987.

RUDDICK, BOB

This Island Isn't Big Enough for the Four of Us by Bob Ruddick and Gery Greer, not illustrated; Crowell, 1987. **Awarded:** Maud Hart Lovelace 1992; South Dakota Prairie Pasque 1990; Utah Children's 1990.

RUDNIK, MARYKA

The Winter When Time Was Frozen by Els Pelgrom, translated by Maryka Rudnik and Raphael Rudnik, not illustrated; Morrow, 1980. **Awarded:** Batchelder 1981.

RUDNIK, RAPHAEL

The Winter When Time Was Frozen by Els Pelgrom, translated by Maryka Rudnik and Raphael Rudnik, not illustrated; Morrow, 1980. **Awarded:** Batchelder 1981.

RUDOLPH, NORMAN GUTHRIE

Bucky Forrester by Leland Silliman, illustrated by Norman Guthrie Rudolph; Winston, 1951. **Awarded:** Boys Club 1952.

RUDSTROM, LENNART

A Farm by Lennart Rudstrom, translated by Ernest Edwin Ryden, illustrated by Carl Larsson; Putnam, 1976. **Awarded:** Children's Book Showcase 1977.

A Home by Lennart Rudstrom, illustrated by Carl Larsson; Putnam, 1974. **Awarded:** Children's Book Showcase 1975; New York Times Best Illustrated 1974.

RUE, LEONARD LEE, III

Cottontail: Children's Pet, Gardener's Pest, and Hunter's Favorite by Leonard Lee Rue III, illustrated with photographs; Crowell, 1965. **Awarded:** New Jersey Institute of Technology (science) 1966.

Meet the Beaver written and illustrated by Leonard Lee Rue III; Dodd Mead, 1986. **Awarded:** New Jersey Institute of Technology 1988.

Meet the Opossum by Leonard Lee Rue III with William Owen, illustrated with photographs by Leonard Lee Rue III; Dodd, Mead, 1983. **Awarded:** New Jersey Institute of Technology 1983.

The World of the White-tailed Deer by Leonard Lee Rue, III, illustrated with photographs; Lippincott, 1962. **Awarded:** New Jersey Institute of Technology (science) 1963.

RUFF, DONNA

Our Golda: The Story of Golda Meir by David A. Adler, illustrated by Donna Ruff; Viking, 1984. **Awarded:** Woodson (Outstanding Merit) 1985.

RUFSVOLD, MARGARET

Awarded: American Association of School Librarians 1988.

RUGH, BELLE DORMAN

Crystal Mountain by Belle Dorman Rugh, illustrated by Ernest Shepard; Houghton, 1955. **Awarded:** Spring Book Festival (middle) 1955.

RUGOFF, MILTON

Hurly Burly and the Knights by Milton Rugoff, illustrated by Emanuele Luzzati; Platt, 1963. **Awarded:** New York Times Best Illustrated 1963.

RUHLIN, ROGER

Behind the Scenes at the Horse Hospital by Fern G. Brown, edited by Kathleen Tucker, photographs by Roger Ruhlin; Whitman, 1981. **Awarded:** Sandburg 1982.

RUSE, MARGARET

The Little Old Woman Who Used Her Head by Hope Newell, illustrated by Margaret Ruse; Nelson, 1966, 1935. **Awarded:** Lewis Carroll Shelf 1972.

RUSH, BARBARA

The Diamond Tree: Jewish Tales From Around the World by Barbara Rush and Howard Schwartz, illustrated by Uri

Shulevitz; HarperCollins, 1991. **Awarded:** Sydney Taylor Book Award (Older) 1992.

RUSH, KEN

Brickyard Summer: Poems by Paul B. Janeczko, illustrated by Ken Rush; Orchard, 1989. **Awarded:** Lupine Award 1990.

RUSSELL, FRANKLIN

Corvus the Cow by Franklin Russell, illustrated by Richard Cuffari; Four Winds, 1972. **Awarded:** New Jersey Institute of Technology 1972.

The Honeybees by Franklin Russell, illustrated by Colette Portal; Knopf, 1967. **Awarded:** New York Times Best Illustrated 1967.

Lotor the Raccoon by Franklin Russell, illustrated by Richard Cuffari; Four Winds, 1972. **Awarded:** New Jersey Institute of Technology 1972.

RUSSELL, HELEN ROSS

Awarded: Eva L. Gordon 1976.

City Critters by Helen R. Russell, illustrated by Marcia Erickson; Meredith, 1969. **Awarded:** New Jersey Institute of Technology 1969.

RUSSELL, JAMES

The Apache Gold Mystery by Eileen Thompson, illustrated by James Russell; Abelard-Schuman, 1965. **Awarded:** Edgar Allan Poe (runnerup) 1966.

RUSSELL, JEAN

Awarded: Eleanor Farjeon 1983.

RUSSELL, JIM

Thunder and Lightnings by Jan Mark, illustrated by Jim Russell; Kestrel, 1976. **Awarded:** Carnegie 1976; Guardian (commended) 1977.

RUSSELL, WILLIAM F.

Animal Families of the Wild edited by William F. Russell, illustrated by John Butler; Crown, 1990. **Awarded:** Book Can Develop Empathy 1991.

RUSSO, MARISABINA

The Line Up Book written and illustrated by Marisabina Russo; Greenwillow, 1986. **Awarded:** International Reading Assn. (primary) 1987.

RUSSON, MARY

The Battle of St. George Without by Janet McNeill, illustrated by Mary Russon; Little, 1968. **Awarded:** Spring Book Festival (middle honor) 1968.

RUTH, ROD

Big Mutt by John Reese, illustrated by Rod Ruth; Westminster, 1952. **Awarded:** Spring Book Festival (older) 1952.

RUTHERFORD, JENNY

Courage, Dana by Susan Pfeffer, illustrated by Jenny Rutherford; Delacorte, 1983. **Awarded:** Parents' Choice (literature) 1983.

RUTLEDGE, JAMES T.

Wisconsin, Forward! by Marion Fuller Archer, edited by James T. Rutledge, illustrated; McRoberts, 1978. **Awarded:** Council of Wisconsin Writers (juvenile runnerup) 1979.

RUY-VIDAL, FRANCOIS

The Secret Journey of Hugo the Brat by Francois Ruy-Vidal, illustrated by Nicole Claveloux; Quist, 1968. **Awarded:** New York Times Best Illustrated 1968.

RYAN, CHELI DURAN

Hildilid's Night by Cheli Duran Ryan, illustrated by Arnold Lobel; Macmillan, 1971. **Awarded:** Caldecott (honor) 1972; Children's Book Showcase 1972; National Book Award (finalist) 1972.

RYCHLICKI, ZBIGNIEW

Awarded: Hans Christian Andersen (illustrator) 1982.

RYDEN, ERNEST EDWIN

A Farm by Lennart Rudstrom, translated by Ernest Edwin Ryden, illustrated by Carl Larsson; Putnam, 1976. **Awarded:** Children's Book Showcase 1977.

RYDEN, HOPE

Wild Animals of Africa ABC by Hope Ryden; Dutton, 1989. **Awarded:** Book Can Develop Empathy 1990.

RYDER, JOANNE

Fireflies by Joanne Ryder, illustrated by Don Bolognese; Harper, 1977. **Awarded:** New Jersey Institute of Technology 1978.

Fog in the Meadow by Joanne Ryder, illustrated by Gail Owens; Harper, 1979. **Awarded:** New Jersey Institute of Technology 1980.

Simon Underground by Joanne Ryder, illustrated by John Schoenherr; Harper, 1976. **Awarded:** Children's Book Showcase 1977.

Snail in the Woods by Joanne Ryder and Harold S. Feinberg, illustrated by Jo Polseno; Harper, 1979. **Awarded:** New Jersey Institute of Technology 1980.

The Snail's Spell by Joanne Ryder, illustrated by Lynne Cherry; Warne, 1982. **Awarded:** New York Academy of Sciences (younger) 1983.

Step Into the Night by Joanne Ryder, illustrated by Dennis Nolan; Four Winds, 1988. **Awarded:** Commonwealth Club of California 1988; Parents' Choice (Picture Book) 1988.

When the Woods Hum by Joanne Ryder, illustrated by Catherine Stock; Morrow, 1991. **Awarded:** Book Can Develop Empathy 1991.

RYLANT, CYNTHIA

Appalachia: the Voices of Sleeping Birds by Cynthia Rylant, illustrated by Barry Moser; Harcourt Brace Jovanovich, 1991. **Awarded:** Boston Globe Horn Book (Nonfiction) 1991; Ohioana 1992; Parents' Choice (Picture Book) 1991.

But I'll Be Back Again: An Album by Cynthia Rylant, illustrated with photos; Orchard, 1989. **Awarded:** Ohioana 1990.

A Fine White Dust by Cynthia Rylant, not illustrated; Bradbury, 1986. **Awarded:** Newbery (honor) 1987; Parents' Choice (literature) 1986.

Henry and Mudge and the Happy Cat by Cynthia Rylant, illustrated by Sucie Stevenson; Bradbury, 1990. **Awarded:** Garden State Children's (easy to read) 1993.

Henry and Mudge Get the Cold Shivers by Cynthia Rylant, illustrated by Sucie Stevenson; Bradbury, 1989. **Awarded:** Garden State (Easy to Read) 1992.

Henry and Mudge in Puddle Trouble by Cynthia Rylant, illustrated by James Stevenson; Bradbury, 1987. **Awarded:** Garden State Children's Book Award (Easy to Read) 1990.

Missing May by Cynthia Rylant, not illustrated; Orchard, 1992. **Awarded:** Boston Globe Horn Book (Fiction) 1992; Hungry Mind (Middle Readers/Fiction) 1993; Newbery 1993; Parents Choice (Story Book) 1992; Reading Magic Award 1992.

The Relatives Came by Cynthia Rylant, illustrated by Stephen Gammell; Bradbury, 1985. **Awarded:** Caldecott (honor) 1986; New York Times Best Illustrated 1985.

Waiting to Waltz by Cynthia Rylant, illustrated by Stephen Gammell; Bradbury, 1984. **Awarded:** Society of Midland Authors 1985.

When I Was Young in the Mountains by Cynthia Rylant, illustrated by Diane Goode; Dutton, 1982. **Awarded:** Caldecott (honor) 1983.

RYPINS, SENTA
Green Wagons by Senta Rypins and Oskar Seidlin, illustrated by Barbara Cooney; Houghton, 1943. **Awarded:** Spring Book Festival (middle honor) 1943.

S

S., SVEND OTTO
Awarded: Hans Christian Andersen (illustrator) 1978; Hans Christian Andersen (highly commended illustrator/Denmark) 1976.

A Christmas Book translated by J. Tate, illustrated by Svend Otto S.; Pelham, 1978. **Awarded:** Biennale Illustrations Bratislava (plaque) 1979.

The Giant Fish and Other Stories written and illustrated by Svend Otto S., translated by Joan Tate; Larousse, 1982. **Awarded:** Parents Choice (illustration) 1982.

SAARI, KAY
The Kidnapping of the Coffee Pot by Kay Saari, illustrated by Henri Galeron; Quist, 1975. **Awarded:** New York Times Notable Books 1975.

SABUDA, ROBERT
Saint Valentine retold and illustrated by Robert Sabuda; Atheneum, 1992. **Awarded:** Hungry Mind (Picturebooks/Nonfiction) 1993.

SACHAR, LOUIS
Awarded: Milner Award 1990.

Dogs Don't Tell Jokes by Louis Sachar, not illustrated; Knopf, 1991. **Awarded:** Parents' Choice (Story Book) 1991.

Sideways Stories from Wayside School by Louis Sachar, illustrated by Dennis Hockerman; Follett, 1978. **Awarded:** Ethical Culture School 1978.

There's a Boy in the Girls' Bathroom by Louis Sachar, not illustrated; Knopf, 1987. **Awarded:** Buckeye (grades 3-5) 1991; Georgia Children's Book Award 1990; Golden Sower (grades 4-6) 1991; Indian Paintbrush 1990; Iowa Children's Choice 1991; Land of Enchantment 1990; Massachusetts Children's 1991; Nene 1991; Nevada Young Reader Award (Intermediate) 1989-90; Parents' Choice (Story Book) 1987; Charlie May Simon 1989-90; Sunshine State (grades 3-5) 1991; Sunshine State (grades 6-8) 1991; Texas Bluebonnet 1990; Mark Twain 1990; Utah Children's 1992; Volunteer State Book Awards (grades 4-6) 1991; West Virginia Children's Book Award 1990-91; Young Reader's Choice 1990.

There's a Boy in the Girls' Washroom by Louis Sachar, not illustrated. **Awarded:** Surrey School 1990.

Wayside School Is Falling Down by Louis Sachar, illustrated by Joel Schick; Lothrop, Lee & Shepard, 1989. **Awarded:**

Arizona Young Readers (chapter book) 1993; Garden State (Fiction) 1992; Land of Enchantment 1992; Parents' Choice (Story Book) 1989.

SACHS, ANNE
Dorrie's Book by Marilyn Sachs, illustrated by Anne Sachs; Doubleday, 1975. **Awarded:** Garden State Children's (young fiction) 1978.

SACHS, MARILYN STICKLE
The Bears' House by Marilyn Sachs, illustrated by Louis Glanzman; Doubleday, 1971. **Awarded:** National Book Award (finalist) 1972; New York Times Notable Books 1971; Stone, George G. 1989.

The Big Book for Peace by Marilyn Sachs and Ann Durrell, with various illustrators; Dutton, 1990. **Awarded:** Addams 1991.

Call Me Ruth by Marilyn Sachs, not illustrated; Doubleday, 1982. **Awarded:** Sydney Taylor Book Award (older children) 1983.

Dorrie's Book by Marilyn Sachs, illustrated by Anne Sachs; Doubleday, 1975. **Awarded:** Garden State Children's (young fiction) 1978.

The Fat Girl by Marilyn Sachs, not illustrated; Dutton, 1984. **Awarded:** Bay Area Book Reviewers Assn. 1985.

Fran Ellen's House by Marilyn Sachs, not illustrated; Dutton, 1987. **Awarded:** Bay Area Book Reviewers Assn. 1988; Parents' Choice (Story Book) 1987; Stone, George G. 1989.

A Pocket Full of Seeds by Marilyn Sachs, illustrated by Ben Stahl; Doubleday, 1973. **Awarded:** Jane Addams (honor) 1974.

Underdog by Marilyn Sachs, not illustrated; Doubleday, 1985. **Awarded:** Christopher (ages 10-12) 1986.

SACRE, MARIE-JOSE
Viktor, das Fliegende Nilpferd by Guy Counhaye, illustrated by Marie-Jose Sacre; Everest, 1982. **Awarded:** Owl Prize 1982.

SADLER, MARILYN
Elizabeth and Larry by Marilyn Sadler, illustrated by Roger Bollen; Simon & Schuster, 1990. **Awarded:** Parents' Choice (Story Book) 1990.

SADLER, PHILIP A.
Awarded: Children's Reading Round Table 1986.

SAETHER, HAAKON
North of Danger by Dale Fife, illustrated by Haakon Saether; Dutton, 1978. **Awarded:** Commonwealth Club of California 1978.

ST. GEORGE, JUDITH
The Brooklyn Bridge: They Said it Couldn't be Built by Judith St. George, illustrated with photographs; Putnam, 1982. **Awarded:** Golden Kite (nonfiction honor) 1982; New York Academy of Sciences (older) 1983; New York Times Notable Books 1982.

Do You See What I See? by Judith St. George, not illustrated; Putnam, 1982. **Awarded:** New Jersey Institute of Technology 1983.

The Halloween Pumpkin Smasher by Judith St. George, illustrated by Margot Tomes; Putnam, 1978. **Awarded:** Edgar Allan Poe (runnerup) 1979.

In the Shadow of the Bear by Judith St. George, not illustrated; Putnam, 1983. **Awarded:** New Jersey Institute of Technology 1983.

The Mount Rushmore Story by Judith St. George, illustrated with photographs; Putnam, 1985. **Awarded:** Christopher (young adult) 1986; Golden Kite (nonfiction honor) 1985.

Panama Canal by Judith St. George, illustrated with photographs; Putnam, 1989. **Awarded:** Golden Kite (nonfiction) 1989; New Jersey Institute of Technology 1989.

What's Happening To My Junior Year? by Judith St. George, not illustrated; Putnam, 1986. **Awarded:** New Jersey Institute of Technology 1988.

Who's Scared? Not Me by Judith St. George, not illustrated; Putnam, 1987. **Awarded:** New Jersey Institute of Technology 1988.

ST. JOHN, WYLLY FOLK
The Secret of the Seven Crows by Wylly Folk St. John, illustrated by Judith Gwyn Brown; Viking, 1973. **Awarded:** Edgar Allan Poe (runnerup) 1974.

Uncle Robert's Secret by Wylly Folk St. John, illustrated by Frank Aloise; Viking, 1972. **Awarded:** Edgar Allan Poe (runnerup) 1973.

SAKURAI, ATSUSHI
Crabs by Sylvia A. Johnson, photographs by Atsushi Sakurai; Lerner, 1982. **Awarded:** New York Academy of Sciences (special award) 1983.

SALAMANCA, LUCY
Lost in the Everglades by Lucy Salamanca, illustrated by Jo Polseno; Western, 1971. **Awarded:** Lucille E. Ogle (ages 8-12) 1970.

SALANT, SAM
The Right Size: Why Some Creatures Survive and Others Are Extinct by Hal Hellman, illustrated by Sam Salant; Putnam, 1968. **Awarded:** New Jersey Institute of Technology (science) 1968.

SALATA, ESTELLE
Blind Date by Estelle Salata in Time Enough edited by Jack Booth; Holt, Rinehart & Winston, 1979. **Awarded:** Vicky Metcalf Short Story 1980.

SALISBURY, GRAHAM
Blue Skin of the Sea: A Novel in Stories by Graham Salisbury, not illustrated; Delacorte, 1992. **Awarded:** Parents Choice (Story Book) 1992.

SALLER, CAROL
The Bridge Dancers by Carol Saller, illustrated by Gerald Talifero; Carolrhoda, 1991. **Awarded:** Carl Sandburg 1991.

SALMON, MICHAEL
The Monster Who Ate Australia written and illustrated by Michael Salmon; Lamont, 1986. **Awarded:** Young Australian Best Book (Picture Book) 1990.

SALTEN, FELIX
Album de Bambi by Felix Salten, illustrated; Societe Nouvelle de Editions Bias, 1966. **Awarded:** Bologna (critici in erba) 1966.

SALTMAN, JUDITH
Awarded: Frances E. Russell 1986.

SALVADORI, MARIO
Building: The Fight Against Gravity by Mario Salvadori, illustrated by Saralinda Hooker and Christopher Ragus; Atheneum, 1979. **Awarded:** Boston Globe Horn Book (nonfiction) 1980; New York Academy of Sciences (older) 1980.

SAM, JOE
The Invisible Hunters by Harriet Rohmer, illustrated by Joe Sam; Children's Book Press, 1987. **Awarded:** Coretta Scott King (Illustration honor) 1988.

SAMPSON, KATHARINE
Dorothea Dix: Hospital Founder by Mary Malone, illustrated by Katharine Sampson; Garrard, 1968. **Awarded:** New Jersey Institute of Technology (biography) 1968.

SAMSON, HANS
A Moment of Silence by Pierre Janssen, translated by William R. Tyler, photographs by Hans Sampson; Atheneum, 1970. **Awarded:** Christopher (ages 8-12) 1971.

SAMSTAG, NICHOLAS
Kay-Kay Comes Home by Nicholas Samstag, illustrated by Ben Shahn; Obolensky, 1962. **Awarded:** New York Times Best Illustrated 1962.

SAMUELS, BARBARA
Duncan & Dolores written and illustrated by Barbara Samuels; Bradbury, 1986. **Awarded:** Christopher (ages 4-6) 1987.

SAN SOUCI, DANIEL
The Legend of Scarface: A Blackfeet Indian Tale by Robert San Souci, illustrated by Daniel San Souci; Doubleday, 1978. **Awarded:** New York Times Best Illustrated 1978.

Potter, Come Fly to the First of the Earth by Walter Wangerin, Jr., illustrated by Daniel San Souci; Chariot Books, 1985. **Awarded:** Gold Medallion 1986.

Trapped in Sliprock Canyon by Gloria Skurzynski, illustrated by Daniel San Souci; Lothrop, 1984. **Awarded:** Western Writers 1985.

SAN SOUCI, ROBERT D.
The Legend of Scarface: A Blackfeet Indian Tale by Robert San Souci, illustrated by Daniel San Souci; Doubleday, 1978. **Awarded:** New York Times Best Illustrated 1978.

Sukey and the Mermaid by Robert D. San Souci, illustrated by Brian Pinkney; Four Winds, 1992. **Awarded:** Hungry Mind (Picturebooks/Fiction) 1993; Coretta Scott King (Illustration Honor) 1993; Reading Magic Award 1992.

The Talking Eggs by Robert D. San Souci, illustrated by Jerry Pinkney; Dial, 1989. **Awarded:** Irma S. and James H. Black 1989; Caldecott (honor) 1990; Colorado Children's 1991; Golden Sower (K-3) 1992; Coretta Scott King (Illustration honor) 1990; Parents' Choice (Picture Book) 1989.

SANCHA, ALICIA
Story of Brother Francis by Lene Mayer-Skumanz, illustrated by Alicia Sancha; Ave Maria Press, 1983. **Awarded:** Catholic Book Awards (Children's) 1984.

SANCHA, SHEILA
The Castle Story written and illustrated by Sheila Sancha; Kestrel, 1979. **Awarded:** Carnegie (highly commended) 1979.

SANCHEZ-SILVA, JOSE MARIA
Awarded: Hans Christian Andersen (highly commended author/Spain) 1966; Hans Christian Andersen (author) 1968.

SANDBURG, CARL
Rainbows Are Made: Poems by Carl Sandburg edited by Lee Bennett Hopkins, illustrated by Fritz Eichenberg; Harcourt, 1982. **Awarded:** New York Times Best Illustrated 1982.

The Wedding Procession of the Rag Doll and the Broom Handle and Who Was in It by Carl Sandburg, illustrated by Harriet Pincus; Harcourt, 1967. **Awarded:** Art Books for Children 1973; Spring Book Festival (picture book honor) 1967.

SANDBURG, HELGA
Joel and the Wild Goose by Helga Sandburg, illustrated by Thomas Daly; Dial, 1963. **Awarded:** Lewis Carroll Shelf 1965.

SANDER, JOELLE

Before Their Time: Four Generations of Teenage Mothers by Joelle Sander, not illustrated; Harcourt Brace Jovanovich, 1991. **Awarded:** Janusz Korczak (About Children) 1992.

SANDERS, PETE

Why Do People Smoke? by Pete Sanders, illustrated with photos; Gloucester Press, 1989. **Awarded:** Times Educational Supplement (Junior) 1989.

SANDERS, RUTH MANNING

Storia di una Volpe (original English *Fox Tales*) by Ruth Manning Sanders, translated by Daniela Camboni; Nuove Edizioni Romane, 1981. **Awarded:** International Board on Books for Young People (translation/Italy) 1984.

SANDERSON, RUTH

The Animal, the Vegetable & John D. Jones by Betsy Byars, illustrated by Ruth Sanderson; Delacorte, 1982; Dell, 1983. **Awarded:** CRABbery 1983; Parents' Choice (literature) 1982.

Caught in the Turtle by Judith Gorog, illustrated by Ruth Sanderson; Philomel, 1983. **Awarded:** New Jersey Institute of Technology 1983.

Don't Hurt Laurie! by Willo Davis Roberts, illustrated by Ruth Sanderson; Atheneum, 1977. **Awarded:** Georgia Children's 1982; West Australian Young Readers (secondary) 1981; Young Hoosier (grades 4-6) 1980.

The Enchanted Wood written and illustrated by Ruth Sanderson; Little Brown, 1991. **Awarded:** Irma S. and James H. Black 1991.

Into the Dream by William Sleator, illustrated by Ruth Sanderson; Dutton, 1979; Scholastic, 1979. **Awarded:** CRABbery (honor) 1980.

Samantha on Stage by Susan Clement Farrar, illustrated by Ruth Sanderson; Dial, 1979. **Awarded:** West Australian Young Readers (primary) 1983.

SANDFORD, DAVID E.

My Village, My World by David E. Sandford, illustrated by Gustave Nebel; Crown, 1969. **Awarded:** Spring Book Festival (middle honor) 1969.

SANDIN, JOAN

Hey, What's Wrong with This One? by Maia Wojciechowska, illustrated by Joan Sandin; Harper, 1969. **Awarded:** Georgia Children's 1973.

The Lemming Condition by Alan Arkin, illustrated by Joan Sandin; Harper, 1976. **Awarded:** New York Times Notable Books 1976.

The Mysterious Red Tape Gang by Joan Lowery Nixon, illustrated by Joan Sandin; Putnam, 1974. **Awarded:** Edgar Allan Poe (runnerup) 1975.

Trouble at the Mines by Doreen Rappaport, illustrated by Joan Sandin; Crowell, 1987. **Awarded:** Addams (Honor) 1988.

SANDOZ, MARI

The Horsecatcher by Mari Sandoz, not illustrated; Westminster, 1957. **Awarded:** Newbery (honor) 1958; Spring Book Festival (older honor) 1957.

The Story Catcher by Mari Sandoz, illustrated by Elsie J. McCorkell; Westminster, 1963. **Awarded:** Western Writers of America (fiction) 1964.

SANDVED, KJELL

Insect Magic by Michael Emsley, photographs by Kjell Sandved; Viking, 1978. **Awarded:** New York Academy of Sciences (older honor) 1979.

Leaves by Ghillean Tolmie Prance, photographs by Kjell B. Sandved; Crown, 1985. **Awarded:** New York Academy of Sciences (older honor) 1986.

SANTORO, CHRISTOPHER

Hominids: A Look Back at Our Ancestors by Helen Roney Sattler, illustrated by Christopher Santoro; Lothrop, Lee & Shepard, 1988. **Awarded:** New York Academy of Sciences (Older Honor) 1989.

The Illustrated Dinosaur Dictionary by Helen R. Sattler, foreword by John H. Ostrom, illustrated by Pamela Carroll, color insert by Christopher Santoro and Anthony Rao; Lothrop, Lee & Shepard, 1983. **Awarded:** Golden Kite (nonfiction) 1983.

SARABASHA, SUSAN

Prune by Ramon Royal Ross, illustrated by Susan Sarabasha; Atheneum, 1984. **Awarded:** Southern California Council (notable work of fiction) 1985.

SARG, TONY

The Cock, the Mouse and the Little Red Hen by Felicite Lefevre, illustrated by Tony Sarg; Macrae, 1947. **Awarded:** Lewis Carroll Shelf 1965.

SARGENT, SARAH

Edward Troy and the Witch Cat by Sarah Sargent, illustrated by Emily McCully; Follett, 1978. **Awarded:** Council of Wisconsin Writers (juvenile) 1979.

Weird Henry Berg by Sarah Sargent, not illustrated; Crown, 1980. **Awarded:** Friends of American Writers (older) 1981.

SARI

(pseudonym for Anne Elizabeth Fleur)

A Bear Named Grumms by Bessie F. White, illustrated by Sari; Houghton, 1953. **Awarded:** Spring Book Festival (4-8 honor) 1953.

SARICK, JUDY

Awarded: Claude Aubry Award 1991.

SASEK, MIROSLAV

This Is London written and illustrated by Miroslav Sasek; Macmillan, 1959. **Awarded:** New York Times Best Illustrated 1959.

This Is New York written and illustrated by Miroslav Sasek; Macmillan, 1960. **Awarded:** Boys Club 1961; New York Times Best Illustrated 1960.

SATO, YUKO

Dragonflies by Cynthia Overbeck, photographs by Yuko Sato; Lerner, 1982. **Awarded:** New York Academy of Sciences (special award) 1983.

Grasshoppers by Jane Dallinger, photographs by Yuko Sato; Lerner, 1981. **Awarded:** New York Academy of Sciences (special award) 1983.

Ladybugs by Sylvia A. Johnson, photographs by Yuko Sato; Lerner, 1983. **Awarded:** New York Academy of Science (special award) 1983.

Swallowtail Butterflies by Jane Dallinger and Cynthia Overbeck, photographs by Yuko Sato; Lerner, 1982. **Awarded:** New York Academy of Sciences (special award) 1983.

SATTLER, HELEN R.

Dinosaurs of North America by Helen R. Sattler, introduction by John H. Ostrom, illustrated by Anthony Rao; Lothrop, Lee & Shepard, 1981. **Awarded:** Boston Globe Horn Book (nonfiction honor) 1982; Golden Kite (nonfiction honor) 1981.

Hominids: A Look Back at Our Ancestors by Helen Roney Sattler, illustrated by Christopher Santoro; Lothrop, Lee & Shepard, 1988. **Awarded:** New York Academy of Sciences (Older Honor) 1989.

The Illustrated Dinosaur Dictionary by Helen R. Sattler, foreword by John H. Ostrom, illustrated by Pamela Carroll, color insert by Christopher Santore and Anthony Rao; Lothrop, Lee & Shepard, 1983. **Awarded:** Golden Kite (nonfiction) 1983.

Tyrannosaurus Rex and Its Kin by Helen Rooney Sattler, illustrated by Joyce Powzyk; Lothrop Lee & Shepard, 1989. **Awarded:** Oklahoma Book Award 1990.

SATTLEY, HELEN R.
Shadow Across the Campus by Helen R. Sattley, not illustrated; Dodd, Mead, 1957. **Awarded:** Edith Busby 1956; Child Study 1957.

SAUER, JAMES
Hank by James Sauer, not illustrated; Delacorte, 1990. **Awarded:** Delacorte Press Prize 1989.

SAUER, JULIA L.
Fog Magic by Julia L. Sauer, illustrated by Lynd Ward; Viking, 1943. **Awarded:** Newbery (honor) 1944.

The Light at Tern Rock by Julia L. Sauer, illustrated by Georges Schreiber; Viking, 1951. **Awarded:** Newbery (honor) 1952.

SAUNDERS, BRIAN
The Black Symbol by Edgar and Annabel Johnson, illustrated by Brian Saunders; Harper, 1959. **Awarded:** Spring Book Festival (older honor) 1959.

SAVAGE, KATHARINE
Story of the Second World War by Katharine Savage, illustrated with maps; Oxford, 1957. **Awarded:** Carnegie (commended) 1957.

SAVAGE, STEELE
The Golden Knight by George Challis, illustrated by Steele Savage; Greystone Press, 1940. **Awarded:** Spring Book Festival (older honor) 1940.

SAVIN, DEBORAH
An Introduction to Insects by Bettina Bird and Joan Short, illustrated by Deborah Savin. **Awarded:** Whitley (Educational Series) 1989.

SAVITT, SAM
Ghost Hound of Thunder Valley by Ewart A. Autry, illustrated by Sam Savitt; Dodd, Mead, 1965. **Awarded:** Edith Busby 1964.

SAVITZ, HARRIET MAY
Awarded: Outstanding Pennsylvania Author 1981.

Run, Don't Walk by Harriet May Savitz, not illustrated; Watts, 1979. **Awarded:** New Jersey Institute of Technology 1980.

SAWYER, RUTH
Awarded: Regina 1965; Laura Ingalls Wilder 1965.

The Christmas Anna Angel by Ruth Sawyer, illustrated by Kate Seredy; Viking, 1944. **Awarded:** Caldecott (honor) 1945.

Journey Cake, Ho! by Ruth Sawyer, illustrated by Robert McCloskey; Viking, 1953. **Awarded:** Caldecott (honor) 1954.

Roller Skates by Ruth Sawyer, illustrated by Valenti Angelo; Viking, 1936. **Awarded:** Lewis Carroll Shelf 1964; Newbery 1937.

SAXBY, MAURICE
Awarded: Dromkeen 1983.

SAY, ALLEN
The Boy of the Three-Year Nap by Dianne Snyder, illustrated by Allen Say; Houghton Mifflin, 1988. **Awarded:** Boston Globe (Picture Book) 1988; Caldecott (honor) 1989; Parents' Choice (Story Book) 1988; Reading Magic Award 1988.

El Chino written and illustrated by Allen Say; Houghton Mifflin, 1990. **Awarded:** Reading Magic Award 1990.

How My Parents Learned to Eat by Ina Friedman, illustrated by Allen Say; Houghton Mifflin, 1984. **Awarded:** Christopher (ages 6-8) 1985.

The Lucky Yak by Annetta Lawson, illustrated by Allen Say; Parnassus/Houghton Mifflin, 1980. **Awarded:** New York Times Best Illustrated 1980.

A River Dream written and illustrated by Allen Say; Houghton Mifflin, 1988. **Awarded:** New York Times Best Illustrated 1988.

Tree of Cranes written and illustrated by Allen Say; Houghton Mifflin, 1991. **Awarded:** Bay Area Book Reviewers Assn. 1992; PEN Center USA West 1992.

SAYERS, FRANCES CLARKE
Awarded: Southern California Council (distinguished contribution of lasting value for children and young people) 1969; Regina 1973.

SAYLES, EDWIN B.
Throw Stone: The First American Boy, 25,000 Years Ago by Edwin B. Sayles and M. E. Stevens, illustrated by Barton Wright; Reilly & Lee, 1960. **Awarded:** Steck-Vaughn 1962.

SAYNOR, MARJORIE
Man Must Measure: The Wonderful World of Mathematics by Lancelot Thomas Hogben, illustrated by Andre and others, maps by Marjorie Saynor; Rathbone, 1955. **Awarded:** Carnegie (commended) 1955.

SAYRE, JOHN WOODROW
Taxation by J. Woodrow Sayre and Edith G. Stull; Watts, 1963. **Awarded:** New Jersey Institute of Technology (children-economics) 1964.

SCAGELL, ROBIN
Jet Journey by Robin Scagell and Mike Wilson, illustrated with photographs and diagrams; Viking, 1978. **Awarded:** New York Academy of Sciences (special award for series on engineering and Technology) 1979.

SCARRATT, ELAINE
After the Bomb: Brother in the Land by Guy Dickens, Elaine Scarratt, and Nick Williams; English & Media Centre, 1991. **Awarded:** Times Educational Supplement (Schoolbook) 1991.

SCARRY, HUCK
How They Built the Statue of Liberty by Mary J. Shapiro, illustrated by Huck Scarry; Random House, 1985. **Awarded:** Garden State Children's (Younger Nonfiction) 1988.

SCARRY, RICHARD
The Great Steamboat Mystery written and illustrated by Richard Scarry; Random House, 1975. **Awarded:** Edgar Allan Poe (runnerup) 1976.

SCHACHNER, ERWIN
Samantha's Masquerade by Charles W. Pierce, illustrated by Erwin Schachner; McKay, 1967. **Awarded:** New Jersey Institute of Technology 1967.

SCHAEFER, JACK WARNER
Old Ramon by Jack Schaefer, illustrated by Harold West; Houghton, 1960. **Awarded:** Aurianne 1962; Newbery

(honor) 1961; Ohioana 1961; Spring Book Festival (older honor) 1960.

The Plainsmen by Jack Schaefer, illustrated by Lorence F. Bjorklund; Houghton, 1963. **Awarded:** Spring Book Festival (older honor) 1963.

SCHAMI, RAFIK
A Hand Full of Stars by Rafik Schami, not illustrated; Dutton, 1990. **Awarded:** Batchelder 1991.

SCHEADER, CATHERINE
Shirley Chisholm: Teacher and Congresswoman by Catherine Scheader, illustrated with photos; Enslow, 1990. **Awarded:** Woodson (Elementary) 1991.

SCHECHTER, BETTY
The Dreyfus Affair: A National Scandal by Betty Schechter, not illustrated; Houghton, 1965. **Awarded:** Jewish Book Council 1965.

The Peaceable Revolution by Betty Schechter, illustrated with photographs; Houghton, 1963. **Awarded:** Child Study 1963; Edison Mass Media (character development in children) 1964.

SCHEELE, WILLIAM E.
Prehistoric Animals written and illustrated by William E. Scheele; World, 1954. **Awarded:** Ohioana 1955.

Prehistoric Man and the Primates written and illustrated by William E. Scheele; World, 1957. **Awarded:** Boys Club 1958.

SCHEER, GEORGE F.
Yankee Doodle Boy: A Young Soldier's Adventure in the American Revolution Told by Himself by Joseph Plumb Martin, edited by George F. Scheer, illustrated by Victor Mays; Scott, 1964. **Awarded:** Edison Mass Media (America's past) 1965.

SCHEER, JULIAN WEISEL
Rain Makes Applesauce by Julian Scheer, illustrated by Marvin Bileck; Holiday, 1964. **Awarded:** Caldecott (honor) 1965; New York Times Best Illustrated 1964.

SCHEFFLER, URSEL
Spatzen Brauchen Keinen Schirm by Ursel Scheffler, illustrated by Ulises Wensell; Methuen Children's, 1984. **Awarded:** Owl Prize 1985.

SCHEFFRIN-FALK, GLADYS
Another Celebrated Dancing Bear by Gladys Scheffrin-Falk, illustrated by Barbara Garrison; Scribner, 1991. **Awarded:** New York Times Best Illustrated 1991; UNICEF-Ezra Jack Keats National Award for Children's Book Illustration 1991.

SCHEFT, MARGARET
Mystery of the Velvet Box by Margaret Scheft, illustrated by Charles Geer; Watts, 1963. **Awarded:** Edgar Allan Poe (runnerup) 1964.

SCHEIB, IDA
The Earth's Satellite: Man's First True Space Adventure by John Lewellen, illustrated by Ida Scheib; Knopf, 1957. **Awarded:** Boys Club 1958.

SCHEIDL, GERDA MARIE
Das Mondgesicht by Gerda Marie Scheidl, illustrated by Lilo Fromm; Obpacher Buch u. Kunstverlag, 1960. **Awarded:** Hans Christian Andersen (runnerup) 1962.

SCHELLIE, DON
Awarded: Outstanding Arizona Author 1986.

SCHERF, WALTER
Awarded: Chandler Reward of Merit 1971.

SCHERTLE, ALICE
William and Grandpa by Alice Schertle, illustrated by Lydia Dabcovich; Lothrop, Lee & Shepard, 1989. **Awarded:** Christopher (ages 8-11) 1990; Parents' Choice (Picture Book) 1989.

Witch Hazel by Alice Schertle, illustrated by Margot Tomes; HarperCollins, 1991. **Awarded:** Parents' Choice (Picture Book) 1991.

SCHICK, ALICE
Kongo and Kumba: Two Gorillas by Alice Schick, illustrated by Joseph Cellini; Dial, 1974. **Awarded:** Friends of American Writers (illustrator) 1975.

SCHICK, JOEL
Bagdad Ate It by Phyllis Green, illustrated by Joel Schick; Watts, 1980. **Awarded:** California Young Reader (primary) 1984.

My Robot Buddy by Robert Slote, illustrated by Joel Schick; Lippincott, 1975. **Awarded:** Nene 1981.

Wayside School Is Falling Down by Louis Sachar, illustrated by Joel Schick; Lothrop, Lee & Shepard, 1989. **Awarded:** Arizona Young Readers (chapter books) 1993; Garden State (Fiction) 1992; Land of Enchantment 1992; Parents' Choice (Story Book) 1989.

SCHILLER, JUSTIN G.
Awarded: L. Frank Baum 1964.

SCHINDEL, MORTON
Awarded: Regina 1979.

SCHINDELMAN, JOSEPH
Charlie and the Chocolate Factory by Roald Dahl, illustrated by Joseph Schindelman; Knopf, 1964. **Awarded:** Books I Love Best Yearly (Read Aloud Primary-12) 1992; New England Round Table 1972; North Dakota Children's Choice (Older) 1985; Surrey School 1973; Young Teens 1991.

Charlie and the Great Glass Elevator by Roald Dahl, illustrated by Joseph Schindelman; Knopf, 1972. **Awarded:** Nene 1978; Surrey School 1975.

The Great Picture Robbery by Leon Harris, illustrated by Joseph Schindelman; Atheneum, 1963. **Awarded:** New York Times Best Illustrated 1963.

SCHINDLER, S. D.
Catwings by Ursula K. Le Guin, illustrated by S. D. Schindler; Orchard, 1988. **Awarded:** Carolyn W. Field 1989; Reading Magic Award 1988.

The First Tulips in Holland by Phyllis Krasilovsky, illustrated by S. D. Schindler; Doubleday, 1982. **Awarded:** Parents' Choice (illustration) 1982.

Is This a House for Hermit Crab? by Megan McDonald, illustrated by S. D. Schindler; Orchard, 1990. **Awarded:** International Reading Assn. (Younger) 1991.

SCHLAGER, NORMA
Predicting Children's Choices in Literature: A Developmental Approach by Norma Schlager in *Children's Literature in Education* Autumn 1978. **Awarded:** Children's Literature Assn. Award for Literary Criticism (runnerup) 1979.

SCHLEE, ANN
Ask Me No Questions by Ann Schlee, not illustrated; Macmillan (London), 1976; Holt, 1982. **Awarded:** Boston Globe Horn Book (fiction honor) 1982; Guardian (commended) 1977.

The Vandal by Ann Schlee, not illustrated; Macmillan, 1979. **Awarded:** Carnegie (commended) 1979; Guardian 1980.

SCHLEIER, CURT
You'd Better Not Tell by Curt Schleier, not illustrated; Westminster, 1979. **Awarded:** New Jersey Institute of Technology 1980.

SCHLEIN, MIRIAM
Fast Is Not a Ladybug: A Book about Fast and Slow Things by Miriam Schlein, illustrated by Leonard Kessler; Scott, 1953. **Awarded:** Boys Club 1954; New York Times Best Illustrated 1953.

Giraffe: The Silent Giant by Miriam Schlein, illustrated by Betty Fraser; Four Winds, 1976. **Awarded:** Children's Book Showcase 1977.

Heavy Is a Hippopotamus by Miriam Schlein, illustrated by Leonard Kessler; Scott, 1954. **Awarded:** New York Times Best Illustrated 1954.

Little Red Nose by Miriam Schlein, illustrated by Roger Duvoisin; Abelard, 1955. **Awarded:** Spring Book Festival (ages 4-8 honor) 1955.

Project Panda Watch by Miriam Schlein, illustrated by Robert Shetterly and with photographs; Atheneum, 1984. **Awarded:** New York Academy of Sciences (younger honor) 1985.

The Raggle Taggle Fellow by Miriam Schlein, illustrated by Harvey Weiss; Abelard-Schuman, 1959. **Awarded:** Spring Book Festival (ages 4-8 honor) 1959.

The Sun Looks Down by Miriam Schlein, illustrated by Abner Graboff; Abelard-Schuman, 1954. **Awarded:** New York Times Best Illustrated 1954.

When Will the World Be Mine? The Story of a Snowshoe Rabbit by Miriam Schlein, illustrated by Jean Charlot; Scott, 1953. **Awarded:** Caldecott (honor) 1954.

SCHLOREDT, VALERIE
Martin Luther King: America's Great Non-Violent Leader by Pam Brown and Valerie Schloredt, illustrated; Exley Publications, 1988; Longman, 1988. **Awarded:** Times Educational Supplement (Senior Information Book) 1988.

SCHMIDERER, DOROTHY
The Alphabeast Book: An Abecedarium written and illustrated by Dorothy Schmiderer; Holt, 1971. **Awarded:** Children's Book Showcase 1972.

SCHMIDT, ANNIE M. G.
Awarded: Andersen (Author) 1988.

Wiplala by Annie Schmidt; Arbeiderspers, 1957. **Awarded:** Hans Christian Andersen (runnerup) 1960.

SCHMIDT, SARAH LINDSAY
New Land by Sarah L. Schmidt, illustrated by Frank Dobias; McBride, 1933. **Awarded:** Newbery (honor) 1934.

SCHMITZ, FRED
Der Gelbe Vogel (original English: *Alan and Naomi*) by Myron Levoy, translated by Fred Schmitz; Benziger, 1981. **Awarded:** International Board on Books for Young People (translation/German Federal Republic) 1984.

SCHNEIDER, GERLINDE
Uncle Harry by Gerlinde Schneider, adapted by Elizabeth Shub, illustrated by Lilo Fromm; Macmillan, 1972. **Awarded:** Children's Book Showcase 1973.

SCHNEIDER, HERMAN
Awarded: Eva L. Gordon 1977.

Laser Light by Herman Schneider, illustrated by Radu Vero; McGraw Hill, 1978. **Awarded:** New York Academy of Sciences (older) 1979.

Let's Find out: A Picture Science Book by Herman Schneider and Nina Schneider, illustrated by Jeanne Bendick; Scott, 1946. **Awarded:** Spring Book Festival (middle honor) 1946.

SCHNEIDER, HOWIE
Amos: The Story of an Old Dog and His Couch by Howie Schneider and Susan Seligson, illustrated by Howie Schneider; Joy Street Books, 1987. **Awarded:** Washington Children's Choice 1990.

SCHNEIDER, NINA
Awarded: Eva L. Gordon 1977.

Let's Find Out: A Picture Science Book by Herman Schneider and Nina Schneider, illustrated by Jeanne Bendick; Scott, 1946. **Awarded:** Spring Book Festival (middle honor) 1946.

SCHOENHERR, JOHN CARL
The Barn written and illustrated by John Schoenherr; Little, Brown, 1968. **Awarded:** New Jersey Institute of Technology 1968.

Gentle Ben by Walt Morey, illustrated by John Schoenherr; Dutton, 1965. **Awarded:** Dutton Junior Animal 1965; Sequoyah 1968.

Incident at Hawk's Hill by Allan W. Eckert, illustrated by John Schoenherr; Little, Brown, 1971. **Awarded:** Newbery (honor) 1972; George G. Stone 1975.

Julie of the Wolves by Jean Craighead George, illustrated by John Schoenherr; Harper, 1972. **Awarded:** National Book Award (finalist) 1973; Newbery 1973.

Owl Moon by Jane Yolen, illustrated by John Schoenherr; Philomel, 1987. **Awarded:** Caldecott 1988; International Board on Books for Young People (Illustration/USA) 1990.

Rascal: A Memoir of a Better Era by Sterling North, illustrated by John Schoenherr; Dutton, 1963. **Awarded:** Aurianne 1965; Lewis Carroll Shelf 1964; Dorothy Canfield Fisher 1965; New Jersey Institute of Technology 1963; Newbery (honor) 1964; Sequoyah 1966; William Allen White 1966; Young Reader's Choice 1966.

Simon Underground by Joanne Ryder, illustrated by John Schoenherr; Harper, 1976. **Awarded:** Children's Book Showcase 1977.

Susy's Scoundrel by Harold Keith, illustrated by John Schoenherr; Crowell, 1974. **Awarded:** Western Heritage 1975.

SCHOLDER, FRITZ
Anpao: An American Indian Odyssey by Jamake Highwater, illustrated by Fritz Scholder; Lippincott, 1977. **Awarded:** Boston Globe Horn Book (fiction honor) 1978; Newbery (honor) 1978.

SCHOLEFIELD, EDMUND O.
Tiger Rookie by Edmund O. Scholefield, illustrated by Paul Frame: World, 1966. **Awarded:** New Jersey Institute of Technology (ages 12-up) 1966.

SCHOLES, KATHERINE
The Blue Chameleon by Katherine Scholes, illustrated by David Wong; Hill of Content, 1989. **Awarded:** Family Award 1989; New South Wales State Literary Awards (Children's) 1990.

SCHOLES, PERCY
Oxford Junior Companion to Music based on the original published by Percy Sholes; 2nd edition by Michael Hurd, illustrat-

ed with photographs; Oxford, 1979. **Awarded:** Times Educational Supplement (senior) 1980.

SCHOMBURG, ALEX
The Challenge of the Sea by Arthur C. Clarke, illustrated by Alex Schomburg; Holt, 1960. **Awarded:** Boys Club 1961.

Marooned on Mars by Lester del Rey, illustrated by Alex Schomburg; Winston, 1952. **Awarded:** Boys Club 1953.

Ships, Shoals, and Amphoras: The Story of Underwater Archaeology by Suzanne de Borhegyi, illustrated by Alex Schomburg; Holt, 1961. **Awarded:** Ohioana 1962.

SCHON, ISABEL
Awarded: Grolier 1986.

SCHONFELDT, SYBIL GRAFIN
Hinter Dem Norwind translated by Sybil Grafin Schonfeldt; Annette Betz, 1981. (Original English: *At the Back of the North Wind*). **Awarded:** International Board on Books for Young People (honour list/translation/German Federal Republic) 1982.

SCHONGUT, EMANUEL
John Henry McCoy by Lillie D. Chaffin, illustrated by Emanuel Schongut; Macmillan, 1971. **Awarded:** Child Study 1971.

SCHOOLLAND, MARIAN M.
Leading Little Ones to God: A Child's Book of Bible Teachings by Marian M. Schoolland, illustrated by Paul Stoub; revised ed.; Eerdmans, 1981, c1962. **Awarded:** Gold Medallion (cowinner) 1982.

SCHOTTER, RONI
Hannukkah by Roni Schotter, illustrated by Marylin Hafner; Little Brown, 1990. **Awarded:** Jewish Book Council (Children's Picture Book) 1991.

SCHOUTEN, ALET
The Sea Lord by Alet Schouten, translated by Patricia Crampton, illustrated by Rien Poortvliet; Methuen, 1977. **Awarded:** International Board on Books for Young People (honour list/translation/Great Britain) 1980.

SCHRAMM, ULRIK
I Marched with Hannibal by Hans Baumann, translated by K. Potts, illustrated by Ulrik Schramm; Walck, 1962. **Awarded:** Spring Book Festival (older honor) 1962.

SCHRANK, JEFFREY
TV Action Book by Jeffrey Schrank, illustrated with charts and drawings; McDougall-Littell, 1974. **Awarded:** Media & Methods (textbook) 1975.

SCHREIBER, GEORGES
Bambino the Clown written and illustrated by Georges Schreiber; Viking, 1947. **Awarded:** Caldecott (honor) 1948.

The Light at Tern Rock by Julia L. Sauer, illustrated by Georges Schreiber; Viking, 1951. **Awarded:** Newbery (honor) 1952.

Pancakes-Paris by Claire Huchet Bishop, illustrated by Georges Schreiber; Viking, 1947. **Awarded:** Newbery (honor) 1948; Spring Book Festival (middle) 1947.

SCHREITER, RICK
The Little Man by Erich Kastner, translated by James Kirkup, illustrated by Rick Schreiter; Knopf, 1966. **Awarded:** Batchelder 1968.

SCHROEDER, ALAN
Ragtime Tumpie by Alan Schroeder, illustrated by Bernie Fuchs; Little Brown, 1989. **Awarded:** Parents' Choice (Picture Book) 1989.

SCHROEDER, BINETTE
Crocodile, Crocodile by Peter Nickl, illustrated by Binette Schroeder; Nord-Sud Verlag, 1975; Tundra, 1976. **Awarded:** Owl Prize 1976.

The Wonderful Travels and Adventures of Baron Munchhausen by Peter Nickl, translated by Elizabeth Buchanan Taylor, illustrated by Binette Schroeder; Chatto & Windus, 1979. **Awarded:** New York Times Best Illustrated 1980.

SCHROEDER, TED
Beware! Beware! A Witch Won't Share by Ida DeLage, illustrated by Ted Schroeder; Garrard, 1972. **Awarded:** New Jersey Institute of Technology 1972.

Paul Bunyan Finds a Wife by Adele deLeeuw, illustrated by Ted Schroeder; Garrard, 1969. **Awarded:** New Jersey Institute of Technology 1970.

What Does a Witch Need? by Ida DeLage, illustrated by Ted Schroeder; Garrard, 1971. **Awarded:** New Jersey Institute of Technology 1971.

SCHROTTER, GUSTAV
Avalanche! by A. Rutgers Van der Loeff, illustrated by Gustav Schrotter; Morrow, 1958. **Awarded:** Boys Club 1959; Spring Book Festival (middle honor) 1958.

Robert Boyle, Founder of Modern Chemistry by Harry Sootin, illustrated by Gustav Schrotter; Watts, 1962. **Awarded:** Boys Club 1963.

SCHULTZ, GWEN M.
Icebergs and Their Voyages by Gwen M. Schultz, illustrated with photographs and maps; Morrow, 1975. **Awarded:** Council for Wisconsin Writers (juvenile) 1976.

SCHUMACHER, CLAIRE
Where Babies Come From by Harriet Ziefert and Martin Silverman, illustrated by Claire Schumacher; Random House, 1989. **Awarded:** New Jersey Institute of Technology 1990.

SCHURFRANZ, VIVIAN
Renee by Vivian Schurfranz; Scholastic, 1989. **Awarded:** Golden Medallion 1990.

SCHWARTZ, ALVIN
Chin Music: Tall Talk and Other Talk by Alvin Schwartz, illustrated by John O'Brien; Lippincott, 1979. **Awarded:** New Jersey Institute of Technology 1980, 1981.

I Saw You in the Bathtub and Other Folk Rhymes by Alvin Schwartz, illustrated by Syd Hoff; Harper & Row, 1989. **Awarded:** New Jersey Institute of Technology 1990.

In a Dark, Dark Room and Other Scary Stories retold by Alvin Schwartz, illustrated by Dirk Zimmer; Harper, 1984. **Awarded:** Buckeye (grades K-2) 1987; Garden State (easy to read) 1987; Virginia Young Readers (primary) 1988; Volunteer State Book Awards (K-3) 1989; Washington Children's Choice 1987.

Kickle Snifters and Other Fearsome Critters by Alvin Schwartz, illustrated by Glen Rounds; Lippincott, 1976. **Awarded:** New Jersey Institute of Technology 1977.

More Scary Stories to Tell in the Dark by Alvin Schwartz, illustrated by Stephen Gammell; Lippincott, 1984. **Awarded:** Buckeye (grades 3-5) 1989; Emphasis on Reading (grades 3-5) 1990-91.

The Night Workers by Alvin Schwartz, photographs by Ulli Steltzer; Dutton, 1966. **Awarded:** New Jersey Institute of Technology (ages 12-16) 1966.

The Rainy Day Book written and illustrated by Alvin Schwartz; Simon & Schuster/Trident, 1968. **Awarded:** New Jersey Institute of Technology (games) 1968.

Scary Stories 3: More Tales To Chill Your Bones retold by Alvin Schwartz, illustrated by Stephen Gammell; HarperCollins, 1991. **Awarded:** Buckeye (grades 3-5) 1993.

Scary Stories to Tell in the Dark by Alvin Schwartz, illustrated by Stephen Gammell; Lippincott, 1981. **Awarded:** Arizona 1987; Buckeye (grades 3-5) 1987.

Tales of Trickery from the Land of Spoof by Alvin Schwartz, illustrated by David Christiana; Farrar, Straus & Giroux, 1985. **Awarded:** New Jersey Institute of Technology 1987.

Telling Fortunes by Alvin Schwartz, illustrated by Tracey Cameron; Lippincott, 1987. **Awarded:** New Jersey Institute of Technology 1988.

Ten Copycats in a Boat and Other Riddles by Alvin Schwartz, illustrated by Marc Simont; Harper, 1980. **Awarded:** New Jersey Institute of Technology 1981.

Tom Foolery, Trickery and Foolery with Words collected by Alvin Schwartz, illustrated by Glen Rounds; Lippincott, 1973. **Awarded:** New York Times Notable Books 1973.

A Twister of Twists, a Tangler of Tongues by Alvin Schwartz, illustrated by Glen Rounds; Lippincott, 1972. **Awarded:** New Jersey Institute of Technology 1972; New York Times Notable Books 1972.

University: The Students, Faculty and Campus Life at one University by Alvin Schwartz, illustrated with photographs; Viking, 1969. **Awarded:** New Jersey Institute of Technology 1969.

When I Grew up Long Ago by Alvin Schwartz, illustrated by Harold Berson; Lippincott, 1978. **Awarded:** New Jersey Institute of Technology 1980.

SCHWARTZ, AMY
The Crack-of-Dawn Walkers by Amy Hest, illustrated by Amy Schwartz; Macmillan, 1984. **Awarded:** Parents' Choice (literature) 1984.

Magic Carpet by Pat Brisson, illustrated by Amy Schwartz; Bradbury, 1991. **Awarded:** Parents' Choice (Story Book) 1991.

Mrs. Moskowitz and the Sabbath Candlesticks written and illustrated by Amy Schwartz; Jewish Publication Society, 1983. **Awarded:** Jewish Book Council (illustrated children's book) 1985; Sydney Taylor Book Award (picturebook) 1985.

The Lady Who Put Salt in Her Coffee by Lucretia Hale, adapted and illustrated by Amy Schwartz; Harcourt Brace Jovanovich, 1989. **Awarded:** Parents' Choice (Picture Book) 1989.

The Purple Coat by Amy Hest, illustrated by Amy Schwartz; Four Winds, 1986. **Awarded:** Christopher (ages 6-8) 1987.

SCHWARTZ, DANIEL
The House of Wings by Betsy Byars, illustrated by Daniel Schwartz; Viking, 1972. **Awarded:** National Book Award (finalist) 1973.

SCHWARTZ, DAVID M.
How Much Is a Million? by David M. Schwartz, illustrated by Steven Kellogg; Lothrop, Lee & Shepard, 1985. **Awarded:** Boston Globe (illustration honor) 1985; Utah Children's Informational Book Award 1988.

SCHWARTZ, HOWARD
The Diamond Tree: Jewish Tales From Around the World by Barbara Rush and Howard Schwartz, illustrated by Uri

Shulevitz; HarperCollins, 1991. **Awarded:** Sydney Taylor Book Award (Older) 1992.

SCHWARTZ, JULIUS
It's Fun to Know Why: Experiments with Things Around Us by Julius Schwartz, illustrated by Edwin Herron and Anne Marie Jauss; McGraw, 1973. **Awarded:** New York Academy of Sciences (older honor) 1974.

SCHWARTZ, SHEILA
Awarded: ALAN 1981.

SCHWARZ, FRANK
Bionic Parts for People: The Real Story of Artificial Organs and Replacement Parts by Gloria Skurzynski, illustrated by Frank Schwarz; Four Winds, 1978. **Awarded:** Golden Kite (nonfiction honor) 1978.

SCHWARZ, LEISELOTTE
Der Traummacher by Leiselotte Schwarz; Verlag Heinrich Ellermann, 1972. **Awarded:** Biennale Illustrations Bratislava (grand prix) 1973.

SCHWEBEIL, GERTRUDE C.
Undine by Friedrich de la Motte Foque, retold and edited by Gertrude C. Schwebeil, illustrated by Eros Keith; Simon & Schuster, 1971, c1957. **Awarded:** Lewis Carroll Shelf 1971.

SCHWEITZER, IRIS
Louie's Lot by E. W. Hildick, illustrated by Iris Schweitzer; Faber, 1965. **Awarded:** International Board on Books for Young People (Great Britain) 1968.

SCIESZKA, JON
The Stinky Cheese Man and Other Fairly Stupid Tales by Jon Scieszka, illustrated by Lane Smith; Viking, 1992. **Awarded:** Caldecott (honor) 1993; New York Times Best Illustrated 1992.

SCOGGIN, MARGARET C.
Awarded: Grolier 1960; Women's National Book Assn. 1952.

SCOPPETTONE, SANDRA
Bang, Bang, You're Dead by Sandra Scoppettone and Louise Fitzhugh, illustrated by Louise Fitzhugh; Harper, 1969. **Awarded:** Art Books for Children 1974; New York Times Best Illustrated 1969.

The Late Great Me by Sandra Scoppettone, not illustrated; Putnam, 1976. **Awarded:** California Young Reader Medal (high school) 1979.

Playing Murder by Sandra Scoppettone, not illustrated; Harper, 1985. **Awarded:** Edgar Allan Poe (runnerup) 1986.

Trying Hard to Hear You by Sandra Scoppettone, not illustrated; Harper, 1974. **Awarded:** New Jersey Institute of Technology 1976.

SCOREY, JOHN
What's Under the Ground? by Susan Mayes, illustrated by Mike Pringle, Brin Edwards and John Scorey; Usborne, 1989. **Awarded:** Science Book Prizes 1990.

Where Does Electricity Come From? by Susan Mayes, illustrated by John Shackell and John Scorey; Usborne, 1989. **Awarded:** Science Book Prizes 1990.

SCOTT, CORA ANNETT PIPITONE
How the Witch got Alf by Cora Annett Scott, illustrated by Steven Kellogg; Watts, 1975. **Awarded:** Christopher (ages 7-11) 1976.

SCOTT, ERIC
Down the River, Westward Ho! by Eric Scott, not illustrated; Meredith, 1967. **Awarded:** Western Heritage 1968.

SCOTT, HUGH
Why Weeps the Brogan? by Hugh Scott, not illustrated; Walker Books, 1989. **Awarded:** Whitbread 1989.

SCOTT, LLOYD
The Great Adventure: An Illustrated History of Canada by Donalda Dickie, illustrated by Lloyd Scott; Dent, 1950. **Awarded:** Governor-General's Literary Award 1950.

SCOTT, LYNN H.
The Covered Wagon & Other Adventures by Lynn H. Scott, illustrated; University of Nebraska Press, 1987. **Awarded:** Western Heritage 1988.

SCOTT, PATRICIA
Awarded: Dromkeen Medal 1988.

SCOTT, SALLY
Benjie and His Family by Sally Scott, illustrated by Beth Krush; Harcourt, 1952. **Awarded:** Boys Club 1953.

SCRIBE, MURDO
Murdo's Story: A Legend from Northern Manitoba by Murdo Scribe, illustrated by Terry Gallagher; Pemmican Publications, 1985. **Awarded:** Governor General (illustrator) 1985.

SCROFANI, JOSEPH
Dr. Beaumont and the Man with the Hole in his Stomach by Sam Epstein and Beryl Epstein, illustrated by Joseph Scrofani; Coward, 1978. **Awarded:** New York Academy of Sciences (younger honor) 1979.

Lost in the Devil's Desert by Gloria Skurzynski, illustrated by Joseph M. Scrofani; Lothrop, Lee & Shepard, 1982. **Awarded:** Utah Children's 1984.

SCRUTON, CLIVE
Sidney the Monster by David Wood, illustrated by Clive Scruton; Walker, 1988. **Awarded:** Nottinghamshire (Acorn) 1989.

SCULLARD, SUE
Miss Fanshawe and the Great Dragon Adventure written and illustrated by Sue Scullard; Macmillan Children's, 1986. **Awarded:** Mother Goose (runnerup) 1987.

SCURO, VINCENT
Wonders of Sheep by Vincent Scuro and Sigmund A. Lavine, illustrated with photographs and old prints; Dodd, Mead, 1983. **Awarded:** New Jersey Institute of Technology 1983.

SEABORG, GLENN T.
Elements of the Universe by Glenn T. Seaborg and Evans G. Valens, illustrated with charts and diagrams; Dutton, 1958. **Awarded:** Edison Mass Media (science book youth) 1959.

SEABROOKE, BRENDA
Judy Scuppernong by Brenda Seabrooke, illustrated by Ted Lewin; Dutton, 1990. **Awarded:** Boston Globe Horn Book (Fiction/Poetry Honor) 1991.

SEALE, CLEM
All the Proud Tribesmen by Kylie Tennant, illustrated by Clem Seale; Macmillan (London), 1959. **Awarded:** Children's Book Council of Australia (book of the year) 1960.

Ash Road by Ivan Southall, illustrated by Clem Seale; Angus & Robertson, 1965. **Awarded:** Children's Book Council of Australia (book of the year) 1966.

SEALOFF, GEORGIA
Awarded: Grolier 1956.

SEARCY, MARGARET
Tiny Bat and the Ball Game by Margaret Searcy, illustrated by Lu Celia Wise; Portals Press, 1978. **Awarded:** Authors Award/Alabama 1980.

SEARLE, CHRIS
Wheel Around the World by Chris Searle, illustrated by Katinka Kew; Macdonald, 1983. **Awarded:** Other Award 1984.

SEARS, PAUL M.
Firefly by Paul M. Sears, illustrated by Glen Rounds; Holiday House, 1956. **Awarded:** New Jersey Institute of Technology (science) 1963.

SEBESTYEN, OUIDA
IOU's by Ouida Sebestyen, not illustrated; Little, Brown, 1982. **Awarded:** Texas Institute of Letters 1983.

Words by Heart by Ouida Sebestyen, not illustrated; Little Brown, 1979. **Awarded:** American Book Award (children's fiction paperback) 1982; International Reading Assn. 1980; New York Times Notable Books 1979.

SECKAR, ALVENA
Zuska of the Burning Hills by Alvena Seckar, illustrated by Kathleen Voute; Oxford, 1952. **Awarded:** Spring Book Festival (ages 8-12 honor) 1952.

SEDACCA, JOSEPH M.
The Language of Life: An Introduction to the Science of Genetics by Muriel Beadle and George Beadle, illustrated by Joseph M. Sedacca and others; Doubleday, 1966. **Awarded:** Edison Mass Media (science books for youth) 1967.

SEEGER, ELIZABETH
The Pageant of Chinese History by Elizabeth Seeger, illustrated by Bernard Watkins; Longmans, 1934. **Awarded:** Newbery (honor) 1935.

SEEGER, PETE
Abiyoyo by Pete Seeger, illustrated by Michael Hays; Macmillan, 1986. **Awarded:** Redbook 1986.

SEEMAN, ELIZABETH
The Talking Dog and the Barking Man by Elizabeth Seeman, illustrated by James Flora; Watts, 1960. **Awarded:** Spring Book Festival (middle honor) 1960.

SEFTON, CATHERINE
Starry Night by Catherine Sefton, not illustrated; Hamilton, 1986. **Awarded:** Guardian (runnerup) 1987; Other Award 1986.

SEGAL, E. A.
A Ring and a Riddle by E. A. Segal and M. Ilin, translated by Beatrice Kinkead, illustrated by Vera Bock; Lippincott, 1944. **Awarded:** Spring Book Festival (younger) 1944.

SEGAL, ELIZABETH
Laura Ingalls Wilder's America: An Unflinching Assessment by Elizabeth Segal in *Children's Literature in Education* Summer 1977. **Awarded:** Children's Literature Assn. Award for Literary Criticism (runnerup) 1978.

SEGAL, JOYCE
It's Time to Go to Bed by Joyce Segal, illustrated by Robin Eaton; Doubleday, 1979. **Awarded:** New Jersey Institute of Technology 1980.

SEGAL, LORE
All the Way Home by Lore Segal, illustrated by James Marshall; Farrar, 1973. **Awarded:** Children's Book Showcase 1974.

The Book of Adam to Moses by Lore Segal, illustrated by Leonard Baskin; Knopf, 1987. **Awarded:** New York Times Notable 1987; Parents' Choice (Picture Book) 1987.

The Church Mice Adrift by Lore Segal, illustrated by Graham Oakley; Macmillan, 1976; Atheneum, 1976. **Awarded:** Greenaway (highly commended) 1976; New York Times Best Illustrated 1977.

The Juniper Tree and Other Tales from Grimm translated by Lore Segal and Randall Jarrell, illustrated by Maurice Sendak; Farrar, 1973. **Awarded:** Children's Book Showcase 1974; New York Times Best Illustrated 1973.

The Story of Mrs. Lovewright and Purrless her Cat by Lore Segal, illustrated by Paul O. Zelinsky; Knopf, 1985. **Awarded:** New York Times Best Illustrated 1985; New York Times Notable 1985.

The Story of Old Mrs. Brubeck and how She Looked for Trouble and where She Found Him by Lore Segal, illustrated by Marcia Sewall; Pantheon, 1979. **Awarded:** New York Times Best Illustrated 1981.

Tell Me a Mitzi by Lore Segal, illustrated by Harriet Pincus; Farrar, 1970. **Awarded:** Spring Book Festival (picture book) 1970.

SEGAWA, YASUO
Awarded: Andersen (Illustrator Highly Commended) 1988.

Taro and a Bamboo Shoot by Masaku Matsuno, illustrated by Yasuo Segawa; Fukuinkan Shoten. **Awarded:** Biennale Illustrations Bratislava (grand prix) 1967.

SEIDEL, HEINRICH
The Magic Inkstand and Other Stories by Heinrich Seidel, translated by Elizabeth Watson Taylor; Jonathan Cape, 1982. **Awarded:** International Board on Books for Young People (translation/Great Britain) 1984.

SEIDEL, HILDE
Auf Endlosen Strassen by Gerhart Ellert, illustrated by Hilde Seidel; Osterreichischer Bundesverlag, 1959. **Awarded:** Hans Christian Andersen (runnerup) 1962.

SEIDLER, ROSALIE
Panda Cake written and illustrated by Rosalie Seidler; Parents, 1978. **Awarded:** Christopher (picture book) 1979.

SEIDLER, TOR
Terpin by Tor Seidler, not illustrated; Farrar, 1982. **Awarded:** New York Times Notable Books 1982.

SEIDLIN, OSKAR
Green Wagons by Oskar Seidlin and Senta Rypins, illustrated by Barbara Cooney; Houghton, 1943. **Awarded:** Spring Book Festival (middle honor) 1943.

SEIGNOBOSC, FRANCOISE
Chouchou written and illustrated by Francoise; Scribner, 1958. **Awarded:** New York Times Best Illustrated 1958.

Jeanne-Marie Counts Her Sheep written and illustrated by Francoise; Scribner, 1951. **Awarded:** Spring Book Festival (picture book) 1951.

SEISSER, JEAN
A Book of A-maze-ments by Jean Seisser; Quist, 1974. **Awarded:** New York Times Best Illustrated 1975.

SELBERG, INGRID
Our Changing World by Ingrid Selberg, illustrated by Andrew Muller; Collins, 1982; Philomel, 1982. **Awarded:** Bologna (critici in erba) 1983.

SELDEN, GEORGE
The Cricket in Times Square by George Selden, illustrated by Garth Williams; Farrar, 1960. **Awarded:** Lewis Carroll Shelf 1963; Massachusetts Children's (grades 4-6) 1979; Newbery (honor) 1961.

Harry Cat's Pet Puppy by George Selden, illustrated by Garth Williams; Farrar, 1974. **Awarded:** William Allen White 1977.

Tucker's Countryside by George Selden, illustrated by Garth Williams; Farrar, 1969. **Awarded:** Christopher (ages 8-12) 1970.

SELIGSON, SUSAN
Amos: The Story of an Old Dog and His Couch by Howie Schneider and Susan Seligson, illustrated by Howie Schneider; Joy Street Books, 1987. **Awarded:** Washington Children's Choice 1990.

SELSAM, MILLICENT E.
Awarded: Eva L. Gordon 1964; Lucky Book Club Four-Leaf Clover 1973; Washington Post/Children's Book Guild Nonfiction 1978.

Benny's Animals and How He Put Them In Order by Millicent E. Selsam, illustrated by Arnold Lobel; Harper & Row, 1966. **Awarded:** Boys Club (certificate) 1966-67.

Biography of an Atom by Millicent E. Selsam and Jacob Bronowski, illustrated by Weimer Pursell; Harper, 1965. **Awarded:** Edison Mass Media (science book) 1966.

How Kittens Grow by Millicent E. Selsam, photographs by Esther Bubley; Four Winds, 1975, 1973. **Awarded:** Garden State Children's (young nonfiction) 1978.

Stars, Mosquitoes, and Crocodiles: The American Travels of Alexander Von Humboldt edited by Millicent E. Selsam, illustrated by Russell Francis Peterson; Harper, 1962. **Awarded:** Boys Club 1963.

Tyrannosaurus Rex by Millicent E. Selsam, illustrated with photographs; Harper, 1978. **Awarded:** Garden State Children's (younger nonfiction) 1981.

SELZNICK, BRIAN
The Houdini Box by Brian Selznick, illustrated; Knopf, 1991. **Awarded:** Rhode Island 1993; Texas Bluebonnet 1993.

SEMEL, NAVA
Becoming Gershona by Nava Semel, not illustrated; Viking, 1990. **Awarded:** Jewish Book Council (Children's Literature) 1991.

SENDAK, JACK
The King of Hermits and Other Stories by Jack Sendak, illustrated by Margot Zemach; Farrar, 1967. **Awarded:** New Jersey Institute of Technology 1967.

The Magic Tears by Jack Sendak, illustrated by Mitchell Miller; Harper, 1971. **Awarded:** Children's Book Showcase 1972; New York Times Best Illustrated 1971.

Martze by Jack Sendak, illustrated by Mitchell Miller; Farrar, 1968. **Awarded:** New Jersey Institute of Technology 1968.

SENDAK, MAURICE BERNARD
Awarded: Hans Christian Andersen (illustrator) 1970; Chandler Reward of Merit 1967; Drexel Citation 1989; Empire State Award 1990; Keene State College 1986; University of Southern Mississippi 1981; Laura Ingalls Wilder 1983.

Along Came a Dog by Meindert DeJong, illustrated by Maurice Sendak; Harper, 1958. **Awarded:** Aurianne 1960; International Board on Books for Young People (USA) 1960; Newbery (honor) 1959.

The Animal Family by Randall Jarrell, illustrated by Maurice Sendak; Pantheon, 1965. **Awarded:** Lewis Carroll Shelf

1970; New York Times Best Illustrated 1965; Newbery (honor) 1966.

The Bat-poet by Randall Jarrell, illustrated by Maurice Sendak; Macmillan, 1964. **Awarded:** New York Times Best Illustrated 1964; North Carolina AAUW 1964.

The Birthday Party by Ruth Krauss, illustrated by Maurice Sendak; Harper, 1957. **Awarded:** New York Times Best Illustrated 1957.

Dear Mili by Wilhelm Grimm, illustrated by Maurice Sendak; Farrar Straus Giroux, 1988. **Awarded:** Bologna (Critici in Erba) 1989; Reading Magic Award 1988.

Dwarf Long-nose by Wilhelm Hauff, translated by Doris Orgel, illustrated by Maurice Sendak; Random House, 1960. **Awarded:** Lewis Carroll Shelf 1963.

Father Bear Comes Home by Else Holmelund Minarik, illustrated by Maurice Sendak; Harper, 1959. **Awarded:** New York Times Best Illustrated 1959.

Fly by Night by Randall Jarrell, illustrated by Maurice Sendak; Farrar, 1976. **Awarded:** Children's Book Showcase 1977; New York Times Best Illustrated 1976.

The Griffin and the Minor Canon by Frank R. Stockton, illustrated by Maurice Sendak; Holt, 1963. **Awarded:** Lewis Carroll Shelf 1963.

A Hole Is to Dig by Ruth Krauss, illustrated by Maurice Sendak; Harper, 1952. **Awarded:** New York Times Best Illustrated 1952.

The House of Sixty Fathers by Meindert DeJong, illustrated by Maurice Sendak; Harper & Row, 1956. **Awarded:** Child Study 1956; International Board on Books for Young People (USA) 1958; Newbery (honor) 1957; Woodward Park School 1958.

Hurry Home, Candy by Meindert DeJong, illustrated by Maurice Sendak; Harper, 1953. **Awarded:** Newbery (honor) 1954.

I Saw Esau by Iona Opie and Peter Opie, illustrated by Maurice Sendak; Candlewick, 1992. **Awarded:** Parents Choice (Picture Book) 1992; Reading Magic Award 1992.

I Want to Paint My Bathroom Blue by Ruth Krauss, illustrated by Maurice Sendak; Harper, 1956. **Awarded:** New York Times Best Illustrated 1956.

I'll Be You and You Be Me by Ruth Krauss, illustrated by Maurice Sendak; Harper, 1954. **Awarded:** New York Times Best Illustrated 1954.

In the Night Kitchen written and illustrated by Maurice Sendak; Harper, 1970; Harper Trophy, 1985. **Awarded:** Art Books for Children 1973, 1974, 1975; Caldecott (honor) 1971; New York Times Best Illustrated 1970; Redbook 1985.

The Juniper Tree and Other Tales from Grimm translated by Lore Segal and Randall Jarrell, illustrated by Maurice Sendak; Farrar, 1973. **Awarded:** Children's Book Showcase 1974; New York Times Best Illustrated 1973.

Kenny's Window written and illustrated by Maurice Sendak; Harper, 1956. **Awarded:** Spring Book Festival (ages 4-8 honor) 1956.

King Grisly-beard: A Tale from the Brothers Grimm translated by Edgar Taylor, illustrated by Maurice Sendak; Farrar, 1973. **Awarded:** Children's Book Showcase 1974; New York Times Best Illustrated 1973.

A Kiss for Little Bear by Else Holmelund Minarik, illustrated by Maurice Sendak; Harper, 1968. **Awarded:** New York Times Best Illustrated 1968.

Let's be Enemies by Janice May Udry, illustrated by Maurice Sendak; Harper, 1961. **Awarded:** Spring Book Festival (ages 4-8 honor) 1961.

The Light Princess by George MacDonald, illustrated by Maurice Sendak; Farrar, 1969. **Awarded:** New York Times Best Illustrated 1969.

Little Bear's Visit by Else Holmelund Minarik, illustrated by Maurice Sendak; Harper, 1961. **Awarded:** Caldecott (honor) 1962.

Mr. Rabbit and the Lovely Present by Charlotte Zolotow, illustrated by Maurice Sendak; Harper, 1962. **Awarded:** Caldecott (honor) 1963.

The Moon Jumpers by Janice May Udry, illustrated by Maurice Sendak; Harper, 1959. **Awarded:** Caldecott (honor) 1960.

Nutcracker by E. T. A. Hoffmann, illustrated by Maurice Sendak, translated by Ralph Manheim; Crown, 1984. **Awarded:** New York Times Best Illustrated 1984.

Open House for Butterflies by Ruth Krauss, illustrated by Maurice Sendak; Harper, 1960. **Awarded:** New York Times Best Illustrated 1960.

Outside Over There written and illustrated by Maurice Sendak; Harper, 1981. **Awarded:** American Book Award (picture book hardback) 1982; Boston Globe Horn Book (illustration) 1981; Caldecott (honor) 1982; New York Times Best Illustrated 1981; New York Times Notable Books 1981.

Shadrach by Meindert DeJong, illustrated by Maurice Sendak; Harper, 1953. **Awarded:** Newbery (honor) 1954.

The Singing Hill by Meindert DeJong, illustrated by Maurice Sendak; Harper, 1962. **Awarded:** New York Times Best Illustrated 1962.

The Tin Fiddle by Edward Tripp, illustrated by Maurice Sendak; Oxford, 1954. **Awarded:** Spring Book Festival (ages 4-8 honor) 1954.

A Very Special House by Ruth Krauss, illustrated by Maurice Sendak; Harper, 1953. **Awarded:** Caldecott (honor) 1954.

What Do You Say, Dear? A Book of Manners for All Occasions by Sesyle Joslin, illustrated by Maurice Sendak; Scott, 1958; Harper Trophy, 1986. **Awarded:** Caldecott (honor) 1959; New York Times Best Illustrated 1958; Redbook 1986.

The Wheel on the School by Meindert DeJong, illustrated by Maurice Sendak; Harper, 1954. **Awarded:** Lewis Carroll Shelf 1963; Newbery 1955.

Where the Wild Things Are written and illustrated by Maurice Sendak; Harper, 1963; Harper Trophy, 1984. **Awarded:** Art Books for Children 1973, 1974, 1975; Caldecott 1964; Lewis Carroll Shelf 1964; Children's Choice [Arizona] (picture book) 1985; International Board on Books for Young People (USA) 1966; New York Times Best Illustrated 1963; Redbook (paperback) 1984.

Zlateh the Goat and Other Stories by Isaac Bashevis Singer, translated by Elizabeth Shub, illustrated by Maurice Sendak; Harper, 1966. **Awarded:** International Board on Books for Young People (translation/United States) 1982; New York Times Best Illustrated 1966; Newbery (honor) 1967.

SENIOR, MARGARET

The Australian Book by Eve Pownall, illustrated by Margaret Senior; Sands, 1953. **Awarded:** Children's Book Council of Australia 1952.

SEREDY, KATE

Caddie Woodlawn by Carol Ryrie Brink, illustrated by Kate Seredy; Macmillan, 1935. **Awarded:** Lewis Carroll Shelf 1959; Newbery 1936.

The Christmas Anna Angel by Ruth Sawyer, illustrated by Kate Seredy; Viking, 1944. **Awarded:** Caldecott (honor) 1945.

An Ear for Uncle Emil by Eva Roe Gaggin, illustrated by Kate Seredy; Viking, 1939. **Awarded:** Spring Book Festival (younger honor) 1939.

The Good Master written and illustrated by Kate Seredy; Viking, 1935. **Awarded:** Newbery (honor) 1936.

Little Vic by Doris Gates, illustrated by Kate Seredy; Viking, 1951. **Awarded:** William Allen White 1954.

The Singing Tree written and illustrated by Kate Seredy; Viking, 1939. **Awarded:** Newbery (honor) 1940.

The White Stag written and illustrated by Kate Seredy; Viking, 1937. **Awarded:** Lewis Carroll Shelf 1959; Newbery 1938.

Winterbound by Margery Bianco, illustrated by Kate Seredy; Viking, 1936. **Awarded:** Newbery (honor) 1937.

The Wonderful Year by Nancy Barnes, illustrated by Kate Seredy; Messner, 1946. **Awarded:** Julia Ellsworth Ford 1945; Newbery (honor) 1947.

Young Walter Scott by Elizabeth Janet Gray, illustrated by Kate Seredy; Viking, 1935. **Awarded:** Newbery (honor) 1936.

SERRAILLIER, ANNE

Florinda and the Wild Bird by Selina Chonz, translated by Anne Serraillier and Ian Serraillier, illustrated by Alois Carigiet; Walck, 1952. **Awarded:** New York Times Best Illustrated 1953.

SERRAILLIER, IAN

Florinda and the Wild Bird by Selina Chonz, translated by Ian Serraillier and Anne Serraillier, illustrated by Alois Carigiet; Walck, 1952. **Awarded:** New York Times Best Illustrated 1953.

The Silver Sword by Ian Serraillier, illustrated by C. Walter Hodges; Cape, 1956; Criterion, 1959. **Awarded:** Boys Club 1960; Carnegie (commended) 1956; Spring Book Festival (older honor) 1959.

SERVELLO, JOE

Songs of the Chippewa adapted by John Bierhorst, illustrated by Joe Servello; Farrar Straus Giroux, 1974. **Awarded:** State Historical Society of Wisconsin 1975.

SERVICE, PAMELA F.

The Reluctant God by Pamela F. Service, not illustrated; Atheneum, 1988. **Awarded:** Golden Kite (Fiction honor) 1988.

SERVICE, ROBERT W.

The Cremation of Sam McGee by Robert W. Service, illustrated by Ted Harrison; Greenwillow, 1987. **Awarded:** New York Times Best Illustrated 1987; Parents' Choice (Picture Book) 1987.SESSHU

Cricket Songs: Japanese Haiku translated by Harry Behn, illustrated by Sesshu and others; Harcourt, 1964. **Awarded:** George G. Stone 1965.

SEUBERLICH, HERTHA

Annuzza, a Girl of Romania by Hertha Seuberlich, translated by Stella Humphries, illustrated by Gerhard Pallasch; Rand, 1962. **Awarded:** Lewis Carroll Shelf 1963.

SEUSS, DR.

(pseudonym for Theodor Geisel)

Awarded: Children's Choice Award (Texas) 1978, 1992; Regina 1982; Southern California Council (special contribution to children's literature) 1974; Laura Ingalls Wilder 1980.

And to Think that I Saw it on Mulberry Street written and illustrated by Dr. Seuss; Vanguard, 1937. **Awarded:** Lewis Carroll Shelf 1961

Bartholomew and the Oobleck written and illustrated by Dr. Seuss; Random House, 1949. **Awarded:** Caldecott (honor) 1950.

The Butter Battle Book written and illustrated by Dr. Seuss; Random House, 1984. **Awarded:** Little Archer 1984; New York Times Notable 1984.

Horton Hatches the Egg written and illustrated by Dr. Seuss; Random House, 1940. **Awarded:** Lewis Carroll Shelf 1958.

I Had Trouble in Getting to Solla Sollew written and illustrated by Dr. Seuss; Random House, 1965. **Awarded:** Boys Club 1966.

If I Ran the Zoo written and illustrated by Dr. Seuss; Random House, 1950. **Awarded:** Caldecott (honor) 1951.

McElligot's Pool written and illustrated by Dr. Seuss; Random House, 1947. **Awarded:** Caldecott (honor) 1948; Young Reader's Choice 1950.

Sefereggel (Original English *The Foot Book*) by Dr. Seuss, translated by Leah Naor; Keter, 1982. **Awarded:** International Board on Books for Young People (Translation/Israel) 1984.

SEVELA, EFRAIM

We Were Not Like Other People by Efraim Sevela, not illustrated, translated by Antonia W. Bouis; Harper & Row, 1989. **Awarded:** International Board on Books for Young People (translation/USA) 1992.

SEVERE, LLOYD

Awarded: Southern California Council (distinguished contribution for outstanding community service in the field of literature) 1972.

SEVERN, DAVID

The Girl in the Grove by David Severn, not illustrated; Harper, 1974. **Awarded:** Edgar Allan Poe (runnerup) 1975.

SEWALL, MARCIA

Crazy in Love by Richard Kennedy, illustrated by Marcia Sewall; Unicorn/Dutton, 1980. **Awarded:** Parents' Choice (illustration) 1980.

The Golden Locket by Carol Greene, illustrated by Marcia Sewall; Harcourt Brace Jovanovich, 1992. **Awarded:** Parents Choice (Picture Books) 1992.

The Marzipan Moon by Nancy Willard, illustrated by Marcia Sewall; Harcourt, 1981. **Awarded:** New York Times Notable Books 1981.

The Nutcrackers and the Sugartongs by Edward Lear, illustrated by Marcia Sewall; Atlantic-Little, 1978. **Awarded:** New York Times Best Illustrated 1978.

Pilgrims of Plimoth written and illustrated by Marcia Sewall; Atheneum, 1986. **Awarded:** Boston Globe Horn Book (nonfiction) 1987.

Saying Goodbye To Grandma by Jane Resh Thomas, illustrated by Marcia Sewall; Clarion, 1988. **Awarded:** Fassler 1989.

Stone Fox by John Reynolds Gardiner, illustrated by Marcia Sewall; Crowell Jr. Books, 1980. **Awarded:** Emphasis on

Reading (grades 4-6) 1986-87; Maud Hart Lovelace 1987; New York Times Notable Books 1980; Southern California Council (notable work of fiction) 1981; George G. Stone 1987; Utah Children's 1985.

The Story of Old Mrs. Brubeck and how She Looked for Trouble and where She Found Him by Lore Segal, illustrated by Marcia Sewall; Pantheon, 1979. **Awarded:** New York Times Best Illustrated 1981.

SEWELL, HELEN MOORE

The Bears on Hemlock Mountain by Alice Dalgliesh, illustrated by Helen Sewell; Scribner, 1952. **Awarded:** Newbery (honor) 1953.

By the Shores of Silver Lake by Laura Ingalls Wilder; illustrated by Helen Sewell and Mildred Boyle; Harper, 1939. **Awarded:** Newbery (honor) 1940; Young Reader's Choice 1942.

Little Town on the Prairie by Laura Ingalls Wilder, illustrated by Helen Sewell and Mildred Boyle; Harper, 1941. **Awarded:** Newbery (honor) 1942.

The Long Winter by Laura Ingalls Wilder, illustrated by Helen Sewell and Mildred Boyle; Harper, 1940. **Awarded:** Newbery (honor) 1941.

On the Banks of Plum Creek by Laura Ingalls Wilder, illustrated by Helen Sewell and Mildred Boyle; Harper, 1937. **Awarded:** Newbery (honor) 1938.

The Thanksgiving Story by Alice Dalgliesh, illustrated by Helen Sewell; Scribner, 1954. **Awarded:** Caldecott (honor) 1955.

These Happy Golden Years by Laura Ingalls Wilder, illustrated by Helen Sewell and Mildred Boyle; Harper, 1943. **Awarded:** Newbery (honor) 1944; Spring Book Festival (middle) 1943.

The Three Kings of Saba by Alf Evers, illustrated by Helen Sewell; Lippincott, 1955. **Awarded:** New York Times Best Illustrated 1955.

SEYDL, ZDENEK

Pribehy by Anna Hostomska, illustrated by Zdenek Seydl; Albatros, 1969. **Awarded:** Bologna (Graphics for Youth) 1968.

SEYMOUR, RICHARD

The Mirrorstone by Michael Palin, illustrated by Alan Lee, design by Richard Seymour; Cape, 1986; Knopf, 1986. **Awarded:** Smarties (innovation) 1986.

SEYTON, MARION

The Hole in the Hill by Marion Seyton, illustrated by Leonard Shortall; Follett, 1960. **Awarded:** Follett Beginning to Read 1960.

SHAAP, DICK

Bo Knows Bo: The Autobiography of a Ballplayer by Bo Jackson and Dick Shaap; Doubleday, 1990. **Awarded:** Young Teens 1991.

SHACKELL, JOHN

Where Does Electricity Come From? by Susan Mayes, illustrated by John Shackell and John Scorey; Usborne, 1989. **Awarded:** Science Book Prizes 1990.

SHACKELL, RODNEY

Enchantress from the Stars by Sylvia L. Engdahl, illustrated by Rodney Shackell; Atheneum, 1970; Collier, 1989. **Awarded:** Newbery (honor) 1971; Phoenix Award 1990.

SHAHN, BEN

A Boy of Old Prague by Sulamith Ish-Kishor, illustrated by Ben Shahn; Pantheon, 1963. **Awarded:** Jewish Book Council 1963.

Kay-Kay Comes Home by Nicholas Samstag, illustrated by Ben Shahn; Obolensky, 1962. **Awarded:** New York Times Best Illustrated 1962.

Ounce, Dice, Trice by Alastair Reid, illustrated by Ben Shahn; Little, Brown, 1958. **Awarded:** Art Books for Children 1973.

SHAHN, BERNARDA BRYSON
see BRYSON, BERNARDA

SHAMIR, MOSCHE

All Together by Mosche Shamir; Hatzair, 1959. **Awarded:** Hans Christian Andersen (runnerup) 1960.

SHANNON, GEORGE

Unlived Affections by George Shannon, not illustrated; Harper & Row, 1989. **Awarded:** Friends of American Writers 1990.

SHANNON, JACQUELINE

Too Much T.J. by Jacqueline Shannon, not illustrated; Delacorte, 1986. **Awarded:** Delacorte (honorable mention) 1984.

SHANNON, MONICA

Dobry by Monica Shannon, illustrated by Atanas Katchamakoff; Viking, 1934. **Awarded:** Newbery 1935.

SHAPIRO, IRWIN

Joe Magarac and His U.S.A. Citizenship Papers by Irwin Shapiro, illustrated by James Daugherty; Messner, 1948. **Awarded:** Julia Ellsworth Ford 1947.

SHAPIRO, MARY J.

How They Built the Statue of Liberty by Mary J. Shapiro, illustrated by Huck Scarry; Random House, 1985. **Awarded:** Garden State Children's Book Award (Younger Nonfiction) 1988.

SHARMAT, MARJORIE WEINMAN

My Mother Never Listens To Me by Marjorie Weinman Sharmat, illustrated by Lynn Munsinger; Whitman, 1984. **Awarded:** Emphasis on Reading (grades 2-3) 1987-88.

Nate the Great and the Missing Key by Marjorie Weinman Sharmat, illustrated by Marc Simont; Coward, McCann, 1981. **Awarded:** Garden State (easy to read) 1984.

Nate the Great and the Snowy Trail by Marjorie Sharmat, illustrated by Marc Simont; Coward, 1982. **Awarded:** Garden State (easy to read) 1985.

The Pizza Monster by Marjorie Sharmat and Mitchell Sharmat, illustrated by Denise Brunkus; Delacorte, 1989. **Awarded:** CRABbery 1990.

Rich Mitch by Marjorie Weinman Sharmat, illustrated by Loretta Lustig; Morrow, 1983. **Awarded:** KC Three 1985-86.

Taking Care of Melvin by Marjorie Weinman Sharmat, illustrated by Victoria Chess; Holiday House, 1980. **Awarded:** Parents' Choice (illustration) 1980.

SHARMAT, MITCHELL

The Pizza Monster by Marjorie Sharmat and Mitchell Sharmat, illustrated by Denise Brunkus; Delacorte, 1989. **Awarded:** CRABbery 1990.

SHARP, EDITH LAMBERT

Nkwala by Edith Lambert Sharp, illustrated by William Winter; Little, Brown Canada, 1958. **Awarded:** Governor-General's Literary Award 1958; International Board on Books for Young People (Canada) 1960; Little Brown Canadian 1957.

SHARP, MARGERY
The Rescuers by Margery Sharp, illustrated by Judith Brook; Collins, 1959. **Awarded:** Carnegie (commended) 1959

SHARP, PEGGY
Awarded: Evelyn Sibley Lampman 1989.

SHARPE, ELAINE
The Rainbow Serpent by Elaine Sharpe, illustrated by Jennifer Inkamala; Yipirinya School Council, 1990. **Awarded:** Australian Multicultural Children's Literature Award (Picture Book) 1991.

SHARRATT, NICK
The Story of Tracy Beaker by Jacqueline Wilson, illustrated by Nick Sharratt; Doubleday, 1991. **Awarded:** Carnegie (Highly Commended) 1991; Nottinghamshire (Oak Tree) 1992.

The Suitcase Kid by Jacqueline Wilson, illustrated by Nick Sharratt; Doubleday, 1992. **Awarded:** Children's Book Award 1993.

SHAW, CHARLES
Stay Put, Robbie McAmis by Frances G. Tunbo, illustrated by Charles Shaw; Texas Christian University Press, 1988. **Awarded:** Western Heritage 1989.

SHAW, SPENCER
Awarded: Grolier 1982.

SHEA, AGATHA
Awarded: Children's Reading Round Table 1954.

SHECTER, BEN
Sparrow Song written and illustrated by Ben Shecter; Harper, 1981. **Awarded:** Parents' Choice (illustration) 1982.

SHELDON, DYAN
The Whales' Song by Dyan Sheldon, illustrated by Gary Blythe; Hutchinson, 1990; Dial, 1991. **Awarded:** Greenaway 1990; Mother Goose (runnerup) 1991.

SHELDON, MYRTLE
Boy of the South Seas by Eunice Tietjens, illustrated by Myrtle Sheldon; Coward, 1931. **Awarded:** Newbery (honor) 1932.

SHELL, RICHARD L.
Sasha, My Friend by Barbara Corcoran, illustrated by Richard L. Shell; Atheneum, 1969. **Awarded:** Willam Allen White 1972.

SHELLEY, JOHN
The Secret in the Matchbox by Val Willis, illustrated by John Shelley; Farrar, Straus Giroux, 1988. **Awarded:** Parents' Choice (Picture Book) 1988.

SHELLEY, NOREEN
Family at the Lookout by Noreen Shelley, illustrated by R. Micklewright; Oxford, 1972. **Awarded:** Children's Book Council of Australia (book of the year) 1973.

SHEMIN, MARGARETHA
The Empty Moat by Margaretha Shemin, not illustrated; Coward, 1969. **Awarded:** Child Study 1969.

SHENTON, EDWARD
Bat: The Story of a Bull Terrier by Stephen W. Meader, illustrated by Edward Shenton; Harcourt, 1939. **Awarded:** Spring Book Festival (older honor) 1939.

Boy with a Pack by Stephen W. Meader, illustrated by Edward Shenton; Harcourt, 1939. **Awarded:** Newbery (honor) 1940.

Renfrew Flies Again by Laurie York Erskine, illustrated by Edward Shenton; Appleton Century Crofts, 1941. **Awarded:** Spring Book Festival (older honor) 1941.

Road to Down Under by Maribelle Cormack, illustrated by Edward Shenton; Appleton Century Crofts, 1944. **Awarded:** Spring Book Festival (older honor) 1944.

SHEPARD, ELIZABETH
No Bones by Elizabeth Shepard, illustrated by Ippy Patterson; Macmillan, 1988. **Awarded:** New York Academy of Sciences (Special Award to Field Guides - Younger) 1989.

SHEPARD, ERNEST H.
Awarded: University of Southern Mississippi 1970.

Crystal Mountain by Belle Dorman Rugh, illustrated by Ernest Shepard; Houghton, 1955. **Awarded:** Spring Book Festival (middle) 1955.

Enter David Garrick by Anna Bird Stewart, illustrated by Ernest H. Shepard; Lippincott, 1951. **Awarded:** Ohioana 1952.

The Reluctant Dragon by Kenneth Grahame, illustrated by Ernest H. Shepard; Holiday, 1953, 1938. **Awarded:** Lewis Carroll Shelf 1963.

The Wind in the Willows by Kenneth Grahame, illustrated by Ernest H. Shepard; Scribner, 1954, c1908. **Awarded:** Lewis Carroll Shelf 1958; Feature a Classic 1983.

The World of Christopher Robin by A. A. Milne, illustrated by E. H. Shepard; Dutton, 1958. **Awarded:** Lewis Carroll Shelf 1962.

The World of Pooh by A. A. Milne, illustrated by Ernest H. Shepard; Dutton, 1957. **Awarded:** Lewis Carroll Shelf 1958.

SHEPARD, MARY
Mary Poppins by Pamela L. Travers, illustrated by Mary Shepard; Harcourt, 1962. **Awarded:** Nene 1965.

SHEPARD, RAY ANTHONY
Sneakers by Ray Anthony Shepard, not illustrated; Dutton, 1973. **Awarded:** Council on Interracial Books (African American) 1970.

SHEPPARD, NANCY
Alitji in Dreamland adapted and translated by Nancy Sheppard, illustrated by Donna Leslie, notes by Barbara Ker Wilson; Simon & Schuster Australia, 1992. **Awarded:** Crichton 1993.

SHERBURNE, ZOA
Jennifer by Zoa Sherburne, not illustrated; Morrow, 1959. **Awarded:** Child Study 1959.

SHERIN, RAY
A Black Bear's Story by Emil Ernest Liers, illustrated by Ray Sherin; Viking, 1962. **Awarded:** Aurianne 1964.

SHERMAN, EILEEN BLUESTONE
Monday in Odessa by Eileen Bluestone Sherman, not illustrated; Jewish Publication Society, 1986. **Awarded:** Jewish Book Council (children's literature) 1987.

SHERMAN, NANCY
Gwendolyn the Miracle Hen by Nancy Sherman, illustrated by Edward Sorel; Golden, 1961. **Awarded:** Spring Book Festival (ages 4-8) 1961.

Gwendolyn and the Weathercock by Nancy Sherman, illustrated by Edward Sorel; Golden, 1963. **Awarded:** New York Times Best Illustrated 1963.

SHERRY, SYLVIA
The Liverpool Cats by Sylvia Sherry, illustrated by Ilse Koehn; Lippincott, 1969. **Awarded:** Spring Book Festival (middle honor) 1969.

SHETTERLY, ROBERT

Earthworms, Dirt and Rotten Leaves: An Exploration in Ecology by Molly McLaughlin, illustrated by Robert Shetterly; Atheneum, 1986. **Awarded:** New York Academy of Sciences (younger honor) 1987.

Project Panda Watch by Miriam Schlein, illustrated by Robert Shetterly and with photographs; Atheneum, 1984. **Awarded:** New York Academy of Sciences (younger honor) 1985.

SHETTLE, ANDREA

Flute Song Magic by Andrea Shettle, not illustrated; Avon, 1990. **Awarded:** Avon Flare Competition 1989.

SHIELDS, CHARLES

Dragon, Dragon and Other Timeless Tales by John Gardner, illustrated by Charles Shields; Knopf, 1975. **Awarded:** New York Times Notable Books 1975.

SHIFFMAN, LENA

Keeping a Christmas Secret by Phyllis R. Naylor, illustrated by Lena Shiffman; Atheneum, 1989. **Awarded:** Christopher (ages 4-7) 1990.

SHIMIN, SYMEON

Gorilla, Gorilla by Carol Fenner, illustrated by Symeon Shimin; Random House, 1973. **Awarded:** Christopher (ages 4-8) 1974.

Grandpa and Me by Patricia Lee Gauch, illustrated by Symeon Shimin; Coward, 1972. **Awarded:** New Jersey Institute of Technology 1972, 1973.

Onion John by Joseph Krumgold, illustrated by Symeon Shimin; Crowell, 1959. **Awarded:** Lewis Carroll Shelf 1960; Newbery 1960.

The Pair of Shoes by Aline Glasgow, illustrated by Symeon Shimin; Dial, 1970. **Awarded:** Child Study (special citation) 1971.

Santiago by Pura Belpre, illustrated by Symeon Shimin; Warne, 1969. **Awarded:** Art Books for Children 1973.

Send Wendell by Genevieve Gray, illustrated by Symeon Shimin; McGraw, 1974. **Awarded:** Art Books for Children 1978.

Zeely by Virginia Hamilton, illustrated by Symeon Shimin; Macmillan, 1967. **Awarded:** Nancy Bloch 1967.

SHIMIZU, KIYOSHI

Carnivorous Plants by Cynthia Overbeck, photographs by Kiyoshi Shimizu; Lerner, 1982. **Awarded:** New York Academy of Sciences (special award) 1983.

Inside an Egg by Sylvia A. Johnson, photographs by Kiyoshi Shimizu; Lerner, 1982. **Awarded:** New York Academy of Sciences (special award) 1983.

SHIPPEN, KATHERINE BINNEY

Men, Microscopes and Living Things by Katherine B. Shippen, illustrated by Anthony Ravielli; Viking, 1955. **Awarded:** International Board on Books for Young People (USA) 1956; Newbery (honor) 1956; Spring Book Festival (older honor) 1955.

New Found World by Katherine B. Shippen, illustrated by C. B. Falls; Viking, 1945. **Awarded:** Newbery (honor) 1946l Spring Book Festival (older honor) 1945.

Passage to America: The Story of the Great Migrations by Katherine B. Shippen, not illustrated; Harper, 1950. **Awarded:** Boys Club 1952.

SHIRES, LINDA M.

Fantasy, Nonsense, Parody, and the Status of the Real: The Example of Carroll by Linda M. Shires in *Victorian Poetry* 26.3 (Fall 1988). **Awarded:** Children's Literature Assn. Criticism Award (runnerup) 1989.

SHIRREFFS, GORDON D.

The Gray Sea Raiders by Gordon D. Shirreffs, not illustrated; Chilton, 1961. **Awarded:** Commonwealth Club 1961.

SHISLER, WILLIAM

Crafting with Newspapers by William Shisler and Vivienne Eisner, illustrated by Guy Brison-Stack; Sterling, 1977. **Awarded:** New Jersey Institute of Technology 1978.

SHOLOKOV, MIKHAIL

Fierce and Gentle Warriors by Mikhail Sholokov, translated by Miriam Morton, illustrated by Milton Glaser; Doubleday, 1967. **Awarded:** Spring Book Festival (older honor) 1967.

SHORE, JUNE LEWIS

What's the Matter with Wakefield? by June Lewis Shore, illustrated by David K. Stone; Abingdon, 1974. **Awarded:** Abingdon 1974.

SHORE, ROBERT

Ramlal by Albert Theodore William Simeons, illustrated by Robert Shore; Atheneum, 1965. **Awarded:** Boys Club 1966.

SHORT, JOAN

An Introduction to Insects by Bettina Bird and Joan Short, illustrated by Deborah Savin. **Awarded:** Whitley (Educational Series) 1989.

SHORTALL, LEONARD

ABC of Buses by Dorothy Shuttlesworth, illustrated by Leonard Shortall; Doubleday, 1965. **Awarded:** New Jersey Institute of Technology 1965.

The Boy Who Would not Say His Name by Elizabeth Vreekin, illustrated by Leonard Shortall; Follett, 1959. **Awarded:** Follett Beginning to Read 1959.

The Bully of Barkham Street by Mary Stolz, illustrated by Leonard Shortall; Harper & Row, 1963. **Awarded:** Boys Club 1964.

Cutlass Island by Scott Corbett, illustrated by Leonard Shortall; Atlantic-Little, 1962. **Awarded:** Edgar Allen Poe 1963.

Encyclopedia Brown Keeps the Peace by Donald J. Sobol, illustrated by Leonard Shortall; Nelson, 1969. **Awarded:** Young Readers Choice 1972.

Encyclopedia Brown Lends a Hand by Donald J. Sobol, illustrated by Leonard Shortall; Nelson, 1974. **Awarded:** Garden State Children's (young fiction) 1977.

The Hole in the Hill by Marion Seyton, illustrated by Leonard Shortall; Follett, 1960. **Awarded:** Follett Beginning to Read 1960.

Pecos Bill and the Mustang by Harold W. Felton, illustrated by Leonard Shortall; Prentice Hall, 1965. **Awarded:** Boys Club (certificate) 1966-67.

Ten Cousins by Wanda Joy Campbell, illustrated by Leonard Shortall; Dutton, 1963. **Awarded:** Steck-Vaughn 1964.

SHOTWELL, LOUISA R.

Roosevelt Grady by Louisa R. Shotwell, illustrated by Peter Burchard; World, 1963. **Awarded:** Nancy Bloch 1963; Lewis Carroll Shelf 1964; Woodward Park School 1964.

SHOWELL, ELLEN HARVEY
Cecelia and the Blue Mountain Boy by Ellen H. Showell, illustrated by Margot Tomes; Lothrop, Lee & Shepard, 1983. **Awarded:** Parents' Choice (literature) 1983.

The Ghost of Tillie Jean Cassaway by Ellen H. Showell, illustrated by Stephen Gammell; Four Winds, 1978. **Awarded:** South Carolina Children's 1982.

SHOWERS, KAY S.
Before You Were a Baby by Kay S. Showers and Paul Showers, illustrated by Ingrid Fetz; Crowell, 1968. **Awarded:** New Jersey Institute of Technology (science) 1968.

SHOWERS, PAUL
Before You Were a Baby by Paul Showers and Kay S. Showers, illustrated by Ingrid Fetz; Crowell, 1968. **Awarded:** New Jersey Institute of Technology (science) 1968.

A Drop of Blood by Paul Showers, illustrated by Don Madden; Crowell, 1967. **Awarded:** New Jersey Institute of Technology (science) 1968.

Find Out by Touching by Paul Showers, illustrated by Robert Galster; Crowell, 1961. **Awarded:** New Jersey Institute of Technology 1961.

Hear Your Heart by Paul Showers, illustrated by Joseph Low; Crowell, 1968. **Awarded:** New Jersey Institute of Technology (science) 1968.

How You Talk by Paul Showers, illustrated by Robert Galster; Crowell, 1967. **Awarded:** New Jersey Institute of Technology (science) 1968.

In the Night by Paul Showers, illustrated by Ezra Jack Keats; Crowell, 1961. **Awarded:** New Jersey Institute of Technology 1961.

The Listening Walk by Paul Showers, illustrated by Aliki; Crowell, 1961. **Awarded:** New Jersey Institute of Technology 1961.

SHREVE, SUSAN
The Flunking of Joshua T. Bates by Susan Shreve, illustrated by Diane de Groat; Knopf, 1984. **Awarded:** KC Three 1986-87.

Lucy Forever & Miss Rosetree, Shrinks by Susan Shreve, not illustrated; Henry Holt, 1987. **Awarded:** Edgar Allan Poe 1988.

SHRIVER, JEAN ADAIR
Mayflower Man by Jean Adair Shriver, not illustrated; Delacorte, 1991. **Awarded:** Delacorte Press Prize (Honorable Mention) 1989.

SHUB, ELIZABETH
About Wise Men and Simpletons: Twelve Tales from Grimm translated by Elizabeth Shub, illustrated by Nonny Hogrogian; Macmillan, 1971. **Awarded:** New York Times Notable Books 1971.

Uncle Harry by Gerlinde Schneider, adapted by Elizabeth Shub, illustrated by Lilo Fromm; Macmillan, 1972. **Awarded:** Children's Book Showcase 1973.

Zlateh the Goat and Other Stories by Isaac Bashevis Singer, translated by Elizabeth Shub, illustrated by Maurice Sendak; Harper, 1966. **Awarded:** International Board on Books for Young People (translation/United States) 1982; New York Times Best Illustrated 1966.

SHUBERT, REINOLD
I Hate Books and Other Stories by Reinold Shubert, illustrated; Vantage, 1975. **Awarded:** New Jersey Institute of Technology 1976.

I Wanna Be a Lady Plumber and Other Stories by Reinold Shubert; Vantage, 1968. **Awarded:** New Jersey Institute of Technology (science) 1968.

No Girls Allowed and Other Stories by Reinold Shubert; Vantage, 1967. **Awarded:** New Jersey Institute of Technology 1966.

The Polished Diamond and other Stories by Reinold Shubert, illustrated; Vantage, 1963. **Awarded:** New Jersey Institute of Technology (ages 6-14 short story) 1964.

Two Straws in a Soda by Reinold Shubert, not illustrated; Vantage, 1970. **Awarded:** New Jersey Institute of Technology 1971.

You Can't Measure My Love with a Teaspoon by Reinold Shubert, illustrated; Vantage, 1965. **Awarded:** New Jersey Institute of Technology (ages 6-14) 1965.

SHULEVITZ, URI
Dawn written and illustrated by Uri Shulevitz; Farrar, 1974. **Awarded:** Art Books for Children 1976, 1977, 1978; Children's Book Showcase 1975; Christopher (preschool) 1975; International Board on Books for Young People (illustration/USA) 1976; New York Times Notable Books 1974.

The Diamond Tree: Jewish Tales From Around the World by Barbara Rush and Howard Schwartz, illustrated by Uri Shulevitz; HarperCollins, 1991. **Awarded:** Sydney Taylor Book Award (Older) 1992.

The Fool of the World and the Flying Ship by Arthur Ransome, illustrated by Uri Shulevitz; Farrar, 1968. **Awarded:** Caldecott 1969.

The Golem by Isaac Bashevis Singer, illustrated by Uri Shulevitz; Farrar, 1982. **Awarded:** New York Times Notable Books 1982; Parents' Choice (literature) 1983.

Hanukah Money by Sholem Aleichem, adapted and illustrated by Uri Shulevitz; Greenwillow, 1978. **Awarded:** New York Times Best Illustrated 1978.

The Magician by I. L. Peretz, adapted and illustrated by Uri Shulevitz; Macmillan, 1973. **Awarded:** Children's Book Showcase 1974; Spring Book Festival (younger) 1973.

Soldier and Tsar in the Forest: A Russian Tale by Richard Lourie, illustrated by Uri Shulevitz; Farrar, 1972. **Awarded:** Spring Book Festival (picture book honor) 1972.

The Treasure written and illustrated by Uri Shulevitz; Farrar, 1979. **Awarded:** Caldecott (honor) 1980; New York Times Best Illustrated 1979.

SHURA, MARY FRANCES
The Search for Grissi by Mary Frances Shura, illustrated by Ted Lewin; Dodd, Mead, 1985. **Awarded:** Sandburg 1985.

SHUSTERMAN, NEAL
Shadow Club by Neal Shusterman, not illustrated; Little Brown, 1988. **Awarded:** Volunteer State Book Awards (grades 7-9) 1990.

What Daddy Did by Neal Shusterman, not illustrated; Little Brown, 1991. **Awarded:** Southern California Council (Outstanding Fiction for Young Adults) 1992.

SHUTTLESWORTH, DOROTHY
Awarded: Eva L. Gordon 1978; Rutgers 1979.

ABC of Buses by Dorothy Shuttlesworth, illustrated by Leonard Shortall; Doubleday, 1965. **Awarded:** New Jersey Institute of Technology 1965.

All Kinds of Bees by Dorothy Shuttlesworth, illustrated by SuZan Noguchi Swain; Random House, 1967. **Awarded:** New Jersey Institute of Technology 1967.

Animal Camouflage by Dorothy Shuttlesworth, illustrated by Matthew Kalmenoff; Doubleday, 1966. **Awarded:** New Jersey Institute of Technology 1966.

Farms for Today and Tomorrow: The Wonders of Food Production by Dorothy E. Shuttlesworth and Gregory J. Shuttlesworth, not illustrated; Doubleday, 1979. **Awarded:** New Jersey Institute of Technology 1980.

The Story of Ants by Dorothy Shuttlesworth, illustrated by SuZan Swain; Doubleday, 1964. **Awarded:** New Jersey Institute of Technology 1965.

SHUTTLESWORTH, GREGORY J.
Farms for Today and Tomorrow: The Wonders of Food Production by Gregory J. and Dorothy E. Shuttlesworth, not illustrated; Doubleday, 1979. **Awarded:** New Jersey Institute of Technology 1980.

SHYER, MARLENE FANTA
Welcome Home, Jellybean by Marlene Fanta Shyer, not illustrated; Granada, 1981. **Awarded:** Other Award 1982.

SIBBICK, JOHN
Creatures of Long Ago: Dinosaurs by Peggy Winston, illustrated by John Sibbick; National Geographic, 1988. **Awarded:** Redbook 1988.

SIBLEY, DON
Fiddler's Fancy by Julia Montgomery Street, illustrated by Don Sibley; Follett, 1955. **Awarded:** North Carolina AAUW 1956.

Skinny by Robert Burch, illustrated by Don Sibley; Viking, 1964. **Awarded:** Georgia Children's 1969; Spring Book Festival (middle honor) 1964.

Snow on Blueberry Mountain by Stephen W. Meader, illustrated by Don Sibley; Harcourt, 1961. **Awarded:** New Jersey Institute of Technology 1961.

SICKELS, EVELYN
Awarded: Grolier 1959.

SIDJAKOV, NICOLAS
Baboushka and the Three Kings by Ruth Robbins, illustrated by Nicolas Sidjakov; Parnassus, 1960. **Awarded:** Hans Christian Andersen (runnerup) 1962; Caldecott 1961; New York Times Best Illustrated 1960.

The Emperor and the Drummer Boy by Ruth Robbins, illustrated by Nicolas Sidjakov; Parnassus, 1962. **Awarded:** New York Times Best Illustrated 1962.

The Friendly Beasts by Laura Baker, illustrated by Nicolas Sidjakov; Parnassus, 1957. **Awarded:** New York Times Best Illustrated 1957.

SIEBERT, DIANE
Sierra by Diane Siebert, illustrated by Wendell Minor; HarperCollins, 1991. **Awarded:** John & Patricia Beatty 1992.

Train Song by Diane Siebert, illustrated by Mike Wimmer; Crowell, 1990. **Awarded:** Redbook 1990.

SIEBERT, SARA
Awarded: Grolier 1971.

SIEGAL, ARANKA
Upon the Head of a Goat: A Childhood in Hungary, 1939-1944 by Aranka Siegal, not illustrated; Farrar, Straus, Giroux, 1981.

Awarded: Boston Globe Horn Book (nonfiction) 1982; Korczak (books for children) 1982; Newbery (honor) 1982.

SIEGEL, HAL
That Was Then, This Is Now by S. E. Hinton, illustrated by Hal Siegel; Viking, 1971. **Awarded:** Massachusetts Children's (grades 7-9) 1978; Spring Book Festival (older honor) 1971.

SIEGEL, ROBERT
Whalesong by Robert Siegel, not illustrated; Crossways Books, 1981. **Awarded:** Golden Archer 1986.

SIEGEL, WILLIAM
Jumping-off Place by Marian Hurd McNeely, illustrated by William Siegel; Longmans, 1929. **Awarded:** Newbery (honor) 1930.

SIEGIEDA, JAN
Where is Bobo? by Susan Hulme, illustrated by Jan Siegieda; Methuen, 1985. **Awarded:** Best Books for Babies 1986.

SIEGL, HELEN
The Dancing Palm Tree and Other Nigerian Folktales by Barbara K. Walker, illustrated by Helen Siegl; Texas Tech University Press, 1990. **Awarded:** New York Times Best Illustrated 1990.

SIEKKINEN, RAIJA
Herra Kuningas by Raija Siekkinen, illustrated by Hannu Taina; Otava, 1986. **Awarded:** Biennale Illustrations Bratislava (grand prix) 1987.

SIGMUNDOVA, JANA
Hodina Nachove Ruze by Maria Krugernova, illustrated by Jana Sigmundova; Albatros. **Awarded:** Bologna (Graphics for Youth) 1973.

SILCOCK, SARA
Me and My Little Brain by John D. Fitzgerald, illustrated by Sara Silcock; Dent, 1974. **Awarded:** Surrey School 1976.

SILLIMAN, LELAND
Bucky Forrester by Leland Silliman, illustrated by Norman Guthrie Rudolph; Winston, 1951. **Awarded:** Boys Club 1952.

SILLS, LESLIE
Inspirations: Stories About Women Artists by Leslie Sills, illustrated with photos; Whitman, 1989. **Awarded:** Reading Magic 1989.

SILMAN, ROBERTA
Somebody Else's Child by Roberta Silman, illustrated by Chris Conover; Warne, 1976. **Awarded:** Child Study 1976.

SILVER, NORMAN
No Tigers in Africa by Norman Silver, not illustrated; Faber, 1990; Dutton, 1992. **Awarded:** Guardian (runnerup) 1991.

SILVERBERG, BARBARA
Phoenix Feathers: A Collection of Mythical Monsters by Barbara Silverberg, illustrated with old prints; Dutton, 1973. **Awarded:** Children's Book Showcase 1974.

SILVERBERG, ROBERT
The Auk, the Dodo, and the Oryx: Vanished and Vanishing Creatures by Robert Silverberg, illustrated by Jacques Hnizdovsky; Crowell, 1967. **Awarded:** Spring Book Festival (older honor) 1967.

Letters from Atlantis by Robert Silverberg, illustrated by Robert Gould; Atheneum, 1990. **Awarded:** Woodward Park 1991.

Lost Cities and Vanished Civilizations by Robert Silverberg, illustrated with photographs; Chilton, 1962. **Awarded:** Spring Book Festival (older honor) 1962.

SILVERMAN, BURT

The Globe for the Space Age by S. Carl Hirsch, illustrated by Burt Silverman; Viking, 1963. **Awarded:** Edison Mass Media (science book) 1964.

Private Eyes: Adventures with the Saturday Gang by Lee Kingman, illustrated by Burt Silverman; Doubleday, 1964. **Awarded:** Edgar Allan Poe (runnerup) 1965.

SILVERMAN, MARTIN

Where Babies Come From by Martin Silverman and Harriet Ziefert, illustrated by Claire Schumacher; Random House, 1989. **Awarded:** New Jersey Institute of Technology 1990.

SILVERSTEIN, ALVIN

Aging by Alvin Silverstein and Virginia Silverstein, illustrated with photographs; Watts, 1979. **Awarded:** New Jersey Institute of Technology 1980.

Glasses and Contact Lenses by Alvin Silverstein and Virginia Silverstein, illustrated with photos; Lippincott, 1989. **Awarded:** New Jersey Institute of Technology 1990.

Guinea Pigs: All about Them by Alvin Silverstein and Virginia Silverstein, photographs by Roger Kerkham; Lothrop, 1972. **Awarded:** New Jersey Institute of Technology 1972.

Potatoes: All about Them by Alvin Silverstein and Virginia Silverstein, illustrated by Shirley Chan; Prentice Hall, 1976. **Awarded:** New York Academy of Sciences (older honor) 1977.

The Robots Are Here by Alvin Silverstein and Virginia Silverstein, illustrated with photographs and drawings; Prentice Hall, 1983. **Awarded:** New Jersey Institute of Technology 1983.

Story of Your Foot by Alvin Silverstein and Virginia Silverstein, illustrated by Greg Wenzel; Putnam, 1987. **Awarded:** New Jersey Institute of Technology 1988.

The Story of Your Mouth by Alvin Silverstein and Virginia B. Silverstein, illustrated by Karen Ackoff; Coward McCann, 1983. **Awarded:** New Jersey Institute of Technology 1983.

Wonders of Speech by Alvin Silverstein and Virginia Silverstein, illustrated by Gordon Tomei; Morrow, 1988. **Awarded:** New York Academy of Sciences (Older Honor) 1989.

SILVERSTEIN, SHEL

A Light in the Attic written and illustrated by Shel Silverstein; Harper & Row, 1981. **Awarded:** Buckeye (grades 4-8 honor) 1983; Buckeye (grades 6-8) 1985; Garden State (younger nonfiction) 1984; George G. Stone 1984; William Allen White 1984.

Where the Sidewalk Ends written and illustrated by Shel Silverstein; Harper, 1974. **Awarded:** Michigan Young Readers (division II) 1981; New York Times Notable Books 1974; George G. Stone 1984.

SILVERSTEIN, VIRGINIA B.

Aging by Virginia Silverstein and Alvin Silverstein, illustrated with photographs; Watts, 1979. **Awarded:** New Jersey Institute of Technology 1980.

Glasses and Contact Lenses by Virginia Silverstein and Alvin Silverstein, illustrated with photos; Lippincott, 1989. **Awarded:** New Jersey Institute of Technology 1990.

Guinea Pigs: All about Them by Virginia Silverstein and Alvin Silverstein, photographs by Roger Kerkham; Lothrop, 1972. **Awarded:** New Jersey Institute of Technology 1972.

Potatoes: All about Them by Virginia Silverstein and Alvin Silverstein, illustrated by Shirley Chan; Prentice Hall, 1976. **Awarded:** New York Academy of Sciences (older honor) 1977.

The Robots Are Here by Alvin Silverstein and Virginia Silverstein, illustrated with photographs and drawings; Prentice Hall, 1983. **Awarded:** New Jersey Institute of Technology 1983.

Story of Your Foot by Virginia Silverstein and Alvin Silverstein, illustrated by Greg Wenzel; Putnam, 1987. **Awarded:** New Jersey Institute of Technology 1988.

The Story of Your Mouth by Alvin Silverstein and Virginia B. Silverstein, illustrated by Karen Ackoff; Coward McCann, 1983. **Awarded:** New Jersey Institute of Technology 1983.

Wonders of Speech by Virginia Silverstein and Alvin Silverstein, illustrated by Gordon Tomei; Morrow, 1988. **Awarded:** New York Academy of Sciences (Older Honor) 1989.

SILVERSTEIN, HERMA

Mad Mad Monday by Herma Silverstein, not illustrated; Dutton, 1988. **Awarded:** Emphasis on Reading (grades 6-8) 1989-90.

SIMBARI, NICOLA

Gennarino written and illustrated by Nicola Simbari; Lippincott, 1962. **Awarded:** New York Times Best Illustrated 1962.

SIMEONS, ALBERT THEODORE WILLIAM

Ramlal by Albert Theodore William Simeons, illustrated by Robert Shore; Atheneum, 1965. **Awarded:** Boys Club 1966.

SIMMONDS, POSY

Fred written and illustrated by Posy Simmonds; Cape, 1987; Knopf, 1987. **Awarded:** W. H. Smith (£500) 1988.

SIMMONS, MARTIN

Introducing Archaeology by Magnus Magnusson, illustrated by Martin Simmons; Bodley Head, 1972. **Awarded:** Times Educational Supplement 1972.

SIMMS, GEORGE OTTO

Brendan the Navigator by George Otto Simms, illustrated by David Rooney; O'Brien Press, 1989. **Awarded:** Bisto (Information Book) 1990.

Exploring the Book of Kells by George Otto Simms, illustrated by David Rooney; O'Brien Press, 1988. **Awarded:** Bisto (Information Book) 1990; Reading Association of Ireland (Special Merit) 1989.

SIMON, CHARLIE MAY

The Far-away Trail by Charlie May Simon, illustrated by Howard Simon; Dutton, 1940. **Awarded:** Spring Book Festival (younger honor) 1940.

Joe Mason, Apprentice to Audubon by Charlie May Simon, illustrated by Henry C. Pitz; Dutton, 1946. **Awarded:** Boys Club 1948.

Martin Buber: Wisdom in our Time by Charlie May Simon, illustrated with photographs; Dutton, 1969. **Awarded:** Jewish Book Council 1969.

SIMON, HILDA

Dragonflies written and illustrated by Hilda Simon; Viking, 1972. **Awarded:** Children's Book Showcase 1973.

SIMON, HOWARD

Chucho: The Boy with the Good Name by Eula Mark Phillips, illustrated by Howard Simon; Follett, 1957. **Awarded:** Charles W. Follett 1957.

The Far-away Trail by Charlie May Simon, illustrated by Howard Simon; Dutton, 1940. **Awarded:** Spring Book Festival (younger honor) 1940.

SIMON, NOEL

The Giant Panda written and illustrated by Xuqi Jin and Markus Kappeler, translated by Noel Simon; Putnam, 1986. **Awarded:** New York Academy of Sciences (younger honor) 1987.

SIMON, NORMA

The Daddy Days by Norma Simon, illustrated by Abner Graboff; Abelard-Schuman, 1958. **Awarded:** New York Times Best Illustrated 1958.

The Wet World by Norma Simon, illustrated by Jane Miller; Lippincott, 1954. **Awarded:** New York Times Best Illustrated 1954.

SIMON, SEYMOUR

Awarded: Eva L. Gordon 1984; Washington Post/Children's Book Guild Nonfiction 1993.

Hidden Worlds: Pictures of the Invisible by Seymour Simon, illustrated with photographs; Morrow, 1983. **Awarded:** New York Academy of Sciences (younger honor) 1984.

Icebergs and Glaciers by Seymour Simon, illustrated; Morrow, 1987. **Awarded:** New York Academy of Sciences (Younger) 1988.

The Paper Airplane Book by Seymour Simon, illustrated by Byron Barton; Viking, 1971. **Awarded:** Children's Book Showcase 1972.

Volcanoes by Seymour Simon, illustrated with photos; Morrow, 1988. **Awarded:** Garden State Children's (Younger Nonfiction) 1991.

Whales by Seymour Simon, illustrated with photos; Crowell, 1989. **Awarded:** Book Can Develop Empathy 1991; New York Times Best Illustrated 1989.

SIMONSEN, THORDIS

You May Plow Here: The Narrative of Sarah Brooks by Thordis Simonsen, illustrated with photos; Norton, 1986. **Awarded:** Woodson (Outstanding Merit) 1988.

SIMONT, MARC

The Dallas Titans Get Ready for Bed by Karla Kuskin, illustrated by Marc Simont; Harper & Row, 1986. **Awarded:** Parents' Choice (literature) 1986.

The Happy Day by Ruth Krauss, illustrated by Marc Simont; Harper & Row, 1949. **Awarded:** Caldecott (honor) 1950.

In the Year of the Boar and Jackie Robinson by Betty Lord, illustrated by Marc Simont; Harper, 1986. **Awarded:** Jefferson Cup 1985.

Jareb by Miriam Powell, illustrated by Marc Simont; Crowell, 1952. **Awarded:** Child Study 1952; Spring Book Festival (ages 8-12 honor) 1952.

Many Moons by James Thurber, illustrated by Marc Simont; Harcourt Brace Jovanovich, 1990. **Awarded:** Redbook 1990.

Nate the Great and the Missing Key by Marjorie Weinman Sharmat, illustrated by Marc Simont; Coward, McCann, Geoghegan, 1981. **Awarded:** Garden State (easy to read) 1984.

Nate the Great and the Snowy Trail by Marjorie Sharmat, illustrated by Marc Simont; Coward, 1982. **Awarded:** Garden State (easy to read) 1985.

The Philharmonic Gets Dressed by Karla Kuskin, illustrated by Marc Simont; Harper, 1982. **Awarded:** New York Times Notable Books 1982.

A Space Story by Karla Kuskin, illustrated by Marc Simont; Harper, 1978. **Awarded:** New York Academy of Sciences (younger) 1980.

The Star in the Pail by David McCord, illustrated by Marc Simont; Little, 1975. **Awarded:** National Book Award (finalist) 1976.

Ten Copycats in a Boat and Other Riddles by Alvin Schwartz, illustrated by Marc Simont; Harper, 1980. **Awarded:** New Jersey Institute of Technology 1981.

Top Secret by John Reynolds Gardiner, illustrated by Marc Simont; Little Brown, 1984. **Awarded:** PEN Center USA West 1986.

The Trail Driving Rooster by Fred Gipson, illustrated by Marc Simont; Harper, 1955. **Awarded:** Steck-Vaughn 1957.

A Tree Is Nice by Janice May Udry, illustrated by Marc Simont; Harper, 1956. **Awarded:** Caldecott 1957.

SIMPSON, CATHY

Groosham Grange by Anthony Horowitz, illustrated by Cathy Simpson; Methuen, 1988. **Awarded:** Lancashire County Library 1989.

SIMPSON, GRETCHEN DOW

Gretchen's ABC written and illustrated by Gretchen Dow Simpson; HarperCollins, 1991. **Awarded:** Parents' Choice (Story Book) 1991.

SIMPSON, KATE

But No Cheese! by Saviour Pirotta, illustrated by Kate Simpson; Hodder & Stoughton, 1992. **Awarded:** Mother Goose (honorable mention) 1993.

SIMS, GRAEME

Rufus the Fox written and illustrated by Graeme Sims; Warne, 1983. **Awarded:** Mother Goose (runnerup) 1984.

SINETI, DON

The Whale Watchers' Guide by Robert Gardner, illustrated by Don Sineti; Messner, 1984. **Awarded:** New York Academy of Sciences (older honor) 1985.

SINGER, ISAAC BASHEVIS

Awarded: Sydney Taylor Book Award (general contributions) 1971.

Alone in the Wild Forest by Isaac Bashevis Singer, illustrated by Margot Zemach; Farrar, 1971. **Awarded:** Children's Book Showcase 1972.

A Day of Pleasure: Stories of a Boy Growing up in Warsaw by Isaac Bashevis Singer, illustrated by Roman Vishniac; Farrar, 1969. **Awarded:** National Book Awards 1970.

The Fearsome Inn by Isaac Bashevis Singer, illustrated by Nonny Hogrogian; Scribner, 1967. **Awarded:** Newbery (honor) 1968.

The Golem by Isaac Bashevis Singer, illustrated by Uri Shulevitz; Farrar, 1982. **Awarded:** New York Times Notable Books 1982; Parents' Choice (literature) 1983.

The Power of Light: Eight Stories for Hanukkah by Isaac Bashevis Singer, illustrated by Irene Lieblich; Farrar, 1980. **Awarded:** Present Tense 1980.

Pundak Ha-Eima by Isaac Bashevis Singer, translated by Yehuda Meltzer; Adam, 1980. (original English: *The Fearsome Inn*) **Awarded:** International Board on Books for Young People (translation/Israel) 1982.

Stories for Children by Isaac Bashevis Singer, not illustrated; Farrar, Straus, Giroux, 1984. **Awarded:** New York Times Notable 1984.

When Schlemiel Went to Warsaw and Other Stories by Isaac Bashevis Singer, illustrated by Margot Zemach; Farrar, 1968. **Awarded:** Newbery (honor) 1969.

Zlateh the Goat and Other Stories by Isaac Bashevis Singer, translated by Elizabeth Shub, illustrated by Maurice Sendak; Harper, 1966. **Awarded:** International Board on Books for Young People (honour list/translation/United States) 1982; New York Times Best Illustrated 1966; Newbery (honor) 1967.

SINGER, MARILYN
It Can't Hurt Forever by Marilyn Singer, illustrated by Leigh Grant; Harper, 1978; Harper Trophy, 1981, c1978. **Awarded:** Maud Hart Lovelace 1983.

Turtle in July by Marilyn Singer, illustrated by Jerry Pinkney; Macmillan, 1989. **Awarded:** New York Times Best Illustrated 1989.

SINGMASTER, ELSIE
Swords of Steel: The Story of a Gettysburg Boy by Elsie Singmaster, illustrated by David Hendrickson; Houghton, 1933. **Awarded:** Newbery (honor) 1934.

SINNEMA, JAC
Vertel Het uw Kinderen by Jac Sinnema and C. M. de Vries; Nederlandsche Zondacsschool Vereniging. **Awarded:** Bologna (Graphics for Youth) 1970.

SIROVATKA, OLDRICH
Slavische Marchen by Vladislav Stanovsky and Oldrich Sirovatka, illustrated by Maria Zelibska; Artia. **Awarded:** Bologna (Graphics for Youth) 1972.

SIS, PETER
Beach Ball written and illustrated by Peter Sis; Greenwillow, 1990. **Awarded:** New York Times Best Illustrated 1990.

Follow the Dream written and illustrated by Peter Sis; Knopf, 1991. **Awarded:** New York Times Best Illustrated 1991.

Komodo! by Peter Sis; Greenwillow, 1993. **Awarded:** Boston Globe (illustration honor) 1993.

The Midnight Horse by Sid Fleischman, illustrated by Peter Sis; Greenwillow, 1990. **Awarded:** Parents' Choice (Story Book) 1990.

An Ocean World written and illustrated by Peter Sis; Greenwillow, 1992. **Awarded:** Parents Choice (Picture Book) 1992.

Rainbow Rhino written and illustrated by Peter Sis; Knopf, 1987. **Awarded:** New York Times Best Illustrated 1987.

The Scarebird by Sid Fleischman, illustrated by Peter Sis; Greenwillow, 1988. **Awarded:** Redbook 1988.

The Whipping Boy by Sid Fleischman, illustrated by Peter Sis; Greenwillow, 1986. **Awarded:** Golden Archer 1987; Nene 1992; Newbery 1987; Charlie May Simon 1988-89.

SISLEY, E. L.
You and Your Brain by Judith Groch, illustrated by E. L. Sisley; Harper, 1963. **Awarded:** Edison Mass Media (science book for youth) 1964.

SIVERS, BRENDA
The Snailman by Brenda Sivers, illustrated by Shirley Hughes; Little Brown, 1978. **Awarded:** Little Brown Canadian 1977.

SKARDINSKI, STAN
You Can't Be Timid with a Trumpet: Notes from the Orchestra by Betty Lou English, illustrated with photographs by Betty Lou English, illustrated by Stan Skardinski; Lothrop, 1980. **Awarded:** Boston Globe Horn Book (nonfiction honor) 1981.

SKINNER, CLEMENTINE
Awarded: Children's Reading Round Table 1976.

SKOGSBERG, INGVAR
Dansa Pa Min Grav (original English *Dance on my Grave*) by Aidan Chambers, translated by Ingvar Skogsberg; Awe/Gebbers, 1983. **Awarded:** International Board on Books for Young People (translation/Sweden) 1984.

SKOLNICK, ARNOLD
Duey's Tale by Pearl Bailey, photographs by Arnold Skolnick and Gary Azon; Harcourt, 1975. **Awarded:** Coretta Scott King 1976.

SKORPIL, JUDY
From Hand Ax to Laser: Man's Growing Mastery of Energy by John Purcell, illustrated by Judy Skorpil; Vanguard, 1982. **Awarded:** New York Academy of Sciences (Elliott Montroll special award) 1984.

SKURZYNSKI, GLORIA
Almost the Real Thing: Simulation in Your High Tech World by Gloria Skurzynski, illustrated with photos; Bradbury, 1991. **Awarded:** American Institute of Physics 1992.

Bionic Parts for People: The Real Story of Artificial Organs and Replacement Parts by Gloria Skurzynski, illustrated by Frank Schwarz; Four Winds, 1978. **Awarded:** Golden Kite (nonfiction honor) 1978.

Lost in the Devil's Desert by Gloria Skurzynski, illustrated by Joseph M. Scrofani; Lothrop, Lee & Shepard, 1982. **Awarded:** Utah Children's 1984.

The Tempering by Gloria Skurzynski, not illustrated; Clarion, 1983. **Awarded:** Golden Kite (fiction) 1983.

Trapped in Sliprock Canyon by Gloria Skurzynski, illustrated by Daniel San Souci; Lothrop, Lee & Shepard, 1984. **Awarded:** Western Writers 1985.

What Happened in Hamelin? by Gloria Skurzynski, not illustrated; Four Winds, 1979. **Awarded:** Christopher (ages 9-12) 1980.

SLADKUS, INGRID
Monica: The Story of a Young Magazine Apprentice by Ingrid Sladkus and Alberta Eiseman, not illustrated; Dodd, Mead, 1957. **Awarded:** Calling All Girls - Dodd, Mead 1957.

SLATE, JOSEPH
Awarded: Ohioana (citation) 1988.

SLEATOR, WILLIAM
The Angry Moon by William Sleator, illustrated by Blair Lent; Atlantic-Little, 1970. **Awarded:** Boston Globe Horn Book (illustration honor) 1971; Caldecott (honor) 1971.

Interstellar Pig by William Sleator, not illustrated; Dutton, 1984. **Awarded:** California Young Reader (Young Adult) 1988.

Into the Dream by William Sleator, illustrated by Ruth Sanderson; Dutton, 1979; Scholastic, 1979. **Awarded:** CRABbery (honor) 1980.

SLEPIAN, JANICE

The Alfred Summer by Janice Slepian, not illustrated; Macmillan, 1980. **Awarded:** Boston Globe Horn Book (fiction honor) 1980; New Jersey Institute of Technology 1981.

The Night of the Bozos by Jan Slepian, not illustrated; Dutton, 1983. **Awarded:** New Jersey Institute of Technology 1983.

Something Beyond Paradise by Jan Slepian, not illustrated; Philomel, 1987. **Awarded:** New Jersey Institute of Technology 1988.

SLIER, DEBORAH

Make a Joyful Sound edited by Deborah Slier, illustrated by Cornelius Van Wright and Ying-Hwa Hu; Checkerboard, 1991. **Awarded:** Hungry Mind (Middle Readers/Fiction) 1992.

SLOAN, ELLEN

ABC Fire Dogs by Ida DeLage, illustrated by Ellen Sloan; Garrard, 1977. **Awarded:** New Jersey Institute of Technology 1978.

Frannie's Flower by Ida DeLage, illustrated by Ellen Sloan; Garrard, 1979. **Awarded:** New Jersey Institute of Technology 1980.

SLOAN, PETER

Australian Animals by Peter Sloan, illustrated by Ross Latham; Mathuen Australia, 1983. **Awarded:** Whitley Awards 1984.

SLOBODKIN, LOUIS

The Hundred Dresses by Eleanor Estes, illustrated by Louis Slobodkin; Harcourt, 1944. **Awarded:** Newbery (honor) 1945.

Many Moons by James Thurber, illustrated by Louis Slobodkin; Harcourt, 1943. **Awarded:** Caldecott 1944.

The Middle Moffat by Eleanor Estes, illustrated by Louis Slobodkin; Harcourt, 1942. **Awarded:** Newbery (honor) 1943.

The Moffats by Eleanor Estes, illustrated by Louis Slobodkin; Harcourt, 1941. **Awarded:** Lewis Carroll Shelf 1961.

Rufus M. by Eleanor Estes, illustrated by Louis Slobodkin; Harcourt, 1943. **Awarded:** Newbery (honor) 1944.

SLOBODKINA, ESPHYR

Caps for Sale: A Tale of a Peddler, some Monkeys and their Monkey Business written and illustrated by Esphyr Slobodkina; Scott, 1947. **Awarded:** Lewis Carroll Shelf 1958.

The Little Cowboy by Margaret Wise Brown, illustrated by Esphyr Slobodkina; Scott, 1949, 1948. **Awarded:** Spring Book Festival (younger honor) 1949.

SLOCUM, JERRY

Puzzles Old and New by Jerry Slocum and Jack Botermans, text by Carla van Splunteren and Tony Burrett; Plenary Publications International, distributed by Univ. of Washington Press, 1986. **Awarded:** New York Academy of Sciences (prize as an exhibition catalogue of excellence and extraordinary interest) 1987.

SLOTE, ALFRED

Clone Catcher by Alfred Slote, illustrated by Elizabeth Slote; Lippincott, 1982. **Awarded:** Edgar Allan Poe (runnerup) 1983.

SLOTE, ELIZABETH

Clone Catcher by Alfred Slote, illustrated by Elizabeth Slote; Lippincott, 1982. **Awarded:** Edgar Allan Poe (runnerup) 1983.

SLOTE, ROBERT

My Robot Buddy by Robert Slote, illustrated by Joel Schick; Lippincott, 1975. **Awarded:** Nene 1981.

SMALL, DAVID

As: A Surfeit of Similes by Norton Juster, illustrated by David Small; Morrow, 1989. **Awarded:** Parents' Choice (Picture Book) 1989.

Box and Cox by Grace Chetwin, illustrated by David Small; Bradbury, 1990. **Awarded:** Parents' Choice (Picture Book) 1990.

Company's Coming by Arthur Yorinks, illustrated by David Small; Crown, 1988. **Awarded:** Redbook 1988.

Imogene's Antlers written and illustrated by David Small; Crown, 1985. **Awarded:** Parents' Choice (literature) 1985.

SMALL, ERNEST

see LENT, BLAIR

SMALLEY, JANET

The School Train by Helen Acker, illustrated by Janet Smalley; Abelard, 1953. **Awarded:** Spring Book Festival (8-12 honor) 1953.

SMARIDGE, NORAH

Manners Matter by Norah Smaridge, illustrated by Imbior Kudrna; Abingdon, 1980. **Awarded:** New Jersey Institute of Technology 1981.

The Mysteries in the Commune by Norah Smaridge, illustrated by Robert Handville; Dodd, Mead, 1982. **Awarded:** New Jersey Institute of Technology 1983.

Only Silly People Waste by Norah Smaridge, illustrated by Mary Carrithers; Abingdon, 1973. **Awarded:** New Jersey Institute of Technology 1977.

Scary Things by Norah Smaridge, illustrated by Ruth Van Sciver; Abingdon, 1969. **Awarded:** New Jersey Institute of Technology 1969.

School Is not a Missile Range by Norah Smaridge, illustrated by Ron Martin; Abingdon, 1977. **Awarded:** New Jersey Institute of Technology 1978.

The Secret of the Brownstone House by Norah A. Smaridge, illustrated by Michael Hampshire; Dodd, Mead, 1977. **Awarded:** New Jersey Institute of Technology 1978.

The Story of Cake by Norah Smaridge, illustrated with photographs; Abingdon, 1979. **Awarded:** New Jersey Institute of Technology 1980.

Watch Out! by Norah Smaridge, illustrated by Susan Perl; Abingdon, 1965. **Awarded:** New Jersey Institute of Technology (ages K-3) 1965.

What a Silly Thing to Do by Norah Smaridge, illustrated by Susan Perl; Abingdon, 1967. **Awarded:** New Jersey Institute of Technology 1967, 1968.

What's on Your Plate? by Norah Smaridge, illustrated by C. Imbior Kudrna; Abingdon Press, 1982. **Awarded:** New Jersey Institute of Technology 1983.

The World of Chocolate by Norah Smaridge, illustrated by Don Lambo; Messner, 1969. **Awarded:** New Jersey Institute of Technology 1969.

SMEDMAN, M. SARAH

Out of the Depths to Joy by M. Sarah Smedman in *Triumphs of the Human Spirit in Children's Literature* edited by Francelia Butler & Richard Rotert, 1986. **Awarded:** Children's Literature Assn. Criticism (runnerup) 1987.

SMEDLEY, CHRIS
Pongwiffy and the Spell of the Year by Kaye Umansky, illustrated by Chris Smedley; Viking, 1992. **Awarded:** Nottinghamshire (oak tree) 1993.

SMEE, DAVID
The Blue Hawk by Peter Dickinson, illustrated by David Smee; Gollancz, 1976. **Awarded:** Carnegie (commended) 1976; Guardian 1977.

Chance, Luck and Destiny by Peter Dickinson, illustrated by David Smee and Victor Ambrus; Atlantic-Little, 1976. **Awarded:** Boston Globe Horn Book (nonfiction) 1977.

Dancing Bear by Peter Dickinson, illustrated by David Smee; Gollancz, 1972. **Awarded:** Carnegie (commended) 1972.

SMITH, AGNES
An Edge of the Forest by Agnes Smith, illustrated by Roberta Moynihan; Viking, 1959. **Awarded:** Aurianne 1961; Lewis Carroll Shelf 1966; Spring Book Festival (older) 1959.

SMITH, ALISON
Reserved for Mark Anthony Crowder by Alison Smith, not illustrated; Dutton, 1978. **Awarded:** International Reading Assn. 1979.

SMITH, ALVIN
Mystery of the Fat Cat by Frank Bonham, illustrated by Alvin Smith; Dutton, 1968. **Awarded:** Edgar Allan Poe (runnerup) 1969.

Shadow of a Bull by Maia Wojciechowska, illustrated by Alvin Smith; Atheneum, 1964. Newbery 1965; Spring Book Festival (older honor) 1964.

SMITH, BEATRICE S.
Awarded: Council for Wisconsin Writers (juvenile) 1973.

The Babe: Mildred Didrickson Zaharias by Beatrice S. Smith, illustrated with photographs; Raintree, 1976. **Awarded:** Council of Wisconsin Writers (juvenile runnerup) 1977.

The Case of the Missing Bills by Beatrice S. Smith, illustrated by George Overlie; Carolrhoda, 1976. **Awarded:** Council of Wisconsin Writers (picture book runnerup) 1977.

SMITH, CATRIONA
The Long Dive written and illustrated by Catriona Smith and Ray Smith; Atheneum/Cape, 1979. **Awarded:** New York Times Best Illustrated 1979.

SMITH, CICELY FOX
The Valiant Sailor by C. Fox Smith, illustrated by Neville Dear; Criterion, 1957. **Awarded:** Boys Club 1958.

SMITH, CRAIG
The Cabbage Patch Fib by Paul Jennings, illustrated by Craig Smith; Puffin, 1988. **Awarded:** Young Australian Best Book (Fiction Younger Reader) 1989.

Sister Madge's Book of Nuns by Doug MacLeod, illustrated by Craig Smith; Omnibus, 1986. **Awarded:** Children's Book Council of Australia (book of the year younger honor) 1987; KOALA (Secondary) 1988; Young Australian Best Book (Fiction Younger Reader) 1987.

Where's Mum? by Libby Gleeson, illustrated by Craig Smith; Omnibus, 1992. **Awarded:** Children's Book Council of Australia (Picture Book of the Year honor) 1993.

Whistle Up the Chimney by Craig Smith and Nan Hunt, illustrated by Craig Smith; Collins, 1982. **Awarded:** New South Wales State Literary Awards (Children's) 1982.

SMITH, DAVID EUGENE
The Wonderful Wonders of One-Two-Three by David Eugene Smith, illustrated by Barbara Irvins; McFarlane, Warde & McFarlane, 1937. **Awarded:** Spring Book Festival (younger honor) 1937.

SMITH, DORIS BUCHANAN
Return to Bitter Creek by Doris Buchanan Smith, not illustrated; Viking Kestrel, 1986. **Awarded:** Parents' Choice (literature) 1986.

A Taste of Blackberries by Doris Buchanan Smith, illustrated by Charles Robinson; Crowell, 1973. **Awarded:** Child Study 1973; Georgia Children's 1975; Sue Hefly 1979.

Tough Chauncey by Doris Buchanan Smith, illustrated by Michael Eagle; Morrow, 1974. **Awarded:** Boston Globe Horn Book (text honor) 1974.

SMITH, E. BOYD
The Farm Book written and illustrated by E. Boyd Smith, introduction by Barbara Bader; Houghton, Mifflin, 1982, c1938. **Awarded:** Parents' Choice (illustration) 1982.

SMITH, EDESSE PEERY
Pokes of Gold by Edesse Peery Smith, not illustrated; Dodd, Mead, 1958. **Awarded:** Boys Life 1957.

SMITH, ELWOOD H.
Zounds! The Kids' Guide to Sound Making by Frederick R. Newman, illustrated by Elwood H. Smith; Random House, 1983. **Awarded:** New York Academy of Sciences (older honor) 1984.

SMITH, EMMA
No Way of Telling by Emma Smith, illustrated with maps; Bodley Head, 1972; Atheneum, 1972. **Awarded:** Boston Globe Horn Book (text honor) 1973; Carnegie (commended) 1972.

Out of Hand by Emma Smith, illustrated by Antony Maitland; Harcourt, 1964. **Awarded:** Spring Book Festival (middle honor) 1964.

SMITH, EUNICE YOUNG
Shoon: Wild Pony of the Moors written and illustrated by Eunice Young Smith; Bobbs-Merrill, 1965. **Awarded:** Indiana Authors Day (children) 1966.

SMITH, HELEN
The Inch Boy adapted by Helen Smith, illustrated by Junko Morimoto; Collins, 1984; Viking Kestrel, 1986. **Awarded:** Children's Book Council of Australia (picture book of the year highly commended) 1985.

Kojuro and the Bears adapted by Helen Smith, illustrated by Junko Morimoto; Collins, 1986. **Awarded:** Ashton Scholastic 1987; Children's Book Council of Australia (picture book of the year) 1987.

A Piece of Straw adapted by Helen Smith, illustrated by Junko Morimoto; Collins, 1985. **Awarded:** Children's Book Council of Australia (picture book of the year highly commended) 1986.

The White Crane written and illustrated by Junko Morimoto, adapted by Helen Smith; Collins, 1985. **Awarded:** Children's Book Council of Australia (picture book of the year commended) 1984.

SMITH, HOWARD GODWIN
Tracking the Unearthly Creatures of Marsh and Pond by Howard G. Smith, illustrated by Anne Marie Jauss; Abingon, 1972. **Awarded:** Christopher (ages 8-12) 1973.

SMITH, HUGH

Reflections on a Gift of Watermelon Pickle and Other Modern Verse by Hugh Smith, Edward Lueders, and Stephen Dunning, illustrated with photographs; Lothrop Lee & Shepard, 1966. **Awarded:** Lewis Carroll Shelf 1968.

SMITH, JESSIE WILLCOX

Little Women by Louisa May Alcott, illustrated by Jessie Willcox Smith; Little, Brown, 1968, c1868. **Awarded:** Lewis Carroll Shelf 1969.

SMITH, JOAN

The Adventures of Nimble, Rumble, and Tumble by Joan Smith, not illustrated; Paul Hamilton, 1950. **Awarded:** Esther Glen 1950.

SMITH, JOSEPH A.

Jim Ugly by Sid Fleischman, illustrated by Joseph A. Smith; Greenwillow, 1992. **Awarded:** Parents Choice (Story Book) 1992.

SMITH, LANE

The Big Pets written and illustrated by Lane Smith; Viking, 1991. **Awarded:** Biennale Illustrations Bratislava (Golden Apple) 1991.

Glasses: Who Needs 'Em? written and illustrated by Lane Smith; Viking, 1991. **Awarded:** Parents' Choice (Picture Book) 1991.

Halloween ABC by Eve Merriam, illustrated by Lane Smith; Macmillan, 1987. **Awarded:** New York Times Best Illustrated 1987.

The Stinky Cheese Man and Other Fairly Stupid Tales by Jon Scieszka, illustrated by Lane Smith; Viking, 1992. **Awarded:** Caldecott (honor) 1993; **Awarded:** New York Times Best Illustrated 1992.

SMITH, LAWRENCE BEALL

Me and Caleb by Franklyn E. Meyer, illustrated by Lawrence B. Smith; Follett, 1962. **Awarded:** Charles W. Follett 1962.

SMITH, LILLIAN

Awarded: Women's National Book Assn. 1945.

SMITH, MARY ROGERS

Awarded: Southern California Council (distinguished contribution to the field of children's literature) 1966.

SMITH, MAVIS

Good Night, Jessie! by Harriet Ziefert, illustrated by Mavis Smith; Random House, 1987. **Awarded:** New Jersey Institute of Technology 1988.

Hurry Up, Jessie! by Harriet Ziefert, illustrated by Mavis Smith; Random House, 1987. **Awarded:** New Jersey Institute of Technology 1988.

SMITH, MIRIAM

Annie & Moon by Miriam Smith, illustrated by Lesley Moyes; Mallinson Rendel, 1988. **Awarded:** AIM Children's Book Award (Picture Book) 1990.

SMITH, RAY

The Long Dive written and illustrated by Ray Smith and Catriona Smith; Atheneum/Cape, 1979. **Awarded:** New York Times Best Illustrated 1979.

SMITH, ROBERT

How the Kookaburra got His Laugh by Aviva Layton, illustrated by Robert Smith; McClelland & Stewart, 1976. **Awarded:** IODE 1976.

SMITH, ROBERT KIMMEL

Chocolate Fever by Robert Kimmel Smith, illustrated by Gioia Fiammenghi; Dell, 1978. **Awarded:** Massachusetts Children's (elementary) 1980.

Jelly Belly by Robert Kimmel Smith, illustrated by Bob Jones; Delacorte, 1981. **Awarded:** Nene 1985; South Carolina Children's 1984; Young Hoosier (grades 4-6) 1984.

The Squeaky Wheel by Robert Kimmel Smith, not illustrated; Delacorte, 1990. **Awarded:** Parents' Choice (Story Book) 1990.

The War with Grandpa by Robert Kimmel Smith, illustrated by Richard Lauter; Delacorte, 1984. **Awarded:** California Young Reader (Intermediate) 1990; Emphasis on Reading (grades 3-5) 1988-89; Dorothy Canfield Fisher 1986; Georgia Children's Book Award 1989; Golden Sower (grades 4-6) 1987; Parents' Choice (literature) 1984; South Carolina Children's 1986; Mark Twain 1987; Volunteer State Book Awards 1988; William Allan White 1987; Young Hoosier (grades 4-6) 1987; Young Reader's Choice 1987.

SMITH, SAMANTHA

Journey to the Soviet Union by Samantha Smith, illustrated with photographs; Little Brown, 1985. **Awarded:** Jane Addams (honor) 1986.

SMUCKER, ANNA EGAN

No Star Nights by Anna Egan Smucker, illustrated by Steve Johnson; Knopf, 1989. **Awarded:** International Reading Assn. (Younger) 1990.

SMUCKER, BARBARA CLAASSEN

Awarded: Vicky Metcalf 1988.

Les Chemins Secrets de la Liberte by Barbara Smucker, translated by Paule C. Daveluy, illustrated by Tom McNeely; Pierre Tisseyire, 1978. **Awarded:** International Board on Books for Young People (translation/Canada) 1980.

Days of Terror by Barbara Claassen Smucker, not illustrated; Herald Press, 1979. **Awarded:** Governor General (author) 1979; Ruth Schwartz 1980.

Incredible Jumbo by Barbara Smucker, not illustrated; Viking, 1990. **Awarded:** National Chapter of Canada IODE Violet Downey 1990.

Underground to Canada by Barbara Smucker; Clarke, Irwin, 1977. **Awarded:** Canadian Library Assn. (runnerup) 1978.

SNEDEKER, CAROLINE DALE

Downright Dencey by Caroline Dale Snedeker, illustrated by Maginel W. Barney; Doubleday, 1927. **Awarded:** Newbery (honor) 1928.

Forgotten Daughter by Caroline Dale Snedeker, illustrated by Dorothy P. Lathrop; Doubleday, 1933. **Awarded:** Newbery (honor) 1934.

SNEVE, VIRGINIA DRIVING HAWK

Jimmy Yellow Hawk by Virginia Driving Hawk Sneve, illustrated by Oren Lyons; Holiday House, 1972. **Awarded:** Council on Interracial Books (American Indian) 1970.

SNOW, DOROTHEA J.

Sequoyah, Young Cherokee Guide by Dorothea J. Snow, illustrated by Frank Giacoia; Bobbs-Merrill, 1960. **Awarded:** Friends of American Writers 1961.

Tomahawk Claim by Dorothea J. Snow, illustrated with maps; Bobbs-Merrill, 1968. **Awarded:** Indiana Authors Day (children) 1969.

SNOW, EDWARD ROWE
True Tales of Buried Treasure by Edward Rowe Snow, illustrated with photographs and maps; Dodd, Mead, 1951. **Awarded:** Boys Club 1953.

SNOW, RICHARD
The Iron Road: A Portrait of American Railroading by Richard Snow, photographs by David Plowden; Four Winds, 1978. **Awarded:** Boston Globe Horn Book (nonfiction honor) 1979.

SNOW, RICHARD F.
Freelon Starbird: Being a Narrative of the Extraordinary Hardships Suffered by an Accidental Soldier in a Beaten Army during the Autumn and Winter of 1776 by Richard F. Snow, illustrated by Ben F. Stahl; Houghton Mifflin, 1976. **Awarded:** New York Times Notable Books 1976.

SNYDER, ANDREW
Anthony Wayne: Washington's General by Cateau DeLeeuw and Adele DeLeeuw, illustrated by Andrew Snyder; Westminster, 1974. **Awarded:** New Jersey Institute of Technology 1975, 1976.

SNYDER, ANNE
First Step by Anne Snyder, not illustrated; Holt, 1975. **Awarded:** Friends of American Writers (older) 1976.

SNYDER, CAROL
Ike and Mama and the Block Wedding by Carol Snyder, illustrated by Charles Robinson; Coward, 1979. **Awarded:** Sydney Taylor Book Award 1980.

Ike and Mama and the Seven Surprises by Carol Snyder, illustrated by Charles Robinson; Lothrop, Lee & Shepard, 1985. **Awarded:** Sydney Taylor Book Award (older) 1986.

Ike and Mama and the Trouble at School by Carol Snyder, illustrated by Charles Robinson; Coward McCann, 1983. **Awarded:** New Jersey Institute of Technology 1983.

Leave Me Alone, Ma by Carol Snyder, not illustrated; Bantam Books, 1987. **Awarded:** New Jersey Institute of Technology 1988.

Memo: To Myself When I Have a Teenage Kid by Carol Snyder, not illustrated; Coward McCann, 1983. **Awarded:** New Jersey Institute of Technology 1983.

SNYDER, DIANNE
The Boy of the Three-Year Nap by Dianne Snyder, illustrated by Allen Say; Houghton Mifflin, 1988. **Awarded:** Boston Globe (Picture Book) 1988; Caldecott (honor) 1989; Parents' Choice (Story Book) 1988; Reading Magic Award 1988.

SNYDER, JEROME
Umbrellas, Hats, and Wheels by Ann Rand and Jerome Snyder, illustrated by Jerome Snyder; Harcourt, 1961. **Awarded:** New York Times Best Illustrated 1961.

SNYDER, ZILPHA KEATLEY
The Birds of Summer by Zilpha Keatley Snyder, not illustrated Atheneum, 1983. **Awarded:** Parents' Choice (literature) 1983; PEN Center USA West 1983.

The Changeling by Zilpha Keatley Snyder, illustrated by Alton Raible; Atheneum, 1970. **Awarded:** Christopher (ages 8-12) 1971.

The Egypt Game by Zilpha Keatley Snyder, illustrated by Alton Raible; Atheneum, 1967. **Awarded:** Lewis Carroll Shelf 1970; Newbery (honor) 1968; Spring Book Festival (middle) 1967; George G. Stone 1973.

A Fabulous Creature by Zilpha Keatley Snyder, not illustrated; Atheneum, 1981. **Awarded:** New York Times Notable Books 1981.

The Headless Cupid by Zilpha Keatley Snyder, illustrated by Alton Raible; Atheneum, 1971. **Awarded:** Christopher (teenage) 1972; International Board on Books for Young People (text/USA) 1974; Newbery (honor) 1972; William Allen White 1974.

Libby on Wednesday by Zilpha Keatley Snyder, not illustrated; Delacorte, 1990; Dell, 1991. **Awarded:** CRABbery Award (Honor) 1991.

Song of the Gargoyle by Zilpha Keatley Snyder, not illustrated; Delacorte, 1991. **Awarded:** CRABbery (Honor) 1992.

The Witches of Worm by Zilpha Keatley Snyder, illustrated by Alton Raible; Atheneum, 1972. **Awarded:** National Book Award (finalist) 1973; New York Times Notable Books 1972; Newbery (honor) 1973.

SOBOL, DONALD J.
Awarded: Edgar Allan Poe (special award for Encyclopedia Brown books) 1975.

Encyclopedia Brown and the Case of the Midnight Visitor by Donald J. Sobol, illustrated by Lillian Brandi; Nelson, 1977. **Awarded:** Buckeye (grades 4-8 honor) 1982.

Encyclopedia Brown Keeps the Peace by Donald J. Sobol, illustrated by Leonard Shortall; Nelson, 1969. **Awarded:** Young Reader's Choice 1972.

Encyclopedia Brown Lends a Hand by Donald J. Sobol, illustrated by Leonard Shortall; Nelson, 1974. **Awarded:** Garden State Children's (younger fiction) 1977.

SOJO, TOBA
The Animals Frolic by Velma Varner, illustrated by Toba Sojo; Putnam, 1954. **Awarded:** New York Times Best Illustrated 1954.

SOKOL, BILL
All Aboard: Poems by Mary Britton Miller, illustrated by Bill Sokol; Pantheon, 1958. **Awarded:** Boys Club 1959; New York Times Best Illustrated 1958.

Alvin's Swap Shop by Clifford Hicks, illustrated by Bill Sokol; Holt, 1976. **Awarded:** Charlie May Simon 1978-79.

Cats, Cats, Cats, Cats, Cats by Beatrice de Regniers, illustrated by Bill Sokol; Pantheon, 1958. **Awarded:** Spring Book Festival (ages 4-8 honor) 1958.

Rockets and Satellites by Franklyn M. Branley, illustrated by Bill Sokol; Crowell, 1961. **Awarded:** New Jersey Institute of Technology 1961.

SOLBERT, ROMAINE G.
see SOLBERT, RONNI

SOLBERT, RONNI
I Wrote my Name on the Wall: Sidewalk Songs written and illustrated by Ronni Solbert; Little Brown, 1971. **Awarded:** Children's Book Showcase 1972.

The Pushcart War by Jean Merrill, illustrated by Ronni Solbert; Scott, 1964. **Awarded:** Boys Club 1965, 1966-67; Lewis Carroll Shelf 1965.

The Superlative Horse by Jean Merrill, illustrated by Ronni Solbert; Scott, 1961. **Awarded:** Lewis Carroll Shelf 1963.

Woody and Me by Mary Neville, illustrated by Ronni Solbert; Pantheon, 1966. **Awarded:** Spring Book Festival (middle honor) 1966.

SOLLIDAY, TIM
Rover and Coo Coo by John Hay, illustrated by Tim Solliday; Green Tiger Press, 1986. **Awarded:** Friends of American Writers ($500) 1987.

SOLOWEY, E. M.
Cubs of the Lion of Judah by E. M. Solowey. **Awarded:** Sydney Taylor Manuscript Awards 1987.

SOMAN, DAVID
Tell Me a Story, Mama by Angela Johnson, illustrated by David Soman; Orchard, 1989. **Awarded:** Ezra Jack Keats New Writer Award 1991; Parents' Choice (Story Book) 1989.

When I Am Old With You by Angela Johnson, illustrated by David Soman; Orchard, 1990. **Awarded:** Coretta Scott King (Illustration honor) 1991.

SOMMER-BODENBURG, ANGELA
My Friend, the Vampire by Angela Sommer-Bodenburg, illustrated by Amelie Glienke; Dial, 1984. **Awarded:** Virginia Young Readers (Elementary) 1987.

SOMMERFELT, AIMEE
My Name is Pablo by Aimee Sommerfelt, illustrated by Hans Norman Dahl; Criterion, 1965. **Awarded:** Spring Book Festival (middle honor) 1966.

The Road to Agra by Aimee Sommerfelt, illustrated by Ulf Aas; Criterion, 1961. **Awarded:** Jane Addams 1962; Boys Club 1962; Child Study 1961; Woodward Park 1962.

The White Bungalow by Aimee Sommerfelt, illustrated by Ulf Aas; Criterion, 1964. **Awarded:** Edison Mass Media (character development in children) 1965.

SOOTIN, HARRY
Robert Boyle, Founder of Modern Chemistry by Harry Sootin, illustrated by Gustav Schrotter; Watts, 1962. **Awarded:** Boys Club 1963.

SOREL, EDWARD
Gwendolyn the Miracle Hen by Nancy Sherman, illustrated by Edward Sorel; Golden, 1961. **Awarded:** Spring Book Festival (ages 4-8) 1961.

Gwendolyn and the Weathercock by Nancy Sherman, illustrated by Edward Sorel; Golden, 1963. **Awarded:** New York Times Best Illustrated 1963.

Pablo Paints a Picture by Warren Miller, illustrated by Edward Sorel; Little, Brown, 1959. **Awarded:** New York Times Best Illustrated 1959.

SORENSEN, VIRGINIA
Miracles on Maple Hill by Virginia Sorensen, illustrated by Beth Krush and Joe Krush; Harcourt, 1956. **Awarded:** Newbery 1957.

Plain Girl by Virginia Sorensen, illustrated by Charles Geer; Harcourt, 1955. **Awarded:** Child Study 1955.

SOTO, GARY
Baseball in April and Other Stories by Gary Soto, not illustrated; Harcourt Brace Jovanovich, 1990. **Awarded:** John and Patricia Beatty 1991; Reading Magic Award 1990; George G. Stone 1993.

Neighborhood Odes by Gary Soto, illustrated by David Diaz; Harcourt Brace Jovanovich, 1992. **Awarded:** Hungry Mind (Middle Readers/Fiction) 1993.

SOUTHALL, IVAN FRANCIS
Ash Road by Ivan Southall, illustrated by Clem Seale; Angus & Robertson, 1965. **Awarded:** Children's Book Council of Australia (book of the year) 1966.

Bread and Honey by Ivan Southall, not illustrated; Angus & Robertson, 1970. **Awarded:** Children's Book Council of Australia (book of the year) 1971.

Fly West by Ivan Southall, not illustrated; Angus & Robertson, 1974. **Awarded:** Children's Book Council of Australia (book of the year) 1976.

Josh by Ivan Southall, not illustrated; Angus & Robertson, 1971. **Awarded:** Carnegie 1971; International Board on Books for Young People (text/Australia) 1974.

The Long Night Watch by Ivan Southall, not illustrated; Methuen, 1983. **Awarded:** National Children's Literature Award 1986.

Matt and Jo by Ivan Southall, not illustrated; Angus & Robertson, 1973. **Awarded:** Writers Award 1974.

Sly Old Wardrobe by Ivan Southall, illustrated by Ted Greenwood; Cheshire, 1968. **Awarded:** Children's Book Council of Australia (picture book) 1969.

To the Wild Sky by Ivan Southall, illustrated by Jennifer Tuckwell; Angus & Robertson, 1967. **Awarded:** Children's Book Council of Australia (book of the year) 1968.

SOUTHEY, ROBERT
The Cataract of Lodore by Robert Southey, illustrated by David Catrow; Holt, 1992. **Awarded:** New York Times Best Illustrated 1992.

SOUTHGATE, MARK
The White Cat by Mark Southgate; to be published by Macmillan. **Awarded:** Macmillan (2nd prize) 1986.

SPANFELLER, JAMES JOHN
Dorp Dead by Julia Cunningham, illustrated by James Spanfeller; Pantheon, 1965. **Awarded:** Lewis Carroll Shelf 1972; Southern California Council (notable) 1966; Spring Book Festival (middle) 1965.

The Malibu and Other Poems by Myra Cohn Livingston, illustrated by James J. Spanfeller; Atheneum, 1972. **Awarded:** Southern California Council (notable) 1973.

The Summer Birds by Penelope Farmer, illustrated by James J. Spanfeller; Harcourt, 1962. **Awarded:** Carnegie (commended) 1962.

Where the Lilies Bloom by Bill Cleaver and Vera Cleaver, illustrated by Jim Spanfeller; Lippincott, 1969. **Awarded:** Boston Globe Horn Book (text honor) 1970; National Book Award (finalist) 1970.

SPARKS, MARY WALKER
Taffy of Torpedo Junction by Nell Wise Wechter, illustrated by Mary Walker Sparks; Blair, 1957. **Awarded:** North Carolina AAUW 1957.

SPEARE, ELIZABETH GEORGE
Awarded: Laura Ingalls Wilder 1989.

The Bronze Bow by Elizabeth George Speare, not illustrated; Houghton, 1961. **Awarded:** International Board on Books for Young People (USA) 1964; Newbery 1962.

The Sign of the Beaver by Elizabeth George Speare, not illustrated; Houghton Mifflin, 1983; Dell, 1984. **Awarded:** Child Study 1983; Christopher (ages 10-12) 1984; New York Times Notable Books 1983; Newbery (honor) 1984; Scott O'Dell 1983.

The Witch of Blackbird Pond by Elizabeth George Speare, not illustrated; Houghton, 1958. **Awarded:** International Board on Books for Young People (USA) 1960; New England Round Table 1976; Newbery 1959.

SPEER, BONNIE
Hillback To Boggy told by Jess Willard Speer, written by Bonnie Speer, illustrated; Reliance Press, 1991. **Awarded:** Oklahoma Book Award 1992.

SPEER, JESS WILLARD
Hillback To Boggy told by Jess Willard Speer, written by Bonnie Speer, illustrated; Reliance Press, 1991. **Awarded:** Oklahoma Book Award 1992.

SPEICHER, HELEN ROSS
Clocks, from Shadow to Atom by Helen R. Speicher and Kathryn K. Borland, illustrated by Robert W. Addison; Follett, 1969. **Awarded:** Indiana Authors Day (children) 1970.

SPENCE, ELEANOR
Deezle Boy by Eleanor Spence, not illustrated; Collins Dove, 1987. **Awarded:** Children's Book Council of Australia (Book of the Year Older Honour) 1988; Family Award 1987.

The Green Laurel by Eleanor Spence, illustrated by Geraldine Spence; Oxford, 1963. **Awarded:** Children's Book Council of Australia (book of the year) 1964.

The Left Overs by Eleanor Spence, not illustrated; Methuen Australia, 1982. **Awarded:** Children's Book Council of Australia (book of the year highly commended) 1983.

Me and Jeshua by Eleanor Spence, illustrated by Shane Conroy; Dove Communications, 1985, c1984. **Awarded:** Children's Book Council of Australia (Book of the Year commended) 1985; Australian Christian Book of the Year Children's Award 1985.

The October Child by Eleanor Spence, illustrated by Malcolm Green; Oxford, 1976. **Awarded:** Children's Book Council of Australia (book of the year) 1977; International Board on Books for Young People (honour list/text/Australia) 1978.

Seventh Pebble by Eleanor Spence, illustrated by Sisca Verwoert; Oxford University Press, 1980. **Awarded:** New South Wales State Literary Awards (Special Children's) 1981.

SPENCE, GERALDINE
The Blue Boat by William Mayne, illustrated by Geraldine Spence; Oxford, 1957. **Awarded:** Carnegie (commended) 1957.

Devil's Hill by Nan Chauncy, illustrated by Geraldine Spence; Oxford, 1958; Watts, 1960. **Awarded:** Children's Book Council of Australia (book of the year) 1959; Boys Club 1961.

The Green Laurel by Eleanor Spence, illustrated by Geraldine Spence; Oxford, 1963. **Awarded:** Children's Book Council of Australia (book of the year) 1964.

SPENCER, CORNELIA
Made in India by Cornelia Spencer, illustrated by Allen Lewis; Knopf, 1946. **Awarded:** Spring Book Festival (older honor) 1946.

SPENCER, PAULA UNDERWOOD
Who Speaks for Wolf by Paula Underwood Spencer, illustrated by Frank Howell; Tribe of Two Press, 1983. **Awarded:** Jefferson Cup 1984.

SPENCER, ROY
The Orchestra and its Instruments by Christopher Headington, illustrated by Roy Spencer; Bodley Head, 1965. **Awarded:** Carnegie (commended) 1965.

SPENDER, STEPHEN
The Magic Flute by Stephen Spender, illustrated by Beni Montresor; Putnam, 1966. **Awarded:** New York Times Best Illustrated 1966.

SPERRY, ARMSTRONG
All Sail Set: A Romance of the Flying Cloud written and illustrated by Armstrong Sperry; Winston, 1935. **Awarded:** Newbery (honor) 1936.

Call it Courage written and illustrated by Armstrong Sperry; Macmillan, 1940. **Awarded:** Newbery 1941.

The Codfish Musket by Agnes D. Hewes, illustrated by Armstrong Sperry; Doubleday, 1936. **Awarded:** Newbery (honor) 1937.

The Rainforest written and illustrated by Armstrong Sperry; Macmillan, 1947. **Awarded:** Boys Club 1949; Spring Book Festival (middle honor) 1947.

Sky Highways: Geography from the Air by Trevor Lloyd, illustrated by Armstrong Sperry; Houghton Mifflin, 1945. **Awarded:** Spring Book Festival (middle honor) 1945.

Storm Canvas written and illustrated by Armstrong Sperry; Winston, 1944. **Awarded:** Spring Book Festival (older) 1944.

Thunderbolt House by Howard Pease, illustrated by Armstrong Sperry; Doubleday, 1944. **Awarded:** Commonwealth Club of California 1944.

SPIER, PETER
Awarded: David McCord Children's Literature Citation 1989; University of Southern Mississippi 1984.

Bored - Nothing to Do written and illustrated by Peter Spier; Doubleday, 1978. **Awarded:** New York Times Notable Books 1978.

The Erie Canal written and illustrated by Peter Spier; Doubleday, 1970. **Awarded:** Christopher (ages 4-8) 1971.

The Fox Went Out on a Chilly Night written and illustrated by Peter Spier; Doubleday, 1961. **Awarded:** Caldecott (honor) 1962.

London Bridge Is Falling Down! written and illustrated by Peter Spier; Doubleday, 1967. **Awarded:** Boston Globe Horn Book (illustration) 1967.

Noah's Ark written and illustrated by Peter Spier; Doubleday, 1977. **Awarded:** American Book Awards (picturebook paperback) 1982; Art Books for Children 1979; Caldecott 1978; Lewis Carroll Shelf 1978; Christopher (picture book) 1978; International Board on Books for Young People (illustration/USA) 1980; National Religious Book Award 1978; New York Times Best Illustrated 1977.

Oh, Were They Ever Happy written and illustrated by Peter Spier; Doubleday, 1978. Little Archer 1978.

People written and illustrated by Peter Spier; Doubleday, 1980. **Awarded:** Christopher (picture book) 1981.

SPINELLI, EILEEN
Story by Eileen Spinelli in Highlights magazine. **Awarded:** Magazine Merit Award (Fiction) 1990.

Somebody Loves You, Mr. Hatch by Eileen Spinelli, illustrated by Paul Yalowitz; Bradbury, 1991. **Awarded:** Christopher Award (Ages 4-6) 1992.

SPINELLI, JERRY
Awarded: Outstanding Pennsylvania Author 1992.

Maniac Magee by Jerry Spinelli, not illustrated; Little Brown, 1990. **Awarded:** Boston Globe (Fiction) 1990; Buckeye (grades 6-8) 1993; Rebecca Caudill 1993; Charlotte Book Award (grades 6-8) 1992; Carolyn W. Field Award 1991; Dorothy Canfield Fisher 1992; Indian Paintbrush 1992; Massachusetts Children's 1993; Newbery 1991; North Dakota

Children's Choice (Juvenile Fiction) 1992; Rhode Island 1992; Mark Twain 1993; William Allen White 1993.

SPINNER, STEPHANIE
Aliens for Breakfast by Jonathan Etra and Stephanie Spinner, illustrated by Steve Bjorkman; Random House, 1988. **Awarded:** Texas Bluebonnet 1991.

SPIRIN, GENNADY
The Fool and the Fish: A Tale From Russia by Alexander Nikolayevich Afanasyev, illustrated by Gennady Spirin; Dial, 1990. **Awarded:** New York Times Best Illustrated 1990.

Once There Was a Tree by Natalia Romanov, illustrated by Gennady Spirin; Dial, 1985. **Awarded:** New York Times Notable 1985.

SPRAGUE, GRETCHEN
Signpost to Terror by Gretchen Sprague, not illustrated; Dodd, Mead, 1967. **Awarded:** Edgar Allan Poe 1968.

SPRAGUE, ROSEMARY
Red Lion and Gold Dragon: A Novel of the Norman Conquest by Rosemary Sprague, not illustrated; Chilton, 1967. **Awarded:** Spring Book Festival (older honor) 1967.

SPRIESTERSBACH, BARBARA
Awarded: American Association of School Librarians 1991.

SPRINGER, MARILYN HARRIS
see HARRIS, MARILYN

SPRINGER, NANCY
Colt by Nancy Springer, not illustrated; Dial, 1991. **Awarded:** Fassler 1992.

SPRINGSTUBB, TRICIA
With a Name Like Lulu, Who Needs More Trouble? by Tricia Springstubb, illustrated by Jill Kastner; Delacorte, 1989. **Awarded:** Ohioana 1991.

SPURRIER, STEVEN
The Circus Is Coming by Noel Streatfeild, illustrated by Steven Spurrier; Dent, 1938. **Awarded:** Carnegie 1938.

SPYNDONOS
Along the Seaside by Themos Potaaianos, illustrated by Spyndonos; Greece. **Awarded:** Hans Christian Andersen (runnerup) 1960.

STADTLER, BEA
The Holocaust: A History of Courage and Resistance by Bea Stadtler, illustrated by David Stone Martin; Behrman, 1974. **Awarded:** Jewish Book Council 1974.

STAFFELBACH, E. H.
Towards Oregon by E. H. Staffelbach, illustrated by Charles Hargens; Macrae Smith, 1946. **Awarded:** Commonwealth Club of California 1946.

STAFFORD, ANN
Five Proud Riders by Ann Stafford, illustrated by Bobri; Knopf, 1938. **Awarded:** Spring Book Festival (older honor) 1938.

STAHL, BEN
Blackbeard's Ghost written and illustrated by Ben Stahl; Houghton Mifflin, 1965. **Awarded:** Sequoyah 1969.

Freelon Starbird: Being a Narrative of the Extraordinary Hardships Suffered by an Accidental Soldier in a Beaten Army during the Autumn and Winter of 1776 by Richard F. Snow, illustrated by Ben F. Stahl; Houghton Mifflin, 1976. **Awarded:** New York Times Notable Books 1976.

A Pocket Full of Seeds by Marilyn Sachs, illustrated by Ben Stahl; Doubleday, 1973. **Awarded:** Jane Addams (honor) 1974.

STAHLER, CHARLES
I Love Animals and Broccoli by Debra Wasserman and Charles Stahler, illustrated; Vegetarian Resource Group, 1985. **Awarded:** Book Can Develop Empathy 1990.

STALDER, VALERIE
Even the Devil Is Afraid of a Shrew retold by Valerie Stalder, adapted by Ray Broekel, illustrated by Richard Brown; Addison Wesley, 1972. **Awarded:** Children's Book Showcase 1973.

STAMATY, MARK ALAN
Who Needs Donuts? written and illustrated by Mark Alan Stamaty; Dial, 1973. **Awarded:** Art Books for Children 1975.

Yellow, Yellow by Frank Asch, illustrated by Mark Alan Stamaty; McGraw Hill, 1971. **Awarded:** Art Books for Children 1973, 1974, 1975.

STAMPNICK, KEN
The Wooden People by Myra Paperny, illustrated by Ken Stampnick; Little, Brown, 1976. **Awarded:** Governor General (author) 1976; Little Brown Canadian 1975.

STANEK, LOU WILLETT
Gleanings by Lou Willett Stanek, not illustrated; Harper & Row, 1985. **Awarded:** Woodward Park 1985.

STANG, WENDY
Hubert, the Caterpillar Who Thought He Was a Moustache by Wendy Stang and Susan Richards, illustrated by Robert L. Anderson; Quist, 1967. **Awarded:** New York Times Best Illustrated 1967.

STANLEY, DIANA
The Borrowers by Mary Norton, illustrated by Diana Stanley; Dent, 1952. **Awarded:** Carnegie 1952.

The Borrowers Afloat by Mary Norton, illustrated by Diana Stanley; Dent, 1959. **Awarded:** Carnegie (commended) 1959; International Board on Books for Young People (Great Britain) 1962.

STANLEY, DIANE
Bard of Avon: The Story of William Shakespeare by Diane Stanley and Peter Vennema, illustrated by Diane Stanley; Morrow, 1992. **Awarded:** Reading Magic 1992.

Good Queen Bess by Diane Stanley and Peter Vennema, illustrated by Diane Stanley; Four Winds, 1990. **Awarded:** Boston Globe Horn Book (Nonfiction Honor) 1991; Reading Magic Award 1990.

Peter the Great written and illustrated by Diane Stanley; Four Winds, 1986. **Awarded:** Golden Kite (nonfiction honor) 1986.

Shaka: King of the Zulus by Diane Stanley and Peter Vennema, illustrated by Diane Stanley; Morrow, 1988. **Awarded:** New York Times Best Illustrated 1988.

STANLEY, JERRY
Children of the Dust Bowl by Jerry Stanley, illustrated with photographs; Crown, 1992. **Awarded:** John and Patricia Beatty 1993; Hungry Mind (Middle Readers/Nonfiction) 1993; Jefferson Cup 1993; Orbis Pictus 1993.

STANLEY, ROBERT
Exploring the Film by Robert Stanley and William Kuhns; Pflaum/Standard, 1969. **Awarded:** Media & Methods (textbook) 1973.

STANOVSKY, VLADISLAV
Slavische Marchen by Vladislav Stanovsky and Oldrich Sirovatka, illustrated by Maria Zelibska; Artia. **Awarded:** Bologna (Graphics for Youth) 1972.

STAPELBROEK, MARLYS G.
Story by Marlys G. Stapelbroek in *Boys Life* magazine. **Awarded:** Magazine Merit (Fiction) 1991.

STAPLES, SUZANNE FISHER
Shabanu: Daughter of the Wind by Suzanne Fisher Staples, not illustrated; Knopf, 1989. **Awarded:** International Board on Books for Young People (writing/USA) 1992; Newbery (Honor) 1990; Sugarman Children's Book Award 1990.

STAPLETON, JANICE
It's BASIC: The ABC's of Computer Programming by Shelley Lipson, illustrated by Janice Stapleton; Holt, 1982. **Awarded:** Garden State (younger nonfiction) 1985; New Jersey Institute of Technology 1983.

STASHIN, LEO
The Lower East Side: A Portrait in Time by Diane Cavallo, photographs by Leo Stashin; Crowell-Collier, 1971. **Awarded:** Children's Book Showcase 1972.

STEADMAN, RALPH
I, Leonardo written and illustrated by Ralph Steadman; Cape, 1983. **Awarded:** W. H. Smith Illustration (1st prize) 1987.

That's my Dad written and illustrated by Ralph Steadman; Andersen Press, 1986. **Awarded:** Bologna (critici in erba) 1987.

STEARNS, MONROE
Kasimir's Journey by Monroe Stearns, illustrated by Marlene Reidel; Lippincott, 1959. **Awarded:** New York Times Best Illustrated 1959.

STEARNS, PAMELA
The Fool and the Dancing Bear by Pamela Stearns, illustrated by Ann Strugnell; Little, Brown, 1979. **Awarded:** Commonwealth Club of California 1979.

STECHER, MIRIAM B.
Max, the Music Maker by Miriam B. Stecher, photographs by Alice S. Kandell; Lothrop, 1980. **Awarded:** New York Academy of Sciences (younger honor) 1981.

STEEL, RICHARD
Skulls! by Richard Steel, illustrated by Gerry Gaskin; Heinemann, 1980. **Awarded:** Times Educational Supplement (senior) 1981.

STEELE, MARY QUINTARD GOVAN
(pseudonym is Wilson Gage)

Arkwright written and illustrated by Mary Steele; Hyland House, 1985. **Awarded:** Children's Book Council of Australia (junior book of the year) 1986.

Big Blue Island by Wilson Gage, illustrated by Glen Rounds; World, 1964. **Awarded:** Aurianne 1966.

Journey Outside by Mary Q. Steele; illustrated by Rocco Negri; Viking, 1969. **Awarded:** Lewis Carroll Shelf 1971; Newbery (honor) 1970.

Mrs. Gaddy and the Ghost by Wilson Gage, illustrated by Marylin Hafner; Greenwillow, 1979. **Awarded:** Garden State Children's (easy to read) 1982.

The Secret of Fiery Gorge by Wilson Gage, illustrated by Mary Stevens; World, 1960. **Awarded:** Spring Book Festival (middle honor) 1960.

STEELE, WILLIAM OWEN
Davy Crockett's Earthquake by William O. Steele, illustrated by Nicolas Mordvinoff; Harcourt, 1956. **Awarded:** Spring Book Festival (ages 4-8 honor) 1956.

Flaming Arrows by William O. Steele, illustrated by Paul Galdone; Harcourt, 1957. **Awarded:** Spring Book Festival (middle honor) 1957; William Allen White 1960.

The Perilous Road by William O. Steele, illustrated by Paul Galdone; Harcourt, 1958. **Awarded:** Jane Addams 1958; Newbery (honor) 1959.

Westward Adventure: The True Stories of Six Pioneers by William O. Steele, with maps by Kathleen Voute; Harcourt, 1962. **Awarded:** Edison Mass Media (America's past) 1963.

Winter Danger by William O. Steele, illustrated by Paul Galdone; Harcourt, 1954. **Awarded:** Lewis Carroll Shelf 1962; Spring Book Festival (middle) 1954.

STEFANSSON, EVELYN SCHWARTZ
Here is Alaska by Evelyn Stefansson, photographs by Frederick Machetanz, maps by Raymond Lufkin; Scribner, 1943. **Awarded:** Spring Book Festival (older honor) 1943.

Within the Circle by Evelyn Stefansson, illustrated by Richard Edes Harrison; Scribner, 1945. **Awarded:** Spring Book Festival (older honor) 1945.

STEFFANS, KLAUS
No Hero for the Kaiser by Rudolf Frank, illustrated by Klaus Steffans, translated by Patricia Crampton; Lothrop, Lee & Shepard, 1986. **Awarded:** Batchelder 1987; Parents' Choice (literature) 1986.

STEFFEN, RANDY
The Western Horse: A Handbook by Natlee P. Kenoyer, illustrated by Randy Steffen; Meredith, 1962. **Awarded:** Western Writers (nonfiction) 1963.

STEIG, WILLIAM
Awarded: Little Archer 1983.

Abel's Island written and illustrated by William Steig; Farrar, 1976. **Awarded:** Lewis Carroll Shelf 1977; Children's Book Showcase 1977; New York Times Notable Books 1976; Newbery (honor) 1977.

The Amazing Bone written and illustrated by William Steig; Farrar, 1976. **Awarded:** Art Books for Children 1978, 1979; Boston Globe Horn Book (illustration honor) 1977; Caldecott (honor) 1977; Children's Book Showcase 1977; New York Times Notable Books 1976.

Amos and Boris written and illustrated by William Steig; Farrar, 1971. **Awarded:** Children's Book Showcase 1972; National Book Award (finalist) 1972; New York Times Best Illustrated 1971; New York Times Notable Books 1971.

Brave Irene written and illustrated by William Steig; Farrar, Straus & Giroux, 1986. **Awarded:** New York Times Best Illustrated 1986; Parents' Choice (Story Book) 1987; Redbook 1986.

Caleb and Kate written and illustrated by William Steig; Farrar, 1977. **Awarded:** National Book Award (finalist) 1978.

Doctor DeSoto written and illustrated by William Steig; Farrar, Straus & Giroux, 1982. **Awarded:** American Book Award (picturebook hardback) 1983; Boston Globe Horn Book (illustration honor) 1983; Georgia Children's Picture Storybook 1985; International Board on Books for Young People (illustration/USA) 1984; New York Times Notable Books 1982; Newbery (honor) 1983; Parents' Choice (illustration) 1983.

Dominic written and illustrated by William Steig; Farrar, 1972. **Awarded:** Christopher (all ages) 1973; National Book Award (finalist) 1973; William Allen White 1975.

Gorky Rises written and illustrated by William Steig; Farrar, 1980. **Awarded:** Irma Simonton Black 1980; New York Times Best Illustrated 1980; New York Times Notable Books 1980.

Shrek! written and illustrated by William Steig; Farrar, Straus, Giroux, 1990. **Awarded:** Parents' Choice (Picture Book) 1990; Reading Magic Award 1990.

Solomon the Rusty Nail written and illustrated by William Steig; Farrar, Straus & Giroux, 1985. **Awarded:** Redbook 1985.

Spinky Sulks written and illustrated by William Steig; Farrar Straus Giroux, 1988. **Awarded:** Redbook 1988.

Sylvester and the Magic Pebble written and illustrated by William Steig; Windmill/Simon & Schuster, 1969. **Awarded:** Caldecott 1970; Lewis Carroll Shelf 1978; Emphasis on Reading (grades K-1) 1982-83; National Book Award (finalist) 1970; Spring Book Festival (picture book honor) 1969.

Yellow & Pink written and illustrated by William Steig; Farrar, Straus & Giroux, 1984. **Awarded:** Redbook (hardback) 1984.

The Zabajaba Jungle written and illustrated by William Steig; Farrar, Straus, Giroux, 1987. **Awarded:** Parents' Choice (Picture Book) 1987.

STEIGLER, JUDITH
Helicopters at Work by Judith Steigler and Mary Elting, illustrated by Ursula Koering; Harvey House, 1972. **Awarded:** New Jersey Institute of Technology 1972.

STEIN, ALEX
The Secret of the Missing Footprint by Phyllis A. Whitney, illustrated by Alex Stein; Westminster, 1969. **Awarded:** Edgar Allan Poe (runnerup) 1971.

STEIN, HARVE
Coronado and His Captains by Camilla Campbell, illustrated by Harve Stein; Follett, 1958. **Awarded:** Steck-Vaughn 1960.

STEIN, SARA
The Evolution Book written and illustrated by Sara Stein, photographs by Rona Beame; Workman, 1986. **Awarded:** New York Academy of Sciences (older) 1987.

STEINEL, WILLIAM
The Living Community: A Venture into Ecology by S. Carl Hirsch, illustrated by William Steinel; Viking, 1966. **Awarded:** Edison Mass Media (best children's science book) 1967; Clara Ingram Judson 1967.

STEINER, BARBARA A.
Stanleigh's Wrong-side-out Day by Barbara A. Steiner, illustrated by George Cloven and Ruth Cloven; Children's Press, 1982. **Awarded:** Colorado (runnerup) 1985.

STEINER, JORG
Rabbit Island by Jorg Steiner, translated by Ann Conrad Lammers, illustrated by Jorg Muller; Harcourt, 1978. **Awarded:** Batchelder 1979.

STEINER, STAN
The Tiguas: The Lost Tribe of City Indians by Stan Steiner, illustrated with photographs; Crowell-Collier, 1972. **Awarded:** Western Writers (nonfiction) 1973.

STELTZER, ULLI
The Night Workers by Alvin Schwartz, photographs by Ulli Steltzer; Dutton, 1966. **Awarded:** New Jersey Institute of Technology (ages 12-16) 1966.

STEMPLE, ADAM
Jane Yolen's Mother Goose Songbook edited by Jane Yolen, illustrated by Rosekrans Hoffman, music by Adam Stemple; Boyds Mills Press, 1992. **Awarded:** Hungry Mind (Picturebooks Nonfiction) 1993.

STEPHANE, NELLY
Roland by Nelly Stephane, illustrated by Andre Francois; Harcourt, 1958. **Awarded:** New York Times Best Illustrated 1958.

STEPHEN, DAVID
String Lug the Fox by David Stephen, illustrated by Nina Scott Langley; Little, Brown, 1952. **Awarded:** Spring Book Festival (older honor) 1952.

STEPHENS, MARY JO
Witch of the Cumberlands by Mary Jo Stephens, illustrated by Arvis Stewart; Houghton, 1974. **Awarded:** Ohioana 1976.

STEPTOE, JOHN
Awarded: Biennale Illustrations Bratislava (Honorable Mention in Memoriam) 1989; Milner Award 1989.

All the Colors of the Race: Poems by Arnold Adoff, illustrated by John Steptoe; Lothrop, Lee & Shepard, 1982. **Awarded:** Jane Addams (special recognition) 1983.

Mother Crocodile = Maman-Caiman by Birago Diop, translated and adapted by Rosa Guy, illustrated by John Steptoe; Delacorte, 1981. **Awarded:** Coretta Scott King (illustrator) 1982.

Mufaro's Beautiful Daughters written and illustrated by John Steptoe; Lothrop, Lee & Shepard, 1987. **Awarded:** Boston Globe Horn Book (illustration) 1987; Caldecott (honor) 1988; Coretta Scott King (Illustration) 1988; Parents' Choice (Picture Book) 1987.

She Come Bringing Me that Little Baby Girl by Eloise Greenfield, illustrated by John Steptoe; Lippincott, 1974. **Awarded:** Irma Simonton Black 1974; Boston Globe Horn Book (illustration honor) 1975.

Stevie written and illustrated by John Steptoe; Harper, 1969. **Awarded:** Art Books for Children 1973; **Awarded:** Lewis Carroll Shelf 1978.

The Story of Jumping Mouse retold and illustrated by John Steptoe; Lothrop, Lee & Shepard, 1984. **Awarded:** Caldecott (honor) 1985.

STERLING, DOROTHY
Captain of the Planter: The Story of Robert Smalls by Dorothy Sterling, illustrated by Ernest Crichlow; Doubleday, 1958. **Awarded:** Nancy Bloch 1958.

Mary Jane by Dorothy Sterling, illustrated by Ernest Crichlow; Doubleday, 1959. **Awarded:** Nancy Bloch 1959; Woodward Park 1960.

The Trouble They Seen: Black People Tell the Story of Reconstruction edited by Dorothy Sterling, illustrated with photographs; Doubleday, 1976. **Awarded:** Woodson 1977.

STERLING, PHILIP
Sea and Earth: The Life of Rachel Carson by Philip Sterling, illustrated with photographs; Crowell, 1970. **Awarded:** Christopher (teenage) 1971.

STERMAN, BETSY

Too Much Magic by Betsy Sterman and Samuel Sterman, illustrated by Judy Glasser; Lippincott, 1987. **Awarded:** Washington Irving (Older Fiction) 1990.

STERMAN, SAMUEL

Too Much Magic by Samuel Sterman and Betsy Sterman, illustrated by Judy Glasser; Lippincott, 1987. **Awarded:** Washington Irving (Older Fiction) 1990.

STERN, MARIE SIMCHOW

The Golden Almanac by Dorothy Agnes Bennett, illustrated by Marie Stern; Simon & Schuster, 1944. **Awarded:** Spring Book Festival (younger honor) 1944.

STEVENS, CARLA

Awarded: Lucky Book Club Four-Leaf Clover 1980.

STEVENS, CHRISTIAN D.

Meagher of the Sword: A Dramatization of the Life of Thomas Francis Meagher by Christian D. Stevens, illustrated with photographs; Dodd, Mead, 1967. **Awarded:** Edith Busby 1966.

STEVENS, M. E.

Throw Stone: The First American Boy, 25,000 Years Ago by M. E. Stevens and Edwin B. Sayles, illustrated by Barton Wright; Reilly & Lee, 1960. **Awarded:** Steck-Vaughn 1962.

STEVENS, MARY

A Canvas Castle by Alice Rogers Hager, illustrated by Mary Stevens; Messner, 1949. **Awarded:** Julia Ellsworth Ford 1948.

Janitor's Girl by Frieda Friedman, illustrated by Mary Stevens; Morrow, 1956. **Awarded:** Spring Book Festival (middle honor) 1956.

Nobody Listens to Andrew by Elizabeth Guilfoile, illustrated by Mary Stevens; Follett, 1957. **Awarded:** Follett Beginning to Read 1958.

The O'Leary's and Friends by Jean H. Berg, illustrated by Mary Stevens; Follett, 1961. **Awarded:** Follett Beginning to Read 1961.

The Secret of Fiery Gorge by Wilson Gage, illustrated by Mary Stevens; World, 1960. **Awarded:** Spring Book Festival (middle honor) 1960.

Tornado Jones by Trella Lamson Dick, illustrated by Mary Stevens; Wilcox & Follett, 1953. **Awarded:** Charles W. Follett 1953.

STEVENSON, AUGUSTA

Awarded: Indiana Authors Day (special citation) 1958.

STEVENSON, JAMES

Clams Can't Sing written and illustrated by James Stevenson; Greenwillow, 1980. **Awarded:** Garden State Children's (easy to read) 1983.

Don't You Know There's a War On? written and illustrated by James Stevenson; Greenwillow, 1992. **Awarded:** Parents Choice (Picture Book) 1992.

Georgia Music by Helen V. Griffith, illustrated by James Stevenson; Greenwillow, 1986. **Awarded:** Boston Globe Horn Book (fiction honor) 1987.

Grandaddy's Place by Helen V. Griffith, illustrated by James Stevenson; Greenwillow, 1987. **Awarded:** Parents' Choice (Picture Book) 1987; Parents' Choice (Story Book) 1987.

Henry and Mudge in Puddle Trouble by Cynthia Rylant, illustrated by James Stevenson; Bradbury, 1987. **Awarded:** Garden State Children's Book Award (Easy to Read) 1990.

Higher on the Door written and illustrated by James Stevenson; Greenwillow, 1987. **Awarded:** Parents' Choice (Picture Book) 1987; Redbook 1987.

Howard written and illustrated by James Stevenson; Greenwillow, 1980. **Awarded:** New York Times Best Illustrated 1980; New York Times Notable Books 1980.

I Know a Lady by Charlotte Zolotow, illustrated by James Stevenson; Greenwillow, 1984. **Awarded:** Redbook (hardback) 1984.

The New Kid on the Block by Jack Prelutsky, illustrated by James Stevenson; Greenwillow, 1984. **Awarded:** Emphasis on Reading (grades 2-3) 1986-87; Garden State (younger nonfiction) 1987.

Oliver, Clarence and Violet written and illustrated by James Stevenson; Greenwillow, 1982. **Awarded:** Parents' Choice (literature) 1982.

Something Big Has Been Here by Jack Prelutsky, illustrated by James Stevenson; Greenwillow, 1988. **Awarded:** Kentucky Bluegrass (grades 4-8) 1992.

We Can't Sleep written and illustrated by James Stevenson; Greenwillow, 1982. **Awarded:** Christopher (ages 4-7) 1983.

What's Under My Bed? written and illustrated by James Stevenson; Greenwillow, 1983. **Awarded:** Little Archer 1985.

STEVENSON, ROBERT LOUIS

Child's Garden of Verses by Robert Louis Stevenson, illustrated by many artists; Chronicle Books, 1989. **Awarded:** Redbook 1989.

A Child's Garden of Verses by Robert Louis Stevenson, illustrated by Brian Wildsmith; Watts, 1966. **Awarded:** Lewis Carroll Shelf 1966.

El Diablillo de la Botella (original English *The Bottle Imp*) by Robert Louis Stevenson, translated by Ellie; Ediciones Ekare-Banco de Libro, 1981. **Awarded:** International Board on Books for Young People (translation/Venezuela) 1984.

STEVENSON, SUCIE

Henry and Mudge and the Happy Cat by Cynthia Rylant, illustrated by Sucie Stevenson; Bradbury, 1990. **Awarded:** Garden State (easy to read) 1993.

Henry and Mudge Get the Cold Shivers by Cynthia Rylant, illustrated by Sucie Stevenson; Bradbury, 1989. **Awarded:** Garden State (Easy to Read) 1992.

STEVENSON, WILLIAM

The Bushbabies by William Stevenson, illustrated by Victor Ambrus; Houghton, 1965. **Awarded:** Woodward Park 1967.

STEWARD, JO

Andrea by Jo Steward, not illustrated; New American Library, 1982. **Awarded:** Golden Medallion 1983.

STEWART, A. C.

Elizabeth's Tower by A. C. Stewart, not illustrated; S. G. Phillips, 1972. **Awarded:** Edgar Allan Poe (runnerup) 1973.

STEWART, ANNA BIRD

Bibi, the Baker's Horse by Anna Bird Stewart, illustrated by Catherine M. Richter; Lippincott, 1942. **Awarded:** Ohioana 1943.

Enter David Garrick by Anna Bird Stewart, illustrated by Ernest H. Shepard; Lippincott, 1951. **Awarded:** Ohioana 1952.

STEWART, ANNE
The Bus Driver by Anne Stewart, photographs by Chris Fairclough; Hamish Hamilton, 1986. **Awarded:** Other Award 1986.

STEWART, ARVIS
The Macmillan Book of Greek Gods and Heroes by Alice Low, illustrated by Arvis Stewart; Macmillan, 1985. **Awarded:** Washington Irving (All Ages) 1988.

Witch of the Cumberlands by Mary Jo Stephens, illustrated by Arvis Stewart; Houghton, 1974. **Awarded:** Ohioana 1976.

STEWART, CHARLES
Lady of the Linden Tree by Barbara Leonie Picard, illustrated by Charles Stewart; Oxford, 1954. **Awarded:** Carnegie (commended) 1954.

STEWART, JOHN
Elephant School written and illustrated by John Stewart; Pantheon, 1982. **Awarded:** New York Academy of Sciences (younger honor) 1983.

STEWART, SARAH-JANE
This Poem Doesn't Rhyme by Gerard Benson, illustrated by Sarah- Jane Stewart; Viking, 1990. **Awarded:** Signal Poetry Award 1991.

STIELER, ROBERT
Narzeczony z Morza by Robert Stieler, illustrated by Ardrezej Strumitto; Nasza Ksiegarnia, 1971. **Awarded:** Biennale Illustrations Bratislava (grand prix) 1971.

STILL, JAMES
Jack and the Wonder Beans by James Still, illustrated by Margot Tomes; Putnam, 1977. **Awarded:** New York Times Best Illustrated 1977.

STIMOLA, MICHAEL
Awarded: Lucile M. Pannell 1991.

STIMOLA, ROSEMARY
Awarded: Lucile M. Pannell 1991.

STINELY, RICHARD
America's First Army by Burke Davis, illustrated by Richard Stinely, photographs by John Crane; Rinehart/Colonial Williamsburg, 1962. **Awarded:** Boys Club 1963.

STINETORF, LOUISE A.
The Shepherd of Abu Kush by Louise A. Stinetorf, not illustrated; Day, 1963. **Awarded:** Indiana Authors Day (children) 1964; Woodward Park School 1963.

STINSON, KATHY
Red Is Best by Kathy Stinson, illustrated by Robin Baird Lewis; Annick Press, 1982. **Awarded:** IODE 1982.

El Rojo es el Major (original English *Red Is Best*) by Kathy Stinson, translated by Kiki and Clarisa de la Rosa; Ediciones Ekare-Banco del Libro, 1985. **Awarded:** International Board on Books for Young People (translation/Venezuela) 1986.

STITT, SUE
Growing Up by Susan Meredith, illustrated by Sue Stitt, Kuo Kang Chen and Rob McCaig; Usborne, 1985. **Awarded:** Times Educational Supplement (senior) 1985.

STOBBS, WILLIAM
Beorn the Proud by Madeleine Polland, illustrated by William Stobbs; Holt, 1962. **Awarded:** Spring Book Festival (middle honor) 1962.

A Bundle of Ballads compiled by Ruth Manning-Sanders, illustrated by William Stobbs; Oxford, 1959. **Awarded:** Greenaway 1959.

Kashtanka by Anton Chekov, translated by Charles Dowsett, illustrated by William Stobbs; Oxford, 1959. **Awarded:** Greenaway 1959.

Knight Crusader by Ronald Welch, illustrated by William Stobbs; Oxford, 1954. **Awarded:** Carnegie 1954.

Return to Freedom by Josephine Kamm, illustrated by William Stobbs; Abelard-Schuman, 1962. **Awarded:** Jewish Book Council 1962.

STOCK, CATHERINE
Justin and the Best Biscuits in the World by Mildred Pitts Walter, illustrated by Catherine Stock; Lothrop Lee & Shepard, 1986. **Awarded:** Coretta Scott King (literature) 1987.

Posy by Charlotte Pomerantz, illustrated by Catherine Stock; Greenwillow, 1983. **Awarded:** Christopher (picturebook) 1984.

When the Woods Hum by Joanne Ryder, illustrated by Catherine Stock; Morrow, 1991. **Awarded:** Book Can Develop Empathy 1991.

STOCKMAN, JACK
Tales of the Kingdom by David Mains and Karen Mains, illustrated by Jack Stockman; David C. Cook, 1983. **Awarded:** Gold Medallion 1984.

STOCKTON, FRANK R.
The Griffin and the Minor Canon by Frank R. Stockton, illustrated by Maurice Sendak; Holt, 1963. **Awarded:** Lewis Carroll Shelf 1963.

The Storyteller's Pack by Frank R. Stockton, illustrated by Bernarda Bryson; Scribner, 1968. **Awarded:** Lewis Carroll Shelf 1969.

STODART, ELEANOR
The Australian Echidna by Eleanor Stodart, illustrated; Houghton Mifflin Australia, 1989; Houghton Mifflin, 1991. **Awarded:** Whitley (Zoological Photo Essay) 1989.

Australian Junior Field Guides (series) by Eleanor Stodart; Weldon. **Awarded:** Whitley 1990.

STODDARD, SANDOL
Free by Sandol Stoddard, illustrated by Jenni Oliver; Houghton, 1976. **Awarded:** Children's Book Showcase 1977.

STOEHR, SHELLEY
Crosses by Shelley Stoehr, not illustrated; Delacorte, 1991. **Awarded:** Delacorte Press Prize (Honorable Mention) 1990.

STOIA, JUDITH
The Hardest Lesson: Personal Accounts of a School Desegregation Crisis by Judith Stoia and Pamela Bullard, not illustrated; Little, Brown, 1980. **Awarded:** Christopher (ages 12-up nonfiction) 1981; Woodson (outstanding merit) 1981.

STOEKE, JANET MORGAN
Minerva Louise written and illustrated by Janet Morgan Stoeke; Dutton, 1988. **Awarded:** Dutton Children's Books Picture Book Competition 1986.

STOLZ, MARY SLATTERY
Awarded: Kerlan Award 1993; George G. Stone 1982.

Because of Madeline by Mary Stolz, not illustrated; Harper, 1957. **Awarded:** Spring Book Festival (older) 1957.

Belling the Tiger by Mary Stolz, illustrated by Beni Montresor; Harper, 1961. **Awarded:** Newbery (honor) 1962.

The Bully of Barkham Street by Mary Stolz, illustrated by Leonard Shortall; Harper & Row, 1963. **Awarded:** Boys Club 1964.

The Day and the Way We Met by Mary Stolz, not illustrated; Harper, 1956. **Awarded:** Spring Book Festival (older honor) 1956.

The Edge of Next Year by Mary Stolz, not illustrated; Harper, 1974. **Awarded:** National Book Award (finalist) 1975.

In a Mirror by Mary Stolz, not illustrated; Harper, 1953. **Awarded:** Child Study 1953.

Night of Ghosts and Hermits by Mary Stolz, illustrated by Susan Gallagher; Harcourt, 1985. **Awarded:** New York Academy of Sciences (younger honor) 1986.

The Noonday Friends by Mary Stolz, illustrated by Louis S. Glanzman; Harper, 1965. **Awarded:** Newbery (honor) 1966.

Ready or Not by Mary Stolz, not illustrated; Harper, 1953. **Awarded:** Spring Book Festival (older honor) 1953.

Storm in the Night by Mary Stolz, illustrated by Pat Cummings; Harper & Row, 1988. **Awarded:** Coretta Scott King (Illustration honor) 1989; Parents' Choice (Story Book) 1988.

STOMANN, ALLAN
Selby Screams by Duncan Ball, illustrated by Allan Stomann; Angus & Robertson, 1989. **Awarded:** West Australian (primary) 1991.

Selby Speaks by Duncan Ball, illustrated by Allan Stomann; Angus & Robertson, 1988. **Awarded:** West Australian (Primary) 1990.

Selby's Secret by Duncan Ball, illustrated by Allan Stomann; Angus & Robertson, 1985. **Awarded:** West Australian (Primary) 1987.

STOMMEL, ELIZABETH
Volcano Weather: The Story of 1816, the Year Without a Summer by Elizabeth Stommel and Henry Stommel; illustrated; Seven Seas Press, 1983. **Awarded:** New York Academy of Sciences (older) 1984.

STOMMEL, HENRY
Volcano Weather: The Story of 1816, the Year Without a Summer by Elizabeth Stommel and Henry Stommel; illustrated; Seven Seas Press, 1983. **Awarded:** New York Academy of Sciences (older) 1984.

STONAKER, FRANCES BENSON
Famous Mathematicians by Frances B. Stonaker, not illustrated; Lippincott, 1966. **Awarded:** New Jersey Institute of Technology 1967.

STONE, DAVID K.
What's the Matter with Wakefield? by June Lewis Shore, illustrated by David K. Stone; Abingdon, 1974. **Awarded:** Abingdon 1974.

STONE, DEREK
Aldita and the Forest by Thelma Catterwall, illustrated by Derek Stone; Dent, 1988; Houghton Mifflin, 1989, c1988. **Awarded:** Whitley (Children's Book) 1989.

STONE, ELBERTA
I'm Glad I'm Me by Elberta Stone, illustrated by Margery W. Brown; Putnam, 1971. **Awarded:** New Jersey Institute of Technology 1971.

STONE, HELEN
All Around the Town by Phyllis McGinley, illustrated by Helen Stone; Lippincott, 1948. **Awarded:** Caldecott (honor) 1949.

Little Witch by Anna Elizabeth Bennett, illustrated by Helen Stone; Lippincott, 1953. **Awarded:** Helen Dean Fish 1953.

The Most Wonderful Doll in the World by Phyllis McGinley, illustrated by Helen Stone; Lippincott, 1950. **Awarded:** Caldecott (honor) 1951.

Taffy and Joe by Earl Burton and Linette Burton, illustrated by Helen Stone; Whittlesey House, 1947. **Awarded:** Spring Book Festival (younger honor) 1947.

STONG, PHILIP DUFFIELD
Captain Kidd's Cow by Phil Stong, illustrated by Kurt Wiese; Dodd, Mead, 1941. **Awarded:** Spring Book Festival (middle honor) 1941.

The Hired Man's Elephant by Phil Stong, illustrated by Doris Lee; Dodd, Mead, 1939. **Awarded:** Spring Book Festival (older) 1939.

Honk the Moose by Phil Stong, illustrated by Kurt Wiese; Dodd, Mead, 1935. **Awarded:** Lewis Carroll Shelf 1970; Newbery (honor) 1936.

STORM, THEODOR
Little John by Theodor Storm, illustrated by Anita Lobel; Farrar, 1972. **Awarded:** Spring Book Festival (picture book) 1972.

STORR, CATHERINE
The Boy and the Swan by Catherine Storr, illustrated by Laszlo Acs; Deutsch, 1987. **Awarded:** Earthworm Award 1987.

STOUB, PAUL
Leading Little Ones to God: A Child's Book of Bible Teachings by Marian M. Schoolland, illustrated by Paul Stoub; revised ed.; Eerdmans, 1981, c1962. **Awarded:** Gold Medallion (cowinner) 1982.

STOUTENBERG, ADRIEN
Out There by Adrien Stoutenberg, illustrated by Donald A. Mackay; Viking, 1971. **Awarded:** Spring Book Festival (older honor) 1971.

STOVER, JO ANN
The Phantom of Walkaway Hill by Edward Fenton, illustrated by Jo Ann Stover; Doubleday, 1961. **Awarded:** Edgar Allan Poe 1962.

STRACHAN, IAN
Moses Beech by Ian Strachan, not illustrated; Oxford, 1981. **Awarded:** Observer Teenage Fiction 1981.

STRAETER, ANGELA
Clarinda by Frances Duncombe, illustrated by Angela Straeter; Holt, 1944. **Awarded:** Spring Book Festival (younger honor) 1944.

STRAND, MARK
Rembrandt Takes a Walk by Mark Strand, illustrated by Red Grooms; Clarkson N. Potter, 1986. **Awarded:** New York Times Best Illustrated 1986.

STRATTON, LUCILLE N.
Wild Wings over the Marshes by Lucille N. Stratton and William D. Stratton, illustrated by Bernard Garbutt; Golden Gate, 1964. **Awarded:** Southern California Council (illustration) 1964.

STRATTON, WILLIAM D.
Wild Wings over the Marshes by Lucille N. Stratton and William D. Stratton, illustrated by Bernard Garbutt; Golden Gate, 1964. **Awarded:** Southern California Council (illustration) 1964.

STRAUSS, JOYCE
Imagine That!! Exploring Make-believe by Joyce Strauss, illustrated by Jennifer Barrett; Human Sciences Press, 1984. **Awarded:** Christopher (all ages) 1985.

STRAVINSKY, IGOR
Petrouchka adapted and illustrated by Elizabeth Cleaver from the work of Igor Stravinsky and Alexandre Benois; Macmillan (Canada), 1980; Atheneum, 1980. **Awarded:** International Board on Books for Young People (illustration/Canada) 1982.

STRAYER, PAUL
The Sword of Roland Arnot by Agnes Danforth Hewes, illustrated by Paul Strayer; Houghton, 1939. **Awarded:** Spring Book Festival (older honor) 1939.

STREATFEILD, NOEL
The Circus is Coming by Noel Streatfeild, illustrated by Steven Spurrier; Dent, 1938. (Published in the U.S. as *Circus Shoes*). **Awarded:** Carnegie 1938.

Movie Shoes by Noel Streatfeild, illustrated by Susanne Suba; Random House, 1949. **Awarded:** Spring Book Festival (under 12 honor) 1949.

A Young Person's Guide to Ballet by Noel Streatfeild, illustrated by Georgette Bordier; Warne, 1975. **Awarded:** Children's Book Showcase 1976.

STREET, JULIA MONTGOMERY
Dulcie's Whale by Julia Montgomery Street, illustrated by Anthony D'Adamo; Bobbs-Merrill, 1963. **Awarded:** North Carolina AAUW 1963.

Fiddler's Fancy by Julia Montgomery Street, illustrated by Don Sibley; Follett, 1955. **Awarded:** North Carolina AAUW 1956.

North Carolina Parade by Julia Montgomery Street and Richard Walser, illustrated by D. B. Browning; University of North Carolina, 1966. **Awarded:** North Carolina AAUW 1966.

STREETER, SHERRY
More Minden Curses by Willo Davis Roberts, illustrated by Sherry Streeter; Atheneum, 1980. **Awarded:** Edgar Allan Poe (runnerup) 1981.

STREN, PATTI
Eating Ice Cream With a Werewolf by Phyllis Green, illustrated by Patti Stren; Harper and Row, 1983. **Awarded:** Maud Hart Lovelace 1989.

STRIEBER, WHITLEY
Wolf of Shadows by Whitley Strieber, not illustrated; Sierra Club/Knopf, 1985. **Awarded:** Friends of American Writers ($350) 1986.

STROGART, ALEXANDER
Maxie, Rosie and Earl: Partners in Grime by Barbara Park, illustrated by Alexander Strogart; Knopf, 1990. **Awarded:** Parents' Choice (Story Book) 1990.

STRUGNELL, ANN
Bongleweed by Helen Cresswell, illustrated by Ann Strugnell; Faber, 1973. **Awarded:** Carnegie (commended) 1973.

The Fool and the Dancing Bear by Pamela Stearns, illustrated by Ann Strugnell; Little, Brown, 1979. **Awarded:** Commonwealth Club of California 1979.

More Stories Julian Tells by Ann Cameron, illustrated by Ann Strugnell; Knopf, 1986. **Awarded:** Parents' Choice (literature) 1986.

Once upon a Time in a Pigpen by Margaret Wise Brown, illustrated by Ann Strugnell; Addison-Wesley, 1980. **Awarded:** Parents' Choice (illustration) 1980.

The Stories Julian Tells by Ann Cameron, illustrated by Ann Strugnell; Pantheon, 1981. **Awarded:** Irma Simonton Black 1981.

STRUMITTO, ARDREZEJ
Narzeczony z Morza by Robert Stieler, illustrated by Ardrezej Strumitto; Nasza Ksiegaa. **Awarded:** Biennale Illustrations Bratislava (grand prix) 1971.

STRYKER, SANDY
Tonia the Tree by Sandy Stryker, illustrated by Itoko Maeno; Advocacy Press, 1988. **Awarded:** Friends of American Writers 1989.

STUART, JESSE
Awarded: Jesse Stuart 1981.

Old Ben by Jesse Stuart, illustrated by Richard Cuffari; McGraw, 1970. **Awarded:** Lewis Carroll Shelf 1970.

STUART, MORNA
Marassa and Midnight by Morna Stuart, illustrated by Janina Ede; Heinemann, 1966. **Awarded:** Carnegie (commended) 1966.

STUBLEY, TREVOR
Old Dog, New Tricks by Dick Cate, illustrated by Trevor Stubley; Hamish Hamilton, 1978. **Awarded:** Other Award 1979.

Storm Surge by David Rees, illustrated by Trevor Stubley; Lutterworth, 1975. **Awarded:** Guardian (commended) 1976.

STULL, EDITH G.
Taxation by Edith G. Stull and J. Woodrow Sayre; Watts, 1963. **Awarded:** New Jersey Institute of Technology (economics children) 1964.

STYLES, S. J.
The American West 1840-1895 by R. A. Rees and S. J. Styles, illustrated with photos; Longman, 1986. **Awarded:** Times Educational Supplement (Schoolbook) 1987.

SUBA, SUSANNE
Lottie's Valentine by Katherine Wigmore Eyre, illustrated by Susanne Suba; Oxford, 1941. **Awarded:** Spring Book Festival (middle honor) 1941.

Movie Shoes by Noel Streatfeild, illustrated by Susanne Suba; Random House, 1949. **Awarded:** Spring Book Festival (under 12 honor) 1949.

Sonny-boy Sim by Elizabeth Baker, illustrated by Susanne Suba; Rand McNally, 1948. **Awarded:** Spring Book Festival (younger honor) 1949; Steck-Vaughn 1951.

SUCHER, MARY
Awarded: ALAN 1978.

SUHL, YURI
Simon Boom Gives a Wedding by Yuri Suhl, illustrated by Margot Zemach; Four Winds, 1972. **Awarded:** Lewis Carroll Shelf 1972; Children's Book Showcase 1973; New York Times Best Illustrated 1972.

Uncle Misha's Partisans by Yuri Suhl, not illustrated; Four Winds, 1973. **Awarded:** Jewish Book Council 1973; Sydney Taylor Book Award 1973.

SULLIVAN, BETTY
A Poetic Look at Aesop's Fables by Betty Sullivan; Carleton Press. **Awarded:** New Jersey Institute of Technology 1977.

Sudden Steps, Small Stones by Betty Sullivan; Carleton Press. **Awarded:** New Jersey Institute of Technology 1977.

SUMMERS, JAMES L.
Girl Trouble by James L. Summers, not illustrated; Westminster, 1953. **Awarded:** Spring Book Festival (older honor) 1953.

SUPREE, BURTON
Harlequin and the Gift of Many Colors by Burton Supree and Remy Charlip, illustrated by Remy Charlip; Parents, 1973. **Awarded:** Irma Simonton Black 1973.

Mother, Mother, I Feel Sick, Send for the Doctor Quick, Quick, Quick by Burton Supree and Remy Charlip, illustrated by Remy Charlip; Parents', 1966. **Awarded:** Boys Club 1966-67.

SUSCHITZY, W.
The Golden Book of Animals by Anne Terry White, photographs by W. Suschitzy; Simon & Schuster, 1958. **Awarded:** New York Times Best Illustrated 1958.

SUTCLIFF, ROSEMARY
Awarded: Hans Christian Andersen (highly commended author/Great Britain) 1974.

Blood Feud by Rosemary Sutcliff, not illustrated; Dutton, 1977. **Awarded:** Boston Globe Horn Book (fiction honor) 1977.

Dawn Wind by Rosemary Sutcliff, illustrated by Charles Keeping; Walck, 1962. **Awarded:** Spring Book Festival (older) 1962.

The Eagle of the Ninth by Rosemary Sutcliff, illustrated by C. Walter Hodges; Oxford, 1954. **Awarded:** Carnegie (commended) 1954.

The Lantern Bearers by Rosemary Sutcliff, illustrated by Charles Keeping; Oxford, 1959. **Awarded:** Carnegie 1959.

The Mark of the Horse Lord by Rosemary Sutcliff, illustrated with maps; Walck, 1965; Oxford, 1975; Penguin, 1983. **Awarded:** Phoenix 1985.

The Road to Camlann by Rosemary Sutcliff, illustrated by Shirley Felts; Dutton, 1982. **Awarded:** Boston Globe Horn Book (fiction honor) 1983.

The Shield Ring by Rosemary Sutcliff, illustrated by C. Walter Hodges; Oxford, 1957, 1956. **Awarded:** Carnegie (commended) 1956; Spring Book Festival (older honor) 1957.

The Silver Branch by Rosemary Sutcliff, illustrated by Charles Keeping; Walck, 1958; Oxford, 1957. **Awarded:** Carnegie (commended) 1957; Spring Book Festival (older honor) 1958.

Song for a Dark Queen by Rosemary Sutcliff, not illustrated; Pelham, 1978. **Awarded:** Other Award 1978.

Tristan and Iseult by Rosemary Sutcliff, illustrated by Victor Ambrus; Bodley Head, 1971. **Awarded:** Carnegie (highly commended) 1971.

Tristan and Iseult by Rosemary Sutcliff, not illustrated; Dutton, 1971. **Awarded:** Boston Globe Horn Book (text) 1972.

Unmei no Kishi (original English: *Knight's Fee*) by Rosemary Sutcliff, translated by Yoko Inokuma; Iwanami-shoten, 1970. **Awarded:** International Board on Books for Young People (translation/Japan) 1986.

Warrior Scarlet by Rosemary Sutcliff, illustrated by Charles Keeping; Oxford, 1958; Walck, 1958. **Awarded:** Carnegie (commended) 1958; International Board on Books for Young People (Great Britain) 1960.

The Witch's Brat by Rosemary Sutcliff, illustrated by Richard Lebenson; Walck, 1970. **Awarded:** Lewis Carroll Shelf 1971.

SUTEYEV, V.
The Chick and the Ducklings by V. Suteyev, translated and adapted by Mirra Ginsburg, illustrated by Ariane Aruego and Jose Aruego; Macmillan, 1972. **Awarded:** Children's Book Showcase 1973.

SUTHERLAND, ROBERT D.
Stickelwort and Feverfew written and illustrated by Robert D. Sutherland; Pikestaff Press, 1980. **Awarded:** Friends of American Writers (juvenile book author/illustrator) 1981.

SUTHERLAND, ZENA
Awarded: Children's Reading Round Table 1978; Grolier 1983.

SUTTON, ANN
Wildlife of the Forests by Ann Sutton and Myron Sutton, illustrated with photographs; Abrams, 1979. **Awarded:** New York Academy of Sciences (special award for a reference book series to a publisher) 1980.

SUTTON, EVE
My Cat Likes To Hide in Boxes by Eve Sutton, illustrated by Lynley Dodd; Hamish Hamilton, 1974. **Awarded:** Esther Glen 1975.

SUTTON, JANE
Me and the Weirdos by Jane Sutton, illustrated by Sandy Kossin; Houghton Mifflin, 1981. **Awarded:** Utah Children's 1986.

SUTTON, MYRON
Wildlife of the Forests by Myron Sutton and Ann Sutton, illustrated with photographs; Abrams, 1979. **Awarded:** New York Academy of Sciences (special award for a reference book series to a publisher) 1980.

SUTTON, SUZANNE
Awarded: American Association of School Librarians 1987.

SUZUKI, DAVID
Looking At Insects by David Suzuki, with Barbara Hehner, illustrated; Stoddart, 1986. **Awarded:** Information Book Award 1987.

SUZUKI, MASAHARU
Potatoes by Sylvia A. Johnson, illustrated by Masaharu Suzuki; Lerner, 1984. **Awarded:** New York Academy of Sciences (younger honor) 1985.

SVENSON, ANDREW
Awarded: New Jersey Institute of Technology (New Jersey author awards special citation) 1969.

SVENSSON, BORJE
Sailing Ships by Ron Van Der Meer and Dr. Alan McGowan, paintings by Borje Svensson; Viking, 1984. **Awarded:** Redbook (popup) 1984.

SWAIN, SU ZAN NOGUCHI
All Kinds of Bees by Dorothy E. Shuttlesworth, illustrated by Su Zan Noguchi Swain; Random House, 1967. **Awarded:** New Jersey Institute of Technology 1967.

The Story of Ants by Dorothy Shuttlesworth, illustrated by Su Zan Swain; Doubleday, 1964. **Awarded:** New Jersey Institute of Technology 1965.

SWAINSON, DONALD
The Buffalo Hunt by Eleanor Swainson and Donald Swainson, illustrated by James Tughan; PMA Books, 1980. **Awarded:** Amelia Frances Howard-Gibbon (runnerup) 1981.

SWAINSON, ELEANOR

The Buffalo Hunt by Eleanor Swainson and Donald Swainson, illustrated by James Tughan; PMA Books, 1980. **Awarded:** Amelia Frances Howard-Gibbon (runnerup) 1981.

SWALLOW, PAMELA CURTIS

Leave It To Christy by Pamela Curtis Swallow, not illustrated; Putnam, 1987; Scholastic, 1988, c1987. **Awarded:** New Jersey Institute of Technology 1988.

SWARTHOUT, GLENDON

Cadbury's Coffin by Glendon Swarthout and Kathryn Swarthout, illustrated by Frank Mayo; Doubleday, 1982. **Awarded:** Edgar Allan Poe (runnerup) 1983.

SWARTHOUT, KATHRYN

Cadbury's Coffin by Glendon Swarthout and Kathryn Swarthout, illustrated by Frank Mayo; Doubleday, 1982. **Awarded:** Edgar Allan Poe (runnerup) 1983.

SWAYZE, FRED

Awarded: Vicky Metcalf 1966.

SWEAT, LYNN

Amelia Bedelia and the Baby by Peggy Parish, illustrated by Lynn Sweat; Greenwillow, 1981. **Awarded:** Buckeye (K-3 honor) 1983.

Amelia Bedelia Goes Camping by Peggy Parish, illustrated by Lynn Sweat; Greenwillow, 1985. **Awarded:** Garden State Children's Book Award (Easy to Read) 1988.

The Garden Is Doing Fine by Carol Farley, illustrated by Lynn Sweat; Atheneum, 1975. **Awarded:** Child Study 1975; Golden Kite 1975.

Merry Christmas, Amelia Bedelia by Peggy Parish, illustrated by Lynn Sweat; Greenwillow, 1986. **Awarded:** Garden State Children's Book Award (Easy to Read) 1989.

Teach Us, Amelia Bedelia by Peggy Parish, illustrated by Lynn Sweat; Greenwillow, 1977. **Awarded:** Garden State Children's (easy to read) 1980.

SWEENEY, JOYCE

Center Line by Joyce Sweeney, not illustrated; Delacorte, 1984. **Awarded:** Delacorte 1983.

SWIFT, HILDEGARDE HOYT

From the Eagle's Wing: A Biography of John Muir by Hildegarde Hoyt Swift, illustrated by Lynd Ward; Morrow, 1962. **Awarded:** Southern California Council (notable) 1963.

Little Blacknose: The Story of a Pioneer by Hildegarde Swift, illustrated by Lynd Ward; Harcourt, 1929. **Awarded:** Newbery (honor) 1930.

North Star Shining by Hildegarde Hoyt Swift, illustrated by Lynd Ward; Morrow, 1947. **Awarded:** Spring Book Festival (older honor) 1947.

The Railroad to Freedom: A story of the Civil War by Hildegarde Swift, illustrated by James Daugherty; Harcourt, 1932. **Awarded:** Newbery (honor) 1933.

SWINDELLS, ROBERT

Brother in the Land by Robert Swindells, not illustrated; Oxford University Press, 1984. **Awarded:** Carnegie (highly commended) 1984; Children's Book Award 1984; Other Award 1984.

Room 13 by Robert E. Swindells, illustrated by Jon Riley; Doubleday, 1989. **Awarded:** Children's Book Award (Federation) 1989-90.

SWITZER, ELLEN

Our Urban Planet by Ellen Switzer, photographs by Michael Switzer and Jeffrey Switzer; Atheneum, 1980. **Awarded:** New York Academy of Sciences (older honor) 1981.

SWITZER, JEFFREY

Our Urban Planet by Ellen Switzer, photographs by Michael Switzer and Jeffrey Switzer; Atheneum, 1980. **Awarded:** New York Academy of Sciences (older honor) 1981.

SWITZER, MICHAEL

Our Urban Planet by Ellen Switzer, photographs by Michael Switzer and Jeffrey Switzer; Atheneum, 1980. **Awarded:** New York Academy of Sciences (older honor) 1981.

SYME, NEVILLE RONALD

Boy of the North: The Story of Pierre Radisson by Ronald Syme, illustrated by Ralph Ray; Morrow, 1950. **Awarded:** Boys Club 1951.

SYMONDS, JOHN

The Magic Currant Bun by John Symonds, illustrated by Andre Francois; Lippincott, 1952. **Awarded:** New York Times Best Illustrated 1952.

SZEKERES, CYNDY

Brimhall Comes To Stay by Judy Delton, illustrated by Cyndy Szekeres; Lothrop, 1978. **Awarded:** Council of Wisconsin Writers (picture book runnerup) 1979.

It's Time to Go to Bed by Joyce Segal, edited by Cyndy Szekeres, illustrated by Robin Eaton; Doubleday, 1979. **Awarded:** New Jersey Institute of Technology 1980.

SZILAGYI, MARY

The Basket by George Ella Lyon, illustrated by Mary Szilagyi; Orchard, 1990. **Awarded:** Kentucky Bluegrass (grades K-3) 1992.

T

TABACK, SIMMS

Please Share that Peanut! A Preposterous Pageant in Fourteen Acts by Sesyle Joslin and Simms Taback, illustrated by Simms Taback; Harcourt, 1965. **Awarded:** New York Times Best Illustrated 1965.

TAFURI, NANCY

Four Brave Sailors by Mirra Ginsburg, illustrated by Nancy Tafuri; Greenwillow, 1987. **Awarded:** Parents' Choice (Picture Book) 1987.

Have You Seen my Duckling? written and illustrated by Nancy Tafuri; Greenwillow, 1984. **Awarded:** Caldecott (honor) 1985.

If I Had a Paka: Poems in Eleven Languages by Charlotte Pomerantz, illustrated by Nancy Tafuri; Greenwillow, 1982. **Awarded:** Jane Addams (honor) 1983.

Junglewalk written and illustrated by Nancy Tafuri; Greenwillow, 1988. **Awarded:** Redbook 1988.

Who's Counting? written and illustrated by Nancy Tafuri; Greenwillow, 1986. **Awarded:** Please Touch 1987.

TAHSE, MARTIN

Awarded: Southern California Council (significant contribution for interpretation of literature through film) 1978.

TAILFEATHERS, GERALD
The White Calf by Cliff Faulknor, illustrated by Gerald Tailfeathers; Little, Brown, 1965. **Awarded:** Little Brown Canadian 1964.

TAINA, HANNU
Herra Kuningas by Raija Siekkinen, illustrated by Hannu Taina; Otava, 1986. **Awarded:** BIB (grand prix) 1987.

TAIT, DOUGLAS
Mouse Woman and the Vanished Princesses by Christie Harris, illustrated by Douglas Tait; McClelland & Stewart, 1976. **Awarded:** Canadian Library Assn. 1977; International Board on Book for Young People (text/Canada) 1978.

The Trouble with Princesses by Christie Harris, illustrated by Douglas Tait; McClelland & Stewart, 1980; Atheneum, 1980. **Awarded:** Canadian Library Assn. (runnerup) 1981; Governor General 1980; Amelia Frances Howard-Gibbon 1981.

TAKASHIMA, SHIZUYE
A Child in Prison Camp written and illustrated by Shizuye Takashima; Tundra, 1971. **Awarded:** Amelia Frances Howard-Gibbon 1972.

TAKEUCHI, BETTY
Awarded: Southern California Council (Dorothy C. McKenzie Award) 1990.

TALBERT, MARC
Dead Birds Singing by Marc Talbert, not illustrated; Little Brown, 1985; Hamilton, 1986. **Awarded:** West Australian (Secondary) 1988.

TALBOTT, HUDSON
We're Back! A Dinosaur Story written and illustrated by Hudson Talbott; Crown, 1987. **Awarded:** Georgia Children's Picture Storybook 1991; Nevada Young Reader Award (Primary) 1990-91.

TALIFERO, GERALD
The Bridge Dancers by Carol Saller, illustrated by Gerald Talifero; Carolrhoda, 1991. **Awarded:** Sandburg 1991.

TALLON, ROBERT
Rhoda's Restaurant written and illustrated by Robert Tallon; Bobbs Merrill, 1973. **Awarded:** Art Books for Children 1975.

TALMADGE, MARIAN
Pony Express Boy by Marian Talmadge and Iris Gilmore, illustrated; Dodd, Mead, 1956. **Awarded:** Boys Life - Dodd Mead 1955.

TAMARIN, ALFRED H.
Voyaging to Cathay: Americans in the China Trade by Alfred Tamarin and Shirley Glubok, illustrated with photographs and old prints; Viking, 1976. **Awarded:** Boston Globe Horn Book (nonfiction) 1976.

TAMCHINA, JURGEN
Dominique and the Dragon by Jurgen Tamchina, translated by Elizabeth D. Crawford, illustrated by Heidrun Petrides; Harcourt, 1968. **Awarded:** Spring Book Festival (picture book honor) 1969.

TANEMURA, HIROSHI
Frogs and Toads by Jane Dallinger and Sylvia A. Johnson, photographs by Hiroshi Tanemura; Lerner, 1982. **Awarded:** New York Academy of Sciences (special award) 1983.

TANNER, JANE
Drac and the Gremlin by Allan Baillie, illustrated by Jane Tanner; Viking Kestrel, 1988; Dial, 1989. **Awarded:** Children's Book Council of Australia (Picture Book of the Year) 1989.

TANNER, LOUISE
Reggie and Nilma: A New York City Story by Louise Tanner, not illustrated; Farrar, 1971. **Awarded:** Spring Book Festival (older) 1971.

TANNINEN, OILI
Muru Menee Kalaan written and illustrated by Oili Tanninen; Otava, 1961. **Awarded:** Hans Christian Andersen (runnerup) 1964.

TANOBE, MIYUKI
Quebec: Je T'aime: I Love You written and illustrated by Miyuki Tanobe; Tundra, 1976. **Awarded:** Children's Book Showcase 1977; Amelia Frances Howard-Gibbon (runnerup) 1977.

TANSLEY, ERIC
The Book of the West: An Epic of America's Wild Frontier by Charles Chilton, illustrated by Eric Tansley; Bobbs-Merrill, 1962. **Awarded:** Western Heritage 1963.

TARTAGLIONE, JOHN
Mother Teresa of Calcutta by Roy M. Gasnick and David Michelinie, illustrated by John Tartaglione; Franciscan Communications Office, 1984. **Awarded:** Catholic Book Awards (Youth) 1985.

TATE, ELEANORA E.
Secret of Gumbo Grove by Eleanora E. Tate, not illustrated; Watts, 1987. **Awarded:** Parents' Choice (Story Book) 1987.

TATE, JOAN
A Christmas Book translated by J. Tate, illustrated by Svend Otto S.; Pelham, 1978. **Awarded:** Biennale Illustrations Bratislava (plaque) 1979.

The Giant Fish and other Stories written and illustrated by Svend Otto S., translated by Joan Tate; Larousse, 1982. **Awarded:** Parents' Choice (illustration) 1982.

TAVO, GUS
Ride the Pale Stallion by Gus Tavo, illustrated by Lorence F. Bjorklund; Knopf, 1968. **Awarded:** Steck-Vaughn 1969.

TAYLOR, ANDREW
The Coal House by Andrew Taylor, not illustrated; Collins, 1986. **Awarded:** Carnegie (commended) 1986; Whitbread 1986.

TAYLOR, CORA
The Doll by Cora Taylor, not illustrated; Western Producer Prairie Books, 1987. **Awarded:** Ruth Schwartz 1988.

Julie by Cora Taylor, not illustrated; Western Producer Prairie Books, 1985. **Awarded:** R. Ross Annett 1986; Canadian Library Assn. 1986; Governor General 1985.

TAYLOR, EDGAR
King Grisly-Beard: A Tale from the Brothers Grimm translated by Edgar Taylor, illustrated by Maurice Sendak; Farrar, 1973. **Awarded:** Children's Book Showcase 1974; New York Times Best Illustrated 1973.

TAYLOR, ELIZABETH BUCHANAN
The Wonderful Travels and Adventures of Baron Munchhausen by Peter Nickl, translated by Elizabeth Buchanan Taylor, illustrated by Binette Schroeder; Chatto & Windus, 1979. **Awarded:** New York Times Best Illustrated 1980.

TAYLOR, ELIZABETH WATSON
The Magic Inkstand and other Stories by Heinrich Seidel, translated by Elizabeth Watson Taylor; Jonathan Cape, 1982. **Awarded:** IBBY (translation/Great Britain) 1984.

TAYLOR, HERB

The Lobster: It's Life Cycle by Herb Taylor, illustrated with photographs; Sterling, 1975. **Awarded:** New York Academy of Sciences (younger honor) 1976.

TAYLOR, KIM

Bird by David Burnie, illustrated by Kim Taylor and Peter Chadwick; Dorling Kindersley/Natural History Museum, 1988; Knopf, 1988. **Awarded:** Greenaway (special Commendation) 1988.

Frog by Angela Royston, illustrated by Kim Taylor; Lodestar, 1991. **Awarded:** Redbook 1991.

TAYLOR, MARK

Awarded: Southern California Council (significant contribution. for excellence in a series for the Henry series) 1976

Bobby Shafto's Gone to Sea by Mark Taylor, illustrated by Graham Booth; Golden Gate Junior Books, 1970. **Awarded:** Southern California Council (contribution to illustration) 1971.

TAYLOR, MILDRED D.

Awarded: CBC Honors Program 1988; Ohioana Award (Alice L. Wood Memorial) 1991.

The Friendship by Mildred D. Taylor, illustrated by Max Ginsburg; Dial, 1987. **Awarded:** Boston Globe (Fiction) 1988; Coretta Scott King (Text) 1988.

The Gold Cadillac by Mildred D. Taylor, illustrated by Michael Hays; Dial, 1987. **Awarded:** Christopher (ages 9-12) 1988; New York Times Notable 1987.

Let the Circle be Unbroken by Mildred D. Taylor, not illustrated; Dial, 1981. **Awarded:** Jane Addams (honor) 1982; Coretta Scott King (author) 1982; New York Times Notable Books 1981; Stone, George G. 1990.

Mississippi Bridge by Mildred Taylor, illustrated by Max Ginsburg; Dial, 1990. **Awarded:** Christopher (Ages 9-12) 1991.

The Road to Memphis by Mildred D. Taylor, not illustrated; Dial, 1990. **Awarded:** Coretta Scott King (Text) 1991; George G. Stone 1991; Young Adult Novel of the Year/Michigan Library Assn. 1990.

Roll of Thunder, Hear my Cry by Mildred D. Taylor, illustrated by Jerry Pinkney; Dial, 1976. **Awarded:** Jane Addams (honor) 1977; Boston Globe Horn Book (fiction honor) 1977; National Book Award (finalist) 1977; Newbery 1977; George G. Stone 1991; Young Reader's Choice 1979.

Song of the Trees by Mildred D. Taylor, illustrated by Jerry Pinkney; Dial, 1975. **Awarded:** Jane Addams (honor) 1976; Children's Book Showcase 1976; Council on Interracial Books for Children (African-American) 1973.

TAYLOR, NEIL

Back-Back and the Lima Bear by Thomas L. Weck, illustrated by Neil Taylor; Winston-Derek, 1985. **Awarded:** Catholic Book Awards (Children's) 1986; New Jersey Institute of Technology 1987.

TAYLOR, SYDNEY

Awarded: Sydney Taylor Body of Work 1979.

All-of-a-Kind Family by Sydney Taylor, illustrated by Helen John; Follett, 1951. **Awarded:** Charles W. Follett 1951; Jewish Book Council 1951.

TAYLOR, THEODORE

Awarded: Southern California Council (distinguished contribution to the field of children's literature & body of work) 1978; George G. Stone (body of work) 1980.

Battle in the Arctic Seas: The Story of Convoy PQ17 by Theodore Taylor, illustrated by Robert A. Parker; Harper, 1976. **Awarded:** New York Times Notable Books 1981.

The Cay by Theodore Taylor, not illustrated; Doubleday, 1969. **Awarded:** Lewis Carroll Shelf 1970; Commonwealth Club of California 1969; Southern California Council (notable) 1970; Woodward Park School 1970.

A Shepherd Watches, a Shepherd Sings by Theodore Taylor and Louis Irigary, illustrated with photographs; Doubleday, 1977. **Awarded:** Commonwealth Club of California 1977; Western Writers of America 1977.

The Sniper by Theodore Taylor, not illustrated; Harcourt Brace Jovanovich, 1989. **Awarded:** California Young Reader (Intermediate) 1992.

The Trouble with Tuck by Theodore Taylor, not illustrated; Doubleday, 1981. **Awarded:** California Young Reader (intermediate) 1984.

TAYLOR, WILLIAM

Agnes the Sheep by William Taylor, not illustrated; Ashton Scholastic, 1990; Scholastic, 1990. **Awarded:** Esther Glen 1991.

TEALE, EDWIN WAY

Awarded: Eva L. Gordon 1965.

TEASON, JAMES G.

The Lion's Whiskers: Tales of High Africa by Russell Davis and Brent Ashabranner, illustrated by James G. Teason; Little, Brown, 1959. **Awarded:** Spring Book Festival (older honor) 1959.

TEICHER, DICK

A Boat to Nowhere by Maureen Crane Wartski, illustrated by Dick Teicher; Westminster, 1980. **Awarded:** Child Study 1981.

TEJIMA, KEIZABURO

Fox's Dream written and illustrated by Keizaburo Tejima; Philomel, 1987. **Awarded:** New York Times Best Illustrated 1987; New York Times Notable 1987.

Swan Sky written and illustrated by Tejima; Philomel, 1988. **Awarded:** New York Times Best Illustrated 1988.

TEMPLE, FRANCES

A Taste of Salt: A Story of Modern Haiti by Frances Temple, not illustrated; Orchard, 1992. **Awarded:** Jane Addams 1993; Hungry Mind (Young Adult/Fiction) 1993.

TEMPLE, HERBERT

The Legend of Africania by Dorothy Robinson, illustrated by Herbert Temple; Johnson, 1974. **Awarded:** Coretta Scott King 1975.

TEMPLE, PHILIP

The Story of the Kakapo Parrot of the Night by Philip Temple, illustrated by Chris Gaskin; Hodder & Stoughton, 1988. **Awarded:** AIM Children's Book Award (Picture Book 2nd prize) 1990.

TEMPLE, ROBERT K. G.

The Genius of China by Robert K. G. Temple, illustrated with photos; Simon & Schuster, 1986. **Awarded:** New York Academy of Sciences (Older honor) 1988.

TENGBOM, MILDRED

Talking Together About Love and Sexuality by Mildred Tengbom, illustrated; Bethany House, 1985. **Awarded:** Gold Medallion 1986.

TENGGREN, GUSTAF
Farm Stories by Kathryn Byron Jackson, illustrated by Gustaf Tenggren; Simon & Schuster, 1946. **Awarded:** Spring Book Festival (younger) 1946.

TENNANT, KYLIE
All the Proud Tribesmen by Kylie Tennant, illustrated by Clem Seale; Macmillan (London), 1959. **Awarded:** Children's Book Council of Australia (book of the year) 1960.

TENNENT, JULIE
The Three and Many Wishes of Jason Reid by Hazel J. Hutchins, illustrated by Julie Tennent; Viking Kestrel, 1988. **Awarded:** Reading Magic Award 1988.

TENNIS, DONNA JEAN
Summer Nanny by Donna Jean Tennis. unpublished manuscript. **Awarded:** Golden Medallion 1992.

TENNYSON, ALFRED
The Charge of the Light Brigade by Alfred Tennyson, illustrated by Alice Provensen and Martin Provensen; Golden, 1964. **Awarded:** New York Times Best Illustrated 1964.

TERRIS, DANIEL
A Twilight Struggle: The Life of John Fitzgerald Kennedy by Daniel Terris and Barbara Harrison, illustrated; Lothrop, Lee & Shepard, 1992. **Awarded:** Parents Choice (Picture Book) 1992.

TERRIS, SUSAN
Nell's Quilt by Susan Terris, not illustrated; Farrar Straus Giroux, 1987. **Awarded:** Commonwealth Club of California 1987.

TESKEY, DONALD
Under the Hawthorn Tree by Marita Conlon-McKenna, illustrated by Donald Teskey; Holiday House, 1990. **Awarded:** International Reading Assn. (Older) 1991; Reading Association of Ireland 1991.

TESTA, FULVIO
If You Take a Pencil written and illustrated by Fulvio Testa; Dial, 1982. **Awarded:** Parents' Choice (illustration) 1983.

TETTMAR, JAQUELINE
Animals of Farthing Wood: Escape from Danger by Colin Dann, illustrated by Jaqueline Tettmar; Heinemann, 1979. **Awarded:** Arts Council of Great Britain 1979.

THACHER, EDITH
see BROWN, MARGARET WISE

THACKER, NOLA
Summer Stories by Nola Thacker, illustrated by William Low; Lippincott, 1988. **Awarded:** Author's Award (Alabama) 1989.

THAMM, PETER
The Little Monster series by Peter Thamm, illustrated by Robert Roennfeldt; Lutheran Publishing House, 1988. **Awarded:** Australian Christian Book of the Year Children's Award 1989.

THAYER, ERNEST L.
Casey at the Bat by Ernest L. Thayer, illustrated by Leonard Everett Fisher; Watts, 1964. **Awarded:** New York Times Best Illustrated 1964.

THAYER, JANE
see WOOLLEY, CATHERINE

THESMAN, JEAN
Appointment With a Stranger by Jean Thesman, not illustrated; Houghton Mifflin, 1989. **Awarded:** Sequoyah Young Adult 1992.

The Rain Catchers by Jean Thesman, not illustrated; Houghton Mifflin, 1991. **Awarded:** Golden Kite (Fiction) 1991.

THIELE, COLIN
Blue Fin by Colin Thiele, illustrated by Roger Haldane; Rigby, 1969. **Awarded:** International Board on Books for Young People (Australia) 1972.

The Fire in the Stone by Colin Thiele, not illustrated; Rigby, 1973; Harper, 1974. **Awarded:** Edgar Allan Poe (runnerup) 1975; Writers Award 1973.

The Magpie Island by Colin Thiele, illustrated by Roger Haldane; Rigby, 1975. **Awarded:** Children's Book Council of Australia (best illustrated) 1975.

Storm Boy by Colin Thiele, illustrated by Robert Ingpen; Rigby, 1963. **Awarded:** Children's Book Council of Australia (best illustrated) 1975.

The Valley Between by Colin Thiele, not illustrated; Rigby, 1981. **Awarded:** Children's Book Council of Australia (book of the year) 1982.

THOMAS, DAWN
A Bicycle from Bridgetown by Dawn Thomas, illustrated by Don Miller; McGraw, 1975. **Awarded:** New Jersey Institute of Technology 1976.

THOMAS, DYLAN
A Child's Christmas in Wales by Dylan Thomas, illustrated by Edward Ardizzone; Godine, 1980. **Awarded:** New York Times Best Illustrated 1980.

THOMAS, ELEANOR
Mr. Totter and the Five Black Cats by Eleanor Thomas, illustrated by Charlotte Becker; Scribner, 1942. **Awarded:** Ohioana (honor) 1943.

THOMAS, FRANCES
The Blindfold Track by Frances Thomas, not illustrated; Macmillan, 1980. **Awarded:** Tir Na n-Og (English) 1981.

The Region of the Summer Stars by Frances Thomas, not illustrated; Barn Owl Press, 1985. **Awarded:** Tir Na n-Og (English) 1986.

Who Stole a Bloater? by Frances Thomas, not illustrated; Seren Books, 1991. **Awarded:** Tir Na n-Og (English) 1992.

THOMAS, HAROLD E.
Coyotes: Last Animals on Earth? by Harold E. Thomas, illustrated by Lorence F. Bjorklund; Lothrop, Lee & Shepard, 1975. **Awarded:** Commonwealth Club of California 1975.

THOMAS, JANE RESH
Saying Goodbye to Grandma by Jane Resh Thomas, illustrated by Marcia Sewall; Clarion, 1988. **Awarded:** Fassler 1989.

THOMAS, JOYCE CAROL
Bright Shadow by Joyce Carol Thomas; Avon, 1983. **Awarded:** Coretta Scott King (honorable mention) 1984.

Marked by Fire by Joyce Carol Thomas, not illustrated; Avon, 1982. **Awarded:** American Book Award (children's fiction paperback) 1983; New York Times Notable Books 1982.

THOMAS, KATRINA
Oh, Boy! Babies! by Jane Lawrence Mali and Alison Cragin Herzig, illustrated by Katrina Thomas; Little, Brown, 1980. **Awarded:** American Book Awards (children's nonfiction hardcover) 1981.

THOMAS, LUCILLE COLE
Awarded: Grolier 1988.

THOMAS, MACK

What Would Jesus Do? by Mack Thomas, not illustrated; Questar Publications, 1991. **Awarded:** Gold Medallion (Preschool) 1992.

THOMAS, RUTH

The Runaways by Ruth Thomas, not illustrated; Hutchinson Children's, 1987; Lippincott, 1989. **Awarded:** Guardian Award 1988.

THOMAS, VALERIE

Winnie the Witch by Valerie Thomas and Korky Paul, illustrated by Korky Paul; Oxford University Press, 1987. **Awarded:** Children's Book Award (Federation of...) 1987.

THOMASMA, KEN

Naya Nuki: Girl Who Ran by Ken Thomasma, illustrated by Eunice Hundley; Baker Book House, 1983. **Awarded:** Indian Paintbrush 1986.

Pathki Nana: Kootenai Girl Solves a Mystery by Ken Thomasma, illustrated by Jack Brouwer; Barker Book House, 1991. **Awarded:** Indian Paintbrush 1993.

THOMPSON, BRIAN

The Story of Prince Rama by Brian Thompson, illustrated by Roy Jeroo and original paintings; Kestrel, 1980. **Awarded:** Garavi Gujarat (children) 1982.

THOMPSON, CAROL

Busy Baby's Day - Afternoon written and illustrated by Carol Thompson; Macdonald, 1987. **Awarded:** Mother Goose (runner-up) 1988.

Busy Baby's Day - Bedtime written and illustrated by Carol Thompson; Macdonald, 1987. **Awarded:** Mother Goose (runnerup) 1988.

Busy Baby's Day - Morning written and illustrated by Carol Thompson; Macdonald, 1987. **Awarded:** Mother Goose (runnerup) 1988.

Busy Baby's Day - Wake up Time written and illustrated by Carol Thompson; Macdonald, 1987. **Awarded:** Mother Goose (runnerup) 1988.

THOMPSON, EILEEN

The Apache Gold Mystery by Eileen Thompson, illustrated by James Russell; Abelard-Schuman, 1965. **Awarded:** Edgar Allan Poe (runnerup) 1966.

THOMPSON, GEORGE SELDEN

see SELDEN, GEORGE

THOMPSON, HARLAN H.

(pseudonym for Stephen Holt)

Prairie Colt by Stephen Holt, illustrated by Wesley Dennis; Longmans, 1947. **Awarded:** Boys Club 1949.

Spook, the Mustang by Harlan Thompson, illustrated by Paul Lantz; Doubleday, 1956. **Awarded:** Commonwealth Club of California 1956.

THOMPSON, MARJORIE

Who Likes the Dark? by Virginia Howell, illustrated by Marjorie Thompson; Howell, Soskin, 1945. **Awarded:** Spring Book Festival (younger honor) 1946.

THOMPSON, MARY WOLFE

Two in the Wilderness by Mary W. Thompson, illustrated by Tom O'Sullivan, McKay, 1967. **Awarded:** Dorothy Canfield Fisher 1969.

THOMPSON, MOZELLE

Lift Every Voice and Sing: Words and Music by James Welson Johnson and J. Rosamund, illustrated by Mozelle Thompson; Hawthorn, 1970. **Awarded:** Lewis Carroll Shelf 1971; New York Times Best Illustrated 1970.

THOMPSON, RALPH

The Golden Impala by Pamela Ropner, illustrated by Ralph Thompson; Criterion, 1958. **Awarded:** Boys Club 1959.

THOMPSON, RUTH PLUMLY

Awarded: L. Frank Baum 1968.

THOMPSON, SHERLEY CLARK

The Official Encyclopedia of Baseball by Hy Turkin and Sherley Clark Thompson, illustrated with photographs and diagrams; A. S. Barnes, 1951. **Awarded:** Boys Club 1952.

THOMPSON, VIVIAN LAUBACH

George Washington by Vivian L. Thompson, illustrated by Frank Aloise; Putnam, 1964. **Awarded:** New Jersey Institute of Technology (biography ages 7-9) 1964.

Sad Day, Glad Day by Vivian L. Thompson, illustrated by Lilian Obligado; Holiday House, 1962. **Awarded:** New Jersey Institute of Technology 1963.

THOMSON, PEGGY

Auks, Rocks and the Odd Dinosaur: Inside Stories from the Smithsonian's Museum of Natural History by Peggy Thomson, illustrated; Crowell, 1985. **Awarded:** Boston Globe Horn Book (nonfiction) 1986.

THOMSON, RUTH

Have You Started Yet? by Ruth Thomson, illustrated by C. Beaton; Heinemann, 1980. **Awarded:** Other Award 1981.

Making a Book by Ruth Thomson, illustrated by Chris Fairclough; Watts, 1987. **Awarded:** Times Educational Supplement (Junior) 1988.

THORNE, JENNY

My Uncle written and illustrated by Jenny Thorne; Atheneum, 1982. **Awarded:** New York Times Best Illustrated 1982; Parents' Choice (illustration) 1982.

THORNHILL, JAN

A Tree in a Forest written and illustrated by Jan Thornhill; Greey de Pencier, 1991; Simon & Schuster, 1992. **Awarded:** Information Book Award 1992.

The Wildlife ABC written and illustrated by Jan Thornhill; Greey de Pencier, 1988. **Awarded:** Alcuin 1989.

The Wild Life 1-2-3: A Nature Counting Book written and illustrated by Jan Thornhill; Greey de Pencier Books, 1989; Simon & Schuster, 1989. **Awarded:** UNICEF-Ezra Jack Keats International Award for Children's Book Illustration 1990.

THORNLEY, TONY

Active Science I by Michael Coles, Richard Gott, and Tony Thornley, illustrated; Collins Educational, 1988. **Awarded:** Times Educational Supplement (Schoolbook) 1988.

THRASHER, CRYSTAL

Between Dark and Daylight by Crystal Thrasher, not illustrated; Atheneum, 1979. **Awarded:** Friends of American Writers (older) 1980.

The Dark Didn't Catch Me by Crystal Thrasher, not illustrated; Atheneum, 1975. **Awarded:** New York Times Notable Books 1975.

THRUELSEN, RICHARD
Voyage of the Vagabond by Richard Thruelsen, illustrated with maps; Harcourt, 1965. **Awarded:** New Jersey Institute of Technology (ages 11-14) 1966.

THUM, MARCELLA
Exploring Black America: A History and Guide by Marcella Thum, illustrated with photographs; Atheneum, 1975. **Awarded:** Children's Book Showcase 1976.

The Mystery at Crane's Landing by Marcella Thum, not illustrated; Dodd, Mead, 1964. **Awarded:** Edith Busby 1963; Edgar Allen Poe 1965.

THURBER, JAMES GROVER
The Great Quillow by James Thurber, illustrated by Doris Lee; Harcourt, 1944. **Awarded:** Ohioana (2nd place) 1945.

Many Moons by James Thurber, illustrated by Louis Slobodkin; Harcourt, 1943. **Awarded:** Caldecott 1944.

Many Moons by James Thurber, illustrated by Marc Simont; Harcourt Brace Jovanovich, 1990. **Awarded:** Redbook 1990.

The White Deer by James Thurber, illustrated by Don Freeman; Harcourt, 1945. **Awarded:** Ohioana 1946.

THURSTON, ROBERT
The Battlestar Galactica Storybook by Robert Thurston and Glen A. Larson, adapted by Charles Mercer, illustrated with photographs; Putnam, 1979. **Awarded:** New Jersey Institute of Technology 1980.

THYGESEN-BLECHER, LONE
The Battle Horse by Harry Kullman, translated by Lone Thygesen- Blecher and George Blecher, not illustrated; Bradbury, 1981. **Awarded:** Batchelder 1982; International Board on Books for Young People (translation/USA) 1984.

TIBO, GILLES
Simon and the Snowflakes written and illustrated by Gilles Tibo; Tundra Books, 1988. **Awarded:** Owl Prize 1989.

TIBONI, GEORGE
Never Say Yes to a Stranger by Susan Newman, photographs by George Tiboni; Putnam, 1985. **Awarded:** New Jersey Institute of Technology 1987.

You Can Say No to a Drink or a Drug: What Every Kid Should Know by Susan Newman, photographs by George Tiboni; Putnam, 1986. **Awarded:** New Jersey Institute of Technology 1987.

TIBOR
Inigo: The Adventures of a Saint by Michael Hansen, illustrated by Tibor; David Lovell, 1991. **Awarded:** Australian Christian Book of the Year (Children's joint winner) 1992.

TIEGREEN, ALAN
Doodle and the Go-Cart by Robert Burch, illustrated by Alan Tiegreen; Viking, 1972. **Awarded:** Georgia Children's 1974.

Ramona and Her Father by Beverly Cleary, illustrated by Alan Tiegreen; Morrow, 1977. **Awarded:** Boston Globe Horn Book (fiction honor) 1978; Garden State Children's (young fiction) 1980; Sue Hefly (honor) 1982; International Board on Books for Young People (text/USA) 1980; Land of Enchantment 1981; Nene 1979; Newbery (honor) 1978; Texas Bluebonnet 1981; Utah Children's Choice 1980; Volunteer State 1980; Young Readers Choice 1980.

Ramona and Her Mother by Beverly Cleary, illustrated by Alan Tiegreen; Dell/Yearling, 1980. **Awarded:** American Book Awards (children's fiction paperback) 1981; Garden State Children's (younger fiction) 1982; Surrey School 1982.

Ramona Forever by Beverly Cleary, illustrated by Alan Tiegreen; Morrow, 1984. **Awarded:** Iowa Children's 1987; New York Times Notable 1984; Parents' Choice (literature) 1984.

Ramona Quimby, Age 8 by Beverly Cleary, illustrated by Alan Tiegreen; Morrow, 1981. **Awarded:** Buckeye (grades 3-5) 1985; Garden State (younger fiction) 1984; Michigan Young Readers 1984; Newbery (honor) 1982; Charlie May Simon 1983-83; Sunshine (runnerup) 1984.

Ramona the Brave by Beverly Cleary, illustrated by Alan Tiegreen; Morrow, 1975. **Awarded:** Golden Archer 1977; Mark Twain 1978.

TIETJENS, EUNICE
Boy of the South Seas by Eunice Tietjens, illustrated by Myrtle Sheldon; Coward, 1931. **Awarded:** Newbery (honor) 1932.

TIGHE, BENJAMIN
Awarded: Chandler Reward of Merit 1972.

TILLY, NANCY
Golden Girl by Nancy Tilly, not illustrated; Farrar, Straus & Giroux, 1985. **Awarded:** North Carolina AAUW 1986.

TIMMERMAN, JOHN H.
Fantasy Literature's Evocative Power by John H. Timmerman in *Christian Century* May 17, 1978. **Awarded:** Children's Literature Assn. Award for Literary Criticism (runnerup) 1979.

TIMMERMANS, GOMMAAR
The Great Balloon Race written and illustrated by Gommaar Timmermans; Addison-Wesley, 1976. **Awarded:** Children's Book Showcase 1977.

TINDALE, NORMAN BARNETT
The First Walkabout by Norman Barnett Tindale and Harold Arthur Lindsay, illustrated by Madeleine Boyce; Longmans, 1954. **Awarded:** Children's Book Council of Australia 1955.

TISCHLER, RAGNA
Lean Out of the Window: An Anthology of Modern Poetry compiled by Sara Hannum and Gwendolyn E. Reed, illustrated by Ragna Tischler; Atheneum, 1965. **Awarded:** Spring Book Festival (middle honor) 1965.

TITCOMB, MARGARET
The Voyage of the Flying Bird by Margaret Titcomb, illustrated by Joseph Feher; Dodd, Mead, 1963. **Awarded:** Edith Busby 1961.

TITHERINGTON, JEANNE
A Place for Ben written and illustrated by Jeanne Titherington; Greenwillow, 1987. **Awarded:** Redbook 1987.

Pumpkin, Pumpkin written and illustrated by Jeanne Titherington; Greenwillow, 1986. **Awarded:** New York Academy of Sciences (younger honor) 1987.

A Taste for Quiet and Other Disquieting Tales by Judith Gorog, illustrated by Jean Titherington; Philomel, 1982. **Awarded:** New Jersey Institute of Technology 1983.

TITUS, EVE
Anatole by Eve Titus, illustrated by Paul Galdone; Whittlesey, 1956. **Awarded:** Caldecott (honor) 1957.

Anatole and the Cat by Eve Titus, illustrated by Paul Galdone; Whittlesey, 1957. **Awarded:** Caldecott (honor) 1958.

TOBIAS, JERRY V.
Awarded: L. Frank Baum 1979.

TODD, JUSTIN

Alice's Adventures in Wonderland by Lewis Carroll, illustrated by Justin Todd; Gollancz, 1984. **Awarded:** Maschler (runnerup) 1984; W. H. Smith Illustration (2nd prize) 1987.

Through the Looking Glass and What Alice Found There by Lewis Carroll, illustrated by Justin Todd; Gollancz, 1986. **Awarded:** W. H. Smith Illustration (2nd prize) 1987.

TODD, ROBERT

Mr. Justice Holmes by Clara Ingram Judson, illustrated by Robert Todd; Follett, 1956. **Awarded:** Edison Mass Media (character development in children) 1957; Newbery (honor) 1957.

TOLAN, STEPHANIE S.

The Great Skinner Strike by Stephanie S. Tolan, not illustrated; Macmillan, 1983; New American Library, 1985. **Awarded:** CRABbery (honor) 1984.

The Liberation of Tansy Warner by Stephanie S. Tolan, not illustrated; Scribner, 1980. **Awarded:** Ohioana 1981.

TOLAND, JOHN

The Battle of the Bulge by John Toland, illustrated by Jerome Kuhl; Random House, 1966. **Awarded:** Boys Club (certificate) 1966- 67.

TOLKIEN, JOHN RONALD REUEL

The Hobbit written and illustrated by J. R. R. Tolkien; Houghton Mifflin, 1938. **Awarded:** Emphasis on Reading (grades 7-9) 1980-81; Spring Book Festival (younger) 1938.

TOM TWO ARROWS

The Whirly Bird by Aylesa Forsee, illustrated by Tom Two Arrows; Lippincott, 1955. **Awarded:** Helen Dean Fish 1955.

TOMEI, GORDON

Wonders of Speech by Virginia Silverstein and Alvin Silverstein, illustrated by Gordon Tomei; Morrow, 1988. **Awarded:** New York Academy of Sciences (Older Honor) 1989.

TOMES, MARGOT

Aaron and the Green Mountain Boys by Patricia L. Gauch, illustrated by Margot Tomes; Coward, 1972. **Awarded:** New Jersey Institute of Technology 1972, 1973.

And Then What Happened, Paul Revere? by Jean Fritz, illustrated by Margot Tomes; Coward, 1973. **Awarded:** Boston Globe Horn Book (text honor) 1974.

Cecelia and the Blue Mountain Boy by Ellen H. Showell, illustrated by Margot Tomes; Lothrop, Lee & Shepard, 1983. **Awarded:** Parents' Choice (literature) 1983.

Chimney Sweeps: Yesterday and Today by James C. Giblin, illustrated by Margot Tomes; Crowell, 1982. **Awarded:** American Book Award (children's nonfiction) 1983; Golden Kite (nonfiction) 1982.

If There Were Dreams to Sell by Barbara Lalicki, illustrated by Margot Tomes; Lothrop, Lee & Shepard, 1984. **Awarded:** New York Times Best Illustrated 1984.

Jack and the Wonder Beans by James Still, illustrated by Margot Tomes; Putnam, 1977. **Awarded:** New York Times Best Illustrated 1977.

The Halloween Pumpkin Smasher by Judith St. George, illustrated by Margot Tomes; Putnam, 1978. **Awarded:** Edgar Allan Poe (runnerup) 1979.

Homesick: My Own Story by Jean Fritz, illustrated with drawings by Margot Tomes and photographs; Putnam, 1982. **Awarded:** American Book Award (children's fiction hardback) 1983; Boston Globe Horn Book (fiction honor) 1983; Child Study 1982; Christopher (ages 8- 12) 1983; New York Times Notable Books 1982; Newbery (honor) 1983.

Little Sister and the Month Brothers by Beatrice Schenk deRegniers, illustrated by Margot Tomes; Seabury, 1976. **Awarded:** Children's Book Showcase 1977.

A Secret House by Patricia Lee Gauch, illustrated by Margot Tomes; Coward, 1970. **Awarded:** New Jersey Institute of Technology 1971.

The Shadowmaker by Ron Hansen, illustrated by Margot Tomes; Harper, 1987. **Awarded:** New York Times Notable 1987.

Witch Hazel by Alice Schertle, illustrated by Margot Tomes; HarperCollins, 1991. **Awarded:** Parents' Choice (Picture Book) 1991.

TOMKINS, JASPER

Nimby written and illustrated by Jasper Tomkins; Green Tiger Press, 1982. **Awarded:** Washington Children's Choice 1985.

TOMOS, ANGHARAD

Y Llipryn Llwyd by Angharad Tomos; Y Lolfa, 1985. **Awarded:** Tir Na n-Og (Welsh) 1986.

TOMPERT, ANN

Charlotte & Charles by Ann Tompert, illustrated by John Wallner; Crown, 1979. **Awarded:** Woodward Park School 1980.

Little Fox Goes to the End of the World by Ann Tompert, illustrated by John Wallner; Crown, 1976. **Awarded:** Friends of American Writers (illustration) 1977.

TONDREAU, SHARON

Pumpkin Personalities by Ruth J. Katz, illustrated by Sharon Tondreau; Walker, 1979. **Awarded:** New Jersey Institute of Technology 1980.

TONG, GARY

Awarded: Lucky Book Club Four Leaf Clover 1982.

TOR, REGINA

Discovering Israel written and illustrated by Regina Tor; Random House, 1960. **Awarded:** Jewish Book Council 1960.

TORJESEN, ELIZABETH FRASER

Captain Ramsey's Daughter by Elizabeth Fraser Torjesen, illustrated by Adrienne Adams; Lothrop, Lee & Shepard, 1953. **Awarded:** Spring Book Festival (ages 8-12) 1953.

TORRES, PAT

Do Not Go Around the Edges: Poems by Daisy Utemorrah, illustrated by Pat Torres; Magabala Books, 1991. **Awarded:** Australian Multicultural Children's Literature Award (Junior Fiction) 1992.

TORREY, MARJORIE

Far From Marlborough Street by Elizabeth Philbrook, illustrated by Marjorie Torrey; Viking, 1944. **Awarded:** Spring Book Festival (middle honor) 1944.

Sing in Praise: A Collection of the Best Loved Hymns by Opal Wheeler, illustrated by Marjorie Torrey; Dutton, 1946. **Awarded:** Caldecott (honor) 1947.

Sing Mother Goose by Opal Wheeler, illustrated by Marjorie Torrey; Dutton, 1945. **Awarded:** Caldecott (honor) 1946.

TOSCHIK, LARRY

Coyote, Come Home by B. F. Beebe, illustrated by Larry Toschik; McKay, 1963. **Awarded:** Boys Club 1964.

TOURRET, SHIRLEY

Two's Company by Jackie Kay, illustrated by Shirley Tourret; Blackie, 1992. **Awarded:** Signal 1993.

TOWNSEND, ANNE, DR.
Marvelous Me by Dr. Anne Townsend, illustrated by Saroj Vaghela; Lion Publishing Co., 1984. **Awarded:** Gold Medallion 1985.

TOWNSEND, JOHN ROWE
Hell's Edge by John Rowe Townsend, not illustrated; Hutchinson, 1963. **Awarded:** Carnegie (commended) 1963.

The Intruder by John Rowe Townsend, illustrated by Joseph A. Phelan; Lippincott, 1970. **Awarded:** Boston Globe Horn Book (text) 1970; Edgar Allan Poe 1971.

The Intruder by John Rowe Townsend, illustrated by Graham Humphreys; Oxford, 1969. **Awarded:** Carnegie (honour) 1969.

The Islanders by John Rowe Townsend, not illustrated; Lippincott, 1981. **Awarded:** Christopher (young adult) 1982.

TOWNSEND, LEE
Lone Star Fight by Irmengarde Eberle, illustrated by Lee Townsend; Dodd, Mead, 1954. **Awarded:** Steck-Vaughn 1956.

Sagebrush Sorrel by Frank C. Robertson, illustrated by Lee Townsend; Nelson, 1953. **Awarded:** Western Writers 1954.

TOWNSEND, SUE
The Growing Pains of Adrian Mole by Sue Townsend, illustrated by Caroline Holden; Methuen, 1984. **Awarded:** West Australian (overseas secondary) 1986.

The Secret Diary of Adrian Mole, Aged 13 3/4 by Sue Townsend, not illustrated; Methuen, 1982. **Awarded:** Books I Love Best Yearly (Read Alone Secondary) 1990; West Australian (Secondary) 1985.

TOWNSEND, TOM
Where the Pirates Are by Tom Townsend, illustrated; Eakin Press, 1985. **Awarded:** Friends of American Writers ($500) 1986.

TOYE, WILLIAM
Awarded: Vicky Metcalf 1972.

Cartier Discovers the St. Lawrence by William Toye, illustrated by Laszlo Gal; Oxford, 1970. **Awarded:** Canadian Library Assn. 1971.

The Loon's Necklace by William Toye, illustrated by Elizabeth Cleaver; Oxford, 1977. **Awarded:** Amelia Frances Howard-Gibbon 1978; IODE 1977.

The St. Lawrence by William Toye, illustrated by Leo Rampen; Oxford, 1959. **Awarded:** Canadian Library Assn. 1961.

Simon and the Golden Sword by Frank Newfeld and William Toye, illustrated by Frank Newfeld; Oxford, 1976. **Awarded:** Canadian Library Assn. (runnerup) 1977.

TRACY, EDWARD B.
King of the Stallions by Edward B. Tracy, illustrated by Paul Brown; Dodd, Mead, 1947. **Awarded:** Boys Club 1949.

TRAMACCHI, JOE
Tjarany Roughtail by Gracie Greene and Joe Tramacchi, illustrated by Lucille Gill; Magabala, 1992. **Awarded:** Children's Book Council of Australia (Eve Pownall) 1993.

TRAVERS, PAMELA LYNDON
Mary Poppins by Pamela L. Travers, illustrated by Mary Shepard; Harcourt, 1962. **Awarded:** Nene 1965.

TREADGOLD, MARY
We Couldn't Leave Dinah by Mary Treadgold, illustrated by Stuart Tresilian; Cape, 1941. **Awarded:** Carnegie 1941.

TREASE, GEOFFREY
This Is Your Century by Geoffrey Trease, not illustrated; Harcourt, 1965. **Awarded:** Spring Book Festival (older) 1966.

TREDEZ, ALAIN
see TREZ, ALAIN

TREDEZ, DENISE
see TREZ, DENISE

TREECE, HENRY
The Dream Time by Henry Treece, illustrated by Charles Keeping; Brockhampton, 1967. **Awarded:** Carnegie (commended) 1967.

TREFFINGER, CAROLYN
Li Lun, Lad of Courage by Carolyn Treffinger, illustrated by Kurt Wiese; Abingdon-Cokesbury, 1947. **Awarded:** Lewis Carroll Shelf 1959; Newbery (honor) 1948; Ohioana 1948.

TREGASKIS, RICHARD
John F. Kennedy and PT-109 by Richard Tregaskis, illustrated with photographs; Random House, 1962. **Awarded:** Young Readers Choice 1965.

TREHERNE, KATIE THAMER
The Little Mermaid by Hans Christian Andersen, illustrated by Katie Thamer Treherne; Harcourt Brace Jovanovich, 1989. **Awarded:** Redbook 1989.

TRELEASE, JIM
Read-Aloud Handbook by Jim Trelease, illustrated by Joanne Rathe; Penguin, 1982. **Awarded:** Jeremiah Ludington 1988.

TRELOAR, BRUCE
Bumble's Dream written and illustrated by Bruce Treloar; Bodley Head, 1981. **Awarded:** Children's Book Council of Australia (picture book of the year commended) 1982.

Kim by Bruce Treloar; Collins, 1978. **Awarded:** Russell Clark 1979.

TRESILIAN, CECIL STUART
see TRESILIAN, STUART

TRESILIAN, STUART
Mystery Island by Enid Blyton, illustrated by Stuart Tresilian; Macmillan, 1945. **Awarded:** Boys Club 1948.

Three and a Pigeon by Kitty Barne, illustrated by Stuart Tresilian; Dodd, Mead, 1944. **Awarded:** Spring Book Festival (middle honor) 1944.

We Couldn't Leave Dinah by Mary Treadgold, illustrated by Stuart Tresilian; Cape, 1941. **Awarded:** Carnegie 1941.

TRESSELT, ALVIN
Bonnie Bess: The Weathervane Horse by Alvin Tresselt, illustrated by Marylin Hafner; Lothrop, Lee & Shepard, 1949. **Awarded:** Spring Book Festival (younger) 1949.

Hide and Seek Fog by Alvin Tresselt, illustrated by Roger Duvoisin; Lothrop, Lee & Shepard, 1965. **Awarded:** Caldecott (honor) 1966; New York Times Best Illustrated 1965; Spring Book Festival (picture book honor) 1965.

Rain Drop Splash by Alvin Tresselt, illustrated by Leonard Weisgard; Lothrop, Lee & Shepard, 1946. **Awarded:** Caldecott (honor) 1947.

White Snow, Bright Snow by Alvin Tresselt, illustrated by Roger Duvoisin; Lothrop, Lee & Shepard, 1947. **Awarded:** Caldecott 1948.

TREVINO, ELIZABETH BORTON DE
I, Juan de Pareja by Elizabeth Borton de Trevino, not illustrated; Farrar, 1965. **Awarded:** Newbery 1966.

Turi's Poppa by Elizabeth Borton de Trevino, illustrated by Enrico Arno; Farrar, 1968. **Awarded:** Boston Globe Horn Book (text honor) 1969.

TREZ, ALAIN
Sophie written and illustrated by Alain Trez and Denise Trez, translated by Douglas McKee; World, 1964. **Awarded:** Spring Book Festival (picture book honor) 1964.

TREZ, DENISE
Sophie written and illustrated by Denise Trez and Alain Trez, translated by Douglas McKee; World, 1964. **Awarded:** Spring Book Festival (picture book honor) 1964.

TREZISE, PERCY J.
The Quinkins written and illustrated by Percy J. Trezise and Dick Roughsey; Collins, 1978. **Awarded:** Children's Book Council of Australia (picture book) 1979; International Board on Books for Young People (illustration/Australia) 1980.

Turramulli the Giant Quinkin written and illustrated by Percy Trezise and Dick Roughsey; Collins, 1982. **Awarded:** Children's Book Council of Australia (picture book of the year commended) 1983.

TRINKLE, SALLY
Eric: The Tale of a Red Tempered Viking by Susan Bond, illustrated by Sally Trinkle; Grove Press, 1968. **Awarded:** New Jersey Institute of Technology 1970.

The Manners Zoo by Susan Bond, illustrated by Sally Trinkle; Follett, 1969. **Awarded:** New Jersey Institute of Technology 1970.

TRIPP, EDWARD
The Tin Fiddle by Edward Tripp, illustrated by Maurice Sendak; Oxford, 1954. **Awarded:** Spring Book Festival (ages 4-8 honor) 1954.

TRIPP, WALLACE
Granfa' Grig Had a Pig and Other Rhymes without Reason from Mother Goose adapted and illustrated by Wallace Tripp; Little, Brown, 1976. **Awarded:** Boston Globe Horn Book (illustration) 1977.

TRIVAS, IRENE
The Doggone Mystery by Mary Blount Christian, illustrated by Irene Trivas; Whitman, 1980. **Awarded:** Edgar Allan Poe (runnerup) 1981.

The Pain and the Great One by Judy Blume, illustrated by Irene Trivas; Bradbury, 1984. **Awarded:** Emphasis on Reading (grades K-1) 1985-86.

TRNKA, JIRI
Awarded: Hans Christian Andersen (highly commended illustrator/USSR) 1966; Hans Christian Andersen (illustrator) 1968.

TROFIMUK, ANN
Babushka and the Pig by Ann Trofimuk, illustrated by Jerry Pinkney; Houghton, 1969. **Awarded:** New Jersey Institute of Technology 1969.

TROUGHTON, JOANNA
How the Birds Changed Their Feathers retold and illustrated by Joanna Troughton; Blackie, 1976. **Awarded:** Greenaway (highly commended) 1976.

TROY, HUGH
Five Golden Wrens written and illustrated by Hugh Troy; Oxford, 1943. **Awarded:** Spring Book Festival (younger) 1943.

TRUSS, JAN
Jasmin by Jan Truss, not illustrated; Douglas & McIntyre, 1982; Atheneum, 1982. **Awarded:** Canadian Library Assn. (runnerup) 1983; Ruth Schwartz 1983.

TRUX, JOHN
Worlds within Worlds: A Journey into the Unknown by John Trux, Michael Marten, John Chesterman and John May, illustrated with photographs; Holt, 1977. **Awarded:** New York Academy of Sciences (older honor) 1979.

TSUCHIYA, YUKIO
Faithful Elephants by Yukio Tsuchiya, illustrated by Ted Lewin; Houghton Mifflin, 1988. **Awarded:** Book Can Develop Empathy 1990.

TSUTSUI, YORIKO
Anna's Special Present by Yoriko Tsutsui, illustrated by Akiko Hayashi; Viking Kestrel, 1988; Puffin, 1990. **Awarded:** Ezra Jack Keats New Writer's Award 1989.

T'U, YENCHI TIAO
The Magic Spear and Other Stories of China's Famous Heroes by Louise Crane, illustrated by Yenchi Tiao T'u and Ching Chi Yee; Random House, 1938. **Awarded:** Spring Book Festival (younger honor) 1938.

TUCHMAN, BARBARA
Awarded: Women's National Book Assn. 1982.

TUCKER, B.
Bugles at the Border by Mary Gillett, illustrated by B. Tucker; Blair, 1968. **Awarded:** North Carolina AAUW 1969.

TUCKER, KATHLEEN
Behind the Scenes at the Horse Hospital by Fern G. Brown, edited by Kathleen Tucker, photographs by Roger Ruhlin; Whitman, 1981. **Awarded:** Sandburg 1982.

TUCKWELL, JENNIFER
To the Wild Sky by Ivan Southall, illustrated by Jennifer Tuckwell; Angus & Robertson, 1967. **Awarded:** Children's Book Council of Australia (book of the year) 1968.

TUDOR, TASHA
Awarded: Chandler Reward of Merit 1963; Regina 1971.

Mother Goose compiled and illustrated by Tasha Tudor; Oxford, 1944. **Awarded:** Caldecott (honor) 1945.

One is One written and illustrated by Tasha Tudor; Oxford, 1956. **Awarded:** Caldecott (honor) 1957.

A Tale for Easter written and illustrated by Tasha Tudor; Oxford, 1941. **Awarded:** Spring Book Festival (younger honor) 1941.

TUGHAN, JAMES
The Buffalo Hunt by Donald Swainson and Eleanor Swainson, illustrated by James Tughan; PMA Books, 1980. **Awarded:** Amelia Frances Howard-Gibbon (runnerup) 1981.

TUNBO, FRANCES G.
Stay Put, Robbie McAmis by Frances G. Tunbo, illustrated by Charles Shaw; Texas Christian University Press, 1988. **Awarded:** Western Heritage 1989.

TUNIS, EDWIN BURDETT
Colonial Craftsmen and the Beginnings of American Industry written and illustrated by Edwin Tunis; World, 1965. **Awarded:** Spring Book Festival (older honor) 1965.

Colonial Living written and illustrated by Edwin Tunis; World, 1957. **Awarded:** Edison Mass Media (America's past) 1958.

Frontier Living written and illustrated by Edwin Tunis; World, 1961. **Awarded:** Newbery (honor) 1962.

Shaw's Fortune: The Picture Story of a Colonial Plantation written and illustrated by Edwin Tunis; World, 1966. **Awarded:** New York Times Best Illustrated 1966.

The Tavern at the Ferry written and illustrated by Edwin Tunis; Crowell, 1973. **Awarded:** Children's Book Showcase 1974.

Wheels: A Pictorial History written and illustrated by Edwin Tunis; World, 1955. **Awarded:** Boys Club 1956.

The Young United States 1783-1830 written and illustrated by Edwin Tunis; World, 1969. **Awarded:** National Book Award (finalist) 1970.

TUNIS, JOHN ROBERTS
Highpockets by John R. Tunis, illustrated by Charles Beck; Morrow, 1948. **Awarded:** Spring Book Festival (older honor) 1948.

Iron Duke by John R. Tunis, illustrated by Johan Bull; Harcourt, 1938. **Awarded:** Spring Book Festival (older) 1938.

Keystone Kids by John R. Tunis, not illustrated; Harcourt, 1943. **Awarded:** Child Study 1943.

The Kid from Tomkinsville by John R. Tunis, illustrated by Jay Hyde Barnum; Harcourt, 1940. **Awarded:** Spring Book Festival (older honor) 1940.

Son of the Valley by John R. Tunis, not illustrated; Morrow, 1949. **Awarded:** Spring Book Festival (older honor) 1949.

TURIN, ADELA
Aurora by Adela Turin and Annie Goetzinger, illustrated with photographs; Dalla Parte delle Bambine. **Awarded:** Bologna (graphics for youth) 1979.

TURKIN, HY
The Official Encyclopedia of Baseball by Hy Turkin and Sherley Clark Thompson, illustrated with photographs and diagrams; A. S. Barnes, 1951. **Awarded:** Boys Club 1952.

TURKLE, BRINTON
The Adventures of Obadiah written and illustrated by Brinton Turkle; Viking, 1972. **Awarded:** Christopher (ages 4-8) 1973.

Danny Dunn on the Ocean Floor by Jay Williams and Raymond Abrashkin, illustrated by Brinton Turkle; McGraw, 1960. **Awarded:** Young Readers Choice 1963.

Deep in the Forest written and illustrated by Brinton Turkle; Dutton, 1976. **Awarded:** Art Books for Children 1978; Children's Book Showcase 1977; Ohioana 1977.

The Far-off Land by Rebecca Caudill, illustrated by Brinton Turkle; Viking, 1964. **Awarded:** Friends of American Writers 1965.

The Fiddler of High Lonesome written and illustrated by Brinton Turkle; Viking, 1968. **Awarded:** Lewis Carroll Shelf 1968.

Granny and the Indians by Peggy Parish, illustrated by Brinton Turkle; Macmillan, 1969. **Awarded:** Emphasis on Reading (grades 2-3) 1981-82.

Island Time by Bette Lamont, illustrated by Brinton Turkle; Lippincott, 1976. **Awarded:** Ohioana 1977.

Poor Richard in France by Ferdinand N. Monjo, illustrated by Brinton Turkle; Holt, 1973. **Awarded:** National Book Award (finalist) 1974.

Thy Friend, Obadiah written and illustrated by Brinton Turkle; Viking, 1969. **Awarded:** Boston Globe Horn Book (illustration honor) 1969; Caldecott (honor) 1970; Spring Book Festival (picture book) 1969.

TURNER, ANNE WARREN
Vultures by Anne W. Turner, illustrated by Marian G. Warren; McKay, 1973. **Awarded:** New York Academy of Sciences (older honor) 1974.

TURNER, BRENDA BAUM
Awarded: L. Frank Baum 1987.

TURNER, GWENDA
The Tree Witches written and illustrated by Gwenda Turner; Kestrel, 1983. **Awarded:** Russell Clark 1984.

TURNER, JOSIE
see CRAWFORD, PHYLLIS

TURNER, PHILIP
The Grange at High Force by Philip Turner, illustrated by William Papas; Oxford, 1965. **Awarded:** Carnegie 1965.

TURNER, STANLEY
Son of the Hawk by Thomas H. Raddall, illustrated by Stanley Turner; Winston, 1950. **Awarded:** Boys Club 1951.

TURNGREN, ELLEN
Shadows into Mist by Ellen Turngren, illustrated by Vera Bock; Longmans, 1958. **Awarded:** Spring Book Festival (older honor) 1958.

TURSKA, KRYSTYNA
Pegasus written and illustrated by Krystyna Turska; Hamilton, 1970. **Awarded:** Greenaway (honour) 1970.

The Woodcutter's Duck written and illustrated by Krystyna Turska; Hamilton, 1972; Macmillan, 1973. **Awarded:** Greenaway 1972; Spring Book Festival (younger honor) 1973.

A Year and a Day by William Mayne, illustrated by Krystyna Turska; Hamish Hamilton, 1976. **Awarded:** International Board on Books for Young People (honour list/text/Great Britain) 1978; New York Times Notable Books 1976.

TUTTLE, MERLIN D.
Batman: Exploring the World of Bats by Laurence Pringle, photographs by Merlin D. Tuttle; Scribner, 1991. **Awarded:** Book Can Develop Empathy 1991.

TWAIN, MARK
see CLEMENS, SAMUEL LANGHORNE

TYLER, WILLIAM ROYALL
A Moment of Silence by Pierre Janssen, translated by William R. Tyler, photographs by Hans Samson; Atheneum, 1970. **Awarded:** Christopher (ages 8-12) 1971.

U

UCHIDA, YOSHIKO
The Happiest Ending by Yoshiko Uchida, not illustrated; Atheneum, 1985. **Awarded:** Bay Area Book Reviewers Assn. 1986.

A Jar of Dreams by Yoshiko Uchida, not illustrated; Atheneum, 1981. **Awarded:** Commonwealth Club of California 1981; FOCAL 1986.

The Magic Listening Cap: More Folk Tales from Japan written and illustrated by Yoshiko Uchida; Harcourt, 1955. **Awarded:** Spring Book Festival (middle honor) 1955.

Samurai of Gold Hill by Yoshiko Uchida, illustrated by Ati Forberg; Scribner, 1972. **Awarded:** Commonwealth Club of California 1972.

The Two Foolish Cats by Yoshiko Uchida, illustrated by Margot Zemach; McElderry, 1987. **Awarded:** Parents' Choice (Story Book) 1987.

UDEN, GRANT
Dictionary of Chivalry by Grant Uden, illustrated by Pauline Baynes; Kestrel, 1968; Crowell, 1969. **Awarded:** Greenaway 1968; Spring Book Festival (older honor) 1969.

UDRY, JANICE MAY
Let's Be Enemies by Janice May Udry, illustrated by Maurice Sendak; Harper, 1961. **Awarded:** Spring Book Festival (ages 4-8 honor) 1961.

The Moon Jumpers by Janice May Udry, illustrated by Maurice Sendak; Harper, 1959. **Awarded:** Caldecott (honor) 1960.

A Tree Is Nice by Janice May Udry, illustrated by Marc Simont; Harper, 1956. **Awarded:** Caldecott 1957.

ULLBERG, NENA GRIGORIAN
Beyond the East Wind: Legends and Folktales of Vietnam by Jewell Reinhart Coburn, told by Duong Van Quyen, illustrated by Nena Grigorian Ullberg; Burn, Hart, 1976. **Awarded:** Southern California Council (special recognition for a contribution of cultural significance) 1980.

Encircled Kingdom: Legends and Folktales of Laos by Jewell Reinhart Coburn, illustrated by Nena Grigorian Ullberg; Burn, Hart, 1979. **Awarded:** Southern California Council (special recognition for a contribution of cultural significance) 1980.

Khmers, Tigers and Talismans: From the History and Legends of Mysterious Cambodia by Jewell Reinhart Coburn, illustrated by Nena Grigorian Ullberg; Burn, Hart, 1978. **Awarded:** Southern California Council (special recognition for a contribution of cultural significance) 1980.

ULLIN, ALBERT
Awarded: Dromkeen 1986.

ULLMAN, JAMES RAMSEY
Banner in the Sky: The Story of a Boy and a Mountain by James Ramsey Ullman, not illustrated; Lippincott, 1954. **Awarded:** Lewis Carroll Shelf 1966; Newbery (honor) 1955.

UMANSKY, KAYE
Pongwiffy and the Spell of the Year by Kaye Umansky, illustrated by Chris Smedley; Viking, 1992. **Awarded:** Nottinghamshire (Oak Tree) 1993.

UNDERHILL, RUTH MURRAY
Antelope Singer by Ruth M. Underhill, illustrated by Ursula Koering; Coward, 1961. **Awarded:** Nancy Bloch 1961.

UNDERWOOD, MARY BETTY
The Tamarack Tree by Mary Betty Underwood, illustrated by Bea Holmes; Houghton Mifflin, 1971. **Awarded:** Jane Addams 1972.

UNGERER, JEAN THOMAS
see UNGERER, TOMI

UNGERER, TOMI
Awarded: Hans Christian Andersen (highly commended illustrator/ France) 1980.

Allumette written and illustrated by Tomi Ungerer; Parents, 1974. **Awarded:** Children's Book Showcase 1975.

The Beast of Monsieur Racine written and illustrated by Tomi Ungerer; Farrar, 1971. **Awarded:** Art Books for Children 1975; Children's Book Showcase 1972; New York Times Best Illustrated 1971.

Crictor written and illustrated by Tomi Ungerer; Harper, 1958. **Awarded:** Spring Book Festival (ages 4-8) 1958.

Emile written and illustrated by Tomi Ungerer; Harper, 1960. **Awarded:** Spring Book Festival (ages 4-8 honor) 1960.

The Great Song Book edited by Timothy John; music editor, Peter Hankey; illustrated by Tomi Ungerer; Doubleday, 1978. **Awarded:** New York Times Best Illustrated 1978.

The Hat written and illustrated by Tomi Ungerer; Parents, 1970. **Awarded:** Spring Book Festival (picture book honor) 1970.

The Mellops Go Flying written and illustrated by Tomi Ungerer; Harper, 1957. **Awarded:** Spring Book Festival (ages 4-8 honor) 1957.

Moon Man written and illustrated by Tomi Ungerer; Harper, 1967; Harper Trophy, 1984. **Awarded:** Art Books for Children 1973; Redbook (paperback) 1984; Spring Book Festival (picture book) 1967.

Snail, Where Are You? written and illustrated by Tomi Ungerer; Harper, 1962. **Awarded:** Spring Book Festival (picture book honor) 1962.

A Storybook edited and illustrated by Tomi Ungerer; Watts, 1974. **Awarded:** New York Times Best Illustrated 1974.

The Three Robbers written and illustrated by Tomi Ungerer; Atheneum, 1962. **Awarded:** Art Books for Children 1973; New York Times Best Illustrated 1962.

UNSELL, MARTIN
The Song of Pentecost by William J. Corbett, illustrated by Martin Unsell; Methuen, 1982. **Awarded:** Whitbread 1982.

UNWIN, NORA SPICER
Amos Fortune, Free Man by Elizabeth Yates, illustrated by Nora S. Unwin; Aladdin, 1950. **Awarded:** Newbery 1951; Spring Book Festival (older) 1950; William Allen White 1953.

Cupola House by Mabel Leigh Hunt, illustrated by Nora S. Unwin; Lippincott, 1961. **Awarded:** Indiana Authors Day (young children) 1962.

Mountain Born by Elizabeth Yates, illustrated by Nora S. Unwin; Coward, 1943. **Awarded:** Newbery (honor) 1944.

A Place for Peter by Elizabeth Yates, illustrated by Nora S. Unwin; Coward, 1952. **Awarded:** Boys Club 1953.

The Secret Garden by Frances Hodgson Burnett, illustrated by N. Unwin; Lippincott, 1938, 1911. **Awarded:** Lewis Carroll Shelf 1959.

UNWIN, PIPPA
The Great Zoo Hunt written and illustrated by Pippa Unwin; Macmillan, 1989; Doubleday, 1990. **Awarded:** Macmillan Prize (3rd Prize) 1988.

UPDEGRAFF, IMELDA
Earthquakes and Volcanoes written and illustrated by Imelda Updegraff and Robert Updegraff; Methuen, 1980. **Awarded:** Times Educational Supplement (junior) 1980.

UPDEGRAFF, ROBERT
Earthquakes and Volcanoes written and illustrated by Robert Updegraff and Imelda Updegraff; Methuen, 1980. **Awarded:** Times Educational Supplement (junior) 1980.

URE, JEAN
Plague 99 by Jean Ure, not illustrated; Methuen Teen Collection, 1989. **Awarded:** Lancashire County Library 1990.

URQUHART, JENNIFER C.
Creatures of the Desert World by Jennifer C. Urquhart, illustrated by Barbara Gibson; National Geographic Society, 1987. **Awarded:** Redbook 1987.

UTEMORRAH, DAISY
Do Not Go Around the Edges: Poems by Daisy Utemorrah, illustrated by Pat Torres; Magabala Books, 1991. **Awarded:** Australian Multicultural Children's Literature Award (Junior Fiction) 1992.

UTTON, PETER
Shhh! by Sally Grindley, illustrated by Peter Utton; ABC, 1991; Little Brown (Joy Street), 1992. **Awarded:** Children's Book Award (Picture Book) 1992.

The Witch's Hand written and illustrated by Peter Utton; Aurum Books for Children, 1989; Farrar Straus Giroux, 1989. **Awarded:** Mother Goose (runnerup) 1990.

V

VAGHELA, SAROJ
Marvelous Me by Dr. Anne Townsend, illustrated by Saroj Vaghela; Lion Publishing Co., 1984. **Awarded:** Gold Medallion 1985.

VAGIN, VLADIMIR
The King's Equal by Katherine Paterson, illustrated by Vladimir Vagin; HarperCollins, 1992. **Awarded:** Irma S. and James H. Black 1992.

VAINIO, PIRKKO
Josie Smith by Magdalen Nabb, illustrated by Pirkko Vainio; Collins, 1988; McElderry, 1989. **Awarded:** Guardian Award (runnerup) 1989.

Josie Smith and Eileen by Magdalen Nabb, illustrated by Pirkko Vainio; Collins, 1991; HarperCollins, 1991; McElderry, 1992. **Awarded:** Smarties (6-8 years) 1991.

VALDES, JOAN
The Media Works by Joan Valdes and Jeanne Crow; Pflaum/Standard, 1973. **Awarded:** Media & Methods (textbook) 1975.

VALEN, NANINE
The Drac: French Tales of Dragons and Demons by Nanine Valen and Felice Holman, illustrated by Stephen Walker; Scribner, 1975. **Awarded:** New York Times Notable Books 1975.

VALENS, EVANS G.
Elements of the Universe by Evan G. Valens and Glenn T. Seaborg, illustrated with charts, diagrams and photographs; Dutton, 1958. **Awarded:** Edison Mass Media (science books for youth) 1959.

Me and Frumpet: An Adventure with Size and Science written and illustrated by Evans G. Valens, illustrated with photographs; Dutton, 1958. **Awarded:** Spring Book Festival (middle honor) 1958.

VALENZUELA, JUAN
I Am Magic by Juan Valenzuela; Indian Historian Press, manuscript. **Awarded:** Council of Interracial Books (Chicano) 1970.

VALINTCOURT, HONORE
The City under the Back Steps by Evelyn Lampman, illustrated by Honore Valintcourt; Doubleday, 1960. **Awarded:** Dorothy Canfield Fisher 1962.

VAN ALLSBURG, CHRIS
Awarded: Regina 1993.

Ben's Dream written and illustrated by Chris Van Allsburg; Houghton Mifflin, 1982. **Awarded:** New York Times Best Illustrated 1982; Parents' Choice (illustration) 1982.

The Garden of Abdul Gasazi written and illustrated by Chris Van Allsburg; Houghton Mifflin, 1979. **Awarded:** Boston Globe Horn Book (illustration) 1980; Irma Simonton Black 1979; Caldecott (honor) 1980; International Board on Books for Young People (illustration/United States) 1982; New York Times Best Illustrated 1979; New York Times Notable Books 1979.

Jumanji written and illustrated by Chris Van Allsburg; Houghton Mifflin, 1981. **Awarded:** American Book Award (graphic art) 1982; Boston Globe Horn Book (illustration honor) 1981; Buckeye (K-3 honor) 1983; Caldecott 1982; Kentucky Bluegrass 1983; New York Times Best Illustrated 1981; New York Times Notable 1981; Washington Children's Choice 1984; West Virginia 1984-85.

The Mysteries of Harris Burdick written and illustrated by Chris Van Allsburg; Houghton Mifflin, 1984. **Awarded:** Irma Simonton Black 1984; Boston Globe Horn Book (illustration honor) 1985; New York Times Best Illustrated 1984; Redbook (hardback special mention) 1984.

The Polar Express written and illustrated by Chris Van Allsburg; Houghton Mifflin, 1985. **Awarded:** Boston Globe Horn Book (illustration honor) 1986; Buckeye (K-2) 1991; Caldecott 1986; Kentucky Bluegrass 1987; Little Archer 1986; Nevada Young Reader Award (Primary) 1987-88; New York Times Best Illustrated 1985; Redbook 1985.

The Stranger written and illustrated by Chris Van Allsburg; Houghton Mifflin, 1986. **Awarded:** Kentucky Bluegrass (grades 4-8) 1990; New York Times Best Illustrated 1986.

Two Bad Ants written and illustrated by Chris Van Allsburg; Houghton Mifflin, 1988. **Awarded:** Colorado Children's (Runnerup) 1990; Georgia Children's Picture Storybook Award 1992; Virginia Young Readers (Primary) 1991; Washington Children's Choice 1991.

The Widow's Broom written and illustrated by Chris Van Allsburg; Houghton Mifflin, 1992. **Awarded:** Parents Choice (Picture Book) 1992.

The Wreck of the Zephyr written and illustrated by Chris Van Allsburg; Houghton Mifflin, 1982. **Awarded:** New York Times Best Illustrated 1983; New York Times Notable Books 1983.

The Z Was Zapped written and illustrated by Chris Van Allsburg; Houghton Mifflin, 1987. **Awarded:** Parents' Choice (Picture Book) 1987.

VAN BILSEN, RITA
Das Schonste Geschenk by Rita Van Bilsen and Cornelius Wilkeshuis, illustrated; Bohem Press, 1977. **Awarded:** Owl Prize 1978.

VAN CAMP, JOHN
Awarded: L. Frank Baum 1981.

VAN DE WETERING, JANWILLEM
Hugh Pine and the Good Place by Janwillem Van De Wetering, illustrated by Lynn Munsinger; Houghton Mifflin, 1986. **Awarded:** New York Times Notable 1986.

VAN DER ESSEN, ANNE
Yok Yok series by Anne van der Essen, illustrated by Etienne Delessert; Gallimard. **Awarded:** Bologna (graphics for children) 1981.

VAN DER HAAS, HENRIETTA
Orange on Top by Henrietta Van der Haas, illustrated by Lucille Wallower; Harcourt, 1945. **Awarded:** Spring Book Festival (middle honor) 1945.

VAN DER LINDE, HENRY
Pit Pony by Joyce C. Barkhouse, illustrated by Henry Van Der Linde; Gage, 1989. **Awarded:** Brimer 1991.

VAN DER LOEFF, A. RUTGERS
Avalanche! by A. Rutgers Van der Loeff, illustrated by Gustav Schrotter; Morrow, 1958. **Awarded:** Boys Club 1959; Spring Book Festival (middle honor) 1958.

VAN DER MEER, ATIE
My Brother Sammy written and illustrated by Atie Van Der Meer and Ronald Van Der Meer; Hamish Hamilton, 1978. **Awarded:** Mother Goose (runnerup) 1979.

Sammy and Mara written and illustrated by Atie Van Der Meer and Ronald Van Der Meer; Hamish Hamilton, 1978. **Awarded:** Mother Goose (runnerup) 1979.

Your Amazing Senses written and illustrated by Ron Van Der Meer and Atie Van Der Meer; Aladdin; Child's Play, 1987. **Awarded:** Utah Children's Informational 1989.

VAN DER MEER, RONALD
My Brother Sammy written and illustrated by Atie Van Der Meer and Ronald Van Der Meer; Hamish Hamilton, 1978. **Awarded:** Mother Goose (runnerup) 1979.

Sailing Ships by Ron Van Der Meer and Dr. Alan McGowan, paintings by Borje Svensson; Viking, 1984. **Awarded:** Redbook (popup) 1984.

Sammy and Mara written and illustrated by Atie Van Der Meer and Ronald Van Der Meer; Hamish Hamilton, 1978. **Awarded:** Mother Goose (runnerup) 1979.

Your Amazing Senses written and illustrated by Ron Van Der Meer and Atie Van Der Meer; Aladdin; Child's Play, 1987. **Awarded:** Utah Children's Informational 1989.

VAN DER ZEE, JAMES
James Van Der Zee: The Picture Takin' Man by Jim Haskins, illustrated with photographs by James Van Der Zee; Dodd, Mead, 1979. **Awarded:** Woodson (outstanding merit) 1980.

VAN EVEREN, JAY
Nicholas: A Manhattan Christmas Story by Anne Carroll Moore, illustrated by Jay Van Everen; Putnam, 1924. **Awarded:** Newbery (honor) 1925.

Truce of the Wolf and Other Tales of Old Italy by Mary Gould Davis, illustrated by Jay Van Everen; Harcourt, 1931. **Awarded:** Newbery (honor) 1932.

VAN ITERSON, SINY ROSE
Pulga by Siny Rose Van Iterson, translated by Alexander Gode and Alison Gode, illustrated with maps; Morrow, 1971. **Awarded:** Batchelder 1973.

VAN KAMPEN, VLASTA
ABC, 123: The Canadian Alphabet and Counting Book written and illustrated by Vlasta van Kampen; Hurtig, 1982. **Awarded:** Governor General (illustrator) 1982.

The Great Canadian Animal Stories written and illustrated by Vlasta Van Kampen; Hurtig, 1978. **Awarded:** Amelia Frances Howard- Gibbon (runnerup) 1979.

The Great Canadian Adventure Stories written and illustrated by Vlasta Van Kampen; Hurtig, 1979. **Awarded:** Amelia Frances Howard- Gibbon (runnerup) 1980.

VAN LAAN, NANCY
Possum Come a-Knockin' by Nancy Van Laan, illustrated by George Booth; Knopf, 1990. **Awarded:** Parents' Choice (Picture Book) 1990.

Rainbow Crow: A Lenape Tale by Nancy Van Laan, illustrated by Beatriz Vidal; Knopf, 1989. **Awarded:** Author's Award (Alabama) 1991.

VAN LEEUWEN, JEAN
The Emperor's New Clothes by Hans Christian Andersen, adapted by Jean Van Leeuwen, illustrated by Jack Delano and Irene Delano; Random House, 1971. **Awarded:** Art Books for Children 1974.

The Great Christmas Kidnapping Caper by Jean Van Leeuwen, illustrated by Steven Kellogg; Dial, 1975. **Awarded:** Ethical Culture School 1975; South Carolina Children's 1979; William Allen White 1978.

I Was a 98-pound Duckling by Jean Van Leeuwen, not illustrated; Dial, 1972. **Awarded:** New Jersey Institute of Technology 1972.

Too Hot for Ice Cream by Jean Van Leeuwen, illustrated by Martha Alexander; Dial, 1974. **Awarded:** New Jersey Institute of Technology 1975, 1976.

VAN LOON, HENDRIK WILLEM
The Story of Mankind written and illustrated by Hendrik Willem Van Loon; Boni & Liveright, 1921. **Awarded:** Newbery 1922.

VAN NUTT, ROBERT
The Ugly Duckling by Hans Christian Andersen, illustrated by Robert Van Nutt; Knopf, 1986. **Awarded:** New York Times Best Illustrated 1986.

VAN QUYEN, DUONG
Beyond the East Wind: Legends and Folktales of Vietnam by Jewell Reinhart Coburn, told by Duong Van Quyen, illustrated by Nena Grigorian Ullberg; Burn, Hart, 1976. **Awarded:** Southern California Council (special recognition for a contribution of cultural significance) 1980.

VAN RAVEN, PIETER
A Time of Troubles by Pieter Van Raven, not illustrated; Scribners, 1990. **Awarded:** Scott O'Dell 1990.

VAN RHIJN, ALEID
The Tide in the Attic by Aleid Van Rhijn, illustrated by Margorie Gill; Criterion, 1962. **Awarded:** Boys Club 1963.

VAN SCIVER, RUTH
Scary Things by Norah Smaridge, illustrated by Ruth Van Sciver; Abingdon, 1969. **Awarded:** New Jersey Institute of Technology 1969.

You Know What? I Like Animals by Bernice Wells Carlson, illustrated by Ruth Van Sciver; Abingdon, 1967. **Awarded:** New Jersey Institute of Technology 1967.

VAN SPLUNTEREN, CARLA
Puzzles Old and New by Jerry Slocum and Jack Botermans, text by Carla Van Splunteren and Tony Burrett; Plenary Publications distributed by University of Washington Press, 1986. **Awarded:** New York Academy of Sciences (special prize as an exhibition catalogue of excellence and extraordinary interest) 1987.

VAN STEENWYCK, ELIZABETH A.
Awarded: Helen Keating Ott 1990.

VAN STOCKUM, HILDA
A Day on Skates: The Story of a Dutch Picnic written and illustrated by Hilda Van Stockum; Harper, 1934. **Awarded:** Newbery (honor) 1935.

VAN WOERKEM, DOROTHY O'BRIEN
Meat Pies and Sausages by Dorothy O. Van Woerkom, illustrated by Joseph Low; Greenwillow, 1976. **Awarded:** Children's Book Showcase 1977.

VAN WRIGHT, CORNELIUS
Make a Joyful Sound edited by Deborah Slier, illustrated by Cornelius Van Wright and Ying-Hwa Hu; Checkerboard, 1991. **Awarded:** Hungry Mind (Middle Readers/Fiction) 1991.

VAN ZWIENEN, ILSE CHARLOTTE KOEHN
see KOEHN, ILSE

VANCE, MARGUERITE
Awarded: Ohioana (body of work) 1962.

Willie Joe and His Small Change by Marguerite Vance, illustrated by Robert MacLean; Dutton, 1959. **Awarded:** Edison Mass Media (character development in children) 1960.

VARIAN, GEORGE
The Great Quest: A Romance of 1826 by Charles Boardman Hawes, illustrated by George Varian; Little Brown, 1921. **Awarded:** Newbery (honor) 1922.

VARLEY, SUSAN
Badger's Parting Gifts written and illustrated by Susan Varley; Andersen Press, 1984; Lothrop Lee & Shepard, 1984. **Awarded:** Kentucky Bluegrass 1986; Mother Goose 1985.

The Monster Bed by Jeanne Willis, illustrated by Susan Varley; Lothrop, 1987. **Awarded:** Redbook 1987.

VARNER, VELMA
The Animal Frolic by Toba Sojo, adapted by Velma Varner; Putnam, 1954. **Awarded:** New York Times Best Illustrated 1954.

VASILIU, MIRCEA
Wings against the Wind by Natalie Savage Carlson, illustrated by Mircea Vasiliu; Harper & Row, 1955. **Awarded:** Boys Club 1956; Spring Book Festival (middle honor) 1955.

VAUGHAN, ANNE
Appleseed Farm by Emily Taft Douglas, illustrated by Anne Vaughan; Abingdon-Cokesbury, 1948. **Awarded:** Spring Book Festival (middle honor) 1948.

VAUGHAN-JACKSON, GENEVIEVE
Epics of Everest by Leonard Wibberley, illustrated by Genevieve Vaughan-Jackson; Ariel, 1954. **Awarded:** Commonwealth Club of California 1954.

VEGLAHN, NANCY
The Spider of Brooklyn Heights by Nancy Veglahn, illustrated with photographs by Andreas Feininger; Scribner, 1967. **Awarded:** Spring Book Festival (middle honor) 1967.

VELASQUEZ, ERIC
Journey to Jo'burg: A South African Story by Beverly Naidoo, illustrated by Eric Velasquez; Lippincott, 1986. **Awarded:** Child Study 1986; Other Award 1985.

VELTHUIJS, MAX
The Painter and the Bird written and illustrated by Max Velthuijs, translated by Ray Broekel; Addison Wesley, 1975. **Awarded:** Children's Book Showcase 1976.

VENDRELL, CARMEN SOLE
Desde el Iris Con Amor (Iris Series) by Miguel Obiols, illustrated by Carme Sole Vendrell; Aura Communicacion (Barcelona). **Awarded:** Bologna (Critici in Erba) 1992.

Un Iris Irritado (Iris Series) by Miguel Obiols, illustrated by Carme Sole Vendrell; Aura Communicacion (Barcelona). **Awarded:** Bologna (Critici in Erba) 1992.

No Mires Aquel Iris (Iris Series) by Miguel Obiols, illustrated by Carme Sole Vendrell; Aura Communicacion (Barcelona). **Awarded:** Bologna (Critici in Erba) 1992.

El Oro de una Iris (Iris Series) by Miguel Obiols, illustrated by Carme Sole Vendrell; Aura Communicacion (Barcelona). **Awarded:** Bologna (Critici in Erba) 1992.

Que Viene el Iris, Leri (Iris Series) by Miguel Obiols, illustrated by Carme Sole Vendrell; Aura Communicacion (Barcelona). **Awarded:** Bologna (Critici in Erba) 1992.

Tantos Iris Como Dragones (Iris Series) by Miguel Obiols, illustrated by Carme Sole Vendrell; Aura Communicacion (Barcelona). **Awarded:** Bologna (Critici in Erba) 1992.

Todos los Iris al Iris (Iris Series) by Miguel Obiols, illustrated by Carme Sole Vendrell; Aura Communicacion (Barcelona). **Awarded:** Bologna (Critici in Erba) 1992.

VENEMA, REINTJE
Joe and Timothy Together by Dorothy Edwards, illustrated by Reintje Venema; Methuen, 1971. **Awarded:** Other Award 1975.

VENNEMA, PETER
Bard of Avon: The Story of William Shakespeare by Diane Stanley and Peter Vennema, illustrated by Diane Stanley; Morrow, 1992. **Awarded:** Reading Magic Award 1992.

Good Queen Bess by Diane Stanley and Peter Vennema, illustrated by Diane Stanley; Four Winds, 1990. **Awarded:** Boston Globe Horn Book (Nonfiction Honor) 1991; Reading Magic Award 1990.

Shaka: King of the Zulus by Diane Stanley and Peter Vennema, illustrated by Diane Stanley; Morrow, 1988. **Awarded:** New York Times Best Illustrated 1988.

VENTURA, PIERO
Great Painters written and illustrated by Piero Venturo; Putnam, 1984. **Awarded:** Utah Children's Informational Book Award 1986.

Piero Ventura's Book of Cities written and illustrated by Piero Ventura; Random House, 1975. **Awarded:** Art Books for Children 1977, 1978, 1979.

VERMEULEN, LO
Manko Kapak by Lo Vermeulen and Karel Jeuninckx, illustrated by Elzavan Hagendoren; De Sikkel, 1957. **Awarded:** Hans Christian Andersen (runnerup) 1960.

VERNEY, JOHN
February's Road written and illustrated by John Verney; Collins, 1961. **Awarded:** Carnegie (commended) 1961.

Friday's Tunnel written and illustrated by John Verney; Collins, 1959; Holt, 1966. **Awarded:** Hans Christian Andersen (runnerup) 1962; Carnegie (commended) 1959; Spring Book Festival (middle honor) 1966.

The Greatest Gresham by Gillian Avery, illustrated by John Verney; Collins, 1962. **Awarded:** Carnegie (commended) 1962.

VERO, RADU
Laser Light by Herman Schneider, illustrated by Radu Vero; McGraw, 1978. **Awarded:** New York Academy of Sciences (older) 1979.

VERWOERT, SISCA
Seventh Pebble by Eleanor Spence, illustrated by Sisca Verwoert; Oxford University Press, 1980. **Awarded:** New South Wales State Literary Awards (Special Children's) 1981.

VERY, JACQUES
Univers a Deux Voix Insecte by Marie Perennou, Claude Nuridsany, Jacques Very, and children of C.E.S.; La Noria. **Awarded:** Bologna (graphics for youth) 1981.

VESEY, AMANDA
Cousin Blodwyn's Visit written and illustrated by Amanda Vesey; Methuen, 1980. **Awarded:** Mother Goose (runnerup) 1981.

VESTAL, HERMAN B.
Scat, the Movie Cat by Justin F. Denzel, illustrated by Herman B. Vestal; Garrard, 1977. **Awarded:** New Jersey Institute of Technology 1978.

Wild Wing: Great Hunting Eagle by Justin F. Denzel, illustrated by Herman B. Vestal; Garrard, 1975. **Awarded:** New Jersey Institute of Technology 1976.

VETTER, CAROLE
The Wishing Night by Carole Vetter, illustrated by Beverly Komoda; Macmillan, 1966. **Awarded:** New Jersey Institute of Technology 1966.

VEVERS, GWYNNE, DR.
Your Body: Skin and Bone by Dr. Gwynne Vevers, illustrated by Sarah Pooley; Bodley Head, 1983. **Awarded:** Mother Goose (runnerup) 1984.

VICKERS, DAVID
The Strollers by Lesley Beake, illustrated by David Vickers; Maskew Miller Longman, 1987. **Awarded:** Percy Fitzpatrick 1988,

VICKERY, ROBERT
The Chocolate War by Robert Cormier, illustrated by Robert Vickery; Pantheon, 1974; Dell, 1975. **Awarded:** Lewis Carroll Shelf 1979; Media & Methods (paperback) 1976.

I Am the Cheese by Robert Cormier, illustrated by Robert Vickery; Pantheon, 1977. **Awarded:** Woodward Park School 1978.

VIDAL, BEATRIZ
Rainbow Crow: A Lenape Tale by Nancy Van Laan, illustrated by Beatriz Vidal; Knopf, 1989. **Awarded:** Author's Award (Alabama) 1991.

VIERECK, ELLEN K.
The Summer I Was Lost by Phillip Viereck, illustrated by Ellen Viereck; Day, 1965. **Awarded:** Lewis Carroll Shelf 1970; Edison Mass Media (character development for children) 1966; Dorothy Canfield Fisher 1967.

VIERECK, PHILLIP R.
The Summer I Was Lost by Phillip Viereck, illustrated by Ellen Viereck; Day, 1965. **Awarded:** Lewis Carroll Shelf 1970; Edison Mass Media (character development for children) 1966; Dorothy Canfield Fisher 1967.

VIGNA, JUDITH
Nobody Wants a Nuclear War written and illustrated by Judith Vigna; Whitman, 1986. **Awarded:** Jane Addams 1987.

VIGUERS, RUTH HILL
Awarded: Women's National Book Assn. 1968.

VIKSTEN, ALBERT
Gunilla, an Arctic Adventure by Albert Viksten, translated by Gustaf Lannestock, illustrated by Rus Anderson; Nelson, 1957. **Awarded:** Spring Book Festival (older honor) 1957.

VILLIERS, ALAN JOHN
Whalers of the Midnight Sun: A Story of Modern Whaling in the Antarctic by Alan Villiers, illustrated by Charles Pont; Angus & Robertson, 1949. **Awarded:** Children's Book Council of Australia 1949.

VINCENT, GABRIELLE
Smile, Ernest and Celestine written and illustrated by Gabrielle Vincent; Greenwillow, 1982. **Awarded:** New York Times Best Illustrated 1982.

VINGE, JOAN D.
Return of the Jedi: The Storybook based on the Movie by Joan D. Vinge, illustrated with photos; Random House, 1983. **Awarded:** North Dakota Children's Choice (Older) 1984.

VINING, ELIZABETH GRAY
see GRAY, ELIZABETH JANET

VINKE, HERMANN
The Short Life of Sophie Scholl by Hermann Vinke, translated by Hedwig Pachter, illustrated with photographs; Harper & Row, 1984. **Awarded:** Jane Addams 1985.

VIORST, JUDITH
Alexander and the Terrible, Horrible, No Good, Very Bad Day by Judith Viorst, illustrated by Ray Cruz; Atheneum, 1972. **Awarded:** Georgia Children's Picture Book 1977; George G. Stone 1988.

The Good-Bye Book by Judith Viorst, illustrated by Kay Chorao; Atheneum, 1988. **Awarded:** Christopher (ages 5-7) 1989; New Jersey Institute of Technology (Children's) 1989.

I'll Fix Anything by Judith Viorst, illustrated by Arnold Lobel; Harper, 1969. **Awarded:** New Jersey Institute of Technology 1970.

Sunday Morning by Judith Viorst, illustrated by Hilary Knight; Harper, 1968. **Awarded:** New Jersey Institute of Technology 1969.

VIPONT, ELFRIDA
see FOULDS, ELFRIDA VIPONT

VISHNIAC, ROMAN
A Day of Pleasure: Stories of a Boy Growing up in Warsaw by Isaac Bashevis Singer, illustrated by Roman Vishniac; Farrar, 1969. **Awarded:** National Book Award 1970.

VITALE, LIDIA
The Donkey from Dorking by Frances F. Neilson, illustrated by Lidia Vitale and Janet Hopkins; Dutton, 1942. **Awarded:** Spring Book Festival (picture book honor) 1942.

VITALE, STEFANO
The World in 1492 by Jean Fritz, Katherine Paterson, Patricia McKissack, Fredrick McKissack, Margaret Mahy and Jamake Highwater, illustrated by Stefano Vitale; Henry Holt, 1992. **Awarded:** Hungry Mind (Young Adult/Nonfiction) 1993.

VIVAS, JULIE
Awarded: Dromkeen 1992.

The Nativity written and illustrated by Julie Vivas; Harcourt Brace Jovanovich, 1988. **Awarded:** Boston Globe (Picture Book honor) 1989.

Possum Magic by Mem Fox, illustrated by Julie Vivas; Omnibus Books, 1983. **Awarded:** Children's Book Council of Australia (picture book of the year highly commended) 1984; International Board on Books for Young People (illustration/Australia) 1986; KOALA (primary) 1987; New South Wales State Literary Awards (Children's) 1984.

The Tram to Bondi Beach by Elizabeth Hathorn, illustrated by Julie Vivas; Methuen, 1981. **Awarded:** Children's Book Council of Australia (picture book of the year highly commended) 1982.

Very Best of Friends by Margaret Wild, illustrated by Julie Vivas; Margaret Hamilton, 1989; Harcourt Brace Jovanovich, 1990. **Awarded:** Children's Book Council of Australia (Picture Book of the Year) 1990.

VIVIER, COLETTE
Awarded: Hans Christian Andersen (highly commended author/France) 1972, 1974.

VOAKE, CHARLOTTE
The Mighty Slide by Allan Ahlberg, illustrated by Charlotte Voake; Viking Kestrel, 1988. **Awarded:** W. H. Smith (Second Prize) 1989.

The Ridiculous Story of Gammer Gurton's Needle by David Lloyd, illustrated by Charlotte Voake; Clarkson N. Potter/Crown, 1987. **Awarded:** New York Times Notable 1987; Parents' Choice (Story Book) 1987.

The Way to Sattin Shore by Philippa Pearce, illustrated by Charlotte Voake; Greenwillow, 1984. **Awarded:** Parents' Choice (literature) 1984.

VO-DINH
First Snow by Helen Coutant, illustrated by Vo-Dinh; Knopf, 1974. **Awarded:** Christopher (ages 8-12) 1975.

VOGEL, RAY
The Other City by Ray Vogel, photographs by William Boyd and others; White, 1969. **Awarded:** Nancy Bloch 1969.

VOGENTHALER, ELIZABETH
Awarded: Children's Reading Round Table 1977.

VOIGHT, LEIGH
The Mantis and the Moon by Marguerite Poland, illustrated by Leigh Voight; Raven Press, 1979. **Awarded:** Percy Fitzpatrick 1979.

VOIGT, CYNTHIA
Awarded: ALAN Award 1989.

The Callendar Papers by Cynthia Voigt, not illustrated; Atheneum, 1983. **Awarded:** Edgar Allan Poe 1984.

Come a Stranger by Cynthia Voigt, not illustrated; Atheneum, 1986. **Awarded:** Judy Lopez 1987.

Dicey's Song by Cynthia Voigt, not illustrated; Atheneum, 1982. **Awarded:** Boston Globe Horn Book (fiction honor) 1983; Newbery 1983.

Homecoming by Cynthia Voigt, not illustrated; Atheneum, 1981. **Awarded:** New York Times Notable Books 1981.

Izzy, Willy-Nilly by Cynthia Voigt, not illustrated; Atheneum, 1986. **Awarded:** California Young Reader (Young Adult) 1990; Virginia Young Readers (high school) 1988; Volunteer State Book Awards (grades 10-12) 1989.

A Solitary Blue by Cynthia Voigt, not illustrated; Atheneum, 1983. **Awarded:** Boston Globe Horn Book (fiction honor) 1984; Newbery (honor) 1984; Parents' Choice (literature) 1983.

Tree by Leaf by Cynthia Voigt, not illustrated; Atheneum, 1988. **Awarded:** Sugarman Children's Book Award 1989.

VON BAEYER, HANS CHRISTIAN
Rainbows, Snowflakes and Quarks: Physics and the World Around Us by Hans Christian Von Baeyer, illustrated by Laura Hartman; McGraw Hill, 1984. **Awarded:** New York Academy of Sciences (older honor) 1985.

VON FALLERSLEBEN, HOFFMANN
Jeder Nach Seiner Art by Hoffmann von Fallersleben, illustrated by Klaus Ensikat; Beltz and Gelberg. **Awarded:** Bologna (Graphics for Youth) 1992.

VON SCHMIDT, ERIC
By the Great Horn Spoon! by Sid Fleischman, illustrated by Eric von Schmidt; Atlantic-Little, 1963. **Awarded:** Boys Club 1964; FOCAL (Friends of Children and Literature) 1983; Southern California Council (notable) 1964; George G. Stone 1972; Western Writers (fiction) 1964.

Champions of Peace: Winners of the Nobel Peace Prize by Edith Patterson Meyer, illustrated by Eric von Schmidt; Little, Brown, 1959. **Awarded:** Jane Addams 1960.

Chancy and the Grand Rascal by Sid Fleischman, illustrated by Eric von Schmidt; Atlantic-Little, 1966. **Awarded:** Commonwealth Club of California 1966.

The Ghost on Saturday Night by Sid Fleischman, illustrated by Eric Von Schmidt; Atlantic-Little, 1974. **Awarded:** Charlie May Simon 1976-77; Mark Twain 1977; Young Hoosier (grades 4-6) 1979.

The Gnu and the Guru Go Behind the Beyond by Peggy Clifford, illustrated by Eric Von Schmidt; Houghton, 1970. **Awarded:** New York Times Best Illustrated 1970.

Humbug Mountain by Sid Fleischman, illustrated by Eric von Schmidt; Atlantic-Little, 1978. **Awarded:** Boston Globe Horn Book (fiction) 1979; National Book Award (finalist) 1979.

Jingo Django by Sid Fleischman, illustrated by Eric von Schmidt; Atlantic-Little, 1971. **Awarded:** Spring Book Festival (middle honor) 1971.

Mr. Mysterious & Co. by Sid Fleischman, illustrated by Eric von Schmidt; Atlantic-Little, 1962. **Awarded:** Spring Book Festival (middle honor) 1962.

Treasure of the High Country by Jonreed Lauritzen, illustrated by Eric von Schmidt; Little, Brown, 1959. **Awarded:** Spring Book Festival (middle honor) 1959.

VON SCHMIDT, HAROLD
Queer Person by Ralph Hubbard, illustrated by Harold Von Schmidt; Doubleday, 1930. **Awarded:** Newbery (honor) 1931.

VON STORCH, ANNE B.
see MALCOLMSON, ANNE B.

VON TEMPSKI, ARMINE
Bright Spurs by Armine von Tempski, illustrated by Paul Brown; Dodd, Mead, 1946. **Awarded:** Spring Book Festival (older honor) 1946.

VOSBURGH, LEONARD

The Boy with Wings by Adele deLeeuw, illustrated by Leonard Vosburgh; Nautilus, 1971. **Awarded:** New Jersey Institute of Technology 1972.

Chingo Smith of the Erie Canal by Samuel Hopkins Adams, illustrated by Leonard Vosburgh; Random House, 1958. **Awarded:** Spring Book Festival (older honor) 1958.

Never Go Anywhere with Digby by Ethelyn M. Parkinson, illustrated by Leonard Vosburgh; Abingdon, 1971. **Awarded:** Abingdon 1970.

VOTAW, SUSAN

A Life of Their Own: An Indian Family in Latin America by Lisa W. Kroeber and Aylette Jeness, photographs by the authors, illustrated by Susan Votaw; Crowell, 1975. **Awarded:** New York Academy of Sciences (older honor) 1976.

VOUTE, KATHLEEN

Westward Adventure: The True Stories of Six Pioneers by William O. Steele, illustrated with maps by Kathleen Voute; Harcourt, 1962. **Awarded:** Edison Mass Media (America's past) 1963.

Zuska of the Burning Hills by Alvena Seckar, illustrated by Kathleen Voute; Oxford, 1952. **Awarded:** Spring Book Festival (ages 8-12 honor) 1952.

VREEKIN, ELIZABETH

The Boy Who Would not Say His Name by Elizabeth Vreekin, illustrated by Leonard Shortall; Follett, 1959. **Awarded:** Follett Beginning to Read 1959.

W

WABER, BERNARD

A Firefly Named Torchy written and illustrated by Bernard Waber; Houghton Mifflin, 1970. **Awarded:** Boston Globe Horn Book (illustration honor) 1971.

The House on East 88th Street written and illustrated by Bernard Waber; Houghton, 1962. **Awarded:** Spring Book Festival (picture book honor) 1962.

Ira Sleeps Over written and illustrated by Bernard Waber; Houghton, 1972. **Awarded:** Children's Book Showcase 1973.

Lyle, Lyle, Crocodile written and illustrated by Bernard Waber; Houghton, 1965. **Awarded:** Lewis Carroll Shelf 1979.

WADDELL, EVELYN MARGARET
see COOK, LYN

WADDELL, MARTIN

Can't You Sleep Little Bear? by Martin Waddell, illustrated by Barbara Firth; Walker, 1988. **Awarded:** Greenaway 1988; Smarties (Grand Prix) 1988; Smarties (Under 5s) 1988.

Farmer Duck by Martin Waddell, illustrated by Helen Oxenbury; Walker, 1991; Candlewick, 1992. **Awarded:** British Book Awards (Illustrated) 1991; Greenaway (Highly Commended) 1991; Reading Magic Award 1992; Smarties (0-5 years) 1991; Smarties (Grand Prix) 1991.

Grandma's Bill by Martin Waddell, illustrated by Jane Johnson; Simon & Schuster, 1990. **Awarded:** Bisto (Books for Young Readers) 1991.

The Hidden House by Martin Waddell, illustrated by Angela Barrett; Walker Books, 1989. **Awarded:** W. H. Smith 1991.

The Park in the Dark by Martin Waddell, illustrated by Barbara Firth; Walker Books, 1989; Lothrop, Lee & Shepard, 1989. **Awarded:** Kurt Maschler 1989.

The Pig in the Pond by Martin Waddell, illustrated by Jill Barton; Walker, 1992. **Awarded:** Greenaway (highly commended) 1992.

Rosie's Babies by Martin Waddell, illustrated by Penny Dale; Walker, 1989. **Awarded:** Best Books for Babies 1990.

Squeak-a-Lot by Martin Waddell, illustrated by Virginia Miller; Walker, 1991; Greenwillow, 1991. **Awarded:** Mother Goose (runnerup) 1991.

WADE, ALAN

I'm Flying! by Alan Wade, illustrated by Petra Mathers; Knopf, 1990. **Awarded:** New York Times Best Illustrated 1990.

WAECHTER, FRIEDRICH KARL

Three Is Company written and illustrated by Friedrich Karl Waechter, translated by Harry Allard; Doubleday, 1979. **Awarded:** Parents' Choice (illustration) 1980.

WAGENKNECHT, EDWARD
Awarded: L. Frank Baum 1985.

WAGNER, JANE

J.T. by Jane Wagner, illustrated by Gordon Parks, Jr.; Van Nostrand, 1969. **Awarded:** Georgia Children's 1972.

WAGNER, JENNY

The Bunyip of Berkeley's Creek by Jenny Wagner, illustrated by Ron Brooks; Longmans Young, 1974. **Awarded:** Children's Book Council of Australia (picture book) 1974.

John Brown, Rose and the Midnight Cat by Jenny Wagner, illustrated by Ron Brooks; Kestrel, 1977; Bradbury, 1978. **Awarded:** Children's Book Council of Australia (picture book) 1978; Guardian (commended) 1978; New South Wales State Literary Awards (Children's) 1979.

WAGNER, LAUREN LYNN McGRAW

Merry Go Round in Oz by Lauren McGraw Wagner and Eloise Jarvis McGraw, designed and illustrated by Dick Martin; Reilly & Lee, 1963. **Awarded:** L. Frank Baum (cowinner) 1983.

WAGSTAFF, SUE

Two Victorian Families by Sue Wagstaff, illustrated with photographs and artists impressions; Black, 1979. **Awarded:** Other Award 1979.

WAHL, JAN

Humphrey's Bear by Jan Wahl, illustrated by William Joyce; Holt, Rinehart and Winston, 1987. **Awarded:** Christopher (ages 6-8) 1988; Redbook 1987.

Little Eight John by Jan Wahl, illustrated by Will Clay; Lodestar Books, 1992. **Awarded:** Coretta Scott King (Illustration honor) 1993.

The Norman Rockwell Storybook by Jan Wahl, illustrated by Norman Rockwell; Windmill/Simon & Schuster, 1969. **Awarded:** Ohioana 1970.

Pocahontas in London by Jan Wahl, illustrated by John Alcorn; Delacorte/Seymour Lawrence, 1967. **Awarded:** Bologna (critici in erba) 1969.

WALDECK, THEODORE J.

Lions on the Hunt by Theodore J. Waldeck, illustrated by Kurt Wiese; Viking, 1942. **Awarded:** Spring Book Festival (middle honor) 1942.

WALDMAN, NEIL

Bring Back the Deer by Jeffrey Prusski, illustrated by Neil Waldman; Harcourt Brace Jovanovich, 1988. **Awarded:** Washington Irving (Illustration) 1990.

The Gold Coin by Alma Flor Ada, illustrated by Neil Waldman; Atheneum, 1991. **Awarded:** Christopher Award (Ages 8-10) 1992.

The Highwayman by Alfred Noyes, illustrated by Neil Waldman; Harcourt Brace Jovanovich, 1990. **Awarded:** Washington Irving (Illustration) 1992.

Nessa's Fish by Nancy Leunn, illustrated by Neil Waldman; Atheneum, 1990. **Awarded:** Parents' Choice (Story Book) 1990.

WALDRON, ANN

The French Detection by Ann Waldron, not illustrated; Dutton, 1979. **Awarded:** New Jersey Institute of Technology 1981.

Integration of Mary-Larkin Thornhill by Ann Waldron, not illustrated; Dutton, 1975. **Awarded:** New Jersey Institute of Technology 1977.

True or False? Amazing Art Forgeries by Ann Waldron, illustrated; Hastings House, 1983. **Awarded:** New Jersey Institute of Technology 1983.

WALFORD, ASTRID

The Story of Albert Schweitzer by Jo Manton Gittings, illustrated by Astrid Walford; Abelard, 1955; Methuen, 1955. **Awarded:** Boys Club 1957; Carnegie (commended) 1955.

WALKER, BARBARA K.

The Dancing Palm Tree and Other Nigerian Folktales by Barbara K. Walker, illustrated by Helen Siegl; Texas Tech University Press, 1990. **Awarded:** New York Times Best Illustrated 1990.

WALKER, BARBARA M.

The Little House Cookbook by Barbara M. Walker, illustrated by Garth Williams; Harper, 1979. **Awarded:** Western Heritage 1980.

WALKER, BOB

Fashion as a Career by Edith Heal, illustrated by Bob Walker; Messner, 1966. **Awarded:** New Jersey Institute of Technology 1966.

WALKER, C.

That Dunbar Boy by Jean Gould, illustrated by C. Walker; Dodd, Mead, 1958. **Awarded:** Edison Mass Media (character development in children) 1959.

WALKER, DAVID

Big Ben by David Walker, illustrated by Victor Ambrus; Houghton, 1969. **Awarded:** Charlie May Simon 1971-72.

WALKER, JANE MURRAY

Rites of Passage Today: The Cultural Significance of The Wizard of Earthsea by Jane Murray Walker in *Mosaic*. **Awarded:** Children's Literature Assn. Awards for Excellence in the field of Literary Criticism (runnerup) 1981.

The Lion, the Witch, and the Wardrobe as Rite of Passage by Jane Murray Walker in *Children's Literature in Education* 58 (Spring 1985). **Awarded:** Children's Literature Assn. Awards for Excellence in the field of Literary Criticism (runnerup) 1986.

WALKER, JOHN

Lorenzo De'Medici and the Renaissance by John Walker and Charles L. Mee, Jr., illustrated with photographs; American Heritage, 1969. **Awarded:** Spring Book Festival (older honor) 1969.

WALKER, KATE

Peter by Kate Walker, not illustrated; Omnibus Books, 1991. **Awarded:** Children's Book Council of Australia (Book of the Year Older Honor) 1992.

Raining Away to Sea by Kate Walker. **Awarded:** Mary Grant Bruce ($100) 1991.

WALKER, MARGARET

Awarded: Lucile M. Pannell 1989.

WALKER, NEDDA

Nathan, Boy of Capernaum by Amy Morris Lillie, illustrated by Nedda Walker; Dutton, 1944. **Awarded:** Spring Book Festival (middle honor) 1945.

WALKER, ROBIN

Awarded: Lucile M. Pannell 1989.

WALKER, STEPHEN

The Drac: French Tales of Dragons and Demons by Felice Holman and Nanine Valen, illustrated by Stephen Walker; Scribner, 1975. **Awarded:** New York Times Notable Books 1975.

WALL, ELIZABETH S.

Story by Elizabeth S. Wall in *Highlights* magazine. Awarded: Magazine Merit (Nonfiction) 1991.

WALLACE, BARBARA BROOKS

Peppermints in the Parlor by Barbara Brooks Wallace, not illustrated; Atheneum, 1980. **Awarded:** William Allan White 1983.

WALLACE, BILL

Beauty by Bill Wallace, not illustrated; Holiday House, 1988. **Awarded:** Sequoyah Children's 1991; William Allen White 1991.

Danger in Quicksand Swamp by Bill Wallace, not illustrated; Holiday House, 1989. **Awarded:** Young Reader's Choice 1992.

A Dog Called Kitty by Bill Wallace, not illustrated; Holiday House, 1980. **Awarded:** Golden Sower (4-6) 1985; Sequoyah 1983; Texas Bluebonnet 1983.

Ferret in the Bedroom, Lizards in the Fridge by Bill Wallace, not illustrated; Holiday House, 1986. **Awarded:** Golden Sower (grades 4-6) 1989; South Carolina Children's 1989.

Snot Stew by Bill Wallace, illustrated by Lisa McCue; Holiday House, 1989. **Awarded:** KC Three 1991-92; South Carolina Children's 1992; Texas Bluebonnet 1992.

Trapped in Death Cave by Bill Wallace, not illustrated; Holiday House, 1984. **Awarded:** Soaring Eagle (Grades 7-9) 1991; Sunshine State Young Reader's Award (grades 6-8) 1990; Utah Children's 1989.

WALLACE, IAN

Chin Chiang and the Dragon's Dance written and illustrated by Ian Wallace; Douglas & McIntyre, 1984. **Awarded:** Amelia Frances Howard-Gibbon 1985; International Board on Books for Young People (illustration/Canada) 1986; IODE 1984.

The Name of the Tree by Celia Barker Lottridge, illustrated by Ian Wallace; Douglas & McIntyre, 1989; McElderry, 1989. **Awarded:** Amelia Frances Howard-Gibbon (2nd runnerup)

1990; Mr. Christie's (English Illustration) 1989; Elizabeth Mrazik-Cleaver 1990.

WALLENTA, E.
Lale, Die Turkin by Karl Bruckner, illustrated by E. Wallenta; Jungend u. Volk, 1958. **Awarded:** Hans Christian Andersen (runnerup) 1960.

WALLES, DWIGHT
Who, What, When, Where Book about the Bible by William L. Coleman, illustrated by Dwight Walles; David C. Cook, 1980. **Awarded:** Gold Medallion 1981.

WALLNER, JOHN
Charlotte & Charles by Ann Tompert, illustrated by John Wallner; Crown, 1979. **Awarded:** Woodward Park School 1980.

Harvey, the Beer Can King by Jamie Gilson, illustrated by John Wallner; Lothrop Lee & Shepard, 1978. **Awarded:** Friends of American Writers (older) 1979.

Little Fox Goes to the End of the World by Ann Tompert, illustrated by John Wallner; Crown, 1976. **Awarded:** Friends of American Writers (illustrator) 1977.

When the Dark Comes Dancing compiled by Nancy Larrick, illustrated by John Wallner; Philomel, 1983. **Awarded:** Parents' Choice (literature) 1984.

WALLOWER, LUCILLE
Awarded: Outstanding Pennsylvania Author 1987.

Orange on Top by Henrietta van der Haas, illustrated by Lucille Wallower; Harcourt, 1945. **Awarded:** Spring Book Festival (middle honor) 1945.

WALSER, RICHARD
North Carolina Parade: Stories of History and People by Richard Walser and Julia Street, illustrated by D. B. Browning; University of North Carolina Press, 1966. **Awarded:** North Carolina AAUW 1966.

WALSH, ANNE BATTERBERRY
A Gardening Book: Indoors and Outdoors written and illustrated by Anne Batterberry Walsh; Atheneum, 1976. **Awarded:** Children's Book Showcase 1977.

WALSH, ELLEN STOLL
Mouse Paint written and illustrated by Ellen Stoll Walsh; Harcourt Brace Jovanovich, 1989. **Awarded:** Reading Magic 1989.

WALSH, JILL PATON
see PATON WALSH, JILL

WALSH, MARY R.
Molly the Rogue by Mary R. Walsh, illustrated by Henry C. Pitz; Knopf, 1944. **Awarded:** Spring Book Festival (younger honor) 1944.

WALT DISNEY STUDIO
The Fox and the Hound by Walt Disney Productions, illustrated; Golden Press, 1981. **Awarded:** North Dakota Children's Choice (younger) 1982.

The Walt Disney Story of Our Friend the Atom by Heinz Haber, illustrated by Walt Disney Studio; Simon & Schuster, 1957. **Awarded:** Spring Book Festival (middle honor) 1957.

WALTER, MARION
The Mirror Puzzle Book written and illustrated by Marion Walter; Tarquin Publications, 1985. **Awarded:** New York Academy of Sciences (younger honor) 1986.

WALTER, MILDRED PITTS
Because We Are by Mildred Pitts Walter, not illustrated; Lothrop, Lee & Shepard, 1983. **Awarded:** Coretta Scott King (honorable mention) 1984; Parents' Choice (literature) 1984.

Brother to the Wind by Mildred Pitts Walter, illustrated by Diane and Leo Dillon; Lothrop, Lee & Shepard, 1985. **Awarded:** Parents' Choice (literature) 1985.

Justin and the Best Biscuits in the World by Mildred Pitts Walter, illustrated by Catherine Stock; Lothrop, Lee & Shepard, 1986. **Awarded:** Coretta Scott King (literature) 1987.

Mississippi Challenge by Mildred Pitts Walter, illustrated with photos; Bradbury Press, 1992. **Awarded:** Christopher (ages 12-up) 1993; Coretta Scott King (Text honor) 1993.

My Mama Needs Me by Mildred Pitts Walter, illustrated by Pat Cummings; Lothrop, Lee & Shepard, 1983. **Awarded:** Coretta Scott King (illustrator) 1984.

Trouble's Child by Mildred Pitts Walter, not illustrated; Lothrop, Lee & Shepard, 1985. **Awarded:** Coretta Scott King (literature honorable mention) 1986.

WALTERS, MARTIN
The Simon & Schuster Young Readers' Book of Animals by Martin Walters; Simon & Schuster, 1991. **Awarded:** Book Can Develop Empathy 1991.

WALTON, LUKE
The Galapagos Kid: or, The Spirit of 1976 by Luke Walton, not illustrated; Nautilus, 1971. **Awarded:** New Jersey Institute of Technology 1971.

WANGERIN, WALTER, JR.
Book of the Dun Cow by Walter Wangerin, Jr., not illustrated; Harper, 1978. **Awarded:** New York Times Notable Books 1978; National Religious Book Award 1979.

Potter, Come Fly to the First of the Earth by Walter Wangerin, Jr., illustrated by Daniel San Souci; Chariot Books, 1985. **Awarded:** Gold Medallion 1986.

WARD, JON
Big Baby by Jon Ward, illustrated by Claudio Munzo; Walker Books, 1986. **Awarded:** Mother Goose (runnerup) 1987.

WARD, KEITH
The Black Stallion by Walter Farley, illustrated by Keith Ward; Random House, 1941. **Awarded:** Young Reader's Choice 1944.

WARD, LYND KENDALL
Awarded: Regina 1975; Rutgers 1969; University of Southern Mississippi 1973.

The American Indian Story by May McNeer, illustrated by Lynd Ward; Ariel, 1963. **Awarded:** New Jersey Institute of Technology 1963.

America's Ethan Allen by Stewart Holbrook, illustrated by Lynd Ward; Houghton Mifflin, 1949. **Awarded:** Caldecott (honor) 1950.

America's Mark Twain by May McNeer, illustrated by Lynd Ward; Houghton, 1962. **Awarded:** New Jersey Institute of Technology 1963.

Armed with Courage by May McNeer and Lynd Ward, illustrated by Lynd Ward; Abingdon, 1957. **Awarded:** Edison Mass Media (character development for children) 1958.

The Biggest Bear written and illustrated by Lynd Ward; Houghton Mifflin, 1952. **Awarded:** Caldecott 1953.

Bright Island by Mabel L. Robinson, illustrated by Lynd Ward; Random House, 1937. **Awarded:** Newbery (honor) 1938; Spring Book Festival (older honor) 1937.

The Cat Who Went to Heaven by Elizabeth Coatsworth, illustrated by Lynd Ward; Macmillan, 1930. **Awarded:** Newbery 1931.

Fog Magic by Julia L. Sauer, illustrated by Lynd Ward; Viking, 1943. **Awarded:** Newbery (honor) 1944.

From the Eagle's Wing: A Biography of John Muir by Hildegarde Hoyt Swift, illustrated by Lynd Ward; Morrow, 1962. **Awarded:** Southern California Council (notable) 1963.

Johnny Tremain by Esther Forbes, illustrated by Lynd Ward; Houghton, 1943. **Awarded:** Newbery 1944.

Little Blacknose: The Story of a Pioneer by Hildegarde Swift, illustrated by Lynd Ward; Harcourt, 1929. **Awarded:** Newbery (honor) 1930.

Martin Luther by Lynd Ward and May McNeer, illustrated by Lynd Ward; Abingdon-Cokesbury, 1953. **Awarded:** Spring Book Festival (ages 8-12 honor) 1953.

North Star Shining by Hildegarde Swift, illustrated by Lynd Ward; Morrow, 1947. **Awarded:** Spring Book Festival (older honor) 1947.

Runner of the Mountain Tops: The Life of Louis Agassiz by Mabel L. Robinson, illustrated by Lynd Ward; Random House, 1939. **Awarded:** Newbery (honor) 1940.

Santiago by Ann Nolan Clark, illustrated by Lynd Ward; Viking, 1955. **Awarded:** Spring Book Festival (older honor) 1955.

The Silver Pony written and illustrated by Lynd Ward; Houghton, 1973. **Awarded:** Boston Globe Horn Book (illustration honor) 1973; Lewis Carroll Shelf 1973; Children's Book Showcase 1974; New York Times Best Illustrated 1973.

Spice and the Devil's Cave by Agnes D. Hewes, illustrated by Lynd Ward; Knopf, 1930. **Awarded:** Newbery (honor) 1931.

The Story of George Washington by May McNeer, illustrated by Lynd Ward; Abingdon, 1973. **Awarded:** New Jersey Institute of Technology 1973.

WARD, MAY McNEER
see McNEER, MAY

WARD, PATRICIA
The Secret Pencil by Patricia Ward, illustrated by Nicole Hornby; Random House, 1960. **Awarded:** Spring Book Festival (middle honor) 1960.

WARE, LEON
The Mystery of 22 East by Leon Ware, not illustrated; Westminster, 1965. **Awarded:** Edgar Allen Poe 1966.

WARFEL, DIANTHA
On Guard! by Diantha Warfel, not illustrated; Dodd Mead, 1961. **Awarded:** Boys Life - Dodd, Mead 1960.

WARNER, GERTRUDE CHANDLER
The Boxcar Children by Gertrude Chandler Warner, illustrated by L. Kate Deal; Whitman, c1942. **Awarded:** Emphasis on Reading (grades 4-6) 1984-85.

WARNER, LUCILLE SCHULBERG
From Slave to Abolitionist: The Life of William Wells Brown adapted by Lucille Schulberg Warner, illustrated by Tom Feelings: Dial, 1976. **Awarded:** Children's Book Showcase 1977.

WARREN, BETSY
Indians Who Lived in Texas written and illustrated by Betsy Warren; Steck-Vaughn, 1970. **Awarded:** Steck-Vaughn 1971.

WARREN, MARIAN G.
Vultures by Anne W. Turner, illustrated by Marian G. Warren; McKay, 1973. **Awarded:** New York Academy of Sciences (older honor) 1974.

WARSHAW, MAL
The Hospital Book by James Howe, illustrated with photographs by Mal Warshaw; Crown, 1981. **Awarded:** Boston Globe Horn Book (nonfiction honor) 1981.

WARSHOFSKY, ISAAC
see SINGER, ISAAC BASHEVIS

WARTSKI, MAUREEN CRANE
Story by Maureen Crane Wartski in *Boys Life* magazine. **Awarded:** Magazine Merit (Fiction Honor) 1990.

A Boat to Nowhere by Maureen Crane Wartski, illustrated by Dick Teicher; Westminster, 1980. **Awarded:** Child Study 1980.

WASSERMAN, DEBRA
I Love Animals and Broccoli by Debra Wasserman and Charles Stahler, illustrated; Vegetarian Resource Group, 1985. **Awarded:** Book Can Develop Empathy 1990.

WATANABE, SHIGEO
Gin No Ude No Otto (original English *Otto of the Silver Hand*) by Howard Pyle, translated by Shigeo Watanabe; Kaisei-sha, 1983. **Awarded:** International Board on Books for Young People (translation/Japan) 1984.

WATERHOUSE, CHARLES
Where the Raritan Flows by Earl Schenck Miers, illustrated by Charles Waterhouse; Rutgers University Press, 1964. **Awarded:** New Jersey Institute of Technology (history) 1964.

WATERSON, MARY
Gypsy Family by Mary Waterson, photographs by Lance Browne; Black, 1978. **Awarded:** Other Award 1978.

WATERTON, BETTY
A Salmon for Simon by Betty Waterton, illustrated by Ann Blades; Douglas & McIntyre, 1978. **Awarded:** Canadian Library Assn. (runnerup) 1979; Governor General (illustrator) 1978; Amelia Frances Howard-Gibbon 1979.

WATKINS, BERNARD C.
The Pageant of Chinese History by Elizabeth Seeger, illustrated by Bernard Watkins; Longman, 1934. **Awarded:** Newbery (honor) 1935.

WATKINS, YOKO KAWASHIMA
So Far from the Bamboo Grove by Yoko Kawashima Watkins, introduction by Jean Fritz; Lothrop, Lee & Shepard, 1986. **Awarded:** Parents' Choice (literature) 1986.

WATKINS-PITCHFORD, DENYS JAMES
(pseudonym is B. B.)

The Little Grey Men: A Story for the Young in Heart written and illustrated by Denys Watkins-Pitchford; Lyre & Spottiswoode, 1942. **Awarded:** Carnegie 1942.

WATSON, CLYDE
Father Fox's Pennyrhymes by Clyde Watson, illustrated by Wendy Watson; Crowell, 1971. **Awarded:** Art Books for Children 1973; Children's Book Showcase 1972; National Book Award (finalist) 1972; New York Times Notable Books 1971.

WATSON, JAMES
Talking in Whispers by James Watson, not illustrated; Gollancz, 1983. **Awarded:** Other Award 1983.

WATSON, JOHN
Ssh! It's the Secret Club! written and illustrated by John Watson; Macmillan Children's, 1987. **Awarded:** Macmillan Prize (1st prize) 1986.

WATSON, RICHARD JESSE
The High Rise Glorious Skittle Skat Roarious Sky Pie Angel Food Cake by Nancy Willard, illustrated by Richard Jesse Jackson; Harcourt Brace Jovanovich, 1990. **Awarded:** KC Three 1992-93.

Tom Thumb written and illustrated by Richard Jesse Watson; Harcourt Brace Jovanovich, 1989. **Awarded:** Golden Kite (Picture- Illustration) 1989.

WATSON, SALLY
To Build a Land by Sally Watson, illustrated by Lili Cassel; Holt, 1957. **Awarded:** Woodward Park School 1959.

WATSON, WENDY
Doctor Coyote: A Native American Aesop's Fable retold by John Bierhorst, illustrated by Wendy Watson; Macmillan, 1987. **Awarded:** Southwest 1986.

Father Fox's Pennyrhymes by Clyde Watson, illustrated by Wendy Watson; Crowell, 1971. **Awarded:** Art Books for Children 1973; Children's Book Showcase 1972; National Book Award (finalist) 1972; New York Times Notable Books 1971.

First Farm in the Valley: Anna's Story by Anne Pellowski, illustrated by Wendy Watson; Philomel, 1982. **Awarded:** State Historical Society of Wisconsin 1983.

WATTS, BARRIE
Conker written and illustrated by Barrie Watts; A & C Black, 1987. **Awarded:** Times Educational Supplement (Junior) 1988.

Duck by Angela Royston, illustrated by Barrie Watts; Lodestar, 1991. **Awarded:** Redbook 1991.

WATTS, BERNADETTE
Das Kleine Madchen mit den Schwefelholzchen by Hans Christian Andersen, illustrated by Bernadette Watts; Nord-Sud, 1983. **Awarded:** Owl Prize 1986.

WATTS, MABEL PIZZEY
While the Horses Galloped to London by Mabel Watts, illustrated by Mercer Mayer; Parents, 1971. **Awarded:** Children's Book Showcase 1974.

WATTS, MARGARET
A Cat for Samantha by Margaret Watts. **Awarded:** Mary Grant Bruce ($100) 1990.

WAY, MARK
Nicholas and the Moon Eggs by Mark Way, illustrated; Collins-Australia, 1977. **Awarded:** Bologna (critici in erba) 1978.

WEATHERBY, MARK ALAN
Call of the Wolves by Jim Murphy, illustrated by Mark Alan Weatherby; Scholastic, 1989. **Awarded:** Nevada Young Reader (Primary) 1991-92.

WEAVER, STELLA
A Poppy in the Corn by Stella Weaver, not illustrated; Pantheon, 1960. **Awarded:** Spring Book Festival (older honor) 1961.

WEBB, JEAN FRANCIS
Kaiulani: Crown Princess of Hawaii by Jean Francis Webb and Nancy Webb, not illustrated; Viking, 1962. **Awarded:** Spring Book Festival (older honor) 1962.

WEBB, KAYE
Awarded: Eleanor Farjeon 1969.

WEBB, MARGOT S.
Letters from Uncle David: Underground Hero by Margot S. Webb, manuscript. **Awarded:** Council on Interracial Books (ages 12-16) 1969.

WEBB, NANCY
Kaiulani: Crown Princess of Hawaii by Nancy Webb and Jean Francis Webb, not illustrated; Viking, 1962. **Awarded:** Spring Book Festival (older honor) 1962.

WECHTER, NELL WISE
Taffy of Torpedo Junction by Nell Wise Wechter, illustrated by Mary Walker Sparks; Blair, 1957. **Awarded:** North Carolina AAUW 1957.

WECK, THOMAS L.
Back-Back and the Lima Bear by Thomas L. Weck, illustrated by Neil Taylor; Winston-Derek Publishers, 1985. **Awarded:** Catholic Book Awards (Children's) 1986; New Jersey Institute of Technology 1987.

WEEKS, KENT R.
X-raying the Pharaohs by Kent R. Weeks and James E. Harris, illustrated with photographs; Scribner, 1973. **Awarded:** New York Academy of Sciences (older honor) 1974.

WEGEN, RON
The Halloween Costume Party written and illustrated by Ron Wegen; Clarion, 1983. **Awarded:** New Jersey Institute of Technology 1983.

WEGNER, FRITZ
The Champion of Merrimack County by Roger W. Drury, illustrated by Fritz Wegner; Little, Brown, 1976. **Awarded:** Christopher (ages 9-12) 1977; Ethical Culture School 1976; Mark Twain 1979.

Heard It In the Playground by Allan Ahlberg, illustrated by Fritz Wegner; Viking Kestrel, 1989. **Awarded:** Signal Poetry Award 1990.

Jacob Two-two Meets the Hooded Fang by Mordecai Richler, illustrated by Fritz Wegner; McClelland & Stewart, 1975. **Awarded:** Canadian Library Assn. 1976; New York Times Notable Books 1975; Ruth Schwartz 1976.

Woof! by Allan Ahlberg, illustrated by Fritz Wegner; Viking Kestrel, 1986. **Awarded:** International Board on Books for Young People (Writing/Great Britain) 1988.

WEIDHORN, MANFRED
Napoleon by Manfred Weidhorn, illustrated; Atheneum, 1986. **Awarded:** New Jersey Institute of Technology 1988.

WEIGAND, PATRICK
The New Oxford School Atlas by Patrick Weigand, illustrated; Oxford University Press, 1990. **Awarded:** Times Educational Supplement (Senior) 1990.

WEIGEL, SUSI
Hannes und Sein Bumpan by Mira Lobe, illustrated by Susi Weigel; Jugend u. Volk, 1961. **Awarded:** Hans Christian Andersen (runnerup) 1964.

WEIHS, ERIKA
Cakes and Miracles: A Purim Tale by Barbara Diamond Goldin, illustrated by Erika Weihs; Viking, 1991. **Awarded:** Sydney Taylor Book Award (Picture Book) 1992.

CHILDREN'S LITERATURE AWARDS AND WINNERS

Days of Awe: Stories for Rosh Hashanah and Yom Kippur adapted by Eric A. Kimmel, illustrated by Erika Weihs; Viking, 1991. **Awarded:** Aesop Prize 1993.

WEIK, MARY HAYS
The Jazz Man by Mary Hays Weik, illustrated by Ann Grifalconi; Atheneum, 1966. **Awarded:** New York Times Best Illustrated 1966; Newbery (honor) 1967.

WEIL, ANN YEZNER
Red Sails to Capri by Ann Weil, illustrated by C. B. Falls; Viking, 1952. **Awarded:** Newbery (honor) 1953.

WEIL, LISL
The Case of the Secret Scribbler by E. W. Hildick, illustrated by Lisl Weil; Macmillan, 1978. **Awarded:** Edgar Allan Poe (runnerup) 1979.

WEILER, DIANA J.
Boy Who Walked Backwards by Diana J. Weiler; Western Producer Prairie, 1985. **Awarded:** Vicky Metcalf Short Story 1986.

WEILER, MARY
The Whale People by Roderick Haig-Brown, illustrated by Mary Weiler; Collins-Canada, 1962. **Awarded:** Canadian Library Assn. 1964.

WEILERSTEIN, SADIE ROSE
Awarded: Jewish Book Council (body of work) 1955; Sydney Taylor Body of Work 1981.

Ten and a Kid by Sadie Rose Weilerstein, illustrated by Janina Domanska; Doubleday, 1961. **Awarded:** Jewish Book Council 1961.

WEIMAN, EIVEEN
Which Way Courage by Eiveen Weiman, not illustrated; Atheneum, 1981. **Awarded:** Southern California Council (distinguished work of fiction) 1982.

WEIR, DOFFY
Knickerless Nicola by Kara May, illustrated by Doffy Weir; Macmillan, 1989. **Awarded:** Nottinghamshire (Acorn) 1990.

WEISGARD, LEONARD JOSEPH
The Courage of Sarah Noble by Alice Dalgliesh, illustrated by Leonard Weisgard; Scribner, 1954. **Awarded:** Lewis Carroll Shelf 1959; Newbery (honor) 1955; Spring Book Festival (middle honor) 1954.

Dorinda by Elizabeth Howard, illustrated by Leonard Weisgard; Lothrop, 1944. **Awarded:** Spring Book Festival (older honor) 1944.

Indian, Indian by Charlotte Zolotow, illustrated by Leonard Weisgard; Simon & Schuster, 1952. **Awarded:** Spring Book Festival (picture book honor) 1952.

The Little Island by Golden MacDonald, illustrated by Leonard Weisgard; Doubleday, 1946. **Awarded:** Caldecott 1947; Children's Choice [Arizona] (picture book) 1982.

Little Lost Lamb by Golden MacDonald, illustrated by Leonard Weisgard; Doubleday, Doran, 1945. **Awarded:** Caldecott (honor) 1946.

Rain Drop Splash by Alvin R. Tresselt, illustrated by Leonard Weisgard; Lothrop, 1946. **Awarded:** Caldecott (honor) 1947.

The Secret River by Marjorie Kinnan Rawlings, illustrated by Leonard Weisgard; Scribner, 1955. **Awarded:** Newbery (honor) 1956.

White Bird by Clyde Robert Bulla, illustrated by Leonard Weisgard; Crowell, 1966. **Awarded:** George G. Stone 1968.

WEISS, ANN EDWARDS
Lies, Deception, and Truth by Ann E. Weiss, not illustrated; Houghton Mifflin, 1988. **Awarded:** Christopher (ages 10-12) 1989.

The Nuclear Arms Race - Can We Survive It? by Ann E. Weiss, not illustrated; Houghton Mifflin, 1983. **Awarded:** Christopher (ages 12-up) 1984.

Save the Mustangs! How a Federal Law Is Passed by Ann E. Weiss, illustrated with photographs; Messner, 1974. **Awarded:** Christopher (ages 8-12) 1975.

WEISS, ELLEN
Heather's Feathers by Leatie Weiss, illustrated by Ellen Weiss; Watts, 1976. **Awarded:** Garden State Children's (easy to read) 1979.

My Teacher Sleeps in School by Leatie Weiss, illustrated by Ellen Weiss; Viking, 1984. **Awarded:** Emphasis on Reading (K-1) 1987-88; Georgia Children's Picture Storybook 1987.

WEISS, EMIL
It's Like This, Cat by Emily Cheney Neville, illustrated by Emil Weiss; Harper, 1963. **Awarded:** Newbery 1964.

Profiles in Courage by John F. Kennedy, illustrated by Emil Weiss; Harper, 1964. (Young readers memorial edition) **Awarded:** Jane Addams 1964.

Seeing Fingers: The Story of Louis Braille by Etta DeGering, illustrated by Emil Weiss; McKay, 1962. **Awarded:** Edison Mass Media (character development in children) 1963.

WEISS, HARVEY
Pencil, Pen and Brush written and illustrated by Harvey Weiss; Scott, 1961. **Awarded:** Spring Book Festival (middle honor) 1961.

The Raggle Taggle Fellow by Miriam Schlein, illustrated by Harvey Weiss; Abelard-Schuman, 1959. **Awarded:** Spring Book Festival (ages 4-8 honor) 1959.

WEISS, JACQUELINE SCHACTER
Awarded: Drexel Citation 1988; Helen Keating Ott 1988.

WEISS, JERRY
Awarded: ALAN 1976.

WEISS, LEATIE
Heather's Feathers by Leatie Weiss, illustrated by Ellen Weiss; Watts, 1976. **Awarded:** Garden State Children's (easy to read) 1979.

My Teacher Sleeps in School by Leatie Weiss, illustrated by Ellen Weiss; Viking, 1984. **Awarded:** Emphasis on Reading (K-1) 1987-88; Georgia Children's Picture Storybook 1987.

WEISS, M. JERRY
Awarded: Landau 1977.

WEISS, MORTON JEROME
see WEISS, M. JERRY

WEISS, RENEE KAROL
The Bird from the Sea by Renee Karol Weiss, illustrated by Ed Young; Crowell, 1970. **Awarded:** New Jersey Institute of Technology 1971.

A Paper Zoo by Renee Weiss, illustrated by Ellen Raskin; Macmillan, 1968. **Awarded:** New Jersey Institute of Technology 1969.

WEISSENBERG, FRAN
The Streets Are Paved with Gold by Fran Weissenberg, not illustrated; Harbinger House, 1990. **Awarded:** Sydney Taylor Manuscript Awards 1988.

WEISSKOPF, VICTOR F.
Knowledge and Wonder: The Natural World as Man Knows It by Victor F. Weisskopf, illustrated by R. Paul Larkin; Doubleday, 1962. **Awarded:** Edison Mass Media (science book for youth) 1963.

WELCH, d'ALTE A.
Awarded: Chandler Reward of Merit 1972.

WELCH, MARTHA McKEEN
Sunflower! written and illustrated by Martha McKeen Welch; Dodd, Mead, 1980. **Awarded:** New York Academy of Sciences (younger honor) 1981.

WELCH, RONALD
Knight Crusader by Ronald Welch, illustrated by William Stobbs; Oxford, 1954. **Awarded:** Carnegie 1954.

WELLER, FRANCES WARD
Boat Song by Frances Ward Weller, not illustrated; Macmillan, 1987. **Awarded:** New Jersey Institute of Technology 1988.

WELLER, FRANCES WARD
Riptide by Frances Ward Weller, illustrated by Robert J. Blake; Philomel, 1990. **Awarded:** Golden Sower (grades K-3) 1993.

WELLER, JOAN
Awarded: Frances E. Russell 1987.

WELLMAN, MANLY WADE
Rifles at Ramsour's Mill: A Tale of the Revolutionary War by Manly Wade Wellman, not illustrated; Washburn, 1961. **Awarded:** North Carolina AAUW 1962.

WELLMAN, PAUL I.
The Greatest Cattle Drive by Paul I. Wellman, illustrated by Lorence F. Bjorklund; Houghton, 1964. **Awarded:** Western Heritage 1965.

WELLS, FRANCES
How Man Discovered his Body by Sarah R. Riedman, illustrated by Frances Wells; Abelard-Schuman, 1966. **Awarded:** New Jersey Institute of Technology (science) 1966.

WELLS, HARU
The Biography of Daniel Inouye by Jane Goodsell, illustrated by Haru Wells; Crowell, 1977. **Awarded:** Carter G. Woodson 1978.

The Master Puppeteer by Katherine Paterson, illustrated by Haru Wells; Crowell, 1976. **Awarded:** National Book Award 1977; Edgar Allan Poe (runnerup) 1977.

WELLS, PETER
Mr. Tootwhistle's Invention written and illustrated by Peter Wells; Winston, 1942. **Awarded:** Spring Book Festival (picture book) 1942.

WELLS, ROBERT
Five-Yard Fuller of the N.Y. Gnats by Robert Wells, illustrated by Harold Eldridge; Putnam, 1967. **Awarded:** Boys Club 1968.

WELLS, ROSEMARY
Awarded: David McCord Children's Literature Citation 1991.

Benjamin and Tulip written and illustrated by Rosemary Wells; Dial, 1973. **Awarded:** Art Books for Children 1975, 1976, 1977.

The Fog Comes on Little Pig Feet written and illustrated by Rosemary Wells; Dial, 1972. **Awarded:** Spring Book Festival (ages 12-16 honor) 1972.

Forest of Dreams by Rosemary Wells, illustrated by Susan Jeffers; Dial, 1988. **Awarded:** Golden Kite (Picture-Illustration) 1988.

Hazel's Amazing Mother written and illustrated by Rosemary Wells; Dial, 1985. **Awarded:** New York Times Best Illustrated 1985.

A Lion for Lewis written and illustrated by Rosemary Wells; Dial, 1982. **Awarded:** New Jersey Institute of Technology 1983.

The Man in the Woods by Rosemary Wells, not illustrated; Dial, 1984. **Awarded:** Virginia Young Readers (High School) 1987.

Max's Chocolate Chicken written and illustrated by Rosemary Wells; Dial, 1989. **Awarded:** Washington Irving (Younger Fiction) 1992.

Max's Christmas written and illustrated by Rosemary Wells; Dial, 1986. **Awarded:** Washington Irving (Illustration) 1988;New Jersey Institute of Technology 1987.

Morris's Disappearing Bag: A Christmas Story written and illustrated by Rosemary Wells; Dial, 1975. **Awarded:** Irma Simonton Black 1975.

Noisy Nora written and illustrated by Rosemary Wells; Dial, 1973. **Awarded:** Children's Book Showcase 1974.

Peabody written and illustrated by Rosemary Wells; Dial, 1983. **Awarded:** Golden Sower (K-3) 1986; Washington Irving (fiction) 1986; New Jersey Institute of Technology 1983.

Shy Charles written and illustrated by Rosemary Wells; Dial, 1988. **Awarded:** Boston Globe (Picture Book) 1989; Parents' Choice (Story Book) 1989.

When No One Was Looking by Rosemary Wells, not illustrated; Dial, 1980. **Awarded:** Edgar Allan Poe (runnerup) 1981.

WELSH, PATRICK J.
Treasure in an Oatmeal Box by Ken Gire, illustrated by Patrick J. Welsh; NavPress, 1990. **Awarded:** Gold Medallion (Elementary) 1991.

WENNERSTROM, GENIA KATHERINE
see GENIA

WENSELL, ULISES
Spatzen Brauchen Keinen Schirm by Ursel Scheffler, illustrated by Ulises Wensell; Methuen Children's, 1984. **Awarded:** Owl Prize 1985.

WENTWORTH, ELAINE
Lighthouse Keeper's Daughter by Arielle North Olson, illustrated by Elaine Wentworth; Little Brown, 1987. **Awarded:** Friends of American Writers 1988.

WENTZ, BUDD
Paper Movie Machines by Budd Wentz, illustrated with photographs; Troubadour, 1975. **Awarded:** New York Academy of Sciences (younger honor) 1976.

WENZEL, GREG
Story of Your Foot by Alvin Silverstein and Virginia Silverstein, illustrated by Greg Wenzel; Putnam, 1987. **Awarded:** New Jersey Institute of Technology 1988.

WENZEL, WALT
A Guide to Nature Projects by Ted S. Pettit, illustrated by Walt Wenzel; Norton, 1966. **Awarded:** New Jersey Institute of Technology 1967.

WERENSKIOLD, ERIK
Norwegian Folk Tales by Peter Christen Asbjornsen and Jorgen Moe, illustrated by Erik Werenskiold and Theodore Kittelsen; Viking, 1961. **Awarded:** Spring Book Festival (middle) 1961.

WERNER, ELSA JANE
The Golden Bible for Children: The New Testament edited by Elsa Jane Werner, illustrated by Alice Provensen and Martin Provensen; Golden Press, 1953. **Awarded:** New York Times Best Illustrated 1953.

The Golden Geography: A Child's Introduction to the World by Elsa Jane Werner, illustrated by Cornelius DeWitt; Simon & Schuster, 1952. **Awarded:** Boys Club 1954.

WERNER, JERRY
The Beginner's Devotional by Stephen T. Barclift, illustrated by Jerry Werner; Questar Publishers, 1991. **Awarded:** Gold Medallion (Elementary) 1992.

WERSBA, BARBARA
Tunes for a Small Harmonica by Barbara Wersba, not illustrated; Harper, 1976. **Awarded:** National Book Award (finalist) 1977.

WERTH, KURT
McBroom Tells the Truth by Sid Fleischman, illustrated by Kurt Werth; Norton, 1966. **Awarded:** Lewis Carroll Shelf 1969.

McBroom the Rainmaker by Sid Fleischman, illustrated by Kurt Werth; Grosset, 1973. **Awarded:** Golden Kite (honor) 1973.

That Jefferson Boy by Earl Schenck Miers, illustrated by Kurt Werth; World, 1970. **Awarded:** New Jersey Institute of Technology 1971.

WESSON, LIS C.
I Am an Orthodox Jew by Laura Greene, illustrated by Lis C. Wesson; Holt, 1979. **Awarded:** Council for Wisconsin Writers (picture book runnerup) 1980.

WEST, HAROLD
Old Ramon by Jack Schaefer, illustrated by Harold West; Houghton, 1960; **Awarded:** Aurianne 1962; Newbery (honor) 1961' Ohioana 1961; Spring Book Festival (older honor) 1960.

WESTALL, ROBERT
Blitzcat by Robert Westall, not illustrated; Macmillan Children's, 1989. **Awarded:** Guardian Award (Special Praise) 1990; Smarties (9-11) 1989.

The Devil on the Road by Robert Westall, illustrated; Macmillan, 1978. **Awarded:** Carnegie (commended) 1978.

Gulf by Robert Westall, not illustrated; Methuen, 1992. **Awarded:** Carnegie (highly commended) 1992; Children's Book Award (longer novel) 1993.

The Kingdom by the Sea by Robert Westall, not illustrated; Methuen Children's, 1990; Farrar Straus Giroux, 1991. **Awarded:** Carnegie (Highly Commended) 1990; Guardian 1991.

The Machine Gunners by Robert Westall, not illustrated; Macmillan, 1975; Greenwillow, 1976. **Awarded:** Boston Globe Horn Book (fiction honor) 1977; Carnegie 1975; Guardian (commended) 1976.

The Scarecrows by Robert Westall, not illustrated; Chatto & Windus, 1981; Greenwillow, 1981. **Awarded:** Boston Globe Horn Book (fiction honor) 1982; Carnegie 1981.

WESTCOTT, NADINE BERNARD
The Emperor's New Clothes by Hans Christian Andersen, retold and illustrated by Nadine Bernard Westcott; Little, Brown, 1984. **Awarded:** Redbook (paperback) 1984.

The Lady With the Alligator Purse written and illustrated by Nadine Bernard Westcott; Little Brown, 1988. **Awarded:** Kentucky Bluegrass (grades K-3) 1990.

Skip To My Lou written and illustrated by Nadine Bernard Westcott; Little Brown, 1989. **Awarded:** Redbook 1989.

WESTERBERG, CHRISTINE
Duane, the Collector by Eleanor J. Lapp, illustrated by Christine Westerberg; Addison Wesley, 1976. **Awarded:** Council for Wisconsin Writers (picture book) 1977.

WESTERBERG, VIRGINIA
Awarded: Landau 1975.

WESTERSKOV, KIM
Albatross Adventure by Kim Westerskov. **Awarded:** New Zealand Library Association Nonfiction 1993.

WESTINGHOUSE RESEARCH LABORATORIES SCIENTISTS
Saturday Science by the Westinghouse Research Laboratories Scientists, edited by Andrew Bluemle, illustrated with diagrams; Dutton, 1960. **Awarded:** Edison Mass Media (science books for youth) 1961.

WESTON, CHRISTINE
Bhimsa, the Dancing Bear by Christine Weston, illustrated by Roger Duvoisin; Scribner, 1945. **Awarded:** Newbery (honor) 1946.

WESTON, JOHN
The Boy Who Sang the Birds by John Weston, illustrated by Donna Diamond; Scribner, 1976. **Awarded:** Commonwealth of California 1976.

WESTON, MARTHA
Bet You Can't! Science Impossibilities to Fool You by Vicki Cobb and Kathy Darling, illustrated by Martha Weston; Lothrop, 1980. **Awarded:** New York Academy of Sciences (younger) 1981.

The Book of Think: or, How to Solve a Problem Twice Your Size by Marilyn Burns, illustrated by Martha Weston; Little, Brown, 1976. **Awarded:** Children's Book Showcase 1977.

The Sierra Club Wayfinding Book by Vicki McVey, illustrated by Martha Weston; Little Brown, 1989. **Awarded:** New York Academy of Sciences (Younger) 1989.

WETERING, JANWILLEM VAN DE
Hugh Pine and the Good Place by Janwillem van de Wetering, illustrated by Lynn Munsinger; Houghton Mifflin, 1986. **Awarded:** New York Times Notable 1986.

WEXLER, JEROME
A Chick Hatches by Joanna Cole, photographs by Jerome Wexler; Morrow, 1976. **Awarded:** Children's Book Showcase 1977.

From Flower to Flower by Patricia Lauber, illustrated by Jerome Wexler; Crown, 1986. **Awarded:** New York Academy of Sciences (Younger honor) 1988.

WEZEL, PETER
The Good Bird written and illustrated by Peter Wezel; Harper, 1966. **Awarded:** Spring Book Festival (picture book honor) 1966.

WHEATLEY, ARABELLE
Questions and Answers about Seashore Life by Ilka Katherine List, illustrated by Arabelle Wheatley and Ilka Katherine List; Four Winds, 1971. **Awarded:** Children's Book Showcase 1972.

WHEATLEY, NADIA
Dancing in the Anzac Deli by Nadia Wheatley, illustrated by Neil Phillips and Waldemar Buczynski; Oxford, 1984. **Awarded:** Children's Book Council of Australia (book of the year com-

mended) 1985; International Board on Books for Young People (Writing/Australia) 1986.

Five Times Dizzy by Nadia Wheatley, illustrated; Oxford, 1982. **Awarded:** Children's Book Council of Australia (book of the year commended) 1983; New South Wales State Literary Awards (Special Children's) 1983.

The House that Was Eureka by Nadia Wheatley, not illustrated; Viking Kestrel, 1984. **Awarded:** Children's Book Council of Australia (book of the year commended) 1986; New South Wales State Literary Awards (Children's) 1985.

My Place by Nadia Wheatley, illustrated by Donna Rawlins; Collins Dove, 1987. **Awarded:** Children's Book Council of Australia (Book of the Year Younger) 1988; International Board on Books for Young People (Writing/Australia) 1990; Young Australian Best Book (Fiction Younger Reader) 1988.

WHEELER, BENSON
My Brother Was Mozart by Benson Wheeler and Claire Lee Purdy, illustrated by Theodore Nadejen; Holt, 1937. **Awarded:** Julia Ellsworth Ford 1937.

WHEELER, CINDY
Marmalade's Christmas Present written and illustrated by Cindy Wheeler; Knopf, 1984. **Awarded:** Author's Award [Alabama] 1986.

WHEELER, OPAL
Sing in Praise: A Collection of the Best Loved Hymns by Opal Wheeler, illustrated by Marjorie Torrey; Dutton, 1946. **Awarded:** Caldecott (honor) 1947.

Sing Mother Goose music by Opal Wheeler, illustrated by Marjorie Torrey; Dutton, 1945. **Awarded:** Caldecott (honor) 1946.

WHEELWRIGHT, SIDNEE
Come Back, Salmon by Molly Cone, photographs by Sidnee Wheelwright; Sierra, 1992. **Awarded:** Orbis Pictus (honor) 1993.

WHELAN, GLORIA
A Clearing in the Forest by Gloria Whelan, not illustrated; Putnam, 1978. **Awarded:** Friends of American Writers (older) 1979.

WHISTLER, THERESA
Rushavenn Time by Theresa Whistler, illustrated by Anne Jope; Brixworth V C Primary School, 1988. **Awarded:** Smarties (9-11) 1988.

WHITBY, JOY
Awarded: Eleanor Farjeon 1978.

WHITCOMB, ADAH
Awarded: Children's Reading Round Table 1955.

WHITE, ANNE H.
A Dog Called Scholar by Anne H. White, illustrated by Lilian Obligado; Viking, 1963. **Awarded:** Spring Book Festival (middle honor) 1963.

Junket by Anne H. White, illustrated by Robert McCloskey; Viking, 1955. **Awarded:** Spring Book Festival (middle honor) 1955.

WHITE, ANNE TERRY
The Golden Book of Animals by Anne Terry White, illustrated by W. Suschitzky; Golden Press, 1958. **Awarded:** New York Times Best Illustrated 1958.

WHITE, BESSIE F.
A Bear Named Grumms by Bessie F. White, illustrated by Sari; Houghton, 1953. **Awarded:** Spring Book Festival (ages 4-8 honor) 1953.

WHITE, DALE
see PLACE, MARIAN T.

WHITE, ELIZABETH Q.
Awarded: Outstanding Arizona Author 1989.

WHITE, E. B. (ELWYN BROOKS)
Awarded: Hans Christian Andersen (highly commended author/U.S.) 1970, 1976; Laura Ingalls Wilder 1970.

Charlotte's Web by E. B. White, illustrated by Garth Williams; Harper, 1952. **Awarded:** Lewis Carroll Shelf 1959; Emphasis on Reading (grades 2-3) 1980-81; Massachusetts 1984; Michigan Young Readers 1979; Newbery (honor) 1953; George G. Stone 1970; Surrey School 1972.

Stuart Little by E. B. White, illustrated by Garth Williams; Harper, 1945. **Awarded:** Emphasis on Reading (grades 4-6) 1982-83.

The Trumpet of the Swan by E. B. White, illustrated by Edward Frascino; Harper, 1970. **Awarded:** Sue Hefly 1975; International Board on Books for Young People (USA) 1972; National Book Award (finalist) 1971; Sequoyah 1973; Spring Book Festival (middle honor) 1970; William Allen White 1973; Young Hoosier (4-6) 1975.

WHITE, FLORENCE MEIMAN
First Woman in Congress: Jeannette Rankin by Florence Meiman White, illustrated; Messner, 1980. **Awarded:** Jane Addams 1981.

WHITE, JACK R.
The Invisible World of the Infrared by Jack R. White, illustrated; Dodd, Mead, 1984. **Awarded:** New York Academy of Sciences (older honor) 1985.

WHITE, ROBB
Deathwatch by Robb White, not illustrated; Doubleday, 1972. **Awarded:** Edgar Allan Poe 1973.

Silent Ship, Silent Sea by Robb White, not illustrated; Doubleday, 1967. **Awarded:** Commonwealth Club of California 1967.

Smuggler's Sloop by Robb White, illustrated by Andrew Wyeth; Little, Brown, 1937. **Awarded:** Spring Book Festival (older) 1937.

WHITE, SANDRA VERRILL
Sterling: The Rescue of a Baby Harbor Seal by Sandra Verrill White and Michael Filisky, illustrated; Crown, 1989. **Awarded:** Book Can Develop Empathy 1990.

WHITEHEAD, BARBARA
Letters To Oma: A Young German Girl's Account of Her First Year in Texas, 1847 by Marj Gurasich, illustrated by Barbara Whitehead; Texas Christian, 1989. **Awarded:** Western Heritage 1990.

WHITEHOUSE, ARCH
John J. Pershing by Arch Whitehouse, not illustrated; Putnam, 1964. **Awarded:** New Jersey Institute of Technology (biography teens) 1964.

WHITETHORNE, BAJE
Monster Slayer: a Navajo Folktale by Vee Browne, illustrated by Baje Whitethorne; Northland Publishing, 1991. **Awarded:** Western Heritage 1992.

WHITFIELD, PHILIP

Can the Whales Be Saved? by Philip Whitfield, illustrated; Viking Kestrel, 1989. **Awarded:** Christopher (ages 10-12) 1990.

Macmillan Illustrated Animal Encyclopedia edited by Philip Whitfield, illustrated; Macmillan, 1984. **Awarded:** New York Academy of Sciences (special award) 1985.

WHITLOCK, RALPH

Spiders by Ralph Whitlock, illustrated with photographs; Wayland & Priory Press, 1975. **Awarded:** Times Educational Supplement (junior) 1975.

WHITMAN, MAURICE

After-harvest Festival: The Story of a Girl of the Old Kankakee by Dorothy Fay Arbuckle, illustrated by Maurice Whitman; Dodd, Mead, 1955. **Awarded:** Indiana Authors Day (children) 1956.

WHITNEY, ELINOR

Tod of the Fens by Elinor Whitney, illustrated by Warwick Goble; Macmillan, 1928. **Awarded:** Newbery (honor) 1929.

WHITNEY, GEORGE G.

Penn by Elizabeth Janet Gray, illustrated by George G. Whitney; Viking, 1938. **Awarded:** Newbery (honor) 1939.

WHITNEY, PHYLLIS AYAME

The Mystery of the Haunted Pool by Phyllis A. Whitney, illustrated by H. Tom Hall; Westminster, 1960. **Awarded:** Edgar Allan Poe 1961; Sequoyah 1963.

The Mystery of the Hidden Hand by Phyllis A. Whitney, illustrated by H. Tom Hall; Westminster, 1963. **Awarded:** Edgar Allan Poe 1964.

Mystery of the Scowling Boy by Phyllis A. Whitney, illustrated by John Gretzer; Westminster, 1973. **Awarded:** Edgar Allan Poe (runnerup) 1974.

The Secret of the Missing Footprint by Phyllis A. Whitney, illustrated by Alex Stein; Westminster, 1969. **Awarded:** Edgar Allan Poe (runnerup) 1971.

The Secret of the Tiger Eyes by Phyllis A. Whitney, not illustrated; Westminster, 1961. **Awarded:** Edgar Allan Poe (runnerup) 1962.

Willow Hill by Phyllis Whitney, not illustrated; Reynal & Hitchcock, 1947. **Awarded:** Spring Book Festival (older honor) 1947.

WHYBROW, IAN

Quacky, Quack-quack! by Ian Whybrow, illustrated by Russell Ayto; Walker, 1991; Four Winds, 1991. **Awarded:** Mother Goose (runnersup) 1992.

WIBBERLEY, LEONARD

A Dawn in the Trees: Thomas Jefferson, the Years 1776 to 1789 by Leonard Wibberley, not illustrated; Ariel, 1964. **Awarded:** Southern California Council (notable) 1965.

Epics of Everest by Leonard Wibberley, illustrated by Genevieve Vaughan-Jackson; Ariel, 1954. **Awarded:** Commonwealth Club of California 1954.

Peter Treegate's War by Leonard Wibberley, not illustrated; Farrar, 1960. **Awarded:** Edison Mass Media (America's past) 1961.

The Treegate Chronicles by Leonard Wibberley, not illustrated; Farrar, 1976. **Awarded:** Southern California Council (excellence in a series) 1977.

WIBERG, HARALD

The Tomten by Astrid Lindgren, illustrated by Harald Wiberg; Coward, 1961. **Awarded:** Art Books for Children 1973; Lewis Carroll Shelf 1970.

WIELER, DIANA

Bad Boy by Diana Wieler, not illustrated; Douglas & McIntyre, 1989; Delacorte, 1992. **Awarded:** Governor General's Literary Award (Text) 1989; International Board on Books for Young People (Writing/Canada) 1990; Ruth Schwartz 1990; Young Adult Canadian 1990.

WIER, ESTER ALBERTI

The Loner by Ester Wier, illustrated by Christine Price; McKay, 1963. **Awarded:** Newbery (honor) 1964.

WIESE, KURT

Captain Kidd's Cow by Phil Stong, illustrated by Kurt Wiese; Dodd, Mead, 1941. **Awarded:** Spring Book Festival (middle honor) 1941.

Daughter of the Mountains by Louise S. Rankin, illustrated by Kurt Wiese; Viking, 1948. **Awarded:** Lewis Carroll Shelf 1962; Newbery (honor) 1949; Spring Book Festival (middle) 1948.

Fish in the Air written and illustrated by Kurt Wiese; Viking, 1948. **Awarded:** Caldecott (honor) 1949; Spring Book Festival (younger honor) 1948.

The Five Chinese Brothers by Claire Huchet Bishop, illustrated by Kurt Wiese; Coward, 1938. **Awarded:** Lewis Carroll Shelf 1959.

Honk the Moose by Phil Stong, illustrated by Kurt Wiese; Dodd, Mead, 1935. **Awarded:** Lewis Carroll Shelf 1970; Newbery (honor) 1936.

Li Lun, Lad of Courage by Carolyn Treffinger, illustrated by Kurt Wiese; Abingdon-Cokesbury, 1947. **Awarded:** Lewis Caroll Shelf 1959; Newbery (honor) 1948; Ohioana 1948.

Lions on the Hunt by Theodore Waldeck, illustrated by Kurt Wiese; Viking, 1942. **Awarded:** Spring Book Festival (middle honor) 1942.

Quest in the Desert by Roy Chapman Andrews, illustrated by Kurt Wiese; Viking, 1950. **Awarded:** Spring Book Festival (older honor) 1950.

Quest of the Snow Leopard by Roy Chapman Andrews, illustrated by Kurt Wiese; Viking, 1955. **Awarded:** Boys Club 1957.

The Return of Silver Chief by Jack O'Brien, illustrated by Kurt Wiese; Holt, 1943. **Awarded:** Young Readers Choice 1946.

The Story About Ping by Marjorie Flack, illustrated by Kurt Wiese; Viking, 1933. **Awarded:** Lewis Carroll Shelf 1965.

The Wizard and his Magic Powder by Alfred S. Campbell, illustrated by Kurt Wiese; Knopf, 1945. **Awarded:** Spring Book Festival (younger honor) 1945.

You Can Write Chinese written and illustrated by Kurt Wiese; Viking, 1945. **Awarded:** Caldecott (honor) 1946.

Young Fu of the Upper Yangtze by Elizabeth Foreman Lewis, illustrated by Kurt Wiese; Winston, 1932. **Awarded:** Lewis Carroll Shelf 1960; Newbery 1933.

WIESEL, ELIE

Awarded: Christopher (special award) 1987.

WIESNER, DAVID

Free Fall written and illustrated by David Wiesner; Lothrop, Lee & Shepard, 1988. **Awarded:** Caldecott (honor) 1989.

June 29, 1999 written and illustrated by David Wiesner; Clarion, 1992. **Awarded:** Parents Choice (Picture Book) 1992.

The Loathsome Dragon retold by David Wiesner and Kim Kahng, illustrated by David Wiesner; Putnam, 1987. **Awarded:** Redbook 1987.

The Rainbow People by Laurence Yep, illustrated by David Wiesner; Harper & Row, 1989. **Awarded:** Boston Globe (Nonfiction honor) 1989; Reading Magic 1989.

Tuesday illustrated by David Wiesner; Clarion, 1991. **Awarded:** Caldecott 1992.

WIESNER, WILLIAM
More Tongue Tanglers and a Rigmarole by Charles Francis Potter, illustrated by William Wiesner; World, 1964. **Awarded:** Spring Book Festival (picture book honor) 1964.

WIGNELL, EDEL
Clever Juice by Edel Wignell. **Awarded:** Mary Grant Bruce (additional $100) 1986.

WIJNGAARD, JUAN
Bear written and illustrated by Juan Wijngaard; Crown, 1991. **Awarded:** Reading Magic Award 1991.

The Blemyahs by William Mayne, illustrated by Juan Wijngaard; Walker, 1987. **Awarded:** W. H. Smith (£500) 1988.

Cat written and illustrated by Juan Wijngaard; Crown, 1991. **Awarded:** Reading Magic Award 1991.

Dog written and illustrated by Juan Wijngaard; Crown, 1991. **Awarded:** Reading Magic Award 1991.

Duck written and illustrated by Juan Wijngaard; Crown, 1991. **Awarded:** Reading Magic Award 1991.

Green Finger House by Rosemary Harris, illustrated by Juan Wijngaard; Eel Pie, 1980. **Awarded:** Mother Goose 1981.

Jelly Belly by Dennis Lee, illustrated by Juan Wijngaard; Macmillan of Canada, 1983; Blackie, 1983. **Awarded:** Canadian Library Assn. (runnerup) 1984.

Sir Gawain and the Loathly Lady retold by Selina Hastings, illustrated by Juan Wijngaard; Walker Books, 1985. **Awarded:** Greenaway 1985.

WIKLAND, ILON
Tills Aventyr I Skorstensgrand by Gunnel Linde, illustrated by Ilon Wikland; Bonnier, 1962. **Awarded:** Hans Christian Andersen (runnerup) 1964.

Broderna Lejonhjarta by Astrid E. Lindgren, illustrated by Ilon Wikland; Raben & Sjogren, 1973. **Awarded:** Janusz Korczak (books for children) 1979.

WILBUR, RICHARD
Opposites written and illustrated by Richard Wilbur; Harcourt, 1973. **Awarded:** Spring Book Festival (middle honor) 1973.

The Persistence of Riddles by Richard Wilbur in Yale Review 78.3 (December 1989). **Awarded:** Children's Literature Assn. Criticism Award 1990.

WILCOX, ELEANOR REINDOLLAR
The Cornhusk Doll by Eleanor Reindollar Wilcox, illustrated by Gerald McCann; Dodd, Mead, 1956. **Awarded:** Edith Busby 1955.

WILD, MARGARET
Very Best of Friends by Margaret Wild, illustrated by Julie Vivas; Margaret Hamilton, 1989; Harcourt Brace Jovanovich, 1990. **Awarded:** Children's Book Council of Australia (Picture Book of the Year) 1990.

WILDE, GEORGE
First Boy on the Moon: A Junior Science Fiction Novel by Clifford B. Hicks, illustrated by George Wilde; Winston, 1959. **Awarded:** Friends of American Writers 1960.

WILDE, OSCAR
The Selfish Giant by Oscar Wilde, illustrated by Dom Mansell; Walker Books, 1986. **Awarded:** Mother Goose (runnerup) 1987.

WILDER, LAURA INGALLS
Awarded: Laura Ingalls Wilder 1954.

By the Shores of Silver Lake by Laura Ingalls Wilder, illustrated by Helen Sewell and Mildred Boyle; Harper, 1939. **Awarded:** Newbery (honor) 1940; Young Readers Choice 1942.

The Little House in the Big Woods by Laura Ingalls Wilder, illustrated by Garth Williams; Harper, 1953. **Awarded:** Lewis Carroll Shelf 1958.

Little Town on the Prairie by Laura Ingalls Wilder, illustrated by Helen Sewell and Mildred Boyle; Harper, 1941. **Awarded:** Newbery (honor) 1942.

The Long Winter by Laura Ingalls Wilder, illustrated by Helen Sewell and Mildred Boyle; Harper, 1940. **Awarded:** Newbery (honor) 1941.

On the Banks of Plum Creek by Laura Ingalls Wilder, illustrated by Helen Sewell and Mildred Boyle; Harper, 1937. **Awarded:** Newbery (honor) 1938.

These Happy Golden Years by Laura Ingalls Wilder, illustrated by Helen Sewell and Mildred Boyle; Harper, 1943. **Awarded:** Newbery (honor) 1944; Spring Book Festival (middle) 1943.

WILDSMITH, BRIAN
Awarded: Hans Christian Andersen (highly commended illustrator/Great Britain) 1966, 1968.

Birds written and illustrated by Brian Wildsmith; Oxford, 1967. **Awarded:** Greenaway (commended) 1967.

Brian Wildsmith's ABC written and illustrated by Brian Wildsmith; Oxford, 1962. **Awarded:** Greenaway 1962.

Brian Wildsmith's Birds written and illustrated by Brian Wildsmith; Watts, 1967. **Awarded:** New York Times Best Illustrated 1967.

Brian Wildsmith's 1,2,3s written and illustrated by Brian Wildsmith; Watts, 1965. **Awarded:** Art Books for Children 1973.

A Child's Garden of Verse by Robert Louis Stevenson, illustrated by Brian Wildsmith; Watts, 1966. **Awarded:** Lewis Carroll Shelf 1966.

Fifer for the Union by Lorenzo Allen, illustrated by Brian Wildsmith; Morrow, 1964. **Awarded:** Spring Book Festival (middle honor) 1964.

The Lion and the Rat: A Fable by Jean de La Fontaine, illustrated by Brian Wildsmith; Oxford, 1963. **Awarded:** Greenaway (commended) 1963.

The Owl and the Woodpecker written and illustrated by Brian Wildsmith; Oxford, 1971. **Awarded:** Greenaway (highly commended) 1971.

The Oxford Book of Poetry for Children compiled by Edward Blishen, illustrated by Brian Wildsmith; Oxford, 1963. **Awarded:** Greenaway (commended) 1963.

Pelican written and illustrated by Brian Wildsmith; Oxford, 1982; Pantheon, 1982. **Awarded:** Maschler (runnerup) 1982; Parents' Choice (illustration) 1983.

Tangara: Let Us Set off Again by Nan Chauncy, illustrated by Brian Wildsmith; Oxford, 1960. **Awarded:** Children's Book Council of Australia (book of the year) 1961; International Board on Books for Young People (Great Britain) 1962.

WILEY, KARLA HUMMEL
Assignment: Latin America - a Story of the Peace Corps by Karla Wiley, not illustrated; McKay, 1968. **Awarded:** New Jersey Institute of Technology 1968.

Styles by Suzy by Karla H. Wiley, illustrated by Genia; McKay, 1965. **Awarded:** New Jersey Institute of Technology 1965.

WILHELM, HANS
Blackberry Ink by Eve Merriam, illustrated by Hans Wilhelm; Morrow, 1985. **Awarded:** Parents' Choice (literature) 1985.

I'll Always Love You written and illustrated by Hans Wilhelm; Crown, 1985. **Awarded:** Book Can Develop Empathy 1990.

What Does God Do? adapted from the *International Children's Bible*, illustrated by Hans Wilhelm; Worthy, 1987. **Awarded:** Gold Medallion (Preschool) 1988.

WILKES, ANGELA
My First Cook Book by Angela Wilkes, illustrated; Knopf, 1989. **Awarded:** Redbook 1989.

WILKES, LARRY
Find the White Horse by Dick King-Smith, illustrated by Larry Wilkes; Viking, 1991. **Awarded:** Children's Book Award (Shorter Novel) 1992.

WILKESHUIS, CORNELIS
Das Schonste Geschenk by Cornelis Wilkeshuis and Rita Van Bilsen, illustrated; Bohem Press, 1977. **Awarded:** Owl Prize 1978.

WILKIN, ELOISE
A Good House for a Mouse by Irmengarde Eberle, illustrated by Eloise Wilkin; Messner, 1940. **Awarded:** Spring Book Festival (younger honor) 1940.

The Tune Is in the Tree by Maud Hart Lovelace, illustrated by Eloise Wilkin; Crowell, 1950. **Awarded:** Spring Book Festival (ages 8-12 honor) 1950.

WILKINSON, BARRY
The Secret of the Missing Boat by Paul Berna, translated by John Buchanan-Brown, illustrated by Barry Wilkinson; Pantheon, 1967, c1966. **Awarded:** Edgar Allan Poe (runnerup) 1968.

WILKINSON, BRENDA
Ludell by Brenda Wilkinson, not illustrated; Harper, 1975. **Awarded:** National Book Award (finalist) 1976; Woodward Park School 1976.

WILKON, JOZEF
Die Geschichte Vom Guten Wolf by Peter Nickl, illustrated by Jozef Wilkon; Nord-Sud Verlag, 1985, c1982. **Awarded:** Owl Prize 1984.

WILKS, MIKE
The Ultimate Alphabet written and illustrated by Mike Wilks; Pavilion, 1987, c1986; Henry Holt, 1986. **Awarded:** Times Educational Supplement (Senior) 1987.

WILL
see LIPKIND, WILLIAM

WILLARD, BARBARA
The Iron Lily by Barbara Willard, not illustrated; Longman, 1973. **Awarded:** Guardian 1974.

The Queen of the Pharisees' Children by Barbara Willard, not illustrated; MacRae, 1983. **Awarded:** Whitbread 1984.

WILLARD, NANCY
Awarded: School Library Media Specialists of South Eastern New York 1992.

The High Rise Glorious Skittle Skat Roarious Sky Pie Angel Food Cake by Nancy Willard, illustrated by Richard Jesse Watson; Harcourt Brace Jovanovich, 1990. **Awarded:** KC Three 1992-93.

The Island of the Grass King: The Further Adventures of Anatole by Nancy Willard, illustrated by David McPhail; Harcourt, 1979. **Awarded:** Lewis Carroll Shelf 1979.

The Marzipan Moon by Nancy Willard, illustrated by Marcia Sewall; Harcourt, 1981. **Awarded:** New York Times Notable Books 1981.

Sailing to Cythera and Other Anatole Stories by Nancy Willard, illustrated by David McPhail; Harcourt, 1974. **Awarded:** Lewis Carroll Shelf 1977.

Simple Pictures Are Best by Nancy Willard, illustrated by Tomie de Paola; Harcourt, 1977. **Awarded:** Art Books for Children 1978.

A Visit to William Blake's Inn: Poems for Innocent and Experienced Travelers by Nancy Willard, illustrated by Alice Provensen and Martin Provensen; Harcourt, 1981. **Awarded:** Boston Globe Horn Book (illustration) 1982; Golden Kite (fiction honor) 1981; Caldecott (honor) 1982; Newbery 1982.

WILLIAMS, BARBARA
Albert's Toothache by Barbara Williams, illustrated by Kay Chorao; Dutton, 1974. **Awarded:** Children's Book Showcase 1975.

Chester Chipmunk's Thanksgiving by Barbara Williams, illustrated by Kay Chorao; Dutton, 1978. **Awarded:** Christopher (ages 7-9) 1979.

WILLIAMS, CAROLE
Holly and the Porpoises by Carole Williams. **Awarded:** Mary Grant Bruce (writer living in Gippsland $200) 1986.

Lisa of the Lyrebird Creek by Carole Williams. **Awarded:** Mary Grant Bruce Story Award (Writer Living in Gippsland $200) 1989.

WILLIAMS, DOROTHY JEANNE
(pseudonyms are Jeanne Williams and J. R. Williams)

Freedom Trail by Jeanne Williams, not illustrated; Putnam, 1973. **Awarded:** Western Writers (fiction) 1974.

The Horse-Talker by J. R. Williams, not illustrated; Prentice, 1960. **Awarded:** Western Writers (fiction) 1961.

Tame the Wild Stallion by J. R. Williams, not illustrated; Prentice Hall, 1957. **Awarded:** Steck-Vaughn 1959.

WILLIAMS, GARTH MONTGOMERY
Beneath a Blue Umbrella by Jack Prelutsky, illustrated by Garth Williams; Greenwillow, 1990. **Awarded:** New York Times Best Illustrated 1990.

Charlotte's Web by E. B. White, illustrated by Garth Williams; Harper, 1952. **Awarded:** Lewis Carroll Shelf 1959; Emphasis on Reading (grades 2-3) 1980-81; Massachusetts 1984; Michigan Young Readers 1979; Newbery (honor) 1953; George G. Stone 1970; Surrey School 1972.

The Cricket in Times Square by George Selden, illustrated by Garth Williams; Farrar, 1960. **Awarded:** Lewis Carroll Shelf 1963; Massachusetts Children's (grades 4-6) 1979; Newbery (honor) 1961.

The Family under the Bridge by Natalie Savage Carlson, illustrated by Garth Williams; Harper, 1958. **Awarded:** Newbery (honor) 1959.

The Golden Name Day by Jennie D. Lindquist, illustrated by Garth Williams; Harper, 1955. **Awarded:** Newbery (honor) 1956.

Harry Cat's Pet Puppy by George Selden, illustrated by Garth Williams; Farrar, 1974. **Awarded:** William Allen White 1977.

The Little House Cookbook by Barbara M. Walker, illustrated by Garth Williams; Harper, 1979. **Awarded:** Western Heritage 1980.

The Little House in the Big Woods by Laura Ingalls Wilder, illustrated by Garth Williams; Harper, 1953. **Awarded:** Lewis Carroll Shelf 1958.

Stuart Little by E. B. White, illustrated by Garth Williams; Harper & Row, 1945. **Awarded:** Emphasis on Reading (grades 4-6) 1982-83.

Tiny Animal Stories (series) by Dorothy Kunhardt, illustrated by Garth Williams; Simon & Schuster, various years. **Awarded:** Spring Book Festival (younger honor) 1948.

Tucker's Countryside by George Selden, illustrated by Garth Williams; Farrar, 1969. **Awarded:** Christopher (ages 8-12) 1970.

WILLIAMS, J. R.
see WILLIAMS, DOROTHY JEANNE

WILLIAMS, JAY
Danny Dunn and the Homework Machine by Jay Williams and Raymond Abrashkin, illustrated by Ezra Jack Keats; Whittlesey House, 1958. **Awarded:** Young Readers Choice 1961.

Danny Dunn on the Ocean Floor by Jay Williams and Raymond Abrashkin, illustrated by Brinton Turkle; McGraw, 1960. **Awarded:** Young Readers Choice 1963.

Everyone Knows What a Dragon Looks Like by Jay Williams, illustrated by Mercer Mayer; Four Winds, 1976. **Awarded:** Irma Simonton Black 1976; New York Times Best Illustrated 1976.

Forgetful Fred by Jay Williams, illustrated by Friso Henstra; Parents, 1974. **Awarded:** Biennale Illustrations Bratislava (plaque) 1977.

The Hawkstone by Jay Williams, not illustrated; Walck, 1971. **Awarded:** Lewis Carroll Shelf 1972.

Petronella by Jay Williams, illustrated by Friso Henstra; Parents, 1973. **Awarded:** Children's Book Showcase 1974.

The Practical Princess by Jay Williams, illustrated by Friso Henstra; Parents, 1969. **Awarded:** Biennale Illustrations Bratislava (golden apple) 1969.

WILLIAMS, JEANNE
see WILLIAMS, DOROTHY JEANNE

WILLIAMS, JENNIFER
Stringbean's Trip to the Shining Sea by Vera B. Williams, illustrated by Vera B. Williams and Jennifer Williams; Greenwillow, 1988. **Awarded:** Boston Globe (Picture Book

honor) 1988; New York Times Best Illustrated 1988; Parents' Choice (Story Book) 1988.

WILLIAMS, JENNY
A Lion in the Meadow by Margaret M. Mahy, illustrated by Jenny Williams; Watts, 1969. **Awarded:** Esther Glen 1970.

WILLIAMS, KIT
[*The Bee on the Comb*] written and illustrated by Kit Williams; Cape, 1984. The book was published without a title. **Awarded:** Bologna (graphics for youth) 1985.

WILLIAMS, LINDA
The Little Old Lady Who Was Not Afraid of Anything by Linda Williams, illustrated by Megan Lloyd; Crowell, 1986. **Awarded:** Colorado Children's (Runnerup) 1988; Keystone to Reading 1988.

WILLIAMS, MABEL
Awarded: Grolier 1980.

WILLIAMS, MARGERY
see BIANCO, MARGERY WILLIAMS

WILLIAMS, NICK
After the Bomb: Brother in the Land by Guy Dickens, Elaine Scarratt, and Nick Williams; English & Media Centre, 1991. **Awarded:** Times Educational Supplement (Schoolbook Award) 1991.

WILLIAMS, PATRICK J.
see BUTTERWORTH, WILLIAM

WILLIAMS, PHYLLIS S.
Science Wizardry for Kids by Margaret Kenda and Phyllis S. Williams, illustrated by Tim Robinson; Barron's, 1992. **Awarded:** Hungry Mind (Middle Readers/Nonfiction) 1993.

WILLIAMS, RHYS
Verity of Sydneytown by Ruth Williams, illustrated by Rhys Williams; Angus & Robertson, 1950. **Awarded:** Children's Book Council of Australia 1951.

WILLIAMS, RICHARD
Herbie Jones by Suzy Kline, illustrated by Richard Williams; Putnam, 1985. **Awarded:** West Virginia Children's 1987-88.

What's the Matter with Herbie Jones? by Suzy Kline, illustrated by Richard Williams; Putnam, 1986. **Awarded:** KC Three 1988-89.

WILLIAMS, RUTH
Verity of Sydneytown by Ruth Williams, illustrated by Rhys Williams; Angus & Robertson, 1950. **Awarded:** Children's Book Council of Australia 1951.

WILLIAMS, SHERLEY ANNE
Working Cotton by Sherley Anne Williams, illustrated by Carole Byard; Harcourt Brace Jovanovich, 1992. **Awarded:** Caldecott (honor) 1993; Coretta Scott King (Illustration honor) 1993.

WILLIAMS, SLIM
The Long Hungry Night by Slim Williams and Elizabeth C. Foster, illustrated by Glo Coalson; Atheneum, 1973. **Awarded:** Friends of American Writers (ages 10-14) 1974; Friends of American Writers (illustration) 1974.

WILLIAMS, SOPHY
When Grandma Came by Jill Paton Walsh, illustrated by Sophy Williams; Viking, 1992. **Awarded:** Mother Goose (runnerup) 1993.

WILLIAMS, TEPPY
What Do Animals Do When it Rains? by J. Fred Dice, illustrated by Teppy Williams; Crescent, 1978. **Awarded:** New York Academy of Sciences (younger honor) 1980.

WILLIAMS, TERRY TEMPEST
The Secret Language of Snow by Terry Tempest Williams and Ted Major, illustrated by Jennifer Dewey; Sierra Club/Pantheon, 1984. **Awarded:** New York Academy of Sciences (younger) 1985.

WILLIAMS, URSULA MORAY
The Three Toymakers by Ursula Moray Williams, illustrated by Shirley Hughes; Nelson, 1971. **Awarded:** Spring Book Festival (middle honor) 1971.

WILLIAMS, VERA B.
A Chair for My Mother written and illustrated by Vera B. Williams; Greenwillow, 1982; MacRae, 1983. **Awarded:** Boston Globe Horn Book (illustration) 1983; Caldecott (honor) 1983; Other Award 1984.

Cherries and Cherry Pits written and illustrated by Vera B. Williams; Greenwillow, 1986. **Awarded:** Boston Globe Horn Book (illustration honor) 1987; New York Times Best Illustrated 1986.

More, More, More, Said the Baby: 3 Love Stories written and illustrated by Vera Williams; Greenwillow, 1990. **Awarded:** Caldecott (Honor) 1991.

Music, Music for Everyone written and illustrated by Vera B. Williams; Greenwillow, 1984. **Awarded:** Jane Addams (honor) 1985.

Stringbean's Trip to the Shining Sea by Vera B. Williams, illustrated by Jennifer Williams and Vera B. Williams; Greenwillow, 1988. **Awarded:** Boston Globe (Picture Book honor) 1988; New York Times Best Illustrated 1988; Parents' Choice (Story Book) 1988.

WILLIAMS-GARCIA, RITA
Awarded: PEN/Norma Klein Award (Citation) 1991.

WILLIAMSON, JOANNE SMALL
Jacobin's Daughter by Joanne S. Williamson, illustrated by Charles Clement; Knopf, 1956. **Awarded:** Spring Book Festival (older honor) 1956.

WILLIS, JEANNE
Dr. Xargle's Book of Earth Tiggers by Jeanne Willis, illustrated by Tony Ross; Andersen Press, 1990; Dutton, 1991. **Awarded:** Greenaway (Highly Commended) 1990.

The Monster Bed by Jeanne Willis, illustrated by Susan Varley; Lothrop, Lee & Shepard, 1987. **Awarded:** Redbook 1987.

WILLIS, ROBERT J.
Model-A Mule by Robert J. Willis, illustrated by Victor Mays; Follett, 1959. **Awarded:** Charles W. Follett 1959.

WILLIS, VAL
The Secret in the Matchbox by Val Willis, illustrated by John Shelley; Farrar, Straus Giroux, 1988. **Awarded:** Parents' Choice (Picture Book) 1988.

WILLMOTT, FRANK
Breaking Up by Frank Willmott, not illustrated; Fontana Lions, 1983. **Awarded:** Children's Book Council of Australia (book of the year commended) 1984.

WILLOW, DIANE
At Home in the Rain Forest by Diane Willow, illustrated by Laura Jacques; Charlesbridge, 1991. **Awarded:** Book Can Develop Empathy 1991.

WILSON, BARBARA KER
Alitji in Dreamland adapted and translated by Nancy Sheppard, illustrated by Donna Leslie, notes by Barbara Ker Wilson; Simon & Schuster Australia, 1992. **Awarded:** Crichton 1993.

In Love and War by Barbara Ker Wilson, not illustrated; World, 1962. **Awarded:** Spring Book Festival (older honor) 1963.

WILSON, BOB
Stanley Bagshaw and the Short-Sighted Goal Keeper by Bob Wilson, illustrated; Hamish Hamilton, 1986. **Awarded:** Maschler (runnerup) 1986.

WILSON, BUDGE
The Leaving by Budge Wilson, not illustrated; Anansi Press, 1990; Philomel, 1992. **Awarded:** Young Adult Canadian 1991.

Oliver's Wars by Budge Wilson, not illustrated; Stoddart, 1992. **Awarded:** Brimer 1993.

WILSON, CHARLES BANKS
River Dragon by Carl D. Lane, illustrated by Charles Banks Wilson; Little, Brown, 1948. **Awarded:** Spring Book Festival (middle honor) 1948.

WILSON, ELLEN JANET
American Painter in Paris: A Life of Mary Cassatt by Ellen Janet Wilson, illustrated with plates; Farrar, 1971. **Awarded:** Indiana Authors Day (young adult) 1972.

WILSON, HAZEL
Herbert by Hazel H. Wilson, illustrated by John N. Barron; Knopf, 1950. **Awarded:** Spring Book Festival (ages 8-12 honor) 1950.

His Indian Brother by Hazel Wilson, illustrated by Robert Henneberger; Abingdon, 1955. **Awarded:** Edison Mass Media (character development in children) 1956.

Island Summer by Hazel Wilson, illustrated by Richard Floethe; Abingdon-Cokesbury, 1949. **Awarded:** Ohioana (honorable mention) 1950.

WILSON, JACQUELINE
The Story of Tracy Beaker by Jacqueline Wilson, illustrated by Nick Sharratt; Doubleday, 1991. **Awarded:** Carnegie (Highly Commended) 1991; Nottinghamshire (Oak Tree) 1992.

The Suitcase Kid by Jacqueline Wilson, illustrated by Nick Sharratt; Doubleday, 1992. **Awarded:** Children's Book Award 1993.

WILSON, JANE B.
Awarded: Grolier 1975.

WILSON, JOHN
Striped Ice Cream by Joan M. Lexau, illustrated by John Wilson; Lippincott, 1968. **Awarded:** Charlie May Simon 1970-71.

WILSON, KATHLEEN ATKINS
The Origin of Life on Earth: An African Creation Myth retold by David A. Anderson, illustrated by Kathleen Atkins Wilson; Sight Productions, 1992. **Awarded:** Coretta Scott King (Illustration) 1993.

WILSON, LEON
This Boy Cody by Leon Wilson, illustrated by Ursula Koering; Watts, 1950. **Awarded:** Lewis Carroll Shelf 1959.

WILSON, MIKE
Jet Journey by Mike Wilson and Robin Scagell, illustrated with photographs, drawings and diagrams; Viking, 1978. **Awarded:** New York Academy of Sciences (special award for series on engineering and technology) 1979.

WILSON, PEGGY
Ananse the Spider: Tales from an Ashanti Village by Peggy Appiah, illustrated by Peggy Wilson; Pantheon, 1966. **Awarded:** New York Times Best Illustrated 1966.

WILSON, W. N.
Hokahey! American Indians Then and Now by Edith Dorian, illustrated by W. N. Wilson; Whittlesey House, 1957. **Awarded:** Boys Club 1958.

WILSON, WILLIAM N.
Jeb Ellis of Candlemas Bay by Ruth Moore, illustrated by William N. Wilson; Morrow, 1952. **Awarded:** Spring Book Festival (older honor) 1952.

WIMMER, HELMUT KARL
Experiments in Sky Watching by Franklyn M. Branley, illustrated by Helmut K. Wimmer; Crowell, 1959. **Awarded:** Edison Mass Media (science book) 1960.

Exploring by Satellite: The Story of Project Vanguard by Franklyn M. Branley, illustrated by Helmut K. Wimmer; Crowell, 1957. **Awarded:** New Jersey Institute of Technology 1961.

The Moon: Earth's Natural Satellite by Franklyn M. Branley, illustrated by Helmut K. Wimmer; Crowell, 1960. **Awarded:** New Jersey Institute of Technology 1961.

WIMMER, MIKE
Flight: The Journey of Charles Lindbergh by Robert Burleigh, illustrated by Mike Wimmer; Philomel, 1991. **Awarded:** Orbis Pictus 1992.

My Teacher Is an Alien by Bruce Coville, illustrated by Mike Wimmer; Pocket Books, 1989. **Awarded:** Nevada Young Reader Award (Intermediate) 1990-91.

Train Song by Diane Siebert, illustrated by Mike Wimmer; Crowell, 1990. **Awarded:** Redbook 1990.

WINBORN, MARSHA
Fat Santa by Margery Cuyler, illustrated by Marsha Winborn; Henry Holt, 1987. **Awarded:** New Jersey Institute of Technology 1988.

WINDHAM, SOPHIE
Twelve Days of Christmas illustrated by Sophie Windham; Putnam, 1986. **Awarded:** Redbook (honorable mention) 1986.

WINDSOR, PATRICIA
Diving for Roses by Patricia Windsor, not illustrated; Harper, 1976. **Awarded:** New York Times Notable Books 1976.

The Sandman's Eyes by Patricia Windsor, not illustrated; Delacorte, 1985. **Awarded:** Edgar Allan Poe 1986.

The Summer Before by Patricia Windsor, not illustrated; Harper, 1973. **Awarded:** Spring Book Festival (older honor) 1973.

WINN, CHRIS
Outlawed Inventions by Chris Winn and Jeremy Beadle, illustrated; Pepper Press, 1982. **Awarded:** Mother Goose (runnerup) 1983.

WINSTON, CLARA
The Ark by Margot Benary-Isbert, translated by Clara Winston and Richard Winston; Harcourt, 1953. **Awarded:** Lewis Carroll Shelf 1968; Spring Book Festival (older) 1953.

Blue Mystery by Margot Benary-Isbert, translated by Clara Winston and Richard Winston, illustrated by Enrico Arno; Harcourt, 1957. **Awarded:** Jane Addams 1957.

Jonah the Fisherman written and illustrated by Reiner Zimnick, translated by Clara Winston and Richard Winston; Pantheon, 1956. **Awarded:** New York Times Best Illustrated 1956.

The Magic Stone by Leonie Kooiker, translated by Clara Winston and Richard Winston, illustrated by Carl Hollander; Morrow, 1978. **Awarded:** International Board on Books for Young People (translation/USA) 1980.

WINSTON, PEGGY
Creatures of Long Ago: Dinosaurs by Peggy Winston, illustrated by John Sibbick; National Geographic, 1988. **Awarded:** Redbook 1988.

WINSTON, RICHARD
The Ark by Margot Benary-Isbert, translated by Clara Winston and Richard Winston; Harcourt, 1953. **Awarded:** Lewis Carroll Shelf 1968; Spring Book Festival (older) 1953.

Blue Mystery by Margot Benary-Isbert, translated by Clara Winston and Richard Winston, illustrated by Enrico Arno; Harcourt, 1957. **Awarded:** Jane Addams 1957.

Jonah the Fisherman written and illustrated by Reiner Zimnick, translated by Clara Winston and Richard Winston; Pantheon, 1956. **Awarded:** New York Times Best Illustrated 1956.

The Magic Stone by Leonie Kooiker, translated by Clara Winston and Richard Winston, illustrated by Carl Hollander; Morrow, 1978. **Awarded:** International Board on Books for Young People (translation/USA) 1980.

WINTER, JEANETTE
Diego by Jonah Winter, illustrated by Jeanette Winter; Knopf, 1992. **Awarded:** Hungry Mind (Picturebooks/Nonfiction) 1992; New York Times Best Illustrated 1991; Parents' Choice (Picture Book) 1991.

Klara's New World written and illustrated by Jeanette Winter; Knopf, 1992. **Awarded:** Parents Choice (Picture Book) 1992.

WINTER, JONAH
Diego by Jonah Winter, illustrated by Jeanette Winter; Knopf, 1991. **Awarded:** Hungry Mind (Picturebooks/Nonfiction) 1992; New York Times Best Illustrated 1991; Parents' Choice (Picture Book) 1991.

WINTER, PAULA
The Bear and the Fly written and illustrated by Paula Winter; Crown, 1976. **Awarded:** Children's Book Showcase 1977; **Awarded:** New York Times Best Illustrated 1976.

WINTER, WILLIAM
Nkwala by Edith Lambert Sharp, illustrated by William Winter; Little, Brown Canada, 1958. **Awarded:** Governor-General's Literary Award 1958; International Board on Books for Young People (Canada) 1960; Little Brown Canadian 1957.

WINTHROP, ELIZABETH
The Castle in the Attic by Elizabeth Winthrop, illustrated by Trina Schart Hyman; Holiday House, 1985. **Awarded:** California Young Reader (Intermediate) 1989; Dorothy Canfield Fisher 1987; West Virginia Children's (Honor book) 1988-89.

WINTON, IAN
Ian and Fred's Big Green Book by Fred Pearce, illustrated by Ian Winton; Kingfisher, 1991. **Awarded:** Times Educational Supplement (Junior) 1991.

WISBECKI, DOROTHY GROSS
The True Story of Okee the Otter by Dorothy Wisbecki, illustrated with photographs; Farrar, 1967. **Awarded:** New Jersey Institute of Technology 1967.

WISE, LU CELIA
Tiny Bat and the Ball Game by Margaret Searcy, illustrated by Lu Celia Wise; Portals Press, 1978. **Awarded:** Author's Award/Alabama 1980.

WISE, WILLIAM
The Two Reigns of Tutankhamen by William Wise, illustrated with photographs; Putnam, 1964. **Awarded:** Boys Club 1965.

WISEMANN, ANN
Rags, Rugs, and Wool Pictures: A First Book of Rug Hooking by Ann Wisemann, illustrated with photographs; Scribner, 1968. **Awarded:** New Jersey Institute of Technology 1968.

WISENFELD, ALISON
The Tree by Judy Hindley, illustrated by Alison Wisenfeld; Aurum, 1990; Potter, 1990. **Awarded:** Times Educational Supplement (Junior) 1990.

WISLER, GARY CLIFTON
Thunder on the Tennessee by Gary Clifton Wisler, not illustrated; Lodestar, 1983. **Awarded:** Western Writers 1984.

WISSMAN, RUTH H.
The Summer Ballet Mystery by Ruth H. Wissman, not illustrated; Dodd, Mead, 1962. **Awarded:** Calling All Girls - Dodd, Mead 1962.

WIZOWATY, SUZI
Borders by Suzi Wizowaty. **Awarded:** Sydney Taylor Manuscript Award 1989.

WOHL, CLIFFORD F.
Awarded: Lucile M. Pannell 1990.

WOHLRABE, RAYMOND A.
Exploring the World of Leaves written and illustrated by Raymond A. Wohlrabe; Crowell, 1976. **Awarded:** New York Academy of Sciences (older honor) 1977.

WOJCIECHOWSKA, MAIA
Awarded: New Jersey Institute of Technology (New Jersey's writer of children's books) 1969.

Don't Play Dead Before You Have to by Maia Wojciechowska, not illustrated; Harper, 1970. **Awarded:** New Jersey Institute of Technology 1970.

Hey, What's Wrong with this One? by Maia Wojciechowska, illustrated by Joan Sandin; Harper, 1969. **Awarded:** Georgia Children's Picture Book 1973.

The Life and Death of a Brave Bull by Maia Wojciechowska, illustrated by John Groth; Harcourt, 1972. **Awarded:** New Jersey Institute of Technology 1972.

Shadow of a Bull by Maia Wojciechowska, illustrated by Alvin Smith; Atheneum, 1964. **Awarded:** Newbery 1965; Spring Book Festival (older honor) 1964.

Through the Broken Mirror with Alice: Including Parts of Through the Looking Glass by Lewis Carroll by Maia Wojciechowska, not illustrated; Harcourt, 1972. **Awarded:** New Jersey Institute of Technology 1972.

WOLCOTT, ELIZABETH TYLER
Out of the Flame by Elois Lownsbery, illustrated by Elizabeth T. Wolcott; Longmans, 1931. **Awarded:** Newbery (honor) 1932.

WOLF, BERNARD
Don't Feel Sorry for Paul written and illustrated by Bernard Wolf; Lippincott, 1974. **Awarded:** Children's Book Showcase 1975.

WOLF, JANET
Rosie & the Yellow Ribbon by Paula De Paola, illustrated by Janet Wolf; Joy Street Books, 1992. **Awarded:** Christopher (ages 6-8) 1993.

WOLF, SUSAN
The Adventures of Albert, the Running Bear by Barbara Isenberg and Susan Wolf, illustrated by Dick Gackenbach; Clarion, 1982. **Awarded:** Emphasis on Reading (Grades 2-3) 1985-86.

WOLF, VIRGINIA
The Magic Circle of Laura Ingalls Wilder by Virginia Wolf in *Children's Literature Assn. Quarterly* 9 (Winter 1984-85). **Awarded:** Children's Literature Assn. Excellence in Criticism (runnerup) 1985.

WOLFE-CUNDIFF, LESLIE
Family Cracks by Leslie Wolfe-Cundiff in Short Story International: Seedlings series No. 24. **Awarded:** Witty Short Story Award 1987.

WOLFF, ASHLEY
Baby Beluga by Raffi, illustrated by Ashley Wolff; Crown, 1990. **Awarded:** Book Can Develop Empathy 1991.

A Year of Beasts written and illustrated by Ashley Wolff; Dutton, 1986. **Awarded:** Redbook 1986.

WOLFF, VIRGINIA EUWER
The Mozart Season by Virginia Euwer Wolff, not illustrated; Henry Holt, 1991. **Awarded:** Hungry Mind (Middle Readers/Fiction) 1992; Janusz Korczak (Children Honorable Mention) 1992; Parents' Choice (Story Book) 1991.

Probably Still Nick Swansen by Virginia Euwer Wolff, not illustrated; Henry Holt, 1988. **Awarded:** International Reading Assn. (Older) 1989; PEN Center USA West 1989.

WOLKSTEIN, DIANE
The Magic Orange Tree and Other Haitian Folktales by Diane Wolkstein, illustrated by Elsa Henriquez; Knopf, 1978. **Awarded:** New York Academy of Sciences (older honor) 1979.

WONG, DAVID
The Blue Chameleon by Katherine Scholes, illustrated by David Wong; Hill of Content, 1989. **Awarded:** Family Award 1989; New South Wales State Literary Awards (Children's) 1990.

WONG, JEANYEE
The Sky River by Fa-Shun Chang, illustrated by Jeanyee Wong; Lothrop, 1950. **Awarded:** Boys Club 1951.

WONSETLER, JOHN
Mounted Messenger by Cornelia Meigs, illustrated by John Wonsetler; Macmillan, 1943. **Awarded:** Spring Book Festival (middle honor) 1943.

WOOD, ANNE
Awarded: Eleanor Farjeon 1968.

WOOD, AUDREY
Heckedy Peg by Audrey Wood, illustrated by Don Wood; Harcourt Brace Jovanovich, 1987. **Awarded:** Irma S. and James H. Black 1987; Christopher (picture book) 1988; Colorado Children's (runner up) 1989; Nevada Young Reader Award (Primary) 1989-90; Virginia Young Readers (primary) 1989; Young Hoosier (Picture Book K-3) 1992.

King Bidgood's in the Bathtub by Audrey Wood, illustrated by Don Wood; Harcourt, 1985. **Awarded:** Caldecott (honor) 1986; Colorado Children's 1986; Little Archer 1987; PEN

Center USA West 1986; Washington Children's Choice 1988; West Virginia Children's (Honor book) 1987-88.

The Napping House by Audrey Wood, illustrated by Don Wood; Harcourt, 1984. **Awarded:** California Young Reader (primary) 1987; Golden Kite (picture illustration) 1984; New York Times Best Illustrated 1984; Southern California Council (significant contribution to illustration) 1985.

Piggies by Audrey Wood, illustrated by Don Wood; Harcourt Brace Jovanovich, 1991. **Awarded:** Southern California Council (Notable Picture Book) 1992.

WOOD, DAVID
Sidney the Monster by David Wood, illustrated by Clive Scruton; Walker, 1988. **Awarded:** Nottinghamshire (Acorn) 1989.

WOOD, DON
Heckedy Peg by Audrey Wood, illustrated by Don Wood; Harcourt Brace Jovanovich, 1987. **Awarded:** Irma S. and James H. Black 1987; Christopher (picture book) 1988; Colorado Children's (runner up) 1989; Nevada Young Reader Award (Primary) 1989-90; Virginia Young Readers (primary) 1989; Young Hoosier (Picture Book K-3) 1992.

King Bidgood's in the Bathtub by Audrey Wood, illustrated by Don Wood; Harcourt, 1985. **Awarded:** Caldecott (honor) 1986; Colorado Children's 1986; Little Archer 1987; PEN Center Usa West 1986; Washington Children's Choice 1988; West Virginia Children's (Honor book) 1987-88.

The Napping House by Audrey Wood, illustrated by Don Wood; Harcourt, 1984. **Awarded:** California Young Reader (primary) 1987; Golden Kite (picture illustration) 1984; New York Times Best Illustrated 1984; Southern California Council (significant contribution to illustration) 1985.

Piggies by Audrey Wood, illustrated by Don Wood; Harcourt Brace Jovanovich, 1991. **Awarded:** Southern California Council (Notable Picture Book) 1992.

WOOD, DOUGLAS
Old Turtle by Douglas Wood, illustrated by Cheng-Khee Chee; Pfeifer-Hamilton, 1992. **Awarded:** American Booksellers Assn (children's Book) 1993; International Reading Assn. (younger) 1993; Minnesota (younger children) 1992.

WOOD, HARRIE
The Boy Who Was by Grace T. Hallock, illustrated by Harrie Wood; Dutton, 1928. **Awarded:** Newbery (honor) 1929.

WOOD, KERRY
Awarded: Vicky Metcalf 1963.

The Great Chief: Maskepetoon, Warrior of the Crees by Kerry Wood, illustrated by John A. Hall; Macmillan Canada, 1957. **Awarded:** Governor General's Literary Award 1957.

The Map Maker by Kerry Wood; Macmillan Canada, 1955. **Awarded:** Governor General 1955.

WOOD, LAURA NEWBOLD
Raymond L. Ditmars: His Exciting Career with Reptiles, Insects and Animals by Laura Newbold Wood, illustrated with photographs; Messner, 1944. **Awarded:** Julia Ellsworth Ford 1944.

Walter Reed: Doctor in Uniform by Laura Newbold Wood, illustrated by Douglas Duer; Messner, 1943. **Awarded:** Spring Book Festival (older honor) 1943.

WOOD, LINDA C.
Windows in Space by Linda C. Wood and Ann Elwood, illustrated; Walker, 1982. **Awarded:** Southern California Council (distinguished work of nonfiction) 1983.

WOOD, MICHAEL
Village Heritage by Miss Pinnell and the children of Sapperton School, introduction by Michael Wood; Alan Sutton, 1986. **Awarded:** Smarties (innovation) 1986.

WOOD, MURIEL
The Olden Days Coat by Margaret Laurence, illustrated by Muriel Wood; McClelland & Stewart, 1979. **Awarded:** Canadian Library Assn. (runnerup) 1980.

WOOD, NANCY
War Cry on a Prayer Feather: Prose and Poetry of the Ute Indians by Nancy Wood, illustrated with photographs; Doubleday, 1979. **Awarded:** Woodson 1980.

WOOD, PHYLLIS ANDERSON
This Time Count Me In by Phyllis Anderson Wood, not illustrated; Westminster, 1980. **Awarded:** Helen Keating Ott 1981.

Win Me and You Lose by Phyllis Anderson Wood, not illustrated; Westminster, 1977. **Awarded:** Helen Keating Ott 1981.

WOODALL, HEATHER
Ytek and the Arctic Orchid: An Inuit Legend by Garnet Hewitt, illustrated by Heather Woodall; Douglas & McIntyre, 1981; Vanguard, 1981. **Awarded:** Canadian Library Assn. (runnerup) 1982; Governor General 1981; Amelia Frances Howard-Gibbon 1982.

WOODBERY, JOAN
Rafferty Rides a Winner written and illustrated by Joan Woodbery; Parrish, 1961. **Awarded:** Children's Book Council of Australia (book of the year) 1962.

WOODRESS, JAMES
Voices from America's Past by James Woodress and Richard B. Morris, illustrated with photographs; Dutton, 1963. **Awarded:** Edison Mass Media (America's past) 1964.

WOODRICH, MARY NEVILLE
see NEVILLE, MARY

WOODRUFF, BARBARA
Keep Singing, Keep Humming: A Collection of Play and Story Songs by Margaret Bradford, illustrated by Lucienne Bloch, accompaniments by Barbara Woodruff; Scott, 1946. **Awarded:** Spring Book Festival (younger honor) 1946.

WOODS, GEORGE A.
Catch a Killer by George A. Woods, not illustrated; Harper, 1972. **Awarded:** Dorothy Canfield Fisher 1974; New Jersey Institute of Technology 1973; Edgar Allan Poe (runnerup) 1973.

WOODS, GEORGE
Myths and Legends of Maoriland by A. W. Reed, illustrated by George Woods and W. Dittmer; Reed, 1946. **Awarded:** Esther Glen 1947.

WOODSON, JACK
For Conspicuous Gallantry: Winners of the Medal of Honor by Donald E. Cooke, illustrated by Jack Woodson; Hammond, 1966. **Awarded:** Boys Club (certificate) 1966-67.

WOODWARD, HILDEGARD
Roger and the Fox by Lavinia R. Davis, illustrated by Hildegard Woodward; Doubleday, 1947. **Awarded:** Caldecott (honor) 1948.

The Wild Birthday Cake by Lavinia R. Davis, illustrated by Hildegard Woodward; Doubleday, 1949. **Awarded:** Caldecott (honor) 1950.

WOODY, REGINA JONES
Wisdom to Know by Regina J. Woody, not illustrated; Funk & Wagnalls, 1964. **Awarded:** New Jersey Institute of Technology (teenage novel) 1964.

WOOLLEY, CATHERINE
(pseudonym for Jane Thayer)

Awarded: New Jersey Institute of Technology (New Jersey's children's book writer of the year) 1964.

Cathy Leonard Calling by Catherine Woolley, illustrated by Liz Dauber; Morrow, 1961. **Awarded:** New Jersey Institute of Technology 1961.

A Drink for Little Red Diker by Catherine Woolley, illustrated by W. T. Mars; Morrow, 1963. **Awarded:** New Jersey Institute of Technology 1963.

Ginnie and her Juniors by Catherine Woolley, illustrated by Liz Dauber; Morrow, 1963. **Awarded:** New Jersey Institute of Technology 1963.

I Like Trains by Catherine Woolley, illustrated by George Fonseca; Harper, 1965. **Awarded:** New Jersey Institute of Technology 1965.

Look Alive, Libby by Catherine Woolley, illustrated by Liz Dauber; Morrow, 1962. **Awarded:** New Jersey Institute of Technology 1963.

WOOLSEY, MARYHALE
The Keys and the Candle by Maryhale Woolsey, illustrated by Donald Bolognese; Abingdon, 1963. **Awarded:** Commonwealth Club of California 1963.

WORMELL, CHRISTOPHER
An Alphabet of Animals written and illustrated by Christopher Wormell; HarperCollins, 1990; Dial, 1990. **Awarded:** Bologna (Graphics for Children) 1991; W. H. Smith (Second Prize) 1991.

WORMSER, RICHARD
The Black Mustanger by Richard Wormser, illustrated by Don Bolognese; Morrow, 1971. **Awarded:** Western Heritage 1972; Western Writers (fiction) 1972.

Ride a Northbound Horse by Richard Wormser, illustrated by Charles Geer; Morrow, 1964. **Awarded:** Western Writers (fiction) 1965.

WORTH, KATHRYN
The Middle Button by Kathryn Worth, illustrated by Dorothy Bayley; Doubleday-Doran, 1941. **Awarded:** Spring Book Festival (older honor) 1941.

They Loved to Laugh by Kathryn Worth, illustrated by Marguerite De Angeli; Doubleday, 1942. **Awarded:** Spring Book Festival (older honor) 1942.

WORTH, VALERIE
Awarded: National Council of Teachers of English 1991.

More Small Poems by Valerie Worth, illustrated by Natalie Babbitt; Farrar, 1976. **Awarded:** Children's Book Showcase 1977.

WORTIS, AVI
see AVI

WOSMEK, FRANCES
Mystery of the Eagle's Claw by Frances Wosmek, not illustrated; Westminster, 1979. **Awarded:** Edgar Allan Poe (runnerup) 1980.

WRIGHT, BARTON
Throw Stone: The First American Boy 25,000 Years Ago by M. E. Stevens and Edwin B. Sayles, illustrated by Barton Wright; Reilly & Lee, 1960. **Awarded:** Steck-Vaughn 1962.

WRIGHT, BETTY REN
Christina's Ghost by Betty Ren Wright, not illustrated; Holiday House, 1985. **Awarded:** Georgia Children's Book Award 1988; KC Three 1987-88; Sequoyah Children's 1988; Texas Bluebonnet 1988; Virginia Young Readers (Elementary) 1990; Young Hoosier (Grades 4-6) 1989.

The Dollhouse Murders by Betty Ren Wright, not illustrated; Holiday House, 1983. **Awarded:** California Young Reader (intermediate) 1987; Caudill Young Reader's Book Award 1989; Emphasis on Reading (grades 4-6) 1987-88; Indian Paintbrush 1988; Iowa Children's Choice 1988; Edgar Allan Poe (runnerup) 1984; Texas Bluebonnet 1986; Mark Twain 1986; Young Readers Choice 1986.

WRIGHT, JOE
Mrs. Plug the Plumber by Allan Ahlberg, illustrated by Joe Wright; Kestrel, 1980. **Awarded:** Other Award 1980.

WRIGHT, SHIRLEY
Awarded: Frances E. Russell 1983.

WRIGHTSON, PATRICIA
Awarded: Hans Christian Andersen (author) 1986; Dromkeen 1984; Golden Cat 1986; New South Wales State Literary Awards (Special Award) 1988.

Behind the Wind by Patricia Wrightson, not illustrated; Hutchinson, 1981. **Awarded:** Children's Book Council of Australia (book of the year highly commended) 1982.

The Crooked Snake by Patricia Wrightson, illustrated by Margaret Horder; Angus & Robertson, 1955. **Awarded:** Children's Book Council of Australia (book of the year) 1956.

The Dark Bright Water by Patricia Wrightson, not illustrated; Atheneum, 1979, c1978. **Awarded:** New South Wales State Literary Awards (Special Children's) 1979.

I Own the Racecourse by Patricia Wrightson, illustrated by Margaret Horder; Hutchinson, 1969. **Awarded:** International Board on Books for Young People (honour list/Australia) 1970.

The Ice Is Coming by Patricia Wrightson, illustrated with maps; Hutchinson Australia, 1977. **Awarded:** Children's Book Council of Australia (book of the year) 1978; Guardian (commended) 1978.

A Little Fear by Patricia Wrightson, not illustrated; Hutchinson, 1983; Atheneum, 1983. **Awarded:** Children's Book Council of Australia (book of the year) 1984; Boston Globe Horn Book (fiction) 1984; Observer Teenage Fiction 1984.

The Nargun and the Stars by Patricia Wrightson, not illustrated; Hutchinson, 1973. **Awarded:** Children's Book Council of Australia (book of the year) 1974; International Board on Books for Young People (honour list/text/Australia) 1976; New York Times Notable Books 1974.

A Racecourse for Andy by Patricia Wrightson, illustrated by Margaret Horder; Harcourt, 1968. **Awarded:** Spring Book Festival (middle) 1968.

WRIGLEY, ELSIE
Life in a Bucket of Soil by Richard Rhine, illustrated by Elsie Wrigley; Lothrop, 1972. **Awarded:** New Jersey Institute of Technology 1972.

WRONKER, LILI CASSEL
see CASSEL, LILI

WU, CHENG-EN
Monkey and the Three Wizards by Cheng-en Wu, translated by Peter Harris, illustrated by Michael Foreman; Collins, 1976. **Awarded:** W. H. Smith (£100) 1977.

WUORIO, EVA-LIS
Detour to Danger by Eva-Lis Wuorio, not illustrated; Delacorte, 1981. **Awarded:** Edgar Allan Poe (runnerup) 1982.

The Island of Fish in the Trees by Eva-Lis Wuorio, illustrated by Edward Ardizzone; World, 1962. **Awarded:** New York Times Best Illustrated 1962.

WYETH, ANDREW
The Lost Baron by Allen French, illustrated by Andrew Wyeth; Houghton, 1940. **Awarded:** Spring Book Festival (older honor) 1940.

Smuggler's Sloop by Robb White, illustrated by Andrew Wyeth; Little, Brown, 1937. **Awarded:** Spring Book Festival (older) 1937.

WYETH, NEWELL CONVERS
Glory of the Seas by Agnes Hewes, illustrated by N. C. Wyeth; Knopf, 1933. **Awarded:** Newbery (honor) 1934.

The Yearling by Marjorie Kinnan Rawlings, illustrated by N. C. Wyeth; Scribner, 1962. **Awarded:** Lewis Carroll Shelf 1963; Feature a Classic 1981.

WYLLIE, STEPHEN
Monkey's Crazy Hotel by Stephen Wyllie, illustrated by Maureen Roffey; Harper, 1987. **Awarded:** Redbook 1987.

There Was an Old Woman by Stephen Wyllie, illustrated by Maureen Roffey, paper engineering by Ray Marshall; Harper, 1985. **Awarded:** Redbook 1985.

WYNANTS, MICHE
The Giraffe of King Charles X written and illustrated by Miche Wynants; McGraw, 1964. **Awarded:** New York Times Best Illustrated 1964.

WYNDHAM, LEE
Awarded: New Jersey Institute of Technology (New Jersey author awards - special citation for husband and wife writers of children's books) 1969.

Beth Hilton: Model by Lee Wyndham, not illustrated; Messner, 1961. **Awarded:** New Jersey Institute of Technology 1961.

Holidays in Scandinavia by Lee Wyndham, illustrated by Gordon Laite; Garrard, 1975. **Awarded:** New Jersey Institute of Technology 1976.

Russian Tales of Fabulous Beasts and Marvels by Lee Wyndham, illustrated by Charles Mikolaycak; Parents, 1969. **Awarded:** New Jersey Institute of Technology 1970.

Tales the People Tell in Russia by Lee Wyndham, illustrated by Andrew Antal; Messner, 1970. **Awarded:** New Jersey Institute of Technology 1970.

The Winter Child by Lee Wyndham, illustrated by Yaroslava; Parents, 1970. **Awarded:** New Jersey Institute of Technology 1970.

WYNDHAM, ROBERT
Awarded: New Jersey Institute of Technology (New Jersey author awards special citation for husband and wife writers of children's books) 1969.

Tales the People Tell in China by Robert Wyndham, edited by Doris K. Coburn, illustrated by Jay Yang; Messner, 1971. **Awarded:** New Jersey Institute of Technology 1971.

WYNNE-JONES, TIM
Zoom at Sea by Tim Wynne-Jones, illustrated by Ken Nutt; Douglas & McIntyre, 1983. **Awarded:** Amelia Frances Howard-Gibbon 1984; IODE 1983; Ruth Schwartz 1984.

Zoom Away by Tim Wynne-Jones, illustrated by Ken Nutt; Douglas & McIntyre, 1985. **Awarded:** Amelia Frances Howard-Gibbon 1986.

X

XANTHOULIS, YANNIS
The Planet Floor written and illustrated by Yannis Xanthoulis; Asteri Bookshop, 1980. **Awarded:** International Board on Books for Young People (honour list/illustration/Greece) 1982.

XARAS, THEODORE A.
The Bears and I: Raising Three Cubs in the North Woods by Robert Frank Leslie, illustrated by Theodore A. Xaras; Dutton, 1968. **Awarded:** Southern California Council (notable) 1969.

Y

YADIN, YIGAEL
The Story of Masada by Yigael Yadin, retold by Gerald Gottlieb, illustrated with photographs; Random House, 1969. **Awarded:** Jewish Book Council 1969.

YAGAWA, SUMIKO
The Crane Wife retold by Sumiko Yagawa, translated by Katherine Paterson, illustrated by Suekichi Akaba; Morrow, 1981. **Awarded:** New York Times Best Illustrated 1981; New York Times Notable Books 1981.

YALOWITZ, PAUL
Somebody Loves You, Mr. Hatch by Eileen Spinelli, illustrated by Paul Yalowitz; Bradbury, 1991. **Awarded:** Christopher Award (Ages 4-6) 1992.

YAMAGUCHI, MARIANNE
The Miracle Tree by Christobel Mattingly, illustrated by Marianne Yamaguchi; Hodder & Stoughton, 1985; Harcourt Brace Jovanovich, 1985. **Awarded:** Australian Christian Book of the Year Children's Award 1986.

The Plum-Rain Scroll by Ruth Manley, illustrated by Marianne Yamaguchi; Hodder & Stoughton Australia, 1978. **Awarded:** Children's Book Council of Australia (book of the year) 1979.

YANG, JAY
The Pai-Pai Pig by Joy Anderson, illustrated by Jay Yang; Harcourt, 1967. **Awarded:** Boys Club (certificate) 1968.

Tales the People Tell in China by Robert Wyndham, edited by Doris Coburn, illustrated by Jay Yang; Messner, 1971. **Awarded:** New Jersey Institute of Technology 1971.

YARBRO, CHELSEA QUINN
Floating Illusions by Chelsea Quinn Yarbro, not illustrated; Harper, 1986. **Awarded:** Edgar Allan Poe (runnerup) 1987.

YARBROUGH, CAMILE

Corn Rows by Camile Yarbrough, illustrated by Carole Byard; Coward, 1979. **Awarded:** Coretta Scott King (illustration) 1980.

The Shimmershine Queens by Camile Yarbrough, not illustrated; Putnam, 1989. **Awarded:** Parents' Choice (Story Book) 1989.

YARDLEY, THOMPSON

Mighty Microbes by Thompson Yardley, illustrated; Cassell, 1992. **Awarded:** Science Book Prizes 1993.

YAROSLAVA

The Winter Child by Lee Wyndham, illustrated by Yaroslava; Parents, 1970. **Awarded:** New Jersey Institute of Technology 1970.

YASHIMA, TARO

Awarded: Southern California Council (distinguished contribution to the fields of illustration and writing) 1964; University of Southern Mississippi 1974.

Crow Boy written and illustrated by Taro Yashima; Viking, 1955. **Awarded:** Caldecott (honor) 1956; Child Study 1955.

Seashore Story written and illustrated by Taro Yashima; Viking, 1967. **Awarded:** Caldecott (honor) 1968; New York Times Best Illustrated 1967; Southern California Council (contribution to illustration) 1968.

Umbrella written and illustrated by Taro Yashima: Viking, 1958. **Awarded:** Caldecott (honor) 1959; Spring Book Festival (ages 4-8 honor) 1958.

YASUDA, CHIZUKO

What the Bible Is All About for Young Explorers by Frances Blankenbaker, illustrated by Chizuko Yasuda; Reagal Books, 1986. **Awarded:** Gold Medallion 1987.

YATES, ELIZABETH

Amos Fortune, Free Man by Elizabeth Yates, illustrated by Nora S. Unwin; Aladdin, 1950. **Awarded:** Newbery 1951; Spring Book Festival (older) 1950; William Allen White 1953.

Mountain Born by Elizabeth Yates, illustrated by Nora S. Unwin; Coward, 1943. **Awarded:** Newbery (honor) 1944.

Patterns on the Wall by Elizabeth Yates, illustrated by Warren Chappell; Knopf, 1943. **Awarded:** Spring Book Festival (older) 1943.

A Place for Peter by Elizabeth Yates, illustrated by Nora S. Unwin; Coward, 1952. **Awarded:** Boys Club 1953.

Rainbow Round the World: A Story of UNICEF by Elizabeth Yates, illustrated by Betty Alden and Dirk Gringhuis; Bobbs Merrill, 1954. **Awarded:** Jane Addams 1955.

YAUKEY, GRACE S.

see SPENCER, CORNELIA

YEAGER, CHUCK

Yeager: An Autobiography by Chuck Yeager and Leo Janos, illustrated with photographs; Bantam, 1985. **Awarded:** Emphasis on Reading (grades 10-12) 1986-87.

YEATS, JACK BUTLER

Big Tree of Bunlahy: Stories of my Own Countryside by Padraic Colum, illustrated by Jack Yeats; Macmillan, 1933. **Awarded:** Newbery (honor) 1934.

YEATS, W. B.

Fairy Tales of Ireland by W. B. Yeats, illustrated by P. J. Lynch; Collins, 1990. **Awarded:** Bisto (illustration) 1991.

YEE, CHING CHI

The Magic Spear and Other Stories of China's Famous Heroes by Louise Crane, illustrated by Ching Chi Yee and Yenchi Tiao T'u; Random House, 1938. **Awarded:** Spring Book Festival (younger honor) 1938.

YEE, PATRICK

Awarded: Macmillan Prize (3rd prize) 1989.

The Tiger and the Traveller by Patrick Yee. **Awarded:** Macmillan Prize (3rd prize) 1990.

YEE, PAUL

Tales From Gold Mountain by Paul Yee, illustrated by Simon Ng; Douglas & McIntyre, 1989; Macmillan, 1989. **Awarded:** Canadian Library Assn.(runnerup) 1990; Egoff 1990; National Chapter of Canada IODE Violet Downey 1990.

YEFREMOV, IVAN

Land of Foam by Ivan Yefremov, not illustrated; Houghton, 1959. **Awarded:** Spring Book Festival (older honor) 1959.

YEOMAN, JOHN

Rumbelow's Dance by John Yeoman, illustrated by Quentin Blake; Hamish Hamilton, 1982. **Awarded:** Maschler (runnerup) 1982.

The Wild Washerwomen: A New Folktale by John Yeoman, illustrated by Quentin Blake; Hamish Hamilton, 1979. **Awarded:** Greenaway (highly commended) 1979.

YEOMANS, DONALD K.

Comet Halley: Once in a Lifetime by Mark Littmann and Donald K. Yeomans, illustrated; American Chemical Society, 1985. **Awarded:** New York Academy of Sciences (Elliott Montroll special award) 1986.

YEP, LAURENCE MICHAEL

Child of the Owl by Laurence Yep, not illustrated; Harper, 1977. **Awarded:** Jane Addams 1978; Boston Globe Horn Book (fiction) 1977.

Dragon of the Lost Sea by Laurence Yep, not illustrated; Harper, 1982. **Awarded:** Ethical Culture School 1982.

Dragonwings by Laurence Yep, not illustrated; Harper, 1975. **Awarded:** Jane Addams (honor) 1976; Boston Globe Horn Book (fiction honor) 1976; Lewis Carroll Shelf 1979; FOCAL 1984; International Reading Assn. 1976; Newbery (honor) 1976; Carter G. Woodson 1976.

The Rainbow People by Laurence Yep, illustrated by David Wiesner; Harper & Row, 1989. **Awarded:** Boston Globe (Nonfiction honor) 1989; Reading Magic 1989.

Sea Glass by Laurence Yep, not illustrated; Harper, 1979. **Awarded:** Commonwealth Club of California (silver medal unclassified) 1979.

The Star Fisher by Laurence Yep, not illustrated; Morrow, 1991. **Awarded:** Christopher Award (Ages 10-up) 1992.

YLLA

Animal Babies by Arthur Gregor, illustrated by Arthur Gregor and Ylla; Harper, 1959. **Awarded:** New York Times Best Illustrated 1959.

I'll Show You Cats by C. N. Bonsall, illustrated by Ylla; Harper, 1964. **Awarded:** New York Times Best Illustrated 1964.

The Little Elephant written and illustrated by Ylla; Harper, 1956. **Awarded:** New York Times Best Illustrated 1956.

YOKOI, DAISUKE

The Little Bookmobile: Colors, Numbers, and Shapes on Wheels by Suzanne Greene, illustrated by Daisuke Yokoi; Doubleday, 1986. **Awarded:** Redbook 1986.

YOLEN, JANE H.

Awarded: Chandler Reward of Merit 1970; Kerlan Award 1988; Regina Medal 1992.

Commander Toad in Space by Jane Yolen, illustrated by Bruce Degen; Coward McCann, 1980. **Awarded:** Garden State (easy to read) 1983.

The Devil's Arithmetic by Jane Yolen, not illustrated; Viking Kestrel, 1988. **Awarded:** Jewish Book Council (Children's Literature) 1989; Sydney Taylor Book Award (Older) 1989.

Dragon's Blood: A Fantasy by Jane Yolen, not illustrated; Delacorte, 1980. **Awarded:** Parents' Choice (literature) 1982.

The Emperor and the Kite by Jane Yolen, illustrated by Ed Young; Collins-World, 1967. **Awarded:** Caldecott (honor) 1968; Lewis Carroll Shelf 1968.

The Girl Who Cried Flowers and Other Tales by Jane Yolen, illustrated by David Palladini; Crowell, 1974. **Awarded:** Golden Kite 1974; National Book Award (finalist) 1975; New York Times Best Illustrated 1974.

The Girl Who Loved the Wind by Jane Yolen, illustrated by Ed Young; Crowell, 1972. **Awarded:** Children's Book Showcase 1973; Lewis Carroll Shelf 1973.

Jane Yolen's Mother Goose Songbook edited by Jane Yolen, illustrated by Rosekrans Hoffman, music by Adam Stemple; Boyds Mills Press, 1992. **Awarded:** Hungry Mind (Picturebook/Nonfiction) 1993.

The Little Spotted Fish by Jane Yolen, illustrated by Friso Henstra; Seabury, 1975. **Awarded:** Children's Book Showcase 1976.

The Minstrel and the Mountain: A Tale of Peace by Jane Yolen, illustrated by Anne Rockwell; World, 1967. **Awarded:** Boys Club (certificate) 1968.

The Moon Ribbon and Other Tales by Jane Yolen, illustrated by David Palladini; Crowell, 1976. **Awarded:** Golden Kite (honor) 1976.

Owl Moon by Jane Yolen, illustrated by John Schoenherr; Philomel, 1987. **Awarded:** Caldecott 1988; International Board on Books for Young People (Illustration/USA) 1990.

Piggins by Jane Yolen, illustrated by Jane Dyer; Harcourt Brace Jovanovich, 1987. **Awarded:** Charlotte Book Award (grades 3-5) 1990; Golden Sower (K-3) 1989; Parents' Choice (Story Book) 1987.

The Seeing Stick by Jane Yolen, illustrated by Remy Charlip and Demetra Maraslis; Crowell, 1977. **Awarded:** Christopher (ages 6-9) 1978.

The Stone Silenus by Jane Yolen, not illustrated; Philomel, 1984. **Awarded:** Parents' Choice (literature) 1984.

The Three Bears Rhyme Book by Jane Yolen, illustrated by Jane Dyer; Harcourt Brace Jovanovich, 1987. **Awarded:** Parents' Choice (Picture Book) 1987.

The Transfigured Hart by Jane Yolen, illustrated by Donna Diamond; Crowell, 1975. **Awarded:** Golden Kite (honor) 1975.

YONEKURA, MASAKANE

Magic for Sale by Tsuguo Okuda, illustrated by Masakane Yonekura; Kaisei-sha Publishing. **Awarded:** Bologna (Graphics for Children) 1976.

YORINKS, ARTHUR

Company's Coming by Arthur Yorinks, illustrated by David Small; Crown, 1988. **Awarded:** Redbook 1988.

Hey, Al! by Arthur Yorinks, illustrated by Richard Egielski; Farrar, 1986. **Awarded:** Caldecott 1987; Kentucky Bluegrass (grades K-3) 1988; Little Archer 1988.

It Happened in Pinsk by Arthur Yorinks, illustrated by Richard Egielski; Farrar, Straus & Giroux, 1983. **Awarded:** BIB (plaque) 1985.

YOSHIDA, TOSHI

Young Lions written and illustrated by Toshi Yoshida; Philomel, 1989. **Awarded:** Reading Magic 1989.

YOSHINO, SHIN

Cats by Cynthia Overbeck, photographs by Shin Yoshino; Lerner, 1983. **Awarded:** New York Academy of Sciences (special award) 1983.

YOUD, C. S.

see CHRISTOPHER, JOHN

YOUMANS, ELEANOR

Mount Delightful: The Story of Ellen Evans and Her Dog Taffy by Eleanor Youmans, illustrated by Sandra James; Bobbs-Merrill, 1945. **Awarded:** Ohioana (3rd place) 1945.

YOUNG, ANDREW

Black as I Am by Zindzi Mandela and Peter Magubane, foreword by Andrew Young, illustrated; Guild of Tudors Press, 1978. **Awarded:** Korczak (for children) 1981.

Quiet as Moss: 36 Poems chosen by Leonard Clark by Andrew Young, illustrated by Joan Hassall; Hart-Davis, 1959. **Awarded:** Carnegie (commended) 1959.

YOUNG, CHIP

The Little Hen of Huronia by Chip Young; G. McLeod, 1971. **Awarded:** Amelia Frances Howard-Gibbon (runnerup) 1972.

YOUNG, DELBERT

Last Voyage of the Unicorn by Delbert Young, illustrated by Mary Cserepy; Clarke, Irwin, 1969. **Awarded:** Beaver Trophy 1967.

YOUNG, ED

The Bird from the Sea by Renee Karol Weiss, illustrated by Ed Young; Crowell, 1970. **Awarded:** New Jersey Institute of Technology 1971.

Cats Are Cats: Poems by Nancy Larrick, illustrated by Ed Young; Philomel, 1988. **Awarded:** New York Times Best Illustrated 1988.

The Double Life of Pocahontas by Jean Fritz, illustrated by Ed Young; Putnam, 1983. **Awarded:** Boston Globe Horn Book (nonfiction) 1984.

Dreamcatcher by Audrey Osofsky, illustrated by Ed Young; Orchard, 1992. **Awarded:** Minnesota (younger children) 1993.

The Emperor and the Kite by Jane Yolen, illustrated by Ed Young; Collins World, 1967. **Awarded:** Caldecott (honor) 1968; Lewis Carroll Shelf 1968.

The Eyes of the Dragon by Margaret Leaf, illustrated by Ed Young; Lothrop, Lee & Shepard, 1987. **Awarded:** California

Young Reader (Primary) 1990; Parents' Choice (Picture Book) 1987; Parents' Choice (Story Book) 1987.

The Girl Who Loved the Wind by Jane Yolen, illustrated by Ed Young; Crowell, 1972. **Awarded:** Lewis Carroll Shelf 1973; Children's Book Showcase 1973.

Lon Po Po written and illustrated by Ed Young; Philomel, 1989. **Awarded:** Boston Globe (Picture Book) 1990; Caldecott 1990.

Seven Blind Mice written and illustrated by Ed Young; Philomel, 1992. **Awarded:** Boston Globe Horn Book (Picture Book) 1992; Caldecott (Honor) 1993; Reading Magic Award 1992.

Up a Tree written and illustrated by Ed Young; Harper, 1983. **Awarded:** New York Times Best Illustrated 1983; Parents' Choice (illustration) 1983.

Yeh-Shen: A Cinderella Story from China retold by Ai-Ling Louie, illustrated by Ed Young; Philomel, 1982. **Awarded:** Boston Globe Horn Book (illustration honor) 1983; New Jersey Institute of Technology 1983.

YOUNG, ELLA
Tangle-Coated Horse and Other Tales: Episodes from the Fionn Saga by Ella Young, illustrated by Vera Bock; Longmans, 1929. **Awarded:** Newbery (honor) 1930.

The Wonder-Smith and His Son: A Tale from the Golden Childhood of the World by Ella Young, illustrated by Boris Artzybasheff; Longmans, 1927. Newbery (honor) 1928.

YOUNG, GEOFFREY
The Sunday Times Countryside Companion by Geoffrey Young, illustrated; Country Life Books, 1985. **Awarded:** Times Educational Supplement (senior) 1985.

YOUNG, MIRIAM
Miss Suzy's Birthday by Miriam Young, illustrated by Arnold Lobel; Parents, 1974. **Awarded:** New York Times Best Illustrated 1974.

YOUNG, NOELA
The Best-Kept Secret by Emily Rodda, illustrated by Noela Young; Angus & Robertson, 1988; Henry Holt, 1990. **Awarded:** Children's Book Council of Australia (Book of the Year Younger) 1989.

Finders Keepers by Emily Rodda, illustrated by Noela Young; Omnibus, 1990; Greenwillow, 1991. **Awarded:** Children's Book Council of Australia (Book of the Year Younger) 1991; Young Australian Best Book (Fiction Younger Reader) 1991.

Pigs Might Fly by Emily Rodda, illustrated by Noela Young; Angus & Robertson, 1986. **Awarded:** Children's Book Council of Australia (book of the year younger) 1987.

Something Special by Emily Rodda, illustrated by Noela Young; Angus & Robertson, 1984. **Awarded:** Children's Book Council of Australia (junior book of the year) 1985.

YOUNG, SELINA
Maybe It's a Pirate by Judy Hindley, illustrated by Selina Young; ABC, 1992. **Awarded:** Mother Goose (runnerup) 1993.

My Grampa has Big Pockets written and illustrated by Selina Young. **Awarded:** Macmillan Prize (1st prize) 1991.

YOUNG WORLD BOOKS
Awarded: Other Award (special commendation) 1981.

YUE, CHARLOTTE
The Igloo written and illustrated by Charlotte Yue and David Yue; Houghton Mifflin, 1988. **Awarded:** New York Academy of Sciences (Younger Honor) 1989.

The Pueblo written and illustrated by Charlotte Yue and David Yue; Houghton Mifflin, 1986. **Awarded:** Southwest 1985.

The Tipi: A Center of Native American Life by Charlotte and David Yue, illustrated by David Yue; Knopf, 1983. **Awarded:** Boston Globe Horn Book (nonfiction honor) 1984.

YUE, DAVID
The Igloo written and illustrated by David Yue and Charlotte Yue; Houghton Mifflin, 1988. **Awarded:** New York Academy of Sciences (Younger Honor) 1989.

The Pueblo written and illustrated by Charlotte Yue and David Yue; Houghton Mifflin, 1986. **Awarded:** Southwest 1985.

The Tipi: A Center of Native American Life by Charlotte and David Yue, illustrated by David Yue; Knopf, 1983. **Awarded:** Boston Globe Horn Book (nonfiction honor) 1984.

YUNUPINGU, DJOKI
Land of the Rainbow Snake by Catherine Berndt, illustrated by Djoki Yunupingu; Collins, 1979. **Awarded:** New South Wales State Literary Awards (Special Children's) 1980.

YVART, JACQUES
The Rising of the Wind: Adventures Along the Beaufort Scale by Jacques Yvart, illustrated by Claire Forgeot; Green Tiger Press, 1984. **Awarded:** New York Academy of Sciences (younger honor) 1985.

Z

ZABRANSKY, ADOLF
Awarded: Hans Christian Andersen (highly commended illustrator/USSR) 1972.

ZACH, CHERYL
The Frog Princess by Cheryl Zach, not illustrated; Silhouette, 1984. **Awarded:** Golden Medallion 1985.

Waiting for Amanda by Cheryl Zach, not illustrated; Silhouette, 1985. **Awarded:** Golden Medallion 1986.

ZACHARIAS, THOMAS
Mikosch, das Karusselpferd written and illustrated by Thomas Zacharias and Wanda Zacharias; Mohn, 1962. **Awarded:** Hans Christian Andersen (runnerup) 1964.

ZACHARIAS, WANDA
Mikosch, das Karusselpferd written and illustrated by Thomas Zacharias and Wanda Zacharias; Mohn, 1962. **Awarded:** Hans Christian Andersen (runnerup) 1964.

ZAFFO, GEORGE J.
The Big Book of Real Building and Wrecking Machines written and illustrated by George J. Zaffo; Grosset, 1951. **Awarded:** Spring Book Festival (picture book honor) 1951.

ZAID, BARRY
Rimes de la Mere Oie: Mother Goose Rendered into French translated by Ormonde deKay, Jr., illustrated by Barry Zaid, Milton Glaser and Seymour Chwast; Little, Brown, 1971. **Awarded:** Children's Book Showcase 1972.

ZAK, DRAHOS
Murgatroyd's Garden by Judy Zavos, illustrated by Drahos Zak; Heinemann, 1986. **Awarded:** Children's Book Council of Australia (picture book of the year honor) 1987.

ZALLINGER, JEAN
Valley of the Smallest: The Life Story of a Shrew by Aileen Fisher, illustrated by Jean Zallinger; Crowell, 1966. **Awarded:** International Board on Books for Young People (USA) 1968; Western Writers (nonfiction) 1967.

ZAMBELLIS, PETROS
Awarded: Hans Christian Andersen (highly commended illustrator/Greece) 1972.

ZAPPLER, GEORGE
Then and Now by George Zappler and Lisbeth Zappler, illustrated by Dorothea Barlowe and Sy Barlowe; McGraw, 1974. **Awarded:** New Jersey Institute of Technology 1976.

ZAPPLER, LISBETH
Then and Now by George Zappler and Lisbeth Zappler, illustrated by Dorothea Barlowe and Sy Barlowe; McGraw, 1974. **Awarded:** New Jersey Institute of Technology 1976.

ZAR, ROSE
In the Mouth of the Wolf by Rose Zar, not illustrated; Jewish Publication Society of America, 1983. **Awarded:** Sydney Taylor Book Award (older readers) 1984.

ZARINS, JOYCE AUDY
How To Survive Third Grade by Laurie Lawlor, illustrated by Joyce Audy Zarins; Whitman, 1988. **Awarded:** KC Three 1990-91.

ZAUNDERS, BO
Max, the Bad-Talking Parrot by Patricia B. Demuth, illustrated by Bo Zaunders; Dodd, Mead, 1986. **Awarded:** Georgia Children's Picture Storybook 1989.

ZAVOS, JUDY
Murgatroyd's Garden by Judy Zavos, illustrated by Drahos Zak; Heinemann, 1986. **Awarded:** Children's Book Council of Australia (picture book of the year honor) 1987.

ZAVREL, STEPAN
Die Blumenstadt by Eveline Hasler, illustrated by Stepan Zavrel; Bohem Press, 1987. **Awarded:** Bologna (Critici in Erba) 1988.

ZAWADSKY, PATIENCE
Mystery of the Old Musket by Patience Zawadsky, illustrated by D. McMains; Putnam, 1967. **Awarded:** New Jersey Institute of Technology 1968.

ZDINAK, WILLIAM
Where Does God Live? by Monsignor Thomas Hartman and Rabbi Marc Gellman, illustrated by William Zdinak; Triumph Books, 1991. **Awarded:** Christopher Award (All Ages) 1992.

ZECCA, CAROLYN
Spaceshots: The Beauty of Nature Beyond Earth by Timothy Ferris and Carolyn Zecca, illustrated with photographs; Pantheon, 1984. **Awarded:** New York Academy of Sciences (older honor) 1986.

ZEI, ALKI
Petros' War by Alki Zei, translated by Edward Fenton, not illustrated; Dutton, 1972. **Awarded:** Batchelder 1974; International Board on Books for Young People (translation/USA) 1986.

The Sound of Dragon's Feet by Alki Zei, translated by Edward Fenton, not illustrated; Dutton, 1979. **Awarded:** Batchelder 1980.

Wildcat under Glass by Alki Zei, translated by Edward Fenton, not illustrated; Holt, 1968. **Awarded:** Batchelder 1970.

ZELDICH, ARIEH
Always, Always by Crescent Dragonwagon, illustrated by Arieh Zeldich; Macmillan, 1984. **Awarded:** Parents' Choice (literature) 1984.

ZELIBSKA, MARIA
Slavische Marchen by Vladislav Stanovsky and Oldrich Sirovatka, illustrated by Maria Zelibska; Artia. **Awarded:** Bologna (Graphics for Youth) 1972.

ZELINSKY, PAUL O.
Buster's World by Bjarne Reuter, illustrated by Paul O. Zelinsky; Dutton, 1989. **Awarded:** Batchelder 1990.

Dear Mr. Henshaw by Beverly Cleary, illustrated by Paul O. Zelinsky; Morrow, 1983. **Awarded:** Christopher (ages 8-10) 1984; Commonwealth Club of California 1983; Dorothy Canfield Fisher 1985; FOCAL 1987; Garden State (younger fiction) 1986; Massachusetts 1986; Nene Award 1989; New York Times Notable Books 1983; Newbery 1984; Parents' Choice (literature) 1982; Sequoyah 1986.

Emily Upham's Revenge: or, How Deadwood Dick Saved the Banker's Niece: A Massachusetts Adventure by Avi, illustrated by Paul O. Zelinsky; Pantheon, 1978. **Awarded:** Edgar Allan Poe (runnerup) 1979.

Hansel and Gretel retold by Rika Lesser, illustrated by Paul O. Zelinsky; Dodd, Mead, 1984. **Awarded:** Caldecott (honor) 1985.

The Maid and the Mouse and the Odd-Shaped House: A Story in Rhyme adapted and illustrated by Paul O. Zelinsky; Dodd, Mead, 1981. **Awarded:** New York Times Best Illustrated 1981.

Ralph S. Mouse by Beverly Cleary, illustrated by Paul O. Zelinsky; Morrow, 1982. **Awarded:** Emphasis on Reading (grades 2-3) 1983-84; Garden State (younger fiction) 1985; Golden Kite (fiction) 1982; Iowa Children's 1985; Parents' Choice (literature) 1982; Sunshine (runnerup) 1985; Surrey School 1986; West Virginia 1986-87.

Rumpelstiltskin retold and illustrated by Paul O. Zelinsky; Dutton, 1986. **Awarded:** Caldecott (honor) 1987; Redbook 1986.

The Story of Mrs. Lovewright and Purrless her Cat by Lore Segal, illustrated by Paul O. Zelinsky; Knopf, 1985. **Awarded:** New York Times Best Illustrated 1985; New York Times Notable 1985.

Strider by Beverly Cleary, illustrated by Paul O. Zelinsky; Morrow, 1991. **Awarded:** Reading Magic Award 1991.

The Wheels on the Bus written and illustrated by Paul O. Zelinsky; Dutton, 1990. **Awarded:** Parents' Choice (Picture Book) 1990; Reading Magic Award 1990; Redbook 1990.

ZEMACH, HARVE
Duffy and the Devil retold by Harve Zemach, illustrated by Margot Zemach; Farrar, 1973. **Awarded:** Caldecott 1974; Lewis Carroll Shelf 1976; Children's Book Showcase 1974; National Book Award (finalist) 1974; New York Times Notable Books 1973; Spring Book Festival (younger honor) 1973.

The Judge by Harve Zemach, illustrated by Margot Zemach; Farrar, 1969. **Awarded:** Caldecott (honor) 1970.

Mommy, Buy Me a China Doll by Harve Zemach, illustrated by Margot Zemach; Farrar, 1966. **Awarded:** Art Books for Children 1977.

A Penny a Look by Harve Zemach, illustrated by Margot Zemach; Farrar, 1971. **Awarded:** Children's Book Showcase 1972.

The Princess and Froggie by Harve and Kaethe Zemach, illustrated by Margot Zemach; Farrar, 1975. **Awarded:** Children's Book Showcase 1976.

Salt: A Russian Tale by Harve Zemach, illustrated by Margot Zemach; Follett, 1965. **Awarded:** Spring Book Festival (picture book) 1965.

Too Much Nose by Harve Zemach, illustrated by Margot Zemach; Holt, 1967. **Awarded:** Spring Book Festival (picture book honor) 1967.

ZEMACH, KAETHE
The Princess and Froggie by Harve and Kaethe Zemach, illustrated by Margot Zemach; Farrar, 1975. **Awarded:** Children's Book Showcase 1976.

ZEMACH, MARGOT
Awarded: Kerlan 1979.

Alone in the Wild Forest by Isaac Bashevis Singer, illustrated by Margot Zemach; Farrar, 1971. **Awarded:** Children's Book Showcase 1972.

Duffy and the Devil retold by Harve Zemach, illustrated by Margot Zemach; Farrar, 1973. **Awarded:** Caldecott 1974; Lewis Carroll Shelf 1976; Children's Book Showcase 1974; National Book Award (finalist) 1974; New York Times Notable Books 1973; Spring Book Festival (younger honor) 1973.

Hush, Little Baby written and illustrated by Margot Zemach; Dutton, 1976. **Awarded:** Art Books for Children 1978, 1979; International Board on Books for Young People (illustration/USA) 1978.

It Could Always Be Worse: A Yiddish Folk Tale written and illustrated by Margot Zemach; Farrar, 1977. **Awarded:** Caldecott (honor) 1978; New York Times Best Illustrated 1977.

Jake and Honeybunch Go to Heaven written and illustrated by Margot Zemach; Farrar, 1982. **Awarded:** Commonwealth Club of California 1982; New York Times Notable Books 1982.

The Judge by Harve Zemach, illustrated by Margot Zemach; Farrar, 1969. **Awarded:** Caldecott (honor) 1970.

The King of Hermits and Other Stories by Jack Sendak, illustrated by Margot Zemach; Farrar, 1967. **Awarded:** New Jersey Institute of Technology 1967.

Mommy, Buy Me a China Doll by Harve Zemach, illustrated by Margot Zemach; Farrar, 1966. **Awarded:** Art Books for Children 1977.

A Penny a Look by Harve Zemach, illustrated by Margot Zemach; Farrar, 1971. **Awarded:** Children's Book Showcase 1972.

The Princess and Froggie by Harve and Kaethe Zemach, illustrated by Margot Zemach; Farrar, 1975. **Awarded:** Children's Book Showcase 1976

Salt: A Russian Tale by Harve Zemach, illustrated by Margot Zemach; Follett, 1965. **Awarded:** Spring Book Festival (picture book) 1965.

Self-Portrait: Margot Zemach written and illustrated by Margot Zemach; Addison-Wesley, 1978. **Awarded:** Boston Globe Horn Book (nonfiction honor) 1979.

Simon Boom Gives a Wedding by Yuri Suhl, illustrated by Margot Zemach; Four Winds, 1972. **Awarded:** Lewis Carroll Shelf 1972; Children's Book Showcase 1973; New York Times Best Illustrated 1972.

Too Much Nose by Harve Zemach, illustrated by Margot Zemach; Holt, 1967. **Awarded:** Spring Book Festival (picture book honor) 1967.

The Two Foolish Cats by Yoshiko Uchida, illustrated by Margot Zemach; McElderry, 1987. **Awarded:** Parents' Choice (Story Book) 1987.

When Schlemiel Went to Warsaw and Other Stories by Isaac Bashevis Singer, illustrated by Margot Zemach; Farrar, 1968. **Awarded:** Newbery (honor) 1969.

ZIEBEL, PETER
Look Closer! written and illustrated by Peter Ziebel; Clarion, 1989. **Awarded:** New Jersey Institute of Technology 1990.

ZIEFERT, HARRIET
Good Night, Jessie! by Harriet Ziefert, illustrated by Mavis Smith; Random House, 1987. **Awarded:** New Jersey Institute of Technology 1988.

Hurry Up, Jessie! by Harriet Ziefert, illustrated by Mavis Smith; Random House, 1987. **Awarded:** New Jersey Institute of Technology 1988.

I Won't Go To Bed by Harriet Ziefert, illustrated by Andrea Baruffi; Little Brown, 1987. **Awarded:** New Jersey Institute of Technology 1988.

Max and Diana and the Beach Day by Harriet Ziefert, illustrated by Lonni Sue Johnson; Harper & Row, 1987. **Awarded:** New Jersey Institute of Technology 1988.

Max and Diana and the Birthday Present by Harriet Ziefert, illustrated by Lonni Sue Johnson; Harper & Row, 1987. **Awarded:** New Jersey Institute of Technology 1988.

Max and Diana and the Snowy Day by Harriet Ziefert, illustrated by Lonni Sue Johnson; Harper & Row, 1987. **Awarded:** New Jersey Institute of Technology 1988.

A New Coat for Anna by Harriet Ziefert, illustrated by Anita Lobel; Harper & Row, 1986. **Awarded:** New Jersey Institute of Technology 1988.

Pet Day by Harriet Ziefert, illustrated by Richard Brown; Little Brown, 1987. **Awarded:** New Jersey Institute of Technology 1988.

Sarah's Questions by Harriet Ziefert, illustrated by Susan Bonners; Lothrop, Lee & Shepard, 1986. **Awarded:** New Jersey Institute of Technology 1987.

The Small Potatoes' Busy Beach Day by Harriet Ziefert, illustrated by Richard Brown; Dell, 1986. **Awarded:** New Jersey Institute of Technology 1987.

So Hungry! by Harriet Ziefert, illustrated by Carol Nicklaus; Random House, 1987. **Awarded:** New Jersey Institute of Technology 1988.

Trip Day by Harriet Ziefert, illustrated by Richard Brown; Little Brown, 1987. **Awarded:** New Jersey Institute of Technology 1988.

Where Babies Come From by Harriet Ziefert and Martin Silverman, illustrated by Claire Schumacher; Random House, 1989. **Awarded:** New Jersey Institute of Technology 1990.

Where's the Cat? by Harriet Ziefert, illustrated by Arnold Lobel; Harper & Row, 1987. **Awarded:** New Jersey Institute of Technology 1988.

Where's the Dog? by Harriet Ziefert, illustrated by Arnold Lobel; Harper & Row, 1987. **Awarded:** New Jersey Institute of Technology 1988.

Where's the Guinea Pig? by Harriet Ziefert, illustrated by Arnold Lobel; Harper & Row, 1987. **Awarded:** New Jersey Institute of Technology 1988.

Worm Day by Harriet Ziefert, illustrated by Richard Brown; Harper & Row, 1987. **Awarded:** New Jersey Institute of Technology 1988.

ZILBOORG, MARGARET STONE
Jeremiah Octopus by Margaret Stone Zilboorg, illustrated by Hilary Knight; Golden, 1962. **Awarded:** Spring Book Festival (picture book honor) 1962.

ZIM, HERBERT
Awarded: Eva L. Gordon 1981.

Snakes by Herbert Zim, illustrated by James G. Irving; Morrow, 1949. **Awarded:** Boys Club 1950.

ZIMMER, DIRK
Felix in the Attic by Larry Bograd, illustrated by Dirk Zimmer; Harvey House, 1978. **Awarded:** Irma Simonton Black 1978.

In a Dark, Dark Room and Other Scary Stories retold by Alvin Schwartz, illustrated by Dirk Zimmer; Harper & Row, 1984. **Awarded:** Buckeye (grades K-2) 1987; Garden State (easy to read) 1987; Virginia Young Readers (primary) 1988; Volunteer State Book Awards (K-3) 1989; Washington Children's Choice 1987.

ZIMNIK, REINER
The Bear and the People written and illustrated by Reiner Zimnik, translated by Nina Ignatowicz; Harper, 1971. **Awarded:** New York Times Notable Books 1971.

The Bear on the Motorcycle written and illustrated by Reiner Zimnik; Atheneum, 1963. **Awarded:** Spring Book Festival (picture book honor) 1963.

Jonah the Fisherman written and illustrated by Reiner Zimnik, translated by Richard Winston and Clara Winston; Pantheon, 1956. **Awarded:** New York Times Best Illustrated 1956.

Little Owl by Reiner Zimnik and Hanne Axmann, illustrated by Hanne Axmann; Atheneum, 1962. **Awarded:** New York Times Best Illustrated 1962.

The Snow Party by Beatrice Schenk de Regniers, illustrated by Reiner Zimnik; Pantheon, 1959. **Awarded:** Boys Club 1960.

ZINDEL, PAUL
The Pigman by Paul Zindel, not illustrated; Harper, 1968; Dell, 1970. **Awarded:** Boston Globe Horn Book (text honor) 1969; Media & Methods (paperback) 1973.

The Pigman's Legacy by Paul Zindel, not illustrated; Harper & Row, 1980. **Awarded:** New York Times Notable Books 1980.

ZION, EUGENE
see ZION, GENE

ZION, GENE
All Falling Down by Gene Zion, illustrated by Margaret Bloy Graham; Harper, 1951. **Awarded:** Caldecott (honor) 1952.

Dear Garbage Man by Gene Zion, illustrated by Margaret Bloy Graham; Harper, 1957. **Awarded:** New York Times Best Illustrated 1957.

Really Spring by Gene Zion, illustrated by Margaret Bloy Graham; Harper, 1956. **Awarded:** New York Times Best Illustrated 1956.

ZISFEIN, MELVIN B.
Flight: A Panorama of Aviation by Melvin B. Zisfein, illustrated by Robert Andrew Parker; Pantheon, 1979. **Awarded:** New

York Times Best Illustrated 1981; **Awarded:** New York Times Notable Books 1981.

ZISKIND, SYLVIA
Awarded: Southern California Council (distinguished contribution for outstanding service in the field of children's literature) 1977.

ZIVKOVIC, NICOLE
Animal A To Z written and illustrated by Nicole Zivkovic. **Awarded:** Macmillan Prize (2nd prize) 1991.

ZOLA, MEGUIDO
Only the Best by Meguido Zola, illustrated by Valerie Littlewood; Julia MacRae, 1981. **Awarded:** Mother Goose (runnerup) 1982.

ZOLOTOW, CHARLOTTE SHAPIRO
Awarded: Kerlan 1986; University of Southern Mississippi 1990.

I Know a Lady by Charlotte Zolotow, illustrated by James Stevenson; Greenwillow, 1984. **Awarded:** Redbook (hardback) 1984.

Indian, Indian by Charlotte Zolotow, illustrated by Leonard Weisgard; Simon, 1952. **Awarded:** Spring Book Festival (picture book honor) 1952.

Mr. Rabbit and the Lovely Present by Charlotte Zolotow, illustrated by Maurice Sendak; Harper & Row, 1962. **Awarded:** Caldecott (honor) 1963.

My Grandson Lew by Charlotte Zolotow, illustrated by William Pene du Bois; Harper & Row, 1974. **Awarded:** Christopher (ages 4-8) 1975.

Some Things go Together by Charlotte Zolotow, illustrated by Karen Gundersheimer; Crowell, 1983. **Awarded:** Carolyn W. Field 1984.

The Storm Book by Charlotte Zolotow, illustrated by Margaret Bloy Graham; Harper & Row, 1952. **Awarded:** Caldecott (honor) 1953.

William's Doll by Charlotte Zolotow, illustrated by William Pene du Bois; Harper Trophy, 1985, c1972. **Awarded:** Redbook 1985.

ZOTTER, GERRI
Das Sprachbastelbuch by Gerri Zotter; Jugend und Volk Verlag. **Awarded:** Bologna (Graphics for Youth) 1975.

ZUBROWSKI, BERNIE
Bubbles by Bernie Zubrowski, illustrated by Joan Drescher, Little Brown, 1979. **Awarded:** New York Academy of Sciences (younger honor) 1980.

Messing Around with Water Pumps and Siphons by Bernie Zubrowski, illustrated by Steve Lindblom; Little Brown, 1981. **Awarded:** New York Academy of Sciences (younger) 1982.

ZUDECK, DARRYL S.
Prairie Songs by Pam Conrad, illustrated by Darryl S. Zudeck; Harper & Row, 1985. **Awarded:** Boston Globe Horn Book (fiction honor) 1986; Golden Kite (fiction honor) 1985; International Reading Assn. 1986; Judy Lopez 1986; Society of Midland Authors 1986; Western Heritage 1986; Western Writers 1986.

ZWEIFEL, FRANCES WIMSATT
Bony by Fran Zweifel, illustrated by Whitney Darrow, Jr.; Harper, 1977. **Awarded:** New Jersey Institute of Technology 1978.

Pickle in the Middle and Other Easy Snacks written and illustrated by Frances W. Zweifel; Harper, 1979. **Awarded:** New Jersey Institute of Technology 1980, 1981.

ZWERGER, LISBETH

Awarded: Hans Christian Andersen (Illustrator) 1990.

Aesop's Fables illustrated by Lisbeth Zwerger; Picture Book Studios, 1989. **Awarded:** Parents' Choice (Picture Book) 1989.

The Gift of the Magi by O. Henry, illustrated by Lisbeth Zwerger, lettering by Michael Neugebauer; Neugebauer Press distributed by Alphabet Press, 1982. **Awarded:** New York Times Best Illustrated 1982.

The Legend of Rosepetal by Clemens Brentano, illustrated by Lisbeth Zwerger; Picture Book Studio, 1985. **Awarded:** New York Times Best Illustrated 1985.

Little Red Cap by Jacob and Wilhelm Grimm, translated by Elizabeth D. Crawford, illustrated by Lisbeth Zwerger; Morrow, 1983. **Awarded:** New York Times Best Illustrated 1983.

The Swineherd by Hans Christian Andersen, translated by Anthea Bell, illustrated by Lisbeth Zwerger; Morrow, 1982. **Awarded:** Parents' Choice (illustration) 1982.

ZYLMAN, MICHELE

Animals that Migrate by Caroline Arnold, illustrated by Michele Zylman; Carolrhoda, 1982. **Awarded:** New York Academy of Sciences (younger honor) 1983.

Part Three

SELECTED
BIBLIOGRAPHY

Selected Bibliography

Aaron, Ira E. and Sylvia M. Hutchinson. "Comparing Award-winning Children's Books from Five English-speaking Countries." *USBBY Newsletter* 14 (1989): 14,16-17.

"ABA Marketing Council to Promote Book Awards." *School Library Journal* 27 (February 1981): 12.

Aborne, Carlene. "The Newberys: Getting Them to Read (It Isn't Easy)." *Library Journal* 99 (April 15, 1974): 1197-99.

Alderman, Belle. "The Impact of Children's Book Awards." *Incite* 11 (August 13, 1990): 1, 11.

"ALSC Banner Contest Celebrates Caldecott." *School Library Journal* 35 (Spring 1988): 104.

"ALSC Fiftieth Anniversary National Banner Contest Awards." *American Libraries* 19 (Spring 1988): 17.

Ashby, A. "CLA Book of the Year for Children Award: What Really Happens?" *Emergency Librarian* 7 (January 1980): 5-6.

"The Association for Library Service to Children Announced Winners of the Caldecott Fiftieth Anniversary Banner Contest." *Journal of Youth Services* 2 (Fall 1988): 11-14.

Averill, Esther. "What Is a Picture Book?" in *Caldecott Medal Books: 1938-1957* edited by Bertha Mahony Miller and Elinor Whitney Field. Boston: Horn Book, 1957. 307-14.

"Award-winning Children's Books Sell Better and Longer." *Publisher's Weekly* 203 (February 26, 1973): 98-99.

Barker, Keith. "All That Glitters..." *Books for Keeps* 39 (1986): 10-11.

Barker, Keith. "The Books Kids Like." *SLG News* 11 (Spring 1985): 20-21.

Barker, Keith. "Fifty Years of Carnegie Medals." *British Book News Children's Books* (June 1986): 6.

Barker, Keith. *In the Realms of Gold: The Story of the Carnegie Medal*. London: Julia MacRae in association with the Youth Libraries Group of the Library Association, 1986.

Barker, Keith. "Researching the Medal." *Youth Library Review* 1 (1986): 15-16.

Barnes, Ruth A. "The Newbery Prize List." *Elementary Education* 6 (March 1929): 74-75.

Barron, E.L. *Trends in the Newbery Award Books from 1960-1987*. Thesis, University of North Carolina at Chapel Hill, 1988.

Batchelder, Mildred L. "Newbery and Caldecott Awards: Authorization and Terms-1966." *Top of the News* 22 (January 1966): 155-57.

Bauer, Carolyn J. and La Vonne H. Sanborn. "The Best of Both Worlds: Children's Books Acclaimed by Adults and Young Readers." *Top of the News* 38 (Fall 1981): 53-6.

Bedenbaugh, Edna M. "South Carolina Children's Book Award Program." *South Carolina Librarian* 20 (Spring 1976): 22-4.

Behrmann, C.A. "The Media Used in Caldecott Picture Books: Notes Toward a Definitive List. *Journal of Youth Services* 1 (Winter 1988): 198-212.

Bell, I. W. *Caldecott Honor Books Search-a-word Learning Guide: The First 25 Years 1938-62*. Littleton, Colo.: Libraries Unlimited, 1990.

Bell, I. W. *Caldecott Search-a-word Learning Guide*. Littleton, Colo.: Libraries Unlimited, 1988.

Beneduce, Ann. "Prizes: Risks Rewarded." *USBBY Newsletter* 17 (Spring 92): 3.

Bodart, Joni. "The Also-rans: or, What Happens to the Ones That Didn't Get Eight Votes?" *Top of the News* 38 (Fall 1981): 70-3.

Bogan, Mary E. "The William Allen White Children's Book Award Program: A Successful State Program." *Top of the News* 36 (Fall 1979): 87-95.

Bologna Fair Prizes 1986. *Bookbird* 24 (1986): 58-9.

Breed, Clara E. "Newbery Medal." *Wilson Library Bulletin* 17 (May 1942): 724-25.

Broderick, Dorothy. "The Newbery Award Is Not a Popularity Contest." *Junior Libraries* 6 (March 1960): 116-18.

Brown, M.W. and R.S. Foudray. *Newbery and Caldecott Medalists and Honor Book Winners*. 2nd ed. New York: Neal-Schuman, 1992.

Burr, Elizabeth. "Newbery and Caldecott Awards." *Top of the News* 16 (December 1959): 67-70.

Callaghan, L.W. "Caldecott Citations: A Selective Bibliography." *Journal of Youth Services* 1 (Winter 1988): 160-67.

Campbell, A.K.D. *Outstanding Children's Books: A List of 554 Books Which Have Won Awards or Official Commendations During the Period from 1930-1988*. Swansea: LISE Publications, 1990.

Cann, Muriel E. "Newbery Prize Books." *Elementary Education* 11 (September 1934): 180-82, 192.

Carter, Betty. "The Library Connection." *The ALAN Review* 19 (Spring 1992): 45-47.

Chatham, Walter L. *Reading Grade Placement of the John Newbery Prize Books from 1945-1965*. Ph.D. dissertation, University of Southern Mississippi, 1967.

"The Children's Book Council of Australia Annual Awards 1992." *Reading Time* 36 (July 1992): 2-7.

"Children's Book Council of Australia Awards: The Past and the Future." *Reading Time* 98 (January 1986): 4-5.

Chosen for Children: An Account of the Books Which Have Been Awarded the Library Association Carnegie Medal, 1936-1965. rev. ed. London: The Library Association, 1967.

Chrisman, Arthur Bowie. "John Newbery: The Father of Children's Books" in *Newbery Medal Books: 1922-1955* edited by Bertha Mahony Miller and Elinor Whitney Field. Boston: Horn Book, 1955. pp. 6-9.

"CLA to Raise Funds to Support Book Awards." *School Library Journal* 27 (February 1981): 12.

Clark, Margaret M. "Children's Book Clubs and Awards." *Elementary Education* 20 (October 1943): 235-39.

Colquhoun, S. "The Geography of Newbery Winners." *The School Librarian's Workshop* 10 (January 1990): 9-10.

Colwell, Eileen H. "Kate Greenaway Medal." *Library Association Record* 57 (December 1955): 481-82.

"Coming of Age." *Junior Bookshelf* 21 (November 1957): 243-50.

Connor, Jenni. "Glittering Prizes?" *Magpies* 5 (September 1990): 10-12.

Cook, P. "CLA Illustrator's Award: Fairy Tale, Myth, or Reality?" *Emergency Librarian* 7 (January 1980): 7-9.

Corcoran, Clodagh. "Ten Years of Mother Goose." *Books for Keeps* 59 (November 1989): 4-6.

Crago, Maureen. "New Values, New Awards." *Magpies* 6 (September 1991): 14-16.

Crago, Maureen. "The Family Award Is Three Years Old." *Orana* 26 (November 1990): 197-201.

Crawford, Elizabeth D. "Mildred L. Batchelder Award-Translation: The Editor's Viewpoint." *Top of the News* 38 (Fall 1981): 87-90.

Criscoe, B.L. *Award-winning Books for Children and Young Adults: An Annual Guide*, 1989. Scarecrow, 1990.

Criscoe, B.L. and P.J. Lanasa, III. *Award-winning Books for Children and Young Adults 1990-91*. Scarecrow, 1993.

Crouch, Marcus. "Salute to Children's Literature and Its Creators: 21st Birthday for Carnegie Medal." *Top of the News* 14 (May 1958): 7-10.

Cullinan, Bernice E. "Books in the Classroom: Teachers' Choices." *Horn Book* 66 (January/February 1991): 109-12.

Danziger, Paula. "Why I Will Never Win the Newbery Medal." *Top of the News* 36 (Fall 1979): 57-60.

Davidson, D. "Booktalking the Bluebonnets." *Wilson Library Bulletin* 65 (May 1991): 1-2.

Davis, D.C. "Tools for the Selection of Children's Books: The Lewis Carroll Shelf Awards." *Elementary English* 39 (December 1961): 549-52.

Doll, Carol A. "Which Book Will Win the Caldecott?" *Publishing Research Quarterly* 7 (Fall 1991): 77-90.

Donohue, Mildred Sileo. *Trends in Choosing Newbery Award Winners*. Master's Thesis, Southern Connecticut State College, 1970.

"Double Challenge at Book Awards." *Library Association Record* 94 (August 1992): 484.

Dresang, Eliza T. "A Newbery Song for Gifted Readers." *School Library Journal* 30 (November 1983): 33-37.

Dresang, E. T. "Discussion for Awards and Distinctions " in *Evaluation Strategies and Technique for Public Library Children's Services*. University of Wisconsin- Madison. School of Library & Information Studies, 1990. pp. 261-6.

Dukler, Margot. "Five Popular Children's Authors." *Elementary Education* 35 (January 1958): 3-11.

Eaglen, Audrey. "Don't Argue with Success." *School Library Journal* 36 (May 1990): 54.

Eaglen, Audrey. "Editor's Note." *Top of the News* 36 (Fall 1979): 15.

Egoff, Shelia and G.T. Stubbs and L.F. Ashley. *Only Connect: Readings on Children's Literature*. Toronto: Oxford University Press, 1969.

Ellis, Alec. "Forty Years of the Carnegie Medal: A Hallmark of Quality." *Library Association Record* 79 (February 1977): 76+.

Field, Carolyn W. "Publishers' Changes in Newbery-Caldecott Books." *Top of the News* 16 (October 1959): 31-2.

Fincher, Beatrice M. "YABBA: The Children's Choice." *Australian School Librarian* 23 (December 1986): 107-08.

Fowler, V.E. "An Editor Recalls: From German to English to the Batchelder Award." *Top of the News* 24 (June 1968): 395-98.

Fox, C. J. "Establishing the Rebecca Caudill Young Reader's Book Award." *Illinois Libraries* 72 (Fall 1990): 129-31.

Frazekas, P. L. "On the Bulletin Board: Have a Happy Newbery..." *School Librarian's Workshop* 9 (January 1989): 10-12.

Fryatt, Norma R. "Picture Books Today." in *Newbery and Caldecott Medal Books: 1956-1965* edited by Lee Kingman. Boston: Horn Book, 1975. pp. 270-80.

Gagliardo, Ruth. "Frederic Melcher and Children's Books." *ALA Bulletin* 57 (June 1963): 549-52.

Gamble, Jill. "A Judge's Comments: Children's Book Awards, 1984." *Lu Rees Archives: Notes, Books and Authors* (5th issue, 1985): 10-12.

Geller, E. "Backstage with the Judges: The Herald Tribune Children's Book Awards." *School Library Journal* 13 (May 1966): 64-8.

Gerhardt, Lillian N. "SLJ & YASD: The Story of an Award." *School Library Journal* 34 (June-July 1988): 4.

Gerhardt, Lillian N. "That Unstoppable Question [Why Not Let the Children Choose the Children's Book Awards]?" *School Library Journal* 28 (May 1982): 5.

Gerhardt, Lillian N. "Tied Up in Washington: SLJ's Report on ALA's Midwinter Meeting, '79." *School Library Journal* 25 (March 1979): 102.

Goodman, Jo. "An Open Letter from a Judge." *Literature Base* 1 (June 1990): 8-9.

Graham, Eleanor. "The Carnegie Medal and Its Winners." *Junior Bookshelf* 8 (July 1944): 59-65.

Green, Irene Smith. "The Newbery-Caldecott Medals: Legacy to Children's Literature." *Top of the News* 20 (March 1964): 191-95.

Greene, David L. "Recent Trends in Children's Books: The Newbery and Caldecott Award Books 1975-1976." *Children's Literature* 6 (1977): 193-95.

Griffin, William. "Refreshment for over 50 Years: Zolotow receives USM's Silver Medallion." *Publishers Weekly* 237 (April 27, 1990): 30.

Gross, Elizabeth H. "Twenty Medal Books: In Perspective " in *Newbery and Caldecott Medal Books: 1956-65* edited by Lee Kingman. Boston: Horn Book, 1975. pp. 3-10.

Hagerty, M. "Mark Twain Is Alive and Growing in Missouri." *Show-Me Libraries* 31 (March 1980): 12-15.

Haigh, Gideon. "Kid Literati: Deciding What Children Should Read." *The Age (Melbourne) Tempo Midweek Magazine* 20 (November 1991): 1, 4.

Hale, Robert D. "Musings." [article concerns the Lucile M. Pannell Award]. *Horn Book* 61 (July/August 1985): 474-77.

Hamilton, Margaret. "The CBC - As I See It." *Australian Bookseller and Publisher* 71 (August 1991): 14.

Hanzl, Anne. "Activities for Use with the Short-listed Books for Children's Book of the Year-Younger Readers Award." *Literature Base* 2 (June 1991): 21-27.

Harman, Lauren. "The Presentation of the Children's Book Council of Australia Book of the Year Awards, Canberra, 19th July 1985." *Reading Time* 97 (October 1985): 6-7.

Harmon, E.A. "Spice of Variety: 1964-65 Sequoyah Children's Book Award Masterlist." *Oklahoma Librarian* 15 (October 1965): 126-28.

Haviland, Virginia. "The New National Book Award for Children's Literature." *Horn Book* 49 (June 1969).

Heeks, Peggy. "Looking for a Winner." *Times Literary Supplement, Children's Books* 66 (June 6, 1968): 578.

Herr, Marian. "Selection of the Newbery-Caldecott Award." *Wilson Library Bulletin* 25 (January 1951): 383.

Herrin, Barbara. *A History and Analysis of the William Allen White Children's Book Award*. Ph.D. dissertation, Kansas State University, 1979.

Hollowell, Lillian. "Children's Book Awards." *Elementary English* 28 (December 1951): 468-74.

Hopkins, Lee Bennett. "Children's Choices: [Awards Determined by Children's Votes]. *School Library Media Quarterly* 10 (Winter 1982): 105-06.

Horowitz, Carolyn. "Only the Best " in *Newbery and Caldecott Medal Books: 1956-1965* edited by Lee Kingman. Boston: Horn Book, 1975. pp. 151-62.

Humphries, Tudor. "Response to a Jaded Jury." *Books for Keeps* 41 (1986): 19.

Huntoon, E. "Caldecott Fiftieth Anniversary Celebration" (special issue) *Journal of Youth Services* 1 (Winter 1988): 127-212.

Hurlimann, B. "Reflections on the First Fifteen Years of the BIB." *Bookbird* 17 (1979 no. 3): 56-60.

Immroth, Barbara. "The Newbery and Caldecott Awards." *Texas Libraries* 50 (Spring 1989): 3-7.

Immroth, Barbara. "Prizing in Children's Literature." *USBBY Newsletter* 17 (Spring 92): 1, 3.

Inglis, J. "Shadowing Carnegie: A Fiction Project for GCSE." *School Librarian* 40: (November 1992): 128-29+.

Izard, Anne R. "Behind Doors with the Newbery-Caldecott Committee." *Top of the News* 22 (January 1966): 160-63.

Jankunis, Myrtice and Winona Anderson. "Art, Literature and the Caldecott Books." *Winona School Libraries in Canada* 10 (Winter 1989): 11-13.

"Jewish Juvenile Book Awards: Survey and Evaluation " in *Jewish Book Annual* vol. 35. Jewish Book Council of America, 1977. pp. 78-91.

"The John Newbery Prize Book." *Journal of the National Education Association* 20 (October 1931): 242.

Johnson, Gill. "How the Medal Was Won." *Books for Keeps* 39 (1986): 10-11.

Johnston, Leah Carter. "Newbery Medal Books." *Horn Book* 32 (February 1956): 45-8.

Jordan, Helen L. "Child-Choice Book Awards in the U.S.A." *Bookbird* (1981 no.1): 15-21.

Jordan, Helen L. "State Awards for Children's Book." *Top of the News* 36 (Fall 1979): 79-86.

Kalb, V. "Curriculum Connections: Around the World with Caldecott Awards." *School Library Media Quarterly* 18 (Fall 1989): 29-30.

Kalkhoff, Ann. "Innocent Children or Innocent Librarians " in *Issues in Children's Book Selection*. New York: Bowker, 1973. pp. 11-19.

Kayden, Mimi and Suzanne M. Glazer. "For Whom the Calls Toll: The Newbery Caldecott Awards from the Publisher's Viewpoint." *Top of the News* 36 (Fall 1979): 35-42.

Kempster, G. "Tomorrow's Politicians Need Libraries Now." *Library Association Record* 94 (August 1992): 522-23.

Kerlan, Irvin. *Newbery & Caldecott Awards: A Bibliography of First Editions*. Minneapolis: University of Minnesota Press, 1949.

Kingman, Lee W. *Newbery and Caldecott Medal Books, 1956-1965*. Boston: Horn Book, 1965.

Kingman, Lee W. *Newbery and Caldecott Medal Books, 1966-1975*. Boston: Horn Book, 1975.

Kingman, Lee. *Newbery and Caldecott Medal Books, 1976-1985*. Boston: Horn Book, 1986.

Lacy, L. E. "Evaluating Picture Book Art." *School Library Journal* 33 (December 1986): 39-40.

Lacy, Lyn Ellen. *Art and Design in Children's Picture Books: An Analysis of Caldecott Award-Winning Illustrators*. Chicago: American Library Association, 1986.

Lacy, Lyn. "Gilly, Turtle, and Ramona: The 1979 Newbery Awards from an Elementary Educator's Viewpoint." *Top of the News* 36 (Fall 1979): 63-71.

Lanes, Selma G. "Sign of the Times: The Caldecott Winner for 1975." *School Library Journal* 22 (November 1975): 28-29.

Langton, J. "Fair or Unfair? Confessions of a Literary Contest Judge." *Publisher's Weekly* 202 (July 17, 1972): 88-90.

Latrobe, K.H. & C. Casey. "On Choosing Young Adult Book Awards." *Journal of Youth Services* 3 (Spring 1990): 227-33.

Lawler, Clare C. *An Analysis and Evaluation of the Newbery Award Books by a Selected Group of Junior Reviewers*. Master's Thesis, Kent State University, 1961.

Lawrence, Frances A. "Facts about the Newbery Books." *Library Journal* 68 (November 1942): 942-43.

Lechner, Judith V. "The Role of Awards in Promoting Quality Science Trade Books for Children." *Journal of Youth Services* 5 (Spring 1992): 287-95.

Levis, Neil and others. "How the Judges Choose the Books We Use." *Contact* (December 7, 1984): 8-9.

Lewis, Geraint. "Tir Na n'Og Awards for Children's Books." *Book News from Wales* (Winter 1988): 4-7.

Livo, Norma J. "The Colorado Children's Book Award." November 1980. [ERIC document number ED 197 376]

Lomas, Derek. *Fifty Years of the Carnegie Medal: A Celebration*. Birmingham: Youth Libraries Group of the Library Association, in conjunction with the Carnegie United Kingdom Trust, 1986.

Lynch-Brown, Carol and Carl M. Tomlinson. "Batchelder Books: International Read-Alouds." *Top of the News* 42 (Spring 1986): 260-66.

Marley, A. "No Prizes for this Award." *Library Association Record* 93 (September 1991): 574-5.

Meek, Margaret and Neil Philip. "The Signal Poetry Award." *Signal* (May 1983): 59-71.

Meeker, Amy. "Do Awards Sell Books?" *Publishers Weekly* 236 (August 25, 1989): 32, 35-36.

Mehringer, Sarah C. "The Appeal of the Newbery Prize Books to Children in the Elementary Grades." *Teachers College Journal* 15 (September 1943): 15-19.

Melcher, Frederic. "The New Day for Children's Books." *Elementary Education* 5 (October 1928): 229-30.

Melcher, Frederic. "The Origin of the Newbery and Caldecott Medals " in *Newbery and Caldecott Medal Books, 1956-1965* edited by Lee W. Kingman. Boston: Horn Book, 1975. pp. 1-2.

Meltzer, Milton. "Where Do All the Prizes Go? The Case for Non-fiction." *Horn Book* 52 (February 1976): 17-23.

Miller, Adele. "Don't Sell Newbery Books Short." *Top of the News* 22 (January 1966): 168-71.

Miller, Bertha Mahony. "Frederic G. Melcher - A Twentieth Century John Newbery " in *Newbery Medal Books, 1922-1955* edited by Bertha Mahony Miller and Elinor Whitney Field. Boston: Horn Book, 1955.

Miller, Bertha Mahony. "Randolph Caldecott - For Whom the Award Is Named " in *Caldecott Medal Books, 1938-1957* edited by Bertha Mahony Miller and Elinor Whitney Field. Boston: Horn Book, 1957. pp. 1-5.

Miller, Bertha Mahony and Elinor Whitney Field. *Caldecott Medal Books, 1938-1957*. Boston: Horn Book, 1957.

Miller, Bertha Mahony and Elinor Whitney Field. *Newbery Medal Books, 1922-1955*. Boston: Horn Book, 1955.

Miller, Leo R. *The Reading Grade Placement of the First Twenty-three Books Awarded the John Newbery Prize*. Ph.D. dissertation, Pennsylvania State University, 1945.

Miller, Leo R. "Reading Grade Placement of the First Twenty-three Books Awarded the John Newbery Medal." *Elementary School Journal* 46 (March 1946): 394-99.

Moulton, Doris H. "Newbery Caldecott Committee." *Wilson Library Bulletin* 37 (October 1962): 190.

"National Book Award for Children's Lit Makes a Comeback." *American Libraries* 6 (December 1975): 636-37.

"National Book Award Winner Stresses Seriousness of Fantasy: Jury Nominees Challenged." *School Library Journal* 18 (April 1971): 14-15.

Nesbitt, Elizabeth. "The Test of Recollection " in *Newbery Medal Books, 1922-1955* edited by Bertha Mahony Miller and Elinor Whitney Field. Boston: Horn Book, 1955. pp. 44-5.

"The Newbery Award, Open Forum." *Elementary English* 117 (April 1940): 160.

Newton, Jennifer. "Newbery Winners Reflect Societal Trends." *Top of the News* 43 (Fall 1986): 97-102.

"The 1992 Hans Christian Anderson Awards Ceremony: A Personal Reminiscence." *USBBY Newsletter* 18 (Fall 1992): 9.

Nist, J.S. "Cultural Constellations in Translated Children's Literature: Evidence from the Mildred L. Batchelder Award." *Bookbird* 17 (1979 no. 2): 3-8.

Nist, Joan. *The Mildred L. Batchelder Award Books 1968-1977: A Decade of Honored Children's Literature in Translation*. Ph.D. dissertation, Auburn University, 1977.

O'Connell, Kathleen A. "The Library Connection: An Interview with Carolyn Caywood " [about the Newbery Medal]. *The ALAN Review* 18 (Winter 1991): 46-51.

"Open Forum on the Newbery Award." *Elementary English* 16 (November 1939): 283.

Patterson, N.E. *Evaluation of the Runners-up for the Newbery Medal, 1949-1959*. Master's thesis, University of North Carolina, 1968.

Paul, Justine. "Look Who Came to Dinner: IBBY Seminar and Celebratory Dinner, Saturday 1st November 1986: Some Thoughts on an Exciting Day." *Orana* 23 (February 1987): 23-24.

Peltola, Bette J. "Choosing the Newbery and Caldecott Medal Winners." *Top of the News* 32 (April 1976): 213.

Peltola, Bette J. "Choosing the Newbery and Caldecott Medal Winners." *Top of the News* 36 (Fall 1979): 43-47.

Peltola, Bette J. "Newbery and Caldecott Medals: Authorization and Terms." *Top of the News* 36 (Fall 1979): 49-54.

Peterson, Linda Kaufmann and Marilyn Leathers Solt. *Newbery and Caldecott Medal and Honor Books: An Annotated Bibliography*. Boston: G.K. Hall, 1982.

Philip, Neil. "The Smarties Prize for Children's Books." *British Book News Children's Books* (December 1985): 35-38.

Pileri, Iris M. "Newbery Medal Books Are Alive and Well at Court Street School." *School Library Journal* 27 (March 1981): 93-95.

Ray, S.G. "Seminar on Children's Book Awards." *Bookbird* 17 (1979 no. 3): 33.

Rhea, R. "Popularizing the Newbery Books." *Library Journal* 85 (May 15, 1960): 2018-20.

Roberts, Patricia L. "The Female Image in the Caldecott Medal Award Books." Monograph Number 2. Stockton, Calif.: Bureau of Educational Research and Field Services, University of the Pacific, 1976. [ERIC document number ED 181 467]

Roginski, Jim. *Newbery and Caldecott Medalists and Honor Book Winners: Bibliographies and Resource Material Through 1977*. Littleton, Colo.: Libraries Unlimited, 1982.

Roll, Dusan. "Twenty Years of BIB, 1967-1987." *Bookbird* 2 (1987): 15-20.

Rosenquist-Buhler, C. "Tenth Anniversary Celebration for Golden Sower Award." *Nebraska Library Association Quarterly* 22 (Fall 1991): 17-8.

Rudnik, Maryka. "Mildred L. Batchelder Award - The Winter When Time Was Frozen and The Art of Translating." *Top of the News* 38 (Fall 1981): 91-5.

Rue, Eloise, and Evrard, Connie. "Student Evaluations of Newbery Award Books." *Elementary Education* 40 (November 1963): 712-15.

Rupp, Mary. *Study of the John Newbery Award with Critical Evaluation of the Award Books*. Master's thesis, University of Washington, 1955.

Saxby, Maurice. "Two Gold Medals to Australia." *Magpies* 1 (September 1986): 15.

Schafer, P.J. "Readability of the Newbery Medal Books." *Language Arts* 53 (May 1976): 557-59.

Schlager, Norma Marion. *Developmental Factors Influencing Children's Responses to Literature*. Ph.D. dissertation, Claremont Graduate School, 1974. [study based on books which have received the Newbery Medal]

Schmidt, D.J. and Osborn, J. "Effect of Literary Awards on Children's Book Recommendations." *Top of the News* 30 (April 1974): 257-66.

Sharkey, P.M.B. *Newbery and Caldecott Medal and Honor Books in Other Media*. New York: Neal-Schuman, 1992.

Silver, Linda R. "One Book to Win: The Continuing Story of the Newbery-Caldecott Awards." *Top of the News* 36 (Fall 1979): 31-34.

Smith, Irene. *A History of the Newbery and Caldecott Medals*. New York: Viking, 1957.

Smith, J. "The Kentucky Bluegrass Award and other State Children's Choice Awards: Their Value and Effect." *Kentucky Libraries* 53 (Winter 1989): 13-16.

Spoerl, D.T. "Research and the Newbery Books." *Wilson Library Bulletin* 26 (June 1952): 818-19.

Stackhouse, J.S. *Study of the Relationship Between Children's Favorite Book Choices and Adult Standards*. Master's Thesis, Southern Connecticut State College, 1974.

Stevens, T. "In Search of the Perfect Golden Pen: or, Java, Donuts and Youth Participation " in *The VOYA Reader*. Scarecrow, 1990. pp. 69-76.

Stewig, J. W. "Choosing the Caldecott Winner: Fifth Graders Give Their Reasons. *Journal of Youth Services* 3 (Winter 1990): 128-133.

Sullivan, Peggy. "Victim of Success? A Closer Look at the Newbery Award " in *Issues in Children's Book Selection*. New York: Bowker, 1983. pp. 31-34.

Sutcliffe, Chris. "Stories, Smiles, and Smarties." *Books for Keeps* 67 (1991): 22-23.

Sutherland, Zena B. "Golden Apples and Blue Ribbons: The Meaning of International Awards " in *Children's Books International, Boston Public Library Proceedings*. Boston: Public Library, 1978. pp. 51-56.

Sutherland, Zena B. "Not Another Article on the Newbery-Caldecott Awards?" *Top of the News* 30 (April 1974): 249-53.

Sutton, Roger. "Ruminations on a YA Literary Award." *School Library Journal* 29 (December 1983): 37.

Thompson, F. "Coming: A New Hoosier Book Award." *Indiana Media Journal* 13 (Spring 1991): 11-13.

Thomson, Pat. "The Children's Book Award." *Bookmark* 13 (1985): 24-26.

Tobin, Barbara. Reader's Choice Book Awards: Trends Across Two Nations." *Orana* 22 (February 1986): 25-29.

Townes, Mary E. "Popularity of Newbery Medal Books." *Library Journal* 60 (November 1, 1935): 839-41.

Townsend, J.R. "Decade of Newbery Books in Perspective " in *Newbery and Caldecott Medal Books, 1966-1975* edited by Lee Kingman. Boston: Horn Book, 1975. pp. 141-53.

Townson, H. "Polishing the Medals." *Public Library Journal* 6 (May/June 1991): 85-86.

Tyrrel, Margot. "Children's Book Council Awards." *Australian Book Review* 123 (August 1990): 45-46.

USBBY Newsletter 16 (Spring 1991): 3-12. Devoted to articles about Mildred L. Batchelder and the award.

Vardell, Sylvia. "A New 'Picture of the World': The NCTE Orbis Pictus Award for Outstanding Nonfiction for Children." *Language Arts* 68 (October 1991): 474-79.

Watts, Doris Ryder. "An Open Letter to John Newbery." *Wilson Library Bulletin* 36 (January 1962): 390-91.

Weibel, K. "What is the Newcott-Calderberry?" *Top of the News* 30 (April 1974): 254-6.

Weiss, Jacqueline Shacter. *Prizewinning Books for Children: Themes and Stereotypes in U.S. Prizewinning Prose Fiction for Children*. Lexington, Mass.: Heath, 1983.

Weller, Anna Elizabeth. *The Portrayal of the Female Character in the Newbery Award Books*. Ph.D. dissertation, Indiana University, 1977.

Wightson, Rosemary. "Children's Book Awards: How and Why." *Australian Book Review* (July 1969): 172-5.

Wignell, Edel. "A Popular or Fun Book Award." *Orana* 28 (February 1992): 30-3.

Wignell, Edel. "Children's Literature Winners and Losers?" *Reading Time* 34 (1990 no. 4): 5-7.

"William Allen White Children's Book Award." *Kansas Library Bulletin* 21 (June 1952): 3-5.

"William Allen White Children's Book Award - 25 Years." *Kansas Association of School Librarians Newsletter* 27 (December 1977): 4.

Wright, Ethel C. "Favorite Children's Books of the Past Decade." *Elementary Education* 12 (April 1935): 101-5.

"Young Hoosier Book Award Committee." *Indiana Media Journal* 1 (Summer 1979): 20.

Zeligs, Rose. "Children's Opinions of Newbery Prize Books." *Elementary English* 17 (October 10, 1940): 218-20, 249.

Part Four

INDEXES

Author/Illustrator Index

Aamundsen, Nina Ring   17, 243
Aardema, Verna   13, 14, 40, 53, 62, 67, 161, 180, 183, 184, 192, 243, 281, 322, 323, 375, 439, 447, 479
Aas, Ulf   3, 32, 55, 78, 235, 243
Abbott, Mary Ogden   30, 243, 344
Abdullah, Aishah S   73, 243
Abel, Ray   33, 243, 392
Abelard   3, 32, 46, 108, 114, 153, 209, 222, 243, 275, 328, 331, 332, 354, 396, 423, 428, 439, 449, 478, 492
Abercrombie, Barbara   21, 192, 243, 360
Abernethy, Robert   78, 243
Abrahams, Hilary   47, 243, 254
Abrashkin, Raymond   239, 243, 402
Abruzzi, Rey   213, 243, 442
Acker, Helen   209, 243
Ackerman, Eugene   106, 243, 285
Ackerman, Karen   41, 199, 244, 348, 349
Ackoff, Karen   144, 244
Acs, Laszlo   77, 244
Ada, Alma Flor   69, 244
Adams, Adrienne   21, 25, 39, 46, 50, 107, 141, 194, 209, 211, 224, 244, 250, 251, 356, 358, 363, 402
Adams, James D.   205, 244, 374
Adams, Jeanie   60, 74, 244
Adams, Julia Davis   165, 244, 314, 458, 467
Adams, Laura   253
Adams, Richard   41, 47, 101, 244
Adams, Samuel Hopkins   210, 244
Adamson, Joy   32, 244
Addison, Robert W.   106, 244, 275
Adkins, Jan   11, 12, 52, 62, 63, 244
Adler, Carole S.   56, 73, 93, 232, 244, 341
Adler, David A.   64, 219, 234, 244, 273, 331
Adoff, Arnold   4, 13, 134, 182, 244, 245, 259, 443
Afanasyev, Alexander Nikolayevich   159, 245
Agard, John   176, 245, 362
Agee, Jon   192, 245
Agueros, Jack   73, 245
Ahlberg, Allan   18, 34, 56, 99, 100, 108, 110, 176, 197, 199, 245
Ahlberg, Janet   18, 99, 125, 245
Aichinger, Helga   10, 61, 71, 245, 274, 284
Aiken, Conrad   11, 245, 355
Aiken, Joan   34, 47, 51, 101, 161, 187, 245, 277, 436
Ajegbo, Keith   245

Akaba, Suekichi   10, 13, 14, 158, 162, 181, 182, 245, 246, 378, 390, 468, 472
Albers, David   185, 246, 296
Albert, Burton   95, 246, 479
Alborough, Jez   23, 246
Alcock, Vivien   48, 246
Alcorn, John   22, 154, 155, 246, 441, 443
Alcott, Louisa May   51, 66, 246, 334, 415
Alda, Arlene   246
Alden, Betty   3, 246, 364
Alderson, Brian   81, 99, 161, 246, 342, 363, 469
Aldous, Kate   49, 172, 246, 312
Aldrich, Mary M.   208, 246, 305
Aldridge, Alan   230, 246, 480
Aldridge, James   59, 102, 246
Aleichem, Sholem   157, 246
Alexander, Frances   216, 246
Alexander, Lloyd   8, 26, 30, 73, 76, 83, 93, 95, 114, 131, 133, 160, 169, 177, 179, 180, 181, 182, 184, 185, 193, 246, 247, 292, 388, 410
Alexander, Martha G.   61, 68, 116, 141, 142, 214, 247
Alexander, Sue   93, 202, 203, 247, 250, 272, 329
Alexander, William P.   205, 247, 305, 399
Alford, Douglas   394
Aliki   33, 63, 76, 88, 135, 136, 148, 155, 177, 247, 260, 278, 354, 373
Allais, A.   23, 299, 462
Allan, Mabel Esther   26, 187, 247
Allard, Harry   11, 35, 42, 63, 70, 90, 96, 156, 172, 179, 188, 247, 437
Allee, Marjorie Hill   55, 165, 247, 248, 271, 316
Allen, Agnes   45, 248
Allen, Eleanor   221, 248
Allen, Eric   47, 248, 402
Allen, Frances C.   248
Allen, Gary   113, 248, 352
Allen, Jack   45, 248
Allen, Jeffrey   63, 248, 437
Allen, Jonathan   225, 248, 434
Allen, Judy   48, 77, 231, 248
Allen, Laura J.   248
Allen, Lorenzo   212, 248
Allen, Pamela   6, 58, 59, 60, 70, 109, 248
Allen, Richard E.   75, 248
Allen, Robert Thomas   194, 248, 472
Allen, Thomas B.   4, 29, 56, 159, 164, 181, 248, 289, 375
Allen, Thomas Benton   33, 248
Allende, Isabel   199, 248, 475

Allison, Bob   31, 248, 348, 377
Allison, Linda   248
Almedingen, E. M.   25, 214, 215, 248, 250
Almquist, Don   138, 249, 307
Aloise, Frank   136, 139, 187, 249, 391
Als, Roald   19, 249, 275
Alter, Judith M.   220, 249, 304
Alter, Robert Edmond   33, 249, 488, 467, 490
Althea   176, 249, 334
Altschuler, Franz   201, 249, 264
Altshuler, Shanne   84, 249, 481
Alvarez, Carlos Maria   10, 249, 412
Alvord, Douglas   25, 249
Ambrus, Victor G.   25, 26, 27, 46, 47, 57, 98, 99, 101, 197, 212, 213, 214, 235, 248, 249, 250, 258, 261, 286, 315, 321, 347, 363, 477, 478
Ames, Evelyn   209, 250, 326
Ames, Lee   88, 106, 210, 250, 463
Ames, Mildred   25, 250
Amundsen, Richard E.   141, 250, 319
Anckarsvard, Karin   211, 212, 250, 348, 433
Ancona, George   93, 148, 151, 159, 234, 247, 250, 295, 450
Anders, Hanns-Jorg   148, 250, 390
Andersen, Doris   44, 250
Andersen, Frederick   205, 250, 318
Andersen, Hans Christian   9, 10, 12, 38, 50, 51, 97, 104, 107, 156, 158, 178, 179, 185, 191, 192, 212, 244, 245, 249, 250, 251, 252, 261, 265, 267, 274, 280, 281, 282, 285, 290, 294, 298, 299, 300, 316, 317, 318, 322, 328, 330, 331, 332, 335, 343, 346, 347, 350, 352, 354, 364, 365, 366, 367, 368, 372, 380, 383, 384, 389, 390, 392, 393, 394, 400, 401, 402, 411, 412, 413, 419, 420, 423, 426, 435, 436, 439, 448, 449, 452, 454, 460, 462, 463, 464. 465. 466, 467, 468, 469, 470, 476, 482, 483, 489, 490, 492
Anderson, Bertha C.   174, 251, 301
Anderson, Clarence W.   204, 251
Anderson, Dave   251
Anderson, David   143, 251, 338
Anderson, David A.   119, 251
Anderson, Joy   33, 94, 251, 449
Anderson, Lonzo   244, 251
Anderson, Lucia   148, 251, 360
Anderson, Madelyn Klein   251
Anderson, Mildred N.   71, 251, 469
Anderson, Norman D.   251, 282
Anderson, Rachel   102, 251, 436

Anderson, Robert L.   *155, 251, 491*
Anderson, Rus   *210, 251, 415*
Ando, Hiroshige   *55, 251, 283, 401*
Andre, John   *162, 251, 346*
Andrews, Mary Evans   *67, 86, 251, 395*
Andrews, Roy Chapman   *32, 208, 251*
Andrist, Ralph K.   *229, 251, 269*
Anfousse, Ginette   *108, 251*
Angell, Judie   *80, 81, 194, 251*
Angelo, Valenti   *15, 51, 166, 252*
Anglund, Joan Walsh   *54, 252*
Anguissola, Giana   *9, 252, 489*
Annett, Cora   *68, 252, 403*
Anno, Masaichiro   *252*
Anno, Mitsumasa   *4, 10, 12, 13, 14, 23, 26, 27, 63, 68, 191, 214, 217, 252*
Anson, Jay   *200, 252*
Antal, Andrew   *252*
Antonucci, Emil   *79, 252, 349*
Appel, Benjamin   *137, 138, 141, 252, 283, 414*
Appiah, Peggy   *252*
Apple, Margot   *95, 126, 181, 224, 252, 292, 318, 465*
Arbuckle, Dorothy Fay   *106, 252*
Archer, Janet   *19, 48, 101, 174, 253, 310, 312, 474*
Archer, Jules   *230, 253*
Archer, Marion Fuller   *72, 92, 215, 253*
Archer, P. C.   *253*
Ardizzone, Edward   *9, 46, 49, 53, 98, 107, 154, 156, 157, 210, 212, 213, 253, 277, 335, 436, 474, 489*
Argent, Kerry   *14, 232, 253, 270, 293*
Argiroff, Louise   *253*
Arkin, Alan   *161, 253*
Armer, Laura Adams   *37, 253*
Armer, Sidney   *253*
Armitage, David   *91, 253*
Armitage, Ronda   *91, 253*
Armstrong, George   *86, 215, 253, 269*
Armstrong, Jennifer   *95, 254*
Armstrong, Patricia   *254*
Armstrong, Richard   *45, 210, 254, 380, 421*
Armstrong, William H.   *52, 103, 222, 254, 260*
Arno, Enrico   *3, 25, 254, 266*
Arnold, Caroline   *94, 149, 151, 203, 254, 361, 376, 377*
Arnold, Elliott   *205, 231, 254, 294, 360*
Arnold, Ralph   *47, 243, 254*
Arnold, Tedd   *71, 80, 90, 226, 254*
Arnold, Tim   *105, 254*
Arnosky, Jim   *69, 96, 227, 254*
Arntson, Herbert E.   *227, 254, 354*
Arora, Shirley L.   *3*
Arora, Shirley Lease   *85, 235, 254, 365*
Arrows, Tom Two   *83, 342*
Arthur, Robert   *138, 254, 413*
Artis, Vicki Kimmel   *72, 254, 385*
Artzybasheff, Boris   *37, 165, 166, 204, 205, 254, 367, 456*
Aruego, Ariane   *12, 13, 26, 61, 63, 160, 254, 255, 354, 410*
Aruego, Jose   *12, 13, 26, 61, 63, 156, 160, 254, 255, 354, 410*

Arundel, Jocelyn   *32, 255, 319*
Asare, Meshack   *109, 255, 489*
Asbjornsen, Peter Christen   *211, 255, 407, 452*
Asch, Frank   *12, 13, 61, 139, 141, 143, 255*
Aschmann, Helen Tann   *36, 255*
Ashabranner, Brent   *4, 29, 69, 204, 211, 227, 234, 255, 303, 315*
Ashabranner, Melissa   *69, 234, 255*
Ash, Russell   *192, 255, 377*
Ashforth, Camilla   *34, 255*
Ashley, Bernard   *48, 176, 255, 402*
Asimov, Isaac   *77, 227, 255*
Aska, Warabe   *104, 255, 315*
Aston, Phillippa   *221, 256, 335*
Atkinson, Joan   *79*
Atkinson, Kathie   *232, 256, 308, 372*
Atkinson, Linda   *115, 256*
Atwater, Florence   *49, 166, 238, 256, 417*
Atwater, Richard   *49, 238, 256, 417*
Atwood, Ann   *26, 201, 202, 256*
Aubry, Claude   *14, 109, 256, 310, 313, 326, 331, 451*
Ault, Phil   *230, 256*
Ault, Phillip H.   *71, 256, 339*
Austin, Neal F.   *256*
Australia, Diabetes   *75, 308, 388, 405, 436, 462*
Autry, Ewart A.   *36, 256*
Averill, Esther   *256*
Avery, Gillian Elise   *46, 47, 101, 256, 371, 392*
Avery, Kay   *207, 256, 280*
Avi   *30, 68, 94, 122, 144, 170, 173, 188, 193, 218, 225, 226, 256, 457*
Avi-Yonah, M.   *22, 246, 256*
Avishai, Susan   *194, 256, 376*
Awret, Irene   *120, 256*
Axelrod, Steve   *59, 256, 372*
Axmann, Hanne   *257*
Ayer, Margaret   *86, 207, 257, 276, 283*
Aylesworth, Jim   *129, 257, 348*
Ayto, Russell   *257*
Azon, Gary   *118, 257*

Babbitt, Natalie   *53, 61, 64, 68, 108, 116, 214, 217, 257*
Bach, Alice   *65, 257*
Bach, Richard   *257*
Bacon, Paul   *192, 235, 257, 357*
Bacon, Ronald Leonard   *5, 70, 257, 392*
Bader, Barbara   *179, 257, 352*
Baer, Edith   *257*
Bagshaw, Ruth   *140, 257, 290*
Bahti, Tom   *40, 216, 257, 263*
Bailey, Carolyn Sherwin   *167, 257, 349*
Bailey, Jean   *231, 257, 309*
Bailey, Margery   *205, 257, 483*
Bailey, Pearl   *118, 257*
Baillie, Allan   *15, 59, 60, 82, 110, 258*
Baity, Elizabeth Chesley   *167, 208, 258, 335*
Baker, Alan   *48, 230, 258, 474*
Baker, Betty   *64, 177, 228, 229, 258, 330, 401*

Baker, Charlotte   *52, 215, 216, 258, 452, 469*
Baker, Elizabeth   *207, 208, 216, 258, 369*
Baker, Jeannie   *29, 59, 60, 77, 110, 117, 190, 237, 258*
Baker, Keith   *223, 258*
Baker, Laura   *153, 258*
Baker, Leslie   *112, 258*
Baker, Margaret Joyce   *46, 208, 258, 262, 404*
Baker, Olaf   *28, 40, 158, 162, 258, 349*
Balch, Glenn   *31, 258, 309*
Balderson, Margaret   *47, 57, 236, 249, 258, 398*
Baldredge, Cyrus L.   *408*
Balet, Jan B.   *153, 258, 363, 364, 398*
Balian, Lorna   *70, 73, 80, 90, 92, 258, 259*
Balkwill, Fran   *195, 259*
Ball, Duncan   *227, 228, 259*
Ball, Robert   *205, 259, 469*
Ball, Zachary   *83, 212, 231, 259, 363, 439*
Bancroft, Bronwyn   *15, 259, 405*
Bancroft, Griffing   *68, 259, 368*
Bang, Molly   *27, 28, 29, 40, 41, 110, 259*
Banks, Lynne Reid   *11, 42, 98, 162, 181, 199, 225, 227, 259, 302, 378, 422*
Banks, Lynn Reid   *54, 105, 126, 164, 239, 352*
Banks, Sandra   *259*
Bannatyne-Cugnet, Jo   *259*
Bannatyne-Gugnet, Jo   *453*
Bannon, Laura   *49, 204, 209, 259, 276*
Barbeau, Charles Marius   *43, 259, 383, 483*
Barber, Antonia   *34, 100, 182, 192, 259, 263, 418*
Barber, Richard   *221, 259, 311*
Barberis, Franco   *22, 259*
Barclay, James   *174, 260, 466*
Barclift, Stephen T.   *92, 260*
Bare, Arnold Edwin   *37, 260, 406*
Barker, Carol   *98, 99, 260, 262*
Barker, Mary   *36, 260, 415*
Barker, Robert   *77, 260, 422*
Barkhouse, Joyce C.   *34, 260*
Barklem, Jill   *260*
Barkley, James   *52, 103, 222, 254, 260*
Barlowe, Dorothea   *260*
Barlowe, Sy   *260*
Barnard, Peggy   *57, 260, 373*
Barne, Kitty   *45, 206, 260, 353*
Barnes, Joseph   *56, 260, 346*
Barnes, Nancy   *86, 167, 260*
Barney, Maginel W.   *165, 260*
Barnhouse, Dorothy P.   *18, 260*
Barnstone, Aliki   *155, 260, 354*
Barnstone, Willis   *106, 260, 408*
Barnum, Jay Hyde   *38, 205, 260, 340*
Barokas, Bernard   *23, 260, 276*
Barrett, Angela   *125, 130, 198, 199, 260, 377, 382, 448, 492*
Barrett, Anne   *46, 260, 408*
Barrett, Jennifer   *69, 261, 481*
Barrett, Judi   *35, 62, 70, 95, 261*
Barrett, Judith   *90*

Barrett, Ron   *35, 62, 70, 90, 95, 157, 161, 261, 330, 466*

Barron, John N.   *208, 261*

Barry, Katharina   *136, 212, 261, 398*

Barry, Robert E.   *32, 261*

Barthelme, Donald   *61, 261*

Bartholomew, Barbara   *95, 261*

Barton, Byron   *61, 62, 156, 159, 162, 186, 214, 261, 361*

Barton, Jill   *100, 261*

Bartos-Hoeppner, Barbara   *212, 249*

Baruffi, Andrea   *261*

Base, Graeme   *59, 60, 117, 237, 261*

Bash, Barbara   *204, 261*

Baskin, Hosea   *12, 13, 40, 261*

Baskin, Leonard   *12, 13, 40, 63, 156, 158, 164, 179, 181, 261, 262, 385*

Bate, Lucy   *41, 262, 316*

Bates, Betty   *194, 262, 330*

Bates, Dianne   *16, 228, 262*

Bates, Herbert E.   *98, 260, 262*

Bates, Leo   *208, 258, 262*

Bates, Robert L.   *150, 262, 391*

Batherman, Muriel   *64, 136, 212, 262, 350*

Bauer, Caroline Feller   *68, 157, 203, 262, 471*

Bauer, Helen   *71, 262, 443*

Bauer, Joan   *75, 262*

Bauer, John   *62, 262, 430*

Bauer, Marion Dane   *4, 81, 92, 93, 105, 228, 232, 262*

Baum, Arline   *262*

Baum, Joseph   *262*

Baum, L. Frank   *17, 18, 51, 262, 280, 318, 319, 334, 339, 345, 347, 349, 361, 366, 369, 370, 381, 409, 423, 433, 435, 438, 443, 444, 449, 466, 468, 483*

Baum, Louis   *100, 262, 276*

Baumann, Hans   *17, 209, 210, 212, 263, 386, 482, 490*

Baumel, Judith Tydor   *120, 263*

Baumgartner, Robert   *85, 263, 415*

Bawden, Nina   *47, 101, 179, 181, 183, 185, 186, 188, 190, 263, 282, 423, 483*

Bayless, Roger   *133, 263, 409*

Bayley, Dorothy   *205, 263, 455*

Bayley, Nicola   *34, 100, 125, 259, 263, 440*

Baylis, Sarah   *263*

Baylor, Byrd   *13, 14, 26, 40, 96, 148, 177, 216, 257, 263, 471, 472*

Baynes, Pauline   *46, 50, 99, 163, 181, 214, 239, 263, 321, 422, 478*

Beadle, George   *78, 263, 264*

Beadle, Jeremy   *264*

Beadle, Muriel   *78, 263, 264*

Beake, Lesley   *84, 264*

Beame, Rona   *151, 264*

Bear, Polar   *192, 290, 438*

Beasley, Dick   *216*

Beaton, C.   *264*

Beattie, Janet   *209, 264, 393*

Beatty, John   *18, 71, 201, 249, 264, 272, 301, 488*

Beatty, Patricia   *4, 18, 71, 72, 93, 173, 201, 202, 203, 249, 264, 272, 301, 451, 486, 488*

Beaude, Pierre Marie   *24*

Bebenroth, Charlotta M.   *174, 264, 292*

Beck, Charles   *135, 207, 264, 447*

Becker, Charlotte   *174, 205, 264, 311*

Becker, Joyce   *264*

Beckman, Delores   *111, 264*

Bedard, Michael   *45, 97, 236, 264*

Beddows, Eric   *29, 44, 104, 110, 111, 131, 170, 264, 315, 340, 392*

Bednarova, Eva   *19, 264*

Bee, Ronald J.   *69, 264, 336*

Beebe, B. F.   *32, 264*

Beech, Carol   *227, 265, 390*

Beeler, Nelson F.   *78, 265, 355*

Begg, Barbara   *212, 265, 393*

Begin, Maryjane   *21, 265, 485*

Begley, Ed   *51, 265, 407*

Behn, Harry   *216, 265*

Behrangi, Samad   *22, 265, 448*

Behrens, Michael   *16, 265*

Behrman, Carol H.   *265*

Beim, Jerrold   *206, 265, 435*

Beim, Lorraine   *206, 265, 435*

Beirne, Barbara   *145, 146, 265, 481*

Bell, Angela   *221, 265, 408*

Bell, Anthea   *17, 84, 108, 109, 161, 179, 250, 265, 330, 387, 439, 461, 464, 483*

Bell, Clare   *111, 265*

Bell, Corydon   *83, 171, 208, 213, 265, 266, 322, 341*

Bell, Edwina   *108, 265, 463*

Bell, Frederic   *161, 265, 466*

Bell, Margaret E.   *78, 208, 265, 492*

Bell, Thelma H.   *83, 265, 266*

Bell, Thelma Harrington   *208, 265, 266*

Bell, William   *195, 236, 266*

Bellairs, John   *128, 160, 180, 224, 225, 266, 331, 358*

Belleguie, Andre   *23, 266, 479*

Belloc, Hilaire   *12, 156, 266, 403*

Belpre, Pura   *12, 266*

Belting, Natalia M.   *39, 63, 155, 216, 266, 283, 300, 322, 323*

Belton, Robyn   *70, 266, 306*

Bemelmans, Ludwig   *37, 38, 208, 210, 266*

Benary-Isbert, Margot   *3, 51, 201, 209, 254, 266*

Ben-Asher, Naomi   *114, 266, 417*

Benchley, Nathaniel   *230, 266*

Bendick, Jeanne   *30, 96, 147, 207, 209, 266, 272*

Benedum, Patricia   *228*

Benjamin, Carol Lea   *25*

Benjamin, Carol Lee   *24, 266*

Benjamin, Hameed   *218, 266, 466*

Bennett, Anna Elizabeth   *83, 267*

Bennett, Dorothy Agnes   *206, 267*

Bennett, Jay   *267*

Bennett, Jill   *42, 82, 182, 218, 267, 311, 406*

Bennett, John   *267*

Bennett, Rainey   *211, 267*

Benson, Gerard   *197, 267*

Benson, Mildred   *33, 267*

Benson, Patrick   *34, 130, 192, 199, 267, 311, 440, 441, 451*

Benson, Robert   *82, 267, 268, 425*

Bentley, Nicolas   *45, 267, 424*

Berenstain, Jan   *76, 122, 267*

Berenstain, Stan   *35, 267*

Berenzy, Alix   *24, 267*

Berg, Jean H.   *86, 267*

Berg, Ron   *104, 267, 418*

Berger, Barbara Helen   *94, 268*

Berger, Larry   *82, 267, 268, 425*

Bergere, Richard   *78, 268, 396*

Berke, Ernest   *33, 268*

Berna, Paul   *268, 283*

Bernal C. Payne, Jr.   *135, 474*

Bernard, George   *221, 268, 469*

Berndt, Catherine   *74, 268*

Bernhard, Josephine B.   *206, 268, 429*

Bernstein, Michael J.   *69, 93, 268, 355*

Bernstein, Zena   *26, 52, 126, 132, 169, 222, 231, 239, 268, 465*

Berridge, Celia   *199, 268*

Berry, Erick   *165, 166, 207, 210, 268, 370, 412*

Berry, James   *30, 118, 197, 198, 268, 277*

Berson, Harold   *61, 143, 268*

Bertelli, Mariella   *111, 268, 347*

Bertin, Gerald   *155, 268, 419*

Bertol, Roland   *214, 268, 483*

Bess, Clayton   *203, 268*

Best, Herbert   *268*

Besterman, Catherine   *167, 268, 294*

Besunder, Marvin   *139, 269, 435*

Betts, Ethel F.   *51, 269, 286*

Betz, Eva K.   *136, 269, 467*

Bevan, Clare   *82, 269*

Beyer, Audrey W.   *25, 269, 322*

Beyer, Audrey White   *269, 323*

Bhend, Kathi   *24, 269, 394*

Bianchi, John   *151, 269, 322*

Bianco, Margery   *166, 269*

Bice, Clare   *43, 123, 269, 298, 419*

Bierhorst, John   *61, 64, 204, 215, 234, 269*

Biesterveld, Betty   *86, 253, 269*

Biesty, Stephen   *34, 269, 480*

Bileck, Marvin   *39, 154, 269*

Bilibin, Ivan   *63, 269, 429, 486*

Billman, Carol   *66, 269*

Billout, Guy   *269*

Binch, Caroline   *100, 269, 380*

Binder-Strassfurt, Eberhard   *22, 269*

Bing, Jon   *109, 269, 419*

Bingham, Edwin R.   *229, 251, 269*

Binns, Archie   *208, 270, 287*

Birch, Reginald   *204, 270, 491*

Bird, Bettina   *232, 270*

Birnbaum, Abe   *38, 270*

Bishop, Claire Huchet   *49, 55, 168, 207, 209, 270, 327*

Bishop, Gavin   *5, 70, 270*

Bixby, William   *78, 270, 320*

Bixler, Phyllis   *65, 270*

Bjorklund, Lorence F.   *71, 86, 106, 136, 168, 174, 195, 212, 216, 228, 270, 345, 350, 399, 402*

Bjorkman, Steve   *184, 220, 270, 334, 421*
Black, Helen   *204, 270, 486*
Black, Irma Simonton   *21, 80, 244, 270, 272, 274, 277, 289, 291, 295, 302, 321, 340, 359, 362, 365, 399, 403, 427, 440*
Black, Mary Martin   *208, 270, 319*
Blackburn, William   *65, 270*
Blackwood, Gary L.   *87, 270*
Blackwood, Mary   *14, 253, 270*
Blades, Ann   *44, 97, 103, 104, 270, 271*
Blair, Helen   *55, 167, 206, 247, 271, 359, 447*
Blair, Mary   *208, 271, 410*
Blaisdell, Elinore   *86, 271*
Blake, Michael   *199, 271*
Blake, Quentin   *25, 34, 54, 56, 81, 98, 99, 105, 108, 125, 126, 135, 157, 163, 172, 190, 196, 198, 224, 225, 227, 228, 230, 231, 271, 311, 379*
Blake, Robert J.   *96, 271*
Blanc, Esther Silverstein   *18, 115, 219, 271, 323*
Blank, Pius   *90, 271, 482*
Blankenbaker, Frances   *91, 271*
Blathwayt, Benedict   *198, 271*
Blegvad, Erik   *63, 157, 168, 170, 174, 187, 216, 271, 272, 274, 307, 403, 414, 425, 426*
Blegvad, Lenore   *272*
Blickenstaff, Wayne   *33, 272, 314*
Blishen, Edward   *47, 98, 99, 272, 350, 402*
Bloch, Lucienne   *154, 207, 272, 277, 387*
Bloch, Marie H.   *210, 272, 436*
Bloom, Lloyd   *21, 29, 87, 93, 115, 170, 203, 247, 272, 359, 397, 399, 426, 433*
Blos, Joan W.   *7, 29, 170, 272, 348*
Blough, Glenn O.   *96, 266, 272*
Bluemle, Andrew   *78, 272*
Blumberg, Rhoda   *18, 85, 94, 272*
Blumberg, Rhonda   *28*
Blume, Judy   *11, 22, 25, 35, 42, 64, 65, 70, 73, 74, 80, 84, 88, 89, 92, 96, 98, 103, 112, 121, 122, 126, 128, 134, 140, 141, 143, 145, 172, 196, 197, 199, 200, 218, 220, 224, 225, 226, 227, 237, 238, 239, 240, 272, 273, 325, 424*
Blundell, Tony   *130, 273, 443*
Blythe, Gary   *100, 130, 273*
Blyton, Enid   *30, 273*
Bobak, Cathy   *89, 273, 288*
Bobri   *152, 204, 210, 273, 284, 425, 491*
Bobri, Vladimir   *152, 210, 273, 284, 425, 491*
Bock, Vera   *138, 165, 206, 210, 273, 389, 406, 490*
Boddy, Joseph   *91, 273, 374*
Bode, Janet   *235, 273*
Bode, Regina   *205, 273, 382*
Bodecker, N. M.   *63, 64, 68, 156, 174, 209, 211, 244, 272, 274, 329*
Bodker, Cecil   *10, 17, 27, 274, 413, 482*
Bodmer, Karl   *95, 185, 190, 274, 344*
Boehm, Linda   *142, 274, 438*
Boeke, Kees   *274*
Bograd, Larry   *21, 274*
Bohdal, Susi   *179, 274, 448*

Bolden, Melvin R.   *139, 274, 398*
Boles, Paul   *106, 274*
Bollen, Roger   *184, 274*
Bolliger, Max   *61, 245, 274, 284*
Bolognese, Donald   *71, 142, 211, 214, 228, 230, 274, 352, 428*
Bolton, Nancy   *90, 274, 454*
Bond, Felicia   *35, 42, 70, 80, 90, 135, 179, 185, 274, 403, 464*
Bond, Nancy   *26, 28, 111, 169, 222, 274, 314*
Bond, Susan   *139, 274, 420*
Bonham, Frank   *187, 202, 216, 235, 274, 275*
Bonners, Susan   *8, 275*
Bonsall, C. N.   *275*
Bonsall, Crosby   *215, 275, 460*
Bontemps, Arna Wendell   *3, 275, 430*
Bonzon, Paul Jacques   *275*
Boock, Paula   *6, 275*
Booth, David   *104, 111, 275, 319, 419*
Booth, George   *183, 275*
Booth, Graham   *148, 202, 275, 373*
Booth, Jack   *443*
Bordier, Georgette   *63, 275*
Borek, Ernest   *78, 275*
Borland, Kathryn K.   *106, 244, 275*
Borner, Hanne   *19, 249, 275*
Bornstein, Ruth   *202, 275, 444*
Borten, Helen   *135, 136, 153, 275, 278, 428*
Bosmajian, Hamida   *66, 275*
Bosse, Malcom J.   *109, 275, 370*
Bostelmann, Else   *174, 275, 308, 348*
Boston, Lucy M.   *46, 51, 213, 275, 276*
Boston, Peter   *46, 51, 213, 275, 276*
Bosworth, Allen R.   *71, 344*
Botermans, Jack   *151, 276, 286*
Bothma, Alida   *127*
Bothwell, Jean   *207, 257, 276*
Boucher, Joelle   *23, 260, 276*
Bougard, Marie-Therese   *222, 276, 450*
Bouis, Antonia W.   *110, 276*
Bouma, Paddy   *100, 262, 276*
Bourgeois, Paulette   *107, 276, 413*
Bourke, Linda   *88, 276, 450, 489*
Boutis, Victoria   *4, 276*
Bowden, Joan Chase   *27, 276, 281*
Bowen, Betsy   *157, 276, 451*
Bowen, Keith   *57, 276, 324*
Bowen, Robert S.   *31, 276*
Bowen, William A.   *276*
Bowman, James Cloyd   *49, 204, 259, 276*
Bowman, Leslie W.   *82, 276, 406*
Boxer, Devorah   *276*
Boyce, Madeleine   *276, 424*
Boyce, Sonia   *197, 268, 277*
Boyd, Candy Dawson   *118, 277*
Boyd, William   *21, 277*
Boyer, Edward   *277*
Boyer, Robert E.   *277*
Boyle, Madeleine   *57*
Boyle, Mildred   *166, 167, 206, 238, 277*
Boynton, Sandra   *21, 277*
Bozzo, Frank   *47, 101, 132, 215, 245, 277, 444*
Bradbury, Christopher   *23, 277, 305*

Bradbury, Ray   *32, 153, 277, 352*
Bradfield, Roger   *33, 91, 277, 478*
Bradford, Karleen   *77, 236, 277*
Bradford, Margaret   *207, 272, 277*
Bradley, Duane   *3, 235, 277, 395*
Bradley, Helen   *11, 277*
Bradley, John   *191, 198, 277, 437*
Brady, Irene   *120, 277*
Braginetz, Donna   *152, 332, 358, 383*
Brancato, Robin   *277*
Brand, Christianna   *212, 253, 277, 423*
Brand, Pippa   *148, 277, 373, 397, 458*
Brand, Stewart   *278*
Brandi, Lillian   *35, 278*
Brandis, G. Brender   *7, 20, 236, 278*
Brandis, Marianne   *7, 20, 236, 278*
Brandt, Katrin   *22, 278, 363, 364*
Branfield, John   *48, 278*
Branley, Franklyn M.   *62, 77, 96, 135, 136, 138, 140, 275, 278, 308, 348, 355, 405*
Bransby, Lawrence   *127*
Branscum, Robbie   *87, 162, 163, 185, 188, 278*
Braun, Kathy   *155, 278, 446*
Braymer, Marjorie   *211, 278*
Breinburg, Petronella   *99, 278, 426*
Brenner, Anita   *33, 152, 205, 209, 278, 279, 295*
Brenner, Barbara   *177, 211, 214, 279, 401*
Brentano, Clemens   *279*
Breslin, Theresa   *82, 279*
Brett, Jan   *191, 279*
Brewster, Patience   *96, 279, 413*
Bridgers, Sue Ellen   *6, 27, 68, 279*
Bridwell, Norman   *64, 279*
Brier, Howard M.   *205, 279, 310*
Brierley, Louise   *159, 279, 317*
Briggs, Katharine   *279, 353*
Briggs, Katherine M.   *130, 279*
Briggs, Raymond   *12, 14, 27, 34, 53, 62, 98, 99, 125, 176, 191, 199, 214, 279, 342*
Bright, Robert   *210, 279*
Brill, Edith   *99, 279, 478*
Brindze, Ruth   *148, 206, 279, 292*
Brink, Carol Ryrie   *49, 117, 166, 201, 279*
Brinsmead, Hesba Fay   *57, 58, 279, 431*
Brison-Stack, Guy   *142, 279, 331, 515*
Brisson, Pat   *146, 184, 279, 282*
Brittain, Bill   *81, 280*
Brittain, William   *170, 197, 280, 355*
Brochman, Odd   *9, 280*
Brock, Emma L.   *204, 280*
Broder, Bill   *64, 280*
Broekel, Ray   *61, 63, 280, 282*
Bromhall, Winifred   *207, 256*
Bronowski, Jacob   *78, 280, 485*
Brook, Judith   *46, 280*
Brooke, L. Leslie   *50, 280, 295*
Brookins, Dana   *202, 280*
Brooks, Bruce   *28, 94, 280*
Brooks, Jerome   *194, 280*
Brooks, Lester J.   *61, 280*
Brooks, Martha   *30, 45, 236, 280*

Brooks, Polly   28, 280
Brooks, Ron   58, 101, 147, 280
Brosseit, Virginia   87, 280
Brouwer, Jack   105, 280
Brown, Bill   71, 280
Brown, Buck   142, 280, 316
Brown, Elizabeth Burton   280
Brown, Fern G.   194, 281
Brown, Irene Bennett   120, 230, 281
Brown, Judith Gwyn   79, 89, 122, 187, 237, 281
Brown, Laurenc Krasny   281
Brown, Lloyd A.   32, 281
Brown, Marbury   137, 281, 447
Brown, Marc   27, 227, 243, 276, 281
Brown, Marcia   26, 38, 39, 41, 51, 154, 193, 214, 224, 233, 250, 281, 293, 476
Brown, Margaret Wise   37, 39, 79, 117, 157, 178, 207, 208, 281, 295, 352, 373, 387, 432
Brown, Margery W.   140, 281
Brown, Mary G.   282
Brown, P.   31, 282, 399
Brown, Palmer   210, 282
Brown, Pam   221, 282
Brown, Paul   30, 86, 206, 207, 282, 325, 329
Brown, Richard   61, 145, 146, 280, 282
Brown, Rick   279, 282
Brown, Roy   108, 282, 370
Brown, Ruth   100, 192, 282, 376
Brown, Walter R.   251, 282
Brown, William F.   282
Browne, Anthony   29, 100, 109, 125, 158, 181, 183, 282, 291, 363
Browne, Lance   282
Browne, Vee   229, 282
Browning, D. B.   171, 282
Bruckner, Karl   9, 10, 282
Bruner, Stephen   151, 282, 383
Brunkus, Denise   74, 283
Bryan, Ashley   103, 118, 119, 178, 183, 185, 224, 283, 414
Bryan, Catherine   206, 283, 433
Bryant, Chester   86, 257, 283
Bryant, Samuel   141, 169, 283, 465
Bryant, Samuel H.   252, 283
Bryson, Bernarda   25, 39, 51, 52, 136, 212, 216, 266, 283, 298
Bubley, Esther   88, 283
Buchanan, Heather S.   283
Buchanan, William J.   200, 283
Buchanan-Brown, John   283
Buchenholz, Bruce   283
Bucholtz-Ross, Linda   283
Buchwald, Art   144, 283, 484
Buchwald, Emilie   215, 283, 341
Buck, Pearl   55, 251, 283, 401
Buck, Pearl S.   109, 283, 353
Buckingham, Simon   283
Buczynski, Waldemar   59, 109, 283, 478
Budbill, David   84, 284
Budney, Blossom   273, 284
Buff, Conrad   31, 37, 201, 284
Buff, Mary   31, 37, 284
Buffett, Jimmy   16, 284, 314
Buffett, Savannah Jane   16, 284, 314

Buffie, Margaret   44, 236, 284
Bull, Angela   284
Bull, Johan   204, 284
Bulla, Clyde Robert   31, 61, 67, 71, 196, 197, 200, 201, 202, 203, 216, 245, 274, 284, 285, 360
Bullard, Pamela   68, 234, 284
Bunn, Alan   6, 284
Bunting, Eve   5, 42, 72, 93, 96, 134, 182, 196, 199, 200, 202, 203, 218, 223, 225, 284, 285, 291, 316, 378, 436
Burch, Robert   3, 27, 55, 89, 186, 212, 217, 285, 417
Burchard, Peter   21, 31, 51, 67, 168, 188, 230, 235, 284, 285, 369, 403, 461
Burgemeestre, Kevin   228, 262
Burger, Carl   15, 44, 52, 82, 83, 106, 107, 134, 137, 168, 195, 231, 239, 243, 285, 286, 354, 463
Burgess, Melvin   48, 285
Burgess-Kohn, Jane   73, 285
Burglon, Nora   165, 285, 313
Burgwyn, Mebane H.   171, 285, 474
Burkert, Nancy Ekholm   22, 30, 40, 51, 53, 126, 160, 183, 190, 212, 250, 285, 311, 363, 364, 393, 419
Burleigh, Robert   285
Burleson, Elizabeth   216, 229, 286
Burn, Doris   140, 286, 351
Burnett, Frances Hodgson   50, 51, 65, 74, 269, 270, 286
Burnford, Shelia Every   15, 44, 52, 82, 83, 107, 231, 239, 285, 286
Burnie, David   100, 195, 286, 293
Burningham, John   24, 26, 61, 64, 98, 99, 125, 156, 157, 158, 160, 182, 183, 239, 286, 340, 360
Burns, Irene   84, 286, 333
Burns, Marilyn   63, 286
Burns, Robert   209, 286, 333
Burrett, Tony   151, 276, 286
Burris, Burmah   137, 286, 290
Burstein, Chaya M.   114, 115, 286
Burstein, John   142, 286, 407
Burt, Roger   82, 286
Burton, Earl   207, 286, 287
Burton, Hester   26, 46, 98, 212, 249, 286
Burton, Jane   24, 192, 287
Burton, Linette   207, 286, 287
Burton, Philip   141, 287, 471
Burton, Virginia Lee   37, 38, 49, 287, 434
Bush, John   192, 287, 473
Bush, Terri   21, 287, 398
Busnar, Gene   287
Busoni, Rafaello   50, 208, 270, 287
Busoni, Raphael   86, 287, 320
Buss, Fran Leeper   5, 105, 287, 309
Butcher, Julia   287
Butler, Beverly   43, 92, 215, 287
Butler, Francelia   54, 65, 66, 287
Butler, John   24, 287
Butterworth, Emma M.   16, 287
Butterworth, Oliver   52, 211, 287, 312, 318
Butterworth, William E.   16, 136, 137, 287, 472

Buxbaum, Susan Kovacs   8, 288, 301
Buxton, Jane H.   192, 288, 479
Byard, Carole   41, 118, 119, 288, 362
Byard, Carole M.   141, 288, 289
Byars, Betsy   7, 27, 42, 52, 56, 74, 80, 84, 89, 92, 109, 116, 124, 132, 134, 162, 163, 169, 179, 181, 183, 184, 193, 196, 197, 200, 218, 222, 226, 232, 235, 273, 288, 301, 362, 364, 384, 428, 468
Byars, Guy   197, 288
Bygott, David   222, 288
Byrd, Robert   63, 288, 410

Caesar, Gene   228, 288
Calabro, Marian   146, 288
Calder, Alexander   155, 288, 421
Calhoun, Mary   27, 70, 92, 93, 226, 288, 389
Callaert, Jacques   36, 288, 469
Callahan, Dorothy   141, 143, 288, 289
Callaway, Kathy   87, 289
Calvert, Patricia   87, 199, 289
Camazine, Cynthia   151, 289
Camazine, Scott   151, 289
Camboni, Daniela   109, 289
Cameron, Ann   4, 21, 56, 181, 248, 289
Cameron, Duncan F.   11
Cameron, Eleanor   26, 71, 85, 117, 132, 160, 179, 180, 183, 187, 201, 214, 289, 389, 411, 468, 469
Cameron, Polly   139, 289
Cameron, Tracey   145, 289
Campbell, Alfred S.   206, 289
Campbell, Camilla   216, 289
Campbell, Marjorie   97, 289
Campbell, Marjorie W.   404
Campbell, Stan   211, 289, 322
Campbell, Wanda Jay   216, 289
Cannon, A. E. (Ann Edwards)   75, 289
Canty, Mary   139, 289, 356
Capron, Jean   138, 289
Caputo, Robert   149, 289, 384
Carey, Joanna   198, 222, 289, 462
Carey, Mary V.   203, 289
Carey, Valerie Scho   94, 181, 290, 427
Carigiet, Alois   10, 152, 290, 296
Carle, Eric   11, 12, 13, 14, 22, 35, 116, 192, 214, 290, 438
Carleton, Barbee Oliver   187, 290
Carley, Wayne   140, 257, 290
Carlson, Bernice Wells   136, 137, 138, 141, 143, 286, 290, 306, 443, 451
Carlson, Dale Bick   68, 215, 290, 461, 462
Carlson, Maria   179, 290, 449, 484
Carlson, Natalie Savage   31, 32, 55, 168, 208, 209, 210, 235, 290, 329, 401, 453, 454, 474
Carmer, Carl L.   208, 290, 304
Carmi, Giori   219, 290, 406
Carner, Chas   162, 290, 291
Caroselli, Remus F.   188, 290
Carpenter, Edmund   52, 290
Carr, Harriet   187, 290
Carr, Mary Jane   166, 291, 381
Carrick, Carol   42, 63, 148, 164, 291

Carrick, Donald   *5, 21, 42, 62, 63, 69,*
128, 148, 162, 164, 182, 203, 284, 285,
290, 291, 302, 345, 416, 436
Carris, Joan   *81, 112, 146, 226, 238, 291,*
456, 461, 475
Carris, Joan Davenport   *146, 291, 461*
Carrithers, Mary   *142, 291*
Carroll, Latrobe   *171, 291*
Carroll, Lewis   *8, 23, 49, 50, 51, 52, 53,*
63, 100, 125, 140, 156, 183, 199, 243,
244, 245, 246, 250, 252, 253, 254, 256,
257, 258, 259, 260, 262, 263, 265, 266,
268, 269, 270, 275, 276, 279, 280, 281,
282, 283, 285, 286, 287, 288, 290, 291,
295, 296, 297, 298, 299, 300, 306, 307,
308, 309,. 310, 311, 312, 314, 315, 316,
317, 319, 321, 322, 323, 324, 326, 328,
330, 331, 332, 333, 334, 335, 336, 338,
340, 341, 342, 343, 345, 346, 347, 348,
349, 350, 351, 352, 354, 355, 356, 357,
360, 362, 363, 364, 365, 366, 368, 370,
371, 372, 373, 375, 379, 381, 382, 386,
392, 393, 395, 397, 398, 399, 400, 401,
402, 403, 404, 405, 406, 407, 409, 410,
411, 413, 415, 416, 417, 418, 419, 420,
421, 422, 423, 424, 428, 430, 432, 436,
440, 441, 443, 444, 445, 446, 447, 448,
451, 455, 456, 459, 460, 461, 462, 463,.
464, 465, 466, 467, 468, 469, 472, 474,
475, 479, 480, 482, 483, 485, 486, 487,
488, 491, 492
Carroll, Pamela   *94, 291, 468, 487*
Carroll, Ruth   *171, 291*
Carson, John F.   *106, 291*
Carter, Alden R.   *80, 199, 292*
Carter, Angela   *100, 125, 292, 342*
Carter, Bebby L.   *184, 247, 292*
Carter, David A.   *183, 192, 292*
Carter, Dorothy Sharp   *62, 292, 388*
Carter, Forrest   *8, 292*
Carter, Helene   *206, 279, 292*
Carter, Peter   *48, 102, 173, 292, 394, 491*
Cartlidge, Michelle   *129, 292*
Cartwright, Pauline   *70, 292, 332*
Cartwright, Reg   *130, 182, 292, 372, 406*
Cartwright, Sally   *148, 292, 366*
Carty, Leo   *73, 292, 439, 458*
Cary   *139, 141, 292, 317, 435*
Cary, Louis F.   *141, 435*
Cassedy, Sylvia   *122, 292*
Cassel, Lili   *235, 292*
Castle, Jane   *208, 292, 335*
Caswell, Edward   *174, 264, 292*
Cate, Dick   *176, 292*
Catling, Patrick   *126, 224, 252, 292*
Catrow, David   *160, 292*
Catterwall, Thelma   *232, 253, 293*
Caudill, Rebecca   *21, 39, 54, 67, 86, 103,*
115, 167, 208, 209, 217, 257, 293, 326,
352, 364, 395, 455, 460
Caufield, Don   *84, 293, 469*
Caufield, Joan   *84, 293, 469*
Cauley, Lorinda Bryan   *87, 293, 421*
Causley, Charles   *125, 197, 293, 342, 402*
Cavallo, Diane   *61, 293*
Cavanah, Frances   *106, 293, 388*

Cavanna, Betty   *137, 141, 187, 207, 293,*
362, 445
Cawley, Winifred   *101, 293*
Cazet, Denys   *42, 293*
Cebulash, Mel   *140, 144, 293, 329, 466*
Cecil, Edward   *155, 293, 472*
Cecil, Laura   *130, 293, 298*
Cellini, Joseph   *85, 87, 226, 293, 367*
Chadwick, Peter   *100, 286, 293*
Chaffin, Lillie D.   *56, 294*
Chagall, Marc   *85, 294, 362*
Chaikin, Miriam   *115, 219, 294, 449*
Chalk, Gary   *121, 228, 294, 392*
Challis, George   *205, 294*
Chalmers, Mary   *137, 142, 210, 294*
Chamberlain, Christopher   *47, 294, 305,*
318
Chamberlain, Margaret   *56, 294, 349, 350*
Chambers, Aidan   *65, 82, 109, 294*
Chambliss, Maxie   *145, 294, 305*
Chan, Chih-Yi   *37, 294*
Chan, Plato   *37, 294*
Chan, Shirley   *148, 294*
Chandler, David   *150, 294, 314*
Chandra, Avinash   *9, 294, 452*
Chang, Fa-Shun   *31, 294, 566*
Chang, Ina   *105, 294*
Chapman, Carol   *42, 90, 294, 465*
Chapman, Frederick T.   *167, 231, 254,*
294, 394
Chapman, Gaynor   *99, 294, 363*
Chapman, Sydney   *78, 294*
Chappell, Warren   *167, 206, 268, 294*
Charbonneau, Eileen   *95, 294*
Charles, Robert H.   *50, 280, 295*
Charley   *99, 103, 208, 257, 264, 290,*
293, 364, 402, 469
Charlip, Remy   *21, 22, 26, 33, 68, 148,*
155, 156, 159, 250, 295, 399, 435, 450
Charlot, Jean   *31, 33, 37, 38, 152, 167,*
168, 205, 209, 278, 279, 281, 295, 297,
411, 491
Chase, Ken   *110*
Chasek, Judith   *62, 295, 457*
Chastain, Madye Lee   *167, 295, 306, 376*
Chauncy, Nan   *32, 54, 57, 107, 295, 305,*
383, 456, 466
Chavez, Edward   *201, 295, 416*
Chee, Cheng-Khee   *8, 112, 129, 295*
Cheefu, students in   *216*
Chekhov, Anton   *98, 295, 325*
Chen, Ju-Hong   *181, 295, 455*
Chen, Tony   *3, 61, 63, 192, 295, 349,*
355, 441, 481
Chermayeff, Ivan   *211, 296, 459*
Cherry, Lynne   *54, 149, 186, 296*
Chess, Victoria   *11, 179, 181, 185, 296,*
358, 374, 397
Chessare, Michele   *81, 296, 404*
Chester, Michael   *33, 296, 368*
Chesterman, John   *149, 296, 437, 440*
Chetwin, Grace   *183, 296*
Chiasson, John   *29, 296*
Chick, Sandra   *177, 296*
Childress, Alice   *3, 53, 132, 160, 162,*
235, 296
Childs, Katherine   *296*

Childs, Kathleen   *123*
Chilton, Charles   *228, 296*
Chilton, Irma   *222, 296*
Ching, Chi Yee   *204, 307*
Ching, Yenchi Tiao T'u   *204, 307*
Chirinos, Lito   *63, 296, 435*
Chisholm, James   *229, 296, 382*
Chittum, Ida   *52, 296*
Chocolate, Deborah Newton   *185, 246,*
296
Chonz, Selina   *152, 290, 296*
Chorao, Kay   *62, 68, 69, 146, 296*
Chrisman, Arthur Bowie   *165, 296, 372*
Christelow, Eileen   *92, 113, 121, 122,*
296, 297, 312
Christensen, Gardell Dano   *71, 297, 453*
Christian, Mary Blount   *188, 297*
Christiana, David   *145, 297*
Christopher, John   *67, 101, 180, 217, 297*
Chubb, Thomas C.   *32, 297, 483*
Churcher, Betty   *221, 297*
Chwast, Jacqueline   *210, 297, 426*
Chwast, Seymour   *61, 115, 155, 182,*
184, 297, 316, 354, 355, 357, 448
Ciardi, John   *32, 134, 135, 137, 138, 153,*
154, 155, 194, 211, 297, 352, 358, 450,
467
Clancy, Joseph P.   *214, 297*
Clapp, Patricia   *51, 131, 145, 297*
Clark, Ann Nolan   *37, 167, 177, 193,*
205, 208, 209, 210, 295, 297, 376, 481
Clark, Brenda   *104, 111, 297, 385*
Clark, Catherine Anthony   *43, 269, 298*
Clark, Emma Chichester   *130, 293, 298*
Clark, Joan   *44, 217, 298*
Clark, Leonard   *46, 65, 99, 298, 372, 385*
Clark, Mary Higgins   *22, 138, 298*
Clark, Mavis Thorpe   *57, 298, 447*
Clark, Phyllis E.   *4, 298, 419*
Clarke, Arthur C.   *32, 298*
Clarke, Gus   *130, 298*
Clarke, Pauline   *46, 51, 107, 212, 283,*
297, 298, 387, 421
Clarke, Peter   *228, 298, 403*
Claveloux, Nicole   *10, 155, 298, 452*
Clay, Will   *119, 298*
Cleary, Beverly   *7, 18, 27, 35, 36, 69, 72,*
79, 83, 84, 85, 88, 89, 92, 93, 98, 103,
108, 112, 121, 122, 126, 128, 134, 163,
170, 179, 180, 190, 193, 196, 197, 217,
218, 220, 222, 224, 226, 228, 231, 233,
239, 298, 299, 313, 411, 423
Cleaver, Bill   *26, 53, 131, 132, 133, 161,*
230, 299, 438
Cleaver, Elizabeth   *10, 44, 97, 103, 108,*
111, 179, 267, 299, 325
Cleaver, Vera   *26, 53, 230, 299, 438*
Clemens, Samuel   *50, 51, 299, 400, 432*
Clement, Charles   *210, 299*
Clement, Frederic   *20, 299, 448*
Clement, Rod   *237, 299*
Clements, Bruce   *132, 299*
Clifford, Eth   *196, 238, 300, 385*
Clifford, Mary Louise   *139, 300*
Clifford, Peggy   *155, 300*
Clifford, Rowan   *102, 300, 478*
Clifford, Sandy   *74, 300*

Clifton, Lucille   *4, 118, 300, 322, 362*
Climo, Lindee   *104, 300*
Cloven, George   *70, 300*
Cloven, Ruth   *70, 300*
Cluff, Tom   *85, 300, 468*
Clymer, Eleanor   *56, 194, 196, 235, 300, 316, 460*
Coalson, Glo   *87, 300, 342*
Coats, Alice M.   *205, 300*
Coats, Laura Jane   *146, 300*
Coatsworth, Elizabeth   *10, 117, 165, 205, 214, 300, 314, 324*
Cobb, Alice   *21, 300, 334*
Cobb, Vicki   *96, 113, 149, 194, 300, 312, 455*
Cober, Alan   *26, 47, 155, 169, 300, 305*
Cober, Alan E.   *155, 266, 300, 350*
Coblentz, Catherine C.   *49, 167, 300, 381*
Coburn, Doris K.   *140, 300*
Coburn, Jewell Reinhart   *202, 301*
CoccaLeffler, Maryann   *8, 248*
CoConis, Ted   *169, 288, 301*
Codye, Corinn   *235, 301, 406*
Coe, Lloyd   *174, 251, 301*
Coerr, Eleanor   *18, 227, 301, 378, 488*
Cogancherry, Helen   *116, 301, 357*
Coggins, Herbert L.   *208, 301, 328*
Cohen, Barbara   *79, 94, 114, 140, 142, 144, 145, 146, 189, 219, 301, 320, 368, 388, 391*
Cohen, Miriam   *180, 301, 337*
Cohen, Peter   *86, 159, 301, 319, 414*
Cohen, Peter Zachary   *61, 301, 456*
Cohn, Dr. Ronald H.   *89, 151, 301, 473*
Cohn, Janice   *182, 301, 468*
Cohn, Myra Livingston   *466*
Cohn, Norma   *206, 301*
Coil, Suzanne M.   *146, 301*
Coit, Margaret L.   *78, 301*
Coker, Paul   *149, 302, 492*
Colabella, Vincent   *139, 302, 317*
Colbert, Edwin H.   *150, 302*
Cole, Babette   *100, 302*
Cole, Bernard   *4, 302, 448*
Cole, Brock   *11, 42, 54, 87, 126, 162, 164, 181, 194, 197, 198, 225, 239, 259, 302, 473*
Cole, Joanna   *21, 29, 54, 64, 70, 85, 89, 94, 96, 225, 226, 227, 291, 302, 316*
Cole, Sheila R.   *93, 302, 488*
Coleman, J. Winston   *217, 302*
Coleman, Pauline H.   *36, 302*
Coleman, William L.   *91, 302*
Coleridge, Ann   *59, 302, 371*
Coles, Michael   *222, 302, 358*
Collard, Derek   *215, 302, 474*
Collier, Christopher   *3, 132, 169, 302*
Collier, James L.   *3, 132, 169, 302*
Collier, James Lincoln   *56, 302*
Collington, Peter   *130, 198, 302*
Collins, Carolyn Strom   *7, 302, 333*
Collins, Fred   *31, 302, 353*
Collins, Meghan   *72, 180, 303, 347*
Collodi, Carlo   *64, 100, 303, 389, 458*
Collura, Mary-Ellen Lang   *77, 79, 236, 303*
Colman, Hila   *55, 88, 303*

Coltman, Paul   *100, 303, 442*
Colum, Padraic   *164, 165, 166, 193, 303, 398, 481*
Colver, Alice Ross   *138, 303*
Commager, Evan Carroll   *211, 303*
Compact   *43*
Company, E.P. Dutton and   *76*
Conder, Pamela   *232, 303, 333*
Cone, Molly   *175, 219, 303*
Conford, Ellen   *42, 80, 180, 181, 200, 201, 218, 239, 303, 347, 468*
Conger, Elizabeth Mallett   *206, 303, 307*
Conklin, Paul   *4, 29, 204, 234, 255, 303*
Conley, Andrea   *24, 303, 435*
Conley, Elizabeth   *126, 303, 374, 490*
Conlon-McKenna, Marita   *20, 112, 189, 303*
Connolly, Peter   *221, 304*
Conoly, Walli   *220, 249, 304*
Conover, Chris   *27, 56, 304*
Conrad, Arthur   *208, 290, 304*
Conrad, Pam   *29, 92, 94, 111, 121, 175, 183, 184, 189, 199, 229, 230, 304, 331*
Conroy, Shane   *15, 59, 304*
Constable, Evhy   *145, 304*
Constant, Dr. Helen   *125*
Constantini, Flavio   *156, 304, 312, 440*
Conta, Marcia Maher   *72, 304, 489*
Cook, Beryl   *100, 304, 466*
Cook, D. C.   *91, 304, 382*
Cook, Fred J.   *143, 304*
Cook, Scott   *183, 304, 445*
Cooke, Donald E.   *33, 304*
Cooke, Tom   *172, 304, 438*
Coolidge, Olivia E.   *26, 168, 209, 213, 304, 396, 429, 487*
Coombs, Patricia   *156, 304*
Coon, Susan   *83, 304*
Cooney, Barbara   *8, 29, 39, 40, 54, 116, 117, 123, 157, 161, 162, 167, 191, 206, 208, 224, 246, 304, 305, 367, 383, 452, 483*
Cooney, Caroline B.   *171, 305, 469*
Cooney, Nancy Evans   *145, 294, 305*
Cooper, Elizabeth K.   *77, 305*
Cooper, Floyd   *184, 305, 347*
Cooper, James Fenimore   *23, 277, 305*
Cooper, Jamie Lee   *106, 305*
Cooper, Martha Kinney   *173*
Cooper, Susan   *26, 47, 48, 120, 163, 169, 179, 180, 222, 223, 300, 305, 376, 388*
Copley, Heather   *47, 294, 305, 318*
Corbett, Scott   *92, 187, 188, 222, 305, 348, 353, 357*
Corbett, William J.   *230, 305*
Corbin, William   *31, 55, 239, 305, 309, 444*
Corcoran, Barbara   *231, 305, 368*
Corentin, Philippe   *61, 305, 390*
Cormack, Maribelle   *204, 205, 206, 247, 305, 399, 417*
Cormier, Robert   *6, 53, 79, 126, 161, 162, 163, 235, 305, 306*
Cornwall, Ian Wolfram   *46, 306, 384*
Corrin, Ruth   *6, 306*
Cosgrove, J. O.   *107, 168, 306, 416*
Cote, Phyllis   *207, 306, 454*

Cothren, Marion B.   *208, 306*
Cottrell, Leonard   *147, 306*
Counhaye, Guy   *178, 306*
Couper, Heather   *149, 221, 306, 375*
Courlander, Harold   *167, 295, 306, 376*
Cousins, Jane   *221, 306, 387*
Cousins, Lucy   *123, 160, 186, 306*
Coutant, Helen   *68, 306*
Coventry, Martha   *17, 306, 348, 359, 389*
Coville, Bruce   *135, 200, 306*
Coville, Katherine   *200, 306*
Covington, Dennis   *75, 306*
Cowcher, Helen   *184, 306*
Cowing, Deborah   *143, 306*
Cowing, Sheila   *143, 306*
Cowley, Joy   *5, 6, 70, 266, 306, 398*
Cox, Charles   *141, 290, 306*
Cox, David   *58, 59, 181, 306*
Cox, Lee Sheridan   *106, 307*
Cox, Sarah   *176, 307, 357*
Cox, Virginia   *73, 307*
Coy, Harold   *77, 307, 456*
Coynik, David   *126, 307*
Craddock, Sally   *130, 307, 475*
Craddock, Sonia   *218, 307*
Craft, Ruth   *63, 178, 272, 307, 365*
Crago, Hugh   *65, 307*
Craig, Eleanor   *120, 307*
Craig, Helen   *116, 307, 381*
Craig, M. Jean   *138, 249, 307*
Craighead, George   *15, 352*
Craighead, Jean   *15, 352*
Craigie, Dorothy   *31, 307, 361*
Crampton, Patricia   *17, 82, 84, 108, 109, 180, 181, 307, 331, 344, 423, 482*
Crane, John   *32, 307, 314*
Crane, Louise   *204, 307*
Crane, Walter   *156, 307*
Craven, Carolyn   *94, 307, 320*
Craven, Thomas   *210, 307*
Crawford, Bill   *206, 303, 307, 355*
Crawford, Deborah   *52, 307*
Crawford, Elizabeth D.   *158, 214, 307, 308, 363, 477*
Crawford, Phyllis   *86, 166, 308, 415*
Crayder, Dorothy   *215, 308, 389*
Creagh, Carson   *232, 256, 308, 372*
Credle, Ellis   *52, 308*
Cresswell, Helen   *47, 186, 230, 308, 326, 337, 341*
Crew, Fleming   *174, 275, 308, 348*
Crew, Gary   *60, 75, 147, 308*
Crew, Linda   *75, 94, 112, 308*
Crews, Donald   *14, 40, 62, 138, 158, 185, 191, 278, 308*
Crichlow, Ernest   *21, 235, 308*
Cricket, Donna Diamond in   *233, 321, 381*
Cricket, Leonard Everett Fisher in   *233, 339, 480*
Crisp, Frank   *209, 308, 483*
Crisp, Steve   *110, 308, 419*
Crisp, William G.   *33, 308*
Crockett, Lucy H.   *205, 308*
Crofford, Emily   *87, 308, 413*
Cross, Gillian   *34, 48, 49, 102, 185, 189, 198, 231, 308, 471*

Cross, Peter   19, 130, 308, 311
Crossley-Holland, Kevin   48, 198, 309, 402, 436
Croswell, Volney   309
Crow, Jeanne   126, 309
Crowell, James   72, 309, 361
Crowell, Pers   31, 231, 239, 257, 258, 305, 309
Crowell, Volney   153
Crowther, Robert   129, 309
Crutcher, Chris   237, 309
Cruz, Ray   90, 217, 309
Cserepy, Mary   18, 309
Cubias, Daisy   105, 287, 309
Cuffari, Richard   52, 62, 63, 68, 140, 141, 169, 202, 309, 333, 397, 406, 467, 476, 482
Culfogienis, Angio   139, 309, 332, 358
Culin, Charlotte   79, 309
Cumbaa, Stephen   34, 309, 413
Cumberledge, Vera   63, 450
Cumberlege, Vera   309
Cumming, Robert   309
Cummings, Alison   31, 309, 360
Cummings, Betty Sue   133, 309
cummings, e.e.   83, 309, 488
Cummings, Pat   30, 118, 119, 175, 183, 309
Cummings, W. T.   153, 310
Cummming, Robert   221
Cunette, Lou   141, 142, 310, 316, 391
Cunette, Louis   205, 279, 310
Cunningham, David   72, 310, 415
Cunningham, John T.   140, 310
Cunningham, Julia   27, 52, 53, 68, 72, 132, 154, 161, 201, 202, 212, 310, 359, 428
Cunningham, Walter   57, 310, 489
Cupples, Pat   106, 310, 365
Curry, Jane L.   188, 201, 310
Curry, Jane Louise   174, 202, 214, 253, 310
Curry, Jennifer   77, 310
Curry, Peggy Simson   229, 310
Curtis, Dr. William J.   70
Cutler, Katherine   136, 310
Cutting, Susan   222, 310, 430
Cuyler, Margery   145, 310
Czekeres, Cyndy   318
Czernecki, Stefan   7, 310

D'Adamo, Anthony   171, 227, 310, 484
Dabcovich, Lydia   69, 157, 183, 184, 310, 335, 364
Dahl, Hans Norman   213, 311
Dahl, Roald   25, 28, 34, 42, 54, 56, 81, 98, 105, 109, 110, 125, 126, 134, 135, 163, 172, 192, 198, 218, 224, 225, 227, 228, 231, 240, 267, 271, 285, 311, 486
Dahl, Sharon   92, 311, 414
Dahl, Tor Edvin   110, 311
Dale, Mitzi   236, 311
Dale, Penny   19, 100, 311
Dalgliesh, Alice   39, 49, 167, 168, 205, 209, 264, 311, 450
Dallas-Smith, Peter   19, 130, 308
Dallinger, Jane   150, 311, 396, 412, 468

Dalrymple, De Wayne   51, 311, 448
Dalton, Anne   221, 259, 311
Dalton, Annie   49, 172, 246, 312
Daly, Maureen   43, 52, 312
Daly, Niki   181, 312
Daly, Thomas   51, 312
Damitz, Charles   145, 312
Dana, Barbara   113, 121, 122, 296, 297, 312
Dana, Dorathea   207, 312, 347
Daniel, Alan   35, 79, 84, 95, 112, 121, 129, 134, 196, 200, 217, 239, 312, 384, 430, 453
Daniels, Guy   156, 304, 312, 440
Daniels, Jonathan   171, 312, 456
Dann, Colin   14, 312
Dann, Max   59, 312, 392
Danska, Herbert   209, 312, 330
Danziger, Paula   42, 74, 80, 126, 128, 134, 141, 143, 179, 181, 183, 200, 225, 235, 312
Daringer, Helen Fern   208, 312, 358
Darke, Marjorie   101, 253, 312, 455
Darling, Kathy   24, 149, 300, 312, 313
Darling, Louis   52, 84, 89, 98, 103, 134, 196, 197, 218, 231, 239, 287, 298, 299, 312, 313
Darling, Tara   24, 312, 313
Darling, Kathy   149, 300, 312
Darrow, Whitney   142, 313
Darwin, Beatrice   92, 231, 299, 313
Darwin, Leonard   135, 313, 449, 450
Dauber, Liz   135, 136, 313
Daudet, Alphonse   213, 313, 459
Daugherty, Charles M.   206, 313
Daugherty, James   31, 37, 39, 86, 165, 167, 313, 331, 386, 483
Daugherty, James H.   166, 313
Daugherty, Richard D.   148, 313, 407
Daughtry, Duanne   186, 313
d'Aulaire, E. Parin   165
d'Aulaire, Edgar Parin   31, 37, 132, 160, 193, 256, 285, 313
d'Aulaire, Ingri   31, 37, 313
Davar, Ashok   4, 68, 313
Daveluy, Paule   14, 109, 313, 314, 452
Daveluy, Paule C.   108, 313, 314, 446
Daves, Michael   216, 314, 413
Davey, Thyrza   15, 314
David, Tibor   15, 314, 369
Davidson, Andrew   125, 314, 385
Davidson, Basil   176, 314
Davidson, Mickie   33, 272, 314
Davie, Helen K.   128, 314, 333
Davies, Andrew   27, 102, 314
Davis, Allen   26, 111, 169, 222, 274, 314
Davis, Bette J.   140, 143, 314, 442
Davis, Burke   32, 307, 314
Davis, Clyde Brion   208, 314
Davis, Daniel S.   28, 314
Davis, Don   150, 294, 314
Davis, Dr. David C.   49
Davis, Jenny   237, 239, 314
Davis, Lambert   16, 119, 284, 314, 368
Davis, Lavinia R.   38, 207, 314
Davis, Marguerite   50, 205, 300, 314, 491
Davis, Mary Gould   165, 314

Davis, Ossie   4, 118, 314
Davis, Paxton   162, 314
Davis, Robert   50, 314, 331
Davis, Russell   211, 255, 315
Davison, Claire   209, 315, 466
Dawlish, Peter   98, 249, 315, 404
Day, David   44, 104, 110, 255, 264, 315
Day, Shirley   70, 315
Dayrell, Elphinstone   39, 213, 315, 420
Deal, L. Kate   79, 315
Dean, Leigh   156, 315, 355, 448
Dean, Leon W.   30, 315
deAngeli, Marguerite   37, 39, 50, 75, 165, 167, 168, 177, 193, 206, 207, 315, 361
Dear, Neville   32, 315
Deaver, Julie Reece   225, 226, 315
De Beer, Hans   24, 178, 265, 315
de Borhegyi, Suzanne   174, 315
de Brunhoff, Jean   50, 282, 366
de Brunhoff, Laurent   153, 282, 366
DeClements, Barthe   35, 42, 64, 70, 79, 89, 92, 96, 112, 121, 122, 126, 128, 134, 172, 186, 218, 220, 239, 315
DeFelice, Cynthia C.   159, 196, 315, 471
DeFeo, Charles   43, 316, 367
Defoe, Daniel   19, 316, 482
DeForest, Charlotte B.   213, 316, 377
Degen, Bruce   29, 54, 70, 85, 88, 89, 96, 225, 226, 302, 316
Degens, T.   26, 111, 316
DeGering, Etta F.   78, 316, 556
deGogorza, Maitland   165, 247, 248, 316
deGroat, Diane   41, 42, 56, 74, 89, 93, 115, 129, 197, 201, 223, 235, 262, 285, 300, 316, 429, 446, 461
Deguine, JeanClaude   148
deHamel, Joan   91, 316, 341
deJenkins, Lyll Becerra   173, 183, 393
deJong, Dola   187, 316, 492
DeJong, Meindert   9, 15, 51, 55, 107, 131, 154, 168, 193, 235, 316, 443
deKay, Ormonde   61, 297, 316, 355
de la Fontaine, Jean   98, 413
DeLage, Ida   138, 139, 140, 141, 142, 143, 280, 310, 316, 317, 324, 409, 433, 436, 446, 451, 459, 465, 470, 475, 478
de la Mare, Walter   45, 50, 159, 279, 317, 373, 404
Delaney, Young Miss Josie   137, 383, 435
Delano, Irene   12, 250, 317
Delano, Jack   12, 250, 317
DeLara, George   317, 391
de la Rosa, Clarisa   110
de la Rosa, Kiki   110
DeLarrea, Victoria   72, 317, 383
DeLeeuw, Adele   136, 137, 138, 139, 140, 141, 142, 292, 302, 317, 404
DeLeeuw, Cateau   139, 141, 317, 318
Delessert, Etienne   10, 12, 13, 23, 24, 155, 156, 318, 390, 407
Delgado, Abelardo B.   73, 318
del Rey, Lester   31, 318
Delton, Judy   72, 143, 172, 181, 252, 318, 336, 347
DeLucca, Geraldine   66, 318

deMalroy, Geneva *205, 250, 318*
DeMare, Eric S. *47, 294, 305, 318*
Demarest, Chris L. *116, 185, 318, 456*
De Mejo, Oscar *158, 159, 160, 179, 318, 352*
Demi *158, 250, 318*
DeMiskey, Julian *210, 211, 287, 318, 400*
Demuth, Jack *199, 318*
Demuth, Patricia B. *90, 199, 318*
Denetsosie, Hoke *55, 318, 416*
Denneborg, Heinrich-Maria *318*
Dennis, Clarence James *60, 318, 359*
Dennis, Morgan *205, 318*
Dennis, Wesley *30, 32, 50, 83, 167, 195, 205, 208, 231, 238, 239, 255, 270, 318, 319, 375, 469*
Denny, Norman *47*
Denslow, Sharon Phillips *87, 319, 401*
Denslow, W. W. *51, 262, 319*
Dent, George *378*
Denton, Kady MacDonald *104, 129, 275, 319, 353*
Denton, Terry *14, 16, 59, 182, 192, 319, 343, 362, 393*
Denzel, Justin F. *140, 141, 142, 143, 250, 319, 388, 468*
DePaola, Paula *69, 319*
dePaola, Tomie *12, 14, 28, 40, 61, 62, 86, 88, 94, 117, 123, 191, 193, 301, 307, 319, 320, 391*
Deraney, Michael J. *114, 144, 219, 301, 320*
de Regniers, Beatrice Schenk *12, 32, 39, 61, 64, 106, 153, 154, 209, 210, 320, 358, 365, 366, 453*
deRoo, Anne *5, 320*
deRoussan, Jacques *103*
Desai, Anita *102, 320*
deSantillana, Giorgio *78, 270, 320*
deTrevino, Elizabeth Borton *25, 254, 320*
Deuker, Carl *200, 320*
Deutsch, Babette *86, 287, 320*
Devaney, John *33, 320*
DeVeaux, Alexis *12, 118, 320, 369*
de V. Lee, Manning *71, 77, 205, 208, 209, 331, 418, 419, 475, 487*
Devlin, Harry *138, 139, 142, 144, 146, 320*
Devlin, Wende *139, 144, 146, 320*
deVries, C. M. *22, 320*
Dewan, Ted *130, 320, 471*
Dewdney, Selwyn *43, 111, 321, 328, 401*
DeWeese, Gene *72, 321*
Dewey, Ariane *26, 63, 254, 255, 410*
Dewey, Jennifer *150, 321, 434*
deWilde, Dick *176, 321, 459*
DeWitt, C. H. *174, 205, 321, 354, 432*
DeWitt, Cornelius *31, 321*
Dhondy, Farrukh *176, 321*
Diamond, Donna *21, 22, 53, 71, 93, 128, 144, 169, 225, 228, 233, 321, 359, 381, 472, 481*
Diaz, David *105, 321*
Dice, J. Fred *149, 321*
Dick, Trella Lamson *85, 321*

Dickens, Charles *20, 100, 159, 321, 389*
Dickens, Guy *222, 321*
Dickie, Donalda *97, 321*
Dickinson, Peter *23, 27, 29, 47, 48, 49, 93, 100, 101, 108, 129, 163, 230, 231, 239, 249, 263, 321, 322, 342, 367, 418, 482*
Dickinson, Terence *106, 151, 269, 322*
Dicks, Terrance *188, 322*
Dickson, Barry *111, 322, 401*
Dietrich, Richard Vincent *149, 322*
Dietzsch-Capelle, Erika *178*
Digby, Desmond *22, 58, 322, 472*
Diggins, Julia E. *213, 265, 322*
DiGrazia, Thomas *4, 300, 322*
Dillon, Diane *13, 14, 25, 26, 27, 30, 40, 53, 62, 63, 109, 118, 119, 212, 217, 243, 266, 269, 322, 323, 359, 362, 368, 372, 439, 458, 473, 484*
Dillon, Eilis *20, 52, 211, 212, 214, 289, 322, 324, 404*
Dillon, Leo *13, 14, 25, 26, 27, 30, 40, 53, 62, 63, 109, 118, 119, 157, 158, 159, 161, 163, 169, 176, 181, 186, 212, 217, 243, 266, 269, 322, 323, 359, 362, 368, 372, 439, 458, 473, 484*
Dimson, Theo *44, 107, 323, 446*
Dinan, Carolyn *48, 176, 323, 403*
Dines, Carol *75, 323*
Dingwall, Laima *127, 383*
Dinnerstein, Harvey *132, 323, 448*
Dinwoodie, Hepburn *205, 323*
Diop, Birago *118, 323, 365*
Disher, Garry *60, 323*
Diska, Pat *152, 323, 393*
Disney, Walt *172, 210, 323, 366*
Distad, Audree *87, 323*
Dittmer, W. *90, 323, 489*
Dixon, Tennessee *18, 115, 219, 271, 323*
Doane, Pelagie *135, 207, 323, 324, 380*
Dobbs, Rose *51, 324, 331*
Dobias, Frank *165, 166, 324, 447*
Dobie, J. Frank *31, 324*
Dobler, Lavinia G. *36, 324*
Dodd, Lynley *5, 6, 91, 324*
Dodds, Gerald *63, 324, 449, 487*
Dodds, Siobhan *19, 324, 364*
Dodge, Mary Mapes *144, 324, 360*
Dodge, Nanabah Chee *73, 324, 430*
Dodgson, Elyse *176, 324*
Dodson, Bert *143, 145, 317, 324, 373*
Dodwell, Christina *151, 324*
Doherty, Berlie *29, 34, 36, 48, 49, 57, 190, 276, 324*
Domanska, Janina *12, 26, 40, 114, 157, 162, 212, 213, 214, 300, 324, 343, 416*
Donahey, Mary Dickerson *207, 323, 324*
Donahue, Vic *212, 322, 324*
Donaldson, Karin *14, 325, 397*
Donovan, Frank *32, 325*
Donovan, John *67, 132, 160, 214, 325*
Doorly, Eleanor *45, 204, 210, 325, 353*
Doremus, Robert *32, 210, 325, 452*
Doren, Marion Walker *69, 325*
Dorian, Edith *32, 325*
Dorn, Daniel *142, 325, 395*
Dornberg, John *63, 325*

Dorris, Michael *173, 325*
Dorros, Arthur *104, 184, 325, 408*
Doty, Roy *11, 89, 98, 126, 140, 172, 196, 197, 200, 227, 239, 240, 273, 325*
Douglas, Emily Taft *207, 325*
Douglas, John Scott *33, 325*
Dow, Katharine *154, 325, 333*
Dowden, Anne Ophelia T. *62, 63, 325*
Downer, Marion *207, 212, 325*
Downey, Fairfax *206, 282, 325*
Downie, Mary Alice *103, 299, 325*
Downing, Julie *185, 325, 419*
Dowsett, Charles *98, 295, 325*
Doyle, Brian *44, 45, 109, 127, 129, 256, 325, 326*
Dragonwagon, Crescent *95, 118, 163, 180, 326, 479*
Drake, W. H. *50, 326, 345, 407*
Drescher, Henrik *158, 159, 179, 326*
Drescher, Joan *149, 326*
Drucker, Malka *105, 120, 203, 326, 379*
Drummond, V. H. *47, 98, 308, 326*
Drumtra, Stacy *16, 326*
Drury, Roger W. *68, 80, 222, 326*
Dubanevich, Arlene *179, 326*
du Bois, Lee Po *12, 326, 480*
du Bois, William Pene *12, 38, 39, 52, 55, 60, 63, 68, 115, 135, 136, 137, 139, 156, 157, 160, 167, 191, 205, 207, 208, 209, 210, 250, 270, 293, 326, 327, 335, 356, 445, 480, 575*
Duca, Bill *91, 327, 457*
Duchac, Kenneth F. *11*
Duckett, Alfred *118, 327*
Duder, Tessa *5, 6, 91, 327*
Duer, Douglas *206, 327*
Duggan, Maurice *90, 327*
Dugo, Andre *152, 327*
Duka, Ivo *31, 327, 409*
Duke, Kate *28, 191, 327*
Dumas, Phillipe *27, 157, 327, 337*
Dunbar, Joyce *102, 327*
Duncan, Frances *218, 327*
Duncan, Gregor *206, 327, 437*
Duncan, Lois *22, 42, 43, 79, 81, 84, 112, 121, 126, 135, 162, 182, 183, 187, 189, 200, 225, 228, 238, 254, 289, 327, 328*
Duncombe, Frances *206, 328*
Dunham, Mabel *43, 321, 328*
Dunn, Mary Lois *196, 328*
Dunnahoo, Terry *202, 203, 328, 382*
Dunne, Jeanette *20, 189, 328, 441*
Dunne, John William *204, 328*
Dunning, Stephen *51, 328, 430*
Dunnington, Tom *194, 328, 377, 396*
Dupasquier, Philippe *48, 172, 198, 328, 338*
Durack, Elizabeth *57, 328, 470*
Duranceau, Suzanne *7, 328, 456*
Durrell, Ann *5, 328*
DuSoe, Robert C. *208, 328, 370*
Duvoisin, Roger *10, 38, 39, 117, 135, 136, 141, 142, 146, 147, 148, 152, 153, 154, 155, 156, 167, 194, 206, 208, 209, 210, 211, 212, 223, 290, 301, 328, 329, 336, 345, 438*
Dwyer, John N. *148, 329*

Dyer, Jane   *54, 96, 181, 182, 329*
Dyer, Thomas A.   *56, 329*

Eager, Edward   *174, 209, 211, 273, 274, 329*
Eagle, Ellen   *203, 247, 329*
Eagle, Michael   *26, 329*
Eames, Genevieve   *329*
Eames, Genevieve T.   *86*
Earle, Vana   *3, 329, 334*
Early, Margaret   *60, 329*
Eaton, Jeanette   *165, 166, 167, 174, 329, 339, 390, 488*
Eaton, Robin   *143, 329*
Eaton, Tom   *140, 293, 329*
Eberle, Irmengarde   *205, 216, 292, 329*
Ebert, Marian   *229, 329, 367*
Eckart, Chuck   *27, 64, 258, 330, 393*
Eckblad, Edith   *72, 330*
Eckert, Allan W.   *169, 217, 330*
Ede, Janina   *47, 330*
Edel, May   *209, 312, 330*
Edgerton, Clyde   *80, 330*
Edmonds, Catharine   *68, 330*
Edmonds, Walter D.   *31, 50, 68, 132, 153, 161, 166, 214, 330, 364, 415, 454*
Edwards, Brin   *195, 330, 440, 484*
Edwards, Catherine   *148, 250, 330, 390*
Edwards, Dorothy   *175, 176, 330*
Edwards, Julie   *74, 330*
Edwards, Linda S.   *35, 196, 218, 239, 330, 354*
Edwards, Linda Strauss   *194, 262, 330*
Edwards, Michelle   *104, 115, 330*
Edwards, Roland   *185, 330, 491*
Efron, Marshall   *161*
Egielski, Richard   *20, 41, 92, 116, 180, 183, 224, 266, 304, 330, 331, 404*
Ehlert, Lois   *30, 36, 41, 116, 159, 190, 191, 192, 253, 331, 438*
Ehrenstrale, Kristina   *109, 307, 331*
Ehrlich, Amy   *84, 160, 192, 251, 331, 393, 471*
Eichenbaum, Rose   *244, 331*
Eichenbaum, Rose A.   *219*
Eichenberg, Fritz   *38, 50, 51, 158, 166, 206, 314, 324, 331, 380, 382, 386*
Eidrigevicius, Stasys   *20, 331, 476*
Eifert, Virginia S.   *77, 209, 331, 418*
Eileen, Aplin   *32, 77, 252, 339, 380*
Einzig, Susan   *46, 51, 107, 331, 354, 355, 474*
Eiseman, Alberta   *43, 331*
Eisen, Anthony T. Fon   *51, 341, 436*
Eisenberg, Azriel   *114, 331, 332, 478*
Eisner, Vivienne   *142, 279, 331*
Ekoomiak, Normee   *175, 331*
Eldridge, Harold   *30, 33, 238, 331, 335*
Elkin, Benjamin   *39, 313, 331*
Elkin, Judith   *82, 176, 331, 412*
Elkington, John   *77, 332, 367*
Elkins, Dov Peretz   *114, 331, 332, 478*
Ellacott, S. Ernest   *46, 332*
Ellentuck, Shan   *137, 213, 332*
Ellerby, Leona   *81, 332*
Ellert, Gerhart   *9, 332*
Ellie   *109, 332*

Elliot, David   *70, 292, 332*
Ellingsen, Kris   *152, 332, 358, 383*
Ellis, Louise   *70, 332*
Ellis, Mel   *72, 84, 332*
Ellis, Melvin Richard   *196, 332*
Ellis, Sarah   *79, 97, 332*
Ellsberg, Edward   *31, 205, 332, 342*
Elting, Mary   *137, 139, 140, 309, 332, 341, 358, 409, 453, 480*
Elwood, Ann   *203, 332*
Emberley, Barbara   *12, 39, 51, 332*
Emberley, Ed   *12, 39, 51, 54, 138, 154, 155, 332, 333, 373*
Embury, Lucy   *86, 333, 368*
Emerson, Donald   *215, 333*
Emrich, Duncan   *52, 333, 466*
Emsley, Michael   *149, 333*
Ende, Michael   *120*
Engdahl, Sylvia L.   *68, 169, 186, 309, 333*
Engel, Marian   *111, 333, 347*
Englander, Alice   *69, 333, 491*
English, Betty Lou   *28, 333*
Enright, Elizabeth   *52, 166, 168, 210, 212, 333, 365, 411*
Ensikat, Klaus   *19, 24, 157, 333, 335, 409, 448*
Epstein, Beryl   *149, 209, 286, 333*
Epstein, June   *232, 303, 333*
Epstein, Sam   *149, 209, 286, 333*
Erdman, Loula Grace   *216, 333*
Erhard, Walter   *154, 325, 333*
Erickson, Marcia   *139, 333*
Erickson, Phoebe   *83, 231, 333*
Eriksson, Christina Wyss   *7, 302, 333*
Eriksson, Eva   *17, 333, 462*
Erskine, Laurie York   *205, 333*
Erwin, Betty K.   *84, 286, 333*
Esbensen, Barbara Juster   *128, 314, 333*
Escourido, Joseph   *21, 300, 334*
Esmaili-E-Soli, Marteza   *334*
Estes, Angela M.   *66, 334, 415*
Estes, Eleanor   *50, 166, 167, 208, 264, 334, 336*
Esteva, Carmen   *110, 334, 420, 447*
Estrada, Ric   *139, 334, 373*
Etra, Jonathan   *220, 270, 334*
Ets, Aurora Labastida   *39, 334, 412*
Ets, Marie Hall   *37, 38, 39, 107, 117, 152, 155, 207, 208, 212, 334, 412*
Evans, Chris   *176, 249, 334*
Evans, Eva Knox   *3, 329, 334*
Evans, Katherine   *207, 334, 346*
Evans, Larry   *148, 334*
Evarts, Hal G.   *187, 197, 334*
Evatt, Harriet Torrey   *174, 334*
Everden, Margaret   *369*
Everett, Gwen   *105, 160, 334, 396*
Evernden, Margaret   *207, 334*
Evers, Alf   *153, 334*
Evers, Leonard Herbert   *57, 335*
Evslin, Bernard   *113, 335*
Ewen, David   *208, 292, 335*
Eyerly, Jeannette   *67, 335*
Eyre, Katherine Wigmore   *71, 205, 335, 448*

Faber, Doris   *215, 335*
Fairbridge, Lynne   *6, 335*
Fairclough, Chris   *176, 221, 256, 335*
Falconer, Elizabeth   *130, 335, 457*
Falconer, Pearl   *211, 335, 395*
Fallersleben, Hoffmann von   *24, 333, 335*
Falls, C. B.   *167, 168, 206, 208, 258, 335, 430*
Falwell, Cathryn   *190, 335*
Fanelli, Sara   *124, 335*
Farber, Norma   *63, 132, 157, 310, 327, 335, 426*
Farjeon, Eleanor   *9, 46, 49, 81, 82, 193, 246, 253, 265, 267, 269, 287, 294, 296, 307, 331, 335, 339, 359, 377, 382, 385, 393, 394, 404, 419, 423, 437, 447, 456, 466*
Farley, Carol   *56, 87, 93, 335, 417*
Farley, Walter   *30, 177, 238, 331, 335*
Farmer, Penelope   *46, 335*
Farrar, Susan Clement   *227, 336*
Fatchen, Max   *59, 336*
Fatio, Louise   *135, 141, 142, 152, 153, 156, 328, 336*
Fatio, Louise   *141, 142, 328, 336*
Faulkner, Jack   *136, 336, 447*
Faulkner, John   *172, 318, 336*
Faulkner, Nancy   *187, 336, 409*
Faulknor, Cliff   *121, 127, 336*
Fava, Rita   *211, 336, 368*
Faville, Barry   *5, 336*
Fax, Elton Clay   *117, 336*
Feelings, Muriel   *12, 13, 26, 40, 76, 177, 336*
Feelings, Tom   *12, 13, 26, 40, 52, 64, 118, 169, 235, 336, 363, 421*
Feher, Joseph   *36, 336*
Feiffer, Jules   *216, 336, 399*
Feinberg, Harold S.   *143, 336, 481*
Feininger, Andreas   *213, 336*
Feldbaum, Carl B.   *69, 264, 336*
Felsen, Henry Gregor   *31, 206, 336, 337*
Felton, Harold W.   *33, 337*
Felts, Shirley   *28, 230, 308, 337*
Fender, Kay   *157, 327, 337*
Fenn, Priscilla Neff   *216*
Fenner, Carol   *68, 337*
Fennimore, Stephen   *208, 337, 432*
Fenton, Carroll Lane   *136, 337, 407*
Fenton, Edward   *17, 110, 187, 337*
Fenton, Mildred A.   *136, 337, 407*
Ferguson, Alane   *189, 337*
Ferguson, Amos   *119, 337, 362*
Fernandez, Laura   *79, 337, 386*
Ferris, Helen   *55, 337*
Ferris, Jean   *203, 337*
Ferris, Jeri   *204, 234, 235, 337, 369*
Ferris, Timothy   *151, 337*
Ferry, Charles   *87, 337*
Fetz, Ingrid   *138, 224, 337, 373*
Feynman, Richard P.   *151, 337, 388, 419*
Fiammenghi, Gioia   *126, 172, 180, 301, 337*
Field, Rachel   *37, 49, 50, 165, 338, 397, 416*
Field, Rachel L.   *422*
Fielding, Grace   *74*

Fienberg, Anna   *60, 74, 338, 348*
Fife, Dale   *71, 174, 338*
Filisky, Michael   *24, 338*
Filmer-Sankey, Josephine   *47*
Films, Oxford Scientific   *221, 268, 469*
Fincher, E. B.   *234, 338*
Fincher, Ernest B.   *143, 338*
Fine, Anne   *34, 48, 49, 102, 172, 182, 198, 328, 338*
Fine, Joan   *143, 251, 338*
Finger, Charles J.   *165, 204, 338, 382, 480*
Finlay, Winifred   *187, 338*
Finley, Fred J.   *43, 97, 338, 373*
Finney, Gertrude E.   *106, 338, 405*
Firth, Barbara   *100, 125, 198, 338*
Fischer-Nagel, Andreas   *225, 338*
Fischer-Nagel, Heiderose   *225, 338*
Fischer, Hans   *152, 338*
Fish, Helen Dean   *37, 83, 267, 338, 342, 416, 417, 436*
Fish, Richard   *114, 338, 450*
Fisher, Aileen   *107, 133, 229, 338, 339*
Fisher, Cyrus   *167, 339, 341*
Fisher, David E.   *151, 339*
Fisher, James   *32, 252, 339*
Fisher, L.   *31, 339, 422*
Fisher, Leonard Everett   *32, 33, 68, 71, 114, 117, 154, 168, 174, 180, 193, 194, 203, 211, 212, 219, 224, 227, 233, 256, 329, 339, 345, 395, 425, 426, 447, 480*
Fisher, Leona W.   *66, 339*
Fisk, Pauline   *198, 339*
Fitch, Florence Mary   *174, 339*
Fitch, Sheree   *129, 339, 452*
Fitzgerald, Joanne   *97, 339, 392*
Fitzgerald, John D.   *89, 218, 239, 339, 440*
Fitzhugh, Louise   *12, 73, 155, 176, 195, 339, 340*
Fitzpatrick, Marie-Louise   *20, 189, 340*
Fitz-Randolph, Jane   *149, 340*
Fix, Philippe   *67, 340, 371*
Flack, Marjorie   *38, 51, 260, 340*
Flanagan, Geraldine Lux   *148, 221, 340, 455*
Fleischer, Rosalie   *220, 340*
Fleischman, Paul   *29, 72, 94, 95, 162, 170, 180, 264, 340, 355, 391*
Fleischman, Seymour   *374*
Fleischman, Sid   *27, 32, 51, 71, 85, 92, 93, 108, 133, 134, 170, 184, 185, 192, 197, 201, 202, 212, 214, 216, 222, 229, 233, 238, 340, 486*
Fleishman, Paul   *93*
Fleishman, Seymour   *80, 92, 270, 340*
Fleming, Denise   *30, 186, 192, 340*
Fleming, Ian   *239, 286, 340*
Fletcher, Claire   *131, 341, 393*
Fletcher, Sydney E.   *31, 341*
Fleutiaux, Pierrette   *147, 341, 457*
Floethe, Richard   *167, 174, 208, 339, 341, 372, 373*
Floherty, J. J.   *205, 341*
Flora, James   *35, 70, 79, 174, 211, 341*
Florian, Douglas   *185, 341*
Flournoy, Valerie   *69, 116, 118, 341, 479*

Floyd, Gareth   *47, 91, 186, 215, 308, 316, 341, 370*
Flynn, Barbara   *215, 283, 341*
Folsom, Frank   *341*
Folsom, Franklin   *137, 139, 230, 332, 341, 409, 453, 480*
Fonseca, George   *137, 341*
Forberg, Ati   *71, 73, 93, 232, 244, 341*
Forbes, Esther   *167, 341*
Forbus, Ina B.   *171, 265, 341*
Ford, Barbara   *143, 145, 312, 341*
Ford, Betty   *149, 341, 342, 471*
Ford, George   *4, 118, 342, 362, 439*
Ford, Lauren   *37, 342*
Ford, Marianne   *125, 342, 485*
Foreman, Michael   *23, 48, 56, 99, 100, 125, 159, 163, 197, 198, 199, 246, 292, 293, 321, 342, 350, 363, 371, 392, 398, 478*
Forest, Antonia   *46, 47, 342, 400*
Forgeot, Claire   *150, 342*
Forman, James   *52, 213, 214, 342*
Forrester, Victoria   *180, 342*
Forsee, Aylesa   *83, 342*
Forshay-Lunsford, Cindy   *342*
Fortnum, Peggy   *46, 342, 399*
Fortune, Amos   *208, 231*
Foster, G.   *205, 332, 342*
Foster, Genevieve   *31, 166, 167, 168, 342*
Foster, Gerald   *31, 332, 342*
Foster, Elizabeth C.   *87, 300, 342*
Foulds, Elfrida Vipont   *45, 342, 343, 345*
Founds, George   *93, 343, 442*
Fouque, Friedrich de La Motte   *52, 343, 402, 508*
Fourie, Corlia   *127*
Fournier, Catharine   *212, 324, 343*
Fowke, Edith   *44, 127, 343, 436*
Fowler, Jim   *24, 343, 364*
Fowler, Thurley   *59, 343*
Fowler, Zinita   *221, 343*
Fox, Carol   *54*
Fox, Mary Virginia   *72, 343*
Fox, Mem   *59, 76, 109, 117, 147, 192, 319, 343*
Fox, Michael   *68, 343*
Fox, Paula   *8, 10, 29, 56, 65, 69, 109, 131, 133, 162, 163, 169, 170, 224, 257, 343, 402, 430*
Fox, Ruth   *30, 343, 428*
Fox, Thomas C.   *132, 343, 423*
Frace, Charles   *68, 343*
Frame, Paul   *31, 74, 79, 137, 343, 444, 470, 475*
Frampton, David   *182, 184, 343, 407, 412*
Frances, Helen   *59, 343*
Franchere, Ruth   *211, 343*
Franco, Marjorie   *199, 343*
Francois, Andre   *152, 153, 154, 156, 344, 372, 419*
Francoise   *153, 208, 344*
Frank, Rudolf   *17, 307, 344*
Frankel, Alona   *186, 344, 490*
Frankenberg, Robert   *32, 71, 106, 167, 276, 344, 399, 456*
Franklin, George Cory   *30, 243, 344*
Franks, Hugh   *119, 344*

Frascino, Edward   *103, 107, 132, 196, 214, 231, 237, 344*
Frasconi, Antonio   *39, 72, 153, 154, 344, 426*
Fraser, Betty   *8, 64, 344, 379*
Frasier, Debra   *104, 184, 344*
Freedman, Florence B.   *115, 219, 344, 471*
Freedman, Russell   *28, 30, 80, 94, 95, 105, 110, 113, 119, 148, 170, 175, 185, 190, 227, 229, 234, 274, 344*
Freehof, Lillian Simon   *114, 345, 400*
Freeman, Bill   *97, 127, 345*
Freeman, Charles   *221, 345*
Freeman, Don   *39, 71, 79, 174, 201, 202, 209, 345*
Freeman, Ira M.   *137, 345, 490*
Freeman, Lydia   *209, 345*
Freeman, Mae Blacker   *136, 270, 345*
Freeman, T. R.   *345*
Freeman, Terence Reginald   *45, 342, 343, 345*
French, Allen   *205, 345*
French, Fiona   *61, 99, 100, 184, 345*
French, Kersti   *51, 213, 345, 364*
French, Michael   *42, 345*
French, Simon   *58, 59, 60, 345*
Frenzeny, P.   *50, 326, 345, 407*
Freschet, Berniece   *21, 62, 147, 291, 329, 345*
Friedman, Estelle   *339, 345*
Friedman, Estelle E.   *32, 345*
Friedman, Frieda   *207, 208, 210, 345, 373, 374*
Friedman, Ina   *69, 346*
Friedman, Rose   *138, 139, 346*
Friermood, Elisabeth H.   *106, 174, 346*
Friis-Baastad, Babbis   *17, 346, 445*
Frimmer, Steven   *140, 346*
Friskey, Margaret   *334, 346*
Friskey, Margaret R.   *207, 346*
Fritz, Jean   *8, 26, 27, 28, 29, 56, 69, 105, 119, 123, 162, 163, 170, 175, 177, 181, 193, 194, 224, 227, 230, 233, 251, 346, 349, 377, 389, 434, 445, 473, 484*
Frizzell, Dick   *70, 346, 356*
Frolov, Vadim   *56, 260, 346*
Fromm, Lilo   *9, 62, 346*
Frost, A. B.   *51, 346, 370*
Froud, Brian   *161, 346, 464*
Fuchs, Bernie   *183, 346*
Fuge, Charles   *123, 130, 346*
Fulfold, Deborah   *221, 346, 466*
Fuller, John G.   *148, 346*
Fuller, Muriel   *207, 312, 347*
Funai, Mamoru   *141, 143, 318, 347*
Funakoshi, Canna   *23, 159, 347, 391*
Furley, Deborah   *164, 347*
Furukawa, Mel   *61, 347, 409*
Fusillo, Archimede   *34, 347*
Fuson, Robert H.   *152, 347*
Fyson, Jenny Grace   *47, 249, 347*

Gackenbach, Dick   *80, 88, 162, 347, 390*
Gaffney-Kessell, Walter   *180, 303, 347, 445*
Gag, Wanda   *37, 49, 117, 165, 347*

Gage, Wilson   15, 88, 211, 347, 366
Gaggin, Eva Roe   166, 347, 366
Gaggin, Eva Rose   205
Gagliardo, Ruth Garver   231
Gal, Laszlo   44, 72, 97, 104, 111, 180, 250, 268, 303, 333, 347, 430, 435, 448
Galbraith, Katherine   184, 305, 347
Galdone, Joanna   90, 347, 348
Galdone, Paul   3, 31, 39, 50, 90, 92, 138, 168, 194, 209, 210, 211, 222, 231, 239, 248, 250, 278, 305, 347, 348, 377, 432, 433, 444
Galeron, Henri   161, 348
Galinsky, Ellen   140, 348
Gall, Alice Crew   174, 275, 308, 348
Gallagher, Susan   151, 348
Gallagher, Terry   97, 348
Gallant, Roy A.   77, 348, 376
Gallaz, Christophe   17, 306, 348, 359, 389
Gallob, Edward   147, 348
Galster, Robert   135, 138, 278, 348
Gamble, Kim   60, 74, 338, 348
Gammell, Stephen   11, 27, 28, 29, 35, 40, 41, 80, 94, 129, 158, 162, 199, 200, 244, 257, 258, 272, 346, 348, 349, 425
Gannett, Ruth C.   38, 349, 491
Gannett, Ruth Chrisman   51, 167, 207, 257, 349
Gannett, Ruth Stiles   51, 167, 207, 349
Gantos, Jack   64, 349
Garbutt, Bernard   201, 206, 208, 349
Garbutt, Katharine   208, 349
Garbutt, Katharine K.   206, 349
Gard, Joyce   213, 349
Gardam, Jane   26, 48, 186, 215, 230, 349, 488
Gardiner, Frederic M.   206, 349
Gardiner, John Reynolds   80, 122, 162, 185, 202, 217, 224, 349
Gardner, Beau   186, 349
Gardner, John   79, 161, 252, 349
Gardner, Robert   150, 349
Garelick, May   63, 295, 349
Garfield, Leon   25, 27, 33, 47, 56, 93, 99, 101, 125, 155, 186, 230, 272, 294, 300, 342, 349, 350, 402, 434
Garland, Nicholas   221, 350, 432, 446
Garland, Peter   164, 350
Garland, Sherry   95, 350
Garner, Alan   10, 47, 52, 66, 101, 130, 350, 402, 431, 478
Garnett, Emmeline   213, 350
Garnett, Eve   45, 350
Garraty, Gail   132, 169, 350, 419
Garret, Wilbur E.   151, 350
Garrison, Barbara   159, 223, 350
Garrison, Christian   202, 350, 357
Garst, Doris Shannon   238, 350, 369
Garten, Jan   136, 212, 262, 350
Garthwaite, Marion   71, 86, 270, 350
Garver, Susan   234, 350, 444
Garvey, Kathleen   95, 350
Gaskin, Chris   6, 70, 350, 432
Gaskin, Gerry   221, 351
Gasnick, Roy M.   53, 351, 449

Gates, Doris   50, 71, 85, 166, 231, 351, 415
Gauch, Patricia Lee   27, 140, 141, 144, 146, 286, 351, 389, 484
Gault, Clare   142, 351
Gault, Frank   142, 351
Gavin, Jamila   102, 351
Gay, Marie-Louise   97, 104, 351, 418
Gay, Zhenya   166, 205, 351, 380, 398
Gee, Maurice   5, 91, 351
Geer, Charles H.   43, 55, 97, 107, 136, 140, 187, 216, 228, 229, 351, 382, 383, 456, 474, 480, 486
Gehm, Charles   128, 351, 475
Gehrts, Barbara   110, 352
Geis, Darlene   32, 352, 476
Geisert, Arthur   159, 163, 257, 352
Gekiere, Madeleine   32, 152, 153, 154, 277, 297, 352, 363
Geldart, William   105, 164, 181, 259, 352
Geller, Mark   145, 352
Gellman, Marc   69, 159, 318, 352, 371
Gemming, Elizabeth   150, 352
Generowicz, Witold   58, 352
Genia   137, 209, 293, 352
George, Jean Craighead   9, 15, 51, 96, 113, 117, 119, 132, 168, 169, 183, 194, 214, 216, 224, 248, 274, 352
George, John Lothar   15, 352
George, Lindsay Barrett   24, 83, 352
George, William T.   24, 83, 352
Geralis, Georgiou   9, 352
Geras, Adele   219, 352, 398
Gergely, Tibor   39, 281, 352
Geringer, Laura   159, 352, 439
Gerlach, Geff   188, 305, 353
Gerrard, Jean   130, 353
Gerrard, Roy   23, 130, 158, 159, 179, 183, 353
Gerson, Corinne   68, 74, 353, 389
Gerson, Mary-Joan   353
Gerstein, Mordicai   159, 163, 164, 181, 184, 353
Gervis, Ruth   45, 260, 353
Ghezelayagh, Soraya   109, 283, 353
Ghikas, Panos   209, 353, 459
Giacoia, Frank   86, 353
Gibbings, Robert   45, 204, 210, 325, 353
Gibbon, Rebecca   124, 353
Gibbons, Gail   8, 227, 353
Gibbs, May   117, 353
Giblin, James C.   8, 94, 353
Giblin, James Cross   29, 94, 353
Gibson, Barbara   191, 353
Gibson, Betty   129, 319, 353
Gilbert, Kenneth   31, 302, 353
Gilbert, Yvonne   130, 279, 353
Gilchrist, Jan Spivey   119, 183, 354, 362, 425
Gilchrist, Marie Emilie   174, 321, 354
Gill, Joan   155, 297, 354
Gill, Lucille   60, 354, 361
Gill, Margorie   32, 354
Gillett, Mary   171, 354
Gillette, Henry S.   227, 254, 354
Gilliland, Judith Heide   105, 354, 374, 422

Gilmore, Iris   33, 354
Gilson, Jamie   35, 67, 87, 194, 196, 197, 218, 239, 330, 354
Ginsburg, Max   29, 69, 118, 354
Ginsburg, Mirra   52, 61, 181, 254, 255, 354, 410
Giorni, Lionelle Zorn   9, 354, 489
Giovanopoulos, Paul   155, 260, 354, 380
Gipson, Fred   134, 168, 195, 216, 231, 239, 285, 354
Gire, Ken   92, 354
Girion, Barbara   79, 144, 354
Girvan, Helen   205, 354, 366
Gittings, Jo Manton   32, 46, 331, 354, 355, 435
Gittings, Robert   46, 331, 354, 355
Giusti, George   78, 265, 355
Gjertsen, Carol   143, 355, 414
Gladstone, M. J.   161, 355
Glanzman, Louis   53, 132, 140, 160, 169, 217, 278, 355, 413
Glanzman, Louis S.   423
Glaser, Milton   11, 61, 156, 213, 245, 297, 315, 316, 355, 448, 455
Glasgow, Aline   51, 56, 61, 295, 355
Glasgow, Bernard   51, 355
Glass, Andrew   170, 280, 340, 355
Glassner, Judy   113, 143, 355, 477
Gleeson, Libby   15, 59, 60, 66, 355, 361
Glegg, Creina   230, 355, 356
Gleit, Maria   55, 355, 488
Gleitzman, Morris   60, 81, 355
Glenn, Mel   69, 93, 268, 355
Glick, Carl   206, 307, 355
Glienke, Amelie   225, 355
Glimmerveen, Ulco   24, 356
Glover, Denis   70, 346, 356
Glubok, Shirley   26, 50, 63, 227, 356, 463
Gnoli, Domenico   155, 356, 399
Gobhai, Mehlli   52, 356
Goble, Dorothy   13, 356
Goble, Paul   13, 14, 40, 356
Goble, Warwick   165, 356
Goddard, Ragna T.   139, 289, 356
Godden, Rumer   46, 107, 180, 208, 211, 230, 244, 326, 355, 356, 484
Gode, Alexander   17, 356
Gode, Alison   17, 356
Godfrey, Martyn   20, 127, 236, 356
Godkin, Celia   106, 356
Goetzinger, Annie   23, 356
Goff, Beth   56, 356, 476
Goffin, Josse   24, 356
Goffstein, M. B.   4, 40, 156, 157, 213, 356
Gohlke, Madelon S.   65, 356
Golden, Robert   176, 307, 357
Goldin, Augusta   152, 357
Goldin, Barbara Diamond   115, 182, 219, 297, 357
Goldman, William   80, 357
Goldstein, Nathan   187, 305, 357
Goldstein, Peggy   184, 357
Golembe, Carla   160, 353, 357
Golenbock, Peter   192, 235, 257, 357
Gondosch, Linda   116, 301, 357

Gonzalez, Lydia Milagros   73, 357
Goodacre, Selwyn H.   8, 291, 357, 406, 455
Goodall, John S.   25, 61, 62, 63, 64, 157, 158, 178, 215, 357
Goode, Diane   41, 180, 191, 202, 350, 357, 422, 467
Goodman, Elaine   67, 357
Goodman, Walter   67, 357
Goodsell, Jane   234, 357
Goodsir, Don   232, 357, 466
Goodwin, Edward   208, 312, 358
Goor, Nancy   29, 358
Goor, Ron   29, 358
Goose, Mother   13, 14, 19, 27, 37, 38, 39, 40, 61, 62, 98, 103, 105, 129, 130, 143, 152, 157, 161, 163, 181, 192, 246, 257, 260, 264, 267, 273, 279, 287, 292, 293, 297, 298, 302, 307, 308, 309, 311, 315, 316, 320, 321, 335, 341, 346, 350, 353, 355, 369, 371, 377, 378, 380, 382, 385, 386, 393, 395, 406, 407, 408, 425, 427, 429, 431, 435, 436, 440, 441, 443, 444, 448, 451, 454, 457, 465, 467, 471, 473, 475, 480, 482, 483, 484, 485, 489, 491
Gordon, Isabel   154, 320, 358
Gordon, Sheila   4, 5, 358
Gorey, Edward   11, 12, 23, 32, 61, 128, 137, 138, 155, 156, 160, 179, 180, 225, 266, 296, 297, 320, 358, 374, 418, 460, 476, 489
Gorman, Carol   81, 358
Gorman, James   152, 277, 332, 358, 383
Gorog, Judith   80, 144, 145, 358
Gorsline, Douglas   208, 358
Gossett, Margaret   139, 309, 332, 358
Gott, Richard   222, 302, 358
Gottlieb, Gerald   114, 358
Gottlieb, William P.   32, 358
Goudey, Alice E.   39, 244, 358
Goudge, Elizabeth   45, 207, 358, 380
Gough, Sue   60, 359
Gould, Jean   77, 359
Gould, Robert   236, 359
Gouldthorpe, Peter J.   60, 318, 359
Govan, Christine Noble   206, 271, 359
Grabianski, Janusz   23, 154, 359, 361
Graboff, Abner   152, 153, 359
Grace, Patricia   5, 359, 399
Graeber, Charlotte T.   21, 112, 115, 134, 196, 218, 228, 238, 321, 359, 370
Graeber, Charlotte Towner   87, 272, 359
Graese, Judy   132, 161, 310, 359
Graglia, Richard   17, 306, 348, 359, 389
Graham, Ada   148, 149, 151, 359, 398, 424
Graham, Al   38, 359, 469
Graham, Amanda   56, 359, 365
Graham, Bob   59, 60, 110, 359
Graham, Frank   148, 149, 151, 359, 398, 424
Graham, Lorenz   27, 55, 63, 85, 201, 214, 322, 323, 359, 360
Graham, Margaret Bloy   38, 153, 360
Graham, Mark   21, 192, 243, 360
Grahame, Kenneth   49, 51, 82, 125, 286, 360

Gramatky, Hardie   51, 360
Grammer, June Amos   144, 324, 360
Granahan, Lolita   205, 254, 360
Granberg, Wilbur J.   31, 309, 360
Grant, Cynthia D.   105, 186, 235, 360
Grant, Donald   44, 360, 490
Grant, Eva   141, 143, 360, 368, 441
Grant, Gwen   172, 360, 451
Grant, Joan   60, 360
Grant, Leigh   84, 87, 122, 143, 148, 196, 197, 200, 202, 251, 284, 360, 377, 424, 477
Grant, Lesley   107, 360, 381
Gray, Bettyanne   53, 360
Gray, Charles A.   78, 360
Gray, Dulcie   221, 360, 370
Gray, Elizabeth Janet   76, 165, 166, 205, 206, 233, 315, 360, 361, 368, 417
Gray, Genevieve   14, 361
Gray, Nicholas Stuart   46, 361
Grebu, Davis   378
Grebu, Devis   219, 361
Greder, Armin   15, 355, 361
Green, Clarence C.   137, 492
Green, Eileen   47, 361, 371
Green, Malcolm   58, 108, 361
Green, Margaret   154, 359, 361
Green, Michelle Y.   74, 361, 442
Green, Phyllis   42, 72, 122, 309, 361, 430
Green, Suzanne   191, 361
Greenberg, Tony   203, 254, 361
Greenblat, Rodney A.   183, 361
Greene, Bette   93, 126, 132, 161, 169, 180, 361, 423
Greene, Carol   185, 361
Greene, Constance   214, 261, 361
Greene, Gracie   60, 354, 361
Greene, Graham   31, 307, 361
Greene, Laura   73, 361
Greene, Shep   200, 361
Greene, Winifred   152, 361, 413
Greenfeld, Howard   62, 85, 294, 361, 362
Greenfield, Eloise   4, 21, 26, 27, 118, 119, 217, 234, 288, 322, 323, 337, 342, 354, 362, 425, 436, 479
Greenleaf, Margery F.   85, 362, 449
Greenwald, Sheila   181, 362
Greenwood, Barbara   127, 362
Greenwood, Ted   14, 58, 107, 319, 362, 393
Greer, Gery   122, 201, 224, 362
Gregor, Arthur   153, 362
Gregory, Kristiana   72, 94, 362
Gregory, Valiska   185, 362, 455
Gretz, Susanna   176, 198, 245, 362
Gretzer, John   187, 207, 362
Gretzner, John   293
Grey, Vivian   139, 362
Grifalconi, Ann   41, 52, 118, 155, 169, 229, 288, 300, 362, 414
Griffen, Elizabeth   155, 362, 471
Griffith, Helen V.   29, 181, 182, 362, 363
Griffith, Julius   43, 97, 363, 413
Griffiths, Anne   176, 363, 374
Griffiths, Helen   47, 249, 250, 363
Griggs, Tamar   156, 363
Grimes, Nikki   118, 336, 363

Grimm, Jacob   22, 23, 25, 40, 41, 53, 82, 94, 99, 100, 108, 109, 153, 158, 160, 180, 212, 244, 258, 278, 282, 285, 294, 307, 342, 352, 363, 364, 380, 388, 393, 398, 418
Grimm, Wilhelm   22, 23, 24, 25, 40, 41, 53, 82, 94, 99, 100, 108, 109, 153, 158, 160, 180, 190, 212, 244, 258, 278, 282, 285, 294, 307, 342, 352, 363, 364, 380, 388, 393, 398, 418
Grimm, William C.   62, 364, 378
Grindley, Sally   19, 56, 324, 364
Gringhuis, Dirk   3, 246, 364
Gripe, Harald   51, 108, 213, 345, 364, 413
Gripe, Maria   10, 51, 108, 213, 345, 364, 413
Grissom, Virgil   106, 364
Griswold, Jerome   65, 364
Groch, Judith   78, 364
Grooms, Red   159, 364
Gropper, William   31, 153, 330, 364
Gross, Michael   31, 364
Grosser, Morton   72, 364
Grossman, Nancy   103, 293, 364
Grossman, Patricia   184, 310, 364
Grossman, Robert   84, 288, 364
Grossman, Virginia   112, 192, 364, 428
Groth, John   140, 364
Grove, Vicki   189, 364
Grover, Wayne   24, 343, 364
Gryski, Camilla   106, 310, 365
Guarino, Deborah   146, 365, 403
Guertik, Helene   205, 365, 488
Guertik, Lida   205, 365, 488
Guggenheim, Hans   3, 85, 235, 254, 365
Guggenmos, Josef   22, 365, 430
Guiberson, Brenda Z.   184, 365, 426
Guilfoile, Elizabeth   85, 365
Guillot, Rene   9, 32, 49, 50, 365, 405, 418, 436
Gulley, Judie   87, 365
Gundersheimer, Karen   83, 365
Guney, Eflatun Gem   9, 365, 460
Gunn, John   57, 365, 404
Gurasich, Marj   229, 365
Gurko, Leo   168, 210, 365, 410
Gustafson, Elton T.   136, 492
Guthrie, Alfred B.   31, 365, 414
Guthrie, Vee   55, 365, 370
Guy, Rosa   118, 160, 162, 176, 180, 323, 365
Gynell, Donna   56, 359, 365

Haas, Dorothy   67, 189, 365
Haas, Irene   21, 63, 153, 178, 209, 212, 307, 320, 333, 365, 366
Haas, Merle   153, 282, 366
Haas, Shelly O.   219, 366, 415
Habenstreit, Barbara   3, 366
Haber, Heinz   78, 210, 366
Hader, Elmer   37, 38, 166, 347, 366
Hadithi, Mwenye   100, 366, 404
Haemer, Alan   205, 354, 366
Hafner, Marylin   88, 115, 148, 207, 292, 366
Hagendoren, Elzavan   9, 366, 394

Hager, Alice Rogers   86, 366
Hague, Michael   70, 90, 180, 226, 366, 390, 440
Hahn, Emily   208, 366
Hahn, Mary Downing   4, 42, 54, 56, 74, 81, 84, 96, 112, 122, 124, 173, 196, 201, 217, 220, 223, 224, 225, 226, 232, 238, 239, 366
Haig-Brown, Roderick   43, 127, 316, 366, 556
Hailes, Julia   77, 332, 367
Haines, Gail Kay   8, 367
Haldane, Roger   58, 107, 367
Hale, Lucretia   183, 367
Hales, Robert   47, 321, 367
Haley, Gail E.   26, 40, 99, 117, 178, 367
Halkin, Hillel   4, 17, 219, 367, 467
Hall, Adele   136, 367
Hall, Anna Gertrude   166, 205, 254, 367
Hall, Barbara   204, 367
Hall, Donald   40, 157, 162, 305, 367
Hall, Douglas   214, 367, 433
Hall, H. Tom   187, 195, 367
Hall, John A.   43, 97, 367, 433
Hall, Kristi D.   124
Hall, Lynn   27, 80, 85, 94, 188, 199, 226, 293, 367
Hall, Pam   103, 367, 480
Hall, Roger   6, 367, 486
Haller, Adolf   9, 367, 380
Hallock, Grace T.   165, 367
Hallock, Robert   206, 361, 368
Hallowell, Priscilla   211, 336, 368
Hall-Quest, Olga W.   229, 329
Halpern, Joan   140, 301, 368
Halverson, Lydia   199, 368, 492
Halvorson, Marilyn   6, 11, 368
Hamanaka, Sheila   5, 89, 116, 129, 200, 218, 228, 368, 387
Hamberger, John   68, 259, 368
Hamil, Tom   33, 296, 368
Hamilton, Carol   204, 368, 421
Hamilton, Russel   86, 333, 368
Hamilton, Virginia   4, 10, 21, 26, 28, 29, 52, 53, 108, 109, 113, 118, 119, 132, 158, 161, 163, 169, 170, 174, 175, 176, 180, 187, 190, 191, 193, 215, 314, 322, 323, 368, 402, 455, 479, 483
Hamm, Diane Johnston   229, 368
Hampshire, Michael   141, 142, 360, 368, 369
Hancock, Ralph   149, 369, 470
Handford, Martin   11, 130, 369
Handforth, Thomas   37, 207, 334, 369
Handville, Robert   33, 36, 144, 369, 376, 435
Haney, Lynn   230, 285, 369
Hanford, Martin   25
Hani, Shabo   150, 369, 468
Hankey, Peter   157, 369, 394
Hanley, Boniface   53, 369
Hanley, Luceille   34, 369
Hanna, Cheryl   118, 320, 369
Hanna, Wayne A.   91, 369, 464
Hannum, Hildegarde   120, 369, 450
Hannum, Hunter   120, 369, 450
Hannum, Sara   213, 369, 489

Hano, Arnold   33, 369
Hansen, Joyce   118, 181, 369
Hansen, Michael   15, 314, 369
Hansen, Ron   164, 369
Hanson, Joseph E.   137, 369
Hanson, Peter E.   234, 337, 369
Harbour, Elizabeth   123, 369
Harding, Lee   58, 369
Hargens, Charles   71, 207, 238, 258, 350, 369, 370
Hargreaves, Brian   221, 360, 370
Harlan, Elizabeth   144, 370
Harlan, Judith   234, 370
Harnden, Ruth P.   55, 365, 370
Harness, Cheryl   112, 115, 134, 196, 218, 228, 238, 359, 370
Harnett, Cynthia   45, 46, 209, 215, 341, 370
Harper, Arthur   208, 328, 370
Harper, Eon   222, 370
Harper, Martha Barnhart   207, 268, 370
Harrah, Madge   230, 370
Harranth, Wolf   108, 109, 275, 282, 370
Harris, Christie   44, 97, 104, 108, 127, 154, 370, 451, 490
Harris, James E.   370
Harris, Janet   143, 370
Harris, Joel Chandler   20, 51, 118, 159, 182, 184, 190, 191, 346, 370, 421, 455, 471, 479
Harris, Leon   154, 370
Harris, Marilyn   53, 126, 371
Harris, Mark Jonathan   85, 230, 371
Harris, Mary Kathleen   47, 361, 371
Harris, Peter   199, 342, 371
Harris, Rosemary   47, 130, 214, 371
Harris, Thomas   126, 371
Harrison, Barbara   185, 371
Harrison, David L.   67, 340, 371
Harrison, Richard Edes   207, 371
Harrison, Ted   104, 109, 159, 182, 371
Hart, Carolyn G.   43, 371
Hart, Dick   46, 256, 371
Hartas, Leo   123, 371
Hart-Davis, Adam   221, 371
Hartelius, Margaret   142, 371
Hartford, John   29, 371
Hartling, Peter   17, 110, 371
Hartman, Laura   150, 371
Hartman, Thomas   69, 352, 371
Hartwick, Harry   61, 371, 466
Harvey, Amanda   123, 130, 371
Harvey, Anne   197, 371, 417
Harvey, Roland   59, 60, 302, 371, 378, 379, 421
Haskins, James   16, 118, 119, 234, 371, 372
Haskins, Jim   105, 185, 234, 372, 471
Hasler, Eveline   23, 372
Hassall, Joan   46, 298, 372
Hassall, Richard   232, 256, 308, 372
Hasselriis, Else   165, 296, 372
Hastings, Selina   100, 182, 292, 372
Hatch, Alden   206, 372
Hathorn, Elizabeth   58, 59, 256, 372
Hathorn, Libby   59, 372, 392
Hatt, E. M.   154, 344, 372, 419

Hauff, Wilhelm   50, 372, 467
Haugaard, Erik Christian   3, 4, 25, 185, 186, 212, 213, 322, 323, 372, 396
Hauman, Doris   49, 372, 480
Hauman, George   49, 372, 480
Hauptmann, Tatjana   23, 372
Hautzig, Esther   3, 25, 52, 131, 214, 219, 372
Havighurst, Marion   167, 174, 206, 208, 341, 372, 384
Havighurst, Walter   167, 174, 206, 208, 341, 372, 384
Havill, Juanita   116, 373, 465
Hawes, Charles Boardman   50, 164, 165, 373, 492
Hawes, Judy   136, 138, 139, 148, 247, 275, 332, 334, 373, 429, 433, 442
Hawes, Louise   145, 324, 373
Hawkins, Arthur   140, 373, 473
Hawkins, Irene   45, 317, 373
Hawkins, Sheila   57, 260, 373
Hawthorne, Hildegarde   71, 206, 373, 390
Hay, David   221, 373
Hay, John   87, 148, 277, 373, 458
Hayashi, Akiko   116, 190, 373
Hayes, Geoffrey   157, 281, 373
Hayes, John F.   43, 97, 127, 338, 373
Hayes, John Francis   338
Hayes, Sarah   373, 467
Hays, Michael   69, 164, 191, 373
Haywood, Carolyn   32, 75, 177, 207, 208, 224, 337, 345, 373, 374
Hazard, David   91, 273, 374
Hazelton, I. B.   205, 244, 374
Hazen, Barbara S.   68, 374, 406
Headington, Christopher   47, 374
Heal, Edith   137, 374
Heaney, Seamus   197, 374, 385
Hearne, Betsy   67, 194, 374, 378
Heaslip, Peter   176, 363, 374
Heaslip, Peter C.   176, 177, 374
Hecht, Jeff   151, 374
Hehner, Barbara   106, 374
Heide, Florence Parry   23, 61, 67, 72, 74, 92, 93, 105, 156, 181, 197, 296, 340, 354, 358, 374, 422
Heimes, Patricia   112, 374
Heine, Helme   28, 157, 160, 162, 178, 182, 374
Heinlein, Robert   195, 374
Heintz, Ann   126, 303, 374, 490
Helfman, Elizabeth S.   93, 374
Heller, Linda   179, 219, 374
Heller, Ruth   149, 375
Hellman, Hal   138, 141, 375
Hemmant, Lynette   74, 375, 406
Hemmings, Susan   176, 375
Henbest, Nigel   149, 221, 306, 375
Hendershot, Judith   29, 159, 164, 181, 248, 375
Henderson, Douglas   104, 375, 416
Hendrickson, David   166, 375
Hendry, Diana   231, 375
Hendry, Frances   116, 375
Hendry, George   83, 375
Henkes, Kevin   117, 375

Henneberger, Robert　*77, 375*

Henriquez, Elsa　*149, 375*

Henry, Marguerite　*50, 66, 117, 167, 195, 196, 202, 228, 231, 238, 239, 318, 319, 375, 428*

Henry, O.　*158, 375, 376, 460, 466*

Henstra, Friso　*19, 62, 63, 175, 184, 243, 375, 423*

Hentoff, Nat　*21, 92, 213, 235, 376*

Hentra, Friso　*19*

Herman, Charlotte　*194, 256, 376*

Herman, Vic　*64, 376*

Herman, William　*31, 376, 432*

Hermes, Patricia　*42, 73, 134, 376*

Hernandez, Antonia A.　*73, 376*

Herrera, Velino　*37, 205, 297, 376*

Herriot, James　*192, 282, 376*

Herron, Edwin　*147, 376, 393*

Herron, Edward A.　*71, 376*

Herzig, Alison Cragin　*7, 376, 434, 435*

Herzog, George　*167, 295, 306, 376*

Heslop, Michael　*48, 169, 222, 305, 376*

Hess, Lowell　*77, 348, 376*

Hesse, Karen　*69, 104, 112, 376*

Hest, Amy　*69, 180, 376*

Heuck, Sigrid　*182, 376*

Heuman, William　*33, 369, 376*

Hewes, Agnes Danforth　*165, 166, 205, 376*

Hewett, Joan　*203, 235, 376*

Hewett, Richard　*94, 151, 203, 235, 254, 376, 377*

Hewitt, Garnet　*44, 97, 104, 377*

Hewitt, Marsha　*194, 377, 432*

Heyduck-Huth, Hilde　*22, 377*

Heyman, Anita　*144, 219, 377*

Hibben, Frank Cummings　*32, 377*

Hickman, Janet　*174, 377*

Hickman, Martha Whitmore　*87, 360, 377*

Hicks, Clifford B.　*86, 197, 377*

Hicyilmaz, Gaye　*102, 105, 377*

Hida, Keiko　*213, 316, 377*

Highwater, Jamake　*4, 27, 105, 169, 346, 377, 434, 445, 473*

Higonnet, Margaret R.　*66, 377*

Higton, Bernard　*192, 255, 377*

Hildebrant, Darrel　*172*

Hildick, E. W.　*107, 188, 377*

Hill, Douglas　*182, 377*

Hill, Eric　*130, 377*

Hill, Frank Ernest　*31, 248, 348, 377*

Hill, Kay　*44, 127, 377, 411, 412*

Hill, Ngaio　*164, 377*

Hill, Olive　*164, 377*

Hill, Susan　*198, 260, 377*

Hiller, Ilo　*221, 377*

Hills, Jonathan　*197, 378, 468*

Hilton, Nette　*59, 60, 378, 450, 483*

Hilton, Suzanne　*76, 230, 378*

Him, George　*199, 259, 378*

Himler, Ann　*141, 378*

Himler, Ronald　*62, 72, 141, 162, 194, 203, 227, 284, 285, 301, 364, 374, 378, 404*

Himmelman, John　*24, 378*

Hindle, Lee J.　*16, 378*

Hindley, Judy　*131, 222, 378*

Hinton, S. E.　*25, 79, 92, 103, 126, 213, 214, 225, 378*

Hirawa, Yasuko　*13, 14, 246, 378, 468*

Hirsch, Karen　*235, 378, 389*

Hirsch, S. Carl　*3, 67, 78, 115, 378*

Hirschfelder, Arlene　*145, 229, 234, 378*

Hirsh, Marilyn　*219, 361, 378*

Hirst, Robin　*60, 371, 378, 379, 421*

Hirst, Sally　*60, 371, 378, 379, 421*

Hiscock, Bruce　*151, 379*

Hissey, Jane　*34, 379*

Hnizdovsky, Jacques　*213, 379*

Ho, Minfong　*73, 105, 184, 379*

Hoban, Brom　*203, 326, 379*

Hoban, Lillian　*33, 52, 67, 379*

Hoban, Russell　*33, 52, 67, 108, 125, 157, 230, 271, 379*

Hoban, Tana　*12, 14, 29, 30, 61, 76, 148, 150, 151, 156, 159, 163, 183, 186, 217, 227, 379*

Hoberman, Mary Ann　*8, 344, 379*

Hockerman, Dennis　*81, 379*

Hodges, C. Walter　*32, 45, 46, 47, 98, 107, 207, 210, 211, 254, 358, 380, 440, 441, 478*

Hodges, Carl G.　*228, 379, 438*

Hodges, Elizabeth J.　*155, 354, 380*

Hodges, Margaret　*39, 41, 83, 106, 154, 158, 177, 380, 389, 420*

Hoeflich, Sherman C.　*71, 380, 485*

Hoff, Carol　*85, 216, 380, 449*

Hoff, Syd　*146, 380*

Hoffman, Mary　*100, 269, 380*

Hoffman, Rosekrans　*105, 380*

Hoffmann, E. T. A.　*158, 380, 435*

Hoffmann, Eleanor　*205, 206, 331, 351, 380*

Hoffmann, Felix　*9, 10, 63, 155, 212, 363, 364, 367, 380*

Hoffmann, William　*138, 380, 481*

Hofmann, Ginnie　*145, 380*

Hogben, Lancelot T.　*32, 46, 77, 251, 252, 380*

Hogben, Lancelot Thomas　*380, 469*

Hogrogian, Nonny　*39, 40, 120, 160, 169, 363, 381, 462*

Hoig, Stan　*175, 381*

Hoke, Helen　*31, 381*

Holabird, Katharine　*116, 307, 381*

Holberg, Richard　*166, 291, 381*

Holbrook, Stewart　*38, 239, 381, 491*

Holcroft, Anthony　*233, 321, 381*

Holdcroft, Tina　*107, 360, 381*

Holden, Caroline　*227, 381*

Hole, Quentin　*58, 381, 472*

Holl, Kristi D.　*381*

Holland, Barbara　*200, 381*

Holland, Isabelle　*132, 177, 381, 411, 445*

Holland, Janice　*49, 167, 300, 381*

Holland, Katrien　*24, 381*

Holland, Viki　*215, 381*

Hollander, Carl　*108, 381, 409*

Hollindale, Peter　*66, 381*

Holling, Holling Clancy　*31, 37, 50, 71, 167, 201, 381*

Holm, Anne S.　*33, 53, 381, 406*

Holman, Felice　*53, 56, 161, 381, 382*

Holmes, Bea　*3, 202, 328, 382*

Holmstrand, Marie　*33, 382*

Holt, Stephen　*30, 319, 382*

Homel, David Toby　*108, 194, 382, 437*

Homsher, Lola M.　*229, 296, 382*

Honey, Elizabeth　*237, 382, 430*

Hong, Lily Toy　*190, 382*

Honore, Paul　*165, 338, 382*

Honour, Alan　*106, 211, 382*

Hood, Robert E.　*138, 382*

Hook, Frances　*91, 304, 382*

Hook, Richard　*91, 304, 382*

Hooker, Saralinda　*27, 149, 382, 487*

Hooper, Byrd　*216, 351, 382*

Hooper, John　*205, 273, 382*

Hoover, H. M.　*174, 182, 382*

Hoover, Helen　*13, 14, 382, 449*

Hoover, Russell　*106, 382, 458*

Hope, Christopher　*130, 260, 382, 448*

Hopkins, Janet　*205, 382, 460*

Hopkins, Lee Bennett　*103, 117, 158, 224, 283, 331, 382, 426*

Hopkins, Lila　*171, 382*

Horder, Margaret　*32, 57, 107, 212, 213, 295, 383, 478*

Horioka, Yasuko　*9, 383, 390*

Hornby, Nicole　*211, 383*

Horne, R. S.　*137, 383, 435*

Horner, John R.　*152, 277, 332, 358, 383*

Hornyansky, Michael　*43, 259, 383, 483*

Horowitz, Anthony　*121, 383*

Horstman, Lisa　*75, 383*

Hort, Lenny　*146, 383, 427*

Horvatic, Anne　*151, 282, 383*

Horwitz, Elinor Lander　*161, 305, 383*

Hosea　*12, 13, 40, 261, 262*

Hosford, Jossie　*228, 351, 383*

Hosmer, Herbert H.　*54*

Hosoe, Eikoh　*214, 383, 423*

Hostomska, Anna　*22, 383*

Hotze, Sollace　*194, 383*

House, Charles　*72, 317, 383*

Houser, Lowell　*165, 383, 435*

Houston, James　*44, 77, 103, 127, 383*

Houston, James D.　*85, 383, 384*

Houston, Jeanne Wakatsuki　*85, 383, 384*

Howard Associates, Ron　*177, 384, 443*

Howard, Elizabeth Fitzgerald　*184, 206, 228, 384, 487*

Howard, Ellen　*94, 185, 384*

Howard, M. Maitland　*46, 306, 384*

Howe, Deborah　*35, 79, 84, 95, 112, 121, 134, 196, 200, 217, 239, 312, 384*

Howe, Gertrude　*206, 372, 384*

Howe, James　*28, 35, 70, 74, 79, 84, 89, 95, 112, 113, 121, 134, 172, 196, 200, 217, 226, 239, 312, 384, 454, 457*

Howell, Frank　*113, 384*

Howell, Troy　*7, 27, 192, 251, 288, 384*

Howell, Virginia　*207, 332, 384*

Howker, Janni　*29, 36, 48, 111, 164, 173, 231, 384*

Howland, Douglas　*137, 384, 388*

Hsia, Miriam　*149, 289, 384*

Hsu-Flanders, Lillian　*147, 384, 488*

Hu, Ying-Hwa　*104, 384*

Hubbard, Harlan   *217, 384*

Hubbard, Ralph   *165, 384*

Huck, Charlotte   *121, 218, 384*

Hudson, Jan   *11, 44, 97, 109, 183, 236, 385*

Hudson, Mark   *123, 385*

Huether, Anne F.   *106, 345, 385*

Huffman, Pamela   *53, 385, 414*

Huffman, Tom   *42, 74, 134, 148, 197, 218, 385, 435, 469*

Hughes, David   *130, 385, 436*

Hughes, George   *196, 238, 300, 385*

Hughes, Jan   *72, 216, 254, 385, 462*

Hughes, Monica   *6, 10, 11, 18, 97, 102, 104, 108, 111, 127, 236, 297, 385*

Hughes, Shirley   *82, 91, 99, 121, 125, 176, 183, 214, 298, 385, 434*

Hughes, Ted   *63, 102, 125, 196, 197, 262, 314, 374, 385, 426*

Hughey, Roberta   *75, 385*

Huigin, Sean O.   *97, 385*

Hull, James   *86, 386*

Hulme, Susan   *18, 386*

Hulsmann, Eva   *202, 386, 488*

Humphrey, Henry   *155, 386*

Humphreys, Graham   *47, 386*

Humphries, Stella   *17, 50, 211, 263, 386, 400, 401, 469, 490*

Hundal, Nancy   *79, 337, 386*

Hundley, Eunice   *105, 386*

Hunt, Nan   *147, 386*

Hunt, Irene   *51, 85, 107, 169, 181, 386, 485*

Hunt, Lawrence J.   *187, 386*

Hunt, Mabel Leigh   *106, 166, 167, 205, 206, 313, 331, 386, 389, 397, 450*

Hunt, Nan   *147, 386, 465*

Hunt, Paul   *131, 386*

Hunter, Bernice Thurman   *111, 127, 386*

Hunter, Evan   *211, 386, 387*

Hunter, Kristin   *52, 68, 73, 76, 132, 215, 386*

Hunter, Llyn   *199, 386, 492*

Hunter, Mark   *211, 386, 387*

Hunter, Mollie   *26, 47, 56, 160, 161, 186, 214, 225, 386, 387, 411, 444*

Hunter, Richard   *211, 386, 387*

Hunter, Susan   *221, 306, 387*

Hunter, Ted   *211, 386, 387*

Hurd, Clement   *26, 61, 79, 207, 213, 214, 281, 387, 483*

Hurd, Edith Thacher   *61, 154, 213, 214, 272, 387*

Hurd, Michael   *221, 387*

Hurd, Peter   *165, 387, 447*

Hurd, Thacher   *28, 61, 154, 213, 214, 272, 387*

Hurle, Garry   *35, 387*

Hurley, Frank   *57, 387*

Hurlimann, Ruth   *17, 22, 265, 387*

Hurmence, Belinda   *94, 171, 179, 387*

Hurten, Bjorn   *148*

Hurwitz, Johanna   *89, 105, 116, 129, 179, 180, 200, 218, 220, 228, 368, 387, 396, 468*

Hutchings, Edward   *337, 388, 419*

Hutchins, Carleen Maley   *137, 384, 388*

Hutchins, Hazel J.   *11, 190, 388*

Hutchins, Pat   *11, 25, 60, 99, 107, 125, 156, 214, 388*

Hutchinson, William   *140, 143, 319, 388, 435*

Hutchison, P. A.   *78, 388*

Hutchison, Paula   *106, 293, 388*

Hutton, Warwick   *28, 158, 159, 163, 179, 180, 181, 305, 388*

Huxley, Dee   *75, 388, 405*

Huynh, Quang Nhuong   *87, 232, 388, 434, 461*

Hyde, Margaret   *78, 388*

Hyman, Trina Schart   *25, 26, 27, 30, 41, 42, 44, 62, 63, 76, 83, 84, 85, 94, 95, 114, 116, 146, 158, 160, 180, 182, 185, 186, 214, 219, 226, 228, 247, 289, 292, 301, 346, 351, 363, 380, 388, 389, 395, 406, 416, 425, 461, 486*

Ibbotson, Eva   *48, 389, 415*

Ignatowicz, Nina   *160, 389*

Ihrig, Robert   *121, 389, 476*

Ilin, M.   *206, 273, 389, 406*

Illinois School Library Media Association, *54*

Ilsley, Velma   *68, 106, 215, 308, 353, 386, 389*

Inderieden, Nancy   *235, 378, 389*

Ingpen, Robert   *10, 58, 76, 389*

Ingpen, Robert R.   *108, 389, 469*

Ingraham, Erick   *20, 27, 70, 92, 93, 179, 226, 288, 389, 434*

Inkamala, Jennifer   *15, 389*

Inkpen, Mick   *34, 56, 172, 389*

Innocenti, Roberto   *17, 20, 100, 159, 303, 306, 321, 348, 359, 389*

Inokuma, Yoko   *110, 389*

Inouye, Carol   *142, 389, 473*

Institute, Phillips   *60, 360*

Inui, Tomiko   *9, 383, 390*

Inyart, Gene   *227, 265, 390*

Ionesco, Eugene   *61, 155, 305, 318, 390*

Ipcar, Dahlov   *209, 390*

Ireland, Timothy   *176, 390*

Irigary, Louis   *71, 230, 390*

Iroh, Eddie   *109, 390*

Irvine, Joan   *224, 390, 490*

Irving, James G.   *31, 390*

Irvins, Barbara   *204, 390*

Irwin, Hadley   *4, 112, 196, 199, 390*

Isaacson, Philip M.   *29, 390*

Isadora, Rachel   *27, 40, 64, 184, 390*

Isele, Elizabeth   *180, 366, 390*

Isenbart, Hans-Heinrich   *148, 250, 330*

Isenberg, Barbara   *80, 347, 390*

Ishii, Momoko   *181, 182, 246, 390*

IshKishor, Sulamith   *390, 427*

Ishmael, Woodi   *167, 206, 329, 373, 390*

Ishmole, Jack   *36, 390*

Italiano, Carlo   *103, 108, 390*

Ito, Toshio   *150, 390, 409*

Ivanov, Anatoly   *144, 301, 391*

Ivens, Dorothy   *97, 391, 446*

Iwago, Tokumitsu   *150, 391, 468*

Izawa, Masana   *150, 391, 396*

Izawa, Yohiji   *23, 159, 347, 391*

Jaber, William   *143, 391*

Jackson, Bo   *240, 391*

Jackson, Jacqueline   *84, 391, 465*

Jackson, Jesse   *234, 391*

Jackson, Julia   *150, 262, 391*

Jackson, Kathryn Byron   *207, 391*

Jackson, Nancy Ruth   *133, 391, 412*

Jackson, Richard Jesse

Jacobi, Kathy   *72, 93, 162, 340, 391*

Jacobs, Allan D.   *142, 317, 391*

Jacobs, Francine   *151, 391*

Jacobs, Joseph   *39, 391, 460*

Jacobs, Leland B.   *113, 138, 139, 140, 141, 142, 249, 310, 317, 319, 391, 430, 435, 458, 465*

Jacques, Brian   *34, 121, 228, 294, 391, 392*

Jacques, Faith   *47, 101, 107, 157, 256, 392, 474*

Jacques, Laura   *24, 392*

Jacques, Robin   *19, 34, 392, 435*

Jaffrey, Madhur   *100, 163, 342, 392*

Jahnke, Robert   *70, 257, 392*

Jahnke, Robert H. G.   *5, 257, 392*

Jam, Teddy   *97, 104, 111, 131, 264, 339, 392*

James, Ann   *59, 312, 372, 392, 408*

James, John   *222, 268, 392, 454*

James, Sandra   *174, 392*

James, Will   *51, 165, 327, 392*

Jameson, Cynthia   *62, 392, 427*

Jameson, Malcolm   *31, 392*

Jampolsky, Gerald G.   *4, 392, 483*

Jane, Mary C.   *33, 243, 392*

Janeczko, Paul B.   *123, 392*

Janos, Leo   *80, 392*

Janosch (Horst Eckert)   *10, 109, 265, 330, 392*

Janssen, Al   *91, 390, 392*

Janssen, Pierre   *67, 392*

Jarrell, Randall   *22, 40, 52, 53, 62, 64, 154, 155, 156, 157, 160, 169, 171, 285, 363, 364, 392, 393*

Jarvis, Robin   *34, 121, 393*

Jaspersohn, William   *27, 330, 393*

Jauss, Anne Marie   *67, 138, 147, 209, 264, 376, 393*

Jeffers, Susan   *8, 13, 19, 40, 62, 94, 143, 144, 184, 192, 251, 296, 331, 393, 423, 428*

Jeness, Aylette   *410*

Jenkin-Pearce, Susie   *131, 341, 393*

Jenkins, Sue   *66, 393*

Jenkyns, Chris   *152, 323, 393*

Jenness, Aylette   *148, 149, 152, 214, 234, 393, 492*

Jenness, Jonathan   *214, 393*

Jennings, Gary   *212, 265, 393*

Jennings, Paul   *14, 25, 117, 228, 237, 319, 362, 393, 394, 443*

Jennings, Terry   *221, 394*

Jensen, Albert C.   *149, 394*

Jensen, Dorothea   *81, 394*

Jernigan, E. Wesley   *177, 204, 394*

Jernigan, Giselda   *204, 394*

Jeroo, Roy   *88, 394*

Jerry Spinelli   29, 35, 54, 83, 84, 105, 193, 223, 232
Jeruchim, Simon   212, 275, 394, 462
Jervis, Richard   173, 292, 394
Jeschke, Susan   87, 394
Jespersen, James   149, 340
Jeuninckx, Karel   9, 366, 394
Jewett, Eleanore Myers   167, 294, 394
Jewett, Sarah Orne   25, 249, 394
Jigsaw, Isabel Reiner   128, 490
Jim Long's Stage   103, 367, 480
Johansen, Margaret   165, 394, 423, 430
Johansen, Hanna   24, 269, 394
John, Angela V.   176, 394
John, Helen   85, 114, 394
John, Mary   222, 394
John, Naomi   179, 394, 472
John, Timothy   157, 369, 394
Johnson, Alexander L.   43, 394
Johnson, Angela   116, 119, 183, 394
Johnson, Annabel   231, 335, 492
Johnson, Avery   86, 251, 395
Johnson, Clifton   204, 395, 490
Johnson, Crockett   206, 395, 410, 419
Johnson, E. Harper   3, 21, 71, 235, 277, 293, 395, 414
Johnson, Edgar   211, 229, 394, 395
Johnson, Edith F.   205, 395, 444
Johnson, Elizabeth   25, 388, 395
Johnson, Enid   204, 395, 475
Johnson, Gerald W.   33, 168, 211, 212, 339, 395
Johnson, Hannah Lyons   142, 325, 395
Johnson, Helen Lossing   206, 395, 396
Johnson, James Weldon   52, 156, 395
Johnson, Jane   20, 130, 395
Johnson, Lois   91, 395, 475
Johnson, Lois Walfrid   215, 216, 395
Johnson, Lonni Sue   145, 395, 396
Johnson, Margaret S.   206, 395, 396
Johnson, Mildred D.   194, 328, 377, 396
Johnson, Milton   3, 25, 26, 168, 169, 213, 304, 372, 396, 465
Johnson, Pamela   179, 387, 396
Johnson, Ryerson   3, 396, 423
Johnson, Sally P.   154, 396, 453
Johnson, Siddie Joe   101, 216, 396, 453
Johnson, Steve   112, 129, 396, 441
Johnson, Sylvia A.   150, 311, 391, 396, 407, 409, 439
Johnson, William H.   105, 160, 334, 396
Johnston, Edith F.   396
Johnston, Johanna   78, 268, 396
Johnston, Julie   97, 133, 396
Johnston, Norma   137, 144, 145, 146, 396, 397
Johnston, Tony   185, 203, 272, 296, 397
Johnston, William   33, 397
Johnstone, David   223, 397, 434
Johnstone, Paul   148, 277, 397
Jonas, Ann   29, 30, 96, 158, 397
Jones, Adrienne   185, 202, 203, 309, 397
Jones, Alun L.   398
Jones, Bob   134, 200, 238, 397
Jones, Cyril   397, 398
Jones, Dan   89, 223, 397, 450

Jones, Diana Wynne   28, 29, 47, 48, 101, 397
Jones, Dorothy Holder   43, 397
Jones, Doug   14, 325, 397
Jones, Elizabeth Orton   37, 49, 206, 338, 386, 397, 398
Jones, Elsie   14, 325, 397
Jones, Eufron Gwynne   149, 397
Jones, Gwen Redvers   397, 398
Jones, Gwyneth A.   102, 398
Jones, Harold   46, 50, 51, 107, 398, 406, 424
Jones, Helen Hinkley   185, 398
Jones, Idwal   166, 351, 398
Jones, Jessie Orton   37, 397, 398
Jones, John Pinion   397, 398
Jones, Malcolm M.   397, 398
Jones, Nikki   236, 258, 398
Jones, Patricia   153, 258, 363, 364, 398
Jones, Penri   398
Jones, Ron   79, 398, 471
Jones, T. Llew   398
Jones, Terry   56, 342, 398
Jones, Weyman   51, 228, 398, 409
Jones, Wilfred   165, 303, 398
Joosse, Barbara M.   95, 398, 417
Jope, Anne   198, 398
Jordan, Drake   149, 359, 398
Jordan, Emil L.   139, 274, 398
Jordan, Jael   219, 352, 398
Jordan, June   21, 132, 287, 398
Jordan, Sherryl   5, 6, 306, 398
Joseph, Lynn   184, 190, 398, 479
Joslin, Sesyle   39, 153, 155, 191, 212, 261, 398, 399
Jowett, Margaret   46, 342, 399
Joyce, William   69, 159, 184, 190, 191, 399, 439
Joyner, Jerry   26, 156, 295, 399
Judkis, Jim   83, 399
Judson, Clara Ingram   31, 66, 77, 106, 115, 167, 168, 199, 233, 270, 282, 293, 326, 344, 378, 399, 477, 486
Jukes, Mavis   21, 29, 170, 272, 399
Jupo, Frank   32, 399
Jurmain, Suzanne   203, 399
Juster, Norton   155, 183, 216, 336, 356, 399
Justis, Lyle   205, 247, 305, 399

Kahl, Virginia   52, 209, 399
Kahng, Kim   191, 399
Kahukiwa, Robin   399
Kahukiwa, Robyn   5, 70, 359, 399
Kakkak, Dale   105, 399, 489
Kalashnikoff, Nicholas   167, 400, 428
Kalb, Jonah   218, 238, 400, 409
Kallay, Dusan   10, 19, 400
Kallin, Tasha   46, 342, 400
Kalman, Maira   159, 183, 400
Kalmenoff, Matthew   93, 137, 400, 472
Kalnay, Francis   168, 210, 318, 400
Kamm, Josephine   114, 400
Kandell, Alice S.   149, 400
Kandoian, Ellen   145, 400
Kane, Henry B.   133, 154, 400, 442
Kanozawa, Susumu   150, 400, 468

Kantrowitz, Mildred   68, 400, 471
Kapelus, Helen   20
Kapelus, Helena   400, 457
Kaplan, Seymour R.   114, 345, 400
Kaplow, Robert   146, 400
Kappeler, Marcus   400
Kappeler, Xuqi Jin   151, 394
Karasz, Ilonka   167, 400, 440
Karl, Herb   75, 400
Karlin, Eugene   211, 386, 400, 401
Karloff, Boris   51, 299, 400
Karma, Maija   9, 400, 462
Karr, Kathleen   185, 400
Kashiwagi, Isami   209, 400, 423
Kasper, Vancy   236, 401
Kass, Pnina   233, 401
Kassian, Olena   111, 321, 322, 401
Kastner, Erich   9, 17, 50, 125, 214, 401, 407, 419, 420, 432, 444
Kastner, Jill   87, 175, 319, 401
Kasza, Keiko   116, 401
Katan, Norma Jean   149, 401, 451
Katchamakoff, Atanas   166, 401
Katsushika, Nokusai   55, 251, 283, 401
Katz, Jacqueline Hunt   63, 401
Katz, Ruth J.   143, 401
Katz, Welwyn Wilton   44, 77, 97, 236, 401
Katz, William Loren   63, 235, 401
Katzoff, Sy   211, 279, 401
Kaufman, William I.   67, 401
Kaufmann, Angelika   108, 401, 426
Kaufmann, Herbert   211, 386, 400, 401
Kaufmann, John   55, 76, 228, 258, 290, 401, 457
Kavanagh, Patrick J.   102, 401
Kay, Jackie   197, 402
Kaye, Geraldine   176, 401, 463
Keating, Bern   228, 270, 402
Keats, Ezra Jack   12, 26, 39, 40, 116, 135, 141, 223, 224, 239, 243, 341, 373, 394, 402, 422, 465, 479, 492
Keehn, Sally M.   83, 402
Keen, Martin   141, 143, 402
Keen, Martin L.   477
Keeping, Charles   10, 19, 46, 47, 48, 99, 100, 107, 125, 198, 199, 210, 212, 248, 255, 272, 293, 309, 350, 402, 464
Kehret, Peg   96, 238, 402
Keigwin, R. P.   50, 244, 250, 402
Keith, Eros   52, 141, 169, 174, 187, 343, 368, 402, 455
Keith, Hal   149, 152, 403, 439
Keith, Harold   51, 168, 197, 228, 229, 285, 403
Kelen, Betty   52, 403
Kelleher, Victor   58, 59, 66, 227, 228, 298, 403, 434
Kelley, Ruth   233, 403
Kellogg, Steven   12, 21, 29, 63, 68, 80, 90, 92, 121, 123, 128, 146, 156, 172, 179, 181, 193, 200, 224, 232, 266, 365, 403, 463
Kelly, Eric P.   33, 165, 403, 485
Kemp, Gene   48, 176, 231, 323, 399, 403
Kendall, Carol   168, 174, 179, 272, 274, 403

Kenly, Henry   205, 403
Kenly, Julie Closson   205, 403
Kennaway, Adrienne   100, 366, 404
Kenneally, Christy   53, 404, 467
Kennedy, John F.   3, 239, 404
Kennedy, Paul   50, 136, 317, 404
Kennedy, Richard   46, 52, 162, 178, 180, 207, 214, 258, 322, 330, 378, 404, 452
Kennedy, X. J.   81, 161, 296, 404, 446
Kennemore, Tim   48, 404
Kenoyer, Natlee P.   229, 404
Kensington, Sarah   221, 404, 431
Kent, Jack   220, 404
Kenyon, Chris   229, 404, 462
Keogh, Brian   57, 365, 404
Kepes, Juliet   38, 152, 153, 154, 155, 212, 404
Kerkham, Roger   140, 404
Kerr, Illingsworth   97, 289, 404
Kerr, Judith   215, 404
Kerr, M. E.   42, 68, 79, 80, 93, 161, 162, 215, 404, 447
Kerr, Tom   146, 405, 459
Kerrod, Roger   195, 405
Kesey, Ken   405, 455
Kessler, Ethel   153, 405
Kessler, Leonard   31, 135, 136, 138, 139, 152, 153, 194, 278, 405, 417
Ketchum, Fred   3, 405
Ketchum, Jean   3, 405
Kettelkamp, Larry   142, 146, 405
Kevles, Bettyann   148, 405
Kew, Katinka   176, 405
Key, Alexander   52, 171, 405
Khalsa, Dayal Kaur   159, 164, 182, 405
Kherdian, David   4, 27, 53, 87, 170, 405
Kidd, Diana   15, 75, 259, 388, 405
Kiddell-Monroe, Joan   32, 46, 50, 405, 436, 489
Kidwell, Carl   106, 338, 405
Kiesel, Stanley   162, 405, 445
Kilbracken, John   221, 405
Kilgore, Susi   235, 301, 406
Kilworth, Garry   49, 406
Kimmel, Eric   41, 120, 219, 226, 233, 290, 388, 406
Kimmel, Eric A.   5, 87, 406
Kimmel, Margaret Mary   63, 389, 406
Kincade, Nancy   68, 374, 406
Kincaid, James R.   8, 291, 357, 406, 455
King, Buzz   75, 406
King, Clive   27, 101, 406
King, Coretta Scott   117, 118, 251, 257, 268, 277, 283, 288, 298, 300, 309, 314, 320, 322, 323, 326, 327, 336, 337, 341, 342, 354, 362, 363, 365, 368, 369, 370, 371, 372, 394, 406, 414, 421, 433, 439, 441, 445, 458, 473, 479, 481, 484, 492
King, Edna   128, 406
King, Stephen   22, 240, 406, 469
Kingman, Lee   37, 62, 187, 260, 309, 406
Kingsland, L. W.   33, 53, 381, 406
Kingsley, Charles   51, 398, 406
King-Smith, Dick   28, 74, 181, 267, 375, 450, 562
Kinkead, Beatrice   206, 273, 389, 406
Kinmouth, Patrick   130, 292, 406

Kinsey-Warnock, Natalie   82, 276, 406
Kipling, J. L.   50, 326, 345, 407
Kipling, Rudyard   50, 51, 156, 181, 184, 265, 318, 326, 343, 345, 407, 471
Kirby, Susan E.   56, 87, 407
Kirk, Louis   148, 313, 407
Kirk, Ruth   148, 313, 407
Kirkup, James   17, 401, 407
Kirn, Ann   153, 407
Kirouac, Paul   142, 286, 407
Kishida, Isao   150, 396, 407
Kismaric, Carole   182, 407, 449
Kitamura, Satoshi   130, 151, 163, 197, 407, 443, 467
Kitchen, Bert   23, 158, 192, 407
Kitchen, Herminie B.   136, 337, 407
Kitchen, David   222, 407
Kittelsen, Theodor   211, 255, 407, 452
Kitzinger, Sheila   29, 221, 407, 462
Kjelgaard, James   229, 407
Kjelgaard, Jim   30, 33, 407, 411, 412
Klass, David   203, 407
Klass, Sheila Solomon   144, 145, 407, 408
Klause, Annette Curtis   196, 237, 408
Klein, Norma   79, 126, 186, 360, 408
Klein, Robin   58, 59, 60, 76, 117, 147, 227, 237, 392, 408, 421
Kleven, Elisa   76, 104, 184, 325, 408
Kliman, Gilbert   120, 408
Kline, Suzy   115, 228, 408
Klipsch, Leona   36, 408
Knaff, Jean Christian   130, 408
Knight, Christopher G.   28, 170, 408, 416
Knight, Clayton   207, 408
Knight, David   46, 260, 408
Knight, Eric   238, 258, 408
Knight, Hilary   139, 211, 408
Knight, Hugh   221, 265, 408
Knoepflmacher, U. C.   65, 408
Knotts, Howard   62, 86, 106, 260, 408
Knutson, Barbara   129, 408
Koch, Michelle   146, 409
Kocsis, J. C.   51, 228, 398, 409
Koehn, Ilse   4, 27, 53, 133, 214, 409
Koenig, Marion   157, 333, 409
Koering, Ursula   21, 50, 137, 140, 332, 341, 409
Koertge, Ron   87, 409
Kohl, Herbert   105, 133, 263, 409
Kohl, Judith   133, 263, 409
Kohn, Bernice   61, 347, 409
Koike, Hiroo   150, 396, 409
Kolda, Helena   31, 327, 409
Komoda, Beverly   137, 409
Komura, Hirotsuga   150, 390, 409
Konigsburg, E. L.   51, 132, 169, 181, 213, 231, 409
Kontstantinov, Fodor   23, 409, 485
Koob, Theodora   409
Kooiker, Leonie   108, 381, 409
Korach, Mimi   141, 142, 187, 317, 336, 409
Koren, Edward   19, 156, 409
Kossin, Sandy   218, 224, 238, 400, 409, 410
Kosterina, Nina   52, 354, 410

Kotzwinkle, William   35, 172, 410, 439
Krahn, Fernando   62, 410
Krasilovsky, Phyllis   179, 410
Kraus, Robert   12, 13, 26, 63, 160, 254, 255, 288, 410
Krause, Pat   236, 410
Krauss, Ruth   38, 152, 153, 154, 206, 208, 271, 395, 410
Krautter, Frances   43, 410
Kredel, Fritz   168, 210, 365, 410
Krementz, Jill   82, 88, 227, 410
Krigstein, Bernard   114, 246, 410
Kroeber, Lisa W.   148, 393, 410
Kroll, Edite   17, 235, 410, 491
Kropp   236, 410
Krugernova, Maria   23, 410
Krull, Kathleen   30, 410
Krumgold, Joseph   31, 50, 168, 295, 411
Krupp, Edwin C.   203, 411
Krupp, Robin Rector   203, 411
Krush, Beth   31, 50, 52, 71, 76, 83, 168, 177, 187, 210, 211, 289, 298, 333, 411, 464
Krush, Joe   31, 50, 52, 71, 76, 83, 168, 177, 187, 210, 211, 289, 298, 333, 411, 464
Kubie, Nora Benjamin   114, 411
Kubinyi, Laszlo   44, 62, 160, 377, 386, 411, 412, 486
Kudrna, C. Imbior   144, 411, 412
Kudrna, Imbior   143, 144, 411, 412
Kuhl, Jerome   33, 411, 412
Kuhn, Bob   30, 407, 411, 412
Kuhns, William   126, 411, 412
Kullman, Harry   10, 17, 109, 271, 411, 412
Kunhardt, Dorothy   207, 412
Kurelek, William   26, 44, 62, 63, 103, 111, 156, 160, 161, 412
Kuribayashi, Satoshi   150, 311, 412, 468
Kurten, Bjorn   412, 413
Kurtz, Carmen   10, 249, 412
Kurusa   176, 331, 412
Kushkin, Karla   64
Kushner, Donn   44, 133, 391, 412
Kuskin, Karla   133, 149, 163, 181, 182, 185, 343, 412
Kyle, Anne   165, 268, 412
Kyle, Elisabeth   212, 328, 412, 456

Labastida, Aurora   39, 334, 412
Lackey, Eunice   152, 361, 413
LaFarge, Margaret   151, 413, 451
LaFarge, Sheila   27, 108, 274, 364, 413
LaFave, Kim   34, 97, 104, 107, 195, 276, 309, 413, 430
Laimgruber, Monika   156, 250, 413
Laird, Christa   120, 413
Laird, Elizabeth   36, 48, 56, 413
Laite, Gordon   141, 216, 314, 413
Lake, David   59, 413
Lake, Denise   15, 413
Lakin, Patricia   96, 279, 413
Laklan, Carli   56, 413
Lalicki, Barbara   158, 413
LaMarche, Jim   87, 308, 413
Lamb, Lynton   46, 413, 440

Lambert, David   *152, 413*
Lambert, Margaret   *148, 412, 413*
Lambert, Richard S.   *43, 97, 363, 413*
Lambert, Saul   *138, 254, 413*
Lambo, Don   *139, 413*
Lamborn, Florence   *53, 355, 413, 423*
Lammers, Ann Conrad   *17, 413, 456*
Lamont, Bette   *174, 414*
Lamont, Priscilla   *125, 414*
Lamorisse, Albert   *153, 414*
LaMotte, Judy Appenzeller   *215, 414, 474*
Lampman, Evelyn Sibley   *64, 83, 120, 229, 277, 280, 281, 336, 362, 381, 406, 414, 419, 444, 451, 454, 486*
Lancaster, Matthew   *53, 385, 414*
Landau, Elaine   *142, 143, 146, 355, 414*
Landau, Jacob   *31, 138, 252, 365, 414*
Landru, Jack   *33, 414*
Landstrom, Lena   *185, 414*
Landstrom, Olof   *159, 185, 301, 414*
Lane, Carl D.   *207, 414*
Lane, Christopher A.   *92, 311, 414*
Lane, Frederick A.   *71, 395, 414*
Lang, Denise V.   *145, 414*
Lange, Suzanne   *219, 414*
Langford, Sondra Gordon   *144, 414*
Langley, Nina Scott   *209, 414*
Langner, Nola   *26, 414, 444*
Langstaff, John   *39, 118, 209, 283, 414*
Langton, Jane   *170, 187, 271, 272, 414*
Lanier, Sterling E.   *85, 263, 415*
Laning, Edward   *86, 166, 308, 415*
Lannestock, Gustaf   *210, 251, 415*
Lant, Kathleen M.   *66, 334, 415*
Lanton, Sandy   *219, 366, 415*
Lantz, Paul   *21, 36, 50, 71, 85, 166, 260, 330, 351, 415, 447*
Lanz, Daniel J.   *215, 415*
Lapedes, Daniel   *138, 415*
Lapp, Eleanor J.   *72, 310, 415*
Large, Annabel   *48, 389, 415*
Larimer, Tamela   *16, 415*
Larkin, R. Paul   *78, 415*
Larrick, Nancy   *159, 177, 180, 415*
Larsen, Glen A.   *143, 415, 448*
Larsen, John   *7, 415*
Larsen, Rebecca   *235, 415*
Larson, Jean Russell   *53, 415, 440*
Larson, Lynn   *215, 415*
Larsson, Carl   *62, 64, 156, 415*
Lasenby, Jack   *91, 415*
Lasker, Joe   *13, 14, 157, 161, 191, 415*
Lasky, Kathryn   *28, 114, 163, 170, 219, 227, 389, 408, 416*
Latham, Barbara   *136, 416, 436*
Latham, Jean Lee   *32, 107, 168, 306, 349, 416, 441*
Latham, John   *208, 216, 416*
Latham, Ross   *232, 416*
Lathrop, Dorothy P.   *37, 50, 165, 166, 208, 338, 416*
Latimer, Jim   *128, 291, 416*
Lattimore, Deborah Nourse   *186, 203, 204, 416*
Lauber, Patricia   *96, 104, 151, 163, 170, 175, 227, 375, 416*

Laure, Ettagale   *132, 416*
Laure, Jason   *132, 416*
Laurence, Margaret   *44, 416*
Lauritzen, Jonreed   *55, 201, 211, 295, 318, 416*
Lauter, Richard   *42, 80, 84, 89, 96, 180, 200, 223, 226, 232, 238, 239, 416*
Lavallee, Barbara   *95, 398, 417*
Lavies, Bianca   *124, 152, 417*
Lavine, Sigmund A.   *144, 417*
Lavrin, Nora   *210, 417, 422*
Law, Mrs. Birdie   *73*
Lawlor, Laurie   *115, 417*
Lawrence, Ann   *102, 417*
Lawrence, Jacob   *12, 13, 155, 417*
Lawrence, James   *139, 405, 417*
Lawrence, John   *63, 197, 198, 371, 417*
Laws, George   *145, 417, 464*
Lawson, Annetta   *157, 417*
Lawson, John   *25, 417*
Lawson, Julie   *104, 417, 454*
Lawson, Patrick   *33, 330, 417*
Lawson, Robert   *31, 37, 49, 50, 166, 167, 168, 204, 205, 238, 256, 305, 338, 360, 417, 418*
Layton, Aviva   *111, 417*
Lazar, Wendy   *142, 417*
Lazare, Jerry   *3, 55, 89, 186, 217, 285, 417*
Lazarevich, Mila   *87, 335, 417*
Leaf, Margaret   *42, 181, 182, 417, 418*
Leaf, Munro   *37, 289, 417, 418*
Leaf, Hayim   *114, 266, 417*
Lear, Edward   *99, 104, 155, 157, 267, 358, 418, 469*
Leatham, Moyra   *49, 365, 418, 436*
Lebenson, Richard   *52, 219, 418, 455*
Le Blanc, Annette   *76, 418*
LeCain, Errol   *99, 100, 108, 109, 182, 192, 259, 363, 364, 418, 428*
Leckie, Robert   *136, 137, 141, 418, 451*
Lee, Alan   *100, 198, 321, 418, 469*
Lee, Ann Thompson   *65, 418*
Lee, Dennis   *44, 97, 103, 107, 108, 111, 127, 129, 194, 351, 418, 446, 460*
Lee, Doris   *174, 205, 418*
Lee, Josephine   *212, 418, 436*
Lee, Mildred   *55, 160, 214, 419*
Lee, Robert C.   *222, 419*
Leedy, Loreen   *182, 419*
Leeming, John F.   *204, 419, 465*
Leeming, Joseph   *30, 419*
Leeson, Robert   *82, 102, 110, 308, 419*
LeFevre, Felicite   *51, 419*
LeFoll, Alain   *155, 268, 419*
LeGallienne, Eva   *51, 212, 419*
LeGuin, Ursula K.   *25, 53, 83, 109, 120, 132, 169, 185, 190, 269, 325, 350, 419*
Lehrman, Robert   *4, 298, 419*
Leight, Edward   *153, 419, 453*
Leighton, Margaret   *71, 202, 418, 419*
Leighton, Margaret C.   *83, 419, 447*
Leighton, Ralph   *151, 337, 388, 419*
Leinwoll, Stanley   *143, 419*
Leitch, Adelaide   *123, 269, 419*
Leman, Martin   *158, 419*
Lemarchand, Jacques   *154, 344, 372, 419*

Lemieux, Michele   *104, 111, 275, 419*
Lemke, Horst   *9, 50, 139, 274, 318, 401, 419, 420, 444*
Lemoine, Georges   *24, 264, 420*
L'Engle, Madeleine   *6, 7, 10, 51, 80, 117, 168, 170, 193, 195, 214, 224, 420*
Lens, Sidney   *4, 420*
Lenski, Lois   *55, 166, 167, 174, 193, 205, 207, 223, 420, 478*
Lent, Blair   *19, 25, 26, 39, 40, 61, 92, 107, 154, 160, 213, 315, 380, 420, 455*
Lenz, Millicent   *66, 420*
Leodhas, Sorche Nic   *39, 50, 168, 247, 381, 460, 462*
Leon, Miguel   *110, 334, 420, 447*
Lerner, Carol   *87, 93, 151, 194, 420, 442*
Leroe, Ellen   *144, 420*
LeRoy, Gen   *141, 142, 420*
Leslie-Melville, Betty   *24, 421*
Leslie, Cecil   *46, 107, 298, 420, 421*
Leslie, Donna   *74, 421*
Leslie, Robert Franklin   *201, 421*
Lessac, Frane   *183, 421, 481*
Lesser, Carolyn   *87, 293, 421*
Lesser, Rika   *41, 421*
Lester, Alison   *14, 58, 59, 408, 421*
Lester, Helen   *42, 70, 96, 421, 457*
Lester, Julius   *52, 53, 118, 132, 169, 179, 182, 184, 190, 336, 370, 421, 479*
Leszczynski, Michael   *45, 254, 421*
LeTord, Bijou   *24, 421*
Leunn, Nancy   *184, 421*
LeVert, John   *237, 421*
Levin, Betty   *122, 421*
Levin, Eli   *114, 421*
Levin, Meyer   *114, 421*
Levin, Ruth   *114, 421, 476*
Levine, Abby   *204, 368, 421*
Levine, Ellen   *184, 270, 421*
Levine, Joe   *60, 371, 378, 379, 421*
Levinger, Elma Ehrlich   *31, 208, 422*
Levinson, Nancy Smiler   *203, 422*
Levinson, Riki   *180, 191, 357, 422*
Levitin, Sonia   *53, 114, 115, 182, 185, 189, 202, 219, 230, 235, 422, 459*
Levoy, Myron   *4, 27, 62, 109, 141, 142, 215, 235, 402, 422, 425*
Lewellen, John B.   *31, 32, 77, 260, 339, 422*
Lewin, Ted   *24, 30, 98, 105, 194, 222, 259, 354, 374, 422, 475*
Lewis, Allen   *165, 207, 338, 422*
Lewis, Barbara A.   *105, 422, 449*
Lewis, C. S.   *46, 50, 239, 263, 422*
Lewis, Elizabeth Foreman   *50, 165, 422*
Lewis, Hilda   *210, 417, 422*
Lewis, J. Patrick   *175, 375, 423*
Lewis, Richard   *213, 423*
Lewis, Robin Baird   *111, 423*
Lexau, Joan M.   *55, 197, 423, 457*
Ley, Willy   *209, 400, 423*
Lide, Alice   *165, 394, 423, 430*
Lieblich, Irene   *189, 423*
Liers, Emil Ernest   *15, 423*
Life, Kay   *89, 298, 423*
Lifton, Betty Jean   *132, 211, 214, 343, 383, 423, 452*

Lightburn, Ron   *97, 104, 131, 133, 423,*
    443
Lightfoot, David   *120*
Lightwood, Donald   *116, 423*
Lignell, Lois   *3, 396, 423*
Liljeberg, Eva Imber   *110, 423, 461*
Lillie, Amy Morris   *206, 423*
Lillington, Kenneth   *102, 423*
Lilly, Charles   *101, 161, 169, 263, 361,*
    423
Lilly, Gweneth   *423*
Lim, John   *104, 423*
Lindbergh, Reeve   *192, 393, 423*
Lindblom, Steve   *149, 423*
Linde, Gunnel   *10, 423*
Lindenbaum, Pija   *160, 423*
Lindgren, Astrid   *9, 12, 17, 32, 52, 53,*
    84, 120, 180, 210, 265, 278, 307, 355,
    413, 423, 424, 470, 492
Lindgren, Astrid E.
Lindman, Maj   *50, 424*
Lindquist, Jennie D.   *168, 424*
Lindsay, Harold Arthur   *57, 276, 424*
Lindsay, Rae   *143, 360, 424*
Lindvall, Ella K.   *91, 424, 485*
Line, David   *189, 424*
Line, Les   *148, 359, 424*
Lines, Kathleen   *46, 50, 107, 398, 424*
Linevski, Aleksandr M.   *17, 424, 481*
Linfield, Esther   *72, 424*
Linklater, Eric   *45, 267, 424*
Lionni, Leo   *4, 12, 13, 19, 39, 40, 50, 67,*
    128, 153, 154, 155, 213, 217, 424
Lipkind, William   *38, 152, 153, 424, 453,*
    454
Lippman, Peter J.   *154, 424*
Lipson, Shelley   *88, 144, 424*
Lipsyte, Robert   *56, 142, 144, 424*
Lisker, Sonia O.   *74, 128, 272, 424, 425*
Lisle, Janet   *180, 425*
Lisle, Janet Taylor   *94, 170, 183, 348,*
    425
Lisowski, Gabriel   *62, 215, 422, 425*
List, Ilka Katherine   *61, 425*
Liston, Robert A.   *68, 425*
Litchfield, Ada B.   *74, 424, 425*
Lithwick, Dahlia   *82, 267, 268, 425*
Litsky, Frank   *143, 425*
Littell, Joseph Fletcher   *126, 425*
Littke, Lael   *204, 425*
Little, Jean   *29, 44, 45, 97, 121, 127, 190,*
    195, 425, 470
Little, Lessie Jones   *27, 183, 234, 354,*
    362, 425, 479
Little, Lisa   *215, 425, 459*
Littlefield, William   *210, 273, 425*
Littlewood, Valerie   *130, 425*
Littmann, Mark   *151, 425*
Litzinger, Roseanne   *144, 425, 439*
Liu, Beatrice   *85, 425, 475*
Lively, Penelope   *47, 108, 215, 230, 425,*
    434
Livingston, Myra Cohn   *72, 93, 115, 133,*
    180, 182, 201, 202, 203, 210, 216, 272,
    297, 339, 344, 388, 425, 426
Livoni, Cathy   *426*
Livoni, Kathy   *203*

Llewellyn, Claire   *222, 426*
Lloyd, Carole   *48, 426*
Lloyd, David   *164, 182, 426*
Lloyd, Errol   *99, 278, 426*
Lloyd, J. Selwyn   *426*
Lloyd, Megan   *70, 117, 184, 365, 382,*
    426
Lloyd, R. J.   *102, 197, 385, 426*
Lloyd, Trevor   *206, 426*
Llywelyn, Morgan   *20, 426*
Lobe, Mira   *9, 108, 401, 426*
Lobel, Anita   *28, 40, 62, 64, 145, 155,*
    157, 162, 215, 426, 427, 486
Lobel, Arnold   *11, 21, 28, 33, 40, 61, 62,*
    63, 64, 67, 68, 88, 94, 114, 122, 131,
    132, 139, 145, 154, 156, 157, 160, 161,
    162, 163, 169, 179, 181, 215, 217, 224,
    290, 335, 390, 392, 426, 427, 455, 467,
    470, 483
Locker, Thomas   *69, 146, 158, 163, 383,*
    427
Lodge, Bernard   *99, 427*
Lofgren, Ulf   *19, 427*
Lofting, Hugh   *49, 165, 428*
Logan, Dwight   *30, 31, 343, 428, 490*
Loh, Jules   *230, 428*
Lohman, Philip   *139, 428, 484*
Lois, Lois Ehlert   *30, 36, 41, 116, 190,*
    191, 192, 253, 331, 438
Loken, Anna Belle   *211, 274, 428*
Lokka, Pirkko   *109, 428*
Long, Sylvia   *112, 192, 364, 428*
Longfellow, Henry Wadsworth   *69, 100,*
    109, 144, 393, 418, 428, 487
Longstreth, Joseph   *153, 275, 428*
Longworth, Polly   *213, 428*
Lopez, Barry   *183, 428, 481*
Lord, Athena V.   *4, 56, 428*
Lord, Betty   *113, 428*
Lord, John Vernon   *199, 428, 449*
Lorenz, Lee   *144, 428*
Loriot   *23, 428, 456, 484*
Lorraine, Walter   *153, 154, 210, 310,*
    428, 489, 490
Lossing, Margaret   *206, 395, 396*
Lottridge, Celia Barker   *45, 104, 129,*
    131, 428
Louden, Claire   *167, 400, 428*
Louden, George   *167, 400, 428*
Lougheed, Robert   *196, 228, 375, 428*
Louie, Ai-Ling   *28, 144, 428*
Louie, AiLing
Lourie, Peter K.   *124, 428*
Lourie, Richard   *215, 429*
Lovejoy, Bahija Fattuhi   *140, 429*
Lovelace, Maud Hart   *122, 208, 281, 297,*
    312, 315, 349, 360, 361, 362, 366, 429,
    470, 474
Low, Alice   *113, 429*
Low, Joseph   *40, 63, 64, 138, 152, 157,*
    209, 211, 304, 373, 429
Low, Ruth   *152, 429*
Low, William   *16, 18, 429, 444, 445*
Lowe, Patricia Tracey   *63, 269, 429*
Lowentowicz, Irena   *206, 268, 429*
Lownsbery, Eloise   *165, 429*
Lowrey, Janette Sebring   *216, 429*

Lowry, Lois   *5, 29, 30, 42, 54, 56, 84, 88,*
    89, 92, 94, 98, 108, 111, 115, 124, 126,
    128, 129, 170, 180, 197, 200, 201, 219,
    223, 316, 429, 466
Lubach, Peter   *123, 429*
Lubin, Leonard   *63, 133, 291, 343, 430*
Lubin, Leonard B.   *53, 156, 430*
Lucas, Celia   *222, 310, 430*
Lucas, George   *172, 430*
Lucas, Mary Seymour   *206, 335, 430*
Lucey, Marilyn   *142, 391, 430*
Lucht, Irmgard   *22, 365, 430*
Lueders, Edward   *51, 328, 430*
Lufkin, Raymond   *3, 165, 167, 206, 275,*
    394, 423, 430, 432
Luiken, Nicole   *236, 430*
Luis, Earlene W.   *36, 430, 450*
Luks, Margaret   *72, 361, 430*
Luling, Virginia   *176, 430*
Lundbergh, Holger   *62, 262, 430*
Lunge, Jeffrey   *73, 324, 430*
Lunn, Janet   *42, 44, 97, 104, 109, 111,*
    127, 129, 133, 195, 236, 312, 347, 413,
    430, 453
Lurie, Alison   *66, 430*
Lurie, Leon   *219, 430, 481*
Lurie, Morris   *58, 237, 382, 430*
Lustig, Arnost   *114, 430, 460*
Lustig, Loretta   *115, 430*
Lutzeier, Elizabeth   *82, 431*
Luzzati, Emanuele   *154, 431*
Lydecker, Laura   *64, 431, 441*
Lynch, P. J.   *20, 431*
Lynch, Patrick James   *130, 350, 431*
Lyon, George Ella   *94, 117, 431*
Lyons, Mary E.   *5, 95, 235, 431*
Lyons, Oren   *73, 431*

Mabey, Richard   *150, 221, 404, 431*
MacAlvay, Nora Tully   *86, 106, 431*
Macarthur-Onslow, Annette   *431, 482*
Macaulay, David   *8, 26, 29, 40, 41, 54,*
    62, 63, 64, 68, 148, 149, 156, 157, 162,
    163, 179, 181, 195, 222, 227, 431, 482
MacCarthy, Patricia   *159, 431, 434*
MacClintock, Dorcas   *62, 147, 431, 452*
MacClintock, Marshall   *205, 432*
MacCloud, Malcolm   *68, 432*
Macdonald, Caroline   *5, 6, 60, 70, 75, 91,*
    102, 350, 432
MacDonald, George   *109, 155, 432*
MacDonald, Golden   *37, 38, 64, 281, 432*
MacDonald, James   *31, 166, 376, 432*
MacDonald, Reby E.   *74, 432*
Macdonald, Shelagh   *230, 432*
MacDonald, Suse   *41, 94, 432*
Macfarlane, Aidan   *221, 350, 432, 446*
MacGibbon, Jean   *175, 432*
MacGregor, Ellen   *239, 348, 432*
MacGrory, Yvonne   *20, 432*
Machetanz, Frederick   *206, 430, 432*
MacIntyre, Elisabeth   *57, 206, 432*
MacIntyre, Rod   *236, 432*
Mack, Stanley   *61, 156, 214, 401, 410,*
    432
MacKain, Bonnie   *124, 432*
Mackay, Claire   *127, 128, 194, 377, 432*

MacKay, Donald   *432*
MacKay, Donald A.   *214, 432*
Macken, Walter   *213, 432*
MacKnight, Ninon   *208, 337, 432*
MacLachlan, Patricia   *28, 69, 89, 93, 94, 110, 113, 163, 170, 173, 183, 197, 272, 433*
MacLean, Robert   *106, 433, 438*
MacLeod, Charlotte   *188, 433*
MacLeod, Doug   *59, 237, 433*
MacMillan, Annabelle   *211, 250, 348, 433, 486*
Macmillan, Cyrus   *43, 367, 433*
Macness, Brian   *232, 433*
Madden, Don   *138, 373, 433*
Madden, Mabra   *206, 283, 433*
Maddock, Reginald   *214, 367, 433*
Madison, Arnold   *93, 187, 433*
Maeno, Itoko   *87, 433*
Maggio, Rosalie   *124, 433*
Magnuson, Diana   *199, 433, 492*
Magnusson, Magnus   *221, 433*
Magorian, Michelle   *48, 102, 111, 225, 227, 228, 433*
Magubane, Peter   *118, 119, 433, 435*
Mahan, Benton   *141, 317, 433*
Maher, Ramona   *43, 229, 433*
Mahy, Margaret   *28, 29, 48, 91, 99, 105, 109, 159, 164, 173, 225, 248, 346, 377, 385, 431, 434, 445, 469, 473*
Mai, Vo-Dinh   *87, 232, 388, 434*
Mains, David   *91, 434*
Mains, Karen   *91, 434*
Maitland, Antony   *25, 33, 47, 98, 99, 101, 108, 186, 212, 223, 227, 230, 349, 350, 397, 403, 425, 434, 474*
Major, Alice   *6, 434*
Major, Beverly   *20, 179, 389, 434*
Major, Kevin   *34, 44, 45, 77, 97, 108, 127, 194, 236, 434*
Major, Ted   *150, 321, 434*
Malcolmson, Anne B.   *38, 287, 434*
Mali, Jane Lawrence   *7, 376, 434, 435*
Malkus, Alida   *165, 383, 435*
Mallory, Kenneth   *24, 303, 435*
Malmgren, Dallin   *75, 435*
Malone, Mary   *36, 137, 138, 139, 140, 141, 269, 292, 369, 383, 388, 435*
Maloney, Margaret Crawford   *97, 104, 250, 347, 435*
Maloney, Ray   *75, 435*
Malsberg, Edward   *140, 141, 391, 435*
Malvern, Corinne   *86, 206, 265, 435*
Malvern, Corrine   *207*
Malvern, Gladys   *86, 207, 435*
Mandela, Zindzi   *119, 433, 435*
Manes, Stephen   *42, 74, 89, 134, 197, 218, 385, 435*
Mangurian, David   *63, 296, 435*
Manheim, Ralph   *158, 380, 435*
Manley, Ruth   *58, 435*
Manning-Sanders, Ruth   *19, 98, 392, 435*
Manos, Helen   *35, 435*
Mansell, Dom   *130, 435*
Manton, Jo   *46, 331, 354, 355*
Maraslis, Demetra   *68, 295, 435*

Marcellino, Fred   *41, 183, 185, 190, 250, 436, 476*
Marcher, Marion W.   *136, 416, 436*
Marchetta, Melina   *15, 60, 436*
Marchiori, Carlos   *44, 343, 436*
Mardon, John   *140, 317, 436*
Margolis, Richard J.   *69, 291, 436*
Mari, Iela   *214, 436*
Marino, Dorothy   *83, 210, 272, 436*
Mark, Jan   *48, 101, 102, 130, 173, 385, 436, 471*
Marks, Alan   *48, 309, 436*
Marlow, Eric   *234, 362, 436*
Marnie, Neal   *222*
Marray, Denis   *436*
Marrin, Albert   *28, 436*
Marriott, Pat   *51, 102, 212, 245, 251, 418, 436*
Mars, W. T.   *51, 85, 136, 202, 284, 341, 436, 451*
Marsden, John   *59, 69, 75, 117, 436*
Marsh, Gwen   *32, 49, 50, 365, 405, 418, 436*
Marshak, Samuel   *190, 436, 486*
Marshall, Archibald   *213, 253, 436*
Marshall, Bernard G.   *164, 437*
Marshall, Catherine   *79, 91, 273, 374, 437*
Marshall, Edward   *42, 70, 226, 437*
Marshall, James   *11, 35, 41, 42, 61, 62, 63, 70, 74, 89, 90, 96, 156, 160, 172, 179, 180, 182, 184, 188, 224, 226, 247, 248, 437, 438, 459, 479*
Marshall, Ray   *191, 198, 277, 437*
Marshall, Rosamund Van der Zee   *206, 327, 437*
Marstall, Bob   *24, 437, 446*
Martchenko, Michael   *195, 437, 457*
Martel, Suzanne   *108, 127, 382*
Martell, Suzanne   *194, 437*
Marten, Michael   *149, 296, 437, 440*
Martin, Ann M.   *144, 145, 238, 239, 437*
Martin, Barry   *71, 438, 492*
Martin, Bill   *30, 116, 192, 253, 290, 331, 438*
Martin, David Stone   *114, 438, 527*
Martin, Dick   *17, 18, 438, 444*
Martin, James Henry   *57, 438*
Martin, Joseph Plumb   *78, 438, 441*
Martin, Patricia Miles   *211, 329, 438, 450*
Martin, Ron   *142, 438*
Martin, Sarah Catherine   *160, 437, 438*
Martin, William Donald   *57, 438*
Martinez, Elizabeth Sutherland   *3, 428, 438*
Martinez, John   *228, 379, 438*
Martini, Teri   *142, 274, 438*
Maruki, Toshi   *4, 17, 28, 438*
Marvin, Frederic   *132, 299, 438*
Maschler, Kurt   *279, 282, 291, 293, 338, 379, 385, 388, 402, 478, 492*
Mason, Evelyn   *172, 304, 438*
Mason, Miriam E.   *106, 433, 438*
Massie, Diane Redfield   *188, 212, 438*
Masuda, Modoki   *150, 396, 439*
Matas, Carol   *20, 235, 236, 439*
Math, Irwin   *149, 152, 403, 439*

Mather, Kirtley F.   *78, 439, 455, 456*
Mather, Cotton   *217, 400, 439*
Mather, P. P. Karen   *217, 400, 439*
Mathers, Petra   *30, 159, 184, 192, 243, 352, 439*
Mathiesen, Egon   *211, 439*
Mathis, Sharon Bell   *26, 73, 118, 161, 169, 292, 322, 323, 342, 439*
Mathison, Melissa   *35, 410, 439*
Matsuno, Masaku   *19, 439*
Mattingly, Christobel   *15, 58, 439, 456*
Maureen Daly. In 1960   *43*
Maurer, Richard   *8, 439*
Maurer, Werner   *108, 265, 439, 464*
Mauser, Pat Rhoads   *84, 223, 439, 468*
Maxner, Joyce   *159, 399, 439*
Maxwell, Florenz Webbe   *73, 439*
Maxwell, John   *210, 439, 443*
Maxwell, William   *167, 400, 440*
May, John   *149, 296, 437, 440*
May, Kara   *172, 440*
Mayakovsky, Vladimir   *156, 304, 312, 440*
Mayer, Marianna   *70, 90, 128, 226, 366, 440*
Mayer, Mercer   *11, 13, 21, 42, 53, 62, 85, 89, 128, 157, 239, 339, 415, 440*
Mayes, Susan   *195, 320, 330, 440, 484*
Mayne, William   *29, 46, 47, 51, 100, 102, 108, 109, 125, 130, 162, 199, 263, 267, 292, 380, 413, 440, 441*
Mayo, Frank   *188, 441*
Mayo, Gretchen   *143, 360, 441*
Mays, Lucinda   *199, 441*
Mays, Victor   *31, 32, 78, 85, 117, 136, 137, 416, 438, 441, 446, 447, 473*
Mazer, Anne   *129, 396, 441*
Mazer, Harry   *162, 228, 441*
Mazer, Norma Fox   *42, 53, 68, 112, 132, 161, 163, 170, 188, 441*
McaLean, Robert   *77*
McBratney, Sam   *20, 441*
McCabe, Eugene   *189, 441, 465*
McCaffrey, Anne   *64, 431, 441*
McCain, Murray   *154, 246, 441*
McCann, Gerald   *36, 441*
McCaughren, Tom   *20, 189, 328, 441*
McCauley, Jane R.   *192, 295, 441*
McClintock, Barbara   *159, 442*
McClintock, Marshall   *321*
McClinton, Leon   *72, 442*
McCloskey, Robert   *37, 38, 39, 64, 134, 174, 193, 208, 209, 231, 238, 239, 442*
McClung, Robert   *199, 442*
McClung, Robert M.   *93, 96, 148, 343, 420, 442*
McClure, Gillian   *100, 303, 442*
McCord, David   *54, 123, 132, 133, 279, 319, 346, 400, 403, 442, 479*
McCord, Jean   *162, 442*
McCorkell, Elsie J.   *229, 442*
McCormick, Dell J.   *238, 442*
McCoy, J. J.   *143, 213, 243, 314, 442*
McCoy, Joseph J.   *143, 243, 314, 442*
McCracken, Steve   *74, 361, 442*
McCrea, James   *139, 373, 442*
McCrea, Ruth   *139, 373, 442*

McCue, Lisa   *24, 200, 220, 442*
McCully, Emily   *11, 13, 41, 61, 72, 92, 112, 126, 131, 134, 196, 200, 222, 226, 237, 245, 316, 442, 443, 489*
McCurdy, Bruce   *71, 262, 443*
McCurdy, Michael   *159, 182, 443, 463*
McCutcheon, Elsie   *102, 443*
McDermott, Beverly Brodsky   *40, 161, 443*
McDermott, Gerald   *12, 13, 26, 30, 40, 52, 443*
McDonald, Megan   *112, 443*
McDonald, Ralph   *141, 290, 443*
McDougall, Marina   *127, 443*
McDowall, David   *177, 384, 443*
McDowell, Dottie   *91, 443, 460*
McDowell, Josh   *91, 443, 460*
McEwan, Keith   *237, 393, 443*
McFall, Christie   *137, 138, 443*
McFarlane, Sheryl   *97, 104, 131, 133, 423, 443*
McGaw, Jessie Brewer   *216, 443*
McGiffin, Lee   *210, 216, 439, 443*
McGillis, Roderick   *66, 443*
McGinley, Phyllis   *38, 155, 246, 443*
McGough, Roger   *130, 197, 273, 407, 443*
McGovern, Ann   *26, 122, 414, 443, 444*
McGowan, Dr. Alan   *191, 444*
McGraw, Eloise J.   *50, 348*
McGraw, Eloise Jarvis   *18, 120, 168, 188, 208, 438, 444*
McGraw, Lauren Lynn   *18, 438, 444*
McGraw, Sheila   *172, 444, 457*
McGuire, Paula   *234, 350, 444*
McHale, Ethel K.   *202, 275, 444*
McHargue, Georgess   *132, 215, 277, 295, 444*
McHugh, Florence   *50, 401, 420, 444*
McHugh, Isabel   *50, 401, 420, 444*
McInnes, John   *79, 343, 444*
McIntosh, Jane   *151, 444*
McKay, Donald   *50, 299*
McKay, Hilary   *102, 444*
McKay, Robert   *174, 444*
McKeating, Eileen   *203, 444*
McKee, Douglas   *212, 444*
McKenna, Nancy Durrell   *221, 444*
McKenna, Terry   *130, 444*
McKenny, Margaret   *205, 395, 396, 444*
McKenzie, Ellen Kindt   *18, 72, 429, 444, 445*
McKillip, Patricia A.   *62, 180, 445, 463*
McKinley, Charles Frederick   *207, 326, 445*
McKinley, Robin   *170, 445*
McKinnon, Lise Somme   *17, 53, 213, 346, 445*
McKissack, Fredrick   *5, 30, 105, 119, 235, 346, 377, 434, 445, 473*
McKissack, Patricia   *5, 30, 41, 105, 119, 170, 183, 235, 304, 346, 377, 434, 445, 473, 479*
McKissack, Patricia   *5, 30, 105, 119, 235, 346, 377, 434, 445, 473*
McKissock, Patricia   *177, 445*
McKown, Robin   *55, 445*

McLaughlin, James   *177, 381, 445*
McLaughlin, Jean   *207, 293, 445*
McLaughlin, Molly   *151, 445*
McLeod, Doug   *117*
McLeod, Emilie   *405, 445*
McLeod, Emilie Warren   *26, 445, 446*
McLoughlin, John C.   *149, 445*
McMains, D.   *138, 445*
McMeekin, Isabel McLennan   *86, 445, 470*
McMillen, Wheeler   *137, 445*
McMullan, Jim   *155, 278, 446*
McMullan, Kate   *74, 316, 446*
McNair, Kate   *106, 446*
McNamara, John   *80, 446*
McNaughton, Colin   *125, 446*
McNeely, Marian Hurd   *165, 446*
McNeely, Tom   *108, 313, 446*
McNeer, May   *77, 136, 141, 193, 209, 446*
McNeill, James   *44, 107, 323, 446*
McNeill, Janet   *213, 446*
McNulty, Faith   *24, 437, 446*
McPhail, David   *26, 53, 129, 161, 179, 404, 418, 445, 446*
McPhedran, Marie   *97, 391, 446*
McPheeters, Bill   *215, 446, 471*
McPherson, Ann   *221, 350, 432, 446*
McRobbie, Narelle   *74*
McSwigan, Marie   *238, 446, 489*
McVay, Tracy   *141, 142, 317, 446*
McVey, Vicki   *151, 446*
Meader, Stephen W.   *135, 136, 137, 138, 166, 205, 264, 281, 441, 446, 447*
Meadow, Charles T.   *148, 447*
Meadowcroft, Enid La Monte   *31, 447*
Means, Elliott   *83, 419, 447*
Means, Florence Crannell   *21, 55, 167, 271, 415, 447*
Meddaugh, Susan   *160, 180, 243, 447*
Mee, Charles L.   *214, 447*
Meeker, Alice M.   *136, 336, 447*
Meeks, Arone Raymond   *74, 223, 447*
Meigs, Cornelia L.   *3, 50, 165, 206, 324, 387, 447*
Melcher, Frederic G. Family of   *164*
Melia, Gerard   *176, 447*
Mellecker, Judith   *184, 447, 471*
Melling, O. R.   *236, 447*
Mellonie, Bryan   *110, 334, 420, 447*
Melrose, Genevieve   *57, 298, 447*
Meltzer, Milton   *4, 5, 26, 28, 36, 56, 67, 68, 78, 94, 113, 114, 131, 132, 133, 219, 227, 234, 302, 323, 339, 447, 448*
Meltzer, Yehuda   *109, 448*
Melville, Herman   *19, 333, 448*
Melwood, Mary   *173, 448*
Melzack, Ronald   *111, 347, 448*
Mendoza, George   *51, 311, 448*
Menuhin, Yehudi   *130, 260, 382, 448*
Meral, C.   *20, 299, 448*
Mercer, Charles   *143, 415, 448*
Meredith, Don   *11, 448*
Meredith, Lucy   *179, 274, 448*
Meredith, Susan   *221, 295, 441, 448*
Merriam, Eve   *133, 155, 159, 180, 297, 448*

Merrill, Jean   *33, 51, 84, 196, 448, 469*
Merson, Elizabeth   *176, 448, 485*
Merwin, Decie   *71, 335, 448*
Mesghali, Farshid   *10, 22, 265, 448*
Messenger, Norman   *192, 449*
Metcalf, Vicky   *253, 254, 280, 304, 307, 325, 336, 343, 345, 354, 356, 362, 366, 370, 373, 377, 383, 385, 386, 406, 418, 425, 430, 432, 434, 437, 443, 445, 456, 457, 482, 490*
Meyer, Carolyn   *63, 324, 449, 487*
Meyer, Edith Patterson   *3, 177, 449*
Meyer, Franklyn E.   *85, 449*
Meyers, Bob   *85, 216, 380, 449*
Meyers, Susan   *43, 449*
Meyrick, Bette   *222, 449*
Michaels, Steve   *105, 422, 449*
Michelinie, David   *53, 351, 449*
Michi, James   *449*
Michie, James   *199, 428, 449*
Mickelsen, A. Berkeley   *91, 449*
Micklethwait, Lucy   *185, 449*
Micklewright, Robert   *58, 449*
Midgley, Andrew   *123, 449*
Miers, Earl Schenck   *135, 138, 140, 313, 449, 450*
Mikaelsen, Ben   *112, 230, 449*
Miklowitz, Gloria   *227, 449*
Mikolaycak, Charles   *13, 14, 63, 85, 94, 115, 117, 139, 158, 179, 182, 251, 290, 294, 309, 362, 382, 407, 449, 450, 484*
Miles, Betty   *89, 223, 397, 450*
Miles, Miska   *11, 67, 71, 169, 235, 438, 450, 471*
Miles, Patricia   *108, 211, 329, 438, 450*
Milgrim, Shirley G.   *114, 338, 450*
Milhous, Katherine   *38, 75, 167, 205, 206, 208, 311, 386, 450*
Mill, Eleanor   *135, 313, 449, 450*
Millar, Barbara F.   *36, 430, 450*
Millard, Kerry   *60, 378, 450*
Miller, Alice   *120, 369, 450*
Miller, Andrew   *450*
Miller, Ann   *222, 276, 450*
Miller, Don   *141, 229, 450, 453*
Miller, Edward   *146, 450*
Miller, Elizabeth C.   *165, 450, 477*
Miller, Frances A.   *42, 450*
Miller, Jane   *153, 154, 297, 450*
Miller, Jon   *183, 406, 450*
Miller, Judi   *225, 450*
Miller, Margaret   *160, 450*
Miller, Mary Beth   *148, 159, 250, 295, 450, 489*
Miller, Mary Britton   *32, 153, 154, 450, 460*
Miller, Mitchell   *61, 138, 156, 451*
Miller, Randy   *157, 276, 451*
Miller, Ruth White   *171, 451*
Miller, Theodore R.   *141, 418, 451*
Miller, Virginia   *130, 451*
Miller, Warren   *153, 451*
Mills, Elaine   *172, 360, 451*
Mills, John Fitzmaurice   *148, 451*
Mills, John Frazer   *154, 370, 451*
Mills, Roger   *176, 451*
Milne, A. A.   *49, 50, 451*

Milne, Lorus J.   *151, 413, 451*
Milne, Margery   *413, 451*
Milton, Hilary   *16, 92, 451*
Milton, Hilary H.   *79, 451*
Minarik, Else Holmelund   *39, 153, 155, 451*
Minnerly, Faith C.   *136, 290, 451*
Minor, Wendell   *18, 451*
Miret, Gil   *139, 317, 451*
Mirsky, Reba Paeff   *85, 436, 451*
Mitchell, Adrian   *199, 267, 451*
Mitchell, Isla   *207, 404, 452*
Mitchell, James   *221, 452*
Mitchell, Jerry   *33, 452*
Mitchison, Naomi   *9, 294, 452*
Mitsui, Eiichi   *211, 423, 452*
Mitton, Simon   *149, 452*
Mizumura, Kazue   *26, 452*
Mochi, Ugo   *62, 147, 431, 452*
Mocniak, George   *213, 452, 460*
Moe, Jorgen   *211, 255, 407, 452*
Moeri, Louise   *186, 452*
Mogilevsky, Alexander   *204, 452*
Mohr, Nicholasa   *3, 132, 141, 142, 160, 452*
Moini, Mahdi   *23, 334, 452*
Mole, John   *197, 452, 463*
Mollel, Tololwa M.   *97, 104, 131, 452, 454*
Moloney, James   *81, 452*
Momaday, Natachee Scott   *229, 452, 476*
Mongeau, Marc   *129, 339, 452*
Monjo, F. N.   *132, 452*
Monreal, Guy   *155, 298, 452*
Monsell, Mary   *92, 452, 457*
Montgomery, Charlotte Baker   *216, 452*
Montgomery, Lucy   *109, 314, 452*
Montgomery, Rutherford   *71, 229, 297, 305, 450, 452, 453*
Montgomery, Rutherford G.   *32, 167, 209, 210, 325, 452, 463*
Montresor, Beni   *39, 106, 154, 155, 160, 168, 184, 320, 396, 452*
Moodie, John   *139, 332, 341, 453*
Moon, Carl   *165, 453*
Moon, Grace P.   *165, 453*
Moon, Henrietta Jones   *216, 396, 453*
Moon, Marjorie   *74, 453*
Moon, Sarah   *23, 453, 476*
Moon, Sheila   *155, 453, 472*
Moore-Slater, Carol W.   *24, 453*
Moore, Anne Carroll   *165, 193, 233, 453*
Moore, Christopher   *129, 312, 430, 453*
Moore, Emily R.   *73, 453*
Moore, Inga   *198, 453*
Moore, Janet Gaylord   *169, 453*
Moore, Joseph Thomas   *234, 453*
Moore, Mary   *188, 453, 473*
Moore, Nancy   *153, 419, 453*
Moore, Ruth   *209, 453*
Moore, Yvette   *129, 259, 453*
Moorhouse, Geoffrey   *99, 453, 470*
Morales, Leslie   *24, 453*
Mordvinoff, Nicolas   *31, 38, 152, 153, 209, 210, 290, 424, 453, 454, 462*
Moreau, Rene   *9, 454, 466*

Morey, Walt   *76, 84, 120, 195, 231, 454, 471*
Morgan, Alison   *102, 454*
Morgan, Charles   *54, 82, 454*
Morgan, Helen L.   *207, 306, 454*
Morgan, Nicola   *79, 454*
Mori, Toshio   *4, 454*
Morice, Stella Margery   *90, 274, 454*
Morimoto, Junko   *14, 59, 454*
Morin, Paul   *97, 104, 131, 417, 452, 454*
Morison, Samuel Eliot   *77, 454, 468*
Morley, Carol   *131, 454*
Morley, Jacqueline   *222, 268, 392, 454*
Morozumi, Atsuko   *159, 454*
Morpurgo, Michael   *102, 230, 454*
Morrill, Leslie   *74, 89, 172, 214, 228, 330, 384, 454*
Morris, Anthony   *101, 312, 455*
Morris, Dudley   *205, 455*
Morris, Howard   *78, 439, 455, 456*
Morris, Jean   *231, 455*
Morris, Richard B.   *78, 455*
Morris, Robert A.   *61, 427, 455*
Morris, Sandra   *70, 455*
Morris, Sean   *148, 221, 340, 455*
Morris, Willie   *216, 455*
Morris, Winifred   *181, 295, 455*
Morrison, Bill   *113, 300, 455*
Morrison, Lucile   *43, 455*
Morrow, Betty   *4, 455, 458*
Morse, Carol   *212, 476*
Morse, Dorothy B.   *167, 208, 293, 455*
Morton, Alexandra   *79, 455*
Morton, Miriam   *141, 213, 355, 402, 455*
Morton, Robin   *79, 455*
Mosel, Arlene   *25, 40, 61, 92, 107, 160, 420, 455*
Moser, Barry   *8, 20, 30, 110, 159, 170, 175, 184, 185, 191, 291, 357, 362, 368, 370, 399, 405, 406, 455, 471*
Moser, Erwin   *178, 455*
Moskins, Marietta   *219, 418, 455*
Moss, Anita   *65, 456*
Moss, Jeff   *116, 318, 456*
Most, Bernard   *113, 456*
Mowat, Farley   *32, 43, 97, 107, 127, 344, 351, 456*
Moyers, William   *77, 171, 307, 312, 456*
Moyes, Lesley   *6, 456*
Moyler, Allan   *86, 301, 456*
Moynihan, Roberta   *15, 51, 211, 456*
Mozley, Charles   *212, 412, 456*
Mueller, Robert E.   *136, 456*
Muench, Josef   *78, 439, 455, 456*
Muhlbauer, Rita   *23, 456, 492*
Mukerji, Dhan Gopal   *165, 254, 456*
Mulkey, Kim   *146, 291, 456*
Mullen, Don   *215, 456*
Muller, Andrew   *23, 456*
Muller, Jorg   *17, 23, 27, 413, 428, 456, 484*
Muller, Robin   *7, 97, 111, 328, 456*
Mullins, Patricia   *58, 439, 456*
Munari, Bruno   *147, 154, 155, 341, 456, 457*
Munoz, Claudio   *130, 457*
Munoz, Rie   *183, 457*

Munro, Roxie   *158, 457*
Munsch, Robert   *127, 195, 437, 457*
Munsch, Robert N.   *172, 444, 457*
Munsil, Janet   *7, 457, 492*
Munsinger, Lynn   *42, 70, 80, 92, 96, 163, 226, 384, 421, 452, 457*
Munthe, Adam John   *130, 335, 457*
Munzo, Claudio
Murawski, Marian   *20, 400, 457*
Murdocca, Sal   *62, 295, 457*
Murphy, Elspeth Campbell   *91, 327, 457*
Murphy, Jill   *18, 100, 457*
Murphy, Jim   *94, 95, 135, 144, 146, 457*
Murphy, Joseph E.   *87, 457*
Murphy, Robert   *76, 401, 457*
Murphy, Shirley Rousseau   *182, 457*
Murray, Denis   *102, 457*
Murray, Don   *135, 457, 490*
Murray, Gladys Hall   *43, 457*
Murray, Irene   *55, 423, 457*
Murray, Jane   *65, 66*
Murray, Peter   *232, 457*
Murray, Ruth E.   *30, 94, 122, 170, 256, 457, 458*
Musgrove, Margaret   *27, 40, 157, 322, 323, 458*
Mussino, Attilio   *303, 458*
Mussino, Attilio   *64*
Myers, Anna   *175, 458*
Myers, Elisabeth P.   *106, 382, 458*
Myers, Mitzi   *66, 458*
Myers, Walter Dean   *5, 30, 54, 74, 95, 118, 119, 144, 146, 170, 171, 175, 179, 180, 182, 183, 185, 188, 200, 235, 458*
Myers, Walter M.   *73, 292, 458*

Nabb, Magdalen   *102, 198, 458*
Nabokov, Peter   *234, 458*
Nadejen, Theodore   *86, 165, 314, 458, 485*
Nadler, Ellis   *77, 458, 482*
Naeem, Shahid   *4, 455, 458*
Nagel, Stina   *138, 391, 458*
Naidoo, Beverly   *56, 176, 458*
Nairac, Rosemonde   *148, 277, 373, 458*
Nakamura, T.   *23, 459*
Nakatani, Chiyoko   *213, 313, 459*
Namioka, Lensey   *188, 459*
Nance, John   *28, 459*
Nankivell, Joice M.   *209, 353, 459*
Naor, Leah   *109, 459*
Narahashi, Keiko   *182, 459*
Nardi, Marcia   *154, 459, 482*
Narell, Irena   *114, 459*
Nash, Ogden   *184, 211, 296, 437, 459*
Nash, Rod   *221, 459, 471*
Natti, Susanna   *68, 459, 477*
Naughton, Bill   *176, 321, 459*
Navarra, John Gabriel   *143, 459*
Navarra, Tova   *146, 405, 459*
Naylor, Penelope   *215, 425, 459*
Naylor, Phyllis R.   *459*
Naylor, Phyllis Reynolds   *56, 69, 81, 93, 170, 184, 188, 200, 217, 226, 236, 237, 459*
Nebel, Gustave   *214, 459*
Nebel, Gustave E.   *139, 317, 459*

Needle, Jan   *48, 102, 459*
Negri, Rocco   *52, 169, 459*
Negron, Bill   *202, 422, 459*
Neilsen, Ann   *91, 443, 460*
Neilson, Frances F.   *205, 382, 460*
Neimark, Anne E.   *86, 460, 471*
Nelsen, Donald   *61, 358, 460*
Nelson, Theresa   *113, 460*
Nemcova, Jeanne   *114, 430, 460*
Nesbitt, Esta   *235, 300, 460*
Neset, Gunal   *9, 365, 460*
Ness, Evaline   *39, 50, 154, 155, 168, 210, 211, 212, 293, 391, 450, 460, 462, 467, 482*
Neugebauer, Michael   *158, 375, 460, 466*
Neville, Emily Cheney   *3, 168, 213, 452, 460*
Neville, Mary   *213, 460*
Nevins, Ann   *144, 460*
Nevins, Dan   *144, 460*
Newberry, Clare Turlay   *37, 38, 460*
Newell, Hope   *52, 206, 460, 475*
Newfeld, Frank   *9, 44, 103, 107, 108, 111, 194, 418, 460, 461*
Newfield, Marcia   *235, 316, 461*
Newkirk, Ingrid   *24, 461*
Newman, Daisy   *214, 461*
Newman, Frederick R.   *150, 461*
Newman, Penny   *6, 461, 472*
Newman, Robert   *188, 285, 461*
Newman, Susan   *145, 461*
Newsom, Carol   *112, 146, 197, 226, 238, 291, 461*
Newton, Suzanne   *163, 171, 461, 486*
Ney, John   *133, 461*
Ng, Simon   *45, 77, 79, 133, 461*
Nhuong, Huynh Quang   *87, 232, 388, 461*
Nichols, Beverly   *110, 423, 461*
Nichols, Ruth   *44, 214, 389, 461*
Nicholson, William   *52, 269, 461*
Nickl, Peter   *157, 178, 461*
Nicklaus, Carol   *17, 68, 145, 265, 290, 461, 462, 464*
Nicolas   *4, 9, 31, 38, 39, 45, 152, 153, 154, 209, 210, 267, 290, 424, 452, 453, 454, 462*
Nicollet, Jean-Michel   *23, 247, 299, 462*
Niehuis, Charles   *229, 404, 462*
Niklaus, Thelma   *212, 275, 394, 462*
Niland, Deborah   *58, 108, 147, 237, 462, 470, 472*
Niland, Kilmeny   *58, 108, 232, 462, 472*
Nilsson, Eleanor   *60, 75, 133, 462*
Nilsson, Lennart   *29, 221, 407, 462*
Nilsson, Ulf   *17, 333, 462*
Nimmo, Jenny   *198, 222, 289, 462*
Nishikawa, Osamu   *150, 462, 468*
Nissinen, Aila   *9, 400, 462*
Nixon, Joan Lowery   *22, 42, 74, 96, 112, 135, 182, 188, 189, 196, 216, 225, 230, 238, 283, 385, 462, 463, 475*
Noakes, Polly   *195, 463*
Noble, Iris   *71, 150, 463*
Noble, Marty   *24, 463, 470*
Noble, Trinka Hakes   *70, 144, 145, 146, 172, 403, 463*

Nodelman, Perry M.   *65, 66, 463*
Nolan, Dennis   *72, 95, 182, 463*
Nolan, Jeannette C.   *106, 250, 463*
Nonnast, Marie   *209, 452, 463*
Nook, Gerald   *50, 63, 356, 463*
Noonan, Julia   *62, 445, 463*
Norman, Howard   *159, 443, 463*
Norman, Lilith   *108, 236, 265, 463*
Norman, Mary   *197, 452, 463*
North, Sterling   *15, 51, 83, 136, 137, 168, 195, 210, 231, 239, 250, 285, 463*
Northway, Jenny   *176, 401, 463*
Norton, Andre   *174, 270, 463*
Norton, Mary   *45, 46, 50, 107, 161, 211, 346, 411, 464*
Norweb, Jeanne K.   *145, 417, 464*
Nostlinger, Christine   *10, 17, 108, 265, 439, 461, 464*
Novak, Matt   *186, 464*
Noyes, Alfred   *100, 113, 402, 464*
Nugebauer, Michael   *460*
Numeroff, Laura J.   *35, 42, 70, 80, 90, 135, 274, 464*
Numeroff, Laura Joffe   *185, 274, 464*
Nutt, Ken   *104, 111, 195, 464*
Nyberg, Morgan   *97, 464*
Nystrom, Carolyn   *91, 369, 464*

Oakley, Graham   *27, 99, 100, 125, 157, 464*
Obiols, Miguel   *24, 464*
Obligado, Lilian   *84, 136, 212, 464, 465*
Obligado, Lillian   *391*
Obo, Shizuko   *233, 465*
O'Brien, Anne Sibley   *116, 373, 465*
O'Brien, Jack   *238, 465*
O'Brien, Katherine   *91, 465*
O'Brien, Robert C.   *4, 26, 52, 126, 132, 169, 188, 222, 231, 239, 268, 304, 465*
Obstfeld, Raymond   *75, 465*
O'Connor, Jane   *95, 149, 252, 465*
O'Donnell, Al   *189, 441, 465*
O'Donnell, James J.   *142, 143, 465*
O'Donnell, Peter   *131, 465*
Oechsli, Kelly   *24, 42, 90, 138, 139, 294, 316, 317, 465, 470*
Oeschli, Kelly   *142, 391*
Offen, Hilda   *198, 465*
Ogden, Betina   *147, 386, 465*
Ogle, Richard B.   *204, 419, 465*
O'Hare, Colette   *27, 100, 304, 466*
Ohi, Ruth   *11*
Ohlsson, Ib   *140, 293, 466*
Ohlsson, Ib Spang   *10, 52, 61, 333, 371, 466*
Okamoto, Dorothy Tomiye   *73, 466*
O'Kelley, Mattie Lou   *179, 466, 486*
Oktober, Tricia   *232, 466*
Okuda, Tsuguo   *23, 466*
Olds, Elizabeth   *38, 466*
Oliver, Jenni   *42, 64, 93, 111, 126, 426, 429, 466*
Oliver, Tony   *232, 357, 466*
Ollivier, Jean   *9, 454, 466*
Olsen, Alfa Betty   *161*
Olson, Arielle North   *87, 466*
Olson, Helen Kronberg   *218, 266, 466*

Ommanney, F. D.   *466*
Ommanney, Francis D.   *221, 346*
O'Moran, Mabel   *209, 315, 453, 466*
Oneal, Zibby   *29, 69, 86, 466, 482*
O'Neill, Joan   *189, 466*
O'Neill, Mary   *174, 260, 466*
Onyshkewych, Zenowij   *161, 265, 466*
Opie, Iona   *66, 185, 190, 192, 466, 467*
Opie, Peter   *66, 185, 190, 466, 467*
Oppenheim, Joanne   *97, 104, 111, 131, 195, 467, 490*
Oppenheim, Sulamith   *202, 357, 467*
Oram, Hiawyn   *130, 407, 467*
Orbaan, Albert   *33, 467*
Orbaan, Robert   *33, 467*
Orgel, Doris   *50, 56, 93, 157, 219, 372, 427, 467*
Orlev, Uri   *4, 17, 115, 120, 189, 219, 367, 467*
Orlowsky, Wallace   *141, 309, 467, 476*
Ormerod, Jan   *58, 100, 130, 373, 467*
Ormondroyd, Edward   *71, 467, 489*
Ortiz, Gloria   *53, 404, 467*
Osborn, Robert   *135, 211, 297, 467*
Osborne, Chester G.   *32, 467*
Osborne, Mary Pope   *235, 467*
Osborne, Maurice Machado   *211, 460, 467*
Osborne, Richard N.   *32, 467*
Osmond, Edward   *45, 467*
Osofsky, Audrey   *129, 467*
Ostendorf, Lloyd   *136, 269, 467*
Ostman, Lempi   *165, 314, 467*
Ostrom, John H.   *28, 93, 94, 291, 467, 468, 487*
O'Sullivan, Tom   *84, 85, 300, 468*
Otava, Merja   *9, 468*
Otsuka, Yuzo   *13, 14, 246, 378, 468*
Ottley, Reginald   *52, 78, 213, 468, 475*
Otto, Svend S.   *10, 19, 179*
Oughton, Taylor   *142, 319, 468*
Overbeck, Cynthia   *150, 311, 369, 391, 400, 412, 462, 468*
Overholser, Wayne D.   *229, 468, 473*
Overlie, George   *72, 468*
Overly, Charles   *77, 454, 468*
Owen, Dyddgu   *468*
Owen, Gareth   *197, 378, 468*
Owen, William   *144, 468*
Owens, Gail   *42, 84, 85, 105, 143, 171, 179, 180, 182, 196, 218, 220, 223, 226, 239, 288, 289, 301, 303, 305, 387, 439, 468, 469*
Owens, Mary Beth   *123, 190, 469, 480*
Owens, Robert   *52, 215, 258, 469*
Oxenbury, Helen   *30, 34, 99, 100, 125, 161, 183, 190, 191, 198, 246, 286, 418, 434, 469*

Pace, Mildred M.   *83, 205, 259, 319, 469*
Pace, Mildred Mastin   *148, 385, 469*
Pachter, Hedwig   *4, 469*
Page, Michael F.   *108, 389, 469*
Page, Valerie King   *36, 288, 469*
Paget-Fredericks, Joseph   *71, 469*
Palazzo, Tony   *38, 208, 359, 469*
Palin, Michael   *198, 418, 469*

Palladini, David   *22, 93, 132, 156, 406, 469*

Pallasch, Gerhard   *50, 386, 469*

Palmer, Jan   *84, 196, 293, 448, 469*

Palmquist, Eric   *9, 32, 423, 470*

Palumbo, Toni   *369, 470*

Pandell, Karen   *24, 463, 470*

Panesis, Nicholas   *86, 445, 470*

Papas, William   *47, 98, 99, 453, 470*

Paperny, Myra   *97, 121, 470*

Paris, Pat   *143, 317, 470*

Parish, Peggy   *24, 35, 74, 79, 88, 89, 128, 343, 427, 465, 470*

Park, Barbara   *81, 89, 122, 128, 180, 182, 183, 185, 220, 224, 226, 228, 238, 470*

Park, Ruth   *28, 58, 102, 108, 147, 179, 237, 462, 470*

Parker, K. Langloh   *57, 328, 470*

Parker, Lewis   *121, 425, 470*

Parker, Nancy   *57, 453, 470*

Parker, Nancy Winslow   *68, 144, 149, 157, 262, 341, 400, 470, 471*

Parker, Robert   *86, 460, 471*

Parker, Robert A.   *141, 160, 161, 216, 263, 287, 331, 471*

Parker, Robert Andrew   *40, 115, 131, 158, 159, 162, 181, 184, 219, 315, 344, 407, 447, 471, 483*

Parker, Steve   *130, 320, 471*

Parker, Tom   *79, 398, 471*

Parkins, David   *48, 102, 221, 308, 436, 459, 471*

Parkinson, Ethelyn M.   *3, 215, 446, 471*

Parks, Gordon   *89, 471*

Parks, Rosa   *105, 234, 362, 372, 436, 471*

Parks, Van Dyne   *20, 159, 191, 455, 471*

Parnall, Peter   *11, 13, 14, 26, 40, 67, 71, 76, 84, 96, 148, 150, 155, 169, 179, 216, 231, 235, 263, 293, 362, 394, 438, 453, 454, 471, 472*

Parnall, Virginia   *179, 394, 472*

Parramore, Barbara M.   *171, 472*

Parrish, Anne   *165, 167, 472*

Parrish, Dillwyn   *165, 472*

Parrish, Helen Rand   *71, 208, 472, 481*

Parry, Caroline   *77, 106, 111, 472*

Parsons, John   *6, 461, 472*

Partridge, Jenny   *23, 472*

Pascal, Francine   *84, 128, 472*

Paschel, Herbert P.   *32, 292, 472*

Pasco, Dallas   *136, 287, 472*

Pascoe, Elaine   *234, 472*

Pasnak, William   *11, 472*

Pastic, George   *194, 248, 472*

Patent, Dorothy Hinshaw   *93, 96, 400, 472*

Paterson, A. B.   *58, 108, 462, 472*

Paterson, Andrew Barton   *22, 58, 322, 381, 472*

Paterson, Diane   *64, 472*

Paterson, Katherine   *4, 6, 21, 22, 30, 53, 68, 73, 88, 89, 105, 112, 116, 117, 126, 128, 132, 133, 158, 159, 162, 163, 169, 170, 180, 181, 188, 193, 218, 224, 225, 232, 245, 321, 322, 323, 346, 377, 434, 445, 472, 473*

Paton, Alan   *209, 473*

Paton, Jane   *46, 473, 489*

Patten, Brian   *188, 453, 473*

Patten, Lewis B.   *229, 468, 473*

Patterson, Charles   *234, 473*

Patterson, Claire   *164, 473, 486*

Patterson, Dr. Francine   *151, 301, 473*

Patterson, Francine   *89, 151, 301, 473*

Patterson, Geoffrey   *198, 473*

Patterson, Ippy   *152, 473*

Patterson, Lillie   *117, 119, 441, 473*

Paul, Aileen   *140, 142, 373, 389, 473*

Paul, Korky   *56, 192, 287, 473*

Paul, Lissa   *66, 473*

Paulsen, Gary   *6, 35, 84, 89, 92, 112, 122, 128, 129, 170, 172, 181, 184, 196, 199, 218, 225, 226, 230, 232, 238, 473, 474*

Paulsen, Ruth Wright   *129, 230, 474*

Pavey, Peter   *58, 474*

Paxton, Arthur   *145, 474*

Paxton, Helen Sive   *145, 474*

Paylin, Jolie   *215, 414, 474*

Payne, Emmy   *79, 474, 491*

Payne, Harry C.   *65, 474*

Payne, Joan Balfour   *208, 209, 474*

Payne, Josephine Balfour   *208, 209, 474*

Payne, Stephen   *229, 351, 474*

Payson, Dale   *171, 235, 285, 290, 474*

Peacock, David   *7, 474*

Pearce, A. Philippa   *46, 48, 49, 51, 98, 107, 210, 212, 215, 230, 253, 258, 302, 331, 392, 434, 474*

Pearce, Fred   *222, 474*

Pearce, Philippa   *46, 48, 49, 51, 93, 98, 107, 180, 210, 212, 215, 230, 253, 258, 302, 331, 392, 434, 474*

Peare, Catherine Owens   *31, 195, 231, 343, 474, 475*

Pearlman, Corinne   *130, 307, 475*

Pearson, Clyde   *52, 78, 213, 468, 475*

Pearson, Gayle   *18, 475*

Pearson, Kit   *20, 44, 45, 77, 129, 475*

Pearson, Tracy Campbell   *182, 462, 475*

Pease, Howard   *30, 55, 71, 205, 418, 475*

Peaver, Walt   *139, 317, 475*

Peck, Anne Merriman   *204, 206, 395, 460, 475*

Peck, Beth   *81, 291, 475*

Peck, Graham   *85, 425, 475*

Peck, Richard   *6, 79, 87, 135, 142, 187, 188, 199, 224, 475*

Peck, Robert Newton   *70, 126, 128, 215, 222, 351, 422, 475*

Peck, Virginia   *91, 395, 475*

Peder, Margarte Sayers   *199*

Pedro   *38, 85, 243, 375, 481*

Peery, Edesse   *33*

Peet, Bill   *41, 42, 70, 90, 92, 94, 106, 190, 201, 203, 217, 225, 475, 476*

Pelgrom, Els   *17, 476*

Pelham, David   *192, 476*

Pellowski, Anne   *101, 215, 233, 476*

Pelta, Kathy   *151, 476*

Penick, Ib   *179, 358, 476*

PenistonBird, Adrian   *476*

Perceval, Don   *229, 452, 476*

Perennou, Marie   *23, 464, 476*

Perera, Thomas B.   *141, 309, 467, 476*

Peretz, I. L.   *62, 215, 476*

Perez, Norah A.   *121, 389, 476*

Perkins, Carol Morse   *212, 476*

Perkins, Richard Marlin   *212, 476*

Perkyns, Dorothy   *20, 476*

Perl, Lila   *28, 184, 476*

Perl, Susan   *56, 137, 138, 356, 476*

Perrault, Charles   *20, 23, 38, 41, 183, 190, 281, 331, 436, 453, 476*

Perrot, Jean   *66, 476*

Pershall, Mary   *81, 147, 476*

Pessin, Deborah   *114, 421, 476*

Petersen, Russell F.   *32, 352, 476*

Petersham, Maud   *37, 165, 450, 476, 477*

Petersham, Miska   *37, 165, 450, 476, 477*

Peterson, Esther Allen   *68, 459, 477*

Peterson, Lorraine   *92, 477*

Peterson, Russell Francis   *32, 477*

Petie, Haris   *141, 402, 477*

Petrides, Heidrun   *214, 307, 477*

Petroski, Catherine   *171, 477*

Pettit, Ted S.   *137, 477*

Pevsner, Stella   *84, 93, 115, 194, 477*

Peyton, K. M.   *25, 46, 47, 101, 213, 249, 250, 376, 477*

Pfeffer, Susan Beth   *84, 180, 194, 196, 200, 360, 477*

Pfister, Marcus   *24, 69, 477*

Phelan, Joseph A.   *26, 187, 477*

Phelan, Terry Wolfe   *143, 355, 477*

Philbrook, Elizabeth   *206, 477*

Philip, Marlene Nourbese   *44, 478*

Philip, Neil   *66, 478*

Phillips, Carolyn E.   *91, 277, 478*

Phillips, Ethel Calvert   *205, 420, 478*

Phillips, Eula Mark   *85, 478*

Phillips, Neil   *59, 109, 283, 478*

Philpott, Heather   *108, 478, 480*

Phipson, Joan   *32, 57, 76, 109, 236, 339, 383, 478*

Phipson, Joan M.   *57, 212, 478*

Piatti, Celestino   *154, 155, 478*

Picard, Barbara Leonie   *46, 47, 380, 478*

Pickard, Charles   *114, 331, 332, 478*

Pienkowski, Jan   *99, 110, 125, 279, 478*

Pierce, Charles W.   *138, 478*

Pierce, Meredith Ann   *42, 111, 163, 179, 180, 478*

Pierce, Tamora   *144, 478*

Piers, Helen   *99, 100, 263, 342, 478*

Pierson, Lori   *143, 317, 478*

Pilling, Ann   *102, 300, 478*

Pincus, Harriet   *12, 213, 214, 479*

Pinguilly, Yves   *23, 266, 479*

Pinkney, Brian   *95, 105, 119, 184, 190, 191, 246, 368, 398, 479*

Pinkney, Gloria Jean   *185, 479*

Pinkney, Jerry   *4, 21, 27, 41, 63, 69, 71, 73, 76, 95, 96, 116, 118, 119, 123, 133, 138, 159, 169, 182, 185, 190, 192, 217, 234, 239, 243, 288, 326, 341, 362, 370, 421, 425, 445, 479*

Pinkwater, Daniel M.   *79, 162, 179, 437, 479*

Pinkwater, Manus   *141, 479*

Pinnell, Miss   *198, 479*

Pinto, Ralph   53, 421, 479
Piper, Watty   49, 372, 480
Pirotta, Saviour   131, 480
Pirsig, Robert M.   126, 480
Pitcher, Caroline   82, 480
Pitcher, Donald T.   139, 480
Pitrone, Jean Maddern   86, 480
Pitt, Nancy   219, 480
Pittaway, Margaret   108, 478, 480
Pittman, Al   103, 367, 480
Pitz, Henry C.   30, 204, 206, 338, 480
Place, Marian T.   88, 223, 480
Place, Marian Templeton   229, 480
Platt, Kin   187, 202, 480
Platt, Richard   34, 269, 480
Pleninger, Diane Brooks   233, 339, 480
Pliskin, Jacqueline   146, 480
Pliskin, Jacqueline Jacobson   146, 480
Plomer, William   230, 246, 480
Plowden, David   27, 64, 480
Plume, Ilse   40, 178, 480
Plummer, Louise   75, 480
Plummer, W. K.   137, 332, 341, 480
Po, Lee   12, 326, 480
Pochocki, Ethel   123, 469, 480
Pogany, Willy   164, 303, 481
Pohrt, Tom   183, 428, 481
Poignant, Axel   57, 481
Poitier, Sidney   118, 481
Polacco, Patricia   5, 72, 95, 112, 219, 481
Poland, Marguerite   84, 249, 481
Pole, James T.   36, 481
Polese, Carolyn   69, 261, 481
Politi, Leo   38, 71, 85, 193, 201, 207, 208, 297, 472, 481
Pollack, Merrill   138, 380, 481
Polland, Madeleine   211, 212, 431, 481
Pollock, Penny   144, 145, 265, 321, 481
Polseno, Jo   62, 143, 173, 336, 481
Polushkin, Maria   17, 424, 481
Pomerantz, Barbara   219, 430, 481
Pomerantz, Charlotte   3, 4, 69, 183, 295, 421, 481
Pond, Roy   15, 482
Pont, Charles   57, 482
Pooley, Sarah   19, 130, 482
Poortvliet, Rien   108, 307, 482
Pope, Allen   207, 482, 492
Pope, Elizabeth M.   63, 169, 309, 482
Pope, Elizabeth Marie   210, 460, 482
Popov, Nikolaj   19, 316, 482
Porcellino, Michael R.   152, 482
Porritt, Jonathon   77, 458, 482
Portal, Colette   154, 459, 482
Porter, David Lord   163, 431, 482
Porter, George   86, 139, 466, 482
Porter, Helen Fogwell   236, 482
Porter, Richard W.   148, 482
Porter, Sheena   47, 431, 482
Porter, Sue   129, 321, 482
Poskanzer, Susan C.   482
Potaaianos, Themos   9, 482
Potter, Beatrix   49, 50, 482
Potter, Charles F.   482
Potter, Charles Francis   212, 482
Potts, K.   212, 263, 482
Potts, Richard   102, 482

Poulenic, Rhone   195
Poulin, Stephane   104, 110, 127, 131, 482
Poulsen, Gunnar   17, 274, 482
Powell, Lesley Cameron   90, 271, 482
Powell, Miriam   55, 209, 482
Powell, Randy   186, 483
Power, Margaret   59, 378, 483
Powers, Alfred   31, 313, 483
Powers, Elizabeth   142, 483
Powers, Richard M.   32, 209, 297, 308, 483
Powers, William   140, 483
Pownall, Eve   57, 60, 354, 361, 483
Powzyk, Joyce   175, 183, 190, 263, 483
Prachaticka, Marketa   23, 291, 483
Pragoff, Fiona   100, 483
Prance, Ghillean Tolmie   483
Prater, John   130, 483
Prather, Hugh   4, 392, 483
Prather, Ray   215, 368, 483
Prelutsky, Jack   64, 80, 88, 117, 157, 159, 162, 427, 483
Preston, Alice B.   205, 257, 483
Preston, Edna Mitchell   26, 40, 131, 161, 305, 387, 471, 483
Prestopino, Gregorio   214, 268, 483
Preussler, Otfried   10, 161, 265, 483
Price, Arthur   43, 259, 383, 483
Price, Christine   43, 168, 483, 484, 492
Price, Leontyne   119, 322, 323, 484
Price, Susan   48, 176, 484
Pride, Marilyn   74, 484
Primavera, Elise   144, 146, 163, 230, 283, 346, 351, 484
Primrose, Jean   46, 211, 356, 484
Pringle, Laurence   25, 96, 139, 149, 428, 484
Pringle, Mike   195, 320, 330, 440, 484
Pringle, Patrick   32, 484
Pritchett, Lulita Crawford   227, 310, 484
Proctor, John   149, 484
Proctor, Susan   149, 484
Prokofiev, Sergei   23, 179, 290, 428, 449, 456, 484
Provensen, Alice   13, 14, 28, 40, 41, 93, 152, 153, 154, 157, 159, 161, 162, 163, 170, 179, 190, 191, 194, 212, 484, 485
Provensen, Martin   13, 14, 28, 40, 41, 93, 191, 212, 484, 485
Provines, Virginia   71, 380, 485
Prusski, Jeffrey   113, 485
Pruszynska, Angela   33, 165, 403, 485
Pryor, Bonnie   21, 265, 485
Pucci, Albert J.   51, 85, 169, 386, 485
Puckett, Kent   91, 424, 485
Pugh, Anna   125, 342, 485
Pullman, Philip   112, 121, 485
Purcell, John   150, 485
Purdy, Claire Lee   86, 458, 485
Purkis, Sallie   176, 448, 485
Pursell, Weimer   78, 280, 485
Pushkin, Alexander Sergeevic   23, 63, 269, 409, 429, 485, 486
Puskas, James   171, 461, 486
Putnam, Peter Brock   62, 411, 412, 486
Pye, Trevor   6, 367, 486
Pyle, Howard   26, 52, 109, 388, 486

Quackenbush, Robert   93, 188, 264, 486
Queval, Jean   108, 340, 486
Quidam, Adam   109, 311, 486
Quilter, Lindsay   164, 473, 486
Quin-Harkin, Janet   64, 162, 426
Quinn, John   20, 486

Rabe, Berniece   93, 115, 486
Rabinowitz, Ann   145, 146, 486
Raddall, Thomas H.   31, 486
Radin, Ruth Yaffe   179, 466, 486
Radius, Emilio   22, 486
Radlov, Nicholas   204, 270, 486
Radunsky, Vladimir   190, 436, 486
Raffi   24, 486
Raftery, Gerald   136, 351, 486
Ragon, Michel   22, 486
Ragus, Christopher   27, 149, 382, 487
Raible, Alton   52, 67, 107, 132, 160, 169, 213, 217, 231, 487
Rampen, Leo   44, 487
Ramsey, Michael   63, 324, 449, 487
Rand, Ann   153, 487
Rand, Paul   153, 487
Rand, Ted   69, 428, 487
Randall, Kenneth Charles   208, 418, 487
Randall, Ruth Painter   86, 487
Rankin, Laura   30, 104, 487
Rankin, Louise S.   50, 167, 207, 487
Ransome, Arthur   39, 45, 487
Ransome, James   184, 384, 487
Rao, Anthony   28, 93, 94, 291, 467, 468, 487
Rapaport, Stella F.   34, 487
Rappaport, Doreen   4, 487
Raskin, Ellen   12, 26, 27, 61, 62, 73, 128, 139, 155, 169, 170, 188, 213, 225, 304, 487, 488
Rathe, Joanne   122, 488
Rattigan, Jama Kim   147, 384, 488
Rau, Margaret   202, 386, 488
Ravielli, Anthony   107, 168, 210, 488
Rawlings, Marjorie   82, 488
Rawlings, Marjorie Kinnan   51, 168, 488
Rawlins, Donna   59, 110, 237, 488
Rawlins, Janet   48, 230, 349, 488
Rawls, Wilson   42, 92, 98, 126, 128, 172, 196, 232, 488
Ray, Deborah Kogan   18, 76, 83, 184, 301, 309, 488
Ray, Jane   34, 192, 198, 488
Ray, Ralph   31, 55, 167, 174, 329, 355, 488
Raymond, Charles   86, 409, 488
Raymond, Louise   205, 365, 488
Rayner, Mary   28, 99, 102, 161, 181, 182, 406, 488
Raynor, Paul   93, 302, 488
Raysor, Joan   71, 467, 489
Read, Piers Paul   489
Reardon, Maureen   72, 304, 489
Reardon, Mary   238, 446, 489
Reaver, Herbert R.   75, 189, 489
Reavin, Sam   61, 442, 489
Recheis, Kathe   109, 255, 489
Redpath, Ian   195, 489
Redvers, Gwen   397

Reed, A. W.   *90, 323, 489*
Reed, Gwendolyn E.   *213, 369, 489*
Reed, Jacqueline   *43, 489*
Reed, Philip   *39, 489*
Reeder, Carolyn   *5, 56, 113, 173, 489*
Rees, David   *48, 101, 176, 489*
Rees, Ennis   *61, 358, 489*
Rees, Leslie   *57, 310, 489*
Rees, R. A.   *221, 489*
Reese, John   *209, 489*
Reeves, James   *46, 98, 210, 253, 405, 473, 489*
Regen, Susan   *88, 450, 489*
Reggiani, Renee   *9, 354, 489*
Regguinti, Gordon   *105, 399, 489*
Regosta, Gastone   *9, 252, 489*
Reich, Hanns   *155, 489*
Reid, Alastair   *12, 153, 210, 428, 489, 490*
Reid, Barbara   *97, 104, 111, 129, 131, 195, 223, 224, 390, 467, 490*
Reid, Bill   *44, 370, 490*
Reid, Dorothy   *44, 360, 490*
Reid, James   *204, 395, 490*
Reid, John   *164, 490*
Reid, Piers Paul   *489*
Reidel, Marlene   *153, 490*
Reidman, Sarah   *365*
Reidman, Sarah R.   *361*
Reilly, Pauline   *232, 490*
Reiner, Isabel   *490*
Reinfeld, Fred   *77, 490*
Reiss, Johanna   *3, 114, 160, 169, 490*
Rekimies, Erkki   *9, 490*
Remini, Robert V.   *87, 490*
Renberg, Dalia H.   *186, 344, 490*
Renick, Marion   *31, 428, 490*
Renick, Marion Lewis   *174, 490*
Renner, Hans Peter   *17, 263, 386, 490*
Resch, George T.   *137, 345, 490*
Rethi, Lili   *135, 457, 490*
Reuter, Bjarne   *17, 490*
Reuter, Carol   *138, 273, 490*
Reuter, M. Lawrence   *126, 303, 374, 490*
Rey, H. A.   *50, 65, 79, 153, 172, 474, 490, 491*
Rey, Margret   *55, 490, 491*
Reyes, Gregg   *130, 491*
Reyher, Becky   *38, 349, 491*
Reynolds, Pat   *232, 491*
Reynolds, Susan Lynn   *236, 491*
Rhind, Mary   *116, 491*
Rhine, Richard   *140, 491*
Rhoads, Dorothy   *168, 295, 491*
Rhodes, Timothy   *7, 310*
Ribbons, Ian   *47, 48, 292, 491*
Ricciuti, Edward R.   *149, 491*
Rice, Eve   *64, 491*
Rice, Inez   *210, 273, 491*
Rich, Louise Dickinson   *208, 491*
Richard, Adrienne   *132, 491*
Richards, Laura E.   *50, 204, 270, 314, 491*
Richards, Lawrence   *91, 491*
Richards, Norman   *151, 491*
Richards, Susan   *155, 251, 491*
Richardson, Ernest   *239, 381, 491*

Richardson, Jean   *69, 333, 491*
Richardson, Robert S.   *147, 491*
Riches, Judith   *185, 330, 491*
Richler, Mordecai   *44, 161, 194, 491*
Richter, Catherine M.   *174, 491*
Richter, Hans Peter   *17, 235, 410, 491*
Ride, Sally   *89, 491*
Ridley, Philip   *184, 198, 491, 492*
Riedel, Manfred G.   *149, 302, 492*
Riedman, Sarah R.   *136, 492*
Riehecky, Janet   *199, 368, 386, 433, 492*
Rienow, Leona   *207, 482, 492*
Riesenberg, Felix   *207, 492*
Riley, Jon   *56, 492*
Riley, Louise   *43, 484, 492*
Rinaldi, Ann   *145, 492*
Ringgold, Faith   *5, 41, 104, 116, 119, 160, 184, 492*
Rink, Hanno   *23, 456, 492*
Rink, Paul   *71, 438, 492*
Riordan, James   *125, 260, 492*
Ripley, A. L.   *50, 165, 373, 492*
Riswold, Gilbert   *187, 231, 316, 395, 492*
Ritchie, Scot   *7, 457, 492*
Ritter, Bob   *78, 265, 492*
Ritter, Bruce   *120, 492*
Rivers, Alice   *152, 234, 393, 492*
Riwkin-Brick, Anna   *210, 423*
Roach, Marilynne K.   *63, 429*
Robbins, Ken   *158, 184*
Robbins, Ruth   *9, 25, 39, 53, 154, 419*
Roberts, Clare   *150, 431*
Roberts, Doreen   *98*
Roberts, Jim   *72, 262, 330*
Roberts, Ken   *218*
Roberts, Willo David   *223*
Roberts, Willo Davis   *42, 74, 89, 135, 189, 200, 223, 227, 228, 238, 454*
Robertson, Barbara   *103, 299, 325*
Robertson, Ellen   *34*
Robertson, Frank C.   *229*
Robertson, Keith   *134, 139, 210, 231, 239, 268, 402, 442, 480, 482*
Robins, Patricia   *70, 315*
Robinson, Aminah Brenda Lynn   *105*
Robinson, Barbara   *79, 89, 122, 177, 237, 281*
Robinson, Charles   *26, 56, 89, 103, 114, 144, 197, 201, 214, 215, 219, 247, 280, 290, 310, 422*
Robinson, Dorothy   *118*
Robinson, Irene   *201, 204, 328*
Robinson, Jackie   *113, 118, 327, 428*
Robinson, Jessie   *30, 419*
Robinson, Jessie B.   *114, 345*
Robinson, Joan G.   *102*
Robinson, Mabel L.   *166, 204*
Robinson, Mark   *198, 492*
Robinson, Michele P.   *73*
Robinson, Tim   *105, 403*
Robinson, Tom   *205, 318*
Robinson, William Powell   *195, 270*
Rocker, F.   *101, 293*
Rocker, Fermin   *176, 255*
Rocklin, Joanne   *203, 444*
Rockwell, Anne   *33, 62, 191*
Rockwell, Harlow   *62*

Rockwell, Norman   *174*
Rockwell, Thomas   *11, 41, 92, 112, 126, 134, 172, 196, 200, 222, 226, 237, 337, 442*
Rodari, Gianni   *10, 22, 269*
Rodda, Emily   *59, 60, 237*
Rodgers, Mary   *41, 68, 89, 134, 215, 218*
Rodgers, Raboo   *87*
Rodman, Bella   *21, 33, 85*
Rodwell, Jenny   *27, 466*
Roe, Eileen   *146*
Roennfeldt, Robert   *15*
Roesch, Roberta F.   *136*
Roffey, Maureen   *99, 191, 192, 427, 437*
Rogers, Fred   *36, 83, 399*
Rogers, Jacqueline   *146, 181, 288*
Rogers, Jean   *183, 457*
Rogerson, James   *199, 378*
Rohmer, Harriet   *118*
Roisman, Lois   *220*
Rojankovsky, Feodor   *39, 168, 209, 270, 414*
Roland, Will   *232, 490*
Rollins, Charlemae   *67, 117*
Rolph, Mic   *195, 259*
Romanov, Natalia   *163*
Rooney, David   *20, 189*
Roos, Stephen   *197, 461*
Roosevelt, Eleanor   *55, 337*
Ropner, Pamela   *32*
Rosamund, J.   *52, 156, 395*
Rose, Anne   *63, 157, 426, 427*
Rose, David   *70, 113, 384*
Rose, Elizabeth   *98, 211*
Rose, Gerald   *98, 211*
Rose, J. M.   *166, 329*
Rose, Margaret   *108, 194, 382, 437*
Rosell, Ingrid   *212, 250*
Rosen, Albert   *120, 408*
Rosen, Billi   *81*
Rosen, Lillian   *235*
Rosen, Michael   *30, 34, 100, 176, 183, 190, 196, 198, 271, 469*
Rosen, Michael J.   *105*
Rosenberg, Maxine B.   *234, 250*
Rosenblum, Richard   *151, 359*
Rosenthal, Jules M.   *72, 304, 489*
Rosenthal, Lynn   *65*
Rosholt, Malcolm   *215, 415, 456*
Rosholt, Margaret   *215, 415, 456*
Rosier, Lydia   *140, 435*
Ross, Christine   *6, 70*
Ross, K. K.   *24, 442*
Ross, Pat   *88, 366*
Ross, Ramon Royal   *203*
Ross, Tony   *70, 77, 100, 145, 172, 191, 332, 367, 463*
Rossi, Kendall   *33, 407*
Rossmoore, Harold W.   *148*
Rossmore, Harold W.   *497*
Rostkowski, Margaret I.   *94, 111, 113*
Rotert, Richard   *54, 65, 66*
Roth, Arnold   *138, 140, 142*
Roth, George   *229, 286*
Roth, Susan L.   *159*
Rothchild, Sylvia   *114, 410*
Rothfuchs, Heiner   *210, 263*

Rothman, Mrs. M E   *127*
Roughsey, Dick   *58, 108*
Rounds, Glen   *15, 33, 49, 50, 52, 53, 87,*
   117, 136, 140, 142, 160, 161, 171, 180,
   181, 205, 278, 296
Rourke, Constance M.   *166, 432*
Rouverol, Jean   *202*
Rowan, Peter   *195, 463*
Rowe, Barry   *173, 292, 394*
Rowe, Jeannette   *15*
Rowe, John   *20, 26, 47, 68, 187, 386, 477*
Rowell, Kenneth   *90, 327*
Rowland, Dolores M.   *143, 290*
Roy, Claude   *10, 155, 268, 419*
Roybal, J. D.   *230, 341*
Royston, Angela   *192, 287*
Rozanov, Sergei   *204, 452*
Rubel, Nicole   *64, 349*
Rubinstein, Gillian   *16, 59, 60, 66, 133,*
   147, 237, 319
Ruckman, Ivy   *96, 112, 122, 196, 200*
Ruddick, Bob   *122, 201, 224, 362*
Rudnik, Maryka   *17, 476*
Rudnik, Raphael   *17, 476*
Rudolph, Norman Guthrie   *31*
Rudstrom, Lennart   *62, 64, 156, 415*
Rue, Leonard Lee III   *136, 137, 144, 145,*
   468
Ruff, Donna   *234, 244*
Rugh, Belle Dorman   *209*
Rugoff, Milton   *154, 431*
Ruhlin, Roger   *194, 281*
Ruse, Margaret   *52, 460*
Rush, Barbara   *219*
Rush, Ken   *123, 392*
Russell, Franklin   *140, 155, 309, 482*
Russell, Helen R.   *96, 139, 333*
Russell, James   *187*
Russell, Jim   *48, 101, 436*
Russell, William F.   *24, 287*
Russo, Marisabina   *111*
Russon, Mary   *213, 446*
Ruth, Rod   *209, 489*
Rutherford, Jenny   *180, 477*
Rutledge, James T.   *72, 253*
Ryan, Cheli Duran   *40, 61, 132, 427*
Ryden, Ernest Edwin   *64, 415*
Ryden, Hope   *24*
Ryder, Joanne   *24, 64, 72, 142, 143, 149,*
   182, 274, 296, 336, 463, 468, 481
Rylant, Cynthia   *30, 41, 89, 105, 158,*
   170, 175, 181, 184, 185, 190, 199, 348,
   349, 357, 455
Rypins, Senta   *206, 304*

Saari, Kay   *161, 348*
Sabuda, Robert   *105*
Sachar, Louis   *11, 35, 81, 89, 96, 105,*
   112, 121, 126, 128, 134, 135, 182, 183,
   184, 197, 218, 220, 223, 224, 226, 228,
   239, 379
Sachs, Anne   *88*
Sachs, Marilyn   *3, 5, 18, 69, 88, 132, 160,*
   182, 217, 219, 328, 355
Sadler, Marilyn   *184, 274*
Saether, Haakon   *71, 338*

St. George, Judith   *69, 94, 144, 145, 146,*
   149, 163, 188
St. John, Wylly Folk   *187, 249, 281*
Sakurai, Atsushi   *150, 396*
Salamanca, Lucy   *173, 481*
Salant, Sam   *138, 375*
Salata, Estelle   *127*
Salisbury, Graham   *185*
Saller, Carol   *194*
Salmon, Michael   *237*
Salten, Felix   *22*
Salvadori, Mario   *27, 149, 382, 487*
Sam, Joe   *118*
Sampson, Katharine   *138*
Sampson, Katherine   *435*
Samson, Hans   *67, 392*
Samstag, Nicholas   *154*
Samuels, Barbara   *69*
Sancha, Alicia   *53, 440*
Sancha, Sheila   *48*
Sandburg, Carl   *12, 158, 194, 213, 256,*
   262, 280, 302, 331, 354, 374, 376, 382,
   383, 420, 479
Sandburg, Helga   *51, 312*
Sander, Joelle   *120*
Sanders, Pete   *222*
Sanders, Ruth Manning   *109, 289*
Sanderson, Ruth   *21, 73, 74, 89, 144,*
   179, 227, 238, 288, 336, 358
Sandford, David E.   *214*
Sandin, Joan   *4, 89, 161, 188, 253, 462,*
   487
Sandoz, Mari   *168, 210, 229, 442*
Sandved, Kjell   *149, 333*
Sandved, Kjell B.   *151, 483*
Sanford, David E.   *459*
San Souci, Daniel   *91, 157, 230*
San Souci, Robert D.   *21, 41, 71, 96, 105,*
   119, 157, 183, 191, 479
Santoro, Christopher   *94, 152, 291, 468,*
   487
Sarabasha, Susan   *203*
Sarg, Tony   *51, 419*
Sargent, Sarah   *72, 87, 442*
Sari   *209, 341*
Sasek, Miroslav   *32, 154*
Sato, Yuko   *150, 311, 396, 468*
Sattler, Helen R.   *28, 93, 94, 291, 467,*
   468, 487
Sattler, Helen Roney   *152, 175, 483*
Sattley, Helen R.   *36, 55*
Sauer, Julia L.   *167*
Saunders, Brian   *211, 394, 395*
Savage, Katherine   *46*
Savage, Steel   *294*
Savage, Steele   *205*
Savin, Deborah   *232, 270*
Savitt, Sam   *36, 256*
Savitz, Harriet May   *143, 177*
Sawyer, Ruth   *37, 38, 51, 166, 193, 233,*
   252, 442
Say, Allen   *18, 29, 41, 69, 157, 159, 182,*
   186, 190, 346, 417
Sayles, Edwin B.   *216*
Saynor, Marjorie   *46, 251, 380*
Sayre, J. Woodrow   *136*
Scagell, Robin   *149, 504*

Scarratt, Elaine   *222, 321*
Scarry, Huck   *89*
Scarry, Richard   *188*
Schachner, Erwin   *138, 478*
Schaefer, Jack   *15, 168, 174, 211, 212,*
   270
Schami, Rafik   *17*
Scheader, Catherine   *235*
Schechter, Betty   *55, 78, 114*
Scheele, William E.   *32, 174*
Scheer, George F.   *78, 438, 441*
Scheer, Julian   *39, 154, 269*
Scheffler, Ursel   *178*
Scheffrin-Falk, Gladys   *223, 350*
Scheft, Margaret   *187, 351*
Scheib, Ida   *32, 422*
Scheidl, Gerda Marie   *9, 346*
Schertle, Alice   *69, 183, 184, 310*
Schick, Alice   *87, 293*
Schick, Joel   *11, 42, 89, 121, 134, 183,*
   361
Schiller, Justin   *17*
Schindelman, Joseph   *25, 134, 135, 154,*
   172, 218, 240, 311, 370
Schindler, S. D.   *83, 112, 179, 190, 410,*
   419, 443
Schlager, Norma   *65*
Schlee, Ann   *28, 48, 101, 102*
Schleier, Curt   *143*
Schlein, Miriam   *31, 38, 64, 150, 152,*
   209, 211, 295, 328, 344, 359, 405
Schloredt, Valerie   *221, 282*
Schmiderer, Dorothy   *60*
Schmidt, Annie   *9*
Schmidt, Eric Von   *3, 27, 32, 71, 85, 133,*
   155, 197, 201, 211, 212, 214, 216, 222,
   229, 238, 300, 340, 416, 449
Schmidt, Harold Von   *165, 384*
Schmidt, Sarah L.   *166, 324*
Schmitz, Fred   *109, 422*
Schneider, Gerlinde   *62, 346*
Schneider, Herman   *96, 149, 207, 266*
Schneider, Howie   *226*
Schneider, Nina   *207, 266*
Schoenherr, John   *15, 41, 51, 64, 76, 83,*
   110, 132, 136, 138, 168, 169, 195, 217,
   228, 231, 239, 330, 352, 403, 454, 463
Scholder, Fritz   *27, 169, 377*
Scholefield, Edmund O.   *137, 287, 343*
Scholes, Katherine   *81, 147*
Scholes, Percy   *221, 387*
Schomberg, Alex   *318*
Schomburg, Alex   *31, 32, 174, 298, 315*
Schonfeldt, Sybil Grafin   *109, 432*
Schongut, Emanuel   *56, 294*
Schoolland, Marian M.   *91*
Schotter, Roni   *115, 366*
Schouten, Alet   *108, 307, 482*
Schramm, Ulrik   *212, 263, 482*
Schrank, Jeffrey   *126*
Schreiber, Georges   *38, 167, 207, 270*
Schreiter, Rick   *17, 401, 407*
Schroeder, Alan   *183, 346*
Schroeder, Binette   *157, 178, 461*
Schroeder, Ted   *139, 140, 317*
Schrotter, Gustav   *32, 210*
Schultz, Gwen M.   *72*

Schumacher, Claire   146
Schurfranz, Vivian   95
Schwartz, Alvin   11, 35, 80, 88, 137, 138, 139, 140, 142, 143, 145, 146, 160, 161, 225, 226, 268, 289, 297, 348, 380, 465
Schwartz, Amy   69, 115, 180, 183, 184, 219, 279, 367, 376
Schwartz, Daniel   132, 288
Schwartz, David   224
Schwartz, David M.   29, 403
Schwartz, Howard   219
Schwartz, Julius   147, 376, 393
Schwarz, Frank   93
Schwarz, Leiselotte   19
Schwebeil, Gertrude C.   52, 343, 402
Schweitzer, Iris   107, 377
Scieszka, Jon   41, 160
Scoppettone, Sandra   12, 42, 142, 155, 189, 339
Scorey, John   195, 440
Scotland, BBC   116
Scott, Cora Annett   68, 252
Scott, Eric   228
Scott, Hugh   231
Scott, Lloyd   97, 321
Scott, Lynn H.   229
Scott, Sally   31, 411
Scribe, Murdo   97, 348
Scrofani, Joseph M.   149, 224, 333
Scruton, Clive   172
Scullard, Sue   130
Scuro, Vincent   144, 417
Seaborg, Glenn T.   77, 509, 546
Seabrooke, Brenda   30, 422
Seeagell, Robin   149, 504
Seale, Clem   57
Searcy, Margaret   16
Searle, Chris   176, 405
Sears, Paul M.   136
Sebestyen, Ouida   8, 111, 162, 220
Seckar, Alvena   209
Sedacca, Joseph M.   78, 263, 264
Seed, Jenny   127
Seeger, Elizabeth   166
Seeger, Pete   191, 373
Seeman, Elizabeth   211, 341
Sefton, Catherine   102, 176
Segal, E. A.   206, 273, 389, 406
Segal, Elizabeth   65
Segal, Joyce   143, 329
Segal, Lore   62, 99, 156, 157, 158, 163, 164, 181, 214, 261, 392, 437, 464, 479
Segal, Lore   62, 156, 392
Segawa, Yasuo   10, 19, 439
Seidel, Heinrich   109
Seidel, Hilde   9, 332
Seidler, Rosalie   68
Seidler, Tor   163
Seidlin, Oskar   206, 304
Seisser, Jean   156
Selberg, Ingrid   23, 450, 456
Selden, George   50, 67, 126, 168, 231
Seligson, Susan   226
Selsam, Millicent   88, 96, 227, 283
Selsam, Millicent E.   32, 33, 78, 88, 122, 280, 427, 477, 485
Selznick, Brian   193, 220

Semel, Nava   115
Sendak, Jack   61, 137, 138, 156, 451
Sendak, Maurice   8, 10, 12, 13, 15, 21, 24, 28, 38, 39, 40, 50, 51, 52, 54, 55, 62, 64, 66, 76, 80, 107, 109, 116, 152, 153, 154, 155, 156, 157, 158, 162, 168, 169, 171, 185, 190, 191, 209, 210, 211, 224, 233, 235, 316, 363, 372, 380, 392, 399, 410, 432, 435, 451, 466, 467, 476
Senior, Margaret   57, 483
Seredy, Kate   37, 49, 50, 86, 166, 167, 205, 231, 260, 269, 279, 347, 351, 361
Serraillier, Anne   152, 290, 296
Serraillier, Ian   32, 46, 152, 211, 290, 296, 380
Servello, Joe   215, 269
Service, Pamela F.   94
Service, Robert W.   159, 182, 371
Seuberlich, Hertha   50, 386, 469
Seuss, Dr.   33, 38, 49, 50, 65, 75, 92, 109, 163, 193, 202, 233, 238, 324, 352, 383, 420, 459
Sevela, Efraim   110, 276
Severn, David   188
Sewall, Marcia   29, 80, 82, 122, 157, 158, 162, 178, 185, 202, 217, 224, 349, 361, 404, 418
Sewell, Helen   39, 153, 166, 167, 206, 238, 277, 311, 334
Seydl, Zdenek   22, 383
Seymour, Richard   198, 418, 469
Seyton, Marion   86
Shaap, Dick   240, 391
Shackell, John   195, 440
Shackell, Rodney   169, 186, 333
Shahn, Ben   12, 114, 154, 390, 490
Shamir, Mosche   9
Shannon, George   87
Shannon, Jacqueline   75
Shannon, Monica   166, 401
Shapiro, Irwin   86, 313
Shapiro, Mary J.   89
Sharmat, Marjorie   74, 88, 283
Sharmat, Mitchell   74, 283
Sharmat, Marjorie Weiman   296
Sharmat, Marjorie Weinman   80, 115, 179, 430, 457
Sharp, Edith Lambert   97, 107, 121
Sharp, Margery   46, 280
Sharpe, Elaine   15, 389
Sharratt, Nick   49, 56, 172
Shaw, Charles   229
Shecter, Ben   179
Sheldon, Dyan   100, 130, 273
Sheldon, Myrtle   165
Shell, Richard L.   231, 305
Shelley, John   182
Shelley, Noreen   58
Shelly, Noreen   449
Shemin, Margaretha   56
Shenton, Edward   166, 205, 206, 305, 333, 446, 447
Shepard, E. H.   50, 451
Shepard, Elizabeth   152, 473
Shepard, Ernest H.   49, 51, 82, 174, 209, 223, 360, 451
Shepard, Mary   134

Shepard, Ray Anthony   73
Sheppard, Nancy   74, 421
Sherburne, Zoa   55
Sherin, Ray   15, 423
Sherman, Eileen Bluestone   115
Sherman, Nancy   154, 211
Sherry, Sylvia   214, 409
Shetterly, Robert   150, 151, 445
Shettle, Andrea   16
Shields, Charles   161, 349
Shiffman, Lena   69, 459
Shimin, Symeon   12, 14, 21, 50, 56, 68, 140, 141, 168, 266, 337, 351, 355, 361, 368, 411
Shimizu, Kiyoshi   150, 468
Shimuzu, Kiyoshi   396
Shippen, Katherine B.   31, 107, 167, 168, 206, 210, 335, 488
Shires, Linda M.   66
Shirreffs, Gordon D.   71
Shisler, William   142, 279, 331
Sholokhov, Mikhail   213, 355, 455
Shore, Robert   33
Short, Joan   232, 270
Shortall, Leonard   32, 33, 86, 88, 137, 187, 216, 239, 289, 305, 337
Shotwell, Louisa R.   21, 51, 235, 285
Showell, Ellen H.   180, 200, 348
Showers, Kay S.   138, 337
Showers, Paul   135, 138, 247, 337, 348, 402, 429, 433
Shreve, Susan   115, 189, 316
Shriver, Jean Adair   75
Shub, Elizabeth   62, 109, 155, 160, 346, 363, 381
Shubert, Reinold   136, 137, 138, 140, 141
Shulevitz, Uri   13, 39, 40, 62, 68, 108, 157, 161, 163, 180, 215, 219, 246, 429, 476, 487
Shura, Mary Frances   194, 422
Shusterman, Neal   204, 226
Shuttlesworth, Dorothy   96, 137, 194, 400
Shyer, Marlene Fanta   176
Sibbick, John   192
Sibley, Don   89, 135, 171, 212, 285, 447
Sidjakov, Nicholas   258
Sidjakov, Nicolas   9, 39, 154
Siebert, Diane   18, 192, 451
Siegal, Aranka   28, 119, 170
Siegel, Hal   126, 214, 378
Siegel, Robert   92
Siegel, William   165, 446
Siegieda, Jan   18, 386
Siegl, Helen   159
Siekkinen, Raija   20
Sigmundova, Jana   23, 410
Silcock, Sara   218, 339
Silliman, Leland   31
Sills, Leslie   190
Silman, Roberta   56, 304
Silver, Norman   102
Silverberg, Barbara   62
Silverberg, Robert   212, 213, 236, 359, 379
Silverman, Burt   78, 187, 378, 406
Silverman, Martin   146

Silverstein, Alvin   *140, 143, 144, 145,*
146, 148, 152, 244, 294, 404
Silverstein, Herma   *80*
Silverstein, Shel   *35, 88, 128, 161, 217,*
232
Silverstein, Virginia   *140, 143, 144, 145,*
146, 148, 152, 244, 294, 404
Simbari, Nicola   *154*
Simeons, Albert Theodore William   *33*
Simmonds, Posy   *199*
Simmons, Martin   *221, 433*
Simms, George Otto   *20, 189*
Simon, Charlie May   *30, 114, 197, 205,*
249, 273, 280, 284, 288, 299, 313, 316,
325, 334, 340, 341, 354, 360, 374, 377,
385, 403, 423, 429, 433, 435, 461, 480
Simon, Hilda   *61*
Simon, Howard   *85, 205, 478*
Simon, Noel   *151, 394, 400*
Simon, Norma   *153, 359, 450*
Simon, Seymour   *24, 61, 89, 96, 150,*
151, 159, 227, 261
Simonsen, Thordis   *234*
Simont, Marc   *38, 39, 55, 88, 113, 132,*
143, 149, 163, 181, 185, 192, 209, 216,
349, 354, 410, 412, 428, 442, 482
Simpson, Cathy   *121, 383*
Simpson, Gretchen Dow   *184*
Simpson, Kate   *131, 480*
Sims, Graeme   *130*
Sineti, Don   *150, 349*
Singer, Isaac Bashevis   *60, 109, 131, 155,*
163, 169, 180, 189, 219, 381, 423, 448
Singer, Marilyn   *122, 159, 360, 479*
Singmaster, Elsie   *166, 375*
Sinnema, Jae   *22, 320*
Sirovatka, Oldrich   *22*
Sis, Peter   *30, 92, 134, 159, 170, 184,*
185, 192, 197, 340
Sisley, E. L.   *78, 364*
Sivers, Brenda   *121, 385*
Sjostrand, Ulla-Britt   *92*
Skardinski, Stan   *28, 333*
Skogsberg, Ingvar   *109, 294*
Skolnick, Arnold   *118, 257*
Skorpil, Judy   *150, 485*
Skurzynski, Gloria   *8, 68, 93, 94, 224,*
230
Sladkus, Ingrid   *43, 331*
Sleator, William   *26, 40, 42, 73, 420*
Slepian, Jan   *143, 144, 145*
Slepian, Janice   *27*
Slier, Deborah   *104, 384*
Sloan, Ellen   *142, 143, 316, 317*
Sloan, Peter   *232, 416*
Slobodkin, Louis   *37, 50, 166, 167, 334*
Slobodkina, Esphyr   *49, 208, 281*
Slocum, Jerry   *151, 276, 286*
Slote, Alfred   *188*
Slote, Elizabeth   *188*
Slote, Robert   *134*
Small, David   *181, 183, 192, 296, 399*
Small, Ernest   *213, 420*
Smalley, Janet   *209, 243*
Smaridge, Norah   *137, 138, 139, 142,*
143, 144, 291, 369, 411, 412, 413, 438,
476

Smedley, Chris   *173*
Smee, David   *27, 47, 48, 101, 249, 321*
Smith, Agnes   *15, 51, 211, 456*
Smith, Alison   *111*
Smith, Alvin   *169, 187, 212, 274, 275*
Smith, Beatrice S.   *72, 468*
Smith, Catriona   *157*
Smith, Cicely Fox   *32, 315*
Smith, Craig   *59, 60, 117, 147, 237, 355,*
386, 393, 433
Smith, David Eugene   *204, 390*
Smith, Doris Buchanan   *26, 56, 89, 103,*
181, 329
Smith, E. Boyd   *179, 257*
Smith, Edesse Peery   *522*
Smith, Elwood H.   *150, 461*
Smith, Emma   *26, 47, 212, 434*
Smith, Eunice Young   *106*
Smith, Helen   *14, 59, 454*
Smith, Howard G.   *67, 393*
Smith, Hugh   *51, 328, 430*
Smith, Jessie Willcox   *51, 103, 246*
Smith, Joan   *90*
Smith, Joseph A.   *185, 340*
Smith, Lane   *20, 41, 159, 160, 184, 448*
Smith, Lawrence B.   *85*
Smith, Lawrence Beall   *449*
Smith, Mavis   *145, 146*
Smith, Miriam   *6, 456*
Smith, Ray   *157*
Smith, Robert   *111, 417*
Smith, Robert Kimmel   *42, 80, 84, 89,*
96, 126, 134, 180, 200, 223, 226, 232,
238, 239, 337, 397, 416
Smith, Samantha   *4*
Smucker, Anna Egan   *112, 396*
Smucker, Barbara   *44, 108, 127, 133,*
313, 446
Smucker, Barbara Claassen   *97, 194*
Snedeker, Caroline Dale   *165, 166, 260,*
416, 468
Sneve, Virginia Driving Hawk   *73, 431*
Snow, Dorothea J.   *86, 106, 353*
Snow, Edward Rowe   *31*
Snow, Richard F.   *27, 161, 480*
Snyder, Andrew   *141, 317*
Snyder, Anne   *87*
Snyder, Carol   *144, 146, 219*
Snyder, Dianne   *29, 41, 182, 190*
Snyder, Jerome   *154, 487*
Snyder, Keatley   *52, 67, 74, 107, 213,*
217, 231, 487
Snyder, Zilpha Keatley   *52, 67, 74, 107,*
132, 160, 162, 169, 180, 185, 213, 217,
231, 487
Sobol, Donald J.   *35, 88, 188, 239, 278*
Sojo, Toba   *152*
Sokol, Bill   *32, 135, 153, 197, 210, 278,*
320, 377, 450
Solbert, Ronni   *33, 51, 61, 213, 448, 460*
Solliday, Tim   *87, 373*
Solowey, E. M.   *220*
Soman, David   *116, 119, 183, 394*
Sommer-Bodenburg, Angela   *225*
Sommerfelt, Aimee   *3, 32, 55, 78, 213,*
235, 243, 311
Sootin, Harry   *32*

Sorel, Edward   *153, 154, 211, 451*
Sorensen, Virginia   *55, 168, 351, 411*
Soto, Gary   *18, 105, 190, 217, 321*
Southall, Ivan   *47, 57, 58, 107, 133, 236,*
362
Southey, Robert   *160, 292*
Southgate, Mark   *123*
Spanfeller, James   *52, 201, 212, 310*
Spanfeller, James J.   *46, 202, 335, 426*
Spanfeller, Jim   *26, 131, 299*
Sparks, Mary Walker   *171*
Speare, Elizabeth George   *56, 69, 107,*
135, 163, 168, 170, 173, 233
Speare, George   *56, 69, 107, 233*
Speer, Bonnie   *175*
Speer, Jess Willard   *175*
Speicher, Helen R.   *106, 244, 275*
Spence, Eleanor   *15, 57, 59, 81, 108, 147,*
304, 361
Spence, Geraldine   *32, 46, 57, 295, 440*
Spencer, Cornelia   *207, 422*
Spencer, Paula Underwood   *113, 384*
Spencer, Roy   *47, 374*
Spender, Stephen   *155, 453*
Sperry, Armstrong   *30, 71, 166, 206, 207,*
376, 426, 475
Spier, Peter   *8, 14, 25, 39, 40, 53, 67, 68,*
92, 108, 123, 134, 157, 162, 224
Spinelli, Eileen   *69, 124*
Spinelli, Jerry   *29, 35, 54, 83, 84, 105,*
126, 170, 172, 177, 193, 223, 232
Spinner, Stephanie   *220, 270, 334*
Spirin, Gennady   *159, 163, 245*
Spook   *71, 182, 284, 291, 415*
Sprague, Gretchen   *187*
Sprague, Rosemary   *213*
Springer, Nancy   *82*
Springstubb, Tricia   *175, 401*
Spurrier, Steven   *45*
Spyndonos   *9, 482*
Stadtler, Bea   *114, 438*
Staffelbach, E. H.   *71, 369, 370*
Stafford, Ann   *204, 273*
Stahl, Ben   *3, 195*
Stahl, Ben F.   *161*
Stahler, Charles   *24*
Stalder, Valerie   *61, 280, 282*
Stamaty, Mark Alan   *12, 13, 255*
Stampnick, Ken   *97, 121, 470*
Stanek, Lou Willet   *235*
Stang, Wendy   *155, 251, 491*
Stanley, Diana   *45, 46, 107, 464*
Stanley, Diane   *30, 94, 159, 190*
Stanley, Jerry   *18, 105, 113, 175*
Stanley, Robert   *126, 411, 412*
Stanovsky, Vladislav   *22*
Stapelbroek, Marlys G.   *124*
Staples, Suzanne Fisher   *110, 170, 217*
Stapleton, Janice   *88, 144, 424*
Stashin, Leo   *61, 293*
Steadman, Ralph   *23, 199*
Stearns, Monroe   *153, 490*
Stearns, Pamela   *71*
Stecher, Miriam B.   *149, 400*
Steel, Richard   *221, 351*
Steele, Mary   *59, 347*
Steele, Mary Q.   *52, 169, 459*

Steele, William O.   *3, 50, 78, 168, 209, 210, 231, 348, 454*

Stefansson, Evelyn   *206, 207, 371, 430, 432*

Steffans, Klaus   *17, 307, 344*

Steffen, Randy   *229, 404*

Steig, William   *8, 13, 14, 21, 27, 28, 39, 40, 53, 60, 63, 65, 68, 79, 90, 92, 109, 131, 132, 133, 156, 157, 159, 160, 161, 162, 163, 169, 170, 180, 181, 182, 183, 190, 191, 192, 214, 231, 456*

Steigler, Judith   *140, 332, 409*

Stein, Alex   *187*

Stein, Harve   *216, 289*

Stein, Sara   *151, 264*

Steinel, William   *78, 115, 378*

Steiner, Barbara A.   *70, 300*

Steiner, Jorg   *17, 413, 456*

Steiner, Stan   *230*

Steltzer, Ulli   *137*

Stemple, Adam   *105, 380*

Stephane, Nelly   *153, 344*

Stephen, David   *209, 414*

Stephens, Mary Jo   *174*

Steptoe, John   *4, 12, 20, 21, 26, 29, 41, 53, 118, 128, 181, 244, 323, 362, 365*

Sterling, Dorothy   *21, 234, 235, 308*

Sterling, Philip   *67*

Sterman, Betsy   *113, 355*

Sterman, Samuel   *113, 355*

Stern, Marie   *206, 267, 438*

Stevens, Christian D.   *36*

Stevens, Mary   *85, 86, 210, 211, 267, 321, 345, 365, 366*

Stevens, M. E.   *216*

Stevenson, James   *29, 68, 80, 88, 89, 92, 117, 157, 162, 179, 181, 182, 185, 191, 362, 363, 483*

Stevenson, Robert Louis   *51, 109, 192, 332*

Stevenson, Sucie   *89*

Stevenson, William   *235, 249*

Stewart, A. C.   *187*

Stewart, Anna Bird   *174, 491*

Stewart, Anne   *176, 335*

Stewart, Arvis   *113, 174, 429*

Stewart, Charles   *46, 478*

Stewart, John   *149*

Stewart, Sarah-Jane   *531*

Stieler, Robert   *19*

Still, James   *157*

Stinely, Richard   *32, 307, 314*

Stinetorf, Louise A.   *106, 235*

Stinson, Kathy   *110, 111, 423*

Stitt, Sue   *221, 295, 441, 448*

Stobbs, William   *45, 98, 114, 212, 295, 325, 400, 435, 481*

Stock, Catherine   *24, 69, 118, 481*

Stockman, Jack   *91, 434*

Stockton, Frank R.   *50, 52, 283*

Stodart, Eleanor   *232*

Stoddard, Sandol   *64, 466*

Stoehr, Shelley   *75*

Stoeke, Janet Morgan   *76*

Stoia, Judith   *68, 234, 284*

Stolz, Mary   *32, 55, 117, 119, 132, 151, 168, 169, 183, 209, 210, 217, 309, 348, 355, 453*

Stomann, Allan   *227, 228, 259*

Stommel, Elizabeth   *150*

Stommel, Henry   *150*

Stonaker, Frances B.   *137*

Stone, David K.   *114, 438, 515*

Stone, Derek   *232, 293*

Stone, Elberta   *140, 281*

Stone, Helen   *38, 83, 207, 267, 286, 287, 443*

Stong, Phil   *52, 166, 205, 418*

Storey, Denise C.   *95*

Storm, Theodor   *215, 426*

Storr, Catherine   *77, 244*

Stoub, Paul   *91*

Stoutenburg, Adrien   *214, 432*

Stover, Jo Ann   *187, 337*

Strachan, Ian   *173*

Straeter, Angela   *206, 328*

Strand, Mark   *159, 364*

Strandvag 22   *92*

Stratton, Lucille N.   *201, 349*

Stratton, William D.   *201, 349*

Strauss, Joyce   *69, 261*

Strayer, Paul   *205, 376*

Streatfeild, Noel   *45, 63, 208, 275*

Street, Julia Montgomery   *171, 310*

Street, Julia   *282*

Streeter, Sherry   *188*

Stren, Patti   *122, 361*

Strieber, Whitley   *87*

Strogart, Alexander   *183, 470*

Studios, Walt Disney   *210, 366*

Strugnell, Ann   *21, 47, 71, 178, 181, 281, 289, 308*

Strumitto, Ardrezej   *19*

Stryker, Sandy   *87, 433*

Stuart, Jesse   *52, 217, 293, 294, 298, 302, 309, 384, 400, 439, 483*

Stuart, Morna   *47, 330*

Stubley, Trevor   *101, 176, 292, 489*

Studios, Caru   *32, 292, 472*

Stull, Edith G.   *136*

Styles, S. J.   *221, 489*

Suba, Susanne   *205, 208, 216, 258, 335*

Sue Gough   *60, 359*

Sugarman, Joan G.   *217*

Suhl, Yuri   *52, 61, 114, 156, 219*

Sullivan, Betty   *142*

Summers, James L.   *209*

Supree, Burton   *21, 33, 295*

Suschitzy, W.   *153*

Sutcliff, Rosemary   *10, 26, 27, 28, 46, 47, 52, 107, 110, 176, 186, 210, 212, 249, 337, 380, 389, 402, 418*

Suteyev, V.   *61, 254, 255, 354*

Sutherland, Robert D.   *87*

Sutton, Ann   *149*

Sutton, Eve   *91, 324*

Sutton, Jane   *224, 410*

Sutton, Myron   *149*

Suzuki, David   *106, 374*

Suzuki, Masaharu   *150, 396*

Svensson, Borje   *191, 444*

Swain, Su Zan Noguchi   *137*

Swainson, Donald   *104*

Swainson, Eleanor   *104*

Swallow, Pamela Curtis   *145*

Swarthout, Glendon   *188, 441*

Swarthout, Kathryn   *188, 441*

Sweat, Lynn   *35, 56, 88, 89, 93, 335, 470*

Sweeney, Joyce   *75*

Swift, Hildegarde   *165, 313*

Swift, Hildegarde Hoyt   *201, 207*

Swindells, Robert E.   *48, 56, 176, 492*

Switzer, Ellen   *149*

Switzer, Jeffrey   *149*

Switzer, Michael   *149*

Syme, Ronald   *31, 488*

Symonds, John   *152, 344*

Szekeres, Cyndy   *72*

Szilagyi, Mary   *117, 431*

Taback, Simms   *155, 398*

Tafuri, Nancy   *4, 41, 181, 186, 192, 354, 481*

Tailfeathers, Gerald   *121, 336*

Taina, Hannu   *20*

Tait, Douglas   *44, 97, 104, 108, 370*

Takashima, Shizuye   *103*

Talbert, Marc   *228*

Talbott, Hudson   *90*

Talifero, Gerald   *194*

Tallon, Robert   *13*

Talmadge, Marian   *33, 354*

Tamarin, Alfred   *26, 356*

Tamchina, Jurgen   *214, 307, 477*

Tanemura, Hiroshi   *150, 311, 396*

Tanner, Jane   *60, 258*

Tanner, Louise   *214*

Tanninen, Oili   *10*

Tanobe, Miyuki   *64, 103*

Tansley, Eric   *228, 296*

Tartaglione, John   *53, 351, 449*

Tate, J.   *19*

Tate, Joan   *179*

Tavo, Gus   *216, 270*

Taylor, Andrew   *48, 231*

Taylor, Cora   *11, 44, 97, 195*

Taylor, Edgar   *62, 156*

Taylor, Elizabeth Buchanan   *157, 461*

Taylor, Elizabeth Watson   *109*

Taylor, Herb   *148, 537*

Taylor, Kim   *100, 192, 286, 293*

Taylor, Mark   *202, 275*

Taylor, Mildred   *36, 69, 175, 354*

Taylor, Mildred D.   *4, 27, 29, 63, 69, 73, 118, 119, 133, 162, 164, 169, 217, 237, 239, 354, 373, 479*

Taylor, Neil   *53*

Taylor, Sydney   *14, 85, 114, 218, 219, 220, 244, 271, 290, 294, 301, 303, 320, 323, 331, 339, 340, 344, 349, 352, 357, 361, 366, 367, 372, 375, 377, 378, 389, 390, 394, 398, 406, 414, 415, 416, 418, 422, 429, 430, 448, 455, 467, 471, 480, 481*

Taylor, Theodore   *42, 52, 71, 161, 201, 202, 217, 230, 235, 390, 471*

Taylor, William   *91*

Teason, James G.   *211, 255, 315*

Tefft, Elden   *231*

Teicher, Dick 56
Tejima, Keizaburo 159, 537
Temple, Frances 5, 105
Temple, Herbert 118
Temple, Philip 6, 350
Temple, Robert K. G. 151, 537
Tempski, Armine von 207, 282
Tengbom, Mildred 91
Tenggren, Gustaf 207, 391
Tennant, Kylie 57
Tennent, Julie 190, 388
Tennis, Donna Jean 95
Tennyson, Lord Alfred 484, 485
Teresinski, Sally 92
Terris, Daniel 185, 371
Terris, Susan 72
Teskey, Donald 112, 189, 303
Tettmar, Jacqueline 14, 312
Thacker, Nola 16, 429
Thamm, Peter 15
Thayer, Ernest L. 154, 339
Thesman, Jean 95, 196
Thiele, Colin 58, 107, 188, 236, 367, 389
Thomas, Dawn 141, 450
Thomas, Dylan 253
Thomas, Eleanor 264
Thomas, Frances 222
Thomas, Harold E. 71, 270
Thomas, Jane Resh 82
Thomas, Joyce Carol 8, 118
Thomas, Katrina 7, 376, 435
Thomas, Mack 92
Thomas, Ruth 102
Thomas, Valerie 56, 473
Thomasma, Ken 105, 386
Thompson, Brian 88, 394
Thompson, Carol 130, 539
Thompson, Eileen 187
Thompson, Harlan 71, 382, 415
Thompson, Marjorie 207, 384
Thompson, Mary W. 84, 468
Thompson, Mozelle 52, 156, 395
Thompson, Ralph 32
Thompson, Sherley Clark 31
Thompson, Vivian Laubach 136, 249, 464, 465
Thomson, Peggy 29
Thomson, Ruth 176, 221, 264, 335
Thorne, Jenny 158, 539
Thornhill, Jan 7, 106, 223
Thrasher, Crystal 87
Thruelsen, Richard 137, 540
Thum, Marcella 36, 63
Thurber, James 37, 174, 192, 345, 418
Thurston, Robert 143, 415, 448
Tibo, Gilles 178, 340
Tiboni, George 145, 461
Tiegreen, Alan 7, 27, 35, 88, 89, 92, 103, 108, 112, 121, 128, 134, 163, 170, 180, 197, 218, 220, 222, 224, 226, 285, 298, 299
Tietjens, Eunice 165
Tiffany's 119
Tilly, Nancy 171, 540
Timmerman, John H. 65
Timmermans, Gommaar 64
Tindale, Norman Barnett 57, 276, 424

Tischler, Ragna 213, 369, 489
Titcomb, Margaret 36, 336
Titherington, Jean 144, 358
Titherington, Jeanne 192
Titus, Eve 39, 348
Todd, Justin 125, 199, 291
Todd, Robert 77, 168, 399
Tolan, Stephanie S. 74
Toland, John 33, 411, 412
Tolkien, J. R. R. 79, 204
Tomei, Gordon 152
Tomes, Margot 8, 26, 28, 56, 64, 69, 94, 140, 141, 157, 158, 163, 164, 170, 180, 184, 188, 320, 346, 351, 353, 369, 413
Tomkins, Jasper 226
Tompert, Ann 87, 235
Tondreau, Sharon 143, 401
Tor, Regina 114
Torjesen, Elizabeth Fraser 209, 244
Torres, Pat 15
Torrey, Marjorie 38, 206, 477
Toschik, Larry 32, 264
Tourret, Shirley 197, 402
Townsend, Dr. Anne 91
Townsend, John Rowe 26, 47, 68, 187, 386, 477
Townsend, Lee 216, 229, 329
Townsend, Sue 25, 227, 381
Townsend, Tom 87
Toye, William 44, 103, 111, 127, 299, 347, 461, 487
Tracy, Edward B. 30, 282
Tramacchi, Joe 60, 354, 361
Travers, Pamela L. 134
Treadgold, Mary 45
Trease, Geoffrey 213
Treece, Henry 47, 402
Treffinger, Carolyn 49
Treherne, Katie Thamer 192, 250
Trelease, Jim 122, 488
Treloar, Bruce 58, 70
Tresilian, Stuart 30, 45, 206, 260, 273
Tresselt, Alvin 38, 39, 155, 207, 212, 328, 329, 366
Tresselt, Alvin R. 38
Trez, Alain 212, 444
Trez, Denise 212, 444
Trezise, Percy 58, 108
Trinkle, Sally 274
Tripp, Edward 209
Tripp, Wallace 27
Trivas, Irene 80, 188, 273, 297
Trofimuk, Ann 138, 479
Troughton, Joanna 99
Troy, Hugh 206
Truss, Jan 44, 194
Tsuchiya, Yukio 24, 422
Tsutsui, Yoriko 116, 373
Tucker, B. 171, 354
Tucker, Kathleen 194, 281
Tuckwell, Jennifer 57
Tudor, Tasha 37, 39, 54, 193, 205
Tughan, James 104
Tunbo, Frances G. 229
Tunis, Edwin 32, 62, 77, 213
Tunis, John R. 55, 204, 205, 207, 208, 260, 264, 284

Turin, Adela 23, 356
Turkin, Hy 31
Turkle, Brinton 13, 26, 40, 51, 64, 67, 79, 86, 132, 174, 214, 239, 243, 293, 414, 452, 470
Turner, Anne W. 147, 544
Turner, Gwenda 70
Turner, Philip 47, 470
Turner, Stanley 31, 486
Turngren, Ellen 210, 273
Turska, Krystyna 99, 108, 162, 215, 441
Tuttle, Merlin D. 25, 484
Twain, Mark 23, 115, 136, 174, 222, 247, 254, 260, 268, 285, 288, 299, 305, 316, 326, 329, 339, 340, 348, 366, 397, 416, 419, 422, 429, 439, 442, 446, 450, 462, 465, 468, 475, 480
Tyler, William R. 67, 392

Uchida, Yoshiko 18, 71, 72, 85, 182, 209, 341
Uden, Grant 99, 214, 263
Udry, Janice May 39, 211
Ullberg, Nena Grigorian 202, 301
Ullman, James Ramsey 51, 168
Umansky, Kaye 173
Underhill, Ruth M. 21, 409
Underwood, Betty 3, 382
Underwood, Mary Betty 3
Ungerer, Tomi 10, 12, 60, 62, 154, 156, 157, 191, 210, 211, 212, 213, 214, 369, 394
Unsell, Martin 230, 305
Unwin, N. 50, 74, 286
Unwin, Nora S. 31, 106, 167, 208, 231, 386
Unwin, Pippa 123
Updegraff, Imelda 221
Updegraff, Robert 221
Ure, Jean 121
Urquhart, Jennifer C. 191, 353
Utemorrah, Daisy 15
Utton, Peter 56, 130, 364

Vaghela, Saroj 91
Vagin, Vladimir 21, 473
Vainio, Pirkko 102, 198, 458
Valdes, Joan 126, 309
Valen, Nanine 161, 381
Valens, Evans G. 77, 210, 546
Valenzuela, Juan 73
Valintcourt, Honore 83, 414
Vallingby 92
Vance, Marguerite 77, 174, 433
Van Allsburg, Chris 8, 21, 27, 28, 29, 35, 40, 41, 71, 90, 92, 108, 116, 135, 157, 158, 162, 163, 179, 181, 185, 191, 193, 225, 226, 228, 248
Van Bilsen, Rita 178, 546
van der Essen, Anne 23, 318
Van Der Meer, Atie 130
Van Der Meer, Ron 191, 224, 444
Van der Haas, Henrietta 206
Van Der Linde, Henry 34, 260
Van der Loeff, A. Rutgers 32, 210
Van Der Zee, James 234, 372
Van de Wetering, Jamwillem 163, 457

Van Everen, Jay   *165, 314, 453*
Van Iterson, Siny Rose   *17, 356*
van Kampen, Vlasta   *97, 103, 104*
Van Laan, Nancy   16, 183, 275
van Leeuwen, Jean   *12, 80, 140, 141, 200, 232, 247, 250, 317, 403*
Van Loon, Hendrik Willem   *164*
Van Nutt, Robert   *158, 250*
Van Quyen, Duong   *202, 301*
Van Raven, Pieter   *173*
Van Rhijn, Aleid   *32, 354*
Van Sciver, Ruth   *138, 139, 290*
Van Splunteren   *151, 276, 286*
Van Stockum, Hilda   *166*
Van Woerkom, Dorothy O.   *64, 429*
Varian, George   *164, 373*
Varley, Susan   *116, 130, 192*
Varner, Velma   *152*
Vasiliu, Mircea   *32, 209, 290*
Vasquez, Enriqueta Longeaux y   *3, 428, 438*
Vaughan, Anne   *207, 325*
Vaughan-Jackson, Genevieve   *71, 548*
Veglahn, Nancy   *213, 336*
Velasquez, Eric   *56, 176, 458*
Velthuijs, Max   *63, 280*
Vendrell, Carme Sole   *24, 464*
Venema, Reintje   *175, 330*
Vennema, Peter   *30, 159, 190*
Ventura, Piero   *13, 14*
Venturo, Piero   *224*
Vermeulen, Lo   *9, 366, 394*
Verney, John   *9, 46, 213, 256*
Vero, Radu   *149*
Verwoert, Sisca   *147*
Vesey, Amanda   *130*
Vestal, Herman B.   *142, 319*
Vetter, Carole   *137, 409*
Vevers, Dr. Gwynne   *130, 482*
Vickers, David   *84, 264*
Vickery, Robert   *53, 126, 235, 306*
Vidal, Beatriz   *16*
Viereck, Ellen   *52, 78, 84*
Viereck, Phillip   *52, 78, 84*
Vigna, Judith   *4*
Viksten, Albert   *210, 251, 415*
Villiers, Alan   *57, 482*
Vincent, Gabrielle   *158*
Vinge, Joan D.   *172*
Vinke, Hermann   *4, 469*
Viorst, Judith   *69, 90, 139, 146, 217, 296, 309, 408, 427*
Vipont, Elfrida   *45, 214, 279, 342, 343, 345*
Vishniac, Roman   *131*
Vitale, Lidia   *205, 382, 460*
Vitale, Stefano   *105, 346, 377, 434, 445, 473*
Vivas, Julie   *29, 58, 60, 76, 109, 117, 147, 343, 372*
Voake, Charlotte   *164, 180, 182, 199, 245, 426, 474*
VoDinh   *68*
Vogel, Ray   *21, 277*
Voight, Leigh   *84, 481*
Voigt, Cynthia   *6, 28, 42, 122, 162, 170, 180, 188, 217, 225, 226*

Von Babar, Die Geschichte   *23*
Von Baeyer, Hans Christian   *150, 371*
Vosburgh, Leonard   *3, 140, 210, 244, 317, 471*
Votaw, Susan   *148, 393, 410*
Voute, Kathleen   *78, 209*
Vreekin, Elizabeth   *86*

Waber, Bernard   *26, 53, 61, 211*
Waddell, Martin   *19, 20, 34, 100, 125, 130, 191, 198, 199, 260, 261, 311, 338, 395, 451, 469*
Wade, Alan   *159, 439*
Waechter, Friedrich Karl   *179, 247*
Wagner, Lauren McGraw   *438, 444*
Wagner, Jane   *89, 471*
Wagner, Jenny   *58, 101, 147, 280*
Wagstaff, Sue   *176, 551*
Wahl, Jan   *22, 69, 119, 174, 191, 246, 298, 399*
Wakatsuki, Jeanne   *85, 383, 384*
Walck   *17, 46, 49, 52, 53, 61, 107, 210, 212, 249, 253, 261, 263, 265, 277, 285, 290, 291, 296, 325, 333, 335, 345, 350, 373, 387, 397, 402, 418, 458, 482*
Waldeck, Theodore J.   *205*
Waldman, Neil   *69, 113, 184, 244, 421, 464, 485*
Walford, Astrid   *32, 46, 354*
Walker, Barbara K.   *159*
Walker, Barbara M.   *229*
Walker, Bob   *137, 374*
Walker, C.   *77, 359*
Walker, David   *197, 249*
Walker, Jane Murray   *65, 66*
Walker, John   *214, 447*
Walker, Kate   *35, 60*
Walker, Nedda   *206, 423*
Walker, Stephen   *161, 381*
Wall, Elizabeth S.   *124, 552*
Wallace, Barbara Brooks   *232*
Wallace, Bill   *96, 115, 196, 199, 200, 218, 220, 224, 232, 239, 442*
Wallace, Ian   *104, 109, 111, 129, 131, 428*
Wallenta, E.   *9, 282*
Walles, Dwight   *91, 302*
Wallner, John   *87, 180, 235, 354, 415*
Wallower, Lucille   *177, 206*
Walser, Richard   *282*
Walsh, Anne Batterberry   *64*
Walsh, Ellen Stoll   *190*
Walsh, Jill Paton   *26, 64, 131, 160, 197, 198, 214, 223, 230, 231, 302, 473*
Walsh, Mary R.   *206, 480*
Walter, Marion   *151, 553*
Walter, Mildred Pitts   *69, 118, 119, 180, 181, 309, 322, 323*
Walters, Martin   *25*
Walter Wangerin, Jr.   *91*
Walton, Luke   *140, 553*
Wangerin, Walter   *91, 134, 162*
Ward, Jon   *130, 457*
Ward, Keith   *238, 335*
Ward, Lynd   *26, 38, 53, 62, 77, 136, 141, 156, 165, 166, 167, 193, 194, 201, 204,*

207, 209, 210, 224, 297, 300, 341, 376, 381, 446
Ward, Patricia   *211, 383*
Ware, Leon   *187, 544*
Warfel, Diantha   *33*
Warner, Gertrude   *79, 315*
Warner, Lucille Schulberg   *64, 336*
Warren, Betsy   *216*
Warshaw, Mal   *28, 384*
Wartski, Maureen Crane   *56*
Wasserman, Debra   *24*
Watanabe, Shigeo   *109, 486*
Waterhouse, Charles   *136, 449*
Waterson, Mary   *282*
Waterton, Betty   *44, 97, 103, 271*
Watkins-Pitchford, Denys   *257*
Watkins, Bernard   *166*
Watkins, Yoko Kawashima   *181, 346*
WatkinsPitchford, Denys James
Watson, Clyde   *11, 60*
Watson, James   *176, 555*
Watson, John   *123, 555*
Watson, Richard Jesse   *94, 115*
Watson, Sally   *235, 292*
Watson, Wendy   *11, 60, 132, 160, 204, 215, 269, 476*
Watts, Barrie   *192, 221*
Watts, Bernadette   *250*
Watts, Mabel   *62, 440*
Watts, Margaret   *35*
Watty, Piper   *49, 372, 480*
Way, Mark   *23*
Weatherby, Mark Alan   *135, 457*
Weaver, Stella   *211*
Webb, Jean Francis   *212*
Webb, Margot S.   *73*
Webb, Nancy   *212*
Wechter, Nell Wise   *171*
Weck, Thomas L.   *53*
Weeks, Kent R.   *147, 370*
Wegen, Ron   *144, 555*
Wegner, Fritz   *44, 68, 80, 110, 161, 194, 197, 222, 245, 326, 491*
Weidhorn, Manfred   *146, 555*
Weigand, Patrick   *222*
Weigel, Susi   *9, 426*
Weihs, Erika   *5, 219, 357, 406*
Weik, Mary Hays   *155, 169, 362*
Weil, Ann   *168, 335*
Weil, Lisl   *188, 377*
Weiler, Mary   *44, 367*
Weilerstein, Sadie Rose   *114, 219, 324*
Weiman, Eileen   *202*
Weir, Doffy   *172, 440*
Weisgard, Leonard   *37, 38, 49, 64, 168, 206, 208, 209, 216, 281, 284, 311, 384, 488*
Weiss, Ann E.   *68, 69*
Weiss, Ellen   *80, 88, 90*
Weiss, Emil   *3, 78, 168, 316, 404, 460*
Weiss, Harvey   *211*
Weiss, Leatie   *80, 88, 90*
Weiss, Renee   *139, 487*
Weissenberg, Fran   *220*
Weisskopf, Victor F.   *78, 415*
Welch, Diana   *125*
Welch, Martha McKeen   *557*

Welch, Ronald   *45, 337*

Weldon, James   *52, 156, 395*

Weller, Frances Ward   *96, 271*

Wellman, Manly Wade   *171, 557*

Wellman, Paul I.   *228, 270*

Wells, Frances   *137, 492*

Wells, Haru   *132, 188, 234, 357, 473*

Wells, Peter   *205*

Wells, Robert   *33, 331*

Wells, Rosemary   *12, 13, 21, 29, 62, 94, 96, 113, 123, 144, 145, 158, 183, 188, 215, 225, 393*

Welsh, Patrick J.   *92, 354*

Wendelin, Karla Hawkins   *95*

Wensell, Ulises   *178*

Wentworth, Elaine   *87, 466*

Wentz, Budd   *148, 557*

Wenzel, Greg   *145*

Wenzel, Walt   *137, 477*

Werenskiold, Erik   *211, 255, 407, 452*

Werner, Elsa Jane   *31, 152, 321, 484, 485*

Werner, Jerry   *92, 260*

Wersba, Barbara   *133, 558*

Werth, Kurt   *51, 93, 140, 340, 449*

Wesson, Lis C.   *73, 361*

West, Harold   *15, 168, 174, 211*

Westall, Robert   *27, 28, 47, 48, 49, 57, 101, 102, 198*

Westcott, Nadine Bernard   *116, 191, 192, 250*

Westerberg, Christine   *72, 415*

Weston, Christine   *167, 328*

Weston, John   *71, 321*

Weston, Martha   *63, 149, 151, 286, 300, 312, 446*

Wexler, Jerome   *64, 151, 302, 416*

Wezel, Peter   *213*

Wheatley, Arabelle   *61, 425*

Wheatley, Nadia   *58, 59, 109, 110, 147, 237, 283, 478, 488*

Wheeler, Cindy   *16*

Wheeler, Benson   *86, 458, 485*

Wheeler, E. King   *128, 406*

Wheeler, J.   *128, 406*

Wheeler, Opal   *38*

Wheelwright, Sidnee   *175, 303*

Whelan, Gloria   *87*

Whistler, Theresa   *198, 398*

White, Anne H.   *209, 212, 442, 464*

White, Anne Terry   *153*

White, Bessie F.   *209*

White, Dale   *229, 351, 480*

White, E. B.   *10, 49, 79, 103, 107, 126, 128, 132, 168, 196, 214, 216, 218, 231, 233, 237, 344*

White, Florence Meiman   *4*

White, Jack R.   *150, 559*

White, Robb   *71, 204*

White, Sandra Verrill   *24, 338*

Whitehead, Barbara   *229, 365*

Whitethorne, Baje   *229, 282*

Whitfield, Philip   *69*

Whitlock, Ralph   *221*

Whitman, Maurice   *106, 252*

Whitney, Elinor   *165, 356*

Whitney, George G.   *166, 361*

Whitney, Phyllis A.   *187, 195, 207, 362, 367*

Whybrow, Ian   *257*

Wibberley, Leonard   *71, 78, 201, 202*

Wiberg, Harald   *12, 52, 424*

Wieler, Diana   *77, 97, 110, 195, 236*

Wier, Ester   *168, 483*

Wiese, Kurt   *32, 38, 49, 50, 51, 52, 165, 166, 167, 174, 205, 206, 207, 208, 238, 251, 270, 289, 340, 422, 465, 487*

Wiesner, David   *29, 41, 190, 191, 399*

Wiesner, William   *212, 482*

Wignell, Edel   *34*

Wijngaard, Juan   *44, 100, 130, 190, 199, 371, 372, 418, 440*

Wikland, Ilon   *10, 423*

Wilbur, Richard   *66, 215*

Wilcox, Eleanor Reindollar   *36, 441*

Wild, Margaret   *60*

Wilde, George   *86, 377*

Wilde, Oscar   *130, 435*

Wilder, Laura Ingalls   *49, 65, 66, 166, 167, 206, 232, 233, 238, 277, 281, 298, 399, 418*

Wildsmith, Brian   *10, 11, 51, 57, 98, 99, 107, 125, 155, 180, 212, 248, 272, 295, 413*

Wiley, Karla H.   *137, 138, 352*

Wilhelm, Hans   *24, 91, 180, 448*

Wilkes, Angela   *192*

Wilkes, Larry   *56, 406*

Wilkeshuis, Cornelius   *178, 546*

Wilkin, Eloise   *205, 208, 329, 429*

Wilkinson, Barry   *268, 283*

Wilkinson, Brenda   *235*

Wilkon, Jozef   *178, 461*

Wilks, Mike   *221*

Willard, Barbara   *101, 231*

Willard, Nancy   *14, 28, 40, 53, 93, 115, 162, 170, 194, 319, 446, 485*

Williams, Barbara   *62, 68, 296*

Williams, Garth   *49, 50, 54, 67, 79, 126, 128, 159, 168, 207, 216, 218, 229, 231, 233, 290, 412, 424, 483*

Williams, J. R.   *216, 229*

Williams, Jay   *19, 21, 52, 62, 157, 239, 243, 375, 402, 440*

Williams, Jeanne   *230*

Williams, Jennifer   *29*

Williams, Jenny   *91, 434*

Williams, Kit   *23*

Williams, Linda   *70, 117, 426*

Williams, Margery   *52, 269, 461*

Williams, Phyllis S.   *105, 403*

Williams, Rhys   *57*

Williams, Richard   *115, 228, 408*

Williams, Ruth   *57*

Williams, Sherley Anne   *41, 119, 288*

Williams, Slim   *87, 300, 342*

Williams, Sophy   *131, 473*

Williams, Teppy   *149, 321*

Williams, Terry Tempest   *150, 321, 434*

Williams, Ursula Moray   *214, 385*

Williams, Vera B.   *4, 28, 29, 41*

Williamson, Joanne S.   *210, 299*

Willis, Jeanne   *100, 192*

Willis, Robert J.   *85, 441*

Willis, Val   *182*

Willmott, Frank   *59*

Willow, Diane   *24, 392*

Wilson, Barbara Ker   *74, 212, 421*

Wilson, Bob   *125, 564*

Wilson, Budge   *34, 236*

Wilson, Charles Banks   *207, 414*

Wilson, Ellen Janet   *106*

Wilson, Hazel   *77, 174, 341, 375*

Wilson, Hazel H.   *208, 261*

Wilson, Jacqueline   *49, 56, 172*

Wilson, John   *197, 423*

Wilson, Kathleen Atkins   *119, 251*

Wilson, Leon   *50, 409*

Wilson, Mike   *149, 504*

Wilson, Peggy   *252*

Wilson, W. N.   *32, 325*

Wilson, William N.   *209, 453*

Wimmer, Helmut K.   *77, 278*

Wimmer, Mike   *135, 175, 192, 285, 306*

Winborn, Marsha   *145, 310*

Windham, Sophie   *191*

Windsor, Patricia   *215*

Winn, Chris   *264*

Winston, Clara   *3, 51, 108, 153, 209, 254, 266, 381, 409*

Winston, Peggy   *192*

Winston, Richard   *3, 51, 108, 153, 209, 254, 266, 381, 409*

Winter, Jeanette   *104*

Winter, Jonah   *104*

Winter, Paula   *63*

Winter, William   *97, 107, 121*

Winthrop, Elizabeth   *42, 84, 228, 388*

Winton, Ian   *222, 474*

Wisbecki, Dorothy   *565*

Wisbeski, Dorothy   *138*

Wise, Lu Celia   *16*

Wise, William   *33*

Wisemann, Ann   *138, 566*

Wisenfeld, Alison   *222, 378*

Wisler, Gary Clifton   *230*

Wissman, Ruth H.   *43*

Wizowaty, Suzi   *220*

Wohlrabe, Raymond A.   *148, 566*

Wojciechowska, Maia   *89, 139, 140, 169, 212, 291, 364*

Wolcott, Elizabeth Tyler   *429*

Wolf, Bernard   *62*

Wolf, Janet   *69, 319*

Wolf, Susan   *80, 347, 390*

Wolf, Virginia   *66*

Wolfe-Cundiff, Leslie   *233, 566*

Wolff, Ashley   *24, 191, 486*

Wolff, Virginia Euwer   *104, 112, 120*

Wolkstein, Diane   *149, 375*

Wong, David   *81, 147*

Wong, Jeanyee   *31, 294*

Wonsetler, John   *206, 447*

Wood, Audrey   *21, 41, 42, 69, 70, 92, 94, 203, 204, 225, 226, 228, 238*

Wood, David   *172*

Wood, Don   *21, 41, 42, 69, 70, 92, 94, 203, 204, 225, 226, 228, 238*

Wood, Douglas   *8, 112, 129, 295*

Wood, Harrie   *165, 367*

Wood, Kerry   *97, 127, 367*

Wood, Laura Newbold   *86, 206, 327*
Wood, Linda C.   *203, 332*
Wood, Michael   *198, 479*
Wood, Muriel   *44, 416*
Wood, Nancy   *234*
Wood, Phyllis Anderson   *177, 567*
Woodall, Heather   *44, 97, 104, 377*
Woodbery, Joan   *57*
Woodress, James   *78, 455*
Woodruff, Barbara   *207, 272, 277*
Woods, George   *90, 323, 489*
Woods, George A.   *84*
Woodson, Jack   *33, 304*
Woodward, Hildegard   *38, 314*
Woody, Regina J.   *136, 568*
Woolley, Catherine   *135, 136, 137, 313, 341, 436*
Woolsey, Maryhale   *71, 274*
Wormell, Christopher   *24, 199*
Wormser, Richard   *228, 229, 230, 274, 351*
Worth, Kathryn   *205, 206, 263, 315*
Worth, Valerie   *64, 257*
Wosmek, Frances   *188, 568*
Wright, Barton   *216*
Wright, Betty Ren   *42, 54, 80, 89, 105, 112, 115, 196, 220, 223, 225, 238, 239*
Wright, Joe   *245*
Wrightson, Alice Patricia   *57, 383*
Wrightson, Patricia   *10, 28, 57, 58, 59, 76, 93, 101, 107, 147, 161, 173, 213, 236, 383*
Wrigley, Elsie   *140, 491*
Wu, Cheng-en   *569*
Wuorio, Eva-Lis   *154, 253, 569*
Wyeth, Andrew   *204, 205, 345*
Wyeth, N. C.   *51, 82, 166, 376, 488*
Wyllie, Stephen   *191, 192, 437*
Wynants, Miche   *154, 569*
Wyndham, Lee   *135, 139, 141, 252, 413, 449*
Wyndham, Robert   *139, 140, 300*
Wynne-Jones, Jim   *104, 195, 464, 569*

Xanthoulis, Yannis   *108*
Xaras, Theodore A.   *201, 421*
Xargle, Professor   *100*

Yadin, Yigael   *114, 358*
Yagawa, Sumiko   *158, 162, 245, 472*
Yalowitz, Paul   *69*
Yamaguchi, Marianne   *15, 58, 435, 439*

Yang, Jay   *33, 251, 300*
Yarbro, Chelsea Quinn   *189, 569*
Yarbrough, Camile   *118, 288*
Yardley, Thompson   *195*
Yashima, Taro   *39, 55, 201, 210, 224*
Yasuda, Chizuko   *91, 271*
Yates, Elizabeth   *3, 31, 167, 206, 208, 231, 246, 294, 364*
Yeager, Chuck   *80, 392*
Yeats, Jack   *166, 303*
Yeats, W. B.   *20, 431*
Yee, Patrick   *123, 570*
Yee, Paul   *45, 77, 79, 133, 461*
Yefremov, Ivan   *211*
Yenchi, Ching Chi Yee   *204, 307*
Yeoman, John   *99, 271*
Yeomans, Donald K.   *151, 425*
Yep, Laurence   *4, 26, 27, 29, 53, 69, 71, 81, 85, 111, 190, 234*
Ylla   *275, 362*
Yokoi, Daisuke   *191, 361*
Yolen, Jane   *33, 39, 41, 51, 52, 54, 61, 63, 68, 88, 93, 96, 105, 110, 115, 117, 132, 156, 179, 180, 181, 182, 193, 219, 295, 316, 321, 329, 375, 380, 435, 469*
Yonck, Barbara Jean   *226*
Yonekura, Masakane   *23, 466*
Yorinks, Arthur   *20, 41, 92, 116, 192, 330, 331*
Yoshida, Toshi   *190*
Yoshino, Shin   *150, 468*
Youmans, Eleanor   *174, 392*
Young, Andrew   *46, 119, 298, 372, 433, 435*
Young, Chip   *103*
Young, Delbert   *18, 309*
Young, Ed   *28, 30, 39, 41, 42, 51, 52, 61, 129, 140, 144, 158, 159, 179, 181, 182, 191, 346, 415, 417, 428, 467*
Young, Ella   *254, 273*
Young, Geoffrey   *221*
Young, Miriam   *156, 427*
Young, Noela   *59, 60, 237*
Young, Selina   *123, 131, 378*
Yue, Charlotte   *28, 204*
Yue, David   *28, 204*
Yunupingu, Djoki   *268*
Yvart, Jacques   *150, 342*

Zach, Cheryl   *95*
Zacharias, Thomas   *10*
Zacharias, Wanda   *10*

Zaffo, George J.   *208*
Zaid, Barry   *61, 297, 316, 355*
Zak, Drahos   *59*
Zallinger, Jean   *107, 229, 339*
Zappler, George   *260*
Zappler, Lisbeth   *260*
Zar, Rose   *219*
Zarins, Joyce Audy   *115, 417*
Zaunders, Bo   *90, 318*
Zavos, Judy   *59*
Zavrel, Stepan   *23, 372*
Zawadsky, Patience   *138, 445*
Zdinak, William   *69, 352, 371*
Zecca, Carolyn   *151, 337*
Zei, Alki   *17, 110, 337*
Zeldich, Arieh   *180, 326*
Zelibska, Maria   *22*
Zelinsky, Paul O.   *17, 41, 69, 72, 79, 84, 85, 88, 93, 112, 126, 134, 158, 163, 170, 179, 180, 183, 188, 190, 191, 192, 196, 218, 228, 256, 298, 299, 421, 490*
Zemach, Harve   *13, 40, 53, 61, 62, 63, 212, 213, 215, 338*
Zemach, Kaethe   *63*
Zemach, Margot   *13, 14, 27, 40, 52, 53, 60, 61, 62, 63, 72, 108, 117, 132, 137, 156, 157, 160, 163, 169, 182, 212, 213, 215*
Ziebel, Peter   *146*
Ziefert, Harriet   *145, 146, 261, 275, 282, 395, 396, 426, 427, 461*
Zilboorg, Margaret Stone   *211, 408*
Zim, Herbert   *31, 96, 390*
Zimmer, Dirk   *21, 35, 88, 225, 226, 274*
Zimnik, Reiner   *32, 153, 154, 160, 212, 257, 320, 389*
Zindel, Paul   *25*
Zion, Gene   *38, 153, 360*
Zisfein, Melvin B.   *158, 162, 471*
Zivkovic, Nicole   *123*
Zola, Meguido   *130, 425*
Zolotow, Charlotte   *38, 39, 68, 83, 117, 191, 208, 224, 326, 327, 360, 365*
Zotter, Gerri   *23*
Zubrowski, Bernie   *149, 326, 423*
Zudeck, Darryl S.   *29, 94, 111, 121, 199, 229, 230, 304*
Zweifel, Fran   *142, 313*
Zwerger, Lisbeth   *10, 158, 179, 183, 250, 265, 279, 307, 363, 375, 460, 466*
Zylman, Michele   *254*

Title Index

Aardvarks, Disembark! 30, 397

Aaron and the Green Mountain Boys 140, 141, 351, 541

Abbey-lubbers, Banshees and Boggarts: An Illustrated Encyclopedia of Fairies 130, 279, 353

Abbie's God Book 177, 381, 445

Abby, My Love 112, 196, 390

ABC, 123: The Canadian Alphabet and Counting Book 97, 547

ABC: The Story of the Alphabet 73, 307

ABC Bunny 165, 347

ABC Fire Dogs 142, 316, 521

ABC Halloween Witch 142, 310, 316

ABC of Buses 137, 515, 516

ABC of Monsters 58, 462

ABC Pigs Go to Market 142, 316, 465

ABC Pirate Adventure 142, 280, 316

ABC Triplets at the Zoo 143, 317, 478

Abel's Island 53, 63, 65, 161, 169, 456, 528

Abe Lincoln: Log Cabin to White House 250

Abe Lincoln Gets his Chance 106, 293, 388

Abiyoyo 191, 373, 509

Aborigines 176, 430

About David 200, 477

About Owls 63, 295, 349

About Wise Men and Simpletons: Twelve Tales from Grimm 160, 363, 381, 516

The Abracadabra Mystery 43, 433

Abraham Lincoln 37, 167, 313, 342, 344, 399

Abraham Lincoln, Friend of the People 167, 344, 399

Abraham Lincoln's World 167, 342

Abuela 104, 184, 325, 408

Ace: The Very Important Pig 74, 375, 406

Achilles the Donkey 98, 260, 262

The Acorn People 79, 398, 471

Across Five Aprils 51, 85, 169, 386, 485

Active Science I 222, 302, 358, 539

Adam's Book of Odd Creatures 211, 429

Adam and Eve: The Bible Story 181, 388

Adam Gray, Stowaway: A Story of the China Trade 227, 254, 354

Adam of the Road 166, 205, 360, 417

Adrift! 82, 99, 157, 258, 464, 510

Adventure Beyond the Clouds 87, 457

The Adventure of Light 32, 399

The Adventure of Pinocchio 458

Adventure on Thunder Island 128, 406

Adventures in the Desert 211, 386, 400, 401

The Adventures of Albert, the Running Bear 80, 347, 390, 566

The Adventures of Huckleberry Finn 50, 299, 432

The Adventures of Isabel 184, 437, 459

The Adventures of King Midas 199, 259, 378

Adventures of Misha 204, 452, 499

The Adventures of Nimble, Rumble, and Tumble 90, 523

The Adventures of Obadiah 67, 544

The Adventures of Paddy Pork 25, 357

The Adventures of Pinocchio 64, 100, 303, 389

The Adventures of Taxi Dog 183, 260, 284

The Adventures of Ulysses 154, 344, 372, 419

Aesop's Fables 142, 183, 192, 199, 255, 377, 428, 449, 533, 576

Aesop and Company 257, 352

Afraid of the Dark 111, 322, 401

Africa Dream 288, 362

African Dream 118

African Journey 29, 296

After-harvest Festival: The Story of a Girl of the Old Kankakee 106, 252, 560

The Afterdark Princess 172, 246, 312

Afternoon of the Elves 170, 183, 425

After the Bomb: Brother in the Land 222, 321, 504, 563

After the Dancing Days 94, 111, 113, 497

After the First Death 162, 305

After the Fortune Cookies 189, 271

After the Rain 170, 441

After the Storm 34, 287

Against the Storm 102, 105, 377

Agave Blooms Just Once 204, 394

The Ageless Story: With It's Antiphons 37

Aging 143, 518

Agnes the Sheep 91, 537

Aida 119, 322, 323, 484

AIME Executive Secretary 237

Ain't Gonna Study War No More: The Story of America's Peace Seekers 4, 56, 447

Airborne: The Search for the Secret of Flight 8, 439

Aircraft of Today and Tomorrow 57, 438

Airport 162, 261

Ajeemah and His Son 30, 268

AK 231, 321

Aki and the Fox 190, 373

Alala 155, 298, 452

Alan and Naomi 4, 27, 109, 142, 235, 422, 506

Alanna: The First Adventure 144, 478

Albatross Adventure 164, 558

Alberic the Wise and other Journeys 155, 356, 399

Albert's Toothache 62, 296, 562

Alberta Culture and Multiculturalism 6

Albert Einstein 31, 208, 422

Album de Bambi 22, 502

Alcuin Society 7

Aldita and the Forest 232, 293, 532

Alec and His Flying Bed 123, 283

Alenka v Kraji Divu 23, 291, 483

Alessandra: Alex in Rome 6, 91, 327

Alessandra In Love 146, 400

Alex 5, 6, 31, 32, 91, 174, 187, 298, 315, 318, 327, 507, 529, 560

Alexander and the Terrible, Horrible, No Good, Very Bad Day 90, 217, 309, 549

Alexander and the Wind-up Mouse 40, 67, 424

Alexandra 79, 180, 455, 465

Alex in Winter 5, 91, 327

The Alfred Summer 27, 143, 521

Alias Madame Doubtfire 182, 338

Alica v Krajine Zazrakov 19, 400

Alice's Adventures in Wonderland 8, 100, 125, 183, 199, 282, 291, 357, 406, 455, 541

Alice in Rapture, Sort of 81, 459

Aliens for Breakfast 220, 270, 334, 527

Alitji in Dreamland 74, 421, 514, 564

Alive 126, 489

Alive & Starting Over 124, 126, 136, 144, 405, 407

All-of-a-Kind Family 85, 114, 394, 537

All Aboard! The Story of Passenger Trains in America 230, 256

All Aboard: Poems 32, 153, 450, 524

All About Anna and Harriet and Christopher and Me 59, 256, 372

All About Books 31

All About Light and Radiation 137, 345, 490

All About Sam 42, 89, 129, 197, 201, 223, 316, 429

All Alone 98, 168, 209, 253, 270, 495

All Around the Town 38, 443, 532

Alla Scoperta Dell'Africa 22

All Because of Jill 142, 438

All Butterflies: An ABC   26, 281
Alle Meine Blatter   22, 365, 430
All Falling Down   38, 360, 575
The Alligator Case   137, 326
Alligator Pie   44, 107, 111, 418, 460
The Alligator Under the Bed   216, 385, 462
All in a Day   4, 252
All in Free but Janey   25, 388, 395
All in the Blue Unclouded Weather   147, 408
All in the Morning Early   39, 460, 462
All Join In   125, 271
All Kinds of Bees   137, 516, 517, 534
All Night, All Day: A Child's First Book of African American Spirituals   119, 283
Allosaurus   199, 386, 492
All Sail Set: A Romance of the Flying Cloud   166, 526
All the Colors of the Race: Poems   4, 244, 529
All the King's Men   109, 440
All the Money in the World   197, 280, 493
All the Proud Tribesmen   57, 509, 538
All the Way Home   62, 437, 509
All Times, All Peoples: A World History of Slavery   68, 339, 447
All Together   9, 27, 68, 162, 279, 513
All Together Now   27, 68, 162, 279
Allumette   62, 545
All Upon a Stone   214, 274, 352
All We Know   59, 345
Almost the Real Thing: Simulation in Your High Tech World   8, 520
Alone in the Wild Forest   60, 519, 574
Alone in Wolf Hollow   188, 202, 280
Along Came a Dog   15, 107, 168, 316, 510
Along the Seaside   9, 482, 527
Alphabatics   41, 94, 432
The Alphabeast Book: An Abecedarium   60, 506
Alphabeasts   34, 271
Alphabet City   123, 385
An Alphabet of Animals   24, 199, 568
The Alphabet Parade   184, 297
The Alphabet Tale   136, 212, 262, 350
Alphavegetabet (poems)   70, 332
Alphonse, That Bearded One   31, 209, 290, 453
Als Ich Ein Kleiher Junge War   9, 419
Als Ich Kleiher Junge War   401
Alvin's Swap Shop   197, 377, 524
Always, Always   180, 326, 573
Always Room for One More   39, 381, 462
Alzheimer's Disease   146, 414
The Amazing Bone   13, 14, 27, 40, 63, 161, 528
Amazing Grace   100, 269, 380
The Amazing Voyage of the Cucumber Sandwich   195, 463, 498
Amelia Bedelia and the Baby   35, 470, 535
Amelia Bedelia Goes Camping   89, 470, 535
Am Ende der Spur   108, 282, 370

America's Endangered Birds: Programs and People Working to Save Them   93, 343, 442
America's Ethan Allen   38, 381, 553
America's First Army   32, 307, 314, 531
America's Mark Twain   136, 446, 553
America's Own Mark Twain   174, 329, 339
America Grows Up: A History for Peter   211, 339, 395
America Is Born: A History for Peter   168, 339, 395
America Moves Forward: A History for Peter   168, 339, 395
An American ABC   37, 476, 477
American Indians Today: Issues and Conflicts   234, 370
The American Indian Story   136, 446, 553
American Painter in Paris: A Life of Mary Cassatt   106, 564
The Americans   77, 307, 456
Americans Before Columbus   167, 208, 258, 335
The American West 1840-1895   221, 489, 533
Amifika   4, 300, 322
Amikuk   209, 452, 463
Amish People: Plain Living in a Complex World   63, 324, 449, 487
Amityville Horror   200, 252
Amos: The Story of an Old Dog and His Couch   226, 506, 510
Amos's Sweater   97, 104, 195, 413, 430
Amos and Boris   60, 132, 156, 160, 528
Amos Fortune, Free Man   167, 208, 231, 545, 570
Amy's Eyes   180, 330, 404
Anancy and Mr. Dry-Bone   184, 345
Ananse the Spider: Tales from an Ashanti Village   155, 252, 565
Anansi the Spider: A Tale from the Ashanti   40, 52, 443
Anastasia, Ask your Analyst   88, 429
Anastasia Has the Answers   89, 429
Anastasia Krupnik   128, 429
Anatole   39, 53, 348, 446, 540, 562
Anatole and the Cat   39, 348, 540
Ancient China   148, 277, 373, 458
Andi's War   81, 496
And Loving It!   33, 397
And Miss Carter Wore Pink: Scenes from an Edwardian Childhood   11, 277
And Now Miguel   31, 168, 295, 411
And One Was a Wooden Indian   228, 258
Andrea   16, 24, 95, 145, 227, 261, 303, 435, 449, 515, 530, 574
Andrew Carnegie: Giant of Industry   139, 269, 435
And Then What Happened, Paul Revere?   26, 346, 541
And Tomorrow the Stars: The Story of John Cabot   44, 377, 411, 412
And to Think that I Saw It on Mulberry Street   50, 512
Andy and the Lion   37, 313
Andy and Willie   106, 307

And You Give Me a Pain, Elaine   93, 115, 477
Andy Says ... Bonjour!   152, 323, 393
Angel's Mother's Boyfriend   181, 252, 318
The Angel and the Soldier Boy   198, 302
Angelina Ballerina   116, 307, 381
Angry Arthur   130, 407, 467
The Angry Moon   26, 40, 420, 520
The Animal, the Vegetable & John D. Jones   74, 179, 288, 503
Animal Alphabet   158, 407
Animal Atlas of the World   139, 274, 398
Animal A To Z   123, 575
Animal Babies   24, 153, 362, 442, 497, 570
Animal Camouflage   137, 400, 517
Animal Clocks and Compasses: From Animal Migration to Space Travel   78, 388
The Animal Fair   484, 485
Animal Families of the Wild   24, 287, 500
The Animal Family   52, 155, 169, 392, 510
The Animal Farm   152
The Animal Frolic   152, 548
Animalia   59, 117, 237, 261
Animal Numbers   23, 407
Animals, Animals   192, 290
The Animals Frolic   524
Animals Made by Me   140, 281
Animals of Farthing Wood: Escape from Danger   14, 312, 538
Animals of Many Lands   155, 489
Animals of the Bible: A Picture Book   37, 338, 416
Animals Showing Off   192, 295, 441
Animals that Migrate   149, 254, 576
Animals that Use Tools   143, 312, 341
Animal Tracks   232, 256, 308, 372
Ann, Aurelia and Dorothy   235, 290, 474
Anna (Anna Khlebnikova de Poltaratzky, 1770- 1840)   248
Anna's Special Present   116, 373, 543
Annabel's House   192, 449
The Anne of Green Gables Treasury   7, 302, 333
Annie & Moon   6
Annie and the Old One   11, 67, 71, 169, 235, 438, 471
Annie and the Wild Animals   191, 279
Annie Sullivan   140, 435, 497
Anno's Alphabet: An Adventure in Imagination   13, 26, 63, 68, 156, 161, 252
Anno's Britain   158, 252
Anno's Counting Book   27, 148, 191, 252
Anno's Italy   162, 178, 252
Anno's Journey   14, 27, 252
Anno's Math Games II   183, 252
Anno's Math Games III   184, 252
Anno's Mysterious Multiplying Jar   150, 179, 252
Anno's Song Book   23, 252
Anno's U.S.A.   163, 252
Anno's Unique World   23, 252

Annuzza: A Girl of Romania　50, 386, 469, 512

Another Celebrated Dancing Bear　159, 223, 350, 505

Another Heaven, Another Earth　174, 382

Another Place, Another Spring　202, 397

Anpao: An American Indian Odyssey　27, 169, 377, 506

The Answer Book of History　137, 332, 341, 480

Answers to Brut　60, 147, 499

An Ant Colony　225, 338

Antelope Singer　21, 409, 545

Anthology Two　127, 385

Anthony Burns: The Defeat and Triumph of a Fugitive Slave　4, 29, 113, 118, 368

Anthony Wayne: Washington's General　141, 317, 524

Antler, Bear, Canoe: A Northwoods Alphabet Year　184, 276

Ants　150, 412, 468

The Apache Gold Mystery　187, 500, 539

Apatosaurus　199, 368, 492

Ape in a Cape: An Alphabet of Odd Animals　38, 331

Appalachia: The Voices of Sleeping Birds　30, 175, 184, 455, 500

The Apple and the Arrow　167, 284

Appleseed Farm　207, 325, 548

Apple Trees　150, 396, 409

Appointment With a Stranger　196, 538

Apprentices of Florence　165, 268, 412

April's Kittens　37, 460

April Fool!　141, 310, 391

April Fools　62, 410

Aquarius　173, 436

Arc-en-ciel 2　222, 276, 450, 496

The Archaeology of Ships　148, 277, 397

Archer's Goon　28, 397

Archosauria: A New Look at the Old Dinosaur　149, 445

Arctic Explorer: The Story of Matthew Henson　235, 337

Arctic Memories　175, 331

Are All the Giants Dead?　161, 346, 464

Are We Nearly There?　100, 262, 276

Are You in the House Alone?　142, 188, 475

Are You There God? It's Me, Margaret　92, 98, 134, 172, 237, 272

The Ark　51, 209, 266, 565

Arkwright　59, 528

Armed with Courage　77, 446, 553

Arm in Arm　22, 155, 295

Armour and Blade　46, 332

Arnold of the Ducks　163, 353

Arnold Roth's Crazy Book of Science　140, 497

The Arrow Book of Backyard Creatures　232, 433

Arrow to the Sun: A Pueblo Indian Tale　12, 13, 40, 443

The Art and Industry of Sandcastles　11, 12, 52, 132, 244

Arthur　56, 359, 365

Arthur, for the Very First Time　93, 272, 433

Arthur's Baby　227, 281

Arthur and the Dragon　70, 292, 332

An Artist　98, 152, 157, 356

The Art of Ancient Egypt　50, 356, 463

The Art of the Northwest Coast Indians　63, 356, 463

Arts Victoria　75

As: A Surfeit of Similes　183, 399, 521

Ashanti to Zulu: African Traditions　27, 40, 157, 322, 323, 458

Ash Road　57, 509, 525

As I Was Crossing Boston Common　63, 132, 335, 426

Aska's Animals　104, 255, 315

Ask Me no Questions　28, 101, 505

Aspire to the Heavens: A Portrait of George Washington　138, 298

As Right as Right Can Be　63, 157, 426, 427, 496

Assignment: Latin America - a Story of the Peace Corps　138, 562

Association for Indiana Media Educators　237

As the Waltz Was Ending　16, 287

Athletic Shorts: Six Short Stories　237, 309

At Home and in the Street in 1900　176, 448, 485

At Home in the Rain Forest　24, 392, 564

At Home in 1900　176, 448, 485

Atlas of Kentucky　217, 400, 439

Atlas of North America　151, 350

At Mary Bloom's　63, 247

The Atoms within Us　78, 275

At School and in the Country in 1900　176, 448, 485

At School in 1900　176, 448, 485

At the Back of the north Wind　109, 432, 507

At the Cafe Splendid　182, 319

At the Crossroads　184, 390

At the Edge　4, 16, 42, 200, 225, 265, 284, 455, 458

At the Palace Gates　71, 208, 472, 481

Audubon　30, 166, 432, 480, 498, 518

Auf Endlosen Strassen　9, 332, 510

The Auk, the Dodo, and the Oryx: Vanished and Vanishing Creatures　213, 379, 517

Auks, Rocks and the Odd Dinosaur: Inside Stories from the Smithsonian's Museum of Natural History　29, 539

Aunt Agatha, There's a Lion under the Couch　138, 320

Aunt Flossie's Hats (and Crab Cakes Later)　184, 384, 487

Aunt Harriet's Underground Railroad in the Sky　5, 492

Aurora　23, 356, 544

Australia's Prehistoric Animals　232, 457

The Australia Book　483

Australian Animals　232, 416, 521

The Australian Book　14, 57, 511

Australian Dinosaurs and Their Relatives　74, 484

The Australian Echidna　232, 531

Australian Junior Field Guides　232, 531

Australian Legendary Tales　57, 328, 470

Australian Museum's Young Naturalist　232

The Australopedia　60, 360

Authorized Autumn Charts of the Upper Red Canoe River Country　61, 86, 301, 319

An Auto Mechanic　185, 341

The Automobile　145, 341

Autumn Street　108, 429

Avalanche!　32, 210, 507, 547

The Avion my Uncle Flew　167, 339, 341

Awaiting Developments　48, 77, 231, 248

Awards Committee　30, 81, 86, 88, 100, 122, 131, 177, 219

Away Went Wolfgang!　209, 399

An Awful Name to Live Up To　228, 351, 383

Ayu and the Perfect Moon　59, 306

Babar's Fair Will Be Opened next Sunday　153, 282, 366

Baba Yaga　213, 420

The Babe: Mildred Didrickson Zaharias　72, 522

Babe: The Gallant Pig　28, 181, 406, 488

Baboushka and the Three Kings　9, 39, 154, 493, 517

Babushka　72, 138, 158, 449, 479, 481, 543

Babushka's Doll　72, 481

Babushka and the Pig　138, 479, 543

Baby-sitting Is a Dangerous Job　223

The Baby's Catalogue　100, 245

Baby Beluga　24, 486, 566

The Baby Project　79, 332

Babysitters on Board!　239, 437

Babysitting Is a Dangerous Job　135, 200, 238, 493

Back-Back and the Lima Bear　53, 144, 537, 555

Back Home　185, 228, 433, 479

Bad Boy　97, 110, 195, 236, 560

Badger's Parting Gifts　116, 130, 548

Badger on the Barge and other Stories　36, 111, 384

The Bad Little Duck-hunter　207, 281, 387

Bagdad Ate It　42, 361, 505

A Bag of Moonshine　130, 350, 431

The Baillie's Daughter　116, 423

The Baker Street Irregulars in the Case of the Cop Catchers　188, 322

The Bakery Factory: Who Puts the Bread on Your Table　1, 149, 393

The Balancing of Child and Adult　65, 408

Balarin's Goat　61, 268

The Ball That Wouldn't Bounce　140, 293, 329

Bambino the Clown　38, 507

The Bamboo Flute　60, 323

Banana Blitz　74, 374

Banana Twist　197, 374

Bang, Bang, You're Dead　12, 155, 339, 508

Banner in the Sky: The Story of a Boy and a Mountain　51, 168, 545

Banner over Me   85, 362, 449

Bard of Avon: The Story of William Shakespeare   190, 527, 548

Bare Bear   130, 246

Barkis   37, 460

The Barn   138, 506

The Baron All at Sea   199, 267, 451

Bartholomew and the Oobleck   38, 512

Barto Takes the Subway   211, 279, 401

Bart Starr   33, 320

Barty   36, 82, 303

Baseball in April and Other Stories   18, 190, 217, 525

The Basket   117, 431, 535

The Bassumtyte Treasure   188, 310

The Bat-Poet   154, 171, 392, 511

Bat: The Story of a Bull Terrier   205, 446, 514

Batman: Exploring the World of Bats   25, 484, 544

The Battle Horse   17, 109, 271, 411, 412, 540

Battle in the Arctic Seas: The Story of Convoy PQ17   161, 471, 537

The Battle of Bubble and Squeak   48, 230, 258, 474

Battle of Gettysburg, 1-3 July, 1863   47, 491

The Battle of St. George Without   213, 446, 500

The Battle of the Bulge   33, 411, 412, 541

The Battlestar Galactica Storybook   143, 415, 448, 540

The Bayeaux Tapestry: The Story of the Norman Conquest: 1066   47, 319, 338

Bayou Suzette   174, 420

Beach Ball   159, 520

Be a Perfect Person in Just Three Days!   42, 385

Bear   190, 561

The Bear: Ship of Many Lives   34, 487

The Bear's Bicycle   26, 445, 446

The Bear's House   160, 355

The Bear and the Fly   63, 157, 565

The Bear and the People   160, 389, 575

Bear Circus   52, 60, 156, 160, 326

Bear Mouse   21, 62, 291, 345

A Bear Named Grumms   209, 503, 559

Be a Rockhound   143, 402

The Bear on the Motorcycle   212, 575

Bear Party   38, 326

The Bears' House   132, 217, 501

The Bears and I: Raising Three Cubs in the North Woods   201, 421, 569

Bears in the Night   128, 267

The Bears on Hemlock Mountain   167, 311, 513

The Beast of Monsieur Racine   12, 60, 156, 545

Beasts and Nonsense   152, 334

Beasts from a Brush   153, 404

Beat the Story-drum, Pum-pum   118, 178, 283

Beauty and the Beast   128, 440

Beaver Business: An Almanac   171, 498

Beaver Valley   214, 330, 454

Beaver Water   32, 210, 325, 452

Because of Madeline   210, 531

Because We Are   118, 180, 553

Becky and her Brave Cat, Bluegrass   106, 433, 438

Becoming Gershona   115, 510

Beef for Beauregard!   216, 351, 382

The Bee on the Comb   23, 563

Bees and Beelines   136, 247, 373

Beetles   150, 217, 226, 396, 407, 451, 459

Beetles, Lightly Toasted   217, 226, 459

Befana: A Christmas Story   62, 494

Before Their Time: Four Generations of Teenage Mothers   120, 503

Before the Lark   230, 281

Before the Supreme Court: The Story of Belva Ann Lockwood   202, 328, 382

Before You Were a Baby   138, 337, 516

The Beggar Queen   180, 246

The Beginner's Devotional   92, 260, 558

Beginnings and Endings with LIFETIMES in Between   110, 334, 420, 447

The Beginning Was a Dutchman   207, 404, 452

Be Good, Harry   137, 294

Behind Barbed Wire: the Imprisonment of Japanese Americans during World War II   28, 314

Behind the Back of the Mountain: Black Folktales from Southern Africa   62, 243, 322, 323

Behind the Scenes at the Horse Hospital   194, 281, 499, 543

Behind the Wheel   19, 156, 409

Behind the Wind   58, 568

Being Born   29, 221, 407, 462

Belinda   60, 94, 171, 179, 248, 387

Belling the Tiger   168, 453, 531

The Bells of Christmas   119, 314, 368

Ben's Dream   158, 179, 546

Ben's Trumpet   27, 40, 390

Ben and Me   50, 417

Beneath a Blue Umbrella   159, 483, 562

Benedict Arnold: Hero and Traitor   139, 318

Benjamin's Barn   192, 393, 423

Benjamin's Three Hundred and Sixty Five Birthdays   62, 261

Benjamin and Tulip   12, 13, 557

Benjamin Franklin   106, 344, 399

Benjamin Rush: Physician, Patriot, Founding Father   137, 361, 492

Benjamin Tabart's Juvenile Library   74, 453

Benjie and His Family   31, 411, 509

The Ben Lilly Legend   31, 324

The Bennington Stitch   145, 407

Benny's Animals and How He Put them in Order   33, 427, 510

Benny's Nose   140, 293, 466

Bently & Egg   190, 198, 208, 213, 396, 399

Beorn the Proud   212, 481, 531

Berchick   18, 115, 219, 271, 323

The Berenstain Bears and the Spooky Old Tree   35, 267

Berenstain Bears Get in a Fight   35, 267

Bernice Knows Best   59, 312, 392

Berries Goodman   3, 460

Bert Breen's Barn   68, 132, 161, 330

Bertie and the Bear   59, 248

The Best-Kept Secret   60, 495, 572

Best and Fairest   35, 435

The Best Christmas Pageant Ever   79, 89, 122, 237, 281, 493

Best Friends   75, 181, 323, 403

Best Friends Tell the Best Lies   75, 323

Bestiare Fableux   20, 299, 448

Beth Hilton: Model   135, 569

Bethie   146, 486

Better Known as Johnny Appleseed   167, 313, 386

Between Dark and Daylight   87, 539

Bet You Can't! Science Impossibilities to Fool You   149, 300, 312, 558

Beware! Beware! A Witch Won't Share   140, 317, 507

The Bewitched Caverns   207, 482, 492

Beyond the Chocolate War   163, 306

Beyond the Divide   163, 416

Beyond the East Wind: Legends and Folktales of Vietnam   202, 301, 545, 547

Beyond the High White Wall   219, 480

Beyond the Labyrinth   60, 133, 499

Beyond the Sun / Au Dela du Soleil   103, 498

Beyond the Weir Bridge   26, 249, 286

Beyond Two Rivers   87, 405

The BFG   25, 56, 109, 110, 227, 271, 311, 486

Bhimsa, the Dancing Bear   167, 328, 558

Bibi, the Baker's Horse   174, 491, 530

Bible Crafts   144, 264

Bible Stories You Can't Forget   161, 261, 330, 466

A Bicycle from Bridgetown   141, 450, 538

Big, Small, Short, Tall   182, 419

The Big Alfie and Annie Rose Storybook   183, 385

Big Baby   130, 457, 553

Big Bad Bruce   42, 90, 475

Big Ben   197, 249, 552

Big Blue Island   15, 498, 528

The Big Book for Peace   5, 328, 501

The Big Book of Animal Stories   154, 359, 361

The Big Book of Real Building and Wrecking Machines   208, 572

Big Dog   15, 355, 361

Bigfoot   88, 197, 223, 334, 480

The Biggest Bear   38, 553

The Biggest House in the World   213, 424

The Big Janosch Book of Fun and Verse   109, 265, 330

Big Mutt   209, 489, 500

The Big Orange Splot   79, 479

The Big Pets   20, 523

Big Red   30, 64, 153, 279, 405, 407, 411, 412

Big Red Bus   153, 405

The Big Rock   151, 379

The Big Sky: An Edition for Younger Readers 31, 365, 414
The Big Sky: An Edition for Young Readers 414
The Big Snow 38, 366
The Big Stretch: The Complete Book of the Amazing Rubber Band 151, 359, 496
Big Tracks, Little Tracks 135, 278, 405
Big Tree 166, 167, 284, 303, 570
Big Tree of Bunlahy: Stories of my Own Countryside 166, 303, 570
The Big Wave 55, 109, 251, 283, 353, 401
Bill's New Frock 48, 172, 198, 328, 338
A Billion for Boris 68, 495
Bill of Rights 143, 338
Bill Peet: An Autobiography 94, 190, 203, 225, 475
Billy Button's Butter'd Biscuit 205, 386, 450
Bimwili and the Zimwi 180, 243, 447
Bingo Brown, Gypsy Lover 184, 273, 288
Binky Brothers and the Fearless Four 139, 405, 417
Biography of an Atom 78, 280, 485, 510
The Biography of Daniel Inouye 234, 357, 557
A Biography of Thomas Wolfe 171, 256
Bionic Parts for People: The Real Story of Artificial Organs and Replacement Parts 93, 508, 520
Bip: The Snapping Bungaroo 74
Bird 100, 286, 293, 537
The Bird from the Sea 140, 556, 571
Birds 99, 155, 404, 561
The Birds of Summer 180, 185, 524
Birds We Live With 136, 337, 407
A Birthday for the Princess 62, 426
The Birthday Party 153, 410, 511
Birthdays of Freedom: America's Heritage from the Ancient World 168, 342
The Birthday Trombone 142, 371
Bitter Herbs and Honey 142, 301
Bittersweet 207, 268, 370
Blabber Mouth 60, 355
Black and British 222, 288
Black and White 41, 131, 431
Black as I Am 119, 433, 435, 571
A Black Bear's Story 15, 423, 514
Blackbeard's Ghost 195, 527
Blackberry Ink 180, 448, 562
The Blackbird in the Lilac 210, 253, 489
The Black Cauldron 169, 246
Black Child 118, 433
Black Dance in America: A History Through Its People 119, 371
The Black Fox of Lorne 168, 315
Black Gold 195, 318, 375
Black Images: The Art of West Africa 215, 425, 459
Black Jack 47, 349, 434
Black Kettle: King of the Wild Horses 141, 250, 319
Black Lives, White Worlds 176, 245
Black Magic, White Magic 212, 265, 393

Black Music In America: A History Through Its People 234, 371
The Black Mustanger 228, 230, 274, 568
The Black Pearl 169, 396, 465
Black Pilgrimage 235, 336
The Black Stallion 30, 238, 331, 335, 553
The Black Stallion Returns 30, 238, 331, 335
Black Star, Bright Dawn 235, 465
The Black Symbol 211, 394, 395, 504
Black Troubador, Langston Hughes 117, 495
Blade of the Poisoner 182, 377
Blaine's Way 11, 385
Blaze and the Gypsies 204, 251
The Blemyahs 199, 440, 561
Blind Colt 50, 498
Blind Date 127, 502
The Blindfold Track 222, 538
Blissymbolics: Speaking Without Speech 93, 374
Blitzcat 102, 198, 558
Blood Feud 27, 534
Blood Red Ochre 45, 77, 236, 434
Bloodroot Flower 87, 289
Blossom Comes Home 192, 282, 376
The Blossom on the Bough: A Book of Trees 63, 325
Blowfish Live in the Sea 131, 343
A Blow for Liberty 137, 446, 447
A Blow for Victory 441
Blubber 141, 172, 239, 272
Blueberries for Sal 38, 174, 442
The Blue Bird 61, 345
A Bluebird Will Do 216, 333
The Blue Boat 46, 440, 526
The Blue Book of Hob Stories 130, 267, 440
The Blue Cat of Castle Town 49, 167, 300, 381
The Blue Chameleon 81, 147, 506, 566
Blue Fin 107, 367, 538
The Blue Hawk 48, 101, 321, 522
The Blue Horse 20, 303
The Blue Lobster: A Life Cycle 63, 148, 291
Blue Mystery 3, 254, 266, 565
Blue Skin of the Sea: A Novel in Stories 185, 502
Blue Skye 204, 425
Bluestones 222, 394
The Blue Sword 170, 445
Blue Willow 50, 71, 85, 166, 351, 415
Boat Song 146, 557
Boats on the River 38, 260, 340
A Boat to Nowhere 56, 537, 554
Bobby Shafto's Gone to Sea 202, 275, 537
Bo Knows Bo: The Autobiography of a Ballplayer 240, 391, 513
The Bollo Caper: A Furry Tale for all Ages 144, 283, 484
The Bomb 4, 222, 321, 420, 504, 563
Bond of the Fire 51, 341, 436
A Bone from a Dry Sea 49, 321

The Bones Book and Skeleton 34, 309, 413
Bones on Black Spruce Mountain 84, 284
Bongleweed 47, 308, 533
Bonifacius the Green 212, 250, 496
Bonnie Bess: The Weathervane Horse 207, 366, 542
Bony 142, 313, 575
Bonzini! the Tattooed Man 248, 437
Boodil my Dog 160, 423
A Book Dragon 133, 412
A Book for Jodan 235, 316, 461
A Book of A-maze-ments 156, 510
The Book of Adam to Moses 164, 181, 261, 509
A Book of Astronauts for You 136, 278, 405
A Book of Dragon 391
A Book of Ghosts and Goblins 19, 392, 435
The Book of Giant Stories 67, 340, 371
A Book of Mars for You 138, 278, 405
The Book of Pets 143, 419
A Book of Stars for You 138, 278, 405
Book of the Dun Cow 134, 162, 553
The Book of the West: An Epic of America's Wild Frontier 228, 296, 536
The Book of Think: or, How to Solve a Problem Twice Your Size 63, 286, 558
A Book of Wild Flowers 205, 395, 396, 444
The Book of Wiremu 90, 274, 454
Books! 154
The Booksellers Association of Great Britain and Ireland 230
Booksellers New Zealand 5
The Boomerang Book of Legendary Tales 57, 453, 470
Boom Town Boy 174, 420
Boo to a Goose 63, 197, 429, 452, 463
Border Hawk: August Bondi 114, 246, 410
Borders 220, 566
Bored - Nothing to Do 162, 526
Borka: The Adventures of a Goose With No Feathers 98, 286
The Borning Room 95, 340
Born to Dance Samba 180, 301, 337
Born To the Land: An American Portrait 204, 255, 303
Borreguita and the Coyote 192, 243, 439
Borrowed Children 94, 431
Borrowed Summer 69, 325
The Borrowers 45, 46, 50, 107, 211, 411, 464, 527
The Borrowers Afloat 46, 107, 211, 411, 464, 527
Bossyboots 181, 306
The Bottle Imp 109, 332, 530
Botton 124, 335
The Boundary Riders 32, 383, 478
Bow Down Shadrach 6, 306
A Bowl of Mischief 72, 444
Box and Cox 183, 296, 521
The Boxcar Children 79, 315, 554

Box Turtle at Long Pond   24, 83, 352
Boy   28
A Boy, a Dog, and a Frog   11, 440
Boy: Tales of Childhood   311
Boy Alone   52, 78, 213, 468, 475
The Boy and the Samurai   185, 372
The Boy and the Swan   77, 244, 532
A Boy Had a Mother Who Bought Him a Hat   64, 412
Boy in the Moon   87, 409
A Boy of Old Prague   114, 390, 513
A Boy of Tache   103, 270
Boy of the North: The Story of Pierre Radisson   31, 488, 535
Boy of the South Seas   165, 514, 540
The Boy of the Three-Year Nap   29, 41, 182, 190, 504, 524
The Boys' War   94, 457
The Boy Scientist   77, 260, 422
Boys Life   124
A Boy Went out to Gather Pears   155, 380
The Boy Who Could Do Anything and Other Mexican Folk Tales   205, 278, 295
The Boy Who Drank Too Much   200, 361
The Boy Who Held Back the Sea   146, 383, 427
Boy Who Owned the School: A Comedy of Love   184, 473
The Boy Who Sang the Birds   71, 321, 558
The Boy Who Saw Bigfoot   223, 480
Boy Who Walked Backwards   127, 556
The Boy Who Was   165, 182, 286, 367, 567
The Boy Who Would not Say His Name   86, 515, 551
Boy with a Pack   166, 447, 514
The Boy with Wings   140, 317, 551
The Brassman's Secret   109, 255, 489
The Brats and Mr. Jack   16, 451
Brave Irene   159, 182, 191, 528
The Brave Little Goat of Monsieur Seguin   213, 313, 459
Bread and Honey   58, 525
Breaking the Chains: African- American Slave Resistance   235
Breaking Up   59, 564
Breakthrough: The True Story of Penicillin   151, 391
The Bremen-Town Musicians   40, 178, 480
Brendan the Navigator   20, 496, 518
Brian Boru: Emperor of the Irish   20, 426
Brian Wildsmith's ABC   98, 561
Brian Wildsmith's Birds   155, 561
Brian Wildsmith's 1, 2, 3s   11, 561
Brickyard Summer: Poems by Paul B. Janeczko   123, 392, 500
The Bridge Between   137, 396
The Bridge Dancers   194, 502, 536
Bridges   184, 493
Bridget and William   48, 349, 488
Bridge to Terabithia   22, 53, 128, 169, 225, 321, 472
Bridging the Golden Gate   151, 476

Bright April   207, 315
Bright Heritage   71, 380, 485
Bright Island   166, 204, 494, 554
Bright Shadow   118, 538
Bright Spurs   207, 282, 550
Brighty of the Grand Canyon   231, 319, 375
Brimhall Comes To Stay   72, 318, 535
Bring Back the Deer   113, 485, 552
Bristle Face   83, 212, 231, 259
Broderna Lejonhjarta   561
The Bronze Bow   107, 168, 525
The Brooklyn Bridge: They Said It Couldn't Be Built   94, 149, 163, 501
Brother, Can You Spare a Dime? The Great Depression, 1929-1933   67, 447
Brother Eagle, Sister Sky: A Message from Chief Seattle   8, 184, 296, 393
Brother in the Land   48, 56, 176, 222, 321, 504, 535, 563
Brother Night   228, 298, 403
Brothers   115, 219, 344, 471
The Brothers Grimm: Popular Folk Tales   99, 246, 342, 363
The Brothers Lionheart   120
Brother to the Wind   181, 322, 323, 553
A Brown Cow   24, 421
Brown Mouse and Vole   72, 254, 385
Bruno Munari's ABC   154, 456
Bubbles   149, 326, 575
Bubby, Me and Memories   219, 430, 481
Buck   16, 415
The Buck Stops Here   190, 484
Bucky Forrester   31, 499, 517
Buddies   81, 180, 470
Buffalo and Beaver   135, 264, 447
Buffalo Bill   31, 313
Buffalo Hunt   94, 104, 104, 234, 344, 534, 535, 543
The Buffalo Trace   77, 209, 331, 418
Bugles at the Border   171, 354, 543
Building: The Fight Against Gravity   27, 149, 382, 487, 502
Building Blocks of the Universe   77, 255
Building Worker   176, 307, 357
Bullard of the Space Patrol   31, 392
The Bully of Barkham Street   32, 515, 532
Bumble's Dream   58, 542
Bummer Summer   144, 437
A Bundle of Ballads   98, 435, 531
A Bundle of Sticks   84, 223, 439, 468
Bunkhouse Journal   229, 368
Bunnicula: A Rabbit Tale of Mystery   35, 79, 84, 95, 112, 121, 134, 196, 200, 217, 239, 312, 384
A Bunny Ride   141, 317, 446
Bunny School   142, 317, 446
The Bunyip of Berkeley's Creek   58, 280, 551
Burglar Bill   99, 245
Burke and Wills   59, 371
The Burning Glass   229, 394, 395
The Burning Questions of Bingo Brown   89, 183, 273, 288
Bury the Dead   173, 292
Busby & Co.   208, 301, 328

The Bus Driver   176, 335, 531
The Bus Girls   47, 361, 371
The Bushbabies   235, 249, 530
Bush Holiday   208, 337, 432
Bush Song   232, 466
Bush Vark's First Day Out   123, 130, 346
A Business of Their Own   36, 324
Buster's World   17, 490, 573
Busy Baby's Day - Afternoon   130, 539
Busy Baby's Day - Bedtime   130, 539
Busy Baby's Day - Morning   130, 539
Busy Baby's Day - Wake up Time   130, 539
The Busy Honeybee   61, 347, 409
But I'll Be Back Again: An Album   175, 500
But No Cheese!   131, 480, 519
The Butter Battle Book   92, 163, 512
Butterflies on my Mind: Their Life and Conservation in Britain Today   221, 360, 370
The Butterfly Ball and the Grasshopper's Feast   230, 246, 480
The Butterfly Jar: Poems   116, 318, 456
By Camel or by Car: A Look at Transportation   157, 269
By Day and By Night   24, 463, 470
By the Great Horn Spoon!   32, 85, 201, 216, 229, 340, 550
By the Sea: An Alphabet Book   104, 131, 270
By the Shores of Silver Lake   166, 238, 277, 513, 561
The Byzantines   32, 297, 483
C.L.O.U.D.S.   118, 309
c/o Arnold's Corners   171, 461
The Cabbage Patch Fib   237, 393, 522
The Cabbage Princess   99, 418
The Cabin at Medicine Springs   227, 310, 484
Cactus   150, 184, 365, 369, 426, 468
Cactus Hotel   184, 365, 426
Cadbury's Coffin   188, 441, 535
Caddie Woodlawn   49, 166, 279, 512
A Cageful of Butterflies   84, 264
Cages of Glass, Flowers of Time   79, 309
Cakes and Custard: Children's Rhymes   161, 246, 469
Cakes and Miracles: A Purim Tale   219, 357, 555
Cal Cameron by Day, Spider-Man by Night   75, 289
Caleb and Kate   133, 528
Calendar Moon   216, 266, 283
Calico Bush   165, 338, 422
The Callendar Papers   188, 550
Call It Courage   166, 526
Call Me Ruth   219, 501
Call of the Wolves   135, 457, 555
Came Back To Show You I Could Fly   60, 408
Campion Towers   71, 264
Can't You Sleep Little Bear?   100, 198, 338, 551
The Canada Geese Quilt   82, 276, 406
Canadian Children's Annual   128, 432

Canadian Garbage Collectors 107, 276, 413
Candidate for Fame 46, 342, 399
Candy Floss 211, 244, 356
Can It Be True? 198, 260, 377
Cannily, Cannily 58, 345
Canterbury Tales 94, 146, 301, 388
Can the Whales Be Saved? 69, 560
A Canvas Castle 86, 366, 530
Can You Catch Josephine? 104, 131, 482
Can You Sue Your Parents for Malpractice? 143, 312
Cap'n Ezra, Privateer 205, 244, 374
A Capital for the Nation 175, 381
Cappyboppy 106, 475
Caps for Sale: A Tale of a Peddler, some Monkeys and their Monkey Business 49, 521
Captain Bilgerbelly's Treasure 123, 371
Captain Carp Saves the Sea 7, 415
Captain Eco and the Fate of the Earth 77, 458, 482
Captain Ghost 83, 171, 265, 266
Captain Hook, That's Me 74, 424, 425
Captain Kidd's Cow 205, 532, 560
Captain of the Planter: The Story of Robert Smalls 308, 529
Captain Ramsey's Daughter 209, 244, 541
The Car: Watch it Work by Operating the Moving Diagrams! 191, 277, 437
Careers in Conservation 149, 359, 398
Cargoes on the Great Lakes 97, 391, 446
A Caribou Alphabet 190, 469
Carlos P. Romulo: The Barefoot Boy of Diplomacy 142, 317
Carnivorous Plants 150, 468, 515
Carolina Caravan 206, 271, 359
The Carp in the Bathtub 140, 301, 368
Carrie's War 47, 186, 263, 282
Carrie Hepple's Garden 178, 307, 365
A Carrot for a Nose 161, 355
The Carrot Seed 206, 395, 410
Carry On, Mr. Bowditch 107, 168, 306, 416
Cartier Discovers the St. Lawrence 44, 347, 542
The Case of the Missing Bills 72, 468, 522
The Case of the Secret Scribbler 188, 377, 556
Casey at the Bat 154, 339, 538
Castaway Christmas 46, 258, 404
The Castaways 106, 305
Castle 40, 148, 431
The Castle in the Attic 42, 84, 228, 388, 565
The Castle of Grumpy Grouch 207, 323, 324
The Castle on Hester Street 179, 219, 374
The Castle Story 48, 502
Castors Away! 46, 249, 286
Cat 190, 561
The Cat and Mouse Who Shared a House 17, 265, 387

The Cataract of Lodore 160, 292, 525
The Cat Ate My Gymsuit 126, 134, 141, 225, 312
Catbird 140, 348
Catch a Killer 84, 141, 187, 567
Catchpenny Street 141, 293
Catfish 214, 387
A Cat for Samantha 35, 555
Cathedral 40, 62, 156, 431
Cathedral: The Story of its Construction 40, 156, 431
Catherine Marshall's Storybook for Children 91, 273, 374
Cathie and the Paddy Boy 86, 106, 431
Cathy Leonard Calling 135, 313, 568
A Cat of Artimus Pride 11
Cat Poems 182, 388, 425
Cats 150, 468, 571
Cats, Cats, Cats, Cats, Cats 210, 320, 524
Cats and Bats and Things with Wings 11, 245, 355
Cats Are Cats: Poems 159, 415, 571
The Cat Who Went to Heaven 165, 300, 554
The Cat Who Wished To Be a Man 26, 246
Catwings 83, 190, 419, 505
Caught in the Turtle 144, 358, 503
The Cautious Carp and other Fables in Pictures 204, 270, 486
The Cave Bear Story: Life and Death of a Vanished Animal 148, 412, 413
The Caves of the Great Hunters 209, 263
Caxton's Challenge 370
The Cay 52, 71, 201, 235, 537
Cecelia and the Blue Mountain Boy 180, 516, 541
Cedric the Forester 164, 437
The Celery Stalks at Midnight 74, 384, 454
Celestino Piatti's Animal ABC 155, 478
Cells Are Us 195, 259, 495
Cells Wars 495
Cell Wars 195, 259
Center Line 75, 535
Ceremony of Innocence 52, 342
A Certain Small Shepherd 115, 293, 326
Chaga 153, 424, 453, 454
Chains for Columbus 31, 483
A Chair for My Mother 28, 41, 176, 564
The Chalk Cross 188, 250
The Chalk Doll 183, 421, 481
The Challenge of the Sea 32, 298, 507
Chameleon the Spy and the Case of the Vanishing Jewels 188, 438
Chameleon Was a Spy 188, 438
The Champion 5, 42, 68, 80, 218, 222, 267, 311, 326, 351, 555
The Champion of Merrimack County 68, 80, 222, 326, 555
Champions of Peace: Winners of the Nobel Peace Prize 3, 449, 550
An Chanail 189, 340
Chance, Luck and Destiny 27, 249, 321, 522

Chancy and the Grand Rascal 71, 340, 550
Chang's Paper Pony 18, 301, 488
The Changeling 67, 487, 524
The Changelings of Chaan 59, 413
The Changeover 28, 48, 91, 109, 434
Changes, Changes 11, 60, 156, 214, 388
Change the Locks 60, 345
The Changing City 27, 456
The Changing Countryside 27, 456
Chanticleer and the Fox 39, 304
The Chanukkah Guest 219, 290, 406
Chapatis, Not Chips 177, 374
The Charge of the Light Brigade 154, 484, 485, 538
Charles Keeping's Classic Tales of the Macabre 199, 402
Charley, Charlotte and the Golden Canary 99, 402
Charley Skedaddle 173, 264
Charley the Horse 208, 469
Charley the Mouse Finds Christmas 140, 257, 290
Charlie Anderson 21, 192, 243, 360
Charlie and the Chocolate Factory 25, 66, 135, 172, 218, 240, 275, 311, 505
Charlie and the Chocolate Factory and Other Excremental Visions 66, 275
Charlie and the Great Glass Elevator 134, 218, 311, 505
The Charlie Barber Treatment 48, 426
Charlie Lewis Plays for Time 231, 399, 403
Charlie Needs a Cloak 12, 62, 319
Charlie the Tramp 33, 379
Charlotte & Charles 235, 541, 553
Charlotte's Web 49, 54, 66, 79, 126, 128, 168, 216, 218, 463, 559, 562
A Charmed Life 48, 101, 397
Chartbreak 48, 308
Chase Me, Catch Nobody! 4, 372
Cheerful 210, 282
Chelsey and the Green-Haired Kid 81, 358
Chen-Li and the River Spirit 233, 321, 381
Cherokee Bill: Oklahoma Pacer 231, 257, 309
Cherries and Cherry Pits 29, 159, 564
Chester's Barn 104, 300
Chester's Way 117, 375
Chester Chipmunk's Thanksgiving 68, 296, 562
The Chicago Tribune 204
Chicka Chicka Boom Boom 30, 116, 253, 331, 438
The Chick and the Duckling 354
The Chick and the Ducklings 61, 254, 255, 534
Chicken Little Count-to-Ten 207, 334, 346
Chicken Man 104, 115, 330
Chickens Aren't the Only Ones 149, 375
Chicken Sunday 72, 95, 481
A Chick Hatches 64, 302, 558
A Child's Christmas in Wales 157, 253, 538

A Child's Garden of Verses 51, 192, 530, 561

A Child's Good Night Book 37, 281, 295

A Child in Prison Camp 103, 536

Child of Fire 161, 465

Child of the Owl 4, 27, 570

The Child of Two Mothers 215, 415, 497

The Child Reader as Sleuth 66, 269

Children's Book Circle 81

Children's Folklore Section 5

Children's Literature: the Bad Seed? 65, 287

Children's Literature Association Quarterly 65, 66, 270, 566

Children's Literature in Education 65, 66, 269, 298, 318, 393, 463, 505, 509, 552

Children's Playmate 124, 452

Children as Teachers of Peace: By Our Children 4, 392, 483

The Children of Green Knowe 46, 51, 65, 275, 276, 497

Children of Long Ago: Poems 183, 354, 425

Children of the Book 173, 292, 394, 498

Children of the Dust Bowl 18, 105, 113, 175, 527

Children of the Maya: A Guatemalan Indian Odyssey 4, 234, 255, 303

Children of the Red King 211, 431, 481

Children of the River 75, 94, 112, 308

Children of the Soil: A Story of Scandinavia 165, 285, 313

Children of the Wild West 28, 229, 344

Children of Vietnam 132, 343, 423

Childtimes 27, 234, 362, 425, 479

The Chimneys of Green Knowe 46, 275, 276

Chimney Sweeps: Yesterday and Today 8, 94, 353, 541

The China Coin 15, 258

Chin Chiang and the Dragon's Dance 104, 109, 111, 552

The Chinese Americans 234, 448

The Chinese Mirror 6, 434

Chinesische Volksmarchen 19, 264

Chingo Smith of the Erie Canal 210, 244, 551

Chin Music: Tall Talk and other Talk 143, 465, 507

Chips and Jessie 125, 385

Chitty-Chitty-Bang-Bang 239, 286, 340

Chloe and Maude 21, 277

Chloris and the Creeps 202, 480

The Chocolate Chip Mystery 79, 343, 444

Chocolate Fever 126, 337, 523

The Chocolate Touch 126, 224, 252, 292

The Chocolate War 53, 126, 161, 163, 306, 549

Choose Your Grandma 128, 254

Choristers' Cake 46, 380, 440

The Chosen Puppy 25, 266

Chouchou 153, 510

Christian Century 65, 540

Christina's Ghost 89, 115, 196, 220, 225, 238, 568

Christina Katerina and the Box 140, 286, 351

Christina Katerina and the Time She Quit the Family 146, 351, 484

Christmas: The King James Version 125, 478

The Christmas Anna Angel 37, 504, 512

A Christmas Book 19, 501, 536

The Christmas Camel 144, 470

A Christmas Carol 20, 100, 159, 321, 389

Christopher Columbus: Voyager to the Unknown 203, 422

The Christophers 67

Christy 53, 79, 106, 145, 386, 389, 404, 437, 467, 535

Chronicles of Narnia 239, 263, 422

Chucaro: Wild Pony of the Pampa 168, 210, 318, 400

Chucho: The Boy with the Good Name 85, 478, 519

The Church 99, 100, 125, 157, 177, 453, 464, 470, 510

The Church Mice Adrift 99, 157, 464, 510

The Church Mice in Action 100, 125, 464

Cinderella: or, The Little Glass Slipper 38, 281, 476

Circle of Giving 94, 384

The Circle of Gold 118, 277

Circles, Triangles, and Squares 148, 379

A Circle Unbroken 194, 383

Circus 191, 331

The Circus in the Mist 155, 457

The Circus is Coming 45, 527, 533

Circus Ruckus 152, 424, 454

Circus Shoes 533

City 62, 431

City Cop 143, 304

City Critters 139, 333, 500

City Leaves, City Trees 147, 348

The City of Gold and Lead 217, 297

City of Gold and Other Stories from the Old Testament 23, 48, 100, 321, 342

City Rocks, City Blocks and the Moon 147, 348

The City Rose 171, 451

The City under the Back Steps 83, 414, 546

Civil War Nurse: Mary Ann Bickerdyke 141, 317

Clams Can't Sing 88, 530

Clara Barton 205, 259, 469

Clarinda 206, 328, 532

Class Clown 116, 129, 200, 228, 368, 387

Class Dismissed: High School Poems 93, 268, 355

Class Dismissed: More High School Poems, No. II 69, 268, 355

Claude and Sun 186, 464

Claudius the Bee 204, 419, 465

The Clay Marble 105, 379

The Clay Pot Boy 62, 392, 427

A Clearing in the Forest 87, 559

Clearing Weather 165, 324, 447

Cleopatra's Revenge 233, 403

Clever Juice 34, 561

Clifford, the Big Red Dog 64, 279

Clive Eats Alligators 59, 421

Clocks, From Shadow to Atom 106, 244, 275, 526

Clone Catcher 188, 521

A Close Call 123, 130, 371

Cloudy with a Chance of Meatballs 35, 70, 90, 95, 157, 261

Cloverdale Switch 203, 284

Clowning Around 190, 335

The Coal House 48, 231, 536

Coalmining Women 176, 394

Cock-a-Doodle-Doo 366

Cock-a-Doodle Doo 37

The Cock, the Mouse and the Little Red Hen 51, 419, 503

Cockleburr Quarters 52, 215, 258, 469

The Coconut Thieves 212, 324, 343

Code Name Kris 235, 439

The Codfish Musket 166, 376, 526

Cold Hazard 210, 254, 380

Collected Stories for Children 45, 317, 373

College English 65, 356

Colonial Craftsmen and the Beginnings of American Industry 213, 543

Colonial Living 77, 544

Colonial New Jersey 140, 310

Color in Plants and Flowers 149, 484

Color Zoo 41, 331

Colt 30, 50, 82, 206, 211, 274, 319, 349, 428, 498, 527, 539

The Colt from the Dark Forest 211, 274, 428

Come Again, Pelican 201, 345

Come a Stranger 122, 550

Come Away from the Water, Shirley 157, 286

Come Back, Salmon 175, 303, 559

Come By Here 26, 304, 396

Come Sing, Jimmy Jo 163, 181, 472

The Comet and You 203, 411

Comet Halley: Once in a Lifetime 151, 425, 570

Come the Morning 85, 371

Come to Mecca and other Stories 176, 321

Come to the Edge 53, 68, 310

Comfort Herself 176, 401, 463

Comick Book of Pets: Found, Raised, Washed, Curried, Combed, Fed, and Cared for in Every other Way 142, 497

A Comick Book of Sports 141, 497

Coming to North America from Mexico, Cuba & Puerto Rico 234, 350, 444

Commanche of the Seventh 83, 419, 447

Commander Toad in Space 88, 316, 571

Commodore Perry in the Land of the Shogun 28, 94, 170, 272

The Common Frog 221, 268, 469

Communism, An American's View 33, 339, 395

Company's Coming 192, 521, 571

The Complete Adventures of Snugglepot and Cuddlepie 117, 353

A Comprehensive Education, 1965-1975 176, 451

Computer Graphics: How It Works, What It Does 146, 405

The Computer Nut 197, 288

Confessions of a Teenage TV Addict 144, 420

Conker 221, 555

Connie Bell, M.D. 36, 255

Conquistadores and Pueblos: The Story of the American Southwest 1540-1848 229, 329, 367

Conrad's War 27, 102, 314

Constance: A Story of Early Plymouth 51, 131, 297

The Contender 56, 424

The Contest 40, 123, 128, 381

Contexts 127, 362

Coping with Television 126, 425

Copycats 125, 143, 342, 485, 508, 519

The Coriander 212, 322, 324

The Corn Grows Ripe 168, 295, 491

The Cornhusk Doll 36, 441, 561

Corn Is Maize: The Gift of the Indians 148, 247

Corn Rows 118, 288, 570

Coronado and his Captains 216, 289, 529

Corporal Keeperupper 206, 450

Corvus the Cow 140, 309, 500

Cosmic View: The Universe in 40 Jumps 148, 274

The Cossacks 212, 249, 261

Cottontail: Children's Pet, Gardener's Pest, and Hunter's Favorite 137, 499

Could You Stop Josephine? 110, 482

Count and See 61, 156, 379

Counting On Frank 237, 299

Count Your Way Around the World 16, 371, 372

Courage, Dana 180, 477, 500

The Courage of Sarah Noble 49, 168, 209, 311, 556

The Court of the Stone Children 132, 289

Cousin Blodwyn's Visit 130, 549

Cousins 113, 123, 160, 186, 190, 216, 221, 289, 306, 368, 387, 456, 515

Covenant House 120, 492

Covered Bridge 45, 129, 325

The Covered Wagon & Other Adventures 229, 509

Cow-tail Switch, and Other West African Stories 167, 295, 306, 376

The Cowboy and His Horse 31, 341

Cowboy Boots 238, 350, 369

Cowboys Don't Cry 6, 368

Cow for Jaya 141, 360, 368

Coyote, Come Home 32, 264, 541

Coyotes: Last Animals on Earth? 71, 270, 538

The Crab Nebula 149, 452

Crabs 73, 150, 396, 502

The Crack-of-Dawn Walkers 180, 376, 508

The Crackajack Pony 171, 285, 474

Cracker Jackson 124, 181, 200, 232, 288

Crackers Magazine 127, 356

Cracking Open the Geode: the Fiction of Paula Fox 65, 257

The Cradle Will Fall 22, 298

Crafting with Newspapers 142, 279, 331, 515

Crafty Chameleon 100, 366, 404

Cranberry Birthday 146, 320

The Cranberry Book 150, 352

Cranberry Valentine 144, 320

The Crane Wife 158, 162, 245, 472, 569

Crazy in Love 178, 404, 512

Creation to Civilization 65, 307

Creatures of Long Ago: Dinosaurs 192, 517, 565

Creatures of the Desert World 191, 353, 546

Credit-Card Carole 145, 408

Creepy Castle 63, 357

The Cremation of Sam McGee 159, 182, 371, 512

Cricket 124, 233, 383

The Cricket in Times Square 50, 126, 168, 510, 563

Cricket Songs: Japanese Haiku 216, 265, 512

Crictor 210, 545

Crimson Anchor: A Sea Mystery 207, 492

The Cripples' Club 236, 266

Crocodile, Crocodile 178, 461, 507

A Crocodile's Tale 61, 254, 255

Crocodile Tears 153, 344

Crocodilians 232

The Crooked Snake 57, 383, 568

Cross-Country Cat 27, 70, 92, 93, 226, 288, 389

Cross-country Runner 72, 442

Crosses 75, 531

Crossfire 81, 452

Crow and Weasel 183, 428, 481

Crow Boy 39, 55, 570

Crown Fire 208, 444

Cruise 31, 332, 342

Cruise of the Jeanette 31, 332, 342

Crusher Is Coming 59, 359

Crutches 17, 110, 371

A Cry from the Earth: Music of the North American Indians 234, 269

The Cry of the Wolf 48, 285

Crystal 11, 87, 98, 119, 161, 182, 209, 227, 458, 499, 514, 539

The Crystal Drop 11

Crystal Mountain 209, 499, 514

Cubs of the Lion of Judah 220, 525

The Cucumber King: A Story with a Beginning, a Middle and an End 108, 265, 439, 464

Cupola House 106, 386, 545

Curious George 50, 55, 65, 153, 172, 490, 491

Curious George Gets a Medal 153, 490

Curious George Goes to the Hospital 55, 490, 491

Curious George Takes a Job 50, 491

Curse of Claudia 146, 450

The Curse of the Blue Figurine 180, 225, 266, 358

Custom Car: A Nuts-and-Bolts Guide to Creating One 146, 457

Cute Is a Four-Letter Word 477

Cute Is a Four Letter Word 194

Cutlass Island 187, 305, 515

Cutover Country: Jolie's Story 215, 414, 474

The Cybil War 196, 226, 288, 468

Cyril: The Quest of an Orphan Squirrel 189, 441, 465

Cyrus, the Unsinkable Sea Serpent 92, 475

D'Aulaires' Trolls 132, 160, 313

Daddy's Chair 219, 366, 415

The Daddy Days 153, 359, 519

Daggie Dogfoot 102, 406, 488

Daisy Chain War 189, 466

Dakota of the White Flats 184, 491

The Dallas Titans Get Ready for Bed 181, 412, 519

The Damselfly 164, 350

Dana Doesn't Like Guns Anymore 24, 453

Dance on my Grave 109, 294, 520

Dances With Wolves 199, 271

Dancing Bear 47, 71, 159, 167, 223, 321, 328, 350, 505, 522, 528, 533, 558

Dancing in the Anzac Deli 59, 109, 283, 478, 558

The Dancing Palm Tree and Other Nigerian Folktales 159, 517, 552

Dancing Skelton 159, 315, 471

Danger at Black Dyke 187, 338

Danger Beats the Drum 187, 433

Danger in Quicksand Swamp 239, 552

The Dangerous Cove: A Story of Early Days in Newfoundland 43, 338, 373

Dangerous Deadline 33, 267

The Dangling Witness: A Mystery 188, 267

Daniel 'Coon: The Story of a Pet Raccoon 231, 333

Daniel Boone 166, 313

Danny: the Champion of the World 218, 267, 311

Danny Dunn and the Homework Machine 239, 243, 402, 563

Danny Dunn on the Ocean Floor 239, 243, 544, 563

Dansa Pa Min Grav 109, 294, 520

Daphne's Book 232, 366

The Dark-Thirty 105, 119, 170, 445, 479

The Dark-Thirty: Southern Tales of the Supernatural 105, 479

The Dark and Deadly Pool 238, 462

The Darkangel 42, 111, 163, 179, 478

The Dark Behind the Curtains 48, 102, 308, 471

The Dark Bright Water 147, 568

The Dark Corridor 146, 267

The Dark Didn't Catch Me 161, 539

The Dark Frigate 50, 165, 373, 492

Dark Harvest: Migrant Farmworkers in America 29, 234, 255, 303

The Dark Is Rising　26, 47, 169, 300, 305
The Dark Shadow　116, 491
The Dark Star of Itza　165, 383, 435
Dark Venture　25, 269, 322, 323
Das Buch Vom Dorf　23
Das Gelbe Haus　23
Dash and Dart　37, 284
Das Kleine Madchen mit den Schwefelholzchen　178, 250, 555
Das Mondgesicht　9, 346, 505
Das Schonste Geschenk　178, 546, 562
Das Sprachbastelbuch　23, 575
Daughter of the Mountains　50, 167, 207, 487, 560
A Daughter of the Seine: The Life of Madame Roland　165, 329
Dave's Song　174, 444
David and the Phoenix　71, 467, 489
David Livingston, Foe of Darkness　174, 329, 488
Davy Crockett　166, 210, 432, 454, 498, 528
Davy Crockett's Earthquake　210, 454, 528
Dawn　13, 28, 62, 68, 108, 161, 259, 516
A Dawn in the Trees: Thomas Jefferson, the Years 1776 to 1789　201, 560
Dawnrider　11, 236, 385
The Dawn Seekers　204, 368, 421
Dawn Wind　212, 402, 534
Day, Night and Nobody's Time　120
The Day and the Way We Met　210, 532
The Daybreakers　201, 214, 310, 493
A Day in the Country　106, 260, 408
The Day Jimmy's Boa Ate the Wash　172, 403, 463
The Day Mother Sold the Family Swords　233, 465
A Day no Pigs Would Die　70, 126, 215, 475
A Day of Pleasure: Stories of a Boy Growing up in Warsaw　131, 519, 549
A Day of Rhymes　19, 482
A Day on Skates: The Story of a Dutch Picnic　166, 548
Days of Awe: Stories for Rosh Hashanah and Yom Kippur　5, 406, 556
Days of Honey: The Tunisian Boyhood of Raphael Uzan　120, 256
Days of Terror　97, 194, 523
The Day the Circus Came to Lone Tree　53, 498
The Day the Sun Danced　213, 387
The Daywatchers　150, 471
The Day We Saw the Sun Come Up　39, 244, 358
A Day with a Miner　221, 256, 335
A Day With Wilbur Robinson　184, 399
Dead Birds Singing　228, 536
A Deadly Game of Magic　238, 462
The Dead Man in Indian Creek　81, 366
Dear Baby　203, 444, 494
Dear Bill, Remember Me? and Other Stories　53, 68, 161, 441
Dear Garbage Man　153, 360, 575
Dear Hill　102, 398
Dear Mili　24, 190, 363, 511

Dear Mr. Henshaw　69, 72, 84, 85, 88, 126, 134, 163, 170, 180, 196, 298, 573
Dear Nobody　49, 324
Dear Rat　154, 310, 428
Death: Everyone's Heritage　142, 414
Deathwatch　187, 559
Debbie of the Green Gate　208, 312, 358
Debutante Hill　43, 327
December Stillness　4, 42, 56, 366
Decouvertes Gallimard　23
Dede Korkut Masallari　9, 365, 460
Deep in the Forest　13, 64, 174, 544
Deezle Boy　59, 81, 526
Defence　221, 345
The Defender　167, 400, 428
The Delphic Choice　146, 396
The Demon Who Would not Die　144, 301, 391
Den Fjerneste Kyst　109, 269, 419
Den Fortrollade Floden　110, 423, 461
Derek and the Dinosaur　14, 253, 270
Der Gelbe Vogel　109, 422, 506
Der Gestiefelte Kater (Puss in Boots)　20, 331, 476
Der Hut des Kaminfegers　23
Der Kleine Daumling　19, 333
Der Page Orteguill　9, 367, 380
Der Rabe Im Schnee　178, 455
Der Traummacher　19, 508
Desde el Iris Con Amor　24, 464, 548
Desert Giant　204, 261
The Desert Is Theirs　13, 14, 26, 40, 148, 216, 263, 471
Destination, Moon　91, 390, 392
Detective Mole and the Halloween Mystery　188, 486
Det Femte Hornet (The Fifth Corner)　307, 331
Detour to Danger　188, 569
The Development of Consciousness in Lucy Boston's The Children of Green Knowe　65, 497
The Devil & Mother Crump　94, 181, 290, 427
Devil-in-the-Fog　101, 349, 434
The Devil's Arithmetic　115, 219, 571
The Devil's Children　47, 321, 367
Devil's Hill　32, 57, 295, 526
The Devil's Other Storybook　182, 257
The Devil's Stone　59, 343
The Devil's Storybook　132, 257
The Devil Did It　87, 394
The Devil in Vienna　56, 93, 219, 467
The Devil on the Road　48, 558
Devils Who Learned To Be Good　182, 443
Diamond　82, 480
The Diamond in the Window　187, 271, 414
The Diamond Tree: Jewish Tales From Around the World　219, 499, 508, 516
The Diary of Nina Kosterina　52, 354, 410
Dic-tion-ar-y Skilz　140, 293
Dicey's Song　28, 170, 550
Dick Whittington and His Cat　38, 281
Dictionary of Chivalry　99, 214, 263, 545

The Diddakoi　230, 355, 356
Did You Carry the Flag Today, Charley?　103, 293, 364
Did You Hear What Happened to Andrea?　227, 449
Die Blumenstadt　23, 372, 573
Die Geschichte Vom Guten Wolf　178, 461, 562
Die Geschichte Von Babar, Dem Kleine Elefanten　23
Die Geschichte Von der Kleinen Gans, Die Nicht Schnell Genug War　24, 269, 394
Diego　104, 160, 184, 565
Die Maus Hat Rote Strumpfe an　265
Die Wichtelmanner　22, 278, 363, 364
The Different One　36, 302
Digby, the Only Dog　171, 291
Digging Dinosaurs　152, 277, 332, 358, 383
Digging into Yesterday　32, 339, 345
Digging up America　32, 377
Dinner At Auntie Rose's　7, 457, 492
Dinosaur Cousins?　113, 456
Dinosaur Dream　95, 463
Dinosaurs, Dinosaurs　186, 261
Dinosaurs: An Illustrated History　150, 302
Dinosaurs and Other Pre-Historic Animals　476
Dinosaurs and Other Prehistoric Animals　32, 352
Dinosaurs Divorce: A Guide for Changing Families　163, 281
Dinosaurs of North America　28, 93, 467, 487, 503
Dinosaur Time　88, 427, 470
Dipper of Copper Creek　15, 352
The Disappearance　162, 365
The Disappearing Stranger　215, 395
Discover Bones　107, 360, 381
Discovering Africa's Past　176, 314
Discovering Cycles　147, 266, 272
Discovering Design　207, 325
Discovering Israel　114, 541
Dismembering the Text: The Horror of Louisa May Alcott's Little Women　66, 334, 415
Displaced Person　58, 369
Dita Saxova　114, 430, 460
Diving for Roses　161, 565
The Divorce Express　80, 179, 200, 235, 312
Dixie Storms　204, 367
Do Bananas Chew Gum?　194, 197, 354
Dobry　166, 401, 513
Doctor Change　21, 291, 302
Doctor Coyote: A Native American Aesop's Fable　204, 269, 555
Doctor De Soto　8, 28, 90, 109, 163, 170, 180, 528
Doctor in the Zoo　132, 148, 283
Doctor Kiss Says Yes　97, 339, 392
Dodger　66, 144, 293, 355
Does God Have a Big Toe? Stories About Stories in the Bible　159, 318, 352
Dog　190, 561

A Dog's Book of Bugs   155, 362, 471

A Dog Called George   236, 258, 398

A Dog Called Kitty   96, 196, 220, 552

A Dog Called Scholar   212, 464, 559

The Dogcatcher's Dog   152, 327

Dogger   99, 385

The Doggone Mystery   188, 297, 543

Dog Runner   11, 448

Dogsbody   47, 397

Dogs Don't Tell Jokes   184, 501

Dog Song   170, 181, 226, 473

A Dog So Small   212, 434, 474

Dog Who Wanted to Die   127, 253

Doing Time: A Look at Crime and Prisons   4, 298, 419

The Doll   124, 195, 196, 201, 223, 225, 232, 366, 536

The Dollhouse Murders   42, 54, 80, 105, 112, 188, 220, 223, 239, 568

The Doll in the Garden   124, 196, 201, 223, 225, 232, 366

Dolphin Adventure: A True Story   24, 343, 364

Dominic   65, 68, 132, 231, 456, 529

Dominique and the Dragon   214, 307, 477, 536

Don't Feel Sorry for Paul   62, 566

Don't Hurt Laurie!   89, 227, 238, 493, 503

Don't Look Behind You   112, 183, 225, 238, 327

Don't Play Dead Before You Have to   139, 566

Don't Say a Word   110, 352

Don't Take Teddy   17, 53, 213, 346, 445

Don't Touch My Room   96, 279, 413

Don't You Know There's a War On?   185, 530

Donald and the Singing Fish   123, 429

Donald Says Thumb Down   145, 294, 305

The Dong with a Luminous Nose   155, 358, 418

Donkey's Crusade   231, 455

The Donkey's Dream   94, 268

The Donkey from Dorking   205, 382, 460, 549

Do Not Go Around the Edges: Poems   15, 541, 546

Doodle and the Go-Cart   89, 285, 540

The Doorbell Rang   125, 388

The Door in the Wall: Story of Medieval London   50, 167, 315

Dorinda   206, 384, 556

Doris Fein Mysteries   203, 269

Dorothea Dix: Hospital Founder   138, 435, 502

Dorp Dead   52, 201, 212, 310, 525

Dorrie's Book   88, 501

Dot for Short   207, 345, 373

A Double Discovery   155, 460

The Double Knights: More Tales from Round the World   44, 323, 446

The Double Life of Pocahontas   28, 346, 571

Double or Nothing   83, 333

The Dove's Letter   182, 258

Down, Down the Mountain   52, 308

Down by Jim Long's Stage: Rhymes for Children and Young Fish   103, 367, 480

Downright Dencey   165, 260, 523

Down Ryton Water   166, 347, 366

Down Street   127

Down the River, Westward Ho!   228, 509

Downtown   21, 163, 441

Do You See Me, God? Prayers for Young Children   91, 327, 457

Do You See What I See?   144, 501

Do You Want To Be My Friend?   214, 290

Dr. Beaumont and the Man With the Hole in His Stomach   149, 333, 509

Dr. Lawrence Reck   237

Dr. Xargle's Book of Earth Tiggers   100, 497, 564

The Drac: French Tales of Dragons and Demons   161, 381, 546, 552

Drac and the Gremlin   60, 258, 536

The Dragon   213, 253, 436

Dragon, Dragon and other Timeless Tales   161, 349, 515

Dragon's Blood: A Fantasy   179, 571

The Dragon's Pearls   454

The Dragon's Robe   186, 204, 416

Dragon Fall   16, 378

Dragonflies   61, 150, 468, 503, 518

Dragon Magazine   124, 377

Dragon of an Ordinary Family   99, 434, 469

Dragon of the Lost Sea   81, 570

Dragonsong   64, 431, 441

The Dragons Pearls   104, 417

Dragonwings   4, 26, 53, 85, 111, 169, 234, 570

The Drawbridge Gate   209, 370

Drawing from Nature   69, 150, 254

Draw 50 Monsters   88, 250

Dreamcatcher   129, 467, 571

Dream Coach   165, 472

Dream Eater   202, 350, 357

Dreamers and Doers: Inventors who Changed our World   151, 491

Dreamland Lake   187, 475

A Dream of Seas   108, 265, 463

The Dream Runner   87, 323

The Dream Time   47, 402, 542

Drei Vogel   22, 377

The Dreyfus Affair: A National Scandal   114, 505

The Driftway   215, 425

A Drink for Little Red Diker   136, 436, 568

A Drop of Blood   138, 433, 516

The Drowners   49, 406

The Druid's Tune   236, 447

The Drummer Boy   47, 154, 349, 434, 493, 517

Drummer Hoff   39, 51, 332

Drusilla   204, 280

Drylongso   191, 368, 479

Duane, the   72, 415, 558

Duane, the Collector   72, 415, 558

The Duchess Bakes a Cake   52, 209, 399

Duck   190, 192, 499, 555, 561

The Duck in the Gun   70, 266, 306

Ducks Fly   183, 310

The Duck Street Gang   102, 436, 457, 457

Duey's Tale   118, 257, 520

Duffy and the Devil   40, 53, 62, 132, 160, 215, 573, 574

Dulcie's Whale   171, 310, 533

Dumpling Soup   147, 384, 488

Duncan & Dolores   69, 502

The Dunderhead War   229, 258

Dupper   64, 258, 330

Durango Street   216, 274

Dust of the Earth   53, 161, 230, 299

Dwarf Long-nose   50, 372, 467, 511

Dwellers of the Tundra: Life in an Alaskan Eskimo Village   214, 393

The Dwindling Party   179, 358, 476

Dying Sun   87, 270

E. Nesbit: Riding the Wave of the Future   66, 430

E.T.: Extra-terrestrial Storybook   35, 172, 410, 439

Each Peach, Pear, Plum   99, 108, 245

The Eagle of the Ninth   46, 380, 534

An Ear for Uncle Emil   205, 347, 512

The Early Eagles   32, 325

Early in the Morning: A Collection of New Poems   125, 197, 293, 342

The Earth's Satellite: Man's First True Space Adventure   32, 422, 505

The Earth Beneath Us   78, 439, 455, 456

Earthfasts   51, 440

Earthquake at Dawn   72, 362

Earthquakes and Volcanoes   221, 545

Earth Songs   203, 339, 425

Earth Tigerlets as Explained by Professor Xargle   100

Earthworms, Dirt and Rotten Leaves   151, 445, 515

East End at Your Feet   176, 321

Easter   21, 98, 110, 205, 244, 326, 478, 543

The Easter Egg Artists   21, 244

Easy Avenue   44, 325

The Easy Way to Bird Recognition   221, 405

Eating Between the Lines   34, 45, 236, 434

Eating Crow   171, 382

Eating Ice Cream With a Werewolf   122, 361, 533

Eating the Alphabet   190, 331

Eclipse: Darkness in Daytime   62, 278, 308

Eddie's Menagerie   224, 337, 373

Eddie and His Big Deals   32, 373

Eddie and Teddy   130, 298

Eddie and the Fairy Godpuppy   228, 454, 493

The Edge of Next Year   132, 532

The Edge of the Cloud   47, 249, 477

An Edge of the Forest   15, 51, 211, 456, 522

Edge of Two Worlds   51, 228, 398, 409

The Education of Little Tree   8, 292

Edward Troy and the Witch Cat   72, 442, 503

Effective English   143, 482

The Egg Tree   38, 208, 450

The Egypt Game   52, 169, 213, 217, 487, 524

Egyptian Adventures   209, 304, 429

An Egyptian Pyramid   222, 268, 392, 454

The Eighteenth Emergency   84, 288, 364

Ein Tag Im Leben der Dorothea Wutz   23, 372

El Bronx Remembered: A Novella and Stories   132, 141, 452

El Chino   190, 504

El Diablillo de la Botella   109, 332, 530

The El Dorado Adventure   182, 246

Eleanor, Elizabeth   59, 355

Element of Time   203, 426

Elements of the Universe   77, 509, 546

The Elephant and the Bad Baby   214, 279, 342

Elephant Rock   91, 432

Elephants   24, 150, 159, 391, 422, 431, 434, 468, 543

Elephant School   149, 531

The Eleventh Hour   60, 117, 237, 261

Eli's Ghost   194, 374, 378

Elidor   47, 350, 402

Eliezer Ben-Yehuda, the Father of Modern Hebrew   120, 326

Elijah's Angel   105

Elijah's Angels   493, 496

Elizabeth's Tower   187, 530

Elizabeth and Larry   184, 274, 501

El Mundo Maravilloso de Macu   73, 357

El Oro de una Iris   24, 464, 548

El Pito de Plata de Pito   73, 245

El Rojo es el Mejor   110, 496, 531

Elsa, the True Story of a Lioness   32, 244

Elvira Everything   12, 139, 255

Emile   211, 545

Emilie de la Nouvelle Lune   109, 314, 452

Emily Dickinson: Her Letter to the World   213, 428

Emily of the New Moon   109, 314, 452

Emily Upham's Revenge: or, How Deadwood Dick Saved the Banker's Niece: A Massachusetts Adventure   188, 256, 573

Emma's Dilemma   141, 420

Emmet Otter's Jug-band Christmas   52, 67, 379

The Emperor's New Clothes   12, 156, 191, 250, 317, 413, 547, 558

The Emperor's New Clothes: A Fairy Tale   156, 250, 413

The Emperor's Panda   44, 110, 264, 315

The Emperor's Winding Sheet   230, 473

The Emperor and the Drummer Boy   154, 493, 517

The Emperor and the Kite   39, 51, 571

Emperor Penguin: Bird of the Antarctic   148, 316

The Empty Moat   56, 514

The Empty Schoolhouse   55, 290, 401

An Enchanted Hair Tale   118, 320, 369

The Enchanted Wood   21, 503

The Enchanter's Daughter   182, 192, 259, 418

Enchantress from the Stars   169, 186, 333, 513

Encircled Kingdom: Legends and Folktales of Laos   202, 301, 545

Encounter at Easton   68, 256

Encyclopedia Brown   35, 88, 188, 239, 278, 515, 524

Encyclopedia Brown and the Case of the Midnight Visitor   35, 278, 524

Encyclopedia Brown Keeps the Peace   239, 515, 524

Encyclopedia Brown Lends a Hand   88, 515, 524

Endless History   120

The Endless Steppe: Growing up in Siberia   3, 25, 52, 131, 214, 219, 372

Energy in the World of the Future   141, 375

Engineer's Dream   400, 423

Engineer's Dreams   209

English At the Back of the North Wind   109, 432, 507

English Fables and Fairy Stories   46, 405, 489

Enigma Variations: What Feminist Theory Knows About Children's Literature   66, 473

Enora and the Black Crane   223, 447

The Enormous Egg   52, 287, 312

Enter David   174, 514, 531

Enter David Garrick   174, 514, 531

Epics of Everest   71, 548, 560

Epidemic! The Story of the Disease Detectives   148, 253

Eric: The Tale of a Red Tempered Viking   139, 274, 543

The Erie Canal   67, 210, 244, 526, 551

Ernst   76, 408

Escape from Nowhere   67, 335

Escape from the Evil Prophecy   62, 309, 406

Escape to Freedom   4, 118, 236, 314, 401

Escape to the Overworld   236, 430

Esio Trot   198, 271, 311

Eva   29, 48, 239, 321

Even If I Did Something Awful   68, 374, 406

Even the Devil Is Afraid of a Shrew   61, 280, 282, 527

Everett Anderson's Goodbye   118, 300, 362

The Everlasting Hills   181, 386

Everybody Here!   176, 496

Everybody Needs a Rock   13, 263, 471

Everyone Else's Parents Said Yes   183, 312

Everyone Knows What a Dragon Looks Like   21, 157, 440, 563

Every Vote Counts: A Teenage Guide to the Electoral Process   142, 465

Everywhere   94, 280

The Evolution Book   151, 264, 529

Evolution Goes on Everyday   93, 400, 472

Exactly Alike   154, 460

Exeter Blitz   48, 489

The Exiles   102, 444

Exit from Home   219, 377

Exodus   115, 294, 449

Experiment in Terror   135, 474

Experiments in Sky Watching   77, 278, 565

Experiments in Sound   78, 265, 355

Explorations in Chemistry   78, 360

An Explorer's Handbook   151, 324

Exploring Black America: A History and Guide   63, 540

Exploring by Satellite: The Story of Project Vanguard   135, 278, 565

Exploring the Book of Kells   20, 189, 496, 518

Exploring the Film   126, 411, 412, 527

Exploring the Night Sky   150, 151, 269, 294, 314, 322

Exploring the Night Sky With Binoculars   150, 294, 314

Exploring the Sky By Day   106, 322

Exploring the Sun   143, 391

Exploring the Universe   77, 348, 376

Exploring the World of Leaves   148, 566

Eyak   73, 466

The Eye of Conscience: Photographers and Social Change   4, 302, 448

The eyes of Karen Connors   228, 327

The Eyes of the Dragon   22, 42, 181, 182, 406, 417, 469, 571

Fables   40, 427

Fables of Aesop   155, 288, 421

A Fabulous Creature   162, 524

The Fabulous Fifty   72, 364

The Fabulous Firework Family   174, 341

Face-off   16, 326

The Face at the Edge of the World   42, 200, 225, 225, 284

Face to Face   105, 129, 262

Facts and Fictions of Minna Pratt   183, 433

Faerie Queene   41, 83, 158, 380, 389

Fair's Fair   56, 294, 349, 350

Fairwater   210, 428, 489

The Fairy Circus   165, 416

The Fairy Doll   46, 107, 244, 356

Fairy Tales of Ireland   20, 431, 570

Faithful Elephants   24, 422, 543

Falcon, Fly Back   86, 271

Falconer's Lure: The Story of a Summer Holiday   46, 342, 400

Fallen Angels   54, 118, 146, 183, 200, 458

False Face   77

Falter Tom and the Water Boy   90, 327, 498

A Family Apart   225, 230, 462

Family at the Lookout   58, 449, 514

Family Bible Encyclopedia   91, 449

The Family Conspiracy   57, 212, 383, 478

Family Cracks   233, 566

Family Farm   69, 427

The Family from One End Street and Some of Their Adventures   45, 350

The Family under the Bridge 168, 290, 563

Famous American Explorers 228, 270, 402

Famous Mathematicians 137, 532

Fantastic Flyer 124, 497

Fantasy, Nonsense, Parody, and the Status of the Real: The Example of Carroll 66, 515

Fantasy Literature's Evocative Power 65, 540

The Far-away Trail 205, 518, 519

The Far-off Land 86, 293, 544

Farewell To Manzanar 85, 383, 384

Farewell to Shady Glade 201, 475

Farewell to the Farivox 61, 371, 466

Far From Marlborough Street 206, 477, 541

Far from Shore 236, 434

A Farm 64, 199, 318, 415, 499, 500

The Farm Book 179, 257, 522

Farm Boy 208, 358

Farmer Duck 34, 100, 191, 198, 469, 551

Farmer Hoo and the Baboons 52, 296, 498

The Farmhouse 34, 347

Farms for Today and Tomorrow: The Wonders of Food Production 143, 517

Farm Stories 207, 391, 538

The Farthest Shore 109, 132, 269, 350, 419

Fashion as a Career 137, 374, 552

Fast Friends: A Tail and Tongue Tale 75, 383

Fast Green Car 137, 287

Fast Iron 31, 441

Fast Is not a Ladybug: A Book about Fast and Slow Things 31, 152, 405, 506

Fast Sam, Cool Clyde and Stuff 235, 458

The Fat and Juicy Place 15, 259, 405

Fat Chance, Claude 182, 462, 475

Fat Eliot and the Gorilla 141

Fat Elliot and the Gorilla 479

The Fat Girl 18, 501

Fat Glenda Turns Fourteen 184, 476

Father Bear Comes Home 153, 451, 511

Father Christmas 12, 62, 99, 199, 279

Father Fox's Pennyrhymes 11, 60, 132, 160, 554, 555

Fat Santa 145, 310, 565

The Favershams 23, 158, 179, 353

The Fearsome Inn 109, 169, 381, 448, 519, 520

Feather in the Wind 215, 287

Feather Mountain 38, 466

Feathers, Fur and Frills 232, 462

Feathers for Lunch 192, 331

February's Road 46, 548

Feelings between Brothers and Sisters 72, 304, 489, 497

Fe Fi Fo Fum: A Picture Book of Nursery Rhymes 98

Felix and Alexander 59, 319

Felix in the Attic 21, 274, 575

Ferret in the Bedroom, Lizards in the Fridge 96, 200, 552

Ferris Wheels 150, 152, 251, 282, 352

Fever: The Hunt for a New Killer Virus 148, 346

Fiddler's Fancy 171, 517, 533

The Fiddler of High Lonesome 51, 544

The Field Guide to Geology 152, 413

Fierce and Gentle Warriors 213, 355, 455, 515

Fifer for the Union 212, 248, 561

Fifteen 34, 37, 83, 95, 106, 220, 227, 238, 298, 411

The Fifth Corner 109, 307, 331

Fifty Useful Americans 137, 445

Figgs and Phantoms 62, 169, 487

The Fight for Union 78, 301

The Fighting Ground 173, 256

A Figure of Speech 132, 441

Film: Real to Reel 126, 307

Final Grades 144, 377

Finders Keepers 38, 60, 237, 424, 454, 495, 572

The Finding 181, 263

Finding a Poem 155, 297, 448

Finding the Forgotten: Adventures in the Discovery of the Past 140, 346

Finding Your First Job 93, 247, 250

Find Out by Touching 135, 348, 516

Find the White Horse 56, 406, 562

A Fine Anger: A Critical Introduction to the Work of Alan Garner 66, 478

A Fine White Dust 170, 181, 500

Finlandia, the Story of Sibelius 205, 254, 360

Fiona Kenshole 81

Fire! It's Many Faces and Moods 143, 465

Fire Came to the Earth People 159, 497

Fireflies 142, 274, 500

Firefly 26, 136, 172, 444, 457, 498, 509, 551

A Firefly Named Torchy 26, 551

The Fire in the Stone 188, 236, 538

The Firelings 179, 274, 403

Fireweed 214, 473

The First Book of Color 32, 292, 472

The First Book of Space Travel 209, 266

First Boy on the Moon: A Junior Science Fiction Novel 86, 377, 561

First Farm in the Valley: Anna's Story 215, 476, 555

The First Lake Dwellers 32, 467

The First Margaret Mahy Story Book: Stories and Poems 91, 385, 434

The First Noel: The Birth of Christ from the Gospel According to St. Luke 153, 484, 485

The First of Midnight 101, 312, 455

First Scientist of Alaska: William Healey Dall 71, 376

First Snow 68, 306, 550

First Step 87, 524

First There Was Frances 59, 110, 359

The First Tulips in Holland 179, 410, 505

The First Two Lives of Lukas-Kasha 133, 246

The First Two Lives of Lukas-Kaska 73

The First Walkabout 57, 276, 424, 540

First Woman Ambulance Surgeon: Emily Barringer 71, 463

First Woman in Congress: Jeannette Rankin 4, 559

The Fisherman and his Wife 153, 352, 363

Fish Eyes: A Book You Can Count On 159, 331

Fish for Supper 40, 356

Fish Friday 18, 475

Fish in the Air 38, 207, 560

Fish Is Fish 128, 424

The Fish of our Fathers 5, 257, 392

The Fish Who Could Wish 192, 287, 473

The Five-Finger Discount 186, 315

Five-Yard Fuller of the N.Y. Gnats 33, 331, 557

The Five Chinese Brothers 49, 270, 560

Five Golden Wrens 206, 543

Five Little Monkeys 38, 152, 404

Five Minutes' Peace 18, 457

Five Proud Riders 204, 273, 527

Five Times Dizzy 58, 147, 559

Five Words 233, 401

Flags of all Nations and the People Who Live under Them 139, 332, 341

Flambards 25, 47, 101, 249, 477

Flamboyan 182, 244, 245, 259

The Flame of Peace: A Tale of the Aztecs 203, 416

Flaming Arrows 210, 231, 348, 528

The Fledgling 170, 272, 414

Fletcher and Zenobia 11, 296, 358

Flight: A Panorama of Aviation 158, 162, 471, 575

Flight: The Journey of Charles Lindbergh 217, 226, 175

The Flight of the Cassowary 237, 421

The Flight of the Doves 213, 432

Flight of the Solar Ducks 82, 454

Flight of the Sparrow 27, 72, 310

Flight of the White Wolf 84, 196, 332

Flip 205, 319

Floating and Sinking 138, 278, 348

Floating Illusions 189, 569

Floating Island 165, 472

Florida 84, 146, 217, 301, 302, 316, 440

Florinda and the Wild Bird 152, 290, 296, 512

Flour Babies 49, 338

Flowers in the Attic 239, 251

The Flunking of Joshua T. Bates 115, 316, 516

Flutes and Cymbals (poems) 99, 298, 385

Flutes and Cymbals (Poems) compiled by Leonard Clark 99, 298, 385

Flute Song Magic 16, 515

Fly Away Home 72, 138, 284, 332, 373, 378

Fly by Night 64, 157, 392, 511

Fly High, Fly Low 39, 345

Flying   33, 36, 39, 123, 158, 159, 166, 210, 277, 283, 308, 336, 439, 487, 516, 526, 540, 545, 551

The Flying Hockey Stick   33, 277

Fly West   58, 525

Foal Creek   86, 301, 456

A Foal Is Born   148, 250, 330, 390

Focus the Bright Land   174, 346

Fog   160, 419, 468

The Fog Comes on Little Pig Feet   215, 557

Fog in the Meadow   143, 468, 500

Fog Magic   167, 504, 554

Folk Tales   82, 99, 136, 205, 209, 211, 246, 255, 295, 299, 317, 325, 342, 363, 404, 407, 452, 545, 557

Folk Tales by Jacob Grimm and Wilhelm Grimm   82, 99, 342, 363

Follow the Dream   159, 520

The Fool and the Dancing Bear   71, 528, 533

The Fool and the Fish: A Tale From Russia   159, 245, 527

The Fool of the World and the Flying Ship   39, 487, 516

The Foot Book   109, 459, 512

Footfalls   144, 370

Footsteps   27, 145, 350, 414

Footsteps in the Ocean: Careers in Diving   145, 414

Forbidden City   195, 236, 266

The Forbidden Door   145, 417, 464

The Forbidden Forest   157, 326

The Forbidden Fountain of Oz   18, 438, 444

Forbidden Paths of Thual   227, 403, 434

For Conspicuous Gallantry: Winners of the Medal of Honor   33, 304, 567

Forest of Dreams   94, 393, 557

The Forest Pool   37, 253

Forgery!   187, 267

Forgetful Fred   19, 375, 563

Forgotten Daughter   166, 416, 523

The Forgotten Door   52, 171, 405

A Formal Feeling   69, 466

The Fortune-tellers   30, 95, 160, 185, 247, 388

The Forty-third War   186, 452

For Your Own Protection: Science Stories Photos Tell   113, 300

Foster Child   93, 262

Four and Twenty Blackbirds: Nursery Rhymes of Yesterday Recalled for Children of Today   37, 338, 417

Four Brave Sailors   181, 354, 535

Four Dollars and Fifty Cents   233, 406

Fourth Down   31, 276

Four Women in a Violent Time   52, 307

Fox's Dream   159, 164, 537

The Fox and the Circus Bear   130, 444

The Fox and the Hound   172, 323, 553

The Fox Busters   183, 406, 450

The Fox in Winter   48, 278

Fox on the Job   89, 437

Fox Tales   109, 289, 503

The Fox Went Out on a Chilly Night   39, 526

Francie   208, 366

Fran Ellen's House   18, 182, 217, 501

Franklin Delano Roosevelt   95, 113, 175, 344

Franklin of the Arctic: A Life of Adventure   43, 97, 363, 413

Frannie's Flower   143, 317, 521

Freaky Friday   41, 68, 89, 134, 215, 218, 495

Freckle Juice   128, 272, 424

Fred   199, 518

Frederick   39, 155, 424

Frederick's Alligator   68, 459, 477

Free   64, 466, 531

Free as a Frog   155, 354, 380

Freedom Builders: Great Teachers from Socrates to John Dewey   138, 139, 346

Freedom Eagle   140, 314

Freedom Trail   230, 562

Free Fall   41, 560

Freelon Starbird: Being a Narrative of the Extraordinary Hardships Suffered by an Accidental Soldier in a Beaten Army During the Autumn and Winter of 1776   161, 524, 527

Freight Train   14, 40, 191, 308

The French Detection   143, 552

Freshie   236, 410

Freunde   178, 374

Frida Kahlo   105

Friday's Tunnel   9, 46, 213, 549

Frido Kahlo   326

Friedrich   17, 52, 179, 235, 247, 343, 402, 410, 491, 508, 551

A Friend Is Someone Who Likes You   153, 252

The Friendly Beasts   28, 153, 258, 319, 517

The Friendly Beasts: An Old English Christmas Carol   28, 319

Friendly Wolf   13, 356

The Friendly Woods   72, 317, 383

The Friends   160, 365

The Friendship   29, 118, 354, 537

The Friends of Burramys   232, 303, 333

The Friends of Emily Culpepper   59, 302, 371

Frog   192, 499, 537

Frog and Toad   11, 40, 61, 68, 131, 160, 161, 169, 215, 217, 427

Frog and Toad All Year   68, 161, 427

Frog and Toad Are Friends   40, 131, 427

Frog and Toad Together   11, 61, 160, 169, 215, 427

Frog Goes to Dinner   13, 440

A Frog Prince   24, 267

The Frog Princess   95, 180, 366, 390, 572

Frogs, Toads and Newts   221, 346, 466

Frogs and Toads   150, 311, 396, 536

Frog Went A-courtin'   39, 209, 414, 495

From Afar it is an Island   147, 341, 457

From Archetype to Zeitgeist: Powerful Ideas for Powerful Thinking   105, 409

From Flower to Flower   151, 416, 558

From Hand Ax to Laser: Man's Growing Mastery of Energy   150, 485, 520

From King Boggen's Hall to Nothing At All   19, 420

From Slave to Abolitionist: The Life of William Wells Brown   66, 336, 554

From the Eagle's Wing: A Biography of John Muir   201, 535, 554

From the Mixed-up Files of Mrs. Basil E. Frankweiler   51, 169, 231, 409

Frontier Living   168, 544

A Frost in the Night: A Childhood on the Eve of the Third Reich   143, 257

Fudge   112, 115, 134, 196, 218, 228, 238, 359, 370

Full of Wonder   153, 407

Funny Bone Dramatics   141, 290, 306

Funny Bone Ticklers in Verse and Rhyme   141, 391, 435

The Funny Little Woman   40, 61, 92, 107, 160, 420, 455

Fun with Puzzles   30, 419, 494

Further Tales of Uncle Remus   184, 370, 421, 479

Gaffer Samson's Luck   197, 198, 302, 473

Gaijain: Foreign Children of Japan   164, 377

Galahad Schwartz and the Cockroach Army   97, 464

The Galapagos Kid: or, The Spirit of 1976   140, 553

Galax-Arena   60, 499

Galaxies and Quasars   221, 306, 375

The Gammage Cup   168, 174, 272, 403

Gandhi, Fighter without a Sword   167, 329, 488

Ganesh   109, 275, 370

Ganesh Oder Eine Neue Welt   109, 275, 370

Garbage Delight   44, 103, 108, 194, 418, 460

Gardd o Gerddi   397, 398

A Gardener's Alphabet   123, 369

A Gardening Book: Indoors and Outdoors   64, 553

The Garden Is Doing Fine   56, 93, 335, 535

The Garden of Abdul Gasazi   21, 27, 40, 108, 157, 162, 546

Garram the Hunter: A Boy of the Hill Tribes   165, 268

Garth Pig and the Ice Cream Lady   99, 488

A Gathering of Days: A New England Girl's Journal, 1830-32   7, 170, 272

The Gats!   213, 356

Gautama Buddha, in Life and Legend   52, 403

Gay-neck: The Story of a Pigeon   165, 254, 456

Gemini: A Personal Account of Man's Venture into Space   106, 364

The Genius of China   151, 537

Genius with a Scalpel: Harvey Cushing   140, 319

Gennarino · 154, 518

Gentle Ben　76, 195, 454, 506
Gentlehands　68, 162, 404
George's Marvellous Medicine　227, 271, 311
George and Martha　61, 156, 160, 437
George and Matilda Mouse and the Floating School　178, 283
George Rogers Clark: Soldier and Hero　106, 250, 463
George Washington　31, 136, 138, 141, 166, 167, 249, 298, 329, 342, 446, 496, 539, 554
George Washington: An Initial Biography　31, 167, 342
George Washington's World　166, 342
Georgia Music　29, 362, 530
Georgie to the Rescue　210, 279
Gertrude Stein: A Biography　62, 361
Gesu Oggi　22, 486
The Get-away Car　196, 300
Getting There: Frontier Travel without Power　230, 378
Ghost's Hour, Spook's Hour　182, 284, 291, 291
The Ghost Belonged to Me　87, 475
The Ghost Downstairs　99, 350, 434
The Ghost Drum　48, 484
The Ghost Horse of the Mounties　97, 385
Ghost Hound of Thunder Valley　36, 256, 504
The Ghost in my Soup　225, 450
The Ghost of Ballyhooly　187, 293
Ghost of Summer　202, 284, 436
The Ghost of Thomas Kempe　47, 108, 425, 434
The Ghost of Tillie Jean Cassaway　200, 348, 516
The Ghost on Saturday Night　197, 222, 238, 340, 550
Ghost Paddle　103, 383
The Ghost Rock Mystery　33, 243, 392
The Ghosts of Austwick Manor　74, 432
Ghosts of Departure Point　203, 284
The Ghosts of Now　188, 462
The Ghosts of Stoney Clove　95, 294
The Giant's Toe　181, 302
The Giant Book of Space　195, 489
The Giant Egg　145, 312
The Giant Fish and other Stories　179, 501, 536
The Giant Panda　151, 394, 400, 519
Gideon Ahoy!　29, 440
A Gift of Mirrorvax　68
A Gift of Mirrovax　432
The Gift of the Magi　158, 375, 460, 466, 576
Gilberto and the Wind　212, 334
Gildaen: The Heroic Adventures of a Most Unusual Rabbit　215, 283, 341
Gilgamesh: Man's First Story　25, 283
Gillespie and the Guards　39, 313, 331
Ginger Pye　167, 208, 334
Ginnie and her Juniors　136, 313, 568
Gin No Ude No Otto　109, 486, 554
Giorgio's Village　94, 319
Giraffe: the Silent Giant　64, 344, 506

The Giraffe and the Pelly and Me　125, 271, 311
The Giraffe of King Charles X　154, 569
The Girl　185, 278
A Girl Called Al　214, 261, 361
A Girl Called Boy　179, 387
The Girl from Puerto Rico　55, 303
A Girl From Yamhill: A Memoir　18, 190, 298
The Girl in the Grove　188, 512
The Girl in the White Hat　153, 310
Girls Are Powerful: Young Women's Writings from Spare Rib　176, 375
Girl Trouble　209, 534
The Girl Who Cried Flowers and Other Tales　93, 132, 156, 469, 571
The Girl Who Had no Name　93, 486
The Girl Who Loved the Wind　52, 61, 571, 572
The Girl Who Loved Wild Horses　14, 40, 356
Girl with a Pen: Charlotte Bronte　212, 412, 456
The Girl with the Silver Eyes　42, 74, 223, 493
Give a Man a Horse　204, 338, 480
Give Me Liberty　206, 373, 390
The Giver　30, 429
Glass and Man　106, 385
Glassblower's Children　108, 364, 413
Glasses: Who Needs 'Em?　184, 523
Glasses and Contact Lenses　146, 518
Gleanings　235, 527
The Globe for the Space Age　78, 378, 518
Glooskap's Country and Other Indian Tales　43, 367, 433
The Glorious Flight: Across the Channel with Louis Bleriot　41, 163, 179, 484, 485
The Glory Girl　80, 288
Glory of the Seas　166, 376, 569
The Gnu and the Guru Go Behind the Beyond　155, 300, 550
The Goalkeeper's Revenge and other Stories　176, 321, 459
Go Ask Alice　126
The Goats　139, 164, 194, 302, 334, 373
The Goats Who Killed the Leopard　139, 334, 373
God, Mrs. Muskrat and Aunt Dot　177, 381, 411
The God Beneath the Sea　47, 99, 272, 350, 402
God Made the World　135, 323
The Gods in Winter　108, 438
Goggle-eyes　48, 102, 338
Goggles　40, 402
Going on Sixteen　207, 293, 362
Going the Moose Way Home　128, 291, 416
The Gold Cadillac　69, 164, 373, 537
The Gold Coin　69, 244, 552
The Golden Almanac　206, 267, 530
The Golden Basket　166, 266
The Golden Bible for Children: The New Testament　152, 484, 485, 558

The Golden Bird　65, 99, 279, 463, 478
The Golden Book of Animals　153, 534, 559
The Golden Fleece and the Heroes Who Lived before Achilles　164, 303, 481
The Golden Geography: A Child's Introduction to the World　31, 321, 558
Golden Girl　171, 540
The Golden Goblet　168, 444
Goldengrove　160, 473
The Golden Impala　32, 496, 539
The Golden Knight　205, 294, 504
The Golden Locket　185, 361, 512
Golden Mare　239, 305, 309
The Golden Name Day　168, 424, 563
The Golden Phoenix and other French Canadian Fairy Tales　43, 259, 383, 483
Goldilocks and the Three Bears　41, 182, 437
The Golem　40, 114, 160, 161, 163, 180, 390, 427, 443, 516, 519
The Golem: A Jewish Legend　40, 161, 443
Gone-away Lake　52, 168, 210, 333
Gone and Back　160, 266
Gone Away Lake　411
Good-Bye, My Wishing Star　189, 364
The Good-Bye Book　69, 146, 296, 549
Good-bye Chicken Little　162, 288
Good-bye My Wishing Star　189, 364
The Good Bird　213, 558
A Good House for a Mouse　205, 329, 562
Good if it Goes　115, 422, 485
Good Luck Horse　37, 294
Good Luck to the Rider　57, 383, 478
The Good Master　166, 512
Good Morning, Lady　141, 317, 446
Good Night, Jessie!　145, 523, 574
Goodnight, Mister Tom　48, 102, 111, 433
Good Night, Mr. Tom　225, 227
The Goodnight Circle　87, 293, 421
Good Old Boy　216, 455
Good Queen Bess: The Story of Elizabeth I of England　30, 190, 527, 548
The Good Side of My Heart　145, 492
Goody Hall　61, 187, 214, 257
The Goof that Won the Pennant　218, 238, 400, 409
The Goose That Laid the Golden Egg　198, 473
Gorilla　29, 68, 100, 125, 141, 158, 159, 202, 275, 282, 337, 454, 479, 515
Gorilla, Gorilla　68, 337, 515
Gorky Rises　21, 157, 162, 529
Go to the Room of the Eyes　84, 286, 333
The Gould League Book of Australian Birds　232, 357, 466
The Gould League Book of Australian Mammals　232, 357, 466
Grabianskis Stadtmusikanten　23, 359
Graham Oakley's Magical Changes　27, 464

Grains: An Illustrated History with Recipes 148, 280

Gran at Coalgate 101, 293, 494

Grandaddy's Place 181, 182, 362, 363, 530

Grandfather's Bridge 73, 494

Grandma's Bill 20, 395, 551

Grandma's Favourite 176, 374

Grandma Cadbury's Trucking Tales 228, 262

Grandpa's Ghost Stories 35, 341

Grandpa and Me 140, 141, 351, 515

Granfa' Grig Had a Pig and Other Rhymes without Reason from Mother Goose 27, 543

The Grange at High Force 47, 470, 544

Grannie Was a Buffer Girl 48

Granny and the Indians 79, 470, 544

Granny Was a Buffer Girl 29, 36, 324

Granpa 125, 158, 286

Grasshopper on the Road 88, 427

Grasshoppers 150, 311, 503

A Grass Rope 46, 413, 440

Graven Images: Three Stories 170, 340, 355

The Gray Sea Raiders 71, 515

The Great Adventure: An Illustrated History of Canada 97, 321, 509

The Great American Gold Rush 18, 85, 175, 272

The Great Balloon Race 64, 540

Great Brain Does It Again 89, 239, 339, 440

The Great Brain Reforms 239, 339, 440

The Great Canadian Adventure Stories 104, 547

The Great Canadian Animal Stories 103, 547

The Great Canoe 123, 269, 419

Great Cat 179, 446

The Great Chief: Maskepetoon, Warrior of the Crees 97, 367, 567

The Great Christmas Kidnapping Caper 80, 200, 232, 403, 547

Great Civilizations of Ancient Africa 61, 280

The Great Dimple Oak 94, 348, 425

Great Discoverers in Modern Science 32

Great Discoveries in Modern Science 484

The Great Dissenters: Guardians of their Country's Laws and Liberties 77, 490

The Great Eggspectations of Lila Fenwick 74, 316, 446

The Great Elephant Chase 49, 198, 231, 308

The Greatest Cattle Drive 228, 270, 557

The Greatest Gresham 46, 256, 549

The Great Games Book [fourteen brilliant board games] 23, 246

The Great Geppy 205, 326

The Great Gilly Hopkins 4, 68, 73, 88, 89, 112, 126, 133, 170, 218, 232, 472

The Great Green Turkey Creek Monster 70, 79, 341

The Great Kapok Tree: A Tale of the Amazon Rain Forest 54, 296

The Great Little Madison 29, 175, 346

Great Men of Medicine 30, 343, 428

Great Painters 224, 548

The Great Picture Robbery 154, 370, 505

Great Quarterbacks of the NFL 137, 251

The Great Quest: A Romance of 1826 164, 373, 548

The Great Quillow 174, 418, 540

The Great Skinner Strike 74, 541

The Great Sleigh Robbery 198, 342

The Great Smile Robbery 130, 273, 443

The Great Song Book 157, 369, 394, 545

The Great Steamboat Mystery 188, 504

Great Swedish Fairy Tales 62, 262, 430

The Great Wheel 168, 417

The Great White Man-Eating Shark 225, 248, 434

Great Wolf and the Good Woodsman 13, 14, 382, 449

The Great Zoo Hunt 123, 545

Greedy Mariana and Other Folktales of the Antilles 388

Greedy Mariani and Other Folktales of the Antilles 62, 292

The Green Book of Hob Stories 130, 267, 440

The Green Bough of Liberty 176, 489

Green Eyes 38, 152, 270

Green Finger House 130, 371, 561

The Green Ginger Jar 31, 282, 399

The Green Isle 141, 287, 471

The Green Laurel 57, 526

The Green Man 178, 367

Green Wagons 206, 304, 501, 510

The Green Wind 59, 343

Greetings From Sandy Beach 60, 359

Greg's Revenge 83, 375

Grendel 79, 252, 349

Gretchen's ABC 184, 519

Grey Cloud 87, 272, 359

The Grey King 48, 169, 222, 305, 376

The Grey Lady and the Strawberry Snatcher 27, 40, 259

The Griffin and the Minor Canon 50, 511, 531

The Griffin Legacy 188, 408

Grishka and the Bear 32, 50, 365, 405, 436

The Grizzly 231, 395, 492

Groosham Grange 121, 383, 519

The Grouch and the Tower and other Sillies 142, 465

Grover 24, 132, 299, 343, 364, 438, 540

Growing Anyway Up 72, 93, 374

The Growing Pains of Adrian Mole 227, 381, 542

Growing Up 221, 295, 441, 448, 531

Growing up in Earthsea 66, 393

The Guardian 97, 101, 385

The Guardian of Isis 97, 385

The Guardians 67, 101, 297

Guess Who My Favorite Person Is 216, 263, 471

Guests in the Promised Land: Stories by Kristin Hunter 68, 132, 215, 386

A Guide to Nature Projects 137, 477, 557

The Guinea Pig ABC 28, 191, 327

Guinea Pigs: All about Them 140, 404, 518

Gulf 49, 57, 206, 279, 292, 558

The Gulf Stream 206, 279, 292

Gunga Din 181, 407, 471

Gunilla, an Arctic Adventure 210, 251, 415, 549

Guns over Champlain 30, 315

Gwendolyn and the Weathercock 154, 514, 525

Gwendolyn the Miracle Hen 211, 514, 525

Gypsy Family 176, 282, 554

Gypsy Moth: Its History in America 148, 442

Hail, Hail, Camp Timberwood 42, 218, 239, 303, 468

Hail, Hail Camp Timberwood 42, 218, 239, 303, 468

Hairy Maclary, Scattercat 5, 324

Hairy Maclary's Caterwaul Caper 5, 324

Hairy Maclary's Rumpus at the Vet 6, 324

Hairy Maclary's Showbusiness 6, 324

Hairy Maclary from Donaldson's Dairy 5, 324

Hakon of Rogen's Saga 212, 322, 323, 372

Hal 175, 432

The Half-a-Moon Inn 72, 93, 162, 340, 391

Half-Breed 362, 414

Half a Moon and One Whole Star 118, 326, 479

Half Breed 229

Half Magic 209, 273, 329

The Halfmen of O 5, 351

Halloween ABC 159, 448, 523

The Halloween Costume Party 144, 555

The Halloween Party 141, 244, 251

The Halloween Pumpkin Smasher 188, 501, 541

The Hand-me-Down Kid 84, 472

A Hand Full of Stars 17, 505

A Handful of Time 44, 77, 475

Handles 48, 436, 471

The Handmade Alphabet 30, 104, 487

Hands On, Thumbs Up 106, 310, 365

Handtalk: An ABC of Finger Spelling and Sign Language 148, 250, 295, 450

Handtalk Birthday 159, 250, 295, 450

Hanging On: How Animals Carry Their Young 148, 344

Hang Toughf 53, 385, 414

Hank 75, 504

Hannes und Sein Bumpan 9, 426, 555

Hannukkah 115, 366, 507

Hans Brinker: Sunny World, Angry Waters 65, 364

Hansel and Gretel 41, 100, 109, 282, 363, 421, 573

Hansy's Mermaid 144, 463

Hanukah Money 157, 246, 516

Hanukkah: Eight Nights, Eight Lights 203, 326, 379
The Happiest Ending 18, 544
Happily May I Walk 145, 229, 234, 378
Happily May I Walk: American Indians and Alaska Natives Today 145, 229, 234, 378
Happy Birthday, Oliver! 157, 421
Happy Christmas, Gemma 100, 373, 467
The Happy Day 38, 410, 519
The Happy Hunter 154, 328
The Happy Lion 135, 152, 153, 328, 336
The Happy Lion's Quest 135, 328, 336
The Happy Lion in Africa 153, 328, 336
The Happy Owls 154, 478
The Happy Place 152, 266
The Hardest Lesson: Personal Accounts of a School Desegregation Crisis 234, 531
The Hardest Lesson: Personal Stories of a School Desegregation Crisis 68, 284
The Hare and the Tortoise and the Tortoise and the Hare 12, 326, 480
Harlekin 19, 427
Harlequin and the Gift of Many Colors 21, 295, 534
Harold and Chester in Scared Silly: A Halloween Treat 172, 384, 454
Harriet 207, 326, 445
Harriet's Daughter 44, 478
Harriet and the Promised Land 12, 13, 155, 417
Harriet the Spy 195, 340
Harry's Mad 42, 182, 267, 406
Harry Cat's Pet Puppy 231, 510, 563
Harry in England 204, 270, 491
Harvey, the Beer Can King 87, 354, 553
Harvey Angell 231, 375
The Hat 214, 545
Hatchet 35, 84, 89, 92, 112, 122, 128, 170, 172, 196, 218, 225, 232, 238, 473
Hating Alison Ashley 117, 227, 237, 408
Hatter Fox 126, 371
Hattie and the Wild Waves 123, 304
Hattie Rabbit 88, 347
Haunted House 74, 99, 343, 470, 478
The Haunted Mountain 160, 386, 411
The Haunted Reef 209, 308, 483
The Haunting 48, 91, 124, 381, 434
The Haunting of Cabin 13 124, 381
Haunting of Safekeep 203, 285
Have Space Suit - Will Travel 195, 374
Have You Ever Seen...? An ABC Book 186, 349
Have You Seen Birds? 97, 104, 111, 131, 195, 467, 490
Have You Seen my Duckling? 41, 535
Have You Seen Tom Thumb? 166, 331, 386
Have You Seen Who's Just Moved in Next Door to Us? 125, 446
Have You Seen Wilhemina Krumpf? 62, 295, 457
Have You Started Yet? 176, 264, 539
Hawaii, the Aloha State 71, 262, 443
Hawk, I'm Your Brother 40, 263, 471
The Hawk of May 102, 417

The Hawkstone 52, 563
Haym Salomon: Liberty's Son 114, 338, 450
Hazel's Amazing Mother 158, 557
Head High, Ellen Brody 106, 346
The Headless Cupid 67, 107, 169, 231, 487, 524
The Headless Horseman Rides Tonight: More Poems to Trouble your Sleep 157, 162, 427, 483
Hear a Different Drummer 138, 409
Heard It In the Playground 197, 245, 555
Heartaches of a French Cat 159, 442
Heart of Danger: A Tale of Adventure on Land and Sea 30, 55, 475
Heart of Danger: A Tale of Adventure on Land and Sea with Tod Moran, Third Mate of the Tramp Steamer Araby 30, 475
Hearts Courageous: Twelve Who Achieved 31, 376, 432
Hear your Heart 138, 429, 516
Heather's Feathers 88, 556
The Heavenly Tenants 167, 400, 440
Heavy Is a Hippopotamus 152, 405, 506
Heckedy Peg 21, 69, 70, 135, 225, 238, 566, 567
Hector and Christina 142, 328, 336
Hector Lives in the United States Now 235, 376
Hector Penguin 156, 328, 336
Hedgehogs in the Closet 146, 291, 461
Helen Keller's Teacher 33, 272, 314
The Helen Keller Story 195, 231, 474
The Helen Oxenbury Nursery Story Book 125, 469
Helicopters at Work 140, 332, 409, 529
Hell's Edge 47, 542
Hello, Clouds! 186, 344, 490
Hello, Come In 140, 317, 436
Hello, People 140, 391, 435
Hello, the Boat! 86, 166, 308, 415
Help! I'm a Prisoner in the Library 238, 300, 385
Help! Let Me Out! 163, 431, 482
Help, Help, the Globolinks! 155, 156, 315, 355, 448
Helpers 99, 176, 385
Helpful Microorganisms 138, 415
Helping Horse 236, 478
Henry 183, 190, 263, 483
Henry-Fisherman 38, 281
Henry's Leg 102, 300, 478
Henry and Mudge and the Happy Cat 89, 500, 530
Henry and Mudge Get the Cold Shivers 89, 500, 530
Henry and Mudge in Puddle Trouble 89, 500, 530
Henry and Ribsy 239, 298, 313
Henry and the Paper Route 239, 298, 313
Henry and the Red Stripes 92, 296
Henry Reed, Inc. 231, 442, 493
Henry Reed's Baby-sitting Service 134, 231, 239, 442, 493

Hepzibah 129, 321, 482
Herbert 208, 261, 564
Herbert Rowbarge 163, 257
Herbie's Troubles 42, 90, 294, 465
Herbie Jones 115, 228, 408, 563
Hercules 113, 335
A Herd of Deer 52, 214, 322, 404
Here Is Alaska 206, 430, 432, 528
Here Lies the Body 188, 305, 353
Here She Is, Ms. Teeny-Wonderful! 127, 356
Herio'r Cestyll 397, 398
A Heritage Restored: America's Wildlife Refuges 76, 457
Herman the Helper 26, 254, 255, 410
A Hero Ain't Nothin' but a Sandwich 3, 53, 132, 160, 235, 296
The Hero and the Crown 170, 445
A Hero by Mistake 152, 209, 278, 295
Hero of Lesser Causes 97, 133, 396
Her Own Song 185
Her Own Story 384
Herra Kuningas 20, 517, 536
Hershel and the Hanukkah Goblins 41, 226, 388, 406
Hew Against the Grain 133, 309
Hey! Get Off Our Train! 286
Hey, Al! 41, 92, 116, 330, 571
Hey, Get Off Our Train 24, 183, 286
Hey, What's Wrong with this One? 89, 503, 566
Hey Willie, See the Pyramids 183, 400
Hi, Cat! 26, 402
Hiawatha 100, 109, 144, 393, 418, 428
Hiawatha's Childhood 100, 109, 418, 428
Hickory, Dickory, Dock 7, 328, 456
Hidden Heroines: Women in American History 142, 414
The Hidden House 199, 260, 551
The Hidden Message 216, 395
The Hidden Treasure of Glaston 167, 294, 394
Hidden Worlds: Pictures of the Invisible 150, 519
Hide and Seek Fog 39, 155, 212, 328, 542
Hieroglyphs: The Writing of Ancient Egypt 149, 401, 451
Higgins of the Railroad Museum 215, 446, 471
Higher on the Door 181, 191, 530
The High King 131, 169, 247
Highlights 124, 356, 428, 526, 552
Highlights. 124, 356, 428, 526, 552
The High Pasture 55, 365, 370
Highpockets 207, 264, 544
High Prairie 206, 372, 384
The High Rise Glorious Skittle Skat Roarious Sky Pie Angel Food Cake 115, 555, 562
High Road Home 31, 55, 305
High Sounds, Low Sounds 138, 278, 348
The Highwayman 100, 113, 402, 464, 552
Hildilid's Night 40, 61, 132, 427, 500
Hilla of Finland 205, 250, 318

Title Index

Hillback to Boggy 175, 526
Him, she Loves? 80, 404
Himmelszelt und Schneckenhaus 23, 456, 492
Him She Loves? 80, 404
Hinter dem Norwind 109, 432, 507
The Hired Man's Elephant 205, 418, 532
Hiroshima no Pika 4, 17, 28, 438
His Indian Brother 77, 375, 564
His Own Where 132, 398
Hispanic Voters: A Voice in American Politics 234, 370
Hist! 60, 318, 359
Histoire du Petit Stephen Girard by Mark Twain 23, 247, 299, 462
Hitty, Her First Hundred Years 50, 165, 338, 416
The Hobbit 79, 204, 541
Hodie 208, 349
Hodina Nachove Ruze 23, 410, 517
Hokahey! American Indians Then and Now 32, 325, 565
Hokkyoku no Mushika Mishika 9, 383, 390
Hold Back the Hunter 229, 480
Hold Fast 44, 97, 108, 194, 434
The Hole in the Hill 86, 513, 515
A Hole Is to Dig 152, 410, 511
A Holiday for Mister Muster 154, 427
Holiday Happenings in Limerick Land 140, 391, 435
Holidays in Scandinavia 141, 413, 569
The Hollow Land 48, 230, 349, 488
Holly and the Porpoises 34, 562
The Holocaust: A History Of Courage and Resistance 114, 438, 527
A Home 62, 104, 120, 156, 415, 499
Homecoming 162, 550
Home in the Sky 59, 258
Home Place 95, 326, 479
Homer Price 238, 442
Homer the Tortoise 208, 258, 262
The Home Run Trick 92, 222, 305, 348
Homesick, My Own Story 8, 28, 56, 69, 163, 170, 346, 541
Hominids: A Look Back at Our Ancestors 152, 503, 504
Honey, I Love and Other Love Poems 217, 322, 323, 362
The Honeybees 155, 482, 500
Honey Girl 230, 370
Hong Kong Altar Boy 137, 369
Honk the Moose 52, 166, 532, 560
The Honorable Prison 173, 183, 393
Honor Bound 187, 274
Honschi 61, 295, 355
Hoops 188, 458
Hoppy the Toad 24, 287
Horatio 198, 342
The Horse-Talker 229, 562
The Horse and his Boy 46, 263, 422
A Horse Called Dragon 85, 293, 367
The Horsecatcher 168, 210, 503
The Horse in the Camel Suit 137, 326
Horses in Battle 99, 249
A Horse to Remember 86, 282, 329

Hortense, the Cow for a Queen 210, 290, 454
Horton Hatches the Egg 49, 512
Hosie's Alphabet 12, 13, 40, 156, 261, 262
The Hospital Book 28, 384, 554
Hospital Worker 176, 307, 357
Hostage to Alexander 86, 251, 395
The Hot and Cold Summer 105, 180, 220, 387, 468
Hotheads 142, 420
Hot Rod 31, 336
The Houdini Box 193, 220, 510
Hound Dog Moses and the Promised Land 31, 330, 364
The House 55, 247, 271
The House Guest 60, 75, 133, 462
A House is a House for Me 8, 344, 379
The House of Dies Drear 174, 187, 368, 402
The House of Four Seasons 210, 328
The House of Sixty Fathers 55, 107, 168, 235, 316, 511
The House of the Fifers 209, 293, 352
The House of the People 70, 257, 392
The House of Wings 132, 288, 508
The House on Charlton Street 187, 316, 492
The House on East 88th Street 211, 551
The House on Walenska Street 194, 256, 376
Houses from the Sea 39, 244, 358
The House that Jack Built: A Picture Book in Two Languages 39, 153, 344
The House that Was Eureka 59, 147, 559
The House With a Clock in its Walls 128, 160, 266, 358
How, Hippo! 214, 281
Howard 157, 162, 530
How Casbo Became a Clown 34, 369
How Dog Began 181, 263
How Droofus the Dragon Lost His Head 41, 70, 476
How Fletcher Was Hatched! 139, 320
How Hospitals Help Us 136, 336, 447
How I Came to be a Writer 93, 459
How I Put My Mother Through College 74, 353
How It Feels To Fight for Your Life 82, 410
How Kittens Grow 88, 283, 510
Howl's Moving Castle 29, 397
Howliday Inn 226, 384, 457
How Man Discovered his Body 137, 492, 557
How Many? From 0 to 20 100, 483
How Many Bugs in a Box? 192, 292
How Medicine Man Cured Paleface Woman: An Easy Reading Story in Indian Picture Writing and Paleface Words 216, 443
How Much and How Many: The Story of Weights and Measures 30, 266
How Much Is a Million? 29, 224, 403, 508
How my Parents Learned to Eat 69, 346, 504

How Nature Works 195, 286
How Pizza Came to Queens 159, 405
How Seeds Travel 150, 369, 468
How St. Francis Tamed the Wolf 211, 496
How Summer Came to Canada 103, 299
How the Birds Changed Their Feathers 99, 543
How the Forest Grew 27, 330, 393
How the Guinea Fowl Got Her Spots 129, 408
How the Kookaburra Got his Laugh 111, 417, 523
How the Mouse Was Hit on the Head by a Stone and so Discovered the World 12, 13, 318
How the Ox Star Fell From Heaven 190, 382
How the Witch Got Alf 68, 403, 508
How They Built the Statue of Liberty 89, 504, 513
How to Eat Fried Worms 11, 41, 92, 112, 126, 134, 196, 200, 222, 226, 237, 442, 494
How To Fight a Girl 172, 337, 494
How to Hide a Hippopotamus 153, 309
How To Make Pop-Ups 224, 390, 490
How Tom Beat Captain Najork and his Hired Sportsmen 108, 230, 271, 379
How To Survive Third Grade 115, 417, 573
How You Talk 138, 348, 516
How You Were Born 94, 302
Hubert, the Caterpillar Who Thought He Was a Moustache 155, 251, 491, 527
Hugh Glass, Mountain Man 199, 442
Hugh Pine and the Good Place 163, 457, 547, 558
Hugo's Zoo 57, 432
Hugo and the Spacedog 144, 428
Human Populations 221, 373
Humbug 27, 133, 185, 263, 340, 550
Humbug Mountain 27, 133, 340, 550
Humphrey's Bear 69, 191, 399, 551
The Hundred Dresses 167, 334, 521
The Hundred Penny Box 26, 161, 169, 322, 323, 439
The Hungry Time 111, 321, 401
The Hunter I Might Have Been 51, 311, 448
Hunter in the Dark 6, 10, 18, 97, 236, 385
Hunters of the Whale: An Adventure in Northwest Coast Archaeology 148, 313, 407
The Hunt for the Whooping Crane 213, 243, 442
Hurly Burly and the Knights 154, 431, 499
Hurray for Captain Jane! 61, 442, 489
Hurry, Hurry, Mary Dear! and Other Nonsense Poems 68, 273
Hurry Home, Candy 168, 316, 511
Hurry Up, Jessie! 146, 523, 574
Hush, Little Baby 13, 14, 108, 574
Hush Little Baby 13, 14, 108, 574
Hyena Day 149, 289, 384

I, Juan de Pareja 169, 543

I, Leonardo 199, 528

I'll Always Love You 24, 562

I'll Be You and You Be Me 152, 410, 511

I'll Fix Anything 139, 427, 549

I'll Get There. It Better Be Worth the Trip 214, 325

I'll Protect You from the Jungle Beasts 68, 247

I'll Show You Cats 154, 275, 570

I'm an Australian: A Class Journal 16, 262

I'm Coming to Get You! 191, 497

I'm Flying! 159, 439, 551

I'm Glad I'm Me 140, 281, 532

I'm Going to Sing: Black American Spirituals, vol. 2 118, 283

I'm Going to Sing: Black American Spirituals vol. 2 118, 283

I'm Hiding 216, 272, 426

I'm Moving 87, 360, 377

I'm OK, You're OK: A Practical Guide to Transactional Analysis 371

I Am an Orthodox Jew 73, 361, 558

I Am Magic 73, 546

I Am Regina 83, 402

I Am Susannah 59, 355

I Am the Cheese 235, 306, 549

Ian and Fred's Big Green Book 222, 474, 565

I Believe in Unicorns 130, 335, 457

Ibis: A True Whale Story 378

I Can Fly 208, 271, 410

I Carve Stone 143, 251, 338

Iceberg Alley 148, 251

Icebergs and Glaciers 151, 519

Icebergs and their Voyages 72, 507

The Ice Cream Store 129, 418, 446

The Ice Is Coming 58, 101, 568

Ice River 72, 309, 361

Ich Schenk Dir Einen Papagei! 22, 259

Ida Early Comes Over the Mountain 27, 285

Ideology and the Children's Book 66, 381

If all the Seas Were One Sea 12, 26, 40, 324

If I Asked You, Would You Stay? 203, 284

If I Asked You Would You Stay 203, 284

If I Built a Village 26, 452

If I Had a Paka: Poems in Eleven Languages 4, 481, 535

If I Love You, Am I Trapped Forever? 215, 404

If I Ran the Zoo 38, 512

If There Were Dreams to Sell 158, 413, 541

If This Is Love, I'll Take Spaghetti 200, 303

If We Could Hear the Grass Grow 120, 307

If Wishes Were Horses and other Rhymes by Mother Goose 143, 393

If You Didn't Have Me 17, 333, 462

If You Give a Moose a Muffin 185, 274, 464

If You Give a Mouse a Cookie 35, 42, 70, 80, 90, 135, 274, 464

If You Lived in the Days of the Wild Mammoth Hunters 139, 332, 341, 453

If You Really Trust Me, Why Can't I Stay Out Later? 92, 477

If You Take a Pencil 179, 538

The Igloo 151, 572

IGY: Year of Discovery: The Story of the International Geophysical Year 78, 294

I Had a Friend Named Peter 182, 301, 468

I Had Trouble in Getting to Solla Sollew 33, 512

I Hate Books and other Stories 141, 516

I Hate English! 184, 270, 421

I Hate My Name 143, 360, 441

I Have a Friend 182, 459

I Have Just Begun to Fight: The Story of John Paul Jones 205, 332, 342

I Heard My Mother Call My Name 79, 337, 386

I Jessie: A Biography of the Girl who Married John Charles Fremont 86, 487

Ike and Mama and the Block Wedding 219, 493, 524

Ike and Mama and the Seven Surprises 219, 493, 524

Ike and Mama and the Trouble at School 144, 493, 524

Ike and Porker 87, 407

I Know a Lady 191, 530, 575

I Know a Lot of Things 153, 487

Il Cavallo di Bronzo 23, 409, 485

Il Etait Une Fois, Les Mots 23, 266, 479

I Lift My Lamp: Emma Lazarus and the Statue of Liberty 203, 422

I Like Trains 137, 341, 568

Illiada 9, 352

The Illustrated Dinosaur Dictionary 94, 291, 468, 487, 503, 504

The Illyrian Adventure 83, 181, 247

I Love Animals and Broccoli 24, 527, 554

Il Principe Felice 23

"Imagine" 69, 123, 221, 261, 309, 449, 533

Imagine That!!! Exploring Make-Believe 69, 261, 533

I Marched with Hannibal 212, 263, 482, 507

I Met a Man 135, 211, 297, 467

Imogene's Antlers 181, 521

The Impact Zone 75, 435

Impeccable Governesses, Rational Dames, and Moral Mothers 66, 458

The Impossible People: A History Natural and Unnatural of Beings Terrible and Wonderful 132, 215, 277, 444

In a Dark, Dark Room and Other Scary Stories 35, 88, 225, 226, 507, 575

In a Mirror 55, 532

In Came Horace 209, 264, 393

The Inch Boy 59, 454, 522

Inch by Inch 39, 50, 154, 424

Incident at Hawk's Hill 169, 217, 330, 506

Incident at Loring Groves 189, 422

In Coal Country 29, 159, 164, 181, 248, 375

The Incredible Journey: A Tale of Three Animals 15, 44, 52, 82, 83, 107, 231, 239, 285, 286

The Incredible Journey of Lewis and Clark 94, 272

Incredible Jumbo 133, 523

The Incredible Painting of Felix Clousseau 192, 245

Incroyables Adventures de Mister MacMiffic 108, 340, 486

In Deutschland 221, 459, 471

Indian, Indian 208, 556, 575

Indian Captive: The Story of Mary Jemison 166, 420

Indian Foe, Indian Friend: The Story of William S. Harney 230, 253

Indian Harvests 62, 364, 378

The Indian in the Cupboard 11, 42, 54, 126, 162, 225, 239, 259, 302

Indians of the Southern Plains 140, 483

Indians Who Lived in Texas 216, 554

An Indian Winter 95, 185, 190, 274, 344

The Indy 500 144, 457

I Never Had It Made 118, 327, 494

Inigo: The Adventures of a Saint 15, 314, 369, 540

In Kindling Flame: The Story of Hannah Senesh, 1921-1944 115, 256

In Love and War 212, 564

In My Mother's House 37, 205, 297, 376

The Innkeeper's Boy 233, 339, 480

In Nueva York 142, 452

In Our House 191, 494

In Prehistoric Seas 136, 337

Insect Magic 149, 333, 503

The Insect Man: Jean Henri Fabre 204, 325, 353

Insect Metamorphosis 29, 358

The Inside-Outside Book of New York City 158, 457

Inside: Seeing Beneath the Surface 63, 244

Inside an Egg 150, 396, 515

Inside my Feet: The Story of a Giant 162, 378, 404

Inside the Whale and Other Animals 130, 320, 471

Inspirations: Stories About Women Artists 190, 517

In Such a Place 6, 335

In Summer Light 29, 466

In Summertime, it's Tuffy 80, 251

Integration of Mary-Larkin Thornhill 142, 552

International Children's Bible 91, 491, 562

The International Children's Bible Handbook 91, 491

Interstellar Pig 42, 520

In the Beginning: Creation Stories from Around the World 170, 368, 455

In the City of the King   11, 472

In the Eye of the Teddy   141, 255

In the Face of Danger   230, 462

In the Forest   13, 37, 64, 87, 106, 174, 215, 334, 429, 516, 544, 559

In Their Own Words: A History of the American Negro, vol. 2, 1865-1916

In the land of Ur: The Discovery of Ancient Mesopotamia   17, 263, 386, 490

In the Middle of a Rainbow   144, 354

In the Mouth of the Wolf   219, 573

In the Night Kitchen   12, 13, 40, 156, 191, 511

In the Shadow of the Bear   144, 501

In the Tall, Tall Grass   30, 186, 192, 340

In the Trail of the Wind: American Indian Poems and Ritual Orations   61, 269

In the Year of the Boar and Jackie Robinson   113, 428, 519

Into a Strange Land   69, 234, 255

Into the Dream   73, 503, 520

Introducing Archaeology   221, 433, 518

Introducing Birds to Young Naturalists   221, 377

An Introduction To Insects   232, 270, 504, 515

Introduction to Tomorrow: The U.S. and the Wider World, 1945- 1965   78

In Trouble Again, Zelda Hammersmith?   80, 367

The Intruder   26, 47, 187, 386, 477, 542

In Two Worlds: A Yup'ik Eskimo Family   152, 234, 393, 492

Inventor's Notebook: Entirely New Do- it-Yourself Toy Inventions   136

Invincible Louisa: The Story of the Author of Little Women   50, 165, 447

Invincible Summer   203, 337

The Invisible Giants: Atoms, Nuclei and Radioisotopes   139, 362

The Invisible Hunters   118, 495, 502

The Invisible World of the Infrared   150, 559

IOU's   220, 509

I Own the Racecourse   107, 383, 568

Ira Sleeps Over   61, 551

Iron Barred Door   127, 385

Iron Duke   204, 284, 544

The Iron Lily   101, 562

The Iron Lion   163, 263, 321

The Iron Man   125, 314, 385

The Iron Road: A Portrait of American Railroading   27, 480, 524

Isaac Campion   29, 48, 164, 384

Is Anybody There?   96, 200, 284

I Saw Esau   185, 190, 466, 467, 511

I Saw You from Afar: A Visit to the Bushmen of the Kalahari Desert   212, 476

I Saw You in the Bathtub and Other Folk Rhymes   146, 380, 507

A Is For Animals: 26 Pop-up Surprises: An Animal ABC   192, 476

A Is for Anything: An ABC Book of Pictures and Rhymes   136, 261

Is It Larger? Is It Smaller?   151, 186, 379

Is It Red? Is It Yellow? Is It Blue?   14, 379

Is It Rough? Is It Smooth? Is It Shiny?   150, 379

Is Kissing a Girl Who Smokes Like Licking an Ashtray?   186, 483

Island Boy   29, 305

The Islanders   68, 542

An Island in a Green Sea   26, 247, 493

The Island of Adventure   273

The Island of Fish in the Trees   154, 253, 569

The Island of Ghosts   20, 322

Island of Peril   87, 495

Island of the Blue Dolphins   50, 85, 107, 134, 168, 201, 225, 231, 465

The Island of the Grass King: The Further Adventures of Anatole   53, 446, 562

The Island of the Skog   128, 403

The Island on Bird Street   4, 17, 120, 189, 219, 367, 467

Island Summer   174, 341, 564

Island Time   174, 414, 544

I Spy: An Alphabet In Art   185, 449

Israel   99, 109, 114, 120, 185, 398, 421, 448, 459, 470, 512, 520, 541

Is That You, Miss Blue?   161, 404

Is This a House for Hermit Crab?   112, 443, 505

Is Your Mama a Llama?   146, 365, 403

It's a Mile from Here to Glory   222, 419

It's an Aardvark-Eat-Turtle World   181, 312

It's BASIC: The ABC's of Computer Programming   88, 144, 424, 528

It's Fun to Know Why: Experiments with Things Around Us   147, 376, 393, 508

It's Like This, Cat   168, 460, 556

It's Not the End of the World   140, 272

It's OK To Be You! Feeling Good About Growing Up   164, 473, 486

It's Raining, Said John Twaining: Danish Nursery Rhymes   68, 273

It's Time to Go to Bed   143, 329, 509, 535

It's Your Turn, Roger!   198, 362

It Can't Hurt Forever   122, 360, 520

It Could Always Be Worse: A Yiddish Folk Tale   157, 574

I Tell a Lie Every So Often   132, 299

It Happened in Pinsk   20, 330, 331, 571

It Is Better Farther On: Laura Ingalls Wilder and The Pioneer Spirit   65, 418

The Ivory Lyre   182, 457

I Walk and Read   163, 379

I Wanna Be a Lady Plumber and other Stories   138, 516

I Want My Potty   100, 497

I Want To Be an Astronaut   159, 261

I Want to Paint My Bathroom Blue   153, 410, 511

I Was a 98-pound Duckling   140, 547

I Will Call it Georgie's Blues: A novel   163, 461

I Will Sing Life   82, 267, 268, 425

I Will Tell You of a Town   153, 428, 490

I Won't Go To Bed   145, 261, 574

I Wrote My Name on the Wall: Sidewalk Songs   61, 524

Izzy, Willy-Nilly   42, 225, 226, 550

J.T.   89, 471, 551

Jabas   398

Jack and the Wonder Beans   157, 531, 541

Jack Holburn   33, 350, 434

Jacko   61, 357

Jack Tar   53, 415, 440

Jack the Treacle Eater   125, 293, 402

Jacky Nobody   5, 320

Jacob Have I Loved   73, 162, 170, 473

Jacobin's Daughter   210, 299, 564

Jacob Two-two Meets the Hooded Fang   44, 161, 194, 491, 555

Jake and Honeybunch Go to Heaven   72, 163, 574

Jamaica's Find   116, 373, 465

Jambo Means Hello: Swahili Alphabet Book   13, 26, 40, 336

James and the Giant Peach: A Children's Story   126, 285, 311

James Van Der Zee: The Picture Takin' Man   234, 372, 547

Jam Magazine   127, 253

Jane's Island   165, 247, 248

Jane Addams: Pioneer for Social Justice, a Biography   3, 447

Jane Yolen's Mother Goose Songbook   105, 380, 529, 571

Janine   55, 445

Janitor's Girl   210, 345, 530

January, February, June, or July   236, 482

Jan und das Wildpferd   9, 318, 420

Jareb   55, 209, 482, 519

A Jar of Dreams   72, 85, 544

Jasmin   44, 194, 543

Jayhawker   72, 264

Jazz Country   21, 213, 235, 376

The Jazz Man   155, 169, 362, 556

Jeanne-Marie Counts Her Sheep   208, 510

Jeb Ellis of Candlemas Bay   209, 453, 565

Jed: The Story of a Yankee Soldier and a Southern Boy   51, 285

Jeder Nach Seiner Art   24, 333, 335, 550

Jelly Belly   44, 134, 200, 238, 397, 418, 523, 561

Jennifer   55, 514

Jennifer, Hecate, Macbeth, William McKinley, & Me   169, 213, 409

Jenny's Birthday Book   152, 256

Jenny's Corner   161, 265, 466

Jenny of the Tetons   94, 362

Jeremiah Octopus   211, 408, 575

Jerusalem Shining Still   182, 343, 412

Jesper   236, 439

Jesus, the Friend of Children   91, 304, 382

Je t'Attends a Peggy's Cove   109, 256, 326

Jet Journey   149, 504, 564

Jets and Rockets and How they Work 32, 358

The Jewish Americans: A History in Their Own Words, 1650- 1950 28, 113

The Jewish Holiday Book 142, 417

The Jewish Holiday Game & Workbook 146, 413, 480

The Jewish Kids Catalog 115, 286

The Jewish People: Book Three 114, 421, 476

Jimmy: The Story of Young Jimmy Carter 143, 288

Jimmy's Boa and the Big Splash Birthday Bash 146, 403, 463

Jimmy Yellow Hawk 73, 431, 523

Jim Ugly 185, 340, 523

Jingo Django 214, 340, 550

Joe and Timothy Together 175, 330, 548

Joel, Growing Up a Farm Man 199, 318

Joel and the Wild Goose 51, 312, 502

Joe Magarac and his U.S.A. Citizenship Papers 86, 313, 513

Joe Mason, Apprentice to Audubon 30, 480, 518

John Brown, Rose and the Midnight Cat 58, 101, 147, 280, 551

John Diamond 230, 350, 434

John F. Kennedy and PT-109 239, 542

John Henry McCoy 56, 294, 507

John J. Pershing 136, 559

John J. Plenty and Fiddler Dan 154, 297, 352

Johnny Crow's Garden: A Picture Book 50, 280

Johnny Jump-up 205, 273, 382

Johnny Texas 85, 216, 380, 449

Johnny Tremain 167, 341, 554

Johnny Wants to be a Policeman 31, 309, 360

John Patrick Norman McHennessey, The Boy Who Was Always Late 182, 286

Joi Bangla! The Children of Bangladesh 132, 416

Join Hands with the Ghosts 139, 289, 356

The Joker and the Thief 75, 465

The Jolly Christmas Postman 100, 245

The Jolly Mon 16, 284, 314

The Jolly Postman: or, Other People's Letters 56, 100, 110, 125, 245

Jolly Snow 34, 379

Jolly Tall 34, 379

Jonah and the Great Fish 28, 71, 158, 163, 245, 284, 388

Jonah the Fisherman 153, 565, 575

Jonathan Down Under 203, 264

Jonathan Livingston Seagull 134, 257

Jonpanda 172, 360, 451

Jorinda and Joringel 25, 244, 363

Josefina February 212, 460

Joseph's Boat 70, 350, 432

Joseph's Yard 99, 402

Joseph and Lulu and the Prindiville House Pigeons 107, 362

Josephine 47, 102, 104, 110, 114, 131, 206, 208, 209, 212, 268, 319, 338, 400, 418, 423, 429, 436, 474, 482, 531

Joseph Strauss - Builder of the Golden Gate Bridge 33, 296, 368

Joseph Strauss: Builder of the Golden Gate Bridge 33, 296, 368

Joseph Who Loved the Sabbath 219, 361, 378

Josh 47, 91, 107, 112, 230, 443, 449, 460, 525

Joshua: Fighter for Bar Kochba 114, 456

Joshua Fortune 235, 360

Josie Smith 102, 198, 458, 546

Josie Smith and Eileen 198, 458, 546

Journal of Madame Royale 142, 483

The Journey: Japanese Americans, Racism and Renewal 5, 368

Journey Cake 38, 86, 442, 445, 470, 504

Journey Cake, Ho! 38, 442, 504

Journey from Peppermint Street 131, 316, 443

The Journey of Josiah Talltatters 209, 474

The Journey of the Eldest Son 47, 249, 347

Journey of the Sparrows 5, 105, 287, 309

Journey Outside 52, 169, 459, 528

Journey to America 114, 422, 494

Journey to Jo'burg 56, 176, 458, 548

Journey to Jo'burg: A South African Story 56, 458, 548

Journey to the Planets 163, 416

Journey to the Soviet Union 4, 523

Joyful Noise: Poems for Two Voices 29, 170, 264, 340

Joy Is Not Herself 212, 418, 436

Juanita 38, 116, 207, 373, 465, 481

Juanito's Railroad in the Sky 64, 376

Juarez: A Son of the People 202, 498

Jud 86, 488

The Judge 40, 573, 574

Judy's Journey 55, 420

Judy and Lakshmi 9, 294, 452

Judy Scuppernong 30, 422, 509

Julia's Magic 180, 289, 468

Julia and the Hand of God 85, 289, 468

Julie 11, 44, 97, 536

Julie's Magic Moment 95, 261

Julie of the Wolves 132, 169, 352, 506

Juma and the Magic Jinn 94, 251, 449

Jumanji 8, 28, 35, 40, 116, 158, 162, 226, 228, 546

Jumbo: Giant Circus Elephant 141, 250, 319

Jump Again! 20, 159, 191, 370, 455, 471

Jump Again! More Adventures of Brer Rabbit 20, 159, 370, 455, 471

Jumping-off Place 165, 446, 517

The Jumping Lions of Borneo 204, 328, 494

June's Island 316

June 29, 1999 185, 561

The Jungle Book 50, 326, 345, 407

A Jungle in the Wheat Field 211, 439

Junglewalk 192, 535

Junior Flower Shows: A Complete Guide to the Planning, Staging and Judging of Children's Flower Shows 136, 310

Junior Jewish Encyclopedia 114, 266, 417

The Juniper Game 6, 398

The Juniper Tree and other Tales from Grimm 62, 156, 392, 510, 511

Junius Over Far 118, 368

Junket 209, 442, 559

Junk Food, Fast Food, Health Food: What America Eats and Why 28, 476

Just As Long As We're Together 145, 272

Just Enough Is Plenty: A Hanukkah Tale 115, 182, 297, 357

Just Imagine - Ideas in Painting 221, 309

Justin and the Best Biscuits in the World 118, 531, 553

Justin Morgan Had a Horse 167, 319, 375

Just Like Everybody Else 235, 496

Just Me 39, 334

Just One More 146, 409

Just So Stories 51, 156, 184, 265, 318, 343, 407

Just Tell Me When We're Dead! 196, 300, 385

Kaiulani: Crown Princess of Hawaii 212, 555

Kangaroo & Kangaroo 13, 155, 232, 278, 440, 446, 490, 495

Kap the Kappa 211, 423, 452

Karen's Curiosity 154, 484, 485

Karen's Opposites 212, 484, 485

Karen Kepplewhite is the World's Best Kisser 134, 284

Kashtanka 98, 295, 325, 531

Kasimir's Journey 153, 490, 528

Katie's Adventure at Blueberry Pond 91, 443, 460

Katy No-Pocket 79, 474, 491

Kavik, the Wolf Dog 76, 84, 231, 454, 471

Kay-Kay Comes Home 154, 502, 513

The Keeper 5, 108, 336, 385

The Keeper of the Isis Light 108, 385

Keeping a Christmas Secret 69, 459, 515

Keeping it Secret 144, 321, 481

The Keeping Quilt 219, 481

Keep Singing, Keep Humming: A Collection of Play and Story Songs 207, 272, 277, 567

Kenny's Window 210, 511

Kentucky: A Pictorial History

Kept in the Dark 179, 188, 263

The Kestrel 179, 247

Kevin 34, 44, 45, 48, 77, 97, 108, 117, 127, 194, 198, 210, 228, 236, 262, 294, 309, 375, 402, 434, 436

The Keys and the Candle 71, 274, 568

Keys to a Magic Door 114, 410, 497

Keystone Kids 55, 544

Khmers, Tigers and Talismans: From the History and Legends of Mysterious Cambodia 202, 301, 545

Kickle Snifters and other Fearsome Critters 142, 498, 507

The Kid's Guide to Social Action   105, 422, 449

The Kid from Tomkinsville   205, 260, 544

The Kid In the Red Jacket   182, 228, 470

Kidnapping of Christine Lattimore   188, 462

The Kidnapping of the Coffee Pot   161, 348, 501

Kid Power   84, 196, 360, 477

Kids Can Save the Animals: 101 Easy Things To Do   142, 389, 473

Kids Cooking Without a Stove: A Cookbook for Young Children

Kids Gardening: A First Indoor Gardening Book for Children   140, 373, 473

The Kid Who Batted 1.000   31, 248, 348, 377

Kildee House   167, 305, 452

Killer-of-Death   228, 258, 401

Killing Mr. Griffin   79, 126, 327

Kim   70, 542

A Kind of Wild Justice   48, 255, 402

The King, the Cat and the Fiddle   130, 260, 382, 448

The King's Daughter   108, 194, 382, 437, 496

The King's Equal   21, 473, 546

The King's Fifth   169, 283, 465

The King at the Door   87, 302

King Bidgood's in the Bathtub   41, 70, 92, 185, 226, 228, 566, 567

The Kingdom by the Sea   48, 102, 558

The Kingdom of the Riddles   127, 443

The Kingdom under the Sea   99, 478

King Grisly-Beard: A Tale from the Brothers Grimm   62, 156, 511, 536

King Krakus and the Dragon   157, 162, 324

King Leonard's Celebration   92, 311, 414

King Midas and the Golden Touch   99, 260

The King of Hermits and Other Stories   137, 510, 574

The King of Men   213, 304, 487

King of the Mountain Men: The Life of Jim Bridger   228, 288

King of the Seventh Grade   114, 189, 301

King of the Stallions   30, 282, 542

King of the Wind   167, 238, 319, 375

Kings, Bishops, Knights and Pawns: Life in a Feudal Society   47, 243, 254

King Solomon's Navy   114, 411

King Stork   26, 388, 486

King Tree   99, 345

King Tut's Game Board   81, 332

The King Who Saved Himself from Being Saved   137, 297, 358

King Wilbur the Third and the Bicycle   199, 378, 495

Kipper   172, 389

A Kiss for Little Bear   155, 451, 511

A Kiss Is Round: Verses   152, 273, 284

Kiss the Dust   56, 413

Kites, the Science and the Wonder   409

Kites: The Science and Wonder   150, 390

Kitten   192, 287, 499

Klara's New World   185, 565

Kleiner Eisbar, Wohin Fahrst Du?   178, 265

Kleiner Eisbar Nimm Micht Mit!   24, 315

Knee-deep in Thunder   155, 453, 472

The Knee-high Man and other Tales   53, 421, 479

Knee-knock Rise   169, 257

Knee Holes   194, 280

Knickerless Nicola   172, 440, 556

Knight's Castle   174, 273, 329

Knight's Fee   110, 389, 534

Knight Crusader   45, 531, 557

Knight on Horseback   145, 486

Knock at the Door, Emmy   21, 415, 447

Knowledge and Wonder: The Natural World as Man Knows It   78, 415, 557

KOALA Committee   117

Kojuro and the Bears   59, 454, 522

Koko's Kitten   151, 301, 473

Koko's Story   89, 301, 473

Komodo!   30, 520

Kongo and Kumba: Two Gorillas   87, 293, 505

Konrad   17, 265, 461, 464

Kopfblumen   22, 269, 494, 495

Krindlekrax   198, 492, 494

Kristli's Trees   43, 321, 328

Kristoffers Rejse   19, 249, 275

Ksiega Bajek Polskich (Book of Polish Fairy Tales)   20, 400, 457

The Kuia and the Spider   5, 359, 399

Kujuro and the Bears   14

The Ku Klux Klan: America's Recurring Nightmare   143, 304

Kwajo und das Geheimnis de Trommelmannchens   109, 255, 489

KwaZulu, South Africa   221, 444

L'Univers a Deux Voix Insecte   23, 464, 476

La Cachette   108, 251

La Chicane (The Wrangle)   108, 251

La Cite de l'an 2000   22, 486

The Lady and the Spider   24, 437, 446

Ladybird, Ladybird   100, 282

Lady Bird, Quickly   212, 404

Ladybug, Ladybug, Fly Away Home   138, 332, 373

Ladybugs   150, 396, 503

Lady for the Defense: A Biography of Belva Lockwood   72, 343

Lady of the Linden Tree   46, 478, 531

Lady Queen Anne: A Biography of Queen Anne of England   106, 380

The Lady Who Put Salt in Her Coffee   183, 367, 508

The Lady With the Alligator Purse   116, 558

The Lake at the End of the World   5, 60, 75, 102, 432

Lale, Die Turkin   9, 282, 553

The Land and People of Malaysia   139, 300

The Land and People of South Africa   209, 473

A Land Divided   97, 338, 373

Land for My Sons: A Frontier Tale of the American Revolution   205, 247, 305, 399

The Land I Lost: Adventures of a Boy in Vietnam   87, 232, 388, 434, 461

Land of Foam   211, 570

Land of the Rainbow Snake   147, 268, 572

Land Rush   228, 379, 438

Langston Hughes: A Biography   131, 448

Langston Hughes: Poet of his People   106, 382, 458

The Language of Life: An Introduction to the Science of Genetics   78, 263, 264, 509

Language of Man   126, 425

The Lantern Bearers   46, 402, 534

The Lark on the Wing   45, 342, 343, 345

Laser Light   149, 506, 549

Lassie Come Home   238, 258, 408

The Last Battle: A Story for Children   46, 263, 422

Last Chance Summer   77

The Last Guru   162, 479

The Last Innocent Summer   221, 343

The Last Mission   162, 441

The Last of the Mohicans   23, 277, 305

The Last of the Really Great Whangdoodles   74, 330

La Storia di Francesco e Chiara (Raccontata dai Bimbi di Croce)   22

The Last Rabbit   77, 310

The Last Run   230, 371

Last Voyage of the Unicorn   18, 309, 571

The Latchkey Children   47, 248, 402

The Late Great Me   42, 508

Laura Charlotte   184, 305, 347

Laura Ingalls Wilder's America: An Unflinching Assessment   65, 509

Lavender's Blue   46, 50, 107, 398, 424

Leader by Destiny: George Washington, Man and Patriot   166, 329, 496

Leading Little Ones to God: A Child's Book of Bible Teachings   91, 507, 532

Lean Out of the Window: An Anthology of Modern Poetry   213, 386, 489, 540

Leave It To Christy   145, 535

Leave Me Alone, Ma   146, 524

Leaves   23, 147, 148, 151, 334, 348, 445, 452, 483, 503, 515, 566

The Leaving   27, 236, 367, 564

Leaving Egypt   220, 495

Leaving Home   102, 454

Le Avventure de Cinque Ragazzi e un Cane   9, 354, 489

The Left Overs   58, 526

The Legend of Africania   118, 494, 537

Legend of Billy Bluesage   201, 295, 416

Legend of Odysseus   221, 304

The Legend of Rosepetal   158, 279, 576

The Legend of Scarface: A Blackfeet Indian Tale   157, 502

Legends and Folk Tales of Holland   136, 317, 404

Le Livre de la Creation   24, 264, 420

The Lemming Condition   161, 253, 503

Lena Horne   118, 372

Lenny Kandell, Smart Aleck 180, 303, 347

Leo, the Late Bloomer 12, 255, 410

Leonard Baskin's Miniature Natural History: First Series 158, 179, 262

Leonardo DaVinci 191, 484, 485

The Leopard 17, 139, 274, 334, 373, 482

Leo the Late Bloomer 12, 255, 410

Le Petit Chaperon Rouge 23, 453, 476

LeRoy and the Old Man 16, 287

Les Chemins Secrets de la Liberte 108, 313, 446, 523

Les Saltimbanques 9, 454, 466

Les Secrets de L'Image 23

Les Yeux de la d'ecouverte 24

Let's Be Enemies 211, 511, 545

Let's Celebrate 77, 106, 111, 472

Let's Celebrate! Canada's Special Days 106, 111, 472

Let's Find Out: A Picture Science Book 207, 266, 506

Let's Make Soup 142, 325, 395

Let's Pretend It Happened to You 141, 290, 443

The Letter, the Witch and the Ring 224, 266, 331

A Letter from India 99, 470

A Letter from Israel 99, 470

Letters from a Slave Girl 5, 95, 431

Letters From Atlantis 236, 359, 517

Letters from Rifka 69, 112, 376

Letters from Uncle David: Underground Hero 73, 555

Letters to a Friend on a Brown Paper Bag 73, 453

Letters To Oma: A Young German Girl's Account of Her First Year in Texas, 1847 229, 365, 559

Let the Circle be Unbroken 4, 118, 162, 217, 537

Let Them Live 208, 416

Let There Be Light: a Book About Windows 94, 353

Lewis Carroll's Alice's Adventures in Wonderland 8, 291, 357, 406, 455

Li'l Sis and Uncle Willie 105, 160, 334, 396

Libby on Wednesday 74, 524

The Liberation of Tansy Warner 174, 541

Lies, Deception, and Truth 69, 556

The Life and Death of a Brave Bull 140, 364, 566

Life in a Bucket of Soil 140, 491, 568

The Life of a Queen 154, 459, 482

A Life of Their Own: An Indian Family in Latin America 148, 393, 410, 551

Lift Every Voice and Sing 52, 156, 395, 496, 539

The Light at Tern Rock 167, 504, 507

Lighthouse Keeper's Daughter 87, 466, 557

The Lighthouse Keeper's Lunch 91, 253

A Light in the Attic 35, 88, 217, 232, 518

The Light Princess 155, 432, 511

Like Jake and Me 29, 170, 272, 399

A Likely Lad 47, 101, 256, 392

Lila on the Landing 203, 247, 329

Liliuokalani: Queen of Hawaii 141, 292, 435

Li Lun, Lad of Courage 49, 167, 174, 542, 560

Lily and the Bears 6, 497

Lily and the Present 70, 497

Lincoln: A Photobiography 94, 110, 113, 170, 344

Lindbergh: Lone Eagle 139, 317

The Line Up Book 111, 500

Lion 39, 210, 326

The Lion, the Witch, and the Wardrobe as Rite of Passage 66, 552

The Lion, the Witch and the Wardrobe 50, 66, 263, 422, 552

The Lion's Whiskers: Tales of High Africa 211, 255, 315, 537

The Lion and the Ostrich Chicks 118, 283

The Lion and the Rat: A Fable 98, 413, 561

The Lion and the Unicorn 65, 66, 275, 339, 418

A Lion for Lewis 144, 557

A Lion in the Meadow 91, 434, 563

A Lion in the Night 70, 248

Lions 150, 391, 468

Lions and Lobsters and Foxes and Frogs: Fables from Aesop 61, 358, 489

Lions in the Way 21, 33, 85, 495

Lions on the Hunt 205, 552, 560

Lisa 20, 439

Lisa of the Lyrebird Creek 34, 562

Listen! and Help Tell the Story 137, 286, 290

Listen - the Birds 154, 450, 460

Listen for the Singing 97, 425

The Listening Man 86, 333, 368

The Listening Walk 135, 247, 516

Listen to This 130, 293, 298

Literary Imagination 66, 443

Lito, the Shoeshine Boy 63, 296, 435

Little Angela and her Puppy 83, 436

A Little at a Time 64, 244, 273

The Little Bookroom 253, 335

Little Bear's Visit 39, 451, 511

Little Big-Feather 153, 275, 428

The Little Black Fish 22, 265, 448

Little Blacknose: The Story of a Pioneer 165, 535, 554

Little Blue and Little Yellow 12, 13, 153, 424

The Little Bookmobile: Colors, Numbers, and Shapes on Wheels 191, 361, 571

The Little Bookroom 9, 46, 49, 253, 335

The Little Bookroom: Eleanor Farjeon's Short Stories for Children Chosen by Herself 46, 49, 253

Little Brother 59, 258

Little by Little: A Writer's Education 29, 425

The Little Cowboy 208, 281, 521

Little Eight John 119, 298, 551

The Little Elephant 50, 153, 282, 366, 570

The Little Engine That Could 49, 372, 480

A Little Fear 28, 59, 173, 568

Little Fingerling: A Japanese Folktale 104, 111, 297, 385

The Little Fishes 3, 25, 213, 372, 396

Little Fox Goes to the End of the World 87, 541, 553

The Little French Farm 205, 365, 488

Little Girls without Their Curls 65, 408

Little Gorilla 202, 275

The Little Grey Men: A Story for the Young in Heart 45, 554

The Little Hen of Huronia 103, 571

The Little Horse Bus 31, 307, 361

The Little House 37, 49, 229, 232, 233, 287, 552, 561, 563

The Little House Cookbook 229, 552, 563

The Little House in the Big Woods 49, 561, 563

A Little House of Your Own 153, 209, 320, 365

The Little Island 38, 64, 281, 556

Little John 215, 426, 532

Little Little 93, 404

Little Lost Lamb 37, 281, 556

Little Love 118, 368

A Little Lower than the Angels 231, 441

The Little Man 17, 214, 401, 407, 432, 507

The Little Man and the Big Thief 214, 401, 432

The Little Mermaid 97, 104, 192, 250, 347, 435, 542

The Little Monster 15, 495, 538

Little Nino's Pizzeria 181, 259, 260

The Little Old Lady Who Was Not Afraid of Anything 70, 117, 426, 563

The Little Old Man Who Could Not Read 80, 270, 340

The Little Old Woman Who Used Her Head 52, 460, 499

Little Owl 141, 154, 257, 378, 575

Little Owl, Keeper of the Trees 141, 378

Little People in a Big Country 206, 301

Little Pickle 130, 302

Little Pieces of the West Wind 202, 350, 357

The Little Pig-a-wig and Other Rhymes About Pigs 272

A Little Princess: Being the Whole Story of Sara Crewe now Told for the First Time 51, 269, 286

Little Rabbit's Loose Tooth 41, 262, 316

Little Rascal 137, 285, 463

Little Red Cap 158, 307, 363, 576

Little Red Nose 209, 328, 506

Little Red Riding Hood 41, 94, 160, 180, 184, 363, 388, 453

A Little Schubert 156, 356

Little Sister and the Month Brothers 64, 320, 541

The Little Spotted Fish 63, 375, 571

The Littlest House 205, 300, 314

The Little Swineherd and other Tales 133, 343, 430

Little Though I Be   157, 429

Little Tim and the Brave Sea Captain   53, 253

Little Toot   51, 360

Little Town on the Prairie   166, 277, 513, 561

Little Tree   8, 83, 292, 309, 488

Little Tricker the Squirrel Meets Big Double the Bear   110

Little Tricker the Squirrel Meets Big Trouble the Bear   405, 455

Little Vic   231, 351, 512

The Little White Horse   45, 207, 358, 380

Little Witch   83, 267, 532

Little Women   50, 51, 66, 165, 246, 334, 415, 447, 523

Little Wu and the Watermelons   85, 425, 475

The Liverpool Cats   214, 409, 514

Lives and Half-Lives: Biographies of Women for Young Adults   66, 318

The Lives of Christopher Chant   48, 397

The Lives of Spiders   93, 472

Lives of the Musicians: Good Times, Bad Times (And What the Neighbors Thought)   30, 410

The Living Community: A Venture into Ecology   78, 115, 378, 529

Living in Two Worlds   234, 250, 496

Living with Dinosaurs   104, 375, 416

Liza Lou and the Yeller Belly Swamp   42, 440

Lizard   75, 306

Lizzy's Lion   97, 351, 418

The Load of the Unicorn   46, 370

The Loathsome Dragon   191, 399, 561

Lobo of the Tasaday   28, 459

The Lobster: It's Life Cycle   148, 537

Locked In Time   135, 189, 200, 327

Log of Christopher Columbus   152, 347

London's River: The Story of a City   47, 284, 305, 318

London Bridge Is Falling Down!   25, 526

Lone Journey: The Life of Roger Williams   167, 329, 390

Lonely Veronica   136, 328

The Loner   168, 483, 560

Lonesome Longhorn   208, 216, 416

Lone Star Fight   216, 329, 542

The Long-nosed Princess   211, 336, 368

A Long, Long Song   24, 318

Long Adventure: The Story of Winston Churchill   71, 373

The Long Black Coat   187, 267

Long Claws   44, 127, 383

The Long Dive   157, 522, 523

A Long Hard Journey: The Story of the Pullman Porter   5, 119, 235, 445

The Long Hungry Night   87, 300, 342, 563

Long Is a Dragon: Chinese Writing For Children   184, 357

Long Journey Home: Stories from Black History   52, 132, 421

Long Neck and Thunder Foot   100, 342, 478

The Long Night Watch   133, 525

The Long Red Scarf   59, 378, 483

The Long Road to Gettysburg   95, 457

Longtime Passing   58, 279

A Long Way From Tipperary   359

A Long Way From Verona   186, 215, 349

A Long Way to Frisco: A Folk Adventure Novel of California and Oregon in 1852   31, 313, 483

A Long Way To Tipperary   60

Long Wharf: A Story of Young San Francisco   205, 418, 475

The Long Winter   166, 277, 513, 561

Lon Po Po   30, 41, 572

Look! Look! Look!   159, 379

Look Again!   12, 13, 61, 156, 379

Look Alive, Libby   136, 313, 568

Look Closer!   146, 574

Look how Many People Wear Glasses: The Magic of Lenses   148, 279

Looking-for-Something   208, 297

Looking At Insects   106, 374, 534

Looking At the Moon   45, 475

Looking for Alibrandi   15, 60, 436

Looking for Something   481

Looking Out   4, 59, 276, 372, 392

Looking Out for Sampson   59, 372, 392

Looking the Tiger in the Eye: Confronting the Nuclear Threat   69, 264, 336

Look Out, Look Out, Mad Animals About   124, 410

Look What I Can Do   61, 156, 255

Loon's Necklace   103, 111, 111, 299, 542

Loosen your Ears   87, 335, 417

Lords of the Earth: The History of the Navajo Indians   230, 428

Lorenzo De'Medici and the Renaissance   214, 447, 552

The Lost Baron   205, 345, 569

Lost Cities and Vanished Civilizations   212, 517, 518

Lost Horse   31, 258, 309

Lost in the Barrens   43, 97, 107, 351, 456

Lost in the Devil's Desert   224, 509, 520

Lost in the Everglades   173, 481, 502

Lost in the Storm   63, 291

The Lost Kingdom   86, 257, 283

The Lothian Run   214, 387

Lotor the Raccoon   140, 309, 500

Lottie's Valentine   205, 335, 533

The Lotus Cup   174, 310

Louie's Lot   107, 377, 508

Love, Bid Me Welcome   216, 429

Love from Aunt Betty   144, 470, 471

Love in a Different Key   199, 343

Lovers' Games   144, 301

Love You Forever   172, 444, 457

The Lower East Side: A Portrait in Time   61, 293, 528

Low Tide   102, 440

The Luck Child   99, 294, 363

Lucky Blacky   152, 361, 413

The Lucky Yak   157, 417, 504

Lucy Forever & Miss Rosetree, Shrinks   189, 516

Ludell   132, 235, 562

Luke and the Van Zandt County War   220, 249, 304

Luke Was There   56, 300, 316

Lumberjack   63, 156, 161, 412

Lupita Manana   4, 264

Lyle, Lyle, Crocodile   53, 551

M.C. Higgins, the Great   26, 53, 108, 132, 161, 169, 368

M.C. Higgins, the Great by Virginia   26, 53, 108, 132, 161, 169, 368

M.E. and Morton   122, 292

M.V. Sexton Speaking: A Novel   171, 461

M & M and the Bad News Babies   88, 366, 497

MacDonald's Encyclopedia of Africa   221

The Machine Breakers: The Story of the Luddites   176, 284

The Machine Gunners   27, 47, 101, 558

The Macmillan Book of Greek Gods and Heroes   113, 429, 531

Macmillan Illustrated Animal Encyclopedia   151, 560

Mad, Mad, Monday   80, 518

Madame Doubtfire   102, 182, 338

Made in India   207, 422, 526

Madeleine and the Bad Hat   210

Madeline   37, 38, 152, 266, 531

Madeline's Rescue   38, 152, 266

Madeline and the Bad Hat   266

Mad Mad Monday   80, 518

The Maggie B.   21, 63, 178, 365

The Magical Adventures of Pretty Pearl   118, 180, 368

The Magic Balloon   214, 436

Magic Beach   14, 421

Magic Carpet   184, 279, 508

The Magic Circle of Laura Ingalls Wilder   66, 566

The Magic Currant Bun   152, 344, 535

The Magic Fan   223, 258

The Magic Feather Duster   153, 424, 454

The Magic Flute   155, 453, 526

Magic for Mary M.   216, 452

Magic for Sale   23, 466, 571

The Magician   62, 215, 476, 516

The Magic Inkstand and other Stories   109, 510, 536

Magic in the Mist   63, 389, 406

Magic in the Movies: The Story of Special Effects   149, 367, 465

The Magic Leaf   181, 295, 455

The Magic Listening Cap: More Folk Tales from Japan   209, 545

Magic Maize   168, 284

The Magic Meadow   171, 405

The Magic of the Glits   73, 93, 232, 244, 341

The Magic Orange Tree and Other Haitian Folktales   149, 375, 566

Magic or Not?   211, 274, 329

The Magic Paintbrush   97, 456

The Magic Rabbit   76, 418

The Magic School Bus at the Waterworks   29, 54, 70, 85, 96, 226, 302, 316

The Magic School Bus Inside the Earth   225, 302, 316

The Magic School Bus Inside the Human Body   89, 302, 316

The Magic School Bus Lost in the Solar System   89, 302, 316

The Magic Spear and Other Stories of China's Famous Heroes   204, 307, 543, 570

The Magic Stone   108, 381, 409, 565

The Magic Tears   61, 156, 451, 510

The Magic Tree   12, 26, 443

Magic With Everything   82, 286

The Magnificent Moo   180, 342

Magnificent Nose & Other Marvels   60, 74, 338, 348

The Magnificent Nose and Other Marvels   74, 338, 348

Magnolia's Mixed-up Magic   74, 283, 462

The Magpie Island   58, 367, 538

The Magpies   70, 346, 356

Mahatma Gandhi: The Father of Nonviolence   31, 343, 475

The Maid and the Mouse and the Odd-Shaped House: A Story in Rhyme   158, 573

Maisy Goes to Bed   186, 306

Major Corby and the Unidentified Flapping Object   72, 321

Major Resolution   127, 362

Make a Joyful Noise unto the Lord! The life of Mahalia Jackson   234, 391

Make a Joyful Sound   104, 384, 521, 548

Make it Happy: What Sex Is All About   221, 306, 387

The Makers   66, 403

Make Way for Ducklings   37, 442

Make Way for Sam Houston   163, 230, 346, 484

Making a Book   221, 335, 539

Making Music   145, 474

The Making of Man   46, 306, 384

Making our Way: America at the Turn of the Century in the Words of the Poor and Powerless   63, 401

Malachi Mudge   155, 293, 472

Malcolm X: By Any Means Necessary   74, 458

The Malibu and other Poems   202, 426, 525

Mama, Do You Love Me?   95, 398, 417

Mama's Going to Buy You a Mockingbird   44, 195, 425

Mama Don't Allow   28, 387

Mame's Cats 1, 2, 3   23

The Man   125, 279

Man Against Earth: The Story of Tunnels and Tunnel Builders   135, 457, 490

Man and Machines. The Mitchell Beazley Joy of Knowledge Library   221, 452

Man and Magic   138, 252, 414

Manatee: On Location   24, 312, 313

MA NDA LA   13, 245, 443

The Man from Ironbark   58, 381, 472

The Man From the Other Side   17, 115, 467

The Mangrove Summer   91, 415

Manhattan   130, 165, 408, 453, 547

Maniac Magee   29, 35, 54, 83, 84, 105, 126, 170, 172, 193, 223, 232, 526

Man in Space to the Moon   140, 278, 355

The Man in the Box: A Story from Vietnam   196, 328

The Man in the Woods   225, 557

Manko Kapak   9, 366, 394, 548

Man Must Measure: The Wonderful World of Mathematics   46, 251, 380, 504

Manners Matter   143, 411, 412, 521

The Manners Zoo   139, 274, 543

A Man of the Family   216, 286

The Mantis and the Moon   84, 481, 550

Manuel Zigenarpojken   9, 463, 497

The Man Who Sang the Sillies   32, 297, 358

The Man Who Took the Indoors Out   63, 156, 427

The Man Who Wanted To Live Forever   182, 292, 372

The Man Who Was Don Quixote: The Story of Miguel Cervantes   50, 287

Manya's Story   53, 360

Many Moons   4, 37, 192, 377, 519, 521, 540

Many Smokes, Many Moons: A Chronology of American Indian History through Indian Art   46, 251, 380, 504

The Many Ways of Seeing: An Introduction to the Pleasures of Art   169, 453

The Maplin Bird   47, 213, 249, 477

The Map Maker   97, 567

Map Making: The Art that Became a Science   32, 281

A Map of Nowhere   48, 308

Marassa and Midnight   47, 330, 533

Marc & Pixie & the Walls in Mrs. Jones' Garden   141, 328

Marc Chagall   85, 294, 362

The March Wind   210, 273, 491

Marguerite de Angeli's Book of Nursery and Mother Goose Rhymes   39, 315

Marian Anderson   234, 473

Marianne Po Sykehus   9, 280

Marie Curie: Woman of Genius   139, 292, 317

Marked by Fire   8, 163, 538

The Mark of Conte   202, 422, 459

The Mark of the Horse Lord   186, 534

Marmalade's Christmas Present   16, 559

Marooned on Mars   31, 318, 507

The Marrow of the World   44, 389, 461

Marshamallow   460

Marshmallow   37

Martha Speaks   160, 447

Martin Buber: Wisdom in our Time   114, 518

Martin Luther   117, 118, 119, 209, 221, 282, 406, 441, 446, 473, 506, 554

Martin Luther King, Jr.: Man of Peace   117, 441, 473

Martin Luther King, Jr. and the Freedom Movement   119, 473

Martin Luther King: America's Great Non-Violent Leader   221, 282, 506

Martze   138, 451, 510

The Marvelous Journey Through the Night   160, 374

Marvelous Me   91, 542, 546

The Marvelous Misadventures of Sebastian: Grand Extravaganza, including a Performance by the Entire Cast of the Gallimaufry-Theatricus   131, 247

Marvin & Me & the Flies   128, 432

Mary Anne   144, 324, 360

Mary Jane   21, 166, 235, 291, 308, 381, 529

Mary of Mile 18   44, 271

Mary Poppins   134, 514, 542

The Marzipan Moon   162, 512, 562

Mass Media   126, 303, 374

The Master of Miracle: A New Novel of the Golem   114, 160, 390, 427

Master of the Grove   58, 403

The Master Puppeteer   132, 188, 473, 557

The Matchlock Gun   50, 166, 330, 415

Matilda   12, 17, 25, 54, 56, 58, 81, 98, 105, 126, 130, 135, 156, 172, 178, 224, 225, 228, 266, 271, 283, 311, 322, 347, 353, 403, 472

Matilda Jane   130, 353

Matilda Who Told Lies and Was Burned to Death   12, 156, 266, 403

Matt and Jo   236, 525

A Matter of Pride   87, 308, 413

Matthew and his Dad   144, 246

Mattimeo   121, 228, 294, 392

Maurice Sendak's Ritual Cooking of the Child in Three Tableaux   66, 476

Max   64, 390

Max, the Bad-Talking Parrot   90, 318, 573

Max, the Music Maker   149, 400, 528

Max's Chocolate Chicken   113, 557

Max's Christmas   113, 145, 557

Max and Diana and the Beach Day   145, 395, 574

Max and Diana and the Birthday Present   145, 396, 574

Max and Diana and the Snowy Day   145, 396, 574

Maxie, Rosie and Earl: Partners in Grime   183, 470, 533

Max Smart and the Perilous Pellets   33, 397

Maybe It's a Pirate   131, 378, 572

Mayday! Mayday!   79, 451

Mayflower Man   75, 516

May I Bring a Friend?   39, 106, 320, 453

McBroom Tells the Truth   51, 340, 558

McBroom the Rainmaker   93, 340, 558

McElligot's Pool   38, 238, 512

McGoogan Moves the Mighty Rock   162, 347

Meagher of the Sword: A Dramatization of the Life of Thomas Francis Meagher   36, 530

Me and Caleb   85, 449, 523

Me and Frumpet: An Adventure with Size and Science   210, 546

Me and Jeshua   15, 59, 304, 526

Me and My Little Brain   218, 339, 517

Me and My Million   27, 101, 406

Me and the Weirdos   224, 410, 534

Meaning Well   93, 302, 488

Meanwhile Back at the Ranch 70, 145, 172, 463, 497

Meat Pies and Sausages 64, 429, 548

The Media Lab: Inventing the Future at MIT 151, 278

The Media Works 126, 309, 546

A Medley of Folk Songs 19, 253

The Meeker Massacre 229, 468, 473

Meeting with a Stranger 3, 235, 277, 395

Meet the Beaver 145, 499

Meet the Opossum 144, 468, 499

Megan's Island 189, 493

Meg and Maxie 102, 494

Meggy MacIntosh 165, 315, 361

Mei Li 37, 369

Melanie and the Night Animal 60, 499

Melissa Finds a Mystery 43, 449

The Mellops Go Flying 210, 545

The Member for the Marsh 46, 413, 440

Memo: To Myself When I Have a Teenage Kid 144, 524

Memory 29, 173, 434

Men, Microscopes and Living Things 107, 168, 210, 488, 515

Men Against War 3, 366

Men of Athens 168, 304, 396

Merchants of the Mysterious East 104, 423

Meriwether Lewis: Boy Explorer 174, 264, 292

Merlin Dreams 100, 321, 418

Merry, Merry FIBruary 157, 427, 467

Merry Christmas, Amelia Bedelia 89, 470, 535

Merry Christmas, Harry 142, 294

Merry Ever After: The Story of Two Medieval Weddings 13, 14, 157, 161, 415

Merry Go Round in Oz 18, 438, 444, 551

Messing Around with Water Pumps and Siphons 149, 423, 575

Mexico and the United States 234, 338

The Mice Came in Early this Year 72, 310, 415

Mice Twice 40, 429

Michael the Colt 206, 349

Mickey, the Horse that Volunteered 206, 307, 355

The Microbes, Our Unseen Friends 148, 497

Micromysteries: Stories of Scientific Detection 8, 367

Middl'un 229, 286, 497

The Middle Button 205, 263, 568

The Middle Moffat 166, 334, 521

The Middle of Somewhere 5, 358

The Midnight Adventures of Kelly, Dot, and Esmeralda 215, 357

Midnight Blue 198, 339

The Midnight Farm 192, 393, 423

The Midnight Fox 52, 288, 362

The Midnight Horse 184, 340, 520

Midnight Is a Place 161, 245, 436

Midshipman Plowright 36, 481

Mightier Than the Sword 82, 269

Mighty Hunter 37, 366

Mighty Microbes 195, 570

The Mighty Slide 199, 245, 550

Migrant Girl 56, 413

Mijn Held 24, 381

Mijn Held (My Hero) 381

Mikosch das Karusselpferd 10, 572

Milenka's Happy Summer 36, 260, 415

The Milkweed and Its World of Animals 148, 359, 424

Mill 135, 161, 171, 179, 265, 313, 431, 449, 450, 483, 557

The Miller, his Son, and their Donkey 136, 329

A Million Guitars and Other Stories 106, 274

Millions of Cats 49, 165, 347

Milton Hershey: Chocolate King 140, 388, 435

Milton the Early Riser 12, 13, 160, 254, 255, 410

The Min-Min 57, 298, 447

Mina Olen Lammenpei 9, 400, 462

Mine's the Best 215, 275

Mine for Keeps 121, 425, 470

Minerva Louise 76, 531

Ming Lo Moves the Mountain 179, 427

Minn of the Mississippi 31, 167, 381

The Minnow Leads to Treasure 49, 210, 253, 474

Minnow on the Say 46, 107, 253, 474

The Minpins 34, 192, 267, 311

The Minstrel and the Mountain: A Tale of Peace 33, 494, 571

Minutemen of the Sea 85, 300, 468

Miracles on Maple Hill 168, 411, 525

The Miracle Tree 15, 439, 569

The Miraculous Hind 44, 299

Mirandy and Brother Wind 41, 119, 445, 479

Mirette on the High Wire 41, 160, 443

The Mirror in the Sea: Treasure Island and the Internalization of Romance 65, 270

The Mirror Puzzle Book 151, 553

The Mirrorstone 198, 418, 469, 513

Mischief in Fez 206, 331, 380

Mischling, Second Degree: My Childhood in Nazi Germany 4, 27, 53, 133, 409

Misery Guts 60, 355

Mishka 99, 249

Misplaced Persons 369

Miss Fanshawe and the Great Dragon Adventure 130, 509

Miss Fix-it 137, 317

Miss Happiness and Miss Flower 46, 211, 356, 484

Miss Hickory 167, 257, 349

Missing May 30, 105, 170, 185, 190, 500

Missing Since Monday 145, 437

Mississippi Bridge 69, 354, 537

Mississippi Challenge 69, 119, 553

Miss Jaster's Garden 156, 274

Miss Nelson Has a Field Day 96, 172, 247, 437

Miss Nelson Is Back 70, 96, 179, 247, 437

Miss Nelson Is Missing! 11, 35, 42, 90, 172, 188, 247, 437

Missouri River Boy 33, 369, 376

Miss Pickerell Goes to Mars 239, 348, 432

Miss Rumphius 8, 123, 191, 305

Miss Suzy's Birthday 156, 427, 572

Mister Corbett's Ghost 155, 300, 350

Mister Magnolia 108, 271

Mistress of the White House 207, 306, 454

Misty of Chincoteague 50, 167, 319, 375

Moccasin Trail 50, 168, 348, 444

Model-A Mule 85, 441, 564

Model Boats that Really Go 164, 490

The Moffats 50, 334, 521

Moffatt's Road 102, 251, 436

Moja Means One: Swahili Counting Book 12, 13, 40, 336

Moke and Poki in the Rain Forest 141, 347

Molly's New Washing Machine 159, 352, 439

Molly's Pilgrim 144, 301, 320

Molly the Rogue 206, 480, 553

A Moment of Silence 67, 392, 502, 544

Mommy, Buy Me a China Doll 13, 573, 574

Monarch Butterfly 136, 416, 436

Monday in Odessa 115, 514

The Money Machine 139, 482, 493

Monica: The Story of a Young Magazine Apprentice 43, 331, 520

Monkey's Crazy Hotel 192, 495, 569

Monkey and the Three Wizards 199, 342, 371, 569

The Monkey and the Wild, Wild Wind 3, 396, 423

Monkey in the Jungle 26, 387, 483

Monkey Puzzle and other Poems 72, 344, 426

Monkeys: The Japanese Macaques 150, 462, 468

Monkey Tricks 34, 255

The Monster's Ring 200, 306

The Monster Bed 192, 548, 564

Monster Den; or, Look What Happened at my House - and To It 138, 155, 297, 358

The Monster Garden 48, 246

Monster Slayer: a Navajo Folktale 229, 282, 559

The Monster Who Ate Australia 237, 502

A Month of Christmases 216, 396, 453

Moon-bells and other Poems 196, 385

Moon-Flash 180, 445

The Moon: Earth's Natural Satellite 135, 278, 565

Moon and Me 199, 390

Moonbeam on a Cat's Ear 104, 351

The Moon in the Cloud 47, 214, 371

The Moon Is Like a Silver Sickle: A Celebration of Poetry by Russian Children 141, 402, 455

The Moon Jumpers 39, 511, 545

The Moonlight Man 163, 343

The Moonlit Journey 131, 465

Moon Man 12, 191, 213, 545

Moon Moth 137, 384, 388

The Moon Ribbon and Other Tales   93, 469, 571

The Moon Seems to Change   135, 275, 278

More, More, More, Said the Baby: 3 Love Stories   41, 564

More Bugs in Boxes: A Pop-up book about Color   183, 292

More Just So Stories   51, 265, 407

More Minden Curses   188, 493, 533

More Scary Stories to Tell in the Dark   35, 80, 348, 507

More Small Poems   64, 257, 568

More Stories Julian Tells   181, 289, 533

More Surprises   117, 382, 426

More Tales of Uncle Remus: Further Adventures of Brer Rabbit   190, 370, 421, 479

More Tongue Tanglers and a Rigmarole   212, 482, 561

More Wires and Watts   152, 403, 439

Morning Arrow   73, 324, 430

Morning Girl   173, 325

The Morning Side of the Hill   43, 489

Morning Song   73, 379

Morning Star, Black Sun: The Northern Cheyenne Indians and America's Energy Crisis   234, 255, 303

The Morning the Sun Refused to Shine   180, 498

Morris's Disappearing Bag: A Christmas Story   21, 557

Morse, Marconi and You: Understanding and Building Telegraph, Telephone and Radio Sets   149, 403, 439

Mosaic   65, 552

Moses Beech   173, 532

Moses in the Bulrushes   163, 388

Mosses   150, 391, 396

Mossflower   228, 294, 392

The Most Amazing Hide and Seek Alphabet Book   129, 309

The Most Beautiful Place in the World   4, 56, 248, 289

The Most Wonderful Doll in the World   38, 443, 532

Mote   75, 189, 489

Mother, Mother, I Feel Sick, Send for the Doctor Quick, Quick, Quick   33, 295, 534

The Mother Beaver   61, 387

Mother Crocodile Maman-Caiman   118, 323, 365, 529

Mother Goose   37, 543

Mother Goose and Nursery Rhymes   39, 489

The Mother Goose Book   13, 14, 157, 161, 484, 485

Mother Goose Riddle Rhymes   152, 429

Mother Goose Treasury   98, 279

Motherland: West Indian Women to Britain in the 1950s   176, 324

Motherstone   91, 351

Mother Teresa of Calcutta   53, 351, 449, 536

Motorcycle on Patrol: The Story of a Highway Officer   203, 376

Motown and Didi: A Love Story   118, 458

The Mouldy   125, 263, 440

Mountain Born   167, 545, 570

The Mountain of Truth   215, 290, 494

Mountains are Free   165, 314, 458

The Mountains of Tibet   159, 164, 353

Mount Delightful: The Story of Ellen Evans and Her Dog Taffy   174, 392, 571

Mounted Messenger   206, 447, 566

Mount Joy   214, 461

The Mount Rushmore Story   69, 94, 501

The Mouse and the Motorcycle   98, 103, 134, 218, 231, 239, 298, 313

The Mouse and the Song   63, 429, 493

Mouse Cafe   156, 304

The Mousehole Cat   34, 100, 259, 263

Mouse Paint   190, 553

The Mouse Rap   183, 458

Mouse Tales   21, 427

The Mousewife   208, 326, 356

Mousewoman and the Vanished Princesses   44, 108, 370, 536

The Moved-outers   55, 167, 271, 447

Move Over, Twerp   116, 247

The Moves Make the Man   28, 163, 170, 280

Movie Shoes   208, 533

Moving Heavy Things   149, 244

Mowje Bozorg   109, 283, 353

Moy Moy   201, 481

The Mozart Season   104, 120, 184, 566

Mr. and Mrs. Noah   207, 420

Mr. and Mrs. Pig's Evening Out   161, 488

Mr. Archimedes' Bath   147, 248

Mr. Fox   5, 270

Mr. Gumpy's Motor Car   64, 286

Mr. Gumpy's Outing   26, 61, 99, 156, 160, 286

Mr. Jordan in the Park   146, 300

Mr. Justice Holmes   77, 168, 399, 541

Mr. Magnolia   56, 99

Mr. McBroom's Wonderful One-Acre Farm   108

Mr. Michael Mouse Unfolds His Tale   156, 307

Mr. Miller the Dog   157, 374

Mr. Moon's Last Case   188, 453, 473

Mr. Mysterious & Co.   197, 208, 212, 328, 340, 347, 361, 542, 546, 550

Mr. Penny's Race Horse   39, 334

Mr. Plunkett's Pool   16, 319, 499

Mr. Popper's Penguins   49, 166, 238, 256, 417

Mr. Potter's Pigeon   130, 292, 406

Mr. Rabbit and the Lovely Present   39, 511, 575

Mr. Revere and I   31, 417

Mr. Slim Goodbody Presents the Inside Story   142, 286, 407

Mr. Squint   23, 472

Mr. T.W. Anthony Woo: The Story of a Cat and a Dog and a Mouse   38, 208, 334

Mr. Tootwhistle's Invention   205, 557

Mr. Totter and the Five Black Cats   174, 264, 538

Mr. Yowder and the Giant Bull Snake   53, 498

Mr. Yowder and the Lion Roar Capsules   171, 498

Mrs. Cockle's Cat   98, 434, 474

Mrs. Easter and the Storks   98, 326

Mrs. Frisby and the Rats of NIMH   26, 52, 126, 132, 169, 222, 231, 239, 268, 465

Mrs. Gaddy and the Ghost   88, 366, 528

Mrs. Hanna Nuba   116

Mrs. Katz and Tush   481

Mrs. McGinty and the Bizarre Plant   70, 270

Mrs. Moskowitz and the Sabbath Candlesticks   115, 219, 508

Mrs. Pig Gets Cross and Other Stories   182, 488

Mrs. Plug the Plumber   176, 245, 568

Mrs. Portree's Pony   199, 367

Mufaro's Beautiful Daughters   29, 41, 118, 181, 529

Muggie Maggie   89, 298, 423

Mulga Bill's Bycycle   58, 108, 462, 472

Mum - I Feel Funny!   221, 350, 432, 446

Mummies Made in Egypt   88, 247

Mundo and the Weather Child   102, 327

The Murder of Hound Dog Bates: a novel   163, 188, 278

Murdo's Story: A Legend from Northern Manitoba   97, 348, 509

Murgatroyd's Garden   59, 572, 573

Muru Menee Kalaan   10, 536

The Mushroom Center Disaster   63, 272, 274

Mushrooms   150, 391, 396

Music, Music for Everyone   4, 564

Mustang: Wild Spirit of the West   97, 196, 228, 375, 428

Mustard   21, 228, 321, 359

My Aunt Mary Went Shopping   6, 367, 486

My Brother Bird   209, 250, 326

My Brother Sam Is Dead   3, 132, 169, 302

My Brother Sammy   130, 547

My Brother Sean   99, 278, 426

My Brother Stevie   235, 300, 460

My Brother Was Mozart   86, 458, 485, 559

My Cat Likes To Hide in Boxes   91, 324, 534

My Cat Maisie   6, 248

My Daddy Was a Soldier: A World War II Story   184, 488

My Daniel   230, 304

My Darling Villain   227, 259

My Enemy, My Brother   214, 342

My Father's Dragon   51, 167, 207, 349

My Father Hijacked a Plane   73, 318

My First Book of Time   222, 426

My First Cook Book   192, 562

My Friend, the Vampire   225, 355, 525

My Grampa has Big Pockets   123, 572

My Grandmother's Stories   219, 352, 398

My Grandson Lew   68, 326, 575

My Horrible Secret   197, 461, 496

My Little Hen   13, 484, 485

My Little Red Car   185, 318

My Mama Needs Me   118, 309, 553

My Mate Shofiq   102, 459

My Mom Hates Me in January   172, 318, 336

My Mom Travels a Lot   68, 157, 262, 471

My Mother Is the Most Beautiful Woman in the World   38, 349, 491

My Mother Never Listens To Me   80, 457, 513

My Name Is Not Odessa Yarker   111, 333, 347

My Name Is Pablo   213, 311, 525

My own Private Sky   111, 264

My Place   59, 60, 110, 237, 371, 378, 379, 421, 488, 559

My Place in Space   60, 371, 378, 379, 421

My Robot Buddy   134, 505, 521

My Side of the Mountain   9, 51, 168, 216, 352

My Sister   92, 215, 235, 287, 378, 389

My Sister's Keeper   92, 215, 287

The Mysteries in the Commune   144, 369, 521

The Mysteries of Harris Burdick   21, 29, 158, 191, 546

The Mysterious Disappearance of Leon (I Mean Noel)   61, 487

The Mysterious Red Tape Gang   188, 462, 503

The Mysterious Tadpole   21, 403

The Mystery at Crane's Landing   36, 187, 540

Mystery at Love's Creek   137, 293

Mystery Cottage in Left Field   188, 290

Mystery in the Frozen Lands   20, 236, 356

Mystery in Wales   187, 247

Mystery Island   30, 273, 542

The Mystery Man   187, 305, 357

The Mystery of Ghost Valley   187, 290

The Mystery of Shadow Walk   43, 455

The Mystery of the Bewitched Bookmobile   92, 340, 374

The Mystery of the Creaking Windmill   174, 334

Mystery of the Eagle's Claw   188, 568

Mystery of the Fat Cat   187, 274, 275, 522

The Mystery of the Haunted Pool   187, 195, 367, 560

The Mystery of the Hidden Hand   187, 367, 560

The Mystery of the Missing Red Mitten   63, 403

Mystery of the Old Musket   138, 445, 573

The Mystery of the Red Tide   187, 275

Mystery of the Scowling Boy   187, 362, 560

Mystery of the Talking Totem Pole   43, 457

The Mystery of the Tarnished Trophy   106, 291

Mystery of the Velvet Box   187, 351, 505

Mystery of the Witch Who Wouldn't   187, 480

The Mystery of 22 East   187, 554

The Mystery Waters of Tonbridge Wells   142, 274, 438

Mystical Fantasy for Children: Silence and Community   66, 339

My Teacher Is an Alien   135, 306, 565

My Teacher Sleeps in School   80, 90, 556

Myths and Legends of Maoriland   90, 323, 489, 567

My Time of Year   154, 325, 333

My Uncle   158, 167, 179, 339, 341, 539

My Very Own Animated Jewish Holiday Activity Book   146, 480

My Village, My World   214, 459, 503

My Village, Sturbridge   157, 276, 451

My War with Goggle- eyes   102

My War With Goggle Eyes   338

Na-ni   12, 320

Nadia the Willful   203, 247, 272

A Name for Obed   205, 420, 478

The Name of the Tree   104, 129, 131, 428, 552

The Namesake: A Story of King Alfred   47, 107, 380

Nansen   166, 205, 254, 367

Naomi   93, 486

Napoleon   146, 555

The Napping House   42, 94, 158, 203, 567

The Nargun and the Stars   58, 107, 161, 568

Narrative Fractures and Fragments   66, 377

Narzeczony z Morza   19, 531, 533

Nate the Great and the Missing Key   88, 513, 519

Nate the Great and the Snowy Trail   88, 513, 519

Nathan, Boy of Capernaum   206, 423, 552

Nathaniel Talking   119, 354, 362

National Mathematics Project: Mathematics for Secondary Schools Year 5   222, 370

Native American Doctor: The Story of Susan LaFlesche Picotte   204, 235, 237

Native American Testimony: An Anthology of Indian and White Relations: First Encounter to Dispossession   234

The Natives Are Always Restless   136, 351, 486

The Nativity   29, 550

Natural Fire: Its Ecology in Forests   149, 484

Natural History   4, 29, 62, 100, 105, 147, 157, 158, 179, 232, 254, 262, 286, 293, 356, 431, 452, 481, 537, 539

Natural History from A to Z   105, 254

A Natural History of Giraffes   62, 147, 431, 452

The Naturalists' Year   151, 289

Nature's Clean-up Crew: The Burying Beetles   150, 451

The Nature of the Beast   48, 173, 231, 384

Naughty Children   212, 253, 277

Naya Nuki: Girl Who Ran   105, 386, 539

A Near Thing for Captain Najork   157, 271, 379

Neighborhood Odes   105, 321, 525

Nell's Quilt   72, 538

Nelson Malone Meets the Man from Mushnut   145, 324, 373

Nessa's Fish   184, 421, 552

Nettie Jo's Friends   183, 304, 445

Never Go Anywhere with Digby   3, 471, 551

Never Say Yes to a Stranger   145, 461, 540

Never Spit on Your Shoes   42, 293

Never Steal a Magic Cat   84, 293, 469

Never to Forget: The Jews of the Holocaust   4, 26, 114, 219, 448

The New Baby   83, 399, 495

A New Coat for Anna   145, 426, 574

The New Creatures   184, 353

New Found Land   180, 297

New Found World   167, 206, 335, 515

New Guys Around the Block   180, 365

New Jersey   493

The New Kid on the Block   80, 88, 483, 530

New Kids on the Block   235, 273

New Land   166, 324, 506

New Moon Cove   26, 201, 256

A New Mother for Martha   72, 361, 430

The New Nutcracker Suite and other Innocent Verses   211, 296, 459

The New Oxford School Atlas   222, 555

New Perspectives Book 1: An English Course   221, 265, 408

The News About Dinosaurs   151, 175, 416

The New York Herald Tribune   204

The New York Kid's Book: 170 Children's Writers and Artists Celebrate New York City   68, 162, 330

The New York Review   66, 430

The New York Times Book Review   152, 160

The New York Time's Choice of Best Illustrated Children's Book of the Year Next, Please   32, 261

Nice Work, Little Wolf!   198, 465

Nicholas: A Manhattan Christmas Story   165, 453, 547

Nicholas and the Moon Eggs   23, 555

Nicholas Cricket   159, 399, 439

Nicolas, Where Have You Been?   4, 424

Night Cars   104, 111, 131, 264, 392

Night Cry   188, 459

Night Fall   187, 245

The Nightingale   51, 158, 212, 250, 285, 318, 419

The Night Journey   114, 219, 389, 416

Night Kites   42, 404

Nightmare Mountain   96, 238, 402

Nightmares: Poems to Trouble your Sleep   64, 427, 483

Night Noises   192, 319, 343

Night Noises by Mem Fox   192, 319, 343

Night of Ghosts and Hermits   151, 348, 532

The Night of the Bozos   144, 521

Night of the Twisters   96, 112, 112, 122, 196, 200, 499

The Night Ones   184, 310, 364

Night on Neighborhood Street   119, 354, 362

Night Owls   87, 319, 401

Night Spell   188, 285, 461

The Night Swimmers   7, 27, 288, 384

Night Talks   144, 351

The Nightwalker   171, 387

The Night Watchmen   47, 186, 308, 341

The Night Workers   137, 507, 529

Nighty-nightmare   89, 384, 454

Nilda   3, 160, 452

Nimby   226, 541

Nine Cry-baby Dolls   206, 268, 429

Nine Days to Christmas   39, 334, 412

Nine Lives of Moses on the Oregon Trail   215, 253

Nineteenth Century Fiction   65, 408

Nino   166, 181, 252, 259, 260

Nkwala   97, 107, 121, 513, 565

The No-Return Trail   53, 230, 422

Noah's Ark   8, 14, 40, 53, 68, 108, 134, 157, 181, 498, 526

Noah and the Rainbow: An Ancient Story   61, 245, 274, 284

Nobody's Family Is Going to Change   176, 340

Nobody Asked Me if I Wanted a Baby Sister   61, 247

Nobody Has to Be a Kid Forever   88, 303

Nobody Listens to Andrew   85, 365, 530

Nobody Said It Would Be Easy   11, 368

Nobody Wants a Nuclear War   4, 549

No Bones   152, 473, 514

No End to Yesterday   230, 432

No Girls Allowed and other Stories   137, 516

No Hero for the Kaiser   17, 181, 307, 344, 528

Noisy Nora   62, 557

No Jumping on the Bed!   71, 80, 90, 172, 226, 254

No Mires Aquel Iris   24, 464, 548

No More Magic   188, 256

No Mules   99, 470

None but the Brave: A Story of Holland   206, 327, 437

The Nonsense Book   52, 333, 466

The Noonday Friends   169, 355, 532

No One Is Going to Nashville   21, 272, 399

No Promises in the Wind   85, 386

The Nor'westers: The Fight for the Fur Trade   97, 289, 404

Nordy Bank   47, 431, 482

The Norman Rockwell Storybook   174, 494, 551

No Room: An Old Story   51, 324, 331

The North American Indians: Life and Lore   33, 268

North Carolina Parade: Stories of History and People   171, 282, 533, 553

A Northern Alphabet   104, 109, 371

North of Danger   71, 338, 501

North Star Shining   207, 535, 554

North to Freedom   33, 53, 381, 406

North Woods Whammy   208, 314

Norwegian Folk Tales   211, 255, 407, 452, 557

The Nose Tree   158, 388

No Shelter   82, 431

No Star Nights   112, 396, 523

No Strangers to Violence, No Strangers to Love   53, 369

No Swimming in Dark Pond and Other Chilling Tales   80, 145, 358

The Not-Just-Anybody Family   181, 288, 495

Nothing's Fair in Fifth Grade   35, 42, 64, 70, 79, 89, 92, 96, 112, 121, 122, 126, 134, 172, 218, 220, 315

Nothing At All   19, 37, 347, 420

Nothing But the Truth   30, 170, 256

Nothing Ever Happens on My Block   12, 155, 213, 487

Nothing to Be Afraid of   48, 102, 436, 471

No Tigers in Africa   102, 517

Not So Fast, Songololo   181, 312

Not Very Much of a House   138, 249, 307

No Way of Telling   26, 47, 522

Nowhere to Play   176, 331, 412

Now Is Your Time! The African-American Struggle for Freedom   5, 95, 119, 175, 458

Nuclear Age Literature for Youth   66, 420

The Nuclear Arms Race: Can We Survive It?   69, 556

The Number on my Grandfather's Arm   219, 244, 331

Number the Stars   5, 54, 84, 92, 98, 115, 170, 197, 219, 429

The Number 24   156, 269

Nutcracker   158, 211, 296, 380, 435, 459, 511

The Nutcrackers and the Sugar-tongs   157, 418, 512

The O'Learys and Friends   86, 267, 530

Oak & Company   150, 431, 493

Oasis for Lucy   43, 394

The Obstinate Land   229, 403

Occult Visions: A Mystical Gaze into the Future   143, 355, 414

An Ocean World   185, 520

The October Child   58, 108, 361, 526

Odette: A Bird in Paris   157, 327, 337

The Official Encyclopedia of Baseball   31, 539, 544

Of Love and Death and Other Journeys   132, 381

Of Love and Shadows   199, 248, 475

Of the Jigsaw   128, 490

Oh!   24, 356

Oh, Boy! Babies!   7, 376, 435, 538

Oh, Kojo! How Could You!   180, 243, 281

Oh, Lizzie: The Life of Elizabeth Cady Stanton   215, 335

Oh, Those Harper Girls!   185, 400

Oh, Were They Ever Happy   92, 526

Ohio   35, 86, 173, 174, 490

Ol' Paul, the Mighty Logger   49, 498

Old Ben   52, 309, 533

Old Black Fly   129, 257, 348

Old Bones, the Wonder Horse   83, 319, 469

Old Dog, New Tricks   176, 292, 533

The Olden Days Coat   44, 416, 567

Old Henry   29, 272, 348

Old Mother Hubbard and Her Wonderful Dog   160, 437, 438

Old Ramon   15, 168, 174, 211, 504, 558

An Old Tale Carved Out of Stone   17, 424, 481

The Old Tobacco Shop   164, 276

Old Turtle   8, 112, 129, 295, 567

Old Wind and Liu Li-San   51, 355

Old Winkle and the Seagulls   98, 496

The Old Witch's Party   142, 317, 409

The Old Witch and the Snores   139, 317, 451

The Old Witch and the Wizard   141, 317, 409

The Old Witch Finds a New House   143, 317, 470

The Old Witch Goes to the Ball   139, 317, 459

Old Yeller   134, 168, 195, 231, 239, 285, 354

Oley the Sea Monster   207, 334

Oliver, Clarence and Violet   179, 530

Oliver's Wars   34, 564

Olson's Meat Pies   159, 301, 414

On a Picnic   143, 318, 347

The Once-upon-a-Time Dragon   220, 404

Once a Mouse   39, 51, 154, 281

Once There Was a Tree   163, 495, 527

Once Upon a Horse   203, 399

Once upon a Time in a Pigpen   178, 281, 533

Once Upon a Totem   154, 370, 451

Ondine: The Story of a Bird Who Was Different   211, 460, 467

One-eyed Cat   56, 69, 109, 163, 170, 343

One-eyed Jake   99, 388

One at a Time: His Collected Poems for the Young   133, 400, 442

One Dancing Drum   61, 156, 410, 432

One Day in the Woods   113, 248, 352

One Dragon's Dream   58, 474

One Fat Summer   142, 424

One Fine Day   40, 381

One God: The Ways We Worship Him   174, 339

One Gorilla: A Counting Book   159, 454

One is One   39, 47, 249, 478, 543

One Lonely Kakapo   70, 455

One Misty Moisty Morning   61, 451

One More Flight   93, 285, 316

One Morning   23, 38, 64, 159, 208, 347, 391, 442

One Morning in Maine   38, 64, 208, 442

One Proud Summer   194, 377, 432

The One That Got Away   6, 461, 472
One Wide River to Cross   12, 39, 332
One Winter Night in August and other Nonsense Jingles   161, 404, 446
On Friday Something Funny Happened   130, 483
On Guard!   33, 554
Onion John   50, 168, 411, 515
Onion Tears   75, 388, 405
Only Earth and Sky Last Forever   230, 266
The Only Earth We Have   139, 428, 484
Only Silly People Waste   142, 291, 521
Only the Best   130, 425, 575
On Market Street   28, 40, 157, 162, 426, 427
On My Honor   81, 92, 170, 172, 228, 232, 262
On My Own   236, 311
On the Banks of Plum Creek   166, 277, 513, 561
On the Day Peter Stuyvesant Sailed into Town   61, 67, 427
On the Day You Were Born   104, 184, 344
On the Devil's Court   200, 320
On the Edge   189, 231, 308
On the Far Side of the Mountain   113, 352
On the Forest Edge   87, 420
On the Pampas   184, 283
On the Track of Bigfoot   88, 480
On to Widecombe Fair   27, 351, 389
Ood-Le-Uk the Wanderer   165, 394, 423, 430
Ooh La La (Max in Love)   159, 400
Open House for Butterflies   154, 410, 511
Operation: Dump the Chump   226, 238, 470
Operation Grizzly Bear   146, 288
Opposites   212, 215, 484, 485, 561
OPT: An Illusionary Tale   151, 262
Optics: Light for a New Age   151, 374
Orange on Top   206, 547, 553
The Orchestra and its Instruments   47, 374, 526
The Ordeal of the Young Hunter   55, 318, 416
The Origin of Life on Earth: An African Creation Myth   119, 251, 564
The Orphan Boy   97, 104, 131, 452, 454
The Orphans   115, 212, 275, 394, 462, 486
The Orphans of Simitra   212, 275, 394, 462
Orvis   182, 382
Oscar, Cosmonauta   10, 249, 412
Oscar deMejo's ABC   160, 318
The Other City   21, 277, 550
The Other Shore   199, 441
The Other Side of Dark   22, 42, 112, 189, 196, 225, 462
Otherwise Known as Sheila the Great   140, 200, 273
Otto in Africa   135, 327
Ottoline at the British Museum   130, 307, 475

Otto of the Silver Hand   52, 109, 486, 554
Ounce, Dice, Trice   12, 490, 513
Our Changing World   23, 450, 456, 510
Our Eddie   169, 219, 390
Our Family Got a Divorce   91, 277, 478
Our Fifty States   135, 313, 449, 450
Our Golda: The Story of Golda Meir   234, 244, 499
Our Kids   176, 456
Our Modern Stone Age   150, 262, 391
Our Urban Planet   149, 535
Our Wild Wetlands   143, 306
Outlawed Inventions   130, 264, 565
Out of Hand   212, 434, 522
Out of the Depths to Joy   66, 521
Out of the Earth I Sing: Poetry and Songs of Primitive Peoples of the World   213, 423
Out of the Flame   165, 429, 566
Outside Over There   8, 28, 40, 158, 162, 511
The Outsiders   25, 126, 213, 225, 378
The Outside Shot   180, 458
Out There   214, 432, 532
Out Walked Mel   6, 275
Over the Hills to Fabylon   46, 361
The Owl-Scatterer   159, 443, 463
The Owl and the Pussycat   104, 267, 418
The Owl and the Woodpecker   99, 561
Owl at Home   88, 161, 427
Owl in the Cedar Tree   229, 452, 476
Owliver   63, 255, 410
Owl Moon   41, 110, 506, 571
The Owl Service   47, 101, 350
Owls in the Family   32, 344, 456
The Owlstone Crown   81, 296, 404
Ox-cart Man   40, 157, 162, 305, 367
The Oxford Book of Poetry for Children   98, 272, 561
Oxford Junior Companion to Music   221, 387, 506
Ox Under Pressure   133, 461
Ozzy on the Outside   75, 248
Pablo Paints a Picture   153, 451, 525
A Pack of Lies: Twelve Stories in One   48, 102, 441
Paddle-to-the-Sea   37, 50, 381
A Paddock of Poems   59, 336
Paddy's Evening Out   62, 357
Paddy's New Hat   178, 357
Paddy Goes Traveling   158, 357
Paddy Pork's Holiday   64, 357
Padre Porko: The Gentlemanly Pig   50, 314, 331
The Pageant of Chinese History   166, 509, 554
The Pai-Pai Pig   33, 251, 569
The Pain and the Great One   80, 273, 543
The Painter and the Bird   63, 280, 548
The Pair of Shoes   56, 355, 515
The Palestinians   177, 384, 443
Palmiero and the Ogre   213, 324
Panama Canal   94, 146, 502
Pancakes-Paris   167, 207, 270, 507
Panda Cake   68, 510
The Paper Airplane Book   61, 261, 519

The Paper Crane   29, 110, 259
Paper Faces   102, 251
Paper Movie Machines   148, 557
The Paper Party   71, 345
A Paper Zoo   139, 487, 556
Pappa Pellerin's Daughter   51, 213, 345, 364
Paradise Cafe and Other Stories   30, 128, 236, 280
A Parcel of Patterns   223, 231, 473
The Park in the Dark   125, 338, 551
Parsley   153, 266
Partners: The United Nations and Youth   55, 337, 496
Partnership of Mind and Body: Biofeedback   142, 405
The Party Book for Boys and Girls   136, 290, 451
Passage to America: The Story of the Great Migrations   31, 515
Passover: A Season of Freedom   203, 326, 379
The Pasture   138, 393
Pastures of the Blue Crane   57, 279, 431
The Patchwork Cat   100, 263, 440
The Patchwork Quilt   69, 116, 118, 341, 479
Pathki Nana: Kootenai Girl Solves a Mystery   105, 280, 539
Path of the Pale Horse   94, 180, 340
Patricia C. DuBois   111
Patterns on the Wall   206, 294, 570
Paul Bunyan Finds a Wife   139, 317, 507
Paul Bunyan Swings His Axe   238, 442
Paul Hunt's Night Diary   131, 386
Paul Revere's Ride   69, 428, 487
Paul Robeson   4, 235, 342, 362, 415
Paul Robeson: Hero Before His Time   235, 415
Paul Tiber, Forester   55, 355, 488
Pawnee   208, 265, 266
The Paw Thing   237, 393, 443
Peabody   96, 113, 144, 557
A Peaceable Kingdom: The Shaker Abecedarius   14, 157, 162, 484, 485
The Peaceable Revolution   55, 78, 505
Peace at Last   100, 457
Peacock Pie: A Book of Rhymes   159, 249, 317
Peanut   155, 171, 291, 398, 535
Pebbles from a Broken Jar: Fables and Hero Stories from Old China   216, 246
Pecos Bill   33, 49, 121, 166, 204, 259, 276, 337, 403, 515
Pecos Bill, the Greatest Cowboy of All Time   49, 166, 204, 259, 276
Pecos Bill and the Mustang   33, 337, 515
The Peddler's Clock   206, 386, 397
Pedro & the Padre   184, 243, 375
Pedro, the Angel of Olvera Street   38, 85, 481
Peeper, First Voice of Spring   93, 420, 442
Peepo!   18, 245
Pegasus   99, 544
Pele, The King of Soccer   142, 351

Pelican　125, 153, 180, 201, 297, 345, 352, 561, 562

Pencil, Pen and Brush　211, 556

Pendragon: Arthur and His Britain　214, 297

Penguins　49, 150, 166, 238, 256, 396, 417

Penguin Small　34, 389

A Penguin Year　8, 275

Penn　166, 361, 560

A Penny a Day　50, 317, 404

A Penny a Look　61, 573, 574

Penny Pollard's Diary　59, 392, 408

Penny Rose　171, 285

Penny Tunes and Princesses　141, 402, 422

People　67, 68, 223, 526

People Are Important　3, 329, 334

People at the Edge of the World: The Ohlone of Central California　4, 455, 458

The People Could Fly　109, 118, 158, 163, 176, 322, 323, 368

People Like Us　145, 301

People Might Hear You　227, 408

The People of North Carolina　171, 472

The Peppermint Pig　101, 263, 423

Peppermints in the Parlor　232, 552

The Perilous Gard　63, 169, 309, 482

The Perilous Road　3, 168, 348, 528

Permanent Connections　171, 182, 279

The Persistence of Riddles　66, 561

Pet Day　145, 282, 574

Pete　191, 205, 222, 318, 373, 494, 503, 509

Peter, the Revolutionary Tsar　62, 411, 412, 486

Peter's Pinto: A Story of Utah　31, 284

Peter's Room　46, 342

Peter and the Wolf　179, 182, 290, 292, 372, 449, 484

Peter Penny's Dance　64, 162, 426, 486

Peter Stuyvesant　61, 67, 139, 302, 317, 427

Peter the Great　94, 369, 527

Peter the Revolutionary Tsar　62, 411, 412, 486

Peter Treegate's War　78, 560

Peter und der Wolf　23, 428, 456, 484

Pet of the Met　209, 345

Petronella　62, 99, 278, 375, 426, 563

Petros' War　17, 110, 337, 573

Petrouchka　97, 108, 179, 267, 299, 533

Pets, Vets and Marty Howard　146, 291, 461

Pet Safety　143, 314, 442

Pet Sematary　22, 406

Pets Without Homes　94, 254, 376

Petunia　146, 329

Phaethon　138, 380, 481

Phantom of the Blockade　136, 441, 447

The Phantom of Walkaway Hill　187, 337, 532

Phantom on Skis　205, 354, 366

The Phantom Tollbooth　216, 336, 399

Pheasant and Kingfisher　74

Phebe Fairchild: Her Book　166, 420

The Philharmonic Gets Dressed　163, 412, 519

Philip Hall Likes Me: I Reckon Maybe　161, 169, 361, 423

Phil Sterling, Salesman　31, 364

Phoenix Feathers: A Collection of Mythical Monsters　62, 517

Piccaninny Walkabout: A Story of Two Aboriginal Children　57, 481

Pick-up Sticks　97, 332

Pick a Peck of Puzzles　138, 497

Pickle in the Middle and Other Easy Snacks　143, 575, 576

Picnic　69, 143, 157, 166, 318, 347, 357, 443, 548

The Picture Life of Tina Turner　146, 287

The Picture Life of Whitney Houston　146, 287

Picture Roo Books　232, 490, 495

Pictures of France by her Children　208, 306

The Piebald Princess　209, 474

A Piece of Straw　59, 454, 522

The Piemakers　47, 308, 326

Piero Ventura's Book of Cities　13, 14, 548

Pierre Pidgeon　37, 260, 406

The Pig-tale　53, 63, 156, 291, 430

The Pig's Wedding　162, 374

Pi Gal　36, 288, 469

Pigeon Post　45, 487

Piggies　204, 567

Piggins　54, 96, 182, 329, 571

Piggybook　181, 282

The Pig in the Pond　100, 261, 551

The Pigman　25, 126, 162, 575

The Pigman's Legacy　162, 575

Pigs and Honey　60, 74, 244

Pigs from A to Z　159, 163, 352

Pigs in Hiding　179, 326

Pigs Might Fly　59, 495, 572

The Pigtail of Ah Lee Ben Loo: With Seventeen Other Laughable Tales and 200 Comical Silhouettes　165, 267

The Pigtail of Ah Lee Ben Loo with Seventeen other Laughable Tales and 200 Comical Silhouettes　165, 267

Pilgrim Children on the Mayflower　143, 317, 324

The Pilgrim Goose　210, 268, 493

Pilgrims of Plimouth　29, 512

The Pinballs　42, 56, 89, 92, 134, 197, 218, 222, 232, 235, 288

Pinchpenny Mouse　63, 288, 410

Pinkerton Behave!　90, 92, 403

Pink Pink　141, 317, 433

Pipin and Pod　292

Pippi Longstocking　53, 355, 413, 423

The Pit　214, 367, 433

Pitcher Plants: The Elegant Insect Traps　194, 420

Pito's House　206, 283, 433

Pit Pony　34, 260, 547

Pitschi: The Kitten Who Always Wanted to be Something Else　152, 338

The Pixie's Invitation　23, 459

The Pizza Monster　74, 283, 513

Place Among the Stones　127

A Place Apart　8, 162, 343

A Place for Allie　203, 289

A Place for Ben　192, 540

A Place for Peter　31, 545, 570

Plague 99　121, 546

Plain Girl　55, 351, 525

The Plainsmen　212, 270, 505

The Planet Floor　108, 569

The Planet of Junior Brown　52, 132, 169, 368

The Plan for Birdmarsh　47, 249, 477

Plant Families　151, 420

Playing Beatie Bow　28, 58, 102, 108, 179, 470

Playing It Smart　146, 405, 459

Playing Murder　189, 508

Play with Me　39, 107, 334

Please Share that Peanut! A Preposterous Pageant in Fourteen Acts　155, 398, 535

The Plum-Rain Scroll　58, 435, 569

Plunkety Plunk　154, 424

Pocahontas and the Stranger　67, 284, 285

Pocahontas in London　22, 246, 551

A Pocket for Corduroy　79, 345

A Pocket Full of Seeds　3, 501, 527

A Pocketful of Cricket　39, 293, 460

Pockets　123, 124, 251, 572

Poems for Jewish Holidays　115, 272, 426

A Poetic Look at Aesop's Fables　142, 533

Poetry and Children　65, 298

Poetry for Autumn　138, 391, 458

Poetry for Chuckles and Grins　138, 319, 391

Poetry for Winter　139, 391, 465

Poetry of Witches, Elves, and Goblins　139, 249, 391

The Pointed Brush　211, 329, 438

Pokes of Gold　33, 522

Polar Bear, Polar Bear, What Do You Hear?　192, 290, 438

Polar Express　29, 35, 41, 92, 116, 135, 158, 191, 546

Polar Regions　221, 394

The Polished Diamond and other Stories　136, 516

Pollen Pie　146, 253

The Polly Cameron Picture Book　139, 289

Pongwiffy and the Spell of the Year　173, 522, 545

Pony Express Boy　33, 354, 536

Pony Soldier　216, 443

The Pool of Fire　217, 297

Poor Richard in France　132, 452, 544

Poor Tom's Ghost　174, 188, 253, 310

Pop Bottles　218, 493

Pop Corn and Ma Goodness　40, 131, 471, 483

A Poppy in the Corn　211, 555

The Porcupine Mouse　21, 265, 485

Porcupine Stew　20, 179, 389, 434

Porko von Popbutton　139, 327

Title Index

Portly's Hat   123, 306
Portrait of Lisette   212, 412, 456
Portraits of Nobel Laureates in Medicine and Physiology   136, 365, 492
Possum Come a-Knockin'   183, 275, 547
Possum Magic   59, 109, 117, 147, 343, 550
The Post Office Cat   99, 367
Posy   69, 199, 481, 518, 531
Potatoes   145, 148, 150, 282, 294, 396, 518, 534, 574
Potatoes: All About Them   148, 294, 518
The Potlatch Family   64, 414
Potter, Come Fly to the First of the Earth   91, 502, 553
Poverty in America   94, 448
Powder and Steel: Notable Battles and Campaigns of the 1800's from New Orleans to the Zulu War   33
The Power of Light: Eight Stories for Hanukkah   189, 423, 519
Power of Three   101, 397
The Practical Archaeologist   151, 444
The Practical Princess   19, 375, 563
A Prairie Alphabet, ABC   129, 259, 453
A Prairie Boy's Summer   44, 63, 103, 111, 412
A Prairie Boy's Winter   26, 44, 62, 103, 156, 160, 412
Prairie Child   351, 383
Prairie Colt   30, 319, 539
Prairie Song   29
Prairie Songs   94, 111, 121, 199, 229, 230, 304, 575
Prairie Visions: The Life and Times of Solomon Butcher   145, 304
The Prancing Pony: Nursery Rhymes from Japan   213, 316, 377
Pran of Albania   165, 450, 477
Prayer for a Child   37, 49, 338, 397
Predicting Children's Choices in Literature: A Developmental Approach   65, 505
Prehistoric Animals   32, 174, 232, 352, 457, 505
Prehistoric Man and the Primates   32, 505
The Presidency   212, 339, 395
The President's Car   149, 341, 471
Pribehy   22, 383, 513
Pride Against Prejudice: The Biography of Larry Doby   234, 453
Pride of Lions   79, 454
The Princess and Froggie   63, 574
The Princess and the Admiral   3, 295, 481
Princess Ashley   135, 199, 475
The Princess Bride   80, 357
The Princesses: Sixteen Stories about Princesses   154, 396, 453
The Princess of Tomsobo   9, 460
Princess Smartypants   100, 302
Principio y Fin Tiempo de Vida que Trancurre Entre el Nacer y el Morir   110, 447

Principio y Fin Tiempo de Vida que Transcurre Entre el Nacer y el Morir   334, 420
Priscilla   9, 125, 211, 216, 252, 336, 368, 414, 489
Priska Kesasta Kesaan   9, 468
Prisoners at the Kitchen Table   200, 381
Private Eyes: Adventures with the Saturday Gang   187, 406, 518
The Private World of Julia Redfern   183, 289
The Prize   5, 9, 22, 127, 186, 195, 197, 222, 296
Probably Still Nick Swansen   112, 185, 566
Profiles in Courage   3, 404, 556
Project Panda Watch   150, 506, 515
Promise Not to Tell   69, 261, 481
A Proud Taste for Scarlet and Miniver   132, 409
Prune   203, 497, 503
The Pueblo   204, 572
Pulga   17, 356, 547
Pumpkin, Pumpkin   151, 540
Pumpkin Personalities   143, 401, 541
Punch and Judy: A Play for Puppets   155, 332
Punch in New York   159, 190, 485
Pundak Ha-Eima   109, 448, 520
The Pup Grew Up!   190, 436, 486
Puppy   25, 83, 192, 231, 266, 287, 436, 499, 510, 563
The Purple Coat   69, 376, 508
Purro and the Prattleberries   171, 461, 486
Pursuit   42, 345
The Pushcart War   33, 51, 448, 524
Push Me, Pull Me   177, 296
Puss in Boots   20, 38, 41, 183, 190, 281, 331, 436, 476
Put the Saddle on the Pig   20, 441
Puzzles Old and New   151, 286, 521, 548
Pyramid   26, 63, 68, 222, 268, 392, 431, 454
Quacky, Quack-quack!   131, 257, 560
The Quaint and Curious Quest of Johnny Longfoot, the Shoe King's Son   167, 268, 294
The Quangle-Wangle's Hat   99, 418, 469
The Quarter-pie Window   133, 236, 278
Quebec, Je T'aime : I Love You   103, 536
Queen Eleanor, Independent Spirit of the Medieval World   28, 280
Queenie Peavy   3, 55, 89, 186, 217, 285, 417
Queen of Hearts   133, 299
Queen of the Gospel Singers   234, 391
The Queen of the Pharisees' Children   231, 562
Queer Person   165, 384, 550
Quentin Blake's ABC   190, 271
The Quest: A Report on Extra-terrestrial Life   248
The Quest: A Report on Extraterrestrial Life   33
Quest for a Kelpie   116, 189, 375

Quest for Freedom: Bolivar and the South American Revolution   71, 438, 492
Quest in the Desert   208, 251, 560
The Question Box   75, 385
A Question of Courage   101, 253, 312
Questions and Answers about Seashore Life   61, 425, 558
The Quest of the Golden Condor   207, 408
The Quest of the Golden Gannet   18, 260
Quest of the Snow Leopard   32, 251, 560
Que Viene el Iris, Leri   24, 464, 548
The Quicksand Book   88, 319
Quick Wits and Nimble Fingers   143, 290, 498
Quiet as Moss: 36 Poems chosen by Leonard Clark   46, 298, 372, 571
The Quiet Flame: Mother Marianne of Molokai   136, 269, 467
The Quinkins   58, 108, 497, 543
Quirky Tails! More Oddball Stories   237, 393
The Rabbi's Girls   179, 387, 396
Rabbit & Pork: Rhyming Talk   63, 198, 417
Rabbit and Wolf   124, 259
Rabbit Hill   50, 167, 417
Rabbit Island   17, 413, 456, 529
Rabbit Makes a Monkey Out of a Lion   183, 243, 479
A Rabbit Named Harris   147, 386, 465
Rabble Starkey   29, 94, 429
Rabble Starky   56
A Racecourse for Andy   213, 383, 568
Rachel's Revolution   20, 476
Racial Prejudice   234, 472
The Racketty Street Gang   57, 335
The Radio Imp   208, 270, 287
The Radium Woman: A Youth Edition of the Life of Madame Curie   45, 210, 325, 353
Rafferty Rides a Winner   57, 567
Ragged Robin (poems)   46, 473, 489
The Raggle-Taggle Fellow   211, 506, 556
Rags, Rugs, and Wool Pictures: A First Book of Rug Hooking   138, 566
Rags, Rugs and Wool Pictures: A First Book of Rug Hooking   138, 566
Ragtime Tumpie   183, 346, 507
Railroads of Southern and Southwestern Wisconsin   215, 415
The Railroad to Freedom: A story of the Civil War   165, 313, 535
Railway Passage   19, 99, 402
Railway Worker   176, 307, 357
The Rainbow Book of Art   210, 307
Rainbow Crow: A Lenape Tale   16, 547, 549
The Rainbow Fish   24, 69, 477
Rainbow Jordan   162, 296
The Rainbow People   29, 190, 561, 570
Rainbow Rhino   159, 520
Rainbow Round the World: A Story of UNICEF   3, 246, 364, 570
Rainbows, Snowflakes and Quarks: Physics and the World Around Us   150, 371, 550

Rainbows Are Made: Poems   158, 331, 382, 502

The Rainbow Serpent   15, 58, 389, 498, 514

The Rain Catchers   95, 538

The Rain Door   125, 271, 379

Rain Drop Splash   38, 542, 556

The Rainforest   30, 108, 207, 478, 480, 526

The Rainforest Children   108, 478, 480

Raining Away to Sea   35, 552

Rain in the Woods and Other Small Matters   33, 498

Rain Makes Applesauce   39, 154, 269, 505

Rain of Fire   4, 262

The Rainy Day Book   138, 508

Rainy Day Magic   97, 104, 351

Ralph S. Mouse   79, 88, 93, 112, 179, 218, 228, 298, 573

Ramlal   33, 515, 518

Ramona and Her Father   27, 88, 103, 108, 121, 134, 170, 220, 224, 226, 239, 298, 540

Ramona and Her Mother   7, 88, 218, 298, 540

Ramona Forever   112, 163, 180, 299, 540

Ramona Quimby, Age 8   35, 88, 128, 170, 197, 218, 299, 540

Ramona the Brave   92, 222, 299, 540

Ramona the Pest   89, 134, 196, 239, 299, 313

Rand McNally Atlas of World Wildlife   148

Randolph's Dream   184, 447, 471

Random House Book of Mother Goose   163, 181, 427

Ranger Rick   124, 233, 348, 375, 403, 417

Ransom   46, 187, 327, 380, 478

Ransom for a Knight   46, 380, 478

Rapscallion Jones   180, 437

Rascal: A Memoir of a Better Era   15, 51, 83, 136, 168, 195, 231, 239, 463, 506

Rasmus and the Vagabond   32, 423, 470

Rasmus Pa Luffen   9, 423, 470

Raspberry One   87, 337

Ratha's Creature   111, 185, 265

Rats on the Roof and Other Stories   74, 184, 437

The Rattle Bag: An Anthology of Poetry   197, 374

Raven: A Trickster Tale from the Pacific Northwest   30, 443

Raven's Cry   44, 370, 490

Ravensgill   47, 440

Ray Charles   118, 342, 439

Raymond L. Ditmars: His Exciting Career with Reptiles, Insects and Animals   86, 567

Re-reading the Secret Garden   65, 356

Read-Aloud Handbook   122, 488, 542

Read Aloud Bible Stories   91, 424, 485

The Reader in the Book   65, 294

Reading the Past: The Story of Deciphering Ancient Languages   147, 306

Ready or Not   127, 137, 209, 397, 443, 532

The Real Book   31, 381

Really Spring   153, 360, 575

A Really Weird Summer   188, 444

The Real Tilly Beany   49, 246, 312

The Real Tin Flower: Poems about the World at Nine   155, 260, 354

The Reason for the Pelican   153, 297, 352

Rebecka   61, 141, 255

Rebels of the Heavenly Kingdom   180, 473

Rebels Ride at Night   97, 338, 373

Rechenka's Eggs   112, 481

Red-dirt Jessie   175, 458

The Red Balloon   153, 414

Red Bird of Ireland   144, 414

The Red Book of Hob Stories   130, 267, 440

Redemption Greenback   223, 397, 434

Red Is Best   110, 111, 423, 496, 531

Red Leaf, Yellow Leaf   30, 36, 331

Red Lion and Gold Dragon: A Novel of the Norman Conquest   213, 527

Red Power on the Rio Grande: The Native American Revolution of 1680   230, 341, 498

Red Riding Hood, Retold in Verse for Boys and Girls to Read Themselves   12, 61, 320, 358

Red Rock Over the River   93, 264, 486

Red Sails to Capri   168, 335, 556

Red Sky in the Morning   36, 48, 413

The Red Swan: Myths and Tales of the American Indians   64, 269

Redwall   121, 228, 294, 392

Redwork   45, 97, 133, 236, 264

Reflections on a Gift of Watermelon Pickle and Other Modern Verse   51, 328, 430, 523

Reggie and Nilma: A New York City Story   214, 536

The Region of the Summer Stars   222, 538

The Reign of King Babar   65, 474

The Relatives Came   41, 158, 348, 501

The Reluctant Dragon   51, 360, 514

The Reluctant God   94, 512

Reluctantly Alice   184, 459

The Remarkable Harry   211, 386, 387

Remarkable Journey of Prince Jen   184, 247, 292

Rembrandt Takes a Walk   159, 364, 532

Remember the Days: A Short History of the Jewish American   132, 323, 448

Renee   9, 95, 139, 140, 354, 487, 489, 507, 556, 571

Renfrew Flies Again   205, 333, 514

Rescue: The Story of How Gentiles Saved Jews in the Holocaust   5, 448

Rescue Josh McGuire   112, 230, 449

Rescue of the Stranded Whales   24, 303, 435

The Rescuers   46, 280, 514

Reserved for Mark Anthony Crowder   111, 522

Responsible Parenthood: The Child's Psyche through the Six-Year Pregnancy   120, 408, 496

The Return   115, 182, 185, 219, 422

The Return of Freddy LeGrand   185, 245

The Return of Silver Chief   238, 465, 560

The Return of the Indian   105, 164, 181, 259, 352

Return of the Jedi: The Storybook   172, 549

The Return of the Twelves   51, 212, 283, 298, 421

Return to Bitter Creek   181, 522

Return to Freedom   114, 400, 531

Return to Hiroshima   214, 383, 423

Return to Morocco   146, 396

Reubella and the Old Focus Home   171, 461

Revenge of the Nerd   80, 446

The Revolutionary Age of Andrew Jackson   87, 490

Rex of the Coast Patrol   206, 395, 396

Rhoda's Restaurant   13, 536

Ribsy   84, 134, 239, 298, 299, 313

Rice Without Rain   184, 379

Richard's Castle   83, 304

Rich Mitch   115, 430, 513

The Riddle of Penncroft Farm   81, 394

The Riddle of Racism   3, 378

Ride 'em Cowgirl   230, 285, 369

Ride a Northbound Horse   229, 351, 568

A Ride on the Red Mare's Back   185, 325, 419

Ride Out the Storm   208, 265

The Rider and His Horse   186, 322, 323, 372

Ride the Pale Stallion   216, 270, 536

Ride with Me through ABC   139, 274, 420

The Ridiculous Story of Gammer Gurton's Needle   164, 182, 426, 550

Rifka Grows Up   114, 286

Rifles and Warbonnets   229, 480

Rifles at Ramsour's Mill: A Tale of the Revolutionary War   171, 557

Rifles for Watie   51, 168, 285, 403

The Righteous Revenge of Artemis Bonner   185, 458

The Right Size: Why some Creatures Survive and others are Extinct   138, 375, 502

The Rights of the People: The Major Decisions of the Warren Court   67, 357

The Right to Know: Censorship in America   68, 425

Rimes de la Mere Oie: Mother Goose Rendered into French   61, 297, 316, 355, 572

Ring-rise Ring-set   102, 385

A Ring and a Riddle   206, 273, 389, 406, 509

Ring of Endless Light   170, 420

Ring the Judas Bell   213, 342

Riptide   96, 271, 557

Title Index

The Rising of the Wind: Adventures Along the Beaufort Scale   150, 342, 572
Rites of Passage Today: The Cultural Significance of The Wizard of Earthsea   65, 552
River and Canal   151, 277
River Dragon   207, 414, 564
A River Dream   159, 504
Riverman   110, 258
River Runners: A Tale of Hardship and Bravery   44, 383
The Road from Home: The Story of an Armenian Girl   4, 27, 53, 170, 405
Roadrunner   179, 394, 472
The Road to Agra   3, 32, 55, 235, 243, 525
The Road to Camlann   28, 337, 534
Road to Down Under   206, 305, 514
The Road to Memphis   119, 217, 237, 537
Roaring River   71, 280
The Robber Ghost   211, 250, 348, 433
Robert Boyle, Founder of Modern Chemistry   32, 507, 525
Robinson Crusoe   19, 316, 482
Robodad   199, 292
The Robots Are Here   144, 518
Rocco   6, 52, 169, 398, 459, 528
The Rock and the Willow   55, 419
The Rock Cried Out   73, 439
Rockets and Satellites   135, 278, 524
Rock Star   56, 302
Rodeo Summer   87, 365
Roger's Umbrella   179, 437, 479
Roger and the Fox   38, 314, 567
Roland   153, 185, 344, 529
Roller Skates   51, 166, 252, 504
Roll of Thunder, Hear my Cry   4, 27, 133, 169, 217, 239, 479, 537
The Romantic Obsessions and Humiliations of Annie Sehlmeier   75, 480
Ronia, the Robber's Daughter   17, 180, 307, 423
A Room Made of Windows   26, 85, 160, 214, 289, 389
Room 13   56, 492, 535
Roosevelt Grady   21, 51, 235, 285, 515
The Rooster Crows   37, 477
The Root Cellar   42, 44, 109, 430
The Roquefort Gang   74, 300
Rosa Parks   105, 185, 234, 362, 372, 436, 471
Rosa Parks: My Story   105, 185, 372, 471
Rose Blanche   17, 306, 348, 359, 389
Rosebud & Red Flannel   123, 469, 480
The Rose in my Garden   28, 426, 427
Rose Meets Mr. Wintergarten   60
Rosh Hashanah and Yom Kippur: Sweet Beginnings   203, 326, 379
Rosie & the Yellow Ribbon   14, 19, 25, 69, 311, 319, 533, 551, 566
Rosie's Babies   19, 311, 551
Rosie's Walk   25, 388
Rosie and the Rustlers   183, 353
Rosie and the Yellow Ribbon   69, 319
Rosie Cole's Great American Guilt Club   181, 362
Rosie Meets Mr. Wintergarten   359

Rosie Sips Spiders   14, 421
Rosie Swanson: Fourth-Grade Geek For President   185, 470
Rotkappchen   23, 363
Rotten Ralph   64, 349, 499
A Roundabout Turn   50, 280, 295
Round Buildings, Square Buildings and Buildings That Wiggle Like a Fish   29, 390
Round the Twist   237, 393
Round Trip   96, 158, 397
Rover and Coo Coo   87, 373, 525
The Royal Dirk   201, 249, 264
The Royal Navy   98, 249, 315
A Royal Pain   181, 201, 303
The Ruby in the Smoke   112, 121, 485
Rue de la Mediterranee   24
Rufus M.   167, 334, 521
Rufus the Fox   130, 519
Rumbelow's Dance   125, 271, 570
Rummage   58, 439, 456
The Rumor of Pavel and Paali   182, 407, 449
Rumpelstiltskin   41, 153, 191, 258, 363, 364, 398, 573
Run, Don't Walk   143, 504
Run, Run, as Fast as You Can   235, 467
The Runaway's Diary   53, 371
Runaway Balboa   204, 395, 475
The Runaway Bunny   79, 281, 387
Runaway Danny   199, 268
Runaway Mittens   183, 457, 495
The Runaway Papoose   165, 453
The Runaway Punt   108, 389, 469
Runaway Ralph   134, 197, 299, 313
The Runaways   102, 539
The Runaway Shuttle Train   207, 312, 347
The Runaway Teddy Bear   145, 380
Runaway Teens   93, 433
Runner of the Mountain Tops: The Life of Louis Agassiz   166, 494, 554
Running Scared   48, 255
Run Swift, Run Free   20, 189, 328, 441
Run to Earth   20, 328, 441
The Runt of Rogers School   197, 403
Run With the Wind   20, 328, 441
Rushavenn Time   198, 398, 559
A Russian Farewell   114, 219, 339
Russian Tales of Fabulous Beasts and Marvels   139, 449, 569
Rusty Timmons' First Million   146, 291, 456
Ruth Marini: Dodger Ace   144, 293
Ruth Marini of the Dodgers   144, 293
The S.S. Valentine   143, 355, 477
Sabrina   214, 247
The Sacramental Programme and Welcome to You   15
The Sacred Harvest: Ojibway Wild Rice Gathering   105, 399, 489
Sadako and the Thousand Paper Cranes   227, 301, 378
Sad Day, Glad Day   136, 464, 465, 539
Safe as the Grave   171, 305, 469
The Saga of Erik the Viking   56, 342, 398
Sagebrush Sorrel   229, 493, 542

Sailing for Gold   204, 395, 490
Sailing Ships   191, 444, 534, 547
Sailing to Cythera and Other Anatole Stories   53, 446, 562
Saint George and the Dragon   41, 83, 158, 380, 389
Saint Valentine   105, 501
The Salamander Room   129, 396, 441
Sally Go Round the Sun   44, 343, 436
A Salmon for Simon   44, 97, 103, 271, 554
Salt: A Russian Tale   212, 574
Sam, Bangs, and Moonshine   39, 431, 460
Sam and Emma   61, 358, 460
Samantha's Masquerade   138, 478, 504
Samantha on Stage   227, 336, 503
Sami and the Time of Troubles   105, 354, 374, 422
Sammy and Mara   130, 547
Sampson: Yankee Stallion   143, 319, 388
Samurai of Gold Hill   71, 341, 545
Sancho of the Long, Long Horns   71, 276, 344
The Sandman's Eyes   189, 565
Sandpipers   154, 272, 387
Sandra and the Right Prince   71, 251, 469
Sandy Koufax   33, 452
Santiago   12, 210, 266, 297, 515, 554
Sara's Granny and the Groodle   155, 297, 354
Sarah's Questions   145, 275, 574
Sasha, my Friend   231, 305, 514
The Satanic Mill   161, 265, 483
Saturday, the Twelfth of October   53, 441
Saturday Science   78, 272, 558
Saturnalia   29, 340
Save the Mustangs! How a Federal Law Is Passed   68, 556
Say Goodnight, Gracie   225, 226, 315
Saying Goodbye to Grandma   82, 512, 538
Say it Again, Granny!   176, 245, 362
Scallywag   15, 498
The Scarebird   192, 233, 340, 520
The Scarecrows   28, 48, 558
Scarf Jack   102, 401
Scary Stories to Tell in the Dark   11, 35, 80, 348, 507, 508
Scary Stories 3: More Tales To Chill Your Bones   35, 348, 508
Scary Things   139, 521, 547
Scat, the Movie Cat   142, 319, 549
School Is not a Missile Range   142, 438, 521
The School Train   209, 243, 521
Schorschi Schrumpft: Geschichte   23, 358, 374
Science Alive: Living Things   195, 405
Science and the Secret of Man's Past   137, 341, 409
Science in your Own Backyard   77, 305
Science Wizardry for Kids   105, 403, 494, 563
Scientific Eye   221, 371
Scorpions   170, 458

Scram, Kid!   26, 414, 444
Scrappy the Pup   154, 297, 450
Screaming High   189, 424
Scruffy   24, 465, 470
Sea and Earth: The Life of Rachel Carson   67, 529
A Sea Between   207, 314
Seabird   71, 167, 381
Sea Boots   208, 328, 370
Sea Change   45, 254, 421
The Sea Egg   213, 276
Sea Glass   71, 570
Seahorse   61
The Sea Lord   108, 307, 482, 507
Sea Menace   57, 365, 404
The Seance   188, 462
The Search for Grissi   194, 422, 516
The Sea Serpent of Grenadier Pond   7, 474
The Seashell Song   131, 341, 393
Seashore   39, 61, 136, 155, 201, 367, 425, 427, 455, 558, 570
Seashore Story   39, 155, 201, 570
Seashore Summer   136, 367
Sea Songs   203, 339, 426
Seasons of Splendour   100, 163, 342, 392
Seasons of Splendour: Tales, Myths, and Legends of India   392
Season Songs   63, 262, 385
Sea Star: Orphan of Chincoteague   239, 319, 375
Seaward   120, 223, 305
Sebastian Lives in a Hat   232, 253, 293
Second-hand Dog   24, 266
The Second-hand Tongue   35, 387
Secretariat   9, 19, 34, 107
The Secret Circle   171, 265, 341
Secret City, USA   56, 382
The Secret Diary of Adrian Mole, Aged 13 3/4   25, 227, 542
The Secret Friends   295
The Secret Friendship   87, 280
The Secret Garden   50, 65, 74, 270, 286, 356, 545
The Secret Hiding Place   211, 267
A Secret House   140, 351, 541
The Secret in the Matchbox   182, 514, 564
The Secret Journey of Hugo the Brat   155, 298, 500
The Secret Language of Snow   150, 321, 434, 564
The Secret Life of Dilly McBean   189, 365
The Secret Life of School Supplies   113, 300, 455
The Secret Life of the Underwear Champ   89, 223, 397, 450
The Secret of Fiery Gorge   211, 528, 530
Secret of Gumbo Grove   182, 536
Secret of Haunted Crags   187, 386
The Secret of Spirit Mountain   218, 266, 466
Secret of the Andes   167, 209, 295, 297
The Secret of the Brownstone House   142, 369, 521
The Secret of the Buried Tomb   207, 408

Secret of the Cards   218, 307
The Secret of the Cellars   43, 371
The Secret of the Indian   98, 259, 422
The Secret of the Missing Boat   187, 268, 283, 562
The Secret of the Missing Footprint   187, 529, 560
The Secret of the Mountain   72, 424
The Secret of the Porcelain Fish   207, 334, 369
The Secret of the Ruby Ring   20, 432
The Secret of the Sea Rocks   138, 273, 490
The Secret of the Seven Crows   187, 281, 502
The Secret of the Simple Code   187, 336, 409
The Secret of the Tiger Eyes   187, 560
The Secret of the Two Feathers   31, 327, 409
The Secret of the Undersea Bell   33, 325
Secret Passage   207, 293, 445
The Secret Pencil   211, 383, 554
The Secret River   168, 488, 556
Secrets   6, 306
Secrets and Sequences in Children's Stories   66, 443
Secrets of a Small Brother   69, 291, 436
Secrets of Minos: Sir Arthur Evans' Discoveries at Crete   106, 211, 382
Secrets of Redding Glen: The Natural History of a Wooded Valley   62, 481
Secrets of the Best Choice   91, 395, 475
The Secret World of Polly Flint   230, 308, 337
See and Say: A Picture Book in Four Languages   153, 344
Seeing Earth From Space   175, 416
Seeing Fingers: The Story of Louis Braille   78, 316, 556
The Seeing Stick   68, 295, 435, 571
See What I Am   148, 329
Sefereggel   109, 459, 512
Selby's Secret   227, 259, 532
Selby Screams   228, 259, 532
Selby Speaks   228, 259, 532
Selchie's Seed   202, 357, 467
Self-Portrait: Margot Zemach   27, 574
The Selfish Giant   130, 435, 561
Selina, The Mouse and the Giant Cat   179, 274, 448
Selina Pumpernickel und die Katz Flora   274
Send No Blessings   236, 459
Send Wendell   14, 361, 515
A Sense of Magic   106, 446
A Sense of Shame and other Stories   48, 459
The Sentinels   102, 292
A Separate Battle: Women and the Civil War   105, 294
Sequoyah, Young Cherokee Guide   86, 353, 523
Seven-day Magic   174, 274, 329
Seven Blind Mice   30, 41, 191, 572
The Seven Ravens   212, 363, 364, 380

Seven Simeons: A Russian Tale   37, 204, 254
Seventeen Black Artists   117, 336
Seventeen Kings and Forty-two Elephants   159, 431, 434
Seventeenth Summer   43, 52, 312
Seventh Pebble   147, 526, 549
Seven Wild Pigs   182, 374
Seven Years and a Day   100, 304, 466
Sex Education   237, 239, 314
Shabanu: Daughter of the Wind   110, 170, 217, 528
Shackleton's Argonauts: A Saga of the Antarctic Ice-Packs   57, 387
Shades of Gray   5, 56, 113, 173, 489
Shades of Green   197, 371, 417
Shadow   281
Shadow Across the Campus   36, 55, 504
The Shadow Book   154, 320, 358
Shadow Boy   56, 407
Shadow Cage and other Tales of the Supernatural   48, 253, 474
Shadow Club   226, 516
Shadow in Hawthorn Bay   44, 97, 110, 133, 236, 430
A Shadow Like a Leopard   235, 422
The Shadowmaker   164, 369, 541
Shadow Man   105, 360
Shadow of a Bull   169, 212, 522, 566
Shadow of a Unicorn   145, 396
Shadow of the Wall   120, 413
Shadows   30, 87, 183, 199, 210, 226, 248, 273, 293, 367, 379, 475, 533, 544
Shadows and Reflections   30, 183, 379
Shadows into Mist   210, 273, 544
Shadrach   6, 144, 168, 188, 256, 306, 316, 511
Shadrach's Crossing   144, 188, 256
Shaka: King of the Zulus   159, 527, 548
Shakespeare's Theatre   98, 380
Shakespeare Stories   125, 342, 350
Shanty Boat   217, 384
Shantymen of Cache Lake   97, 345
Shapes, Shapes, Shapes   151, 379
Shark Beneath the Reef   183, 352
Shaw's Fortune: The Picture Story of a Colonial Plantation   155, 544
She, the Adventuress   215, 308, 389
She Come Bringing Me that Little Baby Girl   21, 26, 362, 529
The Sheep-Pig   102, 406, 488
The Sheep and the Rowan Tree   130, 287
Shen of the Sea: A Book for Children   165, 296, 372
The Shepherd of Abu Kush   106, 235, 531
A Shepherd Watches, a Shepherd Sings   71, 230, 390, 537
The Sherwood Ring   210, 460, 482
Shh! It's the Secret Club!   123
Shhh!   56, 364, 546
A Shield of Clover   229, 310
The Shield Ring   46, 210, 380, 534
Shiloh   170, 459
The Shimmershine Queens   183, 570
A Shining Season   200, 283
The Shining Shooter   31, 428, 490

Ships, Shoals and Amphoras: The Story of Underwater Archaeology 174, 315, 507

The Ship that Flew 210, 417, 422

Shipwreck 63, 309, 450

Shirley Chisholm: Teacher and Congresswoman 235, 505

The Shirt of the Happy Man 111, 268, 347

Shoeshine Girl 196, 197, 200, 202, 284, 360

Shoon: Wild Pony of the Moors 106, 522

Short, Short, Short Stories 184, 243

Shortcut 185, 308

The Short Life of Sophie Scholl 4, 469, 549

A Shovelful of Earth 151, 413, 451

Show Me the Evidence 189, 337

A Show of Hands: Say It in Sign Language 88, 276, 450, 489

Shrek! 183, 190, 529

Shrimps 138, 373, 429

The Shrinking of Treehorn 61, 156, 358, 374

Shy Charles 29, 183, 557

Sia Lives on Kilimanjaro 210, 423, 424, 492

Sidewalk Indian 72, 332

Sidewalk Story 73, 292, 439

Sideways Stories from Wayside School 81, 379, 501

Sidney the Monster 172, 509, 567

Sierra 18, 451, 517

The Sierra Club Wayfinding Book 151, 446, 558

Signal 54 66, 473

Signature Books 31, 447

The Sign of the Beaver 56, 69, 163, 170, 173, 525

The Sign of the Scales 7, 20, 278

Signpost to Terror 187, 527

Silas and Ben-Godik 27, 274, 413

The Silent One 5, 306, 398

Silent Ship, Silent Sea 71, 559

Silicon Songs 75, 406

Silkworms 150, 396, 407

Silver's Revenge 102, 419

The Silver Branch 46, 210, 402, 534

The Silver Cow 163, 179, 180, 305, 388

Silver Days 235, 422

The Silver Kiss 196, 237, 408

Silver on the Tree 222, 305

The Silver Pencil 167, 311, 450

The Silver Pony 26, 53, 62, 156, 554

The Silver Sword 32, 46, 211, 380, 512

Simba of the White Mane 32, 255, 319

The Simon & Schuster Young Readers' Book of Animals 25, 553

Simon's Book 158, 179, 326

Simon's Challenge 82, 279

Simon and the Golden Sword 44, 461, 542

Simon and the Snowflakes 178, 540

Simon Boom Gives a Wedding 52, 61, 156, 533, 574

Simon Underground 64, 500, 506

Simple Machines 151, 282, 383

Simple Pictures Are Best 14, 319, 562

Sinbad and Me 187, 480

Sing Down the Moon 169, 465

The Singing Cave 71, 211, 289, 322, 418, 419

The Singing Game 66, 466, 467

The Singing Hill 154, 316, 511

The Singing Tree 166, 512

Sing in Praise: A Collection of the Best Loved Hymns 38, 541, 559

Sing Mother Goose 38, 541, 559

Sing to the Sun 103, 185, 283

Sir Cedric 158, 353

Sirens and Spies 180, 425

Sir Francis Drake: His Daring Deeds 159, 353

Sir Gawain and the Loathly Lady 100, 372, 561

A Sister for Sam 172, 304, 438

Sister Madge's Book of Nuns 59, 117, 237, 433, 522

Siwiti: A Whale's Story 79, 455

Six Days from Sunday 86, 253, 269

Six Dinner Sid 198, 453

Six Little Ducks 27, 304

Sixth Grade Can Really Kill You 35, 96, 121, 135, 218, 239, 315

Sixth Grade Sleepover 196, 218, 223, 285

The Skating Rink 214, 419

The Skeleton Man 189, 267

Skinny 89, 212, 285, 517

Skinnybones 89, 122, 220, 224, 226, 470

Skipper John's Cook 38, 281

Skip To My Lou 192, 558

Skulls! 221, 351, 528

Sky Highways: Geography from the Air 206, 426, 526

Sky in the Pie 197, 407, 443

The Sky Is Falling 20, 44, 129, 475

The Sky River 31, 294, 566

Sky Songs 180, 203, 339, 426

Slake's Limbo 53, 382

Slambash Wangs of a Compo Gormer 110, 308, 419

The Slave Dancer 169, 343, 402

Slave of Haida 44

Slave of the Haida 250

Slavische Marchen 22, 520, 528, 573

Sled Dog of Alaska 33, 414

Sleep and Dreams 143, 360, 424

Sleepers 182, 405

Sleeping Beauty and other Favourite Fairy Tales 100, 125, 292, 342

The Sleeping Giant 20, 340

The Sleighs of my Childhood / Les Traineaux de mon Enfance 103, 108, 390

The Slightly Irregular Fire Engine: or, The Hithering, Thithering Djinn 61, 132, 261

The Slightly Irregular Fire Engine: or, The Hithering Thithering Djinn 61, 132, 261

Slinky Malinki 6, 324

Slither McCreep and His Brother Joe 185, 296, 397

Sly Old Wardrobe 58, 362, 525

Small Energy Sources 152, 357

The Smallest Life Around Us 148, 251, 360

The Small Potatoes' Busy Beach Day 145, 282, 574

Small Rain: Verses from the Bible 37, 397, 398

A Smart Kid Like You 84, 477

Smile, Ernest and Celestine 549

Smile, Ernestine and Celestine 158

Smile for Auntie 64, 472

Smith 25, 47, 350

Smoke 112, 121, 205, 222, 239, 279, 305, 310, 485, 503

Smoke Eater 205, 279, 310

Smoky, the Cowhorse 51, 165, 392

Smudge of the Fells 213, 349

Smuggler's Road 334

Smuggler's Sloop 204, 559, 569

Smugglers Road 187

Snail, Where Are You? 212, 545

The Snail's Spell 149, 296, 500

Snail and Caterpillar 99, 263, 478

Snail in the Woods 143, 336, 481, 500

The Snailman 121, 385, 520

Snails 150, 396, 439

A Snake-lover's Diary 279

A Snake Lover's Diary 214

Snakes 31, 390, 575

The Snake Tree 171, 498

Sneakers 73, 514

The Sniper 42, 537

Snipp, Snapp, Snurr and the Red Shoes 50, 424

Snot Stew 115, 200, 220, 442, 552

The Snow and the Sun: A South American Folk Rhyme in Two Languages 154, 344

Snowbird 87, 199, 289

Snowfoot: White Reindeer of the Arctic 142, 319, 468

The Snowman 14, 27, 53, 99, 191, 199, 279

The Snow Monkey at Home 202, 386, 488

Snow on Blueberry Mountain 135, 447, 517

The Snow Owl's Secret 174, 334

The Snow Party 32, 320, 575

The Snow Spider 198, 222, 289, 462

Snow Treasure 238, 446, 489

Snow White and the Seven Dwarfs 22, 37, 40, 53, 160, 285, 347, 363, 364, 393

Snow White in New York 100, 345

Snowy 57, 276, 324

The Snowy Day 12, 39, 145, 396, 402, 574

So, Nothing Is Forever 202, 309, 397

Soap Soup and Other Verses 185, 412

Socks 92, 231, 299, 313

The Socksnatchers 80, 258

So Far from the Bamboo Grove 181, 346, 554

Soft as the Wind 72, 330, 493

So Hungry! 145, 461, 574

Sojourner Truth: Ain't I a Woman? 30, 119, 445

Soldier and Tsar in the Forest: A Russian Tale 215, 429, 516

The Solitary 94, 367

A Solitary Blue 28, 170, 180, 550

The Solomon System 56, 459

Solomon the Rusty Nail 191, 529

Sol Solet 23, 292

Somebody Else's Child 56, 304, 517

Somebody Loves You, Mr. Hatch 69, 526, 569

Some Follow the Sea 206, 336, 337

Someone Is Hiding on Alcatraz Island 199, 285

Something Beyond Paradise 145, 521

Something Big Has Been Here 117, 483, 530

Something on My Mind 118, 336, 363

Some Things go Together 83, 365, 575

Something Special 59, 495, 572

Some Things You Should Know about my Dog 64, 262

Something Upstairs: A Tale of Ghosts 193, 218, 226, 256

Somewhere in the Darkness 30, 119, 171, 458

So Much to Tell You ... 59, 69, 75, 117, 436

Son for a Day 68, 353, 389

Song and Dance Man 41, 199, 244, 348, 349

Songberd's Grove 46, 260, 408

Song for a Dark Queen 176, 534

The Song of Pentecost 230, 305, 545

Song of Robin Hood 38, 287, 434

Song of the Boat 27, 63, 322, 323, 359

Song of the Buffalo Boy 95, 350

Song of the Chippewa 269

Song of the City 197, 378, 468

Song of the Gargoyle 74, 524

Song of the Pines: A Story of Norwegian Lumbering in Wisconsin 167, 174, 208, 341, 372

Song of the Swallows 38, 481

Song of the Trees 4, 63, 73, 479, 537

Song of the Voyageur 43, 287

Songs of the Chippewa 215, 512

Sonny-boy Sim 208, 216, 258, 533

Son of the Hawk 31, 486, 544

Son of the Valley 208, 544

Son of Thunder: An Old Lapp Tale 202, 275, 444

Sons of the Hurricane 205, 341

Sons of the Steppe 210, 263, 497

Soot Devil 140, 351

Sophie 4, 30, 184, 191, 212, 439, 444, 469, 543, 549, 565

Sophie and Lou 30, 184, 439

Sophiechen und der Riese 109, 311, 486

The Sorcerer's Apprentice 7, 111, 456

Sorrow's Kitchen: The Life and Folklore of Zora Neale Hurston 235, 431

The Soul Brothers and Sister Lou 52, 73, 386

Sounder 52, 103, 134, 169, 222, 254, 260

A Sound of Chariots 56, 160, 186, 387

The Sound of Dragon's Feet 17, 337, 573

Sounds and Signals: How We Communicate 148, 447

Soup 128, 351, 475

Soup for President 222, 422, 475

South Pass - 1868 (His) Journal of the Wyoming Gold Rush 229, 296, 382

South Town 85, 360

Space Case 42, 70, 226, 437

Space Demons 59, 66, 133, 237, 499

Space Frontiers 149, 306, 375

Spaceshots 151, 337, 573

Spaceshots: The Beauty of Nature Beyond Earth 573

Space Songs 203, 339, 426

A Space Story 149, 412, 519

Space Trap 10, 385

Spaghetti for Breakfast and other Useful Phrases in Italian and English 212, 261, 398

Span Across a River 215, 333

Sparkle and Spin: A Book about Words 153, 487

Sparrow Song 179, 514

Spatzen Brauchen Keinen Schirm 178, 505, 557

Speaking to Miranda 6, 432

The Spear and the Piccolo: Heroic and Pastoral Dimensions of William Steig's Dominic and Abel's Island 65, 456

Spectacles 155, 487

A Spell Is Cast 71, 187, 289, 411

Spice and the Devil's Cave 165, 376, 554

Spice Island Mystery 187, 293

The Spider's Web 19, 402

The Spider of Brooklyn Heights 213, 336, 548

Spiders 14, 93, 150, 221, 311, 412, 421, 472, 560

Spies and More Spies 138, 254, 413

Spinky Sulks 192, 529

A Spirit to Ride the Whirlwind 4, 56, 428

Splash! All About Baths 8, 288, 301

Splasher 174, 275, 308, 348

Spook, the Mustang 71, 415, 539

Spooner or Later 14, 319, 362, 393

Sport 73, 340

Sports and Games in Verse and Rhyme 142, 317, 391

Spotlight for Danny 206, 265, 435

Spring Peepers 148, 275, 373

The Spring Rider 25, 417

Spring Story 178, 260

Spurs for Antonia 71, 335, 448

Spy for the Confederacy: Rose O'Neal Greenhow 106, 463

Squanto, Friend of the Pilgrims 285

Squanto, Friend of the White Man 31, 284, 285

Squashed 75, 262

Squawk to the Moon, Little Goose 161, 305, 483

Squeak-a-Lot 130, 451, 551

The Squeaky Wheel 184, 523

Squid and Spider: A Look at the Animal Kingdom 158, 269

The Squirrel-wife 215, 302, 474

Ssh! It's the Secret Club! 555

The St. Lawrence 44, 347, 487, 542

St. Lawrence Seaway 106, 270, 399

The Stable that Stayed 208, 474

Stadtmaus und Landmaus 22, 387

The Stage-Struck Seal 86, 386

The Stalker 42, 462

Stand By - Mark! The Career Story of a Naval Officer 206, 349

Stanleigh's Wrong-side-out Day 70, 300, 529

Stanley Bagshaw and the Short-Sighted Goal Keeper 125, 564

Star-crossed Stallion 33, 417

Starbuck Valley Winter 43, 316, 367

The Star Fisher 69, 570

Stargazers 8, 353

Stargone John 18, 429, 444, 445

The Star in the Pail 132, 442, 519

Star Light Stories: Holiday and Sabbath Tales 114, 345, 494

Star Maiden: An Ojibwa Legend of the First Water Lily 70, 315, 493

The Star Maiden: An Ojibway Tale 128, 314, 333

Starring Sally J. Freedman as Herself 103, 273

Starry Night 102, 176, 509

Stars, Men and Atoms 78, 366

Stars, Mosquitos and Crocodiles: The American Travels of Alexander von Humboldt 32, 477, 510

The Stars and Serendipity 147, 491

Stars and Stripes: The Story of the American Flag 136, 270, 345

Stars Come Out Within 45, 190, 425

Stars for Christy 106, 386, 389

Start of the Trail: The Story of a Young Maine Guide 208, 491

The Star Wars: From the Adventures of Luke Skywalker 172, 430

Staying With Grandma 146, 495

Stay Put, Robbie McAmis 229, 514, 543

The Steadfast Tin Soldier 38, 185, 250, 281, 436

Steal Away 95, 254

Steamboat in a Cornfield 29, 371

Steamboat Up the Missouri 229, 351, 480

Steel Town Cats 222, 310, 430

Stegosaurus 199, 433, 492

Stephen's Feast 69, 333, 491

Stephen Biesty's Incredible Cross Sections 34, 269, 480

Stephen Crane: The Story of an American Writer 211, 343

Step Into the Night 72, 182, 463, 500

Steppin and Family 206, 460, 475

Stepping on the Cracks 74, 173, 217, 366

Sterling: The Rescue of a Baby Harbor Seal 24, 338, 559

Stevie 12, 53, 118, 235, 300, 372, 460, 529

Stick-in-the-Mud: A Tale of a Village, a Custom and a Little Boy 3, 405

Stickelwort and Feverfew 87, 534

The Stinky Cheese Man and Other Fairly Stupid Tales   41, 160, 508, 523
A Stitch in Time   230, 425
Stocky, Boy of West Texas   207, 258, 369
The Stolen Pony   53, 498
Stone and Steel: A Look at Engineering   157, 269
Stone Fox   80, 122, 162, 202, 217, 224, 349, 512
Stones: Their Collection, Identification and Uses   149, 322
The Stone Silenus   180, 571
Stone Soup   38, 281
Stonewall   27, 162, 171, 312, 346, 349, 456
Stonewall Jackson   171, 312, 456
Stonewords   29, 184, 189, 304
Storia di una Volpe   109, 289, 503
Stories for Children   15, 45, 46, 49, 163, 253, 317, 373, 520
Stories for Children of the Kingdom   15
Stories from the Olympics from 776 B.C. to Now   142, 351
The Stories Julian Tells   21, 289, 533
Stories of King David   114, 345, 400
The Storm Book   38, 360, 575
Storm Boy   58, 389, 538
Storm Canvas   206, 526
Storm in the Night   119, 183, 309, 532
Storms on the Labrador   205, 323
Storm Surge   101, 489, 533
A Story, A Story   26, 40, 367
The Story About Ping   51, 340, 560
A Storybook   156, 545
The Story Catcher   229, 442, 503
Story for a Black Night   203, 268
Story Number 1   155, 318, 390
Story Number 3   61, 305, 390
The Story of Albert Schweitzer   32, 46, 354, 552
The Story of Ants   137, 517, 534
The Story of Appleby Capple   167, 472
The Story of Babar, the Little Elephant   50, 282, 366
Story of Brother Francis   53, 440, 502
The Story of Cake   143, 521
The Story of Canada   129, 312, 430, 453
The Story of Christmas   63, 192, 380, 488
The Story of Christmas: Words from the Gospels of Matthew and Luke   192, 488
The Story of Comock the Eskimo, as Told to Robert Flaherty   52, 290
The Story of Creation   34
The Story of Design   212, 325
The Story of Doctor Dolittle   49, 428
The Story of Edward   27, 327
The Story of Football   137, 418
The Story of George Washington   141, 446, 554
The Story of Horace   205, 300
The Story of Irving Berlin   208, 292, 335
The Story of Israel   114, 421
The Story of John Keats   46, 331, 354, 355
The Story of Jumping Mouse   41, 529

Story of Karrawinga, the Emu   57, 310, 489
The Story of Little Quack   129, 319, 353
The Story of Mankind   164, 547
The Story of Masada   114, 358, 569
The Story of Mrs. Lovewright and Purrless, Her Cat   158, 163, 510, 573
The Story of Oceanography   148, 277
The Story of Old Abe   215, 456, 497
The Story of Old Mrs. Brubeck and How She Looked for Trouble and Where She Found Him   158, 510, 513
The Story of People   209, 312, 330
The Story of Prince Rama   88, 394, 539
The Story of Soul the King   98, 493
The Story of Stevie Wonder   118, 372
The Story of the Creation: Words From Genesis   198, 488
The Story of the Dancing Frog   125, 271
The Story of the Falling Star   14, 325, 397
The Story of the Great Lakes   174, 321, 354
The Story of the Kakapo Parrot of the Night   6, 350, 537
Story of the Mississippi   205, 321, 432
Story of the Negro   3, 167, 275, 430
The Story of the Old Colony of New Plymouth   77, 454, 468
Story of the Second World War   46, 504
The Story of Tracy Beaker   49, 172, 514, 564
The Story of World War II   136, 418
Story of Your Foot   145, 518, 557
The Story of your Home   45, 248
The Story of Your Mouth   144, 244, 518
The Storyteller's Pack   52, 283, 531
Straight Talk about Love and Sex for Teenagers   73, 285
Strandia   236, 491
Strange Animals of the Sea   192, 288, 479
The Strange Appearance of Howard Cranebill, Jr.   158, 326
Strange Objects   60, 75, 147, 308
The Stranger   116, 158, 284, 546
A Stranger at Green Knowe   46, 276
A Stranger Came Ashore: A Story of Suspense   26, 161, 387
Stranger With my Face   42, 81, 126, 162, 200, 238, 327
Strange Summer in Stratford   121, 389, 476
Strat and Chatto   130, 385, 436
Strawberry Girl   167, 420
Streams to the River, River to the Sea   173, 181, 465
The Stream that Stood Still   110, 423, 461
Street Family   185, 397
Street Flowers   221, 404, 431
Street of Ships   206, 313
The Streets Are Paved with Gold   220, 556
Strega Nona   13, 14, 40, 319
Strider   190, 299, 573

String, Straight-edge and Shadow: The Story of Geometry   213, 265, 322
Stringbean's Trip to the Shining Sea   29, 159, 182, 563, 564
A String in the Harp   26, 111, 169, 222, 274, 314
String Lug the Fox   209, 414, 529
A String of Chances   200, 459
Strings and Things: Poems and Other Messages for Children   53, 404, 467
Striped Ice Cream   197, 423, 564
The Strollers   84, 264, 549
A Strong and Willing Girl   176, 330
Strongbow   20, 426
The Stronghold   47, 387
Stuart Little   79, 559, 563
The Stubborn One   229, 450, 453
Studies in the Literary Imagination   66, 443
The Stupids Die   11, 247, 437
The Stupids Step Out   63, 247, 437
Styles   45, 137, 221, 352, 489, 533, 562
Styles by Suzy   137, 352, 562
A Sudden Silence   42, 196, 203, 285
Sudden Steps, Small Stones   142, 533
Sugar Bush   207, 312
Sugaring Time   170, 408, 416
Suho and the White Horse: A Legend of Mongolia   13, 14, 246, 378, 468
The Suitcase Kid   56, 514, 564
Sukey and the Mermaid   105, 119, 191, 479, 502
Sukkot: A Time to Rejoice   203, 326, 379
The Sultan's Bath   99, 249
The Summer After the Funeral   26, 349
The Summer Ballet Mystery   43, 566
The Summer Before   215, 565
The Summer Birds   46, 335, 525
The Summerboy   144, 424
Summerfield Farm   208, 270, 319
Summer Gold: A Camper's Guide to Amateur Prospecting   148, 329
The Summer I Was Lost   52, 78, 84, 549
Summer Nanny   95, 538
Summer of Fear   42, 84, 121, 327
The Summer of Lily and Esme   20, 486
Summer of my German Soldier   93, 126, 132, 161, 361
Summer of the Monkeys   42, 92, 196, 232, 232, 488
Summer of the Swans   169, 288, 301
Summer of the Zeppelin   102, 443
Summer Stories   16, 429, 538
The Summer that Lasted Forever   171, 477
A Summer to Die   42, 111, 126, 429, 466
The Sun: Our Nearest Star   136, 275, 278
A Sundae with Judy   208, 345, 374
Sunday Morning   139, 408, 549
The Sunday Times Countryside Companion   221, 572
Sundiata: The Epic of the Lion King   214, 268, 483
Sunflower!   149, 213, 332, 557
A Sunflower as Big as the Sun   213, 332
Sunflowers   150, 400, 468

The Sun Horse   43, 269, 298

The Sun Is a Golden Earring   39, 266, 283

The Sunken City   107, 323, 446

Sunlight   148, 292, 366

The Sun Looks Down   152, 359, 506

Sunny   65, 79, 129, 303, 364, 490

Sunshine   58, 79, 100, 126, 130, 408, 467

Superbike!   236, 281

Superfudge   11, 25, 35, 42, 64, 65, 70, 73, 80, 88, 89, 96, 98, 103, 112, 134, 143, 172, 199, 218, 220, 224, 225, 226, 227, 238, 239, 273

The Superlative Horse   51, 448, 524

Supermachines   149, 369, 470

Superplanes   143, 459

Super Stitches: A Book of Superstitions   144, 460

Surely You're Joking, Mr. Feynman!   151, 337, 388, 419

Surfer the Seal   24, 287

The Surprise Picnic   157, 357

Surrogate Mothers   146, 414

Susan Cornish   21, 293, 395

Susan Who Lives in Australia   206, 432

Susie, the Cat   208, 469

Susie the Cat   208, 469

Susy's Scoundrel   228, 506

Suzy's Scoundrel   403

Sven's Bridge   155, 426

SVK   110, 311

Swallowtail Butterflies   150, 311, 468, 503

The Swamp Fox of the Revolution   239, 381, 491

Swan Sky   159, 537

A Swarm in May   46, 380, 441

Sweetgrass   44, 97, 109, 183, 385

A Sweetheart for Valentine   73, 259

The Sweet Touch   70, 90, 92, 258

Sweet Whispers, Brother Rush   28, 109, 118, 163, 170, 368

A Swiftly Tilting Planet   7, 420

Swift Rivers   165, 387, 447

The Swimming Pool   21, 300, 334

Swimmy   12, 19, 39, 154, 424

The Swineherd   179, 250, 265, 576

Switcharound   124, 200, 429

Switch on the Night   32, 153, 277, 352

Sword in Sheath   174, 270, 463

The Sword of Roland Arnot   205, 376, 533

Swords of Steel: The Story of a Gettysburg Boy   166, 375, 520

Sybil and the Blue Rabbit   130, 395

Sylvester and the Magic Pebble   39, 53, 79, 131, 214, 529

T-Bone, the Baby Sitter   38, 460

Tacky the Penguin   42, 70, 96, 421, 457

Taffy and Joe   207, 286, 287, 532

Taffy of Torpedo Junction   171, 525, 555

Tail Feathers   192, 467

Tail Feathers from Mother Goose: The Opie Rhyme Book   192, 467

The Tailor of Gloucester   50, 482

The Tailypo: A Ghost Story   90, 347, 348

Taipi   19, 333, 448

Takeru   23

Take the Long Path   91, 316, 341

Taking Care of Melvin   179, 296, 513

Taking Care of Terrific   180, 429

Taking Terri Mueller   42, 188, 441

A Tale for Easter   205, 543

A Tale of Antarctica   24, 356

The Tale of a Wood   154, 400

The Tale of Czar Saltan: or, The Prince and the Swan Princess   63, 269, 429, 485

The Tale of Fancy Nancy: A Spanish Folk Tale   157, 333, 409

The Tale of John Barleycorn: or, From Barley to Beer: A Traditional English Ballad   180, 257

The Tale of Peter Rabbit   49, 482

A Tale of Terror   225, 256

The Tale of the Mandarin Ducks   30, 159, 322, 323, 473

A Tale of Two Kings   131, 454

Tales for the Perfect Child   181, 296, 374

Tales From Gold Mountain   45, 77, 79, 133, 461, 570

Tales from Silver Lands   165, 338, 382

Tales Mummies Tell   151, 416

Tales of a Dead King   144, 458

Tales of a Fourth Grade Nothing   11, 89, 98, 126, 140, 172, 196, 197, 200, 227, 239, 240, 273, 325

Tales of a Gambling Grandma   164, 405

Tales of Christophilos   209, 353, 459

Tales of Nanabozho   44, 360, 490

Tales of Pan   181, 353

Tales of the Kingdom   91, 434, 531

Tales of Thunder and Lightning   142, 320

Tales of Trickery: From the Land of Spoof   145, 297, 508

Tales of Trickery from the Land of Spoof   145, 297, 508

The Tales of Uncle Remus   118, 182, 370, 421, 479

Tales the People Tell in China   140, 300, 569

Tales the People Tell in Russia   139, 252, 569

Talk, Talk: An Ashanti Legend   185, 246, 296

The Talking Cat   208, 290, 329

The Talking Dog and the Barking Man   211, 341, 509

The Talking Eggs   21, 41, 71, 96, 119, 183, 479, 502

Talking in Whispers   176, 555

Talking Together About Love and Sexuality   91, 537

Talking Turkey   171, 382

Talking With Artists   30, 175, 309

Talking Without Words   155, 334

Tallyho, Pinkerton!   179, 403

The Tamarack Tree   3, 145, 297, 382, 545

Tame the Wild Stallion   216, 562

Tan Ar y Comin   398

Tancy   94, 171, 387

Tangara: Let Us Set off Again   57, 107, 295, 562

Tangle-Coated Horse and Other Tales: Episodes from the Fionn Saga   165, 273, 572

Tangle and the Firesticks   198, 271

A Tangle of Roots   79, 354

Taniwha   5, 70, 399

Tantos Iris Como Dragones   24, 464, 548

Tapporahat   9, 490

Tar Beach   41, 104, 116, 119, 160, 184, 492

Taresh the Tea Planter   99, 470

Taro and a Bamboo Shoot   19, 439, 510

Taronga   59, 403

The Tartar's Sword   87, 406

A Taste for Quiet and Other Disquieting Tales   144, 358, 540

A Taste of Blackberries   56, 89, 103, 494, 522

A Taste of Salt   5, 537

The Taste of Spruce Gum   84, 391, 465

Tatsinda   212, 333, 365

The Tattooed Potato and other Clues   188, 487, 488

The Tavern at the Ferry   62, 544

Tawny   162, 290, 291

Taxation   136, 504, 533

Teacher's Pet   89, 218, 368, 387

Teach Us, Amelia Bedelia   88, 470, 535

Teammates   192, 235, 257, 357

The Teen Guide to Dating   143, 414

Teeny-tiny   391, 430

Teeny Tiny   142

Tehanu   190, 419

Television Magic   149, 397

Telling Fortunes   145, 289, 508

Tell Me a Mitzi   214, 479, 510

Tell Me a Story, Mama   116, 183, 394, 525

The Tempering   94, 520

Ten, Nine, Eight   41, 259

Ten and a Kid   114, 324, 556

Ten Copycats in a Boat and other Riddles   143, 508, 519

Ten Cousins   216, 289, 515

Ten Dogs   124, 353

Ten Kids, No Pets   238, 239, 437

Ten Little Rabbits   112, 192, 364, 428

Tenrec's Twigs   192, 407

Ten Tall Texans   210, 439, 443

The Tent Under the Spider Tree   227, 265, 390

Terpin   163, 510

Terraced House Books: Set D   176, 363, 374

The Terrible Tale of the Vanishing Library   34, 476

Terry's Brrrmmm GT   58, 362

Tex   103, 378

Text as Teacher: The Beginning of Charlotte's Web   66, 463

Textile Worker   176, 307, 357

Thanks for Being My Friend   91, 395, 475

The Thanksgiving Story   39, 311, 513

That's My Dad   23, 528

Thatcher Payne-in-the-Neck 194, 262, 330

That Dunbar Boy 77, 359, 552

That Jefferson Boy 140, 449, 558

That Julia Redfern 179, 289, 469

That Mario 205, 308

That Scatterbrain Booky 111, 386

That Was Then, This Is Now 126, 214, 378, 517

Their Shining Hour: Based on Events in the life of Susanna Dickenson at the Siege of the Alamo 229, 433

Them that Glitter and Them That Don't 180, 361

Then Again, Maybe I Won't 140, 273

Then and Now 32, 142, 260, 325, 565, 573

Theodor and Mr. Balbini 159, 439

Theodore Roosevelt, Fighting Patriot 168, 270, 399

There's a Bat in Bunk Five 42, 74, 312

There's a Boy in the Girls' Bathroom 35, 96, 112, 121, 126, 134, 135, 182, 197, 218, 220, 223, 224, 226, 228, 501

There's a Monster Under My Bed 70, 113, 384, 496

There's an Alligator Under My Bed 85, 440

There's a Sound in the Sea: A Child's Eye View of the Whale 156, 363

There Once Was a Woman Who Married a Man 157, 310, 335

There Was an Old Woman 156, 191, 403, 437, 495, 569

There Were Monkeys In My Kitchen! 129, 339, 452

There Will Be Wolves 236, 277

These Happy Golden Years 167, 206, 277, 513, 561

Theseus and the Minotaur 159, 388

They Loved to Laugh 206, 315, 568

They Never Came Home 187, 328

They Put Out To Sea: The Story of the Map 206, 329

They Were Strong and Good 37, 417

A Thief in the Village 118, 198, 268

Thimble Summer 166, 333

Thing 58, 408, 421

Thin Ice 222, 407

The Third-Story Cat 112, 258

The Third Experiment 151, 339

The Third Eye 22, 189, 225, 238, 328, 387

The Third Magic 44, 97, 401

Thirteen 16, 26, 35, 156, 196, 216, 218, 239, 295, 330, 354, 399

The Thirteenth Stone 207, 257, 276

Thirteen Ways to Sink a Sub 35, 196, 218, 239, 330, 354

Thirty-one Brothers and Sisters 85, 436, 451

This Boy Cody 50, 409, 564

This Is a Crocodile 145, 304

This Island Isn't Big Enough for the Four of Us 122, 201, 224, 362, 499

This Is London 154, 503

This Is New York 32, 154, 503

This Is the Desert 71, 256, 339

This Is the Story of Faint George Who Wanted to be a Knight 32, 153, 261

This Is Your Century 213, 542

This Life 118, 481

This Little Pig-a-wig and other Rhymes about Pigs 157

This Poem Doesn't Rhyme 197, 267, 531

This School Is Driving Me Crazy 92, 376

This Star Shall Abide 68, 309, 333

This Strange New Feeling 118, 179, 421

This Time Count Me In 177, 567

Thistle and Thyme: Tales and Legends from Scotland 50, 168, 460, 462

This Was Bridget 36, 369, 435

Thomas' Snowsuit 195, 437, 457

Thomas Jefferson: His Many Talents 78, 268, 396

Thorn Rose 99, 108, 363, 364, 418

Thou Shalt not be Aware: Society's Betrayal of the Child 120, 369, 450

Threadbear 56, 172, 389

Three and a Pigeon 206, 260, 542

The Three and Many Wishes of Jason Reid 190, 388, 538

The Three Bears Rhyme Book 181, 329, 571

The Three Brothers of Ur 47, 249, 347

Three Days 42, 74, 89, 134, 162, 197, 218, 314, 385, 435

Three Gold Pieces 33, 247

Three Hundred and Ninety-seventh White Elephant 49, 365, 418, 436

Three Is Company 179, 247, 551

The Three Jovial Huntsmen: A Mother Goose Rhyme 13, 19, 40, 62, 393

The Three Kings of Saba 153, 334, 513

The Three Policemen 136, 327

Three Poor Tailors 98, 249

The Three Robbers 12, 154, 545

The Three Toymakers 214, 385, 564

The Throne of the Erril of Sherill 62, 445, 463

Through the Broken Mirror with Alice: Including Parts of Through the Looking Glass 140, 291, 566

Through the Looking Glass and What Alice Found There 199, 291, 541

Through the Mickle Woods 185, 362, 455

Through the Telescope 152, 482

Through the Web 34, 493

Throw Stone: The First American Boy 25,000 Years Ago 216, 504, 530, 568

Thumbelina 50, 244, 250, 402

Thunder and Lightnings 48, 101, 436, 500

Thunderbolt House 71, 475, 526

Thunder in the Sky 47, 249, 477

Thunder on the Tennes: The Summer Ballet Mystery

Thunder on the Tennes: Trapped in Sliprock Canyon

Thursday's Child 356

Thursday's Children 180

Thursday's Daughters: The Story of Women Working in America 143, 370

The Thursday Kidnapping 47, 342

Thy Friend, Obadiah 26, 40, 214, 544

Ticket To Curlew 45, 428

The Tide in the Attic 32, 354, 547

The Tiger and the Traveler 123, 570

Tiger Eyes 22, 35, 42, 74, 84, 112, 187, 273, 560

Tiger in the Bush 57, 295, 383

Tiger Rookie 137, 343, 506

Tigers 185, 202, 301, 330, 491, 517, 545

Tigress 184, 306

The Tiguas: The Lost Tribe of City Indians 230, 529

Tikki Tikki Tembo 25, 420, 455

Tikta'liktak: An Eskimo Legend 44, 383

Til All the Stars Have Fallen: Canadian Poems for Children 104, 275, 319

Tills Aventyr I Skorstensgrand 10, 423, 561

Tilly's House 157, 392

Tim's Last Voyage 156, 253

Tim all Alone 98, 253

Time-ago Lost: More Tales of Jahdu 215, 368, 483

Time and Clocks for the Space Age 149, 340, 394

The Time Before Dreams 7, 310

Time Circles 222, 449

Time Enough 127, 145, 492, 502

Time Enough for Drums 145, 492

Time of Trial 46, 98, 212, 249, 286

A Time of Troubles 173, 547

Time of Wonder 39, 174, 442

The Times Educational Supplement 221

Timewarp Summer 144, 397

The Timid Ghost: or, What Would You Do with a Sackful of Gold? 33, 278, 279, 295

Timothy's Horse 156, 304, 312, 440

Timothy Turtle 38, 359, 469

The Tin Fiddle 209, 511, 543

Tingambato: Adventures in Archaeology 150, 463

Tinker, Tailor, Soldier, Sailor: A Picture Book 99, 427, 495

Tinker's Tim and the Witches 174, 251, 301

Tin Lizzie and Little Nell 58, 306

Tintinyane: The Girl Who Sang Like a Magic Bird 127

Tiny 108, 401, 426

Tiny Animal Stories 207, 412, 563

Tiny Bat and the Ball Game 16, 509, 566

The Tiny Visitor 158, 179, 318

The Tipi: A Center of Native American Life 28, 572

Tirra Lirra: Rhymes Old and New 50, 314, 491

Titch 107, 388

Titus in Trouble 98, 253, 489

Tjarany Roughtail 60, 354, 361, 542

The New York Times's Choice of Best Illustrated Children's Book of the Year

To Be a Slave 52, 169, 336, 421

To Become a Man 123, 296

To Build a Land 235, 292, 555

Toby, Granny and George 87, 278, 498

Toby's Millions   58, 430
Tod's Owl   102, 482
Tod of the Fens   165, 356, 560
Todos los Iris al Iris   24, 464, 548
Tog the Ribber: or, Granny's Tale   100, 303, 442
To Live in Two Worlds: American Indian Youth Today   234, 255, 303
Tom's Friend   232, 491
Tom's Midnight Garden   46, 51, 107, 331, 474
Tomahawk Claim   106, 523
Tom and Pippo   190, 469
Tomas and the Red-headed Angel   71, 86, 270, 350
The Tombs of Atuan   132, 169, 350, 419
Tomb Travellers: Beyond the Gateways and Guardians of Egypt's Underworld   15, 482
Tomfoolery, Trickery and Foolery with Words   161, 498, 508
Tomie de Paola's Favorite Nursery Tales   191, 319
Tom Paine, Freedom's Apostle   168, 210, 365, 410
Tom Sawyer   51, 299, 400
The Tomten   12, 52, 424, 560
Tom Thumb   94, 166, 331, 386, 555
Tom Tit Tot   39, 391, 460
The Tongue-Cut Sparrow   181, 182, 246, 390
Tonia the Tree   87, 433, 533
Tonk and Tonka   106, 243, 285
Tony of the Ghost Towns   210, 272, 436
Too Fat? Too Thin? Do You Have a Choice?   203, 254, 361
Too Hot for Ice Cream   141, 142, 247, 547
Toolchest   62, 244
Tools   143, 151, 158, 282, 312, 341, 493
Too Many Pets   208, 246, 305
The Toom County Mud Race   75, 400
Too Much Magic   113, 355, 530
Too Much Nose   213, 574
Too Much T.J.   75, 513
The Toothpaste Genie   218, 327
The Toothpaste Millionaire   84, 196, 448, 469
Topsail Island Treasure   137, 281, 447
Top Secret   185, 349, 519
Topsy Turvies: Pictures to Stretch the Imagination   12, 156, 214, 252
Tormented Angel: A Life of John Henry Newman   213, 350
Tormented Genius: The Struggles of Vincent Van Gogh   106, 382
Tornado!   85, 92, 321, 451, 530
Tornado Jones   85, 321, 530
Torrie   211, 335, 395
To Space and Back   89, 491
To Survive We Must be Clever   106, 338, 405
To the Green Mountains   132, 289
To the Pacific with Lewis and Clark   229, 251, 269
To the Tune of the Hickory Stick   162, 278

To the Wild Sky   57, 525, 543
Touched with Fire: Alaska's George William Seller   78, 265, 492
Touch of Light: The Story of Louis Braille   86, 460, 471
Tough Chauncey   26, 329, 522
A Tournament of Knights   191, 415
Tournaments   221, 259, 311
Towards Oregon   71, 369, 370, 527
Tracker   199, 474
Tracking the Unearthly Creatures of Marsh and Pond   67, 393, 522
Tradition and the Individual Talent of Frances Hodgson Burnett: A Generic Analysis of Little Lord Fauntleroy, A Little Princess, and The Secret Garden   65, 270
Trailblazer: Negro Nurse in the American Red Cross   86, 480
Trail Blazer of the Seas   32, 416, 441
The Trail Driving Rooster   216, 354, 519
Trail of the Little Paiute   209, 315, 466
The Train   58, 352
Train for Tiger Lily   43, 484, 492
Train Song   192, 517, 565
Traitor: The Case of Benedict Arnold   162, 251, 346
The Tram to Bondi Beach   58, 372, 550
The Transfigured Hart   93, 321, 571
translated from Englis
Transport 7-41-R   26, 111, 316
The Trap   31, 302, 353
Trapped in Death Cave   199, 218, 224, 552
Trapped in Sliprock Canyon   230, 502, 520
Trapped in Tar: Fossils From the Ice Age   151, 254, 377
Trapping the Silver Beaver   229, 404, 462
Traveler from a Small Kingdom   213, 452, 460
Travels of a Snail   205, 351, 380
The Treasure   40, 132, 144, 157, 161, 310, 359, 425, 439, 516
Treasure in an Oatmeal Box   92, 354, 557
The Treasure is the Rose   132, 161, 310, 359
Treasure Keepers   148, 451
Treasure of Green Knowe   275, 276
Treasure of the High Country   211, 416, 550
Treasure River   187, 334
Treasures of Time   425
The Treasure Trap   144, 425, 439
Treasure your Love   36, 408
The Tree   222, 378, 566
Tree by Leaf   217, 550
The Treegate Chronicles   202, 560
A Tree in a Forest   539
A Tree in the Forest   106
A Tree Is Nice   39, 519, 545
The Tree of Animal Life: A Tale of Changing Forms and Fortunes   149, 445
Tree of Cranes   18, 186, 504

Tree of Freedom   167, 208, 293, 455
Tree Trunk Traffic   152, 417
The Tree Witches   70, 544
The Trek   29, 397
The Trial of Anna Cotman   48, 246
Triceratops   199, 433, 492
The Tricksters   164, 434
Trip Day   146, 282, 574
Tristan and Iseult   26, 47, 249, 534
Triumphs of the Human Spirit in Children's Literature   66, 521
Trois Petits Flocons   23, 260, 276
Trouble's Child   118, 553
Trouble at the Mines   4, 487, 503
Trouble at Turtle Bay   33, 382
Trouble for Trumpets   19, 130, 308, 311
Trouble Half-way   102, 436, 471
The Troublesome Pig   125, 414
The Trouble They Seen: Black People Tell the Story of Reconstruction   234, 529
The Trouble with Donovan Croft   176, 255, 494
The Trouble with Gramary   122, 421
The Trouble with Jenny's Ear   211, 287, 318
The Trouble with Lucy   138, 289
The Trouble with Princesses   44, 97, 104, 370, 536
The Trouble with Terry   55, 423, 457
The Trouble with Tuck   42, 537
Truce of the Wolf and Other Tales of Old Italy   165, 314, 547
Truck   40, 205, 308, 455
The Truck That Flew   205, 455
The True Confessions of Charlotte Doyle   30, 94, 122, 170, 256, 457
True or False? Amazing Art Forgeries   144, 552
The True Story of Lilli Stubeck   59, 246
The True Story of Okee the Otter   138, 565
The True Story of Spit MacPhee   102, 147, 246
True Tales of Buried Treasure   31, 524
Trumpeter of Krakow   33, 165, 403, 485
The Trumpet of the Swan   103, 107, 107, 132, 196, 214, 231, 237, 344, 559
The Truth about Santa Claus   29, 353
The Truth Trap   42, 450
Trying Hard to Hear You   142, 508
Trysor Bryniau Caspar   426
The Tsar and the Amazing Cow   175, 375, 423
The Tub People   92, 183, 304, 331
Tucker's Countryside   67, 510, 563
Tuck Everlasting   53, 68, 108, 161, 257
Tuesday   41, 561
Tugboat   64, 480
Tuhatkiloinen Kultakala   109, 288, 428
Tulku   48, 108, 230, 322
The Tune Is in the Tree   208, 429, 562
Tunes for a Small Harmonica   133, 558
The Turbulent Term of Tyke Tiler   48, 176, 323, 403
Turi: The Story of a Little Boy   90, 271, 482
Turi's Poppa   25, 254, 543

Turkeylegs Thompson   162, 442

Turramulli the Giant Quinkin   58, 498, 543

A Turtle, and a Loon, and other Fables   212, 438

Turtle in July   159, 479, 520

Turtle Knows Your Name   183, 283

Turtle Tale   143, 255

Turtle Watch   151, 250

The Tutti-Frutti Case: Starring the Four Doctors of Goodge   156, 247, 437

Tutto Su Gerusalemme Biblica   22, 246, 256

TV Action Book   126, 507

The Twelve and the Genii   46, 107, 298, 421

Twelve at War: Great Photographers under Fire   138, 382

Twelve Cats for Christmas   158, 419

The Twelve Dancing Princesses   97, 99, 104, 111, 347, 363, 364, 418, 430

Twelve Days of Christmas   191, 565

The Twenty-five Cent Miracle   113, 460

The Twenty-one Balloons   207, 327

The Twenty-seventh Annual African Hippopotamus Race   237, 382, 430

Twenty-six Ways to Be Somebody Else   154, 276

Twenty and Ten   55, 270, 327

The Twenty Miracles of Saint Nicholas   136, 283

The Twenty One Balloons   167

Twenty Six Ways To Be Somebody Else   154

A Twilight Struggle: The Life of John Fitzgerald Kennedy   185, 371, 538

The Twisted Window   182, 328

A Twister of Twists, a Tangler of Tongues   140, 160, 498, 508

The Two-thousand-pound Goldfish   109, 163, 288, 428

Two's Company   197, 402, 541

Two Bad Ants   71, 90, 225, 226, 546

Two Boys of Baghdad   140, 429

The Two Foolish Cats   182, 545, 574

The Two Germanys   63, 325

Two in the Wilderness   84, 468, 539

Two Little Birds and Three   154, 404

Two Moons in August   45, 236, 280

Twopence a Tub   176, 484

The Two Reds   38, 424, 454

The Two Reigns of Tutankhamen   33, 566

Two Shorts and One Long   17, 243

Two Straws in a Soda   140, 516

Two Victorian Families   176, 551

Two Weeks With the Queen   81, 355

Tyrannosaurus Rex   88, 175, 199, 433, 483, 492, 504, 510

Tyrannosaurus Rex and Its Kin   175, 483, 504

The Ugly Duckling   158, 192, 250, 384, 547

Uhu   58, 431

The Ultimate Alphabet   221, 562

Ulysses and his Woodland Zoo   33, 407, 497

Umbrella   39, 159, 179, 210, 326, 437, 479, 483, 562, 570

Umbrellas, Hats and Wheels   154, 487, 524

Unbelievable! More Surprising Stories   237, 393

Unbuilding   149, 157, 162, 179, 431

Uncanny! Even More Surprising Stories   228, 237, 393

Uncertain Glory   43, 410

Unclaimed Treasures   28, 433

Uncle Ben's Whale   153, 330, 364

Uncle Harry   62, 346, 506, 516

Uncle Misha's Partisans   114, 219, 533

Uncle Remus: His Songs and Sayings   51, 346, 370

Uncle Robert's Secret   187, 249, 502

Uncle Wizzmo's New Used Car   183, 361

Under Christopher's Hat   141, 288, 289

Underdog   69, 501

Under Goliath   48, 292, 491

Underground   5, 44, 64, 73, 313, 431, 492, 500, 506, 523, 555

Underground to Canada   44, 313, 523

Underrunners   91, 434

Understanding Art: the Use of Space, Form, and Structure   297

Understanding Art: The Uses of Space, Form and Structure   221

Under the Eagle's Claw   11, 472

Under the Green Willow   214, 300, 324

Under the Hawthorn Tree   112, 189, 303, 538

Under the Lights: A Child Model at Work   146, 265

Under the Sun   145, 400

Under the Sunday Tree   119, 337, 362

Underwear!   89, 92, 223, 397, 450, 452, 457

Undine   52, 343, 402, 508

Undine by Friedrich de la Motte Fouque   52, 343, 402

Uneasy Money   145, 146, 277

Unfulfilled Promise: Rescue and Resettlement of Jewish Refugee Children in the United States, 1934-1945   120, 263

The Unhappy Hippopotamus   153, 419, 453

UNICEF Book of Children's Legends   67, 401

UNICEF Book of Children's Poems   67, 401

UNICEF Book of Children's Prayers   67, 401

UNICEF Book of Children's Songs   67, 401

The Unicorn and the Lake   70, 90, 226, 366, 440

Unicorns in the Rain   79, 301

Un Iris Irritado   24, 464, 548

Univers a Deux Voix Insecte   23, 464, 476, 549

The Universe of Galileo and Newton   78, 270, 320

University: The Students, Faculty and Campus Life at One University   139, 508

Unleaving   26, 64, 473

Unlived Affections   87, 513

Unlocking the Doors   236, 430

Unmei no Kishi   110, 389, 534

Unmentionable! More Amazing Stories   237, 394

Unreal! Eight Surprising Stories   25, 117, 237, 394

The Unusual Puerto Rican   73, 415

Up a Road Slowly   107, 169, 386

Up a Tree   158, 179, 572

Up From Jericho Tell   181

Up from Jerich Tell   409

Upon the Head of a Goat: A Childhood in Hungary 1939-1944   28, 119, 170, 517

The Upside-down Man   332

Upside Downers, Downside Uppers: More Pictures to Stretch the Imagination   12, 252

The Upside Down Man   137

The Upstairs Room   3, 114, 160, 169, 490

Up the Pier   47, 308, 341

Up to Low   44, 326

Up to the Quarterback   139, 287

Usha the Mouse Maiden   52, 356

Vaino, a Boy of New Finland   165, 314, 467

Valentine   211, 303

Valentine and Orson   30, 183, 190, 285

Valery   206, 303, 307

Valiant Minstrel: The Story of Sir Harry Lauder   86, 435

The Valiant Sailor   32, 315, 522

The Valley Between   58, 538

A Valley Grows Up   45, 467

Valley of the Smallest: The Life Story of a Shrew   107, 229, 339, 573

The Vandal   48, 102, 506

Vanishing Wings: A Tale of Three Birds of Prey   68, 259, 368

Vast Horizons   206, 335, 430

The Velveteen Rabbit: or, How Toys Become Real   52, 269, 461

Verity of Sydneytown   57, 563

Veronica's Smile   136, 329

The Versatile Satellite   148, 482

Vertel Het uw Kinderen   22, 320, 520

Very Best of Friends   60, 550, 561

The Very Hungry Caterpillar   12, 13, 14, 290

The Very Obliging Flowers   155, 268, 419, 498

The Very Quiet Cricket   11, 35, 192, 290

A Very Special House   38, 410, 511

A Very Young Dancer   88, 410

Vicky Barnes, Junior Hospital Volunteer: The Story of a Candy Striper   138, 303

Victorian Poetry   66, 515

Video Fever   95, 350

The View from the Oak   133, 263, 409

Viking Dagger   128, 490

Viktor, das Fliegende Nilpferd 178, 306, 501

Vila: An Adventure Story 176, 263

The Village by the Sea 29, 102, 320, 343

Village Heritage 198, 479, 567

The Village of Round and Square Houses 41, 362

Village of the Vampire Cat 188, 459

Vilma Martinez 235, 301, 406

The Violin 44, 194, 248, 412, 472

The Violin Maker's Gift 44, 412

The Virginia Quarterly Review 65, 287

Visitors 5, 45, 178, 260, 353, 432

Visitors from London 45, 260, 353

A Visit to William Blake's Inn: Poems for Innocent and Experienced Travelers 28, 40, 93, 170, 485, 562

Viva Chicano 235, 275

Viva la Raza! The Struggle of the Mexican-American People 3, 428, 438

Voice of the Children 21, 287, 398

Voices from America's Past 78, 455, 567

Voices from the Grass 205, 403

Voices on the Wind: Poems for All Seasons 104, 111, 275, 419

Volcano: The Eruption and Healing of Mount St. Helens 151, 170, 416

Volcanoes 89, 221, 519, 545

Volcano Weather: The Story of 1816, the Year Without a Summer 150, 532

The Voyage Begun 28, 274

The Voyage of the Flying Bird 36, 336, 540

Voyage of the Vagabond 137, 540

The Voyagers: Being Legends and Romances of Atlantic Discovery 165, 303, 398

The Voyages of Doctor Dolittle 165, 428

Voyaging to Cathay: Americans in the China Trade 26, 356, 536

Vultures 147, 544, 554

W.E.B. DuBois 235, 445

Waddayaknow (Workbook, 1, 2, Teacher's Manual) 15, 413

Wait, Skates! 194, 328, 377, 396

Waiting for Amanda 95, 572

Waiting for Anya 102, 454

Waiting for Moma 219, 418, 455

Waiting for the Rain: A Novel of South Africa 4, 358

Waiting for the Whales 97, 104, 131, 133, 423, 443

Waiting Game 203, 284

Waiting to Waltz 199, 349, 501

Wait Til Helen Comes 54, 84, 96, 112, 122, 220, 224, 225, 226, 238, 239, 366

Wake Up, Dad! 19, 324, 364

Wake Up, Mr. B! 100, 311

The Walck Archaeology 147

Walk a Narrow Bridge 174, 338

Walking Across Egypt 80, 330

Walking the Road to Freedom: A Story about Sojourner Truth 234, 337, 369

Walk in the Sky 36, 390

A Walk Out of the World 214, 389, 461

Walk Through Cold Fire 75, 342

A Walk to the Beach 70, 350

The Wall 50, 61, 120, 167, 203, 206, 285, 294, 315, 378, 413, 524, 570

Wall of Words 48, 404

The Walloping Window Blind 138, 320

Walls: Defenses throughout History 94, 353

The Walls of Windy Troy: A Biography of Heinrich Schliemann 211, 278

The Walt Disney Story of Our Friend the Atom 210, 366, 553

Walter Reed: Doctor in Uniform 206, 327, 567

Walter Warthog 24, 421

Walt Whitman, Builder for America 86, 287, 320

Waltzing Matilda 22, 58, 322, 472

Wanted: One New Dad 146, 265

Wapiti the Elk 71, 297, 453

The War Between the Pitiful Teachers and the Splendid Kids 162, 405, 445

War Boy 100, 159, 199, 342

War Cry on a Prayer Feather: Prose and Poetry of the Ute Indians 234, 567

The Warden's Niece 46, 256, 371

The War for the Lot: A Tale of Fantasy and Terror 85, 263, 415

War Horse 206, 230, 282, 325, 454

The War in Korea, 1950-53 136, 418

Warrior Scarlet 46, 107, 402, 534

Wart, Son of Toad 80, 292

The War with Grandpa 42, 80, 84, 89, 96, 180, 200, 223, 226, 232, 238, 239, 416, 523

War Work 86, 466, 482

Wash and Brush Up 221, 248

Washday on Noah's Ark 181, 498

The Washington Post 204, 226, 227

Was It a Good Trade? 153, 320, 366

The Watcher Bee 173, 448

The Watcher in the Garden 109, 478

Watching the Wild Apes: The Primate Studies of Goodall, Fossey, and Galdikas 148, 405

Watch It Work! The Plane 198, 277, 437

Watch Out! 137, 476, 521

Watch the Stars Come Out 180, 191, 357, 422

The Water Babies 51, 398, 406

Water in the Blood 6, 284

Water is Wet 145, 265, 481

Waterless Mountain 165, 253

Watership Down 41, 47, 101, 126, 244

The Wave 39, 66, 154, 380, 420, 430

A Wave In Her Pocket: Stories From Trinidad 184, 190, 398, 479

Wayside School Is Falling Down 11, 89, 121, 183, 501, 505

The Way Things Are and other Poems 93, 426, 466

The Way Things Work 8, 29, 54, 195, 222, 431

The Way to Sattin Shore 180, 474, 550

The Way to Start a Day 40, 263, 472

We're Back! A Dinosaur's Story 90, 135, 536

We're Going on a Bear Hunt 30, 100, 183, 190, 198, 469, 496

We Are Having a Baby 215, 381

We Are Mesquakie, We Are One 4, 390

We Are the Government 139, 309, 332, 358

Weasel 183, 196, 315, 428, 481

The Weaver's Gift 28, 408, 416

The Web 34, 60, 147, 164, 329, 345, 347, 378, 450, 493

The Web: The Triumph of a New Zealand Girl Over Anorexia 164, 347

The Web in the Grass 147, 329, 345

We Can't Sleep 68, 530

We Couldn't Leave Dinah 45, 542

We Dare Not Go A-Hunting 188, 433

The Wedding Ghost 125, 350, 402

The Wedding Procession of the Rag Doll and the Broom Handle and Who Was in It 12, 213, 479, 502

The Wednesday Surprise 5, 203, 285, 291

Wee Gillis 37, 417, 418

Weeny Witch 138, 317, 465

Wee Willow Whistle 207, 256, 280

Wee Wisdom 124, 431

Weird Henry Berg 87, 503

The Weirdstone of Brisingamen and a Tale of Alderly 52, 350

Welcome Home, Jellybean 176, 517

We Read: A to Z 138, 308

The Western Horse: A Handbook 229, 404, 528

Western Producer Prairie 11, 44, 77, 97, 127, 133, 195, 236, 303, 448, 536, 556

The Westing Game 27, 73, 128, 170, 225, 488

Westmark 8, 247

Westward Adventure: The True Stories of Six Pioneers 78, 528, 551

Westward the Eagle 71, 395, 414

The Wet World 153, 450, 519

We Were Not Like Other People 110, 276, 512

The Whale People 44, 367, 556

Whalers of the Midnight Sun: A Story of Modern Whaling in the Antarctic 57, 482, 549

Whales 24, 69, 97, 100, 104, 130, 131, 133, 159, 273, 303, 423, 435, 443, 514, 519, 560

The Whales' Song 100, 130, 273, 514

The Whalesinger 236, 401

Whalesong 92, 517

The Whale Watchers' Guide 150, 349, 519

What's Happening To My Junior Year? 145, 502

What's Inside? 163, 186, 313, 407

What's on your Plate? 144, 411, 412, 521

What's the Matter with Herbie Jones? 115, 408, 563

What's the Matter with Wakefield? 515, 532

What's Under My Bed? 92, 530

What's Under the Ground? 195, 330, 440, 484, 508

665

What's Your Story? A Young Person's Guide to Writing Fiction   129, 262

What a Morning! The Christmas Story in Black Spirituals   118, 283, 414

What Are You Up To, William Thomas?   171, 461

What a Silly Thing to Do   138, 476, 521

What Can Rabbit Hear?   160, 306

What Daddy Did   204, 516

What Do Animals Do When it Rains?   149, 321, 564

What Does a Witch Need?   140, 317, 507

What Does God Do?   91, 562

What Do You Do with a Kangaroo?   13, 440

What do you Feed Your Donkey On? Rhymes from a Belfast Childhood   27, 466, 495

What Do You Say, Dear?   39, 153, 191, 399, 511

What Happened in Hamelin?   68, 520

What Happened To Patrick's Dinosaurs?   42, 164, 291

What Happens When We Die?   91, 369, 464

What Hearts   171, 280

What if They Knew?   73, 376

What I Heard   145, 352

What I Like about Toads   139, 373, 442

What Is a Union?   176, 249, 334

What Is It For?   155, 386

What is the Truth? A Farmyard Fable for the Young   102, 197, 385, 426

What It's all About   56, 260, 346

What Kind of a House Is That?   139

What Kind of House Is That?   320

What Makes a Fairy Tale Good: The Queer Kindness of the Golden Bird   65, 463

What Makes a Flower Grow?   195, 330, 440, 484

What Makes Day and Night?   136, 275, 278

What Makes It Rain?   195, 320, 440, 484

What Sadie Sang   64, 491

What the Bible Is All About for Young Explorers   91, 271, 570

What the Forest Tells Me: 1977 Sierra Club Calendar for Children   64, 280

What the Mailman Brought   94, 307, 320

What Then, Raman?   3, 85, 235, 254, 365

What the Neighbors Did and Other Stories   107, 392, 474

What Would Jesus Do?   92, 539

Wheel Around the World   176, 405, 509

The Wheel of King Asoka   4, 68, 313

The Wheel of Surya   102, 351

Wheel on the Chimney   39, 281, 352

The Wheel on the School   51, 168, 316, 511

Wheels: A Pictorial History   32, 544

Wheels for Ginny's Chariot   36, 430, 450

The Wheels on the Bus   183, 190, 192, 573

When Clay Sings   40, 216, 257, 263

When Grandma Came   131, 473, 563

When Hitler Stole Pink Rabbit   215, 404

When I Am Old With You   119, 394, 525

When I Dance   197, 268, 277

When I Grew Up Long Ago   143, 268, 508

When I Was a Boy   50, 401, 420, 444

When I Was Young in the Mountains   41, 357, 501

When Jays Fly to Barbmo   47, 57, 249, 258

When No One Was Looking   188, 557

When Schlemiel Went to Warsaw and Other Stories   169, 520, 574

When Sheep Cannot Sleep   151, 407

When the Boys Ran the House   112, 146, 226, 238, 291, 461

When the Dark Comes Dancing   180, 415, 553

When the Moon Is New   209, 259

When the Phone Rang   228, 441

When the Sad Ones Come to Stay   72, 374

When the Sky is Like Lace   161, 305, 383

When the Wind Blew   157, 281, 373

When the Wind Blows   176, 279

When the Wind Changed   147, 237, 462, 470

When the Woods Hum   24, 500, 531

When We First Met   112, 441

When Will the World be Mine? The Story of a Snowshoe Rabbit   38, 295, 506

Where's Al?   62, 156, 261

Where's Florrie?   142, 301, 368

Where's Gomer?   63, 327, 335

Where's Julius?   125, 286

Where's Mum?   60, 355, 522

Where's Spot?   130, 377

Where's the Cat?   145, 427, 574

Where's the Dog?   145, 427, 574

Where's the Guinea Pig?   145, 427, 575

Where's Waldo?   11, 369

Where's Wally   25, 130, 369

Where's Wally?   25, 130, 369

Where's Your Head? Psychology for Teenagers   68, 290, 461, 462

Where Are You When I Need You?   171, 461

Where Babies Come From   146, 507, 518, 574

Where Does Electricity Come From?   195, 440, 508, 513

Where Does God Live?   69, 352, 371, 573

Where Does It Go?   160, 450

Where Does the Day Go?   73, 292, 458

Where Does the Trail Lead?   95, 246, 479

Where Is Bobo?   18, 386, 517

Where is Daddy? The Story of a Divorce   56, 356, 476

Where It Stops, Nobody Knows   84, 331

Where Kite Balloons Come Back   120

Where the Buffaloes Begin   28, 40, 158, 162, 258, 349

Where the Forest Meets the Sea   29, 60, 77, 110, 117, 190, 237, 258

Where the Lilies Bloom   26, 131, 299, 525

Where the Panther Screams   195, 270, 494

Where the Pirates Are   87, 542

Where the Raritan Flows   136, 449, 554

Where the Red Fern Grows   98, 126, 128, 172, 488

Where the River Begins   158, 163, 427

Where the Sidewalk Ends   128, 161, 217, 518

Where the Wild Things Are   12, 13, 39, 51, 64, 107, 154, 191, 511

Which Twin Wins?   177, 374

Which Way Courage   202, 556

Which Way Freedom?   118, 369

Which Witch?   48, 389, 415

While the Horses Galloped to London   62, 440, 555

The Whipman Is Watching   56, 329

The Whipping Boy   92, 134, 170, 197, 340, 520

Whirlwind Is a Ghost Dancing   63, 266, 322, 323

The Whirly Bird   83, 342, 541

Whiskers & Rhymes   163, 427

Whiskers and Rhymes   163

The Whiskers of Ho Ho   210, 273, 425

The Whispered Horse   188, 367

The Whispering Mountain   47, 101, 245, 277

Whispers and other Poems   210, 297, 426

Whispers from the Dead   96, 135, 463

Whistle for Good Fortune   205, 257, 483

Whistler's Van   166, 351, 398

Whistle Up the Chimney   147, 386, 522

The Whitby Witches   121, 393

The White Archer: An Eskimo Legend   44, 383

White Bird   216, 284, 556

The White Bungalow   78, 243, 525

The White Calf   121, 336, 536

The White Cat   123, 525

The White Crane   59, 454, 522

The White Deer   174, 345, 540

White Falcon   231, 254, 294

White Gold in the Cassiar   33, 308

A White Heron   25, 249, 394

The White Mountains   97, 217, 297

Whiteout   77

White Peak Farm   190, 324

White Snow, Bright Snow   38, 329, 542

The White Stag   50, 166, 512

Whitney's First Round-up   205, 498

Who, Said Sue, Said Whoo?   12, 26, 62, 488

Who, What, When, Where Book about the Bible   91, 302, 553

Where Does God Live?   69, 352, 371,

Who's Counting?   186, 535

Who's in Rabbit's House? A Masai Tale   53, 243, 322, 323

Who's Scared, Not Me   145, 502

Who's Sick Today?   186, 296

Who Gave Us . . . Peacocks? Planes? and Ferris Wheels?   152, 352

Who Goes Next? True Stories of Exciting Escapes   33, 249, 467

Who Is Frances Rain?   44, 236, 284

The Whole Nine Yards   75, 435

Who Lies Inside   176, 390
Who Likes the Dark?   207, 384, 539
Who Needs a Bratty Brother?   116, 301, 357
Who Needs Donuts?   13, 527
Who Sank the Boat?   58, 109, 147, 248
Whose Town?   214, 360
Who Speaks for Wolf   113, 384, 526
Who Stole a Bloater?   222, 538
Who Stole the Apples?   182, 376
Who Will Clean the Air?   141, 309, 467, 476
Who Will Speak for the Lamb?   25, 250
Why Am I Grown So Cold? Poems of the Unknowable   180, 426
Why Do People Smoke?   222, 503
Why Frogs Are Wet   138, 373, 433
Why Me?   181, 303
Why Mosquitos Buzz in People's Ears: A West African Tale   13, 14, 40, 161, 243, 322, 323
The Whys and Wherefores of Littabelle Lee   132, 161, 299
Why the Cangaroo Has Such Long Legs   20, 498
Why the Chicken Crossed the Road   181, 431
Why the Chinese Are the Way They Are   138, 141, 252, 283
Why the Man in the Moon Is Happy and Other Eskimo Creation Stories   111, 347, 448
Why the Russians Are the Way They Are   137, 252, 283
Why the Sky Is Far Away   160, 353, 357
Why the Sun and the Moon Live in the Sky: An African Folktale   39, 213, 315, 420
Why the Tides Ebb and Flow   27, 276, 281
Why Weeps the Brogan?   231, 509
The Wider Heart   137, 397
The Widow's Broom   185, 546
Wie Tierkinder Schlafen   178, 322
Wild Animals of Africa ABC   24, 500
Wild Animals of the Five Rivers Country   30, 243, 344
Wild Appaloosa   171, 498
The Wild Birthday Cake   38, 314, 567
Wildcat under Glass   17, 337, 573
Wildflower Girl   20, 303
Wild Geese Calling   76, 401, 457
Wild Green Things in the City: A Book of Weeds   62, 325
The Wild Horse Killers   72, 332
The Wild Horse of Santander   47, 249, 250, 363
Wild Horses of the Red Desert   52, 498
Wild Hunter   208, 418, 487
The Wild Inside: A Sierra Club Guide to the Great Indoors   149, 248
Wild in the World   132, 160, 325
The Wildlife ABC   7, 539
Wildlife of the Forests   149, 534
Wildlife of the Mountains   149, 491
Wildlife of the Oceans   149, 394
The Wild Life 1-2-3: A Nature Counting Book   539

The Wildman   198, 309, 402
Wild Man of the Woods   44, 298
Wild Mouse   148, 277
The Wild Swans   192, 251, 331, 393
The Wild Washerwomen: A New Folktale   99, 271, 570
Wild Wing: Great Hunting Eagle   142, 319, 549
Wild Wings over the Marshes   201, 349, 532
Wiley and the Hairy Man   188, 259
Will's New Cap   185, 414
Will's Quill   202, 345
William's Doll   191, 327, 575
William and Grandpa   69, 183, 310, 505
William Crawford Gorgas: Tropic Fever Fighter   209, 286, 333
William Tell   60, 329
Willie Joe and His Small Change   77, 433, 548
Willie Mays   33, 369
Willie Pearl   74, 361, 442
Will of Iron   176, 447
Willow Hill   207, 560
The Willow Maiden   72, 180, 303, 347
Will to Live   119, 344
Willy Bear   68, 400, 471
Will You Sign Here, John Hancock?   26, 346, 389
Wilted   236, 410
The Wind Blew   99, 157, 281, 373, 388
Windfall   46, 208, 250, 290, 304, 477
Windfall Fiddle   208, 290, 304
The Wind Has Wings: Poems from Canada   103, 299, 325, 493
The Wind in the Willows   49, 82, 125, 286, 360, 514
Wind of the Vikings   204, 305, 417
The Wind on the Moon: A Story for Children   45, 267, 424
Window   60, 237, 258
Window into a Nest   340, 455
Windows in Space   203, 332, 567
Windows Into a Nest   148, 221
Windward Island   77
Windy Hill   165, 447
Winged Girl of Knossos   166, 268
The Wing on a Flea: A Book about Shapes   154, 333
Wings   81, 171, 280
Wings against the Wind   32, 209, 290, 548
Win Me and You Lose   177, 567
Winners   77, 133, 236, 303
Winners on the Ice   143, 425
Winnie the Witch   56, 473, 539
Winning with Numbers: A Kid's Guide to Statistics   179, 302, 492
Winter's Eve   155, 266, 300
The Winter Bear   63, 272, 307
Winterbound   166, 269, 512
The Winter Cat   62, 86, 408
The Winter Child   139, 569, 570
Winter Danger   50, 209, 348, 528
The Winter Fun Book   127, 383
A Winter Place   179, 466, 486
The Winter Room   122, 170, 474

The Winter When Time Was Frozen   17, 476, 499
Wiplala   9, 506
Wisconsin, Forward!   72, 253, 500
Wisdom to Know   136, 568
Wish and the Magic Nut   57, 260, 373
The Wish Giver: Three Tales of Coven Tree   170, 280, 355
The Wishing Night   137, 409, 549
Wish on a Unicorn   104, 376
The Witch's Brat   52, 418, 534
The Witch's Hand   130, 546
Witch Cat   72, 81, 291, 442, 475, 503
Witchery Hill   44, 401
The Witches   132, 139, 160, 163, 169, 174, 187, 227, 231, 248, 251, 271, 290, 301, 311, 487, 524
The Witches' Secret   139, 248
The Witches Bridge   187, 290
The Witches of Worm   132, 160, 169, 487, 524
Witch Hazel   184, 505, 541
The Witch of Blackbird Pond   107, 135, 168, 525
The Witch of Fourth Street and other Stories   62, 215, 422, 425
Witch of the Cumberlands   174, 529, 531
The Witch of the North: Folktales of French Canada   103
The Witchy Broom   139, 317, 475
With a Name Like Lulu, Who Needs More Trouble?   175, 401, 527
Within the Circle   207, 371, 528
Without a Silver Spoon   109, 390
With Westie and the Tin Man   56, 244
The Wizard and his Magic Powder   206, 289, 560
The Wizard of Earthsea   25, 53, 65, 419, 493, 552
The Wizard of Oz   51, 262, 319
A Woggle of Witches   141, 244
Wok's Cooking?   177, 374
Wolf   68, 185, 308, 343
Wolf's Chicken Stew   116, 401
Wolf Brother   229, 407
Wolf Island   106, 356
Wolf of Shadows   87, 533
The Wolves of Willoughby Chase   51, 245, 436
Woman from Hiroshima   4, 454
The Woman in the Moon and other Tales of Forgotten Heroines   125, 260, 492
The Woman who Loved Reindeer   180, 478
Won't Know Till I Get There   179, 458
The Wonder-smith and His Son: A Tale from the Golden Childhood of the World   165, 254, 572
Wonderful Time   155, 246, 443
The Wonderful Travels and Adventures of Baron Munchhausen   157, 461, 507, 536
The Wonderful Wonders of One-Two-Three   204, 390, 522
The Wonderful World of Communication   32, 380

667

The Wonderful World of Energy 77, 252, 380

The Wonderful World of the Sea 32, 252, 339

The Wonderful World Outside 43, 397

The Wonderful Year 86, 167, 260, 512

The Wonders of Astronomy 136, 287, 472

The Wonders of Rockets and Missiles 136, 287

The Wonders of Sand 137, 138, 443

Wonders of Sheep 144, 417, 509

Wonders of Speech 152, 518, 541

The Wood-ash Stars 84, 249, 481

The Woodcutter's Duck 99, 215, 544

The Wooden People 97, 121, 470, 527

Woodsong 129, 230, 474

Woodworks: Experiments with Common Wood and Tools 151, 282

Woody and Me 213, 460, 524

Woof! 110, 124, 245, 555

Woof Miaow 124

The Wool-Pack 45, 370

A Word from our Sponsor: or, My Friend Alfred 81, 251

Words by Heart 8, 111, 162, 509

The Words of Martin Luther King, Jr. 118, 406

Working Cotton 41, 119, 288, 563

World's Fairs: Yesterday, Today and Tomorrow 136, 495

The World Beneath Our Feet: The Story of Soil 141, 402, 477

World Full of Horses 209, 390

The World in 1492 105, 346, 377, 434, 445, 473, 549

The World of Chocolate 139, 413, 521

The World of Christopher Robin 50, 451, 514

World of Our Fathers: The Jews of Eastern Europe 132, 448

The World of Pooh 49, 451, 514

The World of the White-tailed Deer 136, 499

Worlds Lost and Found 114, 331, 332, 478

Worlds within Worlds: A Journey into the Unknown 149, 296, 437, 440, 543

The World Turned Upside Down: The Story of the American Revolution

Worm Day 146, 282, 575

Wrapped for Eternity: The Story of the Egyptian Mummies 148, 385, 469

The Wreck of the Zephyr 158, 163, 546

Wrestling With Honor 203, 407

The Wright Brothers 30, 95, 105, 113, 170, 185, 190, 344

The Wright Brothers: How They Invented the Airplane 30, 95, 113, 170, 185, 190, 344

A Wrinkle in Time 10, 51, 168, 195, 420

The Writing on the Hearth 215, 341, 370

The Wrong Step 120

Wuffles Goes to Town 98, 496

X-raying the Pharaohs 147, 370, 555

Yale Review 66, 561

Yankee Doodle Boy: A Young Soldier's Adventure in the American Revolution Told by Himself 78, 438, 441, 505

Yari 73, 376

Y Drudwy Dewr 423

Yeager: An Autobiography by Chuck Yeager and Leo Janos 80, 392, 570

The Year 219, 414

A Year and a Day 108, 162, 441, 544

A Year in the Woods 23

The Year it Rained 163, 326

The Yearling 51, 82, 488, 569

A Year of Beasts 191, 566

The Year of the Dragon 120

The Year of the Gopher 237, 459

The Year of the Yelvertons 91, 465

The Year Without Michael 200, 477

Yeh-Shen: A Cinderella Story from China 28, 144, 428, 572

Yellow & Pink 191, 529

Yellow, Yellow 12, 13, 255, 527

Yellow Bird and Me 181, 369

The Yellow Book of Hob Stories 130, 267, 441

The Yellow Umbrella 159, 326

Y Flwyddyn Honno 468

Y Llinyn Arian 397

Y Llipryn Llwyd 541

Yok Yok 23, 318, 547

Yonder 203, 272, 397

Yonderbeyond 15, 314

Yonie Wondernose 37, 315

You'd Better Not Tell 143, 506

You're Worth More Than You Think 91, 395, 475

You and Atomic Energy 31, 339, 422

You and Your Brain 78, 364, 520

You Are Ri-di-cu-lous 156, 344

You Are Wonderfully Made 91, 395, 475

You Can't Be Timid with a Trumpet: Notes from the Orchestra 28, 333, 520

You Can't Catch Me! 196, 271, 496

You Can't Measure My Love with a Teaspoon 137, 516

You Can Pick Me Up at Peggy's Cove 109, 256, 326

You Can Say No to a Drink or a Drug 145, 461, 540

You Can Write Chinese 38, 560

You Know What? I Like Animals 138, 290, 547

You May Plow Here: The Narrative of Sarah Brooks 234, 519

You Never Can Tell 80, 303

Young and Alive 124, 249

The Young Aunts 205, 264, 311

Young Fu of the Upper Yangtze 50, 165, 422, 560

The Young Green Consumer Guide 77, 332, 367, 497

Young Hero of the Range 229, 351, 474

The Young Landlords 118, 458

Young Lions 190, 197, 378, 468, 571

Young Mac of Fort Vancouver 166, 291, 381

Young Mark 25, 214, 248, 250

Young Miss Josie Delaney, Detective 137, 383, 435

A Young Person's Guide to Ballet 63, 275, 533

Young Readers Book of Christian Symbolism 216, 314, 413

The Young Unicorn 214

The Young United States 1783-1830 131, 544

Young Walter Scott 166, 361, 512

Young Willkie 206, 372

The Young Unicorns 420

Your Amazing Senses 224, 547

Your Best Friend, Kate 146, 279, 282

Your Body: Skin and Bone 130, 482, 549

Your Kind Indulgence 207, 435

Yours 'til Niagara Falls, Abby 95, 252, 465

Yours Til Niagara Falls, Abby 95, 252, 465

You Shouldn't Have to Say Good-Bye 42, 112, 134, 374, 376

You Take the High Road 81, 147, 476

Youth Town 55

Ytek and the Arctic Orchid: An Inuit Legend 44, 97, 104, 377, 567

Yuletide Blues 236, 432

Yussel's Prayer: A Yom Kippur Story 114, 219, 301, 320

The Zabajaba Jungle 181, 529

Zeek Silver Moon 160, 331, 471

Zeely 21, 368, 515

Zen and the Art of Motorcycle Maintenance: An Inquiry into Values 126, 480

Z for Zachariah 4, 188, 465

Zlateh the Goat and Other Stories 109, 155, 169, 511, 516, 520

Zoar Blue 174, 377

Zoe's Rainy Day 129, 490

Zoe's Snowy Day 129, 490

Zoe's Sunny Day 129, 490

Zoe's Windy Day 129, 490

Zoo 100, 282, 556

Zoom at Sea 104, 111, 195, 464, 569

Zoom Away 104, 464, 569

Zoo Walk 130, 491

Zounds! The Kids' Guide to Sound Making 150, 461, 522

Zucchini 113, 121, 122, 296, 297, 312

Zuska of the Burning Hills 209, 509, 551

The Z Was Zapped 181, 546

Awards Index

A Book Can Develop Empathy
  see Book Can Develop Empathy, A
  24
A Kelpie for the Nineties
  see Kelpie for the Nineties, A   116
Abingdon Press Children's Book Award
  3
Addams Children's Book Award, Jane   3
Aesop Prize   5
AIM Children's Book Awards   5
ALAN Award   6
Alberta Writing for Youth Competition   6
Alcuin Citation for Excellence in Book
  Design in Canada   7
Allie Beth Martin Award
  see Martin Award, Allie Beth   124
Amelia Frances Howard-Gibbon
  Illustrator's Award
  see Howard-Gibbon Illustrator's Award,
  Amelia Frances   103
American Association of School Librarians
  President's Award   7
American Book Awards   7
American Booksellers Book of the Year
  (ABBY)   8
American Institute of Graphic Arts Book
  Show   8
American Institute of Physics Science
  Writing Award   8
Andersen Awards, Hans Christian   9
Ann Connor Brimer Award
  see Brimer Award, Ann Connor   34
Annett Award, R. Ross   10
Arizona Young Readers Award   11
Art Books for Children Citations   11
Arts Council of Great Britain National
  Book Award   14
Ashton Scholastic Award   14
Association of Jewish Libraries Sydney
  Taylor Book Award
  see Taylor Book Award, Sydney   218
Association of Jewish Libraries Sydney
  Taylor Body of Work Award
  see Taylor Body of Work Award,
  Sydney   219
Aubry Award, Claude   14
Aurianne Award   15
Australian Children's Book Award
  see Children's Book Council of
  Australia Book of the Year Awards
  57
Australian Christian Book of the Year
  Children's Award   15
Australian Multicultural Children's
  Literature Awards   15

Author's Awards/Juvenile/Young Adult
  16
Avon/Flare Young Adult Novel
  Competition   16

Batchelder Award, Mildred L.   16
Baum Memorial Award, L. Frank   17
Bay Area Book Reviewers Association
  Award   18
Beatty Award, John and Patricia   18
Beaver Trophy   18
Best Books for Babies   18
Biennale of Illustrations Bratislava   19
Bilson Award for Historical Fiction,
  Geoffrey   20
BISTO Book of the Year Award   20
Black Award, Irma S. and James H.   21
Bloch Memorial Award, Nancy   21
Blue Spruce: Colorado Young Adult Book
  Award   22
Bologna Children's Book Fair Prizes   22
Book Can Develop Empathy, A   24
Books I Love Best Yearly Awards
  (BILBY)   25
Boston Globe-Horn Book Awards   25
Boys Club Junior Book Awards   30
Boys' Life-Dodd Mead Writing Award
  33
Brimer Award, Ann Connor   34
British Book Awards   34
Bruce Story Award for Children's
  Literature, Mary Grant   34
Buckeye Children's Book Award   35
Burnley Express Award   36
Burr Award, Elizabeth   36
Busby Award: Dodd Mead Librarian and
  Teacher Prize Competition, Edith   36

CBC Honors Program   36
Caldecott Medal, Randolph   36
California Young Reader Medal   41
Calling All Girls-Dodd Mead Prize
  Competition   43
Canada Council Children's Literature
  Prizes
  see Governor General's Literary Awards
  96
Canadian Library Association Book of the
  Year for Children Award   43
Carl Sandburg Award
  see Sandburg Award, Carl   194
Carnegie Medal   45
Carolyn W. Field Award
  see Field Award, Carolyn W.   83
Carroll Shelf Award, Lewis   49

Carter G. Woodson Book Award
  see Woodson Book Award, Carter G.
  234
Catholic Book Awards   53
Caudill Young Readers' Book Award,
  Rebecca   54
Chandler Reward of Merit, J. G.   54
Charles W. Follett Award
  see Follett Award, Charles W.   85
Charlie May Simon Children's Book
  Award
  see Simon Children's Book Award,
  Charlie May   197
Charlotte Book Award   54
Chauncy Award, Nan   54
Child Study Children's Book Award   55
Children's Book Award   56
Children's Book Council of Australia Book
  of the Year Awards   57
Children's Book Showcase   60
Children's Choice Award (Arizona)   64
Children's Choice Award (Texas)   65
Children's Literature Association Awards
  for Excellence in Literary Criticism
  65
Children's Peace Literature Award   66
Children's Reading Roundtable Award
  66
Christopher Awards   67
Clara Ingram Judson Award
  see Judson Award, Clara Ingram   115
Claremont Graduate School Recognition of
  Merit Award   216
  see George G. Stone Center Award
Clark Award, Russell   70
Claude Aubry Award
  see Aubry Award, Claude   14
Collier-Macmillan Award   70
Colorado Children's Book Award   70
Commonwealth Club of California Book
  Awards   71
Coretta Scott King Awards
  see King Awards, Coretta Scott   117
Council for Wisconsin Writers Award   72
Council on Interracial Books for Children
  Award   73
CRABbery Award   73
Crichton Award for Children's Book
  Illustration   74

Darton Award, Harvey   74
David McCord Children's Literature
  Citation
  see McCord Children's Literature
  Citation, David   123

Delacorte Press Prize for an Outstanding
   First Young Adult Novel   74
Diabetes Australia Alan Marshall Prize for
   Children's Literature   75
Dr. Seuss Picture Book Award   75
Dorothy Canfield Fisher Children's Book
   Award
   see Fisher Children's Book Award,
   Dorothy Canfield   83
Drexel Citation   75
Dromkeen Medal   76
Dutton Children's Books Picture Book
   Competition   76
Dutton Junior Animal Book Award   76

Earthworm Award   76
Ebel Memorial Award, Max and Greta
   77
Edgar Allan Poe Award
   see Poe Award, Edgar Allan   187
Edison Foundation National Mass Media
   Awards, Thomas Alva   77
Edith Busby Award: Dodd Mead Librarian
   and Teacher Prize Competition
   see Busby Award: Dodd Mead Librarian
   and Teacher Prize Competition, Edith
   36
Edwards Award, Margaret A.   78
Egoff Children's Prize, Sheila A.   79
Eleanor Farjeon Award
   see Farjeon Award, Eleanor   81
Elizabeth Burr Award
   see Burr Award, Elizabeth   36
Elizabeth Mrazik-Cleaver Canadian Picture
   Book Award
   see Mrazik-Cleaver Canadian Picture
   Book Award, Elizabeth   131
Elliott Landau Award
   see Landau Award, Elliott   121
Emphasis on Reading   79
Empire State Award for Excellence in
   Literature for Young People   80
Esther Glen Award
   see Glen Award, Esther   90
Ethical Culture School Book Award   80
Eva L. Gordon Award
   see Gordon Award, Eva L.   96
Evelyn Sibley Lampman Award
   see Lampman Award, Evelyn Sibley
   120
Ezra Jack Keats New Writer's Award
   see Keats New Writer's Award, Ezra
   Jack   116

Faber/Jackanory/Guardian Children's
   Writers Competition   81
Fair Award, Jeanette   81
Family Award   81
Farjeon Award, Eleanor   81
Fassler Memorial Book Award, Joan   82
Feature a Classic   82
Federation of Children's Book Groups
   Awards
   see Children's Book Award   64-65
   Fidler Award, Kathleen   82
Field Award, Carolyn W.   83
Fish Award, Helen Dean   83

Fisher Children's Book Award, Dorothy
   Canfield   84
FIT Astrid Lindgren Translation Prize   84
Fitzpatrick Award, Percy   84
Florida Reading Association (FRA)
   Children's Book Award   84
FOCAL (Friends of Children and
   Literature) Award   85
Follett Award, Charles W.   85
Follett Beginning-To-Read Award   85
Ford Foundation Award, Julia Ellsworth
   86
Frances E. Russell Award
   see Russell Award, Frances E.   193
Franklin Watts Juvenile Fiction Award
   see Watts Juvenile Fiction Award,
   Franklin   227
Friends of American Writers Juvenile Book
   Merit Award   86

G. P. Putnam's Sons Fiction Prize
   see Putnam's Sons Fiction Prize, G. P.
   189
Garavi Gujarat Racial Harmony Book
   Awards   87
Garden State Children's Book Award   88
Geoffrey Bilson Award for Historical
   Fiction
   see Bilson Award for Historical Fiction,
   Geoffrey   20
George G. Stone Center for Children's
   Books Recognition of Merit Award
   see Stone Center for Children's Books
   Recognition of Merit Award, George G.
   216
Georgia Children's Book Award   89
Georgia Children's Picture Storybook
   Award   90
Glen Award, Esther   90
Gold Medallion Book Award   91
Golden Archer Award and Little Archer
   Award   92
Golden Cat Award   92
Golden Kite Award   93
Golden Medallion Award   95
Golden Sower Award   95
Golden Spur
   see Western Writers of America Spur
   Awards   96
Gordon Award, Eva L.   96
Governor General's Literary Awards   96
Great Stone Face Award   97
Greenaway Medal, Kate   98
Grolier Foundation Award   100
Guardian Award for Children's Fiction
   101

Hans Christian Andersen Awards
   see Andersen Awards, Hans Christian
   9
Harvey Darton Award
   see Darton Award, Harvey   74
Hefly Award, Sue   102
Helen Dean Fish Award
   see Fish Award, Helen Dean   83
Helen Keating Ott Award for Outstanding
   Contribution to Children's Literature

see Ott Award for Outstanding
   Contribution to Children's Literature,
   Helen Keating   177
Hopkins Poetry Award, Lee Bennett   103
Howard-Gibbon Illustrator's Award,
   Amelia Frances   103
Hungry Mind Review Children's Books of
   Distinction   104

Indian Paintbrush Award   105
Indiana Authors Day Awards   105
Information Book Award   106
International Board on Books for Young
   People   107
International Brothers Grimm Award
   110
International Order of the Daughters of the
   Empire (IODE) Best Children's Book of
   the Year   110
International Reading Association
   Children's Book Award   111
Iowa Children's Choice Award   112
Iowa Teen Award   112
Irma S. and James H. Black Award
   see Black Award, Irma S. and James H.
   21
Irving Children's Book Choice Award,
   Washington   113

J. G. Chandler Reward of Merit
   see Chandler Reward of Merit, J. G.
   54
Jacobs Award, Leland B.   113
Jane Addams Children's Book Award
   see Addams Children's Book Award,
   Jane   3
Janusz Korczak Literary Awards for
   Children's Books (USA)
   see Korczak Literary Awards for
   Children's Books (USA), Janusz   119
Janusz Korczak International Literary
   Award (Poland)
   see Korczak International Literary
   Award (Poland), Janusz   120
Jeanette Fair Award
   see Fair Award, Jeanette   81
Jefferson Cup Award   113
Jeremiah Ludington Memorial Award
   see Ludington Memorial Award,
   Jeremiah   123
Jesse Stuart Media Award, Jesse
   see Stuart Media Award, Jesse   217
Jewish Book Council National Jewish Book
   Awards   113
Joan Fassler Memorial Book Award
   see Fassler Memorial Book Award, Joan
   82
Joan G. Sugarman Children's Book Award
   see Sugarman Children's Book Award,
   Joan G.   217
John and Patricia Beatty Award
   see Beatty Award, John and Patricia
   18
John Newbery Medal
   see Newbery Medal, John   164
Judson Award, Clara Ingram   115

Judy Lopez Memorial Award
  see Lopez Memorial Award, Judy
  121
Julia Ellsworth Ford Foundation Award
  see Ford Foundation Award, Julia
  Ellsworth 86

Kate Greenaway Medal
  see Greenaway Medal, Kate 98
Kathleen Fidler Award
  see Fidler Award, Kathleen 82
KC Three Award 115
Keats New Writer's Award, Ezra Jack
  116
Keene State College Children's Literature
  Festival Award 116
Kelpie for the Nineties, A 116
Kentucky Bluegrass Award 116
Kerlan Award 117
Keystone To Reading Book Award 117
Kids Own Australian Literature (KOALA)
  117
King Awards, Coretta Scott 117
Knickerbocker Award for Juvenile
  Literature 119
Korczak Literary Awards for Children's
  Books (USA), Janusz 119
Korczak International Literary Award
  (Poland), Janusz 120
Kurt Maschler Award
  see Maschler Award, Kurt 125

L. Frank Baum Memorial Award
  see Baum Memorial Award, L. Frank
  17
Lampman Award, Evelyn Sibley 120
Lancashire County Library/National
  Westminster Bank Children's Book of
  the Year Award 120
Land of Enchantment Children's Book
  Award 121
Landau Award, Elliott 121
Laura Ingalls Wilder Award
  see Wilder Award, Laura Ingalls 232
Lee Bennett Hopkins Poetry Award
  see Hopkins Poetry Award, Lee Bennett
  103
Leland B. Jacobs Award
  see Jacobs Award, Leland B. 113
Lewis Carroll Shelf Award
  see Carroll Shelf Award, Lewis 49
Little Brown Canadian Children's Book
  Award 121
Lopez Memorial Award, Judy 121
Lovelace Book Award, Maud Hart 122
Lucile Micheels Pannell Award
  see Pannell Award, Lucile Micheels
  178
Lucille E. Ogle Literary Awards
  see Ogle Literary Awards, Lucille E.
  173
Lucky Book Club Four-Leaf Clover Award
  122
Ludington Memorial Award, Jeremiah
  123
Lupine Award 122

Macmillan of Canada Contest 123
Macmillan Prize 123
Magazine Merit Award 124
Margaret A. Edwards Award 78
  see Edwards Award, Margaret A. 79
Mark Twain Award
  see Twain Award, Mark 222
Martin Award, Allie Beth 124
Mary Grant Bruce Story Award for
  Children's Literature
  see Bruce Story Award for Children's
  Literature, Mary Grant 34
Maschler Award, Kurt 125Maryland
  Children's Choice Book Award 124
Massachusetts Children's Book Award
  125
Maud Hart Lovelace Book Award
  see Lovelace Book Award, Maud Hart
  122
Max and Greta Ebel Memorial Award
  see Ebel Memorial Award, Max and
  Greta 77
McCord Children's Literature Citation,
  David 123
Media & Methods Maxi Award 126
MER Prize for Youth Literature 127
Metcalf Award, Vicky 127
Metcalf Short Story Award, Vicky 127
Michigan Young Reader's Award 128
Mildred L. Batchelder Award
  see Batchelder Award, Mildred L. 16
Milner Award 128
Minnesota Children's Book Award 128
Mississippi Children's Book Award 129
Mr. Christie's Book Award Program 129
Mother Goose Award 129
Mrazik-Cleaver Canadian Picture Book
  Award, Elizabeth 131

Nan Chauncy Award
  see Chauncy Award, Nan 54
Nancy Bloch Memorial Award
  see Bloch Memorial Award, Nancy
  21
National Book Awards 131
National Chapter of Canada IODE Violet
  Downey Book Award 133
National Children's Literature Award
  133
National Council of Teachers of English
  Achievement Award for Poetry for
  Children 133
National Religious Book Award 134
Nene Award 134
Nevada Young Readers' Award 135
New England Round Table of Children's
  Librarians Awards 135
New Jersey Institute of Technology
  Authors Awards 135
New South Wales State Literary Awards
  147
New Voices, New World 147
New York Academy of Sciences Children's
  Science Book Awards 147
New York Herald Tribune Spring Book
  Festival Awards
  see Spring Book Festival Awards 204

New York Times Choice of Best Illustrated
  Children's Books of the Year 152
New York Times Notable Books 160
New Zealand Library Association Young
  People's Nonfiction Medal 164
Newbery Medal, John 164
North Carolina Division of American
  Association of University Women in
  Juvenile Literature 171
North Dakota Children's Choice Award
  172
Nottinghamshire Children's Book Award
  172

Observer Teenage Fiction Prize 173
O'Dell Award for Historical Fiction, Scott
  173
Ogle Literary Awards, Lucille E. 173
Ohioana Book Awards 173
Oklahoma Book Award 175
Orbis Pictus Award for Outstanding
  Nonfiction for Children 175
Other Award 175
Ott Award for Outstanding Contribution to
  Children's Literature, Helen Keating
  177
Outstanding Arizona Author 177
Outstanding Pennsylvania Author 177
Owl Prize 178

Pannell Award, Lucile Micheels 178
Parents Choice Award for Children's
  Books 178
PEN Center USA West Literary Award in
  Children's Literature 185
PEN/Norma Klein Award 186
Percy Fitzpatrick Award
  see Fitzpatrick Award, Percy 84
Phoenix Award 186
Please Touch Book Award 186
Poe Award, Edgar Allan 187
Present Tense/Joel H. Cavior Literary
  Awards 189
Putnam's Sons Fiction Prize, G. P. 189

Quest for a Kelpie
  see Kelpie for the Nineties, A 116

R. Ross Annett Award
  see Annett Award, R. Ross 10
Randolph Caldecott Medal
  see Caldecott Medal, Randolph 36
Reading Association of Ireland (RAI)
  Children's Book Award 189
Reading Magic Awards 190
Rebecca Caudill Young Readers' Book
  Award
  see Caudill Young Readers' Book
  Award, Rebecca 54
Redbook's Top Ten Children's Picture
  Books 191
Regina Medal 192
Rhode Island Children's Book Award
  193
Russell Award, Frances E. 193
Russell Clark Award
  see Clark Award, Russell 70

Rutgers Award for Distinguished
    Contribution to Children's Literature
    193
Ruth Schwartz Children's Book Award
    see Schwartz Children's Book Award,
    Ruth   *194*

Sandburg Award, Carl   *194*
School Library Media Specialists of South
    Eastern New York (SLMSSNY) Award
    194
Schwartz Children's Book Award, Ruth
    194
Science Book Prizes   *195*
O'Dell Award for Historical Fiction
    see O'Dell Award for Historical Fiction,
    Scott   *173*
Paul A. Witty Short Story Award
    see Witty Short Story Award, Paul A.
    233
Sequoyah Children's Book Award   *195*
Sequoyah Young Adult Award   *196*
Sheila A. Egoff Children's Prize
    see Egoff Children's Prize, Sheila A.
    79
Signal Poetry Award   *196*
Simon Children's Book Award, Charlie
    May   *197*
Smarties Prize for Children's Books   *197*
Smith Illustration Award, W. H.   *198*
Soaring Eagle Book Award   *199*
Society of Midland Authors Award   *199*
South Carolina Children's Book Award
    200
South Carolina Young Adult Book Award
    200
South Dakota Prairie Pasque Award   *200*
Southern California Council on Literature
    for Children and Young People Annual
    Children's Literature Award   *201*
Southwest Book Award   *204*
Spring Book Festival Awards   *204*
State Historical Society of Wisconsin's
    Book Award of Merit   *215*
Steck-Vaughn Award   *216*
Stone Center for Children's Books
    Recognition of Merit Award, George G.
    216
Stuart Media Award, Jesse   *217*
Sue Hefly Award
    see Hefly Award, Sue   *102*

Sugarman Children's Book Award, Joan G.
    217
Sunshine State Young Readers Award
    217
Surrey School Book of the Year Award
    218
Sydney Taylor Book Award
    see Taylor Book Award, Sydney   *218*
Sydney Taylor Body of Work Award
    see Taylor Body of Work Award,
    Sydney   *219*
Sydney Taylor Manuscript Award
    see Taylor Manuscript Award, Sydney
    220

Taylor Book Award, Sydney   *218*
Taylor Body of Work Award, Sydney
    219
Taylor Manuscript Award, Sydney   *220*
Tennessee Children's Choice Book Award
    see Volunteer State Book Award   *225*
Texas Bluebonnet Award   *220*
Texas Institute of Letters Publishers Award
    for Best Book for Children   *220*
Thomas Alva Edison Foundation National
    Mass Media Awards
    see Edison Foundation National Mass
    Media Awards, Thomas Alva   *77*
Times Educational Supplement Information
    Book Award   *221*
Tir Na n'Og Award   *222*
Twain Award, Mark   *222*

UNICEF-Ezra Jack Keats International
    Award for Children's Book Illustration
    223
UNICEF-Ezra Jack Keats National Award
    for Children's Book Illustration   *223*
Universe Literary Prize   *223*
University of Southern Mississippi
    Medallion   *223*
Utah Children's Book Award   *224*
Utah Children's Informational Book Award
    224
Utah Young Adults' Book Award   *225*

Vicky Metcalf Award
    see Metcalf Award, Vicky   *127*
Vicky Metcalf Short Story Award
    see Metcalf Short Story Award, Vicky
    127
Virginia Young Readers Program   *225*

Volunteer State Book Award   *225*

W. H. Smith Illustration Award
    see Smith Illustration Award, W. H.
    198
Washington Children's Choice Picture
    Book Award   *226*
Washington Irving Children's Book Choice
    Award
    see Irving Children's Book Choice
    Award, Washington   *113*
Washington Post/Children's Book Guild
    Nonfiction Award   *226*
Watts Juvenile Fiction Award, Franklin
    227
Weekly Reader Children's Book Club
    Award   *227*
West Australian Young Readers Book
    Award   *227*
West Virginia Children's Book Award
    228
Western Heritage Children's Book Award
    228
Western Writers of America Spur Awards
    229
Whitbread Literary Awards   *230*
White Children's Book Award, William
    Allen   *231*
Whitley Awards   *232*
Wilder Award, Laura Ingalls   *232*
William Allen White Children's Book
    Award
    see White Children's Book Award,
    William Allen   *231*
Witty Short Story Award, Paul A.   *233*
Women's National Book Association
    Award   *233*
Woodson Book Award, Carter G.   *234*
Woodward Park School Annual Book
    Award   *235*
Writers Award   *236*

Young Adult Canadian Book Award   *236*
Young Adult Novel of the Year/Michigan
    Library Association   *236*
Young Australian's Best Book Award
    237
Young Hoosier Book Award   *237*
Young Reader's Choice Award   *238*
Young Teens Children's Literature Award
    239

Subject Index of Awards

ALABAMA
Author's Award/Juvenile/Young Adult *16*
Emphasis on Reading *79*

ANIMALS
Aurianne Award *15*
A Book Can Develop Empathy *25*
Dutton Junior Animal Book Award *76*

ARIZONA
Arizona Young Readers Award *11*
Children's Choice Award (Arizona) *64*
Outstanding Arizona Author *177*
Young Teens Children's Literature Award *239*

ASTRONOMY
American Institute of Physics Science Writing Award *8*

AUSTRALIA
Ashton Scholastic Award *14*
Australian Christian Book of the Year Children's Award *15*
Australian Multicultural Children's Literature Awards *15*
Books I Love Best Yearly (BILBY) Awards *25*
Mary Grant Bruce Story Award for Children's Literature *34*
Nan Chauncy Award *54*
Children's Book Council of Australia Book of the Year Awards *57*
Children's Peace Literature *66*
Crichton Award for Children's Book Illustration *74*
Diabetes Australia Alan Marshall Prize for Children's Literature *75*
Dromkeen Medal *76*
Family Award *81*
Kids Own Australian Literature (KOALA) *117*
National Children's Literature Award *133*
New South Wales State Literary Awards *147*
West Australian Young Readers Book Award *227*
Whitley Awards *232*
Writers Award *236*
Young Australian's Best Book Award *237*

BODY OF WORK
ALAN Award *6*

Hans Christian Andersen Awards *9*
Claude Aubry Award 14 *14*
CBC Honors Program *36*
J. G. Chandler Reward of Merit *54*
Nan Chauncy Award *54*
Children's Reading Roundtable Award *66*
Drexel Citation *75*
Dromkeen Medal *76*
Margaret A. Edwards Award *79*
Empire State Award for Excellence in Literature for Young People *80*
Eleanor Farjeon Award *81*
Golden Cat Award *92*
Eva L. Gordon Award *96*
Grolier Foundation Award *100*
Leland B. Jacobs Award *113*
Keene State College Children's Literature Festival Award *116*
Kerlan Award *117*
Knickerbocker Award for Juvenile Literature *119*
Evelyn Sibley Lampman Award *120*
Lucky Book Club Four-Leaf Clover Award *122*
David McCord Children's Literature Citation *123*
Vicky Metcalf Award *127*
Milner Award *128*
National Council of Teachers of English Achievement Award for Poetry for Children *133*
Ohioana Book Awards *173*
Outstanding Arizona Author *177*
Outstanding Pennsylvania Author *177*
Pen/Norma Klein Award *186*
Regina Medal *192*
Rutgers Award for Distinguished Contribution to Children's Literature *194*
School Library Media Specialists of South Eastern New York Award *194*
Southern California Council on Literature for Children and Young People Annual Children's Literature Award *201*
Sydney Taylor Body of Work Award *218*
University of Southern Mississippi Medallion *223*
Washington Post/Children's Book Guild Nonfiction Award *227*
Laura Ingalls Wilder Award *232*
Women's National Book Association Award *233*

BOOKSELLERS
American Booksellers Book of the Year *8*

BOOKSTORES
Lucille Micheels Pannell Award *178*

CALIFORNIA
Bay Area Book Reviewers Association Award *18*
John and Patricia Beatty Award *18*
California Young Reader Medal *41*
Commonwealth Club of California Book Awards *71*
FOCAL (Friends of Children and Literature) Award *85*
Southern California Council on Literature for Children and Young People Annual Children's Literature Award *201*

CANADA
Alberta Writing for Youth Competition *6*
Alcuin Citation for Excellence in Book Design *7*
R. Ross Annett Award *10*
Claude Aubry Award *14*
Beaver Trophy *18*
Geoffrey Bilson Award for Historical Fiction *20*
Ann Connor Brimer Award *34*
Canadian Library Association Book of the Year for Children Award *43*
Collier-Macmillan Award *70*
Max and Greta Ebel Memorial Award *77*
Sheila A. Egoff Children's Prize *79*
Governor General's Literary Awards *96*
Amelia Frances Howard-Gibbon Illustrator's Award *103*
Information Book Award *106*
International Order of the Daughters of the Empire (IODE) Best Children's Book of the Year *110*
Little Brown Canadian Children's Book Award *121*
Macmillan of Canada Contest *123*
Vicky Metcalf Award *127*
Vicky Metcalf Short Story Award *127*
Mr. Christie's Book Award Program *129*
Elizabeth Mrazik-Cleaver Canadian Picture Book Award *131*
National Chapter of Canada IODE Violet Downey Book Award *133*
Frances E. Russell Award *70*
Ruth Schwartz Children's Book Award *194*

Surrey School Book of the Year Award
218
Young Adult Canadian Book Award   236

CHILDREN'S CHOICE
Arizona Young Readers Award   11
Blue Spruce Award   22
Bologna Children's Book Fair Prizes   22
Books I Love Best Yearly (BILBY)
Awards   25
Buckeye Children's Book Award   35
California Young Reader Medal   41
Rebecca Caudill Young Readers' Book
Award   54
Charlotte Book Award   54
Children's Choice Award (Arizona)   64
Children's Choice Award (Texas)   65
Colorado Children's Book Award   70
CRABbery Award   73
Emphasis on Reading   79
Ethical Culture School Book Award   80
Dorothy Canfield Fisher Children's Book
Award   83
Florida Reading Association Children's
Book Award   84
Garden State Children's Book Award   88
Georgia Children's Book Award   89
Georgia Children's Picture Storybook
Award   90
Golden Archer Award   92
Golden Sower Award   95
Great Stone Face Award   98
Sue Hefly Award   102
Indian Paintbrush Award   105
Iowa Children's Choice Award   112
Iowa Teen Award   112
Washington Irving Children's Book Choice
Award   113
KC Three Award   115
Kentucky Bluegrass Award   116
Keystone To Reading Book Award   117
Kids Own Australian Literature (KOALA)
117
Lancashire County Library/National
Westminster Bank Children's Book of
the Year Award   120
Land of Enchantment Children's Book
Award   121
Little Archer Award   92
Maud Hart Lovelace Book Award   122
Maryland Children's Choice Book Award
124
Massachusetts Children's Book Award
125
Michigan Young Reader's Award   128
Milner Award   128
Mississippi Children's Book Award   129
Nene Award   134
Nevada Young Readers' Award   135
North Dakota Children's Choice   172
Nottinghamshire Children's Book Award
172
Rhode Island Children's Book Award
193
Ruth Schwartz Children's Book Award
194
Sequoyah Children's Book Award   195

Sequoyah Young Adult Book Award   196
Charlie May Simon Children's Book
Award   197
Soaring Eagle Book Award   199
South Carolina Children's Book Award
200
South Carolina Young Adult Book Award
200
South Dakota Prairie Pasque Award   200
Sunshine State Young Readers Award   217
217
Surrey School Book of the Year Award
218
Texas Bluebonnet Award   220
Mark Twain Award   222
Utah Children's Book Award   224
Virginia Young Readers Program   225
Volunteer State Book Award   225
Washington Children's Choice Picture
Book Award   226
West Australian Young Readers Book
Award   227
West Virginia Children's Book Award
228
William Allen White Children's Book
Award   231
Woodward Park School Annual Book
Award   235
Young Australian's Best Book Award
237
Young Hoosier Book Award   237
Young Reader's Choice Award   238
Young Teens Children's Literature Award
239

CLASSICS
Feature a Classic   82
Phoenix Award   186

COLORADO
Blue Spruce Award   22
Colorado Children's Book Award   70

CONCEPT BOOKS
Please Touch Book Award   186

CONTRIBUTIONS TO THE FIELD
American Association of School Librarians
President's Award   7
Claude Aubry Award   14
L. Frank Baum Memorial Award   17
CBC Honors Program   36
J. G. Chandler Reward of Merit   54
Children's Reading Round Table Award
66
Drexel Citation   75
Dromkeen Medal   76
Eleanor Farjeon Award   81
Grolier Foundation Award   100
Evelyn Sibley Lampman Award   120
Elliott Landau Award   121
Jeremiah Ludington Award   123
Allie Beth Martin Award   124
Lucile Micheels Pannell Award   173
School Library Media Specialists of South
Eastern New York Award   194

Women's National Book Association
233

CRITICISM
Children's Literature Association Awards
for Excellence in Literary Criticism
65
Harvey Darton Award   74

DEATH
Joan Fassler Memorial Book Award   82

DESIGN
Alcuin Citation for Excellence in Book
Design   7
Children's Book Showcase   60

ENGLAND
Arts Council of Great Britain National
Book Award   14
Best Books for Babies   18
British Book Awards   34
Burnley Express Award   36
Carnegie Medal   45
Children's Book Award   56
Harvey Darton Award   74
Earthworm Award   76
Faber/Jackanory/Guardian Children's
Writers Competition   81
Eleanor Farjeon Award   81
Garavi Gujarat Racial Harmony Book
Awards   87
Kate Greenaway Medal   98
Guardian Award for Children's Fiction
101
Lancashire County Library/National
Westminster Bank Children's Book of
the Year Award   120
Macmillan Prize   123
Kurt Maschler Award   125
Mother Goose Award   129
Nottinghamshire Children's Book Award
56
Observer Teenage Fiction Prize   173
Other Award   175
Science Book Prizes   195
Signal Poetry Award   196
Smarties Prize for Children's Books   197
W. H. Smith Illustration Award 198
Times Educational Supplement Information
Book Award   221
Universe Literary Prize   223
Whitbread Literary Awards   230

ENVIRONMENT
Earthworm Award   76

FAMILY LIFE
Family Award   81
Ezra Jack Keats New Writer's Award

FLORIDA
Florida Reading Association Children's
Book Award   56
Sunshine State Young Readers Award
217

FOLKLORE
Aesop Prize   *5*

GENERATIONAL UNDERSTANDING
Max and Greta Ebel Memorial Award   *77*

GEORGIA
Georgia Children's Book Award   *56*
Georgia Children's Picture Storybook
   Award   *90*

HANDICAPS
Joan Fassler Memorial Book Award   *82*

HAWAII
Nene Award   *134*

HISTORICAL FICTION
   see LITERATURE, HISTORICAL
   FICTION

HOSPITAL LITERATURE
Joan Fassler Memorial Book Award   *82*

HUMAN RELATIONS
Woodward Park School Book Award
   235

HUMANITARIANISM
Janusz Korczak Literary Awards for
   Children'sBooks (USA)   *119*
Janusz Korczak International Literary
   Award (Poland)   *120*

ILLINOIS
Rebecca Caudill Young Readers' Book
   Award   *54*
Carl Sandburg Award

ILLUSTRATION
American Institute of Graphic Arts Book
   Show   *8*
Hans Christian Andersen Awards   *9*
Art Books for Children Citations   *11*
Ashton Scholastic Award   *14*
Briennale Illustrations Bratislava   *19*
Irma S. and James H. Black Award   *21*
Bologna Children's Book Fair Prizes   *22*
Boston Globe Horn Book Awards
Randolph Caldecott Medal   *36*
Children's Book Showcase   *60*
Christopher Award   *67*
Russell Clark Award   *70*
Council for Wisconsin Writers   *72*
Crichton Award for Children's Book
   Illustration   *74*
Dr. Seuss Picture Book Award   *75*
Dutton Children's Books Picture Book
   Competition   *76*
Georgia Children's Picture Storybook
   Award   *90*
Golden Kite Award   *93*
Governor General's Literary Awards   *96*
Kate Greenaway Medal   *98*
Amelia Frances Howard-Gibbon
   Illustrator's Award   *103*
Hungry Mind Review Children's Books of
   Distinction   *104*

International Board on Books for Young
   People   *107*
Coretta Scott King Awards   *117*
Macmillan Prize   *123*
Kurt Maschler Award   *125*
Mr. Christie's Book Award Program   *129*
Mother Goose Award   *129*
Elizabeth Mrazik-Cleaver Canadian Picture
   Book Award   *131*
New York Times Choice of Best Illustrated
   Children's Books of the Year   *152*
Owl Prize   *178*
Parents Choice Award for Children's
   Books   *178*
Redbook's Top Ten Children's Picture
   Books   *191*
W. H. Smith Illustration Award   198
Southern California Council on Literature
   for Children and Young People Award
   201
Spring Book Festival   *204*
George G. Stone Award   *216*
Sydney Taylor Book Award   *218*
UNICEF-Ezra Jack Keats International
   Award for Children's Book Illustration
   223
UNICEF-Ezra Jack Keats National Award
   for Children's Book Illustration   *223*
Washington Children's Choice Picture
   Book Award   *226*
Weekly Reader Children's Book Club
   Award   *227*

INDIANA
Indiana Authors Day Awards   *105*
Young Hoosier Book Award   *237*

INTERNATIONAL
Jane Addams Children's Book Award   *56*
Hans Christian Andersen Awards   *9*
Briennale Illustrations Bratislava   *19*
Bologna Children's Book Fair Prizes   *22*
FIT Astrid Lindgren Translation Prize   *84*
Golden Cat Award   *92*
International Board on Books for Young
   People   *107*
International Brothers Grimm Award
   110
International Reading Association
   Children's Book Award   *56*
Janusz Korczak International Literary
   Award (Poland)   *120*
Owl Prize   *178*
UNICEF-Ezra Jack Keats International
   Award for Children's Book Illustration
   223
University of Southern Mississippi
   Medallion   *223*

IOWA
Iowa Children's Choice Award   *112*
Iowa Teen Award   *112*

IRELAND
BISTO Book of the Year Award   *20*
Reading Association of Ireland Children's
   Book Award   *56*
Whitbread Literary Awards   *230*

JAPAN
Owl Prize   178

JEWISH LITERATURE
Jewish Book Council National Jewish Book
   Awards   *113*
Present Tense/Joel H. Cavior Literary
   Awards   *189*
Sydney Taylor Book Award   *218*
Sydney Taylor Body of Work Award
   219
Sydney Taylor Manuscript Award   *220*

KANSAS
William Allen White Children's Book
   Award   *56*

KENTUCKY
Kentucky Bluegrass Award   *116*
Jesse Stuart Media Award   *217*

LITERATURE, FICTION
Abingdon Press Children's Book Award
   56
Jane Addams Children's Book Award   *56*
Aesop Prize   *5*
AIM Children's Book Award   *56*
Alberta Writing for Youth Competition   *6*
American Book Awards   *7*
American Booksellers Book of the Year
   8
American Institute of Physics Science
   Writing Award   *8*
Hans Christian Andersen Awards   *9*
R. Ross Annett Award   *10*
Arizona Young Readers Award   *11*
Arts Council of Great Britain National
   Book Award   *14*
Australian Christian Book of the Year
   Children's Book   *15*
Australian Multicultural Children's
   Literature Awards   *15*
Author's Awards/Juvenile/Young Adult
   16
Beaver Trophy   *18*
BISTO Book of the Year Award   *20*
Irma S. and James H. Black Award   *21*
Nancy Bloch Memorial Award   *21*
Boston Globe Horn Book Awards   *25*
Boys Club Junior Book Awards   *30*
Boys Life-Dodd Mead Writing Award
   33
British Book Awards   *34*
Mary Grant Bruce Award   *34*
Canadian Library Association Book of the
   Year for Children Award   *43*
Carnegie Medal   *45*
Lewis Carroll Shelf Award   *49*
Child Study Children's Book Award   *56*
Children's Book Award   *56*
Children's Book Council of Australia Book
   of the Year Awards   *57*
Children's Book Showcase   *60*
Christopher Award   *67*
Commonwealth Club of California Book
   Award   *71*
Council for Wisconsin Writers   72 Award
Dutton Junior Animal Book Award   *76*

Thomas Alva Edison Foundation National Mass Media Award   77
Feature a Classic   82
Carolyn W. Field Award   83
Helen Dean Fish Award   83
Percy Fitzpatrick Award   84
FOCAL (Friends of Children and Literature) Award   85
Charles W. Follett Award   85
Follett Beginning-To-Read Award   85
Julia Ellsworth Ford Foundation Award   86
Friends of American Writers Juvenile Book Merit Award   86
Garavi Gujarat Award   87
Esther Glen Award   90
Golden Archer Award   92
Golden Cat Award   92
Governor General's Literary Awards   96
Guardian Award for Children's Fiction   101
Hungry Mind Review Children's Books of Distinction   104
International Board on Books for Young People   107
Washington Irving Children's Book Choice Award   113
Leland B. Jacobs Award   113
Clara Ingram Judson Award   115
A Kelpie for the Nineties   116
Coretta Scott King Award   117
Little Archer Award   92
Judy Lopez Memorial Award   121
Lucky Book Club Four-Leaf Clover Award   122
Macmillan of Canada Contest   123
Mr. Christie's Book Award Program   129
National Book Awards   131
New England Round Table Award   135
New Jersey Institute of Technology Authors Awards   135
New York Times Notable Books   160
John Newbery Award   164
North Carolina AAUW Award   171
Nottinghamshire Children's Book Award   56
Lucile E. Ogle Award   173
Ohioana Book Awards   173
Parents Choice Award for Children's Books   178
Phoenix Award   186
Reading Association of Ireland Children's Book Award   56
Carl Sandburg Award   194
Smarties Prize for Children's Books   197
Society of Midland Authors Award   199
Southern California Council on Literature for Children and Young People Award   201
Spring Book Festival   204
Steck Vaughn Award   216
George G. Stone Award   216
Tir Na n'Og Award   222
Franklin Watts Award   227
Whitbread Literary Awards   230
Writers Award   236

LITERATURE, HISTORICAL FICTION
Geoffrey Bilson Award for Historical Fiction   20
Scott O'Dell Award for Historical Fiction   173

LITERATURE, MULTICULTURAL
Australian Multicultural Children's Literature Awards   15
Nancy Bloch Memorial Award   21
Max and Greta Ebel Memorial Award   77
Ezra Jack Keats New Writer's Award   116
New Voices, New World   147
Carter G. Woodson Book Award   234

LITERATURE, NONFICTION
American Institute of Physics Science Writing Award   8
Boston Globe Horn Book Awards   30
Garden State Children's Book Award   56
Golden Kite Award   93
Governor General's Literary Awards   96
Hungry Mind Review Children's Books of Distinction   104
Information Book Award   106
International Reading Association Children's Book Award   56
Washington Irving Children's Book Choice Award   113
Jefferson Cup   113
Janusz Korczak Literary Awards for Children's Books   119
National Children's Literature Award   133
New York Academy of Sciences Children's Science Book Awards   147
New Zealand Library Association Young People's Nonfiction Medal   164
Orbis Pictus Award for Outstanding Nonfiction for Children   175
Please Touch Book Award   186
Reading Association of Ireland Children's Book Award   56
Texas Institute of Letters Publishers Award for Best Book for Children   220
Times Educational Supplement Information Book Award   221
Utah Children's Informational Book Award   224
Washington Post/Children's Book Guild Nonfiction Award   227
Western Writers of America Spur Award   228
Carter G. Woodson Book Award   234

LITERATURE, RELIGIOUS
Abingdon Press Children's Book Award   56
Australian Christian Book of the Year Children's Award   15
Catholic Book Awards   53
Christopher Award   67
Golden Medallion Award   91
Jewish Book Council National Jewish Book Awards   113

National Religious Book Award   134
Helen Keating Ott Award for Outstanding Contributions to Children's Literature   177
Present Tense/Joel H. Cavior Literary Awards   189
Sydney Taylor Book Award   218
Sydney Taylor Body of Work Award   219
Sydney Taylor Manuscript Award   220
Universe Literary Prize   223

LITERATURE, YOUNG ADULT
ALAN Award
Arizona Young Readers Award   11
Blue Spruce Award   22
Margaret A. Edwards Award   79
International Reading Association Children's Book Award   56
Iowa Teen Award   112
Observer Teenage Fiction Prize   173
Sequoyah Young Adult Award   196
South Carolina Young Adult Book Award   200
Utah Young Adults' Book Award   225
Virginia Young Readers Program   225
Young Adult Canadian Book Award   236
Young Adult Novel of the Year/Michigan Library Association   236
Young Teens Children's Literature Award   239

LOUISIANA
Sue Hefly Award   102

MAGAZINE LITERATURE
Magazine Merit Award   124

MAINE
Lupine Award   123

MANUSCRIPTS
Abingdon Press Children's Book Award   56
Alberta Writing for Youth Competition   6
Avon/Flare Young Adult Novel Competition   16
Beaver Trophy   18
Boys Life-Dodd Mead Writing Award   33
Mary Grant Bruce Story Award for Children's Literature   34
Edith Busby Award   36
Calling All Girls-Dodd Mead Prize Competition   43
Collier-Macmillan Award   70
Council on Interracial Books for Children Award   73
Delacorte Press Prize for an Outstanding First Young Adult Novel   74
Dr. Seuss Picture Book Award   75
Dutton Children's Books Picture Book Competition   76
Dutton Junior Animal Book Award   76
Faber/Jackanory/Guardian Children's Writers Competition   81
Kathleen Fidler Award   82
Charles W. Follett Award   85

Follett Beginning-To-Read Award   85
Julia Ellsworth Ford Foundation Award
    86
Little Brown Canadian Children's Book
    Award   56
Macmillan of Canada Contest   123
Macmillan Prize   123
New Voices, New World   147
Lucile E. Ogle Literary Awards   173
Sydney Taylor Manuscript Award   220
Franklin Watts Juvenile Fiction Award
    227

MARYLAND
Maryland Children's Choice Book Award
    124
Joan G. Sugarman Award   217

MASSACHUSETTS
Massachusetts Children's Book Award
    56

MICHIGAN
Feature a Classic   82
Michigan Young Reader's Award   128
Young Adult Novel of the Year/Michigan
    Library Association   236

MIDWEST
Society of Midland Authors Award   199

MINNESOTA
Jeanette Fair Award   81
Minnesota Children's Book Award   56
Maud Hart Lovelace Book Award   122

MISSISSIPPI
Mississippi Children's Book Award   56

MISSOURI
KC Three Award   115
Mark Twain Award   222

MULTICULTURAL LITERATURE
    see LITERATURE, MULTI-
    CULTURAL

MYSTERY
Edgar Allan Poe Award   187

NATURE
Eva L. Gordon Award   96

NEBRASKA
Golden Sower Award   95

NEVADA
Nevada Young Readers' Award   135

NEW HAMPSHIRE
Great Stone Face Award   98
Keene State College Children's Literature
    Festival Award   116

NEW JERSEY
Garden State Children's Book Award   56
New Jersey Institute of Technology
    Authors Awards   135

Rutgers Award for Distinguished
    Contribution to Children's Literature
    194

NEW MEXICO
Land of Enchantment Children's Book
    Award   56

NEW YORK
Charlotte Book Award   54
Empire State Award for Excellence in
    Literature for Young People   80
Knickerbocker Award for Juvenile
    Literature   119
School Library Media Specialists of South
    Eastern New York Award   194
Washington Irving Children's Book Choice
    Award   113

NEW ZEALAND
AIM Children's Book Award   56
Russell Clark Award   70
Esther Glen Award   90
New Zealand Library Association Young
    People's Nonfiction Medal   164

NONFICTION
    see LITERATURE, NONFICTION

NORTH CAROLINA
North Carolina Division of American
    Association of University Women in
    Juvenile Literature   171

NORTH DAKOTA
North Dakota Children's Choice Award
    172

OHIO
Buckeye Children's Book Award   56
Ohioana Book Awards   173

OKLAHOMA
Oklahoma Book Award   175
Sequoyah Children's Book Award   56
Sequoyah Young Adult Award   195

OREGON
Evelyn Sibley Award Lampman   120

PACIFIC NORTHWEST
Young Reader's Choice Award   238

PAPERBACKS
Jeremiah Ludington Memorial Award
    123
Media and Methods Maxi Award   126

PEACE
Jane Addams Children's Book Award   56
Children's Peace Literature   66

PENNSYLVANIA
Drexel Citation   75
Carolyn W. Field Award   83
Keystone to Reading Book Award   117
Outstanding Pennsylvania Author   177

PHYSICS
American Institute of Physics Science
    Writing Award   8

POETRY
Lee Bennett Hopkins Poetry Award   103
National Council of Teachers of English
    Achievement Award for Poetry for
    Children   133
Signal Poetry Award   196

PUBLISHER SPONSORED
Abingdon Press Children's Book Award
    3
Avon/Flare Young Adult Novel
    Competition   16
Edith Busby Award   36
Calling All Girls-Dodd Mead Prize
    Competition   43
Collier-Macmillan Award   70
Delacorte Press Prize for an Outstanding
    First Young Adult Novel   74
Dr. Seuss Picture Book Award   75
Dutton Children's Books Picture Book
    Competition   76
Dutton Junior Animal Book Award   76
Kathleen Fidler Award   82
Helen Dean Fish Award   83
Charles W. Follett Award   85
Follett Beginnint -To-Read Award   85
Julia Ellsworth Ford Foundation Award
    86
Little Brown Canadian Children's Book
    Award   56
Lucky Book Club Four-Leaf Clover Award
    122
Macmillan of Canada Contest   123
Macmillan Prize   123
New Voices, New World   147
Lucile E. Ogle Literary Awards   173
G. P. Putnam's Sons Fiction Prize   189
Franklin Watts Juvenile Fiction Award
    227
Weekly Reader Children's Book Club
    Award   227

RACIAL HARMONY
Council on Interracial Books for Children
    Award   73
Garavi Gujarat Racial Harmony Book
    Awards   87
Coretta Scott King Awards   117
Carter G. Woodson Book Award   234

RELIGIOUS LITERATURE
    see LITERATURE, RELIGIOUS

RESEARCH
International Brothers Grimm Award
    110
Frances E. Russell Award   193

RHODE ISLAND
Rhode Island Children's Book Award   56

ROMANCE
Golden Medallion Award   91

SCIENCE
Science Book Prizes *195*

SCOTLAND
Kathleen Fidler Award *82*
A Kelpie for the Nineties *116*

SHORT STORY
Vicky Metcalf Short Story Award *127*
Paul A. Witty Short Story Award *233*

SOCIAL SCIENCES
Carter G. Woodson Book Award *234*

SOUTH AFRICA
Percy Fitzpatrick Award *84*
MER Prize for Youth Literature *127*

SOUTH CAROLINA
South Carolina Children's Book Award *56*
South Carolina Young Adult Book Award *200*

SOUTH DAKOTA
South Dakota Prairie Pasque Award *200*

SOUTHWEST
Southwest Book Award *204*

TENNESSEE
Volunteer State Book Award *225*

TEXAS
Children's Choice Award (Texas) *65*
Steck-Vaughn Award *216*
Texas Bluebonnet Award *220*
Texas Institute of Letters Publishers Award for Best Book for Children *220*

TEXTBOOKS
Media & Methods Maxi Award *126*
Times Educational Supplement Information Book Award *221*

TRANSLATION
Mildred L. Batchelder Award *16*
FIT Astrid Lindgren Translation Prize *84*
International Board on Books for Young People *107*

UTAH
Elliott Landau Award *121*
Utah Children's Book Award *56*
Utah Children's Informational Book Award *224*
Utah Young Adults' Book Program *225*

VALUES
Other Award *175*

VERMONT
Dorothy Canfield Fisher Children's Book Award *56*

VIRGINIA
Jefferson Cup Award *113*
Joan G. Sugarman Children's Book Award *56*
Virginia Young Readers Program *225*

WALES
Tir Na n'Og Award *222*

WASHINGTON
Washington Children's Choice Picture Book Award *226*

WASHINGTON, DC
Joan G. Sugarman Children's Book Award *56*

WEST VIRGINIA
West Virginia Children's Book Award *56*

WESTERN LITERATURE
Western Heritage Children's Book Award *56*
Western Writers of America Spur Award *229*

WHOLESOME BOOKS
Thomas Alva Edison Foundation National Mass Media Awards *77*
Vicky Metcalf Award *127*

WISCONSIN
Elizabeth Burr Award *36*
Council for Wisconsin Writers Award *72*
Golden Archer Award *92*
Little Archer Award *92*
State Historical Society of Wisconsin's Book Award of Merit *215*

WIZARD OF OZ
L. Frank Baum Memorial Award *17*

WYOMING
Indian Paintbrush Award *105*
Soaring Eagle Book Award *199*

YOUNG ADULT LITERATURE
see LITERATURE, YOUNG ADULT

ZOOLOGY
Whitley Awards *232*